INVESTMENT MANAGEMENT

SECURITY ANALYSIS AND PORTFOLIO MANAGEMENT

[For the Students of Management, Commerce, Professional Course of CA, CS, ICWA, Professionals of Financial Institutions and Policy Makers]

V.K. BHALLA
Professor,
Faculty of Management Studies,
University of Delhi,
DELHI

S. CHAND
PUBLISHING
empowering minds

S Chand And Company Limited
(ISO 9001 Certified Company)
RAM NAGAR, NEW DELHI - 110 055

S Chand And Company Limited

(ISO 9001 Certified Company)

Head Office: 7361, RAM NAGAR, QUTAB ROAD, NEW DELHI - 110 055
Phone: 23672080-81-82, 66672000 Fax: 91-11-23677446
www.**schandpublishing**.com; e-mail: **info@schandpublishing.com**

Branches:

Ahmedabad	:	Ph: 27541965, 27542369, ahmedabad@schandpublishing.com
Bengaluru	:	Ph: 22268048, 22354008, bangalore@schandpublishing.com
Bhopal	:	Ph: 4209587, bhopal@schandpublishing.com
Chandigarh	:	Ph: 2625356, 2625546, 4025418, chandigarh@schandpublishing.com
Chennai	:	Ph: 28410027, 28410058, chennai@schandpublishing.com
Coimbatore	:	Ph: 2323620, 4217136, coimbatore@schandpublishing.com (Marketing Office)
Cuttack	:	Ph: 2332580, 2332581, cuttack@schandpublishing.com
Dehradun	:	Ph: 2711101, 2710861, dehradun@schandpublishing.com
Guwahati	:	Ph: 2738811, 2735640, guwahati@schandpublishing.com
Hyderabad	:	Ph: 27550194, 27550195, hyderabad@schandpublishing.com
Jaipur	:	Ph: 2219175, 2219176, jaipur@schandpublishing.com
Jalandhar	:	Ph: 2401630, jalandhar@schandpublishing.com
Kochi	:	Ph: 2809208, 2808207, cochin@schandpublishing.com
Kolkata	:	Ph: 23353914, 23357458, kolkata@schandpublishing.com
Lucknow	:	Ph: 4065646, lucknow@schandpublishing.com
Mumbai	:	Ph: 22690881, 22610885, 22610886, mumbai@schandpublishing.com
Nagpur	:	Ph: 2720523, 2777666, nagpur@schandpublishing.com
Patna	:	Ph: 2300489, 2260011, patna@schandpublishing.com
Pune	:	Ph: 64017298, pune@schandpublishing.com
Raipur	:	Ph: 2443142, raipur@schandpublishing.com (Marketing Office)
Ranchi	:	Ph: 2361178, ranchi@schandpublishing.com
Sahibabad	:	Ph: 2771235, 2771238, delhibr-sahibabad@schandpublishing.com

First Edition 1982
Subsequent Editions and Reprints 1994 (Twice), 95, 96, 97 (Twice), 99, 2000, 2001, 2003, 2004, 2005, 2007, 2008, 2009, 2010, 2011, 2012
Nineteenth Edition 2013
Reprints 2016, 2017
Reprint 2018 (Twice)

ISBN : 978-81-219-1248-8   **Code :** 1007G 223

PRINTED IN INDIA

By Vikas Publishing House Pvt. Ltd., Plot 20/4, Site-IV, Industrial Area Sahibabad, Ghaziabad-201010 and Published by S Chand And Company Limited, 7361, Ram Nagar, New Delhi-110 055.

Preface to the 19th Edition

The security markets are in the process of an ongoing revolution, as evidenced by the internationalisation of trading, introduction of a variety of instruments, and from improved communication abilities. *INVESTMENT MANAGEMENT*: SECURITY ANALYSIS AND PORTFOLIO MANAGEMENT describes techniques, vehicles, and strategies for planning, implementing, and overseeing the optimal allocation of the funds of an investor(s) and/or an institution(s) in the changing investment environment. The book is in *SIX PARTS*, containing *forty-nine* chapters. All the parts are organised into related chapters, which should usually be read in the order presented. However, these parts are fairly independent of each other.

Part I - *Investment Environment* contains nine chapters. These are related to the financial position of the investor and his ability to assume risk. The focus of this part is on the operations of the Indian stock market, covering the organisational structure of the stock markets, regulatory framework, stock markets and financial development in India, over- the-counter exchange of India, national stock exchange of India and overall developments in the secondary capital market. The growth of the new issue market and issues related to the listing requirements and the criteria for selecting a broker, from the individual and institutional point of view, are discussed. Since the structure and magnitude of transaction costs need to be considered when making investment decisions as they affect returns, basic types of transactions have been examined. An exhaustive coverage has been provided on investment companies, both, close-end and open-end; the relevance of market indexes and methodology employed to compute these indexes; and the security credit ratings, covering some of the selected leading Indian security credit rating agencies' operations. Finally, an attempt is made to examine critically the recent reforms introduced in the capital market in the context of integration of world financial markets.

Part II - *Alternative Investment Outlets For Funds* introduced various types of securities that are available to meet the needs of the investor along with an estimation of yield and risk. The main thrust of this part of the book is to enable the reader to formulate objective ideas and philosophies concerning the various types of securities .The opening chapters on fixed income securities provide a basic understanding of bonds and preference shares market .The analysis of bonds includes a detailed discussion of alternative measures for bonds, what factors affect yields on bonds, and what influences the volatility of bond returns. This latter discussion considers the very important concept of the bond duration and immunization aspects to explain the bond price volatility. There is also a related consideration of the convexity of alternative bonds and the impact of convexity on bond price volatility. Finally, there is a discussion on the recent developments in the corporate bond market in India and the various initiatives undertaken by the government to develop the bond market. This is followed by preference share valuation and analysis. Subsequent to the fixed –income securities, an extended coverage is on equity valuation process. Changing attitude towards equity ownership, nature of equity shares, dividend policies and decisions, and various models on equity valuation have been discussed. Starting with the general discounted cash flow approach to security valuation, some of the more widely used approaches to security valuation have been reviewed. Private equity and venture capital have been added in this part to emphasis the new sources of financing and investment. Role of primary dealers, crucial in successfully managing the public debt, has been dealt in detail since the government securities issued from time to time and the yield structure of the government securities, the uses of yield curve, default risk and interest rates, inflation and interest rates, the fisher effect has increased the complexity and excitement. The knowledge of sovereign wealth funds is now essential as it has emerged as an important government–owned investment vehicle in response to the strong accumulation of foreign assets by the official sector. Various non-security forms of investment, which attract a major proportion of the household sector's investment in total investment in financial assets, have also been analysed in this part. Further, since the real estate offers an attractive way to diversify an investment portfolio, an exclusively coverage is on the real estate investments. Finally, as investment in short-term (money market) instruments involves a tradeoff between liquidity, the ability to sell a security quickly without suffering a price decline at a small transactions cost, and the yield, managing the short-term investment requires an accumulation of information about the firm, the markets and instruments, the economic environment, and a selection of investment options—all in a very short period of time. The measurement of liquidity and the factors that lead to a strategy of using marketable securities to provide backup liquidity and yield is a function of the maturity, the marketability, the default risk, and the taxability of the security. In making the trade off between the liquidity and yield, a number of money market securities that are appropriate are available. This part concludes with the principal investment instruments of the money market and review of the recent Reserve Bank of India's initiatives and developments in the money market.

Part III - *Security Analysis* presents a discussion of stock market forecasting, the independence of stock market, and the role market exercises in the investment decision-making. The economic-industry- company analysis is linked in order to reach considered estimates of return and risk on individual securities in the fundamental analysis. A detailed systematic approach has been adopted on technical analysis by focusing on the rationale, methods employed by technical school which concentrates on supply and demand relationships in the market and historical price and volume relationship to predict the movement of the market as well as the movement of the prices of individual securities. The last segment of part is devoted to the idea of efficient markets and the theory of random walk, covering evidence related to the efficient market hypothesis including consideration of the growing number of anomalies and the usefulness of the book value / market value ratio. The efficient market notion questions the validity of technical analysis and raises some serious questions about fundamental analysis.

Part IV - *Portfolio Analysis And Management* directs attention to the problem of portfolio management, both in theory and practice. Many of the models and techniques are complex and difficult but they are effective and are widely employed throughout the investment community by investment and portfolio analysts. A deep understanding of them can mean the difference between success and failure in decision-making. There is an extensive coverage of stock price volatility and its measurement, the concept of portfolio selection by portfolio pioneer, Harry Markowitz and the development of a simplified model for portfolio analysis by William Sharpe. The extensive coverage given to the predictive power of factor models in the industry and, at the same time, paves the way for an easy grasp of the assumptions underlying the arbitrage pricing theory. More specifically, this part covers the *why, what, whose*—and more importantly the subject of investment portfolio-decision making. How can an investor reduce expected risk through diversification, why this risk reduction results from *proper* diversification, and how the investor may estimate the expected risk and return level of a given portfolio of assets, Markowitz's model is widely used to allocate wealth across different types of assets. Markowitz demon-strated how to create a frontier of optimal (or "efficient") portfolios, each having the highest possible expected rate of return for a given level of risk. However, this technique was so computationally demanding (given the available technology) that practical application of his optimal allocation model was difficult. Following the discussion on the application of the utility theory and indifference curve in the portfolio choice, Markowitz Model: Mean -Variance Criterion for the selection of portfolios has been critically examined. William Sharpe developed a simplified version of his mentor's model, one that was less demanding with respect to computational effort. It was based on an approximating formula for portfolio return variance known as the single index model. This model, combined with technological advances, allowed contemporary portfolio theory to be readily applied in the real world. Today, Sharpe's model is widely used to allocate wealth within asset groups, especially equity shares.

Prior to the dissemination of portfolio theory into the real world, the following question has been raised: *Suppose everyone managed his or her investments using portfolio theory and invested in the portfolios on the frontier, how would that affect the pricing of securities? To answer this question, the capital asset pricing model (CAPM) was developed.* This model has reigned as the premier model in the field of finance and been widely used in the real world to measure portfolio performance, value securities, make capital budgeting decisions, and even regulate public utilities. The model was questioned since it is empirically impossible to verify its single economic prediction and an alternative to the capital asset pricing model was being developed, called the *arbitrage pricing theory (APT)*. This theory argued that expected return must be related to risk in such a way that no single-investor could create unlimited wealth through arbitrage. APT is less demanding in terms of its assumptions and it is testable, at least in principle, but still CAPM, though being seriously called into question, is widely used in the real world. In fact, CAPM and APT are just versions of a much older valuation technique—the *risk-premium model*. The risk-premium model assigns increasingly high returns for increasing risks. An investment with the lowest possible return would be an investment with no risk. The return on this risk-free investment compensates the investor for his or her illiquidity (having the invested funds tied up) over the life of the investment. In addition, the bond portfolio management strategies, covering the factors to be considered in the selection of a portfolio, distinction between active portfolio strategies and structured portfolio strategies, and the various techniques applied to measure and evaluate the investment performance of a fixed-income portfolio manager have been discussed. Shortcomings in the asset pricing models led the practitioners to use performance measurement procedures that are free of dependence on particular asset pricing models .The performance measures help in discriminating among those who have skill, those who are lucky, and those who can earn higher returns merely because they take risks. It is imperative to understand how the performance measures work, and the nature of their assumptions, and their relative strengths and weaknesses. Measuring portfolio performance with and without asset pricing models has been given a complete and exhaustive coverage.

Part V – *Derivatives: Risk Management*, an integral part of the world of finance, use has per-meated almost every aspect of domestic and international capital and money markets. They are transforming every aspect of finance from investing to raising capital to manage risk. New products and strategies are being developed at the stunning speed into an enormous, pervasive and controversial force, which is placing an enormous strain on financial professionals who must keep abreast of all the changes. Derivatives have been a very successful innovation in the capital market and as in the modern life financial engineering approach keep investors and business going. The investment manager must be able to use all the tools available to control a company's exposure to financial risk. Hence, a broad-based exposure both to the technical aspects of the main clauses of derivatives and markets in which they are traded is essential. By exploiting derivatives markets, the finance manager can create new instruments that have highly specialised and desirable risk and return characteristics. Some derivatives are traded on exchanges ;others are traded in the over-the-counter market, or added to new issues of debt and equity securities. The successful implementation of various investment strategies necessitates a sound working knowledge of the fundamentals of derivatives trading.

A number of initiatives for the further development of OTC derivatives in India have been initiated. Some of the major ones are:-*New Products:* The product on anvil is the Credit Default Swap (CDS). CDS on corporate bonds issued by single legal residential entities have been proposed, with the underlying bonds to be listed ones, but with two exceptions: unlisted but rated bonds of infrastructure companies and unlisted/unrated bonds issued by the SPVs set up by infrastructure companies. *Trade Repository:* CCIL has been acting as the trade repository for IRS transactions since August 2007. There is no such trade repository structure for the FX derivatives at present. There are proposals to introduce repository structure for USD-INR forwards (including swaps) and options. *Central Counterparty Clearing:* CCIL has put in place guaranteed settlement for FX forward transaction effective from the date of contract since December 2009. In case of IRS, CCIL has been providing non- guaranteed settlement since November 2008. It is expected to transit to guaranteed settlement for IRS transactions shortly. *Portfolio Compression:* An important innovation in OTC derivative markets introduced during the last few years relates to portfolio compression services. Since the only way to exit a position in an OTC derivative is to enter into another with opposite pay-off, the gross notional outstanding multiplies manifold as a result. Huge build-up in gross notional outstanding demands higher capital charges and reduces the available counter-party limits for undertaking other business transactions. Moreover, it does not capture the economic essence of the portfolios. CCIL is in the process of developing trade compression services.

Generally speaking, Indian approach to financial markets development has been calibrated, keeping in mind the overall objectives of financial sector development. Particularly at this juncture, while expanding the set of products and instruments available, the emphasise is on the improvement in the pre and post-trading infrastructure as well as consolidation of the regulatory regime so that financial stability is not threatened. A thorough understanding of the rudiments helps the investors to formulate an appropriate desirable strategy. Determining suitability is nothing new to the stock market investors, for stocks themselves are not suitable for every investor. This part provides a broad-based introduction to both the technical aspects of the main classes of derivatives and the markets in which they are traded, and the underlying concepts. This is a comprehensive, industry- independent exploration of financial derivatives, which offers an insightful look inside a revolutionary field that is sweeping the world of corporate, bank, and investment finance. From reviewing the basic building blocks of financial derivatives to systematically examining the myriad of processes involved in creating innovative financial instruments, three main types of traders identified in these markets are: hedgers, speculators, and arbitrageurs, to provide realist understanding of the derivatives by covering options, futures, swaps, carry trades, convertible securities, warrants and hedging. To analyse the application of derivatives on commodity exchanges, various principles underlying the practices have also been discussed along with the critical view of the strategies adopted. Trading is as a rule fully computerised, so that portfolio switching can be affected on a large scale within the shortest possible time regardless of geography. The contracts volume and trading practices are tailored to the professional market players. Bearing this in mind, it is not a surprising that the derivatives markets are characterised by exceptionally high degree of internationality. The infrastructure of derivatives markets is geared to international transactions. Indeed, they are probably the most important developments in the capital markets since the abandonment of the gold standard.

Part-VI - *International Financial Flows* stresses the global aspects of investing as the financial markets are growing global and global finance is becoming a reality. With globalisation of financial markets, portfolio flows (bonds and equities) have quadrupled in the last few years. While traditionally portfolio managers used to diversify the investment portfolio in domestic securities, there has been an ever increasingly a strong tendency to go global, seeking higher profits and more stable portfolio which benefits from diversification in various economies. Three main factors explain the present global trend of extending financial integration from the developed into the developing countries. *First and* foremost, the improved macroeconomic performance in the recipient countries— the adjustment to structural reforms that have taken place since coming out of the debt crisis—have helped in bringing about this phenomenon. The *second* is a structural shift that has to do with the very same reform process: the dominance of the private sector in the incremental growth in many of these countries accounts for the fact that there is a need for private capital to come into private hands. The *third* is monetary developments in the industrial countries, which have led to favourable interest rate differentials, making it important to find out how much of the flows is hot money, which could also reverse.

The benefit for the developing economies of this type of capital inflow is the greater risk bearing by investors, unlike the syndicated bank lending of the 1970s. The greater diversification of investment finance and the better incentives with this type of finance should help in the management of the investment process. It also helps to foster the development of the local capital markets, which would then enhance the domestic resource mobilisation in these countries. If one looks at the benefits for investors in industrial countries, it is clear that it pays to diversify portfolios—which are still very much home-biased, as returns in different countries are little correlated.

Along with the benefits are costs, warnings, and policy implications. One important concern is hot money. Today, huge amounts of capital can move from one place to another just by pressing a button and the speed of adjustment in asset markets is very quick. But the commodities and factors cannot move much more speedily than before. Extensive capital inflows, accompanied by a real appreciation of the exchange rate, may hurt exports. Since these movements may not be symmetric when capital flows out, the detrimental effects on exports are not easily reversed. In some sense, the phenomenon can be of a small tail that can wag a large dog—a very small change in portfolios of the industrial countries can lead to large changes in the flows to developing countries, with possible detrimental effects on their economies. A warning is that the predominance of the private sector in these flows does not mean that governments don't have an important role. The more integrated capital markets are and the more important portfolio shifts become, the more crucial it is to have the right domestic institutional framework for channeling these flows effectively. Laissez-faire does not mean that the government should not have its hands on some very important regulatory roles.

Financial innovations, internationalisation and institutionalisation of investment activities are different but ultimately inseparable aspects of the radical fundamental changes in the world financial markets. World financial markets provide exposure to the current developments in the developed and emerging financial markets. Foreign portfolio investment is emerging as an alternate source of financing with a higher future potential. The modern portfolio theory-oriented approach provides an assess to the riskiness of foreign claims and techniques of portfolio investment. The nature of foreign portfolio investment, and the various issues and challenges posed by foreign portfolio investment to the policy-makers have been examined. Foreign portfolio investment in India: emerging trends and policy developments in the context of liberalisation and market-oriented process has been discussed subsequently. Manias, panics, crashes in the financial markets has been included in this part to analyse the human expectations and various crashes in world stock markets, covering pyramid and ponzi schemes, speculative bubbles, The Great Crash, Oct.'87 Stock market Crash and its aftermath and the Scam of early 1990s and the Market Scam 2001 in India. Finally, the part ends with the discussion on established behaviour patterns that may influence security prices, the common mistakes that investors make while investing in mutual funds, myths about financial derivatives, winning in options, trading strategies of professionals in futures, and the golden rules to achieve success in investment world.

The 19th edition of the *Investment Management: Security Analysis and Portfolio Management* differs in a significant way from the previous edition. The current volume covers recent changes in the world financial markets and the changing compositions of the portfolios. The recent global financial crisis has brought to light the weaknesses of the OTC derivatives market. The complexity and opacity of the OTC market facilitated excessive risk-taking by the market participants. The lack of information about the counterparties coupled with non-availability of the transaction information with the regulators led to seizure of the market. Further, the bilateral counterparty risks have become complex given the variety of structures and asset classes used by the market participants. With increase in volumes and complexities of the OTC derivatives, the infrastructure for clearing and settlement became a major impediment. To cover exhaustively financial derivatives market in India, a new chapter has been added. The major change between this edition and the previous one has to do with updating the coverage. Each chapter of the book presents information in a logical sequential fashion. Many chapters build on the information presented in the preceding chapters. The reader who is using the text as a reference-perhaps scanning one of the later chapters- may find the terms are being encountered that has been defined in an earlier chapter. The index may be of use since some subjects are described, in varying levels of complexity, in more than one place in the book. The text provides illustrative charts, tables, diagrammes and full worked out examples and cases. The exercises and case studies are designed to help readers understand the practical application of the concepts. All the financial calculations are broken down in a step-by-step process designed to help those who prefer to see numbers rather than formulae.

Since the book is synthesis, it uses findings at various places from the published results. I hope that I have interpreted them correctly. I have made acknowledgments of every idea whose source I have been able to identify, but some writers may have been missed unintentionally. I am indebted to my colleagues, both academic and professional, and to countless students. It would be impossible to list them all. Finally, I wish to express thanks to the members of the S. Chand & Company Pvt. Ltd. for their wholehearted support and cooperation.

V.K. BHALLA

Contents

PART I

THE INVESTMENT ENVIRONMENT

1. Investment: Objectives and Risks   3-22

Introduction; Investment; Speculation; Gambling; Features of an Investment Programme: Safety of Principal; Adequate Liquidity and Collateral Value; Stability of Income; Capital Growth; Tax Benefits; Purchasing Power Stability; Concealability; Risks of Investment: Business and Financial Risk; Purchasing Power Risk; Market Risk; Interest Rate Risk; Social or Regulatory Risk; Other Risks; Finance *vs.* Investments: Interacting Decision Elements; Questions; References.

2. The Stock Markets in India   23-49

Introduction; Nature and Function of Stock Exchange; Organisational Structure of the Secondary Market; Regulatory Framework; Legislations: Capital Issues (Control) Act, 1947; Securities Contracts (Regulation) Act, 1956; Companies Act, 1956; SEBI Act, 1992; Depositories Act, 1996; Prevention of Money Laundering Act, 2002; Stock Markets and Financial Development in India; Over the Counter Exchange of India; National Stock Exchange of India; Developments in the Secondary Capital Market; Major Policy Initiatives in the Secondary Market; Questions; References.

3. New Issue Market   50-66

Introduction; New Issue Market: The Concept; Functions; Role of the New Issue Market; Recent Trends in the Primary Market; Major Policy Initiatives in the Primary Market; Questions; References.

4. Listing of Securities   67-82

Introduction; Advantages of Listing; Listing: Is It a Legal Requirement?; Key Provisions in Listing Agreement; Eligibility Criteria for IPOs/FPOs; Listing Procedures: National Stock Exchange (NSE); Approval of Memorandum and Articles of Association; Approval of Draft Prospectus; Submission of Application (For Issuers listing on NSE for the first time); Submission of Application (Security Deposit); Listing Fees; Delisting; Voluntary De-listing of Companies; Compulsory De-listing of Companies; Questions; References.

5. The Brokerage Business   83-109

Introduction; Functions of a Brokerage Firm; Brokerage Information; Functional

Specialisation of Members; Selecting a Broker and a Brokerage Firm; Execution of Order; Types of Transactions in a Stock Exchange; Mechanics of Share Trading; Features of Share Trading; Transaction Costs; Basic Types of Transactions—Long Purchase: Margin Trading, Making Margin Transactions, Initial Margin, Maintenance Margin, Basic Margin Formula, Return on Invested Capital, Uses of Margin Trading; Short Selling; Essentials of Short Selling; Who Lends the Securities?; Uses of Short Selling; Clearing and Settlement System; Clearing Process; Risk Management; Risk Containment Measures; Settlement Agencies; Carry Forward Facility and the Theory of Badla; Floating Stock and Badla Rates; Brokerage Charges; Review Problems; Questions; Problems; References.

6. Investment Companies   110-139

Introduction; Investment Company: The Concept; Market Design of Investment Companies (Mutual Funds); Structure of Investment Companies (Mutual Funds); Types of Investment Companies; Open-end Investment Companies; Closed-end Investment Companies; Advantages and Disadvantages of Investing in Mutual Funds; Regulation of Mutual Funds; Recent Policy and Regulatory Initiatives; Computation of Net Asset Value (NAV); Measuring Performance; Sources of Return; Measures of Return; Returns on Closed-End Funds; The Matter of Risk; Mutual Funds' Operation in India; Recent Policy Developments; Questions and Problems; References.

7. Market Indexes   140-158

Introduction; Index: The Concept; Methods of Computing the Stock Indexes; Price-Weighted and Quantity-Weighted Indexes; Value-Weighted Indexes; Leading Stock Market Indexes: Sensex - The Barometer of Indian Capital Markets; BSE-100 Index; BSE-200 Index; Dollex Series of BSE Indices; BSE-500 Index and Sectoral Indices; BSE Bankex; BSE TECk INDEX; BSE PSU Index; BSE Mid-Cap and BSE Small-Cap Index; S&P CNX Nifty; CNX Nifty Junior; CNX 100; S&P CNX 500; CNX Midcap; S&P CNX Defty; CNX Midcap 200; CNX IT Index; CNX Bank Index; CNX FMCG Index; CNX PSE Index; CNX MNC Index; CNX Service Sector Index; S&P CNX Industry Indices; Customised Indices; CNX Energy Index; CNX Pharma Index; GOI-Bond Index; Nifty Futures at SGX-DT; RBI Index of Security Prices; Other Index of Security Prices; Users and Uses of Market Indexes; Questions; References.

8. Security Credit Ratings   159-180

Introduction; Definition of Credit Rating; Factors Affecting Assigned Ratings; Credit Rating in India; Functions and Approaches of Credit Rating Agencies; Benefits of Credit Rating; Disadvantages of Credit Rating; Types of Rating; Credit Rating Agencies in India; Analytical Framework Used by CRAs; The Regulatory Framework for CRAs; CRAs Business Models: Issuer Pays Model, Investor-Pays Model, The Government/Regulator-Pays Model, The Exchange-Pays Model; How Do CRAs Address Regulatory Concerns?; Limitations of Credit Ratings; Questions; References.

9. Capital Market Reforms   181-212

Introduction; The Primary Securities Market; The Secondary Securities Market; Capital Market reforms: Policy Initiatives and Developments; New Capital Issues; Book Building; Depository System; Trading Rules; Insider Trading; Unfair Trade Practices; Sweat Equity; Takeovers; Buy Back; Circuit Breakers;

Short Selling and Securities Lending and Borrowing; Introduction of Direct Market Access Facility; Institutional Trades; Promoters to Compulsorily Disclose Details of Shares Pledged by Them; Securities Contracts (Regulation) Amendment Act, 2007; PAN as the Sole Identification Number; Real Estate Mutual Funds; New Derivative Products; Volatility Index; Investment Options for Navaratna and Miniratna Public Sector Enterprises; Investor Protection and Education Fund (IPEF); Cross Margining; ASBA; Questions; References.

PART II

ALTERNATIVE INVESTMENT OUTLETS FOR FUNDS

10. Bond Valuation and Analysis   215-262

Introduction; Definition; Reasons for Issuing Bonds; Bond Features: Indenture, Maturities, Interest Payments, Call Feature, Types of Bonds: Convertible and Non-Convertible Bonds, Sinking Fund Bonds, Serial Bonds, Mortgage or Secured Bonds, Collateral Trust Bonds, Income Bonds, Adjustment Bonds, Assumed Bonds, Joint Bonds, Guaranteed Bonds, Redeeemable and Irredeemable Bonds, Participating Bonds; Risks Associated with Investing in Bonds; Bond Prices, Yields, and Interest Rate; Relationship Among Bond Prices, Time to Maturity and Interest Rates: Malkiel's Theorems; Malkiel's Theorems and Mixed Messages; Duration; Chua's Closed-Form Duration; Bond Duration and Price Volatility; Modified Duration; Duration in Value (DV); Bond Immunization; Developing the Corporate Debt Market in India; Measures Taken to the Corporate Bond Market; Issues Regarding the Development of Corporate Debt Market: Improving Liquidity, Market Making, Credit Derivatives, Interest Rate Derivatives, Repo in Corporate Debt, Credit Enhancement - Bank Guarantee, Smooth Sovereign Yield Curve, Enhancing Transparency, Relaxing Investment Restrictions, Expanding Access to the Foreign Investors, Settlement Systems/Trading Platform, Efficient Bankruptcy Regime; Implementation of BASEL III and Corporate Bond Market; Review Problems; Questions; Problems; References.

11. Preference Share Valuation and Analysis   263-272

Introduction; Features of Preference Shares; Preference Share Yields: Current Yield, Planning or Holding Period Return, Yield to the Call Date; Review Problems; Questions; Problems; References.

12. Equity Shares   273-309

Itroduction; Changing Attitude Towards Equity Ownership; Equity Capital Terminology: Authorised Capital, Issued Capital, Paid Up Capital; Nature of Equity Shares, Dividend: Cash Dividend, Stock Dividend (Bonus Shares); Dividend Policy: Short-term Dividend Policy, Alternative Dividend Policies— Stable Rupee Dividend, Target Payout Ratios, Regular and Extra Dividends, Long-term Dividend Policy; Dividend as a Passive Residual, Irrelavance of Dividends—MM Theory; Relevance of Dividends; Dividend Provisions Under the Companies Act, 1956; Review Problems; Questions; Problems; References.

13. Equity Valuation And Analysis   310-376

Introduction; Active Equity Investment Styles; Equity Valuation Models; Basic Models: Zero Growth Model, Constant Growth Model, Variable Growth Rate of Dividends. Major Indexes; Value Model for Cyctical Stock; Models Based on

Price Ratio Analysis; Price-Earnings (P/E) Ratio (Earnings Multiplier Model; Greenspan Model; Growth at a Reasonable Price (GARP); Price-Cash Flow (P/CF) Ratio; Price-Sales (P/S) Ratio; Price/Book Value (P/BV) Ratio; Valuation Equations to Find Expected Return: Trend, Current—Trend, Analyst's Best Estimate (ABE), Random Valuation Model, Intrinsic Value; Relative Strength Model; Homogeneous Group/Group Relation Models; Multifactor Models; Market Anomaly Models; Capital Asset Pricing Model (CAPM); The Q Ratio; Considerations In Developing and Selecting Quantitative Strategies; Review Problems; Questions; Problems; References.

14. Private Equity And Venture Capital   377-404

Introduction; Rudiments of Private Equity (PE); Players in The Private Equity Market; Business Cycle of Private Equity; Risk Profile of Private Equity Investment; Benefits of Private Equity Finance; Size of Private Equity (PE) Industry; Strategic Secret of Private Equity; Evolution of Private Equity; Evolution of Private Equity in India; Private Equity's New Focus; Private Equity – Implications for India; Prospects for the Private Equity Market in India; Venture Capital; Exit Routes: Corporate Sale/Trade Sale, Take Out, Share Repurchase by the Promoter, Share Buyback of the Company, Listing on the Stock Exchange(s); Difference between Private Equity, Venture Capital and Hedge Funds; Regulation of Private Equity and Venture Capital in India; Questions; References.

15. Government Securities   405-450

Introduction; Government Securities Market in India; Primary Dealers; Objectives and Rationale for a Primary Dealer System; Benefits and Costs of Primary Dealer System; Necessary Conditions for a Primary Dealer System; Primary Dealers in India; PDs Role and Obligations; Operations and Performance of PDs; Sources and Application of Funds of Standalone PDs; Financial Performance of PDs; The Yield Structure of the Government Securities; The Concept of a Yield Curve; YTM *vs.* ZCYC; Shape of the Yield Curves; Sensitivity of the Yield Curve; Default Risk and Interest Rates; Inflation and Interest Rates; Developing Government Securities Market in India; Critical Components for a Well Functioning and Vibrant G-Sec Market; Review Problems; Questions; Problems; References.

16. Sovereign Wealth Funds   451-475

Introduction; Characteristics of SWFs; What Are SWFs; Source of Sovereign Wealth Funds; Home Country Policy Goals; Necessary Conditions for Success; Policy Objectives; Classification of SWFs and its Implications; Theoretical Considerations behind SWFs' Strategic Asset Allocations; Investment Horizon and SAA; Funding Source and SAA; How are SWFS Different from Private Equity Funds?; Growing Concerns about SWFs; Soveriegn Wealth Funds and Financial Crisis; Crisis Implication for Strategic Asset Allocation; SWFs: Indian Perspective; India as a Home Country, SEV for Use of Reserves; Questions; References.

17. Non-Security Forms of Investment   476-503

Introduction; Flow of Funds; Recent Investment and Saving Trends; Indian Banking Sector; Bank Assurance; Indian Insurance Industry: Life Insurance, Non-life Insurance, Insurance Penetration; Pension Sector; Post-office Small Savings Schemes; Deposits with Companies; Bullion: Gold, Silver; Questions; References.

18. Real Estate Investments   504-526

Introduction; Setting Real Estate Investment Objectives; Determinants of Value; Real Estate Valuation; Estimating Market Value: The Cost Approach, The Comparative Sales Approach, The Income Approach; Forecasting Investment Returns; NOI Versus After-tax Cash Flows; Calculating Discounted Cash Flows; Calculating Approximate Yield; Comprehensive Example of Real Estate Valuation; Determinants of Value; Calculating Investment Returns; Synthesis and Interpretation; Review Problems; Questions; Problems; References.

19. Money Market   527-560

Introduction; Characteristics of the Money Market; Money Market Instruments; Convergence Among Financial Market Segments; Changing Monetary Policy Paradigm; Monetary Management in the More Recent Period; Liquidity Management; Money Market Price and Rates: Bank Discount Basis; Bank Discount Yield Values Bond Equivalent Yields; Bond Equivalent Yields, APRs, and EARs, Review Problems; Questions; Problems; References.

PART III

SECURITY ANALYSIS

20. Fundamental Security Analysis   563-603

Introduction; An Analysis of the Economy: The Current State of the Economy; Industry Analysis; The Industrial Growth Cycle; Structure and Operational Characteristics of the Industry; Input-Output Analysis; Reasons for Decline in the Competitive Position of an Industry; Investment Classification of Industries; Selecting an Industry; Company Analysis; Evaluating Management; Fundamental Security Analysis: An Appraisal; Review Problems; Questions; Problems; References.

21. Technical Analysis   604-628

Introduction; The Concept; Basic Technical Assumption; Technical vs. Fundamental Analysis; Old Puzzles and New Developments; Fibonacci Numbers; Dow Theory; Elliott Wave Principle; Kondratev Wave Theory; Chaos Theory; Neutral Networks; Charting as a Technical Tool; Types of Charts: Lince Chart, Bar Chart, Point-and-Figure Chart, Candlestick Chart; Important Chart Patterns: Support and Resistance Levels; Head and Shoulders Configurations; Trend Analysis; Triangles, Pennants, Wedges and Flags; Limitations of Charts; Technical Indicators: The Short Interest-Ratio Theory, Confidence Index, Spreads, Advance-Decline Ratio, Market Breadth Index, The Odd-Lot Ratio, Insider Transactions, Moving Average, Indicators of the Witchcraft Variety; Technical Analysis — An Evaluation; The Future of Technical Analysis; Questions; Problems; References.

22. Efficient Market Theory   629-654

Introduction; Forms of the Efficient Market Hypothesis: A Weak-Form and the Random Walk, Semi-Strong Form, Strong Form; Testing Market Efficiency; Implications; Challenge to Security Analysts; Market Efficiency and Anomalies; So, are the Markets Efficient?; Questions; Problems; References.

PART IV

PORTFOLIO ANALYSIS AND MANAGEMENT

23. **Portfolio Analysis: Risk and Return** 657-691

Introduction; Portfolio and Security Returns; Risk; Portfolio Risk; When Diversification Does Not Help; When Diversification Can Eliminate Risk; The Insurance Principle; Borrowing and Lending; Review Problems; Questions; Problems; References.

24. **Portfolio Investment Process** 692-715

Introduction; Basic Principles; Aspects of The Portfolio Investment Process: Planning, Implementation, Portfolio Monitoring; Objectives of Portfolio Management; The Importance of Primary and Secondary Objectives; Other Factors to Consider in Establishing Objectives; Portfolio Objectives and the Personal Characteristics of the Investor; The Concept of a Strong Financial Position; Portfolio Management Goals and Objectives, and Establishing the Income Portfolio; The Investor's Needs; Articulation of Goals and Objectives; Portfolio Dedication; Portfolio Management Policies; Review Problems; Questions; Problems; References.

25. **Portfolio Choice: Utility Theory and Indifference Curves** 716-730

Introduction; Utility Functions: Linear Utility Function and Risk; Concave Utility Function and Risk, Uncertain Outcomes, Insurance and Expected Returns; Indifference Curves; Review Problems; Questions; Problems; References.

26. **Markowitz: Portfolio Selection Model** 731-767

Introduction; Markowitz Model: The Mean-Variance Criterion Efficient Portfolios: Two-Security Portfolio, Three Security Portfolio, Five - Security Portfolio; A Graphical Approach; Corner Portfolios; Dents in the Efficient Set; Dominance Principle; Modificaiton to the Efficient Frontier: Short Selling; Leveraged Portfolios; Questions; Problems; References.

27. **Sharpe: The Single Index Model** 768-813

Introduction; Characteristic Lines; Probabilistic Characteristic Lines; Market and Nonmarket Risk and Return; Portfolio Characteristic Lines; The Effectiveness of Diversification; Non-Market Return in an Efficient Market; Constructing the Optimal Portfolio: Ranking Securities, Selecting the Cut-off Rate (C*), Calculating the Cut-off Rate, Optional Portfolio Selection Short Sales Allowed; Review Problems; Questions; Problems; References.

28. **Capital Market Theory and The Capital Asset Pricing Model** 814-886

Introduction; Assumptions; Capital Market Theory; Capital Market Line; Capital Asset Pricing Model; The Security Market Line; SML Versus CML; Determination of Systematic Risk; Growth Rates, Accounting Betas, and Variance in EBIT; CAPM *vs.* Market Model; CAPM; Computing Estimates; Estimating Beta; Fundamental and Creative Beta Prediction; Estimating the Risk-free Rate; Estimating the Market Return; The Usual Risk-Premium Estimate; Tests of the

CAPM; Some Applications and Implications of the Capital Asset Pricing Model; Review Problems; Questions; Problems; References.

29. **Factor Models and Arbitrage Pricing Theory**   887-912

Introduction; Single Factor Model; Multiple-Factor Models; Arbitrage Pricing Theory (APT) Model; Practical Applications of APT; Review Problems; Questions; Problems; References.

30. **Bond Portfolio Management Strategies**   913-934

Introduction; Active Bond Portfolio Strategies; Structured Strategies; Bond Indexing; Indexing Methodologies; Logistical Problems in Implementing an Indexing Strategy; Liability Funding Strategies; Bond Performance Measurement and Evaluation; Requirements for a Bond Performance and Attribution Analysis Process; Review Problems; Questions; Problems; References.

31. **Investment Timing and Performance Measurement**   935-956

Introduction; Timing The Purchases of Securities; Complexities of Investment Timing; Alternative Methods to Measure the Return on The Portfolio: Arithmetic Average (Mean) Rate of Return, Internal Method-Rupee Weighted, Time-Weighted Rate of Return; Timing the Sale is Critical; Alternative Solutions to Timing: Formula Plans—Types of Formula Plans, Rupee-cost Averaging, A Buy-and-hold Policy; Questions; Problems; References.

32. **Performance Evaluation**   957-1002

Introduction; Alternative Measures of Performance Evaluation; Total Variance *vs.* Beta as a Risk Index; Treynor Reward-to-Volatility Ratio; Sharpe Reward-to-Variability Ratio; Jensen's Performance Index; Decomposition of Excess Return: Fama's Approach, Measuring Performance Using the Arbitrage Pricing Theory; Measuring Performance Without the Use of an Asset Pricing Model; Application of Evaluation Techniques; Performance Measurement With Changing Portfolio Composition; Performance Attribution Procedures; Style Analysis; Morningstar's Risk-adjusted Rating (RaR); The M^2 Performance Measure; Bond Portfolio Performance Evaluation; Performance Evaluation When Options are Used; Incremental Risk-Adjusted Return (IRAR) From Options; Residual Option Spread (ROS); Review Problems; Questions; Problems; References.

$$\boxed{PART\ V}$$

$$\boxed{\textbf{DERIVATIVES: RISK MANAGEMENT}}$$

33. **Financial Derivatives Markets: A Global Perspective**   1005-1035

Introduction; Managing Derivative Risk; Types of Derivatives Risk; An Integrated Approach to Manage Derivative Risks: Systemic Risk; Market Risk; Credit Risk; Liquidity Risk; Cashflow Management Risk; Legal Risk; Operational Risk; Value- at-Risk (VaR) Analysis: Risk Aggregation; Value-at-Risk (VaR): A Bird's-Eye View; Recent Developments in Global Financial Derivative Markets; Derivatives Market in India; Derivative Trading Mechanism NSE-SPAN; Questions; References.

34. **Options**   1036-1085

Introduction; Option: The Concept; Uses of Options; Types of Options; Option

Valuation and Pricing: The Profit Potential of Puts and Calls, Fundamental Value; Factors Determining Option Price; Characteristics; Binomial Model; Black-Scholes Model; Delta; Theta; Gamma; Vega; Rho; Index Options; Portfolio Insurance; Put-call Parity Relationship; Review Problems; Questions; Problems; References.

35. Convertible Securities
1086-1120

Introduction; Convertible Debentures; Objectives of Convertible Debentures; Valuation of Convertible Debentures: The Convertible Debenture as Equity, Convertible Debenture's Value as an Hybrid Security; Implications of the Convertible Bond Issue for the Issuing Company; Convertible Preference Share; Selecting Convertibles; Future of the Convertible Securities; Review Problems; Questions; Problems; References.

36. Warrants
1121-1132

Introduction; Considerations for Shares Issued Through Warrants; Gearing Effect; Valuation of Warrant; Lapse of Warrants; Warrants Attached to Debenture; Similarities Between Options and Warrants; Review Problems; Questions; Problems; References.

37. Futures
1133-1160

Introduction; Futures Markets; Futures Contracts and Future Trading; Margin; Clearinghouse and Clearing Margins; Stock Index Futures; Hedging Using Index Futures: Naive Hedging Model, Stock Index Price Sensitivity Model, Market Timing; Speculating on Unsystematic Risk; Stock Index Futures Pricing: Carrying-Cost Model; Triple Witching Hour; Futures Versus Options; Synthetic Futures; Futures Versus Forward Markets; Risk Containment Measures for Index Futures in India; Strategies for Futures Markets; Review Problems; Questions; Problems; References.

38. Swaps
1161-1172

Introduction; Swaps—The Concept; Growth of the Swap Market; The Basic Swap Structures: The Interest Rate Swap, The Fixed Currency Swap, The Currency Coupon Swap, The Basis Rate Swap; How to Reduce Swap Risk?; Swaptions; Equity Caps and Floors; Review Problems; Questions; Problems; References.

39. Hedging
1173-1193

Introduction; The Objectives and Benefits of Hedging; Short Hedge and Long Hedge; Contract Choice; Margin Requirements and Marketing to Market; Cross Hedges and Changing Volatilities of an Asset Position; Strategies for Hedging; A Portfolio Hedge; An Asset-Liability Hedge; An Inventory Hedge; The Hedging Process; Review Problems; Questions; References.

40. Derivatives: Carry Trades and Speculative Dynamics
1194-1203

Introduction; Economic Derivatives; Motives for Trading Economic Announcement; Economic Derivatives as Indicators of Market Expectations; Carry Trade: A Speculative Investment Strategy; Measuring the Risk in Carry Trades; OTC Derivatives; Characteristics of OTC Derivatives and Implications for Post-Trade Processing; Questions; References.

41. Financial Derivatives Market in India   **1204-1233**

Introduction; Structure of Derivatives Market in India; The Regulatory Framework; Classification of Derivatives; Reasons for Derivative Transaction; Facilitating Institutions to Reduce Counterparty Risks; Impetus for Development Post-Global Financial Crisis; Developing Comprehensive Reporting Structure for OTC Forex and Interest Rate Derivatives; Consolidating the Reporting Arrangements of the OTC Derivatives; Financial Products Innovations in India: A Critique; Interest Rate Swap Market; Credit Default Swap; Interest Rate Futures; Market Segmentation; Questions.

42. Derivatives and Commodity Exchange   **1234-1264**

Introduction; Evolution and Functioning of Commodity Exchanges; Commodity Futures; Participants of Commodity Derivatives: Hedgers, Speculators, Arbitrage; Objectives of Commodity Futures; Benefits of Commodity Futures Markets; Difference Between Commodity and Financial Derivatives; Working of Commodity Market; Structure of the Commodity Futures Markets in India; Commodity Exchange In India; National Multi-Commodity Exchange of India Limited (NMCE), Multi-Commodity Exchange of India (MCX), National Commodity and Derivatives Exchange (NCDEX) Ltd., Indian Commodity Exchange Limited (ICEX); Turnover on Commodity Futures Markets; Recent Policy Developments; Constraints, Major Challenges and Policy Options of Commodity Futures; Convergence of Securities and Commodity Markets; Divergence, Apprehensions and Concerns; Questions; References.

PART VI

INTERNATIONAL FINANCIAL FLOWS

43. World Financial Markets   **1267-1289**

Introduction; Factors Leading to Financial Crisis; Government Support Measures: What has been done since September 2009?; Cautious Optimism on Gradual Recovery; Recovery in Advanced Economies; Basel III: Shaping the Regulatory Reform; A Case of Fragile Global Recovery; Reform Agenda; How Has India Been Hit By the Crisis?; How has India Responded to the Challenge?; Questions; References.

44. International Portfolio Investment   **1290-1313**

Introduction; Principles of International Portfolio Investment; The Benefits From International Portfolio Investment; Participation in Growth of Foreign Markets; Hedging of Consumption Basket; International Portfolio Diversification; Unique Risks of and Institutional Constraints for International Portfolio Investment; Channels for International Portfolio Investment; Direct Foreign Portfolio Investment; Indirect Foreign Portfolio Investment; Questions; References.

45. Modern Portfolio Theory-oriented Approach to   **1314-1334**
Assess the Riskiness of Foreign Claims and
Techniques of Portfolio Investment

Intorduction; Global Asset Allocation; How to Generate the Distribution of Portfolio Returns; Techniques of Portfolio Investment; Country Funds; American

Depository Receipts; Global Depository Receipts (GDRs); Indian Depository Receipts (IDRs); Questions; References.

46. Issues Posed by Foreign Portfolio Investment　　　　1335-1347

Introduction; Key Issues: Potential Size, Terms of Lending, Macroeconomic Destabilisation, Recipients of Capital Inflows, Financial Innovation; Portfolio Capital Flows: Hot or Cold?; Questions; References.

47. Foreign Portfolio Investment in India:　　　　1348-1360
Emerging Trends and Policy Developments

Introduction; New Economic Policy and Foreign Investment; Foreign Portfolio Investment: Trends in Portfolio Investment Flows; Initiatives to attract foreign investment and External Commercial Borrowings; Expansion of Qualified Foreign Investors Scheme; Initiatives to attract FII Investment; Liberalization in External Commercial Borrowings Policy during 2012-13; Questions; References.

48. Manias, Panics and Crashes: Switching　　　　1361-1380
Policies in Financial Crises

Introduction; Pyramids and Ponzi Schemes; Blind Faith and High Hopes; Aggressive Sales People; False Prophets; Speculative Bubbles; Tulipmania: The Legend; Stock Market Bubbles; The Great Crash; Oct.' 87 Stock Markets Crash and its Aftermath; The Scam; The Global Financial Crisis and Beyond; Questions; References.

49. Success in Investment　　　　1381-1409

Introduction; Characteristics of Success; Behavioural Aspects in Investment Financing; Established Behaviour; Mistaken Statistics; So, What's the Recipe For Success ?; Achieving Success in Financial Derivatives Markets; Achieving Success in Option Markets; Trading Rules in Options; Trading Secrets of the Professionals in Futures; Golden Rules for Success in Stock Markets; A Selected List of Proverbs of Stock Markets; Questions; References.

Index　　　　1410-1420

Part I

THE INVESTMENT ENVIRONMENT

1

Investment: Objectives and Risks

INTRODUCTION

Investment is the sacrifice of certain present value for the uncertain future reward. It entails arriving at numerous decisions such as type, mix, amount, timing, grade etc. of investment and disinvestment. Further, such decision-making has not only to be continuous but rational too. Broadly speaking, an investment decision is a trade off between risk and return. All investment choices are made at points of time in accordance with the personal investment ends and in contemplation of an uncertain future. Since investments in securities are revocable, investment ends are transient and investment environment is fluid, the reliable bases for reasoned expectations become more and more vague as one conceives of the distant future. Investors in securities will, therefore, from time to time, reappraise and reevaluate their various investment commitments in the light of new information, changed expectations and ends.

Investment choices or decisions are found to be the outcome of three different but related classes of factors. The first may be described *as factual or informational* premises. The factual premises of investment decisions are provided by many streams of data which taken together, represent to an investor the observable environment and general as well as particular features of the securities and firms in which he may invest. The second class of factors entering into investment decisions may be described as *expectational* premises. Expectations relating to the outcomes of alternative investments are subjective and hypothetical in any case but their foundations are necessarily provided by the environmental and financial facts available to investors. These limit not only the range of investments which may be undertaken but also the expectations of outcomes which may legitimately be entertained. The third and final class of factors may be described as *valuational* premises. For investors generally these comprise the structure of subjective preferences for the size and regularity of the income to be received from and for the safety and negotiability of specific investments or combinations of investments, as these are appraised from time to time.

In the formulation of a programme for the acquisition and management of investment, the first and most basic step is to understand the basic connotations of *investment*, *speculation and gambling* and to appreciate the fundamental differences between these terms.

INVESTMENT

"Investment" or "investing", like "value" is a word of many interpretations in business management, finance and economics relating to saring or deferring consumption. An investment operation is one which, upon thorough analysis promises safety of principal and an adequate return. There are basically three concepts of investment: (1)

3

economic investment - that is, an economist's definition of investment; (2) investment in a more general or extended sense, which is used by "the man on the street"; (3) the sense in which we are going to be very much interested, namely, financial investment. Let us briefly review these types of investments to get a feel of some of the characteristics they possess.

The term economic investment has a rather precise meaning in the literature of economic theory. Investment, as production over a period of time (per year), is not capital. The time dimension of investment makes it a flow. By contrast, capital is a stock, that is, an accumulation measurable at a point in time. Typically investment includes net additions to the capital stock of society. By 'capital stock of society' is meant those goods which are used in the production of other goods.[1] This is a gross, societal, or aggregate point of view. In society there are a number of goods (such as building and equipment) which are used to produce other goods, and that these means of production are considered part of the capital stock of society. For a number of reasons, economists also include inventories (that is, the goods produced and still in the manufacturer's hands) as part of that capital stock. Thus, a net addition to the capital stock - an investment - means an increase in buildings, equipments or inventories over the amount of equivalent goods that existed, say, one year ago at the same time.

Investment is ovten modeled as a function of Income and Interest rates, given by the relation $I = f(Y, r)$. An increase in income encourages higher investment, whereas a higher interest rate may discourage investment as it becomes more costly to borrow money. Even if a firm chooses to use its own funds in an investment, the interest rate represents an opportunity cost of investing those funds rather than lending out that amount of money for interest.

The everyday usage of the term investment can mean a variety of things, but to the man on the street it usually refers to a money commitment of some sort. For example, a commitment of money to buy a new car is certainly an "investment" from an individual's point of view. But these are so in very general and in very extended sense of the word since no rate of return is involved, nor is a financial return or capital growth expected.

Financial investment is a form of this general or extended sense of the term. It means an exchange of financial claims - stocks and bonds (collectively termed securities), real estate mortgages, etc. The term financial investment is often used by investors to differentiate between the pseudo-investment concept of the consumer and the real investment of the businessman. Semantics aside, there is still a difference between an "investment" in a ticket on a horse and the construction of a new plant; between the pawning of a watch and the planting of a field of corn. Some investments are simply transactions among people, others involve nature. The latter are "real" investments; the former are "financial" investments. The financial assets are expected to provide income or positive future cash flows, and may increase or decrease in value giving the investor capital gains or losses. Trades in contingent claims or derivative securities do not necessarily have future positive expected cash flows, and so are not considered assets, or strictly speaking,

---

1. Examples include tangibles (such as building a railroad or factory) and intangibles (such as a year of schooling or on-the-job training). In measures of national income and output, **gross investment** (represented by the variable I) is also a component of Gross domestic product (GDP), given in the formula $GDP = C + I + G + NX$, where C is consumption, G is government spending, and NX is net exports. Thus investment is everything that remains of production after consumption, government spending, and exports are subtracted. Both non-residential investment (such as factories) and residential investment (new houses) combine to make up I. **Net investment** deducts depreciation from gross investment. It is the value of the net increase in the capital stock per year.

securities or investments. Nevertheless, since their cash flows are closely related to (or derived from) those of specific securities, they are often studied as or treated as investments. Valuation is the method for assessing whether a potential investment is worth its price. Returns on investments will follow the risk-return spectrum.

Investments are often made indirectly through intermediaries, such as banks, mutual funds, pension funds, insurance companies, collective investment schemes, and investment clubs. Though their legal and procedural details differ, an intermediary generally makes an investment using money from many individuals, each of whom receives a claim on the intermediary.

Within personal finance, money used to purchase shares, put in a collective investment scheme or used to buy any asset where there is an element of capital risk is deemed an *investment*. Saving within personal finance refers to money put aside, normally on a regular basis. This distinction is important, as investment risk can cause a capital loss when an investment is sold, unlike saving(s) where the more limited risk is cash devaluing due to inflation.

In many instances the terms *saving* and *investment* are used interchangeably, which confuses this distinction. For example many deposit accounts are labeled as *investment accounts* by banks for marketing purposes. Whether an asset is a saving(s) or an investment depends on where the money is invested: if it is cash then it is savings, if its value can fluctuate then it is investment.

SPECULATION

Speculation is a financial action that does not promise safety of the initial investment along with the return on the principal sum. The art of speculating in one form or another has been around forever. When it comes to speculating, there are always three things that one can be sure of—there will be always people willing to speculate, there will always be people who will love to play the game with the first group. Lastly history can be counted on to repeat itself. Sure the object of speculation may change, the rules may change and the technology may change. But in the end it is always the same. However, what has happened before is 100% sure to happen again. Speculators can count on it. Everyone thinks always that they are so original when it always the same story again and again. Whether it is tulip bulbs, precious metals, mutual funds, lottery tickets or penny stocks human nature is human nature.

Ignorance, greed, fear and hope determine how people react and thus how prices move and markets behave. People have speculated on everything at one time or another. For the last hindered years and certainly into the foreseeable future speculating on stock prices offers liquidity combined with legitimacy and purpose. Stock speculation, trading[2] and investing have become an essential and vital parts of both our economy and our lives. The well known speculator Victor Niederhoffer, in "*The Speculator as Hero*"[3] describes the benefits of speculation:

> Let's consider some of the principles that explain the causes of shortages and surpluses and the role of speculators. When a harvest is too small to satisfy consumption at its normal rate, speculators come in, consumption so that the smaller supply will last longer. Producers

---

2. Trading is just another word for speculating and investing is nothing more than speculating, except that it supposedly encompasses a longer time horizon and for some odd reason implies less risk. Speculators speculate, trader's trade and investors invest to make money. Traders buy stock or any other object of speculation because they anticipate a price appreciation.

3. Victor Niederhoffer: *Daily Speculation*, the Well Street Journal, February 10, 1989.

encouraged by the high price further lessen the shortage by growing or importing to reduce the shortage. On the other side, when the price is higher than the speculators think the facts warrant, they sell. This reduces prices, encouraging consumption and exports and helping to reduce the surplus.

Another service provided by speculators to a market is that by risking their own capital in the hope of profit, they add liquidity to the market and make it easier for others to offset risk, including those who may be classified as hedgers and arbitrageurs.

If a certain market—for example, port bellies—had no speculators, then only producers (hog farmers) and consumers (butchers, etc.) would participate in that market. With fewer players in the market, there would be a larger spread between the current bid and ask price of pork bellies. Any new entrant in the market who wants to either buy or sell pork bellies would be forced to accept an illiquid market and market prices that have a large bid-ask spread or might even find it difficult to find a co-party to buy or sell to. A speculator (e.g. a pork dealer) may exploit the difference in the spread and, in competition with other speculators, reduce the spread, thus creating a more efficient market.

Auctions are a method of squeezing out speculators from a transaction, but they may have their own perverse effects; see winner's curse. The winner's curse is however not very significant to markets with high liquidity for both buyers and sellers, as the auction for selling the product and the auction for buying the product occur simultaneously, and the two prices are separated only by a relatively small spread. This mechanism prevents the winner's curse phenomenon from causing mispricing to any degree greater than the spread.

Speculation can also cause prices to deviate from their intrinsic value if speculators trade on misinformation, or if they are just plain wrong. For example, speculative purchasing can push prices above their true value (real value - adjusted for inflation) simply because the speculative purchasing artificially increases the demand. Speculative selling can also have the opposite effect, causing prices to artificially decrease below their true value in a similar fashion. In various situations, price rises due to speculative purchasing cause further speculative purchasing in the hope that the price will continue to rise. This creates a positive feedback loop in which prices rise dramatically above the underlying value or worth of the items. This is known as an economic bubble. Such a period of increasing speculative purchasing is typically followed by one of speculative selling in which the price falls significantly, in extreme cases this may lead to crashes.

It is a controversial point whether the presence of speculators increases or decreases the short-term volatility in a market. Their provision of capital and information may help stabilize prices closer to their true values. On the other hand, crowd behaviour and positive feedback loops in market participants may also increase volatility at times.

Investment and speculation are somewhat different and yet similar because speculation requires an investment and investments are at least somewhat speculative. Investment usually involves putting money into an asset which is not necessarily marketable in the short run in order to enjoy a series of returns the investment is expected to yield. On the other hand, speculation is usually a more short-run phenomenon. Speculators tend to buy assets with the expectation that a profit can be earned from a subsequent price change and sale. Accordingly, they buy marketable assets which they do not plan to own for very long.

Probably the best way to make a distinction between investment and speculation is by considering the role of expectations. Investments are usually made with the expectation that a certain stream of income or a certain price which has existed will not change in the future. Speculations, on the other hand, are usually based on the expectation that some change will occur. An expected change is a basis for speculation but not for an investment.[4]

Speculation involves a higher level of risk and a more uncertain expectation of returns but in many cases the investors are also in the same boat. The investor who thinks that the market fluctuations of his investments are not of interest to him because he is buying solely for income can very well be compared with the ostrich burying its head in the ground during danger and feeling himself secure.

The trained speculator takes action only when the probabilities are higher in his favour. Though the speculator should not swing with each fresh current but this does not imply inflexible behaviour on his part. When the evidence builds up unmistakeably against his view, he must be able to change it without becoming disorganized. His notions of prestige must not attach irrationality to his opinions. For the speculator, pride of opinion is the costliest luxury. In fact, the spleculator must have the courage to make decisions when the general atmosphere is one of panic, despair, or great optimism — and yet go against the current. The crowd is wildly bullish at tops and in a panic at bottom, and these emotions are highly contagious.

The truth of the matter is that everything we do in this world is a speculation, whether we regard it as such or not, and the man who comes out in the open and uses his judgement to forecast the probable course of events, and then acts on it, is the one who would reap the returns of his endeavour. This is a peculiar psychology that makes many investors avoid certain sound stocks or bonds because their broker speaks of "speculative possibilities". These investors judge safety by yield. If a security pays beyond certain percentage it is classed as "speculative", and is not for them.

What is the solution of the problem of investing primarily for income and yet relating the very important and useful quality of ready marketability without loss. It is best solved by never making an investment that does not appear after investigation, to be an equally good speculation. It follows that speculative investment may be undertaken with the expectation of success only by those specialists who are able, out of their knowledge and experience, to weigh carefully the possible outcomes. Further more, because of the great risk, what is expected by the spleculator is not that he will not make errors of judgement, but that his substantial resources and superior judgement, will permit him on balance to expect to maximize aggregate gains. Thus, at the expert level the late Bernard Baruch, from his experience wrote:

> Success in speculation requires as much specialised knowledge as success in law or
> medicine or any other profession, A skilled operation in any field requires an almost
> instinctive "feel" which enables him to sense many things without being able to explain

---

4. However, a strange situation emerges in this regard because, depending on the techniques used, such speculation may or may not be respectable. For example, if the technical approach to investing is used to anticipate prices (using past price movements), such a speculation has little respectability, because evidence indicates that one can not garner unusual returns for the level of risk assumed when he tries to forecast future prices based on past prices. A second aspect of speculate is anticipating share price investments based in the movement of the market as a whole. The level of overall economic activity is forecasted, and from that forecast the d direction of the market is inferred and the assets in the portfolio are adjusted assuming that portfolio returns will react systematically to changes in the returns on the market. This approach differs from technical analysis in that it is based on analysis of the overall economy rather than on share price movements and/ or price movements of the market. This is considerable difference both conceptually and operationally. Although both approaches hope to obtain unusual returns based on anticipations, the bases for such hope are different. A technical analyst tries to define the future based on past share prices and other technical market indicators, whereas the other anticipates the market based on economic indicators from which he infers what the market will do.

them .... After my first youthful reverses were behind me, I tried my finance never to go into any speculation over my depth - beyond my financial capacity to pay for any error of judgement........ No speculator can be right all the time. In fact, if a speculator is correct half of the time he is hitting a good average. Even being right three or four times out often should yield a person a fortune if he has the sense to cut his losses quickly on the ventures where he has been wrong.

Another point often raised is, *"can the man of limited means afford to speculate ?"* The reply to that question depends on what is inferred by the word 'speculate'. If one means to buy rapidly fluctuating stocks on margin in the hope of getting aboard the right one, the answer is emphatically "No". But if one's idea of speculation is the right one - that is, to buy sound stocks for cash after a careful study of factors apt to affect their future prices, it is certainly good policy. Indeed, no man ever become wealthy without speculating in something.

One interesting issue is the fact that bond rating agencies commonly use the term "speculative" when rating bonds. This issue presents the question: Is buying a junk bond speculation or investing? The answer, of course, depends on the definition of the terms and in this case its important to examine exactly what the ratings represent. Bonds rated lower than BBB by Standard & Poors (or Baa by Moody's) are frequently associated with the term "speculative" (or "junk").[5] With S&P, the term "speculative" refers specifically to the entities "capacity to pay interest and repay principal in accordance with the terms of the obligation." The rating is not meant to imply anything about the bond's price and makes no recommendation regarding its value and whether an investor should buy or sell the security at any given price.

There are any number of other scenarios that present similarly interesting questions.

i) Is an investor that buys a government bond in search of a short term gain (from dropping interest rates) investing or speculating? Government bonds (Treasury Bills, Bonds and Notes) are considered "risk-free" and certainly are not considered speculative securities by most. Yet these securities are used frequently to speculate on the direction of interest rates.

ii) Is an allocation to a venture capital transaction an investment or speculation? The majority of individual venture capital investments result in complete losses. However, venture funds typically yield higher returns than stocks because one or more of the funds' investments commonly yield many times the initial investment (thus more than making up for complete losses of other investments).

Taking the debate a step further, Fridson suggested viewing speculation in the context of "Modern Portfolio Theory."[6] Building on the work of Harry Markowitz, William Sharpe, and others, Fridson concluded that "The common thread between speculation and transactions that seem speculative, yet fail to satisfy all the established criteria, is that they are all bets against the consensus view." In offering a new definition of speculation, Fridson proposed the term "subdiversification" to describe all deviations from the market portfolio. A portfolio can consist of all asset classes or a single specific

5. The use of junk bonds increased dramatically in the 1980's and Michael Milken initially became famous by marketing the securities on an unprecedented scale (and earning hundreds of $ millions for himself in the process). Milken cited research by W. Braddock Hickman from 1958. The rationale for high yield bonds is that their higher yields more than compensate for their added risk. Therefore a strong argument can be made that junk bonds are better investments for some investors than other less risky bonds.

6. Martin Fridson, "Exactly What Do You Mean By Speculation?" Journal of Portfolio Management, Fall 1993.

asset class. Having introduced the new term, Fridson then offered his definition of speculation.

Subdiversification: Ownership of a mix of assets other than a fully diversified, market-weighted portfolio.

Speculation: Subdiversification with the intention of earning a superior risk-adjusted return.

Fridson was quick to point out that definitions can be dangerous and makes two points in attempting to prevent misunderstandings. *First*, there is no inherent contradiction in acknowledging that a deviation from the market portfolio in pursuit of capital gains is, by definition, speculation, while rejecting the claim that securities markets are perfectly efficient. At any given time, however, judging which securities are misvalued involves a certain amount of conjecture. "Speculation' is therefore a fair term for attempts to exploit pricing anomalies. Again, it should be regarded as a description, rather than a pejorative appellation. *Second*, a genuinely usable definition of speculation must take into account that many portfolio managers concentrate within subsets of the universe of assets.

There is no such thing as something for nothing. Those who come to the stock market with visions of easy money are apt to leave it sadder, if not wiser. We get out of things what we put into them, and brains and money used in an honest effort to secure reasonable income on profits in the stock market generally receive a just reward.

From a social stand point speculation must be differentiated from investment on different grounds. Directly, it is of no significance to society whether a given purchase (transfer of ownership of capital) is speculative or non-speculative. So far as the social capital fund is concerned, the same amount of capital is being employed all the time. Indirectly, there must be distinction, for there can be devastating repercussions of the resultant profits or losses. If social definition of a speculation is to be created it must apparently include the four functions of speculation as a process: (i) smoothening of the price fluctuation process; (ii) maintenance of temporary equilibrium between capital supply and demand; (iii) consideration of future business prospects in determining the business value of existing capital funds; and (iv) equating the risk to return in the infinitely varied utilisations of the social capital fund.

The several differences between speculation and investment which have the doubtful merits of public support, may be summarised as under :

Basis	Investment	Speculation
Type of contract	Creditor	Ownership
Basis of acquisition	Usually by outright purchase	Often-on-margin
Length of commitment	Comparatively long term	For a short time only
Source of income	Earnings of enterprise	Change in market price
Quantity of risk	Small	Large
Stability of income	Very stable	Uncertain and erratic
Psychological attitude of participants	Cautious and conservative	Daring and careless
Reasons for purchase	Scientific analysis of intrinsic worth	Hunches, tips "inside dope", etc.

From the foregoing discussion it follows that speculation needs no defence. Sometimes it may run riot and end in disaster, but that is due to its abuse. In fact, good investment management is difficult to distinguish at times from what appears to be speculative activity, and vice versa. However, it would be foolish to suppose from this that speculators are imbued with any idea that on them the responsibility rests of rectifying the injustice of a stagnant market. Their motives may be as selfish as those of any other businessmen, but the speculators of a market are there to act when opportunity arises and their presence is a benefit. The speculator who attempts to corner a market is menace. His aim is to create an artificial value; that in itself is bad.

But speculation when undertaken with a full sense of market responsibilities, of market reputation and of market traditions, falls into a distinctly different category. In fact, speculation may be a service and has its place in the scheme of economics, when the adjustment of prices in responding to the law of supply and demand may be so slow that we would constantly be in a state of "slack-water". In fact, there are days when buying in the market is in homeopathic doses; consumers will not give the lead lest prices should drop still further. When the professional speculators take a stand they buy in quantities that at once affect the market, and the timid consumer also comes in and fills his forward as well as his immediate requirements. Those who have delayed are ready to pay any reasonable advance on the last quotation. Every one is buoyant, everyone is happy again, the speculator has performed his good work, There are some who argue that it is all a matter of degree. If there were no speculators, then there would be nothing to make the consumer's purchase appear too insignificant to influence the market; that the speculator is a parasite whose buying dwarfs the legitimate trading to such an extent that nothing short of exaggerated buying will react on prices.

Let us accept a market without speculation, a market on miniature scale, one that by constant demand has reached prices that have stimulated production so that there is now a surplus offering. Of course, prices should recede, but what would really happen in that case is that the producers would combine to maintain the price. Competition, it is argued, is enough to check the evil of price agreements; but competition is only another of the blessings that can be abused, and it is kept in bounds by the righting arm of speculation. Some will concede all this, but argue that it only establishes the place of the speculator to come in at the two extremes of the statistical position, whereas he is known to be operating almost daily, at any rate much often than during extremes of a statistical position.

That is true, but the law of supply and demand is not the whole of marketing. Prices must fluctuate by variations of credit, and credit alters from moment to moment. The changes are mere fractional changes, and the professional operator is the medium through whom these niceties of the price are introduced. Speculator does not get excessive reward for his invaluable services. His only reward is derived from the differences on the amount he is prepared to risk. Of course, his real task is small. If he is dealing in some commodity the risk is that the price may go up or down contrary to his expectations. There is no chance of the value disappearing entirely or that it may rise without affording him an opportunity to cut his loss. Thus the remuneration is ample, but not excessive.

GAMBLING

Gambling dates back to antiquity. Most dictionaries refer to 'gamble' as an act involving an element of risk. In particular, a gamble involves taking on risk without demanding compensation in the form of increased expected return. Gamblers exhibit some or all of the following characteristics:

(i) Gambling is a typical, chronic and repetitive experience.
(ii) Gambling absorbs all other interests.
(iii) The gambler displays persistent optimism without winning.
(iv) The gambler never stops while winning.

(v) The gambler eventually risks more than he or she can afford.

(vi) The gambler seeks and enjoys a strange thrill from gambling, a combination of pleasure and pain.

The distinction between the conscious and unconscious motivations of the gambler is important. The gambler's conscious response to the question *"Why do you gamble?"* is usually *"Because I want to win money"* or *"the game gives me thrills and excitement"*. Further probing into the gambler's conscious motivation reveals this line of reasoning. The possibility of earning real money by normal work is greatly restricted, if not impossible. On the other hand, there are people who make fortunes through gambling. Why not try that way ?

Despite this rationalisation by gamblers, most psychiatrists believe the answer to compulsive gambling lies in the sub-conscious mind. Gamblers unconsciously want to Jose. This probably seems like a ridiculous desire. But in their own confused way, compulsive gamblers apparently transform pain into pleasure; *i.e.* they suffer from masochism.

INVESTMENT/ SPECULATION/ GAMBLING

People usually makes investments with a future end date in mind . The length of time from the date when investment is purchased to the final date can be called the investor's planning horizon ,investment horizon, or holding period. A financial asset purchased with a very short holding period in mind probably is not really an investment—it may be simply a gamble or a speculation.

A gamble is ususally a very short- term investment in a game of chance. The holding period for most gambles can be measured in seconds. That is, the result of so called investments are quickly resolved by the roll of the dice or the turn of a card. Such activities have planning horizons that are far too brief to do the research that should precede any investment activity.

Speculation typically lasts longer than gambles but are briefer than investments. A speculation usually involves the purchase of a salable assets in hopes of making a quick profit from an increase in the price of the asset which is expected to occur within a few weeks or months. Those involved in speculations are reluctant to refer to this activity as speculation because they dislike the connotations of the word; the prefer to refer to speculations as investment activities.

There is no precise dividing line with respect to the length of investment holding periods that could be used to separate gambles from speculations and speculations from investments. At its best, investment is well grounded and carefully planned speculation whereas it is an ostrich-like form of involuntary and unconscious speculation at its worst. There are no set rules for permanently establishing which securities are investment and which are speculations. Only constant examination and vigilance, against a background of knowledge, can enable us to decrease the risks which are inherent in all forms of ownership

Speculation is not the same as gambling and the two should never be confused. The difference between speculation *and* gambling is that in gambling artificial and unnecessary risks are created whereas in speculation the risks already exist and the question is simple who shall bear them. Gambling is a far cry from the carefully planned research and scientific procedure which underlies the best speculative practice. The gambler plays rumours, tips, hunches and other unreliable intuitions which should not play any but a negative role in the trained speculator's process. Speculation is a reasoned anticipation of future conditions. It does not rely upon hearsay or labels. It attempts to organise the relevant knowledge as a support for judgements. It is as legitimate and moral as any other form of risk-taking business activity.

In fact, the whole fabric of our society revolves around speculation. Those who write and speak most forcibly against speculation are usually guilty of failing to define their terms. Mere risk assumption is not gambling so long as the size of the risk is known, risk taking is speculating. Gambling has to do with acceptance of risks (1) for their own sake, (2) for the object of pecuniary gains, and (3) without knowledge of the exact nature of the risk. It may be truthfully said that by far the majority of men of the street who take a "flier" in the market are sheer gamblers.

The primary difference between speculation and gambling is "commensurate gain." They reason that "a gamble is the assumption of risk for no purpose but enjoyment of the risk itself, whereas speculation is undertaken in spite of the risk involved because one perceives a favorable risk-return trade-off. To turn a gamble into a speculative prospect requires an adequate risk premium for compensation to risk-averse investors for the risks that they bear. Hence *risk aversion and speculation are not inconsistent*.

It's like a crapshoot in Las Vegas, except in Las Vegas the odds are with the house. As for the market, the odds are with you, because on average over the long run, the market has paid off.[7]

Harry Markowitz certainly isn't the first to compare the stock market to gambling. Analogies and metaphors comparing investments with casino games and other games of chance are commonly used in stock markets. Humans of course, have a long history of engaging in and developing addictions for gambling. The earliest form of gambling may date back to 3500 BC when a kind of dice game called astragali was played. "Human beings have always been infatuated with gambling because it puts us head-to-head against the fates, with no holds barred. We enter this daunting battle because we are convinced that we have a powerful ally: Lady Luck will interpose herself between us and the fates (or the odds) to bring victory to our side."

At a time when casino's, lotteries, and sports betting are hugely popular, it's easy to understand why people might confuse speculation with investment.[8] Mega resort Casinos have sprouted in the Las Vegas desert (and all over the map) at an remarkable rate. Larger and more elaborate casinos pop-up one after the other. Perhaps experiences with lotteries can shed some additional light on humans' obsession with risk. Millions of people are willing to stand in lines for hours just to buy a one lottery ticket with worse than "one-in-a-million" odds. The odds of picking all six numbers in a 6/49 lottery are roughly one in fourteen million and the odds of winning the powerball lottery are roughly one in eighty million. For every one dollar lottery ticket purchased, 40 to 60 cents typically goes into the pot and is returned to ticket buyers. Lotteries are therefore negative-sum games because the total payout is less than what goes into the pot. It's not surprising that some have gone so far as to describe state lotteries as a "tax on stupid people."

On the other hand, as Richard Thaler points out in The Winner's Curse, "it is easy to rationalize the purchase of a lottery ticket by saying that for a dollar purchase, the customer is paying 50 cents for a fantasy. That's a pretty good deal."

---

7. Harry Markowitz commenting on the stock market in "Risk Management: Improving your Odds in the Crapshoot" from Bloomberg Personal (July 1996).

8. Lottery games date at least to biblical days. Israel was divided among seven tribes by lot. Christ's robe was given to a lottery winner so it would not have to be cut. The Sistine chapel and its paintings were supported by lotteries. The Italian lottery has been running continuously since 1530. Lotteries are played in over 100 countries.

Perhaps it is the fact that the stock market and other investments generally rise over the long term, that draws speculators to investment markets. As Markowitz points out, stocks in general are a positive-sum game since they rise in the long term. But, while an investor purchasing a stock has a positive expected return, his or her expected return *relative to the market* is zero (before costs). Because investors have the option of investing in index funds, the returns from a specific market (or asset class) and any individual security can be separated. This issue goes to the heart of the passive vs. active management decision.

Let's say an investor measures his performance against an index. If he chooses to overweight or underweight a stock relative to its composition in the index, is this an investment decision or is it speculation? Similar questions can be asked of other investors relative to their benchmarks . The answers of course, depend on definitions.

Regardless of how an investor defines the terms, its likely to be a worthwhile activity to estimate expected returns on both an absolute basis as well as relative to an appropriate benchmark. And if investors find themselves enjoying the activity of investing or if they find themselves addicted to the speed and excitement of the trading game, perhaps they should seriously consider whether they have crossed the line between investing and speculation, or worse yet, maybe they are really gambling with their money. Some of the famous quotes on investment/speculation/gambling are listed below in Box-1.

Box–1

QUOTES ON INVESTMENT/SPECULATE/GAMBLING

"The greatest advantage from gambling comes from not playing it at all."

Girolamo Cardano (Source: Against The Gods)

"A prospect that has a zero risk premium is called a fair game. Investors that are risk-averse reject investment portfolios that are fair games or worse."

Zvi Bodie, Alex Kane, and *Alan J. Marcus* in Investments

"The mathematical expectation of the speculator is zero."

Louis Bachelier in "The Theory of Speculation" (1900)

"It would seem the difference between investment and speculation is not very clear in the minds of most market participants. At market extremes - after prolonged bullish advances or bearish retreats - the confusion between investment and speculation appears to be universal. . . We have no idea what will happen to the market. . . What is certain, however, is that market participants need to be reminded of investment/speculation distinction; confusion over the concepts is as widespread as it has ever been."

"Speculation is an effort, probably unsuccessful, to turn a little money into a lot. Investment is an effort, which should be successful, to prevent a lot of money from becoming a little."

Fred Schwed Jr. in Where Are The Customer's Yachts?

"Games of chance must be distinguished from games in which skill makes a difference. The principles that work in roulette, dice, and slot machines are identical, but they explain only part of what is involved in poker, betting on the horses, and backgammon. With one group of games the outcome is determined by fate; with the other group, choice comes into play. The odds—the probability of winning—are all you need to know for betting in a game of chance, but you need far more information to predict who will win and who will lose when the outcome depends on skill as well as luck. There are cardplayers and racetrack bettors who are genuine professionals, but no one makes a successful profession out of Craps. Many observes consider the stock market itself little more than a gambling casino . . . Cards, coins, dice, and roulette wheels have no memory."

Peter Bernstein in Against the Gods

"Outright speculation is neither illegal, immoral, nor (for most people) fattening to the pocketbook . . . There is intelligent speculation as there is intelligent investing. But there are many ways in which speculation may be unintelligent. Of these the foremost are: (1) speculating when you think you are

investing; (2) speculating seriously instead of as a pastime, when you lack proper knowledge and skill for it; and (3) risking more money in speculation than you can afford to lose. . . everyone who buys a so-called "hot" common-stock issue, or makes a purchase in any way similar thereto, is either speculating or gambling. Speculation is always fascinating, and it can be a lot of fun while you are ahead of the game. If you want to try your luck, put aside a portion—the smaller the better—of your capital in a separate fund for this purpose. Never add more money to this account just because the market has gone up and profits are rolling in. (That's the time to think of taking money out of your speculative funds.) Never mingle your speculative and investment operations in the same account, nor in any part of your thinking.

Benjamin Graham in The Intelligent Investor

In the foregoing numerous academic definitions of investment speculation and gambling, it can be observed that most of them are framed around the following three differentiating factors:

1. *What is the motive of the buyer?* The investor presumably buys to procure an annual return under conditions of safety, whereas others buy for appreciation.
2. *What type of security is bought - high grade or low grade ?* The investor presumably buys high-grade securities, the others low-grade.
3. *How long is the security held?* The investor presumably holds for the long-term, the speculator for the short-term.

FEATURES OF AN INVESTMENT PROGRAMME

In choosing specific investments, investors will need definite ideas regarding features which their portfolios should possess. These features should be consistent with the investors' general objectives and, in addition, should afford them all the incidental conveniences and advantages which are possible under the circumstances. The following are the suggested features as the ingredients from which many successful investors compound their selection policies.

Safety of Principal

The safety sought in investment is not absolute or complete; it rather implies protection against loss under reasonably likely conditions or variations. It calls for careful review of economic and industry trends before deciding types and/or timing of investments. Thus, it recognizes that errors are unavoidable for which extensive diversification is suggested as an antidote.

Adequate diversification means assortment of investment commitments in different ways. Those who are not familiar with the aggressive-defensive approach nevertheless often carry out the theory of hedging against inflation-deflation. Diversification may be geographi-cal, wherever possible, because regional or local storms, floods, droughts, etc. can cause extensive real estate damage. Vertical and horizontal diversification can also be opted for the same. Vertical diversification occurs when securities of various companies engaged in different phases of production from raw material to finished goods are held in the portfolio. On the other hand, horizontal diversification is the holding by an investor in various companies all of which carry on activity in the same stage of production.

Another way to diversify securities is to classify them according to bonds and shares and reclassify according to types of bonds and types of shares. Again, they can also be classified according to the issuers, according to the dividend or interest income dates, according to the products which are made by the firms represented by the securities. But overdiversification is undesirable. By limiting investments to a few issues, the investor has an excellent opportunity to maintain a knowledge of the circumstances surrounding each issue. Probably the simplest and most effective diversification is accomplished by holding different media at the same time having reasonable concentration in each.

Adequate Liquidity and Collateral Value

An investment is a liquid asset if it can be converted into cash without delay at full market value in any quantity. For an investment to be liquid it must be (1) reversible or (2) marketable. The difference between reversibility and marketability is that reversibility is the process whereby the transaction is reversed or terminated while marketability involves the sale of the investment in the market for cash. To meet emergencies, every investor must have a sound portfolio to be sure of the additional funds which may be needed for the business opportunities. Whether money raising is to be done by sale or by borrowing it will be easier if the portfolio contains a planned proportion of high-grade and readily saleable investment.

Stability of Income

Stability of income must be looked at in different ways just as was security of principal. An investor must consider stability of monetary income and stability of purchasing power of income. However, emphasis upon income stability may not always be consistent with other investment principles. If monetary income stability is stressed, capital growth and diversification will be limited.

Capital Growth

Capital appreciation has today become an important principle. Recognising the con-nection between corporation and industry growth and very large capital appreciation, investors and their advisers constantly are seeking "growth stocks". It is exceedingly difficult to make a successful choice. The ideal "growth stock" is the right issue in the right industry, bought at the right time.

Tax Benefits

To plan an investment programme without regard to one's tax status may be costly to the investor. There are really two problems involved here, one concerned with the amount of income paid by the investment and the other with the burden of income taxes upon that income. When investors' incomes are small, they are anxious to have maximum cash returns on their investments, and are prone to take excessive risks. On the other hand, investors who are not pressed for cash income often find that income taxes deplete certain types of investment incomes less than others, thus affecting their choices.

Purchasing Power Stability

Since an investment nearly always involves the commitment of current funds with the objective of receiving greater amounts of future funds, the purchasing power of the future fund should be considered by the investor. For maintaining purchasing power stability, investors should carefully study (1) the degree of price level inflation they expect, (2) the possibilities of gain and loss in the investment available to them, and (3) the limitations imposed by personal and family considerations.

Concealability

To be safe from social disorders, government confiscation, or unacceptable levels of taxation, property must be concealable and leave no record of income received from its use or sale. Gold and precious stones have long been esteemed for these purposes because they combine high value with small bulk and are readily transferable.

RISKS OF INVESTMENT

The Webster's New Collegiate Dictionary definition of risk includes the following meanings: This conforms to the connotations put on the term by most investors. Professionals often speak of "downside risk" and "upside potential." The idea is straightforward enough: risk has to do with bad outcomes, potential with good ones.

In considering economic and political factors, investors commonly identify five kinds of hazards to which their investments are exposed. They are:

Business and Financial Risk

Business risk and financial risk are actually two separate types of risks, but since they are interrelated it would be wise to discuss them together. Business risk, which is sometimes called operating risk, is the risk associated with the normal day-to-day operations of the firm. Financial risk is created by the use of fixed cost securities (that is, debt and preference shares). Looking at the two categories in a sources and uses context, business risk represents the chance of loss and the variability of return created by a firm's uses of funds. Financial risk is the chance of loss and the variability of the owners' return created by a firm's sources of funds.

To clarify this important distinct between business and financial risk, let us examine the income statement contained in Exhibit. Earnings before interest and taxes can be viewed as the operating profit of the firm; that is, the profit of the firm before deducting financing changes and taxes.

EXHIBIT-I

XYZ CORPORATION LIMITED

INCOME AND EXPENDITURE STATEMENT FOR THE FINANCIAL YEAR ENDED
31st MARCH, 201X

(₹ in crores)

Income		
Sales	6052.70	
Other income	104.19	
		6156.89
Expenditure		
Consumption of materials and stores, power and fuel	3167.73	
Payment to and provision for employees	743.21	
Other operating expenses	386.68	
Excise Duty	772.35	
		5069.97
Earning Before Interest and Taxes (EBIT)		**1086.92**
Interest		163.08
Depreciation		145.04
Earnings Before Taxes		**778.80**
Provision for taxation		380.00
Earnings after Taxation		**398.80**
Preferred Dividend		0
Earnings available to equity holders		**398.80**
Number of equity shares (in crores)		40
Earnings per share		*₹ 9.97*

Business risk is concerned with earnings before interest and taxes and financial risk is concerned with earnings available to equity holders. The two components of business risk signify the chance that the firm will fail because of the inability of the assets of the firm to generate a sufficient level of earnings before interest and the variability of such earnings. The two components of financial risk reflect the chance that the firm will fail because of the inability to meet interest and/or principal payments on debt, and the variability of earnings available to equity holders caused by fixed financing changes (that is, interest expense and preferred dividends). Putting it in another way, this second component of financial risk is the extent to which earnings available to equity holders will vary at a greater rate than earnings before interest and taxes. In case the firm does not employ debt, there will be no financial risk.

An important aspect of financial risk is the interrelationship between financial risk and business risk. In effect, business risk is basic to the firm, but the firm's risk can be affected by the amount of debt financing used by the firm. Whatever be the amount of business risk associated with the firm, the firm's risk will be increased by the use of debt financing. As a result, it follows that the amount of debt financing used by the firm should be determined largely by the amount of business risk that the firm faces. If its business risk is low, then it can use more debt financing without fear of default, or a marked impact on the earnings available to the equity share holders. Conversely, if the firm faces a lot of business risk, then the use of a lot of debt financing may jeopardize the firm's future operations.

Purchasing Power Risk

Whenever investors desire to preserve their economic position over time, they utilise investment outlets whose values vary with the price level. They select investments whose market values change with consumer prices which compensates them for cost of living increase. If they do not, they will find that their total wealth has been diminished. Inflation is an economic crippler that destroys the economic power of investors over goods and services. In essence, investors have to be concerned with the command that their invested money has over goods and services on a continuing basis. In fact, we have been living with increasing consumer prices for many years.

The relation between the market rate earned r, the rate of price change $\Delta P/P$, and the investor's rate of change in real purchasing power X is shown in the equation (1):

$$X = \frac{1+r}{1+\Delta P/P} - 1.0 \qquad \qquad \text{...(1)}$$

X represents the percentage change in purchasing power resulting from an investment with a rate of return r. If the investor's rate of interest just equals the rate of inflation, $r = \Delta P/P$, then the investor's real rate of return is zero, X = 0. In a more typical situation, the investor's rate of return r might be 12 per cent while inflation $\Delta P/P$ is 6 per cent. In this case the investor's purchasing power is increasing at (1.12/1.06) - 1 = 5.66 per cent; this is the investor's real rate of return after allowing for inflation. Stock brokers sometimes tell their customers that equity shares are an inflation hedge which will more than protect them from purchasing power risk. This is a bit of overstatement. It is true that equity shares suffer less from purchasing power risk than fixed-income investments, but equity shares are only a hedge against inflation most of the time. It has not always yielded real increases in purchasing power during inflation.

Market Risk

This hazard arises from the fact that market prices and collateral values of securities and real property may vary substantially, even when their earning power does not change. The causes of these price uncertainties are varied. At times many markets are simply thin - that is, buyers and sellers appear only intermittently. More commonly, investment prices vary because investors vacillate in their preference for different forms of investment, or simply because they sometimes have money to invest and sometimes do not have it. But once the equity has developed a particular price pattern, it does not change this pattern quickly. The causes of changes in market price are usually beyond the control of the corporation. An unexpected war or the end of one, an election year, political activity, illness or death of a president, speculative activity in the market, the outflow of bullion - all are tremendous psychological factors in the market. The irrationality in the securities markets may cause losses unrelated to the basic risks discussed before. These losses are the result of changes in the general tenor of the market and are called market risks.

The market risk in equity shares is much greater than it is in bonds. Equity shares value and prices are related in some fashion to earnings. Current and prospective dividends, which are made possible by earnings, theoretically, should be capitalized at a rate that will provide yields to compensate for the basic risks. On the other hand, bond prices are closely related to changes in interest rates on new debt. Equity prices are affected primarily by financial risk considerations which, in turn, affect earnings and dividends. However, equity prices may be strongly influenced by mass psychology, by abrupt changes in financial sentiment and by waves of optimism or pessimism. Whenever emotions run high, speculators and gamblers crave action. They cannot refrain from entering the market arena as their greed for profits becomes their overpowering motivation. They do not hesitate to analyse the market environment. They do not base their judgements on an accurate evaluation of the underlying factors. Instead, they rush into the market and distort prices beyond any semblance of value. Greed pushes prices up, and fear drives them down. In short, the crux of the market risk is the likelihood of incurring capital losses from price changes engendered by a speculative psychology.

Interest Rate Risk

A major source of risk to the holders of high quality bonds is changes in interest rates, commonly referred to as interest rate risk. These high-quality bonds are not subjected to either substantial business risk or financial risk. Consequently, they are referred to as high-quality bonds. But since they are high-quality bonds, their prices are determined mainly by the prevailing level of interest rate in the market. As a result, if interest rates fall, the prices of these bonds will rise, and vice versa.

Interest rate risk affects all investors in high quality bonds regardless of whether the investors hold short-term or long-term bonds. Changes in interest rate have the greatest impact on the market price of long-term bonds, since the longer the period before the bond matures, the greater the effect of a change in interest rates. On the other hand, changes in interest rates will not have much of an impact on the market price of short-term bonds, but the interest income on a short-term bonds portfolio may fluctuate markedly from period to period, as interest rates change. Consequently, changes in interest rates affect investors in long-term as well as in short-term bonds.

Social or Regulatory Risk

The social or regulatory risk arises where an otherwise profitable investment is impaired as a result of adverse legislation, harsh regulatory climate, or in extreme instance nationalisation by a socialistic government: The profits of industrial companies may be reduced by price controls, and rent controls may largely destroy the value of rental property held for income or as a price-level hedge. The social risk is really political and thus unpredictable, but under a system of representative government based on increasing government intervention in business affairs, no industry can expect to remain exempt from it.

Other Risks

Other types of risk, particularly those associated with investment in foreign securities, are the monetary value risk and the political environment risk. The investor who buys foreign government bonds or securities of foreign corporations often in an attempt to gain a slightly higher yield than obtained on domestic issues, runs the calculated risk of (1) a change in the foreign government and repudiation of outstanding debt, (2) nationalisation of business, firms, that is, seizure by government, or (3) the desire but inability of the foreign government or corporation to handle its indebtedness. The investor should weigh carefully the possibility of the additional risks associated with foreign investments against his expected return, either in the form of interest or dividends or capital gains, when investing in foreign securities rather than domestic securities.

FINANCE VS. INVESTMENTS: INTERACTING DECISION ELEMENTS

Investment decisions and finance decisions interact with each other. Like the two blades of a pair of scissors, the investment (and savings) decision interacts with the finance (and spending) decision to cut the pie (called total income) into mutually satisfactory (optimal) proportions.

For many years finance and investment have encompassed the three major areas of spending in the aggregate economy as stated in equation (2):

$$GNP = C + 1 + G + F \qquad \qquad ...(2)$$

where

GNP = Gross national product (total spending in the nation).
 C = Spending by individuals for personal consumption.
 I = Gross private domestic investment by business firms.
 G = Governmental purchases.
 F = Net foreign spending.

One can study specific applications to (1) business or corporate finance and investments, (2) government (sometimes called public) finance and investments, (3) personal finance and investments. But, then, the two are different. Finance and investments traditionally have been viewed as separate and distinct disciplines.

Finance decisions have been concerned primarily with the sources of money. Three major questions must be answered. According to traditional views of finance, these are :

1. *How much money will be required ?*
2. *During what span of time will the money be needed ?*
3. *What is the cheapest source (or combination of sources) for obtaining the required sum of money ?*

Risk is included implicitly in all three parts of the finance decision. Investment decisions, on the other hand, traditionally have been concerned primarily with uses or budgeting of money instead of with locating the cheapest source of money. Elements of typical investment decisions are :

1. *How much total money to invest ?*
2. *What should be the allocation between current consumption (e.g., dividend payout) and re-investment (i.e., retained and reinvested earnings) ?*
3. *What is the optimal rate of total investment (i.e. what should be the rate of increase in*

capacity for production or earnings) ?
4. *What specific assets should be purchased ?*
5. *What proportion of the total money available should be invested in each particular asset?*
6. *How often to evaluate the performance of the portfolio of assets ?*

Thus, on the one hand, optimal investment decisions can be made only after the source, and therefore, the cost of financing has been determined. This is so because total profits can be calculated only if total costs (including cost of financing) are known. On the other hand, since the cost of financing depends upon the expected profit and risk of the project to be financed, total costs can be determined only after the investment decision has been made. Therefore, the two decisions finance and investments, together are required for a solution. Either one alone is insufficient for decision-making purposes. We may benefit and possibly gain additional insight into the difference (if any) between the two disciplines by looking at the complementary nature of jobs of the financial manager and investment manager.

A financial manager is nearly always a borrower of funds and seldom a lender; he is generally the seller of an equity interest in a business and is not often a purchaser. Since each financial asset is a bargain between the business financial manager and the investor, the study of investment management and analysis makes it necessary for the student to reverse his position. As business financial manager, the student has available to him all the information concerning the firm's operations. In contrast, the investor in his relationship with the business with which he is dealing is usually viewing financial transactions as an outsider. His dealings with the business are nearly always as a creditor or an absentee owner. Unless the investor has a substantial interest in the business, the management does not feel compelled to share all the information available.

The investor reinforces his bargaining position by analysing the investment opportunities offered to him by business financial managers. The power of selection or rejection forces the financial manager to offer only those opportunities that will meet their requirements of the mass of investors who make up market. The key to successful investing involves examination and analysis of three chronological segments of the business operation - past performance, present condition and future prospects.

QUESTIONS

1. Define the term 'investment' as it relates to securities investment.
2. "Investment is well grounded and carefully planned speculation".
   In the light of the above statement, explain and differentiate between 'investment' and 'speculation'. How do they differ from 'gambling'?
3. As an investment advisor what features would you suggest to be included in the investment bunch of a client ? Explain these features briefly.
4. "No investment is risk-free".
   In view of the above statement, write an essay on the meaning and types of investment-risk. Can this risk be eliminated or minimised?
5. State the points of similarity and difference between 'investment-decisions' and 'finance-decisions'. Can they go hand-in-hand?
6. Describe how the term risk is used to depict the behaviour of certain investments. Differentiate between low-risk and high -risk investments.
7. Define the term speculation and explain why individuals speculate.
8. Discuss the characteristics of investors , speculators, and gamblers. Explain the impact of each on the investment programme process.
9. "A fool and his money are quickly parted". Do you agree?

10. Discuss the features of an investment programme?
11. Why do individuals invest? What factors contribute to the rate of return that investors require on an investment?
12. Give an example of a liquid investment and an illiquid investment. Discuss why you consider cash of them to be liquid or illiquid?

REFERENCES

1. Bellemore, Phillips, and Ritchie. *Investments*. Cincinnati: South-western Publishing, 1979.
2. Chen, Nui-Fu, Richard Roll, and Stephen A. Ross. "Economic Forces and the Stock Market." *Journal of Business* 59, no. 3 (July 1986).
3. Cohen, J., E. Zinbarg, and A. Zeikel. *Investment Analysis and Portfolio Management*, Richard D Irwin, Home wood, IL, 1987.
4. D'ambrosio, Charles A. *Principles of Modern Investments*. Chicago: Science Research Associates.
5. Fisher, D.E., and R.J. Jordan. *Security Analysis and Portfolio Management*. Englewood Cliffs, N.J.: Prentice-Hall, 1979.
6. Fuller, Russell J. "Behavioral Finance and the Sources of Alpha", Journal of Pension Plan Investing,Winter,1998
7. Graham, B., D.L. Dodd, and S. Cottle. *Security Analysis*. New York: McGraw-Hill, 1962, part 3.
8. Graham, Benjamin. Intelligent Investor, Harper Collins Books, 1973.
9. Graham, Benjamin; and Dand Dodd. *Security Analysis*, McGraw-Hill Book Co., 1951.
10. Grodinsky, Julius. *Investments*. New York: Ronald Press, 1953.
11. Gunther, Max. The Zurich Axious, Souvenir Press, 1992.
12. Hamilton, William P. *The Stock Market Barometer*. New York: Richard Russell Associates, 1960.
13. Hayes D., and W. Bauman. *Investments: Analysis and Management*. New York: Macmillan, 1976,.
14. Kahneman, Daniel,and Amos Tversky. "The Psychology of Preferences,"Scientific American, Jan/June,1982
15. Levin, Laurence. "Are Assets Fungible? Testing Alternative Theories of Life –Cycle Savings", working paper,Santa Clara University,Santa Clara,CA.
16. Lishan, J.M., and D. T. Crary. eds. *The Investment Process*. International Textbook, 1970.
17. Mendelson and Robbins. *Investment Analysis & Securities Markets*. New York: Basic Books, 1976.
18. Moskowitz, Milton. "The 'Intelligent Investor' at 80," *New York Times*. May 5, 1974.
19. Nelson, S.A. *The ABC of Stock Speculation*. Wells, Vt.: Eraser Publishing, 1964.
20. Niederhoffer, Victor. *Practical Speculation*, Willey, 2005.
21. Noddings, Thomas C. *Advanced Investment Strategies*. Homewood, III.: Dow Jones-Irwin, 1978.
22. Robert,R. and N. Schwartz. "Effects of Perceptual Fluency on Judgement of Truth",Consciousness and Cognition 8(1999)
23. Sauvain, Harry C. *Investment Management*, 4th ed. Englewood Cliffs, N.J.: Prentice-Hall, 1973
24. Sharpe, William F., Gordon J. Alexander, and Jeffrey V. Bailey. *Investments*, 5th ed. Englewood Cliffs, N.J.: Prentice-Hall, 1995.
25. Smith, Adam. "The Money Game", Random House: New York,1976

26. Sobel, Robert. The Money Manias: The Erws of Great Speculation in America, 1770-1970, Beard Books, 2000.

27. Statman, Meir. "Behavioral Finance versus Standard Finance, "Behavioral Finance and Decision Theory in Investment Management (Charlottesville, VA: AIMR,1995)

28. Thaler, R. "Mental Acccounting and Consumer Choice,Marketing Science 4,(1995)

29. Tversky, Amos. "The Psychology of Decision Making," Behavioral Finance and Decision Theory in Investment Management (Charlottesville,VA:AIMR,1995)

30. Tversky, Amos. "The Psychology of Risk", Quantifying the Market Risk Premium Phenomenon for investment Decision Making, (Charlottesville, VA: AIMR,1995)

31. Tversky, Amos, and D.Kahneman. "Availability :A Heuristic for Judging Frequency and Probability", Cognitive Psychology 5 (1973)

32. Wood, Arnold S. "Behavioral Risk : Anecdotes and Disturbing Evidence", Investment WorldwideVI,AIMR

2

The Stock Markets in India

INTRODUCTION

Stock exchanges are intricately inter-woven in the fabric of a nation's economic life. Without a stock exchange, the saving of the community—the sinews of economic progress and productive efficiency — would remain underutilised. The task of mobilisation and allocation of savings could be attempted in the old days by a much less specialised institution than the stock exchange. But as business and industry expanded and the economy assumed more complex nature, the need for "permanent finance" arose. Entrepreneurs needed money for long term whereas investors demanded liquidity — the facility to convert their investments into cash at any given time. The answer was a ready market for investments and this was how the stock exchange came into being. Stock exchange means any body of individuals, whether incorporated or not, constituted for the purpose of regulating or controlling the business of buying, selling or dealing in securities. These securities include:

(i) shares, scrips, stocks, bonds, debentures stock or other marketable securities of a like nature in or of any incorporated company or other body corporate;

(ii) government securities; and

(iii) rights or interest in securities.

NATURE AND FUNCTION OF STOCK EXCHANGE

There is an extraordinary amount of ignorance and of prejudice born out of ignorance with regard to the nature and functions of stock exchange. As economic development proceeds, the scope for acquisition and ownership of capital by private individuals also grows. Alongwith it, the opportunity for stock exchange to render the service of stimulating private savings and channelling such savings into productive investment exists on a vastly great scale. These are services which the stock exchange alone can render efficiently. It is no exaggeration to say that in a modern industrialist society, which recognises the rights of private ownership of capital, stock exchanges are not simply a convenience, they are essential. In fact, they are the markets which exist to facilitate purchase and sale of securities of companies and the securities or bonds issued by the government in the course of its borrowing operation. As our country moves towards liberalisation, this tendency is certain to be strengthened. The task facing the stock exchanges is to devise the means to reach down to the masses, to draw the savings of the man in the street into productive investment, to create conditions in which many millions of little investors in cities, towns and villages will find it possible to make use of the facilities, which have so far been limited to the privileged few. This calls for far-reaching changes, institutional as well as operational.

The stock exchanges in India, thus, have an important role to play in the building of a real shareholders' democracy. Aim of the stock exchange authorities is to make it as nearly perfect in the social and ethical sense as it is in the economic. To protect the interests of the investing public, the authorities of the stock exchanges have been increasingly subjecting not only its members to a high degree of discipline, but also those who use its facilities -joint stock companies and other bodies in whose stocks and shares it deals. There are stringent regulations to ensure that directors of joint stock companies keep their shareholders fully informed of the affairs of the company. In fact, some of the conditions that the stock exchange imposes upon companies before their shares are listed are more rigorous and wholesome than the statutory provisions such as those contained in the Companies Act.

Apart from providing a market that mobilises and distributes the nation's savings, the stock exchange ensures that the flow of savings is utilised for the best purpose from the community's point of view. These markets are not simply a matter of many buyers and sellers. If the prices at which stocks and shares change hands are to be 'fair' prices, many important conditions must be satisfied. It is the whole vast company of investors, competing with one another as buyers and sellers, that decides what the level of security prices shall be. But the public is prone to sudden swings of hope and fear. If left entirely to itself, it would produce needlessly violent and often quite irrational fluctuations. The professional dealers inside the stock exchange, and those outside who depend upon them, absorb a large part of the stock of these movements. These are valuable activities. So as to ensure that the investors reap the full benefit of them, they (dealers as well as investors) need to be regulated by a recognised code of conduct. Fair prices and free markets require, above all things, clean dealings both by professionals and by the investors - and dealings based upon up- to-date and reliable information, easily accessible to all.

In case the investment markets are not active and free or adequate information were not available promptly and widely, the unscrupulous people would be able to manipulate particular prices for their own ends. In any of these contingencies, the relative values of securities would no longer be 'true' values, so that the relative yields obtainable from them would be mutually distorted. The signposts which, in a well regulated market, show the way along which savings ought to move, would point in the wrong directions. Good businesses would get less, and indifferent or bad businesses more finance than they deserved. The savings of the community would be misdirected and wasted. In addition, some investors would incur losses which they might otherwise have avoided, and others might reap profits which not otherwise could have been made.

Any such unfairness as between one investor and another is obviously undesirable. Not for a moment, however, should it be supposed that this is the most important evil that may flow from distortion of the security markets. Much more far reaching is the fact that any misdirection of savings forces the whole society to accept a lower standard of living than it could have enjoyed had its resources been rightly used.

Thus a free and active market in stock and shares has become a pre-requisite for the mobilisation and distribution of the nation's savings on the scale needed to support modern business. The stock exchange by a process of prolonged trial and error, which is by no means complete, has been continuously streamlining its structure to meet these wide and ever growing responsibilities to the public. The activities of the stock exchange are governed by a recognised code of conduct apart from statutory regulations. Investors, both actual and potential, are provided, through the daily stock exchange price quotations, with an up-to-the minute approval of the present worth of their holdings, in the light of all the influences that affect the position and prospectus of the companies in question. But the stock market does not determine the health of one company, it merely reflects it. It is thermometer, not the fever. The prices are sometimes distorted by excessive speculation but, by and large, they provide a continuous assessment of the current value of assets, not available to those who invest in houses or land or other assets, not traded on the stock exchange. In fact, whether the demand for a stock is motivated by income or profits, so long as it is related to a corporation, the prices of the securities markets will play a realistic part in determining the corporation's ability to raise funds. For those enterprises that must finance externally, the receptivity of the market to their offerings establishes both the volume and cost of capital raised. For those companies that finance the bulk of their requirements through reinvested earnings, the willingness of stock holders to defer dividends in the expectation of a higher return through capital gains, establishes both the volume and cost of the capital raised. If a company's outlook is very promising and buyers bid up the security's market value, new financing becomes easier whether through external or internal sources - the earnings price ratio is reduced, and the cost of capital becomes correspondingly low.

However, the capacity of a business to raise fresh capital for approved purposes by selling shares to the public, and the cost of capital to the borrower, do not depend simply or even mainly, upon the intrinsic merits of the business. They depend upon the public's estimate of the investment merits of its shares in comparison with those of other comparable securities. But these relative investment merits are measured very largely by the prices at which the new securities are offered and the comparable existing securities quoted in the market. More precisely, they are determined by the relative yields, actual or prospective, that can be obtained in interest or dividends on the capital sum that these market prices represent. The cost of a company of raising new capital is not the price at which the new shares are sold to investors, but the effective rate of interest that investors obtain by buying at that. The 'price' of new capital is the interest yield that has to be offered in order to secure it. Other things being equal, investors will readily accept a lower interest yield for a progressive and promising company than they will demand from a slow moving and inefficient one.

Sometimes, to secure the working capital from the banks, individual businessmen, partnerships and corporations provide the stocks and shares of companies as collateral. Securities which are listed and for which published quotations are readily available make the satisfactory collateral for such short-term loan taken by the industries to serve the purpose of working capital. Industries are therefore, particularly appreciative of the usefulness of collateral value of listed securities. In this respect the stock exchange indirectly helps the industries to secure working capital from the banks.

Expanded business needed permanent finance and could not expand without it. Investors needed 'liquidity' — the ability to turn their investment into cash at any time — and would not invest without it. It was this dilemma that brought the stock exchange into being. As business (and governments, too, for that matter) could not ordinarily return invested capital, an investor could not get cash for his investment unless he found somebody else who was ready to buy it from him — to take over his share in the company's 'Joint Stock', or his holdings of government securities. What was needed was a market for investments. The job of the stock exchange and its members is to satisfy that need — to bring the buyers and sellers of investments together, and to make the 'exchange' of stock between them as simple and fair a process as possible.

The tremendous important and socially useful service that the stock exchange renders to the industries is with regard to the shifting of the burden of financing from the management to those of the investors. It will be realised more so from the fact that there is always a conflict of motives between the industries and the investors, Industries require long-term finance with the end in view of locking it up in land, buildings, plants, etc. Investors, on the other hand, have liquidity preference, that is to say they want to get back the money as and when they would need it. In other words, while the industries require permanent finance, the investors can lend it only for a while because the money that they lend to the industries comes from their savings (part of the income not spent presently) which are made for future spending over contingencies. It is not merely the individual investors alone who suffer from the 'liquidity preference' complex, institutional investors too have the same motive.

It is generally thought that a stock exchange serves only those who have money to invest and securities to sell. But a stock benefits the whole community in a variety of ways. By enabling producers to raise capital, it indirectly gives employment to millions of people and helps consumers to get the goods needed by them. Again, all those who save and put their money either in banks or in life insurance, invest in buying shares and securities, are also helped by stock exchanges, because the institutions with which they place their savings avail themselves of the services of the exchanges to invest the money collected by them.

It is evident from the foregoing analysis that the ready liquidity and constant evaluation of assets, together with the wide range of available investments act as a powerful inducement to save and invest and draw the savings of the community into the channels which are expected to be most productive. It would be difficult to find a more effective method of doing this. In addition, the overall trend of prices and volume of business on the stock exchange serve as an economic barometer which faithfully registers the changing events and opinion about the investment outlook. Even allowing for the aberrations of speculation, this mirror of the investment scene is one that neither economists nor businessmen nor the government, charged with the formulation of economic policy, can afford to ignore.

ORGANISATIONAL STRUCTURE OF THE SECONDARY MARKET

The stock exchanges are the exclusive centres for trading of securities. At present, there are 23 operative stock exchanges in India. Most of the stock exchanges in the country are incorporated as 'Association of Persons' of Section 25 companies under the Companies Act. These are organised as 'mutuals' and are considered beneficial in terms of tax benefits and matters of compliance. The trading members, who provide brooking services also own, control and manage the stock exchanges. They elect their representatives to regulate the functioning of the exchange, including their own activities. Until recently, the area of operation/jurisdiction of an exchange was specified at the time of its recognition, which in effect precluded competition among the exchanges. These are called regional exchanges. In order to provide an opportunity to investors to invest/trade in the securities of local companies, it is mandatory for the companies, wishing to list their securities, to list on the regional stock exchange nearest to their registered office. If they so wish, they can seek listing on other exchanges as well. Monopoly of the exchanges within their allocated area, regional aspirations of the people and mandatory listing on the regional stock exchange resulted in multiplicity of exchanges. As a result, at the end of March 2008, there were 19 stock exchanges registered with SEBI having a total of 8,517 registered brokers and 43,874 registered sub-brokers trading on them.

The stock exchanges need to be recognized under the Securities Contracts (Regulation) Act, 1956. There are 19 stock exchanges in India. The Securities and Exchange Board of India (SEBI), has approved and notified the Corporatisation and Demutualisation Scheme of 19 Stock Exchanges. BSE has successfully completed the process of Demutualisation in terms of The BSE (Corporatisation and Demutualisation) Scheme, 2005 on May 16, 2007. NSE since inception has adopted a demutualised structure and its model of demutualization compares well with the international models of demutualised stock exchanges as seen from (Table 1).

TABLE 1

Comparison of the NSE Model and the International Models of Demutualised Stock Exchanges

Comparators	International Model	NSE Model
Legal Structure	Company	Company
For Profit / Not for Profit	For Profit Company	For Profit Company
Ownership Structure	Owned by Shareholders which includes brokers	Owned by Shareholders which are financial institutions which also have broking firms as subsidiaries.
Listing	Several stock exchanges are listed on themselves after Initial Public Offer.	Not a listed company. No Initial Public Offer made.
Ceilings on shareholding	Mostly 5% of voting rights for a single shareholder	No ceiling
Segregation of ownership, trading rights and management	These are segregated. To become a member of the demutualised stock exchange, it is not necessary to own a share in the company. Thus, members may or may not be shareholders and members who own shares may sell off their trading rights and all shareholders are not necessarily members.	These are segregated. The trading rights and ownership are segregated. The broking firms are not shareholders.
Board Structure	The Governing Board comprises of directors who are elected by shareholders. Some of the directors are brokers but majority do not have stock broking background.	The Board comprises of representatives of shareholders, academics, chartered accountant, legal experts etc. Of these, 3 directors are nominated by SEBI and 3 directors are public representatives approved by SEBI.
Fiscal benefits	As mutual entities, stock exchanges enjoyed fiscal benefits prior to demutualisation, but when converted into for profit companies these are taxed.	NSE was set up as a demutualised for profit company and is taxed. So the question of fiscal benefit prior to demutualisation does not arise.
Transfer of assets	Assets were transferred from the mutual entity to the for-profit demutualised company and shares were given to the members in lieu of the ownership in the old entity. There was no cash consideration paid. Since an Initial Public Offer (IPO) was also made in many cases, the valuation of the shares were done by the market and no separate valuation exercise was required as for example in the case of LSE where a bonus issue was made.	The question of transfer of assets did not arise because NSE was set up by the institutions as a demutualised company itself.
Enactment of legislation to give effect to demutualisation	In several countries a separate legislation was necessary as in the case of Australia, Hong Kong, Toronto and Singapore. In several others no legislation was necessary as in the case of UK.	Not applicable as NSE was set up as a demutualised company.

Source: Report of the SEBI Group on Corporatisation and Demutualisation of Stock Exchanges.

Membership

The trading platform of a stock exchange is accessible only to trading members. They play a significant role in the secondary market by bringing together the buyers and the sellers. The brokers give buy/sell orders either on their own account or on behalf of clients. As these buy and sell order matches, the trades are executed. The exchange can admit a broker as its member only on the basis of the terms specified in the Securities Contracts (Regulation) Act, 1956, the SEBI Act 1992, the rules, circulars, notifications, guidelines, and the byelaws, rules and regulations of the concerned exchange. No stock broker or sub-broker is allowed to buy, sell or deal in securities, unless he or she holds a certificate of registration from the SEBI.

Fees/Eligibility Criteria

The stock exchanges, however are free to stipulate stricter requirements than those stipulated by the SEBI. The minimum standards stipulated by NSE are in excess of those laid down by the SEBI. The admission of trading members is based on various criteria like capital adequacy, track record, education, and experience. With effect from July 1, 2008 a processing fee of ₹ 11,2367- and an admission fee of ₹ 5,61,8007- is charged for taking up new membership. The detailed eligibility criteria for trading membership in the CM, WDM, F&O and CD segment is presented in Table 2. This reflects a conscious decision of NSE to ensure quality broking services.

Corporatisation No of Brokers and Sub brokers

The authorities have been encouraging corporatisation of the broking industry. As a result, a number of brokers-proprietor firms and partnership firms have converted themselves into corporates. As of end March 2008, 4,190 brokers, accounting for nearly 44.1 7 % of total brokers have become corporate entities. Amongst those registered with NSE around 92.03 % of them were corporatised, followed by BSE with 81.08 % corporate brokers.

During 2007-08, 218 new brokers were registered with SEBI, whereas 174 were membership cases of reconciliation/cancellation/surrender.

As at end-March 2008, there were 44,074 sub-brokers registered with SEBI, as compared with 27,540 sub-brokers as at end of previous year. NSE and BSE together constituted 97.02% of the total sub-brokers.

TABLE 2
Eligibility Criteria for Trading Membership

Corporates

(Amount in ₹ lakh)

Particulars/ Segments	CM	CM and F&O	WDM	CM and WD,	CM, WDM and F&O
Minimum Paid-up capital	30	30	30	30	30
Net Worth WDM	100	100 (Membership in CM segment and Trading/ Trading and self-clearing membership in F&O segment) 300 (Membership in CM segment and Trading and Clearing membership in F&O segment)	200	200	200 (Membership in segment, CM segment and Trading/Trading and Self Clearing membership in F&O segment) 300 (Membership in WDM segment, CM segment and Trading and Clearing membership in F&O segment)
Interest Free Security Deposit (IFSD) with NSEIL	85	110	150	235	260
Interest Free Security Deposit (IFSD) with NSCCL	15	15*	NIL	15	15*
Collateral Security Deposit (CSD) with NSCCL	25	25**.	NIL	25	25**
Annual Subscription	1	1	1	2	2
Advance Minimum Transaction Charges for Futures Segment	NIL	1	NIL	NIL	1
Education	Two directors should be graduates. Dealers should also have passed SEBI approved certifi-	Two directors should be graduates. Dealers should also have passed SEBI approved certification test for Derivatives and	Two directors should be graduates. Dealers should also have passed FIMMDA -NSE Debt Market	Two directors should be graduates. Dealers should also have passed FIMMDA-NSE of Debt Market	Two directors should be graduates. Dealers should also have passed FIMMDA-NSE Debt Market (Basic Module) NCFM Capital Market

cation test for Capital Market Module of NCFM.	Capital Market Module of NCFM.	(Basic Module) of NCFM.	(Basic Module) of NCFM .& Capital Market Module of NCFM.	Module of NCFM.& SEBI approved certification test for Derivatives.
Experience	─────────Two year's experience in securities market───────			
Track Record	The Directors should not be defaulters on any stock exchange. They must not be debarred by SEBI for being associated with capital market as intermediaries They must be engaged solely in the business of securities and must not be engaged in any fund-based activity.			

Net worth requirement for Professional Clearing members in F&O segment is ₹300 lakhs. Further a Professional Clearing member needs to bring IFSD of 25 lakhs with NSCCL and Collateral Security Deposit (CSD) of 25 lakhs with NSCCL as deposits.

* *Additional IFSD of 25 lakhs with NSCCL is required for Trading and Clearing (TM-CM) and for Trading and Self clearing member (TM/SCM).*

** *Additional Collateral Security Deposit (CSD) of 25 laksh with NSCCL is required for Trading and Clearing (TM-CM) and for Trading and Self clearing member (TM/SCM).*

In addition, a member clearing for others is required to bring in IFSD of ₹2 lakh and CSD of ₹8 lakh per trading member he undertakes to clear in the F&O segment.

Requirements for Professional Clearing Membership

(All values in ₹lakh)

Particulars	CM Segment	F&O Segment	CM and F&O Segment
Eligibility	Trading Member of NSE/SEBI Registered Custodians/Recognised Banks		
Net Worth	300	300	300
Interest Free Security Deposit (IFSD) *	25	25	34
Collateral Security Deposit (CSD)	25	25	50
Annual Subscription	2.5	Nil	2.5

* *The Professional Clearing Member (PCM) is required to bring in IFSD of ₹2 lakh and CSD of ₹8 lakh per trading member whose trades he undertakes to clear in the F&O segment and IFSD of ₹6 lakh and CSD of ₹17.5 lakh (₹9 lakh and ₹25 lakh respectively for corporate Members) per trading member in the CM segment.*

Eligibility Criteria for Trading Membership-Individuals/Partnership Firms

(Amount in ₹ lakh)

Particulars/ Segments	CM	CM and F&O	WDM	CM and WD	CM,WDM and F&O
Net Worth	75	75 (Membership in CM segment and Trading membership in F&O segment) 100 (Membership in CM segment and Trading and Self clearing membership in the F&O segment) 300 (Membership in CM segment and Trading and Clearing membership in F&O segment)	200	200	200 (Membership in WDM segment, CM segment and Trading/ Trading and Self Clearing membership in F&O segment) 300(Membership in WDM segment,CM segment and Trading and clearing membership on F&O segment)
Interest Free Security Deposit (IFSD) with NSEIL	26.5	51.5	150	176.5	201.5
Interest Free Security Deposit (IFSD) with NSCCL	6	6*	NIL	6	6*
Collateral Security Deposit (CSD) with NSCCL	17.5	17.5 **	NIL	17.5	17.5 **
Annual Subscription	0.5	0.5	1	1.5	1.5
Advance Minimum Transaction Chareaes for Futures Segment	NIL	1	NIL	NIL	1

* *Additional IFSD of 25 lakhs with NSCCL is required for Trading and Clearing (TM-CM) and for Trading and Self clearing member (TM/SCM).*

** *Additional Collateral Security Deposit (CSD) of 25 lakh with NSCCL is required for Trading and Clearing (TM-CM) and for Trading and Self clearing member (TM/SCM).*

Currency Derivatives–Corporates, Individuals and Firms

(Amount in ₹ Lakh)

Particulars	NSE Members		NCDEX Members		New Applicants		
	Trading Members	Trading cum Clearing Membership	Trading Member-ship	Trading cum Members	Trading Clearing	Trading cum Member-ship	Professional Clearing Membership
Networth	100	1000	100	1000	100	1000	1000
Cash to NSEIL	10	10	12.5	15	15	20	–
Cash to NSCCL	–	25	–	25	–	25	25
Non cash to NSCCL	–	25	–	25	–	25	25

Clearing member pays ₹10 lakhs for clearing every trading member's trades in cash & non-cash form. In case the member is opting for membership of any other segment(s) in combination with the membership of Currency Derivatives segment, the applicable net worth will be the minimum net worth required for the other segment(s) or the minimum net worth required for Currency Derivatives Segment, whichever is higher.

REGULATORY FRAMEWORK

The four main legislations governing the securities market are: (a) the SEBI Act, 1992 which establishes SEBI to protect investors and develop and regulate securities market; (b) the Companies Act, 1956, which sets out the code of conduct for the corporate sector in relation to issue, allotment and transfer of securities, and disclosures to be made in public issues; (c) the Securities Contracts (Regulation) Act, 1956, which provides for regulation of transactions in securities through control over stock exchanges; and (d) the Depositories Act, 1996 which provides for electronic maintenance and transfer of ownership of demat securities.

Legislations

Capital Issues (Control) Act, 1947

The Act had its origin during the war in 1943 when the objective was to channelise resources to support the war effort. It was retained with some modifications as a means of controlling the raising of capital by companies and to ensure that national resources were channelled into proper lines, *i.e.*, for desirable purposes to serve goals and priorities of the government, and to protect the interests of investors. Under the Act, any firm wishing to issue securities had to obtain approval from the Central Government, which also determined the amount, type and price of the issue. As a part of the liberalisation process, the Act was repealed in 1992 paving way for market-determined allocation of resources.

Securities Contracts (Regulation) Act, 1956

It provides for direct and indirect control of virtually all aspects of securities trading and the running of stock exchanges and aims to prevent undesirable transactions in securities. It gives Central Government regulatory jurisdiction over (a) stock exchanges, through a process of recognition and continued supervision, (b) contracts in securities, and (c) listing of securities on stock exchanges. As a condition of recognition, a stock exchange complies with conditions prescribed by Central Government. Organised trading activity in securities takes place on a specified recognised stock exchange. The stock exchanges determine their own listing regulations, which have to conform with the minimum listing criteria set out in the Rules.

Companies Act, 1956

It deals with issue, allotment and transfer of securities and various aspects relating to company management. It provides for standards of disclosure in public issues of capital, particularly in the fields of company management and projects, information about other listed companies under the same management, and management perception of risk factors. It also regulates underwriting, the use of premium and discounts on issues, rights and bonus issues, payment of interest and dividends, supply of annual report and other information.

SEBI Act, 1992

The Securities and Exchange Board of India (SEBI) is the regulatory authority established under the SEBI Act 1992, in order to protect the interests of the investors in securities as well as promote the development of the capital market. It involves regulating the business in stock exchanges; supervising the working of stock brokers, share transfer agents, merchant bankers, underwriters, etc; as well as prohibiting unfair trade practices in the securities market.

Initially SEBI was a non statutory body without any statutory power. However in 1995, the SEBI was given additional statutory power by the Government of India through an amendment to the securities and Exchange Board of India Act 1992. In April, 1998 the SEBI was constituted as the regulator of capital market in India under a resolution of the Government of India.

Basic objectives of the Board were identified as: to protect the interests of investors in securities; to promote the development of Securities Market; to regulate the securities market; and, for matters connected therewith or incidental thereto.

Responsibilities: SEBI has to be responsive to the needs of three groups, which constitute the market: the issuers of securities the investors; and, the market intermediaries.

Role or functions of SEBI are: i) To protect the interests of investors through proper education and guidance as regards their investment in securities. For this, SEBI has made rules and regulation to be followed by the financial intermediaries such as brokers, etc. SEBI looks after the complaints received from investors for fair settlement. It also issues booklets for the guidance and protection of small investors. ii) To regulate and control the business on stock exchanges and other security markets. For this, SEBI keeps supervision on brokers. Registration of brokers and sub-brokers is made compulsory and they are expected to follow certain rules and regulations. Effective control is also maintained by SEBI on the working of stock exchanges. iii)To provide suitable training to intermediaries. iv) To register and regulate the working of mutual funds including UTI (Unit Trust of India). SEBI has made rules and regulations to be followed by mutual funds. The purpose is to maintain effective supervision on their operations & avoid their unfair and anti-investor activities. v) To promote self-regulatory organization of intermediaries. SEBI is given wide statutory powers. However, selfregulation is better than external regulation. Here, the function of SEBI is to encourage intermediaries to form their professional associations and control undesirable activities of their members. vi) To regulate and control the fraudulent & unfair practices which may harm the investors and healthy growth of capital market. vii) To issue guidelines to companies regarding capital issues. Separate guidelines are prepared for first public issue of new companies, for public issue by existing listed companies and for first public issue by existing private companies. SEBI is expected to conduct research and publish information useful to all market players (i.e. all buyers and sellers). viii) To conduct inspection, inquiries & audits of stock exchanges, intermediaries and self-regulating organizations and to take suitable remedial measures wherever necessary. This function is undertaken for orderly working of stock exchanges & intermediaries. ix) To restrict insider trading activity through suitable measures. This function is useful for avoiding undesirable activities of brokers and securities scams.

For the discharge of its functions efficiently, SEBI has been invested with the necessary powers which are : to approve by laws of stock exchanges; to require the stock exchange to amend their by laws; inspect the books of accounts and call for periodical returns from recognized stock exchanges; inspect the books of accounts of financial intermediaries; levy fees and other charges on the intermediaries for performing its functions; delegate powers exercisable by it; and, prosecute and judge directly the violation of certain provisions of the companies Act.

Depositories Act, 1996

The Depositories Act, 1996 provides for the establishment of depositories in securities with the objective of ensuring free transferability of securities with speed, accuracy and security by (a) making securities of public limited companies freely transferable subject to certain exceptions; (b) dematerialising the securities in the depository mode; and (c) providing for maintenance of ownership records in a book entry form. In order to streamline the settlement process, the Act envisages transfer of ownership of securities electronically by book entry without making the securities move from person to person. The Act has made the securities of all public limited companies freely transferable, restricting the company's right to use discretion in effecting the transfer of securities, and the transfer deed and other procedural requirements under the Companies Act have been dispensed with.

Prevention of Money Laundering Act, 2002

The primary objective of the Act is to prevent money-laundering and to provide for confiscation of property derived from or involved in money-laundering. The term money-laundering is defined as whoever acquires, owns, possess or transfers any proceeds of crime; or knowingly enters into any transaction which is related to proceeds of crime either directly or indirectly or conceals or aids in the concealment of the proceeds or gains of crime within India or outside India commits the offence of money-laundering. Besides providing punishment for the offence of money-laundering, the Act also provides other measures for prevention of Money Laundering. The Act also casts an obligation on the intermediaries, banking companies etc. to furnish information, of such prescribed transactions to the Financial Intelligence Unit-India, to appoint a principal officer, to maintain certain records etc.

STOCK MARKETS AND FINANCIAL DEVELOPMENT IN INDIA

The role of stock markets as a source of economic growth has been widely debated. It is well recognised that stock markets influence economic activity through the creation of liquidity. Liquid financial market was an important enabling factor behind most of the early innovations that characterised the early phases of the Industrial Revolution. Recent advances in this area reveal that stock markets remain an important conduit for enhancing development. Many profitable investments necessitate a long-term commitment of capital, but investors might be reluctant to relinquish control of their savings for long periods. Liquid equity markets make investments less risky and more attractive. At the same time, companies enjoy permanent access to capital raised through equity issues. By facilitating longer-term and more profitable investments, liquid markets improve the allocation of capital and enhance the prospects for long-term economic growth. Furthermore, by making investments relatively less risky, stock market liquidity can also lead to more savings and investments.

Over the years, the stock market in India has become strong. The number of stock exchanges increased from 8 in 1971 to 9 in 1980 to 21 in 1993 and further to 23 as at end-March 2000. The number of listed companies also moved up from 4739 in 2004-05 to 5151 in 2011-12. The market capitalisation at BSE as a percentage of GDP at current market prices also improved considerably from around 57.2 per cent in the in 2008-09 to over 91.6 per cent at the end of 2010-11. Though the Indian stock market was founded more than a century ago, it remained quite dormant with a capitalisation ratio (market capitalisation to GDP) touching to 106.3 in 2007-08. However, the patterns of demand for capital have undergone significant changes during the last two decades and improved stock market activity. It may be recalled that till the 'nineties, institutional term-lending acted as the primary source of Industrial finance in India. Financial Institutions raised money through Government-guaranteed bonds at low rates of interest, which, in turn, lent funds at concessional rates of interest. This system provided corporates a cushion to absorb the relatively high risk of Implementing new projects. This, in turn, discouraged the corporates to raise risk capital from equity markets. On this account, the debt market segment, which is sensitive to 'economic information' also remained underdeveloped and illiquid. With the onset of the reforms process in the 'nineties. Institutions had to raise resources at market related rates. At the same time, the market has witnessed the introduction of several new customised bonds at maturities tailored to suit Investor needs and with market-driven coupons. Along with this development, a number of measures were initiated to reform the stock markets, which helped to improve the overall activity in the stock market significantly.

The Indian capital market has experienced a significant structural transformation over the years. It now compares well with those in developed markets. This was deemed necessary because of the gradual opening of the economy and the need to promote transparency in alternative sources of financing. The regulatory and supervisory structure has been overhauled with most of the powers for regulating the capital market having been vested with the Securities and Exchange Board of India (SEBI). Apart from changes in the fundamental factors, information asymmetries and the associated constraints to efficient price discovery remain at the heart of the volatile movements in stock prices. The extent of stock price volatility is also influenced by the extent of integration between the domestic and international capital markets as well as the regulatory framework governing the stock market. In India, two most important factors which had a significant bearing on the behaviour of stock prices since 'nineties are the net investments by FIIs and trends in the international stock exchanges. Asset price bubbles entail significant risks in the form of higher inflation when the bubble grows in size and in the form of financial instability and lost output when the bubble bursts. Monetary and fiscal authorities, therefore, closely watch the asset market developments. The positive wealth effect resulting from bull runs could impart a first round of risk to inflation. If the bull run is prolonged, a second round of pressure on prices may result from subsequent upward wage revisions. Since financial assets are used as collaterals, asset booms may also give rise to large credit expansion. When domestic supply fails to respond to the rising demand, it could give rise to higher external current account deficit. The asset price cycles may follow. When the asset prices collapse, firms may face severe financing constraints as a result of declining value of their collaterals, making lenders reluctant to lend at a scale they do when asset prices are rising. Recognising these alternative complexities emanating from asset market bubbles, information on asset prices is being increasingly used as a critical input for the conduct of public policies.

Exchanges in the country offer screen based trading system. There were 9,487 trading members registered with SEBI as at end March 2008. Over the period, the market capitalization has grown indicating more companies using the trading platform of the stock exchange. The All-India market capitalization was around ₹ 64,003 billion in 2011-12. The trading volumes on stock exchanges have been witnessing phenomenal growth over the past years. However, the trading volume declined both in BSE and on NSE during 2010-11 due to global financial market uncertainties. The CMIE Overall Share Price Index (COSPI) rose by 1.7 per cent in December 2012. The market capitalisation of the index scaled a 20-month high of ₹ 68. 6 lakh crore during the month.

On 13 December 2012, market regulator SEBI announced a set of pre-trade risk controls to be imple-mented by stock exchanges. It placed quantitative limits on individual orders to prevent errors from leading to a disruption of trading on exchanges. Henceforth, any order with value exceeding ₹ 10 crore per order will not be accepted by stock exchanges in the normal market. Further, it asked stock exchanges to ensure that appropriate checks for value and quantity are imple-mented by stock brokers based on the respective risk profile of their clients.

SEBI also asked stock exchanges to ensure that stock brokers put in place a mechanism to limit the cumulative value of all unexecuted orders placed from their terminals to below a threshold limit set by the stock brokers. Stock exchanges shall ensure that such limits are effective.

The market regulator tightened the dynamic price bands (commonly known as dummy filters or operating range) for stocks on which derivative products are available. Stock exchanges shall now set the dynamic price bands at ten per cent of the previous closing price for stocks on which derivatives products are available, stocks included in indices on which derivatives products are available, index futures and stock futures. However, exchanges may revise these dynamic price bands in increments of five per cent in case of a market trend in either direction.

TABLE 3
COSPI and Key Secondary Market Indicators

	No. of Cos COSPI	Mkt. Cap of COSPI Cos (Rs.crore)	P/E of COSPI Cos (Times)	Returns on COSPI (%)	Volati-lity (%)	Liqui-dity (Times)	Returns on Equally Wtd. COSPI (%)	Mkt cap. all listed Cos. (Rs.crore)	No. of listed Cos.
Dec 2011	2,423	53,11,81,268	16.61	-5.80	1.27	0.63	-7.89	55,09,646	5,142
Jan 2012	2,382	60,23,31,295	18.96	13.60	1.04	0.55	17.54	62,24,777	5,145
Feb 2012	2,557	63,27,06,116	19.89	4.95	1.20	0.53	3.85	65,24,129	5,145
Mar 2012	2,533	62,01,51,347	19.49	-2.16	1.22	0.55	-5.03	64,00,306	5,151
Apr 2012	2,419	61,54,43,444	1912	-0.68	0.80	0.54	3.29	63,57,705	5,150
May 2012	2,331	57,69,62,116	16.57	-5.93	0.83	0.57	-5.64	59,79,034	5,154
Jun 2012	2,348	61,07,59,753	17.57	6.07	0.92	0.53	3.88	63,12,281	5,151
Jul 2012	2,385	60,35,10,428	17.45	-1.05	0.78	0.54	-0.44	62,37,679	5,160
Aug 2012	2,403	60,32,45,777	19.48	-0.02	0.49	0.53	-1.93	62,29,909	5,164
Sep2012	2,434	65,23,83,764	21.04	8.15	0.69	0.49	9.04	67,24,724	5,165
Oct 2012	2,519	64,36,76,525	20.16	-1.42	0.65	0.51	0.44	6635,758	5,166
Nov 2012	2,447	66,98,11,602	18.84	4.15	0.61	0.49	3.27	69,06,264	5,172
Dec 2012	2,535	68,59,84,943	19.26	1.69	0.53	0.49	2.19	70,77,089	5,180

Source: Monthly Review of Indian Economy, CMIE, January, 2013.

SEBI also mandated the exchanges to ensure that brokers are put in the risk-reduction mode when 90 per cent of the stock brokers collateral available for adjustment against margins gets utilised on account of trades that fall under a margin system. Under the risk-reduction mode, all unexecuted orders will be cancelled once the stock broker reaches 90 per cent collateral utilisation level. The broker will be moved back to the normal risk management mode as and when the collateral of the broker is lower than 90 per cent utilisation level.

OVER THE COUNTER EXCHANGE OF INDIA (OTCEI)

Securities markets in developed countries are multi-tiered with an element of in-built competition amongst various layers. This prevents monopolisation of securities exchange and makes the markets more efficient. In India, however, the situation has been altogether different because of the virtual monopoly enjoyed by stock exchanges till recently. The multi-tier securities exchange model was adopted in our country in October 1990 with the establishment of the Over the Counter Exchange of India (OTCEI). The object of the OTCEI "is to provide an alternate market for the securities of smaller companies, public-sector companies, closely-held companies desirous of listing, etc. It has been promoted jointly by UTI, ICICI, IDBI, SBI Capital Markets Ltd., IFCI, GIC and Canbank Financial Services Ltd. The Government has conferred it the status of a 'recognised stock exchange' under Sec. 4 of the Securities Contracts Regulation Act. Consequently, companies listed with OTCEI will practically be at par with companies listed on any stock exchange in the country.

The OTCEI is *floor-less exchange* where all the activities are computerised be it trading, billing, payments, etc. OTC designated dealers operate through their computer terminals which are hooked to a central computer. All quotes and transactions are recorded and processed here. The dealers are spread over the country and have access to the central computer. Besides, PTI OTC scan is available to each dealer which displays the best bids and offers of the market makers in respect of each scrip. A transaction can be effected by entering the bid or offer in a dealer's computer counter. The exact transaction price alongwith other details is also displayed in the counter computer.

The trading documents of OTCEI include : (a) Counter Receipt (CR) which is handed over to the buyer when a deal is made. It is a tradeable document and hence must be preserved carefully. It is akin to a share certificate so far as its contents are concerned; (b) Sale Confirmation Slip (SCS) which is passed on to the seller when a deal is made. The seller also must preserve it carefully since he gets the payment against this slip later on.

Trading at OTCEI will be permitted only in respect of the securities of the listed companies. Listing may be obtained by (i) Companies with issued equity capital between ₹ 30 lacs to 25 crores; (ii) Closely held companies interested in listing; (iii) Venture capital companies; (iv) Companies which are not listed on any other recognised stock exchange provided: (a) they offer to the public at least 40% of the issued equity or ₹ 20 lacs, whichever is higher, where the issued equity ranges between ₹ 30 lacs to less than ₹ 300 lacs (i.e. 3 crores), (b) they offer to the public at least 60% of the issued equity where issued equity is between 3 crores to 25 crores of rupees, (c) they offer at least 25% of the issued equity to the public in case of a venture capital company, (d) where the issued equity ranges between 3 crores to 25 crores of rupees, the norms for listing on a recognised stock exchange must be satisfied, (e) the company is not carrying on the business of investment, leasing, finance, hire-purchase or amusement parks.

OTCEI promoters have been designated as 'sponsor members' and they alone are entitled to sponsor a company for listing here. Before recommending a company for enlistment, such members have to carry out the appraisal of the project to ensure its technological and financial viability. They also ensure that all government rules and regulations have been complied with. They are required to clarify the investment worthiness of the company and its project. Finally, they would value the shares of the company, comply with SEBI guidelines for the issue of securities and manage the public issue. OTCEI requires such sponsor members to act as 'market makers' in that scrip for at least 3 years and also to appoint an additional market maker for that scrip for a period of at least one year.

NATIONAL STOCK EXCHANGE OF INDIA

National Stock Exchange was set up in April 1993 with the objectives of (a) establishing a nationwide trading facility for all types of securities, (b) ensuring equal access to all investors all over the country through an appropriate communication network, (c) providing a fair, efficient and transparent securities market using electronic trading system, (d) enabling shorter settlement cycles and book entry settlements and (e) meeting the international benchmarks and standards. Within a short span of time, above objectives have been realized and the Exchange has played a leading role as a change agent in transforming the Indian Capital Markets to its present form.

NSE has set up infrastructure that serves as a role model for the securities industry in terms of trading systems, clearing and settlement practices and procedures. The standards set by NSE in terms of market practices, products, technology and service standards have become industry benchmarks and are being replicated by other market participants. It provides screen-based automated trading system with a high degree of transparency and equal access to investors irrespective of geographical location. The high level of information dissemination through on-line system has helped in integrating retail investors on a nation-wide basis. The Exchange currently operates four market segments, namely Capital Market Segment, Wholesale Debt Market Segment, Futures an Options segment and the Currency Derivatives Segment.

NSE has been playing the role of a catalytic agent in reforming the market in terms of microstructure and market practices. Right from its inception, the exchange has adopted the purest form of demutualised set up whereby the ownership, management and trading rights are in the hands of three different sets of people. This has completely eliminated any conflict of interest and helped NSE to aggressively pursue policies and practices within a public interest framework. It has helped in shifting the trading platform from the trading hall in the premises of the exchange to the computer terminals at the premises of the trading members located country-wide and subsequently to the personal computers in the homes of investors. Settlement risks have been eliminated with NSE's innovative endeavors in the area of clearing and settlement viz., reduction of settlement cycle, professionalisation of the trading members, fine-tuned risk management system, dematerialisation and electronic transfer of securities and establishment of clearing corporation. As a consequence, the market today uses the state-of-art information technology to provide an efficient and transparent trading, clearing and settlement mechanism.

NSE provides a trading platform for of all types of securities-equity and debt, corporate government and derivatives. On its recognition as a stock exchange under the Securities Contracts (Regulation) Act, 1956 in April 1993, it commenced operations in the Wholesale Debt Market (WDM) segment in June 1994, in the Capital Market (CM) segment in November 1994, in Futures & Options (F&O) segment in June 2000 and in Currency Derivative Segment (CDS) in August 2008. The Exchange started providing trading in retail debt of Government Securities in January 2003. During the year 2007-08, it accounted for over 90 % of total trading value (debt, derivatives and equity) in the stock exchanges and 69% in equities and more than 98% in derivatives.

The *Wholesale Debt Market* segment provides the trading platform for trading of a wide range of debt securities. Its product, which is now disseminated jointly with FIMMDA, the FIMMDA NSE MIBID/MIBOR is used as a benchmark rate for majority of deals struck for Interest Rate Swaps, Forwards Rate Agreements, Floating Rate Debentures and Term Deposits in the country. Its 'Zero Coupon Yield Curve' as well as NSE-VaR for Fixed Income Securities have also become very popular for valuation of sovereign securities across all maturities irrespective of its liquidity and facilitated the pricing of corporate papers and GOI Bond Index.

NSEs *Capital Market* segment offers a fully automated screen based trading system, known as the National Exchange for Automated Trading (NEAT) system, which operates on a strict price/time priority. It enables members from across the country to trade simultaneously with enormous ease and efficiency.

NSEs *Futures & Options* segment provides trading of a wide range of derivatives like Index Futures, Index Options, Stock Options and Stock Futures.

NSEs *Currency Derivatives* segment provides trading on currency futures contracts on the USD-INR which commenced on August 29, 2008.

Technology and Application Systems in NSE

Technology has been the backbone of the Exchange. Providing the services to the investing community and the market participants using technology at the cheapest possible cost has been its main thrust. NSE chose to harness technology in creating a new market design. It believes that technology provides the necessary impetus for the organisation to retain its competitive edge and ensure timeliness and satisfaction in customer service. In recognition of the fact that technology will continue to redefine the shape of the securities industry, NSE stresses on innovation and sustained investment in technology to remain ahead of competition. NSE is the first exchange in the world to use satellite communication technology for trading. It uses satellite communication technology to energize participation from about 2,956 VSATs from nearly 245 cities spread all over the country.

Its trading system, called National Exchange for Automated Trading (NEAT), is a state of-the-art client server based application. At the server end all trading information is stored in an in-memory database to achieve minimum response time and maximum system availability for users. It has uptime record of 99.7%. For all trades entered into NEAT system, there is uniform response time of less than 1.5 seconds. NSE has been continuously undertaking capacity enhancement measures so as to effectively meet the requirements of increased users and associated trading loads. NSE has also put in place NIBIS (NSEs Internet Based Information System) for on-line real-time dissemination of trading information over the Internet.

As part of its business continuity plan, NSE has established a disaster back-up site at Chennai along with its entire infrastructure, including the satellite earth station and the high-speed optical fibre link with its main site at Mumbai. This site at Chennai is a replica of the production environment at Mumbai. The transaction data is backed up on near real time basis from the main site to the disaster back-up site through the 2 mbps high-speed link to keep both the sites all the time synchronised with each other.

The various application systems that NSE uses for its trading as well clearing and settlement and other operations form the backbone of the Exchange. The application systems used for the day-to-day functioning of the Exchange can be divided into (a) Front end applications and (b) Back office applications.

In the front office, there are 6 applications:

(i) NEAT - CM system takes care of trading of securities in the Capital Market segment that includes equities, debentures/notes as well as retail Gilts. The NEAT - CM application has a split architecture wherein the split is on the securities and users. The application runs on two Stratus systems with Open Strata Link (OSL). The application has been benchmarked to support 15,000 users and handle more than 3 million trades daily. This application also provides data feed for processing to some other systems like Index, OPMS through TCP/IP. This is a direct interface with the trading members of the CM segment of the Exchange for entering the orders into the main system. There is a two way communication between the NSE main system and the front end terminal of the trading member.

(ii) NEAT - WDM system takes care of trading of securities in the Wholesale Debt Market (WDM) segment that includes Gilts, Corporate Bonds, CPs, T-Bills, etc. This is a direct interface with the trading members of the WDM segment of the Exchange for entering the orders/trades into the main system. There is a two way communication between the NSE main system and the front end terminal of the trading member.

(iii) NEAT - F&O system takes care of trading of securities in the Futures and Options (F&O) segment that includes Futures on Index as well as individual stocks and Options on Index as well as individual stocks. This is a direct interface with the trading members of the F&O segment of the Exchange for entering the orders into the main system. There is a two way communication between the NSE main system and the front end terminal of the trading member.

(iv) NEAT - IPO system is an interface to help the initial public offering of companies which are issuing the stocks to raise capital from the market. This is a direct interface with the trading members of the CM segment who are registered for undertaking order entry on behalf of their clients for IPOs. NSE uses the NEAT IPO system that allows bidding in several issues concurrently. There is a two way communication between the NSE main system and the front end terminal of the trading member.

(v) NEAT- MF system is an interface with the trading members of the CM segment for order collection of designated Mutual Funds units

(vi) NEAT - CD system is trading system for currency derivatives. Currently currency futures are trading in the segment.

The exchange also provides a facility to its members to use their own front end software through the CTCL (computer to computer link) facility. The member can either develop his own software or use products developed by CTCL vendors.

In the back office, the following important application systems are operative:

(i) NCSS (Nationwide Clearing and Settlement System) is the clearing and settlement system of the NSCCL for the trades executed in the CM segment of the Exchange. The system has 3 important interfaces - OLTL (Online Trade loading) that takes each and every trade executed on real time basis and allocates the same to the clearing members, Depository Interface that connects the depositories for settlement of securities and Clearing Bank Interface that connects the 13 clearing banks for settlement of funds. It also interfaces with the clearing members for all required reports. Through collateral management system it keeps an account of all available collaterals on behalf of all trading/clearing members and integrates the same with the position monitoring of the trading/clearing members. The system also generates base capital adequacy reports.

(ii) *FOCASS* is the clearing and settlement system of the NSCCL for the trades executed in the F&O segment of the Exchange. It interfaces with the clearing members for all required reports. Through collateral management system it keeps an account of all available collaterals on behalf of all trading/clearing members and integrates the same with the position monitoring of the trading/clearing members. The system also generates base capital adequacy reports.

(iii) *CDCSS* is the clearing and settlement system for trades executed in the currency derivative segment. Through collateral management system it keep an account of all available collateral on behalf of all trading / clearing members and integrates the same with the position monitoring of the trading/cleaning members. The System also generate base capital adequacy report.

(iv) *Surveillance system* offers the users a facility to comprehensively monitor the trading activity and analyse the trade data online and offline.

(v) *OPMS*-the online position monitoring system that keeps track of all trades executed fora trading member vis-a-vis its capital adequacy.

(vi) *PRISM* is the parallel risk management system for F&O trades using Standard Portfolio Analysis (SPAN). It is a system for comprehensive monitoring and load balancing of an array of parallel processors that provides complete fault tolerance. It provides real time information on initial margin value, mark to market profit or loss, collateral amounts, contract-wise latest prices, contract-wise open interest and limits. The system also tracks online real time client level portfolio base upfront margining and monitoring.

(vii) *PRISM-CD* is the risk management system of the currency derivatives segment. It is similar in features to the PRISM of F&O segment.

(viii) *Data warehousing* that is the central repository of all data in CM as well as F&O segment of the Exchange.

(ix) *Listing system* that captures the data from the companies which are listed in the Exchange for corporate governance and integrates the same to the trading system for necessary broadcasts for data dissemination process and

(x) *Membership system* that keeps track of all required details of the Trading Members of the Exchange.

The exchange operates and manages a nationwide network. This network of over 2000 VSATs and 3000 Leased Lines is being migrated from X.25 to IP from 2008 onwards and is expected to complete by early 2009. In the new IP network, members have an advantage of a more generic and latest IP protocol and an overall better design, in terms of bandwidth and resilience. Currently the network has over 2000 VSATs, 1500 Leased Lines and 9 POPs (Point of Presence) across the country.

NOW

NSE is also offering internet based trading services to NSE members. This facility is branded as NOW 'NEAT on Web'. NOW provides an internet portal for NSE members and their authorized clients to transact orders and trades to the various market of NSE viz. CM, F&O and Currency. The members can also access NOW through their existing VSAT/Leased line, in addition to internet links. The various features provided by NOW are:

(a) Comprehensive Administration features
(b) Flexible Risk Management System
(c) High speed dealer terminals
(d) Online trading facility for investors

DEVELOPMENTS IN THE SECONDARY CAPITAL MARKET

The stock market development is often usefully measured in terms of three ratios, viz., the *market capitalisation ratio*, the *total value traded ratio*, and the *turnover ratio*. The market capitalisation ratio, which is measured as market capitalisation divided by GDP indicates the size of the market. Liquidity is measured by two ratios, viz., total value traded ratio and turnover ratio. The total value traded ratio is measured as total value traded divided by GDP. The total value traded ratio complements the market capitalisation ratio in that the market capitalisation may be high without there being much trading. The turnover ratio is measured by the value of total shares traded divided by market capitalisation. Whereas the traded value ratio captures trading in relation to the size of the economy, the turnover ratio captures trading in relation to the size of the stock market.

The domestic stock markets, which remained generally firm up to early January 2008, witnessed a sharp correction beginning January 11, 2008. Liquidity support from foreign institutional investors (FIIs), strong macroeconomic fundamentals, healthy corporate earrings, upward trend in emerging market economies (EMEs) equity markets and other sector and stock specific news helped to boost the market sentiment during April-December 2007. Although the domestic stock markets during this period witnessed corrections in mid-August, mid-October and mid-December 2007, they again recovered to reach new high. Reflecting this, the BSE Sensex reached an all-time high of 20873.33 on January 8, 2008.

Beginning January 11, 2008, the domestic stock markets witnessed severe bouts of volatility due to heightened concerns over the severity of sub-prime lending crises in the US and its spill-over to other market segments and in other countries. Fears of recession in the US economy on account of contraction in the US service industry, weak earnings growth reported by some of the leading US companies, home foreclosures climbing to record high levels and lacklustre retail sales in the US also impacted the sentiment. Liquidity squeeze from the secondary market in the wake of the IPO issuances, heavy sales by FIIs in the Indian equity market, hike in short-term capital gains tax from 10 per cent to 15 per cent announced in the Union Budget 2008-09, increase in domestic inflation rate, rise in global crude oil prices to record highs and decline in ADR prices in the US markets were some of the other factors that adversely affected the market sentiment. Between end-March 2007 and March 31, 2008, the BSE Sensex moved in a wide range of 12455.37-20873.33. The BSE Sensex and the S&P CNX Nifty, closed at 15644.44 and 4734.50, respectively, on March 31, 2008 registering gains of 19.7 per cent and 23.9 per cent, respectively, over end-March 2007. The BSE sensex was 16698.04 on April 23, 2008. FIIs invested ₹ 52,574 crore (US $ 12.7 billion) in the Indian stock markets during 2007-08 as compared with net purchases of ₹ 26,031 crore (US $ 5.7 billion) during 2006-07. Between April 1, 2007 and January 8, 2008, FIIs invested ₹ 66,898 crore (US $ 16.3 billion) in the Indian stock markets. However, FIIs made net sales of ₹ 14,324 crore (US $ 3.6 billion) between January 9, 2008 and March 31, 2008. Mutual funds made net investments of ₹ 15,775 crore during 2007-08 as compared with net investments of ₹ 9,062 crore during 2006-07.

The domestic stock markets after remaining weak and volatile during January-February 2009, witnessed gains during March 2009. The losses during the first two months of 2009 were mainly due to the downward trend in international equity markets on account of more than expected contraction of economic growth in the US, the UK, Japan and China pointing towards deepening of recession. Other factors that led to weak equity markets were heavy net sales by FIIs in the Indian equity market, slowdown in industrial and export growth, depreciation of the rupee against the US dollar, fall in ADR prices, lower than expected corporate earnings in the third quarter of 2008-09, revelations about financial irregularities in a particular information technology company and other sector and stock specific news.

In line with the behaviour of equity markets across the world, the Indian stock markets have been showing improvement since March 2009. The reasons for the improvement are announcement of the details of US$ 1 trillion public private investment program by the US Treasury, some major US banks posting profits for the first two months of 2009, extension of the deadline for buy back of foreign currency convertible bonds (FCCBs) by the Reserve Bank to December 31, 2009, domestic consumer durable and capital goods output increasing by 2.5 per cent and 15.4 per cent, respectively, in January 2009, lower domestic inflation rate, strengthening of the rupee against the US dollar and net purchases by FIIs and mutual funds in domestic equity market. The BSE Sensex and the S&P CNX Nifty closed at 9709 and 3021 at end-March 2009 registering losses of 37.9 per cent and 36.2 per cent, respectively, over end-March 2008.

Indian equity markets witnessed a revival in the secondary market segment, which had recorded a sharp decline in the wake of the global financial crisis during the later half of 2008. The secondary market staged a handsome recovery in 2009 following stimulus measures implemented by the Government and resurgence of foreign portfolio flows displaying renewed interest by foreign investors. The subdued global commodity prices in the beginning of 2009 also lifted the sentiments in the Indian capital market. Furthermore, election results announced in May 2009 removed uncertainty on economic policies and as such boosted Indian equity markets and both benchmark and sectoral indices rallied. The equity markets gained further till September 2009 on positive cues from the global markets, before declining during October 2009. Market sentiments improved during November-December 2009, leading to gains in equity prices and an uptrend in equity market indices.

Amongst the National Stock Exchange (NSE) indices, both Nifty and Nifty Junior recorded positive annual equity returns (current year-end index divided by previous year-end index multiplied by 100) of 75.8 per cent and 128.6 per cent in 2009 as against negative annual equity returns of 51.8 per cent and 63.5 per cent respectively during the calendar year 2008.

In terms of month-to-month movement, the NSE S&P CNX Nifty index showed improvements during March-May, July-September and November–December 2009. The S&P CNX Nifty index moved up from its previous year's closing level of 2,959 to 5,201 on December 31, 2009, recording an increase of 75.8 per cent over the year. Nifty junior was on an uptrend in terms of month-end values from March to December 2009, except a marginal decline in its value in end-October 2009. The rise in the Nifty Junior index, on a point-to-point basis, was 128.6 per cent in end-December 2009. The movement in the BSE Sensex and BSE 500 indices was more or less in the same direction as in the case of Nifty indices during the year 2009.

During 2009, the Asian stock markets were on a recovery path. The cumulative change in global indices in end-December 2010 over the end-December 2003 level revealed a significant rise in these indices across countries. As on 31 December 2010, Indian benchmark indices, the BSE Sensex and Nifty, increased by 17.0 per cent and 17.9 per cent respectively over the closing value of 2009-10. Nifty Junior and BSE 500 also increased by 17.8 per cent and 15.1 per cent respectively over their values in the previous financial year. The free float market capitalization of Nifty, the Sensex, Nifty Junior, and BSE 500 stood at ₹ 18,27,097 crore, ₹ 16,32,236 crore, ₹ 3,37,573 crore, and ₹ 29,52,135 crore respectively, showing an increase of 19.8 per cent, 22.8 per cent, 15.5 per cent and 20.8 per cent respectively over their values in financial year 2009-10.

The price to earnings (P/E) ratios of Nifty, the Sensex, Nifty Junior, and BSE 500 as on 31 December 2010 were 24.5, 23.6, 17.6 and 21.4 respectively, indicating an increase of 10.1 per cent, 10.5 per cent, 11.6 per cent and 4.5 per cent respectively over their 2009-10 values. In the capital market segment, the total turnover of the BSE stood at ₹ 8,93,839 crore and of the NSE at ₹ 27,87,862 crore as on 31 December 2010 as compared to ₹ 13,78,809 crore and ₹ 41,38,024 crore respectively in 2009-10. In the equity derivative segment, the NSE witnessed a total turnover of ₹ 2,05,99,192 crore as on 31 December 2010 as compared to ₹ 1,76,63,665 crore during 2009-10. Similarly, the total turnover in the equity derivative segment of BSE stood at ₹ 35 crore in 2010-11 (so far) as compared to ₹ 234 crore during 2009-10.

The year 2010 has been one of strong growth for the Indian capital markets . Bulls tossed off the markets in the year 2010 to a net gain of 18 per cent, following global recovery and with FIIs pumping money in to the market on account of solid domestic growth coupled with a resurging corporate sector. Indices achieved record highs during the special one-hour *muhurut* trading on 5 November 2010 with the Sensex touching 21004.96 and Nifty 6312.45. As on 31 December 2010, the markets stand just 3 per cent away from this alltime peak and closed at 20509.09 (+ 17.43 per cent from 31 December 2009 for the Sensex-) and 6134.5 (+ 17.95 per cent for Nifty).

Indian markets have been making gains for eight quarters in a row, their longest winning run in at least 20 years. While 2009 was basically a year of recovery from the crisis year of 2008, 2010 was one of consolidation of gains. From 9647 on 31st Dec 2008, the Sensex climbed to ₹ 17464.81 on 31 December 2009 and further consolidated its rally at 20509.09 on 31 December 2010. The total market capitalization as on 31 December 2010 stands at ₹ 72,96,725 crore compared to ₹ 60,81,308 crore as on 31 December, 2009.

In terms of month-on- month movement, indices witnessed a consolidation phase till September 2010. While individual stocks saw many ups and downs, the indices were mostly range bound. The maximum monthly gains were recorded in September when the Sensex and Nifty made 11.67 per cent and 11.62 per cent respectively against the closing price in August. Compared globally, while the Jakarta Composite in Indonesia gained the most among indices with about 45 per cent rise, US' Dow Jones and UK's FTSE 100 have each risen by around 11 per cent and 9 per cent respectively. NASDAQ composite Index was up 16.91 per centwhile S&P rose by 13 per cent. However, Japan's Nikkei 225 and China's Shanghai Composite dipped 3 per cent and 14 per cent respectively during the year, reflecting the rising yen and monetary tightening in the respective countries.

Stock prices continued the bullish trend during July-September 2010 on the back of strong FII investments in equities. India, along with other EMEs experienced strong portfolio inflows as interest rate differential between these countries and advanced economies turned more lucrative. Strong macroeconomic fundamentals in the Indian markets, buoyancy in the industrial and services sector as also possibility of further increase in rural demand on expected better performance of the agricultural sector were some of the pull factors responsible for the FII inflows. As at end-September 2010, the Sensex and the Nifty both registered gains of 14.5 per cent and 14.9 per cent, respectively, over end- March 2010.

In 2011, taking cues from the global turmoil, Indian financial market segments that have a high degree of cross-border linkages turned volatile, while the other segments without strong linkages remained orderly. As a result, increased volatility was evidenced in the equity market since September 2011. Hence, in line with the global markets, the Indian equity prices continued their declining trend in Q2 of 2011-12. The rise in equity indices at the beginning of Q2 due to FII inflows could not sustain the momentum owing to global developments and net sales by FIIs ensued. The two key Indian equity indices, Sensex and Nifty, declined (y-o-y) by about 14.5 per cent and 14.7 per cent, respectively, as on October 19, 2011. Nonetheless. the decline in Indian equity markets was relatively less than that in many emerging and developing economies (EDEs). P-E ratio of Indian equities remained higher than other EDEs as at end September 2011.

Fll investment declined during Q2 of 2011-12. Flls made net sales in the equity segment while making net purchases in the debt segment. Mutual funds (MFs) made net purchases in both equity and debt segments. The turnover in equity derivatrves segmet increased substantially over the year. FII investments in equity derivatives increased significantly during Q2 as compared to the previous quarter.

On 31 December 2011, Indian benchmark indices, BSE Sensex and Nifty, decreased by 20.4 per cent and 20.7 per cent respectively over the closing value of 2010-11. Nifty Junior and BSE 500 also decreased by 22.6 per cent and 26.1 per cent respectively during the same period. The free float market capitalization of Nifty, Sensex, Nifty Junior, and BSE 500 stood at ₹ 14,05,066 crore, ₹ 12,66,639 crore, ₹ 2,47,531 crore, and ₹ 21,66,947 crore respectively in 2011-12 (upto 31 December 2011), indicating a decrease of 20.0 per cent, 18.6 per cent, 21.8 per cent, and 22.0 per cent, respectively over 2010-11.

The P/E ratios of Nifty, Sensex, Nifty Junior, and BSE 500 as on 31 December 2011 were 16.8, 16.4, 13.5, and 16.2 respectively, indicating a decrease of 24.2 per cent, 23.4 per cent, 22.4 per cent, and 15.9 per cent respectively over 2010-11. In the capital market segment, during 2011-12 (up to 31 December 2011), the total turnover of the BSE stood at ₹ 4,88,133 crore and of the NSE at ₹ 19,73,730 crore as compared to ₹ 11,05,027 crore and ₹ 35,77,410 crore respectively in 2010-11.

At the end of December 2011, there were 1,767 registered FIIs as compared to 1,722 on 31 March 2011. The number of registered sub-accounts also increased to 6,278 from 5,686 during the same period. In the Indian equity market, FIIs withdrew ₹ 213 crore during 2011-12 (April-December) compared to ₹ 110,121 crore investment in 2010-11. During the same period they invested ₹ 30,590 crore in the debt segment as compared to ₹ 36,317 crore in 2010-11. During 2011-12, (up to 31 December 2011), total investment in equity and debt by FIIs stood at ₹ 30,376 crore as compared to ₹ 146,438 crore in 2010-11.

Among selected Asian Indices, the Jakarta Composite Index posted a maximum cumulative return of 419.5 per cent in 2011-12 (April-December) over 2003-04 followed by the BSE Sensex Index (176.4 per cent), S&P CNX Nifty Index (161.0 per cent), Kospi Index (107.4 per cent), Kuala Lumpur Comp Index (69.7 per cent), Hang Seng Index (45.4 per cent), SSE Composite Index (26.3 per cent), and TSEC weighted Index (8.4 per cent).

As on 30 December 2011, the markets stood 26 per cent down from the all-time peak achieved during the special one-hour muhurut trading on 5 November 2010 when the Sensex had touched 21004.96 and Nifty 6312.45. The indices closed at 15454.92 (-24.64 per cent for the Sensex) and 4624.3 (-24.62 per cent for Nifty) in the calendar year. During financial year 2011-12 (up to 30 December 2011), the decline stood at 20.73 per cent in case of Nifty and 20.52 per cent for the Sensex.

Subdued FII inflows into the country led to a decline in Indian markets and contributed to the sharp depreciation of the rupee in the forex market, though much of the depreciation was due to 'flight to safety' by foreign investors, given the troubled European and inflation-hit emerging market economies. Moderation in the growth rate of the economy has also affected market sentiments. This moderation in growth is on account of several factors, including the uncertainty in the global environment and lag effect of monetary policy tightening. Monetary tightening in India has led to some correction in stock markets, just as it happened in other emerging market economies as their central banks tightened their grips.

Globally, the deepening European debt crisis and a historic downgrade of the US by S&P triggered fears of another recession. The euro zone imbroglio kept the global markets fluctuating throughout the year. Unless the crisis in Europe is settled, volatility in global markets including India will tend to persist. However, the Indian economy has been less affected as compared to other major indices in the world. Further, the resilience of Indian markets is evident from the ratings given by some of the investment banks and financial firms.

Secondary equity markets improved with reform measures and FI inflows in third quarter of 2012. Up to October 25, 2012, the Indlan equity market witnessed gains on a y-o-y basis. At a level of 18,758, the BSE Sensex is 8.7 per cent higher than it was at the same time last year. Market sentiments, turned positive due to improved global liquidity conditions, FII inflows and the recent policy measures announced by the government. However, governance issues and mixed Q2 results of some major companies pared some of the gains recorded eariler. During 2012-13 so far (up to October 23, 2012), Flls made net investments of about 497 billion in the Indian equity market.

As on January 24, 2013, the domestic equity markets witnessed a y-o-y gain of 17.2 per cent with a 6.2 per cent gain over end- September 2012. Following the global equity market rally driven by a spate of generally better international economic data and policy actions, the Indian bourses also picked up. The BSE Sensex and S&P CNX Nifty crossed the 20,000 and 6,000 mark, respectively after two years. The BSE Sensex closed at 19,924 on January 24, 2013.

Various factors, including recent reform measures such as the diesel price hike, cap on subsidised LPG, permission for FDI retail and aviation and the passing of the Banking Laws (Amendment) Bill, 2011 in Parliament, along with hopes of a cut in the policy rate by the Reserve Bank in January 2013, and sustained FII inflows helped revive the domestic equity market.

Market indicators, such as market capitalisation and daily turnover, have shown an increasing trend in 2012, reflecting the positive sentiment in the Indian stock market. Further, the PE ratio of the BSE Sensex increased in 2012, indicating a rise in the valuation of Indian-stock over the year.

FIIs continued to remain bullish on Indian equities for the seventh consecutive month in December 2012. Their purchases exceeded sales by Rs.24,299 crore in the month. This was the largest amount of net FII inflows into Indian equities in the last 10 months. Overall, FII inflows exceeded outflows in 19 of the 20 trading sessions that were held during the month. A stable ratings outlook by Moody's, approval of FDI in multi-brand retail and the passing of the banking and companies bills in the parliament is likely to have boosted sentiments during the month.

During 2012-13 (up to 23, 2013), Flls made net investments of l,190 billion in the capital market (both equity and debt) compared with that of ₹ 520 billion during the corresponding period in the previous year. Flls made net investments of ₹ 1,011 billion in the equity markets compared with ₹ 27 billion last year. Whereas, the domestic institutional investors (Dlls) (comprising banks, domestic financial institutions, Insurance companies, new pension fund and mutual funds) made net sales during 2012-13 (up to January 23, 2013).

As at end-December 2012, the BSE Bankex, which represents major banks in India, recorded much higher y-o-y gains of 57 per cent than the BSE Sensex (26 per cent), despite concerns about modest loan growth, deterioration in asset quality and alleviated risks. The factors that influenced the BSE Bankex favourably are the strong balance sheet performance by some private sector banks, stable net interest margin owing to a reduction in the CRR by 175 basis points of NDTL and expectation of treasury profit as bonds rallied. The Bankex also benefitted from the positive sentiments in the overall Indian equity markets.

Indian benchmark indices, i.e. the BSE and NSE closed at 19426.7 and 5905.1 (as on 31 December 2012), gaining 25.70 per cent and 27.70 per cent respectively over the closing value of 15454.9 (Sensex) and 4624.3 (Nifty) on 30 December 2011 (Table 4). On 9 February 2013, the trading in equity and equity derivative segment by MCX-SX and the Exchange officially commenced trading in these segments on 11 February 2013.

Further, during the current financial year (up to 31 December 2012), the rise in the indices stood at 11.62 per cent for the Sensex and 11.51 per cent in case of Nifty. Among the major Asian and markets, Indian markets have been the best performing in terms of returns.

TABLE 4

Performance of Major Markets in the World (level and percentage change)

Index	Last trading day of 2010 (31 Dec. 2010)	Last trading day of 2011 (30 Dec. 2011)	Last trading day of 2012 (31 Dec. 2012)	% change in 2012 over 2011
BSE SENSEX	20509.09	15454.92	19426.71	25.7
NSE NIFTY	6134.5	4624.3	5905.1	27.7
S&P 500	1257.64	1257.6	1426.19	13.4
DAX	6914.19	5898.35	7612.39	29.1
FTSE 100	5899.94	5572.28	5897.81	5.8
NIKKEI 225	10228.92	8455.35	10395.18	22.9
HANG SENG	23035.45	18434.39	22656.92	22.9
BRAZIL BOVESPA	69304.81	56754.08	60952.08	7.4
KOSPI	2051	1825.74	1997.05	9.4
DJIA	11577.51	12217.56	13104.14	7.3
Straits Times	3190.04	2646.35	3167.08	19.7
SHANGHAI SE COMPOSITE	2808.077	2199.417	2269.128	3.2
CAC 40	3804.78	3159.81	3641.07	15.2

Source: Bloomberg.

Reinvigorated foreign institutional investor (FII) inflows into the country during the year 2012 helped the Indian markets become one of the best performing in the world in 2012, recovering sharply from their dismal performance in 2011. FIIs make investments in markets on the basis of their perceptions of expected returns from such markets. Their perceptions among other things are influenced by the prevailing macroeconomic environment, the growth potential of the economy, and corporate performance in competing countries. At the end of December 2012, 1,759 FIIs were registered with SEBI, with the number of registered sub-accounts increasing to 6,359. The total net FII flows to India in 2012 stood at US $ 31.01 billion. These flows were largely driven by equity inflows (80 per cent of total flows) which remained buoyant, indicating FII confidence in the performance of the Indian economy in general and Indian markets in particular. The economic and political developments in the Euro zone area and United States had their impact on markets around the world including India. The resolution of the 'fiscal cliff' in the US had a positive impact on the market worldwide including in India. Further, the reform measures recently initiated by the government have been well received by the markets.

Market turnover has also increased during the current year. In the cash segment of the equity market, the total turnover of the BSE and NSE stood at ₹ 4,10,230 crore and ₹ 19,73,624 crore during 2012-13 (April-December) as compared to ₹ 6,67,498 crore and ₹ 28,10,893 crore respectively in 2011-12 (Table 5).

TABLE 5

Market Turnover

(₹ crore)

Market	2009-10	2010-11	2011-12	2012-13#
BSE				
Cash	1378809	1105027	667498	410230
Equity derivatives	234	154	808476	5741593
NSE				
Cash	4138024	3577410	2810893	1973624
Equity derivatives	17663665	29248221	31349732	22879486

Source: BSE and NSE.
Note: # as on 31 December 2012.

In the equity derivatives segment, the NSE witnessed a total turnover of ₹ 2,28,79,486 crore during 2012-13 (April-December) as compared to ₹ 3,13,49,732 crore during 2011-12. The total turnover in the equity derivatives segment of the BSE stood at ₹ 57,41,593 crore in 2011-12 (April-December).

In the currency derivatives segment, the NSE witnessed a turnover of ₹ 37,25,842 crore in 2012- 13 (April-December). The turnover in the currency derivatives segment of the Multi-Commodity Exchange (MCX-SX) stood at ₹ 23,63,819 crore in 2012-13 (April-December).. Further, the United Stock Exchange (USE) witnessed a turnover of ₹ 32,109 crore during the same period (Table 6).

TABLE 6

Trends in Currency Derivatives

Year	NSE		MCX- SX		USE	
	2011-12	2012-13#	2011-12	2012-13#	2011-12	2012-13#
No. of contracts (lakh)	9733	6772	7703	4272	3153	57
Trading value (₹ crore)	4674990	3725842	3732446	2363819	1488978	32109
Average daily trading value (₹ crore)	18775	20140	14990	12777	5980	174

Source: NSE, MCX-SX and USE.
Note: # as on 31 December 2012.

Together with an increase in the turnover in the securities markets, there was also a decline in volatility of both the Nifty and Sensex. Volatility which had increased in 2010-12 (two years), moderated considerably (Table 7).

TABLE 7

Volatility of Weekly Returns on Indian Equity Markets

Index	2009-10	2010-11	2011-12	2012-13#
Nifty	3.8	2.5	2.9	1.8
Nifty Junior	4.5	2.7	2.9	2.0
Sensex	3.6	2.5	2.9	1.8
BSE 500	3.9	2.4	2.8	1.8

Source : BSE and NSE.
Note : # As on 31 December 2012

MAJOR POLICY INITIATIVES IN THE SECONDARY MARKET

Following initiatives have been taken during 2012-13 to integrate the Indian stock market with global financial markets.

1. Rajiv Gandhi Equity Savings Scheme

On 23rd November 2012, the government notified a new tax saving scheme called the Rajiv Gandhi Equity Savings Scheme (RGESS), exclusively for first-time retail investors in the securities market. This scheme provides 50 per cent deduction of the amount invested from taxable income for that year to new investors who invest up to ₹ 50,000 and whose annual income is below ₹ 10 lakh. The operational guidelines were issued by SEBI on 6 December 2012 (Box-1).

2. Electronic Voting Facility made Mandatory for Top Listed Companies

As mandated in the Union Budget 2012-13 for top listed companies to offer electronic voting facility to their shareholders, SEBI has come out with the necessary amendments in this regard on 13 July 2012, to be incorporated in the equity listing agreement by stock exchanges. To make a beginning, based on market capitalization, electronic voting is now mandatory for the top 500 listed companies at the BSE and NSE, in respect of those businesses to be transacted through postal ballot.

3. SME Exchange / Platform

Separate trading platforms for SMEs were launched and became functional at the BSE and NSE in March 2012 and September 2012 respectively. As on 14 January 2013, the number of equities listed on the BSE and NSE SME platforms is 12 and 2 respectively.

4. Reduced Securities Transaction Tax for Cash Delivery Transactions

Following the announcement in Union Budget 2012-13, the rate of the securities transaction tax (STT) has been revised downwards by 20 per cent to 0.1 per cent from 0.125 per cent for delivery-based transactions in the cash market, effective 1 July 2012.

5.. Regulatory Framework for Governance and Ownership of stock exchanges, clearing corporations, and depositories

Based on the recommendations of the Dr. Bimal Jalan Committee, new Securities Contracts (Regulation) (Stock Exchanges and Clearing Corporations) Regulations 2012 were notified on 20 June 2012 to regulate recognition, ownership, and governance in stock exchanges and clearing corporations. Further, the Securities and Exchange Board of India (Depositories and Participants) (Amendment) Regulations 2012 have been brought into effect from 11 September 2012 to regulate ownership and governance norms of depositories.

Box 1

RGESS

The Rajiv Gandhi Equity Saving Scheme (RGESS) will give tax benefits to new investors whose annual income is up to ₹ 10 lakh for investments up to a maximum of ₹ 50,000. The investor will get 50 per cent deduction of the amount invested from taxable income for that year. Salient features of the scheme are as follows:

- The scheme is open to new retail investors identified on the basis of their permanent account numbers (PAN).
- The tax deduction allowed will be over and above the ₹ 1 lakh limit permitted allowed under Section 80 C of the Income Tax Act.
- In addition to the 50 per cent tax deduction for investments, dividend income is also tax free.
- For investments up to ₹ 50,000 in the sole RGESS demat account, if the investor opts for a basic service demat account, annual maintenance charges for the demat account are zero and for investments up to ₹ 2 lakh, ₹ 100.

- Stocks listed under BSE 100 or CNX 100, or stocks of public-sector undertakings (PSUs) that are Navratnas, Maharatnas, and Miniratnas will be eligible under the scheme. Follow-on public offers (FPOs) of these companies will also be eligible.
- IPOs of PSUs, which are scheduled to get listed in the relevant financial year and whose annual turnover is not less than ₹ 4,000 crore for each of the immediate past three years, will also be eligible.
- Exchange-traded funds (ETFs) and MFs that have RGESS-eligible securities as their underlying and are listed and traded in the stock exchanges and settled through a depository mechanism have also been brought under the RGESS to provide the advantage of diversification and consequent risk minimization.
- To benefit the small investors, investments are allowed in instalments in the year in which tax claims are made.
- The total lock-in period for investments will be three years including an initial blanket lock-in of one year.
- After the first year, investors will be allowed to trade in the securities. Investors are free to trade / churn their portfolios for around 90 days in each of the years following the first year of investment.
- Investors would, however, be required to maintain their level of investment during these two years at the amount for which they have claimed income tax benefit or at the value of the portfolio before initiating a sale transaction, whichever is less, for at least 270 days in a year.
- The general principle under which trading is allowed is that whatever is the value of stocks / units sold by the investor from the RGESS portfolio, RGESS-compliant securities of at least the same value are credited back into the account subsequently. However, the investor is allowed to take benefit of the appreciation of his RGESS portfolio, provided its value remains above the investment for which he has claimed income tax benefit.
- In case the investor fails to meet the conditions stipulated, the tax benefit will be withdrawn. The broad provisions of the Scheme and the income tax benefits under it have already been incorporated as a new Section-80CCG- of the Income Tax Act 1961, as amended by the Finance Act 2012. The operational guidelines were issued by SEBI on 6 December 2012.

QUESTIONS

1. React to the following statements: (a) "The stock exchange is a legalised gambling den". (b) "The stock exchange is the pulse of the economy".
2. What are the main functions of a stock exchange? In what ways is a stock exchange indispensable for an economy?
3. How do operations on a stock exchange affect the economic life of a nation? Is it necessary to control the stock exchange?
4. Outline the drawbacks and defects in the working of stock exchanges in India. How far, and in what ways has the Securities Contracts (Regulation) Act, 1956 removed them?
5. Briefly trace the history of stock markets in India.
6. State the regulations pertaining to the membership of a stock exchange.
7. Why is it necessary to maintain a liquid secondary market in securities in India?
8. Write an essay on OTCEI bringing out the rationale, functions and scope of this institution.
9. Write a note on the functioning of the National Stock Exchange of India.
10. Discuss the automation of stock exchanges in India.

REFERENCES

1. Baumol, W.J. *The Stock Market and Economic Efficiency*. New York: Fordham University Press, 1965.
2. Black, Fisher. "Toward a Fully Computerized Stock Exchange," *Financial Analysts Journal*. Nov.-Dec. 1971.
3. Fisher, D.E., and R. J. Jordan. *Security Analysis and Portfolio Management*. Englewood Cliffs, N.J.: Prentice-Hall, 1979, chapter 7.

4. Fosback, Norman G. *Stock Market Logic*. Fort Lauderdale, Fla.: The Institute for Economic Research, 1976.

5. Friend, Irwin. "The Economic Consequences of the Stock Market," *American Economic Review*. May 1972.

6. Graham, B., D. Dodd, and S. Cottle: *Security Analysis*, 4th ed., McGraw-Hill, New York, 1962.

7. Hayes, D., and W. Bauman. *Investments: Analysis and Management*, 3rd ed. New York: Macmillan, 1976, chapters 16-17.

8. Huang, Stanley S.C. *Techniques of Investment Analysis*. New York; Intext Educational Publishers. 1972, chapters 7-8.

9. Ibbotson, Roger G., Judy Sindelar, and Jay R. Ritter. "Initial Public Offerings." *Journal of Applied Corporate Finance* 1, no. 3 (Summer 1988).

10. Jensen, Michael, and Richard Ruback: "The Market for Corporate Control," *Journal of Financial Economics*, April 1983, pp. 5-50.

11. Latane, H., D. Tuttle, and C. Jones. *Security Analysis and Portfolio Management*, 2d ed. Ronald, 1975, chapter 16.

12. Loll, Leo M. Jr., and Julian G. Buckley. *The Over-the-Counter Security Markets*. Englewood Cliffs, N.J.: Prentice-Hall, 1986.

13. Lorie, James H., and Mary T. Hamilton. *The Stock Market: Theories and Evidence*. 2d ed. Homewood, 111.: Richard D. Irwin, 1985.

14. Miller, Robert E., and Frank K. Reilly. "Examination of Mispricing, Returns, and Uncertainty for Initial Public Offerings." *Financial Management* 16, no. 2 (January 1987).

15. Moskowitz, Milton. "The `Intelligent Investor' at 80," *New York Times*. May 5, 1974.

16. National Association of Securities Dealers. *The NASDAQ Handbook*. Rev. ed. Chicago: Probus Publishing, 1992.

17. Peake, Junius W. "The National Market System," *Financial Analysts Journal*. July-Aug. 1978.

18. Robbins, Sidney. *The Securities Markets: Operations and Issues*. New York: Free Press, 1966.

19. Samuelson, Paul A. "Economics of the Stock Market and the Investor," *Commercial & Financial Chronicle*. Oct.

20. Schaefer, J.M., and A.J. Warner. "Concentration Trends and Competition in the Securities Industry," *Financial Analysts Journal*. Nov.-Dec. 1977.

21. Skousen, K. Fred. *An Introduction to the SEC*. 5th ed. Cincinnati: South-Western Publishing, 1990.

22. Sobel, Robert. *The Big Board: A History of the New York Stock Market*. New York: The Free Press, 1965.

23. Stoll, Hans, and Robert E. Whaley. Stock *Market Structure, Volatility, and Volume*. Charlottesville, Va.: Institute of Chartered Financial Analysts Research Foundation, 1990.

3

New Issue Market

INTRODUCTION

The Industrial financing system in India consists of a network of basically two types of institutions:

(i) 'Financial intermediaries' like Unit Trust of India, Commercial Banks, Investment Companies, Life Insurance Organisation, Development Banks and so on, and

(ii) 'Facilitating organisations' comprising the New Issue Market (MM) and the stock exchanges. It is in this latter category that we are more interested here, though their relationships with the first category form an integral part of the whole analysis.

NEW ISSUE MARKET: THE CONCEPT

While discussing the concept of the new issue market, the distinction between the NIM and the stock exchanges must always be kept in mind since they differ from each other organisationally and as regards the nature of functions performed by them. In the first place, New Issue Market deals with 'new' securities, *i.e.* securities which were not previously available and are offered to the investing public for the first time. The market, therefore, derives its name from the fact that it makes available a new block of securities for public subscription. The stock market on the other hand, is a market for 'old' securities *i.e.* those which have already been issued and have been granted stock exchange listing. These are purchased and sold continuously among investors without involvement of the companies whose securities constitute the stock-in-trade except in the strictly limited sense of having to register the transfer of ownership of the securities.

A related aspect of these two parts is the nature of their contribution to industrial financing. The New Issue Market provides the issuing company with additional funds for starting a new enterprise or for either expansion or diversification of an existing one, and thus its contribution to company financing is direct. The role of the stock exchange *vis-a-vis* supply of capital is indirect.

Apart from this, the two parts of the market differ organisationally, *e.g.* the stock exchanges have physical existence and are located in particular geographical areas. The New Issue Market enjoys neither any tangible form nor any administrative organisational setup, and nor is subject to any centralised control and administration for the execution of its business - it is recognised by the services that it renders to the lenders and borrowers of capital funds at the time of any particular operation.

Despite this difference, the New Issue Market and stock exchanges are inseparably connected :

1. The securities issued in the New Issue Market are invariably listed on a recognised

stock exchange, subsequent to their issue. This is of immense utility to potential investors who feel assured that should they receive an allotment of new issues, they will subsequently be able to dispose them of at any time. The facilities provided by the secondary markets, thus, widen the initial market for them.

2. *Secondly*, the stock exchanges exercise considerable control over the organisation of new issues. In terms of the regulatory framework relating to dealings in securities, new issues, which seek stock exchange quotation have to comply with statutory rules as well as regulations framed by the stock exchanges with the object of ensuring fair dealings in them.

3. *Fundamentally*, the markets for new and old securities are, economically, an integral part of a single market- the industrial securities market. Thus they are susceptible to common influence and act and react upon each other. Broadly, new issues increase when stock values are rising and vice versa.

Also, the quantitative predominance of old securities in the market usually ensures that it is these which set the tone of the market as a whole and govern the prices and acceptability of new issues.

Thus, we see that the capital market, with particular reference to company scrips, performs two distinct functions — providing funds for trading in existing securities and funds for fresh issues of capital by the companies either through public issue or right issue or by private placement.

While in many respects, the market mechanism for capital markets is the same as for commodities, there is a fundamental difference that renders the former more complex, *i.e.* in the case of an ordinary commodity, it may be bought or sold several times, but it is used up in consumption after some time. In the case of the capital market nothing is consumed away. Every year there is new supply and so the cumulative total of funds dealt with goes on rising and the New Issue Market provides a common ground for facilitating this transfer process of funds from the suppliers (comprising investors, individual, corporate and institutional) to the companies attempting to raise fresh capital.

The exact amount available for investment in a particular company, however, depends on macro factors like rate of growth of the economy, total money supply, savings potential and the marginal propensity to save; and micro factors like performance of a particular class of companies, facilities available for liquidation of investment and the individual preference of an investor, etc.

There are basically three methods that could be adopted for marketing shares/services. These are:

(a) Private subscription
(b) Right issues
(c) Public issues

Private subscription envisages private sale of securities. The promoters subscribe to the shares themselves or request their relations/friends to associate with them, *i.e.* there is an attempt to affect collection of savings directly from the saving - surplus units without the intermediation of financial institutions. This is known as direct financing.

Right issues to raise capital can be employed by existing companies. Whenever the capital of an existing company is to be increased it should offer right issues to the existing shareholders, unless they themselves decide otherwise.

When a company is new and has to raise huge funds which cannot be done by the previous two methods, it has to go in for public issue. Companies have also gone for public issue so as to get their shares listed in a stock exchange. The issue of capital to the public involves a number of steps, starting from obtaining consents from SEBI to opening/

closing of subscription lists. Consequently, managing the issue becomes a specialised job, for which a number of concerns like underwriters, brokers, issue houses etc. have sprung up in the issue market rendering this type of financing to be an indirect one. The flow of savings from the savers is diverted through intermediary financial institutions to the entrepreneurs.

Functions

The main function of the New Issue Market is to facilitate the 'transfer of resources' from savers to users. Conceptually, however, the New Issue Market should not be conceived as a platform only for the purpose of raising finance for new capital expenditure. In fact, the facilities of the market are also utilised for selling existing concerns to the public as going concerns through conversions of existing proprietary enterprises or private companies into public companies.

It, therefore, becomes imperative at this stage to classify new issues. One classification suggested by R.F. Henderson (c.f. The New Issue Market & Finance for Industry, 1951), categorises new issues into those by:

(a) *New companies* - also called 'initial issues' and

(b) *Old companies* - also called 'further issues'.

These bear no relation to the age of the company, but are based on the fact whether the company already has stock exchange listing. This classification is thus concerned only with the flow of 'new money'.

Another classification (c.f. Merrett, Howe &Newbould — "Equity Issues and the London Capital Market" 1967) distinguishes between flow of funds into the market and flow of "new money" — hence we have 'new money issues' or issues of capital involving newly created share and 'no new money issues' *i.e.* sale of securities already in existence and sold '' by their holders.

This is more an "exclusive" classification in that two types of issues are excluded from the category of new issues.

(a) Bonus/capitalisation issues which represent only book keeping entries.

(b) Exchange issues : by which shares in one company are exchanged for securities of another.

Now, the main function of the New Issue Market, *i.e.* channelling of investible funds, can be divided, from the operational stand-point, into a triple-service function :

(a) Origination

(b) Underwriting

(c) Distribution

The institutional setup dealing with these can be said to constitute the New Issue Market organisation. Let us elucidate a little on all of these.

(a) Origination : refers to the work of investigation and analysis and processing of new proposals. This in turn may be:

(i) A preliminary investigation undertaken by the sponsors (specialised agencies) of the issue. This involves a careful study of the technical, economic, financial and legal aspects of the issuing companies to ensure that it warrants the backing of the issue house.

(ii) Services of an advisory nature which go to improve the quality of capital issues. These services include advice on such aspects of capital issues as :

 • determination of the class of security to be issued and price of the — issue in terms of market conditions;

- the timing and magnitude of issues;
- method of flotation; and
- technique of selling and so on.

The importance of the specialised services provided by the New Issue Market organisation in this respect can hardly be over-emphasized. On the thoroughness of investigation and soundness of judgement of the sponsoring institution depends, to a large extent, the allocative efficiency of the market.

The origination, however, thoroughly done, will not by itself guarantee success of an issue. A second specialised service *i.e.* "Underwriting" is often required.

(b) Underwriting : The idea of underwriting originated on account of uncertainties prevailing in the capital market as a result of which the success of the issue becomes unpredictable. If the issue remains undersubscribed, the directors cannot proceed to allot the shares, and have to return money to the applicants if the subscription is below a minimum amount fixed under the Companies Act. Consequently, the issue and hence the project will fail.

Underwriting entails an agreement whereby a person/organisation agrees to take a specified number of shares or debentures or a specified amount of stock offered to the public in the event of the public not subscribing to it, in consideration of a commission - the underwriting commission. If the issue is fully subscribed by the public, there is no liability attaching to the underwriters; else they have to come forth to meet the shortfall to the extent of the under- subscription.

The underwriters in India may broadly be classified into the following two types :
  (i) Institutional Underwriters;
  (ii) Non-Institutional Underwriting.

Institutional Underwriting in our country has been development oriented. It stands as a major support to those projects which often fail to catch the eye of investing public. These projects rank high from the points of view of national importance *e.g.* steel, fertilizer, and generally receive higher priority by such underwriters. Thus institutional underwriting may be broadly recognised, in the context of development credit, as playing a decisive role in directing the economic resources of the country towards desired activities. This does not mean that they are barred entrance in the issue market from so called glamorous issues to which public can be expected to readily subscribe. They may be underwriting in such cases, but what is expected of them is their support to projects in the priority sector.

One of the principal advantages they offer is that resource-wise they are undoubted. They are in a position to fulfil their underwriting commitments even in the worst foreseeable situations.

The public financial institutions namely IDBI, IFCI, ICICI, LIC and UTI, underwrite a portion of the issued capital. Usually, the underwriting is done in addition to granting term finance by way of loans on debentures. These institutions are usually approached when one or more of the following situations prevail:
  (i) The issue is so large that broker-underwriting may not be able to cover the entire issue.
  (ii) The gestation period is long enough to act as distinctive.
  (iii) The project is weak, inasmuch as it is being located in a backward area.
  (iv) The project is in the priority sector which may not be able to provide an attractive return on investment.

(v) The project is promoted by technicians.

(vi) The project is new to the market.

The quantum of underwriting assistance varies from institution to institution according to the commitments of each of them for a particular industry.

However, institutional underwriting suffers from the following two drawbacks :

1. The institutional handling involves procedural delays which sometimes dampen the initiative of the corporate managers or promoters.

2. The other disadvantage is that the institutions prefer to wait and watch the results to fulfil their obligations only where they are called upon to meet the deficit caused by undersubscription.

(c) Distribution: The sale of securities to the ultimate investors is referred to as distribution, it is another specialised job, which can be performed by brokers and dealers in securities who maintain regular and direct contact with the ultimate investors.

The ability of the New Issue Market to cope with the growing requirements of the expanding corporate sector would depend on this triple-service function.

ROLE OF THE NEW ISSUE MARKET

The analysis of the role of the new issue market in financing companies can be undertaken by the study of the statistics of the annual volume of new issues. The data may be broken down in various ways, for example, according to the type of security issued, the kind of organisation making the issue, the method of flotation of issue and so on. The Reserve Bank of India, for instance, has been following this method in its regular studies of capital issues in the private corporate sector. However, this approach is partial, and to that extent, an inadequate method of appraisal in that it does not explain the full significance of the role of the New Issue Market.

(i) Its first shortcoming is that the technique to aggregate the amount of all prospectus and right issues, to arrive at the new issues made in a particular year does not reveal the true picture, as the entire sum is not necessarily raised by the issuing companies from the investing public in the same year because they are collected through various calls which may be spread over five years. This, of course, is a minor point.

(ii) The method presents absolute figures, unrelated to the use to which these funds are put.

(iii) The method leads to the treatment of the New Issue Market in isolation from the rest of the capital market and consequently to a distorted view as to its real functions.

(iv) Further, it does not disclose as to what kind and size of firms are obtaining funds, nor at what cost they are doing so, and, therefore, gives no clue as to efficiency. To explore such questions, obviously, a different approach is necessary.

Another approach that tries to remedy the weaknesses of the first, is the 'source - and - use - of - funds' approach of analysis of company balance sheets. In this connection, two possibilities suggest themselves:

(a) A possible method is to make a direct comparison between new issues and industrial fixed capital formation. But this suffers from a serious limitation to the extent it is based on the implicit assumption that long-term source of funds ought roughly to match long-term investment, for it is not virtually impossible for the analysts to relate the sums raised on the market to the uses that are made of those funds by the organisation making those issues, but it is also misleading to link specific sources of funds to specific uses. True, investment in tangible fixed assets is the most important long-term use of funds but is certainly not the only important use to which funds are put when a group of companies is expanding output. The expenditure on fixed assets is, therefore, not a good yardstick to measure the importance of capital issues. It is particularly misleading when studying different industries in which the relative importance of investment in stock and in fixed assets varies considerably. What is needed is a much wider and a more comprehensive approach in order to get different source and uses of funds into perspective. However, since it is not always possible to have the correct data forthcoming, we have to make use of that which is available.

RECENT TRENDS IN THE PRIMARY MARKET

Average annual capital mobilisation from the primary market, which used to be about ₹ 70 crore in the 1960s and about ₹ 90 crore in the 1970s, increased manifold during the 1980s, with the amount raised in 1990-91 being ₹ 4,312 crore. It received a further boost during the 1990s with the capital raised by non-government public companies. There is a preference for raising resources in the primary market through private placement of debt instruments. Private placements accounted for about 91% of total resources mobilised through domestic issues by the corporate sector during 2000-01. Rapid dismantling of shackles on institutional investments and deregulation of the economy are driving growth of this segment. There are several inherent advantages of relying on private placement route for raising resources (Box-1). While it is cost and time effective method of raising funds and can be structured to meet the needs of the entrepreneurs, it does not require detailed compliance with formalities as required in public or rights issues. It is believed in some circles that private placement has crowded out public issues. However, to prevent public Issues from being passed on as private placement, the Companies (Amendment) Act, 2001 made offer of securities to more than 50 persons a public issue.

Box 1

PRIVATE PLACEMENT MARKET

In the primary capital market corporates can raise resources through public issues and tights issues and 'private placement'. While public issues involve alloting securities to the general public, tights issues entail allotment of securities to the shareholders. Private placement, in contrast, refers to direct sale of newly issued securities by the issuer to a small number of investors. Private placement of issues is arranged through merchant bankers, with the issuer entering into an arrangement regarding the various features of the issue being privately placed with the selected clients, which are financial institutions, corporates and high net-worth individuals. The time taken as well as the cost of issue for the private placement route is much less for the issuer as compared with a public issue. Thus, the private placement is a cost and time effective way of raising funds for the corporates. The privately placed issues offer greater flexibility to the issuers as the instruments can be structured according to the needs of the entrepreneurs. Moreover, private placement does not require detailed complaince of formalities as required in public or rights issues.

Due to the inherent advantages of the private placement route, this market is quite popular in some of the developed economies, especially the US. The private placement market in the US, where predominantly debt instruments are privately placed, has been providing access to domestic as well as international issuers for a very long time. The foreign issuers are mostly from Canada, UK, France, Sweden, other European countries and Mexico. Of late, developing countries like Korea, Indonesia, Phillippines, Malaysia, Thailand and India have been accessing the private placement market in the US. The private placement market is also a significant source of funding for corporates in the US, in particular the medium sized companies. During

1994- 96, gross issuance of private placements of bonds by non-financial corporations was almost 40 per cent of the public issuance. At end-December, 1996, the non-financial corporate sector had about $450 billion of private placements outstanding, roughly 70 per cent of the amount of bank loans ($ 640 bn) and almost 50 per cent of the amount of public bonds ($ 950 bn) outstanding. The life insurance companies of the US are the most active investors in this market. Section 4(2) of Securities Act of 1933 exempts from registration with Securities Exchange Commission (SEC) "transactions by an issuer not involving any public offering" but does not provide definite rules as to what constitutes a private placement. In early 1982, however, the SEC adopted Regulation D (Rules 501-506), which does provide specific guidelines. The type of information that must be furnished under Regulation D varies, depending on the size of the offering and the nature of the issuer. The private placement memorandum can be compared with an initial registration statement filed for a public offering. The major difference is that the private placement memorandum is not subject to the SEC review process and does not require disclosure of certain non-material information that is otherwise required in a prospectus. The merchant banker should have adequate due diligence before a private placement offering, on the issuer of securities, and Its financial statements as is the case with public offering. SEC introduced Rule 144 in 1972, which allows resale of privately placed instruments after a two-year lock-in-period. SEC further introduced Rule 144A in April 1990, which permitted Qualified Institutional Investors (those with assets in excess of $ 100 million) to trade In privately placed securities without a two-year holding restriction. By removing the two-year requirement, Rule 144A added liquidity to the private placement market thereby increasing the attractiveness of these securities. In November 1992, SEC modified Rule 144A to allow bank trust funds and master trusts for pension funds to buy unregistered bonds and stocks. In comparison with the US market, the private placement market in the UK is not well established, as the sale of bonds under private placement involves small amounts and the deals are entered into directly with the purchaser. In addition, debt issues in private placement market of the UK are nót listed. In Japan too, the private placement market does not form a significant part of the primary market and is accessed mostly by the issuers from Third World countries and private companies of Japan which do not have enough credibility to float public issues. The private placement market in Japan is regulated by guidelines prescribed by the Trustee Banks Committee, 1977, which prescribes the minimum issue amount, the number of times an issuer can enter the market and norms with regard to dividend and certain accounting ratios. In addition to this, In accordance with the directives of the Ministry of Finance, the number of participants in the private placement is restricted to 50 persons per issue and the purchasers of private placements are required to hold the securities for a minimum lock-in period of two years. In Germany, the private placement of securities is made in the form of certificates of indebtendness, which are transferable instruments and are traded on OTC market with bankers making market for it. The private placement of securities in Germany requires the concurrence of the Ministry of Finance. In sharp contrast to this, the private placements in India are not bound by any regulatory system. Information relating to various details of private placement is contained in "Memorandum of Information" and deals are struck through negotiations between the ultimate borrowers and lenders. In the case of equity issues, companies are free to fix the quantum of private placement and only follow the rule of pricing for preferential allotment as stipulated by SEBI. Such private placements have no lock-in-period excepting those in favour of promoters. There is no compliance system for merchant bankers in private placement as in the case of public issues. In view of this, the private placement has become a favoured route for corporates and financial institutions in India for mobilising resources during the last few years. However, private placements are information- intensive securities that require substantial monitoring by the intermediaries and the leaders in order to ascertain their value. With limit on bank's investment on debt removed, one can expect the private placement market to be very active in future Given the informal nature of this market, the need for regulatory norms and standards is imperative for the healthy development of the private placement market. The regulatory aspects should cover disclosure requirements in the memorandum of information, protection of investors' interests, transparency in the event of retailing private placement issues, etc. Policy intervention is also desirable for the growth of secondary market for privately placed issues.

The reforms in the capital markets during the 1990s in terms of market microstructure and transactions have ensured that the Indian capital market in particular is now comparable to the capital markets in most developed markets. The early 1990s saw a greater willingness of the saver to place funds in capital market instruments, on the supply side as well as an enthusiasm of corporate entities to take recourse to capital market instruments on the demand side. The size of the capital market is now comparable to other developing countries but there is still a long way to go. It is important to note that developed economies with bank-based systems, such as Germany and Japan, also have capital markets with substantial market capitalisation in relation to GDP.

While there was a sharp increase in market capitalisation as a percentage of GDP during the 1990s, the share of capital issues to GDP, a measure of resource mobilisation by the capital markets, followed an inverted U curve during the 1990s. The spurt in capital issues beyond 1.0 per cent of GDP during 1993-96 could not be sustained with the onset of the economic slowdown in the latter half of the 1990s. As a result, capital issues, especially equity issues, dwindled to the 1970s' levels (as a proportion of GDP) in the latter half of the 1990s. In fact, public capital issues by non-Government public limited companies declined to 0.2 per cent of GDP during 1998-2002 from 1.9 per cent during 1992-97 and 0.6 per cent during the 1980s. Besides, public equity issues by non-Government public limited companies declined to 0.1 per cent of GDP during 1998-2002 from 1.1 per cent during 1992-97 and 0.7 per cent during the 1980s.

The market for corporate debt is still in the process of development in the Indian economy, as is the case with most developing economies. The private placement market has emerged as an important source of resource mobilisation in the Indian debt market. The first steps in development of the debt market have been taken through development of the government securities market. The issue of government bonds through auction, and their active trading by banks has led to the emergence of a sovereign yield curve. Steps have also been taken, though still in their infancy, to enable active trading of government securities in the stock exchanges. As this market grows and as steps are taken to regulate the private placement market, the corporate bond market will also develop. Creditworthy corporate borrowers will then be able to raise longer term funds for financing their growth.

After the exuberance of the stock market in the mid-1990s and its decline thereafter, a large number of individual investors took flight to safety in bank deposits, safe retirement instruments and insurance. It remains to be seen when and how fast such savers return to the capital market so that it performs its intermediary function efficiently.

Overall, the 1990s have been remarkable for the Indian equity market. The market has grown exponentially in terms of resource mobilisation, number of stock exchanges, number of listed stocks, market capitalisation, trading volumes, turnover and investors' base. Along with this growth, the profile of the investors, issuers and intermediaries have changed significantly. The market has witnessed a fundamental institutional change resulting in drastic reduction in transaction costs and significant improvement in efficiency, transparency and safety. In the 1990s, reform measures initiated by SEBI, market determined allocation of resources, rolling settlement, sophisticated risk management and derivatives trading have greatly improved the framework and efficiency of trading and settlement. Almost all equity settlements take place at the depository. As a result, the Indian capital market has become qualitatively comparable to many developed and emerging markets.

Although the Indian capital market has grown in size and depth in the post reform period, the magnitude of activities is still negligible compared to those prevalent internationally. India accounted for 0.40 per cent in terms of market capitalisation and

0.59 per cent in terms of global turnover in the equity market in 2001. The liberalisation and consequent reform measures have drawn attention of foreign investors and led to rise in the FIIs investment in India. During the first half of the 1990s, India accounted for a larger volume of international equity issues than any other emerging market. Presently, there are nearly 500 registered FIIs in India, which include asset management companies, pension funds, investment trusts, and incorporated institutional portfolio managers. FIIs are eligible to invest in listed as well as unlisted securities.

The stock markets mirrored the growing confidence in the strong fundamentals of the Indian economy as ebullient investor sentiment strained against intermittent technical corrections. Primary market activity gathered momentum during the year, particularly in the equity segment. Foreign institutional investors (FIIs) remained net buyers in each month of the year barring May 2004. Although market sentiment was dampened by political uncertainties in the early part of the year, the surge in international crude oil prices and the edging up of inflation domestically, a strong rally in the secondary market pushed the domestic stock indices to new highs. Investor interest in the public issues segment strengthened during 2004-05, encouraged by the upbeat sentiment in the secondary market. Resourcing mobilisation through public issues (excluding offers for sale) increased sharply to ₹ 19,666 crore from 56 issues as compared with ₹ 7,190 crore from 35 issues during 2003-04. Non-Government public limited companies (private sector) accounted for 65.3 per cent of total resource mobilisation by way of public issues. Of the 56 issues in the current financial year, 23 issues were initial public offering (IPOs), of which 22 were by non-financial companies in the private sector. Public issues by six companies, *viz.* ICICI Bank Ltd., TCS Ltd., Sterlite Industries (India) Ltd., National Thermal Power Corporation Ltd., Jet Airways (India) Ltd. and Punjab National Bank, together accounted for 72.9 per cent of total resource mobilisation.

During 2004-05, equity issues dominated the market constituting 88.7 per cent of the total resource mobilisation. Resource mobilisation through private placements aggregated ₹ 49,255 crore during April-December 2004 as compared with ₹ 42,372 crore a year ago. In all 141 entities entered the market in April-December 2004 with 651 floatations as compared with 133 entities with 678 floatations during the first three quarters of the previous year. All issues in the private placement market barring one were debt issues. Financial institutions continued to dominate the private placement market with a share of 58.2 per cent (as compared with 63.3 per cent in the preceding year) in total resource mobilisation.

Indian companies raised ₹ 3,353 crore through 15 Euro issues during 2004-05 as compared with ₹ 3,098 crore through 18 issues during the previous year. There was no American Depository Receipts (ADR) issue during 2004-05, while resources mobilised by way of Global Depository Receipts (GDRs) registered a sharp increase.

Resource mobilisation by mutual funds declined by 95.3 per cent to ₹ 2,200 crore during 2004-05 mainly on account of redemption pressures on income, gilt and equity-linked saving schemes due to sharp of resource in favour of small saving schemes which offered attraction tax adjusted rates of return. The UTI Mutual Fund recorded net outflows of ₹ 2,722 crore during 2004-05 as compared with net inflows of ₹ 1,667 crore during 2003-04. The public sector mutual funds also recorded net outflows of ₹ 2,677 crore during 2004-05 as compared with net inflows of ₹ 2,597 crore in the previous year. Resource mobilisation by private sector mutual funds was substantially lower at ₹ 7,600 crore as compared with ₹ 42,545 crore in the previous year. The bulk of the resources mobilised by mutual funds were under liquid/money market schemes and growth/equity oriented schemes, while resource mobilisation under debt schemes declined sharply due to change in the interest rate scenario.

Securities markets' performance in terms of information-processing, risk management and liquidity-provision functions improved further in 2005. In December 2005, there were 2,540 companies, where stock market trading took place on at least two-thirds of the days. These companies had a market capitalisation of ₹ 24.7 lakh crore or $550 billion. Household and institutional investor participation increased through growing confidence in the transparency and robustness of the market design which was put in place over the period 1993-2001. Such participation was also assisted by stock market index returns of 11 per cent in 2004 followed by 36 per cent in 2005.

The primary market for equity, which consists of both the 'initial public offering' (IPO) market and the 'seasoned equity offering' (SEO) markets, experienced considerable activity in 2004 and 2005. In 2005, ₹ 30,325 crore of resources were raised on this market, of which ₹ 9,918 crore were made up by 55 companies which were listed for the first time (IPOs). The number of IPOs per year has risen, steadily from 2002 onwards. A level of 55 IPOs in the year translates to roughly 4 IPOs every month. The mean IPO size, which was elevated in 2004, returned to ₹ 180 crore, which is similar to the value prevalent in 2003. The primary issuance of debt securities, as per SEBI, fell to a low of around ₹ 66 crore in 2005, which is one facet of the far-reaching difficulties of the debt market. Unlike equity securities, debt securities issued at previous dates were redeemed by companies every year. Hence, a year with a low issuance of fresh debt securities is a year in which the stock of outstanding debt securities drops.

The primary capital market grew in 2006 and 2007 after the set back of 2005. The amounts raised and the number of new issues which entered the market increased in 2007. The total amount of capital raised through different market instruments during 2007 was 31.5 per cent higher than during 2006, which itself had seen a rebound of 30.6 per cent over the lows of 2005. Component-wise, private placement at ₹ 1,11,838 crore (up to November 2007) accounted for the major share during 2007. The total equity issues mobilized was ₹ 58,722 crore, of which ₹ 33,912 crore was accounted for by the Initial Public Offerings (IPOs). During 2007, the total number of IPOs issued was 100 as compared to 75 in the previous year.

In line with the rising trend in resources raised in the primary market, the net inflow of savings into mutual funds increased by over 30 per cent in 2007 to ₹ 1,38,270 crore. The sharp increase in funds flowing into mutual funds during 2007 was partly due to buoyant equity markets and partly to efforts made by the Indian mutual funds to introduce innovative schemes. Income/debt-oriented schemes fared relatively better during the year compared to other schemes. The private sector mutual funds outperformed the public sector mutual funds in terms of resource mobilization in 2007. The share of UTI and other public sector mutual funds in total amount mobilized gradually declined over the years to 17.8 per cent in 2006 and further to 12.7 per cent in 2007. The resources raised through public issues by the corporate sector increased sharply by 158.5 per cent to ₹ 83,707 crore during 2007-08 over those in last year. The number of issues remained unchanged at 119 in 2007-08. The average size of public issues, however, increased from ₹ 272 crore in 2006-07 to ₹ 703 crore in 2007-08. All public issues during 2007-08 were in the form of equity, barring three which were in the form of debt. Out of 119 issues, 82 issues were initial public offerings (IPOs), accounting for 47.7 per cent of total resource mobilisation.

Mobilisation of resources through private placement increased by 34.9 per cent to ₹ 1,49,651 crore during April-December 2007 over the corresponding period of the previous year. Resources mobilised by private sector entities increased by 49.4 per cent, while those by public sector entities increased by only 15.5 per cent during April-

December 2007. Financial intermediaries (both from public sector and private sector) accounted for the bulk (68.3 per cent) of the total resource mobilisation from the private placement market during April-December 2007 (69.0 per cent during April-December 2006).

Cumulatively, resources raised through public issues declined sharply to ₹ 14,671 crore during 2008-09 from ₹ 83,707 crore during 2007-08. The number of issues also declined considerably from 119 to 45. Out of the 45 issues during 2008-09, 21 were initial public offerings (IPOs) issued by private sector companies, constituting 13.9 per cent of total resource mobilisation. Furthermore, all the issues during 2008-09 were equity issues by private non-financial companies except two by private financial companies. The average size of public issues declined from ₹ 703.4 crore during 2007-08 to ₹ 326.0 crore during 2008-09.

Mobilisation of resources through private placement declined by 25.1 per cent during April-December 2008 as against an increase of 35.2 per cent during April-December 2007. Public sector entities accounted for 58.4 per cent of total mobilisation as compared with 37.2 per cent during the corresponding period of the previous year. Resource mobilisation through financial intermediaries (both from public and private sector) registered a decline of 40.5 per cent over the corresponding period of last year and accounted for 54.4 per cent of the total mobilisation during April-December 2008. However, resources raised by non-financial intermediaries registered an increase of 8.1 per cent (45.7 per cent of total resource mobilisation) during April-December 2008 over the corresponding period of the previous year.

During 2008-09, resources raised through Euro issues -American Depository Receipts (ADRs) and Global Depository Receipts (GDRs) - by Indian corporates declined significantly by 82.0 per cent to ₹ 4,788 crore as compared with the corresponding period of the previous year. All the Euro issues during the financial year were GDR issues.

Though resource mobilization from the primary market through equity investments was sluggish in 2009 both in terms of number of issues and amount raised through public rights issues and follow-on public offerings, there was an increase in debt market activity and private placements. The total number of initial public offerings (IPOs) declined to 20 in 2009 from 37 in 2008. The total amount mobilized through equity issues in 2009 was lower at ₹ 23,098 crore as compared to ₹ 49,485 crore raised in 2008. The amount raised through IPOs, however, increased slightly in 2009 to ₹ 19,296 crore from ₹ 18,393 crore in 2008. The mean IPO size increased to ₹ 965 crore in 2009 from ₹ 497 crore in 2008. There was no debt issue in 2008. The total amount mobilized through three debt issues during 2009 was ₹ 3,500 crore. The total amount raised through private placement of debt in 2009 at ₹ 2,38,226 crore was higher by 53.0 per cent than its previous year's level of ₹ 1,55,743 crore. Total resources mobilized through the primary market at₹ 2,80,090 crore recorded an increase of 32.4 per cent in 2009.

The year 2010-11 has seen the Indian capital market put the worst behind and move towards strong growth. The cumulative amount mobilized as on 30 November 2010-11 through initial public offers (IPOs), follow on public offers (FPOs) and rights issues stood at ₹ 46,701 crore as compared to ₹ 46,737 crore in 2009-10.

During 2010-11, 40 new companies (IPOs) were listed both at the NSE and BSE amounting to ₹ 33,068 crore as against 39 companies amounting to ₹ 24,696 crore in 2009. The mean IPO size for the financial year was ₹ 827 crore as compared to ₹ 633 crore in the previous financial year, shovving an increase of 30.6 per cent. Further, ₹ 2197 crore was mobilized through debt issue as compared to ₹ 2500 crore in 2009-10. The amount of capital mobilized through private placement in 2010-11 (as on 30 November 2010) is ₹ 1,47,400 crore as compared'to ₹ 2,12,635 crore in 2009-10.

During financial year 2011-12 (up to 31 December 2011) resource mobilization through the primary market witnessed a sharp decline over the year 2010-11. The cumulative amount mobilized as on 31 December 2011 through equity public issues stood at ₹ 9,683 crore as compared to ₹ 48,654 crore in 2010-11. During 2011-12, (up to 31 December 2011), 30 new companies (initial public offers—IPOs) were listed at the National Stock Exchange (NSE) and Bombay Stock Exchange (BSE) amounting to ₹ 5,043 crore as against 53 companies amounting to ₹ 35,559 crore listed in 2010-11. The mean IPO size for the year 2011-12 was ₹ 168 crore as compared to ₹ 671 crore in 2010-11. Further, only ₹ 4,791 crore was mobilized through debt issue as compared to ₹ 9,451 crore in 2010-11. The amount of capital mobilized through private placement in corporate debt in 2011-12 (AprilDecember) was ₹ 1,88,530 crore as compared to ₹ 2,18,785 crore in 2010-11.

The primary market showed mixed trends during 2012-13. Indian corporates raised ₹ 26,135.4 crore via the primary capital markets in December 2012. This was 20 per cent higher than the amount raised in the preceding month. The amount raised via equity issues was substan-tially higher at ₹ 16,759.8 crore as compared to the monthly average of ₹ 2,167 crore during April-November 2012. Overall during financial year 2012-13 (up to 31 December, 2012) resource mobilization through primary market (equity issue) witnessed an upward movement (Table 1). The cumulative amount mobilised as on 31 December 2012 through equity public issues stood at ₹ 13,050 crore. During 2012-13, 20 new companies [initial public offers (IPOs)] with resource mobilisation amounting to ₹ 6,043 crore were listed at the National Stock Exchange (NSE) and Bombay Stock Exchange (BSE) with mean IPO size of ₹ 302 crore. However, in the public issue of corporate debt category, ₹ 4,974 crore was mobilised through debt issue in 2012-13 compared to ₹ 35,611 crore in 2011-12.

TABLE 1

Resource Mobilization through the Primary Market

(₹ crore)

Mode	2009-10	2010-11	2011-12	2012-13#
1. Debt	2500	9451	35611	4974
2. Equity	46736	48654	12857	13050
Of which IPOs	24696	35559	5904	6043
Number of IPOs	39	53	34	20
Mean IPO size	633	671	174	302
3. Private placement	212635	218785	261282	263644
4. Euro issues (ADR/GDR)	NA	NA	NA	NA
Total (1+2+3+4)	261871	276890	309750	281667

Source: Securities and Exchange Board of India (SEBI) and RBI (for Euro issues).
Notes: NA indicates Not Available;
as on 31 December 2012 (Provisional); the Equity issues are considered only equity public issues; ADR is American Depository Receipts and GDR is Global Depository Receipts.

Private placement and MFs witnessed substantial pick-up during 2012-13, while the IPO market remained sluggish. Both the number of issues and the amount raised through IPO issues are very low in comparison to the peak resource mobilisation achieved in 2007-08. Even the offer document i.e., Draft Red Herring Prospectus, filed with SEBI during April-September 2012 declined by 90 per cent over the corresponding period in

2011-12- Many companies which had filed their offer document to raise funds have withdrawn their proposals and two IPOs have not been fully subscribed in 2012-13 (till Jan., 2013). During April-August 2012, the total resources mobilised through private placement grew by about 73 per cent (y-o-y), while the net inflow of funds into MFs schemes grew by around 41 per cent on account of the base effect. The MF inflows to the liquid and income schemes were higher, on the back of improved liquidity conditions while they were net sellers in the equity segment.

The IPO market remained subdued due to weak investment demand arising from the slowdown in overall economic growth, persistent inflation and high fiscal and current account deficits. The IPO activity mirrored the trends in the secondary market, in line with cautious investor sentiments in the recent past. Second, many of the IPOs listed during 2011-12 are currently trading below their issue once. As on October 25, 2012, of the 34 IPOs listed in the equity market in 2011-12, 20 were trading below their issue price. Negative returns on IPO investments have adversely affected investor sentiments Third global IPO activities have also been subdued since 2011. During Q2 of 2012-13, the resources raised through global IPO markets were 48 per cent lower than in the previous quarter, even though the secondary equity market posted huge gains during this period. Various measures taken by SEBI, such as allowing qualified foreign investor (QFIs) to invest in the primary as well as secondary market, electronic initial offers (e-IPOs), requiring companies to attain the minimum public shareholding of 25 per cent by June 2013, introduction of the Rajiv Gandhi Equity Savings Scheme, 2012 and the disinvestment programme by the government may also enhance primary market activity. During September-December 2012, ₹ 110 billion was mobilised through 18 issues compared to ₹ 23 billion mobilised through 11 issues during the corresponding period last year.

Policy changes have been contemplated to support the capital market during 2012-13. Apart from the policy reform measure, the Kelkar Committee on Roadmap for Fiscal Consolidation has made suggestions to review the disinvestment programme. The Deepak Parekh Committee suggested setting up infrastructure debt funds to boost infrastructure financing.

Along with these initiatives, SEBI has also taken various measures to revive mutual fund investments and IPO activity. MF companies will now have to shift to the 'one plan per scheme' model. Also, a proposal has been made for a mandatory 'safety net' to protect the interests of small investors. Further, substantial QE programmes of AEs along with low interest rates will boost global liquidity and revive FII inflows to the IPO market. FII inflows and reform measures that are fuelling the uptrend in the secondary market, may also have a positive impact on the IPO market. Finally, SEBI brought out a paper proposing modifications to the share buy back framework. SEBI observed that buy back through open market has failed to achieve its objectives of returning surplus cash to shareholders, increasing underlying share value and supporting share price during periods of temporary weakness. Besides, many companies did not buy back even a single share or failed to achieve the minimum buy back quantity even though the buy back window was open for a year.

SEBI proposed to increase the minimum buy back quantity to 50 per cent of the maximum quantity proposed for buy back. Currently, companies have to buy back a minimum of 25 per cent of the maximum quantity proposed for buy back. SEBI also suggested that the period to complete the buy back be shortened to three months from one year at present.

To ensure that only serious companies launch the buy back programme, SEBI proposed that these companies be mandated to put 25% of the maximum amount pro-posed for buy back in an escrow account. Further, SEBI also recommended that companies coming out with buy back programmes may not be allowed to raise further capital for a period of two years.

To prevent companies from launching buy back programmes to stabilise their share price, SEBI asserted that companies that are unable to buy back 100 per cent of the proposed amount (or the proposed maximum number of shares) may not be allowed to come out with another buy back for at least a year.

MAJOR POLICY INITIATIVES IN THE PRIMARY MARKET

In the overall context of the evolving macroeconomic situation in the country and global financial developments, the government in close collaboration with the RBI and SEBI has recently taken a number of initiatives to meet the growing capital needs of the Indian economy. Some of the initiatives are as follows:

1. SEBI (Alternative Investment Funds) Regulations 2012: With a view to extending the reach of regulation to unregulated funds, ensuring systemic stability, increasing market efficiency, encouraging new capital formation, and providing investor protection, SEBI has notified new regulations covering alternate investment funds (AIFs) under three broad categories:

Category 1: AIFs with positive spillover effects on the economy, for which certain incentives or concessions might be considered by SEBI or the Government of India or other regulators in India; and which shall include venture capital funds, small and medium enterprises (SME) funds, social venture funds, and infrastructure funds.

Category 2: AIFs for which no specific incentives or concessions are given by the government or any other regulator; which shall not undertake leverage other than to meet dayto-day operational requirements as permitted in these regulations

Category 3: AIFs with funds (including hedge funds) that are considered to have negative externalities.

2. The recent initiatives taken to develop the Indian corporate bond markets are summarized in Box 2.

Box 2

RECENT INITIATIVES FOR FURTHER DEVELOPMENT OF
CORPORATE BOND MARKETS

- To permit banks to take limited membership in SEBI-approved stock exchanges for the purpose of undertaking proprietary transactions in the corporate bond markets.
- To enhance liquidity in the corporate bond markets the Insurance Regulatory and Development Authority (IRDA) has permitted insurance companies to participate in the repo market. The IRDA has also permitted insurance companies to become users of credit default swap (CDS).
- In consultation with the Technical Advisory Committee on Money, Foreign Exchange, and Government Securities Markets, it has been decided to reduce the minimum haircut requirement in corporate debt repo from the existing 10 per cent/12per cent/15per cent to 7.5 per cent/8.5per cent/10 per cent for AAA/AA+/AA-rated corporate bonds.
- MFs have been permitted to participate in CDS in corporate debt securities, as users. MFs can participate as users in CDS for eligible securities as reference obligations, constituting from within the portfolio of only fixed maturity plans (FMP) schemes having tenor exceeding one year.
- Revised guidelines on CDS for corporate bonds by the RBI provide that in addition to listed corporate bonds, CDS shall also be permitted on unlisted but rated corporate bonds even for issues other than infrastructure companies.
- Users shall be allowed to unwind their CDS-bought position with the original protection seller at a mutually agreeable or Fixed Income Money Market and Derivatives Association

of India(IMMDA) price. If no agreement is reached, then unwinding has to be done with the original protection seller at FIMMDA price.

• CDS shall be permitted on securities with original maturity up to one year like CPs, certificates of deposit, and nonconvertible debentures with original maturity less than one year as reference/deliverable obligations.

3. Financial Literacy: With the objective of promoting financial education in a synergistic manner, under the aegis of the Financial Stability and Development Council (FSDC) Sub-Committee a draft National Strategy on Financial Education has been formulated and public consultation on the same has been undertaken. The document is in the stage of finalization.

4. Two-way fungibility in Indian Depository Receipts (IDRs): Pursuant to the budget announcement of 2012-13, the Ministry of Corporate Affairs (MCA) [1 October 2012], the RBI, and SEBI (28 August 2012) have carried out amendments to the existing legal framework to facilitate two-way fungibility in Indian depository receipts.

5. Revisions to the Guidelines on Securitization Transactions: Securitisation is a process by which assets are sold to a bankruptcy remote special purpose vehicle (SPV) in return for an immediate cash payment. The cash flow from the underlying pool of assets is used to service the securities issued by the SPV. While there is sale of single asset or pool of assets to a 'bankruptcy remote' SPV in return for an immediate cash at the first stage of Securitisation, the second stage involves repackaging and selling the security interests representing claims on incoming cash flows from the asset or pool of assets to third party investors by issuance of tradable debt securities. In order to prevent unhealthy practices surrounding securitization, viz. origination of loans for the sole purpose of securitization and in order to align the interest of the originator with that of the investors and with a view to redistributing credit risk to a wide spectrum of investors, it was felt necessary that originators should retain a portion of each securitization originated and ensure more effective screening of loans. In addition, a minimum period of retention of loans prior to securitization was also considered desirable, to make the investors more comfortable regarding due diligence exercised by the originator.

QUESTIONS

1. Explain the meaning of the term 'New Issue Market'. How does it differ from the 'Secondary Market'? Are they connected to each other?

2. Write an essay on the functions of the New Issue Market and importance thereof in the context of industrial finance.

3. Critically examine the recent trends in primary market in India.

4. Analyse the role of new issue market in financing companies.

5. Discuss the recent developments in the primary capital market in India

6. Discuss the role of private placements in raising resources in the primary capital market.

7. Critically examine the recent resource mobilisation in the primary capital market.

REFERENCES

1. Baumol, W.J. *The Stock Market and Economic Efficiency.* New York: Fordham University Press, 1965.

2. Bellemore, Phillips, and Ritchie. *Investments.* Cincinnati: South-western Publishing, 1979.

3.   Black, Fisher. "Toward a Fully Computerized Stock Exchange," *Financial Analysts Journal*. Nov.-Dec. 1971.

4.   Chen, Nui-Fu, Richard Roll, and Stephen A. Ross. "Economic Forces and the Stock Market." *Journal of Business* 59, no. 3 (July 1986).

5.   Cohen, J., E. Zinbarg, and A. Zeikel: *Investment Analysis and Portfolio Management*, Richard D Irwin, Home wood, IL, 1987.

6.   D'ambrosio, Charles A. *Principles of Modern Investments*. Chicago: Science Research Associates.

7.   Fisher, D.E., and R. J. Jordan. *Security Analysis and Portfolio Management*. Englewood Cliffs, N.J.: Prentice-Hall, 1979, chapter 7.

8.   Fosback, Norman G. *Stock Market Logic*. Fort Lauderdale, Fla.: The Institute for Economic Research, 1976.

9.   Friend, Irwin. "The Economic Consequences of the Stock Market," *American Economic Review*. May 1972.

10. Fuller, Russell J., "Behavioral Finance and the Sources of Alpha", Journal of Pension Plan Investing, Winter, 1998.

11. Graham, B., D. Dodd, and S. Cottle: *Security Analysis*, 4th ed., McGraw-Hill, New York, 1962.

12. Grodinsky, Julius. *Investments*. New York: Ronald Press, 1953.

13. Hamilton, William P. *The Stock Market Barometer*. New York: Richard Russell Associates, 1960.

14. Hayes, D., and W. Bauman. *Investments: Analysis and Management*, 3rd ed. New York: Macmillan, 1976, chapters 16-17.

15. Huang, Stanley S.C. *Techniques of Investment Analysis*. New York; Intext Educational Publishers. 1972, chapters 7-8.

16. Ibbotson, Roger G., Judy Sindelar, and Jay R. Ritter. "Initial Public Offerings." *Journal of Applied Corporate Finance* 1, no. 3 (Summer 1988).

17. Jensen, Michael, and Richard Ruback: "The Market for Corporate Control," *Journal of Financial Economics*, April 1983, pp. 5-50.

18. Kahneman, Daniel, and Amos Tversky, "The Psychology of Preferences," Scientific American, Jan/June, 1982

19. Latane, H., D. Tuttle, and C. Jones. *Security Analysis and Portfolio Management*, 2d ed. Ronald, 1975, chapter 16.

20. Levin, Laurence ,"Are Assets Fungible? Testing Alternative Theories of Life – Cycle Savings", working paper, Santa Clara University, Santa Clara, CA.

21. Lishan, J.M., and D. T. Crary, eds. *The Investment Process*. International Textbook, 1970.

22. Loll, Leo M. Jr., and Julian G. Buckley. *The Over-the-Counter Security Markets*. Englewood Cliffs, N.J.: Prentice-Hall, 1986.

23. Lorie, James H., and Mary T. Hamilton. *The Stock Market: Theories and Evidence*. 2d ed. Homewood, 111.: Richard D. Irwin, 1985.

24. Mendelson and Robbins. *Investment Analysis & Securities Markets*. New York: Basic Books, 1976.

25. Miller, Robert E., and Frank K. Reilly. "Examination of Mispricing, Returns, and Uncertainty for Initial Public Offerings." *Financial Management* 16, no. 2 (January 1987).

26. Moskowitz, Milton. "The 'Intelligent Investor' at 80," *New York Times*. May 5, 1974.

27. Noddings, Thomas C. *Advanced Investment Strategies*. Homewood, III.: Dow Jones-Irwin, 1978.

28. Peake, Junius W. "The National Market System," *Financial Analysts Journal*. July-Aug. 1978.

29. Robbins, Sidney. *The Securities Markets: Operations and Issues*. New York: Free Press, 1966.

30. Robert, R. and N.Schwartz," Effects of Perceptual Fluency on Judgement of Truth", Consciousness and Cognition 8(1999)

31. Samuelson, Paul A. "Economics of the Stock Market and the Investor," *Commercial & Financial Chronicle*. Oct.

32. Sauvain, Harry C. *Investment Management*, 4th ed. Englewood Cliffs, N.J.: Prentice-Hall, 1973

33. Schaefer, J.M., and A.J. Warner. "Concentration Trends and Competition in the Securities Industry," *Financial Analysts Journal*. Nov.-Dec. 1977.

34. Sharpe, William F., Gordon J. Alexander, and Jeffrey V. Bailey. *Investments*, 5th ed. Englewood Cliffs, N.J.: Prentice-Hall, 1995.

35. Skousen, K. Fred. *An Introduction to the SEC*. 5th ed. Cincinnati: South-Western Publishing, 1990.

36. Smith, Adam, "The Money Game", Random House: New York, 1976

37. Sobel, Robert. *The Big Board: A History of the New York Stock Market*. New York: The Free Press, 1965.

38. Statman, Meir, "Behavioral Finance versus Standard Finance ,"Behavioral Finance and Decision Theory in Investment Management (Charlottesville, VA: AIMR, 1995)

39. Stoll, Hans, and Robert E. Whaley. Stock *Market Structure, Volatility, and Volume*. Charlottsville, Va.: Institute of Chartered Financial Analysts Research Foundation, 1990.

40. Thaler ,R. ,"Mental Accounting and Consumer Choice, Marketing Science 4,(1995)

41. Tversky, Amos , "The Psychology of Decision Making," Behavioral Finance and Decision Theory in Investment Management (Charlottesville, VA: AIMR, 1995)

42. ————— , and D. Kahneman, "Availability: A Heuristic for Judging Frequency and Probability", Cognitive Psychology 5 (1973)

43. Wood, Arnold S., "Behavioral Risk : Anecdotes and Disturbing Evidence", Investment Worldwide VI, AIMR

4

Listing of Securities

INTRODUCTION

A security is said to be 'listed' when its name is added to the list of securities in which trading on a particular exchange is permitted. The principal objectives of listing are :

(i) to provide ready marketability, liquidity and free negotiability to stocks and shares;

(ii) to ensure proper supervision and control of dealings therein; and

(iii) to protect the interests of shareholders and of general investing public.

ADVANTAGES OF LISTING

The advantages of listing may be viewed from two angles :

(i) from the point of view of the management of companies; and

(ii) from the point of view of the shareholders.

The advantages derived by the management as a result of listing are many. Apart from the distinct advertising value, listing enables the management to broaden and diversify shareholding. It is the general consensus of opinion that a company with a broad-based share ownership is better suited for growth and stability than a company with shares concentrated in few hands. Ensuring thus a broadening of share ownership, listing not only brings a company's shares to the attention of hundreds and thousands of new investors, but also encourages institutional investors to be interested in them. It helps the company to gain national importance and widespread recognition.

There is difference between a listed and a non-listed security (particularly from the point of view of the psychological motivation of the investors in applying for subscription to shares) in as much as Section 73 of the Companies Act requires that every company intending to offer shares or debentures to the public for subscription through issue of a prospectus, must seek enlistment with one or more stock exchanges. If such listing is riot granted or applied for then the company must return all money to the applicants. This, in other words, implies that prospective listing prompts the investors to apply for the shares and failure to secure listing entitles the investors to claim refund of the money. In fact, listing has its tremendous value to a company in regard to the raising of additional capital for expansion or other purposes. Section 81 of the Companies Act provides that any further issue of share, unless waived by them in a general meeting, must in the first instance be offered to the existing shareholders. Now in the case of a non-listed company, if this right of subscribing to the additional shares is not exercised by the shareholders, the company concerned will be in great difficulty, and will also have to incur great expense in selling them. But in the case of a listed company, there is neither this difficulty nor the additional expenses, for this right can be disposed of by the shareholders through the Stock Exchange. Further, when a listed company makes such offer of further shares to the shareholders, the shareholders in their turn get better estimation of the value of the shares from the price at which the shares of the company are quoted on the Stock Exchange. Lasting, thus affords a great advantage to the management in ensuring a saving in the cost of raising new capital. This advantage is also utilised by the management in connection with the acquisition of additional business or assets or mergers with the companies because listing enables it to offer its securities iri exchange for those of a closely held or of an unlisted company.

The shareholders or investors too derive manifold benefits if the shares held or owned by them are listed on the Stock Exchange. The main benefits are :

(i) It affords liquidity to their holdings.

(ii) It affords them to obtain the best prices for the securities they want to sell off.

(iii) It helps them to avoid the botheration of canvassing from door to door to sell the securities. A mere telephonic or verbal order to a stock broker will help them to buy or sell a listed security.

(iv) Transactions on the Stock Exchange are done by auction bids, so there is no hide or seek about the price at which the investor buys or sells the share.

(v) The Stock Exchange quotation helps the investors to keep themselves abreast of the price changes of the securities owned or held by them.

(vi) The investors get maximum protection in regard to their holdings, because the Stock Exchange rules and regulations have been formulated with the end in view.

(vii) Listing gives an added collateral value to the securities held by investors, for banks in making loans and advances prefer a security quoted on the Stock Exchange.

(viii) Listing is also advantageous in the matter of income-tax, wealth-tax, estate duty and other taxes payable by shareholders in their capacity as assessees. However, from the foregoing discussion, it should not be concluded that the Stock Exchange vouches for the listed securities. In fact, price determination and value judgements involve constant scrutiny and assessment of each company from business, financial, accounting, legal and technical points of view, and these are primarily the functions of the buyers and sellers in the market. The Stock Exchange can not and does not stand sponsor for the listed securities or guarantee their investment value; but it does ensure continuing sponsorship and assistance in the establishment arid development of sound and progressively higher standards of corporate practice and procedure. For these reasons, listing carries the hallmark of prestige and confers on the listed company, its securities and its shareholders a privileged position.

LISTING : IS IT A LEGAL REQUIREMENT ?

There is no statutory obligation that a public limited company should get its shares enlisted on a recognised Stock Exchange unless it seeks to raise funds from the public by issue of a prospectus. Also, a company declaring in the prospectus its intention of applying for enlistment is required under Section 73 of the Companies Act to make listing application to the Stock Exchange concerned. Further, government has the power under Section 21 of the Securities Contracts (Regulation) Act, 1956, to compel a public limited company, when it is so necessary or expedient in the interest of the trade or the public to comply with the prescribed requirements and list its shares on a recognised Stock Exchange. Similarly, public financial institutions and nationalised banks make similar stipulations when agreeing to underwrite or subscribe to a new issue of capital.

KEY PROVISIONS IN LISTING AGREEMENT

Listing of securities on Indian stock exchanges is essentially governed by the provisions in the Companies Act, 1956, SCRA, SCRR, rules, bye-laws and regulations of the concerned stock exchange, the listing agreement entered into by the issuer and the stock exchange and the circulars/guidelines issued by Central Government and SEBI. A company intending to have its securities listed on the Exchange has to comply with the listing requirements prescribed by the Exchange. Some of the requirements are as under :-

[I] *Minimum Listing Requirements for New Companies*

The following revised eligibility criteria for listing of companies on the Exchange, through Initial Public Offerings (IPOs) & Follow-on Public Offerings (FPOs), effective August 1, 2006.

Eligibility Criteria for IPOs/FPOs

A. Companies have been classified as large cap companies and small cap companies. A large cap company is a company with a minimum issue size of ` 10 crores and market capitalization of not less than ` 25 crores. A small cap company is a company other than a large cap company.

  (a) In respect of Large Cap Companies

     (i) The minimum post-issue paid-up capital of the applicant company (hereinafter referred to as "the Company") shall be ` 3 crores; and

    (ii) The minimum issue size shall be ` 10 crores; and

   (iii) The minimum market capitalization of the Company shall be ` 25 crores (market capitalization shall be calculated by multiplying the post-issue paid-up number of equity shares with the issue price).

  (b) In respect of Small Cap Companies

     (i) The minimum post-issue paid-up capital of the Company shall be ` 3 crores; and

    (ii) The minimum issue size shall be ` 3 crores; and

   (iii) The minimum market capitalization of the Company shall be ` 5 crores (market capitalization shall be calculated by multiplying the post-issue paid-up number of equity shares with the issue price); and

   (iv) The minimum income/turnover of the Company should be ` 3 crores in each of the preceding three12-months period; and

    (v) The minimum number of public shareholders after the issue shall be 1000.

   (vi) A due diligence . udy may be conducted by an independent team of Chartered Accountants or Merchant Bankers appointed by the Exchange, the cost of which will be borne by the company. The requirement of a due diligence study may be waived if a financial institution or a scheduled commercial bank has appraised the project in the preceding 12 months.

B. For all companies:

(i) In respect of the requirement of paid-up capital and market capitalisation, the issuers shall be required to include in the disclaimer clause forming a part of the offer document that in the event of the market capitalisation (product of issue price and the post issue number of shares) requirement of the Exchange not being met, the securities of the issuer would not be listed on the Exchange.

(ii) The applicant, promoters and/or group companies, should not be in default in compliance of the listing agreement.

(iii) The above eligibility criteria would be in addition to the conditions prescribed under SEBI (Disclosure and Investor Protection) Guidelines, 2000.

[II] Minimum Listing Requirements for Companies listed on Other Stock Exchanges

The Governing Board of the Exchange at its meeting held on 6th August, 2002 amended the direct listing norms for companies listed on other Stock Exchange(s) and seeking listing at BSE. These norms are applicable with immediate effect.

1. The company should have minimum issued and paid up equity capital of ` 3 crores.

2. The Company should have profit making track record for last three years. The revenues/profits arising out of extra ordinary items or income from any source of non-recurring nature should be excluded while calculating distributable profits.

3. Minimum networth of ` 20 crores (networth includes Equity capital and free reserves excluding revaluation reserves).

4. Minimum market capitalisation of the listed capital should be at least two times of the paid up capital.

5. The company should have a dividend paying track record for the last 3 consecutive years and the minimum dividend should be at least 10%.

6. Minimum 25% of the company's issued capital should be with Non-Promoters shareholders as per Clause 35 of the Listing Agreement. Out of above Non Promoter holding no single shareholder should hold more than 0.5% of the paid-up capital of the company individually or jointly with others except in case of Banks/Financial Institutions/Foreign Institutional Investors/Overseas Corporate Bodies and Non-Resident Indians.

7. The company should have at least two years listing record with any of the Regional Stock Exchange.

8. The company should sign an agreement with CDSL & NSDL for demat trading.

[III] Minimum Requirements for Companies Delisted by this Exchange Seeking Relisting of this Exchange

The companies delisted by this Exchange and seeking relisting are required to make a fresh public offer and comply with the prevailing SEBI's and BSE's guidelines regarding initial public offerings.

[IV] Permission to Use the Name of the Exchange in an Issuer Company's Prospectus

The Exchange follows a procedure in terms of which companies desiring to list their securities offered through public issues are required to obtain its prior permission to use the name of the Exchange in their prospectus or offer for sale documents before filing the same with the concerned office of the Registrar of Companies. The Exchange has since last three years formed a "Listing Committee" to analyse draft prospectus/offer documents of the companies in respect of their forthcoming public issues of securities and decide upon the matter of granting them permission to use the name of "Bombay Stock Exchange Limited" in their prospectus/offer documents. The committee evaluates the promoters, company, project and several other factors before taking decision in this regard.

[V] Submission of Letter of Application

As per Section 73 of the Companies Act, 1956, a company seeking listing of its, securities on the Exchange is required to submit a Letter of Application to all the Stock Exchanges where it proposes to have its securities listed before filing the prospectus with the Registrar of Companies.

[VI] Allotment of Securities

As per Listing Agreement, a company is required to complete allotment of securities offered to the public within 30 days of the date of closure of the subscription list and approach the Regional Stock Exchange, i.e. Stock Exchange nearest to its Registered Office for approval of the basis of allotment.

In case of Book Building issue, Allotment shall be made not later than 15 days from the closure of the issue failing which interest shall be paid to the investors.

[VII] Trading Permission

As per Securities and Exchange Board of India Guidelines, the issuer company should complete the formalities for trading at all the Stock Exchanges where the securities are to be listed within 7 working days of finalisation of Basis of Allotment.

A company should scrupulously adhere to the time limit for allotment of all securities and dispatch of Allotment Letters/Share Certificates and Refund Orders and for obtaining the listing permissions of all the Exchanges whose names are stated in its prospectus or offer documents. In the event of listing permission to a company being denied by any Stock Exchange where it had applied for listing of its securities, it cannot proceed with the allotment of shares. However, the company may file an appeal before the Securities and Exchange Board of India under Section 22 of the Securities Contracts (Regulation) Act, 1956.

[VIII] Requirement of 1% Security

The companies making public/rights issues are required to deposit 1% of issue amount with the Regional Stock Exchange before the issue opens. This amount is liable to be forfeited in the event of the company not resolving the complaints of investors regarding delay in sending refund orders/share certificates, non-payment of commission to underwriters, brokers, etc.

[IX] Payment of Listing Fees

All companies listed on the Exchange have to pay Annual Listing Fees by the 30th April of every financial year to the Exchange as per the Schedule of Listing Fees prescribed from time to time.

The schedule of Listing Fees for the year 2011-12, is given in Table-1

TABLE-1A

Securities *other than Privately Placed Debt Securities and Mutual Funds

Sr. No.	Particulars	Amount
1	Initial Listing Fees	₹ 20,000/-
2	Annual Listing Fees	
(i)	Upto ₹ 5 Crs.	₹ 15,000/-
(ii)	₹ 5 Crs. to Rs.10 Crs.	₹ 25,000/-
(iii)	₹ 10 Crs. to ₹ 20 Crs.	₹ 40,000/-
(iv)	₹ 20 Crs. to ₹ 30 Crs.	₹ 60,000/-
(v)	₹ 30 Crs. to ₹ 100 Crs.	₹ 70,000/- plus ₹ 2,500/- for every increase of ₹ 5 crs or part thereof above ₹ 30 crs.
(vi)	₹ 100 Crs. to ₹ 500 Crs.	₹ 125,000/- plus ₹ 2,500/- for every increase of ₹ 5 crs or part thereof above ₹ 100 crs.
(vii)	₹ 500 Crs. to ₹ 1000 Crs.	₹ 375,000/- plus ₹ 2,500/- for every increase of ₹ 5 crs or part thereof above ₹ 500 crs.
(vi)	Above ₹ 1000 Crs.	₹ 625,000/- plus ₹ 2,750/- for every increase of ₹ 5 crs or part thereof above ₹ 1000 crs.

Note: In case of debenture capital (not convertible into equity shares), the fees will be 75% of the above fees.

* includes equity shares, preference shares, indian depository receipts, fully convertible debentures, partly convertible debentures and any other security convertible into equity shares.

TABLE-1(B)

Privately Placed Debt Securities

Sr. No.	Particulars	Amount
1	Initial Listing Fees	NIL
2	Annual Listing Fees	
(i)	Issue size up to ₹5 Crs.	₹ 2,500/-
(ii)	Above ₹ 5 Crs. and up to Rs.10 Crs.	₹ 3,750/-
(iii)	Above ₹10 Crs. and up to ₹ 20 Crs.	₹ 7,500/-
(iv)	Above ₹20 Crs.	₹ 7,500/- plus ₹ 200/- for every increase ₹ 1 Cr. or part thereof above ₹ 20 crs. Subject to a maximum of ₹ 30,000/- per instrument.

Note: Cap on the annual listing fee of debt instruments per issuer is ₹ 5,00,000/- per annum.

TABLE-1(C)

Mutual Funds

Sl. No.	Particulars	Amount (₹)
1	Initial Listing Fees	NIL
2	Annual Listing Fee for tenure of the scheme	Payable per 'month or part thereof
i.	Issue size up to ₹ 50 Crs.	₹ 1,000/-

ii.	Above ₹ 50 Crs.and up to ₹ 100 Crs.	₹ 2,000/-
iii.	Above ₹ 100 Crs.and up to ₹ 300 Crs.	₹ 3,600/-
iv.	Above ₹ 300 Crs.and up to ₹ 500 Crs.	₹ 5,900/-
v.	Above ₹ 500 Crs.and up to ₹ 1000 Crs.	₹ 9,800/-
vi	Above 1000 Crs.	₹15,600/-

Note: 1. For tenure beyond One month, fees are payable for one month or any part thereof.

2. Asset Under Management (AUM) of all such listed schemes of the Fund House exceed ₹ 10,000 crs, discount of 10% will be offered on future annual listing fees for all listed schemes of that Fund House. For eligibility of 10% discount on listing fees, the corpus of AUM will be taken as on March 31st of every year.

Applicability

The above schedule of Listing Fee is uniformly applicable for all companies irrespective of whether BSE is the designated stock exchange or not.

Payment Date

The last date for payment of Listing Fee for the year 2011-12 is April 30, 2011. Failure to pay the Listing Fee (for equity debt segment and/or Mutual Fund) by the due date will attract interest @ 12% per annum w.e.f. May 1, 2011.

Service Tax

Service Tax is payable on the listing fee at the applicable rates.

[X] Compliance with the Listing Agreement

Companies desirous of getting their securities listed at BSE are required to enter into an agreement with BSE called the Listing Agreement, under which they are required to make certain disclosures and perform certain acts, failing which the company may face some disciplinary action, including suspension/delisting of securities. As such, the Listing Agreement is of great importance and is executed under the common seal of a company. Under the Listing Agreement, a company undertakes, amongst other things, to provide facilities for prompt transfer, registration, sub-division and consolidation of securities; to give proper notice of closure of transfer books and record dates, to forward 6 copies of unabridged Annual Reports, Balance Sheets and Profit and Loss Accounts to BSE, to file shareholding patterns and financial results on a quarterly basis; to intimate promptly to the Exchange the happenings which are likely to materially affect the financial performance of the Company and its stock prices, to comply with the conditions of Corporate Governance, etc.

The Listing Department of BSE monitors the compliance by the companies with the provisions of the Listing Agreement, especially with regard to timely payment of annual listing fees, submission of results, shareholding patterns and corporate governance reports on a quarterly basis . Penal action is taken against the defaulting companies.

[XI] Cash Management Services (CMS) - Collection of Listing Fees

In order to simplify the system of payment of listing fees, BSE has entered into an arrangement with HDFC Bank for collection of listing fees from 141 locations all over the country.

Companies intending to utilize this facility for payment of listing fee should furnish the information (as mentioned below) in the Cash Management Cash Deposit Slip. These slips are available at all the HDFC Bank branches.

TABLE 2

S.No	Head	Information to be Provided
1.	Client Name	Bombay Stock Exchange Limited
2.	Client Code	BSELIST
3.	Cheque No.	mention the cheque No & date
4.	Date	date on which payment is being deposited with the bank.
5.	Drawer	state the name of the company and the company code No. The last digits mentioned in the Ref. No. on the Bill is the company code No.e.g If the Ref. No in the Bill is mentioned as : Listing/Alf-Bill/2004-2005/4488,/hen the code No of that company is 4488
6.	Drawee Bank	state the bank on which cheque is drawn
7.	Drawn on Location	Mention the location of the drawee bank.
8.	Pickup Location	Not applicable
9.	No. of Insts	Not applicable

The cheque should be drawn in favour of Bombay Stock Exchange Limited , and should be payable locally. Companies are requested to mention in the deposit slip, the financial year(s) for which the listing fee is being paid. Payment made through any other slips would not be considered. The above slips will have to be filled in quadruplicate. One acknowledged copy would be provided to the depositor by the HDFC Bank.

LISTING PROCEDURES: NATIONAL STOCK EXCHANGE (NSE)

An Issuer has to take various steps prior to making an application for listing its securities on the NSE. These steps are essential to ensure the compliance of certain requirements by the Issuer before listing its securities on the NSE. The various steps to be taken include:

Approval of Memorandum and Articles of Association

Rule 19(2) (a) of the Securities Contracts (Regulation) Rules, 1957 requires that the Articles of Association of the Issuer wanting to list its securities must contain provisions as given hereunder.

The Articles of Association of an Issuer shall contain the following provisions namely:
  a. that there shall be no forfeiture of unclaimed dividends before the claim becomes barred by law;
  b. that a common form of transfer shall be used;
  c. that fully paid shares shall be free from all lien and that in the case of partly paid shares the Issuer's lien shall be restricted to moneys called or payable at a fixed time in respect of such shares;
  d. that registration of transfer shall not be refused on the ground of the transferor being either alone or jointly with any other person or persons indebted to the Issuer on any account whatsoever;
  e. that any amount paid up in advance of calls on any share may carry interest but shall not in respect thereof confer a right to dividend or to participate in profits;
  f. that option or right to call of shares shall not be given to any person except with the sanction of the Issuer in general meetings,
  g. permission for Sub-Division/Consolidation of Share Certificate.

The Relevant Authority may take exception to any provision contained in the Articles of Association of an Issuer which may be deemed undesirable or unreasonable in the case of a public company and may require inclusion of specific provisions deemed to be desirable and necessary. If the Issuer's Articles of Association is not in conformity with the provisions as stated above, the Issuer has to make amendments to the Articles of Association. However, the securities of an Issuer may be admitted for listing on the NSE on an undertaking by the Issuer that the amendments necessary in the Articles of Association to bring Articles of Association in conformity with Rule 19(2)(a) of the Securities Contract (Regulation) Rules, 1957 shall be made in the next annual general meeting and in the meantime the Issuer shall act strictly in accordance with prevalent provisions of Securities Contract (Regulation) Act, 1957 and other statutes. It is to be noted that any provision in the Articles of Association which is not in tune with sound corporate practice has to be removed by amending the Articles of Association.

Approval of Draft Prospectus

The Issuer shall file the draft prospectus and application forms with NSE. The draft prospectus should have been prepared in accordance with the statutes, notifications, circulars, guidelines, etc. governing preparation and issue of prospectus prevailing at the relevant time. The Issuers may particularly bear in mind the provisions of Companies Act, Securities Contracts (Regulation) Act, the SEBI Act and the relevant subordinate legislations thereto. NSE will peruse the draft prospectus only from the point of view of checking whether the draft prospectus is in accordance with the listing requirements, and therefore any approval given by NSE in respect of the draft prospectus should not be construed as approval under any laws, rules, notifications, circulars, guidelines etc. The Issuer should also submit the SEBI acknowledgment card or letter indicating observations on draft prospectus or letter of offer by SEBI.

Submission of Application (For Issuers listing on NSE for the first time)

Issuers desiring to list existing/new securities on the NSE shall make application for admission of their securities to dealings on the NSE in the forms prescribed in this regard as per details given hereunder or in such other form or forms as the Relevant Authority may from time to time prescribe in addition thereto or in modification or substitution thereof.

Issuers whose securities are already listed on the NSE shall apply for admission to listing on the NSE of any further issue of securities made by them. The application for admission shall be made in the forms prescribed in this regard or in such other form oɪ forms as the Relevant Authority may from time to time prescribe in addition thereto or in modification or substitution thereof.

Submission of Application (Security Deposit)

(Payable only for new and fresh issues and only when IMSE is the Regional Stock Exchange)

The Relevant Authority shall not grant admission to dealings of securities of an Issuer which is not listed or of any new (original or further) issue of securities of an Issuer excepting Mutual Funds, which is listed on the NSE unless the Issuer deposits and keeps deposited with the NSE (in cases where the securities are offered for subscription, whether through the issue of a prospectus, letter of offer or otherwise, and NSE is the Regional Stock Exchange for the Issuer) an amount calculated at 1% of the amount of securities offered for subscription to the public and or to the holders of existing securities of the Issuer, as the case may be for ensuring compliance by the Issuer within the prescribed or stipulated period of all requirements and conditions hereinafter mentioned and shall be refundable or forfeitable in the manner hereinafter stated:

1. The Issuer shall comply with all prevailing requirements of law including all requirements of and under any notifications, directives and guidelines issued by the Central Government, SEBI or any statutory body or local authority or any body or authority acting under the authority or direction of the Central Government and all prevailing listing requirements and conditions of the NSE and of each recognized Stock Exchange where the Issuer has applied for permission for admission to dealings of the securities, within the prescribed or stipulated period;

2. If the Issuer has complied with all the aforesaid requirements and conditions including, wherever applicable, its obligation under Section 73 (or any statutory modification or re-enactment thereof) of the Companies Act, 1956 and obligations arising therefrom, within the prescribed or stipulated period, and on obtaining a No Objection Certificate from SEBI and submitting it to NSE , NSE shall refund to the Issuer the said deposit without interest within fifteen days from the expiry of the prescribed or stipulated period;

3. If on expiry of the prescribed or stipulated period or the extended period referred to hereafter, the Issuer has not complied with all the aforesaid requirements and conditions, the said deposit shall be forfeited by the NSE, at its discretion, and thereupon the same shall vest in the NSE. Provided the forfeiture shall not release the Issuer of its obligation to comply with the aforesaid requirements and conditions;

4. If the Issuer is unable to complete compliance of the aforesaid requirements and conditions within the prescribed or stipulated period, the NSE, at its discretion and if the Issuer has shown sufficient cause, but without prejudice to the obligations of the Issuer under the laws in force to comply with any such requirements and conditions within the prescribed or stipulated period, may not forfeit the said deposit but may allow such further time to the Issuer as the NSE may deem fit; provided that

   a. the Issuer has at least ten days prior to expiry of the prescribed or stipulated period applied in writing for extension of time to the NSE stating the reasons for non-compliance, and

   b. the Issuer, having been allowed further time by the NSE, has before expiry of the prescribed or stipulated period, published in a manner required by the NSE, the fact of such extension having been allowed; provided further that where the NSE has not allowed extension in writing before expiry of the prescribed or stipulated period, the request for extension shall be deemed to have been refused; provided also that any such extension shall not release the Issuer of its obligations to comply with the aforesaid requirements and conditions.

5. 50% of the above mentioned security deposit should be paid to the NSE in cash. The balance amount can be provided by way of *a* bank guarantee, in the format prescribed by or acceptable to NSE. The amount to be paid in cash is limited to `3 crores.

Listing Fees

The listing fees depend on the paid up shares capital of the Company:

TABLE 3

Particulars	Amount (₹)
Initial Fees	7,500
Annual Listing Fees Companies with paid up share and/or debenture capita:	
Or ₹ 1 crore	4,200
Above ₹ 1 crore and up to ₹ 5 crores	8,400
Above ₹ 5 crors and up to ₹ 10 crores	14,000
Above ₹ 10 crores and up to ₹ 20 crores	28,000
Above ₹ 20 crores and up to ₹ 50 crores	42,000
Above ₹ 50 crores	70,000

Comapnies which have a paid up capital of more than ₹ 50 crores will pay additional listing fees of ₹ 1400 for ever increase of ₹ 5 crore or part thereof in the paid up share/debenture capital.

As per SEBI provision, the basic norms of listing on the stock exchanges should be uniform across the exchanges. However, the stock exchanges can prescribe additional norms over and above the minimum, which should be part of their byelaws. SEBI has been issuing guidelines/circulars prescribing certain norms to be included in the listing agreement and to be complied by the companies. The listing requirements for companies in the CM segment of NSE are presented in (Table 3).

TABLE 4

Listing Criteria for Companies on the CM Segment of NSE

Criteria	Initial Public Offerings (IPOs)	Companies listed on ther exchanges
Paid-up Equity Capital (PUEQ/Market Capitalisation (MC)/Net Worth	PUEC > ` 10cr. and MC > ` 25 Cr.	PUEC > ` 10cr. and MC > ` 25 Cr. Or PUEC > ` 25cr.OR PUEC > ` 50cr.OR The company shall have a net worth of not less than ` 50 crores in each of the preceding financial years.
Company/Promoter's Track Record	Atleast 3 years track record of either a) the applicant seeking listing OR b) the promoters/promoting company incorporated in or outside India OR c) Partnership firm and subsequently converted into Company not in existence as a Company for three years) and approaches the Exchange for listing. The Company subsequently formed would be considered for listing only on fulfillment of conditions stipulated by SEBI in this regard.	Atleast three years track record of either a) the applicant seeking listing; OR b) the promoters/promoting company, incorporated in or outside India.

Dividend Record / Net worth /
                                                                    Dividend paid in at least 2 out of
                                                                    the last 3 financial years
                                                                    immediately preceding the year in
                                                                    which the application has been
                                                                    made OR The networth of the
                                                                    applicants atleast ` 50 crores OR
                                                                    The applicant has distributable
                                                                    profits in at least two out of the
     last   three financial years.

Listing
                                                                    Listed on any other stock exchange
                                                                    for at least last three years OR
                                                                    listed on the exchange having
                                                                    nationwide trading terminals for
                                                                    at least one year.

Other Requirements   (a) No disciplinary action by other   (a) No disciplinary action by
      other

                              stock exchanges/regulatory   stock exchanges/regulatory
                              authority in past 3 yrs.   authority in past 3 yrs.
                              (b) Satisfactory redressal   (b) Satisfactory redressal
                              mechanism for investor   mechanism for investor
                              grievances,   grievances,
                              (c) distribution of shareholding   (c) distribution of shareholding
                              and   and
                              (d) details of Mitigation record   (d) details of Mitigation record of
                              of the promoting company, if any.   the promoting company, if any.
                              (e) Track record of Directors of   (e) Track record of Directors of
                              the Company   the Company

                                                                    (f) Change in control of a
                                                                    Company/ Utilisation of funds
                                                                    raised from public

Note:

1. (a)   In case of IPOs, Paid up Equity Capital means post issue paid up equity capital.
   (b)   In case of Existing companies listed on other exchanges, the existing paid up equity capital
         as well as the paid up equity capital after the proposed issue for which listing is sought shall
         be taken into account.

2. (a)   In case of IPOs, market capitalisation is the product of the issue price and the post-issue
         number of equity shares.
   (b)   In case of case of Existing companies listed on other stock exchanges the market capitalisation
         shall be calculated by using a 12 month moving average of the market capitalisation over a
         period of six months immediately preceding the date of application. For the purpose of
         calculating the market capitalisation over a 12 month period, the average of the weekly high
         and low of the closing prices of the shares as quoted on the National Stock Exchange during
         the last twelve months and if the shares are not traded on the National Stock Exchange such
         average price on any of the recognised Stock Exchanges where those shares are frequently
         traded shall be taken into account while determining market capitalisation after making
         necessary adjustments for Corporate Action such as Rights / Bonus issue/Split.

3.   In case of Existing companies listed on other stock exchanges, the requirement of ` 25 crores
         market capital shall not be applicable to listing of securities issued by Government Companies,
         Public Sector Undertakings, Financial Institutions, Nationalised Banks, Statutory Corporations
         and Banking Companies who are otherwise bound to adhere to all the relevant statutes,

guidelines, circulars, clarifications etc. that may be issued by various regulatory authorities from time to time

4. Net worth means paid-up equity capital + reserves excluding revaluation reserve - miscellaneous expenses not written off -negative balance in profit and loss account to the extent not set off.

5. Promoters mean one or more persons with minimum 3 years of experience of each of them in the same line of business and shall be holding at least 20 % of the post issue equity share capital individually or severally.

6. In case a company approaches the Exchange for listing within six months of an IPO, the securities may be considered as eligible for listing if they were otherwise eligible for listing at the time of the IPO. If the company approaches the Exchange for listing after six months of an IPO, the norms for existing listed companies may be applied and market capitalisation be computed based on the period from the IPO to the time of listing.

In the whereable debt market (WDM) segment, all government securities, state development loans and treasury bills are 'deemed' listed as and when they are issued. The other categories of securities are traded either under the 'permitted to trade' category or under the 'listed' category. All eligible securities whether publicly issued or privately placed can be made available for trading in the WDM segment. Amongst other requirements, privately placed debt paper of banks, institutions and corporates require an investment grade credit rating to be eligible for listing. The listing requirements for securities on the WDM segment are presented in Table 5.

DELISTING

The securities listed on NSE can be de-listed from the Exchange as per the SEBI (Delisting of Securities) Guidelines, 2003 in the following manner:

Voluntary De-listing of Companies

Any promoter or acquirer desirous of delisting securities of the company under the provisions of these guidelines shall obtain the prior approval of shareholders of the company by a special resolution passed at its general meeting, make a public announcement in the manner provided in these guidelines, make an application to the delisting exchange in the form specified by the exchange, and comply with such other additional conditions as may be specified by the concerned stock exchanges from where securities are to be de-listed. Any promoter of a company which desires to de-list from the stock exchange shall also determine an exit price for delisting of securities in accordance with the book building process as stated in the guidelines. The stock exchanges shall provide the infrastructure facility for display of the price at the terminal of the trading members to enable the investors to access the price on the screen to bring transparency to the delisting process.

Compulsory De-listing of Companies

The stock exchanges may de-list companies which have been suspended for a minimum period of six months for non-compliance with the listing agreement. The stock exchanges have to give adequate and wide public notice through newspapers and also give a show cause notice to a company. The exchange shall provide a time period of 15 days within which representation may be made to the exchange by any person who may be aggrieved by the proposed delisting. Where the securities of the company are de-listed by an exchange, the promoter of the company shall be liable to compensate the security holders of the company by paying them the fair value of the securities held by them and acquiring their securities, subject to their option to remain security-holders with the company.

TABLE 5

Eligibility Criteria for Securities on WDM Segment

Issuer	Listing Criteria	
	Public Issue	*Private Placement*
(a) Public Sector Undertakings / Statutory Corporations		
— Minimum 51% holding by Govt.	As applicable to corporates	As applicable to corporates
— Less than 51% holding by Govt	As applicable to corporates	
(b) Statutory Corporation/Local Bodies/Authorities		
— Minimum 51% holding by Govt.	As applicable to PSUs	—
— Less than 51% shareholding	As applicable to corporates	As applicable to corporates
(c) Financial Institutions (SLR Bonds & Non-SLR Bonds)	Eligible	— Credit Rating
(d) Scheduled Commercial Banks (SCBs)	Net worth of ₹ 50 crore or above	Net worth of ₹ 50 crore or above
(e) Infrastructure Companies (Tax Exemption and recognition as infrastructure company under related statutes/ regulations)	— Credit Rating	Credit Rating
(f) Corporates OR	— Minimum Paid-up capital of ₹ 10 crore, OR	— Minimum Paid-up capital of ₹ 10 crore,
	— Market Capitalisation of ₹ 25 crore (Net worth in case of unlisted companies)	Market Capitalisation of ₹ 25 crore (Net worth in case of unlisted companies)
)g) Mutual Funds	SEBI registered Mutual Fund /Scheme having an investment objective to invest predominantly in debt instruments.	— Credit Rating

QUESTIONS

1. What is meant by 'listing of securities'? What are its advantages from the point of view of the company and investors?

2. Is listing a statutory requirement? What type of companies are required to seek enlistment? Explain.

3. Why is it riskier to buy unlisted securities?

4. Enumerate the listing requirements and explain these with respect to Memorandum and Articles of Association, Minimum Public Offer and Standard Denomination.

5. Discuss the rules applicable to 'prospectus' under the standard requirements.

6. "The shares of a company will not be listed on a stock exchange unless the conditions relating to minimum public offer and minimum number of shareholders are satisfied". Explain and elucidate.

7. Describe the rules to be followed with regard to the allotment of shares for the purpose of obtaining enlistment.

8. Explain the procedure for listing of shares by a company.

9. Why would an investor prefer a listed stock to an unlisted one? Are there any advantages to the corporation in having a listed market?

REFERENCES

1. Bellemore, Phillips, and Ritchie. *Investments.* Cincinnati: South-western Publishing, 1979.

2. Black, Fisher. "Toward a Fully Computerized Stock Exchange," *Financial Analysts Journal.* Nov.-Dec. 1971.

3. D'ambrosio, Charles A. *Principles of Modern Investments.* Chicago: Science Research Associates.

4. Fosback, Norman G. *Stock Market Logic.* Fort Lauderdale, Fla.: The Institute for Economic Research, 1976.

5. Friend, Irwin. "The Economic Consequences of the Stock Market," *American Economic Review.* May 1972.

6. Graham, B., D. Dodd, and S. Cottle: *Security Analysis,* 4th ed., McGraw-Hill, New York, 1962.

7. Grodinsky, Julius. *Investments.* New York: Ronald Press, 1953.

8. Hamilton, William P. *The Stock Market Barometer.* New York: Richard Russell Associates, 1960.

9. Ibbotson, Roger G., Judy Sindelar, and Jay R. Ritter. "Initial Public Offerings." *Journal of Applied Corporate Finance* 1, no. 3 (Summer 1988).

10. Jensen, Michael, and Richard Ruback: "The Market for Corporate Control," *Journal of Financial Economics,* April 1983, pp. 5-50.

11. Levin, Laurence ,"Are Assets Fungible? Testing Alternative Theories of Life –Cycle Savings", working paper, Santa Clara University, Santa Clara, CA.

12. Lishan, J.M., and D. T. Crary, eds. *The Investment Process.* International Textbook, 1970.

13. Mendelson and Robbins. *Investment Analysis & Securities Markets.* New York: Basic Books, 1976.

14. Noddings, Thomas C. *Advanced Investment Strategies.* Homewood, III .: Dow Jones-Irwin, 1978.

15. Robbins, Sidney. *The Securities Markets: Operations and Issues.* New York: Free Press, 1966.

16. Samuelson, Paul A. "Economics of the Stock Market and the Investor," *Commercial & Financial Chronicle.* Oct.

17. Sauvain, Harry C. *Investment Management*, 4th ed. Englewood Cliffs, N.J.: Prentice-Hall, 1973

18. Sharpe, William F., Gordon J. Alexander, and Jeffrey V. Bailey. *Investments*, 5th ed. Englewood Cliffs, N.J.: Prentice-Hall, 1995.

5

The Brokerage Business

INTRODUCTION

In order to transact business in the securities market, an investor has to route his/her orders through a brokerage firm as only member-brokers are allowed to enter the trading floor. Trading among the members of a recognised stock exchange is carried on within the framework of the rules, bye-laws and regulations of the exchange. Only listed securities can be traded on the floor of a stock exchange.

FUNCTIONS OF A BROKERAGE FIRM

The business of brokers consists of searching out buyers when their customers wish to sell and locating sellers when their customers wish to buy so as to execute transactions as per customers' instructions. Usually deals are arranged with other brokers representing their customers. The brokers do not function as principals in the transactions; they are agents only. Brokers charge a commission on each purchase and sale which they execute which varies among brokerage houses.

It is important that the brokerage firm exercises care and demonstrates a reasonable amount of skill in fulfilling the customer's order. The brokerage firm may be held liable for any losses resulting from its mistakes. The care with which the brokerage firm executes orders is determined by what is reasonable practice in their business. The exercise of care and skill requires that the broker follows instructions and places the order in the market ***wru.ii the security is traded in the fastest possible time. The brokerage firm is also obligated to refrain from making secret profits on transactions or from crossing orders in its office by acting as both broker and dealer in the same transaction. All securities listed on an exchange ought to be traded on the floor of that exchange. They cannot be extended off the floor by the broker. The brokerage firm cannot act as both broker and dealer in the same transaction because there could be conflict of interest or a double commission might result. If the securities are not listed on an exchange but traded in the over-the-counter market, the broker might own the shares himself. He would be acting as a principal or dealer in the transaction. Many brokerage firms specialise in making a market in certain securities. Here the brokerage firm would sell the security to the customer at the asking price and would not charge a commission for handling the transaction. The broker makes his fee from the difference between the price at which he buys the shares for his own account and the price at which he sells them to customers. The difference between the asked price and bid price by the brokerage firm is known as spread and is the compensation for making a market in that security.

BROKERAGE INFORMATION

In order to fulfil their functions and earn commissions, brokers must develop their businesses along the following lines.

Firstly, they must provide an office with adequate financial information sources, current quotation facilities and sales representative - advisers to enable investors to make the decisions.

Secondly, they must know when to find, where to find the best unlisted markets for their customers and how to obtain new securities currently being offered by underwriters and distributors.

Thirdly, they must arrange memberships in or contacts with the principal stock exchange of the country, for a very large percentage of all securities buying and selling is done on the stock exchanges. They must also offer their customers incidental services in the financing of their transactions and in the storage of their securities.

FUNCTIONAL SPECIALISATION OF MEMBERS

Functional specialisation of members at the stock exchanges helps a lot in making it a free, active and continuous market. It is, therefore, common at the leading foreign stock exchanges. In India, the stock exchange rules, by-laws and regulations do not prescribe any functional distinction between members. However, as a matter of fact, there is a fairly well-established specialisation under the following main categories :

1. **Commission broker:** Almost all members act as commission brokers. The commission broker executes buying and selling orders on the floor of the exchange. For that, he charges a commission not exceeding the official scale of brokerage.

2. **Floor broker:** The floor brokers are not officially attached to other members. The floor broker executes orders for any members and receives as his compensation a share of the brokerage charged by the commission broker to his constituent. Such brokers are not found on Indian stock exchanges.

3. **Taravniwalla or jobber:** The taravniwalla may be a jobber or specialist who specialises in stocks located at the same trading post. He trades in and out of the market for a small difference in price and as such is an important factor in "making a market", *i.e.* maintaining a continuous and liquid market in stock in which he specialises.

4. **Dealers in non-cleared securities:** The dealer in non-cleared securities specialises in buying and selling on his own account shares which are not in the active list. He is generally prepared to buy what is on offer and sell what is required but the price at which he deals varies with the activity of the particular stock.

5. **Odd-lot dealer:** The odd-lot dealer specialises in buying and selling in amount less than the prescribed trading units or lots. He buys odd lots and makes them up into marketable trading units. He likewise sells odd-lots obtained by buying or by splitting up round lots. The odd-lot dealer does not rely on commission but earns his profit on the difference between the prices at which he buys and sells.

6. **Budliwalla:** The budliwalla or financier lends money to the market by taking up delivery on the due date at the end of the clearing for those who wish to carry over their purchases; or loans securities to the market when it is short by giving delivery on the due date at the end of the clearing for those who wish to carry over their sales. His purchases or sales on the last date of the current clearing are matched by corresponding concurrent sales to or purchase from the same party for the ensuing clearing. The difference between the two is contango or the backwardation charge for the continuation facility offered to the market, *i.e.* for loaning money or stock for a short period of two to three weeks. The loan is fully secured and the return is governed by the technical position of the market and the ruling rate of interest.

7. **Arbitrageur:** The arbitrageur specialises in making purchases and sales in different markets at the same time and profits by the differences in prices between the two centres. Arbitrage depends on the number of securities dealt in the common on more than one stock exchange and the existence of ready means of communication.

8. **Security dealer:** The security dealer specialises in buying and selling gilt- edged securities, that is, securities issued by the Central and State Governments and by statutory public bodies such as Municipal Corporation, Improvement Trusts and Electricity Boards. He acts mainly as jobber and is prepared to take risks inherent in the ready purchase and sale of securities to meet current requirements. The gilt-edged market is over-the-counter market, and each purchase and sale has to be separately negotiated. The market, therefore, tends to be restricted. Moreover, as a result of their active touch with RBI as well as with commercial banks, the LIC and other institutional investors, gilt-edged securities enjoy the benefit of extremely fine quotations.

SELECTING A BROKER AND A BROKERAGE FIRM

It is very difficult for the investor to differentiate between the broker and the brokerage firm. Both the broker and the firm he represents must both be suitable for the investor because they cannot work independently of each other. The conscientious investor should look for a reliable broker who works for a reliable firm. This may seem obvious, but for the individual investing for the first time, selecting a broker may be difficult. Many individuals are hesitant to interview a broker and his firm.

It is most important that the investor selects a broker who can give prompt and efficient service. This means he must be able to confirm a purchase or sale within minutes and provide price quotes quickly. If the individual is new in the investment business, it is important that a broker willing to spend time educating him in the fundamentals of investing.

A broker's integrity must be unquestioned and it should be reflected in the community. Lawyers, bankers and independent investment counsellors can provide the investor with a list of reputed brokers.

For most investors, it is important to select a broker who is experienced in the brokerage business and who is working for a firm with an established record of good services. The new broker often lacks the necessary perspective to help the new investor. A seasoned broker will generally suggest long-term investments instead of suggesting that the client be active trader moving in and out of securities. Active trading can be very expensive because commissions eat away most of the profit. Therefore, it is important that the broker should have the best interest of the investor uppermost in his mind.

A brokerage firm that has an unquestioned credit rating and sufficient size and experience to provide the necessary investment service should be selected. It is perhaps difficult for the novice investor to determine the credit rating and the reputation of a brokerage firm. However, through discreet questioning in the financial community, the relative financial position of a brokerage firm can be determined.

Selecting a brokerage firm that provides information and research facilities is para-mount to a successful investment programme. The information should contain data on general economic conditions, industry analysis, company analysis, and securities appropriate for the individual. The data should also include an historical analysis and economic and business forecasts for the industries selected.

In the final analysis, the brokerage firm should be able to deal in securities listed on the major national and regional exchanges as well as shares traded in the over-the-counter market. In addition, the brokerage firm should have a reputation that enables it to participate in underwriting syndicates, thus, giving clients an opportunity to purchase new security issues.

Institutional investors have a somewhat different set of criteria for selecting a broker, depending upon their needs and the capability of their research staff. The first criterion is the broker's ability to transact business quickly and at a favourable price. Ability to handle larger order is also important. The second criterion for selecting a brokerage firm is the quality of information it supplies. To be competitive, the brokerage firm must provide profitable information; it will be compensated by brokerage commissions. Usually a reciprocal arrangement is made between the broker and the institutional investor. The investor receives the research and the brokerage firm receives the commissions. The firm's proximity to the investor — whether it is local firm - and its proximity to the over-the-counter market are often considered in the selection process, but these are secondary.

EXECUTION OF ORDER

Orders may be communicated to a broker either orally or in writing. Oral orders will be accepted by a broker only if the client is well known. Acceptance of order may be communicated to the client orally or through 'Order Confirmation Note'

If the order pertains to a security listed in Bombay while the order has been given to a broker in Delhi, the Delhi broker will approach a member of the Bombay Stock Exchange to execute the order on his behalf. Thus a broker can execute orders even for those securities which are not listed on the stock exchange where he is a member.

In case the order pertains to a security listed in the stock exchange of the broker, the order is executed in the following manner. There are certain prescribed hours on each working day of the stock exchange when the brokers meet in the trading hall to transact business on behalf of their clients. In the trading hall, the broker calls out the name of the security which he is ordered to buy or sell. If any other broker is interested he will respond to the call by either giving rates at which he is prepared to buy and sell respectively or ask the calling broker regarding the rate at which he is prepared to buy or sell. When the rate and number of shares of the security are decided, the transaction is complete. The transaction is then written on the 'chopri' or 'transaction book'. Both the brokers initial the transaction in each other's transaction book in confirmation of the same.

At the end of trading hours, each broker prepares a 'Daily Transaction Report' which is submitted to the stock exchange. This gives a detail of the transactions transacted by the broker during that day.

In case of cleared securities (and in case of non-cleared securities if so required by the stock exchange authorities) the broker has also to give his net position till date in each of the cleared scripts. This is submitted in the form of 'Consolidated Daily Position.'

The broker intimates his client of the transactions done on his behalf by sending him a 'Contract Note'. This contract note is sent in duplicate. The original is retained by the client and the copy returned with the client's signatures to the broker in confirmation of that contract.

TYPES OF TRANSACTIONS IN A STOCK EXCHANGE

The members of recognised Stock Exchanges are permitted to enter into transactions in securities as under:

(a) For "spot delivery", i.e. for delivery and payment on the same day as the date of the contract or on the next day.

(b) For "hand delivery", *i.e.*, for delivery and payment within the time or on the date stipulated when entering into the bargain, which time or date shall not be more than 14 days following the date of the contract.

(c) For "special delivery", *i.e.* for delivery and payment within any time exceeding 14 days following the date of contract as may be stipulated when entering into the bargain and permitted by the Governing Board or the President.

MECHANICS OF SHARE TRADING

The rules and procedures for buying and selling securities are the same in all the recognised stock exchanges in India. The procedures are listed below:

A. Purchase of Shares

Purchasing of shares can be divided into two parts, namely purchase of existing shares from the market (*i.e.* secondary market) and purchase of shares of companies issuing fresh shares (*i.e.* primary market).

(a) Purchase of existing shares from the market

In the case of purchasing shares of existing companies, the order must be placed with the broker. The broker will require certain sum of money as margin money to be given along with the order. When the shares are purchased a contract note is sent to the I client as to the number, rate and date of purchase. Many brokers require their clients to pay the balance amount (Purchase Price minus Margin Money) on receipt of contract.

(b) Purchase of hares being issued by a company

The company issuing the shares circulates printed application forms on which the intending purchaser has to fill-in the details like Name, Address, Occupation, Age, Specimen signatures etc. Application money per share multiplied by the number of shares applied for has to be paid alongwith this application. Depending on response the company announces an allotment procedure. If the shares are allotted on investor's application, he will receive the allotment letter otherwise a refund order of the amount applied for will be received. The face value of the share is not asked for with application in case of some companies. The company fixes allotment money and call money per share which it asks the shareholders to pay at certain intervals decided by the board of directors of that company. The company makes an endorsement on the share to show that how many calls have been paid by the shareholders.

B. Sale of Shares

The order of the sale of shares has to be placed with the broker, as an individual cannot sell or purchase shares at the stock exchange directly. Only members of that particular stock exchange can transact business at that stock exchange either for themselves or on behalf of their clients. On the sale of shares the broker issues a Contract Note. A contract indicates the number of shares sold, the rate per share, the date of sale and the terms and conditions governing the sale. A contract note binds the broker and his client. In case the client is not satisfied he must notify his broker immediately on receipt of the contract. The payment is made according to the rate appearing on the contract as the rate is calculated after deducting the commission payable to the broker.

FEATURES OF SHARE TRADING

i) Types of Orders

Orders for the sale and purchase of shares are valid for a certain time period, usually a day. Theoretically, investor can have an order with no time limit but in actual practice the broker requires investor to renew the order every day.

The orders are largely classified on the basis of the price limits that it imposes. They can be divided into :

(i) *Nett rate orders :* Nett rate is purchase or sale rate minus brokerage "Buy 100 Hindustan Motor at ₹ 31 Nett" would mean that the client is willing to buy 100 Hindustan Motor for no more than ₹ 31 per share including brokerage payable to the broker.

(ii) *Market rate orders:* Market Rate is Nett Rate plus brokerage for purchase and miuns brokerage for sale. So an order "Buy 100 ABC Ltd. at ₹ 11 market" means that the client is willing to pay ₹ 11 plus brokerage for each share of ABC Ltd.

(iii) *Limited discretionary order :* "Buy 100 ABC Ltd. around ₹ 11" gives a discretion to the broker. The price can be a little above ₹ 11. How much discretion is implied depends on how the broker and client define "around".

(iv) *Best rate order:* "Buy 100 ABC Ltd." means buy ABC Ltd. at the prevailing market price. Obviously these orders tend to be executed very fast as there is no price limit.

(v) *Stop loss order :* "Buy 100 ABC Ltd. at ₹ 11 stop loss ₹ 10" means that buy 100 ABC Ltd. at the market rate of ₹ 11 but if on the same day the price falls to ₹ 10 immediately sell off the shares. Thus an attempt is made to limit the loss of sudden unfavourable shift in the market.

ii) Effect of Book Closing on Delivery

Book closing refers to the closure of the Register of shareholders by the company. As the shares of a company are purchased and sold continuously there are changes in the Register of shareholders maintained by that company. To determine the shareholders at a particular point of time, for example at the time of sending the annual report or distributing dividends, bonus or issuing right shares the Register of Shareholders is closed. Notice of such book closure is given 21 days in advance.

The book closing significantly effects the validity of the transfer deed(s) meant for transferring shares of that company.

All transfer deed(s) bear a date. If the transfer deed(s) carry a date prior to the date of book closing they are no longer valid *e.g.* Book Closing of XYZ Ltd. took place on 5-9-2011 so all transfer deeds bearing dates upto 4-9-2011 are invalid. Transfer deeds dated 5-9-2011 or later will be valid. And if the transfer deed is invalid delivery of those shares cannot be effected in the stock market but the holder of such shares can get it transferred in his name from the company within 12 months of the date borne by the transfer deed(s).

Another point that must be kept in mind is that if as a purchaser investor has not submitted the shares for transfer and a book dosing in those shares takes place then it may be very difficult to obtain a new transfer deed from the seller and to receive the dividend or bonus, if any.

iii) Effect of Bonus Rights, Dividends after Transaction Date but before Delivery Date

This can be best explained by an example. Suppose an investor purchased or sold 100 XYZ Ltd. at ₹ 66 on 14-10-2011 delivery of shares is given to him on 4-11-2011. Then if

(i) Books closed for dividend at Re.l per share on 31-10-2011 he should be charged ₹ 66 - ₹ 1 (i.e. ₹ 66) in case he is a buyer. In case he is a seller, he will be paid at the rate of ₹ 66 - ₹ 1 (*i.e.* ₹ 65).

(ii) Book closed for bonus in the ratio 1:1 on 31-10-2011. 1:1 bonus means that for every share held a new fully paid share is issued by the company. So, as a purchaser, he should get 200 shares of XYZ Ltd. Therefore, if an investor gets 100 shares, he will be charged 36 x 100/200 = ₹ 18 per share.

A seller would similarly be paid ₹ 18 per share.

(iii) Book closed for right shares at ₹ 60 per share, in the ratio 2 shares for every 5 shares held, on 31-10-2011. The seller will have to give 40 shares (100 x 2/5) alongwith 100 shares of XYZ Ltd. He will be paid ₹ 66 per share for 100 shares and ₹ 60 per share for 40 shares.

iv) Cleared, Non-cleared and Permitted Securities

Cleared and Non-cleared securities are those securities which are listed on the stock exchange. Permitted securities are those shares and debentures which are not listed on that stock exchange but permission for trading in them is granted by the stock exchange in public interest.

Cleared securities are those listed securities in whom broker to broker settlement is made on every delivery day, of all transactions that have taken place during the fortnight. In cash or non-cleared securities there is no such settlement.

Transaction Costs

Rather than going through the trouble of direct negotiation trying to find someone who wants to buy that which they want to sell (or vice versa), investors make transactions through brokers or dealers. Transaction costs are paid by the investor to compensate the broker for executing the transaction. Such costs are usually levied on both the purchase and the sale of securities. The structure and magnitude of transaction costs need to be considered when making investment decisions, since they affect returns.

BASIC TYPES OF TRANSACTIONS

An investor can make a number of basic types of security transactions. Each type is available to those who meet certain requirements established by various government agencies as well as by brokerage firms. Although the various types of transactions can be used in a number of ways to meet investment objectives, only the most popular use of each transaction is described here. The three most common types of transaction are the long purchase, margin trading, and short selling.

Long Purchase

The long purchase is a transaction in which investors buy securities in the hope that they will increase in value and can be sold at a later date for profit. The object, then, is to buy low and sell high. A long purchase is the most common type of transaction. Each of the basic types of orders described above can be used with long transactions. Because investors generally expect the price of the security to rise over the period of time they plant to hold it, their return comes from any dividends or interest received during the ownership period, plus the difference between the price at which they sell the security and the price paid to purchase it (capital gains). This return, of course, is reduced by the brokerage fees paid to purchase and sell the securities.

Ignoring any dividends (or interest) and brokerage fees, the long purchase can be illustrated by a simple example. After studying various aspects of Gay Manufacturing, Inc., Ravi Kant is convinced that its equity shares, which currently sells for ₹ 20 per share, will increase in value over the next few years. Based on his analysis, Ravi Kant expects the share price to rise to ₹ 30 per share within two years. He places a limit order and buys a round lot (100 shares) of Gay for ₹ 20. If the share price rises to, say ₹ 40 per share. Ravi Kant will profit from his long purchase; if it drops below ₹ 20 per share. He will experience a loss on the transaction. Obviously, one of the major motivating factors in making a long transaction is an expected rise in the price of the security.

Margin Trading

Most security pruchases do not have to be made on a cash basis; borrowed funds can be used instead. This activity is referred to as margin trading, and it is used for one basic reason: to magnify returns. This is possible because the use of borrowed funds reduce the amount of capital that must be put up by the investor. As peculiar as it may sound, the term *margin* itself refers to the amount of *equity* in an investment, or the amount that is not borrowed. If an investor uses 75 percent margin, for example, it means that 75 percent of the investment position is being financed with the person's own capital and the balance (25 percent) with borrowed money.

A simple example will, help to clarify the basic margin transaction. R. Venkat wishes to purchase 70 shares of Universal Fiber, which is currently selling for ₹ 63.50 per share. If the margin requirement is 50 percent, Venkat must put up only 50 percent of the total purchase price of ₹ 4,445 (₹ 63.50 per share x 70 shares), or ₹ 2,222.50, in cash. The remaining ₹- 2,222.50 will be lent to Venkat by his brokerage firm. Venkat will, of course, have to pay interest on the ₹ 2,222.50 he borrows, along with the application brokerage fees. It should be clear that with the use of margin an investor can purchase more securities than he or she could afford on a strictly cash basis. In this way investors can magnify their returns.

Essentials of Margin Trading

Margin tranding can be used with most kinds of securities. It normally leads to increased returns, but there are also some substantial risks. One of the biggest is that the issue may not perform as expected. If this in fact occurs, no amount of margin trading can correct matters. Margin trading can only *magnify returns,* not *produce* them. Because the security being margined is always the ultimate source of return, *the security selection process is critical to this trading strategy.*

Magnified profits and losses: Using an investor's equity as a base, the idea of margin trading is to employ *financial leverage,* or debt, to maginfy returns. Here is how it works: Suppose an investor has ₹ 5,000 to invest and are considering the purchase of 100 equity shares (at ₹ 50 per share) because he feels, the share in question will go up in price. If he does not margin, he can buy outright (ignoring brokerage commissions) 100 shares. However, if he margins the transaction-for example at 50 percent - he could acquire the same ₹ 5,000 position with only ₹ 2,500 of his own money. This would leave him with ₹ 2,500 to use for other investments, or to buy another 100 shares of the same stock. Either way, he will reap greater benefit from the share's price appreciation by margining.

The concept of margin trading is more fully illustrated in Table 1. An unmargined (100 percent equity) transaction is depicted along the same transaction using various margins. Remeber the margin rates (such as 65 per cent) indicate the equity in the investment, or the amount of capital the investor must put up. When the investment is unmargined and the price of the stock goes up by ₹ 30 per share, the investor enjoys a very respectable 60 percent rate of return. However, observe what happens when margin is used : The rate of return shoots up to as high as 120 per cent, depending on the amount of equity in the investment. This is so because the gain is the same (₹ 3,000) *regardless of how the transaction is financed.*

Clearly, as the investor's equity in the investment *declines* (with lower margins), rate of return *increases* accordingly.

TABLE 1

The Effect of Margin Trading on Security Returns

	Without Margin (100% Equity)	With Margins of		
		80%	*65%*	*50%*
Number of ₹ 50 shares purchased	100	100	100	100
Cost of Investment	₹ 5,000 0	₹ 5,000 0	₹ 5,000 0	₹ 5,000 0
Less : Borrowed money	0	1,000	1,750	2,500
Equity in investment	5,000	₹ 4,000	₹ 3,250	₹ 2,500
A. Investor's Position — if Price Rises by ₹ 30 to ₹ 80 per Share				
Value of stock	₹ 8,000	₹ 8,000	₹ 8,000	₹ 8,000
Less : Cost of investment	5,000	5,000	5,000	5,000
Capital gain	₹ 3,000	₹ 3,000	₹ 3,000	₹ 3,000
Return on investor's equity (capital gain/equity in investment	60%	75%	92.5%	120%
B. Investor Position — if Price falls by ₹ 30 to ₹ 20 per Share				
Value of Stock	₹ 2,000	₹ 2000	₹ 2,000	₹ 2,000
Less : Cost of investment	5,000	5,000	5,000	5,000
Capital loss	₹ 3,000	₹ 3,000	₹ 3,000	₹ 3,000
Return on investor's equity (capital loss/equity in investment)*	(60%)	(75%)	(92.3%)	(120%)

* With a capital loss, return on investor's equity is *negative.*

There facets of margin trading become obvious from the table: (1) The price of the stock will move in whatever way it is going to regardless of how the position is financed. (2) The lower the amount of the investor's equity in the position, the greater the rate of return the investor will enjoy when the price of the security rises. (3) The risk of loss is also magnified (by the same rate) when the price of the security falls.

Advantages and Disadvantages

As already stated, a magnified return is the major advantage of margin trading. The size of the magnified return will depend on both the price behavior of the security being margined and the amount of margin being used. Another, more modest benefit of margin trading is that it allows for greater diversification of security holdings, since investors can spread their capital over a greater number of investments.

The major disadvantage of margin trading, of .course, is that the price of the security may fall rather than rise, resulting in maginfied losses rather than gains. Another disadvantage is the cost of the margin loans themselves. A margin loan is the official vehicle through which the borrowed funds are made available in a margin transaction. Such loans are sued with most types of margin transaction. All margin loans are made at a stated interest rate, which depends on prevailing market rates and the amount of money being borrowed. This cost, which must be absorbed by the investor, will mount daily, reducing the level of profits (or magnifying losses) accordingly.

MAKING MARGIN TRANSACTIONS

To execute a margin transaction, it is necessary to establish a *margin account*. It is opened either in the form of cash or securities. Margin credit can be obtained from a broker or a banker, although nearly all margin trading is done through brokers. The broker will retain any securities purchased on margin as collateral for the loan. There are basically two types I of margin requirements : initial margin and maintenance margin.

Initial Margin

Initial margin stipulates the minimum amount of equity that must be provided by the investor *at the time of purchase*. It is used to prevent overtrading and excessive speculation. Generally, it is this margin requirement that investors refer to when discussing margin trading. Any security that can be margined has a specific initial requirement, although these can be changed by the authorities from time to time.

As long as the margin in an account remains at a level equal to or greater than prevailing initial requirements, the investor is free to use the account in any way he or she sees fit. If the value of the investor's holdings declines, the margin in his or her account will also drop. This situation can lead to what is known as a restricted account, one whose equity is less than the initial margin requirement. It does not mean that the investor must put up additional cash or equity, but it does require the investor to bring the margin back to the initial level when securities are sold while the account is restricted.

Maintenance Margin

Maintenance margin is the absolute minimum amount of margin (equity) that an investor must maintain in the margin account at all times. If the margin falls below the maintenance margin, the broker is authorized to sell enough of the securities to bring the account back up to standard. When an insufficient amount of maintenance margin exists, an investor will receive a margin call to remedy the situation. This call gives the investor a short period of time to find some means to bringing the equity up to the required level. If this is not done, the broker has no alternative but to sell enough of the investor's margined holdings to bring the equity in the account up to this level. The maintenance margin protects both the brokerage house and investors : Brokers avoid having to absorb excessive investor losses, and investors avoid being wiped out. The maintenance margin on equity securities rarely changes, although it is often set slightly higher by brokerage houses for the added protection of both brokers and their customers. For straight debt securities, generally there is no official maintenance margin except that set by the brokerage houses themselves.

Basic Margin Formula

The amount of margin is always measured in terms of its relative amount of equity, which is considered the investor's collateral. A simple formula can be used with all types of *long purchases* to determine the amount of margin in the transaction (or account) at any given point. Basically, only two pieces of information required : (1) the prevailing market value of the securities being margined, and (2) the amount of money being borrowed, or the size of the margin loan, which is known as the debit balance. Given this information, we can compute margin according to Equation 1:

$$\text{Margin} = \frac{\text{value of securities-debit balance}}{\text{value of securities}} \tag{1}$$

$$= \frac{V - D}{V}$$

To illustrate its use, consider the following example. Assume you want to purchase 100 equity shares at ₹ 40 per share, using a 70 percent intial margin. First we must determine how this ₹ 4,000 transaction will be financed. If the 70 percent of it (the initial margin requirement) be financed with equity, the balance (30 percent) can be financed with a margin loan. Therefore investor will borrow ₹ 1,200 (₹ 4,000 x .30 = ₹ 1,200); this, of course, is the debit balance. The remainder (₹ 2,800) represents investor's equity in the transaction. This amount is measured as the difference between the value of the securities being margined (₹ 4,000) and the amount being borrowed (₹ 1,200). In other words, *equity* is represented by the numerator *(V-D)* in the margin formula. If over time the price of the stock moves to ₹ 65, the margin would then be :

$$\text{Margin} = \frac{V - D}{V} = \frac{₹\,6,500 - ₹\,1,200}{₹\,6,500} = .815 = 81.5\%$$

It can be observed that the margin (equity) in the investment position has now risen to 81.5 percent. When the price of the stock goes up, the investor's margin also increases. When the price of security goes down, so does the amount of margin. For instance, if the price of the stock in our illustruction drops to ₹ 30 per share, the new margin would equal only 60 percent. In that case we would be dealing with a restricted account, since the margin level has dropped below the prevailing initial margin. Finally, the same margin formula as used for individual transaction is used with margin *accounts*. The only difference is that we would be dealing with input that applies to the account as a whole- the value of all securities held in the account and the total amount of margin loans.

Return on Invested Capital

When assessing the return on margin transactions, we must take the fact that the individual puts up only part of the funds, the balance being borrowed. Therefore, we are concerned with the rate of profit earned *on only that portion of the funds provided by the investor*. Using both current income received from dividends or interest and total interest paid on the margin loan, we can use Equation 2 to determine the *return on invested capital* from margin transaction:

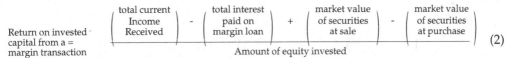

$$\substack{\text{Return on invested}\\ \text{capital from a} =\\ \text{margin transaction}} \frac{\left(\substack{\text{total current}\\ \text{Income}\\ \text{Received}}\right) - \left(\substack{\text{total interest}\\ \text{paid on}\\ \text{margin loan}}\right) + \left(\substack{\text{market value}\\ \text{of securities}\\ \text{at sale}}\right) - \left(\substack{\text{market value}\\ \text{of securities}\\ \text{at purchase}}\right)}{\text{Amount of equity invested}} \tag{2}$$

This equation can be used to compute either the expected or actual return from a margin transaction. To illustrate : consider an investor who wants to buy 100 equity shares at ₹ 50 per share because he feels it will rise to ₹ 75 within six months. The equity share pays ₹ 2 per share in annual dividends (though with the six-month holding period, the investor will receive only half of that amount, or ₹ 1 per share. The investor is going to buy the equity shares with 50 percent margin and pay 10 percent interst on the margin loan. Thus, he is going to put up ₹ 2,500 equity to buy ₹ 5,000 worth of equity share that the hopes will increase to ₹ 7,500 in six months. Since the investor will have a ₹ 2,500 margin loan outstanding at 10 percent for six months, he will pay ₹ 125 in total interest costs (₹ 2,500 x. 10 x 6/12 = ₹ 125). We can substitute this information into Equation 2 to find the expected return on invested capital for this transaction:

$$\text{Return on invested capital from a Margin transaction} = \frac{₹\ 100 - ₹\ 125 + ₹\ 7,500 - ₹\ 5,000}{₹\ 2,500} = \frac{₹\ 2,475}{₹\ 2,500} = .99 = 99\%$$

It should be noted that the 99 percent figure represents the rate of return earned over a six-month holding period. If we wanted to compare this rate of return to other investment opportunities, we could determine the transaction's *annualised* rate of return by multiplying by 2 (the number of six-month periods in a year). This would amount to 198 percent (99% x 2 = 198%).

Uses of Margin Trading

Margin trading is most often used in one of two ways. As we have seen, one of its uses is to magnify transaction returns. Another major margin tactic is called pyramiding, which takes the concept of magnified returns to its limits. Pyramiding uses the paper profits in margin accounts to partly or fully finance the acquisition of additional securities. This allows such transactions to be made at margins below prevailing initial margin levels, and some-times substantially so. In fact, with this technique, it is even possible to buy securities with no new cash at all; rather, they can all be financed entirely with margin loans. The reason is that the paper profits in the account lead to excess margin, more equity in the account than necessary. For instance, if a margin account holds ₹ 60,000 worth of securities and has a debit balance of ₹ 20,000, it is at a margin level of $66^2/_3$ per cent [(₹ 60,000-₹ 20,000) + ₹ 60,000]. This account would hold a substantial amount of excess margin if the prevailing initial margin requirement were only 50 percent.

The principle of pyramiding is to use the excess margin in the account to purchase additional securities. The only constraint, and the key to pyramiding, is that when the additional securities are purchased, the investor's margin account must be at or above the prevailing required initial margin level. Remember that it is the account, and not the individual transactions, that must meet the minimum standards. If the account has excess margin, the investor can use it to build up security holdings. Pyramiding can continue as long as there are additional paper profits in the margin account and as long as the margin level exceeds the prevailing initial requirement when purchases are made. The tactic is somewhat complex but also profitable, especially because it minimise the amount of new capital required in the investor's account.

In general, margin trading is simple, but it is also risky. It should therefore be used only by investors who fully understand its operation and appreciate its pitfalls.

Short Selling

Short selling is used when a decline in security prices is anticipated. The technique enables investors to profit from falling security prices. However, it can also be used to *protect* investors from falling security prices. Almost any type of security can be oshortedo, the short-selling activities of most investors are limited almost exclusively to equity shares and to put and call options.

Essentials of Short Selling

Short selling is generally defined as the practice of selling borrowed securities. Short sales start when securities that have been borrowed from a broker are sold in the market-place. Later, when the price of the issue has declined, the short seller buys back the securities, which are then returned to the lender. The lender's primary concern in a short-sale is that the securities being shorted are provided total and constant protection.

Making money when security prices fall is what short selling is all about. Short sellers to make money by buying low and selling high. The only difference is that they reverse the investment process by starting the transaction with a sale and ending it with a purchase. Table-2 shows how a short sale works and how investors can profit from such transactions. In the illustration, we assume the investor has found a stock he feels will drop from its present level of ₹ 50 per share to about ₹ 25. As a result, it has all the ingredients of a profitable short sale. The amount of profit or loss generated in a short sale is dependent on the price at which the short seller can buy back the stock. Short sellers make money only when the proceeds from the sale of the stock are greater than the cost of buying it back.

TABLE 2
The Mechanics of a Short Sale

1. 100 shares of stock are *sold* at ₹ 50/share:	
Proceeds from sale to investor	₹ 5,000
2. Later, 100 shares of the stock are *purchased* at ₹ 25/share :	
Cost to investor	2,500
Net profit	₹ 2,500

A fact of many short-sale transaction is that the investor must settle for high-risk exposure in the face of limited return opportunities. The price of a security can fall only so far (to a value of or near zero), yet there is really no limit to how far such securities can rise in price. (Remember, when a security goes up in price, a short seller loses). For example, Table 2 shows that the stock in question cannot possibly fall by more than ₹ 50, yet who is to say how high its price can go?

Another less serious disadvantage is that short sellers never earn dividend (or interest) income. In fact, short sellers are responsible for making up the dividends (or interest) that are paid while the transaction is outstanding. That is, if a dividend is paid during the course of a short-sale transaction, the *short seller* must pay an equal amount to the lender of the stock (the mechanics of which are taken care of automatically by the short seller's broker).

The major *advantage* of selling short is, of course, the chance to profit from a price decline. In addition, the technique can be used by investors to protect profits that have already been earned and to defer the taxes on such profits. And as we will see, when used in this manner, short selling becomes a highly conservative investment strategy.

Who Lends the Securities?

Acting through their brokers, short sellers obtain securities from brokerage houses or from other investors. Of the two, brokers are the principle source of borrowed securities. As a service to their customers they lend securities held in the brokers' portfolios or in street name accounts. Street name securities are those held by brokers for their customers; the stock certificate are issued in the brokerage house's name but held in trust for their clients. This is actually a common way of buying securities, since many investors do not want to be bothered with handling and safeguarding stock certificates. In such cases, the certificates are issued in the street name of the broker, who then records the details of the transaction and keeps track of these investments through a series of bookkeeping entries.

When dividends, notices and so on, are received by the broker, they are automatically forwarded to the proper owner of the securities. It is important to recognise that the broker lends the short seller the securities of other investors, and the short seller sells these borrowed securities with the expectation that he can later purchase them at a lower price and return them to the lender.

Uses of Short Selling

Investors short sell for one of two reasons : to seek speculative profits when the price of a security is expected to drop, or to protect a profit and defer taxes by "hedging" their position. The first use is the standard short-sale transaction. The hedge tactic, in constrast, is a conservative use of short selling, employed to lock in a given profit level. *All shorts are executed on margin,* so it seems appropriate to begin our discussion of uses of short selling by looking at how margin fits into a short sale and affects returns.

Shorting on Margin: There are no borrowed funds with margined short sales. With short selling, the term omargino simply indicates the size of the equity deposit the investor must make in order to initiate the transaction. Margined short sales are executed in the same margin account as margined long transactions. They are subject to initial margin requirements and have maintenance margin levels. In fact, the only thing that we do not have to be concerned about with a margined short sale is the account's debit balance. Margining a short sale, then, is much like margining a long transaction. Many of the investment principles, margin features, and behavioral characteristics we discussed previously apply equally here.

Of course, if the price of the security being shorted goes up, the investor loses money. If the price of the security being shorted goes up too much, the account can become restricted or subject to a margin call. To demonstrate, consider the following situation : Assume an investor wants to short 100 equity shares at ₹ 60 per share by using 70 percent initial margin. In this instance, the value of the securities amounts to ₹ 6,000 (100 x ₹ 60). The sales proceeds would also be ₹ 6,000, as this is the amount of money that would be realised by selling 100 shares at ₹ 60 per share. The margin (equity deposit) is ₹ 4,200, 70 percent of the value of the transaction. Now see what happens when the price of the stock rises ₹ 10 to ₹ 70 per share : In this case a potential loss of ₹ 1,000 (100 x ₹ 10) results. The investor will have to pay ₹ 10 more per share ₹ 70 rather than ₹ 60) to buy back the stock at today's price. This will lower the investor's equity position from ₹ 4,200 to ₹ 3,200. The investor would now have ₹ 3,200 equity on a ₹ 7,000 market value — a 46 percent (₹ 3,200 - ₹ 7,000) margin percentage. As the price of the stock goes up, the investor loses money and the amount of margin in the position drops. Because (at 46 percent) the amount of margin has dropped below the initial margin requirement (70 percent), the investor would be faced with a *restricted account.* But since it is above the 30 percent maintenance margin for short sales, a margin call would not *be* issued.

The reverse would happen if, instead of rising, the price of the stock were to fall ₹ 10 to ₹ 50 per share. In this case, the investor's equity would increase by ₹ 1,000 to ₹ 5,200, which would then represent 104 percent (₹ 5,200 ₹ 5,000) of the then-prevailing market value. Clearly an excess of equity would exist in this case.

Return on Invested Capital

Because short sales are executed on margin, the amount of invested capital is limited to investor's equity deposit. This amount therefore is the basis for figuring the rate of return. The only complication in this return measure is that any dividends paid by the short seller to the lender of the securities must be netted out of the profit. Other than that, no dividends are received by the short seller and no interest is paid, so the return formula in Equation 3 is fairly straightforward.

$$\begin{array}{c}\text{Return on invested}\\\text{capital from}\\\text{short sale}\end{array} = \dfrac{\text{proceeds from sale} - \begin{array}{c}\text{purchase cost}\\\text{of securities}\end{array} - \begin{array}{c}\text{dividends paid}\\\text{by short seller}\end{array}}{\text{equity deposit}} \qquad (3)$$

To illustrate, assume an investor uses 70 percent initial margin to short a stock at ₹ 60 per share he feels will drop to ₹ 50 within a six-month period. Because the company pays annual dividends of ₹ 2 per share, the short seller estimates he will probably be liable for about ₹ 1 per share over the expected six-month holding period. Using Equation 3 to compute the return on a per-share basis, we see that the expected return on invested capital for this short sale is about 45 percent:

$$\begin{array}{c}\text{Return on invested}\\\text{capital from}\\\text{short sale}\end{array} = \dfrac{₹\,60 - ₹\,40 - ₹\,1}{₹\,42} = \dfrac{₹\,19}{₹\,42} = .45 = 45\%$$

The figure will be the same regardless of how many shares are actually involved in the transaction. This high rate of return results not only from the profit earned when the price of the stock drops, but also from the limited amount of capital provided by the investor (a margin of only 70 percent).

SPECULATING WITH SHORT SALES

Selling short for speculative purposes is perhaps the most common use of this technique. Because the short seller is betting against the market, this approach is highly speculative and subject to a considerable amount of risk exposure. It works like this: Assume an investor has uncovered a stock that he feels is about to tumble over the next eight months from its present level of ₹ 50 per share to somewhere around ₹ 30. He therefore decides to short sell 300 equity shares at ₹50 by using 50 per cent margin (the prevailing initial margin requirement). Table 3 shows the basics of this hypothetical transaction. Note that the transaction generates a profit of ₹ 6,000 to the investor (ignoring dividends and brokerage commissions). Since it can be executed with an equity deposit of only ₹ 7,500, the transaction should yield a return on invested capital of 80 per cent. However, if the market moves against the short seller, all or most of his ₹ 7,500 investment could be lost.

TABLE 3

Speculating with a Short Sale

Short sale initiated : 300 equity shares sold at ₹ 50/share	₹ 15,000
Short sale covered · 300 equity shares bought back at ₹ 30/share	9,000
Net Profit	₹ 6,000
Equity deposit (.50 x ₹ 15,000)	₹ 7,500

$$\begin{array}{c}\text{Return on}\\\text{invested capital*}\end{array} = \dfrac{₹\,15,000 - ₹\,9,000}{₹\,7,500} = \dfrac{₹\,6,000}{₹\,7,500} = 80\%$$

* Assume the stock pays no dividends and therefore the short seller has no dividend liability.

Shorting-against-the-Box. This exotic-sounding term describes a conservative technique used to protect existing security profits. Like insurance, the purpose of this hedge is to minimise or eliminate exposure to loss. Shorting-against-the-box is done after an investor has generated a profit through an earlier long transaction by following it with a short sale. An investor who already owns 100 equity shares (the long transaction) would short an equal number of equity shares in the same company. By doing this, he or she is able to protect the profit already made in the long transaction, and as a by-product, can defer the taxes on this profit until the next taxable year.

Here is how it works: Suppose that early last year, an investor bought 100 equity shares of Gupta Industries, Inc., at ₹ 20 per share and have since watched the price of Gupta Industries rise to ₹50. He presently has a ₹3,000 net profit. Although he does not want to sell the stock right now, he does not want to lose any of his profit either. In essence, he would like to ride things out for a while and still protect the profit he has earned up to now. A simple short sale against the box will allow him to do this. By shorting 100 shares of Gupta Industries at ₹ 50 per share, and he has 'locked in' his profit of ₹3,000. No matter what happens to the price of the stock, he is guaranteed a profit of ₹ 3,000. He now has two positions u one long and one short u both involving an equal number of shares. Table 4 summarises this tactic and demonstrates how the profit becomes locked in. Note, however, that although this short sale transaction is executed with borrowed securities, it is not necessary to put up an equity deposit, because his current holdings of the stock serve this purpose. Thus, the cost of shorting-

TABLE 4
Shorting-against-the-Box (Hedging with a Short Sale)

Transaction 1 : Purchase 100 equity shares at ₹ 20		₹ 2,000
Price of the equity rises to ₹ 50 per Share		
Current value of stock		₹ 5,000
Cost of transaction		(2,000)
Net profit		₹ 3,000
Transaction 2 : Short sell 100 shares at ₹ 50		
A. Now Price of the.equity rises to ₹ 80 per Share		
Current profit in both transactions :		₹ 8,000
Value of stocks owned (trans. 1)		(2,000)
Cost of transaction		₹ 6,000
Profit		
Less loss on short sale :		
Short sale initiated	₹ 5,000	
Short sale covered	(8,000)	
Net profit		(3,000)
		₹ 3,000)
B. Price of the equity falls to ₹ 30 per Share		
Current profit in both transactions :	₹ 3,000	
Value of stocks owned (trans. 1)	(2,000)	
Cost of transaction	₹ 1,000	
Profit		
Plus profit from short sale :		
Short sale initiated	₹ 5,000	
Short sale covered	(3,000)	2,000
Net profit		₹ 3,000

against-the-box is reasonably low and involves only the brokerage commissions associated with initiating and covering the short sale.

CLEARING AND SETTLEMENT SYSTEM

The Indian stock market has, historically, adopted an account period settlement system whereby positions of brokers are accumulated till the end of a specified period and only the netted out positions with respect to every security are settled. The accumulation of position during the settlement cycle has given scope for speculative activities and, thus, increasing the possibility of default by participants. By combining the features of both cash and futures markets, the account period settlement also impeded the price discovery process. Further, the end of the settlement period, in the absence of significant borrowing and lending facility, has often witnessed erratic price movements. Although the account period settlement system through increased volume of trade, has tended to add to the liquidity in the system, there have been concerns over its ill-effects. As a partial remedy, the period of trading cycle was reduced from a fortnight to one week uniformly across all stock exchanges. The long-term solution to the trading system, however, rests with the alternative system of rolling settlement (RS), which is accepted and has been adopted in a phased manner.

CLEARING PROCESS

The transactions in secondary market are processed through three distinct phases, *viz. trading, clearing* and *settlement*. While the stock exchange provides the platform for trading to its trading members, the clearing corporation determines the funds and securities obligations of the trading members and ensures that trading members meet their obligations. The clearing banks and depositories provide the necessary interface between the custodians/clearing members (who clear for the trading members or their own transactions) for settlement of funds and securities obligations of trading members.

The clearing process involves determination of what counter-parties owe, and what counter-parties are due to receive on the settlement date. It is essentially the process of determination of obligations, after which the obligations are discharged by settlement.

Several entities, like clearing corporation, clearing members, custodians, clearing banks, depositories, are involved in the process of clearing. The roles of each of these entities are explained below:

  i) *Clearing Corporation:* The clearing corporation is responsible for post-trade activities of a stock exchange. Clearing and settlement of trades and risk management are the central functions for a clearing corporation.

  ii) *Clearing Members:* Clearing members can be of two types: (i) those who are trading as well as clearing members; these members trade as well as take the responsibility to settle their trades, and (ii) those who act only as clearing members; these members do not trade but take on the responsibility to settle the trades of other trading members. They are responsible for settling their obligations as determined by the clearing corporation. They have to make available funds and/or securities in the clearing account or pool account, as the case may be, to meet their obligations on the settlement day.

  iii) *Custodians:* Custodians are clearing members but not trading members. They settle trades on behalf of other trading members. A trading member may assign a particular trade to a custodian for settlement. The custodian is required to confirm whether he is going to settle that trade or not. If it confirms to settle that trade, then clearing corporation assigns that particular obligation to that custodian and the custodian is required to settle it on the settlement day.

iv) *Clearing Banks:* Clearing banks are a key link between the clearing members and clearing corporation for funds settlement. Every clearing member is required to open a dedicated clearing account with one of the clearing banks. Based on the clearing member's obligation as determined through clearing, the clearing member makes funds available in the clearing account for the pay-in and receives funds in case of a pay-out.

v) *Depositories:* Depository helps in the settlement of the dematerialised securities. It holds dematerialised securities of the investors in the beneficiary accounts. Each clearing member is required to maintain a clearing pool account with all the depositories. Separate accounts are required to be opened for the settlement of trades on different stock exchanges. The clearing members are required to provide the securities as per their obligations in the clearing pool account on settlement day. At a pre-determined time, the depository sends the information about the availability of securities in the clearing pool accounts of the clearing member to the clearing corporation.

RISK MANAGEMENT

A sound risk management system is integral to an efficient clearing and settlement system. The clearing corporation ensures that trading members' obligations are commensurate with their net worth. It has put in place a comprehensive risk management system, which is constantly monitored and upgraded to pre-empt market failures. It monitors the track record and performance of members and their net worth; undertakes on-line monitoring of members' positions and exposure with the market, collects margins from members and automatically disables members if the limits are breached. To safeguard the interest of the investors, NSE administers an effective market surveillance system to curb excessive volatility, detect and prevent price manipulation and follows a system of price bands. Further, the exchange maintains strict surveillance over market activities in illiquid and volatile securities.

Risk Containment Measures

There have been a number of experiments with different risk containment measures in the recent pasts. NSE, being aware of the importance of the risk containment measures has a dedicated Risk Group which looks into aspects relating to the risk management. These measures have been repeatedly reviewed and revised. The risk containnment measures in vogue are discussed below:

Capital Adequacy

The capital adequacy requirements stipulated by the NSE are substantially in excess of the minimum statutory requirements as also in comparison to those stipulated by other stock exchanges. A person seeking membership in the CM and F&O segment is required to have a net worth of ₹ 1 crore (₹ 3 crore in case of clearing member), and keep an interest free security deposit of ₹ 1.25 crore and collateral security deposit of ₹ 0.25 crore with the Exchange/NSCCL. The deposits kept with the Exchange as part of the membership requirement are taken as base minimum capital of the member to determine the member's intra-day trading limit and/or gross exposure limit. Additional base capital is required to be deposited by the member for taking additional exposure.

Trading and Exposure Limits

NSCCL imposes limits on turnover and exposure in relation to the base minimum capital or additional base capital of a member, which is the amount of funds, and securities that a member keeps with the Exchange/NSCCL.

The members are subject to limits on trading volumes in a day as well as exposure at any point of time. Gross intra-day turnover of a member shall not exceed 25 times the net capital (cash deposit plus security deposit). Gross exposure (aggregate of net cumulative outstanding positions in each security) of a member at any point of time shall not exceed 8.5 times the total base capital (not utilised towards margin) up to ₹ 1 crore. If a member has free capital in excess of ₹ 1 crore, his exposure shall not exceed ₹ 8.5 crore plus 10 times of the capital in excess of ₹ 1 crore. Members exceeding these limits are automatically and instantaneously disabled by the automated trading system. A penalty of ₹ 5,000 is levied for margin violation.

Margin requirements

NSCCL imposes stringent margin requirements as a part of its risk containment measures. The categorisation of stocks for imposition of margins has the structure as given here:

 i) The stocks which have traded at least 80% of the days for the previous 18 months shall constitute the Group I and Group II.
 ii) Out of the scrips identified above, the scrips having mean impact cost of less than or equal to 1% shall be categorised under Group I and the scrips where the impact cost is more than 1, shall be categorised under Group II.
iii) The remaining stocks shall be categorised under Group III.
 iv) The impact cost shall be calculated at 15th of each month on a rolling basis considering the order book snapshots of the previous six months. On the calculated impact cost, the scrip shall move from one group to another group from the 1st of the next month. The impact cost is required to be calculated for an order value of ₹ 1.00 lakh.

The daily margin comprises of the sum of Mark to Market Margin (MTM margin) and Value at Risk-based Margin (VaR-based margin). VaR margin is applicable for all securities in rolling settlement. All securities are classified into three groups for the purpose of VaR margin.

VaR based margins

For the securities listed in Group I Scrip wise daily volatility calculated using the exponentially weighted moving average methodology that is used in the index futures market and the scrip wise daily VaR would be 3.5 times the volatility so calculated.

For the securities listed in Group II the VaR margin shall be higher of scrip VaR (3.5 sigma) or three times the index VaR, and it shall be scaled up by root 3.

For the securities listed in Group III , the VaR margin would be equal to five times the index VaR and scaled up by square root of ($\sqrt{3}$).

VaR margin rate for a security constitute the following:

 1. Value at Risk (VaR) based margin, which is arrived at, based on the methods stated above. The index VaR, for the purpose, would be the higher of the daily Index VaR based on S&P CNX NIFTY or BSE SENSEX. The index VaR would be subject to a minimum of 5%.
 2. Additional VaR Margin: 6% as specified by SEBI.
 3. Security specific Margin : NSCCL may stipulate security specific margins for the securities from time to time.

The VaR based margin is rounded off to the next higher integer (For example, if the VaR based Margin rate is 10.01, it would be rounded off to 11.00) and capped at 100%. The VaR margin rate computed as mentioned above will be charged on the net outstanding position (buy value-sell value) of the respective clients on the respective securities across all open settlements. The net positions at a client level for a member are arrived at and thereafter, it is grossed across all the clients for a member to compute gross exposure for margin calculation.

Mark-to-Market Margin

Mark to market margin is computed on the basis of mark to market loss of a member. Mark to market loss is the notional loss which the member would incur in case the cumulative net outstanding position of the member in all securities, at the end of the relevant day were closed out at the closing price of the securities as announced at the end of the day by the NSE. Mark to market margin is calculated by marking each transaction in scrip to the closing price of the scrip at the end of trading. In case the security has not been traded on a particular day, the latest available closing price at the NSE is considered as the closing price. In the event of the net outstanding position of a member in any security being nil, the difference between the buy and sell values would be considered as notional loss for the purpose of calculating the mark to market margin payable.

MTM profit/loss across different securities within the same settlement is set off to determine the MTM loss for a settlement. Such MTM losses for settlements are computed at client level.

Non-payment of the margin attracts penal charge @ 0.07% per day of the amount not paid throughout the period of non-payment. Trades done by trading embers on behalf of institutions are, however, exempt from margin and exposure requirements.

Index-based Circuit Filters

An index based market-wide circuit breaker system applies at three stages of the index movement either way at 10%, 15% and 20%. These circuit breakers bring about a coordinated trading halt in all equity and equity derivatives markets nation wide. The breakers are triggered by movement of either S&P CNX Nifty or Sensex, whichever is breached earlier.

i) In case of a 10% movement of either of these indices there would be a one-hour market halt if the movement takes place before 1:00 p.m. In case the movement takes place at or after 1:00 p.m. but before 2:30 p.m. there would be trading halt for ½ hour. In case movement takes place at or after 2:30 p.m. there will be no trading halt at the 10% level and market shall continue trading.

ii) In case of a 15% movement of either index, there shall be a two-hour halt if the movement takes place before 1 p.m. If the 15% trigger is reached on or after 1:00 p.m. but before 2:00 p.m., there shall be a one-hour halt. If the 15% trigger is reached on or after 2:00 p.m. the trading shall halt for remainder of the day.

iii) In case of a 20% movement of the index, trading shall be halted for the remainder of the day.

NSE may suo moto cancel the orders in the absence of any immediate confirmation from the members that these orders are genuine or for any other reason as it may deem fit. The Exchange views entries of non-genuine orders with utmost seriousness as this has market-wide repercussion. As an additional measure of safety, individual scrip-wise price bands have been fixed as below:

i) Daily price bands of 2% (either way) on a set of specified securities,

ii) Daily price bands of 5% (either way) on a set of specified securities,

iii) Price bands of 20% (either way) on all remaining securities (including debentures, warrants, preference shares etc. which are traded on CM segment of NSE),

iv) No price bands are applicable on scrips on which derivative products are available or on scrips included in indices on which derivatives products are available.

For Auction market the price bands of 20% are applicable. In order to prevent members from entering orders at non-genuine prices in such securities, the Exchange has fixed operating range of 20% for such securities.

NSCCL settled trades for ₹ 15,16,839 crore of which 26.99% were settled by delivery during 2005-06. However, these deliveries include only the net deliveries made by the trading members to the clearing corporations. Of total delivery, nearly 100% of securities were delivered in demat form in 2005-06. The segment is witnessing substantial reduction in the share of short deliveries. Short deliveries averaged around 0.39% of total delivery in 2005-2006.

While NSE provides a platform for trading to its trading members, the National Securities Clearing Corporation Ltd. (NSCCL) determines the funds/securities obligations of the trading members and ensures that trading members meet their obligations. The core processes involved in clearing and settlement are:

(a) *Trade Recording:* The key details about the trades are recorded to provide basis for settlement. These details are automatically recorded in the electronic trading system of the exchanges.

(b) *Trade Confirmation:* The parties to a trade agree upon the terms of trade like security, quantity, price, and settlement date, but not the counterparty which is the NSCCL. The electronic system automatically generates confirmation by direct participants.

(c) *Determination of Obligation:* The next step is determination of what counter-parties owe, and what counter-parties are due to receive on the settlement date. The NSCCL interposes itself as a central counterparty between the counterparties to trades and nets the positions so that a member has security wise net obligation to receive or deliver a security and has to either pay or receive funds.

(d) *Pay-in of Funds and Securities:* The members bring in their funds/securities to the NSCCL. They make available required securities in designated accounts with the depositories by the prescribed pay-in time. The depositories move the securities available in the accounts of members to the account of the NSCCL. Likewise members with funds obligations make available required funds in the designated accounts with clearing banks by the prescribed pay-in time. The NSCCL sends electronic instructions to the clearing banks to debit member's accounts to the extent of payment obligations. The banks process these instructions, debit accounts of members and credit accounts of the NSCCL.

(e) *Pay-out of funds and Securities:* After processing for shortages of funds/securities and arranging for movement of funds from surplus banks to deficit banks through RBI clearing, the NSCCL sends electronic instructions to the depositories/clearing banks to release pay-out of securities/funds. The depositories and clearing banks debit accounts of the NSCCL and credit accounts of members. Settlement is complete upon release of pay-out of funds and securities to custodians/members.

(f) *Risk Management:* A sound risk management system is integral to an efficient settlement system. The NSCCL ensures that trading members' obligations are commensurate with their net worth. It has put in place a comprehensive risk management system, which is constantly monitored and upgraded to pre-empt market failures. It monitors the track record and performance of members and their net worth; undertakes on-line monitoring of members' positions and exposure in the market, collects margins from members and automatically disables members if the limits are breached. The risk management methods adopted by NSE have brought the Indian financial market in line with the international markets.

SETTLEMENT AGENCIES

The NSCCL, with the help of clearing members, custodians, clearing banks and depositories settles the trades executed on exchanges. The roles of each of these entities are explained below:

(a) *NSCCL:* The NSCCL is responsible for post-trade activities of a stock exchange. Clearing and settlement of trades and risk management are its central functions. It clears all trades, determines obligations of members, arranges for pay-in of funds/securities, receives funds/ securities, processes for shortages in funds/ securities, arranges for pay-out of funds/ securities to members, guarantees settlement, and collects and maintains margins/collateral/ base capital/other funds. It is the counterparty to all settlement obligations of the members.

(b) *Clearing Members:* They are responsible for settling their obligations as determined by the NSCCL. They have to make available funds and/or securities in the designated accounts with clearing bank/depositories, as the case may be, to meet their obligations on the settlement day.

(c) *Custodians:* Custodian is a clearing member but not a trading member. He settles trades assigned to him by trading members. He is required to confirm whether he is going to settle a particular trade or not. If it is confirmed, the NSCCL assigns that obligation to that custodian and the custodian is required to settle it on the settlement day.

(d) *Clearing Banks:* Every clearing member is required to open a dedicated clearing account with one of the clearing banks. Based on his obligation as determined through clearing, the clearing member makes funds available in the clearing account for the pay-in and receives funds in case of a pay-out.

(e) *Depositories:* Depositories help in the settlement of the dematerialised securities. Each custodian/clearing member is required to maintain a clearing pool account with the depositories. He is required to make available the required securities in the designated account on settlement day. The depository runs an electronic file to transfer the securities from accounts of the custodians/clearing member to that of NSCCL. As per the schedule of allocation of securities determined by the NSCCL, the depositories transfer the securities on the pay-out day from the account of the NSCCL to those of members/custodians.

(f) *Professional Clearing Member:* NSCCL admits special category of members namely, professional clearing members. Professional Clearing Member (PCM) may clear and settle trades executed for their clients (individuals, institutions etc.). In such an event, the functions and responsibilities of the PCM would be similar to Custodians. PCMs may also undertake clearing and settlement responsibility for trading members. In such a case, the PCM would settle the trades carried out by the trading members connected to them. A PCM has no trading rights but has only clearing rights, i.e. he clears the trades of his associate trading members and institutional clients.

Settlement Cycles

NSCCL clears and settles trades as per well-defined settlement cycles. Since the beginning of the financial year 2003, all securities are being traded and settled under T+2 rolling settlement. The NSCCL notifies the consummated trade details to clearing members/

custodians on the trade day. The custodians affirm back the trades to NSCCL by T+1 day. Based on the affirmation, NSCCL nets the positions of counterparties to determine their obligations. A clearing member has to pay-in/pay-out funds and/or securities. A member has a security-wise net obligation to receive/deliver a security. The obligations are netted for a member across all securities to determine his fund obligations and he has to either pay or receive funds. Members' pay-in/pay-out obligations are determined latest by T+1 day and are forwarded to them on the same day so that they can settle their obligations on T+2 day. The securities/funds are paid-in/ paid-out on T+2 day and the settlement is complete in 3 days from the end of the trading day.

Settlement Guarantee Fund

The Settlement Guarantee Fund (SGF), provides the cushion for any residual risk. It operates like a self-insurance mechanism where members contribute to the Fund. In the event of failure of a trading member to meet settlement obligations or committing a default, the Fund is utilised to the extent required for successful completion of the settlement. This has eliminated counter-party risk of trading on the Exchange. The market has full confidence that settlement shall take place in time and shall be completed irrespective of isolated trading members.

CARRY FORWARD FACILITY AND THE THEORY OF BADLA

Ordinarily, a buyer/seller of securities is supposed to take/provide delivery thereof and pay/receive the consideration at the end of each settlement period. But, on Indian stock markets, he enjoys an option of carrying forward his transaction. The carry forward facility enables him to defer or postpone his commitments to the next settlement period The process may be repeated several times subject to the rule that it will not be permitted beyond 90 days and at the end of this period, the transaction must be completed either by restoring to squaring up' or by receiving/effecting actual delivery. This facility is available in respect of Category 'A'/cleared/forward shares only. It has often been abused by the leading market players to either jack up or push down the prices of their favourite scripts resulting in undue heavy speculation and securities scam. It would, thus, be pertinent to understand the 'forward trading system' and how it operates.

Let us take a scrip, say Reliance, which is on the specified list on the Delhi Stock Exchange, and assume that during any 14 day settlement period, 50,000 shares were bought/sold by the various brokers operating in this scrip. At the end of the settlement period, all those who had purchased Reliance during the preceding 14 days are required to make payment in full for the shares purchased by them while the sellers are required to effect delivery of all the 50,000 shares sold by them.

Let us also assume that out of the 50,000 shares transacted, 10,000 shares have been purchased for taking delivery. The rest 40,000 shares have been bought with the intention of not making payment but for carrying forward. On the other hand, 50,000 shares sold, 30,000 shares have been sold by actual holders of the scrip with the intention of effecting delivery in the market. The balance 20,000 shares have been sold by people who either do not possess the scrip or do not have the intention of effecting delivery (these 20,000 are the short sales).

It is dear that while 30,000 shares have actually been delivered in the market, buyers for only 10,000 shares are ready to take delivery and make payment in full for them. This implies that for the balance 20,000 shares there are no takers and payment cannot be effected to their sellers. Under the existing system payment for these extra 20,000 shares is made by obtaining loans from financiers (known as badla financiers), and the scrips are delivered to them on a temporary basis as security for the loan. The amount charged by them as interest for the loan is called badla or contango and the rate of interest is obviously governed by the amount of finance available in the market and the demand for it, *i.e.* the number of shares for which finance is required (in our example 20,000) as well as the price of the scrip. The more the number of shares required to be financed, the higher will be the interest charges given a constant amount of availability of finance and vice versa.

Let us assume that for financing the 20,000 extra shares an amount of ₹30 lakhs is required (the price of Reliance being ₹ 150 per share). If the financiers are ready to charge interest at 24 per cent p.a. *i.e. 1* per cent for a 14 day settlement period, the total amount of interest to be paid to them would be ₹ 30,000 which has obviously to be recovered from the purchasers who are not willing to take delivery of the shares.

However, since there are in all 40,000 shares which have been bought without intention of taking delivery, it would be practically not possible to differentiate between them and charge interest on 20,000 and exempt from payment the balance 20,000. What is done is, that the interest amount of ₹ 30,000 is divided by only the extra number of shares (for which finance was required - in this case 20,000 and the amount is recovered from the entire 40,000 shares purchased for carry forward purchases. Thus the badla rate is fixed at ₹1.50 and a total amount of ₹ 60,000 is thus collected. Out of this ₹ 30,000 goes to the financiers while the balance ₹ 30,000 is distributed amongst the 20,000 sellers at the rate of ₹1 .50 per share. The net effect of all this, as far as the operators are concerned, is that all forward purchasers are required to pay a badla charge of ₹1 .50 per share and all short sellers receive an amount of ₹ 1.50 per share as badla for carrying forward their short sales.

Thus, the buyers who are not willing to pay for their purchases are penalised by charging interest from them (which is quite justifiable as they are actually operating on borrowed funds), the short selllers are not for selling something which they do not possess. They actually rewarded in the form of receipt of interest or badla charages.

Floating Stock and Badla Rates

The floating stock refers to the shares which have been sold and delivered in the market, but for which there are no buyers to take immediate delivery. When there is very high floating stock, badla financiers have to lift all of them and badla rates go up. If this stock completely vanishes, 'undha Badla' or 'backwardation charges' occurs.

Are Badla Rates Regulated ?

Till today, Badla is a free market operation. It is decided amongst share brokers and other market operators themselves, depending upon the supply and demand for funds. There are no government restrictions. The stock exchange authorities do not interfere in fixation of badla rates. It is done by the brokers themselves.

Badla trading has been banned and practically all trading stocks are now in the rolling settlement mode.

BROKERAGE CHARGES

As per SEBI Regulations, every stockbroker, on the basis of his total turnover, is required to pay annual turnover charges, which are to be collected by the stock exchanges. In order to share the benefits of efficiency, NSE has been reducing the transaction charges over a period of time.

A member is required to pay the exchange, transaction charges at the rate of 0.0035% (₹ 3.5 per ₹ 1 lakh) of the turnover. Trading members are also required to pay securities transaction tax (STT) on all delivery based transaction at the rate of 0.125% (payable by both buyer and seller) and in case of non-delivery transactions at the rate of 0.025% for equities payable by the seller only).

The maximum brokerage chargeable by trading member in respect of trades effected in the securities admitted to dealing on the CM segment of the Exchange is fixed at 2.5% of the contract price, exclusive of statutory levies like, securities transaction tax, SEBI turnover fee, service tax and stamp duty. However, the brokerage charges as low as 0.15% are also observed in the market

Stamp duties are payable as per the rates prescribed by the relevant states. In Maharashtra, for brokers having registered office in Maharashtra, it is charged at @ Re. 1 for every ₹ 10,000 or part thereof (i.e", 0.01 %) of the value of security at the time of purchase/sale as the case may be. However, if the securities are not delivered, it is levied at @ 20 paise for every ₹ 10,000 or part thereof (i.e. 0.002%).

As per the Finance Bill, 2008 Stock Exchanges and Clearing House Services would be charging a service tax on services rendered by them in relation to assisting, regulating or controlling the business of buying, selling or dealing in securities and including services provided in relation to trading, processing, clearing and settlement of transactions in securities , goods and forward contracts w.e.f 16th May, 2008.

REVIEW PROBLEMS

1. On Monday, July 13, you ask your broker to buy 200 shares of RDX at market, using the 50% allowed initial margin. The broker charges a commission of 2% and the brokerage firm has a 30% maintenance margin. The broker later calls you and says that the trade was executed at ₹ 70 per share. (Note that July 14 is not a business day.)

(a) Why might you use a market order as opposed to a limit or stop order?
(b) On what date must you pay the brokerage firm? How much must be paid?
(c) Since the stock was bought on margin, below what stock price will a margin call be required?
(d) If the stock falls to ₹ 40 and you intend to deposit more cash into the account to bring it back to the maintenance margin, how much cash must you deposit?
(e) If the stock falls to ₹ 40 and you intend to sell stock to repay some of the debt to bring it back to the maintenance margin, how many shares must you sell?

Ans.:

(a) A market order assures that a trade takes place at the existing best price. A limit order would be transacted only if prices are at the limit price or better. A stop order specifies a price at which the trade becomes a market order.
(b) The settlement day on which cash is paid and securities received is five *business* days after the trade date. Since July 14 is a business holiday, settlement will take place on Tuesday, July 21. At that time you will pay: Value of securities bought

200 × ₹ 70	=	₹ 14,000
Plus commission		
₹ 14,000 × 0.02	=	280
Total	=	₹ 14,280
Less margin loan		
0.50 × ₹ 14,000 =		7,000
Net due		₹ 7,280

(c) Maintenance margin $\quad = \quad \dfrac{\text{Security value} - \text{Loan}}{\text{Security Value}}$

$$= \dfrac{(P \times 200) - ₹\,7,000}{(P \times 200)}$$

$$P \quad = \quad ₹\,35$$

(d) Maintainance margin $\quad = \quad \dfrac{\text{Security Value} - \text{Loan} + \text{Cash}}{\text{Security Value} + \text{Cash}}$

$$0.30 \quad = \quad \dfrac{(₹\,40 \times 200) - ₹\,7,000 + \text{Cash}}{(₹\,40 \times 200) + \text{Cash}}$$

$$\text{Cash} \quad = \quad ₹\,2,000$$

(e) Maintainance margin $\quad = \quad \dfrac{\text{New Security Value} - \text{New Loan}}{\text{New Security Value}}$

$$0.30 \quad = \quad \dfrac{₹40 \times (200 - N) - (₹\,7,000 - ₹\,40 \times N)}{₹\,40\,(200 - N)}$$

$$N \quad = \quad 116.23 \text{ shares (117 actually)}$$

QUESTIONS

1. Describe the functions and role of a brokerage firm in the context of capital market.
2. "There is a fairly well-established specialisation of brokers". Do you agree ? Outline the different types of brokers and their usefulness in the stock market trading.
3. How would you go about selecting a broker and a brokerage firm ?
4. Illustrate the stock market trading mechanism.
5. Elaborate the various types of orders and how are they executed ?
6. What brokerage facilities would seem most important to you as an investor in securities?
7. Do you envisage any conflict of interest when a stock broker functions as both a sales representative aiming to maximise his commission and an investment advisor trying to give clients advice on how to trade securities ? Explain.
8. Discuss the function of commission brokers, floor brokers and odd-lot dealers.
9. How is a stop order different from the limit order ? Under what circumstances would you incline to place a limit order to buy ? Discuss the possible disadvantages of limit orders.
10. Can a brokerage business be conducted by a firm which owns no stock exchange membership?
11. Short sellers can theoretically lose an infinite amount of money but, at most, earn 100%
    (a) True or False? Explain.
    (b) How might stop orders be used to reduce the risks of short selling?
12. Discuss the advantages and disadvantages of:
    (a) Market orders

(b) Limit orders

(c) Stop orders

13. What role does the stockbroker play in the overall investment process? Describe the types of services offered by brokerage firms, and discuss the criteria tot selecting a suitable stock-broker.

14. Differentiate between a market order, a limit order, and a stop-loss order. What is the rationale for using a stop-loss order rather than a limit order?

15. Describe margin trading, and explain how profits (and losses) are magnified with margin trading.

16. What advantages and disadvantages does margin trading hold for the individual investor?

17. Critically examine the role of settlement agencies in the stock market operations.

18. Analyse the margin requirement in rolling settlement.

19. Discuss the clearing and settlement process and risk management system in the secondary capital market.

20. Critically discuss the use of VaR-based margin in rolling settlement in the secondary capital market.

21. Discuss the trading rules, instruments, and market participants' operations in the Indian capital market.

22. Discuss the role of Index-Based Circuit Filters in trading system.

PROBLEMS

1. BB Brokers specialises in underwriting new issues by small firms. On a recent offering of SS Enterprises, the terms were as follows:

Price to public	₹ 10 per share
Number of shares	30,00,000
Proceed to SS Enterprises	₹ 2.90 crore

The out-of-pocket expenses incurred by BB Brokers in the design of distribution of the issue were ₹ 3,00,000. What profit or loss would BB Brokers incur if the issue were sold to the public at an average price of (a) ₹ 10 per share?, (b) ₹ 12 per share?, (c) ₹ 8 per share?

REFERENCES

1. Curran, Ward S., "Some Thoughts on the Stock Exchange Specialist," *Quarterly Review of Economics and Business,* Spring 1965, pp. 55 62.

2. Engel, Louis. *How to Buy Stocks,* 5th ed. Boston: Little, Brown, 1971.

3. Groth, John C., Wilbur G. Lewellen, Gary G. Schlarbaum, and Ronald C. Lease. "How Good Are Broker Recommendations?" *Financial Analysts Journal,* January-February 1979.

4. Logue, D.E., and D.L. Tuttle. "Brokerage House Investment Ad-vice," *The Financial Review.* 1973.

5. Loomis, Philip A., Jr. "Broker Research after May Day." *Financial Analysts Journal,* July-August 1975, pp. 14-18.

6. Sobel, Robert. *The Curbstone Brokers: The Origins of the American Stock Exchange.* New York: Macmillan, 1970.

6

Investment Companies

INTRODUCTION

The management of an investment portfolio requires knowledge, experience, constant research; appraisal and reappraisal of securities markets, sectors within the market, and individual securities. One has to keep trace of the trends in the national economy and the competitive position of different industries. He must be familiar with not only those industries in which he invests, but also those in which he does not invest, since they might, in the future, offer attractive outlets for funds. To be successful one requires to combine the skills of a professional analyst with those of a portfolio manager. Not many investors possess the training and experience to carry out an investment programme. Hence arises the management problem and it is in answer to this problem of managing investment portfolios that investment companies have come up.

INVESTMENT COMPANY: THE CONCEPT

Investment companies — or investment trusts as they are often known — are financial institutions which obtain funds from a large number of investors through the sale of shares. These funds are then placed in a pool under professional management, and securities (financial assets) are purchased for the benefit of all shareholders. While investments in the fund may be made by either large or small savers, the investment company exists primarily to offer the small saver a means to diversify asset portfolio in a manner not attainable except with a very large portfolio.

The purpose of any investment company is to diversify the small outlays of its shareholders or unit holders, as the case may be, by operating the collective fund so accumulated through the medium of a large portfolio. Given its ability to build up a portfolio using its professional managers, such a company is able to diversify away the unsystematic risk, thereby reducing the risk exposure of its shareholders. In effect, as the investment is spread over a large number of securities, the risk of loss due to a fall in the value of any one of them is minimised.

Investment companies provide investors with the best overall results. The picture of the individual as a direct owner of securities has been romanticized almost beyond recognition. They offer a partial solution to portfolio management by providing expert research and professional management of funds over which they have control. In many ways investment companies resemble corporations which invest in land, machinery, building, etc. — only they invest in bonds, preference shares and equity shares of other corporations. Their assets are the securities owned, which give income from two sources: dividends or interest, and capital gains.

A notable and very attractive feature of investment companies is the wide scope offered by their field of operations to follow different investment objectives involving varying degree of emphasis on current income and future growth. Each investment company tries to satisfy in the largest possible measure the special needs of a particular class of investors. As a result growth of large number of companies is required for meeting the needs of many different classes of investors and tapping isolated sources of funds. The spectacular success of such companies in the U.K. and the U.S.A. is due in no small measure to this factor, indicating an aggressive search for what will be the best to serve and find acceptance with the investors. This factor is of particular interest to us in India, for in our country potential sources of funds stay untapped because of non-availability of matching terms from saving institutions. In view of the fact that the average Indian, with a small savings, stay at an arm's length from the Stock Exchange and holds it in certain amount of awe as also mistrust for he believes it to be a den of speculators though such a thing is long gone by. In other words, he lacks confidence in it. And as a result, the Indian corporate sector starves off much needed capital. A way to beat this is to build up investment companies—so as to infuse people's confidence in them and in corporate companies. Investment companies appeared on the Indian scene much later than in U.K. and U.S.A. Several factors were responsible for this among which mention may be made of delayed industrial investment, low volume of savings available for investment and the absence of adequate outlets for investment owing to the slow growth of joint stock companies.

In India, the investment trusts or the investment companies are of the management type and are formed under the Companies Act. Like joint-stock companies engaged in commercial or industrial business, investment companies raise their capital by issuing shares and debentures to the public. They invest the fund thus raised in securities of various companies, and also in gilt-edged securities keeping in mind that "all eggs should not be put in the same basket". The Articles of Association define the powers and duties of Directors and other officers. The investment and administration of funds is entrusted to the Board of Directors who may form a small sub-committee to look after this job. The responsibilities and status of the directors are similar to those of other joint stock companies formed under the Companies Act. The profits of such companies comprise the dividends and interest received on the various securities purchased out of the raised capital. Like other companies, they create reserves and distribute dividends out of the current profits. Not being a holding company, such an investment company should have nothing to do with the management and control of those concerns in which it has employed its funds. But it is hardly the case in India. Most of the investment companies are controlled, owned and managed by important managing agency houses which transform the character of such institutions from investment companies to holding companies. Their funds are locked up in pet corporations of managing agents. It can now be realised that the word "investment trust" is a misnomer in India as it does not create any trustee relationship between the investment company and its shareholders. It should better be called an investment company.

MARKET DESIGN OF INVESTMENT COMPANIES (MUTUAL FUNDS)

MFs operate as collective investment vehicles (CIV) on the principle of accumulating funds from a large number of investors and then investing in a diversified manner, thus limiting the risks involved. The process gathered momentum in view of regulatory protection, fiscal concession and change in preference of investors. The MF industry in India is governed by SEBI (Mutual Funds) Regulations, 1996, which lay the norms for the MF and its Asset Management Company (AMC). All MFs in India are constituted as trusts. A MF is allowed to issue open-ended and closed-ended schemes under a common legal structure. There were a total 39 MFs as on March 31, 2001. This includes UTI, which is set up under the UTI Act and is not required to be registered with SEBI. There is however, an arrangement of voluntary compliance by UTI for the schemes launched after July 1994. UTI has made a voluntary compliance with MF regulations in respect of many schemes. Five schemes including US-64 do not yet come under the MF regulations.

Structure of Investment Companies (Mutual Funds)

A typical MF in India has the following constituents:

Fund Sponsor: A 'sponsor' is any person who, acting alone or in combination with another body corporate, establishes a MF. The sponsor of a fund is similar to the promoter of a company. In accordance with SEBI Regulations, the sponsor forms a trust and appoints a Board of Trustees, and also generally appoints an AMC as fund manager. In addition, the sponsor also appoints a custodian to hold the fund assets. The sponsor must contribute at least 40% of the net worth of the AMC and possess a sound financial track record over five years prior to registration.

Mutual Fund: A MF in India is constituted in the form of a trust under the Indian Trusts Act, 1882. The fund invites investors to contribute their money in the common pool, by subscribing to 'units' issued by various schemes established by the trust. The assets of the trust are held by the trustee for the benefit of unitholders, who are the beneficiaries of the trust. Under the Indian Trusts Act, the trust or the fund has no independent legal capacity, it is the trustee(s) who have the legal capacity.

Trustees: The MF or trust can either be managed by the Board of Trustees, which is a body of individuals, or by a Trust Company, which is a corporate body. Most of the funds in India are managed by Board of Trustees. The trustees being the primary guardians of the unitholders funds and assets, a trustee has to be a person of high repute and integrity. The trustees, however, do not directly manage the portfolio of securities. The portfolio is managed by the AMC as per the defined objectives, in accordance with Trust Deed and SEBI (Mutual Funds) Regulations.

Asset Management Company: The AMC, which is appointed by the sponsor or the trustees and approved by SEBI, acts like the investment manager of the trust. The AMC functions under the supervision of its own Board of Directors, and also under the direction of the trustees and SEBI. AMC, in the name of the trust, floats and manages the different investment 'schemes' as per the SEBI Regulations and as per the Investment Management Agreement signed with the Trustees.

Apart from these, the MF has some other fund constituents, such as custodians and depositories, banks, transfer agents and distributors. The custodian is appointed for a safe keeping of securities and participating in the clearing system through approved depository. The bankers handle the financial dealings of the fund. Transfer agents are responsible for issue and redemption of units of MF. AMCs appoint distributors or brokers who sell units on behalf of the Fund, and also serve as investment advisers. Besides brokers, independent individuals are also appointed as 'agents' for the purpose of selling fund schemes to investors. The regulations require arm's length relationship between the fund sponsors, trustees, custodians and AMC.

Types of Investment Companies

Investment companies fall into two general categories:
(1) Open-end; and
(2) Closed-end companies

Open-end Investment Companies

These companies raise capital through issue of shares, which are NOT TRADED ON STOCK EXCHANGES, but handled by specified dealer in over-the-counter transactions. The money obtained from the sale of share is invested directly in the shares of other companies. Usually, no leverage occurs in the open-end fund, unless the company can borrow money to invest, as some companies do.

An example of open-end investment company in India is the Unit Trust of India. It came into existence on 1 February 1964 under the Unit Trust of India Act, 1963. The actual sale of units commenced by the UTI from 1 July, 1964. The sale is conducted through branches of banks and through members of recognised stock exchanges.

The UTI is declared to be a balanced fund, investing in both equity and fixed-income securities. Its investment policy is conservative in nature — it deals only in actively traded securities. Not more than 5 per cent of its total investible funds can be invested in initial issues of any industrial undertakings. This considerably narrows down its scope of operation, and its investment in the channelisation of funds for development purposes. The policy is aimed at securing a high current income as against capital appreciation.

Closed-end Investment Companies

These companies operate in much the same fashion as any industrial company. It issues a fixed number of shares, which may be listed on a stock exchange and bought and sold like any company's shares. If the management desires, it might revise additional equity issues, bonds or preferred stock issues. Majority of such companies have bonds and preferred stocks outstanding as a part of their capital structure.

The use of fixed income securities results in financial leverage for equity shareholders. Such a company will have both asset leverage as well as earnings leverage. Asset leverage is said to occur when the price of equity owned by the company (company's assets) increases or decreases. If the value of the total assets increases, there is greater proportional increase in the value of the equity shares of the investment company and being fixed claims, against assets, any increase in assets goes to equity shareholders. Thus, as the value of investment of an investment company increases the value of its equity shares increases faster. However, as the asset value increases without a corresponding increase in debt capital, the leverage effect is diminished. The interest of debts and the dividends on preference shares represent a fixed charge on the company's earnings. Any increase in earnings over the interest payments and dividends goes to the equity shareholders. As long as company earns more than is needed to pay the interest and dividends, the owner will benefit owing to the earning leverage. As earnings increase, the rate of increase of the return to the equity shareholder increases faster than the rate of increase of the return on the total assets, but, it may have adverse effects when earnings fall and assets decline in value. A closed-end company that raises a substantial portion of its capital by way of debt will be susceptible to wider fluctuations in value, than a company with a relatively small amount of debt. These leverage effects also tend to accentuate the cylical movement of stock prices.

Closed-end investment companies offer various advantages to an investor. Some of these may be listed as follows:

1. Their investment policies are highly flexible and hence, they provide an opportunity for greater diversification of investment than open-end companies.
2. Due to greater diversification and a higher scope for gearing of capital, they offer better returns to investors.
3. They have an additional advantage of ploughing back profit and, hence increasing

returns to their members. Risk of loss is minimised due to above reasons. Given that most such companies are listed on the stock exchange, shareholders face no problems in disposing of their holdings.

In addition to the above, there are many **other types of mutual funds** which may be classified on the basis of their objectives and portfolios. These mutual funds are:

(i) *Equity funds* : Those funds which invest only in equity shares and undertake the associated risk;

(ii) *Income funds:* Those funds which invest in securities which will earn high income;

(iii) *Growth funds* : Those funds which invest in growth oriented securities so as to assure appreciation in their value in the long run;

(iv) *Liquid funds:* Those funds which specialise in investing in short-term money market instruments with emphasis on liquidity with a low rate of return;

(v) *Special funds* : Those funds which invest only in specialised channels like (a) gold and silver, (b) a specific country (Japan Fund, India Fund, etc.), (c) a specific category of companies (Technology Fund);

(vi) *Index-linked funds:* Those funds which invest only in those shares which are included in the market indices and in the same proportion. They move with the market index;

(viii) *Leveraged funds:* Leveraged funds are those which increase the size of the value of the portfolio and benefit the shareholders by gains exceeding the cost of the borrowed funds;

(viii) *Real Estate fund:* Such funds are meant for the real estate ventures;

(ix) *Balanced funds* : Those which divide their investments between equity shares and bonds in order to meet the objectives of safety, growth, and regularity of income;

(x) *Hedge funds:* Funds that buy shares whose prices are likely to go up and sell short, shares whose prices are expected to go down; and finally

(xi) *Offshore funds:* These specialise in investing in foreign companies.

ADVANTAGES AND DISADVANTAGES OF INVESTING IN MUTUAL FUNDS

ADVANTAGES

Investing in mutual has various benefits, which makes it an ideal investment avenue. Following are some of the primary benefits.

1. Diversification

Diversification involves holding a wide variety of investments in a portfolio so as to mitigate risks. Mutual funds usually spread investments across various industries and asset classes, constrained only by the stated investment objective. Thus, by investing in mutual fund. investors can avail of the benefits of diversification and asset allocation, without investing the large amount of money that would be required to create an individual portfolio.

2. Professional Management

Many investors do not have the time or expertise to manage their personal investments every day, to efficiently reinvest interest or dividend income, or to investigate the thousands of securities available in the financial markets. Mutual funds are manager! by professionals who are experienced in investing money and who have the education, skills and resources to research diverse investment opportunities.

3. Liquidity

In an open-ended scheme, unit holders can redeem their units from the fund house anytime, by paying a small fee called an exit load, in some cases. Even with close-ended schemes, one can sell the units on a stock exchange at the prevailing market price. Besides, some close-ended and interval schemes allow direct repurchase of units at NAV related prices from time to time.

4. Return Potential

Over a medium to long-term, Mutual Funds have the potential a higher return in they invest in a diversified basket of selected securities .

5. Cost Effective

Since mutual funds have a number of investors, the fund's transaction costs, commissions and other fees get reduced to a considerable extent. Thus, owing to the benefits of larger scale, mutual funds are comparatively less expensive than direct investment in the capital markets.

6. Transparency

Information available through fact sheets, offer documents, annual reports and promotional materials helps provide the investor with the knowledge about their investments.

7. Choice of Schemes

The investors can chose from various kinds of schemes available to them. The investors with a higher appetite for risk can go for more aggressive schemes while those needing a fixed sum every month can go for MIPs and so on.

8. Tax Benefits

For equity funds, dividends received from equity schemes of Mutual Funds (i.e. schemes with equity exposure of more than 65%) are completely tax-free. Neither does the Mutual Fund have to pay dividend distribution fee nor does the investor have to pay income tax.

9. Convenience and Flexibility

Investing in mutual funds has its own convenience. While an investors owns just one security rather than many but still enloys the benefits of a diversified portfolio and a wide range of services. Fund managers decide what securities to trade, collect the interest payments and see that dividends on portfolio securities are received and investors rights exercised. It also uses the services of a high quality custodian and registrar. Another big advantage is that investors can move funds easily from one fund to another within a mutual fund family. This allows the investor to easily rebalance his portfolio to respond to significant fund management or economic changes. In addition investing in a Mutual Fund reduces paperwork and help the investors avoid many problems such as bad deliveries, delayed payments and follow up with brokers and companies. Mutual Funds save investors time and make investing easy and convenient.

10. Well Regulated

Mutual funds in India are regulated and monitored by the Securities and Exchange Board of India (SEBI), which strives to protect the interests of investors. Mutual funds are required to provide investors with regular information about their investments, in addition to other disclosures like specific investments made by the scheme and the proportion of investment in each asset class.

DISADVANTAGES

When investors invest in a mutual fund, he place his money in the hands of a professional manager. The return on investment depends heavily on that manager's skill and judgment. Since very few portfolio managers are able to out-perform the market; therefore before poarting the fund manager's track record over a period of time must be seen when selecting a fund.

Fees for fund management services and various administrative and sales costs can reduce the return on your investment. These are charged, in almost all cases, whether the fund performs well or not.

Redeeming mutual fund investment in the short-term could significantly impact return due to sales commissions and redemption fees.

REGULATION OF MUTUAL FUNDS

The primary authority for regulating MFs in India is SEBI. SEBI requires all MFs to be registered with it. The SEBI (Mutual Funds) Regulations, 1996 outlined the broad framework of authorisation process and selection criteria. Accordingly, the authorisation for the mutual fund will be granted in two steps. The first step will involve approval and eligibility of each of the constituents of the mutual fund *viz.* sponsors, trustees, asset management company (AMC) and custodian. For this purpose the interested parties would be required to submit necessary information only in on prescribed formats). The second stage will involve formal authorisation of the mutual funds for business. For this purpose the sponsor or the AMC would be required to apply to SEBI in an application form for authorisation alongwith an application fee to be specified later.

The authorisation shall be granted subject to conditions as may be considered necessary by SEBI and payment of authorisation fee as may be specified. It shall be SEBI's endeavour to advise an applicant within 10 to 15 working days of receipt of his letter/ application form regarding status of his application.

The eligibility of the sponsor will be examined with respect to the following: (a) Sponsor could be a registered company, scheduled bank or all India or State level financial institution; (b) More than one registered company can also act as sponsor for a mutual fund; (c) Joint sponsorship with any of the entities in (a) above will also be eligible, and (d) Sponsoring registered companies could be private or public limited companies either listed or unlisted.

Sponsor and where there is more than one sponsor, each of the sponsoring entities, must have a sound track record as evidenced by (a) Audited balance sheet and profit and loss account for last five years; (b) A positive net worth and consistent record of profitability and a good financial standing during the last five years; (c) Good credit record with banks and financial institutions; (d) General reputation in the market; (e) Organisation and management, and (f) Fairness in business transactions.

Sponsor or more than one sponsor put together should have at least a 40 per cent stake in the paid-up equity of the AMC.

The AMC will be authorised by SEBI on the basis of the criteria indicated in the guidelines.

SEBI regulations clearly state that all funds and schemes operational under them would be bound by their regulations. SEBI has recently taken following steps for the regulation of mutual funds:

(1) **Formation:** Certain structural changes have also been made in the mutual fund industry, as part of which mutual funds are required to set up asset management

companies with fifty percent independent directors, separate board of trustee companies, consisting of a minimum fifty percent of independent trustees and to appoint independent custodians. This is to ensure an arm's length relationship between trustees, fund managers and custodians, and is in contrast with the situation prevailing earlier in which all three functions were often performed by one body which was usually the sponsor of the fund or a subsidiary of the sponsor.

Thus, the process of forming and floating mutual funds has been made a tripartite exercise by authorities. The trustees, the asset management companies (AMCs) and the mutual fund shareholders form the three legs. SEBI guidelines provide for the trustees to maintain an arm's length relationship with the AMCs and do all those things that would secure the right of investors.

With funds being managed by AMCs and custody of assets remaining with trustees, an element of counter-balancing of risks exists as both can keep tabs on each other.

(2) **Registration:** In January 1993, SEBI prescribed registration of mutual funds taking into account track record of a sponsor, integrity in business transactions and financial soundness while granting permission. This will curb excessive growth of the mutual funds and protect investor's interest by registering only the sound promoters with a proven track record and financial strength.

(3) **Documents:** The offer documents of schemes launched by mutual funds and the scheme particulars are required to be vetted by SEBI. A standard format for mutual fund prospectuses is being formulated.

(4) **Code of advertisement:** Mutual funds have been required to adhere to a code of advertisement.

(5) **Assurance on returns:** SEBI has introduced a change in the Securities Control and Regulations Act governing the mutual funds. Now the mutual funds were prevented from giving any assurance on the land of returns they would be providing. However, under pressure from the mutual funds, SEBI revised the guidelines allowing assurances on return subject to certain conditions. Hence, only those mutual funds which have been in the market for at least five years are allowed to assure a maximum return of 12 per cent only, for one year. With this, SEBI, by default, allowed public sector mutual funds an advantage against the newly set up private mutual funds.

As per basic tenets of investment, it can be justifiably argued that investments in the capital market carried a certain amount of risk, and any investor investing in the markets with an aim of making profit from capital appreciation, or otherwise, should also be prepared to bear the risks of loss.

(6) **Minimum corpus:** The current SEBI guidelines on mutual funds prescribe a minimum start-up corpus of ₹ 50 crore for a open-ended scheme, and ₹ 20 crore corpus for closed-ended scheme, failing which application money has to be refunded.

The idea behind forwarding such a proposal to SEBI is that in the past, the minimum corpus requirements have forced AMCs to solicit funds from corporate bodies, thus reducing mutual funds into quasi-portfolio management outfits. In fact, the Association of Mutual Funds in India (AMFI) has repeatedly appealed to the regulatory authorities for scrapping the minimum corpus requirements.

(7) **Institutionalisation:** The efforts of SEBI have, in the last few years, been to institutionalise the market by introducing proportionate allotment and increasing the minimum deposit amount to ₹ 5000 etc. These efforts are to channel the investment of individual investors into the mutual funds.

(8) **Investment of funds mobilised:** In November 1992, SEBI increased the time limit from six months to nine months within which the mutual funds have to invest resources raised from the latest tax saving schemes. The guideline was issued to protect the mutual funds from the disadvantage of investing funds in the bullish market at very high prices and suffering from poor NAV thereafter.

(9) **Investment in money market:** SEBI guidelines say that mutual funds can invest a maximum of 25 per cent of resources mobilised into money-market instruments in the first six months after closing the funds and a maximum of 15 per cent of the corpus after six months to meet short term liquidity requirements. Private sector mutual funds, for the first time, were allowed to invest in the call money market after this year's budget.

As SEBI regulations limit their exposure to money markets, mutual funds are not major players in the call money market. Thus, mutual funds do not have a significant impact on the call money market. SEBI also conclude that mutual funds were not responsible for the unprecedented shooting up of call money rates.

Some funds exceeded their limits in an effort to improve their sagging net asset values (NAVs). Usually, funds can early only about 9-12 per cent. Thus, the prospect of earning more than 40 per cent may have been tempting.

(10) **Valuation of investment:** SEBI should work in tandem with the Institute of Chartered Accountants of India (ICAI) to take up a fresh look at mutual fund regulations enacted in 1993. The valuation of investments, a key aspect of fund accounting, as on balance sheet date, needs review. SEBI regulations 1993, give discretionary powers to the fund managers as far as the valuation of the investment portfolio on the balance sheet date is concerned. There are no accounting standards or guidelines prescribed by the ICAI for the valuation of a mutual fund's investment portfolio.

The mutual funds are clearly taking advantage of this situation and valuing the portfolio at cost of acquisition. The subsequent depreciation or appreciation in the investment portfolio are not accounted for. Thus, the mutual funds may be able to show profits in the balance sheet even if there is a severe erosion in the value of the investment portfolio. This erosion in the values of the investment portfolios is clearly seen in the net asset values (NAV) as on the balance sheet date. But the accounts of the mutual funds do not reveal the same.

The objective of the accounting in case of a mutual fund should be besides showing details of income, expenses, assets and liabilities, has to reveal the true value of the fund. The value of the fund is already reflected in its NAV and the balance sheet is expected to be in consonance with this value. This requires that the investment portfolio be calculated at market values, providing for any depreciation or appreciation.

The transparent and well understood declaration or Net Asset Values (NAVs) of mutual fund schemes is an important issue in providing investors with information as to the performance of the fund. SEBI had warned some mutual funds earlier of unhealthy market practices, and is currently working on a common format for *calculating the net asset values (NAVs)* of mutual funds, which are done in various ways by them at present.

(11) **Inspection:** SEBI inspect mutual funds every year. A full SEBI inspection of all the 27 mutual funds was proposed to be done by the March 1996 to streamline their operations and protect the investor's interests. Mutual funds are monitored and inspected by SEBI to ensure compliance with the regulations.

(12) **Underwriting:** In July 1994, SEBI permitted mutual funds to take up underwriting of primary issues as a part of their investment activity. This step may assist the mutual funds in diversifying their business.

(13) **Conduct:** In September 1994, it was clarified by SEBI that mutual funds shall not

offer buy back schemes or assured returns to corporate investors. The Regulations governing Mutual Funds and Portfolio Managers ensure transparency in their functioning.

(14) **Voting rights:** In September 1993, mutual funds were allowed to exercise their voting rights. Department of Company Affairs has reportedly granted mutual funds the right to vote as full-fledged shareholders in companies where they have equity investments.

RECENT POLICY AND REGULATORY INITIATIVES

(i) Rationalisation of Initial Issue Expenses and Dividend Distribution Procedure: In order to contain frequent churning of the investors in mutual fund schemes and to clarify expense structure in SEB1 (Mutual Funds) Regulations, 1996 with greater precision, SEBI decided to rationalise the initial issue expenses. Accordingly, for the purpose of meeting the expenses connected with sales and distribution of schemes, close ended schemes were permitted to charge initial issue expenses to the scheme. In order to bring in more transparency and clarify to the investors in terms of the expenses charged to them in close end schemes, SEBI Board decided that: a) Henceforth, there would not be provision of charging initial issue experises and amortization of the same. b) All mutual fund schemes would now meet the sales, marketing and such other expenses connected with sales and distribution of schemes from the entry load.

It was further clarified that in close-ended schemes where initial issue expenses are amortised, for an investor exiting the scheme before amortisation is completed, the asset management company (AMC) shall redeem the units only after recovering the balance proportionate unamortised issue expenses.

Also, as a step towards introducing uniform practices in procedure for dividend distribution by the mutual funds, the AMCs were advised to issue a notice to the public within one calendar day of the decision by the trustees on dividend distribution.

(ii) Undertaking from Trustees for New Scheme Offer Document: To address the concerns regarding launch of similar products, mutual fund trustees were required to certify that the scheme approved by them is a new product and is not a minor modification of an existing scheme/ product. However, the said certification shall not be applicable to fixed maturity plans and close-ended schemes but shall be applicable to close-ended schemes with a feature of conversion into open-ended scheme on maturity.

(iii) Revised Monthly Cumulative Report (MCR) and Annual Statistical Report (ASR): In order to capture the trends in unit capital, the formats of MCR and ASR submitted by the mutual funds were revised.

(iv) Introduction of Capital Protection Oriented Schemes and Revision in Fees: The SEBI (Mutual Funds) Regulations, 1996 were amended so as to permit the launch of Capital Protection Oriented schemes. The proposed portfolio structure indicated in the offer document and Key Information Memorandum (KIM) must be rated by a SEBI registered credit rating agency as per Regulation 38A of mutual fund Regulation. Moreover, the rating should be reviewed on a quarterly basis. In this regard, the trustees should also continuously monitor the structure of the portfolio of the capital protection oriented scheme and should report the same in the half-yearly trustee report. It should also be ensured that the debt component of the portfolio structure has the highest investment grade rating.

The fees payable by mutual funds to SEBI was also revised. This would be applicable to those schemes whose offer documents were filed with SEBI on or after the issue of Gazette Notification dated August 03, 2006.

(v) Uniform Cut-off Timing for Applicability of Net Asset Value (NAV): Due to various systemic changes brought out by RBI in money market, the cut-off timings for

applicability of NAV in case of purchases and redemptions of liquid schemes were revised and comprehensive. Guidelines were issued. It was decided that the time limit for uploading of NAV for fund of fund schemes would be extended to 10:00 am the following business day. In view of this, the NAVs of these Schemes would appear in the newspapers with one day time lag. The published NAVs would be made available with an asterix explaining that the NAVs were with one day/ or the actual time lag. All delays beyond 10:00 am would be reported to AMFI and SEBI as already stipulated.

(vi) Dispatch of Statement of Accounts: SEBI directed mutual funds to dispatch the statement of accounts to the unit holders under Systematic Investment Plan (SIP) / Systematic Transfer Plan (STP) / Systematic Withdrawal Plan (SWP) once every quarter ending March, June, September and December within ten working days of the end of the respective quarter. However, the first statement of accounts under SIP/STP/ SWP shall be issued within ten working days of the initial investment.

In case of specific request received from investors, mutual funds shall provide the statement of accounts to the investors within five working days from the receipt of such request without any charges. Further, soft copy of the account statement shall be mailed to the investors under SIP/STP/SWP to their e-mail address on a monthly basis, if so desired by the investors.

SEBI further advised mutual funds to provide account statements to the unit holders who have not transacted during the last six months to ensure better information flow.

(vii) Launch of Gold Exchange Traded Funds: SEBI amended the SEBI (Mutual Funds) Regulations, 1996 to specify the methodology for the valuation of gold for the purpose of Gold Exchange Traded Funds (GETFs). Accordingly, the gold held by a GETF scheme shall be valued at the AM fixing price of London Bullion Market Association (LBMA) in US dollars per troy ounce for gold having a fineness of 995.0 parts per thousand, subject to prescribed adjustments. During the year two GETF schemes were launched.

(viii) Real Estate Mutual Fund (REMF): Draft Regulations for REMF were approved by SEBI. REMF Scheme means a scheme of a mutual fund which has investment objective to invest directly or indirectly in real estate property and shall be governed by the provisions and guidelines under SEBI (Mutual Funds) Regulations. The structure of the REMFs, initially, shall be close-ended. The units of REMFs should be compulsorily listed on the stock exchanges and NAV of the scheme should be declared daily. The final framework is being worked out given the special nature of real estate as an asset class and various concerns expressed on this issue (Box 1).

The first guidelines for Real estate Mutual funds were approved by the SEBI in June 2006. A real estate mutual fund scheme refers to mutual fund which has investment objective to invest directly or indirectly in real estate asset and would be governed by the provisions and guidelines under SEBI (Mutual Funds) Regulations, 1996. During 2007-08, steps were taken to address residual issues in discussion with AMFI, ICAI and Credit Rating Agencies. The necessary amendments to the SEBI (Mutual Fund), Regulations 1996, were thereafter notified on April 16, 2008.

Box 1

REAL ESTATE INVESTMENT SCHEMES FOR MUTUAL FUNDS IN INDIA

Real estate is an important asset class, which is generally not available to investors in India, except through direct ownership of properties. Investment in real estate provides opportunity for capital gains as well as periodic incomes. Over a longer term real estate provides returns that are comparable with returns on equities. The volatility in prices of real estate is lower than equities leading to a better risk-return trade off for the investment. Real estate investments made over long periods of time provide an inflation hedge and yield real returns. However, real estate is distinct from other assets. The real estate investments are lumpy in nature and unaffordable to many. The specific risk is high and personal diversification is very difficult. The legal issues and lack of transparency make the probability of a mistake high. The illiquid nature of the markets makes the undoing of a wrong real estate investment a tedious and painful process. Distress sales generate much lower returns than the fair value of the property.

Professional management attempts to limit the risks in real estate investment and, at the same time, brings in such advantages as legal expertise, information on prices and regular maintenance and repairs.

Real estate investment schemes provide affordability to small investors enabling their participation in the property market. They help investors to diversify their investment portfolio across various asset classes and reduce the property specific risk. The benefits include professional management and liquidity for the investment.

Real Estate Investment Trusts (REITs) have been in existence in the United States of America since 1960. In the beginning, REITs were constrained because of the limited permission to own real estate and not operate or manage it. The provisions of the tax code which made real estate investment tax shelter-oriented also hindered the growth of REITs. The Tax Reform Act of 1986 reduced the potential for real estate investment to generate tax shelter opportunities and permitted the REITs to also operate and manage most types of income producing commercial properties. REITs became a popular way of accessing the markets during the early 1990s when property values dropped between 30-50 per cent. While the sector experienced credit crunch, REITs became the source of capital to many private real estate companies and a convenient mode for investors to gain exposure to the sector. There are about 190 publicly traded REITs in the USA and registered with the SEC, with assets totaling over USD 500 billion.

In the United Kingdom, real estate investments are done through pooled managed vehicles (PMVs), which are in the form of Trusts, having a variable capital and are similar to open-ended funds. PMVs may get tax benefits based on the investor profile. REITs are a relatively new entrant in the Asia Pacific region in Singapore, Malaysia, Hong Kong, Taiwan, Korea and Thailand.

Association of Mutual Funds in India (AMFI) had set up a Committee to study the introduction of real estate schemes for mutual funds in India. The Committee submitted its report in October 2000. AMFI subsequently appointed a Sub-Committee to formulate a working plan for launching ofREMFs in India, which submitted its report in August 2002. SEBI examined the proposals and took into consideration certain concerns raised by investor associations and the Institute of Chartered Accountants of India (ICAI). On account of the well developed stage of the mutual fund industry in India, SEBI decided to allow the existing mutual funds in India to float real estate investment schemes. In June 2006, the guidelines for Real Estate Mutual Funds were approved by the SEBI Board. A real estate mutual fund scheme means a mutual fund which has investment objective to invest directly or indirectly in real estate property and shall be governed by the provisions and guidelines under SEBI (Mutual Funds) Regulations, 1996. Certain residual issues relating to valuation and accounting are being addressed.

(ix) Parking of Funds in Short-term Deposits of Scheduled Commercial Banks by Mutual Funds - Pending Deployment: In order to ensure that the funds collected in a scheme are invested as per the investment objective stated in the offer document, SEBI issued guidelines for parking of funds in short-term deposits of scheduled commercial banks - pending deployment. The following were some of the features of the guidelines:

a) "Short-Term" for such parking of funds by mutual funds would be treated as a period not exceeding 91 days.

b) No mutual fund scheme would park more than 15 per cent of the net assets in short-term deposit(s) of all the scheduled commercial banks put together. However, it may be raised to 20 per cent with prior approval of the trustees. Also, parking of funds in short-term deposits of associate and sponsor scheduled commercial banks together would not exceed 20 per cent of total deployment by the mutual fund in short-term deposits.

c) No mutual fund scheme would park more than 10 per cent of the net assets in short-term deposit(s), with any one scheduled commercial bank including its subsidiaries.

d) Asset Management Company (AMC) would not be permitted to charge any investment management and advisory fees for parking of funds in short-term deposits of scheduled commercial banks in case of liquid and debt oriented schemes.

It was clarified that the tenure of the term deposits placed as margin for trading in derivatives shall not exceed 182 days.

(x) Reduction in Filing Fees for Offer Documents and Deployment of Funds in Short-Term Deposits of Scheduled ercial Banks: Filing fees for offer documents i.e. 0.03 per cent of the amount raised in the new fund offer (NFO), subject to a minimum of ₹ one lakh and a maximum of ₹ one crore along with pending deployment of funds of a scheme in terms of investment objectives of the scheme was notified on April 16, 2007. However, filing fees for offer documents was further reduced to 0.005 per cent of amount raised in New Fund Offer (NFO) subject to minimum ₹ one lakh and maximum ₹ 50 lakh w.e.f. April 01, 2008. Also, the registration fees payable by the mutual funds was also reduced to ₹ 25 lakh in place of ₹ 50 lakh earlier.

(xi) Bi-monthly Compliance Test Reports (CTRs): With an objective of effective and relevant disclosure to SEBI, it was decided that instead of filing complete CTR with SEBI, the AMCs shall only do exceptional reporting on a bi-monthly basis i.e., the AMCs would report for only those points in the CTR where it had not complied with the same. This exception report would also be placed before the board of trustees.

(xii) Investment in ADRs/GDRs/ Foreign Securities and Overseas ETFs by Mutual Funds: The aggregate ceiling for overseas ments by mutual funds was raised to USD four billion and subsequently to USD five billion as an industry vide ceiling and within this overall limit, mutual funds can make overseas investments subject to a maximum of USD 300 million. The permissible investments in which overseas investments could be made by mutual funds were expanded. Accordingly, a mutual fund can invest in the following:

a) ADRs/ GDRs issued by Indian or foreign companies;

b) Equity of overseas companies listed on recognised stock exchanges overseas;

c) Initial and follow-on public offerings for listing at recognised stock exchanges overseas;

d) Foreign Debt Securities in the countries with fully convertible currencies, short-term as well as long-term debt instruments with rating not below investment grade by accredited/ registered credit rating agencies;

e) Money market instruments rated not below investment grade;

f) Repos in the form of investment, where the counterparty was rated not below investment grade; repos would not, however, involve any borrowing of funds by mutual funds;

g) Government securities where the countries were rated not below investment grade;

h) Derivatives traded on recognised stock exchanges overseas only for hedging and portfolio balancing with underlying as securities;

i) Short-term deposits with banks overseas where the issuer was rated not below investment grade; and

j) Units/securities issued by overseas mutual funds or unit trusts registered with overseas regulators and investing in (a) aforesaid securities, (b) Real Estate Investment Trusts (REITs) listed in recognised stock exchanges overseas or (c) unlisted overseas securities (not exceeding 10 per cent of their net assets).

(xiii) Reduction in Expenses charged by Index Fund Scheme: The limit on investment and advisory for index fund schemes was reduced to 0.75 per cent of weekly average net assets and the total expenses of the scheme including the investment and advisory fees to 1.5 per cent of the weekly average net assets. The reduced expenses and investment and advisory fees was made applicable to exchange traded index funds also.

(xiv) Short Selling and Securities Lending and Borrowing (SLB): Enabling provisions were made for a mutual fund to engage in short selling of securities as well as lending and borrowing of securities.

(xv) Waiver of Load for Direct Applications: Keeping in view the interest of the investors, it was decided that no entry load should be charged for direct applications received by the asset management company (AMC) i.e., applications received through the internet, submitted to AMC or collection centre/ Investor Service Centre that were not routed through any distributor/ agent/ broker. This would be applicable for investments in existing schemes with effect from January 04, 2008 and in new schemes launched on and after the said date. It would also be applicable to additional purchases done directly by the investor under the same folio and switch-in to a scheme from other schemes, if such a transaction was done directly by the investor.

(xvi) Standard Warning in Advertisements by Mutual Funds: The rapid fire manner in which the standard warning "Mutual Fund investments are subject to market risks, read the offer document carefully before investing" recited in the audio visual and audio media rendered it unintelligible to the viewer/ listener. In order to improve the manner in which the said message was conveyed to the investors, it was decided in consultation with AMFI that with effecHrom April 1, 2008: a) The time for display and voice over of the standard warning be enhanced to five seconds in audio visual ertisements; and b) In case of audio advertisements, the standard warning would be read in an easily understandable manner over a period of five seconds.

(xvii) Load on Bonus Units and Units Allotted on Reinvestment of Dividend: The practice of charging entry load on bonus units issued to unit holders by mutual funds was taken up with AMFI. Based on the recommendations of AMFI Working Group on Standardisation of Key Operational Areas, it was decided that AMCs would not charge entry as well as exit load on bonus units and on units allotted on reinvestment of dividend.

(xviii) Dedicated Infrastructure Funds: Finance Minister in his Budget speech for 2007-08, announced that to promote the flow of investment to the infrastructure sector, mutual funds would be permitted to launch and operate dedicated infrastructure funds.

(xix) Simplification of Offer Documents: Presently Offer Documents (OD) and Key Information Memorandum (KIM) of mutual fund schemes are prepared as per format prescribed by SEBI. It was felt that due to regulatory and other changes over a period of time, the ODs not only became lengthy and complex but also highly technical and

legalistic. Consequently, ODs appeared to have become less-user friendly. SEBI in consultation with AMFI is working on the modalities for simplification of OD. The simplified version of OD would help the investor in making investment decision by concentrating on the scheme specific details.

COMPUTATION OF NET ASSET VALUE (NAV)

The share price of the mutual fund is based on its net asset value (NAV) per share, which is found by subtracting from the market value of the portfolio the mutual fund's liabilities and the dividing by the number of mutual fund shares issued. That is:

$$\text{Net asset value per share} = \frac{\text{Market value of portfolio} - \text{Liabilities}}{\text{Number of mutual fund shares issued}}$$

In August 1994, SEBI had formed a six-member committee to suggest disclosure practices and standardised procedures for computation of net asset values for mutual fund schemes. The committee finalised its report on 12 December 1995 and the same was released on 1 January 1996.

The major guidelines are discussed below :

There has been a major shift in the valuation of securities used for the calculation of the net asset value (NAV) of the mutual fund scheme. Earlier, calculation of the NAV was done by valuing the securities at cost. This has now been changed to marking all securities at market value. The investments which are shown in balance sheet should also be shown at market value so that this comparable with the net asset value. Further, marking all investments at market prices also permits inter- scheme comparison to some extent.

It has been recommended that the NAVs of both open-end and close-end scheme be calculated on a weekly basis, at least.

The fees paid by the mutual fund to the asset management company should be linked to the performance of the mutual fund schemes as against a flat rate charged earlier which did not take into account the mutual fund scheme's performance. It is now suggested that mutual funds would be paying a basic annual fee to the AMC computed as a percentage of the average weekly net asset value of the scheme and an additional fee calculated as a percentage of the net growth of the scheme.

The AMC will have the discretion of floating no load or load schemes or a mixture of the two. Presently, mutual funds are permitted to deduct upto 6% from the net asset value to account for issue expenses.

The report has suggested that repurchase and resale price of open-end schemes should be linked to the NAV of the scheme. Accordingly, the repurchase price of an open-end scheme should not be lower than 93 per cent of the net asset value and the resale price should not be more than 1.07 times the net asset value. Also, the spread between the repurchase and re-sale price should not exceed seven percentage points.

It has been suggested that the failure of a mutual fund scheme to give the minimum assured returns should be met out of the funds of the asset management company and not the corpus of the mutual fund scheme.

The report has suggested that the AMC should disclose custodian and registration fees and has done away with the distinction of short term and long term capital gains.

The committee has suggested the disclosure of ratio of expenses to net assets and gross income to net assets.

These guidelines would apply to all the mutual fund schemes launched in the future but it is not yet decided if these guidelines should be made applicable to existing schemes. Some members of the committee feel that existing schemes should adhere to these guidelines with effect from 1 April 1997. Mutual fund shares are quoted on a bid-offer basis. The offer price is the price at which the mutual fund will sell the shares. It is equal to the NAV per share plus any sales commission that the mutual fund may charge. The sales commission is referred to as a *load*.

Within a short span of four to five years, mutual funds operation has become integral part of the Indian financial system. Investors in India look at mutual funds as a substitute of fixed deposits in banks rather than as a substitute for investment in securities. Mutual funds provide an opportunity for the *risk-averse* investors to share their risk and yet go in for high return equities in the capital market. The popularity of mutual funds has soared so have their diversity and complexity. Despite the many advantages (e.g. diversification, continuous professional management, low operating costs, shareholder services, liquidity, safety from loss due to unethical practices etc.), mutual funds are not for everyone. Critics argue that funds are boring, since shareholders do not have any say as to which stocks are selected. Some people have been able to strike it rich with the right stock. That, then is also a danger of getting carried away and ending up with a big stake in a promising company that is suddenly runs into deep trouble, plunges in value, and takes the life savings down with it. The chances of that happening with the mutual funds are much lower since they are diversified and professionally managed.

The reason most investors do not excell in stock picking is that they succumb to certain common errors, many of which can be avoided or minimised with mutual funds. However, successful investing being a serious business requiring a well thought-out plan, investors do not need to be familiar with the characteristics of the different types of mutual funds. Too many investors do not understand what they are buying - or even what they are paying. With so many choices, investors risk making the wrong ones. Besides investing in inappropriate and high-cost mutual funds, investors also buy laggards. There is no shortage of mediocre performers.

Key Differences Between Closed-End and Open-End Funds

Because close-end funds trade like stocks, an investor must deal with a broker to buy or sell shares, and the usual brokerage commissions apply. Open-end funds, in contrast, are bought from and sold to the fund operators themselves. Another important difference between open-and closed-end funds is their liquidity. As investor can buy and sell relatively large amounts of an open-end mutual fund at its NAV without worrying about affecting the price. However, a relatively large buy or sell order for close-end fund could easily bump its price up or down. Thus, the greater liquidity of open-end funds gives them a distinct advantage. Like open-end funds, most CEFs offer dividend reinvestment plans, but in many cases, that's about it. CEFs simply don't provide the full range of services that mutual fund investors are accustomed to.

All things considered, probably the most important difference is the way these funds are priced in the market place. This is important because it *directly affects* investor costs and returns. Whereas open-end funds can be bought and sold at NAV (plus any front-end load or minus any redemption charge), CEFs have two values—a market value (or stock price) and net asset value (NAV). The two are rarely the same, because CEFs typically trade at either a premium or a discount. A *premium* occurs when a fund trades for more than its NAV; a *discount* occurs when it trades for less. As a rule, CEFs trade at discounts.

The premium or discount is calculated as follows:

Premium (or discount) = (Share price - NAV) / NAV

Suppose Fund A has a NAV of ₹ 10. If its share price is ₹ 8, it will sell at a 20% discount. That is,

Premium (or discount) = (₹ 8 - ₹ 10)/ ₹ 10
= - ₹ 2/ ₹ 10 = - .20 = -20%

Because this value is negative, the fund is trading at a *discount* (or below its NAV). On the other hand, if this same fund were priced at ₹ 12 per share, it would be trading at a premium of 20%—that is, (₹ 12 - ₹ 10)/₹ 10 = ₹ 2/₹ 10 = 0.20. Because the value is positive, the fund is trading at a premium (above its NAV).

MEASURING PERFORMANCE

As in any investment decision, return performance is a major dimension in the mutual fund selection process. The level of dividends paid by the fund, its capital gains, and its growth in capital are all important aspects of return. Such return information enables an investor to judge the investment behaviour of a fund and to appraise its performance in relation to other funds and investment vehicles. Here we will look at different measures that mutual fund investors use to assess return. Also, because risk is so important in defining the investment behaviour of a fund, we will examine mutual fund risk as well.

Sources of Return

An open-end mutual fund has three potential sources of return: (1) dividend income, (2) capital gains distribution, and (3) change in the price (or net asset value) of the fund. Depending on the type of fund, some mutual funds derive more income from one source than another. For example, we would normally expect income-oriented funds to have much higher dividend income than capital gains distributions.

Open-end mutual funds regularly publish reports that recap investment performance. An hypothetical report of a company showing the *Summary of Income and Capital Changes* is provided in Table 1. This statement is found in the fund's profile or prospectus. It gives a brief overview of the fund's investment activity, including expense ratios and portfolio turnover rates. Of interest to us here is the top part of the report (which runs from "net asset value, beginning a period" to "net asset value end of period"—lines 1 to 10). This part reveals the amount of dividend income and capital gains distributed to the shareholders, along with any change in the fund's net asset value.

TABLE 1

A Report of Mutual Fund Income and Capital Changes
(For a Share Outstanding Throughout the Year)

		2011	2010	2009
1.	Net asset value, beginning of period	₹ 24.47	₹ 27.03	₹ 24.26
2.	**Income from investment operations:**			
3.	Net investment income	₹ 0.60	₹ 0.66	₹ 0.50
4.	Net gains on securities (realised and unrealised)	6.37	(1.74)	3.79
5.	Total from investment operations	6.97	(1.08)	4.29
6.	**Less distributions:**			
7.	Dividends from net investment income	₹ (0.55)	₹ (0.64)	₹ (0.50)
8.	Distributions from realised gains	(1.75)	(.84)	(1.02)

9. Total distributions	(2.30)	(1.48)	(1.52)
10. Net asset value, end of period	₹ 29.14	₹ 24.47	₹ 27.03
11. Total return	28.48%	(4.00%)	17.68%
12. Ratios/supplemental data			
13. Net asset value, end of period (₹ '000)	₹ 3,07,951	₹ 1,53,378	₹ 1,08,904
14. Ratio of expenses to average net assets	1.04%	0.85%	0.94%
15. Ratio of net investment income to average net assets 1.47%		2.56%	2.39%
16. Portfolio turnover rate*	85%	144%	74%

* Portfolio turnover rate relates the number of shares bought and sold by the fund to the total number of shares held in the fund's portfolio. A high turnover rate (in excess of 100%) means the fund has been doing a lot of trading.

Dividend income (see line 7 of Table 1) is derived from the dividend and interest income earned on the security holdings of the mutual fund. It is paid out of the *net investment income* that's left after all operating expenses have been met. When the fund receives dividend or interest payments, it passes these on to shareholders in the form of dividend payments. The fund accumulates all of the current income it has received for the period and then pays it out on a prorated basis. If a fund earned, say, ₹ 2 crore in dividends and interest in a given year and if that fund had 1 million shares outstanding, each share would receive an annual dividend payment of ₹ 2.

Capital gains distributions (see line 8) work on the same principle, except that these payments are derived from the capital gains earned by the fund. It works like this: Suppose the fund brought some stock a year ago for ₹ 50 and sold that stock in the current period for ₹ 75 per share. Clearly, the fund has achieved capital gains of ₹ 25 per share. If it held 50,000 shares of this stock, it would have realised a total capital gain of ₹ 12,50,000 (₹ 25 x 50,000 = ₹ 12,50,000). Given that the fund has 1 million shares outstanding, each share is entitled to ₹ 1.25 in the form of a capital gains distribution. Note that this capital gains distribution applies only to *realised* capital gains (that is, the security holdings were actually sold and the capital gains actually earned).

Unrealised capital gains (or paper profits) are what make up the third and final element of a mutual fund's return. When the fund's holdings go up or down in price, the net asset value of the fund moves accordingly. Suppose an investor buys into a fund at ₹ 10 per share and sometime later the fund is quoted at ₹ 12.50. The difference of ₹ 2.50 per share is the unrealised capital gains. It represents the profit that shareholders would receive (and are entitled to) if the fund were to sell its holdings. (Actually, as Table-1 shows, some of the change in net asset value can also be made up of undistributed income).

The return on *closed-end* investment companies is derived from the same three sources as that of open-end funds and from a *fourth source* as well: changes in price discounts or premiums. But because discount or premium is already embedded in the share price of a fund, it follows that, for a close-end fund, the third element of return—change in share price—is made up not only of change in net asset value but also of change in price discount or premium.

What About Future Performance? There's no doubt that a statement like the one in Table-1 provides a convenient recap of a fund's past behaviour. Looking at past performance is useful, but it doesn't tell what the future will be. Ideally, an indication is expected of what the same three elements of return—dividend income, capital gains distribution, and change in NAV—*will be*. But it's extremely difficult—if not impossible—to get a firm grip on what the future holds in dividends, capital gains, and NAV. This is because a mutual fund's future performance is directly linked to the *future make-up of the securities in its portfolio,* something that is next to impossible to get a clear reading on. It's not like evaluating the expected performance of a share of stock in which case an investor may be keying in on one company. With mutual funds, investment performance depends on the behaviour of many different stocks and bonds.

Where, then, do the investors look for insight on future performance? Most market observers suggest that the first place to look is the market itself. In particular, try to get a fix on the future direction of *the market as a whole.* This is important because the behaviour of well-diversified mutual fund tends to reflect the general tone of the market. Thus, if the feeling is that the market is going to be drifting up, so should the investment performance of mutual funds. Also investors should evaluate the *track records* of mutual funds in which they are interested. Past performance has a lot to say about the investment skills of the fund's money managers.

Measures of Return

A simple but effective measure of performance is to describe mutual fund return in terms of the three major sources noted above: dividends earned, capital gains distributions received, and change in price. When dealing with investment horizons of 1 year or less, we can easily convert these fund payoffs into a return figure by using the standard holding period return (HPR) formula. The computations necessary are illustrated below using the 2011 figures from Table 1. Referring to the exhibit, we can see that in 2011, this hypothetical no-load, open-end fund paid ₹ 0.55 per share in dividends and another ₹ 1.75 in capital gains distributions. It had a price at the beginning of the year of ₹ 24.47 that rose to ₹ 29.14 by the end of the year. Table-2 summarises this investment performance.

TABLE-2

Price (NAV) at the *beginning* of the year	₹ 24.47
Price (NAV) at the *end* of the year	29.14
Net increase	₹ 4.67
Return for the year:	
Dividends received	₹ .55
Capital gains distributions	1.75
Net increase in price (NAV)	4.67
Total return	₹ 6.97
Holding period return (HPR) (total return/beginning price)	28.5%

This HPR measure (which is shown in Table 1 as "Total Return" on line 11) not only captures all the important elements of mutual fund return but also provides a handy indication of yield. Note that the fund had a total return of ₹ 6.97. On the basis of beginning investment of ₹ 24.47 (the initial share price of the fund), the fund produced an annual return of 28.5%.

HPR with Reinvested Dividends and Capital Gains

Many mutual fund investors have their dividends and/or capital gains distributions reinvested in the fund. How, then, does an investor obtain a measure of return when he receives his (dividend/capital gains) payout in additional shares of stock rather than cash? With slight modifications, he can continue to use holding period return. The only difference is that he has to keep track of the number of shares acquired through reinvestment. To illustrate, let's continue with the example above and assume that he initially bought 200 shares in the mutual fund. Assume also that he was able to acquire shares through the fund's reinvestment programme at an average price of ₹ 26.50 a share. Thus, the ₹ 460 in dividends and capital gains distributions [(₹ 0.55 + ₹ 1.75) x 200] provided him with another 17.36 shares in the fund (₹ 460/₹ 26.50). Holding period return under these circumstances would relate the market value of the stock holdings at the beginning of the period with holdings at the end:

$$\text{Holding period return} = \frac{\left(\begin{array}{c}\text{Number of}\\ \text{shares at } end \times \frac{\text{Ending}}{\text{price}}\\ \text{of period}\end{array}\right) - \left(\begin{array}{c}\text{Number of}\\ \text{shares at } beginning \times \frac{\text{Initial}}{\text{price}}\\ \text{of period}\end{array}\right)}{\begin{array}{c}\text{Number of shares}\\ \text{at } beginning \text{ of period}\end{array} \times \begin{array}{c}\text{Initial}\\ \text{price}\end{array}}$$

Thus the holding period would be

$$\text{Holding period return} = \frac{(217.36 \times ₹\ 29.14) - (200 \times ₹\ 24.47)}{(200 \times ₹\ 24.47)}$$

$$= \frac{(₹\ 6{,}333.87) - (₹\ 4{,}894.00)}{₹\ 4{,}894.00} = 29.4\%$$

This holding period return, like the preceding one provides a rate-of-return measure that can now be used to compare the performance of this fund to those of other funds and investment vehicles.

Measuring Long-Term Returns

Rather than using 1-year holding periods, it is sometimes necessary to assess the performance of mutual funds over extended periods of time. In these cases, it would be inappropriate to employ holding period return as a measure of performance. When faced with multiple-year investment horizons, we can use the present-value-based *internal rate of return* (IRR) procedure to determine the fund's average annual compound rate of return. To illustrate, refer once again to Table 1. Assume that this time we want to find the annual rate of return over the full 3-year period (2009 through 2011). In this case, we see that the mutual fund had the following annual dividends and capital gains distribution.

	2011	2010	2009
Annual dividends paid	₹ .55	₹ .64	₹ .50
Annual capital gains distributed	₹ 1.75	₹ .84	₹ 1.02
Total distribution	₹ 2.30	₹ 1.48	₹ 1.52

Now, given that the fund had a price of ₹ 24.26 at the beginning of the period (1/1/2009) and was trading at ₹ 29.14 at the end of 2011 (3 years later), we have the following time line of cash flows:

| | Subsequent Cash Flows | | |
Initial Cash Flow	Year 1	Year 2	Year 3
₹ 24.26	₹ 1.52	₹ 1.48	₹ 2.30 + ₹ 29.14
(Beginning Price)	(Distributions)	(Distributions)	Distributions + Ending Price

The idea is to find the discount rate that will equate the annual dividends/capital gains distributions *and* the ending price in year 3 to the beginning price of the fund (₹ 24.26).

Using standard present-value calculations, we find that the mutual fund in Table 1 provided its investors with an annual rate of return of 13.1 percent over the 3-year period from 2009 to 2011. That is, at 13.1%, the present values of the cash flows in years 1, 2, and 3 equal the beginning price of the fund (₹ 24.26). Such information helps us assess fund performance and compare the return performance of one fund to other funds and investment vehicles.

Returns on Closed-End Funds

The returns of CEFs are customarily reported on the basis of their NAVs. That is, *price premiums and discounts are ignored when computing various returns measures.* At the same time, it's becoming increasingly common to see return performance expressed in terms of actual market prices, a practice that captures the impact of changing market premiums or discounts on holding period returns. The greater the premiums or discounts and the greater the changes in these values over time, the greater their impact on reported returns. It's not at all uncommon for CEFs to have different market-based and NAV-based holding period returns. When NAVs are used, the returns on CEFs are found in exactly the same way as the returns on open-end funds. In contrast, when market values are used to measure return, the investors are to *substitute the market price of the fund* (with its embedded premium or discount) *for the corresponding NAV in the holding period or internal rate of return* measure. Some CEF investors like to run *both* NAV-based and market-based measures of return to see how changing premiums (or discounts) have added to or hurt the returns on their mutual fund holdings. Even so, as a rule, NAV-based return numbers are generally viewed as the preferred measures of performance. Because fund managers often have little or no control over changes in premium or discounts, NAV-based measures are felt to give a truer picture of the performance of the fund itself.

The Matter of Risk

Because most mutual funds are so diversified, their investors are largely immune to the business and financial risks normally present with individual securities. Even with extensive diversification, however, the investment behaviour of most funds is still exposed to a considerable amount of *market risk.* In fact, because mutual fund portfolios are so well diversified, they often tend to perform very much like the market—or some segment of the market that's being targeted by the fund. Although a few funds, tend to be defensive (countercyclical), market risk is an important behavioural ingredient in a large number of mutual funds, both open- and closed-end. Investors should be aware of the effect the general market has on the investment performance of a mutual fund. For example, if the market is trending downward and they anticipate that trend to continue, it might be best to place any new investment capital into something like a money fund until the market reverses itself. At that time, they can make a more long-term commitment.

Another important risk consideration revolves around the management practices of the fund itself. If the portfolio is managed conservatively, the risk of a loss in capital is likely to be much less than for aggressively managed funds. Obviously, the more speculative the investment goals of the fund, the greater the risk of instability in the net asset value. But, a conservatively managed portfolio does not necessarily eliminate all price volatility. The securities in the portfolio are still subject to inflation, interest rate, and general market risks. However, these risks are generally reduced or minimised as the investment objectives and portfolio management practices of the funds become more conservative.

MUTUAL FUNDS' OPERATIONS IN INDIA

Mutual funds provide households an option for portfolio diversification and relative risk-aversion through collection of funds from the households and make investments in the stock and debt markets. Resources mobilised by mutual fund (UTI was the only mutual fund until 1987-88) grew at a steady rate until 1992-93; since then they showed some variations. Resources mobilised by mutual funds which was just 0.04 per cent of GDP (at current market prices) during the period of 1970-71 to 1974-85 increased to 1.59 per cent during 1990-91 to 1992-93. Total resources mobilised as proportion of GDP declined to 1.12 per cent by 1994-95 but nevertheless remained positive. During the period from 1995-97, there was a net outflow of funds form mutual funds, especially UTI, as a result of which the ratio turned negative. From 1997-98 onwards, the ratio again turned positive and stood at 1.13 per cent during 1999-2000.

The mutual fund industry registered significant growth in the last few years. The investible resources of mutual funds rose form ₹ 68,200 crore in 1998-99 to ₹ 1,09,114 crore in 1999-2000. Net resource mobilisation by mutual funds declined to ₹ 6,846 crore in April-December, 2000 from ₹ 12,193 crore in the corresponding previous period. This was on account of the steep increase in redemption/repurchase during this period. The outflow of funds via repurchase/redemption constituted 88.7 per cent of gross resource mobilisation during April-December, 2000 compared with 66.0 per cent in the corresponding previous period. In the case of public sector mutual funds, redemption/repurchase exceeded gross resource mobilisation, thereby making their net resource mobilisation negative.

Mutual funds were net sellers of equity in April-December, 2000. Gross purchase of equity amounted to ₹ 12,612 crore while gross sales amounted to ₹ 12,884 crore, thereby making their net investment in equity negative during April-December, 2000. However, they were net buyers in debt during this period. As against their gross purchase at ₹ 8066 crore, their net sale amounted to only ₹ 4968 crore, thus resulting in net investment in debt amounting to ₹ 3098 crore.

Recent policy initiatives in the mutual fund industry. (i) A common format was prescribed for all mutual fund schemes to disclose their portfolios at half-yearly intervals; (ii) Mutual Funds are required to disclose investment in various types of instruments and percentage of investment in each scrip to the total NAV, illiquid and non-performing assets, investment in derivatives and in ADRs / GDRs; (iii) All Asset Management Companies are required to maintain records in support of each investment decision etc., registered significant growth during April-December 2001.

Mutual funds were net sellers in equities to the extent of ₹3,796 crore during 2001-02 as compared with net sales of ₹ 2,767 crore in the previous year. There has been a shift in portfolio allocations towards debt instruments (₹ 10,959 crore during 2001-02 as compared with ₹ 5,023 crore during 2000-01). Mutual funds were net sellers in equities by ₹ 917 crore in the first quarter of 2002-03 as compared with net sales of ₹ 884 crore during the comparable quarter of-2001-02.

Over the last few years, mutual funds are an important avenue through which households participate in the securities market. Intermediation through mutual funds is particularly attractive from the viewpoint of systemic stability, because mutual funds only hold transparent assets, do daily marking to market, have no leverage, and all losses are instantly passed on to the balance sheets of households. While assets under management of all mutual funds had stagnated at roughly ₹ 1.5 lakh crore between 2003 and 2004, there was a significant rise to a level of roughly ₹ 2 lakh crore in 2005. Overall the total assets under management of the mutual funds industry increase to ₹ 2,07,979 crore in January 2006, the highest in recent times up by a robust 36.6 per cent over the year ago levels. January, 2006 also witnessed a net inflow of ₹ 6,031 crore in the mutual fund industry after two consecutive months of outflow. This was largely due to liquid/money market schemes. They recorded the highest net inflow of ₹ 7,485 crore. Schemes that recorded outflow in January, 2006 were income (–₹ 908 crore), growth (–₹ 754 crore) and gilt (–₹ 142 crore). 21 new schemes were launched in January, 2006 out of which 18 were income schemes (one open-ended and 17 closed-ended), one growth (closed) scheme, one liquid/money market (open) scheme and one ELSS (open) scheme. Together these garnered ₹ 5,696 crore. Out of these schemes, liquid money market schemes continue to be the most preferred. As of 31 January 2006, they had a 35 per cent share in the total assets under management of the interest fund industry, followed by growth funds (34 per cent share) and income funds (24 per cent share).

Mutual fund remained net sellers in equities for the third consecutive month in February, 2006. They were net sellers to the tune of ₹ 245.6 crore, following net sales of over ₹ 1,000 crore in the preceding two months. Assets under management of the mutual fund industry during 2002-05 show an over all increase of 62.5 per cent, the maximum growth of 32.36 per cent took place in 2005 as against 7.46 per cent and 14.2 per cent respectively in 2004 and 2003 during this period.

Net mobilisation of resources by mutual funds increased by more than four-fold to ₹ 104,950 crore in 2006 from ₹ 25,454 crore in 2005. The sharp rise in mobilisation by mutual funds was due to buoyant inflows under both income/debt oriented schemes. June, September and December will the only three months when mutual fund industry witnessed net outflow of funds during the calender year 2006.

New investment avenues are opening up for mutual funds. On 4 January 2007, the Securities and Exchange Board of India raised the aggregate ceiling on investments of mutual funds in ADRs and GDRs of Indian companies, equity and rated debt of overseas companies from US$ 2 billion to US$ 3 billion. These investments cannot exceed 10 per cent of the net assets managed by individual mutual funds as on 31 March of each relevant year and subject to a maximum of US$ 150 million per mutual fund. Earlier, in July 2006, the SEBI had removed the restriction on investments by mutual funds in overseas companies with less than 10 per cent share holding in Indian listed companies and had raised the ceiling for overseas investments by them to US$ 2 billion from US$ 1 billion earlier.

Mutual funds made net purchases of ₹ 1.627 crore of Indian equities in December, 2006, after being the net sellers in the preceding two months. Their net investments in debt were ₹ 1,329 crore, the lowest in a single month since March 2006. However, the first quarter of 2007 again witnessed a slump in the mutual fund investment activities. The mutual funds were not sellers in equities, for the third consecutive month in March 2007. There net sales rose to ₹ 1342 crore in January 2007 which fell to ₹ 274 crore in February 2007. However, again in the subsequent month March, 2007, there was a steep increase in the net equity sales which touched to ₹ 1,885 crore. But with the equity markets witnessing an impressive gain which had begun in March 2007, the mutual funds entered in the market and purchased equities aggressively from the secondary market. Whereas net equity purchase by mutual funds amounted to ₹ 1,032 crore in April 2007, it stood at ₹ 1,889 crore, an impressive 83% growth, in the month of May, 2007 over the previous month.

The Indian equity markets, declined sharply during 2008, reflecting the volatility in international financial markets and foreign institutional investment outflows. The market remained range bound during April-March 2009 but exhibited signs of recovery from April 2009. With the revival of foreign institutional investors' (FIIs) interest in emerging market economies including India, the equity markets gained strength during May-July 2009. FIIs made not purchase of US $ 19.0 billion in the Indian equity market during April-December 2009, as against net sales US $ 9.1 billion in the comparable period of the previous year. In contrast, mutual funds' net sales in stock markets during April-December 2009 amounted to ₹ 4,421 crore as against net purchases of ₹ 7,867 crore in the same period of previous year.

During 2009, total net resources mobilized by MFs increased to ₹ 1,43,775 crore as compared to net redemptions amounting to ₹ 624 crore in 2008. Private-sector mutual funds, which had witnessed heavy redemption pressure in 2008, recorded a turnaround with total net resource mobilization of ₹ 1,14,095 crore in 2009 as against a net redemption of ₹ 12,506 crore in 2008. Total funds mobilized by public-sector mutual funds were marginally higher at ₹ 17,624 crore in 2009 (₹ 14,587 crore in 2008). The Unit Trust of India (UTI), which had recorded net redemptions of ₹ 2,704 crore in 2008, mobilized ₹ 12,056 crore in 2009. During 2010-11 (as in November 2010), mutual funds mobilized ₹ 12,185 crore from the market as compared to ₹ 83,080 crore in 2009-10. The market value of assets under management stood at ₹ 6,65,282 crore as on 30 November 2010 compared to ₹ 6,13,979 crore as on 31March 2010, showing an increase of 8.4 per cent. During 2011-12 (up to 30 November 2011), MFs mobilized ₹ 1,00,338 crore from the market as compared to ₹ 49,406 crore liquidation in 2010-11. The market value of assets under management stood at ₹ 6,81,655 crore as on 30 November 2011 compared to ₹ 6,65,282 crore as on 31 March 2011, indicating an increase of 2.5 per cent.

After two years of redemption pressures, mutual funds (MF) mobilized ₹ 1,20,269 crore from the market in 2012-13 (Table 3). The market value of their assets under management stood at ₹ 7,59,995 crores as on 31 December 2012 compared to ₹ 5,87,217 crore as on 31 March 2012, indicating an increase of 29.4 per cent.

TABLE 3

Trends in Resource Mobilization (net) by Mutual Funds

(₹ crore)

Sector	2009-10	2010-1	2011-12	2012-13#
1. UTI	15653	-16636	-3184	10617
2. Public	12499	-13555	-3394	8748
3. Private	54928	-19215	-22024	100906
Total (1+2+3)	83080	-49406	-28602	120269

Source: SEBI.

Note: # As on December 31, 2012.

The number of registered FIIs rose to 1,706 at the end of 2009 from 1,594 in 2008. The number of sub-accounts also increased to 5,331 from 4,872 during the same period. The FII in the spot market increased to ₹ 83,424 crore in 2009 as compared to withdrawals of ₹ 52,987 crore in 2008. Further, net investment in debt was lower at ₹ 4,563 crore in 2009 as compared to ₹ 11,772 crore in 2008. Total net investment by FIIs in equity and debt markets taken together, increased considerably to ₹ 87,987 crore in 2009 compared to a net decline of ₹ 41,216 crore in 2008. Further, the number of registered FIIs increased to 1718 as on 31 December 2010 from 1713 on 31 March 2010. The number of registered subaccounts also increased to 5503 from 5378 during the same period. In the Indian equity market, FIIs invested ₹ 1,12,622 crore during 2010-11 (as on 31 December 2010) as compared to ₹ 1,10,221 crore in 2009-10. In the debt segment, FIIs invested ₹ 24,839 crore in 2010-11 (as on 31 December 2010) as compared to ₹ 32,438 crore in 2009-10. So far during 2010-11, total investment in equity and debt by FIIs stood at ₹ 1,37,461 crore as compared to ₹ 1,42,658 crore in 2009-10.

During April-December 2011, net investments of the mutual fund industry in Indian equities stood at ₹ 4,569.5 crore. This was a complete turnaround from the year ago period when their sales exceeded purchases by ₹ 21,738.3 crore. However, first five months of 2012 saw mutual funds pulling out money. Again after June, 2012 there was a negative net investment for the sixth consecutive months in 2012. Their net withdrawals stood are ₹ 2,615 crore in December 2012.

TABLE 4
Equity Transactions by Mutual Funds (₹ cr)

	Purchase	Sales	Net Investment
Dec 2011	8,808.3	8,228.1	580.2
Jan 2012	10,421.4	12,279.5	-1,858.1
Feb 2012	14,940.4	17,111.5	-2,171.1
Mar 2012	10,585.0	12,134.1	-1,549.1
Apr 2012	9,054.2	9,593.2	-539.0
May 2012	8,871.6	9,269.7	-398.1
Jun 2012	8,5615	8,077.2	484.3
Jul 2012	8,100.3	9,955.5	-1,855.2
Aug 2012	8,128.3	9,986.9	-1,858.6
Sep 2012	9,768.3	12,776.4	-3,008.1
Oct 2012	8,309.3	10,563.2	-2,253.9
Nov 2012	6,299.3	7,571.9	-1,272.6
Dec 2012	8,387.5	11,002.3	-2,614.8
	Apr-Dec	Apr-Dec	Apr-Dec
2011-12	96,190-0	91,968.8	4,221.2
2012-13	75,480.3	88,796.3	-13,316.0
	Apr-Mar	Apr-Mar	Apr-Mar
2011-12	1,32,136.8	1,33,493.9	-1,357.1

Data is provisional and subject to revision/correction.

Source: SEBI.

The cumulative assets under management of mutual funds increased by 60.9 per cent to ₹ 6,65,146 crore as on December 31, 2009 from ₹ 4,13,365 crore as on December 31, 2008. The share of income- /debt-oriented schemes in total assets under management was higher at 54.2 per cent in 2009 as against 47.7 per cent in 2008. The assets under management of equity- /growth-oriented schemes during 2009 accounted for 26.3 per cent of the total assets under management (23.9 per cent during 2008). However, the share of assets under money market schemes in total assets under management declined to 12.0 per cent during 2009 from 20.0 per cent during 2008.

Average assets under management (AUMs) of the mutual fund industry declined by two per cent in November 2011 to ₹ 6.8 lakh crore compared to the preceding month. The fall in total AUMs was on account of a drastic decline in the AUMs of equity schemes, which fell by 8.1 per cent in November 2011 over the preceding month. The share of equity schemes in total AUMs also declined during the last one year. They accounted for 22 per cent of total AUMs in November 2011 as against 27 per cent in November 2010. Net investments in mutual funds increased for the second consecutive month in November 2011. However, the increase was entirely on account of a rise in investments in liquid and money market schemes as all other schemes witnessed outflows during the month. Liquid and money market schemes accounted for around 85 per cent of the net investment in mutual funds in April-November 2011.

Assets under management (AUM) of the mutual fund industry rose by 3.2 per cent to ₹ 7.9 lakh crore at the end of November 2012 as compared to the preceding month (Table-5). This was the highest level of the AUM in the last two-and-a-half years. The rise in total AUM was on account of a sharp rise in AUM of liquid & money market funds.

TABLE 5

	Schemes Launched (in Nos.)	New Schemes Sales (₹ crore)	Existing Schemes Sales (₹ crore)	Total Sales (₹ crore)	Total Redemption (₹ crore)	Total Net investments (₹ crore)	Assets Under Management (₹ crore)
Nov. 2011	54	9,032	5,35,980	5,45,012	5,41,239	3,773	6,81,655
Dec. 2011	89	11,098	5,24,140	5,35,238	5,98,659	-63,421	6,11,402
Jan. 2012	52	8,501	5,43,406	5,51,907	5,28,354	23.553	6,59,153
Feb. 2012	70	11,867	5,12,564	5,24,431	5,23,160	1,271	6.75,238
Mar. 2012	157	36,361	6,24,135	6,60,496	7,44,261	-83,765	5,87,217
Apr. 2012	34	4,434	5,67,631	5,72,065	4,79,319	92,746	6,80,154
May 2012	46	4,429	5,78,087	5,82,516	5 55 774	26.742	6,99,284
Jun. 2012	61	4,516	5,90,479	5,94,995	6,18,964	-23,969	6,88,825
Jul. 2012	30	2,723	6,47,003	6,49,726	6,11,270	38,456	7,30,361
Aug. 2012	24	1,632	6,42,143	6,43,775	6,23,968	19,807	7,52,548
Sep. 2012		1,642	6,13,084	6,14,726	6.66,634 "	-51,908	7,20,113
Oct. 2012	10	745	5,92,127	5,92,872	5,46,151	46,721	7,68,158
Nov. 2012	9	1,555	4,96,423	4,97,978	4,87,370	10.608	7,93,152
	Apr-Nov	Apr-Nov	Apr-Nov	Apr-Nov	Apr-Nov	Apr-Nov	Apr-Nov
2011-12	394	53,530	44,94,077	45,47,607	44,47,268	1,00,339	
2012-13	236	21.676	47,26,977	"47,48,653	45,89,450	1,59,203	
	Apr-Mar	Apr-Mar	Apr-Mar	Apr-Mar	Apr-Mar	Apr-Mar	Apr-Mar
2011-12	762	1,21.357	66,98,322	68.19,679	68,41,702	-22,023	

AUM of liquid & money market funds rose by 7.7 per cent to ₹ 1.8 lakh crore at the end of November 2012 on the back of healthy inflows. Investors pumped in ₹ 11,440 crore into these funds during the month. AUM of equity funds rose by 3.5 per cent to ₹ 1.65 lakh crore as compared to the preceding month. This was in spite of net outflows of ₹ 1,300 crore from equity funds during the month. Equity markets had posted healthy gains in November. This is expected to have led to the rise in AUM of equity funds during the month. AUM of income funds rose by one per cent to ₹ 3.9 lakh crore at the end of November 2012 as compared to the preceding month.

AUM of the mutual fund industry have risen by a healthy 35.1 per cent since the beginning of 2012-13 as compared to a 15.1 per cent rise seen in the same period of the preceding year. Average monthly AUM are 3.5 per cent higher at ₹ 7.3 lakh crore during April-November 2012 as compared to the year-ago period.

RECENT POLICY DEVELOPMENTS

Some of the recent salient policy initiatives relating to the mutual funds are listed below:

i) In order to empower investors to decide the commission to be paid to distributors in accordance with the level of service received, to bring about more transparency in payment of commissions and to incentives long-term investment, it was decided that there should be no entry load for all mutual fund schemes; the scheme application forms should carry a suitable disclosure to the effect that the upfront commission to distributors will be paid by the investor directly to the distributor, based on his assessment of various factors including service rendered; of the exit load charged to the investor, a maximum of 1 per cent of the redemption proceeds should be maintained in a separate account which can be used by the Asset Management Companies to pay commissions to the distributor and to take care of other marketing and selling expenses. Any balance should be credited to the scheme immediately.

ii) It was decided that no distinction among unit holders should be made based on the amount of subscription while charging exit loads.

iii) Considering the importance of a systems audit in the technology-driven asset-management activity, it was decided that mutual funds should have a systems audit conducted by an independent CISA/CISM-qualified or equivalent auditor once in two years. For the financial years April 2008–March 2010, the systems audit should be completed by September 30, 2010.

iv) Units of mutual fund schemes were permitted to be transacted through registered stockbrokers of recognized stock exchanges.

v) All intermediaries of mutual funds units have been advised to follow the code of conduct strictly.

vi) It was decided that no mutual fund should invest more than 30 per cent of net assets in money market instruments of an issuer. In case of existing schemes where the investments in money market instruments of an issuer are not in compliance with this guideline, the AMC should ensure compliance within a period of three months from the date of notification.

vii) It was clarified that mutual funds can invest in IDRs [Indian Depository Receipts as defined in Companies (Issue of Indian Depository Receipts) Rules 2004] subject to compliance with SEBI (Mutual Funds) Regulations 1996 and guidelines issued thereunder, specifically investment restrictions as specified in the Seventh Schedule of the Regulations.

viii) With a view to ensuring that the value of debt securities reflects the current market situation in the calculation of net asset value, it was decided to indicate the discretionary markup and markdown in the case of rated and unrated debt securities. It was also decided that the discretionary mark up or down limit should be applied for valuation of securities purchased after its issuance.

QUESTIONS AND PROBLEMS

1. Discuss the rationale of investment companies. Do they beat the market ?

2. Discuss the concept of investment company. What is the difference between closed-end and open-end investment companies ?

3. Many people advocate mutual funds for small investors. They suggest that best strategy for small investors is to buy shares in a good mutual fund and put them away. What do you think of this advice ?

4. Why may the small investor prefer mutual funds to other investments ? Discuss the SEBI guidelines for mutual fund authorisation.

5. Should an investor expect a mutual fund to outperform the market ? If not, why should the investor buy the shares ?

6. Define net asset value (NAV) for share and discuss how the market price per share relates to the net asset value per share for (a) open ended mutual fund and (b) close ended mutual fund. Illustrate your answer with examples.

7. What factors would you consider in selecting a mutual fund?

8. Critically examine the recent transaction by Mutual funds in the secondary capital market.

9. What is the difference between open-end and closed-end mutual funds? Which of them tend to for more specialised?

10. Why do mutual funds require regulations? How does the regulate of mutual funds differ from that of other financial institution.

11. If you were concerned about the liquidity of mutual fund shares that you hold, would you rather hold shares in a closed-end or open-end fund? Why?

12. If an investor buys shares in a no-load mutual fund for ₹ 31.40 and the shares appreciate to ₹ 44.60 in two years, what would be the rate of return on the investment? If the fund charges an exit fee of 1 percent, what would be the rate of return on the investment?

Ans: Approximately 19 percent before the exit fee.

13. If a mutual fund's net asset value is ₹ 23.40 and the fund sells its shares for ₹ 25.00, what is the load fee as a percentage of the net asset value (i.e., the amount actually invested in the shares)?

Ans.: 6.8%

14. What is the net asset value of an investment company with ₹ 100 crore in assets, ₹ 7.90 crore in current liabilities and 1.2 crore shares outstanding?

Ans.: ₹ 767.50

15. An investor buys shares in a mutual fund for ₹ 200. At the end of the year, the fund distributes a dividend of ₹ 5.80, and after the distribute the net asset value of a share is ₹ 234.10. What would be the investor's return on the investment? Ans: ₹ 39.90/₹ 200 = 20%

16. A mutual fund has 200 share of XYZ Co., currently trading at ₹ 14, and 200 shares of ABC Co., currently trading at ₹ 140. The fund has issued 100 shares.

    i)   What is the NAV of the fund?

ii)   If investors expect the price of the XYZ Co.'s shares to increase to ₹ 18 and price of ABC Co. to decline ₹ 110 by the end of the year, what is the expected NAV at the end of the year?

ii)   What is the maximum that the price of ABC Co. can decline to maintain the NAV as estimated in (i)?

REFERENCES

1. Blume, Marshall, "On the Assessment of Risk," *Journal of Finance,* 26 (March 1971), 1-10.

2. Bower, Richard, and Donald Wippern, "Risk-Return Measurement in Portfolio Selection and Performance Appraisal Models: Progress Report," *Journal of Financial* and *Quantitative Analysis 4,* no. 4 (December 1969): 417-447.

3. Brealey, Richard A. "How to Combine Active Management with Index Funds." *Journal of Portfolio Management* 12, no. 2 (Winter 1986).

4. Brinson, Gary P., L. Randolph Hood, and Gilbert L. Beebower. "Determinants of Portfolio Performance." *Financial Analysts Journal,* July/August 1986, 39-44.

5. Chang, E.C., and W.G. Lewellen. "Market Timing and Mutual Fund Performance," *Journal of Business,* 1984, 57-72.

6. Chen, N., T E. Copeland, and D. Mayers. "A Comparison of Single and Multifactor Portfolio Performance Methodologies." *Journal of Financial and Quantitative Analysis* 22, no. 4 (December 1987).

7. Cornell, Bradford, and Kevin Green. "The Investment Performance of Low-Grade Bond Funds." *Journal of Finance* 46, no. 1 (March 1991).

8. Cranshaw, T. E., "The Evaluation of Investment Performance," *The Journal of Business.* October 1977, pp. 462-485.

9. Dietz, Peter O., and Jeannette R. Kirschman. "Evaluating Portfolio Performance." In *Managing Investment Portfolios,* 2d ed., edited by John L. Maginn and Donald L. Turtle. Boston: Warren Gorham and Lament, 1990.

10. Economic Survey (GOI), Various issues

11. Ellis, Charles D. "Performance Investing." *Financial Analysts Journal,* September-October 1968, p. 117.

12. Evans, John L., and Stephen H. Archer: "Diversification and the Reduction of Dispersion: An Empireical *Analysis," Journal of Finance,* December 1968, pp. 761-67.

13. Fama, Eugene F. "Components of Investment Performance." In James Lorie and Richard Brealey, *Modern Developments in Investment Management,* 2nd ed. Hinsdale, III.: Dryden Press, p. 448.

14. Farrell, James L., Jr. "Homogenous Stock Groupings." *Financial Analysts Journal,* May-June 1975, p. 50.

15. Frankfurter, George M., "The Effect of Market Indexes on the Ex-Post Performance of the Sharpe Portfolio Selection Model," *Journal of Finance,* 31 (June 1976).

16. ——————, Herbert Phillips, and John Seagle, "Performance of the Sharpe Portfolio Selection Model: A Comparison," *Journal of Financial and Quantitative Analysis* 11. No. 2 (June 1976): 195-204.

17. Friend, Irwin, and Marshall Blume, "Measurement of Portfolio Performance Under Uncertainty," *American Economic Review* 60, no. 4 (September 1970): 561 -576.

18. Grinblatt, Mark, and Sheridan Titman: "Mutual Fund Performance: An Analysis of Quarterly Portfolio Holdings," *Journal of Business.* July 1989, pp. 393-416.

19. ——and ——: "Performance Measurement without Benchmarks: An Examination of Mutual Fund Returns." *Journal of Business,* January 1993, pp. 47-68.

20. Haugen, B., and N. Baker: "The Inefficiency of the Value-Weighted Index," *Journal of Portfolio Management*, 1989, pp. 42-55.

21. Ibbotson, R.L. Siegel, and K. Love: "World Wealth: Market Values and Returns," *Journal of Portfolio Management*, Fall 1985, pp. 4-23.

22. Jensen, Michael C: "The Performance of Mutual Funds in the Period 1945-1964," *Journal of Finance*, May 1968, pp. 389-416.

23. Klemkosky, Robert C., "The Bias in Composite Performance Measures," *Journal of . Financial and Quantitative Analysis* 8, no. 3 (June 1973): 505-514.

24. Korschat, Benjamin. "Measuring Research Analysts Performance." *Financial Analysts Journal*, July-August 1978.

25. Lehman, Bruce, and David Modest: "Mutual Fund Performance Evaluation: A Comparison of Benchmarks and Benchmark Comparisons," *Journal of Finance*, June 1987, pp. 233-265.

26. Leibowitz, Martin: "Horizon Analysis for Managed Portfolios," *Journal of Portfolio Management* Spring 1975, pp. 23-34.

27. Markowitz, Harry M., "Investment for the Long Run: New Evidence for an Old Rule," *Journal of Finance*. December 1976, pp. 1273 1286.

28. Matulich, Serge, "Portfolio Performance with Lending and Borrowing," *Journal of Business Finance and Accounting* 2, no. 3 (Autumn 1975): 341-348.

29. Reinganum, Marc: "Abnormal Returns in Small Firm Portfolios," *Financial Analysts Journal*, March-April 1981, pp. 52-57.

30. Roll, Richard. "Ambiguity When Performance Is Measured by the Securities Market Line." *Journal of Finance* 33, no. 4 (September 1978).

31. Schneider, Theodore H. "Measuring Performance." *Financial Analysts Journal*, May-June 1969, p. 105.

32. Sharpe, William F. "Are Gains Likely from Market Timing?" *Financial Analysts Journal*, March-April 1975, p. 60.

33. Sharpe, William F. "Mutual Fund Performance." *Journal of Business* 39, no. 1, Part 2 (January 1966).

34. Shulka. Ray, and Charles Trzcinka. "Performance Measurement of Managed Portfolios." New York: New York University Salomon Center. *Financial Markets, Institutions, and Investments*, Vol. 1. No. 4, 1992).

35. Spigelman, Joseph H. "What Basis for Superior Performance?" *Financial Analysts Journal*, May-June 1974, p. 32.

36. Treynor, J.L. "How to Rate Management of Investment Funds." *Harvard Business Review*, January-February 1965, pp. 63-75.

37. Vandell, Robert F., D. Harrington, and S. Levkoff, "Cyclical Timing: More Return for Less Risk," Darden School Working Paper No. 78-12. Charlottesville, Va.: Darden Graduate School of Business Administration, 1978.

38. Williams, Arthur: *Managing Your Investment Manager*, Dow Jones-Irwin, New York, 1990.

39. Williamson, Peter J. "Measuring Mutual Fund Performance." *Financial Analysts Journal*, November-December 1972, p. 78.

7

Market Indexes

INTRODUCTION

Market indexes have always been of great importance in the world of security analysis and portfolio management. People from different walks of life use and are affected by market indicators. Investors, both individual and institutional, use the market index as a benchmark against which they evaluate the performance of their own or institutional portfolio. The technicians or the chartists often base their decisions to buy and sell on the patterns emerging out of the time series data of market indexes. Even the economists and statisticians use stock market indexes to study the trend of growth patterns in the economy, to analyse as well as forecast business cycles and to correlate stock market indexes to economic activities.

INDEX: THE CONCEPT

An index is a number used to represent the changes in a set of values between a base time period and another time period. A Stock Index is a number that helps measure the levels of the market.* Most stock indices attempt to be proxies for the market they exist in. Returns on the Index thus are supposed to represent returns on the market i.e. the returns that an investor can get if he has the portfolio representing the entire market.

Methods of Computing the Stock Indexes

Different indexes are computed and compiled for use by the investors. While some indexes employ an equal weighting approach (equal amounts assumed to be invested in each component), the others are either price weighted or value weighted. Both these methods are employed in the compilation of stock and consumer price (cost) indexes. Stock indexes are directly used in security analysis and portfolio management, and consumer-price (cost) indexes are used in measuring the change of purchasing power but are also useful in security analysis and portfolio management.

Price-Weighted and Quantity-Weighted Indexes

In a price-weighted index, the basic approach is to sum the prices of the component securities used in the index and divide this sum by the number of components. In other words, we compute a simple arithmetic average. To allow for the impact of stock splits and stock dividends, which could destroy the consistency and comparability of price-weighted index data over time, an adjustment of either the reported price data or the divisor itself is required.

---

* A stock Index is a Derivative asset because it derives its existence and value from independent stocks issued by corporations. It is the simplest Derivative because it is structured as merely some average of specified underlying stocks without any complicated payoff.

A price-weighted index strictly speaking is not an index at all — it is an average. The concept of indexing involves the comparison of currently computed averages with some base value. For example, the current levels of Bombay Stock Exchange National Index of equity prices are compared with the average level for the base period of 1983-84 and are the most widely used example of a value-weighted stock index. In such an index the weight of each component stock is equal to its market value in relation to that of all the stocks included. The use of market value (price per share multiplied by the number of shares outstanding *i.e.* number of shares issued obviates the necessity of adjusting for stock splits or stock dividends.

Two classical forms of indexes are the *Paasche Index* and the *Laspeyres Index*. Both of these are used as methods for determining the consumer price index. They measure price inflation because quantity is held constant

$$\text{Paasche price index} \quad = \quad \frac{\Sigma P_{jt} Q_{jt}}{\Sigma P_{jo} Q_{jt}} \qquad \qquad ....(1)$$

$$\text{Laspeyres price index} \quad = \quad \frac{\Sigma P_{jt} Q_{jo}}{\Sigma P_{jo} Q_{jo}} \qquad \qquad ....(2)$$

where: P_{jt} = price per unit for *j*th commodity in period *t*;
$\quad\quad\;\; P_{jo}$ = price per unit for *j*th commodity in period *o*;
$\quad\quad\;\; Q_{jt}$ = the quantity of *j*th commodity in period *t*; and
$\quad\quad\;\; Q_{jo}$ = the quantity of *j*th commodity in period *o*.

Equations (1) and (2) can be used to construct Fisher's ideal price index:

$$\text{Fisher's ideal price index} = \left(\frac{\sqrt{\Sigma P_{jt} Q_{jt}}}{\Sigma P_{jo} Q_{jt}} \right) \left(\frac{\sqrt{\Sigma P_{jt} Q_{jo}}}{\Sigma P_{jo} Q_{jo}} \right) \qquad ...(3)$$

Similarly, quantity-weighted indexes can be defined:

$$\text{Laspeyers quantity index} \quad = \quad \frac{\Sigma Q_{jt} P_{jo}}{\Sigma Q_{jo} Q_{jo}} \qquad \qquad .... (4)$$

$$\text{Paasche quantity index} \quad = \quad \frac{\Sigma Q_{jt} P_{jt}}{\Sigma Q_{jo} Q_{jt}} \qquad \qquad ....(5)$$

$$\text{Fisher's ideal quantity index} \; = \; \left(\frac{\sqrt{\Sigma P_{jt} Q_{jo}}}{\Sigma P_{jo} Q_{jo}} \right) \left(\frac{\sqrt{\Sigma P_{jt} Q_{jt}}}{\Sigma P_{jo} Q_{jt}} \right) \qquad ....(6)$$

Value-Weighted Indexes

After having discussed indexes of quantity as well as price, it would be appropriate to define total cost of the consumer's purchases in terms of cost index as:

$$\text{Cost Index} \quad = \quad \frac{\Sigma P_{jt} Q_{jt}}{\Sigma P_{jo} Q_{jo}} \qquad \qquad ....(7)$$

The cost index is the basic form used for compiling the value-weighted stock index.

The Paasche index tends to underestimate the inflation rate while the Laspeyres index tends to overestimate the true inflationary impact over time. Stock indexes are intended to be a measure of value growth. The standard form of value-weighted stock indexes is expressed.

$$\text{Stock index} \quad = \quad \frac{\Sigma P_{jt} \, \Sigma Q_{jt}}{\Sigma P_{jo} \, \Sigma Q_{jo}}$$

Therefore, changes in the index level could be the result of either price changes or volume changes. The price effect can be separated out by using one of the constant-quantity approaches as defined in Equations (1), (2), (4), (5), (6) or (8). The quantity effect is also not really an exogenous factor. It can be separated out by using one of the constant-price approaches as defined in equations.

LEADING STOCK MARKET INDEXES

Some of the leading stock market indexes are discussed below:

SENSEX - THE BAROMETER OF INDIAN CAPITAL MARKETS

SENSEX is scientifically designed and based on globally accepted construction and review methodology. First compiled in 1986, SENSEX is a basket of 30 constituent stocks representing a sample of large, liquid and representative companies. The base year of SENSEX is 1978-79 and the base value is 100.[1] The index is widely reported in both domestic and international markets through print as well as electronic media.

The Index was initially calculated based on the "Full Market Capitalization" methodology but was shifted to the free-float methodology with effect from September 1, 2003. The "Free-float Market Capitalization" methodology of index construction is regarded as an industry best practice globally. All major index providers like MSCI, FTSE, STOXX, S&P and Dow Jones use the Free-float methodology.[2]

SENSEX Calculation Methodology

SENSEX is calculated using the "Free-float Market Capitalization" methodology. As per this methodology, the level of index at any point of time reflects the Free-float market value of 30 component stocks relative to a base period. The market capitalization of a company is determined by multiplying the price of its stock by the number of shares issued by the company. This market capitalization is further multiplied by the free-float factor to determine the free-float market capitalization.

To determine Free-float factors of companies, BSE has designed a Free-float format, which is filled and submitted by all index companies on a quarterly basis with the Exchange. The Exchange determines the Free-float factor for each company based on the detailed information submitted by the companies in the prescribed format. Free-float factor is a multiple with which the total market capitalization of a company is adjusted to arrive at the Free-float market capitalization. Once the Free-float of a company is determined, it is rounded-off to the higher multiple of 5 and each company is categorized into one of the 20 bands given below. A Free-float factor of say 0.55 means that only 55% of the market capitalization of the company will be considered for index calculation.

---

1. The financial year 1978-79 has been chosen as the base year. Considerations for the choice were the price stability during that year and the proximity to the current period.
2. Standard & Poor's Composite 500 Index (S & P 500) is a value weighted index of 400 industrial stocks, 40 utility stocks, 20 transportation stocks, and 40 financial stocks. It is computed as follows:

$$S \text{ and } P_1 = \frac{\Sigma P_{jt} \, \Sigma Q_{jt}}{\Sigma P_{jo} \, \Sigma Q_{jo}} \times \text{IO}$$

where : P_{it} = Price of stock i in period t;
$\quad\quad\quad Q_{it}$ = Number of shares outstanding for stock i in period t;
$\quad\quad\quad P_{io}$ = Price of stock i in the base period 0; and
$\quad\quad\quad Q_{io}$ = Number of shares outstanding for stock in base period 0.

% Free-Float	Free-Float Factor	% Free-Float	Free-Float Factor
>0 – 5%	0.05	>50 – 55%	0.55
>5 – 10%	0.10	>55 – 60%	0.60
>10 – 15%	0.15	>60 – 65%	0.65
>15 – 20%	0.20	>65 – 70%	0.70
>20 – 25%	0.25	>70 – 75%	0.75
>25 – 30%	0.30	>75 – 80%	0.80
>30 – 35%	0.35	>80 – 85%	0.85
>35 – 40%	0.40	>85 – 90%	0.90
>40 – 45%	0.45	>90 – 95%	0.95
>45 – 50%	0.50	>95 – 100%	1.00

The closing SENSEX on any trading day is computed taking the weighted average of all the trades on SENSEX constituents in the last 30 minutes of trading session. If a SENSEX constituent has not traded in the last 30 minutes, the last traded price is taken for computation of the Index closure. If a SENSEX constituent has not traded at all in a day, then its last day's closing price is taken for computation of Index closure. The use of Index Closure Algorithm prevents any intentional manipulation of the closing index value.

During market hours, prices of the index scrips, at which trades are executed, are automatically used by the trading computer to calculate the SENSEX every 15 seconds and continuously updated on all trading workstations connected to the BSE trading computer in real time.

The arithmetic calculation involved in calculating SENSEX is simple, but problem arises when one of the component stocks pays a bonus or issues rights shares. If no adjustments were made, a discontinuity would arise between the current value of the index and its previous value despite the non-occurrence of any economic activity of substance. At the Index Cell of the Exchange, the base value is adjusted, which is used to alter market capitalization of the component stocks to arrive at the SENSEX value.

The Index Cell of the Exchange keeps a close watch on the events that might affect the index on a regular basis and carries out daily maintenance of all the 14 Indices.

- **Adjustments for Rights Issues**
  When a company, included in the compilation of the index, issues right shares, the free-float market capitalisation of that company is increased by the number of additional shares issued based on the theoretical (ex-right) price. An offsetting or proportionate adjustment is then made to the Base Market Capitalisation.
- **Adjustments for Bonus Issue**
  When a company, included in the compilation of the index, issues bonus shares, the market capitalisation of that company does not undergo any change. Therefore, there is no change in the Base Market Capitalisation, only the 'number of shares' in the formula is updated.
- **Other Issues**
  Base Market Capitalisation Adjustment is required when new shares are issued by way of conversion of debentures, mergers, spin-offs etc. or when equity is reduced by way of buy-back of shares, corporate restructuring etc.
- **Base Market Capitalisation Adjustment**
  The formula for adjusting the Base Market Capitalisation is as follows:

$$\text{New Base Market Capitalisation} = \text{Old Base Market Capitalisation} \times \frac{\text{New Market Capitalisation}}{\text{Old Market Capitalisation}}$$

To illustrate, suppose a company issues right shares which increases the market capitalisation of the shares of that company by say, ₹100 crores. The existing Base Market Capitalisation (Old Base Market Capitalisation), say, is ₹2450 crores and the aggregate market capitalisation of all the shares included in the index before the right issue is made is, say ₹ 4781 crores. The "New Base Market Capitalisation " will then be:

$$\frac{2450 \times (4781+100)}{4781} = ₹\ 2501.24 \text{ crores}$$

This figure of 2501.24 will be used as the Base Market Capitalisation for calculating the index number from then onwards till the next base change becomes necessary.

SENSEX - Scrip selection Criteria

The general guidelines for selection of constituents in SENSEX are as follows:

1. **Listed History:**The scrip should have a listing history of at least 3 months at BSE. Exception may be considered if full market capitalisation of a newly listed company ranks among top 10 in the list of BSE universe. In case, a company is listed on account of merger/ demerger/ amalgamation, minimum listing history would not be required.

2. **Trading Frequency:** The scrip should have been traded on each and every trading day in the last three months. Exceptions can be made for extreme reasons like scrip suspension etc.

3. **Final Rank:**The scrip should figure in the top 100 companies listed by final rank. The final rank is arrived at by assigning 75% weightage to the rank on the basis of three-month average full market capitalisation and 25% weightage to the liquidity rank based on three-month average daily turnover & three-month average impact cost.

4. **Market Capitalization Weightage:** The weightage of each scrip in SENSEX based on three-month average free-float market capitalisation should be at least 0.5% of the Index.

5. **Industry Representation:** Scrip selection would generally take into account a balanced representation of the listed companies in the universe of BSE.

6. **Track Record:** In the opinion of the Committee, the company should have an acceptable track record.

The Index Committee meets every quarter to discuss index related issues. In case of a revision in the Index constituents, the announcement of the incoming and outgoing scrips is made six weeks in advance of the actual implementation of the revision of the Index.

BSE-100 INDEX

A need was felt for a more broad-based index, which can also reflect the movement of stock prices on a national scale because the BSE Sensitive Index has only 30 scrips. Bombay Stock Exchange Limited, started compilation and publication of an index series called "BSE National Index" since 3rd January, 1989.

Coverage : The equity shares of 100 companies from the "Specified" and the "Non-Specified" list of the five major stock exchanges, viz. Mumbai, Calcutta, Delhi, Ahmedabad and Madras have been selected for the purpose of compiling the BSE National Index. The criteria for selection had been market activity, due representation to various industry-groups and representation of trading activity on major stock exchanges.

Base-Year : The financial year 1983-84 has been chosen as the base year. The price stability during that year and proximity to the index series were the main consideration for choice of 1983-84 as the base year.

Method of Compilation : The basic method of compilation is the same as the one used in the case of the BSE Sensitive Index. However, in the case of BSE National Index, a distinction is made between "local scrips" for which prices were taken from only one exchange and "Inter-Exchange scrips" for which an average of the prices quoted on two or more exchanges were considered for index compilation.

Designation of the BSE 100 National Index to the BSE 100 Index

As noted above, the BSE 100 National index used to take prices of certain scrips from other exchanges or weighted average of some scrips which were popular on other exchanges in order to reflect market movements at the national level. However, changes in trading technology, longer trading period and almost instantaneous availability of information across the country have ensured that there is little or no difference in prices of the index scrips. Therefore, the Exchange administration has decided to redesignate the BSE 100 National index as the 'BSE 100' index. Since October 14, 1996, the prices of the BSE are taken to calculate the index.

Shifting of BSE-100 Index to Free-Float Methodology of Index Maintenance

In line with the shift of the BSE Indices to the globally accepted Free-Float methodology, BSE-100 was shifted to Free-Float methodology effective from April 5th, 2004. The method of computaion of Free-Float Index and determination of Free-Float Factors is similar to the methodology described in SENSEX.

BSE-200 INDEX

The number of companies listed on the Bombay Stock Exchange has registered a phenomenal increase from 992 in the year 1980 to about 3,200 companies by the end of March 1994 and their combined market capitalisation rose from ₹ 5,421 crores to around ₹ 5,63,748 crores as on 31st March, 1996. This necessitated compilation of a new broad-based index series reflecting the present market trends in a more effective manner and providing a better representation of the increased equity stocks, market capitalisation as also the newly emerged industry groups. Towards this end, the Exchange constructed and launched on 27th May 1994, two index series viz. the BSE-200 and the Dollex-200.

The equity shares of 200 selected companies from the specified and non-specified lists of this Exchange have been considered for inclusion in the sample for 'BSE-200'. The selection of companies has primarily been done on the basis of current market capitalisation of the listed scrips on the exchange. Besides market capitalisation, the market activity of the companies as reflected by the volumes of turnover and certain fundamental factors were considered for the final selection of the 200 companies.

The financial year 1989-90 has been chosen as the base year for the price stability exhibited during that year and due to its proximity to the current period. BSE-200 index was initially calculated on full market capitalization methodology. Effective August 16, 2005, the calculation methodology was switched to free-float methodology in line with other BSE indices.

DOLLEX SERIES OF BSE INDICES

All BSE indices reflects the growth in market value of constituent stocks over the base period in rupee terms, a need was felt to design a yardstick by which these growth values are measured in dollar terms. Such an index would reflect, in one value, the changes in both the stock prices and the foreign exchange variation. This is facilitated by the introduction of a dollar-linked index in which the formula for calculation of index is suitably modified to express the current and base market values in dollar terms. The scope for dollar-linked index emerged from the background of Indian equity markets increasingly getting integrated with global capital markets and the need to assess the market movements in terms of international benchmarks. This dollar-linked index is useful to overseas investors, as it helps them measure their 'real returns' after providing for exchange rate fluctuations.

BSE presently calculates dollar-linked version of SENSEX and BSE-200. Dollex-30 was launched on July 25, 2001 whereas Dollex-200 on May 27, 1994. These indices were initially calculated at the end of the trading session by taking into consideration day's rupee/ US$ reference rate as announced by India 's Central Bank i.e. Reserve Bank of India .

BSE announced introduction of Dollex-100, a dollar linked version of BSE-100 index effective from May 22, 2006 and from this date onwards Dollex-30, Dollex-100 and Dollex-200 are calculated and displayed through BSE On-line trading terminals (BOLT) by taking into account real-time Re./US$ Exchange rate. The formula for calculating the index is:

$$\text{Dollex} = \frac{\text{Index Value (In local currency)} * \text{Base rupee-US\$ rate}}{\text{Current rupee-US\$ rate}}$$

BSE-500 INDEX AND SECTORAL INDICES

Bombay Stock Exchange Limited has constructed a new index, christened as BSE-500, consisting of 500 scrips in its basket w.e.f. August 9, 1999 (announced on July 8, 1999 vide its press release). The changing pattern of the economy and that of the market have been kept in mind while constructing this index.

BSE-500 index represents nearly 93% of the total market capitalisation on Bombay Stock Exchange Limited. This means BSE-500 index ideally represents total market. This index represents all 20 major industries of the economy. The BSE-500 index had been calculating on a full market capitalization methodology and effective August 16, 2005 calculation methodology was shifted to a free-float methodology in line with SENSEX.

Simultaneously, BSE also started 5 sectoral indices viz. BSE IT Sector index, BSE FMCG Sector index, BSE Capital Goods Sector Index, BSE Consumer Durables Sector Index and BSE Healthcare Sector Index. All these Sectoral indices are calculated and displayed on the BOLT system on the real time basis.

Effective Monday, August 23, 2004 BSE launched "Sector Series (90/FF)" indices with the view to provide the Indian Capital Market with quality sector benchmarks. The "Sector Series (90/FF)" Indices are a set of indices across 9 significant sectors listed on the BSE. They are constructed and maintained as per the global best practices. Existing 5 sectoral indices i.e. BSE IT, BSE FMCG, BSE Capital Goods, BSE Consumer Durables and BSE Healthcare were shifted to Free-Float methodology and have become part of the "Sector Series (90/FF)" indices. BSE BANKEX launched during June 2003 is being calculated on Free-Float methodology and has also become part of "Sector Series (90/FF)". Three new sectors viz. BSE Auto, BSE Metal and BSE Oil & Gas index were launched effective August 23, 2004 as part of the new series. "90/FF" implies that the index covers 90% of the sectoral market capitalisation and is based on the Free-Float methodology.

Scrip Selection Criteria for BSE Sectoral Indices

(i) Scrips classified under various sectors that are present constituents of BSE-500 index would form the eligible universe.

(ii) Scrips should have a minimum of 90% trading frequency in preceding six months.

(iii) Scrips with a minimum of 90% market capitalisation coverage in each sector based on free-float final rank will form the index.

(iv) A buffer of 2% both for inclusion and exclusion in the index is considered so that movements in and out of the index are minimized. For example, a company can be included in the index only if it falls within 88% coverage and an existing index constituent cannot be excluded unless it falls above 92% coverage. However, the above buffer criterion is applied only after the minimum 90% market coverage is satisfied.

BSE BANKEX

Indian banking is riding on a major recovery both in terms of strength and soundness. In the year 2002, return on assets in Indian banking was higher compared to many emerging economies and the Moody's Bank Financial Strength Index (2002) placed India at 27.5, which is much better than 16.7 of Korea, 15.8 of Thailand and 12.5 of Japan. Similar to experience in other rapidly growing countries, India is making sizeable gains in expanding into consumer credit with tightening of credit administration procedures. Major policy actions that led to sharp fall in the interest rates enabled banks to post significant rise in operational profits. For instance trading profits of the public sector banks shot up by ₹ 3749 crores taking their net profits to an all time high of ₹ 8301 crores in FY 02. This year too banks are showing sizeable gains in their profitability. The enactment of Securitization Bill offered great opportunities to step up loan recoveries that could further enhance the scope of greater profitability.

These developments have impacted the performance of bank stocks significantly. Since bank stocks are emerging as a major segment in the equity markets, BSE considered it important to design an index exclusively for bank stocks. The index is computed on the basis of the globally accepted free float methodology. Earlier BSE had launched its first free float index on TMT stocks now popularly known as the BSE TECk Index.

A few important features of the BANKEX are: (i) BANKEX will track the performance of the leading banking sector stocks listed on the BSE; (ii) BANKEX is based on the free float methodology of index construction; (iii) The base date for BANKEX is 1st January 2002; (iv) The base value for BANKEX is 1000 points; (v) BSE has calculated the historical index values of BANKEX since 1st January 2002; (vi) 12 stocks which represent 90 percent of the total market capitalization of all banking sector stocks listed on BSE are included in the Index; (vii) The Index will be disseminated on a real-time basis through BSE Online Trading (BOLT) terminals from 23rd June, 2003; and (viii) Stocks forming part of the BANKEX along with the particulars of their free float adjusted market capitalization are listed.

Scrips classified under banking sector that are present constituents of BSE-500 index would form the eligible universe. Scrips should have a minimum of 90% trading frequency in preceding six months. Scrips with a minimum of 90% market capitalisation coverage in each sector based on free-float final rank will form the index.

A buffer of 2% both for inclusion and exclusion in the index is considered so that movements in and out of the index are minimized. For example, a company can be included in the index only if it falls within 88% coverage and an existing index constituent cannot be excluded unless it falls above 92% coverage. However, the above buffer criterion is applied only after the minimum 90% market coverage is satisfied.

BSE TECK INDEX

The Technology orientation of the current economy has primarily marked a paradigm shift from manufacturing based activities to knowledge based activities. In the present economic scenario, tangible assets like land, plant & machinery are losing their significance to intangibles like intellectual property, knowledge base and technology. This has resulted in the dominance of emerging sectors like Information Technology, Media, & Telecom.

Scrip Selection Criteria for BSE TECkIndex

It is felt that in the absence of a proper benchmark, the performance of the TMT sectors remained inadequately tracked. In order to fill this void, the BSE-TECk index is being positioned as a reliable index for benchmarking the performance of the TMT sectors.

The launch of BSE-TECk index can be justified on rational grounds which include inter-alia: (i) globally a lot of investment is being committed to the TMT sectors. Even in India, the last few years have seen a lot of international and local money flowing into the TMT sectors; (ii) the TMT sectors are currently dominating the trading pattern on the bourses worldwide. In India, the TMT sectors account for around 68% of the total daily turnover; (iii) with a lot of domestic retail money committed to the TMT sectors and existence of many mutual funds dedicated to one or more of the TMT sectors in India, a need for a quality benchmark to track the performance of such funds has been long felt; (iv) the global and domestic investment community monitors eagerly the performance of the TMT sectors to discern typical trends in the economy.; (v) to provide a ready basket of quality TMT stocks for passive investors; and, finally, (vi) reference for Index futures, options and other derivative products in times to come

BSE PSU INDEX

Bombay Stock Exchange Limited launched "BSE-PSU Index" on Monday, 4th June 2001. The index consists of major Public Sector Undertakings listed on the Exchange. The BSE-PSU Index is displayed on-line on the BOLT trading terminals nationwide. The BSE - Public Sector Undertaking (PSU) Index is a stock index that will track the performance of the listed PSU stocks on the Exchange and provide a suitable benchmark for the Central Government to monitor its wealth on the bourses.

Index Specifications

	Base Date	Base Value	No.of Constituents
BSE- PSU Index	1st Feb, 1999	1000	All PSU stocks in BSE-500 Index

The Base Date for the BSE-PSU Index would be 1st February 1999 when the BSE-500 was launched. Being a subset of BSE-500, the BSE-PSU Index will ensure a reasonable history of how the Central Government wealth fluctuated on the bourses. The Base Value for the BSE-PSU Index has been set at 1000 to ensure adequacy in terms of Daily Index movement.

For consideration scrips for inclusion in BSE PSU index, Public Sector Undertaking refers to any undertaking wherein the Central Government holding is equal to or more than 51%. Since BSE PSU index is a subset of BSE-500 index, scrips that form part of BSE-500 index will automatically be included in BSE PSU index.

BSE MID-CAP AND BSE SMALL-CAP INDEX

BSE introduced the new index series called 'BSE Mid-Cap' index and 'BSE Small-Cap' index to track the performance of the companies with relatively small market capitalization that would exclusively represent the mid and small cap companies listed on the Stock Exchange. BSE-500 index - the broad based index that is considered as a BSE Composite index represents more than 93% of listed universe. Companies with large market capitalization bias the movement of BSE-500 index. This necessitated construction of a separate indicator to capture the trend in the specific class of companies (with lower market capitalisation). BSE Mid-Cap and BSE Small-Cap index would prove to be a great utility to the investing community as they would truly capture the movement of the segments that they represent (mid and small).

Salient feature of these indices are:

(i)   Base year of these indices would be 2002-2003;
(ii)   Base index value would be 1000 for each of these indices;
(iii) Based on a free-float methodology;
(iv)   Scrips that are classified as Z group, scrips traded under permitted category and scrips with the trading frequency of less than 60% days in preceding three months are not considered for inclusion in these indices;
(v)   Constructed on 80%-15%-5% method whereby companies aggregating 98.5% of average market capitalization are categorized under large, mid and small cap segment respectively from the list of eligible universe of BSE;
(vi)   BSE Mid-Cap tracks the performance of scrips between 80 & 95% of aggregate market capitalisation and BSE Small-Cap index tracks the performance of remaining 5% scrips (95-100%);
(vii) Number of companies in each of these indices would be variable. On the date of launch (April 11, 2005), these indices comprised of 231 and 425 constituents in BSE Mid-Cap and BSE Small-Cap index respectively;
(viii) Correlation of 0.98 and 0.93 for BSE Mid-Cap and BSE Small-Cap index respectively with broad based BSE-500 index; and finally,
(ix)   Constituents of these indices are reviewed on a quarterly basis

S&P CNX NIFTY

S&P CNX Nifty is owned and managed by India Index Services and Products Ltd. (IISL), which is a joint venture between NSE and CRISIL. IISL is India's first specialised company focused upon the index as a core product. IISL have a consulting and licensing agreement with Standard & Poor's (S&P), who are world leaders in index services.

S&P CNX Nifty is a well diversified 50 stock index accounting for 22 sectors of the economy. It is used for a variety of purposes such as benchmarking fund portfolios, index based derivatives and index funds. S&P CNX Nifty is professionally maintained and is ideal for derivatives trading. The average total traded value for the last six months of all Nifty stocks is approximately 45.24% of the traded value of all stocks on the NSE. Nifty stocks represent about 57.92% of the total market capitalization as on April 10, 2007. Impact cost of the S&P CNX Nifty for a portfolio size of ₹ 5 million is 0.08%

CNX NIFTY JUNIOR

The next rung of liquid securities after S&P CNX Nifty is the CNX Nifty Junior. It may be useful to think of the S&P CNX Nifty and the CNX Nifty Junior as making up the 100 most liquid stocks in India. As with the S&P CNX Nifty, stocks in the CNX Nifty Junior are filtered for liquidity, so they are the most liquid of the stocks excluded from the S&P CNX Nifty. The maintenance of the S&P CNX Nifty and the CNX Nifty Junior are synchronised so that the two indices will always be disjoint sets; i.e. a stock will never appear in both indices at the same time. Hence it is always meaningful to pool the S&P CNX Nifty and the CNX Nifty Junior into a composite 100 stock index or portfolio.

CNX Nifty Junior represents about 8.69 % of the total market capitalization as on April 10, 2007. The average traded value for the last six months of all Junior Nifty stocks is approximately 10.82 % of the traded value of all stocks on the NSE. Impact cost for CNX Nifty Junior for a portfolio size of ₹ 2.50 million is 0.16%

CNX 100

CNX 100 is a diversified 100 stock index accounting for 35 sector of the economy. The index is owned and managed by India Index Services & Products Ltd. (IISL). CNX 100 represents about 66.61 % of the total market capitalization as on April 10, 2007. The average traded value for the last six months of all CNX100 stocks is approximately 56.02 % of the traded value of all stocks on the NSE. Impact cost for CNX 100 for a portfolio size of ₹ 8 million is 0.11%

S&P CNX 500

The S&P CNX 500 is India's first broad-based benchmark of the Indian capital market for comparing portfolio returns vis-a-vis market returns. The S&P CNX 500 represents about 90.30% of total market capitalization and about 80.02% of the total turnover on the NSE as on March 30, 2007. The S&P CNX 500 companies are disaggregated into 72 industry indices viz. S&P CNX Industry Indices. Industry weightages in the index reflect the industry weightages in the market. For e.g. if the banking sector has a 5% weightage in the universe of stocks traded on NSE, banking stocks in the index would also have an approx. representation of 5% in the index.

CNX MIDCAP

The medium capitalised segment of the stock market is being increasingly perceived as an attractive investment segment with high growth potential. The primary objective of the CNX Midcap Index is to capture the movement and be a benchmark of the midcap segment of the market.

The CNX Midcap Index has a base date of Jan 1, 2003 and a base value of 1000. CNX Midcap is computed using market capitalisation weighted method, wherein the level of the index reflects the total market value of all the stocks in the index relative to a particular base period. The method also takes into account constituent changes in the index and importantly corporate actions such as stock splits, rights, etc without affecting the index value.

The criteria for the selection of constituent stocks in the CNX Midcap has following features: (i) All the stocks, which constitute more than 5% market capitalization of the universe (after sorting the securities in descending order of market capitalization), shall be excluded in order to reduce the skewness in the weightages of the stocks in the universe. (ii) After step (i), the weightages of the remaining stocks in the universe is determined again. (iii) After step (ii), the cumulative weightage is calculated. (iv) After step (iii) companies which form part of the cumulative percentage in ascending order unto first 75 percent (i.e. upto to 74.99 percent) of the revised universe shall be ignored.

(v) After, step (iv), all the constituents of S&P CNX Nifty shall be ignored. (vi) From the universe of companies remaining after step (v) i.e. 75th percent and above, first 100 companies in terms of highest market capitalization, shall constitute the CNX Midcap Index subject to fulfillment of the criteria mentioned below.

All constituents of the CNX Midcap Index must have a minimum listing record of 6 months. In addition, all candidates for the Index are also evaluated for trading interest, in terms of volumes and trading frequency. on financial perference side, all companies in the CNX Midcap Index have a minimum track record of three years of operations with a positive net worth. A company which comes out with a IPO will be eligible for inclusion in the index, if it fulfills the normal eligibility criteria for the index for a 3 month period instead of a 6 month period.

S&P CNX DEFTY

Almost every institutional investor and off-shore fund enterprise with an equity exposure in India would like to have an instrument for measuring returns on their equity investment in dollar terms. To facilitate this, a new index the S&P CNX Defty-Dollar Denominated S&P CNX Nifty has been developed.S&P CNX Defty is S&P CNX Nifty, measured in dollars. The salient features of this are: (i) Performance indicator to foreign institutional investors, off shore funds, etc. (ii) Provides an effective tool for hedging Indian equity exposure. (iii) Impact cost of the S&P CNX Nifty for a portfolio size of ₹ 5 million is 0.07%. (iv) Provides fund managers an instrument for measuring returns on their equity investment in dollar terms.

For S&P CNX Defty, computations are done using the S&P CNX Nifty index calculated on the NEAT trading system of NSE and USD Rupee exchange rate that is based on the real time polled data feed

$$S\&P\ CNX\ Defty = \frac{S\&P\ CNX\ Nifty\ at\ time\ t * Exchange\ rate\ as\ on\ base\ date}{Exchange\ rate\ at\ time\ t}$$

CNX MIDCAP 200

The medium capitalised segment of the stock market is being increasingly perceived as an attractive investment segment with high growth potential. The primary objective of the CNX MidCap 200 Index is to capture the movement and be a benchmark of the midcap segment of the market.

CNX Midcap 200 represents about 72% of the total market capitalization of the Mid-Cap Universe and about 70% of the total traded value of the Mid-Cap Universe (Mid-Cap Universe is defined as stocks having average six months market capitalization between ₹ 75 crores and ₹ 750 crores). Industry weightages in the index dynamically reflect industry weightages in the market The index provide investors a broad based benchmark for comparing portfolio returns vis-à-vis market returns in the midcap segment.

CNX IT INDEX

Information Technology (IT) industry has played a major role in the Indian economy during the last few years. A number of large, profitable Indian companies today belong to the IT sector and a great deal of investment interest is now focused on the IT sector. In order to have a good benchmark of the Indian IT sector, IISL has developed the CNX IT sector index. CNX IT provides investors and market intermediaries with an appropriate benchmark that captures the performance of the IT segment of the market.

Companies in this index are those that have more than 50% of their turnover from IT related activities like software development, hardware manufacture, vending, support and maintenance. The average total traded value for the last six months of CNX IT Index stocks is approximately 91% of the traded value of the IT sector. CNX IT Index stocks represent about 96% of the total market capitalization of the IT sector as on March 31, 2005. The average total traded value for the last six months of all CNX IT Index constituents is approximately 14% of the traded value of all stocks on the NSE. CNX IT Index constituents represent about 14% of the total market capitalization as on March 31, 2005.

Selection of the index set is based on the following criteria: 1) Company's market capitalisation rank in the universe should be less than 500. 2) Company's turnover rank in the universe should be less than 500. 3) Company's trading frequency should be at least 90% in the last six months. 4) Company should have a positive networth. 5) A company which comes out with a IPO will be eligible for inclusion in the index, if it fulfills the normal eligibility criteria for the index for a 3 month period instead of a 6 month period.

CNX BANK INDEX

CNX Bank Index is an index comprised of the most liquid and large capitalised Indian Banking stocks. It provides investors and market intermediaries with a benchmark that captures the capital market performance of Indian Banks. The index initially consist of 12 stocks from the banking sector which trade on the National Stock Exchange. On March 31, 2005, CNX Bank Index stocks were representing about 79% of the total market capitalization of the banking sector and the average total traded value for the last six months of all the CNX Bank Index constituents was approximately 10% of the traded value of all stocks on the NSE. CNX Bank Index constituents represent about 9% of the total market capitalization as on March 31, 2005.

The index is a market capitalization weighted index with base date of January 01, 2000, indexed to a base value of 1000. Selection of the index set is based on the following criteria: i) Company's market capitalisation rank in the universe should be less than 500. i) Company's turnover rank in the universe should be less than 500. iii) Company's trading frequency should be at least 90% in the last six months. iv) Company should have a positive networth. v) A company which comes out with a IPO will be eligible for inclusion in the index, if it fulfills the normal eligiblity criteria for the index for a 3 month period instead of a 6 month period.

CNX FMCG INDEX

FMCGs (Fast Moving Consumer Goods) are those goods and products, which are non-durable, mass consumption products, available off the shelf. The CNX FMCG Index is a 15 stock Index from the FMCG sector that trade on the National Stock Exchange.

The CNX FMCG Index is calculated using the market capitalisation weighted aggregate method. The base period is the month of December 1995, index to a value 1000. The selection of the index set is based on the following criteria: i) Company's market capitalisation rank in the universe should be less than 500. ii) Company's turnover rank in the universe should be less than 500. iii) Company's trading frequency should be at least 90% in the last one year. iv) Company should have a minimum track record of 3 years of operations with a positive networth. v) A company which comes out with a IPO will be eligible for inclusion in the index, if it fulfills the normal eligiblity criteria for the index for a 3 month period instead of a 6 month period.

CNX PSE INDEX

As part of its agenda to reform the Public Sector Enterprises (PSE), the Government has selectively been disinvesting its holdings in public sector enterprises since 1991. With a view to provide regulators, investors and market intermediaries with an appropriate benchmark that captures the performance of this segment of the market, as well as to make available an appropriate basis for pricing forthcoming issues of PSEs, IISL has developed the CNX PSE Index, comprising of 20 PSE stocks. The CNX PSE Index includes only those companies that have over 51% of their outstanding share capital held by the Central Government and/or State Government, directly or indirectly.

The CNX PSE Index is calculated using the market capitalisation weighted aggregate method. The base period is the month of December 1994, index to a value 1000. The selection of the index set is based on the following criteria: i) Company's market capitalisation rank in the universe should be less than 500 ii) Company's turnover rank in the universe should be less than 500. iii) Company's trading frequency should be at least 90% in the last six months. iv) Company should have a minimum track record of 3 years of operations with a positive networth. v) A company which comes out with a IPO will be eligible for inclusion in the index, if it fulfills the normal eligibility criteria for the index for a 3 month period instead of a 6 month period.

CNX MNC INDEX

The CNX MNC Index comprises 50 listed companies in which the foreign shareholding is over 50% and / or the management control is vested in the foreign company.

The CNX MNC Index is calculated using the market capitalisation weighted method, wherein individual stocks are weighted by market value. The base period is the month of December, 1994 indexed to a value 1000. The selection of the index set is based on the following criteria: i) Company's market capitalisation rank in the universe should be less than 500. ii) Company's turnover rank in the universe should be less than 500. iii) Company's trading frequency should be at least 90% in the last six months. iv) Company should have a minimum track record of 3 years of operations with a positive networth. v) A company which comes out with a IPO will be eligible for inclusion in the index, if it fulfills the normal eligibility criteria for the index for a 3 month period instead of a 6 month period.

CNX SERVICE SECTOR INDEX

To capture the performance of the companies belonging to this sector, IISL has developed CNX Service Sector Index. The index is 30 stocks index and includes companies belonging to services sector like Computers – Software, Banks, Telecommunication – services, Financial Institutions, Power, Media, Courier, Shipping etc.

The CNX Service Sector Index is calculated using the market capitalization weighted aggregate method. The base period is the month of May 1999, index to a value 1000. Selection of the index set is based on the following criteria : 1) Company's market capitalisation rank in the universe should be less than 500. 2) Company's turnover rank in the universe should be less than 500. 3) Company's trading frequency should be at least 90% in the last six months. 4) Company should have a positive networth. 5) A company which comes out with a IPO will be eligible for inclusion in the index, if it fulfills the normal eligiblity criteria for the index for a 3 month period instead of a 6 month period.

S&P CNX INDUSTRY INDICES

S&P CNX 500 Equity Index is desegregated into 72 Industry sectors which are separately maintained by IISL. The industry indices are derived out of the S&P CNX 500 and care is taken to see that the industry representation in the entire universe of securities is reflected in the S&P CNX 500. For example, if in the entire universe of securities, Banking sector has a 5% weightage, then the Banking sector (as determined by the Banking stocks in S&P CNX 500) would have a 5% weightage in the S&P CNX 500. The Banking sector index would be derived out of the Banking stocks in the S&P CNX 500. The changes to the weightage of various sectors in the S&P CNX 500 would dynamically reflect the changes in the entire universe of securities.

CUSTOMISED INDICES

IISL undertakes development & maintenance of customised indices for clients as well as offers consultancy services for developing indices. Customised indices can be used for tracking the performance of the client's portfolio of stocks vis-à-vis objectively defined benchmarks, or for benchmarking NAV performance to customised indices.

The customised indices can be sub-sets of existing indices or a completely new index. Some of the indices that can be constructed include: i) Sector Indices, ii) Individual Business Group Indices; iii) Portfolios, and iv) Industry Indices. These customised indices are computed as per the methodology specified by the client, if it is not a market capitalisation weighted index.

CNX ENERGY INDEX

Energy sector Index includes companies belonging to Petroleum, Gas and Power sub sectors. The CNX Energy Index represents about 85.06% and 82.03% of the market capitalization and aggregate turnover of the last six months for the period October 31, 2006 of the Energy Sector Universe respectively . The average total traded value for the last six months of all CNX Energy Index constituents is approximately 13.91% of the traded value of all stocks on the NSE. CNX Energy Index constituents represent about 18.75% of the total market capitalization as on October 31, 2006.

The index is a market capitalization weighted index with base date of January 1, 2001, indexed to a base value of 1000. The selection of the index set is based on the following criteria : 1) Company's market capitalisation rank in the universe should be less than 500. 2) Company's turnover rank in the universe should be less than 500. 3) Company's trading frequency should be at least 90% in the last one year. 4) Company should have a minimum track record of 3 years of operations with a positive networth. 5) A company, which comes out with an IPO, will be eligible for inclusion in the index, if it fulfills the normal eligibility criteria for the index for a 3 month period instead of a 6 month period.

CNX PHARMA INDEX

CNX Pharma Index has been developed to capture the performance of the companies in this sector. It represents about 65% and 64.9% of the market capitalization and aggregate turnover of the last six months for the period October 31, 2006 of the Pharmaceuticals Sector Universe respectively. The average total traded value for the last six months of all CNX Pharma Index constituents is approximately 3.7% of the traded value of all stocks on the NSE. CNX Pharma Index constituents represent about 3% of the total market capitalization as on October 31, 2006.

The index is a market capitalization weighted index with base date of January 1, 2001, indexed to a base value of 1000. The selection of the index set is based on the following criteria : 1) Company's market capitalisation rank in the universe should be less than 500. 2) Company's turnover rank in the universe should be less than 500. 3)

Company's trading frequency should be at least 90% in the last one year. 4) Company should have a minimum track record of 3 years of operations with a positive networth. 5) A company, which comes out with an IPO, will be eligible for inclusion in the index, if it fulfills the normal eligiblity criteria for the index for a 3 month period instead of a 6 month period.

GOI-BOND INDEX

The increased activity in the government securities market in India and simultaneous emergence of mutual (gilt) funds has given rise to the need for a well defined Bond Index to measure returns in the bond market. The NSE-Government Securities Index prices components off the NSE Benchmark ZCYC so that the movements reflect returns to an investor on account of change in interest rates The index provides a benchmark for portfolio management by various investment managers and gilt funds It also forms the basis for designing index funds and for derivative products such as options and futures. Some of the salient features of this index are: The index uses all Government of India bonds issued after April 1992. There were issued on the basis of an auction mechanism that imparted some amount of market-relatedness to their priceing. Bonds issued prior to 1992 were on the basis of administered interest rates. The index uses a chain-link methodology i.e. today's values are based on the previous value times the change since the previous calculations. This gives the index the ability to add new issues and remove old issues when redeemed. Coupons and redemption payments are assumed to be re-invested back into the index in proportion to the constituent weights. The constituents are weighted by their market capitalization.

Nifty Futures at SGX-DT

With commencement of derivatives trading in India, foreign bourses have evinced interest to introduce trading in derivatives based on Indian indices. Under an agreement, Singapore Exchange Derivatives Trading Limited (SGX-DT) was granted a license to trade futures and options contracts based on S&P CNX Niifty Index.

SGX-DT launched the SGX S&P CNX Nifty Index futures contract on September 25, 2000. The contract is based on the S&P CNX Nifty Index, which is owned by IISL, a subsidiary of NSE. The SGX S&P CNX Nifty Index futures is traded in US $, with a contract size equivalent to US $ 20 multiplied by the S&P CNX Nifty Index. Based on the closing index value of 1358.05 on August 18, 2000, the size of each futures contract is about US$ 27,161 (approximately 5 times that of the contract traded in NSE). The contract is cash settled and is traded on the Exchange's electronic trading platform (SGX ETS) from Monday to Friday. The trading of Nifty futures in SGX was introduced for enabling international market participants gain exposure to the Indian stock market in a highly cost-effective manner. With the growing number of global investors getting exposure to the Indian market place, especially in stocks related to technology, internet and pharmaceuticals, the contract will help participants to effectively trade as well as hedge their portfolio.

RBI Index of Security Prices

The Reserve Bank of India started compiling indices of security prices in 1949. These were classified under the following heads: (*a*) Government and Semi-government securities; (*b*) Debentures of companies; and (*c*) Equity shares of companies.

The RBI introduced several modifications in the computation of the security prices indices necessitated on account of passage of time such as shifting of base, enlarging the coverage of securities and industries, etc. Presently, the RBI compiles the indices of prices of equity shares of companies only and has discontinued such compilation in respect of debentures and government securities after December 1979 as these were not actively traded. The ongoing RBI series covers 338 equity shares (base 1980-81 = 100) out of which 32 per cent belong to Mumbai, 26 per cent, to Calcutta, 17 per cent to Madras, 10 per cent to Ahmedabad and the rest 15 per cent to Delhi. It provides weekly averages for months, years, etc. on an all-India as well as regional basis for five centres, namely, Mumbai, Calcutta, Madras, Ahmedabad and Delhi.

Scrip selection in an industry: The selection of component scrips in each industry group has been made on the basis of (i) the size of the average market value of the share capital of the company during the base year; and (ii) the market activity of the scrip as disclosed by the number of price changes during the base year.

Number of scrips in a region : The number of scrips selected at each region has been fixed keeping in view (i) the total number of shares listed there, and (if) their paid-up capital with a further rider that the selected scrips accounted for 60-70 per cent of the aggregate market value of all the scrips in the region.

Weightage: The weights given to each company (and also to each industry group) are proportional to their share in the aggregate average market value of share capital of total companies listed on each stock exchange or stock exchanges in the region (in case of regional weights) or all stock exchanges (in case of all-India weights).

Method of compilation: The weekly average price of each scrip is obtained as the arithmetical average of daily closing quotations in a week. The price relative[3] or index for each scrip during a particular week is computed as the ratio of the average price for the current week to the average price of that scrip in the base year. But the price relative for a sub-group is worked out as the unweighted geometric mean of price relatives of all scrips selected in that sub-group.

Other Index of Security Prices

Besides the above mentioned indices, the Financial Express, the Economic Times, the Business Standard, etc. also publish their own share price indices.

USERS AND USES OF MARKET INDEXES

People from many walks of life use and are affected by market indexes. Economists and statisticians use stock-market indexes to study long-term growth patterns in the economy, to analyze and forecast business-cycle patterns, and to relate stock indexes to other time-series measures of economic activity. Investors, both individual and institutional, use the market index as a benchmark against which to evaluate the performance of their own or institutional portfolios. The answer to the question, "Did you beat the market?" has important ramifications for all types of investors. Market technicians in many cases base their decisions to buy and sell on the patterns that appear in the time series of the market indexes. The final use of the market index is in portfolio analysis. In discussions of the market model and systematic it will be evident that the relevant riskiness of a security is determined by the relationship between that security's return and the return on the market. Among economists and statisticians one of the major uses of stock-market indexes is to use them as a leading economic indicator. Judging by how long they have been employed, leading indicators of economic activity must be considered in a forecasting success. Unlike econometric modeling, the leading economic indicator approach to forecasting does not require assumptions about what causes economic behaviour. Instead,

---

3. Price relative is obtained by expressing current year price (P_1) as a percentage of the base year price (P_0) and is computed as under: Index Numberr or Price Relative = $P_1/P_0 \times 100$.

it relies on statistically detecting patterns among economic variables that can be used to forecast turning points in economic activity.

QUESTIONS

1. What is a market index ? Outline its utility for security analysis. Give two different methods used to weight indexes.

2. Compare the Paasche and Laspeyres price indexes. What are the benefits and disadvantages of each index ? Suggest a method to overcome these disadvantages.

3. What is the RBI index of share prices ? How many stocks are included in it ? What method is used to weight the stocks ?

4. What stocks make up the BSE National Index ? How is it computed ? Why do so investors consider it to.be a better measure of market performance than the other indexes?

5. Write a note on the predictive capabilities of a market indexes.

6. Returns on various security indexes are often used to judge the performance of an actively managed portfolio. What potential problems do you see in such comparisons?

7. Give two different methods used to weight indexes.

8. "The most important index in financial market is the stock index, which uses a set of stock that are representation of the whole market, or a specified sector, to measure the change in the overall behaviour of the market or sector over a period of time." Do you agree?

REFERENCES

1. Ahearn, Daniel S. "Investment Management and Economic Research," *Financial Analysts Journal.* Jan.-Feb. 1964.

2. Bailey, Jeffrey: "Evaluating Benchmark Quality," *Financial Analysts Journal*, May-June 1992, pp. 33-39.

3. Baumol, W.J. *The Stock Market and Economic Efficiency.* New York: Fordham University Press, 1965.

4. Black, Fisher. "Toward a Fully Computerized Stock Exchange," *Financial Analysts Journal.* Nov.-Dec. 1971.

5. Bostian, David B., Jr. "The Impact of Institutions on the Market," *Financial Analysts Journal.* Nov.-Dec. 1973.

6. Bratt, E.C. *Business Cycles & Forecasting*, 5th ed. Homewood, III .; R.D. Irwin, 1961.

7. Butler, W.F., and E.C. Kavesh. *How Business Economists Forecast*, part 3. Englewood Cliffs, N.J.: Prentice-Hall, 1966.

8. Calderfield, Stanford. "The Truth about Index Funds." *Financial Analysts Journal*, July 1977.

9. Chen, N., R. Roll, and S. Ross. "Economic Forces and the Stock Market." *Journal of Business*, July 1986, 383-403.

10. Clark, Lindley H., Jr. "Model Building Game," *The Wall Street Journal.* Aug. 2, 1977.

11. Cohen, J., E. Zinbarg, and A. Zeikel. *Investment Analysis & Management.* Homewood, III.: R.D. Irwin, 1977, chap. 12.

12. D'Ambrosio, Charles A. *A Guide to Successful Investing.* Englewood Cliffs, N.J.: Prentice-Hall, 1970.

13. Ellis, Charles D. "The Loser's Game," *Financial Analysts Journal.* July-Aug. 1975.

14. Ellis, Charles D. "The Loser's Game." *Financial Analysts Journal*, July-August 1975, pp. 19-28.

15. Financial Analysts Research Foundation. *The Economic Frame-work for Investors.* 1975, University of Virginia.

16. Fisher, Lawrence. "Determinants of Risk Premium on Corporate Bonds," *Journal of Political Economy*. June 1959.

17. Fisher, Lawrence. "Some New Stock Market Indexes," *Journal of Business*. Jan. 1966.

18. Friend, Irwin. "The Economic Consequences of the Stock Market," *American Economic Review*. May 1972.

19. Gastineau, Gary L. "An Index of Listed Option Premiums." *Financial Analysts Journal*, May-June 1977.

20. Good, Walter R. "Interpreting Analysts' Recommendations," *Financial Analysts Journal*. May-June 1975.

21. Graham, Benjamin. *The Intelligent Investor*, 4th ed. New York: Harper & Row, 1972.

22. Hickman, W.B. *Corporate Bond Quality and Investor Experience*. Cambridge, Mass.: National Bureau of Economic Research, 1958.

23. Kahn, Irving. "Lotteries Always *Lose*." *Financial Analysts Journal*, March 1977.

24. King, Benjamin: "Market and Industry Factors in Stock Price Behavior," *Journal of Business*, January 1966, pp. 139-190.

25. Latane, H.A., D.L. Tuttle, and W.E. Young. "Market Indexes and the Implications for Portfolio Management," *Financial Analysts Journal*. Sept.-Oct. 1971.

26. Lorie, J.H., and M.T. Hamilton. *The Stock Market: Theories and Evidence*. Homewood, Ill.: Irwin, 1973.

27. Mendelson, M., and J.W. Peake. "Which Way to a National Market System? " *Financial Analysts Journal*. Sept.-Oct. 1979.

28. Mendelson, Morris. "Automated Quotes to Automated Trading: Re-structuring the Stock Market in the U.S.," *Bulletin of the Institute of Finance*. Graduate School of Business Administration, New York University, March 1972.

29. Moor, Roy E. "The Use of Economics in Investment Analysis," *Financial Analysts Journal*. Nov.-Dec.

30. Moore, Geoffrey H., and julius shiskin. *Indicators of Business Expansions and Contractions*. National Bureau of Economic Re-search, 1967.

31. Robbins, Sidney. *The Securities Markets: Operations and Issues*. New York: Free Press, 1966.

32. Samuelson, Paul A. "Economics of the Stock Market and the Investor," *Commercial & Financial Chronicle*. Oct.

33. Schaefer, J.M., and A.J. Warner. "Concentration Trends and Competition in the Securities Industry," *Financial Analysts Journal*. Nov.-Dec. 1977.

34. Stoll, Hans, and Robert E. Whaley. Stock *Market Structure, Volatility, and Volume*. Charlottsville, Va.: Institute of Chartered Financial Analysts Research Foundation, 1990.

35. Umstead, David A. "Forecasting Stock Market Prices," *The Journal of Finance*, vol. XXXII. May 1977.

36. Wolfe, Harry D. *Business Forecasting Methods*. New York: Holt, Rinehart and Winston, 1966.

8

Security Credit Ratings

INTRODUCTION

The origins of credit rating can be traced to the 1840's. Following the financial crisis 1837, Louis Tappan established the first mercantile credit agency in New York in 1841. The agency rated the ability of merchants to pay their financial obligations. It was subsequently acquired by Robert *Dun* and its first rating guide was published in 1859. Another similar agency was set up by John Bradstreet in 1849, which published a rating book in 1857.' These two agencies were merged together to form Dun & Bradstreet in 1933, which became the owner of Moody's Investors Service in 1962. The history of Moody's itself goes back about a 100 years. In 1900 Joyn Moody founded Moody's Investors Service, and in 1909 published his 'Manual of Railroad Securities'. This was followed by the rating of utility and industrial bonds in 1914, and the rating of bonds issued by U.S. cities and other municipalities in the early 1920s.

Further expansion of the credit rating industry took place in 1916, when the Poor's Publishing Company published its first rating followed by the Standard Statistics Company in 1922, and Fitch Publishing Company in 1924. The Standard Statistics Company merged in 1941 to form Standard & Poor's which was subsequently taken over by McGraw Hill in 1966. For almost 50 years, since the setting up of Fitch Publishing in 1924, there were no major new entrants in the field of credit rating and then in the 1970s, a number of credit rating agencies commenced operations all over the world. These included the Canadian Bond Rating Service (1972), Thomson Bankwatch (1974), Japanese Bond Rating Institute (1975), McCarthy Crisani & Maffei (1975 acquired by Duff & Phelps in 1991), Dominican Bond Rating Service (1997), IBCA Limited (1978), and Duff & Phelps Credit Rating Company (1980).

There are credit rating agencies in operation in many other countries such as Malaysia Philippines, Mexico, Indonesia, Pakistan, Cyprus, Korea, Thailand and Australia. In India the Credit Rating & Information Services of India Ltd. (CRISIL) was set up as the first rating agency in 1987, followed by ICRA Ltd. (formerly known as Investment Information and Credit Rating Agency of India Limited) in 1991, and Credit Analysis & Research Ltd. (CARE) in 1994. The ownership pattern of all the three agencies is institutional. Duff and Phelps has tied up with two Indian NBFCs to set up Duff and Phelps Credit Rating India (P) Limited in 1996.

DEFINITION OF CREDIT RATING

Rating, usually expressed in alphabetical or alphanumeric symbols, are a simple and easily understood tool enabling the investor to differentiate between debt instruments on the basis of their underlying credit quality. The credit rating is thus a symbolic indicator of the current opinion of the relative capability of the issuer to service its debt obligation in a timely fashion, with specific reference to the instrument being rated. It is focused on communicating to the investors, the relative ranking of the defaults loss probability for a given fixed income investment, in comparison with other rated instruments.

In fact, the rating is an opinion on the future ability and legal obligation of the issue to make timely timely payments of principal and interest on a specific fixed income security. The Biting measures the probability that the issuer will default on the security over its life, which depending on the instrument, may be a matter of days to 30 years or more. In addition, long term rating incorporates an assessment of the expected monetary loss should a default occur.

Credit rating help investors by providing an easily recognisable, simple tool that couples a possible unknown issuer with an informative and meaningful symbol of credit quality. Credit rating can be defined as an expression, through use of symbols, of the opinion about credit quality of the issuer of security/instrument. Credit rating does not amount to any recommendation to purchase, sell or hold that security. It is concerned with an act of assigning values by estimating worth or reputation of solvency, and honesty so as to repose the trust in persons ability and intention to repay.

The ratings assigned are generally regarded in the investment community as an objective evaluation of the probability that a borrower will *default* on a given security issue. Default occurs whenever a security issuer is late in making one or more payments that it is legally obligated to make. In the case of a bond, when any interest or principal payment falls due and is not made on time, the bond is legally in default. While many defaulted bonds ultimately resume the payment of principal and interest, others never do, and the issuing company winds up in bankruptcy proceedings. In most instances, holders of bonds issued by a bankrupt company receive only a margined amount on his investments, invested, once the company's assets are sold at auction. Thus, the investor who holds title to bankrupt bonds typically loses both principal and interest. It is no wonder, then, that security ratings are so closely followed by investors. In fact, many investors accept the ratings assigned by credit agencies as a substitute for their own investigation of a security's investment quality.

Factors Affecting Assigned Ratings

Each rating assigned to a security issue is a reflection of at least three factors : (i) the character and terms of the particular security being issued; *(ii)* the probability that the issuer will default on the security and the ability and willingness of the issuer to make timely payments as specified in the indenture (contract) accompanying the security; and (iii) the degree of protection afforded investors if the security issuer is liquidated, reorganised, and/or declares bankruptcy. As a matter of practice, the investment agencies focus principally upon: (a) the past and probable future cash flows of the security issuer as an indication of the institution's ability to service its debt; (b) the volume and composition of outstanding debt; and (c) the stability of the issuer's cash flows over tie. Other factors influencing quality ratings are the value of assets pledged as collateral for a security and the security's priority of claim against the issuing firm's assets. Quality analysts also place heavy emphasis upon interest-coverage ratios and liquidity of the issuing firm.

The rating agencies stress that their evaluations of individual security issues are not recommendations to buy or sell or an indication of the suitability of any particular security for the investor. The agencies do not act as financial advisers to the businesses or units of government whose securities they rate, which helps to promote objectivity in assigning quality ratings. Both domestic and foreign securities are rated using the same criteria.

CREDIT RATING IN INDIA

In Indian context, the scope of credit rating is limited generally to debt, commercial paper, fixed deposits and of late mutual funds as well. So it is the instrument which is rated and not the company. In other words credit quality is not general evaluation of issuing organisation, *i.e.*, if debt of company *XYZ* is rated *AAA* and debt of company *ABC* is rated *EBB*, then it does not mean firm *XYZ* is better than firm *ABC*. However the issuer company gets strength and credibility with the grade of rating awarded to the credit instrument it intends to issue to public for raising funds. Rating, in a way, reflects upon the issuers strength and soundness of operations, management, organisation behaviour and expresses a view on its prospective composite performance and also the organisational behaviour based on the study of past results.

Further the rating will differ for different instruments to be issued by the same company, within the same time span. For example, credit rating for debenture issue will differ to that of commercial paper or certificate of deposit for the same company because nature of obligation is different in each case.

In India, credit ratings started with the setting up of The Credit Rating Information Services of India Limited 1987 CRISIL was promoted by premier financial institutions like ICICI, HDFC, UTI, SBI, LIC and Asian Development Bank. Now CRISIL is an S&P company with a majority shareholding. Apart from CRISIL four more rating agencies have been registered by SEBI in India. These are 1991 promoted by IFCI and now controlled by Moody's, (1993) promoted by IDBI, Fitch India (1996) a 100% subsidiary of Fitch, and a new born Brickworks (2008). In India, CRAs that rate capital market instruments are governed by Securities and Exchange Board of India (Credit Rating Agencies) Regulations, 1999.

FUNCTIONS AND APPROACHES OF CREDIT RATING AGENCIES

A credit rating a comment on the relative likelihood of default in comparison to other rated instruments. In other words, a rating indicates the probability of default of the rated instrument and therefore provides a benchmark for measuring and pricing credit risk. A credit rating compresses an enormous amount of diverse information into a single rating symbol. A simple alphanumeric symbol, such as AAA' or P2+', is normally used to convey a credit rating. Currently rating agencies have standardised rating nomenclatures for long term ratings, short term instruments, medium term ratings, fixed deposits, corporate/issuer credit rating, long and short term debt fund portfolios, IPO grading etc. The rating symbols for the various instruments used by the five rating agencies in India are given at Table-1.

TABLE-1

Comparative Rating Symbols for Long Term Ratings

RATINGS	CRISIL	CARE	ICRA	FITCH	BRICKWORKS
Highest degree of safety with regard to timely payment of financial obligations	AAA	CAREAAA	LAAA	AAA(Ind)	BWR AAA
High degree of safety with regard to timely payment of financial obligations.	AA	CAREAA	LAA	AA(Ind)	BWR AA
Adequate degree of safety with regard to timely payment of financial obligations. .However, changes in circumstances can adversely affect such issues more than those in the higher rating categories.	A	CARE A	LA	A(Ind)	BWR A
Moderate safety with regard to timely payment of financial obligations for the present; changing circumstances are more likely to lead to a weakened capacity to pay interest and repay principal.	BBB	CAREBBB	LBBB	BBB(Ind)	BWR BBB

Inadequate safety with regard to timely payment of financial obligations; less likely to default in the immediate future.	BB	CARE BB	LBB	BB(Ind)	BWR BB
Greater likelihood of default; while currently financial obligations are met, adversebusiness or economic conditions would lead to lack of ability or willingness to pay interest or principal.	B	CARE B	LB	B(Ind)	BWR B
Vulnerable to default; timely payment of financial obligations is possible only if favourable circumstances continue.	C	CARE C	LC	CCC(Ind), CC(Ind),	BWR C
In default or are expected to default on scheduled payment dates. Such instrumentsare extremely speculative and returns from these instruments may be realised only on reorganisation or liquidation.	D	CARE D	LD	DDD(Ind), DD(Ind), D(Ind)	BWR D
Instruments rated 'N.M' have factors present in them, which render the rating outstandingmeaningless. These include reorganisation or liquidation of the issuer, the obligation is under dispute in a court of law or before a statutory authority etc.	NM				

CRAs may apply '+' (plus) or '-' (minus) signs for ratings from 'AA' to 'C' to reflect comparative standing within the category.

Rating Related Products and Activities

CRAs in India rate a large number of financial products: (1) Bonds/ debentures- [the main product]; (2) Commercial paper; (3) Structured finance products; (4) Bank loans; (5) Fixed deposits and bank certificate of deposits; (6) Mutual fund debt schemes; and, the (7) Initial Public Offers (IPOs).

CRAs also undertake customised credit research of a number of borrowers in a credit portfolio, for the use of the lender. CRAs use their understanding of companies' business and operations and their expertise in building frameworks for relative evaluation, which are then applied to arrive at performance grading. For example developer gradings are carried out to assess the ability of the developers to execute projects on a timely basis and promised quality while maritime institute gradings are carried out to assess quality of education imparted to the students vis a vis DGS (Directorate General of Shipping) objectives.

Non-rating Related Activities

CRAs often undertake a variety of non rating related activities. These include the following:

1. **Economy and Company Research**: Some Indian CRAs have set up research arms to complement their rating activities. These arms carry out research on the economy, industries and specific companies, and make the same available to external subscribers for a fee. In addition, they disseminate opinions on the performance of the economy or specific industries, available through releases to the media. The research would also be used internally by the rating agencies for arriving at their rating opinions. SEBI permits CRAs to carry out this activity subject to relevant firewalls.

2. **Risk consulting**: With the application of Basel II regulations for banks, there is considerable demand for tools and products that will allow banks to compute their capital adequacy ratios under the revised guidelines. The risk consulting groups of credit rating agencies would leverage the agencies' understanding of credit risk to develop and provide the tools and data that banks would require. The products in this area include tools for internal ratings, operational risk evaluation, and overall capital calculation.

3. **Funds research**: Some CRAs have diversified from mutual fund ratings into mutual fund research. The services that are available under this head include fund rankings, performance attribution tools (to help users understand the reasons for funds' performance), desktop tools, and fixed income research.

4. **Advisory services**: CRAs offer various kinds of advisory services, usually through dedicated advisory arms. Most of this is in the nature of developing policy frameworks, bid process management, public private partnership consulting, and creating an enabling environment for business in India and globally.

5. **Knowledge Process Outsourcing**: Some Indian CRAs (CRISIL and ICRA) have KPO arms that leverage their analytical skills and other process and manpower capabilities. These arms provide services to the CRAs' affiliates in developed markets, and also to other clients outside India.

BENEFITS OF CREDIT RATING

For different class of persons different benefits accrue from use of rated instruments. Such benefits directly accruing to investors through rated instruments are:

(A) Benefits to Investors

Investors are benefitted in very many ways if the corporate security in which they intend to invest their saving has been rated by credit rating agency. Some of the benefits are as:

(1) *Safeguards against bankruptcy:* Credit rating of an instrument done by credit rating agency gives an idea to the investors about degree of financial strength of the issuer company which enables him to decide about the investment. Highly rated instrument of a company gives an assurance to the investors of safety of instrument and minimum risk of bankruptcy.

(2) *Recognition of risk:* Credit rating provides investors with rating symbols which carry information in easily recognisable manner for the benefit of investors to perceive risk involved in investment. It becomes easier for the investors by looking at the symbol to understand the worth of the issuer company because the instrument is backed by the financial strength of the company which in detail cannot be provided at the minimum cost to each and every one and at the same time they cannot also analyse or understand such information for taking any investment decisions. Rating symbol gives them the idea about the risk involved or the expected advantages from the investment.

(3) *Credibility of issuer:* Rating gives a clue to the credibility of the issuer company. The rating agency is quite independent of the issuer company and has no business connections or otherwise any relationship with it or its Board of Directors, etc. Absence of business links between the rater and the rated firm establish ground for credibility and attract investors.

(4) *Easy understandability of investment proposal:* Rating symbol can be understood by an investor which needs no analytical knowledge on his part. Investor can take quick decisions about the investment to be made in any particular rated security of a company.

(5) *Saving of resources:* Investors rely upon credit rating. This relieves investors from the botheration of knowing about the fundamentals of a company, its actual strength, financial standing, management details, etc. The quality of credit rating done by professional experts of the credit rating agency reposes confidence in him to rely upon the rating for taking investment decisions.

(6) *Independence of investment decisions:* For making investment decisions, investors have to seek advice of financial intermediaries, the stock brokers, merchant bankers, the portfolio managers etc. about the good investment proposal, but for rated instruments, investors need not depend upon the advice of these financial intermediaries as the rating symbol assigned to a particular instrument suggests

the credit worthiness of the instrument and indicates the degree of risk involved in it.

(7) *Choice of investments:* Several alternative credit rating instruments are available at a particular point of time for making investment in the capital market and the investors can make choice depending upon their own risk profile and diversification plan.

(8) *Benefits of rating surveillance:* Investors get the benefit of credit rating agency's on-going surveillance of the rating and rated instruments of different companies. The credit rating agency downgrades the rating of any instrument if subsequently the company's financial strength declines or any event takes place which necessitates consequent dissemination of information on its position to the investors.

In addition to above, investors have other advantages like : Quick understanding of the credit instruments and weigh the ratings with advantages from instruments; quick decisions making for investment and also selling or buying securities to take advantages of market conditions; or, perceiving of default risk by the company.

(B) Benefits of Rating to Company

Company which had its credit instrument or security rated by a credit rating agency is benefited in many ways as summarised below :

(1) *Lower cost of borrowing :* A company with highly rated instrument has the opportunity to reduce the cost of borrowing from the public by quoting lesser interest on fixed deposits or debentures or bonds as the investors with low risk preference would come forward to invest in safe securities though yielding marginally lower rate of return.

(2) *Wider audience for borrowing:* A company with a highly rated instrument cap approach the investors extensively for the resource mobilisation using the press media. Investors in different strata of the society could be attracted by higher rated instrument as the investors undestands the degree of certainty about timely payment of interest and principal on a debt instrument with better rating.

(3) *Rating as marketing tool:* Companies with rated instrument improve their own image and avail of the rating as a marketing tool to create better image in dealing with its customers feel confident in the utility products manufactured by the companies carrying higher rating for their credit instruments.

(4) *Reduction of cost in public issues :* A company with higher rated instrument is able to attract the investors and with least efforts can raise funds. Thus, the rated company can economise and minimise cost of public issues by controlling expenses on media coverage, conferences and other publicity stunts and gimmicks. Rating facilitates best pricing and timing of issues.

(5) *Motivation for growth :* Rating provides motivation to the company for growth as the promoters feel confident in their own efforts and are encouraged to undertake expansion of their operations or new projects. With better image created though higher credit rating the company can mobilise funds from public and instructions or banks from self assessment of its own status which is subject to self-discipline and self-improvement, it can perceive and avoid sickness.

(6) *Unknown issuer :* Credit rating provides recongnition to a relatively unknown issuer while entering into the market through wider investor base who rely on rating grade rather than on 'name recognition'.

(7) *Benefits to brokers and financial intermediaries :* Highly rated instruments put the brokers at an advantage to make less efforts in studying the companys credit

position to convince their clients to select an investment proposal. This enables brokers and other financial inter-mediaries to save time, energy, costs and man-power in convincing their clients about investment in any particular instrument.

DISADVANTAGES OF CREDIT RATING

(1) *Biased rating and misrepresentations:* In the absence of quality rating, credit rating is a curse for the capital market industry, carrying out detailed analysis of the company, should have no links with the company or the persons interested in the company so that their reports impartial and judicious recommendations for rating committee. The companies having lower grade rating do not advertise or use the rating while raising funds from the public. In such cases the investor cannot get information about the riskness of instrument and hence is at loss.

(2) *Static study :* Rating is done on the present and the past historic data of the company and this is only a static study. Prediction of the company's health through rating is momentary and anything can happen after assignment of rating symbols to the company. Dependence for future results on the rating, therefore defeats the very purpose of risk indicativeness of rating. Many changes take place in economic environment, political situation, government policy framework which directly affect the working of a company.

(3) *Concealment of material information:* Rating company might conceal material information from the investigating team of the credit rating company. In such cases quality of rating suffers and renders the rating unreliable.

(4) *Rating is no guarantee for soundness of company:* Rating is done for a particular instrument to assess the credit risk but it should not be construed as a certificate for the matching quality of the company or its management. Independent views should be formed by the user public in general of the rating symbol.

(5) *Human bias:* Finding off the investigation team, at times, may suffer with human bias for unavoidable personal weakness of the staff and might affect the rating.

(6) *Reflection of temporary adverse conditions:* Time factor affects rating, sometimes, misleading conclusions are derived. For example, company in a particular industry might be temporarily in adverse condition but it is given a low rating. This adversely affects the company's interest.

(7) *Down grade:* Once a company has been rated and if it is not able to maintain its working results and performance, credit rating agencies would review the grade and down grade the rating resulting into impairing the image of the company.

(8) *Difference in rating of two agencies:* Rating done by the two different credit rating agencies for the same instrument of the same issuer company in many cases would not be identical. Such differences is likely to occur because of value judgement differences on qualitative aspects of the analysis in tow different agencies.

TYPES OF RATING

Following are the different kinds of rating:

(1) *Bond/debenture rating :* Rating the debentures/ bonds issued by corporates, government etc. is called debenture or bond rating.

(2) *Equity rating:* Rating of equity shares issued by a company is called equity rating.

(3) Preference share rating: Rating of preference share issued by a company is called preference share rating.

(4) *Commercial paper rating:* Commercial papers are instruments used for short term borrowing. Commercial papers issued by manufacturing companies, finance companies, banks and financial institutions and rating of these instruments is called commercial paper rating.

(5) *Fixed deposits rating:* Fixed deposits programmes are medium term unsecured borrowings. Rating of such programmes is called as fixed deposits rating.

(6) *Borrowers rating:* Rating of borrowers is refered as borrower rating.

(7) *Individuals rating:* Rating of individuals is called as individuals credit rating.

(8) *Structured obligation :* Structured obligation are also debt obligation different to debenture or bond or fixed deposit programmes and commercial papers. Structured obligation is generally asset backed security. Credit rating agencies assessed the risk associated with the transaction with the main trust on cash flows emerging from the asset would be sufficient to meet committed payments, to the investors in worst case scenario.

(9) *Sovereign rating :* Is a rating of a country which is being considered whenever a loan is to be extended or some major investment is envisaged in a country.

CREDIT RATING PROCESS IN INDIA

Rating is a multilayered decision making process. The process of rating starts with a rating request from the issuer, and the signing of a rating agreement. The rating agreement has important clauses like confidentiality, agreement by the issuer to share information with the CRA for the purpose of assigning the rating and thereafter on an ongoing basis when the rating is under surveillance. The rating agency undertakes discussion with the management of the issuing entity. Discussions during a management meeting are wide-ranging, covering competitive position, strategy, financial policy, historical performance, and near- and long-term financial and business outlook. Discussions with company managements help rating analysts evaluate management capability and risk appetite, which is an important aspect of the evaluation. After discussion with the issuer's management, a report is prepared detailing the analyst team's assessment of the business risk, financial risk, and management risk associated with the issuer. The report is then presented to the rating committee. This is the only aspect of the process in which the issuer does not directly participate. Drawing on the knowledge and expertise of the participants, the rating committee determines the rating. The process is an attempt to ensure objectivity of the rating, since the decision results from the collective thinking of a group of experts analysing the risks pertaining to the issuer vis-a-vis its competitors in the industry and markets in which they operate. On finalisation of a rating at the rating committee meeting, the rating decision is communicated to the issuer. As the decision to get an initial rating is at the issuer's discretion (except, in India, for public issues of debt), the global best practice is to allow the issuer to decide whether to accept the rating. If the issuer disagrees with the rating, it can also appeal for a fresh look at the rating assigned. The rating committee then discusses the information submitted; it may or may not decide to modify the rating, depending on the facts of the case. If the rating is not changed and the issuer continues to disagree with the rating, it can choose not to accept the rating, which then does not get published.

ANALYTICAL FRAMEWORK USED BY CRAs

A credit rating is an opinion on the relative credit risk (or default risk) associated with the instrument being rated, where a failure to pay even one rupee of the committed debt service payments on the due dates would constitute a default. For most instruments, the process involves estimating the cash generation capacity of the issuer through operations (primary cash flows) in relation to its requirements for servicing debt obligations over the tenure of the instrument. The analysis is based on information obtained from the issuer, and on an understanding of the business environment in which the issuer operates; it is carried out within the framework of the rating agency's criteria.

The analytical framework involves the analysis of business risk, technology risk, operational risk, industry risk, market risk, financial risk and management risk. Business risk analysis covers industry analysis, operating efficiency, market position of the company whereas financial risk covers accounting quality, existing financial position, cash flows and financial flexibility. Under management risk analysis an assessment is made of the competence and risk appetite of the management.

CHART-1
ANALYTICS BEHIND CREDIT RATING

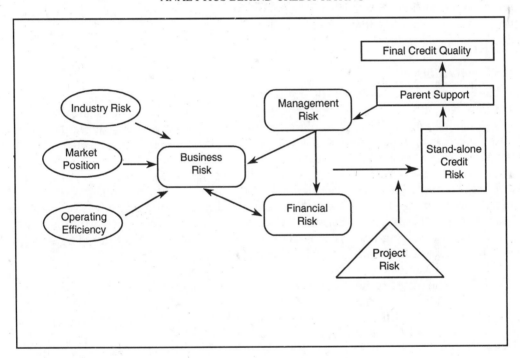

Source: CRISIL Ratings

In addition to the basic framework, rating agencies also have detailed criteria/ methodologies for various industries which take into account the specific features of that industry.

The CRA might also look at the sufficiency of other means of servicing debt in case the primary cash flows are insufficient: for instance, in a securitised instrument, the credit enhancement and structure will be examined, while in case of a guaranteed bond the credit strength of the guarantor could drive the rating.

The quality of ratings is also affected by the timeliness of adjustment of the ratings. The issue is whether there should be aggressive rating changes – such as downgrading a rating by several notches immediately in reaction to adverse news rather than responding to a fundamental change increditworthiness. CRAs need to balance between the dual objectives of accuracy of ratings and their stability. In other words, the point is whether ratings should reflect changes in default risk even if they are likely to be reversed within a very short period of time – whether ratings should focus on the long term or should they fluctuate with near term performance?

CRAs are known to be using Through The Cycle (TTC) methodology and Point In Time (PIT) approach for assigning credit ratings. TTC methodology has two aspects: a focus on the permanent component of default risk and rating change policy. This methodology disregards short term fluctuations in default risk. It filters out the temporary component of default risk and retains only the permanent, long term and structural component. Only substantial changes in the permanent component of default risk lead to rating migrations. In contrast, PIT approach ensures change in credit rating immediately as the fortunes change irrespective of the cause. The basic difference between these two approaches perhaps lies on the relative weight that is assigned to the temporary and permanent components of credit quality. The relative weights are influenced by the time horizons for which the rating is valid. For a one year horizon, the temporary component may get more weightage than for longer time horizon.

THE REGULATORY FRAMEWORK FOR CRAs

Sebi Regulations

The Securities and Exchange Board of India (Credit Rating Agencies) Regulations, 1999 empower SEBI to regulate CRAs operating in India. In fact, SEBI was one of the first few regulators, globally, to put in place an effective and comprehensive regulation for CRAs. In contrast, the US market saw CRA regulations only recently (in 2007), and the European Union is still in the process of framing its regulations. SEBI's CRA regulations have been used as model by other regulators in the emerging economies. In terms of the SEBI Regulations, a CRA has been defined as a body corporate which is engaged in or proposes to be engaged in, the business of rating of securities offered by way of public or rights issue. SEBI has also prescribed a Code of Conduct to be followed by the rating agencies in the CRA Regulations. However, SEBI administers the activities of CRAs with respect to their role in securities market only.

SEBI regulation for CRAs has been designed to ensure the following:
- Credible players enter this business (through stringent entry norms and eligibility criteria)
- CRAs operate in a manner that enables them to issue objective and fair opinions (through well- defined general obligations for CRAs)
- There is widespread investor access to ratings (through a clearly articulated rating dissemination process).
- The applicant should be registered as a company under the Companies Act, 1956 and possess a minimum network of Rs.5 crore.

CRAs are amongst the very few market intermediaries for which such detailed operating guidelines have been prescribed under the regulations. The following are some of the General Obligations specified in the CRA regulations:

SEBI Code of Conduct

SEBI's code of conduct for CRAs addresses some of the basic issues relating to conflicts of interest. The Code of Conduct is designed to ensure transparent and independent functioning of CRAs.

Some of the salient provisions of the Code of Conduct are:
i) A CRA shall make all efforts to protect the interests of investors.

   ii) A CRA shall at all times exercise due diligence, ensure proper care and exercise independent professional judgment in order to achieve and maintain objectivity and independence in the rating process.

  iii) A CRA shall have in place a rating process that reflects consistent and international rating standards.

  iv) A CRA shall keep track of all important changes relating to the client companies and shall develop efficient and responsive systems to yield timely and accurate ratings. Further a CRA shall also monitor closely all relevant factors that might affect the creditworthiness of the issuers.

   v) A CRA shall disclose its rating methodology to clients, users and the public.

  vi) A CRA shall not make any exaggerated statement, whether oral or written, to the client either about its qualification or its capability to render certain services or its achievements with regard to the services rendered to other clients.

Provisions Relating to Conflict of Interest

Credibility is the cornerstone of acceptability of credit rating services in the market. SEBI has prescribed certain provisions in the Code of Conduct to ensure credible rating devoid of conflict of interest. The important ones are as follows.

   i) A CRA shall, wherever necessary, disclose to the clients, possible sources of conflict of duties and interests, which could impair its ability to make fair, objective and unbiased ratings. Further it shall ensure that no conflict of interest exists among any member of its rating committee participating in the rating analysis, and that of its client.

  ii) A CRA or any of its employees shall not render, directly or indirectly, any investment advice about any security in the publicly accessible media.

  iii) A CRA shall not offer fee-based services to the rated entities, beyond credit ratings and research.

  iv) A CRA shall maintain an arm's length relationship between its credit rating activity and any other activity.

   v) A CRA shall develop its own internal code of conduct for governing its internal operations and laying down its standards of appropriate conduct for its employees and officers in the carrying out of their duties within the CRA and as a part of the industry. Such a code may extend to the maintenance of professional excellence and standards, integrity, confidentiality, objectivity, avoidance of conflict of interests, disclosure of shareholdings and interests, etc. Such a code shall also provide for procedures and guidelines in relation to the establishment and conduct of rating committees and duties of the officers and employees serving on such committees.

Despite maintaining a Chinese Wall between advisory services and rating services criticism persists as rating and non-rating entities have common ownership and top management. Recognising the merit in such criticism, CARE's Board decided to discontinue its advisory service business and their activities are confined to only credit rating and research activities.

CRAs in general maintain that while non rating services do pose conflict of interest challenges on one hand, revenues from other services reduce dependence on rating service revenues thereby enabling them to maintain objectivity and independence.

Multiplicity of Regulators

A significant portion of CRAs' revenues are from products that come under the

caacac

purview of SEBI. However, there are rating agency products that are regulated by RBI (such as bank loans, fixed deposits, and commercial paper). RBI carried out a detailed and rigorous evaluation of Indian CRAs before granting them External Credit Assessment Institution status for rating of bank loans under Basel II. Further, some regulators (such as IRDA and PFRDA) have incorporated ratings into the investment guidelines for the entities they regulate. The list of various products, and the relevant regulators, are as noted below:

TABLE 2

Products/Instruments Requiring Mandatory Rating before Issuance

Sl.No	Instrument	Regulator
1.	Public / Rights/ Listed issue of bonds	SEBI
2.	IPO Grading	SEBI
3.	Capital protection oriented funds	SEBI
4.	Collective Investment Schemes of plantation Companies	SEBI
5.	Commercial Paper	RBI
6.	Bank loans	RBI (Basel II capital computation for banks)
7.	Security Receipts	RBI (For NAV declaration)
8.	Securitised instruments (Pass Through Certificates)	RBI ((Basel II capital computation for banks)
9.	Fixed Deposits by NBFCs & HFCs	RBI
10.	LPG/SKO Rating	Ministry of Petroleum and Natural Gas
12.	Maritime Grading	Directorate General of Shipping (for somecourses)

TABLE 3

Regulatory Prescription of Use of Ratings for Investment Purposes

S. No	Product	Regulator
1.	Banks' investments in unrated non-SLR portfolio	RBI
2.	Investments by Insurance companies	IRDA
3.	Provident Fund investments	Government of India

TABLE 4

Products that are Not Mandated or Covered

Performance gradings (non financial instruments	Ratings (Financial instruments)
Real Estate Developer/Project rating	Privately-placed bonds and debentures
Broker grading	Short term debt/Fixed deposits invested by non-banks and bank CD's
Governance and Value Creation ratings	Bond Fund ratings (except Capital protection oriented funds)
MFI Grading (encouraged by SIDBI, Nabard)	Financial strength ratings for insuranceCompanies
NSIC rating for SSI/SME ratings (encouraged by NSIC)	
Contractor gradings	

International Regulations

IOSCO has formulated a Code of Conduct Fundamentals for the working of CRAs. The Code Fundamentals are designed to apply to any CRA and any person employed by a CRA in either in full time or part time capacity. The Code of Conduct focuses on transparency and disclosure in relation to CRA methodologies, conflicts of interest, use of information, performance and duties to the issuers and public, the role of CRA in structured finance transactions etc. It does not dictate business models or governance but rather seeks to provide the market with information to judge and assess CRA activities, performance and reliability. The IOSCO Code of Conduct broadly covers the following areas;

   i) Quality and integrity of the rating process – This includes the measures to ensure quality of the rating process and monitoring and updating by the CRAs.
   ii) CRA's independence and avoidance of conflicts of interest – The procedures and policies to ensure the same.
   iii) CRA's responsibilities to the investing public and issuers – These address issues such as transparency and timeliness of ratings disclosure and the treatment of confidential information.
   iv) Disclosure of the code of conduct and communication with market participants – This requires CRAs to disclose to the public, inter alia, its code of conduct, how the code of conduct is in accordance with the IOSCO Principles regarding the activities of Credit Rating Agencies and the IOSCO Code of Conduct Fundamentals for Credit Rating Agencies and in case of deviation, reasons for the same.

It is observed that all SEBI regulated CRAs in India have framed their internal code of conduct, which have provisions, inter alia, of conflict of interest management, avoidance and disclosures of conflict of interest situations etc. and such provisions prescribed are by and large in accordance with the IOSCO Code of Conduct Fundamentals for CRAs. The internal code of conduct formulated by the CRAs is in addition to the Code of Conduct prescribed under the SEBI(CRA) Regulations – 1999.

CRAS BUSINESS MODELS

The various business models used by CRAs are discussed below:

ISSUER PAYS MODEL

Under issuer-pays-model' the entity that issues the security also pays the rating agency for the rating. Conceptually, the issuer-pays model may appear to imply an inherent bias which may lead to CRAs assigning higher-than-warranted ratings to issues they rate. CRAs have argued that they have several checks and balances and robust operating guidelines and procedures to ensure that the quality of ratings is high and objective. One example of this is separation of business development, analytical, criteria, and quality teams. CRAs point to a long-term track record of default and transition statistics which demonstrate that higher ratings are consistently more stable and have a lower probability of default than lower ones. Specifically it is argued that

   i) Ratings are ordinal; that is the higher the rating, the lower are the observed default levels.
   ii) Ratings have been assigned across the entire rating scale, with no bias in their distribution towards higher ratings, which would be the pattern expected had the CRAs been influenced by the issuer-pays model.
   iii) Rating actions are distributed across both upgrades and downgrades, which is also a different pattern from the one expected where the issuer-pays model

might influence the decision to upgrade rather than downgrade and also work to prevent downgrades.

CRAs have a strong incentive to maintain the highest quality of rating, since issuers will approach a CRA for ratings only if its opinions carry credibility with investors whom they are trying to access. Nevertheless, there are questions about whether all CRAs adopt uniformly high governance and process standards.

Widespread availability of ratings is the strength of the issuer-pays model. The goal of ratings is to reduce information asymmetry. Because issuers/borrowers pay for ratings, the market and lenders significantly benefit from the wide availability of credit ratings. Today, all ratings and rating changes are available to the entire market — including retail investors -- free of charge, as they are widely disseminated by rating agency websites and the media. An investor can compare the ratings of a wide array of instruments before making an investment decision, and can continuously evaluate the relative creditworthiness of a wide range of issuers and borrowers.

Other features of the issuer-pays model are listed below:

Access to information enhances quality of analysis: The issuer-pays model provides CRAs access to company managements on a regular basis. CRAs submit that this allows them to provide superior quality and depth of analysis to the market, which would be difficult under public information-based and model-driven approaches. The CRA's contract with the issuer/borrower places an obligation on the issuer's management to cooperate in sharing information, which is critical for maintaining continuous surveillance on rated credits. Because the issuer's management has commissioned the rating exercise, its level of engagement in providing information to the CRA is high. Issuer managements often provide CRAs insights into future strategy that might not be in the public domain. Moreover, interactions also help rating agencies evaluate management capabilities better. For rating structured finance issuances, the question assumes even greater criticality, since it is virtually impossible to rate these instruments without access to information from the originator of the underlying assets.

Cost of ratings is kept low: Currently, rating fees are the smallest element in the cost of raising money. With large and frequent issuers of debt, rating agencies typically work on the basis of fee caps (negotiated lump-sum fees as opposed to issue-by-issue or loan-by-loan pricing). Not only does this keep rating fees low, it also results in smaller issuers being, in effect, subsidised by larger ones.

INVESTOR-PAYS MODEL

Under investor-pays model the user of rating pays for the ratings. According to CRAs this model does not eliminate the conflict of interest- it only shifts the source of conflict from issuer to investors. Under the investor-pays model, CRAs could give lower ratings than indicated by the actual credit quality of the rated debt, so that investors would get a higher yield than warranted. Pressures from investors to avoid rating downgrades would increase considerably under the investor-pays model, since downgrades result in mark-to-market losses on rated securities. In fact, even under the current issuer-pays model, CRAs face a high level of pressure from investors to not downgrade ratings. In particular, it is possible that a large investor who has a large exposure on an issuer would like to have a more favourable rating for that issuer. On the other hand, a short seller would prefer if the rating is lowered. Internationally, the experience with the investor-pays models has not been successful. Nevertheless, the potential conflicts seem substantially less severe than for the issuer pays model. One example of a rating agency that operates today on the basis of subscription by investors is Egan-Jones Ratings; it is now recognised by the US SEC, but its coverage and impact have been low.

Widespread availability of ratings: The investor-pays model is weak on this count. If investors pay for ratings, only investors who pay will get access to ratings. The goal of reduced information asymmetry is therefore compromised under this model. Investors would also not be able to benchmark the quality of their investments against other companies, since they may not be willing to pay for ratings of companies in which they do not invest. This model also favours large investors who can afford to pay for ratings. The biggest losers are the smaller institutional investors and the retail investors, who would have had free access to all ratings under the issuer-pays model or the Government/regulator pays model.

Other advantages and limitations of the investor-pays model

Greater responsiveness to investor concerns: Under the investor-pays model CRAs could be more responsive to investor concerns and further the investor protection agenda as they would be positioned as quasi-investor representatives. Also, an investor paying for a specific rating could demand customised analysis from the rating agency which is attuned to their goals or organisational requirements.

Investor is not known at the time of assigning ratings: Issuers/borrowers intending to raise money approach CRAs for an independent evaluation, based on which they approach prospective investors. This means that typically, when the rating is assigned, the investor is not known. If the investor were to commission and pay for ratings, it would lead to huge inefficiencies and practical problems in the fund-raising programmes of issuers/borrowers.

Bias against smaller issuers/borrowers: The problem of investors not being known can be addressed by rating agencies assigning ratings *suo-moto* to large/frequent issuers and borrowers; investors can later pay for this on a subscription basis. However, this system creates a strong bias against smaller issuers which would not get rating coverage, and their funding programmes could be severely impaired. *Suo-moto* ratings also suffer the disadvantage of not getting a meaningful interaction with the management to make an assessment about them and their strategy. In fact, this is the main reason why rating agencies that operate on the investor-pays model have limited coverage and impact.

Costs of ratings would increase: Investors would choose to pay for ratings of those companies that they are interested in, and even here, only for rating specific issuances by a particular company. The benefits of fee caps as described above would be lost and the overall rating costs could go up. From the point of view of investors, it will increase information asymmetry as ratings opinion will be available only with a few large investors which is detrimental to the liquidity and development of the market.

Limited access to information could affect quality of analysis: If investors were to pay for ratings, issuers would not be contractually bound to provide rating agencies access to information and regular management interactions. This is important if the rating agency has to carry out surveillance on an ongoing basis. Moreover, regular meetings with management and insights on company strategy enable rating agencies to make a thorough evaluation of management capabilities and risk appetite. It is hard to envisage the same level of access, information and sharing of insights as exists under the issuer-pays model. Further this may also involve rating of the same issue by multiple agencies resulting in the issuer being required to meet and share information with all agencies.

The Reserve Bank of India, under Basel II guidelines, has stipulated that even though ratings are used by the banks for determining their capital requirements, the ratings should be solicited by the companies themselves, and not by the banks.

THE GOVERNMENT/REGULATOR-PAYS MODEL

In this model the Government funds the rating costs. Conceptually, this model would carry less inherent bias, since in most cases there is no incentive to provide either higher-than-warranted or lower-than-warranted ratings. The one exception that could arise would be in case of public sector enterprises; the perception could be that the government could influence rating outcomes in this case. Further, widespread availability of ratings can also be easily ensured under the government/regulator pays model as they could stipulate that rating agencies make all ratings and rating changes freely available on their websites and disseminate them through the media as happens currently.

Other positive and negative aspects of the Government/regulator pays model are listed below:

Control over/guidance of rating agencies becomes simpler: If Government/regulators pay for ratings, it becomes easier to monitor and control the activities of rating agencies

Moral hazard: Rating opinions being seen as being endorsed by the Government: This is a major limitation of the Government/regulator pays model. Investors and markets could see the opinions provided by rating agencies as having government endorsement. This carries the serious risk of expectation of Government support in the event of default by a rated entity. This risk is larger than it may seem as evident in recent actions across the globe.

Use of public money for companies and institutional investors who can afford to pay for ratings

It is questionable whether paying for ratings is the best use of public funds as compared to other objectives like improving financial literacy and small investor protection. Both issuers and institutional investors can well afford to pay for ratings. As explained above, under the issuer-pays model, the small retail investor too benefits as ratings are freely available in the public domain. India has emerged as the second-largest rating market, with the widespread acceptance of rating by the regulators and the markets. The budget for supporting this industry could be quite substantial.

Limited access to companies could affect quality of analysis: If Government/regulators pay the rating agencies, issuers would not be contractually bound to provide rating agencies access to information, and regular management interactions, which could affect the quality of analysis.

Several practical problems in implementation: The challenge under the Government/regulator pays model is: how would the choice of rating agency for a rating a specific issuer/company be made, and by whom? How would the rating fees be decided? If a company desiring to raise money approaches the regulator to request that a rating be commissioned, would they also specify which rating agency they would prefer? This in effect, would make it an issuer-driven choice. Would companies or issues be allocated on a random basis amongst all rating agencies? This would lead to huge inefficiencies and the costs of ratings would increase from a system perspective. Adequate safeguards also need to be put in to ensure that the oversight of the work allocation to the rating agencies remains objective, lest any subversion of rating outcomes take place as a result of undue influence.

These measures could also breed complacency amongst CRAs, who will begin to see it as a steady assured business, rather than the current situation of fending for themselves. For example, if the selection of rating agencies is done on a random basis, then rating agencies will have no incentive to produce the most analytical rigorous, independent, objective rating on a timely basis which will provide best insights for investors.

THE EXCHANGE-PAYS MODEL

Under this model the exchanges pay for the ratings and recover the cost through an additional trading fee. The major advantage of this model is that the investors would be paying for the rating thereby eliminating the conflict of interest inherent in 'issuer pays model' and at the same time the rating agencies would not be influenced either by the rated company or the investors. The major disadvantage of this model is that this model can work only for securities that are listed.

The above discussion indicates why the issuer-pays model has prevailed over other possible alternative models. Recent regulatory initiatives in the United States and Europe aim to address the issue of conflict of interest presented by this model, but do not recommend a move to any other model. What they recognise is that rating agencies should be subject to scrutiny to ensure that conflicts of interest do not influence rating decisions. Their recommendations to manage this conflict include greater transparency and disclosures, and better governance practices to ensure independence.

Regulatory Concerns about CRAs Business Models

Internationally in view of the inadequacies observed in the functioning of CRAs, particularly in the wake of the sub-prime financial crisis, there is a growing concern among the regulators about the potential gap between expectation and realisation- between reliance on credit ratings and the reliability of such ratings. The concern emanates from the fact that inaccurate credit ratings could disturb the market allocation incentives, cost structures and competition. In view of the multiple activities performed by the rating agencies and the complexity of certain instruments for which the CRAs render their service, there are apprehensions about regulatory arbitrage, non-maintenance of arm's length distance, porosity of Chinese Walls, inappropriate conflict management etc arising out of the activities of the rating agencies. In short there is real regulatory (and market) apprehension that the self-regulation model of conflict regulation has failed substantively in the CRA realm and that the model of multiple businesses of CRAs is riddled with inherent conflict that cannot be solved with internal Chinese walls and codes of conduct alone. The gate-keepers' commercial aspirations appear to be too high so that they have become just enterprises driven by the profit / revenue only agenda like other market intermediaries, rather than the ethos of institutions.

CRAs have been highly criticized for understating the risk involved with instruments like Mortgage Backed Securities (MBS). CRAs have given investment grade ratings to securitization transactions viz. Collateralized Debt Obligations (CDOs) and MBS based on sub prime mortgage loans. Higher ratings were justified by the rating agencies by citing various credit enhancements, including over collateralization (i.e pledging collateral in excess of the debt issues). In the USA, CRAs had failed to warn the public of imminent bankruptcies in case of Enron and WorldCom, as well as the recent sub-prime loan crisis. It is alleged that the lenient standards adopted by rating agencies for MBS segment could possibly be because the rating fees were twice as high for the mortgage-backed bonds as for the corporate bonds. It is also possible that the dealers regularly sought the inputs from the CRAs when creating new issues, which effectively put the rating agencies in a position to influence the size of the market from which they drew lucrative revenues. At the same time, the dealers were shopping around for ratings, inviting a race to the bottom , leading to inflated ratings. Mortgage-backed bonds being a relatively recent innovation, assessments of creditworthiness by the rating agencies ended up relying on data and techniques provided by the dealers. But these were all reflections of the underlying conflicts arising from their business models-the opportunity to help structure and rate millions of complex derivative products just magnified it, exposing both the conflicts and capabilities of the CRAs.

In India CRAs rate money market instruments and also play an important role in the pension and insurance sector. For example, in the context of implementation of the Basel II Framework in India, from March 2008, for the capital adequacy regime of the banks, it has been decided to adopt, initially, the Standardized Approach for determining the capital charge for the credit risk inherent in the operations of banks. The Standardized Approach relies almost entirely on the ratings assigned by the CRAs, accredited for the purpose by the RBI. These ratings are mapped into the corresponding regulatory risk weights applicable to the credit risk exposures on the counterparties, which form the basis of computation of the capital adequacy ratio of the banks. Besides, the capital charge for specific risk under the Market Risk Framework for interest rate-related instruments is also governed by the ratings assigned by the CRAs to the instrument concerned. Similarly IRDA and PFRDA recognize the ratings approved by rating agencies for prescribing their investment guidelines. SEBI regulates the CRA activities from the securities market point of view. Thus activities performed by CRAs which fall under the jurisdiction of other regulators should also be governed by appropriate guidelines and principles relevant to them.

Following are potentially the major regulatory concerns of the Indian regulators. It must be noted that some of these are generic to the industry.

1. Regulatory arbitrage resulting from activities of CRAs being governed/ used by various regulators.
2. Inadequacy of existing methodologies adopted by CRAs for structured products given their complexity, multiple tranches and their susceptibility to rapid, multiple-notch downgrades which are pro-cyclical.
3. A basic conflict of interest which is partly inherent, since the sponsor/issuer of new instruments pays the CRA for being rated.
4. A general lack of accountability as CRAs do not have a legal duty of accuracy and are often protected from liability in case of inaccurate ratings.
5. CRAs sometimes provide ancillary services in addition to credit ratings. The issuer may use the incentive of providing the CRA with more ancillary business in order to obtain higher ratings. There is a clear conflict of interest in offering advisory services or consulting services to entities rated by the CRA.
6. Oligopolistic nature of the rating industry because of natural barriers or propriety barriers of entry leading to lack of competition.

HOW DO CRAs ADDRESS REGULATORY CONCERNS?

Investor over- reliance on credit ratings has been long recognised as undesirable, although by embedding ratings in various regulations some authorities have inadvertently encouraged their overuse. For example the longstanding use of credit ratings to screen eligible collateral for various central bankliquidity backstop facilities is viewed as encouraging rating shopping. Regulations relating to pension fund holdings, for example, typically restrict fixed-income investment to those with investment-grade ratings (i.e. BBB and higher). Furthermore, although the differentiation of structured credit ratings is welcome, the ratings remain based on one-dimensional metrics (default probabilities or expected losses) that fail to capture all of the risk dimensions peculiar to tranched products. Currently rating for complex products like structured obligations are indicated by using special symbols. It also highlights the need for greater awareness generation.

CRAs follow a reputational model. Users will approach CRAs for ratings only if its opinions carry creditability with investors whom the issuers are trying to signal. Ratings which undergo frequent downgrades may not inspire confidence of the market. This incentivizes CRAs to maintain high quality of ratings.Rules, regulations, statutes as well as compliance with international covenants ensure that CRAs behave in a transparent manner. Misdemeanour can be punished through tight regulations. Regulatory arbitrage can be resolved by following lead regulatory model or greater inter agency coordination.

CRAs argue that advisory or consulting services are offered by different legal entities with whom physical, organizational and functional separation is maintained. CRISIL and ICRA have separated the advisory business into separate companies, managed by separate teams with separate organisation structures.

CARE though until recently carried out this business as part of its rating business, has now decided to exit advisory business. With respect to individuals, CRAs ensure that common directors do not attend rating committee meeting and disclosures to that effect are made. Further analyst compensation is not linked to rating fees. Each rating by the CRA passes though a multi-layer process and there is a team approach to avoid individual bias. Rating fees are not linked to issue success or rating level and are decided upfront and there is separation of business development and analytical teams. Another leading CRA stated that in order to avoid conflicts of interest, their advisory and consulting services division have been spun off into a separate company and has its own independent management, staff rules and personnel policies.

The SEBI CRA Regulations state that a CRA cannot rate an entity with common chairman, directors, or employee of credit rating agency or its rating committee. A CRA can rate a company with which it shares an independent director, but the existence of the common independent director and the fact that he or she did not participate in the rating process needs to be disclosed.

The entry requirements into the Credit Rating industry is stringent but does not act as a barrier to entry of new funds.

LIMITATIONS OF CREDIT RATINGS

Specifically, a credit rating, in the words of the CRAs, is:

i. Not a recommendation to buy, hold or sell any shares, bonds, debentures or other instruments issued by the rated entity, or derivatives thereof. A rating is one of the many inputs that is used by investors to make an investment decision.

ii. Not Intended to measure many other factors that debt investors must consider in relation to risk such as yield offered, liquidity risk, pre-payment risk, interest rate risk, taxation aspects, risk of secondary market loss, exchange loss risk, etc.

iii. Not a general-purpose credit or performance evaluation of the rated entity, unless otherwise specified. The rating is usually specific to the instrument and is not the rating of the issuer.

iv. Not an opinion on associate, affiliate or group companies of the rated entity, or on promoters, directors or officers of the rated entity.

v. Not a statutory or non-statutory audit of the rated entity

vi. Not an indication of compliance or otherwise with legal or statutory requirements

vii. Not a guarantee against default of the rated instrument. Even the highest-rated instrument faces some risk of default, although the risks associated with this are lower than lower-rated instruments.

Credit Ratings are typically ordinal in nature – for example we know that a rating of BB has a higher likelihood of default than BBB, but we do not know how much higher. It is not until each rating is assigned a probability of default that we can say how much more risky a BB rated instrument is thus making the system cardinal. Cardinality is more useful for pricing an instrument. Translation of credit ratings to default probabilities is, however, not a straight forward task.

Some of the serious limitations of credit rating are its backward looking nature (depends on past data) which in a dynamic market framework can have serious consequences including accentuating a systemic crisis like the current global crisis, and its failure and unwillingness to capture/cover market risks. Estimating market risk can potentially make the rating exercise forward looking, could avoid sudden, multiple downgrades and reduce the pro-cyclicality of rating. A really informed forward looking rating could potentially also capture tail risks and forewarn the system to help take systemic steps well in advance to avoid panic and knee-jerk reactions. If rating is to straddle the high ground it aspires to hold rating exercise has to achieve this dynamism to really help measure all the risks of the market, rather than sticking to a partial methodology of expressing an opinion on a few aspects of the product they rate. No product can be usefully rated in a vacuum, isolated from the caprices of the market as a whole.

Whither Credit Rating Agencies?

The informational value of credit rating and informational effect of credit ratings are matters of continuing debate. The central issue is whether institutions of credit rating are in a better position to decipher the default risk present in financial instruments than the financial markets. Empirical evidence from some countries have suggested that markets do this information processing better than credit rating institutions. Academic studies argue that by looking at the market price it would be easy to infer an effective credit rating of each instrument. Since market prices are available at near zero cost , there would appear to be no role for credit rating.

The rationale for credit rating may be expressed on the following counts:

1. If markets do not trade a particular instrument actively , then there is an informational challenge. In general impact cost on the market is lowered when more is publicly known about the securities being traded. In such cases a good credit rating (for eg. one which forecasts the interest rate at which bonds are traded on the secondary market. If issue A is rated above B then markets should demand a lower interest from A than B) helps reduce informational asymmetry and enhance liquidity in the market.

2. Suppose a company wants to do a primary market issue of bonds/ equity. At the time of issue, in the absence of trading , the default risk may not be clearly known to the market. This could generate a phenomenon like IPO underpricing. Hence it is optimal for the issuer to obtain a credit rating so as to place the bonds/equity at a superior price.

3. International obligations like Basel II require prudential provisioning of capital on the basis of risk weights attached to assets. Computation of capital required to be maintained by banks then requires rating of its assets.

In practice, by nudging more trades to the exchange platform the problem of informational challenge can be addressed. Till such time greater disclosure of reliable information can help the market in pricing the issue. Recent financial crisis has shown that ratings provided by credit rating agencies despite access to non public information have been faulty.However where market asymmetries are strong and financial literacy low, sound credit rating can continue to bridge the information gap considerably.

QUESTIONS

1. Define credit rating. What are the advantages and disadvantages of credit rating.
2. Discuss the factors affecting assigning the credit rating to securities.
3. Critically examine the role and rationale of credit rating agencies.
4. Discuss the functions and approaches of credit rating agencies.
5. Discuss the rating process and analytical framework used by CRAs.
6. "Credit rating agencies use the same criteria in evaluating, both the domestic and foreign securities". Comment.
7. Discuss the role of credit rating agencies in promoting objectivity in assigning quality ratings.
8. Critically examine the analytical framework used by CRAs for rating process..
9. Evaluate the different types of credit rating. What are the limitations of credit ratings?
10. Discuss the regulatory framework for CRAs. What are the regulatory concerns about CRAs business models.

REFERENCES

1. Ang, James S., and K.A. Patel. "Bond Rating Methods: Comparison and Validation." *Journal of Finance*, May 1975, 631-640.
2. Cantor, R. and F. Packer: "The credit rating industry", *Federal Reserve Bank of New York Quarterly Review*, Summer-Fall, 1994.
3. Drehmann, M. and N. Tarashev: "Systemaic importancce: some simple indicators", *BIS Quarterly Review*, March, 2011.
4. Fender, I., N. Tarashev and H. Zhu: "Credit fundamentals, ratings and value-at-risk: CDOs versus corporate exposures", *BIS Quarterly Review*, March, 2008.
5. Financial Stability Board: *Principles for reducing reliance on CRA ratings*, October, 2010.
6. Fitch Ratings: "Global financial institutions ratings criteria", *Master Criteria*, 16 August, 2010.
7. Moody's Investors Service: *Calibrating bank rating in the context of the global financial crisis*, Febrary, 2009.
8. Morgan, D.: "Rating banks: risk and uncertainty in the opaque industry", *American Economic Review*, vol. 92, 2012, pp. 874-88
9. Packer, F., R. Sterver and C. Upper: "The covered bond market", *BIS Quarterly Rview*, September, 2007.
10. Pogue. Thomas F. and Robert M. Soldofsky: "What's in a Bond Rating.'" *Journal of Financial and Quantitative Analysis*, June 1969, pp. 201-228.
11. Reilly, Frank K., and Michael D. Joehnk. "The Association between Market-Determined Risk Measures for Bonds and Bond Ratings." *Journal of Finance* 31, no. 5 (December 1976).

12. Reilly. Frank, G. Werehi Kao, and David Wright: "Alternative Bond Market Indexes." *Financial Analysts Journal*, May-June 1992, pp. 47-58.

13. Standard & Poor's: *Methodology for determining banking industry country risk assessment*, 13 May, 2010.

14. Weinstein, Mark I. "The Effect of a Rating Change Announcement on Bond Price." *Journal of Financial Economics 5*, no. 3 (December 1977).

9

Capital Market Reforms

INTRODUCTION

Investment decisions are taken within the framework provided by a complex of financial institutions and intermediaries which together comprise the capital market. It has a vital role in promoting efficiency and growth. It intermediates the flow of funds from those who want to save a part of their income from those who want to invest in productive assets. It is this market which provides the mechanism for channeling current savings into investment in productive facilities, that is, for allocating the country's capital resources among alternative uses. In effect, the capital market provides an economy's link with the future, since current decisions regarding the allocation of capital resources are a major determining factor of tomorrow's output. The crucial role played by the capital market in shaping the pattern and growth of real output imparts a social significance to individual investment and portfolio decisions. The efficiency of intermediation depends on the width, depth and diversity of the capital market. Till about two decades ago, a large part of household savings was either invested directly in physical assets, or put in bank deposits and government small saving schemes. It is only since the late eighties that the equity market has started to play a role in this intermediation process.

THE PRIMARY SECURITIES MARKET

The primary market for securities is the *new issues* market which brings together the "supply and demand" or "sources and uses" for new capital funds. In this market the principal source of funds is the domestic savings of individuals and businesses; other suppliers include foreign investors and governments. The principal uses of funds are: the long-term financing of the investment in housing (mortgages), the long-term investment of corporations and other businesses, and the long-term borrowing of government. The ultimate suppliers of funds are those sectors with a surplus of current income over expenditure (savings); and these funds flow to their ultimate users, namely, economic units which issue securities to finance a surplus of expenditures over their current incomes.

In a highly developed capital market by far the largest proportion of individuals' savings reaches the new issues market *indirectly* via a financial intermediary. For example, the savings of most individuals are channeled to an ultimate user, say a corporation desiring to finance an expansion of its productive facilities, via an investment company or a similar institution. Moreover, most individual investors are unfamiliar with the new issues market and its institutions, such as underwriters and selling syndicates which serve as middlemen between the corporate demanders of funds and the individual investors and financial institutions which supply the funds. To most investors the term *securities market* is synonymous with the "stock exchange".

THE SECONDARY SECURITIES MARKET

The purpose of a stock exchange or *secondary* securities market, like any other organised market, is to enable buyers and sellers to effect their transactions more quickly and cheaply than they could otherwise. However, since a stock exchange typically deals in *existing* securities rather than in new issues, its economic significance may be misunderstood.

As we noted above, the primary function of the capital market relates to the channeling of savings into capital formation; hence the capital market's economic significance stems from its impact on the allocation of capital resources among alternative uses. But an increase in the volume of securities trading in the stock market does not represent an increase in the economy's aggregate savings, every purchase of an *existing* security being exactly offset by the sale of the same security.

To place the capital market in proper perspective it is useful to distinguish between the "primary" and "secondary" securities markets. For the economy as a whole, an increase in savings in the form of securities ownership is measured by the volume of net new issues of securities, while transactions in existing securities represent shifts among owners, which always cancel out in the aggregate. Similarly, transactions in existing securities do not provide additional funds to finance capital formation; here again it is the volume of net new issues which provides additional financing to business enterprises. An analogy can readily be drawn from the automobile market. The sales of new Maruti cars (new issues) by the Maruti Udyog (issuing firm) provide revenue (investment funds) to the company; transactions in older models of Maruti cars (existing securities) in the used car market (stock exchange) do not. But just as the existence of a resale market for cars affects the willingness of consumers to purchase new Marutis, the availability of an efficient secondary market for securities is one of the more important factors inducing investors to acquire new issues of securities. And the connection between the primary and secondary markets is even stronger in the case of the securities market, since new issues are often close, or even perfect, substitutes for outstanding securities.

The basic economic function of a stock exchange is to provide marketability for long-term investments, thereby reducing the personal risk incurred by investors and broadening the supply of equity and long-term debt capital for the financing of business enterprise. For example, even though the investment in equity shares is fixed for the life of the firm, the ability to shift ownership to others during the course of this period permits more individuals to participate in the long-term financing of companies. In an economy with a well developed secondary securities market, the fixed investment of firms is provided by a changing group of individuals, none of whom may have been willing to commit his personal resources for the entire or even a substantial part of the life of the enterprise. Thus in an efficient stock exchange the supply of credit, which from the private investor's viewpoint is often inherently short-term, is transformed into a supply of long-term investment fund for the financing of capital formation. The ability to transfer the risks of investment forges a link between the stock exchange and the new issues market, and this greatly enhances the ability of business enterprises to mobilise additional long-term capital to finance the creation of new, or the expansion of existing production facilities.

To effectively fulfill its functions as an allocator of capital, the securities market should be influenced solely by economic considerations; the prices of the various securities should reflect their expected returns and risk characteristics. In an efficient market current prices for a company's securities will reflect the investors' best estimates of the firm's anticipated profitability and of the risks attaching to these profits. And since - other things being equal-rising stock prices attract investors, the allocation of capital will be *biased* in favour of firms with relatively high levels of risk-adjusted profits. On the other hand, firms with low profitability or excessive riskiness will find it difficult, expensive, or on occasion even impossible to raise additional capital for expansion.

The prerequisites for such an efficient securities market are roughly the same as those of any 'perfect" or purely competitive market: (a) the products traded in the market must be homogeneous; (b) the market must be comprised of many relatively small buyers and sellers; and (e) there must be free entry and exit into and out of the market.

Although a securities market is made up of many types of securities of a large number of companies, each class of securities is homogeneous in the sense that the risk-adjusted rates of return of the various classes of securities comprise homogeneous commodities. One share of a given risk class is as good as any other and therefore they must sell at the same price. In addition, a modem securities market is made up of a large number of relatively small buyers and sellers so that it is difficult for any individual to influence prices.

This rather sanguine view of the stock market and its impact on the allocation of capital is not universally held. To some the *Stock Exchange is a den of iniquity;* to other, more sophisticated, observers stock market prices reflect mass psychology with little if any connection to underlying economic values. The case against the stock exchange was most forcibly expressed during the 1930s by the most famous economist of the time, John Maynard Keynes. In a characteristically brilliant passage which goes a long way towards explaining his own success as an investor, Keynes described the stock exchange as a place where most investors attempt to guess what average opinion thinks average opinion will be like one month hence, while others practice the "fourth, fifth and higher degrees" of this art.'

It should be recalled that Keynes was writing at a time when a worldwide financial crisis had so undermined public confidence that stock prices did often appear to be unconnected with any underlying economic values. Taking a somewhat longer view, however, there is really no inherent contradiction between the kind of speculative behaviour which Keynes described and the thesis that stock prices, in the long run, reflect economic values. For this purpose it is sufficient that some investors become conditioned to the fact that stock prices rise when profits and dividends increase, so that it "pays" to exploit all available information in an attempt to anticipate such possibilities. The available statistical evidence suggest that Keynes notwithstanding, the pure speculator does *not* rule the roost, and therefore the quest for quick capital gains has not divorced the trend in the price of a company's stock from the expectation of future profits.

CAPITAL MARKET REFORMS: POLICY INITIATIVES AND DEVELOPMENTS

The Indian capital market, which has a long history spanning over 100 years, is currently passing through the most radical phase. Although the Indian capital market witnessed some significant changes during the eighties, both the primary and the secondary segments continued to suffer from some serious deficiencies. Many unhealthy practices prevailed in the primary market to attract the retail investors. Another disturbing feature was the high cost of new issues. Although over the years, a number of agencies came into existence offering different types of services in connection with the new issues of capital, their activities were not overseen by any regulatory authority.

The problems were even more serious in the secondary market. The general functioning of stock exchanges was not satisfactory. The exchanges were governed by their internal bye-laws and managed by their Governing Bodies, which were dominated by elected member-brokers. Trading members were also not adequately capitalised. Insider trading was rampant and was one of the major causes of excessive speculative activity, leading to default by stock brokers, frequent payment crises and disruption of market activity. The stock exchanges followed inefficient and outdated trading systems. This, in turn, led to lack of transparency in trading operations, besides resulting in long and uncertain settlement cycles. The risk management system in the market was also not satisfactory. Though the margin system was operative, the margins were inadequate and the system of collection of margins was not enforced strictly. Post-trade settlement procedures also suffered from some serious drawbacks, such as, high share of bad deliveries, delayed settlements, sometimes clubbing of settlements, etc. The procedures relating to investor protection were also not satisfactory.

Some of the major developments/changes, which have radically transformed the structure of the Indian capital market since 1992, are set out below:

New Capital Issues

Raising of capital from the securities market before 1992 was regulated. Under the Capital Issues (Control) Act, 1947, firms were required to obtain approval from the Controller of Capital Issues (CCI) for raising resources in the market. New companies were allowed to issue shares only at par. Only the existing companies with substantial reserves could issue shares at a premium, which was based on some prescribed formula. In 1992, the Capital Issues (Control) Act, 1947 was repealed and with this ended all controls relating to raising of resources from the market. Since then the issuers of securities could raise the capital from the market without requiring any consent from any authority either for making the issue or for pricing it. Restrictions on rights and bonus issues have also been removed. New as well as established companies are now able to price their issues according to their assessment of market conditions. However, issuers of capital are required to meet the guidelines of SEBI on disclosure and investor protection. Companies issuing capital are required to make sufficient disclosures, including justification of the issue price and also material disclosure about the 'risk factors' in their offering prospectus. These guidelines have served as an important measure for protecting investor's interest and promoting the development of the primary market along sound lines.

Book Building

Book building, introduced in 1995, is basically *a* capital issuance process used in Initial Public Offer (IPO) which aids price and demand discovery. It is a process used for marketing a public offer of equity shares of a company. It is a mechanism where, during the period for which the book for the IPO is open, bids are collected from investors at various prices, which are above or equal to the floor price. The process aims at tapping both wholesale and retail investors (Box-1). The offer/issue price is then determined after the bid closing date based on certain evaluation criteria.

Box-1

PROCESS OF BOOK BUILDING

i)   The Issuer who is planning an IPO nominates a lead merchant banker as a 'book runner'.

ii) The Issuer specifies the number of securities to be issued and the price band for orders.

iii) The Issuer also appoints syndicate members with whom orders can be placed by the investors.

iv) Investors place their order with a syndicate member who inputs the orders into the 'electronic book'. This process is called 'bidding' and is similar to open auction.

v)   A Book should remain open for *a* minimum of 5 days.

vi) Bids cannot be entered less than the floor price.

```


vii) Bids can be revised by the bidder before the issue closes.

viii) On the close of the book building period the book runner evaluates the bids on the basis of the evaluation criteria which may include -
— Price Aggression
— Investor quality
— Earliness of bids, etc.

ix) The book runner and the company conclude the final price at which it is willing to issue the stock and allocation of securities.

x) Generally, the number of shares are fixed, the issue size gets frozen based on the price per share discovered through the book building process.

xi) Allocation of securities is made to the successful bidders.

xii) Book Building is a good concept and represents a capital market which is in the process of maturing.

Rules governing book building is covered in Chapter XI of the Securities and Exchange Board of India (Disclosure and Investor Protection) Guidelines 2000. BSE offers the book building services through the Book Building that runs on the BSE Private network. This system is one of the largest electronic book building networks anywhere spanning over 350 Indian cities through over 7000 Trader Work Stations via eased lines, VSATs and Campus LANS. The softwere is operated through book-runners of the issue and by the syndicate member brokers. Through this book, the syndicate member brokers on behalf of themselves or their clients' place orders.

Bids are placed electronically through syndicate members and the information is collected on line real-time until the bid date ends. In order to maintain transparency, the software gives visual graphs displaying price v/s quantity on the terminals. Corporates may raise capital in the primary market by way of an initial public offer, rights issue or private placement. An Initial Public Offer (IPO) is the selling of securities to the public in the primary market. This Initial Public Offering can be made through the fixed price method, book building method or a combination of bothy. In case the issuer chooses to issue securities through the book building route then as per SEBI guidelines, an issuer company can issue securities by: (a) 100% of the net offer to the public through the book building route. (b) 75% of the net offer to the public through the book building process and 25% through the fixed price portion. Box-2 shows the difference between shares offered through book building and offer of share through normal public issuer.

Box-2

| Features | Fixed Price process | Book Building process |
|---|---|---|
| Pricing | Price at which the securities are offered/allotted is known in advance to the investor. | Price at which securities will be offered / allotted is not known in advance to the investor. Only an indicative price range is known. |
| Demand | Demand for the securities offered is known only after the closure of the issue | Demand for the securities offered can be known everyday as the book is built. |
| Payment | Payment if made at the time of subscription wherein refund is given after allocation. | Payment only after allocation. |

Both BSE and NSE offer their infrastructure for conducting on-line IPOs through book building. A related development has been the efforts to market IPOs through the existing secondary market infrastructure (trading terminals of stock exchanges, brokers, etc.). A number of initiatives were taken to further rationalise the Initial Public Offer (IPO) norms. These are set out in Box-3.
```

Box 3

IPO NORMS

i) SEBI (Disclosure and Investor Protection) Guidelines require a minimum offering of 25 per cent of post issue capital to public. This requirement was relaxed to 10 per cent, first for companies in the Information Technology sector, and then in the entertainment, media and telecom sectors.

ii) In December 2000, this relaxation was extended to companies in all sectors. SEBI also kept the minimum offering size at ₹ 100 crore and retained the existing limit of minimum public offer of 20 lakh shares. Companies not meeting the prescribed conditions need to make a minimum public offering of 25 per cent.

ii) With a view-to enhancing the quality of issues in the primary market, SEBI tightened the entry norms for IPOs. Accordingly, IPOs of issue size upto 5 times the pre-issue networth shall be allowed only if the company has track record of profitability and networth as specified in the Guidelines.

iv) The book building route has been made compulsory for companies, which do not have such track record. Further, 60 per cent of the offer made by them should be allotted to Qualified Institutional Buyers (QIBs) comprising financial institutions, banks, mutual funds, FIIs and VCFs registered with SEBI. Inability to meet this condition would mean failure of the issue.

v) The book-building route has also been made compulsory for IPOs with issue size more than 5 times the pre-issue networth and for public issues by listed companies worth more than 5 times the pre-issue networth. In these cases also success of the issue requires allocation of 60 per cent of the offer to QIBs.

vi) The lock-in provisions applicable to IPOs have been rationalised. While the lock-in period for minimum promoters' contribution of 20 per cent shall continue to be 3 years, the balance of the entire pre- IPO capital held by promoters or others shall be locked in for 1 year from the date of allotment of the IPO.

vii) It has also been decided to lock in the shares issued on preferential basis by a listed company to any person for one year from the date of their allotment except in respect of issues involving share swap for acquisition.

viii) The procedures for allotment of shares and refunds were streamlined. The time for finalising the allotment has been reduced from 30 to 15 days in book-built issues so as to minimise the risk arising from volatility.

SEBI decision to amend. The IPO regulations on August 26, 2005 would take the IPO process another step towards being transparent, equitable and investor friendly. Allotment to the category of Qualified Institutional Biodders (QIB) comprising on proportionate basis as in the case of retail investors would put an end to the controversies raised by certain domestic mutual funds and financial institution over the alleged prefered allotment to the FIIs. Of course, investment bankers were not too happy with the change and felt that the post-listing price may drop as QIBS with a short-term outlook — namely hedge funds — might book profits on listing. If indeed this happens, it may not be a bad thing after all, as it will make IPO investment a serious business rather than a lottery game. Long-term investors never look for listing gains anyway and are not going to be disturbed by a low listing price.

SEBI has also addressed the other important issue of QIBs not being required to make advance payment *a la* retail investors while applying for an IPO. Once the new regulations are in place, the QIBs will have to pay 10 per cent of the value of the shares they are applying for, along with the application.

The existing system discriminated between institutional and retail investors; while the former did not have to pay any money upfront, the latter had to pay the full value of the shares they were applying for. The result was that in their desire to secure maximum allotment, institutional bidders collectively bid for disproportionately high numbers of shares in relation to those on offer, exploiting the fact that there was no need to commit money upfront. Such speculative bidding had had the twin effect of skewing the response pattern to the offer and influencing the pricing decision. When the number of shares bid for at the upper end of the price band exceeded those on offer, the temptation was to price the IPO at that level.

SEBI's endeavour to correct this situation must be appreciated but it is doubtful if a 10 per cent margin will be enough to curb speculative bidding by the QIBs. A higher margin may be necessary to ensure that institutional bidders do not resort to speculative bidding. However, a start has been made and, hopefully, SEBI will review this threshold based on responses to future IPOs.

While the issues addressed now are important, SEBI may have to soon focus on yet another aspect of the IPO process —— funding by banks and other institutions. At present, with funds easily available, a number of investors, particularly in the high net worth (HNI) category, and also some retail investors, borrow short term to invest in IPOs. Their strategy is to secure allotment and dump the shares on the listing day to book profits. This category of non-serious bidders end up skewing the picture as they put in disproportionately high bids to maximise their speculative gains. They have to make enough profit when they dump their shares to cover the interest charge they pay the financier. The vested interest that they, therefore, have in the stock listing at a price substantially higher than the allotment price, has led to allegations of rigging of the listing price.

SEBI has made it compulsory for companies coming out with IPOs of equity shares to get their IPOs graded by at least one credit rating agency registered with SEBI from May 1, 2007. This measure is intended to provide the investor with an informed and objective opinion expressed by a professional rating agency after analyzing factors like business and financial prospects, management quality and corporate governance practices etc. The grading would be disclosed in the prospectus, abridged prospectus and in every advertisement for IPOs.

Depository System

A depository is an organisation, which assists in the allotment and transfer of securities, and securities lending. The shares in a depository are held in the form of electronic accounts, i.e., in dematerialised form and the depository system revolves around the concept of paper-less or scrip-less trading. An effective and fully developed securities depository system is essential for maintaining and enhancing the market effeciency, which is one of the core characteristics of a mature capital market. In March 1989, the 'Group of Thirty' had emphasised the importance of a central depository by highlighting the adverse effect on global investment brought about by the inefficiencies of international settlement and clearing facilities in their Report on "Clearance and Settlement Systems in the World's Securities Markets". The depository and custodial service is one of the key ingredients of the developed markets like Japan, UK and the USA. Some of the developing countries like Korea, Hong Kong, Malaysia, Sri Lanka, Taiwan and Thailand have also set up depository systems. The depository system provides a wide range of service, viz., primary market services, secondary market services and ancilliary services.

In the case of primary market services, the depository through its participants works as a link between issuers and prospective shareholders. In the secondary market, the depository through participants as a link between the investor and dealing house of the exchange to facilitate settlements of the security transactions through book- keeping entries. Further, the depository can provide ancillary services like collecting dividends and interests and reporting corporate information.

In India the need for setting up a depository was realised after the large scale irrgularities in securities transactions of 1992 exposed the limitations of the prevailing settlement system. The need for depository system was also realised for the healthy growth of primary market, which would reduce the time between the allotment of shares and transfer of entitlements arising out of each allotment. As India has a large number of listed companies involving a massive amount of paper work, there have been stolen share., forged/fake certificates, etc., which pose a threat to the security of investment. The idea of setting up a depository and the introduction of scripless trading and settlement were thus conceived for improving the efficiency of the markets and eliminating the various problems associated with dealing in physical certificates. A depository system benefits the investing public, the issuers of securities, the intermediates and the nation as a whole.

The move on depository system in India was initiated by the Stock Holding Corporation of India Limited (SHCIL) in July 1992 when it prepared a concept paper on "National Clearance and Depository System" in collaboration with Price Waterhouse under a programme sponsored by the U.S. Agency for International Development. Thereafter, the Government of India constituted a Technical Group under the Chairmanship of Shri R. Chandrasekaran, Managing Director, SHCIL, which submitted its Report in December 1993. The Securities and Exchange Board of India (SEBI) constituted a seven-member action squad subsequently to discuss the various structural and operational parameters of Depository System. Considering the various problems and issues, the Government of India promulgated the Depositories Ordinance in September -1995, thus paving the way for setting up of depositories in the country. The Depositories Act was passed by the Parliament in August 19%, which lays down the legislative framework for facilitating the dematerialisation and book entry transfer of securities in a depository. The Act provides that a depository, which is required to be a company under the Companies Act, 1956, and depository participants (i.e. agents of the depository) need to be registered with SEBI. The depository shall carry out the dematerialisation of securities and the transfer of beneficial ownership through electronic book entry. The investors, however, have the option to hold securities in physical or dematerialised form, or to rematerialise securities previously held in dematerialised form SEBI issued a Consultative Paper No. X on the draft regulations for depositories and participants in October 1995 for wider consultation and notified the regulations in May 1996, which, *inter alia*, cover the norms for registration of depositories and participants, the eligibility criteria for admission of securities to a depository, the specific rights and obligations of depositories, participants and issuers, the periodic reports to and inspections by SEBI. The Deposits Related Laws (Amendment) Ordinance, 1997 issued in January 1997 enabled units of mutual funds and UTI, securities of statutory corporations and public corporations to be dealt through depositories.

The National Securities Depository Limited (NSDL), the first depository in India which has been promoted by three premier institutions in India, viz., IDBI, UTI and NSE, started operating from November 8,1996. NSDL carries out its operations through participants and the clearing corporation of the stock exchange, with participants acting as market intermediaries through whom NSDL interacts with the investors and the clearing members. To begin with, only the capital market segment of the National Stock Exchange of India Limited (NSE) has been associated with the NSDL as only the NSE has a clearing corporation (NSCCL), which guarantees performance of trade obligations and has been admitted into the depository.

The Depository Act provides for multiple depository system. Many other organisations are in the process of setting up depositories. The BSE has decided to set up its own depository (with capital of ₹ 100 crores). As the network of depositories expands and the proportion of securities dematerialised increases, the benefits would percolate to the vast majority of market participants and investors.

Safe and quick transfer of securities is an important element for smooth and efficient functioning of the securities market. Apart from the problems involved in the movement of physical security certificates, bad deliveries due to faulty paper work, theft, forgery etc. added to the transaction cost and restricted liquidity. To overcome these difficulties, legislative changes were carried out for maintaining ownership records in an electronic book-entry form. Under this mode, securities are transferred in a speedy and safe manner without interposition of issuers in the process, except in few circumstances. In order to catalyse the process of dematerialisation of securities and dematerialised trading, an element of compulsion was Introduced by requiring the individual and institutional investors to settle trades compulsorily in dematerialised form in shares of select companies.

The efficiency of automated *vis-a-vis* floor-based trading system in the secondary segment of the market is widely debated, although the evidence around the world suggests that markets are moving away from the floor-based trading system. Over time, floor-based trading is likely to disappear, going by the trends noticed so far. Transparency is the major factor in debates over floor-based system *versus* electronic system and proponents of the automated system contend that floor-based trading is inefficient and less transparent. Many major international stock markets, such as, London, Paris, Toronto, Frankfurt and Sydney, conduct electronic trading.

Till recently, trading on the Indian stock exchanges took place through open outcry system barring NSE and OTCEI, which adopted screen-based trading system from the beginning (*i.e.*, 1994 and 1992, respectively). At present all other stock exchanges have adopted on-line screen-based electronic trading, replacing the open outcry system. Of the two large stock exchanges, the BSE provides a combination of order and quote driven trading system, while NSE has only an order driven system. In an order driven system, orders from all over India are entered into the electronic system and matched directly on a continuous basis without the involvement of a jobber or market maker. In a quote driven system, the market makers offer two way quotes and are ready to buy and sell any quantity. With the introduction of computerised trading, members could enter their orders/quotes on work stations installed in their offices instead of assembling in the trading ring.

There are three main advantages of electronic trading over floor-based trading as observed in India, *viz.*, transparency, more efficient price discovery, and reduction in transaction costs. Transparency ensures that stock prices fully reflect available information and lowers the trading costs by enabling the investor to assess overall supply and demand. Owing to computer-based trading, the speed with which new information gets reflected in prices has increased tremendously. The quantity and quality of Information provided to market participants during the trading process (pre-trading and post-trading) having significant bearing on the price formation has also improved. Besides, the screen-based trading has the advantage of integrating different trading centres all over the country into a single trading platform. It may be noted that prior to screen-based trading, the very presence of stock markets in different regions implied segmentation of markets affecting the price discovery process. Investors in other locations were, under such conditions, unable to participate in the price formation process at the major stock exchange, namely the BSE. However, with screen-based trading spread across various locations, the process of price discovery has improved in the Indian stock markets. Screen-based trading has also led to significant reduction in the transaction cost since it enabled the elimination of a chain of brokers for execution of orders from various locations at BSE and NSE.

The Depositories in India provide depository services to investors through Depository Participants (DPs). The Depositories do not charge the investors directly, but charge their DPs who in turn charge the clients. DPs are free to have their own charge structure for their clients. However, as per SEBI directive, DPs cannot charge investors towards opening of a Beneficiary Owner (BO) account (except statutory charges), credit of securities into BO account and custody charges. It may be added that the depositories have been reducing its charges along with the growth in volumes. The charges levied on DPs by NSDL and CDSL are presented in (Table 1).

TABLE 1

Service Charges levied by the Depositories end of June 2008

Depositories Services	NSDL	CDSL
Dematerialisation	Nil	Nil
Rematerialisation	a) ₹ 10 for every hundred securities or part thereof; or b) a flat fee of ₹ 10/- per certificate which ever is higher,	A fee of ₹ 10/- for every 100 securities or part thereof; or a Flat fee of ₹ 10/- per certificate, whichever is higher. (However, no fee shall be collected in case of government securities where rematerialisation is used for transfer to other SGL participant account and units of UTI and other mutual funds where rematerialisation is used for redemption / repurchase.)
Custody	Nil	Nil
Settlement Fee	₹ 5 per debit instruction	₹ 500 per month on Clearing Members' settlement related accounts. ₹6/- per transaction is levied on Beneficial Owner accounts only for debit transactions.
Pledge Creation	₹ 25 per instruction	12 /- per request (only Pledgor)
Pledge Closure	Nil	121- per request (only Pledgor)
Pledge Invocation	Nil	Nil
Securities Borrowing		Facility not currently used

Source: NSDL & CDSL.

Trading Rules

Trading by member brokers is subject to some restrictions. These relate to margining system, intra-day trading limit and exposure limit. Each broker is subject to margins and to the trading limit. Various types of margins, such as, daily margins, mark to market margin, ad hoc margin and volatility margins to contain price volatility, are in place.

There is also an intra-day trading limit, which is the limit to volume. Each broker's trading volume during a day is not allowed to exceed the intra-day trading limit. In case a broker wishes to exceed this limit, he or she has to deposit additional capital with the exchange. Thus, brokers are now required to have adequate capital in relation to their positions. With a view to enhancing market safety, the upper limit for gross exposure of the member-broker of the stock exchange has been fixed at 20 times of his capital. These restrictions have an iImpact on daily transaction volume and daily volatility.

Thus, SEBI has put in place an elaborate risk management system in consultation with both stock exchanges and market participants. However, over time the system acquired complexity and rigidity. SEBI therefore reviewed the entire risk management system comprising the margin system, exposure norms, circuit filter, capital adequacy, etc. and designed a simplified system without in any way diluting safety and efficiency aspects. The salient features of the system implemented by SEBI are: price band of 200 scrips and scrips under the compulsory rolling settlement has been relaxed to 16 per cent; scrip-limit in carry forward position under the Modified Carry Forward System (MCFS) or on the trade positions in the Automated Lending and Borrowing Mechanism (ALBM) has been placed at ₹ 5 crore per scrip for a member in account period and also in rolling settlement; member-wise carry forward position under MCFS or on the trade positions under ALBM has been raised from ₹ 20 crore to ₹ 40 crore as an aggregate exposure of account period and rolling settlement; the slabs for volatility margins and the margin rates for account period have been revised: for volatility range of more than 80 per cent but up to 100 per cent at 10 per cent, more than 100 per cent but up to 150 per cent at 15 per cent and more than 150 per cent at 25 per cent; no volatility margin has been prescribed under compulsory rolling settlement system; the minimum cash component to be deposited by the broker has been fixed at 30 per cent of the total margin; and, finally, to encourage delivery-based transactions, it has been decided that the margins can be provided as bank guarantee, cash component need not be insisted. Further, the Negotiated Dealing System (NDS) (Phase I) was operationalised with effect from February 15,2002 with 41 participants.The NDS provides on-line electronic bidding facility in the primary auctions of Central/State Government securities and OMO/LAF auctions. It enables screen-based electronic dealing and reporting of transactions in money market instruments, secondary market transactions in government securities and facilitates dissemination of information on trades with the minimal time lag. It also permits "paperless settlement of transactions in government securities with electronic connectivity to the Clearing Corporation of India Limited (CCIL) and the delivery *versus* payment (DVP) settlement system at the Public Debt Office.

The CCIL also commenced its operations from February 15, 2002 in clearing and settlement of transactions in government securities. Acting as a central counterparty through novation, the CCIL provides guaranteed settlement and has in place risk management systems to limit settlement risk. It operates a settlement guarantee fund (SGF) made up of contributions from its members and backed by lines of credit from commercial banks (Box-4). All repo transactions have to be necessarily put through the CCIL while all outright transactions up to ₹ 20 crore have to be settled through the CCIL. The option to settle outright transactions in government securities above the face value of ₹ 20 crore either directly with the Reserve Bank or through the CCIL is available to NDS members.

Box-4

RISK MANAGEMENT BY THE CLEARING CORPORATION OF INDIA LIMITED (CCIL)

The CCIL has been set up to function as an industry service organisation for clearing and settlement of trades in foreign exchange, government securities and other debt instruments. It is owned by major banks (58.5 per cent of the equity), financial institutions (24 per cent of equity) and primary dealers (17.5 per cent of equity). As the Central Counter Party (CCP) to all trades executed by its members, the CCIL is required to have a sound system for risk management since the failure of a CCP would have serious systemic consequences, especially where multiple markets are served by one CCP. The CCIL manages various risks and reallocates risk among its participants as set out below.

1. Credit and Market risk

(i) Securities Transactions-The operation of the CCIL through a delivery *versus* payment (DVP) mechanism in the books of the Reserve Bank eliminates any principal risk (loss of assets purchased) of default. In case of any default, the CCIL's risk is essentially limited to market risk arising from any adverse change in the price of the security. The CCIL covers this risk by making members maintain initial margins to cover future adverse movements of prices of the securities as well as mark-to-market margin to cover the notional loss, *i.e.*, the difference between the current market price and the contract price in respect of the outstanding trades. The margins are computed trade-wise. The initial margin requirement for each trade is calculated by multiplying the value of the security by a margin factor (calculated on the basis of security-specific VaR) for the security. The mark-to-market margin is required to be maintained by members holding adverse positions; no credit is allowed for positions with notional gains. Members are required to maintain adequate balances in the Settlement Guarantee Fund (SGF) in the form of eligible government securities/Treasury Bills and cash (minimum 10 per cent) to cover the margin requirements in respect of their trades. For securities deposited into the SGF, a 'haircut' is applied which is currently at 5 per cent.

(ii) Foreign Exchange Transactions - Unlike in securities transactions which settle on a DVP basis, default in foreign exchange transactions because of time zone differences results in the loss of the asset purchased. The CCIL does not, however, bear this principal risk which is borne by the members; in its role as the CCP, CCIL ensures the liquidity of the system by delivering the counter-value funds to the buyer on the value date. Credit risk arising on account of a member's default in settlement of its obligation in a currency is managed by the CCIL by resorting to its loss allocation mechanism (*i.e.*, by apportioning the loss arising out of such default, net of the margin collected from the defaulting member, to its counterparties in proportion of their net buy position *vis-a-vis* the defaulting member in the currency of default). To ensure that the members are in a position to absorb any loss due to default in a foreign exchange trade, membership is restricted to authorised dealers with a threshold level of financial strength assessed by using a model based on criteria like capital, profitability, asset quality, liquidity size, *etc*. The maximum exposure to be taken by the CCIL on a member or Net Debit Cap (NDC), is arrived at on this basis. The margin factor of a member is decided on the basis of the financial standing. The margin factor also includes a factor for Rupee/US dollar exchange rate volatility (VaR at 99 per cent confidence level for three-day holding period). The actual exposure taken by the CCIL to a member is decided by the margin factor and the value of SGF contribution, with NDC acting as the outer limit. Utilisation of the Exposure Limit by member banks is monitored to ensure that there is no breach of limit. Any exposure in excess of NDC is entirely covered by deposits by the member in US dollars. It is ensured (through appropriate computation of the margin factors) that the collateral collected from the members is sufficient to secure a line of credit (fully collateralised) large enough to absorb at least the default by the member having the largest NDC. The settlement bank would provide the credit line.

2. Liquidity Risk - The CCIL's primary commitment is to ensure uninterrupted settlement and therefore it is required to provide adequate liquidity in terms of government securities, rupee funds and US dollar funds for completion of settlements. To cover its liquidity risk, CCIL has arranged

(i) rupee securities through members' contribution to the SGF;

(ii) rupee funds through lines of credit with various banks; the securities in the SGF could also be used for repo operations in the market with PDs/banks which, in turn, could use the securities for repos with the Reserve Bank under the Liquidity Adjustment Facility (LAF);

(iii) US dollar funds by way of a fully collateralised line of credit with the settlement bank, (collateralised by members' contribution to the SGF in US dollars) which would be enough to absorb at least the default by the member having the largest NDC. An additional clean committed line of credit of substantial amount has also been arranged from the settlement bank. In case these lines are not enough for completion of settlement at the time designated, a Shortfall Allocation Procedure, along the lines of the Loss Allocation Mechanism is initiated.

3. Operational Risk - To deal with operational risk, the CCIL is developing a fully automated system for processing trades. CCIL's computer systems are robust with sufficient redundancies built in to support; uninterrupted operations. The trade data are received from the Negotiated Dealing System in an automated process avoiding possible human errors. A Disaster Recovery Site is being set up at the Institute for Development and Research in Banking Technology (IDRBT), Hyderabad to ensure business continuity *in* case of a disaster. High level of data security has been implemented using latest technologies like Firewall and PK! based encryption. Suitable personnel have been recruited and appropriate authority structure, workflow design and control systems are in place.

Source: Clearing Corporation of India Ltd.

Insider Trading

Insider Trading is considered as an offence and is hence prohibited as per the SEBI (Prohibition of Insider Trading) Regulations, 1992. The same was amended in the year 2003. The act prohibits an insider from dealing (on his behalf or on behalf of any other person) in securities of a company listed on any stock exchange, when in possession of any unpublished price sensitive information. Further, it has also prohibited any insider from communicating, counseling or procuring directly or indirectly any unpublished price sensitive information to any person who while in possession of such unpublished price sensitive information should not deal in securities. Price sensitive information means any information which is related directly or indirectly to a company and which if published is likely to materially affect the price of securities of a company. It includes information like periodical financial results of the company, intended declaration of dividends (both interim and final), issue of securities or buy-back of securities, any major expansion plans or execution of new projects, amalgamation, merger or takeovers, disposal of the whole or substantial part of the undertaking and significant changes in policies, plans or operations of the company. SEBI is empowered to investigate on the basis of any complaint received from the investors, intermediaries or any other person on any matter having a bearing on the allegations of insider trading. SEBI can also investigate suo motu upon its own knowledge or information in its.

Unfair Trade Practices

The SEBI (Prohibition of Fraudulent and Unfair Trade Practices relating to the Securities Market) Regulations 2003 enable SEBI to investigate into cases of market manipulation and fraudulent and unfair trade practices. The regulations specifically prohibit fraudulent dealings, market manipulations, misleading statements to induce sale or purchase of securities, unfair trade practices relating to securities. When SEBI has reasonable ground to believe that the transaction in securities are being dealt within a manner detrimental to the investor or the securities market in violation of these regulations and when any intermediary has violated the rules and regulations under the act then it can order to investigate the affairs of such intermediary or persons associated with the securities market. Based on the report of the investigating officer, SEBI can initiate action for suspension or cancellation of registration of an intermediary.

Sweat Equity

As per provisions of the Companies (Amendment) Ordinance, companies can issue sweat equity shares subject to authorisation by a resolution passed by a general meeting. The expression 'Sweat Equity' refers to equity shares issued by a company to directors or employees at a discount or for consideration other than cash for providing know-how or making available rights in the nature of intellectual property rights or value additions. All limitations, restrictions and provisions relating to equity shares are applicable to sweat equity shares. It is worth noting here that Guidelines were issued in June 1998 to facilitate issue of GDR/ADR linked stock option to its employees by a company engaged in manufacture or production of software where not less than 80 per cent of the company's turnover is from software activities.

Takeovers

The restructuring of companies through takeover is governed by SEBI (Substantial Acquisition of shares and Takeover) Regulations, 1997. These regulations were formulated so that the process of acquisition and takeovers is carried out in a well-defined and orderly manner following the fairness and transparency.

In context of this regulation 'acquirer' is defined as a person who directly or indirectly acquires or agrees to acquire shares or voting rights in the target company or acquires or agrees to acquires 'control'over the target company, either by himself or with any person acting in concert with the acquirer. The term 'control' includes right to appoint majority of the directors or to control the management or policy decisions exercisable by any person or persons acting individually or in concert, directly or indirectly, including by virtue of their shareholding or management rights or shareholders agreements or voting agreements or in any other manner. This implies that where there are two or more persons in control over the target company, the cesser of any one of such persons from such control should not be deemed to be in control of management.

Certain categories of persons are required to disclose their shareholding and/or control in a listed company to that company. Such companies, in turn, are required to disclose such details to the stock exchanges where shares of the company are listed. In case of acquisition of 5 percent and more share or voting rights of a company, an acquirer would have to disclose at every stage the aggregate of his shareholding or voting rights in that company to the company and to the stock exchange where shares of the target company are listed.

No acquirer either by himself or through/with persons acting in concert with him should acquire, additional shares or voting rights unless such acquirer makes a public announcement to acquire shares in accordance with the regulations. As per the regulations, the mandatory public offer is triggered on:

i) Limit of 15 percent or more but less than 55 percent of the shares or voting rights in a company.

ii) Limit of 55 percent or more but less than 75 percent of the shares. In a case where the target company had obtained listing of its shares by making an offer of at least ten percent of issue size to the public in terms of the relevant clause mentioned in the Securities Contracts (Regulations) Rules 1957 or in terms of any relaxation granted from strict enforcement of the said rule, then the limit would be 90 percent instead of 75 percent. Further, if the acquire (holding 55 % more but less than 75 percent) is desirous of consolidating his holding while ensuring that the public shareholding in the target company does not fall below the minimum level permitted in the listing agreement, he may do so only by making a public announcement in accordance with these regulations.

Irrespective of whether or not there has been any acquisition of shares or voting rights in a company, no acquirer should acquire control over the target company, unless such person makes a public announcement to acquire shares and acquires such shares in accordance with the regulations.

The regulations give enough scope for existing shareholders to consolidate and also cover the scenario of indirect acquisition of control. The applications for takeovers are scrutinised by the Takeover Panel constituted by the SEBI.

Buy Back

Buy Back is done by the company with the purpose to improve liquidity in its shares and enhance the shareholders' wealth. Under the SEBI (Buy Back of Securities) Regulations, 1998, a company is permitted to buy back its shares or other specified securities by any of the following methods:-

i) From the existing security holders on a proportionate basis through the tender offer

ii) From the open market through (i) book building process (ii) stock exchange

iii) From odd-lot holders.

The company has to disclose the pre and post-buy back holding of the promoters. To ensure completion of the buy back process speedily, the regulations have stipulated time limit for each step. For example in the cases of purchases through tender offer an offer for buy back should not remain open for more than 30 days. The company should complete the verifications of the offers received within 15 days of the closure of the offer and shares or other specified securities. The payment for accepted securities has to be made within 7 days of the completion of verification and bought back shares have to be extinguished and physically destroyed within 7 days of the date of the payment. Further, the company making an offer for buy back will have to open an escrow account on the same lines as provided in takeover regulations.

Circuit Breakers

Volatility in stock prices is a cause of concern for both the policy makers and the investors. To curb excessive volatility, SEBI has prescribed a system of circuit breakers. The circuit breakers bring about a nation-wide coordinated halt in trading on all the equity and equity derivatives markets. An index based market-wide circuit breaker system applies at three stages of the index movement either way at 10%, 15% and 20%. The breakers are triggered by movement of either Nifty 50 or Sensex, whichever is breached earlier.

Further, the NSE views entries of non-genuine orders with utmost seriousness as this has market-wide repercussion. It may suo-moto cancel the orders in the absence of any immediate confirmation from the members that these orders are genuine or for any other reason as it may deem fit. As an additional measure of safety, individual scrip-wise price bands has been fixed as below:

i) Daily price bands of 2% (either way) on a set of specified securities,

ii) Daily price bands of 5% (either way) on a set of specified securities,

iii) Price bands of 20% (either way) on all remaining securities (including debentures, warrants, preference shares etc which are traded on CM segment of NSE),

iv) Daily price bands of 10% (either way) on specified securities,

v) No price bands are applicable on scrips on which derivative products are available or on scrips included in indices on which derivatives products are available.

For auction market the price bands of 20% are applicable. In order to prevent members from entering orders at non-genuine prices in these securities, the Exchange has fixed operating range of 20% for such securities.

Short Selling and Securities Lending and Borrowing

Pursuant to the recommendations of the Secondary Market Advisory Committee (SMAC) of SEBI and the decision of the SEBI Board

To operationalise Short selling and securities lending and borrowing from Monday, April 21, 2008, it was decided to permit all classes of investors to short sell. It was also decided in consultation with Government of India and SEBI, to permit Foreign Institutional Investors (FIls) registered with SEBI and sub-accounts of FIls to short sell, lend and borrow equity shares of Indian companies. Short selling, lending and borrowing of equity shares of Indian companies would be subject to such conditions as may be prescribed in that behalf by the Reserve Bank and the SEBI / other regulatory agencies from time to time.

The above permission would be subjected to the following conditions:

(i)   The FIl participation in short selling as well as borrowing / lending of equity shares would be subject to the current FDI policy and short selling of equity shares by FIls would not be permitted for equity shares which are in the ban list and / or caution list of Reserve Bank.

(ii) Borrowing of equity shares by FIls would only be for the purpose of delivery into short sale.

(iii) The margin / collateral would be maintained by FIls only in the form of cash. No interest would be paid to the FIl on such margin/collateral.

The designated custodian banks would separately report all transactions pertaining to short selling of equity shares and lending and borrowing of equity shares by FIls in their daily reporting with a suitable remark (short sold / lent / borrowed equity shares) for the purpose of monitoring by RBI

Introduction of Direct Market Access Facility

Direct Market Access (DMA) is a facility which allows brokers to offer clients direct access to the exchange trading system through the broker's infrastructure without manual intervention by the broker. Some of the advantages offered by DMA are direct control of clients over orders, faster execution of client orders, reduced risk of errors associated with manual order entry, greater transparency, increased liquidity, lower impact costs for large orders, better audit trails and better use of hedging and arbitrage opportunities through the use of decision support tools / algorithms for trading. While ensuring conformity with the provisions of the Securities Contract (Regulations) Act, 1956 (42 of 1956), Stock Exchanges are required facilitate Direct Market Access for investors subject to the following conditions:

i) Application for Direct Market /Access (DMA) Facility

- Brokers interested to offer DMA facility would be required to apply to the respective stock exchanges giving details of the software and systems proposed to be used, which should be duly certified by a Security Auditor as reliable.

- The stock exchange would have to grant approval or reject the application as the case may be, and communicate its decision to the member within 30 calendar days of the date of completed application submitted to the exchange.

- The stock exchange, before giving permission to brokers to offer DMA facility would have to ensure the fulfillment of the applicable conditions

ii) Operational Specifications

- All DMA orders are required to be routed to the exchange trading system through the broker's trading system. The broker's server routing DMA orders to the exchange trading system should be located in India.

- The broker are required to ensure sound audit trail for all DMA orders and trades, and be able to provide identification of actual user-id for all such orders and trades. The audit trail data should available for at least 5 years.
- Exchanges should be able to identify and distinguish DMA orders and trades from other orders and trades. Exchanges should maintain statistical data on DMA trades and provide information on the same to SEBI on a need basis.
- The DMA system should have sufficient security features including password protection for the user ID, automatic expiry of passwords at the end of a reasonable duration, and reinitialisation of access on entering fresh passwords.
- Brokers would be required to follow the similar logic/priorities used by the Exchange to treat DMA client orders. Brokers would have to maintain all activities/alerts log with audit trail facility. The DMA Server should have internally generated unique numbering for all such client order/trades.
- A systems audit of the DMA systems and software should be periodically carried out by the broker as may be specified by the exchange and certificate in this regard should be submitted to the exchange.
- The exchanges and brokers would have to provide for adequate systems and procedures to handle the DMA trades.

iii) Client Authorization and Broker - Client Agreement

- Exchanges should specify from time to time the categories of investors to whom the DMA facility can be extended. Initially, the permission is restricted to institutional clients.
- Brokers should specifically authorize clients for providing DMA facility after fulfilling Know Your Client requirements and carrying out due diligence regarding clients' credit worthiness, risk taking ability, track record of compliance and financial soundness.
- Brokers should ensure that only those clients who are deemed fit and proper for this facility are allowed access to the DMA facility. Brokers should maintain proper records of such due diligence. Individual users at the client end would also be authorized by the broker based on minimum criteria. The records of user details, user-id and such authorization would be maintained by the broker. Details of all user-ids activated for DMA should be provided by the broker to the exchange.
- The broker should enter into a specific agreement with the clients for whom they permit DMA facility. This agreement should include the following safeguards:
  a) The client shall use the DMA facility only to execute his own trades and shall not use it for transactions on behalf of any other person / entity.
  b) Electronic/Automated Risk management at the broker's level before release of order to the Exchange system. The client should agree to be bound by the various limits that the broker should impose for usage of the DMA facility.
  c) Right to withdraw DMA facility if the limits set up are breached or for any other such concerns
  d) Withdrawal of DMA facility on account of any misuse or on instructions from SEBI/Exchange.
      Exchanges should prepare a model agreement for this purpose. The broker's agreement with clients should not have any clause that is less stringent/contrary to the conditions stipulated in the model agreement.

iv) Risk Management

The broker should ensure that trading limits/ exposure limits/ position limits are set for all DMA clients based on risk assessment, credit quality and available margins of the client. The broker system should have appropriate authority levels to ensure that the limits can be set up only by persons authorized by the risk / compliance manager.

The broker should ensure that all DMA orders are routed through electronic/automated risk management systems of the broker to carry out appropriate validations of all risk parameters including Quantity Limits, Price Range Checks, Order Value, and Credit Checks before the orders are released to the Exchange. All DMA orders should be subjected to the following limits:

a) Order quantity / order value limit in terms of price and quantity specified for the client.
b) All the position limits which are specified in the derivatives segment as applicable.
c) Net position that can be outstanding so as to fully cover the risk emanating from the trades with the available margins of the specific client.
d) Appropriate limits for securities which are subject to FII limits as specified by RBI.

The broker may provide for additional risk management parameters as they may consider appropriate.

v) Broker to be Liable for DMA Trades

The broker should be fully responsible and liable for all orders emanating through their DMA systems. It shall be the responsibility of the broker to ensure that only clients who fulfill the eligibility criteria are permitted to use the DMA facility

vi) Cross Trades

Brokers using DMA facility for routing client orders should not be allowed to cross trades of their clients with each other. All orders must be offered to the market for matching.

vii) Other Legal Provisions

In addition to the requirements mentioned above, all existing obligations of the broker as per current regulations and circulars should continue without change. Exchanges may also like to specify additional safeguards / conditions as they may deem fit for allowing DMA facilities to their brokers.

Institutional Trades

Trades by Mutual Funds and Foreign Institutional Investors are termed as Institutional trades. Transactions by MFs in the secondary market are governed by SEBI (Mutual Funds) Regulations, 1996. A MF under all its schemes is not allowed to own more than 10% of any company's paid-up capital. They are allowed to do only 'delivery-based' transactions. With effect from 21st April, 2008 a MF may engage in short selling of securities in accordance with the framework relating to short selling and securities lending and borrowing specified by SEBI. A MF cannot invest more than 10% of the NAV of a particular scheme in the equity shares or equity related instruments of a single company.

The investment by FIIs are governed by the rules and regulations of the RBI and the SEBI. As per the RBI guidelines, total holding of each FII/sub-accounts should not exceed 10 % of the total paid up capital or paid up value of each series of convertible debentures. Further total holding of all the FIIs/sub-accounts put together should not exceed 24 % of the paid up capital or paid up value of each series of convertible debentures. This limit of 24 % can be increased to the sectoral cap / statutory limit as applicable to the Indian Company concerned, by passing a resolution of its Board of Directors followed by a special resolution to that effect by its General Body.

Promoters to Compulsorily Disclose Details of Shares Pledged by Them

To enhance the disclosure requirements, the SEBI made it mandatory for promoters (including promoter group) to disclose the details of pledge of shares held by them in listed entities promoted by them. According to the regulator, such disclosures shall be made as and when the shares are pledged as well as *by* way of periodic disclosures. According to SEBI. details of pledge of shares and release/ sale of pledged shares will have to be made to the company and the company shall in turn inform the same to the public through the stock exchanges. However, promoters do not need to disclose whether they have pledged shares of the holding company of a listed entity. Instead, they will have to make adequate disclosures if the lenders sell the pledged shares in the open market. These rules will also apply to offshore transactions.

This decision was taken as lenders ask promoters to pay additional margins when the value of the shares pledged as collateral falls. The lenders then sell these shares in the market if promoters fail to pay margins. This could negatively impact the company's scrip on the bourses.

While this move by the regulator would improve corporate governance, it may impact M&A activities, particularly leveraged buyouts. A leveraged buyout refers to the acquisition of another company using a significant amount of borrowed money (bonds or loans) to meet the cost of acquisition. Often, the assets of the company being acquired are used as collateral for the loans in addition to the assets of the acquiring company. In international markets where no regulators require such disclosures, funding of leveraged buyouts is mostly done by pledging shares of the company to be acquired.

The market regulators also took the following decisions to further safeguard investor interest:

(i) *Listed companies are to declare dividend on per share basis only.* Earlier companies used to declare dividend either as a percentage of the face value or on per share basis. Dividend decalration as percentage of face value were misleading investors in cases where the face value of shares of two companies are different. In order to facilitate easy comparison of the quantum of dividends declared by different companies the SEBI mandated that all listed entities will have to declare dividend on per-share basis only.

(ii) *Timelines for bonus issues reduced:* SEBI reduced the timeline to complete a bonus issue to 15 days, if no share holder approval is required, and sixty days if shareholder approval is required. Indian companies have to complete bonus issue within 6 months from the dale of the board approval.

(iii) *Time frame for announcing the price band for Initial Public Offering (IPO) shortened:* The market regulator reduced the time frame for announcing the price band for an initial public offering to two working days prior to the issue opening for subscription the price band was required to be disclosed in the Red Herring Prospectus i.e. about two weeks before the date of opening of the IPO. The current volatile market conditions as well as the regulators drive towards overall reduction in time scale prompted this move.

(iv) *Review of preferential allotment guidelines for warrants:* The regulator decided to increase the upfront margin paid by allotees of warrants to 25 per cent from 10 per cent.

Securities Contracts (Regulation) Amendment Act, 2007

It was recognized that in India, the market for securitised debt remains underdeveloped. Despite two major initiatives, namely, the amendment of the National Housing Bank Act, 1987(NHB Act) in 2000; and enactment of the Securitisation and Reconstruction of Financial Assets and Enforcement of Security Interest Act, 2002 (SARFAESI Act), the market did not pick up because the facility of trading on stock exchanges was not available. This was, in part due to the fact that securitisation transactions under the NHB Act were not covered under the definition of 'securities' in the SCR Act. As a result, buyers of securitised financial instruments have few exit options.

Thus, the Securities Contracts Regulation Act, 1956 was amended in 2007 to include securitised instruments under the definition of 'securities' and provide for disclosure based regulation for issue of the securitized instruments and the procedure thereof. This has been done keeping in view that there is considerable potential in the securities market for the certificates or instruments under securitisation transactions. The development of the securitised debt market is critical for meeting the huge requirements of the infrastructure sector, particularly housing sector, in the country. Replication of the securities markets framework for these instruments would facilitate trading on stock exchanges and in turn help development of the market in terms of depth and liquidity.

PAN as the Sole Identification Number

The need for a Unique Identification Number (UIN) for market participants in the securities markets was felt in the interest of enforcement action. Presently, a person has variety of identification numbers such as Permanent Account Number (PAN) from CBDT, Depository Account Numbers from respective depositories, Bank Account Numbers from respective banks, MAPIN from SEBI, Unique Client Code from Exchanges, Director Identification Number from MCA, etc. and there is no arrangement to link these numbers.

It was felt that the PAN issued by the CBDT could be a UIN for market participants. A PAN could identify all participants and the account managers (Depositories, Banks, Exchanges, Insurance Companies, Pension Fund Managers, Post Offices, and Intermediaries etc.) must use these numbers. Following a budget announcement to this effect in the budget of 2007-08, SEBI has declared PAN the sole identification number for all transactions in securities market. It is an investor friendly measure as he does not have to maintain different identification numbers for different kinds of transactions/ different segments in financial markets.

In the Budget of 2008-09 it was proposed that the requirement of PAN be extended to all transactions in the financial market subject to suitable threshold exemption limits.

Real Estate Mutual Funds

After careful and detailed deliberations and consultation process, SEBI approved the launch of Real Estate Mutual funds (REMFs) and accordingly made necessary amendments to the SEBI (Mutual Fund) Regulations 1996 in April, 2008.

This product would allow retail investors to invest in real estate in a much more flexible and convenient manner. A REMF has investment objective to invest directly or indirectly in real estate property. Real estate the largest asset class in the world, may serve as a hedge against other asset classes like debt or equity. By including it in ones portfolio, an investor reduces risk and can achieve stable returns. Unlike other asset classes, real estate rarely earns negative returns, and does not suffer high volatility. Over years, the value of real estate usually increases manifold. This also makes it a good hedge against inflation. Real estate is a good long-term investment.

New Derivative Products

The Mini derivative Futures & Options contract was introduced for trading on S&PCNX Nifty on January 1, 2008 while the long term option contracts on S&P CNX Nifty were introduced for trading on March 3, 2008.

Volatility Index

With rapid changes in volatility in securities market from time to time, a need was felt for an openly available and quoted measure of market volatility in the form of an index to help market participants. On January 15, 2008, Securities and Exchange Board of India recommended Exchange to construct and disseminate the volatility index. Volatility Index is a measure, of the amount by which an underlying Index is expected to fluctuate, in the near term, (calculated as annualised volatility, denoted in percentage e.g. 20%) based on the order book of the underlying index options. On April 08, 2008, NSE launched the Volatility Index, India VIX, based on the Nifty 50 Index Option prices. From the best bid-ask prices of Nifty 50 Options contracts, a volatility figure (%) is calculated which indicates the expected market volatility over the next 30 calendar days. The India VIX is a simple but useful tool in determining the overall volatility of the market

Investment Options for Navaratna and Miniratna Public Sector Enterprises

The Navaratna and Miniratna Public Sector Enterprises have been allowed to invest in public sector mutual funds subject to the condition that they would not invest more than 30% of the available surplus funds in equity mutual funds and the Boards of PSEs would decide the guidelines, procedures and management control systems for such investment in consultation with their administrative Ministries.

Investor Protection and Education Fund (IPEF)

SEBI has set up the Investor Protection and Education Fund (IPEF) with the purpose of investor education and related activities. SEBI has contributed a sum of ₹ 10 crore toward the initial corpus of the IPEF from the SEBI General Fund. In addition following amounts will also be credited to the IPEF namely: (i) Grants and donations given to IPEF by the Central Government, State Governments or any institution approved by SEBI for the purpose of the IPEF;(ii) Interest or other income received out of the investments made from the IPEF; and (iii) Such other amount that SEBI may specify in the interests of the investors.

Cross Margining

Many trading members undertake transactions on both the cash and derivative segments of an Exchange. They keep separate deposits with the exchange for taking positions in two different segments. In order to improve the efficiency of the use of the margin capital by market participants SEBI introduced cross margining for institutional investors in May 2008.

In December 2008, SEBI extended the cross margin facility across Cash and F&O segment to all the market participants. The salient features of cross margining are as under:

1. Cross margin is available across Cash and F&O segment and to all categories of market participants.
2. The positions of clients in both the Cash and F&O segments to the extent they offset each other shall be considered for the purpose of cross margining as per the following priority.

    a) Index futures and constituent stock futures in F&O segment.
    b) Index futures and constituent stock positions in Cash segment.
    c) Stock futures in F&O segment and stock positions in Cash segment.

3. In order to extend the cross margin benefit as per 2 (a) and (b) above, the basket of constituent stock futures/ stock positions shall be a complete replica of the index futures.

4. The positions in F&O segment for stock futures and index futures shall be in the same expiry month to be eligible for cross margin benefit.

5. Positions in option contracts shall not be considered for cross margining benefit.

6. The Computation of cross margin shall be at client level on an on-line real time basis.

7. For institutional investors the positions in Cash segment shall be considered only after confirmation by the custodian on T+1 basis and on confirmation by the clearing member in F&O segment.

8. The positions in the Cash and F&O segment shall be considered for cross margining only till the time the margins are levied on such positions.

9. The positions which are eligible for offset, shall be subject to spread margins. The spread margins shall be 25% of the applicable upfront margins on the offsetting positions

ASBA

To make the existing public issue process more efficient, SEBI introduced a supplementary process of applying in public issues, viz, the 'Applications Supported by Blocked Amount (ASBA) in July 2008. ASBA is an application containing an authorization to block the application money in the bank account, for subscribing to an issue. If an investor is applying through ASBA, his application money is debited from the bank account only if his/her application is selected for allotment after the basis of allotment is finalized, or the issue is withdrawn/failed. In case of rights issue his application money is debited from the bank account after the receipt of instruction from the registrars. The ASBA process is available in all public issues made through the book building route. In September 2008, the ASBA facility was extended to Rights Issue.

ASBA facility has been extended to institutional investors in public issues from May 1, 2010. SEBI also made it compulsory for institutional investors to pay 100% money upfront for public issues as against 10%

On April 6, 2010, SEBI proposed to reduce the time between public issue closure and listing to 12 days from the existing (upto) 22 days. This would be applicable to public issues opening on or after May 1, 2010. With this ASBA process would have suitable modifications to make it consistent with the new timelines. This will make the public issue process more efficient.

POLICY INITIATIVES & REGULATORY DEVELOPMENTS DURING 2010-11

To bring transparency and to integrate Indian capital market with world markets policy initiatives have been taken to regulate the developments. Box-5 present the recent measures to regulate the development more effectively in the capital market.

Box - 5

KEY POLICY INITIATIVES & REGULATORY DEVELOPMENTS DURING 2010-11

Securities Contracts(Regulation) (Amendment) Rules, 2010 (June 04, 2010)

This amendment changed the face of Rule 19(2)(b) by making it more simpler. The said clause was substituted to provide that:

For the purpose of listing of securities on a recognized stock exchange, the stock exchange has to be satisfied that

    i.   At least 25 % of each class or kind of equity shares or debentures convertible into equity shares issued by the company was offered and allotted to public in terms of an offer document; or

    ii. At least 10 % of each class or kind of equity shares or debentures convertible into equity shares issued by the company was offered and allotted to public in terms of an offer document if the post issue capital of the company calculated at offer price is more than four thousand crore rupees

The second proviso provided that companies which have offered and allotted 10 % of each class of equity shares or debentures convertible into equity shares to public in terms of an offer document, shall increase the public shareholding to 25% by increasing it to the extent of at least 5% per annum beginning from the date of listing of the securities, in the manner specified by the SEBI.

The amendment also made it mandatory to make an application for listing in respect of all new issues of any class or kind of securities to be offered to the public and for all further issues of securities that are already listed on a recognized stock exchange.

Rule 19A was inserted to provide the following:

1) Every listed company shall maintain public shareholding of at least twenty five per cent. Any listed company which has public shareholding below twenty five percent, shall bring the public shareholding to twenty five percent by increasing its public shareholding to the extent of atleast five percent per annum.

2) Where the public shareholding in a listed company falls below 25% at any time, such company shall bring the public shareholding to 25% within a maximum period of 12 months from the date of such fall.

Securities Contracts(Regulation) (Second Amendment) Rules, 2010
(August 09, 2010)

This amendment made further changes which are as under:

(a) In Rule 19(2)(b), the second proviso was substituted to provided that companies which has offered and allotted 10 % of each class of equity shares or debentures convertible into equity shares to public in terms of an offer document, shall increase its public shareholding to at least 25% within a period of 3 years from the date of listing of the securities,

(b) Clause (c) was inserted to provide that a public sector company ("public sector company" means a body corporate constituted by an Act of the Parliament or any State Legislature and includes a government company) shall offer and allot at least 10% of each class or kind of equity shares or debentures convertible into equity shares to public in terms of an offer document

(c) Public sector companies were excluded from the scope of Rule 19A (d) Sub rule (1) of Rule 19A was amended as follows: Every listed company shall maintain public shareholding of at least twenty five per cent. Any listed company which has public shareholding below twenty five percent, shall increase its public shareholding to at least 25% within a period of 3 years

(e) In Rule 19A, sub- rule (3) was inserted to provide that

    i.   Every listed public sector company shall maintain public shareholding of at least 10%.

    ii. a listed public sector company has public shareholding below 10% on the date of commencement of this amendment shall increase its public shareholding to at least 10% within a period of 3 years from the date of such commencement

    iii. a listed public sector company whose public shareholding reduces below 10% after the date of commencement of this amendment, shall increase its public shareholding to at least 10% within a period of 12 months from the date of such reduction

SEBI (ISSUE OF CAPITAL AND DISCLOSURE REQUIREMENTS) REGULATIONS, 2009

ICDR Regulations were amended twice during the previous year by enactment of the Third Amendment and the Fourth Amendment Regulations. The major changes made are as under:

Change in definition of "Employee" in clause (m) of Reg 2, 13th April, 2010

The definition of employee has been made wider to include permanent and full-time employees of the holding company or subsidiary company or of that material associate(s) of the issuer whose financial statements are consolidated with the issuer's financial statements as per Accounting Standard 21.

Lock-in provisions in case of exempted category of preferential allotment

SEBI has restricted the lock-in provisions in case of exempted category of preferential allotment to allotments in terms of the rehabilitation scheme approved by the BIFR under the Sick Industrial Companies (Special Provisions) Act, 1985. Thus, lock-in requirements shall not apply in case of issue of shares pursuant to a scheme approved by a High Court under section 391 to 394 of the Companies Act, 1956.

Enlargement of Retail Individual Investors category in case of issue of IDR

The allocation to Retail Individual Investors in case of issue of IDRs has been increased from 15 % to 30%.

EMPLOYEES RESERVATION

SEBI has reduced the aggregate of employee reservation from ten percent to 5 percent of post issue capital of the company.

Chapter XA inserted: Issue of Specified Securities by Small and Medium Enterprises SEBI has provided relief to small and medium companies from hefty compliances required for issue of shares to public by introducing **Chapter XA** and SME Exchange. The main provisions of the said

Applicability: Compulsory for issuer whose post-issue face value capital does not exceed ten crore rupees• Optional for issuer, whose post issue face value capital is more than ten crore rupees and upto twenty five crore rupees

Definition of SME Exchange: A trading platform of a recognised stock exchange having nationwide trading terminals permitted by the Board to list the specified securitiesissued in accordance with this Chapter and includes a stock exchange granted recognition for this purpose but does not include the MainBoard

Issuer need not file draft prospectus with the Board: The issuer shall file a copy of the offer document with the Board through a merchant banker, simultaneously with the filing of the prospectus withthe SME exchange and the ROC or letter of offer with the SMEExchange and that the Board shall not issue any observation on the offer document.

Underwriting: The issue made under this Chapter shall be 100% underwritten.

Minimum Application Value & Minimum number of Allottees: To be stipulated in the offer document. However, the same shall not be less than one lakh rupees per application. Prospective allottees cannotbe less than fifty.

Migration to SME Exchange: A listed issuer whose post-issue face value capital is less than 25 crore rupees may migrate its specified securities to SME exchange if itsshareholders approve such migration by passing a special resolution tothis effect and if such issuer fulfils the eligibility criteria for listing laid down by the SME exchange.

Migration to MainBoard: Where the issuer's post issue face value capital is more than 10 crore and upto 25 crore, the issuer has an option to migrate its specifiedsecurities to Main Board if its shareholders approve such migration by passing a special resolution through postal ballot to this effect and ifsuch issuer fulfils the eligibility criteria for listing laid down by the Main Chapter are stated hereunder:

Board

Where the issuer's post issue face value capital is likely to increasebeyond 25 crore rupees by virtue of any further issue of capital, the issuer shall migrate its specified securities listed on SME

CAPITAL MARKET REFORMS

exchange to Main Board and seek listing of specified securities proposed to be issued on the Main Board subject to the fulfilment of the eligibility criteria for listing of specified securities laid down by the Main Board.

Change in definition of Retail Individual Investors

In case of retail individual investors/shareholders, the amount of application or the monetary bid has been enhanced from one lakh rupees to two lakh rupees

Addition to manner of making draft offer document public

Reg 9(3) has been inserted to provide that the issuer either on the date of filing the draft offer document with the Board or on the next day shall make a public announcement in one English national daily newspaper with wide circulation, one Hindi national daily newspaper with wide circulation and one regional language newspaper with wide circulation at the place where the registered office of the issuer is situated, disclosing to the public the fact of filing of draft offer document with the Board and inviting the public to give their comments to the Board in respect of disclosures made in the draft offer document."

Additional obligation for Merchant Banker, 12th November, 2010

The merchant bankers shall also be required to submit a compliance certificate in the prescribed format, for the period between the date of filing the draft offer document with the Board and the date of closure of the issue, in respect of news reports appearing in the newspapers, major business magazines and print and electronic media controlled by a media group where the media group has a private treaty/shareholders' agreement with the issuer or promoters of the issuer

SEBI (SUBSTAN T IAL ACQ UISI TI O N OF S HARES AND TAKEOVER S) REGULATIONS, 1997

The major changes that have taken place since the last budget in SEBI (SAST) Regulations, 1997 are enumerated and explained as under:

Addition to the list of exemption in Regulation , April 13, 2010

Amendment in Takeover Regulation was a consequential change that was made pursuant to inclusion of Chapter XA in the SEBI ICDR Regulations. A merchant banker or nominated investor in the process of market making and subscription by the nominated investor to the unsubscribed portion of issue, in terms of Chapter XA of the Securities and Exchange Board of India (Issue of Capital and Disclosure Requirements) Regulations, 2009 were exempted from applicability of Regulation 10 and 11 of the Takeover Regulations. The Takeover Regulations have been amended from time to time in response to events and developments in the marketplace, regulatory and judicial rulings as well as evolving global practices. However, to address the growing corporate restructuring by Indian companies, increasing level of M&A activity in India, the increasing sophistication of takeover market, the decade-long regulatory experience and various judicial pronouncements, SEBI, vide its order dated September 4, 2009, constituted the Takeover Regulations Advisory Committee under the Chairmanship of Mr. C. Achuthan with the mandate to examine and review the Takeover Regulations of 1997.

Takeover Regulation Advisory Committee (TRAC) Report on Takeover Regulations

The TRAC submitted its Report to SEBI on 19th July 2010 which was open for public comments upto 31st August 2010. The same is under consideration of the concerned Ministry and we look forward to it with the hopes and aspiration of having a more comprehensive takeover regime in India.

SIGNIFICANT AMENDMENT IN CLAUSE 24, 41 AND 49 OF THE LISTING AGREEMENT, APRIL 05, 2010

The major changes that have taken place since the last budget in the Listing Agreement are enumerated and explained as under: SEBI notified amendments to the Equity Listing Agreement as part of a review of the extant policies of disclosure requirements for listed entities and also to bring more transparency and efficiency in the governance of listed entities. Main features of the said notification are discussed below:

Clause No.	Subject matter of Amendment
Clause 24	SEBI has brought in an additional requirement of submitting auditors'certificate while submitting the scheme of amalgamation / merger / reconstruction, etc. (schemes) to the stock exchanges under clause 24(f) of the Equity Listing Agreement to the effect that the accounting treatmentcontained in such schemes is in compliance with all the applicableAccounting Standards.
Clause 41	• Timelines for submission and publication of financial results by listed entities have been amended to provide that quarterly (audited or un- audited with limited review) financial results shall be submitted within 45 days of the end of every quarter.
	• Audited annual results on stand-alone as well as consolidated basis, shall be disclosed within 60 days from the end of the financial year for those entities which opt to submit their annual audited results in lieu of the last quarter unaudited financial results with limited review.
	• Clause 41(I) (g) has been inserted to provide for Voluntary adoption of International Financial Reporting Standards (IFRS) by listed entities having subsidiaries.
	• Clause 41(1) (h) has been inserted which requires a valid peer review certificate for statutory auditors.
	• Clause 41(V) (h) and Annexure IX have been inserted which require disclosure of statement of assets and liabilities in the specified format within forty-five days from the end of the half-year as a note to their half-yearly financial results.
Clause 49	The appointment of the CFO shall now be required to be approved by theAudit Committee before finalization of the same by the management. TheAudit Committee, while approving the appointment, shall assess the qualifications, experience & background etc. of the candidate.

Discontinuation of Electronic Data Information Filing and Retrieval (EDIFAR) System. April 16, 2010

SEBI discontinued the EDIFAR system w.e.f from April 1, 2010. Consequently, the Equity Listing Agreement was amended by removal of words, "and also through the EDIFAR website" from Clause 32 and omission of Clause 51

Making Annual Reports of Listed Companies easily accessible, May 07, 2010

By this Circular, all Stock Exchanges were advised to make the Annual Reports for the financial year 2009-10 onwards, submitted to Stock Exchange as per Clause 31 of Equity Listing Agreement, available on their respective websites.

Conditions of listing for issuers seeking listing on SME Exchange - Model SME Equity Listing Agreement, May 17, 2010

In continuation of inclusion of Chapter XA in the ICDR Regulations and to facilitate listing of specified securities in the SME exchange, "Model Equity Listing Agreement" to be executed between the issuer and the Stock Exchange, to list/migrate the specified securities on SME Exchange, was notified through this circular.

Significant amendment made to the Listing Agreement, 16th December 2010

SEBI notified amendments to the Equity Listing Agreement with respect to various disclosures to be made by listed companies with an objective to streamline the disclosures made by listed companies with the ever increasing need of transparency and public interest. Main features of the said notification are discussed below:

Clause No.	Subject matter of Amendment
Clause 5A	The procedure contained in existing Clause 5A has also been madeapplicable to shares issued in physical form. Prior to this, it only resolved the practical difficulties of companies which have issued shares in electronic mode and which remained unclaimed and lying in the escrow account.
Clause 20 and22	In order to enable investors to manage their cash/securities flow efficiently,Listed Companies shall pre-announce and intimate to the stock exchange, the fixed date for payment of dividends and credit of bonus shares. Consequential changes have been made in Clause 21.
Clause 35	In addition to disclosing the shareholding pattern to the Stock Exchangeswithin 21 days from the end of each quarter, the same has to be disclosed on two more occasions: i. One day prior to listing of its securities on the stock exchangesii. Within 10 days of any capital restructuring of the company resulting in a change exceeding +/-2% of the total paid-up share capital. The formats for making disclosure under Clause 35 have also been amended.
Substitution of Clause 40A	Clause 40A has been substituted to include the following: i. The issuer company agrees to comply with the requirements specified inRule 19(2) and Rule 19A of the Securities Contracts (Regulation) Rules,1957. ii. Where the issuer company is required to achieve the minimum level of public shareholding specified in Rule 19(2)(b) and/ or Rule 19A of the Securities Contracts (Regulation) Rules, 1957, it shall adopt any of the following methods to raise the public shareholding to the required level: a. issuance of shares to public through prospectus; or b. offer for sale of shares held by promoters to public through prospectus; orc. sale of shares held by promoters through the secondary market. Provided that for the purpose of adopting the method specified at sub-clause(c) above, the issuer company agrees to take prior approval of the Specified Stock Exchange (SSE) which may impose such conditions as it deems fit.
Insertion of Clause 53	The disclosure norms have been extended to cover agreements made withmedia companies and/ or their associates. The issuer company has to notify the stock exchange and also disseminate

	certain prescribed information on the same through its own website
Insertion of Clause 53	It has been made mandatory for the issuer company to maintain a functionalwebsite for disseminating basic information about the company. The website shall remain updated at any given point of time.

Amnesty Schemes Introduced by MCA: Company Law Settlement Scheme, 2010

Company Law Settlement Scheme has been issued by the Ministry to give an opportunity to the defaulting companies to enable them to make their default good by filing belated documents and become a regular compliant by
- condoning the delay in filing documents with the Registrar,
- granting immunity from prosecution
- charging additional fee of 25 % of actual additional fee payable for filing belated documents

The Scheme remained in effect for a period of three months from 30th May 2010 to 31st August 2010.

Amnesty Schemes Introduced by MCA: Easy Exit Scheme, 2010

The MCA has introduced Easy Exit Scheme to give an opportunity to the defunct companies to get their name strike off from the Register of Companies under section 560 of the Companies Act, 1956. Eligible companies may after complying with the requirements of the Scheme, exit from the Register of Companies. The Scheme remained in effect for a period of three months from 30th May 2010 to 31st August 2010

Modification for Government Companies in EES 2010

For smooth implementation of Easy Exit Schemes in case of Government Companies the MCA decided that if no Board is in existence, an officer not below the rank of Deputy Secretary of the concerned administrative Ministry may be authorized to enter his name and other details in place of directors and sign the relevant documents

Revision in additional fee to be levied for delays in filing forms

Almost after fifteen years, the MCA revised the additional fees to be charged on delayed filing of forms by the corporate, thereby making the negligence on the part of corporate really expensive for them

Period of delay	Fixed rate of additional fee
Upto 30 days	Two times of normal fee
More than 30 days and upto 60 days	Four times of normal fee
More than 60 days and upto 90 days	Six times of normal filing fee
More than 90 days	Nine times of normal filing fee

Reopening/ revision of annual accounts after their adoption

The Ministry instructed Registrar of Companies to keep a check on revised filing of accounts by the companies. The financial statements of the company once approved by the shareholders at the Annual General Meeting cannot be normally revised except in exceptional circumstances mentioned in the Ministry's Circular Number 1/2003 (F. No. 17/75/2002) dated 13.01.2003.

Companies, were thus being made cautious so as to ensure that correct set of accounts are uploaded in the MCA site to avoid any inconvenience.

Re-introduction of Easy Exit Scheme 2010

This Scheme was re-introduced as Easy Exit Scheme 2011 by the Ministry to give an opportunity to all those who missed the chance of closing down their inoperative companies without going into the long drawn hassles of winding up procedures during June- August Easy Exit Scheme 2010.

The major difference with the 2010 Scheme was that while there was no fees to apply under 2010 Scheme, a company applying under 2011 Scheme was required to pay a fees of Rs. 3,000/-.

The Scheme came into force on the 1st January 2011 and remained in force up to 31st January

2011.

Rectification in Approved Forms 1, 1A and 44 made possible

MCA for the first time provided scope for rectification in forms which were already approved by the online systems. A new e-Form 68 was notified by way of Rule no. 20G for making an application for rectification of mistakes made while filing e-Form 1, e-Form 1A and e-Form 44 electronically on the Ministry's website. The application for rectification was possible within 365 days from the date of approval of respective form.

Note that e-Form 1 was for the purpose of making 'Application or declaration for incorporation of a company', e-Form 1A for 'Application for availability or change of a name' and e-Form 44 is filed for 'Documents delivered for registration by a foreign company'.

Easy Exit Scheme 2011

The Ministry extended the time for availing Easy Exit Scheme introduced by General Circular No. 6/2010 dated 3rd December 2010 by a period of three months, i.e., upto 30th April 2011.

Direction under Section 212(8) of the Companies Act, 1950

In terms of the section 212, companies were required to attach Annual Report of subsidiaries with the Annual Report of the holding company. The Central Government however was empowered, on application, to direct that in relation to any subsidiary, the provisions of this section shall not apply, or shall apply only to such extent as may be specified in the direction.

The Ministry has granted general exemption to all companies having subsidiaries from complying with the provision of section 212 of the Companies Act. By the present circular, the MCA has granted general exemption to companies in this respect subject to complying with the conditions mentioned therein.

Exemption under section 211 of the Companies Act, 1956 for Public Financial Institutions Feb .8,2011

MCA granted exemption to Public Financial Institutions as specified under section 4A of the Companies Act, 1956 from disclosing Investments as required under paragraph (1) of Note (1) of Part-I of Schedule VI in their balance sheet subject to fulfillment of the certain conditions mentioned therein.

Exemption under section 211 of the Companies Act, 1956 to certain class of companies February 8, 2011

Section 211 of the Companies Act, 1956 requires that the balance sheet and profit and loss account of a company shall be in the form set out in Part I of Schedule VI or in such other form as may be approved by the Central Government either generally or in any particular case. However, considering the need to align the disclosure requirements of our country with those of foreign companies and to generate competitive advantage to Indian corporate, MCA granted general exemption to the certain categories of companies like Companies producing Defence Equipments including Space Research, Export Oriented company, Shipping companies, Hotel companies, Manufacturing companies and Trading Companies from compliance with the disclosures requirement of Part II of Schedule VI as specified in the said Circular.

Amendment to Schedule XIII to the Companies Act,1956, 8th February 2011

Public limited companies (listed and unlisted) with no profits/ inadequate profits were required to approach the Ministry for approval in cases where the remuneration of Directors/ equivalent managerial personnel exceeds certain limits. In the light of the evolving economic and regulatory environment, MCA has notified that:

- Unlisted companies (which are not subsidiaries of listed companies) shall not require Government approval for managerial remuneration in cases where they have no profits/ inadequate profits, provided they meet the other conditions stipulated in the Schedule.
- Remuneration Committee has been defined to mean:
  o In case of listed companies, consisting of three non-executive independent directors
  o In case of any other company, a Remuneration Committee of Directors.

Transfer of Shares/Preference shares / Convertible debentures by way of sale

Transfer of Shares by way of sale, by Resident to Non-Resident

For Quoted shares shall be at a price not less than the price at which a preferential allotment of shares can be made under SEBI guidelines.

For Unquoted Shares shall be at a price not less than the fair value to be determined by a SEBI registered category I Merchant Banker or a Chartered Accountant. For transfer by Non Resident to a Resident, the transfer price of shares shall not be more than the minimum price at which the transfer of shares can be made from a Resident to a Non Resident as stated above

Reporting under Foreign Direct Investment (FDI) Scheme ,14 September 2010)

Indian companies are required to report, the details of the amount of consideration received for issue of FDI instruments, viz. equity shares, fully and mandatorily convertible preference shares and debentures under the FDI scheme, in the Advance Reporting Format along with the KYC report on the non-resident investor, to the Regional Office of the Reserve Bank in whose jurisdiction the Registered Office of the company operates, within 30 days of receipt of the amount of consideration. Further, the Indian company is required to issue the FDI instruments to the non-resident investor within 180 days of the receipt of the inward remittance and report the same in Form FC-GPR, to the Regional Office concerned of the Reserve Bank, within 30 days from the date of issue of shares.

Guidelines on trading of Currency Options on Recognized Stock / New Exchanges

Persons resident in India were permitted to participate in the currency futures market in India subject to directions contained in the Currency Futures (Reserve Bank) Directions, 2008. It has been decided to permit trading of currency options on spot USD-INR rate in the currency derivatives segment of the stock exchanges, recognized by SEBI as per directions, guidelines, etc issued by the RBI and the SEBI from time to time. Persons resident in India are permitted to participate in the currency options market.

Foreign Currency Convertible Bonds (FCCBS): Buyback / Prepayment

Indian companies were allowed to buyback their Foreign Currency Convertible Bonds (FCCBs) under the approval route, up to June 30, 2010, which is now extended up to 30.06.2011subject to the issuers complying with all the terms and conditions of buyback/ prepayment of FCCBs.

Overseas Investments -Liberalisation

Indian entities are permitted to invest in overseas unincorporated entities in the oil sector, up to 400 per cent of the net worth of the Indian company, under the automatic route. As a measure of further liberalisation, it has now been decided, to allow Indian companies to participate in a consortium with other international operators to construct and maintain submarine cable systems on co-ownership basis under the automatic route. Accordingly, banks may allow remittances by Indian companies for overseas direct investment subject to compliance of terms and conditions.

Foreign Exchange Management Act (FEMA),1999 - Current Account Transactions – Liberalisation Release of Foreign Exchange for Visits Abroad – Currency Component

Authorised Dealer Banks may permit drawal of foreign exchange by persons for payment of royalty and lump-sum payment under technical collaboration agreements without the approval of Ministry of Commerce and Industry, Government of India. uthorised Dealers and Full Fledged Money Changers are permitted to sell foreign exchange in the form of foreign currency notes and coins, up to USD 2,000 or its equivalent, to the travellers proceeding to countries other than Iraq, Libya, Islamic Republic of Iran, Russian Federation and other Republics of Commonwealth of Independent States. The existing limits of USD 2,000 now been increased to USD 3000. The other terms and conditions remaining unchanged.

QUESTIONS

1. How do stock market prices affect the allocation of capital resources in the economy?
2. Discuss the role of depositories in upgrading the existing stock trading system into a modern one.

3. Distinguish between primary and secondary securities markets.
4. Discuss the recent policy initiatives and developments in the capital market in India.
5. "Stock market prices reflect the mass psychology with little if any connection to the underlying economic values". Comment.
6. Discuss the role of capital market in an economy.
7. Comment on the recently introduced takeover code in India.
8. Evaluate the modified framework for book building.
9. Critically examine the role of Clearing Corporation of India Limited (CCIL) in risk management.
10. Discuss the impact of changing capital market structure on the volatility, liquidity and transaction cost.

REFERENCES

1. Bellemore, Phillips, and Ritchie. *Investments.* Cincinnati: South-western Publishing, 1979.
2. Black, Fisher. "Toward a Fully Computerized Stock Exchange" *Financial Analysts Journal.* Nov.-Dec. 1971.
3. Bollerslev, T.: "Generalized Autoregressive Conditional Heteroscedasticity," *Journal of Econometrics* 31, 1986, pp. 307-327.
4. Chen, Nui-Fu, Richard Roll, and Stephen A. Ross. "Economic Forces and the Stock Market." *Journal of Business* 59, no. 3 (July 1986).
5. Cohen, A.W. *How to Use the Three-Point Reversal Method of Point and Figure Stock Market Trading.* Larchmont, N.Y.: Chartcraft, 1972.
6. Cohen, J., E. Zinbarg, and A. Zeikel: *Investment Analysis and Portfolio Management,* Richard D Irwin, Home wood, IL, 1987.
7. Crounch, Robert L. "Market Volume and Price Changes," *Financial Analysts Journal,* July-Aug. 1970.
8. D'Ambrosio, Charles A. *A Guide to Successful Investing.* Englewood Cliffs, N.J.: Prentice-Hall, 1970
9. Dines, James. *How the Average Investor Can Use Technical Analysis for Stock Profits.* New York: Dines Chart Corporation, 1974.
10. Edwards, R.D., and J. Magee. *Technical Analysis of Stock Trends.* Springfield, Mass.: John Magee, 1958.
11. Evans, Richard L. "Technical Analysis," *AII Journal* (January 1994): 19-22.
12. Fama, Eugene F., and Arthur B. Laffer, "Information and Capital Markets," *Journal of Business,* July 1971, pp. 289 -298.
13. Fisher, D.E., and R.J. Jordan. *Security Analysis and Portfolio Management.* Englewood Cliffs, N.J.: Prentice-Hall, 1979.
14. Fisher, Lawrence. "Some New Stock Market Indexes," *Journal of Business.* Jan. 1966.
15. Gibbons, Jean Dickinson, *Nonparametrical Methods for Quantitative Analysis* (New York: Holt, Rinehart and Winston, 1976), Chap. 8.
16. Gordon, William. *The Stock Market Indicators.* Palisades Park, N.J.: Investors' Press, 1968.
17. Graham, B., D.L. Dodd, and S. Cottle. *Security Analysis.* New York: McGraw-Hill, 1962, part 3.
18. Granville, Joseph E. *Granville's New Strategy of Daily Stock Market Timing for Maximum Profit.* Englewood Cliffs, N.J.: Prentice-Hall (Parker), 1976.
19. Grodinsky, Julius. *Investments.* New York: Ronald Press, 1953.
20. Hamilton, William P. *The Stock Market Barometer.* New York: Richard Russell Associates, 1960.

21. Hardy, C. Colburn. *Investor's Guide to Technical Analysis.* New York: McGraw-Hill, 1978.

22. Hayes D., and W. Bauman. *Investments: Analysis and Management.* New York: Macmillan, 1976.

23. Huang, Stanley S.C. *Techniques of Investment Analysis.* New York: Intext Educational Publishers, 1972, chapter 9.

24. Jiler, William L. *How Charts Can Help You in the Stock Market,* Trendline, Standard & Poor's Corp., 1962.

25. Kerrigan, Thomas J. "Behavior of the Short-Interest Ratio," *Financial Analysts Journal.* Nov.-Dec. 1974.

26. Kritzman, Mark: "A Simple Solution for Optimal Currency Hedging," *Financial Analysts Journal,*

27. Leuthold, Steven C. "Upside Breakout?—Technicians are Enjoying A Bull Market of Their Own," *Barron's,* May 29, 1978.

28. Levy, Robert A. *The Relative Strength Concept of Common Stock Price Forecasting.* Investors Intelligence, 1968.

29. Lishan, J.M., and D. T. Crary, eds. *The Investment Process.* International Textbook, 1970.

30. Loll, Leo M. Jr., and Julian G. Buckley. *The Over-the-Counter Security Markets.* Englewood Cliffs, N.J.: Prentice-Hall, 1986.

31. Mendelson and Robbins. *Investment Analysis & Securities Markets.* New York: Basic Books, 1976.

32. Moskowitz, Milton. "The 'Intelligent Investor' at 80," *New York Times.* May 5, 1974.

33. Murphy, John J. *Technical Analysis of the Futures Markets.* 2d ed. New York: McGraw Hill, 1985.

34. Nelson, S.A. *The ABC of Stock Speculation.* Wells, Vt.: Eraser Publishing, 1964.

35. Noddings, Thomas C. *Advanced Investment Strategies.* Homewood, III .: Dow Jones-Irwin, 1978.

36. ————— *Principles of Modern Investments.* Chicago: Science Research Associates.

37. Pring, Martin J. *Technical Analysis Explained.* 2d ed. New York: McGraw Hill, 1985.

38. Rich, Steven P., and William Reichenstein. "Market Timing for the Individual Investor: Using the Predictability of Long-Horizon Stock Returns to Enhance Portfolio Performance." *Financial Services Review* (1993/1994): 29-43.

39. Robbins, Sidney. *The Securities Markets: Operations and Issues.* New York: Free Press, 1966.

40. Russell, Richard. *The Dow Theory Today.* New York: Richard Russell Associates, 1961.

41. Sauvain, Harry C. *Investment Management,* 4th ed. Englewood Cliffs, N.J.: Prentice-Hall, 1973.

42. Schaefer, J.M., and A.J. Warner. "Concentration Trends and Competition in the Securities Industry," *Financial Analysts Journal.* Nov.-Dec. 1977.

43. Schultz, John W. *The Intelligent Chartist.* New York: WRSM Financial Service Corp., 1962.

44. Selihman, Daniel. "Playing the Market with Charts," *Fortune,* Feb. 1962; "The Mystique of Point-and-Figure," *Fortune,* March 1962.

45. Sharpe, William F., Gordon J. Alexander, and Jeffrey V. Bailey. *Investments,* 5th ed. Englewood Cliffs, N.J.: Prentice-Hall, 1995.

46. Shaw, Alan R. "Market Timing and Technical Analysis." In *Financial Analysts Handbook.* 2d ed., edited by Summer N. Levine. Homewood III.: Dow Jones-Irwin, 1988.

47. Stein, Lawrence. *The Fundamental Stock Market Technician.* Chicago: Probus, 1986.

48. West, Stan, and T.J. Murphy. "Caveats for Market Technicians," *Financial Analysts Journal.* Sept.-Oct. 1978.

Part II

ALTERNATIVE INVESTMENT
OUTLETS FOR FUNDS

10

Bond Valuation and Analysis

INTRODUCTION

The investment media includes, *inter alia*, bonds and debentures. This form of investment represents the most usual way of borrowing by a company. It is intended to suit the investment needs of a risk avertor who is primarily interested in steady returns coupled with safety of the principal sum. It would be worthwhile to comprehend the salient features, kinds, risk-return relationship, etc. of debentures and bonds.[1]

DEFINITION

A debenture is a legal document containing an acknowledgement of indebtedness by a company. It contains a promise to pay a stated rate of interest for a defined period and then to repay the principal at a given date of maturity. In short, a debenture is a formal legal evidence of debt and are termed as the senior securities of a company.

The position of a bond-holder contrasts sharply with that of a equity-holder. Whereas the former are creditors, the latter are the ultimate owners of a company. Bond-holders assume risk but comparatively lower than the equity holders in the same organisation.

Unlike equity holders, the bond investor does not share in the growth of a company to any appreciable extent. Thus, although serious losses can accrue to bond holders if a company suffers financial reverses, they cannot profit to any significant degree by a spectacular improvement in the company's position. It is a case of heads they lose and tails they cannot win. Therefore, their primary role in an investment portfolio is to provide continuity of income under all reasonably conceivable economic conditions.

The debenture holder, it is assumed, is a happy being who is totally unconcerned with fluctuation in earning power. For preference and ordinary share holders the hard rule is : No profits, no dividends. The debenture-holder, however, if he receives no interest, has usually the right to foreclose, sell the company's assets, and recover his principal. To put the matter crudely, if a company makes profits, he receives his interest; if it ceases to make them, he gets his money back.

---

1. In U.S.A. the bonds differ from debentures in the sense that bonds can be either secured or unsecured whereas the debentures are only unsecured ones. This makes the distinction between the debentures and preference shares much more subtle. Most writers declare that the two differ not only in degree but in kind. Preference shares, the argument runs, are entitled to dividend only when profits are available and directors have resolved to pay them. Legally, debentures, however, are not part of a given company's capital but of its funded debt. Debenture holders, being creditors and not proprietors, are entitled to payment of their full rate of interest whether profits are available or not. The liability to remit interest on debentures is created automatically with the passage of an agreed interval of time, and directors have no discretional powers in the matter.

The consequences of the universal acceptance of this legal dogma have been, first, that a halo of sacrosanctity has surrounded the debenture, and secondly, that companies and industries with a large proportion of "fixed" capital assets (which can readily be mortgaged) have obtained much cheap capital by debenture issues.

The longer high profits last, the greater the liability of the debenture-holder to capital depreciation, not in spite of the fact that industry is prosperous, but because it is prosperous. This is the theory of the matter. To sum up, it may be suggested that while periods of good trade improve the "backing" of industrial debentures, the high money rates usually associated with such epochs act as an effective brake on any incipient upward movement in the market value. When trade turns downwards, the converse applies, low interest rates tending to raise the market price of debentures. If industrial depression becomes extreme, however, the security market may be intimidated by the "industrial risk" which attaches to all securities whose service is dependent on the earnings of industry. Investors may become actually anxious as to the entire financial position of certain companies, and there may be, consequently, in any severe depression "dead point" at which debentures are almost unsaleable, because the public has over-hastily included them in a general condemnation of all industrial securities. This abnormal condition, however, is more of long duration. Sooner or later, the public proceeds to separate the industrial sheep from the goats, and to value individual debentures, like other securities approximately on their merits. It is then that the difference between good and bad debentures becomes painfully apparent.

In the stringent money market conditions, companies find it difficult to attract equity capital or even preference capital. Since banks generally advance only on the security of floating assets, issue of debentures is regarded as the only other suitable alternative for raising capital. In India, for proposals of debentures issues, companies have to obtain a specific consent and not merely an acknowledgement from the appropriate authority, but no such permission is required in the case of convertible debentures exclusively placed with the financial institution.

In general, the issue of bearer debentures is not permitted. Issue of debentures only to prevent an undertaking from closing down because of recurring losses is also not allowed. Consent to the postponement of debentures already issued is given only on the specific condition that any debenture holder who expresses his dissent to the postponement, whether in person or at a meeting of the debenture-holders held for the purpose or if he has not attended the meeting, in writing before the due date of redemption. The maximum permissible rates of interest on debentures are notified by government from time to time.

In view of the inability of some companies to borrow on straight debentures issues at reasonably low rates of interest, the appropriate authority does not withhold his consent of the conversion feature if introduced as an inducement to investors, because convertible debentures not only confer a fixed income and sense of security but also carry the right to participate in future profits and hold out prospects of future growth. Financial institutions like the International Finance Corporation, Washington, and the Commonwealth Development Finance Corporation, London, also favour this method of financing projects in India.

When sanctioning the issue of convertible debentures, generally three to four dates and rates of conversion are allowed to be fixed. New companies and companies whose shares are quoted at par are permitted to issue convertible debenture. Permission is also given to companies engaged in reconstruction of their capital when they desire to fund some debt for the time being but feel that they could not be able to maintain dividend on the new capital if the reconstruction were financed by equity capital only.

However, when the shares of a company are quoted at a premium, expansion of equity capital is favoured in preference to issue of convertible debentures so as not to leave any scope for undesirable manipulation.

REASONS FOR ISSUING BONDS

Governments have no choice but to borrow when they are unable to meet their expenses from current revenue. Corporations, on the other hand, have a wider choice in the matter of financing their operations *e.g.,* retained earnings, new equity issues, etc. But they still prefer to go in for borrowing for the following reasons :

1. To Reduce the Cost of Capital

Bonds are the cheapest source of financing. A corporation is willing to incur the risk of borrowing in order to reduce the cost of capital by financing a portion of its assets with securities bearing a fixed rate of return in hope of increasing the ultimate return to the equity holder.

2. To Gain the Benefit of Leverage

The presence of debt and/or preference shares in the company's financial structure means that it is using financial leverage. When financial leverage is used, changes in earnings before interest and tax (EBIT) translate into the larger changes in earnings per share. However, leverage is a two-edged sword as EBIT can rise or fall. If it falls, and financial leverage is used, the equity holders endure negative changes in EPS that are larger than the relative decline in EBIT. For example, if a company can borrow at 10% and put the funds to works to earn more than 10%, the earnings on the equity holders are increased and vice versa.

3. To Effect Tax Saving

Unlike dividends on equity, the interest on bonds is deductible in figuring up corporate income for tax purposes. Hence, the EPS increases if the financing is through bonds rather than with preference or equity shares.

4. To Widen the Sources of Funds

By issuing bonds, the corporation can attract funds from individual investors and especially from those investing institutions which are reluctant or not permitted to purchase equity shares.

5. To Preserve Control

An increase in debt does not diminish the voting power of present owners since bonds ordinarily carry no voting right.

However, a manager must be concerned with the effect of fixed cost securities on both EPS and the price earnings ratio. An increase in risk has a depressing influence on a price-earnings ratio, while an increase in growth will tend to increase the price-earnings ratio. Fixed cost securities affect both risk and growth. If the risk effect outweighs the growth effect, then the price-earnings ratio will decline. If the growth effect outweighs the risk effect, then the price earnings ratio will increase.

BOND FEATURES

Indenture

The indenture is a long, complicated legal instrument containing the restrictions, pledges and promises of the contract. Bond indenture involves three parties. The first party is the debtor corporation that borrows the money, promises to pay interest, and promises to repay the principal borrowed. The bond holders are the second party; they lend the money. They automatically accept the indenture by acquiring their bonds. The trustee is the third party with whom the bond contract is made. The trustee ensures that the corporation keeps its promises and follows the provisions contained in the indenture. In other words, the trustee does the "watchdog" job form all the bond holders.

Maturities

Maturities vary widely. Bonds are usually grouped by their maturity classes. Short-term bonds are usually bonds maturing within 5 years. They may be secured or unsecured. These are common in industrial financing. Medium-term bonds mature in 5 to 10 years. If a bond is originally issued on a medium-term bond, it is usually secured by a real estate or equipment mortgage, or it may be backed by other security. Long-term bonds may run 20 years or more. Capital-intensive industries with long expectation of equipment life are the greatest users of this for of bond financing.

Interest Payments

Bond interest is usually paid semi-annually, though annual payments are also popular. The method of payment depends upon whether the bond is a coupon (bearer) or registered bond.

A coupon bond is one to which has been attached a number of coupons. A coupon is an agreement of the corporation to pay a stipulated amount of money as the interest which will be due upon the bond at a specified date; the respective coupons fall due upon the interest dates. If the interest is payable semi-annually, there will be two coupons for each year the bond has to run. As a matter of fact, the coupons are simply printed along with the bond on a large sheet of paper. To "cash" a coupon, one cuts it from the bond and presents it for payment. The severance of the coupon preparatory to presentation for payment is called "clipping". Each coupon is a sort of sub-promissory note carrying the serial number of the bond as well as its own number.

On the other hand, a registered bond does not have coupons. Each registered bond is numbered, has a payee on its face, and the debtor corporation or its agent maintains a ledger of the bond holders. As the interest on registered bonds is paid to the holder of bonds, therefore, the holder must be registered with the trustee to ensure proper payment. Registered bond can be transferred only by registering the name of the new owner with the trustee and cancelling the name of the previous owner.

In some instances, the virtues of coupon bonds are combined with those of registered bonds. These bonds are registered as to principal for their owner's protection, but they still pay interest by the convenient and economical coupon method. Combination bonds are transferred by endorsement.

Call Feature

Most modern corporate bonds are callable at the discretion of the issuer. This gives the issuing company the right to recall a bond before it reaches maturity. For example, suppose a corporation originally issues bonds for ` 1,000 each at a high rate of interest but, since the date of issue, market interest rates have fallen and the market value of the bond has risen. It may be to the benefit of the company to recall the bonds, retire them, and then issue new bonds at a lower rate. In that case, the investor would be unable to continue to receive an interest rate that is higher than the prevailing market rate. To compensate for the undesirable callable features, a new issue of callable bonds will carry a higher interest rate than a comparable issue of uncallable bonds.

The call privilege serves corporate managements in still another way used with convertible issues to force bond holders to exchange their bonds for common stock. In this case, management can retire a bond issue without expanding cash. Thus loan is made for another bond issue that will finance some new capital project.

TYPES OF BONDS

Convertible and Non-Convertible Bonds

Convertible bonds can be one of the finest holdings for the investor looking for both appreciation of investment and income of bond. A convertible bond is a cross between a bond and a stock. The holder can at his option, convert the bond into a predetermined number of shares of common stock at a predetermined price. Sometimes there is a provision for compulsory conversion of bonds into shares at specified date. The rate may also be left to be decided by the appropriate authority (SEBI) on the date of conversion. In all convertible bonds the indenture contract specifies the terms of conversion and the period during which the conversion privilege can be exercised, which is usually for the life of the bond.

Sinking Fund Bonds

Sinking fund bonds arise when the company decides to retire its bond issue systematically by setting aside a certain amount each year for the purpose. The payment, usually fixed annual rupees amount or percentage instalment, is made to the sinking fund agent who is usually the trustee. This person then uses the money to call the bonds annually at some call premium or to purchase them on the open market if they are selling at a discount.

Sinking fund bonds have been common in industrial financing that involved some risk because debt issues are more attractive to investor with a promise of faster repayment. Where risk is lower, sinking fund bonds are less frequently used.

Serial Bonds

Like sinking fund bonds, serial bonds are not special types of bonds but just names given to describe the method of repayment. Thus, any bond can be such by merely specifying it in the indenture.

Serial bonds are appropriate for companies that wish to divide their issues into a series, each part of the series maturing at a different time. Ordinarily the bonds are not callable, and the company pays each part of the series as it matures.

Mortgage or Secured Bonds

The term mortgage generally refers to a lien on real property or buildings. Mortgage bonds may be open-end, close-end, and limited open-end. An open-end mortgage means that a corporation under the mortgage may issue additional bonds. But the open-end mortgage indenture usually provides that the corporation can issue more bonds only if the earnings or additional security obtained by selling the new securities meet certain tests of earnings and asset coverage. In a close-end mortgage, the company agrees to issue at one time a stated amount of bonds. After these bonds have been issued no more may be issued under the mortgage. Additional bonds may be sold but they rank as junior to the first mortgage bonds. In other words, the original issue has priority on claims and may not be issued beyond the specified amount of the issue. In a limited open-end mortgage, the indenture provides that corporation may issue a stated amount of bonds over a period of years in series.

Debentures which do not create a change on the assets of a company are termed as unsecured or naked debentures. The holders of these debentures, like ordinary unsecured creditors, do not have any cover to guarantee the safety of their investment.

Collateral Trust Bonds

Instead of being secured by a pledge of tangible property, as are mortgage bonds, collateral trust issues are secured by a pledge of intangibles, usually in the form of stocks and bonds of corporation. Collateral trust issues are thus secured by (1) shares, representing ownership in corporation, (2) bonds, representing the indirect pledge of assets, or a combination of both. Usually, the pledged securities are those of other corporations. The shares pledged frequently represent control of a subsidiary corporation, and such control often materially adds to or detracts from the intrinsic value of collateral issues secured thereby. The place occupied by the subsidiary concern in the corporate system may be the key which enhances or depreciates the investment value of collateral trust issues. In the analysis these bonds are to be presumed to equal a first mortgage bond upon the properties owned by the corporation whose securities are pledged only when all issues of the company are pledged.

Income Bonds

Income bonds are bonds on which the payment of interest is mandatory only to the extent of current earnings. If earnings are sufficient to pay only a portion of the interest, that portion usually is required to be paid, but if the corporation is able to pay the unearned balance out of its cash resources, it is of course free to do so. Income bonds are not offered for sale as new financing but are often issued in reorganization or recapitalization to replace other securities.

Adjustment Bonds

Adjustment bonds are issued in the reorganization of companies in financial difficulties. In practically all cases, interest is payable only if earnings permit. They are a leading type of income bond.

Assumed Bonds

Assumed bonds are issues in respect of a company that has been acquired by another by way of merger or as a result of the re-organization. In taking over the property of the original issuer the debts of the issuer are assumed by the successor company

Joint Bonds

Joint bonds are loan certificates that are jointly secured by two or more companies. Two companies that use a common facility and have raised money to finance it through the sale of debt would provide a good example of a situation where the bonds might be jointly secured. The investor has the additional security of another corporation's pledge.

Guaranteed Bonds

Bonds may be guaranteed by firm other than the debtors. Some guarantors assure payment of both principal and interest whereas some assure interest only. An effect somewhat similar to a guarantee is achieved when a lessee company agrees to pay a long-term rental which is more than sufficient to service the lessor's bonds. A guaranty or lease contract will add assurance to a bond if the guarantor or lessee is financially strong. However, the legal effects of guaranties and lease contracts are not usually so potent as those of outright assumptions, and an assumption undertakes only an unsecured obligation.

Redeeemable and Irredeemable Bonds

A redeemable debenture is a bond which has been issued for a certain period on the expiry of which its holder will be repaid the amount thereof with or without premium. A bond without the aforesaid redemption period is termed as an irredeemable debenture. These may be repaid either in the event of the winding-up of company or the happening of certain specified uncertain or contingent events.

Participating Bonds

Companies with poor credit positions issue participating bonds. They have a guaranteed rate of interest but may also participate in earnings up to an additional specified percentage.

Because of this very characteristic of increased dividends with increased earnings, these are unpopular bonds with the common stockholders of the company who prefer to keep all earnings for themselves.

RISKS ASSOCIATED WITH INVESTING IN BONDS

Although bonds have much to offer investors, buying bound is not without risk. Some bonds expose investors to more risk than other bonds. For example, government bonds do not have any default risk but still expose investors to other risks.

Credit Risk

Credit Risk (technically called default risk) is the biggest concern of the creditor. Essentially, credit risk involves the possibility that the bond's issuer will not make interest and principal payments when due. The level of credit risk vary widely. For instance, government bonds have no credit risk whereas other bonds have much greater probability of default. To avoid credit risk, the bondholders should look at a set of qualitative and quantitative standards of safety. Qualitative standards include stability, issue size, and issue terms. More-stable companies with better interest coverage ratios and profitability over several business cycles are better credit risks. For example, a company whose interest coverage ratio stays near 3.0 over several business cycles is a better credit risk than one whose interest coverage ranges from, say,, 1.5 to 4.5, depending on the economic environment, Larger issues are safer than small issues since the historical default rate is higher for small issues (measured in terms of total assets) than the rate for larger issues. Finally the term of the issue are also important. Shorter maturities, more secure type of securities, and protective provisions make for safer bonds. For example, bonds with sinking funds are better, safer investment compared to bonds without sinking funds. In addition to qualitative standards, there are certain quantitative standards for investment grade-bonds. For example the issuer of investment grade bonds should have net total current assets (current assets minus current liabilities) equal to, say, at least 100% of outstanding long-term debt. Further there should be reasonable stability of earning power, with no or infrequent loss years, reasonable protect against excessive dilution of the priority of claim on earnings power, positive tends in growth an profitability relative to trends in the economy and in the company's industry, a quick ratio of say 1:1, retained earning equal to say 40% of assets, except in capital-intensive business where 25% may be adequate, a working capital ratio of say at least 1.75:1, an equity cushion of 200% total debt as measured by the 5-year average of the market value of the borrower's net worth etc.

Interest Rate Risk: Bond prices varies inversely with interest rates. If an investor is forced to sell a bond when interest rates are high, he or she, could suffer a capital loss, even if the seller does not sell before maturity, rising interest rates also create an opportunity cost. For example, if the interest rates rise to 12% but an investor has a bond with a coupon rate of 8%, he loses the opportunity to get the higher rate because the bond is locked in at 8%. Furthermore, some bonds are more price sensitive than others. Bonds with low coupon rates, for example, are more price sensitive than similar bonds with high coupon rates. Therefore, some bond expose investors to more interest risk (i.e., are more price sensitive than other bonds.

Reinvestment Risk: Reinvesting the coupon payments at a rate higher than the bond's yield to maturity could raise the actual rate of return above the promised return when the bond was initially purchased. Note that interest rate risk and reinvestment risk tend to offset each other to some extent and the immunization techniques are based on this offsetting effect.

Purchasing Power Risk: Purchasing power risk deals with the impact of future rate of inflation on cash flows. If a bond has a coupon rate of 8% when inflation is raging at 10%, the purchasing power of the invested money actually declines. Purchasing power risk hurts a bond investor if actual inflation exceeds the rate the investor expected when he or she first purchased the bond. Further, as the purchasing power risk and interest risk are closely related, the rising expected inflation would lead to higher interest rates.

Call Risk: A call provision gives the issuer the option to buy back the bond from the investor at a specified price during a specified period of time, before maturity. An issues is most likely to call a bond when interest rates are low or have fallen substantially from when the bond was initially issued. To replace the called bond in such an environment, the investor could probably have to accept a lower coupon rate. A bond may offer investors a period of call protection during which the bond is not callable.

Liquidity Risk: Some bonds trade in poor secondary markets, so the spreads between their respective bid prices and ask prices could be quite high. It may be difficult for investors to sell certain bonds before maturity for anything approaching their true values.

Foreign Exchange Risk: In recent years, the investors have been attracted to bonds issued by foreign governments and corporations since many foreign issuers' bond have offered yields well above those offered by domestic bonds. Many foreign bonds are denominated in foreign currencies, however, so their returns depends on both interest rates and foreign exchange rates.

Bond investors should focus primarily on avoiding losses. Bond selection is primarily a negative art. It is a process of exclusion and rejection, rather than (of) search and acceptance. Give that bonds exposes investors to several different types of risk, we can relate the promised (required or expected) return on bond to several factors, as follows:

$$r = f(i, \Delta p, ir, rr, dr, cr, lr, fxr) \tag{1}$$

When:

i	=	real rate of interest
Δp	=	expected rate of inflation over the bond's term,
ir	=	interest rate risk
rr	=	reinvestment risk
dr	=	default risk/credit risk
cr	=	call risk
lr	=	liquidity risk
fxr	=	foreign exchange risk

Equation-1 represents a general model of determinants of bond yields. As each risk factor rises (or falls), the promised return on a bond also rises (or falls). The two factors, change interest rate and change in purchasing power, make up the required return on a risk-free bond. (The closest thing to a truly risk-free security is a short-term T-bll). The other factor can be thought of as compensation (or risk premiums) for investing in bonds that expose investors to various types of risk. For some bonds, certain risk premiums may be zero, or close to zero. For example T–securities have no credit risk, thus investors can demand on risk premium to the bond's required return to compensate investors for credit risk. However, T-securities do expose investors to other types of risk (e.g., interest rate risk), and thus those risk premiums will be added to the bond's promised returns.

BOND PRICES, YIELDS, AND INTEREST RATE

There are a number of risks in bond investment. One is the business risk, that a decline in earning power may impair the corporation's ability to service debt. The second is the purchasing power risk, the prospect that a severe inflation may impair the purchasing power of interest on debt as well as of the principal itself. The third is the so-called interest rate risk. If interest rate rises the market price of the security will decline until its yield becomes competitive with the new higher interest rate. Usually near the peak of the expansion, when the boom seems about to top out, when the Central Bank authorities are enforcing a tight money policy which has driven interest rates up and bond prices down, shrewd portfolio managers may switch from shares to high grade bonds. As a recession develops, tight money will be eased; interest rates may fall; and high grade bonds rise. In fact the deeper the recession, the higher will go the price of high grade bonds, as investment demand switches to favour them and bids up their prices.

The inflation and efforts to control it drive interest rates up. Borrowing corporations and governmental bodies have to pay much higher interest on new issues and older outstanding bonds with lower fall in price, even in a recession period. To understand the nature of the inverse relationship between price and yield, it is necessary to know something about the methods of yield calculations.

Current Yield

The current yield on a bond is the annual interest due on it dividend by the bond's market price. The current yield is a reliable measure of returns earned by perpetual bonds and/or almost any bond with a long time remaining to maturity.

$$\text{Current yield} = \frac{\text{Annual interest}}{\text{Market price}}$$

Thus a 15 per cent interest bond selling at 90 has a current yield of:

$$\text{Current yield} = \frac{15}{90} \times 100 = 16.67\%$$

Investors use the current yield to determine the rate of return earned on each invested rupee, but they know this yield has some handicaps. It means bond returns over an indefinite time period. In theory, the current yield assumes bonds are without a maturity date when interest payments cease or that a bond will be sold at the same price as the purchase price. The current yield, in other words, assumes interest will be paid forever or that a bond will not appreciate or depreciate in price over a holding period.

The Planning or Holding Period Return

The current yield is based on the assumption that the stream of interest income from bond investments will continue indefinitely while the holding period return confirms total returns to a definite investment period. This planning or holding period can be any length of time. The holding period yield for a bond is

$$HPY_b = \frac{I_t + \Delta P}{P_o}$$

t = The subscript t stands for time and refers to a holding period.
It = The bond's coupon interest payment during holding period t
P_a = The bond's price at the beginning of holding period t.
ΔP = Change in bond price over the period.

The HPY can be broken down into an "income yield" measure and a percentage price change measure. As an example, for a bond the formulation would be :

$$HPY_b = \frac{I_t}{P_o} + \frac{\Delta P}{P_o}$$

where the first term on the right of the equation is the familiar coupon yield, and the second term is the percentage change in bond price.

To illustrate the holding period for one year and for two years, following example of ABC company can be taken:

(A) A one year investment period

I_t =   ₹ 80
P_e =   ₹ 1000
P_t =   ₹ 1200
ΔP =   ₹ 1200 – ₹ 1000 = ₹ 200

$$HPR_b = \frac{I_t + \Delta P}{P_o} = \frac{₹\ 80 + ₹\ 200}{₹\ 1000}$$

HPR_b = 28%

(B) A two year investment period

$$HPR_b = \frac{I_t + DP}{P_o}$$

I_t = $I_1 + I_2$
P_0 =   ₹ 1000
P_1 =   ₹ 1300
ΔP =   ₹ 1300 - ₹ 1000 = ₹ .300
I_t =   ₹ 80 + ₹ 80 = ₹ 160

$$HPR_b = \frac{₹160 + ₹300}{₹\ 1,000}$$

HPR_b = 46%

The holding period return was 28.0 per cent for one year and 46.0% for two years. The two year holding period return averages out to 23 per cent per year which is smaller than the 28.0 per cent one year holding period return. The reason is simple — the one year price gain was ₹200 while the two year price gain was ₹ 300, not ₹ 400. The 46.0 per cent holding period return is not a geometric mean or a time consuming accumulation return. The effective annual return (IRR) is solved by setting:

$$0 = 1000 + 80 (1 + i)^{-1} + 80 (1 + i)^{-2} + 650 (1 + i)^{-2}$$

and solving for 'i'.
In this case "i" = 21.5%.

Yield to Maturity

The yield measure most commonly used for bonds is not current but yield to maturity (YTM) — the percentage yield that will be earned on the bonds from purchase date to maturity date. The yield to maturity puts bonds income into a common denominator that permits investors to make yield comparisons. The yield to maturity need not consider capital gains; bonds are redeemed at their face value at maturity. Indeed, the yield to maturity has several other virtues. It considers the time value of money, market discounts and premium, and is the return earned over the remaining life of a bond issue.

The yield to maturity is a complex computation based upon a rather simple idea. It is the discount rate that equals the present value of all cash flows from a bond to the cost (current market price).

$$P_0 = \sum_{t-1}^{n} \frac{I_t}{(1+r)^t} + \frac{P_t}{(1+r)^n}$$

P_0 = Cost of bond
P_t = Terminal price or value
I_f = Annual interest in rupees
r = Discount rate which is the yield to maturity
t = Time period.

With this formula, investors can utilise the present value technique. Applying the formula to calculate the yield to maturity of bond with, say, a 4-1/2 per cent coupon and 10 years remaining to maturity, selling at a price of 90 (90 per cent of par or ₹ 900 on a ₹ 1000 bond), the yield to maturity in this case is equivalent to the rate of interest, compounded semi-annually, which a savings institution would have to guarantee to enable one to deposit ₹ 900 today, withdraw ₹ 22.50 every half year, and have ₹ 1000 in a passbook 10 years hence. In more technical terms, it is that discount rate which will cause the present values of ₹ 1000, to years hence, plus a 10 year semi- annual annuity of ₹ 22.50 to total ₹ 900. To avoid these cumbersome calculations, yields to maturity have been reduced to tables. However, bond tables are not complete. Complete table would show the net yield on every amount invested at every possible rate of yield for every possible maturity. Such a compilation is, of course, out of question. A large assortment of tables is available, with a wide range in coupon rates, maturities, and prices. The more modern tables reflect the use of low and fractional coupon rates and provide means by which prices and yields for maturities involving monthly periods can be determined with a minimum of interpolation. Interpolation is a matter of proportion, as it is based upon the assumption that the changes in the bond table values are proportionate. The assumption is not absolutely correct, but the degree of variance is too small to be serious.

The formula for approximating the yield to maturity is :

$$\frac{\text{Annual coupon interest} + (\text{Discount}/\text{Number of years to maturity})}{(\text{Current price} + \text{Parvalue})/2}$$

Or

$$\frac{\text{Annual coupon interest - (Premium/Number of years to maturity)}}{\text{(Current price + Par value)}/2}$$

To illustrate the application of the formula, using the previous example of the bond selling at 900:

$$\frac{45+100/10}{(900+1000)/2} = \frac{45+10}{950} = \frac{55}{950} = 5.79\%$$

Thus the yield to maturity is about 5.79%. If the same bond were selling at 1100 instead of 900, applying the formula as follows :

$$\frac{45-100/10}{(900+1000)/2} = \frac{45-10}{1050} = \frac{35}{1050} = 3.33\%$$

giving a yield to maturity of about 3.33%.

The yield to maturity calculation may not be an appropriate measure of the is expected rate of return if a bond is callable for refunding purposes. The corporation may exercise the call privilege in case there is a significant chance that interest rates may fail to level which makes refunding attractive to the issuer. Then the investment manager will be faced with the necessity of reinvesting at lower rates, if the quality is not to be reduced. In addition to reinvesting at lower rates, he will incur the annoyance and expense of having to make a new search for an acceptable issue. At offset against this expense will be the "call premium" which the issuer must pay in order to exercise the call privilege. The end results of all these factors may be a realized yield that is substantially different from the originally calculated yield to maturity.

RELATIONSHIP AMONG BOND PRICES, TIME TO MATURITY AND INTEREST RATES: MALKIEL'S THEOREMS

There is a set of relationships among bond prices, time to maturity, and interest rates known as *Malkiel's theorems*. Understanding these price patterns is a must for an investment professional.

Theorem One: Bond Prices Move Inversely with Yields

If the general level of interest rates rises, the price of an existing bond will go down. Conversely, if the level of interest rates declines, the price of an existing bond will increase. The reason this happens stems directly from the fixed income stream associated with a particular bond, and the effect of the time value of money.

Suppose that currently investors will pay par for a 7-year, 12%, AA-rated bond. The owner of ₹ 10,000 par will receive ₹ 1,200 every year until the bond matures. Two months later if the Resrve Bank of India lowers the discount rate by 1%, the change will generally result in a downward shift in the yield curve. Newly issued AA-rated bond with a 11% coupon would provide 1,100 per year in interest. Given a choice between two AA-rated bonds of equal maturity, one of which pays ₹ 1,200 per year and the other paying ₹ 1,100 per year, an investor would not pay the same price for these bonds.

Because the 12% bond is preferable, its price will rise until its yield falls to the current

11% level. This new price is ₹ 10,909. At this price its investment appeal is generally comparable to the new 11% coupon bonds.

Theorem Two: Long-Term Bonds Have More Risk

If two bonds are similar in every respect except for the time remaining until they mature, the bond with the longest life will fluctuate most as interest rates change. Consider three bonds: (1) a 12% coupon bond that matures tomorrow, (2) a 12% perpetual bond and (3) a 12% bond maturing in one year. Regardless of what interest rates do, the first bond is worth ₹ 10,000 tomorrow. It makes no difference if market rates go up or down. The holder of the perpetual bond, however, is very concerned about interest rate movements. If interest rates rise, he will be stuck with a security paying a below-market rate, conceivably forever. The consol has no maturity date to eventually pull the bond price up.

The holder of the one-year bond faces a situation that lies between these extremes. If interest rates rise tomorrow, the price of this bond will fall because it will pay a below-market rate for the next 12 months. In one year, though, it will be redeemed at par. In this sense investors experience no loss from the fall in the bond price because the "loss" is eventually recovered at maturity. If the bond is sold before maturity, however, there *would* be a loss in this instance.

Theorem Three: Higher Coupon Bonds Have Less Risk

The yield on a bond comes from two sources: the interest received and return of the principal at maturity. Consider a 12.5% bond, maturing 7 years, selling for ₹ 900, with a yield to maturity of 15%. With annual coupon payments, its pricing equation is as follows:

$$₹896 = \sum_{t-1}^{7} \frac{₹125}{(1+.15)^t} + \frac{₹1000}{(1+.15)^7}$$

If there is a another bond with zero coupon bond maturity in 7-year and yield to maturity 15% having annual period for consistency, its valuation equation is:

$$₹ 375.94 = \sum_{t=1}^{7} \frac{0}{(1+.15)^t} + \frac{₹ 1,000}{(1+.15)^7}$$

Suppose interest rates fall and 7-year bonds of similar risk now yield just 14.00%. The 12.5% coupon bond will rise to ₹ 935.68 of its market value (a 4.43% increase) while the zero coupon bond will rise by to 23.70 (6.30% of market value) to ₹ 399.63. As required by the theorem, the higher coupon pond was least affected by the change in interest rates.

Theorem Four: The Importance of Theorem Two Diminishes with Time

Theorem two tells us the longer the bond held until its maturity, the more its price will fluctuate. Theorem four tells us when comparing two bonds, the relative importance of Theorem two diminishes as the maturities of the two bonds increase.

To illustration this theorem, assume we have two bonds with identical coupons of 9.5%. Bond A matures in 7 years; Bond B matures in 10. If interest rates rise, we know from Theorem one that the price of both bonds will fall. Theorem two tells us that Bond B, with its longer time until maturity, will fall in price the most.

Consider two other bonds, C and D. Bond C matures in 15 year, while Bond D matures in 18. Rising interest rates will cause the prices of these two bonds to fall also, and Bond D will fall more than Bond C. Theorem Four tells us that the price differential between the bonds will be larger with Bonds A and B than with C and D. In other words, the 3-year difference in maturity is more important with the short-term bonds than with the long-term bonds.

Table 1 indicates that if market interest rates rise from 11 % to 12%, the prices of all four bonds fall. Note the longer the term of the bond, the greater the price decline. Bonds A and B are 3 years apart in their maturities; the difference in their price changes is ₹ 9.53. Bonds C and D are also 3 years apart, but the difference in their price changes is only ₹ 3.32. As Theorem Four indicates, the extra 3 years make little difference for long-term bonds.

TABLE 1

Yield to Maturity	Bond A: 7 Years	Bond B: 10 Years	Bond C: 15 Years	Bond D: 18 Years
	₹ 929.30	₹ 911.66	₹ 892.13	₹ 884.47
	₹ 885.91	₹ 858.74	₹ 829.73	₹ 818.75
	₹ 43.39	₹ 52.92	₹ 62.40	₹ 65.72
	<———> ₹ 9.53 difference		<———> ₹ 3.32 difference	

Theorem Five: Capital Gains from an Interest Rate Decline Exceed the Capital Loss from an Equivalent Interest Rate Increase

This last theorem does not influence the portfolio manager's decisions. It is simply a mathematical fact of life. In Table 1, we see that if interest rates rise by 1% (from 11% to 12%), the price of Bond A declines to ₹ 43.39. If, instead, interest rates had fallen by 1% (to10%), Bond A (7 years) would sell at ₹ 998.66, a price rise of ₹ 69.36. The capital gain rom a 1% drop in interest rates exceeds the capital loss (₹ 43.39) from a 1 % rise in interest rates

Malkiel's Theorems and Mixed Messages

According to the first theorem, bond prices move inversely with interest rates, so both bond prices will rise. A more interesting question is determining which will rise the *most*. Because the first bond has the shortest maturity, Theorem Two indicates it should change in value *less* than the other bond. But the first bond also has a lower coupon than its counterpart. By Theorem Three, it should change the *most*.

How do we reconcile this apparent contradiction? We do so by computing a statistic called duration, one of the handiest tools available to the fixed income portfolio manager.

DURATION

One of the problems with yield-to-maturity is that it assumes investor can reinvest bond's periodic coupon payments at the same rate over time. But if investor reinvest his interest coupon at a lower rate (or spend it, his real return will be much lower than that indicated by YTM. The assumption that interest rates will remain constant is a key weakness of YTM. Another flaw with YTM is that it assumes the issues will make all payments on time and would not call the bonds before maturity, as often happens when interest rates drop. For bonds that are not held to maturity, prices will reflect prevailing interest rates, which will likely differ from YTM. If rates have dropped, it will sell at a premium. The sales price will obviously have a big impact on the total return earned.

The problem with YTM, in effect, is that it fails to take into account the effects of reinvestment risk and price, or market risk. To see how reinvestment and price risk behave relative to one another, consider a situation in which market interest rates have undergone a sharp decline. Under such conditions, a lot of investors might be tempted to cash out their holdings and take some gains (in other words, to do a little "profit taking"). The fact is that selling before maturity is the only way to take advantage of falling interest rates, since a bond will pay its par value at maturity, regardless of prevailing interest rates. The problem is that the interest rates fall, so too do opportunities to invest a high rates. Thus, whereas the investor gain on price side, he loses on the reinvestment side. Even if the investor does not sell out, he is still faced with increased reinvestment risk, because in order to earn the YTM promised on bonds, investor must be able to reinvest each coupon payment at the - same YTM rate. Investor will find it increasingly difficult to reinvest the stream of coupon payments at or above the YTM rate as rates fall. When market rates rise, just the opposite happens.

What is needed is a yardstick or measure or performance that outcomes these deficiencies and takes into account both price and reinvestment risks. Such a yardstick is provided by something called *duration*, which captures in a single measure the extent to which the price of a bond will react to different interest rate environments. Because duration gauges the price volatility of a bond, it gives a better idea of how like the expected return (YTM) is to be earned. That, in turn, will help in tailoring holdings to match expectations of interest rate movements.

The Concept of Duration

The concept of duration was first outlined in 1938 by actuary Frederick Macaulay to help insurance companies match their cash inflows with payments. When applied to bonds, duration recognising that the amount and frequency of the interest payments, yield-to-maturity, and time to maturity all affect the *time dimension* of a bond. The time to maturity is important because it influences how much abend's price rises or falls as interest rate changes. In general, bonds with longer maturities fluctuate more than shorter-term issues when rates move. However, maturity alone is not sufficient measure of time dimension of bonds. Maturity says nothing about interim payments as it is concerned with the time of last payment to be made. The amount of reinvestment risk is also directly related to the size of a bond's coupons. Bonds paying high coupons have greater reinvestment risk simply because there is more to reinvest.

Any change in interest rates will cause price risk and reinvestment risk to push and pull bonds in opposite directions. An increase in rates will produce a drop in price but will lessen reinvestment Tisk by making it easier to reinvest coupon payments at or above the YTM rate. Declining rates, in contrast, will boost prices but increase reinvestment risk. At some point in time, these two forces should exactly offset each other. *That point in time is the bond's duration.*

In general, bond duration possesses the following properties :
- Higher coupons result in shorter durations.
- Longer maturities mean longer durations.
- Higher yields (YTMs) lead to shorter durations.

Together, a bond's coupon, maturity, and yield interact with one another to produce the issue's measure of duration. Knowing a bond's duration is helpful because it combines price and reinvestment risks in such a way that it captures the underlying volatility of a bond. *A bond's duration and volatility are directly related :* the shorter the duration, the less volatility there is in the bond.

Measuring Duration

Duration is a measure of the effective maturity of a fixed- income as opposed to actual maturity. Only those bonds which promise a single payment to be received at maturity (*i.e.*, no yearly coupons) have duration equal to their actual years to maturity. Zero coupon bonds are such bonds. For all others, *duration measures are always less than their actual maturities.*

Duration may be thought of as the *weighted-average life of a bond*, where the weights are the relative future cash flows of the bond, all of which are discounted to their present values. Duration can be de-termined for any cash flow stream; it need not be limited to bond analysis. The original measure, not surprisingly, is known as *Macaulay duration.*[1] Wheh applied to a noncallable security, Macaulay duration is the time-value-of-money-weighted, average number of years necessary to recover the initial cost of the security. Duration's principal value to the financial manager or industrial engineer is that it is a direct measure of interest rate risk; the higher the duration, the higher is the interest rate risk.

Macaulay duration is calculated via equation (2).

$$D = \frac{\sum_{t=1}^{N} \frac{C_t}{(1+Y)^t} \cdot t}{P} \tag{2}$$

where D = duration
  C_t = cash flow at time t
  Y = yield to maturity (per period)\
  P = current price of bond
  N = number of periods until maturity
  t = period in which cash flow is received

Equation (2) provides some intuition into the duration statistic in that it shows time t weighted by the present value of the cash flows received in each period. Each cash flow has a weight, $1/(1+Y)^t$, associated with it. That weight represents a proportion of the present value of the bond cash flows. The sum of all the discounted cash flows from the bond will yield the bond price. Note that the denominator of equation (2) is the bond price. The sum of all the weights equals one; the sum of all the weighted cash flows equals the bond price.

The above equation can be translated into the following four steps:

Step 1: Find the present value of each annual coupon or principal payment. Use the prevailing YTM on the bond as the discount rate:

Step 2: Divide this present value by the current market price of the bond.

Step 3: Multiply the relative value by the year in which the cash flow is to be received.

Step 4: Repeat step 1 through 3 for each year in the life of the bond, and then add up the values computed in Step 3.

---

1.   Macaulay, F.R., "Some Theoretical Problems Suggested by the Movement of Interest Rates, Bond Yields, and Stock Prices in the United States Since 1856." National Bureau of Economic Research (New York: Columbia, 1938).

Table-2 illustrates this procedure, as it presents the duration calculations for 15 per cent, 10-year bond price (at ₹ 944) to yield 18 per cent. Note that this particular 10-year bond has a duration of less than 5-1/4 years - 5.02 years, to be exact. Here is how we find this value: Along with the current market price of the bond (₹ 944), the first 3 columns of Table-2 provide the basic input data: Column (1) is the year *(t) of* the cash flow, Column (2) is the amount of annual cash flow (from coupons and principal); and Column (3) is the appropriate present value interest factors, give an 18% discount rate (which is equal to the prevailing YTM on the bond). *Firstly,* Step 1 is to find the present value of each of the annual cash flows (Column 4), and then - Step 2 - divide each of these present values by the current market price of the bond (Column 5). *Finally,* multiplying the relative cash flows from (Column 5) by the year (t) - in which the cash flows occur - Step 3 - results in a time- weighted value for each of the annual cash flow streams (Column 6). When we add up all the values in Column (6). Step 4 is the duration of the bond which is much less than its maturity in this case - a condition that would exist with any coupon-bearing bond. However, the duration of any bond will change over time as YTM and term to maturity change. For example, the duration on this 15 per cent, 10-year bond will fall as the bond nears maturity and/or as the market yield (YTM) on the bond increases.

TABLE 2

Duration Calculation for a 15%, 10-Year Bond Priced at 18%

Year	Annual Cash Flow	PV at 18%	PV of Annual Cash Flows	PV divided by current market price of the Bond (4) ÷ ₹ 944	Time-weigh- ted Relative Cash Flow (1) x (5)
(1)	(2)	(3)	(4)=(2) x (3)	(5)	(6)
1.	₹ 150	.847	₹127.1	.1346	.1346
2.	150	718	107.7	.1141	.2282
3.	150	.609	91.4	.0968	.2904
4.	150	.516	77.4	.0819	.3276
5.	150	.437	65.6	.0695	.3475
6.	150	.370	55.5	.0588	.3528
7.	150	.314	47.1	.0499	.3493
8.	150	.266	39.9	.0423	.3404
9.	150	.225	33.8	.0358	.3222
10.	1150	.191	219.6	.2326	2.3263
				Duration	5.0193

Duration is not merely a single security concept; rather it also applies to whole portfolio of fixed income securities. The duration of an entire portfolio is extremely easy to calculate — all that is required is the duration of the individual securities in the portfolio and the proportion that each security contributes to the overall value of the portfolio. Thus, *the duration of a portfolio is simply the weighted average of the duration of each security in the portfolio,* where the weights are the wealth proportions of each of the individual securities.

With a *noncallable* bond, duration is a weighted average of time until the cash flows occur. However, in the increasingly complex world of fixed income securities, investors should avoid thinking of duration as a measure of time. Many debt instruments contain embedded options that may alter the security's cash flow stream. If the life or the payments of the bond are uncertain, thinking of duration as a measure of time can be mis-leading.

Chua's Closed-Form Duration

Solving for duration via equation (2) is cumbersome because of the summation requirement. Without a spreadsheet template or a programmable calculator, the calculation, while not difficult, is tedious. Fortunately, Chua's closed-form duration formula is a simpler method.[2] It is presented in equation (3):

$$D = \frac{C_t \left[\frac{(1+Y)^{N+1} - (1+Y) - YN}{Y^2(1+Y)^N} \right] \frac{FN}{(1+Y)^N}}{P} \tag{3}$$

where F equals face value (par value) of the bond and all other variables are as previously defined in equation (2).

Bond Duration and Price Volatility

A bond's price volatility is in part a function of its term to maturity and in part of its coupon yield. Unfortunately, there is no exact relationship between bond maturities and bond price volatilities with respect to interest rate changes. There is, however, a fairly close relationship between bond duration and price volatility — at least, so long as the market does not experience wide swings in yield. That is, duration can be used as a viable prediction of price volatility so long as the yield swings are relatively small. The problem is, because the price- yield relationship of a bond is convex in form (but duration is not), when the market (or bond) undergoes a big change in yield, duration will *understate* price appreciation when rates fall and will *overstate* the price decline when rates increase. Assuming that is not the case (i.e., that the investor is dealing with relatively small changes in the market yield), then multiplying a bond's duration value by -1 results in its price elasticity with respect to interest rate changes. Thus, by calculating a bond's duration, it is possible to obtain a fairly accurate measure of how much its price will change relative to a given (reasonably small) change in market interest rates.

Modified Duration

The mathematical link between bond price and interest rate changes involve the concept of modified duration. Since the price of a bond equals the present value of the cash flows associated with the bond:

$$P = \sum_{t=1}^{N} \frac{C_t}{(1+Y)^t} = \frac{C_1}{(1+Y)} + \frac{C_2}{(1+Y)^2} + \dots + \frac{C_N}{(1+Y)^N} \tag{4}$$

An investment manager is interested in how a bond price changes as interest rates change. Investigating rates of change is a calculus problem. We can take the derivative of equation (5) with respect to the interest rate, giving the following:

$$\frac{dP}{dY} = \frac{-C_1}{(1+Y)^2} + \frac{-2C_2}{(1+Y)^3} + \dots + \frac{-NC_N}{(1+Y)^{N+1}} \tag{5}$$

---

2.   Chua, Jess, "A Closed Form Formula for Calculating Bond Duration," Financial Analysis Journal (May/June 1984), 76-78.

A common term, $-1/(1+Y)$, is on the right-hand side of equation (5). Factoring it out, the equation becomes

$$\frac{dP}{dY} = \frac{-1}{(1+Y)}\left[\frac{C_1}{(1+Y)^1} + \frac{2C_2}{(1+Y)^2} +.... + \frac{-NC_N}{(1+Y)^N}\right] \qquad (6)$$

Equation (6) shows the amount change in the value of the bond associated with a small change in the yield of the bond. Dividing both sides of the equation by the bond price gives the *percentage* change in the price of the bond for a unit percentage change in interest rates:

$$\frac{dP}{dY}\cdot\frac{1}{P} = \frac{-1}{(1+Y)}\left[\frac{C_1}{(1+Y)^1} + \frac{2C_2}{(1+Y)^2} +.... + \frac{NC_N}{(1+Y)^N}\right]\cdot\frac{1}{P} \qquad (7)$$

Equation (7) is called *modified duration*. The term in brackets on the right side of equation (7) equals the numerator of the expression for Macaulay duration shown in equation (2). Modified duration, then, equals Macaulay duration divided by the quantity 1 plus the yield to maturity.

$$\text{Modified duration} = \frac{\text{Duration in years}}{1 + \text{Yield to maturity}}$$

Thus, the modified duration value for the 10 year bond discussed above is as follows:

$$\text{Modified duration} = \frac{5.0193}{1+0.18}$$

$$= 4.2536$$

To determine the bond's percentage price change resulting from an increase is market interest rates for say 18% to 20%, the modified duration value calculated above is first multiplied by -1 (due to inverse relationship between bond price and interest rate) and then by the change in the level of the market interest rates, that is

Percent change in bond price = -1 x modified duration x change in interest rates
= - 1 x 4.2536 x 2.0 = –8.5072%

Thus, a 2% change in market interest rates will lead to 8.50% drop in the price of 10 - year bond. Such information is useful to bond investors seeking (or trying to avoid) high price volatility.

Modified duration shows the percentage price change associated with a one-point change in interest rates. In other words, the percentage change associated with a small change in the bond's yield to maturity; it is the price elasticity with respect to changes in interest rates. If interest rates rise by 0.25% for instance, a bond with a modi-fied duration of 10.0 should decline in price by about 2.5%.

In accordance with Malkiel's Theorem One, the duration derivative is negative. Rising interest rates reduce bond prices and vice versa. Although this relationship is well known, in practice, investors quote duration as a positive number simply for ease of expression.

Effective Duration

In one of his excellent books, Frank Fabozzi describes another measure of duration that stems directly from the implications of modified duration.[3] *Effective duration* is a

3. Fabozzi, Frank J., *Bond Markets, Analysis and Strategies*, 2d ed. (Englewood Cliffs, NJ: Prentice-Hall, 1993).

measure of price sensitivity calculated from actual bond prices associated with different interest rates. It is a close approximation of modified duration for small yield changes. Effective duration is especially useful with callable bonds or other securities whose life is uncertain (like a mortgage, for instance).

Equation (9) calculates effective duration:

$$D_{effective} = \frac{P_a - P_b}{P_0(Y_b - Y_a)} \qquad (9)$$

where P_a = price of bond associated with a decline of x basis points
$\quad\quad\quad P_b$ = price of bond associated with a rise of x basis points
$\quad\quad\quad Y_a$ = initial yield minus x basis points
$\quad\quad\quad Y_b$ = initial yield plus x basis points
$\quad\quad\quad P_0$ = initial price of the bond

We now calculate effective duration for Bond X using a .05% change in yield. If its current yield to maturity is 11.44%, at a yield of 11.49%, the associated bond price is 89.77%. At a yield of 11.39%, the bond price is 90.25%.

$$D_{effective} = \frac{90.25 - 89.77}{90(.1149 - .1139)} = 5.33$$

Comparing this answer with Chua's closed-form duration we find

$\quad\quad C$ = ₹ 47.50
$\quad\quad F$ = ₹ 1,000
$\quad\quad P$ = ₹ 900
$\quad\quad Y$ = 11.44% per year, or 5.72% per half-year period
$\quad\quad N$ = 8 years, or 16 half-year periods

$$D = \frac{47.5\dfrac{(1+.0572)^{16+1} - (1.0572) - 0.0572(16)}{0.0572^2 \, (1.0572)^{16}} + \dfrac{1000(16)}{(1.0572)^{16}}}{900}$$

$\quad\quad$ = 11.29 semiannual periods, or 5.64 years

The closed-form duration equation produces Macaulay duration. To convert to modified duration, divide by the quantity 1 plus half the annual yield to maturity, or 1.0572:

$$D_{modified} = \frac{5.64}{1.0572} = 5.33$$

In this instance effective duration exactly equals modified duration, at least to two decimals.

Duration in Value (DV)

The duration measures seen thus far determine *percentage* price change for a small change in interest rates. Sometimes we are interested in the absolute amount value associated with a percentage price change. **Duration** in value does this. Given modified duration, duration in value is easy to calculate, as shown below.

$\quad\quad$ DV = -Modified duration x Bond price as a percentage of par $\qquad (10)$

In the preceding example we saw a bond with modified duration of 5.33 and a market price of ₹ 900 (90% of par). Remember the modified duration value is actually *minus* 5.33. This bond has a duration in value of -5.33(90) = -479.70. Duration in value can be associated with a change in yield to estimate the change in bond price as shown in equation (10).

$$P_{new} = P_{old} + (DV \times \text{Change in yield}) \tag{11}$$

For instance, if the bond's yield rises by .05 % the new bond price is estimated as 90 + (-479.70 x .0005) = 89.76, or ₹ 897.60 per ₹ 1,000 par.[4]

Another concept is related to duration. The *price value of a basis point* is the price change in a bond associated with a single basis point change in the bond's yield. In the previous example we determined a duration value of --₹ 479.70. The price value of a basis point is therefore (-479.70) (.0001) = -0.0480. For the bond at hand with an initial price of 90%, its price would change to 90.048% or 89.952% depending on whether rates fell or rose.[5] Like modified duration, duration in value is negative, but the minus sign is often dropped when discussing the statistic.

Applying Duration

Duration is especially useful in determining the relative riskiness of two or more bonds when visual inspection of their characteristics makes it unclear which is most vulnerable to changing interest rates. Consider, for instance, the two bonds in Table-3.

Malkiel's theorems indicate the prices of bonds with higher coupons fluctuate less than those of bonds with lower coupons, and that bonds with shorter maturities fluctuate less than bonds with longer maturities. With Bonds X and Y, though, it is not immediately obvious which will fluctuate most with changing intrest rates because the higher coupon bond also has the longest time remaining until maturity. Calculation of the durations indicates that Bond Y, with a duration of 7.42, has more risk than Bond X with a duration of 5.64.

TABLE 3
Using Duration to Compare Two Bond

Bond	Annual Interest	Remianing Life	Price	Yield to Maturity	Duration
X	₹ 95	8 years	₹ 900	11.44%	5.64
Y	₹ 110	15 years	₹ 930	12.00%	7.42

A mathematical example will confirm this result. Suppose the entire yield curve shifts upward by 50 basis points. When yields across the entire maturity spectrum change by the same amount, it is called a *parallel shift*. Again, the yield curve expereinces a parallel shift when interest rates at each maturity change by the same amount. If we calculate, the new price of Bond X will be ₹ 876, which is 2.67% lower than before the rate change. For Bond Y, the new price will be ₹ 899, a drop of 3.33%. As expected, the bond with the largest duration changed in value by the greatest percentage.

Another, perhaps more important, use of duration is in the *structuring of bond portfolios*. For example, if a bond investor believes that interest rates are about to increase, he could calculate the expected percentage decrease in the value of his portfolio, given a certain change in the market interest rates, and the overall duration of the portfolio by selling

4. The actual new price would be 89.77, nearly identical to that predicted by duration. All duration measures are most accurate for small changes in interest rates. This is a general characteristic of calculus first derivatives.

5. A related, but less common, concept is the *yield value of a price change*. It measures the change in yield for a small change (such as 1/8%) in the bond price.

higher-duration bonds and buying those of shorter duration. Such a strategy would prove quite profitable since short-duration instruments do not decline in value to the same degree as longer bonds. Of course, if the investor believed that interest rates were about to decrease, the opposite strategy would be optimal.

Although active short-term investors frequently use duration analysis in their day-today operations, longer-term investors have also employed duration analysis in planning their investment decisions. Indeed, a strategy known as *bond portfolio immunization* represents one of the most important uses of duration.

BOND IMMUNIZATION

Some investors holding portfolios of bonds do not actively attempt to *beat the market* but, rather, seek to accumulate a specified level of wealth at the end of a given investment horizon. For these investors, bond portfolio immunization often proves to be of great values. Immunization allows an investor to derive specified rate of return from bond investments over a given investment interval *regardless of what happens to market interest rates over the course of the* holding *period*. In essence, an investor is able to immunize bis portfolio from the effects of changes in market interest rates over a given investment horizon.

To understand how and why bond portfolio immunization is possible, it is necessary to know that changes in market interest rates lead to two distinct and. opposite changes in bond valuation. The first effect, known as the *price effect*, results in portfolio valuation changes when interest rates change before the end of the desired investment horizon. This is true since interest rate decreases lead to bond price increases, and vice versa. The second effect, known as the *reinvestment effect* arise because YTM calculations assume that all of a bond's coupon payments will be reinvested at the prevailing YTM or the bond when it was purchased. If interest rates increase, however, the forthcoming coupons may be reinvested at a higher rate than the expected by the investor, leading to increase in investor wealth. Of course, the opposite is true when the interest rate falls. Thus, whereas an increase in rates has a negative effect on a bond's price, it has a positive effect on the re investment of coupons. Taken together, when interest rate changes do occur, the price and reinvestment effects work against each other from the investor's wealth standpoint. When *do these counteracting effects exactly offset each other and leave the investor's wealth position unchanged?* When the average duration of the portfolio just equals the investment horizon of the investor because such a property is already embedded in and is fundamental to duration itself. Accordingly, if it applies to a single bond, it should also apply to the weighted-average duration of a bond portfolio. Such a condition (of offsetting price and reinvestment effects) is said to exist when a bond portfolio is immunized. More specifically, an investor's wealth position is immunized from the effects of interest rate changes when the *weighted -average duration of the bond portfolio is exactly equal* to the desired *investment horizon*.

Although bond immunization is a powerful investment tool it is clearly not a passive investment strategy as it requires a continual portfolio rebalancing on the part of the investor in order to maintain a fully-immunized portfolio. Indeed, invtstor pursue a contingent immunization strategy to identify both the available immunization target rate and a lower safety-net level return. This calls for an active portfolio strategy until an adverse investment experience drives the then - available potential return - the combined active return from past experience and immunized return from expected future experience - down to the safety-net level. When that point is reached, the investor is obliged to immunize the portfolio completely and lock in the safety-net return. As long as the safety net is not violated, the investor can continue to actively manage the portfolio. Once the immunization made is activated because the safety net is violated, the investor can no longer return to the active mode, unless of course, the contingent immunization plan is abandoned.

The three key factors in implementing a contingent immunization strategy are (i) establishing accurate immunized initial and ongoing available target returns, (ii) identifying a suitable and immunizable safety-net return, and (iii) designing an effective monitoring procedure to ensure that the safety-net return is not violated.

To illustrate this strategy, suppose that a client investing ₹ 5 million to accept a 10% rate of return over a 4-year planning horizon at a time when a possible immunized rate of return is 12 per cent. The 10 per cent return is called the safety-net return. The difference between the immunized return and the safety-net return is called the *safety cushion*. In our example, the safety evasion is 2% (12% minus 10%).

Because the initial portfolio value is ₹ 5 million, the minimum target value at the end of 4 years, based on semiannual compounding, is ₹ 73,87,277 [₹ 50,00,000 X $(1.05)^8$]. The rate of return at the time is 12 per cent, so the assets required at this time to achieve the nunimum target value of ₹ 73,87,277 represents the present value of ₹ 73,87,277 discounted at 12 per cent on the semiannual basis, which is ₹ 43,34,869 [₹ 73,87,277/ $(1.06)^8$]. Therefore the safety cusion of 2% translates into an initial safety margin of ₹ 6,65,131. Had the safety net of return been 11% instead of 10%, the safety cusion would have been 1 per cent points and the initial safety margin ₹ 1,85,594. In other words, the smaller the safety cusion, the smaller the current of safety margin. Table-4 illustrates the contingency immunization strategy by showing the portfolio's value at initial investment and for two scenarios six months later.

TABLE 4
Contingency Immunization: Two Scenarios

Initial Condition		Initial Investment	
Investment		20-years, 12% coupon bond, sellenig at par to yield 12%	
Achievable immunization rate =		12%	
Safety- net reurn	= 10%		
Planning horizon	= 4years		

Scenario/Interest rates	Initial rate	Drops to 9% in 6 months	Rises in 6 months to 14.26%
Minimum target value to horizon	₹ 73,87,277	₹ 73,87,277	₹ 73,87,277
Current portfolio value	₹ 50,00,000	₹ 66,67,000	₹ 45,61,578
Present value minimum target	₹ 43,34,869	₹ 54,28,389	₹ 45,61,489
Safety margin	₹ .6,65,131	₹ 1,23,861	₹ 88
(Current value-present value of minimum target)			
Management strategy	ACTIVE	ACTIVE	ACTIVE

The investor initially puisnes an active portfolio strategy within the contingent immunization strategy. Suppose that the investor puts all the funds into a 20 year 12 per cent coupon bond selling at par to yield 12 per cent. If the market falls to 9 per cent at the end of 6 months, the value of the portfolio at the end of 6 months would consist of (1) the value of the 19.5 - year, 12 per cent coupon bond at a 9 per cent market yield and (2) 6 month's coupon interest. The price of the bond would increase from 100 to ₹ 127.34, so the price of ₹ 5 million of these bonds would rise to ₹ 6367 million. Coupon interest is ₹ 0.3 million (0.50 x 0.12 x ₹ 5 million). Thus the portfolio value at the end of 6 months is ₹ 6.667 million.

How much would it be necessary to achieve the minimum target return of ₹ 73,87,277 if a portfolio can be immunized at the current interest rate of 9 per cent ? The required value is found by computing the present value of the minimum target return at 9 per cent for 3.5 years. The required amount is ₹ 54,28,389 (₹ 73,87,277/((1.045)^7].

The portfolio value of ₹ 6.667 million is greater than the required portfolio value of ₹ 5.428 million. The investor can therefore continue to manage the portfolio actively. The safety margin is now ₹ 12,38,611 (₹ 66,67,000- ₹ 54,28,389). As long as the safety margin is positive (that is, the portfolio value is greater than the required portfolio value to achieve the minimum target value at the prevailing interest rate), the portfolio is actively managed.

Suppose that instead of declining to 9 per cent in six months, interest rates rose to 14.26 per cent The market value of the bond would decline to ₹ 42,61,578. The portfolio value would then equal to ₹ 45,61,578 (the market value of the bonds plus ₹ 3,00,000 of coupon interest). The required amount to achieve the minimum target value of ₹ 73,87,277 at the current interest rate (14.26 per cent) would be ₹ 45,61,489 [₹ 73,87,277/(1.0713)^7]. The required amount is approximately equal to the portfolio value (that is, the safety margin is almost zero). Thus the investor would be required to immunize the portfolio in order to achieve the minimum target value (safety-net margin) over the investment horizon.

Finally, when multiperiod liabilities are to be satisfied, either multiperiod immunization or cash flow matching can be used. Multiperiod immunization is a duration-watching *strategy* that exposes the portfolio to immunization risk. In cash flow strategy, matching does not impose any duration requirement. With the only risk that the liabilities will not be satisfied is that issue will be called or will default, the cost of a cash flow-matched portfolio may be higher than that of a portfolio constructed using a multiperiod immunization strategy.

DEVELOPING CORPORATE DEBT MARKET IN INDIA

Capital market comprising equity and debt market is one of the most important segments in the financial system of any country. While India has a very advanced G-sec market, its corporate bond market is relatively under developed. Developing a more vibrant corporate bond market has therefore become an important agenda among the concerned stakeholders, i.e., Government of India (GoI), the Reserve Bank of India, the Securities and Exchange Board of India (SEBI), the Insurance Regulatory and Development Authority (IRDA), etc. and in the recent times they have made co-ordinated efforts to achieve this objective.

GROWTH OF INDIAN DEBT MARKET

The growth of corporate bond market in India has been aided by existence of a well-developed G-sec . market which provides a benchmark yield curve for bond pricing, a well- functioning depository system, credible system of rating agencies and adequate legal framework. Measures, such as, rationalising the listing norms, standardisation of market conventions, reduction in the shut period, setting up of reporting platforms, and implementation of DvP settlement of corporate bond trades have had an encouraging impact on the market resulting in considerable increase in issuance as well as secondary market trading of corporate bonds. Total issuance has increased from ₹ 1,747.8 1 billion in 2008-09 to ₹ 2,968.94 billion in 2011-12. Similarly trade volume has increased from

₹ 1,481.66 billion in 2008-09 to ₹ 5,937.83 billion in 2011-12. During the current fiscal year upto September 2012, the trade volumes have been ₹ 3261.14 billion. The share of bonds issued through public issues has increased from 0.86 per cent in 2008- 09 to 7.3 per cent in 2011-12. Out of the four modes of resource mobilisation namely, IPOs, FPOs, bonds and rights issues, the share of bonds have increased from 9.2 per cent in 2008-09 to 73.5 per cent in 2011-12 indicating greater reliance of entities on bonds for resource mobilisation in the recent period.

STRUCTURE OF CORPORATE DEBT MARKET IN INDIA

The primary market for corporate debt is mainly dominated by private placements (93 per cent of total issuance in 2011-12) as corporates prefer this route to public issues because of operational ease, i.e., minimum disclosures, low cost, tailor made structures and speed of raising funds. Banks/Fis (42.3 per cent of total issuances) followed by finance companies (26.4 per cent) were the major issuers in 2011-12. India lacks a long-term debt market for pure project finance. Corporate bonds issued in India usually carry a rating of AAA indicating Iack of interest in bonds of lower rated borrowers in the debt market. Institutional participants, such as, banks, primary dealers, mutual funds, insurance companies, pension funds, corporates, etc. are the major players in this market. Retail investors are also gradually entering this market. Their participation is, however, minuscule. As regards regulation of corporate debt market, the regulatory involvement is clearly delineated between the Reserve Bank of India and the SEBI. The Reserve Bank is responsible for the market for repo transactions and OTC credit derivatives besides framing prudential regulations for banks, etc. in respect of their exposure to corporate bonds. In all other cases, SEBI has the regulatory jurisdiction except in case of unlisted privately placed bonds.

NEED FOR A WELL-DEVELOPED CORPORATE BOND MARKET IN INDIA

India's financial system has been bank-dominated, supplemented by the Development Financial Institutions (DFIs). However, the financial system has undergone several changes during the recent years and DFIs have been converted into banks. Commercial banks, by nature, are not able to fill the gap in long-term finance, given the asset- liability management issues. India's infrastructure funding requirements (estimated at around 10 per cent of GDP annually) need a robust corporate bond market for diversifying risk, enhancing financial stability, and for better matching of risk-return preferences of the borrowers.

A well-developed corporate bond market is critical for Indian economy since the 2008 Global Financial Crisis (GFC) highlighted the need to reduce the dominance of the banking system in financing corporate sector by developing a good corporate bond market. Accordingly, development of the corporate bond market has been high on the agenda for the regulators to enhance the Indian economy growth rate as its development will enable:.

Efficient Allocation of Fesources

A well-developed corporate bond market provides additional avenues to corporates for raising funds in a cost effective manner and reduces reliance of corporates on bank finance. A deep and liquid debt market augments financial savings and helps match the savers to the borrowers in an efficient manner. By enlarging the financial sector, capital markets promote Innovation in financial Instruments. In addition, it instils discipline in behaviour of firms leading to increased efficiency of the system. The existence of a well-functioning bond market can lead to the efficient pricing of credit risk as expectations of all bond market participants are incorporated into bond prices. In order to achieve the objective, it is desirable to have diversified issuer and investor base. Issuer profile in India, however, is concentrated among a few category of market participants dominated by financial sector firms including banks, Non-Banking Financial Companies (NBFCs), financial institutions, housing finance companies (HFCs) and Primary Dealers (PDs)(81 per cent) while other non-finance corporates account for only 19 per cent of total issuances made in 2011-12. Similarly, on demand side, majority of Investment are made by banks and institutions including Foreign Institutional Investors (FIIs) with very little or negligible part played by retail investors. Thus, there is an urgent need to further develop the Indian corporate debt market.

Infrastructure Financing

The Committee on Infrastructure Financing has estimated that ₹ 51.46 trillion would be required for infrastructure development during the 12th Five Year Plan (2012-17) and that 47 per cent of the funds could come through the PPP route. If we add the potential financing needs for upgrading railways, urban and rural infrastructure, the financing needs could be much larger. As much as the G-sec market development has provided a boost to the development of the corporate bond market, the municipal bond market could derive similar benefits from a well-developed corporate bond market. This would provide boost to financing the urban infrastructure in an assured and sustainable manner. In this context, it is important to note that GoI's capital expenditure has remained stagnant during the last two years at around 13 per cent. Hence, the role of private sector assumes greater importance in the context of infrastructure development.

Health of the Corporate Balance Sheet

External borrowings of the corporate sector have increased substantially in the last decade, in part due to the falling implicit cost of the external commercial borrowings (ECBs). While the external debt could help the corporate sector diversify the funding sources, excessive reliance on the same could pose balance sheet risks when the availability of funding liquidity is subject to sharp volatility in the international markets, making the debt rollovers difficult or rollovers are possible only at high interest rates. A Standard & Poors (S&P) forecast in June 2012 had warned that more than half of the 48 companies that are due to redeem an estimated US$ 5 billion of convertible bonds in 2012 may default, while the others may redeem by borrowing at high cost or stiffer terms. The recent phenomenon of sharp fluctuation in the exchange rate, particularly sharp depreciation of Rupee has imparted severe pressure on the profitability of many Indian firms having large foreign exchange obligations. A well-developed domestic corporate bond market could, thus, reduce such vulnerability of corporates to both currency and liquidity risks besides reducing external sector vulnerabilities as share of ECBs as per cent of foreign exchange reserves has been declining in the recent years. A perusal of the various sources of raising resources in the domestic market reveals that the large non-financial corporates have been raising only about 4 per cent through the debt route while the bank borrowings and foreign currency borrowings account for 17.8 per cent and 3.2 per cent, respectively as on March 31, 2011.

Financial Inclusion of the SMEs and Retail Investors

Corporate debt can provide our SMEs with an avenue for sourcing funds. Since this would require rating and would result in greater external scrutiny, it would help SMEs become more transparent and follow proper accounting, governance and disclosure practices. It would also increase their understanding of this important market for sourcing funds in addition to banks and other alternative funding options. It is expected that Chambers of Commerce and SME associations would take this up on a priority basis so that SMEs too could access the corporate debt market in the coming years as has been the experience in the US, Europe and some Asian countries. This would also go a long way in fulfilling financial inclusion objectives for the SMEs, most of whom do not have access to formal financial sector. Corporate debt can also provide an excellent long term investment avenue for retail investors, who lack knowledge and understanding of this important asset class. One hopes that, market bodies, such as, the Fixed Income Money Market and Derivatives Association of India (FIMMDA). the Primary Dealer Association of India (PDAI), etc. together with the stock exchanges take up the task of spreading awareness with all sincerity that it deserves.

This is very relevant as Indian households have one of the highest savings rate in the world but the household wealth in India is generally parked in bank deposits, gold and real estate with almost negligible investment in corporate bonds. If retail investors prefer to invest in shares of certain companies, there should be no reason why they should be hesitant to also consider investing in its debt.

Financial Stability

Various financial crises have highlighted that even well regulated, supervised, capitalised and managed banking systems may have limitations in mitigating financial vulnerabilities. The crises have underscored that the banking systems cannot be the predominant source of long-term investment capital without making an economy vulnerable to external shocks. In other words, bond markets could act like a 'spare tyre'. substituting for bank lending as a source of corporate funding at times when banks' balance sheets are weak and banks are rationing credit. The capital inflows to the country through ECBs, while helping the country fund the current account deficits and corporate to raise resources at a lower cost, could become a source of the transmission of severe external shocks to the domestic economy. Therefore, it is important to develop the domestic corporate bond market to enable corporates to meet a substantial part of their funds requirement domestically. Further, credit flow to infrastructure sector by banks has grown manifold in last few years. There is, however, a risk of exposure attached to banks with such long term financing considering ALM mismatch. Moreover, banks' ability to withstand stress is critical, especially in the context of the recent increase in banks' non-performing assets on account of their exposure to the infrastructure sector, bond markets also aids financial stability by spreading credit risks across the economy and thereby shielding the banking sectors in times of stress. Further, a well-developed bond market can also help banks raise funds to strengthen their balance-sheets. Viewed in the above context, a vibrant debt market is critical to meet the funding requirement for infrastructure sector. Hence, going forward, there is a need to increase the reliance on the corporate bond financing so as to reduce macro-economic vulnerability to shocks and mitigate systemic risks.

Development of Municipal Bond Market

It is estimated that India will need to invest ₹ 39,187 billion between 2012 and 2031 to meet its urban infrastructure requirements. Municipal bonds could be an important source of financing for this requirement. Since 1997, only 25 municipal bond issues have taken place in India mobilising only ₹ 14 billion. An active corporate bond market could enable market for municipal bonds issued by the Urban Local Bodies (ULBs). In this context, a World Bank study (October 2011) on "Developing a Regulatory Frame work for Municipal Borrowing in India' has focused on such bonds. Keeping in view sustainability it has recommended that there should be interest cap on such bonds and they should be treated as tax-free bonds in the same manner as other tax free instruments. The study has also recommended that a new asset class called 'rated municipal securities' needs to be added instead of "non-government securities' to both the IRDA and the Pension Fund Regulatory and Development Authority's (PFRDA) investment guidelines.

MEASURES TAKEN TO DEVELOP THE CORPORATE BOND MARKET

Government, SEB1 and other stakeholders have initiated several measures to develop the corporate debt market. Reserve Bank of India has also taken various initiatives in this regard. Some of these are recounted below:

i) To promote transparency in corporate debt market, a reporting platform was developed by FIMMDA and it was mandated that all RBI-regulated entities should report the OTC trades in corporate bonds on this platform. Other regulators have also prescribed such reporting requirement in respect of their regulated entities. This has resulted in building a credible database of all the trades in corporate bond market providing useful information for regulators and market participants.

ii) Clearing houses of the exchanges have been permitted to have a pooling fund account with RBI to facilitate DvP-1 based settlement of trades in corporate bonds.

iii) Repo in corporate bonds was permitted under a comprehensive regulatory framework.

iv) Banks were permitted to classify their investments in non-SLR bonds issued by companies engaged in infrastructure activities and having a minimum residual maturity of seven years under the Held to Maturity (HTM) category;

v) The provisioning norms for banks for infrastructure loan accounts have been relaxed.

vi) The exposure norms for PDs have been relaxed to enable them to play a larger role in the corporate bond market.

vii) Credit Default Swaps (CDS) have been introduced on corporate bonds since December 01, 2011 to facilitate hedging of credit risk associated with holding corporate bonds and encourage investors participation in long term corporate bonds.

viii) FI1 limit for investment in corporate bonds has been raised by additional US$ five billion on November 18, 2011 taking the total limit to US $20 billion to attract foreign investors into this market. In addition to the limit of US$ 20 billion, a separate limit of US$ 25 billion has been provided for investment by Flls in corporate bonds issued by infrastructure companies. Further, additional US$ one billion has been provided to the Qualified Financial Institutions (QFI).

ix) The terms and conditions for the scheme for FII investment in infrastructure debt and the scheme for non-resident investment in Infrastructure Development Funds (IDFs) have been further rationalised in terms of lock-in period and residual maturity.

x) Further, as a measure of relaxation, QFls have been now allowed to invest in those MF schemes that hold at least 25 per cent of their assets (either in debt or equity or both) in the infrastructure sector under the current US$ three billion sub-limit for investment in mutual funds related to infrastructure.

xi) Revised guidelines have been issued for securitisation of standard assets so as to promote this market. The guidelines focus on twin objectives of development of bond market as well as provide investors a safe financial product. The interest of the originator has been aligned with the investor and suitable safeguards have been designed.

xii) Banks have been given flexibility to invest in unrated bonds of companies engaged in infrastructure activities within the overall ceiling of 10 per cent; and

xiii) Bank has issued detailed guidelines on setting up of IDFs by banks and NBFCs. It is expected that IDFs will accelerate and enhance the flow of long- term debt for funding the ambitious programme of infrastructure development in country.

xiv) Of late, the retail investors have been showing interest in corporate bonds, especially bonds issued by the infrastructure companies that entail tax incentive. While investors are not shy of debts issued by the top-rated firms, they are reluctant to subscribe to the lower-rated instruments. This is an anomaly because lower-rated companies do have access to bank financing. Credit enhancement by banks can perhaps make such instruments attractive to investors. But on the flip side, credit enhancement essentially involves transfer of the credit risk to banks and this will not only hamper the development of corporate bond market by stunting the price discovery process but also increase the risk in the banking system. The focus must be on de-risking banking system and, at the same time, building/encouraging institutions that provide credit enhancement.

ISSUES AND CHALLENGES IN CORPORATE BOND MARKET·

Corporates in many developed markets - predominantly in the US and increasingly in other jurisdictions - have a marked preference to tap the bond market rather than to seek bank loans for meeting their external finance requirements. In India, however, companies continue to depend on the banking system for funds because of ease of availing bank finance, absence of credit risk mitigation mechanisms and a host of other factors, such as, absence of sound bankruptcy framework and lack of active interest of long-term investors like insurance companies.

An examination of the issuer profile of corporate bonds reveals that issuances are dominated by banks and public sector companies. Private sector, non-financial corporate issuers represent a smaller proportion. Issuers with triple-A ratings raise funds with ease from the markets as compared to firms with lower ratings. Private placements mostly dominate the primary segment of the corporate debt market accounting for more than 98 per cent of the total issuance of corporate debt (2010-11) in India. Corporates prefer raising funds through private placements as against public issuances because of operational ease of issuance under private placements with minimum disclosures, low cost of issuance and the speed of raising funds. The issuance process is also impacted by costs, such as, stamp duties, transfer costs, etc. which needs rationalisation. Preference for private placement is also dictated by the profile of investors which is mostly institutional and a narrow base at that.

While the measures taken so far have generated the momentum needed to develop the market, the indicators are suggesting that the market is yet to develop to its potential in relation to needs of macro-economy. The size of the Indian corporate bond market at 11.8 per cent of GDP is lower than the average for Emerging East Asia and for Japan at 17.2 and 19.8 per cent respectively, There are potential risks associated with this market, such as, absence of robust bankruptcy framework, insufficient liquidity, narrow investor base, refinancing risk, lack of better market facilities and standardisation. Some of the issues and challenges which need attention are:

    i) Taking measures to improve liquidity, such as, consolidation of particularly the privately placed bonds, etc.;

    ii) Setting up a suitable framework for market making in corporate bonds;

    iii) Providing tools to manage credit, market and liquidity risks {e.g. CDS, Interest Rate Futures (1RF), Repo in corporate bonds, etc.};

    iv) Introducing a suitable institutional mechanism for credit enhancement to enable SMEs and other corporates with lower credit rating to access the corporate bond market;

    v) Developing a smooth yield curve for thegovernment securities market for efficient pricing of the corporate bonds;

    vi) Enhancing transparency by setting up of centralised database for tracking rating migration, issue size, etc.;

    vii) Increase the scope of investment by provident/pension/gratuity funds and Insurance companies in corporate bonds;

    viii) Calibrated opening of the corporate bond market to the foreign investors;

    ix) Developing safe and sound market infrastructure;

    x) Establishing a sound bankruptcy regime;

    xi) Rationalisation of stamp duty across States;

    xii) Developing the securitisation market under the new regulatory framework;

    xiii) Wider participation of retail investors in the market through stock exchange s and mutual funds.

Reserve Bank is connected directly or indirectly particularly with some of these issues listed below:

Improving Liquidity

Low liquidity is an issue that needs to be addressed urgently. Several reports have suggested consolidation , of the corporate bond issues through reissues to promote liquidity. RBI needs to make a beginning in this ärea by involving PSUs and large corporate with significant volumes of bonds outstanding in devising asuitable scheme of consolidation oftheir issues. There are suggestions to the effect that in respect of regular issuers that there could be restriction on the number of securities they can issue in a year so that reissues would become necessity.

Market Making

Banks and PDs have played the role of market making in the G-Sec with reasonable success and there is need to explore the possibility of replicating the experience in the corporate debt market as well, albeit with the realisation that primary dealers would be exposed to greater credit risk if they carry a sufficiently large inventory of corporate bonds that is needed for market making. Moreover, their limitation to increase exposure to corporate bonds with the context of growing issuance size of Government bonds has to be kept in view. Further, there is a need for a debate on creation of a separate agency/ institution to promote market making in corporate bonds, on the lines of institutions established to promote government securities market.

Credit Derivatives

In the context of development of the corporate bond market and promoting infrastructure funding, CDS has been introduced with ali safeguard, such as, not allowing naked CDS for the users, mandating position limits for the market makers, compulsory reporting of transactions to the trade repository in CCIL, etc. and high expectations. CDS could provide an avenue for participants to mitigate credit risk and enable effective redistribution of credit risk within the system. With the necessary infrastructure that included trade repository, documentation, publication of CDS curve for valuation, standardisation of contracts, etc.in place, participants were permitted to enter into CDS with effect from December 1, 2011. However, so far only few trades have taken place since the launch of the product. Some of the reasons being attributed are difficulty in signing separate Credit Support Annex (CSA for India), non-availability of netting benefits and posting of collateral on daily basis. Both SEBI and 1RDA are likely to permit their regulated entities to participate in CDS as users soon. These are not major operational issues and should not deter market participants from undertaking trades. Stringent capital adequacy guidelines are also being termed as stumbling block. Since CDS is a complex derivative product and downside risk is very high, Reserve Bank intends to follow a cautious and gradual approach in the nascent stage of development of the market. As far as capital adequacy guidelines are concerned, Reserve Bank has broadly followed Basel norms. Hence, it is imperative that market participants use the product to suit their business and risk management requirements.

Interest Rate Derivatives

Interest rate derivatives (IRD)products like Interest Rate Swaps (IRS) and (Interest Rate Futures (IRF) enable market participants to hedge their interest rate risk and take a trading call in the market, leading to the development of the underlying cash market in terms of enhancing liquidity and price discovery. Thus, success of IRDs will be key to the development of corporate debt market. Though the market for IRS has evolved over the past decade and is fairly liquid with average daily trade volumes comparable with the volume traded in the G-Sec market, same is not true for exchange traded IRF. Reserve Bank is examining the possibilities to introduce IRF based on overnight call borrowing rate, fine tuning the product design of the delivery-based 10-yr IRF by permitting single-bond contracts, larger contract size, etc. to revive IRF market. As regards IRS, Reserve Bank has already taken various initiatives like setting up of a reporting platform for IRS transactions and enabling non-guaranteed central clearing of IRS trades. The process for introduction of guaranteed settlement of IRS transactions is underway. H is expected that market participants will make use of various IRD products for hedging interest rate risk in their portfolio. There is also a need for altering the skewed participation profile in the IRS market given that majority of the participants are foreign and private sector banks with minuscule interest from public sector banks.

Repo in Corporate Debt

Among the various initiatives taken by RBI, introduction of repo in corporate bonds has been one that is aimed to impart secondary market liquidity to the corporate bond market. The guidelines permitting repo incorporate bonds were issued in March 2010 and the same were fine-tuned in December 2010. However, except for a handful of trades, the market has not taken off. The reasons cited for lack of interest include non-signing of the Global Market Repo Agreement (GMRA), lack of lenders, such as, mutual funds and insurance companies in repo market, etc. Reserve Bank is engaging with other regulators to address these issues. While SEBI has permitted the mutual funds to participate in this repo market, authorisation from IRDA is expected soon. There is a view that an exchange traded tripartite repo structure could enhance attractiveness of corporate bonds and improve trading volumes. There are, however, concerns, among others, relating to the capacity of central counterparty (CCP) to handle the risk, particularly given the low level of liquidity in the underlying cash market and liquidity accessing capacity of the CCP under extreme situations when settlement obligations have to be met in an orderly manner. The efficacy of these instruments (CDS, IRF and repo) hinges around the crucial issue of whether market participants would use the instrument to hedge risks or they remain as available instruments not used.

Credit Enhancement - Bank Guarantee

Other issue which market has been demanding is allowing banks to provide credit enhancement/partial credit enhancement to corporate bonds by means of guarantee, credit facility, liquidity facility, etc. The measure may appear to be expedient but the underlying objective of de-risking the bank balance sheets through development of corporate debt market will not be met as such a product will place the entire risk on the banking system. Further, banks providing credit enhancements/partial credit enhancement like issuing guarantees for corporate bonds will distort the pricing of the corporate bonds, discourage institutional and retail investors to appraise and assume credit risk and add to the reputational and financial risk of banks. Further, if guarantees are offered by public sector banks, investors tend to form an impression that the bonds have implicit Government support. Thus, provision of bank guarantee will impinge on the genuine development of corporate bond market. In fact, there is hardly any parallel in the world of credit enhancements being provided by the banking sector to corporate bonds. In this regard, some structure for partial credit enhancement, outside banking, could, however, be considered. Under the extant regulations of the Foreign Exchange Management Act (FEMA), entities like multi- lateral/regional financial institutions, government and financial institutions, foreign equity holders, etc. have been enabled to provide credit enhancement and for this guarantee fees upto 200 bps could be paid by the Indian issuers. Some international and domestic financial institutions have in fact shown some interest in this regard and these initiatives could be taken forward.

Smooth Sovereign Yield Curve

The absence of a risk-free term structure of interest rates makes it difficult to price credit risk of instruments issued by the private sector and quasi- sovereign. In the Indian context, however, with issuance of Government bonds for different maturities upto 30 years the sovereign risk free curve does exist. There is, however, an issue relating to having a smooth yield as also almost flat nature of the curve beyond 10 years since trading is confined to a few points, particularly in the 10 to 14 year segment. Fixed Income Money Market Derivatives Association (FIMMDA) has, however, taken steps to create a yield curve by taking available trade data from different points. In addition to passive consotidation being adopted by the Reserve Bank over the years, it is, in consultation with the Government, considering the process for active consolidation involving buybacks/switch operations besides regular issuances at different points of the curve.

Enhancing Transparency

It is desirable that the level of information dissemination available in G-Sec and money market is replicated in corporate debt market. This is required as there is paucity of information on individual issuances as there is no comprehensive database which constrains policy-making. The proposed measures of SEBI to simplify the disclosure norms for debt listing will definitely improve the situation. However, there is an urgent need to design and create such centralised database with more details like issue size, option availability, rating, etc. for better market transparency and improve regulation. It may also be noted that there is also abias towards issuance of bonds through private placement which is not a very transparent method and thus, is impacting the secondary market liquidity in corporate debt. Hence, there is need to encourage public issuance of bonds.

Relaxing Investment Restrictions

Keeping in view the long term funding requirements of infrastructure sector, insurance, provident funds (PFs) and pension companies are best suited for making investment in such bonds. Hence, there is a need to revisit the investment guidelines of such institutional investors since the existing mandates of most of these institutions do not permit large investment in corporate bonds. Prudential requirements of the sectoral regulations would, however, need to be balanced with the need for a developed bond market which ultimately would be in the interest of ali the financial market participants.

Expanding Access to the Foreign Investors

There is a growing demand to open up the corporate debt market and, in particular infrastructure debt segment to the FIIs/QFIs. There is also a demand for fiscal concession to the FIIs. However in the wake of global financial crisis, RBI has adopted a cautious approach. Nevertheless, the limits and conditions for investments by the FIIs have been liberalised particularly for the infrastructure bond . The limits available so far, however, have not been used up significantly. The recent announcement regarding reduced withholding tax to five per cent for foreign currency denominated infrastructure bonds and its likely extension for the Rupee infrastructure bond investments by the FIIs may lead to greater utilisation of the available limits.

Settlement Systems/Trading Platform

The success of order matching trading platform in G-Sec market can act as guidance for setting up of order-matching trading platforms for the corporate debt market. Considering that the trading platforms on exchanges are non-functional, a quote driven anonymous screen based trading platform could possibly bring about the desired focus on trading in corporate debt market due to reduction in transaction cost and improved time efficiency in execution of trades.

Efficient Bankruptcy Regime

A robust, timely, effective and efficient bankruptcy regime is essential to development of corporate debt market from investors' point of view. Steps, such as, reforming bankruptcy law, early resolution of bankruptcy cases and streamlining the procedures relating to insolvency would go a long way in achieving the same. The issue of insolvency of financial institutions established under statutes and bi-lateral netting among them during bankruptcy also need resolution. Possibly, as recommended by the Committee on Financial Sector Assessment, a comprehensive insolvency regime for banks and other financial institutions need to be expedited.

IMPLEMENTATION OF BASEL III AND CORPORATE BOND MARKET

Many steps have been taken to promote bank lending to infrastructure sector like liberalisation of credit exposure norms, liberal dispensation for classification of investments under HTM category, expansion of list of businesses included under infrastructure sector, etc. As a result, banks'exposure to infrastructurelending has grown bymore than fourtimes between 2005 and 2011. However, two factors are limiting the ability of the banks. First, in the context of Basel III guidelines for the banks, the additional capital requirement is esliinated at ₹ 5 tri l lion for the banks, of which non-equity capital will be of the order of ₹ 3.25 trillion while equity capital will be of the order of ₹ 1.75 trillion.

Capital augmentation of banks in future could be a challenge and this could constrain them from increasing their lending to infrastructure in line with the financing needs of the sector. Therefore, there is a clear need for a corporate debt market to serve as a source of long-term finance for corporates and as an alternate to a bank-dominated financial system. The specific characteristics of infrastructure bonds like long duration and high coupon make these bonds attractive for insurance and pension companies who should step up their investments given the limitations on banks' capacity. Steps being contemplated by IRDA for insurance companies may provide necessary boost. The second constraint faced by the banks is that of ALM mismatches that limits the banks role in lending to infrastructure. For banks it would be difficult to assume bulk of the project risk and capital costs indefinitely in infrastructure projects without a commensurate development of the corporate bond market. Therefore, the importance of long-term debt financing for infrastructure projects can hardly be overstated owing to the longer pay-back period, multiplicity of approvals required, delays due to complexities in the design, safety and environmental aspects, etc. It may, however, be noted that we may see large issues of bonds by the banks to augment capital requirements for Basel III and this, in turn, add to the volumes in the corporate bond market.

A vibrant corporate bond market provides an alternative to conventional bank finances and also mitigates the vulnerability of foreign currency sources of funds. From the perspective of financial stability, there is a need to strengthen the corporate bond market. Limited investor base, limited number of issuers and preference for bank finance over bond finance are some of the other obstacles faced in development of a deep and liquid corporate bond market. The regulators have taken proactive steps and provided the market with tools of risk management. Efforts are on to enable wider paiticipation in the market and create scope for market making.This would enable growth of the corporate bond market and cater to the needs of the real economy and the financial sector.

REVIEW PROBLEMS

1. An investor is considering the purchase of the following debenture:

Maturity	Coupon	Par
3 years	11%	₹ 100

(a) If the investor requires a YTM of 13 per cent on debentures of equivalent risk and maturity, what does he believe is a fair market price ?

(b) If the debenture is selling for a price of ₹ 97.59, what is its promised YTM?

(c) If the investor expect the debenture to provide a final payment of ₹ 105 in year 3 instead of the promised ₹ 11 (par plus coupon). Using the debenture's market price of ₹ 97.59, what is his expected annual return ? If the return on three-year risk-free securities is equal to 10.0 per cent, why might this debenture sell at a higher expected return ?

(d) Why is the expected return different from the yield to maturity calculated in part (b) ?

(e) What is the duration of this debenture ?

(f) If an investor 'X' has a horizon date of 4.0 years, why is this debenture risky to investor 'X' ?

(g) If an investor 'Y' has a horizon date of 2.0 years, why is this debenture risky to investor 'Y' ?

Ans.:

(a) $\dfrac{₹11}{(1+.13)} + \dfrac{₹11}{(1+.13)^2} + \dfrac{₹111}{(1+.13)^3} = ₹95.28$

(b) By trial and error, YTM is found to be 12 per cent :

$\dfrac{₹11}{(1+.12)} + \dfrac{₹11}{(1+.12)^2} + \dfrac{₹11}{(1+.12)^3} = ₹97.59$

(c) Again, by trial and error, the expected return is 10.16 per cent :

$\dfrac{₹11}{(1.1016)} + \dfrac{₹11}{(1.1016)^2} + \dfrac{₹105}{(1.1016)^3} = ₹97.59$

If the default risk on this debenture is systematic (undiversifiable), a risk premium above the risk-free rate of 10 per cent will be required.

(d) The yield to maturity is the return which is expected only if all promised payments are indeed expected. If this is not the case, YTM will be upwardly biased measure of the true expected return.

(e) Consider the debenture to be a portfolio of three zero- coupon debentures:

Debenture	Duration	Value	Xi		Weighted Duration
1	1 Year	₹ 9.82*	10.06	per cent	0.1006= (1 × 0.1006) = 10.06 %
2	2 Year	₹ 8.77**	8.99	per cent	.1798 = (2 × 0.0899) = 17.98%
3	3 Year	₹ 79.01***	80.95	per cent	2.4285 = (3 × 0.8095) = 24.29%
		₹ 97.60	100.00		2.7087

* ₹.11/1.12 = ₹ 9.82
** ₹ 11/1,12² = ₹ 8.77
*** ₹ 111/1.12³ = ₹ 97.01

(f) Investor 'X' faces net reinvestment risk since the average date at which cash is to be received (2.7 years) is sooner than the date when cash is needed (4.0 years). The portfolio will have to be reinvested at unknown future interest rates.

(g) Investor 'Y' faces a price risk since cash is needed in 2.0 years but the portfolio measures (on average) is 2.7 years. To obtain this cash, the portfolio will have to be sold at unknown future prices.

2. R.D. Gupta recently purchased a bond with a ₹ 1000 face value, a 10 per cent coupon rate, and four years to maturity. The bond makes annual interest payments, the first to be received one year from today. Mr. Gupta paid ₹ 1,032.40 for the bond.

(i) What is the bond's yield-to-maturity ?

(ii) If the bond can be called two years from now at a price of ₹ 1,100, what is its yield-to-call ?

Ans.:

(i) A bond YTM is that interest rate that equates the bond's price to the discounted value of its promised cash flows. In this case:

$₹ 1032.40 = \dfrac{₹ 100}{(1 + YTM)} + \dfrac{₹ 100}{(+ YTM)^2} + \dfrac{₹ 100}{(1 + YTM)^3} + \dfrac{₹ 1.100}{(1+YTM)^4}$

YTM = 9 per cent

(ii) If the bond can be called in two years for ₹ 1,100 ite yield-to-call is found by solving for the YTM assuming the receipt of only two coupon payments and a call price of ₹ 1,100. That is:

$$₹1032.40 = \frac{₹100}{(1+YTC)^1} + \frac{₹1,200}{(1+YTC)^2}$$

where   :   YTC = Yield-to-call
By solving :   YTC = 125 per cent

3. Venkat purchased at par a bond with a face value of ₹ 1,000. The bond had five years to maturity and a 10 per cent coupon rate. The bond was called two years later for a price of ₹ 1,200, after making its second annual interest payment. Venkat then reinvested the proceeds in a bond selling at its face value of ₹ 1,000, with three years to maturity and a 7 per cent coupon rate. What was Venkat's actual YTM over the five-year period ?

Ans.:

The actual YTM is :

$$YTM = \frac{₹100}{(1+YTM)^1} + \frac{₹1,300}{(1+YTM)^2} + \frac{₹1,000}{(1+YTM)^2} + \frac{₹70}{(1+YTM)^3} + \frac{₹70}{(1+YTM)^4}$$

$$+ \frac{₹70}{(1+YTM)^5} + \frac{₹1,000}{(1+YTM)^6}$$

YTM = 12.9 per cent

4. R.S. Verma is considering investing in a bond currently selling for ₹ 8,785.07. The bond has four years to maturity, a ₹ 10,000 face value, and a 8 per cent coupon rate. The next annual interest payment is due one year from today. The approximate discount factor for investments of similar risk is 10 per cent.

(i) Calculate the intrinsic value of the bond. Based on this calculation, should Verma purchase the bond?

(ii) Calculate the YTM of the bond. Based on this calculation, should Verma purchase the bond ?

Ans.:

(i) The intrinsic value of a bond is equal to the discounted value of the cash flows . In this particular problem :

$$V = \frac{₹800}{(1+10)^1} + \frac{₹800}{(1+10)^2} + \frac{₹800}{(1+10)^3} + \frac{₹10,800}{(1+10)^4}$$

$$= ₹727.27 + ₹66116 + ₹601.05 + ₹7,376.55$$

$$= ₹9,366.03$$

Because the bond is actually selling for ₹ 8,785.07, the bond is underpriced and Verma should purchase it.

(ii) The YTM is the interest rate that equates the price of the bond to the discounted value of the bond's cash flows. In mis particular problem :

$$₹8785.07 = \frac{₹800}{(1+YTM)^1} + \frac{₹800}{(1+YTM)^2} + \frac{₹800}{(1+YTM)^3} + \frac{₹10,800}{(1+YTM)^4}$$

YRM = 12 per cent
Because the YTM (12 per cent) is greater than the appropriate discount rate (10 per cent) for this bond, Verma should purchase it.

5. Ashok Sen acquired at par a bond for ₹ 1,000 that offered a 15 per cent coupon rate. At the time of purchase, the bond had four years to maturity. Assuming annual interest payments, calculate Sen's actual yield-to-maturity if all the interest payments were reinvested in an investment earning 18 per cent per year. What would Sen's actual yield-to-maturity be if all interest payments were spend immediately upon receipt ?

Ans.:

Sen receives four ₹ 150 coupon payments from the bond. Assuming that they are reinvested at 18 per cent, those coupon payments plus the principal repayment will, after four years, have grown to an accumulated value of:

Acc. value = ₹ 150 × $(1.18)^3$ + ₹ 150 × $(1.18)^2$ + ₹ 150 × $(1.18)^1$ + ₹ 1,150 $(1.18)^0$
= ₹ 246.45 + ₹ 208.86 + ₹ 177 + ₹ 1,150 = ₹ 1,782.31

As the bond had a purchase price of ₹ 1,000, Sen's actual YTM over the four years is:

Actual yield = (₹ 1,782.31 / ₹ 1,000)$^{1/4}$ = ,15.54 per cent

If the coupon payments were spend immediately upon receipt, men the effective reinvestment rate is 0 per cent. Thus the accumulated value of the cash flow is:

Ace. value = ₹ 150 × $(1.0)^3$ + ₹ 150 × $(1.0)^2$ + ₹ 150 × $(1.0)^1$ + ₹ 1,150 $(1.0)^0$
= ₹ 1600

Therefore, Sen's actual YTM over the four years is :

Actual yield = (₹ 1600 / ₹ 1000)$^{1/4}$ = 1.1246828 = 12.47 per cent

6. From the price data that follow, compute the holding period returns:

Ans.:

Time	Stock Price
1	₹ 25
2	30
3	24
4	32

Time	Stock Price	Holding-Period Return
1	₹ 25	
2	30	(₹ 30/₹ 25) - 1 = 20 per cent
3	24	(₹ 24/₹ 30) - 1 = - 20 per cent
4	32	(₹ 32/₹ 24) - 1 =333 per cent

7. A.D. Sachdev is considering buying a 13 percent, five- year bond that pays interest once per year. The bond sells for ₹ 1,036, which represents a 12 per cent yield to maturity. What is the bond's duration?

Ans.:

$$\text{Duration} = 5 - \frac{1301\triangleright - (1+.12)\ 3.6]}{1036\ (.12)} = 3.99$$

8. Refer to problem (7) (price = ₹ 1,036, duration = 3.99), A.D. Sachdev plans to purchase a bond whose price is ₹ 873 and whose duration is 8.62. What is the duration of a portfolio of one of each of these bonds?

Ans.:

The total value of the portfolio:
$$= ₹ 1036 + ₹873$$
$$= ₹1909$$

The duration of the portfolio
$$D_p = 3.99\ (1036/1909) + 8.62\ (873/1909)$$
$$= 2.17 + 3.94$$
$$= 6.11$$

9. Calculate the value and duration for the following bonds:

Bond	Years of Maturity	Annual Interest	Maturity value
ABC	10	₹ 80	₹ 1,000
XYZ	15	₹ 65	₹ 1,000)

Ans.:

Bond		ABC Bond	XYZ Bond		
Bond value		₹ 1000	₹ 872		
Year	Interest	PV of Interest		Interest	PV of Interest
1	₹ 80	₹ 74		₹ 65	₹ 60
2	80	137		65	111
3	80	191		65	155
4	80	235		65	191
5	80	272		65	221
6	80	302		65	246
7	80	327		65	265
8	80	346		65	281
9	80	360		65	293
10	1080	5002		65	301
11				65	307
12				65	310
13				65	311
14				65	310
15				1065	5036
Sum of PV of Interest		₹ 7,247			₹ 8,398
Duration		7.25			9.63

10. What *is* the elasticity of a ten-year zero-coupon bond priced to yield 10 percent?

Ans.:

Because it is a zero-coupon bond, its duration is equal to its maturity.

$$= \frac{10(.10)}{(1+.10)} = -.9091$$

This means that for a 1 per cent rise in interest rates (not a rise of one percentage point), the price of the bond should fall by 0.9091 percent.

11. ABC Company has just sold a ₹ 10 crore, 10-year, 12 per cent bond issue. A sinking fund will retire the issue over its life. Sinking fund payments are of equal

amount and will be made is *semiannually*, and the proceeds will be used to retire bonds as the payments are made. Bonds can be called at par for sinking fund purposes, or the funds paid into the sinking fund can be used to buy bonds in the open market.

(a) How large must each semiannual sinking fund payment be?

(b) What will happen, under the conditions of the problem thus far, to the company's debt service requirements per year for this issue over time?

(c) Now suppose ABC Ltd. set up its sinking fund so that *equal annual amount*, payable at the end of each year, are paid into a sinking fund trust held by a bank, with the proceeds being used to buy government bonds that pay 9 per cent interest. The payments, plus accumulated interest, must total ₹ 10 crore at the end of 10 years, and the proceeds will be used to retire the bonds at the time. How large must the annual sinking fund payment be now?

(d) What are the annual cash requirements for covering bond service costs under the trusteeship arrangement described in part c?

(e) What would have to happen to interest rates to cause the company to buy bonds on the open market rather than call them under the original sinking fund plan?

Ans.

(a) ₹ 10,00,00,000/10 = ₹ 1,00,00,000 per year or ₹ 50,00,000 each 6 months. Since the ₹ 50,00,000 will be used to retire bonds immediately, no interest will be earned on it.

(b) The debt service requirements will decline. As the amount of bonds outstanding declines, so will the interest requirements:

Semiannual Payment Period	Outstanding Bonds on Which Interest is Paid	Interest Payment[3]	Sinking Fund Payment	Total Bond Service
(1)	(2)	(3)	(4)	(3) + (4) = (5)
1	₹ 10 crore	₹ 0.6 crore	₹ 0.5 crore	₹ 1.10 crore
2	9.5	0.57	0.5	1.07
3	9.0	0.54	0.5	1.04
.	.	.	.	.
.	.	.	.	.
.	.	.	.	.
20	0.5	0.03	0.5 crore	0.53

a. Interest is calculated as (0.5)(0.12)(Column 2); for example: interest in Period 2 = (0.5)(0.12)(₹ 9.5 crore) = ₹ 0.57 crore

The company's total cash bond service requirement will be ₹ 2.17 crore per year for the first year. The requirement will decline by 0.12 (₹ 1,00,00,000) = ₹ 12,00,000 crore per year for the remaining years.

(c) Here we have a 10-year, 9 per cent annuity whose compound value is ₹ 10 crore, and we are seeking the annual payment, PMT. The solution can be obtained by using this equation:

$$₹1,00,000,000 = \sum_{t=1}^{10} PMT(1+k)^t$$

$$= PMT \ (FVIFA_{9\%,\ 10})$$

$$= PMT \left[\frac{(1+0.09)^{10} - 1}{0.09} \right]$$
$$= PMT \, (15.193)$$
$$PMT = ₹ \, 65,81,979 = \text{Sinking fund payment.}$$

(d) Annual debt service costs will be ₹ 10,00,00,000 (0.12) + ₹ 65,82,009 = ₹ 18,582.009.

(e) If interest rates rose, causing the bonds' price to fall, the company would use open market purchase. This would reduce its debt service requirements.

QUESTIONS

1. What types of investors are interested in debentures in general ?

2. What is meant by yield-to-maturity (YTM)?

3. What comprises the appropriate discount rate for a given debenture ?

4. Market interest rates and debenture prices are inversely related. Explain why.

5. Explain the following statement : "The risk-free real rate of interest is a function of time preference of consumption and the long-term productivity of investment".

6. Explain the variables that determine the present value of a debenture. Explain how each variable relates to the present value.

7. Other things being equal, why should an investor prefer a discount Bond over a bond selling above par.

8. Distinguish between current yield, yield to maturity and coupon-rate. Discuss the concept involved.

9. Why must the duration of a coupon-bearing bond always be less than the time to its maturity date?

10. What does the term *duration* mean to bond investor, and how does the duration on a bond differ from its maturity ? What is the modified duration and how is it used ?

11. Explain how market yield affect the price of a bond. Could you value (price) a bond without knowing its market yield ? Explain.

12. Describe the process of bond portfolio immunization and note why an investor would want to immunize a portfolio. Would you consider portfolio immunization to be a passive investment strategy, comparable to, say, a buy-and-hold approach ? Explain.

13. Explain why interest rates are more important to both constructive and aggressive bond investors. What causes interest rates to move, and how can individual investors monitor such movements.

14. A bond with annual coupon payments of ₹ 150 has a YTM of 15 per cent. Find its price.

15. The rate of return you would get if you bought a bond and held it to its maturity date is called the bond's yield to maturity. If interest rate in the economy rise after a bond has been issued , what will happen to the bond's price and to its YTM? Does this length of time to maturity affect the extent to which a given change in interest rates will affect the bond's price?

16. Does current yield more strongly overstate yield to maturity for long-term maturity or short-maturity premium bonds?

17. Explain how an investor realises an interest when he purchases a zero coupon bond?

18. What are the limitations of using duration as a measure of bond's price sensitivity to interest rate changes?

19. Explain why the total return from holding a bond to maturity will be between the yield to maturity and the reinvesttment ratte.

20. Discuss the recent developments in the corporate bond market in India.

21. What are the risks associated with investing in bonds? To which type (s) of risk are all bond investors exposed?

22. Define duration. How does duration relate to interest rate risk? What is a duration tracking error? What causes it?

PROBLEMS

1. R.K. Gupta purchases debentures that mature in 7 years. Because he intended to hold them until maturity, he claims he is not exposed to interest rate risk. He notes that even if market interest rates rise and the price of the bonds fall, he will still collect the par value on the maturity date. Does Gupta's argument valid ? Explain.

2. You are thinking about buying a 15 per cent coupon issue which matures in 7 years. Interest is paid semi-annually, and investors require a 20 per cent YTM. What price will you pay to purchase the debenture ?

3. Novex debentures have three years remaining to maturity. A 15 per cent coupon is paid annually on ₹100 par value. What *is the* promised YTM if the debentures are selling at ₹ 88?

4. On January 1, 2010, a debenture with 15 per cent coupon which matures on December 31, 2010 sold for par to yield 15 per cent. A relevant price index was 100.00 on January 1, 2010 and 108.7 on December 31, 2010. Assuming the interest was paid at the end of the year, what are the nominal and real interest yields? What is the effect of inflation on the principal received at year end.

5. Consider a bond selling at its par value of ₹ 1,000 with six years to maturity and a 12 per cent coupon rate (with annual interest payments). Calculate the bond's duration.

6. Rank order the following bonds in terms of duration. Explain the rationale behind your ranking

Bond	Time-to-Maturity	Coupon Rate	Yield-to-Maturity
1	30 years	16.0	16.0
2	30	0.0	16.0
3	30	16.0	12.0
4	5	16.0	16.0

7. Find a duration and modified duration of a 10-year, 15 per cent corporate bond that is being priced to yield 12 per cent. According to the modified duration of this bond, how much of a price change would this bond incur if market yields rose to 18 per cent in one year? Using annual compounding, calculate the price of this bond in one year if rates do arise to 18 per cent. How does this price change compare to that predicted by the modified duration ? Explain the difference.

8. Consider two ₹ 1000/ bonds a 18 per cent, 7-year bond and a 15 per cent, 5-year bond, both with annual coupon . Find the duration of the two bonds , assuming 12 per cent discount rate coupon. Compare your results.

9. The following table gives the current price of four discount bonds with different maturities. Calculate the current spot rates for each maturity.

Time to maturity	1	2	3	4
Price	₹ 925.93	₹ 849.46	₹ 773.25	₹ 645.48

Ans.: Current spot rates : (1) = 0.08; (2) = 0.085; (3) .= 0.09; (4) = 0.115

10. Assume that on January 1, 1998, Sudha Industries issued bonds with semi-annual payment, with an annual coupon of 18 percent, call protection for 10 years, a 30-year maturity, and a ₹ 1,000 par value. The bonds are callable at ₹ 1,120 on January 1, 2008, the first call date, and the call price declines thereafter at the rate of ₹ 6 per year until maturity. By January 1, 2003, interest rate on bonds had fallen to these levels: 5-year maturity: 8 percent; 20- to 30-year maturity: 10 percent.

   (a) Within what general price range do you think the bonds will sell on January 1, 2003? (b) Toward which and of this range do you think the actual price would lie ?

   (c) If the bonds actually sold at a price of ₹ 1,500 on January 2003, what pre-tax rate of return could a mutual fund expect if it bought the bond?

   (d) Suppose, on January 1, 2003, you were the mutual fund's investment manager, and you had a choice between the Sudha Industries bond at a price of ₹ 1,500 and a new issue of 5-year, non-callable, 7.75 per cent coupon semiannual payment, ₹ 1,000 bond also issued by Sudha Industries that sell at par. Which would you prefer, the 18 per cent bond of 2028 or the 7.75 per cent bond of 2008?

   (e) Does your answer to part (d) suggest that you might want to change your answer to part (a) ?

Ans.: (a) ₹ 1487 to ₹ 1730; (b) Closer to ₹ 1487, call is likely (c) 7.76 per cent, the YTC

11. What is the price of a discount bond maturing in 3 years if the interest rate is 25 per cent and the bond has a face value of ₹ 10,000?

12. What will be the price of a five-year discount bond that pays ₹ 1,000 at maturity if interest rate suddenly rise to 11 per cent ?

13. Refer to problem (12), what will be its price if interest rate suddenly falls to 9 per cent ?

14. A bond with a six years left to maturity has a coupon rate of 9 per cent and a par value of ₹ 1,000. How much is an investor willing to pay for the bond if he requires the following annual rates of return?

   (a) 7 per cent   (b) 10 per cent   (c) 12 per cent

Ans.: (a) ₹ 1,095.29; (b) ₹ 956.48; (c) ₹ 876.63

15. ABC Company's semiannual bonds pay ₹ 100 in interest (₹ 10 every six months), mature in 15 years, and pay ₹ 1,000 at maturity.

   (a) What is the value of these bonds when the following rate of interest is : (1) 6 percent, (2) 9 percent, and (3) 12 percent.

   (b) Now suppose ABC Company has some other bonds that also pay ₹ 50 interest every six-months and ₹ 1,000 at maturity, but mature in 1 year. What is the value of these bonds at a growing rate of interest of (1) 6 percent, (2) 9 percent, and (3) 12 per cent ?

Ans.: (a) 1. ₹ 1,392.01; 2. ₹ 1,081.44; 3. ₹ 862.35

   (b) 1. ₹ 1,038.27; 2. ₹ 1,009.36; 3. ₹ 981.67

16. A ₹ 1,000 bond has a coupon rate of 10 per cent and matures after eight years. Interest rates are currently 7 percent.

   (a) What will the price of this bond be the interest is paid annually ?

   (b) What will the price be if investors expect that the bond will be called with no call penalty after two years ?

   (c) What will the price be if the investors expect that the bond will be called after 2 years and there will be a call penalty of one year's interest ?

Ans.: (a) ₹ 1,179; (b) ₹ 1,054. (c) ₹ 1,142

17. You own a bond that pays ₹ 140 in annual interest with a ₹ 1,000 par value. It matures in ten years. Your required rate of return is 16 percent.

(a) Calculate the value of the bond.

(b) How does the value change if your required rate of return (i) increased to 18 percent, or (if) decreased to 12 per cent ?

(c) Explain the implications of your answers in part (b) as they relate to interest rate risk, premium bonds, and discount bonds.

(d) Assume that the bond matures in seven years instead of ten years. Recompute your answer in part (b).

(e) Explain the implications of your answers in part (d) as they relate to interest rate risk, premium bonds, and discount bonds.

18. On September 1, 2011, you are considering buying stock of General Star Company, which has just announced a new type of biodegradable container. EPS in 2010 were ₹ 1.20. The company's expected earnings growth rate is 50 per cent for 2011 and 2012, 25 per cent for the following 2 years, and 10 per cent thereafter. Its payout ratio is expected to be zero in 2011 and 2012, to rise to 20 per cent for the following 2 years, and then to stabilise at 50 per cent. Return on market = 15 per cent, Risk-free rate of return = 10 per cent, and General Star's beta = 1.2.

(a) What is General Star's intrinsic value, if the assumptions set forth previously are those of the marginal investor?

(b) Suppose that the investor was offered an opportunity to purchase ₹ 1,000 par value "junk bond" issued by Silver Star Company, a competitor of General Star. The issue has a 4-years remaining until maturity, and carries a coupon rate of 12 per cent. What price could the investor pay for this bond and earn the same before-tax return as the General Star stock (16 per cent) ? What is the after-tax yield to an investor with a 40 per cent marginal tax rate ?

(c) Assume that you (i) are in the 40 per cent tax bracket, (ii) can buy General Star for ₹ 22.26, and (iii) can buy the Silver Star Company junk bond for ₹ 888.07. Your investment horizon is 4 years hence, as you would like to buy a house at that time. Which investment would be a better choice for you ?

(d) Try varying the purchase price of the Silver Star bond, while keeping the tax rate at 40 per cent. How long must the price of the bond before you could consider choosing it over the General Star ?

Ans.: (a) ₹ 22.26; (b) ₹ 888.07; 9.74 per cent; (d) ₹ 863.

19. Consider a five-year discount bond with a face value of ₹ 1,000 that yields 10 per cent compounded annually. What is its price ?

Ans.: ₹ 620.92

20. A bond has the following features - Principal amount: ₹ 1,000; Interest rate (the coupon): 11.5 per cent; Maturity date: 10 years; Sinking fund: None; Call feature: After two years; call penalty: One year's interest.

(a) If comparable yields are 12 per cent what should be the price of this bond?
(b) Would you expect the firm to call the bond if yields are 12 per cent ?
(c) If comparable yields are 8 per cent, what should be the price of the bond ?
(d) Would the firm call the bond today if yields are 8 per cent?
(e) If you expected the bond to be called after 3-years, what is the maximum price you would pay for the bond if the current interest rate is 8 per cent ?

21. Assume that the liquidity preference hypothesis holds and that the annual spot rates are expected to stay constant at 10 per cent. The liquidity premium is 1 per cent per year.

Calculate the implied forward rates for years 2 and 3. Also, calculate the yields for pure discount bonds with maturities of 1 year, 2 years, and 3 years.

Ans.: Year(1) =0.10; Year (2) =0.105; Year (3) =0.1067

22. Suppose ABC Company needs to raise ₹ 40 crore, and its financial advisor has indicated that 10-year zero coupon bond could be sold at a YTM of 12 per cent while a 14 per cent yield would be required on annual payment coupon bonds sold at par. The company's tax rate is 34 per cent (Assume that the discount can be amortised by the issuer using the straight line method. This cannot be done under current tax laws, but assume it anyway).

   (a) How many ₹ 1000 par value bonds would ABC Company have to sell under each plan?

   (b) What would be the after-tax YTM on each type of bond (i) to a holder who is tax exempt, and (ii) to a tax payer in the 50 per cent bracket ?

   (c) What would be the after-tax cost of each type of bond to ABC Company ? (d) Why would investors be willing to buy the zero coupon bond? (e) Why might ABC Company turn down the offer to issue zero coupon bonds ?

Ans.: (a) Zero: 12,42,236; Annual coupon: 4,00/XX)

   (b) Zero: 12.0 per cent; 5.69 per cent; Annual coupon: 14.0 per cent; 7 per cent

   (c) Zero: 7.63 per cent; Annual coupon: 9.24 per cent

23. What is the price of the following split coupon bond if comparable yields are 12 per cent?

   Principal : ₹ 1,000
   Maturity : 12 years
   Coupon : 0 per cent for year 1-3 ₹ 100 for years 4-12

If comparable yields decline to 10 per cent, what is the appreciation in the price of the bond?

Ans.: ₹ 636.

24. A bond pays interest annually and sells for ₹ 835. It has six years left to maturity and a par value of ₹ 1,000. What is its coupon if its promised yield to maturity is 12 per cent?

Ans.: The coupon rate is 7.99 per cent.

25. It is now August 1, 2008 and you are considering the purchase of an outstanding bond that was issued on August 1, 2006. The bond has a 105 per cent annual coupon and a 30-year original maturity (it matures in 2026). There was originally a 5-year call protection (until December 31, 2010) after which time the bond could be called at ₹ 110 (that is, at 110 per cent of par, or for ₹ 1,100). Interest rates have declined since the bond was issued, and the bond is now selling at ₹ 115.174 percent, or ₹ 1,151.74. You want to determine both the yield to maturity and the yield to call for this bond.

   (a) What is the yield to maturity on August 1, 2008, for this bond? What is its yield to call ?

   (b) If you bought this bond, which return do you think you would actually earn? Explain your reasoning.

   (c) Suppose the bond had sold at a discount would the yield to maturity or the yield to call have been more relevant?

   (d) Suppose the bond's price suddenly jumps to ₹ 1,250. What is the yield to maturity now, and the yield to call ?

   (e) Suppose the price suddenly falls to ₹ 800, now what would the YTM and YTC be?

Ans.: (a) YTM = 9.00 per cent; YTC = 7.73 per cent

   (d) YTM = 8.20 per cent; YTC = 458 per cent

   (c) YTM= 13.23 per cent; YTC = 23.13 per cent

26. If a bond sells at ₹ 975 and has a coupon rate of 12 per cent, what is the most you can say about its YTM ?

Ans.: YTM > 1232 per cent

27. In February 1990, Arvind Group issued a series of 3.4 per cent annual coupon payment, 30-year bonds. Interest rates rose substantially in the years following the issue, and as rates rose, the price of the bond declined. In February 2003, 13 years later, the price of the bond had dropped from ₹ 1,000 to ₹ 650.

   (a) Each bond originally sold at its ₹ 1,000 par value. What was the yield to maturity of these bonds at their time of issue?
   (b) Calculate the yield to maturity in February 2003.
   (c) Assume that interest rate stabilised at the 2003 level and remain at this level for the remainder of the life of the bonds. What will be their price in February 2015, when they have 5 years remaining to maturity?
   (d) What will the price of the bond be the day before they mature in 2020?
   (e) In 2003, Arvind Group bonds were called "discount bonds". What happens to the price of discount bonds as they approach maturity? Is mere a "built-in capital gain" on discount bonds?
   (f) The conpon interest divided by the market price of a bond is defined as the bond's current yield. What is the current yield of an Arvind Group bond (1) in February 2003 and (2) in February 2015? What are its expected annual capital gains yields and total yields (total yield equals yield to maturity) on those same two dates?

Ans.: (a) 3.40 per cent; (b) 6.98 per cent; (c) ₹ 853.13; (d) ₹ 1,000 plus accrued interest; (f) Current yield (83) = 5.23 %, Current yield (95) = 3.99 %, Capital gains yield (83) = 1.75 %, Capital gains yield (95) = 2.99%, Total Yield (83) = Total Yield (95) = 6.98 %

28. What is the price of a three year 8 per cent annual coupon bond yielding 11 per cent and having a face value of ₹ 1000 ?

Ans.: ₹ 926.69

29. R.P. Ghosh wishes to find the yield to maturity (YTM) on his company's ten-year 10 per cent bond that sells for ₹ 106.38 per cent of the par value of ₹ 1,000.

   (a) Calculate the YTM by trial and error.

   (b) Find the YTM using the approximation equation.

Ans.: (a) 9.01 per cent (b) 9.07 per cent

30. A bond with a coupon rate of 15 per cent is currently selling at par. Find its YTM.

Ans.: 15 per cent

31. PAWAN Enterprises issued a new series of bonds on January 1, 1978. the bonds were sold at par (₹ 1,000), had a 12 per cent coupon, and had an original maturity of 30 years. Coupon payments are made semiannually (on June 30 and December 31).

   (a) What was the yields to maturity of the bond on January 1, 1978 ?
   (b) What was the price of the bond on January 1, 1983, 5 years later, assuming that the level of interest rates had fallen to 10 per cent ?
   (c) Find the current yield and the capital gains on the bond on January 1,1983, given the price as determined in part (b).
   (d) On July 1, 1998, the bonds sold for ₹ 8%.64. What was the YTM at that date? What was the effective annual rate?
   (e) What was the current yield and capital gain on July 1, 1998?
   (f) What was the after-tax yield on July 1,1998 for an investor in the 40 per cent tax bracket?

Ans.: (a) 12 per cent; (b) ₹ 1,182.56; (c) 10.15; - 0.15 per cent; (d) 14 per cent; 14.49 per cent; (e) 13.38 per cent; 0.62 per cent; (f) 8.52 per cent

32. A bond pays a coupon of 12 per cent per annum on a face value of ₹ 1,000 and matures in 3 years. If it has a yield of 9 per cent, what is its price?

33. A bond pays a coupon of 12 per cent per annum on a face value of ₹ 1,000 and matures in 3 years. If it has a yield of 12 per cent, what is its price?

Ans.: ₹ 1,000

34. A bond pays a coupon of 12 per cent per annum on a face value of ₹ 1,000 and matures in 3 years. If it has a yield of 15 per cent, what is its price?

Ans.: ₹ 931.50

35. Consider the last three problems (from 32 to 34). What can you say about the relationship between bond prices and bond yields? Be specific.

36. A bond is currently selling for ₹ 700 and has eight years left to maturity, and a par value of ₹ 1,000. The bond has a 7 per cent coupon (payable annually). What is its promised yield to maturity to the nearest tenth of a percent?

Ans.: 13.32 per cent

37. It is now August 1,1998. CBA Enterprises has a 15 per cent semiannual coupon, noncallable bond issue outstanding which matures on December 31, 2018. Each bond currently sells for 112 per cent of its ₹ 1,000 par value.

(a) What is the bond's before-tax yield to maturity?
(b) What is the bond's effective annual YTM?
(c) What is the bond's after-tax YTM to an investor in the 28 per cent marginal tax bracket?
   (i) Assume that the premium is treated as a long-term capital loss at maturity?
   (ii) Assume that the premium is amortized over the life of the issue and used to offset the interest income.

Ans.: (a) 13.28 per cent; (b) 13.72 per cent; (c) (i) 9.51 percent, (ii) 9.61 per cent

REFERENCES

1. Alexander, Gordon J. "Applying the Market Model to Long-Term Corporate Bonds." *Journal of Financial and Quantitative Analysis* 15, no. 5 (December 1980).
2. Altman, E.: "Financial Ratios, Discriminant Analysis and the Prediction of Corporate Bankruptcy," *Journal of Finance,* September 1968, pp. 589-609.
3. ————. "Defaults and Returns on High Yield Bonds: An Update Through the First Half of 1991." *Financial Analysts Journal* (November/December 1991): 67-77.
4. ————. "Revisiting the High-Yield Bond Market." *Financial Management* (sum-mer 1992): 78-92.
5. ————. "The Anatomy of the High-Yield Bond Market." *Financial Analysts Journal* (July/August 1987): 12-25.
6. ————, ed. *The High Yield Debt Market.* Homewood, IL. Dow Jones-Irwin, 1990.
7. ———— and Scott A. Nammacher. *Investing in Junk Bonds.* New York: John Wiley & Sons, 1987.
8. Ang, J.S., and K.A. Patel. "Bond Rating Methods: Comparison and Validation." *The Journal of Finance,* May 1975, pp. 631-40.
9. Babcock, Guilford C. "Duration as a Link between Yield and Value." *Journal of Portfolio Management,* Summer 1984, 58-65.
10. Blume, Marshall, and Donald Keim: "Lower-Grade Bonds: Their Risks and Return," *Financial Analysts Journal,* July-August 1987, pp. 26-33.
11. Brennan, Michael, and Eduardo Schwartz: "Bond Pricing and Market Efficiency," *Financial Analysts Journal,* September-October 1982, pp. 49-56.
12. Cheung, Rayner, Joseph C. Bencivenga, and Frank J. Fabozzi, "Original Issue High-Yield Bonds: Historical Return and Default Experiences, 1977-1989," *The Journal of Fixed Income* 2, no. 2 (September 1992).

13. Darst, David M. *The Complete Bond Book.* New York: McGraw-Hill, 1975.

14. —————. *The Handbook of the Bond and Money Markets.* New York: McGraw-Hill, 1981.

15. Fabozzi, Frank J. "Bond Pricing and Return Measures," in Frank J. Fabozzi, ed. *The Handbook affixed Income Securities,* 3rd ed. Homewood, IL: Business One-Irwin, 1991.

16. —————, Mark Pitts, and Ravi E. Dattatreya. "Price Volatility Characteristics of Fixed Income Securities," in Frank J. Fabozzi, ed. *The Handbook of Fixed Income Securities,* 3rd ed. (Homewood, IL: Business One-Irwin, 1991).

17. ————— and Franco Modigliani. Mortgage *and Mortgage-Backed Security Markets.* Boston, Mass.: Harvard University Press, 1994.

18. ————— and T. Dessa Fabozzi: *Bond Markets, Analyses and Strategies.* Prentice-Hall, Engle-wood Cliffs, NJ, 1989.

19. Fama. E.F.: "Short-Term Interest Rates as Predictors of Inflation." *American Economic Review,* June 1975, pp. 269-282.

20. Feldstein, Sylvan G. *The Dow Jones-Irwin Guide to Municipal Bonds.* Homewood, 111.: Dow Jones-Irwin, 1986.

21. Findlay, M.C., and E.E. Williams. "Better Debt Service Coverage Ratios." *Financial Analysts Journal,* November-December 1975, pp. 58-62.

22. Finnerty, John D. "Evaluating the Economics of Refunding High-Coupon Sinking-Fund Debt." *Financial Management* 12, no. 1 (Spring 1983).

23. Fisher, Irving, *The Theory of Interest.* New York: Macmillan, 1930.

24. Fisher, Lawrence, and Roman L. Weil. "Coping with the Risk of Interest-Rate Fluctuations: Returns to Bondholders from Naive and Optimal Strategies." *Journal of Business* 44, no. 4 (October 1971).

25. ————— "Determinants of Risk Premium on Corporate Bonds," *Journal of Political Economy.* June 1959.

26. French, Kenneth R. "Stock Returns and the Weekend Effect." *Journal of Financial Economics* 8, no. 1 (March 1980).

27. Fridson, Martin. *High Yield Bonds: Assessing Risk and Identifying Value in Speculative Grade Securities.* Chicago: Probus Publishing, 1989.

28. Fuller, Russell J., and John W. Settle. "Determinants of Duration and Bond Volatility." *Journal of Portfolio Management,* Summer 1984, 66-72.

29. Gentry, James A., David T. Whitford, and Paul Newbold. "Predicting Industrial Bond Ratings with Probit Model and Funds Flow Components." *The Financial Review* 23, no. 3 (August 1988).

30. Grey, W.S., "Discount Rates and Return Forecasts," *Financial Analysts Journal,* 30 (May-June 1974), 53-61.

31. Grier, Paul, and Steven Katz: "The Differential Effects of Bond Rating Changes among Industrial and Public Utility Bonds by Maturity." *Journal of Business.* April 1976, pp. 226-239.

32. Gross, William H. "The Effects of Coupons on Yield Spreads." *Financial Analysts Journal,* July-August 1979.

33. Hickman, W. Braddock. *Corporate Bond Quality and Investor Experience.* A study by the National Bureau of Economic Research. Princeton, N.J.: Princeton University Press, 1958.

34. Homer, Sidney. "Total Money Management with Specific Illustrations from the Bond Market." New York: Salomon Brothers, 1973.

35. ————— and M.L. Liebowitz; *Inside the Yield Book.* Prentice-Hall. Englewood Cliffs. NJ, 1972.

36. Hopewell, Michael H., and George Kaufman. "Bond Price Volatility and Term to Maturity: A Generalized Respecification." *American Economic Review,* September 1973, 749-753. .

37. Howe, Jane Tripp. *Junk Bonds: Analysis and Portfolio Strategies.* Chicago: Probus Publishing, 1988.

38. Hradsky, Gregory, and Robert D. Long. "High-Yield Default Losses and the Return of Bankrupt Debt." *Financial Analysts Journal* (July/August 1989): 38-49.

39. Ibbotson, R. ., and R. Sinquefield, *Stocks, Bonds, Bills and Inflation. 1985 Yearbook: Market Results for 1926-1984* (Chicago: Capital Market Re-search Center, 1985).

40. Jenkins, James W. "Taxes, Margining, and Bond Selection." *Financial Analysts Journal,* May-June 1980.

41. Kalotay, A.J. "On the Structure and Valuation of Debt Refundings." *Financial Management* 11, no. 1 (Spring 1982).

42. Kaplan, Robert S., and Gabriel Urwitz. "Statistical Models of Bond Ratings: A Methodological Inquiry." *Journal of Business* 52, no. 2 (April 1979).

43. Keim, Donald B., and Robert F. Stambaugh. "Predicting Returns in Stock and Bond Markets." *Journal of Financial Economics* 17, no. 2 (December 1986).

44. Lenderman, Richard. "The Sinking Fund Bond Game." *Financial Analysts Journal,* November-December 1980.

45. Mayer, Kenneth R. "Yield Spreads and Interest Rate Bonds." *Financial Analysts Journal,* November-December 1978.

46. McConnell, J.J., and G.G. Schlarbaum. "Returns, Risks, and Pricing of Income Bonds, 1956-1976 (Does Money Have an Odor?)." *Journal of Business,* January 1981, 33-64.

47. Merton, Robert. "On the Pricing of Corporate Debt: The Risk Structure of Interest Rates." *The Journal of Finance,* May 1974, pp. 449-70.

48. Perry, Kevin S., and Robert A. Taggart, Jr. "The Growing Role of Junk Bonds in Corporate Finance," *Journal of Applied Corporate Finance* 1, no. 1 (Spring 1988).

49. Pinches. George E., and Kent A. Mingo: "A Multivariate Analysis of Industrial Bond Ratings," *Journal of Finance,* March 1973, pp. 1-18.

50. Pogue, Thomas F., and Robert M. Soldofsky. "What's in a Bond Rating?" *Journal of Financial and Quantitative Analysis.* June 1969, 201-228.

51. Rosen, Lawrence R., *Investing in Zero Coupon Bonds.* New York : John Wiley & Sons, 1986.

52. Sherwood, Hugh C. *How Corporate Debt, Is Rated,* New York; John Wiley & Sons, 1976.

53. Stigum, Marcia, and Frank Fabozzi, *The Dove Jones-Irwin Guide to Bonds and Mony Market Instruments.* Homewood III.: Dow Jones-Irwin, 1987.

54. Tuttle, Donald., ed. *The Revolution in Techniques for Managing Bond Portfolios.* Charlottesville, Va.: The Institute of Chartered Financial Analysts, 1983.

55. Wilson, Richard S. *Corporate Senior Securities.* Chicago: Probus Publishing, 1987.

56. ——————, and Frank J. Fabozzi. *The New Corporate Bond Market.* Chicago: Probus Publishing, 1990.

57. Winkelmann, Kurt. "Uses and Abuses of Duration and Convexity." *Financial Analysts Journal* 45, no. 5 (September-October 1989).

58. Yago, Glenn. *Junk Bonds.* New York: Oxford University Press, 1991.

11

Preference Share Valuation and Analysis

INTRODUCTION

Preference shares are a *hybrid security* that is not heavily utilized by corporations as a means of raising capital. It is hybrid because it combines some of the characteristics of debt and some of equity. Legally a preference share represents a position of the ownership of the company, and thus is shown in the balance sheet with the equity shares as making up the capital stock or equity interest. In the investment practice, however, preference share is basically a weak corporate security as it has the limitation of bonds with few to the advantages. Like any fixed-income security, preference shares offer no protection from inflation. If inflation were to increase, the real purchasing power of the dividend would be diminished. In addition, increased inflation would probably, lead to higher interest rates, which would derive down the market value of the preference shares. Thus, higher rate of inflation doubly curse the preference shares, as the purchasing power of the dividend and the market value of the shares both will be diminished. This disadvantage, of course, applies to all fixed-income securities. Further, the preference share are also tend to be less marketable then other securities. Marketability of a particular preference share depends on the size of the issue. However, most preference shares are brought by institution. The market for remaining shares may be quite thin, so there can be substantial spread between the bid and he ask prices. Moreover, the preference shares are of inferior position to debt obligations. The investor must realize that preference share is perceptibly riskier then bonds. In addition the yield offered on preference share are probably insufficient to justify the additional risk. The yield on preference shares are not necessarily higher than those available on bonds because of the tax advantage. It does not enjoy strong legal position of a bond when the corporation is required to pay return to the investor and refund the principal amount at maturity. As the returns to the holders are discretionary, the corporation is under much less compulsion to pay preference dividends than to pay bond interest because preference share is merely given the right to receive its specific dividend before any dividends are paid on the equity. When a corporation fails to meet interest charges on bonds, the result is receivership, which may result in liquidation or (more probably) a re-organisation with a complete turnover of management. Therefore, it may be presumed that a company will pay bond interest as long as it is possible to do so. But the penalty resulting from a failure to declare dividends to preference share holders is not particularly onerous. Such a default merely means that the company cannot pay dividends on the equity until the preference dividends have been paid in full. Preference shares do have, however, certain preferences which makes it similar to bonds since both bonds and preference shares usually have (1) a limited return and (2) a prior claim on assets and income of the corporation. In fact, some of the disadvantages of the preference shares can be offset if following qualifications of a well performed preference share are taken care of:

(i) It must meet all the minimum requirements of a safe bond.

(ii) It must exceed these minimum requirements by a certain added margin to offset the discretionary feature in the payment of dividends, *i.e.* the margin of safety must be so large that the directors may always be expected to declare the dividend as a matter of course.

(iii) The stipulation of investment stability in the business itself must be more stringent than in the case of a bond investment, because a company subject to alternation between large profits and temporary losses is likely to suspend dividends to the preference shareholders during the latter periods even though its average earnings may far exceed the annual requirements.

FEATURES OF PREFERENCE SHARES

The features of preference shares, like those of bonds, cover a wide range. Each individual preference share will vary as to the features it includes. Corporation financial managers usually emphasize one or the other set of features while issuing them. The main features of preference shares are listed below :

1. Dividends

Preference shares have dividend provisions which are either cumulative or non-cumulative. Most shares have the cumulative provisions, which means that any dividend not paid by the company accumulates. Normally, the firm must pay these unpaid dividends prior to the payment of dividends on the equity. These unpaid dividends are known as dividends in arrears or arrearages.

Non-cumulative dividends do not accumulate if they are not paid when due. An investor contemplating the purchase of preference shares with a non-cumulative dividend provision needs to be especially diligent in the investigation of the company because of the investor's potentially weak position *vis-a-vis* those preference shares with a cumulative dividend provision. In case of cumulative preference shares, even if the arrears of the preference dividend are cleared in full, the investor would be loser as he is to get less in net worth.

2. Participating Preference Shares

Most preference shares are non-participating, meaning that the preference shareholder receives only his stated dividend and no more. The theory is that the preference shareholder has surrendered claim to the residual earnings of his company in return for the right to receive his dividend before dividends are paid to equity shareholders. The participating preference shareholder receives stipulated dividend and shares additional earnings with the equity shareholders. But this share is usually non-cumulative which confirms the view that preference share does have both protective and profit participating provisions.

3. Voting Rights

Preference shares do not normally confer voting rights. The basis for not allowing the preference shareholder to vote is that the preference shareholder is in a relatively secure position and, therefore, should have no right to vote except in the special circumstances. In India, for instance, the non- cumulative type qualifies for voting rights if preference dividends have been in arrears for the two financial years preceding the meeting or for any three years during a period of six years (ending with the financial year) preceding the meeting. The cumulative preference shares can vote if their dividend is in arrears for

2 years. The voting right of each preference shareholder is to be in the proportion which the paid-up share capital on his shares bears to the total equity share capital of the company.

4. Convertible

Convertible preference share means that the owner has the right to exchange a preference share for a share of equity share of the same company. As in the case of bonds, sometimes the number of shares of equity are given. There are times when conversion is determined on the basis of par value. For example, a ₹100 per preference share may be convertible into equity shares at ₹ 50 a share or 2 shares of equity for each share of ₹100 per preference share. The holder of convertible preference share has a stronger claim than the holder of an equity share to earnings and assets. In addition, if a company earnings increase, the convertible preference shares will rise in value.

A company might wish to call preference shares. Then the preference shareholder must be given the required number of days notice. This will enable him to either convert into equity or sell the stock. Since the preference share is registered in the name of the holder, the company will notify him of the call.

5. Par Value

Most preference shares have a par value. When it does, the dividend rights and call price are usually stated in terms of the par value. However, those rights would be specified even if there were no par value. It seems, therefore, as with equity shares, the preference share that has a par value has no real advantage over preference share that has no par value.

6. Redeemable or Callable Preference Shares

Typically, preference shares have no maturity date. In this respect it is similar to equity shares. Redeemable or callable preference shares may be retired by the issuing company upon the payment of a definite price stated in the investment. Although the "call price" provides for the payment of a premium, the provision is more advantageous to the corporation than to the investor. When money rates decline, the corporation is likely to call in its preference shares and refinance it at a lower dividend rate. When money rates rise, the value of the preference shares declines so as to produce higher yield, the call price acts as an upper peg or plateau through which the price will break only in a very strong market. Non-callable preference shares are issued in periods of high interest rates. The issue is barred from redeeming them later in the event of generally falling yields or for a certain period so the investor has important protection against declining income.

7. Sinking Fund Retirement

Preference share issue are often retired through sinking funds. In these cases, a certain percentage of earnings (above minimum amounts) is allocated for redemption each year. The shares required for sinking fund purposes can be called by lot or purchased in the open market.

The owners of preference shares called for sinking fund purposes must seek alternative investments. In this sense, preference sinking funds have unfavourable overtones for these investors. But sinking funds have favourable overtones for the owners of shares that are not retired. Sinking fund requirements reduce preference shares outstanding which will give the remaining shares a strong income position. Hence, dividend payments are more certain. The investment status of preference shares will improve gradually where sinking fund arrangements exist.

8. Preemptive Right

Common law statute gives shareholders, equity or preference, the right to subscribe to additional issues to maintain their proportionate share of ownership. However, the existence of the preemptive right depends on the law and the provisions of the company's articles of incorporation. The right is a bit more likely to be waived for preference shares than for equity, particularly if preference shares are non-voting.

It can be observed from foregoing analysis that though the word "preference" in everyday life always means something that is better but in investment parlance preference shares are not better than equity shares. They are preferred as to dividends in the case of trouble and they are preferred as to assets in case of liquidation or reorganization, but actually it is better to buy equity shares that is going to stay out of trouble and improve and if it gets into trouble sell it than to buy a preference share and stand on legal rights. On the preference shares of the straight, ordinary kind, income is limited but loss is unlimited. The only kind of preference shares that are attractive are those in trouble but going out of it. They can often be bought at a large discount, sometimes with arrears, or when they have the advantage of a conversion privilege. Preference shares are not usually a better investment than equity shares stocks, as some people incorrectly believe.

PREFERENCE SHARE YIELDS

To determine the rates of return earned, the preference share holders use following three yields :

Current Yield

When preference shares do not have a maturity date, the investors use the current yield to measure the return available from dividends. They merely divide the annual dividend payment by the current market price to calculate this yield as follows :

$$\text{Current Yield} = \frac{\text{Annual dividend}}{\text{Market price}}$$

For example, if the 9% preference shares of XYZ Company are sold for ₹ 72, the current yield is 12.5 per cent.

$$\text{Current Yield} = \frac{₹\,9}{₹\,72} = 12.5\%$$

However, the planning or holding period return would be more useful if the investment horizons are known.

Planning or Holding Period Return

To calculate the gross receipts expected to be earned from holding a preference share, the formula used is:

$$\text{HPR} \quad = \quad \frac{D_t + \Delta P}{P_i}$$

and $\Delta P = P_t - P_i$

HPR	=	Planning or holding period return.
D_t	=	Dividend to be paid during the planned investment period.
P_i	=	Initial Price
P_t	=	Terminal price.
Δ_p	=	Change in prices during the planned investment period.

For example, suppose the XYZ company 9 percent cumulative preference share (₹ 100 par) is sold for ₹ 72. An investor expects this to increase in price by ₹ 18 due to expected decline in interest rates. This change, he feels, would take about two years. On this basis, the holding period return would be :

$$\text{HPR} = \frac{D_i + \Delta P}{P_i}$$

$$= \frac{₹ 18 + ₹ 18}{₹ 72} = \frac{₹ 36}{₹ 72}$$

Yield to the Call Date

If the issues are callable, their dividend payments cannot be expected to continue indefinitely. In this case, the probable call date is used as an investment terminal date to evaluate.

$$Y_c = \frac{D_t + \dfrac{C_P - P_i}{n}}{(P_i + C_P)/2}$$

As an example, we can assume that 9 per cent (₹ 100 par) will be called in 3 years at ₹ 108. The current market price of this issue is ₹ 72. The yield to call date is :

$$
\begin{aligned}
D_t &= & .09 \times 3 \times ₹ 100 &= ₹ 27 \\
C_p &= & ₹ 108 \\
P_i &= & 72 \\
n &= & 3 \text{ years}
\end{aligned}
$$

$$Y_c = \frac{D_t + \dfrac{C_P - P_i}{n}}{\frac{1}{2}(P_i + C_P)}$$

$$Y_c = \frac{₹ 27 + \dfrac{₹ 108 - ₹ 72}{3}}{1/2(₹ 72 + ₹ 108)} = \frac{₹ 27 + ₹ 12}{1/2 \text{ of } ₹ 180}$$

$$Y_t = \frac{₹ 39}{₹ 90} = \frac{₹ 13}{₹ 30} = 43.13\%$$

The approximate annual yield to a three year call date is 43.13%. Most probably, this call would not be undertaken. Under the conditions outlined above, the management would prefer to purchase in the open market at ₹ 63.48 rather than issue a call at ₹ 108.

REVIEW PROBLEMS

1. Consider a share of preferred stock with a par value of ₹ 100 that pays an 12% annual dividend, or ₹ 12. If the discount rate for this share is 15%, what would the preference share be worth?

Ans:

$$V_P = \frac{₹ 12}{0.15} = ₹ 80$$

2. PHIND pays a ₹ 2.76 dividend on each preference share. What is the value of each preference share if the required rate of return of investors is 12 percent?

Ans:

$$V_P = \frac{₹\ 2.76}{0.12} = ₹\ 23$$

3. What is the value of a preference share where the dividend rate is 18 percent on a ₹ 100 par value? The appropriate discount rate for a stock of this risk level is 15%.

$$V_P = \frac{0.18 \times ₹\ 100}{0.15}$$

$$= \frac{₹\ 18}{0.15} = ₹\ 120$$

4. The preference shares of KD Group are selling for ₹ 47.50 per share and pays a dividend of ₹ 2.35 in dividends. What is your expected rate of return if you purchase the security at market price?

Ans.

$$\text{Expected rate of return} = \frac{\text{Dividend}}{\text{Market Price}}$$

$$= \frac{₹\ 2.35}{₹\ 47.50}$$

$$= 4.95\%$$

5. You own 250 preference shares of XYZ company which currently sells for ₹ 38.50 per share and pays annual dividends of ₹ 6.50 per share.
   (a) What is your expected return?
   (b) If you require a 13% return, given the cu8rrent price, should you sell or buy more preference shares?

Ans:

(a) $\text{Expected return} = \dfrac{\text{Dividend}}{\text{Market Price}}$

$$= \frac{₹\ 6.50}{₹\ 38.50}$$

$$= 16.88\%$$

(b) Given 13 percent required rate of return, the stock is worth:

$$V_P = \frac{\text{Dividend}}{\text{Required Rate}}$$

$$= ₹\ 50.00$$

Because the expected rate of return (16.88%) is greater than the required rate of return (13%) or because the current market price (₹ 38.50) is less than ₹ 50.00, the stock is undervalued and it is worth buying.

6. Pioneer's preference shares are selling for ₹ 44 per share in the market and pays a ₹ 4.40 annual dividend.
   (a) What is the expected rate of return on the preference shares?
   (b) If an investor's required rate of return is 12 percent, what is the value of a preference share for that investor?
   (c) Should the investor acquire the preference shares?

Ans:

(a) Expected rate of return on preference

$$= \frac{₹\ 4.40}{₹\ 44.00}$$

(b) $V_P = \dfrac{\text{Dividend}}{\text{Required rate of return}}$

$$= \frac{₹\ 4.40}{0.12}$$

$$= ₹\ 36.67$$

(c) The investor's required rate of return (12%) is more than the expected rate of return for the investment (10%). Also, the value of the preference share to th2 investor (₹ 36.67) is less than the existing market price (₹ 44). Therefore, the investor should not acquire the preference shares from the market.

QUESTIONS

1. What are some of the general characteristics found in preference shares ?
2. Discuss the nature of preference shares and indicate the attributes that make it unique.
3. Comment upon the stability of the current yield on preference share.
4. What should an investor emphasis in analysis of preference share ?
5. Describe the usual features of a preference share with respect to the typical rights given to it in the agreement.
6. How can we determine whether the preference dividend is secured?
7. What risks are associated with the purchase for investment of preference share, and how can they be estimated ?
8. Contrast the stability or variability of yields on preference share with those of bonds.
9. Explain why preference shares are less actively traded than equity shares. Does preference share represent debt or equity to the issuing corporation ?
10. Under what circumstances would a preference share with dividends in arrears be an attractive investment ?
11. Do individual investors find preference shares attractive as a vehicle of investment?
12. In trying to explain the concept of preference share to a novice investor, they are referred as a 'hybrid security'. What does 'hybrid' mean? What are the advantages and disadvantages of investing in preference shares?

PROBLEMS

1. Assume that a preference share is currently priced to provide a 10% required rate of return and pays a ₹ 8 dividend.
    (a) Calculate the value of the preference share.
    (b) Assume that the required rate of return declines to 8%. Calculate the new value for the preference share.
    (c) Calculate the holding period return, assuming that the investor purchased the preference share when it was priced to provide a 10% rate of return and sold when required rate of return reached 9%. Also assume that the investor held the share long enough to receive an annual dividend.
2. Consider the following two investment alternatives :_____

	Preference Share	Debenture
Terms-to-maturity	7 years	

Annual dividend/Interest	₹ 12	₹ 15
Required rate of return	15%	20%

(a) Calculate the intrinsic values for the preference shares and the debenture.
(b) Assume that the required rate of return on the preference share declines to 13% and the debenture's return declines to 16%. Calculate the intrinsic values for both securities.
(c) Calculate the percentage changes in the intrinsic values for the preference share and the debenture.
(d) For an individual pursuing an active investment strategy, which security appears more attractive on a return basis ?

3. Consider the following data on a preference share:

Par value		₹ 100
Price on January 1,2011	:	₹ 80
Price on January 1,2010	:	₹ 70
Dividend rate	:	11%

(a) Calculate the dividend yield on January 1, 2010 and on January 1, 2011.
(b) Calculate the holding period return for 2010.

4. G AMA Series is considering refunding its preference share. The dividend rate on this share is ₹ 15 and it has a par value of ₹ 100 a share. The call price is ₹ 120 a share, and 50,00,000 shares are issued. The company feels that it can issue new preference shares in the current market at an interest rate of 12 per cent. With this rate, the new issue could be sold at par : the total par value of the issue could be ₹ 100 crore. Floatation costs ₹ 5 crores are tax deductible; but the call premium is not tax deductible; the company's marginal tax rate is 50 per cent. A 90-day period of overlap is expected between the time the new preference share is issued and the time the old preference share is retired. Should the company refund its preference shares ?

6. DMX company could sell preference shares with a dividend cost of 12 per cent. If it were to sell debentures in the current market, the interest-rate cost would be 15 per cent. The company is in 40 per cent tax bracket.
(a) What is the after-tax cost of each of those methods of financing?
(b) MXD holds a limited number of preference shares in its marketable security portfolio. It is in a 50% tax bracket. If it were to invest in the preference shares of DMX company, what would be its after-tax return ? What would be its after-tax return if it were to invest in the debentures ?

6. Gujarat Industries needs to raise ₹ 950 crores for capital improvements. One possibility is a new preference share issue: 12 per cent, ₹ 100 par value preference share that would yield 15 per cent to investors. Flotation costs for an issue of this size amount to 5 per cent of the total amount of preference shares sold; these costs are deducted from gross proceeds in determining the net proceeds to the company.
(a) At what price per share will the preference shares be offered to investors ?
(b) How many shares must be issued to raise ₹ 950 crores for Gujarat Industries?

7. An investor on a preference share has an annual dividend of ₹ 5. If he requires a 12% return, how much is he willing to pay for a share?
Ans: ₹ 41.67

8. Determine the times-dividends-earned ratio for the following information: 30% corporate income tax rate ₹ 10,00,000 EBIT (Earnings before interest and taxes) ₹ 2,00,000 interest owed ₹ 2,00,000 dividends on preference shares.
Ans: Times-dividend earned : 2.8

9. What should be the price of a preference share if the appropriate discount rate is 13% and the annual dividend is ₹ 6?
Ans: ₹ 46.15

10. Super Company has a perpetual preference share issue outstanding that pays a 10 percent dividend. The par value of each share is ₹ 100 and the dividend is paid quarterly.

The shares are currently trading for ₹ 85.
   (a) What is the expected nominal rate of return on the issue?
   (b) What is the expected effective annual rate of return?
   (c) What is the expected after-eax return (i) to an individual investor in the 28% marginal tax bracket? To a corporate investor in the 34% marginal tax bracket?
   (d) Assume that the issue has a sinking fund provision whereby the firm redeems 10 percent of the issue in each year over the next 10 years at a share price equal to par value, or ₹ 100, what is the expected pre-tax rate of return with a sinking fund provision?

Ans: (a) 11.76%
   (b) 12.29%
   (c) 14.41%

11. Assume that you are in the 40% tax bracket and that the capital gain taxes are deferred until maturity. Assuming equal investment risk and a horizontal yield curve, rank the following investment opportunities on the basis of their effective annual yields:
   (a) A ₹ 100 par value perpetual preference share with an annual coupon of 12%, quarterly payments, and selling at ₹ 105.
   (b) A ₹ 100 par value, 20-year, non-callable, semiannual bond with a coupon of 12%, currently selling at ₹ 1050.
   (c) A ₹ 1,000 par value, 20-year, non-callable, semiannual bond with a coupon of 6% selling at a price of ₹ 637.
   (d) How would the situation change if the ranker had been (i) a mutual fund investment manager, or (ii) a corporation that is in the 40 percent tax bracket? Explain in words but demonstrate that you could quantify your answer.

Ans: (a) 7.03%
   (b) 6.90%
   (c) 6.61%
   (d) (i) 11.93%, (ii) 11.68%, (iii) 10.59%

12. W.W. Watch Company is expected to skip its annual preferred dividend payments of ₹ 9 for the next three years; however, it is expected to resume its normal payment pattern starting four years from now. At that time, the three delayed dividends will also be paid in full. If the required rate on the preference share is 12%, find the current price of the preference share.

Ans: ₹ 70.54.

13. Refer to problem (12), assume that W.W. Watch Company must pay 10% interest, compounded annually on any delayed preferred dividends. What is the current preference share price in that case? Ans: ₹ 74.21.

REFERENCES

1. Bellemore, Phillips, and Ritchie. *Investments.* Cincinnati: South-western Publishing, 1979.

2. Cohen, J., E. Zinbarg, and A. Zeikel: *Investment Analysis and Portfolio Management,* Richard D Irwin, Home wood, IL, 1987.

3. Curran, Ward S. "Preferred Stock for Public Utilities." *Financial Analysts Journal,* July-August 1969, p. 112.

4. D'ambrosio, Charles A. *Principles of Modern Investments.* Chicago: Science Research Associates.

5. Donaldson, G. "In Defense of Preferred Stock." *Harvard Business Review,* 40 (July-August 1962). Reprinted in *Foundations for Financial Management,* ed. James Van Home, pp. 194-218. Homewood, III.: Irwin, 1966.

6. Grodinsky, Julius. *Investments.* New York: Ronald Press, 1953.

7. Hayes D., and W. Bauman. *Investments: Analysis and Management.* New York: Macmillan, 1976,.

8. Mendelson and Robbins. *Investment Analysis & Securities Markets.* New York: Basic Books, 1976.

9. Noddings, Thomas C. *Advanced Investment Strategies.* Homewood, III .: Dow Jones-Irwin, 1978.

10. Sauvain, Harry C. *Investment Management,* 4th ed. Englewood Cliffs, N.J.: Prentice-Hall, 1973

11. Sharpe, William F., Gordon J. Alexander, and Jeffrey V. Bailey. *Investments,* 5th ed. Englewood Cliffs, N.J.: Prentice-Hall, 1995.

12

Equity Shares

INTRODUCTION

Equity represents an ownership position in a corporation. It is a residual claim, in the sense that creditors and preference shareholders must be paid as scheduled before equity shareholders can receive any payment. In bankruptcy equity holders are in principle entitled only to assets remaining after all prior claimants have been satisfied. Thus, risk is highest with equity shares and so must be its expected return. When investors buy equity shares, they receive certificates of ownership as proof of their being part owners of the company. The certificate states the number of shares purchased and their par value.-

CHANGING ATTITUDE TOWARDS EQUITY OWNERSHIP

With a broadening of the corporate sector, volume of business on the exchanges in India is likely to increase. The greater interest shown in recent years by investors is partly reflected in the over-subscription of new issues. There has been a great demand for "growth" issues *i.e.* shares of companies with growth prospects (companies floated with foreign collaboration fall into this category). It has been observed that the wider the distribution of corporate securities among investors, the greater the reception accorded to new or additional issues of capital; the more mobile the additional issues of capital; the more mobile the market, the greater the participation of investors and traders in the raising of corporate capital.

The available data about share ownership in the country show that there is gradual widening of ownership. The increasing participation in stock market activities by financial and non-financial intermediaries, particularly of institutions which are mainly investors has tended to create an orderly and stable market. Further, the various growth-permitting factors — including regulatory measures, progressive spread of literacy and dissemination of investment information — all tend to contribute to a healthy growth of the stock market. In the security market, equity shares are the most romantic of all the form of securities. Further-more, equity analysis is more complicated than bond appraisal, and greater skill is required in selecting equity shares than fixed income securities. The attitude towards equity shares has varied from extreme pessimism to optimism from time to time. It is equity shares that entice most investors, and some investors have been known to feel a greater sympathy for their equity than their spouses. Presence of market and business risks associated with such investments fails to keep the investing public and institution out of the market because of their confidence in the ultimate success of the equity shares, *i.e.* towards overshadow risks. In fact the advantages of equity shares ownership are enough to lure the investors and change their attitude towards securities.

The main advantages of equity shares are listed below :

1. Potential for Profit

The potential for profit is greater in equity share than in any other investment security. Current dividend yield may be low but potential of capital gain is great. The total yield or yields to maturity, may be substantial over a period of time.

2. Limited Liability

In corporate form of organisation, its owners have, generally, limited liability. Equity Share is usually fully paid. Shareholders may lose their investment, but no more. They are not further liable for any failure on the part of the corporation to meet its obligation.

3. Hedge Against Inflation

The equity share is a good hedge against inflation though it does not fully compensate for the declining purchasing power as it is subject to the money-rate risk. But, when interest rates are high, shares tend to be less attractive, and prices tend to be depressed.

4. Free Transferability

The owner of shares has the right to transfer his interest to someone else. The buyer should ensure that the issuing corporation transfers the ownership on its books so that dividends, voting rights, and other privileges will accrue to the new owner. Although the individual has the right to sell his shares, there is little or no trading in the shares of many corporations due to the lack of interested buyers. For this reason, equity shares of many small businesses are nonliquid and difficult to market.

5. Share in the Growth

The major advantage of investment in equity shares is its ability to increase in value by sharing in the growth of company profits over the long run.

6. Tax Advantages

Equity shares also offer tax advantages to the investor. The larger yield on equity shares results from an increase in principal or capital gains, which are taxed at lower rate than other incomes in most of the countries.

EQUITY CAPITAL TERMINOLOGY

The important terms used in equity capital are listed below:

Authorised Capital

The authorised capital is the maximum number of shares of each type that may be issued by a company. To change this number, or the provisions of any class of shares, the company requires the formal approval of shareholders.

Issued Capital

Issued capital is that part of the authorised capital that has been issued for cash, property, or service.

Paid up Capital

Fully paid shares are those shares for which the corporation has received full payment up to par-value, or up to the amount established as the selling price of no-par-shares. Partly-paid shares are those shares that have been issued for less than par-value or the agreed subscription price.

NATURE OF EQUITY SHARES

Equity shares represent an ownership of a corporation. It is true that the equity shares must bear first impact of any adversity, but it is also true that the equity shares is the only class of securities privileged to enjoy the maximum participation in an extensive growth of the company. The risk of the one may be regarded as commensurate with the opportunity of the other. There is nothing certain about earnings on equity shares, and the investor can lose as well as earn a profit.

1. Evidence of Ownership

When investors buy equity shares, they receive certificates of ownership as proof of their part as owners of the company. The certificate states the number of shares purchased, their par value, if any, and usually the transfer agent. When equity shares are purchased on the market (that is, when it is not a new issue which is purchased from the company), the new owner and the number of shares bought are noted in the record book of the transfer agent.

Although all equity shares represent an ownership interest in the company, the investment characteristics of these shares differ widely. Hence stocks are grouped into largely subjective categories including *blue chip, growth, income defensive, cyclical, and penny stocks*. These categories are not mutually exclusive, nor are they precise. Of all the categories of stock, blue chip stocks might be best known. *Blue chip is a colloquial term used to imply high quality*. It is generally associated with a company being a long, uninterrupted history of dividend payments. Another popular category is *income stocks*. These are those stocks that have *historically paid a larger than - average percentage of their net income after taxes (NIAT). Cyclical stocks, whose fortune is directly tied to the state of the overall national economy often have higher- than - average market risk*. The term cycle has nothing to do with its chart pattern, nor does the term imply that stock prices are more predictable than other issues. *Defensive stock* largely immune to changes in the macroeconomy, continue to sell. These stock have nothing to do with national defense. *Growth stocks* is one in which the company reinvests most of its earnings into profitable investment opportunities return than returning them directly to the shareholders in the form of cash dividends. The growth stock is expected to show above-average capital appreciation in the future. *Speculative stock* is one with the potential to make its owners a lot of money quickly. At the same time it carries a higher than normal degree of risk. In other words, a speculative stock has a high probability of a loss and a small probability of a large profit. The potential for a large profit is the attraction. *Penny Stocks* fell into a catchall category that refers to unusually risky, especially inexpensive shares.

2. Maturity of Equity Shares

Equity Shares have no maturity date. Their life is limited by the length of time stated in the corporate charter known as 'Memorandum of Association'. The corporate life might be for a stated or limited period, or it might be perpetual. Most corporations have a perpetual charter.

For investment purposes, equity shares can be purchased and sold at any time. The date on which the equity is sold by the investor is the maturity date, and the price at which the equity is sold is the maturity price. In fact, the investor is vitally concerned with the yield earned over the period that the equity is owned, since the yield for the holding period represents the total earnings to the investor and is a measure of performance to be compared to those of other securities investments.

3. Par Value

Par value is the face value of a share. Equity shares have a par value, a nominal stated value. The par value of an equity share indicates the amount of capital originally subscribed by the shareholders. New shares cannot be sold for less than par value. If the equity shares are sold for more than par, the excess is transferred to 'Share Premium Account'.

4. Net Asset Value and Book Value

Distrust of present value formulae, the quest for objectivity and perhaps even nontalgia lead some analysts to place greater emphasis on the asset value factor when evaluating the investment worth of a company's equity shares. Net assets or net worth can be calculated from either the asset or liability side of the balance sheet. For example, Company X has a net worth of ₹ 13,15,94,000 which we got by deducting the total liabilities worth ₹ 30,29,99,000 from the total assets of ₹ 43,45,93,000 for the same year. And since the annual report for that year indicates that 5,44,072 shares of shares were outstanding at the end of the year, net assets per share can readily be calculated by dividing the number of shares into total net assets (net worth):

$$\frac{₹\ 13,15,94,000}{5,44.072} = 241.86\ \text{Per share}$$

What significance can be attributed to the figure 241.86 per share ? Does it represent the "value" of the share in some objective sense ? In particular, if a share is selling for more than ₹ 241.86, are we justified in concluding that it is overpriced ? On the other hand, what if the price of the equity is significantly below the book value; does it then represent a "bargain"?

Unfortunately, an unequivocal answer cannot be given to either of these questions. In general, a systematic relationship between book value and market price can be established. The estimate of net assets per share reflects the accounting conventions used in drawing up the balance sheet and this accounting practice deviates significantly from economic theory, so that there is little reason to suppose that an accounting valuation, will have a meaningful relationship to an economic valuation of the same property. It is sufficient for this purpose to consider the use of historical costs in accounting. A plant which was erected five years ago might be worth double the amount on the open market today, owing to inflation, rises in property values, changes in local taxes, etc. But at the same time there is no guarantee that it is not worth half of its book value, owing to innovations, a fall in property values, of the like. Furthermore, the possibility of converting into more profitable assets (or liquidating) may be very small because of regulatory constraints. Manufacturing concerns that have substantial assets that produce little cash flow frequently cannot liquidate these assets, except at distress prices. Hence, for all practical purposes, their asset "values" have no real significance.

Shares of some companies sell at too low a price because their cash assets are too large. This sounds like a paradox, but moment's thought will show that the statement can be true. Market price depends chiefly on earnings; cash assets bring in no or very little earnings. A company with nothing but cash in bank could not possibly earn to support a market price equal to its cash-asset value. It has been by no means unusual to find companies that are so rich in cash that they are necessarily poor in earning power as related to book value.

Thus, the net book value of a firm does not measure its value as a growing concern, but neither does it measure its "break-up" value, or the realizable value of the assets in case of liquidation. Of course, there are exceptions to the rule and some companies have a high correlation between the current market values and book values of their assets. But in such cases, one must recall that the growing concern value may well be higher. All of the firm's valuable assets do not always appear on the balance sheet. For example, the productivity of assets and a specific combination of assets and entrepreneurial ability often create greater earnings and greater values than the book value of the assets suggests.

5. Financial Analysis and Accounting Data

The historical numbers that analyst uses to prepare rates and forecasting equations are generally based on figures that have been taken from the published financial statements of the firm being analysed. Although these statements may have been prepared "according to generally accepted accounting principles", there may be significant variation in the real economic meaning of financial reports. Obvious inconsistencies in the methodology of preparation (for example, when a firm switches from LIFO to FIFO inventory valuation, or from accelerated depreciation to straight line) require adjustments to the documents pre-pared by the accounting community. More subtle problems may exist, however, which cannot easily be handled by making simple adjustments. One of the more plaguing difficulties with financial statements is that they are prepared on the assumption of stable prices. To the extent that price changes over time, the reported asset value on the firm's balance sheet (and perhaps the liability values as well) will be inaccurate. Further, because accounting costs are usually based on historical prices, a misstatement about the value of an asset may well result in an inaccurate depiction of net income. Moreover, net income in one period may not be equivalent to an identical net income in another if the value aggregate level of prices has changed.

Another problem is that the market values of a firm's assets have no relationship to their book values. Price-level changes, variances from depreciation estimates, and the insistence of accountants upon valuing assets at the lower of cost or market (an example of doctrine of 'conservatism') make the balance sheet an unreliable statement about the value of the enterprise. Of course, the accountants themselves beg off, claiming that financial analysts expect too much from published statements. One respected practitioner has observed:

> "...accountants in their most solemn pronouncements have made it quite clear that the financial statements they prepare do not even purport to provide, information about solvency and profitability. For instance, anyone might be pardoned for thinking that a conventional balance sheet is prepared to show the financial strength of a company by listing its obligations against its resources and to establish its net value. But this is not at all how a balance sheet is defined in accounting texts."

Thus, when the analyst finds that return on total investment has increased from 20 per cent to 21 per cent, it is not clear that an improvement has taken place. Earnings figures from one year to the next (and across firms for any given year) are not strictly comparable, and total investment can become completely incomparable over time.

What should the unfortunate analyst do under such circumstances ? The answer, of course, is to make the best of the situation. Adjustments to published statements should be made whenever there is good justification to do so. Otherwise, the analyst should bear in mind always the limitations of the data that he has used in making his appraisal. A report based on less-than-perfect data is better than no report at all. Security analysis has always been a tentative undertaking. It is perhaps less so today that it was a few years ago. Nevertheless, all the powerful statistical tools that the analyst now has at his disposal have not reduced the process to a scientific procedure. Analysis is an artful endeavour. It has been in the past and will always be a matter of rational guess work.

6. Pre-emptive Right

A pre-emptive right, simply means the inherent right of the shareholder, to maintain his proportionate share of the assets, earnings, and control of the corporation. It is a common-law right. In other words, the corporation offers new shares to its own shareholders before offering it to the public. This is to prevent the company from offering shares to the public at a price substantially below its worth, thus lessening the interest of the old shareholders in the corporate pie. When a company offers new shares to its old shareholders, its price to them is usually set below the current market. A shareholder has a right to subscribe for new shares, proportionately for each share held. A letter of offer is sent to the shareholder stating the number of rights owned which corresponds to the number of shares held. It will also specify the number of new shares to which the shareholder is entitled to subscribe and the per share price of such subscription. This privilege to subscribe is of short-term nature, usually expiring in few weeks.

(a) Mechanics of Rights Offering

The mechanics of a rights offering are quite simple. The company announces a rights offering to shareholders listed on the books as of the record date. These shareholders will receive rights to buy additional shares that may be exercised any time between the date of the rights distribution and the expiration date. In the period between the announcement and the last date one may purchase the equity to become a shareholder by the record date. Till such time, the equity is said to be selling "rights-on" or "cum-rights". This means that any purchase of the equity shares between those days carries with it the right to buy additional new shares. After the record date, the equity shares sell "rights-off' or "ex-rights".

Exhibit-1 and the following example will make more clear the mechanics of a equity share rights offering.

EXHIBIT-1

Meeting Day 'Rights-on' period September 1st	Record Day September 15th	Rights Expire 'Rights-off ' period September 30th

At their meeting on September 1, the board of directors of a corporation announce that investors owning shares on September 15 (the record day) will be eligible to participate in a forthcoming distribution of new equity shares.

The period between the announcement day and the record day is the 'rights-on' period between September 1 and September 15. The period between the record day and the day the rights expire is the 'rights-off period — September 15 to September 30. In this latter period, the rights may be exercised.

Many a perplexed shareholder in a company making a rights issue wonders what to do about 'rights' - whether to take up the rights or not ? For this, the following points are noteworthy:

(b) Why Rights Issue?

Essentially companies make rights issues to shareholders in order to raise finance with which to underpin an investment programme (money for new plant etc.) or to reduce the burden of company debt. Alternatively a company could be hard-pressed for cash and have to come to its shareholders to put more cash because the necessary finance cannot be raised elsewhere. This latter case could be termed as 'involuntary' rights issues because the company has no alternative open to it of raising the ready cash. The former case is basically a Voluntary' rights issue because the company has the other options open to it of raising the necessary cash by selling equity to the investing public, or by arranging a term loan.

(c) What About the Shareholders

Normally, rights issues are bad news for shareholders and tend to have been disliked. A rights issue can (and most probably will) dilute the shareholders' return from the company in which he has invested because the rise in net profit on the new capital raised will usually be less than the increase in shareholders' capital.

It is first necessary to clear up a popular misconception which has probably been caused by the cosmetic effect of the new rights issues. There are still many investors who believe that a rights issue by the company in which they hold shares offers them the opportunity of subscribing capital on preferential terms — in other words the shareholder is getting something for nothing. What is not fully understood, or perhaps not understood at all, is that the apparent discount between the price of new shares being issued by way of rights, as against the price of the old shares, is eliminated when the shares go 'ex-rights'.

The rights will only have a value if the market believes that the new capital being raised will earn a rate of return which is the same as, or greater than, the existing share capital. In order to evaluate a rights issue, it is necessary for the shareholder to know to what purpose the capital being raised by the company's rights issue is to be put, and what sort of return will be earned from it.

Having made the case for the commonsense approach to a rights issue — remember that it is rare that rights issue capital will earn the same rate of return as the shareholders' existing capital in a company, particularly if the new money is only being used to fund existing debt.

(d) Calculating the Value of a Right

To calculate the theoretical value of rights in 'on' and 'off period, following formulae have been developed:

(i) *The Value for the 'Rights-on' Period:* Anyone acquiring shares after the meeting day and before, the record day receives the privilege of subscribing to new shares. Consequently, the privilege represented by a right has value in the 'rights-on' period. This value, furthermore, is reflected in the market price of an equity share. The theoretical value of one equity share right in the right-on period can be described by the following formula :

$$V = \frac{M_1 - S}{R + 1} \qquad (1)$$

V = Theoretical value of one equity share right.

M_1 = Market value of one share of equity in the 'right- on period.

S = Subscription price of one share of new equity.

R = Ratio of old to new equity; that is, the number of shares an investor must own to receive one new share.

To illustrate, assume that XYZ Corporation intends to raise ₹ one crore through pre-emptive rights. The equity shares of the XYZ Corporation has been selling at ₹ 30 a share so the subscription price is expected to be ₹ 25 a share. In addition, the shareholders of record will be able to purchase one new share for every four shares owned. What is the theoretical value of one right in the rights-on period?

$$V = \frac{M_1 - S}{R + 1}$$

$$V = \frac{₹\ 30 - ₹\ .25}{4 + 1}$$

$$V = ₹\ 1.$$

(ii) *The value in the 'Rights-off Period :* The subscription right issues to shareholders following the record day has a value completely divorced from its equity share during the 'rights-off' period. And this value is determined by supply and demand in the stock market during the life of the rights issue. The theoretical value of one right can be calculated as follows:

$$V = \frac{M_2 - S}{R}$$

Where

M_2 = Market value of one share of equity in the rights-off period. By substituting the XYZ .Corporation's values, we get:

$$V = \frac{M_2 - 25}{4}$$

$1 \times 4 = M_2 - 25$

$M_2 = 25 + 4$

$M_2 = 29$

(iii) *The theoretical value of the Equity:* In planning investment strategies, investors are concerned with the theoretical value of the equity share after the rights issue has expired. With such information available, they can estimate the worth of their holdings ex-rights.

To calculate the theoretical value of an equity stock ex-rights, following formula can be used:

$$V = \frac{M_1 R + S}{R + 1} \qquad (2)$$

where:

P = Value of the equity share ex-rights.

The XYZ Corporation case can be used to illustrate the value of an equity share (P) ex-rights. The theoretical value of the XYZ Corporation equity share ex-rights is :

$$P = \frac{30 \times 4 + 25}{4 + 1} = ₹\ 29$$

The XYZ Corporation equity shares can be expected to sell around ₹ 29 a share after the proposed rights offering has been completed. Of course, the actual market price of the XYZ Corporation equity shares will be determined by supply and demand in the stock market.

7. Share Prices and Issuance of New Shares

When a firm goes to the market to sell additional shares, the obvious short-run consequence is a reduction of current earnings per share. 'Dilution' is the term applied to this phenomenon, and many analysts feel that the effect of issuing new shares (and the consequent dilution) will depress share prices. Thus, if XYZ has issued 10 lakh shares outstanding selling at ₹ .20 per share and it issues another 10 lakh shares, one might suppose that the price per share would fall (see figure). Suppose XYZ earned ₹ 1 .00 per share (₹ 10 lakh). If another one lakh shares were issued, the adjusted earning per share would be 100000/110000 = ₹ 0.91.

If a multiple of 20 x were applied to the adjusted earnings, a price of (20) (.91) = ₹ 18.20 would prevail. Thus the shift in the XYZ share supply curve from S to S would tend to depress the stock's price.

Of course, only part of the story has been told. It is usually the case that the secondary effects of selling new shares are very positive, and the real position of the firm may improve rather than deteriorate as a result of the issue. The sale of new shares may allow the firm to raise needed capital to expand facilities, improve sales, and increase long-run profits. If long-run earnings per share increase by an amount larger than the short-run dilution produced by the creation of new shares, the price of the firm's stock should rise rather than fall. Suppose XYZ earnings increased to a long-run EPS of ₹ 1.05 as a result of the new share issue. It might be expected here that demanders would bid up share prices given these improved expectations. In fact, if the multiple of 20 X holds, we might expect the price to rise to :

$$(20) \ (₹ \ 1.05) = ₹ \ 21$$

This would be effected by a shift in the demand curve from D to D^1 (see Figure 1). Although it cannot be argued that every new issue of share will produce increase in long-run earnings sufficient to offset the dilution effect, one should not merely assume that a new issue will always depress prices. Rather, one should attempt to assess the long-run impact on earnings resulting from raising new capital.

8. Voting Rights

The shareholders have the right to select the board of directors, as well as vote on any fundamental changes in the corporation such as dissolution, consolidation, or amendments to the chapter or bylaws. But this right is largely theoretical. In most cases, the management determines the board of directors, and the basic changes to be made at annual or offer meetings. In advance of the meetings, the shareholders are sent notices of the meeting, statements setting forth the directors to be elected, other business to be approved, and proxies which they are asked to sign. The proxy is a document by which the shareholder authorises another person to attend and to vote at the meeting. In short, a proxy is a power of attorney granted by a shareholder authorising another person to act as per his instructions.

The board of directors is elected either under a majority voting system or under a cumulative voting system depending upon the corporate charter. Under majority voting system, each shareholder has one vote against each share that he owns and he must vote for each director position that is open. For example, if a shareholder owns 100 shares then he can cast 100 votes for each director's position open. This system precludes minority interests from electing directors as each person seeking a position on the board must win a majority of the total votes cast for that position. The management can elect the entire board in case they have votes or can obtain proxies, for over 50 per cent of the shares voted.

However, the cumulative voting system takes into account the minority interest as under this system the shareholder is able to accumulate his votes. For example, if a shareholder owns 100 shares and 10 directors are to be elected then he will be entitled to cast 1000 votes. He can cast these votes in whatever way he likes to choose the directors.

The minimum number of shares to elect a specific number of directors is determined by:

$$\frac{\text{Total shares issued times specific number of directors to be elected}}{\text{Total number of directors to be elected plus one}} + 1$$

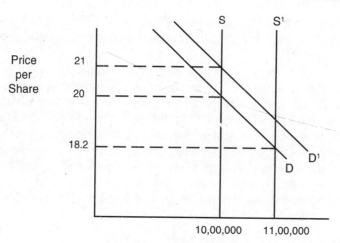

FIGURE 1: SHARES OUTSTANDING

For example, if the number of shares outstanding are five lakhs, the total number of directors to be elected is ten, and if a minority group wishes to elect two directors, it will need at least the following number of shares :

$$\frac{5,00,000 \times 2}{10+1} + 1 = 90,910$$

Even with cumulative voting, however, management sometimes can preclude minority interests for obtaining a seat on the board of directors by reducing the number of directors or by staggering the terms of the directors so that only a portion is elected each year.

DIVIDEND POLICIES AND DECISIONS

Dividend, in the normal use of the word, refers to that portion of earnings that is paid to equity shareholders. The management has three choices with respect to its net income. Firstly, income may be distributed in part or whole to the owners of the business. Secondly, earnings may be retained in the business for any use the management may decide on in the future. Thirdly, income may be retained for one or more specific purposes, and designated as reserves for these ends. However, the disposal of net income will be governed by number of considerations. The first consideration is necessarily the legal rights of the corporation to distribute net income. Government laws limit payment of dividend by corporations and even without statutory restrictions there are common law limitations upon dividend declarations. In the second place, the distribution of income to the owners of business is influenced by the tax consequences, both to the enterprise and to the owners personally. A third factor affecting dividend distributions is the working capital position of a corporation, for it would obviously be short-sighted to pay dividends where the effect is to undermine the financial strength of the enterprise and even to threaten its future solvency. A fourth basic consideration is the long term capital requirements of the business and availability of other sources of funds for expansion. Fifth, corporations may have specific objectives in view, such as merger with another business, that would be furthered by liberal dividend distributions that would make their stock more attractive if offered in exchange for the shares of other business, and the desire to achieve such a purpose may offset other considerations in shaping dividend policy.

Cash Dividend

The large majority of dividends are payable in cash. Corporations incorporated abroad usually pay dividends in their own countries, and in some cases restrictions apply to transfer of dividends out of a country. Cash dividends are recommended by the board of directors and paid to the equity shareholders. Normally cash dividend is paid out of the current year's net profit and rest is appropriated to the reserves and surplus account.

Normally cash dividend is declared after few months of the dosing of accounts as in these months the accounting is done and profit and loss statement and also balance sheet is prepared. After these have been compiled and completed, the board of directors sit for a meeting in which they consider the accounts for the year and also declare dividends. Besides these, the other matters such as resolution for changing the authorised capital etc. are considered.

The records of the meetings are noted by the Company Secretary and balance sheet is printed. These are sent to the equity shareholders and also notice is given to them about the annual general meeting where the dividend is declared and other resolutions are approved by shareholders or their proxies through voting. After the approval has been obtained the company in due course sends dividend warrants to the shareholders. The dividend paid to each shareholder depends on the number of shares held by him and the amount of dividend declared by the company.

Stock Dividend (Bonus Shares)

A stock dividend occurs when the board of directors authorise a distribution of bonus shares to existing shareholders. This has effect of increasing the number of shares of the firm. For example, if a shareholder owns 100 shares of equity at a time when the firm distributes a 5 per cent stock dividend, the shareholder will receive 5 additional shares.

Several favourable aspects of stock dividend are:

1. To Conserve Cash: The stock dividend allows the firm to declare a dividend without using up cash that may be needed for operations or expansion. Rather than seek additional external financing the firm can retain its funds that would otherwise be distributed to shareholders.

2. To Indicate Higher Future Profits: Normally a stock dividend is an indication of higher future profits. If the profits do not rise, the firm would experience a dilution of earnings as a result of the additional shares outstanding. Since a dilution of earnings is not desirable, stock dividends are usually declared only by board of directors who expect rise in earnings to offset the additional shares.

3. To Raise Future Dividends: If the regular cash dividend is continued after an extra stock dividend is declared, the shareholders will receive an increase in cash dividends in the future. For example, a firm may declare ₹1 regular dividend and a 5 per cent extra stock dividend. A shareholder with 100 shares will receive ₹100 and 5 additional shares. If the firm continues its ₹1 dividend, this investor would receive ₹105, an increase of ₹5 in the next period.

4. To have Positive Psychological Value: Because of the positive aspects of stock dividends, the dividend declaration is usually received positively by the market. This tends to encourage investment in the stock thus supporting or raising its market price. Instead of experiencing a drop in value after a stock dividend, the price may actually rise.

5. To Retain Proportional Ownership for Shareholders: The stock dividend differs from an issue of a new equity. If the existing shareholders do not have the funds to purchase a new equity, their proportion of the ownership in the firm will decline as new investors purchase shares. This is avoided by a stock dividend which is, in effect, nothing more than a recapitalization of the firm.

THE FIRM'S DIVIDEND POLICY

Short-Term Dividend Policy

Dividend policy, like all business decisions, can be optimised only in terms of objectives that the financial management of the company is trying to achieve. The objective of financial management should be to maximise the market value of shares of the existing equity shareholders or more simply to maximise the *net present worth* (NPW) of the company. This objective provides a rational guide for running a business and for efficient allocation of resources of society. This objective is a valid guide to financial decisions for all transactions not involving transfer of assets between the corporate entity and the shareholders. For these external transactions like maximisation of the firm's NPW naturally results in the maximisation of the shareholder's wealth. However, in case of dividend policy, since cash is transferred from the corporate entity to its shareholders, the wealth of the shareholders is measured not only by the value of their shares but also by the amount of cash dividends they receive. Therefore, the maximisation of the firm's net present worth may not result in maximisation of shareholders wealth. For example, it is not possible that a company can maximise its NPW (and therefore share prices) by not paying any dividend at all. But such dividend policy could actually reduce the wealth of the shareholders, if the return on retained earnings is less than the rate at which investors capitalise the earnings of the company.

In the ensuing discussion, dividend stability i.e. whether dividend remains fixed or fluctuates from period to period, a factor that a firm must consider in determining its optimal dividend policy is discussed. Overwhelming majority of mature corporations have dividend policies that emphasize regular and steady dividend declarations. Although earnings may fluctuate from year to year, the dividend will not. A number of arguments may be advanced to underline the importance of steady dividend payments including:

1. Perception of Stability: When a firm declares a regular dividend, investors accept the declaration as a sign of continued normal operations. At the same time, a reduction in the declared dividend will draw immediate attention and will be taken by many as a sign of potential or expected trouble in future. Many investors will immediately sell their stock without checking further and this selling will cause a decline in the market price of the stock. Stable dividend declarations avoid this reaction on the part of investors.

2. Preference of Investors: The equity shareholders of mature corporations generally prefer to receive steady dividends. They expect to receive an approximate amount of cash each year and they may make advance commitment to investment or spend the money. If a firm fails to declare a dividend, these investors will seek to invest in firms that provide a steady cash payment.

3. Routinising of Dividend Decisions: By establishing a stable dividend policy, the board of directors avoid lengthy discussions during annual general meeting. Unless circumstances warrant a possible change, regular dividend can be declared. This policy avoids wasting the time of the board and allows its members to concentrate on more important matters facing the firm.

4. Flexibility of the Extra Dividend: With a steady dividend policy, the firm can flexibly handle a period of temporarily high earnings. This is accomplished by declaring an extra dividend in the year. This allows a larger distribution of earning without raising the expectation of investors.

From the investors angle, long term stability of dividends and growth prospects are two major determinants for a blue chip. Very few companies in India have enjoyed the reputation of maintaining an uninterrupted record of dividends and holding on to certain traditions laid down by their founder directors.

Alternative Policies

Regardless of the policy determining the long-run dividend payment ratio, year-to-year fluctuations in dividend may follow any one of the several guidelines listed below :

1. Stable Rupee Dividend

The rupee level of dividend, under this scheme, is relatively stable from period to period. There are companies which maintain a steady dividend even though they issue bonus shares. They have issued bonus shares only after being confident that after enlargement of capital base they will be in position to maintain dividend. These companies win the investor's confidence.

2. Target Payout Ratios

It would appear that a number of companies follow the policy of a target dividend-payout ratio over the long run. Lintner contends that dividends are adjusted to changes in earnings, but only with a lag. When earnings increase to a new level dividends are increased only when it is felt that the increase in earnings can be maintained. In addition, there appears to be a definite reluctance on the part of companies to cut the absolute amount of their cash dividend changes behind changes in earnings. Given a large relationship, retained earnings will increase relative to dividends in an economic upturn. In a contraction, however, retained earnings will decrease relative to dividends.

3. Regular and Extra Dividends

One way for a company to increase its cash distribution in periods of prosperity is to declare an extra dividend in addition to the regular annual dividend. By declaring an extra dividend, the company attempts to prevent investors from expecting that the dividend represents an increase in the established dividend rate. The declaration of an extra dividend is particularly suitable for companies with fluctuating earnings. Trading companies, for example, frequently declare dividend in good trading years. The use of extra dividend enables the company to maintain a stable record of regular dividends but also to distribute to shareholders some of the rewards of prosperity. By paying extra dividends only when earnings are higher than usual, the company will not lead investors to count on the increased dividends in future periods. However, a company can pay extra dividend continuously without conveying to the market some impression of permanency. As soon as a certain level of dividend is required, investors begin to expect that level regardless of the distinction between regular and extra dividends.

Dividend as a Passive Residual

The treatment of dividend policy as a passive residual determined strictly by the availability of acceptable investment proposals implies that dividends are irrelevant; the investor is indifferent between dividends and capital gains. If investment opportunities promise a return greater than their required return, the investor is happy to have the company retain earnings. Contrarily, if the return is less than the required return, he prefers dividends. Supposedly, if the firm can earn more on projects than the required return, then investors are perfectly happy to let the firm retain as much in earnings as it needs to finance the investments.

A residual theory of dividend policy does not necessarily mean that dividends need fluctuate from period to period in keeping with fluctuation in investment opportunities. A firm may smooth out actual payments by saving some funds in surplus years in anticipation of deficit ones. If forecasting is relatively accurate, the firm can establish its dividend payment at a level which the cumulative distribution over time corresponds to cumulative residual funds over the same period. The fact that dividends do riot correspond to residual funds period by period do not negate the residual theory of dividends. The critical question is whether dividends are more than just a means of distributing unused funds. Should dividend policy be active decision variable as opposed to a passive 'one ? To answer these questions, the arguments that dividends are irrelevant so that changes in the payout ratio (holding investment opportunities constant) do not affect shareholders' wealth are examined thoroughly below.

Irrelavance of Dividends - M M Theory

The most comprehensive argument for the irrelevance of dividends is given by Miller and Modiglian. They assert that, given the investment decision of the firm, the dividend-payout ratio is merely detail. It does not affect the wealth of shareholders. MM argue that the value of the firm is determined solely by the earning power on the firm's assets or its investment policy and that the manner in which the earnings stream is split between dividends and retained earnings does not affect the value. The critical assumption of MM are:

1. Perfect capital markets in which all investors are rational. Information is available to all at no cost; transactions are instantaneous and without cost; securities are infinitely divisible; and no investor is large enough to affect the market price of a security.
2. An absence of flotation costs on securities issued by the firm.
3. A world of no taxes.
4. A given investment policy for the firm, not subject to change.
5. Perfect certainty by every investor as to future investments and profits of the firm. MM dropped this assumption later.

Under these assumptions the valuation of all shares would be governed by the following fundamental principle: the price of each share must be such that the rate of return (dividend plus capital gains) on every share will be the same throughout the market over any given interval time. Another way to say this is that with perfect markets and no personal taxes, dividend policy changes the form in which investors receive their return but not the amount. Thus the internal rate of return to an investor for holding a share of stock one period is defined as the discount rate that equals the present value of the dividends received during the period, plus the end of period selling price, to the current share price:

$$P_0 = \frac{D_1 + P_1}{1 + k_1} \tag{3}$$

where:

P_0 = current share price
D_1 = dividends per share during the period
P_1 = end of period share price
k_e = internal rate of return, on in equilibrium the cost of equity capital
Solving for k_e

$$k_e = \frac{D_1}{P_0} + \frac{P_1 - P_0}{P_0} \tag{4}$$

which states that the return to the investor equals the dividend yield, plus the percent-age increase or decrease in share price over the period.

Then Miller and Modigliani consider what will happen if the company pays a dividend and at the same time make a new share issue equal to the amount of that dividend. Let n equal the number of shares at t_0 and let m equal the number of new shares sold at tj. Rewriting equation (4) to reflect the total market value of equity at t_t they get:

$$nP_0 = \frac{1}{P_0} [nD_1 + (n + m)P_1 - mP1] \qquad (5)$$

The total value of the new issue of shares (mP_1) will depend on the amount of new investment (I), the net profit earned during the period (Y), and the dividends paid on the equity shares (nD_1). Thus:

$$mP_1 = I - (Y - nD_1) \qquad (6)$$

Substituting equation (6) into equation (3) they find that

$$nP_0 = nP_0 = \frac{1}{(1+k_e)} (n + m) P_1 - I + Y \qquad (7)$$

As the nDi term has cancelled out, Dj, does not appear in equation (7). Furthermore, as the other variables in equation are assumed to be independent of D_1 Miller and Modigliani conclude that P_0 is not a function of the company's dividend decision.

Following Professors Miller and Modigliani, we can state the above reasoning more rigorously by referring to what is known as the earnings-investment model. Assuming an all-equity firm, and multiplying equation (3) by the current number of shares outstanding, n_0, the total market value of the firm can be written as :

$$V_0 \, nP_0 = \frac{D_1 n_0 + P_1 \, n_0}{1 + k_e} \qquad (8)$$

But since dividend policy affects the amount of new equity financing required, P_1 in the above equation depends on D_1. To unravel this dependence, let us equate sources of company's cash to use during period I.

$$\begin{aligned} &\text{Sources} &&= \text{Uses} \\ &Y_1 + P_1 (n_1 - n_0) &&= D_1 \, n_0 + I_1 \end{aligned}$$

where Y_1 and I_1 are earnings and investment in period I, and P_1 is the total number of shares outstanding at time 1. This identity says that for an all-equity firms, earnings plus receipts from the sale of new shares must equal dividend plus investment. Solving this identity for $n_0 P_1$ and combining it with equation (8) yields :

$$V_0 = \frac{V_1 - I_1}{1 + k_e} + \frac{V_1}{1 + k_e} \qquad (9)$$

This expression is not quite the earning-investment model, but it does enable us to see the logic of the irrelevance argument. Since D_1 does not appear in the equation directly, the only way current dividends can influence firm value (or share price) is if they affect one of the variables : Y_1 depends on the profitability of past investments and hence is independent of dividends in any period; similarly k_e depends only on the risk borne by equity shareholders and not on the firm's dividend policy. V_1 might depend on dividends, but if so the dependence will be on dividends in period 2 and beyond, not on current dividends. This is because current dividends will be part of history by the end of period and therefore cannot affect V_1. So the only possible candidate for dependence is Jj. However, if management follows the recommended policy of accepting all investments above the Market Line, I_1 will also be independent of current dividends. We conclude therefore, that firm value and share price are independent of current dividends — at least under present assumptions.

To demonstrate that V_0 is also independent of all subsequent dividends, we need only apply the above logic to future periods. Since equation (9) expresses V_0 as a function of Vj we can simply increment the time subscripts one period to write V_1 as similar function of V_2. Thus :

$$V_1 = \frac{Y_2 - I_2}{1 + k_e} + \frac{V_2}{1 + k_e} \tag{10}$$

so that substituting into equation (9)

$$V_0 = \frac{Y_1 - I_1}{1 + k_e} + \frac{Y_2 - I_2}{(1 + k_e)} + \frac{V_2}{(1 + k_e)} \tag{11}$$

Repeating the exercise for all future periods yields the desired earnings-investment model:

$$V_0 = \sum_{t=1}^{\infty} \frac{Y_1 - I_1}{(1 + k_e)^t} \tag{12}$$

$$P_0 = \frac{1}{n_0} \sum_{t=1}^{\infty} \frac{Y_1 - I_1}{(1 + k_e)^t}$$

Since the variables on the right h and side of these equations are independent of dividends in any period, V_0 and P_0 must be similiarly independent.

In addition to the irrelevance of dividends, the earnings- investment model also illustrates several interesting facts about equity-share values. *First,* it characterises the firm as a giant capital-expenditure project, with Y_t representing cash inflows and I_t cash outflows. Consistent with the capital budgeting techniques, the value of the project (firm) is the present value of these inflows, minus the present value of the outflows-discounted at an appropriate rate. In other words, the market value of an all equity firm equals the difference between the present value of its earnings and its investment, discounted at the cost of equity capital. *Second,* the model re-emphasises the fact that the value of a share is not simply the present value of future earnings per share. This would be true only in the extreme case where the firm made no new investments and issued no new shares.

Thus, it is not the firm's dividend policy that is important; rather, the value of the firm is influenced only by its expected future earnings stream. Fischer Black-and Myron Scholes also studied dividend policy by using the capital asset pricing model (CAPM) to empirically relate a stock's market behaviour to its dividend payout ratio. They found that stocks with high payout ratios did not provide return that were significantly different from those with low payouts. As a result, they concluded that such evidence tended to be consistent with the idea that dividend policy does not matter. If dividend policy is irrelevant, what does this imply about the basic valuation model, which states that the price of a share of stock is equal to the present value of expected future dividends ? The answer is that dividend policy affect only the timing of the expected dividend, not their present value. The irrelevance position maintains that the present value of expected future dividend will remain un-changed, even though dividend policy may change the timing of payments. Thus, rather than contradictory, the dividend-capitalisation and the earning-investments models are actually equivalent valuation expressions.

Relevance of Dividends

A number of arguments have been advanced in support of the contrary position namely the dividends are relevant under conditions of uncertainty. In other words, the investor is not indifferent as to how the earning stream is split between dividends and retained earnings. These arguments are examined under conditions of uncertainty but keeping intact MM and other assumptions — no transaction or flotation costs, the absence of taxes, and a given fixed policy of the firm.

(i) **Resolution of Uncertainty:** It has been argued that the payment of current dividends resolves uncertainty in the minds of investors, and, therefore, an investor is not indifferent between dividends and capital gains. He prefers dividends. *Gordon*, for example, contends that uncertainty on the part of investors increases at an increasing rate with the distance in the future of prospective cash payments. When the company cuts its dividend to finance investments, its near dividend is reduced, while distant dividends are increased. If the discount rate rises with the length of time in the future, the reduction in the near dividend is said to lead to a lower share price, all other things the same.

(ii) **Informational Content of Dividends:** The argument above is allied closely to the "informational content of dividends" argument. The latter argument implies that dividends have an impact on share price because they communicate information to investors about the firm's profitability. When a firm has a target payout ratio that is stable overtime, and it changes this ratio, investors may believe that management is announcing a change in the expected future profitability of the firm. Accordingly, the price of the stock may react to this change in dividends. MM do not deny the possibility of the information effect but continue to maintain that present and future earnings are what determine value. They assert that dividends are merely a reflection of these factors and do not in themselves determine value, therefore, the irrelevance proposition holds.

(iii) **Preference for Current Income:** Another aspect of the uncertainty question involves investors who have a preference for current income. Under the irrelevance proposition, MM would argue that these investors can sell stock on a periodic basis to obtain income. With perfect markets, the investor always could sell part of his holdings or reinvest the dividends to satisfy his desire for consumption. Over the long run, the investor should be able to obtain the same income as he would with regular dividends. However, with uncertainty, stock prices fluctuate. Certain investors may regard as unsatisfactory the alternative of selling a portion of their stock for income at fluctuating prices. As a result they may have a definite preference for current dividends. In addition to the uncertainty of the selling price, the inconvenience of selling a small portion of stock periodically for income may be factor. For this reason alone, certain investors might prefer current dividends to capital gains.

(iv) **Sale of Stock at Lower Price:** The irrelevance doctrine also rests upon the assumption that the sale of stock by the firm to replace the dividend will be at the current price. In order to sell the stock, however, the firm must appeal to new investors or to the existing investors to increase their holdings. With divergent investor expectations, *Lintner* contends that the equilibrium price of a share stock will decline as the firm sells additional stocks to replace dividends. In other words, there is a downward-sloping demand curve for the stock.

(v) **Market Imperfections:** Some of the factors assumed away are discussed below:
  (a) *Tax Effect:* When we allow for taxes there are variety of effects. The most important is due to capital gains being taxed at lower rate than dividends. Moreover, the capital gains tax is deferred until the investor actually sells his stock. Thus, there is a strong bias in favour of capital gains as opposed to dividends, and this bias

favours the retention of earnings. Suppose a corporation pays a substantial dividend and expands by selling shares on a rights basis to existing shareholders. These shareholders receive dividends, which are taxed at the ordinary income tax, and then purchase more stock. If the corporation has retained the earnings the tax would have avoided. The shareholder could realise value on his investment by selling some of his shares and paying only a capital gains tax. The effect of the differentials must be qualified to take account of the growing number of taxfree institutional investors. For these investors, the tax effect would not influence their preference for dividends or capital gains.

(b) *Flotation Costs :* The irrelevance proposition is based upon the idea that given the investment policy of the firm, funds paid out by the firm be replaced by funds acquired through external financing. The introduction of flotation costs favours the retention of earnings in the firm. For each rupee paid out in dividends, the firm nets less than a rupee after flotation costs per rupee of external financing. Moreover, the smaller the size of the issue, the greater in general the flotation costs as a percentage of the total amounts of funds raised.

(c) *Transaction Costs and Divisibility of Securities:* Transaction costs involved in the sale of securities tend to restrict the arbitrage process. The shareholder who desires current income must pay a brokerage fee on the sale of a portion of his shares if the dividend paid is not sufficient to satisfy his current desire for income. This fee varies universally, per rupee of shares sold. For a small sale, the brokerage fee can be rather significant percentage-wise. Because of this fee, shareholders with consumption desires in excess of currant dividends will prefer that company pay additional dividends. Perfect capital market also assume that securities are infinitely divisible. The fact that the smallest integer is one share in any result in Tumpiness' with respect to selling shares for current income. This too acts as a deterrent to the sale of shares in lieu of dividends. On the other hand, the shareholder not desiring dividends for current consumption purposes will need to reinvest his dividends. Here again transaction costs and divisibility problems work to disadvantage of the shareholder, although in the opposite direction.

(d) *Other Legal Impediments :* Certain investors are restricted by law as to types of equity shares in which they can invest. The prescribed list of eligible securities is determined in part by the duration over which dividends have been paid. If a company does not pay dividend or has not paid dividends over a sufficiently long period of time, certain institutional investors are not able to invest in the stock.

DIVIDEND PROVISIONS UNDER THE COMPANIES ACT, 1956

While laying down its dividend policy, a company has to comply with the following legal provisions too:

(1) No dividend shall be declared or paid by a company for any financial year except (a) out of the profits of the company for that year arrived at after providing for depreciation, (b) out of the profits of the company for any previous financial year or years and remaining undistributed, or (c) out of both, or (d) out of moneys provided by the Central Government or a State Government for the payment of dividend in pursuance of a guarantee given by that Government.

(2) If the company has not provided for depreciation for any previous financial year or years it shall, before declaring or paying dividend for any financial year, provide for

such depreciation out of the profits of that financial year or out of the profits of any other previous financial year or years.

(3) If the company has incurred any loss in any previous financial year or years, then the amount of the loss or an amount which is equal to the amount provided for depreciation for that year or those years, whichever is less, shall be set off against the profits of the company for the year for which dividend is proposed to be declared or paid or against the profits of the company for any previous financial year or years, arrived in both cases after providing for depreciation or against both.

(4) The Central Government may, if it thinks necessary so to do in the public interest, allow any company to declare or pay dividend for any financial year out of the profits of the company for that year or any previous financial year or years without providing for depreciation.

(5) Depreciation shall be provided either :
(a) to the extent specified in Section 350; or
(b) in respect of each item of depreciable asset, for such an amount as is arrived at by dividing ninety-five per cent of the original cost thereof to the company by the specified period in respect of such asset; or
(c) on any other basis approved by the Central Government which has the effect of writing off by way of depreciation ninety-five per cent of the original cost to the company of each such depreciable asset on the expiry of the specified period; or
(d) as regards any other depreciable asset for which no rate of depreciation has been laid down by this Act or any rules made thereunder, on such basis as may be approved by the Central Government by any general order published in the Official Gazette or by any special order in any particular case.

(6) No dividend shall be declared or paid by a company for any financial year out of the profits of the company for that year arrived at after providing for depreciation, except after the transfer to the reserves of the company of such percentage of its profits for that year, not exceeding ten per cent, as may be prescribed.

(7) No dividend shall be payable except in cash. Provided that nothing in this sub-section shall be deemed to prohibit the capitalization of profits or reserves of a company for the purpose of issuing fully paid-up bonus shares or paying up any amount for the time being unpaid on any shares held by the members of the company.

(8) Any dividend payable in cash may be paid by cheque or warrant sent through the post direct to the registered address of the shareholder entitled to the payment of the dividend or in the case of joint shareholders, to the registered address of that one of the joint shareholders which is first named on the register of members, or to such person and to such address as the shareholder or the joint shareholders may in writing direct.

(9) Dividend not to be paid except to registered shareholders or to their order or to their brokers (Sec.206)
(i) No dividend shall be paid by a company in respect of any share therein except:
(a) to the registered holder of such share or to his order or to his bankers; or
(b) in case a share warrant has been issued in respect of the share in pursuance of Section 114, to the bearer of such warrant or to his bankers.
(ii) Nothing contained in sub-section (z) shall be deemed to require the bankers of a registered shareholder to make a separate application to the company for the payment of the dividend.

REVIEW PROBLEMS

1. Global Enterprises is considering a rights offering to raise ₹ 50 crore. Currently this firm has 2,50,00,000 share selling for ₹ 50 per share. The subscription price on the new share would be ₹ 40 per share.
   (a) How many shares must be sold to raise the desired funds?
   (b) How many rights are necessary to purchase one equity share ?
   (c) ₹ 50 crore

Ans:

(a) New shares to be sold $= \dfrac{₹\ 50\ \text{crore}}{₹\ 40} = 1.25$ crore shares

(b) Number of rights necessary to purchase one equity share

$$\dfrac{2,50,00,000}{1,25,00,000} = 2 \text{ rights}$$

(c) Value of one right $= \dfrac{₹\ 50 - ₹\ 40}{2+1} = ₹\ 3.33$

2. RND Industries is planning to raise ₹ 35 crore through the sale of new equity under a rights offering. The subscription price is ₹ 70 per share while the share currently sells for ₹ 80 per share, rights on. Total outstanding shares equal 10 crore. Of this amount, Kamal Kant owns 1,00,000 shares.
   (i) How many equity shares will each right permit its owner to purchase ?
   (ii) What will be the total value of Kamal Kant's rights a day before the ex-rights date, assuming that the market price of RND Industries stock remain ₹ 80 per share ?
   (iii) After the ex-rights date, if the market value of each RND Industries equals ₹ 0.25, what must be the ex- rights market price RND Industries?

Ans:

(i) Number of shares to be Issued =

$$\dfrac{\text{Funds be raised}}{\text{Price per share to be change}} = \dfrac{₹\ 35\ \text{crore}}{₹\ 70} = 50,00,000$$

With 10 crore equity shares of currently issues, the owner of RND Industries one share (right) will be permitted to purchase:

$50,00,000/10,00,00,000 = .05$ new shares

(ii) Prior to the ex-rights date, the value of right is given by:

$$V = \dfrac{M_1 - S}{N + 1}$$

Because each right permits the owner to buy .05 new shares, 20 rights are needed to purchase one new share. Therefore each right is worth :

$$V = \dfrac{(₹\ 80 - ₹\ 70)}{(20 = 1)} = 0.476$$

Because Kamal Kant will receive 1,00,000 rights, the total value of RND Industries these rights is:

1,00,000 x ₹ 0.476 = ₹ 47,600

(iii) After the ex-rights date, the value of the right is :

$$V = (M_2 - S)/N$$

Given the ex-rights value of a right is ₹ 0.25, the ex-rights value of RND Industries equity is:

M_2 = (₹ 0.25 x 20) + ₹ 70 = ₹ 75

3. K.D. Group has 1,00,000 equity shares outstanding. Last year it had earnings per share of ₹ 3 and paid dividends of ₹ 1 per share. If the company's equity share is selling for ₹ 40.00 per share, how many equity shares would the company need to sell if all of the earnings had been paid as dividends?

Ans:

Additional equity shares	= (3 - 1)/40
	= 0.05
Total equity shares	= 0.05 (1,00,000 existing equity shares)
	= 5,000 equity shares

4. D.P. Manufacturing pays a current dividend of ₹ 2.00 which should grow at a 0.05 rate in the future. D.P.'s required rate of return is 0.12. What is the value of a share of D.P.'s stock?

Ans:

Dividend in period 1:	D_1	= ₹ 2.00 (1 + 0.05)
		= ₹ 2.10
Value of the stock:	V_0	= ₹ 2.10/ (0.12 - 0.05)
		= ₹ 30

5. Manav Industries declares a 5 percent stock dividend. What should be the ex-dividend price of the stock, if the price on the day before ex-dividend is ₹ 50? What is the net wealth of an investor with 100 shares before and after the dividend?

Ans:

The ex-dividend stock price:	= ₹ 50 / (1 + 0.05)
	= ₹ 47.62
Net worth before dividend	= ₹ 50 (100)
	= 5000
Net worth ex-dividend	= ₹ 47.62 (105)

6. XYZ Company is conducting the annual election for its 5- member Board of directors. The company has 15,00,000 equity shares.
   (i) Under a majority voting system, how many shares must a shareholder own to ensure being able to elect him or her choices to each of the five director seats?
   (ii) Under a cumulative voting system, how many shares must a shareholder own to ensure being able to elect his or her choices to two of the director seats ?
   (iii) Anil Sharma holds 20% of XYZ Company's shares. How many directors can Anil elect under a cumulative voting system?

Ans:
   (i) Under a majority voting system, a majority of the shares is required to ensure election of one or all of the directors of the board. In the case of XYZ Company, 7,50,001 shares (i.e. 50% plus one of the shares) are needed,
   (ii) The number of shares required to elect directors under a cumulative voting system is given by :
   n = [(2 x 15,00,000) / (5 + 1)] + 1 = 5,00,001
   (iii) With 20% of XYZ Company's shares (3,00,000), the number of directors that Anil can be sure of electing is formed by solving :

$$d \;=\; [(n\text{-}l)\mathrm{x}(D+l)]/S$$

when
$d \;=\;$ director(s) elected
$n \;=\;$ number of shares to be held
$s \;=\;$ number of shares

By substituting, we get:

$$d \;=\; [(3,00,000\ \text{-}1) \times (5+1)]/15,00,000 = 1.2$$

Thus Anil is assured of being able to elect at least one director.

7. K.C. Sharma owns equity shares in Novex Auto. Novex is planning a rights offering in which 7 shares must be owned by one additional share at a price of ₹15. Novex's equity shares are currently selling for ₹ 63 per share.
   (a) What is the value of a Novex right ?
   (b) At the time of offering announcement, Sharma's assets consisted of ₹ 1,50,000 in cash and 4900 shares of Novex. List and show the value of Sharma's assets prior to the ex-rights date.
   (c) List and show die value of Sharma's assets on the ex- rights date if Novex equity sells for ₹ 60 per share on date.
   (d) List and show the value of Sharma's assets if Sharma sells the Novex rights on the ex-rights date.

Ans:

(a) The value of the right is
$$V = (M_1 - S)/(N+1)$$
In the case of Novex :
$$V = (₹\ 63 - ₹\ 15)/(7+1) = ₹\ 6.00$$

(b) At the time of the offering announcement, Sharma's assets consisted of:
   Cash   ₹ 1,50,000
   Stock   ₹ 3,08,700 (₹ 63 x 4900)
   Rights   ₹ 29,400 (₹ 6 x 4900) ₹ 4,88,100

(c) On the ex-rights date, Sharma's assets consisted of :
   Cash   ₹ 1,50,000
   Stock   2,94,000 (₹ 60x4900)
   Rights   31,510 (₹ 6.43 x 4900) = 4,75,510
   when $V= (M_2 - S)/N = (60 - IS)/7 = ₹\ 6.43$

(d) If Sharma sells the rights on the ex-rights date then Sharma's total assets will remain the same at ₹ 4,75,510. However, cash will increase by ₹ 31,510 and the value of Sharma's rights will be zero, as all will have been sold.
   $$= ₹\ 5000$$

8. ABC Company expects some degree of certainty to generate the following net income and to have the following capital expenditure during the next five years (in thousands).

(₹ in thousands)

Years	1	2	3	4	5
Net Income	₹ 5,000	₹ 4,000	₹ 2,500	₹ 2,000	₹ 1,500
Capital expenditure	2,000	2,500	3,200	4,000	5,000

The company currently has 10,00,000 shares of equity and pays dividends of ₹ 5 per share.

(a) Determine dividends per share if dividend policy is treated as a residual decision.

(b) Determine the amounts of external financing that will be necessary if the present dividend per share is maintained.

(c) Determine dividends per share and the amounts of external financing that will be necessary if a dividend payout ratio of 50% is maintained.

(d) Under which of the three dividend policies are aggregate dividends maximised? External financing minimised ?

Ans:

(a)

Year	Income Available for Dividends	Dividends Per Share	External Financing
1	₹ 30,00,000	₹ 3	0
2	15,00,000	1.5	0
3	0	0	₹ 70,00,000
4	0	0	20,00,000
5	0	0	35,00,000
	₹ 45,00,000		₹ 1,25,00,000

(b)

Year	Net Income	Dividends	Capital External	External Financing
1	₹ 50,00,000	₹ 50,00,000	₹ 20,00,000	₹ 20,00,000
2	40,00,000	50,00,000	25,00,000	35,00,000
3	25,00,000	50,00,000	32,00,000	57,00,000
4	20,00,000	50,00,000	40,00,000	70,00,000
5	15,00,000	50,00,000	50,00,000	85,00,000
	₹ 2,50,00,000			₹ 2,67,00,000

(c)

Year (1) =(1)	Net Income (2)	Dividends (3)	Dividends Per Share (4)	Capital Expenditure (5)	External FRinancing $6=(3)+(5)$
1	₹ 50,00,000	₹ 25,00,000	₹ 2.50	₹ 20,00,00	—
2	40,00,000	20,00,000	2.00	25,00,000	₹ 5,00,000
3	25,00,000	12,50,000	1.25	32,00,000	19,50,000
4	20,00,000	10,00,000	1.00	40,00,000	30,00,000
5	15,00,000	7,50,000.	0.75	50,00,000	42,50,000
		₹ 75,00,000			₹ 97,00,00

(d) Aggregate dividends are highest under alternative b, external financing is minimised under alternative c, a constant dividend payout policy.

9. A firm has new investment opportunities requiring an aggregate outlay of ₹ 10,00,000. The firm has decided that the appropriate debt/equity ratio, given the nature of its business and its operating risk, is 0.30. Historically, it has paid out 65% of its earnings as dividends. Its earnings for the period just ended were ₹ 12,00,000. Determine for each of the four policy alternatives the external financing requirements (debt and equity) and the debt and equity levels after external financing is completed.

Ans.

The solution table shows the firm treats all three decisions as active, that is, it sets each at the desired level.

(₹ in thousands)

| | No residual | No external equity | | |
		Investment residual	Debt/equity residual	Dividends residual
Before external financing				
Debt	3,000	3,000	3,000	3,000
Equity	10,000	10,000	10,000	10,000
Debt/equity	0.30	0.30	0.30	0.30
Investment				
Opportunities	1,000	550	1,000	550
Earnings	1,200	1,200	1,200	1,200
Payout ratio	0.65	0.65	0.65	0.36
Dividends	780	780	780	430
Earnings retained	420	420	420	770
External Financing				
Debt	230	130	580	230
Equity	350	0	0	0
After external financing				
Debt	323	313	358	323
Equity	1,077	1,042	1,042	1,077
Debt/equity				
(optimum = 0.30)	0.30	0.30	0.34	0.30

10. Super Industries had capitalisation as shown :

Equity share capital (₹ 10 par, 10,00,000 shares)	₹ 1,00,00,000
Paid-up capital	5,00,00,000
Retained earnings	14,00,00,000
Total owners' equity	₹ 20,00,00,000

Super paid a 20 per cent stock dividend. At the time of the stock dividend, the stock was selling at ₹ 60 per share. Show the new capitalisation.

Ans:

A 20 per cent stock dividend would represent 2,00,000 new shares (20% of 10,00,000 shares outstanding). At ₹ 60 per share, the toted amount would be ₹

1,20,00,000. The amount is transferred from retained earnings into the equity share capital and paid-up capital accounts. The equity share capital account is allocated ₹ 10 per share (the par value) or a total of ₹ 20,00,000. The paid-up capital account is allocated the remaining ₹ 1,00,00,000. The result is shown below :

Equity share capital (₹ 10 par, 12,00,000 shares)	₹ 1,20,00,000
Paid-up capital	6,00,00,000
Retained earnings	12,80,00,000
Total owners' equity	₹ 20,00,00,000

The total remains constant, and only the distribution of amounts by accounts changes.

11. Sudha Textiles earned ₹ 30,00,000 after taxes in 2009 and paid out 50% of this in cash dividends. The price of the firm's equity share on December 31, 2009 was ₹ 50. The capital structure of Sudha's on December 31, 2009 was as follows

Equity share capital (₹ 10 par, 10,00,000 shares)	₹ 1,00,00,000
Capital surplus	30,00,000
Retained earnings	1,70,00,000
Net worth	₹ 3,00,00,000

(a) If the firm declared a stock dividend of 20 per cent on December 31, 2009, what would the reformulated capital structure be ?

(b) If the firm declared a 50 per cent stock dividend rather than 20% dividend, what would the reformulated capital structure be ?

(c) Assuming the firm paid no stock dividend, how much would earnings per share for 2009 be ? How much dividends per share be ?

(d) Assuming a 20 per cent stock dividend, what would the EPS and DPS be for 2009 ? Assuming a 50 per cent dividend ?

(e) What would the price of the share be after 20% dividend ? After the 50% dividend ?

Ans.:

(a) 20% of 10,00,000 shares = 2,00,000
2,00,000 × ₹ 20   = ₹ 40,00,000

Equity share capital (12,00,000 shares)	₹ 1,20,00,000
Capital Surplus	50,00,000
Retained Earnings	1,30,00,000
Net worth	₹ 3,00,00,000

(b) 50% X 10,00,000 shares = 5,00,000
5,00,000 X ₹ 20   = ₹ 1,00,00,000

Equity share capital (15,00,000 shares)	₹ 1,50,00,000
Capital Surplus	80,00,000
Retained earnings	70,00,000
Net worth	₹ 3,00,00,000

(c) Earnings per share would be :
EPS = ₹ 30,00,000/10,00,000 shares   = ₹ 3.00
Dividends per share would be :
DPS = ₹ 15,00,000/10,00,000 shares   = ₹ 1.50
(d) For 20% stock dividends :
EPS = ₹ 30,00,000/12,00,000 shares   = ₹ 2.50
DPS = 15,00,000/12,00,000   = ₹ 1.25
For 50% stock dividends :
EPS = ₹ 30,00,000/15,00,000 shares   = ₹ 2.00
DPS = ₹ 15,00,000/15,00,000 shares   = ₹ 1.00
(e) Price of the share after 20% dividends :

$$50 \left[1 = \frac{1.00}{1.20} \right] = 8.33$$

50-8.33 = 41.67
Price of the share after 50% dividends :

$$50 \left[1 = \frac{1.00}{1.50} \right] = 50(.333) = 16.67$$

12. Aman Enterprises has issued 10 crore shares at ₹ 100 per value in 1998. The current share price is ₹ 550 and the current market capitalisation is ₹ 5,500 crore. Aman needs ₹ 1500 crore for further expansion. The company is willing to offer the existing shareholders the new equity shares at ₹ 500 per share, what is the value of the shares after the rights issue, i.e. the 'ex-rights' price? What could the investor sell his 'right' for?

Ans.

Number of new shares issued:

$$\frac{₹ \ 1500 \ crore}{₹ \ 500} = 3 \text{ crore shares}$$

Hence, we have to issue one-new share for every 3.33 existing shares.
This is 3 for 10, rights issue:
10 old shares @ ₹ 5.50 = ₹ 5,500
3 new shares @ ₹ 500 = ₹ 1,500
Hence, 13 shares are worth = ₹ 7,000
Value of 1 share (ex-rights) = ₹ 538.46
Hence, value of 1 right = ₹ 38.46 (₹ 538.46 - ₹ 500)

13. Gujarat Textiles Industries (GTI) plans to sell an additional 5 crores equity shares through a rights offering. The company currently has issued 40 crore equity shares. Each equity shareholder will receive one right for each share currently held. Therefore, each right will enable shareholders to purchase 0.125 shares. GTI's equity is currently selling ₹ 37 per share and the subscription price of the rights will be ₹ 28 per share.
    (i)   Calculate the value of the right for both the rights—on and ex-rights cases.
    (ii) Determine the amount that the market price of the GTI's equity is expected to drop on the ex-rights date, assuming all other things are equal.
    (iii) If the market price of GTI's equity increases to ₹ 42 per share, determine the value of the rights-on case.

Ans.

(i) Rights - on case:

$$V = \frac{M_o - S}{N+1}$$

$$= \frac{₹\ 37 - ₹\ 28}{8+1} = \frac{9}{9} = ₹\ 1.00$$

Ex-rights case:

$$V = \frac{M_e - S}{N} = \frac{₹\ 36 - ₹\ 28}{8} = ₹\ 1.00$$

(ii) ₹ 1.00

(iii) $$V = \frac{M_o - S}{N+1}$$

$$= \frac{₹\ 42 - ₹\ 28}{8+1} = \frac{₹\ 19}{9}$$

$$= ₹\ 1.56$$

14. PLC is about to raise finance by increasing its 12 crore equity shares with a one for three rights issue. Total debt in the capital structure comprises the following:

	Book value (₹ crores)
16% debentures	10.0
16% bank loan	10.0
Various short-term loans and overdrafts	0.2

The debentures have a further life of seven years and are redeemable at par. The fixed-interest 16% bank loan is guaranteed by the bank to be available for a further nine years. Both the debentures and the bank loan were initially arranged several years ago when interest rates were high. Interest rates have since fallen. The money raised by the rights issue will be used as follows :

1. To fund a new contract to which PLC already committed and which requires an initial outlay of ₹1 crore. The contract has a profitability index (ratio of present value [PV] of future net cash inflows to PV of initial capital outlay) of 1.4, and fill details of the contract have been public knowledge for several months.

2. To reduce borrowings by buying back, at current market value, and cancelling the ₹ 10 crore debenture issue. The debentures are currently priced in the market to yield 8% per annum, the current yield on such corporate debt. Total finance required in 1 and 2 will be rounded up to the next whole ₹ 10,00,000 for the purpose of the rights issue. The excess funds raised will be used to reduce short-term borrowings and overdrafts.

The company intends to announce full details of the rights issue on 1 July when the market price per share prior to the announcement is expected to be ₹ 50. The company is confident that the whole issue will be purchased, but the managing director is concerned that the discount at which the issue is made may raise the cost of equity capital and hence the weighted-average cost of capital.

(a) Calculate

(i) the issue price per share;

      (ii)   the theoretical ex-rights price per share;

     (iii)   the value of the right attached to each P.L.C. share before being traded ex-rights.

(b)   Briefly explain whether the concern of the managing director is justified.

(c)   Discuss whether this rights issue could be expected to alter the cost of equity and/or the weighted-average cost of capital in any way.

(d)   After setting the issue price (calculated in (a) but before announcing the rights issue, PLC decides to reduce borrowings by redeeming the 16% bank loan at its face value of ₹ 10 crore rather than buying back the debentures at market value. The possibility of the redemption at face value is now known only to the company and its bankers but will become public knowledge when the rights issue is announced on 1 July. The market had expected the bank loan to run for its full remaining seven years of life.

The excess cash generated by the rights issue, after reducing borrowings and funding the ₹ 1 crore contract, will be invested in a project which has a profitability index of 1.2. The market is not aware of this project and will remain unaware until its details become public knowledge when the rights issue is announced.

Calculate:

(i)   the share price on 1 July immediately after the announcement of the rights issue but before the shares are traded ex-rights;

(ii)   the theoretical ex-rights price per share.

     Briefly explain your calculations and also explain whether they assume that the market is displaying the weak, simi-strong or strong level of market efficiency.

Ans:

Part (a) The total funds to be raised are to be used to fund a new contract and to buy back the debentures. The market price of the debentures is not known, but can be estimated. It is assumed that the market is rational and is valuing a debenture at the PV of the cash flow that will be received over the debenture's life. Therefore the total funds to be raised are as follows.

	PV Factor 8%		₹ crore
To fund contract			1.0
Market value of debentures:			
Interest payments, ₹ 1.6 crore p.a.for seven years	6.247	9.995	
Redemption, ₹ 10 crores in nine years	0.500	5.000	14.995
Total			15.995
Rounded to ₹ 16 crores_			

(i)   A one for three rights issue will increase the number of shares by 40 lacs. Hence the issue price per share must be ₹ 40.

     As details of the contract are already public knowledge any impact on share price will already have taken place. Similarly, as the repurchasing of the debenture is at market value based on current rates of interest, this is unlikely to affect the share price.

(ii)   The total value of equity after rights issue is as follows:

Existing shares	1.2 crore	at ₹ 50 = ₹ 60 crore
New shares	40,00,000	at ₹ 40 = ₹ 16 crores
1.6 crores = 76 crores		

The theoretical ex-rights price per share is ₹ 760/16 = ₹ 47.5

(iii) Each three shares currently held give the right to purchase for ₹ 40.00, a share which will be worth ₹ 47.5. The value of such rights attached to three existing shares is ₹ 7.50 (i.e. ₹ 47.5 - ₹ 40.00). Hence the value of the right attached to one share is ₹ 2.50.

Part (b) The fact that the shares are being offered under the rights issue at a discount on the current price should not affect the cost of equity provided either that the market is efficient in valuing the securities or the existing shareholders take up the entire rights issue. If the market misinterprets the way in which the funds are to be used and some existing shareholders sell the rights, then there could well be a wealth transfer, with a possible reduction in the wealth of existing shareholders.

Part (c) The weighted average cost of capital will change as there is a change in the debt-to-equity ratio. The rights issue is increasing the equity base and the funds raised being used to reduce the level of leverage.

Part (d) (i) Rights issue announcement will provide new information which will cause the market to revise its valuation of the firm and also of the firm's equity. The revision will be caused by the following:

Reduction of debt liability

The market's perceptions of a seven year life for the bank loan will cause its value, as calculated in part (a)(i) to be (approx.)	₹ 15 crore
The liability can be cancelled for the sacrifice of its face value of	₹ 5 crore
Leaving a benefit of equity of:	₹ 10 crore

Profitable use of excess cash

The excess cash of ₹ 5 crores placed in a project with NPV ₹ l crore.

This NPV accrues to equity:	₹ 1 crore
Total revision of equity value :	₹ 6 crore
Previous equity value :	₹ 60 crore
Revised equity value	₹ 66 crore

The share price after the revision of expectation should move towards ₹ 66 crore/1.2 crore = ₹ 55..

(ii) Total equity value after the rights issue:

Existing shares after revision of expectations:	1.2 crore at ₹ 55	₹ 66 crore
New shares	40,00,000 at ₹ 40	₹ 16 crore
1.6 crore	₹ 82 crore	

The theoretical ex rights price per share is ₹ 82/16 = ₹ 51.25.

It is assumed that the market is efficient in the semi- strong form and reacts to publicly available information, but is not efficient in the strong form and requires information to be made public before it can be incorporated into market valuations.

QUESTIONS

1. Outline the features of a rights issue of equity capital and suggest why this method of issuing fresh equity may be preferred by shareholders.

2. What are the main advantages and disadvantages to a company of raising finance by issuing the ordinary shares ?

3. What are the factors that have to be taken into account when pricing a new issue of shares?

4. Why is it more difficult to determine the value of an equity share as opposed to finding the value of a bond ?

5. Under what conditions will the market of equity be the same as its accounting book value ? Explain.

6. Since a rights offering allows equity shareholders to purchase equity shares at a price below the current market price, why is it not of value to the equity shareholders ?

7. With respect the payment of the dividends, distinguish between declaration date, ex-dividend date, and date of record ?

8. If you bought an equity share, you would typically expect to get dividends plus capital gains. Would you expect the distribution between dividend yield and capital gains to be influenced by the firm's decision to pay more dividends rather than to retain and reinvest more of its earnings?

9. What is the *residual dividend theory* 1 Why is this theory operational only in long term?

10. What are the advantages of a bonus share over a cash dividend ?

11. What legal restrictions may limit the amount of dividend to be paid ?

12. Why might investor prefer capital gains to the same amount of dividend income ?

13. Explain the trade-off between internally generated funds and paying cash dividends.

14. Explain the differences between the following dividend policies : (a) regular dividend, (b) regular dividend plus extras; and (c) irregular dividend.

15. For each of the companies described below, would you expect it to have a medium/high or a low dividend-payout ratio ? Explain.

(a) A growth company with an abundance of good investment opportunities.

(b) A company with a volatile earnings and high business risk.

(c) A company experiencing ordinary growth that has high liquidity and much numbered borrowing capacity.

(d) A company with a large proportion of inside ownership, all of whom are high-income individuals.

(e) A dividend-paying company that experiences an unexpected drop in earnings from a trend.

16. Why is an individual equity shareholder indifferent between the firm retaining earnings or of paying out the earnings as dividend, assuming that the shareholder maintains a constant debt-equity ratio ?

17. Reported earnings typically differ, sometimes considerably from economic earnings. Nevertheless, it is often argued that reported earnings are intended simply to provide a "source of information" to investors about the value of the firm. If so, might there not be many alternative accounting procedures of equal use to investors ? How might one go about evaluating the usefulness of such procedures ?

18. How are dividends used as a signelling device by corporate management ? To the extent that dividends are a signelling device, how are dividend changes related to equity share prices ?

19. Why might the price of an equity share react only partially to an "earnings surprise" on the first day or two after the earnings announcement ?

20. For a given level of earnings (E), net new investment (I) and dividend (D), explain why a firm must issue new shares if E is less than D + I and it desires to maintain a constant debt-equity ratio.

21. Evaluate the following statement :"Because investors purchase a security for its expected cash flows, the dividend policy of a firm will affect the value of the firm's stock".

22. Discuss the dividend provisions under the Companies Act, 1956.

PROBLEMS

1. XYZ Company is considering raising ₹ 25 crore through a right offering. Currently, it has 1 crore shares in the market which are selling for ₹ 84 per share. The subscription price on the new equity will be ₹ 60 per share. How many shares must be sold to raise the desired hinds ? How many rights are necessary to purchase one equity share? What is the value of one right ?

2. Golden Star is in the process of selling equity through rights offering. Prior to the rights offering, the firm has 60,00,000 equity shares in the market. Through the rights offering it plans on issuing an additional 10,00,000 shares at a subscription price of ₹ 45. After the equity went ex- rights, the market price was ₹ 52. What was the price of the Golden Star equity share just prior to the rights offering ?

3. General Store has 300 shares of XYZ Industries. The market price per share is ₹ company now offers to equity shareholders 1 new share to be purchased at ₹ 60 4 shares held.

   (a) Determine the value of each right.

   (b) Assume that General Store (i) uses 80 rights and sells the other 220, or (ii) sells 300 rights at the market price you have calculated. Prepare a statement showing the changes in her position in each case.

Ans.: (a) ₹ 3.00

4. Daman Group of Industries (DGI) needs to raise ₹ 5 crore of new equity to support its expansion programme. The firm's stock uncertainty currently sells for ₹ 100 per share, and it has 1 crore shares issued. Its charter does not include the preemption right, so the new equity can be raised by a public offering or a rights offering.

   (a) What are the pros and cons of each type of offering?

   (b) If the public offering is to be used, what would be the appropriate price to the public and the percentage of underwriting cost to the firm?

   (c) If a rights offering is to be used:

   (i) What subscription price would you recommend and at what price, what would be the value of each right and the ex-rights price of the stock?

   (ii) How would the percentage floatation cost under the rights offering compare with that under the public offering?

5. United Industries' equity share is priced at ₹ 72 a share in the market. Notice is given that equity shareholders may purchase 1 new share at a price of ₹ 40 for every 7 shares held. You hold 120 shares at the time of notice.

   (a) At approximately what price will each right sell in the market?

   (b) Why will this be the appropriate price?

   (c) What effect will the issuance of rights have on the original market price? Why?

Ans.: (a) ₹ 4.00

6. PXY finances new investments by 40 per cent debt and 60 per cent equity. The firm needed ₹ 65 crore for financing new investments. If retained earnings equal ₹ 42 crore, how much money will be available for dividends in accordance with residual dividend theory ?

7. If flotation costs for an equity issue are 12 per cent, how large might the issue be so that the firm will net ₹ 2580 crore ? If the equity share sells for ₹ 85 per share, how many shares must be issued ?

8. The earnings for Bindra Agro has been predicted for the next five years and are listed below. There are 1 crore shares in the market. Determine the yearly dividend per share to be paid if the following policies are enacted :

   (a) Constant ividend payout ratio of 25 per cent.

   (b) Stable dividend target at 40 per cent of the earnings over the five-year period.

   (c) Small, regular dividend of ₹ 1.50 per share plus a year-end extra when the profits in any year excees ₹ 15 crore. The year-end extra dividend will equal 50% of profits exceeding ₹ 15 crore.

Years	1	2	3	4	5
Profits after tax	₹ 14 crore	₹ 20 crore	₹ 18 crore	₹ 9 crore	₹ 25 crore

9. If you own 80 shares of RRR Industries equity with a current price of ₹ 50 per share and the firm announces a three-for-two bonus share, how many new shares will you have? What is the price of each share after the bonus?

Ans.: 120 shares; ₹ 33.33

10. ABC company, whose stock price is now ₹ 25, needs to raise ₹ 2.0 crore in equity. Underwriters have informed the firm's management that they must price the new issue to the public at ₹ 22 per share because of downward-sloping demand curve. The underwriters compensation will br 5% of the issue price, so ABC company will net ₹ 20.90 per share. The company will also incur expenses in the amount of ₹ 1,50,000. How many shares must the firm sell to net ₹ 2 crore after underwriting and flotation expenses?

Ans.: 9,64,115

11. A broker expects the equity shares of CKD Group to earn a 20% return during the coming year. The share price is currently ₹ 150, and the dividend is expected to be ₹ 5.00 per share. What does the broker expect the share price to be at the end of the year?

Ans.: ₹ 175.00

12. Desai Group's equity shares are trading for ₹ 230 each. Annual dividends are expected to be ₹ 7.50 for each of the next five years. If the share price is expected to be ₹ 400 at the end of five years, what annual rate of return is anticipated during this five-year period?

Ans.: 14.36%

13. KR Group pays an annual dividend of ₹ 1.80 and is expected to do so permanently. If an investor requires a 15% return on his investment, how much is he willing to pay for a share?

Ans.: ₹ 12.00

14. Shares of Chandra Industries just paid a ₹ 16.00 dividend, and the dividend was ₹ 8.90, 12 years ago. What has been the annual growth rate in dividends during this time? If the growth rate remains the same, how much should an investor be willing to pay for a share if the following returns are required: (a) 10%, (b) 12%, (c) 14%, (d) 16%.

Ans.: (a) ₹ 336; (b) ₹ 240; (c) ₹ 186.70; (d) ₹ 152.70

15. SSS Company *paid* a dividend of ₹ 6.80 five years ago and has just paid an annual divider of ₹ 10.00. S. Kumar expects dividends to grow at the same annual rate for the next for years. After that, he expects dividends to grow at an annual rate of 12%. How much willing to pay for a share if he requires a 16% rate of return?

Ans: ₹ 24350

16. Golden Tools recently paid an annual dividend of ₹ 2.50. Analyst for XYZ Inv believes that the dividend will grow at an average rate of 4% in perpetuity.

    (a) What is the value of the stock if the discount rate is 10%?

    (b) If tomorrow the discount rate falls to 8%, what is the effect on the stock price?

Ans.: (a) ₹ 43.33   (b) ₹ 65.00

17. The required return on an investment is 12%. You estimate that firm XYZ's dividends will grow as follows:

Year	1	2	3	4
Dividend	₹ 1.20	₹ 2.00	₹ 3.00	₹ 4.50

For the subsequent years, you expect the dividend to grow but at the more modest rate of 7% annually. What is the maximum price that you should pay for this stock?

Ans.: Present value of dividend payments: ₹ 7.66 Value of stock :₹ 68.91

18. An investor requires a return of 12%. A stock sells for ₹ 25, it pays a dividend of ₹ 1.00, and the dividends compound annually at 7%. Will this investor find the stock attractive? What is the maximum amount that this investor should pay for the stock?

Ans.: ₹ 21.40, which is less than ₹ 25 (Don't buy).

19. The annual risk-free rate of return is 9% and the investor believes that the market will rise annually at 15%. If a stock has a beta coefficient of 1.5 and its current dividend is ₹ 1.00, what should be the value of the stock if its earnings and dividends are growing annually at 6%?

Ans.: Required return: 8%

20. You are considering the purchase of 100 shares of Anupam General Store. The shares pay an annual dividend of ₹ 1 (which you expect to remain constant for the next sevral years) and have a beta of 1.25. Although you expect the risk-free rate to remain at 10% for the next three years, you believe that the share price will be ₹ 25 immediately after paying the dividend three years from today, how much are you willing to pay for a share today?

Ans.: ₹ 18.69

REFERENCES

1. Aber, John. "Industry Effects and Multivariate Stock Price Behavior." *Journal of Financial and Quantitative Analysis* 11, No. 5 (November 1976).

2. Ahlers, David M., "SEM: A Security Analysis Model," in Kalman J. Cohen and Frederick S, Hammer, eds., *Analytical Methods in Banking* (Homewood, III. Irwin, 1966).

3. Akemann, Charles A., and Werner E. Keller, "Relative Strength Does Persist!" *Journal of Portfolio Management*, Fall 1977, pp. 38-45.

4. Akgeray, V.: "Conditional Heteroscedasticity in Time Series of Stock Returns: Evidence and Forecasts," *Journal of Business*, January 1989, pp. 55-70.

5. Bajkowski, John. "From Theory to Reality: Applying the Valuation Models," *AAII Journal* (January 1993):34-38.

6. Baker, H. Kent, Aaron L. Phillips, and Gary E. Powell. "The Stock Distribution Puzzle: A Synthesis of the Literature on Stock Splits and Stock Dividends." *Financial Practice and Education* (spring/summer 1995): 24-37.

7. Baker, H. Kent, and Patricia L. Gallagher. "Management's View of Stock Splits." *Financial Management* (summer 1980): 73-77.

8. Baker, H. Kent, Gail E. Farrelly, and Richard B. Edelman. "A Survey of Management Views on Dividend Policy." *Financial Management* (autumn 1985): 78-84.

9. Ball, Clifford, and Walter Tarous: "The Maximum Likelihood Estimation of Security Price Volatility: Theory, Evidence, and Application to Option Pricing," *Journal of Business,* January 1984, pp. 97-112.

10. Ball, Ray, and Ross Watts. "Some Time Series Properties of Accounting Earnings Numbers." *Journal of Finance* 27, No. 3 (June 1972).

11. Banz, R.W. "The Relationship Between Return and Market Value of Common Stocks." *Journal of Financial Economics 9,* No. 1 (March 1981

12. Beaver, W., P. Ketler, and M. Scholes: "The Association Between Market Determined and Accounting Determined Risk Measures," *Accounting Review,* October 1970, pp. 654-682.

13. Beaver, William, and Dale Morse. "What Determines Price-Earnings Ratios?" *Financial Analysts Journal* 34, No. 4 (July-August 1978).

14. Benesh, Gary A., and Pamela P. Peterson. "On the Relation Between Earnings Changes, Analysts' Fore-casts and Stock Price Fluctuations." *Financial Analysts Journal* 42, No. 6 (November-December 1986).

15. Black, Fischer, "The Dividend Puzzle," *Journal of Portfolio Management,* Winter 1976, pp. 5-8.

16. Born, Jeffery, James Moses, and Dennis Officer. "Changes in Dividend Policy and Subsequent Earnings." *Journal of Portfolio Management* 14, No. 4 (Summer 1988).

17. Brealey, Richard A., *Security Prices in a Competitive Market* (Cambridge, Mass.: M.I.T. Press, 1971).

18. Brigham, Eugene F., and Myron J. Gordon, "Leverage, Dividend Policy, and the Cost of Capital," *Journal of Finance,* March 1968, pp. 85-103.

19. Chen, Nui-Fu, Richard Roll, and Stephen A. Ross. "Economic Forces and the Stock Market." *Journal of Business* 59, No. 3 (July 1986).

20. Christie, Andrew: "The Stochastic Behavior of Common Stock Variances: Value, Leverage and Inter-est Rate Effects," *Journal of Financial Economics,* December 1982, pp. 407-432.

21. Cottle, Sidney, Roger F. Murray, and Frank E. Block. *Graham and Dodd's Security Analysis.* 5th ed. New York: McGraw-Hill, 1988.

22. Cowen, Scott, and Jeffrey Hoffer: "Usefulness of Financial Ratios in a Single Industry," *Journal of Business Research,* March 1982, pp. 103-118.

23. Cusatis, Patrick, James Miles, and Randall Woolridge: "Restructuring through Spin-offs," *Journal of Financial Economics,* June 1993, pp. 293-312.

24. Dann, Larry Y. "Common Stock Repurchases: An Analysis of Returns to Bondholders and Stockholders." *Journal of Financial Economics* (June 1981): 113-138.

25. Donaldson, G. "In Defense of Preferred Stock." *Harvard Business Review,* 40 (July-August 1962). Reprinted in *Foundations for Financial Management,* ed. James Van Home, pp. 194-218. Homewood, III.: Irwin, 1966.

26. Drew, Garfield A. *New Methods for Profit in the Stock Market.* Wells, Vt.: Fraser Publishing, 1966.

27. Durand, David. "Growth Stocks and the Petersburg Paradox." *Journal of Finance* XII (September 1957), pp. 348-63.

28. Eiteman, David K.., "A Computer Program for Common Stock Valuation," *Financial Analysts Journal,* July-August 1968, pp. 107-111.

29. Fama, Eugene F., and Kenneth French. "Dividend Yields and Expected Stock Returns." *Journal of Financial Economics* 22, No. 1 (October 1988).

30. Farrell, James L. "The Dividend Discount Model: A Primer." *Financial Analysts Journal* 41, No. 6 (November-December 1985).

31. Fewings, David: 'The Impact of Corporate Growth on the Risk of Common Stocks," *Journal of Finance,* May 1975, pp. 525-531.

32. Foster, George, Chris Olsen, and Terry Shevlin. "Earnings Releases, Anomalies, and the Behavior of Security Returns." *Accounting Review* 59, No. 4 (October 1984).

33. Franks, Julian, Robert Harris, and Sheridan Titman: "The Postmerger Share-Price Performance of Acquiring Firms," *Journal of Financial Economics*, March 1991, pp. 81-96.

34. Friend, Irwin, and Marshall Puckett, "Dividends and Stock Prices," *American Economic Review*, September 1964, pp. 656-682.

35. Fuller, Russ: "Programming the Three-Phase Dividend Discount Model," *Journal of Portfolio Management*, Summer 1979, pp. 28-32.

36. Holt, Charles C.: "The Influence of Growth Duration on Share Price," *Journal of Finance*, September 1961, pp. 465-475.

37. Houston, John L. "Common Stock Repurchases: A Bane or Boon to Shareholders." AAII *Journal* (February 1984): 7-10.

38. Jahnke. William: 'The Growth Stock Mania," *Financial Analysts Journal*, May-June 1973, pp. 65-69.

39. Jennings, Robert. *Reaction of Financial Analysts to Corporate Management Earnings per Share Fore-casts.* Financial Analysts Research Foundation, Monograph No. 20, (New York, 1984).

40. Johnson, Lewis: "The Role of Convexity in Equity Pricing," *Financial Analysts Journal*, September-October 1992, pp. 69-73.

41. ———: "Equity Duration: Another Look," *Financial Analysts Journal*, March-April 1989, pp. 73-75.

42. Johnson, R.S., Lyle Fiore, and Richard Zuber. "The Investment Performance of Common Stocks in Relation to Their Price-Earnings Ratios: An Update of the Basu Study." *Financial Review* 24, No. 3 (August 1989).

43. Joy, O. Maurice, and Charles P. Jones, "Predictive Value of P/E Ratios." *Financial Analysts Journal*, September-October 1970, p. 61.

44. Kaplan, R., and R. W. Roll. "Accounting Changes and Stock Prices." *Financial Analysts Journal*, January-February 1973, p. 48.

45. Kaplan, R., and R.W. Roll. "Accounting Changes and Stock Prices." *Financial Analysts Journal*, January-February 1973, pp. 48-53.

46. Keenan, W. Michael. "Toward a Positive Theory of Equity Valuation." *The Journal of Finance*, March 1968, p. 197.

47. Keim, Donald B. "Dividend Yields and Stock Returns: Implications of Abnormal January Returns." *Journal of Financial Economics* 14, No. 3 (September 1985).

48. Keim, Donald B. "Size-Related Anomalies and Stock Return Seasonality." *Journal of Financial Economics* 12, No. 1 (June 1983).

49. Keim, Donald B., and Robert F. Stambaugh. "Predicting Returns in Stock and Bond Markets." *Journal of Financial Economics* 17, No. 2 (December 1986).

50. King, Benjamin F. "Market and Industry Factors in Stock Price Behavior." *Journal of Business* 39, No. 1, Part II (January 1966).

51. Leibowitz, Martin, and Stanley Kogelman: "Resolving the Equity Duration Paradox," *Financial Analysts Journal*, January-February 1993, pp. 51-67.

52. ———: Eric Sorenson, Robert Arnott, and Nicholes Hanson: "A Total Differential Approach to Equity Duration," *Financial Analysts Journal*, September-October 1989, pp. 30-37.

53. Levy, Robert A. "On the Safety of Low P/E Stocks." *Financial Analysts Journal*, January-February 1973, pp. 57-63.

54. Lintner, John. "Distribution of Incomes of Corporations among Dividends, Retained Earnings and Taxes." *The American Economic Review*, May 1956.

55. Litzenberger. Robert H., and O. Maurice Joy. "Further Evidence on the Persistence of

Corporate Profitability Rates." *Western Economic Journal,* June 1970, pp. 209-212.

56. Livingston, Miles. "Industry Movements of Common Stocks." *Journal of Finance* 32, No. 3 (June 1977).

57. Malkiel, B.G., and R.E. Quandt. "The Supply of Money and Common Stock Prices: Comment." *The Journal of Finance,* September 1972, pp. 921-26.

58. Malkiel, Burton G.: "Equity Yields, Growth, and the Structure of Share Prices," *American Economic Review,* December 1963, pp. 467-494.

59. —— and John G. Cragg: "Expectations and the Structure of Share Price," *American Economic Review,* September 1970, pp. 601-617.

60. Mao. James C.T., "The Valuation of Growth Stocks: The Investment Opportunities Approach." *Journal of Finance.* March 1966, pp. 95   102.

61. Masson. Robert, "Executive Motivations, Earnings, and Consequent Equity Performance," *Journal of Political Economy.* November-December 1971, pp. 127,8-1292.

62. McGough, Eugene F. "Anatomy of a Stock Split." *Management Accounting* (September 1993): 58-61.

63. McNichols, M., and A. David. "Stock Dividends, Stock Splits, and Signalling." *Journal of Finance* (July 1990): 857-879.

64. Meyers, Stephen L. "A Re-Examination of Market and Industry Factors in Stock Price Behavior." *Journal of Finance* 28, No. 3 (June 1973).

65. Miller, Merton H., and Franco Modigliani. "Dividend Policy, Growth and the Valuation of Shares." *The Journal of Business* XXXIV (October 1961), pp. 411-33.

66. Mitchell, Mark: "The Value of Corporate Takeovers," *Financial Analysts Journal,* January—February 1990, pp. 21-31.

67. ——: and Harold Mulhern: "The Stock Price Response to Pension Terminations and the Relation of Terminations with Corporate Takeovers," *Financial Management,* Autumn, 1989, pp. 41-56.

68. Murphy, Joseph E., Jr., and J. Russell Melson. "Stability of P/E Ratios." *Financial Analysts Journal,* March-April 1969, p. 77.

69. Nagorniak, John J. "Thoughts on Using Dividend Discount Models." *Financial Analysts Journal* 41, No. 6 (November-December 1985).

70. Niederhoffer, Victor, and Patrick J. Regan. "Earnings Changes, Analysts' Forecasts, and Stock Prices." *Financial Analysts Journal,* May-June 1972, pp. 65-71.

71. Ofer, Aharon R.. "Investors' Expectations of Earnings Growth. Their Accuracy and Effects on the Structure of Realized Rates of Return," *Journal of Finance* May 1975, pp. 509-523.

72. Pettit, R. Richardson, "Dividend Announcements, Security Performance, and Capital Market Efficiency," *Journal of Finance,* December 1972, pp. 993-1008.

73. Pinches, George E., and William R. Kinney, Jr. "The Measurement of the Volatility of Common Stock Prices." *The Journal of Finance,* March 1971, p. 119.

74. Porter, Michael E. "How to Conduct an Industry Analysis." In *The Financial Analysts Handbook.* 2nd ed., edited by Sumner N. Levine. Homewood, III.: Dow Jones-Irwin, 1988.

75. Porter, Michael E. "Industry Structure and Competitive Strategy: Keys to Profitability." *Financial Analysts Journal* 36, No. 4 (July-August 1980).

76. Radcliffe, R.C., and W.G. Gillespie. "The Price Impact of Reverse Splits." *Financial Analysts Journal,* January-February 1979.

77. Reilly, Frank K. "Stock Price Changes by Market Segment." *Financial Analysts Journal,* March-April 1971, p. 54.

78. ——, "The Misdirected Emphasis in Security Valuation." *Financial Analysts Journal* 29, No. 1 (January-February 1973).

79. Reilly, Frank K., and Eugene Drzycimski. "Alternative Industry Performance and Risk." *Journal of Financial and Quantitative Analysis* 9, No. 3 (June 1974).

80. Sharpe, W.F., and H.B. Sosin. "Risk Return and Yield on Common Stocks." *Financial Analysts Journal,* March-April 1976, pp. 33-42.

81. Shiskin, Julius. "Systematic Aspects of Stock Price Fluctuations." Reprinted in James Lorie and Richard Brealey, *Modern Developments in Investment Management.* 2nd ed. Hinsdale, Ill.: The Dryden Press, 1978.

82. Spudeck, R.E., and R. Charles Moyer. "Reverse Splits and Shareholder Wealth: The Impact of Commissions." *Financial Management* (winter 1985): 52-56.

83. Staubus, George J., "Earnings Periods for Common Share Analysis," *Journal of Business,* October 1968, pp. 472-476.

84. Stewart, Samuel S. "Forecasting Corporate Earnings." In *The Financial Analysts Handbook.* 2nd ed., edited by Sumner N. Levine. Homewood, Ill.: Dow Jones-Irwin, 1988.

85. Walter, James E. "Dividend Policies and Common Stock Prices." *The Journal of Finance,* March 1965.

86. —————, *Dividend Policy and Enterprise Value* (Belmont, Calif.: Wadsworth Publishing Co., Inc., 1967).

87. Williams. J. B., *The Theory of Investment Value* (Cambridge, Mass.: Harvard University Press, 1938).

88. Woolridge, J.R., and D.R. Chambers. "Reverse Splits and Shareholder Wealth." *Financial Management* (autumn 1983): 5-15.

13

Equity Valuation and Analysis

INTRODUCTION

The security analyst, when faced with the problem of making a buy, hold, or sell decision, must first evaluate the past performance of the security and then coupled with his personal experience, predict its future performance and relative market position. The detailed data available to the analyst for this task far exceed his human capabilities of assimilation. The analyst, therefore, will normally base his predictions on several basic attributes of the security and modify these results in the light of his intuitive beliefs. While the process may be generally successful, its intuitive segments make the evaluation of errors and improvements of this technique very difficult, if not impossible.

The valuation task is relatively straightforward in case of bond and preference share, because benefits are generally constant and reasonably certain. Equity valuation is different, because the return on equity is uncertain and can change from time to time. It is the size of the return and the degree of fluctuation (i.e. risk) which together determine the value of a share to the investor. Therefore, forecasting abilities of the analyst are far more crucial in the equity analysis. Infact, active equity management is based on the notion, explicitly stated or implied, that the stock market is not totally efficient. Put another way, active equity management assumes that all historical and current information is not *fully and correctly* reflected in the current price of every stock. Hence, there exist stocks that are *undervalued, fairly valued,* and *overvalued.* The task of the active equity manager is to decide which stocks are which and invest accordingly. By contrast, an investor/equity manager who believes the market is efficient tends to favour a passive strategy, with indexing being the most common form of passive strategy.

A useful way of thinking about active versus passive strategy is in terms of three activities performed by the manager : (1) portfolio construction (deciding on the equity to buy or sell), (2) trading of securities, and (3) portfolio monitoring. Figure-1 summarises the differences in the three activities for active management and passive management. Generally active managers devote the majority of their time to portfolio construction. In contrast, with passive strategies such as indexing, managers devote less time to this activity.

ACTIVE EQUITY INVESTMENT STYLES

The primary styles of active equity management are *top-down* and *bottom-up.* Even though there are few pure examples of these two styles, they serve as a useful point of reference. A manager who uses a top-down equity management style begins with an assessment of the overall economic environment and a forecast of its near-term outlook and makes a general asset allocation decision regarding the relative attractiveness of the

EQUITY MANAGEMENT

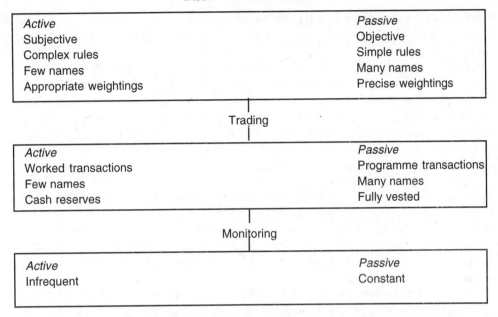

FIGURE 1: ACTIVE EQUITY MANAGEMENT VERSUS PASSIVE EQUITY
MANAGEMENT

various sectors of the financial markets (e.g., equity, bond, real estate, bullion, and cash
equivalents). The top-down manager then analyses the stock market in an attempt to
identify economic sectors and industries that stand to gain or lose from the manager's
economic forecast. After identifying attractive and unattractive sectors and industries,
the top-down manager finally selects a portfolio of individual stocks. This process is
presented in Figure-2.

A manager who uses a *bottom-up equity management style* de-emphasises the significance
of economic and market cycles and focuses instead on the analysis of individual securities.
Using financial analysts and/or computer screening techniques, the bottom-up manager

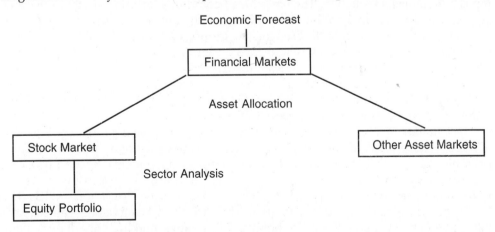

FIGURE 2: TOP-DOWN INVESTMENT PROCESS

seeks out stocks that have certain characteristics that are deemed attractive (e.g., low price-earnings ratio, small capitalisation, low analyst coverage).

Subcategories of Active Equity Management

Some of the major subcategories of the two major styles of active equity management are listed below:

Growth Managers: Growth managers can be classified as either top-down or bottom-up. Growth managers are often divided into large capitalisation and small capitalisation subgroups. The growth managers seek to buy securities that are typically selling at relatively high P/E ratios due to high earnings growth, with the expectation of continued high (or higher) earnings growth. The portfolios of growth managers are characterised by relatively high betas, price-book and P/E ratios, high returns or equity and growth rates, and relatively low dividend yields.

Market Timers: The market timer is typically a set category of the top-down investment style and comes in many varieties. The basic assumption of the market timer is that he can forecast when the stock market will go up (or continue to go up) and when it will go down (or continue to go down). In this sense, the market timer is not-too-distant relative to the technical analyst. The portfolio of the market timer is not fully invested in equity. Rather, he/she moves in and out of the stock market as his/her economic, analytical and technical work dictates.

Hedgers: The hedger seeks to buy equity shares, but also to place well-defined limits on investor's investment risk. One popular hedging technique involves simultaneously purchasing a stock and a put option on that stock The put option sets a floor on the amount of loss that can be sustained (if the stock price goes down), while the potential profit (if the stock price goes up) is diminished only by the original cost of the put. This is an example of a relatively simple hedge. However, practitioners follow much more complicated hedge strategies.

Value Managers: Value managers sometimes called *Contrarians* because they see value where many other market participants do not. The value manager seeks to buy securities that are at a discount to their *face value* and sell them at or in excess of that value. Value managers can fall into either the top-down or the bottom-up category. Value managers use dividend discount

Group Rotation Managers: The group rotation manager is in a subcategory of the top-down management style. The basic idea behind this technique is that the economy goes through reasonably well-defined phases of the business cycle, namely, recession, recovery, expansion, and credit crunch. The group rotator believes that he can discern the current phase of the economy and forecast into which phase it will evolve. He can then select those economic sectors and industries that are about to benefit. For example, if the economy were perceived to be on the verge of moving from recession to recovery, the group rotator would begin to purchase stocks in the appropriate sectors and specific industries that are sensitive to a pickup in the economy.

Technicians: Technicians (sometimes called *technical analysts* or *chartists)* discern market cycles (not economic cycles) and pick securities solely on the basis of historical price movements as they related to the projected price movements. By reading a chart of the price action of a stock (or a group of stocks) and artfully discerning patterns, the technician hopes to be able to predict the future path of the price action models (DDM), P/E ratios, earnings surplus etc. In terms of portfolio characteristics, value managers have relatively low betas, low price-book and P/E ratios, and high dividend yields.

EQUITY VALUATION MODELS

Having discussed some of the various styles of equity management, we turn now to some of the actual models of equity valuation. The purpose of these models is to identify whether a stock is misplaced. Underpriced stocks need to be purchased, overpriced stocks should be shorted. As most modern equity valuation models are based upon the present value theory, set forth in detail by John B. Williams in *Theory of Investment Value*. Investment analyst must turn first to the present value estimation to know the intrinsic value of the equities.

Present Value Estimation

Present value is simply the inverse of future value. If we have opportunity to receive a given sum in the future, and we know the appropriate interest rate, we can calculate its value today.

$$\text{Present value} = \frac{\text{Future}}{(1+i)^n} \tag{1}$$

More formally, by rewriting (1), we get

$$W_t = \frac{W_{t+n}}{(1+i)^n} \tag{2}$$

where W is the amount at any time t, W_{t+n} is the amount n periods later, n is the number of periods, and i is the interest rate per period.

Let us consider an example. Suppose we have an opportunity to receive ₹ 100 a year from now. What is its value today if the interest rate is 12 per cent ? Applying equation-2, we have

$$W_0 = \frac{₹\,100}{(1+.12)} = 89.28$$

Likewise, the value today of ₹ 100 to be received 2 years in the future would be given by

$$W_0 = \frac{₹\,100}{(1+.12)^2} = 79.72$$

Whereas we spoke of compounding cash flows forward in time, we speak of discounting back in time. In calculating a present value, the interest rate is reflected to as the discount rate.

In order to develop a consistent system of security valuation theory, it has become fashionable to apply the techniques of present value theory to the equity valuation. To illustrate this method of evaluation, let us assume an investor, whose cost of capital equals k, is to decide whether to invest in the equity of a particular company. As a first step he calculates the adjusted earnings per share (EPS) over the past few years, examines the stability of the earnings and their growth, and on the basis of these findings and of an analysis of the company's outlook derives an estimate of future earnings per share. For convenience let us assume that the expected earnings are constant, and equal to E per share; that these earnings will be received on the last day of each year; and that the earnings will continue indefinitely into the future. What is the value of such a share to this particular investor ? Given his cost of capital of k, the present value of such a share of equity can be calculated as follows:

$$W = \frac{E}{(1+k)} + \frac{E}{(1+k)^2} + \ldots\ldots\ldots + \frac{E}{(1+k)^t} \tag{3}$$

$$\sum_{t=1}^{\infty} \frac{E}{(1+k)^t}$$

where:

V - the present value of the earning stream

Equation (3) can be rewritten as an infinite geometric progression with a common term $\dfrac{1}{(1+k)}$

$$V = \frac{E}{1+k} \left[1 + \frac{1}{(1+k)} + \frac{1}{(1+k)^2} + \ldots\ldots\right] \tag{4}$$

Summing the geomertic progression with the brackets yields

$$V = \frac{E}{1+k} \cdot \frac{1}{1 - \dfrac{1}{1+k}} = \frac{E}{k}$$

Thus the expected stream of earnings, capitalised at the investor's cost of capital, measures the share "intrinsic" value to him. Invoking the present value, we find that if the share's market price (P) is below its intrinsic value (V) the investor should purchase the share, since the net present value is positive $(V-P > 0)$. On the other hand, if the shares' market price is greater than its intrinsic value he should not make this investment since its net present value is negative $(V - P < 0)$.

Different investors can be expected to evaluate the investment differently. Some will decide to buy the equity while others will decide not to buy, or to sell it if they already own some. This differential behaviour reflects two principal factors

(a) Different individuals have different costs of capital so that a calculation using one discount rate may result in negative NPV while the use of another discount rate may give a positive NPV for the same expected earnings.

(b) Even if both investors have the same cost of capital, differences in their estimates of the firm's profitability may result in different investment decisions.

To illustrate the logic of the present value approach, the case of ABC Company can be taken. The EPS of the ABC Company were ₹ 12.72 and the market price per share was ₹ 85.00 in 2011. Assume that on the basis of an analysis of the company's outlook we reach the conclusion that the rate of profit will continue indefinitely. *Does it pay to buy the share of ABC Company, given the market price ?*

Clearly the answer to the question depends on an investor's cost of capital. Table-1 calculates the value of ABC Company given the constant expected earnings of ₹ 12.72

TABLE 1

Intrinsic Value of Share (12.72/k)	Discount Rate (Percentage)
122.76	10.36
85.00	14.96
61.38	20.79
40.94	30.69

per share, for a variety of alternative assumptions regarding the discount rate. If we subtract from all transaction costs and transfer taxes, only investors whose costs of capital are lower than 14.96% will find the investment attractive. For higher discount rates, the purchase price, ₹ 85.00 exceeds the value of the capitalised earnings.

BASIC MODELS

One of the most widely used equity valuation model is the dividend discount model (DDM). In its simplest form, the DDM defines the intrinsic value of a share as the present value of future dividend. There are several variations of the DDM because of different assumptions about the growth rate of dividend and its relationship to the discount rate used to calculate present values.

Zero Growth Model

The most basic of all the DDMs is the zero growth model. This mode assumes that dividend will *be* constant over time, so that growth is zero, and that the investor's required rate of return is constant. This model is:

$$V_0 = \frac{D_1}{(1+k)^1} + \frac{D_2}{(1+k)^2} + \frac{D_3}{(1+k)^3} + \frac{D_4}{(1+k)^4} + \ldots + \ldots \tag{5}$$

where V_0 = intrinsic value of equity today or at time period 0.
            D_1 = dividend per share in period t.
            k = investor's required rate of return.

Given $D_1 = D_2 = D_3 = \ldots\ldots = D$ assumption, the time subscript can be dropped. The dividend income stream is essentially a perpetuity, and the value can be calculated as:

$$V_0 = \frac{D}{k} \tag{6}$$

For example, assume that the dividend per share are estimated to be ₹ 4.00 per year indefinitely and the investor requires a 20 per cent of return. The intrinsic value of the equity share is ₹ 4/.20 = ₹ 20. (This model is more appropriate for an analysis of preference share because of the constant dividend assumption).

Constant Growth Model

In this model, the cash dividends are expected to increase at constant (percentage) rate each year. In order to find the discounted present value of the stream of constantly rising dividends, the investors can use equation-7 which is the constant growth model where:

$$V_0 = \sum_{t=1}^{\infty} \frac{D_0 \, ((1+g)^t}{(1+k)^t} \tag{7}$$

and further simplfted to:

$$V_0 = \frac{D_1}{(k-g)} \tag{8}$$

This equation tells us that the value or an equity share is equal to the cash dividend in time period I discounted by the difference between the required rate of return required by equity investors and growth rate of dividends (g). In using equation-7 for a constantly growing series of cash dividends, we must use the cash dividends expected one year hence, or D_1. To illustrate, if an investor has a share whose current cash dividend (at time $t = 0$) is ₹ 4.00, the constant compound growth rate in dividends is 15 per cent per year and the required rate of return is 20 per cent, the value of this share is :

$$V_0 = V_0 = \frac{D_1}{(k-g)}$$

$$= \frac{D_0 (1+g)}{(k-g)}$$

$$= \frac{₹ 4.00 (1+.15)}{0.20-0.15}$$

$$= ₹ 92.00$$

Note that this current price of ₹ 92.00 is substantially higher than the ₹ 20 when no growth in future cash dividends was assumed. This is expected since, other things being equal, an investor would value a growing cash flow stream at a higher rate than a non-growing stream.

Variable Growth Rate of Dividends

Consider a firm which grows at a fast rate for a few years and then reverts to a constant or no growth situation. This might occur because a firm made previous investments that produced high cash flows, but increasing competition is expected to reduce the future growth rate. In this case, the value of firm whose growth rate of dividends varies over time can be determined by the following equation-9.

$$V_0 = \sum_{t=1}^{n} \frac{D_0 (1+g_x)^t}{(1+k)^t} + \sum_{t=n+1}^{\infty} \frac{D_n (1+g_y)^{t-n}}{(1+k)^t} \qquad (9)$$

where : g_x = growth rate of dividends for n year
g_y = growth rate of dividends for years n +1 and beyond

This equation can be expanded any number of growth rate or time periods, the ability to change growth rates allows one to value a share over the life cycle of a firm on the rates of growth change. If the growth rate of dividends is expected to grow at one rate for a period of time and then a constant rate, the equation for the variable growth rate model is :

$$V_0 = \sum_{t=1}^{n} \frac{D_0 (1+g_x)^t}{(1+k)^t} + \frac{D_{n+1}}{(k-g_y)} \left[\frac{1}{(1+k)^n} \right] \qquad (10)$$

To illustrate the use of the multiple growth rate dividend valuation model in valuing a firm, consider the case of a hypothetical XYZ Company. The company paid its first cash dividend of ₹ 2.50 today and dividends are expected to grow at a rate of 30 per cent per year for the next 3 years. Thereafter, cash dividends will grow at a 10 per cent rate per year. Shareholders expect to earn a 15 per cent return on their investments. Based on these assumptions the steps necessary to calculate the value of share of XYZ Company are presented below:

STEP 1:

Calculate the present value of dividends for the first 3 years.

$$\sum_{t=1}^{n} \frac{D_0 (1+g_x)^t}{(1+k)^t}$$

$= ₹\ 8.3473$

Year	Dividend $D_0(1+g_x)$ ₹ 2.50$(1+0.30)'$ X	x	Capitalisation Rate $k=0.15$	=	Present Value
(1)	(2)		(3)		(4) = (2)X(3)
0	₹ 2.500				
1	3.250		0.870		3.7356
2	4.225		0.756		5.5886
3	5.493		0.658		8.3473

STEP 2:

Value at the end of 3 years for the remaining life of the company

Dividend in 4th year $D_4 = D_3(1 + g_y)$

$$= ₹\ 5.493\ (1 + 0.10) = ₹\ 6.0423$$

Value at the end of the third year

$$V_3 = \frac{D_4}{K - g_y}$$

$$= \frac{6.0423}{0.15 - 0.10}$$

$$= ₹\ 120.846$$

STEP 3:

The present value at the end of 3 years (V_3) discounted by the required rate of return $k = 0.15$

$$(V_3) \times \frac{1}{(1 + k)^3}$$

$$= ₹\ 120.846\ (0.658)$$

$$= ₹\ 79.516668$$

STEP 4:

The value per share today equals the present value of dividends for the first 3 years (Step-1) plus the present value of the share price at the end of year 3 (Step-3).

Step 1		Step 2
V_0 = ₹ 8.343 = ₹ 87.8639668	+	₹ 79.516668

STEP 5:

Multiply the number of shares by the price per share to determine the total value of the equity. If there are 10,00,000 ordinary shares the total value of the firm is ₹ 8,78,63,967.

Applying Major Indexes

One way to analyse the data on relative price levels is by extracting information from a popular index like the NIFTY or the SENSEX. By substituting the earnings for dividends, and, with minor adjustments, the analyst can apply the basic DDM valuation model to indexes. Assuming that earnings grow at some long-term average, their present value can be found. Suppose the following information as given in Table-2 is available.

TABLE 2

Index level	5024
Divided Yield	2.75%
P/E Ratio	45.50
Expected Earnings	₹ 84.50

Give an index level of 5024 and expected earnings of ₹ 84.50, we can determine the denomination of equation-8

$$V_o = \frac{D_o(1+g)}{k-g}$$

By substituting these values as:

$$5024 = \frac{₹\ 84.50}{X}$$

Investors call the quantity k-g the capitalization rate, is just the 'cap rate'. Even though the shareholders' required rate of return (k) or the future growth rate for certain (g) is not known, but the investors know the difference between them as implied in the DDM.

According to financial theory, over the long-term a firm's earnings and dividends grow at the same rate. This rate, called the sustainable growth rate, equals the firm's earnings retention rate times its return on equity. If the P-E ratio remains unchanged the stock price will also grow at this rate. From a corporate perspective:

Growth rate = (1-Payout ratio) x Return on equity

Equation-8 has important implication. With a 100% payout ratio, dividends equal earnings and growth equals zero. We can restate it as

$$P_o = \frac{E_o}{K} \qquad\qquad (11)$$

Rearranging,

$$K = \frac{E_o}{P_o}$$

This is the expression for earnings yield. Note that the earnings yield is simply the reciprocal of the P-E ratio and that is grounded in time value of money relationships.

Following William's theory, John C. Clendenin has developed a method for determining the justifiable price-dividend multiplier for a growth stock, given alternative assumptions as to rates of growth, duration of growth and stock rates. He presents a series of present value tables which can be used either to determine the assumptions concerning growth rate and duration which are implicit in the current market value of a stock, given certain assumptions about growth and appropriate discount rates. The value of a share of stock to a long-term investor is contained entirely in the future dividends the share (or its successors following mergers, bonus shares or spin- offs) may pay, plus the value of occasional rights or small miscellaneous distribution which do not dilute the basic equity.

In describing the use of his technique, Clendenin shows that it can be applied to short-term investments as well. A person who' plans to hold a share of stock for only three years, for example, will arrive at today's value by discounting to its present value (a) the dividends he expects to receive during the next three years and (b) the price he expects to receive at the time of sale, which will be determined by all future dividends the stock is expected to yield from year 3 to infinity.

Three factors are basic to Clendenin's valuation method: (1) the rate of dividend growth, (2) the duration of the growth trend, and (3) the discount or capitalisation rates (or yield rates as he calls them). Cautioning investors concerning over-optimism about growth rates and duration, he advocates a system of progressively higher discount rates to be applied to expected dividend returns in the distant future.

Clendenin suggests that 20 years are "not beyond the scope of reasonable estimation in the case of well established concerns". Beyond that time he advises caution but illustrates that the largest part of the value of any stock attaches to dividends of the first twenty years because of the increasing effect of discounting as time progresses. He also suggests application of the method to groups of stocks rather than single issue, to obtain greater reliability in long-term projections. The analyst using Clendenin's method of growth stock valuation still faces a major task, namely, that of deciding what values to assign to Clendenin's basic three factors : growth rate, duration and discount rates. Clendenin offers limited help on how to estimate future growth rate duration. He arrives at a discount rate by checking what the norm is among high-grade stocks, add 1 per cent to expected real terms growth rate to take into account average inflationary forces, and suggests a discount rate which depends on the quality of the corporation whose stock is considered. Clendenin avoids being any more specific in assigning values to his factors because in all instances, the investor has a subjective analysis to make.

Valuation Model for Cyclical Stock

Bauman used, as did Clendenin, the present value concept of arriving at a stock value by discounting at an appropriate yield rate all future cash incomes or dividends. He spells out the factors that determine future dividend income, namely, the growth rate and the growth duration, and argues that a company with a growth rate in excess of the average shown in an industry will sooner or later find its growth rate declining to the average level. How long this "transitional" period lasts depends on the company, the industry, the product, the competition, etc. A guide to follow is to determine the probable position of the company in its life cycle. For example, if a company has been experiencing an abnormally high growth rate, Bauman suggests,"...... *unless there is sufficient evidence to the contrary, the best earnings and dividend projection is probably one based on a decreasing rate of growth, until it eventually approximates the secular growth rate for the majority of companies in the company*". For reasons of convenience, and for lack of evidence to the contrary, Bauman makes the assumption in his model that the growth rate will decline by equal amounts over the span of the transitional period.

According to Bauman, therefore, in order to make a good estimate of future dividends, the investor must ascertain (a) the current growth rate of dividends (and earnings), and (b) how long will it take until the growth rate has declined to the average typical for the majority of corporations.

Once the investor has determined the pattern for future dividend incomes, he must discount them to arrive at a present value. *What shall be the discount rate* ? It depends on the risk involved. The discount rate applied to the first year's expected dividends is usually the lowest, and it increases with time as income of more distant years becomes more and more uncertain. That is, the risk premium added to the discount rate increases with time. Although he does not advise the investor exactly on how much higher future discount rate should be than initial rates, he gives a very strong clue by showing what rates were representative for a majority stock average. Bauman relies heavily upon historical data, and believes this action is justified by absence at present of any indicators which point to large changes ahead. He reminds the investor, however, to be on guard constantly to recognise signs of changes.

Obviously, the cyclical model is difficult to formulate even on a simple configuration, but it does point out the variables that must be considered. The power of time and compounding is great with high rates being difficult to achieve for long periods of time. Let us assume that a stock has a four year business cycle from trough to peak to trough; that the stock pays a regular dividend; and that the investor is willing to trade in and out of the stock but; since the risks are great, he must earn a 20 per cent rate of return (k) rather than 10 per cent if he bought the stock at the low and sold at the high the equation would be :

$$V_0 = \frac{D_1}{(1+k)} + \frac{D_2+P_2}{(1+k)^2} \tag{12}$$

where D_1 and D_2 are dividends, and P_2 is the expected price, including capital gains, at the top of the cycle. If D_1 and D_2 are ₹ 1, and P_2 is ₹ 80, the net present value of the stream of income at 20 per cent is :

$$V_0 = \frac{1}{(1+.20)} + \frac{1.80}{(1+.20)^2} = ₹ 57.08$$

Therefore, if the stock could be purchased at ₹ 57.08 or lower, it would provide the speculative investor with a yield of 20 per cent. But what valuation model would we employ if the speculative investor wished to continue trading in shares, did not wish to sell short, and therefore was temporarily out of the market. May be his funds were placed in saving accounts. The equation would be as follows

$$V_0 = \frac{D_1}{(1+k)} + \frac{D_2+CG_2}{(1+k)^2} + \frac{I_3}{(1+k)^3} + \frac{D_4}{(1+k)^4} + \frac{D_5}{(1+k)^5} + \frac{D_6+P_6}{(1+k)^6} \tag{13}$$

Where CG_2 is capital gains in year 2, 1_3 and I_4 are interest income, and D_1, D_2 ...... are dividends. The equation covers a successful trade from the purchase of stock at the cyclical low, then to a sale at the high and a move to a say, 8 per cent savings account, then to a repurchase at the low, and a final sale at the peak in year 6. It is obvious that this is difficult to do in practice and that the cycle might be substantially shorter than six years.

MODELS BASED ON PRICE RATIO ANALYSIS

Price ratios are widely used by financial analysts, more so even than dividend discount models. Of course, all valuation methods try to accomplish the same thing, which is to appraise the economic value of a company's stock. However, analysts readily agree that no single method can adequately handle this task on all occasions. The most popular price ratio methods, used in the financial analysis, are discussed below:

Price-Earnings (P/E) Ratio (Earnings Multiplier Model)

The most popular price ratio used to assess the value of equity is a company's price-earnings ratio, also referred as the earnings multiplier. P/E ratio is calculated as the ratio of a firm's current stock price divided by its annual earnings per share (EPS). P/E ratio is specified as follows:

Price/Earnings Ratio = Earnings Multiplier

$$= \frac{\text{Current market price}}{\text{Expected 12-month earnings}} = \frac{P}{E} \tag{14}$$

The inverse of a P/E ratio is called an earning yield, and it is measured as earnings per share divided by a current stock price (E/P). Clearly, an earnings yield and a price-earnings ratio are simply two ways to measure the same thing. In practice, earnings yields are less commonly stated and used than P/E ratios.

Since most companies report earnings each quarter, annual earnings per share can be calculated either as the most recent quarterly earnings per share times four or as the sum of the last four quarterly earnings per share figures. Most analysts prefer the first method of multiplying the latest quarterly earnings per share value times four. However, the' difference is usually small, but it can sometimes be a source of confusion.

Financial analysts often refer to high-P/E stocks as growth stocks. To see why, notice that a P/E ratio is measured as a *current* stock price over *current* earnings per share. Now, consider two companies with the same current earnings per share, where one company is a high-growth company and the other is a low-growth company. Which company should have a higher stock price, the high-growth company or the low-growth company?

This question is a no-brainer. All else equal, we would be surprised if the high-growth company did not have a higher stock price, and therefore a higher P/E ratio. In general, companies with higher expected earnings growth will have higher P/E ratios, which is why high-P/E stocks are often referred to as growth stocks.

The reasons high-P/E stocks are called growth stocks seems obvious enough; however, in a seeming defiance of logic, low-P/E stocks are often referred to as value stocks. The reason is that low-P/E stocks are often viewed as "cheap" relative to *current earnings*. This suggests that these stocks may represent good investment values, and hence the term value stocks. However, it should be rated that the terms "growth stock" and "value stock" are mostly just commonly-used labels. Of course, only time will tell whether a high-P/E stock turns out to actually be a high-growth stock, or whether a low-P/E stock is really a good value.

The P/E ratio, used in the valuation equation, is influenced by (i) P/E ratios, for a group of companies, tend to change little from one period to the next. Therefore an investor cannot expect a dramatic change in future P/E ratios. The future level of the P/E ratio could be viewed as a function of the current P/E ratio or an average P/E ratio over some period of time; (ii) The P/E ratio is a function of future expected earnings. The higher the growth rate of earnings expected, higher the P/E ratio. An investor will be willing to pay a higher price for the current earnings if earnings are expected to grow at a much higher rate in the future; (iii) A normal P/E for the market is difficult to determine. A normal P/E ratio is established for each company, but it can be compared to the market P/E ratio to provide some idea of risk. The higher the P/E ratio relative to the market, the higher the risk. This is true in spite of the fact that investors are willing to pay more; iv) Inflationary expectations tend to reduce P/E ratios; (v) Higher interest rates tend to reduce P/E ratio; (vi) P/E ratios vary by industry; (vii) An investor should examine the trend of P/E ratios over time for each company; (viii) The level of P/E ratios is not an absolute value but a relative one; (ix) Speculative companies and cyclical companies have relatively low P/E ratio; (x) Growth companies tend to have higher P/E ratios; (xi) Companies with a large portion of debt in the capital structure tend to have lower P/E ratios; (xii) A company that pays a higher dividend tend to have a higher P/E ratio; and finally, (xiii) the P/E ratios can change radically and suddenly because of a change in the expected growth rate of earnings. Therefore, the greater the expected stability of the growth rate of earnings per share, the higher the P/E ratios.

How can the P/E ratio be used as guide in making an investment decision ? For this the analyst is to apply various rules of thumb on company's earnings selecting an appropriate P/E ratio to determine the value for its shares. The resulting price is to be compared with current market price to assess the relative magnitude of the ratio. Taken from historical record of the equity in question, the determination of the current P/E must be followed by a standard of comparison. For this, the analyst may ascertain the median or mean P/E for the equity as well as its range over time. More weight can be given to the recent past. This provides boundaries within which the P/E should fall (range) and indicates whether the equity is tending to sell at the upper limits of expectation (high end of P/E range) or lower limits. Industry P/E's provide some guidelines, however, different companies in the same industry frequently carry quite different P/E's. And when Firm's P/E ratio differs from the industry average, the investor may want to ask why and analyse the firm further before making an investment decision.

P/E ratio may be used to compare firms and help to select individual stocks. This approach appears to be quite different from the dividend-growth model. They are, however, essentially very similar. The dividend-growth modes is:

$$V = \frac{D_o(1+g)}{k-g}$$

Since the firm's current dividend (D_o) is related to its current earnings (E_o) and the proportion of the earnings that are distributed (d), then

$$D_o = dE_o$$

When this is substituted back into the dividend-growth model, the model becomes:

$$V = \frac{dE_o(1+g)}{k-g}$$

If both sides of the equation are divided by E_o, the stock's valuation is expressed as a P/E ratio:

$$\frac{V}{E_o} = \frac{d(1+g)}{k-g}$$

From this perspective, a P/E ratio depends on the same fundamental financial variables as the stock's valuation achieved through use of the dividend-growth model.

The use of P/E ratios instead of dividend-growth model offers one major advantage and one major disadvantage. The advantage is that P/E ratio may be applied to equity that are not currently, paying cash dividends. The dividend growth model assumes that the firm will eventually pay cash dividends and that these future dividends that give the stock current value. The major weakness of the use of P/E ratios is that these ratios do not tell the analyst if the security is under–or overvalued. The ratio may indicate whether the firm's stock is selling near its historic high or low P/E ratio and then the investor draws an inference form this information. The dividend-growth model establishes a value based on the investor's required rate of return, the firm's dividends, and the future growth in those dividends. This valuation is then compared to actual price to answer the question of whether the stock is under–or overvalued.

GREENSPAN MODEL

An analyst can adapt the Greenspan model for use with individual equity securities. In this application, compute the ratio of the company's estimated earnings per share for the next 12 months to the current yield on a 10-year treasury security. If this ratio is less than the current stock price, the stock is overvalued. If it is more, the stock is undervalued.

Greenspan stock value = Estimated Annual Earnings ÷ 10-year treasury rate

While this heuristic is not perfect (nor is any stock selection tool), it provides some historical perspective on share value. Many analysts routinely calculate this figure on the stocks they follow.

Grrowth At a Reasonable Price (GARP)

GARP technique seeks to combine elements of both growth and value investing. It advocates shares for good growth prospects that simultaneously sell for a price near or less than the firm's estimated intrinsic value. Value investors like low price-earnings ratios; growth investors like high growth rates. The Price - earnings - to - growth (PEG) ratio, combines both perspectives. This is the principal yard-stock which GARP investors use in their analysis.

$$\text{PEG Ratio} = \frac{\text{P/E Ratio}}{\text{Annual Earnings Per Share Growth Rate}} \qquad (15)$$

While there no magic benchmark, GARP investors like a number, and many seek stocks with a PEG ratio less than one.

There are many ways to calculate the PEG Ratio.

Robert Ferguson presents a method of determining justifiable price /earnings ratios for growth stocks as compared with more standard. His objectives are to answer the following questions :

(a) How many years of the present high growth rate are assumed by today's market price before the growth rate of the company will drop to the "standard" rate ?

(b) What price /earnings ratio is justified given a certain rate of growth which is higher than the standard rate for a certain number of years ?

Ferguson takes the market price as a base and then tries to determine what estimates of the basic factors (growth rate and growth duration) the market makes. He then leaves the investor to decide whether these estimates are too low or too high in his judgement. Ferguson develops a nomograph which eliminates the need for complicated calculation on the part of the investor. The nomograph is a graphical solution to the equation:

$$\frac{D_a}{P^1_a} + \frac{(1+R_a)^n}{(1+R_b)^n} \qquad (16)$$

Where :

D_a = Some standard price /earnings ratio; P^1_a Growth stock price /earnings ratio;

R_a = Standard growth rate assumed; R_b - Rate of growth assumed for growth stock.

Although, it appears that Ferguson ignores the discount rate, closer examination reveals that the use of a standard growth rate in the denominator of his equation, implies that investors will apply uniform discount rates to all equity earnings and that difference in price /earnings ratios arise only from differences in assumed growth rates and duration.

A further assumption is made implicitly that the quoted growth rates stay on the same level until period t and then drop off suddenly to a rate equivalent to the "standard rate". An analysis based on the foregoing assumption differs, of course, very strongly from Bauman's Variable Rate Method, which assumes evenly declining growth rates and increasing discount rates for incomes with longer futurity. In the last paragraph of his article, Ferguson states :

> "We have not considered the fact that many stocks pay dividends which are an important source of profit, in addition to price appreciation. This is especially true in situations where the growth rate is of the same order of magnitude as the dividend yield. In these instances, the neglect of dividends may well result in an incorrect calculation. An approximate adjustment for dividend income, useful in many instances, would be to add the yield to the per share earnings growth rate and use the resultant figure in place of the growth rate".

This implicitly assumes that the current market price of stocks completely disregards dividend payments. Moreover, this procedure would represent double counting and overstate justifiable price/earnings ratios for growth stocks, since dividend payout is already implicitly in the standard price/earnings ratio used in his equation.

Nicholas Molodovsky believes that any standardized selections of future periods, such as ten years, for instance, could serve illustrative purposes only. He stressed that in actual analytical practice, projections of future earnings trends of different stock would have to be made for whatever varying period might be specifically indicated. The nature of the industry to which a company belongs — as well as that corporations's particular characteristics — should in reality determine both the length of the period for which earnings are projected into the future and also the delicate process of the "spicing" with an overall historical rate. Depending on each individual case, such a transition may well take the form of mathematical curves with very different gradations of diminishing rates of growth. Such gradual transition can be easily performed by a computer, which could also carry out the valuation formula's requirement of an infinite time horizon. According to Molodovsky, this later condition can be easily met by combining the compound interest formula used for complying a bond's yield maturity with the expression of a geometric progression for an infinite number of terms which constitute a mathematical description of a equities' natural habitat.

According to Molodovsky, the appropriate rate will take into consideration the risks involved, which are influenced by the growth of earnings or dividend expected in the future, and the future expected price. In short, risk is a function of the variability of return. A higher discount rate will be employed where the risk is greater, and a lower one where risks are lower.

One commonly used approach is based on the multiple growth model and a view that companies typically evolve through three stages during their lifetime. These stages are : (i) Growth stage: The stage is characterised by rapidly expanding sales, higher profit margins, and abnormally high growth in EPS. Because the expected profitability of new investment opportunities is high, the payout ratio is generally low. The unusually high earnings enjoyed in this stage attracts competitors leading to a gradual decline in the growth rate; (ii) Transition stage: In the later years of a company's life, increased profit saturation begins to reduce its growth rate, and its profit margins comes under pressure. Since there are fewer new investment opportunities, the company-begins to payout a larger percentage of earnings; *(Hi)* Maturity stage (or steady- state stage): Generally, the company reaches a position where its new investment opportunities offer, on average, slightly attractive returns on equity. At that time, its earnings growth rate, payout ratio, and average return on equity stabilise for the remaining life of the company.

In applying the multiple growth model, a security analyst must estimate a number of variables for each security being evaluated. One method involves estimating values for the following variables: (i) Expected earnings and dividend for the next five years, (ii) The growth rate of earnings and the payout ratio for the start of the transition stage, which is assured to be in year six. (iii) The duration of the transition *stags* — that is, the number of years until the company reaches the maturity stage, (iv) Growth patterns for EPS and the payout ratio during the transition stage, (v) The combination of an earnings growth rate and payout ratio that provides the desired average return on equity for next investments during the maturity stage.

Jeremy C. Jenks criticises methods of comparative valuation because they are either based on price/earnings ratios or on price dividend ratios. He argues that *"no one approach will give satisfactory results in a wide variety of common stocks .... because there are two 'investment reasons for owning common stock ... dividend income and hope of capital appreciation if the company grows'. Thus there really is no sharp dividing line between an 'income stock' and a 'growth stock'"*.

In this technique, two different multipliers are computed, one to be applied to the dividend from one set of factors, and another multiplier from another set of factors to be applied to the earnings retained in the business. The two resultant values are added together in order to obtain "the value" of the equity.

Price-Cash Flow [P/CF] Ratio

Instead of price-earnings (P/E) ratios, many analysts prefer to look at price cash flow (P/CF) ratios. A price-cash flow [P/CF] ratio is measured as a company's current stock price divided by its current annual cash flow per share. The P/CF ratio is specified as follows:

$$P/CF_x = \frac{P_t}{CF_{t+1}} \qquad (17)$$

When:

P/CF_x = the price cash flow ratio per firm x
P_t = the price of the stock in period t
CF_{t+1} = the expected cash flow per share per firm x

There are a variety of definitions of cash flow. In this context, the most common measure is simply calculated as net income plus depreciation, so this is the one we use here. Cash flow is usually reported in a firm's financial statements and labeled as cash flow from operations (or operating cash flow).

The difference between earnings and cash flow is often confusing, largely because of the way that standard accounting practice defines net income. Essentially, net income is measured as revenues minus expenses. Obviously this is logical. However, not all expenses are actually cash expenses. The most important exception is depreciation.

When a firm acquires a long-lived asset such as a new factory facility, standard accounting practice does not deduct the cost of the factory all at once, even though it is actually paid for all at once. Instead, the cost is deducted over time. These deductions do not represent actual cash payments, however. The actual cash payment occurred when the factory was purchased.

Most analysts agree that in examining a company's financial performance, cash flow can be more informative than net income. To see why, consider the hypothetical example of two identical companies: ABC Co. and XYZ Co. Suppose that both companies have the same constant revenues and expenses in each year over a three-year period. These constant revenues and cash expenses (excluding depreciation) yield the same constant annual cash flows, and they are stated as follows:

	ABC Co.	XYZ Co.
Revenues	₹ 5,00,000	₹ 5,00,000
Cash expenses	₹ 3,00,000	₹ 3,00,000
Cash flow	₹ 2,00,000	₹ 2,00,000

Thus, both companies have the same ₹ 2,00,000 cash flow in each of the three years of this hypothetical example.

Next, suppose that both companies incur total depreciation of ₹ 3,00,000 period out over the three-year period. Standard accounting practice sometimes allows a manager to choose among several depreciation schedules. ABC Co. chooses straight-line depreciation and XYZ Co. chooses accelerated depreciation. These two depreciation schedules are tabulated below:

	ABC Co.	XYZ Co.
Year 1	₹ 1,00,000	₹ 1,50,000
Year 2	1,00,000	1,00,000
Year 3	1,00,000	50,000
Total	₹ 3,00,000	₹ 3,00,000

Note that total depreciation over the three-year period is the same for both companies. However, ABC Co. has the same ₹ 1,00,000 depreciation in each year, while XYZ Co. has accelerated depreciation ₹ 1,50,000 in the first year ₹ 1,00,000 in the second, year, and ₹ 50,000 depreciation in the third year.

Now, let's look at the resulting annual cash flows and net income figures for the two companies, recalling that in each year, Cash flow = Net income + Depreciation:

	ABC Co.		XYZCo.	
	Cash Flow	Net Income	Cash Flow	Net Income
Year 1	₹ 2,00,000	₹ 1,00,000	₹ 2,00,000	₹ 50,000
Year 2	2,00,000	1,00,000	2,00,000	1,00,000
Year 3	2,00,000	1,00,000	2,00,000	1,50,000
Total	₹ 6,00,000	₹ 3,00,000	₹ 6,00,000 :	₹ 3,00,000

Note that XYZ Co.'s net income is lower in the first year and higher in the third year than ABC Co.'s net income. This is purely a result of XYZ Co.'s accelerated depreciation schedule, and has nothing to do with XYZ Co.s actual profitability. However, an inexperienced analyst observing XYZ Co.'s rapidly rising annual earnings figures might incorrectly label XYZ as a growth company. An experienced analyst would observe that there was no cash flow growth to support this naive conclusion.

Financial analysts typically use both price-earnings ratios and price-cash flow ratios. They point out that when a company's earnings per share is not significantly larger than its cash flow per share (CFPS), this is a signal, at least potentially, of good-quality earnings. The term "equality" means that the accounting earnings mostly reflect actual cash flow, not just accounting numbers. When earnings and cash flow are far from each other, this may be a signal of poor quality earnings.

Price-Sales (P/S) Ratio

An alternative view of a company's performance is provided by its price-sales (P/S) ratio. A price-sales ratio is calculated as the current price of a company's stock divided by its current annual sales revenue per share.

The specific P/S ratio is:

$$P/S_x = \frac{P_t}{S_{t+1}} \tag{18}$$

Where

P/S_x	=	the price to salses ratio for firm x
P_t	=	the price of the stock in period t
S_{t+1}	=	The expected sales per share for price x

P/S ratio is useful and meaningful for two reasons. First, strong and consistent sales growth in the requirement for a growth company. Although above average profit margin is important, the growth process must begin with sales. Second, given all the data in financial statement, sales information is subject to less manipulation than any other data item.

However it is important to match the current price with the firm's expected sales per share, which may be difficult to derive for a large cross section of stocks. Two caveats are relevant to the price to sales ratio. First, this particular valuation ratio varies dramatically by industry. The second consideration is the profit margin on sales. For instance, the retail food stores low- high sales per share which will cause a low P/S ratio, which is considered good until one realizes that these firms have low net profit margin.

Price/Book Value [P/BV] Ratio

A very basic price ratio for a company is its price-book [P/BV] ratio, sometimes called the market-book value ratio. A price-book ratio is measured as the market value of a company's equity issued divided by its book value of equity.

P/BV ratio is specified as follows:

$$P/BV_x = \frac{P_t}{BV_{t+1}} \tag{19}$$

Where:

	P/BV_x	=	the price/book value ratio for firm x
	P_t	=	the price of the stock in period t
	BV_{t+1}	=	the estimated end-of-year book value per share for firm x

P/BV ratios are appealing because book values represent, in principle, historical costs. The stock price is an indicator of current value, so a P/BV ratio simply measures what the equity is worth today relative to what it cost. A ratio bigger than 1.0 indicates that the firm has been successful in creating value for its stockholders. A ratio smaller than 1.0 indicates that the company is actually worth less than it cost.

This interpretation of P/BV ratio seems simple enough, but the truth is that because of varied and changing accounting standards, book values are difficult to interpret. For this and other reasons, P/BV ratios may not have as much information value as they once did.

Price-earnings ratios, price-cash flow ratios, and price-sales ratios are commonly used to calculate estimates of expected future stock prices. This is done by multiplying a historical average price ratio by an expected future value for the price-ratio denominator variable. For example, Table-3 summarises such a price ratio analysis for Rico Group based on mid-year 2010 information.

In Table-3, the current value row contains midyear 2010 values for earning per share, cash flow per share, and sales per share (SPS). The five-year average ratio row contains five-year average P/E, P/CF, and P/S ratios, and the growth rate row contains five-year historical average EPS, CFPS, and SPS growth rates.

TABLE-3
Price Ratio Analysis for Rico Group Mid-year 2010 Stock Price ₹ 89.88

	Earnings [P/E]	Cash Flow [P/CF]	Sales [P/S]
Current value per share	₹ 3.49	₹ 4.62	₹ 12.67
Five-year average price ratio	13.5	9.6	3.0
Growth rate	42.7%	39.6%	34.3%
Expected stock price	₹ 67.23	₹ 61.92	₹ 51.05

The expected price row contains expected stock prices one year hence. The basic idea is this. Since Rico has had an average P/E ratio of 13.5, we will assume that Rico's stock price will be 13.5 times its earnings one year from now. To estimate Rico's earnings one year from now, we note that Rico's earnings have typically grown at a rate of 42.7 per cent per year. If earnings continue to grow at this rate, then next year's earnings will be equal to this year's earnings multiplied by 1.427. Putting it all together, we have:

Expected price = Historical P/E Ratio x Projected EPS

= Historical P/E Ratio x Current EPS + Historical EPS

= 13.5 x ₹ 3.49 x 1.427

= 67.23

The same procedure is used to calculate an expected price based on cash flow per share:

Expected price = P/CF ratio x CFP x (1 + Cash Flow Growth Rate)

= 9.6 x ₹ 4.62 x 1.396

= ₹ 61.92

Finally, an expected price based on sales per share is calculated as:

Expected Price = P/S ratio x SPS x (1 + Sales Growth Rate)

= 3.0 x ₹ 12.67 x 1.34

= ₹ 51.05

Notice that each price ratio method yields a different expected future price. This is normal. Since each method uses different information, each makes a different prediction.

VALUATION EQUATIONS TO FIND EXPECTED RETURN

To get optimal risk-return on an investment, the investors are to find the expected returns (r)[1]. This is done by substituting the current price (P_0) for equity value (V_0) and solving r by trial and error with the present value or discount rate is found that equates the present value of the income stream to current price. The equation then becomes:

$$P_0 = \frac{D_0(1+g_d)^1}{(1+r)^1} + \frac{D_0(1+g_d)^2}{(1+r)^2} + \frac{D_0(1+g_d)^3 P_3}{(1+r)^3} \qquad (20)$$

or, as it is stated alternatively,

$$P_0 = \sum_{t=1}^{3} \frac{D_0(1_-g_d)^t}{(1=r)^t} + \frac{E_0(1_-g_e)^3 (P/E)_3}{(1=r)^3}$$

where P_Q is the current price, E_Q is the earnings per share in year O, D_0 is divident in year O and all are known; g_f and g_d are estimated annual growth rate of earnings and dividends respectively; P_3 is the price expected in year 3, which is the function of E_3 (EPS in year 3) times $(P/E)_3$ (price-earnings ratio in year 3 based on the growth of earnings in year 4, 5, 6, ... n). The equation for P_3 may be written $P_3 = E_0 (1 + g_e)^3 (P/E)_3$, where E_Q is the EPS in year O, g_e is the expected growth rate of EPS, and $(P/E)_3$ is the P/E ratio expected in year 3.[2]

To solve the equation and get the estimates of earnings growth rate, and the price-earnings ratio expected in year 3, several approaches are identified such as (z) Trend, (z'z) Trend-Current, (Hi) Analyst's Best Estimate (ABE), and (zY;) Random.

Trend

In applying the trend model, the investor assumes that past trend of earnings growth, dividend growth, and P/E ratio will continue. The trend is based on the past ten years of experience, a period that is used to obtain the unknowns of ge(expected earnings growth), g_d (dividend growth rate), and $(P/E)_3$ for the next three years holding period. To illustrate, assume an XYZ Index was 125 at the end of 2007. In 2006, the index earned ₹ 14.75 per share and had ₹6.55 dividends per share. For the purpose of valuation, 125 is PO, ₹ 14.75 is E_0, and ₹ 6.55 is D_0. For the ten-year period ending in 2006, the growth rate of earnings was 10.85, the dividend growth rate was 9.2 per cent, and the ten-year price earnings ratio was 11. Therefore, $g_{e,10}$ = 10.85 per cent; $g_{d,10}$ 9-20 per cent; and $(P/E)_{3\,10}$= 11. Substituting these estimates into the valuation equation gives:

$$₹\ 125 = \frac{₹\ 5.55(1.092)}{(1+r)} + \frac{₹\ 6.55(1.092)^2}{(1+r)^2} + \frac{₹\ 6.55(1.092)^3}{(1+r)^3} + 14.97 \times \frac{(1.185)^3 \times 11}{(1+r)^3}$$

$$₹\ 125 = \frac{₹\ 7.15}{(1+italcir)} + \frac{₹\ 7.81}{(1+r)^2} + \frac{₹\ 8.53}{(1+r)^3} + \frac{₹\ 221.60}{(1+r)^3}$$

$$₹\ 125 = \frac{₹\ 7.15}{(1+r)} + \frac{₹\ 7.81}{(1+r)^2} + \frac{₹\ 230.13}{(1+r)^3}$$

1. The emphasis on the solution of the valuation equation for r is appropriate because the investor shall focus on the return and risk that are expected. The calculation of the r for the holding period of equity then allows investors to compare the returns for each type of investments, including debentures and preference shares.
2. Three-year future time is used since it is more realistic; long enough to eliminate market cycles and short enough to be predictable - or at least estimatable by the analyst.

Using trial and error method for r, the value of r at 26 per cent provides the present value of ₹ 125.68. The conclusion drawn on the basis of Trend Valuation is that the investor would earn a return of 26 per cent for the three-year holding period through the end of 2010.

Trend-Current

Trend-Current equation uses the current P/E ratio for $(P/E)_3$. XYZ Index will continue to be used along with 10-Year growth rate of earnings per share and dividends as the estimate for the future three-year holding period. So, only change made in the equation is that the $(P/E)_3$ estimate is changed from 11 to 8 and the new valuation equation becomes :

$$₹\ 125 = \frac{₹7.15}{(1+r)} + \frac{₹7.81}{(1+r)^2} + \frac{₹8.53}{(1+r)^3} + \frac{₹14.79(1.085)^5\,8}{(1+r)^3}$$

$$₹\ 125 = \frac{₹7.15}{(1+r)} + \frac{₹7.81}{(1+r)^2} + \frac{₹169.69}{(1+r)^3}$$

$$= ₹\ 126.82 \text{ at } 14\%$$

$$= ₹\ 123.78 \text{ at } 15\%$$

Thus, the r value is found in between 14 and 15 per cent. Based on these estimates for the three-year future period, it may be concluded that the investor would not rush into the market at the 125 level of the XYZ Index if the return is comparable to what the investor might earn with less risk on long-term fixed income securities available in 2007.

Analyst's Best Estimate (ABE)

ABE is based on what an informed security analyst thinks will be earned in the future, what dividends will be paid, and what P/E multiple to assign in year 3 in the future. The expected annual return for the period is obtained by putting the estimates from the analyst into the valuation equation. For instance, if the analyst expects the XYZ Index earnings to increase 10 per cent annually from 2007 to 2010. That would mean that earnings per share would increase to ₹ 18.15 in 2008 from the estimated ₹ 16.50 per share in 2007. Earnings in 2009 and 2010 are estimated to be ₹ 19.97 and ₹ 21.96 respectively. The dividends would increase 9 per cent per year over the forecast period. The 2007 dividend was ₹ 7.14. The analyst expects a P/E ratio of 11 in 2010. Based on these estimates, the equation is:

$$₹\ 125 = \frac{₹6.55\,(1.09)}{(1+r)} + \frac{₹6.55\,(1.09)^2}{(1+r)^2} + \frac{₹6.55\,(1.09)^3}{(1+r)^3} + \frac{₹16.50\,(1+.10)^3\,11}{(1+r)^3} +$$

$$₹\ 125 = \frac{₹7.14}{(1+r)} + \frac{₹7.14}{(1+r)^2} + \frac{₹263.48}{(1+r)^3}$$

$$r = 31.6 \text{ per cent}$$

The 31.6 would be an excellent return over the next three years period, given the risks involved and compared to long-term fixed income securities.

Random Valuation Model

The Random Valuation model begins with the premise that the next three years' growth of earnings, dividends, and price will be similar to those of the past ten years. This is similar to Trend Valuation equation for estimating the rate of return, r. In Random, the ten year growth rate of earnings and dividends is used, alongwith the ten-year P/E ratio. But instead of assuming that the 10-year rates will continue in the future, it is assumed that the rate is unknown but it is likely to be within the value established by the ten-year mean value and the standard deviation around the mean value of its estimate. This applies to each variable that is to be substituted into the valuation equation to solve for r. Three variables must be estimated in the valuation equation to establish r. They are the expected dividend growth rate, g_d; the expected earnings growth rate, g_e and the expected P/E ratio in the third year $(P/E)_3$. The value for each variable assume to be around the historic mean plus one standard deviation of the estimate.[3]

Let us apply this to the XYZ Index. As an example, the growth rate of EPS for the XYZ Index is 11 per cent annually for the ten-year period. The standard deviation of this mean value is 12 per cent. The dividend growth rate is 9.2 per cent with a standard deviation of 22 per cent and the P/E ratio averaged 11 with a standard deviation of 3.7 per cent. It implies that the past growth rates cf earnings were 11 ± 12 per cent; the past growth rate of dividends were 9.2 + 22 per cent; and the past P/E ratios were 11 ± 3.7. RANDOM is then formed in the following way : An earnings growth rate is selected at random from the limits of -1 to +23 per cent. Then a dividend rate is selected at random between -12.8 and 31.2 per cent. Finally, a P/E ratio is selected at random between 7.3 and 14.7 per cent. The equation is solved for $\tilde{r}$ A second set of variable is again selected at random within tine limits of the data, and $\tilde{r}_2$ is calculated. This process continues until $\tilde{r}$ has been calculated 100 times, $\tilde{r}_{100}$. The resulting $\tilde{r}$ values are averaged and the standard deviation calculated. The average $\tilde{r}$ value becomes the estimate of the random return, and the standard deviation, the variability of random return, is the measure of risk. This process is summarised below:

$\tilde{g}_{el}$	$\tilde{g}_d$	$\tilde{p}/E$	$\tilde{r}$
$\tilde{g}_{e1}$	$\tilde{g}_{d1}$	$(\tilde{p}/E)_1$	$\tilde{r}_1$
$\tilde{g}_{e2}$	$\tilde{g}_{d2}$	$(\tilde{p}/E)_2$	$\tilde{r}_2$
"	"	"	"
"	"	"	"
"	"	"	"
$\tilde{g}_{e100}$	$\tilde{g}_{d100}$	$(\tilde{p}/E)_{100}$	$\tilde{r}_{100}$

Where $\tilde{g}_e$, $\tilde{g}_d$ and $\tilde{p}/E$ are the first set of randomly selected variables, and $\tilde{g}_{e100}$, $\tilde{g}_{e100}$ $(\tilde{p}/E)_{100}$ are the one-hundredth set of randomly selected variables. The 100 calculations

---

3. The Random model assumes that the future three years will yield growth rates within the limits and certainty assumed by the respective probability distributions. In applying Random, it is understood that no one knows accurately what the future will bring, but it is assumed that the outcome will be within the specified statistical limits. The proxy for the unknown future is the random selection of each of the key variables in the valuation equation and the solution of the equation to find the rate of return. This process is done repeatedly, the results are averaged, and the standard deviation is calculated. The average rate of return is the expected annual return for the next three years, and the standard deviation is the expected variation of return and represents risks.

of $\tilde{r}$ are then averaged and the variability of the r values is calculated. The tilda ($\tilde{r}$) indicates that the variables are randomly established.

The estimated average Fvalues from Random do not differ substantially from Trend. The significant difference in the valuation methods is that Random established the variability of return, which becomes an estimate of risk. In fact, this measure allows for the calculation of the return-to-risk ratio which is found by subtracting the risk free rate of return from the estimated return divided by the standard deviation of the return. This is written $\tilde{r}_u - \tilde{r}_f + \sigma_r$ where $\tilde{r}_u$ is the mean of the $\tilde{r}$ values, $\tilde{r}_f$ is the risk-free yield, and σ_r is the standard deviation of the mean of the $\tilde{r}$ values. The return-to- risk ratio indicates the level of return to risk, which helps the investor establish the relative riskiness of an investment. A return-to risk ratio of 1.0 or higher is acceptable; those less than 1.0 are unacceptable.

With a knowledge of the expected return ($\tilde{r}_u$ and the estimate of the standard deviation (σ_r) and the return-to-risk ratio, the investor has two excellant measures of investment attractiveness — return and risk.

The use of Random model does not change the investment conclusion. The XYZ Index ar 122.5 offers a fair return. The $\tilde{r}$ value from the computer output is 28.05 per cent, with a standard deviation of 16.4. The expected return ($\tilde{r}_u$) for the next three years using Random is 28.05 per cent, which suggests that the XYZ Index offer the investor an excellent return compared to historic standards. However, the return to risk ratio [(28.05-12) / 18.42] = .87 is a bit low, suggesting that there is slightly more risk for each unit of return which would cause in investor to be cautious. The same conclusions was reached in the result of the other relation models.

Intrinsic Value

For equity analysis, Graham and Dodd noted that there were three approaches. The first they called the *anticipation approach*. This involved selecting and recommending that equity shares "out perform" the market over a given span of time, usually the ensuing 12 months. This approach they noted did not involve seeking an answer to the question : "*What is the stock worth ?*" The second concept stands in *market contrast*. It attempts to value a share independently of its current market price. If the value found is substantially above or below the current price, the analyst concludes that the issue should be bought or disposed off. This independent value has a variety of names, the most familiar of which is the intrinsic value. It may also be called indicated value, central value, normal value, investment value, reasonable value, fair value and appraised value. Graham, Dodd and Cottle's third approach is concerned with *relative rather than with intrinsic value from* the current level of the equity prices. In estimating relative value, the analyst more or less accepts the prevailing market level and seeks to determine the value of an equity in terms of it. His efforts, therefore, are devoted fundamentally to appraising the relative attractiveness of individual issues in terms of the then existing level of equity prices and not to determine the fundamental worth of an equity. Graham, Dodd and Cottle favour the intrinsic value approach as they say :

> *A general definition of intrinsic value would be "that value which is justified by the facts, e.g. assets, earnings, dividends, definite prospects, including the factor of management". The primary objective in using the adjective "intrinsic" is to emphasize the distinction between value and current market price, but not to invest this "value" with an aura of performance............. The most important single factor determining a stock's value is now held to be the indicated future earning power i.e., the estimated average earnings for a*

future span of years. Intrinsic value would then be found by first forecasting this earning power and then multiplying that prediction by an appropriate "capitalization factor".

Graham, Dodd and Cottle were explicit that their intrinsic value approach would not apply to high growth rate stocks or inherently speculative issues since they do not admit of a "soundly ascertained value". They consider only growth stocks at high price earnings ratios basically in this category. In other words, a genuine growth stock will typically appear to be selling too high by one evaluation standards and the true investor may do well to avoid it for this reason. But both the price and the ultimate value may often develop independently of, and contrary to, any given valuation.

Intrinsic Value vs. Market Price

The model for assessing the value of a firm as a going concern takes off from the observation that an investor in stock expects a return consisting of cash dividends and capital gains or losses. We begin by assuming a 1-year holding period and supposing that ABC stock has an expected dividend per share, $E(D_1)$, of ₹ 4, the current price of a share (P_0) is ₹ 48, and the expected price at the end of a year, $E(P_1)$, is ₹ 52.

The holding period return that the investor expects is $E(D_1)$ plus the expected price appreciation, $E(P_1) - P_0$, all divided by the current price P_0:

Expected HPR = $E(r)$

$$\frac{E(D_1)+[(EP_1)-P_0]}{P_0} \tag{21}$$

$$\frac{4+(52-48)}{48}$$

$$= 0.167 \ 16.7\%$$

Note that E() denotes an expected future value. Thus $E(P_1)$ represents the stock price 1 year from now. $E(r)$ is referred to as the stock's expected holding period return. It is the sum of the expected dividend yield, $E(D_1)/P_0$, and the expected rate of price appreciation, the capital gains, $[(P_1) - P_0] / P_0$.

But what is the investor's required rate of return on the stock? From the CAPM we know that the required rate, k, is equal to $R_f + \beta (E(R_m) - R_f)$. Suppose $R_f = 6\%$, $\beta = 1.2$, and $E(R_m) - T = 5\%$. Then the value of k is

$$k = 6\% + 1.2 \times 5\% = 12\%$$

For ABC the rate of return that the investor expects exceeds the required rate based on ABC's risk by a margin of 4.7 per cent. Naturally, the investor will want to include more ABC stock in the porfolio than a passive strategy would dictate.

Another way to see this is to compare the intrinsic value, V_0, of a share of stock to its current market price:

$$V_0 = \frac{E(D_1 + P)}{1+k} \tag{22}$$

In the case of ABC the intrinsic value based on present value of expected cash flows to the stockholder is

$$V_0 = \frac{₹ \ 4 + ₹ \ 52}{1.12} = ₹ \ 50$$

In other words, the intrinsic value is the present value of the expected future cash inflow (that is, the dividend plus the terminal price at which the stock can be sold) discounted by the required rate of return. Whenever the intrinsic value, or the investor's estimate of what the stock is really worth, exceeds the market price, the stock is undervalued. In the ABC case, $V_0 > P_0$ (₹ 50 > ₹ 48), so the stock is undervalued by the market. Investors will want to buy more ABC than they would following a passive strategy.

If the intrinsic value turns out to be lower than the current market price, investors should buy less of it than under the passive strategy. It might even pay to go short ABC stock. It is useful to think of shorting a stock as a way to hold a negative number of shares of a firm.

In market equilibrium the current market price will reflect an average of the intrinsic value estimates of all market participants. This means that the individual investor whose intrinsic V_0 estimate differs from the market price, P_0, in effect must disagree with some or all of the market consensus estimates of D_1, P_a, or k. Another way to refer to the market consensus value of k is by the term market capitalization rate.

Relative Strength Model

Relative strength models come in several varieties, but the basic idea is that stocks that have had better-than-average price performance in the recent past will continue (for some time in the future) to have above-average price performance. These models generally calculate percentage changes in stock price over some recent period, rank-order the percentages from high to low, and purchase the stocks with the largest percentage increases. Though not a pure version of the relative strength model but still the well-known Value Line timeliness ranking system includes a relative strength component of its calculations.

In value line rankings, the investors use information, contained in either a quarterly earnings announcement or a revision of an earnings forecast by security analysts, to make abnormal returns. The ranking system is a complicated process which is based on three components: (i) a relative valuation based on 'earnings momentum', (ii) an 'earnings surprise factor', and (iii) a value index. Points are given for each of these three components, with the total points determining the stock's ranking.

The relative earnings momentum' is determined as follows: Each company's year-to-year change in quarterly earnings is computed (for example, fourth quarter 20011 EPS compared with fourth-quarter 2010 EPS, and this percentage change is divided by the average year-to-year quarterly earnings change for all stocks. (Analysts make some adjustments for quarterly affected by unusual factors such as labour strikes or changes in accounting procedures.) The respected return are based on strategy of forming portfolios at the beginning of each year based on the rank of each stock at that time and then holding the portfolios constant for the entire year. The next year new portfolios are formed based on the ranks of the stock at the start of the second year, and so on.

The 'earning surprise' factor is added to the ranking system Abnormal return are associated with the stocks of companies which report unusually large changes in quarterly earnings. The earnings surprise factor is based on the difference between actual reported quarterly earnings and the estimate of the quarterly earnings.

The most complex of the three components which determines the Value Line timeliness rankings is the nonparametric value position. This value position (V) is calculated from the following equation:

$$V = a + b_1 z_1 + b_2 x_2 + b_3 x_3 \qquad (23)$$

Where

x_1 = a score of from 1 to 10, depending on how the current year's earnings divided by the average earnings of all companies ranks, compared with the company's same ratio for the last 10 years.

x_2 = a score from 1 to 10 based on the stock's relative price, where the ratios are calculated as above with the stock prices substituted for earnings

x_3 = a price momentum index which is the ratio of the stock's latest 10-week average relative price, where relative price is the stock price divided by the average price for all stocks.

a, b_1, b_2, b_3 = coefficient from a multiple regression based on over 12 years of stock market data.

All companies are then given a rank based upon their value.

Finally, the points for each of the three major components (relative earnings momentum, earnings surprise factor, and V value) are added and the stocks are classified into group 1, group 2, etc., based upon their total points. Thus, the Value Line ranking system is a complex procedure. It is heavily weighted toward relative P/E ratios, earnings momentum, and earnings surprises. Interestingly, it also includes a component (x_3 in the above equation) which would fall under the purely 'technical' category. This variable is based strictly on historical price data. Value line ranking 'work' primarily because they use quarterly earnings in both the earnings momentum and surprise elements that go into the Value Line ranking procedure. After all, it has been noted that there are abnormal price movements subsequent to the announcement of quarterly earnings.

To summarise, there is a two-part puzzle associated with Value Line risks. First, Value Line appears to have superior precenting ability that is based on public information. Second, the market takes time to adjust to the Value Line rankings. Both of these observation are puzzling because they are inconsistent with the notion of efficient markets. To further complicate matters, most rank charges occur shortly after earnings announcements are made. Superior performance is attributable to the 'post-earnings-announcement drift.' Hence the two anomalies appear to be related.

Homogeneous Group/Group Rotation Models

The homogeneous group model uses *cluster analysis*, a statistical technique which identifies clusters of stocks whose returns are highly correlated within each cluster and relatively uncorrelated between clusters. Using this technique, at least four clusters of the stocks may be noted in the market : growth, cyclical, stable and energy. A substantial reward awaits the manager who can select valid clusters and then correctly forecast those the market will favour.

Multifactor Models

Factor models are concerned with identifying systematic factors that affect security returns. Investor is to estimate the factor exposures in order to identify companies that will be most affected by these factors. Equity prices can be described by an econometric model with a small number of well-chosen explanatory variables. These variables are simply financial data or the regression coefficients attached to them but because of an equity allusion to variables that were generated by a statistical procedure called factor analysis, such variables are currently labeled *factors/attributes/indexes*. By using various factors, it seems plausible to create models such as :

$$R_i = B_{i/0} + B_{i/1}(BETA) + B_{i/2}(SIZE) + B_{i/3}(P/E) + e_i \qquad (24)$$

which merely states that stock i's return (R_i) is a function of its beta (BETA), capitalization (SIZE), P/E ratio (P/E), and sensitivities to each variable (B_i, j), as well as other unmeasured effects that are assumed to act as independent errors *fa)*.

How many factors are there ? Most studies suggest at least three to five systematic factors. However, some factor may be important at some time. If the risk of such factors can be diversified away, these transient factors might affect returns periodically. However, no risk premium would attach to them, because risk premiums are only related to nondiversifiable risk.

One multifactor model for use of institutional investors has been developed by the consulting firm BARRA of Berkeley, California. The BARRA model contains 13 common factors (called *risk indexes* in their terminology): (1) variability, (2) success, (3) size, (4) trading activity, (5) growth, (6) earnings/price, (7) book/price, (8) earnings variation, (9) financial leverage, (10) foreign income, (11) labour intensity, (12) yield, and (13) low capitalisation. Another multifactor model has been developed by Chen, Roll and Ross. Their model is consistent with the arbitrage pricing theory (APT) developed by Stephen Ross and expanded by several others. This model is important because it serves as the prototype for almost all subsequent APT-based, multifactor investment models. The basic models proposed by Chen, Roll and Ross asserts that asset prices depend upon their exposure to the *state variables* which describe the economy.

Market Anomaly Models

If the stock markets were totally efficient, then there would be no systematic gain from investing in stocks with certain easily identifiable characteristics such as low P/E, small capitalisation, and low analyst coverage. Market anomalies do in fact exist. Five sources of anomalous return prevails in the stock market are: high-dividend stocks, small capitalisation stocks, low P/E stocks, abnormally high returns for the month of January, and abnormally high returns for stocks rated "1" in the Value Line timeliness rank. Generally, it is noted that there are abnormally low rates of return for stocks on Monday, as compared with the rest of the week.

Capital Asset Pricing Model (CAPM)

Those who use the CAPM for active equity management employ its prediction that, in equilibrium, the expected return on a stock is an exact linear function of the risk-free rate, the beta for the stock, and the expected return on the market portfolios. This linear relationship is called the *security market line*. In theory, a stock whose expected return from a valuation model (such as the DDM) equals the expected return from the CAPM is to be *in equilibrium*. If the expected return from the DDM were greater than the expected return from the CAPM, then the market would adjust the price of the stock upward and hence lower its expected return. If the expected return from the DDM were less than the expected return from the CAPM, then the market would adjust the price of the stock downward and hence raise its expected return.

The capital asset pricing model has said very little so far about prices. The discussion has revolved almost completely around risk and expected returns. It didn't have to. Concentrating on risk and expected return was simply a convenient way to approach the problem. Nonetheless, it is a security's price which is transacted in the markets and which determines whether speculative opportunities exist.

The equilibrium price should provide no opportunity for speculative profits. It should be set at such a level that *expected returns from buying the security are identical to those available on an efficient portfolio of equivalent nondiversifiable risk.* For example, if risk free rate (R_f) = 10%, risk premium which expects to be earned above the risk free rate for bearing the market portfolio's risk, RP_M = 6%, and the beta of a stock = 0.7, then the stock should be priced to provide an expected return of 14.2%:

$$E(R_i) = R_f + \beta_{im} (RP_m) \tag{25}$$
$$14.2\% = 10.0\% + 0.7 (6.0\%)$$

If this security is trading at a price lower than equilibrium, then a speculative profit is possible and excess demand will exist until the price is forced up to equilibrium. If the security is trading at a higher than equilibrium price, speculators will sell (short sell if there are no restrictions on doing so) until the price is at equilibrium. In short, expected return from owning the security should be:

Equilibrium Required Return
$$E(R_i) = R_f + \beta_i (RP_m)$$

The return which will actually be earned consists of any increases (or decreases) in the security's price plus any cash payoff, such as dividends on a stock or coupons on a bond. In the case of a stock:

Actual Security Return

$$R_{i1} = \frac{P_{i1} - P_{i0} + D_{i1}}{P_{i0}} \tag{26}$$

Where: R_{i1} = Price of security at the end of period 1
P_{i0} = Price of i at the beginning of period 1
D_{i1} = dividends received during period 1

For the security to be priced at equilibrium, the expected outcome of equation-26 should be equal to the fair return expressed in equation-25:

Equilibrium Required Return = Expected Security Return

Equilibrium Market Return

$$R_f + \beta_i (RP_M) = \frac{E(P_{i1}) + ED_{i1}}{P_{i0}} \tag{27}$$

Rearranging this quite logical statement and letting P*$_{i0}$ represent the equilibrium price of i, we see that this equilibrium price is simply the present value of the expected end-of-period price and dividend discount at a return appropriate for its level of non-diversifiable risk:

Equilibrium Security Price

$$P_{i0}^* = \frac{E(P_{i1}) + E(D_{i1})}{1.0 + R_f + \beta_i (RP_M)} \tag{28}$$

For example, let's compute the equilibrium price of XYZ stock given the following data:

$RP_M = 6\%$ $\beta_x = 0.5$ $E(P_{xl}) = ₹ 52.70$ $R_f = 10\%$ $E(D_x) = ₹ 3.80$

According to the Security Market time (SML) one should expect a 13.0% return on any investment in a security having the amount of nondiversifiable risk present in XYZ share: 10.0% + 0.5 (6.0%) = 13.0%

Since the expected price at the end of the period (say, one year) is ₹ 52.70 and the expected dividend is ₹ 3.80, the equilibrium price must be ₹ 50.00:

$$\frac{₹\ 52.70 + ₹\ 3.80}{1.13} = ₹\ 50.00$$

The equilibrium pricing formula stated in equation-28 strictly applies to a single-period world. There is no warranty on its validity when it is used in other situations. In practice, however, the principal features of the model are used widely. Security analysts forecast expected future dividends and prices on a stock and discount them to the present using a discount rate generated from the SML.

The Q Ratio

So far we have focused on approaches for valuing expected income and cash flows to assess an appropriate value for the corporation. We might refer to these as income might classify as asset oriented, which focus on directly valuing the assets of the companies. Though both approaches are ultimately intertwined, because an asset essentially derives value from the cash flow it can generate, the distinction in useful as a means of sharpening the analytical perspective. Furthermore, some valuation approaches are primarily associated with practioners who are commonly viewed as asset-value-oriented.

Having an alternative approach is important because income-based approaches do not work consistently well over all ties and may be particularly deficient in valuing certain kinds of companies, industries, or even broad sectors of the market. The deficiency of income-based approaches occurred when there are considerable restructuring of corporations through merges leveraged buyouts (LBOs), and share buybacks, indicating that their underlying value has not been correctly assessed. In this context, the Q Ratio is both a concept and a measure that provides a useful perspective for discussing asset-based valuation.

The Q Ratio approach, devised by Tobin, explains the linkage between the real economy and the financial markets. It is simply defined as the ratio of the market value of the firm, as reflected in the financial markets, to the replacement value of the assets:

$$q = \frac{\text{Market Value}}{\text{Replacement Value}} \tag{29}$$

It was originally developed as a macroeconomic concept to assess whether additional capital investments by corporations would add to or detract from the market value of the corporation and thereby provide a signal as to whether or not to invest. With a Q Ratio below 1, capital investments detracts from the value of the corporation and is not warranted. On the other hand, when the ratio is above 1, then investment is warranted because it would add value to the corporation. Investing would also continue under this circumstances until Q Ratio declined to its equilibrium ratio of 1.

The notion also has application to valuation and offers another perspective, which can be shown to be consistent with the dividend discount model (DDM), on appraising 'growth' opportunities. Using a simplified version of DDM and redefining the retention rate (b), return on assets (r), growth rate (g), and payout ratio (1-b), we express assets as (A) and write:

$$P = \frac{rA(1-b)}{k-g} \tag{30}$$

We can, in turn, divide by the asset value A, and recognizing that q = P/A, we obtain

$$q = \frac{P}{A} = \frac{r(1-b)}{k-g} \tag{31}$$

It can be observed from the expression that when the return on assets (r) is greater than the discount rate or cost of capital (k), g will be greater than 1. This is evidence of true growth and that investment is warranted because it will increase the value of the company. Correspondingly, investment is warranted until the marginal return (r) is equal to the discount rate (k), at which point the Q Ratio becomes 1. In terms of valuation models, this represents a condition of expansion, where additional investment neither adds to or detrects from the value of the corporation.

In addition to providing a link between the real economy and financial markets, as well as another perspective on evaluating growth opportunities, the Q Ratio can represent a standard for asset valuation of individual stock. The theoretical equilibrium value of the Q Ratio 1 might also be considered as fair value. A Q above 1 can be viewed as indicator of overvaluation, depending on the particular stock. Correspondingly, values below 1 could indicate a deficiency of prospects for the company or, alternatively, could be a sign of undervaluation, depending on the particular circumstances. For pragmatic uses, market Q's, industry Q's, or index Q's could be considered the equilibrium value.

To properly assess the valuation of individual stocks, appraising the replacement value of the company assets is the most critical, though difficult, task. Book value may provide a useful guideline, but this measure is less than adequate guage of replacement value. In example, plant and equipment on books at historic cost may be severely, understated in value because of subsequent high inflation. Conversely, plant and equipment may be overstated in value because of obsolescence.

CONSIDERATIONS IN DEVELOPING AND SELECTING QUANTITATIVE STRATEGIES

These approaches are not mutually exclusive. Rather, many of these models can be used in combination with each other and especially in combination with sound judgement. The quantitative strategy in valuation models may be defined as *engineered investment strategies*. In developing these strategies, consideration must be given at least to three characteristics.

First, the strategy should be based on a sound theory. That is, there should be not only a reason why the strategy worked in the past, but, more importantly, a reason why it should be expected to work in the future. Second, the strategy should be put in quantified terms. Finally, a determination should be made of how the strategy would have performed in the past. This last characteristic is critical and is the reason why investment strategies are back-tested.

An equity manager encounters many potential problems in the design, testing and implementation of engineered investment strategies. These include:

1. *Insufficient rationale:* There is insufficient rationale for why a strategy worked in the past and why it is anticipated that it will work in the future.
2. *Blind assumptions:* Some strategies are based on blind assumptions that certain factors are always *good* or always *bad*.

3. *Data mining:* Data mining occurs when so many strategies are tested that, by the laws of chance, one works. This is related to the problem of insufficient rationale and investment analyst uncovers statistical relationships that are not related to any investment theory or substantive model and may well be just a result of the type of data or statistical model used or per se chance.

4. *Quantity of Data :* In searching for investment strategies, managers use computer-based historical data. These data bases often suffer from problems of inaccuracy, omissions, and survivor bias. Survivor bias occurs when the companies that disappeared are eliminated from the data base. As a result, any testing of potential strategy that includes only surviving companies would be biased in favour of *survivors.*

5. *Look-ahead bias :* This bias involves testing an investment strategy using data that would not have been available at the time the strategy was implemented. For example, suppose that a manager is testing a strategy involving the price-earnings ratio and performs the following test: If the P/E ratio is greater than a specified value on December 31, then sell the stock on January 1. If it is less than a specified value, then buy the stock on January 1. The look-ahead bias here is that the P/E ratio based on actual earnings for the year ending December 31 cannot be calculated on December 31 because actual earnings for the year ending December 31 are reported in the first quarter (or later) of the following year. Thus, in conducting this back test, the manager would be using data on December 31 that were not available on that date. To have a valid back test of this investment strategy, the equity manager will have to design the test so as to use earnings data that would have been avaiable on December 31 (e.g., an analyst's *estimate* of earnings as of December 31).

6. *Multiple factors :* Many of the market anomalies may be highly correlated. Adding highly correlated factors to a model neither enhances returns nor lowers risk. Factors that by themselves seem not to be important may be important when combined with other factors. An equity manager must be able to untangle these relationships.

7. *Statistical assumptions and techniques:* A product of a test of a strategy using historical data is predicted investment returns or excess returns. These returns are then subjected to statistical tests to determine if they are statistically different from zero (i.e., they did not result merely by chance). Statistical tests require that assumptions be made about the probability distribution for the return of the stocks. For example, it is common to assume that returns are normally distributed. Yet empirical evidence does not support this assumption. Therefore, in this case, the equity manager must assess the extent to which the test of a strategy is affected by the underlying assumption about the probability distribution of returns.

8. *Linear models:* In the valuation models, it is assumed that there is a linear relationship between a factor and the expected return. Though empirical evidence does seem to suggest that factors conform to a linear model; yet an equity manager may test a linear model and find it not to be statistically significant. A more complex nonlinear model infect may produce a highly significant correlation between return and the factors.

9. *Market Impact :* In implementing a strategy, one of the transactions costs faced is market impact cost. This must be recognised in conducting test of strategies. Predicted excess returns can be wiped out by market impact.

10. *'Reference'* or *'normal'* portfolio: Finally, in designing a test of the historical performance of a strategy, performance should be measured against a suitable benchmark called the *reference* or *normal* portfolio.

Comparative selection decisions for most industrial equity shares can usually be intelligently reached through the appropriate use of one or more of the valuation techniques. The data on individual equity derived from these techniques should ordinarily be compared with bench mark for a representative stock market average or index to give an indication of the comparative values that are currently available in the market. In all cases, however, a subjective interpretation of the various quality features is inherently a part of the decision process.

However, it might be noted that even the most sophisticated appraisal techniques cannot assure superior long- term investment results. Because results entirely depend upon the realization of future earnings and dividends, it is possible that they will be seriously affected by dynamic new developments. Such possibilities are one reason for portfolio diversification of reasonable proportions. But at the same time, it would seem only reasonable that selection decision derived from a penetrating analytical process of the quality of the company and its earnings and dividend potential in relation to the price of the stock should substantially increase the probabilities of obtaining satisfactory long-term investment results.

REVIEW PROBLEMS

1. Suppose that a stock pays three annual dividends of ₹ 10 per year and the discount rate is 15 per cent. What is the present value (V_o) of th stock?

Ans.:

The present value of the stock is:

$$V_o = \frac{₹\ 10}{(1+.15)^1} + \frac{₹\ 10}{(1+.15)^2} + \frac{₹\ 10}{(1+.15)^3}$$

$$= ₹\ 48.16$$

2. Suppose ABC Co, stock pays three annual dividends of ₹ 10, ₹ 20 and ₹ 30 in year 1, 2, and 3, respectively, and the discount rate is 10 per cent. What is the present value (V_o) of the stock?

Ans.:

The present value (V_o) of the stock is:

$$(V_o) = \frac{₹\ 10}{(1+.10)^1} + \frac{₹\ 20}{(1+.10)^2} + \frac{₹\ 30}{(1+.10)^3}$$

$$= ₹\ 48.16$$

3. Suppose that the dividend growth rate is 10 per cent, the discount rate is 8 per cent, there are 20 years of dividends to be paid, and the current dividend is ₹ 10. What is the value of the stock based on the constant growth model?

Ans.:

The present value (V_o) of the stock is:

$$V_0 = \frac{₹\ 10(1+.10)}{.08-.10}\left[1-\left(\frac{1+.10}{1+.08}\right)20\right]$$

$$= ₹\ 243.86$$

4. D.K. Rao has invested in Apex Auto. The capitalisation rate of the company is 15 per cent and the current dividend is ₹ 2.00 per share. Calculate the value of the company's equity share if the company is slowly sinking with an annual decline rate of 5% in the dividend.

Ans:

The value of the firm stock is :

$$V_e = \frac{D_1}{k-g}$$

$$= \frac{₹\ 2(1-.05)}{.15-(-0.05)}$$

$$= \frac{₹\ 1.90}{0.20}$$

$$= ₹\ 9.50$$

5. What would be the value of the equity share of Apex Auto of previous problem if the company shows no growth but is able to maintain its dividend.

Ans:

The value of the equity is:

$$V_e = \frac{D_1}{k-g}$$

$$= \frac{₹\ 2.00(1+0)}{0.15-(-0.00)}$$

$$= \frac{₹\ 200}{0.15}$$

$$= ₹\ 13.33$$

6. Repeat the Apex Auto problem (4) and assume that it grows at an average rate, which is taken to be an average annual increase in dividend of 7 per cent. Compute the value of equity share.

Ans:

The value of the equity share is :

$$V_e = \frac{D_1}{k-g}$$

$$= \frac{₹\ 2.00(1+0.07)}{0.15-(-0.07)}$$

$$= \frac{₹\ 2.14}{0.08}$$

$$= ₹\ 26.75$$

7. Suppose dividends for a particular company are projected to grow at 5 per cent

forever. If of the discount rate is 15 per cent and the current dividend is ₹ 10, what is the value of the stock?

Ans.:

The value of the Stock is:

$$V_0 = \frac{₹\ 10(1+.10)}{.15-.05}$$

$$= ₹\ 105$$

8. Padma currently earns ₹ 3 per share. His return on equity is 25 per cent and he retains 50% of its earnings (both figures are expected to be maintained indefinitely). Stocks of similar risk are priced to return 15%. What is the intrinsic value of Padma's stock ?

Ans:

If Padma will earn 25 per cent on its equity and pay out 50 per cent of its earnings indefinitely, then the growth rate is

$$\begin{aligned} g &= r(1\text{-}d) \\ &= 25\ (1 - .50) \\ &= 25 \times .50 \\ &= .1250 = 12.50\% \end{aligned}$$

In the case of a constant growth :

$$\begin{aligned} V &= [(1\text{-}d)xE_0x(1+g)]/(k\text{-}g) \\ &= [(1 - .50) \times ₹\ 3 \times (1 + .1250)]/(.15 - .1250) \\ &= ₹\ 1.\ 6875/.025 = ₹\ 67.50 \end{aligned}$$

9. BPT paid ₹ 2.75 in dividends on its equity shares last year. Dividends are expected to grow at 12 per cent annual rate for an indefinite number of years.

   (a) If BPT's current market price is ₹ 37.50, what is the stock's expected rate of return?
   (b) If your required rate of return is 14 per cent, what is the value of the stock for you?
   (c) Should you make the investment?

Ans:

   (a) Expected Rate of Return $= \dfrac{₹\ 2.75(1.12)}{₹\ 37.50} + .12 = 20.21\%$

   (b) Investor s value $= \dfrac{₹\ 2.75(1.12)}{.14-.12} = ₹\ 154$

   (c) The expected rate of return is greater than the required rate of return (20.21% versus 14%). Also, the value of the stock (₹ 154) is larger than the current market price (₹ 37.50). The share is undervalued and should be purchased.

10. The market price for Super Iron's equity is ₹ 65 per share. The price at the end of one year is expected to be ₹ 90, and dividends for next year should be ₹ 2.90. What is the expected rate of return (ERR)?

Ans:

If the expected rate of return is represented by ERR:

Dividend in year 1 Price in year 1

Current price $= \dfrac{D_1}{(1+ERR)} + \dfrac{P_1}{(1+ERR)}$

$ERR = \dfrac{D_1 + P_1}{\text{Current Price}} - 1$

$ERR = \dfrac{₹\ 2.90 + ₹\ 90}{65} - 1 = 0.30$

$ERR =\ 30.0\%$

11. Gandhi Petro is expected to pay ₹ 3.00 in dividends next year, and the market price is projected to be ₹ 75 by year end. If the investor's required rate of return is 20 percent, what is the current value of the stock?

Ans:

$V_e = \dfrac{D_1}{(1+k)} + \dfrac{P_1}{(1+k)}$

$= \dfrac{₹\ 3.00}{(1+.20)} + \dfrac{₹\ 75}{(1+.20)}$

$=\ ₹\ 2.50 + ₹\ 62.50$

$=\ ₹\ 65.00$

12. On Sudha Enterprises' equity shares, the dividend paid at ₹ 1.32 per equity share last year and this is expected to grow indefinitely at an annual 7 per cent rate. What is the value of each equity share of Sudha Enterprises if the investor requires an 11 percent return?

Ans:

$V_e = \dfrac{D_0\ (1+g)}{(k-g)}$

$= \dfrac{₹\ 1.32(1.07)}{0.11-0.07} = ₹\ 35.31$

13. An investor holds an equity share giving him an annual dividend of ₹ 30. He expects to sell the share for ₹ 300 at the end of a year. Calculate the value of the share if the required rate of return is 10%.

Ans:

The market price of a share in the beginning of the period is equal to the present value of the dividends paid at the end of the period plus the market price of the share at the end of the period. Symbolically:

$$P_0 = \frac{D_1}{1+k} + \frac{P_1}{1+k}$$

or $$P_0 = \frac{D_1 + P_1}{(1+k)}$$

where,

$P_0 =$ The current price of the share

$k =$ The required rate of return or the cost of equity

$D_1 =$ Dividend to be received at the end of the period

$P_1 =$ Market price of share at the end of the period Substituting the values, we get:

$$P_0 = \frac{₹\ 30 + ₹\ 300}{(1+0.10)}$$

$$= \frac{₹\ 330}{1.10} = ₹\ 300$$

14. Ahuja Textile's equity share currently sells for ₹ 23 per share. The company's finance manager anticipates a constant growth rate of 10.5 per cent and an end-of-year dividend of ₹ 2.50.

    (a) What is the expected rate of return?

    (b) If the investor requires a 17% return, should he purchase the stock?

Ans:

    (a) Expected rate or return $= \dfrac{D_1}{\text{Current Price}} + g$

$$= \frac{₹\ 2.50}{23.00} + 0.105$$

$$= 21.37\%$$

    (b) $V_e = \dfrac{₹\ 2.50}{.17 - .105}$

$$= ₹\ 38.46$$

The value of the stock would be ₹ 38.46. Thus, the expected rate of return exceeds the required rate of return, which means that the value of the security is greater than the current market price. Thus the investor should buy the stock.

15. RAJ's equity shares currently sells for ₹ 22.50 per share. The finance manager of RAJ anticipates a constant growth rate of 12 per cent and an end-of-year dividend of ₹ 2.50.

    (a) What is your expected rate of return if you buy the stock for ₹ 25?

    (b) If you require a 18 percent return, should you purchase the stock?

Ans:

(a) Expected Rate of Return $= \dfrac{\text{Dividend in year 1}}{\text{Market price}} + \text{Growth rate}$

$$= \dfrac{₹\ 2.50}{₹\ 25} + .12$$

$$= .22 = .22\%$$

(b) $\qquad\qquad\qquad V_e = \dfrac{₹\ 2.50}{.18 - .12}$

$$= ₹\ 41.67$$

Yes, purchase the equity shares of RAJ.

16. Firms A, B and C are similar. Firm A is the most progressive and trades at a 18/1 P/E multiple. Firm B is less progressive, is not publicly traded, and has an EPS of ₹ 1.20. Firm C is least progressive and trades at a 15/1 P/E ratio. What is the intrinsic value of firm B?

Ans:

Average P/E $=\ 16.5$

Intrinsic value $=\ 16.5 \times 1.20$

$$=\ ₹\ 19.80$$

17. Companies R, S and T are similar. Company R is privately held, and has a book value of ₹ 40 per share. Company S has a market price of ₹ 15 and a book value of ₹ 12. Company T has a market value (MV) of ₹ 82 and a book value of ₹ 62. What is a possible value for company R?

Ans:

Ratio of book value to market value :

Company R $=\ ₹\ 40/\ MV - .78$

$\qquad$ MV $=\ ₹\ 51$

Company S $=\ ₹\ 12/₹\ 15 = .8$

Company T $=\ ₹\ 62/₹\ 82 = .76$

18. A firm's current EPS is ₹ 6, its dividend payout is 40 percent, and its growth rate of EPS is 10%. The normal P/E multiple is 15/1. What is the stock's value using the capitalisation of earnings method? What is its value in 3 years using the same method?

Ans:

$P/ExEPS_{cumrtt} = PV$

PV $= 15 \times 6 = ₹\ 90$

$EPS_3 = ₹\ 6\ (1.10)^3$

$\qquad = ₹\ 7.986$

Value in 3 years $= 15 \times ₹\ 7.986$

$\qquad\qquad\qquad = ₹\ 119.79$

19. For the firm in problem 18, what is the current value and the value in 4 years

using the centralisation of dividends method? If an investor expects a dividend payout of ₹ 75 per cent, what is the firm's current value and value in 3 years using the capitalisation of earnings-and- dividends method?

Ans:

Dividends = EPS x Dividend payout

= ₹ 6x40%

= ₹ 2.40 dividend per share

Normal P/D multiple = P/Enm. /Dividend payout

= 15/75% = 20/1

Capitalisation of dividend value

= $D/SxP/D_{norm}$

= ₹ 2.40x20

= ₹ 48

In four years dividend

= ₹ 2.40 (1.10) = 3.5138

= 3.5138x20 = ₹ 70.28

Capitalisation of earnings and dividend:

(P/E) (D/S + .25 EPS)

Value = (15) (₹ 2.40 + .25 x ₹ 6)

= ₹ 58.50

Value in three years

= (15) (₹ 3.59 + .25 x ₹ 7.986)

= ₹ 77.85

20. Companies X, Y and Z are in the same industry . Company X has a 5 per cent growth rate, pays a ₹ 2.00 dividend, and sells for ₹ 25 per share. Company Y pays a ₹ 4 dividend, has an 8 per cent growth rate, and is not publicly traded. Company Z sells for ₹ 60, pays a ₹ 6 dividend, and has a 2 per cent growth rate. What is the value of the stock of Company Y?

Ans:

V_X = ₹ 2/₹ 25 + .05 = 13%

V_Z = ₹ 6/₹ 60 + .02 = 12%

V_{xz} = 12.5%

Value of V_y = ₹ 4/(12.5% - 8%)

= ₹ 89

21. Given the following: current dividend, ₹ 4; dividend payout, 40 per cent; normal capitalization rate, 12 per cent; actual capitalization rate, 15 per cent. What is the current value of the stock? If it increases its dividend payout to 60 per cent, how much will the current value go up or down? Why did it do this?

Ans:

V_e $= ₹ 4 / (12\% - 15\% \times 60\%)$
       $= ₹ 133$

Change in Dividend Payout Ratio and V_e:
V_e $= ₹ 6 / (12\% - 15\% \times 40\%)$
       $= ₹ 100$

A drop of ₹ 33 because raising dividend decreases present value when firm is more profitable than norm.

22. Prem Nath is a conservative investor who demands 10 percent interest on his fixed investment but 20 percent from his equity investments. He has been considering the purchase of an equity that pays ₹ 2.50 in dividends this year and whose dividends are expected to grow at 10 percent per year for the next three years. Earnings this year are ₹ 5 per share and are expected to grow at 20 percent for the next seven years. Stocks growing at this rate generally sell at 40 times earnings. What price Prem pays for this equity?

Ans.:

Using the three year valuation formula:

$$P_0 = \frac{D(1=g)}{1=K} + \frac{D(1+g)^2}{(1+K)^2} + \frac{D(1+g)^3 + P_3}{(1+K)^3}$$

where:

P_3 = $(E)(P/E)(1+g)^3$
P_3 = $(₹ 4)(40)(1 + 20\%)^3 = ₹ 276.48$

$$P_0 = \frac{₹ 2.50(1+.10)}{(1+.20)} + \frac{₹ 2.50(1+.10)^2}{(1+.20)^2} + \frac{₹ 2.50(1+.10)^3 + ₹ 276.48}{(1+.20)^3}$$

$$= \frac{₹ 2.50}{(1.20)} + \frac{₹ 3.035}{(1.44)} + \frac{₹ 3.3275 = ₹ 276.48}{(1.728)}$$

$= ₹ 2.292 + ₹ 2.107 + ₹ 161.926$
$= ₹ 166.32$

23. Refer to problem 22, Sanjay Jain, another investor, would consider investment in this equity that Prem Nath is interested in, but he thinks he should earn a yield of 15 percent rather than 20 percent. What price would Sanjay consider fair?

$$P_0 = \frac{D(1+g)}{1+K} + \frac{D(1+g)^2}{(1+K)} + \frac{D(1+g)^3 + P_3}{(1+K)^3}$$

P_3 = $(E)(P/E)(1+g)^3$
P_3 = $(₹ 4)(40)(1 + 20\%)^3 = ₹ 276.48$

$$P_0 = \frac{₹ 2.50(1+.10)}{(1+.15)} + \frac{₹ 2.50(1+.10)^2}{(1+.10)^2} + \frac{₹ 2.50(1+.10)^3 + ₹ 276.48}{(1+.15)^3}$$

$$= ₹ 2.39 + ₹ 2.29 + ₹ 183.98$$
$$= ₹ 188.66$$

24. R.K. Sinha is suspicious of the estimates prepared by Prem Nath and Sanjay Jain. He has carefully examined the company and thinks dividends will grow at 6 percent, earnings growth will be 16 percent, and the future P/E ratio will be 25. Like Sanjay Jain, he thinks the discount rate should be 15 percent (Refer to problem 22 and 23). What should Sinha pay for the equity?

Ans:

Using the three year valuation formula:

$$P_3 = (₹\ 4)\ (25)\ (1 + .16)^3 = ₹\ 156$$

$$P_0 = \frac{₹\ 2.50(1+.06)}{(1+.15)} + \frac{₹\ 2.50(1+.06)^2}{(1+.15)^2} + \frac{₹\ 2.50(1+.60)^3 + ₹\ 156}{(1+.15)^3}$$

$$= ₹\ 2.30 + ₹\ 2.12 + ₹\ 104.53$$
$$= ₹\ 108.95$$

25. J.D. Kapoor just learned that he can buy the stock under discussion for ₹ 200 per share (refer to problems 22 to 24). Based upon Sanjay Jain's assumption, what yield will Kapoor earn? Should he buy?

Ans:

Using the three year valuation formula:

$$P_3 = (₹\ 4)\ (40)\ (1 + 20\%)^3 = ₹\ 276.48$$

$$200 = \frac{₹\ 2.50(1+.10)}{(1+r)} + \frac{₹\ 2.50(1+.10)^2}{(1+r)^2} + \frac{₹\ 2.50(1+.10)^3 + ₹\ 276.48}{(1+r)^3}$$

$$200 = \frac{₹\ 2.75}{(1+r)} + \frac{₹\ 3.25}{(1+r)^2} + \frac{₹\ 279.81}{(1+r)^3}$$

If $r = 40\%$
$$200 = ₹\ 203.40$$

The PV of the expected income when discounted by an r of .40 results in a present value of ₹ 203.40. This means that actual r value is slightly higher than 40 per cent.

26. Refer to problems 22 to 25, what yield will J.D. Kapoor earn if he buys on the basis of R.K. Sinha's estimates? Should he buy?

Ans:

15%. A yield of 15% is attractive but J.D. Kapoor must decide if the risks are commensurate with the yield.

27. R. Khan can buy an equity that will pay ₹ 2.00 in dividends annually over the next 3 years. The earnings of the company are expected to grow and the equity is expected to reach a price of ₹ 70 per share at the end of three years. This is a conservative investment and Khan expects a yield of 18 percent. What price should Khan pay for the equity if he wishes to earn 18 percent?

Ans:

Approximate method:

$$\text{Yield (Y)} = \dfrac{\dfrac{D + P_3 - P_0}{3}}{\dfrac{P_3 + P_0}{2}}$$

Solving for P_0: $\dfrac{(Y)(P_3) + P_0)}{2} + D + \dfrac{P_3 - P_0}{3}$

$$(3)\,(Y)\,(P_3 + P_0) = (2)\,(3)\,(D) + (2)\,(P_3 - P_0)$$

$$3YP_3 + 3YP_0 = 6D + 2P_3 - 2P_0$$

$$3YP_0 + 2P_0 = 6D + 2P_3 - 3YP_3$$

$$P_0 = \dfrac{6D + P_3(2 = 3Y)}{3Y + 2}$$

Substituting:

$$P_0 = \dfrac{(6 \times ₹\,2)\,(₹\,75[(2 - 3)(0.18)]}{(3)(0.18) + 2}$$

$$= \dfrac{₹\,12 + i\,70\,[2.54]}{.54 + 2}$$

$$P_0 = \dfrac{₹\,12 + i\,102.20}{2.54}$$

$$P_0 = ₹\,45$$

Verification:

$$.18 = \dfrac{₹\,2.00 \dfrac{(70 - 45)}{3}}{\dfrac{70 - 45}{2}}$$

$$= \dfrac{₹\,2 + 8.33}{57.50}$$

$$= 18\%$$

28. Abdul wants to buy stock in Karim Enterprises. It traded yesterday at ₹ 405. The company paid a dividend last year ₹ 2.40 per share. Dividends have grown at 15 per cent per year, and earnings at 20 percent per year, for the last 5 years. Earnings per share were ₹ 4.75 last year and are expected to be ₹ 6.50 this year. Earnings are expected to grow at a 20 percent rate next year and the year after, and that stock should enjoy a P/E of 35. The company announced that the stock was to be split 2 for 1 shortly. Dividends should increase as they have in the past.

What yield would Abdul earn for the investment if he purchased it at ₹ 405 and held it for three years?

Ans:

Using the three year valuation equation:

$$P_3 = (₹\ 6.50)\ (35)\ (1 + .20)3 = ₹\ 393.12$$

$$405 = \frac{(₹\ 2.40)(1+.15)}{(1+r)} + \frac{(₹\ 2.40)(1+.15)^2}{(1+r)^2} + \frac{(₹\ 2.40)(1+.15)^3}{(1+r)^3}$$

$$+ \frac{(₹\ 393.12)}{(1+r)^3}$$

$$405 = \frac{₹\ 2.76}{(1+r)} + \frac{₹\ 3.174}{(1+r)^2} + \frac{₹\ 3.650}{(1+r)^3} + \frac{₹\ 393.12}{(1+r)^2}$$

If r = .18

405 = ₹ 246.10

The stock is selling at a negative yield. It may be noticed that even if we use a discount rate of 0, the present value would not equal 405, but ₹ 402.70. Obviously, it would be unattractive for investment on the basis of this valuation.

29. Given the following: EPS, ₹ 5; Market price ₹ 60; Growth rate of sales, 6%, and of EPS, 9%; Dividend payout, 70%; Normal capitalisation rate ,12%. Using the capitalisation and dividend growth methods, what is the value of the stock?

Ans:

Capitalisation of earnings: ₹ 5 (8.33)*= ₹ 41.67

  *1/.12 = 8.33

Capitalisation of dividends: ₹ 2 (11.9)* = ₹ 23.80

  *833(70) = 119

Capitalisation of earnings and dividends:

  8.33 (₹ 2+30% (₹ 5) = ₹ 29.16

Capitalisation of growth: ₹ 7.06 (8.5+2(9))= ₹ 187

  5(10+1.5(6))=₹ 95 Dividend growth model:

  ₹ 2/(12%-8.33%*(60%)) = ₹ 28.57

  *5/60 = 8.33%

30. Gujrat Agro Industries (GAI), an ungeared company operating in the processed food industry, is contemplating the takeover of Punjab Agro Produces (PAP), but is unsure how to value its target. GAI's analysts have assembled the following information:

(i) Punjab's Balance Sheet as at Dec. 31, 2011

Fixed Assets (net)		1400
Current Assets:		
Equity	-400	
Debtors	-800	
Cash	—	
Current Liabilities:		
Trade creditors	1000	
Bank Overdraft	300	
Net current Assets		-100
Net Assets		1300
Financed by:		
Issued share capital (₹ 100)		1,000
Profit & Loss Account		300
Shareholders' fund		1300

(ii) In its most recent period, ending Dec., 2011, PAP's sales were ₹ 5,000 crore, but after operating costs and other expenses, including a depreciation charge of ₹ 200 crore, its profit after tax was ₹ 200 crore. This figure includes an extraordinary item (sale of property of ₹ 50 crore). The full year dividend was ₹ 50 crore in total, paid about a year ago.

(iii) PAP has recently followed a policy of increasing dividends by 12% p.a. Its shareholders required rate of return is 17%

(iv) GAI's P/E Ratio is 14:1, PAP's is 8:1.

(v) More efficient utilisation of PAP's assets could generate annual operating savings of ₹ 50 crore p.a. after tax.

Required:

(a) What is the current market value of PAP's shares?

(b) Why might the market value differ from book value?

(c) What rate of return does PAP currently achieve for its shareholders?

(d) As Financial Director of GAI, you are required to assess the value of PAP using discounted cash flow approach. (Carefully specify any assumptions which you make.)

Ans.:

(a) P/E Ratio for PAP = 8:1

PAP's profit after tax (PAT) = ₹ 150 crore (after deducting the exceptional item)

Hence, market value = 8 x ₹ 150 crore = ₹ 1200 crore.

The price per share is ₹ 1200 crore/(₹ 1000 crore +100) = ₹ 120

Since the last dividend was paid a year ago this appears to be cum-dividend share price.

Last year's dividend per share was

(₹ 50 crore/₹ 1000 crore - 100) = ₹ 5

Given 12% growth, this year dividend would be ₹ 5 x (1.12) = ₹ 5.60.

Therefore ex-dividend price would be about 114.

(b) Book value is based on historic cost. Market value depends on earning power. Value stated in the accounts may be suspect, e.g. fixed assets under-valued, stock over-valued.

(c) Book value of net assets = ₹ 1300 crore

Shareholder earnings after tax = ₹ 150 crore

Return on book value = ₹ 150 crore/₹ 1300 crore = 11.5%

Alternatively,

Return on market value = ₹ 150 crore/₹ 1200 crore = 12.5%

(d) PAP's normal cash flow

= (PAT-exceptional item + depreciation)

= ₹ 200 crore - ₹ 50 crore + ₹ 200 crore = ₹ 350 crore

Assume

— Infinite life, use perpetuity formula

— no growth

— Cost of equity for GAI given as 17%

— annual replacement investment for PAP = depreciation charge of ₹ 200 core Allowing for operating savings of ₹ 5000 crore, free cash flow = ₹ 350 crore - ₹ 200 crore + ₹ 50 crore

= ₹ 200 crore p. a.

With no growth, value of PAP

= ₹ 200 crore/. 17

= ₹ 1176 crore

31. On April 1, 2011 the equity share of Gitam stood at ₹ 469. The traded options market in the shares quotes May ₹ 500 puts at ₹ 47. If the share price falls to ₹ 450, how much, if any, profit would be investor make? What will the option be worth if the share price moves up to ₹ 510?

Ans.:

Traded options give the holder right, but not the obligation, to buy (a call option) or sell (a put option) a quantity of shares at a fixed price on an exercise date in the future. They are usually in contracts of 1,000 shares and for three, six or nine moths.

Holders of a put option in Gitam have the right to sell shares in May at ₹ 500.

For this right they currently have to pay a premium of ₹ 47, or ₹ 470 on a contract of 1000 shares.

If the share price falls below ₹ 453 (i.e. ₹ 500-₹ 47), the shares become profitable and the holder is in the money. So if they fall to ₹ 450, the investor can buy shares at this price, and exercise his put option to sell shares for ₹ 500.

A profit of ₹ 50 per share which, after the initial cost of the option gives a net profit of ₹ 3 per share or ₹ 3000 per contract.

If the share price moves up to ₹ 510 by May, the option becomes worthless, and the investor loses his ₹ 47 premium.

Option such as these can be used to either speculate or hedge on share price changes for a relatively low premium.

32. An investor has invested in a company which is growing at an above-average rate, translated to an annual increase in dividends of 20 per cent for 15 years. Thereafter dividend growth returns to an average rate of 7 per cent. The capitalisation rate of the company is 9 per cent and the current dividend per equity share is ₹ 1.00 per share. Determine the value of the equity share.

Ans:

A two-stage approach must be employed to determine value in this case. For the next 15 years the dividend is expected to grow from $D_0 = ₹ 1.00$ to $D_{15} = ₹15.407$ for a total of ₹ 86.44. If our discount rate is 9%, this 15-year stream has a present value of ₹ 35.276. All the necessary dividend computations are shown in following table.

Year	Dividend $1(1+0.20)^t$	Discount Factor $1(1+09)^t$	Dividend Present Value
1	1.200	0.917	1.100
2	1.440	0.842	1.212
3	1.728	0.722	1.248
4	2.074	0.708	1.469
5	2.488	0.650	1.617
6	2.986	0.596	1.780
7	3.583	0.547	1.960
8	4.300	0.502	2.159
9	5.160	0.460	2.374
10	6.192	0.442	2.734
11	7.430	0.388	2.883
12	8.916	0.356	3.174
13	10.696	0.326	3.487
14	12.839	0.299	3.839
15	15.407	0.275	4.237
	₹ 86.442		₹ 35.276

The value of the equity share at the end of 15 years is :

$$V_{15} = \frac{D_{16}}{k-g}$$

$$= \frac{D_{15}(1+0.07)}{k-g}$$

$$= \frac{₹ 15.407 (1+0.07)}{0.09-0.07}$$

$$= \frac{₹\,16.49}{0.02}$$

$$= ₹\,824.50$$

The present value of ₹ 824.50 to be received in 15 years discounted at 9 per cent is ₹ 226.74 (₹ 824.50 X 0.275). Combining this value with the present value of the expected dividend stream for the next 15 years (₹ 35.276), an investor would be willing to pay ₹ 262.02 per share.

33. Abhishek Industries currently pays a dividend of ₹ 2.00 per share and this dividend is expected to grow at a 15% annual rate for 3 years, then at a 12% rate for the next three years, after it is expected to grow at a 5 per cent rate forever.

    (a) What value would you place on the equity if 9% rate of return were required?
    (b) Would your calculation change if you expect to hold the equity only 3 years?

Ans:

End of Year	Dividend	Present value of Dividends —— 9 per cent	
1	₹ 2.00 (1.15) =	₹ 2.30 X 0.9174 =	₹ 2.11
2	2.00 (1.15)^2 =	2.64X0.8417 =	2.22
3	2.00 (1.15)^3 =	3.04 X 0.7722 =	2.35
4	3.04(1.12) =	3.40 X 0.7084 =	2.41
5	3.04 (1.12)^2 =	3.81 X 0.6499 =	2.48
6	3.04 (1.12)^3 =	4.27X0.5963 = Total =	2.55 ₹ 14.12

Year 7 dividend $\quad = \quad ₹\,4.27\,(1.05)$

$\qquad\qquad\qquad\quad = \quad ₹\,4.48$

Market value at end of year 6 $\quad = \quad \dfrac{₹\,4.28}{.09-.05} = ₹\,112$

(a) Present value of ₹ 1 12 with 9% discount rate

$\qquad\qquad\qquad = \quad 112\text{X}0.5963$

$\qquad\qquad\qquad = \quad ₹\,66.78$

Valuation $\qquad\qquad = \quad ₹\,14.12 + ₹\,66.78$

$\qquad\qquad\qquad = \quad ₹\,80.90$

(b) Present value of Market Value at end of year 3

$\qquad\qquad\qquad = \quad ₹\,2.41 + ₹\,2.48 + ₹\,2.55 + ₹\,66.78$

$\qquad\qquad\qquad = \quad ₹\,74.22$

Present value of expected dividend to be received at end of year 1, 2 and 3

$\qquad\qquad\qquad = \quad ₹\,2.11 + ₹\,2.22 + ₹\,2.35$

$\qquad\qquad\qquad = \quad ₹\,6.68$

Total value $\qquad\quad = \quad ₹\,74.22 + ₹\,6.68$

$\qquad\qquad\qquad = \quad ₹\,80.90.$

Thus, the value is the same for an investor with a 2-year time horizon.

34. Aman Group recently paid an annual dividend of ₹ 3.50 per share. Earnings for the same year were ₹ 7.00 per share. The required return on equity with similar

risk is 12%. Dividends are expected to grow 10 percent per year indefinitely. Calculate Aman's 'normal' price-earning ratio.

Ans:

Assuming constant dividend growth, the 'normal' price- earning ratio for equity is

$V/Eo = D \times (1+g)/(k-g)$

In the case of Aman, the company is paying out 50% of its earnings, the

$V/E_0 = .50 \times (1 + .10)/(.12 - .10) = ₹ 27.50$

35. As a firm is operating in a mature industry, Novex Industries is expected to maintain a constant dividend payout ratio and constant growth rate of earnings for the foreseeable future. Earnings were ₹ 4 per share in the recently completed fiscal year. The dividend payout ratio has been constant 50 per cent in recent years and is expected to remain so. Novex's return on equity is expected to remain 15 per cent in the 'future, and you require 12 per cent return on the equity.

(a) Using the constant growth dividend discount model, calculate the current value of Novex equity share.
After an aggressive acquisition and marketing programme, it now appears that Novex's EPS and ROE will grow rapidly over the next two years. You are aware that the dividend discount model can be useful in estimating the value of equity even when the assumption of constant growth does not apply.

(b) Calculate the current value of Novex's equity, using the dividend discount model, assuming that Novex dividend will grow at a 20% rate for the next two years, returning in the third year to the historical growth rate for the foreseeable future.

Ans:

(a) Constant Growth (single-stage) dividend discount model:

V_0 = $D_1(k-g)$
V_Q = Value at the beginning
D_1 = Next year's dividend
k = Required rate of return
g = constant growth rate
D = $[EPS_0] (1+g)$ D/P Ratio
= $(4.00) (1 + .06) (.50)$
= ₹ 2.12
k = given at 12% or .12
g = (ROE) (1 - D/P Ratio)
= $(.15) (1 - .50)$
= $.075$ $V_0 = ₹ 2.12/(.12 - .075)$
= ₹ 47.11

(b) Multistage dividend discount model (where $g_1 = 20\%$ and $g_2 = V_1 - D_1/(1 + k) + D_2/(1+k)^2 + D_3/(k-g_2)/(1+k)^2$

$$
\begin{aligned}
D_1 &= (EPS_0)\,(1+g)\,D/P\ \text{Ratio} \\
&= (4.00)\,(1.20)\,(.50) = ₹\ 2.40 \\
&= (₹\ 2.40)\,(1.20) = ₹\ 2.88 = \text{given at } 12\% \text{ or } .12 = .075\ D_3 = D_2(1+g) \\
&= (₹\ 2.88)\,(1.075) = ₹\ 3.096\ \text{Value}_0 = ₹\ 2.40/(1.12) + (₹\ 2.88) \\
&\quad (1.12)^2 + [₹\ 3.096] \\
&= ₹\ 2.143 + ₹\ 2.296 + ₹\ 54.847 = ₹\ 59.29
\end{aligned}
$$

36. In 2011, the United Group paid a ₹ 2.08 dividend. Using the current dividend (Do) = ₹ 2.08, discount rate (k) = 8.75 per cent, and growth rate (g) = 20 per cent, calculate a present value estimate for United Group. Compare this with the 2011 United Group stock price of ₹ 29. If return on equity (ROE) of United Group is 7.9 per cent and earnings per share (EPS) of ₹ 1.87, what is he value of the stock?

Ans.:

The present value (V_0) of the United Group stock is:

$$
V_0 = \frac{₹\ 2.08[1+.02]}{.0875-.02}
$$

$$
= ₹\ 31.43
$$

We see that estimated price is a little lighter than the ₹ 29 stock price.

If United Group's payout ratio is ₹ 2.08 / ₹ 1.87 = 1.112. Hence, the retention ratio is:

$$
1-1.112 = -.112, \text{ or } -11.2 \text{ per cent.}
$$

United Group's sustainable growth rate is :

$$
-.112 \times 7.9\%
$$

$$
= -.00885
$$

$$
= -0.885 \text{ per cent.}
$$

Using the Constant growth model, we obtain a value of :

$$
\frac{₹\ 2.08[.99115]}{[.0875-(-.0085)]}
$$

$$
= ₹\ 21.47
$$

This value (₹ 21.47) is much less then United Group's 2011 stock price of ₹ 29, suggesting that United Group's stock is perhaps overvalued, or, more likely, that a -.885 per cent growth rate underestimates United Group's future dividend growth.

37. You are considering buying the stock of two companies that operate in the same industry; they have similar characteristics except for their dividend payout policies. Both companies are expected to earn ₹ 6.00 per share this year. However, Company D (for "dividend") is expected to pay out all of its earnings as dividends, while Company G (for "growth") is expected to pay out only one third of its

earnings, or ₹ 2.00 per share. D's stock price is ₹ 40. G and D are equally risky. Which of the following is most likely to be true?

(a) Company G will have a faster growth rate than Company D. Therefore, G's stock price should be greater than ₹ 40.

(b) Although G's growth rate should exceed D's, D's current dividend exceeds that of G, and this should cause D's price to exceed G's.

(c) An investor in Stock D will get his or her money back faster because D pays out more of its earnings as dividends. Thus, in a sense, D is like a short-term bond, and G is like a long-term bond. Therefore, if economic shifts cause k_D and k_e to increase, and if the expected streams of dividneds from D and G remain constant, both stock D and G will decline, but D's price should decline further.

(d) D's expected and required rate of return are 15%. G's expected return will be higher because of its higher expected growth rate.

(e) If we observe that G's price is also ₹ 40, the best estimate of G's growth rate is 10 per cent.

Ans.

(a) This is not necessarily true. Because G plows back two-thirds of its earnings, its growth rate should exceed that of D, but D pays higher dividends (₹ 6 versus ₹ 2). We cannot say which stock should have the higher price.

(b) Again, we just do not know which price would be higher.

(c) This is false. The changes in k_d and k_e would have a greater effect on G; its price would decline more.

(d) The total expected return for D is $\tilde{k}_D = D_1/P_0 + g = 15\%$. The total expected return from G will have D_1/P_0 less than 15 per cent and g greater than 0 per cent, but $\tilde{k}_G$ should be nether greater nor smaller than D's total expected return, 15 per cent, because the two stocks are stated to be equally risky.

(e) We have eliminated a, b, c, and d, so e should be correct. On the basis of the available information, D and G should sell at about the same price, ₹ 40; thus, $\tilde{k}_e = 15\%$ for both D and G. G's current dividend yield is ₹ 2/₹ 40 = 5%. Therefore, g = 15%-5% = 10%.

38. XYZ Company's current stock price is ₹ 36, and its last dividend was ₹ 2.40. In view of company's strong financial position and its consequent low risk, its required rate of return is only 12 per cent. It dividends are expected to grow at a constant rate, g, in the future, and if k_e is expected to remain at 12 per cent, what is XYZ's expected stock price 5 years from now.

Ans.

The first step is to solve for g, the unknown variable, in the constant growth equation. Since D_1 is unknown but D_0 is known, substitute $D_0(1+g)$ as follows:

$$\hat{P} = P_0 = \frac{D_1}{k_e - g} = \frac{D_0(1+g)}{k_e - g}$$

$$₹\,36 = \frac{₹\,2.40(1+g)}{0.12 - g}$$

Solving for g, we find the growth rate to be 5 per cent.

$$₹ 4.32 - ₹ 36g = ₹ 2.40 + ₹ 2.40g$$
$$₹ 38.4g = ₹ 1.92$$
$$g = 0.05 = 5\%$$

The next step is to use the growth rate to project the stock price 5 years hence:

$$\hat{P}_5 = \frac{D_0(1+g)^6}{k_e - g}$$

$$\frac{₹ 2.40(1.05)^6}{0.12 - 0.05}$$

$$= ₹ 45.95.$$

[Alternatively, $\hat{P}_5 = ₹ 36(1.05)^5 = ₹ 45.95.$]

Therefore, XYZ Company's expected stock price 5 years from now is ₹ 45.95.

39. At midyear 2011, Axle Auto Power (AAP) had a return on equity (ROE) = 12.5 per cent, earnings per share (EPS) = ₹ 3.09, and a per share dividend (Do) = ₹ 2.40. What was AAP's retention ratio and its sustainable growth rate? What is the value of AAP's stock assuring a discount rate of 8.75 per cent?

Ans.:

AAP's dividend payout was:

₹ 2.40/₹ 3.09 = .777 or 77.7 per cent.

Hence, AAP's retention ratio is:

1 - .777 = .223 or 22.3 per cent.

The AAP's sustainable growth rate was:

.223 x 12.5% = 2.79%

The value of AAP's stock at a discount rate of 8.75 per cent is :

$$\frac{₹ 2.40[1+0279]}{[.0875 - 0279]}$$

$$= ₹ 41.39$$

40. Zen Group's equity shares are currently selling for ₹ 45 per equity share. The company paid ₹ 2.70 dividend on per share and has a projected constant growth rate of 12%.If you purchase the equity shares at market price, what is your expected rate of return?

Ans:

Expected rate of return = $\dfrac{₹ 27 \ (1 + .12)}{₹ 15} + .12 = 18.72\%$

41. Consider the following inspiration on two securities. Which has greater total risk, greater systematic risk, greater unsystematic risk, and a higher risk premium?

	Standard Deviation	Beta
Security ABC	40%	.50
Security XYZ	20	1.50

Ans.:

Security ABC has greater total risk, but it has substantially *less* systematic risk. Because the total risk is the sum of systematic and unsystematic risk, security ABC must have greater unsystematic risk. Finally, from the systematic risk principle, Security XYZ will have a higher risk premium and a greater expected return, despite the fact that it has less total risk.

42. Suppose a firm has a current dividend (Do) of ₹ 5, which is expected to 'shrink' at the rate $g_t = -10$ per cent for n = 5 years and thereafter grow at the rate $g_2 = 4$ per cent. With discount rate (k) of 10 per cent, what is the value of the stock?

Ans.:

Using the two-stage model, present value (V_o), is calculated as:

$$\frac{₹\ 5(.90)}{.10-(-.10)}\left[1-\left(\frac{.90}{1+.10}\right)\right] + \left[\frac{.90}{1+.10}\right]\frac{₹\ 5(1.04)}{.10-.04}$$

$$= ₹\ 14.25 + ₹\ 31.78$$

$$= ₹\ 46.03$$

The total present value of ₹ 46.3 is the sum of a ₹ 14.25 per cent value of the first five dividends plus a ₹ 31.78 present value of all subsequent dividends.

43. In 2011, ABC's previous five-year growth rate was 19.6 per cent and analysts were forecasting a 13.2 per cent long-term growth rate. Suppose ABC grows as 19.6 per cent rate for another five years, and thereafter grows at a 13.2 per cent. What value would you place on ABC by assuming a 14.5 per cent discount rate? ABC's 2011 dividend was ₹ 0.92.

Ans.:

Using the two stage model, the value (V_0) of ABC is:

$$V_0 = \frac{₹\ 0.92(1+.196)}{.145-.196}\left[1-\frac{(1+.196)}{(1+.145)}\right] + \left(\frac{(1+.196)}{(1+.145)}\right)\frac{₹\ 0.92(1+.196)}{.145-.196}$$

$$= ₹\ 5.25 + ₹\ 99.61$$

$$= ₹\ 104.86.$$

44. Arvind Auto's equity shares are selling for ₹ 67 a share in the market. The company is planning to introduce new products next week which will support the company's overall growth rate of 20% for about two years. After that, the growth is to fell and level off at about 8%. The company currently pays an annual dividend of ₹ 5, which can be expected to grow with the company. The rate of return on stocks like Arvind Auto is approximately 12%. Is Arvind Auto a good buy at ₹ 67?

Ans.

The first year future dividend is:

$D_1 = D_o (1 + g_1)$

$\quad = ₹\ 5.00 (1.20)$

$\quad = ₹\ 6.00$

To get the second year's dividend:

$D_2 = D_1(1 + g_1)$

$= ₹\ 6.00\ (1.20)$

$= ₹\ 7.20$

And, for the 3rd year:

$D_3 = D_2(1 + g_2)$

$= ₹\ 7.20\ (1.08)$

$= ₹\ 7.776$

Using the Gordon Model at the point in time when the growth rate changes and constant growth begins. That's year 2 in this case, so

$$P_2 = \frac{D_3}{k - g_2}$$

$$= \frac{₹7.776}{.12 - .08}$$

$$= ₹\ 194.40$$

Calculating a price in present value

$P_0 = ₹\ 6.00\ (PV_{12\%,}{}^1) + ₹\ 7.20\ (PV_{12\%,}{}^2)$

$\quad + ₹\ 194.40\ (PV_{12\%,}{}^2)$

$\quad = ₹\ 6.00\ (.89286) + ₹\ 7.20\ (.79719)$

$\quad + ₹\ 194.40\ (.79719)$

$\quad = ₹\ 5.3572 + ₹\ 5.7398 + ₹\ 154.9737$

$\quad = ₹\ 166.07$

If we compare the ₹ 166.07 with the market price of ₹ 67, clearly the valuation is larger. If the assumption are correct, the stock is worth almost ₹ 96 more than its current market price, hence, the stock is likely to rise substantially in a relatively short time. It would be advisable to buy the stock.

45. In 2011, P.K. Handa, a security analyst, forecasted a long-term 12.0 per cent growth rate for XYZ Co., although its recent five-year growth was only 1.2 per cent. Assume a 16.0 per cent discount rate, what value would you place on XYZ Co.? The 2011 dividend was ₹ 0.47.

Ans.:

The value (V_0 of the XYZ Co. is:

$$V_0 = \frac{₹\ 0.47(1.012)}{.16 - .012}\left[1 - \left(\frac{1.012}{1.16}\right)\right] + \left[\frac{1.012}{1.16}\right] * \frac{₹\ 0.47(1.12)}{.16 - .12}$$

$$= ₹\ 1.59 + ₹\ 6.65 = ₹\ 8.24.$$

46. Apex Industries is considering acquisition of RG Group in an equity for equity exchange. Assume that no immediate synergistic benefits are expected. Table below gives the select financial data on the two companies:

	Apex Industries	RG Group
Sales (₹ crore)	₹ 2000	₹ 1500
Earnings after taxes (₹ crore)	₹ 260	₹ 140
Equity issued (in crores)	₹ 100	₹ 60
EPS	₹ 2.50	₹ 3.50
Price per equity share	₹ 50	₹ 40
Dividends per share	₹ 1.50	₹ 1.00

(i) If Apex is not willing to incur an initial dilution in its EPS — that is, not have the postmerger EPS below ₹ 2.50— and if Apex also feels that it will have to offer the RG Group equity shareholders a minimum of 25% over RG Group's current market price, what is the relevant range of RG Group's per equity share price with which Apex is working?

(ii) Calculate Apex's postmerger EPS if the RG Group's shareholders accept an offer by the Apex of ₹ 50 in an equity - for - equity exchange.

Ans.

(i) Low end of range:

₹ 40 x 1.25 = ₹ 50

High end of range:

P_{nax} = (P/E) (EPS)

= (50/2.50) (3.50)

= ₹ 70

$$EPS_{Apex} = \frac{₹\ 260\ crore + ₹140\ crore}{100\ crore + 60\ crore} = \frac{₹\ 400\ crore}{160\ crore}$$

= ₹ 2.50

47. An investor expects the earnings and dividends on Apex Autos equity to gross at a rate of 20% per annum for the next five years. Following the period of above-normal growth, dividend are expected to grow at the slower rate of 12% for the foreseeable future. The firm currently pays a divided, Do, of ₹ 2.5 per share. What is the value of Apex's equity share to an investor who requires 24% rate of return?

Ans.

The PV of the dividends received during the growth period, year 1 through 5, is:

Value of Apex Autos Equity Share

Year	Dividend	PV Factor	PV
1.	₹ 2.5 $(1 + .20)^1 = 3$	0.806	2.42
2.	₹ 2.5 $(1 + 20)^2 = 3.6$	0.650	2.34
3.	₹ 2.5 $(1 + .20)^3 = 4.32$	0.524	2.26
4.	₹ 2.5 $(1 + .20)^4 = 5.18$	0.423	2.19
5.	₹ 2.5 $(1 + .20)^5 = 6.22$	0.341	2.12
			₹ 11.33

Value of Equity and End of years 5,

$$P_5 = \frac{D_6}{K_e - g_2}$$

$D_6 = D_5(1 + g_2)$

$= 6.22(1 + 0.12)$

$= ₹ 6.97$

$$\frac{₹ 6.97}{0.24 - 0.12}$$

$= ₹ 58.08$

$$PV(P_s) = \frac{₹ 58.08}{(1 + 0.24)^5}$$

$₹ 58.08(0.341)$

$= ₹ 19.81$

Value of Equity share, $P_0 = PV$ [First 5 years dividend $+ PV(P_s)$]

$P_0 = ₹ 11.33 + 19.81$

$= ₹ 31.14$

48. Super Computer Chips is experiencing a period of rapid growth. Earnings and dividends are expected to grow at a rate of 15 per cent during the next 2 years, at 13 per cent in the third year, and at a constant rate of 6 per cent thereafter. Super's last dividend was ₹ 1.15, and the required rate of return on the stock is 12 per cent.
   (a) Calculate the value of the stock today.
   (b) Calculate P_1 and P_2.
   (c) Calculate the dividend yield and capital gains yield for Years 1, 2, and 3.

Ans.

(a) (1) Calculate the PV of the dividends paid during the supernormal growth period:

$$D_1 = ₹ 1.1500(1.15) = ₹ 1.3225.$$
$$D_2 = ₹ 1.3225(1.15) = ₹ 1.5209.$$
$$D_3 = ₹ 1.5209(1.13) = ₹ 1.7186$$

$PV\ D = ₹ 1.3225(0.8929) + ₹ 1.5209(0.7972) + ₹ 1.7186(0.7118)$

$= ₹ 1.18909 + ₹ 1.2125 + ₹ 1.2233$

$= ₹ 3.6167 \approx ₹ 3.62.$

(2) Find the PV of Super's stock price at the end of Year 3:

$$\hat{P}_3 = \frac{D_4}{k_e - g} = \frac{D_3(1 + g)}{k_e - g}$$

$$= \frac{₹ 17186(1.06)}{0.12 - 0.06}$$

$= ₹ 30.36.$

$$PV\ \hat{P}_3 = ₹ 30.36(0.7118) = ₹ 21.61.$$

(3) Sum the two components to find the value of the stock today:

$$\hat{P}_0 = ₹ 3.62 + ₹ 21.61 = ₹ 25.23.$$

Alternatively, the cash flows can be placed on a time line as follows:

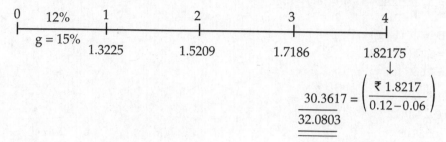

$$30.3617 = \left(\frac{₹\,1.8217}{0.12-0.06} \right)$$

$$\underline{32.0803}$$

Enter the cash flows into the cash flow register, I = 12, and press the NPV key to obtain $P_0 = ₹\ 25.23$.

(b) $\hat{P}_1$ = 1.5209(0.8929) + ₹ 1.7186(0.7972) + ₹ 30.36(0.7972)

    = ₹ 1.3580 + ₹ 1.3701 + ₹ 24.2030

    = ₹ 26.9311 ≈ ₹ 26.93

    $\hat{P}_2$ = ₹ 1.7186(0.8929) + ₹ 30.36(0.8929)

    = ₹ 1.5345 + ₹ 27.1084

    = ₹ 28.6429 ≈ ₹ 28.64

c. Year | Dividend Yield | + | Capital Gains Yield | = | Total Return

1. $\dfrac{₹\,1.3225}{25.23} \approx 5.24\%$ + $\dfrac{₹\,26.93 - ₹\,25.23}{₹\,25.23} \approx 6.74\%$ ≈   12%

2. $\dfrac{₹\,1.5209}{₹\,26.93} \approx 5.65\%$ + $\dfrac{₹\,28.64 - ₹\,26.93}{₹\,26.93} \approx 6.35\%$ ≈   12%

3. $\dfrac{₹\,1.7186}{₹\,28.64} \approx 6.00\%$ + $\dfrac{₹\,30.26 - ₹\,28.64}{₹\,28.64} \approx 6.00\%$ ≈   12%

49. XYZ Co. currently (Do) pays a ₹ 2 per share dividend is expected to grow at 25% annual rate over next three years and then to grow at 10% per year for the foreseeable future. What would you pay for a share of this stock if you demand a 40% rate of return?

Ans.

Present value of first 3 years dividends:

$D_0 = ₹\ 2.00\ g_1 = 0.25\ K_e = 40\%$

Year (1)	Dividend (2)	PV Interest factor (3)	PV 4 = (2) (3)
t	$D_t = ₹\ 2.00\ (1 + 0.25)^t$	$PV_{0.40}^t = 1$	$(1 + 0.40)^t$
1	₹ 2 $(1 + 0.25)^1 = 2.50$	0.714	1/79
2	₹ 2 $(1 + 0.25)^2 = 3.125$	0.514	1.61
3	₹ $(1 + 0.25)^3 = 3.906$	0.364	1.42
	PV (first three year dividend		4.82

Value of share at end of year 3

$$P_3 = \frac{D_4}{K_e g_2} \quad g_2 = 10$$

$$D_u = D_3 (1 + g_2) = ₹\ 3.906\ (1 + .10) = 4.297$$

$$P_3 = \frac{₹\ 4.297}{[(.40)-(.10)]} = ₹\ 14.322$$

PV of P_3

$$PV\ (P_3) = \frac{P_3}{(1+k)^3} = \frac{₹\ 14.32}{(1+0.40)^3}$$

$$= ₹\ 14.322\ PV_{0.40}t) = ₹\ 14.322\ (0.364)$$
$$= ₹\ 5.213$$

Value of equity share:

$$P_o = PV\ (\text{first 3 years dividend}) + PV\ (P_3)$$
$$= ₹\ 6 + ₹\ 5.213 = ₹\ 11.21s$$

53. Varun Textiles has expected dividend growth of 7% and the average market return is 12% per annum. Dividend expected end-year on Varun is ₹ 2.50. The company stock has $\beta = 2.00$ and the risk-free rate is 6%. What is the risk-adjusted rate of return on Varun assuming the CAPM holds? What is the fair price of the equity share if the current market price is ₹ 20? What are the risks attached to the investment strategy?

Ans.

Risk adjusted rate of return on Varun, using CAPM is:

$$ER_i = R_f + \beta_i\ (ER_m - R_f)$$
$$= 6\% + 2.00\ (12\% - 6\%)$$
$$= 18\%$$

Fair Value of Varun is:

$$V = D\ /\ (ER_i - g)$$
$$= ₹\ 2.50\ /\ (0.18 - 0.7)$$
$$= ₹\ 22.73$$

Since the Varun's equity is underpriced, the investor should buy the equity shares. But the CAPM measure ER_i may not hold for all future periods. If the market price diverge from the fair value, the demand for the Varun will shot up till there is equilibrium.

54. Following table contains some information about ABC Co. Calculate expected share prices using the P/E ratio, Price Cash Flow Ratios and Price Sales Ratios. Price Ratio Analysis for ABC Co. 2011 Mid-year Stock Price : ₹ 79.31

	Earnings [P/E]	Cash Flow [P/CF]	Sales [P/S]
Current value per share	₹ 2.66	₹ 9.92	₹ 32.21
Five=year average price ratio	35.2	10.3	2.4
Growth rate	10.4%	25.4%	25.1%

Ans.:

Applying the P/E approach, we come up with the following estimate of the price of ABC Co. in one year:

- Expected price = Average P/E x Current EPS x (1 + Growth Rate) = 35.2 x ₹ 2.66 x 1.104 = ₹ 103.37

Check that the price-cash flow and price-sales approaches give estimates of ₹ 128.13 and ₹ 96.71, respectively. All of these prices suggest that ABC Co. is potentially undervalued.

55. The risk free rate of return in 7.5%, based on an expected inflation premium of 4%. The expected rate of return on the market portfolio is 14%.

    (i) Determine the required rate of return on Chaman Group's equity share where rate is 1.25.

    (ii) Assume that the expected rate of return on the market portfolio remains constant but that the expected inflation premium increased from a current level of 4% to 5%. Determine the required rate of return on equity share of the Group.

    (iii) Assume that the expected inflation premium remain at 4% but that the expected return on the market portfolio increases to 16%. Determine the required rate of return on the group's equity share.

Ans.

    (i) $R_i = + \beta_i (R_m - R_f)$
        $= 7.5 + 1.25 (14 - 7.5)$
        $= 15.625$

    (ii) $R_i = 8.5 + 1.25 (14 - 8.5)$
        $= 15.375$

    (iii) $R_i = 7.5 + 1.25 (16 - 7.5)$
        $= 18.125$

56. Venkat Chemicals' equity has market risk premium is 5% over the risk-free rate (10%) and the spot rates from the yield curve are 12%, 15%, and 12%. Current dividend is ₹ 1.50 and expected dividend at end of year 1, 2 and 3 are ₹ 2.00, ₹ 2.75, ₹ 3.25 respectively. After year 3, expected dividend growth is likely to be 8.50%. Calculate the fair price of Venkat Chemicals. If the market price is ₹ 27.50 would you purchase / sell Venkat's equity.

Ans. The risk-adjusted rates of return is each year are give by:

$R_i = R_f + (R_m - R_f)$
$R_1 = 12\% + 5\% = 17\%$
$R_2 = 15\% + 5\% = 20\%$
$R_3 = 12\% + 5\% = 17\%$

The fair value (FV) using these required rates of return is:

$FV_o = ₹ 2.00/(1.17)1 + ₹ 2.75/(1.20)^2 + FV_3/(1.17)^3$
$FV_3 = D_3 (1+g)/(R_i - g)$
       $= 3.25 (1.085) / (0.17 - 0.085) = ₹ 41.485$

Hence:

$V_o = ₹ 2.00/((1.17)^1 + ₹ 2.75/(1.20)^2 + ₹ 41.485/(1.17)^3$
    $= ₹ 1.709 + ₹ 1.909 + ₹ 25.902$
    $= ₹ 29.52$

Sell the Venkat Chemical's equity since the current market price exceeded the fair value of ₹ 27.50.

QUESTIONS

1. Why is the valuation of equity different from that of debentures or preference shares, and what is the purpose of equity valuation?

2. What part do the growth rate of earnings, dividend, and the future P/E play in the valuation equation?
3. What would be the main emphasis in valuing a cyclical equity?
4. Explain and contrast: (a) Trend valuation equation; (b) Trend-Current valuation equation; (c) ABE valuation equation; and (d) Random valuation equation.
5. What is the significance of the P/E ratio, and how can it help determine whether the current price of an equity share is reasonable?
6. What is the relationship between the P/E ratio and risk?
7. (a) What P/E would be expected from the growth company ? Relate this to the discussion about the P/E ratios.
   (b) Would the P/E ratio of a speculative company be expected to be high, low, or normal? Explain.
   (c) What are the dangers involved in purchasing a high P/E ratio equity?
   (d) What kind of P/E ratio would be expected for a company with cyclical earnings?
   (e) What kind of P/E ratio would be expected for a company with a large amount of debt in capital structure?
   (f) The average P/E ratio permits a forecast of future price of the-equity based on future estimated earnings. Discuss
   (g) Would a high or low P/E ratio be expected if the company had a stable dividend policy?
8. Can one pay too much for a quality company?
9. Discuss the difference between the Top-down and Bottom-approaches. What is the major assumption that causes the difference in these two approaches?

PROBLEMS

1. Investors in the XYZ Company were paid ₹ 2.40 in dividends per share last year on their equity and these are expected to grow indefinitely at 12% rate. What is the value of the equity if the investors require an 18% return?
2. Ajanta Arts is expected to pay ₹1.75 in dividends to its equity shareholders next year and the market price is projected to be ₹52.50 by year end. If the investor required rate of return is 15%, what is the current value of the equity share?
3. S.D. Khera can buy equity shares that will pay ₹ 2.50 in dividends per share annually over the next three years. The earnings of the company are expected to grow, and the equity is expected to reach a price of ₹ 80 per share at the end of three years. This is a conservative investment, and Khera expects a return of 18%. What price should Khera pay for the share if he wants to earn 18%?
4. The market price for KDT equity shares is ₹ 43 per share. The price at the end of the year is expected to be ₹ 57, and dividends for next year should be ₹ 3.25. What is the expected rate of return?
5. An investor wants to buy equity shares of Sadhna Enterprises. The shares were traded at ₹ 284 yesterday. The company paid a dividend of ₹ 24 per share last year. Dividends have grown at 12% per year, and earning at 18% per year for the last five years. Earnings per share were ₹ 27.50 last year and are expected to be ₹ 35.00 this year. Earnings are expected to grow at a 20% rate next year and the year after, and the equity shares would enjoy a price earning ratio of 15. The company is likely to announce the bonus shares 2 for 1 shortly. Dividend should increase as they have in the past. What return would the investor earn for the investment if he purchased at ₹ 284 and held it for three years?.

6. FTX's equity shares are selling for ₹ 48.50 per share. Recently ₹ 2.85 were paid as dividend on per equity share and has a projected growth rate of 11.5%. If the investor purchases the equity shares at the market price, what is the investor's expected rate of return?

7. ABC Group paid ₹ 1.65 in dividends on its equity shares last year. Dividends are expected to grow at an 12% annual rate for an in definite number of years. If ABC Group's current market price is ₹ 32.50, what would be the expected rate of return on the equity share ? If the investor required rate of return is 17.50%, what is the value of the equity share for the investor? Should an investor make the investment?

8. Gold Star has been generating 10% less earnings for its equity shareholders in last few years. Given this depressing stage of affairs, all the earnings are paid to the equity shareholders. Earnings for this year just finished were ₹ 8 per share, and the corresponding dividend were just paid. If investors require 18% return from Gold Star, what is the current equity price? What will be its price in two years?

Ans: ₹ 25.71

9. C-Tech has decided not to pay any dividends on its equity for the next six years, but direct all its resources to R&D. In year seven, it will pay a dividend of ₹ 4.50 per share, and each year thereafter, it will increase its dividend by 3%. If the required rate on C-Tech equity is 17%, what is its current stock price?

Ans: ₹ 12.53.

10. RFC Industries is experiencing a period of very fast growth and expects to increase its earnings by 12% annually for the next 10 years. After that period, earnings will increase by 5% forever. Next year's earnings are expected to be ₹ 12 per share. If the annual discount rate is 10%, what is RFG's current price?

Ans: ₹ 387.89

11. An equity share is currently worth ₹ 60. Dividend payments are expected to grow at 6% forever. What do you expect the price of this share to be in five ears.

Ans: ₹ 80.29

12. An investor estimates that a firm will have the following dividend for the next three periods: ₹ 1.17, ₹ 1.44 and ₹ 1.88. After these, the investor expects dividends to grow at their long-term rate of 3%. What is the share price according to the dividend valuation model? What would it be if the long-term growth rate were 5%? Assume a discount rate of 10%.

Ans: ₹ 33.32

13. Consider a firm that pays a dividend of ₹ 5 in the next period and has a growth rate of 11% for the next 4 years. What are the dividends for these periods? Assume that the firm will never pay any dividends beyond the fifth year. According to the dividend valuation model, what would be the price of this share? The discount rate is 15%.

Ans: ₹ 28.50

14. It is now August 1, 2010. Last year, National Coal suffered a major strike which had a disastrous effect on the firm's financial condition, forcing management to temporarily suspend dividend payments. It is expected that the firm will not pay a dividend in 2010 or 2011, but it will declare a ₹ 5.00 dividend in 2012. Dividend growth is expected to be 3% in 2013 and 2014, and thereafter dividends are expected to grow indefinitely at the same rate as the national economy, 6 percent. The required rate of return on the stock is 15 percent.

    (a)   Calculate the expected dividends for 2010 through 2015.

    (b)   Find the value of the stock today.

    (c)   Calculate the current yield, the capital gains yield expected in 2010. Also, calculate these same three yields for 2011 and 2012. Assume that the stock is in equilibrium.

    (d)   What is the impact of zero dividends on the return mix, that is, on the relative values of dividend yield versus capital gains yield? Would an investor's tax situation influence the value of such stocks?

Ans: (a) ₹ 0; ₹ 0; ₹ 5.0; ₹ 5.15; ₹ 5.30; ₹ 5.62.

     (b) ₹ 39.9.

     (c) 0.0%; 15.0%; 15.0% 0.0%; 15.0%; 15.0% 9.5%; 5.5%; 15.0%

15. ABC Company's ore reserves are being depleted, and its cost of recovering a declining quantity of ore are rising each year. As a result, company's earnings and dividends are declining at the constant rate of 10 percent per year.

    (a)   If $D_0 = ₹ 6$ and cost of equity (Ke) = 15%, what is the value of ABC Company's stock?

    (b)   Explain why any one would be willing to buy a stock whose price is expected to fall over time.

Ans: (a) ₹ 21.60

16. Vinay Auto's next annual dividend is forecast to be ₹ 2.00, and the firm is expected to grow at a constant annual rate of 6 percent indefinitely. Investors require a return of 15% on this stock.

    (a)   What is the stock's intrinsic value?

    (b)   What is Vinay's intrinsic, value using the quarterly growth model?

    (c)   Explain why your answers to part (a) and part (b) are different.

Ans: (a) ₹ 22.22

     (b) ₹ 23.44

17. It is now August 1, 2011. Ventura Engineering has just developed a solar panel capable of generating 200 percent more electricity than any solar panel currently on the market. As a result, the firm is expected to experience a 10 percent annual growth rate for the next 5 years. By the end of 5 years, other firms will have developed comparable technology, and Ventura's growth rate will slow to 8 percent per year indefinitely. Stockholders require a return of 12 percent on the firm's stock. The most recent annual dividend (D_0) which was paid last week, was ₹ 1.50 per share.

    (a)   Calculate the expected dividends for 2011 through 2016.

    (b)   Calculate the value of the stock today.

    (c)   Calculate the current dividends yield. D_0/P_0, the capital gains yield expected in 2011 and the expected total return (dividend yield plus capital gains yield) for 2011. Also, calculate these same three yields for 2015.

    (d)   Suppose your boss tells you that he believes that the firm's annual growth rate will be only 15% over the next 5 years, and that the firm's normal growth rate is only 6%. Calculate the expected dividend stream and the value of the stock today under these assumptions.

    (e)   Suppose your boss also tells you that he regards Ventura as being quite risky, and that he feels that the required rate of return is 15%, not 12%. Calculate the value of the firm's stock. Do the calculations with cost of equity value of 20% and 25% to see how cost of equity value affects the stock price.

Ans: (a) ₹ 1.95; ₹ 2.54; ₹ 3.30; ₹ 4.28; ₹ 5.57; ₹ 6.01.

(b) ₹ 97.32

(c) 2.0%; 10.0%; 12.0%; 4.0%; 8.0%; 12.0%

(d) ₹ 1.73; ₹ 1.98; ₹ 2.28; ₹ 2.62.; ₹ 3.02; ₹ 3.20; ₹ 38.37.

(e) ₹ 25.17; ₹ 15.79; ₹ 11.40.

REFERENCES

1. Aber, John. "Industry Effects and Multivariate Stock Price Behavior." *Journal of Financial and Quantitative Analysis* 11, no. 5 (November 1976).

2. Ahlers, David M., "SEM: A Security Analysis Model," in Kalman J. Cohen and Frederick S, Hammer, eds., *Analytical Methods in Banking* (Homewood, III. Irwin, 1966).

3. Akemann, Charles A., and Werner E. Keller, "Relative Strength Does Persist!" *Journal of Portfolio Management*, Fall 1977, pp. 38-45.

4. Akgeray, V.: "Conditional Heteroscedasticity in Time Series of Stock Returns: Evidence and Forecasts," *Journal of Business*, January 1989, pp. 55-70.

5. Alexander, Gordon J. "Applying the Market Model to Long-Term Corporate Bonds." *Journal of Financial and Quantitative Analysis* 15, no. 5 (December 1980).

6. Altman, Edward I., and Scott A. Nammacher. *Investing in Junk Bonds.* New York: John Wiley & Sons. 1987.

7. Altman. Edward I., ed. *The High Yield Debt Market.* Homewood, III.: Dow Jones-lrwin. 1990.

8. Babcock, Guilford C. "The Concept of Sustainable Growth." *Financial Analysts Journal* 26, no. 3 (May-June 1970).

9. ————————————-"When Is Growth Sustainable?" *Financial Analysts Journal,* May-June 1970, p. 108.

10. Bajkowski, John. "From Theory to Reality: Applying the Valuation Models," *AAII Journal* (January 1993):34~38.

11. Baker, H. Kent, Aaron L. Phillips, and Gary E. Powell. "The Stock Distribution Puzzle: A Synthesis of the Literature on Stock Splits and Stock Dividends." *Financial Practice and Education* (spring/summer 1995): 24-37.

12. Baker, H. Kent, and Patricia L. Gallagher. "Management's View of Stock Splits." *Financial Management* (summer 1980): 73-77.

13. ————————————, Gail E. Farrelly, and Richard B. Edelman. "A Survey of Management Views on Dividend Policy." *Financial Management* (autumn 1985): 78-84.

14. Ball, Clifford, and Walter Tarous: "The Maximum Likelihood Estimation of Security Price Volatility: Theory, Evidence, and Application to Option Pricing," *Journal of Business,* January 1984, pp. 97-112.

15. Ball, Ray, and Ross Watts. "Some Time Series Properties of Accounting Earnings Numbers." *Journal of Finance* 27, no. 3 (June 1972).

16. Banz, R.W. "The Relationship Between Return and Market Value of Common Stocks." *Journal of Financial Economics 9, no.* 1 (March 1981). Basu, Senjoy. "Investment Performance of Common Stocks in Relation to Their Price-Earnings Ratios: A Test of the Efficient Market Hypothesis." *Journal of Finance* 32, no. 3 (June 1977).

17. Bar Yosef, S., and R. Kolodny, "Dividend Policy and Capital Market Theory," *Review of Economics and Statistics* (May 1976), 181-90.

18. Basu, S., "Investment Performance of Common Stocks in Relation to Their Price-Earnings Ratios: A Test of the Efficient Market Hypothesis," *Journal of Finance* 32 (June 1977)-.663-682.

19. Basu, Senjoy. "The Relationship Between Earnings Yield, Market Value and Return for NYSE Common Stocks." *Journal of Financial Economics* 12, no. 1 (June 1983).

20. Beaver, W., P. Ketler, and M. Scholes: "The Association Between Market Determined and Accounting Determined Risk Measures," *Accounting Review,* October 1970, pp. 654-682.

21. —————————, and Dale Morse. "What Determines Price-Earnings Ratios?" *Financial Analysts Journal* 34, no. 4 (July-August 1978).

22. Beidleman. Carl. ed. *The Handbook of International Investing.* Chicago: Probus Publishing. 1987.

23. Belkaoui, Ahmed. "Industrial Bond Ratings: A New Look." *Financial Management* 9. no. 3 (Autumn 1980).

24. Benesh, Gary A., and Pamela P. Peterson. "On the Relation Between Earnings Changes, Analysts' Forecasts and Stock Price Fluctuations." *Financial Analysts Journal* 42, no. 6 (November-December 1986).

25. Black, Fischer, "The Dividend Puzzle," *Journal of Portfolio Management,* Winter 1976, pp. 5-8.

26. —————————, and M. Scholes, "The Effects of Dividend Yield and Dividend Policy on Common Stock Prices and Returns," *Journal of Financial* Economics, 20 (May 1974), 1-22.

27. Boquist, John, George Racette, and Gary Schlarbaum, "Duration and Risk Assessment for Bonds and Common Stocks," *Journal of Finance,* 30 (December 1975), 1360-1365.

28. Born, Jeffery, James Moses, and Dennis Officer. "Changes in Dividend Policy and Subsequent Earnings." *Journal of Portfolio Management* 14, no. 4 (Summer 1988).

29. Bower, Dorothy H., and Richard S. Bower. "Test of a Stock Valuation Model." *The Journal of Finance,* May 1970, p. 483.

30. Brealey, Richard A., *Security Prices in a Competitive Market* (Cambridge, Mass.: M.I.T. Press, 1971).

31. Brigham, Eugene F., and Myron J. Gordon, "Leverage, Dividend Policy, and the Cost of Capital," *Journal of Finance,* March 1968, pp. 85-103.

32. Brown, Philip, and Ray Ball. "Some Preliminary Findings on the Association Between the Earnings of a Firm, Its Industry, and the Economy." *Empirical Research in Accounting: Selected Studies 1967,* supplement to vol. 5. *Journal of Accounting Research.*

33. Chen, Nui-Fu, Richard Roll, and Stephen A. Ross. "Economic Forces and the Stock Market." *Journal of Business* 59, no. 3 (July 1986).

34. Christie, Andrew: "The Stochastic Behavior of Common Stock Variances: Value, Leverage and Interest Rate Effects," *Journal of Financial Economics,* December 1982, pp. 407-432.

35. Churchman, C. West, "An Analysis of the Concept of Simulation," in Austin C. Hoggatt and Frederick E. Balderston, eds.. *Symposium on Simulation Models Methodologv and Applications to the Behavioral Sciences* (Cincinnati: South-Western 1963).

36. Clayman, Michelle. "In Search of Excellence: The Investor's Viewpoint," *Financial Analysts Journal* 43, no. 3 (May-June 1987).

37. Cohen, Kalman J., and Richard M. Cyert, "Computer Models in Dynamic Economic *Quarterly Journal of Economics,* February 1961, pp. 112-127.

38. Cole, James F. "What About the Anatomy of the Stock." *Financial Analysts Journal,* November-December 1977.

39. Copeland, Tom, Time Koller, and Jack Murrin. *Valuation: Measuring and Managing the Value of Companies.* 2d ed. New York: John Wiley & Sons, 1994.

40. Cottle, Sidney, Roger F. Murray, and Frank E. Block. *Graham and Dodd's Security Analysis.* 5th ed. New York: McGraw-Hill, 1988.

41. Cowen, Scott, and Jeffrey Hoffer: "Usefulness of Financial Ratios in a Single Industry," *Journal of Business Research,* March 1982, pp. 103-118.

42. Cragg. John G., and Burton G. Malkiel, "The Consensus and Accuracy of Some Predictions of the Growth of Corporate Earnings," *Journal of Finance,* March 1968, pp. 67-84.

43. Curran, Ward S. "Preferred Stock for Public Utilities." *Financial Analysts Journal,* July-August 1969, p. 112.

44. Cusatis, Patrick, James Miles, and Randall Woolridge: "Restructuring through Spin-offs," *Journal of Financial Economics,* June 1993, pp. 293-312.

45. Dann, Larry Y. "Common Stock Repurchases: An Analysis of Returns to Bondholders and Stockholders." *Journal of Financial Economics* (June 1981): 113-138.

46. Donaldson, G. "In Defense of Preferred Stock." *Harvard Business Review*, 40{July-August 1962). Reprinted in *Foundations for Financial Management*, ed. James Van Home, pp. 194-218. Homewood, Ill.: Irwin, 1966.

47. Drew, Garfield A. *New Methods for Profit in the Stock Market.* Wells, Vt.: Fraser Publishing, 1966.

48. Durand, David. "Growth Stocks and the Petersburg Paradox." *Journal of Finance* XII (September 1957), pp. 348-63.

49. Eisemaun, Peter C., and Edward A. Moses. "Stock Dividend: Management View." *Financial Analysts Journal*, July-August 1978.

50. Eiteman, David K.., "A Computer Program for Common Stock Valuation," *Financial Analysts Journal*, July-August 1968, pp. 107-111.

51. Elton Edwin J.. and Martin J. Gruber: "Estimating the Dependence Structure of Share Prices— Implications for Portfolio Selection," *Journal of Finance.* December 1973. pp. 1203-1232.

52. —————————————-, "The Effect of Share Repurchase on the Value of the Firm," *Journal of Finance.* March 1968.

53. Fama, Eugene F. "Stock Market Price Behavior, Efficient Capital Markets: A Review of Theory and Empirical Work." *The Journal of Finance*, September 1970, p. 383.

54. —————————————-, "Components of Investment Performance." *The Journal of Finance*, June 1972, p. 551.

55. ——————-, and Kenneth French. "Dividend Yields and Expected Stock Returns." *Journal of Financial Economics* 22, no. 1 (October 1988).

56. —————————————-, "The Cross-Section of Expected Stock Returns." *Journal of Finance* 47, no. 2 (June 1992).

57. Farrell, James L. "The Dividend Discount Model: A Primer." *Financial Analysts Journal* 41, no. 6 (November-December 1985).

58. Ferguson, Robert. "How to Beat the Index Funds." *Financial Analysts Journal*, May-June 1975, pp. 63-72.

59. Fewings, David: 'The Impact of Corporate Growth on the Risk of Common Stocks," *Journal of Finance*, May 1975, pp. 525-531.

60. Fisher, Lawrence, and James H. Lorie. *A Half Century of Returns on Stock and Bonds.* Chicago: The University of Chicago School of Business, 1977.

61. Foster, George, Chris Olsen, and Terry Shevlin. "Earnings Releases, Anomalies, and the Behavior of Security Returns." *Accounting Review* 59, no. 4 (October 1984).

62. Franks, Julian, Robert Harris, and Sheridan Titman: "The Postmerger Share-Price Performance of Acquiring Firms," *Journal of Financial Economics*, March 1991, pp. 81-96.

63. French, Kenneth R. "Stock Returns and the Weekend Effect." *Journal of Financial Economics* 8, no. 1 (March 1980).

64. Friend, Irwin, and Marshall Puckett, "Dividends and Stock Prices," *American Economic Review*, September 1964, pp. 656-682.

65. Fruhan, William E., Jr. *Financial Strategy.* Homewood, Ill.: Richard D. Irwin, 1979.

66. Fuller, Russ: "Programming the Three-Phase Dividend Discount Model," *Journal of Portfolio Management*, Summer 1979, pp. 28-32.

67. Giberti, Daniela, Marcello Mentini, and Pietro Scabellone, "The Valuation of Credit Risk in Swaps: Methodological Issues and Empirical Results." *The Journal of Fixed Income* 2, no. 4 (March 1993).

68. Gordon, Myron J. *The Investment, Financing, and Valuation of the Corporation.* Homewood, Ill.: Richard D. Irwin, 1962.

69. Graham, Benjamin. "The Future of Common Stocks." *Financial Analysts Journal*, September-October 1974, p. 20.

70. Hackel, Kenneth S., and Joshua Livnat. *Cash Flow and Security Analysis* (Homewood, Ill.: Business One-Irwin, 1992).

71. Hamada, Robert: "The Effect of the Firm's Capital Structure on the Systematic Risk of Common Stocks," *Journal of Finance,* May 1971, pp. 435-452.

72. Hassel, J., and Robert Jennings. "Relative Forecast Accuracy and the Timing of Earnings Forecast Announcements." *The Accounting Review* 61, no. 1 (January 1986).

73. Hertz, David B., "Risk Analysis in Capital Investment," *Harvard Business Review* January-February 1964, pp. 95-106.

74. Hillier, Frederick S., "The Derivation of Probabilistic Information for the Evaluations of Risky Investments," *Management Science,* April 1963, pp. 443-457.

75. Holmes, John R. "Growth, Risk, and Stock Valuation." *Financial Analysts Journal,* May-June 1976, pp. 46-55.

76. Holt, Charles C.: "The Influence of Growth Duration on Share Price," *Journal of Finance,* September 1961, pp. 465-475.

77. Homer, Sidney, and Martin L. Leibowitz. *Inside the Yield Book.* Englewood Cliffs, N.J.: Prentice-Hall, 1972.

78. Houston, John L. "Common Stock Repurchases: A Bane or Boon to Shareholders." AAII *Journal* (February 1984): 7-10.

79. Howe, Jane Tripp. *Junk Bonds: Analysis and Portfolio Strategies.* Chicago: Probus Publishing, 1988.

80. Imhoff, Eugene, and G. Lobo. "Information Content of Analysts Composite Forecast Revisions." *Journal of Accounting Research* 22, no. 3 (Autumn 1984).

81. Jaffe, Jeffery, Donald Keim, and Randolph Westerfield. "Earnings Yields, Market Values, Stock Returns." *Journal of Finance* 44, no. 1 (March 1989).

82. Jahnke. William: 'The Growth Stock Mania," *Financial Analysts Journal,* May-June 1973, pp. 65-69.

83. ———": What's Behind Stock Prices?" *Financial Analysts Journal,* September-October 1975, pp. 69-76.

84. Jennings, Robert. *Reaction of Financial Analysts to Corporate Management Earnings per Share Forecasts.* Financial Analysts Research Foundation, Monograph No. 20, (New York, 1984).

85. Johnson, Lewis: "The Role of Convexity in Equity Pricing," *Financial Analysts Journal,* September-October 1992, pp. 69-73.

86. ———, "Equity Duration: Another Look," *Financial Analysts Journal,* March-April 1989, pp. 73-75.

87. Johnson, R.S., Lyle Fiore, and Richard Zuber. "The Investment Performance of Common Stocks in Relation to Their Price-Earnings Ratios: An Update of the Basu Study." *Financial Review* 24, no. 3 (August 1989).

88. Joy, O. Maurice, and Charles P. Jones, "Predictive Value of P/E Ratios." *Financial Analysts Journal,* September-October 1970, p. 61.

89. Kaplan, R., and R. W. Roll. "Accounting Changes and Stock Prices." *Financial Analysts Journal,* January-February 1973, p. 48.

90. Keenan, W. Michael. "Toward a Positive Theory of Equity Valuation." *The Journal of Finance,* March 1968, p. 197.

91. Keim, Donald B. "Dividend Yields and Stock Returns: Implications of Abnormal January Returns." *Journal of Financial Economics* 14, no. 3 (September 1985).

92. ———, "Size-Related Anomalies and Stock Return Seasonality." *Journal of Financial Economics* 12, no. 1 (June 1983).

93. Keim, Donald B. "The CAPM and Equity Return Regularities." *Financial Analysts Journal* 41, no. 3 (May-June 1986).

94. ———, and Robert F. Stambaugh. "Predicting Returns in Stock and Bond Markets." *Journal of Financial Economics* 17, no. 2 (December 1986).

95. King, Benjamin F. "Market and Industry Factors in Stock Price Behavior." *Journal of Business* 39, no. 1, Part II (January 1966).

96. Lang, L., Rene Stulz, and Ralph Walking: "A Test of the Free Cash Flow Hypothesis: The Case of Bidder Returns," *Journal of Financial Economics,* October 1991, pp. 315-336.

97. Leibowitz, Martin, and Stanley Kogelman: "Resolving the Equity Duration Paradox," *Financial Analysts Journal,* January-February 1993, pp. 51-67.

98. ————————————, and Eric Sorenson, Robert Arnott, and Nicholes Hanson: "A Total Differential Approach to Equity Duration," *Financial Analysts Journal,* September-October 1989, pp. 30-37.

99. Levine, Sumner N. *The Financial Analysts Handbook.* 2d ed. Homewood, Ill.: Dow Jones-Irwin, 1988.

100. Levy, Robert A. "Beta as a Predictor of Return." *Financial Analysts Journal,* January-February 1974, p. 61.

101. ————————————, "On the Safety of Low P/E Stocks." *Financial Analysts Journal,* January-February 1973, pp. 57-63.

102. Lintner, John. "Distribution of Incomes of Corporations among Dividends, Retained Earnings and Taxes." *The American Economic Review,* May 1956.

103. Litzenberger, Robert H., and K. Ramaswamy, "The Effect of Personal Taxes and Dividends Capital Asset Prices," *Journal of Financial* Economics, 7 (1979), 1653-95.

104. ————————————, "Dividends, Short Selling Restrictions, Tax-Induced Investor Clienteles and Market Equilibrium," *Journal of Finance,* 35 (May 1980), 469-82.

105. ————————————, and O. Maurice Joy. "Further Evidence on the Persistence of Corporate Profitability Rates." *Western Economic Journal,* June 1970. pp. 209-212.

106. Livingston, Miles. "Industry Movements of Common Stocks." *Journal of Finance* 32, no. 3 (June 1977).

107. Malkiel, Burton G.: "Equity Yields, Growth, and the Structure of Share Prices," *American Economic Review,* December 1963, pp. 467-494.

108. ————————————, and R.E. Quandt. "The Supply of Money and Common Stock Prices: Comment." *The Journal of Finance,* September 1972, pp. 921-26.

109. ————————————, and John Cragg. "Expectations and the Structure of Share Prices." *American Economic Review* 60, no. 4 (September 1970).

110. Mao. James C.T., "The Valuation of Growth Stocks: The Investment Opportunities Approach." *Journal of Finance.* March 1966, pp. 95   102.

111. Markese, John. "A Fundamental Guide to Common Stock Valuation," *AAII Journal* (January 1993):30-33.

112. Masson. Robert, "Executive Motivations, Earnings, and Consequent Equity Performance," *Journal of Political Economy.* November-December 1971, pp. 127,8-1292.

113. McGough, Eugene F. "Anatomy of a Stock Split." *Management Accounting* (September 1993): 58-61.

114. McNichols, M., and A. David. "Stock Dividends, Stock Splits, and Signalling." *Journal of Finance* (July 1990): 857-879.

115. Meyers, Stephen L. "A Re-Examination of Market and Industry Factors in Stock Price Behavior." *Journal of Finance* 28, no. 3 (June 1973).

116. Miller, Merton H., and Franco Modigliani. "Dividend Policy, Growth and the Valuation of Shares." *The Journal of Business* XXXIV (October 1961), pp. 411-33.

117. ————————————, and M. Scholes, "Dividends and Taxes," *Journal of Financial Economics, 7* (December 1978), 333-64.

118. ————————————, "Rate of Return in Relation to Risk: A Reex-amination of Some Recent Findings," in Studies m *the Theory of Capital Markets,* ed. M. Jensen, pp. 47-78. New York: Praeger, 1972.

119. Mitchell, Mark: "The Value of Corporate Takeovers," *Financial Analysts Journal,* January—February 1990, pp. 21-31.

120. ——————————, and Harold Mulhern: "The Stock Price Response to Pension Terminations and the Relation of Terminations with Corporate Takeovers," *Financial Management*, Autumn, 1989, pp. 41-56.

121. Modigliani, Franco, and M. Miller, "Corporate Income Taxes and the Cost of Capital: A Correction," *American Economic Review*, 52 (June 1963), 433-42.

122. ——————————, "The Cost of Capital, Corporation Finance, and the Theory of Investment," *American Economic Review*, June 1958, pp. 261-297.

123. Murphy, Joseph E., Jr., and J. Russell Melson. "Stability of P/E Ratios." *Financial Analysts Journal*, March-April 1969, p. 77.

124. Nagorniak, John J. "Thoughts on Using Dividend Discount Models." *Financial Analysts Journal* 41, no. 6 (November-December 1985).

125. Niederhoffer, Victor, and Patrick J. Regan. "Earnings Changes, Analysts' Forecasts, and Stock Prices." *Financial Analysts Journal*, May-June 1972, pp. 65-71.

126. Ofer, Aharon R.. "Investors' Expectations of Earnings Growth. Their Accuracy and Effects on the Structure of Realized Rates of Return," *Journal of Finance* May 1975, pp. 509-523.

127. Olsen, John A., and Terry A. Blaney, "Forecasting by Probabilities: The Copper Industry," *Financial Analysts Journal*, March-April 1968, pp. 36-40.

128. Orcutt, Guy H., "Simulation of Economic Systems," *American Economic Review*, December 1960, pp. 893-907.

129. Peterson, Pamela P., and D. R. Peterson, "Divergence of Opinion and Return," *Journal of Financial Research*, 5 (Summer 1982), 125-34.

130. Pettit, R. Richardson, "Dividend Announcements, Security Performance, and Capital Market Efficiency," *Journal of Finance*, December 1972, pp. 993-1008.

131. Pinches, George E., and William R. Kinney, Jr. "The Measurement of the Volatility of Common Stock Prices." *The Journal of Finance*, March 1971, p. 119.

132. Pozeu, Robert C. "When to Purchase a Protective Put." *Financial Analysts Journal*, July-August 1978.

133. Price, Lee H. "Choosing Between Growth and Yield." *Financial Analysts Journal*, July-August 1979.

134. ——————————, "Growth or Yield: The Choice Depends on Your Tax Rate." *Financial Analysts Journal*, July-August 1979.

135. Radcliffe, R.C., and W.G. Gillespie. "The Price Impact of Reverse Splits." *Financial Analysts Journal*, January-February 1979.

136. Redington, F. M. "Review of the Principle of Life—Office Valuations." *Journal of the Institute of Actuaries.* 78 (1952).

137. Reilly, Frank K. "Stock Price Changes by Market Segment." *Financial Analysts Journal*, March-April 1971, p. 54.

138. —————————— "The Misdirected Emphasis in Security Valuation." *Financial Analysts Journal* 29, no. 1 (January-February 1973).

139. ——————————, and Eugene Drzycimski. "Alternative Industry Performance and Risk." *Journal of Financial and Quantitative Analysis* 9, no. 3 (June 1974).

140. Richards, R. Malcolm. "Analysts Performance and the Accuracy of Corporate Earnings Forecasts." *Journal of Business* 49:3 (July 1976). pp. 350-357.

141. Rie, Daniel, "How Trustworthy Is Your Valuation Model?" *Financial Analysts Journal* 41, no. 6 (November-December 1985).

142. Robichek, Alexander A., and Marcus C. Bogue. "A Note on the Behavior of Expected Price/Earnings Ratio over Time." *The Journal of Finance*, June 1971, p. 731.

143. Rodriguez, Tita N. "Measuring Multinationals Exchange Risk." *Financial Analysts Journal*, November-December 1979.

144. Shaked, Israel. "International Equity Markets and the Investment Horizon." *Journal of Portfolio Management* 11, no. 2 (Winter 1985).

145. Sharpe, W; F., *Investments, 2nd* ed. Englewood Cliffs, N.J.: Prentice-Hall, 1981.

146. ——————————, and H.B. Sosin. "Risk Return and Yield on Common Stocks." *Financial Analysts Journal,* March-April 1976, pp. 33-42.

147. Shiskin, Julius. "Systematic Aspects of Stock Price Fluctuations." Reprinted in James Lorie and Richard Brealey, *Modern Developments in Investment Management.* 2d ed. Hinsdale, III.: The Dryden Press, 1978.

148. Shubik, Martin, "Simulation of the Industry and the Firm," *American Economic Review,* December 1960, pp. 908-919.

149. Slivka, Ronald T. "Risk and Return for Option Investment Strategies." *Financial Analysts Journal,* September-October 1980.

150. Spudeck, R.E., and R. Charles Moyer. "Reverse Splits and Shareholder Wealth: The Impact of Commissions." *Financial Management* (winter 1985): 52-56.

151. Staubus, George J., "Earnings Periods for Common Share Analysis," *Journal of Business,* October 1968, pp. 472-476.

152. Stekler, H.O., *Profitability and Size of Firm* (Berkeley: University of California Institute of Business and Economic Research, 1963).

153. ____, "The Variability of Profitability with *Size* of Firm, 1947-1958," *Journal of the American Statistical Association,* December 1964, pp. 1183-1193.

154. Stewart, Samuel S. "Forecasting Corporate Earnings." In *The Financial Analysts Handbook.* 2d ed., edited by Sumner N. Levine. Homewood, III.: Dow Jones-Irwin, 1988.

155. Van Home, James C. *Financial Market Rates and Flows.* 3d ed. Englewood Cliffs, N.J.: Prentice-Hall, 1989.

156. Vandell, R.F., and J. Stevens, "Personal Taxes and Equity Security Pricing," *Financial Management,* Spring 1982, pp. 31-40.

157. Vandell, Robert F., and J.L. Stevens, "Personal Taxes and Equity Security Pricing," *Financial Management,* 11 (Spring 1982), 31-40.

158. Viner, Aron. *Inside Japanese Financial Markets.* Homewood, III.: Dow Jones-lrwin, 1988.

159. Walter, James E. "Dividend Policies and Common Stock Prices." *The Journal of Finance,* March 1965.

160. Walter, James E. "Dividend Policies and Common Stock Prices." *The Journal of Finance,* March 1965.

161. Walter. James E., "Dividend Policy: Its Influence on the Value of the Enterprise," *Journal of Finance,* May 1963, pp. 280-291.

162. Warren, James M., and John P. Shelton, "A Simultaneous Equation Approach to Financial Planning." *Journal of Finance.* December 1971. pp. 1123 -1142.

163. Waymire, G. "Additional Evidence on the Information Content of Management Earnings Forecasts." *Journal of Accounting Research* 22, no. 3 (Autumn 1984).

164. Wendt, Paul F. "Current Growth Stock Valuation Methods." *Financial Analysts Journal,* March-April 1965, pp. 91-103.

165. Whitbeck, Volkert S., and Manown Kisor. "A New Tool in Investment Decision-Making." *Financial Analysts Journal,* May-June 1963, pp. 55-62.

166. Whittall, David, "A Simulation Model for Estimating Earnings," *Financial Analysts Journal.* November December 1968. pp. 115- 118.

167. Williams, John Burr. *The Theory of Investment Value.* Cambridge, Mass.: Harvard University Press, 1938.

168. Wilson, Richard S. *Corporate Senior Securities.* Chicago: Probus Publishing, 1987.

169. ——————————, and Frank J. Fabozzi. *The New Corporate Bond Market.* Chicago: Probus Publishing, 1990.

170. Winkelmann, Kurt. "Uses and Abuses of Duration and Convexity." *Financial Analysts Journal* 45, no. 5 (September-October 1989).

171. Woolridge, J.R., and D.R. Chambers. "Reverse Splits and Shareholder Wealth." *Financial Management* (autumn 1983): 5-15.

172. Yago, Glenn. *Junk Bonds.* New York: Oxford University Press, 1991.

14

Private Equity and Venture Capital

INTRODUCTION

India is on the threshold of a high technology revolution and new entrepreneurial growth. The last years of the twentieth century created a technology base which propel us towards dramatic unanticipated achievements. Much of the drive for this technical surge is due to the technical entrepreneur. They are taking concepts from the laboratories and turning them into products and markets. Breakthrough developments in biotechnology, electronics, robotics, materials, computer science, artificial intelligence and medicine, will soon change the way. In the context, the advent of private equity (PE) and venture capital (VC) industry has energized the entrepreneurial climate in India. They have been facilitating the productive use of existing assets and resources, usually by identifying companies with untapped potential and reorganizing their operations in ways that increase their value. In fact, the concept of financial inclusion agents may be extended beyond the purview of banks to include enterprises like 'private equity firms' which can commit much needed and timely financial assistance to sectors like small and medium industries, infrastructure sector with long gestation periods and excess capacities in the short run, high value agriculture investments *etc*. With India aiming at more than 9.0 per cent growth and a lot more scope remaining for infrastructure development, private equity investment will have a seminal role to play in the coming years. However, the rapid growth and globalization of the PE industry has raised demands for increased regulation and disclosure within the sector due to concerns regarding anti-competitive behavior, excessive tax benefits and stock manipulation. However, there is a popular discourse as how much restriction is optimum restriction for an evolving industry. This question is particularly important for India. At present the industry is largely self regulated. In India, the quality and end-use of foreign PE capital is well regulated under foreign direct investment (FDI) norms.

RUDIMENTS OF PRIVATE EQUITY (PE)

Private equity is a broad term that commonly refers to any type of equity investment in an asset in which the equity is not freely tradeable on a stock market. More accurately, private equity refers to the manner in which the funds have been raised, namely on the private markets, as opposed to the public markets. Private equity firms were commonly misunderstood to invest in assets which were not in the public market. However this is not necessarily the case—larger private equity firms invest in companies listed on exchanges and take them private. Passive institutional investors may invest in private equity funds, which are in turn used by private equity firms for investment in target companies over medium or long-term—to nonquoted companies with high growth potential. It is also called *'patient capital'* as it seeks to profit from long-term capital gains rather than short-term regular disbursements. Categories of private equity investment include *leveraged buyout, venture capital, growth capital, angel investing, mezzanine (bridge) capital* and others. Private equity funds typically control management of the companies in which they invest, and often bring in new management teams that focus on making the company more valuable.

Market Structure and Activities of PE

Virtually, all private equity firms are organized as limited partnerships where private equity firms serve as general partners and large institutional investors and high net worth individuals providing bulk of the capital serve as limited partners. Typically such partnerships last for 10 years and partnership agreements signed at the funds inception clearly define the expected payments to general partners.

Types of private equity activities in terms of the stages of corporate development, where PE financing is called for, can be categorised as follow:

1. *Seed Financing*: Providing small sums of capital necessary to develop a business idea.

2. *Start-up financing*: Providing capital required for product development and initial marketing activities.

3. *First-stage*: Financing the commercialization and production of products.

4. *Second-stage*: Providing working capital funding and required financing for young firms during growth period.

5. *Third-stage*: Financing the expansion of growth companies.

6. *Bridge financing*: Last financing round prior to an initial public offering of a company.

7. *PIPE deals*: A private investment in public equity, often called a PIPE deal, involves the selling of publicly traded equity shares or some form of preferred stock or convertible security to private investors.

8. *Leveraged Buyout (LBO)*: It entails the purchase of a company by a small group of investors, especially buyout specialists, largely financed by debt.

9. *Management Buyout (MBO)*: It is a subset of LBO whereby incumbent management is included in the buying group and key executives perform an important role in the LBO transactions.

PE firm may further be classified by the stages of corporate development in terms of revenues generated and the corresponding growth potential, finance requirement and access to various sources of finance of the firm. For example, an early stages new venture company is visualized as a firm generating small but have a revenues a high growth potential with limited access to bank credit and greater dependence on alternative sources of finance such as the private equity. Private equity investments in firms in financial distress includes firms which are over-leveraged or suffer from operating problems with very limited access to other financial markets and the objective is to effect a turnaround.

PLAYERS IN THE PRIVATE EQUITY MARKET

Three major participants in a private equity market are:

(i) *Issuers or firms where private equities invest in:* As private equity is an expensive form of finance, issuers are generally firms that do not have recourse to an alternative source of financing such as a bank loan, private placement or the public equity market. These firms vary in their size and reasons for raising capital. Firms seeking venture capital include young firms that are expected to show high growth rates, early stage capital for companies that have commenced trading but have not moved into profitability as well as later stage investments where the product or service is widely available but capital is required for further growth. Non-venture private equity investments include middle-market companies that raise private equity finance for expansion or change in their capital structure.

(ii) *Intermediaries which are private equity funds themselves:* These are mostly organized as limited partnerships where investors who contribute to the fund's capital are limited partners, while the professional managers running the fund serve as the general partners. About four fifths of the private equity investments flow through specialized intermediaries, while the remainder is invested directly in firms through co-investments.

(iii) *Investors who are contributing capital to private equity firms:* These may include public and corporate pension funds, endowments, foundations, bank holding companies, investment banks, insurance companies and wealthy families and individuals. Most institutional investors contribute capital to private equity funds because they expect the risk-adjusted returns in private equity to be higher than the risk-adjusted returns on other investments and because of the potential benefits of diversification.

How Private Equity (PE) Works?

Private equity firms raise funds from institutions and wealthy individuals and then invest that money in buying and selling businesses. After raising a specified amount, a fund will close to new investors; each fund is liquidated, selling all its businesses, within a preset time frame, usually no more than ten years. A firm's track record on previous funds drives its ability to raise money for future funds.

Private equity firms accept some constraints on their use of investors' money. A fund management contract may limit, for example, the size of any single business investment. Once money is committed, however, investors-in contrast to shareholders in a public company - have almost no control over management. Although most firms have an investor advisory council, it has far fewer powers than a public company's board of directors.

The CEOs of the businesses in a private equity portfolio are not members of a private equity firm's management. Instead, private equity firms exercise control over portfolio companies through their representation on the companies' boards of directors. Typically, private equity firms ask the CEO and other top operating managers of a business in their portfolios to personally invest in it as a way to ensure their commitment and motivation. In return, the operat-ing managers may receive large rewards linked to profits when the business is sold. In accordance with this model, operating managers in portfolio businesses usually have greater autonomy than unit managers in a public company. Although private equity firms are beginning to develop operating skills of their own and thus are now more likely to take an active role in the management of an acquired business, the traditional model in which private equity owners provide advice but don't intervene directly in day-to-day operations still prevails.

With large buyouts, private equity funds typically charge investors a fee of about 1.5% to 2% of assets under management, plus, subject to achieving a minimum rate of return for investors, 20% of all fund profits. Fund profits are mostly realized via capital gains on the sale of portfolio businesses.

Because financing acquisitions with high levels of debt improves returns and covers private equity firms' high management fees, buyout funds seek out acquisitions for which high debt makes sense. To ensure they can pay financing costs, they look for stable cash flows, limited capital investment requirements, at least modest future growth, and, above all, the opportunity to enhance performance in the short to medium term.

Private equity firms and the funds they manage are typically structured as private partnerships. In some countries -particularly the United States-that gives them important tax and regulatory advantages over public companies.

BUSINESS CYCLE OF PRIVATE EQUITY

A private equity business cycle consists of *four stages*. The *first stage* of a private equity business cycle is to establish investment funds that collect capital from investors or limited partners. Limited partners include pension and provident funds, hedge funds, sovereign wealth funds, multilateral development banks like the Asian Development Bank and bilateral development financial institutions. These institutions, with the exception of hedge funds, do not have the professional staff nor the expertise to make such investments themselves and hence channel capital to private equity funds.

The partners commit funds for a set period (on average 10 years). The fund raising period lasts for six months to one year. There can be three types of private equity funds *viz., Independent, Captive* and *Semi-captive funds.* Independent private equity funds are those in which third parties are the main source of capital and in which no one shareholder holds a majority stake. In a captive fund, one shareholder contributes most of the capital.

At the *second stage*, the capital thus raised is used to buy equity stakes in high-potential companies following a clearly defined strategy. The private equity management team makes investments essentially in the first five years of the fund. A private equity investment takes place through one of the four investment vehicles *viz.*, direct investments, funds, fund-of-funds and more exotic products like collateralized fund obligations (CFOs), publicly quoted entities or mixed portfolios. Under *direct investments*, venture capital funds and informal private equity investors align interests with the founders or early round investors to avoid adverse selection and opportunistic behaviour. A private equity fund, on the other hand, collects capital from investors to choose and manage about 10 to 20 direct investments on their behalf. Investors decide to pool in funds based on due diligence including the quality of the management team, its track record, investment strategy and fund structure. Capital is drawn down as needed in order to pay set-up costs and management fees and to invest in a number of companies over an investment period of 4-5 years. Over the following years, the companies in the portfolio are further financed and managed for exit *via* trade sales, public offerings or secondary markets. Under the *fund of funds*, capital is collected from investors to invest in 20 or more funds on their behalf. They typically charge a management fee of around 0.5 per cent per year and participate in the profits upto 5 per cent to 10 per cent. Collateralised fund obligations are effectively securitization of mainly private equity fund-of-funds. Publicly traded products refer to those entities that raise capital from the public market like mutual funds and invest into private equity. Their net asset value is published regularly and the market price reflects the market's judgement on their fair value. These include listed companies whose core business is private equity quoted investment funds and specially structured investment vehicles.

Private equity funds generally do not intend to maintain indefinite control of the target company. Instead they seek to acquire control of companies, implement value adding changes and then realize the resulting capital gain by disposing of their investment within a relatively short time frame which is generally 3-5 years. Hence the penultimate stage of a private equity business cycle is to exit the investment. They require timely and profitable exits not only to redeem capital and returns to their investors and themselves but also to establish and maintain their reputation, which in turn enable them to raise capital again for future funds from existing and new limited partners. Hence it is extremely important that there exists a smooth and functional public issues market where they can divest and capitalize their gains.

Finally, the capital recovered from the exit is redistributed to original investors on a pro-rata basis depending on the size of their initial investment. These reimbursements along with the capital gains, allow the institutional investors to honour their insurance contracts, pensions and savings deposits. This completes one private equity business cycle. When all the capital collected from the investors has been invested and when certain investments have already been exited, the fund managers may launch a second fund. Their credibility in attracting new investors depends on their historical performance because they will be in competition with other managers in the asset management market. Successful private equity firms stay in business by raising a new fund every 3 to 5 years.

Risk Profile of Private Equity Investment

Private equity is regarded as a risky asset given the amount of leverage involved in the deals. However, private equity investments are not necessarily risky. The risk profiles of private equity investment varies with the investment vehicle used in the process. For example, a direct investment has a high probability of total loss whereas a fund has a very small probability of total loss. In sum, private equity originally evolved as a conduit to finance young entrepreneurial firms which require substantial capital to drive growth and innovation. These enterprises are characterized by significant intangible but limited tangible assets, expect a period of negative earnings and have uncertain prospects which makes debt financing difficult. Similarly, private equity organizations finance firms trapped in troubled waters which typically find it difficult to raise debt finance. Private equity organizations finance these high risk situations and expect high rewards in return. They protect the value of their equity investments by conducting careful and extensive due diligence before making an investment regarding business, financial, regulatory and environmental issues relevant for the company in question.

BENEFITS OF PRIVATE EQUITY FINANCE

Private equity finance has become popular in recent times as it confers various benefits on the companies concerned, as well as the industry, economy and society at large. Most private equities conceptualise 'provision of capital' as their most important contribution to growth of business followed by optimizing company's financing structure, general management guidance at the board level, ability to recruit the best managers to run the business, improve corporate governance and improvement of business processes. Host companies also benefit from international network of contracts, injection of international know-how, etc. The private equity/venture capitalists speed up product commercialization, adoption of human resource development policies and strengthens companies commercialization strategies.

Private equity also provide 'venture capital' and therefore PE funds are looked upon as 'company builders'. They favour build-up of absorptive capacity preparing firms with the ability to identify, evaluate and absorb internally different forms of know-how which have been generated outside the firm. By investing in the build-up of absorptive capacity through in-house R&D, companies may therefore increase their ability to generate future innovations by remaining actively tuned on what others are doing and ready to exploit opportunities that scientific and technological advances create. In fact, firms receiving private equity investments has shown that PE investors encourage collaboration with universities in R&D. They shape portfolio companies innovative strategies by investing at the right time and making them public at the right moment and thus freeing of capital to reinvest it in new ventures. Incentivisation of management coupled with control function of debt are prone to making executives rethink existing business models and inspire new ideas. They stimulate management for add-on acquisitions or for launch of new higher margin products or markets. Further, companies improved since the private equity helps companies to perform better in several ways. The post-buyout operating performance of LBOs pressure of servicing a debt load eased coupled with changes in incentive. Monitoring and governance structure of firm also lead to improved performance. It has also been found that post-IPO, majority ownership by a PE-sponsor is associated with better long-term stock performance. Besides, PE-firms are said to extend several social benefits such as improving environment, building infrastructure, encouraging R&D and upgrading human capital.

Above all, private equity firms are known as natural system stabilizers. During a systemic crisis, while those with short term funding may indulge in risk trading, private equity firms can balance the system by being a risk trader because of their long term funding requirements. Private equity firms get the bulk of their funds from long term investors like pension funds and invest in illiquid assets.

In the same letter and spirit, the role of private equity in developing countries like India may broadly be described as 'enabling capital' given the potential support it can provide to capital starved sectors such as small and medium enterprises (SMEs) and infrastructure, emerging sectors like realty, telecom, IT, *etc.*, restructuring of loss making companies as well as the high value agriculture sector. With policy support, private equity can revolutionise the disinvestment process in India. This will require policy support such as relaxation of archaic labour laws and land legislations that have hitherto disabled transfer of capital and other resources into more productive pursuits.

SIZE OF PRIVATE EQUITY (PE) INDUSTRY

The very term private equity continues to evoke admiration, envy, and fear. In recent years, private equity firms have pocketed huge - and controversial - sums, while stalking ever larger acquisition targets. Indeed, the global value of private equity buyouts bigger than $1 billion grew from $28 billion in 2000 to $502 billion in 2006. Despite the private equity environment's becoming more challenging amid rising interest rates and greater government scrutiny, that figure reached $501 billion in just the first half of 2007.

Private equity firms' reputation for dramatically increasing the value of their investments has helped fuel this growth. Their ability to achieve high returns is typically attributed to a number of factors: high-powered incentives both for private equity portfolio managers and for the operating managers of businesses in the portfolio; the aggressive use of debt, which provides financing and tax advantages; a determined focus on cash flow and margin improvement; and freedom from restrictive public company regulations.

But the fundamental reason behind private equity's growth and high rates of return is something that has received little attention, perhaps because it's so obvious: the firms' standard practice of buying businesses and then, after steering them through a transition of rapid performance improvement, selling them. That strategy, which embodies a combination of business and investment-portfolio management, is at the core of private equity's success.

STRATEGIC SECRET OF PRIVATE EQUITY

Buying to sell can't be an all-purpose strategy for public companies to adopt, it doesn't make sense when an acquired business will benefit from important synergies with the buyer's existing portfolio of businesses. It certainly isn't the way for a company to profit from an acquisition whose main appeal is its prospects for long-term organic growth.

However, as private equity firms have shown, the strategy is ideally suited when, in order to realize a one-time, short to medium-term value-creation opportunity, buyers must take outright ownership and control. Such an opportunity most often arises when a business hasn't been aggressively managed and so is underperforming. It can also be found with businesses that are undervalued because their potential isn't readily apparent. In those cases, once the changes necessary to achieve the uplift in value have been made usually over a period of two to six years — it makes sense for the owner to sell the business and move on to new opportunities.

The benefits of buying to sell in such situations are plain-though, again, often overlooked. Consider an acquisition that quickly increases in value-generating an annual investor return of, say, 25% a year for the first three years — but subsequently earns a more modest if still healthy return of, say, 12% a year. A private equity firm that, following a buy-to-sell strategy, sells it after three years will garner a 25% annual return. A diversified public company that achieves identical operational performance with the acquired business — but, as is typical, has bought it as a long-term investment — will earn a return that gets closer to 12% the longer it owns the business. For the public company, holding on to the business once the value-creating changes have been made dilutes the final return.

In the early years of the current buyout boom, private equity firms prospered mainly by acquiring the noncore business units of large public companies. Under their previous owners, those businesses had often suffered from neglect, unsuitable performance targets, or other constraints. Even if well managed, such businesses may have lacked an independent track record because the parent company had integrated their operations with those of other units, making the businesses hard to value. Sales by public companies of unwanted business units were the most important category of large private equity buyouts until 2004, and the leading firms' widely admired history of high investment returns comes largely from acquisitions of this type.

More recently, private equity firms-aiming for greater growth — have shifted their attention to the acquisition of entire public companies. This has created new challenges for private equity firms. In public companies, easily realized improvements in performance often have already been achieved through better corporate governance or the activism of hedge funds. For example, a hedge fund with a significant stake in a public company can, without having to buy the company outright, pressure the board into making valuable changes such as selling unnecessary assets or spinning off a noncore unit. If a public company needs to be taken private to improve its performance, the necessary changes are likely to test a private equity firm's implementation skills far more than the acquisition of a business unit would.

Many also predict that financing large buyouts will become much more difficult, at least in the short term, if there is a cyclical rise in interest rates and cheap debt dries up. And it may become harder for firms to cash out of their investments by taking them public; given the current high volume of buyouts, the number of large IPOs could strain the stock markets' ability to absorb new issues in a few years.

Even if the current private equity investment wave recedes, though, the distinct advantages of the buy-to-sell approach - and the lessons it offers public companies-will remain. For one thing, because all businesses in a private equity portfolio will soon be sold, they remain in the spotlight and under constant pressure to perform. In contrast, a business unit that has been part of a public company's portfolio for some time and has performed adequately, if not spectacularly, generally doesn't get priority attention from senior management. In addition, because every investment made by a private equity fund in a business must be liquidated within the life of the fund, it is possible to precisely measure cash returns on those investments. That makes it easy to create incentives for fund managers and for the executives running the businesses that are directly linked to the cash value received by fund investors. That is not the case with business unit managers or even for corporate managers in a public company.

Furthermore, because private equity firms buy only to sell, they are not seduced by the often alluring possibility of finding ways to share costs, capabilities, or customers among their businesses. Their management is lean and focused, and avoids the waste of time and money that corporate centers, when responsible for a number of loosely related businesses and wishing to justify their retention in the portfolio, often incur in a vain quest for synergy. Finally, the relatively rapid turnover of businesses required by the limited life of a fund means that private equity firms gain know-how fast.

EVOLUTION OF PRIVATE EQUITY IN INDIA

Historical Background

The seeds of the Indian private equity industry was laid in the mid 80's. The first generation venture capital funds, which can be looked at as a subset of private equity funds were launched by financial institutions like ICICI and IFCI. In 1984, ICICI decided to launch its venture capital scheme to encourage start-up ventures in the private sector and emerging technology sectors. This was followed by the establishment of 'Technology Development and Information Company Ltd' and IFCI sponsored 'Risk Capital and Technology Finance Corporation of India Ltd'. Commercial banks like Canara Bank also came up with their own venture capital funds. Subsequently, various regional venture capital funds came up in Andhra Pradesh and Gujarat. In late 80's and early 90's, various private sector funds also came into being. Between 1995-2000, several foreign PE firms like Baring PE partners, CDC Capital, Draper International, HSBC Private Equity and Warbug Pincus also started coming in. Firms like Chrys Capital and West Bridge Capital set up by managers of Indian origin with foreign capital also embarked into India with a focus on IT and internet related investments in tune with the technology boom in US during the period (Venture Intelligence, 2005). During the mid 1990's, laws for venture capital funds formally started taking shape. The Securities and Exchange Board of India issued the SEBI (Venture Capital Funds), Regulations, 1996. These regulations were amended in 2000.

The PE industry slowed down between 2001-03 after the technology boom burst in US in 2000. Many foreign PE investors fled India during that period. Investment activity revived in 2004 with the upward trend in domestic stock market. Six PE-backed companies went public successfully. Investment focus also turned towards non-IT investments like manufacturing, healthcare and those dependent on domestic consumption growth. However, despite a long history, the penetration of PE capital into India remains a miniscule 0.61 per cent of GDP today.

Performance of Private Equity in India

In India too, private equity has been emerging as a potential source of corporate finance supplementing the traditional sources of resource mobilization such as public equity issues, private placements, euro issues and external commercial borrowings.

The key driving factors behind the flow of PE capital into India are its strong macro-economic fundamentals characterized by high growth rate, high gross domestic investment and a booming stock market. In fact, private equity interest in India grew from 2003 onwards when the domestic stock markets recorded higher returns. A booming secondary market and regulatory reforms in the primary market widened the exit possibilities for private equity firms and hence attracted them to India. Over the last few years, private equity has emerged as a potential source of finance for the cash strapped small and medium enterprises, infrastructure sector, education and environment sensitive sectors too. The number of private equity deals in India increased from 82 in 2004 to 439 in 2007 with the total investment rising from US$ 1,719 million in 2004 to US$ 13,269 million in 2007.

Private equity mainly flowed into banking and financial services, construction and real estate, information technology, media and entertainment and other sectors. During 2007, the financial services sector accounted for around a quarter of the total investments and around 75.0 per cent of the investments in that sector is made by foreign private equity firms. Most of the deals were PIPE deals. The infrastructure sector also accounted for a good chunk of investments. Telecom sector in particular accounted for around 16.0 per cent of the total PE investments in India in 2007 and over 70.0 per cent of the investments were made by joint ventures between Indian and foreign private equity firms. The construction and real estate sector accounted for over 13.0 per cent of the investments, mostly by foreign private equity firms in late stage and PIPE deals. During 2008, private equity investments recorded a decline of 23.0 per cent to US$ 10.8 billion due mainly to the adverse impact of global financial turmoil. Between 2000 and 2008, PE-backed companies registered comparatively better performance over non-PE-backed companies in terms of sales, profit after tax, foreign exchange earnings, job creation and growth in research and development.

FDI by private equity funds increased 18 per cent to $77 billion – measured by the net value of cross-border M&As (table 1). They once were emerging as a new and growing source of international investment but have lost momentum. Before the crisis, some private equity firms (e.g. Apollo Management, RHJ International and KKR) had listed their shares in stock markets and successfully raised funds for investments. Most of the money stemmed from institutional investors, such as banks, pension funds and insurance companies. Hence, the deterioration of the finance industry in the recent crisis has led to difficulties in the private equity fund industry and slowed the dynamic development of such funds' investment abroad. The supply of finance for their investments has shrunk. As a result, funds raised by private equity have fallen by more than 50 per cent since the peak in 2007, to about $180 billion in 2011. The scale of investment has also changed. In contrast to the period when large funds targeted big, publicly traded companies, private equity in recent years has been predominantly aimed at smaller firms.

While the private equity industry is still largely concentrated in the United States and the United Kingdom, its activity is expanding to developing and transition economies where funds have been established. Examples include Capital Asia (Hong Kong, China), Dubai International Capital (United Arab Emirates), and H&Q Asia Pacific (China). Asian companies with high growth potential have attracted the lion's share of spending in developing and transition regions, followed by Latin America and Africa. In 2009–

2010, private equity activity expanded in Central and Eastern Europe (including both new EU member States such as Poland, the Czech Republic, Romania, Hungary and Bulgaria, in that order, and transition economies such as Ukraine). This activity was driven by venture and growth capital funds, which are becoming important in the financing of small and mediumsized enterprises in the region.

TABLE 1
Cross-Border M&As by Private Equity Firms, 1996–2011
(Number of Deals and Value)

	Gross cross-border M&As				Net cross-border M&As			
	Number of deals		Value		Number of deals		Value	
Year	Number	Share in total (%)	$ billion	Share in total (%)	Number	Share in total (%)	$ billion	Share in total (%)
1996	932	16	42	16	464	13	19	14
1997	925	14	54	15	443	11	18	10
1998	1 089	14	79	11	528	11	38	9
1999	1 285	14	89	10	538	10	40	6
2000	1 340	13	92	7	525	8	45	5
2001	1 248	15	88	12	373	9	42	10
2002	1 248	19	85	18	413	13	28	11
2003	1 488	22	109	27	592	20	53	29
2004	1 622	22	157	28	622	17	76	33
2005	1 737	20	221	24	795	16	121	26
2006	1 698	18	271	24	786	14	128	20
2007	1 918	18	555	33	1 066	15	288	28
2008	1 785	18	322	25	1 080	17	204	29
2009	1 993	25	107	19	1 065	25	58	23
2010	2 103	22	131	18	1 147	21	65	19
2011	1 900	19	156	15	902	16	77	15

Source: UNCTAD, cross-border M&A database (www.unctad.org/fdistatistics).

Note: Value on a net basis takes into account divestments by private equity funds. Thus it is calculated as follows: Purchases of companies abroad by private equity funds (-) Sales of foreign affiliates owned by private equity funds. The table includes M&As by hedge and other funds (but not sovereign wealth funds). Private equity firms and hedge funds refer to acquirers as "investors not elsewhere classified". This classification is based on the Thomson Finance database on M&As.

The private equity market has traditionally been stronger in the United States than in other countries. The majority of private equity funds invest in their own countries or regions. But a growing proportion of investments now cross borders. Private equity funds compete in many cases with traditional TNCs in acquiring foreign companies and have joined with other funds to create several of the largest deals in the world.

In terms of sectoral interest, private equity firms invest in various industries abroad but are predominantly represented in the services sector, with finance playing a significant part. However, the primary sector, which was not a significant target in the mid-2000s, has become an increasingly important sector in the past few years. Private equity has targeted mining companies and firms with a strong interest in the mining sector, such as Japanese transnational trading houses (sogo shosha). Interest in manufacturing has also been increasing, particularly since 2011.

Differences have also emerged between the patterns of FDI by private equity firms in developing countries and in developed ones. In developing countries, they focus largely on services (finance and telecommunications) and mining. In developed countries, private equity firms invest in a wide range of industries, from food, beverages and tobacco in the manufacturing sector to business activities (including real estate) in the services sector.

The increasing activity of private equity funds in international investment differs from FDI by TNCs in terms of the strategic motivations of the investors, and this could have implications for the long-run growth and welfare of the host economies. On the upside, private equity can be used to start new firms or to put existing firms on a growth path. For example, it has been shown that firms that receive external private equity financing tend to have a greater start-up size and can therefore better exploit growth potential. In developing countries, where growth potential is high but perceived risks are equally high, traditional investors are often deterred or unfamiliar with the territory. Some private equity funds specialize in developing regions to leverage their region-specific knowledge and better risk perception. For example, Helios Investment Partners, a pan-African private equity group with a $1.7 billion investment fund, is one of the largest private equity firms specializing in the continent. BTG Pactual, Avent International and Vinci Partners, all based in Brazil, are major investors in Latin America, an $8 billion plus market for private equity funds.

On the downside, some concerns exist about the sustainability of high levels of FDI activity by private equity funds. *First*, the high prices that private equity funds paid for their investments in the past have made it increasingly difficult for them to find buyers, increasing further the pressure that private equity firms normally exert to focus on short-run profit targets, often leading to layoffs and restructuring of companies. *Second*, acquiring stock-listed companies deviates from the private equity funds' former strategy of investing in alternative asset classes (e.g. venture capital, unlisted small firms with growth potential).

Furthermore, there are concerns related to transparency and corporate governance, because most funds are not traded on exchanges that have regulatory mechanisms and disclosure requirements. And there are differences in the investment horizons of private equity funds and traditional TNCs. Private equity funds, often driven by short-term performance targets, hold newly acquired firms on average for five to six years, a period which has declined in recent years. TNCs, which typically are engaged in expanding the production of their goods and services to locations abroad, have longer investment horizons.

Despite the implications of these differences for the host economy, many private equity firms have nevertheless demonstrated more awareness about long-term governance issues and disclosure; for example, environmental and social governance. In fact, more than half of private equity firms have implemented programmes on environmental and social governance in their investments.

PRIVATE EQUITY'S NEW FOCUS

As private equity has gone from strength to strength, public companies have shifted their attention away from value-creation acquisitions of the sort private equity makes. They have concentrated instead on synergistic acquisitions. Conglomerates that buy unrelated businesses with potential for significant performance improvement have fallen out of fashion. As a result, private equity firms have faced few rivals for acquisitions. Given the success of private equity, it is time for public companies to consider whether they might compete more directly in this space.

These are two options. The first is to adopt the buy-to-sell mode I. The second is to take a more flexible approach to the ownership of businesses, in which a willingness to hold on to an acquisition for the long term is balanced by a commitment to sell as soon as corporate management feels that it can no longer acid further value.

Buy to Sell

Companies wishing to try this approach in its pure form face some significant barriers. One is the challenge of overhauling a corporate culture that has a buy-to-keep strategy embedded in it. That requires a company not only to shed deeply held beliefs about the integrity of a corporate portfolio but also to develop new resources and perhaps even dramatically change its skills and structures.

The emergence of public companies competing with private equity in the market to buy, transform, and sell businesses could benefit investors substantially. Private equity funds are illiquid and are risky because of their high use of debt; furthermore, once investors have turned their money over to the fund, they have no say in how it's managed. In compensation for these terms, investors should expect a high rate of return. However, though some private equity firms have achieved excellent returns for their investors, over the long term the average net return fund investors have made on buyouts is about the same as the overall return for the stock market.

Private equity fund managers, meanwhile, have earned extremely attractive rewards, with little up-front investment. As compensation for taking the initiative in raising money, managing investments, and marketing their benefits, they have structured agreements so that a large portion of the gross returns around 30%, after adding management and other fees - flows to them. And that figure doesn't take into account any returns made on their personal investments in the funds they manage. Public companies pursuing a buy-to-sell strategy, which are traded daily on the stock market and answerable to stockholders, might provide a better deal for investors.

From where might a significant number of publicly traded competitors to private equity emerge? Even if they appreciate the attractions of the private equity strategy in principle, few of today's large public industrial or service companies are likely to adopt it. Their investors would be wary. Also, few corporate managers would slip easily into a more investment-management-oriented role. Private equity partners typically are former investment bankers and like to trade. Most top corporate managers are former business unit heads and like to manage.

Public financial firms, however, may find it easier to follow a buy-to-sell strategy. More investment companies may convert to a private equity management style. More private equity firms may decide to float an entire investment portfolio on the public markets. More experienced investment banks may focuses on buy-to-sell opportunities. In addition, some experienced private equity managers may decide to raise public money for a buyout fund through an IPO.

Flexible Ownership

A strategy of flexible ownership could have wider appeal to large industrial and service companies than buying to sell. Under such an approach, a company holds on to businesses for as long as it can add significant value by improving their performance and fueling growth. The company is equally willing to dispose of those businesses once that is no longer clearly the case. A decision to sell or spin off a business is viewed as the culmination of a successful transformation, not the result of some previous strategic error. At the same time, the company is free to hold on to an acquired business, giving it a potential advantage over private equity firms, which sometimes must forgo rewards they'd realize by hanging on to investments over a longer period.

Flexible ownership can be expected to appeal the most to companies with a portfolio of businesses that don't share many customers or processes. At present, there are not money large public companies in the industrial or service sector that explicitly pursue flexible ownership as a way to compete in the private equity sweet spot. Although many companies go through periods of actively selling businesses, the purpose is usually to make an overly diversified portfolio more focused and synergistic, not to realize value from successfully completed performance enhancements. Even the acquisitive conglomerates that successfully targeted performance improvement opportunities ultimately weren't willing enough to sell or spin off businesses once they could no longer increase their value-and thus found it difficult to sustain earnings growth. But given the success of private equity's model, companies need to rethink the traditional taboos about selling businesses.

PRIVATE EQUITY – IMPLICATIONS FOR INDIA

Trade off between Private Equity and other Non-bank Sources of Finance

There is no gainsaying that private equity is a boon for capital constrained developing economies as they help to bridge large saving-investment gaps. However, does easy access to private equity funds delay firms' decision to go for public offers? Similarly, does it compete away investments/suck liquidity from the domestic debt market? In other words, does private equity compete with traditional non-bank sources of finance like public issues and private placement or supplement them?

Some traces of trade off between non-bank sources of resource mobilization by corporates was found in the first half of 2008-09 in the Indian equity market. With the Indian equity markets on a downswing, the public issues virtually dried up during the first half of 2008-09. Resource mobilization through public issues market declined by 61.2 per cent to ₹ 12,361 crore during April-September 2008-09 in tandem with the subdued conditions in the secondary market. Similarly, resource mobilization through private placement market declined by 31.2 per cent during April-June 2008-09 to ` 34,719 crore. The number of issues also declined as several companies either withdrew their issues from the market due to lacklustre response from investors or postponed their fund raising indefinitely. Under uncertainty, such firms had been induced to tap alternative investment sources like private equity. 'Worckhardt' is one such example to conjure with. However, it is difficult to establish whether private equity funds delay initial attempts at public issues because PE firms themselves seek exit from an investment 4-5 years down the line by handing over its stake either through public offer or sell-off to another company. Further, after investing in a company, PE firms emphasise organizational changes and encourage the host company to go for raising of debt. In view of that, it is natural to expect a positive relationship between private equity and other non-bank sources of finance such as public/ rights issues and resources raised through private placement of debt. This is important because any tendency to compete away or delay public issue by companies may not be a healthy trend as resource mobilization through public offers is more transparent as it involves a number of public disclosures as opposed to private equity.

Trade Off between PE Regulation and Non-Regulation

Private equity regulation has raised some typical issues in recent times. For example, the activities that private equity firms indulge in, mainly activities like leveraged buyouts (LBOs) may not be compatible with the corporate laws of the state. In European corporate law, for example, leveraged buyouts are perceived as an indirect and fraudulent instance of financial assistance and are as such not immune to the ban imposed by Article 23 of Directive 77/91/EEC under which a company may not provide 'financial assistance' for the purchase of its own shares. In Italy, the legality of LBOs has always been under dispute. Until February 2000, the legitimacy of buyouts were uncertain in Italy. On February 04, 2000, the Italian Supreme Court sentenced LBOs to be illegal. Critics have alleged that LBOs fall within the scope of the provisions of Italian Civil Code that prescribes criminal sanctions for directors who damage the integrity of a company's share capital through an acquisition or subscription of shares of the company, or in case of a merger cause harm to the company's creditors. In 2001, the Italian parliament specifically requested to reconsider the buyout regulation and hence in January 2004, a new legislative decree was issued where LBOs were legitimized subject to the fulfillment of additional disclosure requirements and provided they do not violate any financial assistance law. The American law, on the other hand, stresses on the social utility of LBOs. The US legal treatment draws an ex-post distinction between 'illegal' and 'legal' LBOs on the basis of whether or not such transfers are intentionally fraudulent. Such disputes indicate the need for some universal laws for the operation of private equity such as Basel norms for banks.

Another issue emerging from this relates to whether regulations should be made applicable uniformly to banks, hedge funds and private equity firms, irrespective of the diversity of their risk behavior. Each of these institutions have different investment objectives, different capacity to bear various sets of risks and hence different risk behaviour. Under similar kinds of transparency, valuation, accounting and risk management rules, these players would behave homogenously in case of eventuality thereby reducing financial market liquidity and enhancing systemic fragility.

PROSPECTS FOR THE PRIVATE EQUITY MARKET IN INDIA

The shift in financial conditions since the US sub-prime crisis in August 2007 has magnified vulnerabilities that extend beyond the mortgage markets. Tangentially related markets like the leveraged buyout market are being affected through second and third order effects as concerns in structured finance markets triggered a broad-based increase in risk premia and induced a reluctance to lend, a reduced distinction between investments and other changes in market psychology. At higher leverage and price multiples, the LBO business of private equity firms are facing high economic risks today. The private equity deals are most sensitive to situations of high growth and high interest rates. Rising interest rates have been squeezing the interest coverage ratios (cash flows relative to cash interest payments) and consequently narrowing the gains to private equity holders on LBO targets. The medium term prospects also appear challenging for LBO market because most recent deals are likely to face financing difficulties. Private equity firms may not be able to secure financing on attractive terms and may also have to carry more demanding debt service burden than anticipated in the coming months. Given this gloomy scenario in the rest of the world, what are the prospects for the private equity inflow into India?

The correlation between developed world markets and emerging markets have increased in recent years due to opening up of the trade and financial sector. But due to the gradual pace of opening of the economy, efficient regulatory supervision, strong domestic demand and comparatively limited dependence on foreign trade, economies like India have been able to partially shield themselves from the uncertainties in the rest of the world economy. Thus when the rest of the world has submerged into a recession after the global financial crisis, India has revived relatively faster from the initial contagion of global downturn. India's growth prospects remain robust with the growth forecast for 2009-10 at 6.5 per cent and gross domestic investment expected to be steady at 36.5 per cent of GDP. India's industrial and service sector growth remains resilient. Given this congenial investment climate and sound business outlook, India remains a relatively high-return and low risk source of diversifying returns for private equity investments.

However, fresh private equity inflows may witness some re-arrangement in portfolio allocations in the near term. Thus while there may be a trend away from sectors like manufacturing and export oriented IT sectors because of slowdown, banking and financial institutions, media and entertainment and telecom sectors may see more inflows in the coming years given the Government's proposal to infuse more reforms into these sectors. Further, capital market reforms may also reinforce growth of private equity finance. SEBI has amended SEBI (Disclosure and Investor Protection) guidelines and listing agreement to reduce the time duration for Rights issue to 43 days from the present 109 days. Efforts are on to squeeze the IPO process to the international best practice of 7 days from the current 12 days. SEBI has also eased SEBI (Substantial Acquisitions of Shares and Takeovers) Regulations, 1997 to extend the creeping acquisitions limit beyond 55 per cent. Under this, SEBI has done away with the requirement of public announcement by non-promoters before acquiring stake in any company. The efforts towards setting up of stock exchange for small and medium enterprises and easing of several public listing norms including reduction of the time period for listing would go a long way in attracting private equity investment into India. Emphasis on infrastructure development and affordable housing will also attract private equity investment into India in a big way. However, tougher trading conditions throughout most economic sectors would shift the way private equity firms create value. Whereas previously private equity firms have achieved high returns through acquisitions, balance sheet restructuring and rising valuations, today they may have to emphasise on growth improvements for which organizational changes and operational improvements would become essential.

VENTURE CAPITAL

Venture capital is considered to be a subset of private equity on investments in new and maturing companies. In other words, the venture capital means the investment of long term risk equity finance where the primary reward for its provider, the venture capitalist, is an eventual capital gain, rather than interest income or dividend yield. It is also different from the development capital provided by several Central and state level Government bodies in that the profit objective is the motive behind the financing and not employment generation or balanced regional growth or any other social objective, though all these do result indirectly due to setting up of successful new business.

Venture Capital a risky business, rather like a Bollywood studio, the venture capitalist relies on a few big hits for nearly all the profits on the funds he manages. Another peculiar feature of this financing is that the venture capitalist usually has a continuing involvement in the business of the customer after making an investment. This does not mean management interference but a venture capitalist will seek to protect and enhance his investment by keeping close to the entrepreneur and his team in an active supportive role. This style of operation is in marked contrast to that of a banker or other lenders. It also differs radically from the approach of a stock market investor who can buy or sell at will without ever meeting the management of his investee company.

A venture capital investment is illiquid, i.e. not subject to repayment on demand as with an overdraft or following a loan repayment schedule. The investment is realised only when the company is sold or achieves a stock market listing. It is lost when an sometimes occurs, the company goes into liquidation. Venture Capital is risk financing at its extreme.

Valuing and Financing a Venture

As entrepreneurs and potential financiers consider pursuing a venture the critical question is, *What is the business worth?* The value of a typical publicly traded firm can readily be estimated by examining the firm's past earnings or dividends, forecasting its future earnings or dividends, and then applying a rational discount rate. For a venture, the task of valuation is much more difficult for two reasons. *First,* the typical venture has no history of earnings, and in many cases a market does not yet exist for the proposed venture's product or service. Thus, earnings estimates are often little more than wild guesses. *Second,* the venture may be planning to operate in a new or young industry in which comparable companies are scarce or nonexistent, so establishing a rational discount rate is also highly problematic.

Nevertheless, the value of a venture must be established through some type of rational *valuation process.* One popular, though admittedly ad hoc, approach to valuing a venture that is financed with equity shares involves four steps:

1. Project a future horizon date at which the venture will be a stable, profitable firm, assuming that the firm's long-term business goals are achieved. Forecast the venture's earnings and earnings growth as of that date.
2. Calculate the fair value of the firm as of this horizon date. A normal discount rate, market-to-book equity ratio, or price-earnings ratio (P/E) can be used for this purpose.
3. Calculate the current value of the venture by discounting the calculated horizon-date value of the firm to the present, using an appropriate risk-adjusted discount rate. The annual discount rate for early-stage ventures are higher than discount rate for later-stage ventures. Adjustments are made for the probability of the venture's success, the length of time to the horizon date, current interest rates, and risk premiums in the market.
4. Finally, use the estimated current value of the venture to partition the venture's shares among the firm's entrepreneurs and investors.

In reality, valuation and financing issues are more complex. The entrepreneurs and the financier may disagree on (a) the amount of financing required at the current stage of development (b) the amount of time that will be required to bring the venture to fruition (c) The future earnings that the firm will realise given that the business plan is successful, and (d) the appropriate discount rate to use in the valuation (especially as this discount rate depends on the probability of the vanture's success). To the extent that they disagree on the current value of the venture, the entrepreneurs and the potential financier will disagree on the appropriate percentage of the venture's equity that the financier should receive.

Venture Capital Specialisation

Most venture capital funds operate with some degree of *specialisation* in the investments they seek or are prepared to consider. These specialisation are based on:

(A) The *state of development* of the investee company, which defines the financing stage as perceived by the venture capitalist. This has been explained in details later on.

(B) The Funds *Investments size range*. The players in the venture capital market place do not all invest in a similar size of company, nor do they all operate within a common range of amount invested. The minimum/maximum equity percentages also vary from fund to fund.

(C) *Financing instruments and rewards mix*: Equity investment, the core of any venture capital transaction, can involve one or more of a wide range of financing instruments. These include ordinary shares, preferred ordinary shares, deferred ordinary shares, preference shares and convertible loan stock.

(D) *Technological Focus*: Most Venture Capitalists do not claim to specialise only in high technology investments, although their portfolios may well include a significant proportion of business which operate in areas of advanced technology. There are however a number of venture capital funds which deliberately set out to concentrate on advanced technology investments. Many of those concentrate on a particular segment like biotechnology, information technology, etc. The reason is practical. The impossibility, economically, of keeping up with the rapid pace of development in more than a few specialist segments.

(E) *Time Scale To Realisation*: Capital realisation is the essence of venture capital - to recycle funds for new investments, to demonstrate performance to the funds investors, and to achieve the fund management's own incentives. Even where a fund is open ended, such as most bank sponsored capital funds and there is no need for realisations to make new investments it is a natural motivation in professional venture capitalists to achieve successful realisations.

Funds investing at the early stage financing are inevitably taking a medium to long term (5-7 years) view of their eventual pay back or realisation. Later stage financing will have a 3-5 years time scale.

(F) *Geographical Limitations*: The funds say also specialise regionally.

The course of business growth cannot be described in a strictly compartmentalised way. There are however, identifiable *stages* in corporate development each of which has distinct characteristics, although the stages merge in the continuous process of growth.

Stages of Investment

The venture capital industry recognises these different stages to the extent that most funds specialise in one or more. These are as follows:

(A) Equity Share

(a) Seed Capital & R & D Projects

One area which the venture capital industry is keen to encourage is seed finance - the provision of very small amounts for finance needed to turn into a business.

Before a product based business can be established, there is often a lengthy process of Research and Development (R & D) starting with the initial concept. This concept will form the basis of a research project. The financial risk mounts progressively as the research phase moves into the development phase, where a prototype product is tested prior to commercialisation. It is during this phase that external finance is often sought by the investor/entrepreneur as his own capital is consumed.

(b) Start Ups

The start up is widely recognised as the essence of venture capital activity, so such so that many people use term start up and venture capital interchangeably. Perhaps the most exciting and risky aspect of venture capital is the launch of a new business, often after a period of R&D. At the start up stage the entrepreneur and his products or services are as yet untried, the finance required usually dwarfs his own resources. Not all start ups are of the first-time investor or greenfield variety, so beloved of transatlantic venture capital myths. Many new enterprises are formed by experienced people wishing to launch their own business in an industry they know well. Others are spin offs from research bodies or large corporations, where a venture capitalist joins with an industrially experienced or corporate partner. Still other start ups occur when an existing generally smaller company wishes to licence new technology from a research source or overseas based business and does not have adequate financial resources.

(B) Second Round Finance

There are positive and negative reasons why early stages of development may require further funding after start up but before the business is established. Among the positive reasons for second round finance is that the business may be growing at such a rate (or have such potential) that even where only small profits, if any, are being achieved, new investors can be attracted to provide this first stage of expansion finance. Among the negative reasons is that there is often a period of loss after start up, during which the start up capital is consumed and debt incurred which out grows the equity base of the business.

(a) Expansion Finance

This phase embraces two basic paths of developments for an existing business - Organic growth or growth by acquisition. Organic expansion implies bigger factory, larger warehouse, new factories, new products or new markets. Acquisition seeks to achieve the same through purchase of existing businesses.

TABLE - 2
Venture Capital Spectrum

Early Stage Investment	Time Scale (yrs.)	Risk
Seed Capital	7-10	Extreme
Start up	5-10	Very High
Second Round	3-7	High
Later Stage Investment		
Expansion	1-3	Medium
Replacements	1-3	Low
Turnarounds	3-5	Medium
Buy Outs	3-5	Low

(b) Replacement Capital

A major part of investment by venture capitalists is to purchase the existing shares of owners. This may be due to a variety of reasons including personal need of finance, conflict in the family, or need for association of a well known name. Though initially it may not result in any new business, a partnership in future growth does result in development of new businesses.

(c) Turnarounds

A turnarounds or recovery case requires very specialised skills. It may need a renegotiation of all the company's borrowings, change in management or even a change in ownership. A very active hands on approach is required in the initial crisis period where the venture capitalist may appoint its own chairman or nominate its directors on the board.

(d) Buy Outs

It involves the creation of a separate business by separating it from their existing owners. A buy out will involve the existing or a new management team and a set of assets which may be just a trade name or a group of people. The buy-outs continue to dominate the UK venture capital industry. Some idea of the scale of by-out activity can be gained from the fact that there were more buy-outs in 1991 than acquisition of independent companies.

Management buy-outs have dominated investment strategy in recent years. Buy outs have been a bull market phenomenon. But in the long term it is impossible to get high returns without high risks. Venture Capitalists must concentrate on start ups and early stage financing at the small end, and buy-ins and restructuring at the big end.

The Entrepreneur's Choice

Just as the venture capitalist has to be careful in selecting his investment, the entrepreneur should also take several *factors into account* while selecting the venture capitalist. The venture capital industry's rapid growth over the past decade has meant that equity capital is available in unprecedented amounts. It has also meant that the entrepreneur is faced with a bewildering choice between various sources of finance. Following factors are important in taking the decision.

1. Hands on or Hands off Approach

The hands on style of management will normally involve a representation on the board. It would involve very active interaction between the entrepreneur and the venture capitalist. An attempt is made to value add the services in an advisory role or active involvement in marketing, recruitment and finding technical collaborators. It will be a kind of active partnership between the two.

The hands off approach on the other hand would be passive and venture capitalist would just receive a periodic statement of financial and other information. Normally a right to appoint a director would be reserved but seldom exercised.

There is an intermediate style where the approach is passive except in major decisions like change in top management, large expansion, or major acquisition. A board appointee, if made, would in this case, perform a role of a financial watchdog rather than involving in active management decisions.

2. Deal Structuring Flexibility

The entrepreneur should seek out the fund which gives a package that best meets his needs. Some funds are very flexible in this matter and any surprise the entrepreneur with their generosity. Others have some rigid rules and there are various approaches between these two extremes.

3. Exit Aspirations

If the exit aspirations of the venture capitalist, whether it is buy back, or quotation or trade sale, are not clarified in the beginning, it may result in conflict later on. There should be a clear understanding between the two in this matter and entrepreneur should make sure that exit aspirations does not compromise his interest.

4. Fund Viability and Liquidity

The entrepreneur must sure that the fund has committed backers and not someone interested in just a quick realisation of capital gains. This is very important in raising follow up finance.

5. Track Record of the Fund and Its Team

Entrepreneur must look at the period for which the fund has been operational, the backed successful projects in the past or not, the objective of reward and return, and the experience of the team.

There should be good chemistry between the two. Also the team must be committed full time and preferably have general management experience. This will ensure continuous guidance specially in bad times.

Most venture capital companies do not want an introduction from anyone. A business proposal, that is well prepared is the best introduction that one can have. Most venture capital companies are interested in good investments and not in social contacts or introductions

A detailed and well organised business plan is the only way to gain a venture capitalists attention and obtain funding. They do not invest on a two page summary. They want a summary as a start but not as a substitute for a sound plan. A well prepared business proposal serves two functions. *First* it informs the venture capitalist about entrepreneurs ideas. *Second*, it shows that the entrepreneur has thought out the intended business, and knows the industry and have thought through all the potential problems.

The summary should contain the name, address and telephone number of the contact person in a conspicuous location. Briefly the type of business or nature of industry should be discussed. This should be followed by a thumbnail sketch of the company's history todate. The experience of the entrepreneur and the top management should be mentioned. A short description of product and service is required. The amount of funds required and the form in which required should also be mentioned. Summary of five years financial projections and five year history of existing group companies should be appended. Also the exit plans must be mentioned.

Exit Routes

Corporate Sale/Trade Sale

This involves two basic questions. (i) why and (ii) at what price/ the sale of the whole undertaking will take place only if it is advantageous for both the parties. From the point of view of the acquirer, the acquisition might offer advantage of forward/ backward integration, availability of new technology, availability of the established marketing channels, etc. From the point of the entrepreneur, it may afford him an opportunity to realise a good price for the efforts (successful) so far made by him, and to use the resources so raised in implementing some other project, with or without the assistance of the Venture capitalist. It is also possible that the unit has reached a stage where it is unable to feed the market, without substantial expansion at a cost beyond his capacity in any form. It would be best for him to consider corporate sale as one of the solutions. From the point of view of the venture capitalists, the corporate sale is the best thing which can happen. The price is normally higher than what he can otherwise get for this investment. Moreover, he gets ready cash, which he can employ profitably elsewhere. For him this is win-win situation.

Coming to the question of pricing, several theories have been advanced. One way can be the Net Asset Value of the company. But what value? The book value or the replacement value? What about the valuation of some intangible assets e.g. brands, goodwill, capable management etc., the value of which may far exceed the value of all other assets put together. Another theory speaks of Discounted Cash Flow. But can the future cash flows be measured accurately. If it is possible to do so, the theory can work. If not, it is doubtful if the calculations can satisfy either the buyer or the seller.

Much will therefore depend upon the negotiations and the need. The price will depend upon hard bargaining. The payment for the price may take the form of immediate cash, or the shares in the acquirer company, in which case the entrepreneur will have the benefit of enjoying the fruits of future growth. The agreement may also include a provision for utilising the services of the entrepreneur in a suitable capacity. The pre-condition for such an agreement will, however, be the mental preparedness of the entrepreneur to play a lesser role in the same until which was established and nursed and commanded.

Take Out

This term is used where the venture capitalist transfers his interest in the unit to another venture capitalist. He may consider the option for variety of reasons, but in most of the cases this is resorted to when he needs funds for financing some other unit. However, this form of exit is not very popular. The buyer venture capitalist is bound to look upon the offer with misgivings, and there can never be a foolproof system to satisfy him. The seller venture capitalist is unlikely to reduce the price below a certain level. Under these circumstances, the bargain is most unlikely to be struck.

Share Repurchase by the Promoter

Almost all the agreements of venture capital assistance contain the clause that, at the end of the given period the venture capitalist, at the direction will be free to dispose of his stake but will have to make the first offer to the promoter (s). The original promoters are best suited for buying back the shares of their own company as it is they who can motivate the employees thereof, and also because they are expected to run the company efficiently in future. The price at which the shares are transferred by the venture capitalist is mutually agreed, and is determined on the basis of commercial criteria which reflects profit potential of the venture, share's book-value, future earning potential, and P/E ratio of similar listed companies. The share purchase route gives the entrepreneur the advantage of retaining or even strengthening control over the company.

Share Buyback of the Company

Under the provisions of Section 77 of the Companies Act the buyback of own shares by the companies is prohibited. However, some relaxation in these provisions has recently been made a good number of companies, of course in the big league have already amended their Articles of Association to facilitate the buyback of their shares. It is, however, doubtful if the Venture capitalists will be able to take advantage of the buyback route, for the companies finances by them are normally of the small size, and are not expected to have sufficient free reserves to avail of this route. Buybacks are an expensive way of assuring investment investment an exit route. If the project is beginning to generate returns share prices will appreciate substantially. Internal accruals alone may not be enough to pay for the repurchase. As far as institutions funding for such buyouts are concerned, they are rarely forthcoming.

Listing on the Stock Exchange(s)

Listing of the company's shares on the stock exchange is another route through which the venture capitalist can hope to get back his investment and exit. However, this route has its own problems. *Firstly*, the listing guidelines require that 60% of the offer should be made to the public. The promoter's stake gets substantially diluted, and in certain cases, there can be the possibility of losing control over the company, which he had nursed. The reluctance of the promoter to take this route is therefore quite understandable. *Secondly*, the Stock exchange guidelines require a company to have minimum paid up capital of ₹ 3 crores for obtaining stock exchange listing. Most of the venture capital investee companies are small sized, and do not qualify for getting listed. *Thirdly*, the listing fee charged by the stock exchange, is at times beyond the means of the small companies to pay. *Finally*, even if the shares of a company are listed on the stock exchange, that in itself is no guarantee that they will be traded. There are a number of factors due to which almost 80% of the shares of the companies listed on the stock exchange are not traded. We may therefore treat this route as non-existent, as an exit route for venture capitalist.

To overcome the difficulties faced by new enterepreneurs in raising equity capital, it has been decided to formulate a scheme under which venture capital companies/funds will be enabled to invest in new companies and be eligible for the concessional treatment of capital gains available to non-corporate entities. Venture capital companies/funds which want to avail of concessional treatment of capital gains, would be required to comply with the following guidelines:

1. Establishment

(i)   Funds, companies or schemes wishing to undertake venture capital finance activities may be established using the term venture capital if they come within and agree to abide by these guidelines.

(ii) Approvals should be given for the establishment of the venture capital companies/ funds by the Department of Economic Affairs, Ministry of Finance, or such authority as may be nominated by the Government, and applications for such approvals should be made with a suitable explanatory note and details of the proposal and addressed to CCI/Joint Secretary (Investments) in the Department of Economic Affairs.

(iii) Applications for issue of capital by companies should be made under the Capital Issues (Control) Act to the Controller of Capital Issues. Composite applications for approval to establish the fund for the issue of capital can also be made.

(iv) All-India public sector financial institutions, State Bank of India and other scheduled banks, including foreign banks operating in India and the subsidiaries of the above would be eligible to start venture capital funds/companies, subject to such approval as may be required from the Reserve Bank of India in respect of banking companies. Joint venture between them, or between non-institutional promoters and them would be permitted, but the equity holding of such promoters shall not exceed a total of 20 per cent, and must not be the largest single holding.

2. Management

(i)   It is required that the venture capital funds/companies are managed by professional such as bankers, managers and administrators and persons with adequate experience of industry, finance, accounts, etc., if established by subsidiaries of banks/institutions, or in-house schemes they should maintain their independence and an arms length relationship. They would, however, be free to draw upon the professional expertise and infrastructure of the parent organisation in the interests of their shareholders and clients and minimising costs.

(ii) No person would be permitted to be the full time chairman/president/chief executive, or executive director or a whole-time director of a VCC/VCF. If he holds any of the above positions in any other company except that he may hold such a position in assisted company by virtue of his position in the VCC/VCF.

3. Venture Capital Assistance

(i) It is intended that venture capital assistance should go mainly to enterprise where the risk element is comparatively high due to the technology involved being relatively new, untried or very closely-held, and/or the entrepreneurs being relatively new and not effluent though otherwise qualified, and the size being modest. For successful units, the possibility of high returns would exist, but the projects would initially find it difficult to raise equity from the market, especially when public issues are no longer readily available for small, green field companies. The assistance should mainly be for equity support, though loan support to supplement this may also be done.

Venture capital assistance, therefore, should cover those enterprises which fulfil the following parameters:

(A) *Size:* Total investments not to exceed ₹ 10 crores.

(B) *Technology:* New or relatively untried or very closely-held or being taken from pilot to commercial stage, or which incorporates some significant improvements over the existing ones in India.

(C) *Promoters/entrepreneurs:* Relatively new, professionally or technically qualified, with inadequate resources or backing to finance the project.

Investment in enterprises engaged in trading, broking, investment or financial services, agency or liaison work, shall not be permitted. Further investment in assisted units for their expansion or strengthening or investments for the revival of sick units, would be permitted as a part of venture capital activity and the above parameters will not apply.

(a) The recipient venture should be established as a limited company and must employ professionally qualified persons to maintain its accounts.

(b) The VCC/VCF should invest at least 60 per cent of its funds into venture capital activity.

(c) During the first 12 months, any permissible investment may be made (including leasing up to 15 per cent of the funds), but a level of 30 per cent, should be reached for venture capital activity by the end of the second year, and 60 per cent, by the end of the third year, and 75 per cent, by the end of the fifth year of operations.

The balance amounts may be invested in any new issue, by an existing or a new company, of equity CCPS, debentures, bonds or other securities approved for this purpose by CCI. A part of this may also be employed for leasing but this should not, at any stage, exceed 15 per cent, of the total funds deployed, including in the first year. Activities such as money market operations, bills rediscounting, broking, portfolio investments and fund management, financial services and consultancy, inter-corporate lending would not be permitted to VCC/VCF. Specific approval of CCI should be taken for activities not prohibited, but also not included in the permitted list above.

(d) *Size:* The minimum size of a VCC/VCF would be ₹ .10 crores. If it desires to raise funds from the public, the promoters stage shall not be less than 40 per cent.

(e) Capital Issues:

(i) Funds may be raised through public issues and/or private placements to finance VCF/VCCs.

(ii) Foreign equity up to 25 per cent, multilateral/international financial organisations, development finance institutions, reputed mutual funds etc. would be permitted, provided these are management neutral and are for medium to long-term investments.

(iii) NRI investment would be permitted up to 74 per cent, on a non-repatriable basis and up to 25 per cent/40 per cent on a repatriable basis.

(iv) An application should be addressed to Ministry of Finance, Investment Division, North Block, New Delhi, with a copy to Chairman, Securities & Exchange Board of India for foreign NRI participation in capital issues.

(f) *Debt-equity ratio:* Debt-equity ratio may be maximum 1:1.5.

(g) *Underwriting/listing:*

(i) The VCC/VCF may be listed according to the prescribed norms. Its issue may be underwritten at the discretion of the promoters.

(ii) For assisted units also listing guidelines would apply. Investment by widely-held VCF would be treated as public participation for this purpose.

(h) *Exit:* Pricing of the shares at the time of disinvestment by a public issue or general offer of sale by the VCC/VCF may be done them, subject to this being calculated on objective criteria like book value, profit earning capacity, etc., and the basis is adequately disclosed to the public.

(i) Eligibility of tax concession: The preferential tax treatment would be available to the approved venture capital company/fund only in respect of financing of such assisted units as are eligible to the treated as venture capital. For this purpose, the unit seeking equity support from the VCC/VCF should obtain a letter of eligibility from IDBI/ICICI, or any such agency that may be nominated by the Government.

DIFFERENCE BETWEEN PRIVATE EQUITY, VENTURE CAPITAL AND HEDGE FUNDS

Presently there is lot of ambiguity surrounding the concepts of private equity and alternative investment channels like venture capital and hedge funds. Venture capital is a subset of private equity and refers to equity investments made for the launch, early development, or expansion of a business. It has a particular emphasis on entrepreneurial undertakings rather than on mature businesses. In fact, in most of the literature on private equity and venture capital, these two concepts are used interchangeably. Hedge Funds differ from private equity firms in terms of their time-to-hold, liquidity, leverage and strategic direction of investments which in turn dictates differences in their exit strategy, risk tolerance and desired rate of return of the two types of funds. Hedge funds seek a quick flip of their investments with the average length of their investments being 6-18 months, whereas private equity firms stay invested for around 3-5 years. Hedge funds are also inclined towards volatile withdrawal of investments as opposed to private equity firms which are focussed on long term returns. However, of late, it has been observed that the arena of activities of such institutional investors are not mutually exclusive. Many private equity groups own hedge funds and make long term investments in hedge funds. Further, attracted by the significant returns in buyout deals, many hedge funds have joined hands with private equity players to make large buyout deals. Given the differences in activities and risk tolerance of the two players coupled with the absence of any public reporting norms of their activities, the synergy between the two players has raised regulatory concerns, of recent.

REGULATION OF PRIVATE EQUITY AND VENTURE CAPITAL IN INDIA

In India, private equity is not a regulated activity, *per se*. However, indigenous and foreign venture capital funds are regulated by SEBI (Venture Capital Funds) Regulations, 1996 and Foreign Venture Capital Funds Regulations, 2000. Further, private equity/venture capital funds investments from abroad have to adhere to the restrictions on foreign capital inflows. In other words, although there may not be any explicit regulations for private equity fundraising and investment in India like in US and UK, private equity funds are regulated within the ambit of existing regulations.

SEBI (Venture Capital Funds) Regulations, 1996

Venture capital, which can be looked at as a subset of private equity, has been under regulatory oversight since 1996 when the SEBI (Venture Capital Funds) Regulations, 1996 came into existence. This legislation enumerated the norms for registration of venture capital funds, investment conditions and restrictions, general obligations and responsibilities and investigation and inspection. Under this, venture capital funds are prohibited from inviting subscription from public. They can only obtain funds through private placement of units. Further, no venture capital funds shall be eligible to list on a recognised stock exchange till the expiry of three years from the date of issuance of its units. Restrictions on investment conditions include disclosure of investment strategy at the time of registration of funds, investment in a particular undertaking shall not exceed 25 per cent of the corpus of the fund, *etc.*

Foreign Venture Capital Funds Regulations, 2000

Subsequently, SEBI introduced Foreign Venture Capital Investors (FVCI) Regulations in 2000 to enable foreign funds to register with SEBI and avail of some benefits which are otherwise not available under FDI route. Some of these benefits include no lock up of shares held by registered investors and exemption from applicability of valuation norms, thereby enabling investors to buy and sell shares in Indian unlisted companies at prices they deem appropriate, upon mutual agreement between buyers/sellers. However, they cannot invest more than 33.3 per cent of the investible funds in shares of listed companies or debt instruments. Further, the provisions of SEBI (Substantial Acquisitions of Shares and Takeover) Regulations, 1997 do not apply to shares transferred from an FVCI to the promoters of the company or the company itself. Thus if the promoters intend to buy-back their shares from FVCI, they will not be required to comply with the public offering requirements of the Takeover Code. FVCIs registered with SEBI are 'Qualified Institutional Buyers' under SEBI (Disclosure and Investor Protection) Guidelines, 2000 and hence are eligible to participate in the primary issuance process. They are subject to regular inspection and investigation by SEBI. Further, Indian venture capital funds (VCFs) are entitled to tax benefits under Section 10(23FB) of the Income Tax Act (1961) under which any income earned by SEBI registered VCF, established either as a trust or company, to raise funds for investment in VCF, is exempt from tax. Further, FVCIs particularly benefit from the Section 90(2) of Income Tax Act which provides relief from double taxation to non-resident investors residing in countries with whom India has Double Tax Avoidance Agreement such as Mauritius. Mauritius is now increasingly used by foreign investors to establish offshore entities and invest into Indian VCFs, thus benefiting from the tax avoidance treaty. However, while considering an FVCI application, SEBI reviews the applicants track record, professional competence, financial soundness, experience, general reputation, whether the applicant is regulated by an appropriate foreign regulatory authority or is an income tax payer, amongst other factors. However, it is not manadatory for a foreign venture capital fund to register with SEBI. They can still invest in India *via* the foreign direct investment route subject to compliance with applicable securities pricing norms.

Restrictions on Inflow of Foreign Private Equity

Foreign venture and private equity funds came to invest in India through the FDI route. Foreign investments, either through FII route or FDI route, are subject to sectoral caps. Government of India has imposed investment limits for FIIs of 10 per cent and the maximum FII investment in each publicly listed company may at times be lower than the sectoral cap for foreign investment in that company. Under the FDI route, FIPB approval is required for foreign investments where the proposed shareholding is above the prescribed sector cap or for investments in sectors where FDI is not permitted or where it is mandatory that proposals be routed through the FIPB. Very recently, the Foreign Investment Promotion Board has ruled that foreign investment can flow into private equity funds registered as trusts. The Department of Industrial Policy and Promotion is framing the guidelines for allowing investments in trusts that invest in companies, especially start-ups, with the aim of long-term capital gains.

Prudential Regulations for Private Equity

As of now, there are no prudential regulations on private equity unlike Indian banks. However, keeping in view that Indian financial sector is largely bank-intermediated and there have been recent cases of Indian banks engaging in sponsoring and managing private pools of capital such as venture capital funds and infrastructure funds, the Reserve Bank of India had mandated maintenance of certain level of economic capital in some of the cases approved in the recent past.

However, legal caution still prevails with respect to private equity investment into leveraged buyouts and exit through foreign listing. The laws for leveraged buyout of Indian companies are not conducive. Companies Act 1956, Section 77(2) prohibits a public company (or a private company which is a subsidiary of a public company) from providing any financial assistance whether by means of guarantee, provision of security in connection with purchase of their shares or shares of their holding companies. Further, if a public company is listed, prior to being acquired in a LBO, the company must delist and convert itself to a private company. FIPB's Press Note 9 bars a foreign investment company from borrowing from an Indian bank to buy into a company in India.

While exit of private equity investment through domestic public listing is under the process of liberalization, laws still hold back exit through foreign listing. SEBI guidelines require mandatory listing of Indian companies on domestic exchange prior to foreign listing. Bulk of the private equity transactions in India are minority transactions. This is because in a large number of Indian companies, management control rests with promoters who may not want to divest their controlling stake for additional capital. In the absence of control, it may be difficult to finance a minority investment using leverage given the control over the cash flows of the target company to service the debt. Further, a minority private equity investor, will be unable to sell it's holding to a strategic buyer, thereby limiting the exit options available for the investment.

Besides, there are restrictions on the use of investment instruments. Funds investing in Indian companies have the option of investing in equity shares, preference shares, debentures and other instruments depending on the status of the portfolio company i.e. whether it is a private limited company, public unlisted or public listed company. Usage of innovative customized instruments while investing in private limited companies require the prior approval of Government. Hence, private equity investors mostly subscribe to traditional instruments while investing in private companies. Even within the available instruments, investing in preference shares and debentures raises several regulatory restrictions. For example, proceeds raised by non convertible/ optionally convertible debentures or preference shares cannot be used for general corporate purposes. Also such instruments need to have a minimum maturity period and cap on the coupon payable, if they are to be issued without approval.

QUESTIONS

1. Explain the concept of Private Equity. What are the factors responsible for the phenominal growth of the private equity market.
2. Discuss the basics of private equity ownership and the current change in shift to new focus from buying business units of public companies to taking entire public companies private.
3. "The strategy, which embodies a combination of business and investment portfolio management, is at the case of private equity's success." Do you agree?
4. Discuss the business cycles of private equity. Does easy access to private equity funds delay firms' decision to go for public offer?
5. Discuss the concept of Venture Capital. What are the major recommendations of the SEBI Committee on Venture Capital Fund (VCF)?
6. Critically examine the different stages of investment which the venture capital industry recognises.
7. Discuss the various factor which are responsible for the slow growth of the venture capital industry in India.
8. Analyse the factors which the entrepreneur should take into account while selecting the venture capitalist
9. Critically examine the role of SEBI as a nodal agency for VCFs.
10. Distinguish between private equity, venture capital and hedge funds. Discuss the prospects for the Private equity market in India.
11. Critically examine the implication of private equity for India. Does private equity compete with traditional non-bank sources of finance like public issues and private placement or supplement them?
12. Explain the working of private equity. What are the most common types of private equity ctivities in terms of stages of corporate development.

REFERENCES

1. Chokshi (2007): "Challenges in Executing Leveraged Buyouts in India, The Evolution of the Growth Buyout", Glucksman Institute of Research in Securities Markets, April 2007.
2. EVCA (2007): 'Guide on Private Equity and Venture Capital for Entrepreneurs', An EVCA Special Paper, November 2007.
3. Fenn, G, Liang, N and Prowse, S (1995): 'The Economics of the Private Equity Market', Working Paper No. 168, Board of Governors of the Federal Reserve System.
4. Gandhi, V (2008): Private Equity and Venture Capital Investments in India, Certain Legal Aspects, IVCA, September 2008.
5. GFSR (2008): 'Assessing Risks to Global Financial Stability', Global Financial Stability Report, April 2008
6. Gopinath, S (2009): 'Addressing Regulatory Perimeter Issues – Indian Experience', Speech by Deputy Governor, RBI at the Ninth Annual International Seminar on Policy Challenges for the Financial Sector, co-hosted by The Board of Governors of the Federal Reserve System, The IMF, and The World Bank on "Emerging from the Crisis - Building a Stronger International Financial System", June 3-5, 2009, Washington, D.C.
7. Hellman, T and Puri, M (2000): 'The Interaction between Product Market and Financing Strategy: The Role of Venture Capital, Review of Financial Studies, 13(4).
8. IFSL Research (2008): Private Equity 2008, August 2008.

9. Kaplan, S. N. (1989): 'The Effects of Management Buyouts on Operations and Value, Journal of Financial Economics, Vol.24, pp: 217-254.

10. Katz, S (2008): 'Earnings Quality and Ownership Structure: The Role of Private Equity Sponsors', NBER Working Paper No. 14085, June 2008.

11. KPMG (2008): "Private Equity: Implications for Economic Growth in Asia Pacific".

12. Lerner, J (1999): 'Venture Capital and Private Equity – A Casebook', New York, John Wiley and Sons, Inc.

13. Ljungqvist, A and Richardson (2003): The Cash Flows, Return and Risk Characteristics of Private Equity, CEPR, January 2003.

14. McKinsey Global Institute (2007): The New Power Brokers: How Oil, Asia, Hedge Funds, and Private Equity Are Shaping Global Capital Markets, October 2007.

15. Metric, A and Yasuda, A (2008): 'The Economics of Private Equity Funds' , Journal of Economic Literature, September 2008.

16. Michelacci, C and Suarez, J (2004): 'Business Creation and the Stock Market, Review of Economic Studies, 71(2), 459-81.

17. Morgan, J (2007): Private Equity Finance: How it works, what its effects are, can it be justified? Working Paper No.3, The Center of Excellence in Global Governance Research, July 2007.

18. Persaud (2008):"Regulation, Valuation and Systemic Liquidity", Bank of France Working Papers, 2008.

19. Povaly, S (2007): 'Private Equity Exits', Springer.

20. Pratt, S (1981): 'Guide to Venture Capital Sources', 5th Edition, Wellesley, MA, Capital Publishing.

21. Private Equity Valuation (2006): "International Private Equity and Venture Capital Guidelines", October 2006.

22. PwC (2008): 'The Global Private Equity Report', Price WaterHouseCooper.

23. Rin, M (2007): 'The Effect of Venture Capital on Innovation Strategies', NBER Working Paper No. 13636, November 2007.

24. Rin, M and Penas, M (2007): 'The Effect of Venture Capital on Innovation Strategies', NBER Working Paper No.13636.

25. Venture Intelligence (2005 and 2006): 'Private Equity Impact Report', Venture Intelligence.

26. Weidig and Mathonet (2004): 'The Risk Profiles of Private Equity', January 2004.

15

Government Securities

INTRODUCTION

Fiscal policy encompasses the taxation, expenditure, and debt management of the government. It is used to pursue national economic goals: full employment, price stability and economic growth. When government expenditure exceeds revenues, this deficit must be financed. In order to do so, the government issues a variety of securities. This helps the government to tap the different sources of funds that are available in the money and capital markets. In fact. the existence of an efficient government securities debt market is usually seen as an essential precursor for the corporate debt market. Following a developmental model rather than a regulatory and supervisory model, the Reserve Bank of India took up the task of developing the government securities market, so as to facilitate overall improvement in the strength of financial and economic system of the country.

GOVERNMENT SECURITIES MARKET IN INDIA

As the debt manager to the Government, the development of a deep and liquid market for Government securities is of critical importance to the Reserve Bank for facilitating the process of price discovery and reducing the cost of Government debt. The Reserve Bank has taken several structural and development measures for deepening and widening the Government securities market. During the last two decades, the size of the G-Sec market has grown from Rs.76,908 crore (in 1991-92) to Rs.25,93,328 crore (2011-12) – an almost 34 fold increase; recording a compounded annual growth of over 19% (Table 1). The average maturity of the outstanding G-Sec has risen from 5.50 years (in 1996-97) to 12.66 years (2011-12) with issuances ranging from 2 years to up to 30 years in maturity.

TABLE 1

G-Sec Market: A snapshot

	1992	2005	2012
Outstanding stock (₹ crore)	76,908	7,58,995	25,93,328
Outstanding stock as ratio of GDP (per cent)	11.75	23.41	28.88
Weighted average cost of the securities issued during the year (Per cent)	11.78	6.11	8.52
Min. and max. maturities of stock issued during the year (Years)	N.A.	5-30	5-30
Average maturity of the securities issued during the year (Years)	—	14.13	12.66
Secondary market volume (₹ crore)	—	8,62,820	30,99,107
Volume / GDP (per cent)	—	26.61	34.51
Volume / Outstanding Stock (per cent)	—	113	120

While the market for G-Sec has grown since 1992, the liquidity in secondary market has not been high and commensurate with the growth in the economy, size of the market, widening of institutional investor-base, etc. In spite of passive consolidation through reissuance of G-Sec, the number of outstanding securities has remained high (92 GoI dated securities as of Jan 2012). This has led to fragmentation of liquidity in the secondary market. The objective of the issuer to elongate the maturity profile of outstanding debt, keeping in view the redemption pressures and to minimize rollover risk, has resulted in lack of primary issuances in the short-end of the yield curve, i.e. tenors below 5 years.

The annual settlement volumes of outright trades in GoI dated securities have increased from Rs.8,62,820 crore in 2004-05 to Rs.30,99,108 crore in 2011-12 (Table 2). The average daily volumes during this period have increased from about Rs.3,400 crore to over Rs.10,000 crore. However, a closer look at the trade data reveals a not so encouraging picture of the secondary market. The settlement volume has shown a secular rising trend since 2005-06 and has more than trebled since then but the growth in volume during the last few years has not matched the same during the period 2005-10. The turnover ratio in the G-Sec market averaged little over 1 during the period 2004-12 and has not crossed 1.5 during this period. In fact, the turnover ratio declined in 2010-11 vis-à-vis 2009-10 and has remained constant in 2011-12 as the trade volume could not keep pace with the rise in the outstanding stock of G-Sec. While there are signs of fall in trading interest of late, albeit marginal, the secondary market volume is not broad-based across securities and tenors.

TABLE 2
Secondary Market Activity in GoI Dated Securities

Year	Settlement Volume (₹Cr)	Turnover Ratio	Share in volume traded		Avg. tenor of Top security (yrs)
			Top 5 securities	Top security	
2003-04	14,58,665	2.1	39%	11%	14
2004-05	8,62,820	1.1	50%	29%	11
2005-06	6,57,213	0.8	64%	31%	11
2006-07	8,83,248	0.9	75%	36%	9
2007-08	14,67,704	1.3	66%	36%	10
2008-09	19,55,412	1.5	61%	44%	10
2009-10	24,80,850	1.4	61%	36%	9
2010-11	25,52,181	1.2	72%	39%	11
2011-12	30,99,108	1.2	86%	51%	10

The share of the top 5 traded securities in total volume has increased from 39% (in 2003-04) to over 86% (in 2011-12), which indicates that the entire trade volume is concentrated in a few securities. In fact, a more serious issue is that the share of a single security averages about 35% during this period (and is at 51% during 2011-12). Trading is predominant in the 9-11 year segment of the yield curve leaving the other segments of the yield curve illiquid. With the total number of G-Sec at 92, the availability of market-determined prices is restricted to 5 securities thereby resulting in a scenario where the remaining securities have to be priced/valued on derived prices, based on a model, which may not reflect the true price of the security. The other important outcome of this skewness in secondary market is the lack of benchmark yields for pricing of non-sovereign debt across the maturity spectrum (excluding the few liquid securities).

The repo market in G-Sec, which is critical for funding of positions by the traders, has also witnessed considerable growth during the last 10 years (Table 3). The leverage of technology and the availability of a robust clearing and settlement mechanism have been instrumental in the migration of the repo market from a pure OTC market to an electronic environment where order-matching systems are available for standard basket repos as well as 'special' repos.

TABLE 3

Market Repo Transactions in G-Sec

(₹ in cr)

Year	Dated Securities	T-Bills	SDLs	Total	CBLO
2002-03	4,03,971	64,238	20	4,68,229	-
2003-04	8,74,438	59,222	9,530	9,43,190	-
2004-05	12,62,149	2,86,955	8,803	15,57,907	9,76,789
2005-06	13,69,411	2,77,687	47,411	16,94,509	29,53,132
2006-07	21,26,634	3,79,165	50,677	25,56,475	47,32,272
2007-08	35,69,960	3,23,984	54,807	39,48,751	81,10,828
2008-09	34,75,348	5,83,335	35,603	40,94,286	88,24,784
2009-10	52,33,295	8,12,537	26,996	60,72,828	1,55,41,378
2010-11	32,53,965	8,32,632	12,688	40,99,284	1,22,59,745
2011-12	21,86,877	15,54,121	22,878	37,63,876	1,11,55,428

The CBLO, since its introduction, has come to occupy an important place in the repo market. The tripartite nature of the instrument has been an attractive feature of this lending/borrowing instrument and this is reflected in the dominance of the CBLO in the collateralized market. The annual value of repo trades in G-Sec has increased from Rs.4,68,229 crore (in 2002-03) to Rs.37,63,876 crore in 2011-12 with the annual volume transacted through CBLO in 2011-12 at Rs.1,11,55,428 crore. Correspondingly, the annual volume of repo trades in CROMS was Rs.25,67,038 crore (during 2011-12).

PRIMARY DEALERS (PDs)

A primary dealer system is an agreement between two major stakeholders in the domestic government debt market — the debt manager and a group of dealers — to pursue a common strategy in support of the functioning and development of primary and secondary markets for government securities. Primary dealers (PD) are financial intermediaries that, generally in exchange for specific privileges, agree to perform specific obligations or functions in the operation of markets for government securities. Following from this definition, the roles include

(i) acting as a channel *between debt manager and investor* in the primary market (for example, by participating in auctions);

(ii) performing as *bookmakers and distributors* by having dealers that canvass investors' interest and distribute securities ahead of auctions through when-issued markets.

(iii) acting as *providers of immediacy* of liquidity to primary and secondary markets;

(iv) acting as *providers of asset transformation and market-making services* by being willing to hold inventories of government securities and allowing investors to swap between various outstanding issues of government securities on a continuous basis helps bring liquidity to the market;

   (v)   promoting *continuous markets and efficient price discovery* by organizing dealers within an appropriate market structure that can encourage efficient price discovery;

  (vi) acting as *agents and relationship managers* educating investors about the attractiveness of government securities as an investment; and

 (vii) being *advisors to the government* by formulating and adopting appropriate strategies for the development of products and markets.

Selection criteria for primary dealers typically include financial strength as indicated by adequate capitalization; an active role in government securities markets and financial expertise, such as skilled management and staff, together with access to appropriate technology. Obligations generally include one or more of the following: (i) participating in the primary market in a substantial and consistent manner; (ii) serving as a market maker in the secondary market by providing two-way quotes, either indicative or firm, for specified groups of securities; and (iii) providing market-related information to the public debt manager, whose main objective is to ensure that the government's financing needs and its obligations are met at the lowest possible cost, consistent with a prudent degree of risk. Privileges, or supporting arrangements, which vary widely among countries, generally involve the granting of some aspect of exclusivity—for example, the exclusive right to participate in the auction for treasury bills, and/or the right to serve as a counterparty to the central bank when it conducts open market operations, and/or access to a line of credit or permission to borrow particular issues from the central bank.

OBJECTIVES AND RATIONALE FOR A PRIMARY DEALER SYSTEM

The main purposes of a primary dealer system include strengthening the primary market by helping to build a stable, dependable source of demand for securities, by providing liquidity in title secondary market, devoting capital resources to underwriting (as a proprietary buyer) to absorb an occasional shortfall of liquidity, building distribution channels (to act as intermediaries) and providing market information, including prices, volumes, and spreads between bids and offers. These objectives in turn, serve the overall goals of: (i) lowering the cost and associated risk of servicing the public debt, (ii) developing financial markets, (iii) enabling the central bank to use indirect instruments of monetary policy, and (iv) encouraging saving by providing a relatively risk-free investment with attractive returns.

Development of financial markets involves a broader set of policies than just establishing a primary dealer system. In particular, some countries may have set up primary dealer systems without necessary supporting policies, including a commitment to a market-clearing outcome. Based on empirical observation, establishment of a primary dealer system can be an efficient way to develop and execute a coordinated approach to market development and thereby accelerate the development of market structure. Practical experience shows that primary dealer systems are in many cases a very helpful and efficient way to build up a market as well as maintain the functioning of the market in later stages. Other ways to set up markets, however, do exist, and in the choice of different setups country specificity and historical (path-dependence), considerations might well play a role, in addition to theoretical considerations.

In addition, setting up a system of primary dealers can be interpreted as a response to a market failure, if the government perceives that the existing market structure is not performing efficiently or if the market does not yet exist or is very thin. This happens typically in many developing countries, where the rationale for primary dealers may rest not only on efficiency arguments but also on developmental reasons. Additionally, the creation of a primary dealer system can be seen as a commitment to sound debt management practices. By selecting a specialized set of institutions, the authorities might be signaling to the financial community and the public at large their commitment to a liberalized market and a sustainable public debt strategy. Therefore, defining such a group of qualified dealers might increase investors' confidence in government securities as an investment.

In analyzing the issue of primary dealers, it is important to include considerations of securities market structure and development, and coordination of the various players involved. A decision whether to set up a primary dealer system, and the associated design, can be considered not only from a developmental point of view but also, in more advanced economies, from a market structure point of view. In this context, design of the mix of obligations and privileges must be an integral part of the strategy for developing and improving a government securities market, and the design itself can target market development (create a market, accommodate public sector borrowing requirements) and/or market structure (competition, efficiency, financial instruments).

From a developmental point of view, in the early stages of development the authorities might view the existence of a group of specialized institutions as instrumental in supporting their efforts to develop a market for government securities. These institutions would concentrate limited expertise and scarce resources in a limited number of players, thereby facilitating coordination among players and supporting a smooth market process. For instance, in the absence of liquid funding markets, a broad and well-informed investor base, available and well-developed trading platforms, and a supporting infrastructure, a primary dealer system can be a very useful platform upon which to develop the government securities market. In this context, it is clear the developmental role that a coordinated set of players can have in supporting government-borrowing strategy, while at the same time creating some of the conditions for the use of indirect instruments of monetary policy.

The design of the primary dealer system as a developmental objective should aim at a mix of obligations, privileges, and supporting arrangements that help the authorities to achieve their objectives. Equally important, other supporting markets or infrastructures are likely to be missing in this context, so there must be a commitment from the authorities to implement policies to put in place necessary infrastructure (e.g., book-entry system, DVP, and bidding technology) and to develop other markets (interbank market and local capital market, for instance). Given this background, the performance of primary dealers can be expected to be less than optimal, but mechanisms should be put in place to limit possible non-competitive behavior and moral hazard.

In more advanced economies, where developmental issues become less pressing, a market structure approach is also useful. When a country has already developed market intermediaries and infrastructures, the reasons for having a primary dealer system are different from the ones highlighted above. Arguments for specialization and economies of scale tend to prevail, and country experience in advanced economies (France, Italy) indicates that a primary dealer system accomplishes several objectives: (i) decreases market and refinancing risk, (ii) improves knowledge of the market, (iii) strengthens product and process innovations, (iv) provides better access to end investors, (v) improves promotion of debt, and (vi) provides skillful advisory support in building and following the debt management policy. One could also argue that some potential threats to an efficient market functioning must be taken into account—for instance, by selecting a preferential group of intermediaries, the authorities might reduce competitive neutrality and limit contestability. In addition, when the authorities have introduced on-line trading systems and financial markets and intermediaries are extremely sophisticated, as in the

United States, which has had a system of primary dealers for a long time, the case for a primary dealer system becomes less clear. When there are substantial fiscal deficits and financing needs, however, primary dealers may continue to play a positive role in the primary market even in developed markets.

The practice of selecting a specialized group of intermediaries for government securities can be seen as similar to the practice of private commercial borrowers that implement their financing strategy via placements through a specific group of investment banks for the same reasons highlighted above (advisory, access investors, lower market and financing risk and so forth). However, there are additional risks in taking this approach by a government with a specific group of primary dealers. One risk is increased moral hazard, or the possibility that designated primary dealers will engage in more risky behavior because they have been selected by the authorities. Also, customers may assume in error that primary dealers are guaranteed by the government or central bank. In addition, compared with the private market solution, selection by the authorities may risk reduced contestability and possible anti-competitive behavior.

Therefore, it is essential that in deciding for the adoption of a primary dealer system, the authorities design mechanisms to reduce these risks, while preserving as much of the benefits as possible. Contestability can be supported by rotating primary dealers based on performance (Mexico), while the risk of anti-competitive behavior must be addressed by strengthening supervision. The argument for moral hazard/implicit guarantees must also be addressed in the context of liquidity/crisis management policies by designing an appropriate structure of incentives and controls.

In deciding for the adoption of a primary dealer system, the authorities should simultaneously address these issues to achieve their debt management objectives while maximizing market efficiency. Countries that have fairly advanced markets and intermediaries, but that for some reason would not be able to address the negative effects induced by the introduction of a primary dealer system, should strengthen their capacity of intervention in these areas before putting the system in place, or phase in supervisory and regulatory reforms at the same time. While in developing economies the developmental aspects can outweigh downsides related to market structure, in more advanced economies the authorities should clearly evaluate whether the market would not be able to perform the same functions without introducing a selected subgroup of specialized intermediaries.

Another aspect of a primary dealers activity in the secondary market is to serve as an intermediary between the debt manager, often the central bank, and retail investors. In this regard, primary dealers are often expected to serve as partners with the debt manager and central bank in developing the institutional and retail markets. This function may include educating the public about investing in government securities.

In recent years, a number of debt managers in developed economies have been moving into direct retail sales of securities over the internet. More generally, modernization of markets and automation are making some of the functions traditionally performed by primary dealers less important or redundant. For example, automation gives a means to handle large numbers of participants in auctions that was not previously possible. Electronic markets offer information on market conditions and prices that might formerly have been possible to have only directly from dealers. Whether this recent trend in developed economies also applies for the needs of developing countries depends on country-specific situations, given the technological possibilities and constraints that different countries face.

BENEFITS AND COSTS OF PRIMARY DEALER SYSTEM

By selecting certain firms as primary dealers and not others, authorities concentrate market activity in a smaller number of firms, which has both positive and negative implications. On the positive side, especially in the early phases of market development, there can be important efficiencies associated with larger volumes of financial transactions, including automation and more advanced technology, and the use of specialized, highly skilled personnel. Acquiring these resources has substantial fixed costs, and spreading these costs over a larger volume makes them more economical. Competition and efficiency can also increase if foreign firms are allowed to become primary dealers, if as seems likely those firms are advanced and have an international clientele. In addition, there are advantages to the debt manager in limiting the number of institutions with which it has to deal in conducting auctions of government securities and (if it is the central bank) in its open market operations. A general benefit of a primary dealer system is that it reduces both risks and the risk management burden. The quality criteria reduce credit, execution, settlement and operational risks; and the limited number of dealers makes the administrative and credit monitoring burden more manageable.

The most significant possible problem of setting up a primary dealer system is the risk of promoting a less than efficient market structure. A primary dealer system is a dealer market structure; developing one involves choosing (by the issuer) this particular market structure for the trading and issuance of debt. If alternative market structures are more efficient or appropriate, then a primary dealer system is best avoided and a different and more appropriate country-specific strategy developed.

A second drawback of a primary dealer system is that it can potentially limit competition and contribute to oligopolistic behavior. Since selection is fundamental to a primary dealer system, it can in some respects run counter to the principle of establishing a level playing field. To a considerable extent, however, these potential "negatives" can be avoided by careful design of the system, for example, by not unduly limiting the number of market participants.

In addition, by selecting a group of financial firms to serve as primary dealers, there is a risk that the public may view them as possessing an implicit guarantee by the government. There may also be moral hazard in that guarantee, in that once selected as a primary dealer, the primary dealer may engage in more risky behavior, believing that the government would not stand by and let it fail. In this regard, the primary dealer might be induced to take on more risks than it otherwise would. Authorities should try to reduce this moral hazard by supervision and by allowing contestability. For example, periodically, authorities may reassess and reselect the group of primary dealers.

Since establishing a system of primary dealers has its pros and cons, an important question concerns whether, or under what conditions it is helpful to have such a system. In general, the answer depends on the authorities' overall strategy for developing the government securities market and the appropriate microstructure for the market. In particular, if authorities envision a secondary market structure in which there are competing dealers and market makers, then a primary dealer system may be an appropriate choice. However, authorities may opt for an auction system with direct buy and sell orders to a single location or electronic matching system, in which case a primary dealer system might not be appropriate. Or, alternatively, the secondary market may be too small to support an effective number of primary dealers, in which case the authorities may decide as a transitional measure to open a secondary window at the central bank.

The justification for establishing a system of primary dealers is that the system satisfies public goals that might otherwise not be met. One of the main goals in this regard is to maintain or enhance the liquidity of secondary markets. A liquid market may involve external benefits that accrue to other parties that are not directly involved in the government securities market.

It may be useful to consider whether the tradeoff between the advantages and the disadvantages of a primary dealer system changes during the course of economic development. In the early stages, for instance, not all of the key conditions may be present for an effective primary dealer system. In particular, there may not be enough dealers who are active in the government securities market. Moreover, in those early stages, the commercial banks, which are some of the most likely candidates for primary dealership, may have a vested interest in not developing the government securities market, since they have competing products and may profit from the scarce opportunities of their depositors. In addition, the size of the financial system, and of the government securities market in particular, may play an important role, with smaller countries finding it more difficult to justify a primary dealer system. In this context, the potential for specialization on the part of dealers in government securities is limited by the small size of the financial market. At the same time, the potential contributions of a primary dealer system—developing the primary and secondary markets and developing the retail base for government securities—are most relevant for developing and emerging-market countries.

In the latter stages of financial development, especially in large diversified financial systems (Germany or Switzerland), the need for, or potential contributions from a primary dealer system may be less important. In many developed countries, there may be a relatively large number of active participants in the primary market; and there may be an active and highly competitive secondary market, while retail investors have a number of attractive alternatives. Thus, some industrial countries, such as Australia, Germany, Japan, New Zealand, and Switzerland, do not have primary dealer systems, while the United States with the largest and most diversified financial system in the world does have such a system. The United States, however, has reduced the privileges of primary dealers over time, and opened the system to more competition. Now, aside from being recognized as a primary dealer, the main privilege is to be one of the counterparties to the Federal Reserve when it conducts its open market operations. More generally, the role and specific features of a primary dealer system may change during the course of economic development.

NECESSARY CONDITIONS FOR A PRIMARY DEALER SYSTEM

Important prerequisites for establishing a primary dealer system are listed below:
i) **A government must have a strategy for issuing government securities:** A government must accurately plan its debt issuance strategy so as to provide a medium-term horizon for the investment strategy of primary and secondary market agents.
ii) **Interest rates should be liberalized:** It is essential, that interest rates on government securities reflect actual demand and supply, in both the primary and secondary markets, to guarantee efficient price discovery.
iii) **An adequate number of end investors is necessary:** This means that the government should try to estimate potential demand among individuals and the financial sector and be able to fine-tune its own supply, arising from its financing needs, to be able to meet potential demand. Preliminary discussions with banks will help the government gauge this potential absorption capacity.

iv) **A minimum set of attractively designed securities should be available:** In deciding its debt strategy, the government should plan for a certain number of different types of securities, taking into account different maturities and trying to establish benchmarks. In addition, other instruments could include index-linked securities, inflation-linked securities, to mention just some simple examples that can help investors diversify their portfolios of instruments and provide instruments for risk management.

v) **The government must be committed to secondary market development:** This is important condition because it guarantees the primary dealers and other market participants that they will not compete directly with the government in the placement of securities in the retail market. The authorities should refrain from intervening directly in the market, for instance, limiting or avoiding, direct sale of securities.

vi) **The government must also be committed to market-determined outcomes:** The authorities should make efforts to stimulate a setup of the primary and secondary market to allow competitive forces to play a dominant role. In this context, primary dealers should not be seen as a captive group that can be burdened with government securities, but rather as the initiators of a market or a group providing additional liquidity and transparency to the market for the purpose of better price discovery and resource allocation.

vii) **Arrangements between primary dealers and the debt managers in support of the auction system should be carefully arrived at:** This is an important prerequisite, since the auction is the central mechanism for securities allocation in the primary market. The auction design must allow an efficient price discovery. Problems in auction design are bound to have a strong negative effect on subsequent segments of the market, since inefficient price discovery or inefficient allocation will impact the secondary market both at wholesale and retail level.

viii) **Sufficient debt and a potential volume of secondary market trade should be available to support a profitable group of competing dealers without subsidies for the operations:** With respect to the size of the market, it is important to have an adequate number of active participants in the market, and enough volume in government securities issued to justify a primary dealer system. In addition to authorities' commitment to market-determined prices and attainment of a minimum size of the market for government securities, there are other highly desirable conditions for establishing a primary dealer system, including a legal framework for government securities, a regulatory/supervisory system for government securities dealers, and an adequate payment and settlement system. However, the primary dealers can be used as a platform and an integral part of the building of such systems. In many developing and emerging market countries for instance, primary dealers have been used as custody agents as part of the book entry system. They have been given accounts with central banks to clear and settle on a Delivery versus Payment (DvP) basis. In addition, in some countries, the setting up of primary dealers has been the cornerstone of developing efficient primary markets.

In the early stages of development and for many small developing countries, there may not be enough participants in the government securities auctions to reduce the number further by establishing a primary dealer system. Having an adequate number of participants in the auction may be a particular problem if the authorities are trying to limit participants to commercial banks for clearing and settlement purposes. If the main objective is to be as inclusive as possible for bidding at the auctions, then limiting the numbers further in order to start a primary dealer system may be inappropriate.

PRIMARY DEALERS IN INDIA

Primary dealers/wholesalers of government securities can be loosly referred to as Merchant bankers to Government of India, comprising the first tier of the government securities market. In 1996 RBI framed guidelines for a enlistment and operations of Primary Dealers (PDs) is accordance with the announcement in the Monetary and Credit policy on May 14, 1994 to introduce a system of PDs in the government securities market.

There were 21 Primary Dealers (PDs) operating in the financial markets as on June 30, 2012. Of them, 13 were run by banks as a department called Bank-PDs, and the remaining 8 were non-bank entities known as standalone PDs registered as NBFCs under Section 45 IA of the RBI Act, 1934.

The objectives of the PD systems are: (i) To strengthen the infrastructure in the government securities market in order to make it vibrant, liquid and broad based, (ii) To ensure development of underwriting and market making capabilities for government securities outside the RBI so that the latter will gradually shed these functions, (iii) To improve secondary market trading system, which would contribute to price discovery, enhance liquidity and turnover and encourage voluntary holding of government securities amongst a wider investor base, (iv) To make PDs an effective conduit for conducting open market operations (OMO).

The decision to enlist Primary Dealers is taken by Reserve Bank of India based on its perception of market needs, suitability of the applicant and the likely value addition to the system. The classes of institutions eligible to apply for Primary Dealership are: (i) Subsidiary of scheduled commercial bank/s and all India financial institution/s dedicated predominantly to the securities business and in particular to the government securities market, (ii) Company incorporated under the Companies Act. 1956 and engaged predominantly in the securities business and in particular the government securities market, (iii) Subsidiaries/ joint ventures set up by entities incorporated abroad under the approval of Foreign Investment Promotion Board (FIPB).

The applicant shall have net owned funds of a minimum of ₹ 50 crore. The owned funds will consist of paid-up equity capital, free reserves, balance in share premium account and capital reserves representing surplus arising out of sale proceeds of assets but not reserves created by revaluation of assets. From this the aggregate of the following items will be deducted (i) accumulated balance of loss; (ii) deterred revenue expenditure; and (iii) other intangible items.

PDs Role and Obligations

PDs are expected to play an active role in government securities market, both in its primary and secondary segments. A Primary Dealer will be required to have a standing arrangement with RBI based on the execution of an undertaking and the authorisation letter issued by RBI covering inter-alia the following aspects;

(i) A Primary Dealer will have to commit to aggregatively bid for Government of India dated securities on an annual basis of not less than a specified amount and auction Treasury Bills for specified percentage for each auction. The agreed minimum amount/ percentage of bids would be separately indicated for dated securities and Treasury Bills.

(ii) A Primary Dealer would be required to achieve a minimum success ratio of 40 per cent for dated securities and 40 per cent for Treasury Bills.

(iii) Underwriting of Dated Government Securities: Primary Dealers will be collectively offered to underwrite up to 100% of the notified amount in respect of all issues where the amounts are notified.

A Primary Dealer can offer to underwrite an amount not exceeding five times of its net owned funds. The amount so arrived at should not exceed 30% of the notified amount of the issue. If two or more issues are floated at the same time, the limit of 30% is applied by taking the notified amounts of both the issues together.

In the case of revolvement, allotment of securities will be at the competitive cut-off price/yield decided at the auction or at par in the case of pre-determined coupon floatation. Obligations under items (i) to (iii) above would be confined for the present only to Central Government dated securities and obligations under items (i) to (ii) to Treasury Bills.

(iv) Treasury Bills

Treasury bill issues are not underwritten. Instead, Primary Dealers are required to commit to submit minimum bids at each auction. The commitment of Primary-Dealer's participation in treasury bills subscription works out as follows:

(a) Each Primary Dealer individually commits, at the beginning of the year, to submit minimum bids as a fixed percentage of the notified amount of treasury bills, in each auction.

(b) The minimum percentage of the bids for each Primary Dealer is determined by the Reserve Bank through negotiation with the Primary Dealer so that the entire issue of treasury bills is collectively apportioned among all Primary Dealers.

(c) The percentage of minimum bidding commitment determined by the Reserve Bank remains unchanged for the entire financial year or till furnishing of undertaking on bidding commitments for the next financial year, whichever is later. In determining the minimum bidding commitment, the Reserve Bank takes into account the offer made by the Primary Dealer, its net owned funds and its track record.

(v) A Primary Dealer shall offer firm two-way quotes either through the Negotiated Dealing System or over the counter telephone market or through a recognised Stock Exchange of India and deal in the secondary market for Government securities and take principal positions.

(vi) A Primary Dealer shall maintain the minimum capital standards at all points of time.

(vii) A Primary Dealer shall achieve a sizeable portfolio in government securities before the end of the first year of operations after authorisation.

(viii) The annual turnover of a Primary Dealer in a financial year shall not be less than 5 times of average month end stocks in government dated securities and 10 times of average month end stocks in Treasury Bills. Of the total, turnover in respect of outright transactions shall not be less than 3 times in respect of government dated securities and 6 times in respect of Treasury Bills. The target should be achieved by the end of the first year of operations after authorisation by RBI.

(ix) A Primary Dealer shall maintain physical infrastructure in terms of office, computing equipment, communication facilities like Telex/Fax, Telephone, etc.

and skilled manpower for efficient participation in primary issues, trading in the secondary market, and to advise and educate the investors.

(x) A Primary Dealer shall have an efficient internal control system for fair conduct of business and settlement of trades and maintenance of accounts.

(xi) A Primary Dealer will provide access to RBI to all records, books, information and documents as may be required.

(xii) A Primary Dealer shall subject itself to all prudential and regulatory guidelines issued by RBI.

(xiii) A Primary Dealer shall submit periodic returns as prescribed by RBI.

(xiii) A Primary Dealer's investment in G-Secs and Treasury Bills on a daily basis should be at least equal to its net call borrowing plus net RBI borrowing plus net owned funds of ₹ 50 crore.

The Reserve Bank would extend the following facilities to PDs to enable them to effectively fulfill their obligations: (i) Access to Current Account facility with Reserve Bank Of India, (ii) Access to Subsidiary General Ledger (SGL) Account facility (for Government securities). (iii) Permission to borrow and lend in the money market including call money market and to trade in all money market instruments, (iv) Access to liquidity support through Repo operations with RBI in Central Government dated securities and Auction Treasury Bills up to the limit fixed by RBI. The Scheme is separately notified every year, (v) Access to Liquidity Adjustment Facility (LAF) of Reserve Bank of India, (v) Favoured access to open market operations by Reserve Bank of India.

RBI will have access to records and accounts of an authorised Primary Dealer and the right to inspect its books. A Primary Dealer will be required to submit prescribed returns to RBI, IDM Cell a daily report on transactions and market information, monthly report of transactions in securities, risk position and performance with regard to participation in auctions, quarterly return on capital adequacy, an annual report on its performance together with annual audited accounts and such other statements and returns as are prescribed either specifically or generally by Reserve Bank of India vide any of its intitutions/circulars/directives. Further, PDs are required to meet such registration and other requirements as stipulated by Securities and Exchange Board of India (SEBI) including operations on the Stock Exchanges. Authorised PDs are expected to join self-regulatory organisations (SROs) like Primary Dealers Association of India (PDAI) and Fixed Income Money Market and Derivatives Association (FIMMDA) and abide by the code of conduct framed by them and such other actions initiated by them in the interests of the securities markets.

In respect of transactions in government securities, a Primary Dealer should have a separate desk and should maintain separate accounts and have an external audit of annual accounts. The Primary Dealer should maintain separate accounts in respect of its own position and customer transactions. A Primary Dealer should bring to the RBI's attention any major complaint against it or action initiated/taken against it by authorities such as the Stock Exchanges, SEBI, CBI, Enforcement Directorate, Income Tax. etc. Reserve Bank of India reserves the right to cancel the Primary Dealership if, in its view, the concerned institution has not fulfilled any of the prescribed performance criteria contained in the authorisation letter. Reserve Bank of India reserves its right to amend or modify these guidelines from time to time, as may be considered necessary.

The primary dealer (PD) system underwent significant changes during 2006-07. PDs, as underwriters to the Government's market borrowing and market makers in Government securities, are exposed to significant market risk. In order to diversify the risks inherent in the PD business, PDs were permitted to diversify into other business lines while retaining the requirement of maintaining predominance in Government securities business. PDs were allowed to diversify their investments into corporate debt, equity and securitisation instruments, subject to certain prudential limits so as to enable them to diversify their balance sheet risks. They were also allowed to offer certain fee based services.

Concomitantly, it was decided that PDs would not be permitted to set up step-down subsidiaries. Those PDs that already had step-down subsidiaries (in India and abroad) were advised to restructure the ownership pattern of those subsidiaries. This was done to ensure that the balance sheet of the PD does not get affected by the spillover of risks from other businesses/ subsidiaries and that the business of the PDs is focused on their primary dealership activities. Consequently, five out of eight stand-alone PDs. which either had step-down subsidiaries or undertook businesses other than those specifically permitted, were required to restructure their operations.

Keeping in view the increased responsibility of PDs in the wake of the FRBM Act, 2003, changes were made in the system of underwriting the issues of dated Government securities by PDs. The revised system envisages underwriting the entire issue in an auction. The twin policy measures of expanding the permitted structure of the PD system to include banks and revising the scheme of underwriting have contributed to successful debt management in the post-FRBM scenario. Stand-alone PDs'continued to remain adequately capitalised. Although the CRAR of PDs at 33 per cent as on March 31, 2007 declined from the previous year's level, it was much in excess of the stipulated minimum of 15 per cent of aggregate risk-weighted assets.

During the year 2008-09, many policy initiatives were taken to strengthen the PD system. First, in order to enable the PDs to raise more capital from the market through issue of subordinated debts, the extant ceiling of 200 basis points on the interest rate spreads at the time of issue of the subordinated instruments for the purpose of Tier II and Tier III capital requirements, was removed. Primary Dealers are now allowed to issue subordinated Tier II and Tier III bonds at coupon rates as decided by their Boards of Directors. Second, stand-alone PDs were allowed to hold up to 100 per cent of their paid up capital in Held- to- Maturity (HTM) category to insulate their financials from the price fluctuations caused during extreme stress times. Third, in the context of the Interest Rate Futures (Reserve Bank) Directions, 2009 dated August 28, 2009, stand-alone Primary Dealers (PDs) were allowed to deal in Interest Rate Futures (IRFs) for both hedging and trading on own account and not on client's account, subject to adherence to the prescribed prudential norms. Fourth, the limit on borrowing by the PDs from the call / notice money market, on an average in a reporting fortnight, was increased from the existing ceiling of 200 per cent of their NOF to 225 per cent of NOF, as at the end March of the preceding financial year. Fifth, to ensure stability of Primary Dealers in times of volatile interest rates, the minimum capital requirement increased from ₹ 50 crore to ₹ 150 crore. PDs which intend to diversify into other permissible activities need to have net owned funds of ₹ 250 crore as against ₹ 100 crore earlier.

The recommendations of the Internal Working Group on Auction Process of Government of India Securities, such as reduction of the time gap between the bid submission and the declaration of auction results, withdrawal of the facility of bidding in physical form and submission of competitive bids only through the NDS; and submission of a single consolidated bid on behalf of all its constituents by the bank/PD in respect of non-competitive bids have been implemented. In response to the Government borrowing programme in 2008-09 and 2009-10 so far, the underwriting income of PDs has registered a steady growth (Box 1).

Box-1

UNDERWRITING OF CENTRAL GOVERNMENT DATED SECURITIES

Concomitant with the objectives of Primary Dealer (PD) system, PDs are required to support auctions for issue of Government dated securities, through underwriting the dated securities and meeting the underwriting/bidding commitments. In terms of the Fiscal Responsibility and Budget Management (FRBM) Act, 2003, the Reserve Bank of India's participation in the primary issues of Government securities stood withdrawn with effect from April 1, 2006, except under exceptional circumstances. To address the emerging needs, an Internal Technical Group on Central Government Securities Market was constituted, which recommended the restructuring of the institutional process of bidding commitment by introducing a revised methodology for Primary Dealers' obligations. Under the new scheme, Primary Dealers are required to meet 100 per cent underwriting commitment in each auction, replacing the earlier requirement of bidding commitment and voluntary underwriting. The scheme of underwriting was put in place from April 1, 2006. The Scheme was further reviewed in November, 2007 and it was decided that the minimum bidding requirement for each PD in the ACU auction would be equal to the amount of MUC.

Under the scheme, the underwriting commitment on dated securities of Central Government is divided equally into two parts - Minimum Underwriting Commitment (MUC) and Additional Competitive Underwriting (ACU). The MUC of each PD is computed to ensure that at least 50 percent of the notified amount of each issue is mandatorily underwritten equally by all PDs. The share under MUC will be uniform for all PDs, irrespective of their capital or balance sheet size. The remaining portion of the notified amount is underwritten through an Additional Competitive Underwriting (ACU) auction. The commission payable on the amount accepted in the ACU is discriminatory (multiple-price) whereas the commission payable on the MUC amount is made differential in order to make the ACU bidding competitive. The PDs which are successful in the ACU auction for 4per cent or more of the notified amount are eligible to receive the commission on the MUC at the weighted average rate of all the accepted bids in the ACU auction whereas the PD which are successful by less than 4per cent or not successful in the ACU auction, get the commission on the MUC at the weighted average rate of lowest three bids in the ACU.

The amount so allotted in the underwriting auction becomes the minimum bidding obligation for the PD in the main auction. Devolvement of securities, if any, on PDs takes place on pro-rata basis, depending upon the amount of underwriting obligation of each PD after setting off the successful bids in the main auction. As on June 30, 2010, there were twenty Primary Dealers (PDs), of which twelve were banks carrying on Primary Dealership business departmentally (Bank-PDs) and the remaining eight were non-bank entities, known as standalone PDs, registered as NBFCs under section 45 IA of the RBI Act, 1934. During the year 2009-10, DSP Merrill Lynch Securities Trading Limited ceased to be a PD pursuant to the agreement for merger between Bank of America Corporation, the parent company of Bank of America, N. A. and Merrill Lynch & Co. in terms of which the PD business of DSP Merrill Lynch Securities Trading Limited, was taken over by the Bank of America. Further, Morgan Stanley India Primary Dealer Pvt. Ltd and Nomura Fixed Income Securities Pvt. Ltd. were given authorisation to undertake Primary Dealership with effect from July 20, 2009 and September 7, 2009 respectively. Axis Bank was given authorisation to undertake PD business departmentally with effect from April 5, 2010.

Operations and Performance of PDs

During 2011-12, the bid to cover ratio of PDs in both dated Government of India securities (G-Sec) and Treasury Bills (T-Bills) was marginally lower than in the previous year. PDs were required to achieve a minimum success ratio (bids accepted to the bidding commitment) of 40 per cent for T-Bills and Cash Management Bills (CMBs) put together, usually reviewed on a half-yearly basis. All the PDs achieved the stipulated minimum success ratio in both the first and second half of 2011-12. The success ratio in T-Bill auctions, however, was marginally lower during the year.

During 2011-12, all the dated G-Secs were fully underwritten. In the auctions of dated securities, the share of the PDs (bids accepted to the securities issued) decreased marginally (Table 4). Partial devolvement on the PDs took place on 14 instances.

TABLE 4

Performance of the PDs in the Primary Market

(As at End-March)

(Amount in ₹ billion)

Item	2011	2012
1	2	3
Treasury Bills & CMBs		
Bidding Commitment	3,808	7,296
Actual Bids Submitted	7,260	13,505
Bid to Cover Ratio	2.3	2.2
Bids Accepted	2,353	4,271
Success Ratio (in per cent)	61.8	58.6
Central Govt. Securities		
Notified Amount	4,370	5,100
Actual Bids submitted	6,239	6,932
Bid to Cover Ratio	1.4	1.3
Bids of PDs Accepted	2,165	2,432
Share of PDs (in per cent)	49.6	47.7

Note: Percentage variation could be slightly different because absolute numbers have been rounded off to ₹ billion.

1. Turnover ratio is computed as the ratio of total purchase and sales during the year in the secondary market to average monthend stocks.

Performance of Standalone PDs

In the secondary market, PDs have individually achieved a minimum annual total turnover ratio[1] (outright and repo transactions) of 5 times in dated G-Sec and 10 times in T-Bills during 2011-12. PDs had also achieved the minimum annual outright turnover ratio of 3 times in dated G-Sec and 6 times in T-Bills (Table 5.)

TABLE 5

Performance of Standalone PDs in the Secondary Market

(As at End-March)

(Amount in ₹ billion)

Item	2011	2012
1	2	3
Outright		
Turnover of standalone PDs	10,900	18,381

Turnover of market participants	57,419	69,764
Share of PDs (in per cent)	19.0	26.3
Repo		
Turnover of standalone PDs	11,460	15,245
Turnover of market participants	81,986	75,278
Share of PDs (in per cent)	14.0	20.3
Total		
Turnover of standalone PDs	22,359	33,625
Turnover of market participants	1,39,405	1,45,042
Share of PDs (in per cent)	16.0	23.2

Notes:1. Percentage variation could be slightly different because absolute numbers have been rounded off to ₹ billion.

2. Components may not add up to the whole due to rounding off.

Source: Clearing Corporation of India Limited.

Sources and Application of Funds of Standalone PDs

Investment by PDs in corporate bond market has decreased. The net owned fund (NOF) of the PDs has increased marginally. Reserves and surplus of the PDs had increased significantly. Both the secured and unsecured loans of the PDs also increased significantly during 2011-12. Investments in corporate bonds decreased marginally during the year (Table 6).

TABLE 6

Sources and Applications of Funds of Standalone Primary Dealers

(Amount in ₹ million)

Item	As at end-March			Percentage Variation	
	2010	2011$	2012	2011	2012
1	2	3	4	5	6
Sources of Funds	1,03,080	130,320	2,03,810	26.4	56.4
1 Capital	15,410	15,210	15,080	-1.3	-0.8
2 Reserves and Surplus	19,250	18,890	20,490	-1.9	8.4
3 Loans (a + b)	68,420	96,220	168,240	40.7	74.9
a) Secured	25,220	63,520	113,970	151.9	79.4
b) Unsecured	43,200	32,700	54,260	-24.3	66.0
Application of Funds	1,03,080	1,30,320	2,03,810	26.4	56.4
1 Fixed Assets	140	380	370	171.4	-2.6
2 Investments (a + b + c)	72,800	98,520	1,45,080	35.3	47.3
a) Government Securities	62,518	86,430	1,33,320	38.1	54.2
b) Commercial Papers	1,420	100	250	-92.9	149.4
c) Corporate Bonds	8,800	11,990	11,510	36.2	-4.0
3 Loans and Advances	7,410	4,260	19,380	-42.5	354.9

4	Non-current Assets	0	0	2,970	-	-
5	Equity, Mutual Funds, etc.	680	250	160	-63.2	-36.0
6	Others*	22,050	26,910	35,850	22.0	33.2

* Others include cash + certificate of deposits + bank balances + accrued interest + deferred tax assets – current liabilities and provisions.

$: Except Morgan Stanley Deutsche Sec and IDBI Gilts.

*Notes:*1. Percentage variation could be slightly different because of rounding off.

    2. Components may not add up to the whole due to rounding off.

Source: Annual Reports of PDs.

Financial Performance of Standalone PDs

Sharp increase in expenses led to reduction in profit. The net profit of the PDs reduced marginally during 2011-12. The total income of the PDs increased significantly. However, the PDs reported a sharp increase in their interest expenses mainly due to the increased cost of borrowings (Table 7). As a result, the costincome ratio (i.e., operating expenses to net total income) increased during the year. The return on net worth (RONW) and return on average assets (ROAA) for the year ended March 2012 were down marginally (Table 8). The CRAR of the PDs increased from 46.2 per cent to 53.8 per cent during the year as against a minimum prescribed requirement of 15 per cent (Table 9).

TABLE 7

Financial Performance of Standalone Primary Dealers

(Amount in ₹ million)

Item	2010-11	2011-12	Variation	
			Amount	Percentage
1	2	3	4	5
A. Income (i to iii)	10,790	15,470	4,680	43.4
i)Interest and discount	9,700	13,820	4,120	42.5
ii)Trading Profit	580	640	60	10.3
iii)Other income	510	1,010	500	98.0
B. Expenses (i+ii)	8,070	13,070	4,560	62.0
i)Interest	6,530	11,180	4,650	71.2
ii)Other expenses including Establishment and Adminis-trative Costs	1,540	1,890	350	22.7
Profit Before Tax	2,720	2,400	-320	-11.8
Profit After Tax	1,780	1,540	-240	-13.5

*Notes:*1. Percentage variation could be slightly different because absolute numbers have been rounded off to ₹ billion.

    2. Components may not add up to the whole due to rounding off.

Source: Returns submitted by PDs.

TABLE 8

Financial Indicators of Standalone PDs

(Amount in ₹ million)

Indicator	2010-11	2011-12
1	2	3
i) Net profit	1,780	1,540
ii) Average Assets	1,66,970	1,97,460
iii) Return on Average Assets (in per cent)	1.1	0.8
iv) Return on Net Worth (in per cent)	5.1	4.4

TABLE 9

CRAR of the standalone PDs

(As at end-March)

(Amount in ₹ million)

Particulars	2011	2012
1	2	3
1. Total Net Capital Funds	36,260	39,290
2. Total Risk Weighted Assets	78,580	72,980
a) Credit Risk	33,500	37,420
b) Market Risk	45,080	35,560
3. CRAR (in percent)	46.2	53.8

THE YIELD STRUCTURE OF THE GOVERNMENT SECURITIES

A loan carries a yield as a compensation for the loss of liquidity which ready money can provide. In an integrated market, under equilibrium situation, therefore, the yield on a loan should be a direct function of its illiquidity and an index series of relative liquidity of different maturities should be nothing but the ratios of the reciprocals of such yields. The term yield, however, is not equivalent to just *the coupon* on a loan, since the very feature of marketability of an asset implies that the market price is a variable factor and hence its acquisition and disposal can entail capital gain /loss. The market price of a loan need not be at par; nor should the coupon rate have any definite relationship with its remaining terms to maturity — the coupon was decided upon at the time when the loan was floated subject to the then terms to maturity and the accompanying circumstances. It should, therefore, be more relevant to use a yield measure inclusive of expected capital gain/loss.

The Concept of a Yield Curve

In the market, there is nothing like the rate of interest, nor for that matter, is there anything like the long-term or the short-term rate of interest. Each rate of interest is at least two-dimensional. It is related on the one hand to the type of asset or loan for which it is being quoted and on the other to its term to maturity. Thus at any point of time, the whole system of interest rates in the market can be represented in the form of a set of vector of interest rates in such a way that each vector pertains to one particular asset and consists of rates quoted for that asset for different maturities.

Thus, for example, for assets A, B, C, D, ... the vectors of interest rates as at time t will be:

$$_t R_{1a}, _t R_{2a}, _t R_{3a}......,$$

$$_t R_{1b}, _t R_{2b}, _t R_{3b}......,$$

$$_t R_{1c}, _t R_{2c}, _t R_{3c}......,$$

where the top-script denotes the type of asset under consideration, the subscript denoted the maturity and the prescript denotes the time when the rate would become effective.

One such vector of interest rate is called a term structure of Interest rates — it is a set of interest rates that pertain, at any point of time t, to a given type of assets such that the rate differentials within this set are solely due to the differences in the term to maturity. In the case of public debt, we have a term structure of yield rates — where yield refers to the yield to redemption inclusive of capital gain/loss. The theory of term structure of interest rates may analyse and explain the determiration and changes in the absolute level of interest rates in such a term structure as also the rate differentials contained therein. It does not explain, however, the rate differentials between different types of assets of a given maturity.

Typically, the studies of term structure have tended to concentrate their attention on *risk-free* government securities or first class corporate bonds, the yield on which may be assumed to differ from each other only on account of term to maturity. Such an approach enables the analyst to pick up that vector (Or term structure) of yield rates in which the risk of default on the part of the issuer of the loan is not a function of the maturity of the loan. Such a condition is supposed to be satisfied in the case of marketable public loans which are subject to similar tax and call conditions. The analysis of the interdependence and determination of the constituent rates of the term structure as pertaining to the government securities is therefore not sullied by considerations irrelevant to the pure argument.

The term structure of yield rates on public debt can be represented graphically in the foam of yield curve. In such a graph, along X-axis we measure the term to maturity and along Y-axis we measure the per cent per annum yield to redemption. It is to be noted that in such a yield curve, the assumption is that the purchaser of a security today will pay the current market price for it, will get the periodic coupon payments and will retain the security till its redemption, when he will be paid its face value plus the last Instalment of the coupon. In actual practice, the debt holders do purchase and sell the securities without holding them till redemption, but the expected changes in their prices would influence the current market prices thereof and hence the yield structure as such.

YTM Vs. ZCYC

Fixed income instruments, both government securities and corporate paper, constitute sizeable proportion of the investment portfolios of most financial sector entities. The change in the value of these portfolios arising out of shifts in the interest rate structure is of immense concern — both for the purpose of ascertaining the mark-to-market value of the portfolio and in view of concerns related to risk management. This in turn underscores the need for a sound and consistent norms for valuation of fixed income instruments.

Unlike equities for which prices are available on a daily basis which can be used to value any portfolio, the secondary debt market does not provide market quotes for all securities on a regular basis for valuation of fixed income portfolios. Traditionally, the valuation norms for such instruments have been announced from time to time by the regulator for the particular segment, for instance, by SEBI for mutual funds and RBI for banks. These are yield to maturity (YTM)-based norms, with pre-specified credit spreads distinguishing between sovereign and corporate paper. With the objective of moving towards more market-determined — as opposed to mandated — valuation norms, RBI recently discontinued its practice of prescribing year-end YTMs for unquoted government securities; these are now put out by PDAI/FIMMDA.

A sound valuation methodology should: (i) have a firm conceptual base, (ii) provide a framework that allows consistent valuation of all similar instruments, and (iii) be available at high frequency (preferably daily) so as to enable players to constantly value and, if required, reshuffle their portfolios.

YTM is the single rate, which equates the quoted price of a security to the sum of the present discounted value of its cash flows. For a given market price, cash flows and time to cash flows, the YTM of a security can be computed from the present value (PV) relation. Conversely, one could derive the price of a security for given cash flows, discounting them using the YTM. However, the latter would involve the assumption of a constant discount rate for all cash flows from a security, irrespective of when they fall due, violating the notion of time value of money'. Further, the corollary to this is that two cash flows due at the same time, but coming from two different instruments, are discounted at different (security-specific) YTM rates. This makes it difficult to conceptualise a unique relation between YTM and maturity alone, the so-called Yield Curve. From the perspective of a user, this, in turn, makes' it difficult to derive the YTM for a new security with a different coupon rate, even if its maturity matches that of an existing security. Similarly, it is difficult to interpolate the YTM for a new security with a different maturity, even if its coupon rate matches that of an existing security. Hence, there exists a need for an alternative to YTM for valuation of portfolios of fixed income securities that is invariant to security-specific characteristics and provides a unique discount rate-maturity relation. The Zero Coupon Yield Curve (ZCYC) provides such an alternative.

The ZCYC, also referred to as the term structure of interest rates, depicts the relationship between interest rates in the economy and the term to maturity. On any particular day, the ZCYC is estimated using the present value (PV) relation. However, unlike in derivation of PVs using YTMs, the discount rate used for computing the PV of each cash flow is the interest rate associated with the time to maturity of the given cash flow. Derivation of the entire set of interest rates requires prior specification of an interest rate-maturity relation (the model) that is estimated using market prices and corresponding PVs for all traded securities. Once estimated, the ZCYC can be used to derive the underlying 'fundamental' price of any fixed income instrument, including non-traded instruments, by discounting its cash flows using the interest rate for the associated 'time to cash flow'. Further, with interest rates being a function of maturity alone, cash flows due at the same time are discounted using the same rate even if they were due from two different instruments.

A usually held argument against ZCYC vis-a-vis YTM is that the former is more complicated both in terms of computation and interpretation. While the computation of YTMs is certainly less time-consuming, it takes far more time and ingenuity to use YTMs as a pricing/valuation methodology for/portfolios of securities that include non-traded instruments. In addition, YTM would have limited applicability as the debt market develops and new instruments like Seperate Trading of Registered Interest and Principal of Securities (STRIPS) and other derivative products are introduced. ZCYC, on the other hand, is eminently suitable for valuation of such instruments. With sufficient number of secondary market trades in Government securities available to estimate a chosen model, it is possible to estimate the sovereign term structure daily, thus making it a useful valuation methodology to track changes in the value of portfolios of Government securities on a day-to-day basis. Once the ZCYC parameters are available, suitably designed software, such as the NSE Zero Curve Calculator, can easily handle the bond-pricing calculations that a treasury would be interested in. Finally, the ZCYC can be used to price all non-sovereign fixed income instruments after adding an appropriate credit spread related to the credit rating and tenor of the instrument. A readily available database of ZCYC would be of immense help for primary dealers, banks and other entities to compute Value at Risk (VaR) of their fixed income portfolios in a consistent manner.

In view of the above, the regulatory authority should consider ZCYC as an alternative to the YTM in setting valuation and risk management systems for fixed income portfolios.

Shape of the Yield Curves

While the interest rate measure the price the borrower is agreed to pay for a loan, the yield or rate of return on the loan, from the lender's point of view, may be quite different since it depends on the total rate of return on the transaction, i.e. yield takes into account number of factors e.g. change in market value of the security, default rate, deferring of payment etc. The relationship between the rates of return (or yield) on financial instruments and their maturity is labeled the term structure of interest rates. The term structure of rates may be represented visually by drawing a yield curve for all securities of equivalent grade or quality. The yield curve considers only the relationship between the maturity or term of a loan and its yield at one moment in time, with all other factors held constant. For example, we cannot draw a yield curve for securities bearing different degrees of risk or subject to different tax laws because both risk and tax rates affect relative yields along with maturity. We may, however, draw a yield curve for government securities of varying maturities because they all have minimal default risk, the same tax status, and so on. Similarly, yield curves could be constructed for all corporate bonds having the same credit rating.

Yield curves change their shape over time in response to changes in the public's interest-rate expectations, fluctuations in the demand for liquidity in the economy, and other factors. Several different shapes have been observed, but most yield curves may be described as upward sloping, down-ward sloping, or horizontal (flat). An upward-sloping yield curve, of course, indicates that borrowers must pay higher interest rates for longer-term loans than for shorter-term loans. A downward sloping yield curve means that long-term loans and securities presently carry lower interest rates than shorter-term financial assets. However, each shape of the yield curve has important implications for lenders and savers, borrowers and investors, and the financial institutions that serve them.

What determines the shape or slope of the yield curve? One view is the expectations hypothesis. The expectation hypothesis assumes equality between the expected holding-period yields irrespective of the maturities of the loans held. It also assumes perfect substitutability between various maturities, maximisation of the present value on the part of the investors on the basis of single-valued expectations, absence of transaction costs and quick mobility of funds as between different maturities. It was the long-term forecasting of the short-term rates such that: (1) the current interest rates contain the expectation for the future one-period, rates as well; and (2) the current n-period rate is an average of the current one-period rate and the expected one-period rates in the remaining n-1 periods. The traditional approach expounded by Meiselman was that of using the extrapolative ability of the past expectations on the assumption that forward rates are, on an average, unbiased estimates of future spot rates. It is important to note that according to the expectation hypothesis current interest rate structure contains and fully represents the actual expectations held by the market; additionally, the new expectations hypothesis says that since the of level expectations need not turn out to be always correct, they are revised on the basis of an error-learning process. It may be claimed, however, that:

> *Firstly*, the expectation hypothesis appears incomplete because expectations need not be only extrapolative; they can also be regressive towards a *normal level of yield rates. Secondly,* the error-learning approach is not deduced from any optimising behaviour assumptions. *Thirdly, though it is mostly agreed that the expectations are an important explanatory factor of the current structure of interest rates, this hypothesis ignores the supply side of the debt. Therefore, unless it is recognised that the management of public debt may have a direct bearing on the formation of the expectations, this hypothesis cannot be used for testing the sensitivity of the yield structure to debt management. As it is, the expectations hypothesis in its present form only implies that the authorities are not able to twist the term structure of yields.*

This theory, therefore, leads us to the conclusion that the shape of the yield curve would be solely a function of the present one period rate and the expectations regarding the future one period rates. The determination of one-period rate itself and actual changes therein, period after period, are not explained. One would have expected that at least in the stage of formation of expectations, a positive role of debt management would appear. But this is not the case. Even the new expectations theory bases the revision of expectations only on an error learning process — a kind of autoregression. Thus, the expectations hypothesis is not able to define any constraints on, or predict changes in, the shape of the yield curve.

Does the liquidity premiums approach fare better in this regard? It appears so to some extent at least, the liquidity premiums approach could maintain that the yield to redemption would be a monotonically rising function of maturity irrespective of the maturity distribution of the public debt. Hicks and other exponents of the liquidity premiums approach, on the assumption of the risk aversion by debt holders, were assigning a weightage to the interest rate risk which is more on longer maturity securities. This necessitates a higher yield level for the longer securities. This then imposes one major constraint on the shape of the yield whereby the longer end of the yield will always be higher than the shorter one. This would lead us to a dead end of this line of investigation as per as a debt management policy towards changes in relative liquidity of different maturities is concerned, provided the liquidity preference, of each investor is constant and uniform, since in that case changes in relative supplies of shorts and longs will not change the initial equilibrium yield structure. However, this does not pose a serious threat to the use of this approach for testing the debt management sensitivity of the yield curve since in practice different investors are most likely not to have a uniform and constant liquidity preference and therefore it should be possible to bring about a change in the yield structure of the public debt by changing its maturity composition. Historically, also, the yield curve has not shown an equal variability in all its segments.

There are two important considerations that arise in this connection. *Firstly*, as Newlyn's analysis of *encashment* and *requirement* periods will imply, liquidity premiums need not exist all along this line, nor need they arise monotonically with respect to term to maturity; their existence and quantum will depend upon the relevant differences between the *encashment* and *requirement* periods in the market. Secondly, the exact relationship between the liquidity premiums and the general level of yield rates itself is not clear. From Kessel and Malkeil one finds that liquidity premium is a direct function of the level of interest rates, and the gap between the short and long rates widens with the height of the yield curve. Van Horne found that liquidity premiums were universally related to the level of interest rates relative to an accustomed range. Richard Roll, however, points out that Van Horne's conclusion is based upon unconvincing evidence, as he was using the "beginning forward rates". Richard Roll could establish the proposition that liquidity premiums vary directly with the level of interest rates. Thus the consideration of an acceptance of liquidity premiums as such does not enable us to lay down the recognised constraints that management policies would face while trying to influence the yield structure of public debt. Since the very shape of the yield curve is in doubt, and since the response of the yield curve of change in the level of interest rates is not definite it remains a question of empirically verifying the fact. The concepts of encashment and requirement periods in this connection appear quite relevant provides the same can be ascertained. A sufficient knowledge of requirement and encashment periods in the market would enable us to test its responsiveness to debt management operations. But even here we have to work under limitations of lack of information. On the encashment side (i.e. on the side of debt holders providing the demand for debt), a definite information is not likely to be available. But the Modigliani and Sutch approach suggests a way out. The market is neither likely to be a perfectly integrated one nor a perfectly segregated one. It would have debt holders with preferred maturity habitats implying that debt holders would be normally moving along within limited ranges and would move away from them only when there is adequate inducement to that effect. The existence of arbitragers etc. would dilute the effect of maturity habitats but would not eliminate it. Thus the existence of maturity habitats would make the yield curve sensitive to the debt management operations — which can represent the requirement or supply side of the public debt. It should be possible to test the nature and extent of the yield sensitivity as also the ability of the authorities to change the relative liquidity of different structure.

Box-2

THE TERM STRUCTURE OF INTEREST RATES

The term structure of Interest rates Is the relationship between interest rates and term to maturity. However, financial Instruments differ not only In terms of their maturity characteristic, but also other characteristics, most notably the risk. Therefore, the term structure is best estimated through yields on the default risk free government securities. A yield curve that charts yield-to-maturtty (YTM) for Treasury securities (on the vertical axis) of various maturities (on the horizontal axis) as of a particular date captures the term structure. The yield curve changes from day to day as the YTM changes. While yields on other money market Instruments, such as those on commercial papers of varying maturity could also be considered for the term structure, the risk element in these Instruments would need to be considered. Yield curves, today, are popularly estimated in parametric forms using the methodology of Nelson and Siegel or its extension by Svensson.

Three alternative paradigms are usually used to explain the term structure of interest rates. The unbiased expectations theory (or the pure expectations theory) suggests that the expected future spot rate equals the forward rate. If, say, current economic conditions (say rise in current inflation or a speculative pressure on domestic currency) make short-term spot rates high, then the term structure represented by the yield curve should turn downward sloping in accordance with the expectations theory.

The liquidity preference theory is based on the premise that investors prefer short-term securities because of the interest rate risk or because the investors fear that if needed, they may not be able to realise their funds earlier than anticipated because of liquidity problems. Investors, therefore, prefer short-term securities and try to roll over these securities. Rollovers, however. Involve transaction costs. The investors, therefore, evaluate the expected returns from holding long-term bonds and compare them with those on the short-term bonds. They generally tend to charge a liquidity premium for holding long-term bonds, which Is the difference between the forward rate and the expected future spot rate. In this case downward sloping yield curves would occur only when the market expectations are that interest rates would decline substantially. A flat term structure in itself indicates that Interest rates are expected to decline somewhat. The upward sloping yield curve would indicate an expected rise or fall In interest rates depending upon the steepness of the slope. Steeper the slope, more likely is that market expects interest rates to rise In future.

Another alternative explanation for observed term structure is provided by the market segmentation theory. It points to Institutional and legal constraints that often exist in markets so that some investors and , borrowers are restricted to certain maturities alone. Psychological factors, customs and habits may also restrict them from Investing only in certain classes of maturities. For example, pension and insurance funds generally prefer longer maturity debt instruments in relation to banks and other financial institutions. Besides, trading restrictions, lack of Instruments and institutional structures may also result in the term structure getting disjointed. It is possible that the short-end, the long-end and the intermediate-term of the markets may be segmented. With spot rates In each of these segments getting determined by respective demand and supply conditions, the yields In each segment may remain misaligned. The yield curve could be upward or downward sloping depending upon whether the intersection of short-end demand and supply curves are lower or higher than that for the long-end.

The term structure or the yield curves have considerable information content. They could be used to value a wide range of fixed Income Instruments, including coupon paying bonds, interest rate forwards and swaps and other derivative Instruments. The coupon paying bonds, for example, can be stripped into zero coupon instruments .corresponding to various cash flows, with the redemption amount getting added to the terminal coupon. The underlying price of this fixed income security can then be calculated as the net present value of the stream of all these cash flows using this zero coupon yield curve. In practice, however, yields of various securities of various maturities are affected by several factors, other than coupon rates and maturity period. The risk factor, marketability and tax rates are important considerations In pricing that a yield curve may not easily capture.

The term structure also has information content on future inflation and future real economic activity. The value of this information content to a large extent depends upon the stability and predictability of the yield curve with respect to non-financial activity. The information content in the yield curve depends largely on the Fisher equation and the expectations theory of the yield curve. Fisher equation decomposes one period nominal Interest rate roughly Into one period *ex ante* real interest rate and the one period ahead expected Inflation. Combining this with expectations theory, the YTM could be explained by the expected real Interest rate and the expected Inflation. Following liquidity preference theory, a risk premium could be added to the two expected variables determining YTM if investors are believed to charge the same for holding the bond of a certain maturity. Under the expectations theory, however, the risk premium is constant for all maturities. The yield spread or the slope of the yield curve provides information on expected real Interest rate spread and on market's inflation expectations. The yield curve provides the best measure of market's expected Inflation path if expectations are formed rationally, risk premium is constant over time and the real term structure is flat denoting constant expected real interest rate for all maturities. If prices are fixed, nominal yield spreads capture the expectations regarding the future real economic activity. However, in practice, the information content of the yield spread for the future real economic activity depends on the nature of macro economic shocks. If the shocks are largely of a monetary nature, a positive yield spread could indicate expectations of an economic slowdown. If shocks ate real and price rigidities exist, a positive yield spread could indicate a future economic upswing.

In India, the predictive power of the yield curve is yet to be established. The term structure was largely segmented and though a great deal of integration has taken place over the last few years, yields of various maturities are still not perfectly correlated with one another or with the movements in expected 'inflation. As a result, the predictive power of the yield spread is curtailed by the noise in the forecasts. The term structure is segmented with liquidity considerations affecting the short-end and expectations dominating the long-end of the market. The growing integration of the term structure is, however, reflected in the co movement of interest rates. The correlation coefficients among the set of interest rates is positive (Report on Currency and Finance, 1998-99). For the banking sector, the short-term deposit rates, long-term deposit rates and the prime lending rates have shown strong co-movement with the Bank Rate in the recent years. More importantly, the inter-linkages across the term structure for gilts in India is reflected in cointegration between call money rates and cut off yield on short term 91 day T-bills, medium term 364 days T-bills arid redemption yield on long-term Government of India securities. However, as unique common stochastic trend is not observed in this set, the complete integration of the term structure or the efficiency of trading across maturities is still to evolve. As such, it is difficult to identify a reference rate that could be used as a policy instrument to guide the course of the entire term structure. The cut off yield on 91 day T-bills could qualify as a reference rate for India among the set of other available rate variables since that excluding call money rates and return on equity, all other interest rates exhibited co-movement with the 91 days Treasury bills. It is possible that with further widening and deepening of the gilt market, a smooth yield curve may emerge in the years ahead. The term structure ranging from the overnight call rate to the long-end may get aligned, so that the central bank can more effectively operate at the short-end for its monetary policy objectives. The yield curve could then have a considerable predictive power.

Sensitivity of the Yield Curve

This brings us to the question of the sensitivity of the yield curve to debt management operations and policies. The supply side of the public debt has both size and maturity composition dimensions. The normal approach would be to regress the changes in the yield structure upon variables covering these two dimensions. The amount of the public debt outstanding in the market is given by the historically determined size of the debt plus the current budgetary debt issue and debt-retirement policies as also the open market operations of the Reserve Bank. The maturity composition of the public debt outstanding in the market is determined by the historically given maturity composition, new floatations, retirements and the open market operations of the Reserve Bank. If we could assume that the authorities could provide the size and maturity composition of the outstanding debt in the market as factors exogenous to the market, the yield curve could be expected to be sensitive to such exogenous changes if :

(a) the market was a completely segmented one, or if
(b) there were maturity habitats in the market.

In the absence of a complete integration of the market, the authorities should be able to "twist" the yield structure and thereby effect the relative liquidity of different maturities. The extent of such "twisting" ability of the authorities is a function of many factors including the constitution of the market, the expectations that the debt management policies generate in the market, the scale of operations and the sensitivity of the liquidity premiums to the level of the yield curve and so on. If the market is completely segmented, the yield rate in different maturity ranges would depend upon only the demand and supply forces working within each segment. There will be no spill-over effects and as such the authorities will be able to manage the market in parts. When the market is not completely segmented but the maturity habitats exist, the spill-over effects are expected in the neighbourhood of the region being operated in, since in that case the debt holders could be ready to move to and from the neighbouring maturities if sufficient inducement exists.

In the case of fully integrated market, or when all the debt holders have a consistent and uniform liquidity preference, the market will respond evenly in all its segments. Under such circumstances, it may be maintained that the *relative* liquidity of different maturities would remain unchanged, though all the maturities might acquire (or lose) liquidity in relation to money.

If, however, when the market is not fully integrated, but the authorities tailor new issues to the market preferences for different maturities, then to that extent the debt operations would be only counter-balancing the changing demand pattern. The effects of supply changes on term structure in that case will be mixed up with demand effects and regressing the changes in the yield structure on the size and maturity composition of the government securities would probably yield insignificant co- efficients.

Uses of the Yield Curve

Forecasting Interest Rates

First, if the expectations hypothesis is correct, the yield curve gives the investor a clue concerning the future course of interest rates. If the curve has an upward slope, the investor may be well advised to look for opportunities to move away from bonds and other long-term securities into investments whose market price is less sensitive to interest-rate changes. A downward-sloping yield curve, on the other hand, suggests the likelihood of near-term declines in interest rates and a rally in bond prices if the market's forecast of lower rates turns out to be true.

Uses for Financial Intermediaries

The slope of the yield curve is critical for financial intermediaries, especially commercial banks, savings and loan associations, and savings banks. A rising yield curve is generally favorable for the these institutions because they borrow most of their funds by selling short-term deposits and lend a major portion of those funds long term. The more steeply the yield curve slopes upward, the wider the spread between borrowing and lending rates and the greater the potential profit for a financial intermediary. However, if the yield curve begins to flatten out or slope downward, this should serve as a warning signal to portfolio managers of these institutions.

A flattening or downward-sloping yield cure squeezes the earnings of financial inter-mediaries and calls for an entirely different portfolio-management strategy than an upward-sloping curve. For example, if an upward-sloping yield curve starts to flatten out, portfolio managers of financial institutions might try to "lock in" relatively cheap sources of funds by getting long-term commitments from depositors and other funds-supplying customers. Borrowers, on the other hand, might be encouraged to take out long-term loans at fixed rates of interest. Of course, the financial institution's customers also may be aware of impending changes in the yield curve and resist taking on long-term loans or deposit contracts at potentially unfavourable interest rates.

Detecting Overpriced and Underpriced Securities

Yield curves can be used as an aid to investors in deciding which securities are temporarily overpriced or underpriced. This use of the curve derives from the fact that, in equilibrium, the yields on all securities of comparable risk should come to rest along the yield curve at their appropriate maturity levels. In an efficiently functioning market, however, any deviations of individual securities from the yield curve will be short-lived; so the investor must move quickly upon spotting a security whose yield lies temporarily above or below the curve.

If a security's rate of return lies above the yield curve, this sends a signal to investors that particular security is temporarily underpriced relative to other securities of the same maturity. Other things equal, this is a buy signal which some investors will take advantage of, driving the price of the purchased security upward and its yield back down toward the yield curve. On the other hand, if a security's rate of return is temporarily below the yield curve, this indicates a temporarily overpriced financial instrument, because its yield is below that of securities bearing the same maturity. Some investors holding this security will sell it, pushing its price down and its yield back up toward the curve.

Indicating Trade-Offs between Maturity and Yield

Still another use of the yield curve is to indicate the current trade-off between maturity and yield confronting the investor. If the investor wishes to alter the maturity of a portfolio, the yield curve indicates what gain or loss in rate of return may be expected for each change in the portfolio's average maturity.

With an upward-sloping yield curve, for example, an investor may be able to increase a bond portfolio's expected annual yield by extending the portfolio's average maturity. However, the prices of longer-term bonds are more volatile, creating greater risk of capital loss. Moreover, longer-term securities tend to be less liquid and less marketable than shorter-term securities. Therefore, the investor must weigh the gain in yield from extending the maturity of his or her portfolio against added price, liquidity, and marketability risk. Because yield curves tend to flatten out for the longest maturities, the investor bent on lengthening the average maturity of a portfolio eventually discovers that gains in yield get smaller and smaller for each additional unit of maturity. At some point along the yield curve it dearly does not pay to further extend the maturity of a portfolio.

Riding the Yield Curve

Finally, some active security investors, especially dealers in government securities, have learned to "ride" the yield curve for profit. If the curve is positively sloped, with a slope steep enough to offset transactions costs from buying and selling securities, the investor may gain by timely portfolio switching. For example, if a securities dealer purchases securities six months from maturity, holds them for three months, converts the securities into cash, and buys new six-month securities, he or she can profit in two ways from a positively sloped yield curve. Because the yield is lower on three-month than on six-month security, the dealer experiences a capital gain on the sale. Second, the purchase of new six-month securities replaces a lower-yielding security with a higher-yielding one at a lower price. Riding the yield curve can be risky, however, since yield curves are constantly changing their shape. If the curve gets flatter or turns down, a potential gain can be turned into a realised loss. Experience and good judgment are indispensables in using the yield curve for investment decision making.

DEFAULT RISK AND INTEREST RATES

Another important factor causing one interest rate to differ from another is the degree of default risk carried by individual securities. Investors face many different kinds of risk, of course, but one of the most important is default risk—the risk that a borrower will not meet all promised payments at the times agreed upon. All securities except government securities are subject to varying degrees of default risk. If you purchase a 7- year corporate bond with a ₹ 100 par value and a coupon rate of 15 per cent, the issuing company promises in the indenture (i.e., bond contract) that it will pay you ₹ 15 a year for 7- years plus ₹ 100 at the end of the 7-year period. Failure to meet any of these promised payments on time puts the borrower in default, and the investor may have to go to court to recover at least some of the monies owed.

The Premium for Default Risk

The market yield on a security is positively related to the risk of borrower default as perceived by investors. Specifically, the market yield on a risky security is composed of at least two elements:

Market yield on risky	=	Risk-free interest rate	+	Risk premium security

where:

Risk premium	=	Promised yield on a risky security	−	Risk-free Interest rate

The promised yield on a risky security is the yield to maturity that will be earned by the investor if the borrower makes all the payments that are pledged, when they are due. The higher the degree of default risk associated with a security, me higher the risk premium on that security and the greater the required rate of return (yield) attached to that instrument in the marketplace. Any adverse development—a downturn in the economy, natural disaster, ill health, serious financial difficulties, etc.—which makes a borrower appear more risky will lead the market to assign a higher risk premium to his or her security. And, if the risk-free rate remains unchanged, the security's market yield must rise and its price must decline.

The Expected Rate of Return or Yield

Volatile changes in business and consumer spending, interest rates, and commodity prices frequently have led to serious miscalculations by both large and small firms, with sometimes fatal results. For this reason, many investors today have learned to look at the *expected rate of return*, or yield, on a security as well as its promised yield.

The expected yield is simply the weighted average of all possible yields to maturity from a security. Each possible yield is weighted by the probability that it will occur. Thus, if there are m possible yields from a given risky security.

$$\text{Expected Yield} = \sum_{i=1}^{m} P_i \, Y_i$$

Where Y_i represents the its possible yield and P_i is the probability that yield will be obtained.

Expected Default Loss and Market Risk Premiums

For a risk-free security held to maturity, the expected yield equals the promised yield. However, in the case of a risky security, the promised yield may be greater than the expected yield, and the difference between them is usually labeled the anticipated loss due to default. This is:

Anticipated loss on a risky security = Promised yield – Expected yield

The concept of anticipated loss is important because it represents each investor's view of what the appropriate risk premium on a security should be. To illustrate, let's suppose that an investor carries out a careful financial analysis of a company in preparation for purchasing its bonds and decides that the firm is a less-risky borrower than perceived by the market as a whole. Perhaps the market has assigned the firm's bonds a risk premium of 4 percent; however, the investor feels the true anticipated loss due to default is only 3 percent. Because the market-risk premium exceeds this investor's anticipated loss, he would be inclined to buy the security. As he sees it, the security's market yield (including its risk premium) is too high, and therefore its price is too low.

Consider the opposite case. An investor calculates the anticipated loss on bonds issued by a PSU to finance a new project. He concludes that a risk premium of 5 percent is justified because of a significant number of uncertainties associated with the future success of the project. However, the current yield on the security is only 10 percent, and the risk-free interest rate is 6 percent. Because the market has assigned only a 4 percent risk premium, while the investor prefers a 5 percent premium, it is unlikely that he will purchase the PSU bond. As the investor views this bond, its market yield is too low, and therefore its price is too high.

Major financial institutions employ large numbers of credit analysts for the express purpose of assessing the anticipated loss on a wide range of securities they would like to acquire. These institutions feel they have a definite advantage over the average investor in assessing the true degree of default risk associated with any particular security. This high level of technical expertise may permit major institutional investors to take advantage of underpriced securities where, in their judgment, the market has overestimated the true level I of default risk.

What facors influence the risk premiums assigned by the market to different securities? Several studies in recent years have addressed the question of what factors influence risk premiums on securities (especially corporate bonds) and the factors which security rating companies use to evaluate default risk. Among the factors identified for corporate securities are variability in company earnings, the period of time a firm has been in operation, and the amount of leverage employed (i.e., the amount of debt relative to equity). A company with volatile earnings runs a greater risk of experiencing periods when losses will exceed the firm's ability to raise funds. Moreover, the longer a firm has been operating without default, the more investors come to expect continued successful performance. Greater use of financial leverage (debt) in the capital structure of a firm offers the potential for greater earnings per share of stock, because debt is a relatively cheap source of funds (measured on an aftertax basis). However, financial leverage is a two-edged sword. As the proportion of borrowed funds rises relative to equity, the risk of significant declines in earnings is increased.

Thus the relationship between default risk and interest rates points to a fundamental principle in the field of finance: risk and expected return are positively related. The investor expected returns must also be willing to accept greater risk of ruin. Moreover default risk is correlated with both internal (or borrower-specific) factors associated with a loan and external factors, especially the state of the economy and changing demands for a particular industry's product or service.

INFLATION AND INTEREST RATES

The most serious problem confronting most economies in the world today is inflation. Inflation is defined as a rise in the average level of prices for all goods and services. Some prices of individual goods and services are always rising, while others are declining.

However, inflation occurs when the average level of all prices in the economy rises.

Interest rates represent the "price" of credit. Are they also affected by inflation? The answer is yes, though there is considerable debate as to exactly how Inflation affects interest rates.

The Normal and Real Interest Rate

To examine the relationship between inflation and interest rates, several key terms must be defined. First, we must distinguish between *nominal and real interest rates*. The nominal rate is the published or quoted interest rate on a security or loan. For example, an an-nouncement in the financial press that major commercial banks have raised their prime lending rate to 15 percent per annum indicates what nominal interest rate is now being quoted by banks to their most credit-worthy customers. In contrast, the real rate of interest is the return to the lender or investor measured in terms of its actual purchasing power. In a period of inflation, of course, the real rate will be lower than the nominal rate. Another important concept is the *inflation premium*, which measures the rate of inflation expected by investors in the marketplace during the life of a financial instrument.

These three concepts are all related to each other. Obviously, a lender of funds is most interested in the real rate of return on a loan—that is, the purchasing power of any interest earned. For example, suppose you loan ₹ 1,000 to a business firm or individual for a year and expect prices of goods and services to rise 10 per cent during the year. If you charge a nominal interest rate of 12 percent on the loan, your real rate of return on the ₹ 1,000 face amount of the loan is only 2 percent, or ₹ 20. However, if the actual rate of inflation during the period of the loan turns out to be 13 per cent, you have actually suffered a real decline in the purchasing power of the monies loaned. In general, lenders will attempt to charge nominal rates of interest which give them desired real rates of return on their loanable funds. And nominal interest rates will change as frequently as lenders alter their expectations regarding inflation.

The Fisher Effect

In a classic article written just before the turn of the century, economist living Fisher argued that the nominal interest rate was related to the real rate by the following equation:

$$\text{Nominal interest Rate} = \left(\text{Real rate}\right) + \left(\text{Inflation premium}\right) + \left(\text{Real rate} \times \text{Inflation premium}\right)$$

The cross-product term in this equation is normally ignored because it is usually quite small.

Does the above equation suggest that an increase in expected inflation automatically increases nominal interest rates? Not necessarily. There are at least two different views on the matter, Fisher argues that the real rate of return tends to be stable over time because it depends on such long-run factors as the productivity of capital and the volume of savings in the economy. Therefore, a change in the inflation premium is likely to influence only the nominal interest rate. The nominal rate will rise as the expected rate of inflation increases, and decline with a drop in expected inflation. For example, suppose the real rate is 3 percent and the expected rate of inflation is-10 percent. Then the nominal rate will be calculated as follows:

$$\text{Nominal interest rate} = 3\% + 10\% = 13\%$$

According to Fisher's hypothesis, if the expected rate of inflation now rises to 12 percent, the real rate will remain unchanged at 3 per cent, but the nominal rate will rise to 15 percent.

If this view (known today as the Fisher effect) is correct, it suggests a method of judging the *direction* of future interest- rate changes. To the extent that rise in the actual rate of inflation causes investors to expect greater inflation, in the future, higher nominal interest rates will soon result. Conversely a decline in the actual rate of inflation may cause investors to revise downward their expectations of future inflation, leading to lower nominal interest rates.

AN ALTERNATIVE VIEW

The Fisher effect conflicts with another view of the inflation-interest rate phenomenon, developed originally by the British economist Sir Roy Harrod. It is based upon the liquidity preference theory of interest, Harrod argues that the real rate will be affected by inflation, but the nominal rate need not be. Following the liquidity preference theory, the nominal interest rate is determined by the demand for and supply of money. Therefore, unless inflation affects either the demand for or supply of money, the nominal rate must remain unchanged regardless of what happens to inflationary expectations.

What, then, is the link between inflation and interest rates according to this view? Harrod argues that a rise in inflationary expectations will lower the real rate of interest. In liquidity preference theory, the real rate measures the inflation-adjusted return on bonds. However, conventional bonds, like money, are not a hedge against inflation, because their rate of return is fixed by contract. Therefore, a rise in the expected rate of inflation lowers investors' real return from holding bonds. While the nominal rate of return on bonds remains unchanged, the real rate is squeezed by expectations of rising prices.

This so-called Harrod effect does not stop with bonds, however. There are two other groups of assets in the economy which, unlike bonds, often provide a hedge against inflation—equity shares and real estate. Inflationary expectations often lead to rapidly rising prices for homes, farmland, and commercial structures and to rallies in the stock market Allegedly, an increase in the rate of inflation causes the demand for these inflation-hedged assets to increase as well. Real estate and stock prices rise and, of course, their nominal rates of return fall until an equilibrium set of returns on stocks, bonds, real estate, and other assets is achieved.

While theories of interest-rate determination typically assume there is a single interest rate in the economy, in point of fact there are thousands of different interest rates confronting investors at any one time. The investors must focus upon several factors — the maturity or term of a loan, the risk of borrower default, and inflationary expectations — which cause rates to vary on different types of securities. Knowledge of each of these factors is of critical importance to security investors in making intelligent portfolio decisions.

DEVELOPING GOVERNMENT SECURITIES MARKET IN INDIA

The Indian bond market is dominated by government securities both in terms of outstanding stock as well as borrower. The G-Secs. market play a vital role as it provides the benchmark of determining the level of interest rates through the yields on government securities which are referred to as the rrisk-free rate of return in on economy. The relevance of government securities can be viewed from three points of view, namely from the Government which wants to borrow; from their role in financial markets especially debt markets and from the operation of monetary policy. *First,* from the viewpoint of the Government/fiscal authorities, the development of a deep and liquid government securities market facilitates public borrowings at reasonable costs and avoidance of automatic monetisation of government deficit by the central bank. Broad and well-functioning secondary markets are particularly important where the Government's borrowing needs are substantial. A well developed government securities market provides flexibility to the debt management authorities to exercise various options to optimise maturity as well as interest cost to the Government, to minimise the market impact of large or lumpy government debt operations and, facilitate better coordination between monetary policy and debt management.

Second, the government securities market provides the backbone of most fixed income markets across the world since it helps pricing of various debt instruments through creation of a benchmark, enables a proper evaluation of risk and acts a conduit for convergence of interest rates in other markets. In addition, the gilts market acts as the channel for the integration of various segments of the domestic financial market and help establish inter-linkages between internal and external financial markets. It is sometimes argued that it is not always necessary to develop a government securities market. Some countries do not have government securities market because their Governments have no funding requirements and in such countries, alternate benchmarks have developed so that price discovery has shifted from a single Government market to a range of non-Government markets. Thus, inter bank repo rates, collateralised obligations, interest rate swaps and top rated corporate bonds have gained acceptance as benchmarks in such markets.

Third, a number of countries are moving away from the use of direct instruments to indirect instruments such as repos and direct open market operations. Government securities facilitate the development of implementing indirect instruments of monetary policy. Typically, Treasury Bills and Government Dated Securities are ideal instruments for conducting repos in many emerging economies. While the T-Bills market serves the objective of raising finances for the Government, it also spurs the development of the money market. An important ingredient in the development of money market is the terms under which liquidity is available from the central bank. If liquidity adjustment support is available with certainty in regard to quantity and price, it could impede the development of the money market as banks will desist from entering into transactions with each other. In fact, the link between development of money market and the government securities is an important aspect of development of debt markets.

The reform of the G-Sec market has been a part of the economic reforms process undertaken by India to attain high growth and support the nation's socio-economic objectives. A well-developed G-Sec market plays a critical role in the overall economic development of the country by ensuring stable funding to the Government through effective channelization of the savings in the economy, improving the effectiveness of monetary policy through availability of additional channels and instruments and providing a benchmark in terms of instruments and infrastructure for broader development of the financial/capital market and robust management of financial risks. Finally, a well-developed G-Sec market improves the resilience of the economy to the possible domestic and external shocks. In this context, the reform process that began in 1992 was aimed at building an institutional framework to facilitate the evolution and smooth functioning of the G-Sec market. The setting up of infrastructure for demat holding of G-Sec, electronic platforms for auction, trading & settlement, establishment of the PD System, setup of CCIL as CCP for guaranteed settlement and a strong legal framework through amendments to existing laws (SCRA, Reserve Bank Act, 1934 etc.) and passing of new laws (FRBM Act, 2003, GS Act, 2006) have provided a solid foundation for the development of the G-Sec market. Some of the important measures aimed at improving the secondary market for G-Sec by developing the market microstructure are highlighted below:

The development of the primary market for G-Sec had been important part of the reform process as it was essential for discovery of price through an efficient market mechanism. Prior to the reforms period, the G-Sec market was characterized by administered interest rates and captive investors. Such administered rates affected the yield structure of financial assets in the system, and led to a high interest rate environment. The automatic accommodation to Central Government by the Reserve Bank, through *ad hoc* Treasury Bills, led to an increase in the volume of Government debt, particularly short-term debt. The introduction of auction process for primary issuance, abolition of ad hoc treasury bills, withdrawal of Reserve Bank from the primary market (as a consequence of the FRBM Act) have been instrumental in the development of the primary market for G-Sec that gradually led to an efficient process for price discovery and consequently, encouraged the development of a secondary market for these securities. Along with these measures, the gradual reduction in the prescriptions for CRR and SLR also aided the price discovery mechanism in G-Sec market. Another important contributing factor towards secondary market liquidity has been the passive consolidation undertaken by the Reserve Bank since 1999.

NDS was operationalized in February 2002 and soon after (in April 2002) guaranteed settlement of trades in G-Sec was provided by CCIL. The settlement of G-Sec trades on DvP-III basis was introduced in April 2004 and the electronic platform for anonymous trading in G-Sec (NDS-OM) was launched in August 2005. The setting up of NDS and NDS-OM brought in pre-trade and post-trade transparency in the G-Sec market that led to efficient price discovery. The electronic platform with net settlement of trades (on DvP-III basis) and CCP guarantee have played an important role in positively impacting the secondary market volumes in G-Sec. The standardization of market conventions like settlement cycle, computation of accrued interest, etc. was also instrumental in improving trading volumes.

Trades in the G-Sec market have been characterised by high volumes recorded during phases of 'bull-runs', with the same tapering-off during 'bear-phases'. In order to encourage market participants to trade freely during 'bear-phases' and to express negative views on the interest rate, intraday short selling in G-Sec was permitted in 2006, which was extended to 5 days in 2007 and to 3 months in 2011. Activity in short selling, at present, is restricted to banks and PDs in view of the risks involved in running short positions and the obligation to deliver securities against short positions to settle the 'short' transitions through reverse repo. Further, participant-level quantitative limits have also been prescribed on the amounts that can be short sold to obviate risk of 'squeeze' in the securities and to cap the overall risk in the market due to short selling. Short selling activity was tepid during the initial phase but it has been observed that the same has been high during 'bear-phases'. Of late, however, it has been noticed that short sale volumes have been gradually rising indicating the presence of 'bears' along with the 'bulls' in the market at all times, which is a sign of a maturing market.

The role and importance of a well-developed derivatives market for the development of the financial markets in general (including G-Sec market) and market volume in particular is well recognized. IRDs in the OTC market (IRS) were permitted in 1999 and exchange traded IRFs were introduced in 2003 and reintroduced in 2008 with modifications to the product design, valuation mechanism, etc. (10-year IRF). Over a period of time the market for IRS has evolved into a reasonably active market especially for institutional participants like banks and PDs. In this direction the Reserve Bank has taken steps to improve transparency and market microstructure and obviate the associated risks. Reporting of all interbank OTC trades in IRS to CCIL was introduced in August 2005 and non-guaranteed settlement was introduced in 2008. The non-interbank trades, i.e., trades between banks and their clients are being reported on a weekly-basis to the Reserve Bank since Oct 2009. Thus, the Reserve Bank has exercised close oversight over the OTC market for IRDs where all trades are being captured by the regulator and the same is also being disseminated across the market to promote post-trade transparency and efficient price-discovery. Attempts are on to activate the market for IRFs through changes to the settlement mechanism (cash-settled contracts) and introduction of short-tenor contracts but the activity in this segment has remained subdued due to various factors.

CRITICAL COMPONENTS FOR A WELL FUNCTIONING AND VIBRANT G-SEC MARKET

A well-developed G-Sec market plays a critical role in the overall economic development of the country by ensuring stable funding to the Government through effective channelization of the savings in the economy, improving the effectiveness of monetary policy through availability of additional channels and instruments and providing a benchmark in terms of instruments and infrastructure for broader development of the financial/capital market and robust management of financial risks. Finally, a well-developed G-Sec market improves the resilience of the economy to the possible domestic and external shocks. In this context, some of the **critical components for a well functioning and vibrant g-sec market** to draw the contours of future developments are discussed below:

Investors

High savings rate, large set of domestic institutional investors and active interest from foreign investors can create a large and heterogeneous group that is necessary for an efficient bond market. The traditional investor base for G-Sec in India comprised banks, provident funds, and insurance companies. With the entry of co- operative banks, regional rural banks, pension funds, mutual funds and non-banking finance companies, the institutional investor base has been reasonably diversified. Notwithstanding the predominantly institutional character of the G-Sec market, the Reserve Bank has recognised merit in promoting retail participation and has initiated certain policy measures to this end. Some of these include enabling small and medium-sized investors to participate in the primary auction of G-Sec through a 'Scheme of Non-competitive Bidding', improving access to the market for mid-segment investors by permitting well- managed and financially sound Urban Co-operative Banks (UCBs) to become members of NDS-OM and revision of authorisation guidelines for the Primary Dealers (PDs) mandating achievement of minimum retailing targets. To ease the process of investment by retail/mid-segment investors, a web-enabled platform which would seamlessly integrate their funds and securities accounts has been planned by the Reserve Bank. Some major banks have also initiated measures like on-line trading portal for the retail investors.

An important feature of investor profile of the G-sec market is the dominance of domestic investors and limited foreign participation but this is an aspect of a policy framework rather than indicative of lack of interest by overseas investors. Investment limits for the Foreign Institutional Investors (FIIs) have been enhanced in a phased manner to US$ 15 billion in G-sec and US$ 45 billion in the case of corporate bonds (including US$ 25 billion for infrastructure sector bonds/units). Some observers argue that in the absence of significant investments by foreign investors, markets are deprived of not only a large and liquid pool of savings but also active global trading strategies which can contribute to the much-needed trading liquidity. The counter-argument is that the willingness of foreign investors to take a long-term view and remain engaged is highly sensitive to global economic factors and possible sudden reversals arising from 'hot money' strategy of foreign investors has potential to impact the systemic stability. Let me add that the participation of foreign investor in the domestic bond markets also needs to be examined in the light of our policy stance relating to calibrated approach to capital account convertibility and the possibility of interest rate and exchange rate volatility due to large-scale reversal of capital flows.

A recurrent theme in the government bond market is the lack of liquidity as seen from the low trading volumes. The daily trading volume is less than one per cent of the outstanding stock. The banks and insurance companies between themselves hold about 70 per cent of the outstanding stock. The investment strategy of insurance companies and pension funds are usually dictated by Asset-Liability Management (ALM)/actuarial considerations. In India, because banks are mandated to hold as much as 24 per cent of their liability in the form of government securities, under Statutory Liquidity Ratio (SLR) framework, they have been permitted to classify these holdings as held-to-maturity (HTM) with a view to protecting their balance-sheets from volatility arising out of interest rate fluctuations. With a dominant part of the outstanding stock thus residing in HTM portfolio and out of the market, the low volume of trading is but natural. The term HTM, however, appears to be an illusion as securities are almost never held till they mature but are sold at an opportune time. Such an investment strategy impacts liquidity of the security, in particular, and the market, in general. While the changes imminent in accounting norms under the International Financial Reporting Standards (IFRS) may force transformation of the strategies of banks, there is a need for debate on the issue of reduction in the HTM category dispensation, albeit in a phased manner.

Investor interest in the interest rate derivatives market ought to be dictated by their exposure to the cash market. While investors' cash market exposure is substantial and has been increasing over time, the accounting hedge through HTM classification insulates the holders against market risk. Therefore, we observe skewed and limited participation, resulting in shallow markets. Though the interest rate swaps (IRS) was launched in 1999, the only product where the market volumes have grown substantially is the overnight index swap based on the overnight money market index. Here too the participation is not significantly broad-based. Foreign banks (owning only 7 per cent of the banking sector assets) are the most dominant players in the IRS market followed by the private sector banks while the participation of the public sector banks who own as much as 74 per cent of the banking sector assets remain miniscule. Notwithstanding the large trading volume and value of contracts outstanding, the skewed participation leads to pricing anomalies and also puts a question mark on the economic utility of the product.

Issuers

Sovereign securities dominate the fixed income markets almost everywhere. In India too, the central and state governments remain the main issuers. Two observations are in order. Traditionally, marketable securities of the Central and the State Governments constituted only a part of their respective liabilities and, therefore, the size of the government bond market as measured by the outstanding stock was relatively small compared to the debt-to-GDP ratio. Secondly, if one excludes the securities held by the Reserve Bank under the Open Market Operations (OMO) and other buy-and-hold entities, the market size becomes even smaller.

In recent times, market borrowings have emerged as the largest source of financing fiscal deficit. The auction-based issuance process is transparent with publication of auction calendars well in advance enabling the market participants to plan their investments. The large supply of securities, due to enhanced borrowings, has enabled creation of benchmark securities with sufficient outstanding stock and issuances across the yield curve. The issuances across the risk-free yield curve in turn have provided benchmarks for valuation of other bonds/ financial assets.

Despite economic recovery in 2010-11 and resumption of fiscal consolidation path, the market borrowing of the Government has remained at elevated levels in India. The Union Budget of India 2011-12 estimated gross fiscal deficit (GFD) at Rs.4,128.17 billion and budgeted gross market borrowings of Rs.4,170.00 billion. The market borrowings, however, through dated securities for the current year has been increased by about Rs.930.00 billion due to shortfall in other financing items, primarily due to moderation in the growth rate of the economy and increased expenditure. Besides inflationary implications, such large overhangs of debt and increasing annual borrowings have impeded the growth of flow of resources to the private sector by way of both loans and bonds. More importantly, lack of fiscal flexibility has not facilitated creation of limited number of benchmarks and active consolidation of illiquid securities. This fragmented G-Sec market has neither been beneficial to the issuer nor the investors.

In spite of some passive consolidation of government securities undertaken by the Reserve Bank, the market remains fragmented with many stocks with relatively small size. Nearly fifty per cent of the outstanding stocks has volume less than '200 billion. There is merit in pursuing active consolidation with focus on buy-backs and switches to build volumes and improve liquidity.

Instruments

For a market to meet the diverse funding and hedging needs of the participants, there is need for a wide array of instruments and products which would also offer benefits of diversification in the portfolio. In the process of development of new instruments, the Reserve Bank's endeavour has been to ensure calibrated and orderly development of the markets with emphasis on prudent risk management and promotion of financial stability.

Over the years, several instruments like zero- coupon bonds, capital-indexed bonds, floating rate bonds, separate trading of registered interest and principal securities (STRIPS) and bonds with call and put options have been introduced after wide consultations with market participants and with product features comparable to those of the most popular and liquid instruments elsewhere. In the case of short-term instruments cash management bills (CMBs) have emerged as a new class of instrument providing opportunities for secured, shorter term investment in sovereign paper. The size and frequency of issuance of CMBs are likely to increase given the uncertainty in cash inflows and outflows of the Government whose income and expenditure has been growing rapidly. Issues, such as, very short notice for issue of CMBs, more demand for treasury bills, which have structured tenors, may come in the way of large demand for CMBs. There is a plan to launch a new long-term instrument – the inflation indexed bonds (IIBs) wherein both capital and interest would be provided protection against inflation. It is expected that institutional investors, such as, pension funds and insurance companies would exhibit interest in investing in the IIBs. The expectation is based on the fact that the IIBs give investors long-term assets with a fixed long-term real yield, insulating them against inflation as their real yields are indexed to actual inflation. Further, it is also being contemplated to increase the non-competitive portion for IIBs to have significant participation of retail investors in these instruments.

Plain vanilla fixed coupon bonds, however, remain the mainstay of issuances. With the exception of an innovative product like collateralised borrowing and lending obligations (CBLO), the market has not displayed any appetite for instruments with varied structure.

A similar response pattern has been observed in respect of products such as interest rate futures (IRFs) (based on 10-year bond and 91-day T-Bill), repo in corporate bonds and new issuance of Floating Rate Bond (FRB). One plausible reason for lack of interest is illiquidity in the underlying bond market. The dilemma is that while participants do not want to trade till liquidity improves, liquidity will not improve till the participants trade giving rise to the typical 'chicken and egg problem'. The bottomline is that the market participants need to be more active in trading across the yield curve and across products and this requires an urgent and serious introspection by them.

Recently, the guidelines on the interest rate futures of two and five year tenors have been issued. These futures will be cash-settled with settlement price computed through a polling process managed by the FIMMDA. As the product design has been finalised after due consultation with the market participants and the issue of illiquidity in underlying cash market has been dealt with by permitting cash settlement, it is expected that the product will attract active interest. Another significant step is the extension of the period of short sale to three months, effective from February 1, 2012. This will enable the participants to express their interest rate views more effectively and is expected to give fillip to term repo market. Similarly, the credit default swap (CDS) on corporate bonds has been introduced to facilitate hedging of credit risk associated with corporate bonds. Introduction of credit enhancement for corporate bonds through CDS may also increase investors' interest in corporate bonds.

Several episodes in international markets underscored the importance of risk management in the use of financial products. Learning from these episodes, the approach of the Reserve Bank of India towards regulation and risk management has been oriented to ensure orderly development of financial markets and products. This objective is achieved by establishing efficient infrastructure, addressing systemic stability issues and also supporting market development. The pre-dominant motivation has been to strike a balance between systemic stability and financial market development.

Infrastructure

Market infrastructure is a comprehensive term that includes the entire gamut of arrangements for the transactions to be carried out and settled in an efficient and safe manner. Infrastructure plays an important role in development of markets and want of an efficient, transparent and robust infrastructure can keep market participants away on one extreme or cause market crisis on the other. Reserve Bank of India has pursuing a strategy for creation of an efficient market infrastructure to enhance market activity and also to create a supporting institutional framework. In the government bond market, a state of the art primary issuance process with electronic bidding and fast processing capabilities, an efficient, completely dematerialised depository system, Delivery-versus-Payment (DvP) mode of settlement, Real Time Gross Settlement (RTGS), electronic trading platforms (Negotiated Dealing Systems and Negotiated Dealing Systems – Order Matching) and a Separate Central Counter Party (CCP) in the Clearing Corporation of India Ltd (CCIL) for guaranteed settlement are among the steps that were taken by the Reserve Bank over the years towards this end. In fact, thanks to these efforts, India can boast of being one of the few emerging countries with such a state-of-the-art financial market infrastructure for the G-Sec market. Creating a robust risk management structure for the CCP to mitigate its increasing concentration risk and enabling an assured liquidity support framework for meeting its emergency liquidity needs are some of the challenges before the Reserve Bank.

Intermediaries

Intermediaries play an important role in development of the market by facilitating the transactions, providing value-added services and increasing efficacy of the processes. With regard to bond markets in India, the role of four major intermediaries, viz. PD system, industry associations like FIMMDA/PDAI, Gilt Mutual Funds and the Infrastructure Development Funds (IDFs), which are in the offing has been discussed below:.

The system of Primary Dealers (PDs) was established to provide support to the market borrowing programmes of the Government and also to impart liquidity in the secondary markets. Subsequent to the withdrawal of the Reserve Bank from the primary market, as mandated by Fiscal Responsibility and Budget Management Act 2003, the PD System has been underwriting the entire Government of India market borrowing. PDs have actively supported the bond issuances and their role in successful completion of sizeable issuance programmes over the past three years has been commendable. Recently, Reserve Bank has revised the guidelines on authorisation of PDs with focus on their market experience as well as increase in retail/mid-segment investor participation so as to widen the investor base. The revised guidelines prescribe a seasoning requirement of at least one year prior to submission of application, reasonable experience in G-Sec market with at least 15 per cent of their assets and turnover in G-Sec and a commitment to achieve a minimum turnover of 75 per cent of their minimum NOF in G-Sec on behalf of retail/mid-segment clients. PDs are expected to continue to support the market borrowing programmes, act as market-makers by providing fillip to secondary markets and retail investors and proactively deal in the financial products such as CDS, IRF, etc. Reserve Bank is also exploring the possibility of enabling banks/PDs to make markets in corporate bonds through appropriate supportive measures.

Changing nature of financial markets necessitate that organisations, such as, FIMMDA and PDAI, play a more proactive role in bringing orderliness in market activities and desired level of discipline amongst market participants. The Reserve Bank regularly engages with FIMMDA and PDAI on various issues of policy and provides inputs and perspectives of the market participants. FIMMDA has been entrusted with responsibilities, such as, publishing model prices for G-Sec and non-G-Sec to be used in valuations, formulation of model code of conduct for market participants, development and operationalisation of critical market infrastructure like reporting platform for corporate bonds, repo in corporate bonds, CPs and CDs, accreditation of brokers in the OTC interest rate derivatives market, development of the daily CDS curve for valuation of open positions, etc. The entrusted responsibilities and activities/functions of FIMMDA in the underlying market clearly indicate its potential for self-regulatory role. There is, however, an urgent need for FIMMDA to further strengthen itself, build competencies, both technical and financial, and broaden its mission to carry out tasks commensurate with the developments in the market and to undertake additional responsibilities as Self-Regulatory Organisation (SRO).

Gilt Mutual Fund industry has grown manifold but the Mutual Funds (MFs) continue to invest predominantly in short-tenor fixed income assets, thereby exhibiting low demand in the G-Sec market. This is a cause of concern and there is an urgent need to examine ways for promoting investment by MFs in G-Sec.

Huge requirement of investment in infrastructure sector underscores the importance of the IDFs. The Reserve Bank has, as a special case, has permitted several prudential relaxations for setting up IDFs including enhanced exposure norms, assigning lower risk weights for capital adequacy purposes, etc. Reserve Bank of India has also allowed investment on full repatriation basis by new class of eligible non-resident investors (viz.

Sovereign Wealth Funds, multilateral agencies, pension funds, insurance funds, endowment funds) in Rupee and Foreign Currency-denominated bonds to be issued by IDF- NBFCs registered by the Reserve Bank of India and Rupee-denominated units issued by IDF-MFs set up as SEBI-registered Mutual Funds. Given our calibrated approach towards opening up of our debt markets to foreign investors, all such investments (excluding those by NRIs) will, however, be within an overall cap of US$ 10 billion (which would be within the overall cap of US$ 25 billion for FII investment in infrastructure debt). IDFs will, in days to come, act as a major source of channelising huge quantum of funds from long- term domestic and foreign investors to the corporate debt markets in the critical infrastructure sector of the country and will indeed be a gamechanger with a potential of redefining various facets of the markets.

Incentives

Incentives, both positive and negative, play a major role in shaping human behaviour and markets are no exception to this rule. The regulatory dispensation of HTM classification has protected balance sheets of the banks and encouraged them to invest in G-Sec but promoted illiquidity in government bonds. Different incentive structures in treasuries of public sector banks and private/foreign bank treasuries partly explains the level of participation in derivative markets in spite of existence of similar risks on the balance sheets. While differences in incentives in public and private banks with regard to treasury operations exist, the reasons for lack of interest shown by most of the public sector in spite of the fact that they hold very high interest rate sensitive portfolio and have the balance sheet capability to participate in the market needs to be examined in depth and debated.

An understanding of the incentives is essential for both policymakers and market participants so that the market activities can be directed towards attainment of objectives of efficiency and effectiveness. While the Reserve Bank tries to align incentives by regulation and supervision, regulation itself could create unintended incentives/disincentives as in the case of requirement regarding 'HTM'. For instance, the ability to buy CDS without an underlying has resulted in perverse incentives in the developed markets. The Reserve Bank, while framing the CDS policy, has designed regulation to curb such skewed incentives by restricting users to buy CDS only to hedge an underlying exposure. Physical settlement has been mandated after the credit event. A nuanced understanding of the incentives would help in design of regulation that promotes market development without jeopardising financial stability.

Innovation

With the world still smarting under the financial crisis believed to have been unleashed by 'innovative' products, one has to talk about innovation with some degree of caution. Financial innovation is an essential feature in the history of development of financial markets. Bypassing the tax or the regulatory regime has, of course, been a major motivation for innovation, the social and economic utility of which is often questionable. An example is the Negotiable Order of Withdrawal (NOW) accounts in the US that were a result of Regulation Q restrictions on interests on demand deposits. But innovations that are motivated by the need to match the needs of the investor and the issuer or made possible by advancement in technology or knowledge are essential for evolution of financial markets. One can cite many examples–demat accounts, ATMs, credit and debit cards, explosion of options contracts, inflation-indexed bonds, Fixed Rate Capital Securities, IRS, CDS and so on. It is true that financial innovation has also resulted in complex products which package and redistribute risks in a way that is scarcely understood. As observed by Lord Turner of the UK Financial Services Authority, financial innovation has produced some products of very dubious social value. It is vital to understand that financial innovation is not an objective in itself but a process and has to cater to the products to the felt need of the market in particular and wider economy in general without compromising on financial stability. The old adage 'Innovate or Perish' should read 'Innovate with Caution or Perish' in so far as the financial sector is concerned.

Innovation and risk are two aspects of financial markets between which there is a great deal of tension. As such, inadequate risk management framework can make the difference between survival and death for an institution, particularly a financial institution. Several episodes in international markets have repeatedly underscored this – Orange County, LTCM, BCCI, Enron, Barings, Northern Rock – one can go on. We have just seen that innovative products like the CDOs and innovative institutional arrangements like the SPVs without adequate appreciation of embedded risk and an appropriate regulatory framework for risk management could wreak havoc. Nearer home, ill- judged use of some exotic foreign exchange derivative by some corporates led to substantial losses and created fracas between them and the banks that had sold them the products.

In India, innovation has been rather muted and even the reception for new products has been rather insipid. The regulators are not against innovative products; their concern is that neither should the innovation be oriented towards skirting the regulatory regime nor should they lead to build-up of systemic risk. It is imperative for the market participants and the industry association to ensure that adequate risk management systems and corporate governance structures are in place before embarking on innovations. As you all may have observed, the Reserve Bank has followed and will continue to follow a measured approach in the introduction of innovative products through adoption of appropriate risk management framework suitable to our eco-system.

However , it should be realised that development and adoption of new products in emerging market economies is not often easy. It requires considerable amount of patience, hand- holding and fine-tuning depending on the needs of the respective eco-system. It is equally important to remember that market liquidity is a consequence of active participation of market players. New financial products and instruments are designed to cater to funding and hedging needs but the need to be actively used by the market participants without, of course, increasing the risks to the financial stability and jeopardising the interest of the ultimate end-users/ customers. The lack of market interest, if any, must be introspected and debated seriously to draw up remedial action plan.

REVIEW PROBLEMS

1. If the two-year interest rate is 12.5 percent per annum, and the one-year interest rate is 10.50 per cent, what does the market expect the one year interest rate to be a year from now?

Ans:

$$\frac{(1.1250)^2}{1.1050}$$

$= (1.1454) \times 100$

$= 11.454$ per cent per annum.

2. The current price of the security of par value of ₹ 1000 has fallen to ₹ 623.213 in the market. If there are still 6 years to maturity, calculate the spot yield, r.

Ans.

The spot rate of interest (or spot yield) is:

$r = (₹ 1000/₹ 623.213)^{1/6} - 1$

$= 0.082$

$= 8.2\%$ p.a.

3. The market price of the security of par value ₹ 1000 with a 10% coupon bond has fallen to ₹ 900. There are still three years to maturity and semi-annual coupon payments are on to be made. Compute the YTM.

Ans.

The YTM is:

₹ 900 = (₹ 50/(1+y/2) + ₹ 50/(1+y/2)^2
+ .... + ₹ 50/(1+y/2)^5 + ₹ 1050/(1+y/2)^6

YTM = 14.2% p.a.

4. Government issues two securities at par ₹ 1000 each for two years, a security XYZ bearing annual coupon 8.75% and a security ABC with 9.50%. Given the spot rate of interest (or spot yield) r_1 = 6% and r_2 = 7% for two years. Calculate the market price of two securities.

Ans.

Price (Security XYZ):

₹ 8.75/(1.06) + ₹ 108.75 (1.07)^2
    = ₹ 8.25 + ₹ 94.99 = ₹ 103.24

Price (Security (ABC):

    = ₹ 9.50/(1.06) + 109.50 (1.07)^2
    = ₹ 8.96 + ₹ 95.64 = ₹ 104.60

5. (i) If the sport one-year interest rate is 20 per cent per annum and the one-year rate expected to be available one year from now is 8 percent per annum, what will the two-year interest rate be?

(ii) If the rates in (i) are nominal rates and inflation is expected to be 12 per cent and 5 per cent in years one and two respectively, what is the expected two-year real rate of interest?

(iii) If the two-year nominal rate is 10 percent per annum and the one-year rate is 9 per cent per annum, what one-year rate is expected to be available one year from now?

(iv) If the two-year rate in (iii) contains a 1 percent risk premium (and the one-year rate contains no risk premium), how would the answer change?

Ans:

(i) (1.2) (1.08)   = 1.296

     $\sqrt{1.296}$ = 1.1384

(ii) 1.1384-1   = 0.1384 or 13.84% per annum

     (1.0714) (1.0286) = 1.1020

     $\sqrt{1.1020}$ = 1.0498

     1.0498 - 1   = 0.0498

                              = 4.98% per annum

(iii) (1.09) (1 + x)   = (1.10)^2

      So   (1 + x)   = (1.10)^2/(1.09) = 1.1101

      Hence   x   = 11.10 per cent per annum

(iv) Remove the risk premium fro the two-year rate. Then

     (1.09) (1 + x)   = (1.09)^2

            (1 + x)   = (1.09)^2/(1.09) = 1.09

     Hence   x   = 10.9 percent per annum.

6. A 20-year bond with a coupon of 10 has been issued at per value of ₹ 1000. Yield-to-maturity is 11% per annum and semi-annual coupons are to be made. Calculate the price of the bond.

Ans. Semi-annual coupon payment (C) is:

$= 0.5 [0.10 (₹ 1000)] = ₹ 50$

Semi-annual yield-to-maturity (r) is:

$= 0.11/2 = 0.055$

Number of payments are:

$n = 2(20) = 40$

The discounted present value of the coupon payments is given by the an annuity formula:

$A = C [1-1/(1+r)^n]/r$

$= ₹ 50 [1-1/(1.055)^{40}] / 0.055$

$= ₹ 802.31$

Present value of 'one off' single payment:

$₹ 1000 / (1.055)^{40}$

$= ₹ 117.45$

Hence:

Price of Bond $= ₹ 802.31 + ₹ 117.45$

$= ₹ 919.77$

7. Government issues two zero coupon bonds (6 months and 1 year) with spot interest rate $r_1 = 8.0\%$ p.a., $r_2 = 8.30\%$ p.a. Bond ABC has maturity of 1.5 years, coupon rate 8.50%, coupons paid semi annually, market price ₹ 994.50 and par value of ₹ 1000. Calculate the 18-month spot rate of interest, r_3.

Ans.

The correct price of Bond ABC is given by:

$$₹ 994.50 = \frac{₹\ 42.50}{(1+r_1/2)} + \frac{₹\ 42.50}{(1+r_2/2)^2} + \frac{₹\ 1042.50}{(1+r_3/2)^3}$$

Given spot rate of interest on 6 month and 12 month are:

$r_1 = 0.08$ and $r_2 = 0.083$

Hence:

$994.50 = 40.865 + 39.180 + 1042.50 / (1+r_3/2)^3$

$r_3 = 0.0893$ (8.93%) p.a. on a bond equivalent yield basis.

8. If the current one year rate is 6% and the two- year yield to maturity is 8% , what is the one- year forward expectation, according tho the Expectation Hypothesis.

Ans:

One-year forward expectation is

$\quad (1.06) (1 + r)=(1.08)^2$

$\quad (1 + r)=(1.08)^2 /1.06 \qquad =1.1664/1.06$

$\qquad\qquad\qquad\qquad\qquad = 1.1004$ Thus:

$\qquad\qquad\qquad\qquad\qquad r = 10.04\%$

9. The current three-month interest rate is 11 per cent per annum and market expectations of the next seven three-month rates are 11, 11, 10, 10, 10, 9 and 9 percent, (a) what, according to the pure expectation theory, would the current two-years rate be? (b) What would be the effect of a 0.5 percent risk premium on two-year investments?

Ans:

(a) $\sqrt{(1.0275)^3 \ (1.025)^3 \ (1.0225)^3 - 1} \times 100$

= 10.52 per cent per annum.

(b) 10.52 + 0.5 = 11.02 percent per annum.

10. A 5 year bond of par value of ₹ 1,000 with 10% coupon (annual) bond has been issued. It is trading at par (i.e. YTM 10%). Calculate the Holding Period Return (HPR) assuming a horizon of 2 years, a reinvestment rate of 6% and a YTM in 2 years time of 7%.

Ans. Two Coupons + interest on Interest:

= ₹ 100 + ₹ 100 (1.06) = ₹ 206

Interest-on-interest is lower for an assumed investment rate of either 10% or 12%.

After 2 years the bond will have 3 years to maturity:

Expected price after 2 years:

$$\frac{₹ 100}{(1+.07)} + \frac{₹ 100}{(1+.07)^2} + \frac{₹ 100}{(1+.07)^3} + \frac{₹ 100}{(1+.07)^3}$$

= 93.46 + ₹ 87.34 + ₹ 81.63 + ₹ 816.29

= ₹ 1078.72

A fall in the YTM producer a capital gain on the bond.

Terminal Value (TV) = ₹ 206 + ₹ 1078.72

= ₹ 1284.72

Approximate return = (₹ 1284.72 / ₹ 1000) 100

= 28.47% over 2 years (about 14.235% p.a.)

HPR (at compound annual rate) = $(1+r)^2$

= ₹ 1284.72 / ₹ 1000 = 1,284.72

r = 0.13.34 = 13.34

QUESTIONS

1. Distinguish between internal and external debt. Discuss the internal debt obligations of the Government of India.

2. Explain the term *structure of yield rates* on public debt. What is the yield structure of the Government securities in India?

3. What is the expectation hypothesis? How sensitive are the yield curves of the government securities? Illustrate with suitable Indian examples.

4. Discuss the various types of securities issued by the Government of India.

5. Elaborate on the general shape of the yield curve of the Government of India's securities

6. Explain the term *structure of yield rates on the public debt.* What is the yield structure of the Government securities in India.

7. Explain the concept of yield curve and the interrelationship between different components of the yield curve.

8. Discuss the debt obligations of the government of India.

9. Define the term marketablility. Explain its importance to the securities investor and its replationship to the yield on a financial instrument.

10. What are the different roles of the rate of interest in the economy?

11. Explain the meaning of the phrase "term structure of interest rates." What is a yield curve? What assumptions are necessary to construct a yield curve?

12. Explain the differences between the expectations, market-segmentation, and liquidity-

premium views of the yield curve. Depending upon which of these views is correct, what are the implications of each for investors? For public policy?

13. Define default risk. What factors appear to influence the degree of default risk possesssed by a security? In what ways are security ratings designed to reflect default risk?

14. Explain how inflation affects interest rates. What is the Fishereffect and the Harrod effect?

15. The correlation between the inflation rate and market interest rates appears to have interested considerably in recent years. Can you explain.

16. What is the normal, or typical, slope of the yield curve for T-bills? What other slopes have been observed, and why do you think there occur?

17. Briefly describe the implications of each of the three hypothesis - (1) expectations (2) liquidity, and (3) segmentation - when the yeield curve is upward sloping and downward sloping.

19. Distinguish between expected holding-period return and yield to maturity.

20. "The existence of an efficient government securities debt market is an essential precursor for the corporate debt market."

21. Critically examine the role of Primary Dealers (PDs) in government securities an important intermediaries to promote activity in government securities.

22. "Development, sustenance and expansion of the debt markets is a very complex activity." Do you agree?

PROBLEMS

1. The spot three month interest rate is 10 per cent annum and the subsequent three-month rates are to be 10.50,10.75 and 11.00 per cent per annum.

   (i)   What one-year interest rate is suggested by the pure expectancy model?

   (ii) If the spot six-month rate was 11.00 per cent per annum and the one-year rate was 12.50 per cent per annum, what forward-forward rate is implied for the six-month period commencing six months from the present.

   (iii) How would the answers to (i) and (ii) change if there was a risk or liquidity premium?

   (iv) In the case of (if) if the price of three months futures maturing six-months from now indicated a future interest rate of 13.00 per annum, what might you expect the three-month interest rate available in nine months time to be?

REFERENCES

1. Ahu, C., and Howard Thompson: "Jump Diffusion and the Term Structure of Interest Rates," *Journal of Finance* 73. March 1988, pp. 155-74.

2. Altman. Edward, and Duen Kao: "The Implications of Corporate Bond Rating Profit," *Financial Analysts Journal*, May-June 1992, pp. 64-75.

3. Ayres, H.F., and John Barry: "Dynamics of the Government Yield Curve." *Financial Analysts Journal*, May-June 1979, pp. 31-39.

4. Brown, Stephen, and Philip Dybrig: "The Empirical Implications of the Cox. Ingersoll. Ross Theory of the Term Structure of Interest Rates," *Journal of Finance* 41. July 1986. pp. 617-30.

5. —————————, and Stephen Schaefer: "The Term Structure of Real Interest Rates and the Cox. Ingersoll, and Ross Model," *Journal of Financial Economics*, February 1994, pp. 3-42.

6. Burik. Paul, and Richard Ennis: "Foreign Bonds in Diversified Portfolios: A Limited Advantage." *Financial Analysts Journal*, March-April 1990, pp. 31-40.

7. Campbell, John: "A Defense of Traditional Hypotheses about the Term Structure of Interest Rates," *Journal of Finance* 41, March 1986, pp. 183-193.

8. Carlton, Willard T., and Ian A. Cooper: "Estimation and Uses of the Term Structure of Interest Rates," *Journal of Finance*, September 1976. pp. 1076-1083.

9. Carr, Richard: "The Rationale for Investing in International Bonds and Currencies— Historical Re-turns, Risk, and Diversification." *International Bonds and Currencies*, CFA Institute, 1986. pp.11-21.

10. Conard, Joseph W. *The Behavior of Interest Rates.* New York: Na-tional Bureau of Economic Research, 1966.

11. Dattels, Peter, 1997, "Microstructure of Government Securities Market," in *Coordinating Public Debt and Monetary Management*, edited by V. Sundararajan, Peter Dattels, and H. J. Blommestein (Washington: International Monetary Fund).

12. European Union, 2000, "Progress Report on Primary Dealership in EU Public Debt Management" (unpublished; Brussels: Economic and Financial Committee).

13. Evans, Martin, and Paul Wachtel: "Interpreting the Moments in Short-Term Interest Rates," *Journal of Business*, July 1992, pp. 395-423.

14. Fair, Ray C., and Burton G. Malkiel. "The Determinants of Yield Differentials between Debt Instruments of the Same Maturity." *Journal of Money, Credit and Banking*, November 1971, 733-749.

15. Fama. Eugene: "The Information in the Term Structure," *Journal of Financial Economics* 13, December 1984. pp. 509-546.

16. ———: "Short-Term Interest Rates as Predictors of Inflation." *American Economic Review*, June 1975, pp. 269-282.

17. ———: "Term Premiums in Bond Returns." *Journal of Financial Economics*, December 1984, pp. 529-46.

18. Fielitz, Bruce D. "Calculating the Bond Equivalent Yield for T-Bills." *Journal of Portfolio Management*, Spring 1983, 58-60.

19. Froot, Kenneth: "New Hope for the Expectations Hypothesis of the Term Structure of Interest Rates." *Journal of Finance*, June 1989, pp. 283-305.

20. Gray, Simon, 1997, "Government Securities: Primary Issuance," in *Handbooks in Central Banking* No. 11 (London: Center for Central Banking Studies, Bank of England).

21. Homer, Sidney, and M.L. Liebowitz: *Inside the Yield Book*, Prentice-Hall, Englewood Cliffs, N.J.1972.

22. Johnson, Brian and Kenneth Meyer: "Managing Yield Curve Risk in an Index Environment," *Financial Analysts Journal*, November-December 1989, pp. 51-59.

23. Kane, Edward J., and Burton G. Malkiel. "The Term Structure of Interest Rates: An Analysis of a Survey of Interest Rate Expectations." *Review of Economics and Statistics*, August 1967, 343-355.

24. Kessel, Reuben: "The Cyclical Behavior of the Term Structure of Interest Rates," Occasional Paper 91, *National Bureau of Economic Research*, New York, 1965.

25. Lioue, Hirotaka, 1999, "The Structure of Government Securities Markets in G10 Countries: Summary of Questionnaire Results" (unpublished; Basel: Bank for International Settlements).

26. McConnachie, Robin, 1996, "Primary Dealers in Government Securities Markets," in *Handbooks on Central Banking* (London: Center for Central Banking Studies, Bank of England).

27. Meiselman, D.: *The Term Structure of Interest Rates*, Prentice-Hall, Englewood Cliffs, N.J., 1962.

28. Meyer, Kenneth: "Yield Spreads and Interest Rate Levels," *Financial Analysts Journal*, November-December 1978, pp. 58-63.

29. Modigliani, Franco, and Richard Sutch: "Debt Management and the Term Structure of Interest Rates; An Empirical Analysis of Recent Experience," *Journal of Political Economy*, August 1967 Supplement, pp. 569-589.

30. Nelson, Charles, and Andrew Siegel: "Parsimonious Modeling of Yield Curves," *Journal of Business.* October 1987, pp. 473-490.

16

Sovereign Wealth Funds

INTRODUCTION

Sovereign Wealth Funds (SWFs), also refered as Govrnment-owned Investment Vehicles (GIVs), existed for long but they have acquired significance very recently due to their proliferation, growth in size and, above all, active participation in capital infusion in the aftermath of the recently observed financial turbulance. This growth of SWF-type institutional arrangements can be seen as a policy response to the strong accumulation of foreign assets by the offi cial sector. However, SWFs are not new, especially in countries rich in natural resources (e.g., oil). SWFs have recently gained prominence in several (non- oil) emerging markets and commodity-based developing countries, reflecting large balance of payments surpluses.

CHARACTERISTICS OF SWFs

Various governments have created special investment funds to hold foreign assets for long-term purposes. In recent years, a number of these SWFs have emerged as direct investors. There is no universally agreed-upon definition of such funds, but their original objective was wealth preservation. Their objectives vary, but their investment strategies tend to be quite different from those of traditional TNCs and private equity funds.

What are SWFs?

SWFs are government investment vehicles that are funded by the accumulation of foreign exchange assets and managed separately from the official reserves of the monetary authorities. They usually have a higher risk tolerance and higher expected returns than traditional official reserves managed by the monetary authorities. They aim at systematic professional portfolio management to generate a sustainable future income stream. Their portfolio investment includes bonds, equities and alternative asset classes.

Although there is no universally agreed-upon definition, SWFs can generally be defined as special investment funds created or owned by governments to hold foreign assets for long-term purposes. SWFs can be classified according to at least two criteria: (1) the sources of sovereign wealth, and (2) their policy objectives.

Sources of Sovereign Wealth Funds

The funding of SWFs comes from different sources, which can be combined. Some funds are byproducts of fi scal budget surpluses accumulated due to a combination of revenues from exports and spending restraint. Fiscal surpluses and public savings generated domestically, such as privatization receipts, can also be sources for SWFs, as can large balance of payment surpluses, with or without a corresponding budget surplus.

They have existed since the 1950s, especially in countries that were rich in natural resources (particularly oil), but had largely gone unnoticed until the middle of the present decade. Two of the largest of these funds, Kuwait Investment Authority and Temasek Holdings of Singapore, were founded in 1953 and 1974 respectively. In recent years, the assets of SWFs have grown considerably, reflecting the rapidly growing current account surpluses of many developing countries and the accompanying accumulation of foreign exchange reserves.

Sovereign funds (SWFs) from public savings and privatization are more akin to nonrenewable resource funds, as they represent an increase in net financial wealth. The reporting of sovereign financial assets has focused thus far on the appropriate methodological treatment of reserve assets. In 1990, sovereign funds probably held, at most, $500 billion; the current total is an estimated $2-3 trillion and, thereby exceeding assets managed by hedge funds (US$ 1.9 trillion). In fact, such Funds today account for between 1/4 -1/3 of all foreign assets held by sovereigns. SWF assets are projected to surpass the stock of global foreign exchange reserves in the not so distant future and to top US$ 7-11 trillion by 2013.

Is $3 trillion a lot of money? It depends on the comparison. U.S. GDP is $12 trillion, the total value of traded securities (debt and equity) denominated in U.S. dollars is estimated to be more than $50 trillion, and the global value of traded securities is about $165 trillion. In that context, $3 trillion is significant but not huge.

It is, however, large relative to the size of some emerging markets. The total value of traded securities in Africa, the Middle East, and emerging Europe combined is about $4 trillion; this is also roughly the size of these markets in all of Latin America. And total assets under management by private hedge funds — a broad category of private investment funds that seek high returns and, as a consequence, often take on considerable risks — are estimated to be around $2 trillion.

Home Country Policy Goals

While SWFs share the goal of efficiently and effectively managing their country's official financial wealth, they have specific economic policy roles.

(i)   For example, for countries exporting nonrenewable resources, the principal challenge is to transform such resources into sustainable and stable future income, compensating for the reality of volatile commodity prices and finite supplies. Placing commodity revenue in a Sovereign Wealth Fund is a means to avoid boom/ bust cycles, such as those experienced during the 1970s, by accumulating adequate international assets. Moreover, a well- managed and effective SWF can help protect the economy's non-commodity sectors from destabilizing currency fluctuations while helping to spread the country's wealth more equitably across generations.

(ii) Indeed, 30 of the 38 existing SWFs have been established by commodity-exporting countries for stabilization and/or saving purposes. The Fund for Social and Economic Stabilization (FESS) that the government of Chile established long ago is now being managed as just such a Sovereign Wealth Fund. The purpose of this Fund is to smooth government spending by putting aside fiscal surpluses that are in excess of a structural target, so as to be used in periods of weak terms of trade.

(iii) Some Sovereign Wealth Funds also aim explicitly at developing a broader base for economic growth. Developing an efficient and diversified economy reduces the impact of commodity price volatility and helps to prepare the economy for a post-commodity era. This has been one of the stated purposes of 5 recently established SWFs.

(iv) Ageing populations create a need to fund future social obligations.

(v) Finally, reserve accumulation is putting pressure on some central bank balance sheets in terms of carry cost and currency mismatches, driving the need for higher risk-adjusted asset returns. Some countries are seeking prudent and effective management of such type of foreign currency accumulation via Sovereign Wealth Funds.

Necessary Conditions for Success

While Sovereign Wealth Funds can help generate long-term economic benefits, several important conditions must be fulfilled in order to produce the intended results.

First, appropriate budget and monetary policies represent the most important of these preconditions. Thus, the operations of the SWF must be well integrated in the overall policy framework. Failing this, an SWF could produce potential policy pitfalls, such as creating parallel budgets, or—through ill-timed withdrawals—undermining the operations of the central bank.

Second, for the Fund's operations to be properly integrated into the home country economic policy framework, it is critical that adequate information is reported to the relevant agencies, and that accurate data are included in national accounts, as well as monetary, government finance, and external sector statistics.

Third, recent cross-country evidence suggests that SWFs are successful in achieving efficient resource management when they have well-designed funding and withdrawal rules that are consistent with their stated goals. Most recently, following such rules, the government of Chile has established its two existing SWFs as an integral part of Chile's macroeconomic framework. The fiscal framework adopted in 2006 apportioned fiscal surpluses between the SWFs within a fiscal rule designed to smooth government expenditures across the business cycle.

Fourth, an SWF should be underpinned by well-framed corporate governance arrangements. These include the government as its owner setting the Fund's objectives, its governance structure, and an effective accountability framework. Governance structures typically articulate clear roles, responsibilities, and interrelationships between the different bodies involved in the SWF's administration and management with the goal of facilitating operational independence in making investment decisions.

Fifth, clear accountability procedures among the different levels of SWF governance, and to the public, are important in order to prevent misuse of public resources and to gain public support for the Fund and its objectives. These arrangements can generate public support for saving resources rather than spending them, inform the public about the accumulated revenue, and provide the economic rationale for the buildup of SWF resources. Transparency arrangements, in this regard, entail regular public disclosure of the investment objectives of the SWF, its funding, the withdrawals and spending on behalf of the government, the governance framework, and the Fund's asset size and its allocation, and return.

Finally, the success of a Sovereign Wealth Fund is contingent upon responsible investment policies that are consistent with its policy purpose. These include care, skill, and prudence in investment practices, and a robust framework to identify, assess, and manage the risks of its operation. For instance, stabilization funds—that are the most common form of SWF and have shorter investment horizons—are more likely to invest conservatively and may hold relatively large stocks of liquid assets. In contrast, savings funds seek to earn higher returns over a longer horizon, and may invest across all major asset classes, including alternative investments. Pension reserve funds may even determine their investment policies in an asset and liability context to match entitlement payments, thereby choosing portfolios similar to those of funds with direct pension liabilities.

Policy Objectives

The following types of funds can be distinguished, based on their dominant objectives:

i) *Stabilization funds* are set up by countries rich in natural resources to insulate the budget and economy from volatile commodity prices (usually oil). The funds build up assets during the years of ample fiscal revenues to prepare for leaner years.

ii) *Savings funds* are intended to share wealth across generations. For countries rich in natural resources, savings funds transfer nonrenewable assets into a diversified portfolio of international financial assets to provide for future generations, or other long-term objectives .

iii) *Reserve investment corporations* are funds established as a separate entity either to reduce the negative cost-of-carry of holding reserves or to pursue investment policies with higher returns. Often, the assets in such arrangements are still counted as reserves.

iv) *Development funds* allocate resources for funding priority socioeconomic projects, such as infrastructure.

v) *Pension reserve funds* have identified pension and/or contingent-type liabilities on the government's balance sheet. To some extent, development funds and even pension reserve funds can be considered as subsets of SWFs that are (explicitly or implicitly) linked to long-term fi scal commitments.

Additional objectives include enhancing transparency in the management of revenues from (commodity) exports and fiscal policy. In practice, SWFs typically have multiple or gradually changing objectives. For example, some countries set up funds for both stabilization and savings objectives. As circumstances change, the objectives of the funds may also change. This is especially true for countries that export natural resources. Initially, a stabilization fund is established to smooth fiscal revenue or sterilize foreign currency inflows. As the assets in the fund continue to grow beyond the level needed for the purpose of stabilization, country authorities may revisit the objectives and redesign the structure of the fund to broaden the objective. This often leads to assets being split into several branches for different objectives, or to the creation of separate funds with different objectives.

The institutional arrangements for managing these different types of arrangements are broadly of three categories. The first two pertain to those managed by the central bank and/or an independent agency. A third category of SWFs consist of those funds already established that acquire the modality of "tiers of accounts," that is, separate funds for different purposes. In some instances, the central bank transfers funds to the SWF, while in other cases funds are transferred to the central bank for management purposes.

CLASSIFICATION OF SWFS AND ITS IMPLICATIONS

SWFs are typically categorized as stabilization funds, savings funds, pension reserve funds, or reserve investment corporations

The majority of established SWFs are either savings funds for future generations or fiscal stabilization funds (Table 1). There are only a handful of pension reserve funds (Australia's Future Fund, Chile's Pension Reserve Fund (Chile-PRF), Ireland's National Pensions Reserve Fund, New Zealand's Superannuation Fund, and the Russia Federation's National Wealth Fund (Russia-NWF)) operating today, and even fewer reserve investment corporations (China Investment Corporation (CIC), Korea Investment Corporation (KIC), and Government Investment Corporation of Singapore (GIC)). Some SWFs have multiple objectives (e.g., State Oil Fund of Azerbaijan, Kuwait Investment Authority, and Norway's Government Pension Fund-Global), and a number of countries also have more than one SWF with different objectives, including Chile, the Russian Federation, and Singapore.

TABLE 1
Sovereign Wealth Fund Classification

Source	Year established	Country	Policy Purpose			
			Macro stabilization	Saving	Pension reserve	Reserve investment
Oil & Natural Gas	1953	Kuwait	Kuwait Investment Authority, General Reserve Fund	Kuwait Investment Authority, Future Generations Fund		
	1976	Canada		Alberta Heritage Savings Trust Fund		
	1976	United Arab Emirates		Abu Dhabi Investment Authority		
	1976	United States		Alaska Permanent Fund		
	1980	Oman State		General Reserve Fund		
	1983	Brunei Darussalam		Brunei Investment Agency		
	1996	Norway	Government Pension Fund-Global	Government Pension Fund-Global	Government Pension Fund-Global	
	1999	Azerbaijan	State Oil Fund	State Oil Fund		
	2000	Iran, Islamic Republic of	Oil Stabilization Fund			
	2000	Mexico Oil	Revenues Stabilization Fund			
	2000	Qatar		Qatar Investment Authority		
	2000	Trinidad and Tobago	Heritage and Stabilization Fund	Heritage and Stabilization Fund		
	2001	Kazakhstan	National Fund			
	2002	Equatorial Guinea		Fund for Future Generations of Equatorial Guinea		
	2004	São Tomé and Príncipe		National Oil Account		
	2005	Timor-Leste	Petroleum Fund	Petroleum Fund		
	2006	Bahrain	The Future Generations Reserve Fund	The Future Generations Reserve Fund		
	2006	Libya		Libyan Investment Authority		
	2008	Russian Federation	Reserve Fund		National Wealth Fund	
Other Commodity	1956	Kiribati		Kiribati, Revenue Equalization Fund		
	1996	Botswana		Botswana, Pula Fund		
	2006	Chile			Pension Reserve Fund	
	2007	Chile	Economic and Social Stabilization Fund (ESSF)			

	1974	Singapore	Singapore, Temasek	
	1981	Singapore		Government of Singapore Investment Corporation
	1993	Malaysia	Khazanah Nasional BHD	
Fiscal Surpluses	2000	Ireland		Ireland, National Pensions Reserve Fund
	2001	New Zealand		New Zealand Superannuation Fund
	2004	Australia		Australia, Future Fund
	2005	Korea, Republic of		Korea Investment Corporation
	1981	Singapore		Government of Singapore Investment Corporation
FX Reserves	2005	Korea, Republic of		Korea Investment Corporation
	2007	China		China Investment Corporation

The different types of SWFs have important differences in their investment objectives and behavior

A reserve investment corporation, for example, will need to consider the possible repercussions of balance of payments risks, and will want to hold a portion of its portfolio in liquid assets. The SWF's type and its objectives will also influence its investment horizon. For instance, savings SWFs are expected to have longer investment horizons than stabilization SWFs, whereas pension reserve funds can derive their investment horizons from the timing of the future anticipated liabilities falling due, which can be decades in the future.

SWFs' investment objectives may also be influenced by the source of their funds and may take into consideration other assets and liabilities on the wider government balance sheet.

THEORETICAL CONSIDERATIONS BEHIND SWFS' STRATEGIC ASSET ALLOCATIONS

The type of SWF, its investment horizon and funding source, and other balance sheet characteristics should all affect its strategic asset allocation (SAA).

INVESTMENT HORIZON AND SAA

The investment horizon is a critical factor for any investor in determining the SAA. A long investment horizon is traditionally associated with the ability to take more risk. Usually, risk is defined as the probability of a loss or underperformance relative to a reference asset, such as T-bill or a government bond, over a given horizon. The traditional SAA literature suggests that, on longer horizons, equities are less volatile than short-term instruments because of the reinvestment risks associated with short-term investments. In addition, historical data suggest a fairly consistent equity return premium over longer horizons. Hence, a larger share in equities for investors with long investment horizons is appropriate.

Another factor associated with investors with long investment horizons is the ability to invest in illiquid assets to enjoy the illiquidity premium. For many asset classes, such as infrastructure, real estate, and private equity, it may take a long time and a lot of planning to exit the investment without unduly affecting that asset's price. Therefore, only SWFs with truly long horizons (i.e., those that are very unlikely to have to divest in a hurry) would be expected to venture into these asset classes, which, for the purposes of this paper, are classified as "alternative assets."

Conversely, investors with short or very uncertain investment horizons, such as stabilization SWFs, would be expected to have a larger share of their investment portfolios in cash and relatively liquid bonds to be able to meet potential and sometimes unexpected outflows without incurring large losses in the process. In that sense, the SAAs of stabilization funds should be very similar to those of central bank reserve managers. Such SWFs could potentially have some allocation to equities—allowing a part of the portfolio to be longer term—but should acknowledge the associated risk of having to divest these assets at fire sale prices when the liquidity requirement kicks in.

FUNDING SOURCE AND SAA

Whether the source of the funds should affect the SAA depends, to a certain extent, on the type of SWF. For instance, for stabilization and savings SWFs that derive their funds from a commodity this question seems self-evident. If a country's income is dependent on one (or even a few) real assets, it would be natural according to portfolio theory to diversify this dependency by investing in financial assets that have a negative or low correlation with the real asset. Thus, for instance, SWFs funded from oil resources would need to take oil price risk, cycles, and assets in the ground into consideration when determining their SAAs. However, there is little evidence of countries explicitly taking into account the assets in the ground (and uncertainty about the amount, the timing of extraction, and other factors) in their optimization models when deriving their SAAs. Alternatively, a small country could outright hedge the commodity price risk. For example, in Mexico the hedging volume corresponds to the amount of revenue that the national oil company (PEMEX) transfers to the budget, and the option premiums are paid out of the stabilization SWF. This cushions the outlays that have to be made from the SWF in downturns, and reduces the windfall revenues in upturns, thereby smoothing the profile of the revenue flows over the cycle.

In general, if a stabilization SWF is sourced from fiscal surpluses, its investment objectives are likely to be influenced by the dynamics of the government budget. SWFs sourced from international reserves may also be influenced by the dynamics of private capital flows and the composition of private external debt—just as international reserves are— depending on the institutional arrangement and the funding and withdrawal rules of the SWF. For example, the Government of Singapore Investment Corporation states that its resources may be called upon during times of crisis. Finally, the original source of pension reserve funds is unlikely to enter into the SAA process, which is more likely to be driven by the investment horizon and the nature of the liabilities.

Additionally, the vulnerability of other assets and liabilities of the wider balance sheet may also need to be taken into consideration when determining an SWF's SAA. Thus, for instance, countries with more than one SWF, or those that are considering establishing additional SWFs, may want to take the SAAs of their other funds into account when allocating their SAA.

HOW ARE SWFs DIFFERENT FROM PRIVATE EQUITY FUNDS?

Both SWFs and private equity firms have become increasingly important players in global investment activities. However, since SWFs hold more financial resources than private equity or hedge funds, they could have a significant influence on financial markets worldwide.

They have diversified the investor base and contributed to a better environment for managing risks and absorbing shocks during crises. They can play a complementary role to TNCs as important sources of much-needed investment in the developing world. Potentially, this could have a positive impact in helping to reduce disparities in the global economy. Taken as a whole, the activities of SWFs are also increasing the stake of developing countries in the global economy.

Both SWFs and private equity funds have generated significant benefits through their investments, but they have also given rise to some important concerns. Significant challenges at both the systemic and national levels relate largely to regulatory issues and the need to strengthen transparency and oversight without undermining the benefits that these institutions generate. This requires policy development at both national and multilateral levels.

There are some major differences between SWFs and private equity funds:

(i) Unlike private equity funds, SWFs are controlled directly by the home country government.
(ii) SWFs can hold stakes for a longer period than private equity funds.
(iii) Non-economic rationale sometimes combines with economic motivations in investment decisions by SWFs.

These differences manifest themselves in the investment strategies of SWFs.

TABLE 2

Comparison between SWFs and Private Equity Funds, 2007

Item	SWFs	Private equity funds
Volume	$5,000 billion	$540 billion
FDI	$10 billion	$460 billion a
Main source economies of FDI	United Arab Emirates, Norway, Saudi Arabia, Kuwait, Singapore, China, Hong Kong (China) and Russian Federation	United States, United Kingdom
Largest funds involving FDI	Istithmar PJSC (United Arab Emirates), Dubai Investment Group, Temasek Holdings(Pte) Ltd (Singapore), GIC (Singapore)	KKR, Blackstone, Permira, Fortress, Bain Capital, Carlyle (United States)
Investment strategy	Shifting from passive to active investors. Have tended to hold investment-grade, short-term, liquid sovereign assets in the major currencies, particularly United States treasury securities, but are now becoming strategic investors, with a preference for equities. Also investing in bonds, real estate, hedge funds, private equity and commodities. Still limited involvement in FDI. Concentrated in developed countries.	Shorter time frame (exit within 5-8 years) than public companies and traditional TNCs, but play a more active role in the management of invested companies than SWFs. At the same time, inclined to look for options that offer quick returns, akin to those of portfolio investors. Buy larger and also publicly listed companies, but also invest in venture capital. Undertake FDI through buyouts. FDI is expanding in developing countries.

Capital Flows by Private Equity Funds and Sovereign Wealth Funds Compared

Private equity funds and SWFs gained a significant share in cross-border FDI during the previous M&A boom in 2003–2007. Both funds drew widespread attention in international financial markets, which focused on their investment behaviour and the effects of their investments on host countries. Discussion on these issues led to some political disputes. The crisis in financial markets has seriously affected both funds, initially private equity funds, followed with some time lag by SWFs. It is useful for policymakers to have a good understanding of these funds' role in FDI transactions and the differences between them in terms of their investment patterns and performance. Private equity funds invest in venture capital, growth capital, distressed capital, and buyouts, among other forms. In recent years, crossborder M&As by private equity funds and other collective investment funds have extended across all sectors, and originated mainly in North America and Europe. While there is little doubt that venture capital financing may spur economic growth by providing capital to firms that otherwise would have only limited possibilities to raise capital or loans, the effects of private equity investments in the form of LBOs are not clear. Some contend that LBOs can improve economic welfare by increasing efficiency and productivity; but other studies have found that the performance of private equity funds, has been overstated. The collapse of cross-border LBOs by private equity funds in the second half of 2008 depressed the performance of those funds in 2009, seriously affecting their fund-raising capabilities.

This, combined with the hesitant lending policy of the financial sector, will further depress cross-border M&As by private equity funds and other collective investment funds in the near future.

SWFs have some similarities with private equity funds, but there are also large differences in their investment behaviour and the financing of FDI. There are over 50 such funds in more than 40 countries, but "there is no such thing as an average SWF". Some funds are new (e.g. China Investment Corporation, established in 2007), while others are very old (e.g. Kuwait Investment Authority, founded in 1953). Some SWFs are very big (e.g. Abu Dhabi Investment Authority, with assets of more than $500 billion), and others are very small in size (e,g, Sao Tome and Principe, with assets of $20 million). Some are passive investors, while others are active investors (e.g. Singapore's Temasek Holdings). Their growth has reflected rising oil and non-oil commodity prices and the fast growing current-account surpluses of their home countries.

Sovereign Wealth Funds on the Rise

The growth of SWFs has been impressive even during 2007-2011, a period spanning the global financial crisis. Cumulative FDI by SWFs amounts to only $125 billion, on an asset base of nearly $5 trillion at the end of 2011, suggesting significant potential for further investment in sustainable development. Despite losses on individual holdings, the total cumulative value of SWF assets rose at an annual rate of 10 per cent, compared with a 4 per cent decline in the value of international banking assets. That growth is likely to continue as the emerging-market owners of most funds keep outperforming the world economy, and as high commodity prices further inflate the revenue surpluses of countries with some of the largest SWFs.

SWFs are for the most part portfolio investors, with the bulk of their funds held in relatively liquid financial assets in mature market economies. Only a small proportion of their value (an estimated $125 billion) is in the form of FDI. FDI thus accounts for less than 5 per cent of SWF assets under management and less than 1 per cent of global FDI stock in 2011. However, evidence shows a clear growth trend since 2005 – when SWFs invested a mere $7 billion – despite a steep decline in annual flows in 2010 in response to global economic conditions.

FDI by SWFs in developed countries has grown faster than that in developing countries (table 3), also reflecting the availability of acquisition opportunities in North America and Europe during the crisis. However, SWF FDI in developing countries is rising steadily. Some countries in developing Asia that have more advanced capital markets are already significant recipients of investment by SWFs, but in forms other than FDI.

TABLE 3

FDI by SWFs by Host Region/Country, Cumulative Flows, 2005–2011

(Millions of dollars)

Target economy	2005	2006	2007	2008	2009	2010	2011
World	11186	19005	39673	63085	93476	106534	125152
Developed economies	5738	12582	26573	38354	62016	71722	84346
Europe	4394	9438	17775	23429	39078	42148	53143
European Union	4394	9438	17746	23399	39049	42118	53113
United States	125	1925	5792	10210	10335	12007	14029
Developing economies	5449	6423	12926	23544	29277	31210	35868
Africa	900	900	1304	7560	7560	8973	11418
Latin America and the Caribbean	228	228	1149	1216	1291	1696	3118
East and South-East Asia	4278	5040	5270	7366	9845	9930	10721
South Asia	43	143	1092	1209	1239	1268	1268
West Asia	-	112	4112	6193	9343	9343	9343
Transition economies	-	-	174	1187	2183	3602	3938

Source: UNCTAD, cross-border M&A database (www.unctad.org/fdistatistics) and information from the Financial Times Ltd, fDi Markets (www.fDimarkets.com).

Note: Data refer to net M&A cumulative flows since 1992 and greenfield cumulative flows since 2003. Only data on investments by SWFs that are the sole and immediate investors are included, not those made by entities established by SWFs or those made jointly with other investors.

FDI by SWFs is concentrated on specific projects in a limited number of industries, finance, real estate and construction, and natural resources (table 4). In part, this reflects the strategic aims of the relatively few SWFs active in FDI, such as Temasek (Singapore), China Investment Corporation, the Qatar Investment Authority and Mubadala (United Arab Emirates). Even these four SWFs have devoted only a fraction of their total holdings to FDI. For example, Temasek is the most active SWF investor in developing countries, where it holds roughly 71 per cent of all its assets located abroad (S$131 billion or $102 billion in 2011). Yet, only $3 billion of those assets are FDI (acquisitions of more than 10 per cent equity).

TABLE 4

FDI by SWFs by Sector/Industry, Cumulative Flows, 2005–2011

(Millions of Dollars)

Target industy	2005	2006	2007	2008	2009	2010	2011
Total industry	11186	19005	39673	63085	93476	106534	125152
Primary	1170	1512	1682	3055	9645	10945	11899
Agriculture, hunting, forestry and fisheries	-	-	170	170	170	170	170
Mining, quarrying and petroleum	1170	1512	1512	2885	9475	10775	11729
Manufacturing	3114	4369	10675	16357	30122	31470	31594
Publishing and printing	-	-	-	248	248	248	248
Coke, petroleum and nuclear fuel	-	-	5146	10253	13449	13457	13457
Chemicals and chemical products	2800	2800	2800	2800	3301	4641	4765
Rubber and plastic products	-	-	1160	1160	1160	1160	1160

Non-metallic mineral products	-	-	-	-	150	150	150
Metals and metal products	47	47	47	374	374	374	374
Machinery and equipment	15	15	15	15	15	15	15
Electrical and electronic equipment	-	15	15	15	364	364	364
Motor vehicles and other transport equipment	251	1492	1492	1492	11061	11061	11061
Services	6903	13124	27316	43673	53709	64120	81659
Electricity, gas and water	1396	1396	2317	2317	2532	4112	8789
Construction	19	19	19	2738	3994	5227	13081
Hotels and restaurants	508	2300	3132	4174	4249	4337	4997
Trade	20	320	2125	2125	3011	5309	5380
Transport, storage and communications	14	303	3197	3499	3652	4532	6280
Finance	754	1296	4171	14878	15199	18667	19596
Business services	2697	5994	9282	10385	12413	12698	14299
Real estate	2697	5994	8872	9975	12002	12287	13889
Health and social services	-	-	1578	2062	2062	2062	2062
Community, social and personal service activities	1495	1495	1495	1495	6598	7174	7174

Source: UNCTAD, cross-border M&A database (www.unctad.org/fdistatistics) and information from the Financial Times Ltd, fDi Markets (www.fDimarkets.com).

Note: Data refer to net cumulative flows through cross-border M&As since 1992 and cumulative flows through greenfield projects since 2003. Only data on investments by SWFs that are the sole and immediate investors are included, not those made by entities established by SWFs or those made jointly with other investors.

Despite SWFs' current focus on developed countries, and the concentration of their activities with their long-term and strategically oriented investment outlook, SWFs may be ideally well placed to invest in productive activities abroad, especially in developing countries, including in particular the LDCs that attract only modest FDI flows from other sources. The scale of their holdings enables SWFs to invest in large-scale projects such as infrastructure development and agricultural production – key to economic development in many LDCs – as well as industrial development, including the build-up of green growth industries.

For both developing and developed countries, investment by foreign State-owned entities in strategic assets such as agricultural land, natural resources or key infrastructure assets can lead to legitimate policy concerns. Nonetheless, given the huge gap across the developing world in development financing for the improvement of agricultural output, construction of infrastructure, provision of industry goods as well as jobs, and generation of sustainable growth, FDI by SWFs presents a significant opportunity.

As SWFs become more active in direct investments in infrastructure, agriculture or other industries vital to the strategic interests of host countries, controlling stakes in investment projects may not always be imperative. Where such stakes are needed to bring the required financial resources to an investment project, SWFs may have options to work in partnership with host-country governments, development finance institutions or other private sector investors that can bring technical and managerial competencies to the project – acting, to some extent, as management intermediaries.

SWFs may set up, alone or in cooperation with others, their own general partnerships dedicated to particular investment themes – for example, infrastructure, renewable energy or natural resources. In 2010, Qatar Holding, the investment arm of the Qatar

Investment Authority, set up a $1 billion Indonesian fund to invest in infrastructure and natural resources in Indonesia. In the same year, the International Finance Corporation (IFC) committed up to $200 million as a limited partner in the IFC African, Latin American and Caribbean Fund, in which the anchor investors, with total commitments of up to $600 million, include SWFs such as the Korea Investment Corporation and the State Oil Fund of the Republic of Azerbaijan, as well as investors from Saudi Arabia. In 2011, Morocco's Tourism Investment Authority established Wissal Capital, a fund that aims to develop tourism in the country, through a partnership with the sovereign funds of Qatar, the United Arab Emirates and Kuwait, with investment funds of $2.5–4 billion.

Where SWFs do take on the direct ownership and management of projects, investments could focus on sectors that are particularly beneficial for inclusive and sustainable development, including the sectors mentioned above – agriculture, infrastructure and the green economy – while adhering to principles of responsible investment, such as the Principles for Responsible Agricultural Investment, which protect the rights of smallholders and local stakeholders. Expanding the role of SWFs in FDI can provide significant opportunities for sustainable development, especially in less developed countries. Overcoming the challenges of unlocking more capital in the form of FDI from this investment source should be a priority for the international community.

GROWING CONCERNS ABOUT SWFs

Increasing investments of SWFs in the banking industry have been generally welcomed in view of their stabilizing effect on financial markets. Opponents of FDI by SWFs further argue that the funds might invest in companies that were privatized in recent years and that the improvements in their efficiency from such privatizations may be rolled back as a result of SWF investment. In addition, some are sceptical about investments by SWFs from countries that lack a free market or respect for human rights and sound environmental standards. However, it should be pointed out that SWFs have to conform to national and international labour and environmental standards, and that if there is a high degree of competition in the market, SWFs have no monopoly power to control or exploit that market. But they have also aroused some negative public sentiment in several developed countries, provoking new fears of protectionism and policy moves to change legislation on FDI. In particular, concerns by developed as well as developing countries that SWFs could gain control of infrastructure and other strategic industries (e.g. energy, national defence, oil, gas and electricity supply, and other sensitive activities such as sea ports and airports) have led some governments to tighten regulations (or propose such changes) relating to investments by SWFs.

It has been argued that since SWFs could pose a threat to national security, governments should erect barriers against these investors. But most countries already reserve the right to refuse M&As for national security reasons, even if, overall, they are very open to foreign investors. National security exceptions mainly relate to economic activities in the military and other strategic sectors. A prominent example is the United States Exon-Florio provision which allows the blocking of an acquisition by a foreign entity if national security is endangered. In Japan, Germany, France, the United Kingdom and many other countries, the legal framework similarly allows the restriction or withdrawal of a foreign investment for national safety and security reasons.

The cross-border asset holdings of SWFs raise issues similar to those faced by other international market participants, including their role in global financial markets. One view is that SWFs enhance market liquidity and financial resource allocation. This view recognizes that SWFs, especially the larger ones, typically use a mix of well-trained in-house expertise and well-regarded international external fund managers, and have longer investment horizons that can accommodate short-term volatility. Consequently, their investment operations may dampen asset price volatility and lower liquidity risk premia, compared with a situation in which these assets were to be managed with shorter duration. Another view holds, however, that the limited publicly available information on some SWFs, their multiplicity of objectives, and a lack of clarity on their institutional structure and investment management, make it diffi cult to assess the SWFs' asset management activities and their impact on the capital markets. Without more public accountability, funds may alter their governance structures, perhaps as a result of losses, which, in turn, could lead to sharp changes in investment policies, possibly exacerbating market volatility in some asset classes. The public ownership of SWFs (and other state-owned entities) also raises questions about possible capital account restrictions initiated in recipient countries, especially to avoid certain types of foreign direct investment

As their size, number, and use grows, and as domestic and international public attention directed toward them increases, SWFs may be faced with several institutional and operational challenges, including:

(i) *Defining objectives and setting and implementing sovereign asset allocation.* A well-defined SAA within a clearly articulated investment policy is a critical operational component for public investment funds, and as new developments arise, a reassessment of existing objectives and constraints might be needed and reflected in the overall risk tolerance.

(ii) *Institutional arrangements*, including withdrawal and accumulation rules that reflect risksharing arrangements between the government and the SWF, or the central bank, and establishing responsibility for investment decisions and their outcomes. For instance, in the case of some oil-related SWFs, it is often diffi cult to determine on which institutions' balance sheet the assets appear.

(iii) *Accountability arrangements,* including fiduciary duty to citizens, the legal foundation, and the internal governance structure. In practice, the public disclosure of SWFs varies significantly in terms of the nature of information and its timeliness, providing for more or less public scrutiny of the sovereign assets.

The real danger is that sovereign wealth funds (and other forms of government-backed investment vehicles) may encourage capital account protectionism, through which countries pick and choose who can invest in what. Of course, there are always some national security limitations on what foreigners can own. But recent developments in the world suggest there may be a perception that certain foreign governments shouldn't be allowed to own what are regarded as an economy's "commanding heights." This is a slippery slope, which leads quickly and painfully to other forms of protectionism. It's important to preempt such pressures.

Sovereign funds are not likely to go away. They're based on current account surpluses and will become less important only if the countries with large surpluses begin to run prolonged current account deficits. Major countries have committed to reducing their current account imbalances, and this would limit the growth of sovereign funds. But the world economy evolves continuously in ways that make it hard to be sure current account imbalances will shrink. For example, global growth may accelerate or decelerate, and this is likely to affect commodity prices. But if commodity prices remain high, commodity exporters will have large surpluses for the foreseeable future. If commodity prices fall, the surpluses of Asian countries that export manufactures may increase.

What should the IMF do about this situation? There's no apparent reason to see the continued existence of these funds as destablizing or worrying. In fact, the IMF has strongly encouraged exporters of nonrenewable resources to build up exactly such funds in prepertion for a rainy day. Infact there's certainly no need for dramatic action. For one thing, the situation involves sensitive issues of national sovereignty. For another, at their current level of $3 trillion, sovereign funds aren't a pressing issue. But as the level creeps closer to $10 trillion—although even $10 trillion isn't a huge amount of money—the phenomenon will likely attract greater attention

On the other hand, the changing investment strategy of SWFs may imply considerable opportunities as well. For example, they recycle the huge dollar inflows of the countries concerned, thereby contributing to the financing needs of the deficit countries, and therefore to stabilization of the global financial system, by injecting more capital. The passive investments of SWFs in dollar-denominated fixed assets in the past were connected with low returns; today their governments are seeking higher returns on their investments. Enhancing transparency and accountability of SWFs is important. If such conditions were to be met, there would be little reason to treat SWFs less favourably than other fund management companies, private equity groups or hedge funds.

Several initiatives are already under way to establish principles and guidelines relating to FDI by SWFs. At the multilateral level, the IMF has been called upon to develop guidelines for SWFs and has created, with some member States, the International Working Group of Sovereign Wealth Funds to agree on a common set of voluntary principles and practices for SWFs; the European Commission (EC) is exploring plans for an EU-wide law to monitor SWFs; and the OECD is developing guidelines for recipient countries. Ministers of OECD countries, at the Council at Ministerial Level on 5 June 2008, endorsed the following policy principles for countries receiving SWF investments:

> *"Recipient countries should not erect protectionist barriers to foreign investment. Recipient countries should not discriminate among investors in like circumstances. Any additional investment restrictions in recipient countries should only be considered when policies of general application to both foreign and domestic investors are inadequate to address legitimate national security concerns.*

Where such national security concerns do arise, investment safeguards by recipient countries should be: transparent and predictable, proportional to clearly-identified national security risks, and subject to accountability in their application"

At the SWF level, the Abu Dhabi Investment Authority (ADIA), GIC and Norges Bank Investment Management (NBIM) are working with the IMF to develop a code of conduct for their activities. Singapore's Temasek Holdings has stated that it will avoid investing in "iconic" companies in developed markets. Clear procedures and guidelines by governments, identifying which industries are regarded as strategically important, should be established to make the investment environment more predictable. Such guidelines will have important implications for the regulatory and legal frameworks of host countries.

SOVERIEGN WEALTH FUNDS AND FINANCIAL CRISIS

The size and rapid growth of Sovereign Wealth Funds is placing them front and center with regard to public attention, as well as for international financial and economic policy deliberations. Thus far, the role of SWFs in the context of the past year's turmoil in advanced economy financial markets has been notably positive. If anything, the Funds' actions have shown that they can play a shock-absorbing role in global financial markets, at least in terms of dampening short-term market volatility. This is a reflection of their typically long-term investment horizons, limited immediate redemption needs, and mainly unleveraged positions. In addition, many of these Funds' managers are highly skilled and experienced investors. As such, they understand clearly their long-term interest in preserving well-functioning, open, liquid global markets.

Nevertheless, some concerns about SWF investments have been raised in recipient countries. Worries have been expressed that SWF investments could affect national security, or that SWF investments could be based on noncommercial motives. Although it is clear that these concerns have little or no basis in the way SWFs have operated up to now, it is important to avoid negative perceptions or run the risk of a protectionist backlash. Such outcomes would be damaging for all parties concerned. It could curtail the scope for SWF investment, increase the investment risk SWFs face, and lead to retaliatory measures: Also, such negative dynamics could undermine the efficient flow of global capital and even diminish the stability of the international financial and monetary system.

The global financial crisis affected SWFs worldwide. The sharp downturn in asset prices, particularly prices for equity and alternative investments, resulted in large losses for many SWFs especially those with longer investment horizons. In some cases, the losses reached 30 percent of the portfolio values for 2008, thereby impairing SWFs' long-term returns as well.

These losses have sparked domestic debates on SWFs' investment strategies. Some have been criticised for entering the equity market at the wrong time, some blamed for a lack of insight for investing in financial institutions at the early stage of the crisis and suffering heavy losses, and others reproached for investing abroad when their support for domestic markets was highly needed. These criticisms have put SWFs' investment outlooks and strategies under increased scrutiny and their managers under pressure to avoid further losses.

Moreover, the crisis has led some SWFs to take prominent roles in financing government operations, as per their mandate. For instance, stabilization funds have been drawn upon to finance rising fiscal deficits, as per their mandate, and some of them have also supported stimulus packages to prop up economic activity. Rising sovereign or quasi-sovereign liabilities can be expected to weigh on demand for SWF resources for some time to come.

Some SWFs have also taken on new roles, beyond their original mandates. For example, several countries have used SWF resources to support domestic banks or corporations through the banking system. Some SWFs have provided liquidity to the banking system by depositing their assets in domestic banks, and others have helped with bank recapitalisation. SWF assets have also been earmarked in some countries to support deposit insurance schemes and some SWFs have purchased domestic stocks to boost markets and investor confidence.

The heavy demands on SWF resources and the uncertainty in the economic environment have led many SWFs to take a more cautious approach toward investing. SWFs are wary about supporting further bail-outs of distressed companies, as a result of the heavy unrealized or realized losses some experienced after investing in financial institutions in developed countries. Nonetheless, as financial market conditions started to improve in early 2009, some SWFs achieved record profits.

These developments are reflected also in the dynamics of SWFs' assets under management during the crisis. The value of stabilization fund assets remained on a steady growth path until the end of 2008, when it became evident that the implications of the crisis for domestic liquidity and fiscal conditions would be greater than originally anticipated. These funds declined by about 50 percent between the end-2008 and end-2009 after withdrawals. Pension reserve funds and savings funds suffered equity valuation losses during the period September 2008 through March 2009, but have since recovered. Finally, SWFs with both stabilization and savings objectives—which are mostly invested in fixed-income assets— have weathered the crisis relatively unscathed.

CRISIS IMPLICATION FOR STRATEGIC ASSET ALLOCATION

The implications of the crisis for asset allocations going forward will be fundspecific, and some of the driving factors are discussed below.

i) The crisis has affected SWFs' asset allocations in different ways

Several SWFs with stabilization objectives have reduced their shares of cash holdings either because of the use of cash resources (Chile-ESSF), or because of moving to fixed income (Trinidad and Tobago). Alaska Permanent Fund and Ireland National Pension Reserve Fund have increased the share of their cash holdings. SWFs with previous investment in alternative assets have increased their investments in such assets, presumably with a view to further diversifying their portfolios. The KIC has introduced alternative assets investment and increased their equity shares. Notwithstanding the impact of the crisis, some SWFs have also continued with the implementation of previously approved SAAs—for example, Norway has increased equity shares, and the Australian Future Fund has introduced fixed-income and increased equity and alternative assets investments in its portfolio. In the case of Norway, the continuous implementation of the SAA helped it to benefit greatly from the rebound of risk assets since early 2009.

ii) Geographic reallocation also seems to be occurring

Confidence in emerging markets' recovery prospects, along with concerns about advanced economies, has prompted some SWFs to tilt their investments toward these markets. For example, Singapore's Temasek reportedly plans to focus on emerging markets in Asia, Brazil, and the Russian Federation and reduce emphasis on OECD countries (from one-third to one-fifth of assets). Norway's SWF has also increased its operations in Asia and plans to open an office in Singapore after opening one in Shanghai.

iii) Shifts are fund-specific and reflect individual circumstances

In some cases, SWFs with longer-term mandates have encountered unexpected liquidity needs, thereby effectively shortening their investment horizons. In some cases, increased scrutiny and pressure to minimize future losses may have contributed to shifts to relatively more conservative investment positions whereas some SWFs may have concluded that the market provided them with opportunities for upside value, even over the medium-term.

iv) Changes in their domestic economic and financial environments may have caused some SWFs to temporarily deviate from their original mandates

To address such concerns, some SWFs are thoroughly reviewing their investment strategies and risk management frameworks. These reviews involve clarifying SWF objectives, potential liquidity needs, and related investment horizons and risks.

v) Some SWFs are re-examining the traditional asset class-based approach to SAA and have started to use, or are considering using, a risk factor-based approach

The Board of the Alaska Permanent Fund, for example, decided to choose an approach to asset allocation "that is a good fit for the goal of building an all-weather portfolio" and decided to group investments by their risk and return profiles, and by the market condition or liability that each group is intended to address.

vi) Still, in many cases a profound change in an SWF's SAA may not be justified

Instead, SWFs may need to improve their communication strategies and put more effort into educating stakeholders about their operations and risks. In the case of savings-type SWFs, this direction requires that owners and other stakeholders understand the likelihood of encountering short-term losses and have the ability to tolerate them. This may be easier to achieve in an environment of overall political and economic stability, with well-engrained frameworks for medium- and long-term planning, and good crisis management planning and coordination.

It is not surprising, therefore, that public and private leader in both SWF sponsor countries and recipient countries recognized that the international system would benefit from enhanced clarity regarding the principles and practices followed by both side convened the International Working Group (IWG) of SWFs to collaborate with General Accepted Principles and Practices (GAPP) International Monetary Fund, the World Bank, and the OECD in drafting the GAPP framework. The GAPP recommends 24 voluntary principles that, if adopted, will enable countries to better manage their SWFs while promoting investor confidence. Although the current financial crisis has given SWFs a boost in popularity—these days nations are happy to get capital from any source—the implementation of GAPP practices should help prevent a return to the hostile investment environment of the recent past.

During development of the GAPP, IWG nations collaborated with policymakers from recipient countries. Consequently, these nations were afforded a greater understanding of the real issues surrounding sovereign wealth funds, which, in turn, allowed participating countries to balance their open markets with national security concerns. The GAPP should not only result in greater transparency and sounder investment decisions in SWFs but also mitigate the biggest threat to the world's economic and national security—protectionist investment policies.

Although these funds represent only a relatively small share of the total global financial market, the rise of sovereign wealth funds carries implications for worldwide market stability, corporate governance, and national interests. The GAPP helps to address these concerns by establishing the following objectives for SWFs :

   (i) To invest in assets that deliver a rate of return on the basis of sound economic and financial variables that appropriately accounts for risk. Additionally, SWFs should implement transparent governance structures that clearly establish the roles and responsibilities—while enhancing the accountability—of management. These objectives establish the importance of using economic rather than political criteria as the foundation of an effective SWF investment strategy.
   (ii) To comply with laws, regulations, and disclosure requirements of the countries receiving SWF investment. This critical objective identifies the important role that disclosure of a fund's investment policy, asset allocation, approach to risk management, and other financial data play in mitigating governments' and markets' uncertainty about the purpose of that fund.

(iii) To help maintain a stable global financial system and the free flow of capital. By clearly stating the need and criteria for SWFs to act as responsible players in the world's asset markets and to promote sound macroeconomic and investment policies, the GAPP addresses larger concerns regarding the distorting effect SWFs can have on markets.

While market pressures are already working to prompt improved transparency from some sovereign investors, GAPP guidance that clearly describes methods of implementing good governance practices, greater measures of accountability, and sound financial investment strategies will help countries to structure and operate their funds more effectively and responsibly. Equally as important, these principles delineate a path for SWFs to ensure that their investments do not distort or destabilize markets in a way that reduces their return on investment or harms the economies in which they invest.

Moreover, the IWG/IMF process promoted meaningful debate and research about sovereign wealth funds. As a result, participating nations gained an increased understanding of SWFs' impact on U.S. and world markets in addition to sovereign investors themselves. This forum should remain active, providing a means to discuss the effectiveness and impact of the GAPP on SWF management and to address new concerns that may arise from global debate on international financial regulation or from countries receiving new sovereign wealth investment. Keeping channels open for cooperation will make it easier for nations to stand firm against implementing protectionist barriers against foreign investment.

The rise of sovereign wealth funds carries implications for global financial market stability and the national interests of countries receiving these funds.

The "shock-absorbing role" that the SWFs had played by providing capital during the year's financial turmoil in advanced-economy markets, has reflected the funds' typically long-term investment horizons, limited liquidity needs, and mainly unleveraged positions, Also, the funds clearly understand their long-term interest in preserving well-functioning, open, liquid markets. However, recipient countries have raised concerns about the potential noncommercial motives of SWF investments. Such negative perceptions could be damaging to all parties as well as diminish the stability of the global financial and monetary system by undermining the efficient flow of global capital. In this context, both SWF sponsor and recipient countries would benefit from the enhanced clarity provided by the voluntary principles and practices. The GAPP would improve the understanding of SWFs and allow the newly established funds to benefit from the experience of others. Newly released principles should help to ensure that SWFs are managed effectively, make sound investment decisions, and are more transparent. As the collaborative process to establish the GAPP indicates, the growing trade and investment ties that bind the economies of the world together are more likely to promote responsible economic behavior than to entice mayhem. Investment is about creating wealth, not destroying it. Erecting barriers to foreign investment would stifle that creative process, leaving all countries poorer.

Sovereign funds are not likely to go away. They're based on current account surpluses and will become less important only if the countries with large surpluses begin to run prolonged current account deficits. Major countries have committed to reducing their current account imbalances, and this would limit the growth of sovereign funds. But the world economy evolves continuously in ways that make it hard to be sure current account imbalances will shrink. For example, global growth may accelerate or decelerate, and this is likely to affect commodity prices. But if commodity prices remain high, commodity exporters will have large surpluses for the foreseeable future. If commodity prices fall, the surpluses of Asian countries that export manufactures may increase.

The crisis demonstrates the importance of conducting regular macro-level risk assessments and weighing carefully the sovereign's financing options, both in normal times and during financial stress. First, having thorough reserve adequacy assessments and stress testing the foreign exchange liquidity needs when setting SWF objectives can prevent having to suffer losses in crisis situations. This is particularly relevant for countries establishing SWFs with long investment horizons, because having to sell assets under stress could be extremely costly, especially when the assets have been allocated to cover specific liabilities. For example, pension reserve SWFs that have been drawn down or reallocated to finance public interventions during the crisis may have to be recapitalized eventually, or the government may need to avail itself of other resources to meet the associated liabilities as they fall due. Second, automatically using SWF assets to cover liquidity needs may not be the best strategy; issuing debt may be a cheaper option. In some cases, an assessment can be made beforehand whether borrowing is feasible and would be cost-effective in times of stress. This needs to consider that in times of stress, the cost of issuing debt may be higher or debt issuance may not be feasible. Going a step further, if a country has excellent debt management capacity, a commensurate credit rating, and deep and liquid local markets, establishing a largescale stabilization fund may not be necessary in the first place; though for some countries, if the SWF can effectively sterilize large receipts that are cyclical, it may still be a good macro management tool.

By the same token, the government can lower the cost of macro stabilization by issuing more debt even without having a financing need when times are good and investor risk appetite is strong, to either finance an existing stabilization fund or establish a new one. When financing is needed during downturns, the government would not have to issue at high cost, but would draw down the stabilization fund. Such an approach can also have positive externalities, and if the SWF is properly set up, can help with developing local debt markets.

Hence, the international financial markets are likely to face increased regulation and demands for greater transparency and accountability, which may affect SWFs' cross-border operations. Increased regulation in the financial sector, for example, may alter the relative attractiveness of some asset classes or industries in which SWFs invest. More directly, new transparency and disclosure requirements for financial institutions and investment vehicles or regulations could generate similar demands on SWFs.

At the same time, SWFs have actively participated in the discussion on the evolving global regulatory environment. Since the regulatory environment could potentially affect their operations and the value of their investments, SWFs are eager to see well-targeted and good quality financial regulation that is unlikely to inflict unintended consequences. SWFs have also shown considerable interest in interested in promoting good corporate governance principles. Some SWFs have chosen to do this through active shareholder involvement, while some have chosen to take a less active approach to exercising their ownership rights and therefore are more reliant on recipient country governments promoting good corporate governance principles and monitoring their effective implementation.

The SAAs of SWFs reflect their inherent characteristics, notably including the type of SWF and its funding source. At the same time, differences among similar-type SWFs are evident, resulting from differences in views about the investment horizon and asset class performance, the size of the SWF, the ability to tolerate losses, the amount of untapped funding sources, and the maturity and sophistication of the SWF. The crisis has affected SWFs' SAAs in different ways, with some SWFs increasing liquidity, and others opting for more conservative or less conservative portfolios depending on individual country circumstances. Still others have taken on new roles beyond their original mandates. The shift, however, may not be ideal or justified in all cases, and some SWFs are thoroughly reviewing their investment strategies and risk management frameworks. SWFs may also need to enhance their communication strategies to ensure consistency of their SAAs with their fundamental investment objectives.

More generally, the crisis demonstrates the importance of macro-stability risk assessment and careful consideration of the financing options of the sovereign both in normal times and during financial stress. Thorough reserve adequacy and liquidity assessments are needed, as are cost-risk assessments of funding sovereign asset and liability operations.

Looking ahead, the scope for SWFs' stabilizing role in international capital markets will remain substantial. Despite their losses during the crisis and greater domestic focus, SWFs' relative size and influence in the global market will remain large. Furthermore, SWFs' longer-term investment strategies relative to most other investors will continue to play an important stabilizing role in the global economy.

Regulatory considerations also will become increasingly important to SWFs, as changes to the international regulatory environment are developed in response to the crisis. In this regard, active involvement by SWFs in the period ahead will be required. There's no apparent reason to see the continued existence of these funds as destabilizing or worrying. In fact, the IMF has strongly encouraged exporters of nonrenewable resources to build up exactly such funds in preparation for a "rainy day." In fact, sovereign wealth funds are major state-owned players of the 21st century. Hedge funds, while becoming more prominent in this century, are in some sense a throw back to the end of the 19th century, when large pools of private capital moved around the world with unregulated ease— and generally contributed to a long global boom, rapid productivity growth around the world, and a fair number of crises. What happens when the 21st-century state meets the 19th-century private sector? The outcome remains to be seen.

SWFs: INDIAN PERSPECTIVE

India as a Host Country

In India, the regulatory regime governing capital inflows does not recognise SWFs as a distinct category. Hence, their investments are subject to normal regulations governing capital flows under the category of Foreign Direct Investment (FDI) and Foreign Institutional Investments (FII). In regard to some sectors, such as banking and financial market infrastructure companies, there are limits on individual holdings and the investment proposals are subject to an element of due diligence processing with regard to fit and proper requirements. For this purpose, no discrimination is made between a domestic investor and a foreign investor, or between SWFs and others, as long as the policy criteria are met.

The existing FDI policy permits investments under the 'automatic route' and the 'approval route' in most, though not all, of the activities. Under the automatic route, the investors are allowed to invest in the identified sectors up to the threshold specified for those sectors, without the need for a prior approval from regulators or the Foreign Investment Promotion Board (FIPB). In respect of the other sectors, the investors will need a prior approval of the FIPB, before undertaking any investment. The FIPB is functioning under the aegis of the Ministry of Finance and comprises representatives of various government departments, who are expected to ensure that the proposed investment addresses the administrative and other concerns before allowing investments in the concerned activity. Similarly, under the FII route, the FIIs registered with the securities market regulator (the Securities and Exchange Board of India - SEBI) can invest in the secondary market, without prior approval, subject to certain limits on individual FIIs and an overall aggregate limit for all FIIs, as a category, as well as the sectoral thresholds and other conditions applicable to FDI. SWFs can also invest directly as an FII or indirectly as a 'sub- account' of a registered FII, which include hedge funds and investment funds. Accordingly, any SWF can invest under the FDI route (automatic or approval routes, as the case may be) or under FII route either directly or indirectly. Thus, on the inflows, there is generally no discrimination on the basis of the country of origin of the foreign investor or on the basis of category of foreign investors.

The policy, however, does provide for a framework in regard to ownership and management of the entity investing in some sectors, particularly the financial sector, which is applicable equally to resident as well as non-resident investors. In respect of banks, acknowledgement from the Reserve Bank for acquisition/ transfer of shares is required for all cases of acquisition of shares which will take the aggregate holding (direct and indirect, beneficial or otherwise) of an individual or group to equivalent of 5 per cent or more of the paid-up capital of the bank. The relevant factors for 'fit and proper' assessment of the investor include the source of funds for the acquisition and, where the investor is a body corporate, its track record of reputation for operating in a manner that is consistent with the standards of good corporate governance, financial strength and integrity. The process also envisages a higher level of due diligence when the share holding of the investor exceeds 10 per cent in the investee bank's paid up capital, which includes fit and proper status of the investor entity.

An amendment to the Banking Regulation Act has been proposed which envisages prior approval of the Reserve Bank for acquisition of more than five per cent of the paid up share capital of a bank by any investor 'directly or indirectly, by himself or acting in concert with any person'. The approval will be accorded after ensuring that the investor would be 'fit and proper' from the perspective of public interest, interest of banking policy, emerging trends in banking and international best practices, and the interest of banking and financial system in India.

In the case of investments in financial market infrastructure companies, such as stock exchanges, the guidelines stipulate a desirable dispersal of ownership. Investment by individual entities, including investments by persons acting in concert, is subject to a threshold of five per cent of the equity in these companies.

In regard to Securitisation and Reconstruction Companies (SRC), the Reserve Bank conducts due diligence on the sponsors / investors before giving a certificate of registration to the SRC. Any subsequent investment by any individual entity in excess of 10 per cent of the paid up equity capital of the SRC also acquires the status of a 'sponsor' and requires prior permission of the Reserve Bank which, as the regulator, is required to satisfy itself, among other things, of the 'fit and proper' credentials of the investor.

Foreign investment in an Indian company in the financial services sector, through acquisitions, requires prior permission of the Reserve Bank which allows such investments only after ensuring that the regulatory concerns, if any, are appropriately addressed and that the bonafides of the overseas investor are satisfactory. Wherever necessary, the clearance or comments of the home country regulators of the investing entity are also sought while examining the requests.

In case of investments by foreign investors in activities other than the financial services sector, where there are security or other administrative concerns, for instance, in defence and strategic industries, and print media and broadcasting sectors, investments are allowed only under the "approval route".

In order to assess the eligibility of an entity to be registered as FII or as Foreign Venture Capital Investor, SEBI takes into account all factors relevant to the grant of a certificate and in particular the applicant's track record, professional competence, financial soundness, experience, general reputation of fairness and integrity as well as the fact whether the applicant is regulated by an appropriate foreign regulatory authority.

In brief, India is yet to consider a policy addressing investments by SWFs, except as a part of due diligence in regard to all investors.

India as a Home Country

In India, the foreign exchange reserves are on the balance sheet of the Reserve Bank of India (RBI) and are managed as per the provisions of the RBI Act, consistent with the global best practices. The Reserve Bank adheres to appropriate prudential norms and the transparency and data dissemination standards in regard to reserves management.

Given the significant increase in the level of foreign exchange reserves, there is an increasing expectation in regard to returns. The returns on the foreign exchange reserves, under the present framework, are constrained by the mandate to the Reserve Bank of India, which understandably lays a greater emphasis on safety and liquidity.

It may, however, be possible to argue that a part of the reserves, which may be considered to be in excess of the usual requirements, be managed with the primary objective of earning higher returns. Given the limitations placed on the central bank by its mandate, it can be held that it will be appropriate to bestow this responsibility on a different sovereign entity. If and when the country considers setting up of a SWF for the purpose, one of the methodologies could be to fund SWF by purchasing the foreign exchange from the central bank, to the extent required. These foreign currency funds could then be used by the sovereign entity for seeking higher returns by investing in assets, which a central bank's mandate may not permit. As the SWF will be a public enterprise, it will be required to conform to the applicable governance, transparency and disclosure standards.

While it is possible to make a case for an Indian SWF, there are also weighty arguments for caution in this regard. First, it would be very difficult to reckon in the Indian context - as is the case with many other countries, the 'reserve adequacy' in a dynamic setting and on that basis divert a part of 'excess' reserves for a higher return from riskier assets. The current reserves management policy recognises this, based on experience during periods of both net inflows and outflows and, therefore, the overall approach to the management of India's foreign exchange reserves takes into account the changing composition of the balance of payments and endeavours to reflect the 'liquidity risks' associated with different types of flows and other requirements.

Second, while most other countries that have set up SWFs have amassed large reserves either on account of persistent current account surpluses or due to revenue gains from commodity exports, in particular of oil and gas, the Indian economy has twin deficits-a current account deficit as also a fiscal deficit. India's export basket is diversified and does not have any dominant "exportable" natural resource output, which might promise significant revenue gains at the current juncture.

Third, India has experienced consistent but manageable current account deficits barring very few years of a modest surplus. India is also having a negative international investment position (IIP) with liabilities far exceeding the assets. The large reserves have been built, over time, mostly on account of capital flows like foreign direct investments (FDI), portfolio flows through foreign institutional investors (FII), external commercial borrowing (ECB) and short-term credit. Further, the increasing reserves also reflect, in part, the lower absorption capacity of the economy, which may pick up with the economy moving on to a higher growth trajectory.

In brief, the public policy is yet to take a conscious view on the desirability of establishing a SWF.

SPV for Use of Reserves

In the context of growing developmental needs, particularly of the infrastructure sector, a step in the direction of using a small part of reserves for development has recently been taken after considerable deliberations. An announcement was made by the Finance Minister in the budget Speech 2007-2008 on February 28, 2007 to "use a small part of the foreign exchange reserves without the risk of monetary expansion" for the purpose of financing infrastructure development projects. Accordingly a scheme has been finalised which envisages the Reserve Bank investing, in tranches, up to an aggregate amount of USD 5 billion in fully Government guaranteed foreign currency denominated bonds issued by an overseas SPV of the India Infrastructure Finance Corporation Ltd. (IIFCL), a wholly owned company of Government of India. The funds, thus raised, are to be utilised by the company for onlending to the Indian companies implementing infrastructure projects in India and/or to co-finance the ECBs of such projects for capital expenditure outside India without creating any monetary impact. The lending by the SPV under the arrangement would be treated as external commercial borrowings (ECB) and would be subject to the prescribed reporting and disclosure requirements. The bonds will carry a floating rate of interest. The investment by the Reserve Bank in the foreign currency denominated bonds issued by the SPV will not be reckoned as a part of the foreign exchange reserves, but will be a foreign currency asset on the Reserve Bank balance sheet.

It is noteworthy that this arrangement is distinct in the sense that India is both a home and a host for the IIFCL's subsidiary, as it is basically a SPV for channelising foreign exchange funds for meeting the requirements of the Indian private sector for infrastructure projects in India by drawing upon the foreign exchange reserves of the country available with the central bank.

To sum up, India has not yet considered regulatory initiatives specifically addressing SWFs. Existing provisions in regard to fit-and-proper or take-over code are, however, applicable to all investors, including SWFs. Currently, the pros and cons for the establishment of an Indian SWF, as generally understood now, are still under debate. India is monitoring recent developments in regard to enhancing transparency and disclosure in respect of hedge funds, private equity and SWFs. In particular, India is watching with great interest the development of global codes, standards and practices in regard to SWFs, both in view of the presence of SWFs in the Indian financial markets and the ongoing debate on establishing an Indian SWF. The hope is that both host countries and SWFs see that their interest lies in building confidence. The hosts stand to benefit from the funds' capital. Meanshile the fund are ruled by the politics of the places where they invest. One is sovereign only at home; abroad, someone else worlds the power.

QUESTIONS

1. Define Sovereign Wealth Fund (SWFs). Critically examine the criteria to classify these funds.
2. Discuss the impact of Sovereign Wealth Funds on global financial market.
3. Critically examine the major consideration which usually guide the allocation and distribution of SWF assets.
4. Discuss the SWFs from Indian perspective.
5. Critically examine the growing concerns about Soveriegn Wealth Fund (SWFs) which need urgent consideration.
6. How are SWFs different from private equity funds? Discuss the size and structure of major SWFs.

REFERENCES

1. Beck, Roland, and Michael Fidora, 2008, *"The Impact of Sovereign Wealth Funds on Global Financial Markets,"* ECB Occasional Paper Series No. 91 (Frankfurt: European Central Bank).
2. Chhaochharia, Vidhi, and Luc Laeven, 2008, *"Sovereign Wealth Funds: Their Investment Strategies and Performance,"* CEPR Discussion Paper No. 6959 (London: Center for Economic Policy Research).
3. Fotak, Veljko, Bernardo Bortolotti, and William Megginson, 2008, *"The Financial Impact of Sovereign Wealth Fund Investments in Listed Companies"* (unpublished; University of Oklahoma).
4. George R. Hoguet, 2008, "The Potential Impact of Sovereign Wealth Funds on Global Asset Prices," *Vision*, Vol. 3, Issue 2, pp. 23–30.
5. Hammer, Cornelia, Peter Kunzel, and Iva Petrova, 2008, *"Sovereign Wealth Funds: Current Institutional and Operational Practices,"* IMF Working Paper 08/254.
6. Jen. Stephen and David K. Miles, 2007, "Sovereign Wealth Funds and Bond and Equity Prices," Morgan Stanley Research (31 May, 2007).
7. Alaska Permanent Fund Corporation, 2009, *"Asset Allocation."* Available via the Internet: http://www.apfc.org/home/Content/investments/assetAllocation2009.cfm.
8. Bernstein, Peter L., 1996, "Are Stocks the Best Place to Be in the Long Run? A Contrary Opinion," *The Journal of Investing*, Vol. 5, No. 4, pp. 9–12.
9. Bodie, Zvi, 1995, "On the Risks of Stocks in the Long Run," *Financial Analysts Journal*, Vol. 51, No. 3, pp. 18–22.
10. Brown, Aaron, Michael Papaioannou, and Iva Petrova, 2010, *"Macrofinancial Linkages of the Strategic Asset Allocation of Commodity-Based Sovereign Wealth Funds"*, IMF Working Paper WP/10/9 (Washington: International Monetary Fund).
11. Das, Udaibir S., Yinqiu Lu, Christian Mulder, and Amadou Sy, 2009, *"Setting up a Sovereign Wealth Fund: Some Policy and Operational Considerations,"* IMF Working Paper WP/09/179 (Washington: International Monetary Fund).
12. Dimson, Elroy, Paul Marsh, and Mike Staunton, 2003, "Irrational Optimism," LBS Institute of Finance and Accounting Working Paper No. IFA 397 (London Business School).
13. Financial Dynamics, 2009, "Sovereign Wealth Fund Survey" (London and New York: Financial Dynamics). Available via the Internet: http://www.fd.com/admin/upload/uploaded_files/Survey_of_leading_SWFs.pdf.
14. Hammer, C., P. Kunzel, and I. Petrova, 2008, *"Sovereign Wealth Funds: Current Institutional and Operational Practices,"* IMF Working Paper WP/08/254 (Washington: International Monetary Fund).
15. International Forum of Sovereign Wealth Funds, 2009, "Baku Statement." Available via the Internet: http://www.ifswf.org/pr/pr2.htm.

16. International Forum of Sovereign Wealth Funds, 2010, "Sydney Statement." Available via the Internet: http://www.ifswf.org/pr/pr4.htm.

17. IMF (International Monetary Fund), 2007, Global Financial Stability Report, October 2007 (Washington). Available via the Internet: http://www.imf.org/external/pubs/ft/gfsr/2007/02/pdf/annex12.pdf.

18. ——, 2008, "Sovereign Wealth Funds—A Work Program" (Washington). Available via the Internet: http://www.imf.org/external/np/pp/eng/2008/022908.pdf

19. ——, 2009, "Crisis-Related Measures in the Financial System and Sovereign Balance Sheet Risks" (Washington). Available via the Internet: http://www.imf.org/external/np/pp/eng/2009/073109.pdf.

20. Scherer, B., and A. Gintschel, 2008, "Optimal Asset Allocation for Sovereign Wealth Funds," Journal of Asset Management, Vol. 9, No. 3, pp. 215–238.

17

Non-Security Forms of Investment

INTRODUCTION

The financial system intermediates part of a country's total investment through financial institutions, while firms, households and the government finance a part of the investment directly through their own savings. Financial intermediaries perform the important task of moving financial resources from the units in surpluses to those which are in deficit and need finance from other units for their investments. Financial development is, therefore, to some extent reflected in the inter-sectoral movements of funds.

FLOW OF FUNDS

The extent and process of evolution of financial development can be gauged from the flow of funds account of the Indian economy, which provides information on instrument-wise and sector-wise financial flows. The flow of funds accounts for the Indian economy provide information on the following six sectors of the economy: households, corporates, government, banks, other financial institutions (OFIs) and the rest of the world (ROW). Of the six sectors of the economy, household is the only sector which is in consistent surplus, while government and corporates are the deficit sectors. The deficit sectors meet their requirements mainly from the households and occasionally, and to a *smaller extent* from the ROW.

RECENT INVESTMENT AND SAVING TRENDS

In India, the household sector's investment in non-security forms constitutes a major proportion of its total investment in financial assets. One of the basic channels of influence of financial development on growth is the saving rate. An investor is the backbone of the capital markets of any economy as he is the one lending his surplus resources for funding the setting up of or expansion of companies, in return for financial gain. The rate of Gross Domestic Saving (GDS) had steadily risen since 2002-03 to a peak of 37.7 per cent of GDP in 2007-08, mainly due to improved performance of the private corporate sector, enhanced contribution of public sector and the progress made in fiscal consolidation. Gross domestic saving as per cent of GDP at current market prices increased from 35.7 per cent in 2006-07 to 37.7 per cent in 2007-08. The private corporate saving rate improved for the sixth consecutive year, reflecting better corporate performance and higher retained earnings. Saving of the household sector also increased, *albeit*, marginally. Public sector saving—which had witnessed a turnaround from dis-saving prior to 2003-04 to positive saving, was largely the result of higher savings of non-departmental as well as departmental enterprises, which recorded gradual but significant improvement in 2007-08.

There has been a decline in the average saving rate since 2008-09, led by a sharp decline in public sector saving rate that has not been offset by private savings (Table-1). The reduction in the average public sector savings rate in the post-global crisis period largely reflects the impact of fiscal stimulus measures as well as the decline in the contribution of non-departmental enterprises. Average investment rate has also declined in the post-crisis period.

TABLE-1

Gross Domestic Saving nd Investment

Item	Per cent of GDP at current market prices				Amount in ? billion		
	Average 2003-04 to 2007-08	2008-09	2009-10 P	2010-11*	2008-09	2009-10 P	2010-11*
1	2	3	4	5	6	7	8.
1. Household Saving (Net) (a+b)	23.2	23.6	25.4	22.8	13,309	16,390	17,493
a) Financial Assets	11.2	10.1	12.9	10.0	5,710	8,356	7,677
b) Physical Assets	12.0	13.5	12.4	12.8	7,598	8,035	9,816
2. Private corporate sector	7.2	7.4	8.2	7.9	4,175	5,321	6,025
3. Public sector	2.9	1.0	0.2	1.7	543	118	1,302
4. Gross Domestic Saving	33.3	32.0	33.8	32.3	18,026	21,830	24,819
5. Net capital inflow	2.1	2.3	2.8	2.7	1,288	1,807	2,101
6. Gross Domestic Capital Formation (7+8)	33.6	34.3	36.6	35.1	19,314	23,637	26,920
7. Errors and Omissions	0.3	-1.2	0.5	-0.7	-687	313	-572
8. Gross Capital Formation	33.4	35.5	36.1	35.8	20,001	23,324	27,492
of which :							
a) Public sector	7.8	9.4	9.2	8.8	5,317	5,916	6,762
b) Private corporate sector	12.5	11.3	12.7	12.1	6,363	8,210	9,285
c) Household sector	12.0	13.5	12.4	12.8	7,598	8,035	9,816
d) Valuables»	1.1	1.3	1.8	2.1	722	1,163	1,628
Memo:							
Total Consumption Expenditure (a+b)		69.4	69.4	68.4	38,646	44,824	52,491
a) Private Final Consumption Expenditure		58.4	57.4	56.5	32,493	37,081	43,384
b) Government Final Consumption Expenditure		11.0	12.0	11.9	6,153	7,743	9,107
Saving-Investment Balance (4-6)	-2.1	-2.3	-2.8	-2.8			
Public Sector Balance #	-4.9	-8.4	-9.0	-7.1			
Private Sector Balance #							
a) Private Corporate Sector	-5.3	-3.9	-4.5	-4.2			
b) Household Sector	11.2	10.1	13.0	10.0			
GDP at Market Prices (at current prices)	38,111	55,826	64,574	76,741			

P: Provisional Estimates.   *: Quick Estimates.
#: Valuables cover the expenditures made on acquisition of valuables, excluding works of art and antiques.
Source: Central Statistics Office.

Preliminary estimates show that the net financial saving of the household sector declined further to 7.8 per cent of GDP at current market prices in 2011-12 from 9.3 per cent in the previous year and 12.2 per cent in 2009-10 (Table-2). The moderation in the net financial saving rate of the household sector during the year mainly reflected an absolute decline in small savings and slower growth in households' holdings of bank deposits, currency as well as life funds. At the same time, the persistence of inflation at a high average rate of about 9 per cent during 2011-12 further atrophied financial saving, as households attempted to stave off the downward pressure on their real consumption/ lifestyle.

TABLE-2

Financial Saving of the Household Sector (Gross)

Item	Per cent to Gross Financial Saving			₹ billion		
	2009-10 R	2010-11 R	2011-12 P	2009-10 R	2010-11 R	2011-12 P
1	2	3	4	5	6	7
A. Change in Financial Assets (Gross Financial Saving)	100.0	100.0	100.0	9,898.0	9,913.1	9,690.8
a) Currency	9.8	13.8	11.3	969.4	1,371.3	1,090.2
b) Deposits	41.9	45.6	52.8	4,148.7	4,516.8	5,120.3
i) With Commercial Banks	36.6	41.3	48.5	3,620.0	4,093.6	4,704.2
ii) With Non-banking Companies	1.9	0.4	1.5	185.2	43.9	148.5
iii) With Cooperative Banks and Societies	3.7	3.1	2.3	361.4	311.1	222.5
iv) Trade Debt (Net)	-0.2	0.7	0.5	-17.8	68.2	45.1
c) Share and Debentures	4.5	0.2	-0.7	448.4	17.3	-65.1
of which :						
i) Private Corporate Business	0.7	0.7	0.1	70.5	67.8	13.2
ii) Banking	0.1	0.1	0.1	9.5	8.1	9.1
iii) Bonds of public Sector undertakings	0.1	0.1	0.1	6.1	8.3	11.3
iv) Mutual Funds (including UTI)	3.3	-1.2	-1.1	330.4	-115.6	-106.2
d) Claims on Government	4.4	4.1	-2.1	434.8	410.6	-205.1
i) Investment in Government Securities	0.0	0.0	0.0	3.9	3.4	3.9
ii) Investment in Small Savings, etc.	4.3	4.0	-2.3	424.8	399.0	-220.3
e) Life Insurance Funds	26.2	22.3	23.1	2,598.2	2,207.3	2,234.3
of which :						
i) Life Funds of LIC and private Insurance companies	25.6	22.2	23.2	2,536.3	2,200.0	2,250.0
f) Provident and Pension Funds	13.1	14.0	15.6	1,298.5	1,389.7	1,516.1
B. Change in Financial Liabilities				2,034.5	2,783.2	2,741.7
C. Net Financial Saving of Household Sector				7,863.5	7,129.9	6,949.2

R: Revised.

P: Preliminary Estimates.

Note: Components may not add up to the totais due to rounding off.

Furthermore, with real interest rates on bank deposits and instruments such as small savings remaining relatively low on account of the persistent high inflation, and the stock market adversely impacted by global developments, households seemed to have favoured investment in valuables, such as gold. In the post-global crisis period, valuables have increased from 1.3 per cent of GDP at current market prices in 2008-09 to 2.8 per cent in 2011-12; the share of valuables in investment (gross capital formation) has also increased from 3.7 per cent to 7.9 per cent, over this period. The apparent proclivity of households towards investment in valuables such as gold could have also impacted the pace of their investment in physical assets such as housing in 2011-12.

The trend of falling savings rate, particularly that of public sector savings, needs to be reversed for adequate resources to be available to support a high growth trajectory during the Twelfth Plan.

The rate of gross fixed capital formation (investment) has declined persistently from a peak of 32.9 per cent in 2007-08 to 30.4 per cent in 2010-11 .The slackening of overall fixed investment was largely reflected in the private corporate sector as a result of both monetary and non-monetary factors. Sluggish growth rate of capital raised through initial public offerings (IPOs) during 2011-12 further impacted investment. The correlation between IPOs as a ratio to GDP and the fixed investment rate between 2000-01 and 2011-12 was 0.71.

INDIAN BANKING SECTOR

A growing economy needs investment to sustain its growth process. Such investments can be quickly and efficiently undertaken if investors have access to well-developed financial sysem and markets. Historically, banks have played the role of intermediaries matching savers with investors. In the post-reform era, the transition of the Indian economy to a higher growth trajectory, the provision of adequate and timely availability of bank credit to the productive sectors of the economy has acquired importance. As public sector banks still own about 71 per cent of the assets of the banking system, they continue to play an important role in responding to the changes in the economic environment. As the banking regulator and supervisor and as the monetary policy authority, the Reserve Bank of India (RBI) continues to guide the banking system, including foreign, private sector and public sector banks, to meet emerging economic challenges.

Indian banks can be broadly classified into public sector banks (those banks in which the Government of India holds a stake), private banks (government does not have a stake in these banks; they may be publicly listed and traded on stock exchanges) and foreign banks. Some of the selected schemes to mobilise the funds by banks in India are listed below:

1. Savings Banks Account

Savings Bank Accounts are meant to promote the habit of saving among the citizens while allowing them to use their funds when required. The main advantage of Savings Bank Account is its high liquidity and safety.

2. Current Account

Current Account is primarily meant for businessmen, firms, companies, public enterprises etc. that have numerous daily banking transactions. Current Accounts are cheque operated accounts meant neither for the purpose of earning interest nor for the purpose of savings but only for convenience of business hence they are non-interest bearing accounts

3. Recurring Bank Deposits

Under a Recurring Deposit account (RD account), a specific amount is invested in bank on monthly basis for a fixed rate of return. The deposit has a fixed tenure, at the end of which the principal sum as well as the interest earned during that period is returned to the investor.

4. Bank Fixed Deposits

Bank Fixed Deposits are also known as Term Deposits. In a Fixed Deposit Account, a certain sum of money is deposited in the bank for a specified time period with a fixed rate of interest. The rate of interest for Bank Fixed Deposits depends on the maturity period. It is higher in case of longer maturity period. There is great flexibility in maturity period and it ranges from 15 days to 5 years.

5. Demat Account

Demat refers to a dematerialised account. Demat account is just like a bank account where actual money is replaced by shares. Just as a bank account is required if we want to save money or make cheque payments, we need to open a demat account in order to buy or sell shares.

6. Senior Citizen Saving Scheme 2004

The Senior Citizen Saving Scheme 2004 had been introduced by the Government of India for the benefit of senior citizens who have crossed the age of 60 years. However, under some circumstances the people above 55 years of age are also eligible to enjoy the benefits of this scheme.

BANK ASSURANCE

Banks account for a significant share in the distribution of products in the life insurance segment. IRDA issued, in October 2012, a revised exposure draft on bancassurance. The proposed regulations allow banks to sell insurance products by either becoming a broker or a corporate agent. Banks selling insurance products offer several benefits viz., it encourages customers of banks to purchase insurance policies and further helps in building better relationship with the bank; reach of insurance products could improve through the widely distributed networks and better marketing channels of banks; and the increased competition could facilitate better premium rates and services for the customer. However, many instances of mis-selling of insurance products through this channel have been evidenced. The exposure draft seeks to leverage on the benefits of bancassurance while addressing the concerns of mis-selling through stipulations such as imposition of a ceiling on number of tie ups a bank can enter into as bancassurance agent, improved grievance redressal systems, prescription of a code of conduct and enhanced due diligence and compliance of KYC (Tables 3 and 4).

TABLE 3

Premium Under Life Sector: Bancassurance Vs Other Channels

| Financial Year | Individual Category | | | | Group Category | | | |
| | Banks | | Others | | Banks | | Others | |
	No. of Policies (million)	Premium (₹ billion)	No. of Policies (million)	Premium (₹ billion)	No. of Schemes	Premium (₹ billion)	No. of Schemes	Premium (₹ billion)
2009-10	2.1	86.9	52.3	758.9	444	6	28224	272.8
2010-11	1.9	110.7	46.7	729.5	1834	13.2	28765	418.7
2011-12	2.2	97	42	551.1	936	31.0	30593	459.8

Sourcs: IRDA

Several aspects of the exposure draft will need careful consideration. Extant regulations do not permit banks to become insurance brokers. Banks assuming the role of insurance brokers may also lead to conflict of interests where the bank is also the promoter of an insurance company. Further, some provisions of the exposure draft, if implemented, may expose the banks to reputational risks.

Table 4

Premium Under Non Life Sector: Bancassurance Vs Other Channels

Financial Year	Banks		Others	
	No. of Policies (million)	Premium (₹ billion)	No. of Policies (million)	Premium (₹ billion)
2009-10	6.5	2819.3	82.5	35650.0
2010-11	6.5	2849.3	101.2	44258.4
2011-12	7.1	3273.3	81.6	54690.7

Source: IRDA.

As the banking system has been liberalised and become increasingly market-oriented and financial markets have developed concurrently, the conduct of monetary policy has also been tailored to take into account the realities of the changing environment (switch from direct to indirect instruments). Given the predominance of bank-based finance in India, questions arise about the advantages and disadvantages of bank-based financial systems vis-a-vis (stock) market-based financial systems. The banking system avoids some of the information-deficiencies associated with the securities markets. Put differently, banks perform screening and monitoring functions on behalf of investors, which, left to themselves, can be undertaken only at a high cost. As a consequence, resource allocation and credit availability are considered to be superior under a bank-based as opposed to a market-based financial system. On the contrary, lower transaction costs in the absence of intermediation, may favour market-based sources of finance (see Exhibit-1).

EXHIBIT-1

Bank-Based and Market-Based Financial Systems

Financial systems differ not only with respect to their degree of sophistication, but also with respect to the type of the system. An important aspect of the growth process that has been widely discussed in recent time is the type of the financial system that is most conducive to growth. At one extreme, there is Germany, where a few large banks play a dominant role and stock market is not very important. At the other extreme is the US, where financial markets play an important role and the banking industry is much less concentrated.

Recent work in this area, using company balance sheet data, have demonstrated that internal sources of finance constituted the major portion of corporate (physical) investment in major OECD countries and that the role of the stock market (net of redemption) was limited in the majority of these countries. This can be traced to the fact that in the early stages of development, adequate incentives exist to bring borrowers' and lenders interests into line. An efficient banking system may act as an important conduit for channelling scarce resources from the surplus to the deficit sectors. The role of disintermediation in such circumstances is likely to be limited. In the longer term, as markets develop and the financial infrastructure is in place, intermediaries may be less central to the development of firms.

Traditional explanations of differences in financing patterns (such as tax treatment) attracted little empirical support. Recent advances have attempted to endogenously determine the emergence of bank-based or market-based financial system. In the presence of informational problems, if banks are initially competent monitors of firms, then a bank-based financial system emerges, and banks become more productive due to learning-by-doing and the financial sector continues to be dominated by banks. If, on the other hand, the productivity of the banking sector is initially low then a market-dominated regime emerges: banks become even more unproductive because there are no learning effects in banking, and market-based sources of finance gain in prominence.

Experiences of the, two most successful industrialised countries - Germany and Japan -reveal that the dominance of bank-based system has been the most successful financial vehicle for late industrialisation. While the institutional arrangements underlying bank-based systems vary, the basic contours are that banks establish long-term relationships with industrial companies, often reinforced by cross-holdings. For example, in Japan, banks had preferential access to transaction deposits of the firms, while the firms had secured access to loans from the banks, especially in situations of cyclical downturns. This ensured a steady supply of long-term finance to the firm, irrespective of the phase of cyclical fluctuation and built up a synergy between investment and growth. On the other hand, in countries, such as, the US and the UK, financial markets have played an important role in the development of these economies. A cross-country comparison reveals that both bank-based and market-based systems are in vogue.

This leads to two important and inter-related questions: (i) how do these marked differences in ownership emerge, and (ii) how are they related to the structure of financial systems? It has been argued that, there are two classes of economies: (a) *banking economies*, which have a small proportion of quoted companies, high concentration of ownership and long-term relations between banks and industry, and (b) market economies which have a high proportion of quoted companies, low concentration of ownership and short-term relations between banks and industry. In case of the former, firms have long-standing relationship with banks. This is ascribed to closer involvement of banks in corporate activities, for example, bank representation on corporate boards, bank holdings of corporate equity, etc. in case of the latter, the banking industry is much less important. In these countries, securities market share centre-stage with banks in terms of channelling society's savings to firms, exerting corporate control and easing risk management.

The global economy showed deeper signs of stress during the past year. With the deteriorating macroeconomic situation in the euro area interacting with a loss of growth momentum in the US and in emerging and developing economies (EDEs), the risks of potentially large negative spillovers have increased. Domestically, the macroeconomic situation continues to raise concerns. Even as growth has slowed significantly, inflation remains well beyond the comfort level of the Reserve Bank. The headwinds from domestic and international economic developments posed challenges to the banking sector during the year 2011-12. While banks maintained their profitability, their asset quality was impaired. During the year 2011-12, the NPA stock has risen. The slippage ratio of the banking system, which showed a declining trend during 2005-08, increased during 2008-12. Banks need to, not only utilise effectively, the various measures put in place by the Reserve Bank and the Government of India for the resolution and recovery of bad loans, but also have to strengthen their due diligence, credit appraisal and post sanction loan monitoring systems to minimise and mitigate the problem of increasing NPAs. Going forward, banks will need to move towards the mandated higher capital standards, stricter liquidity and leverage ratios and a more cautious approach to risk. This implies that Indian banks will need to improve efficiency even as their costs of doing business go up. They will need to refine their risk management skills for enterprisewide risk management. In addition, banks need to have in place a fair and differentiated risk pricing of products and services since capital comes at a cost. This involves costing, a quantitative assessment of revenue streams from each product and service and an efficient transfer-pricing mechanism that would determine capital allocation. As things stand, several initiatives are under way to strengthen the regulatory and accounting frameworks aimed at increasing the resilience of the institutions. However, higher capital standards, stricter liquidity and leverage ratios and a more cautious approach to risk is likely to raise the funding costs of banks. Compliance with Basel III stipulations along with the credit needs of a growing economy will require banks to tap various avenues to raise capital. Broad estimates suggest that for public sector banks, the incremental equity requirement due to implementation of Basel III norms by March 2018 is expected to be approximately ₹ 750-800 billion. Meeting these capital requirements will entail the use of innovative and attractive market based funding channels by the banks. The convergence with the International Financial Reporting Standards (IFRS) may also place additional demands on the banks' technical as well as human resources. Considering the granularity of data required for effective supervisory review, efforts should be to automate data flow from reporting entities through the adoption of straight-through processing systems. With regard to financial inclusion, quantitative coverage has improved, but meaningful financial inclusion through the evolution of sustainable business and delivery models needs to be achieved.

Going ahead, banks need to tap into untapped business opportunities for resources to power the growth engine. This requires harnessing resources and fortune at the bottom of the pyramid. Small customers are an important key to big business opportunities waiting to be tapped. The challenge before banks is to make the best use of technology and innovation to bring down intermediation costs while protecting their bottom lines. The recent regulatory initiatives like the deregulation of savings bank deposit interest rates and opening up government business to more banks, imminent steps, such as licensing of new banks and subsidiarisation of the foreign bank branches, on the one hand, and the changing profile and simultaneously rising aspirations and expectations of customers on the other, should make the turf more competitive and increasingly, a buyers' market. As the Indian banking sector is propelled forward to a higher orbit, banks would have to strive to remain relevant in the changed economic environment by reworking their business strategy, designing products with the customer in mind and focussing on improving the efficiency of their services. The challenge for Indian banks is to reduce costs and pass on the benefits to both depositors and lenders.

Notwithstanding the multitude of challenges to be braved by the Indian banking sector against the backdrop of a difficult domestic and global macroeconomic environment, the regulatory responses and the inherent strengths underlying the Indian economy would ensure that the banking system withstands the transitory difficult phase and plays a positive intermediation role in supporting the financing needs of a growing economy.

INDIAN INSURANCE INDUSTRY

In an increasingly competitive world economy the need for economy against risks is well recognised. In India, the insurance sector was opened up for private participation with the enactment of the Insurance Regulatory and Development Authority (IRDA) Act, 1999. While permitting foreign participation in the ventures set up by the private sector, the Government restricted participation of the foreign joint venture partner through the FDI route. Since opening up, the vast network of insurance offices including micro or oneman offices reaching out to several towns and villages principle access to a pointer to the availability of sales touch points in smaller places. With a view to ensuring special attention to the rural, economically and socially vulnerable segments of the population, the IRDA (Rural and Social Obligations) Regulations cast obligations on insurers to cover these segments under insurance.

Since the opening up of the insurance sector, the number of participants in the insurance industry has gone up from seven insurers (including the Life Insurance Corporation of India [LIC], four public-sector general insurers, one specialized insurer, and the General Insurance Corporation as the national re-insurer) in 2000 to 52 insurers as on 30 September 2012 operating in the life, non-life, and re-insurance segments (including specialized insurers, namely the Export Credit Guarantee Corporation and Agricultural Insurance Company [AIC]). Four of the general insurance companies, viz. Star Health and Alliance Insurance Company, Apollo Munich Health Insurance Company, Max BUPA Health Insurance Company, and Religare Health Insurance Company function as standalone health insurance companies. Of the 23 insurance companies that have set up operations in the life segment post opening up of the sector, 21 are in joint ventures with foreign partners. Of the 21private insurers who have commenced operations in the nonlife segment, 18 are in collaboration with foreign partners.

Life Insurance

From being the sole provider of life insurance till financial year 1999-2000, LIC is today competing in an industry with 23 private-sector insurers who have commenced operations over the period 2000- 12. The industry which reported an annual growth rate of 19.8 per cent during the period 1996-7 to 2000-1 has, post opening up of the sector, reported an annual growth rate of 18.85 per cent during 2001-2 to 2011-12. The life insurers underwrote new business of ₹ 1,13,942 crore during financial year 2011-12 as against ₹ 1,26,398 crore during the year 2010-11, recording a decline of 9.85 per cent. Of the new business premium underwritten, the LIC accounted for ₹ 81,862.25 crore (71.85 per cent market share) and private insurers for ₹ 32,079.92 crore (28.15 per cent market share). The market share of these insurers was 68.84 per cent and 31.16 per cent respectively in the corresponding period of 2010-11.

Non-life Insurance

The industry which reported a growth rate of around 10 per cent during the period 1996-7 to 2000- 1 has, post opening up of the sector, reported average annual growth of over 15 per cent over the period 2001-2 to 2011-12. In addition, the specialized insurers Export Credit Guarantee Corporation and AIC are offering credit guarantee and crop insurance respectively. The premium underwritten by the nonlife insurers during 2011-12 was ₹ 52,875.8 crore as against ₹ 42,576.5 crore in 2010-11, thus recording a growth of 24.19 per cent. The growth was satisfactory, particularly in view of the across-theboard cuts in tariff rates. The private insurers underwrote premium of ₹ 22,315.03 crore as against ₹ 17,424.6 crore in 2010-11, reporting growth of 28.07 per cent vis-a-vis 24.67 per cent in 2010-11. The publicsector insurers, on the other hand, underwrote a premium of ₹ 30,560.74 in 2011-12 as against ₹ 25,151.8 crore in 2010-11, i.e. a growth of 21.5 per cent as against 21.84 per cent in 2010-11. The market shares of the public and private insurers are 57.80 and 42.20 per cent in 2011-12 as against 59.07 and 40.93 in the previous year

Insurance Penetration

The growth in the insurance sector is internationally measured based on the standard of insurance penetration defined as the ratio of premium underwritten in a given year to the gross domestic product (GDP). Insurance density is another wellrecognized benchmark and is defined as the ratio of premium underwritten in a given year to total population (measured in US dollars for convenience of comparison). The Indian insurance business has in the past remained underdeveloped with low levels of penetration. Post liberalization, the sector has succeeded in raising the levels of insurance penetration from 2.7 (life 2.15 and non-life 0.56) in 2001 to 4.1 (life 3.4 and non-life 0.7) in 2011.

IRDA has pioneered the issuance of Micro Insurance Regulations which encourage simple and low ticket premium products covering the risks of life as well as livelihood. Many categories of individuals and entities that were considered by the Reserve Bank to act as BCs are under consideration of IRDA for according Micro Insurance Agency eligibility, with a few exceptions. Further a number of District Cooperative Banks, Regional Rural Banks and urban co-operative banks that are working in rural and semi urban areas are also being considered for permitting to act as Micro Insurance Agents. In addition to one Life Insurance Company and one General Insurance Company, a Micro Insurance Agent is now proposed to be permitted to work with Agriculture Insurance Company of India Ltd for the limited purpose of distributing crop insurance. The proposed modified regulations also entitle the individual insurance agents, who were already licensed to act as insurance agents, in rural areas where population is not more than 2000, to the higher percentage of Micro Insurance Remuneration. Further, it is also proposed to link the higher remuneration / commission rates payable on Second and Subsequent years' premium to the persistency rate of Micro Insurance business portfolio of Micro Insurance Agent so as to encourage and emphasize on the quality of business.

As regards the scope of Micro Insurance Products, in the existing regulations, non life Micro Insurance (MI) products are covering retail risks faced by individuals. They do not address the institutional risks faced by Micro, Small and Medium enterprises that are playing a significant role in the country's growth. Therefore, a proposal is under consideration that General (Non Life) Insurance policies issued to Micro, Small and Medium Enterprises as defined in Section 7 of Micro, Small and Medium Enterprises Development (MSMED) Act, 2006 under various classes of non-life insurance business will be qualified as non-life micro insurance business up to a premium of ₹ 25000 per annum per policy. However, the non life insurance companies will have enough discretion to decide whether to appoint MI Agents, if so to which sector / enterprises of MSME Sector.

Initiatives Taken by the Authority in the Insurance Sector

The initiatives taken by the authority in the insurance sector include the following:

1) Amendment to Insurance Legislation

The Insurance Laws (Amendment) Bill 2008 introduced in Parliament recently proposes to amend the Insurance Act 1938, the Insurance Regulatory and Development Authority (IRDA) Act 1999, and the General Insurance Business (Nationalization) Act 1972. The amendments to the Insurance Act and the IRDA Act focus on the current regulatory requirements; the proposed changes provide for greater flexibility in operations and are aimed at deletion of clauses that are no longer relevant in the present context. The amendments also provide for enhancement of enforcement powers and levy of stringent penalties.

2) Micro Insurance

The IRDA has formulated the Micro Insurance Regulations to distribute insurance products that are affordable to the rural and urban poor and to enable micro insurance to become an integral part of the country's wider insurance system. The main thrust of these regulations is to provide low income people with affordable insurance products as a hedge against unforeseen risks. Total premium income in the micro insurance portfolio of life insurers for the year 2009-10 is ₹ 402 crore. Fourteen life insurers have so far launched 28 micro insurance products and by the end of March 2010 there were 8676 individual micro insurance agents in India.

3) Guidelines on the AML Programme

The IRDA issued guidelines on the AML Programme to the insurance industry on 31 March 2006, whereby insurers were advised to put a proper AML policy framework in place in case of life insurance companies and non-life insurance companies effective from 1 August 2006 and 1 January 2007 respectively. An updated master circular on Anti-Money laundering/Counter-financing of terrorism has been issued by the Authority on 24 September 2010. The AML/CFT guidelines were reviewed by the Authority to align certain stipulations with those of the 40 +9 recommendations of the FATF and additional stipulations/clarifications were issued to insurers vide circular dated 12 November 2010 to be complied with by 31 December 2010.

4) Data Warehouse

The IRDA has initiated steps to design, build, and manage a data warehouse for the insurance industry recognizing that data will help the insurers design new products and allow scientific underwriting, further calculations of actuarial risks, price setting, and various aspects relating to claims settlement, management of hazards, etc. As a first step, the IRDA has designed a data set relating to health and motor vehicle insurance. The IRDA also proposes to put in place a formal data warehouse to enable access by various stakeholders across the industry.

5) Consumer Grievance Redressal Cell

The Grievance Redressal Cell of the IRDA looks into complaints from policyholders. Complaints against life and non-life insurers are handled separately. This Cell plays a facilitative role by taking up complaints with the respective insurers.

6) Public Awareness Campaigns/Programmes

The IRDA's strategy for consumer awareness/ education includes campaigns through external media, i.e. mass media, mainly print, television and the Internet, and internal initiatives such as an exclusive consumer education web page and sample booklets on various insurance-related topics, containing generic information, which insurers would also be advised to publish and distribute.

7) Cap on Unit-Linked Insurance Plans (ULIP) Charges

The insurance industry has introduced ULIPs which have found favour with customers in India. These products prescribe certain charges which are deducted either from contributions or from the fund. In order to simplify and to ensure that the charges are reasonable, relevant to the services being provided, and clear to customers, the IRDA has mandated an overall cap on all charges put together. Care has been taken to ensure that the insurers have freedom to distribute charges across the term of the policy. This also imparts flexibility and facilitates product innovation.

8) Corporate Governance Guidelines

Corporate governance guidelines have been rolled out for insurance companies, effective from 1 April 2010. The objective of the guidelines is to ensure that the structure, responsibilities, and functions of the Boards of Directors and senior management of companies fully recognize the expectations of all stakeholders as well as those of the regulator. The guidelines broadly cover major structural elements of corporate governance.

9) Initiatives in the Area of Policyholders Grievances Redressal

   a) Grievance redressal guidelines effective from 1 August 2010 specific to both life and general insurance companies have been issued by the IRDA fixing the turnaround time for various grievances.

   b) The IRDA has during July 2010 inaugurated the nationwide toll-free grievance call centre no.'155255' for policyholders to lodge complaints against insurance companies. The Grievance Redressal Cell of the IRDA looks into complaints from policyholders. This Cell plays a facilitative role by taking up complaints with the respective insurers for speedy disposal.

   c) Guidelines have been issued by the IRDA effective from 1 June 2009 on renewability of health insurance policies clearly defining the procedure while declining a renewal or imposing a loading and also regarding upfront disclosures in Prospectuses. Insurers were also guided tocondone delay in renewal up to 15 days.

   d) The IRDA has also instructed insurers on the terms and conditions of health insurance to senior citizens and made it mandatory for products filed after the circular date to allow entry at least till 65 years of age. The IRDA vide its circular dated 2 September 2009 has also advised insurers to provide a 'free look period' for health insurance policies with term three or more years.

   e) The IRDA is in the process of developing the new Integrated Grievance Management system (IGMS) which will not only facilitate policyholders to register/track their complaints online with insurance companies but also facilitate the IRDA to monitor the grievance redressal procedure of insurance companies

   f) The IRDA being in receipt of several complaints from policyholders relating to agency identification and servicing, keeping the interests of policyholders in view, has directed all insurers to display the agency code, agency name, and nobile number (landline if mobile number not available) and other contact details prominently on the first page of the policy document to be implemented on or before 1 November 2010.

   g) In respect of medical insurance policies, if there is a change in Preferred Provider of Network (PPN) of Hospitals, the insurers have been directed on 24 August 2010 to inform the policyholders at all times of the nearest possible alternative hospitals where the cashless facility is available and the conditions thereof.

   h) Guidance notes have been issued by the IRDA on 28 June 2010 on recent regulatory changes on ULIPs.

10) For the Orderly Growth of Insurance and Reinsurance Industry

   (i) As the inter-company balances in reinsurance and coinsurance are growing, the IRDA, noting that these balances can have serious implications for the liquidity of several entities in the insurance sector, has decided to induce insurers and brokers to move over to a computer system of administration and settlement of accounts in respect of all inter-company transactions.

   (ii) The IRDA (Sharing of Database for Distribution of Insurance Products) Regulations 2010 have been issued and all insurers advised to terminate all the referral arrangements entered into prior to the coming into effect of these regulations that are not in conformity with the provisions of these regulations.

   (iii) The IRDA (Insurance Advertisements and Disclosures) (Amendment) Regulations 2010 have been issued to ensure the orderly growth of the insurance industry.

(iv) The IRDA (Treatment of Discontinued Linked Insurance Policies) Regulations 2010 have been issued detailing the procedure on policy discontinuance and imposing a cap on charges on policy discontinuation.

(v) Authority revamped its present agency licensing portal with a new Agency portal in order to widen the scope of the portal and to integrate the various stakeholders with the agency licensing system. The portal commenced its operations on 5/1/2010.

11) Credit Insurnace

New guidelines on trade credit insurance policies have been issued by the IRDA effective from 13 December 2010, with a view to standardizing the features of these products. All insurers have to revise their products in line with file & use guidelines and trade credit insurance guidelines. These guidelines specify that a policyholder should necessarily be a supplier of goods and services and his loss should be by nonreceipt of trade receivables and can only be issued on whole turnover basis covering all buyers.

12) Variable Insurance Products

Guidelines have been issued by the IRDA on variable insurance products (VIP) on 23 November 2010. As per these guidelines, all VIP products shall only be offered under non-unit-linked platform either as participating or non-participating and shall not be permitted under unit-linked platform. Benefit is payable on these policies either on death or maturity and only regular premiums with minimum policy and payment terms of five years are allowed. Single premium, limited premium, and group insurance contracts are not allowed under these products.

13) Consumer Education

Consumer education and policyholder protection being two sides of the same coin, the Regulator encourages and supports consumer bodies to conduct seminars on insurance, thereby not only educating the consumer but also providing a platform for the consumer to interact with representative(s). The IRDA itself conducts/ participates in and supports national-level seminars on different topics and is also proposing to launch a consumer portal shortly.

14) Persistency of Life Insurance Policies

In order to increase persistency in the interests of the insurance industry and to create professionalism amongst agents and encourage them to build a longterm career, the IRDA has issued an exposure draft to set certain minimum standards and requirements for agents and mandate insurers to review the performance of agents periodically. These proposals would be a step forward in protecting the interests of policyholders, who in the ultimate analysis stand to gain if persistency is high, both in terms of protection of life and profitability of the life insurance business which would benefit them in the long run.

15) IPO Guidelines

Several insurance companies will be completing 10 years of their operations shortly, after which they may be allowed by the Regulator to go in for an IPO. It is essential that the investors be made fully aware of the financial performance, company profile, financial position, risk exposure, elements of corporate governance in place, and the management of such insurance companies. The IRDA is participating in the meetings of the Standing Committee on Disclosures and Accounting Issues (SCODA) set up by SEBI to finalize the disclosure requirements for insurance companies in their prospectus documents. While laying down the stipulations on disclosure requirements, the IRDA has drawn on international best practices. It is proposed that the disclosure requirements for life and non-life companies would be separately mandated given the nature of their respective businesses.

16) Other Activities

The IRDA along with National Disaster Management Authority (NDMA) has conducted a seminar on Disaster Management in New Delhi on 11 August 2010 to lay down a plan for devising products for catastrophe perils and also to discuss the collective role of the Government, NDMA, and IRDA representing insurance companies, on disaster management.

Alongwith the above mentioned initiatives, the capital market solutions for catastrophe risk insurance are another area that needs focus. This essentially transfers insurance risk of natural calamities like earthquakes, hurricanes and floods to the capital markets through issue of catastrophe bonds. The instrument is widely used in advanced countries and there is scope for introducing it in countries like India to provide insurance against contingencies.

PENSION SECTOR

The pension sector essentially encompasses the organized sector. The majority of the country's workforce in the unorganized sector has no access to formal channels of old-age income support. Only about 12 per cent of the working population in India is covered by some form of retirement benefit scheme. Besides the problem of limited coverage, the existing mandatory and voluntary pension system has been characterized by limitations like fragmented regulatory framework, lack of individual choice and portability, lack of uniform standards, low real rate of returns, etc. India's need for comprehensive reforms in the pension system is thus self-evident.

Pension reforms in India have evolved primarily in response to the need of reform in the Government pension system. This had been designed to make a shift from defined-benefit to defined-contribution by putting a cap on Government's liability towards civil servants' pension. As a result of implementation of the New Pension System (NPS), all employees of the Central Government and Central autonomous bodies, with the exception of the armed forces, are now covered by this defined-contribution scheme with effect from 1 January 2004. Subsequently, 27 State Governments have notified and joined the NPS for their employees. Till January 5, 2013, the subscriber base for the mandatory Government sector has crossed 42.17 lakhs with a corpus approaching to ₹ 26,189 crore. With opening up of the NPS to all citizens of India from 1 May 2009, on voluntary basis, the challenge is to spread the message of the NPS and old age income security to people in the unorganized sector across the country. This involves spreading the NPS distribution network such that NPS is easily accessible to all, and there is adequate awareness about it for people to decide voluntarily to open pension accounts.

NPS Design

The NPS architecture essentially involves a set of financial institutions, called points of presence (PoP), which are authorized to open NPS accounts and receive contributions; the Pension Fund Managers (PFMs), or the PFMs, which are appointed by the Pension Funds Regulatory and Development Authority (PFRDA) and are authorized to manage the pension corpus of the subscribers; and the Central Recordkeeping Agency (CRA), which does the record keeping.

A centralized record keeping for the NPS ensures that the individual pension account is completely portable across the country, professions, and employment. The management of the NPS is highly technology driven; the transmission of information and funds is done in an electronic environment ensuring speed, accuracy, and efficiency. The investment of the pension funds is done in accordance with prescribed norms which specify different categories of investment instruments along with prudential limits on the quality and quantity of investments. The pension fund managers manage three separate scheme, consisting of three asset classes, namely (i) equity, (ii) Government securities, and (iii) credit risk- bearing fixed income instruments, with the investment in equity subject to a cap of 50 per cent. In the equity scheme, the fund managers will invest only in index funds that replicate either the BSE Sensex or NSE Nifty 50 index. The subscriber will have the option to decide the investment mix of his pension wealth. In case the subscriber is unable or unwilling to exercise any choice regarding asset allocation, his contribution will be invested in accordance with the 'auto choice' option with a predefined portfolio.

Recent Initiatives

Although the NPS is perhaps one of the cheapest financial products available in the country, in order to make it affordable for economically disadvantaged people, the PFRDA has recently introduced a lower cost version of the NPS, known as NPS-Lite, which enables groups of people to join the NPS at substantially reduced cost. The PFRDA has so far authorized nine aggregators to implement NPS-Lite. One of the distinguishing features of NPS has been unstinted Government support in popularizing the concept of old age income security. In this regard, the announcement of the Swavalamban scheme in budget 2010 by the Finance Minister was significant. Swavalamban is an incentive scheme for the NPS. Under this any citizen in the unorganized sector, who joins NPS in 2010-11, with a minimum annual contribution of ₹ 1000 and maximum of ₹ 12,000 will receive a Government contribution of ₹ 1000 in his NPS account. With this announcement, the Government of India has become a direct stakeholder in the old age income security of every citizen. The scheme is presently available for another three years beyond 2010-11 and will go a long way in promoting pension culture in the country.

Efforts are under way to expand the reach of the NPS to new segments like Central and State autonomous bodies and the organized sector. The PFRDA is in dialogue with several State Government autonomous bodies and undertakings for extending the NPS to their employees.

Performance of the NPS

In the unorganized sector, nearly 34,000 subscribers had jointed the NPS as of December 2010 on voluntary basis. The subscriber base in the newly launched NPS-Lite is around 5000. For all citizens including workers of the unorganized sector, the NPS is currently available through nearly 5000 service provider branches of 35 PoPs.

Despite all its good features, popularization of the NPS remains a challenge. To address this challenge, the PFRDA has appointed an expert committee, called the Committee to Review implementation of Informal Sector Pension (CRIISP), to look into a range of issues connected with the NPS, such as reasons of sluggish public response, viability of the NPS as a financial product, ways and means of marketing/proper popularizing of the NPS and the agency best suited to perform this role, a sustainable and viable economic incentive model for the NPS, and the role of NPS fund managers in the entire NPS architecture, and suggest remedial measures. Important challenges before the PFRDA are to expand the distribution network of the NPS so that it is available within easy reach of all citizens, educate the citizens to take appropriate investment decisions based on their risk and return profiles, and contribute to improving financial literacy levels. The PFRDA is doing every bit to ensure that the complete distribution network of the NPS is fully galvanized so that access to the NPS is improved It is expected that the success of pension reforms will not only help in facilitating the flow of long-term savings for development, but also help establish a credible and sustainable social security system in the country.

Although the NPS is perhaps one of the cheapest financial products available in the country, in order to make it affordable for the economically disadvantaged, the government in September 2010 introduced a lower cost version, known as Swavalamban Scheme, which enables groups of people to join the NPS at a substantially reduced cost. As per existing scheme under NPS, Swavalamban could be availed either in unorganized sector or in NPS Lite. NPS Lite is a model specifically designed to bring NPS within easy reach of the economically disadvantaged sections of the society. NPS Lite is extremely affordable and viable due to its optimized functionalities available at reduced charges. Under the Swavalamban scheme, the government provides subsidy to each NPS account holder and the scheme has been extended until 2016-17. A customized version of the core NPS model, known as the NPS Corporate Sector Model was also introduced from December 2011 to enable organized-sector entities to move their existing and prospective employees to the NPS under its Corporate Model. All the PSBs have been asked to provide a link on their website to enable individual subscribers to open online NPS Accounts.

POST-OFFICE SMALL SAVINGS SCHEMES

To moblise the small savings various small savings schemes through post office savings banks were included in the Union List vide item No. 39 of Seventh Schedule of the Constitution of India. Various Schemes framed by the Central Government under; Government Savings Certificate Act, 1959 and the Public Provident Fund Act, 1968. The object of small savings schemes was to provide safe & attractive investment options to the public and at the same time to mobilise resources for development. These schemes are operated through about 1.54 Lakh post offices throughout the country. Public provident Fund Schemels also operated through about 8000 branches of public sector banks in addition to the post offices. Deposit Schemes for Retiring Employees are operated through selected branches of public sector banks only.

National Savings Organisation (NSO) is responsible for national level promotion of these schemes through publicity campaigns and advertisements in audio, video as well as print media. A large network of over 5 lakh small savings agents working under different cateaories viz: Standardised Agency System (SAS), Mahila Pradhan Kshetriya Bachat Yojana (MPKBY), Public Provident Fund Agency Scheme, Payroll Saving Groups, School Savings Banks (Sanchayikas) etc help in the mobilisation process. In addition, the Extra Departmental Branch Postmasters (EDBPMs) also help in mobilising savings, especially in rural and remote/far flung areas.

Institutional Investment in Small Savings Schgemes

These schemes being primarily meant for small urban and rural investors; institutions are not eligible to invest in major small savings schemes. The Non-Resident Indians (NRIs.) are not eligible to invest in small savings schemes including Public Provident Fund (PPF) and Deposit Schemes For Retiring Employees. Box-1 pesent current the small savings schemes with main features.

Box-1

CURRENT SMALL SAVINGS SCHEMES WITH MAIN FEATURE

Post Office Savings Accounts

These schemes can be opened by: a single adult or two-three adults jointly; a pensioner to receive/credit his monthly pension; Group Accounts by Provident Fund, Superannuation Fund or Gratuity Fund; public Account by a local authority/body; an employee, contractor, or agent of a government or of a government company or of a university for depositing security amounts; a Gazetted Officer or an officer of a government company or Corporation or Reserve Bank of India or of a local authority in his official capacity; and, a cooperative Society or a cooperative bank for payment of pay, leave salary, pension contribution of government servants on deputation with such society or bank at any post office.

In these schemes; account can be opened with a *mlnimum* of ₹ 20. It is *maxlmum* of Rupees *One Lakh* for single holder and ₹ *Two lakhs* for joint holders. If depositors have more than one account (single, pension or joint), the balances or shares of balances in ali such accounts taken together should not exceed ₹ One Lakh for each of the depositors. There is no lock-in / maturity period prescribed. Withdrawals can be of any amount subject to keeping a minimum balance of ₹ 50 in simple and ₹ 500 for cheque facility accounts. Interest at the rate (s) 'as decided by the Central Government from time to time', is calculated on monthly balances and credited annually.

Depositor is provided with a pass book with entries of ali transactions duly stamped by the post Office. An account, not operated during three complete years, shall be treated as 'Silent Account'. A service charge @ ₹ 20 per year is charged on the last day of each year until it is reactivated. In a silent account from which after deduction of service charge, the balance becomes NIL, the account stands automatically closed. Final withdrawal/ closure of account shall be allowed by Sub Postmaster/Extra departmental Sub/Branch Postmaster on obtaining sanction from Head Postmaster.

Income tax relief is available on the amount of interest under the provisions of section SOL of Income Tax Act.

Post Office Time Deposit Accounts

Types of accounts under this are: 1 Year maturity; 2 Years maturity; 3 Years maturity & 5 Years maturity. This can be opened by a single adult or two adults jointly; a pensioner to receive/credit his monthly pension; group Accounts by Provident Fund, Superannuation Fund or Gratuity Fund, Authority controlling funds of the Sanchayika; Public Account by a local authority/body; Institutional Accounts by the Treasurer of Charitable Endowments for India, Trust Regimental Fund & Welfare Fund; A cooperative society / cooperative bank or scheduled bank on behalf of its members, clients or employees; and, a Gazetted Officer in his official capacity at any post office.

The account can be opened with a deposit with a *minimum* of ₹ 200 with *no maximum limit*. The deposited amount is *repayable after explry of the period* for which it is made viz: 1 year, 2 years, 3 years or 5 years. Interest is 'calculated on quarterly compounding basis', is payable annually. Interest rates applicable w.e.f. the 1st day of March, 2003 are :

Period of deposit	Rate of Interest per cent / per annum
1 YEAR	6.25
2 YEARS	6.50
3 YEARS	7.25
5 YEARS	7.50

Depositor is provided with a pass book with entries of the deposited amount and other particulars duly stamped by the post office. Income tax relief is available on the amount of interest under the provisions of section SOL of Income Tax Act. Premature withdrawals from ali-types of Post Office Time Deposit accounts are *permlssible after explry of 6 months* with certain conditions. Post maturity interest "at the rate applicable to the post office savings accounts from time to time", is payable for a maximum period of 2 years.

Post Office Recurring Deposit Accounts

The account can be opened by a single adult or two adults jointly; a guardian on behalf of a minor or a person of unsound mind; or a minor who has attained the age of ten year, in his own name at any post office.

Period of maturity of an account is five years.Sixty equal monthly deposits shall be made in an account in multiples of ₹ five subject to a minimum of ten rupees. Accounts with not more than four defaults in deposits can be regularized within a period of two months on payment of a default fee. Account becomes discontinued after more than four defaults.

On maturity of the accounts opened on or after 1ˢᵗ March, 2003, an amount (Inclusive of Interest) of ₹ 728.90 is payable to a subscriber of Rupees: Ten denomination account. Amount repayable, inclusive of interest, on an account of any other denomination shall be proportionate to the amount specified above. Depositor is provided with a pass book with entries of the deposited amount and other particulars duly stamped by the post Office. Premature closure of accounts is permissible after expiry of three years provided that interest at the rate applicable to post office savings account shall be payable on such premature closure of account. Continuation after maturity in permissible for a maximum period of five years.

Post Office Monthly Income Account

This can be opened by a single adult or 2-3 adults jointly and more than one account can be opened subject to maximum deposit limits at any post office. Period of maturity of an account is six years. Only one deposit shall be made in an account. Minimum deposit limit is rupees one thousand; and maximum: rupees **three lakhs** in case of single and rupees **six lakhs** in case of Joint account. Deposits in ali accounts taken together shall not exceed ₹ three lakhs in single account and ₹ six lakhs in joint account. The depositor's shares in the balances of joint accounts shall be taken as one half or one third of such balance according as the account is held by 2 or 3 adults.

Interest @ **8 per cent/** per annum, **payable monthly** in respect of the accounts opened on or after the 1ˢᵗ March, 2003. In addition, **bonus** equal to **ten per cent** of the deposited amount is payable at the time of repayment **on maturity.** Depositor is provided with a pass book with entries of the deposited amount and other particulars duly stamped by the post Office. Premature closure facility is available after one year subject to condition. Further the account shall be closed after expiry of 6 years, bonus equal to ten per cent of deposits shall be paid alongwith principle amount. Income tax relief is available on the interest earned as per limits fixed vide section 8oL of Income Tax, as amended from time to time.

National Savings Certificate (Viii Issue)

These can be purchase by an adult in his own name or on behalf of a minor, a minor; a trust; two adults jointly; and, Hindu Undivided Family. These are available for purchase/issue at Post Offices. Period of maturity of a certificate is six Years. Nomination facility is available. Certificates can be transferred from one post Office to any other post Office. Transfer from one person to another person is permissible in certain conditions.

Certificates are available in denominations (face value) of ₹ 100, ₹ 500, ₹ 1000, ₹ 5000 &. ₹ 10,000. There is *no maximum* limit for purchase of the Certificates. With effect from 1ˢᵗ March, 2003, **Maturity value** a certificate of ₹ 100 denomination is ₹ **160.10.** Maturity value of a certificate of any other denomination shall be at proportionate rate. Interest accrued on the Certificates every year is liable to income tax but deemed to have been reinvested. Premature encashment of the certificate is not permissible except at a discount in the case of death of the holder(s), forfeiture by a pledgee and when ordered by a court of law. These can be encashed/discharged at the post office where it is registered or any other post office.

Income Tax rebate is available on the amount invested and interest accruing every year under Section 88 of Income tax Act, as amended from time to time. Income tax relief is also available on the interest earned aspelimits fixed vide section SOL of Income Tax, as amended from time to time.

Kisan Vikas Patra

These can be purchased by an adult in his own name or on behalf of a minor; minor; a Trust; two adults jointly. These are available for purchase/issue at Post Offices. With effect from 1st March, 2003, invested amount **doubles** on **maturity** after **Eight Years and Seven months.** Nomination facility is available.

Certificates are available in denominations (face value) of ₹ 100, ₹ 500, ₹ 1000, ₹ 5000, ₹ 10,000 & ₹ 50,000. There is *no maximum limit* for purchase of the certificates. No income tax benefit is available under the scheme. However the deposits are exempt from Tax Deduction at Source (TDS) at the time of withdrawal. Premature encashment of the certificate is not permissible except at a discount in the case of death of the holder(s), forfeiture by a pledgee and when ordered by a court of law. These can be encashed/discharged at the post Office where it is registered or any other post office on maturity.

Public Provident Fund Scheme

This scheme is available to an individual in his own name, on behalf of a minor of whom he is a guardian, and, Hindu Undivided Family.

The accounts can be opened at designated post offices throughout the country, and at designated branches of Public Sector Banks throughout the country.

The account matures for closure after *15 years*. Account can be continued with or without subscriptions after maturity for block periods of five years. Nomination facility is available. *Minimum* deposit required is ₹ *500* in a financial year. *Maximum* deposit limit is ₹ *70,000* in a financial year. *Maximum* number of deposits is *twelve* in a financial year.

Loans from the amount at credit in PPF account can be taken after completion of one year from the end of the financial year of opening of the account and before completion of the 5th year. The amount of withdrawal cannot exceed 40% of the amount that stood to credit at the end of fourth year preceding the year of withdrawal or at the end of preceding year whichever is lower. Premature withdrawal is permissible every year after completion of 5 years from the end of the year of opening the account. Account can be transferred from one post office to another post office, from a bank to another bank; and from a bank to post office and vice-versa.

Depositor is provided with a pass book with entries of the deposited amounts, interest credited every year and other particulars duly stamped by the post Office. Interest at the rate, notified by the Central Government from time to time, is calculated and credited to the accounts at the end of each financial year. Present rate of interest is **eight** *per cent/per year* since: 1st March, 2003. **Income Tax rebate** is available 'on the deposits made', under Section 88 of Income tax Act, as amended from time to time. Interest credited every year is tax-free.

Deposit Scheme for Retiring Government Employees

The account can be opened by Retired Central and State Governments' employees. Retired Judges of the Supreme Court and High Courts, and at designated branches of Public Sector Banks throughout the country.\

The account matures for closure after *3 years*. Account can be continued with the whole or a part of the deposits after maturity. The account can be opened individually or jointly with his/ her spouse. Nomination facility is available in respect of individual accounts. The deposit limit is *One* time deposit with a *mInImum* of ₹ *1000* to the *maximum* of the total retirement benefits in multiple of one thousand rupees.

Retirement benefits mean: balance at the credit of employee in any of the Government Provident Funds; retirement/Superannuation gratuity; commuted value of pension; cash equivalent of leave; savings element of Government insurance scheme payable to the employee on retirement. Arrears of retirement benefits, as defined in (i) to (v) above on implementation of Fifth Pay Commission's recommendations.

Whole or a *part* of the deposits can be withdrawn at any time after expiry of the normal maturity period of 3 years. Withdrawal is not permissible before completion of one year. They are *permissible* after completion of one year and before completion of three years *on reduced Interest rate.*

Interest at the rate, notified by the Central Government from time to time, is creditedand payable on half yearly basis at any time after 30th June and 31st December every year. Present rate of interest is *Seven per cent/ per annum* since: 1st March, 2003. Account can be transferred from one public sector bank to another public sector bank operating the scheme due to change of residence. Depositor is provided with a pass book with entries of the deposited amount, interest etc. and other particulars by the bank. *Interest* accrued / credited / paid is fully *tax-free. Amount deposited* under the scheme is *free* from *wealth tax.* Selected branches of the following banks are auithorised to accept deposits under the scheme:

Deposit Scheme for Retiring Employees of Public Sector Companies

This scheme is availability to retired/retiring employees of Public Sector Undertakings, Institutions, Corporations, **viz:** Public Sector Banks; Life Insurance Corporation of India; General Insurance Corporation; and public Sector Companies, etc.; at designated branches of Public Sector Banks throughout the country. The account matures for closure after *3 years.* Account can be continued with the whole or a part of the deposits after maturity. The account can be opened individually or jointly with his/her spouse. Nomination facility is available in respect of individual accounts.the deposit limit is *one* time deposit with a *mlnlmum* of ₹ 1000 to the *maximum* of the total retirement benefits in multiple of one thousand rupees. Retirement benbefits means Balance at the credit of employee in any of the Government Provident Funds. Retirement/Superannuation gratuity. Commuted value of pension. Cash equivalent of leave, Savings element of Government Insurance scheme payable to the employee on retirement. Arrears of retirement benefits, as defined in (i) to (v) above on implementation of Fifth Pay Commission's recommendations. *Whole* or a part of the deposits can be withdrawn at any time after expiry of the normal maturity period of *3 years.* Premature withdrawal is, not permissible before completion of one year. It is *permissible* after completion of one year and before completion of three years on *reduced interest rate.*

Interest at the rate, notified by the Central Government from time to time, is credited and payable on half yearly basis at any time after 30th June and 31st December every year. Present rate of interest is *Seven per cent/ per annum* since: 1st March, 2003. Account can be transferred from one public sector bank to another public sector bank operating the scheme due to change of residence. Depositor is provided with a pass book with entries of the deposited amount, interest etc. and other particulars by the bank. Interest accrued / credited / paid is fully tax-free. *Amount deposited* under the scheme is free from *wealth tax.* Selected branches of banks are authorised to accept deposits under the scheme.

DEPOSITS WITH COMPANIES

These deposits are accepted by the companies under relevant Government regulations. But these regulations do not mean any great safety to the depositor. The interest rates are quite attractive but there is no tax exemption on interest earned. The interest income is subject to tax deduction at source, at the rates in force under Section 194-A of the Income Tax Act.

In company deposits element of risk is the real problem as these deposits are unsecured loans. Of course, companies are required to fulfil certain norms such as — deposits for a period of 3-6 months should not exceed 10% of the aggregate paid up share capital and free reserves of the company. According to Section 58-A and 58-B of Companies Amendment Act of 1974 and the Companies (Acceptance of Deposits) Rules 1975 as amended in April, 1979, a company has to reveal certain required information while inviting deposits from the public. An investor should go through that information very carefully.

While investing in reputed companies may be safe to a great extent, an investor must be doubly cautious while investing in less reputed companies, particularly private limited companies who may misguide the public by advertising a phenomenal return for a deposit of 3 years. In fact, there are not many companies in which the public may deposit their money without anxiety.

BULLION

The bullion reserve of a country is the indicator of the amount of wealth a country possesses. Bullion is defined as a bulk quantity of precious metals consisting of gold, silver and others that can be assessed by weight and cast as a lump. Bullion is valued by its purity and mass rather than its face value which is applicable in the case of money. India Bullion Market is a recognizable index that highlights the economic growth of the nation.

GOLD

Gold is one of the chemical elements. Gold's chemical symbol is Au and its atomic number is 79. Its chief characteristics are that it is inert and malleable. Inert means gold does not interact with other chemicals or compounds. Gold doesn't tarnish and even the strongest acids have no effect. Thus, gold lasts forever - and stays shiny the whole time!

Gold as an Investment

Of all the precious metals, gold is the most popular as an investment. Investors generally buy gold as a hedge or safe haven against any economic, political, social or currency-based crises. These crises include investment market declines, currency failure, inflation, war and social unrest. Investors also buy gold during times of a bull market in an attempt to gain financially.

Gold has many industrial uses, but its main historical uses have been jewellery and money - both are a store of value. Gold has been used as a store of value for at least 5000 years. Gold is measured and prices are quoted in Troy Ounces and Grams. As an example of gold's ability to store value, 2000 years ago one ounce of gold would buy a fine man's outfit. Today one ounce of gold will still buy a good quality man's wool suit with enough left over to buy a few shirts, a tie, some underwear, socks, a pair of shoes and *a* belt!

Gold has been called a "barometer of fear." When people are anxious about the economy - they turn to gold and bid the price up. The two main things that make people anxious are deflation and inflation. Most think that deflation is "falling prices" and inflation is "rising prices." Actually, rising and falling prices are symptoms. The root causes are decreases (deflating) or increasing (inflating) of the money supply. Gold has the remarkable ability to store value in both deflationary and inflationary times.

Gold Price

Gold throughout history has been used as money, and therefore, instead of gold having a fixed "price," other goods and services had been priced in relation to a proportional & compatible quantity of gold per economic region. After World War II a gold standard was established following the 1944 Bretton Woods conference, fixing the gold price at $35 per troy ounce (or, in effect, pricing the U.S. dollar as 1/35th of an ounce of gold).

The system held up until the 1971 Nixon Shock, when the US stopped the direct convertibility of the United States dollar to gold. Since 1968 the usual benchmark for the price of gold is known as the London Gold Fixing, a twice-daily (telephone) meeting of representatives from five bullion-trading firms. Furthermore, there is active gold trading based on the intra-day spot price, derived from gold-trading markets around the world as they open and close throughout the day.

International gold prices have risen almost unabatedly in the last few years, though there was one large correction in 2008. From July 2011 the pace of increase in gold prices has, however, accelerated further and in 2012, gold prices rose much faster. The spectacular rise in gold, which is reflected in its price rise, in the recent period can be attributed to several reasons. Firstly, during periods of geopolitical risks, the commodity has a great appeal as a haven. The unrest in Libya and Middle East provided the initial impetus for its rise in 2011. Secondly, measures like quantitative easing have weakened *fiat* money *vis-a-vis* commodities in general and gold in particular. With the US and European economy weakening again, there is speculation of a third round of quantitative easing and fears over further debasement of the US dollar in which gold is denominated. The US dollar is the reserve currency in which most countries hold their foreign exchange reserve assets. A country with a reserve currency has to run current account and fiscal deficits in order to provide enough reserves to meet the demand of the investing countries. Thirdly, it has come to represent a safe harbour in times of fall in risk appetite when sovereign debt sustainability on both sides of the Atlantic is being questioned. The political disagreement over how to address the large and growing sovereign debt and the resultant downgrade of US treasuries by S&P has quickened the pace of appreciation of gold. Some analysts and investors feel that in the current muddled political and economic scenario, gold is the only "hard currency" left. Lastly, short-term trend followers notice that a declining US dollar (in which gold is denominated) and negative real interest rates which reflects that gold price can only rise (may be till it reaches the psychological US$ 2000 mark) have contributed to the feeling that it has emerged as the best performing asset in 2011 .

As regards India, the DRG study by the Reserve Bank of India titled "Gold Mobilisation Instrument as an External Adjustment" (1992) has listed five factors for their influence on demand for gold *viz.*, generation of large market surpluses in rural area as a result of all round increase in agricultural production, unaccounted income/wealth generated mainly in the service sector, comparative rate of return available on alternative financial assets like bank deposits, units of mutual funds, small savings schemes etc., price variation of gold and prices of other commodities.

Inter-linkage between Domestic and International Gold Prices

Indians have a yearning for gold since the inception of civilisation. Gold demand has not only remained high but has shown sharp rise in the recent period especially since 2001 as reflected in the increase in volume of imports. The demand has shown no signs of abating despite incessant price rise. Lord John Maynard Keynes famously commented that India's gold consumption reflects the 'ruinous love of a barbaric relic'. Incidentally, India's gold production continues to be minimal in nature. Almost all of India's demand for gold is met by imports. It would be appropriate to review the gold policy in India since the time of initiation of the economic reforms in 1991. One of the characteristic of gold was the prevalence of a large unofficial market for gold in India on account of restrictions in import of gold at the time. There was a considered view that unrestricted import of gold causes diversion of household savings from productive assets and the consequent diversion of precious foreign exchange resources. At that time, excess demand for gold was considered as one of the reasons for the then external constraint which hindered development and technical progress. This policy in turn led to a dual price for gold – one prevailing in the unofficial market and another one being the official gold price. The restrictive policy of gold resulted in smuggling of a large scale of gold into India.

The economic reform process initiated in 1991 influenced a shift in gold policy from "regulations" towards "deregulations". The major shift towards the deregulation of gold policy was reflected in the various recommendations of the Committee on Capital

Account Convertibility (CCAC) in early 1997. The committee, *inter alia*, recommended the removal of restrictions on import of gold, which it hoped will curb smuggling and hoarding of gold. The committee further recommended the development of gold- related financial instruments; developments of markets for physical and financial gold and encouragement of banks and non-banks to participate in the gold market. In line with these recommendations, the Reserve Bank authorised commercial banks to join the ranks of a few state enterprise like MMTC as nominated agencies for importing gold. As a result of these policy shifts, the import of gold through the official channel increased significantly. By 2011, almost entire import of gold has been taking place through the official channel leading to the integration of domestic gold prices with that of international gold prices.

Domestic gold prices tend to swing with international gold prices. It is expected that on account of the liberalisation of gold, changes in domestic gold prices should be of almost the same magnitude as that of international gold prices adjusted for the exchange rate. With Rupee depreciation/appreciation, domestic gold prices should increase/decrease. Another factor which could have some impact on the domestic gold prices could be changes in domestic equity prices. In terms of its role as a "safe haven" during downturns in equity market, there could be increase in gold demand in the domestic market leading to a rise in domestic gold prices. However, in view of the liberalised environment, such an effect should be limited in magnitude as well as duration.

Gold Price Bubble and Relevance for Financial Stability

With the price of gold surging to record highs there are concerns in academic and policy forums as to whether gold is in a state of bubble and, if so, what could be its macroeconomic consequences in general and with reference to the financial system in particular.

The word "bubble" conjures up the image of an object growing steadily until it finally pops. *A bubble as 'an upward price movement over an extended range that then explodes'* ,*i.e.* that part of asset price movement that is unexplainable based on what we call fundamentals. A speculative bubble exists when the price of something exceeds by a big margin its market fundamentals for some period of time for reasons other than random shocks. Fundamental is usually argued to be a long-term equilibrium consistent with a general equilibrium . It is well known that the price of an asset is the present value of all future *expected* cash flows. Ultimately this means that to define a bubble there must be an implications about the expectations of the cash flows of an asset.

In this context, it is analytically difficult to value the gold because unlike equity or fixed income securities, it does not have coupon or a dividend tied to it. There are no future cash flows that could be discounted using interest rates to arrive at a fair value as is done for financial assets. In fact, investing in gold requires some cash outflows in terms of rent for storage, insurance and other expenses.More important than the determination of gold as a bubble or not, from the financial stability point of view, it is the knowledge about the extent of macroeconomic and macro- financial damage a sharp correction in gold prices can cause that matters more.

The Implications of an Asset Price Bubble on Real Economic Activity and Financial Stability

In general, the key channel through which asset price bubble impacts the real economy is through consumption and investment. In terms of economic paradigms, the fundamentals of any bubble are that the asset price bubble leads to the impression of creating wealth which through the wealth effect and other channels has negative effects on the macro economy when prices fall sharply. There may also be a major impact of asset price bubble, especially, in case of equity price, on corporate fixed investment. A steep fall in the equity prices may affect the net worth of the corporate sector and business houses, which in turn, impacts real economic activity having serious implications for stability of banking sector. An asset price bubble may pose problems to the stability of the banking system through variety of channels. As a result of asset price bubbles, banks may face credit risk, *i.e.* the risk of a severe reduction in collateral values and of increasing defaults of customers who have taken leveraged position. Banks may also encounter market risk, *i.e.* the risk banks incur as direct investors in the affected assets. Thus, the asset price bubble is likely to affect households through the consumption channel, corporate sector through the investment channel and the banking sector through the credit risk and market risk channels.

Asset bubbles burst and lead to contraction of the economy. But the impact of all types of bubbles has not been observed to be identical. Some asset price bubbles have devastating effect on the economy whereas impact of others is minimal. Many episodes of boom-bust financial cycles but not all of them result in a costly economic contraction. Some boom-bust cycles, such as those in Japan and Scandinavian countries in the 1990s, and the sub-prime crisis of 2007-2009, led to banking crises and a severe recession. But on well known occasions such as 1987 stock market crash or the dot-com bubble of 1999-2000, the collapse of asset price did not result in any banking crisis.

A pertinent question thus arises as to why some bubbles cause severe contraction of economic activities while others do not. Why did the dot-com bubble not lead to a serious banking crisis while the sub-prime bubble did? An additional policy dilemma from the financial stability angle, is whether policy makers should react to any sharp increase in asset prices or are there occasions when the market can be left safely to it own devices even when financial prices look to have departed from the fundamentals.

With these theoretical backgrounds, we take a look at the ownership of gold by housholds, central governments and others and make a qualitatitive assessment of the gold price bust, if any, on the real activities. Chart 7 reveals that about 50 percent of the global gold holdings are meant for jewellery purposes which could be ascribed largely to the household sector. Another 12 percent global gold holdings are meant for industrial use wheras 17 percent are official holdings of the Central banks/other government bodies. Thus, a major part of the global gold holdings are not directly held by the banking/financial sector. Finally, there is a lack of leverage in purchasing of gold. Bubbles require large leverage and there is no evidence yet that investors are borrowing to invest in gold. Moreover, gold had been falling as a proportion of total global financial assets.

Gold price bubble, if at all, is likely to have a mild impact on the economic activities. Rather, gold price bust may have certain positive implications for economic activities. There is a general consensus that the present gold price spurt is taking place against the background of global uncertainties and gold is substituting other risky assets like equities in asset portfolios. This in turn could lead to the fall in the entrepreneur's net worth having adverse impact on the economic activities. Fall in consumption expenditure by the household due to the wealth effect induced by fall in gold prices is likely to be minimal as the usage of gold as a collateral for obtaining financial assistance from the banks and non-banks is still limited in nature. Even if used as a collateral, there is considerable anecdotal evidence suggesting that financial institutions have raised margins fearing correction in gold prices.

Whether a deep correction in the gold prices as in 2008 has any financial instability implications to the Indian financial system depends on: (a) whether gold is in a state of bubble or not and (b) the nature and significance of gold in the overall financial architecture. Gold, unlike a financial asset, is not associated with cash inflows. This makes it somewhat difficult to judge on a historical basis whether it is in a state of bubble or not and thus to predict the nature of correction in gold prices in the immediate future. Theoretically, severity of a correction in any asset prices (including gold) on the financial system would depend upon the nature of the ownership of the asset. Specifically, if those assets are held by banks and financial institutions, (collectively financial intermediaries), either directly or indirectly through collateral, the severity of impact of a bursting of a bubble would be severe.

Viewed from this perspective, the likely financial stability implications of a correction in gold prices would be less severe on the financial system. Holding of gold among financial intermediaries is currently low though rising. It is bought mostly by the household sector as an alternative saving avenue and to meet social/cultural needs and not for speculative purposes.

It is important to note that the developments in gold market in 2012-13 are taking place against the backdrop of global and economic uncertainties caused by the downgrading of sovereign debts and the debt crisis in many of the European countries. The crisis has quickly spread to the banking sector in Europe. The scenario that would require gold to fall sharply would entail a turnaround in the global economy, subsiding of geopolitical tensions and a reversal of monetary accommodation. In that scenario, equity and other risky assets ought to recover as investors move money away from "safe haven" assets like gold and US treasuries. In other words, a sharp reversal in gold prices would in fact be reflective of improvement in global conditions, especially, those in the US. The substitution of gold for equity and other riskier assets would thus offset the systemic impact of gold prices, if any.

Methods of Investing in Gold

Investment in gold can be done directly through bullion or coin ownership, or indirectly through gold exchange-traded funds.

Investment Strategies

Fundamental Analysis

Investors using fundamental analysis analyze the macroeconomic situation, which includes international economic indicators, such as GDP growth rates, inflation, interest rates, productivity and energy prices. They would also analyze the yearly global gold supply versus demand. Over 2005 the World Gold Council estimated yearly global gold supply to be 3,859 tonnes and demand to be 3,754 tonnes, giving a surplus of 105 tonnes. While gold production is unlikely to change in the near future, supply and demand due to private ownership is highly liquid and subject to rapid changes. This makes gold very different from almost every other commodity.

Gold versus Stocks

The performance of gold bullion is often compared to stocks. They are fundamentally different asset classes. Gold is regarded by some as a store of value (without growth) whereas stocks are regarded as a return on value (i.e. growth from anticipated real price increase plus dividends). Stocks and bonds perform best in a stable political climate with strong property rights and little turmoil.

The specific comparison between a share of Google and an ounce of gold, two very different investments, seems to have captured the imagination of may in the investment community and is serving to crystallize the broader debute. On January 4 2008, an ounce of gold outpaced the share price of Google by 30.77%, with gold closing at $859.19 per ounce and a share of Google closing at $657 on U.S. market exchanges. On January 24 2008, the gold price broke the $900 mark per ounce for the first time. The price of gold topped $1,000 an ounce for the first time ever on March 13, 2008 amid recession fears in the United States. Google closed 2008 at $307.65 while gold closed the year at $866. The cost of holding onto tangible gold yields risk. Because of gold's value, that risk must be hedged by secure protection. Because of this additional cost and security risk, some opt for mutual funds.

Technical Analysis

As with stocks, gold investors may base their investment decision partly on, or solely on, technical analysis. Typically, this involves analyzing chart patterns, moving averages, market trends and/or the economic cycle in order to speculate on the future price.

Using Leverage

Bullish investors may choose to leverage their position by borrowing money against their existing [gold] assets and then purchasing [more] gold on account with the loaned funds. This technique is referred to as a carry trade. Leverage is also an integral part of buying gold derivatives and unhedged gold mining company shares (see gold mining companies). Leverage via carry trades or derivatives may increase investment gains but also increases the corresponding risk of capital loss if/when the trend reverses.

SILVER

Silver, like other precious metals, may be used as an investment. For more than four thousand years, silver has been regarded as a form of money and store of value. However, since the end of the silver standard, silver has lost its role as legal tender in the United States. (It continued to be used in coinage until 1964, when the intrinsic value of the silver overtook the coins' face values.)

The price of silver has been notoriously volatile as it can fluctuate between industrial and store of value demands. At times this can cause wide ranging valuations in the market, creating volatility. Generally, Silver tracks the gold price due to store of value demands, although the ratio can vary. The gold/silver ratio is often analyzed by traders and investors and buyers. In 1792, the gold/silver ratio was fixed by law in the United States at 1:15, which meant that one troy ounce of gold would buy 15 troy ounces of silver; a ratio of 1:15.5 was enacted in France in 1803. The average gold/silver ratio during the 20th century, however, was 1:47.

India hardly produces any silver and is basically a silver importing country. It holds the 20th place in the list of silver producing countries and the total production of silver in India in 2004 was around 2.1 million ounces. The three major silver producing states in India are: Rajasthan; Gujarat; and Jharkand. Rajasthan is the leading silver producing state in India with a production of around 32 thousand tons. Gujarat follows on the second place with a production of around 20 thousand tons.

Indian Silver Market

India is primarily a silver importing country, as the production of India is not sufficient to satisfy the ever-growing domestic demand. The production of silver in India stands out at the figure of around 2.1 million ounces placing it at the 20th position in the list of major silver producing countries. The import of silver in India hovers over 110 million ounces that shows the huge size of Indian domestic demand.

However, this import level fell sharply as a result of the decline in demand due to rise in silver prices and inconsistent monsoon on which the income of the rural sector depends. But, even this sharp decline could not affect India's reputation of being one of the largest consumer countries of silver in the world. India stands third after United States and Japan among the leading consumers of silver in the world. The countries from which India imports silver and maintain the flow of silver in the market are: China, United Kingdom, European Union, Australia, and Dubai, Over 50% share of import of silver in India is held by Chinese silver. The major importing center of silver in India was Mumbai but now it has been shifted to Ahmedabad and Jaipur due to high sales tax and octroi charges.

State Price is in influencently , number of traders, e.g. price movements of other metals, income level of the rural sector of the economy, available supply verses, fabrication demand, fluctuation in deficits and interest rates, inflation, etc.

Major Trading Centers of Silver are London, Zurich, New York (COMEX), Chicago (CBOT), Hong Kong, and Tokyo Commodity Exchange (TOCOM). In India, silver is traded at the number of places e.g., Delhi, Indore, Rajasthan, Madhya Pradesh, Uttar Pradesh, etc, States is also is traded in the Indian commodity exchanges like National Commodity & Derivatives Exchange Ltd., Multi Commodity Exchange of India ltd. and National Multi Commodity Exchange of India Ltd.

QUESTIONS

1. Why should an investor include non-security forms of investment in his portfolio?
2. Discuss the various saving schemes promoted by Post Office which are available to the investors presently.
3. Outline the various investment avenues offered by the LIC
4. Should an investor commit his funds in bullion? What are the advantages and disadvantages of such an investment?
5. Distinguish between bank-based and market-based financial systems. What are the advantages and disadvantages of each sysem?
6. Critically examine the composition of financial savings of the household sector in India
7. Discuss the role of social security bonds in the mobilising financial savings.
8. Critically examine the recent flow of funds in India.
9. Discuss the various schemes floated by banks to mobilise the savings.
10. Discuss the growth of Indian insurance Industry in recent times.
11. Discuss the role of pension-sector reforms in establishing a robust and sustainable security arrangement in India.
12. Why should the investment in bullion be an important media? What are the factors influencing the price of bullion in recent times?

REFERENCES

1. Cavelti, Peter C. *How to Invest in Gold.* Chicago: Follett Publishing, 1979.
2. Government of India , Economic Survey of various years
3. Haldane, Andrew (2009), "Why Banks Failed The Stress Test?", Bank of England.
4. Kohn, Donald (2008), "Monetary Policy and Asset Prices Revisited", Remarks at the Cato Institute's 26th Annual Monetary Policy Conference, November 19.
5. Mohan, Rakesh (2007), "Recent Financial Market Developments and Implications for Monetary Policy", Reserve Bank of India Bulletin, October
6. Mühleisen, Martin (1997), Improving India's Saving Performance, IMF Working Paper No. 97/4, International Monetary Fund, January.
7. Regan, Patrick J. "The Shattering of the Diamond Market." *Financial Analysts Journal,* July-August 1981.

8. Reserve Bank of India (2009a), "India's Financial Sector: An Assessment" Committee on Financial Sector Assessment (Chairman: Rakesh Mohan), March.

9. Warnock, Veronica Cacdac and Francis E. Warnock (2008), Markets and housing finance, Journal of Housing Economics.

10. World Bank (2008), Global Development Finance 2008: The Role of International Banking, World Bank.

18

Real Estate Investments

INTRODUCTION

Real estate offers an attractive way to diversify an investment portfolio. In addition, it offers favourable risk-return tradeoffs due to the uniqueness of properties and the localised and relatively inefficient market in which they are traded. Real estate differs from security investments in two ways: (1) it involves ownership of a tangible asset - *real property* rather than a financial claim — and (2) managerial decisions about real estate greatly affect the returns earned from investment in it. Investing in real estate means more than just "buying right" or "selling right". It also means managing the property right. In real estate one must answer questions such as: What rents should be charged? How much should be spent on maintenance and repairs? What advertising media should be selected? What purchase, lease, or sales contract provisions should be used? Along with market forces, it is the answers to such questions that determine whether or not investor will earn the desired return on a real estate investment. Like other investment markets, the real estate market changes over time. It also differs from region to region.

SETTING REAL ESTATE INVESTMENT OBJECTIVES

Setting objectives involves three steps. First, the investor should consider how the investment characteristics of real estate differ. Second, the investor should establish investment constraints and goals. Third, the investor should analyse important features.

Investment Characteristics

Individual real estate investments differ in their characteristics even more than individual people differ in theirs. So, just as an investor would not marry without thinking long and hard about the type of person he would be happy with, he should not select an investment property without some feeling for whether or not it is the right one for the investor. To select wisely, the investor needs to consider the available types of properties and whether the investor wants an equity or a debt position.

We can classify real estate into two investment categories: income properties and speculative properties. Income properties are residential and commercial properties that are leased out and expected to provide returns primarily from periodic rental income. Residential properties include *single-family* properties (houses, cooperatives). Commercial properties include office buildings, shopping centres, warehouses, and factories. Speculative properties typically include raw land and investment properties that are expected to provide returns primarily from appreciation in value due to location, scarcity, etc., rather than from periodic rental income.

Income properties are subject to a number of sources of risk and return. Losses can result from tenant carelessness, excessive supply of competing rental units, or poor management. On the profit side, however, income properties can provide increasing rental incomes, appreciation in the value of the property, and possibly even some shelter from taxes. Speculative properties, as the name implies, given their owners a chance to make a financial killing, but also the chance for heavy loss due to high uncertainty. For instance, rumours may start that a new model industrial complex is going to be build on the edge of town. Land buyers would jump into the market, and prices soon would be bid up. The right buy-sell timing could yield returns of several hundred percent or more. But people who bought into the market late, or those who failed to sell before the market turned, might lose the major part of their investment. Before investing in real estate, the investor should determine the risks various types of properties present and then decide which risks the investor can afford.

Constraints and Goals

When the investor decides to invest in real estate, he faces a number of choices. In light of these options, the investor needs to set both financial and nonfinancial constraints and goals. One financial constraint is the risk-return relationship he finds acceptable. In addition, the investor must consider how much money he wants to allocate to the real estate portion of his portfolio. Furthermore, he should define a quantifiable financial objective. Often this financial goal is stated in terms of *net present value* (also referred to as *discounted cashflow)* or approximate yield.

Although the investor will probably want to invest in real estate for its financial rewards, he also needs to consider how his technical skills, temperament, repair skills, and managerial talents fit a potential investment. *Does he want a prestige, trouble-free property? Or would he prefer a fix-up special on which he can release his imagination and workmanship? Would he enjoy living in the same buildings as his tenants or would he like as little contact with them as possible?* Just as he would not choose a career solely on the basis of money, neither should he buy a property just for money.

Analysis of Important Features

The investor while estimating a property's investment potential. Yet first he must consider four general features relating to real estate investment:

1. *Physical Property.* When buying real estate, make sure to get both the quantity and quality of property. Problems can arise if the investor fails to obtain a site survey, an accurate square-footage measurement of the buildings, or an inspection for building or site defects. When signing a contract to buy a property, make sure it accurately identifies the real estate and lists all items of personal property (such as refrigerator) that he expects to receive.

2. *Property Rights.* Strange as it may seem, when buying real estate when the investor buys a bundle of legal rights that fall under concepts in law such as deeds, titles, easements, liens, and encumbrances. When investing in real estate, make sure that along with various physical inspections, to get a legal inspection from a qualified attorney. Real estate sale and lease agreements should not be the work of amateurs.

3. *Time Horizon.* Like a roller coaster, real estate prices go up and down. Sometimes, market forces pull them up slowly but surely; in other periods prices can fall so fast they take an investor's breath away. Before judging whether a prospective real estate investment will appreciate or depreciate. The investor must decide what time period is relevant. The short-term investor might count on a quick

drop in mortgage interest rates and buoyant market expectations, whereas the long-term investor might look more closely at population-growth potential.

4. *Geographic Area.* Real estate is a spatial commodity, which means that its value is directly linked to what is going on around it. With some properties, the area of greatest concern consists of a few square blocks; in other instances an area of hundreds or even thousands of miles serves as the relevant market area. As a result of these spatial differences. The investor must delineate boundaries before he can productively analyse real estate demand and supply.

DETERMINANTS OF VALUE

When analysing real estate investment, value generally serves as the central concept. Will a property increase in value? Will it produce increasing amounts of cash flows? To address these questions, the investor should evaluate the four major determinants of real estate value: demand, supply, the property, and the property transfer process.

Demand

Demand refers to people's willingness and ability to buy or rent a given property. In part demand stems from a market area's economic base. In most real estate markets, the source of buying power comes from jobs. Property values follow an upward path when employment is increasing, and values typically fall when employers begin to lay off personnel. Therefore, the first question the investor should ask about demand is "What is the outlook for jobs in the relavent market area?" Are schools, colleges, and unversities gaining enrollment? Are major companies planning expansion? And are wholesalers, retailers, and financial institutions increasing their sales and services? Upward trends in these indicators often signal a rising demand for real estate.

Population characterstics also influence demand. To analyse demand for a specific property. The investor should look at an area's population demographics and psychographic. Demographics refers to such things as household size, age structure, occupation, sex, and marital status. Psychographics are those characterstics that describe people's mental dispositions, such as personality, lifestyle, and selfconcept. By comparing demographic and psychographic trends to the features of a property. The investor can judge whether it is likely to gain or lose favour among potential buyers or tenants.

Mortgage financial is also a key factor. Tight money can choke off the demand for real estate. Rising interest rates and the relative unavailability of mortgages may cause investor of unsold properties to grow and real estate prices to fall.

Supply

Supply analysis means sizing up the competition. Nobody wants to pay more for a property than the price they can pay for competing property. An integral part of value analysis requires to identify sources of potential competition and then inventory them by price .and features.

In general, people in real estate think of competitors in terms of similar properties. If one is to sell a house, then it seems natural to see in competitions the other houses for sale in the same neighborhood. For longer- term investment decisions, however one should expand his concept of supply. That is he should identify competitors through the principle of substitution. This principle holds that people do not really buy or rent real estate per se. Instead, they judge properties as different sets of benefits and costs. Properties fill people's needs, and it is really these needs that create demand. Thus an analysis of supply should not limit potential competitors to geographically and physically similar properties. In some markets, for example, low-priced single-family houses might compete with condominium units, manufactured homes and even with rental apartments. So before investing in any property, one should decide what market that property appeals to, and then define its competitors as other properties that its buyers or tenants might also typically choose from.

The Property

The price that people will pay is governed by their needs and the relative prices of the properties available to meet those needs. For example, a parent can buy a house on its college student son's campus for several students to share and hire their son to act as live-in rental manager. This strategy can create college housing for a son while acting as a real estate investment for the parents. Yet in real estate the property itself is also a key ingredient. To try to develop a property's competitive edge, an investor should consider five items: (1) restrictions on use; (2) location; (3) site characteristics; (4) improvements; and (5) property management.

Restrictions on Use

In today's highly regulated society, both state and local laws and private contracts limit the rights of all property owners. Government restrictions derive from zoning laws, building and occupancy codes, and health and sanitation requirements. Private restrictions include deeds, leases, and condominium bylaws and operating rules. Because of all these restrictions, the investor should not invest in a property until he determines that what he wants to do with the property *fits within* applicable laws, rules, and contract provisions.

Location Analysis

The three most important determinants of real estate value are *location, location,* and *location.* Of course, location is not only the factor that affects value; yet a good location unquestionably increases a property's investment potential. A good location rates highly on two key dimensions: *convenience* and *environment.* Convenience refers to how accessible a property is to the places the people in *a* target market frequently need to go. Any selected residential or commercial market segment will have a set of preferred places its tenants or buyers will want to be close to. Another element of convenience is transportation facilities. Availability of buses, taxis, subways, and commuter trains is of concern to both tenants and buyers of commercial and residential property. Commercial properties need to be readily accessible to their customers and vice versa.

In the analysis of real estate, the term environment has broader meaning than trees, rivers, lakes and air quality. When one invests in real estate, he considers not only the natural environment, but also the esthetic, socioeconomic, legal and fiscal environments. Neighbourhoods with an *esthetic environment* are those where buildings and landscaping are well executed and well maintained. There is no intrusion of noise, sight, or air pollution, and encroaching unharmonious land uses are not evident. The *socioeconomic environment* refers to the demographics and lifestyles of the people who live or work in nearby properties. The *legal environment* relates to the restrictions on use that apply to nearly properties. And last, the investor needs to consider a property's /feca/ *environment:* the amount of property taxes and municipal assessments he will be required to pay, and the government services he will be entitled to receive (police, fire, schools, parks, waters, sewers, trash collection, libraries). Property taxes are a two-sided coin. On the one side they pose a cost, but on the other they give a property's users the right to services that may be of substantial benefit.

Site Characteristics

One of the most important features of a property site is its size. For residential properties, such as houses, condominiums, and apartments, some people want a large yard for children to play in' or for a garden. Others may prefer virtually no yard at all. For commercial properties, such as office buildings and shopping centers, adequate parking space is necessary. Also, with respect to site size, if the investor is planning a later addition of space, make sure the site is large enough to accommodate it, both physically and legally. Site quality such as soil fertility, topography, elevation and drainage capacity is also important. For example, sites with relatively low elevation may be subject to flooding.

Improvements

In real estate, the term improvements refers to the man-made additions to a site, such as buildings, sidewalks, and various on-site amenities. Typically building size is measured and expressed in terms of square footage. Because square footage is so important in building and unit comparison, the investor should get accurate square footage measures on properties to be considered for investing in.

Another measure of building size is room count and floor plan. For example, a well-designed 1250-square-foot apartment unit might in fact be more livable and therefore easier to rent and at a higher price, than one of 1850 square feet. The investor should make sure that floor plans are logical, that traffic flows throughout a building will pose no inconveniences, that there is sufficient closet, cabinet and other storage space, and that the right mix of rooms exists. For example, in an office building he should not have to cross through other offices to get to the building's only bathroom, or as an exclusive access to any other room; small merchants in a shopping center should not be placed in locations where they do not receive the pedestrian traffic generated by the large (anchor) tenants.

Attention should also be given to amenities, style and construction quality. Amenities such as air conditioning, swimming pools, and elevators can significantly impact the value of investment property. In addition, the architectural style and quality of construction materials and workmanship are important factors influencing property value.

Property Management

In recent years real estate owners and investors have increasingly recognised that investment properties (apartments, office buildings, shopping centers, and so on) do not earn maximum cash flows by themselves. They need to be guided toward that objective, and skilled property management can help. Without effective property management, no real estate investment can produce maximum benefits for its users and owners. Today property management requires the professional managers to run the entire operation as well as to perform day-to-day chores. The property manager will segment buyers, improve a property's site and structure, keep tabs on competitors, and develop a marketing campaign. Management also assumes responsibility for the maintenance and repair of buildings and their physical systems (electrical, heating, air conditioning, and plumbing) and for keeping revenue and expense records. In addition, property managers decide the best ways to protect properties against loss from perils such as fire, flood, theft, storms, and negligence. In its broadest sense, property management means finding the optimal level of benefits for a property, and then providing them at the lowest costs. Of course, for speculative investments such as raw land, the managerial task is not so pronounced and the manager has less control over the profit picture.

The Property Transfer Process

In efficient markets, information flows so quickly among buyers and sellers that it is virtually impossible for an investor to outperform the average systematically. As soon as something good or something bad occurs, the price of the affected company's stock adjusts to reflect its current potential for earnings or losses. Some people accept the premise that securities markets are efficient, while others do not. But one thing is sure: No *one believes real estate markets are efficient*. What this means is that real estate market research pays off. Skillfully conducted analysis can help in beating the averages. The reasons real estate markets differ from securities market is that no good system exists for complete information exchange among buyers and sellers, and among tenants and lessors. There is no central marketplace where transactions are conveniently made by equally well-informed investors who share similar objectives. Instead, real estate is traded in generally *illiquid markets* that are regional or local in nature and where transactions are made by investors, using information they have gathered and developed, in order to achieve their often unique investment objectives. The cash flows a property earn can be influenced significantly through promotion and negotiation.

REAL ESTATE VALUATION

In real estate the concept of market value, or actual worth, must be interpreted differently from its meaning in stocks and bonds. This difference arises for a number of reasons: (1) each property is unique; (2) terms and conditions of sale may vary widely; (3) market information is imperfect; (4) properties may need substantial time for market exposure, time that may not be available to any given seller; and (5) buyers, too, sometimes need to act quickly. All these factors mean that no one can tell for sure what a property's "true" market value is. As a result, many properties sell for prices significantly above or below their estimated (or appraised) market values. To offset such inequities, many real estate investors forecast investment returns in order to evaluate potential property investments. Here we look first at procedures for estimating the market value of a piece of real estate, and then describe methods for forecasting real estate investment returns.

ESTIMATING MARKET VALUE

In real estate, estimating the current market value of a piece of property is done through a process known as a real estate appraisal. Using certain techniques, an appraiser will set the value on a piece of property. Using three complex techniques and then correlating results to come up with one best estimate. These three imperfect approaches to real estate market value are (1) the cost approach, (2) the comparative sales approach, and (3) the income approach.

The Cost Approach

The cost approach is based on the notion that an investor should not pay more for a property than it would cost to rebuild it at today's prices for land, labour, and construction materials. This approach to estimating value generally works well for new or relatively new buildings. Older properties, however, often suffer from wear and tear and outdated materials or design, making the cost approach more difficult to apply. To value these older properties, one would have to subtract some amount for physical and functional depreciation from the replacement cost estimates. Most experts agree that the cost approach is a good method to use as a check against a price estimate, but rarely should it be used exclusively.

The Comparative Sales Approach

The comparative sales approach uses as the basic input variable the sales prices of properties that are similar to a subject property. This method is based on the idea that the value of a given property is about the same as the prices for which other similar properties have recently sold. Of course, the catch here is that all properties are unique in some respect. Therefore the price that a subject property could be expected to bring must be adjusted upward or downward to reflect its superiority or inferiority to comparable properties.

Nevertheless, because the comparable sales approach is based on *selling* prices, not asking prices, it can give the investor a good feel for the market. As a practical matter, if the investor can find at least one sold property slightly better than the one he is looking at, and one slightly worse, their recent sales prices can serve to bracket an estimated market value for a subject property.

The Income Approach

Under the income approach a property's value is viewed as the present value of all its future income. The most popular income approach is called *direct capitalisation*. This approach is represented by the formula in Equation 1.

$$\text{Market value} = \frac{\text{Annual net operating income}}{\text{Market capitalisation rate}}$$

$$V = \frac{NOI}{R}$$

Annual net operating income (NOI) is calculated by subtracting vacancy and collection losses and property operating expenses, including property insurance and property taxes, from an income property's *gross potential* rental income. As estimated capitalisation rate -which technically means the rate used to convert an income stream to a present value — is obtained by looking at recent market sales figures and seeing what rate of return investors currently require. Then, by dividing the annual net operating income by the appropriate capitalisation rate, one gets an income property's estimated market value. An example of the application of the income approach is given in Table 1.

TABLE 1
Applying the Income Approach

Comparable Property	(1) NOI	(2) Sale Price	(3) (1) ÿ (2) Capitalization Rate (R)
A	₹ 16,250	₹ 1,82, 500	.0890
B	15,400	1,67,600	.0919
C	19,200	1,98,430	.0968
D	17,930	1,89,750	.0945

Subject property   ₹ 18,480

From this market-derived information an appraiser would work through Equation-1:

$$V = \frac{NOI}{R}$$

$$V = \frac{₹\ 18,480}{R}$$

$$V = \frac{₹\ 18,480}{.093*}$$

$$V = ₹\ 198.710$$

---

* Based on an analysis of the relative similarities of the comparables and the subject property, the appraiser decided the appropriate R equals .093.

Real estate valuation is a complex and technical procedure that requires reliable information about the features of comparable properties, their selling prices, and applicable terms of financing. As a result, rather than relying exclusively on their own judgement, many investors hire a real estate agent or a professional real estate appraiser to advise them about the market value of a property. As a form of insurance against overpaying, the use of an expert can be well worth the cost.

FORECASTING INVESTMENT RETURNS

Estimates of market value play an integral role in real estate decision making. Yet today more and more investors supplement their market value appraisals with investment analysis. This extension of the traditional approaches to value (cost, comparative sales, and income) gives investors a better picture of whether a selected property is likely to satisfy their investment objectives.

Market Value versus Investment Analysis

The concept of market value differs from investment analysis in four important ways: (1) retrospective versus prospective; (2) impersonal versus personal; (3) unleveraged versus leveraged; and (4) net operating income (NOI) versus after-tax cash flows.

Retrospective versus Prospective

Market value appraisals look backward; they attempt to estimate the price a property will sell for by looking at the sales prices of similar properties in the recent past. Under static market conditions such a technique can be reasonable. But if, say, interest rates, population, or buyer expectations are changing rapidly, past sales prices may not accurately indicate the current value or the future value of a subject property. In contrast, an investment analysis not only considers what similar properties have sold for, but also looks at the underlying determinants of value. An investment analysis tries to forecast such factors as economic base, population demographics and psychographics, availability and cost of mortgage financing, and potential sources of competition.

Impersonal versus Personal

As defined by professional appraisers, a market value estimate represents the price a property will sell for under certain specified conditions — in other words, a sort of market average. But in fact each buyer and seller has a unique set of needs, and each real estate transaction can be structured to meet those needs. So an investment analysis looks beyond what may constitute a "typical" transaction and attempts to evaluate a subject property's terms and conditions or sale (or rent) as they correspond to a given investor's constraints and goals.

For example, a market value appraisal might show that with normal financing and conditionsof sale, a property is worth ₹ 18,00,000. Yet because of personal tax consequences, it might be better for *a* seller to ask a higher price for the property and offer owner financing at a below-market interest rate.

Unleveraged versus Leveraged

The returns a real estate investment offers will be influenced by the amount of the purchase price that is financed. But simple income capitalisation $[V = (NOI/R)]$ does not incorporate alternative financing plans that might be available. It assumes either a cash or an unleveraged purchase.

The use of financing, or leverage, gives differing risk-return parameters to a real estate investment. Leverage automatically increases investment risk because borrowed funds must be repaid. Failure to repay a mortgage loan results in foreclosure and possible property loss. Alternatively, leverage may also increase return. If a property can earn a return in excess of the cost of the borrowed funds, the investor's return will be increased to a level well above what could have been earned from an all- cash deal. This is known as positive leverage. Conversely, if return is below debt cost, the return on invested equity will be less than from an all-cash deal. This is called negative leverage. The following example shows how leverage affects return and provides insight into the possible associated risks.

Assume an investor purchases a piece of land for ₹ 20,00,000. The investor has two financing choices. Choice A is all cash; that is, no leverage is employed. Choice B involves 80 percent financing (20 percent down payment) at 12 per cent interest. With leverage (choice B), the investor signs a ₹ 16,00,000 note (.80 x ₹ 20,00,000) at 12 percent interest with the entire principal balance due and payable at the end of one year. Now suppose the land appreciates during the year to ₹ 30,00,000 (A comparative analysis of this occurrence is presented in Table-2). Had the investor chosen the all-cash deal, the one-year return on the investor's initial equity is 50 per cent. The use of leverage would have magnified that return, no matter how much the property appreciated. The leveraged alternative (choice B) involved only a ₹ 4,00,000 investment in personal initial equity, with the balance financed by borrowing at 12 per cent interest. The property sells for ₹ 30,00,000 of which ₹ 4,00,000 represents the recovery of the initial equity investment, ₹ 16,00,000 goes to repay the principal balance on the debt, and

TABLE 2

The effect of Positive Leverage on Return: An Example*

Purchase price : ₹ 20,00,000
Sale price : ₹ 30,00,000
Holding period : one year

Item Number	Item	Choice A No Leaverage	Choice B 80% Financing
1	Initial equity	₹ 20,00,000	₹ 4,00,000
2	Loan principal	0	16,00,000
3	Sale price	30,00,000	30,00,000
4	Capital gain [(3) -()- (2)]	10,00,000	10,00,000
5	Interestcost[.12x(2)]	0	1,92,000
6	Net return [(4) - (5)]	10,00,000	8,08,000
	Return on investor's equity	₹ 10,00,000	₹ 8,08,000
	[(6)+(1)]	₹ 20,00,000 (+50%)	₹ 4,00,000 (+202%)

* To simplify this example, all value are presented on a before-.tax basis. To get the true return, taxes on the capital gain and the interest expense would be considered.

another ₹ 1,92,000 of gain is used to pay interest (₹ 16,00,000 x 0.12). The balance of the proceeds ₹ 8,08,000 represents the investor's return. The return on the investor's initial equity is 202 percent — over four times that provided by the no-leverage alternative, choice A.

We used 12 per cent in the above example, but it is important to understand that the cost of money has surprisingly little effect on comparative (leveraged versus unleveraged) returns; for example, using 6 per cent interest, the return on investor's equity rises to 226 percent, still way above the unleveraged alternative. Granted, using a lower interest cost does improve return, but, other things being equal, the thing that is really driving return on equity is the *amount* of leverage being used.

There is another side to the coin, however. For no matter what the eventual outcome, risk is *always* inherent in leverage; it can easily turn a bad deal into a disaster. Suppose the ₹ 20,00,000 property discussed above dropped in value by 25 per cent during the one-year holding period. The comparative results are presented in Table-3. The unleveraged investment has resulted in a negative return of 25 per cent. This is not large, however, compared to the leveraged position in which the investor loses not only the entire initial investment of ₹ 4,00,000 but an additional ₹ 2,92,000 (₹ 1,00,000 additional principal on the debt + ₹1,92,000 interest). The total loss of ₹ 6,92,000 on the original ₹ 4,00,000 of equity results in a (negative) return of 173 percent. Thus the loss in the leverage case is nearly seven times the loss experienced in the unleveraged situation.

TABLE 3

The Effect of Negative Leverage on Return (An Example*)

Purchase price : ₹ 20,00,000
Sale price : ₹ 15,00,000
Holding period : one year

Item Number	Item	Choice A No Leaverage	Choice B 80% Financing	
1	Initial equity	₹ 20,00,000	₹ 4,00,000	
2	Loan principal	0	16,00,000	
3	Sale price	15,00,000	15,00,000	
4	Capital gain [(3) -(1)- (2)]	5,00,000	5,00,000	
5	Interest cost [.12 x (2)]	0	1,92,000	
6	Net return [(4) - (5)]	5,00,000	6,92,000	
	Return on investor's equity	₹ 5,00,000 -25%	₹ 6,92,000	-173%
	[(6)+(1)]	₹ 20,00,000	₹ 4,00,000	

*   To simplify this example, all value are presented on a before-tax basis. To get the true return, taxes on the capital gain and the interest expense would be considered.

NOI versus After-Tax Cash Flows

Recall that to estimate market value, the income approach capitalises net operating income (NOI). To most investors, though, the NOI figure holds little meaning. The reason is that the majority of real estate investor finance their purchases. In additibn, few investors today can ignore the effect of tax law on their investment decisions. Investors want to know how much cash they will be required to put into a transaction, and how much cash they are likely to get out. The concept of NOI does not address these equations. In real estate the familiar finance measure of investment return — discounted cash flow — is a prime criterion for selecting real estate investments. Sometimes approximate yield also used to assess the suitability of a prospective real estate investment).

Calculating Discounted Cash Flow

Calculating discounted cash flow involves tne techniques of present value. From the net present value (NPV) — the difference between the present value of the cash flows and the amount of equity required to make the investment — the investor can find whether the proposed investment looks good (a positive net present value) or bad (a negative net present value).

This process of discounting cash flows to calculate the net present value (NPV) of an investment can be represented by the following equation:

$$\text{NPV} = \left[\frac{CF_1}{(1-r)^1} + \frac{CF_2}{(1-r)^2} + \dots + \frac{CFn-_1}{(1-r)^{n-1}} + \frac{CF_n + CF_{R_n}}{(1-r)^n} \right] - I_0$$

where

I_0 = the original required investment

CF_i = annual after-tax cash flow for year

CF_{R_n} = the after-tax net proceeds from sale (reversionary after-tax cash flow) occurring in year n.

r = the discount rate and $[1/(1+r)i]$ is the present-value interest factor for Re. 1 received in year z using an r percent discount rate.

In this equation the annual after-tax cash flows, CFs, may be either inflows to investors or outflows from them. Inflows would be preceded by a plus (+) sign, and outflows by a minus (-) sign.

Calculating Approximate Yield

An alternate way of assessing investment suitability would be to calculate the approximate yield. Restating the formula in terms of the variables defined above, we have:

$$\text{Approximate yield} = \frac{\overline{CF} + \dfrac{CF_{R_n} - I_0}{n}}{\dfrac{CF_{R_n} + I_0}{2}}$$

$$\text{where } \overline{CF} = \begin{array}{c} \text{average annual} \\ \text{after-tax cash} \\ \text{flow} \end{array} = \frac{CF_1 + CF_2 + CF_{n-1} + CF_n}{n}$$

If the calculated approximate yield is greater than the discount rate appropriate for the given investment, the investment would be acceptable. In that case, the net present value would be positive.

When consistently applied, the net present value and approximate yield approaches will always give the same recommendation for accepting or rejecting a proposed real estate investment.

COMPREHENSIVE EXAMPLE OF REAL ESTATE VALUATION

The Academic Apartments

S.K. Verma is deciding whether or not to buy the Academic Apartments. Verma believes he can improve his real estate investment decision making if he follows a systematic procedure. He designs a schematic framework of analysis. Following this framework, Verma (1) sets out his investment objectives, (2) analyses important features of the property, (3) investigates the determinants of the property's value, (4) calculates investment returns, and (5) synthesises and interprets the results of his analysis.

Investor Objectives

Verma is a tenured associate professor of management at GAM College. He is single, age 40, and earns an income of ₹ 75,00,000 per year from salary, consulting fees, stock dividends, and book royalties. His applicable tax rate on ordinary income is 30 percent. Verma wants to further diversify his investment portfolio. He would like to add a real estate investment that has good appreciation potential and also provides a positive yearly after-tax cash flow. For convenience, Verma requires the property to be close to his office, and he feels his talents and personality suit him for ownership of apartments. Verma has ₹ 60,00,000 cash to invest. On this amount he would like to earn a 13 per cent rate of return; toward this end, he has his eye on a small apartment building, the Academic Apartments.

Analysis of Important Features

The Academic building is located six blocks from the college student union. The building contains eight 2-bedroom, 2-bath units of 1,100 square feet each. It was built in 1995, and all systems and building components appear to be in good condition. The present owner gave Verma an income statement reflecting the property's 2009 income and expenses. The owner has further assured Verma that no adverse easements or encumbrances affect the building's title. Of course, if Verma decides to buy the apartment, he would have a lawyer verify the quality of the property rights associated with the property. For now, though he accepts the owner's word.

In this instance, Verma considers a five-year holding period reasonable. At present he is happy at GAM and thinks he will stay there at least until age 45. Verma defines the market for the property as a one-mile radius from campus. He reasons that students who walk to campus (the target market) would limit their choice of apartments to those that fall within that geographic area.

DETERMINANTS OF VALUE

Once Verma has analysed the important features, he next thinks about the factors that will determine the property's investment potential. As noted, these factors include: (1) demand, (2) the property, (3) supply, and (4) the transfer process.

Demand

The major institution, indeed the lifeblood institution in the market area, is GAM College. The base of demand for the Academic Apartments will grow (or decline) with the size of the college's employment and student enrollment. On this basis, Verma judges the prospects for the area to be in the range of good to excellent. During the coming five years, major funding (due to a ₹ 25 crore gift) will increase GAM's faculty by 35 percent, and expected along with faculty growth is a rise in the student population from 3,200 full- time students to 4,600 full-time students. Through further investigation Verma learns that 70 percent of the *new* students will live away from home. In the past GAM largely served the local market, but with its new affluence - and the resources this affluence can buy - the college will draw students from a wider geographic area. Furthermore, because GAM is a private college with relatively high tuition, the majority of students come from upper-middle- income families. Parental support can thus be expected to heighten students' ability to pay. Overall, then, Verma believes the major indicators of demand for the market are look promising.

The Property

Now the question becomes, *Will the Academic Apartments appeal to the desired market segment?* On this issue, Verma concludes the answer is yes. The property is zoned multifamily, and its present (and intended) use complies with all pertinent ordinances and housing codes. Of major importance, though, is the property's location. Not only does the site have good accessibility to the campus, but it is also three blocks from the Campus Town shopping district. In addition, the esthetic, socioeconomic, legal and fiscal environments of the property are compatible with student preferences.

On the negative side, the on-site parking has space for only few autos. Still, the building itself is attractive, and the relatively large 2-bedroom, 2-bath units are ideal for roommates. And although Verma has no experience managing apartments, he feels that if he studies several books on property management and applies his formal business education, he can succeed.

Supply

Verma realises that even strong demand and a good property cannot yield profits if a market suffers from oversupply. Too much competition has pushed many property owners and real estate developers into bankruptcy. Fortunately, Verma thinks that Academic Apartments is well insulated from competing units. Most important is the fact that the designated market area is fully built up, and as much as 80 percent of the area is zoned single-family residential. Any efforts to change the zoning would be strongly opposed by neighbourhood residents. The only potential problem that Verma sees is that the college; might build more student housing on campus. There has been some administrative talk about it, but as yet no funds have been allocated to such a project In sum, Verma concludes that the risk of oversupply in the Academic Apartment market area is low.

The Transfer Process

Since the real estate markets are *not efficient*, therefore before a property's sales price or rental income can reach its potential, an effective means to get information to buyers or tenants must be developed. Here, of course, Verma has great advantage. Notices on campus bulletin boards and announcements to his classes should be all he needs to keep the property rented. Although he might experience some vacancy during the summer months, Verma feels he could overcome this problem by requiring students to sign 12-month leases, but then grant them the right to sublet as long as the sublessees meet the tenant-selection criteria.

CALCULATING INVESTMENT RETURNS

Real estate cash flows depend on the underlying characteristics of the property and the market. Often real estate investors lose money because they "run the numbers" without doing their homework. So as we go through our investment calculations, remember that the numbers coming out will be no better than the numbers going in.

The Numbers

At present R.K. Nanda, the owner of the Academic Apartments, is asking ₹ 2.60 crore for the property. To assist in the sale, he is willing to offer owner financing to a qualified buyer. The terms would be 20 percent down, 11.5 percent interest, and full amortization of the outstanding mortgage balance over 30 years. The owner's income statement for 2009 is shown in Table-4. After talking with Nanda, Verma believes he would probably accept an offer of ₹ 60,00,000 down, a price of ₹ 2.45 crore and a 30-year mortgage at 11 percent. On this basis, Verma prepares his investment calculations.

TABLE 4

Income Statement, Academic Apartments, 2009

Gross rental income		₹ 32,16,000
(8 x₹ 33,500x12)		
Operationg expenses:		
Utilities	₹ 2,83,000	
Trash collection	67,500	
Repairs and maintenance	50,000	
Promotion and advertising	15,000	
Property insurance	84,000	
Property taxes	3,20,000	
Less : Total operating expenses		8,19,500
Net operating income (NOI)		₹ 23,96,500

Cash Flow Analysis

As a first step in cash flow analysis, Verma reconstructs the owner's income statement (as shown in Table-5). This reconstruction reflects higher rent levels, higher expenses, and a lower net operating income. Verma believes that due to poor owner management and deferred maintenance, the present owner is not getting as much in rents as the market could support. In addition, however, Nanda expenses understate those Verma is likely to incur. For one thing, a management expense should be deducted. Verma wants

TABLE 5

Reconstructed Income Statement, Academic Apartment, 2010

Gross rental income	₹ 37,80,000	
Less : Vacancy and collection losses at 4%	1,51,200	
Effective gross income (EGI)		₹ 36,28,800
Operating expenses:		
Management at 5% of EGI	₹ 1,81,400	
Utilities	3,10,000	
Trash collection	75,000	
Repairs and maintenance	2,40,000	
Promotion and advertising	15,000	
Property insurance	96,000	
Property taxes	4,29,200	
Less : Total operating expenses		13,46,600
Net operating income (NOI)		₹ 22,82,200

to separate what is rightfully a return on labour from his return on capital. Also, once the property is sold, a higher property tax assessment will be levied against it. Except for promotion and advertising, other expenses have been increased to adjust for inflation and a more extensive maintenance programme. With these adjustments, the expected NOI for Academic Apartments during 2010 is estimated at ₹ 22,82,200.

To move from NOI to after-tax cash flows (ATCFs), we need to perform the calculations shown in Table-6. From this table one can see that to calculate ATCF, one must first compute the income taxes or income tax savings Verma would incur as a result of property ownership. In this case potential tax savings accrue during the first three years because the allowable tax deductions of interest and depreciation exceed the property's net operating income; in the final two years, income exceeds deductions and as such, taxes are due. The 'magic' of simultaneously losing and making money is caused by depreciation. Assuming that the tax statutes incorporate this tax deduction, which is based on the original cost of the building, to reflect its declining economic life. However, since this deduction does not actually require a current cash outflow by the property owner, it acts as a *noncash expenditure* which reduces taxes and increases cash flow. In other words, in the 2010-12 period the property ownership provides Verma with a *tax shelter*; that is, Verma uses the income tax losses sustained on property to offset the taxable income he receives from salary, consulting fees, stock dividends, and book royalties.

TABLE 6

Cash Flow Analysis, Academic Apartment, 2010-2014

	2010	2011	2012	2013	2014
	INCOME TAX COMPUTATIONS				
NOI	₹ 22,82,200	₹ 24,41,900	₹ 26,12,800	₹ 27,95,700	₹ 29,91,400
— Interest*	20,35,000	20,25,900	20,14,600	20,14,600	19,87,700
— Depreciation**	6.54,500	6,54,500	6,54,500	6,54,500	6,54,500
Taxable income (loss)	(₹ 4,07,300)	(₹ 2,38,500)	(₹ 56,300)	₹ 1,39,000	₹ 3,49,200
Marginal tax rate	.3,000	.3,000	.3,000	.3,000	.3,000
Taxes (-) or tax savings (+)	+₹ 1,262,200	+₹ 71,500	+₹ 16,900	-₹41,700	- ₹ 1,04,800
	AFTER-TAX CASH FLOW (ATCF) COMPUTATIONS				
NOI	₹ 22,82,200	₹ 24,41,900	₹ 26,12,800	₹ 27,95,700	₹ 29,91,400
- Mortgage payment	21,28,000	21,28,000	21,28,000	21,28,000	21,28,000
Before-tax cash flow	₹ 1,54,200	₹ 3,13,900	₹ 4,84,800	₹ 6,67,700	₹ 8,63,400
+ Tax saving or - taxes	+ 1,26,200	+ 71,500	+ 16,900	-41,700	-1,04,800
After-tax cash flow (ATCF)	₹ 2,76,400	₹ 3,85,400	₹ 5,01,700	₹ 6,26,000	₹ 7,58,600

$$\text{average annual after-tax} = \frac{₹\,2,46,400 + ₹\,3,85,400 + ₹\,5,01,700 + ₹\,6,26,000 + ₹\,7,58,600}{5} = \frac{2,518,100}{5} = ₹\,5,03,620$$

cash flow

*   Based on a ₹ 1,85,00,000 mortgage at 11 percent compounded annually. Some rounding has been used.
**   Based on straight-line depreciation over 27.5 years and a depreciable basis of ₹ 1,80,00,000. Land value is assumed to equal ₹ 65,00,000.
*** Found by substituting values for ATCF.

Once the amount of taxes (or tax savings) is known, this amount is substracted (or added) to the before-tax cash flow. Because Verma qualifies as an "active manager" of the property and since his income is low enough, he can use the real estate losses to reduce his other income.

Proceeds from Sale

In this next step in his evaluation of the Academic Apartments, Verma must estimate the net proceeds he will receive when he sells the property. For purposes of this analysis, Verma has assumed a five-year holding period. Now he must forecast a selling price for the property. From that amount he must subtract selling expenses, the outstanding balance on the mortgage, and applicable taxes. The remainder equals Verma's after-tax net proceeds from sale. These calculations are shown in Table-7. (Note that although Verma's ordinary income is subject to a 30 per cent tax rate, the maximum rate of 28 per cent is applicable to the capital gain expected on sale of the property.)

TABLE 7

Estimated After-Tax Net Proceeds from Sale, Academic Apartments, 2015.

INCOME TAX COMPUTATIONS	
Forecasted selling price (at 5% annual appreciation)	₹ 3,12,62,000
— Selling expenses at 7%	21,88,300
— Book value (purchase price less accumulated depreciation)	2.12.27.500
Gain on sale	₹ 78,46,200
X Tax rate on gain*	28%
Tax payable	₹ 21,96,900

COMPUTATION OF AFTER-TAX NET PROCEEDS	
Forecasted selling price	₹ 3,12,62,000
— Selling expenses	21,88,300
— Mortgage balance outstanding	1.79.2.5400
Net proceeds before taxes	₹ 1,11,48,300
— Taxes payable (calculated above)	21,96,900
After-tax net proceeds from sale	₹ 89,51,400

*   Although Verma's ordinary income is taxed at 30 pecent rate, this gain would be taxed at the 28 percent.

Verma wants to estimate his net proceeds from sale conservatively. He believes that at a minimum, market forces will push up the selling price of the property at the rate of 5 percent per year beyond his assumed purchase price of ₹ 2,45,00,000. Thus he estimates the selling price in 5 years will be ₹ 3,12,62,000; he does this by multiplying the ₹ 2,45,00,000 by the future-value interest factor of 1.276 (that is ₹ 2,45,00,000 x 1.27,600 = ₹ 3,12,62,000). Making the indicated deductions from the forecasted selling price, Verma computes an after-tax net proceeds from the sale equal to ₹ 89,51,400

Discounted Cash Flow

In this step, Verma discounts the projected cash flows to their present value. In making this calculation (see Table-8) Verma finds that at his required rate of return of 13 percent the net present value of these flows equals ₹5,48,200.

TABLE 8

Net Present Value, Academic Apartments*

$$NPV = \left[\frac{CF_1}{(1+r)^1} + \frac{CF_2}{(1+r)^2} + \frac{CF_3}{(1+r)^3} + \frac{CF_4}{(1+r)^4} + \frac{CF_5\, CF_{R5}}{(1+r)^5}\right] = -10$$

$$NPV = \left[\frac{276{,}400}{(1+13)^1} + \frac{385{,}400}{(1+13)^3} + \frac{501{,}700}{(1+13)^3} + \frac{626{,}000}{(1+13)^4} + \frac{758{,}600 + 89{,}51{,}400**}{(1+1.3)^5}\right] - ₹\,60{,}00{,}000***$$

$$NPV = ₹\,2{,}44{,}600 + ₹\,3{,}01{,}800 + ₹\,3{,}47{,}700 + ₹\,3{,}83{,}900 + ₹\,52{,}70{,}200 - ₹\,60{,}00{,}000$$

$$NPV = ₹\,65{,}48{,}200 - ₹\,60{,}00{,}000$$

$$NPV = +₹5{,}48{,}200$$

---

*   All inflows are assumed to be end-fo-period receipts.

**   Includes both the fifth year annual after-tax cash flow of ₹ 758,600 and the after-tax net proceeds from sale of ₹ 89,51,400.

*** Calculated using present-value interest factors.

Approximate Yield

Alternatively, the approximate yield formula could be applied using the initial equity, I_0 of ₹ 60,00,000, along with the average annual after-tax cash flow, CF, of ₹ 5,03,600 (calculated at the bottom of Table 6), and the after-tax proceeds from sale, $CF_{R5'}$ of ₹ 89,51,400 (calculated in Table 7). Substituting these values into the approximate yield formula:

$$\text{Approximate yield} = \frac{₹5{,}03{,}600 + \dfrac{₹\,89{,}51{,}400 - ₹\,60{,}00{,}000}{5}}{\dfrac{₹\,89{,}51{,}400 + ₹\,60{,}00{,}000}{2}} = \frac{₹5{,}03{,}600 + ₹5{,}90{,}300}{₹\,74{,}75{,}700}$$

$$= \frac{₹10{,}93{,}900}{₹74{,}75{,}700} = 14.63\%$$

Since the approximate yield of 14.7 percent is in excess of Verma's required rate of return of 13 percent, the investment meets (and exceeds) his acceptance criterion. Although we have merely approximated his return here, this technique, when consistently applied, should always result in the same conclusion as to acceptability as that obtained using net present value.

SYNTHESIS AND INTERPRETATION

Now comes the time for Verma to review his work. He evaluates his market analysis, checks all the facts and figures in the investment return calculations, and then evaluates the results in light of his stated financial and nonfinancial objectives. He must ask himself: All things considered, is the expected payoff worth the risk? In this case, he decides it is. The property looks good. Even a positive finding, however, does not necessarily mean Verma should buy this property. He might still want to shop around to see if he can locate an even better investment. Furthermore, he might be wise to hire a real estate appraiser to confirm that the price he is willing to pay seems reasonable with respect to the recent sales prices of similar properties in the market area. Nevertheless, being an academic, Verma realises that any problem can be studied to death; no one ever can obtain all the information that will bear on a decision. He gives himself a week to investigate other properties and talk to a professional appraiser. If nothing turns up to cause him second thoughts, he decides that he will offer to buy the Academic Apartments. On the terms presented, he is willing to pay up to a maximum price of ₹ 2.45 crore.

Thus, the starting point for real estate investment analysis is setting objectives. This includes straints and goals, and analysing important features such as the physical property, its associated legal rights, the relevant time period, and the geographic area of concern. Investment real estate includes income properties and speculative properties. Income properties can be residential, which includes single-family and multi- family properties, or commercial, which includes office buildings, shopping centres, etc. Speculative properties, such as raw land, are expected to provide returns from appreciation in value rather than from periodic rental income as it the case for income properties. The four determinants of real estate value are demand, supply, the property, and the transfer process. *Demand* refers to people's willingness and ability to buy or rent, and *supply* includes all those properties from which potential buyers or tenants can choose. To analyse a property, applicable restrictions on its use, its location, site characteristics, improvements and property management should be evaluated. The transfer process involves promotion and negotiation of a property. A market value appraisal can be used to estimate real estate value. It relies on the cost approach, the comparative sales approach, and the income approach. An expert can be hired to give advice with regard to property's market value. Investment returns can be estimated by forecasting cash flows and calculating either the net present value or the approximate yield. Risk and return parameters vary depending on the degree of leverage employed in financing a real estate investment. Of course, any quantitative analysis of real estate value and returns must be integrated with various subjective and market considerations prior to making the investment decision.

REVIEW PROBLEMS

1. An individual borrows ₹ 10,00,000 for ten years and agrees to make annual payments that retire the loan and pay 12 percent interest on the declining balance owed. What is the annual payment?

Ans:

$$₹\,10{,}00{,}000 = \frac{X}{(1+0.12)^1} + \ldots + \frac{X}{(1+0.12)^{10}}$$

Since the periodic payments will be equal, this equation may be solved by the use of the present value of an annuity table. Thus:

₹10,00,000   = X times the interest factor for the present value of an annuity at 12% for 10 years

₹10,00,000   = X (5.650)

$$X \;=\; \frac{₹\,10{,}00{,}000}{5.650} = ₹\,1{,}76{,}991$$

2. Refer to problem 1, if the individual is to make monthly payments to retire the loan, what would be the monthly payment?

Ans:

$$\text{₹}10,00,000 = \frac{X}{\left[1+\dfrac{0.12}{12}\right]} + \dots + \frac{X}{\left[1+\dfrac{0.12}{12}\right]} \, 10\times12$$

₹10,00,000	=	X times the interest factor for the present value of an annuity at 1 per cent for 120 time periods
₹10,00,000	=	X (69.698)
X	=	₹ 14,348

The monthly payment is ₹ 14,348. Notice that this amount is less than ₹ 1,76,991 divided by 12 months (₹ 14,749 per month). Since the loan is being retired more rapidly (i.e. every month the principal is reduced), the effect is to reduce the total amount of interest paid and thus decrease the total monthly payment.

QUESTIONS

1. Why should real estate investment analysis start with a definition of objectives?
2. How can adding real estate to your investment portfolio decrease your overall risk? Explain.
3. Define and differentiate between income properties and speculative properties. Differentiate between and give examples of residential and commercial income properties.
4. Which are more important when considering real estate investments, financial or nonfinancial considerations?
5. Briefly describe the important factors to consider when making a real estate investment.
6. Why is property management important to a real estate investor?
7. Are real estate markets efficient? Why or why not?
8. Comment on the following: Market value is always the price at which a property sells.
9. Briefly describe the approaches commonly used by real estate appraisers to estimate the market value of investment properties.
10. Real estate investments can be structured to meet a variety of investment goals. Explain various investment needs and the types of properties that best meet them.
11. What is leverage and what role does it play in real estate investment? How does it effect the risk-return parameters of a real estate investment?
12. Define: (a) net operating income (NOI) and (b) after- tax cash flow (ATCF) as they apply to income from rental properties.
13. Explain why, in spite of being acceptable based on NPV or approximate yield, a real estate investment might still not be acceptable to a given investor.
14. Describe the procedures for setting real estate investment objectives, including consideration of investment characteristics, constraints and goals, and analysis of important features.
15. Explain the key determinants of value in real estate: demand, supply, the property, and the property transfer process.
16. Discuss the valuation techniques commonly used to estimate the market value of real estate.
17. Discuss the investment characterisics of a real estate.
18. Compare and contrast the major ways in which individuals can invest in real estate.

19. What are the risks associated with investing in real estate? In what ways are they similar to the risks associated with investments in financial assets? Why may an investment in real estate be more risky than an investment in an equity or a bond?

PROBLEMS

1. Consider the following potential real estate investment:

Year	After-tax Cash Flow	After-tax Reversal Value
0	₹10,00,000	
1	11,50,000	
2	2 6,00,000	
3	34,00,000	₹12,50,000

(a) Assume an after-tax required rate of return on equity of 15%. Calculate the NPV and indicate whether the real estate appears to be an acceptable investment.
(b) Calculatew the IRR and indicate whether the real estate appears to be an acceptable investment.

2. Consider the following information on a small apartment complex that is being considered as an investment:

Purchase price	₹25,00,000
Holding period	4 Years
Estimate of annual net operating income	₹5,00,000
Annual debt service	₹1,00,000
Estimated annul tax liability	₹80,000
Estimated of after-tax reversion values	₹30,00,000
After tax required rate of return on equity	15%

(a) Calculate the annual after-tax flow.
(b) Calculate the NPV and indicate whether the property is an acceptable investment based on the analysis.
(c) Calculate the IRR and indicate whether the property is an acceptable investment based on the analysis.
(d) Discuss the factors that need to be analysed before a final investment decision is made.

3. In 1984, the average and medium price of a single- family home were approximately ₹ 48,700 and ₹ 55,100 respectively. Ten years later, these prices had risen to ₹ 88,700 and ₹ 1,12,000. During the same period the XYZ Stock Index rose from 805 to 2149, and the ABC Stock Index rose from 96 to 271. Compare the annual rate of increase in house prices to the rate of growth in these two popular aggregate measures of the stock market.

Home:	6.2%
ABC Stock Index:	10.9%

4. What is the expected cash flow and tax liability (or savings) for the first two years for an investment in an apartment building given the following information:

Cost of the building	₹ 8,00,000
Cost of the land	2,00,000
Required from payment	25%

Interest on balance owed	10%
Annual principal repayment	20,000
Annual operating expenses	30,000
Rent, yearly	1,20,000
Annual depreciation expense	40,000
Individual owner's income tax rate	30%

Ans: Earnings before taxes/year 2: - ₹ 3,000

Cash flow year 1: ₹ 2,500 after tax savings and principal repayment

5. Determine the annual repayment schedule for the first two years (i.e., interest owed, principal repayment, and balance owed) for a ₹ 60,000 conventional mortgage for 25 years at 10 per cent. Assume that only one payment is made annually.

Ans: Interest payment: ₹ 6,000

Principal repayment: ₹ 610.11

Balance owed :   ₹ 59,3889.99

6. C.C. Mehta, an investor, is considering two alternative financing plans for purchasing a parcel of real estate costing ₹ 50,00,000. Alternative X involves paying cash alternative Y involves obtaining 80 percent financing at 10.5 percent interest. If the piece of real estate appreciates in value by ₹ 7,50,000 in one year, calculate: (a) Mehta's net return and (b) his return on equity for each alternative. If the value dropped by ₹ 7,50,000, what effect would this have on your answers to (a) and (b)?

7. In the coming year, G.S. Sundram expects a potential rental property investment costing ₹ 12,00,000 to have gross potential rental income of ₹ 2,00,000, vacancy and collection losses equalling 5 percent of gross income, and operating expenses of ₹ 1,00,000. The mortgage on the property is expected to require annual payments of ₹ 85,000. The interest portion of the mortgage payments as well as depreciation is given below for each of the next three years. The G.S. Sundram is in the 30-percent marginal tax bracket.

Year	Interest	Deprec
1	₹ 83,000	₹ 45,000
2	₹ 82,000	₹ 45,000
3	₹ 81,000	₹ 45,000

The net operating income is expected to increase by 6 percent each year beyond the first year

(a) Calculate the net operating income (NOI) for each of the next three years.
(b) Calculate the after-tax cash flow (ATCF) for each of the next three years

8. Ashok Sharma is contemplating selling rental property originally costing ₹ 40,00,000. He believes that it has appreciated in value at an annual rate of 6 percent over its four-year holding period. He will have to pay a commission equal to 5 percent of the sale price to sell the property. Currently the property has a book value of ₹ 2,74,000. The mortage balance outstanding at the time of sale currently is ₹ 31,00,000. Sharma will have to paya 28 percent tax on any capital gains.

(a) Calculate the tax payable on the proposed sale.
(b) Calculate the after-tax net proceeds associated with the proposed sale, CF_R.

9. R.V. Raman has estimated the annual after-tax cash flows (ATCFs) and after-tax net proceeds from sale (CF$_R$) of a proposed real estate investment as noted below for the planned four-year ownership period

Year	ATCF	CF$_R$
1	62,000	
2	80,000	
3	83,000	
4	85,000	
4		5,90,000

The initial required investment in the property is ₹ 5,50,000, at minimum, must earn 14 percent on the investment.

(a) Calculate the net present value (NPV) of the proposed investment.
(b) Calculate the approximate yield from the investment.
(c) From your findings in (a) and (b) what recommendations would you give to Raman? Explain.

10. G.N. Shah wants to estimate the market value of the HRT Apartments, on 18-unit building with nine 1-bedroom units and nine 2-bedroom units. The present owner of HRT provided Shah with the following annual income statement. Today's date is March 1, 2011.

OWNER'S INCOME STATEMENT HRT APARTMENTS, 2010

Gross Income		₹ 65,88,000
Less : Expenses		
Utilities	₹ 14,26,000	
Property insurance	2,73,000	
Repairs & Maintenance	1,39,000	
Property taxes	4,79,000	
Mortgage payments	18,38,000	
Total expenses:		41,55,000
Net Income		₹ 24,33,000

Current rental rates of properties similar to HRT typically run from ₹ 30,000 to ₹ 31,500 per year for 1- bedroom units and ₹ 34,000 to ₹ 36,000 per year for 2- bedroom units. From a study of the market, Shah determined that a reasonable required rate of return for HRT would be 9.62 percent and that vacancy rates for comparable apartment buildings are running around 4 percent. Since Shah has studied economics and knows all about demand and supply, yet he does not understand how to apply it.

1. Advise Shah in a practical way how he might incorporate demand and supply into an investment analysis of the HRT Apartments.
2. Should Shah accept the owner's income statement as the basis for an income appraisal of HRT Apartments. Why or why not?
3. In your opinion what is the reasonable estimate of the market value for the HRT?
4. If Shah could buy HRT for ₹ 10,00,000 less than its market would it be a good investment for him ? Explain.

REFERENCES

1. Blankenship, Frank J. *The Prentice-Hall Real Estate Investor's Encyclopedia.* Englewood Cliffs, N.J.: Prentice-Hall, 1989.

2. Case, Fred E. *The Investment Guide to Home and Land Purchase.* Englewood Cliffs, N.J.: Prentice-Hall, 1978.

3. Corley, Robert N., Peter J. Shedd, and Charles F. Floyd. *Real Estate and the Law.* New York: Random House, 1982.

4. Creedy, Judith, and Norbert F. Wall. *Real Estate Investment by Objectives.* New York: McGraw-Hill, 1979.

5. English, Wesley John, and Grey Emerson Cardiff. *The Coming Real Estate Crash.* New Rochelle, N.Y.: Arlington House, 1979.

6. Floyd, Charles F. *Real Estate Principles.* 3d ed. Chicago: Dearborn Trade, 1992.

7. Greenebaum, Mary. "A Golden Opportunity to Pass Up." *Fortune,* September 1981.

8. Grissom, Terry V., James L. Kuhle, and Carl H. Walther. "Diversification Works in Real Estate, Too." *Journal of Portfolio Management* (winter 1987): 66-71.

9. Gyourko, Joseph, and Donald B. Keim. "Risk and Return in Real Estate: Evidence from a Real Estate Stock Index." *Financial Analysts Journal* (September/October 1993): 39-46.

10. Kimmel, Kenneth M. *Real Estate Investment.* New York: Cornerstone Library, 1980.

11. Parcey, Robert W., and Stuart K. Webster. "City Leases: Up Front, Out Back, In the Closet." *Financial Analysts Journal,* September-October 1980.

12. Sheerin, James J. *The Complete Guide to Buying, Selling and Investing in Undeveloped Land.* Chicago: Probus, 1986.

13. Shiratsuka, S. (1999), Asset Prices Fluctuation and Price Indices, Monitary and Economic Studies.

14. Sutton, G. (2002), 'Explaining Changes in House Prices, BIS Quarterly Review

15. Unger, Maurice A., and George R. Karvel. *Real Estate: Principles and Practice.* 9th ed. Cincinnati: South-Western Publishing Co., 1990.

19

Money Market

INTRODUCTION

Money markets are markets for short-term financial assets that are close substitutes for money usually with maturities of less than a year. The deregulation of money markets and their development are an essential component of financial sector reform. Well-functioning money markets provide a relatively safe income- yielding outlet for the short-term investment of funds both for banks and firms and can also be an important source of short term funds to banks in need of quick liquidity. Well developed money markets are an essential prerequisite for the efficacy of monetary policy in a deregulated financial environment with the central bank having to increasingly use indirect tools of monetary control such as open market operations to equilibrate the demand and supply of bank reserves. The effective use of open market operations greatly depends on an active secondary market for T-bills and the linkages between the T-bill market and other key money markets, in particular the Inter-Bank call money market.

Indian money markets were fairly underdeveloped till the mid- eighties. The most prominent of money markets during this time was the Inter-Bank call money market which was a restricted market with a narrow base and a limited number of participants. The T-bill market was also very narrow with Reserve Bank of India holding most of the T-bills outstanding. Key money market instruments which are common in the developed markets of the advanced market economies such as certificates of deposit and commercial paper did not exist. Since the mid-eighties, however, money markets in India have undergone a great deal of change. Instrumental in this change has been the recommendations of two influential committee reports commissioned by the Reserve Bank of India in the mid-eighties, the Chakravarty committee which submitted its report in 1985 and the Vaghul committee which submitted its report in 1987.

The Chakravarty committee was mostly concerned with reviewing the working of the monetary system. Therefore, with respect to money markets, its attention was mostly centered around the Treasury bill market and ways to develop the latter so as to gradually use the T-bill as an important instrument of monetary policy. The objective of the Vaghul committee, on the other hand, was to examine the entire spectrum of money markets in India and to recommend specific measures for their development. The Chakravarty and Vaghul committees reports provided a blueprint to the Reserve Bank of India on how best to deregulate and develop Indian money markets and most of the reforms that have occurred in the latter since the mid-eighties can be seen as an outcome of the recommendations of these two reports.

CHARACTERISTICS OF THE MONEY MARKET

To the causal observer, the nation's financial markets appear to be one vast cauldron of borrowing and lending activity in which some individuals and institutions are seeking credit while others supply the funds needed to make be basically the same borrowers issue securities which lenders purchase. When the loan is repaid, the borrower retrieves the securities and returns funds to the lender. Closer examination of financial institutions reveals, however, that beyond the simple act of exchanging securities for funds, there are major differences between one financial transaction and another. The purposes for which money is borrowed within the financial system vary greatly from person to person, institution to institution, and transaction to transaction. And the different purposes for which money is borrowed result in the creation of different kinds of financial assets, having different maturities, yields, default risks, and other features.

In the nation's money market, loans have an original maturity of one year or less. Money market loans are used to help corporations and governments pay the wages and salaries of their workers, make repairs, purchase inventories, pay dividends and taxes, and satisfy other short-term working-capital needs. In this respect the money market stands in sharp contrast to the capital market. The capital market deals in long-term credit that has over a year to maturity and is usually used to finance capital investment projects whereas the money market deals with the market for short-term credit.

The broad objectives of the money market are threefold: First, it should provide an equilibrating mechanism for evening out short- term surpluses and deficits. Secondly, the money market should provide a focal point for central bank intervention for influencing liquidity in the economy. Thirdly, it should provide reasonable access to users of short-term money to meet their requirements at a realistic price.

The third objective is particularly important from the point of view of an efficient banking system. In the existing money market with tightly administered interest rates restricted entry and limited Reserve Bank refinance, banks having liquidity problems to obtains cannot, in the short-run, equilibrate their position. In the absence of adequate liquidities for obtaining very short- term funds defaults in the maintenance of reserve requirements pose a real danger and banks face a dilemma of deciding between maintaining large excess liquidity or facing the consequences of defaults, both of which impinge on the profitability of banks. As such it is imperative to develop a money market which can genuinely equilibrate in the short term and provide a viable alternative to defaults in the maintenance of reserve requirements.

To achieve these objectives, the Reserve Bank has accorded prime attention to the development of the money market as it is the key link in the transmission mechanism of monetary policy to financial markets and finally, to the real economy. (See Exhibit-1). In the past, development of the money market was hindered by a system of administered interest rates and lack of proper accounting and risk management systems. With the initiation of reforms and the transition to indirect, market-based instruments of monetary policy in the 1990s, the Reserve funk made conscious efforts to develop an efficient, stable and liquid money market by creating a favourable policy environment through appropriate institutional changes, instruments, technologies and market practices. Accordingly, the call money market was developed into primarily an inter-bank market, while encouraging other market participants to migrate towards collateralised segments of the market, thereby increasing overall market integrity.

EXHIBIT-1

Money Market Instruments For Liquidity Management

The Reserve Bank has been making efforts to develop a repo market outside the LAF for bank and nonbank participants, so as to provide a stable collateralised funding alternative with a view to promoting smooth transformation of the call/notice money market into a pure inter-bank market and for deepening the underlying government securities market. Thus, the following new instruments have been introduced.

Collateralised Borrowing and Lending Obligation (CBLO)

i) Developed by the Clearing Corporation of India Limited and introduced on January 20, 2003, it is a discounted instrument available in electronic book entry form for the maturity period ranging from one day to ninety days (can be made available up to one year as per RBI guidelines).

ii) In order to enable the market participants to borrow and lend funds, CCIL provides the Dealing System through Indian Financial Network (INFINET), a closed user group to the Members of the Negotiated Dealing System (NDS) who maintain Current account with Reserve Bank and through Internet for other entities who do not maintain Current account with Reserve Bank.

iii) Membership (including Associate Membership) of CBLO segment is extended to banks, financial institutions, insurance companies, mutual funds, primary dealers, NBFCs, non-Government Provident Funds, Corporates, *etc.*

iv) Eligible securities are Central Government securities including Treasury Bills.

v) Borrowing limits for members is fixed by CCIL at the beginning of the day taking into account the securities deposited by borrowers in their CSGL account with CCIL. The securities are subjected to necessary hair-cut after marking them to market.

vi) Auction market is available only to NDS Members for overnight borrowing and settlement on T+0 basis. At the end of the auction market session, CCIL initiates auction matching process based on Uniform Yield principle.

vi) CCIL assumes the role of the central counter party through the process of novation and guarantees settlement of transactions in CBLO.

vii) Automated value-free transfer of securities between market participants and the CCIL was introduced during 2004-05.

viii) Members can reckon unencumbered securities for SLR calculations.

ix) The operations in CBLO are exempted from cash reserve requirement (CRR).

Market Repo

i) To broaden the repo market, the Reserve Bank enabled non-banking financial companies, mutual funds, housing finance companies and insurance companies not holding SGL accounts to undertake repo transactions with effect from March 3, 2003. These entities were permitted to access the repo market through their 'gilt accounts' maintained with the custodians.

ii) Subsequently, non-scheduled urban cooperative banks and listed companies with gilt accounts with scheduled commercial banks were allowed to participate.

iii) Necessary precautions were built into the system to ensure 'delivery versus payment' (DvP) and transparency, while restricting the repos to Government securities only.

iv) Rollover of repo transactions in Government securities was facilitated with the enabling of DvP III mode of settlement in government securities which involves settlement of securities and funds on a net basis, effective April 2, 2004. This provided significant flexibility to market participants in managing their collateral.

Some Assessments

i) CBLO and market repo helped in aligning short-term money market rates to the LAF corridor.

ii) Mutual funds and insurance companies are generally the main supplier of funds while banks, primary dealers and corporates are the major borrowers in the repo market outside the LAF.

In line with the objective of widening and deepening of the money market and imparting greater liquidity to the market for facilitating efficient price discovery, new instruments, such as collateralised lending and borrowing obligations (CBLO), have been introduced. Money market instruments such as market repo and CBLO have provided avenues for non-banks to manage their short-term liquidity mismatches and facilitated the transformation of the call money market into a pure inter-bank market. Furthermore, issuance norms and maturity profiles of other money market instruments such as commercial paper (CP) and certificates of deposit (CDS) have been modified over time to encourage wider participation while strengthening the transmission of policy signals across the various market segments. The abolition of *ad hoc* Treasury Bills and introduction of regular auctions of Treasury Bills paved the way for the emergence of a risk free rate, which has become a benchmark for pricing the other money market instruments. Concomitantly, with the increased market orientation of monetary policy along with greater global integration of domestic markets, the Reserve Bank's emphasis has been on setting prudential limits on borrowing and lending in the call money market, encouraging migration towards the collateralised segments and developing derivative instruments for hedging market risks. This has been complemented by the institutionalisation of the Clearing Corporation of India Limited (CCIL) as a central counterparty. The upgradation of payment system technologies has also enabled market participants to improve their asset liability management. All these measures have widened and deepened the money market in terms of instruments and participants, enhanced transparency and improved the signalling mechanism of monetary policy while ensuring financial stability.

These policy initiatives over time have led to the development of a relatively deep, liquid and vibrant money market in the country. Activity in all the segments has increased significantly, especially during the last three years. With the development of market repo and CBLO segments, the call money market has been transformed into a pure inter-bank market from August 2005. A recent noteworthy development is the substantial migration of money market activity from the uncollateralised call money segment to the collateralised market repo and CBLO markets. Thus, uncollateralised overnight transactions are now limited to banks and primary dealers in the interest of financial stability.

In order to improve transparency and efficiency in the money market, reporting of all call/notice money market transactions through negotiated dealing system (NDS) within 15 minutes of conclusion of the transaction was made mandatory. Furthermore, a screenbased negotiated quote-driven system for all dealings in the call/notice and the term money markets (NDS-CALL), developed by the Clearing Corporation of India Limited (CCIL), was operationalised in September 2006 to ensure better price discovery.

In the development of various constituents of the money market, the most significant aspect was the growth of the collateralised market vis-à-vis the uncollateralised market. Over the last decade, while the daily turnover in the call money market either stagnated or declined, that of the collateralised segment, market repo plus CBLO, increased manifold.

Since 2007–08, both the CP and CD volumes have also increased very significantly. Furthermore, issuance of 91-treasury bills has also increased sharply. The overall money market now is much larger relative to GDP than a decade ago.

Alongside, the rates of return on various instruments in the money market have shown greater co-movement, especially since the introduction of LAF (Table 1).

TABLE 1

Interest Rates in the Money Market

(Percent Per Annum: Annual Averages)

	Repo Rate	Call Rate	CBLO Rate	Market Repo Rate	91 day T-Bills	364-day T-Bills	CP Rate	CD Rate
1	2	3	4	5	8	9		
2000-01	11.2	9.1	-	-	9.0	9.8	10.8	9.6
2001-02	8.5	7.2	-	-	7.0	7,3	9.2	8.0
2002-03	7.7	5.9	-	-	5.8	5.9	7.7	6.6
2003-04	7.0	4.6	-	-	4.6	4.7	6 J	5.3
2004-05	6,0	4.7	-	-	-4.9	5.2	5.g	5.0
2005-06	6,2	5.6	5.5	5.4	5.7	6.0	6.7	6.1
2006-07	7.0	7.2	6,2	6.3	6.6	7.0	8.5	7.9
2007-08	7,8	6.1	5.2	5.5	7.1	7.5	9.3	9 1
2008-09	7,4	7.1	6.1	6.5	7.1	7.2	10.7	9.2
2009-10	4.8	3.2	2.7	2.8	3.6	4.4	5.3	5.4
2010-11	5.9	5.7	5.4	5.5	6.2	6.6	8.7	7.7
2011-12	8.0	8.1	7.8	7.9	8.4	8.4	10.1	9.6
2013-14 (so far)	8.0	8.1	7.9	8.0	8.2	8.1	9.3	9.0

The operating framework of monetary policy has been the maintenance of overnight market rates within an interest rate corridor defined by the floor of the reverse repo (absorption) rate and ceiling of the repo (injection) rate. During periods of system wide excess liquidity, overnight rates tend to hug the bottom of the corridor, while touching the ceiling during other periods of liquidity shortage, as might be expected. Increased volatility in capital flows, tending to inject excess liquidity into the system, and in government cash balances resulting from bunching of tax payments that suck liquidity out of the system, make the task of liquidity management somewhat more difficult. Consequently, volatility in overnight rates has increased in recent months relative to previous years, with overnight rates breaching both ends of the corridor.

As a result of various reform measures, the money market in India has undergone significant transformation in terms of volume, number of instruments and participants and development of risk management practices. In line with the shifts in policy emphasis, various segments of the money market have acquired greater depth and liquidity. The price discovery process has also improved. The call money market has been transformed into a pure inter-bank market, while other money market instruments such as market repo and CBLO have developed to provide avenues to non-banks for managing their short-term liquidity mismatches. The money market has also become more efficient as is reflected in the narrowing of the bid-ask spread in overnight rates. The abolition of *ad hoc* Treasury Bills and introduction of Treasury Bills auction have led to the emergence of a risk free rate, which acts as a benchmark for the pricing of other money market instruments.

MONEY MARKET INSTRUMENTS

Call/Notice Money Market

The overnight inter-bank call money market, in which banks trade positions to maintain cash reserves, is the key segment of the money market in India. It is basically an 'over the counter' (OTC) market without the intermediation of brokers. Participation has been gradually widened to include other financial institutions, primary/satellite dealers, mutual funds and other participants in the bills rediscounting market and corporates (through primary dealers) besides banks, LIC and UTI. While banks and primary dealers are allowed two-way operations, other non-bank entities can only participate as lenders. As per the announced policies, once the repo market develops, the call money market would be made into a pure inter-bank market, including primary dealers.

The call money market is influenced by liquidity conditions (mainly governed by deposit mobilisation, capital flows and the Reserve Bank's operations affecting banks' reserve requirements on the supply side and tax outflows, government borrowing programme, non-food credit off-take and seasonal fluctuations, such as, large currency drawals during the festival season on the demand side). At times of easy liquidity, call rates tend to hover around the Reserve Bank's repo rate, which provides a ready avenue for parking short-term surplus funds. During periods of tight liquidity, call rates tend to move up towards the Bank Rate and more recently the Reserve Bank's reverse repo rate (and sometimes beyond) as the Reserve Bank modulates liquidity in pursuit of-monetary stability. Besides, there are other influences, such as, (i) the reserve requirement prescriptions (and stipulations regarding average reserve maintenance), (ii) the investment policy of non-bank participants in the call market which are among the large suppliers of funds in the call market, and (iii) the asymmetries of the call money market, with few lenders and chronic borrowers.

In recent times, money market rates edged up, broadly moving in line with the policy rates, with intra-year movements depending upon the evolving liquidity conditions. Since the outbreak of the global financial crisis in September 2008, the RBI has followed an accommodative monetary policy. In the course of 2009-10, this stance was principally geared towards supporting early recovery of the growth momentum, while facilitating the unprecedented borrowing requirement of the Government to fund its fiscal deficit. The fact that the latter was managed well with nearly two-thirds of the borrowing being completed in the first half of the fiscal year not only helped in checking undue pressure on interest rates, but also created the space for the revival of private investment demand in the second half of the year.

The transmission of monetary policy measures continues to be sluggish and differential in its impact across various segments of the financial markets. The downward revisions in policy rates announced by the RBI post-September 2008 got transmitted into the money and G-Sec markets; however, the transmission has been slow and lagged the in the case of the credit market. Though lending rates of all categories of banks (public, private and foreign) declined marginally from March 2009 (with benchmark prime . lending rates [BPLR] of scheduled commercial banks [SCBs] having declined by 25 to 100 basis points), the decline was not sufficient to accelerate the demand for bank credit. Consequently, while borrowers have turned to alternate sources of possibly cheaper finance to meet their funding needs, banks flush with liquidity parked their surplus funds under the reverse repo window.

There has been continuous moderation in the growth in broad money (M3) from around 21 per cent at the beginning of the fiscal year to 16.5 per cent as of mid-January 2010 and it has remained below the indicated growth projection for the period. While in the first half of the year, credit to the Government remained the key driver of money growth, since the third quarter of 2009-10 that too has moderated.

The money market remained by and large orderly during 2009-10, due to the prevailing surplus liquidity conditions. Call rate continued to hover around the reverse repo rate during Q1 of 2009-10 and averaged 3.2 per cent as compared to 4.2 per cent during the last quarter of 2008-09. During the second quarter of 2009-10, the call rate averaged 3.25 per cent. Even in the third quarter, the call rate continued to hover around the lower bound of the informal LAF corridor. The average call rate was placed at 3.20 per cent during this period.

The money market generally remained orderly during 2010-11. At the commencement of the financial year 2010-11, the call rate mostly remained around the lower bound of the informal LAF corridor up to May 2010. With the tightening of liquidity conditions since end-May 2010, reflecting migration of liquidity to the Central Government account with the RBI on account of 3G auction/ advance tax payments, the call rate firmed up. The average daily call rate for the first quarter was at 4.16 per cent. It hovered around the upper bound of the LAF corridor till July 2010 as deficit liquidity conditions persisted due to the high Central Government cash balances. The call rate declined towards the end of August and early September with the change in liquidity conditions. However, it again firmed up from the middle of September 2010 and breached the upper bound of the informal LAF corridor in the second half of the month reflecting the onset of high deficit liquidity conditions. The average call rate increased to 5.40 per cent in the second quarter (Table 1). The call rate has mostly remained above the upper bound of the corridor in the third quarter of 2010-11 so far, reflecting the increased liquidity stress in the system. The average call rate was 6.59 per cent in the third quarter of 2010-11 (till 20 December 2010).

Interest rates in the collateralized segments of the money market-the market repo (outside the LAF) and the collateralized borrowing and lending obligation (CBLO)—also moderated in tandem with the behaviour of the call rate and remained below the call rate during 2009-10. The weighted average interest rate in the collateralized segment of the money market marginally increased from 2.4 per cent in the first quarter of 2009-10 to 2.7 per cent during the second quarter. During the third quarter of the year, it averaged 2.8 per cent. Transaction volumes in the CBLO and market repo segments remained at a relatively high level during 2009-10. Around 75 per cent of the lending in the collateralized segment was contributed by mutual funds, which reflected their enhanced lending capacity. The collateralized market remained the predominant segment of the money market and accounted for more than 80 per cent of its total volume.

The rates in the collateralized segments have continued to move in tandem with the call rate, albeit below it, so far during 2010-11. The weighted average interest rate in the collateralized segment of the money market increased to 5.20 per cent during the second quarter from 3.97 per cent in the first quarter of 2010-11. Transaction volumes in the collateralized borrowing and lending obligation (CBLO) and market repo segments remained high during this period, reflecting active market conditions. Banks continued to remain the major group of borrowers in the collateralized segments whereas mutual funds (MFs) remained the major group of lenders of funds in these segments. The collateralized segment of the money market continued to remain the dominant segment, accounting for more than 80 per cent of the total volume so far during the year.

Money markets have remained orderly during 2012-13 so far. As a result of the reduction in the policy (repo) rate in the Annual monetary policy statement 2012-13 (released on April 17, 2012) and improvement in liquidity conditions, the average daily call money rate declined to 7.92 per cent in September 2012 from 8.14 per cent in June 2012 (9.17 per cent in March 2012). Call money rates in latter months have moved in a narrow range. Interest rates on commercial paper and certificate of deposits also peaked in March 2012 and decelerated thereafter in line with the moderation in interest rates for other instruments.

Banks and primary dealers remained the major groups of borrowers in the collateralized segments, while mutual funds (MFs) remained the major group of lenders in the collateralized borrowing and lending obligation (CBLO) segment. But, recently, the share of MFs in total lending has declined in the market repo segment, and nationalized banks have emerged as the major group of lenders in this segment. The collateralized segment continued to remain the predominant segment of the overnight money market; its share was around 78 per cent during the financial year (till December 2012). Table-2 shows the volume in money market of various instruments.

TABLE 2

Volume in Money market

(in ₹ billion)

Month	LAF Average of the month		Call money		Market Repo		CBLO		CP Outstanding (as on last day of the month)		CP Outstanding (as on last reporting friday)	
	2011	2012	2011	2012	2011	2012	2011	2012	2011	2012	2011	2012
January	-929	-1292	78	173	115	89	448	280	1018	1499	3776	3909
February	-786	-1405	104	142	132	122	423	331	1013	1618	4185	4029
March	-810	-1574	113	175	151	112	432	380	803	912	4247	4195
April	-188	-1029	134	250	144	143	562	377	1250	1310	4474	4448
May	-546	-986	110	185	159	151	409	339	1212	1498	4333	4394
June	-741	-913	116	152	167	180	413	376	1047	1258	4238	4252
July	-438	-481	115	146	117	173	410	382	1337	1732	4122	4155
August	-407	-462	113	129	148	183	391	459	1488	1879	4057	4030
September	-559	-517	138	143	139	185	451	502	1446	1706	3835	3572
October	-541	-671	129	150	132	218	416	436	1688	1941	3859	3531
November	-916	-941	110	141	133	207	329	368	1735	1994	3784	3066
December	-1167	-1231	149	142	99	147	265	398	1341	1818	4030	3031

Source : RBI

Repos

Repo is a money market instrument, which enables collateralised short-term borrowing and lending through sale/purchase operations in debt instruments. Under a repo transaction, a holder of securities sells them to an investor with an agreement to repurchase at a pre-determined date and rate. In the case of a repo, the forward clean price of the bonds is set in advance at a level which is different from the spot clean price by adjusting the difference between repo interest and coupon earned on the security. *Repo is also called a ready forward transaction as it is a means of funding by selling a security held on a spot (ready) basis and repurchasing the same on a forward basis. Reverse repo is a mirror image of repo as in the case of former, securities are acquired with a simultaneous commitment to resell.*

Commercial Paper

Commercial Paper (CP) is issued by non-banking companies and all-India Financial Institutions (AIFIs) as an unsecured promissory note or in a demateriaslied form at a rate of discount not tied to any transaction. It is privately placed with investors through the agency of banks. Banks act as both principals (i.e., as counter parties in purchases and sales) and agents in dealership and placement. Banks are not allowed to either underwrite or co-accept issue of CP.

Conditions relating to issuing of CPs have been relaxed gradually with a view to broad-basing the market. For instance, the maturity period has been changed from 91 days-6 months earlier to 15 days-1 year. The minimum size of CPs has also been reduced from ₹ 1 crore to ₹ 5 lakh. The issuer base has been widened by allowing PDs, SDs and AIFIs, apart from corporates, to issue CPs to access short-term funds.

The limit for issuance of CP, which was initially carved out of the maximum permissible bank finance (MPBF), was later linked to the cash credit component of MPBF. With the cash credit component gradually shrinking and, thereby, restricting the development of CP, the issuance limit was delinked from the cash credit limit in October 1997. Initially, banks were required to restore the cash credit limit on the maturity of the paper, guaranteeing the issuer funds at the point of redemption. This "stand-by" facility was withdrawn in October 1994 to impart a measure of independence to CP as a money market instrument. Banks could be approached for a restoration of the original cash credit limit at a later date, the sanction of which was left to their discretion. The credit rating requirement, initially an enabling condition for issuing CP, gradually turned to signal the issuer's position in the market. The Reserve Bank converted CP into a stand-alone product effective October 2000, with a view to enabling the issuers in the services sector to meet short-term working capital requirements and, at the same time, according banks and FIs the flexibility to fix working capital limits after taking into account the resource pattern of companies' finances including CPs. Trading in the dematerialised form, which was introduced recently, is likely to reduce transactions costs.

The pricing of CP usually lies between the scheduled commercial banks' lending rate (since corporates do not otherwise have the incentive to issue CP) and some representative money market rate (which represents the opportunity cost of bank funds). The Indian CP market is driven by the demand for CP by scheduled commercial banks, which, in turn, is governed by bank liquidity. Banks' investments in CP, despite a positive interest rate differential between the bank loan rate and the CP rate, may be explained by two factors, *viz.*, (i) the higher transactions costs of bank loans, and (ii) the relative profitability of CP as an attractive short-term instrument to park funds during times of high liquidity. As inter-bank call rates are typically lower than the CP rates, some banks also fund CP by borrowing from the call money market and, thus, book profit through arbitrage between the two money markets. Most of the CPs-seem to have been issued by the manufacturing companies for a maturity period of approximately three months or less, mainly due to the fact that investors do not wish to lock funds for long periods of time. In most international markets, CP is issued on a short-term basis with a roll-over facility; this facility, however, is not allowed in the Indian CP market.

The secondary activity is subdued in most CP markets on account of the investors' preference to hold the instrument due to higher risk-adjusted return relative to those of other instruments. However, mutual funds find the secondary market relatively remunerative; since stamp duty for the issuer will be higher in case the buyer is a mutual fund rather than a bank. Hence, there is a tendency to route a CP through an institution (usually a bank), which attracts lower stamp duty in the primary market, to a mutual fund in the secondary market.

During 2009-10, the commercial paper (CP) market also picked up with the easing of liquidity conditions and the size of fortnightly issuance increased significantly. The outstanding amount of CP issued by corporates has shown an increasing trend from ₹ 44,171 crore in end-March 2009 to ₹ 1,03,915 crore as in end -November 2009, marginally coming down to a level of ₹ 90,305 crore in end-December 2009 . The weighted average discount rate (WADR) of CP declined from 9.79 per cent as in end-March 2009 to 4.71 per cent as in end-July 2009 and increased to 5.17 per cent in end-November 2009. The shares of "manufacturing companies" and "other financial institutions" in total outstanding CPs have increased in the recent period while the share of "leasing and finance companies" has declined. "Manufacturing companies" accounted for 45 per cent in the share in end-November 2009.

During 2010-11 so far, the commercial paper (CP) market has also picked up and the size of fortnightly issuance increased significantly. The outstanding amount of CP issued by corporates has shown an increasing trend from ₹ 75,506 crore at the end of March 2010 to ₹1,12,003 crore at the end of September 2010 and ₹1,17,793 crore at the end of November 2010. The weighted average discount rate (WADR) of aggregate CP issuances increased from 6.29 per cent at the end of March 2010 to 7.82 per cent at the end of September 2010, and reached 12.22 per cent at the end of November 2010.The shares of 'leasing and finance companies', 'manufacturing companies', and 'other financial institutions' in total outstanding CPs were at around 50 per cent, 39 per cent, and 11 per cent respectively at the end of November 2010

During 2012-13 so far, the commercial paper (CP) market also picked up and the average size of fortnightly issuance increased significantly to ₹ 317 billion (till end December 2012). The weighted average discount rate decreased to 9.04 per cent in December 2012 from 12.2 per cent in March 2012.

Certificates of Deposit

Certificates of Deposit (CD), introduced in June 1989, are essentially securitised short-term time deposits issued by banks during periods of tight liquidity, at relatively high interest rates (in comparison with term deposits). But the transaction cost of CDs is often lower as compared with that of retail deposits. When credit picks up, placing pressure on banks' liquidity, banks try to meet their liquidity gap by issuing CDs, often at a premium. The required amounts are mobilised in larger amounts through CD, often for short periods in order to avoid interest liability overhang in the subsequent months when credit demand slackens. As banks offer higher interest rates on CDs, subscribers find it profitable to hold CDs till maturity. As a result, the secondary market for CDs has been slow to develop.

The Reserve Bank initially limited the issuance of CDs at a certain percentage of the fortnightly average of the outstanding aggregate deposits of 1989-90. Over-time, bank-wise limits were raised and subsequently abolished, effective October 16, 1993, enabling the CD to emerge as a market determined instrument. The reduction in the minimum maturity of time deposits and the permission to allow banks to pay different interest rates based on deposit size reduced the relative attractiveness of CDs. With a view to broadening the CD market, the minimum issuance size was gradually scaled down to ₹ 5 lakh and the minimum maturity reduced to 15 days in April 2000. Again, in order to provide flexibility and depth to the secondary market, the restriction on transferability period for CDs issued by both banks and financial institutions was withdrawn effective October 10, 2000.

On the same lines, the FIMMDA has prepared and made public the guidelines and documentation procedures for issuing CDs. The minimum denomination of a CD was reduced to ₹ 1 lakh in June 2002 in order to increase the investor base. As a further step towards transparency, banks and FIs were required to issue CDs only in the dematerialised form with effect from June 30, 2002, without prejudice to the provisions of Depositories' Act 1996. Existing; outstandings of CDs need to be converted into the demat form by October 2002.

With the persistence of surplus liquidity conditions, the fortnightly average issuance of certificates of deposit (CD) also remained high during much of 2009-10. The amount of outstanding CDs issued by SCBs increased from ₹ 1,92,867 crore in end-March 2009 to ₹ 2,43,584 crore as on December 4, 2009. The outstanding amount constituted 7.84 percent (as on December 4, 2009) of aggregate deposits of CD-issuing banks with significant inter-bank variation. During April-December 4, 2009, the average issuance was of the order of ₹ 11,000 crore as compared to ₹ 6,131 crore during the corresponding period of the previous year. Most of the CDs issued were of more than six months duration. The weighted average discount rate declined from 7.53 per cent in end-March 2009 to 4.84 per cent as on December 4, 2009.

Though the average gross issuance of CDs was high during 2010-11 so far, the amount of CDs outstanding declined, indicating decline in net issuances. The amount of outstanding CDs issued by SCBs declined marginally from ₹ 3,41,054 crore at the end of March 2010 to ₹ 3,32,982 crore at the end of November 2010. The outstanding amount constituted 7.45 per cent (as on 19 November 2010) of aggregate deposits of CD-issuing banks with significant inter-bank variation. During April- November 2010, the average issuance was of the order of around ₹ 22,000 crore as compared to around ₹11,000 crore during the same period of the last financial year. The effective interest rate in respect of aggregate CD issuances increased from 6.07 per cent at the end of March 2010 to 8.16 per cent as on 19 November 2010.

The amount of outstanding CD declined from around ₹ 4195 billion at end-March 2012 to around ₹ 3030 billion at midDecember 2012, which indicates decline in net issuances. The weighted average effective interest rate (WAEIR) of CDs declined to 8.6 per cent at mid-December 2012 from 11.1 per cent at endMarch 2012. .

Commercial Bills Market

The commercial bill market in India is very limited, as evidenced by the fact that commercial bills rediscounted by commercial banks with financial institutions stay often well below ₹ 1,000 crore. The commercial bills market was constricted by the cash credit system of credit delivery where the onus of cash management rested with banks. The Reserve Bank withdrew the interest rate ceiling of 12.5 per cent on rediscounting of commercial bills, effective May 1, 1989. The success of the bills discounting scheme is contingent upon financial discipline on the part of borrowers. As such discipline did not exist, the Reserve

Bank, in July 1992, restricted the banks to finance bills to the extent of working capital needs based on credit norms. However, in order to encourage the 'bills' culture, the Reserve Bank advised banks in October 1997 that at least 25 per cent of inland credit purchases of borrowers should be through bills.

Money Market Mutual Funds (MMMFs)

In April 1992, scheduled commercial banks and public financial institutions were allowed to set up MMMFs, subject to certain terms and conditions. The prescribed restrictions were relaxed subsequently between November 1995 and July 1996 in order to impart more flexibility, liquidity and depth to the market. MMMFs are allowed to invest in rated corporate bonds and debentures with a residual maturity of one year. The minimum lock-in period for units of MMMFs was relaxed from 30 days to 15 days in May 1998. In 1999-2000, MMMFs were allowed to offer 'cheque writing facility' in a tie-up with banks to provide more liquidity to unit holders. MMMFs, which were regulated under the guidelines issued by the Reserve Bank, have been brought under the purview of the SEBI regulations since March 7,2000. Banks are now allowed to set up MMMF only as a separate entity in the form of a trust.

Treasury Bills

The T-bill market was relatively free upto the early sixties. However, the seventies and the eighties were a period of widening fiscal imbalances. Consequently, "the resources of banks came to be incorporated in the fiscal allocation process". To keep the borrowing costs of the government down, the yield on T-bills were kept artificially low, often negative in real terms. The demand for T-bills was restricted to the capative market of banks, the letter investing in T-bills as a means of maintaining SLR requirements. As the Chakravarty committee noted, purchasers of T-bills did not hold them till maturity because of their low yield but rediscounted the bills with the RBI before maturity. This led to a concentration of holdings of T-bills with the RBI, the latter holding 92.9 per cent of T bills outstanding in 1994. With excessive monetisation of the deficit in the 1990s, the issue of ad hoc 91 days T bills to finance the budget deficit became the norm during this period.

T-bills issuances during the year 2009-10 were dynamically managed, keeping in view the emerging requirements of the Government and the market conditions. The T-bills issued for enhanced amounts in 2008-09 which became due for repayment both in the first and second quarters of 2009-10 were fully rolled over. The primary market yields for TBs of different tenors (91 days, 182 days and 364 days) remained by and large stable during 2009-10 as compared to the pattern observed in 2008-09.

The introduction of a new short-term instrument, known as cash management bill (CMB), was announced in August 2009 to meet the temporary cash-flow mismatches of the Government. CMBs are non-standard, discounted instruments issued for maturities of less than 91 days. However, issuance of CMBs has not so far been resorted to during the year.

T-Bills issuances during the year 2010-11 were modulated according to the cash management requirements of the Government as well as evolving market conditions. The notified amounts for competitive auctions of T-Bills were reduced during the first two quarters of the fiscal year. The outstanding stock of T- Bills went down from ₹ 1,34,500 crore on 31 March 2010 to ₹ 1,26,269 crore on 31 December 2010, after taking into account a rise in non-competitive allotment. The primary market yields for T-Bills of different tenors (91 days, 182 days, and 364 days) moved up during the year largely influenced by the liquidity conditions and monetary policy action by the RBI.

Cash Management

During the year, a new short-term instrument, named cash management bill (CMB), was introduced in May 2010. CMBs are non-standard, discounted instruments issued for maturities of less than 91 days, to meet the temporary cash-flow mismatches of the Government. During 2010-11, CMBs were issued twice in May 2010 for an aggregate amount of ₹12,000 crore, with a maturity of five and four weeks, respectively.

Foreign Exchange Market

The Indian foreign exchange market has witnessed far reaching changes since the early 1990s following the phased transition from a pegged exchange rate regime to a market determined exchange rate regime in 1993 and the subsequent adoption of current account convertibility in 1994 and substantial liberalisation of capital account transactions. Market participants have also been provided with greater flexibility to undertake foreign exchange operations and manage their risks. This has been facilitated through simplification of procedures and availability of several new instruments. There has also been significant improvement in market infrastructure in terms of trading platform and settlement mechanisms. As a result of various reform measures, liquidity in the foreign exchange market increased by more than five times between 1997-98 and 2006-07.

In fiscal 2009-10, with the signs of recovery and return of FII flows after March 2009, the rupee has been strengthening against the US dollar. The movement of the exchange rate in the year 2009-10 indicated that the average monthly exchange rate of the rupee against the US dollar appreciated by 9.9 per cent from ₹ 51.23 per US dollar in March 2009 to ₹ 46.63 per US dollar in December 2009. mainly on account of weakening of the US dollar in the international market.

Foreign exchange reserves increased from US$ 252 billion at the end of March 2009 to US$ 279.1 billion at the end of March 2010, showing a rise of US$ 27.1 billion. Of the total increase, US$ 13.6 billion was on account of valuation gain (due to decline of the US dollar in the international market) and the remaining US$ 13.5 billion on account of the BoP. During the current fiscal, reserves increased from US$ 279.6 billion at the end of April 2010 to US$ 292.4 billion at the end of November 2010. The reserves stood at US$ 297.3 billion at the end of December 2010, showing an increase of US$ 18.2 billion over the end-March 2010 level mainly on account of valuation changes.

During the current fiscal the montly average exchange rate of the rupee has generally been range bound, moving in the range of ₹ 44-47 per US dollar betwwn April and December 2010. The exchang rate of the rupee depreciated by 1.5 per cent against the US dollar, from ₹ 44.50 per US dollar in April 2010 to ₹ 34.16 per US dollar in December 2010. The rupe also depreciated against other major international currencies such as the pound sterling (3.2 per cent) and Japanese yen (12.2 per cent) during the period.

CONVERGENCE AMONG FINANCIAL MARKET SEGMENTS

Over a period, RBI has taken a keen interest in the development of the money, the government securities and the foreign exchange markets in view of their critical role in overall growth and development of the economy and particularly in the transmission mechanism of monetary policy. The approach has been one of simultaneous movement on several fronts, graduated and calibrated, with an emphasis on institutional and infrastructural development and improvements in market microstructure. The pace of reforms was contingent upon putting in place appropriate systems and procedures, technologies and market practices. Initiatives taken by the Reserve Bank have brought about a significant transformation of various segments of the financial market. These developments, by improving the depth and liquidity in domestic financial markets, have contributed to better price discovery of interest rates and exchange rates, which, in turn, have led to greater efficiency in resource allocation in the economy. The increase in size and depth of financial markets has paved the way for flexible use of indirect instruments. Greater depth and liquidity and freedom to market participants have also strengthened the integration of various segments of the financial market. Increased integration not only leads to more efficient dispersal of risks across the spectrum but also increases the efficacy of monetary policy impulses. Evidence suggests that growing integration of various financial market segments in India has been accompanied by lower volatility of interest rates.

Financial market reforms in India have enabled a greater integration of various segments of the financial market, reducing arbitrage opportunities, achieving higher level of efficiency in market operation of intermediaries and increasing efficacy of monetary policy in the economy. Growing integration of financial markets beginning 2000 could be gauged from cross correlation among various market interest rates. The correlation structure of interest rates reveals several notable features of integration of specific market segments.

First, in the money market segment, there is evidence of stronger correlation among interest rates in the more recent period 2000-06 than the earlier period 1993-2000, suggesting the impact of policy initiatives undertaken for financial deepening. The enhanced correlation among interest rates also indicates improvement in efficiency in the operations of financial intermediaries trading in different instruments. *Second*, the high correlation between risk free and liquid instruments such as Treasury Bills, which serve as benchmark instruments, and other market instruments such as certificates of deposit and commercial papers and forward exchange premia, underlines the efficiency of the price discovery process. *Third*, the sharp improvement in correlation between the reverse repo rate and money market rates in the recent period implies enhanced effectiveness of monetary policy transmission. *Fourth*, the high degree of correlation between long-term government bond yield and short-term Treasury Bills rate indicates the significance of term-structure of interest rates in financial markets. *Fifth*, the correlation between interest ratesln money markets and three-month forward premia was significantly high, indicating relatively high horizontal integration. Integration of the foreign exchange market with the money market and the government securities market has facilitated closer co-ordination of monetary and external sector management. The impact of foreign exchange market intervention can be carefully coordinated with monetary management encompassing constant monitoring of the supply of banking system liquidity and an active use of open market operations to adjust liquidity conditions. *Sixth*, the equity market appears to be segmented with relatively low and negative correlation with money market segments.

A growing integration between the money, the gilt and the foreign exchange market segments was also discernible in the convergence of financial prices, within and among various segments and co-movement in interest rates.

The degree of integration of the foreign exchange market with other markets is largely determined the degree of openness. One of the indicators of foreign market integration is the differential in covered interest rates.[1] In the Indian context, the forward price of the rupee is

---

1. The Covered Interest Parity (CIP) implies that the rates of return on homogenous financial instruments that are denominated in same currency, but traded domestically as well as offshore must be equal under efficient market conditions, provided exchange controls do not exist and country risk premium is similar in two markets. The CIP implies that yield on foreign investment that is covered in forward markets equals the yield on domestic investment. The interest differential is offset by premium or discount on the forward rate. The absence of covered interest differential indicates that there are some impediments to financial integration, attributable to some element of market imperfection, transaction costs, market liquidity conditions, margin requirements, taxation and market entry exit conditions.

not essentially determined by the interest rate differentials, but it is also significantly influenced by: (a) supply and demand of forward US dollars; (b) interest differentials and expectations of future interest rates; and (c) expectations of future US dollar-rupee exchange rate. Empirical evidence supports this view, as the three month forward premia (FP3) has less than perfect co-movement with interest rate differential (between 91-day treasury bill rate and three-month LIBOR), indicative of the time varying nature of the risk premium. The inter-linkage becomes stronger when the interest rate differential is based on the monthly average call money rate and one-month LIBOR. The relationship improves still further, when the difference between the CP rate in India and the 3-month US dollar LIBOR rate is considered for interest parity assessments. The deviation of the forward premia from the interest parity condition appears to increase during volatile conditions in the spot segment of the foreign exchange market.

From the monetary policy perspective, there has been convergence among market segments, with a significant decline in the spread of market interest rates over the reverse repo rate. The spread was the lowest for the inter-bank call money rate followed by rates on Treasury Bills, certificates of deposit, commercial paper and 10-year government bond yield. The benefit of financial market development percolating to the real sector is also evident from the moderation in the spread of commercial paper over the policy rate. The narrowing of the spread between the policy rate and other market rates suggests the increasing efficiency of the transmission mechanism of monetary policy.

Thus, integration among various market segments has grown, especially in the recent period. This is reflected in the increase in the depth of the markets and higher correlation among interest rates in various market segments. Growing integration among various financial market segments was accompanied by lower volatility of interest rates. The narrowing of the interest rate spread over the reverse repo rate reflects an improvement in the monetary policy transmission channel and greater financial market integration.

CHANGING MONETARY POLICY PARADIGM

The monetary policy stance of the Reserve Bank continued to be the provision of adequate liquidity to meet credit growth and support investment demand in the economy while continuing a vigil on movements in the price level. *Liquidity Management in India* is a subject that is not widely discussed but is the bread and butter of daily monetary management.

Conduct of monetary policy and management in the context of large and volatile capital flows has proved to be difficult for many countries. As India became convertible on the current account, and liberalised its capital account in a carefully sequenced manner since the balance of payment crisis of 1991, it too has been faced with similar problems. The evolving policy mix involved careful calibration that took into account diverse objectives of central banking, changes in the monetary policy framework and operating procedures, and widening of the set of instruments for liquidity management.

Before opening of the economy through the 1990s, both the current and capital accounts were controlled. However, despite trade restrictions the current account was in constant deficit, which had to be financed mostly by debt, both official aid flows and private debt. Portfolio flows were not permitted and foreign direct investment was negligible. The only largely "uncontrolled" flows were NRI deposits, which waxed and waned according to macro-economic conditions. The exchange rate was also controlled: it was linked to a basket of currencies and moved as a crawling peg. Consequently, monetary policy management, such as it was, did not pose serious problems, particularly since most interest rates were fixed administratively.

It is only after substantial opening of the economy, and deregulation of interest rates

542

INVESTMENT MANAGEMENT

that price discovery of the rate of interest has become important. Consequently the Reserve Bank has had to experiment on a continuous basis. It has had to operate simultaneously on the external account in the foreign exchange market to contain volatility in the exchange rate, and in the domestic market to contain volatility in interest rates. Since both the exchange rate and interest rate are the key prices reflecting the cost of money, it is particularly important for the efficient functioning of the economy that they be market determined and be easily observed. Excessive fluctuation and volatility masks the underlying value and gives rise to confusing signals. The task of liquidity management then is to provide a framework for the facilitation of forex and money market transactions that result in price discovery sans excessive volatility.

Liquidity Management and Management of Capital Flows

While in the macroeconomic context, liquidity management refers to overall monetary conditions, reflecting the extent of mismatch between demand and supply of overall monetary resources, for a central bank, the concept of liquidity management typically refers to the framework and set of instruments that the central bank follows insteering the amount of *bank reserves* in order to control its price, consistent with the ultimate goals of monetary policy. *What is the price of bank reserves?* The price of bank reserves is fixed in terms of short term interest rates. This is set in terms of overnight inter-bank borrowing and lending rates either secured or unsecured which affect the reserves that the banks keep. As markets do not clear often on their own the central bank itself steps in by influencing the short-term interest rates by affecting short-term repurchase obligations with banks

The need for liquidity management arises from central banks' concept of liquidity measured in terms of the monetary base, of which it is the monopoly supplier. The supply of monetary base by the central bank depends on (i) the public's demand for currency, as determined by the size of monetary transactions and the opportunity cost of holding money and, (ii) the banking system's need for reserves to settle or discharge payment obligations. In fulfilling these needs, central banks also attempt to control and modulate liquidity conditions by varying the supply of bank reserves to meet its macroeconomic objectives subject to the constraint of financial stability. Bank reserves are, therefore, influenced through reserve requirements or open market operations. In so doing, central banks attempt to affect the level of short-term interest rates in a manner in which market movements of these interest rate movements are smoothened out as volatility of any monetary or non-monetary asset prices can be costly in terms of real output and investment decisions. It is from this standpoint that a central bank decides to modulate its market operations over a chosen time horizon to reflect its policy stance.

The importance of central bank liquidity management lies in its ability to exercise considerable influence and control over short-term interest rates by small money market operations. This ability is determined by the credibility of the central bank itself. The interventions that the central bank makes have a pronounced signaling affect. Consequently, developed country central banks typically aim at a target overnight interest rate, which acts as a powerful economy wide signal. As a result, the impact of these transactions is fundamentally different from those undertaken by private market participants. The liquidity management function of a central bank involves a larger economy-wide perspective. Central bank liquidity management has short-term effects in financial markets. However, the long-term implications for the real sector and on price level are more important.

By operating on the current account balances that the commercial banks maintain with the central bank or by directly operating on the short-term money market rate, central banks attempt to influence money market liquidity in order to exercise control over the short-term interest rate. The central bank may directly set at least one of the short-term interest rates that acts as its policy rate. By controlling the short-term interest rate while letting markets determine the rest of the yield curve, the central bank attempts to transmit monetary policy impulses across the yield curve. The sovereign yield curve in turn influences the lending and deposit rates in the economy. Mortgage rates are found to be particularly sensitive to the policy rate changes through the interest rate as well as the credit channel. Once bank lending gets affected, interest rates impact real variables such as consumption and investment, which in turn impact output and inflation levels. So while active liquidity management has a localised objective of keeping short-term interest rates range bound, it also has a long-term meta objective of implementing monetary policy goals of inflation and output.

The difficulty is that monetary policy is formulated and implemented under considerable uncertainty. Injections or absorptions made over extended periods as an intended part of policy have implications on output and prices through changes in interest rates and aggregate demand. Typically, the transmission effects tend to differ across countries depending on country specific factors and institutional and regulatory frameworks. As transmission occurs with long and variable lags in all countries, the long-run impact is often unpredictable.

While liquidity management in most advanced country central banks is conducted in a setting where daily demand for money typically exceeds its supply, liquidity management in emerging markets is more varied, with surplus and shortage conditions alternating and with perhaps greater fluctuations in their external accounts In recent years, capital flows have been a major factor affecting liquidity management in a large number of countries, particularly in Asia, which have faced large and volatile capital flows. Capital flows have little effect on liquidity in the presence of equivalent current account deficits that result in the absorption of capital flows in the economy and they help to accelerate growth in investment, employment and in technology imports, contributing to productivity growth. In situations where they exceed the current account deficit, they result in a build up of foreign exchange reserves, which themselves act as a positive signaling device indicating financial stability.

But unsterilised capital inflows can result in inflation, currency appreciation, loss of competitiveness and attenuation of monetary control. The loss of monetary control could be steep if such flows are large. Even when these flows are sterilised through open market operations the costs could be large when sterilisation operations raise domestic interest rates and result in the trap of even greater capital flows. The fiscal impact of sterilisation also requires to be factored in, specially when a large stock of securities is required to be issued for the purpose.

Clearly, macroeconomic policy options for managing capital flows are difficult. The options also require taking into account the high volatility often associated with such capital flows. These flows are marked by sudden surges and reversals, which in some cases, could occur in a week's time or less. In other cases, surges could be followed by stoppages in a short span of time. Stoppages could also give way to reversals at slight triggers. There are also cases where capital flows are sustained over a long period of time or a drought in flows occurs over a medium-term. In sum, these flows are somewhat unpredictable and it is very difficult to assess the liquidity scenario even over a quarter, far less over a year. At the same time, monetary policy operates with transmission lags that could run 3-4 quarters or longer and these lags are often unpredictable.

Typically, countries that are in the quest for capital flows fall under the impossible trinity problem,. Notwithstanding the theoretical basis, history is replete with examples of countries falling under the temptation to achieve all these goals when faced with opportunities for benefiting from global asset portfolio allocations Generally, countries seek to retain their monetary policy independence as they face asymmetric shocks and common currency area conditions are not pervasive. They are also tempted to keep their exchange rates stable for financial stability or for inflation containment objectives. In most cases countries end up making a costly exit from a hard peg. With greater financial openness, many countries have to move towards greater exchange rate flexibility or accept the subordination of monetary policy goals to goals of global capital market integration. The latter, however, could be costly.

In these circumstances, the problem for monetary management was two-fold. First, it had to distinguish implicitly between durable flows and transient flows. If capital flows are deemed to be durable and indefinite, questions arise regarding foreign exchange management. If the flows are deemed to be semi-durable, essentially reflecting the business cycle, the task of monetary and liquidity management is to smoothen out their impact on the domestic economy, finding means to absorb liquidity in times of surplus and to inject it in times of deficit. Second, in the short term, daily, weekly or monthly volatility in flows needs to be smoothened to minimise the effect on domestic overnight interest rates. In practice, *ex-ante*, it is difficult to distinguish what is durable, what is semi-durable and what is transient. Hence policy and practice effectively operates in an environment of uncertainty and a variety of instruments have to be used to manage liquidity in this fluid scenario.

Shift from Direct to Indirect Instruments

There has been a worldwide trend for shifting from direct instruments of monetary control to indirect instruments. India is one of the emerging market countries, where such a change has distinctly occurred. A major transformation has occurred in the monetary policy framework in the 1990s. In response to the changing financial landscape, the Reserve Bank started using the information content in interest rates and rates of return in different markets along with currency, credit, fiscal position, trade, capital flows, inflation rate, exchange rate, refinancing and transactions in foreign exchange, juxtaposing it with output data for drawing policy perspectives. As part of the financial sector reforms launched in mid-1991, India began to move away from direct instruments of monetary control to indirect ones. The transition of this kind involves considerable efforts to develop markets, institutions and practices. In order to facilitate such transition, India developed a Liquidity Adjustment Facility (LAF) in phases considering country-specific features of the Indian financial system. LAF is based on repo reverse repo operations by the central bank.

In 1998 the Committee on Banking Sector Reforms (Narasimham Committee II) recommended the introduction of a Liquidity Adjustment Facility (LAF) under which the Reserve Bank would conduct auctions periodically, if not necessarily daily. The Reserve Bank could reset its Repo and Reverse Repo rates which would in a sense provide a reasonable corridor for the call money market. In pursuance of these recommendations, a major change in the operating procedure became possible in April 1999 through the introduction of an Interim Liquidity Adjustment Facility (ILAF) under which repos and reverse repos were formalised. With the introduction of ILAF, the general refinance facility was withdrawn and replaced by a collateralised lending facility (CLF) up to 0.25 per cent of the fortnightly average outstanding of aggregate deposits in 1997-98 for two weeks at the Bank Rate. Additional collateralised lending facility (ACLF) for an equivalent amount of CLF was made available at the Bank Rate plus 2 per cent. CLF and ACLF availed for periods beyond two weeks were subjected to *a* penal rate of 2 per cent for an additional two week period. Export Credit refinance for scheduled commercial banks was retained and continued to be provided at the bank rate. Liquidity support to PDs against collateral of government securities at the bank rate was also provided for. ILAF was expected to promote stability of money market and ensure that the interest rates move within a reasonable range.

The transition from ILAF to a full-fledged LAF began in June 2000 and was undertaken in three stages. In the first stage, beginning June 5, 2000, LAF was formally introduced and the Additional CLF and level II support to PDs was replaced by variable rate repo auctions with same day settlement. In the second stage, beginning May 2001 CLF and level I liquidity support for banks and PDs was also replaced by variable rate repo auctions. Some minimum liquidity support to PDs was continued but at interest rate linked to variable rate in the daily repos auctions as determined by RBI from time to time. In April 2003, the multiplicity of rates at which liquidity was being absorbed/injected under back-stop facility was rationalised and the back-stop interest rate was fixed at the reverse repo cut-off rate at the regular LAF auctions on that day. In case of no reverse repo in the LAF auctions, back-stop rate was fixed at 2.0 percentage point above the repo cut-off rate. It was also announced that on days when no repo/reverse repo bids are received/accepted, back-stop rate would be decided by the Reserve Bank on an *ad-hoc* basis. A revised LAF scheme was operationalised effective March 29, 2004 under which the reverse repo rate was reduced to 6.0 per cent and aligned with bank rate. Normal facility and backstop facility was merged into a single facility and made available at a single rate. The third stage of full-fledged LAF had begun with the full computerisation of Public Debt Office (PDO) and introduction of RTGS marked a big step forward in this phase. Repo operations today are mainly through electronic transfers. Fixed rate auctions have been reintroduced since April 2004. The possibility of operating LAF at different times of the same day is now close to getting materialised. In that sense we have very nearly completed the transition to operating a full-fledged LAF.

With the introduction of Second LAF (SLAF) from November 28, 2005 market participants now have a second window to fine-tune the management of liquidity. In past, LAF operations were conducted in the forenoon between 9.30 a.m. and 10.30 a.m. SLAF is conducted by receiving bids between 3.00 p.m. and 3.45 p.m. The salient features of SLAF are the same as those of LAF and the settlement for both is conducted separately and on gross basis.

The introduction of LAF has been a process and the Indian experience shows that phased rather than a big bang approach is required for reforms in the financial sector and in monetary management.

The introduction of LAF had several advantages. *First* and foremost, it helped the transition from direct instruments of monetary control to indirect and, in the process, certain dead weight loss for the system was saved. *Second*, it has provided monetary authorities with greater flexibility in determining both the quantum of adjustment as well as the rates by responding to the needs of the system on a daily basis. *Third*, it enabled the Reserve Bank to modulate the supply of funds on a daily basis to meet day-to-day liquidity mismatches. *Fourth*, it enabled the central bank to affect demand for funds through policy rate changes. *Fifth* and most important, it helped stabilise short-term money market rates.

The call rate has been largely within a corridor set by the repo and reverse repo rates, imparting greater stability in the financial markets.

LAF has now emerged as the principal operating instrument of monetary policy. Although there is no formal targeting of overnight interest rates, the LAF is designed to nudge overnight interest rates within a specified corridor, the difference between the fixed repo and reverse repo rates, currently 100 basic points. The LAF has enabled the Reserve Bank to de-emphasise targeting of bank reserves and focus increasingly on interest rates. This has helped in reducing the CRR without loss of monetary control.

MONETARY MANAGEMENT IN THE MORE RECENT PERIOD

The money markets operated in liquidity surplus mode since 2002 due to large capital inflows and current account surplus. The initial burden of sterilisation was borne by the outright transaction of dated securities and T-bills. However, due to the depletion in stock of government securities, the burden of liquidity adjustment shifted on LAF, which is essentially a tool of adjusting for marginal liquidity. Keeping in view the objective of absorbing the liquidity of enduring nature using instruments other than LAF, the Reserve Bank appointed a Working Group on Instruments of Sterilisation. The Group recommended issue of T-bills and dated securities under Market Stabilisation Scheme (MSS) where the proceeds of MSS were to be held by the Government in a separate identifiable cash account maintained and operated by RBI. The amounts credited into the MSS Account would be appropriated only for the purpose of redemption and / or buy back of the Treasury Bills and / or dated securities issued under the MSS. In pursuance of the recommendation the Government of India and RBI signed a Memorandum of Understanding (MoU) on March 25, 2004. As part of the MoU, the scheme was made operational since April 2004. It was agreed that the Government would issue Treasury Bills and/or dated securities under the MSS in addition to the normal borrowing requirements, for absorbing liquidity from the system. These securities would be issued by way of auctions by the Reserve Bank and the instruments would have all the attributes of existing T-bills and dated securities. They were to be serviced like any other marketable government securities. MSS securities are being treated as eligible securities for Statutory Liquidity Ratio (SLR), repo and Liquidity Adjustment Facility (LAF).

The payments for interest and discount on MSS securities are not made from the MSS Account. The receipts due to premium and/or accrued interest are also not credited to the MSS Account. Such receipts and payments towards interest, premium and discount are shown in the budget and other related documents as distinct components under separate sub-heads. The T-bills and dated securities issued for the purpose of the MSS are matched by an equivalent cash balance held by the Government with the Reserve Bank. Thus, they only have a marginal impact on revenue and fiscal balances of the Government to the extent of interest payment on the outstanding under the MSS.

For mopping up enduring surplus liquidity, policy choice exist between central bank issuing its own securities or government issuing additional securities. A large number of countries, such as, Chile, China, Colombia, Indonesia, Korea, Malaysia, Peru, Philippines, Russia, Sri Lanka, Tawian and Thailand have issued central bank securities. However, central banks of many of these countries faced deterioration in their balance sheets. As such, there are merits in issuing sterilisation bonds on government account. This is more so, in case of an already well established government debt market, where issuing of new central bank bills of overlapping maturity could cause considerable confusion and possible market segmentation which could obfuscate the yield curve, reduce liquidity of the instruments and make operations that much more difficult.

MSS has considerably strengthened the Reserve Bank's ability to conduct exchange rate and monetary management operations. It has allowed absorption of surplus liquidity by instruments of short term (91-day, 182-day and 364-day T-bills) and the medium-term (dated Government securities) maturity. Generally, the preference has been for the short-term instruments. This has given the monetary authorities a greater degree of freedom in liquidity management during transitions in liquidity situation.

The RBI's monetary policy stance has continued to focus on the twin objectives of containing inflation and facilitating growth (a flow chart depicting the transmission of monetary policy is at Box 1). Mounting inflationary pressures during January 2010 to October 2011 required adoption of a tight monetary policy by the Reserve Bank of India (RBI). During this period, RBI raised policy rates (repo rates) by 375 basis points, from 4.75 per cent to 8.5 per cent. There was a moderation in inflation from its peak of 10.9 per cent in April 2010, to an average of 7.6 per cent during AprilDecember 2012. However, increasing

risks to growth from external as well as domestic sources and tight monetary policy in face
of persistent inflationary pressures has contributed to a sharper slowdown of the economy
than anticipated. There has been a shift in the policy stance of RBI since October 2011
wherein it has attempted to balance growth and inflation dynamics. It reduced repo rates by
50 basis points in April, 2012 and again in January 2013 by 25 basis points and reduced the
Cash Reserve Ratio (CRR) and Statutory Liquidity Ratio (SLR) to improve liquidity conditions
(Table 3).

TABLE 3

Revision in Policy Rates (per cent)

Effective date	Repo rate	Reverse repo rate	CRR	SLR	MSF rate*
2010-11					
20 Apr. 2010	5.25	3.75	5.75	25.00	
24 Apr. 2010	5.25	3.75	6.00	25.00	
2 Jul. 2010	5.50	4.00	6.00	25.00	
27 Jul. 2010	5.75	4.50	6.00	25.00	
16 Sep. 2010	6.00	5.00	6.00	25.00	
2 Nov. 2010	6.25	5.25	6.00	25.00	
18 Dec. 2010	6.25	5.25	6.00	24.00	
25 Jan. 2011	6.50	5.50	6.00	24.00	
17 Mar. 2011	6.75	5.75	6.00	24.00	
2011-12					
3-May-11	7.25	6.25	6.00	24.00	
9-May-11	7.25	6.25	6.00	24.00	8.25
16 Jun. 2011	7.50	6.50	6.00	24.00	8.50
26 Jul. 2011	8.00	7.00	6.00	24.00	9.00
16 Sep. 2011	8.25	7.25	6.00	24.00	9.25
25 Oct. 2011	8.50	7.50	6.00	24.00	9.50
28 Jan. 2012	8.50	7.50	5.50	24.00	9.50
10 Mar. 2012	8.50	7.50	4.75	24.00	9.50
2012-13					
17 Apr. 2012	8.00	7.00	4.75	24.00	9.00
18 Jun. 2012	8.00	7.00	4.75	24.00	9.00
11 Aug. 2012	8.00	7.00	4.75	23.00	9.00
22 Sep. 2012	8.00	7.00	4.50	23.00	9.00
03 Nov. 2012	8.00	7.00	4.25	23.00	9.00
18 Dec. 2012	8.00	7.00	4.25	23.00	9.00
29 Jan. 2013	7.75	6.75	4.25	23.00	8.75
09 Feb 2013	7.75	6.75	4.00	23.00	8.75

Source: Reserve Bank of India (RBI). * Note: The MSF commenced from 9 May 2011

As per the assessment of RBI, global economic and financial conditions have continued
to remain too fragile to provide any external growth stimulus to the economy. On the other
hand, inflationary pressures originating from within the country and outside, particularly

BOX 1

Trasmission of Monetary Policy

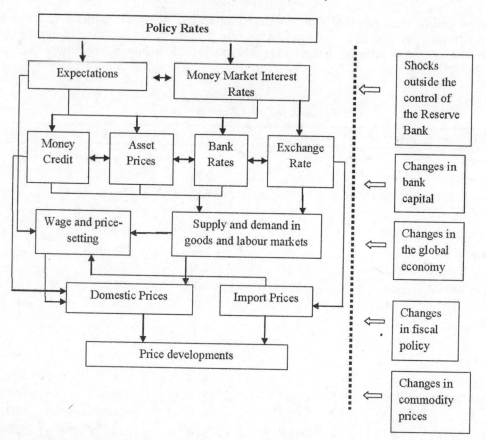

the depreciating rupee exerting its pressure on tradables, may make any reduction in policy rates counterproductive. Furthermore, tight liquidity conditions emerged as a risk to adequate flow of credit to productive sectors. Monetary policy therefore has continued to follow a cautious stand, which, while keeping liquidity comfortable to support growth, had to pause in its policy rate reduction during April-December 2012 due to persistent inflation risks. This cautious monetary policy stance was also considered necessary by RBI in view of mounting subsidies and deteriorating fiscal situation. Government in September 2012, however, announced a road map of fiscal consolidation with a clearly defined midterm fiscal target. It also attempted to improve the investor perception and create a favourable environment for investment. In January 2013, the Government also announced an increase in diesel prices to indicate its resolve to reduce fiscal deficit consistent with the medium term fiscal target announced earlier in September, 2012. There has been some moderation in inflation in the Q3 of 2012- 13 and with the expected fiscal consolidation, the current macroeconomic situation creates room for a somewhat accommodative monetary policy.

The monetary policy stance of Reserve Bank of India in the current year was based on its projection of macroeconomic parameters for 2012- 13. In its Monetary Policy Statement 2012-13 released on April 17, 2012, RBI expected GDP growth at 7.3 per cent and WPI inflation to gradually moderate to 6.5 per cent by March 2013. In its First Quarter Review of

July 31, 2012 while the growth projection was revised downwards to 6.5 per cent, the WPI inflation projection was revised upwards to 7.0 per cent. Consistent with this growth and inflation expectation, it set a target of M3 and non-food credit growth of 15 per cent and 17 per cent, respectively. In its Second Quarter Review on October 30, 2012, RBI reduced its projection of GDP growth further to 5.8 per cent and revised its inflation projection upwards to 7.5 per cent. The indicative targets of M3 and credit growth, therefore, were revised downwards to 14 per cent and 16 per cent, respectively. RBI in its Third Quarter Review of monetary policy on January 29, 2013 reduced its GDP projection to 5.5 per cent with expected inflation also moderating to 6.8 per cent by March 2013. Further, M3 growth projections were lowered to 13.0 per cent even though credit growth was retained at 16.0 per cent. Movement of the monetary aggregates, however, indicate that the growth of broad money and credit have been below the indicative levels set by RBI.

The moderation in growth and nearly flat inflation at around 7-8 per cent in the current year also affected the growth of aggregate deposits, from an average of 17.4 per cent in Q1 of 2011-12 to 12.9 per cent in Q3 of 2012-13. The rate of growth of bank credit also moderated from its peak of 21.7% in Q1 of 2011-12 to around 16-17% in the last 2 quarters. A lower deposit growth, notwithstanding the moderation in credit growth has given rise to an asset-liability gap, which is also indicated by the increase in the credit-deposit ratio (Table 4) Moderating growth and deceleration in capital formation, however, increased the flow of banking sector funds to investment in government and other securities.

TABLE 4

Movement of Key Monetary Aggregates (y-o-y growth rates in per cent)

	2010-11	2011-12	2011-12				2012-13		
			Q1	Q2	Q3	Q4	Q1	Q2	Q3
GDP (at current market prices)	18.8	15.4	18.9	16.6	14.8	12.2	12.2	11.3	-
Reserve Money (Mo)	21.5	14.1	17.6	15.9	14.7	8.7	7.3	6.5	4.3
Broad Money (M3)	16.2	15.8	17.3	16.8	15.4	13.8	14.2	13.6	12.6
Aggregate Deposits	15.7	16.2	17.4	17.2	16.0	14.3	14.7	14.0	12.9
Bank Credit	21.3	18.7	21.7	19.6	17.6	16.4	18.1	16.8	16.5
Investments	9.4	14.3	10.3	15.5	15.5	15.7	16.1	14.4	15.2
Velocity of Money (M3/GDP)	1.28	1.27	1.22	1.20	1.31	1.35	1.20	1.17	-
Money Multiplier (M3/M0)	5.0	5.0	4.92	5.03	5.07	5.12	5.24	5.37	5.44
CD Ratio (per cent)	73.3	74.7	74.3	73.5	74.3	76.4	76.5	75.4	76.7

Source: RBI

What has been the lesson from the Indian experience of coping with liquidity management under large and volatile capital flows? First, by putting reforms on a more stable footing by adopting gradualism but avoiding reversals, it has been able to sustain capital inflows on a more stable basis with lower volatility than has been seen in some other emerging markets. This has helped central banks in smoothening out interest rates under cyclical transition. Second, in cases where money and debt markets have depth, development of open market operations through repo operations is particularly important for building up microeconomic capacities for macroeconomic objective of liquidity management. In India, the emergence of LAF was a single biggest factor which helped to manage liquidity amidst large and volatile capital flows and to keep short-term interest rates stable in this environment. It widened the range of instruments for monetary policy and enabled the Reserve Bank to operate on shorter range of interest rates. Restricting the maturities of interest rates at which central bank operates to a smaller range at the short-end has reinforced market functioning. Third, in the face of constraints on sterilisation arising from paucity of instruments, the monetary authorities in India adopted a careful strategy which preserved the strength of the central bank balance sheet and the credibility of the central bank, while causing minimal frictions in the debt markets. MSS was not contemplated of initially even while capital flows had distinctly increased since 1993-94. However, in face of large surplus liquidity since 2000, MSS was evolved as a very useful instrument of monetary policy to sustain open market operations. MSS has marginal costs, but it has helped the monetary authorities manage business and liquidity cycles through the surpluses and the deficits. With MSS, the monetary authorities now have the option of assigning LAF for day-to-day liquidity management, using MSS for addressing semi-durable liquidity mismatches, while using outright sales/purchases of dated securities for truly long-term liquidity surpluses or deficits. The MSS experience tells us that operating framework and procedures undergo changes and one need to kZXeep innovating to calibrate market operations to the evolving liquidity conditions.

Fourth, by focusing on the microstructure of the markets and by facilitating development of a wider range of instruments such as Collateralised Borrowing and Lending Obligation (CBLO)[2], market repo, interest rate swaps, Certificates of Deposit (CDs) and Commercial Papers (CPs), in a manner that avoided market segmentation while meeting demand for various products, liquidity management could be placed on a much firmer footing. Market and central bank practices evolved to institutional developments. However, the payment and settlement system proved to be the most difficult area, but one which delivered the enabling environment for micro and macro developments supportive of the liquidity management procedures now in place. The focus on micro-aspects reinforced the central bank's ability to signal and transmit policy changes.

Fifth, with efforts to build up indirect instruments for liquidity management, the transmission of monetary policy has improved. The link between overnight interest rates and yields on T-bills and liquid dated securities has become far stronger. While the lending rates and even more so deposit rates have been taking considerable time to adjust, the strength of the transmission has been in evidence in recent periods. It is important to note that in a situation of large surplus liquidity, the transmission is understandably weaker. However, in the more recent period as considerable amount of excess liquidity was mopped up by the central bank, the rate signal efficacy has gone up substantially.

Sixth, monetary policy setting through signalling improves, as the central bank's liquidity management is able to establish its control over short-term interest rate by reducing volatility in these rates. By removing working balance constraints for the banks, it can influence the term structure of interest rates as reflected in money market rates of various maturities and the sovereign yield curve.

---

2   CBLO is a money market instrument developed by Clearing Corporation of India Limited (CCIL) under RBI regulations. The instrument is issued as a discounted instrument in electronic book entry form to enable eligible market participants to undertake collateralised borrowing or lending from overnight to 90 days maturity. It is in the nature of tripartite repo in which CCIL holds the underlying charge on securities. The product was developed mainly for the non-banks, who were phased out from the uncollateralised call money market during 2001-06. Currently, banks, financial institutions, insurance companies, mutual funds, primary dealers, non-bank financial companies, Non-Government Provident Funds and some corporates are participating in the CBLO market.

Lastly, while temporary mismatches in liquidity conditions do pose a problem for maintaining immediate goals of monetary operations, the overall objective of liquidity management needs to accorded primacy. In India, in spite of difficulties posed by sudden transitions in liquidity conditions, macroeconomic success of overall policies are reflected in delivering low inflation, which at 4.7 per cent, has averaged below 5.0 per cent over last five years in terms of the headline rate. Consumer price inflation has averaged still lower at around 4.0 per cent on a point-to-point basis and 3.9 per cent on an average basis.

In spite of the relative success in liquidity management in India, several challenges remain ahead. *First,* notwithstanding the large size of the debt markets, absence of *a* vibrant term market, the illiquidity of *a* large set of securities and limitations of corporate debt market continue to come in way of further contemplated changes. *Second,* while the Reserve Bank now enables market participants to meet their marginal liquidity demand twice a day on each working day, there is a moral hazard that passive operations by central bank in the market may be resulting in some market players not doing enough for their own liquidity management. *Third,* as the system moves to maintenance of SLR securities at statutory minimum levels, liquidity provision would become more difficult unless the instrument set is widened to facilitate market players to even out their liquidity mismatches. *Fourth,* as RBI withdraws from the primary market in accordance with the FRBM Act, 2003, there is an urgent need to bridge the institutional gap with minimal necessary changes so that market operations retain their efficiency, both from the view point of central bank and the market participants. *Finally,* further improvements in liquidity management would substantially depend on our abilities to improve forecasting of liquidity in the system. The short span within which liquidity conditions have been changing by a large amount has been the biggest constraint in targeting short-term interest rates. More effort for understanding the fiscal position and the government cash balances, as also the timing of foreign capital flows are of paramount importance in this context.

LIQUIDITY MANAGEMENT

One of the objectives of the monetary policy is to provide adequate liquidity to the economy. A liquidity deficit, however, is considered necessary for quicker and correct signaling of the monetary policy stance. The medium term trend indicates a widening liquidity deficit, requiring liquidity injection often exceeding the 1 per cent level of net demand and time liabilities considered comfortable by RBI. During 2011-12, liquidity conditions had remained benign until mid-November, but pressures intensified in the subsequent part of the year, with average net borrowing under the liquidity adjustment facility (LAF) reaching as high as ₹ 1,570 billion in March 2012, with an all-time high of ₹ 2,028 billion on March 30, 2012. Both structural and frictional factors – such as foreign exchange market interventions by the RBI, divergence between credit and deposit growth and build-up of government cash balances with RBI– contributed to the liquidity pressures. Responding to the tight liquidity conditions, the RBI had conducted open market operations (OMOs) aggregating ₹ 1.3 trillion between November 2011 and March 2012, besides sequentially reducing CRR, injecting thereby primary liquidity of around ₹ 0.8 trillion into the banking system.

Liquidity conditions eased gradually during the first half of 2012-13. The turnaround in liquidity conditions was due to a decline in government's cash balances, injection of liquidity of about ₹ 860 billion by way of OMOs purchases of securities and increased use of the export credit refinance facility by banks. Reduction in SLR by one percentage point also improved the access of banks to potential liquidity. In September and October 2012 liquidity conditions, however, tightened taking the average net LAF borrowing to ₹ 904 billion since

October 15, 2012, which was well above the (+/-) one per cent of net demand and time liabilities (NDTL) comfort level for liquidity. On the basis of prevailing macroeconomic situation, the Reserve Bank (in the Second Quarter Review of Monetary Policy 2012- 13, announced on October 30, 2012) reduced the cash reserve ratio (CRR) of scheduled banks by 25 basis points from 4.50 per cent to 4.25 per cent of their net demand and time liabilities (NDTL) effective from the fortnight beginning November 3, 2012. Consequently, an estimated amount of around ₹ 175 billion of primary liquidity was injected into the banking system. The average daily net liquidity injection under the LAF increased to around ₹ 670 billion in October 2012 from around ₹ 520 billion in September 2012. The liquidity stress continued in November 2012 with average daily net liquidity injection under the LAF increasing to ₹ 940 billion. The liquidity conditions tightened further in the second-half of December 2012 on account of quarterly advance tax outflows, and the average daily net liquidity injection under the LAF increased significantly to around ₹ 1230 billion during the month.

The liquidity conditions remained above the Reserve Bank's comfort zone during most of the third quarter of 2012-13. Consistent with the stance of monetary policy and based on the current assessment of prevailing and evolving liquidity conditions, the Reserve Bank resumed Open Market Operations (purchase of government securities) on December 4, 2012 after a gap of nearly five months. Total purchase under OMO auctions stood at around ₹ 1060 billion during 2012-13 so far (till January 7, 2013), while total purchases through the anonymous trading platform (NDS-OM) stood at around ₹ 228.7 billion during this period. Although the Reserve Bank lowered the cash reserve ratio, CRR, successively in September and October 2012, and carried out open market operations (OMO) injecting systemic liquidity of ₹470 billion during December and January to augment liquidity, the average net LAF borrowings at ₹929 billion in January were above the Reserve Bank's comfort level. This tightness could potentially hurt credit flow to productive sectors of the economy. The structural deficit in the system provided a strong case for injecting permanent primary liquidity into the system. Accordingly, the RBI lowered the CRR from 4.25 per cent to 4.0 per cent in its third quarter review of Monetary Policy, effective from February 9, 2013. By the end of first week of February, LAF borrowings had declined to the RBI's comfort level

MONEY MARKET PRICE AND RATES

Money market securities typically make a single payment of face value at maturity and make no payments before maturity. Such securities are called pure discount securities because they sell at a discount relative to their face value. There are several different ways market participants quote interest rates. This presents a problem when we wish to compare rates on different investments. But before we can do this we must put them on a common footing. The relationship between the price of a money market instrument and the interest rate quoted on it is discussed below:

Bank Discount Basis

Interest rates for some key money market securities, including Treasury bills and banker's acceptances, are quoted on **a bank discount basis,** or simply discount basis. An interest rate quoted on a bank discount basis is often called discount yield. If we are given an interest rate quoted on a bank discount basis for a particular money market instrument, then we calculate the price of that instrument as follows:

$$\text{Current price} = \text{Face value} \times \left[1 - \frac{\text{Days to Maturity}}{360} \times \text{Discount yield}\right]$$

The term "discount yield" here simply refers to the quoted interest rate.

To give an example, suppose a banker's acceptance has a face value of ₹ 10 crore that will be paid in 90 days. If the interest rate, quoted on a discount basis, is 5 per cent, what is the current price of the acceptance?

As the following calculation shows, a discount yield of 5 per cent and maturity of 90 days gives a current price of ₹ 9,87,50,000.

$$₹\ 9,87,50,000 = ₹\ 10,00,00,000 \times \left[1 - \frac{90}{360} \times .05\right]$$

The difference between the face value of ₹ 10 crore and the price of ₹ 9,87,50,000 is ₹ 12,50,000 and is called the "discount." This discount is the interest earned over the 90-day period until the acceptance matures.

Notice that the formula used to calculate the acceptance price assumes a 360-day business year. This practice dates back to a time when calculations were performed manually. Assuming a 360-day business year, with exactly four 90-day quarter rather than a true 365-day calendar year, made manual discount calculations simpler and less subject to error. Consequently, if ₹ 10 crore is discounted over a full calender year of 365 days using a bank discount year of 5 per cent and an assumed 360-day business year, the resulting price of ₹ 9,49,30,556 is calculated as follows:

$$₹\ 9,49,30,556 = ₹\ 10,00,00,000 \times \left[1 - \frac{365}{360} \times .05\right]$$

Bank Discount Yield versus Bond Equivalent Yields

A bank discount yield is converted to a bond equivalent yield using the following formula

$$\text{Bank Equivalent yield} = \frac{365 \times \text{Discount yield}}{360 - \text{Days to Maturity} \times \text{DIscount yield}}$$

This conversion formula is correct for maturities of six months or less. Calculation of bond equivalent yield for maturities greater than six months is more complicated, and we will not discuss it here.

For example, supposed the asked discount rate on a T-bill with 170 days to maturity is 6.50 per cent. What is the bond equivalent yield? Plugging into the conversion formula, 6.50 per cent discount is converted into a bond equivalent yield as follows:

$$6.7\% = \frac{365 \times .065}{360 - 170 \times .065}$$

The bond equivalent yield is thus 6.7 per cent.

One common cause of confusion about bond equivalent yield calculations is the way that leap years are handled. The rule is that we must use 366 days if February 29 occurs within the next 12 months. For example, 2004 will be a leap year. So, beginning on March 1, 2003, we must use 366 days. Then beginning on March 1, 2004 we must revert back to using 365 days.

We can calculate a Treasury bill asked price using the asked yield, which is a bond equivalent yield, as follows:

$$\text{Bill Price} = \frac{\text{Face Value}}{1 + \text{Bond Equivalent Yield} \times \text{Days to Maturity} / 365}$$

For example, just above we calculated the 6.7 per cent bond equivalent yield on a T-bill with 170 days to maturity and a 6.50 per cent asked discount rate. If we calculate its price using this bond equivalent yield, we get

$$\text{Rs. } 76,21,18,903 = \frac{\text{Rs. } 1,00,00,000}{1+.067 \times 170 / 365}$$

Check that, ignoring a small rounding error, you get the same price using the bank discount formula.

Bond Equivalents, Yields, APRs, and EARs

Money market rates not quoted on a discounted basis are generally quoted on a "simple" interest basis. Simple interest rates are calculated just like the annual percentage rate (APR) on a consumer loan. So, for the most part, money market rates are either bank discount rates or APRs.

In fact, the bond equivalent yield on a T-bill with less than six months to maturity is also an APR. As a result, like any APR, it understates the true interest rate, which is usually called the effective annual rate, or EAR. In the context of the money market, EARs are sometimes referred to as effective annual yields, effective yields, or annualised yields. Whatever it is called to find out what a T-bill, or any other money market instrument, is *really* going to pay, yet another conversion is needed.

First, however, recall that an APR is equal to the interest rate per period multiplied by the number of periods in a year. For example, if the rate on a car loan is 1 per cent per month, then the APR is 1% x 12 = 12%. In general, if we let m be the number of periods in a year, an APR is converted to an EAR as follows:

$$1 + EAR = \left[1 + \frac{APR}{M}\right]^M$$

For example, on our 12 per cent APR car loan, the EAR can be determined by:

$$1 + EAR = \left[1 + \frac{12}{12}\right]^{12}$$

$$= [1.01]^{12} = 1.126825$$

$$EAR = 12.6825\%$$

Thus, the rate on the car loan is really 12.6825 per cent per year.

Now, to see that the bond equivalent yield on a T-bill is just an APR, we can first calculate the price on the bill we considered earlier 6.50 per cent asked discount, 170 days to maturity). Using the bank discount formula, the asked price, for ₹ 10 crore in face value, is

$$\text{Asked Price} = 9,69,30,000 = ₹\ 10,00,000,00 \times \left[1 - \frac{170}{360} \times .065\right]$$

The discount is ₹ 30,70,000. Thus on the 170-day investment, an investor earns ₹ 30,70,000 in interest on a an investment of ₹ 9,69,30,000. On a percentage basis, he earned

$$3.17\% = \frac{\text{Rs. } 30,70,000}{9,69,30,000}$$

In a 365-day year, there are $365/170 = 2.147$ periods of 170 day length. So if we multiply what he earned over the 170-day period by the number of 170-day periods in a year, we get

$$6.80599 = 2.147 \times 3.17\%$$

This is precisely the bond equivalent yield we calculated earlier.

Finally, for the T-bill we can calculated EAR using this 6.80599 per cent:

$$1+EAR = \left[1 + \frac{6.80599}{2.147}\right]^{2.417}$$

In the end, we have three different rates for this simple T-bill. The last one, the EAR, finally tells us what we really want to know: What are we actually going to earn?

REVIEW PROBLEMS

1. The rate on a particular money market instrument, quoted on a discount basis, is 6 per cent. The instrument has a face value of ₹ 1,00,00,000 and will mature in 71 days. What is its price? What if it had 51 days to maturity?

Ans.:

Using the bank discount formula, we have

$$\text{Current price} = \text{Face value} \times \left[1 - \frac{\text{Days to Maturity}}{360} \times \text{Discount Rate}\right]$$

$$₹\,98,81,667 = ₹\,1,00,00,000 \left[1 - \frac{71}{360} \times .06\right]$$

2. Suppose a T-bill has 45 days to maturity and an asked discount of 5 per cent. What is the bond equivalent yield?

Ans.:

Using the bond equivalent yield conversion formula, we have

$$5.101\% = \frac{365.05}{360 - 45 \times .05}$$

The bond equivalent yield is this 5.101 per cent.

3. Refer to problem-2, calculate the asked yield (bond equivalent) for a T-bill price quoted in December 2003 with 119 days to maturity and an asked discount of 6.00 per cent.

Ans.:

Since the 12-month period following the date of the price quote includes February 29, we must use 366 days. Plugging this into the conversion formula, we get:

$$6.22\% = \frac{366 \times .06}{360 - 119 \times .06}$$

This 6.22 per cent is the ask yield stated as bond equivalent yield.

4. A typical credit card may quote an APR of 18 per cent. On closer inspection, you will find that the rate is actually 1.5 per cent per month. What annual interest rate are your *really* paying on such a credit card?

Ans.:

With 12 periods in a year, an APR OF 18 per cent is converted to an EAR a follows:

$$1 + EAR \left[1 + \frac{18}{12}\right]^{12}$$

$$= [1.015]^{12} = 1.1956$$

$$EAR = 19.56\%$$

Thus, the rate on the credit card is really 19.56 per cent per year.

5. A money market instrument with 60 days to maturity has a quoted ask price of 99, meaning ₹ 99 per ₹ 100 face value. What are the banker's yield, the bond equivalent yield, and the effective annual return?

Ans.:

First, to get the discount yield, we have to use the bank discount formula and solve for the discount yield.

$$Rs.\ 90 = Rs.\ 100 \times \left[1 - \frac{60}{360} \times \text{Discount yield}\right]$$

With a little algebra, we see that the discount yield is 6 per cent.
We convert this to a bond equivalent yield as follows:

$$6.145\% = \frac{365 \times .06}{360 - 60 \times .06}$$

The bond equivalent yield is this 6.145 per cent.
Finally, to get the EAR, note that there are 6.0833 sixty-day periods in a year, so

$$1 + EAR = \left[1 - \frac{.6145}{6.0833}\right]^{6.0833}$$

$$= 1.06305$$

$$EAR = 6.305\%$$

This EAR illustrate the general result that the discount rate is lower than the bond equivalent yield, which is turn is less than the EAR.

QUESTIONS

1. What is the money market? Explain why there is a critical need for money market instruments.

2. Who are the principal lenders and borrowers active in the Indian money market?

3. Why do interest rates on the various money market instruments tend to move together the same direction at approximately the same time?

4. Describe the structure of interest rates in the Indian money market. Which instrument anchors the market and appears to be the foundation for other interest rates? Can you explain why this is so?

5. What is commercial paper? What features make it attractive to money market investors?

6. What are the principal advantages accruing to a company large enough to tap the commercial paper market for funds? Are there any disadvantages to issuing commercial paper?

7. Discuss the different types of interest rate quotes that are important for money market instruments?

8. Discuss certificate of deposits and commercial bills. What are the major benefits and costs of these instruments to the operators in the money market?

9. Critically examine the certain specific measures with respect of priority sector lending keeping in view the recent developments in the credit flow.

10. Define the following: *(i)* Money risk, *(ii)* Credit risk, *(iii)* Inflation risk, *(iv)* Currency risk and the, *(v)* Political risk. Which of these risks are minimised by investing in money market instruments? Can a money market investor avoid all of the above risk factors?

11. Critically examine the changing monetary policy paradigm in India.

12. What has been the lessons from the Indian experience of coping with liquidity management under large and volatile capital flows?

13. "Development of the money, the government securities and foreign exchange markets is critical for the overall growth and development of the economy and particularly in the transmission mechanism of monetary policy." Comment.

14. Discuss the money market instruments for liquidity management.

15. "Financial market reforms in India have enabled a greater integration of various segments of the financial markets, reducing arbitrage opportunities, achieving higher level of efficiency in market operations of intermediaries and increasing efficiency of monetary policy." Comment.

PROBLEM

1. A credit card company states an annual percentage (APR) of 12 percent, which is actually a rate of 1 percent per month? What is the EAR?

REFERENCES

1. Bank for International Settlements (2007), The Triennial Central Bank Survey of Foreign Exchange and Derivatives Market Activity.

2. Bank for International Settlements (2008), 78th Annual Report, 2007-08.

3. Bernanke, Ben (2009), "The Crisis and the Policy Response", Stamp Lecture at London School of Economics, January 13.

4. Bhattacharyya, I and P. Ray (2007): "How do we assess Monetary Policy Stance? Characterization of a Narrative Monetary Measure for India", special issue on Money, Banking and Finance, Economic and Political Weekly, March 31, 2007.

5. Borio, C and I. Shim (2007): "What Can (Macro-) Prudential Policy do to Support Monetary Policy?" BIS Working Paper No. 242, December.

6. Goldman Sachs (2007), India's Rising Growth Potential, January 2007, Government of India , Economic Survey of various years.

7. Greenspan, Alan (2001), "Monetary Policy in the face of Uncertainty", Cato Journal, Vol. 21.

8. Group of Thirty (2009), "Financial Reform: A Framework for Financial Stability" (Chairman: Paul A . Volcker), Washington D.C.

9. Haldane, Andrew (2009), "Why Banks Failed The Stress Test?", Bank of England.

10. Henry, Peter Blair (2007), "Capital Account Liberalization: Theory, Evidence, and Speculation", Journal of Economic Literature, Vol. XLV, December.

11. International Monetary Fund (2009a), "Group of Twenty: Note by the Staff of International Monetary Fund", January.

12. ————— (2009b), "Initial Lessons of the Crisis", February.

13. ————— (2009c), World Economic Outlook Database, April.16.html.

14. Issing O. (2004).: Inflation targeting: A View from the ECB. Federal Reserve Bank of St. Louis Review, Vol. 86, No. 4, July/August.

15. Kohn, Donald (2008), "Monetary Policy and Asset Prices Revisited", Remarks at the Cato Institute's 26th Annual Monetary Policy Conference, November 19.

16. Levine, R . (2004), "Finance and Growth: Theory and Evidence". NBER Working Paper No. 10766.

17. Lane, Philip (2009), "Global Imbalances and Global Governance", Paper presented at the `Global Economic Governance: Systemic Challenges, Institutional Responses and the Role of the New Actors', Brussels, February.

18. Mohan, Rakesh (2007), "Recent Financial Market Developments and Implications for Monetary Policy", Reserve Bank of India Bulletin, October.

19. ————— (2006a), "Coping With Liquidity Management in India: A Practitioner's View", Reserve Bank of India Bulletin, April.

20. ————— (2007b), " Monetary Management in Emerging Market Economies: Concerns and Dilemmas", comments made at Policy Panel at the NBER Conference on International Dimensions of Monetary Policy at S'Agaro, Catalino, Spain on June 12, 2007.

21. ————— (2008), "The Growth Record of the Indian Economy, 1950-2008: A Story of Sustained Savings and Investment", Keynote Address at the Conference "Growth and Macroeconomic Issues and Challenges in India" organised by the Institute of Economic Growth, New Delhi on February 14.

22. ————— (2000): "Fiscal Correction for Economic Growth. Data Analysis and Suggestions", Economic and Political Weekly, June 10.

23. ————— (2005), "Some Apparent Puzzles for Contemporary Monetary Policy", paper presented at the Conference on China's and India's Changing Economic Structures: Domestic and Regional Implications, Beijing, China, RBI Bulletin, December.

24. ————— (2006), "Monetary Policy and Exchange R ate Frameworks: The Indian Experience", paper presented at the Second High Level Seminar on Asian Financial Integration organised by the International Monetary Fund and Monetary Authority of Singapore, in Singapore on May 25, 2006, RBI Bulletin.

25. ————— (2008), "The Growth Record of the Indian Economy, 1950-2008: A Story of Sustained Savings and Investment", RBI Bulletin, March.

26. ————— (2006): "Financial Sector Reforms and Monetary Policy: The Indian Experience", Reserve Bank of India Bulletin, July.

27. ————— (2006b), "Evolution of Central Banking in India", Reserve Bank of India Bulletin, June Mühleisen, Martin (1997), Improving India's Saving Performance, IMF Working Paper No. 97/4, International Monetary Fund, January.

28. Prasad, Eswar S., Raghuram G. Rajan and Arvind Subramanian (2007), "Foreign Capital and Economic Growth", Brookings Papers on Economic Activity, 1.

29. Rajan. R., and L. Zingales (2003), "Saving Capitalism from the Capitalists: Unleashing the Power of Financial Markets to Create Wealth and Spread Opportunity". Crown Business, New York.

30. Rangarajan, C (1993): "Autonomy of Central Banks" – Tenth M.G. Kutty Memorial Lecture delivered at Calcutta on September 17, 1993 also printed in 50 years of Central Banking, Governor Speak, Reserve Bank of India, 1997.

31. Reddy, Y.V. (2007), "Monetary Policy Developments in India an Overview", address made at the Sveriges Riksbank, Stockholm, Sweden on September 7, 2007.

32. —————————— (2008), "Global Financial Turbulence and Financial Sector in India: A Practitioner's Perspective", Reserve Bank of India Bulletin, August.

33. —————————— (2007) "Some Perspectives on the Indian Economy", Reserve Bank of India Bulletin, November.

34. —————————— (2008b), "Management of the Capital Account in India: Some Perspectives", Inaugural address delivered at the Annual Conference of the Indian Econometric Society, Hyderabad on January 3, 2008.

35. —————————— (2008a), "Financial Globalisation, Growth and Stability: An Indian Perspective", Lecture delivered at the International Symposium of the Banque de France on Globalisation, Inflation and Monetary Policy, held in Paris on March 7, 2008.

36. —————————— (2009b), "Macroeconomic and Monetary Developments during 2008-09", April. And Methodology of Compilation" (Chairman: Dr. Y.V. Reddy).

37. —————————— (2008): "The Indian Economy and the Reserve Bank of India: Random Thoughts", Reserve Bank of India Bulletin, April.

38. —————————— (2005), "Overcoming Challenges in a Globalising Economy: Managing India's External Sector", lecture delivered at the Indian Programme of The Foreign Policy Centre, London on June 23,2005.

39. Reserve Bank of India (1985): Report of the Committee to Review the Working of the Monetary System (Chairman: Prof. Sukhamoy Chakravarty).

40. Reserve Bank of India (2003): "Report of the Working Group on Instruments of Sterilisation (Chairperson: Smt Usha Thorat).

41. Reserve Bank of India (2004): Report on Currency and Finance, 2003-04.

42. Richard Portes (Ed.), "Macroeconomic Stability and Financial Regulation: Key Issues for the G20", Centre for Economic Policy Research, London.

43. Rodrik, Dani and Arvind Subramanian (2004), Why India Can Grow at 7 Percent a Year or More: Projections and Reflections, IMF Working Papers 04/118, International Monetary Fund.

44. Sheridan N.. (2003) :"Does inflation Targeting Matter?". NBER Working Paper No 9577.

45. Taylor, John (2009), "The Financial Crisis and the Policy Responses: An Empirical Analysis of What Went Wrong", Working Paper 14631, January, National Bureau of Economic Research.

46. Turner Review (2009), "The Turner Review: A Regulatory Response to the Global Banking Crisis" by Lord Turner, Chairman, Financial Services Authority, UK.

47. Vickers, John (2000), "Monetary Policy and the Supply Side", Bank of England Bulletin. Government of India (1993), High Level Committee on Balance of Payments (Chairman: C. Rangarajan), Ministry of Finance. Government of India (2007), Mid-Year Review 2007-08.

48. Warnock, Veronica Cacdac and Francis E. Warnock (2008), Markets and housing finance, Journal of Housing Economics.

49. White, W.R , (2004): "Are Changes in Financial Structure Extending Safety Nets?" BIS Working Paper No. 145, January.

50. World Bank (2008), Global Development Finance 2008: The Role of International Banking, World Bank.

Part III

SECURITY ANALYSIS

20

Fundamental Security Analysis

INTRODUCTION

The objective of fundamental security analysis is to appraise the 'intrinsic value' of a security. The intrinsicvalue is the true economic worth of a financial asset. The fundamentalists maintain that at any point of time every share has an intrinsic value which should in principle be equal to the present value of the future stream of income from that share discounted at an appropriate risk related rate of interest. The actual price of the security, therefore, is considered to be a function of a set of anticipated capitalization rate. Price changes as anticipation changes which in turn change as a result of new information. The fundamentalists then argue that in case there is something less than complete information, the actual price of the stock is generally away from its intrinsic value. Thus they believe that market can often be wrong in appraising the value of a share of a company. Hence, the job of the fundamental security analyst is to sort out the temporary disequilibrium from the true shifts in the national economy and the accounting gimmics from true changes in the firm's income in order to arrive at an unbiased estimate of the intrinsic value.

Relying upon this reasoning, the fundamentalists attempt to estimate the real worth of a security by considering the earning potential of a firm which in turn will depend on investment environmental factors such as state and growth of national economy, monetary policies of the Reserve Bank of India, corporate laws, social and political environment and the factor relating to the specific industry such as state of product and the growth potential of the industry. It will depend to a large extent, on the firm's competitiveness, its quality of management, operational efficiency, profitability, capital structure and dividend policy. However, the firm or the stock market cannot be analysed in vaccum. All firms work within the economic environment, their survival will depend on how the economy as a whole is faring. During periods of economic prosperity the demand for goods and services of the firm is likely to result in increased sales and higher profits. The expectation of the growth of economy is favourable for the stock market.

In order to obtain investment perspective, we must determine the state of the economic environment in which we invest. Essentially, we must determine the current condition of the economy, where it is headed, and the implications for investment decisions. Such an analysis allows us to select the sectors of the economy that appear to offer profitable opportunities. This analysis will also help establish what type of investment should be undertaken among real assets, riskless investments, intermediate or long term bonds, or common stocks.

AN ANALYSIS OF THE ECONOMY

Investment in fixed-income and ownership securities is intimately associated with the economic activity of the nation. An investment in the equity of any company is likely to be more profitable if the economy is strong and prosperous; so the expectation of the growth of the economy is favourable for the stock market. By the same token, strength in an industry that has evidenced rapid growth in the past suggests that companies within that industry and on the periphery of it will benefit from this growth and that, in the end, they will provide substantial rewards.

Not all industries grow at the same rate, nor do all companies. The growth of a company or an industry depends basically on its ability to satisfy human wants through production of goods or performance of a service. How people earn their living and where they spend their money will, in the last analysis, determine which companies and industries will grow and prosper and which will decline.

In contrast, if expectations of a decline in the national economy are strong, the overtones and implications for investment in equity or debt instruments are serious. If we could be certain that the next three years would bring a recession, this fact would be reflected in our investment position. Certainly it would suggest greater attention to fixed-income obligations, because these would offer considerably more safety than equity. It is important, therefore, to analyse the national economy, attempt to determine its course over the next twelve months to three years and to obtain some investment perspective determine what the longer-term possibilities are.

Once this has been accomplished, the growth of the national economy can be used to forecast the growth of an industry or company and thus to determine those areas offering good opportunities. This process will also help to point out industries and companies that should be avoided because they appear to offer less attractive opportunities. As a principle, a strong and stable economy with real growth is favourable for investment.

THE CURRENT STATE OF THE ECONOMY

For investment perspective, the current state of the nation's economy must first be determined. Even the process of determining the state of economic development is not easy, simply because not all the facts and figures are always available. Reporting methods provide an automatic lag in data and information. At best, the investor has only estimates. The improvement in reporting techniques from computerisation of the data collected for the government by private enterprises that predict the future help to tell where the economy is with greater certainty. If the economy is expected to grow in the future at a substantial rate compared with that of the past decade, then one course of action is obviously to invest in equity. If one segment of the economy is expected to grow faster than the economy as a whole, then the investor will attempt to concentrate in this rapidly growing area.

If, on the other hand, the economy is expected to begin a period of cyclical or secular decline, the investor must be more defensive. Under these conditions, bonds would be much more appealing than equity.

Investment climate in an economy can be observed from the GNP and its components. GNP stands for gross national product, the broadest measure of economic activity used to determine where the national economy is, where it has been, and where it is going. It represents the aggregate amount of goods and services produced in the national economy for a period of time, usually one year. Economists and investors deal in terms of the GNP, and have developed the game of "growthmanship" using GNP as a measure of economic activity.

The process of development of the economy gained momentum during the 'nineties with the initiation of major economic reforms in 1991. The economy has since then been successfully launched on to a higher growth trajectory and has registered an improvement in a number of macro-economic indicators in a short span of less than a decade.

A V-shaped recovery from the balance of payments crisis of 1990-91 was followed by phase of uninterrupted expansion at the average rate of 7.0 per cent per annum during 1993-97. The average annual growth rate during the Ninth Five Year Plan (1997-2002) is now estimated at 5.4 per cent which is lower than the plan target of 6.5 per cent. Although this raises new challenges for reinvigorating growth in the Tenth Five Year Plan, the In⁻¹ in growth record is one of the highest among the major economies in the world in recent years. The Indian economy has been resilient in the face of several external shocks during this period such as the East Asian crisis of 1997-98, the oil price increase of 2000-01, and the most recent world economic slowdown. Domestic shocks in the shape of an adverse security environment, natural disasters like the Orissa cyclone and Gujarat earthquake, and two consecutive years of poor agricultural performance, have also been faced successfully by the economy.

The Indian economy is now poised for a higher growth profile. The distinguishing feature of India's macroernnomic performance in recent year has been the strong acceleration of growth. Industry and services, comprising 82 per cent of the economy, registered double-digit growth. The step-up in the overall growth momentum, setbacks to agriculture notwithstanding, occurred, *inter alia*, in an environment of building international interest, and rising business and consumer confidence domestically, in the strength and dynamism of the economy. Real GDP growth, which averaged under three per cent in the 1970s picked up to 5.8 per cent in the 1980s and 1990s but lost pace in the subsequent period and slowed to 4.6 per cent in 2000-03. Since then, however, there seems to have occurred an upward shift in trajectory, with real GDP growth averaging 8.5 per cent in the period 2003-04 to 2006-07.

During 2007-08, the Indian economy continued to expand at a robust pace for the fifth consecutive year, although there was some moderation in the growth momentum during the course of the year. According to the advance estimates released by Central Statistical Organisation (CSO), the real GDP growth rate moderated to 8.7 per cent in 2007-08 from 9.6 per cent in 2006-07. The moderation in growth occurred in all the three sectors. viz., agriculture and allied activities, industry and services. Notwithstanding the moderation, the growth performance was in tune with the high average real GDP growth of 8.7 per cent per annum during the five-year period, 2003-04 to 2007-08. India also continued to be one of the fastest growing economies of the world.

The Indian economy, which was on a robust growth path up to 2007-08, averaging at 8.9 per cent during the period 2003-04 to 2007-08, witnessed moderation in 2008-09, with the deceleration turning out to be somewhat sharper since the third quarter. While the growth deceleration was primarily driven by the knock on effects of the global economic crisis, it also reflected to some extent the slowdown associated with cyclical factors. Industrial growth experienced a significant downturn and the loss of growth momentum was evident in all categories, viz., the basic, capital, intermediate and consumer goods. A hitherto key growth driver, services sector, witnessed some moderation, notwithstanding a counter-cyclical rise in the growth of community, social and personal services on the back of implementation of the Sixth Pay Commission recommendations. Although agriculture also recorded a deceleration in growth, the agricultural outlook remains satisfactory, with the sowing in the rabi season being higher than that in the previous year.

The global financial crisis interrupted the growth momentum of India, despite the strong dominance of domestic sources of growth. There was clear moderation in growth by the third quarter of 2008-09. The Real GDP growth during the third quarter of 2008-09 was lower at 5.3 per cent as compared with 8.9 per cent in the corresponding period of 2007-08, reflecting deceleration of growth in all its constituent sectors. The cumulative position reveals that the real GDP growth was 6.9 per cent during 2008-09 (April-December) as compared with 9.0 per cent during the corresponding period of 2007-08.

There was apprehension that this trend would persist for some time, as the full impact of the economic slowdown in the developed world worked through the system. It was also a year of reckoning for the policymakers, who had taken a calculated risk in providing substantial fiscal expansion to counter the negative fallout of the global slowdown. Inevitably, India's fiscal deficit increased from the end of 2007-08, reaching 6.8 per cent of GDP in 2009-10. A delayed and severely subnormal monsoon added to the overall uncertainty. The continued recession in the developed world, for the better part of 2009-10, meant a sluggish export recovery and a slowdown in financial flows into the economy. Yet, over the span of the year, the economy posted a remarkable recovery, not only in terms of overall growth figures but, more importantly, in terms of certain fundamentals, which justify optimism for the Indian economy in the medium to long term.

It is important to note that during the past three years ,the Indian economy has been severely buffeted by, but has successfully withstood two shocks in rapid succession: (a) a collapse in world growth, finances, and trade with the onset of the global financial crisis in 2007-2009 whose ripple effects continued into 2009-10 and persisted into 2010-11 (with fiscal stresses in Europe) and (b) domestically ,following a year of negative growth in agriculture and allied sectors in 2008-09, erratic monsoons resulted in a severe drought in 2009-10 and unseasonal late rains affecting the winter season crops in 2010-11. This period of economic stress has severely tested policymakers. Yet the Indian economy is coming through with resilience and strength.GDP growth during 2010-11 reverted to the high growth trajectory. Growth had moderated in the preceding two years as the global economy slowed down as a result of global financial crisis. The growth during 2010-11 reflects a rebound in agriculture and sustained levels of activity in industry and services. Aggregate demand accelerated further in 2010-11 even as rebalancing took place from government consumption spending to private consumption and investment. Momentum in overall demand conditions was reflected in indicators like corporate sales growth, improving capacity utilisation, higher employment and pricing power with the producers. Based on the performance of the economy over the last five years and analysis of the underlying trends in critical variables, India's real GDP was expected to grow by 9 percent (+/-0.250) in 2011-12, almost reverting to the pre-crisis levels achieved during the three-year period 2005-06 to 2007-08. The optimum was driven by the fact that the economy had achieved a growth rate of 8.4 per cent during the years 2009-10 and 2010-11 and the savings and investment rates had begun rising once again. However, during the course of 2011-12 it became clear that growth rate would fall short by a significant margin for various reasons. As it happened, the economy was able to register only 6.5 per cent in 2011-12. Like in 2008-9, a part of the reason for the slowdown lies in global, factors, particularly the crisis in the eurozone area and near-recessionary conditions prevailing in Europe; sluggish growth in many other industrialized countries, like the USA; stagnation in Japan; and hardening international prices of crude oil, which always has a large effect on India. Domestic factors, namely the tightening of monetary policy, in particular raising the repo rate in order to control inflation and anchor inflationary expectations, resulted in some slowing down of investment and growth, particuiarly in the industrial sector.

Managing growth and price stability are the major challenges of macro-economic policymaking. In 2012-13, India found itself in the heart of these conflicting demands. The Indian economy is expected to grow by 5.5 percent in 2012-13 since the economy further decelerated in the first half of 2012-13, with moderation in all three sectors of the economy. The weak monsoon dented agricultural performance. Policy constraints, supply and infrastructure bottlenecks and lack of sufficient demand continued to keep industrial growth below trend. Subdued growth in other sectors and weak external demand pulled down the growth of services as well. During 2012-13, the industrial sector is expected to grow by 3.4 per cent against the previous forecast of 4%. Mining sector is expected to record a decline of 0.9 per cent. Utility sector growth is revised downwards to 6.8 percent from the precious forecast of 8.7 per cent. However, projection for agriculture and services remained unchanged at 1.3 per cent and 8.1 per cent, respectively. Though a modest recovery may set in from Q4 of 2012-13 as reforms get implemented, sustaining recovery through 2013-14 would require all-round efforts in removing impediments to business activity.

Demand weakened in the first half of 2012-13. There was significant moderation in consumption as private consumption decelerated even as government expenditure accelerated. On the fiscal side, near-term risks have diminished due to the government's repeated avowal of commitment to the revised fiscal deficit target of 5.3 per cent of gross domestic product (GDP) for the year. However, sustainable fiscal consolidation would require bringing current spending, especially on subsidies, under control and protecting, if not enhancing capital expenditure. Going forward, the key to demand revival lies in improving the investment climate as well as investor sentiments through sustained reforms.

The current account deficit (CAD) to GDP ratio reached a historically high level of 5.4 per cent in Q2 of 2012-13. Low growth and uncertainty in AEs as well as EMDEs continued to adversely impact exports in Q3 of 2012-13. This, combined with continuing large imports of oil and gold, resulted in a deterioration of the trade balance. For the time being, strong capital flows have enabled financing of CAD without a significant drawdown of foreign exchange reserves. However, the possibility of volatility in these flows, which may put further pressure on the external sector, cannot be ruled out. A two-pronged approach, of lowering CAD in the medium term while ensuring prudent financing of CAD in the interim, is necessary from the policy perspective.

Monetary policy in India has sought to balance the growth-inflation dynamics that included a frontloaded policy rate cut of 50 basis points (bps) in April 2012 and several liquidity enhancing measures. These included lowering of the cash reserve ratio (CRR) by 50 bps on top of a 125 bps reduction in Q4 of 2011-12 and the statutory liquidity ratio (SLR) by 100 bps in a bid to improve credit flows. The Reserve Bank also infused liquidity of over ₹ 1.3 trillion through outright open market operation (OMO) purchases during 2012-13 so far. However, growth in monetary aggregates remains below the indicative trajectory.

Improved global sentiments along with recent policy reforms by the government beginning September 2012, and market expectations of a cut in the policy rate in the face of moderation in inflation, aided FII flows into the domestic market. The equity markets showed significant turnaround, while the rupee remained range-bound. In addition, revival is witnessed in the IPO segment. Although Indian financial market sentiments improved significantly in Q3 of 2012-13, some macroeconomic concerns persist, as witnessed in the inverted yield curve. Sustained commitment to curtail twin deficits and nurture growth without fuelling inflation is critical to support investor confidence.

Headline inflation moderated in Q3 of 2012-13 with significant moderation in nonfood manufactured products inflation. Both weakening domestic demand and lower global commodity prices contributed to the softening of headline inflation. Though the recent hike in diesel prices will put some pressure on the overall price level, the near-term inflation outlook indicates that the moderation may continue through Q4 of 2012-13. While the pressure from generalised inflation remains muted at the current juncture, risks from suppressed inflation, pressure on food prices and high inflation expectations getting entrenched into the wage-price spiral need to be reckoned with. The inflation path for 2013- 14 could face downward rigidity as some of the risks from suppressed inflation materialise.

Reforms since September 2012 have reduced immediate risks, but there is a long road ahead to bring about a sustainable turnaround for the Indian economy. Business sentiments remain weak despite reform initiatives and consumer confidence is edging down. The Reserve Bank's survey of professional forecasters anticipates a slow recovery in 2013-14 with inflation remaining sticky. Fiscal risks have somewhat moderated in 2012-13, but a sustained commitment to fiscal consolidation is needed to generate monetary space. Widening CAD, which is at historically high level, remains a constraint on monetary easing. Against this backdrop, while growth can be supported by monetary policy if inflation risks recede, credible fiscal correction with improved execution in infrastructure space to boost investment would be needed for a sustained revival. The balance of macroeconomic risks suggest continuation of the calibrated stance while increasingly focussing on growth risks.

Growth remains subdued due to a combination of external and domestic factors. Business and consumer confidence remain subdued Government's commitment to reforms is expected to instill confidence among investors and support gradual recovery. Inflation has moderated but remains high. The decline has not been commensurate with the slowdown in growth and upside risks remain from suppressed inflation. While government has embarked on a fiscal adjustment path, staying on this course over the medium-term is necessary for providing sufficient space for monetary policy to stimulate growth. The widening current account deficit also remains a major source of concern. While domestic and global conditions are expected to improve slowly, calibration of the policy stance is important due to prevailing uncertainties.

Reforms reduce immediate risks, but long road ahead. The fresh round of reforms that were initiated in September 2012, after a hiatus, has reduced the immediate risks facing the Indian economy. The recent measures taken, especially in January 2013 have further reinforced this momentum. Triere are signs that growth may have bottomed out, though recovery may take some more time and is likely to be paced gradually. However, on an immediate footing, the recent reforms and measures to debottleneck infrastructure and other sectors have reduced the rnacroeconotnic and financial risks facing the Indian economy. These measures need to be carried forward as certain key constraints continue to impede investments in road and power sectors. As the envisaged measures are implemented to remove the impediments, the economy can start turning around in 2013-14. However, weak global economic conditions, domestic business constraints and low confidence levels may keep the recovery modest next year, while the near-term risks to the economy emanating from fiscal and external imbalances remain.

Clearly, there is a long road ahead to regain the pre-crisis potential growth. Traversing this requires tough economic and political decisions that do not fritter away the recent modest gains as the compulsions of poltical cycles mount in the run-up to the 2014 general elections.

Leading, Coincidental, and Lagging Indexes

The economic indicator are grouped into leading, coincidental and lagging indexes to help in analysis and forecasting. The coincidal indicators include GNP in constant or "real" terms, corporate profits, industrial production, unemployment and the producer price index. There are many coincidental indexes, but these are the most common. These indicators tell us what is happening in the economy, but they do not forecast the future.

The leading indicators tell us what to expect in the future. Some of the popular leading indexes are fiscal policy, monetary policy, GNP deflator, productivity, consumer spending, residential construction and stock prices as measured by the RBI etc.

The lagging indicators turn after the movement in the coincidental indicators. The best-known lagging indicator is the prime rate, which usually turns down a few months or quarters after a turndown in the economy. Commercial paper rates, capital expenditures, the inventory sales ratio, retail sales, and the consumer price index are other important lagging indicators.

Significance and Interpretation of the Economic Indicators

The investor makes an analysis of the economy primarily to determine an investment strategy. It is not necessary to make their own economic forecasts. The primary responsibility is to identify the trends in the economy and adjust the investment position accordingly. Many of the published forecasts are excellent and provide the necessary perspective.

The variables for analysis have their own significance. The GNP is nominal and real terms is a useful economic indicator. Inflation and price increases are detrimental to equity prices. Therefore, a real growth of GNP without inflation is favourable and desirable. Higher rates are unfavourable for investment in both bonds and most equities; if inflation is expected to be very high next year, this fact will have an unfavourable effect on the stock market now.

Business investment's a key economic variable to watch. The expectation of an increase in business investment is an optimistic condition for the stock market and the economy.

The leading indicator index is very useful. A rising indicator is bullish for the economy and the stock market. A Federal Reserve Bank of Dallas economist, Wallace H. Duncan, has developed what he considers to be a better leading indicator. He divides quarterly GNP minus business inventories into consumer durables plus residential and business fixed investment. As the ratio rises, this is a sign that the economy will strengthen and that the stock market should turn up. A high level of housing starts is a good indicator of business conditions. A high level of auto production and the expectation growth are favourable indicators. The figures must be interpreted realistically, however: In inflationary conditions, a decline in housing starts and auto production would be a welcome sign, for it would signal reduced pressure on prices. An increase in business inventories is good for the economy under conditions of inflation. But under stable conditions, it signifies the economy is slowing down, which would be unfavourable. increase in employment and a decrease in unemployment are favourable for the economy; the opposite situation is unfavourable. An increase in personal income, coupled with substantial consumer confidence, is a favourable economic indicator. An increase in savings is a negative indicator in depressed times, but positive under inflationary conditions. A deficit is positive for a depressed economy, but negative for an inflationary economy.

Another indicator to be examined is the balance of trade and the price of the currency in the foreign exchange market. A deficit in trade and balance-of-payments position depreciate the currency in foreign exchange markets and it has a negative influence on the economy and the securites market. Further, high short-term interest rates and long-term interest rates are unfavourable for hte economy under normal conditions. They are quite unfavourable for equity prices. High interest rates, then, would be negative influence on the stock market.

A high level of corporate profit and the expectation for increased corporates profits are favourable for the economy and the stock market. Generally, corporate profits and low when the GNP in real terms in low, and vice versa.

A rising stock market suggests that the economy, nine months to a year ahead, will be growing. A declining stock market suggests the economy will not grow substantially in the year ahead.

An examination of these variables will give an investor a handy reference in interpreting the direction of the economy and the stock market. This, coupled with professional economic opinion, should lead to the establishment of a sound investment policy.

INDUSTRY ANALYSIS

The industries that contribute to the output of the major segments of the economy vary in their growth rate and in their overall contribution to economic activity. Some have grown more rapidly than the GNP and offer the expectation of continued growth. Others have maintained a growth comp[arable to that of the GNP. A few have been unable to expand and have declined in economic significance. If we are to succeed as investors, we must analyse the economic significance of industries and invest in those that offer continued success, measured by the industry's ability to compete for its appropriate share of the GNP.

Seeking industries that are expected to grow at faster than the "real" rate of GNP for the future seems to be a logical starting position. We can find successful companies in industries that are not growing. On the other hand, investment success is more likely to be found in growing and strongly competitive industries. The danger in this thesis is that investors tend to bid up the price of these assets in the market place. An over-enthusiastic investor might pay too much for a share of stock in such industries.

The Concept of an Industry

In a broad sense, an industry might be considered a community of interests. This concept would reflect the idea of a group of people coming together because they do a certain type of work or produce a similar type of product. Such groups would include agriculture as well as manufacturing, mining and merchandising. In an economic sense, these groups from into industries because of the nature of what is produced and the processes involved in its production. We tend to think of an industry as a product- or process-oriented unit. The automobile industry, for example, reflects both the concept of the end product—the automobile—and the method of production—the manufacturing process. The banking industry also illustrates the industry concept. It consists basically of commercial banks that makes business and consumer loans. The product, of course, is money, and the process is the lending process.

The classes of industries are unlimited. If we classify industries by the process of manufacture, then we can divide them according to the nature of their function; for example, the manufacturing industry, the transportation industry, and the public utility industry. These broad functional groups can then be further broken down by end product. The manufacturing industry, for instance, would include such diverse products as autos, pianos, tin cans, shoes and cribs. It would include all products that are manufactured. The transportation industry would include railroads, airlines, trucks, shops and possibly pipe-lines. Automobiles would be excluded because, although they are a form of transportation, they are not available as a common carrier except as taxis. However, private transportation companies via the auto with other forms of transportation. In this case, the auto would fall into two classes of industry: the manufacturing class and the transportation class. For practical purposes, autos is placed in the manufacturing industry.

The classification of an industry is important when we analyse its growth. Each industry takes its share of the GNP and competes with every other industry. Thus, the manufacturing industry compete with agriculture, transportation and public utilities. This intere-industry competition is important. And within each major industry classification, the product- or service-oriented segments compete for a share of the GNP. We are mainly interested in these service and product-oriented industries. We define an industry, then, as a limited set of productive functions or activities measured by the output of an end product or service, we can observe changes much more easily than if we used a broader classification. These changes and expectation of change should cause the investor to react favourably or unfavourably toward an industry for investment.

For careful analysis, each industry is broken down into its logical product classes. The drug industry, for example, is usually divided into proprietary drugs and ethical drugs, the auto industry into passenger autos and trucks, and the rubber industry into tiers and rubber products.

The growth of an industry usually begins with a major technological change. In recent years, robots, personal computers, electronic equipment and communication devices, office equipment, automated control equipment and ionic propulsion have created new industries and rapid technological change, resulting in rapid industrial growth. As an industry expands, the following growth pattern emerges, according to Simon Kuznets: In the beginning, rapid growth takes place at extremely high rates. As the industry expands over long periods of time, the percentage rate of growth diminishes. Industries never experience unretarded or accelerated growth for long periods of time.

Kuznets gives several reasons for the decreasing rate of growth of an industry. First, the major technological changes that created the industry are concentrated in the early stages of the life of the industry. These major changes are reinforced by minor changes and improvements, also made early in the development of the product as the bugs are being worked out. If we have a limited number of production functions to use in the industry and their use is changed rapidly, strong economic pressures bring about rapid upward growth. A good illustration of this is the auto industry, whose rate of growth was extremely high in the early years of its development, between 1900 and 1920. Production rates increased rapidly, and the percentage rate of change was extremely high as techniques and products improved. After the early period of development, the growth rate subsided. The industry has become a cyclical growth industry, as well.

A second reason for a diminution in the industry growth rate is the nature of the technological change itself. The basic types of major technological changes help to produce an old product more cheaply or an completely new product on mass basis. This has happened in the pocket-calculator field and in the production of digital watches. A high-priced commodity or service is changed into a low-priced one, making it available to a larger market. A luxury good might be changed into a necessity good. Using the auto industry as an example, both changes increase the immediate demand for the product. In the early years of technological development, these changes have a remarkable impact on growth. Beyond the early years and the immediate reduction in costs and price, the changes have little effect on the growth of the market and the output of the industry.

The relative growth of other industries tends to reduce the impact of cost reductions which, in turn, tends to limit the continued growth of a market. If other industries do not grow as fast as that in which the rapid expansion takes place, prices will not drop in the other industries. This will limit the decline in price in the rapidly expanding industry. Assume, for example, that a technological innovation occurs, such as the development of automated equipment, that permits a reduction in the price of transistors from ` 500 to ` 200 per unit. The demand for transistors expands, and the number produced increase dramatically. However, germanium, a raw material for the transistor, does not undergo a corresponding expansion in demand, since there are no new economies or developments that will allow germanium to be produced at a lower prices, and the amount used in producing transistors is not sufficient to bring about mass-production economies. Since the raw material cannot be lowered in price, there is also a lower limit to the price of the transistor. Any price changes that would help increase output in the future will be negligible, and the accompanying rate of expansion will be diminished. The general effect of this example can be transferred to the economy as a whole: An industry growing at a rapid rate, faster than the national economy, will eventually have its growth dampened because of the slower growth of the economy.

A third factor that tends to limit the growth of an industry is competitive pressure from other industries. The industry that first experienced a technological change may be restrained by the development of a new industry, competing directly for raw materials and thus tending to raise costs for the original industry and limit its expansion potential. Sometimes, new industries are directly competitive with the old product or original product. For example, one material becomes a substitute for each other, depending upon their use. One type of power can be substituted for another, as aluminium was substituted for steel, stainless steel for chromium, and plastics for aluminium or metal. For that matter, all metals can be substituted for other types of power, depending upon the cost-price relationship involved. Nuclear power is even now being substituted for oil-generated steam to produce electricity. The woolen industry lost part of its market to cotton. The cotton lost part of its market to silk and rayon. Then rayon and silk began losing their market to nylon, and so on. The net of these changes is that the competitive position of one product or service is often lost to a rival product that indirectly or directly does a better job than the old one. This competition tends to diminish the growth of the industry.

Another manifestation of this competition is international competition that develops for a national product. Television set production can be used as an illustration. The Japanese developed production techniques allowing TV sets to be cheaply mass-produced. Virtually overnight, the market price was reduced and the competitive position of the industry in the United States was diminished.

A fourth and final factor that might reduce the rate of growth of an industry is a decrease in population growth. In order for a product to expand its output at an increasing rate, per capita output would have to grow at an increasing rate. For this to occur, consumers would have to spend more of their income. The consumer's income does not increase as fast as the growth of the product, because the economy grows more slowly than an industry experiencing rapid growth, and so it is unlikely that the industry's growth rate can be sustained.

The diminishing percentage rate of growth of the output of an industry is depicted in Figure-1. The solid curved line on the semilog graph represents a constantly decreasing rate of growth. If the same data were plotted on regular graph paper, the line would be straight. If the line in Figure-1 were straight, the growth rate would be constant. A constant growth rate is possible over short periods of the growth life of an industry, but not over long periods.

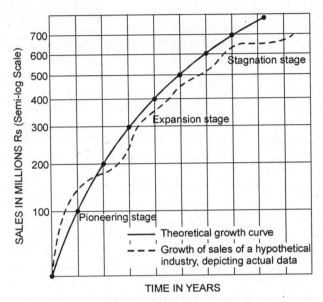

TIME IN YEARS

FIGURE 1: THE INDUSTRIAL GROWTH CURVE

The time intervals in the chart do not represent any specific number of years, since the life cycle of an industry cannot be shown in uniform time periods.

THE INDUSTRIAL GROWTH CYCLE

The growth of an industry is sometimes divided into stages. Grodinsky, in his book on investments, divided the growth cycle into the pioneering stage, the expansion stage, and the stagnation stage - a division quite similar to Kuznet's concept. Figure-1 demonstrates the growth of an industry graphically by the dotted line, which is divided into the three stages. Grodinsky, however, relates the stages of growth more to the characteristics of the company than to the industry as a whole. His concepts should be of interest to the investor.

The Pioneering Stage

The pioneering stage, as presented by Grodinsky, is comparable to Kuznet's discovery stage, the stage when the technological development takes place. Its primary characteristics are a rapid increase in production and rapidly expanding demand for the product. Many companies enter the market to produce the product, and the market is extremely competitive. Profits are large for those firms that first introduce the product, but as competition increases, prices decline rapidly and profits fall. This tends to force out the less efficient firms. There is little price stability in the pioneering stage, and risk capital is supplied more by speculators and promoters than by investors.

As competition forces out some of the firms, they are acquired by the competitively strong companies. As a result, at the end of the pioneering stage, only a few leading companies remain in the industry. In Figure-1, the dip in sales at that point represents the circumstances that force many firms out of the industry. The auto, radio, television, and electronic industries offer excellent illustrations of the pioneering stage as part of the growth cycle.

The Expansion Stage

The expansion stage in the growth cycle is charaterised by an expanding demand for the product, but the rate of growth is less than in the pioneering stage. There is greater stability of prices, and production during this phase. Competition is keen, and a small number of larger firms dominate the industry. These large firms have been put together through merger and acquisition and by their competitive superiorly. The companies that remain have successfully weathered the financial adversity of the later phases of the pioneering stage and remain in business. They are well financed, they have strong financial structures, and their current financial position is excellent. They have an established dividend policy and are able to expand from internally generated funds, making them independent of the long-term capital markets except for major capital-expenditure programmes.

Investors can invest funds during the expansion stage in the knowledge that substantial growth potential remains in the industry. Yet there is safety and security, since the larger companies have been able to retain a sizeable share of the market. The competitive position of the firm is not automatically ensured by its initial success, but it is in a strong position to maintain its status in the industry. Investors have some assurance that they will profit from investment without the threat of a complete loss of principal. This stage of industry growth is sometimes referred to as the period of investment maturity, because of the stability and status of the firms within the industry.

The Stagnation Stage ·

In the later phase of the growth cycle of an industry, the rate of growth subsides. For some industries there is no growth at all in this phase, and output actually declines. In this phase, the industry simply loses its power to expand. When the national economy shows economic strength, the growth of an industry in the stagnation stage does not keep pace, and its output falls faster than the economy increases. The transition from the expansion to the stagnation stage comes about gradually, and unless investors and aware of the changes taking place in the industry, they will be taken by surprise.

The general description of the stages of development of industries by the life-cycle theory tits quite well with the past experience of many industries. Several investment implications of the theory are well worth investors' attention.

(a) The risk in the pioneering stage is too high. Speculators may find it exciting and profitable, but investors should stay away.

(b) The investors should look for opportunities in an industry when the industry enters into the second stage of fast growth.

(c) Industry selection should receive consideration prior to an investment decision.

The theory offers a general description of the industry life cycle. Individual industries have varied substantially from the norm in the stage of developments as portrayed by the theory. What can be most safely said of the development of industries is the common trend toward *retardation in growth rates*. Most industries mature and decline relatively, but do not die as individuals. Not a few industries after reaching the mature stage often go through a long period of alternate prosperity and recession. In retrospect it is often easy to define the stages a mature industry has gone through, but it is not an easy matter to identify the current stage of many industries. Finally, while the life-cycle theory offers the valuable investment implications mentioned, it can cause financial losses to the unwary believer in this industry approach to investment. Even during the stage of fast growth, the actual performance will vary substantially among the surviving corporations. Moreover, not infrequently the prices of the shares of these corporations can be bid up much too high because of an impressive past record and bright prospects. Purchases at such high price levels can easily turn into substantial losses for a long period of time, and there is a good possibility that the investor may be disillusioned and sell out during the interval. If one insists on speculation in this early stage, he should spread his funds over several leading companies, hoping that the ones which will survive and prosper will more than offset the losses on other companies which will be eliminated.

STRUCTURE AND OPERATIONAL CHARACTERISTICS OF THE INDUSTRY

Each industry has its own unique characteristics. A careful review of these unique features should always form an important part of an industry study. The analysis of an industry usually covers several important areas.

1. The structure and the state of competition in the industry.
2. The nature and prospect of demand for the products and services of the industry.
3. Cost conditions and profitability.
4. Technology and research.
5. Immediate and long-term outlook for sales and profits.

Structure of Industry and State of Competition

A study of the structure of an industry should cover these aspects:

1. The number of firms in the industry.
2. The size of each major firm in terms of sales and assets.
3. The concentration ratios for the largest few firms in the industry, measuring the extent of output accounted for by several large firms.
4. The stability of the concentration ratios over an extended period of time.
5. Subdivision of the industry, for example, the steel industry can be classified into major integrated firms, smaller integrated firms, stainless steel, other specialty steel firms, ore producers, merchant pig iron, and refractories.
6. Trend toward merger and diversification outside the industry.

With respect to the state of competition, the analysis should include these questions:

1. What are the price policies of the firms? Do they compete in price? Do they "follow the leader" in announcing price changes?
2. Are products of the industry relatively homogeneous in nature or highly differentiated?
3. Do firms compete actively in offering supplementary services and in advertising?
4. With which domestic industries is the industry in competition? How are the products of the industry compared with substitutes in terms of quality, price, appearance, and other features?
5. What is the state of competition with foreign producers in domestic and foreign markets? Is the industry losing or gaining in the competition with foreign producers?

The pertinent questions to be raised in the inquiry of the nature and prospect of demand for the industry are:

1. Which classification does this industry fall into: growth, cyclical, defensive, or relative decline industry?
2. What are the major markets by customers? What is the distribution of markets by geographical areas including foreign demand?
3. What are the determinants of demand?

4. What factors will likely affect the demand from each major group of customers?
5. What is the immediate and long-run outlook of demand, taking into consideration both the secular and cyclical prospects of general business?

Cost Considerations and Profitability

The "intrinsic value" or normal worth of a security is determined by the profitability, current and prospective, which it represents. Fast growing demand for an industry does not automatically guarantee higher profits for the industry as a whole or individual companies in the industry. Profitability depends no less on cost control and state of competition than on growth in demand. The cost factors and concepts which the analyst should examine in an industry study are:

1. Distribution of costs for the industry among wages, raw materials, and overhead.
2. The rate of increase of labor cost per hour and labor productivity.
3. Rate of increase of prices for finished products.
4. Extent and control of excess capacity.
5. Requirement for new capital expenditures to maintain productive efficiency and keep up competition with producers outside the industry.
6. Turnover of invested capital.

To measure profitability, the following ratios should be computed, compared over time, and analyzed for indications of the causes of changes:

1. Gross profit margin, which relates gross income (sales less cost of goods sold) to sales to indicate profitability at the manufacturing level.
2. Net profit margin, which relates income before income taxes to sales.
3. Rate of return on equity, which relates net income after income taxes to stockholders' equity.
4. Rate of return on total capital, which relates net income after income taxes plus interest charges to total capital invested including loans from creditors.

Technology and Research

Changes in technology often have important impacts on the prospects of an industry. Advances in technology can either broaden and accelerate the growth of an already fast-growing industry or rejuvenate an industry that is on the decline. As far as information is available, the analyst should try to answer a few pertinent questions as follows:

1. Is the technology of the industry relatively stable and mature? Or is it still in a stage of rapid change?
2. Are there any important technological changes on the horizon? And what will their effects be?
3. What percent of sales growth of the industry can be attributed to introduction of new products?
4. What has been the relationship between capital expenditures and sales?
5. What percent of industry sales has been spent on research and development?

Immediate and Long-Run Outlook for Sales and Profits for the Industry

The analyst should assess the findings on the various factors mentioned and translate them into two basic statistics for two time periods. They are:

1. Estimate of rate of growth of sales for the industry
    (a) in the year ahead
    (b) in the next three to five years
2. Estimate of rate of growth of profits after tax

TABLE-1

Hypothetical Transactions Table

Outputs** \ Inputs*	Processing Sector						Final Demand					(12) Total Gross Output
	(1) A	(2) B	(3) C	(4) D	(5) E	(6) F	(7) Gross Inventory Accumulation (+)	(8) Exports to Foreign Countries	(9) Government Purchases	(10) Gross Private Capital Formation	(11) Households	
(1) Industry A	10	15	1	2	5	6	2	5	1	3	14	64
(2) Industry B	5	4	7	1	3	8	1	6	3	4	17	59
(3) Industry C	7	2	8	1	5	3	2	3	1	3	5	40
(4) Industry D	11	1	2	8	6	4	0	0	1	2	4	39
(5) Industry E	4	0	1	14	3	2	1	2	1	3	9	40
(6) Industry F	2	6	7	6	2	6	2	4	2	1	8	46
(7) Gross inventory depletion (-)	1	2	1	0	2	1	0	1	0	0	0	8
(8) Imports	2	1	3	0	3	2	0	0	0	0	2	13
(9) Payments to government	2	3	2	2	1	2	3	2	1	2	12	32
(10) Depreciation allowances	1	2	1	0	1	0	0	0	0	0	0	5
(11) Households	19	23	7	5	9	12	1	0	8	0	1	85
(12) Total gross outlays	64	59	40	39	40	46	12	23	18	18	72	431

Industry Purchasing

Processing Sector Industry Poducing Payment Sector

SOURCE: William H. Miernyk, *The Elements of Input-Output Analysis* (New York: Random House, Inc., 1965), p. 9. * Sales to industries and sectors along the top of the table from the industry listed in each row at the left of the table, t purchases from industries and sectors at the left of the table by the industry listed at the top of each column.

(a)   in the year ahead

(b)   in the next three to five years

For short-term investors, the year-ahead figures for sales and profits growth are likely given more weight, whereas the longer-run oriented investors would profitably treat the three- to five-year estimates as no less important than the year-ahead estimates.

If the analyst has compiled estimates of growth for the whole economy for the two time periods, a comparison should be made between the industry and the economy to see how much better or worse the relative position of the industry will be in the year ahead and in three to five years hence.

INPUT-OUTPUT ANALYSIS

For purposes of developing forecasts of industry sales, many analysts in recent years have turned to a type of interindustry analysis known as input-output analysis. For purposes of illustration, a highly simplified hypothetical input-output relationship is shown in Table. The processing sector of the economy is divided into six basic industries labeled A to F. They can be agriculture, mining, manufacturing, transportation, wholesale and retail trade, and so on. In an actual table there may be 50 or more industries. In addition, there is a payments sector composed of inventory changes, imports or exports, governments, private capital formation, and households. Altogether, there are eleven departments for the economy into which all transactions representing production, distribution, transporta-tion, and consumption are grouped.

Each horizontal row of figures in the table shows the distribution of the output of one sector among other sectors of the economy including itself. The vertical columns show how each sector obtains its inputs from other sectors. Take industry B, for example. The total output is 59 units worth of goods or services. They are distributed as follows: 4 for intraindustry consumption, 5 for A, 7 for C, I for D, 3 for E, 8 for F, 1 for addition to inventory, 6 for exports to foreign countries, 3 for governments, 4 for private capital formation, and 17 for consumption by households. In order to enable industry B to produce 59 units of goods, it obtains inputs from other sectors as follows: 15 from A, 4 from intra-industry firms, 2 from C, 1 from D, 6 from F, 2 from depletion of inventory, 1 from imports, 3 from government services, 2 from wear and tear of equipment, and 23 from services rendered by households.

As shown in the table-1, the total inputs of each industry in the processing sector must equal its total outputs. For the payments sector, however, receipts and expenditures of each department can vary. For example, the households received a total of 85 units but spent only 72 units. Of course, the total receipts of all departments in the payments sector must be the same as their total expenditures for the whole payments sector.

Possible application of the input-output table depend not only on the ingenuity of the user but also on the table's amount of desegregation of industries and on its timeliness. However, several obvious uses can be noted:

1. To indicate:

    (a)   the amount of direct purchases required from other industries per unit of output for each industry, and,

    (b)   the total direct and indirect requirements for inputs from other sectors in order to satisfy an additional unit of final demand for any industry.

2. To estimate not only the distribution of output of one sector but probably also the type of uses the product enters into.

3. To help avoid some inconsistencies that may otherwise develop in economic projections, both long term and short term.

4. To evaluate market prospects for -established products, to identify potential markets for new products, to spot prospective shortages in supplies, and to enable them to evaluate investment prospects in various industries.
5. To help make a forecast of the total sales of an industry. The analyst can estimate the demands from individual sectors and then the total demand for the industry. He can also start from an assumed level of GNP for the economy and work backward to individual industries.

REASONS FOR DECLINE IN THE COMPETITIVE POSITION OF AN INDUSTRY

In the stagnation stage, demand for the product is reduced by competition from other products or by factors mat influence the profits of the industry by increasing costs. Grodinsky refers to these as factors of latent obsolescence that tend to destroy the competitive position of an industry. Included in this category are increasingly high labour costs, changes in social changes in government regulation, and improved technology or automation.

High-Labour Costs

High labour costs might force an industry out of a profitable existence. With a lessening of demand for a product, prices must be reduced to keep the product competitive. However, if prices cannot be reduced because of relatively high production costs, the labour costs in particular, the industry will decline in. economic significance.

Changes in Social Habits

The tobacco industry suffers from latent obsolescence because of a change in social habits. Cancer and cigarette smoking have been closely linked, as demonstrted by several studies in the United States and England. While this has not yet had a significant effect upon cigarette sales, the relationship between lung cancer and other fatal diseases and smoking has become more positive. The long-range result should be a diminishment in smoking. The per capita rate of use has declined in spite of the increase in total use of cigarettes.

Changes in Government Regulation

A change in government regulation, or new regulations, might operate against an industry and cause it to lose its competitive position. The outstanding example of this was Prohibition, which made an industry obsolete almost overnight. Price-support programmes undertaken by the Government will also influence the competitive position of an industry. The enactment of minimum wage legislation affects an industry's wage costs and reduces its competitive effectiveness. A change in the method of depreciating or depleting an asset or a change in costing an asset also affect the economic position of an industry. And, of course, protecting the environment may force some chemical companies to go out of business.

Automation

Because it can bring about changes that will influence the competitive position of an industry, automation is a problem; it is a social problem as well, and demands an answer to the question, "what can we do with workers who are displaced by the computers ?" Computers could lead to a tremendous benefits for the nation and for scientific industries, because it allows us to be competitive in world markets. At present, India is undergoing a technological explosion in the field of automated equipment. One automated machine, for example, can take material from a press and transfer it to another machine for fabrication. The one machine replaces 20 workers, and this is only one phase of the assembly operation. The results, when magnified throughout a plant, achieve considerable savings. At the same time, the new machine replaces older types of machines and causes a decline in demand in other industries. Technological change is not an unmixed blessing; yet improved productivity and automation are necessary if we are to survive in world markets against strong competition.

Other Factors

Other signs pointing to a worsening of the competitive position of an industry include concessive productive capacity and rising prices. An industry that is no longer expanding will not need new plant and equipment. If the industry needs only 60 per cent of its capacity to meet the demand for its product, it may be operating close to its breakeven point. The only course remaining will be to raise prices, or even seek government help or protection. The overcapacity suggests, too, that the growth of the industry is not keeping pace with the national economy. With unused capacity and rising costs, an industry has difficulty in maintaining its competitive position.

INVESTMENT CLASSIFICATION OF INDUSTRIES

The discussion upto this point has been about the economic classification of industries. Investment services provide basic industry information more closely related to our needs and concentrate more on companies within the industry. Most of the services discuss the economic significance of the industry and its future outlook. If an industry appears to offer attractive future benefits, we can easily translate this into the probability that a company's equity will allow us to share in the industry's prosperity.

The investor must know the industry classification used by the investment services. It is vital to learn in detail the characteristic, problems and practices of each industry - its present and future development and operating features - in order to establish the proper perspective in attemping to determine the future of the industry and of a specific company within that industry.

SELECTING AN INDUSTRY

An understanding of the growth pattern of an industry and of the stages of growth - pioneering, expansion and stagnation - as well as the signs of obsolescence, should help us reach a solution to the problem of where to invest. As a matter of principle, the investor should select industries that are in the expansion stage of the growth cycle and should concentrate on these areas. Except for special circumstances brought about by individual portfolio needs, an investor should not invest in industries in the pioneering stage unless he or she is prepared to accept a great deal of speculative risk, comparable to that assumed by the innovator or speculator. By the same token, the investor should ignore industries that are in the stagnation stage or are actually declining in economic importance. Investors should invest in those industries that have developed a strong competitive position, and under little threat of obsolescence. A careful analysis of industries is important to determine which are competitively strong.

This recommendation does not suggest that the investor should ignore industries that are not growing more rapidly than the national economy. The "growth concept" may seem to suggest a rate of growth much greater than that of the national economy. But the recommendation that the investor invent during the expansion stage of the growth cycle refers not only to growth- type industries, but also to those that are growing at a rate equal to that of the national economy. The selection of an industry that is expected to maintain is competitive position on a par with the GNP is entirely consistent with the recommendation.

The growth concept can also be applied to cyclical stocks. Since the economy is cyclical in character, the investor would concentrate on depressed cyclicals when the economy is in a recession. At such a time, cyclical stocks have all the characteristics of a growth during the recovery phase.

The competitive position of an industry can be measured in one of two ways : (1) by comparing the industry growth over time with the growth of the national economy, or (2) by measuring the growth rate of the industry itself. The first step would be to obtain reliable estimates of the physical output, shipments, or sales of the industry. This is relatively easy where the product involved is homogeneous and the data are available. From these figures annual percentage changes can be calculated to reflect the relative growth of the industry. Industry growth can then be compared with the growth of GNP, national income (NI), or disposable personal income (DPI), whichever is more appropriate for the industry in question. If an industry is growing at the same rate as or more rapidly than the GNP or other components, this will be apparent from a comparison.

For the selection of the potential growth industry, its competitiveness with the other industries for its share of gross national product, the stage of the industry, and its stability of sale at the time of economic recession are the three important factors that need to be analysed. Perhaps the ideal investment would be in a firm in a growing industry. Demand for the firms output can be anticipated to grow and even if more companies enter the market itself will permit the firm to maintain its profits in the face of increased competition. However, it is very difficult to identify such industries. At a point of time one industry may be growth- oriented but it is not for always. To have a meaningful analysis of the company, we need to breakdown its operations into product classes in case of diversified product-mix companies and we need to analyze all these classes of the industries before the company's analysis can be done.

COMPANY ANALYSIS

The specific market and economic environment may enhance the performance of a company for a period of time, it is ultimately the firm's own capabilities that will judge its performance over a long period of time. For this reason the firms in the same industry are compared to one another to ascertain which one is the best performer, i.e. which firm earns the most and outperforms its competitors. To analyse a company, ratio analysis is are the most frequently used tools. Ratios are popular because they are easily understood and can be computed with ease. Ratios may be computed and interpreted from two positions. They may be compiled over a number of years to perceive trend. This is called time series analysis. An alternative is to compute ratios at a given time for several firms within an industry. This is called cross-section analysis. Time series and cross- section series may be used together but rarely will all the ratios indicate the same general tendency. When they are taken as a group, the ratios give the investigator an indication of the direction in which the firm is moving and its financial position in comparison with other firms in the industry.

Since a large number of ratios may be calculated the individual should select those that are best suited to his or her specific purpose. This selection will depend on the type of industry and the objective interest of the investigator in the firm.

(A) Marketing

The first variable that influences future earnings in terms of both quality and quantity is the marketing results of the firm in comparison to industry. This in turn is determined by the share of the company in the industry, growth of its sales and stability of sales. A company in a strong competitive position will provide greater earnings with more certainty than a company in a poor competitive position. The company with diversified activity should be competitive in all areas of its production activity.

1. Sales

The rupee amount of annual sales and its share of market helps to determine a company's relative competitive position within the industry and how successful it has been in meeting competition. Here to rank the company, the companies should be compa-rable in like-product groups. Also size is an excellent guide to competitive position. Leading companies are most likely to be leaders of future whereas small companies may not survive the competition. The selection criterion is to select large companies to reduce business risk which tends to reduce variability of the yield of the country.

2. Growth in Sales

The annual growth in sales is equally if not more important than the amount of sale in determining the competitive position of the company. Expanding annual sales and adequate financing firm will be in a better position to earn money. Whereas size of sales protects firm from economic fluctuations, growth in sales gives growth in profits.

3. Stability of Sales

Stability of sales will provide stable earning for a firm, other things being equal. A stability in sales will allow for better financial planning and plant utilisation of plant. Aggregate sales of various industries vary in their degree of stability and company's sale should have same pattern as that of the industry.

One thing that needs to be noted here is that the sale is dependent on two other major factors, namely, the operating efficiency of the plant and the input constraints. One needs to analyse these also before the market competitiveness can be concluded.

(B) Accounting Policies

Before we start analysis of company we should see its accounting policies. There is a risk of faulty interpretation of corporate earnings and consequent bad judgement in pur-chasing, keeping or selling stock. The accounting variations in reporting cost, expenses and extraordinary items could change earnings to a great extent, some of the accounting variations or policies are:

1. Inventory Pricing

Due to change in prices, the value of the inventory may change greatly during an operating period. Several methods of inventory pricing have been developed. These are:

   (i) Cost or market value methods in which case inventory is priced at lower of average cost of inventory or the market price.
   (ii) FIFO, i.e. first in first out, method in which the inventory is priced at the cost of last purchases and the cost of goods first acquired are adjusted in cost of sales.
   (iii) 'LIFO' or last in first out method is just opposite of the FIFO method. Here cost of inventory is on basis of first purchases and last purchases cost is adjusted in cost of sales.

The inventory pricing method affects profitability and inventory costs, i.e. assets of the company as reported in balance sheet. In an inflationary situation FIFO will reflect higher profits because of increase in the carrying inventory cost whereas 'LIFO' method will make the inventory costs only historical cost and thus will under-evaluate the assets of the company and will reflect lesser profits.

2. Depreciation Methods

The depreciation for wear and tear of the machinery and so reduction in value of assets is provided as fixed expenses. The change in providing provision for depreciation will thus affect net income and also affect the valuation of the assets. Higher depreciation will reduce income and undervalue the fixed assets of the firm. The three depreciation methods used are:

    (i) **Straight Line method:** The depreciation amount for a particular item is constant over years till it has nil book value.

    (ii) **Sum of the years digit:** The depreciation amount is initially more and will reduce year to year. Its value is proportion to the balance life of the machinery.

    (iii) **Double declining balance:** The depreciation amount is double in the first year and double the straight line percentage in subsequent years, thus providing a fast rate of depreciation.

3. Non-operating Income

Non-Operating income such as dividend income, interest, etc., generally occur to the firms. To avoid error of judgement these incomes should be studied. In certain accounting period the non-operating income for reasons such as gains or losses due to sale of fixed assets of the company, may affect the working of the company appreciably. Therefore, while analysing the company, non-operating income should also be analysed.

4. Tax Carryover

The company while providing for the provision of corporate tax may not have taken full provision. Moreover, certain refunds or demands of previous years might have been adjusted in the current year profit allocation. The inappropriate provision will affect the profitability as well as total assets and net worth of the company. The incidence of corporate tax and tax carryover should be analysed and taken into consideration.

(C) Profitability

When we buy a security, we are buying the right to future earnings. We are interested in income amount stability and growth of these earnings particularly the amount and when they Will be received. We usually select those companies that have stable and growing sales as we presume earning will follow the growth of sales. This rests on the assumption that the profitability — the relationship between the sales and earnings, will remain constant. To study the relationship of expenses and sales, one needs to study the trends of the profitability ratios, namely, gross profit margin, net profit margin, earning power return on equity and earnings per share. 1.

1. Gross Profit Margin

Gross Profit Margin is operating income divided by sales. An increasing trend in gross profit margin will indicate the increase in operating income because of reduction in operating expenses.

2. Net Profit Margin

Net profit margin is the net profit after tax represented as percentage of sale for a period. This shall normally have the same trend as the Gross Profit Margin and represents directly investors' gain relationship to sales of the firm.

Computation of both these ratios may seem unnecessary but because of variation of incidence of corporate tax and capital structure both ratios will represent a better picture. The reduction in corporate tax will increase net profit margin and this in turn will influence the intrinsic value of the share. This is the reason why share prices increase when Govern-ment announces tax reductions.

3. Earning Power

Earning power is the earning of company net of taxes, measured as a percentage of total assets. Thus earning power is gross profit margin on sales times the ratio of sales to total assets. To study the variation of earning power, one needs to study both gross profit margin and sales to total assets ratio.

4. Return on Equity

Return on equity is the most important ratio to determine the intrinsic value of the security. This ratio represents how the firm is performing for the shareholders. This is the ratio of profit after tax to equity. For the firms having preference shares this ratio must be adjusted by subtracting the dividend paid to the preference share holders from profits after tax. This gives the earning available to the equity shareholders. In addition the contribution of the preference shares to the firm's equity must be subtracted to obtain the investment of the equity shareholders.

5. Earning Per Share

Earning per share is the ratio of firm's total earnings, net of taxes minus the preference dividend over the number of equity shares. This in in turn a multiple of return on equity and the book value of the share. It is ultimately the earnings per share expected in future years and the risk related capitalisation rate that is used to determine the intrinsic value of book. The book value of the share is the ratio of equity capital plus surplus in reserves to the number of shares. This indicates the amount of surpluses and reserves that the company has generated and retained from its profits over the years. This is not to be mixed with intrinsic value since the latter a dependent on the equity and quantity of refunds on equity in addition to the book value. The growth in book value indicates the surplus generated for the period and shows firm's capacity to internal source generation and as a sign of growth prospects.

6. Cash Earning Per Share

The term cash flow is used to describe the cash generated from operation that remains after all cash expenses have been subtracted. The cash flow is obtained by adding non-cash expenses such as depreciation to the profit after taxes minus the preference shares dividend. Cash earning per share is the cash flow-cum-operations divided by number of equity shares. Cash earnings are significant because they give an estimate of discretionary funds over which management has control.

(D) Dividend Policy

In most of the cases it is observed that the management tries to have a stable dividend policy and increase the dividends only when they expect they will be able to maintain the higher rate of dividends in future.

(E) Capital Structure

The return on the equity holders' investment can be magnified by using financial leverage, i.e. using debt financing instead of equity financing. This use of financial leverage may be measured by capitalisation ratios which indicates the extent to which the firm finances its assets by use of debt or preference shares. These ratios are also referred as debt ratios.

(F) Financial Analysis

In the financial analysis, the liquidity and solvency positions of the company are examined. No company can be considered good for investment unless it has a good current financial position. To assess the current financial position, the current assets, its composition and its relationship with current liabilities and cash flow analysis need to be carried out.

1. Current Ratio

The current ratio is the ratio, of current assets to current liabilities and helps us to determine the ability of a company to pay its short-term debt. The higher the current ratio the better is the firm's ability to pay short-term debt.

2. Quick Ratio or Acid Test Ratio

It is a ratio of assets that can be liquidated into a cash in a relatively shorter time to the current liabilities and it gives an idea of cash position of the firm in the short run.

3. Collection Period

It is a ratio of receivables to sales represented in terms of number of days of sales. This ratio indicates the cash management and the credit policy of the firm.

4. Inventory Turnover

Inventory turnover is a ratio of sales to inventory and reflects on the inventory management of the firm.

5. Working Capital Turnover

This is the ratio of net sales to net working capital and reflects on the working capital management of the firm. These ratios are significant in determining the ability of the company to finance sale growth. A declining ratio will indicate the need for a more efficient use of a previously invested capital. A ratio that is too high would reflect that more working capital was needed.

(G) Operating Efficiency

The operating efficiency and the earnings of the company are directly influenced by company's operating characteristics. A company that is constantly expanding its physical facilities and continues to operate at full capacity is more likely to produce profits and earnings in future. A company that is expanding and maintaining a high operating rate with a low break-even point will be a profitable company. A company with the stable operating rate will have more stable revenues, income from sales is the result of efficient use of capital assets combined with raw material, labour and management. For growth of sales the capital asset base should expand preferably from funds generated internally through company's reputation

EXHIBIT - 1

Management Process

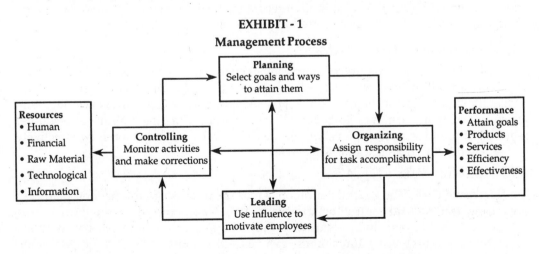

1. Operating Rate

The operating efficiency can be judged from the utilisation of the plant capacity also known as the operating rate. The higher the operating rate the higher the earning per share. Moreover, a change in the operating rate of a company from one level to another differs in its effects depending upon the present operating rate. As a company moves towards a full capacity a given increase in output, other things being equal, will have a smaller effect upon earning.

2. Capital Expenditure

Future earning depends on the ability of the management to invest new corporate funds wisely and to manage the old efficiency. The investment of capital funds is referred to as capital expenditure. This serves as a guide to determine the future profitability of the company. A positive and definite relationship exists between capital equipment and sales and future earnings. Once the operating efficiency has improved to around 100%, the firm cannot expand without more expenditure for the new plant. A better indication of capital expenditure is the relationship between capital expenditure and the existing fixed assets.

(H) Management

Having established the competitive position of a company within its industry (or industries), qualitative company analysis turns next to an evaluation of the quality of a company's management. Some experts believe that the quality of a company's management may be the single most important influence on its future profitability and overall success. A company can have strong financial statements, for example, and yet be overly bureaucratic and incapable of responding quickly to changing business conditions.

To assess management quality, the analyst must understand what the work of management involves, starting with a definition. One leading expert defines *management* as follows:

Management is the attainment of organisational goals in an effective and efficient manner through planning, organising, leading, and controlling organisational resources:

This general definition of management conveys two important ideas: (1) managers are responsible for the attainment of various organisational objectives both effectively and efficiently, and (2) management includes four basic functions: planning, organising, leading, and controlling. The management process of deploying resources to achieve objectives (i.e., promoting organisational performance), within the context of the four basic functions, is illustrated in Exhibit 1. Interpreting the figure requires some elaboration on organisational performance and the four management functions.

ORGANISATIONAL PERFORMANCE

The first part of the definition of management deals with **organisational performance.** Managers are ultimately responsible for applying company resources effectively and efficiently to accomplish the company's goals. *Effectiveness* is defined as the degree to which the company achieves its goals; *efficiency* is defined as the amount of resources required to produce a certain level of output. Performance depends on how effectively and efficiently the company attains its goals.

MANAGEMENT FUNCTIONS

The second part of the general definition of management lists four functions: planning, organising, leading, and controlling. The planning function involves setting future goals for the organisation and then identifying the tasks and resource necessary to obtain those goals. The organising function assigns tasks to various parts of the organisation and allocates resources within the organisation. The leading function involves the motivation of employees to achieve the goals of the organisation. Finally, the controlling function is concerned with the monitoring performance, keeping the organisation moving toward its goals, and correcting deficiencies.

MANAGEMENT SKILLS

What kinds of skills must managers exercise? Most experts identify three essential types of managerial skills: technical, conceptual, and human skills. Technical skills involve knowledge and mastery of such disciplines as engineering manufacturing, basic science, and finance. Conceptual skills involve the ability to think and plan, to see the company as a whole as well as the relationships among all its parts. Finally, human skills involve the ability to work with and through other people. Some human skills include leadership, motivation, communication, and conflict resolution.

Management experts argue that all managers need all three skills; however, the relative importance of each changes as a manager moves up the organisational hierarchy. For example, technical skills may be very important for lower-level managers, but they are less important than conceptual and human skills for top managers.

EVALUATING MANAGEMENT

The discussion of the nature of management leads to the critical question that investors must answer: how well managed is the company? Determining the quality of management is neither easy nor totally objective. In a nutshell, the fundamental issue is how well the company's management performs the four basic functions. Of course, this analysis cannot stop with an assessment of how well management has performed in the past; it must extend to their likely future performance, as well.

Many experienced analysts have trouble defining *good management*, but they often know it when they see it. Generally, to distinguish between good and bad management, the analysts can evaluate management by getting information on some specific questions such as listed below:

1. *What Are the Age and Experience Characteristics of Management?*
   Information on senior management appears in the company's annual report. This usually includes ages, current titles, and brief biographic sketches of each individual. Experts look for a senior management group that appears to have some depth of experience. At the same time, the group should exhibit some variation in terms of age, length of service with the company, and background. For example, some should have marketing backgrounds, whereas others have technical backgrounds. A group of senior managers that appear to be carbon copies of one another should raise concerns.
   Evaluating the senior management group includes considering likely successors to current leaders. This is especially important if the company bears the stamp of one individual. The analyst should ask, could someone take over for the current CEO immediately? If the current CEO were to step down, would possible successors engage in a power struggle? Has the current CEO stayed too long? Some think that the struggle to replace may distract the company and hurt efforts to improve the business.
2. *How Effective Is the Company's Strategic Planning?* Strategic planning (or *strategic management*) is defined as *the set of decisions and actions used to formulate and implement strategies that will provide a competitively superior fit between the organisation and its environment so as to achieve organisational goals.*
   Management experts suggest that strategic planning may be the single most

important function of senior management because success or failure of this work determines much of the future prosperity of the company. Therefore, the effectiveness of the company's strategic planning efforts can reveal a great deal about the overall quality of a company's management. Some questions to ask about a company's strategic planning include whether the strategy is identifiable, consistent (both internally and externally), and feasible.

Management experts contend that effective strategic planning may be even more important for multinational corporations (MNCs). The strategic planning horizon for such a firm is much broader, of course, and planning must accommodate differences among multiple cultural, economic, and political environments. Some of the strategic decisions MNCs must make include whether to pursue global strategies (selling set product lines worldwide) or multidomestic strategies (designing products for individual markets). MNCs must also decide between product-based and geographically-based organisation structures.

3. *Has the Company Developed and Followed a Sound Marketing Strategy?*

An investor's analysis should not discount the importance of a clear, well-planned marketing strategy. To prosper, every company must satisfy the demands of consumers. The basic components of marketing strategy: the target market and the marketing mix variables (distribution, price, product, and promotion) along with the environmental factors form the framework for the marketing strategy. An investor must evaluate how well the company has delineated its target market (or markets). Further, although each marketing mix is another important question variable should be examined individually, the analyst should also assess how well the company has blended the four variables together to satisfy chosen target markets.

4. *Does the Company Understand That It Is Part of a Global Environment?*

Even a company that is not classified as multinational must operate in a global environment. How well a company has adapted to this fact may give some important insight into the quality of its management. Has the company recognised that it sells its products in a single worldwide market and that competitors come from all over the world today? Does the company treat the entire world as a source of supply, as well as a market? Has it accepted the possibility that people in India do not necessarily know best in every situation?

5. *Has the Company Effectively and Nimbly Adapted to Changes in the External Business Environment?*

The contemporary business environment is marked by rapid and sometimes unpredictable changes. How well a company anticipates and reacts to changes in its external business environment depends on the quality of its management. One thing to look at is the company's adoption of modern management techniques, especially those that have succeeded in other, similar companies. One example is the trend to adopt many of the Japanese production techniques and organisational structure characteristics (e.g., work teams) by auto makers.

6. *Has Management Maintained, or Improved, the Company's Overall Competitive Position?*

The company's competitive position is a prime responsibility of management. Well-run companies maintain or improve the competitive positions of all their business units. If a specific business unit cannot compete, a well-run company promptly reduces its investment in that unit, perhaps withdrawing from the business entirely.

7. *Has the Company Grown in an Organised, Sustainable Manner?*

EXHIBIT -2
Selected Ratios for Investors

A. IMPORTANT RATIOS:

Liquidity Ratio

(i) Current ratio $= \dfrac{\text{Current Assets}}{\text{Current Liabilities}}$

(ii) Quick or Acid Test Ratio $= \dfrac{\text{Current Asset - Inventories}}{\text{Current Liabilities}}$

(iii) Interest Earned $= \dfrac{\text{Earning Before Taxes + Interest Charges}}{\text{Interest Charges}}$

(iv) Average Collection Period $= \dfrac{\text{Earning Before Taxes + Sales}}{\text{Interest Charges}}$

Profitable Ratio

(i) Profit on Sales $= \dfrac{\text{Net Profit}}{\text{Sales}}$

(ii) Return on Total $= \dfrac{\text{Net Profit}}{\text{Total Assets}}$

Leverage Ratio

(i) Debt to Total Assets $= \dfrac{\text{Total debt}}{\text{Total assets}}$

(ii) Fixed Charges Coverage $= \dfrac{\text{Income available for fixed charges}}{\text{Fixed charges}}$

(iii) Inventory Turnover $= \dfrac{\text{Sales}}{\text{Inventory}}$

Activity Ratio

(i) Fixed Asset Turnover $= \dfrac{\text{Sales}}{\text{Fixed assets}}$

(ii) Total Asset Turnover $= \dfrac{\text{Sales}}{\text{Fixed charges}}$

B. USEFUL RATIOS FOR INVESTORS:

(1) Equity Per Share (EPS) $= \dfrac{\text{Profit after tax - Preference dividend}}{\text{Number of equity shares}}$

(2) Price Earning (P/E) Ratio $= \dfrac{\text{Market price per equity share}}{\text{Earning per share}}$

(3) Dividend Yield $= \dfrac{\text{Dividend per share}}{\text{Market price per share}} \times 100$

(4) Cover for Equity Dividends $= \dfrac{\text{Earning after tax - Preference dividend}}{\text{Total amount of equity dividend}}$

(5) Pay-out Ratio $= \dfrac{\text{Dividend per equity share}}{\text{Earnings per equity share}}$

(6) Pay-out Ratio $= \dfrac{\text{Equity share capital + Reserves}}{\text{Total number of equity shares}}$
$= \dfrac{\text{Net worth - Preference share capital}}{\text{Total number of equity shares}}$

History teaches that bigger is not always better. America West Airlines is one of many companies that have grown too quickly, outstripping their managerial and financial resources. Founded in the early 1980s, America West tried to reproduce the success of Southwest Airlines as a low-cost regional airline. Its strategy had started to show signs of working by the mid-1980s. Unfortunately, America West embarked on an ambitious expansion program, including initiating service to Hawaii and Japan. Although its revenues more than doubled between 1987 and 1990, America West did not have either the financial or managerial resources to compete effectively with the large airlines, such as Delta and United.

8. *Has the Company Been Financed Adequately and Appropriately?*
A company's financial statements reflect on the quality of its management; as a general rule, better-run companies have better financials than poorly run companies. For Example, prudent financial policy suggests that a company limit its financial risk(i.e., leverage) if it faces a high degree of business risk.

9. *Does the Company Have Good Relations with Its Unions and Employees?*
Managers have to lead and motivate employees; good and successful managers develop extremely effective human skills. Managers cannot achieve the company's goals by themselves; they need employees working with them, not against them. As a general rule, well-run companies have better employee relationships than poorly run companies.

10. *What Is the Company's Public Image?*
Well-run companies know the importance of public Image. Does a company's name convey a positive or negative image? Of course, well-run companies do not neglect their other responsibilities while cultivating positive public images.

11. *How Effective Is the Board of Directors?*
Investors have begun to recognise that well-run companies generally have effective boards of directors. It may be no coincidence that these companies also produce better returns to shareholders on average. In fact, some large institutional investors are examining corporate governance first and then performance when making stock investment decisions. What is an effective board of directors? Ideally, an effective board is one that evaluates the performance of the CEO annually, links executive pay to specific performance goals, pays retainers to directors in the form of company stock— and requires board members to own a significant amount of stock, has fewer than three inside members, and is elected annually.

Summary of Ratios

Selected ratios for investors are presented in Exhibit-2.

FUNDAMENTAL SECURITY ANALYSIS: AN APPRAISAL

The fundamental approach to security analysis is to compare the current observable market value of a particular security with its theoretical or "intrinsic" value that is based on a variety of factors such as growth trend, earnings stability, and dividend history as well as based on subjective estimtes of future earnings and capitalisation rates. Decision rules for buying and selling individual securities result from these comparisons of relative value. The degree of sophistication of these fundamental approach to investments ranges from the classic, qualitative discussions of investment values to highly refined, technically complex valuation modesl.

Regardless how sophisticated the techniques used, a complete, painstaking fundamental analysis, based on relevant facts, is a logical way to estimate the true value of a going concern. Understandably, fundamental analysis is the most widely used method of estimating security prices. Erroneous intrinsic value estimates can be attributed to several facts: (1) The analyst did not have all the relevant information, (2) the analyst simply did not do his work thoroughly, or (3) the market was in a temporary disequilibrium. Hind sight is always better than foresight in these matters. But even under ideal conditions, fundamental analysis can suggest only a range of prices rather than a specific value. Opposition to the fundamental or security analysis approach comes from followers of the technical or chartist school who maintain that all financial data and market information of a given security is already reflected in the market price of the security. As a result, chartists attempt to identify particularly price movement patterns for which wthere are corresponding decision rules for investment action. Although there is little theoretical basis for the technical approach, there are enough charting practioners and their actions cannot be ignored. Most large investment organisations employ both a fundamental and a technical approach.

REVIEW PROBLEMS

1. After thoroughly adjusting H.D.. Engineers, you project the company's dividend to from at a 0.20 rate for the next two years and at 0.14 for the following three years, and to level off at 0.07 thereafter. You estimate a required rate of 0.12. H.D. Engineers currently pays a dividend of ₹ 1.20 per share, what is the fundamental value of a share of H.D/S stock?

Ans:

The fundamental value of H.D. Engineers :

Year	Previous Dividend	Growth Rate	Projected Dividend	Present Value Factor	Present Value
1	₹1.20	-.20	₹1.44	.8928	₹1.29
2	1.44	.20	1.73	.7972	1.38
3	1.73	.14	1.97	.7118	1.40
4	1.99	.14	2.25	.6355	1.43
5	2.25	.14	2.56		

Price based on projected year's dividend .... .5674 .... ₹ 29.05

$$= \frac{₹\ 2.56}{(.12 - .97)} = ₹\ 51.20$$

Value of stock = ₹ 34.55

2. D.T.Verma bought 100 shares of R.D. Enterprises at ₹ 100 per share. He held the shares for 3 years and sold at ₹ 160 per share. The company paid ₹ 12.50 dividend per share in each of the three years .What total return did Verma earn from his investment?

Ans:

Applying the approximate method:
Average investment = (₹ 100 + ₹ 160)/2=₹ 130
Average annual income = ₹ 22.50(₹ 60 capital gain over 3 years plus 2.50 in dividends).

$$= \frac{₹22.50}{₹\ 130} = .173 = 17.3\%$$

Total return to Verma is 17.3%.

3. R.G.Gupta bought 100 equity shares of XYZ Company at ₹ 10 per share three years back. The company has paid no dividend during the period. Gupta is

interested inknowiong the total return he earned and ind indicated risk he assumed. The quarterly prices were as follows:

Year	Quarterly	Prices
1	1	₹ 10
1	2	11
1	3	12
1	4	13
2	1	14
2	2	15
2	3	14
2	4	11
3	1	13
3	2	14
3	3	16
3	4	15

(a) What was the average quarterly return over the investment period?
(b) What was the annual return earned on the investment?
(c) What was the standard deviation of the annual average return?
(d) Should Gupta continue to invest in the equity of the company? Why or why not

Ans:

To compute the average quarterly yield, use the formula:

$$\text{Yield} = \frac{(P_1 - P_0) + D_0}{P_0}$$

where PI is the endind period, P_0 is the beginning price, and D_0 is the quarterly dividend in rupees.
Applying the formula:
(11-10)/10+(12-11)/11+(13-12)/12+(14-13)/13+(15-14)/14+(14-15)/15+(11-14)/14+(13-ll)/13+(14-13)/13+(16-14)/14+(15-16)/15 = 4.36

(b) The annual yield earned on the investment by using the approximate method:
= 104.15/12 = ₹ 12.5

Average annual income:
₹ 1.67 (₹ 5 capital gain over three years=₹ 1.67 per year), ₹ 1. 67/12.5 =.1336

(c) The standard deviation of the average quaterly yield is: V(.13857/ll) = ± .112=11.2%

(d) Gupta, although made a good return, should probably take his money out of this risky holding because of the variability of yield and lack of dividend.

4. Given below are the basic data relating to seven scrips listed in the Stock Exchange. You are required to structure a portfolio with four scrips for a total investment amount of ₹ 1.00 lakh. Also explain the reasons for selecting the same.

SCRIPS PARTICULARS

	A	B	C	D	E	F	G
Backgrond	60 years since inception, good track record, growth oriented	100 years since inception, growth orented, good track record.	60 years since inception, good grack record.	20 years since inception, medium growth, good track record.	30 years since inception, good track record.	55 years since inception, good track record.	80 years since inception, growth oriented, good track, record.
Industry	Power	Textile	Personal	Fertilisers	Food Care	Chemicals	Diversified Product
Face Value (₹)	10.00	10.00	10.00	10.00	10.00	10.00	10.00
Current market price (₹)	189.00	122.00	226.00	12.00	232.00	201.00	253.00
EPS for 2009-10	12.84	26.56	5.28	5.28	6.30	12.31	833
(₹) 2010-11	12.71	30.36	5.61	6.66	9.26	21.83	2.50
DPS for	2.60	5.50	7.50	1.80	5.00	6.50	5.50
2009-10 (₹) 2010-11 (₹)	2.80	5.50	4.80	1.80	6.50	6.50	2.50
High value in 52 weeks (₹)	227.00	375.00	315.00	27.00	434.00	305.00	333.00
P/E Ratio (₹)	15.00	4.10	50.00	1.86	42.00	9.00	25.00
Sensitivity to Govt. Policy	High	High	Medium	High	Medium	High	Medium
Market Lot (No. of Shares)	100	100	100	100	100	100	100

Ans:

The objective of portfolio management is to maximize the return and minimise the risk. The selection of scrips or assets in a portfolio depends on the amount of funds available, investor's goal, risk tolerance and their preferences and a host of other factors.

In this particulars question, we have to select a portfolio of four securities out of the seven available. The total funds available for investment are ₹ one lakh.

With the present given information, our decision would be based upon -

(1) Current trends in the industry
(2) Earning yield
(3) Dividend yield
(4) Potential for capital appreciation in terms of price fluctuation (High/low)

The reason for using earning yield as a decision criteria instead of EPS is that EPS does not recognise the effect of increase in equity capital as a result of retention of earnings.

Ranking for different scrips for the year 2010-11

Company	Industry	EPS (₹)	Ranking	DPS (in ₹)	Ranking	P/E Ratio (₹)	Ranking
A	Power	12.71	3	2.80	4	15.00	4
B	Textile	30.36	1	5.50	2	4.10	2
C	Personal Care	5.61	7	4.80	3	50.00	7
D	Fertilizers	6.66	6	1.80	6	1.86	1
E	Food Products	9.26	5	6.50	1A	42.00	6
F	Chemicals	21.83	2	6.50	1	9.00	3
G	Diversified	10.08	4	250	5	25.00	5

Note: P/E ratio has been ranked in the order of lowest to highest

Company Mkt.	Current	Ranking		Sensitivity to External uncontroliable factors	D/P ratio	Ranking
A	189/-	3	5	High	22%	7
B	122/-	2	6	High	18.11%	7
C	226/-	5	3	Medium	85.56%	1
D	12/-	1	7	High	27.02%	4
E	232/-	6	2	Medium	70.19%	2
F	201/-	4	4	High	29.77%	3
G	253/-	7	1	Medium	24.90%	5

5. Given below are the financial data relating to two scrips in the pharmaceutical industry with a paid-up value of ₹ 10 per share. Based on the data presented, identify the scrip you would select, giving reasons:

Year	2005 Company		2006 Company		2007 Company		2008 Company		2009 Company	
Particulars	A ₹	B	A ₹	B	A ₹	B	A ₹	B	A ₹	B
Face Value	10	10	10	10	10	10	10	10	10	10
Book Value	15.12	26.29	17.60	28.99	19.98	36.73	23.26	41.05	25.04	47.18
EPS	2.78	2.26	5.48	2.96	5.87	8.97	8.06	6.90	6.28	9.13
Dividend per share	2.40	1.00	3.00	2.00	3.50	3.00	4.00	1.50	4.50	3.00

Ans:

Paid up value of both scrips is ₹ 10/- per share. It is assumed that investors are rational and risk averse. They prefer the security that provides the highest return for a given level of risk or the lowest amount of risk for a given level of return; and they want more and more risk premium for given additional risk. In the question, we are given with the data related to return to the equity holders which is reflected by Earning per share (EPS). Therefore, for this given level of return that scrip would be preferred which is less risky and yield more consistent returns. Standard deviation is a measure of risk. Let us first calculate the risk of two securities based on EPS. Let X be the stream of Earning per share (EPS) generated by Company A. Let Y be the stream of Earning per share (EPS) generated by company B. Calculation of Risk (a)

Year	X	Y	X	x^2	y	y^2
2005	2.78	2.26	-2.914	8.49	-3.784	14.32
2006	5.48	2.96	-0.214	0.05	-3.084	9.51
2007	5.87	8.97	0.176	0.03	2.926	8.56
2008	8.06	6.90	2.366	5.60	0.856	0.73
2009	6.28	9.13	0.586	0.34	3.086	9.52
	$\Sigma x = 28.47$	$\Sigma y = 30.22$	$\mathrm{E}x = 0$	$\mathrm{E}x^2 = 14.51$	$\mathrm{E}y = 0$	$\mathrm{E}y^2 = 42.64$

Mean of Scrip A

$$\overline{X}_A = \frac{EX}{N}$$

$$= \frac{28.47}{5} = 5.694$$

Mean of Scrip B

$$\overline{X}_B = \frac{EY}{N}$$

$$= \frac{30.22}{5} = 6.044$$

Standard deviation of scrip A   Standard deviation of Scrip B

$$\sigma_x = \sqrt{\frac{EX^2}{N}}$$

$$= \sqrt{\frac{14.51}{5}} = 1.703$$

$$\sigma_y = \sqrt{\frac{EX^2}{N}}$$

$$= \sqrt{\frac{14.64}{5}} = 2.92$$

In terms of risk, security of company A is better as it is having a lower S.D. of 1.70 as compared to S.D. of 2.92 of company B.

$$\text{C.V.} = \frac{\sigma_x}{X} \times 100$$

$$= \frac{1.703}{5.694} = 29.85$$

$$\frac{\sigma_y}{Y} \times 100$$

$$= \frac{2.92 \times 100}{6.044} = 48.31$$

Morover as we compare the co-efficient of variation of the two scrips, it can be concluded that the scrip A yields less variable (more consistent and stable) returns as compared to scrip B because the C.V. (coefficient of variation) of scrip A is less than that of scrip B. Also, from the data of the Book Value and EPS, it seems that B is more leveraged firm as comapred to A. Hence, those who do not want to expose to higher risk, are advised to go for Scrip A.

Another criteria for the selection of scrip is, the company which pay the higher average dividend per share would be preferred. It may be preferred by those who are interested in regular income. For this the average of dividend per share for the past five years would be calculated because the mean value or the average is the, single value that describes the characteristics of the entire group.

X	Y
2.40	1.00
3.00	2.00
3.50	3.00
4.00	1.50
$EX = 17.40$	$\Sigma Y = 10.50$

$$\overline{X} = \frac{\Sigma X}{N} \qquad\qquad \overline{Y} = \frac{\Sigma Y}{N}$$

$$\overline{X} = \frac{17.40}{5} \qquad\qquad \overline{Y} = \frac{16.50}{5}$$

$$= 3.48 \qquad\qquad\qquad = 2.10$$

Let DPS of company A be denoted by X and DPS of company B be denoted by A
The average dividend per share is more for Company A.

Based on above analysis we would select the scrip of company A for investment as:
(1) It is less risky
(2) It yield stable and consistent returns
(3) It pay more average dividend per share
(4) Another thing to be noticed is that DPS paid by company. A is showing an increasing trend.

Still another criteria may be there for those who are interested only in the capital appreciation to take advantage of the lower tax liability resulting from the long term capital gain. For such investor, a security is preferred if it is ensuring a capital appreciation in future. To decide which scrip is having a prospect of higher capital appreciation in future, one should look at the data of book value. The book value of the scrip-B is increasing very rapidly and it is much higher than that of the scrip-A. Therefore, those who ar ּ looking for capital gains should go for the scrip-B.

6. As a holder of ABC Company equity shares, you are given a right to subscribe to the new issue of equity that is being sold to raise capital to expand plant facilities. The announcement of the offering was made on August 1 for owners of record August 31. The rights expire September 15. Subscription price for the new stock was set at ₹ .45 per share Each equity shareholder is allowed to buy one new equity share at the subscription price for each eight shares of equity owned. The market price on August 7 was ₹ 54.

(a) What was the theoretical value of rights on August 7?
(b) If nothing disturbed the price, what would be the value of the right on September 1?
(c) What value would the rights have on September 16?
(d) Would we expect the market price and theoretical price to be the same in this case? Why ,or why not?

Ans.:

The theoretical value of the right of August 1 was ₹ 1 from the following calculations:

(₹ .54 - ₹ .45)/(8+l) = ₹ 1

(b) On September 1, the right would be expected to still have a value of ₹ 1.
(c) The right would have no value on September16, since the rights expired on the previous day.
(d) Generally, we would not expect the market price and the theoretical price to be identical due to demand conditions for the particular stock.

Table A-1

CORPORATE SCORE BOARD

Company Name	Year End	Equity ₹Cr.	Book Value	Sales ₹Cr.	GPM	NP ₹Cr.	Div	Price 5/6/2011	CPS ₹	EPS ₹	PC Ratio	PE Ratio	Half yearly Sales	Half yearly GP	Half yearly NP	Unaudited EPS	Unaudited PE
95 TYRES/TUBES																	
Appollo Tyres	9103(17)	27.88	41.89	274.77	11.0	20.36	28.2	390.00	6.53	5.13G	59.7	76.8	172.31	12.3	17.07	12.25	31.3
Bombay Tyres	9103	4.50	18.58	207.06	3.7	5.30	6.0	105.00	16.96	11.78A	6.2	8.9	114.59	1.6	48	12.5	8.4
CEAT	9106	23.26	72.54	564.33	6.7	22.66	33.0	200.00	14.23	9.74B	14.1	20.5	340.73	7.5	16.98	14.60	13.7
Dewas Rubber	9106 (15)	1.77	28.93	50.43	7.3	2.37	20.0	137.50	14.46	10.71A	9.5	12.8	—	—	—	—	—
Dewas Tyres	9106(15)	3.34	9.73	23.92	2.3	.14	37.50	1.34	.34	28.0	—	—	—	—	—	—	—
Dunlop	9103	18.99	45.18	604.19	4.3	5.34	30.0	130.00	9.05	2.79E	14.0	46.6	302.00	2.4	.38	.40	—
Falcon Tyres	9103	3.05	14.49	22.57	3.1	.49	47.50	2.30	1.61	20.7	29.5	16.26	6.2	.85	5.57	8.5	—
Goodyear	9112	14.97	34.78	273.74	7.3	7.34	30.0	140.00	8.27	4.90C	16.9	22.6	—	4.5	1.30	22.33	1.03
Govind Rubber	9103	1.50	32.80	67.52	5.2	2.66	17.0	230.00	23.33	17.73G	9.9	13.0	41.36	10.5	13.55	19.30	12.2
JK Inds.	9106	14.04	50.12	373.92	9.9	18.92	30.0	235.00	31.32	13.25D	11.0	17.7	130.37	—	—	—	—
MRF Typres	9109	3.86	215.57	741.91	7.5	19.00	75.0	1225.00	104.15	49.22D	11.8	24.9	294.96	4.5	4.69	7.53	16.8
Modi Rubber	9103	10.38	68.03	518.60	5.3	7.10	25.5	125.00	15.00	6.84D	7.9	11.3	58.65	5.8	2.97	183.90	4.9
Premier Tyres	9103	3.24	574.69	106.77	3.1	2.61	—	900.00	102.47	80.56	8.8	11.3	—	1.9	.11	—	—
Sri Chakra	9012(18)	4.75	19.84	32.63	1.3	.24	—	21.25	.56	.D	37.9	—	25.56	—	—	—	—
Vikrant Tyres	9103	15.60	19.76	244.63	6.3	11.08	17.5	115.00	9.91	7.06A	11.6	16.3	126.88	5.4	4.12	8.79	13.1
IND. COMPOSITE		151.13		4106.99	6.6	125.13					16.4	27.7		6.1			

Also mention the logic for your recommendation

QUESTIONS

1. State the meaning, rationale, procedure and limitations of the Fundamental Analysis.
2. "A fundamental analyst's estimate of intrinsic value is different from the present value of all income". Is this statement true, false, or uncertain ? Explain.
3. Does an increase in a firm's growth rate of earnings always mean an increase in its intrinsic value ? Explain.
4. "An increase in a firm's liquidity ratio means the firm is well-managed and safe. This will always increase its multipliers". Is this statement true, false or uncertain? Explain.
5. What is the benefit in analysing the market and alternative industries before individual securities?
6. Discuss whether you would expect all industries to have a similar relationship to be economy. Give an example of two industries that have different relationship to the economy?
7. Is there a difference between the returns for alternative industries during specific time periods and what is the implication of these results?
8. Is there consistency in the returns for industries overtime and what do these results imply regarding industry analysis?
9. Discuss the recent changes in the financing pattern of Indian companies.
10. In seeking to make a long-term commitment of funds, why is it important to seek a growth industry?
11. Despite the fact that investors are ultimately concerned with earnings and dividends, why do security analysts place so much emphasis on the sales of the firm and growth prospects for the industry?
12. What is an input -output table? Why is it useful in industry forecast?
13. Discuss the life-cycle theory of industry selection. What arguments are there for and 'against placing primary emphasis on this consideration even selecting investments?
14. As an investment consultant which scripts would you recommend to your client for purchase in the tyre industry on the basis of the data given in Table A-1.
15. What are some of the reasons why industries show differing rates of growth?
16. Why must an analyst always investigate the industry when looking at a particular security?

PROBLEMS

1. Atul Glass has issued 2 crore equity shares. The share price is currently ₹ 200, and the annual dividend paid at the end of the year will be ₹ 7.50 per share. What is the expected rate of return on a share under these conditions?
   (a) The share price will be ₹ 210 at the end of the year.
   (b) The share price will be ₹ 225.00 at the end of the year.

Ans: (a) 8.75%, (b) 16.25%

2. After examining the financial statements of Jyoti Ltd., you note that the company consistently pays out 30 percent of its earnings as dividends. You forecast earnings to be ₹ 3.00 per share next year and to grow at a 0.09 rate for the foreseeable future. Your required rate of return for the stock is 0.11. Estimate Jyoti's multiple and stock value.

Ans: $m = 0.30 / (0.11 - 0.09) = 15$
$V_0 = 15 (3.00) = 45$

3. Consider a firm that has issued zero-coupon bonds with a face value of ₹ 4.50 crore. The firm has an asset value of ₹ 6.50 crore, and the asset returns have a standard deviation of 0.35. If the debt matures in one year and the riskless interest-rate is 10%, find the value of firm's equity. Suppose the firm's asset structure can be altered so that the standard deviation of the assets increases to 0.65. Calculate the equity value in this scenario. Provide an intuitive explanation for the differences in the equity values.

Ans: ₹ 2,50,33,089 and ₹ 2,87,66,284.

4. What is the return on a stock according to the security market line if the risk-free rate is 6%, the return on the market is 10%, and the stock's beta is 15?

Ans: Return = 12%

5. Suraj Gem Company (SGC) has been successful and has enjoyed a good growth trend. Now SGC is planning to go public with an issue of equity, and it faces the problem of setting an appropriate price on the equity. The company and its bankers believe that the proper procedure is to select several similar firms with publicly traded equity and to make relevant comparisons. Several gem companies are reasonably similar to SGC with respect to product mix, asset composition, and debt/equity proportions. Of these companies, Super Gem and Suman Gem are most similar. When analysing the following data, assume that 2004 and 2009 were *reasonably* "normal" years for all the three companies - that is, these years were neither especially good nor especially bad in terms of sales, earnings and dividends. At the time of analysis, risk-free rate of return was 8% and market return was 12%.

		Super		Suman		Suraj (Total)
EPS	2004	₹	4.50	₹	7.50	₹ 12 crore
	2009		3.00		5.50	8.16 crore
Price per share						
	2009	₹	36.00	₹	65.00	
Dividend per share						
	2002	₹	2.25	₹	3.75	₹ 6 crore
	2009	1.50			2.75	4.2 crore
Book value per share 2009		₹	30.00	₹	55.00	₹ 90 crore
Market/Book ratio, 2009			120%		118%	—
Total assets, 2009		₹	280 crore	₹	820 crore	₹ 200 crore
Total debt, 2009		₹	120 crore	₹	300 crore	₹ 110 crore
Sales 2009		₹	410 crore	₹	1400 crore	₹ 370 crore

(a) Assume that SGC has 1 crore shares outstanding. Use this information to calculate EPS, DPS and book value per share for SGC.

(b) Calculate earnings and dividends growth rates for the three companies.

(c) On the basis of your answer to Part (a), do you think SGC's shares would sell at a price in the same range as that of Super and Suman?

(d) Assuming that SGC's management can split the stock so that 1 crore shares could be changed to 10 crore shares or any other number, would such an action make sense in this case? Why?

(e) Assume that SGC did split its stock and has 4 crore shares. Calculate new Values for EPP, DPS and book value per share.

(f) Return on equity (ROE) can be measured as EPS/book value per share or as total earnings/ total equity. Calculate ROE's for the three companies for 2009.

(g) Calculate dividend payout ratios for the three companies for both years.

(h) Calculate debt/total asset ratios for the three companies for 2009.

(i) Calculate the PIE ratios for the Super and Suman for 2009. Are these P/Es reasonable in view of relative growth, payout, and ROE date? If not, what other factors might explain them?

(j) Determine a range of values for SGC's stock price, with 4 crore shares outstanding, by applying Super's and Suman's P/E ratios, price/dividend ratios, and price/book value ratios to your data for SGC.

(k) Using the constant growth stock price model, find a price for SGC's stock.

(l) At what price do you think SGC's shares should be offered to the public? You will want to select a price that will be low enough to induce investors to buy the stock but not so low that it will rise sharply immediately after it is issued, consider relative growth rates, ROEs,dividend yields, and total return

Ans.   (a) 2009. ₹.12; ₹ 6; ₹ 90.

(b) SGC: Geps = 8%; GDP = 7.4%

(e) 2009. ₹ 3.00; ₹ 1.50; ₹ 22.50

(f) Super: 15.00%; Suman; 13.64%

(g) 2009: Super 50%; Suman 50%

(h) Super 43%; Suman 37%

(i) Super 8 times; Suman 8.67 times

6. You expect the price of CDP stock to be ₹ 59.77 per share from now. Its current market price is ₹ 50, and you expect it to pay a dividend 1-year from now of ₹.2.15 per share.

(a) What is the stock's expected dividend yield, rate of price appreciation and HPR?

(b) If the stock has a beta of 1.15, the risk-free rate is 6% per year, and the expected rate of return on the market portfolio it 14% per year, what is the required rate of return on the CPD stock?

(c) What is the Intrinsic Value of the CDP stock, and how does it compare to the current market price?

REFERENCES

1. Aber, John. "Industry Effects and Multivariate Stock Price Behavior." *Journal of Financial and Quantitative Analysis* 11, no. 5 (November 1976).

2. Ahearn, Daniel S. "Investment Management and Economic Re-search," *Financial Analysts Journal.* Jan.-Feb. 1964.

3. Arditti, Fred D., "Risk and the Required Return on Equity," *Journal of Finance,* 22 (March 1967), 19-36.

4. Banz, Rolf W., "The Relationship between Return and Market Value of Common Stocks," *Journal of Financial Economics, 9* (1981), 3-18.

5. Basu, S., "Investment Performance of Common Stocks in Relation to their Price-Earnings Ratios: A Test of the Efficient Market Hypothesis," *Journal of Finance,* 32 (June 1977), 663-82.

6. Beaver, W., P. Kettler, and Myron Scholes, "The Association Between Market Determined

and Accounting Determined Risk Measures," *Accounting Review*, October 1970, pp. 654-682.

7. Bernstein, Leopold A., "In Defense of Fundamental Investment Analysis," *Financial Analysts Journal*, January-February 1975, pp. 57-61.

8. Blume, Marshall E. "On the Assessment of Risk." *The Journal of Finance* XXVI (March 1971), pp. 1-10.

9. ————, and Irwin Friend, "Risk, Investment Strategy and the Long-Run-Rates of Return," *The Review of Economics and Statistics* LVI, August 1974, pp. 259 269.

10. Bratt, E.C. *Business Cycles & Forecasting*, 5th ed. Homewood, Ill.; R.D. Irwin, 1961.

11. Brealey. Richard A.. *An Introduction to Risk and Return from Common Stacks* (Cambridge. Mass.: M.I.T.. Press, 1969).

12. Butler, W.F., and E.C. Kavesh. *How Business Economists Forecast*, part 3. Englewood Cliffs, N.J.: Prentice-Hall, 1966.

13. Carleton, Willard T., and J. Lakonishok, "Risk and Return on Equity: The Use and Misuse of Historical Estimates," *Financial Analysts Journal*, 41 (January-February 1985), 38-47.

14. Chambers, E.J., R.H. Scott, and R.S. Smith. *National Income Analysis & Forecasting*. Glenview, Ill.: Scott, Foresman, 1975.

15. Clark, Lindley H., Jr. "Model Building Game," *The Wall Street Journal*. Aug. 2, 1977.

16. Cohen, J., E. Zinbarg, and A. Zeikel. *Investment Analysis & Management*. Homewood, Ill.: R.D. Irwin, 1977, chap. 12.

17. Cowen, Scott, and Jeffrey Hoffer: "Usefulness of Financial Ratios in a Single Industry," *Journal of Business Research*, March 1982, pp. 103-118.

18. Dauten, C.A., and L.M. Valentine. *Business Cycles & Forecasting*. Cincinnati: South-Western Publishing, 1968.

19. Douglas, George, "Risk in the Equity Markets: An Empirical Appraisal of Market Efficiency," *Yale Economic Essays*, 9 (Spring 1969), 3-45.

20. Ehrbar, A.F. "Unraveling the Mysteries of Corporate Profits," *Fortune*. Aug. 27, 1979.

21. Ellis, Charles D. "Performance Investing." *Financial Analysts Journal*, September-October 1968, p. 117.

22. Elton Edwin J., and Martin J. Gruber: "Estimating the Dependence Structure of Share Prices— Implications for Portfolio Selection," *Journal of Finance*. December 1973, pp. 1203-1232.

23. Fama, Eugene F., and Kenneth French. "Business Conditions and Expected Returns on Stocks and Bonds." *Journal of Financial Economics* 25, no. 1 (November 1989).

24. Farrell, J.L., Jr., "Analyzing Covariation of Returns to Determine Homogeneous Stock Groupings," *Journal of Business*, 47 (April 1974), 186-207.

25. ————, "Homogeneous Stock Groupings," *Financial Analysts Journal*, 31 (May-June 1975), 50-62.

26. Fouse, William L., "Risk & Liquidity: The Keys to Stock Price Behavior," *Financial Analysts Journal*, 32 (May-June 1976), 35-45.

27. Fruhan, William E., Jr. *Financial Strategy*. Homewood, Ill.: Richard D. Irwin, 1979.

28. Gargett, Dave R. "The Link between Stock Prices and Liquidity." *Financial Analysts Journal*, January-February 1978.

29. Gooding, Arthur E., "Quantification of Investors' Perceptions of Common Stocks: Risk and Return Dimensions," *Journal of Finance* 30, no. 5 (December 1975): 1301-1316.

30. Gordon, Myron, *The Investment, Financing and Valuation of the Corporation* (Home-wood, Ill.: Irwin, 1962).

31. Graham, Benjamin. "The Future of Common Stocks," *Financial Analysts Journal*. Sept.-Oct. 1974.

32. Gray, William S. III. "The Anatomy of a Stock Market Forecast." *Journal of Portfolio Management* 16, no. 1 (Fall 1989).

33. Grossman, S.J. and Merton H. Miller, "Liquidity and Market Structure." *Journal of Finance*. 43, no. 2 (June 1988).

34. Hall, Marshall, and Leonard Weiss, "Firm Size and Profitability," *Review of Economics and Statistics*, August 1967, pp. 319-331.

35. Hamada, Robert S., "The Effect of the Firm's Capital Structure on the Systematic Risk of Common Stocks," *Journal of Finance*, 18 (May 1972), 435-52.

36. Hassel, J., and Robert Jennings. "Relative Forecast Accuracy and the Timing of Earnings Forecast Announcements." *The Accounting Review* 61, no. 1 (January 1986).

37. Hayes, D.D., and W. Bauman. *Investments: Analysis & Management*. New York: Macmillan, 1976, chap. 5.

38. Ibbotson, R.G., and R.A. Sinquefield. *Stocks, Bonds, Bills and Inflation: Historical Returns (1926-1978)*. The Financial Analysts Research Foundation, 1979, University of Virginia.

39. Imhoff, Eugene, and G. Lobo. "Information Content of Analysts Composite Forecast Revisions. *Journal of Accounting Research* 22, no. 3 (Autumn 1984).

40. Jaffe, Jeffery, Donald Keim, and Randolph Westerfield. "Earnings Yields, Market Values, Stock Returns." *Journal of Finance* 44, no. 1 (March 1989).

41. Jahnke, William W. "The Growth Stock Mania Revisited." *Financial Analysts Journal*, January-February 1975, p. 42.

42. Jennings, Robert. *Reaction of Financial Analysts to Corporate Management Earnings per Share Fore-casts*. Financial Analysts Research Foundation, Monograph No. 20, (New York, 1984).

43. Johnson, R.S., Lyle Fiore, and Richard Zuber. "The Investment Performance of Common Stocks in Relation to Their Price-Earnings Ratios: An Update of the Basu Study." *Financial Review* 24, no. 3 (August 1989).

44. Joy, O. Maurice, "A Simulation Test of the Industry Analysis Hypothesis," *Journal of Business Research*, October 1974, pp. 373-384.

45. Keran, Michael W. "Expectations, Money, & the Stock Market," *Review*. Federal Reserve Bank of St. Louis, Jan. 1971.

46. King, Benjamin F., "Market and Industry Factors in Stock Price Behavior," *Journal of Business* 39, no. 1, part II (January 1966, Supplement): 139-190.

47. Larsen, Robert A. "New Insight into Changes in Earnings Per Share," *Financial Analysts Journal*. March-April 1975.

48. Latane, H., and D. Tuttle, "Industry Analysis Framework for Forming Probability Beliefs." *Financial Analysts Journal*. July -August 1968, pp. 51 -61.

49. ————————, and Charles Jones. *Security Analysis and Portfolio Management*. 2d ed. (New York: Ronald Press. 1975).

50. Levy, Robert A. "On the Safety of Low P/E Stocks." *Financial Analysts Journal*, January-February 1973, pp. 57-63.

51. Lewellen, Wilber G., and J. S. Ang, "Inflation, Security Values, and Risk Premia." *Journal of Financial Research*, 5 (Summer 1982), 105-123.

52. ————————, Ronald C. Lease, and Gary G. Schlarbaum, "The Individual Investor : Attributes and Attitudes," *Journal of Finance* 29, no. 2 (May 1974) : 413-433.

53. ————————, "Patterns of Investment Strategy and Behavior among Individual Investors," *Journal of Business*, July 1977, pp. 296-333.

54. Lintner, John, "Inflation and Security Returns," *Journal of Finance*, 30 (May 1975). 259-80.

55. Livingston, Miles. "Industry Movements of Common Stocks." *Journal of Finance* 32, no. 3 (June 1977).

56. Lorie, James H., and Mary T. Hamilton: *The Stock Market: Theories and Evidence*, Richard D. Irwin, Homewood, IL, 1988.

57. Lys, Thomas, and Jowell Sabino: "Research Design Issues in Grouping-Based Tests," *Journal of Financial Economics*, December 1992, pp. 355-388.

58. Malkiel, B.G., and R.E. Quandt. "The Supply of Money and Common Stock Prices: Comment." *The Journal of Finance*, September 1972, pp. 921-26.

59. ——————, and John Cragg. "Expectations and the Structure of Share Prices." *American Economic Review* 60, no. 4 (September 1970).

60. McCandlish, Randolph W. "Security Analysts I Have Known," *Financial Analysts Journal.* Jan.-Feb. 1971.

61. Mcenally, Richard W., and Edward A. Dyl. "Risk of Selling Short." *Financial Analysts Journal*, November-December 1969, p. 73.

62. Mennis, Edmund A. "An Integrated Investment System." *Financial Analysts Journal*, March-April 1974, p. 38.

63. Meyers, Stephen L. "A Re-Examination of Market and Industry Factors in Stock Price Behavior." *Journal of Finance* 28, no. 3 (June 1973).

64. Modigliani. Franco, and Merton Miller, "The Cost of Capital, Corporation Finance, and the Theory of Investment," *American Economic Review*, June 1958, pp. 261-297.

65. Moor, Roy E. "The Use of Economics in Investment Analysis," *Financial Analysts Journal.* Nov.-Dec. 1971.

66. Moore, Geoffrey H., and Julius Shiskin. *Indicators of Business Expansions and Contractions.* National Bureau of Economic Re-search, 1967.

67. Murphy, Joseph E., Jr., and J. Russell Melson. "Stability of P/E Ratios." *Financial Analysts Journal*, March-April 1969, p. 77.

68. Niederhoffer, Victor, and Patrick J. Regan. "Earnings Changes, Analysts' Forecasts, and Stock Prices." *Financial Analysts Journal*, May-June 1972, pp. 65-71.

69. Okun, Arthur, "On the Appraisal of Cyclical Turning-Point Predictions," *Journal of Business* 33, no. 2 (April 1960): 101-120.

70. Pinches, George, and William Kinney, Jr., "The Measurement of the Volatility of Common Stock Prices," *Journal of Finance* 26 (March 1971): 119-125.

71. Porter, Michael E. "How to Conduct an Industry Analysis." In *The Financial Analysts Handbook.* 2d ed., edited by Sumner N. Levine. Homewood, Ill.: Dow Jones-Irwin, 1988.

72. Reilly, Frank K., and Eugene Drzycimski. "Alternative Industry Performance and Risk." *Journal of Financial and Quantitative Analysis* 9, no. 3 (June 1974).

73. ——————, Frank T. Griggs, and Wenchi Wong. "Determinants of the Aggregate Stock Market Earnings Multiple." *Journal of Portfolio Management* 10, no. 1 (Fall 1983).

74. Schwartz, Robert A. *Equity Markets: Structure, Trading, and Performance.* New York: Harper & Row, 1988.

75. Schwert, William: "Stock Market Volatility," *Financial Analysts Journal.* May-June 1990, pp. 23-34.

76. Shiller, Robert J., and John Campbell. "Stock Prices, Earnings, and Expected Dividends." *Journal of Finance* 43, no. 3 (July 1988).

77. Siegel, Jeremy J. "Does It Pay Stock Investors to Forecast the Business Cycle?" *The Journal of Port-folio Management* 18, no. 1 (Fall 1991).

78. Soldofsky, Robert, and Roger Miller, "Risk Premium Curves for Different Classes of Long Term Securities, 1950-1966," *Journal of Finance* 24 (June 1969): 429-445.

79. Spigelman, Joseph H. "What Basis for Superior Performance?" *Financial Analysts Journal*, May-June 1974, p. 32.

80. Stewart, Samuel S. "Forecasting Corporate Earnings." In *The Financial Analysts Handbook.* 2d ed., edited by Sumner N. Levine. Homewood, Ill.: Dow Jones-Irwin, 1988.

81. Tobin, James: "Liquidity Preference as Behavior towards Risk." *Review of Economic Studies*, February 1958, pp. 65-85.

82. Umstead, David A. "Forecasting Stock Market Prices," *The Journal of Finance*, Vol. XXXII. May 1977.

83. Wallich, Henry C. "Investment Income during Inflation." *Financial Analysts Journal*, March-April 1978.

84. Waymire, G. "Additional Evidence on the Information Content of Management Earnings Forecasts." *Journal of Accounting Research* 22, no. 3 (Autumn 1984).

85. Wolfe, harry D. *Business Forecasting Methods.* New York: Holt, Rinehart and Winston, 1966.

21

Technical Analysis

INTRODUCTION

Technical analysis is probably the most controversial aspect of investment management. That technical analysis is a delusion, that it can never be any more useful in predicting stock performance than examining the insides of a dead sheep, in the ancient Greek traditions. In this chapter, the focus is upon some of the major technical indicators employed to assess the direction of the general market and the direction of individual stocks. Investors should be aware of the principles and practice of technical analysis irrespective of whether they want to base their investment decisions on fundamental analysis, technical analysis, or a belief in efficient markets.

THE CONCEPT

The term *Technical analysis* is used to mean fairly wide range of techniques, all based on the concept that past information on prices and trading volume of stocks gives the enlightened investor *a picture* of what lies ahead. It attempts to explain and forecast changes in security prices by studying only the market data rather than information about a company or its prospects as is done by fundamental analyst. John Magee, whose book Technical Analysis of Stock Trends is considered a classic for technical analysts, says :

> "The technician has elected to study, not the mass of fundamentals, but certain abstraction, namely the market data alone. He is fully aware that is not all..... also he is aware that what he is looking it is indeed a fairly high order of abstraction and that on the back of it lies the whole complicated world of things and events. But this technical view provides a simplified and more comprehensible picture of what is happening to the price of a stock. It is like a shadow or reflection in which can be seen the broad outline of the whole situation. Furthermore, it works."

The technical analysts believe that the price of a stock depends on supply and demand in the market place and has little relationship to value, if any such concept even exits. Price is governed by basic economic and psychological inputs so numerous and complex that no individual can hope to understand and measure them correctly. The technician thinks that the only important information to work from is the picture given by price and volume statistics.

The technician sees the market, disregarding minor changes, moving in discernible trends which continue for significant periods. A trend is believed to continue until there is definite information of a change. The past performance of a stock can then be harnessed to predict the future. The direction of price change is as important as the relative size of the change. With his various tools, the technician attempts to correctly catch changes in trend and take advantage of them.

Basic Technical Assumptions

Before we embark on the actual methods themselves, let us review the basic and necessary assumptions regarding the technical analysis :

1. The market and/ or an individual stock acts like a barometer rather than a thermometer. Events are usually discounted in advance with movements as the likely result of informed buyers and sellers at work. We should never forget, as we explore the technical implications of market analysis that the price formations or patterns (as they are called by some) that evolve due to supply demand behaviour are, for the most part, the result of fundamentalists or speculators putting their money to work based upon their established convictions.

2. Before a stock experiences a mark-up phase, whether it be minor or major, a period of accumulation usually will take place. Conversely, before a stock enters into a major/a minor downtrend, a period of distribution usually will be the preliminary occurrence. Accumulation or distribution activity can occur within natural trading trends. Obviously an uptrend in prices denotes a balance buying, while a down trend is indicative of extreme supply. The ability to analyse accumulation or distribution within net neutral price patterns will be, therefore, a most essential pre-requisite. Such analysis is the technician's mam challenge. He should anticipate, not react.

3. The third assumption is actively tied into the first two. It is an observation that deals with the scope and extend of market movements in relation to each other. As an example, in most cases, a small phase of stock price consolidation — which is really phase of backing and filling — will be followed by a relative short-term movement, up or down, in the stock's price. On the other hand a larger consolidation phase can lead to a greater potential stock price move.

How can a stock give a buy signal when perhaps the news is bad, its earnings are down and it is otherwise unattractive ? To ensure this, two broad approaches to investment, namely, the fundamental analysis and the technical analysis can be applied. Both have strong champions in the stock market. Both can earn money for investors who do their homework, get the facts, watch developments carefully and act quickly, decisively and with commonsense. The orthodox synthesis between the two basic approaches is that once fundamental analysis has found the stocks, their purchases or sale can be at best times through technical analysis. However, a broad comparison between these two approaches is a must to appreciate the role of technical analysis in the stock market.

TECHNICAL VS. FUNDAMENTAL ANALYSIS

With a view to making a broad comparison between technical analysis and fundamental analysis, let us assume that the fundamentalist is a conservative who invests for the long term and the technician is a trader who buys and sells for short-term profits. Actually, of course, the value of technical analysis lies between these extremes.

Fundamentalists study the cause, not the "should". They make their decisions on quality, value and depending on their specific investment goals, the yield or growth potential of the security. They are concerned with the basis, the corporation's financial strength, record of growth in sales and earnings, profitability, the investment acceptance and so on. They also take into account the general business and market conditions. Finally they interpret these data inductively to determine the current value of the stock and then to project its future price. Fundamentalists are patient and seldom expect meaningful profits in less than one year.

In the long run, the fundamentalist who selects quality stocks when they are undervalued and sells them when they become fully priced will make substantial profits. But as John Maynard Keynes often noted, *"In the. long run, we'll all be dead"*.

Compared with long-term investors, technicians seek to keep their money working as profitably as possible at all times. When trading, they want to score profits quickly, and if the stock or market does not perform as anticipated, they are willing to take a small, fast loss.

Technically oriented investors start by checking the market action of the stock. If it is favourable, they examine the fundamentals to be sure the company is sound and profitable. At all times their focus is on the market, generally, on the performance of all listed stocks; specifically, on the price/ volume movements of the stock they are considering buying. They make their decision on technical, not fundamental, data.

Technicians believe that (1) the stock market is rooted 15 per cent in economics and 85 per cent in psychology; (2) the record of past and present performance of a stock, not necessarily of the corporation, is the key factor; and (3) stock market dominated by institutional investors, operates on the Wolf pack theory of following the leaders. When major money managers start to buy, regardless of the reason, the price of the stock will go up. When they start to sell, it will go down. All such moves are shown by technical indicators.

In more detailed terms, here are several ways the technician thinks and acts :

1. Technicians believe that behind the fundamentals are important factors

At any given time, some investors have gains in the stock, and usually some have losses. Those with gains want to safeguard them and if possible, build them higher, they will hold the stocks.

Those with losses will adopt different tactics; some will cut their losses short by selling out early when the stock price begins to decline others will sell when a minor rally has moved the stock up to their cost price; and still others will hold on doggedly until there is a turnaround.

Each of these decision points can be sported on charts : current configuration to show the action of the past week or so; intermediate - and long-term patterns to find the previous important price levels at which selling is likely; and interim and long-term high points from which the stock started to move down in the past.

In this method of analysis, a vital factor is volume. Volume is favourable on the upside when the number of shares traded is greater than before, and on the down side when the number of shares traded dwindles. Volume is unfavourable when volume dips as prices rise or increases when there is a decline. None of these indicators are concerned with the fundamentals of the corporation.

2. Technicians act on the what not the why

They recognise that formations and patterns signify changes in real value as the result of investor expectations, hopes, fears, industry developments and so on. They are not as impressed with the fundamental value of any security as they are with the current and prospective values reflected by market action.

3. Technicians are not committed to a buy-and-hold policy

As long as the trend is up, they will hold a stock. This may be for months or even years. But if there is a reversal, they will sell within hours of purchase. They recognise that, to achieve the greatest gains, they must never let sentiment or emotion override facts (as shown by technical indicators) and should always get out of situation which, on available evidence, is no longer profitable.

4. Technicians do not separate income from capital gains

They look for total returns, that is, the realised price less the price paid plus dividends received. This is a sharp contrast to most long-term investors who buy a high-dividend paying stock and hold it for years, through up-and-down fluctuations. To the technicians, such strategy is foolish. A stock may continue to pay liberally but lose 50% of its value. If a stock is to be judged solely on its income, a non-dividend payer would have no value at all.

5. Technicians act more quickly to make commitments and to take profits and losses

They are not concerned with maintaining a position in any market, any industry or any stock. As a result they are willing to take smaller gains in an up market and accept quick losses in a down market. Traders/technicians want to keep their money working at maximum efficiency.

Technicians know that there is no real value to any stock and that price reflects supply and demand which are governed by hundreds of factors, rational and irrational. No one can grasp and weigh them all, but to a surprising degree, the market does so automatically.

6. Technicians recognise that the more experience one has with the technical indicators, the more alert one becomes to pitfalls and failure of investing

To be rewarding, technical analysis requires attention and discipline, with quality stocks held for the long terms, time can make up for timing mistakes. With technical approaches, the errors become clear quickly.

7. Technicians insist that the market always repeats

What has happened before will probably be repeated again, therefore, current movements can be used for future projections. In other words, with all markets and almost all securities, there are cycles and trends which will occur again and again. Technical analysis, especially charts, provide the best and most convenient method of comparison.

8. Technicians believe that breakouts from previous trends are important signals

They indicate a shift in that all-important supply and demand. When confirmed, breakouts are almost always accurate signals to buy or sell.

9. Technicians recognise that the securities of a strong company are often weak and those of a weak company may be strong

Technical analysis can quickly show when such situations occur. These indicator always delineate between the company and the stock.

10. Technicians use charts to confirm fundamentals

When both agree, the odds are favourable for profitable movement if the trend of the overall stock market is also favourable.

In view of the above comparison between technical and fundamental analysis, let us consider some of the tools used by technical analysts to measure supply and demand and forecast security prices.

OLD PUZZLES AND NEW DEVELOPMENTS

FIBONACCI NUMBERS

Fibonnacci numbers have intrigued mathematicians and scientists for hundred of years. Leonardo Fibonacci (1170-1240) was a medieval mathematician who discovered the series of numbers while studying the reproductive behaviour of rabbits. The beginning of the Fibonacci series is shown below:

1,1,2,3,5,8,13,21,34,55,89,144,233,...

After the initial pair of ones, each succeeding number is simply the sum of the previous two.

The remarkable thing about these numbers is the frequency with which they appear in the environment. Sunflowers have seed spiraling around the center of the plant. Some spirals contain seeds leaning counterclockwise, ith other spirals going the other way. On most sunflowers, the number of clockwise spirals and the number of counterclockwise spirals are adjacent Fibonacci numbers. A blossom might have 34 counterclockwise spirals and 55 clockwise spirals. The structure of pine cones, the number of chambers in a nautilus seashell, the topology of spiraling galaxies, and the ancestry of bees all reveal Fibonacci numbers. Even a professional journal, the *Fibonacci Quarterly*, is devoted to the study of this series.

Technical analysts who follow Fibonacci numbers usually make use of the number 1.618. This number is called *the golden mean* and appears in ancient writings and architecture. (The golden mean features prominently in the dimensions of the Parthenon). After the first ten or so numbers in the series, each Fibonacci number divided by its immediate predecessor equals 1.618. For example, 89/55 = 1.618,134/89 = 1.6189, and so on. This magic number is used to calculate Fibonacci *ratios* as shown in Table 1.

TABLE 1

Fibonacci Ratios

0/618	1	0.618	1.000	1.618	2.618
-	-	X	X	X	X
1.618	1.618	1.618	1.618	1.618	1.618
0.382	0.618	1.000	1.618	2.618	4.236

Many Fibonacci advocates in the investment business use the first two ratios, 0.382 and 0.618, to "compute retracement levels of a previous move." For instance, a stock that falls from ₹ 50 to ₹ 35 (30 per cent drop) will encounter resistance to further advances after it recoups 38.2 per cent of its loss (that is, after it rises to ₹ 40.73).

Some technical analysts keep close-tabs on resistance and support levels as predicted by the Fibonacci ratios. Even people who do not subscribe to this business know that many other people do, and that when stock prices approach important Fibonacci levels, unusual things can occur.

A male bee (a drone) has only a mother; it comes from an unfertilized egg. A female be a queen) comes from a fertilized egg and has both a mother and a father. This means one drone has one parent, two grandparents, three great-grandparents, five great-great grandparents, and so on. The number of ancestors at each generation is the Fibonacci series.

DOW THEORY

The Dow Theory (not to be confused with the Dow Jones Averages), proposed by charles Dow shortly after the turn of the century and extended in a book by Samuel Nelson after Dow's untimely death, is one of the oldest technical method still widely followed, There are many versions of this theory, but essentially it consists of three types of market movements : the major market trend, which can often last a year or more; a secondary intermediate trend, which can move against the primary trend for one to several months; and minor movements lasting only for hours to a few days. The determination of the major market trend is the most important decision to the Dow believer.

Although Charles Dow believed in fundamental analysis, the Dow theory has evolved into a primarily technical approach to the stock market. It asserts that stock prices demon-strate patterns over four to five years and these patterns are mirrored by indices of stock prices. The Dow Theory employs two of the Dow Jones averages, the industrial average and the transportation average. The utility average is generally ignored.

The Dow theory is built upon the assertion that measures of stock prices tend to move together. If the Dow Jones industrial average is rising, then, the transportation average should also be rising. Such simultaneously price movements suggest a strong bull market. Conversely, a decline in both the industrial and transportation averages are moving in opposite directions, the market is uncertain as to the direction of future stock prices.

If one of the averages starts to decline after a period of rising stock prices, then the two are at odds. For example, the industrial average may be rising while the transportation average is falling. This suggests that the industrials may not continue to rise but may soon start to fall. Hence, the market investor will use this signal to sell securities and convert to cash.

The converse occurs when after a period of falling security prices one of the averages starts to rise while the other continue to fall. According to the Dow Theory, this divergence suggests that this phase is over and that security prices in general will soon start to rise. The astute investor will then purchase securities in anticipation of the price increase.

These signals are illustrated in Figure-1. Part A illustrates a buy signal. Both the industrial and transportation average have been declining when the industrial starts to rise. Although the transportation index is still declining, the increase in industrial average suggests that the declining market is over. This change is then confirmed when the transportation average also starts to rise.

Part B illustrates the opposite case in which both the industrial and transportation averages have been rising. Then the industrial average starts to decline while the transportation average continues to rise. This suggests that the market is going through an unsettled period and until they start moving together again there is uncertainty as to the future direction of stock prices. However, in the case illustrated in Fig.l, Part B, the transportation average also starts to fall, which confirms the direction of the industrial average and indicates that a bear market is underway. Of course, this implies that investors should try to liquidate security holdings.

If investors believe this theory, they will try to liquidate when a sell signal becomes apparent, which in turn will drive down prices. Buy signals have the opposite effect. Investors will try to purchase securities, which will drive up their prices. This points out an interesting phenomenon concerning technical analysis in general. If investors believe the signals and act accordingly, the signals will become self-fulfilling properties. Unfortunately, by the time many investors perceive the signal and act, the price change will have already occurred, and much of the potential profit from the alteration in the portfolio will have evaporated.

There are several problems with the Dow Theory. The first is that it is not a theory but an interpretation of known data. It does not explain why the two averages should be able to forecast future stock prices. In addition, there may be a considerable lag between actual turning points and those indicated by the forecast. It may be months before the

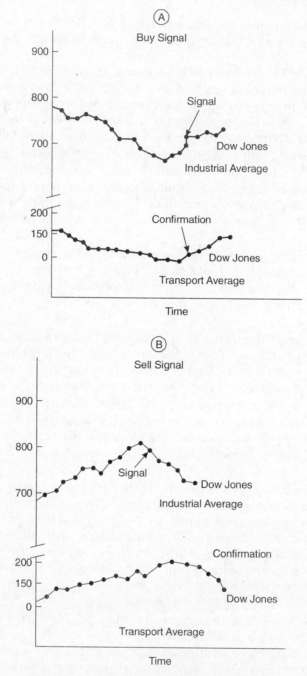

FIGURE 1: THE DOW JONES AVERAGES

two averages confirm each other, during which time individual stocks may show substantial price changes.

The accuracy of the Dow Theory and its predictive power have been the subject of much criticism. Greiner and Whitcomb assert that "the Dow Theory provides a time tested method of reading the stock market barometer". However, between 1929 and 1960 the Dow theory made only 9 correct predictions out of 24 buy or seli signals. Such results are less accurate than the investor may obtain by flipping a coin and have considered diminished support for the technique.

The DOW Theory might work only when a long, wide, upward or downward movement is registered in the market. It is mostly unsuitable as a market predictor when the market trend frequently reverses itself in the short or the intermediate term. Another major drawback is that the theory does not attempt to explain a consistent pattern of the stock price movements.

ELLIOTT WAVE PRINCIPLE

One theory that attempts to develop a rationale for a long- term pattern in the stock price movements is the Elliott Wave Principle (EWP), established in the 1930s by R.N. Eliott and later popularized by Hamilton Bolton. The EWP states that major moves take place in five successive steps resembling tidal waves. In a major bull market, the first move is upward, the second downward, the third upward, the fourth downward and the fifth and final phase upward. The waves have a reverse flow in a bear market. The EWP, claimed to be a valuable tool for market prediction, is demonstrated in Figure - 2.

Figure 2-A is a simple demonstration of the EWP when the stock market advance goes through five clearly marked stages. In Figure 2-B, we see that a major five-stage advance, indicated by broken lines, may run concurrently with several mini five-stage advances (indicated by a solid line). The EWP is applied to an actual situation in Figure 2-C, where it is demonstrated that past movements in the DJIA have followed the five-stage advance principle. For example, the major advance in the DJIA between 1896 and 1929 can be viewed as two minor five-rwwww3stage advances, one covering the penod 1896 to 1909 and the other covering the years 1921 through 1929.

Proponents of the EWP claim that it offers investors a basis for developing important market strategies. However, even they do not deny the fact that the EWP has two major limitations. First, it is difficult to identify the turning point of each stage. Second, investors frequently cannot distinguish between a major and a minor five-stage movement.

KONDRATEV WAVE THEORY

Nikolay Kondratev was a Russian economist and statistician born in 1892. He helped develop the first Soviet five-year plan. From 1920 to 1928 he was Director of the Study of Business Activity at the Timiriazev Agricultural Academy. While there he devoted his attention to the study of Western capitalists economies. In the economies of Great Britain and the United States, he identified long-term business cycles with a period of 50-60 years. He became well known after the U.S. market crash of 1929, which Kondratev predicted would follow the U.S. crash of 1870. His hypothesis of a long-term business cycle is called the *Kondratev Wave Theory.*

Note that the market crash for 1987 occurred 58 years after the crash of 1929, a period consistent with Kondratev's theory. Some modern economists believe Kondratev's theory has merit. Many others believe that significant macroeconomic changes, such as floating exchange rates, the elimination of the gold standard, and the reduction of barriers to free trade, make the decision cycle less predictable. Still, many market analysts consider Kondratev's work in their assessment of the stock market and its risks.

CHAOS THEORY

At recent finance conferences, a few researchers have presented papers on *chaos theory* and its application to the stock market. In physics, chaos theory is a growing field of study examining instances in which apparently random behaviour is, in fact, quite

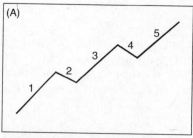

A. Graph Showing a Major Move
in Five Successive Steps

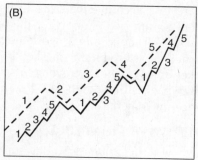

B. A Close-up of the Five-Setp
Market Moves

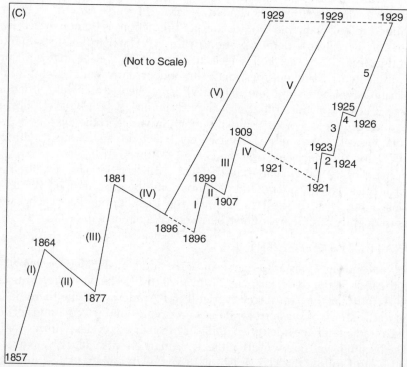

C. Waves, Subwaves, and the DJIA

NOTE : Each of waves (I) (III) (V) breaks down into five subwaves, as do waves I, III, V, and waves 1, 3, 5, Corrective
waves (II) (IV), II, IV, and 2, 4 break down into three subwaves.

FIGURE 2

systematic or even deterministic. Scientists apply this theory to weather prediction,
population growth estimates, and fisheries biology.

As an example of the latter application, a given volume of ocean water, left free from
human interference, will not necessarily reach an equilibrium population of the various
species that inhibit it. As fish grow, they consume the smaller fry (of their own or a

different species) in increasing numbers. Fewer younger fishes are left to mature; this, coupled with the natural death of the older fish, eventually results in a sudden drastic reduction in fish population, causing dismay to fishermen and excitement in the local media. At the same time, it results in reduced predation and food competition by the surviving fry, so the population begins to grow dramatically, and the cycle continues. Interactions -between species add complexity to the process.

Investment analysts have sought a pattern in stock market behaviour since the origin of the exchanges. Much remains unknwon about how security prices are determined, and chaos theory may eventually provide some potential answers. If the apparent randomness of security price changes, can be shown to be nonrandom, much of the theory of finance would need revision.

NEUTRAL NETWORKS

A *neutral network* is a trading system in which a forecasting model is *trained* to find a desired output from past trading data. By repeatedly cycling through the data, the neutral network eventually learns the pattern that produces the desired output. If the desired output remains elusive, more data is included until a pattern is found. Neutral networks may also include a feedback mechanism whereby experience a gained from past errors.

This topic is a hot one in the investment community. National conferences have been organised dealing exclusively with this topic, and the trade literature publishes many articles on the topic. A problem with the concept of a neutral network is that the stock market is seldom deterministic. Situations constantly change, and what may have been true a few years ago will not necessarily prevail tomorrow. Financial academics are especially leery of *backtests,* or research that tests a hypothesis using past data. Mining the data will almost always result in some apparent cause and effect between past events and stock market performance. Research that tests a hypothesis using *subsequent* data is much more useful. AN article in the popular press describes Wall Street's response to this criticism:

One way to get around this hazard is to build something called a genetic algorithm into your neutral network. A sexy term that currently causes Wall Street rocket scientists to swoon, genetic algorithms enable neutral nets to adapt to the future by spawning schools of baby nets, each of which is sent to swim against the changing flow of data, where only the fittest survive to take over the role of the mother.

No matter what someone's field of study, they are interested in the search for a better mousetrap. Essentially, what all security analysts seek to do is find improvements in their methodology for security selection.

CHARTING AS A TECHNICAL TOOL

Most technicians rely heavily on charts of prices and trading volume for their analysis of the market and individual stocks. The purpose of "chart reading" or "chart analysis" is to determine the probable strength of demand versus pressure of supply at various price levels, and thus to predict the probable direction in which a stock will move, and where it will probably stop. The clues are provided by the history of a stock's price movements, as recorded on a chart. In the market, history does repeat itself — often. On the charts, price fluctuations tend, with remarkable consistency, to fall into a number of patterns, each of which signifies a relationship between buying and selling pressures. Some patterns or "formations", indicate that demand is greater than supply, others suggest that supply is greater than demand, and still others imply that they are likely to remain in balance for some time. Technical analysts claim that stock price fluctuations generally form characteristic patterns which have important predictive value. No one of experience doubts that prices move in trends and trends tend to continue until something happens to change the supply — demand balance. Such changes are usually detectable in the action of the marker itself. Certain patterns of formation, levels or areas, appear on the chart which have a meaning that can be interpreted in terms of probable future trend development. They are not infalliable, it must be noted, but the odds are definitely in their favour. There are countless chart systems, but most of them attempt to correlate a relationship between market price action and the volume of trading. The idea is that it is a sign of strength when a stock advances on a large volume of shares traded. Conversely, when volume in the market or on one stock enlarges as a stock declines, it shows that the pessimism is mounting and that the trend is for lower prices. In essence the chartists contend that a study of a stock's behaviour not only tells where a stock has been but also where it is going.

Types of Charts

The three basic types of charts are line, bar and point-and- figure. In each case, the type of chart chosen to record price activity is determined by the amount of information available.

(A) Line Chart

On a line chart, the closing prices of successive time periods are connected by straight lines, with no notice taken of the highs and lows of stock prices for each period. Figure - 3 presents a line chart of ABC Corporation.

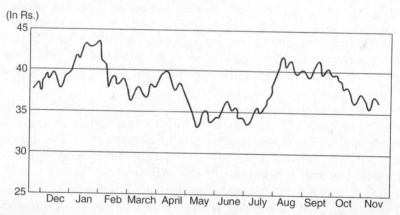

FIGURE 3

(B) Bar Chart

Most investors interested in charting use bar charts — primarily because they have meanings familiar to a technical analyst, but also because these charts are easy to draw. The procedure for preparing a vertical line or bar chart is simple. Suppose an investor is to draw on graph on logarithmic paper a series of vertical lines, each line representing the price movements for a time period — a day, a week, or even a year. The vertical dimensions of the line represent price; the horizontal dimension indicates the time involved by the chart as a whole. In a daily chart, for example, each vertical line represents the range of each day's price activity, and the chart as a whole may extend for a moth. For this, extend the line on the graph paper from the highest transaction of each day drawn to the lowest and make a cross mark to indicate the closing price. (Figure 4)

(C) Point-and-Figure Chart

Bar chartists count on discovering certain buying and selling forces in the market, on the basis of which they predict future price trends. These forces consist of three factors - time, volume and price. Members of another school, known as the point-and-figure chartists, question the usefulness of the first two factors. They argue that the way to predict future price fluctuations is to analyse price changes only. Consequently, they assert, no volume action need be recorded, and the time dimension (day, week, or

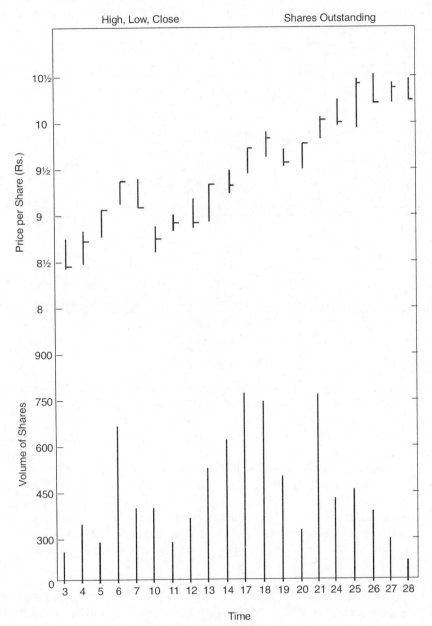

FIGURE 4

month) should also be ignored. If only significant price changes are important, then one need only capture the significant (say, one point or more, ignoring all fractions) price changes in a stock, no matter how long it takes for the stock to register this change.

The first step in drawing a point-and-figure chart is to put an X in the appropriate price column of a graph. Then enter successive price increases (of one point or more, ignoring fractions) in an upward column as long as the uptrend continues. If the price drops by one point or more, the figures move to another column and the O's are entered in a downward progression until the downtrend is reversed Use of such a chart over a reasonable period of time gives a "king-size-tic-tac-toe game" which can be used for prediction. Note, however, a fairly long period should be covered so that definite shapes can be observed on the graph paper. Figure - 5 is a sample point-and-figure chart for ABC Company.

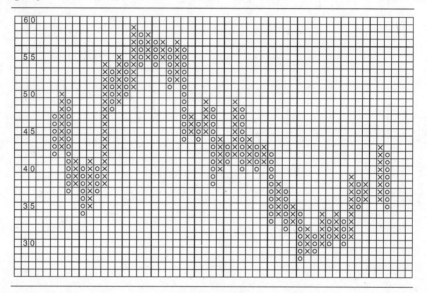

FIGURE 5: THE POINT-AND-FIGURE CHART AND ITS CONSTRUCTION

Candlestick Chart

A candlestick chart is an enhanced version of a bar chart. These charts began to appear in the United States in the mid- 1980s. Such a chart shos a stock's open, close, high, and low in a modified three-dimensional format. The vertical, axis shows stock price, while the horizontal axis reflects the passage of time. The principal difference between a daily candlestick chart and a bar chart are the white and black *candles* augmenting the daily trading range lines. If the opening price exceeds the closing price (the stock is down for the day), the body of the candle is black. When the stock is up (the close exceeds the open), the candle is clear. White candles represent stock advances, with black candles representing declines. The thick portion of an entry is called the *real body*, with the vertical line representing the *wick*. Various clusters of candles have exotic names, such as *dark cloud cover, doji star, hanging mm, harami cross,* and *two-day tweezer tops.*

IMPORTANT CHART PATTERNS

Charts are a means to an end. They help a technical analyst not only to identify stocks which are technically strong or weak but to decide when to buy or sell a stock. Figure - 6

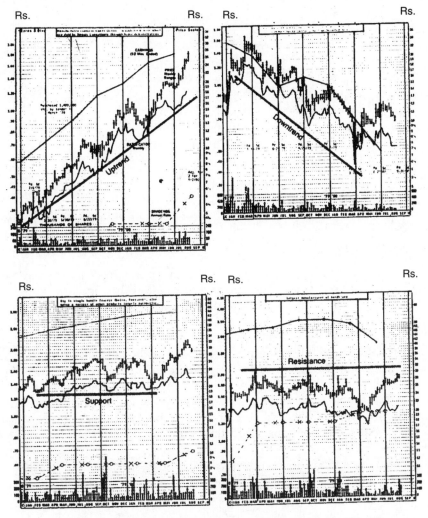

Source: 3-Trend Security Charts, January, 1980, pp. 25, 39, 148, 192.

FIGURE 6: ILLUSTRATIVE BAR CHARS OF STOCK PRICES

shows illustrative bar charts of stork prices. Analysts, of course, use several techniques to examine various chart patterns.

Support and Resistance Levels

One of the most important aspects of chart analysis is the identification of support and resistance levels, as shown in Figure - 7. A support level is a barrier to price decline; a resistance level is a barrier to price advancement. Although the barrier is an obstruction, it is by no means impassable; stock prices do break support and resistance barriers.

Assume ABC stock is currently trading at 35. In the recent past, it has been as low as 30 and as high as 43. When the stock approaches 30, it becomes an attractive investment. A flurry of buying activity follows, and the stock begins to advance in price. Should the stock cross its previous high of 40, however, investors will probably view it as overpriced and begin to liquidate their investment in the stock. Based on these observations, the ABC stock has a support level at 30, with a potential resistance level at 40. The predictive

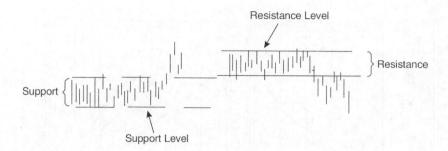

FIGURE 7

value of these levels should be noted : A stock breaking its support level is technically weak; conversely, a stock breaking the resistance level is technically strong.

Head and Shoulders Configurations

Basic reversal patterns help analysts identify the turning points so that they can decide when to buy or sell stock. The key reversal pattern is popularly known as the head and shoulders configuration. This configuration, shown in Figure - 8, is merely another name for an uptrend or a downtrend in a stock; the "neckline" is the familiar resistance or support level.

Head and shoulders formation should be analysed against the background of volume trend. As the head and shoulders top is formed, resistance to further price increases dampens investor enthusiasm; therefore the volume decreases on each of the rally phases within the top formation. The reverse is trye when the head and shoulders bottom is under formation. It should be emphasised that the completion of a head and shoulders top or bottom is not considered final until the penetration of the neckline is apparent.

There are many variations of such reversal formations. Of these, the so-called double and triple tops and bottoms, shown in Figure-9, are particularly interesting.

Trend Analysis

Establishing a major trend is one of the most vexing problems encountered by a technical analyst. Following seven questions may be helpful in analysing the major trend of a stuck:

Question 1 : Does the stock have a move of substance to reverse? The major reversal formation certainly would not be looked for in a stock that has only moved from 20 to 26, but if a move from 20 to 45 had been experienced, any reversal in trend could be major.

Question 2: Has the stock fulfilled readable price objectives ? A major trend is usually preceded by notable advancement in price.

Question 3 : Has the stock violated its trends ? If a trend violation does occur, it could be the forerunner or an early warning of a reversal in the major direction of the stock's price movement.

Question 4 : Are signs of distribution or accumulation evident? A major uptrend is preceded by accumulation, whereas distribution is generally followed by a downturn.

Question 5: If distribution or accumulation is evident, is it significant enough to imply that more than a minor movement in price could be in the offing ?

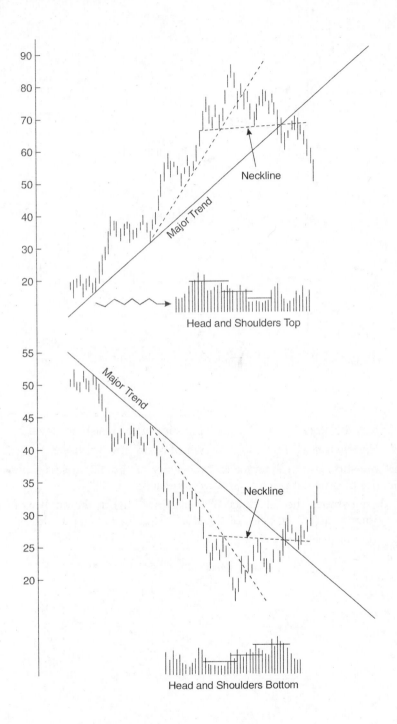

Head and Shoulders Top

Head and Shoulders Bottom

FIGURE 8

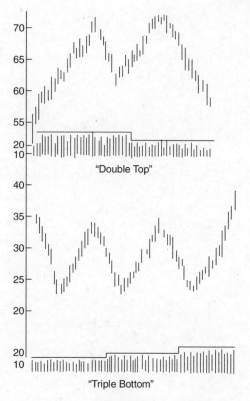

"Double Top"

"Triple Bottom"

FIGURE 9

Question 6 : Has the stock violated a readable support or resistance level ?

Question 7 : Has the stock initiated a downward or an upward trend ?

A "floater" question can be inserted between any of the above seven questions: Is there any evidence of unusual price and/or volume action ?

Figure 10 demonstrates the relevance of these questions to the analysis of a major uptrend and a downtrend in the price of the stock. Note, for example, the reversal of a

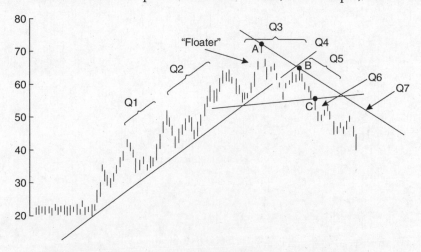

FIGURE 10: THE 7 QUESTIONS (WITH *A* "FLOATER")

major uptrend at point A; this suggests that the stock has violated its trend (Question 3). Furthermore, point B is the beginning of a significant distribution which, according to Question 5, signals a significant decline in the stock's price. Similarly, at point C the stock penetrates its support level (Question 6) and therefore becomes technically weak.

Triangles, Pennants, Wedges and Flags

Certain price configurations are more easily identified than head and shoulders configurations. These configurations, known as triangles, are shown in Figure -11. In addition, a number of other technical configurations qualify as consolidation patterns.

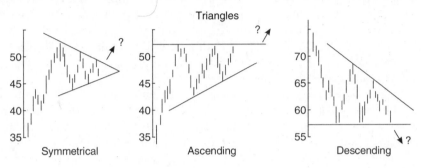

FIGURE 11: TRIANGLES

These patterns, known as wedge, flat, and pennant, are shown in Figure - 12. For example, a falling wedge of the type shown here usually occurs in a major uptrend pattern for the following reason. Sellers in this case are aggressive, as is evident from the steel decline of line A. In contrast, buyers are not quite as discouraged as sellers, as revealed by the relative flatness of the declining line B. Incidently, all three types of formations shown here are short-term in nature and occur early in an upward or a downward trend phase.

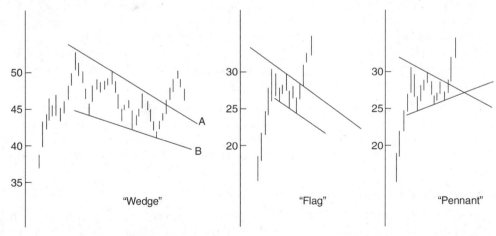

SOURCE: Alan R. Shaw, "Technical Analysis" in Financial Anslyst's Handbook. ed. Summer N. Levine (Homewood, III.: Dow Jones-Irwin, 1975), p. 967.

FIGURE 12

LIMITATIONS OF CHARTS

The technical analyst may have charts of all the principal shares in the market. But all that is necessary is a proper interpretation of charts. Interpretation of charts is very much like a personal offer. In a way, it is like abstract art. Take an abstract painting and show it to ten people and you will get at least eight different interpretations of what is seen. Take one set for chart figures and show it to ten chartists and you are liable to get almost as many interpretations of which way the stock is going.

The trouble with most chart patterns is that they cause their followers to change their opinion so frequently. Most chart services change like the wind. One day they put out a strong buy signal, two weeks later, they see a change in the pattern and tell their clients to sell, then two weeks later, they tell them to buy again. The result is that these patterns force their followers in and out of the market time and time again. Though this is great for brokers' commission, but not so great for the investor.

Another disadvantage - and a great one - which exists in charting is that decisions are almost always made on the basis of the chart alone. Most buyers under this method have no idea why they are buying a company's stock. They rely alone on a stock's action, assuming that the people who have caused or are currently causing this action really know something about the company. This is generally negative thinking—simply because, as more and more chartists are attracted to a stock, there are simply more and more owners who know little or nothing about the company.

TECHNICAL INDICATORS

Most of the technical indicators make sense when examined individually but when one examines many technical indicators simultaneously, the interpretation of their collective meaning is often contradictory and confusing. One technical analyst issued the following report:

> "The breadth of the market remains pretty bearish, but the odd-lot index is still in balance and is more bullish than bearish. While the short interest is not bearish, brokers' loans are at a dangerously high level. Business indices are beginning to turn sharply upward and most psychological indicators are generally uptrend. The index of 20 low-priced stocks remains in a general uptrend, but the confidence index still is in a long- term downtrend. The Canadian gold price index is still in a downtrend which normally implies a higher stock market ahead. Professional and public opinion remains cautiously optimistic, which is also an indication of a higher stock market, but on a decline below 800 the Dow Jones Industrial averages would give a definite sell signal."

The author of this technical report presented numerous technical indicators that collectively add up to organized confusion. Some of the major technical indicators are described in the following sections. Each indicators makes sense by itself, but interpreting all of them at the same time may yield the same type of confusion found in the passage quoted above.

The Short Interest Ratio Theory

The short interest ratio is derived by dividing the reported short interest or the number of shares sold short, by the average volume for about 30 days. When short sales increases relative to total volume, the indicator rises. A ratio above 150 per cent is considered bullish, and a ratio below 100 per cent is considered bearish.

The logic behind this ratio is that speculators and other investors sell stocks at high prices in anti pation of buying them back at lower prices. Thus, increasing short selling is viewed as a sign of general market weakness, and short-covering (as evidenced by decreasing short positions) as a sign of strength. An existing large short interest is considered a sign of strength, since the covers (buying) are yet to come; whereas an estabolished slight short interest is considered a sign of weakness (more short sales are to come).

Confidence Index

It is the ratio of a group of lower-grade bonds to a group of higher-grade bonds. According to the theory underlying this index, when the ratio is high, investors' confidence is likewise high, as reflected by their purchase of relatively more of the lower-grade securities. When they buy relatively more of the higher grade securities, this is taken as an indication that confidence is low, and is reflected in a low ratio.

Spreads

Large spreads between yields indicate low confidence and are bearish; the market appears to require a large compensation for business, financial and inflation risks. Small spreads indicate high confidence and are bullish. In short, the larger the spreads, the lower the ratio and the less the confidence. The smaller the spreads, the greater the ratio, indicating greater confidence.

Advance-Decline Ratio

The index relating advances to declines is called the advance decline ratio. When advances persistently outnumber decline the ratio increases. A bullish condition is said to exist, and vice versa. Thus, advance decline ratio tries to capture the market's underlying strength by taking into account the number of advancing and declining issues.

Market Breadth Index

The market breadth index is a variant of the advance decline ratio. To compute it, we take the net difference between the number of stocks rising and the number of stocks falling, added (or subtracted) to the previous. For example, if in a given week 600 shares advanced, 200 shares declined, and 200 were unchanged, the breadth would be 2[(600-200)/200]. The figure of each week is added to previous week's. These data are then plotted to establish the pattern of movement of advances and declines.

The purpose of the market breadth index is to indicate whether a confirmation of some index has occurred. If both the stock index and the market breadth index increase, the market is bullish; when the stock index increases but the breadth index does not, the market is bearish.

The Odd-Lot Ratio

Odd-lot transactions are measured by odd-lot changes in index. Odd-lots are stock transactions of less than, say, 100 shares. The odd-lot ratio is sometimes referred to as a yardstick of uniformed sentiment or an index of contrary opinion because the odd-lot theory assumes that small buyers or sellers are not very bright especially at tops and bottoms when they need to be brightest. The odd-lot short ratio theory assumes that the odd-lot short sellers are even more likely to be wrong than odd- letters in general. This indicator relates odd-lot sales to purchases.

Insider Transactions

The hypothesis that insider activity may be indicative of future stock prices has received some support in the academic literature. Since insiders may have the best picture of how the firm is faring, some believers of technical analysis feel that these inside transactions offer a clue, to future earnings, dividend and stock price performance. If the insiders are selling heavily, it is considered a bearish indicator and vice versa. Stock holders do not like to hear that the president of a company is selling large blocks of stock of the company. Although the president's reason for selling the stock may not be related to the future growth of the company, it is still considered bearish as investors figurethe president, as an insider, must know something bad about the company that they, as outsiders, do not know.

Moving Average

A moving average is a smoothed presentation of underlying historical data. Each data point is the arithmatic average of a portion of the previous data. A ten-day moving average measures the average over the previous ten trading days; a twenty-day moving average measures average values over the previous twenty days, and so on. Regardless of the time period used, each day a new observation is included in the calculation and the oldest is dropped, so a constant number of points are always being averaged.

Advocates of moving averages in stock selection believe that changes in the slope of the line are important. A stock whose twenty-day moving average line has been trending up might become a candidate for sale if the line turn downward.

Fundamental analysts and technical analysts both use market indicators. Indicators can help present data in a more intuitive way and may suggest areas for further investigation. Tools such as the advance-decline line and relative strength figures may even help some people make decisions, but they should not be more than that. Managers make decisions, not black boxes or technical indicators. It is dangerous, though, to believe that a collection of market indicators of any kind will function as an oracle predicting future movements of a stock or of the overall market.

INDICATORS OF THE WITCHCRAFT VARIETY

Even in this era of political correctness, some indicators are less worthy than others. If there is no logical connection between what an indicator measures and what it purports to show, the indicator probably should not receive much study time. A few such indicators are well established in market folkfore, and while they may have no logical place in the investment decision- making process, an awareness of them is helpful.

The Super Bowl Indicator

This well-known market statistic will bring a smile to the face of many American investment professionals when asked about it. The *super bown indicator* states that the stock market will advance the following year if the super bowl football game is won by a team from the original National Football League. This indicator was correct 27 out of 30 times over the period 1967 through 1996. Such a percentage might seem unlikely to have occurred by chance.

There is a statistical problem with this indicator, however. For one thing, there are more original NFL teams that there are teams in the other conference, the American Football Conference (AFC). The Indianapolis Colts, Pittsburgh Steelers, and Cleveland Browns (all AFC teams) are original NFL teams. Couple this information with the fact that the stock market rises more often than it falls and the odd favour the indicator.

Few people admit to being persuaded by the super bown indicator; most will agree it is unlikely that any trye cause- and-effect relationship exists between the game and the market. Still, many professional investment managers and individual investors alike subconsciously root for the NFL team, just in case.

Sunspots

The public began to associate sunspots with the stock market through five works of William Stanley Jevons published between 1862 and 1897. While the notion of using the eleven-year solar cycle as a forecasting device has few advocates today, it was the focus of much discussion 100 years ago.

Jevons found that rainfall and temperature appeared to be related to solar activity:

> *The success of the harvest in any year certainly depends upon the whether, especially that of the summer and autumn months. Now if this weather depends upon the solar period, it follows that the harvest and the price of grain will depend more or less upon the solar period, and will go through periodic fluctuations in periods of time equal to those of the sun spots.*

The essence of his theory is that increased sunspot activity leads to warmer temperature and more rain, leading to an improved harvest and a stronger economy, and finally to higher stock prices. He tested this theory on English grain prices between 1259 and 1400. Jevons concludes:

> *I do not venture to assert positively that the average fluctuations are solely due to variations of solar power. They seem to show that the subject deserves further investigation.*

Jevons observed a ten to eleven-year cycle in the money market and believed this might be, at least in part, because of the solar influence on crops and the economy.

Hemline Indicator

Like the super bowl indicator, the hemline indicator is market folkfore that few people take seriously, but many like to talk about it. The essence of the hemline indicator is this: as shorter dresses for women because the fashion, the market advances, and vice versa. Simultaneously plotting skirt lengths and market levels reveals a remarkable correlation. In the 1920s the market rose and so did hemlines. During the Great Depression, dresses touched the ground. There was a gradual rise in the market and in hemlines through World War II; the rest of the forties and the fifties peaked in the go-go days of the 1960s with miniskirts. The 1970s saw peasant dresses and maxiskirts and an economic recession. During the prosperity of the 1980s things moved back up. During one stretch in the early 1990s the market was nearly flat for over a year. What was the dress fashion? *Slits* on the side of skirts. Presumably the market did not know what to make of them.

All these "indicators", of course, are likely to be purely spurious correlations. What economic cause and effect could possibly be at work? The lack of an economic underpinning is the reason technical indicators of this type are called witchcraft.

TECHNICAL ANALYSIS — AN EVALUATION

Studies have been made to determine the statistical validity of technicians' theories and technical indicators, but the result of the studies gives no definite answer as to whether these are effective predictors of stock market prices. On the basis of these technical theories, many have endeavoured to forecast the future of the stock market. Some have been moderately successful but the records are full of people who have lost money trying to forecast the future of the stock market. It is believed that the averages are useful and interesting in showing the course of the market and for measuring changes but not for forecasting the future.

Cohen, Zinbarg, and Zeikel stated that:

> " *We can understand the characterization of technical analysis as 'crystal ball gazing'. But we consider this characterization to be rather unfortunate, for it casts aside the goods with bad. The more scholarly and sophisticated technical analyst uses his tools with a proper*

sense of proportion..... if a stock looks attractive to him on technical grounds he probes into its fundamentals ..... he is certainly not unmindful of earnings growth, of values, or of the impact of business cycles."

Thus the technical analysis is not by itself, the road to riches. It is a tool which should be used with fundamental analysis and, most important, with commonsense. Despite assertions of some technicians, technical analysis is still an art. Successful use requires talent, intution and experience. Add a little luck, and it can be the difference between modest and good profits.

Some technical theories are more plausible than profitable. They may work under some conditions but can cause substantial losses under others. In many cases, there is a little margin for safety. The signals are either right or wrong.

Some other disadvantages of technical analysis include the following :

1. All data used in technical analysis is past. Therefore, these indices cannot take into account unexpected events such as natural disasters and economic crisis. Charts can, however, show, activity by insiders well before privileged information becomes public knowledge.
2. With actively traded stocks, the prices may be the result of a battle of wits. For the most part, trading profits are realised at the expense of others who are trying to achieve gains on their own terms. In such cases, the technicians must be cleverer and luckier than his or her rivals.
3. False signals can occur. A chart may show a sudden, deep decline which by strict interpretation, is a signal to sell. But this may be the result of one large trade of a lower-than-market price. The value of the stock may bounce back quickly. If the technicians failed to wait for confirmation, commissions would have to be paid for the sale and probably, for repurchase.

THE FUTURE OF TECHNICAL ANALYSIS

Although there is much in finance that we do not completely understand, technical analysis has persisted for more than 100 years, and it is not likely to disappear from the investment scene anytime soon. Improved quantitative methods coupled with improved behavioural research will continue to generate ideas for analysts to test. The well-known financial behaviourist Warner De Bondt, for instance, recently reported substantial evidence that the public expects the continuation of past price trends. That is, they are bullish in bull markets and pessimistic in bear markets.

Perhaps within a decade or more, the fragmentation of technical analysis into such a wide-ranging array of increasingly comnplex, widely differing formulae will cause a gradual movement away from the entire quasi-science back to some form of more fundamental evaluation.

QUESTIONS

1. Explain the difference between a 'fundamental' approach to investment or trading decisions and the 'technical' approach.
2. "A technical analyst explains that the stock market acts like a barometer rather than a thermometer". Elaborate.
3. Explain in detail the Dow Theory and how it might be used to determine the direction of the stock market ?
4. Briefly describe the eseence of fundamental and technical analysis. Would you advise an investor to use technical analysis as the only basis for investment decisions ?

5. Explain the nature and methodology of trend analysis. What is the primary difference between 'bar charting' and 'point and figure' charting ?
6. Are future market prices predictable on the basis of past price behaviour ?
7. Critically examine the Elliot Wave Principle(EWP) on stock market prediction.
8. Discuss the various types of charts used by chartists to predict the prices and volumes for their analaysis of the stock market and individual stocks.
9. "Most of the technical indicators make sense when examined individually but when one examines many technical indicators simultaneously, the interpretation of their collective meaning is often contradictory and confusing." Comment.
10. The technical analyst places a great deal of importance on supply and demand in stock pricing. Presumably the fundamental analyst also believes that supply and demand are important. In what ways do the two groups disagree on the subject?
11. A support level is the price range at which a technical analyst would expect the:
    (a) supply of a stock to increase substantially.
    (b) supply of a stock to decrease substantially.
    (c) demand for a stock to increase substantially.
    (d) supply for a stock to decrease substantially.
12. List two factors that determine the magnitude of the increment on a point and figure chart.
13. "Chaos theory sees systematic behaviour amidst apparent renderness". Do you agree?
14. Discuss any two witchcraft variety indicators used by the technicians.
15. Discuss why most technicians follow several technical rules and attempt to derive a consensus.
16. Technical analysts believe that one can use past price changes to predict future price changes. How do they justify this belief?

PROBLEMS

1. A stock reached a high point two months ago, closing at ₹ 48. It sold for ₹ 34 two weeks ago, and today the stock sells for ₹ 37. According to the Fibonacci resistance level philosophy, at what price is the stock likely to encounter resistance to further advances?
2. Draw a ₹ 1 point and figure chart for the following series of stock prices: 15.25, 15.75, 15.50, 16, 16.25, 16.75,16.90, 14.50, 14.75, 15.25,15, 14,14.25, 14.60, 15.25,15.50.

REFERENCES

1. Cohen, A.W. *How to Use the Three-Point Reversal Method of Point and Figure Stock Market Trading*. Larchmont, N.Y.: Chartcraft, 1972.
2. Crounch, Robert L. "Market Volume and Price Changes," *Financial Analysts Journal*, July-Aug. 1970.
3. Dines, James. *How the Average Investor Can Use Technical Analysis for Stock Profits*. New York: Dines Chart Corporation, 1974.
4. Edwards, R.D., and J. Magee. *Technical Analysis of Stock Trends*. Springfield, Mass.: John Magee, 1958.
5. Evans, Richard L. "Technical Analysis, *A All Journal* (January 1994): 19-22.
6. Gordon, William. *The Stock Market Indicators*. Palisades Park, N.J.: Investors' Press, 1968.
7. Granville, Joseph E. *Granville's New Strategy of Daily Stock Market Timing for Maximum Profit*. Englewood Cliffs, N.J.: Prentice-Hall (Parker), 1976.

8. Hamilton, William P. *The Stock Market Barometer.* New York: Richard Russell Associates, 1960.

9. Hardy, C. Colburn. *Investor's Guide to Technical Analysis.* New York: McGraw-Hill, 1978.

10. Huang, Stanley S.C. *Techniques of Investment Analysis.* New York: Intext Educational Publishers, 1972, chapter 9.

11. ————. *A New Technical Approach to Stock Market Timing.* Larch-mont, N.Y.: Investors Intelligence, Inc., 1973.

12. Jiler, William L. *How Charts Can Help You in the Stock Market,* Trendline, Standard & Poor's Corp., 1962.

13. Kerrigan, Thomas J. "Behavior of the Short-Interest Ratio," *Financial Analysts Journal.* Nov.-Dec. 1974.

14. Leuthold, Steven C. "Upside Breakout?—Technicians are Enjoying A Bull Market of Their Own," *Barron's,* May 29, 1978.

15. Levy, Robert A. *The Relative Strength Concept of Common Stock Price Forecasting.* Investors Intelligence, 1968.

16. ————. "Conceptual Foundations of Technical Analysis," *Financial Analysts Journal,* July-Aug. 1966.

17. Murphy, John J. *Technical Analysis of the Futures Markets.* 2d ed. New York: McGraw Hill, 1985. Pring, Martin J. *Technical Analysis Explained.* 2d ed. New York: McGraw Hill, 1985.

18. Pinches, George E. "The Random Walk and Technical Analysis," *Financial Analysts Journal.* March-April 1970.

19. Pistolese, Clifford. Using *Technical Analysis.* Rev. ed. Chicago: Probus, 1994.

20. Rhea, Robert. *The Dow Theory.* Boulder, Colo.: Rhea, Greiner, 1959.

21. Rich, Steven P., and William Reichenstein. "Market Timing for the Individual Investor: Using the Predictability of Long-Horizon Stock Returns to Enhance Portfolio Performance." *Financial Services Review* (1993/1994): 29-43.

22. Russell, Richard. *The Dow Theory Today.* New York: Richard Russell Associates, 1961.

23. Schultz, John W. *The Intelligent Chartist.* New York: WRSM Financial Service Corp., 1962.

24. Selihman, Daniel. "Playing the Market with Charts," *Fortune,* Feb. 1962; "The Mystique of Point-and-Figure," *Fortune,* March 1962.

25. Shaw, Alan R. "Technical Analysis," *Financial Analysts' Handbook,* vol. 1. Homewood, III.: Dow Jones-Irwin, 1975.

26. ———— "Market Timing and Technical Analysis." In *Financial Analysts Handbook.* 2d ed., edited by Sumner N. Levine. Homewood III.: Dow Jones-Irwin, 1988.

27. Stein, Lawrence. *The Fundamental Stock Market Technician.* Chicago: Probus, 1986.

28. West, Stan, and T.J. Murphy. "Caveats for Market Technicians," *Financial Analysts Journal.* Sept.-Oct. 1978.

22

Efficient Market Theory

INTRODUCTION

Market efficiency implies that all known information is immediately discounted by all investors and reflected in share prices in the stock market. As such, no one has an information edge. In the ideal efficient market, every one knows all possible-to-know information simultaneously, interprets it similarly, and behaves rationally. But, human beings what they are, this of course rarely happens.

In such a world, the only price changes that would occur are those which result from new information. Since there is no reason to expect that information would be non-random in its appearance, the period-to-period price changes of a stock should be random movements, statistically independent of one another. The level of stock prices will, under these conditions, describe what statisticians call a 'random walk' and physicists call Brownian motion. In the normal course of events, the level of prices, i.e., the summation of these random movements, will show movements that look like cycle but in fact are not.

The explanation of the apparent randomness of stock prices lies in understanding the market-making mechanisms. In an efficient market, liquid capital will channel quickly and accurately where it will do the community the most good. Efficient markets will provide ready financing for worthwhile business ventures and drain capital away from corporations which are poorly managed or producing obsolete products. It is essential that a country have efficient capital markets if that country is to enjoy highest possible level of wealth, welfare and education for population. One of the main reasons that some undeveloped countries do not advance is that they have insufficient capital markets. In inefficient capital markets prices may be fixed or manipulated rather than determined by supply and demand. Capital may be controlled by a few wealthy people and not be fluid and flow where it is needed. Graft, corruption, and public distrust can cause money to be hoarded rather than invested in the capital market; or investors may be ignorant and unable to distinguish between worthwhile business ventures and bad investment.

In an efficient market, all the relevant information is reflected in the current stock price. Information cannot be used to obtain excess return: the information has already been taken into account and absorbed in the prices. In other words, all prices are correctly stated and there are no "bargains" in the stock market. James H. Lone explained what is meant by efficient security market in these words:

> "Efficiency in this context means the ability of the capital markets to function so that prices of securities react rapidly to new information. Such efficiency will produce prices that are 'appropriate in terms of current knowledge, and investors will be less likely to

make unwise investments. A corollary is that investors will also be less likely to discover great bargains _____and thereby earn extraordinary high rates of return."[1]

The requirements for a securities market to be efficient market are: (1) Prices must be efficient so that new inventions and better products will cause a firm's securities prices to rise and motivate investors to supply capital to the firm (i.e., buy its stock); (2) Information must be discussed freely and quickly across the nations so all investors can react to new information; (3) Transactions costs such as sales commissions on securities are ignored; (4) Taxes are assumed to have no noticeable effect on investment policy; (5) Every investor is allowed to borrow or lend at the same rate; and, finally, (6) Investors must be rational and able to recognise efficient assets and that they will want to invest money where it is needed most (i.e., in the assets with relatively high returns).

FORMS OF THE EFFICIENT MARKET HYPOTHESIS

Tests of the market efficiency are essentially tests of whether the three general types of information - past prices, other public information, and inside information - can be used to make above-average returns on investments. In an efficient market, it is impossible to make above-average return regardless of the information available, unless abnormal risk is taken. Moreover, no investor or group of investors can consistently outperform other investors in such a market. These tests of market efficiency have also been termed as weak-form (price-information), semistrong form (other public information), and strong-form (inside information) tests.

A. Weak-Form and the Random Walk

This is the oldest statement of the hypothesis. It holds that present stock market prices reflect all known information with respect to past stock prices, trends, and volumes. Thus, it is asserted, such past data cannot be used to predict future stock prices. Thus, if a sequence of closing prices or successive days for XYZ stock has been 43,44,45,46,47, it may seen that tomorrow's closing price is more likely to be 48 than 46, but this is not so. The price of 47 fully reflects whatever information is implied by or contained in the price sequence preceding it. In other words, the stock prices approximate a random walk. (That is why sometimes the terms Random Walk Hypothesis and Efficient Market Hypothesis are used interchangeably). As time passes, prices wander or walk more or less randomly across the charts. Since the walk is random, a knowledge of past price changes does nothing to inform the analyst about whether the price tomorrow, next week, or next year will be higher or lower than today's price.

The weak form of the EMH is summed up in the words of the pseudonymous "Adam Smith", author of *The Money Game* :"Prices have no memory, and yesterday has nothing to do with tomorrow". It is an important property of such a market, so that one might do as well flipping a coin as spending time analysing past price movements or patterns of past price levels.

Thus, if the random walk hypothesis is empirically confirmed, we may assert that the stock market is weak-form efficient. In this case any work done by chartists based on past price patterns is worthless.

Random walk theorists usually take as their starting point the model of a perfect securities market in which a relatively large number of investors, traders, and speculators conpete in an attempt to predict the course of future prices. Moreover, it is further assumed that current information relevant to decision- making process is readily available

---

1. James A. Lorie, "Public Policy for American Capital Markets", Department of the Treasury, 1974, p. 3.

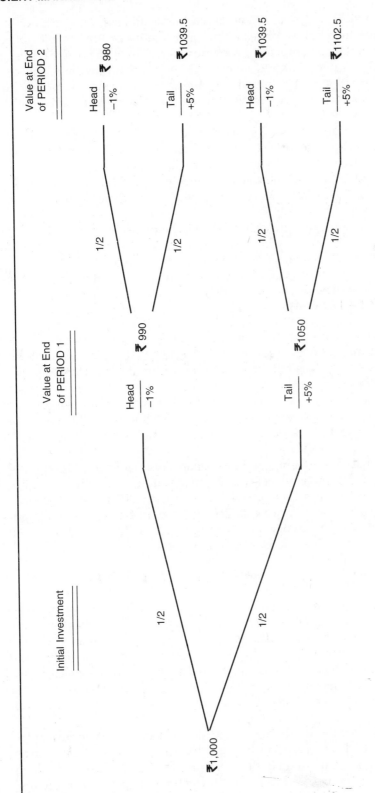

FIGURE 1: RANDOM WALK WITH DRIFT (TWO-PERIOD- CASE)

to all at little or no cost. If we "idealize" these conditions and assume that the market is perfectly competitive then equity prices at any given point of time would reflect the market's evaluation of all currently available information. In such ideal markets, prices would change solely as new, hitherto unavailable information becomes known. And unless the new information is distributed over time in a non-random fashion, and we have no reason to presume this, price movements in a perfect market will be statistically independent of one another.

If stock price changes behave like a series of results obtained by flipping a coin, does this mean that on average stock price changes have zero mean ? Not necessarily. Since stocks are risky, we actually expect to find a positive mean change in stock prices. To see this, suppose an investor invests ₹ 1,000 in a share. Flip a coin; if head comes up he loses 1%, and if tail shows up he makes 5 per cent. The value of investment will be as shown in Figure -1.

Suppose that an investor flips the coin (looks up the prices) once a week and it is his decision when to stop gambling (when to sell). If he gambles only once, his average return is: $1/2 \times ₹ 990 + 1/2 \times ₹ 1050 = ₹ 1020$ since the probabilities of "head" or "tail" are each equal to 1 /2. The investor may decide to gamble for another week. Then the expected terminal value of his investment will be:

$$1/2 \times 980.1 + 1/4 \times 1039.5 + 1/4 \times 1039.5 + 1/4 \times 1102.5 = ₹ 1040.4$$

Now assume that these means are equal to the value of the given shares at the end of the first week and at the end of the second week. The fact that the shares went up in the first period, to ₹ 1050 say, does not affect the probability of the price going up 5% or going down 1% in the second period, which remains 1/2 for each outcome. Thus, share price changes in each period are independent of the share price changes in the previous period. In each period, we would obtain the results which one could obtain by flipping a coin, and it is well known that the next outcome of flipping a coin is independent of the past series of "heads" and "tails".

Note, however, that on an average we earn 2 per cent if we invest for one week and 4.04 per cent if we invest for two weeks. Thus, the random walk hypothesis does not contradict the theory which asserts that risky assets must yield a positive mean return. We say in such a case that share price changes can be characterised by a random walk process with a "positive drift". In our specific example, the drift is equal to :

$$1/2 \times 5\% + 1/2 \times (-1\%) = 2\%$$

Which implies that on average the investment terminal value increases every period by 2%.

Thus, reflecting the historical development, the weak form implies that the knowledge of the past patterns of stock prices does not aid investors to attain improved performance. Random walk theorists view stock prices as moving randomly about a trend line which is based on anticipated earnings power. Hence they contend that (1) analysing past data does not permit the technician to forecast the movement of prices about the trend line and (2) new information affecting stock prices enters the market in random fashion, i.e. tomorrow's news cannot be predicted nor can future stock price movements be attributable to that news.

In its present context, the weak form of the efficient market hypothesis is a direct challenge to the chartist or technician. It was the earliest focus of interest and has received by far the greatest attention in the literature. The main statistical investigations to provide support for the weak form of the efficient market hypothesis are discussed hereinunder.

(i) Filter Rules

The use of charts is essentially a technique for. filtering out the important information from the unimportant. Alexander and Fama and Blume took the idea that price and volume data are supposed to tell the entire story we need to know to identify the important "action" in stock prices. They applied filter rules to see how well price changes pick up both trends and reverses - which chartists claim their charts do. The filters work something like this:

"If a stock moves up X per cent, buy it and hold it long; if it then reverses itself by the same percentage, sell it and take a short position in it. When the stock reverse itself again by X per cent cover the short position and buy the stock long".

The size of the filter varied from 0.5 to 50 per cent. The results showed that the larger filter did not work well. The smaller ones worked better, since they were more sensitive to market swings. However, when trading costs (commissions) are included in the analysis, no filter worked well. In fact, substantial losses would have been incurred using these filter rules.

In essence the result of using the filter technique turn out to be that stock prices do not have momentum from which one can make returns in excess of those warranted by the level of risk assumed. In fact, because of trading costs, we would have been substantially better off buying a random set of stocks and holding them during the same trading period.

(ii) Serial Correlations

Security price changes do not appear to have any momentum or inertia which causes changes of a given sign to be followed by changes of that same sign; the filter rules should have detected this pattern if it existed. However, security prices may follow some sort of a reversal pattern in which price changes of one sign tend to be followed by changes of the opposite sign. Filter fules might not detect a pattern of reversals. Serial correlation (or autocorrelation) measures the correlation co-efficient between a series of numbers with lagging numbers in the same time series. Trends or reversal tendencies in security price changes can be detected with serial correlation. We can measure the correlation between security price changes in period t (denoted P) and price changes in the same security which occur k periods later and are denoted $P_t + k$; k is the number of periods of lag.

Of course they are long-term upward trend in security prices; so if one "period" covers a number of years, a positive serial correlation should be observed. But long-term trends are of no interest, since they are already known to exist. In question here is the existence of patterns in short term (for example, daily, weekly, or monthly) price changes which can be used to earn a larger trading profit after commissions than what the naive buy and hold strategy would yield. If such patterns exist, this would tend to indicate that security prices do not adjust to follow their randomly changing intrinsic values.

(iii) Run Test

Filter rules and serial corelation may not pick up the sensitive price changes that technicians say they use for making decisions. That is, price changes may be random most of the time but occassionally become serially correlated for varying periods of time. To examine this possibility, run tests may be used to determine if there are "runs" in the price changes.

A run is a set of consecutive prices of the same sign. A rime series, such as prices of stocks, can be tested to see whether there are dependencies among the data merely by looking at the number of runs in the series.

If a price increase of any size is designated by "+" and decrease in price by "-" any pattern might be observed over time.

Hypothetical Shares	Number of Runs
A	+ + + + + - - - - - 2
B	+ - + - + - + - + - 10
C	- - + - + + + - - + 6

The pattern for Share A reflects continuing trends : if the price of the share has been increasing (decreasing) it will probably continue to move up (or down). Share B shows the opposite behaviour, a tendency of price reversal from the preceding period. Share A has very few runs but Share B has many. Share C represents an unpredictable sequence, evidenced by a number of runs equal to the number expected by chance in a totally random series. Since each observation is counted equally regardless of size, run analysis removes potential problems of non-normality in identifying independence. To illustrate, and have stronger economic implication assume the price of a stock is as follows : 60,60-1 /8,60-1 /4, 60-3/8, 60- 3/8, 60-3/8, 60-1/2, 60-3/8, 60-1/4, 60-1/8. To determine the number of runs for the entire series, we place a plus sign under each price that is higher than the previous one, a zero under a price that is the same as the previous one, and a minus sign under a price decline. In this case, we have a total of four runs, the first three pluses constituting a run, the next two zeros constituting a second run, the next plus another run, and three minus a fourth run. A test statistics is used to determine whether the resulting number of runs approximates those that might have been generated by random selection. It may be pointed however, that run analysis is not a powerful test and, similar to serial correlation, results have stronger statistical than economic implications. Table 1 shows the procedures for the test.

TABLE 1

The Runs Test

$$Z = \frac{R-x}{\sigma}$$

Where   R = number or runs

$$X \quad = \quad x = \frac{2n_1 n_2}{n_1 + n_2} + 1$$

$$\sigma^2 \quad = \quad \frac{2n_1 n_2 (2n_1 n_2 - n_1 - n_2)}{(n_1 + n_2)^2 (n_1 + n_2 - 1)}$$

n_1, n_2 = the number of observations in each category

Z = standard market variable. This comes from a normal distribution with a mean of zero and a standard deviation of one. Approximately 95% of distribution lies within two standard deviation of the mean. Z status lies with large absolute values do not often occur by chance.

X = mean number of runs given n_1 and n_2

In testing the weekly efficient markets hypothesis, alongwith the filter rules, serial correlations and runs tests, other tests have also been employed. However, their findings are the same. There are scientific studies which tell us one very important thing: there are no price dependencies.

Yesterday's prices do not tell us much about tomorrow's or at least not enough to.consistently make unusual returns based merely on price data.

This conclusion is what statisticians call a random walk. The walk is the time series of prices. Its random aspect is the nature by which the numbers are generated. Yesterday's prices by themselves apparently do not tell us any thing of value for forecasting tomorrow's prices.

B. Semi-Strong Form

The semisrrong form of the efficient market hypothesis centres on how rapidly and efficiently market prices adjust to new publically available information, including :

(1) Expectations regarding contents of future financial reports from individual corporations, for example, future changes in earnings, dividends, capital structure, sales, etc. Current prices, according to the theory, should reflect rational expectation regarding these future realisations.

(2) Incompatibilities between many competing published data series and revision of data series previously published, for example, by governmental departments and agencies, particularly corporate profits and related data series. Efficiency, implies, among other things, that the markets correctly expect and act now upon planned or possible future revisions of either published data or accounting method.

(3) Increasing politicisation of economic data, particularly price inflation rate or cost of living data and unemployment rates.

The shift from the weak, i.e. random walk form, to the semisrrong form of the efficient market hypothesis represents a quantum jump. In other words, semi-strong form suggests the fruitlessness of efforts to earn superior rates of return. This very stronger assertion of the semi-strong form represents a direct challenge to traditional financial analysis based on the evaluation of publicly available data.

Research effort on market efficiency has mainly turned to an examination of the effect of the release of public information on share prices. The studies of the semi-strong form of market efficiency have involved different methods that used to test weak form of efficiency. The tests have typically been based on the use of the capital assets pricing model or variation of it. The residuals of the market model, the empirical analogue of the capital asset pricing model, have been used to determine whether or not a piece of information has had a specific effect on share price independently of other general economic or marketwide effects.

Overall, the evidence to data support market efficiency with respect to publicly available information. This is not to say that there has not been or will not be a breakdown in this form of market efficiency. However, what it does suggest is that it is not common. Moreover, if there has been some degree of inefficiency, it is likely that by the stage there are sufficient data for a thorough examination, it has been recognised by share traders and its effect has been eliminated.

Similarly, any future development of inefficiency with respect to public information is not likely to last long once its presence is recognised. There are usually sufficient rewards to encourage investors to trade on the inefficiency and thus remove it from the market.

C. Strong Form

The strong form is concerned with whether or not certain individuals or groups of individuals possess inside information which can be used to make above average profits. If the strong form of the efficient capital market hypothesis holds, then any day is as good as any other day to buy any stock.

The rationale for the strong tests lies in a combination of the semi-strong tests (information assimilated in a rapid and unbiased fashion) and the fact that a great many supposedly knowledgeable and trained people are engaged in the securities business. It is argued that with so many people and so much information there should be few if any true "sleepers". Studies have indicated that corporation insiders and specialists on the floor of the exchanges (because their "book" contains unfilled orders) may have superior information and thus higher expected returns. Other investors, however, have not been shown to produce consistently higher returns. In particular, numerous studies have shown that the investor could do better by picking securities at random than with the institutional investor. It is extremely unlikely, in principle, that the efficient market hypothesis is strictly true, particularly in its strongest form. For example, as long as information is not wholly free, one might expect investors to require some offsetting gain before they are willing to purchase it. Nor does the empirical evidence justify unqualified acceptance of the efficient market- hypothesis even in its weakest form. The important question, therefore, is not whether the theory is universally true, but whether it is sufficiently correct to provide useful insights into market behaviour. There is now overwhelming evidence to suggest that the random walk hypothesis is such a close approximation to reality that technical analysis cannot provide any guidance to the investment manager. When one turns to the stronger forms of the hypothesis the evidence becomes less voluminous and the correspondence between theory and reality less exact Nevertheless, the overriding impression is that of a highly competitive and efficient market place in which the opportunities for superior performance are rare.

TESTING MARKET EFFICIENCY

There are several ways to test the EMH. Analysts have devised direct and indirect tests of market efficiency. Direct tests assess the success of specific investment strategies or trading rules. An example of a direct test would be a test of the accuracy of predictions by some specific technical indicator. Indirect tests are statistical tests of prices or returns. For example, if prices follow a random walk, the *serial correlation* of returns should be close to zero.

One can also test the efficient markets hypothesis by some scientific methodology or simply by looking for anecdotal evidence. A scientific experiment develops a research design based on a proven methodology. For example, we could scientifically examine market reactions to unexpected earnings announcements using a large sample over time. Results from the study would determine how rapidly the market responds to new public information. Anecdotal evidence involves looking for examples consistent, or inconsistent, with the EMH.

The conundrum, of course, is that all types of tests can be criticised. Critics can argue that the test was applied improperly, was inadequate to measure its target, or both. For example, direct tests of technical trading rules can always be criticised because testing these trading rules requires applying them mechanically. These tests cannot hope to capture the subjective portion of technical analysis that, technicians argue, helps investors exploit historical price patterns. Even if a test provides evidence consistent with the EMH, critics can always argue that the results were due to the test used, not necessarily the truth of the EMH.

Establishing a Benchmark

Tests of the EMH must usually establish some sort of a benchmark. For example, to say that some trading rule works, giving evidence inconsistent with the EMH, a test must find that a portfolio using the trading rule outperformed a similar portfolio that did not use the trading rule, generating abnormal profits. Like the type of test used, critics can always question whether the benchmark chosen was appropriate. The most common benchmark is the so-called buy-and-hold portfolio. As an example, a test may want to evaluate a trading rule that indicates when to switch between a stock index fund and a money market fund. How well does the trading rule perform? It would have to earn higher profits (or returns) than the profits from simply buying and holding the stock index fund over the same period of time. Of course, the test would have to account for differences in risk and transaction costs between the two investment strategies as well. Active trading strategies usually involve higher transaction costs, and they often expose a portfolio to more risk as well.

The Time Factor

The time period(s) selected can, of course, always be criticised. A trading rule partisan may respond to a conclusion that the rule did not work by saying, *"Of course my trading rule didn't work over that period; everyone knows that period was an aberration in the market. The rule works fine during normal markets."* There is no way to prove or disprove that assertion without testing it over every single possible time period, a rather daunting task.

Kiss and Tell

Suppose that someone discovered an investment strategy that really worked and made a lot of money. Why would this person want to tell anyone. He or she could try to make money writing a book or an investment newsletter describing the strategy, but it would probably generate more money if kept secret. Suppose an analyst discovers mat stocks beginning with the letter K rise on Wednesdays and fall on Fridays. Buying K stocks on Tuesdays and selling them on Thursdays makes the analyst lots of money. The dilemma, of course, is that once others know about the strategy, it will likely stop working. K stocks will probably start rising on Mondays and falling on Wednesdays as other investors try to anticipate the market. To avoid this, the analyst would probably keep the strategy a secret for as long as possible.

Seriously, some argue that the inclination to keep successful strategies secret introduces a bias into tests of market efficiency and trading rules. (It is called *sample selection bias.)* Only those strategies that do not work are widely reported and, consequently, tested. Strategies that do work are not reported, so the results are biased in favour of the EMH, showing that trading rules do not produce abnormal profits by testing inferior trading rules. If the successful trading rules are kept secret, perhaps we can never fairly test the true ability if investors or the validity of the EMH.

Qualitative versus Quantitative Efficiency

We know that some investors pay more to trade than others. We also know that some investors can obtain information more cheaply than others. Perhaps we should replace the quantitative question *"are the markets efficient!"* with the more qualitative question *"how efficient are the markets'!"* In other words, market efficiency may mean different things to different investors. Some of the traditional tests of the three forms of the EMH, most of which appear to support the concept of market efficiency, at least in its weak and semistrong forms,[2] are based on historical prices, market reactions to new public information, and the value of private, or inside, information.

Usefulness of Historical Prices

Tests of trading based on historical prices essentially evaluate the weak-form theory of market efficiency: that security prices fully reflect all historical information. These tests fall into two general categories: tests of the random nature of security prices and returns, and tests of specific trading rules.

Tests of the randomness of securities prices over time have relied primarily on two statistical techniques: serial correlation, and a so-called runs test. Serial correlation measures the strength of the relationship between the current value of a time series (e.g., stock returns) and past share values. If stock prices follow something like the random walk, serial correlation coefficients should be close to zero. A runs test counts the number of times that price changes, each one designated positive or negative, change sign over a specific time period. For example, say ten days of price changes produce this series: +, +, +, —, —, —, +, —, +, +. This sequence has five runs (the first three positive changes, the next three negative changes, a positive change, a negative change, and the final two positive changes). Now consider the following sequence of ten price changes: +, +, +, +, +, +, —, —, —, —. This sequence has just two runs (the first six positive changes and the final four negative changes). Too many, or too few, runs suggests that a series is not random.

The result of these statistical tests from many studies have strongly suggested that stock prices and returns are essentially random, thus providing evidence in support of weak-form market efficiency.

In addition to tests of the randomness of security prices and returns, several studies have examined trading rules based on historical prices to see if they produce abnormal profits. Weak-form efficiency, of course, states that such trading rules cannot produce abnormal profits. Again, the extensive evidence generally supports weak-form efficiency. Let's look at one example of a trading rule, filter rules.

Filter rules are closely analogous to the support and resistance levels that we discussed in conjunction with the Dow Theory and technicians' charts. Essentially, a filter rule states that if a stock rises X per cent from its most recent low (its support level), buy it because it has defined an up trend. Similarly, if a stock declines by Y per cent from its most recent high (its resistance level), then sell the stock and hold cash (or sell the stock short if you do not own it) because the stock has defined a down trend.

How well do filter rules perform? Not very well, suggests some of the scientific evidence. One study compared buy-sell filters between 0.5 per cent and 5 per cent on each of the Dow Jones Industrial Average's 30 stocks against a simple buy-and-hold portfolio of those stocks. Only the smallest filter, 0.5 per cent, outperformed the buy-and-hold portfolio, on average. The difference in performance, however, disappeared because of higher transaction costs associated with the actively managed portfolio.

2. These studies are listed in a variety of sources. See, for example, Thomas Copeland and J. Fred Weston, *Financial Theory and Corporate Policy* (Reading, MA: Addison-Wesley, 1992); Edwin Elton and Martin Gruber, *Modern Portfolio Theory and Investment Analysis,* 4th edition (New York: Wiley, and Sons, 1992); and Burton Malkiel, *A Random Walk Down Wall Street* (New York: W.W. Norton, 1995).

Portfolios based on the larger filters all underperformed the buy-and-hold portfolio, even before accounting for higher transaction costs.

Although much of the scientific evidence suggests the markets are weak-form efficient, and thus technical analysis cannot work, there is a growing amount of evidence emerging that may suggest otherwise. In the last chapter, we found that breaking through support and resistance levels produced good sell and buy signals, respectively. It is easy to conclude that a series is random even when important patterns exist. The investor has to know where to look and what to look for.

Market Reaction to New Public Information

A huge amount of widely varying new public information enters the financial markets each day. Companies regularly make significant announcements with both negative and positive implications, and their stock react very quickly to the new information. In many cases, much of the reaction takes place before the announcement is made. Semistrorig-form market efficiency states that security prices reflect all this information and react quickly to it. The reaction is so fast, in fact, that no one can consistently earn abnormal profits simply by buying or selling in response to new public information. Several studies have examined market reactions to almost every conceivable type of new public information. Results of these studies generally support semistrong-form market efficiency.

To find stronger evidence in support of semistrong-form market efficiency, we need to turn to the various scientific studies. These studies, often called *event studies*, typically examine market reactions to specific kinds of announcements. They analyse a large group of similar announcements using a statistical methodology that measures returns different from what would be expected, given no new information (called *abnormal returns* or *residuals*). Semistrong-form market efficiency implies that no abnormal returns should consistently occur after the announcement date.

To illustrate this approach, and the evidence presented by the vast majority of these studies, let's look at a classic study that examined market reactions to merger/takeover announcements.[3] The shareholders of public companies that are taken over (often referred to as *target shareholders*) receive premium prices for their shares (prices higher than the existing market price). As a result, we would logically expect stock prices to jump in response to a takeover announcement. If the market is semistrong-form efficient, then this jump should occur before, and/or on, the announcement date, not afterward. No one can earn an abnormal profit by acting on this new public information after it enters the market. This study's results are, therefore, consistent with semistrong-form market efficiency.

One has to be careful not to over-interpret the results of this and other event studies. Assume that company A offers to buy company B for Rs. 50 cash per share. The price of company B's stock will jump on the announcement. If it does not jump to Rs. 50 per share, does that mean that the market is not semistrong-form efficient? Not necessarily; think of all the things that can happen once a takeover offer becomes public. For one, company A's bid may fail. Even if A does buy B, who knows, when the announcement is first made, just how long it will take to complete the deal. For another alternative, company A may be forced to raise its offer price. The point is that takeovers, and many

3. Arthur Keown and John Pinkerton, "Merger Announcements and Insider Trading Activity," *Journal of Finance*, September 1981, pp. 855-870.

other transactions, are complex and uncertain. As this uncertainty is resolved after the announcement, significant price reactions are likely to occur. The resolution of uncertainty can be thought of as new public information.

Value of Private Information

Tests of the value of inside, or private, information seek to evaluate strong-form market efficiency. These tests are perhaps the most difficult to conduct because there is no way to pinpoint exactly when new private information, or inside information, enters the market. Further, the definition of *inside information* is ambiguous. Not surprisingly, the results from these studies are quite mixed.

One group of studies began with the assumption that mutual fund managers and securities analysts may have access to information before the general investing public-Securities analysts, for example, constantly talk to the companies they follow and may be able to learn some new information before it is made public. These studies then examined the performance of mutual funds or securities analysts' recommendations, compared with some benchmark.

Results from these studies generally show that neither mutual fund managers nor securities analysts appear, on average, to be capable of consistently outperforming the overall market, after adjusting for risk. Does this evidence support strong-form market efficiency, or does it cast doubt on the assumption that mutual fund managers have access to private information? Obviously, there is no way to answer this question.

IMPLICATIONS

There is still a great deal of controversy over the efficient market theory. On the one hand, statisticians continue to provide evidence in favour of the theory and, on the other hand, economists and financial analysts continue to state that they do not believe in the correctness of the theory. This problem highlights the lack of contact between many of the academic workers and real financial analysts or market operators. One gets an impression of mistrust, partly due to the barrier formed by the different technical languages used by both sides. It is to be hoped that this gap will decrease as each side recognises the advantages of closer co-operation. Anyhow, from the examination of the evidence relating to stock market efficiency, following implications in three different areas for share market investment strategies can be observed:

1. Value of the Analyst

The most general implication of the efficient market hypothesis is that most security analysis is logically incomplete and valueless. For true believers in efficient markets, an analyst's recommendations to buy or sell must be predicted on a significant difference between the analyst's views and those of other investors whose opinions have established the stock's current market price.

2. Economics of Scale in Security and Portfolio Management

The question of efficient allocation of human resources is also stepped up by increasing competition. Analysis of securities costs about same whether the amount available for investment is Rs. 1,000 or Rs. 10 crores. Thus if each endeavour could produce superior returns of, say, 0.5 per cent, they state this would produce additional returns of Rs. 5 on the investment of Rs. 1,000 and of Rs. 5 crores on the investment of Rs. 1,000 crores. On this basis they conclude that security research might make sense for large financial institutions having crores of rupees to manage while it would not make sense for investors with smaller sums.

3. Consistently Superior Performance

Another implication of the efficient markets theory is the extreme unlikelihood that one can consistently earn superior rate of return by analysing public information in conventional ways. The only hope for superiority in results lies in seeking unique ways of forming expectations about the prospects for individual companies.

CHALLENGE TO SECURITY ANALYSTS

Efficient market hypothesis challenges the conventional security analysts in two ways:

1. Challenge to the Chartist

If the random walk model is a valid description of reality, the work of the chartist is of no real value in stock market analysis. The only way the chartist can counter this argument is to show that he can consistently use his techniques to make better than chance prediction of stock prices. It is not enough for him to talk mystically about patterns that he sees in the data. He must show that he can consistently use these patterns to make meaningful predictions of future price.

2. Challenge to the Fundamental Analyst

Again if the random walks theory is valid and if security exchanges are 'efficient' markets, then stock prices in any point in time will represent good estimates of intrinsic or fundamental values. On this basis, it can be concluded that additional fundamental analysis is of value only when the analyst has information or new insights not already embedded in a stock's current market price. Thus, if the analyst has neither better insights nor better information, he may as well forget about fundamental analysis and choose securities by some random selection procedure.

MARKET EFFICIENCY AND ANOMALIES

In recent years, several so-called *anomalies* have been identified. Anomalies are situations that appear to violate the traditional view of market efficiency, suggesting that it may be possible for careful investors to earn abnormal returns.

The better-known anomalies are listed in Exhibit-1. Most of these anomalies appear to revolve around four themes:
- Markets tend to overreact to news, both good and bad.
- Value investing is contrarian in nature and is beneficial because markets overreact.
- The market consistently ignores certain stocks, especially small stocks.
- All things being equal, there are times when it is more advantageous to buy stocks whereas there are other times when it is better to avoid stocks.

Let's examine what anomalies mean for investors and the concept of market efficiency.

EXHIBIT-1

Some Stock Market Anomalies

Low Price-Earnings Ratio	Stock that are selling at price earnings ratios that are low relative to the market
Low Price-Sales Ratio	Stocks that have price-to-sales ratios that are lower compared with other stocks in the same industry or with the overall market
Low Price-to-Book Value Ratio	Stocks whose stock prices are less than their respective book values

High Dividend Yield	Stocks that pay high dividends relative to their respective share prices
Small Companies	Stocks of companies whose market capitalisation is less than $100 million
Neglected Stocks	Stocks followed by only a few analysts and/or stocks with low percentages of institutional ownership
Stocks with High Relative Strength	Stocks whose prices have risen faster relative to the overall market
January Effect	Stocks do better during January' than during any other month of the year
Day of the Week	Stocks do poorer during Monday than during other days of the week

Source: "Picking Stocks: Techniques That Stand the Test of time," American Association of Individual Investors, 1994.

Financial Market Overreaction

One of the most intriguing issues to emerge in the past few years is the notion of market overreaction to new information (both positive and negative). Many practitioners have insisted for years that markets to overreact. Recent statistical evidence for both the market as a whole and individual securities has shown errors in security prices that are systematic and therefore predictable. Overreactions are sometimes called reversals. Stocks that perform poorly in one period suddenly reverse direction and start performing well in a subsequent period, and vice versa.

Several studies have found that stock returns over longer time horizons (in excess of one year) display significant *negative* serial correlation. This means that high returns in one time period tend to be followed by low returns in the next period, and vice versa.

Other studies have tested for market overreaction by forming portfolios of winners and losers based on performance over a specific time period and then measuring these portfolios' performance records over subsequent periods of time. One study, for example, found that over the next year a portfolio of "losers" earned about 15 per cent more on average than did a portfolio of "winners."[4]

Market overreaction may offer the best explanation for several of the anomalies listed in Exhibit-1. For example, low price-to-earnings ratio (P /E) stocks may be analogous to the losers we described above, or they may be stocks that are out of favour with investors. However, high P/E stocks may be the current investor favourites, or winners.

As the market demonstrates almost daily, today's favourite stocks can fall from grace and reverse direction very quickly.

Profiting from Reversals: Contrarian and Value Investing

Market overreactions or reversals suggest several possible investment strategies to produce abnormal profits. Some possibilities include buying last year's worst performing stocks, avoiding stocks with high P/E ratios, or buying on bad news. At the risk of oversimplifying, any investment strategy based on market overreaction represents a *contrarian* approach to investing, buying what appears to be out of favour with most investors. But does value investing work? Can you do better following the value-oriented anomalies listed in Exhibit-1?

---

4. See, Werner DeBondt and Richard Thaler, "Does the Stock Market Overreact?" *journal of Finance* July 1985, p. 800.

There are many studies, done by both academics and practitioners, that suggest that buying stocks with low price-to-sales ratios, low price-to-book ratios, or low P/E ratios produced returns that were higher, on average, than those from the overall market, even after adjusting for higher transactions costs. These findings support the notion that contrarian/value investing may indeed work.

Although value investing appears to work, it requires several caveats. First, stocks with low P/E ratios are not necessarily cheap, nor are stocks with high P/E ratios necessarily expensive. The inverse relationship between value and P/E (or market-to-book value) ratios is far from perfect. Some stocks may have low (or high) P/E ratios for very good reasons. Further, value is definitely in the eye of the beholder; one person's bargain is another person's overvalued pariah.

For another ceveat, remember that very good economic reasons may drive some reversals. Reversing prices may be responding to new information and correcting an overreaction. Also, a poor performer may continue to perform poorly as the company continues to slide downhill. The fact that a company had a lousy year this year does not mean it will automatically have a good one next year. Further, the timing of a reversal can be very difficult to predict. Investors have shunned some individual stocks and groups of stocks for long periods of time, whereas other stocks have reversed direction quickly.

Finally, think about what would happen if every investor suddenly became a contrarian. If contrarian investing really does offer abnormal profit opportunities, we would expect the wise investors to exploit opportunities aggressively. Soon competition would eliminate these opportunities. Remember, apparent past success of value investing is no guarantee that it will work in the future.

Calendar-Based Anomalies

Are there better times to own stocks than others? Should you avoid stocks on certain days? The evidence seems to suggest that several calendar-based anomalies exist. The two best known, and widely documented, are the weekend effect and the January effect.

Weekend Effect

Studies of daily returns began with the goal of testing whether the markets operate on calendar time or trading time. In other words, are returns for Mondays (i.e., returns over Friday-to-Monday periods) different from the other day of the week returns? The answer to the question turned out to be *yes*, the trend was called the weekend effect. Monday returns were substantially lower than other daily returns.

One study found that Mondays produced a mean return of almost —35 per cent. By contrast, the mean annualised returns on Wednesdays was more than +25 per cent.[5]

The January Effect

Stock returns appear to exhibit seasonal return patterns as well. In other words, returns are systematically higher in some months than in others. Initial studies found that returns were higher in January for all stocks (thus this anomaly was dubbed the January effect) whereas later studies found the January effect was more pronounced for small stocks than for large ones.[6]

One widely accepted explanation for the January effect is tax-loss selling by investors at the end of December. Because this selling pressure depresses prices at the end of the

---

5. See, for example, Kenneth French, "Stock Returns and the Weekend Effects," *Journal of Financial Economics*, March 1980, pp. 30-65.

year, it would be reasonable to expect a bounce-back in prices during January. Small stocks, the argument goes, are more susceptible to the January effect because their prices are more volatile, and institutional investors (many of whom are tax-exempt) are less likely to invest in shares of small companies.

Calendar-Based Trading Strategies

Both seasonal and day-of-the-week effects are inconsistent with market efficiency because both suggest that historical information can generate abnormal profits. As will all anomalies, however, a more important issue is whether seasonal and/or day-of-the-week effects can create profit opportunities for investors. Should you, for example, always buy stocks at the close of trading on Mondays and sell them at the close of trading on Wednesdays?

Although differences in daily returns appear impressive, they are probably much too small to offset transaction costs. The January effect appears to have far more profit potential. However, once profitable investment strategies are recognised, it is reasonable to expect other investors to aggressively exploit them, eventually eliminating the profit potential. This may be happening to the January effect. Entire books have been published about this widely recognised anomaly, and it may be disappearing.

Small-Firm Effect

Generally the stocks of small companies substantially outperform stocks of large companies. Of course, history has also shown that small stocks have exhibited more year-to-year variation than large stocks. However, even after correcting for differences in risk, some studies suggest that investors can earn abnormal profits by investing in shares of small companies, exploiting the small-firm effect.

Two explanations for the small-firm effect seem plausible to us. The first is that analysts have applied the wrong risk measures to evaluate returns from small stocks. Small stocks may well be riskier than these traditional risk measures indicate. If proper risk measures were used, the argument goes, the small-firm effect might disappear, Small-firm stocks may not generate larger risk-adjusted returns than large stocks. Although the risk of small stocks may not be adequately captured by standard risk measures, it is hard to believe that better measures of risk would eliminate the entire small-firm effect.

Another explanation for the small-firm effect is that large institutional investors often overlook small-firm stocks. Consequently, less information is available on small companies. (They are also followed by fewer analysts.) One could argue that this information deficiency makes small-firm stocks riskier investments, but one could also argue that discovery of a neglected small-firm stock by the institutions could send its price rising as the institutions start buying it. The small-firm effect may arise from the continuous process of discovery of neglected small-firm stocks leading to purchases by institutional investors.

Whatever the explanation, small-firm stocks, although riskier than large-firm stocks, have historically provided substantial returns to investors, far higher than those produced by large-firm stocks. Of course, we can only speculate about whether this relationship will continue in the future.

Performance of Investment Professionals

Investments professionals such as mutual fund managers seem to have a difficult

6. For specific references to studies on the January effect, see Elton and Gruber, *Modern Portfolio Theory*; and Copeland and Weston, *Financial Theory*.

time beating the overall market. In a particular year, some professionals will beat the market, whereas others will not. The key question is whether some professionals can *consistently* outperform the market. Some evidence suggests that the answer to this question may be *yes.*

SO, ARE THE MARKETS EFFICIENT?

Today, it is fashionable to discuss the pending demise of the old EMH. Well, we are not quite yet ready to bury it, but a considerable amount of evidence does contradict it, and more evidence seems to emerge daily. However, a considerable amount of evidence also supports the concept of market efficiency. And even if the markets are not efficient in an academic sense, they may be efficient in a more practical sense. In most parts of the world, the financial markets are well-functioning, competitive institutions in which consistent abnormal profits based on public or historical information are rare.

There is an often-repeated joke about a trader and a finance professor walking down the street. The trader notices a Rs. 500 note lying on the street and stops to pick it up. "Why bother?" the finance professor says," "If it had really been a Rs. 500 note, someone would already have grabbed it."

In one sense, this joke sums up the debate over market efficiency. An unquestioning acceptance of the EMH, and subsequent rejection of all investment analysis and research as worthless, can leave a lot of money lying on the street for someone else. Real-world situations defy a strict view of market efficiency often enough to justify the careful search for undervalued (and overvalued) securities. However, one should always be very skeptical of someone who claims to have a clever system or special insight to consistently beat the market. There are not too many Rs. 500 note lying on the sidewalk, waiting to be picked up. Making money consistently in the stock market is darned hard, but it is possible.

Why should one care if the market is efficient? This is a crucial issue for a security analyst. He may well be hired to find mispriced securities to produce an additional increment of return on the portfolios. If the market is truly efficient, in making it that way, professional investors have performed a valuable service for society.

The investment decisions of the managers of business firms are based to a large extent on signals they get from the capital market. If the market is efficient, the cost of obtaining capital will accurately reflect the prospects for each firm. This means the firms with the most attractive investment opportunities will be able to obtain capital at a fair price which reflects their true potential. The "right" investments will be made, and society will be better off. To the extent that professional security analysts played a role in making it this way, they have served society well, and the total benefit of their services may be very large.

The *marginal* benefit of any one analyst is another matter, however. If the market is efficient, any one financial institution can fire at all their analysts without affecting its expected investment performance. Rather than doing analysis, they can select their investments at random, knowing each security selected has been priced correctly by the remaining analysis. In an efficient market, the *total* product of professional investors may be positive, but the *marginal* product of any one analyst is close to zero. Unfortunately, the amount any one firm is willing to pay an analyst is based on the marginal product. Thus, unless investment analyst can convince people the market is inefficient, he will make very little money as a security analyst. If the market is truly efficient then success will be a matter of chance. The expected probability of "beating" the market in any 1 year will be 50 per cent, and there is nothing a security analyst, personally, can do to improve these olds.

Of what significance is market efficiency to a corporate financial manager? Companies frequently repurchase their own stock because they feel it has been undervalued by the market. If the market is strong form efficient, this rationale is untenable. The stock is never undervalued by the market. If financial manager disagree with the valuation, it may be because his estimate of the company's prospects are overly optimistic. Perhaps he has neglected to consider carefully the implications of some macroeconomic variable, such as the future course of interest rates, on the future prospects and valuation of his firm.

Frequently, investment projects are postponed or financing is done with debt rather than with equity because management feels the entire stock market is depressed. If by the term *depressed* they mean stock prices have fallen below their intrinsic value based on available public information, this rationale is also inappropriate if the market is semistrong form efficient. In a semistrong form efficient market stocks are never "depressed" in the sense their values are less than the present value of the best estimate, based on publicly available information, of the future stream of dividends. In an efficient market, the cost of equity capital to the firm is both fair and reasonable in bear as well as bull markets. Future prospects may not appear as good in bear markets, but in an efficient market the prospects upon which stock prices are set are based on rational analysis of all publicly available information.

In an efficient market, one can also question the rationale for including complexities, such as call provisions in bond indentures. A call provision gives the firm a call option to buy the bonds back from the bondholders at a specific price. This call option held by the stockholders has an implicit market value. The market value of a callable bond will be less than the market value of a comparable noncallable bond by the market value of this call option. If the only rationale for including the call provision is to provide the firm with the opportunity to reissue the bond at a lower interest cost should interest rates fall, this rationale should be questioned if the market is taken to be efficient. In an efficient market, the callable bond will be priced as the difference between the market value of an identical noncallable issue and the market value of the call option held by the stockholders. Both market values will be based on the best available forecast of the future course of interest rates. Given the firm's forecast can't be better than the best forecast available, the firm is no better off by including the call provision in the bond indenture than it would be by selling the bond as a noncallable issue. One can look at it this way: If the call option is priced correctly by the market, the firm should be indifferent toward buying it (including it in the bond indenture) or not buying it.

One can frequently see advertisements by firms announcing that the firm has achieved a remarkable growth record in earnings and dividends. These advertisements frequently appear in financial publications. If these advertisements were placed to cast a favourable light on the firm's equity so as to support its market price, the money to purchase the ad was unwisely spent, given that the market *is* semistrong form efficient. The information contained in the ad has already been publicly disclosed, fully analysed by the army of professional analysts, and is also reflected in the stock price. If the market is efficient, the ad will have absolutely no impact on the market value of the equity.

Managers sometimes express concern over the effect that a change in accounting procedure will have on reported earnings per share. If the market is semistrong form efficient, they should not be concerned. Informed, rational analysts will adjust for different accounting procedures used by different firms and assess prospects on the basis of standardised numbers. The adjustment in accounting technique will have no effect on the opinions of those analysts or on the price of the firm's equity.

If the market is efficient, it should exhibit the following characteristics:

1. Security prices should respond quickly and accurately to the receipt of new information that is relevant to valuation. Every day a rich flow of bits and pieces of information pours into the market. The information pertains to general economic conditions, weather, strikes, shortages of raw materials, international tension, and product demand. This information is relevant to security valuation, and it affects the prices of securities. If the market is efficient, security prices should respond to the information as soon as it is received. Naturally, the response can't be instantaneous, but the gap between the receipt of the information and the reaction of the price should reflect the best available procedures and techniques for receiving and processing the information. The reaction of market prices should also be unbiased. The initial reaction should accurately reflect the true implications of the information on the value of the security. There should be no need for a subsequent correction, for example, of an overreaction to a piece of information.

2. The changes in expected security returns from one period to the next should be related only to changes in the level of the risk-free rate and changes in the level of the risk premium associated with the security.[7] Returns associated with factors other than these should be unpredictable.

3. It should be impossible, by examining the characteristics of current investments, to discriminate between profitable and unprofitable investments in the future (profitable in the sense that the returns are greater than you would normally expect to see, given the risk).

4. If we separate investors who are knowledgeable from those who are not, we should discover we are unable to find a significant difference between the average investment performance of the two groups. Moreover, it should be the case that differences in the performance of individual investors within each group should be insignificant. In other words, differences in performance between groups and within groups should be due to chance, and not something systematic and permanent like differences in ability to find information not already reflected in stock prices.

Systematic Patterns in Stock Prices Related Only to Time-Varying Interest Rates and Risk Premia

In an efficient market the expected returns to stocks may change over time. However, changes in expected returns must result from changes in (a) the risk-free rate of interest or (b) the magnitude of the risk premium in the stocks expected return. Changes in the risk premium may result from changes in the risk of the stock or from changes in the level of risk aversion reflected in investor behaviour.

Interest rates, risk, and risk aversion can all be expected to change with the business

---

7. In most multiperiod equilibrium models, you would expect to find some serial correlation in equilibrium prices and expected rates of return. Within the context of these models, it is technically correct to say that market efficiency is consistent with the case where future *deviations* from equilibrium rates of return can't be predicted on the basis of past *deviations* from equilibrium rates of return. Moreover, in a more general context, an increase in the value of a levered firm body will reduce its debt-to-equity ratio. This may result in a lower required and expected rate of return tomorrow. Thus we may have a slight tendency for negative correlation in stock returns even in an efficient market.

cycle. As the level of economic activity declines, we would expect a decline in the real rate of interest and the expected rate of inflation. Both these factors should produce a decline in the nominal risk-free. At the same time, investors may revise upward their perception of the risk associated with the stock, as the company may begin to experience recession-related trouble in its lime of business. Lower levels of economic activity may also mean lower wealth levels for investors, making them less willing to take on risk they expose themselves to. All these factors may cause the expected returns to stocks to fluctuate with the business cycle. To the extent that changes in the level of economic activity are not purely random, the business cycle may induce nonrandom patterns in stock prices through its effect on the rates that investors use to discount future expected dividends to present values.

However, abstracting from the influence of time-varying interest rates and risk premia on stock prices, the changes in stock prices related to other factors, like changes in expectations about future earnings and dividends, should be random in an efficient market.

Why should security price changes unrelated to changes in equilibrium expected return be random in an efficient market? If the market is efficient, today's stock price should already reflect all the information about future earnings and dividends that is both relevant to the valuation of the stock and "knowable." By knowable we mean all information that has been announced and can be predicted based on past announcements. The only information not reflected in the stock price is that which hasn't been received and can't be predicted. This kind of information, by its very nature, must come into the market in an unpredictable, random fashion. As the market price responds instantly and accurately to its receipt, the price, itself changes in a random, unpredictable fashion over time.

Failure of Simulated Trading Strategies

If the market is efficient, there should be no way to discriminate between profitable and unprofitable investments based on information that is currently available. A *profitable* investment is one that is expected to produce a rate of return that is higher than it should be, given an appropriate benchmark.

One way to test for market efficiency is to test whether a specific trading rule, or investment strategy, would have produced profitable rates of return in the past. Suppose, for example, an investor thinks the market is slow to react to the announcement of new information, such as the release of the firm's earnings reports. In this case, the investment strategy might be to always invest in the top 10 companies that have reported the highest increases in earnings per share for the year. To test the hypothesis, one may go back to a past period of time and try to simulate the results of investing on the basis of this trading rule. The question is: "Would this strategy have produced profitable returns in the past?" If the market is truly efficient, all strategies should fail in this regard.

The first problem in testing any strategy is defining the profitable rate of return. By profitable one must mean that the expected, or realised, rate of return is greater than what the investment should have, given some benchmark. If one choses the capital asset pricing model as a benchmark, the expected rate of return should be the rate given by the beta factor of the investment and the security market line. If the choice is arbitrage pricing theory as a benchmark, the expected rate of return should be equal to the risk-free rate plus the sum of the products of the factor betas of the investment and the factor prices. The test of the performance of the trading rule, in this sense, can be viewed as a joint test of two hypotheses:

1. One has chosen the correct benchmark to measure profitability.

2. The market is efficient relative to the information employed by the trading rule.

In constructing simulation experiment, one has to be careful about a number of other potential pitfalls. First, one must be sure of formulating investment strategy on the basis of information which is actually available at the time of buy or sell the securities. If the strategy is to invest in the stocks that have the greatest increases in earnings per share for the previous year, in simulating the results of executing this strategy in the past, one must be sure of having the earnings number for the year at the time one assume to buy the stock.

In testing the profitability of investment strategy, it's also important to consider the costs involved in finding and processing the required information as well as the differential costs involved in transacting in the market. In a passive investment strategy, one would invest at the very beginning of the period and hold on to the instruments until the very end. The extra commissions and extra taxes may serve to neutralise completely the performance of trading rule. In addition, the investor is to determine whether any extra return produced by his strategy is due to chance or due to his having successfully exploited some systematic inefficiency in pricing by the market. To do this, the investor must determine whether the magnitude of the extra return is significant in a statistical sense.

The issue of whether the extra return is merely compensation for bearing extra risk must also be addressed. This gets back to the question of selecting the appropriate benchmark. Even if the investor has employed information that was actually available at the time he made his investments, even if he has factored in the additional costs associated with transacting and taxes, and even if he still find a statistically significant increment of extra return associated with his trading rule, he must be prepared to defend what he means by *extra*.

Mediocrity in The Performance of Informed Investors

If security prices don't reflect all available information, those investors who are fully informed should be able to construct portfolios that produce superior returns. If the true market pricing structure is that of the capital asset pricing model (CAPM) and if security prices reflect publicly available information alone, traders who possess private information should see investments positioned relative to the security market line. Infact, they should be able to construct portfolios that are also positioned above the security market line. If we use the CAPM-based risk-adjusted performance measures to assess their performance, we should find their performance is superior relative to that of other investors.

If, on the other hand, the market is efficient, no investment is truly positioned above or below the security market line. An investment in such a position, implies that estimates of expected return and risk on the basis of less than the complete set of available information. One may construct a portfolio composed of securities that he *thinks* are above the security market line, but since their true expected returns are all positioned on the line, his risk-adjusted investment performance will be indistinguishable from that of any other investor. It should also be true that within the group of professional investors, there should be no significant differences in their performance. Even if some are more intelligent, or have more resources, than others, if security prices reflect all relevant information, intelligence and capital will be ineffective in searching for undervalued securities.

Thus, we can assess the efficiency of the market by first separating those investors who are likely to be most informed and then measuring their investment performance. If these investors exhibit records of superior performance, they must be investing on the basis of information that is both relevant and not reflected in security prices.

Professional investors are likely to be most informed. They are trained in security and portfolio analysis, and they spend their working days searching for, and analysing, information. Thus, in attempting to resolve the question of market efficiency, we should determine whether professionals as a group are distinguished in terms of their performance and whether we can find significant differences in the performance of individual professional investors.

Thus, we find the findings of the various studies vary widely as to the efficient market theory. Some studies accept the efficient market in toto; others reject it on all counts. This is due to the basic differences with respect to the following listed assumptions:

1. Perfect Markets

The efficient market theory holds that at any time stocks sell at the best estimates of their intrinsic values. The problem is that the time of reasoning is unconfortably close to that used by proponents of the greater-fool theory. Moreover, there has been ample evidence that stocks sometimes are not priced on estimates of actual value but are often swept up in waves of frenzy.

2. Speed of News Dissemination

News does not travel instantaneously, as the efficient market theory suggests. Moreover, the theory implies that no one possesses monopolistic power over the market and the stock recommendations based on unfounded beliefs do not lead to large buying. But in practice, neither of these assumptions accords with reality in today's markets. Brokerage firms specialising in research services institutions wield enormous power in the market and can direct tremendous money flows in and out of stocks. Many speculators may buy and sell a stock simply because they believe that an Influential brokerage house may recommend buying or selling it. Consequently, it is entirely possible that erroneous beliefs about a stock by some professionals can, for a considerable time, be self-fulfilling.

3. Evaluation of Information

Major determinants of a stock's value concern the extent and duration of its growth path far into the future. To convert information of a stock into specific estimates of true value requires expertise in security analysis. In such an environment there is considerable scope for a financial manager to exercise his superior intellect and judgement to turn in superior professional investment performance. However, the number of such competent financial managers is very rare.

QUESTIONS

1. Define the Efficient Market Hypothesis in each of its three farms.
2. Define the Random Walk Hypothesis. What basic assumptions underlying technical analysis is at odds with the weak form of the EMH?
3. Does the Random Walk theory suggest that security price levels are random? Explain.
4. What kinds of empirical evidence were produced to reject the EMH?
5. How do you characterise the nature of the securities markets? Which of the three forms of efficient market hypothesis do you think is valid? Why?
6. What does the efficient market hypothesis imply with respect to (a) technical market analysis, (b) fundamental analysis, and (c) portfolio policy of investors?
7. What is the role of new information in the pricing, of securities? Explain how the concept of new information relates to the EMH.

8. Discuss the rationale for expecting the existence of an efficient capital market. Explain the random welk theory of stock market prices.

9. (a) What evidence (if any) is there to support the random-walk theory of stock market prices?

   (b) What are the arguments against the theory?

10. The random walk hypothesis is fallacious because price is a present value which is not random at all. True or False ? Explain. How was the runs test used to test the efficient market hypothesis?

11. Can you reconcile the evidence of randomness with the fundamental theories of share price determination?

12. Why does the weak form of the EMH cost doubt in technical analysis?

13. Define the Efficient Market Hypothesis in each of its three forms. What are its implications?

14. Explain what is meant by saying that the market behaves as a random walk. What is the relationship between random walk and efficient markets?

15. Define and discuss the strong form EMH. Why do some observers contend that the strong form hypothesis really requires a perfect market in addition to efficient markets. Be specific.

16. Explain the relationship between fundamental analysis and efficient markets. What is the relationship between technical analysis and efficient markets?

17. What sequence of events might bring about an "efficient market"? What are the implications of EMH for use of Technical Analysis?

18. What is the role of new information in the pricing of securities? Explain how the concept of new information relates to the efficient market hypothesis.

19. Define and discuss the semi-strong efficient market hypothesis.

20. What is the implication of an efficient security market for the return an investor will earn over a period of time.

21. How can an investor identify an analyst with "superior" abilities? If an investor does not possess "superior" abilities, what investment strategy might be advisable?

22. If the security markets are infact strong -form efficient, should anyone decide to become a security analyst or an active portfolio manager? What would the impact of such a decision be on the strong-form efficiency?

23. Discuss what is meant by weak-form, semi-strong form, and strong form efficiency.

24. The efficient market theory has major implications for the practice of portfolio management. One obvious implication is the determination of superior analysts. Another is how to carry out the management of portfolios, assuming no success to superior analysts. Assume that none of the analysts to whom you have access is superior what specific investment practices you would implement for your clients

25. "The concept of a random walk in stack prices is bizarre and implies totally irrational behaviour by the investing public. Nothing could be further from the truth than random walk. Prices are related to fundamental economic worth." Comment.

26. (a) "Speculation is a zero-sum game across the market at any point in time as well as for any single speculator over time." How is this statement related to EMT.

   (b) For the market to be efficient, speculators must trade on any price disequilibrium. If speculators earn profits from doing so, is this inconsistant with market efficiency?

27. Recent empirical tests of the efficient market theory has uncovered a numbers of results suggesting the inefficiencies may exist.

   (a) List and briefly discuss those presented in the chapter.

   (b) Assume that you wish to defend EMT in the light of these apparent inconsistencies how would you do so?

28. Technicians often say that trading condition change in the market such that rule that

works during one period might not work during another period. They believe trading rules shouldn't be flexible but, instead, should be adjusted as the new market conditions arise. Comment.

29. Several factors contribute to an efficient market. What factors would you look for to differentiate the market or two alternative stocks? Specifically why should the efficiency of the markets for the stocks differ?

30. It is often argued (especially by active managers) that passive management implies settling for mediocre performance. Is this statement necessarily true? Why?

31. Describe the arguments and evidence of efficient market proponents, many investors pay attention to technical analysis in some form. Speculate as to why these investors use this kind of research?

32. Is if true that in a perfectly efficient market no investor would consistently be able to earn a profit?

33. Distinguish between three forms of market efficiency.

34. Would you expect that a fundamental security analysis makes security markets more efficient? Why?

35. Does the fact that a market exhibits weak-form efficiency necessarily imply that it is also strong-form efficient? How about the converse statement? Explain.

36. The portfolio manager's job can be defined as identifying the portfolio with the highest certainty equivalent return. Explain.

37. Suppose you discovered a systematic relationship between the price-earnings ratios of stocks and the performance of stocks. In other words, knowledge of a firm's price-earnings ratio proved helpful in predicting which stocks would show superior performance. Would this evidence be consistent with any of three versions of the efficient markets hypothesis?

38. If the market adheres to the strong form of the efficient markets hypothesis, what is the implication for the usefulness of the activities of gathering and analysing data about companies? What sort of logical paradox seems to result?

39. For each of the following kinds of information, indicate which form of the efficient markets hypothesis is supported if that information is reflected in security prices:

    (a) Government-released data on the money supply
    (b) A corporate quarterly earnings report
    (c) A public release of information from the Securities and Exchange Commission on insider trading.
    (d) Confidential discussions of a corporate board of directors on dividend policy
    (e) A history of a bond's prices

40. Suppose there is a consistent seasonal movement in stock prices. Why might this be inconsistent with the efficient markets hypothesis?

41. Consider the following statement: In an efficient market, today's price will have no systematic relationship to tomorrow's price. Is that true or false? Explain.

42. Tests of market efficiency are often referred to as *joint tests* of two hypotheses. Explain the meaning of this. Further, try to speculate on the difficulty this poses for tests of market efficiency.

PROBLEMS

1. Compute the number of runs in the following series of 20 daily stock proces. Do the price changes appear to be rendom?

Day	Price	Day	Price
1	Rs. 30.25	11	33.00

2	30.50	12	33.25
3	30.75	13	33.00
4	32.25	14	33.50
5	32.75	15	33.75
6	31.25	16	33.50
7	32.30	17	34.00
8	32.25	18	34.25
9	32.00	19	34.75
10	32.75	20	35.00

REFERENCES

1. Arbit, Harold L., and James E. Rhodes, "Performance Goals in a Generally Efficient Market," *Journal of Portfolio Management*, Fall 1976, pp. 57-61.

2. Beaver, William, and James Manegold, "The Association Between Market-Determined and Accounting-Determined Measures of Systematic Risk: Some Further Evidence," *Journal of Financial and Quantitative Analysis*, June 1975, pp. 231-284.

3. Black, Fisher, "Implications of the Random Walk Hypothesis for Portfolio Management," *Financial Analysts Journal*, March-April 1971, pp. 16-22.

4. Blume, Marshall E., "On the Assessment of Risk," *Journal of Finance* 26, no. 1 (March 1971): 1-10.

5. Boudreaux, Kenneth J., "Competitive Rates and Market Efficiency," *Financial Analysis Journal*, March-April 1975, pp. 18-25.

6. Cranshaw, T. E., "The Evaluation of Investment Performance," *The Journal of Business*. October 1977, pp. 462-485.

7. Dann, Larry Y., David Mayers, and Robert J. Raab, Jr., 'Trading Rules, Large Blocks and the Speed of Price Adjustment," *Journal of Financial Economics*, January 1977, pp. 3-22.

8. Dietz, Peter O., and Jeannette R. Kirschman. "Evaluating Portfolio Performance." In *Managing Investment Portfolios*, 2d ed., edited by John L. Maginn and Donald L. Turtle. Boston: Warren Gorham and Lament, 1990.

9. Ellis, Charles D. "Performance Investing." *Financial Analysts Journal*, September-October 1968, p. 117.

10. Ibbotson, R-L. Siegel, and K. Love: "World Wealth: Market Values and Returns," *Journal of Portfolio Management*, Fall 1985, pp. 4-23.

11. Fama, Eugene F., Lawrence Fisher, Michael Jensen, and Richard Roll, "The Adjust-ment of Stock Prices to New Information," *International Economic Review*, February 1969, pp. 1 21.

12. —————————. "Efficient Capital Markets: A Review of Theory and Empirical Work," *Journal of Finance*, May 1970, pp. 3X3 417.

13. —————————"Random Walks in Stock Market Prices," *Financial Analysts Journal*, September- October, 1965, pp. 55 59.

14. ————————— and Arthur B. Laffer, "Information and Capital Markets," *Journal of Business*, July 1971, pp. 289 -298.

15. Gibbons, Jean Dickinson, *Nonparametrical Methods for Quantitative Analysis* (New York: Holt, Rinehart and Winston, 1976), chap. 8.

16. Jensen. Michael C.. ed., *Studies in the Theory of Capital Markets* (New York' Praeger 1972).

17. —————————, and George Barrington, "Random Walks and Technical Theories: Some Additional Evidence," *Journal of Finance*, May 1970, pp. 469-482.

18. King, Benjamin F., "Market and Industry Factors in Stock Price Behavior," *Journal of Business* 39, no. 1, part II (January 1966, Supplement): 139-190.

19. Korschat, Benjamin. "Measuring Research Analysts Performance." *Financial Analysts Journal*, July-August 1978.

20. Lloyd-Davies, Peter, and Michael Canes, "Stock Prices and the Publication of Second-Hand Information," *Journal of Business*, January 1978, pp. 43-56.

21. Malkiel, Burton G. *A Random Walk Down Wall Street*. New York: W. W. Norton & Co., 1996.

22. Pinches, George E., "The Random Walk Hypothesis and Technical Analysis," *Financial Analysts Journal*, March-April 1970, pp. 104-110.

23. Roll, Richard, *The Behavior of Interest Rates: An Application of the Efficient Market Model to U.S. Treasury Bills* (New York: Basic Books, 1970).

24. Schneider, Theodore H. "Measuring Performance." *Financial Analysts Journal*, May-June 1969, p. 105.

25. Spigelman, Joseph H. "What Basis for Superior Performance?" *Financial Analysts Journal*, May-June 1974, p. 32.

26. Smidt, Seymour, "A New Look at the Random Walk Hypothesis," *Journal of Financial and Quantitative Analysis*, September 1968, pp. 235-261.

27. Vasicek, Oldrich, and John A. McQuown, "The Efficient Market Model," *Financial Analysts Journal*, September-October 1972, pp. 71-84.

28. Williams, Arthur: *Managing Your Investment Manager*, Dow Jones-Irwin, New York, 1990.

Part IV

PORTFOLIO ANALYSIS AND MANAGEMENT

23

Portfolio Analysis: Risk and Return

INTRODUCTION

The portfolio analysis begins where the security analysis ends and this fact has important consequences for investors. Portfolios, which are combinations of securities, may or may not take on the aggregate characteristics of their individual parts.

Portfolio analysis considers the determination of future risk and return in holding various blends of individual securities. Portfolio expected return is a weighted average of the expected return of individual securities but portfolio variance, in sharp contrast, can be something less than a weighted average of security variances. As a result an investor can sometimes reduce portfolio risk by adding another security with greater individual risk than any other security in the portfolio. This seemingly curious result occurs because risk depends greatly on the covariance among returns of individual securities. We will show how an investor can reduce expected risk through diversification, why this risk reduction results from *proper* diversification, and how the investor may estimate the expected return and expected risk level of a given portfolio of assets.

PORTFOLIO AND SECURITY RETURNS

A portfolio is a collection of securities. Since it is rarely desirable to invest the entire funds of an individual or an institution in a single security, it is essential that every security be viewed in a portfolio context. Thus, it seems logical that the expected return of a portfolio should depend on the expected return of each of the security contained in the portfolio. It also seems logical that the amounts invested in each security should be important. Indeed, this is the case. The example of a portfolio with three securities shown in Table-1(A) illustrates this point. The expected holding period value- relative for the portfolio is clearly:

$$\frac{₹\ 23,100}{₹\ 20,000} = 1.155$$

giving an expected holding period return of 15.50%.

Table-1 (B) combines the information in a somewhat different manner. The portfolio's expected holding-period value-relative is simply a weighted average of the expected value-relative of its component securities, using current market values as weights.

The procedure can be used as easily with holding-period returns. Table-l(C) provides an illustration. Holding period return is simply 100 times the value obtained by subtracting one from the holding period value-relative. Thus a weighted average of the former will have the same characteristics as a weighted average of the latter.

TABLE 1

(a) Security and Portfolio Values

Security	No. of Shares	Current Price Per Share	Current Value	Expected End-of Period Share Value	Expected End-of-Period Share Value
1	2	3	4	5	6
XYZ	100	₹ 15.00	₹ 1,500	₹ 18.00	₹ 1,800
ABC	150	20.00	3,000	22.00	3,300
RST	200	40.00	8,000	45.00	9,000
KNF	250	25.00	6,250	30.00	7,500
DET	100	12.50	1,250	15.00	1,500
			₹ 20,000		₹ 23,100

(b) Security and Portfolio Value-Relatives

Security	Current Value	Proportion of current value of Properties	Current Price per share	Expected End-of-period value per share	Expected Holding-period value-Relative	Contribution to Portfolio Expected Holding-period value-Relative
(1)	(2)	3 = (2) ₹ 20,000	(4)	(5)	(6) = (5) / (4)	(7) = (3)×(6)
XYZ	₹ 1,500	.0750	₹ 15.00	₹ 18.00	1.200	0.090000
ABC	3,000	.1500	20.00	22.00	1.100	0.165000
RST	8,000	.4000	40.00	45.00	1.125	0.450000
KNF	6,250	.3125	25.00	30.00	1.200	0.375000
DET	1,250	.0625	12.50	15.00	1.200	0.075000
	₹ 20,000	1.0000				1.155000

(c) Security and Portfolio Holding-period Returns

Security	Proportion of Current Value of Portfolio	Expected Holding Period Return (%)	Contribution to Portfolio Expected Holding Period Return (%)
(1)	(2)	(3)	(4)
XYZ	.0750	20.00	1.50
ABC	.1500	10.00	1.50
RST	.4000	12.50	5.00
KNF	.3125	20.00	6.25
DET	.0625	20.00	1.25
	1.0000		15.50

Since portfolio's expected return is a weighted average of the expected returns of its securities, the contribution of each security to the portfolio's expected returns depends on its expected returns and its proportionate share of the initial portfolio's market value. Nothing else is relevant. It follows that an investor who simply wants the greatest possible expected return should hold one security: the one which is considered to have the greatest expected return. Very few investors do this, and very few investment advisers would counsel such an extreme policy. Instead, investors should diversify, meaning that theirportfolio should include more than one security. This is because diversification can reduce risk.

RISK

Of all possible questions which the investor may ask, the most important one is concerned with the probability of actual yield being less than zero, that is, with the probability of loss. This is the essence of risk. A useful measure of risk should somehow take into account both the probability of various possible "bad" outcomes and their associated magnitudes. Instead of measuring the probability of a number of different possible outcomes, the measure of risk should somehow estimate the extent to which the actual outcome is likely to diverge from the expected.

Two measures are used for this purpose: the average (or mean) absolute deviation and the standard deviation. Table 2(A) shows how the average absolute deviation can be calculated. First the expected return is determined. In this case it is 10.00 per cent. Next, each possible outcome is analysed to determine the amount by which the value deviates from the expected amount. These figures shown in Column (5) of the table, include both positive and negative values. As shown in Column (6), a weighted average, using probabilities as weights, will equal zero. This is a mathematical necessity, given the way expected value is calculated. To assess the risk the signs of deviations can simply be ignored. As shown in column (7), the weighted average of the absolute values of the deviations, using the probabilities as weights, is 10 per cent This constitutes the first measure of "likely" deviation.

TABLE 2

A. Calculating the Mean Absolute Deviation

Event	Probability	Return %	Probability X Return	Deviation	Probability X Deviation	Probability X Absolute Deviation
(1)	(2)	(3)	(4)	(5)	(6)	(7)
a	.20	-10	-2.0	-25.0	-5.0	5.0
b	.40	25	10.0	10.0	4.0	4.0
c	30	20	6.0	5.0	1.5	1.5
d	.10	10	-1.0	-5.0	-0.5	0.5
		Expected Return =	15.0	0	Average = Absolute Deviation	10.0

B. Calculating the Standard Deviation

Event	Probability	Deviation	Deviation Squared	Probability X Deviation Squared
(1)	(2)	(3)	(4) = (3)2	(5) = (2)×(4)
a	.20	-25.0	625.0	125.0
b	.40	10.0	100.0	40.0
c	.30	5.0	25.0	7.5
d	.10	-5.0	25.0	2.4

Variation = Weighted average squared deviation   =   175.0

Standard Deviation = square root of variance   =   13.2287

Table 2(*B*) presents slightly more complex but preferably analytical measure. In this, the deviations are squared (making the value all positive); then a weighted average of these amounts is taken, using the probabilities as weights. The result is termed the variance. It is converted to the original units by taking the square root. The result is termed the standard deviation.

Although the two measures are often interchangeable in this manner, the standard deviation is generally preferred for investment analysis. The reason is simple. The standard deviation of a portfolio's return can be determined from (among other things) the standard deviations of the returns of its components securities, no matter what the distributions. No relationship of comparable simplicity exists for the average absolute deviations.

When an analyst predicts that a security will return 15% next year, he or she is presumably stating something comparable to an expected value. If asked to express the uncertainty about the outcome, he or she might reply that the odds are 2 out of 3 that the actual return will be within 10% of the estimate (i.e., 5% and 25%). The standard deviation is a formal measure of uncertainty, or risk, expressed in this manner, just as the expected value is a formal measure of a "best guess" estimate. Most analysts make such predictions directly, without explicitly assessing probabilities and making the requisite computations.

PORTFOLIO RISK

In order to estimate the total risk of a portfolio of assets, several estimates are needed: the variance of each individual asset under consideration for inclusion in the portfolio and the covariance, or correlation co-efficient, of each asset with each of the other assets.

Table 3(A) shows the returns on two securities and on a portfolio that includes both of them. Security X constitutes 60 per cent of the market value of the portfolio and security Y the other 40 per cent. The predicted return on the portfolio is simply a weighted average of the predicted returns on the securities using the proportionate values as weights. Summary measures show values computed from the estimates in Table-3(B). The expected return for the portfolio is simply the weighted average of the expected returns on its securities, using the proportionate values as weights (17.0% =.6 × 15% +.4 × 20%). However; this is not true for either the variance or the standard deviation of return for the portfolio are smaller than the corresponding values for either of the component securities. This rather surprising result has a simple explanation. The risk of a portfolio depends not only on the risk of its securities, considered in isolation,

TABLE 3

Portfolio and Security Risks

(A) Returns

Event	Probability	Return on Security X	Return on Security Y	Return on Portfolio
(1)	(2)	(3)	(4)	(5)=.6×(3)+.4×(4)
a	.20	-10%	5.0%	-4.0%
b	.40	25	30.0	27.0
c	.30	20	20.0	20.0
d	.10	10	10.0	10.0

(B) Summary Measures

	Security X	Security Y	Portfolio
Expected Return	15.0	20.0	17.0
Variance of Return	175.0	95.0	135.8
Standard deviation of Return	13.2287	9.7468	11.65

(C) Covariance and Correlations

Event	Probability	Deviation of Return for Security X	Deviation of Return for Security Y	Product of Deviation	Probability Times Product of Deviations
(1)	(2)	(3)	(4)	(5)=(3)×(4)	(6) = (2)×(5)
a	.20	-25.0%	-15.0%	375	75.00
b	.40	10.0	10.0	100	40.00
c	.30	5.0	0	0	0
d	.10	-5.0	-10.0	50	5.00

$$\text{Correlation Coefficient} = \frac{120.00}{13.2287 \times 9.7468} = 0.9307 \qquad \text{Covariance} \qquad 120.00$$

but also on the extent to which they are affected similarly by underlying events. To illustrate this, two extreme cases are shown in Table 4. In the first case both the variance and the standard deviation of the portfolio are the same as the corresponding values for the securities. Then diversification has no effect at all on risk. In the second case the situation is very different. Here the security's returns offset one another in such a manner that the particular combination that makes up this portfolio has no risk at all. Diversification has completely eliminated risk. The difference between these two cases concerns the extent to which the security's returns are correlated i.e., tend to "go-together". Either of two measures can be used to state the degree of such a relationship: the covariance or the correlation co-efficient.

The computations required to obtain the covariance for the two securities are presented in Table 3(C). The deviation of each security's return from its expected value is determined and the product of the two obtained (column 5). The variance is simply a weighted average of such products, using the probabilities of the events as weights. A positive value for the covariance indicates that the securities returns tend to go together - for example, a better-than-expected return for one is likely to occur alongwith a better-than-expected return for the other. A negative covariance indicates a tendency for the returns to offset the another—for example, a better-than- expected return for one is likely to occur alongwith a worse-than-expected return for the other. A small or zero value for the covariance indicates that there is little or no relationship between the two returns. The correlation coefficient is obtained by dividing the covariance by the product of the two security's standard deviation. As shown in Table-3(c), in this case the value is 0.9307.

TABLE 4

Risk and Return for a Two-Security Portfolio

(A) Two Securities with Equal Returns

Event	Probability	Return on Security X%	Return on Security Y%	Return-on Portfolio
(1)	(2)	(3)	(4)	(5) =.6 × (3) + .4 × (4)
A	.20	-10.0	-10.0	-10.0
B	.40	25.0	25.0	25.0
C	.30	20.0	20.0	20.0
D	.10	10.0	10.0	10.0
Expected Return		15.0	15.0	15.0
Variance of Return		175.0	175.0	175.0
Standard deviation of Return		13.2287	13.2287	13.2287

(B) Two Securities with Offsetting Returns

Event	Probability	Return on Security X%	Return on Security Y%	Return on Portfolio
(1)	(2)	(3)	(4)	(5)
a	.20	-10.	40.0	10.0
b	.40	25.0	-20.0	10.0
c	.30	20.0	-5.0	10.0
d	.10	10.0	10.0	10.0
Expected return (%)		15.0	-0.5	10.0
Variance of return		175.0	37.47	0
Standard deviation		13.228	6.1217	0

Correlation coefficients always lie between +1.0 and -1.0, inclusive. The former value represents perfect positive correlation, of the type shown in the example in Table-4(A). The latter value represents perfect negative correlation in Table- 4(B). The relationship between the covariance and the correlation coefficient can be represented as follows:

$$C_{XY} = r_{XY}\, \sigma_X\, \sigma_Y \tag{1}$$

or
$$r_{XY} = \frac{C_{XY}}{\sigma_X \sigma_Y} \tag{2}$$

where:

C_{XY} = covariance between return on X and return on Y.

r_{XY} = coefficient of correlation between return on X and return on Y.

σ_X = standard deviation of return for X.

σ_Y = standard deviation of return for Y.

For two securities, X and Y, the relationship between the risk of a portfolio of two securities and the relevant variables, the formula is:

$$\sigma_P^2 = W_X \sigma_X^2 + 2 W_X W_Y C_{XY} + W_Y^2 \sigma_Y^2. \qquad (3)$$

where:

σ_P^2 = the variance of return for the portfolio.

σ_X^2 = the variance of return for security X,

σ_Y^2 = the variance of return for security Y.

C_{XY} = the covariance between the return on security X and the return on security Y.

W_X = the proportion of the portfolio's value invested in security X.

W_Y = the proportion of the portfolio's value invested in security Y.

For the case shown in Table-3

W_X = 0.6; W_Y =0.4

σ_X^2 = 175.0 σ_Y^2 = 95.0

C_{XY} = 120.00

Inserting these values in formula (3), we get the variance of the portfolio as a whole:

$$\sigma_P^2 = (0.6)^2 \times 175.0 + 2 \times .6 \times .4 \times 120 + (0.4)^2 \times 95.0$$
$$= 63.00 + 57.60 + 15.20$$
$$= 135.80$$

The relationship that gives the variance for a portfolio with more than two securities is similar in nature but more extensive. Both the risks of the securities and all their correlations have to be taken into account. The formula is:

$$\sigma_P^2 = \sum_{x=1}^{N}\sum_{y=1}^{N} W_X W_Y C_{XY} \qquad (4)$$

$$= \sum_{x=1}^{N}\sum_{y=1}^{N} W_X W_Y r_{XY} \sigma_X \sigma_Y$$

where:

σ_P^2 = the variance of return for the portfolio.

W_X = the proportion of the portfolio's value invested in security X.

W_Y = the proportion of the portfolio's value invested in security Y.

C_{XY} = the covariance between the return on security X and the return on security Y.

N = the number of securities.

The two summation signs mean that every possible combination must be included in the total, with a value between 1 and N substituted where x appears and a value between 1 and N substituted where Y appears. In those cases in which the value are the same, the relevant covariance is that between a security's return and itself.

WHEN DIVERSIFICATION DOES NOT HELP

Perfectly Positively Correlated Returns

The return from two securities are perfectly positively correlated when a cross-plot gives points lying precisely on a upward-sloping straight line, as shown in Figure - 1(A). Each point indicates the return on security A (horizontal axis) and the return on security B (vertical axis) corresponding to one event. The example shown in Table-4 (A) confirms to this pattern.

What is the effect on risk when two securities of this type are combined ? The general equation is:

$$\sigma_P^2 = W_X^2 \sigma_X^2 + 2W_X W_Y C_{XY} + W_X^2 \sigma_Y^2$$

The covariance term can, of course, be replaced, using formula (1):

However, in this case there is perfect positive correlation, so $r_{XY} = +1$ and $C_{XY} = \sigma_X \sigma_Y$. Substituting all these values in general formula gives :

$$\sigma_P^2 = W_X^2 \sigma_X^2 + 2W_X W_Y \sigma_X \sigma_Y + W_Y^2 \sigma_Y^2$$

$$\sigma_P^2 = (W_X \sigma_X + W_Y \sigma_Y)^2$$

$$\sigma_P = W_X \sigma_X + W_Y \sigma_Y \text{ when } r_{XY} = +1 \tag{5}$$

This is an important result. When two securities returns are perfectly positively correlated, the risk of a combination, measured by the standard deviation of return, is just a weighted average of the risks of the component securities, using market value as weights. The principle holds as well if more than two securities are included in a portfolio. In such cases, diversification does not provide risk reduction but only risk averaging.

WHEN DIVERSIFICATION CAN ELIMINATE RISK

Perfectly Negatively Correlated Returns

Diversification can eliminate risk in case of perfectly negatively correlated returns. Since $r_{XY} = -1$, the general formula becomes :

$$\sigma_P^2 = (W_X^2 \sigma_X^2 - 2 W_X W_Y \sigma_X \sigma_Y + W_Y^2 \sigma_Y^2$$

This can be factored to obtain :

$$\sigma_P^2 = (W_X \sigma_X - W_Y \sigma_Y)^2 \text{ when } r_{XY} = -1. \tag{6}$$

Assuming a portfolio in which the proportionate holdings are inversely related to the relative risks of the two securities, i.e. :

$$\frac{W_X}{W_Y} = \frac{\sigma_Y}{\sigma_X} \text{ or } W_X = \frac{\sigma_Y W_Y}{\sigma_X}$$

For this combination the parenthesized term in formula (6) will be:

$$W_X \sigma_X - W_Y \sigma_Y = \frac{\sigma_Y W_Y}{\sigma_X} \sigma_X - W_Y \sigma_Y = 0$$

If this term is zero, of course, the portfolio's standard deviation of return must be zero as well. When two securities returns are perfectly negatively correlated, it is possible to combine them in a manner that will eliminate all risk. Figure- 1(b) shows the returns from two securities perfectly negatively correlated, a cross-plot gives points lying precisely on a downward-sloping straight line. The example shown in Table-4(b) confirms to this pattern. This principle motivates all hedging strategies. This object is to take position that will offset each other with regard to certain kinds of risk, reducing or completely eliminating such sources of uncertainty.

THE INSURANCE PRINCIPLE

Uncorrelated Returns

Some risks can be substantially reduced by pooling. This has crucial implications for investment management. Most importantly, it provides the basis for understanding the relationship between risk and return. A special case of extreme importance arises when a cross-plot of security returns shows no pattern that can be represented even approximately by an upward- sloping or downward-sloping line (See Figure-l(c)). In such an instance, the returns are uncorrelated. The correlation coefficient, r_{XY}, is zero, as is the covariance. In this situation, the general formula becomes:

$$\sigma_P^2 = W_X^2 \sigma_X^2 + W_Y^2 \sigma_Y^2 \text{ when } r_{XY} = 0 \qquad (7)$$

To illustrate the diversification effect, consider a portfolio divided equally between two securities of equal risk, say 20.0%. That is:

$$W_X = .5, W_Y = .5; \quad \sigma_X = 20; \quad \sigma_Y = 20$$

Substituting these values in equation (7) we get:

$$(.5)^2 (20)^2 + (.5)^2 (20)^2 = (.25)(400) + (.25)(400)$$

Thus:

$$\sigma_P^2 = 200 \text{ and } \sigma_P = 14.14$$

Diversification has helped as the risk of the portfolio is less than the risk of either of its component securities. The result will remain same irrespective of the number of securities. However, when all returns are uncorrelated the complete formula becomes:

$$\sigma_P^2 = W_1^2 \sigma_1^2 + W_2^2 \sigma_2^2 + \ldots\ldots + W_N^2 \sigma_N^2$$

where:

$$
\begin{aligned}
\sigma_{P\ldots\ldots} &= \text{The standard deviation of the return on portfolio.} \\
W_1, W_2\ldots &= \text{The proportions invested in securities 1,2, etc.} \\
\sigma_1, \sigma_2 \ldots &= \text{The standard deviation of the returns for securities 1,2, etc.} \\
N &= \text{The number of securities included.}
\end{aligned}
$$

This is an extremely important relationship for investment analysis and also provides the bases for insurance, or *risk pooling*. This can be seen by extending the previous example and assuming a portfolio of equal parts of a number of securities, each with a risk (standard deviation of return) of 20%. If two securities are included:

$$\sigma_P^2 = (1/2)^2 \, 20^2 + (1/2)^2 \, 20^2$$
$$= 2(1/2)^2 \, 20^2$$

If three securities are included:

$$\sigma_P^2 = (1/3)^2 \, 20^2 + (1/3)^2 \, 20^2 + (1/3)^2 \, 20^2$$
$$= 3(1/3)^2 \, 20^2$$

To generalise, represent the number of securities by N. Then:

$$\sigma_P^2 = (1/N)^2 \, 20^2 + (1/N)^2 20^2 + \ldots\ldots$$
$$= N(1/N)^2 \, 20^2$$

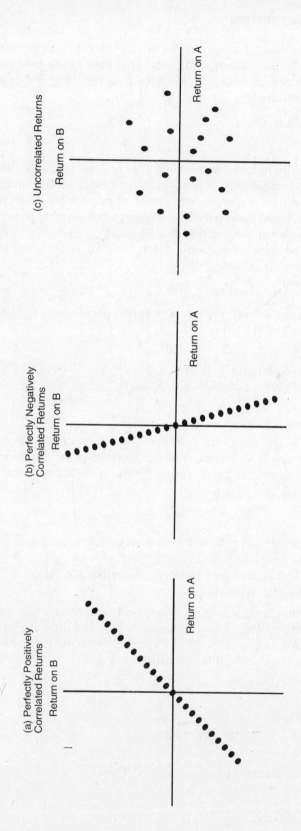

FIGURE 1: RETURN ON TWO SECURITIES

Simplifying:

$$\sigma_P^2 = (N/N)^2 \, 20^2 = 20^2/N$$

$$\sigma_P = 20/\sqrt{N}$$

Diversification provides substantial risk reduction if the components of a portfolio are uncorrelated. In fact, if enough securities are included, the overall risk of the portfolio will be almost (but not quite) zero. This is why insurance companies attempt to write many individual policies and spread their coverage so as to minimise overall risk.

BORROWING AND LENDING

Combining Risky and Riskless Securities

What happens to risk when a riskless security is combined with a risky security (or portfolio). If security A return is certain, while that of security B is uncertain, $\sigma_A = 0$, as does C_{AB}; and the relationship becomes:

$$\sigma_P = W_A^2 0 + 2W_A W_B 0 + W_B^2 \sigma_B^2$$

Thus:

$$\sigma_P = W_B \, \sigma_B \text{ when } \sigma_A = 0$$

In other words, when a risky security or portfolio is combined with a riskless one, the risk of the combination is proportional to the amount invested in the risky component. An obvious case of this sort arises when an investor splits his funds between an equity portfolio and a savings account. Table - 5 shows some representative values, case C and D involve splitting funds between the risky alternative B and the riskless one A. Investing in a riskless security is equivalent to lending money.

TABLE 5

Combining a Riskless and a Risky Investment

	Security A (Savings Account)	Security B (Equity Portfolio)	Combination C	Combination D	Combination E
Proportion in A(W_A)	1.0	0	.7	.3	-.2
Proportion in B(W_B)	0	1.0	.3	.7	1.2
Expected return	8%	23%	12%	18%	26%
Standard deviation of return	0%	25%	6%	14%	30.0%

Alongwith the original alternatives A and B, Figure - 2 portrays the combinations C and D. Each alternative shows the expected return and risk of an alternative combination. Since both risk and return will be proportional to the investment proportions in C case of this sort, both point C and point D lie on the straight line connecting points A and B. All these alternatives have positive individual proportions except E. As shown in Table - 5 and Figure-2, combination E and point E have W_A equal -.20 and W_B equal + 1.20.

What does this mean ? Imagine an investor with ₹ 10,000 to invest. But in order to take advantage of profitable opportunity, he may take additional risk and invest his own ₹ 10,000 and borrow ₹ 2000 at 8% interest. A total of ₹ 12,000 could then be invested in the project. The effect of this sort of leverage may be favourable/unfavourable depending upon the circumstances. Table 6 (a) shows the return on investor's capital may go up to 26%. The final column of the table showed a similar set of computations for combination. Leverage increases the expected return on investor's capital if borrowed funds are invested in a risky alternative. Point E lies above point B in Figure 2. However, the expected return may decline with an unfavourable outcome. Return on investor's capital falls to 4.4 per cent from 26 per cent. (See Table 6 (B)). The effect of leverage on risk is shown in the fourth line of the table. Borrowing increases risk. This is also shown in Figure 2 point E is to the right of point B.

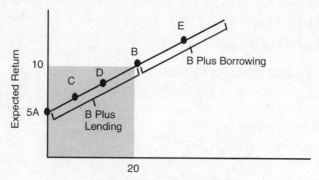

FIGURE 2: RISK AND RETURN FOR COMBINATION OF A RISKY AND A
RISKLESS INVESTMENT

TABLE 6

Effect of Leverage

(A) *With a Favourable Outcome:*			
Investment return		23%	
Return on total investment	.23 × ₹ 12,000	= ₹ 2,760	
Interest rate on loan		8%	
Amount of interest	.08 · × ₹ 2,000	= 160	
	Net proceeds	= ₹ 2,600	
	Return on investor's capital	$=\dfrac{2,600}{10,000}=26\%$	
(B) *With an Unfavourable Outcome:*			
Investment return		5%	
Return on total investment	.05 · ₹ 12,000	= ₹ 600	
Interest rate on loan		8%	
Amount of interest	.08 · ₹ 2,000	= 160	
	Net proceeds	= 440	
	Return on investor's capital	$=\dfrac{₹\,440}{10,000}=4.40\%$	

Leverage generally increases both risk and expected return. It is commonly used by corporations. For example, point B in Figure 2 might represent the risk and return obtained by a firm on its total assets. If, however, the corporation has issued debt, both the risk and return of its investment should be greater than this. Combination E conforms to the example shown in Table 5 and Figure 2.

Like corporations, the individual investors can and do borrow from a number of sources. At any time the interest charged may depend on the borrower, the lender, the collateral, the purpose of loan, the length of time involved, the amount of money borrowed, etc. If there is a chance that the loan will not be repaid in full and on time, the rate charged will, of course, be higher, and the loan will not be repiad in full and on time, the rate charge will of cource be higher, and the loan will not be riskless. But in these cases in which the leverage is used within the limits required to keep the loan riskless, the relationship will be that shown in Figure 2. Margined or leveraged purchase of any risky investment (e.g., B) can be used to obtain a combination of risk and return plotting on the straight line connecting the points representing the two components (e.g., A and B). The prospect obtained in this manner will depend on the amount of leverage: the greater the leverage, the farther to the right of the risky investments point will be the point representing the new combination.

REVIEW PROBLEMS

1. We have the following stocks' returns, $E(R_i)$, and standard deviations (SDi)

Stock	$E(R_1)$	SDi
A	10%	15%
B	10%	12%
C	18%	20%

(i) Does anyone stock dominates another? Explain why.

(ii) Calculate the coefficient of variation for stock B and stock C? Does one dominate the other? If not, what type of investor would choose C over B?

Ans.:

(i) Yes, stock B dominates A because it has a lower risk for the same level of return.

(ii) The coefficient of variation, CV, equals: SD_i/ER_i

   Stock B's CV = 0.12 / 0.10 = 1.2

   Stock C's CV = 0.20 / 0.18 = 1.11.

Based on the CV, stock C has less risk per one per cent of return, but it does not dominate stock B. The choice between stocks B and C depends on the investor's risk preference.

2. Consider the two stocks ABC and XYZ with a standard deviation 0.05 and 0.10, respectively. The correlation coefficient for these two stocks is 0.8

(a) What is the diversification gain from forming a portfolio that has equal proportions of each stock?

(b) What should be the weights of the two assets in a portfolio that achieves a diversification gain of 3%?

Ans.:

(a) The gain from diversification is:

$$\frac{0.075 - 0.0716}{0.75} = 4.53\%$$

(b) To obtain a diversification gain of 3%, the weighting of the portfolio should be 30% to 70%.

3. T.S. Shekhar has a portfolio of five securities. The expected rate and amount of investment in each security is as follows:

Security	A	B	C	D	E
Expected return	.14	.08	.15	.09	.12
Amount invested	₹ 20,000	₹ 10,000	₹ 30,000	₹ 25,000	₹ 15,000

Compute the expected return on Shekhar's portfolio.

Ans.:

The expected return on Shekhar's portfolio is:
$$E(R_p) = (20,000/1,00,000).14 + (10,000/1,00,000).08 + (30,000/1,00,000).15$$
$$+ (25,000/1,00,000).09 + (15,000/1,00,000).12$$
$$= .028 + .008 + .045 + .0225 + .018 = .1215$$
$$= 12.15\%$$

4. XYZ Industries returns for the last five years are given below:

Year	2005	2006	2007	2008	2009
Return	24.85%	5.51%	6.33%	-7.91%	52.10%

(a) Calculate XYZ Industries' ex-post (historical) mean return over the 1996 to 2000 period.
(b) Calculate XYZ Industries' standard deviation risk.

Ans.:

Mean Return $= [(24.85) + (5.51) + (6.33) + (- 7.91) + (52.10)]/5$
$$= 16.18\%$$
Standard deviation $= [(0.2485 - 0.1618)^2 + (0.0551 - 0.1618)^2$
$$+ (0.0633 - 0.1618)^2 + (- 0.0791 - 0.1618)^2 + (0.5210 = 0.1618)^2]^{1/2}$$
$$= 0.232$$

5. Suppose on investor prefers to invest 30 per cent in portfolio ABC and 70 per cent in the risk-free asset. If expected return on market, $E(R_m)$, equals 16 per cent and R_f equals 6 per cent, what is his portfolio's expected return, $E(R_p)$? What is his portfolio risk, σ_p, if market risk, σ_m equals 8 per cent?

Ans.:

$$E(R_p) = (0.30) (0.16) + (1 - 0.30) (0.06)$$
$$= 0.09$$
$$\sigma_p = (0.30) (0.08) = 0.024$$

6. Using the mean returns, standard deviation, and correlation displayed in the following table, calculate the portfolio return and portfolio standard deviation if an investor invests 40 per cent in ABC Co. and 60 per cent in XYZ Co.

	ABC Co.		XYZ Co.
Mean	0.0216		0.0155
Standard deviation (σ)	0.0448		0.0509
CV		0.0007	
Corr. (r)		0.31	

Ans.:

$$E(R_p) = \quad (0.40)\ (ER_{ABC}) + (0.60)\ (ER_{XYZ})$$
$$= \quad (0.40)\ (0.0216) + (0.60)\ (0.0155)$$
$$= \quad 0.0179$$
$$SD_p = \quad [(0.40)^2\ (0.0448)^2 + (1-0.40)^2\ (0.0509)^2 + 2\ (0.40)\ (1 - 0.40)\ (0.0007)]^{\frac{1}{2}}$$
$$= \quad 0.0354$$

7. T.S. Kumar holds a two-stock portfolio. Stock ABC has a standard deviation of returns of .6 and stock XYZ has a standard deviation of .4. The correlation coefficient of the two stocks' returns is 0.25. Kumar holds equal amounts of each stock. Compute the portfolio standard deviation for the two-stock portfolio.

Ans.:

$$\sigma_p \ = \sqrt{.5^2 \times .6^2 + 2 \times .5 \times .5 \times .6 \times .4 \times 25 + 5^2 \times .4^2}$$
$$= \sqrt{.09 + .03 + .04}$$
$$= \sqrt{.16}$$
$$= .4$$

8. National Corporation is planning to invest in a security that has several possible rates of return. Given the following probability distribution returns, what is the expected rate of return on investment? Also compute the standard deviation of the returns. What do the resulting numbers represent?

Ans.:

Probability (P)	Return (R)	Expected Return	Weighted Return
(1)	(2)	$(E(R)]$ $(3) = (1) \cdot (2)$	$[E(R)-R1^2\ P$
0.10	-10%	-1%	52.9%
0.20	5%	1%	12.8%
0.30	10%	3%	2.7%
0.40	25%	10%	57.6%
		$E(R) = 13\%$	$\sigma^2 = 126.0$ $\sigma = 11.22\%$

From our studies in statistics, we know that if the distribution of returns were normal, then National could expect a return of 13% with a 67% possibility that this return would vary up or down by 11.22% between 1.78% (13% -11.22%) and 24.22% (13% +11.22%). However, it is apparent from the probabilities that the distribution is not normal.

9. K.S. Bhatt holds a well-diversified portfolio of stocks in XYZ Group. During the last 5 years returns on these stocks have averaged 20.0% per year and had a standard deviation of 15.0%. He is satisfied with the yearly availability of his portfolio and would like to reduce its risk without affecting overall returns. He approaches you for help in finding an appropriate diversification medium. After a lengthy review of alternatives, you conclude : (i) future average returns and volatility of returns on his current portfolio will be the same as he has historically expected, (ii) to provide a quarter degree of diversification in his portfolio, investment could be made in stocks of the following groups:

Groups	Expected Return	Correlation of Returns with Group XYZ	Standard Deviation
ABC	20%	+1.0	15%
KLM	20%	-1.0	15%
RST	20%	+ 0.0	15%

(a) If Bhatt invests 50% of his funds in ABC Group and leaves the remainder in XYZ Group, would this affect both his expected returns and his risk ? Why ?

(b) If Bhatt invests 50% of his funds in KLM Group and leaves the remainder in XYZ Group, how would this affect both his expected return and his risk ? Why?

(c) What should he do ? Indicate precise portfolio weighting.

Ans.:

(a) Risk and return of ABC Portfolio are the same as those of XYZ portfolio and the correlation coefficient is 1.0, so there is no diversification gain.

(b) Return would remain at 20% but risk would fall to zero since $r = -1.0$

(c) Invest 50/50 in Group XYZ portfolio and group KLM portfolio.

10. Vinay Gautam is considering an investment in one of two securities. Given the information that follows, which investment is better, based on risk (as measured by the standard deviation) and return?

Security ABC		Security XYZ	
Probability	Return	Probability	Return
0.30	19%	0.20	22%
0.40	15%	0.30	6%
0.30	11%	0.30	14%
		0.20	-5%

Ans.:

Investment in security ABC				Investment in security XYZ			
Probability	Return	Expected Return	Weighted Deviation	Probability	Return	Expected Return	Weighted Deviation
				0.20	22%	4.4	31.752%
0.30	19%	5.7%	4.8%	0.30	6	1.8	3.468
0.40	15	6.0	1.0	030	14	4.2	6.348
0.30	11	3.3	4.8	0.20	5	-1.0	41.472
		$E(R) = 15.0\%$	$\sigma^2 = 9.6\%$			$E(R) = 9.4\%$	$\sigma^2 = 83.04$
			$s = 3.09$				$\sigma = 9.113$

11. You have been asked by a client for advice in selecting a portfolio of assets based on the following data:

Year	Return		
	A	B	C
2008	0.14	0.18	0.14
2009	0.16	0.16	0.16
2010	0.18	0.14	0.18

You have been asked to create portfolios by investing equal proportions (i.e., 50%) in each of two different securities. No probabilities have been supplied.

(a) What is the expected return on each of these securities over the three-year period?

(b) What is the standard deviation on each security's return?

(c) What is the expected return on each portfolio?

(d) For each portfolio, how would you characterise the correlation between the returns on its two assets?

(e) What is the standard deviation of each portfolio?

(f) Which portfolio do you recommend? Why?

Ans.:

(a) $E(R_A) = E(R_B) = E(R_C) = .16$

(b) $\alpha_A = (.00027)^{.5} = 0.0164$
$\alpha_B = (.00027)^{.5} = 0.0164$
$\alpha_C = (.00027)^{.5} = 0.0164$

(c) $E(R_{AB}) = E(R_{AC}) = E(R_{BC}) = .16$

(d) A and B are perfectly negatively correlated. A and C are perfectly positively correlated. B and C are perfectly negatively correlated.

(e) $\sigma_{AB} = 0; \sigma_{AC} = 0.0164$
Since A and C are identical,
$\sigma_{BC} = 0$

(f) Choose either AB or BC. All three portfolios have $E(R_P) = .16$, but AB and BC have no risk, while AC has $\sigma_{AC} = .0164$. Therefore, AB and BC provide the most reward for the least amount of risk.

12. Suppose you have ₹ 10,000 to invest and would like to sell ₹ 5000 in stock XYZ short to invest in ABC. Assuming no correlation between the two securities, compute the expected return and the standard deviation of the portfolio from the following characteristics:

Security	ABC	XYZ
E(R)	.12	.02
σ(R)	.08	.10

Ans.:

Expected Return:
$$E(R_P) = W_{ABC} E(R_{ABC}) + W_{XYZ} E(R_{XYZ})$$
$$= \frac{15,000}{10,000} .12 - \frac{5,000}{10,000} .02$$
$$= .18 - .01 = .17$$

Standard deviation:

$$[W^2_{ABC} \sigma^2 (R_{ABC}) + W^2_{XYZ} \sigma^2 (R_{XYZ})]^{\frac{1}{2}} = \sigma_P$$
$$= [(1.5)^2 \times (.08)^2 + (-.5)^2 \times (.10)^2]^{1/2}$$
$$= .130$$

13. A stock that pays no dividends is currently selling at ₹ 100. The possible prices for which the stock might sell at the end of one year, with associated probabilities, are:

End-of-year Price	Probability
₹ 90	0.1
100	0.2
110	0.4
120	0.2
130	0.1

(a) Calculate the expected rate of return by year-end.
(b) Calculate the standard deviations of the expected rate of return.

Ans.:

(a)

Probable	0.1	0.2	0.4	0.2	0.1
Return	−10	0	10	20	30

$$E(R) = 0.1 (-10) + 0.2(0) + 0.4(10) + 0.2(20) + 0.1(30)$$
$$= -1.0 + 0 + 4.0 + 4 + 3.0$$
$$= 10.0\%$$

(b) $$\sigma = [0.1 (-10 - 10)^2 + 0.2(0-10)^2 + 04(10-10)^2 + 02 (20-10)^2 + 0.1 (30-10)^2]^{.5}$$
$$= 10.95\%$$

14. The monthly returns for two assets are given below:

	Period			
	1	2	3	4
Security 1	3%	-3%	6%	-2%
Security 2	2	1	3	-1

Calculate the expected monthly return and variance for each asset and the covariance and correlation coefficients between the returns of the two assets.

Ans.:

The expected returns are equal to

$$E(R_1) = (.03 - .03 + .06 - .02) \div 4 = 0.01$$
$$E(R_2) = (.02 + .01 + .03 - .01) \div 4 = 0.0125.$$

The variances are equal to

$$\sigma_1^2 = \frac{(.03-.01)^2 + (-.03-.01)^2 + (.06-.01)^2 + (.02-.01)^2}{4-1} = .0018$$

$$\sigma_2^2 = \frac{(.02-.0125)^2 + (.01-.0125)^2 + (.03-.0125)^2 + (-.01-.0125)^2}{4-1} = .00029$$

The covariance between the returns of the two assets is

$$COV(R_1, R_2) = (.03 - .01)(.02 - .0125) + (-.03 - .01)(.01 - .0125) +$$
$$(.06 - .01)(.03 - .0125) + (-.02 - .01)(-.01 - .0125)/4 - 1$$
$$= .0006.$$

15. Two assets have the following possible returns and probabilities:

	Asset 1		Asset 2	
	Return	Probability	Return	Probability
	-5%	.20	-10%	.20
	10	.50	15	.50
	20	.30	25	.30

Calculate the portfolio expected return and variance for the weight of asset 1 equal to - 2, 0, .25, and .75

Ans.:

First calculate the expected returns of the two assets:
$$E(R_1) = (.20)(-.50) + (.50)(.10) + (.30)(.20) = .10$$
$$E(R_2) = (.20)(-.10) + (.50)(.15) + (.30)(.25) = .13$$
Calculate the variance and standard deviations of the two assets:
$$\sigma_1^2 = (-.05 - .10)^2 .20 + (.10 - .10)^2 .50 + (.20 - .10)^2 . 30 = .0075$$
$$\sigma_1 = .087$$
$$\sigma_2^2 = (-.10 - .13)^2 .20 + (.15 - .13)^2 .50 + (.25 - .13)^2 . 30 = 0151$$
$$\sigma_2 = .1229$$
The covariance between the returns of the two assets is
$$COV(R_1, R_2) = (-.05 - .10)(-.10 - 13) .20 +(-.10 - .10)(-.15 - 13) .50$$
$$+(-.20 - .10)(-.25 - 13) .30 = 0105$$
The correlation coefficient is .0105 ÷ (.087)(.1229) = .982.
The portfolio expected return is
$$E(R_p) = .10w_1 + .13w_2$$
The portfolio variance is
$$\sigma_p^2 = w_1^2 .0075 + w_2^2 .0151 + 2w_1^2 w_2^2. 0105$$
The portfolio expected return and variance can be obtained for the weights of interest:

w_1	w_2	$E(R_p)$	σ_p^2
-1.00	2.00	0.160	0.02590
0.00	1.00	0.130	0.01510
0.25	0.75	0.123	0.01290
0.75	0.25	0.108	0.00908

16. Consider a portfolio of these stocks, X, Y, Z, with weights w_x, w_y, and w_z. Show the portfolio variance is:
$$w_x^2 \sigma_x^2 + w_y^2 \sigma_y^2 + w_z^2 \sigma_z^2 + 2 w_x w_y \text{Cov}(r_x, r_y)$$
$$+ 2 w_x w_z \text{Cov}(r_x, r_y) + 2 w_y w_z \text{Cov}(r_y, r_z)$$

Ans.:

The bordered covariance metrix is

	w_x	w_y	w_z
w_x	σ_x^2	$\text{Cov}(r_x, r_y)$	$\text{Cov}(r_x, r_z)$
w_y	$\text{Cov}(r_y, r_x)$	σ_y^2	$\text{Cov}(r_y, r_z)$
w_z	$\text{Cov}(r_z, r_x)$	$\text{Cov}(r_z, r_y)$	σ_z^2

There are nine terms in the covariance metrix portfolio variance is calculated, from these nine terms:

$$\sigma_P^2 = w_X^2\sigma_X^2 + w_Y^2\sigma_Y^2 + w_Z^2\sigma_Z^2$$
$$+ w_X w_Y Cov(r_X, r_Y) + w_Y w_X Cov(r_Y, r_X)$$
$$+ w_X w_Y Cov(r_X, r_Z) + w_Z w_X Cov(r_Z, r_X)$$
$$+ w_Y w_Z Cov(r_Y, r_Z) + w_Z w_Y Cov(r_Z, r_Y)$$
$$= w_X^2\sigma_X^2 + w_Y^2\sigma_Y^2 + w_Z^2\sigma_Z^2$$
$$+ 2w_X w_Y Cov(r_X, r_Y) + 2w_X w_Z Cov(r_X, r_Z) + 2w_Y w_Z Cov(r_Y, r_Z)$$

17. Assume that the current rate on a one-year security is 7 per cent. You believe that the yield on a one-year security will be 9 per cent one year from now and 10 per cent 2 years from now. According to the expectations hypothesis, what should the yield be on a three-year security?

Ans.:

Find the geometric mean by averaging the continously compounded rates,
[In (1.07) + In (1.09) + In (1.10)]/3
(0.06766 + 0.08618 + 0.09531/3
= 0.24915/3
= 0.08305

Then converting to nmominal rate:
Exp. (0.08305)-1 = 0.0866

Your expectation imply that the current rate on a three-year security shall be 8.66 per cent.

18. A.K. Kapoor is evaluating a security. One year Treasury bills are currently paying 9.1 per cent. Calculate the below investment's expected return and its standard deviation. Should Kapoor invest in this security?

Probability	.15%	.30%	.40%	.15%
Return	15%	7%	10%	5%

Ans.:

Probability (P)	Return (R)	Expected Return	Weighted deivation
(1)	(2)	(3) = (1)x(2)	
0.15	15%	2.25%	5.22
0.30	7	2.10	1.32
0.40	10	4.00	0.32
0.15	5	0.75	2.52
		E(R) = 9.1%	σ^2 = 9.39%
			σ = 3.06%

Kapoor should not invest in this security. The level of risk is excessive for a return which is equal to the rate offered on treasury bills.

19. Ravi Shankar has prepared the following information regarding two investments under consideration. Which investment should be accepted?

Security ABC		Security XYZ	
Probability	Return	Probability	Return
0.30	27%	0.21	15%
0.50	18%	0.30	6%
0.30	-2%	0.40	10%
—	—	0.10	4%

Ans.:

Investment in security ABC				Investment in security XYZ			
Proba-bility	Return	Expected Return	Weighted Deviation	Proba-bility	Return	Expected Return	Weighted Deviation
0.30	27%	8.1%	31.8%	0.20%	15%	3.0%	6.728%
0.50	18	9.0	0.8	0.30	6	1.8	3.072
0.20	-2	-0.4	69.9	0.40	10	4.0	0.256
				0.10	4	0.4	

$$E(R) = 16.7\% \quad \sigma^2 = 102.5\%$$
$$\sigma \ 10.12\%$$

$$E(R) = 9.2\% \quad \sigma^2 = 12.76\%$$
$$\sigma = 3.57\%$$

20. Suppose you invest in four securities. Company ABC has on expected return of 20 per cent, Company BCD has on expected return of 10 per cent, Company CDE has on expected return of 12 per cent, and Company DEF has an expected return of 9 per cent. You have invested ₹ 40,000. What is the expected rate of return on your portfolio?

Ans.:

The expected rate of return is the weighted average of expected rates in the portfolio:

$$E(R_p) = \sum_{i=1}^{n} W_i \ E(R_i)$$

The portfolio weights are first determined by the formula

$$W_A = \frac{₹ \ \text{invested in ABC}}{\text{Total equity investment}}$$

Since you have invested equally in four securities and total investment is ₹ 40,000, the portfolio weight are equal ($W_{ABC} = W_{BCD} = W_{CDE} = W_{DEF}$) and are determined:

$$W_{ABC} = \frac{₹ \ 10,000}{₹ \ 40,000} = .25$$

Hence, the expected return on the individual securities and the expected rate of return on the portfolio is:

$$\begin{aligned} R_p &= (W_{ABC} \times r_{ABC}) + (W_{BCD} \times r_{BCD}) + (W_{CDE} \times r_{CDE}) \\ &+ (W_{DEF} \times r_{DEF}) \\ &= (.25 \times .20) + (.25 \times .10) + (.25 \times .12) + (.25 \times .09) \\ &= .1275 = 12.75\% \end{aligned}$$

21. Nenny, a Korean-based auto manufacturer, is evaluating two overseas locations for a proposed expansion of production facilities, one site in Neerland and another on Forexland. The likely future return form investment in cash site depends to great extent on future economic conditions. These scenarios are postulated, and the internal rate of return form cash investment is computed under each scenario. The results with their estimated probabilities are shown below:

Probability	Internal Rate of Return (%)	
	Neerland	Forexland
0.3	20	10
0.3	10	30
0.4	15	20

Required:

Calculate the expected value of the IRR and the standard deviation of the return of investments in each location. What would be the expected return and the standard deviation of the following split investment strategies:

(i) committing 50% of the available funds to the site in Neerland and 50% to Forexland.

(ii) committing 75% of the available funds to the site in Neerland and 25% to Forexland site?

(Assume zero correlation between the returns form the two sites?)

Ans.:

Neeroland:

Expected Value of IRR

$= (0.3 \times 20\%) + (0.3 \times 10\%) + (0.4 \times 15\%)$

$= 6\% + 3\% + 6\%$

$= 15\%$

Outcome (1)	Deviation (2)	Sq'd Dev. (3)	p (4)	Sq'd Dev. × p 5) = (3) (4)
20	+ 5	25	.3	7.5
10	-5	25	.3	7.5
15	0	0	.4	0
			Variance = Total =	15
			σ = 3.87	

Forexland:

Expected Value of IRR

$= (0.3 \times 10) + (0.3 \times 30\%) + (0.4 \times 20\%)$

$= 3\% + 9\% + 8\%$

$= 20\%$

Outcome (1)	Deviation (2)	Sq'd Dev. (3)	p (4)	Sq'd Dev. × p 5) = (3) (4)
10	- 10	100	.3	30
30	+ 10	100	.3	30
20	0	0	.4	0
			Variance = Total =	60
			σ= 7.75	

(b)

    (i) For a 50/50 split investment

        EV for IRR

$$= (0.5 \times 15) + (0.5 \times 20\%)$$
$$= 17.5\%$$
$$\sigma = 4.33$$

    (ii) For a 75/25 split investment

        EV of IRR

$$= 10.75 \times 15\%) + (0.25 \times 20\%)$$
$$= 16.25\%$$
$$\sigma = 3.49, \text{ i.e. Lower Risk, Lower Return}$$

22. You have invested ₹ 50,000, 30 per cent of which is invested in Company A, which has a expected rate of return of 15 per cent, and 70 per cent of which is invested in Company B, with an expected return of 12 per cent. What is the return on you portfolio? What is the expected percentage rate of return?

Ans.:

    (a) The rate of return is the percentage of the amount invested in a stock multiplied by its expected rate of return. Thus, of the ₹ 50,000 invested:

        Company A—30 per cent of total with 15 per cent rate of return:

        $.30 \times ₹ 50,000 \times .15 = ₹ 2,250$

        Company B - 70 per cent with a 12 per cent rate of return:

        $.70 \times ₹ 50,000 \times .12 = ₹ 4,200$

        The total return is ₹ 6450 (i.e., ₹ 2250 + ₹ 4200).

    (b) The expected percentage rate of return is the total return divided by the amount invested:

$$r = \frac{\text{Total Return}}{\text{Total amount invested}}$$

$$r = \frac{₹ 6450}{₹ 50,000} = 12.90\%$$

23. Assume the investor in Problem 20 wants to determine how risky his portfolio and wants you to compute the portfolio variance. If the expected correlations and variances of the stocks are as follows, what is the variance of the portfolio?

Correlations		ABC	BCD	CDE	DEF
	BCD	.50			
	CDE	.60	.30		
	DEF	-.30	-.20	-.10	
Variances:		.04	.16	.02	.10

Ans.:

    To compute the variance, you need to make a covariance matrix . Using the square roots of the variances and correlations given, the covariances are calculated:

$$\text{Cov } (r_{ABC}, R_{BCD}) = .500 \times .200 \times .400 = .040$$
$$\text{Cov } (r_{ABC}, R_{CDE}) = .600 \times .200 \times .141 = .070$$
$$\text{Cov } (r_{ABC}, R_{DEF}) = -.300 \times .200 \times .316 = -.019$$
$$\text{Cov } (r_{BCD}, R_{CDE}) = .300 \times .400 \times .141 = .017$$
$$\text{Cov } (r_{BCD}, R_{DEF}) = -.200 \times .400 \times .316 = -.025$$

$$Cov\ (r_{CDE},\ R_{DEF}) = -.100 \times .141 \times .316 = -.004$$

With the given variance and the portfolio weights, the covariance matrix is as follows:

Securities	Weights	ABC	BCD	CDE	DEF
		.25	.25	.25	.25
ABC	.25	.04	.040	.017	−.019
BCD	.25	.040	.16	.017	−.025
CDE	.25	.017	.017	.02	−.004
DEF	.25	−.019	−.025	−.004	.10

Multiplying each covariance by the weight at the top of the column and at the left of the row and summing, we get:

$.25 \times .25 \times .04 = .0025$
$.25 \times .25 \times .040 = .0025$
$.25 \times .25 \times .017 = .0011$
$.25 \times .25 \times -.019 = -.0012$
$.25 \times .25 \times .040 = .0025$
$.25 \times .25 \times .160 = .0100$
$.25 \times .25 \times .017 = .0011$
$.25 \times .25 \times -.025 = .0016$
$.25 \times .25 \times .017 = .0011$
$.25 \times .25 \times .017 = .0011$
$.25 \times .25 \times .020 = .0013$
$.25 \times .25 \times -.004 = -.0003$
$.25 \times .25 \times -.019 = -.0012$
$.25 \times .25 \times -.025 = -.0016$
$.25 \times .25 \times -.004 = -.0003$
$.25 \times .25 \times .100 = .0063$

Total portfolio variance = .0223

24. Given the data on Exhibit - 1:

EXHIBIT - 1

Covariance

1 State of Nature	2 Return on Probability	3 Return on Investment A	4 Investment B	5 $R_N - E(R_A)$	6 $R_{Bi} - E(R_B)$	7 $P_i(R_{Ai} - E(R_A))][R_{Bi} - R_B)]$
Very poor	.1	.10	.18	−.11	.03	.1(−.11)(.03) = −.00033
Poor	.2	.16	.17	−.05	.02	.2 (−.05)(.02) = −.0002
Average	.4	.22	.15	.01	0	.4(.01)(0) = 0
Good	.2	.25	.13	.04	−.02	.2(.04)(−.02) = −.00016
Very good	.1	.30	.12	.09	−.03	.1(.09)(−.03) = −.00027
	1.0					−.00096
E(R)		.21	.15			
σ^2		.00288	.00034			
σ		.05366	.01844			

(i) Calculate the variance and standard deviation of a portfolio formed by the two investments whose returns are given in Exhibit-1. The portfolio was formed by equal investment in each security.

(ii) Calculate the variance and standard deviation of a portfolio formed by the two investments whose returns are given in Exhibit 1. However, this time weigh Investment A as .25 and Investment B as .75.

(iii) Interpret the results by weighing 0 to 1.

Ans.:

(i) Let Investment 1 be A and Investment 2 be B.

$w_1 = .5; w_2 = .5$

$\text{cov}(R_1, R_1) = \text{variance}(R_1) = .00288$

$\text{cov}(R_2, R_2) = \text{variance}(R_2) = .00034$

$\text{cov}(R_1, R_2) = -.00096$

$\sigma_p^2 = w_1 w_1 \text{cov}(R_1, R_1) + w_2 w_2 \text{cov}(R_2, R_2) + 2w_1 w_2 \text{cov}(R_1, R_2)$

$\quad = (.5)(.5)(.00288) + (.5)(.5)(.00034) + 2(.5(.5)(-.00096)$

$\quad = .00072 + .000085 - .00048$

$\quad = .000325$

$\sigma_p = \sqrt{.000325} = .01803$

(ii) $\sigma_p^2 = w_1 w_1 \text{cov}(R_1, R_1) + w_2 w_2 \text{cov}(R_2, R_2) + 2w_1 w_2 \text{cov}(R_1, R_2)$

$\quad = (.25)(.25)(.00288) + (.75)(.75)(.00034) + 2(.25)(.75)(-.00096)$

$\quad = .00018 + .000191 - .00036$

$\quad = .000011$

$\sigma_p = \sqrt{.000011} = .00332$

(iii) Exhibit 2 summarises the results if we weigh from 0 to 1. It shows the expected return and risk on five different portfolios obtained by changing the proportions of the portfolio invested in Securities A and B. Portfolio 1 was 100 per cent investment in Security A while Portfolio 5 was 100 per cent investment in Security B. The other three portfolios were obtained by investing in both securities. Notice that Portfolios 3 and 4 would be preferred to 5 because they offer more return and less risk. In fact, because the two investments have negative correlation between them, Portfolio 4 has very little risk. If the investments had been positively, but not perfectly, correlated, risk reduction through diversification would still have been possible, but it would not have been as dramatic. In the case of perfect correlation, diversification does not reduce portfolio risk.

EXHIBIT - 2

Return and Risk of a Two Security Portfolio

Portfolio Number	Per cent in Security A	Per cent in Security B	$E(R_p)$	σ_p
1	100	0	.21	.05366
2	75	25	.195	.03570
3	50	50	.18	.01803
4	25	75	.165	.00332
5	0	100	.15	.01844

QUESTIONS

1. When is the standard deviation of a portfolio identical to the weighted average standard deviation of the securities held?

2. Is it always possible to construct a portfolio having zero return variable from two component securities having return covariance of minus one?

3. If portfolio expected return is equal to the weighted expected returns of the component securities, why is not portfolio variance-of-return necessarily equal to the weighted sum of component variance?

4. Show how the correlation coefficient is calculated from covariance and standard deviation.

5. What will usually happen to the variance of a very large portfolio?

6. Can all risk be eliminated if a sufficiently large portfolio is held?

7. Explain the significance of the covariance in calculating portfolio risk.

8. In what circumstances will the variance of a very large portfolio diminish to zero?

9. Explain the significance of the covariance in calculating porfolio risk?

PROBLEMS

1. The equity shares of XYZ Company and ABC Company have expected returns of 15 per cent and 20 per cent respectively, while the standard deviations are 25 per cent and 40 per cent. The expected correlation coefficient between the two shares is .45. What is the expected value of return and standard deviation of a portfolio consisting of 60 per cent XYZ and 40 per cent ABC?

2. The expected return on Stock A is 10%; the expected return on Stock B is 8%. If you put 80% of your investment money in Stock A and 20% in Stock B, what is your expected return?

3. The expected return on Stock A is 12%; the expected return on Stock B is 16%. If you put 25% of your investment money in Stock A and 75% in Stock B, what is your expected return?

4. Security KDR has expected returns of 18% and a standard deviation of 24%; and security KHM has expected returns of 15% and a standard deviation of 23%. If they are perfectly negatively correlated, how much money would you put in each to have a zero risk portfolio? What would be the expected return of the portfolio?

5. Security X has an expected return of 0.25 and a standard deviation of returns of 0.20. Security Y has an expected return of 0.18 and a standard deviation of return of 0.18. Find the expected return of a portfolio with 30% invested in security X and 70% invested in security Y?

Ans.: 20.1%.

6. Two investments X and Y have the following returns for the specified events:

Event	Probability	Security X	Security Y
1	.5	4	0
2	.4	2	3
3	.1	0	3

Calculate the variance of σ_X^2 and σ_Y^2 and covariance C_{xy}.

7. Novex Chemicals is considering three possible capital projects for next year. Each project has a 1-year life, and project return depend on next year's state of the economy. The estimated rates of return are shown in the table:

State of the Economy	Probability of each State occurring	Rate of Return if State occurs		
		X	Y	Z
Recession	0.25	10%	9%	14%
Normal	0.50	14	13	12
Boom	0.25	16	188	10

(a) Find each project's expected rate of return, variance, standard deviation, and co-efficient of variation.

(b) Rank the alternatives on the basis of (i) expected return and (ii) risk. Which alternative would you choose?

Ans.:

X: 13.5%; 4.75; 2.2%; 0.16
Y: 13.25%; 10.19; 3.2%; 0.25
Z: 12.0%; 2.0; 1.4%; 0.12

8. You own four stocks. The expected return on each and the proportion of your money invested in each are given.

Stock	Proportion	Expected Return
A	.3	.06
B	.3	.08
C	.2	.04
D	.2	.04

What is the expected return on your portfolio?

9. Compute the standard deviation of portfolio of two stocks using the following data.

$w_1 = .7$ var $(R_1) = .03$ cov $(R_1, R_2) = -.02$
$w_2 = .3$ var $(R_2) = .06$

10. Your eccentric uncle died and left ₹ 1 crore for you. However, the will stipulated that the entire amount must be invested in equity shares. Specifically, 50 per cent of the funds must be invested in a single stock (one-stock portfolio) and the other 50 per cent must be invested in a 100- stock portfolio. You are very risk averse, so you want to minimise the riskiness of each 50 per cent of the investment.

(a) How would you choose your single-stock portfolio?

(b) How would you choose the stock in your 100-stock portfolio?

(c) Should you view the riskiness of your one-stock portfolio in isolation, or should you consider the fact that you really own 101 stocks?

11. Stocks ABC and XYZ have the following probability, distributions of expected future returns:

Probability	ABC	XYZ
0.1	-25%	-40%
0.2	5	0
0.4	15	16
0.2	30	40
0.1	45	66

(a) Calculate the expected rate of return for stock ABC.

(b) Calculate the standard deviation and coefficient of variation of expected returns for stock ABC (Those for stock XYZ are 27.0% and 1.59). Is it possible that most investors might regard stock XYZ as being less risky than stock ABC? Explain.

Ans.:

    (a) 17.0%

    (b) $\sigma ABC = 17.75\%$; $CV_{ABC} = 1.18$

12. Compute the standard deviation of a portfolio of two stocks using the following data.

    $w_1 = .6$ var $(R_1) = .06$ cov $(R_1, R_2) = .04$

    $w_2 = .4$ var $(R_2) = .05$

13. Compute the standard deviation of a portfolio of three stocks using the following data.

    $w_1 = .5$ var $(R_1) = .04$ cov $(R_1, R_2) = .04$

    $w_2 = .25$ var $(R_2) = .06$ cov $(R_1, R_3) = .03$

    $w_3 = .25$ var $(R_3) = .09$ cov $(R_2, R_3) = .07$

14. You are given the following set of data:

Historical Rate of Return

Year	NSE	Stock XYZ
1	-26.5%	-14.0%
2	37.2	23.0
3	23.8	17.5
4	-7.2	2.0
5	6.6	8.1
6	20.5	19.4
7	30.6	18.2

    (a) Determine the arithmatic average rates of return for stock XYZ and the NSE over the period given. Calculate the standard deviations of returns for both stock XYZ and NSE.

    (b) Assuming (i) that the situation during years 1 to 7 is expected to hold time in the future and (ii) that the stock XYZ is in equilibrium (that is, it plots on the security market line). What is the risk-free rate?

Ans.:

    (a) Arithmatic average rate of return of Stock XYZ = 10.6%

        Arithmatic average rates of return of NSE = 12.1%

        $\sigma_{XYZ} = 13.1\%$

        $\sigma_{NSE} = 22.6\%$

    (b) 8.6%

15. ABC portfolio had a following rate of return: -15%, 23%, 11 %, -3%, and 37% over the last five-year period. What were the arithmetic mean rate of return and the variance of the returns?

Ans.: Variance = 338.24

16. Your economic analysis has given you the following possible returns on two investments under three different scenarios:

Scenario	Possibility	Return ABC	Return XYZ
S1	0.30	0.10	0.08
S2	0.40	0.16	0.15
S3	0.30	0.12	0.20

(a) Calculate the expected return on each investment.

(b) Calculate the variance and standard deviation of ABC and XYZ.

(c) Compute the covariance and correlation coefficient between ABC and XYZ.

(e) If you create a portfolio 67% ABC and 33% XYZ, what will be the expected return, and standard deviation of the portfolio?

Ans.:

(a) $E(R_{ABC}) = .13; E(R_{XYZ}) = .144$

(b) $\sigma^2_{ABC} = .00066; \sigma_{ABC} = .0257$

$\sigma^2_{XYZ} = -00218; \sigma_{XYZ} = .0467$

(c) $C_{ABC.XYZ} = -00048;$ Correlation $(r_{ABC.XYZ}) = -40$

(e) $E(R_p) = .1346; \sigma_p = .0273$

17. Compute the standard deviation of a portfolio of three stocks using the following data.

$w_1 = .4$	var $(R_1) = .08$	cov $(R_1, R_2) = .05$
$w_2 = .3$	var $(R_2) = .05$	cov $(R_1, R_3) \neq .04$
$w_3 = .3$	var $(R_3) = .04$	cov $(R_2, R_3) = .03$

18. A research firm's economists predict five possible states of the economy and the probabilities of these states occurring. The firm's security analysts have predicted the rates of return of Stocks A and B for each state of the economy. Here are the predictions.

$w_1 = .4$	var $(R_1) = .08$	cov $(R_1, R_2) = .05$
$w_2 = .3$	var $(R_2) = .05$	cov $(R_1, R_3) = .04$
$w_3 = .3$	var $(R_3) = .04$	cov $(R_2, R_3) = .03$

State of the Economy	Probability	Return on Stock A	Return on Stock B
Very poor	.1	.00	.05
Poor	.2	.06	.06
Average	.4	.10	.08
Good	.2	.14	.09
Very good	.1	.20	.13

(a) Compute the expected return and variances of the two stocks.

(b) Compute the return of portfolios with 80%, 60%, 40%, and 20% invested in Stock A. In each case the remainder of the portfolio is invested in Stock B.

(c) Compute the correlation coefficient between Stock A and B.

(d) Compute the standard deviations of portfolios with 80%, 60%, 40%, and 20% invested in Stock A. In each case the remainder of the portfolio is invested in Stock B.

19. Security ABC has an expected return of 0.15 and a standard deviation of 0.2. Security XYZ has an expected return of 0.1 and a standard deviation of 0.15. Use the following information to solve:

(i) If the correlation between securities ABC and XYZ is 0.8, what is the expected return of a portfolio with half of the funds invested in each security?

(ii) What is the standard deviation of the portfolio in part (i)?

(iii) If 30% of the funds are put in security ABC, what is the expected return of the portfolio made up of ABC and XYZ?

(iv) What is the standard deviation of the portfolio in part (iii)?

(v) The correlation between security DBF and the market is 0.8. If the standard deviation of security DEF is 0.2 and the standard deviation of the market is 0.17, what is the beta of security DEF?

(*vi*) Solve part (*v*), except assume that the standard deviation of security DEF is 0.14. (*vii*) Solve part (*vi*), except assume that the standard deviation of security DEF is 0.17.

Ans.: (*i*) 125%; (*ii*) 16.61%; (*v*) 0.9412; (*vii*) 0.8

20. A research firm's economists predict five possible states of the economy and the probabilities of these states occurring. The firm's security analyst have predicted the rates of return of Stock A and B for each state of the economy. Here are the predictions.

State of the Economy	Probability	Return on Stock A	Return on Stock B
Very Poor	.1	−.10	.06
Poor	.2	.00	.07
Average	.3	.10	.08
Good	.3	.20	.10
Very good	.1	.30	.12

(*a*) Compute the expected return and variance of the two stocks.

(*b*) Compute the return of portfolios with 80%, 60%, 40%, and 20% invested in Stock A. In each case the remainder of the portfolio is invested in Stock B.

(*c*) Compute the correlation coefficient between Stock A and B.

(*d*) Compute the standard deviations of portfolios with 80%, 60%, 40%, and 20% invested in Stock A. In each case the remainder of the portfolio is invested in Stock B.

21. A reputable firm. Students Fast Food, is considering expanding its food-franchising operation by opening another store to sell its smash hit food products. Already operating 150 stores nationwide, the firm knows that the beta of these previous projects is 1.2. With risk-free interest rates at 12%, and assuming the standard market risk premium of 8.9%, what required rate of return should be applied to the new store project?

22. If Students Fast Food goes ahead with the new store, it expects sales of ₹ 1 crore per year, with total costs of ₹ 0.8 crore per year, all stated on after-tax basis. The project will last 20 years. Investment for the new store should be ₹ 0.08 crore. Using the information from problem (21), should they open the new store?

Ans.: ₹ 6,70,460.

23. K.H. Gupta earns returns of 8%, 11 % and 15 % over the last three years. What is the arithmatic mean for these annual returns over the three-year period?

Ans.: 11.33%

24. The proportion of assets X, Y and Z in a portfolio are 25%, 25% and 50%, respectively. The correlation is 0.5 for the three possible pairs of securities. The variance are equal to 100 for all three securities. Find the standard deviation of this portfolio.

Ans.: $\sigma = 8.29\%$

25. You are considering three stocks with the following expected dividend yields and capital gains:

	Dividend Yield	Capital Gain
A	14%	0%
B	8	6
C	0	14

(*a*) What is the expected return on each stock?

(*b*) How may transactions costs and capital gains taxes affect your choices among the three securities?

Ans.: 14 per cent in all three cases.

26. Suppose you are considering the following two investment opportunities:

	Probability	Return
Security ABC		
Does well	0.10	0.30
Does average	0.80	0.15
Does poorly	0.10	0.0
Security XYZ		
Does well	0.30	0.25
Does average	0.40	0.15
Does poorly	0.30	0.05

(a) What is the range of security ABC and of security XYZ?
(b) What is the expected return on security ABC and on security XYZ?
(c) What is the standard deviation of returns on security ABC and security XYZ?
(e) Would you select ABC or XYZ if you were using range as a measure of risk? If you were using standard deviation as a measure of risk?
(e) Why is the range a poor measure of risk?

Ans.

(a) Range$_{ABC}$ = 30%; Range$_{XYZ}$ = 20%
(b) (R_{ABC}) = .15; $E(R_{XYZ})$ = .15
(c) σ_{ABC} = .0671; σ_{XYZ} = .0775

27. A portfolio consists of assets with the following expected returns:

	Expected Return	Weight in Portfolio
Real estate	16%	20%
Low-quality bonds	15	10
XYZ stock	12	30
Savings account	5	40

(a) What is the expected return on the portfolio?
(b) What will be the expected return if the individual reduces the holdings of the XYZ stock to 15 per cent and puts the funds into real estate investments?

Ans.:

(a) 10.3%

28. Your are given the following information concerning two stocks:

	A	B
Expected return	10%	14%
Standard deviation of the expected return	± 3.0	± 5.0
Correlation coefficient of the returns	-.1	

(a) What is the expected return on a portfolio consisting of 40 per cent in stock A and 60 per cent in stock B?
(b) What is the standard deviation of this portfolio?
(c) Discuss the risk and return associated with investing (a) all of your funds in stock A, (b) all of your funds in stock B, and (c) 40 per cent in A and 60 per cent in B.

Ans.:

(a) 12.4 per cent
(b) Standard deviation = 3.12

29. Consider a portfolio of four assets: A, B, C, D. The weights of the assets in a portfolio are 0.2, 0.3, 0.3 and 0.2, respectively. The variance of the assets are 0.01, 0.02, 0.04 and 0.08, respectively. The covariance matrix is shown below. Calculate the variance of the portfolio.

	A	B	C
B	-0.01		
C	0.00	0.00	
D	0.025	0.01	0.00

Ans.: $\sigma_P^2 = .011$

30. You are given the following information:

Expected return on stock A	12%
Expected return on stock B	20%
Standard deviation of returns:	
Stock A	+ 1.0
Stock B	+ 6.0
Correlation coefficient of the returns on stocks A and B	+ .2

(a) What are the expected returns and standard deviations of a portfolio consisting of:
   (1) 100 per cent in stock A?
   (2) 100 per cent in stock B?
   (3) 50 per cent in each stock?
   (4) 25 per cent in stock A and 75 per cent in Stock B?
   (5) 75 per cent in stock A and 25 per cent in Stock B?

(b) Compare the above returns and the risk associated with each portfolio.
    Redo the calculations assuming that the correlation coefficient of the returns on the two stocks is - 0.6. What is the impact of this difference in the correlation coefficient?

Ans.:
   (a) 50% A/50% B: Return = 16%; Standard Deviation = 3.14
   (c) 25% A/75% B: Return = 18%; Standard Deviation = 4.36

31. A stock has a Beta$_i$ of 1 5, and the risk-free rate is 10%. What is the expected return on the stock in the following cases:
   (a) The expected return on the market is 14%.
   (b) The expected return on the market is 16%.
   (c) The expected return on the market is 18%.

Ans.: (a) = .16; (b) = .19; (c) = .22.

32. Stocks ABC and XYZ have the following historical dividend and price data:

Year	Stock ABC		Stock XYZ	
	Dividend	Year-end price	Dividend	Year-end price
2005	—	₹ 22.50	—	₹ 43.75
2006	₹ 2.00	16.00	₹ 3.40	35.50
2007	2.20	17.00	3.65	38.75
2008	2.40	20.25	3.90	51.75
2009	2.60	17.25	4.05	44.50
2010	2.95	18.75	4.25	45.25

(a) Calculate the realised rate of return (or holding period return) for each stock in each year. Then assume that someone had held a portfolio consisting of 50% of ABC and 50% of XYZ (the portfolio was rebalanced at the end of each year). What would the realised rate of return on the portfolio have been in each year from 2006 through 2010? What would the average returns have been for each stock and for the portfolio?

(b) Calculate the standard deviation of returns for each stock and the portfolio.

(c) Add stock RTS to the portfolio; RTS has the following historical dividend and price data:

Stock RTS

Year	Dividend	Year-end price
2005	—	₹ 23.40
2006	₹ 1.85	23.90
2007	1.95	31.50
2008	2.05	27.20
2009	2.15	32.25
2010	2.25	26.00

Assume that the portfolio contains 33.33% of ABC, 33.33% of XYZ and 33.33% of RTS. How does this affect the portfolio return and standard deviation?

(e) Would you rather have a portfolio consisting of one- third of each stock or a portfolio with 50% ABC and 50% XYZ? Explain.

Ans.:

(a) Average Return ABC   = 11.41%
     Average Return XYZ   = 11.40%
     Average Return for portfolio of ABC and XYZ   = 11.41%

(b) $\sigma_{ABC} = 21.9\%$
     σ_{XYZ} $= 21.9\%$
     $\sigma_{PABC.XYZ}$ $= 21.9\%$

33. Consider an equally weighted portfolio of 100 assets, each of which has variance equal to 0.01. Also assume that the covariance between every pair of assets is the same, 0.005. What is the variance of the portfolio? What are the portfolio variances if the number of assets is increased to 1,000 and then to 10,000?

34. An investor combines two risky securities in equal proportions. If both securities have the same variance, and the resulting portfolio has a variance equal to one-fourth the variance of each security, what is the correlation between the two?

Ans.: $r = -0.5$

35. An investor combines securities X and Y and the resulting portfolio is risk-free. The variance of security Y is four times larger than the variance of security X. Also, the expected return on X and Y are 10% and 18%, respectively. Find the expected return on the portfolio.

Ans.: 12.67%

36. Radhika held a portfolio with three stocks. She invested 20% of her funds in stock X, 45% in stock Y and 35% in stock Z. The respective rates of return were 13%, -5%, and 9%. What was the rate of return for the entire portfolio?

37. Over three years, security STY had returns of 10%, 14%, and -3%. For the same three years, security YST had returns of 12%, 10% and 5%. What are the variance and standard deviation of returns for these two securities? What is the covariance of returns between them? What is the correlation of returns?

Ans.:   Variance (STY)   = 52.67;
                  Variance (YST)   =   8.67;
                  Covariance (STY, YST)   = 18.67

38. ROMPY Cement had developed the following data regarding the rates of return available on a potential project and the market:

State of the Economy	Probability of each state occurring	Rate of Return if State occurs	
		Market	Project
Deep Recession	0.05	-20%	-30%
Mild Recession	0.25	10	5
Normal	0.35	15	20
Mild boom	0.20	20	25
Strong boom	0.15	25	30

Further, ROMPY's financial analysts estimate the risk- free rate at 8 per cent.
(a) What are the expected rates of return on the market and the project?
(b) What are the market's beta and the project's beta?
(c) Should the project be accepted?

Ans.:

(a) 14.5%; 16.25%
(b) 1.0; 1.43
(c) 17.3%

39. An investor undertakes a series of one-year investments starting with ₹ 70,000. After the first year, the investment is worth ₹ 78,400; after two years, ₹ 87,810; after three years, ₹ 98,340; and after four years, ₹ 11,015. Calculate the annual arithmatic mean rate of return.

Ans.: 12%.

40. Securities ABC and XYZ have the following historical dividend and price data:

Year	Year Stock ABC		Stock XYZ	
	Dividend	Year-end price	Dividend	Year-end price
2004	—	₹ 12.25	—	₹ 22.00
2005	₹1.00	9.75	₹ 2.40	18.50
2006	1.05	11.00	2.60	19.50
2007	1.15	13.75	2.85	25.25
2008	1.30	13.25	3.05	22.50
2009	1.50	15.05	3.25	24.00

(a) Calculate the realised rate of return (or holding period return) for each security in each year. Then assume that someone had held a portfolio consisting of 50 per cent of ABC and 50 per cent of XYZ. (The portfolio is rebalanced every year so as to maintain these percentages). What would the realised rate of return on the portfolio have been in each year from 2006 through 2010? What would the average returns have been for each security and for the portfolio?
(b) Now calculate the standard deviation of returns for each security and for the portfolio.
(c) On the basis of the extent to which the portfolio has a lower risk than the securities held individually, would you guess that the correlation coefficient between returns on the two securities is closer to 0.9 or to - 0.9?
(e) If you added more stocks at random to the portfolio, what is the most accurate statement of what would happen to σ_p? (i) σ_p would remain constant. (ii) σ_p would decline to somewhere in the vicinity of 15 per cent. (iii) σ_p would decline to zero if enough securities were included.

REFERENCES

1. Arnott, Robert D., "Cluster Analysis and Stock Price Comovement," *Financial Analysts Journal*, 36 (November-December 1980), 56-62.

2. Cohn, R.A., W.G. Lewellen, R.C. Lease, and G.G. Schlaibaum. "Individual Investor Risk Aversion and Investment Portfolio Composition." *The Journal of Finance*, May 1975, p. 605.

3. Estep, Tony, N. Hanson, and Cal Johnson, "Sources of Value and Risk in Common Stocks," *Journal of Portfolio Management*, Summer 1983, pp. 5-13.

4. Evans. John L., "An Examination of the Principle of Diversification." *Journal of Business Finance and Accounting*. Summer 1975, pp. 243 - 255.

5. Evans, J., and S. H. Archer, "Diversification and the Reduction of Dispersion: An empirical Analysis." *Journal of Finance*, December 1968, pp. 761-767.

6. Farrell, J.L., Jr., "Analyzing Covariation of Returns to Determine Homogeneous Stock Groupings," *Journal of Business*, 47 (April 1974), 186-207

7. Fogler, H. Russell, K. John, and J. Tipton, "Three Factors, Interest Rates Differentials and Stock Groups," *Journal of Finance*, 36 (May 1981), 323-35.

8. Frost, Peter A., and James E. Savarino. "Portfolio Size and Estimation Risk." *Journal of Portfolio Management*, Fall 1985, 60-64.

9. Gibbons, M., S. Ross, and J. Shanken: "Test of the Efficiency of a Given Portfolio," *Econometric* 57, 1989, pp. 1121-1152.

10. Goldsmith, David. "Transactions Costs and the Theory of Portfolio Selection." *The Journal of Finance*, September 1976, p. 1127.

11. Green, R., and B. Hollifield: "When Will Mean-Variance Efficient Portfolios Be Well Diversified? *Journal of Finance* 47, 1992, 1785-1809.

12. Harlow, W.V.: "Asset Allocation in a Downside-Risk Framework," *Financial Analysts Jo* September-October 1991, pp. 28-40.

13. Leibowitz, Martin: "Imputing Expected Security Returns from Portfolio Composition." *Journal of Financial and Quantitative Analysis*, June 1974, p. 463.

14. Lintner, J. "Security Prices, Risk and Maximal Gains from Diversification." *Journal of Finance*, December 1965, 587-615. Elton, Edwin J., and Martin J. Gruber. "Risk Reduction and Portfolio Size: An Analytical Solution." *Journal of Business*, October 1977, 415-437.

15. Maginn, John L., and Donald L. Tuttle, eds. *Managing Investment Portfolios: A Dynamic Process*. 2d ed. Sponsored by The Institute of Chartered Financial Analysts. Boston: Warren, Gorham and Lamont, 1990.

16. Phillips, Herbert E., and J.P. Segal, "Data: A Mixed Blessing in Portfolio Selection?" *Financial Management*, 4 (Autumn 1975), 50-53.

17. Pogue, Gerald A., "An Intertemporal Model for Investment Management," *Journal of Bank Research* 1 (Spring 1970): 17-33.

18. Stambaugh, R.: "On the Exclusion of Assets from Tests of the Two-Parameter Model," *Journal of Financial Economics*, November 1982, pp. 237-268.

19. Whitmore, G.A. "Diversification and the Reduction of Dispersion." *Journal of Financial and Quantitative Analysis*, May 1970, 263-264.

24

Portfolio Investment Process

INTRODUCTION

A major thesis of investment is the need to consider individual investments as components of an overall investment plan. Without limiting the range of instruments covered, it is convenient to call individual investments *securities* and the totality the *portfolio*. Since it is rarely desirable to invest the entire funds of an individual or an institution in a single security, it is essential that every security be viewed in a portfolio context. This implies, for example, that a security's *total* risk is not of prime importance, only its *contribution* to the total risk of a portfolio.

The basic problem of portfolio management is to establish an investment goal or objective and then decide how best to reach that goal with the securities available. This has been stated as an attempt by the investor to obtain the maximum return with minimum risk. In order to do a proper job of portfolio management, the investor must be aware of the *investment* process.

The process of portfolio management involves a logical set of steps common to any decision: *plan, implement,* and *monitor.* Yet applying this process to actual portfolios can be complex, and opinions are divided on how best to do so. Large gaps exist in current investment theory, and empirical tests often yield contradictory results. Certain basic principles should be applied to all portfolio decisions:

BASIC PRINCIPLES

1. It is the portfolio that matters

Individual securities are important only to the extent that they affect the aggregate portfolio. For example, a security's risk should not be based on the uncertainty of a single security's return but, instead, on its contribution to the uncertainty of the total portfolio's return. In addition, assets such as a person's career or home should be considered together with the security portfolio. In short, all decisions should focus on the impact the decision will have on the aggregate portfolio of all assets held.

2. Larger expected portfolio returns come only with larger portfolio risk

The most important portfolio decision is the amount of risk which is acceptable, which is determined by the asset allocation within the security portfolio. This is not an easy decision, since it requires that we have some idea of the risks and expected returns available on many different classes of assets. Nonetheless, the risk/return level of the aggregate portfolio should be the first decision any investor makes.

3. The risk associated with a security type depends on when the investment will be liquidated

A person who plans to sell in one year will find equity returns to be more risky than a person who plans to sell in 10 years. Alternatively, the person who plans to sell in 10 years will find one year maturity bonds to be more risky than the person who plans to sell in one year. Risk is reduced by selecting securities with a payoff close to when the portfolio is to be liquidated.

4. Diversification works

Diversification across various securities will reduce a portfolio's risk. If such broad diversification results in an expected portfolio return or risk level which is lower (or higher) than desired, then borrowing (or lending) can be used to achieve the desired level.

5. Each portfolio should be tailored to the particular needs of its owner

People have varying tax rates, knowledge, transaction costs, etc. Individuals who are in a high marginal tax bracket should stress portfolio strategies which increase after-tax returns. Individuals who lack strong knowledge of investment alternatives should hire professionals to provide needed counseling. Large pension portfolios should pursue strategies which will reduce brokerage fees associated with moving capital between equity and non-equity managers (for example, by using options on futures). In short, portfolio strategy should be molded to the unique needs and characteristics of the portfolio's owner.

6. Competition for abnormal returns is extensive

A large number of people are continuously using a large variety of techniques in an attempt to obtain abnormal returns — returns larger than should be expected given a security's risk. Securities which art believed to be undervalued are bought until the price rises to a proper level, and securities which are believed to be overvalued are sold until the price falls to a proper level. If the actions of these speculators are truly effective, security prices will adjust instantaneously to new information — the efficient market theory (EMT) will be correct.

The extent to which EMT is correct as well as the extent to which one has unique information determiners whether a passive "investment" strategy or an active "speculative" strategy should be used.

ASPECTS OF THE PORTFOLIO INVESTMENT PROCESS

The process used to manage a security portfolio is conceptually the same as that used in any managerial decision. One should (1) plan; (2) implement the plan; and (3) monitor the results. This portfolio investment process is displayed schematically in Exhibit 1. Each aspect of the process is discussed in some detail below.

A. PLANNING

Planning is the most important element of proper portfolio investment process. In the planning stage, a careful review should be conducted of the investor's financial situation and current capital market conditions. Taken together, these will suggest a set of investment and speculative policies to be followed. These policies should then be formally documented in a written *statement of investment policy* (SIP). The statement of investment policies will document: (1) the portfolio objective, (2) strategies which may (or may not) be used, and (3) various other investment and speculative constraints. An output of proper planning will be a clearly defined *strategic asset allocation* (SAA). The strategic asset allocation represents the optimal combination of various asset classes in an efficient market. The strategic asset allocation is an indexed portfolio which would actually be held if a passive, pure-investment strategy is to be employed. The strategic

EXHIBIT 1

The Portfolio Investment Process

A. Planning
 1. Investor Conditions
 2. Market Conditions
 3. Investment/Speculative Policies
 4. Statement of Investment Policy
 5. Strategic Asset Allocation

B. Implementation
 1. Rebalance Strategic Asset Allocation
 2. Tactical Asset Allocation
 3. Security Selection

C. Monitoring
 1. Evaluate Statement of Investment Policy
 2. Evaluate Investment Performance

asset allocation portfolio might never actually be held, since adjustments in line with various speculative strategies may be made, but it represents the basic pure "investment" portfolio against which actual portfolio returns can be compared in order to determine whether speculative strategies are actually "adding value".

Aspects of the planning stage are shown in Exhibit 2. Investor and capital market conditions are blended in order to determine a set of investment and speculative policies as well as a long-run strategic asset allocation. These are formally expressed in the statement of investment policy.

Investor Conditions

The first question which must be answered is this - "What is the purpose of the security portfolio?" Understanding the purpose for trading in financial securities will help to: (1) define the expected portfolio liquidation date, (2) aid in determining an acceptable level of risk, and (3) indicate whether future consumption (liability needs) are to be paid in nominal or real money, etc. For example, a 60 year old woman with small to moderate savings probably (1) has a short investment horizon, (2) can accept little investment risk, and (3) needs protection against short-term inflation. In contrast, a young couple investing for retirement in 30 years have (1) a very long investment horizon, (2) an ability to accept moderate to large investment risk because they can diversify over time, and (3) a need for protection against long-term inflation. This suggests that the 60 year old woman should invest solely in low-default- risk money market securities. The young couple could invest in many other asset classes for diversification and accept greater investment risks. In short, knowing the eventual purpose of the portfolio investment makes it possible to begin sketching out appropriate investment/speculative policies.

Financial Situation: Complete financial status of the investor must be understood. Portfolio investment and speculation decisions are too often based solely on potential security portfolio payoffs with no attention given to interactions between the security portfolio and other economic assets and liabilities of the individual or investment organisation. This is the wrong approach. The total economic position of the individual must be examined. The unique short-term risks inherent in major assets and liabilities must be understood. Although this is difficult to quantify, the problem is important and deserves careful thought.

Knowledge: The investor's knowledge of various securities also has an important impact on the types of security classes which should be held and the speculative strategies employed. The investor must understand that yearly equity returns are quite variable, short-term returns on bonds are sensitive to the bonds' duration, international investment entails considerable exchange rate risk, etc. If the investor does not truly understand the nature and extent of a security's short and long-term risk, the security should not be held.

EXHIBIT-2

Portfolio Planning Stage

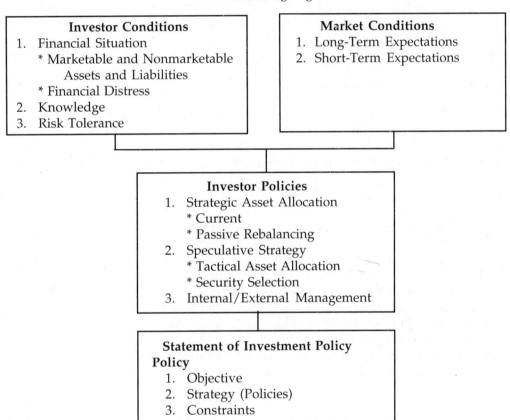

Risk Tolrence: Finally, the tolerance which the investor has for investment risk must be considered. This is clearly a difficult aspect of developing a proper investment strategy. Investment theories are largely based on a single future date at which the portfolio will be liquidated; theory speaks to the standard deviation of the security portfolio's value at that date. But this neglects a number of very important practical investment considerations. These include: i) The relationship between investment horizon date payoffs from the marketable security portfolio and payoffs from other assets or liabilities of the investor (both marketable and non-marketable). Two examples of this were presented above. ii) The investor's reaction to portfolio results during periods of time which are shorter than the investor's true investment horizon. For example, even though an investor is investing for retirement and should be relatively unconcerned about yearly portfolio returns, a year or two with particularly good or bad returns might cause him to make short-term decisions which are not in his best long-term interest — for example, selling stock after it has fallen in value to buy gold at high prices. Long-term investors must be able to bear up to the despair or euphoria that temporary price swings can cause.

Market Conditions

An assessment of potential future returns on various classes or marketable securities must also be made. In this context, two points need to be made. First, short-term (say, one year) expectations might differ considerably from longer-term expectations. If so, the portfolio's tactical asset allocation (TAC) will differ from the long-term strategic asset allocation. Both short and long-term market forecasts must be made if one has any intent of engaging in tactical asset allocation. The forecasts might turn out to be identical. But if tactical asset allocation is allowed, both forecasts should be explicitly made. Second, forecasts should be stated in real money terms if future consumption and liabilities are tied to inflation. If consumption and liabilities are unaffected by inflation, then nominal return forecasts are appropriate.

Investor Policies

The most important investment decision which the owner of a portfolio must make is the portfolio's asset allocation. Asset allocation refers to the percentage invested in various security classes. Security classes are simply the type of securities : (1) Money market investment; (2) Fixed-income obligations; (3) Equity shares; (4) Real estate investment; and (5) International securities.

Strategic Asset Allocation: Strategic asset allocation represents the asset allocation which would be optimal for the investor if all security prices trade at their long-term equilibrium values — that is, if the markets are efficiently priced.

Deciding what the investor's current strategic asset allocation can be a difficult task. In theory, it requires predictions of future return distributions for various security classes, es-timates of the major economic risks faced by the investor, and estimates of the extent to which all of these factors are intercorrelated. In practice, however, simple common sense is often the best guide. If the economic situation of the investor is carefully considered together with reasonable estimates of capital market conditions, then common sense estimates of the current strategic asset allocation can be made.

Few investment strategies are static. They require changes as time passes, as the investor's wealth changes, as security prices change, as the investor's knowledge expands, etc. Thus, the optimal strategic asset allocation will also change. Even if the investor continues to believe that all security prices are fair, the strategic asset allocation will probably require periodic rebalancing. Such changes are passive changes to the portfolio. These are not active changes made in the hopes of earning excess risk-adjusted returns from potential security price disequilibriums. Instead, they represent logical shifts in the investor's strategic asset allocation in response to changes in the investor's condition or (fairly priced) market conditions.

Conceptually, we could think of investors as continuously revising their strategic asset allocation. Thus, there would be no need to plan for a passive rebalancing strategy. At each moment in time, investors would evaluate their personal investment needs and market expectations to develop a current strategic asset allocation. As a practical matter, however, the costs of doing this are too large. For example, mutual funds spend large sums of money and months of efforts to develop a strategic asset allocation. They simply cannot afford to engage in a continuous analysis of what their strategic asset allocation should be. Individual investors who have much less capital and knowledge face even larger problems. As a result it makes sense that part of the strategic asset allocation decision should be a decision about how the strategic asset allocation is to be changed as certain important economic variables change.

Thus, the strategic asset allocation decision should actually contain two elements: (1) definition of a current strategic asset allocation, and (2) specification of a rebalancing strategy which passively adjusts the current strategic asset allocation to changes in the investor's situation and security market conditions.

Three passive rebalancing decisions which the investor should make deal with how the strategic asset allocation decision should change as time passes. The other two passive rebalancing decisions are associated with shorter time spans. They deal with how the strategic asset allocation might be affected by (1) changes in the investor's wealth level and (2) changes in the level of securities price.

Why should there be shift in optimal investment risk as time passes? The reason that the investor's acceptable risk exposure and the investment horizon of the portfolio are closely tied is simple to understand-time diversification. The longer one has before a portion of the portfolio must be liquidated, the greater the ability for good return years to offset bad return years.

The next type of passive rebalancing strategy which should be planned for relates to changes in the investor's net worth (wealth). Given the potential variability of security returns over relatively short time spans, a predetermined passive rebalancing strategy would be wise. However, this strategic rebalancing decision is clearly difficult to make. But, given the potential volatility of equity and debt markets over a two- to-three year period, it is a matter which deserves to be explicitly considered.

The last type of rebalancing strategy focuses not on time or on the investor's net worth, but on the level of prices of a given asset class. This is based on the need for portfolio insurance or the ability to provide it. But decisions such as these are, indeed, difficult to make. In many cases precisely defined portfolio adjustments may not be possible. Yet they must be thought about — unless the investor intends to stumble blindly into the future.

Speculation Strategy: After the investor has determined a current strategic asset allocation and decided how the allocation would be passively rebalanced as time passes, net worth changes, or share prices vary, a decision must be made as to the types and amounts of security speculation which will be allowed. Speculative strategies can be classified as either tactical asset allocation (timing) decisions or security selection decisions.

Internal-External Management: If no speculative strategies are to be used, the management of the portfolio is relatively easy. One simply purchases a number of index portfolios which emulate the desired strategic asset allocation. Small investors can do this by purchasing mutual funds which are indexed to a stock Index such as the National index. If speculative traders are to be allowed, however, one must decide whether the investor will make such decisions or employ an outside professional. Individuals with little investible capital can obtain outside management skills by purchasing shares of actively managed mutual funds. Individuals and organisations with large capital can also employ investment management firms to make their speculative trading decisions. If one wishes to engage in speculative strategies through timing and security selection, outside professional managers are more likely to provide better performance net of all costs than investors could by developing their own opinions.

The Statement of Investment Policy

The portfolio objective, constraints and strategy should always be stated explicitly in a written document. This is not a nicety which only large portfolios need - it is a necessity for all portfolios. This statement of investment policy (or whatever one elects to call it) can be amended periodically as economic conditions or the portfolio owner's needs change. In face, the statement of policy should probably include the requirement that the statement itself be reviewed at least every two to three years. There are at least four advantages to having a written statement of policy: 1. Requiring that a written document be prepared forces the investor to make difficult decisions which might otherwise be set aside. 2. A well-thought-out statement of investment policies can add discipline and stability to the long-run management of the portfolio, reducing whipsaw reactions to temporary price swings. By acting as documentation and education for why particular decisions were made, it should reduce capricious changes in investment strategies. 3. A well-drafted statement of investment policies defines the investor's strategic asset allocation and passive rebalancing strategies. 4. Future performance evaluation is simply impossible without a clear benchmark against which a comparison can be made. The strategic asset allocation serves as the benchmark.

In a sense, the statement of investment policy is the constitution under which the investor's assets are to be managed. As such, it should be prepared only after the investor has fully investigated all major aspects of managing an investment portfolio.

Strategy Policies: Finally, the statement of policy should discuss the forms of active speculation which will be allowed. In the broadest sense, speculative transactions can be related to either *timing* or *selection.*

In *timing-related speculation,* a given asset class is over- or underweighted in comparison to the proportion called for in the baseline investment portfolio. For example, if the baseline portfolio calls for a 40/60 bond/equity mix, and the portfolio owner elects to temporarily use a 50/50 mix in the belief that equities are currently overvalued relative to bonds, this is a timing decision. To date, there is little evidence that professional investment advisers are able to consistently earn abnormal profits from speculative timing decisions. In addition, considerable care must be given to adjustments to the portfolio's asset allocation between bonds, equities etc., since it is this allocation which has the greatest impact on the portfolio's risk position. Both factors cause many investors to restrict the amount of timing which will be allowed in the portfolio.

In *selection-related speculation,* an individual security is over or underweighted in comparison to the proportion called for in the baseline investment portfolio. For example, if the baseline equity portfolio is similar to the National Index and XYZ Company represents 3% of the total value of the National Index, then a decision to place 10% of all equity into XYZ Company is a selection decision to overweight XYZ Company. Whether speculative selection decisions can consistently lead to abnormal profits is unclear. Efficient market theory would suggest not, but empirical tests have failed to provide conclusive evidence that this is true. Based on one's belief in the usefulness of timing and selection speculation, the statement of policy should identify the extent. to which they may be used.

B. IMPLEMENTATION

In the implementation stage, three decisions need to be made, if the percentage holdings of various asset classes are currently different from the desired holdings as stated in the SIP, "the portfolio should be rebalanced to the desired SAA. If a pure-investment strategy is required by the statement of investment policy, this is the only thing which is done in the implementation stage. However, many portfolio owners engage in speculative transactions in the belief that such transactions will generate excess risk-adjusted returns. Such speculative transactions are usually classified as "timing" or "selection" decisions. Timing decisions over or under weight various asset classes, industries, or economic sectors from the strategic asset allocation. Such timing decisions have come to be known as tactical asset allocation decisions. Selection decisions deal with securities within a given asset class, industry group, or economic sector and attempt to determine which securities should be over or under-weighted.

EXHIBIT-3

Portfolio Implementation Stage

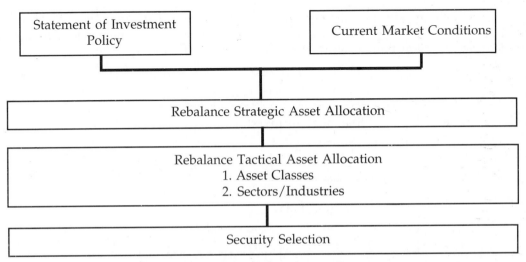

Implementation stage is shown schematically in Exhibit 3. One begins by periodically adjusting the asset mix to the desired mix called for in the strategic asset allocation. Next, any tactical asset allocation and security selection decisions are made.

Tactical Asset Allocation

If one believes that the price levels of certain asset classes, industries, or economic sectors are temporarily too high or too low, actual portfolio holdings should depart from the asset mix called for in the strategic asset allocation. Such a *timing* decision is referred to as tactical asset allocation. As noted, TAA decisions could be made across aggregate asset classes, industry classifications (steel, food), or various broad economic sectors (basic manufacturing, interest- sensitive, consumer durables).

Traditionally, most tactical asset allocation has involved timing across aggregate asset classes. For example, if equity prices are believed to be too high, one would reduce the portfolio's equity allocation and increase the allocation to, say, risk-free securities. If one is indeed successful at tactical asset allocation, the abnormal returns which would be earned are certainly enticing.

Security Selection

The second type of active speculation involves the selection of securities within a given asset class, industry, or economic sector. The strategic asset allocation policy would call for broad diversification through an indexed holding of virtually all securities in the asset class. For example, if the total market value of XYZ Corporation share currently represents 1% of all issued equity capital, then 1% of the investor's portfolio allocated to equity would be held in XYZ Corporation shares. The only reason to overweight or underweight particular securities in the strategic asset allocation would be to offset risks the investor faces in other assets and liabilities outside the marketable security portfolio. Security selection, however, actively overweights and underweights holding of particular securities in the belief that they are temporarily mispriced.

C. PORTFOLIO MONITORING

The last stage in the portfolio investment process consists of monitoring portfolio returns in order to determine which speculative decisions seem to be adding value to the portfolio and to ascertain that the portfolio's objective and constraints are being met and have not changed.

The portfolio monitoring stage is shown schematically in Exhibit-4. There are three aspects to this monitoring. First, the actual portfolio held should be examined to ascertain that it is in compliance with the statement of investment policy and to

EXHIBIT-4

Portfolio Monitoring Stage

Statement of Investment Policy
1. Compliance
2. Periodic Revision

Portfolio Performance
1. Aggregate Portfolio
2. Asset Classes and Managers
3. Speculative Strategy Returns

Actions Required Control
1. Statement of Investment Policy
2. Manager Selection

determine whether any passive rebalancing of the asset mix is required. Second, investment performance should be reviewed. This should consist of a review of returns on (1) the aggregate portfolio, (2) each asset class and investment manager, and (3) the returns from any speculative strategies employed. Finally, adjustments to the statement of investment policies and investment managers should be made if necessary.

OBJECTIVES OF PORTFOLIO MANAGEMENT

Setting objectives is a critical and sometimes difficult part of the process of portfolio management. Problems in setting objectives include confusion over the meaning of terms, inability of the client to make a meaningful decision, and different attitudes toward relative riskiness. Some want income, some capital gains, and some a combination of both. In spite of these varia-tions, several objectives should be considered as basic to a well-executed investment programme. These guiding principles establish the indifference curve of risk versus return for the investor.

1. Security of Principal

The first consideration in establishing investment objec-tives is the security of principal—

the preservation of the value of the investment account for the sake of future income and growth. There are two kinds of people to whom this principle should be especially emphasized. One is the investor with a small fund who says, "I'm interested in quick growth, and it really doesn't make any differ-ence if I lose my entire investment, because I don't have too much to lose." This think-ing can lead to unwise decisions and the acceptance of unnecessary risk, with the inevitable result that the investor may lose all the capital.

The other investor is the wealthy person with the large investment account. This person's position is the same as the small investor's, but for a different reason. This investor rationalizes, "I'm wealthy; therefore I can afford to lose some of my prin-cipal." This thinking may also lead to undue risk, resulting in a large capital loss that would be difficult to replace. Perhaps the wealthy person can assume more risk with a portion of the investment fund, but this thought process should not govern the entire fund.

Protection of principal should be the *dominant force* in portfolio management. Without capital, investment cannot take place, and capital is difficult to raise. It seems unwise to save for years to build an investment fund and then lose it in one careless, risky venture. However, security, of principal means more than just maintaining the original fund. It means the prelection of the purchasing power of the fund. The purchasing-power risk is a very real risk assumed by investors, because of inflation. The necessary steps must be taken to maintain the purchasing power of the fund by buying equity are expected to increase in value if the purchasing power of currency Though investment in equity shares is not a perfect hedge against inflation, but they can be better at the task than fixed-income securities such as bonds or preferre shares.

2. Stability of Income

In establishing an investment fund, an investor should attempt to achieve stability of income as a practical goal. Income received in the form of dividends and interest is somewhat more valuable than a promise of future dividends and interest. Stability of revenues allows the investor to plan more accurately and logically, whether the goal is reinvestment or consumption. Stability of revenue is also more valuable than sporadic, unstable, or uncertain income.

Stability of income is obviously most important for the income investor, but it is equally important for the growth investor. Reinvested income is one way to achieve capital growth.

3. Capital Growth

As a general rule, growth of capital is a desirable objective of portfolio management. This does not mean that every investor must invest in growth stocks; this would be inconsistent with many investors' needs. A fund can be built up from reinvested income as well as through the purchase of growth shares, as was illustrated above. A large fund does provide more income for the investor than a small fund. Many investors have increased the capital value of their funds through reinvested dividends and interest income. Capital growth is necessary to improve the long-range security of the investor, to maintain purchasing power, and to offer flexibility of management. Unfortunately, the search for capital growth by increase in share price is risky.

4. Marketability

Another desirable objective of a sound investment portfolio is marketability. "Marketability refers to whether a security can be bought or sold easily and quickly. It is a function of price and the size of the market for a given stock. The size of the market is determined in turn by the size of the company, the number of shareholders, and general public interest in the stock. High-priced stocks, for exam-ple, are less marketable than low-priced. It is logical to expect that the marketability for a stock at the ₹ 50 level is less than for stock selling at ₹ 3000.

Stocks of small companies tend to have less marketability than those of larger companies, simply because the larger companies have a greater number of shares outstanding. The increased number of shares traded allows a continuous market for the stock. The concept of continuous marketability refers to the number of transac-tions and the close relationship in price between one sale and the previous sale.

The size of the company influences marketability in another way. The larger com-panies tend to be more stable and of higher quality; and size, stability, and quality tend to make their stocks more marketable than those of smaller companies that often lack these investment characteristics.

5. Liquidity

As stated before, one problem for the investor is to balance liquidity with profitability. Liquidity, or nearness to money, is desirable in the portfolio because it offers the investor an opportunity to take advantage of attractive opportunities that arise — such as lower prices or special situations. Conservative portfolio management suggests that some liquidity be maintained, either by setting aside a portion of the investment fund for such purposes or by arranging to use interest and dividends to purchase new shares.

6. Diversification

There is really one main reason for diversification — reduction f loss of the risk of loss of capital and income. Investors face an unknown and uncertain future. Since no one can predict the future most investors diversify their investments. There are many ways to diversify investments. A list of ways to diversify includes: Debt vs. equity; maturity; industry; company; nation; time; and real or physical assets.

Most of the diversification forms are obvious but an explanatory word seems in order.

i) Debt and Equity Diversification

Debt and equity diversification is quite common. Debt provides income with some debt securities, selling at a discount, also providing capital gains. Equity provides income, growth of income and capital gains. They are combined to compli-ment each other since bond yields and returns are not highly correlated to returns on common stocks.

ii) Maturity

Maturity diversification of bonds reduces the risk of loss created by rising yields. Usually short term yields are lower than long term yields. In cases of extreme monetary restraint, however, short term rates rise well above long term rates. Long term bonds will decline in price as market yields rise; therefore, in conditions of rising yields investors should invest in short term bonds. In periods of falling yields investors should invest in long term bonds. The problem, of course, is to determine which way yields are going. To avoid the problem investors invest in a range of maturities to maintain income and protect capital.

iii) Industry

Industry diversification suggests that several industries be selected for investment consideration.

iv) *Company*

Company diversification among risky securities suggests that a few securities be purchased to reduce risk. Technical analysis suggests that investors focus on a few securities. Fundamental analysis suggests selectivity and only a few stocks. After all an investor can buy more, over time, of each security. Modern portfolio theory suggests a large enough number of issues of eqity shares to reduce the risk to the level of market risk or some multiple of the market risk. The market risk is measured

v) *Nation*

As the world competitive environment changes, industry leadership can move to other countries. The competitive leader is not always found in one nation. Therefore, some foreign securities might be part of an investment portfolio. In addP" tion, a gain in return might be achieved because of the increased value of the foreign currency.

vi) *Time*

It doesn't make investment sense to put money into risky assets all at once. If an investor were to in herit ₹ 1 crore, should all the money be committed to risky assets? Absolutely not. This first step would probably be to buy short-term securities while figuring out where and in what assets to invest. The notion of not putting your assets to work at the same time is a corollary to "don't put all your eggs in one basket."

vii) *Real Assets*

Investors might consider real assets (gold, diamond, real estate etc.). Some years might be years of good performance for real assets. It wouldn't hurt to keep informed.

These forms of diversification will help the investor avoid risk or accept risk. Knowledge of these forms will let investors know their risk position.

7. Favourable Tax Status

One factor of importance in the management of invest-ment portfolios is the tax position of the investor. Many financial decisions in today's income tax consideration. Interest or dividends received re immediately taxable. Capital gains are not taxed until they are actually realized. This means that unless income is actually needed, a rupee capital gain is really worth more than a rupee of income. The key point is that unrealized capital gains are not taxed, whereas dividend or interest income is. Taxes can be deferred for many years by successful long-term growth stock investing.

THE IMPORTANCE OF PRIMARY AND SECONDARY OBJECTIVES

Establishing the *primary objective* of the portfolio is a major accomplishment for the fund manager and the fund beneficiary. Little can occur until this is done. But it is also prudent and enormously helpful to establish a *secondary objective* in addition to a primary objective (an objective in addition to a pri-mary objective). The secondary objective, as the name suggests, indicates what is next in importance after specification of the primary objective. The portfolio manager is ultimately going to have to decide what percentage of the investment funds to put into equities. Most of the remainder will go into debt securities; real estate or hard assets may also play a role in some cases. If the fund manager can play psychologist and get the client to talk about secondary objectives, it is much easier to pin down a reasonable range for the equity percentage.

Consider an investor who has discovered that current income should be primary objective of the portfolio. This could be accomplished by in-vesting in money market securities, in long-term debt, or in dividend-pro-ducing common stock. The client might make statements like "I really don't want to take any risk with this money," or "Is there any chance I am going to lose any of this?" In this case, stability of principal is probably the client's secondary objective, and little, if any, of the portfolio will be in-vested in stock.

In contrast, the client might ask, "Is the income I get going to keep up with inflation?" This implies growth of income as a secondary objective. To accomplish this, the fund manager must attempt to get some appreciation in the principal of the fund, and this requires a greater investment in equities.

OTHER FACTORS TO CONSIDER IN ESTABLISHING OBJECTIVES

Inconsistent Objectives

Equally important is the fact that certain primary/secondary objective combinations are incompatible. An example of such *inconsistent objectives* are stability of principal as a primary objective and capital appreciation as a secondary objective. This, in effect, says, "I want no chance of a loss, but I do want capital gains." The world does not work this way.

Note also that growth of income cannot be paired with stability of prin-cipal. There are two ways in which income can continue to rise. One way is for interest rates to increase continually. This occurs during inflationary times, but the government does everything it can to keep this from continuing. An investor cannot rely on increasing inflation to produce continually inceasing income. It is also the case that the actual purchasing power of the higher income has not increased. The other way in which income can increase is through an increased value of the principal amount from which the income is generated. This means that some capital appreciation is necessary. Investment activities that potentially could provide capital appreciation are risky, though, and this is inconsistent with an objective of stability of principal.

Infrequent Objectives

Some investment objective combinations are infrequent. For instance, capital appreciation as a primary goal and stability of principal as a secondary goal appear at first glance to be patently incompatible. In most cases they are, but it is possible to construct a very specific type of portfolio that would generally accomplish this mission. For example, a wealthy individual in a high tax bracket might have no need for addi-tional current income and might not be comfortable with the risk of equity investments. For this individual, investments in traditional fixed-income securities would produce unneeded income that would be heavily taxed in the year received.

An alternative would be to invest in low coupon bonds that were selling in the marketplace at a substantial discount from par. These bonds would produce less income than comparable grade issues with higher coupons. This means less tax liability would be incurred. As they approached their maturity date, these bonds would rise in value and, barring default, would be retired at par. The client would see this as a capital gain, which, depending on current tax laws, might receive favorable tax treatment. In any event, the tax liability would be incurred in the future, and its present value would be much smaller than if it were incurred this year.

A material consideration to such a portfolio is the fact that low coupon bonds face substantial interest rate risk. If interest rates rise, the market value of low coupon bonds falls substantially. This might be considered in- consistent with an objective of stability of principal. The bonds, though, will eventually recover as they approach maturity, and it is also the case that stability of principal was the secondary objective rather than the primary.

Perhaps the important thing to keep in mind with combinations be termed as infrequent is largely philosophical: a portfolio manager should look for ways to do things instead of explaining why they cannot be done. If clients want something unusual, do not begin the conversation by telling them that their needs are bizarre and uncommon. It is better to verify that their situ-ation does indeed call for something a bit out of the ordinary, and if this is the case, try to work out a compromise. This is far better than throwing up hands and saying, "It can't be done!"

Portfolio Splitting

Occasionally a fund manager will receive instructions that require that the portfolio be managed in more than one part. Perhaps a trust endowment fund has grown over the years to a current value of around ₹ 100 crore. One-fourth of this amount might be associated with restricted gifts providing that the annual income be used for a specific purpose. The remaining ₹ 75 crore might have no restrictions as to its use.

In such a case, the fund manager and the board of trustees might decide to prorate the investment of the fund into two components with different objectives. Income is important with the restricted portion, and income might be established as the primary objective of this portion of the fund. Income may be less important with the unrestricted portion, and capital appreciation might be established as the primary objective of these remaining funds. Such *portfolio splitting* is occasionally a more convenient way of administering the fund than trying to establish a single, overall ob-jective

Still, portfolio splitting has the potential to give people the opportunity to avoid making tough decisions about fund management. A board of trustees might get wishy-washy and decide it wants "a little of everything." Unless there is a good reason to do otherwise, the portfolio should be man-aged as a unit.

PORTFOLIO OBJECTIVES AND THE PERSONAL CHARACTERISTICS OF THE INVESTOR

In order to achieve the objectives that minimize risk and maximize reward, the investor must have personal qualifications to achieve these goals. One's financial position determines to a great extent one's ability to assume risk and gain the perspective for investment success. A strong financial position tends to minimise risk and maximize the opportunity for rewards in the future.

THE CONCEPT OF A STRONG FINANCIAL POSITION

A strong financial position is mandatory before investment takes place, particularly before risky assets are purchased. In order to meet the financial prerequisites of investment, an investor should have have adequate life or term insurance; have a plan for the purchase of a home or own a home; maintain a control over consumer credit and instalment debt; and maintain adequate savings. Meeting these conditions will put the investor in an excellent position to consider investment in risky assets.

PORTFOLIO MANAGEMENT GOALS AND OBJECTIVES, AND ESTABLISHING THE INCOME PORTFOLIO

Attitude will determine the indifference curve that establishes investment preferences. Usually, a young, wealthy, healthy single person is best able to accept the risks of equity investment. If youth, health, and single status all disappear, then money alone will allow the investor to accept the risk of common stock ownership.

i) The Age of the Investor

It is difficult to make generalisations about this variable, but in general, the younger the investor, the more the interest in growth investments, and the older the investor, the more interested in income. But there are always exceptions. A gentleman in his late seventies came to see a broker about buying stock. The broker suggested a well-diversified income portfolio. The elderly gentleman said in astonishment, "I don't want income stocks, I want something with growth potential." Obviously, he was not investing to meet his own current needs. Younger investors usually tend to be less cautious than older ones. This might be because of willingness to accept risk, but it also might be because of lack of experience. No one should take unnecessary risks.

ii) Marital Status and Family Responsibilities

MARITAL STATUS AND FAMILY RESPONSIBILITIES The marital status of the investor has an impact on investment needs. Married persons must provide for the physical and educational needs of the family, tending to make them more conservative and less likely to speculate. The investment needs of single persons are much simpler, usually because their financial needs are less complex. The financial commitments of the married investor are much greater, other things being equal, than those of the single person. The cost of establishing a home often makes investment difficult for the family, other than investment in real estate.

iii) The Health of the Investor

The health of investor and family also affects investment policies. An investor in poor health will be in a position in which income is in jeopardy, so demands for current income will be great, precluding investment for growth. A healthy family's investment decisions can be determined by more important investment criteria.

iv) Personal Habits

The personal habits of an individual also influence investment needs. A frugal person will have no problem establishing a fund. Current and future financial needs will be minimal, suggesting a growth policy. Of course, the very frugal person will have less need for future income as well. At the other extreme is the spend-thrift, who needs more current income. Current income demands might be so great that part of capital in addition to income is spent. Obviously, this investor must follow an investment program that maximizes current income. However, to ensure the maintenance of the investment fund, it might be wise to limit expenditures.

v) Willingness to Accept Risks

The emotional makeup of a person will dictate the ability to assume the risks of intvestment. The risks are real; we must understand their nature and significance, we must be willing to accept them and provide against them. People vary as to their willingness to assume the purchasing-power risk, market risk, business risk, or money-rate risk. Some eagerly accept risk and are not alarmed if they actually lose large sums of money. These people are prepared financially and emotionally to invest. Others are so security-conscious that they could not risk the loss of a single penny. They are emotionally unable to accept the risk of loss, and should stay out of the stock market.

One of the important points to remember about investment is that while we can usually obtain results consistent with our objectives, there is no place for greed in the investment equation. If we are motivated by greed, we will often take unnecessary risks to achieve unrealistic goals unconnected with economic reality.

v) The Money Psychology of the Individual

The overriding question the inves-tor must ask is, "What is my psychological attitude about money. Some people just can't beat the thought of parting with a single rupees, even if they have more money than they will ever need. Such people could not buy equity. By the same token, a person should not be so careless about money'that he or she actually tries to lose. Psychopathic gamblers, as an extreme case, are hell-bent for financial and personal destruction. Anyone with this psychological attitude toward stocks should stay away from the market. A person needs a sound psychological attitude toward money in order to make money. Few are outstandingly successful and shrewd when it comes to money matters. Before anyone begins an investment program, he or she must find out about his or her money psychology.

THE INVESTOR'S NEEDS

Whether theory or practice is followed, it must be recognized that when money is invested for an individual, needs must be met. Some of the needs will be financial, some will be emotional and psychological. Certainly, the primary motive for investment is profit. It might be for retirement, for education, to improve one's standard of living, or to be benevolent and leave something for one's alma mater; nonetheless, the goal is profit. Other motives are equally strong for some people. For instance, the wealthy frequently want power, and they continue investing simply to maintain economic power and control over assets for their own benefit. Some people invest for status, so they can tell their friends they own stock.

The point is that the investor must know himself and therefore know his own needs—financial, emotional, and psychological—in order to determine his own requirements for risk and reward.

ARTICULATION OF GOALS AND OBJECTIVES

It is extremely important that investors be as specific as possible about their goals and attitudes if they hope to meet them and be comfortable with their investments. In fact, investors should articulate their objectives by being specific about the rate of return and the amount of risks they expect. An investor should state, "I need a 10 percent return with little or no risk and stability of income." The statement should be written down and reviewed periodically. If an investor knows that risk-free assets, offer a yield of 13 percent, longer-term bonds offer 14 to 17 percent yield and/or return with a standard deviation of 6 percent, and common stock offers returns of 18 to 23 percent with a standard deviation of 14 percent, he or she can determine where to invest funds.

If an investor says, "I need at least 10 percent with no risk," this could be achieved with investments inrisk-free securities. There is no certainty that risk-free securities provide a yield of 10 per cent. In that case, the investor knows that longer-term bonds or income stock will be needed. The investor can combine risk-free securities with longer-term bond and income common stocks to make up a portfolio of.

Even when investors seek help from the professional community, they must be able to tell their investment manager, counselor, or broker what they require. A trust com-pany under a trust agreement, common trust fund, short-term trust, or investment management account must be able to work in terms of specific goals, and client-investors must be able to articulate their aims. An investor must understand the retirement goals and the types of securities that will help meet those goals. Communication between invest-ment management and customer is critical.

PORTFOLIO DEDICATION

Portfolio dedication involves managing an asset portfolio such that it services the requirements of a corresponding liability or portfolio of liabilities. Sometimes called *liability funding*, this is a specialised requirement overlaying the primary and secondary investment objectives. There are two principal methods of portfolio dedication: *cash matching* and *duration* matching.

Cash matching is the most common form of portfolio dedication. With this technique, a portfolio of bonds is assembled such that the cash flows from the portfolio match as nearly as possible the requirements of a particular liability. To illustrate, assume a wealthy university alumnus might endow his or her alma mater with a set of ten four-year scholarships, each of which pays the recipient ₹ 20,000 every six months. This has an annual income requirement of ₹ 4,00,000. Assume for the sake of this example that the ₹ 20,000 payout will remainconslant with no adjustment for inflation. Such an endowment could be structured as a cash-matched, dedicated portfolio. Here the portfolio manager would choose bonds that pay interest semiannually and pay it just before it needs to be distributed to the scholarship recipients.

The general idea of *duration matching* is constructing a portfolio of assets such that it "pays the bills" associated with a liability or portfolio of liabilities. In a duration-matched bond portfolio, a rise in interest rates results in a decline in the value of the portfolio, but reinvestment rates will be higher, and the coupon cheques received will generate enough additional in- come to offset the decline in market value. Similarly, if market rates fall, the increase in the market value of the portfolio will offset the decline in income from reinvested funds. The two keys to duration matching are: First, the duration of the asset portfolio must match the duration of the liabilities. Second, the present value of the liabilities to be paid must equal the market value of the asset portfolio.

PORTFOLIO MANAGEMENT POLICIES

Some of the more common policies that might be followed in the management of an investment fund are income, growth, and a combination of the two. This way of clas-sifying portfolio policy stresses whether returns to the investor will be in the form of current income or capital gains.

The income fund places emphasis on the maximization of current income. Capital gains and growth are given minimum significance in the income portfolio. The securi-ties that provide income are the medium-grade bonds, preferred stocks, dividend-paying equity shares and, for investors in a high tax bracket, tax-exempt securities. The growth portfolio emphasizes the capital growth of the investment fund. The purpose of the growth fund is to postpone current income so that the fund increases in value. The increased value will allow the investor to improve income and growth at a later date. Investors interested in growth would buy stocks that offer appreciation potential and a low cash dividend.

The income-growth fund attempts to balance current income with some growth. The investor desires some current income, yet wishes to build the value of the fund. The problem is whether to balance the securities in the fund between income securities and growth securities, or to choose a security that possesses both growth potential and income—sometimes referred to as a straddle stock. A well-diversified list of comparable stocks would make an excellent combination income and growth portfolio.

Once the facts are reviewed, a suitable goal is established at this point in portfolio building process. This means thought and preparation in establishing a list of securities to meet the needs of the investor. If an investor needs capital growth now and insure in later years, the plan must reflect these needs. When investments are made without regard to any plan, the investor may suddenly find he or she owns a group of securities that do not meet the objective. In investing this way, the investor could make error that would lead to a financial loss.

To handle the problem intelligently, the investor must have objectives dearly defined and a plan established to meet them. It might be proper to list the objectives and then originate a plan to meet them. In this way, a well defined course of action is determined in advance.

Planning is a part of risk-aversion process. The investor must determine how much risk is to be taken and then plan how to achieve these goals. The goal may be growth or income or some combination of both, or as much income as moderately safety of principal will allow and so on, through many possibilities. The investor must realise that high current income and high appreciation hardly ever go together. To improve the chances of getting one, the investor must usually reduce the chances of getting the other.

Portfolio objectives will largely determine the investment strategy. The different objectives may be achieved by: (a) balancing fixed interest securities against equities; (b) balancing high dividend payment companies against high earnings growth companies as required; (c) finding the income or growth portfolio as required; (d) balancing transaction costs against capital gains from rapid switching; (e) balancing income tax payable against capital gains tax; and finally, (f) retaining some liquidity to seize upon bargains.

The investor should be conservative and act rationally when making investment decisions. The concept of conservatism is extremely important. One of the essential aspects of investment is to minimise risk. The investor wishes to accept risk consistent with gains, but not beyond, it would be imprudent to accept risk beyond what is necessary. Risk and return are correlated. It is proper to establish a trade-off between risk and return, rather than undue risk for a strong possibility of gains and loss.

An average traditional portfolio reflects a mixture of two opposing attitudes: concentration and diversification. Within a general investment policy such as "buy equity shares only", investors may decide to buy growth shares only. They may further concentrate on speculative growth shares rather than quality growth shares. If they have great knowledge about highly speculative industry, this knowledge will offset the disadvantages of non-diversification. However, most investors may opt for diversification to reduce the volatility of returns. Ten per cent of the equity portfolio in ten different industries provides adequate equity diversification. Investors may balance equities against fixed-interest bearing securities.

After objectives and strategies have been established, the portfolio must be put together. Security analysis may come into play at this point. For this:

(a) Devise methods for selecting successful investment by calculating the true or intrinsic value of a share and comparing that value with the current market value (Fundamental Analysis). Alternatively, try to predict further share prices from price movements (Technical Analysis).

(b) Get expert advise, for example, stock broker, merchant banker etc.

(c) Study published accounts closely and try to predict the intrinsic value.

(d) Seek out widely diversified growth companies.

(e) Switch quickly from losers to winners.

(f) Try to obtain inside information to beat the market.

(g) Follow newspaper tipsters with a good track record.

(*h*) Locate those companies with the right packaging, that is, appropriate dividend and leverage policies.

(*i*) Locate companies with good asset banking, dividend growth, good earnings record, high quality of management.

For investment success, timing is necessary, this is also considered when the investment plan in being undertaken. The market fluctuates according to the economic and political climate, Individual securities vary in price, in time establishing a price range. In the process of analysis, the investor must decide when a security is high or low. Though it is difficult to buy securities always at their low price and sell them at their high price, but limits can be established to show a security is underpriced or overpriced. If money is available for investment but securities are overpriced, the investor should wait for the right time to buy. There is no relationship, necessary, between the availability of funds and the attractiveness of stock prices. If money is available for investment but stocks are overpriced, the investor should invest in short-term fixed-income investments.

Portfolio management assumes periodic supervision of the security in the portfolio. Buy-and-hold philosophy, in present competitive society and in view of the fluctuations of the stock market, is not a very prudent, conservative, or a rational plan of action for sound portfolio management. The investor should frequently analyse the company and the security to make certain that it meets needs. Investor must be quickly responsive to market changes, and when expected return is too low or the risk too high in relation to return, action must be taken. The investor must take advantage of situations in which securities are over-or-underpriced.

REVIEW PROBLEMS

1. N. T. Rao has ₹ 2,00,000 of wealth, ₹ 1,00,000 of it in a tax-qualified provident fund. He has decided to invest half of its wealth in bonds and half in equity, so he allocates half of his provident fund and half of his funds to each. Suppose Rao earns a 10% per year rate of interest on bonds and 15% per year on equity, all in the form of price appreciation. In 5 years, he will withdraw all his funds and spend them. By how much will he increase his final accumulation if he shifts all bonds into the provident fund and holds all equity outside the provident fund? He is in a 28% tax bracket.

Ans:

If Rao keeps his present asset allocation, he will have the following amounts to spend after taxes 5 years from now:

Tax-qualified account:

Banks: ₹ 50,000 $(1.1)^5 \times 0.72$	=	₹ 57,978.36
Equity: ₹ 50,000 $(1.15)^5 \times 0.72$	=	₹ 72,408.86
Sub-total	=	₹ 1,30,387.22

Non provident fund account

Bonds:	₹ 50,000 $(1.072)^5$	=	₹ 70,785.44
Equity:	₹ : 50,000 $(1.15)^2$ - 0.28 x		
	[50,000 $(1.15)^5$ - 50,000]	=	₹ 86,408.86
Sub-total		=	₹ 1,57,194.30

Total		₹ 2,87,581.52

If Rao shifts all of the bonds into the provident fund account and all of the equity into the non-provident fund account, he will have the following amounts to spend after taxes 5 years from now.

Tax-qualified account:
Bonds: ₹ 1,00,000 (1. 1)^5 × 0.72   = ₹ 1,15,957
Non-provident fund account:
Equity: ₹ 1,00,000 (1.15)^5 - 028 (1,00,000 (1.15)5. 1,00,000)
                    = ₹ 1,72,817.72

           Total   ₹ 2,88,774.72
Rao spending budget will increase by ₹ 1,19320.

2. Ram is a successful business executive who retired at age sixty-five after forty years of service to a privately owned firm. He is married and has three adult children who are self-supporting. At the time of his retirement the Ram owned his own home, had   savings   of ₹ 50,000 in bank deposits, and had a miscellaneous list of good quality stocks and bonds. Ram is entitled to a yearly taxable pension of ₹ 30,000. Upon retirement, he liquidated shares he had acquired in his company over a span of twenty-five years under a stock purchase plan. The proceeds were ₹ 1,70,000 after taxes. Ram require an annual pre-tax income of ₹ 45,000-₹ 50,000 to maintain his present living standard. The following table indicates various categories of securities available in the market, together with assumed yields. Based upon these opportunities three portfolios have been constructed for Ram. Indicate the portfolio from the accompanying table that best meets the needs of the Ram as you perceive them to be. Provide a brief list of substantive reasons to support this portfolio mix.

Category of Security	Assumed Current Yields*	Portfolio 1	Portfolio 2	Portfolio 3
Money market securities	9.5%	₹ 10,000		₹ 10,000
Government bonds:				
Short-term	9.00			₹ 20,000
Intermediate-term	9.50		₹ 20,000	₹ 30,000
Long-term	10.00			₹ 50,000
Long-term corporate bonds:				
AAA Rated	11.25			₹ 30,000
AA Rated	11.40			
A Rated	11.60		₹ 30,000	
BBB Rated	10.00		₹ 20,000	
Post-Office Schemes	6.00	₹ 80,000	₹ 20,000	
Preferred stocks	9.00			₹ 20,000
Transportation stocks	5.00			
FMCG stocks	9.00	₹ 10,000	₹ 30,000	₹ 20,000
Financial stocks	5.50	₹ 10,000	₹ 20,000	₹ 20,000
Industrial stocks	5.00	₹ 1,10,000	₹ 80,000	₹ 20,000
Total		**₹ 2,20,000**	**₹ 2,20,000**	**₹ 2,20,000**
Current Yield (₹)		**₹ 12,700**	**₹ 15,780**	**₹ 19,825**

Ans.:

Ram's capital resources for investment totals ₹ 2,20,000. To augment his pension of ₹ 30,000 a year to attain a total pre-tax income of ₹ 45,000 to ₹ 50,000 a year, it is suggested that these funds be invested in a balanced portfolio of quality fixed-income securities for income and safety of principal and good quality equity shares for current income and the possibility of higher income and capital appreciation. The portfolio should not include speculative securities because of his age. Ram would have difficulty in recovering any heavy losses that might be incurred.

Portfolio #2 is balanced between 40 per cent fixed income securities and 60 per cent equities, reflects a fairly conservative investment policy, and produces a pre-tax annual income of ₹ 15,780 which, together with Ram's annual pension of ₹ 30,000, results in an annual pre-tax income of ₹ 45,000, in line with Ram's income objective. Additional income could be expected from increased dividends over time from the equity portion of his portfolio if individual stocks are carefully selected to produce the desired result.

Obviously, higher annual income could be obtained by putting a larger portion of the portfolio in fixed income securities, but it would be at the expense of restricting the future growth of income and capital gains from the equity portion of the portfolio, i.e., a trade-off between the portfolio's objectives.

Intermediate-term Government bonds provide liquidity to the portfolio in case there is an immediate need for cash at a time when the market conditions are such that other securities could only be sold at a loss.

Corporation bonds provide stability of income and security of principal in the fixed income category of securities in the portfolio. From the standpoint of an investor who is in a high tax bracket, as would be the case for Ram, some tax-exempt post office saving schemes are included in the portfolio for the advantage of minimising taxes on income and obtaining a higher after-tax yield than would be obtainable for other taxable fixed income securities.

A-and BBB-rated corporation bonds are included in the portfolio for the higher yields they offer without undue risk to capital, but AAA- and AA-rated bonds could be included with some sacrifice in income but a larger perceived degree of safety to principal.

The portion of the portfolio invested in FMCG and industrial stocks provides current income with opportunities for increased income and capital appreciation over time to offset the effects of inflation on the investor's standard of living as well as to increase the value of the estate. FMCG stocks are included for their higher yields vis-a-vis other stocks as well for their stability of dividend income and potential for modest future increases in dividends and capital value.

Portfolio #2 meets the general criteria of (a) providing some liquidity for immediate cash needs, (b) offering some reasonable overall balance between fixed income securities and equities, (c) providing annual pre-tax income in line with the investor's requirements, (d) protecting capital and avoiding undue risk to the corpus of the portfolio, and (e) providing opportunities to increase income and capital appreciation over time through a reasonably diverse list of selected quality equity shares to increase the value of the portfolio.

QUESTIONS

1. What is meant by planning portfolio objectives?
2. Discuss the process and principles employed in setting up the income portfolio.

3. Explain how expected return and standard deviation are used to establish the risk level in an income portfolio.

4. Why should an investor diversify between short-term and long-term securities ? Is it difficult in today's market to obtain a generous income from an investment portfolio without sacrificing quality ? Explain.

5. Can an investor ignore safety of principal? Why is knowledge of tax-status important for the investor ?

6. Why is diversification important, and what form does it take in view of the different needs, age groups, marital status, health and attitudes of the investors?

7. What role does equity shares have in a portfolio whose primary objective is stability of principal? Would your answer be different if stability of principal were the secondary rather than the primary objective?

8. As a portfolio advisor advisor what features would you suggest to be included in the investment bunch of a client ? Explain these features briefly.

9. What is the difference betwen the income objective and that of growth of income?

10. Why is it useful to establish a secondary portfolio objective?

11. A client is definitely more interested in income than in capital appreciation. How would you help him or her discover whether the primary objective should be income or growth of income?

12. Does the income objective mean that the fund manager should seek to generate the maximum possible income from the fund? Why or why not?

13. When selecting bonds for a portfolio, what factors should be considered before chosing specific maturities and quality ratings?

14. Comment on the following statment: "In evaluating the suitability of a bond for a portfolio, I don't care about its maturity. Duration is all that matters."

15. When income is important, which is more relevant to the fund manager: current yield or yield to maturity?

PROBLEMS

1. You are being interviewed for a job as a portfolio manager at an investment counselling partnership. As part of the interview, you are asked to demonstrate your ability to develop investment portfolio policy statements for the clients listed below:

   (a) A research institute endowment fund that is described as conservative, with investment returns being utilised alongwith gifts and donations to meet current expenses. The spending rate is 10% per year and inflation in costs is expected at 12% annually.

   (b) A finance company that is described as specialising in annuities. Policy premium rates are based on a minimum annual accumulation rate of 20% in the first year of the policy and a 15% minimum annual accumulation rate in next five years.

   (c) A pension fund mat is described as a mature defined benefit plan, with the work force having an average age of 52. There are no unfunded pension liabilities, and wage-cost increases are forecast at 10% annually.List and discuss the objectives and constraints that will determine the portfolio policy that you would recommend for each client.

2. A widow in her sixties and in good health comes to you for advice about her investments. Her husband left her a portfolio that consists mostly of low-yielding growth securities that are now at prices that approximate their adjusted cost. She has found that the increase available is not nearly enough to help her maintain a comfortable standard of living. She needs ₹ 10,000 monthly income before taxes from her investments. The current market value of the portfolio is ₹ 5,00,000 and its current yield is 4%. Since she will need this higher income for perhaps the next ten years, you have suggested that she place at least half of the portfolio in high-yielding securities.

(a) List the assumption you made regarding the investment environment and the widow's situation in order to consider the immediate investment of one-half of the portfolio in debentures as a 'prudent' decision.

(b) Describe the types of investment you would select for the remainder of the portfolio that is not invested in corporate debentures.

3. Ram Lal, an associate in your firm, has asked you to help him establish a financial plan for his family's future. Ram Lal is 27 years old and has been with your firm for 5 years. Kanta, his 22-year old wife, is employed as a secretary in a MNC. They are childless but may have children in a few years. They have accumulated ₹ 1,00,000 in savings and recently inherited ₹ 5,00,000 in cash. They believe they can save at least ₹ 20,000 yearly. They are currently, in a 35% income tax bracket and both have excellent career opportunities. They are eager to develop a financial plan and understand that it will need to be periodically adjusted as their circumstances change. You tell Ram Lal that you would be happy to meet them and discuss their financial plans.

(a) Identify and describe an appropriate investment objective and investment constraints for the couple and prepare a comprehensive investment policy statement that is based on the objective and constraints.

(b) State and explain your asset all location recommendations for Ram Lal and Kanta based on the policy statement you developed in part (a).

4. As an investment advisor, describe an appropriate investment programme for the following:

(a) An associate's parents, aged sixty-three and sixty-one, have ₹ 5,00,000 to invest They have pension income in the amount of ₹ 20,000 annually, although they have been accustomed to an income of ₹ 1,00,000. This sum and their owned home are their only assets.

(b) An unmarried career woman is approaching forty, has no dependents, and has a secure and well-paying job as an advertising art director which is supplemented by an alternative retirement benefits. She saves ₹ 2,000 to ₹ 2,500 per month but is bored with talk about investments and the stock market. She has just inherited ₹ 10,00,000.

(c) A couple in early thirty with three daughters has an annual income of ₹ 10,00,000. They have their own house and farms worth ₹ 50,00,000.

5. K.D. Verma was a successful senior executive with a MNC. Two years back, he voluntarily retired at age 48 after 25 years of service. He has three self-supporting married children. At time of retirement, Verma owned his own house, held ₹ 15,00,000 investment in securities. As he reviews his financial position, Verma considers himself quite well off, but he believes he should obtain some professional advice about the proper management of his capital resources at this age of his life. Accordingly he makes an appointment with you as an investment counsellor to discuss the financial affairs. During an initial conversation, you learn that he requiem an annual pre tax income of ₹ 20,000 to ₹ 30,000 per month to maintain his present standard of living, and he would like to have as large an estate as possible for his three children. He is concerned about the effects that inflation and taxation may have on his desired income and asset objectives.

(a) Discuss the general investment policy Verma should follow to attain his financial objectives.

(b) Suggest a portfolio that can justify the recommended appropriate risk-return on the available securities and non-security forms of investment.

REFERENCES

1. Bailey, Jeffrey, V. "Evaluating Benchmark Quality." *Financial Analysts Journal* 48, no. 3 (May-June 1992).

2. —————— and David E. Tierney. "Gaming Manager Benchmarks." *Journal of Portfolio Management* 19, no. 4 (Summer 1993).

3. ——————, Thomas M. Richards, and David E. Tierney. "Benchmark Portfolios and the Manager/Plan Sponsor Relationship." *Current Topics in Investment Management.* New York: Harper and Row, 1990.

4. Baumann, W. Scott. *Performance Objectives of Investors.* Charlottesville, Va.: Research Foundation of Financial Analysts, 1975.

5. Black, Frank E., "Elements of Portfolio Construction," *Financial Analysts Journal* 25 (May-June 1969): 123-129. Lorie, James H.. "Diversification: Old and New," *The Journal of Portfolio Management* Winter 1975, pp. 25 28.

6. Fama, Eugene. "Components of Investment Performance." *Journal of Finance* 27, no. 3 (June 1972).

7. Frankfurter, George M., "The Effect of Market Indexes on the Ex-Post Performance of the Sharpe Portfolio Selection Model," *Journal of Finance*, 31 (June 1976).

8. Jensen. Michael C., "Risk, the Pricing of Capital Assets, and the Evaluation of Investment Portfolios," *Journal of Business* 42, no. 2 (April 1969): 167-247.

9. Latane, Henry. Don Tuttle, and Charles Jones. *Security Analysis and Portfolio Management.* 2d ed. (New York: Ronald Press, 1975).

10. Mao, James, "Essentials of Portfolio Diversification Strategy," *Journal of Finance* 25, no. 5 (December 1970): 1109-1124.

11. Mossin, Jan. "Equilibrium in a Capital Asset Market." *Econometrica* 34, no. 4 (October 1966).

12. Sharps, W.F. *Portfolio Theory and Capital Markets.* New York: McGraw-Hill, 1970.

13. Statman, Meir. "How Many Stocks Make a Diversified Portfolio?" *Journal of Financial and Quantitative Analysis* 22, no. 3 (September 1987).

14. Vandell, Robert F., D. Harrington, and S. Levkoff, "Cyclical Timing: More Return for Less Risk." Darden School Working *Paper* No. 78-12. Charlottesville, Va.: Darden Graduate School of Business Administration, 1978.

25

Portfolio Choice: Utility Theory and Indifference Curves

INTRODUCTION

Utility theory is the foundation for the theory of choice under uncertainty. Cardinal and ordinal theories are the two alternatives used by economists to determine how people and societies choose to allocate scarce resources and to distribute wealth among one another over time. A *cardinal utility* implies that a consumer is capable of assigning to every commodity or combination of commodities a number representing the amount of degree of utility associated with it. An *ordinal utility* implies that a consumer needs not be able to assign numbers that represent the degree or amount of utility associated with commodity or combination of commodity. The consumer can only rank and order the amount or degree of utility associated with commodity.

UTILITY FUNCTIONS

Economists define the relationship between psychological satisfaction and wealth as "utility". An upward sloping relationship, as shown in Figure 1, identifies the phenomena of increasing wealth and increasing satisfaction as being directly related. These relationships can be classified into linear, concave, and convex utility functions.

In Figure 1 (a), for each unit change in wealth, there is a linear utility, function, an equal increase in satisfaction or utility. A drilling of wealth will double satisfaction, and so on This is probably not very realistic, an increase in wealth from Rs. 100 to Rs. 200 is probably more important than an increase from Rs. 1 crore to Rs. 2 crore, because the marginal utility diminishes with increased wealth. In Figure-1(b) the concave utility function shows the relationship of an increase in wealth and a less than proportional

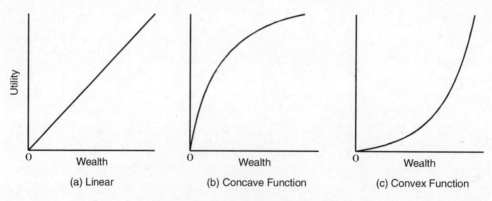

(a) Linear   (b) Concave Function   (c) Convex Function

FIGURE 1: UTILITY FUNCTIONS

increase in utility. In other words, the marginal utility of wealth decreases as wealth increases. As mentioned above, the Rs. 100 increase from Rs. 100 to Rs. 200 of wealth is more important to the individual than the increase from Rs. 1 crore to Rs. 2 crore. Each successive increase in wealth adds less satisfaction as the level of wealth rises. Finally, Figure 1(c) is a convex utility function, which denotes a more than proportional increase in satisfaction for each increase in wealth. Behaviourally, the rich you are the more satisfactions you receive in getting an additional of wealth.

Figure 2 illustrates three wealth-preferences orderings which all show increasing utility with wealth. The solid line represents a constant, or linear, relationship between wealth and the utility attached to it. If wealth doubles, so does utility. For each unit change in wealth, the change in utility remains constant. An increment Rs.1,000 provides the same amount of additional utility at an initial wealth level of Rs. 10,000 as it does at an initial wealth level of Rs. 1,00,000. In the parlance of economics, the solid line depicts a case of *constant marginal utility* of wealth. The dashed curve also shows an increase in utility as wealth increases but illustrates the case of *decreasing marginal utility*. An incremental Rs. 1,000 provides less utility to a person with an initial wealth of Rs. 1,00,000 than it would if the same person's initial wealth were Rs. 10,000. Finally, the dotted curve illustrates the case of *increasing marginal utility*. An incremental Rs. 1,000 provides more utility to a person with an initial wealth level of Rs. 1,00,000 than it would if the same person's initial wealth were Rs. 10,000.

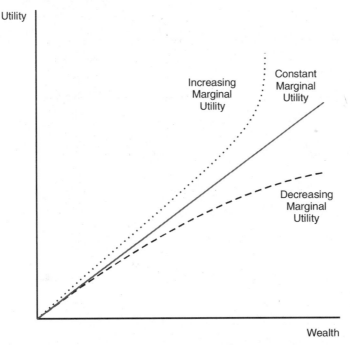

FIGURE 2: WEALTH AND UTILITY

The manner in which people order wealth preferences (the shape of the utility of wealth curve) has profound implications on security pricing and risk measurement. In explaining how investment decisions of portfolio choices are made, utility theory is used here not to imply that individuals actually make decisions using a utility curve, but rather as an expository vehicle that helps explain how investors presumably act In general, human behave as if more is better than less.

In an uncertain environment it becomes necessary to ascertain how different individuals will react to risky situation. The risk is defined as the probability of success or failure. Alternatively, risk could be described as variability of outcomes, payoffs, or returns. This implies that there is a distribution of outcomes associated with each investment decision. What is needed is a linkage between utility or expected utility and risk. Expected utility has been defined as the numerical value assigned to the probability distribution associated with a particular portfolio return. This numerical value is calculated by taking a weighted average of the utilities of the various possible returns. The weights are the probabilities of occurrence associated with each of the possible returns. It is calculated by the following formula:

$$E(U) = \sum_{i}^{n} U(w_i)P_i$$

where:

$\quad E(U)$ = expected utility;
$\quad U(w_i)$ = the utility of the ith outcome w_i; and
$\quad\quad P_i$ = the Probability of the ith outcome.

To illustrate, assume investments A and B as shown in the table, determine the utilities of A and B for the given utility functions.

A		B	
Outcome w_i	Probability	Outcome w_i	Probability
10	2/5	9	2/3
5	2/5	3	1/3
1	1/5		

1. $U(w) = w$
2. $U(w) = w^2$
3. $U(w) = w^2 - w$

By solving, we get:

1. For $U(w) = w$

$\quad\quad$ Utility A $= \frac{2}{3}(10) + \frac{2}{5}(5) + \frac{1}{5}(1) = 6\frac{1}{5}$

$\quad\quad$ Utility B $= \frac{2}{3}(9) + \frac{1}{3}(3) = 7$

2. For $U(w) = w^2$

$\quad\quad$ Utility A $= \frac{2}{5}(100) + \frac{2}{5}(25) + \frac{1}{5}(1) = 50\frac{1}{5}$

$\quad\quad$ Utility B $= \frac{2}{3}(81) + \frac{1}{3}(9) = 57$

3. For $U(w) = w^2 - w$ (use results from 1 and 2)

$\quad\quad$ Utility A $= 50\frac{1}{5} - 6\frac{1}{5} = 44$

$\quad\quad$ Utility B $= 57 - 7 = 50$

In all three cases, B has the higher degree of utility because it has a higher expected value as well as a smaller dispersion than A.

Linear Utility Function and Risk

The shape of an individual's utility function affects his or her reaction to risk. Assume that an individual has Rs. 5,000 and whose behaviour is linear utility function, is offered a chance to gain ₹ 10,000 with a probability of 1/2 or to lose ₹ 10,000 with a probability of 1/2. What should he or she pay for such an opportunity? The answer is nothing, for as can be seen in Figure-3, this individual would be no better or worse off accepting or rejecting this opportunity, his wealth would remain at ₹ 5,000 with utility U_1. Any payment for this chance could reduce his wealth and therefore be undesirable. This is so because the expected value of the fair game is zero.

$$\frac{1}{2}(10,000) + \frac{1}{2}(-10,000) = 0$$

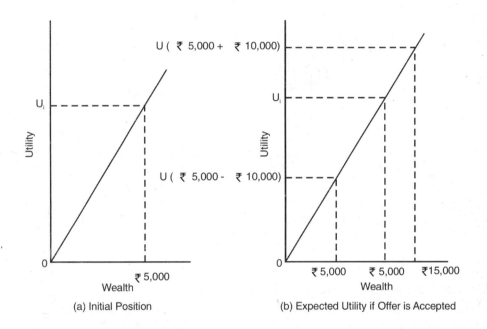

FIGURE 3: RISK, NEUTRAL INVESTORS AND FAIR GAMES

Concave Utility Function and Risk

In case of a concave utility function, if an individual participates and wins his or her utility is shown by point U_w in Figure 4. But if he/she loses, his/her position is shown by U_L. The expected value of this fair game, having a 50 percent chance of winning and a 50 percent chance of losing, is shown by point A. The utility of the fair game is U_F. A comparison of U_F with his/her initial position U_F shows that the investor should not accept this fair game. As shown in Figure 4, the utility of winning $(U_w - U_i)$ is less than the utility of losing $(U_i - U_L)$. Therefore, the utility of doing nothing is greater than the expected utility of accepting the fair game. In fact, the individual should be willing to pay up to the difference between the utility of winning and the utility of losing $(U_i - U_L)$ − $(U_w - U_i)$ to avoid being involved in this situation. Hence, investor with concave utility functions are said to be risk averse. That is, they would reject a fair game because the utility derived from winning is less than the utility lost should they lose the game. In other words, the expected utility of participating in a gair game is negative.

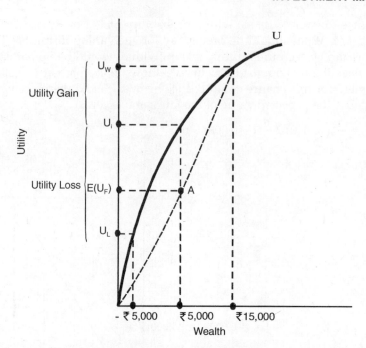

FIGURE 4: RISK-AVERSE INVESTORS AND FAIR GAMES

The convex utility function is not realistk in real-world decision, therefore, it is not worth exploring.

Uncertain Outcomes, Insurance and Expected Returns

Figure 5 plots the utility of wealth curve for an individual who prefers more wealth to less but can be characterised as having decreasing marginal utility. An extra rupees increases his utility but not by as much as a loss of a rupee would decrease his utility. Assume that this individual is a fairly well-off person with a current wealth. Assume that this individual is a fairly well-off person with a current wealth (W_0) of ₹ 1,00,000 which provides a corresponding utility of wealth (U_0). If he is offered by a broker to play a usual coin-tossing game. If head comes, the individual will pay the broker ₹ 5,000. If tails comes up, the broker will pay the individual ₹ 5,000. Though the odds of winning or losing are identical since it is a fair coin but still the individual declines to expose himself to a risk without a corresponding return. *Why?*

To see the truth and insight of the individual's stand, refer again to Figure 5. The individual has two choice: to play the game or not to play the game. If he decides not to play the game, his wealth remains the same and his utility remains at U_0. If he plays the game, his wealth will be either ₹ 95,000 or ₹ 1,05,000, with respective utilities of U_L and U_w. If he decides to play the game with a fair coin, his expected utility of wealth is lower than his expected utility if he does not play. Why? The reason that expected utility is less than U_0 lies in the fact that the individual has decreasing marginal utility of wealth. The increased satisfaction obtained by a ₹ 5,000 increase in his wealth is more than offset by the decreased satisfaction associated with a ₹ 5,000 loss. Individuals with decreasing marginal utility are risk-averse.

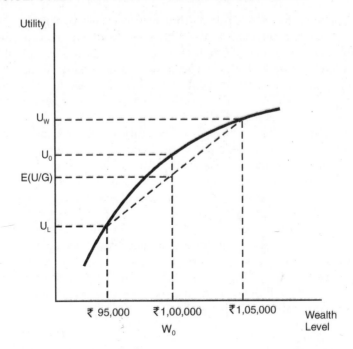

FIGURE 5: UTILITY THEORY AND RISK AVERSION

There are some events in life over which individuals have no control. They are not given the choice to play the game or not but they are forced to play. For example, assume that an individual's wealth is in the form of farm acreage which will either be productive during the next year or suffer little productivity if a drought occurs. Figure 6 plots each possibility as either wealth with productivity (W_p) or wealth with a drought (W_D) together with their respective utilities (U_p and U_D). Assume the probability of either is again 50%, so the expected wealth E(W) lies midway between W_p and W_D. Note that if the wealth level were at point C with no uncertainty at all, the expected

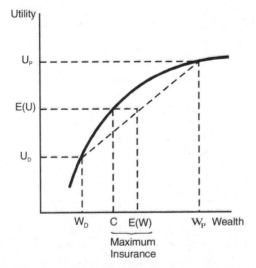

FIGURE 6: CERTAINTY EQUIVALENTS AND INSURANCE

utility would be the same as it is now with her uncertain farm acreage. Point C is referred than C would increase her expected utility. As a result, if an individual could assure himself against uncertainties (both favourable and unfavourable), the maximum he would be willing to pay is $E(W)$-C. Faced with unavoidable wealth risks, people are willing to buy insurance as long as the cost of the insurance does not reduce their expected utility of wealth, this is the basis of the insurance industry as well as of hedging behaviour in the securities markets.

When deciding whether to buy or sell securities, however, one consciously accepts risks, and a positive expected return is required in order for the expected utility of wealth not to fall (and, one hopes, to increase). This idea is shown in Figure 7. To illustrate, assume that an individual has fully insured the risks in his wealth, resulting in a current certain wealth of C and corresponding utility of U_C. Now if a broker offers to play the game again. If he plays, the outcomes would result in wealth levels W_L and W_w. Clearly, the individual will play only if his expected utility does not fall-if his expected wealth is equal to $E(W)$. *The* individual will demand an expected return to freely take on the change outcome. The broker can provide this return either by changing the odds of winning and losing or by paying him to play. The form of return is unimportant The important fact is that the individual demands a positive expected return simply because he has a decreasing marginal utility of wealth curve.

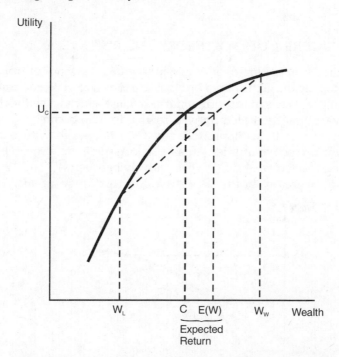

FIGURE 7: SECURITY RISK AND EXPECTED RETURNS

The return which must be paid to induce people to accept the uncertain outcomes associated with securities is known as the risk premium. As the Figure 7 shows that the size of the risk premium will depend upon both the risk aversion of an individual (the slope of his/her utility of wealth curve) and the size of the risk (the distribution of possible wealth levels). And, the method that should be used in selecting the most desirable portfolio involves the use of indifference curves.

INDIFFERENCE CURVES

Indifference (utility function) curves are abstract theoretical concepts. They cannot as a practical matter be used to actually measure how individuals make investment decisions-or any other decisions, for that matter. They are, however, useful for building models that illustrate the relationship between risk and return. An investor's utility function can be utilised conceptually to derive a indifference curve, which shows individual preference for risk and return. (By definition, an indifference curve shows all combinations of products (investments). A and B that will yield same level of satisfaction or utility to consume. This kind of analysis is based upon ordinal rather than cardinal utility theory). Any indifference curve can be plotted in the risk-return space such that the investor's utility is equal all along its length. The investor is indifferent to various combinations of risk and return, hence the name indifference curve. The slope of the indifference curve is a function of the investor's particular preference for a lower but safer return versus a larger but riskier return.

Figure 8 illustrates a 'map' of indifference curves that a hypothetical investor might possess. Each curved line indicates one indifference curve for the investor and represents all combinations of portfolios that provide the investor with a given level of desirability. For example, the investor with the indifference curves in Figure 8 would find portfolios A and B equally desirable, even though they have different expected returns and risk because they both lie on the same indifference curve, I_2. Portfolio B has a higher risk than portfolio A and is therefore less desirable on that dimension. However, exactly offsetting this loss of desirability is the gain in desirability provided by the higher expected return of BC relative to A. All portfolios that lie on a given indifference curve are equally desirable to the investor. An implication of this is that indifference curves cannot intersect. To Illustrate, consider the two indifference curves intersecting as shown in Figure 9. Here the point of intersection is represented by K. Given that K is on both indifference curves, all the portfolios on I_1 must be as desirable as those on I_2. But this presents a contradiction, because I_1 and I_2 are two curves that are supposed to represent different levels of desirability. Thus, in order for there to be no contradiction, these curves cannot intersect. Again, although the investor represented in Figure 8 used find portfolio A and B equally desirable, he or she find portfolio C preferable to both of them. This is because portfolio C happens to be on an indifference curve, I_3. C has a sufficiently larger expected

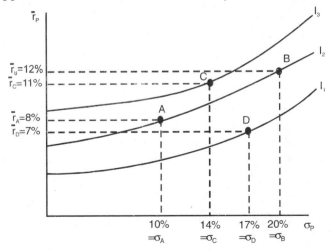

FIGURE 8: MAP OF INDIFFERENCE CURVE FOR A RISK-AVERSE INVESTOR

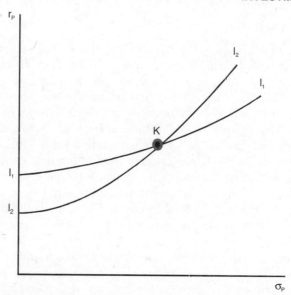

FIGURE 9: INTERSECTING INDIFFERENCE CURVES

return relative to *A* to more than offset its higher standard deviation and, on balance, make it more desirable than *A*. Equivalently, *C* has a sufficiently smaller risk than *B* to more than offset its smaller expected return and, on balance, make it more desirable than *B*. Thus, an investor will find any portfolio that is lying on higher indifference curve to be more desirable than any portfolio lying on lower indifference curves. Finally, it should be noted that an investor has an infinite number of indifference curves. It means that whenever there are two indifference curves on a graph, it is possible to plot a third indifference curve that lies between them. For instance, given indifference curves I_1 and I_2, it is possible to graph a third curve I', lying between them. It also means that another indifference curve can be plotted above I_2 and yet another below I_1 as shown in Figure 10.

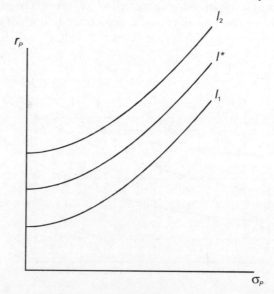

FIGURE 10: PLOTTING A THIRD INDIFFERENCE CURVE BETWEEN TWO OTHER

Two assumptions are implicit in this discussion of indifference curves. First, it is assumed that investor, when given a choice between two otherwise identical portfolios, will always choose the one with the higher level of expected return. More fundamentally, an assumption of *non-satiation* is made in utilising the Markowiz approach' meaning that investors are summed to prefer higher levels of terminal wealth to lower levels of terminal wealth. This is because higher levels of terminal wealth allow the investor to spend more on consumption in the more distant future. Thus given two portfolios with the same risk, such as R and S in Figure 11, the investor will choose the portfolio with

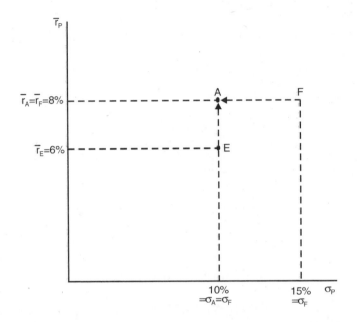

FIGURE 11: NONSATIATION, RISK AVERSION, AND PORTFOLIO CHOICE

the higher expected return. In this case, it is portfolio R. However, when the two portfolios having the same level of expected return but different levels of risk, such as R and S. This is where the second assumption that investors are risk-averse enters. The risk-averse investor will choose to avoid *fair game* of flipping the coin. The reason is that the potential loss represents an amount of *displeasure* that is greater than the amount of *pleasure* associated with the potential gain.

The two assumptions of nonsatiation and risk aversion cause indifference curves to be positively sloped and convex. Although it is assumed that all investors are risk-averse, it is not assumed that they have identical degrees of risk aversion. Some investors may be highly risk averse, whereas others may be only slightly so. This means that different investors will have different maps of indifference curves. Panels (a), (b), and (c) of Figure-12 displays maps for investors who are highly risk-averse investors, aggressive investor, risk-neutral investor

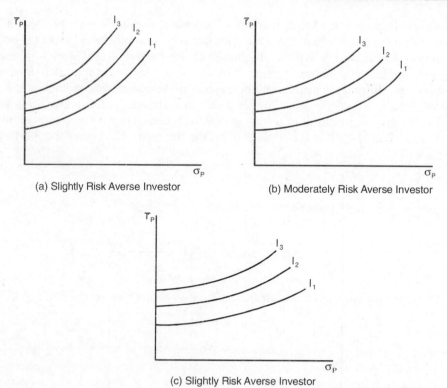

(a) Slightly Risk Averse Investor

(b) Moderately Risk Averse Investor

(c) Slightly Risk Averse Investor

FIGURE 12: INDIFFERENCE CURVES FOR DIFFERENT TYPES AND RISK-AVERSE INVESTORS AND RISK-SEEKING INVESTOR RESPECTIVELY.

REVIEW PROBLEMS

1. Suppose the utility function is $U(W) = \sqrt{W}$
   - (a) What is the uutility level at wealth levels Rs. 50,000 and Rs. 1,50,000?
   - (b) What is expected utility if probability still equals .5?
   - (c) What is the certainty equivalent (CE) of the risky prospect?
   - (d) Does this utility function also display risk aversion?

Ans.

   (a) $U(W) = \sqrt{W}$

   $$U\,(50{,}000) = \sqrt{50{,}000}$$
   $$= 223.61$$
   $$U\,(1{,}50{,}000) = 387.30$$

   (b) $E(U) = .5 \times 223.61 + .5 \times 387.30$
   $$= 305.45$$

   (c) We must find W_{CE} that has utility level 305.45. Therefore:
   $$W_{CE} = 305.45$$
   $$W_{CE} = (305.45)^2$$
   $$= Rs.\ 93{,}301$$

   (d) Yes. the certainty equivalent of the risky venture is less than the expected outcome of Rs. 1,00,000.

2. Given the following utility functions for four investors, what can you conclude about their reaction towards a fair game?

(a) $w^3 - 4w^2$
(b) w^4
(c) e^{-2w} and
(d) $e^{2w} - 4w^2$

Evaluate the second derivative of the utility functions according to the following rules.

$$w''(0) < 0 \text{ implies risk averse}$$
$$w''(0) = 0 \text{ implies risk neutral}$$
$$w''(0) > 0 \text{ implies risk seeker}$$

Ans.:

(a) $\quad u(w) = w^3 - 4w^2$
$\quad u'(w) = 3w^2 - 8w$
$\quad u''(w) = 6w - 8$
$\quad u''(0) = -8 < 0$

This implies the investor is risk averse and would reject a fair gamble.

(b) $\quad u(w) = w^4$
$\quad u'(w) = 4w^3$
$\quad u''(w) = 12w^2$
$\quad u''(0) = 0$

This implies risk neutrality, hence indifference to a fair gamble.

(c) $\quad u'(w) = -2e^{2w}$
$\quad u''(w) = 4e^{2w}$
$\quad u''(0) = 4 > 0$

This implies risk preference; the investor would seek a fair gamble.

(d) $\quad u(w) = e^{2w} - 4w^2$
$\quad u'(w) = 2e^{2w} - 8w$
$\quad u''(w) = 4e^{2w} - 8$
$\quad u''(0) = -4 < 0$

This implies risk aversity; the investor would reject a fair gamble.

3. Given the following data on the utility of wealth function, assume you are at a current wealth level of 30, calculate the expected utility if the probability of winning 10 were 0.70 and the probability of losing 10 were only 0.30

Wealth level	Utility of wealth	Percentage Change in utility
1	0	—
10	2.30	—
20	3.00	30
30	3.40	30
40	3.69	9
50	3.91	6

Ans.:

$\quad$ Expected utility (EV) $\quad = 0.7U (40) + 0/30U (20)$
$\quad\quad = 0.7 (3.69) + 0.3 (3.0)$
$\quad\quad = 3.483$

QUESTIONS

1. Why are people risk-averse? How does the utility theory suggest that we measure risk?

2. Explain why people are willing to purchase insurance and what determines the maximum amount of insurance they will pay for.

3. What is a fair game? Will risk-averter investors/risk-neutral investors/risk-preferring investors enter into a fair game?

4. Why are indifference curves of typical investors assumed to slope upward to the right?

5. What does a set of convex indifference curves imply about an investor's trade-off between risk and return as the amount of risk varies?

6. Do you agree with the assumption of nonsatiation and risk aversion. Make a cause for or against these assumptions.

7. What is meant by the statement that risk avert investors exhibit diminishing marginal utility of income? Why does diminishing marginal utility cause an investor to refuse to accept a fair bet?

8. Explain why an investor's indifference curves cannot intersect?

9. "An indifference curve represents the various combinations of risk and return that the investors find equally desirable." Comment.

10. Why are indifference curves of more risk-averse investors more steeply sloped than those of investors with less risk aversion.

11. "A risk averter will never enter a fair game of chance. "Prove this statement graphically. In your answer indicate the risk premium necessary to induce him to agree to play.

12. Explain what is meant by a utility function which is defined up to a linear transformation. What is the significance of such a function for decision-making? Analyse the impact of such a transformation on the origin and the scale of the utility function.

13. (a) Draw the appropriate indifference curves in the mean variance plane for the following types of individuals: (i) a risk averter; (ii) a risk lover; (Hi) a risk-neutral investor; (iv) an investor who will never take a risk; (b) Can the indifference curves of a risk lover and a risk averter intersect? (c) Can the indifference curves of the same individual intersect? (d) Can the indifference curves of two risk averters intersect?

14. The "risk premium" that is, the maximum amount that an individual is prepared to pay to convert a random distribution into a perfectly certain income, measures the degree of risk associated with such a distribution for all risk averters. Moreover, two risk averters would rank any pair of options by their risk in the same order. Is this statement correct? Prove your answer graphically using a hypothetical numerical example.

15. Why are investor's utility curves important in portfolio theory?

16. Prove graphically that a risk-averse investor will never enter into a fair gamble.

17. Demonstrate graphically that a risk-neutral investor makes investment decisions according to the expected-return criterion.

18. Draw an efficient frontier and possible equilibrium portfolios for risk-neutral and risk-averse investors.

19. Discuss desirable and undesirable features of the quadratic, logarithmic, and power utility functions.

20. Distinguish between utility and expected utility. When do agents act to maximise their expected utility?

21. Explain the concepts of insatiability, diminishing marginal utility, and diminishing marginal substitutability.

22. Explain the meaning of the slope of an investor's indifference curve at any particular point. For a typical risk-averse investor, describe how the investor's risk-return trade-off changes at different points along one of his or her indifference curves.

23. Discuss the problems with the expected-return framework for selecting risky alternatives.

PROBLEMS

1. Consider the following investment opportunities:

INVESTMENT A		INVESTMENT B	
Outcome	Probability	Outcome	Probability
-Rs. 20	.33	-Rs. 500	.33
40	.33	10	.33
100	.33	1,000	.33

Which alternative would you select if you utilised the expected-return criterion? Which alternative would you select if your utility function were $U = x^{\frac{1}{2}}$, $U = x$. or $U = x2$.

2. Consider me following gamble:

OUTCOME	PROBABILITY
Rs. 50	.50
250	.50

What is the certainty equivalent and risk premium if your utility function is $U = x^{\frac{1}{2}}$? Draw a graph illustrating the utility function, expected utility, and risk premium. Also do the same for the logarithmic function $U = 1n\ (x)$. Now assume a linear utility function, $U = 2x$, and graph the situation.

3. One individual has Rs. 2 crore and another has Rs. 10,000. Both are considering an investment that will pay either Rs. 3,000 or Rs. 2,000, with equal likelihood. If both agents have logarithmic utility functions, what is the maximum amount both are willing to pay for the gamble?

4. Consider the following gambles:

	Win	Lose	Probability Win
A	Rs. 102	Rs. 98	.5
B	110	90	.5
C	150	50	.5
D	200	0	.5

What are the certainty equivalents for each of the gambles for the utility functions $U = x^{\frac{1}{2}}$, $U = x^2$, and $U = x$?

5. Suppose you were offered (i) Rs. 1 crore or (ii) a gamble where you would get Rs. 2 crore if a head were flipped but zero if a tail come up.

(a) What is the expected value of the gamble?

(b) Would you take the sure Rs. 1 crore or the gamble?

(c) If you choose the sure Rs. 1 crore, are you a risk averter or a risk seeker?

(d) Suppose you actually take the sum of Rs. 1 crore, you can invest it in either Treasury bills that will return Rs. 1.075 crore at the end of a year or an equity that has a 50-50 chance of being either worthless or worth Rs. 2.30 crore at the end of the year.

(i) What is the expected profit on the stock investment?

(ii) Would you invest in the T-bills or the equity?

(iii) Just how large would the expected profit (or the expected rate of return) have to be on the stock investment to make you just invest in the stock?

    (iv) What is the expected rate of return on the equity?

    (v) How might your decision be affected if, rather than buying one stock per Rs. 1 crore, you could construct a portfolio consisting of 1000 equity shares with Rs. 10,000 in each? Each of these shares has the same return characteristics as the one stock, that is, a 50-50 chance of being worth either zero or Rs. 23,000 at year-end. Would the correlation between returns on these stocks matter?

Ans.: Rs. 1 crore.

REFERENCES

1. Arrow, Kenneth J.: "Essays in Theory of Risk-Bearing", Markham, Chicago (1971.

2. Kritzman, Mark P.: "... About Uncertainty," Financial Analysts Journal, 47, no. 2 (March/April 1991).

3. Kritzman, Mark P.: "... About Utility," Financial Analysts Journal, 47, no. 2 (May/June, 1992).

4. Markowitz, Harry, "Portfolio Selection." Journal of Finance 1, no. 1 (March 1952).

5. ———. Portfolio Selection: Efficient Diversification of Investments. New York: John Wiley and Sons, 1959.

6. Neumann, John von and Oskar Morgenstem: "Theory of Games and Economic Behaviour," (John-Wiley: New York) 1994.

7. Pyle, Devid, and Stephen Turnvosky, "Safety First and Expected Utility Maximization in Mean-Standard Deviation Portfolio Analysis" The Review of Economics and Statistics 52, no. 1 (February 1970): 75-81.

8. Schoemaker, Paul. J.H., "The expected Utility Modelets Variant, Purposes, Evidence and Limitations," Journal of economic Literature, 20. no. 2 (June 1982).

26

Markowitz :
Portfolio Selection Model

INTRODUCTION

As far back as the 18th century, Bernoulli and Cramer reached the conclusion that decisions under condition of uncertainty could not be made solely on the basis of expected (mean) return. Subsequently, various economists have tried to evaluate investments with the aid of two (or more) indicators based on the distribution of returns. Generally one index reflects the profitability of the investment while the other is based on the dispersion of the distribution of returns and reflects the investment's risk. The most common profitability index used is the expected return, that is, the mean of the probability distribution of returns; the risk index is usually based on the variance of the distribution, its range, and on. Until Dr. Harry M. Markowitz infused a high degree of sophistication into portfolio construction by developing a Mean—Variance Model for the selection of portfolios, portfolio managers used rules of thumb and intuitive judgement.

MARKOWITZ MODEL: THE MEAN-VARIANCE CRITERION

Dr. Harry M. Markowitz is credited with developing the first modern portfolio analysis model since the basic elements of modern portfolio theory emanate from a series of propositions concerning rational investor behaviour set forth by Markowitz, then of the Rand Corporation, in 1952, and later in a more complete monograph sponsored by the Cowles Foundation. It was this work that has attracted everyone's perspective regarding portfolio management. Markowitz used mathematical programming and statistical analysis in order to arrange for the optimum allocation of assets within portfolio. To reach this objective, Markowitz generated portfolios within a reward-risk context. In other words, he considered the variance in the expected returns from investments and their relationship to each other in constructing portfolios. In so directing the focus, Markowitz, and others following the same reasoning, recognised the function of portfolio management as one of composition, and not individual security selection — as it is more commonly practiced. Decisions as to individual security additions to and deletions from an existing portfolio are then predicated on the effect such a maneuver has on the delicate diversification balance. In essence, Markowitz's model is a theoretical framework for the analysis of risk-return choices. Decisions are based on the *concept of coefficient portfolios.*

A portfolio is efficient when it is expected to yield the highest return for the level of risk accepted or, alternatively, the smallest portfolio risk for a specified level of expected return. To build an efficient portfolio an expected return level is chosen, and assets are substituted until the portfolio combination with the smallest variance at the return level is found. As this process is repeated for other expected returns, *set* of efficient portfolios is generated.

Box-1

THE FATHER OF PORTFOLIO THEORY

Before the work of Harry Markowitz the field of investments focused on valuing individual securities, primarily through the use of balance sheets and income statements. Ad hoc accounting rules, may outlined in Benjamin Graham's and William Dodd's book Security Analysis, were designed to identify securities that were temporarily selling below or above intrinsic (book) value.

Markowitz changed the field's focus to an analysis of portfolios of assets in his 1952 paper "Portfolio Selection," published in the Journal of Finance. Rather than using accounting information, Markowitz employed a statistical approach to measure the risk and return of portfolios. The major result of this work is that a rational investor will diversify because a portfolio of assets will have less risk than any of the component securities, provided that the assets are less than perfectly positively correlated. His approach also allowed investors to calculate a series of efficient portfolios, each having the highest expected return for a given level of risk.

Assumptions

The Markowitz model is based on several assumptions regarding investor behaviour:
   (*i*) Investors consider each investment alternative as being represented by a probability distribution of expected returns over some holding period.
   (*ii*) Investors maximise one period expected utility and possess utility curve, which demonstrates diminishing marginal utility of wealth.
   (*iii*) Individuals estimate risk on the basis of the variability of expected returns.
   (*iv*) Investors base decisions solely on expected return and variance (or standard deviation) of returns only.
   (*v*) For a given risk level, investors prefer high returns to lower returns. Similarly, for a given level of expected return, investor prefer less risk to more risk.

Under these assumptions, *a single asset or portfolio of assets is considered to be "efficient" if no other asset or portfolio of assets offers higher expected return with the same (or lower) risk or lower risk with the same (or higher) expected return.*

The Specific Model

In developing his model, Markowitz first disposed of the investment behaviour rule that the investor should maximise expected return. This rule implies that the non-diversified single-security portfolio with the highest expected return is the most desirable portfolio. Only by buying that single security can expected return be maximised. The single-security portfolio would obviously be preferable if the investor were perfectly certain that this highest expected return would turn out to be the actual return. However, under real world conditions of uncertainty, most risk averse investors join with Markowitz in discarding the role of calling for maximising expected returns. As an alternative, Markowitz offers the *expected returns/variance of returns* rule.

The goal of the portfolio manager should be to *minimise portfolio risk for any level of expected returns* and suggested that this can be accomplished by solving the following logical set of equations:

Minimise Portfolio Risk

$$\sigma_p = \left[\sum_{x=1}^{N} W_x^2 \sigma_x^2 + \sum_{x=1}^{N} \sum_{y=1}^{N} W_x W_y C_{xy} \right]^{\frac{1}{2}} \qquad (1)$$
$$x \neq y$$

Subject to:
A Minimum Stated Expected Return:

$$R^* \leq E(R_p) = \sum_{x-1}^{N} W_x E(R_X) \tag{2}$$

Equation-I is simply the statistical definition of the portfolio risk, which can be expressed as:

$$V_p = \sum_{x=1}^{N} \sum_{y=1}^{N} W_x W_y C_{xy}$$

Equation-2 defines how the portfolio's expected return is calculated and states that when solving for the optimal portfolio W_x values, the resulting expected portfolio return must be equal to (or greater than) some desired R^*. Usually the model is solved for a number of R^* values so that one has a variety of *efficient portfolios* to choose from which differ in risk/return characteristics.

To solve the above set of equations, the analyst need the data estimates on standard deviation and expected returns for all N securities alongwith correlation coefficient between all possible security pairs. Different levels of risk and return are evaluated for securities and portfolios when a decision must be made concerning which security or portfolio is better than another. It is at that point in the analysis that indifference curves of hypothetical individuals are employed to help determine which securities or portfolios are desirable and which ones are not. Basically, values for return and risk will be plotted for a number of portfolios as well as indifference curves for different types of investors. The investor's optimal portfolio will then be the one identified with the highest level of utility for the various indifference curves.

Given the measures of risk and return for individual securities developed, the measures of risk and return may be used for portfolios of risky assets. Risk-averse investors hold portfolios rather than individual securities as a means of eliminating unsystematic risk; hence the examination of risk and return will continue in terms of portfolios rather than individual securities. Indifference curves can be used to indicate investors' *willingness* to trade risk for return; now investors' ability to trade risk for return needs to be represented in terms of indifference curves and efficient portfolios.

EFFICIENT PORTFOLIOS

Efficient portfolios may contain any number of asset combinations. Two examples are shown, a two-asset combination, a three-asset portfolio, and a five-asset portfolio.

TWO-SECURITY PORTFOLIO

The degree to which a two-security portfolio reduces variance of returns depends on the degree of correlation between the returns of the securities. This can be best illustrated by expressing the variability in terms of standard deviation (the square root of the variance):

$$\sigma_p = \sqrt{W_A^2 \, \sigma_A^2 + W_B^2 \, \sigma_B^2 + 2W_A \, W_B \, r_{AB} \, \sigma_A \, \sigma_B} \tag{3}$$

First, assume that $r_{AB} = 1.0$, which would mean that Securities A and B are perfectly positively correlated. Then:

$$\sigma_p = \sqrt{W_A^2 \, \sigma_A^2 + W_B^2 \, \sigma_B^2 + 2W_A \, W_B \, \sigma_A \, \sigma_B}$$

or:

$$\sigma_p = \sqrt{(W_A\sigma_A + W_B\sigma_B)^2}$$

so:

$$\sigma_p = W_A \sigma_A + W_B \sigma_B \tag{4}$$

With the securities perfectly positively correlated, the standard deviation of the portfolio combination is equal to the weighted average of the standard deviation of the component securities. Since the correlation coefficient cannot be greater than 1.0, the weighted average represents the highest possible values of the portfolio standard deviation. In this case, there is no diversification taking place. With any correlation coefficient less than 1.0, there will be a diversification effect, and this effect will be larger the lower the value of the correlation coefficient.

The ultimate diversification impact occurs if $r_{AB} = -1.0$, perfect negative correlation.

$$\sigma_p = \sqrt{W_A^2\,\sigma_A^2 + W_B^2\,\sigma_B^2 - 2W_A\,W_B\,\sigma_A\,\sigma_B}$$

This can be reduced to:

$$\sigma_p = \sqrt{(W_A\sigma_A - W_B\sigma_B)^2} \tag{5}$$

$$= W_A \sigma_A - W_B \sigma_B$$

To illustrate, *two-security portfolio diversification,* assume that R_A -= 10 per cent, $R_B = 8$ per cent, $\sigma_A = 4$ per cent, and $\sigma = 3$ per cent. Since the values for both R_A and σ_A, are greater than those for R_B and σ_B, respectively, there is no dominant choice between the two securities. Higher return is associated with higher risk. Additionally, assume that $r_{AB} = 1.0$ and that the securities are equally weighted in the portfolio. It follows then that:

$$\sigma_p = \sqrt{(0.5)^2(4)^2 + (0.5)^2(3)^2 + (2)(0.5)(0.5)(1.0)(4)(3)}$$

$$= \sqrt{(0.25)(16) + (0.25)(9) + (2)(0.25)(12)}$$

$$= \sqrt{4 + 2.25 + 6}$$

$$= \sqrt{12.25}$$

$$= 3.5$$

Notice that this is the same result that would have been achieved using Equation, (4), $\sigma p = (0.5)\ (4) + (0.5)\ (3) = 2 + 1.5 = 3.5$ per cent. If $r_{AB} = 0.5$ there still is positive correlation, but as it is not perfect positive correlation, there is a diversification effect.

$$\sigma_p = \sqrt{(0.5)^2(4)^2 + (0.5)^2(3)^2 + (2)(0.5)(0.5)(0.5)(4)(3)}$$

$$= \sqrt{4 + 2.25 + 3}$$

$$= \sqrt{9.25}$$

$$= 3.04$$

This reduction of σ_p from 3.50 to 3.04 is the effect of diversification. Notice that the first two terms under the square root radical were unaffected and that the third term was only half the size it was with no diversification. The diversification impact from a lower correlation coefficient occurs in the covariance term only. If security A and B were independent of one another, that is, $r_{AB} = 0$, it is clear that the covariance term would equal zero.

$$\sigma_p = \sqrt{4 + 2.25 + (2)(0.5)(0.5)(0)(4)(3)}$$

$$= \sqrt{4+2.25+0}$$
$$= \sqrt{6.25}$$
$$= 2.5$$

and the diversification impact reduces σ_{AB} to 2.50.

If security A and B were perfectly and negatively correlated, that is, $r_{AB} = -1$, substituting the numbers from the example, first into Equation (3), gives

$$\sigma_p = \sqrt{4+2.25+(2)(0.5)(0.5)(-1.0)(4)(3)}$$

$$= \sqrt{6.25-6}$$

$$= \sqrt{0.25}$$

$$= 0.5$$

and into Equation (5):

$$\sigma_p = (0.5)(4) - (0.5)(3) = 2 - 1.5 = 0.5$$

With the appropriate weighting factors, the σ_p may be reduced to zero if there is negative correlation. For example, if $W_A = 3/7$ and $W_B = 4/7$ in this

$$\sigma_p = (3/7)(4) - (4/7)(3)$$
$$= 0$$

THREE - SECURITY PORTFOLIO

To illustrate the Markowitz portfolio model application in three assets, assume the following three assets have the characteristics:

Asset	Mean Expected Return $E(\overline{R})$	Proportion in the Portfolio (w)
A	20%	50%
B	20	20
C	20	30

the expected return for the portfolio would be
Portfolio mean return = .50 (.20)+ .20 (.20)+ .20 (.30)
$$= .20 \text{ or } 20\%$$

The portfolio variance is not the simple average of the variances of each of the assets. The general formula for variance to be used with a portfolio containing any number of assets is

$$\sigma_p^2 = \sum_{i=1}^{n}\sum_{j=1}^{n} w_i w_j r_{ij} \sigma_i \sigma_j$$

where

w = proportion in portfolio
σ = standard deviation
r_{ij} = correlation between i and j
p = the portfolio
n = the number of assets
i, j = specific assets,

Thus, the variance of a portfolio containing *three* assets must be calculated using this expanded version of the formula:

$$\sigma_p^2 = w_1^2\sigma_1^2 + w_2^2\sigma_2^2 + w_3^2\sigma_3^2 -$$

$$2w_1w_2 \, cov_{1,2} + 2w_1 \, w_3 \, cov_{1,3} + 2w_2w_3 \, cov_{2,3}$$

Calculation of the Expected Risk and Return for a Three-Asset Portfolio

Security	Mean Expected Return E( )	Variance (σ^2)	Standard Deviation (σ)	Propor- tion in Portfolio (ω)
A	20%	20.0	4.5%	50%
B	20	64.4	8.0	20
C	20	225.0	15.0	30

Correlation Paired Assets	coefficient (r_{ij})	Covariance (cov_{ij})
A, B	.48	21.6
A, C	.30	22.5
B, C	.60	81.0

Portfolio variance = $(.5)^2(20)+ (.2)^2(64.4)+ (.3)^2(225)+$

2 (.5) (.2) (21.6)+ 2 (.5) (.3) (22.5)+ 2 (.3) (.2) (81)

σ_p^2 = 48.6

σ_p = 6.97%

FIVE - SECURITY PORTFOLIO

If the number of securities is more than three, say five. To illustrate, Table-3 presents the relevant data of 5 securities. R represents the annualised return on each security. The *a* values are annualised standard deviations of monthly returns. The diagonal in the correlation matrix is filled with 1.0s, reflecting the fact that a given security is perfectly positively correlated with itself.

As a starting point, let us consider a single security. From the risks and returns for each of the five securities shown in Table 2, it may be observed that D and E are clearly dominated by the others. C also appears to be dominated, though to a less significant degree, by a security with less risk and greater return. If we were to stop here, it is doubtful that C, D, or E would be purchased. But this neglects the important role that diversification and security correlation play in portfolio selection. For example, C and E have a negative correlation equal to -0.12, which suggests that a combination of the two might reduce their combined risk to the point where they should be held.

For a two-security portfolio consisting of, say, C and E,
Equation-1 becomes :

$$\sigma_p = [W_c^2\sigma_c^2 + W_E^2\sigma_E^2 + 2(W_cW_E \, \sigma_c \, \sigma_E r_{CE})]^{1/2}$$

and equation-2 becomes :

$$E(R_p) = W_c \, E \, (R_c) + W_E \, E \, (R_E)$$

But these can be further simplified by recognising that whatever is not invested in one security is invested in the other : for example, $W_c = (1 - W_E)$. As a result, both the standard deviaiton and expected return can be expressed in terms of the percent invested in only one of the stocks :

$$\sigma_p = [W_c^2 \sigma_c^2 + (1 - W_c)^2 \sigma_E^2 + 2(W_c (1 - W_c)] \sigma_c \sigma_E r_{CE})]^{1/2} \qquad (6)$$

$$E(R_p) = W_c E(R_c) + (1-W_c)E(R_E) \qquad (7)$$

TABLE 1

Information on Five Securities From Seven Years of Monthly Return

Security	Annualised	
	Return (R)	Standard Deviation (σ)
A	36.2%	25.2%
B	31.2	21.8
C	26.9	22.3
D	20.2	39.4
E	17.5	51.0

Correlation Matrix

	A	B	C	D	E
A	1.0				
B	0.45	1.0			
C	0.18	0.26	1.0		
D	0.23	0.14	0.25	1.0	
E	-0.01	0.50	-0.12	0.26	1.0

For example, consider a 0.812 is invested in C and a 0.188 investment in E. The standard deviation and expected return will be 19.45 per cent and 25.13 per cent respectively:

$$[(0.812)^2 (0.223)^2 + (1.0 - 0.812)^2 (0.510)^2 + 2(0.812)(1.0 - 0.812) (0.223)(0.510)(-0.12)]^{.5}$$
$$= 0.1945$$
$$(0.812)(0.269) + (1.0 - 0.812)(0.175)$$
$$= 0.2513$$

The percentages of the investments in this example were chosen with a purpose. They happen to be the percentages which lead to a minimum variance (or standard deviation) portfolio. If W_1 is invested in security 1 and $W_2 = (1 - W_2)$ is invested in security 2, then the value of W_1 which produces the minimum possible standard deviation is found as follows:

Minimum Variance:

Using the C −E data: $W_1 = \dfrac{\sigma_2^2 - \sigma_1 \sigma_2 r_{1,2}}{\sigma_1^2 + \sigma_2^2 - 2\sigma_1 \sigma_2 r_{1,2}}$ \qquad (8)

$$W_c = \frac{\sigma_E^2 - \sigma_c \sigma_E r_{CE}}{\sigma_c^2 + \sigma_E^2 - 2\sigma_c \sigma_E r_{CE}}$$

$$= \frac{(0.51)^2 - (0.223)(0.51) - (0.12)}{(0.223)^2 + (0.51)^2 - 2(0.223)(0.51) - (0.12)}$$

$$= 0.812$$
$$W_E = 1.0 - W_C$$
$$= 1.0 - 0.812$$
$$= 0.188$$

Equation 8 applies to a two-security portfolio, but it is useful in finding what proportion in each security will lead to a minimum variance.

When all five securities are considered together the portfolio variance becomes more complex to calculate. But its calculation follows a straightforward logic. First, the variance of each security are weighted by W_x^2 and summed together. Second, the covariances for every possible security combination are weighted by W_x and W_y and added to the summed variances.

σ_P^2, is equal to : $\sigma_p^2 =$

Weighted Security Variances $W_A^2 \, \sigma_A^2 + W_B^2 \sigma_B^2 + ... + W_E^2 \, \sigma_E^2.$

Plus: +

Covariance of A with all others

$2 (W_A \, W_B \, \sigma_A \, \sigma_B \, r_{AB}) + 2 (W_A \, W_C \, \sigma_A \, \sigma_C \, r_{AC}) + ... + 2 (W_A \, W_E \, \sigma_A \, \sigma_E \, r_{AE})$

Plus: +

Covariance of B with others

$2 (W_B \, W_C \, \sigma_B \, \sigma_C \, r_{BC}) + 2 (W_B \, W_D \, \sigma_B \, \sigma_D \, r_{BD}) + ... + 2 (W_B \, W_E \, \sigma_B \, \sigma_E \, r_{BE})$

Plus: +

.

.

.

Plus: +

Covariance of D $2 \quad (W_D \, W_E \, \sigma_D \, \sigma_E \, r_{DE})$

Since each covariance between x and y is the same between y and x, calculating the number once and doubling it saves times.

A Graphical Approach

A graphical representation of the Mean-Variance Criterion is presented in **Figure 1**, the vertical axis denotes expected return while the horizontal axis measures the standard deviation (or variance) of the returns. Given its expected return and standard deviation, any investment option can be represented by a point on such a plane and the set of all potential options can be enclosed by an area such as shown in Figure 1. The efficient, given by the arc AB, is a boundary of the attainable set. In Figure 1 the shaded area represents the attainable set of portfolio considerations, with their own risks and expected returns. (Two different portfolios may have the same expected return and risk). Any point inside the shaded area is not as efficient as a corresponding point on the efficient frontier — the arc AB. For instance, point X_1 offers the same expected returns as X_2 but has a smaller standard deviation. Any point below X_1 such as X_3, has the same standard deviation as X_1 but a smaller expected return. The portfolios on the efficient frontier are said to dominate those within the shaded area representing all possible portfolios.

After the efficient set is defined, an investor can maximise the expected returns or minimise the risk by selecting a portfolio from the set. Any other portfolio would not meet the investor's objective, as long as the objective is either maximum expected return for a pre-selected level of risk or minimum risk for a pre-selected level of expected return. Again, an efficient portfolio is one compared to which no other portfolio has the same returns and a lower risk, or the same risk and a high return.

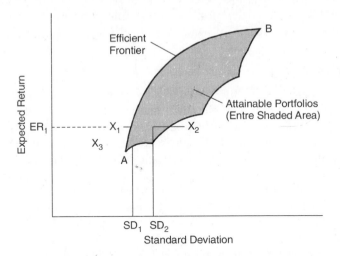

FIGURE 1: MARKOWITZ EFFICIENT FRONTIER

An investor's final choice out of the efficient set depends on his tastes. Figure 2 shows how an investor might select an optimal portfolio. Figure 2 superimposes the individual indifference map on the opportunity set of investments. The investor would prefer an option which would allow him to reach indifference curve I_1 but no attainable investment option of this kind exists (indifference curve l_1) does not intersect or touch the set. The best that he can do, given the potential options, is to choose option N out of the efficient frontier, that is the option which is tangent to indifferences curve l_3. Since no other choice will permit him to reach a higher level of utility, option N is the investor's optimal choice, the one which maximises his utility. Should he choose another alternative

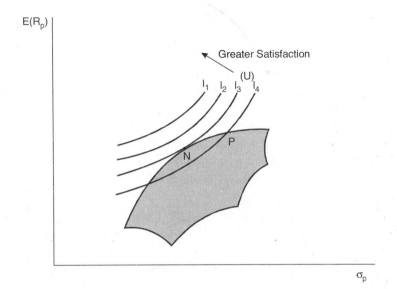

FIGURE 2

out of the efficient frontier, say Points M and P, his utility will fall since these options permit him to reach indifference curve l_4, which represents a lower level of satisfaction. The number of physical portfolio is nearly infinite and the identification of portfolios along the efficient frontier is therefore a form-dable conceptual and computational problem. This requires a solution of a mathematical programming problem on a high speed computer.

CORNER PORTFOLIOS

A number of portfolios on the efficiency frontier are *corner portfolios.* A corner portfolio is defined as one in which either (1) the new security is added to a previously efficient portfolio or (2) a security is dropped from a previously efficient portfolio. For example, assume that a population of 50 screened securities are analysed to identify the set of efficient portfolios. The single security with the highest risk-return value, point A in Figure-3, provides a starting point. Next, expected returns, variances and covariances are pairwise compared for the point A security and each of the remaining 49 securities to identify the one to be added to the portfolio at the second corner point. The security to be added is the one that minimises the slope of the efficiency frontier at that corner point. Given the second corner portfolio, consisting of two securities, each of the remaining 48 will be examined similarly to determine if one security should be added, or one of the previously selected ones dropped from, the next corner portfolio. In every case, when the slope of the efficient frontier is minimised, maximum gain from diversification is realised. This process is continued until each corner portfolio is identified along efficiency frontier.

Part (*a*) of Table 2 illustrates three hypothetical corner portfolios corresponding to points B, D, and F in Figure-3. Corner portfolio B consists of three securities with assumed identification numbers 20,13, and 47. The next corner portfolio occurs at point D where when security number 9 is added. At F security number 20 is dropped from the set and the corner portfolio consists of three remaining securities—13, 47, and 9. Portfolio weights Wj of part (*a*), Table 2, are arbitrary and illustrative.

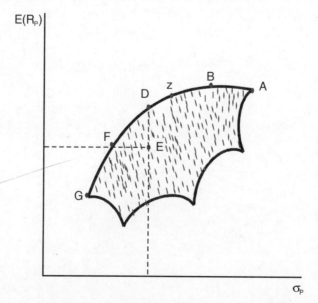

FIGURE 3: INVESTOR'S EFFICIENT FRONTIER : ALL RISKY SECURITIES

Any two portfolios can be combined to form a third in the same manner that two individual securities can be combined to form a portfolio. If portfolios B and D are combined to form a new portfolio z, expected return and risk will be measured in a similar manner to the two security measures of expected returns and standard deviation which are defined

$$E(R_p) = W_1 E(R_1) - W_2 E(R_2) \qquad\qquad W_1 + W_2 = 1$$

$$\sigma_p = \sqrt{W_1^2 \sigma_1^2 + 2 W_1 W_2 \sigma_1 \sigma_2 r_{1,2} + W_2^2 \sigma_2^2}$$

TABLE 2
Corner and Non-corner Efficient Portfolios

(a) Corner Portfolios (Security j)

Portfolio B		Portfolio D		Portfolio F	
j	Wi	j	Wi	j	Wi
20	.333	20	.167		
13	.334	13	.333	13	.100
49	.333	47	.333	47	.300
		9	.167	9	.600
	1.000				
			1.000		1.000

(b) Non-corner Portfolios (Z)
$W_B = .50; W_D = .50$

j	$W_B W_{B,j}$		$W_D W_{D,j}$		W_z
20	(.50 × .333)	+	(.50 × .167)	=	.251
13	(.50 × .334)	+	(.50 × .333)	=	.333
47	(.50 × .333)	+	(.50 × .333)	=	.333
9	(.50 × .000)	+	(.50 × .167)	=	.083
					1.000

Specifically, if W_B percentage of wealth is invested in portfolio B and W_D percentage is invested in portfolio D, expected return and standard deviation for portfolio Z will be defined :

$$E(R_z) = W_B E(R_B) + W_D E(R_D), \qquad\qquad W_B + W_D = 1$$

$$\sigma_z = \sqrt{W_B^2 \sigma_B^2 + 2 W_B W_D \sigma_B \sigma_D r_{BD} + W_D^2 \sigma_D^2}$$

Every security held in either B or D will be held in combination Z in proportions determined by the weighted average of percentages committed to each security in each of the adjacent portfolios. For example, for security 20 of Table 2 and with $W_B = W_D = .50$

$$\begin{aligned} W_{z'20} &= W_B W_{B,20} + W_D W_{D,20} \\ &= (.50)(.333) + (.50)(.167) \\ &= .251 \end{aligned}$$

Part (b) of Table-2 illustrates all four securities in combined portfolio z. The relationship examined there holds in general; weights for each security in any portfolio constructed from two other portfolios can be determined in this manner.

By swapping one security with other, the portfolio's expected return could not be increased with no change in its risk. This leads to an important conclusion : *If two securities in a portfolio have the same marginal variance and different expected returns, the portfolio is not optimal.* Put more positively :If a portfolio is optimal, all securities with a given marginal variance (relative to the portfolio) will have the same expected return. The efficient frontier of Figure-3 consists of expected return-risk loci for corner portfolios and other portfolios which are constructed from adjacent corner portfolios. The frontier is continuous since investors can allocate wealth among risk-return possibilities to achieve any desired point on the efficient arc.

DENTS IN THE EFFICIENT SET

Efficient set is a concave. It can not have any other shape and it is impossible to have dents in an efficient set shown in Figure-4. There is a dent in it between points A and B, showing that there is a region on the efficient set where it is not concave. This can not be an efficient set because an investor would put part of funds in the portfolio located at A and rest of the finds in the portfolio located at B. The resulting portfolio, a combination of A and B , would have to be at the left of the alleged efficient set. It is indicated at point T. If it truly is at efficient portfolio, then it would be impossible to form a portfolio with the same expected returns as T with a lower standard deviation. However, by putting 60 % of his or her funds in A and 40% in B, the investor may have a portfolio that dominates T, since it would have the same expected return but a lower standard deviation ? This portfolio would lie on the straight line connecting A and B if the correlation between A and B were + l. This portfolio has a lower standard deviation than T. Z denotes this point in Figure-4. Because the actual correlation is less than or equal to +1, it would have a standard deviation as low as or lower than Z's standard deviation. This means that the alleged efficient set was constructed in error because it is easy to find more efficient portfolio in the region where it is not concave.

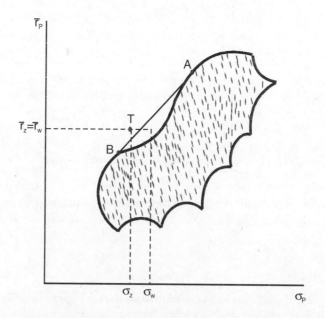

FIGURE 4: INVESTOR'S EFFICIENT FRONTIER: ALL RISKY SECURITIES

DOMINANCE PRINCIPLE

The dominance principle has been developed to understand the risk-return trade-off conceptually. As in efficient frontier analysis, it is assumed that investor prefers returns and dislikes risks. For example, in Figure-5, if a individual experience the higher expected return with portfolio 'K', than with portfolio 'M' but the risk associated with both the portfolios is the same, he would prefer portfolio 'K'. In other words, portfolio 'K' would dominate portfolio 'M'. Infact all the portfolios lying along the lower part of the *dog-leg* are dominated by portfolios lying along upper part. Portfolio that lie along the boundary between points S and L are therefore termed as efficient in that each represented the maximum expected return for a given level of risk.

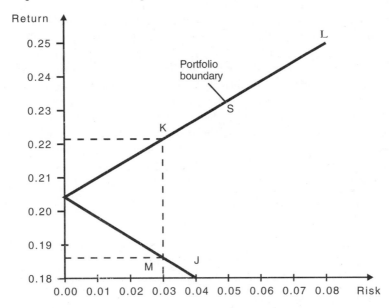

FIGURE 5: REMOVING A 'DENT' FROM THE EFFICIENT SET

It may be observed from Figure 5 that points K and M are directly comparable because they have a common standard deviation. How does risk versus return compare with the other portfolios ? It is difficult to say because the risk and return are not directly comparable using the dominance principle. This is the basic limitation of the dominance principle — the portfolios without a common risk or return factor are not directly comparable.

MODIFICAITON TO THE EFFICIENT FRONTIER

Two modificaiton to the efficient frontier must be discussed: what happens when short selling is added, and what happens when leveraged portfolios are added?

A. Short Selling

Short selling (or "going short") is a very regulated type of market transaction. It involves selling shares of a stock that are borrowed in expectation of a fall in the security's price. When and if the price declines, the investor buys an equivalent number of shares of the same stock at the new lower price and returns to the lender the stock that was borrowed. The minimum-variance set provides the set of portfolio that minimise portfolio variance for a given portfolio expected return and efficient frontier furnishes portfolios that maximise portfolio return for a given level of risk. In Figure-6 the efficient frontier is bounded on both ends by Y *and* the minimum variance portfolio V, respectively. Point Y is called the maximum-return portfolio, since there is no other portfolio with a higher return. This point is normally an efficient security or portfolio with the greatest level of risk and return. It could also be a portfolio of securities, all having the same highest levels of risk and return. Point Z is normally a single security with the lowest level of return, although it could be a portfolio of securities, all having the same low level of return, identical to the Markowitz model except that it allows for short selling.

A negative value for the weight invested in a security is allowed, tantamount to allowing a short sale of the security. An investor could sell the lowest-return security short (X) and take the proceeds and invest them in the highest-return security (Y). If the number of short sales is unrestricted, then by a continuous short selling of X and reinvesting in Y the investor could generate an infinite expected return. Hence the upper bound of the highest-return portfolio would no longer be Y but infinity (shown by the arrow on the top of the efficient frontier). Likewise the investor could short sell the highest-return security Y and reinvest the proceeds into the lowest-yield security X, thereby generating a return less than the return on the lowest-return security. Given no restriction on the amount of short selling, an infinitely negative return can be achieved, thereby removing the lower bound *of* X on the efficient frontier. But rational investors will not short sell a high-return stock and buy a low-return stock. The portfolios on VZ' always dominate those of VX, as shown in Figure 6.

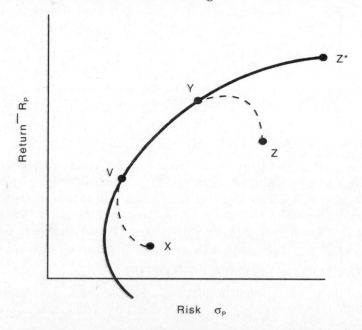

FIGURE 6: THE EFFICIENT FRONTIER WITH SHORT SELLING

Whether an investor engages in any of this short-selling activity depends on the investor's own unique set of indifference curves. Hence, short selling generally will increase the range of alternative investments from the minimum-variance portfolio to plus or minus infinity.

Short Selling With Margin Requirements

Dyl introduced short selling with margin requirements by creating a new set of risky securities, the ones sold short, which are negatively correlated with the existing set of risky securities. These new securities greatly enhance the diversification effect when they are placed in portfolios. The Dyl model affects the efficient frontier in two ways: (1) If the investor were to combine in equal weight any long position in a security or portfolio with a short position in a security or a portfolio, the resulting portfolio would yield zero return and zero variance and (2) any combination of unequal weighted long or short positions would yield portfolios with higher returns and lower risk levels. Overall, these two effects will yield an efficient frontier that dominates the Markowitz efficient frontier. Figure-7 compares the Dyl and Markowitz efficient frontiers.

Even though the inclusion of short selling changes the location and boundaries of the efficient frontier, the concavity of the curve is still intact. This is important in that it preserves the efficient frontier as the locus of optimal portfolios for risk-averse investors. As long as the efficient frontier remains concave, by using indifference curves it will be possible to locate the optimal portfolio for each investor.

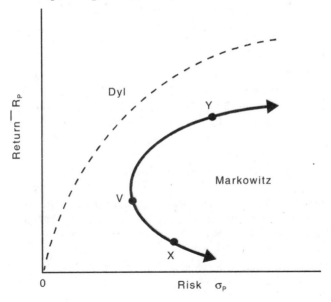

FIGURE 7: EFFICIENT FRONTIERS WITH AND WITHOUT SHORT SELLING AND
MARGIN REQUIREMENTS

B. Leveraged Portfolios

Markowitz Model, which recognised the existence of both systematic and unsystematic risk, did not allow for borrowing and lending opportunities. The investor is assumed to have a certain amount of initial wealth to invest for a given holding period. Of all the periods that are available, the optimal one is shown to correspond to the point where one of the investor's indifference curves is tangent to the efficient set. At the end of the holding period, the investor's initial wealth will have either increased or decreased, depending on the portfolio's rate of return. The resulting end-of-period wealth could then be either completely reinvested, completely spent on consumption, or partially reinvested and partially consumed. Again, in the Markowitz's approach, it is assumed that the assets being considered for investment are individually risky. That is, each one of the N risky assets has an uncertain return over the investor's holding period. Since none of the assets has a perfectly negative correlation with any other asset, all the portfolios also have uncertain returns over the investor's holding period, and these are risky. Furthermore, in the Markowitz approach, the investor is not allowed to use borrowed money, alongwith his or her initial wealth, to purchase a portfolio of assets. This means that the investor is not allowed to use financial leverage.

To expand the Markowitz approach investor can consider risk free assets and financial leverage by first investing in not only risky assets but also in a riskfree assets, and second by borrowing money at a given rate of interest.

(i) Riskfree Asset

Investment in riskfree asset is often referred to as riskfree lending. But what exactly is a riskfree asset in the context of Markowitz's approach ? Since this approach involves investing for a single holding period, it means that the return of the riskfree asset is certain. That is, if the investor purchases this asset at the beginning of the holding period, then the investor knows exactly what the value of the asset will be at the end of the holding period. Since there is no uncertainty about the terminal value of the riskfree asset, the standard deviation of the riskfree asset is, by definition, zero. In turn, this means that the covariance between the rate of return on the riskfree asset and the rate of return on any risky asset is zero.

Since a riskfree asset has, by definition, a certain return, this type of asset must be some kind of fixed-income security with no possibility of default. Since all corporate securities have some chance of default, the riskfree asset cannot be issued by a corporation. This leaves only one type of security as a riskfree asset, i.e. Treasury security. Again, it may be noted that only those specific Treasury bills with a maturity that match the length of the investor's holding period.

With the introduction of a riskfree asset, the investor is now able to put part of his or her money in this asset and the remainder in any of the risky portfolios that are in Markowitz's feasible set. Adding these new opportunities expands the feasible set significantly and, more importantly, changes the location of part of Markowitz's efficient set. The nature of these changes needs to be analysed, since investors are concerned with selecting a portfolio from the efficient set. In doing so, consideration is given initially in determining the expected return and standard deviation for a portfolio that consists of combining an investment in the riskfree asset with an investment in a single risky security.

(ii) Investing in Both the Riskfree Asset and a Risky Asset

The efficient frontier would be altered substantially if a riskfree security is included among available investment opportunities. While a risk free security does not exist in the strict sense of the word, there are securities which promise return with relative certainty. They are characterised by an absence of default risk and interest rate risk; full payment of principal (and interest) is assured without serious prospect of capital loss arising from changes in the level of interest rates. Risk free securities of this type include cash, short-term treasury bills, and time deposits in banks or savings and loan associations; cash would be dominated by the other positive return investments.

Given the opportunity to either borrow or lend at the riskfree rate, an investor proceed to identify the optimal portfolio by plotting his or her indifference curves on graph and noting where one of them is tangent to the indifference efficient set. Figure-8 presents the CML from R to Z with the efficient arc A to B. The ellipse in the graph represents all possible combinations of securities into portfolios that can be put together from all the securities in the market. Each point represents a portfolio with specific risk and return characteristics. Portfolio *e*, for example, has an expected return of 11 per cent and a standard deviation of 12.5 per cent. However, portfolio *e* is not efficient, since portfolio *B* has the same expected return but a standard deviation of only 8 per cent. Portfolio *h* has a higher return and the same risk as portfolio *e*. It is more attractive than portfolio *e* but not efficient, since portfolio *f* has a still higher return with the same degree of risk as *e* and *h*.

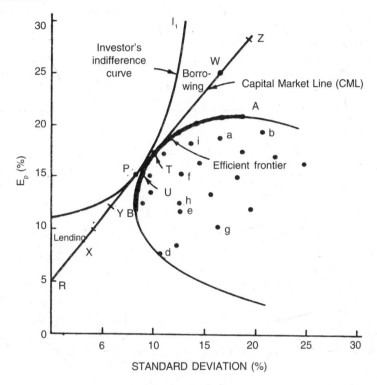

FIGURE 8

Portfolio *A* is a single-equity portfolio that has the highest return and risk; in no way can investor improve on its return-to-risk ratio. If investor moves to the right on the curve, return decreases and risk increases; if investor moves to the left on the curve, return decreases and risk decreases. Hence, investor is on the efficient frontier. It represents all possible portfolios that are *efficient* as investor moves to the left and down. The only way the investor can obtain a higher return on the efficient frontier is to accept a higher amount of risk.

Which of the portfolios should the investor choose ? Should portfolio *A* be choosen, with an expected return of 22 per cent and a risk of 18 per cent (and a reward-to-risk ratio of 0.94) ? Or should it be portfolio *T*, with 17.5 ± 11 per cent (reward to risk equals [17.5 -5] ÷ 11 = (12.5 ÷ 11) = 1.14, or portfolio B, with 12 ± 8 per cent and a reward-to-risk ratio of 0.88? The risk-free return of 5 per cent is for illustrative purposes only. The rate varies in practice with the yield on Treasury bills.

Actually, the investor would invest somewhere on the line *R TZ*, which represents all possible combinations of portfolio *T* and risk free securities. This is similar to the portfolio combination in the two-security cases, but now there are many more portfolios. By combining the securities in portfolio T with risk-free securities at R, the investor would actually reduce risk more than the reduction in return. The reduction of risk makes the combination of securities T and R more attractive at point P than an all-equity portfolio at U. The portfolio at P on the market line, consisting of 70 per cent of portfolio T and 30 per cent of risk free securities, R has the same return but the lower risk than portfolio U and therefore would be more acceptable to the investor, or more efficient.

That part of the capital market line from R to T is called a *lending portfolio*, in that the investor is willing to buy riskless securities or lend a portion of the total portfolio at the risk free yield. The investor can invest all funds in portfolio T, all funds in portfolio R, or some combination of T and R; for example :

Point on CML	Portfolio Combination %		Approximate Return (%)	Approximate Standard Deviation %	Reward-to-Risk Ratio
	r_f	T			
r_f	100	0	5.0	0.0	—
X	50	50	11.25	5.5	1.15
Y	40	60	12.5	6.6	1.14
T	0	100	17.5	11.0	1.14
W	-20	125	21.875	13.75	1.14
Z	-33	150	26.25	16.5	1.14
A	-50	200	36.00	19.25	1.14

Or the investor could invest at the request of the capital market line between T and Z, which represents a *borrowing* portfolio. The investor would buy the securities in portfolio T and would borrow money at the riskless rate to purchase more of the securities in portfolio T. A practical limit on the amount of money borrowed is 50 per cent of the value of portfolio T. Portfolio Z on the CML represents 150% of portfolio T and a loan of 50% of the value of the equities. Portfolio W on the CML represents approximately 125% of portfolio T, with the amount borrowed representing 25% of the value of the equities. The maximum amount borrowed would be 100%, where 200% was invested in portfolio at T. If the investor can borrow at a risk-free yield and invest in portfolio T, then the move would be to point Z on the capital-market line, when the reward would be proportional to the risk rather than less proportional, as a point A on the efficient frontier on equity. Therefore, in theory, it pays investors to borrow and buy equity of an efficient portfolio, since it improves the reward-to-risk ratio *so* that reward and risk are proportional

Where investors operate on the capital market line depends on their attitudes towards risk and return. Investors must determine their own preferences for risk and return by way of an indifference curve. In theory, the investor will invest in the combination of securities found at that point where the highest indifference curve just touches the capital market line. That is portfolio P in Figure-8. Investors might have higher return and lower risk goals, but they can obtain those combinations only on the capital market line, and will invest at some point that gives the combination of return and risk that allows them to maximise net worth and make a satisfactory investment.

To be realistic, assume that the investor's borrowing rate is above the lending rate. Combination of lending or borrowing with a portfolio of risky assets lie along a straight line. With lending and borrowing the efficient frontier looks like Figure-9. Notice that for all investors, except for those whose risk-return trade-offs cause them to hold portfolios between portfolios L and B, the ability to lend and borrow improves their opportunities. The ability to lend (putting part of the funds in the fixed-income securities) is hardly controversial. The borrowing part may be more controversial. Note from Figure-16 that by choosing point X rather than point Y, the investor earns the same return with less risk. Borrowing and buying a less risky portfolio can give higher returns and less risk than buying a more risky portfolio. Comparing Y^1 and Y in Figure-15 shows that it is possible to achieve a higher expected return at the same risk level by borrowing. Of course, borrowing, like short sales or almost any financial mechanism, can be abused. It can be used to take extreme and imprudent risk positions. On the other hand, it can be used to enhance performance. Rejecting borrowing entirely would throw out positive opportunities. For example, consider an investor wishing to have a high portfolio with higher expected return than offered by Portfolio B (e.g. the expected return of Y). This investor would have the same expected return and less risks by buying portfolio B and borrowing than by buying Portfolio Y, which does not involve borrowing.

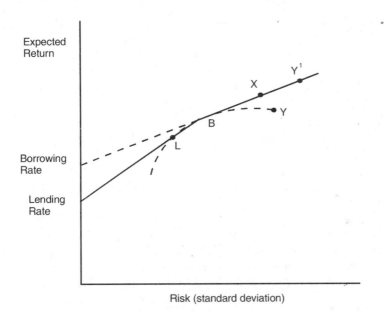

FIGURE 9: THE EFFICIENT FRONTIER WITH DIFFERENTIAL LENDLING AND BORROWING RATES

CRITIQUE

Several criticisms were made of the Markowitz appraisal, both from theoretical and practical point of view. One criticism had to do with the assumption that rational investors can actually risk averters. To illustrate, consider the Table-5 estimated return of alternative portfolios. Markowitz's theory will consider portfolio 4, with a minimum return of 2 per cent, a maximum of 18 per cent, and a mean of 10 per cent, to be superior to portfolio 5, with a minimum of 0 per cent, a maximum of 20 per cent, and the same 10 per cent mean as portfolio 4. But the question is whether or not this necessarily represent a rational choice. *Why should it be irrational for an investor to be willing to chance a zero return in exchange for the possibility of a 20 per cent return ?*

TABLE 5

Estimated Returns of alternative Portfolios

Portfolio	Expected Average Rate of Return	Expected Standard Deviation	Expected Range of Returns at Two Standard Deviations level	
			Lowest	Highest
1	4%	1/4%	3-1/2%	4-1/2%
2	6%	1-1/2%	3%	9%
3	8%	2-3/4%	2-1/2%	13-1/2%
4	10%	4%	2%	18%
5	10%	5%	0%	20%
.	.	.	.	.
.	.	.	.	.
.	.	.	.	.
100	20%	15%	−10%	50%

A closely related question is whether variance as such is the most appropriate portfolio measure of risk. Most of the work stimulated by Markowitz uses short term volatility to determine whether the expected rate of return from a security should be assigned a high or low expected variance. But if an investor has limited liquidity constraints, and is truly a long-term holder, then price volatility per se does not really pose a risk. Rather in this case, the question of concern is one of ultimate price realisation and not interim volatility.

There were (and still are) some very practical obstacles that restricted the use and development of the techniques suggested by Markowitz model. An obvious drawback was that practicing investment managers-unable to understand the conceptual mathematics involved became immediately suspicious that an academic approach to portfolio management was essentially unsound. Second, while security analysts and portfolio managers are accustomed to thinking about expected rates of return, they are much less comfortable in assessing the possible ranges of error in their expectations, and are generally totally unaccustomed to estimating covariances among securities. Another limitation in the use of the Markowitz model is that each time a change in the existing portfolio comes under consideration, the entire population of possible securities must be revaluated in order to preserve the desired risk-return balance. This, in turn, requires a large number of mathematical calculations. Markowitz himself point this out by observing that "an analysis of 100 securities required 100 expected returns, 100 variances, and almost 500 covariances". He then suggested a simple procedure — relating the returns on each security to the returns on an overall index of market prices, thereby implicitly relating the return on each security to each other security.

Even more significantly than the voluminous mathematical computations required to apply the Markowitz technique, is that the portfolio alteration required to achieve constant portfolio efficiency may be so numerous that they can give rise to large, uneconomic transaction costs. This could be true even if portfolio managers reviewed their holdings less often than daily or weekly.

Despite these shortcomings, Markowitz's contribution to contemporary portfolio theory cannot be minimised. The presentation of his technique was a stimulating statement of portfolio selection theory and the benefits that could be derived from efficient diversification. It should be considered as a package of guidelines immediately transferable for use by practicing portfolio manager. A small amount of diversification can result in substantial reduction in risk. Second, Markowitz forced others to consider that some measure of risk and not just the expected rate of return, should be considered when dealing with investment decisions. The focus of the investor's dicision is based on the correct variables expacted return, expected risk, and the relationship of one security return to another. Finally, given the fundamental propositions, others became interested in the theory and began to adjust the basic framework so that practical application could be more readily considered. It suggests that under certain circumstances investors can borrow money to buy stocks.

REVIEW PROBLEMS

1. P. Kar owned five securities at the beginning of the year in the following amounts and with the following current and expected end-of-year prices :

Security	Share	Current Price	Expected Year-End Price
A	100	₹ 50	₹ 65
B	150	30	40
C	75	20	25
D	100	25	32
E	125	40	47

What is the expected return on Kar's portfolio for the year ?

Ans:

The initial value of Kar's portfolio is:
$$= (₹\ 50 \times 100) + (₹\ 30 \times 150) + (₹\ 20 \times 75) + (₹\ 25 \times 100) + (₹\ 40 \times 125)$$
$$= ₹\ 5000 + ₹\ 4500 + ₹\ 1500 + ₹\ 2500 + ₹\ 5000$$
$$= ₹\ 18{,}500$$

The proportion that each security constitutes of Kar's initial portfolio is:

$$\begin{aligned}
X_A &= (₹\ 50 \times 100)/(₹\ 18{,}500) = .27 \\
X_B &= (₹\ 30 \times 150)/(₹\ 18{,}500) = .24 \\
X_C &= (₹\ 20 \times 75)/(₹\ 18{,}500) = .08 \\
X_D &= (₹\ 25 \times 100)/(₹\ 18{,}500) = .14 \\
X_E &= (₹\ 40 \times 125)/(₹\ 18{,}500) = .27
\end{aligned}$$

The expected returns on the portfolio securities are:

$$\begin{aligned}
\tilde{R}_A &= (₹\ 65 - ₹\ 50)/₹\ 50 = 30.0\% \\
\tilde{R}_B &= (₹\ 40 - ₹\ 30)/₹\ 30 = 33.3\% \\
\tilde{R}_C &= (₹\ 25 - ₹\ 20)/₹\ 20 = 25.0\% \\
\tilde{R}_D &= (₹\ 32 - ₹\ 25)/₹\ 25 = 28.0\% \\
\tilde{R}_E &= (₹\ 47 - ₹\ 40)/₹\ 40 = 17.5\%
\end{aligned}$$

The expected return on a portfolio is given by:

$$\tilde{R}_p = \sum_{i=1}^{n}(X_i \times R_i)$$

In the case of Kar's portfolios:
$$\begin{aligned}
\tilde{R}_P &= (.27 \times 30.0\%) + (.24 \times 33.3\%) + (.08 \times 25.0\%) + (.14 \times 28.0\%) + (.27 \times 17.5\%) \\
&= (0.81\%) + (7.992\%) + (2.0\%) + (3.92\%) + (4.725\%) \\
&= 19.447\%
\end{aligned}$$

2. Given the following information about two securities on joint probability distribution

of returns for investments in the security of XYZ Co. and ABC Co., calculate the covariance and correlation coefficient between two investments :

Probability	XYZ Co.	ABC Co.
.10	-12%	12
.15	-7	15
.20	5	20
.25	10	10
.30	12	5

Ans.:

The covariance between two securities is given by :

$$\sigma_{XY} = \sum_{i=1}^{n}(R_X - \tilde{R}_X) \times (R_Y - \tilde{R}_Y)$$

In the case of XYZ Co. and ABC Co. stocks, their expected returns are :

$\tilde{R}_{XYZ}$ = $(-10 \times -12\%) + (.15 \times -7\%) + (.20 \times 5\%) + (.25 \times 10\%) + (.30 \times 12\%)$

         =   -1.2-1.05 + 1.00 + 2.5 + 3.6

         =   4.85

$\tilde{R}_{ABC}$ = $(.10 \times 12\%) + (.15 \times 15\%) + (.20 \times 20\%) + (.25 \times 10\%) + (.30 \times 5\%)$

         = 1.2% + 2.25% + 4% + 2.5% + 1.5%

         = 11.45%

Therefore :

σ_{XYZ} =$[.10 \times (-12\%-4.85) \times (12\%-11.45\%)] + [.15 \times (-7\%-4.85\%) \times (15\%-11.45\%)] +$
       $[.20 \times (5\%-4.85\%) \times (20\%-11.45\%)] + [.25 \times (10\%-4.85\%) \times (10\%-11.45\%)] +$
       $[.30 \times (12\% - 4.85\%) \times (5\% - 11.45\%)]$
       =−.92675 − 6.310125 + .2565 − 1.8669 − 13.8353 = −22.68

The correlation coefficient between two securities is :

     $r_{XY} = C_{XY}/(\sigma_X \times \sigma_X)$

In the case of XYZ and ABC stocks, their standard deviations are:

σ_{XYZ} = $\{[.10 \times (-12\% - 4.85\%)^2] + [.15 \times (-7\% - 4.85\%)^2] +$
       $[.20 \times (5\% - 4.85\%)^2] + [.25 \times (10\% - 4.85\%)^2] + [.30 \times (12\% - 4.85\%)^2]\}^{1/2}$
       = 8.45

σ_{XYZ} = $\{[.10 \times (12\%-11.45\%)^2] + [.15 \times (15 \times (15\% -11.45\%)^2]$
       $+ [.20 \times (20\% -11.45\%)^2] + [.25 \times (10 - 11.45\%)]$
       $+ [.30 \times (5\%-11.45\%)^2]\}^{1/2}$
       = $[0.03025 +1.8904 +14.6205 + .5256 +12.4808]^{1/2}$
       = $[29.5475]^{1/2}$
       = 5.44%

Therefore,

     $r_{XYZ,ABC}$ = -22.687/(8.45x5.44) = -0.49

3. An investor saw an opportunity to invest in new security with excellent growth potential. He wants to invest more than he had, which was only ₹ 10,000, he sold another security short with an expected rate of return of 15 per cent. The total amounthe sold short of was ₹ 40,000, and his total amount invested in the growth security, which had an expected rate of return of 30 per cent, was thus ₹ 50,000. Assume no margin requirements, what is his expected rate of return on this portfolio.

Ans.: Computing the portfolio weights for each security with the formula:

$$W_A = \frac{\text{Investment in A (sold short)}}{\text{Total equity investment}}$$

We find

$$W_A = \frac{-₹\,40,000}{₹\,10,000} = -4.0$$

$$W_B = \frac{-₹\,50,000}{₹\,10,000} = -5.0$$

$$
\begin{aligned}
R_P &= (-4.0 \times 15) + (5.0 \times .24) \\
&= -.60 + 1.2 \\
&= .60 = 60\%
\end{aligned}
$$

4. Suppose we have two portfolios known to be on the minimum variance set for a population of three securities, A,B, and C. There are no restrictions on short sales. The weights for each of the two portfolios are as follows:

	W_A	W_B	W_C
Portfolio X	.24	.52	.24
Portfolio Y	-.36	.72	.64

(a) What would the stock weights be for a portfolio constructed by investing ₹ 2,000 in portfolio X and ₹ 1,000 in portfolio Y?

(b) Suppose you invest ₹ 1,500 of the ₹ 3,000 in Security X. How will you allocate the remaining ₹ 1,500 between Securities X and Y to ensure that your portfolio is on the minimum variance set?

Ans.:

(a) Given a ₹ 2,000 investment in portfolio X and ₹ 1,000 investment in portfolio Y, the investment committed to each security would be:

	A	B	C	Total
Portfolio X	₹ 480	₹ 1,040	₹ b480	₹ 2,000
Portfolio Y	-360	720	640	1,000
Confirmed Portfolio	₹ 120	₹ 1,760	₹ 1,120	₹ 3,000

Since we are investing a total of ₹ 3,000 in the combined portfolio, the investment position in three securities are consistent with the folowing portfolio weights:

	W_A	W_B	W_C
Combined portfolio	.04	.59	.37

(b) Since the equation for the critical line takes the following form:

$$W_B + a + bw_A$$

Substituting in the values for W_A and W_B from portfolio X and Y, we get

$$.52 = a + .24\ b$$
$$.72 = a + =.36b$$

By solving these equations simultaneously, we can obtain the slope and the intercept of the critical line

$$W_B = .6 - \frac{1}{3}\ W_A$$

Using this equation, we can find W_B for any given value W_A if we invest half of the funds in security A $(W_A = .5)$, then

$$W_B = .6 - 1/3\ (.5) = .43$$

Since $W_A + W_B + W_C = 1$, $W_C = 1 - W_A - W_B$

Substituting in our value for W_A and W_B we find

$$W_C = 1 - .5 - .43 = .07$$

5. H.D. Verma owns a portfolio of two securities with the following expected returns, standard deviations, and weights :

Security	Expected Return	Standard Deviation	Weight
A	12%	15%	.40
B	15%	20%	.60

What are the maximum and minimum portfolio standard deviations for varying levels of correlation between two securities?

Ans.:

$$\sigma_p = \left[x_A^2\ \sigma_A^2 + x_B^2\ \sigma_B^2 + 2x_A\ x_B\ r_{AB}\ \sigma_A\sigma_B \right]^{1/2}$$

In Verma's case :

$$\sigma_p = [(.40)^2\ (15)^2 + (.60)^2\ (20)^2 + 2\ (.60)\ (.40)\ (15)\ (20)\ r_{AB}]^{\frac{1}{2}}$$
$$= [36 + 144 + (144)\ r_{AB}]^{.5}$$

The portfolio's standard deviation will be at a maximum when the correlation between securities X and Y is + 1.0. That is

$$\sigma_p = 136 + 144 + (144 \times I)]^{1}/^2$$
$$= 18\%$$

The portfolio's standard deviation will be at a minimum when the correlation between securities X and Y is -1.0. That is :

$$\sigma_p = [36 + 144 + (144 \times -I)]^{\frac{1}{2}}$$
$$= 6\%$$

6. S. Rao buys ₹ 30,000 of stock A and sells short ₹ 10,000 of stock B, using all of the proceeds to buy more of stock A. The correlation between the two securities is .45. The expected returns of stock A and B are 15% and 10% with the standard deviation of 10% and 12% respectively. What are the expected return and standard deviation of Rao's portfolio?

Ans.:

The expected return on a portfolio is given by :

$$\tilde{R}_p = \sum_{i=1}^{n}(x_i \times R_i)$$

Rao has invested ₹ 40,000 in stock A and -₹ 10,000 in stock B. Thus X_A = +1.33 and X_B = -0.33. Therefore:

$$\tilde{R}_p = (1.33 \times 15.0) + (-0.33 \times 10\%)$$

$$= 19.95 - 3.3$$

$$= 16.65$$

The standard deviation of a two-security portfolio is :

$$\sigma_p = [x_A^2 \sigma_A^2 + x_B^2 \sigma_B^2 + 2x_A x_B r_{AB} \sigma_A \sigma_B]^{1/2}$$

For Rao's case :

$$= [(1.33)^2(10)^2 + (-.33)^2(12)^2 + 2(1.33)(-.33)(.45)(10)(12)]^{1/2}$$

$$= [(176.89) + (15.6816) + (-47.4012)]^{1/2}$$

$$= [145.1704]^{1/2}$$

$$= 12.0487$$

7. Suppose that you revised your assessment of the probabilities of each of the five economic scenarios listed below:

State of Economy	Probability	Holding Period Return		
		Stocks %	Bonds %	Cash%
Bonds with low inflation	0.05	74	4	6
Bonds with high inflation	0.2	20	-10	6
Normal growth	0.5	14	9	6
Recession with low inflation	0.2	0	35	6
Recession with high inflation	0.05	-30	0	6

What are your estimates of expected return, standard deviation and correlations?

Ans.:

The new estimates are as follows:

State of Economy	Probability	Holding Period Return		
		Stocks %	Bonds %	Cash%
Bonds with low inflation	0.05	74	4	6
Bonds with high inflation	0.2	20	-10	6
Normal growth	0.5	14	9	6
Recession with low inflation	0.2	0	35	6
Recession with high inflation	0.05	-30	0	6
Expected Return [$E(R)$]		13.2	9.7	6
Standard Deviation (σ)		17.96	14.57	0

Correlation coefficient between stocks and bonds is -0.3449.

8. A portfolio consisting five securities is listed below. Calculate each stock's expected return. Then, using these individual security's expected returns, compute the

portfolio's expected return.

Stock	Initial Investment Value	Expected End-of-Period Investment Value	Value Proportion of Portfolio's Initial Market Value
A	Rs. 5,000	Rs. 7000	20.0%
B	2,500	4,000	10.0
C	4,000	5,000	16.0
D	10,000	12,000	40.0
E	3,500	5,000	12.0

Ans:

Stock	Expected Return	Proportion of Portfolio's Initial Market Value
A	Rs.7,000/Rs.5,000 = 40.00%	20.0%
B	Rs.4,000/Rs.2,500 = 60.00%	10.0
C	Rs.5,000/Rs.4,000 = 25.00%	16.0
D	Rs.12,000/Rs.10,000 = 20.00%	40.0
E	Rs.7,000/Rs.3,500 = 42.86%	12.0

The portfolio's expected return is given by:

$$= \sum_{i=1}^{5}(X_i \times R_i)$$

$$= (.200 \times 40.0\%) + (.10 \times 60.0\%) + (.16 \times 25.0) + (.40 \times 20.0\%) + (.14 \times 42.86)$$
$$= 8 + 6 + 4 + 8 + 6.0004$$
$$= 32.0004\%$$

9. P Sen owns three securities and has estimated the following joint probability distribution of returns :

Outcome	Security X	Security Y	Security Z	Probability
1	15	-12	0	.15
2	12	-2	10	.20
3	5	0	12	.30
4	-3	4	15	.20
5	-8	10	7	.15

Calculate the portfolio's expected return and standard deviation if Sen invests 40% in security X, 25% in security Y and 35% in security Z. Assume that each security's return is completely uncorrelated with the returns of the other securities.

Ans.:

The expected returns on the five securities in Sen's portfolio are:

$$\tilde{R}_X = (.15 \times 15) + (.20 \times 12) + (.30 \times 5) + (20 \times -3) + (.15 \times -8)$$
$$= 2.25 + 2.40 + 1.50 + (-.6) + (-1.20)$$
$$= 4.35$$

$$\tilde{R}_Y = (.15 \times -12) + (.20 \times -2) + (.30 \times 0) + (.20 \times 4) + (.15 \times 10)$$
$$= (-1.8) + (-.40) + (0) + (.80) + (1.5)$$

$$= 0.10$$

$$\tilde{R}_z = (.15 \times 0) + (.20 \times 10) + (.30 \times 12) + (.20 \times 15) + (.15 \times 7)$$
$$= (0) + (2) + (3.6) + (3.0) + (1.05)$$
$$= 9.65$$

The expected return on Sen's portfolio is therefore:

$$\tilde{R}_P = (.40 \times 4.35\%) + (.25 \times .10\%) + (.35 \times 9.65\%)$$
$$= 1.74 + .025 + 3.3775$$
$$= 5.1425\%$$

The standard deviations of the portfolio's three securities are:

$$\sigma_X = \{[.15 \times (15 - 4.35)^2] + [.20 \times (12 - 4.35)^2] + [.30 \times (5 - 4.35)^2] +$$
$$[.20 \times (-3 - 4.35)^2] + [.15 \times (-8 - 4.35)^2]\}^{1/2}$$
$$= [(17.0134) + (11.7045) + (0.1268) + (10.8045) + (22.8784)]^{1/2}$$
$$= [62.5276]^{1/2}$$
$$= 7.91$$

$$\sigma_Y = \{[.15 \times (-12 - .10)^2] + [.20 \times (-2 - .10)^2] + [.30 \times (0 - .10)^2] + [.20 \times (4 - .10)^2]$$
$$+ [.15 \times (10 - .10)^2]\}^{\frac{1}{2}}$$
$$= [(21.9615) + (0.882) + (0) + (3.362) + (15.3015)]^{\frac{1}{2}}$$
$$= [41.507]^{\frac{1}{2}}$$
$$= 6.44$$

$$\sigma_Z = \{[.15 \times (0 - 9.65)^2] + [.20 \times (10 - 9.65)^2] + [.30 \times (12 - 9.65)^2] +$$
$$[.20 \times (15 - 9.65)^2] + [.15 \times (7 - 9.65)^2]\}^{1/2}$$
$$= [(0) + (0.0245) + (1.65675) + (5.7245) + 1.0534)]^{1/2}$$
$$= [8.4591]^{1/2}$$
$$= 2.91$$

The fact that the three securities are each uncorrelated with each other simplifies the calculation of the portfolio's standard deviation. Specifically:

$$\sigma_P = [(.40)^2 \times (7.91)^2 + (.25)^2 \times (6.44)^2 + (.3S)^2 (2.91)^2]^{1/2}$$
$$= [(10.0109) + (2.5921) + (1.0373)]^{1/2}$$
$$= [13.640342]^{1/2}$$
$$= 3.69\%$$

10. Three assets have the expected returns $E(R_1) = 22\%$ $E(R_2) = 10\%$ $E(R_3) = 17\%$ and the following covariance matrix:

	Asset		
	1	2	3
1	.3600	.0200	.0000
2	.0200	.0225	.0400
3	.0000	.0400	.1225

(i) Construct several portfolios with a portfolio expected return of 15%.

(ii) Construct portfolios with weights of $w_1 = 1$ and $w_1 = 0$ with a portfolio variance of .40.

(iii) Use the calculus method to determine MVPs for expected returns of 15% and 20%.

Ans.:

(i) The equation of an isomean line is

$$w_2 = \frac{E(R_3) - E(R_P)}{E(R_3) - E(R_2)} + \frac{E(R_1) - E(R_3)}{E(R_3) - E(R_2)} w_1$$

The equation for the isomean line for an expected portfolio return of 15% is $w_2 = .2857 + .714\, w_1$.

Portfolios that have an expected return of 15% include

$$w_1 = 0,\ w_2 = .2857,\ w_3 = .7143.$$
$$w_1 = .5,\ w_2 = .6427,\ w_3 = -.1427.$$

(*ii*) The portfolio variance is

$$\sigma_p^2 = w_1^2[.36 - 2(0) + .1225] + w_2^2[.0225 - 2\,(.04) + .1225]$$
$$+ 2w_1 w_2[.02 - 0 - .04 + .1225] + 2w_1[0 - .1225]$$
$$+ 2w_2[.04 - .1225] + .1225$$

or

$$\sigma_p^2 = .4825\, w_1^2 + .065\, w_2^2 + .205\, w_1 w_2 = .245\, w_1 - .165\, w_2 + .1225.$$

Hence, to obtain portfolios with a variance of 40%, replace σ_p^2 with .40 and find solutions that satisfy the equation:

$$.40 = .4825\, w_1^2 + .065\, w_2^2 + .205\, w_1 w_2 - .245\, w_1 - .165\, w_2 + .1225$$

or

$$0 = .4825\, w_1^2 + .065\, w_2^2 + .205\, w_1 w_2 - .245\, w_1 - .165\, w_2 - .2775.$$

When w_1 is equal to 0, the above equation is given by the following quadratic:

$$0 = .065\, w_2^2 - .165\, w_2 - 2775.$$

Thus, -1.156 and 3.694 are two values of w_2 that satisfy the above equation. Hence, two portfolios that deliver a portfolio variance of 40% are

$$w_1 = 0,\ w_2 = -1.156,\ w_3 = 2.1556;\ \text{and}\ w_1 = 0,\ w_2 = 3.694,\ w_3 = -2.694.$$

When $w_2 = 0$, the quadratic equation is

$$0 = .2375\, w_1^2 - .245\, w_1 - .2775.$$

The weights that satisfy this equation are $w_1 = 1.0536$ and -546.

Thus, two portfolios that deliver a portfolio variance of 40% are

$$w_1 = 1.0536,\ w_2 = 0,\ w_3 = -.05361\ \text{and}\ w_1 = -.5459,\ w_2 = 0,\ w_3 = 1.5459.$$

(iii) To find portfolios that minimise the variance for expected returns of 15% and 20%, first set up the following matrix:

A					w		B
0.72	0.040	0.00	0.22	1	w_1		0
0.04	0.045	0.080	0.10	1	w_2		0
0.00	0.080	0.245	0.17	1	w_3	$=$	0
0.22	0.100	0.170	0.00	0	λ_1		$E(R_P)$
1.00	1.000	1.000	0.00	0	λ_2		1

The inverse of the A matrix is equal to

0.755	0.539	-1.295	3.213	-0.272
0.539	0.385	0.925	-11.990	2.234
-1.295	-0.925	2.219	8.777	-0.962
3.213	-11.990	8.777	-12.857	0.995
-0.272	2.234	-0.962	0.995	-0.112

Portfolios on the minimum-variance set can be obtained by multiplying the inverse by the B vector. For a portfolio expected return of 15%, the weights that minimise the portfolio variance are: $w_1 = .21$, $w_2 = .44$, $w_3 = .35$. For an expected return of 20%, the weights are $w_1 = .37$, $w_2 = -.16$, $w_3 = .79$.

11. Find the portfolio variance of a portfolio consisting of equities, bonds, and real estate, if the portfolio weights are 25%, 50%, and 25%. The standard deviations are 0.1689,0.0716 and 0.0345 respectively. And, the correlations are 0.45 for equity and bonds, 0.35 for equities and real estate, and 0.20 for bonds and real estate.

Ans.:

The portfolio variance is:

$\sigma^2 p = (0.25)^2(0.1689)^2 + (0.50)^2(0.0716)^2 + (0.25)^2 (0.0345)^2 + 2 (0.25) (0.50) (0.45)$
$(0.1689) (0.0716) + 2 (0.25) (0.25) (0.35) (0.1689) (0.0345) + 2 (0.50)(0.25)$
$(0.20) (0.0716) (0.0345)$

$= 0.00488$

$\sigma_p = 0.0698$

$= 6.98\%$

12. Refer to problem-11,if the expected rate of return for equity, bonds, and real estate are 0.15, 0.10 and 0.05 respectively, what is the expected rate of return and standard deviation of a portfolio of 20% equity, 35% bonds, and 40% real estate?

Ans.:

The expected rate of return of the portfolio is:

$E(R_p) = 0.2 (0.15) + 0.35 (0.10) + 0.40 (0.05)$

$= 0.085$

$= 8.5\%$

The portfolio variance is:

$\sigma^2_p = (0.2)^2 (0.1689)^2 + (0.35)^2 (0.0716)^2 + (0.40)^2 (0.0345)^2$
$+ 2 (0.2 \times 0.35)(0.45)(0.1689)(0.0716) + 2 (0.2) (0.4) (0.35) (0.1689) (0.0345)$
$+ 2 (0.35) (0.40) (0.20) (0.0716) (0.0345)$

$= 0.00319$

$\sigma_p = 0.0565488$

$= 5.65\%$

13. Assume that asset 1 has an expected return of 15% with a standard deviation of 30% and asset 2 has an expected return of 10% and a standard deviation of 20%. Calculate the portfolio expected return and standard deviation for various portfolios. Assume correlation coefficients of 1, 0, and -1. Also calculate the minimum variance portfolios, assuming short sales are not allowed.

Ans.:

w_1	$E(R_p)$	σ_p CORR = 1	σ_p CORR = 0	σ_p CORR = -1
0.00	10.00%	20.00%	20.00%	20.00%
0.25	11.25	22.5	16.8	7.5
0.50	12.50	25.0	18.0	5.0
0.75	13.75	27.5	23.0	17.5
1.00	15.00	30.0	30.0	30.0

When the correlation between returns is equal to 1, the MVP occurs when the weight of asset 1 is equal to 1. The weight of asset 1 that produces the MVP in the case of perfect negative correlation:

$$\frac{\sigma_2}{(\sigma_1+\sigma_2)} = \frac{.20}{.30+.20} = .40$$

If the correlation coefficient is equal to 0, weight of asset 1 that gives the MVP:

$$\frac{\sigma_2^2}{\sigma_1^2+\sigma_2^2} = \frac{.04}{.09+.04} = .3077$$

14. Consider a portfolio of three stocks, X, Y, Z, with weights w_x, w_y, and w_z. Show the portfolio variance is:

$$w_x^2\,\sigma_x^2 + w_y^2\,\sigma_y^2 + w_z^2\,\sigma_z^2 + 2\,w_x w_y\,Cov\,(r_x,\,r_y)$$
$$+ 2\,w_x\,w_z\,Cov\,(r_x,\,r_y) + 2\,\,w_y\,w_z\,Cov\,(r_y,\,r_z)$$

Ans.:

The bordered covariance metrix is

	w_x	w_y	w_z
w_x	σ_x^2	$Cov\,(r_x,\,r_y)$	$Cov\,(r_x,\,r_z)$
w_y	$Cov(r_y,r_x)$	σ_y^2	$Cov\,(r_y,\,r_z)$
w_z	$Cov(r_z,\,r_x)$	$Cov\,(r_z,\,r_y)$	σ_z^2

There are nine terms in the covariance metrix portfolio variance is calculated, from these nine terms:

$$\sigma_P^2 = w_X^2\sigma_X^2 + w_Y^2\sigma_Y^2 + w_Z^2\sigma_Z^2$$
$$+ w_X w_Y Cov(r_X,r_Y) - w_Y w_X Cov(r_Y,r_X)$$
$$+ w_X w_Y Cov(r_X,r_Z) - w_Z w_X Cov(r_Z,r_X)$$
$$+ w_Y w_Z Cov(r_Y,r_Z) - w_Z w_Y Cov(r_Z,r_Y)$$
$$= w_X^2\sigma_X^2 + w_Y^2\sigma_Y^2 + w_Z^2\sigma_Z^2$$
$$+ 2w_X w_Y Cov(r_X,r_Y) + 2w_X w_Z Cov(r_X,r_Z) + 2w_Y w_Z Cov(r_Y,r_Z)$$

15. Asset 1 has an expected return of 10% with a standard deviation of 25%, and asset 2 has an expected return of 15% and a standard deviation of 35%. The correlation coefficient between the returns is .2 and the risk-free rate is 8%. What is the optimal portfolio of risky assets?

Ans.:

The covariance between the returns is equal to .2 × .25 × .35 = .0175. The optimal weight of asset 1:

$$W_1 = \frac{[.10-.08].1225 - [.15-.08].0175}{[.10-.08].1225 + [.15-.08].0625 - [.10-.08+.15-.08].0175}$$
$$= .233$$

and

$$w_{2^*} = .767.$$

16. Given the following data compute the portfolio opportunity set for Dinesh and Esha when

Descriptive Statistics for Two Stocks

	Dinesh	Esha
Expected return, $E(r)$	.20	.15
Standard deviation, σ	.45	.32
covariance, $Cov(r_D, r_E)$		.475
Correlation coefficient, P_{DE}		0.25

Ans.:

From the standard deviations and the correlation coefficient we generate the covariance matrix:

Covariance Matrix

		Covariances	
Portfolio Weights		w_D	w_E
w_D		σ_D^2	$Cov(r_D, r_E)$
w_E		$Cov(r_E, r_D)$	σ_E^2

Stock	Z	D	E
D		.2025	.0360
E		0.360	.1024

The *global minimum-variance* portfolio is constructed so that

$$w_D = [\sigma_E^2 - Cov(r_D, r_E)] \div \sigma_D^2 + \sigma_E^2 - 2\, Cov(r_D, r_E)]$$
$$= (.1024 - .0360) \div (.2205 + .1024 - 2 \times .0360) = .2851$$
$$w_E = 1 - w_D = .7149.$$

Its expected return and standard deviation are

$$E(r_p) = .2851 \times .20 + .7149 \times .15 = .1643$$
$$\sigma_p = [w_D^2 \sigma_D^2 + w_E^2 \sigma_E^2 + 2 w_D w_E\, Cov\,(r_D, r_E)]^{\frac{1}{2}}$$
$$= [.2851^2 \times .2025 + .7149^2 \times .1024 + 2 \times .2851 \times .7149 \times .0360]^{\frac{1}{2}}$$
$$= .2889$$

For the other points we simply increase w_D from .10 to .90 in increments of .10; accordingly, W_E ranges from .90 to .10 in the same increments. We substitute these portfolio proportions in the formulas for expected return and standard deviation. Note that for W_D or W_E equal to 1.0, the portfolio parameters equal those of the stock.

We then generate the following table :

The parameters of the opportunity set are $E(r_D) = .20$, $E(r_E) = .15$, $\sigma_D = .45$, $\sigma_E = .32$, and correlation between D and E = .25, we get

w_D	w_E	$E(R)$	σ
.00	1.00	.1500	.3200
.10	.90	.1550	.3024
.20	.80	.1600	.2918
.2851	.7149	.1643	.2889 (min)
.30	.70	.1650	.2890
.40	.60	.1700	.2942
.50	.50	.1750	.3070

.60	.40	.1800	.3264
.70	.30	.1850	.3515
.80	.20	.1900	.3811
.90	.10	.1950	.4142
1.00	.00	.2000	.4500

QUESTIONS

1. Explain how the efficient frontier is determined using the Markowitz approach. Use a two-security approach.

2. What are the characteristics of assets that lie on the efficient frontier ? What is the difference between the efficient frontier and the attainable set of investment opportunities ? What role does the dominance principle play in this difference ?

3. What are the strengths and weaknesses of the Markowitz approach ?

4. Define what is meant by an efficient portfolio and an inefficient portfolio. How can the dominance principle be used to define the concept of efficient portfolio.

5. How does the efficient set differ from the minimum variance set ? If you could not obtain a portfolio on the efficient set, would you prefer a portfolio of the same expected standard deviation on the remaining minimum variartce set ?

6. Intuitively, why should it be true that, when short selling is allowed, most securities will have either a positive or a negative weight ?

7. Define 'efficient frontiers'. How does the efficient frontier change when the short selling is not allowed ?

8. It is often said that "diversification always pays". Do you agree?

9. What do you understand by the term portfolio management? Explan with the help of suitable examples the "matrix approach" in investment decisions.

10. What is the connection between gains from diversification and the correlation of the returns of securities?

11. "An investor who ignores risk will not diversify his portfolio; an investor who ignores the portfolio's expected return will diversify his portfolio." What is your opinion of these two statements? Support your answer by a graphical presentation.

12. Under what conditions is it possible to construct a portfolio of two risky securities which ensures riskless return? Find the proportions of two securities in such a portfolio.

13. What is the relationship between the number of available securities and the gains from diversification? Does this have any implications for the small investor?

14. Explain the following statement" The stand-alone risk of an individual project may look quite high, but viewed in the context of a project's effect on shareholders' risk, the project's risk may not be very large". How would the correlation between returns on a project and the returns on the firm's other assets' return affect the project's risk?

15. Comment on the following statement "Since Markowitz portfolio theory requires so many assumptions, the notion that investors should be concerned with the risk of the overall portfolio rather than the risk of the individual securities Is misleading."

16. Illustrate why the capital market line dominates the Markowitz efficient frontier.

17. In terms of Markowitz model, explain, using words and graphs, how an investor goes about identifying his or her optimal portfolio. What specific information does an investor need to identify this portfolio?

18. Why does diversification lead to a reduction in unique risk ?Explain both intuitively and mathematically.

19. What is a corner portfolio? Why are corner portfolios important for identifying the composition of efficient set?

20. Draw a properly labeled graph of the Markowitz efficient frontier. Describe the efficient frontier in exact terms. Discuss the concept of Dominant portfolios and show an example of one on your graph.

21. Assume that you and a business associate develop an efficient frontier for a set of investments. Why might the two of you select different portfolios on the frontier?

22. Two portfolio managers are discussing modern portfolio theory. Manager A states that the objective of marketing portfolio analysis is to construct a portfolio that maximises expected return for a given level of risk. Manager B disagrees. He believes that the objective is to contract a portfolio that minimises risk for a given level of return. Which portfolio manager is correct?

23. Indicate why you agree or disagree with the following statement: "Because it is difficult to determine an investor's utility function, Markowitz portfolio theory can not be employed in practice to construct a Markowitz efficient portfolio."

24. What is meant by the optimal portfolio, and how is it related to an efficient portfolio?

25. Explain why most investors prefer to hold a diversified portfolio of securities as opposed to placing all of their wealth in a single asset. Use an illustration of the feasible and efficient sets to explain your answer.

PROBLEMS

1. Given the following market value of equities in your portfolio and their expected rates of return, what is the expected rate of return for you equity portfolio?

Security	Market value	$E(Ri)$
ABC	₹ 15,000	0.14
BCD	17,000	-0.04
DEF	32,000	0.18
FGH	23,000	0.16
KLM	7,000	0.05

2. Given : $E(R_1) = .10$
$E(R_2) = .03$
$E(R_3) = .15$
$E(R_3) = .15$
$E(R_4) = .05$

Calculate the expected returns and expected standard deviation of a two-security portfolio in which security has a weight of 75 per cent under the following conditions:

a = 1.00
b = .75
c = .25
d = .00
e = -.25
f = -.50
g = -.75
h = -1.00

3. The mean annual rates of return and the standard deviations for three groups of risky assets—Equity shares, term Government Bonds, and Long-term corporate bonds—were calculated using 2006-2010 data. The ex-post estimates and the corresponding correlation coefficients are given below:

(i)	Equity Shares (1)	Long-term Bonds Government (2)	Long-term Bonds Corporate (3)
Mean return (%)	16.5	85	12.5
Standard deviation (%)	287	10.5	12.6

Sample Correlation Coefficients

j/i	Equity Shares (1)	Government Bonds (2)	Corporate Bonds (0)
Equity Shares (1)	1.00	0.03	0.24
Govt. Bonds (2)	0.03	1.00	0.76
Corporate Bonds (3)	0.24	076	1.00

The riskless interest rate for the period is estimated at 5%.

Assume that an investor decides to invest in two risky assets out of the three, with or without the risk-free asset.

(a) Determine the optimal proportions to be invested for each of the three possible pairs of risky assets. Assume that there are no constraints on the investment proportions and that any of the assets may be held short.

(b) Which of the three pairs of assets will the investor choose from mean-variance considerations?

(c) Now assume that no short-sales are allowed (so that all the investment proportions are always non-negative). Answer (b) without making any additional calculations.

4. The following table lists the returns available on four securities between 2006 and 2010:

		Return on Securities		
Year	ABC	DEF	GHI	JKL
2006	18.5	-6.5	-4.8	5.8
2007	20.4	12.7	9.7	18.7
2008	35.9	20.8	28.9	38.9
2009	27.6	26.6	27.5	40.5
2010	7.2	-4.8	-7.4	-12.6

(a) Assume that the investor is constrained to a single security portfolio, what are the MV efficient options?

(b) Assuming that the investor can invest in a portfolio composed of equal proportions in two securities, determine the MV efficient option.

(c) Assuming that the investor can invest in a portfolio composed of two securities, with the objective of minimising the portfolio variance, which pair of securities will he choose from mean-variance considerations? What are the particular investment proportions minimising the variance? What are the mean return and the variance of the chosen portfolio?

5. Assume that four securities have an equal probability of earning the following rates of return:

A	B	C	D
30	-18	.50	10
-15	40	-30	10
25	-15	80	10
-10	25	-42	10

(a) Assuming that the investor is constrained to a single- security portfolio, what are the MV efficient options? Draw the efficient set for this case.

(b) Answer part (a) assuming that the investor also can construct portfolios which include two securities in equal proportions. Assume that the returns on the four securities always occur in combination as shown in the above table, i.e., a return of 30 on security A is always observed when security C has a return of 50, etc.

(c) Determine the efficient set for the case when the investor is allowed to construct portfolios consisting of three securities in equal proportions.

(d) Draw the three efficient sets from (a), (b), and (c) on one diagram. Explain and analyse your results.

6. The following are the expected returns, standard deviations and correlation between returns on ABC and XYZ stock:

	ABC	XYZ
Expected return	12.18%	18.68%
Standard Deviation	33.19%	43.65%
Correlation Coefficient	0.40	

(a) Calculate six points on the efficient frontier for xi= 0. 0.1,0.4,0.7,0.9,1.0, where xi is the proportion invested in ABC stock. Draw the efficient frontier in the mean-standard deviation plane.

(b) Find the investment proportions which minimise the portfolio variance. What is the variance and the expected return of the minimum-variance portfolio?

(c) How would your answer to (b) change if the correlation coefficient were negative, -0.40?.

7. Consider the following two securities ABC and XYZ:

	ABC	XYZ
Expected return (ER)	20	40
Variance (σ^2)	10	80

(a) Will an individual (using the Mean-Variance Criterion) ever concentrate all of his investments in security ABC?

(b) Will he ever concentrate his entire interest in security XYZ? Answer under two alternative assumptions: (j) The correlation coefficient between ABC and XYZ is zero, (if) The correlation coefficient between the two securities is +1.

8. There are 565 securities in the portfolio of a mutual fund. How many covariances would have to be computed in order to use the Markowitz full-covariance model?

9. Consider the economic outlook for the coming year and the estimates of sales and earnings for the pharmaceutical industry, you expect the rate of return for ABC Pharma equity shares to fall between -20 per cent and +40 per cent with the following range of probabilities:

Probability	Possible Returns
.10	-0.15
.15	-0.20
.20	0.10
.25	0.05
.20	0.15
.10	0.40

Compute the expected rate of return $[E(R_i)]$ for ABC Pharma.

REFERENCES

1. Beaver, William, and James Manegold, "The Association Between Market-Determined and Accounting-Determined Measures of Systematic Risk: Some Further Evidence," *Journal of Financial and Quantitative Analysis*, June 1975, pp. 231-284.

2. Black, Fischer, "Capital Market Equilibrium with Restricted Borrowing," *Journal of Business* 45, no. 3 (July 1972): 444-454.

3. Black, Fisher, Michael Jensen, and Myron Scholes. "The Capital Asset Pricing Model: Some Empirical Tests." In *Studies in Theory of Capital Markets*, edited by M.C. Jensen. New York: Praeger, 1972.

4. Blume, Marshall E., "Betas and Their Regression Tendencies," *Journal of Finance* 30, no. 3 (June 1975): 785-796.

5. ————, "On the Assessment of Risk," *Journal of Finance* 26, no. 1 (March 1971): 1-10.

6. Cheng, Pao, and M. King Deets, "Systematic Risk and the Horizon Problem," *Journal of Financial and Quantitative Analysis* 8, no. 2 (March 1973): 299-316.

7. Hamada. Robert S., "Investment Decision with a Mean-Variance Approach," Quarterly *Journal of Economics* 85 no. 4 (November 1971): 667-683.

8. Hodges, Steward D., and Richard A. Brealey. "Dynamic Portfolio Selection." *Financial Analysts Journal,* November-December 1972, p. 58.

9. Jensen. Michael C., ed., *Studies in the Theory of Capital Markets* (New York' Praeger 1972).

10. Jobson, J.D.: "Estimating the Mean-Variance Efficient Frontier: The Markowitz Criterion is Not Enough." Presented to the Q Group, Fall Seminar, 1994.

11. Markowitz, Harry, "Portfolio Selection." *Journal of Finance 1,* no. 1 (March 1952).

12. ————, *Portfolio Selection: Efficient Diversification of Investments.* New York: John Wiley and Sons, 1959.

13. ————, "Markowitz Revisited," *Financial Analysts Journal,* September-October 1976

14. Olsen, Robert, "Sample Size and Markowitz Diversification." *Journal of Portfolio Management,* Winter 1984, 18-22.

15. Reilly, Frank K., and David J. Wright. "A Comparison of Published Betas." *Journal of Portfolio Management,* Spring 1988, 64-69.

16. Reilly, Frank K., "Evidence Regarding a Segmented Stock Market," *Journal of Finance* 27, no. 3 (June 1972): 607 625.

17. Renshaw, E. F., "Portfolio Balance Models in Perspective: Some Generalizations That Can Be Derived from the Two Asset Case," *Journal of Financial and Quantitative Analysis,* June 1967, pp. 138-139.

18. Robichek. Alexander A., and Richard A. Cohn, "The Economic Determinants of Systematic Risk," *Journal of Finance* 29, no. 2 (May 1974): 439-447.

19. Roenfeldt, R., G. Griepentrog, and C. Pflaum. "Further Evidence on the Stationarity of Beta Coefficients." *Journal of Finance and Quantitative Analysis,* March 1978, 117-121.

20. Rosenberg, Barr, and James Guy. "Beta and Investment Fundamentals." *Financial Analysts Journal,* May/June 1976, 60-72.

21. Samuelson, Paul, "General Proof that Diversification Pays," *Journal of Financial and Quantitative Analysis,* June 1967, pp. 107-22.

22. ————, "The Fundamental Approximation Theorem of Portfolio Analysis in Terms of Means, Variances, and Higher Moments," *Review of Economic Studies,* October 1970, pp. 537 542.

23. Schneller, Meir, "Mean-Variance Portfolio Composition When Investors' Revision Horizon is Very Long." *Journal of Finance* 30 (December 1975): 1293-1300.

24. Smith, Keith, "Stock Price and Economic Indexes for Generating Efficient Portfolios," *Journal of Business* 42, no. 3 (July 1969): 326 -336.

25. Tobin, James, "Liquidity Preference as Behavior Towards Risk." *Review of Economic Studies 15* (February 1955): 65 86.

26. Upson, Roger, Paul Jessup, and Keishiro Matsumoto. "Portfolio Diversification Strategies." *Financial Analysts Journal.* May June 1975, pp. 86 88.

27. Wallingford, B.A., "A Survey and Comparison of Portfolio Selection Models." *Journal of Financial and Quantitative Analysis.* June 1967, pp. 85 106.

27

Sharpe: The Single Index Model

INTRODUCTION

The Markowitz Model was theoretically elegant and conceptually sound. However, its serious limitation was that it related each security to every other security in the portfolio, demanding the sophistication and volume of work well beyond the capacity of all but a few analysts. Consequently, its application remained severely limited until William F. Sharpe published a model simplifying the mathematical calculations required.

Sharpe assumed that, for the sake of simplicity, the return on a security could be regarded as being linearly related to a single index like the market index. Theoretically, the market index should consist of all the securities trading on the market. However, a popular average can be treated as a surrogate for the market index. Acceptance of the idea of a market index, Sharpe argued, would obviate the need for calculating thousands of covariances between individual securities, because any movements in securities could be attributed to movements in the single underlying factor being measured by the market index. The simplification of the Markowitz Model has come to be known as the Market Model or Single-Index Model (SIM).

CHARACTERISTIC LINES

An old and rather quaint Wall Street aphorism asserts that *when they raid the brothel they take all the girls.* The reference is to a so-called *bear raid,* in which bears (pessimists) raid the market, driving prices down. Completing the translation: the statement asserts that when the market falls dramatically, all stocks go down together.

This sort of view is subject to criticism on several grounds besides taste. The market is rarely divided into bears (pessimists) and bulls (optimists). A decline is more likely to come about when the consensus opinion about the future simply becomes more pessimistic or less optimistic. Moreover, such changes in opinion seldom apply equally to all securities. Pessimism about the prospects for automobiles may accompany optimism about the prospects for railroads, etc.

Nonetheless, there is an element of truth in the assertion. In major market moves, most securities move in the same direction, although at different rates. Moreover, the sensitivity of a security's price to changes in the overall market is of crucial importance, for it constitutes the major component of the security's contribution to portfolio risk.

These concepts can be made more precise. The relationship between a security's prospects and those of the market portfolio can be summarized by means of a *characteristic line.* Figure-1 shows an example. The vertical axis plots the *excess return* on the security in question. This is the difference between the holding-period return on the security and the riskless rate of interest for that period. In symbols:

excess return on security $i = \tilde{R}_i - R_f$

where: $\tilde{R}_i$ = holding-period return on security i
   R_f = riskless rate of interest

For clarity, variables whose actual value is uncertain before the fact (ex ante) are indicated by tildes (i.e., squiggly lines such as ~).

The horizontal axis in Figure 1 plots the excess return on the market portfolio; in symbols:

excess return on the market portfolio $= \tilde{R}_m - R_f$

where: $\tilde{R}_m$ = holding-period return on the market portfolio
   R_f = riskless rate of interest

The market portfolio includes all securities, each in proportion to market value outstanding.

The characteristic line, summarizing the relationship between the two excess returns, can be written as follows:

$$\tilde{R}_i - R_f = \alpha_i + \beta_{im}(\tilde{R}_m - R_f) + \tilde{r}_i \tag{1}$$

The values *of alpha* (α_i) and *beta* (β_{im}) indicate the vertical intercept and slope, respectively, of the line, as shown in Figure-1. The value of α_i can be thought of as excess return on the security that goes with an excess return of zero on the market portfolio. Intuitively, one would think that a positive value would be desirable and a negative value undesirable. This is indeed the case.

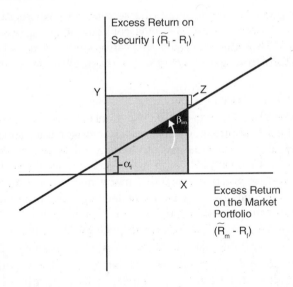

FIGURE 1: A SECUIRTY CHARACTERISTIC LINE

The value of β_{im} measures the *sensitivity* or *responsiveness* of the security's excess return to that of the market portfolio. (It is common practice to simply refer to "beta" whenever one means "beta relative to the market portfolio.") A beta of one indicates that if the market portfolio's excess return is 1% larger than expected, then the best guess is that the security's excess return is also likely to be 1% larger than expected. A beta of .5 indicates that if the market portfolio's return is 1% larger than expected, the best guess is that the security's excess return is likely to be ½ of 1% larger than expected. A beta of 2.0 indicates that if the market portfolio's excess return is 1 % larger than expected, the best guess is that the security's excess return is likely to be 2% larger than expected. And so on.

Securities with beta values less than one are termed *defensive:* in up markets their prices tend to rise at a slower rate than the average security. On the other hand, they tend to fall at a slower rate in down markets. Securities with beta values greater than one are termed *aggressive:* in up markets their prices tend to rise at a faster rate than the average security. On the other hand, they tend to fall at a faster rate in down markets.

The final value in formula (1), $\tilde{r}_i$, represents the uncertain portion of the *nonmarket* component of the excess return on security. This can be seen more clearly by dividing the total into two parts, as follows:

$$\tilde{R}_i - R_f = \left(\begin{array}{c} [\beta_{im}(\tilde{R}_m - R_f) \\ \text{market component} \\ \text{of excess return} \end{array} \right) + \left(\begin{array}{c} [\alpha_i \tilde{r}_i] \\ \text{nonmarket component} \\ \text{of excess return} \end{array} \right) \quad (2)$$

The term in the first set of brackets is the market-related portion of excess return; the term in the second set is the nonmarket portion. By convention, α_i represents the *expected* nonmarket excess return, while $\tilde{r}_i$ represents the deviation from this expectation. Before the fact, the best guess is that $\tilde{r}_i$ will be zero. After the fact, it almost certainly will not be. Unexpected good news will cause $\tilde{r}_i$ to be positive, while unexpected bad news will cause it to be negative.

How far might the nonmarket component of a security's excess return diverge from its expected value? As with other estimates, it is convenient to express the answer in standard deviation terms. Thus the *nonmarket risk* is measured by the likely divergence of nonmarket excess return from its expected value. Formally, the estimated standard deviation of $\tilde{r}_i$, is used:

$S(\tilde{r}_i)$ = the nonmarket risk of security i

Graphically, nonmarket risk measures the likely distance, measured vertically, between the point representing the actual outcome and the characteristic line. Thus in Figure-1, if the excess return on the market portfolio turns out to be X, while that on the security is Y, the actual nonmarket excess return is Z. Non-market risk is an estimate of the likely amount of this difference. For practical purposes many analysts estimate this directly, thinking in terms of a divergence likely to be exceeded only one time out of three (i.e., the chances are two out of three that the actual difference will be less).

Three key measures summarize a security's prospects in this type of analysis: α_i, β_{im}, and $S(\tilde{r}_i)$. Estimates of these variables should be the responsibility of the security analyst. He or she may utilise statistical analysis of historical data in the process, but fundamental knowledge of the company and industry in question can usually be employed to considerable advantage.

Different means may be utilised to obtain such estimates from analysts. Some organizations simply request the three values directly. Others ask for an estimate of dividends and end-of-period security price for two assumed end-of-period market levels.

This fixes two points on the characteristic line, and thus the values of α_i and β_{im}. The analyst may then be asked for a measure of the likely divergence from the estimates, to obtain $S(\tilde{r}_i)$. Another procedure, used by several organizations, asks for nine estimates: three for each of three assumed market conditions. In each case the estimates are thought of as "pessimistic," "likely," and "optimistic." Depending on the interpretations given these terms, the values are then used to estimate α_i, β_{im}, and $S(\tilde{r}_i)$. Figure-2 illustrates this procedure.

Whatever the method used, two features are central in this type of analysis. First, the security analyst is asked to make *conditional* estimates: all forecasts are conditional on market levels. This leaves the task of estimating the expected excess return on the market portfolio, and the attendant uncertainty about it, to others with (hopefully) more appropriate skills. It also facilitates consistency in the estimates obtained for different securities. If analysts are asked to make *unconditional* estimates, they must make their own implicit forecasts of market moves, and each one is likely to make a different forecast, leading to unsatisfactory results when such estimates are combined and compared by a portfolio manager.

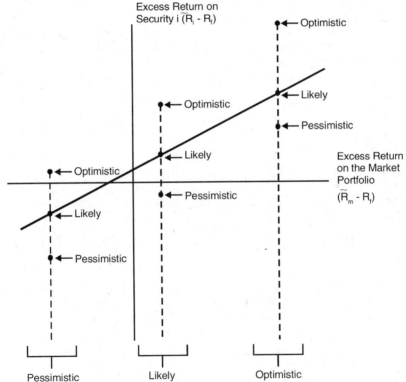

FIGURE 2: THE USE OF "PESSIMISTIC," "LIKELY,' AND "OPTIMISTIC" FORECASTS TO OBTAIN A CHARACTERISTIC LINE

The other hallmark of this approach is the explicit recognition *of uncertainty*. In a sense, the analyst is not expected to draw a clear characteristic line, but a fuzzy one. The line drawn is simply a "best guess." The estimate of nonmarket risk indicates the likely precision of that guess. The greater the nonmarket risk, the wider is the band around the characteristic line within which the analyst feels the actual result might fall.

Not every organization uses such procedures to estimate security returns. People continue to ask for, and get, single estimates, ignoring the influence of overall market moves and the presence of uncertainty. Such procedures are, however, too simplistic: most returns *are* uncertain, and they *do* depend on market moves. These two factors are too important to be ignored.

PROBABILISTIC CHARACTERISTIC LINES

Analysts asked to provide information on characteristic lines usually do so explicitly, or nearly so. However, such relationships rest, at base, on estimates of the outcomes associated with events and the probabilities of such events. While few people actually make these detailed estimates, it is useful to see how the key attributes of a characteristic line can be derived from them, for this provides the conceptual foundation for the entire procedure.

Table 1 shows an analyst's estimates of the excess returns for a security (column) and the market portfolio (column 4) associated with each of several events, as well as estimates of the probabilities of the events (column 2). In columns 5 and 6 the expected values are computed in the usual way; each outcome is multiplied by its probability, then summed. The variance of the excess return on the market portfolio is computed in column 9. Finally, in column 10 the covariance between the two excess returns is computed by taking a weighted average of the products of the deviations from the expectations, using probabilities as weights.

Given these figures, the value of β_{im} for the security can be easily found. The formula is:

$$\beta_{im} = \frac{\text{Cov}\,(\tilde{R}_i - R_f,\ \tilde{R}_m - R_f)}{\text{Var}\,(\tilde{R}_m - R_f)} \qquad (3)$$

where: Cov $(\tilde{R}_i - R_f,\ \tilde{R}_m - R_f)$ = the covariance between the excess return on security i and the excess return on the market portfolio

Var $(\tilde{R}_m - R_f)$ = the variance of the excess return on the market portfolio

Formula (3) is the rigorous definition of a security's beta relative to the market portfolio. In this case it is 119.80/101.0, or 1.186. The security is thus aggressive: its excess return is 18.6% more sensitive to market swings than is that of the average, security.

The value of α_i is the expected value of the nonmarket component of a security's excess return. The expected value of the market component will equal the security's beta times the expected excess return on the market portfolio. The value of alpha is thus the difference between the security's total expected excess return and this amount. In symbols:

$$\alpha_i = \text{Exp}\,(\tilde{R}_i - R_f) - \beta_{im} \text{Exp}\,(\tilde{R}_m - R_f) \qquad (4)$$

where: Exp $(\tilde{R}_i - R_f)$ = the expected excess return on security i

Exp $(\tilde{R}_m - R_f)$ = the expected excess return on the market portfolio

In this case: α_i 10.30 $-(1.186 \times 6.00) = 3.184$.

The analyst thus considers the security underpriced, since the value of alpha is positive.

TABLE 1

Estimating beta from probabilistic predictions

(1) Event	(2) Probability	(3) Excess Return on Security i (%)	(4) Excess Return on the Market Portfolio (%)	(5) = (2) × (3)
a	.10	18.0	13.0	1.8
b	.20	13.0	0.0	2.6
c	.10	8.0	11.0	.8
d	.30	-8.0	-6.0	-2.4
e	.30	25.0	18.0	7.5
				10.3 Expected excess return on security i

(6) = (2) × (4)	(7) Deviation of Excess Return on security i = (3) − 10.3	(8) Deviation of Excess Return on the Market Portfolio = (4) − 6.0	(9) Weighted Deviation for Market Portfolio squared = (2) × (8)²	(10) Weighted Products of Deviations = (2) × (7) x(8)
1.3	7.7	7.0	4.9	5.39
0.0	2.7	-6.0	7.2	-3.24
1.1	-2.3	5.0	2.5	-1.15
-1.8	-18.3	-12.0	43.2	65.88
5.4	14.7	12.0	43.2	52.92
6.0			101.0	119.80
Expected excess return on the market portfolio			Variance of excess return on the market portfolio	Covariance between the excess return on security i and the excess return on the market portfolio

$$\beta_{im} = \frac{119.80}{101.0} = 1.186$$

We come finally to the estimation of nonmarket risk. This is shown in Table-2. Columns 1 through 4 repeat the initial estimates from the previous table. Column 5 shows the excess return on the security accompanying each level of the excess return on the market, using the characteristic line obtained earlier for the estimates. The next column shows the difference between this estimate and the actual one: if the event in question takes place, this will be the actual deviation (r_i). To calculate the nonmarket risk we must find the standard deviation of these values. This is accomplished in the usual manner, as shown in the final column in Table 2.

TABLE 2

Estimating nonmarket risk from probabilistic predictions

(1) Event	(2) Probability	(3) Excess Return on Security i (%)	(4) Excess Return on the Market Portfolio (%)
a	.10	18.0	13.0
b	.20	13.0	0.0
c	.10	8.0	11.0
d	.30	-8.0	-6.0
e	.30	25.0	18.0

(5) Characteristic Line Value of Excess Return on Security i $= 3.184 + 1.186 \times (4)$	(6) Deviation of Nonmarket Return $= (3) - (5)$	(7) Probability Times Nonmarket Deviation squared $= (2) \times (6)^2$
18.602	-.602	.036
3.184	9.816	19.271
16.230	-8.230	6.773
-3.932	-4.068	4.965
24.532	.468	.066

$$\text{Var}(\tilde{r}_i) = \text{Variance of } \tilde{r}_i = 31.111$$

$$S(\tilde{r}_i) = \text{Standard deviation of } \tilde{r}_i = \sqrt{31.111} = 5.578$$

MARKET AND NONMARKET RISK AND RETURN

The characteristic line procedure, summarized in formula (1), dichotomizes a security's return into two components, one market-related and one not. Since the expected value of the latter is α_i, it is a simple matter to relate a security's expected excess return to the expected values of the two parts. In symbols:

$$\text{Exp}(\tilde{R}_i - R_f) = \alpha_i + [\beta_{im} \text{Exp}(\tilde{R}_m - R_f)]$$

Expected value of security i's excess return	Expected value of the nonmarket component of security i's excess return	Expected value of the market component of security i's excess return

$$(5)$$

What about risk? By definition, the nonmarket component of excess return is uncorrelated with the market component. Hence, the variance of the sum will thus equal the sum of the variances of the parts:

$$\underset{\substack{\text{Variance of security}\\ \text{i's excess return}}}{\text{Var}(\tilde{R}_i - R_f)} \quad = \quad \underset{\substack{\text{Variance of the non-}\\ \text{market component of}\\ \text{security i's excess}\\ \text{return}}}{\text{Var}(\tilde{r}_i)} \quad + \quad \underset{\substack{\text{Variance of the}\\ \text{market component}\\ \text{of security i's}\\ \text{excess return}}}{\text{Var}[\beta_{im}(\tilde{R}_m - R_f)]} \qquad (6)$$

Since the variance of a constant times a variable equals the constant squared times the variance of the variable, this can be rewritten as follows:

$$\text{Var}(\tilde{R}_i - R_f) = \text{Var}(\tilde{r}_i) + \beta_{im}^2 \,\text{Var}(\tilde{R}_m - R_f) \qquad (7)$$

Both formulas (6) and (7) show that risk, measured by variance, can also be broken into two parts: one that is not related to market risk and one that is. Moreover, the latter will be larger, the more sensitive the security's return is to market moves (i.e., the greater is β_{im}).

The proportion of a security's total risk attributable to market risk is measured as follows:

$$R\text{-squared} = \frac{B_{im}^2 \,\text{Var}(\overline{R}_m - R_f)}{\text{Var}(\tilde{R}_i - R_f)} \qquad (8)$$

where: R-squared = the proportion of security i's total risk (measured by variance) attributable to market risk

PORTFOLIO CHARACTERISTIC LINES

A characteristic line for a portfolio can be constructed in the manner used for a security. The result can be represented as follows:

$$\underset{\substack{\text{Excess return on}\\ \text{portfolio } P}}{(\tilde{R}_P - R_f)} \quad = \quad \underset{\substack{\text{Nonmarket component}\\ \text{of portfolio } P\text{'s}\\ \text{excess return}}}{[\alpha_p + \tilde{r}_p]} \quad + \quad \underset{\substack{\text{Market component of}\\ \text{portfolio } P\text{'s excess}\\ \text{return}}}{[\beta_{pm}(\tilde{R}_m - R_f)]} \qquad (9)$$

where: $\tilde{R}_p$ = return on portfolio P

α_p = expected value of the nonmarket component of portfolio P's excess return

$\tilde{r}_p$ = deviation of the actual nonmarket component of portfolio P's excess return from its expected value

β_{pm} = the sensitivity of portfolio P's excess return to the excess return of the market portfolio

While a portfolio's characteristic line may be estimated directly, it is much more common to do this indirectly, using estimates obtained for the securities in the portfolio. This is simpler and also avoids potential inconsistencies. By and large, the relationships are straightforward. A portfolio's alpha value is a weighted average of the alpha values for its component securities, using relative market values as weights:

$$\alpha_p = \sum_{i=1}^{N} X_i \alpha_i \qquad (10)$$

where: α_p = value of alpha for portfolio P
X_i = proportion of the market value of portfolio P invested in security i
α_i = value of alpha for security i
N = the number of securities in the portfolio

Similarly, a portfolio's beta value is a weighted average of the beta values of its component securities, using relative market values as weights:

$$\beta_{pm} = \sum_{i=1}^{N} X_i \beta_{im} \tag{11}$$

where: β_{pm} = value of beta for portfolio P
$\quad\quad\quad X_i$ = proportion of the market value of portfolio P invested in security;
$\quad\quad\quad \beta_{im}$ = value of beta for security ;
$\quad\quad\quad N$ = the number of securities in the portfolio

The nonmarket risk of the portfolio is not as easy to estimate, since its magnitude depends on the correlations among the values of $\tilde{r}_i$ for the component securities. If all the securities in a portfolio come from the same industry, non-market risk is likely to be higher than if each security comes from a different industry. At the other extreme, it may be possible to reduce nonmarket risk considerably by hedging, that is, constructing a portfolio of positions with negatively correlated nonmarket returns.

One procedure often used to estimate nonmarket risk assumes that all the values of $\tilde{r}_i$, are uncorrelated. Formula (10) can thus be used to obtain:

$$[S(\tilde{r}_p)]^2 = \sum_{i-1}^{N} X_i^2 [S(\tilde{r}_i)]^2 \qquad \text{when all values of } \tilde{r}_i \text{ are uncorrelated.} \tag{12}$$

This works well for highly diversified portfolios (i.e., those with many securities and no concentration of holdings in any one industry, economic sector, geographic area, etc.). For portfolios not meeting these conditions it *may* seriously under- or overestimate nonmarket risk, and a more complicated procedure should be used.

THE EFFECTIVENESS OF DIVERSIFICATION

Formula (12) can be used to gauge the potential effectiveness of diversification. Consider a portfolio of equity shares, chosen randomly, with investment spread evenly over the securities. Presumably, the greater the number of securities included in the portfolio, the smaller will be its risk.

For simplicity, assume that all securities have a beta of one. Then the market component of risk will be the same, no matter how many securities are included (since β_{pm} will always equal 1.0). But the nonmarket component of risk will generally decline as more and more securities are included. If holdings are equal, each value of X_i will equal $1/N$, and formula (12) can be written:

$$S(\tilde{r}_p)^2 = \sum_{i-1}^{N} = \left(\frac{1}{N}\right)^2 S(\tilde{r}_i)^2 \tag{13}$$

$$= \frac{1}{N} \left[\frac{1}{N} \{ S(\tilde{r}_i)^2 + S(\tilde{r}_2)^2 + \dots + S(\tilde{r}_N)^2 \} \right]$$

The value in the square brackets is simply the average nonmarket risk, measured by variance, for the component securities. But the nonmarket risk (measured by variance) for the portfolio is only one-Nth as large as this.

For a well-diversified portfolio of equal holdings of N securities, then:

$$S(\tilde{r}_p)^2 \approx \frac{\overline{S(\tilde{r}_i)^2}}{N} \tag{14}$$

where: $\overline{S(\tilde{r}_i)^2}$ = the average value of $S(\tilde{r}_i)^2$ for the N securities

Diversification does reduce risk, and the redution can be greater the wider the range of possible investments. But there is a limit: nonmarket risk can be lowered by diversification, but market risk generally remains.

NONMARKET RETURN IN AN EFFICIENT MARKET

The characteristic line for a portfolio that is the market portfolio itself is particularly simple.

$$\tilde{R}_p - R_f = \tilde{R}_m - R_f$$

Casting this in terms of formula (1):

$$\tilde{R}_p - R_f = (0 + 0) + 1(\tilde{R}_m - R_f)$$

For the market portfolio, then:

alpha = 0

beta = 1

nonmarket return = 0

The market portfolio clearly has no nonmarket risk. While nonmarket components of security returns are generally not uncorrelated, the overall market-weighted combination of securities has risk characteristics even better than those that would be obtained if such components were uncorrelated. With respect to nonmarket return, then, the insurance model is closer to reality than it might first seem to be.

To see the impact of this on security returns, we can rewrite the characteristic line formula as follows:

$$\tilde{R}_i \quad = \qquad (R_f + \alpha_i + \tilde{r}_i) \qquad + \qquad \beta_{im}(\tilde{R}_m - R_f) \tag{15}$$

return on investment in security *i*'s nonmarket characteristics	return on a financed investment in the market portfolio

For concreteness, consider a security with a beta of .8. An investment of Re. 1 in the security will give a return that can be considered the sum of two returns. The first results from an investment of Re. 1 in the security's nonmarket characteristics. This gives a return of:

$$1 \times (R_f + \alpha_i + \tilde{r}_i) \tag{16}$$

The second return can be thought of as the investment of ₹ .80 in the market portfolio, using money borrowed at the riskless rate of interest. This will return $(.80 \times \tilde{R}_m)$ and cost $(.80 \times R_f)$ for a net return of

$$.80 \times (\tilde{R}_m - R_f)$$

To gernalise, an investment of ₹ 1 in any security can be characterised as two inveestments: (1) ₹ 1 in the nonmarket characteristics of the security, and (2) β_{im} fund's borrowed at the riskless rate, then invested in the market portfolio.

The implicit "financed investment in the market" associated with a security should be neither better nor worse than an explicit investment of the same type. But what about the other component? What should be the expected return on investment in a security's nonmarket characteristics?

The answer is not difficult to determine. In an efficient market, one should expect to earn the riskless rate of interest on this component. This is *not* because it is riskless. The risk involved can be reduced or completely eliminated via diversification. Careful selection of securities for a portfolio can reduce such risk, and inclusion of all securities, to obtain the market portfolio, can eliminate such risk entirely. Moreover, if the market portfolio is indeed the only truly efficient combination of risky securities, the elimination of nonmarket risk will be both possible and also highly desirable.

If the expected value of $(R_f + \alpha_i + \tilde{r}_i)$ is to equal R_f then α_i must be zero. We reach, then, the key result of the efficient market theory. *A security that is priced correctly will have an ex ante alpha of zero in the eyes of well-informed analysts.* And in an efficient market, all securities are priced correctly.

A security with a positive alpha and beta of 1 and with $\tilde{r}_i$ of zero is expected to do better than the market index. If the market is expected to rise, the best set of variables would be for a positive alpha, a beta higher than one, and a $\tilde{r}_i$ of zero. If the market is expected to fall, the investor would want a positive alpha, a lower beta, and a zero $\tilde{r}_i$. And if the investor wanted a security to perform exactly like the market, the equation would have a zero alpha, a beta of 1 and a $\tilde{r}$ of zero. Thus, a positive alpha and zero $\tilde{r}_i$ are to be desired. A high or low beta must be judged on the expectation of the market. If the market is expected to rise, then a high beta is desirable; if it is expected to fall, then a low beta stock is desirable. In addition, both the alpha and $\tilde{r}_i$ for securities relative to the market tend to be low. A high alpha for securities would be desirable but difficult to obtain.

How should an investor go about selecting the best portfolio? Or, more explicitly, how should an investor go about selecting securities to purchase and how much to invest in each ? The construction of an optimal portfolio is simplified if there is a single number that measures the desirability of including a security in the optimal portfolio. If we accept the single index model, such a number exists.

CONSTRUCTING THE OPTIMAL PORTFOLIO

The calculation of the optimal portfolio would be greatly facilitated, and the ability of practicing security analysts and portfolio managers to relate to the construction of optimal portfolios greatly enhanced, if there is a single number that measured the desirability of including a stock in the optimal portfolio. If one is willing to accept the standard from of the single-index model as describing the comovement between securities, such a number exists.

In this case, the desirability of any security is directly related to its excess return to Beta ratio. Excess return is the difference between the expected return on the stock and the riskless rate of return on a security such as the rate of return on a treasury bill. The excess return to Beta ratio measures the additional return on a security (beyond the offered by a riskless asset) per unit of undiversifiable risk. The form of this ratio should lead to its easy interpretation and acceptance by security analysts and portfolio managers for they are used to thinking in term of the relationship between potential rewards and risk. The numerator of this ranking device is the extra return over the riskless asset that an investor earn from holding a security other than the riskless asset. The denominator is the undiversifiable risk that an investor is subject to by holding a risky security return than the riskless asset.

More formally, the index used to rank stocks is "excess return to Beta," or

$$\frac{\tilde{R}_i - R_f}{\beta_{im}}$$

$\tilde{R}_i$ = the expected return on stock i
R_f = the return on riskless asset
β_{im} = the expected change in the rate on stock in associated with a 1% change in the market return.

If stocks are ranked by excess return to Beta (from highest to lowest), the ranking represents the desirability of any stock's inclusion in a portfolio. In other words, if a stock with a particular ratio of $(\tilde{R}_i - R_f)/\beta_{im}$ is included in an optimal portfolio, all stocks will a higher ratio will be included. On the other hand, if a stock with a particular $(\tilde{R}_i - R_f)/\beta_{im}$ is excluded from an optimal portfolio, all stocks with lower ratios will be excluded (or if short selling is allowed, sold short). When the single-index model is assumed to represent the covariance structure of security returns, then a stock is included or excluded, depending only on the size of its excess return to Beta ratio. How many stocks are selected depended on a unique cut-off rate such that all stocks with higher ratios of $(\tilde{R}_i - R_f)/\beta_{im}$ will be included and all stocks with lower ratios excluded. This is called cut-off ratio C*.

The determine which stocks are included in the optimum portfolio, the necessary steps to follow are:

i) Calculate the "excess return to Beta" ratio for each security under consideration, and rank from higher to lowest.
ii) The optimum portfolio consists of investing in all similar for which $(\tilde{R}_i - R_f)/\beta_{im}$ is greater than a particular cut-off print C*.

Ranking Securities

To illustrate the ranking mechanism, table 3 and 4 represent an example of the ranking procedure. Table -3 contains the data necessary to apply simple ranking device to determine an optimal portfolio. It is the normal output generated from a single index model, plus the ratio of excess return to beta. There are seven securities in the tables. They are already ranked. Selecting the optimal portfolio involves the comparison of $(\tilde{R}_i - R_f)/\beta_{im}$ with C*. For the moment, assume that C* = 5.45. Examining Table 3 shows that for securities 1 to 5, $(\tilde{R}_i - R_f)/\beta_{im}$ is greater than C*, while for security 6 and 7, it is less than C*. Hence, an optimal portfolio consists of securities 1 to 5.

Selecting the Cut-off Rate (C*)

All securities whose excess return-to-risk ratio are above the cut-off rate are selected and all those whose ratios are below are rejected. The value of C* is computed from the characteristics of all of the securities that belong in the optimum portfolio. To determine C*, it is necessary to calculate its values as if there were different numbers of securities in the optimum portfolio. Suppose C_i is candidate of C*. The value of C_i is calculated when i securities are assumed to belong to the optimal portfolio.

Since securities are ranked from highest excess return to beta to lowest, we know that if a particular security belongs in the optimal portfolio, all higher ranked securities also belong in the optimal portfolio. We proceed to calculate values of a variable C_i as if the first-ranked security were in the optimal portfolio (i=l), then the first and second ranked securities were in the optimal portfolio (i= 2), and so on. These C_i are candidates for C*. We have found the optimum C_i, that is, C*, when all securities used in the calculation of C_i have excess returns to beta above C_i and all securities not used to calculate C_i have excess return to betas below C_i. C_5 serves the role of a cut-off rate. In particular, C_5 is the only C_i that when used as a cut-off rate selects only the securities used to construct it. There will always be one and only one C_i with this property and it is C*.

TABLE 3
Data Needed to Find Optimal Portfolio

$(R_f = 5\%)$

Security No. i,	Mean Return $\tilde{R}_i$	Excess Return $\tilde{R}_i - R_f$	Beta β_{im}	Unsystematic Risk $\sigma e^2{}_i$	Excess Return over Beta $(\tilde{R}_i - R_f)/\beta_{im}$
(1)	(2)	(3)	(4)	(5)	(6)
1	15.0	10.0	1.0	50	10.0
2	17.0	12.0	1.5	40	8.0
3	12.0	7.0	1.0	20	7.0
4	17.0	12.0	2.0	10	6.0
5	11.0	6.0	1.0	40	6.0
6	7.0	2.0	0.8	16	2.5
7	5.6	0.6	0.6	6	1.0

Calculating the Cut-off Rate C*

For a portfolio of i securities, C_i is given by :

$$C_i = \frac{\sigma_m^2 \sum_{i=1}^{i} \frac{(\tilde{R}_i - R_f)\beta_{im}}{\sigma_{ei}^2}}{1 + \sigma_m^2 \sum_{i=1}^{i} \frac{\beta_{im}^2}{\sigma_{ei}^2}} \qquad (17)$$

where :

σ_m^2 = variance of the market index

σ_{ei}^2 = variance of a security's movement that is not associated with the movement of the market index; this is the security's unsystematic risk.

The value of C_i for the first security in our list is thus:

Expression	Calculation	Date Locations Table
$\dfrac{(\tilde{R}_i - R_f)\beta_{im}}{\sigma_{ei}^2}$	$\dfrac{(15-5)1}{50} = \dfrac{2}{10}$	Column (3)
$\sum_{i=1}^{I} \dfrac{(\tilde{R}_i - R_f)\beta_{im}}{\sigma_{ei}^2}$	Same as above (since i=1)	Column (5)
$\dfrac{\beta_{im}^2}{\sigma_{ei}^2}$	$\dfrac{(1)^2}{50} = \dfrac{2}{100}$	Column (4)
		[cumulated in column (6)]

TABLE 4

Calculations for Determining Cut-off rate with $\sigma_m^2 = 10$

Security	$(\tilde{R}_i - R_f)/\beta_{im}$	$\dfrac{(\tilde{R}_i - R_f)\beta_{im}}{\sigma_{ei}^2}$	$\dfrac{\beta_{im}^2}{\sigma_{ei}^2}$	$\sum\limits_{i=1}^{i}\dfrac{(\tilde{R}_i - R_f)\beta_{im}}{\sigma_{ei}^2}$	$\sum\limits_{i-1}^{i}\dfrac{\beta_{im}^2}{\sigma_{ei}^2}$	C
(1)	(2)	(3)	(4)	(5)	(6)	(7)
1	10	2/10	2/100	2/10	2/100	1.67
2	8	4.5/10	5.625/100	6.5/10	7.625/100	3.69
3	7	3.5/10	5/100	10/10	12.625/100	4.42
4	6	24/10	40/100	34/10	52.625/100	5.43
5	6	1.5/10	2.5/100	35.5/10	55.125/100	**5.45**
6	2.5	1/10	4/100	42.5/10	76.625/100	4.91
7	1.0	.6/10	6/100	44.1/10	87.625/100	4.52

Putting all this information together yields:

$$C_i = \frac{10(2/10)}{1+10(2/100)} = 1.67$$

For security 2 (i=2) column (3) is

$$\frac{(17-5)1.5}{40} = \frac{4.5}{10}$$

Now column (5) is the sum of column (3) for security 1 and security 2 or

$$\frac{2}{10} + \frac{4.5}{10} = \frac{6.5}{10}$$

Column (4) is

$$\frac{(1.5)^2}{40} = \frac{5.625}{100}$$

Column (6) is the sum of column (4) for security 1 and 2, or

$$\frac{2}{100} + \frac{5.625}{100} = \frac{7.625}{100}$$

and C_2 is

$$C_2 = \frac{\sigma_m^2 [\text{Column(5)}]}{1+\sigma_m^2 [\text{Column(6)}]}$$

$$= \frac{10\left(\dfrac{6.5}{10}\right)}{1+10\left(\dfrac{7.625}{100}\right)} = 3.69$$

Proceeding in the same fashion, we can find all the C_i's.

Optimum Portfolio Selection

To construct the optimum portfolio, the per cent invested for each selected security in the optimal portfolio is to be calculated. The percentage invested in each security is:

$$X_i^0 = \frac{Z_i}{\sum\limits_{j=1}^{n} Z_j}$$

(18)

where:

$$Z_i = \frac{\beta_{im}}{\sigma_{ei}^2} \left[\frac{(\tilde{R}_i - R_f)}{\beta_{im}} - C* \right]$$

(19)

The second expression determines the relative investment in each security, and the first expression simply scales the weights on each security so that they sum to 1 (ensure full investment). The residual variance on each security σ_{ei}^2 plays an important role in determining how much to invest in each security. Applying this formula to our example, we have:

$$Z_1 = \frac{2}{100} (10 - 5.45) = .091$$

$$Z_2 = \frac{3.75}{100} (8 - 5.45) = .095625$$

$$Z_3 = \frac{5}{100} (7 - 5.45) = .0775$$

$$Z_4 = \frac{20}{100} (6 - 5.45) = .110$$

$$Z_5 = \frac{2.5}{100} (6 - 5.45) = .01375$$

$$\sum_{i=1}^{5} Z_i = 0.3878755$$

Dividing each security Z_i by the sum of the Z_i, we would invest 23 .5 per cent of our funds in security 1, 24.6 per cent in security 2, 20 per cent in security 3, 28.4 per cent in security 4, and 3.5 per cent in security 5.

The characteristics of a security that make it desirable can be determined before the calculations of an optimal portfolio is begun. The desirability of any security is solely a function of its excess return to beta ratio.

Up to this point, all stocks assumed have positive Betas. There are sound economic reason to expect all stocks to have positive Betas and the few negative Beta stocks that are found in large samples which are due to measurement errors. However, as negative Beta stocks (and zero Beta stocks) can easily incorporated in the analysis.

Table 5 and 6 present an example to illustrate the use of these formulas. One again, securities are ranked by excess return to Beta. Examining Table 5 shows that the C_i associated with security 4 is the only C_i consistent with the cut-off rate $C*$. That is, it is the only value of C_i not that stocks ranked i or higher will have excess return to Beta above C_i and all stocks ranked below i have excess return to Beta below C_i. Thus the cut-off rate is 8.29.

$$C* = C_4 = \frac{58}{7} = 8.29$$

TABLE 5

Date Required to Determine Optimal Portfolio; $R_f = 5$

Security No. 1	Mean Return $\overline{R}_i$	Excess Return $(\overline{R}_i - R_f)$	Beta β_{im}	Unsystematic Risk σ_{ei}	Excess Return over Beta $(\overline{R}_i - R_f)/\beta_{im}$
1	2	3	4	5	6
1.	19	24	1.0	20	14
2.	23	18	1.5	30	12
3.	11	6	0.5	10	12
4.	25	20	2.0	40	10
5.	13	8	1.0	20	8
6.	9	4	0.5	50	8
7.	14	9	1.5	30	6
8.	10	5	1.0	50	5
9.	9.5	4.5	1.0	50	4.5
10.	13	8	2.0	20	4
11.	11	6	1.5	30	4
12.	8	3	1.0	20	3
13.	10	5	2.0	40	2.5
14.	17	2	1.0	20	2

The optimum amount to invest in determined using equation-18:

$$X_i^o = \frac{Z_i}{\sum\limits_{j=1}^{n} Z_j} \tag{20}$$

For this example, it is

$$Z_1 = \frac{1}{20} = (14 - \frac{58}{7}) = \frac{40}{140} = \frac{240}{840}$$

$$Z_2 = \frac{1.5}{30} = (12 - \frac{58}{7}) = \frac{39}{210} = \frac{156}{840}$$

$$Z_3 = \frac{0.5}{10} = (12 - \frac{58}{7}) = \frac{13}{70} = \frac{156}{840}$$

$$Z_4 = \frac{2}{40} = (10 - \frac{58}{7}) = \frac{24}{280} = \frac{72}{840}$$

Scaling the Z's so that they add to one we have

$$X_1 = \frac{240}{240 + 156 + 156 + 72} = \frac{240}{624} = 0.38$$

$$X_2 = \frac{156}{240 + 156 + 156 + 72} = \frac{156}{624} = 0.25$$

$$X_3 = \frac{156}{240 + 156 + 156 + 72} = \frac{156}{624} = 0.25$$

$$X_4 = \frac{72}{240 + 156 + 156 + 72} = \frac{72}{624} = 0.12$$

Thus in this example optimum portfolio consists of 4 securities with largest investment in security -1 and the smallest in security 4.

TABLE 6

Calculations for Determining Cut-off Rate with $\sigma_m^2 = 10$

Security	$\dfrac{\overline{R}_i - R_f}{\beta_i}$	$\dfrac{(\overline{R}_i - R_f)}{\sigma_{ei}^2}$	$\dfrac{\beta_{im}^2}{\sigma_{ei}^2}$	$\sum\limits_{j=1}^{i}$	$\dfrac{(\overline{R}_i - R_f)\beta_{im}}{\sigma_{ej}^2}$	$\sum\limits_{j=1}^{i} \dfrac{\beta_{im}^2}{\sigma_{ej}^2}$	C_i
No. 1						
1	2	3	4	5	6	7
1.	14	70/100	5/100	70/100	5/100	4.67
2.	12	90/100	7.5/100	160/100	12.5/100	7.11
3.	12	30/100	2.5/100	190/100	15/100	7.6
4.	10	100/100	10/100	290/100	25/100	8.29
5.	8	40/100	5/100	330/100	30/100	8.25
6.	8	4/100	0.5/100	334/100	30.5/100	8.25
7.	6	45/100	7.5/100	379/100	38/100	7.9
8.	5	10/100	2/100	389/100	40/100	7.78
9.	4.5	9/100	2/100	398/100	42/100	7.65
10.	4	80/100	20/100	487/100	62/100	6.64
11.	4	30/100	7.5/100	508/100	69/100	6.39
12.	3	15/100	5/100	523/100	74.5/100	6.19
13.	2.5	25/100	10/100	548/100	84.5/100	5.8
14.	2	10/100	5/100	558/100	89.5/100	5.61

Short Sales Allowed

The procedures used to calculate the optimal portfolio when short sales are allowed related to the procedures in the no short sales case. As a first step all stocks are ranked by excess return to Beta just as they were in the previous case. However the cut-off point for stocks, C^*, non has a different meaning, as well as different procedure for calculation. When short sales are allowed, all stock will either he held long or sold short. Thus, all stocks center into the optimum portfolio and all stocks affect the cut-off point. Equation (17) still represents the cut-off point, but now the number and denominator of the equation are summed over all stocks. In addition, although equation (17) and (19) still hold (with respect to the new C^*), the meaning of Z_i is now changed. Now Z_i for each stock is to be calculated. A positive value of Z_i indicates the stocks will be held long, and a negative value indicates it will be sold short. Thus, the impact of C^* has changed. Stocks that have an excess return to Beta above C^* are held long (as before), but stocks with an excess return to Beta below C^* are now sold short.

To illustrate if we take Table 3, the C^* was calculated by employing equation (17) with i set equal to the number of stocks under consideration. In this case we have population of 7 securities so that

$$C^* = C_7 = 4.52$$

Employing equation (19) for each security, we compute:

$$Z_1 = \frac{2}{100} (10.0 - 4.52) = 0.110$$

$$Z_2 = \frac{3.75}{100} (8.0 - 4.52) = 0.131$$

$$Z_3 = \frac{5}{100} (7.0 - 4.52) = 0.124$$

$$Z_4 = \frac{20}{100} (6.0 - 4.52) = 0.296$$

$$Z_5 = \frac{2.5}{100} (6.0 - 4.52) = 0.037$$

$$Z_6 = \frac{5}{100} (2.5 - 4.52) = 0.101$$

$$Z_7 = \frac{1}{100} (1.0 - 4.52) = 0.335$$

The last step the procedure involves the scaling of the Z_i's so they represent the optimum proportion to invest in each stock (X_i's). There are act well, two ways to do this scaling. These methods exactly parallel the two definition of short sales. First, under the standard definition of short sales, which presumes that a short sales of a stock is a source of fund to the investor, the appropriate scaling factor is given by

$$X_i = \frac{Z_i}{\sum_{j-1}^{n} Z_i}$$

When Z_i can be positive or negative. This scaling is arrived at by realising that under this definition of short sales the constraint on the X_i's is that

$$\sum_{i=1}^{n} X_i = 1$$

The second definition of short sales refer to the use of the investor's fund, however, the investor receives the riskless rate of the fund involved in the short sale. This translates into the constraint

$$\sum_{i=1}^{n} |X_i| = 1$$

The analogous scaling factor is

$$X_i = \frac{Z_i}{\sum_{j=1}^{n} |Z_i|}$$

Under the two alternative definitions of short sales, not only are the same stocks always held long and sold short, but any two stocks are always held in the same ratio to each other. This is time because the two solutions differ by only a scale factor. From the foregoing analysis it is obvious that this scale factor is simply

$$\frac{\sum\limits_{i=1}^{n} |Z_i|}{\sum\limits_{i=1}^{n} Z_i}$$

REVIEW PROBLEMS

1. How many inputs are needed for a portfolio analysis involving 75 securities if covariances are computed using (a) the Markowitz approach and (b) the Sharpe index model ?

Ans.:

Markowitz :
$$N(N + 3)/2$$
$$75(75 + 3)/2 = 2,925$$
Sharpe :
$$(N \times 3) + 2$$
$$(75 \times 3) + 2 = 227$$

2. Three securities and the National Index have had the following annual returns for the past ten years :

Year	National Index	Securities		
		X	Y	Z
1	0.8	1.0	-0.5	1.0
2	1.2	15	-1.0	1.0
3	1.9	1.7	2.0	1.0
4	-2.0	-1.0	3.0	2.0
5	1.8	3.0	0.5	2.0
6	0.9	1.0	0.5	2.0
7	0.3	0.5	1.0	2.1
8	0.5	1.0	1.0	2.2
9	-1.0	-0.5	4.0	-2.3
10	0.5	1.0	0.5	1.5

(a) What is the ten-year average annual return for each security and the National Index?
(b) What is the standard deviation of each security and of the National Index ?
(c) Rank each security on the basis of its total return and risk.
(d) Rank each .security by its beta.
(e) Rank each security by its alpha.
(f) Which security is most volatile, and why ?

Ans.:

(a) The ten-year average yields are:
National Index = .49, X = .92, Y = .30 and Z = 1.25
(b) The standard deviations are: National Index = 1.137; X = 1.057; Y = 1.803; Z = 1.273
(c)

National Index	Yield	S.D.	Reward-to-Risk
.49		1.137(2)	3
X	.92(2)	1.057(1)	2
Y	.30(4)	1.803(4)	4
Z	1.25 (1)	1.273 (3)	1

Securities X and Z are significantly less risky than either the National Index or security Y for the given levels of return.

(d)

Security	Beta	Rank
X	0.87	2
Y	1.33	3
Z	0.71	1

(e)

Security	Alpha	Rank
X	0.465	1
Y	0.365	3
Z	0.845	2

(f) Security Y is the most volatile due both to its high beta and high standard deviation of return.

3. The policy committee of Suntex Finance recently used reports from various security analysts to develop inputs for the single-index model. Output derived from the single-index model consisted of the following efficient portfolios:

Portfolio	Expected Return E(R)	Standard Deviation
1	8%	3%
2	10%	6%
3	13%	8%
4	17%	13%
5	20%	18%

(a) If the prevailing risk-free rate is 6%, which portfolio is the best ?

(b) Assume that the policy committee would like to earn an expected 10% with a σ of 4%. Is this possible ?

(c) If a σ of 12% were acceptable, what would the expected portfolio return be and how would Suntex Finance achieve it ?

Ans.:

Portfolio	$[E(R)-R_f]/\sigma$
1	$(8-6)/3 = 0.67$
2	$(10-6)/6 = 0.67$
3	$(13-6)/8 = 0.875$
4	$(17-6)/13 = 0.846$
5	$(20-6)/18 = 0.77$

Portfolio 3 is the optimal portfolio

(b) A standard deviation of 4% results in an expected return of only 9.5% :

$$9.5\% = 6\% + 4\% (0.875)$$

(c) $E(R) = 6\% + 12\%(0.875) = 16.5\%$

Borrow Re.0.50 for each Re.1.00 equity

$$\sigma_p = 1.5 (8\%) = 12\%$$

4. You are given the following estimates of stock i's and stock j's characteristic lines plus estimates of each stock's σ of returns :

$$(\tilde{R}_{it}-R_f) = 1\% + 1.5(R_f)$$

$$(\tilde{R}_{jt}-R_f) = 4\% + 1.0(R_m-R_f)$$

$$\sigma(\tilde{R}_{it}-R_f) = 20\%;$$

$$\sigma(\tilde{R}_{jt}-R_f) = 10\%$$

(a) One-year T-bills are now yielding 8%. If the market portfolio is expected to return 13% during the year, what is the expected return on each stock as of the beginning of the year ?

(b) The year goes by and the market portfolio actually provides a 10% rate of return during the year. Given this, what is your expectation of the return earned on each stock during the year?

(c) If stock i actually returned 15% and stock j actually returned 11%, what was the residual error return for each stock ?

(d) Why might a residual error return arise, and what is its role in diversified ?

(e) If the standard deviation of stock i's residual error term is 10%, what is your best estimate of the σ of excess returns – i.e., $\sigma(\tilde{R}_i - R_f)$ on the market portfolio?

Ans.:

	Security	Expected Excess Return	Risk-free rate R_f	= E(R)
(a)	i	1.0 + 1.5 (5)	+ 8	= 16.5%
	j	4.0 + 1.0 (5)	+ 8	= 17.0%
(b)	i	1.0 + 1.5 (2)	+ 8	= 12.0%
	j	4.0 + 1.0 (2)	+ 8	= 14.0%
(c)	i	15 – 12	= 3%	
	j	11 – 14	= 3%	

(d) Residual errors net out (approach zero) in diversified portfolios.

(e) $20^2 = 1.5^2 \sigma_m^2 + 10^2$

$\sigma_m = 11.55\%$

5. Using five years of monthly returns, the following regression statistics were generated using the market model and a broad equity index:

Security	α_1	σ	r_{it}
ABC	-0.21	14.7%	0.48
DEF	0.15	6.3%	0.25
GHI	0.01	11.3%	0.51
JKL	0.20	5.2%	0.95
INDEX	0.00	4.3%	1.00

Historical correlation between i and 1.

(a) Calculate an estimate of β for each.

(b) Do you think that the market model betas during next five-year period will be the same, higher, or lower ?

(c) Assuming that the index used is the market portfolio, and the return on market portfolio is 7%; and that risk-free rate is 9.0%, calculate the equilibrium expected return on each.

(d) Assume that each security is the only holding of the portfolio, calculate required expected returns and explain why these are not the same as the answer to part (c).

(e) Calculate the beta of a portfolio consisting of an equal investment in each security.

Ans.:

Security	Beta
ABC	(14.7+ 4.3) (0.48)= 1.64
DEF	(6.3 + 4.3) (0.25) = 0.37
GHI	(11.3+4.3) (0.51)= 1.34
JKL	(5.2+ 4.3) (0.95) = 1.15
INDEX	(4.3+ 4.3) (1.00) = 1.00

(b) Beta estimates smaller than 1.0 will probably increase towards 1.0. Beta estimates larger than 1.0 will probably decrease towards 1.0

(c)

Security	E(R)
ABC	20.48 = 9 + 1.64 (7)
DEF	11.59 = 9 + 0.37 (7)
GHI	18.38 = 9 + 1.34 (7)
JKL	17.05 = 9 + 1.15 (7)
INDEX	16.00 = 9 + 1.00 (7)

(d)

Security	E(R)
ABC	32.93 = 9 + 14.7(7/4.3)
DEF	19.26 = 9+ 6.3(7/4.3)
GHI	27.40 = 9 + 11.3 (7/4.3)
JKL	17.46 = 9+ 5.2(7/4.3)
Index	16.00 =9+ 4.3(7/4.3)

(e) β_{pm} = 0.25(1.64) + 0.25(0.37) + 0.25(1.34) + 0.25(1.15) = 1.125

6. What is the optimum portfolio in choosing among the following securities and assuming the risk-free return is = 8% and variance in the market index (σ_m^2) = 12%?

Security	Expected Return	Beta	Security's unsystematic risk
No.i	$\tilde{R}_i$	β_{im}	σ_{ei}^2
A	20	1.0	40
B	18	2.5	35
C	12	1.5	30
D	16	1.0	35
E	14	0.8	25

F	10	1.2	15
G	17	1.6	30
H	15	2.0	35

Ans.:

Solving by ranking $(\tilde{R}_i - R_f)/\beta_{im}$, $R_f = 8\%$ and $\sigma_m^2 = 12$

Security	$\tilde{R}_i$	$(\tilde{R}_i - R_f)$	β_{im}	$(\tilde{R}_i - R_f)/\beta_{im}$	Rank	σ_{ei}^2
1	2	3	4	5	6	7
A	20	12	1.0	12.00	1	40
B	18	10	25	4.00	5	35
C	12	4	1.5	2.67	7	30
D	16	8	1.0	8.00	2	35
E	14	6	0.0	750	3	25
F	10	2	12	1.67	8	15
G	17	9	16	5.63	4	30
H	15	7	2.0	350	6	35

Comparing the ratio of excess return to β_{im} to the cut-off rate, C^*

Security	$(\tilde{R}i - R_f)/\beta_{im}$	$\dfrac{(\tilde{R}_i - R_f)\beta_{im}}{\sigma_{ei}^2}$	$\dfrac{\beta_{im}^2}{\sigma_{ei}^2}$	$\sum\limits_{i-1}^{i} \dfrac{(\tilde{R}_i - R_f)\beta_{im}^2}{\sigma_{ei}^2}$	$\sum\limits_{i-1}^{i} \dfrac{\beta_{im}^2}{\sigma_{ei}^2}$
A	12.00	0.300	.025	0.300	0.025
D	8.00	0.229	.029	0.529	0.054
E	7.50	0.179	.026	0.708	0.080
G	5.63	0.480	.085	1.188	0.165
B	4.00	0.714	.179	1.902	0.344
H	3.50	0.400	.114	2.302	0.458
C	2.67	0.200	.064	2.502	0.522
F	1.67	0.160	.096	2.662	0.618

Possible Cut off Rates C

$$C_i = \dfrac{\sigma_m^2 \sum\limits_{i=1}^{i} \dfrac{(\tilde{R}_i - R_f)\beta_{im}}{\sigma_{ei}^2}}{1 + \sigma_m^2 \sum\limits_{i=1}^{i} \dfrac{\beta_{im}^2}{\sigma_{ei}^2}}$$

A		2.769	1
D		3.852	2
E		4.414	3
G		4.836	4
B		4.481	5
H		4.276	6
C		4.155	7
F		3.814	8

The value of cut-off rate, C* is 4.836 and equal to G cut off rate. Finding the percentage in each security :

$$Z_1 = \frac{\beta_{im}}{\sigma_{ei}^2}\left[\frac{\tilde{R}-R_f}{\beta_{im}} - C^*\right]$$

$$Z_2 = \frac{1}{40}\sum_{i=1}^{4} Z_i \ (12-4.836) = 0.1791$$

$$Z_3 = \frac{1}{35}(8\text{-}4.836) = 0.0904$$

$$Z_3 = \frac{0.8}{25}\ (7.50\text{-}4.836) = 0.0853$$

$$Z_4 = \frac{1.6}{30}\ (5.63\text{-}4.836) = 0.0423 \ .$$

$$\sum_{i=1}^{4} Z_i = 0.3971$$

Dividing each Z_i by the sum of Z_i, we get the fund to be invested in each security, in A = 45.10%; in D = 22.77%; in E = 21.48%; and in G = 10.65%

7. Arvind stock has a beta of 1.50. Over six years, the following returns were produced by Arvind stock and a market index. Assuming a market model intercept term of 0 per cent, calculate the standard deviation of the market model return error term over this period.

Year	1	2	3	4	5	6
Arvind Return	9.8%	28.5%	13.3%	-6.1%	-3.4%	16.5%
Market Index	6.0%	25.0%	10.2%	-4.0%	-2.5%	12.5%

Ans.:

Assuming a 0% intercept term, the random error term of Arvind stock over the six years can be calculated as follows:

$\tilde{r}_1 = 9.8 - [(1.50) \times (6.0)] = 0.8$

$\tilde{r}_2 = 28.5 - [(1.50) \times (25.0)] = -9.0$

$\tilde{r}_3 = 13.3 - [(1.50) \times (10.2)] = -2.0$

$\tilde{r}_4 = -6.1 - [(1.50) \times (-4.0)] = -0.1$

$\tilde{r}_5 = -3.4 - [(1.50) \times (-2.5)] = 0.35$

$\tilde{r}_6 = 16.5 - [(1.50) \times (12.5)] = -2.25$

The average random error term is:

Average $= (0.8 - 9.0 - 2.0 - 0.1 + 0.35 - 2.25)/6$

$= -2.033$

The standard deviation of the random error term is therefore :

σ_{ei} = $[\{(0.8) - (-2.03)\}^2 + [(-9.0) - (-2.03)]^2 + [(-2.0) (-2.03)]^2$
$+ [(-0.1) - (-2.03)]^2 + [(0.35) - (-2.03)]^2 + [(-2.25) - (-2.03)]^2 /(6-1)]^{1/2}$
$= [\{(2.83)^2 + (-6.97)^2 + (0.03)^2 + (1.93)^2 + (2.38)^2 + (-0.22)^2\}/(5)]^{1/2}$
$= [\{8.0089 + 48.5809 + 0.0009 + 3.7249 + 5.6644 + 0.0484)\}/(5)]^{1/2}$
$= 3.6339\%$

8. Assume that two securities X and Y constitute the market portfolio. Their proportions and variances are 0.49, 150, and 0.51, 324 respectively. The covariances off two securities is 175. Calculate the betas of the two securities

Ans.:

Given the two securities' market model, its variance is :

$$\sigma_m^2 = X_A^2\,\sigma_A^2 + X_B^2\,\sigma_B^2 + 2X_A X_2 C_{AB}$$
$$= (.49)^2\,(150) + (.51)^2\,(324) + 2(.49)\,(.51)\,(175) = 207.75$$

Further, the covariance of a security with the market portfolio equals

$$\sigma_m^2 = \sum_{1=1}^{n} X_{jm}\sigma_{ij}$$

In the two-security market model case :

$$\sigma_{Am} = .49 \times 150 + .51 \times 175$$
$$= 73.50 + 89.25$$
$$= 162.75$$
$$\sigma_{Bm} = .51 \times 324 + .49 \times 175$$
$$= 165.24 + 85.75$$
$$= 250.99$$

The beta of the security is defined as :

$$\beta_i = \sigma_{im}/\sigma_m^2$$

Therefore :

$$\beta_A = 167.75/207.75$$
$$= .81$$
$$\beta_B = 250.24/207.75$$
$$= 1.21$$

9. Shiva owns a portfolio composed of four securities with the following characteristics

:

Security	Beta	Standard Deviation Random Error Term	Projection
A	1.05	12	.30
B	0.90	10	.30
C	1.20	15	.25
D	1.00	11	.15

If the standard deviation of the market index is 20%, what is total risk of Shiva's portfolio?

Ans.:

$$\beta_P = \sum_{i=1}^{4} X_i\beta_i$$

$$= (.30 \times 1.05) + (.30 \times 0.90) + (.25) \times 1.20) + (.15 \times 1.0)$$
$$= [0.315 + 0.27 + 0.3 + .15]$$
$$= 1.035$$

The standard deviation of the portfolio is:

$$= [(1.035)^2\,(20)^2 + (.30)^2\,(12)^2 + (.30)^2\,(10)^2 + (.25)^2\,(15)^2 + (.15)^2\,(11)^2]^{\frac{1}{2}}$$
$$= [428.49 + 12.96 + 9 + 14.0625 + 2.7225]^{1}/^{2}$$
$$= 21.62\%$$

10. Consider an efficient portfolio with expected return of 15% and standard deviation of 12%. Suppose that the lowest variance portfolio with 0 correlation with the efficient portfolio has an expected rate of return of 5%. Next assume that security i has a standard deviation of 20% and a correlation coefficient of 0.6 with the efficient portfolio. What does the expected rate of return on the asset have to be in order to be consistent with the mathematical relationship for efficient portfolios?

Ans.:

Since
$$\beta_i = 0.6\,(0.20)/0.12 = 1.00$$

We find
$$E(R_i) = 0.5 + 1.0\,[0.15\text{-}0.05]$$
$$= 0.15$$
$$= 15\%$$

11. Given the following information and the assumption of the single-index model, SIM, what is the beta factor of stock 1?
$$\beta_2 = 1.20$$
$$\sigma_M^2 = 0.3162$$
$$\text{Cov.}(R_1,R_2) = 0.09$$

Ans.:

Given the assumption of the single-index model, we can write the covariance between any two stocks as
$$\text{Cov. }(R_1, R_2) = \beta_1\,\beta_2\,\sigma_M^2$$
By rearranging the terms, we can solve for:
$$\beta_1 = \frac{\text{Cov.}(R_1,R_2)}{\beta_2 \sigma_m^2}$$

$$= \frac{0.09}{1.20(0.3162)} = 0.0237$$

12. Given the assumption of the single-index model, what is the residual variance of each of the following stocks:

Stock	Portfolio Weight	Beta Return	Expected Variance	Total
X	0.25	0.50	0.40	0.07
Y	0.25	0.50	0.25	0.05
Z	0.50	1.00	0.21	0.07

$$\sigma_m^2 = 0.06$$

Ans.:

We know
$$\sigma_i^2 = \beta^2 \sigma_m^2 + \sigma_{ei}^2$$
$$\sigma_{ei}^2 = \sigma_i^2 - \beta^2 \sigma_m^2$$

or

$$\sigma_{ei}^2 = 0.07 - (0.50)^2\,(0.06) = 0.055$$

$$\sigma_{ey}^2 = 0.05 - (0.50)^2 \ (0.06) = 0.035$$

$$\sigma_{ez}^2 = 0.07 - (1.0)^2 \ (0.06) = 0.010$$

13. Refer to the problem-12, what is the beta factor of the three-stock portfolio?

Ans.:

The beta factor for the portfolio is simply the weighted average beta of the three stocks. Therefore,

$$\beta_p = X_x \beta_x + X_y \beta_y + X_z \beta_z$$
$$= (0.25)(0.50) + (0.25 \times 0.50) + (0.50)(1.00)$$
$$= 0.75$$

14. Given the information in problem-12, compute the variance of the portfolio.

Ans.:

The variance of the portfolio can be splitted into two components, systematic risk and residual variance.

$$\sigma_p^2 = \beta_p^2 \ \sigma_m^2 + \sigma_{ep}^2$$

$$\beta_p^2 \ \sigma_m^2 = (0.75)^2 \ (0.06) = 0.338$$

$$\sigma_{ep}^2 = (0.25)^2 \ (0.55) + (0.25)^2 \ (0.35) + (0.50)^2(0.010) = 0.0081$$

So $\quad \sigma_p^2 = 0.0338 + 0.0081 = 0.419$

15. Given the information in problem-12, what is the expected return on the portfolio?

Ans.:

$$E(R_p) = X_x E(R_x) + X_y E(R_y) + X_z E(R_z)$$
$$= (0.25) \ (0.40) + (0.25) \ (0.25) + (0.50) \ (0.21)$$
$$= 0.2675$$
$$= 26.75\%$$

16. Refer to the problem-12 and given the actual (Markowitz) covariance between the stocks' returns, what is the actual portfolio variance?

$$\text{Cov. } (r_x, r_y) = 0.020$$
$$\text{Cov. } (r_y, r_z) = 0.035$$
$$\text{Cov. } (r_x, r_z) = 0.035$$

Ans.:

$$\sigma_p^2 = \sum_{x=1}^{n} \sum_{y=1}^{n} W_x \, W_y \, C_{xy}$$

$$= (0.25)^2 \ (0.07) + (0.25)^2 \ (0.05) + (0.50)^2 \ (0.07) + 2 \ (0.25) \ (0.25) \ (0.020) +$$
$$2(0.25 \times 0.50 \times 0.035) + 2 \ (0.25 \times 0.50)(0.035)$$
$$= 0.0450$$

17. Radha Raman owns a portfolio containing four stocks. His broker gave him the estimates of each stock's beta. Compute *the* portfolio beta using the following data:

Stock	A	B	C	D
Beta	0.73	1.86	1.45	1.15
Amount	Rs. 20,000	Rs. 40,000	Rs. 10,000	Rs. 30,000

Ans.:

β_p = (20,000/1,00,000)0.73 + (40,000/1,00,000)1.86 + (10,000/1,00,000)1.45 + (30,000/1,00,000)1.15

= 0.146 + 0.744 + 0.145 + 0.345 = 1.38

18. The standard deviation of return is 4.5 percent on equity shares of ABC Company, 3.5% for XYZ company, and 2.5% for the market portfolio. The correlation coefficient of ABC company for the market is +0.075 and XYZ to the market is - 0.5. What is the beta coefficient for ABC and XYZ?

Ans.:

$$\beta_{ABC} \quad \frac{(0.75)\ (0.045)}{0.025} = 1.35$$

$$\beta_{XYZ} \quad \frac{(\text{-}0.5)\ (0.035)}{0.025} = \text{-}0.70$$

19. (a) Determine the expected return and beta for the following portfolio:

Stock	Percentage of Portfolio	Beta	Expected Return
1	35%	1.20	15%
2	25	0.75	11
3	40	1.00	12

(b) Given the information above, if you are to draw the security market live and show when the securities fit on the graph, assuming that the risk-free rate is 8 percent and that the expected return on the market portfolio is 12 percent, how would you interpret these findings?

Ans.:

(a) Portfolio expected return:

(0.35 × 15%) + (0.25 × 11%) + (0.40 × 12%)

= 5.25+2.75+4.80

= 12.80%

Portfolio beta:

(0.31 × 120) + (0.25 × 0.75) + (0.40 × 1.00)

= 0.420 + 0.1775 + 0.400

= 0.9975

(b) Stocks 3 and 2 would be right in line with the security market line, suggesting that they are earning a fair return, given their systematic risk. Stock 1, on the other hand, would be earning more than a fair return (above the security market line). One may be tempted to conclude that security 1 is undervalued. However, it may be an illusion, it is possible to misspecify the security market line by using bad estimates in given data.

20. Lotus is a diversified company with three operating divisions—North, South, and West. The operating characteristics of North are 50% more risky than South, while West is 25% less risky than South. In terms of financial valuation, South is thought to have a market value twice that of North, which has the same market value as the West.

Lotus is all equity financed with a beta of 1.06. The overall return on the BSE Index is 25%, with a standard deviation of 16%. Recently, South has been underperforming and Lotus management plan to sell it and use its entire proceeds to purchase Reeva Ltd., an unquoted company. Reeva is all-equity financed and Lotus' financial strategists reckon that while Reeva is operating broadly in similar markets and industries as South, Reeva has a revenue sensitivity of 1.4 times that of South, an operating gearing ratio of 1.6 compared to the current operating gearing in South of 2.0.

Assume:

No synergistic benefits form the divestment and acquisition. Taxation any be ignored.

Required:

  (a) Calculate the asset betas for the North, South, and West divisions of Lotus. Specify any assumptions which you make.
  (b) Calculate the asset beta for East.
  (c) Calculate the asset beta for Lotus after the divestment and acquisition.
  (d) What discount rate should be applied to any new investment projects in East division?

Ans.:

  (a) Since the asset Beta is a weighted average of the component segment Betas:

$$\beta_A = (1/4 \times \beta_N) + (1/4 \times \beta_W) + (1/2 \times \beta_S) = 1.06$$

Where

$\beta_N = \beta$ of North, $\beta_W = \beta$ of West, $\beta_S = \beta$ of South.

Since North is 50% more risky than South, and West is 25% less risky than South, it follows that

$$(1.5 \; \beta_S)/4 + (0.75 \; \beta_S)/4 + (\beta_S)/2$$
$$= 1.06$$

Whence

$$\beta_S = 1.00, \; \beta_N = 1.50, \; \beta_W = 0.75$$

  (b) The asset beta for East (β_E) is:

$\beta_E = \beta_S \times$ Relative risk factor
$\quad = \beta_S \times$ Revenue sensitive factor $\times$ Operational gearing factor
$\quad = 1.0 \times 1.4 \times (1.6/2.0) = 1.12$

  (c) The asset beta for Lotus after the divestment and acquisition is again a weighted average of the componant asset betas:

$$\beta_A = (1/2 \times \beta_E) + (1/4 \times \beta_W) + (1/4 \times \beta_N)$$
$$(1/2 \times 1.12) + (1/4 \times 0.75) + (1/4 \times 1.5)$$
$$= 0.56 + 0.1875 + 0.375 = 1.12$$

  (d) If we evaluate projects in East on the assumption of all-equity financing, the cut-off rate is:

$R_f + \beta_E \; E(R_m - R_f)$
$= 10\% + 1.12 \, (15\%)$
$= 26.8\%$

21. Suppose that the index model for stock A and B is estimated with the following results:

$$R_A = .01 + .9R_M + e_A$$
$$R_B = -.02 - 1.1R_M + e_B$$
$$\sigma_M = .20$$

$$c(e_A) = .3$$
$$c(e_B) = .1$$

Find the standard deviation of each stock and the covariance between them.

Ans.:

The variance of each stock is $\beta^2 \sigma_M^2 + \sigma^2(e)$

For stock A, we obtain
$$\sigma_A^2 = .9^2(.20)^2 + .3^2 = .1224$$
$$\sigma_A = .35$$

For stock B,
$$\sigma_B^2 = 1.1^2(.20)^2 + .1^2 \, \sigma$$
$$= .0584$$
$$\sigma_B = .24$$

The covariance is
$$\beta_A \beta_B \sigma_M^2 = .9 \times 1.1 \times .2^2 = .0396$$

22. Refer to previous question and suppose we form an equally weighted portfolio of A and B. What will be the non-systematic standard deviation of that portfolio?

Ans.:

$$\sigma^2(e_p) = (1/2)^2 [\sigma^2(e_A) + \sigma^2(e_B)]$$
$$= 1/4(.3^2 + .1^2)$$
$$= 1/4(.09 + .01)$$
$$= .025$$

Therefore
$$\sigma^2(e_p) = .158$$

23. The data below is drawn from a three-stock financial market that satisfies the single index model.

Stock	Capitalisation	Beta	Mean Excess Return	Standard Deviation
A	Rs. 3,000	1.0	.10	.40
B	Rs. 1,940	.2	.02	.30
C	Rs. 1,360	1.7	.17	.50

The single factor in this economy is perfectly correlated with the value-weighted index of the stock market. The standard deviation of the market index portfolio is 25%.
 (a) What is the mean excess return of the index portfolio?
 (b) What is the covariance between stock A and the index?
 (c) Break down the variance of stock B into its systematic and firm-specific components.

Ans.:

 (a) Total market capitalisation is $3000 + 1940 + 1360 = 6300$. Therefore the mean excess return of the index portfolio is

$$\frac{3000}{6300} \times .10 + \frac{1940}{6300} \times .02 + \frac{1360}{6300} \times .17 = .10$$

(b) The covariance between stocks A and the index portfolio equals,

$$\text{Cov}(R_A, R_M) = \beta_A \sigma_M^2 = .2 \times .25^2 = .0125$$

(c) The variance of B equals

$$\sigma_B^2 = \text{Var}(\beta_B R_M + e_B) = \beta_B^2 \sigma_M^2 + \sigma^2(e_B)$$

Thus, the firm specific variance of B equals

$$\sigma_b^2 - \beta_B^2 \sigma_M^2 = .30^2 - .2^2 \times .25^2 = .0875$$

24. Asset 1 has an expected return of 20%, a beta of 1.4, and a residual variance of .015. Asset 2 has an expected return of 13%, a beta of .9, and a residual variance of .010. Find the minimum variance portfolio corresponding to a target portfolio return of 18 per cent. The expected market return is 13.5 per cent and the market variance is equal to .04.

Ans.:

Although the intercept terms are not given, they can be obtained. We know that $E(R_i) = a_i + b_i E(R_i)$ Thus, the intercept for asset 1 is equal to $a_1 = .20 - (1.4 \times .135) = .011$. The intercept for asset 2 is

$a_2 = .13 - (.9 \times .135) = 0085.$

Plugging in the relevant information into the matrices, we have

$$\begin{bmatrix} 0.030 & 0.0000 & 0.000 & 0.0110 & 1 & 1.4 \\ 0.000 & 0.0200 & 0.000 & 0.0085 & 1 & 0.9 \\ 0.000 & 0.0000 & 0.080 & 0.1350 & 0 & -1.0 \\ 0.011 & 0.0085 & 0.135 & 0.0000 & 0 & 0.0 \\ 1.000 & 1.0000 & 0.000 & 0.0000 & 0 & 0.0 \\ 1.400 & 0.9000 & -1.000 & 0.0000 & 0 & 0.0 \end{bmatrix} \begin{bmatrix} w_1 \\ w_2 \\ w_3 \\ \lambda_1 \\ \lambda_2 \\ \lambda_2 \end{bmatrix} = \begin{bmatrix} 0 \\ 0 \\ 0 \\ .18 \\ 1 \\ 0 \end{bmatrix}$$

Thus, $w_1 = .7142$ and $w_2 = .2857$. The portfolio beta equals 1.257, and the portfolio standard deviation is .2677.

25. An investor is considering four securities with the following betas and residual variances:

	$E(R_i)$	b_i	σ_{Ei}^2
1	20%	5.0	30%
2	15%	3.0	15%
3	12%	1.5	3%
4	8%	0.8	1%

The risk-free interest rate is 5 per cent and the market variance is 5 per cent. Use the Elton, Gruber and Padberg (EGP) model to determine the weights for the optimal portfolio, with and without short sales.

Ans.:

In this problem, $\Sigma (b_i^2/\sigma_{Ej}^2) = 25/30 + 9/15 + 2.25/3 + .64/1 = 2.8233$, and $\Sigma [(E(R_i) - R_i] b_i/\sigma_E^2$ is equal to 10.4. Thus the cutoff point will equal $5[10.4/1 + 5(2.8233)] = 3.44$. The Z values:

$$Z_1 = (5/30)\,(3 - 3.44) = -.0733$$
$$Z_2 = (3/15)\,(3.33 - 3.44) = .0213$$
$$Z_3 = (1.5/3)\,(4.66 - 3.44) = .6133$$
$$Z_4 = (.8/1)\,(3.75 - 3.44) = .248$$

If short sales are not allowed, only securities 3 and 4 will be held. The sum of the Z values equals .8613 and the weight of asset three equals $.6133/.8613 = .712$. The weight of asset 2 equals $.248/.8613 = .288$. If short sales are allowed, the sum of the Z values equals .7667. The optimal portfolio contains the four securities in the following proportions: $w_1 = -.0956,\ w_2 = -.0278,\ w_3 = .80,$ and $w_4 = .3235$.

26. Annual returns for the Sensex, Grand Yarn, and Manik Cotton are provided below:

Year	Sensex Returns	Grand Yarn	Manik Cotton
1	-50%	-10%	-5%
2	15%	7	10
3	25	40	30
4	-10	0	-20
5	25	20	25

(i) Calculate the β-coefficients for Grand Yarn and Manik Cotton.
(ii) What is the single-index covariance between the Grand Yarn and Manik Cotton returns? Compare this result with the actual covariance.

Ans.:

	$[r_S - E(r_S)]^2$	$[r_{GY} - E(r_{GY})]^2$	$[r_{MC} - E(r_{MC})]^2$	$[r_S - E(r_P)] \times [r_S - E(r_{GY})]$	$[r_S - E(r_S)] \times [r_{MC} - E(r_{MC})]$	$[r_{GY} - E(r_{GY})] \times (r_{MC} - E(r_{MC})]$
1	225	457.96	169	321	195	278.2
2	25	19.36	4	-22	10	-8.8
3	225	817.96	484	429	330	629.2
4	400	129.96	784	228	560	319.2
5	225	73.96	289	129	255	146.2
*	1100	1499.2	1730	1085	1350	1364

(i) $E(r_S) = 50 \div 5 = 10\%$ $\quad \sigma_S^2 = 1100 \div (5-1) = 275 \quad \sigma_S = 16.58\%$

$E(r_{GY}) = 57 \div 5 = 11.4\%$ $\quad \sigma_{GY}^2 = 1499.2 \div (5-1) = 374.8 \quad \sigma_{GY} = 19.36\%$

$E(r_{MC}) = 40 \div 5 = 8\%$ $\quad \sigma_{MC}^2 = 1730 \div (5-1) = 432.5 \quad \sigma_{MC} = 20.80\%$

$COV(r_{SY}, r_{GY}) = 1085 \div (5-1) = 271.27 \quad\quad b_{GY} = 271.25/275 = .986$

$COV(r_S, r_{MC}) = 1350 \div (5-1) = 337.50 \quad\quad b_{MC} = 337.50/275 = 1.23$

(ii) The single-index model estimate of the covariance between Grand Yarn and Manik Cotton's returns is equal to the product of the two β-coefficients and the market variance. Thus the covariance estimate is equal to $(1.23)(.986)(275) = 333.51$. The actual covariance is equal to $1364 \div 4 = 341$.

27. What will be the nonsystematic standard deviation of the equally weighted portfolio if the average value of $\sigma^2(e_i)$ equals .30, (a) $n = 10$, (b) $n = 100$, (c) $n = 1,000$, and

(d) $n = 10,000$. What do you conclude about the non-systematic risk of large, diversified portfolios?

Ans.:

$$\sigma(e_P) = \sqrt{\sigma^2(e_i)/n}$$

(a) $\sqrt{30/10} = 1.732\%$

(b) $\sqrt{30/100} = .548\%$

(c) $\sqrt{30/1,000} = .173\%$

(d) $\sqrt{30/10,000} = .055\%$

We conclude that non-systematic volatility can be driven to arbitrarily low levels in well-diversified portfolios.

28. You are attempting to construct an optimum portfolio. Over your holding period you have forecast an expected return on the market of 13.5 per cent with a market variance of 25 per cent. The Treasury security rate available is 7 per cent (risk-free). The following securities are under review:

Stock	Alpha	Beta	Residual Variance
A	3.72	.99	9.35
B	0.60	1.27	5.92
C	0.41	.96	0.79
D	-0.22	1.21	5.36
D	0.45	.75	4.52

What is the optimum portfolio?

Ans.:

PORTFOLIO SUMMARY:

Portfolio Beta	1.06
Expected Return	15.66%
Standard Devn.	31.08%

Security	% of Port	Mean Return (1)	Excess Return (2)	Alpha (2A)	Beta (3)	Unsys Risk (4)	Excess Rtn/Bet (5) (2)/	Beta/ Res Var (6) = (2)(3)/(4)	Beta Sod /R.V. (7) = (3)/(4)	Beta /R.V. (8) = sum (6)	Beta^2 /R.V. (9) = (3)^2/ (4)	Cutoff Value (10)
A	73.7%	15.6	10.6	3.72	0.99	9.35	10.707	1.122	0.10482	1.122	0.10482	7.25
B	26.3%	15.8	10.8	0.6	1.27	5.92	8.535	2.325	0.27245	3.448	0.37727	8.07
C	0.0%	14.3	9.3	-0.22	1.21	5.36	7.686	2.099	0.27315	5.547	0.65043	7.92
D	0.0%	11.9	6.9	0.41	0.96	9.79	7.219	0.680	0.09414	6.227	0.74456	7.84
E	0.0%	9.5	4.5	0.45	0.75	4.52	5.933	0.738	0.12445	6.965	0.86901	7.58

29. The following questions relate to the Sharpe and Markowitz methodology. Suppose we had the following data on four stocks:

Stock	Markowitz Expected Return	Alpha	Systematic	Unsystematic	A	B	C	D	Market
			Variance		*Correlation matrix**				
A	17%	-.06	5%	4%	A	1	.4	.7	.2	.74
B	13	.10	2	6	B		1	.6	.5	.50
C	9	.00	3	1	C			1	.9	.87
D	7	-.14	3	2	D				1	.78

(a) "Markowitz would argue that a portfolio consisting of equal investments in stocks A, B, C, and D should provide an expected return of 11.5 per cent and an expected risk (standard deviation of return) of 2.52 per cent" Do you agree or disagree? Why?

(b) Suppose the market is expected to have a return over a forward period of 12 per cent with a return variance of 6 per cent. Calculate the expected return and risk for a portfolio consisting of equal portions of stocks A and C.

Ans.:

(a) The expected return will be 11.5 per cent but the expected risk will no doubt be a number different from 2.52 per cent since the standard deviations of the securities are not additive in a portfolio.

(b) Portfolio risk $= [(.5)(.9) + (.5)(.71)^2 \times (.06) + (.5)^2(.04) + (.5)^2(.01)]$

Variance $= 5.1\%$

Portfolio return $= (.5)[(-.06) + .9\ (.12)] + (.5)[(0) + .71(.12)]$

$= 6.66\%$

$$\text{Beta A} = \frac{(.74)(3)(2.45)}{6} = .9$$

$$\text{Beta C} = \frac{(.87)(2)(2.45)}{6} = .71$$

30. What is the optimum portfolio in choosing among the following securities and assuming $R_F = 5$ per cent, and $\sigma_m^2 = 10$ per cent?

Security	Expected Return	Beta	σ_m^2
A	15	1.0	30
B	12	1.5	20
C	11	2.0	40
D	8	.8	10
E	9	1.0	20
F	14	1.5	10

Ans.:

Solve by ranking $(R_j - R_F)/\beta_j$, $R_F = 5\%$, and $\sigma_m^2 = 10$

Security	Expected Return	Excess Return	Beta	$(R_j - R_F)b_i$	Rank	σ^2_{ej}
A	15	10	1.0	10.0	1	30
B	12	7	1.5	4.67	3	20
C	11	6	2.0	3.0	6	40
D	8	3	0.8	3.75	5	10
E	9	4	1.0	4.0	4	20
F	14	9	1.5	6.0	2	10

Compare the ratio of excess return to beta to the cutoff, C.*

Security	$[R_j - R_F]/\beta_j$	$[R_j - R_y)\beta_j/\sigma_j^2]$	$\beta_j^2\sigma_j^2$	$\Sigma[R_j - R_y)\beta_j^2 1\sigma_{ej}^2$	$\Sigma\beta_j^2/\sigma_j^2$
A	10.00	0.333	0.0333	0.333	0.0333
F	6.00	1.350	0.2250	1.683	0.2583
B	4.67	0.525	0.1125	2.208	0.3708
E	4.00	0.200	0.0500	2.408	0.4208
D	3.75	0.240	0.0640	2.648	0.5848
C	3.00	0.300	0.100	2.948	0.5848

Passible Cutoff Rates C.	Security Risk
2.500	1
4.697	2
4.690	3
4.624	4
4.528	5
4.306	6

The value of C* is 4.697 are equal to C_2. Next, find the percentage in each security.

$Z_1 = (1/30)(10 - 4.697) = 0.17874333$

$Z_2 = (1.5/10)(6 - 4.697) = 0.19545$

$\Sigma Z_i = 0.3721933$

$X_1 = 0.1767433/0.3721933 = 0.4748697$ or 47.5%

$X_2 = 0.19545/0.3721933 = 0.52513028$ or 52.5%

Hence, 47.5 per cent in Security A and 52.5 per cent in Security F will be optimal.

31. SSS Consultants is an investment counseling firm headquatered in Delhi. SSS primary activity is to provide portfolio management services to individuals and institutions with portfolios of ₹ 1 crore or more. The firm also performs related custodial and performance monitoring services. Annuals fees are based upon a percentage of the market value of a client's portfolio.

Since its founding in 1990, the firm has enjoyed phenomenal growth. Today it has well over ₹ 2,500 under management. The professional staff consists of financial and research analysts, information systems personnel, and regional portfolio managers. Most of the analysts are graduates in finance, economics, or computer science.

The heart of the portfolio-management process at is the application of modern portfolio theory and related quantitative techniques. The construction and selection of optimum portfolios is performed using the basic Sharpe model.

K.B. Verma, a businessman, rose rapidly to fame and fortune by developing and marketing a successful line of children's toys. He visited the SSS office in October, 1991 to discuss the placement of Rs. 10 crore in the hands of the firm for investment purposes. Verma had successful real estate holdings in addition to the equity in his toy business. He had liquidated his stock investments in an account with HB Consultants, a Delhi brokerage firm. The portfolio had performed at a mediocre level at best, providing him with an annual rate of return of 8.3 per cent over the past three years.

EXHIBIT 1

List of Candidate Stocks

Security	Alpha	Beta	Unsystematic Risk
A	1.20	0.99	9.25
B	0.60	1.27	5.92
C	0.00	1.35	11.61
D	0.68	1.14	5.37
E	0.58	1.09	10.81
F	-0.22	1.21	5.36
G	1.26	0.93	6.74
H	-0.14	1.12	6.08
I	-0.33	1.13	6.97
J	0.29	1.02	3.86
K	0.87	0.93	6.52
L	0.34	1.00	6.19
M	0.41	0.96	9.79
N	0.60	0.84	3.92
O	1.35	0.71	10.33
P	-0.23	0.88	6.53
Q	0.45	0.75	4.52
R	1.04	0.58	8.56

Expected Market Return	13.50
Risk-Free Return	7.00
Market Variance	25.00

Verma had heard of the success SSS had for its clients using sophisticated models and had decided that his investments certainly could do no worse than they had in the hands of HB Consultants. He asked SSS for a simple demonstration of how SSS created portfolios for clients. The portfolio manager, Venkat Raghavan, prepared a list of stocks with the essential ingredients used by the firm in the selection of efficient combinations of candidate stocks. (See Exhibit 1). He felt that these stocks would provide a useful base for demonstrating the process to Verma.

Construct an optimum portfolio.

Ans.:

Security	% of Port	Mean Return (1)	Excess Return (2)	Alpha (2A)	Beta (3)	Unsys Risk (4)	Excess Retn/Beta (2)(3)
A	59.5%	17.7	10.7	0.6	1.27	5.92	8.641
B	25.3%	18.2	11.2	0.0	1.35	11.61	8.315
C	15.2%	16.1	9.1	0.68	1.14	5.37	7.956
D		14.6	7.6	1.2	0.99	9.35	7.641
E		15.3	8.3	0.58	1.09	10.81	7.610
F		16.1	9.1	-0.22	1.21	5.36	7.533
G		13.8	6.8	1.26	0.93	6.74	7.328
H		15.0	8.0	-0.14	1.12	6.19	7.125
I		14.9	7.9	-0.33	1.13	6.97	7.013
J		14.1	7.1	0.29	1.02	3.86	6.922
K		13.4	6.4	0.87	0.93	6.52	6.909
L		13.8	6.8	0.34	1.00	6.19	6.840
M		13.4	6.4	0.41	0.96	9.79	6.635
N		11.9	4.9	0.6	0.84	3.92	5.881
O		10.9	3.9	1.35	0.71	10.33	5.542
P		11.7	4.7	-0.23	0.88	6.53	5.284
Q		10.6	3.6	0.45	0.75	4.52	4.767
R		8.9	1.9	1.04	0.58	8.56	3.224

Security	Beta/ Res Var	Sqd/ Res Var	Beta/ Res Var	Beta Sqd/ Res Var	Cutoff Value
A	2.305	0.27245	2.305	0.27245	7.38
B	1.305	0.15698	3.610	0.42943	7.69
C	1.925	0.24201	5.536	0.67144	7.78
D	0.801	0.10482	6.337	0.77626	7.76
E	0.836	0.10991	7.173	0.88617	7.75
F	2.058	0.27315	9.231	1.15932	7.70
G	0.940	0.12832	10.171	1.28764	7.66
H	1.444	0.20265	11.615	1.49029	7.59
I	1.285	0.18320	12.900	1.67349	7.53
J	1.866	0.26953	14.766	1.94303	7.45
K	0.916	0.13265	15.682	2.07568	4.41
L	1.105	0.16155	16.787	2.23723	7.37
M	0.625	0.09414	17.412	2.33137	7.34
N	1.059	0.18000	18.470	2.51137	7.24
O	0.270	0.04880	18.741	2.56017	7.21
P	0.627	0.11859	19.367	2.67876	7.12
Q	0.593	0.12445	19.961	2.80321	7.02
R	0.127	0.03930	20.087	2.84251	6.97

The optimal portfolio is:

A	59.5%
B	25.3%
C	15.2%

QUESTIONS

1. What assumptions do beta theorists make in their solution to portfolio management problems.
2. What is beta? Why is beta a better measure of risk than the standard deviation?
3. What does a beta coefficient measure? How is it calculated for an individual asset and for a portfolio of assets? Are individual securities and portfolio betas stable and reliable?
4. Carefully explain the relationship between the single-index model and the Markowitz model of portfolio theory. How many different terms must be calculated in a portfolio consisting of securities using the Markowitz model and the single-index model?
5. In terms of a beta coefficient measure, define what is meant by an "aggressive" and "defensive" security or portfolio? What are the criticism of beta analysis?
6. "Under the SIM we can safely assert that $b_i = 0$ then necessarily all $s_{ij} = 0$". Appraise this statement.
7. What do the Markowitz and single-index models assume about the source of comovement between securities?
8. Why is the single-index model used to estimate the portfolio variance when the Markowitz model provides a correct measure of the portfolio variance?
9. In the single-index framework, what happens to the portfolio residual variance as the number of securities in the portfolio increases?
10. Suppose that residuals tend to be positively correlated. Will the single-index model estimate of the portfolio variance be less than, equal to, or greater than the true portfolio variance? What if they are negatively correlated? Explain.
11. If investor's aversion to risk increased, would the risk premium on a high beta stock increase more or less than that on a low beta stock? Explain.
12. Differentiate between systematic and unsystematic risk.
13. How is beta derived from a security's model? Why are high beta securities termed aggressive? Why are low beta securities termed defensive?
14. What are the difficulties in the direct estimation of the optimal investment proportions in a portfolio, and how can these difficulties be resolved by the SIM?
15. Compute the variance of stock 1.
16. Assume you had constructed an equally weighted portfolio of stocks 1 and 2, Complete the residual variance of this portfolio in two ways:
    (a) Making the simplifying assumption of the two-factor model about residual covariance.
    (b) Without making the simplifying assumption about residual covariance.
17. Compute the market beta and the growth beta for an equally weighted portfolio of stocks 1 and 2.
18. For an equally weighted portfolio of stocks 1 and 2, compute the variance of the portfolio in two ways:
    (a) Making the simplifying assumption of the two-factor model about residual covariance.
    (b) Without making the simplifying assumption about residual covariance.
19. Why would you want to compute portfolio variance by a single- or multifactor model rather than by the Markowitz model?

PROBLEMS

1. Following are data for several securities. The data result from correlating returns on these securities versus returns on a market index:

Securities	α_i	β_i	e^2
XYZ	-.08	+2.5	.05
ABC	+.07	-0.5	.00
KLD	.00	+1.2	.15

(a) Which single security would you prefer to own from a risk-return view point if the market index are expected to have a return of +25 and a variance of return of .20?

(b) What does the variance (e) value for ABC imply? The alpha value for KLD?

2. If a portfolio has a beta of 2.5 and earns 28 percent and the market return is 24 per cent, has it out performed the market?

3. The market return has an expected return of 20 per cent and a standard deviation of 30 per cent. The standard deviation of Silver Star Company's stock is 25 per cent and its correlation coefficient with the market portfolio is .60. Compute the beta of Silver Star's stock. What would happen to the beta if the Company's standard deviation were 35 per cent and the correlation coefficient were .75? What would happen to the total variance of a portfolio if a portion of the Silver Star stock were sold and the proceeds were invested in unrelated stocks having the same beta?

4. Suppose that a portfolio consisting of 500 assets is considered. To utilise the Markowitz risk measure, how many correlation coefficients must be calculated? What inputs *are* necessary to calculate the single-index risk measure?

5. The number of assets under consideration increases from 500 to 501. Discuss the additional inputs necessary in the Markowitz and single-index frameworks.

6. You are given the following set of data:

	Historical Rate of Return	
Year	NSE	Stock XYZ
1	4.0%	3.0%
2	14.3	182
3	19.0	9.1
4	-14.7	--.0
5	-26.5	-15.3
6	372	33.1
7	23.8	6.1
8	-72	32
9	6.6	14.8
10	20.5	24.1
11	30.6	18.0
	Mean = 9.8%	9.8%
	σ=19.6%	13.8%

(a) Construct a scatter diagram showing the relationship between returns on Stock XYZ and the market, and then draw a free hand approximation of the regression line. What is the approximate value of the beta coefficient?

(b) Give an interpretation of what the regression line and the beta coefficient show about stock XYZ's volatility and relative riskiness as compared with those of other stocks.

(c) Suppose the scatter points had been more spread out, but the regression line was exactly where your present graph shows it. How would this affect (i) the firm's risk if the stock is held in a one-asset portfolio, and (ii) the actual risk premium on the stock if the CAPM holds exactly?

(d) Suppose the regression line had been downward-sloping and the beta coefficient had been negative. What would this imply about (i) Stock XYZ's relative riskiness, (ii) its correlation with the market, and (iii) its probable risk premium?

(e) Construct an illustrative probability distribution graph of returns on portfolio consisting of (i) only stock XYZ, (ii) 1 percent each of 100 stocks with beta coefficients similar to that of stock XYZ, and (iii) all stocks (that is, the distribution of returns on the market). Use as the expected rate of return the arithmatic mean as given previously for both stock XYZ and the market and assume that the distribution are normal. Are the expected returns "reasonable"; that is, is it reasonable that both the expected return on market are equal to 9.8?

Ans.: (a) 0.62

7. You are given monthly return for two securities and the National Stock Index (NSI) as shown below:

Month	K (per cent)	H (per cent)	NSI (per cent)
1	5.30	7.3	4.5
2	6.25	8.2	52
3	-2.12	-10.2	1.1
4	12.75	15.4	10.3
5	-3.40	-2.0	-1.3
6	8.60	9.5	10.5
7	9.20	8.2	7.6
8	-2.10	- 1.0	0.0
9	8.30	-10.2	-7.4
10	10.20	11.5	9.3
11	5.40	5.9	4.42
12	6.20	7.2	8.5

(a) Calculate the alpha and beta for each security.
(b) Compute the variance of residuals of each regression.
(c) Calculate the correlation between each security and the market.
(d) Compute the mean return and variance of an optimal portfolio consisting of these two securities in terms of the single-index model.

8. If the β-coefficient for AMCO stock is equal to 1.2 and the intercept term is equal to 02%, what is the expected return for the stock if the expected market return is equal to 10%? Suppose the actual return is equal to 14%. What events might have caused the deviation of the actual and expected returns?

9. If the β-coefficient for DUMA is equal to 1.05, the DANIX residual variance is .02 and the market variance is .04, what is the single-index estimate of the variance of IBM stock?

10. Suppose that DUMA stock has a β of .85. What is the single-index model estimate of the covariance between DUMA and DANIX returns? (See question 16 for DANIX variance information.)

11. Below is return and variance information for four securities:

SECURITY	BETA	INTERCEPT	RESIDUAL VARIANCE
1	0.90	-.01	.030
2	1.10	.02	.025
3	1.60	.01	.015
4	1.05	.02	.020

What are the portfolio expected return and standard deviation if the weights for the securities are as follows: 1 - .40, 2 - .20, 3 - .35, 4 - .05. Assume that the market variance is equal to .04 and an expected return of 10%.

12. Monthly returns for the market portfolio, ABC, and XYZ are given below:

Month	BSE Index Returns	ABC Returns	XYZ Returns
1	1.5%	0.5%	1.7%
2	0.0	0.2	-0.5
3	-2.0	-4.0	-3.0
4	-0.4	1.0	-0.6
5	2.3	1.5	4.0

Calculate the ABC and XYZ and intercept terms and calculate the single-index variance, assuming an equally weighted portfolio and a market variance of .0625. Then use the above information to calculate the Markowitz variance.

13. What is the beta of a portfolio consisting of one share of each of the following stocks given their respective prices and beta coefficients?

Stock	Price	Beta
A	Rs. 10	1.4
B	24	0.8
C	41	1.3
D	19	1.8

How would the portfolio beta differ if (a) the investor purchased 200 shares of stocks B and C for every 100 shares of A and D and (b) equal amounts were invested in each stock?

14. What is the return on a stock according to the security market line if the risk-free rate is 6 per cent, the return on the market is 10 per cent, and the stock's beta is 1.5? If the beta had been 2.0, what would be the return? Is this higher return consistent with the portfolio theory? Why?

Ans.:

Return = 12% when beta = 1.5

15. The following information is given:

	Return on		
Period	Market	Stock X	Stock Y
1	10%	- 2%	13%
2	26	13	41
3	- 2	3	3
4	- 14	- 7	- 7
5	7	9	9
6	14	5	19
7	- 5	2	- 8
8	19	13	13
9	8	- 3	17
10	- 5	8	- 14

(a) Using regression analysis, compute the estimated equations relating the return on stock X to the return on the market and the return on stock Y to the return on the market. According to the equations, what is each stock's beta coefficient? What does each beta coefficient imply about the systematic risk associated with each stock?

(b) What is the difference between the return on each stock given by the estimated equation for period 10 and the actual return? What may account for any differences in the estimated return and the actual return?

(c) What is the R square for each equation? Interpret the R square. What does the R square imply about the other sources of risk as they apply to stocks X and Y?

Ans.:

(a) Beta stock X = 0.352

(b) Beta Stock Y: R²: 0.82

16. The following hypothetical data related to security i and to the market portfolio:

Year	Rate of Return (%)	
	Security i	Market portfolio (m)
1994	20	10
1995	10	6
1996	-20	0

Calculate the systematic risk ($\beta^2\sigma^2_m$) and the non-systematic risk (σ^2_{ei}) of the security. How do these components relate to the with security's own variance σ^2_i?

17. First Growth Mutual Fund has a total investment of Rs. 40 crore in five securities:

Securities	Investment	Security's Beta Coefficient
A	Rs. 12 crore	0.5
B	10 crore	2.0
C	6 crore	4.0
D	8 crore	1.0
E	4 crore	3.0

The beta coefficient for a fund such as this can be found as a weighted average of the betas of the fund's investments. The current risk-free rate is 7%, and the market return has the following estimated probability distribution for the next year:

Probability	Market Return
0.1	8%
0.2	10
0.4	12
0.2	14
0.1	16

(a) What is the estimated equation for the Security Market Line (SML)?

(b) Compute the required rate of return on the First Growth Mutual Fund.

(c) Suppose management receives a proposal to buy a new security. The investment needed to take a position in the security is Rs. 5 crore, it will have an expected return of 16 percent; and its estimated beta coefficient is 2.5. Should the new security be purchased? At what expected rate of return would management be indifferent to purchasing the security?

Ans.: (b) 15.75%

18. If XYZ Company has the same variance as the market, and the correlation between the two is 0.7, what is the XYZ's beta?

Ans.: 0.7

19. A stock has a beta of 12 and an expected return of 15% when the market's expected return is 14%. What must the risk-free rate be?

Ans.: 0.09

20. A firm is considering a project that will generate after-tax cash flows of Rs. 3,00,000 for 5 years. The beta is 1.3 and the investment cost is Rs. 8,50,000. Should the firm undertake the project?

21. Dilshad is a major departmental store chain. Its stock has a beta of 0.8, the risk-free rate is 8.0 percent, and the required rate of return on the market is 13.0 percent.
    (a) What is the market risk premium?
    (b) What is the required rate of return on Dilshad's stock?
    (c) Graph the Security Market Line (SML) and indicate Dilshad's required rate of return on the graph.
    (d) What would Dilshad's required rate of return be if inflation expectations increased by 2 percentage points? (Assume no change in risk aversion.)
    (e) Return to the 8 percent risk-free rate. What would Dilshad's required rate of return be if investors' risk aversion increased, and the market risk premium rose to 7 percentage points?
    (f) Return to the 5 percentage point market risk premium. What would the firm's required rate of return be if Dilshad's beta increased to 12?

22. You are considering an investment in XYZ company. Your statistical analysis has shown that the variance of XYZ company is 0.4928, while that of the market is 0.2982. The correlation coefficient between XYZ company's return and that of the market is + 0.83. What is the XYZ company's beta?

Ans.: Beta = 1.067

23. A firm is considering a project that will generate after-tax cash flows of Rs. 3,00,000 for 5 years. The beta is 0.8 and the investment cost is Rs. 9,00,000. Should the firm undertake the project?

24. Suppose risk-free rate is 10%, market rate of return to be 14% and the $\beta = 1.4$
    (a) What is required rate of return on security A?
    (b) Now suppose risk-free rate (i) increases to 11 percent or (ii) decreases to 9 percent. The slope of the SML remains constant. How will this effect market rate of return and the required rate of return on security A?
    (c) Now assume risk-free rate of return remains at 10%, but market rate of return (i) increases to 15 percent or (ii) falls to 12%. The slope of the SML does not remain constant. How will this effect the required rate of return on security A?
    (d) Now assume that risk-free rate of return remains at 10% and market rate of return at 14%, but beta (1) rises to 1.6 or (ii) falls to 0.75. How will this effect the required rate of return on security A?

Ans.:

(a) 15.6%;	(b) (i) 16.6%, (ii) 14.6%
(c) (i) 17.0%, (ii) 12.8%	(d) (i) 16.4% (ii) 13.0%

25. Suppose you split your money 50-50 between the following two securities:

	Security XYZ	Security ABC
Expected Return	14%	17%
Standard Deviation	- 0.24	0.32
β	1.25	1.50

    (a) What is the expected return of the two-security portfolio?
    (b) What is the portfolio beta?

26. Consider the information in the following table:

Stock	β	Value
1	1.07	10,675
2	0.95	9,845
3	0.80	11,995
4	1.20	9,675
5	1.10	10,475
6	1.50	12,560
7	0.70	11,540
8	1.25	8.975
9	1.18	10,075
10	0.65	11,085
Total	1,06,900	

(a) What is the beta of this portfolio?
(b) What steps might you take to bring this portfolio back to a target beta of 1.10?
27. You are given the following historical data on market returns, R and the returns on securities X and Y, R_x and R_y:

Year	R_m	R_x	R_y
1	29.00	29.00	20.00
2	15.20	15.20	13.10
3	-10.00	-10.00	.50
4	3.30	3.30	7.15
5	23.00	23.00	17.99
6	31.70	31.70	21.35

The risk free rate, R_f is 9%. Your probability distribution for market return for next year is as follows:

Probability	R_m
0.1	-14
0.2	0
0.4	15
0.2	25
0.1	44

(i) Determine graphically the beta coefficient for securities X and Y.
(ii) Graph the Security Market Line and give its equation.
(iii) Calculate the required rates of return on securities X and Y.
(iv) Suppose a new security Z, with Rz =18% and beta Z=2.00, becomes available. Is this security in equilibrium; that is, does the required rate of return on security Z equal its expected return ? Explain if the security is not in equilibrium, explain how equilibrium will be restored.

REFERENCES

1. Beaver, William, and James Manegold, "The Association Between Market-Determined and Accounting-Determined Measures of Systematic Risk: Some Further Evidence," *Journal of Financial and Quantitative Analysis,* June 1975, pp. 231-284.

2. Blume, Marshall E., "Portfolio Theory: A Step Toward Its Practical Application," *Journal of Business,* April 1970, pp. 152-173.

3. ——————, "Betas and Their Regression Tendencies," *Journal of Finance* 30, no. 3 (June 1975): 785-796.

4. ——————, "On the Assessment of Risk," *Journal of Finance* 26, no. 1 (March 1971): 1-10.

5. Casabona, Patrick A., and A. Vora, "The Bias of Conventional Risk Premiums in Empirical Tests of the Capital Asset Pricing Model," *Financial Management,* 11 (Summer 1982).

6. Cheng, Pao, and M. King Deets, "Systematic Risk and the Horizon Problem," *Journal of Financial and Quantitative Analysis* 8, no. 2 (March 1973): 299-316.

7. Cohen, K.J., and J. Pogue, "An Empirical Evaluation of Alternative Portfolio Selection Models," *Journal of Business,* April 1967, pp. 166-93.

8. Elton, Edwin J., M.J. Gruber, and M.W. Padburg, "Simple Criteria for Optimal Portfolio Selection," *Journal of Finance,* 31 (December 1976), 1341-57.

9. Eubank, Arthur A., Jr., and J.K. Zumwalt, "Impact of Alternative Length Estimation and Prediction Periods on the Stability of Security and Portfolio Betas," Journal *of Business Research,* 9 (September 1981) .

10. Fabozzi, Frank J., and Jack C. Francis, "Stability Tests for Alphas and Betas Over Bull and Bear Market Conditions," *Journal of Finance,* September 1977, pp. 1093-1099.

11. Fama, Eugene F., "Short Term Interest Rates as Predictors of Inflation," *American Economic Review,* 65 (June).

12. ——————, "Tests of the Multiperiod Two Parameter Model," *Journal of Financial Economics,* 1 (May 1974), 43-66.

13. ——————, and J.D. MacBeth, "Risk Return and Equilibrium: Empirical Tests," *Journal of Political Economy,* 81 (May-June 1973).

14. Farrell, James L., Jr. *Guide to Portfolio Management.* New York: McGraw-Hill, 1983.

15. Farrell, Jr., James L., "Analyzing Covariation of Returns to Determine Homogeneous Stock Groupings," *Journal of Business* 47, no. 2 (April 1974): 186-207.

16. ——————, "Homogeneous Stock Groupings," *Financial Analysis Journal,* May-June 1975, pp. 50-56.

17. Fisher, Lawrence, and Jules Kamin, "Forecasting Systematic Risk: Estimates of 'Raw' Beta That Take Account of the Tendency of Beta to Change and the Heteroskedasticity of Residual Returns," Journal *of Financial and Quantitative Analysis,* 20 (June 1985).

18. Gonedes, Nicholas, "A Note on Accounting-Based and Market-Based Estimates of Systematic Risk," *Journal of Financial and Quantitative Analysis* 10, no. 2 (June-1975): 355-366.

19. Hodges, Steward D., and Richard A. Brealey. "Dynamic Portfolio Selection." *Financial Analysts Journal,* November-December 1972, p. 58.

20. Jacob, Nancy L., "A Limited Diversification Portfolio Selection Model for the Small Investor," *Journal of Finance* 29, no. 4 (June 1974): 847-856.

21. Jensen, Michael C., ed., *Studies in the Theory of Capital Markets* (New York' Praeger 1972).

22. King, Benjamin F., "Market and Industry Factors in Stock Price Behavior," *Journal of Business* 39, No. 1, part II (January 1966, Supplement): 139-190.

23. Mao, James C.T., "Essentials of Portfolio Diversification Strategy," *Journal of Finance* 25, no. 5 (December 1970): 1109-1131.

24. Reilly, Frank K., and David J. Wright. "A Comparison of Published Betas." *Journal of Portfolio Management*, Spring 1988, 64-69.

25. Renshaw, E.F., "Portfolio Balance Models in Perspective: Some Generalizations That Can Be Derived from the Two Asset Case," *Journal of Financial and Quantitative Analysis*, June 1967, pp. 138-139.

26. Robichek, Alexander A., and Richard A. Cohn, "The Economic Determinants of Systematic Risk," *Journal of Finance* 29, no. 2 (May 1974): 439-447.

27. Roenfeldt, R., G. Griepentrog, and C. Pflaum. "Further Evidence on the Stationarity of Beta Coefficients." *Journal of Finance and Quantitative Analysis*, March 1978, 117-121.

28. Rosenberg, Barr, and James Guy. "Beta and Investment Fundamentals." *Financial Analysts Journal*, May/June 1976, 60-72.

29. Sharpe, William, *Portfolio Theory and Capital Markets* (New York: McGraw-Hill, 1970).

30. Upson, Roger, Paul Jessup, and Keishiro Matsumoto. "Portfolio Diversification Strategies." *Financial Analysts Journal*. May June 1975, pp. 86 88.

31. Wallingford, B.A., "A Survey and Comparison of Portfolio Selection Models." *Journal of Financial and Quantitative Analysis*. June 1967, pp. 85 106.

28

Capital Market Theory and the Capital Asset Pricing Model

INTRODUCTION

The mechanical complexity of the Markowitz's portfolio model kept both practitioners and academics away from adopting the concept for practical use. Its intuitive logic, however, spurred the creativity of a number of researchers who began examining the stock market implications that would arise if all investors used this model. As a result, what is referred to as the Capital Asset Pricing Model (CAPM) was developed.

In order to show how assets are priced, a model must be constructed. This requires simplification, in that the model builder must abstract from the full complexity of the situation and focus only on the most important elements. The way this is achieved is by making certain assumptions need to be simplistic in order to provide the degree of abstraction that allows for some success in building the model. The "reasonableness" of the assumption is of little concern. Instead, the test of a model is with ability to help one understand and predict the process being modeled.

ASSUMPTIONS

The CAPM rests on eight assumptions. The first five assumptions are those that underlie the efficient market hypothesis and thus underlie both modern portfolio theory (MPT) and the CAPM. The last three assumptions are necessary to create the CAPM from MPT. The eight assumptions are the following:

I. The Investor's objective is to maximise the utility of terminal wealth

For MPT and the CAPM, the investor is maximising the utility of wealth, not maximising wealth (or return) itself. Each increment of wealth is enjoyed less than the last because each increment is less important in satisfying the basic needs and desires of the individual. A diminishing marginal utility for wealth is the most frequently described utility function.

II. Investors make choices on the basis of risk and return

Risk and return are measured by the variance and the mean of the portfolio returns. In using MPT and the CAPM, portfolio variance is assumed to be an appropriate measure of risk because it allows use two factors, mean and variance, to describe each asset's relative attractiveness. In moving from MPT to the CAPM, it is presumed that since rational investors diversify away diversifiable risk (unsystematic risk), beta is a measure of the remaining risk (the variance) of the portfolio. Thus, it is presumed that beta and return are directly and linearly related.

When the first two assumptions are joined — that the investor's goal is to maximise the utility of terminal wealth and that the investor's decisions are based on expected risk and rates of return—it can be concluded that investors choose only those portfolios with the highest rate of return for their preferred level of risk (variance), or those with the lowest risk for their preferred rate of return.

III. Investors have homogeneous expectations of risk and return

This assumption simply states that all investors' estimates of risk and return are the same. To have the single efficient frontier of modern portfolio theory, there must be consensus estimates of the mean and variance and thus of the relative value of each investment. Without a consensus, each investor or group of investors could have very different forecasts for variance and for mean return. Consequently, the efficient portfolio for one investor could be quite different from that for another.

IV. Investors have identical time horizon

This assumption suggests that investos form portfolios to achieve wealth at a single, common-terminal rate. That single, common horizon allows us to construct a single-period model. The model implies that investors buy all the assets in their portfolios at one point in time and sell them at some undefined but common point in the future.

Although necessary, this assumption is also obviously unrealistic. The world of investors is composed of short-term speculators, buy-and-holders, and everyone in between. Further, the investors act as if they are to make a series of investments rather than a single period by-and-hold decision. For this, the use of continuous model may be more appreciate, but they are more complex than the single-period models. The single-period model can approximate to multiperiod investor behaviour if the following conditions are true: (i) *Returns are independent over time. For the stock market, this is equivalent to saying that the weak form of the efficient market hypothesis holds. (ii) Expectations are independent of past or current information. For instance, if it is possible to say that the returns from a retail store chain are independent of such things as past and current inflation.* However, these two conditions are clearly not realistic to the investment practitioners. Hence, continuous time adaptations are intriguing, but complex.

V. Information is freely and simultaneously available to investors

If group of investors were privy to special, not widely available, information on which they could make superior decisions, markets would not be efficient and MPT and the CAPM would be affected. Without a set of common forecasts, a single efficient frontier could not exist.

Is this assumption realistic ? Some may disagree but still most of the market value of the stock market consists of stocks of the most carefully analysed firms. And the information about these companies is broadly available to managers of large portfolios. For other assets, such as the stocks and bonds of smaller firms, information is not as widely available.

The last three assumptions, necessary to create the CAPM from MPT, are listed below:

VI. There is a risk-free asset, and investors can borrow and lend unlimited amounts at the risk-free rate

This may be the most crucial assumption of the CAPM. The risk-free asset is needed to simplify the complex pair wise covariance of Markowitz's theory. The risk-free asset simplifies the curved efficient frontier of MPT to the linear efficient frontier of the

CAPM, and the investor has ceased to be concerned with the characteristics of individual assets. Instead, the investor can create a portfolio from his or her own risk-preferred combination. Risk is decreased or increased by adding a portion of the risk-free asset or by borrowing at the risk-free rate to invest additional funds in the market portfolio. This lavies two questions. Firstly, is *there such a thing as a risk-free asset* ? *And, second, can all investors both borrow and lend at the risk-free rate* ?

Several studies have questioned the very existence of a truly risk-free asset and models have been developed that do not depend on the existence of a risk-free security. Fisher Black demonstrated that neither the existence of a risk-free asset nor the requirement that investors can borrow and lend at the risk-free rate is necessary for the theory to hold. However, without the risk-free asset a different firm of the CAPM will result.

Black's argument is as follows. *The beta of the risk-free asset is zero.* That is, since there is no variability of the return on a risk-free asset, it cannot co-vary with the market. If a portfolio can be created such that it is uncorrelated with the market, this portfolio would have a beta of zero which to be called zero-beta portfolio. Figure-1 shows the situation graphically. A tangent is drown from the expected return axis (i.e., the vertical axis) starting at the expected return for the zero portfolio to the Markonitz efficient formula. This line will dominate the Markonitz efficient formula and can be viewed as the capital market line when there is no risk-free asset.

Black demonstrated that if zero-beta portfolio can be constructed, then the CAPM would be modified as follows:

$$E(R_p) = E(R_z) + \beta_p \, [E(R_m) - E(R_z)] \tag{1}$$

where $E(R_z)$ is the expected return on the zero - beta portfolio and $[E(R_m) - E(R_z)]$ is the risk premium. This version of the CAPM is the some as equation

$$E(R_i) = R_f + \beta_i \, [E(R_m) - R_f] \tag{2}$$

except that the expected return for the zero-beta portfolio is substituted for the risk-free rate. Black's zero-beta version of the CAPM is called the two-factor model.

Assuming that many zero-beta portfolio can be created, which zero-beta portfolio should be selected? The situation is depicted in Figure-1. Two zero-beta portfolios, P_1

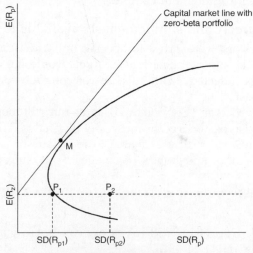

P_1 = Minimum variance zero-beta portfolio

FIGURE 1: THE CAPITAL MARKET LINE WITH NO RISK-FREE ASSET BUT ZERO-BETA PORTFOLIOS

and P$_2$, are shown. Neither portfolio is on the Markonitz's efficient frontier, but both are feesible/attainable portfolios. (The feasible set includes all the portfolios that are attainable, having the maximum expected return for a given risk). Hence, given the choice of the zero-beta portfolio P$_1$ and P$_2$, which one will the investor select? Since both have the same expected return, the investor will select the one with the minimum risk. That is P$_1$. Hence, an investor will select in general the one with the minimum risk of all the possible zero-beta portfolios. The portfolio's selected (i.e. P$_1$) is called the minimum-variance zero-beta portfolio.

How does an investor obtain a portfolio that has a zero-beta? The basic assumption is that by means of short-selling, a zero-beta portfolio can be created from a combination of securities. Short selling involves selling an asset that is not owned in order to benefit from an anticipated decline in the asset's price. Since the asset is presold at a price today, a decline in the asset's price means that an investor can buy the asset in the future at a lower price.

Short-selling is necessary assumption since assets such as stocks are positively correlated, the only way to get a portfolio that is uncorrelated with the market portfolio is to create a portfolio in which stocks are owned and stocks are shorted. Thus, when the price of stocks increases, there will be a gain on the stocks owned in the portfolio, giving a positive return; however, there will be a loss on the stocks that have been shorted and therefore a negative return. The zero-beta portfolio is created much that this combination of stocks owned and stocks shorted will have a beta of zero. Thus two-factor version of the CAPM avoids relying on the myth of borrowing and lending at a risk-free rate.

VII. There are no taxes, transection costs, restrictions on short sales, or other market imperfections

This assumption has several implications for the CAPM. First, the assumption about short sales complements the assumption about a risk-free asset. There must be either a risk-free asset or a portfolio of short-sold securities for the capital market line to be straight; if there were no risk-free asset, the investor could create one by short-selling securities. If there are no risk- free asset, and the investor could not create a proxy risk-free asset, the capital market line would not be a linear and the direct linear relationship between risk (beta) and return would not exist. In reality, there are considerable restrictions on short sales in most portfolios. Second, of the three assumptions specific to the CAPM, this one removes the real world problem of transactions costs and taxes. The CAPM treats dividends and capital gains as equivalent and transaction costs as irrelevant. Assuming that all returns are equally desirable allows us to use the simple CAPM.

VIII. Total asset quantity is fixed, and all assets are marketable and divisible

This assumption suggests that we can ignore liquidity and new issues of securities. If such things cannot be ignored, then the simple CAPM cannot capture all that is important in pricing securities. The fact is that liquidity is a serious concern for investors. Hence, some investors have begun to add liquidity as a factor in making their market estimates. The adaptation produces multiple capital market lines—one line for each particular group of investors (or each desired level of liquidity). Other firms have used the market value (the size) of the company as another factor in determining returns.

In addition to ignoring investors' objectives concerning liquidity,this assumption also ignores the existence of nonmarketable assets—such as human capital or individuals' employability. The fact is that a large portion of most portfolio is made up of either very illiquid assets or unmarketable assets. To exclude these would mean ignoring important parts of "the markets".

These *eight assumptions* are basic to create the simple CAPM. Since these assumptions are critical to understanding the CAPM, let us review their implications. The following list describes the logical sequence of these assumptions:

(*i*) Risk is the variance of expected portfolio returns.

(*ii*) Risk can be broken into two components: diversifiable (unsystematic) risk and nondiversifiable (systematic) risk.

(*iii*) Proper diversification can reduce unsystematic risk.

(*iv*) Beta is the relevant measure of risk for investors with diversified portfolios.

(*v*) Risk and return are linearly related by beta—that is, risk and return are in equilibrium.

(*vi*) Return is total return.

(*vii*) An investor holds portion of two portfolios. The risk-free asset and the market portfolio.

(*viii*) The return that an investor actually receives is derived from only two sources: risk proportional market return plus nonsystematic random return. No other factor is consistent in its effect on security returns.

These are not the assumptions in their strict sense. Instead, they are statements that describe the model and its meaning. None strictly reflects reality, it is simpler to proceed to the implications and then consider their relevance.

What would happen in such a world ? The CAPM would reduce the situation to an extreme case. Every investor can devise an appropriate strategy alone and determine a set of efficient risky portfolios, but everyone would obtain the same set i.e., a combination of all securities, each in proportion to market value called the *market portfolio.* Since markets for securities are perfect, meaning there are no "frictions" to impede investing; potential impediments such as finite divisibility, taxes, transaction costs, and different riskfree borrowing and lending rates have been assumed away. Every investor would have the same proportionate holdings of risky securities.

But what if it won't work ? *What if shares of the ABC Company are not included on the list?* No one will want to hold them, and orders to sell will be received in substantial quantities. Prices will crash. This will make the new analysis necessary if the future prospects of the ABC Company remains unchanged, the current lower prices will push up the expected return. Eventually, when the price has fallen far enough, investors will start investing in ABC Company after all.

The converse situation could also arise. *What if all investors conclude that 20% of every investor's funds at risk should be invested in ABC Company, but at current prices ABC shares constitute considerably less than 20% of total market value* ? Orders to buy will flood in. Hence, there would be rise in price. This will alleviate the problem in two ways. *First,* ABC will represent an increasing share of market value. *Second,* it will be less and less attractive as its price rises, causing investors to reduce its proportionate holdings.

How can everything balance out ? *When would all the adjustment stop, bringing the market into equilibrium* ? *First,* when mere is consistency between the total amount one group of investors wishes to borrow the amount and another group wishes to lend. *Second,* when the preferred combination of risky securities contains every such security, each in proportion to its market value.

CAPITAL MARKET THEORY

Capital market theory is a major extension of the portfolio theory of Markowitz. *Portfolio theory is a description of how rational investors should build efficient portfolio. Capital market theory tells us how assets should be priced in the capital market if indeed, everyone behaved in the way portfolio theory suggests.* In the absence of a risk-free rate, portfolio theory tells us that Markowitz efficient portfolios can be constructed based on expected return and variance and that the optimal portfolio is the one that is tangent to the investor's indifference curve. Once a risk-free asset is introduced and assuming that investors can borrow and lend at the risk-free rate (assumption 6, above), the conclusion of Markowitz portfolio theory can be qualified as illustrated in Figure-2.

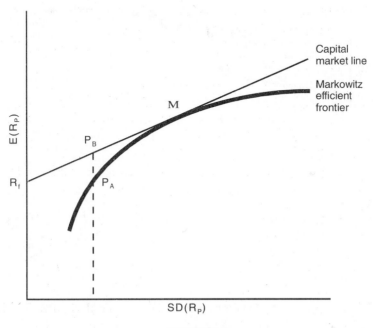

FIGURE-2

CAPITAL MARKET LINE

Every combination of the risk-free asset and the Markowitz efficient portfolio M is shown on the capital market line (CML). The line is drawn from the vertical axis at the risk-free rate tangent to the Markowitz efficient frontier. The point of tangency is denoted by M. All the portfolios on the capital market line are feasible for the investor to construct. Portfolios to the left of M represent combinations of risky assets and the risk-free asset. Portfolios to the right of M include purchases of risky assets made with funds borrowed at the risk-free rate. Such a portfolio is called a leveraged portfolio since it involves the use of borrowed funds.

Now compare a portfolio on the capital market line to the portfolio on the Markowitz efficient frontier with the same risk. For example, compare portfolio P_A, which is on the Markowitz efficient frontier, with portfolio P_B, which is on the capital market line and therefore some combination of the risk-free asset and the Markowitz efficient portfolio M. Notice that for the same risk the expected return is greater for P_B than for P_A. A risk-averse investor will prefer P_B to P_A. That is, P_B will dominate P_A. In fact, this is true for all but one portfolio on the line: portfolio M, which is on the Markowitz efficient frontier.

Recognizing this, we must modify the conclusion from portfolio theory that an investor will select a portfolio on the Markowitz efficient frontier, the particular portfolio depending on the investor's risk preference. With the introduction of the risk-free asset, we can now say that an investor will select a portfolio on the line, representing a combination of borrowing or lending at the risk-free rate and purchases of the Markowitz efficient portfolio M.

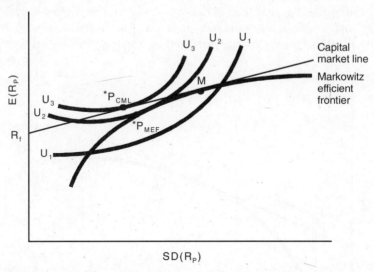

U_1, U_2, U_3 = indifference curves with $U_1 < U_2 < U_3$
M = Market portfolio
R_f = risk-free rate
P^*_{CML} = optiaml portfolio on capital market line
P^*_{MEF} = optiaml portfolio on Markowtiz efficient frontier

FIGURE 3: OPTIMAL PORTFOLIO AND THE CAPITAL MARKET LINE.

The particular efficient portfolio that the investor will select on the line will depend on the investor's risk preference. This can be seen in Figure-3, which is the same as Figure-2 but has the investor's indifference curves included. The investor will select the portfolio on the line that is tangent to the highest indifference curve, U_3. In the absence of a risk-free asset, it would not be possible to construct the portfolio needed to get to the indifference curve indicated by us. Instead, the investor could only get to U_2, which is the indifference curve that is tangent to the Markowitz efficient frontier.

It was Sharpe, Lintner, Treynor, and Mossin who demonstrated that the opportunity to borrow or lend at the risk-free rate implies a capital market where risk-averse investors will prefer to hold portfolios consisting of combinations of the risk-free asset and some portfolio M on the Markowitz efficient frontier. Sharpe called the line from the risk-free rate to portfolio M on the efficient frontier the *capital market line,* and this is the name that has been adopted in the industry.

One more key question remains: *How does an investor construct portfolio M?* Eugene Fama answered this question by demonstrating that M must consist of all assets available to investors, and each asset must be held in proportion to its market value relative to the total market value of all assets. So, for example, if the total market value of some asset is ₹ 20 crore and the total market value of all assets is ₹ X, then the percentage of the portfolio that should be allocated to that asset is ₹ 20 crore divided by ₹ X. Because portfolio M consists of all assets, it is referred to as the market portfolio.

Now we can restate how a risk-averse investor who makes investment decisions as suggested by Markowitz and who can borrow and lend at the risk-free rate should construct efficient portfolios. This should be done by combining an investment in the risk-free asset and the market portfolio. *The theoretical result that all investors will hold a combination of the risk-free asset and the market portfolio is known as the two-fund separation theorem*—one fund consists of the risk-free asset and the other is the market portfolio. Of course, leveraged portfolios hold a negative position with respect to the risk-free asset, but they still make use of this resource. While all investors will select a portfolio on the capital market line, the optimal portfolio for a specific investor is the one that will maximize that investor's utility function.

CAPITAL ASSET PRICING MODEL

The capital asset pricing model (CAPM) is a relationship explaining how assets should be priced. It uses the results of the capital market theory to derive the relationship between the expected returns and systematic risk of individual securities and portfolios. Up to this point, we know how a risk-averse investor who makes decisions based on two parameters (expected return and variance) should construct an efficient portfolio: using a combination of the market portfolio and the risk-free rate. Based on this result, we can derive a model that shows how a risky asset should be priced. In the process of doing so, we can fine-tune our thinking about the risk associated with an asset. Specifically, we can show that the appropriate risk that investors should be compensated for accepting is not the variance of an asset's return but some other quantity. In order to do this, let's take a closer look at the risk.

Systematic and Unsystematic Risk

In the development of portfolio theory, Markowitz defined the variance of the rate of return as the appropriate measure of risk. However, this risk measure can be divided into two general types of risk: systematic risk and unsystematic risk.

Systematic risk is the portion of an asset's variability that can be attributed to a common factor. It is also sometimes called undiversifiable risk or market risk. Systematic risk is the minimum level of risk that can be obtained for a portfolio by means of diversification across a large number of randomly chosen assets. As such, systematic risk is that which results from general market and economic conditions that cannot be diversified away. On the other hand, *unsystematic risk is that the portion of an asset's variability that can be diversified away as unsystematic risk. It is also sometimes called diversifiable risk, unique risk, residual risk, or company-specific risk.* This is the risk that is unique to a company, such as a strike, the outcome of unfavourable litigation, or a natural catastrophe.

How diversification reduces unsystematic risk for portfolios can be illustrated with a graph. Figure-4 shows that at a portfolio size of about 20 randomly selected assets (in this case, equity shares), the level of unsystematic risk is almost completely diversified away. Essentially, all that is left is systematic, or market, risk.

Therefore the total risk of an asset can be measured by its variance. To an asset which would be:

$$\sigma^2 (R_i) = \beta^2_i (R_M) + \sigma^2 (\varepsilon_i) \tag{3}$$

Equation (3) says that the total risk as measured by $\sigma^2 (R_i)$ is equal to the sum of:
(1) The market or systematic risk as measured by $\beta^2_i \sigma^2(R_M)$
(2) The unique risk as measured by $\sigma^2 \varepsilon_i$

THE SECURITY MARKET LINE

The capital market line represents an equilibrium condition in which the expected return on a *portfolio* of assets is a linear function of the expected return on the market portfolio. A directly analogous relationship holds for *individual security* expected returns:

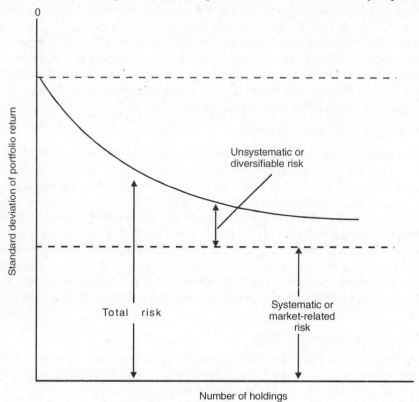

FIGURE 4

$$E(R_i) = R_f \frac{[E(R_M) - R_f]}{\sigma(R_M)} \tag{4}$$

Equation-4 simply uses risk and return variables for an individual security in place of the portfolio values in the formula for the CML. This version of the risk-return relationship for individual securities is called the security market line (SML). As in the case of the CML, the expected return for an asset is equal to the risk-free rate plus the product of the market price of risk and the quantity of risk in the security.

Another more common version of the SML relationship uses the beta of a security. To see how this relationship is developed, look back at equation-3. In a well-diversified portfolio (*i.e.*, Markowitz diversified), the unique risk is eliminated. Consequently, equation-3 can be rewritten as

$$\sigma^2(R_i) = \beta_i^2 \ \sigma^2(R_M).$$

and the standard deviation as

$$\sigma(R_i) = \beta_i \sigma(R_M)$$

Therefore,

$$\beta_i = \frac{c(R_i)}{\sigma(R_M)}$$

If β_i is substituted into Equation (4), we have the beta version of the SML or capital asset pricing model, as shown in equation-2:

$$E[R_i] = R_f + \beta_i [E(R_M) - R_f] \tag{4}$$

This equation states that, given the assumptions of the CAPM, the expected (or required) return on an individual asset is a positive linear function of its index of systematic risk as measured by beta. The higher the beta, the higher the expected return. Notice that it is only an asset's beta that determines its expected return.

Let's look at the prediction of the CAPM for several values of beta. The beta of a risk-free asset is zero, because the variability of the return for a risk-free asset is zero and therefore it does not covary with the market portfolio. So if we want to know the expected return for a risk-free asset, we would substitute zero for β_i in Equation (2):

$$E(R_i) = R_f + 0 [E(R_M) - R_f] = R_f$$

Thus, the return on a risk-free asset is simply the risk-free return. Of course, this is what we expect.

The beta of the market portfolio is 1. If asset i has the same beta as the market portfolio, then substituting 1 into Equation (2) gives

$$E(R_i) = R_f + 1 [E(R_M - R_f)] = E(R_M)$$

In this case, the expected return for the asset is the same as the expected return for the market portfolio. If an asset has a beta greater than the market portfolio (i.e., greater than 1), then the expected return will be higher than for the market portfolio. The reverse is true if an asset has a beta less than the market portfolio. A graph of the SML is presented in Figure-5.

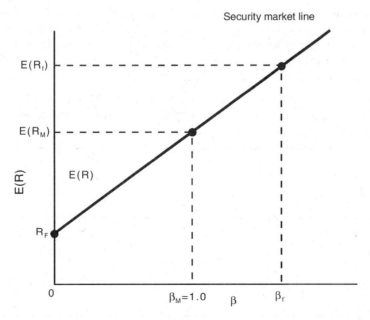

FIGURE 5

In equilibrium, the expected return of individual securities will lie on the SML and *not* on the CML. This is true because of the high degree of unsystematic risk that remains in individual securities that can be diversified out of portfolios of securities.

It follows that the only risk that investors will pay a premium to avoid is market risk. Hence, two assets with the same amount of systematic risk will have the same expected return. In equilibrium, only efficient portfolios will lie on both the CML and the SML. This underscores the fact that the systematic risk measure, beta, is most correctly considered as an *index* of the contribution of an individual security to the systematic risk of a well-diversified portfolio of securities.

There is one more version of the SML that is worthwhile to discuss. Beta for an asset using the statistical technique turns out as follows:

$$\beta_i = \frac{\text{Cov}(R_i, R_M)}{\text{Var}(R_M)} \tag{5}$$

Substituting Equation (5) for β_i in the beta version of the SML results in another version of the SML:

$$E(R_i) = R_f + \frac{\text{Cov}(R_i, R_M)}{\text{Var}(R_M)}[E(R_M) - R_f]$$

This version of the SML emphasizes that it is not the variance or standard deviation of an asset that affects its return. It is the *covariance* of the asset's return with the market's return that affects its return. An asset that has a positive covariance will have a higher expected return than the risk-free asset; an asset with a negative covariance will have a lower expected return than the risk-free asset. If the covariance is positive, this increases the risk of an asset in a portfolio and therefore investors will only purchase that asset if they expect to earn a return higher than the risk-free asset. If an asset has a negative covariance, this will reduce the portfolio risk and investors would be willing to accept a return less than the risk-free asset.

SML Versus CML

To illustrate the application of both the SML and CML and, in the process, to remove any confusion, about to when to use which one, consider the following data on two portfolios and a single stock:

Security	σ	r_{im}	β	$\left[\dfrac{E(P_1 + D_1)}{P_0} - 1.0\right]$
(1)	(2)	(3)	(4)	(5)
Portfolio ABC	15.0%	1.0	0.75	16.0%
Portfolio XYZ	19.0%	0.8	0.90	17.2%
WWW Equity	22.0%	0.5	0.75	16.0%
Market Portfolio	20.0%	1.0	1.0	18.0%
Risk-free Rate (R_f)	0.0	0.0	0.0	10.0%

The Column-5 indicates the return which is expected on each. This might or might not be equal to the equilibrium expected return. Consider holding any of these three as your total portfolio. In that case you would apply the CML, since it identifies expected returns which are available on efficient portfolios of all possible risk levels.

CML	$E(R_p) = R_f + \sigma_p \left[\dfrac{R_{pm} - R_f}{\sigma} \right]$

Portfolio ABC	16.0%= 10.0%+15%(18%-10%)/20%
Portfolio XYZ	17.6%= 10.0%+19%(18%-10%)/20%
WWW Equity	18.8%= 10.0%+22%(18%-10%)/20%

Returns which would be expected on each (if they represent total portfolio) are shown above. Only Portfolio *ABC* can be bought at a current price and later received an expected dividend and price which provide satisfactory return. Only Portfolio ABC is efficient. Portfolio XYZ is expected to provide a 17.2 per cent return, whereas an efficient portfolio with a standard deviation similar to that of a Portfolio XYZ (σ =20%) is expected to provide a 17.6 per cent return. Clearly Portfolio XYZ is not an efficient portfolio. WWW Equity is even worse, providing an expected return of 16 per cent when a similar risk-portfolio would provide 18.8 per cent.

If the market is in equilibrium, this is not a surprising conclusion. Look at the correlation coefficient (r) on each. Portfolio *ABC* is perfectly correlated with the market portfoilio. It has not unsystematic, diversifiable risk. In fact, you may have guess what Portfolio ABC really is. There is only one way in which such a perfectly diversified portfolio can be constructed-by placing a portion of the portfolio in the market portfolio and then lending and borrowing at R_f. Portfolio XYZ is a 70/30 combination of market and risk-free. The other two investments , however , have correlations with portfolio market of less than 1.0. Each has a unsystematic, diversifiable, risk. If the market is at equilibrium, such investments simply would not qualify as efficient portfolios because they would not be satisfactorily diversified.

Now let's look at these investments again, not as total portfolios but as an individual securities which are to be placed into a portfolio containing many other securities also. To evaluate the return which should be expected on a security if it is to be part of a much larger portfolio SML is used.

SML	$E(\tilde{R}_i) = R_f + \beta_{im} \, (\tilde{R}_m - R_f)$
Portfolio ABC	16.0%= 10.0%+ .75 (18%-10%)
Portfolio XYZ	17.6%= 10.0%+ .90 (18%-10%)
WWW Equity	18.8%= 10.0%+ .75 (18%-10%)

In this context each investment is fairly priced. As shown above, each is expected to provide a return equal to what equilibrium conditions suggest should be earned. Notice that SML is able to identify the fair expected returns on an efficient such as Portfolio ABC. Even though, the SML is intended to evaluate single securities, it may also be used on portfolios. Infact WWW Equity is a relatively diversified company and could be easily thought as a portfolio composed of each of its business lines. *The SML, however, asks only whether the security or portfolio fairly priced. It does not indicate whether the investment is an efficient portfolio. To determine whether a portfolio is efficient, the CML must be used.*

DETERMINATION OF SYSTEMATIC RISK

There are two dimensions of risk that affect a firm's systematic risk. The *first* is financial risk, the additional risk placed on the firm and its stockholders due to the firm's decision to be leveraged—that is, to take on additional debt. The *second*, business risk, is the riskiness involved with a firm's operations, if it takes on no debt.

A particular firm's capital structure affects the riskiness inherent in the company's equity and thus affects its required rate of return and the price of the stock. A company's capital-structure policy requires choosing between risk and return. Taking on increasing levels of debt increases the riskiness of the firm's earning stream, but it usually also results in a higher expected rate of return. High levels of risk tend to lower an equity share price, but a high level of expected rates of return tends to raise it. Therefore, striking a balance with the optimal capital structure maximises the price of the stock.

Business risk is the risk inherent in a firm's operations. It can also be defined as the uncertainty inherent in projection of future operating income or earnings before interest and taxes (EBIT). Fluctuations in EBIT can result from a number of factors. On the national level these can be economic factors such as inflationary or recessionary times. At the industry level some factors may be the level of competition between similar industries, natural or manmade catastrophes, labour strikes, price controls, and so on. There are a host of possibilities that affect EBIT by raising or lowering its level.

Uncertainty regarding future income flows is a function of the company's business risk. It may fluctuate among industries, among firms, and across time. The extent of business risk is dependent upon the firm and the industry. Cyclical industries have especially high business risks because they are dependent upon the strength of the economy. The retail food industry is considered to be quite stable because food is a necessary good that will be purchased regardless of the state of the economy.

When a firm uses debt or financial leverage, business risk and financial risk are concentrated on the shareholders. For example, if a firm is capitalised only with equity then the investors share business risk in proportion to their ownership of equity. If, however, a firm is 50 percent levered (50 percent of the corporation is financed by debt, the other half by equity), the investors who put up the equity will then have to bear all business risk and some financial risk.

The effect of leverage upon return on assets (ROA) and return on equity (ROE) and its effect upon the shareholders can be generalised as follows:

1. The use of leverage or debt generally increases ROE.
2. The standard deviation of ROA (σ_{ROA}) is a measure of business risk while the standard deviation of ROE (σ_{ROE}) is a measure of the risk borne by shareholders. $\sigma_{ROA} = \sigma_{ROE}$ if the firm is not levered; otherwise with the use of debt $\sigma_{ROE} > \sigma_{ROA}$, indication that business risk is being borne by stockholders.
3. The difference between σ_{ROE} and σ_{ROA} is the actual risk shareholders face and a measure of the increased risk resulting from financial leverage. Thus

$$\text{Risk of financial leverage} = \sigma^2_{ROE} - \sigma^2_{ROA}$$

GROWTH RATES, ACCOUNTING BETAS, AND VARIANCE IN EBIT

Besides leverage, other financial variables associated with the firm can affect the beta coefficient. These are the growth rate, accounting beta, and variance in EBIT.

Growth Rates

The growth rate can be measured in terms of the growth in total assets or the growth in sales. It is determined by the percentage change between two periods.

$$\frac{\text{sales}_t - \text{sales}_{t-1}}{\text{sales}_{t-1}} \times 100\% \text{ or } \frac{\text{total assets}_t - \text{total assets}_{t-1}}{\text{total assets}_{t-1}} \times 100\%$$

From a financial perspective growth is not always a blessing. Rapid growth can put considerable strain on a company's resources, and unless management is aware of this effect and takes active steps to control it, rapid growth can lead to bankruptcy. It becomes necessary, therefore, to define a company's sustainable growth rate:

$$\frac{\Delta S}{S} = g^* = \frac{P(1-D)(1-L)}{T-P(1-D)(1+L)} \tag{6}$$

where:

P = the profit margin on all sales;
D = the target dividend payout ratio;
L = the target debt to equity ratio;
T = the ratio of total assets to sales;
S = annual sales; and
ΔS = the increase in sales during the year.

How is Equation (6) derived? Assuming a company is not raising new equity, the cash to finance growth must come from retained profits and new borrowings:

Retained profits = Profits — Dividends
= Profit margin × Total sales –Dividends
= $P (S+ \Delta S) (1 -D)$

Further, because the company wants to maintain a target debt-to-equity ratio equal to L, added to the owners' equity enables it to increase its indebtedness by Rs. L. Since the owners' equity will rise by an amount equal to retained profits:

New borrowings = Retained profit × Target debt-to-equity ratio
= $P (S+ \Delta S) (1 -D) L$

The use of cash represented by the increase in assets must equal the two sources of cash (retained profits and new borrowings):

Uses of cash = Sources of cash
Increases in assets = Retained profits+ New borrowings
ΔST = $P(S + \Delta S) (1 + D) + P(S + \Delta S) (1 -D)L$
ΔST = $P(1 -D) (1 + L)S + P(1 -D) (1 + L) \Delta S$
$\Delta S[T -P(1 -D)(1 + L)]$ = $P(1 -D)(1 + L)S$

$$\frac{\Delta S}{S} = \frac{P(1 -D) (1 + L)}{T -P(1 -D)(1 + L)}$$

In Equation (6) the $\Delta S/S$ or g^* is the firm's sustainable growth rate assuming no infusion of new equity. Therefore, a company's growth rate in sales must equal the indicated combination of four ratios, $P, D, L,$ and T. In addition, if the company's growth rate differs from g^*, one or more of the ratios must change. For example, suppose a company grows at a rate in excess of g^*. Then it must either use its assets more efficiently or it must alter its financial policies. Efficiency is represented by the profit margin and asset-to-sales ratio. It therefore would need to increase its profit margin (P) or decrease its asset-to-sales ratio (T) in order to increase efficiency. Financial policies are represented by payout or leverage ratios. In this case, a decrease in its payout ratio (D) or an increase in its leverage (L) would be necessary to alter its financial policies to accommodate a different growth rate. It should be noted that increasing efficiency is not always possible and altering financial policies not always wise.

Accounting Beta

The accounting beta can be calculated from earnings-per-share data. Using EPS as an example, beta can be computed as follows:

$$EPS_{i,t} = \alpha_i + \beta_i\,EPS_{m,t} + e_{i,t} \tag{7}$$

where:

$EPS_{i,t}$ = earnings per share of firm i at time t;

$EPS_{m,t}$ = earnings per share of market average at time t; and

$e_{i,t}$ = error term.

The estimate of β_i, is the EPS type of accounting beta.

Variance in EBIT

The variance in EBIT (X) can be defined as:

$$\frac{\sum_{t=1}^{n}(X_t - \overline{X})^2}{n-1} \tag{8}$$

in which X_t = earnings before interest and taxes in period t, and $\overline{X}$ = average EBIT.

The total variance of EBIT can be used to measure the overall fluctuation of accounting earnings for a firm.

Capital-Labour Ratio

The capital-labour ratio has an impact upon the magnitude of the beta coefficient. Capital intensity results in increased total risks and generally results in an increase in beta. Large investments are often needed to fully automate or to computerise a plant completely. Taking on debt or issuing securities is normally how these capitalisation increases are financed. If the capital-labour ratio is greater than one a firm is capital intensive and if the capital-labour ratio is less than one, then there is a reduction in capital intensity and a shift towards human-resource investment.

Fixed Costs and Variable Costs

Business risk is dependent upon the extent a firm builds fixed costs into its operations. If a large percentage of a firm's costs are fixed, costs cannot decline proportionally when demand falls off. If fixed costs are high, then a slight drop in sales can lead to large declines in EBIT. Therefore, the higher a firm's fixed costs are, the greater its business risk and, generally, the higher its beta.

Beta Forecasting

Analysts and investment managers who use the CAPM and beta are interested in whether the beta coefficient and the standard-deviation statistics for different securities and portfolios are stable through time or whether they change in a predictable fashion. If the beta coefficient and standard deviation are stable, then using a beta derived from current and historical price data is fine, because the beta today is the same as the beta in the future. However, if the beta coefficient and standard deviation are unstable or vary through time, the analyst or manager must forecast a beta's future value before employing it.

Beta on an individual security is generally not stable, while portfolios have stable betas. Hence, the problem is of forecasting future betas in order to use the CAPM for individual securities. Beta forecasting refers to using the historical beta estimates or other historical financial information to forecast future betas.

Market-Based versus Accounting-Based Beta Forecasting

Market-based beta forecasts are based upon market information alone. Historical betas of firms are used as a proxy for their future betas. *Accounting-based beta forecasts* rely upon the relationships of accounting information such as the growth rate of the firm, EBIT, leverage, and the accounting beta as a basis for forecasting beta. To use accounting information in beta forecasts, the historical beta estimates are first cross-sectionally related to accounting information such as growth rate, variance of EBIT, leverage, accounting beta, and so on.

CAPM VS. MARKET MODEL

A. Risk-Premium Form

For a meaningful comparison of the two models, it is desirable to recast each of them in a risk-premium form.

CAPM

According the the CAPM, in equilibrium, the expected return of a portfolio is equal to the risk-free rate plus a risk premium that is proportional to its beta. Because at any given time the risk-free rate can be assumed to be given and can be treated as constant, investors frequently are interested in calculating the *risk premium* that is included in the expected return of the portfolio. The risk premium can be obtained by subtracting the risk-free rate from the expected rate of return.

That is, the expected portfolio risk premium is determined :

$$\tilde{R}_p - R_f = \beta_{pm}(\tilde{R}_m - R_f)$$

where:

$\tilde{R}_p$ = return on portfolio P

R_f = risk-less rate of interest

β_{pm} = sensitivity of portfolio p's excess return to the excess return of the market portfolio.

Figure-6 presents the CAPM both in its general form and the risk-premium form with a beta of 2 and an assumed risk-free rate of 6 per cent. Note that the y-intercepts is -6; that is, the expected portfolio return is -6 per cent when the expected market return is zero in Figure-6 (A). The risk-premium form of CAPM, given in Figure 6(B), relabels both axis so as to measure the expected market and portfolio risk premiums. In this form, the origin is defined as the point where the expected excess return (over the riskless rate) is zero for both the portfolio and the market. The result is that the characteristic line, which still has the slope (β_{pm} = 2) now passes through the origin.

Market Model

Recasting of the Market Model into the risk-premium form involves a different operation. When the model is presented in the risk-premium form the equation becomes:

$$(\tilde{R}_p - R_f) = \beta_p - R_f (1 - \beta_{pm}) + \beta_{pm} (\tilde{R}_m) - R_f) \tilde{R}_p$$

The derivation of this new form deserves a more elaborate explanation. The Market

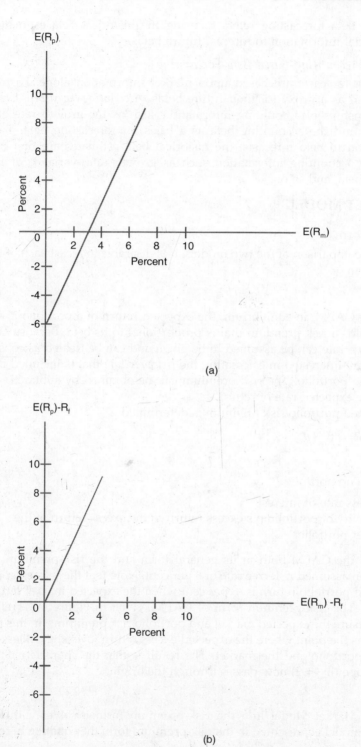

(a)

(b)

FIGURE 6

Model is essentially a regression model. When a regression or characteristic line is developed with $\tilde{R}_m$, on the X- axis and $\tilde{R}_p$ on the Y-axis, the β_{pm} is determined by the sensitivity of the portfolio's return to the market return, and the Y-intercept of the characteristic line is called the (α_p) of the portfolio. When the axes are changed to $\tilde{R}_m - R_f$ and $\tilde{R}_p - R_f$ to present the model in a risk-premium form, however, a new regression or characteristic line is developed. Because the risk of the portfolio remains uneffected, the β_{pm} of the new characteristic line remains unchanged, but the α_p, or the Y-intercept, changes to α^*_p as follows :

$$\alpha^*_p = \alpha_p - R_f (1 - \beta_{pm})$$

where

α^*_p = risk-adjusted excess return

α_p = return on the portfolio when the market return is zero.

Specifically, α^*_p represents the excess return that the portfolio earns when the market return equals the riskless rate — that is, when the excess market returns is zero. Figure-7 presents three positions of α^*_p. Note that the α^*_p can be positive (Figure-7 [A]), negative (Figure-7[B]) and zero (Figure-7[C]). It should also be noted that α^*_p can be lower, higher, or identical with α_p.[1]

An important observation is apropos here. If a portfolio has a positive risk-adjusted excess return [$\alpha^*_p > 0$, or equivalently $\alpha_p > R_f (1 - \beta_{pm})$, then it will yield a return greater than its expected return consisting of the riskless rate plus a risk premium proportional to its beta. This can be observed from the following.

Becomes $\qquad \tilde{R}_p - R_f = \alpha_p - R_f (1 - \beta_{pm}) + \beta_{pm} (\tilde{R}_m - R_f) + \tilde{r}_p$

$\qquad\qquad\qquad \alpha^*_p = \alpha_p - R_f (1 - \beta_{pm})$, the equation becomes :

$$\tilde{R}_p - R_f = \alpha^*_p + \beta_{pm} (\tilde{R}_m - R_f) + \tilde{r}_p$$

Rearranging, and assuming that the mean of the distribution of $\tilde{r}_p$ (the error term) equal zero, we have :

$\tilde{R}_p =$	α^*_p	+	R_f	+	$\beta_{pm} (\tilde{R}_m - R_f)$
	Risk-adjusted excess return		Risk-less return		Market or systematic risk premium

This is an extremely important result affecting portfolio management. It states that if the risk-adjusted excess return of a portfolio is positive ($\alpha^*_p > 0$), then the portfolio return will be greater than normally expected; that is, an investor holding a portfolio with a positive α^*_p has succeeded in *beating the market*. Likewise, a portfolio with a negative α^*_p has under-performed the market.

B. Security in Equilibrium

A closer examination of the Market Model and the CAPM reveals that, except when the portfolio is in equilibrium, the expected excess return or risk premiums on a portfolio

---

1. The relationship of a_p and a^*_p can be categorically stated as

$\qquad\qquad a^*_p < a_p \qquad\qquad$ when $b_{pm} < 1$

$\qquad\qquad a^*_p > a_p \qquad\qquad$ when $b_{pm} > 1$

$\qquad\qquad a^*_p = a_p \qquad\qquad$ when $b_{pm} = 1$

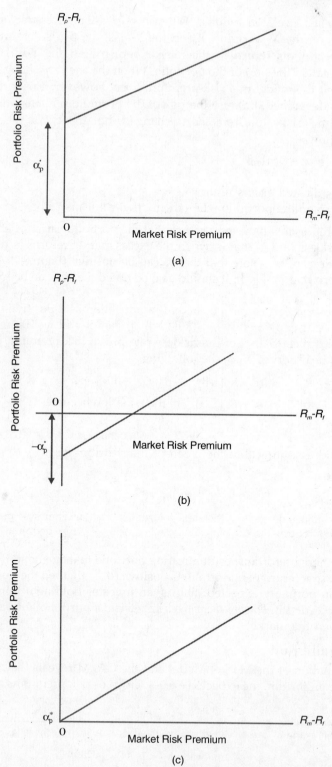

FIGURE 7

are different under two models. Assume the alpha is 4 per cent ($\beta_p = 4$), the riskless rate is 6 per cent ($R_f = 6$), the beta is 2 ($\beta_{pm} = 2$), and the expected market return is 10 per cent ($\tilde{R}_m = 10$). The expected risk premiums on the portfolio under the two models in their risk-premium forms are as follows :

Market Model

$$(\tilde{R}_p - R_f) = \alpha^*_p + \beta_{pm}(\tilde{R}_m - R_f)$$

$$(\tilde{R}_p - R_f) = 4 - 6(1 - 2) + 2(10 - 6)$$

$$= 4 + 6 + 8 = 18\%$$

CAPM

$$\tilde{R}_p - R_f = \beta_{pm}(\tilde{R}_p - R_f)$$

$$= 2(10 - 6)$$

$$= 20 - 12 = 8\%$$

The only time the expected risk premium of a portfolio under both models is identical is when the portfolio is in equilibrium. That happens when the risk-adjusted excess return is expected to be zero ($\alpha^*_p = 0$) or when the alpha (α_p) is expected to equal the riskless rate multiplied by the quantity of one minus beta $\alpha_p = R_f(1 - \beta_{pm})$.[2] In this example, when $\alpha_p = 6(1 - 2)$ or -6, or equivalently $\alpha^*_p = 0$, then the expected risk premiums under both models are identical :

Market Model

$$(\tilde{R}_p - R_f) = -6 - 6(1-2) + 2(10 - 6)$$

$$= -6 + 6 + 8 = 8\%$$

CAPM

$$(\tilde{R}_p - R_f) = 2(10 - 6) = 8\%$$

C. Change in Market Model

Although the two models generate the same expected portfolio risk premiums only when the portfolio is in equilibrium, or when $\alpha^*_p = 0$, the relationship between changes

---

2. The relationship can be clearly seen from the following deviation.

For a portfolio, assuming $\tilde{r}_p = 0$, the two models are:

$\tilde{R}_p = \alpha_p + \beta_{pm}(\tilde{R}_m)$------ Market Model

$\tilde{R}_p = R_f + \beta_{pm}(\tilde{R}_m - R_f)$------ CAPM Model

Assuming the R_p in both models is the same, we have

$$\alpha_p + \beta_p(R_m) = R_f + \beta_{pm}(\tilde{R}_m - R_f)$$

$$\alpha_p = R_f + \beta_{pm}(\tilde{R}_m - R_f) - \beta_{pm}(\tilde{R}_m)$$

$$= R_f + \beta_{pm}(\tilde{R}_m) - \beta_{pm}R_f - \beta_{pm}(\tilde{R}_m)$$

$$= R_f - \beta_{pm}R_f$$

$$= R_f(1 - \beta_{pm})$$

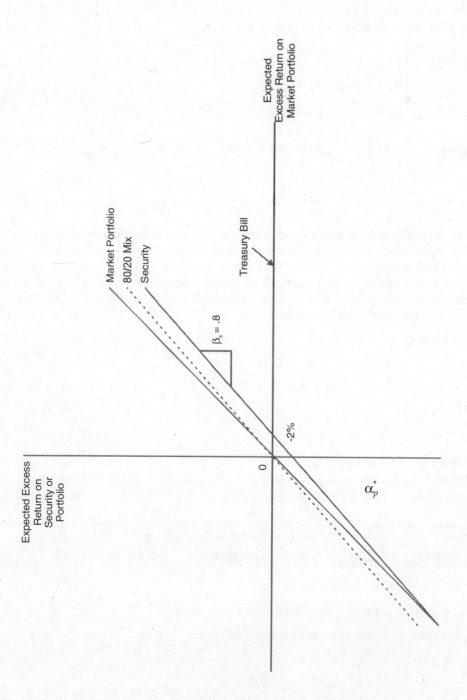

FIGURE 8

in a portfolio risk premium and changes in the market returns is always identical. Assume that the expected market return increase to 12 per cent. The changes in the expected portfolio premium under two models are:

Market Model

$$\tilde{R}_p - R_f = 4\text{-}6\,(1\text{-}2) + 2\,(12\text{-}6)$$
$$= 4 + 6 + 12 = 22$$
$$\Delta\,(\tilde{R}_p - R_f) = 22\text{-}18 = 4\%$$

CAPM

$$(\tilde{R}_p - R_f) = 2(12\text{-}6) = 12$$
$$\Delta\,(\tilde{R}_p - R_f) = 12\text{-}8 = 4\%$$

Risk-Adjusted Excess Return

A comparison of the two models reveals that, with the Market Model, the value of risk-adjusted excess return (α^*_p) can be positive, zero, or negative. However, the CAPM asserts that the value of α^*_p is zero. Reasons for this assertion can be discussed in terms of the risk-premium forms of both models.

Figure-8 presents the profile of a risky security relative to the market portfolio and a portfolio consisting of a riskless security (treasury bill) and a risky security. Note that the figure is presented in the risk-premium form; therefore, the origin measures a zero expected excess return (over the riskless rate).

Let us begin with the characteristic line of the market portfolio. By definition, the expected excess return on the security or portfolio (vertical axis) must always be equal to the expected excess return on the market portfolio (horizontal axis). Consequently, the value of α^*_p of this portfolio must be zero and the value of the beta must be one. The characteristic line of the market portfolio is therefore a 45 degree line passing through the origin.

Next, we turn to a security which is less volatile than the market ($\beta_{im} = 0.8$), but which also has unsystematic risk because its α^*_i is -2 per cent. In this case, it is not clear if this security is preferable to the market portfolio.

Finally, let us consider the third alternative. An investor could split funds between the market portfolio and riskless security in a manner designed to give the same level of systematic risk as that associated with the security. In this case, the appropriate division would result is 80% invested in the market portfolio and 20% in riskless security. This strategy would have a characteristic line passing through the origin (that is, an β_p of zero) with a beta of 0.8 and it would clearly be a better investment than the single security. This is because the beta of the riskless security is zero, the mixed portfolio would have the same level of systematic risk, would have no unsystematic risk, and would offer an expected advantage of 2 per cent, because the α^*_p is zero as compared to the security α^*_i of -2% regardless of how the market performs. The result is predictable. Investors will begin to switch from the single security to a mixed portfolio. The security would be subjected to heavy selling pressure. The price could fall, causing its characteristic line to rise until β becomes zero.

In this example, the beta of the single security was assumed to be less than one. The result will be the same if a security has a beta greater than one. In such a case, however, the appropriate strategy for purposes of comparison would require marginal purchase of the market portfolio, the drawing down of an investor's saving account, or some other action of this type. To keep the analysis simple, it is assumed that this can be accomplished at a cost equal to the risk-free rate.

Thus, it may be pointed that in case the market is efficient, no security will be priced to have a negative risk-adjusted excess return, or $-\alpha^*_i$ irrespective of the beta of a security. Furthermore, because the α^*_p of the market portfolio is simply the weighted average of the α^*_i values of the component securities, and because by definition the a^*_p of the market $\tilde{R}_p - R_f$

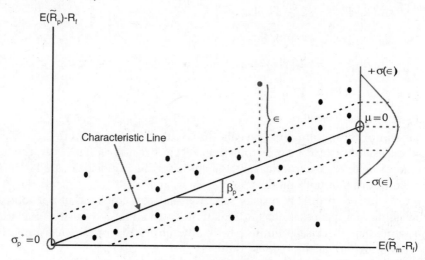

FIGURE 9

portflio is zero, no security can have a positive α^*_i. That is, in an efficient market, the α^*_i of every security and thus the α^*_i of any given portfolio must be zero.

Figure-9 present the profile of perfectly diversified portfolio in the CAPM. The right-hand corner of the figure shows that the error term is normally distributed and its mean is zero. It also shows that the expected risk-adjusted excess return, α^*_i of the portfolio is zero and that the slope of the characteristic line is the beta of the portfolio.

COMPUTING ESTIMATES

ESTIMATING BETA

In the capital asset pricing model, beta is the sole asset-specific or portfolio-specific factor. If the asset's returns tend to move up and down more dramatically than do the market returns, the asset is considered relatively more volatile—more risky—and it will have a higher beta.

Since at any given time the forecasts for the risk-free rate and the market premium are the same for every asset or portfolio, beta alone links the investor's expectations or returns from the asset or portfolio with his or her expectations of returns from the market. Because beta is such a crucial element in the CAPM, its estimation must be accurate.

BETA BASICS

Returns for any security are not "caused" by the market. Rather, returns are driven by macroeconomic events. The effect that these economic events have on investors' expectations will depend on three main factors:

1. The responsiveness of the asset's or portfolio's returns to economic events. This responsiveness is measured as the covariance of the asset's rate of return with that of the market [covariance R_i, R_m].
2. The relationship of the firm's basic characteristics (such as its debt level) with the average characteristics of firms in the market {covariance (R_i, R_m).
3. The general uncertainty attached by investors to macroeconomic events (such as changes in the level of oil prices), described as the variance of the market (R_m).

The expected beta for a firm will change if any of the underlying relationships change. For example, if the firm increases its leverage relative to that of the market or undertakes unusually risky ventures, the change would be a real change in the systematic risk of the firm and should be reflected in beta.

Mathematically, beta is

$$\beta_i = \frac{\text{covariance } (R_i, R_m).}{\text{variance } (R_m)}$$

where

variance (R_m) = the uncertainty attached to economic events
covariance (R_i, R_m) = the responsiveness of an asset's rate of return (R_i) to those things that also change the market's rate of return (R_m)
i = an asset, stock, or portfolio
m = the market

Covariance itself is defined as $r_{im} \, \sigma_i \sigma_m$

where

r_{im} = the correlation coefficient, a measure of the correlation of the returns of i with the returns of m
σ = the standard deviation of the returns

The mathematical relationship is fairly simple, but each variable is expectational. Much of the difficulty we have had in estimating beta has come as a result of compromise— of our using inadequate proxies for expectational factors. Most often the proxy has been the historical relationship of the rate of return to that of a broad-based index of returns on equity.

Using returns on equity represents a major compromise, and using an index that represents only a portion of the stock market is a further compromise. The market portfolio should be a collection of all risky assets, but equity shares represent only one portion of the universe.

Basic Regression Technique

The simplest way to examine the historical relationship between the returns from any asset and those from the market is simply to plot the relationship over time. This relationship can be described by using the formula for a line ($y = a + bx$). The intercept (a in the formula) is the minimum return from the asset if the return from the market were zero. The slope (b) is the incremental return expected from the asset as the market return becomes higher or lower.

Although this is the basic regression technique those estimating beta from history use a somewhat more elegant version of the formula for a straight line. This version is called the *market model. Because the market model and the CAPM look remarkably alike, many people presume that they are the same. They are not. The market model does not rely on any of the assumptions inherent in the CAPM. It simply states that the returns-generating process is a linear relationship between the returns from the asset and the returns from the market. In relying on historical data, these regression techniques assume that history is an accurate predictor of the future. The assumption may or may not be true.*

PRACTICAL PROBLEMS IN REGRESSION METHODOLOGY

Measurement Period

The length of time over which we calculate beta is important. The measurement or holding period must be long enough to allow a statistically significant sample, but it must not be so long as to include information that does not reflect the relationships likely to persist in to the future.

The length of the holding period does affect beta. However, CAPM does not help us in choosing the appropriate holding period. History, as always, is a difficult proxy for the future.

Interval Choice

The length of the intervals within the chosen holding period can affect the beta estimate. For instance, we might use weekly, monthly, quarterly, or annual intervals within the chosen period. Many experts contend that the interval is irrelevant; however, the betas estimated using different intervals are different.

Perhaps even more interesting than the interval problem is of the starting period. The same interval and the same total period (five years) beta estimates may not give the same estimates of beta. The cause of the discrepancy may be that one use data from the third week of each month to calculate beta, whereas the other data from the fourth week.

The Market Proxy

In earlier CAPM history, many believed that the index choice was not a particularly important issue. Indexes were highly correlated; hence, they were assumed to be virtually interchangeable. But two indexes could be highly correlated with each other and still not be correlated with the underlying market for all risky assets. Thus, finding a true proxy may be impossible, and tests using an incorrect index would be useless. The change in some of the simple parameters that are necessary for estimating a beta using historical data change the result. The choice of each input changes the output, and the size of the difference is enough to cause concern. How should betas be measured, using history? Finding the best way to measure beta requires trial-and-error experimentation.

TESTING THE STABILITY OF HISTORICAL BETAS

Since the use of historical data to predict the future assumes that betas are stable over time, most tests of the usefulness of historical betas have focused on the issue of the stability of historical betas. If historical betas remain relatively unchanged overtime, then historical betas may be useful surrogates for forecasted (ex ante) betas. If, however, historical betas vary over time, then they will have little predictive ability.

What are the results of tests of the stability of historical betas?

1. Analysis of Individual Securities Betas

Application of a sophisticated statistical approach to look at the stability of the betas of public utility and industrial stocks shows that mean betas and the proportion stationary for indificual (not portfolios) utility stocks for different industries. However, the ordinary-least-squares (OLS) betas change quite dramatically from period to period—they were not stable. Further, if the amount of variance explained by the market varied from one period to the next, then betas would not be stationary from one period to another. Increasing the size of the portfolio may or may not increase the stability of beta. Beta is more stable in more diversified portfolios. The improvement in beta stability occurred by the point where there were few (say 10) securities in the portfolio. Added securities lent small improvements. It appears that portfolio betas are relatively stable, and, by inference, easier to predict than the betas for individual stocks.

2. Analysing Risk Classes

Another way of assessing beta stability is to look at beta rankings. The hypothesis is that if the firm stays in the same beta class from period to period betas could be said to be relatively stable and thus reasonable predictors. Use of transition matrix indicates the stability of securities' risk class from one period to the next. Larger changes in the betas occur in the extreme pentiles than in the interior pentiles. Betas for randomly generated portfolios were more stable than were betas for individual securities.

3. Analysing Standard Errors

Typically Beta is estimated from history, using a fixed coefficient model like ordinary-least-squares regression. These models estimate beta over time. Using a time-varying model, one where the beta is allowed to vary over time, the use of the OLS method (or fixed-coefficient model) will overestimate the portfolio residual risk if individual security beta coefficients are changing over time. Once beta variability is removed from the residual risk, the residual risks all stationary and the relationship between residual risk and beta is eliminated.

The time-varying models do appear to eliminate some of the problems that unstable betas create. As for creating a beta coefficient that can be used to estimate future returns, however, these models have their limitations. Much of the cause of beta instability is not real instability at all. Estimates of betas using time-series analysis of historic data rely on the past returns, whereas beta is a function of the expected return. The betas estimated using *ex-post* return data can be expected to exhibit intertemporal non-stationarity, even when the underlying *ex-ante* security returns are serially independent and obey a stationary distribution over time.

4. Stability of Correlation Coefficient

A correlation coefficient is an ingredient needed to estimate a beta. If the correlation coefficient is unpredictable, then it would be difficult to say that the beta is stable or predictable.

In different periods the overall means (a simple average correlation coefficient for the stocks included in the test) is a superior method of predicting correlations—better than the more sophisticated methods. However, the *overall mean* is a very cynical method of forecasting. It is tantamount to saying that the best forecast is just an average for the whole sample. Any added efforts to refine the estimate for a single security are fruitless.

The betas for individual securities are not particularly stable, nor do most securities remain in the same risk class from one period to another. Analysis of mean-squared errors shows that although some components of error can be reduced, the major portion of standard error can be lessened only by adding more securities to the portfolio. Finally, the best way to estimate a correlation coefficient is to use the average coefficient for an entire universe of stocks. If historical betas are not particularly stable and cannot be refined significantly, then they cannot be very useful in estimating future betas.

5. Impact of Macroeconomic Change on Beta: The Impact of Interest Rates

If beta changes over time, perhaps it is due to fundamental shifts in the structure of the economy—major political, social, or economic events, not just randomness. The major structural changes are accompanied by major changes in economic scenario. Some firms and the returns from their securities are profoundly influenced by these changes. Other firms' returns are (and perhaps will continue to be) dominated by micro-economic, firm-specific factors: superior management, market power, patent protection, or process innovation. Nonetheless, no firm and thus no security can escape the direct or indirect effects of events in the larger world. It is the desire to find a way to measure this macroeconomic sensitivity that spurs the search for a better beta. Despite the instability of historical betas, the concept of beta is not easily dismissed.

FUNDAMENTAL AND CREATIVE BETA PREDICTION

Many analysts believe that we are simply putting too much emphasis on history. Beta is likely to appear non-stationary because a firm's risk conditions change. The problem with instability is that it is difficult to know whether risk is changing or whether statistical techniques are at fault. History, as usual, presents problems and the future remains unknown. Other methods of estimating beta have also been devised to analyse the determinants of beta by using ratios from the firms' financial statements. These ratios are regressed against betas, derived using the market model. This method, called *multivariate analysis,* is similar to the market model, but the regression includes a larger number of variables. Some researchers have developed fundamental betas, based on many of the firm-specific variables which can affect a security's risk. Although called fundamental, the factors of primary importance were those derived from the market model using historical returns. An attempt to predict unsystematic (micro-economic) risk, a source of a substantial portion of the total risk for individual assets, has also been made. However, the error from the regressions is usually so large that we might suspect that unsystematic risk could instead be systematic or predictable.

Corporate financial experts have long believed that financial leverage (the amount of debt financing a company's assets) and operating leverage (the relationship of fixed and variable costs) are fundamental factors that affect the risk of a company. Hence, the leverage should also be determinants of the risk of a stock.

1. Can Analysts Add Value?

Fundamental betas are still being derived from *historical* measures of return and/or firms' risk characteristics and return changes relative to the market. In analysing historical returns or considering the firm's future risk characteristics, can the analyst add value to the beta estimate by forecasting some of the conditions that will affect future fundamental beta measurement?

To answer this, a beta from earnings forecasts has been developed. It is argued that if the standard error of the beta from a historical regression analysis and/or the analysts's forecast variance is small, estimation risk is not important. This is the case with the stocks of large, well-researched firms. In fact, they estimation error is inversely related to market value size—and the number of analysts following the firm. Each stock into a portfolio is to be placed according to the number of analysts that followed it. It is believed that if unlinkely results could be eliminated, such as a size effect, then adjusted beta would be superior.

In addition to this mechanical adaptation of beta analysts' forecasts, practitioners have been using beta and adapting it for some time. However, in their attempts to implement the CAPM, they ignored price formation in order to concentrate on the behaviour and construction of portfolios. Since models can be tested only with *ex post* data, data that could never convince professional investors. One must note that beta is an expectational estimate based on (1) the financial risk and business risk of a firm and

(2) the degree to which a firm's business covaries with the total economy, beta should be predictable. It is expected that since analysts had traditionally been concerned with these problems, their estimates should add value.

2. Can Betas be Used for Practical Purpose?

Strategies based on investing in stocks with low price-to-book ratios and small-capitalisation firms produce better long-term performance than strategies based on beta. Beta is no longer regarded as sacred. There is merit to ranking performance but the investors should not be misled. To say beta is dead may seem to be biased. Even if beta may be pronounced dead, it does not invalidate the importance of risk/return relationship. The use of betas depend on the analyst's skill at predicting the future. The beta is one of the curious uses of efficient-market theory. A theoretical concept based on market efficiency is used to identify market inefficiencies—undervalued and overvalued securities. In fact, *beta is a summary measure and may prove to be too austere. Much that underlies the movements of returns in the marketplace may be better described by a richer model than the CAPM. Unsystematic risk may not be irrelevant even in the portfolio context.*

ESTIMATING THE RISK-FREE RATE

The risk-free rate is usually used twice in the CAPM. It is first used as the minimum rate of return (R_f), and it is used again to create the risk premium ($R_m - R_f$). Thus, an error in estimating the risk-free rate of return would lead to a misestimate of the expected rate of return for an asset or portfolio. The risk-free rate can also be used in the market model for examining historical results—for estimating the historical betas and alphas. Choosing an incorrect risk-free rate would mean that the analyst would misunderstand the sources of the asset's returns, the quality of its performance, or have poor data on which to make forecasts. As a result, it is important to examine the risk-free proxy choices and not to accept the customary 90-day Treasury bill rate without due consideration. However, there are practical and theoretical problems in choosing a proxy for the risk-free asset.

THEORETICAL PROBLEMS WITH THE TREASURY BILL AS A PROXY

In CAPM theory, the risk-free asset is one of the two asset choices available to the investor. The investor can reduce the risk of a portfolio by increasing the amount of the risk-free asset in that portfolio, or the investor can increase the risk by reducing the risk-free asset position or by borrowing at the risk-free rate to further invest. In effect, the risk-free rate is the rate that will entice investors to choose between current or future consumption—between savings or investment. The price required to induce an investor to forgo current consumption for a certain future sum, to forgo liquidity, is the price of time, or the riskless or risk-free rate of return.

If the CAPM is to be accurate, the investor's choice of assets must, in essence, depend *solely* on expected returns and on his or her aversion to risk. This concept is known as the *Tobin separation theorem*. Essentially, *the theorem states that investors make portfolio choices solely on the basis of risk and return, separating that decision from all other characteristics of the securities.* If the Tobin separation theorem is to work, two things must be true about the risk-free rate of return. The R_f proxy must have no variance and no covariance with the returns from the market. These required characteristics for R_f cause some problems when choosing a proxy. *First,* zero variance can exist only for a single period—the single period of this one-period model. In a multiperiod world, there would be variance in proxies for R_f from period to period. For instance, if 90-days Treasury Bills were chosen an proxy for R_f and the single period were longer than 90-days the rate on those bills would change from period to period. The change is variance, or risk: the rate of return on the reinvestments would be uncertain. *Second*, with variance comes potential covariance. If R_f and R_m covary, the beta for R_f would not equal zero, and the line connecting the R_f and R_m, the capital market line, would not be straight but would be convex (as measured by mean and variance). In either instance, the 90-day Treasury Bills were chosen as proxy for R_f and the single period were longer than 90 days, treasury bill would not be risk free. Another problem with using the Treasury bill as a proxy for the risk-free asset an asset's liquidity is critical to investors: highly liquid assets are particularly attractive to investors. Consequently, these assets would be available at a premium price (that is, their returns would somewhat lower than their prices would imply). The return expected from portfolios of above-average risk may be overestimated if the investor is not able to borrow at the risk-free rate.

The only capital instrument that would seem to fit all the theoretical criteria would be an instantaneous or microsecond Treasury bill. With that kind of security there is not variance and no covariance or default risk. The choice of a proxy for R_f represents an extreme position of pure Tobin liquidity theory, and because the CAPM is a single-period model, the choice implies that investors have virtually instantaneous horizons. If investors' horizons exceed an instant, then an instantaneous bill would have variance due to the constant reinvestment. While minimising default risk and the impacts of inflation, this security would nonetheless exacerbate reinvestment risk—unless economic conditions were perfectly stable.

It is obvious that the rate on any available asset will violate one or more of these theoretical requirements. But such a problem is frequent in implementing a theory. Often the best solution is to use the least flawed of the choices.

PRACTICAL PROBLEMS WITH USING THE TREASURY BILL RATE

1. Central Bank Intervention

The first problem in choosing the Treasury bill rate is that it is not a pure market rate. Rather, these rates are influenced, either directly through interest rate control, or indirectly by controlling the money supply, by the Central Bank in its pursiut of such things as employment, economic growth, and the international stability and value of the currency. Thus, the rates reflect more than the investors' required compensation for illiquidity and their expectations concerning inflation.

The action of the Central Bank certainly affect bond (and equity) prices and thus their yields. However, the effect of rising Treasury rates is to force down equity and bond prices. But are equity and bond prices reduced by the same magnitude? The joint movement of equity and bond prices indicates a covariance between Treasury securities and the equity and bond markets. Because R_f and R_m are theoretically independent, this covariance is not good news for this proxy.

2. Short-Term Rate Volatility

A second practical problem with using a Treasury security is that short-term Treasury securities show significant variability over time. When the rates of return are calculated over longer periods of time, the variability between periods is quite dramatic. Furthermore, for Treasury securities of different maturuties the shift can be quite dramatic in a short time. This variability could come from either of the two components of the risk-free rate: the nominal rate of return or the return to compensate for expected inflation.

The basis component of the risk-free rate is the investor's real return to compensate for illiquidity, although there is some disagreement among academics about the factor or factors that determine the real rate of return. Whether it depends on the balance between the forces of supply and demand for capital, perhaps due to the relative savings rate of a society as it matures (more capital is available for savings in societies with more mature populations), or the rate of growth in the economy, the very high interest rates raise considerable controversy over the true, real rate of return.

Finally, there is another phenomenon that must concern the practitioner. As the horizon lengthens, short-term risks tend to cancel out. Longer cycles, with lower volatility, becomes important.

The volatility of Treasury bill rates underlies a broader problem for the CAPM practitioner. That problem is that small changes in R_f translate directly into changes in the cost-of-equity estimate. If we use a very volatile proxy, the estimated cost of equity may vary substantially over relatively short periods of time. Equity rates are unstable, but are they that volatile? Are they that closely tied to the Treasury bill rate?

3. The Treasury Rate and the Minimum Rate of Return

Although Treasury bill rates are volatile, they may still provide an adequate proxy for risk-free rate if they are found to be comparable with the minimum rates of return required in the past. Are Treasury rates comparable with ex-post minimum rates of return?

In theory, the appropriate rate of discount for an investment would include a risk-free rate plus some risk premium. Because Treasury bills are usually considered to be the closest available approximation to a risk-free investment, the discount rate on Treasury bills is often used as the risk-free rate. This creates some very serious problems, however, because the rate of Treasury bills, like that on most short-term marketable instruments, is quite volatile. One way to approach the problem of dealing with the risk premium factor is to use the long-term interest rate instead of the risk-free rate. The long-term interest rate for investment grade bonds should still be less than the discount rate on equity because the latter are riskier.

The longer-term rates (such as the rate for a high-grade intermediate-term corporate bond) fit in tests of history better than Treasury bill rates. Although these rates are not as volatile as Treasury bills, using such a rate begs the issue: the longer-term rate is still just an approximation and is not based on theory.

There are more questions that the analyst must answer. It is not simply a choice between alternative instruments—Treasury bills versus bonds, some other debt instrument, or a zero-beta portfolio. The analyst must also decide whether to use compound (geometric) or simple (arithmetic) rates of return.

It is argued that the CAPM being a single-period model, the simple (arithmetic) method is appropriate. But the simple method ignores the capital market custom of quoting bond yields or growth rates as geometric averages. The geometric average produces a lower stimulated market return. There is no clear answer to get an estimate for the risk-free rate. What we do have are some warnings abut easy acceptance of conventional wisdom. Anyone using the CAPM must choose the R_f proxy with great care. The most widely used proxies, 30 or 90-day Treasury bill rates, are empirically inadequate and theoretically suspect. A mechanic who simply takes the current 90-day Treasury bill rate as the R_f choice ignores the facts: no single, defensible choice for R_f exists. Moreover, the substitution of the intercept from a historical period is fraught with the problems that history consistently presents: *which period is the one that will be most like the future?*

ESTIMATING THE MARKET RETURN

Many practitioners estimate future market returns in much the same way that they estimate beta. History is assumed to be relatively stable, and the future is not expected to be very different from the past. Consequently, these practitioners assume that the past is an adequate mirror of the investor's expected market premium. The inherent problems of using history to calculate beta and to make forecasts, the same problems arise in the use of history to estimate the market return. Following four of the questions an analyst must answer in the process of estimating the market's rate of return: 1. How should the return be calculated? 2. If an index is used, should it be value-or equal-weighted? 3. Over what period should the return be calculated? 4. What proxy should be used for the market?

1. Calculating the Market Return: Simple or Compound Returns

Two techniques are used for calculating returns: simple (arithmetic) averages or compound (geometric) averages. Obviously there is a difference between simple and compound rates of return. Which should we use in looking at past performance? The truth is, each is appropriate under particular circumstances. The geometric mean measures changes in wealth over more than one period on a buy and hold (with dividends reinvested) strategy. If the average investor rebalanced his portfolio every period, the geometric mean would not be a correct representation of his portfolio's performance over time. The arithmetic mean would provide a better measure of typical performance over a single historical period. But this does not help us in deciding what to use in forecasting the market return.

2. Calculating The Market Return: Value Or Equally Weighted Returns

There are two schools of thought on over whether to use a value-weighted index, where each return in the index is weighted by the market value of the stock, or an equally weighted index, where the returns are simply averaged. The proponents of equally weighted index noted a higher return over each of holding periods due to the heavier weighting of smaller companies' stocks in the use of equally weighted index. The value-weighted index is a reflection of what occurred in the markets and of investors' experience. Equally weighted indexex, make no more sense than that of an index constructed of their names."

3. Time Period

In implementing the CAPM, many contend that investors view the market return as a long-term concept. This suggests that investors' opinions about individual assets may change, but that the expected market returns show long-term stability. However, certain periods of history have a greater impact on individuals than do other periods. For example, the Black Monday and the recent global financial crisis had a profound and prolonged effect on the behaviour of individuals as well as business firms.

Hence, while choosing a period, the major consideration may be not only the level of the rates but their variability. The choice of time period must satisfy by two criteria: *First,* the period should include sufficient number of months to allow the construction of meaningful frequency distributions, and *second,* the choice must take into account the earlier finding that the the variability of returns is higher in the periods concerned (past) than in the subsequent periods.

4. Market Proxy

There are number of indexes which can be used as a proxy for the market. However, there are problems with each index, because all indexes are just fragments of the real market for all risky assets. It is difficult, and probably impossible, to know whether an index is an adequate proxy for the unknown world. Furthermore, since each index is composed of different kinds of stocks, the result can be, and should be, quite different.

In addition to this problem, any single index may not represent the circumstances of individual investors, e.g., liquidity preference. Moreover, once an index is chosen, the other problems arise. Should it be value- or equal-weighted? The index, and the means by which it is calculated, affect the beta and the historical return. Still, to use the CAPM, a market proxy is to be used.

An alternative to using an index is to apply the method used for offsetting beta instability. To use this technique to estimate the risk premium, all securities available are broken into beta-grouped portfolios—the highest betas in portfolio and the lowest betas in portfolio. All securities are regrouped each year into beta-ranked (high to low) portfolios. The betas are calculated using the preceding five years' data. The return for each beta-ranked portfolio is then calculated for each time period. The portfolio returns for all portfolios are then regressed against the returns of the market using the market model. From this regression, two pieces of useful information can be obtained: the risk premium (the increment in return for each increment of risk) and the intercept (the return on any asset when the market return in zero). The intercept, or alpha, can also be interpreted as the return on the risk-free (zero-beta) portfolio. The zero-beta return and risk premium are those for the particular universe being evaluated.

THE USUAL RISK-PREMIUM ESTIMATE

To calculate the market premium, the risk-free rate is subtracted from the market's total rate of return. This method is often called *calculating the spread* and was used long before the CAPM was developed. In fact, in many public utility rate cases, experts present testimony regarding the cost of equity based on the spread between the return (realised yield) on the firm's bonds and its stock. To use this approach, we assume that the spread is assumed to be relatively constant. If the spread is erratic, it will not provide a good proxy for expected spread-for the risk premium.

Typically, the CAPM is implemented by using a long period of history to estimate the market return, and a short spot Treasury rate (such as that on 90-day bills) is used as a proxy for R_f. These choices assume the following conditions.

1. *That a long period of history is the best proxy for investors' expectations of future market returns.* In addition, current market conditions and trends are assumed to be not relevant. Although it is true that investors consider present and past market history in determining what the future will hold, how the investor (or analyst) adapts history for current market circumstances and uses it to make future market forecasts is a matter of his or her own judgment.

2. *That the risk premium required by investors at any point in time depends almost exclusively on changes in R_f.* Because R_m is usually estimated from a large amount of data over a long period of time, changes in the level of this rate occur only slowly—especially when compared with changes in spot Treasury bill rates. The difference between the two, the derived risk premium, thus depends primarily on R_f. In times of very high short-term Treasury rates, the premium for risk would be small, but the cost of equity would be high.

3. *That there is a single risk premium—a single expected capital market line.* In almost every application, a single risk premium or narrow risk-premium band is developed, even though there are factors that suggest that multiple capital market line may exist.

TESTS OF THE CAPM

The assumptions underlying the capital asset pricing model are restrictive. They abstract from reality in ways that are untrue. Investors do pay taxes and at different rates; there are transaction costs; there is inflation; and borrowing and lending at the risk-free rate are unlikely. Hence, the world is quite different from that postulated by the CAPM.

The CAPM's form is simple. It is vulnerable to two potential sources of error. The first potential problem is that the form of the model may simply be wrong. Instead of being linear, the actual risk-return relationship could be nonlinear (for example, the "true" market line could be J-shaped). A model that is wrong is termed *misspecified*. The second potential problem is austerity; the model may not include all the relevant factors. If a certain factor (or factors) does influence the way the investors determine the price of an asset, and if this factor (or factors) is not included in the simple CAPM, the model would be termed *inadequate* to describe the real behaviour of investors.

If the model is either misspecified or inadequate, it would be difficult to use. An example of the real and practical result of misspecification is shown in Figure 10. The line R_fX is the theoretical capital market line. The intercept is at Rf, just as the theory says it should be, and the slope indicates the incremental return for each additional unit of risk. The line R_zY indicates the sort of market line postulated by some of the adaptations: the intercept is above Rf and the slope is less steep.

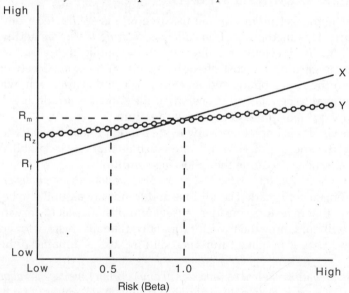

FIGURE 10: THEORETICAL MARKET LINE

Now, looking at the two lines in Figure-10, let us put ourselves in the position of setting rates for a public utility. In determining the allowed rate of return, generally the attempt is to set the rates charged from customers at a level that will cover all the costs of providing the electricity, gas, or telephone service—including the costs of capital. This requires an estimate of the firm's cost of equity. Because utilities typically have betas of less than 1.0, the effect of a misspecified market line is to underestimate the cost of equity. (Of course, for stocks with betas exceeding the market's, the effect is the opposite— an overestimation.) For the utility in question, the allowed rate of return would be lower than the true cost of equity for the firm, that is, the rates the company would be allowed to charge would be lower than those needed to cover its costs.

The same sort of problem can have other impacts. For instance, if a portfolio manager of a company estimating the cost of capital (the hurdle rate) for an investment (even an acquisition), if the investment has a beta less than 1.0, a misspecified market line would underestimate the return it should provide to be acceptable. For an investment with a beta greater than 1.0, the rate chosen would exceed that which should have been used. The effect of these errors is to penalise riskier projects unnecessarily, and to make low-risk projects seem overly attractive.

Let us look at the effect of misspecification from another viewpoint. If a portfolio manager in an investment management organisation is attempting to keep or lure clients over the long term, where should he position his portfolio regarding risk? What if he knows that theory incorrectly draws the capital market line, as shown in Exhibit 1? If the clients will eventually be evaluating his performance against this incorrect, theoretical capital market line, would he choose to position his portfolio with a low beta or a high beta? If his portfolio were low risk, the simple CAPM would forecast a return lower than that forecast by the respecified model. If the return was exactly like the return forecast by the respecified model, on the line $R_z Y$, he would appear to have outperformed the average. This superior performance is not a sleight of hand but simply the result of comparing actual results with a forecast made from the wrong model. Conversely, the risk-taking portfolio manager would consistently look bad when evaluated against the respecified CAPM's capital market line.

There are other possible market lines, curves, slopes, and intercepts. Figure-10 merely demonstrates the practical problems that can result from a model that is wrong. An erroneous model can lead investors, and those evaluating performance, to wrong conclusions and wrong decisions.

SOME APPLICATIONS AND IMPLICATIONS OF THE CAPITAL ASSET PRICING MODEL

Since its development, the uses of the capital asset pricing model (CAPM) have extended into all areas of corporate finance and investments. The CAPM can be applied to two aspects of the capital-budgeting problem: (1) determining the cost of capital and (2) assessing the riskiness of a project under consideration. The CAPM can also be useful in a real-estate problem, deciding to lease or buy.

The use of the CAPM can be extended into valuation of the entire firm. Because of its impact upon firm valuation, the CAPM has been of great use in the merger-analysis area of financial analysis. The CAPM has also been used to test various financial theories. By including a dividend term and considering its effects, the CAPM can be used to test the effects of the firm's dividend policy. An area that has received a great deal of attention is the use of the CAPM in testing the efficient-market hypothesis.

An application of the CAPM to the capital-budgeting process concerns the valuation of risky projects. If accurate estimates can be made about the systematic risk of a project, then the CAPM can be used to determine the return necessary to compensate the firm for the project's risk. If the sum of the estimated cash flows discounted by the CAPM-calculated required rate of return is positive, then the firm should undertake the project.

CAPM can be used to value securities and to calculate their risk-adjusted equilibrium price. CAPM may be rewritten:

$$E(R_i) = \frac{P_1 - P_0}{P_0}$$

where:

R_i = the expected returns for the ith firms;
P_1 = the price of stock in time 1; and
P_0 = the price of stock in the previous period.

Thus, the CAPM is redefined:

$$\frac{E(P_1) - P_0}{P_0} = R_{f,t} + [E(R_m) - R_f]\frac{\sigma_{im}}{\sigma_m^2}$$

or, rearranging Equation:

$$P_0 = \frac{E(P_1)}{1 + R_f + [E(R_m) - R_f]\frac{\sigma_{im}}{\sigma_m^2}}$$

Thus the rate of return used to discount the expected end-of-period price contains a risk premium dependent upon the security's systematic risk.

CAPM has also been applied in the analysis of mergers. As the risks of a portfolio can be substantially reduced with the inclusion of securities that are not perfectly correlated in terms of returns, this principle also applies with respect to the mergers between firms. The merging of two firms with different product lines, called a *conglomerate merger*, creates diversification, considered of great benefit. Suppose that one firm sells a product that is recession resistant; then a decrease in earnings of one division of the conglomerate will be offset by the steady earnings of another division. The overall result will be a relatively stable income stream despite shifting trends in the economy.

Managers often use the corporate cost of capital (usually a weighted average of the marginal costs of debt and equity) as the required rate of return for new corporate capital investments. To develop this overall cost of capital, the manager must have an estimate of the cost of equity capital. To calculate a cost of equity, some managers estimate the firm's beta (often from historical data) and use the CAPM to determine the firm's required return on equity.

Using the CAPM to estimate the cost of equity for the firm is relatively common. Because other equity cost methods require the use of a market determined equity price and estimates of future growth rates and dividends for the firm, the CAPM is of special interest to managers whose firms are closely held, pay no dividends, or have uncertain future rates of growth.

Some managers are not satisfied with a single corporate hurdle rate as the required rate of return. For firms that have diverse business with different risks, a single rate is believed inadequate to represent a fair return for each business segment As a result, some managers have developed multiple hurdle rate — one for each business unit or line of business. The CAPM has been adapted to determine directly these multiple rates.

To do this, some managers first choose a group of similar but publicly traded firms as proxies for the untraded business unit or division. The average of the betas for these proxy firms is used as the divisional beta. The divisional required rate of return is then determined in the same manner as the corporate equity cost. Other managers simulate the returns for the division, using several macro economic scenarios. The beta is a measure of the sensitivity of the returns to changes in the macro economic factors

In addition to calculating hurdle rates for use in evaluating capital investments, including acquisitions, the corporate strategic planner has become aware of the benefits that can be derived by introducing a more consistent and systematic method of risk analysis into the strategic planning process. At least conceptually, the distinction between systematic and unsystematic, macro-economic and micro-economic, risk is very useful as a basis for developing this systematic approach to risk analysis in corporate strategic planning.

The same sort of analysis can be used to evaluate past performance and to determine whether the business unit earned its cost of capital created value or not. The concept of the marginal cost of capital captures the risk position of the firm in its entirety. However, when used as a hurdle rate in the selection of capital projects, it does not reflect the risk of the particular project or projects under consideration. One potential difficulty encountered with the application of conventional methods for risk adjustment is increasing, or racheting upward, the firm's cost of capital. This could come about by accepting projects having risk postures in excess of the firm's risk complexion and thereby increasing the firms risk posture. If this were to happen, the firms marginal cost of capital would increase to reflect the firms new risk structure. If, however, the conventional methods are correctly applied, the firm will also accept projects having a lower risk complexion than the firm overall, and the racheting effect should not take place. Put another way, the average cost of capital represents a strategic rate that management strives to earn on the totality of the operation; management accepts some projects with higher and others with lower risk-return levels, but the average risk-return posture approximates that embodied in the marginal cost of capital.

The capital asset pricing model (CAPM) can also be used to calculate a market-based hurdle rate, risk-adjusted to the project under evaluation. The methodology relates a projects expected returns to an index representing a broad-based measure of economic activity. To illustrate the application of CAPM in project appraisal, the following Exhibit-1 present in a project's expected return, $E(R_j)$, and the expected return on the index, $E(R_m)$, which are computed based upon different states of the economy and their respective probability of occurrence.

In Table A of Exhibit-1, the returns from the index, R_m, and four projects (a, b, c, and d) are shown for four possible states of the economy. The probability of each state of the economy is denoted by P_s. All of the forecasted returns (R_m, R_a, R_b, R_c, and R_d) and probabilities in Table A represent estimates for single periods for each of the projects and the market index. Estimates may be the result of projections from historical data or simulation. The data in Exhibit-A are the results of economic forecasts.

EXHIBIT-1

EXHIBIT-A
Project Evaluation Using CAPM

State of the Economy	P_s	R_m	R_a	R_b	R_c	R_d
Revival (S_1)	0.20	20%	15%	40%	15%	10%
Prosperity (S_2)	0.50	30%	20%	30%	40%	15%
Recession (S_3)	0.20	6%	13%	00%	00%	-6%
Depression (S_4)	0.10	0%	3%	-30%	00%	-3%
	1.00					

EXHIBIT-B

State of the Economy	P_s	R_m	$P_s \times R_m$	$[R_m - E(R_m)]$	$[R_m - E[R_m]]^2$	$[R_m - E(R_m)]^2 P_s$
S_1	0.20	0.20	0.040	-0.002	0.000004	0.0000008
S_2	0.50	0.30	0.150	$+0.098$	0.009604	0.004802
S_3	0.20	0.06	0.012	-0.142	0.020164	0.0040328
S_4	0.10	0.00	0.000	-0.202	0.040804	0.0040804
		$E(R_m)$ = 0.202			σ_m^2 = 0.0129160	
					σ_m = 0.1136485	

EXHIBIT-C

State of the Economy	P_s	R_a	$P_s \times R_a$	$\dfrac{d_a}{R_a - E(R_a)}$	$\dfrac{d_m}{R_m - E(R_m)}$	$d_a\, d_m$	$d_a\, d_m P_s$
S_1	0.20	0.15	0.030	-0.009	-0.002	$+0.000018$	$+0.0000036$
S_2	0.50	0.20	0.100	$+0.041$	$+0.098$	$+0.004018$	$+0.0020090$
S_3	0.20	0.13	0.026	-0.029	-0.142	$+0.004118$	$+0.0008236$
S_4	0.10	0.03	0.003	-0.129	-0.202	$+0.026058$	$+0.0026058$
		$E(R_a)$ = 0.159				Cov (R_a, R_m) = $+0.0005442$	

$$\beta_a = \frac{\text{Cov}(R_a, R_m)}{\sigma_m^2} = \frac{-0.005442}{0.012916} = 0.421$$

EXHIBIT-D

$E(R_a)$ = 0.159	Cov (R_a, R_m) = $+0.005442$	β_a = 0.421
$E(R_b)$ = 0.20	Cov (R_b, R_m) = $+0.02062$	β_b = 1.596
$E(R_c)$ = 0.23	Cov (R_c, R_m) = $+0.019543$	β_c = 1.513
$E(R_d)$ = 0.08	Cov (R_d, R_m) = $+0.00962$	β_d = 0.745

Exhibit-B is a summary of the calculations needed to obtain the expected return, variance, and standard deviation for the market index. Note that the estimated returns for the market index, R_m, are expressed in decimal form in Exhibit-D rather than as percentages as in Exhibit-A. The results show that the expected return on the market index is 20.2%, with a standard deviation of 11.36%.

Exhibit-C derives the necessary inputs to determine the required return from investment a, consistent with its risk characteristics. The results for all four projects are shown in Exhibit-D. The required return as determined using equation is compared with the project's expected return. The project's expected return is the weighted average of the estimated returns of each of the possible states of the economy. If the expected return equals or exceeds the required return, the project is accepted; otherwise, it is rejected.

Based on he inputs of Exhibit-D, it is possible to compute the required return for each project, R_j. In our computation we will assume that the risk-free rate of return, R_f is 8%:

		R_j	$E(R_j)$
$R_a =$	$0.08 + (0.202 -0.08)0.421$	$= 13.14\%$	15.0%
$R_b =$	$0.08 + (0.202 -0.08)1.596$	$= 27.47\%$	20%
$R_c =$	$0.08 + (0.202 -0.08)1.513$	$= 26.46\%$	23%
$R_d =$	$0.08 + (0.202 -0.08)0.745$	$= 17.09\%$	8%

Using the CAPM approach, only project A would be accepted, since its expected return exceeds its required return.

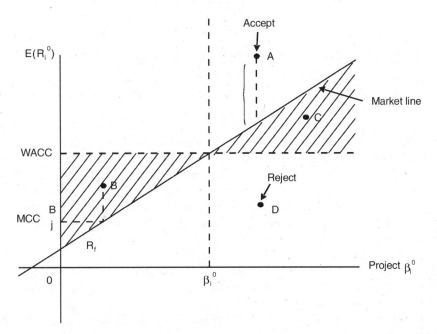

FIGURE 11: PROJECT SELECTION USING CAPITAL ASSET PRICING

Figure-11 shows where each project falls relative to the market price of risk line [i.e., the security market line (SML)]. Only project A falls below the SML, indicating that it offers a rate of return sufficient to compensate for its risk. The other three projects fall above the SML, since their returns are not sufficient to cover the market-related risk.

Several aspect of the capital asset pricing approach illustrated above warrant attention.

1. The possible states of the economy over the life span of the projects must be forecasted. It should be noted that intermediate and long-term forecasting as commonly practiced by business firms have larger variances than do short-term projections.

2. The probabilities related to different states of the economy can be derived from historical data on cyclical behaviour and/or by simulation.

3. Based upon these variables, the forecaster can project returns on the broad-based market index. It will suffice that the market index consists of assets comparable or meaningfully related to the projects. Alternatively, the analysis could have employed historical data on the relationship between similar projects and the market index to calculate Beta.

4. The forecasted returns of the index and the projects are correlated to derive the Beta on each project. Managers seek projects such as project A, with returns in excess of

the levels required by the risk-return market relation illustrated in Figure-11. When such projects are added to the firm's portfolio, the expected returns on the firm's equity (at its previous existing price) will be higher than those required by the market line.

5. In practical implementation, the success of the method hinges on the stability of Beta. Empirical evidence here points to instability when a few time periods are utilised in the calculation, but the variance in Beta tends to decrease as the number of time periods increases.

6. CAPM provides an alternative approach for estimating the firm's cost of equity capital. If we know the Beta of the firm, then the cost of equity capital can be defined as:

$$K_e = R_f + \beta_j \ [E(R_m - R_f]] \tag{9}$$

The above equation may be used to determine the firm's cost of equity capital in place of the dividend valuation model.

7. The project's acceptance or rejection is a function of the investment's own systematic risk. Thus, since the contribution of the project to the firm's variance of equity rate does not affect the accept or reject decision given by the security market line, diversification can be ignored in capital budgeting decisions. Each project is evaluated on its own merits without reference to the firm's existing investments.

The CAPM can also be used by the regulations of public utilities. Utilities rates can be set so that all costs, including costs of debt and equity capital, are covered by rates charged to consumers. In determining the cost of equity for the public utility, the CAPM can be used to estimate directly the cost of equity for the utility in question. The procedure is like that followed for any other firm: the beta and risk-free and market rates of return are estimated, and the CAPM is used to determine a cost of equity.

Beta, independent of the CAPM, can also be used in utility regulation as a measure of risk. The beta for a given utility is used to choose a group of comparable firms (firms with similar betas). These proxy firms are usually in non-regulated businesses. The historical return or equity for this group of firms is then used as a forecast of the required equity return for the given utility.

Investment practitioners have been more enthusiastic and creative in adapting the CAPM for their uses. The CAPM has been used to select securities, construct portfolios, and evaluate portfolio or equity share performance. Securities for which super-normal returns are forecast are considered under-valued, that is, attractive candidates for purchase. Overvalued securities are those with below-normal anticipated returns and are thus candidates for sale. The degree of over-valuation or under-valuation is determined by the security's alpha, or the distance that the risk-return plot for the security lies from the market line. Securities with positive alphas are attractive while negative alpha securities were considered (over-valued). Attractive (under-valued) securities are those whose risk-return characteristics are plotted above the security market line. Fair priced securities lie directly on the line. The degree of under- valuation or over-valuation (the alpha) is simply the distance from the security's plot to the line, represents the analysts forecast of the security's relative attractiveness. In prospect, all forecasts should fall on the market line because beta and expected return are directly and linearly related (theoretically). In practice forecasts do not fall on the market line, and practitioners believe that this process can be used effectively to select securities. In addition to selecting securities, beta has been used to control the risk level of a portfolio. Although the desired level of risk will depend upon each investor's preference, many portfolio optimisation models use a linear-programming approach with a particular beta as the risk-level constraint In using a linear-programming technique, some variable returns, for instance is maximised while another factor or factors (risk, for instance) is controlled. Although this is a simplistic description of the more complex portfolio optimisation methods, it does convey the essence of how beta is used in managing the level of portfolio risk.

Using historical returns and beta, we can evaluate the performance of the portfolio or asset. Portfolios with negative risk-adjusted returns (negative alphas) are said to have under-performed, and those with positive risk-adjusted returns (positive alphas) are said to have shown superior performance. Before using risk-adjusted returns to evaluate performance, the magnitude of returns was most important. We now know that all assets with equivalent returns are equal only if they are equally risky. The beauty of using risk-adjusted performance is that more reasonable information is available.

More sophisticated performance analysis systems take into account restrictions that are placed on portfolios. For instance, if a portfolio manager is restricted to investing in growth securities, the portfolio results are compared to the results from other growth security portfolios. To do otherwise would be to give an unfair advantage or penalty to those who are kept from investing in the broadest possible universe.

The relationship between the expected return of a security and its contribution to a particular characteristic depends on the attitudes of investors to the characteristics. If, on the average, a characteristic is liked by investors, then those securities that contribute more to that characteristic will, other things being equal, offer lower expected returns. Conversely, if a characteristic (such as beta) is disliked by investors, then those securities that contribute more to that characteristic will offer higher expected returns.

In a capital market with may relevant characteristics, to tailor a portfolio for a specific investor is more complicated because only an investor with average attitudes and circumstances should hold the market portfolio. In general, if an investor like a characteristic more than the average investor, he or she should generally hold a portfolio with relatively more of mat characteristic than is provided by holding the market portfolio and vice versa.

The right combination of "tilt" away from market proportions will depend on the extent of the differences between the investor's attitudes and those of the average investor and on the added risk involved in such a strategy. A complex capital market requires all the tools of modem portfolio theory for managing the money of any investor who is significantly different from the "average investor".

The assumption of homogeneous expectation may be replaced with an assumption of heterogeneous expectations if we are to examine the implications of different perceptions about expected return and risk of different investors. In such a case investor will face a unique efficient set. This means that the tangency portfolio is unique for each investor since the optimal combination of risky assets for an investor depends on that investor's perceptions about expected returns and risks. An investor may likely determine that his or her tangency portfolio does not involve an investment in some securities. Nevertheless, the SML will still exist since in aggregate of holdings of all investors each security's price has to be at equilibrium. From the point of an average, or representative, investor, each security is priced fairly, so its expected return (as perceived by investor) will be linearly and positively related to its beta.

Further, the original CAPM assumes that investors are concerned only with risk and return. However, other characteristics may also be important to investors. For example, liquidity may be important Here, liquidity refers to the cost of selling or buying a security "in a hurry". Liquidity may be measured by the size of the spread between the bid and the asked price. Smaller spreads suggesting greater liquidity and vice versa. Though, generally, non liquid securities are more attractive, keeping everything else as constant. However, investors differ in their attitudes towards liquidity. Hence, liquidity is a relative concept. Under these circumstances, security prices would adjust until, overall, investors would be content to hold the outstanding securities.

The expected return of a security would be based on two characteristics of the security:

  (i) The marginal contribution of the security to the risk of an efficient portfolio, measured by beta (Price) of the security.
  (ii) The marginal contribution of the security to the liquidity of an efficient portfolio, measured by the liquidity (L,) of the security.

Investors would like large values of LI and prefer small value of price, ceteris paribus. It means that two securities with different liquidities but with the same beta would have different levels of expected return. Higher demand for more liquid securities would push then price and vice versa till the equilibrium. In equilibrium, the securities with the greater liquidity would have a relatively lower expected return. Similarly, two securities with the same liquidity but different betas would not have the same level of expected returns. Security with a lower beta would have a lower expected return. Figure-12 shows the equilibrium relationship expected among Ri, Price, and Li. The Figure-12 is three-dimensional because expected returns are related to two securities of

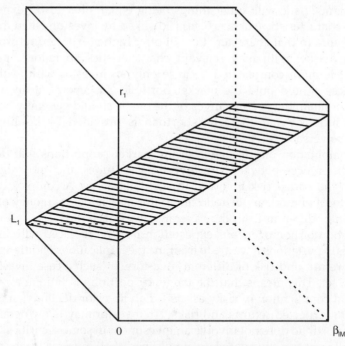

FIGURE 12: SECURITY MARKET PLANE

securities. Accordingly, it is sometimes referred to as a Security Market Plan. There are securities with various levels of Price and Li that provide the same level of R,. And for a given level of Price, more liquid securities have lower expected returns. As in the original CAPM, the more risky securities would have higher expected returns for a given level of L,.

A four-dimensional CAPM would be necessary if expected returns are based on beta, liquidity and a third characteristic to describe the corresponding equilibrium. Although a diagramme cannot be drawn for this type of extended CAPM, an equaktion can be written for it. Such an equation is termed as hyperplane. And, in equilibrium, all securities will plot on a Security Market Hyperplane, when each axis measures the contribution of a security to a characteristic of efficient portfolios that matter (on average) to investors.

Though the CAPM has been regarded as a useful tool for both analysts of financial securities and financial managers; it is not without its critics. It is perhaps worth pointing out at this stage that, although the CAPM has been seen by many as a reasonable approximation of reality, there are a number of problems that exist in adopting the theoretical model for practical use. This factor also causes problems when empirical tests of the model are undertaken. The first point to make is that the model is *ex ante*, i.e., it is based on expectations about the future. We cannot observe expectations but we do have access to actual returns. Hence empirical tests and data for practical use tend to be based almost exclusively on historical returns (*ex post* information). Another point to make is that in theory the CAPM market portfolio includes all risky investments world-wide, while in practice this is replaced by a surrogate which relating to a particular national stock market. The use of national surrogate can be questioned as the movement of investment fund increases in the current deregulated international markets.

The latter point is central to a powerful criticism of the CAPM advanced by Richard Roll who argued that tests performed with any portfolio other than the true market portfolio were not tests of the CAPM but merely tests of whether proxy market portfolio was efficient or not. Hence, the CAPM cannot be tested unless the exact composition of the market is known and used in the tests.

Work on deriving alternatives to the CAPM is underway. The arbitrage pricing theory is an alternative that capture the appealing intuition of the CAPM while purporting, at least by some to be testable at the empirical level.

REVIEW PROBLEMS

1. If the risk-free return is 10% and the expected return on BSE index is 18% (and risk measurement by standard deviation is 5%), how would you construct an efficient portfolio to produce a 16% expected return and what would be its risk ?

Ans.:

An efficient portfolio consists of investing in the market portfolio and risk-free securities,

Thus, using :

$$(R_p) = w (R_m) + (1 - w)R_f$$
$$16\% = w \times 18\% + (1 - w) \ 10\%$$
$$16 = 18w + 10 - 10w$$
$$6 = 8w$$
$$6/8 = w$$
$$w = 75\%$$

Therefore, 75% of the fund should be placed in market portfolio and the balance 25% should be invested in risk-free securities. The resulting portfolio risk can be calculated from:

$$(R_p) = R_f + \frac{(R_m - R_f)}{\sigma_m} \sigma_p$$

$$16\% = 10\% + \frac{18\% - 10\%}{5\%} \sigma_p$$

$$16\% - 10\% = \frac{8\%}{\sigma_p}$$

$$6\% = \frac{8\%}{5\%} \sigma_p$$

$$\frac{30}{8} = \sigma_p$$

$$= 3.75$$

2. Given the information in question (1), and the fact that you have personal funds of Rs.1,00,000 to invest, how would you construct a portfolio giving an expected return of 20% and what would be its risk ?

Ans.:

$$20\% = w \times 18\% + (1 - w)\, 10\%$$
$$20\% = 18w + 10 - 10w$$
$$20 - 10 = 18w - 10w$$
$$10 = 8w$$
$$w = 1.25$$

Therefore borrow 25% of own personal funds at the risk-free interest rate of 10%. Borrow Rs.1,00,000 × 0.25 = Rs. 25,000. Invest your own funds (Rs.10,000) plus the borrowed funds (Rs.25,000) in the market portfolio. Risk of the portfolio would be:

$$20\% = 10\% + 18\% - \frac{10\%}{5\%} \sigma_p$$

$$20\% - 10\% = \frac{8\%}{5\%} \sigma_p$$

$$10\% = \frac{8\%}{5\%} \sigma_p$$

$$\sigma_p = 6.25\%$$

3. After a thorough analysis of both the aggregate stock market and the stock of XYZ Company, you develop the following opinion:

Economic Conditions	Likely Returns			Probability
	Aggregate Market	XYZ		
Good	16%	20%		0.4
Fair	12%	13%		0.4
Poor	3%	-5%		0.2

At present the risk-free rate is equal to 7%. Would an investment in XYZ be wise?

Ans.:

$$R_m = 0.4\,(16) + 0.4\,(12) + 0.2\,(3) = 11.8\%$$
$$R_{xyz} = 0.4\,(20) + 0.4\,(13) + 0.2\,(-5) = 12.2\%$$
$$\sigma_m^2 = 0.4(16-11.8)^2 + 0.4\,(12-11.8)^2 + 0.2\,(3-11.8)^2$$
$$= 22.56$$
$$\sigma_m = \sqrt{22.6}$$
$$= 4.75$$
$$\sigma_{xyz}^2 = 0.4\,(20-12.2)^2 + 0.4\,(13-12.2)^2 + 0.2\,(-5-12.2)^2$$
$$= 83.76$$
$$\sigma_{xyz} = \sqrt{83.76} = 9.15$$

Covariance between m and XYZ

$$0.4\,(16-11.8)(20-12.2) + 0.4\,(12-11.8)(13-12.2) + 0.2\,(3-11.8)(-5-12.2)$$
$$= 43.44$$

$$r_{XYZ} = \frac{43.44}{(4.75)(9.15)}$$
$$= 1.0$$

$$\beta_{XYZ} = \frac{9.15}{4.75}(1.0)$$
$$= 1.93$$

Fair return $= 7\% + 1.93\,(11.8 - 7)$
$$= 16.26\%$$

Since this is larger than the expected 12.2% return, don't buy.

4. Assume that the risk-free rate of interest is 8 per cent, the market has an estimated risk premium of 6 per cent, and the market's standard deviation of return is 10 per cent Calculate the variance (or SD) of return for each portfolio below :

Portfolio I: 30% risk-free fund, 70% the market
Portfolio 2: diversified portfolio with beta 1.5

Ans.:

Portfolio 1:
$$\sigma_1 = 0.7(10.0\%) = 7\%$$

Portfolio 2:
$$\sigma_2^2 = \beta_2^2\sigma_m^2 + 0.0$$
$$\sigma_2^2 = (1.5)^2\,(10)^2 + 0.0$$
$$\sigma_2 = 15\%$$

5. You expect the stock of Firm X to sell for ₹ 70 a year from now and to pay a ₹ 4.00 dividend. If the stock's correlation with portfolio M is -0.3, $\beta_x = 40.0\%$, $\sigma_m = 20.0\%$, $R_f = 5\%$, and Rp_m 50, what would the stock be selling for ? Explain

Ans.:

$$\beta_x = \frac{40}{20}(-0.3)$$
$$= -0.60$$

The expected return would be:

$E(R) = 5\% + (-0.60) (5\%) = 2\%$

The stock should be selling for:

$P_0 = (₹\ 70 + ₹ 4.00) / 1.02$
$= ₹\ 72.55$

6. Assume there are three major classes of risky securities available, as follows:

Security Class	Total Market	σ	Correlation with RE	E	D	Total
Real Estate (RE)	10,000	20%	1.0			0.65
Equity (E)	6,000	30%	0.3	1.0		0.60
Debt (D)	4,000	15%	0.3	0.3	1.0	0.30

(a) What is the market portfolio ? How much of its risky assets should the mutual fund invest in each security type ? What is a the of such a portfolio ?
(b) If riskfree rate is 8.0% and return on market portfolio is 5.0%, what are the CML and SML equations ?
(c) If investment portfolio should have a long-run expected return of 12%, how would this be obtained ?
(d) If a company beta is 12, what should the equity expected to earn to qualify for a purchase?
(e) The local representative of a mutual fund has been pressing the investor to invest solely in the fund. One reason which the representative offers is that the fund has a beta of 1.0 and thus its risk is the same as the market portfolio's risk. Comment.

Ans.:

(a) The optimal portfolio is:

Security	X
Real Estate Equity Debt	0.50
	0.30
	0.20

$\sigma p = [(0.5)^2 (20)^2 + (0.3)^2 (30)^2 + (0.2)^2 (15)^2 + 2(0.3) (0.5) (0.3) (20) (30)$
$+ 2(0.3)(0.5)(0.2)(20)(15) + 2(0.3)(0.3)(0.2)(30)(15)]^{1/2} =$
$= 16.7\%$

(b) CML equation :

$$E(R_p) = 8.0\% + \sigma_p \frac{5.0\%}{16.7\%}$$

SML equation :

$$ER_i = 8.0\% + \beta_i (5.0\%)$$

(c) For each σ_p of an efficient portfolio, a return of 0.3% is earned above the 8.0% risk-free rate. Thus, to have an expected return of 12.0%, σ_p must be (12 -8)/0.3, or 13.33% :

$8.0\% + 13.33\% (0.30) = 12.0\%$

Efficient portfolios would be combination of market portfolio and risk free securities. To get a σ_p = 13.33% when σ_{AM} = 16.7%, they should invest 80% of the portfolio in the market portfolio :

$$\frac{13.33}{16.7} = 0.80$$

The remaining 20% would be placed in risk-free securities.

(d) The equity is expected to earn
$$= 8.0\% + 1.2\ (5.0\%)$$
$$= 14.0\%\ [\text{the SML}]$$

(e) The mutual fund's beta may be 1.0, but this only says that the fund has non-diversifiable (systematic) risk identical to that of the market portfolio. However, unless the mutual fund's percentages of holdings are identical to the percentage weights of the market portfolio, the fund still has some diversifiable (unsystematic) risk and shall not be held as the investor's only investment.

7. Management of a mutual fund has considered three alternative strategies :

Plan	% investment in T-Bonds	Stocks	T-Bonds	Beta of Stocks	Portfolio
1	0.0	100	0	1.0	?
2	20	80	0	1.0	?
3	30	70	0	1.0	?

(a) Which is the most risky strategy ?

(b) If R_f =7% and the expected return under plan 1 is 14%, what is the market risk premium ?

(c) Management believes that this risk premium is too low and that the market will soon adjust it upward. Given this, which plan might management wish to persue?

(d) Would this be a speculative or an investment strategy ?

Ans.:

Plan	Beta
1	0.0(0.0) + 1.0(1.0) = 1.0
2	0.2(0.0) + 0.8(1.0) = 0.8
3	0.3(0.0) + 0.7(1.0) = 0.7

Plan 1 has the greatest market risk-beta.

8. Based on the risk and return relationships of the CAPM, supply values for the seven missing data in the following table:

Security	Expected Return	Beta	Standard Deviation	Non-market risk (σ^2_{ei})
A	— %	0.8	— %	85
B	19.0	1.5	—	.49
C	15.0	—	8	0
D	7.0	0	12	—
E	21.0	—	15	—

Ans.:

The relationships are necessary to identify the missing data in the table :

1) $\tilde{R} = R_f + \beta_i (R_m - R_f)$

2) $\sigma_i^2 = \beta_p^2 \, \sigma_m^2 + \sigma_{ei}^2$

Using these equations, then considering first security D :

$$7.0 = R_f + 0\,(\tilde{R}_m - R_f)$$

$$R_f = 7.0$$

Next consider security B :

$$19.0 = 7.0 + 1.5\,(\tilde{R}_m - 7.0)$$

$$19.0 - 7.0 + 10.5 = 1.5\tilde{R}_m$$

$$22.5 = 1.5\tilde{R}_m$$

$$\tilde{R}_m = 15.0\%$$

Next consider security C :

$$15.0 = 7.0 + \beta_C\,(15.0 - 7.0)$$

$$\beta_C = 1$$

Further:

$$(8)^2 = (1.0)2 \times \sigma_m^2 + 0$$

$$64 = 1\sigma_m^2$$

$$\sigma_m^2 = 64$$

$$\sigma_m = 8$$

Next consider security A :

$$\tilde{R}_A = 7.0 + 0.8(15-7.0)$$

$$\tilde{R}_A = 13.4\%$$

Further :

$$\sigma_A = [(.8)^2 \times (8)^2 + 85]^{1/2}$$

$$= [.64 \times 64 + 85]^{1/2} = 11.22\%$$

Finally, for security E :

$$21.0 = 7.0 + \beta_E\,(15.0 - 7.0)$$

$$\beta_E = 1.75$$

Further :

$$(15)^2 = (1.75)^2 \times (8)^2 + \sigma_{ei}^2$$

$$\sigma_{ei}^2 = 29.0$$

9. B.B. Puri is considering several investments. The risk-free rate of return is currently 6.75 percent, and the expected return for the market is 12 percent. What should be the required rates of return for each investment (using the CAPM)?

Security	A	B	C	D	E
Beta	1.20	0.80	1.50	0.60	1.25

Ans.:

Security	Risk-free Rate of Return (R_f)	Expected Market Return $[E\ (R_m)]$	Beta	Required Rate of Return
(1)	(2)	(3)	(4)	(5)
A	6.75%	12%	1.20	14.85%
B	6.75%	12%	0.80	10.95
C	6.75%	12%	1.50	16.63
D	6.75%	12%	0.60	6.90
E	6.75%	12%	1.00	12.00

10. Using the CAPM, estimate the appropriate required rate of return for the three stocks listed below, given that the risk- free rate is 6 per cent, and the expected rate of return for the market is 18 per cent.

Stock	Beta
A	1.40
B	0.90
C	0.75

Ans.:

Stock A: 6% +1.40 (18% – 6%) = 22.8%
Stock B: 6% + 0.90 (18% – 6%) = 16.8%
stock C: 6% + 0.75 (18% – 6%) = 15%

11. An investor is seeking an efficient portfolio with a correlation of 0.7 between the portfolio and the market and a standard deviation of 2.5%. The market standard deviation is 1.4% and the market rate of return is 16%, a rate that is double the return on risk-free securities. What is the required rate of return being sought by the investor?

Ans.:

Required rate of return:

$$= 0.8 + \left(\frac{0.7 \times 0.25}{0.014}\right)(0.16 - 0.08)$$

$$= 18.04\%$$

12. Y.P. Yadav is considering the purchase of a stock that has a beta coefficient of 0.75. He estimates the expected market return to be 0.12 while T-bills yield 0.08. What rate should the expect and require on this stock, according to the SML?

Ans.:

$$E(R) = 0.08 + 0.75\ (0.12 - 0.08)$$
$$= 0.11$$

13. Riskless securities are currently offering a return of 7.25 percent at a time when the expected market return on all securities is 14.75. The market standard deviation is 2.0%. An investor is seeking a portfolio with a correlation coefficient of 0.85 and a standard deviation of not more than 1.5%. What would be the required return on such a portfolio?

Ans.:

Required Return

$$= 0.0725 + \frac{(0.85)(0.015)}{0.02}(0.1475 - 0.0725)$$

$$= 0.0725 + \frac{(0.01275)}{0.02}0.0750$$

$$= 7.73\%$$

14. R.S. Singh owns a diversified portfolio securities, which he estimates to have a standard deviation of 0.37. The return on short-term T-bills is 0.09, and Singh estimates the expected market return to be 0.14 and the market standard deviation to be 0.28. What is the expected return on the Singh's portfolio according to CML?

Ans.:

$$E(R_p) = 0.09 + (0.14 - 0.09)\frac{0.37}{0.28}$$

$$= 0.09 + 0.066$$

$$= 0.156$$

15. The expected market return for the general market is 15.50 percent; and the risk premium is 7.50 percent ABC, XYZ, RDX have betas of 0.75, 0.87 and 1.20 respectively. What are the appropriate required rates of return for the three securities?

Ans.:

If the expected market return is 15.50 percent and the risk- premium is 7.50%, the riskless rate of return is 8.00% (15.50% − 7.50%). Therefore:

ABC = 8.00% + (15.50% − 7.50%) × 0.75 = 14.00%
XYZ = 8.00% + (15.50% − 7.50%) × 0.87 = 14.96%
RDX = 8.00% + (15.50% − 7.50%) × 1.20 = 17.60%

16. Anand Auto has a beta of 0.865. If the expected market return is 17.50 and the risk free rate of return is 8.50 percent, what is the appropriate required return of Anand Auto (using the CAPM)?

Ans.:

Required rate of return =[Risk-free rate of return + (Market Return − Risk-free rate of return) × Beta

= 8.50% + (17.5% − 8.50%) × 0.865
= 8.50% +9.0% × 0.865
= 8.50% + 7.785%
= 16.285%

17. An asset has been offered for sale to a real estate investment trust at a time when the expected market return is 15% and the riskless rate of return is 8%. The correlation coefficient between the asset and the market is 0.85 and the market standard deviation is 4 percent. The asset can be purchased today for ₹ 10 crore and could be sold next year for an estimated ₹ 10.75 crore. Meanwhile, during the year the asset should earn ₹ 16,00,000. The expected return on the asset overall will have a standard deviation of ₹ 91,000. What is the required return on this investment? What is the expected return? Is the investment efficient?

Ans.:

Expected return is:

(₹ 10.75 crore – ₹ 10 crore + ₹ 0.16 crore)/₹ 10 crore

= (₹ 0.91 crore)/₹ 10 crore = 0.091

Standard deviation:

= (₹ 91,000/₹ 91,00,000).091

= 0.01 × 0.091 = 0.00091

Expected Return Required

$$= 0.08 \frac{(0.85)(0.009)}{0.04} \quad (0.15\text{-}0.08)$$

=.8.134%

Expected return is 9.1%, required return is 8.134%. The investment is slightly not efficient.

18. Refer to the following data for computing betas for (i) Security X, (b) security Y, (iii) for an equally weighted portfolio of securities X and Y.

Security i	Correlation Coefficients i with market	Standard Deviation of i
X	0.5	0.25
Y	0.3	0.30

$E(R_m) = 0.12$, $R_f = 0.05$, $\sigma_m^2 = 0.01$

Ans.:

$$C_{xy} = r_{xy}\sigma_x\sigma_y$$

or $$r_{xy} = \frac{C_{xy}}{\sigma_x\sigma_y}$$

and $$\beta_{im} = \frac{\text{Cov}(R_i, R_m)}{\sigma_m^2}$$

(i) Cov.$(R_x, R_m) = (0.5)(0.25)(0.30) = 0.0375$

$$\beta_x = \frac{0.0375}{0.010} = 3.75$$

(ii) Cov.$(R_y, R_m) = (0.30)(0.30)(0.25) = .0225$

$$\beta_y = \frac{0.0225}{0.010} = 2.25$$

(iii) $\beta_p = (0.5(3.75) + 0.5(2.25) = 3.00$

19. Refer to the data given in problem-18 and compute the equilibrium expected return according to the CAPM for (0 Security X, (ii) Security Y, and (iii) for an equally weighted portfolio of securities X and Y.

Ans.:

(i) $E(R_X) = 0.05 \left[\dfrac{0.12 - 0.05}{(0.01)^{0.5}} (0.5) \right] 0.25 = 0.1375$

(ii) $E(R_Y) = 0.05 + \left[\dfrac{0.12 - 0.05}{(0.01)^{0.5}} (0.3) \right] 0.30 = 0.1130$

(iii) $E(R_p) = (0.5)(0.1375) + (0.5)(0.1130) = 0.1253$

20. The return on the market portfolio is 14 percent and the return on zero β portfolio is 8 percent. The market's standard deviation is 40 percent. Assume the CAPM with risk-free lending but no risk-free borrowing, complete the following table:

Stock	Expected Return Variance	Standard	Beta	Residual
	Deviation			
A	0.20	—	—	0.0475
B	0.26	—	—	0.0650

Ans.:

$\beta_A = \dfrac{0.20 - 0.80}{0.14 - 0.08}$

$= 2.0$

$\beta_B = 0..26 - 0.08$

$= 3.0$

With the security ps, we can now solve for the standard deviations:

$\sigma^2(R_A) = (2.0)^2 (0.40)2 + 0.0475$

$= 0.6875$

$\sigma(R_A) = 0.83$

$\sigma^2(R_B) = (3.0)^2 (0.40)^2 + 0.0650$

$= 1.3450$

$\sigma(R_B) = 1.16$

21. Based on your answer to problem 20 and Cov. $(R_A, R_B) = 0$, what is the expected return on portfolio and standard deviation of a portfolio with equal amounts in stocks A and B?

Ans.:

$E(R_p) = (.5)(.20) + .5(.26)$

$= .23$

$\beta_p = .5(2.0) + .5(3.0)$

$= 2.5$

$\sigma_p^2 = (2.5)^2(.40)^2 + (.5)^2(.0475) + (.5)^2(.0650)$

$= 1.00 + .011875 + .016250$

$= 1.028125$

$\sigma_p = (1.028125)^{.5}$

$= 1.014$

22. Anand Malik has ₹ 1,00,000 to invest. He is a fairly conservative person, so he sets a target β for his portfolio of 0.8. He then proceeds to analyse stocks and select them based on his analysis. After careful analysis, he arrives at a group of 18 stocks with mean β of 1.6. Determine how he can weight his portfolio to reach his risk target.

Ans.:

$$W_p = \frac{0.8}{1.6}$$
$$= 0.5$$

Malik should invest half his money, ₹ 50,000 in the portfolio of stocks. He should invest the other half in T-bills or some other appropriately low-risk security such as a money market fund.

23. Complete the blanks in the following table, assuming the elevant equilibrium model in the CAPM with unlimited borrowing and lending at the riskless rate of return.

Stocks	Expected Return	Standard Deviation	Beta	Residual Variance
A	0.18	—	1.5	0.12
B	0.15	0.50	0.75	0.05
C	—	—	0.60	0.14

Ans.:

From the information we have for securities A and B, we know the risk premium accorded the market portfolio must be:

$$(R_m - R_f) = \frac{(R_A) - (R_B)}{\beta_A - \beta_B} = \frac{0.18 - 0.15}{1.5 - 0.75}$$

$$= \frac{0.03}{0.75} = 0.04$$

Knowing thus, we can use the information we have for stock A to find the risk-free rate:

$$R_A = R_f + (R_m - R_f)\,\beta_A$$
$$R_f = R_A - (R_m - R_f)\,\beta_A$$
$$= 0.18 - (0.04)(1.5)$$
$$= 0.18 - 0.06$$
$$= 0.12$$

We can now find the expected return for stock C:

$$R_c = 0.12 + (0.04)(0.75)$$
$$= 0.15$$

The information given for stock B allows us to estimate the variance of returns to the market

$$\sigma_B^2 = \beta_B^2\,\sigma_m^2 + \sigma_{eB}^2$$

$$\sigma_m^2 = \frac{\sigma_B^2 - \sigma_{eB}^2}{\beta_B^2}$$

$$= (0.50)^2 - (0.05)$$
$$= 0.022$$

The standard deviation of securities A and C can now be found:

$$\sigma_A^2 = (1.5)^2 (0.04) + 0.12$$
$$= 0.21$$
$$\sigma_A = (0.21)^{0.5}$$
$$= 0.43$$
$$\sigma_C^2 = (0.60)^2 (0.04) + (0.14)$$
$$= 0.1544$$
$$\sigma_C = 0.393$$

The complete table should be:

Stock	Expected Return	Standard Deviation	Beta	Residual Variance
A	0.18	0.43	1.5	0.12
B	0.15	0.50	0.75	0.05
C	0.12	0.39	0.60	0.14

24. The management of Super Cement Company (SCC) has been examining the market behaviour of the firm's equity. The equity is generally favoured by the institutional investors. The price fluctuates within a relatively narrow range and appears to be closely linked to the firm's policy of steady dividend payments. This linkage has been weakening in recent years. Though since the mid-1990s, the contribution of dividends plus rises in market value produced average "Return on Asset" of 11 to 18 percent annually for equity shareholders, as shown in Exhibit-1. This return has now declined to below 9 per cent in the 2005-2009 period. This concerns management since it may mean that shareholders may sell their shares to seek better investments and thus depress the equity prices.

EXHIBIT-1

Return on Asset Achieved by SCC Equity Shareholders (2005-09)

Year	ROA*	Year	ROA	Year	ROA
1995	18.0%	2000	12.1%	2005	12.4%
1996	14.1	2001	11.8	2006	10.6
1997	11.0	2002	9.2	2007	-3.5
1998	12.9	2003	8.9	2008	11.6
1999	14.0	2004	14.0	2009	12.4
Average	14.0		13.0%		8.7%

* Measured by sum of dividends and equity share price increase divided by January 1st equity price

The degree of risk inherent in a stock clearly influences how investors perceive the stock's value. To have some basis for comparison, management hired ABC consultants to provide some statistical data on the equity. This is shown in Exhibit-2. Note that the firm's standard deviation of return, correlation coefficient, and β coefficient are given for three periods of five years each. Also, ABC Consultants created a market of 20 similar stocks and calculated a market standard deviation for this group.

EXHIBIT - 2

Statistical Data on SCC that can be used to Measure and Analyse Dispersion of Return and Market Correlations

	1995-1999	2000-2004	2005-2009
Standard Deviation of Return on Asset	8.9%	5.6%	6.8%
Correlation Coefficient, SCC to Market*	0.36	0.80	0.75
Beta Coefficient for SCC	0.60	0.70	0.75
Standard Deviation of Market	6.5%	7.5%	9.0%

* 20 selected securities comparable to SCC, selected by ABC Consultants

The SCC management is aware of the fact that the return to the shareholders involves two factors. The first is the firm's level of dividend payments, which reflects the fundamental operating and financial strength of the company. The second is market activity that causes rises or declines in the firm's stock aside for the company's basic business. ABC Consultants was asked to provide data on these two factors and ABC produced the items in Exhibit-3.

EXHIBIT - 3

Fundamental and Market Data, Actual and Forecast for SCC and Comparable securities

	1995-1999 (Actual)	2000-2004 (Actual)	2005-2009 (Actual)	2010-2014 (Forecast)
SCC Dividend Yield	102%	14.5%	15.0%	17.0%
Market Rate of Return	155%	12%	18.5%	20%
Return on Medium-Term Government Bond	8.5%	9.0%	9.5	10.0%

The management of SCC is concerned with the adequacy of a 17.0% dividend yield to holders of its equity. If 17.0% is less than the required return for equity shareholders, the equity price will drop in the 2010-2014 period. This is not desirable. What is the required return on the SCC for the 2010-2014 period.

Ans.:

Required Return:

During the most recent 5-year period, SCC has had a β co-efficient of 0.75. The forecast of riskless return is 10.0% (medium-term government bonds) and the market rate of return is forecast at 20.0%. Therefore, required rate of return is

$$=0.10+0.75(0.20 - 0.10)$$
$$=0.10+0.75(0.10)$$
$$= 17.50\%$$

Actual Return

The return on asset calculation shows a decline in the 2005-2009 period, as compared to earlier periods. At the same time, management is forecasting a 17% dividend yield in the 2010-2014 period. The dividend yield alone is dose to the return that is required for the next period.

Past Efficiency

Was SCC an efficient investment in prior period? The answer is yes for 1995-1999 and 2000-2004; no for 2005-2009.

	Expected Return Required	Expected Return Actual
1995-1999 : 0.085+0.60(0.155 – 0.085) =	12.70	14%
2000-2004 : 0.09+0.70(0.120 – 0.090) =	11.10%	13%
2005-2009 : 0.095+0.75(0.185 – 0.095)	15.25%	12.5%

With small rises in equity during each year in 2010-2014, SCC will offer an efficient return to investors. Therefore, it appears that the purchase of SCC equity is an efficient investment.

25. Meghna Tex, an all equity financed multinational, is contemplating an expansion into an overseas market. It is considering whether to invest directly in the countary concerned by building a greenfield—site factory. The expected pay-off from the project would depend on the future state of the economy of Zeroland, the host country, as shown below:

State of Zeroland economy	Probability (P)	IRR from projects (%)
S1	0.1	10
S2	0.2	20
S3	0.5	10
S4	0.2	10

Meghna's existing activities are expected to generate an overall return of 30% with a standard deviation of 14%. The correlation coefficient of Meghna's returns with that of the new projects -0.36, Meghna's returns have a correlation coefficient of 0.80 with the return of the market portfolio, while the new project has a correlation coefficient of -0.10 with the Indian market portfolio.

The beta coefficient for Meghna is 1.20.

The risk-free rate is 12%.

Required:

(a) Determine the expected rate of return and standard deviation of return from the new roject.

(b) If the new project requires the capital funding equl to 25% of the value of the existing assets of Meghna, determine the risk-return characteristics of Meghna after the investment.

(c) What effect will the adoption of the project have on the beta of Meghna? Ignore all taxes.

Ans.:

Expected Value of Return
= (0.6 × 10%) + (0.4 × 20%)
= 14%

Outcome (1)	Deviation (2)	Sq'd Dev. (3)	P (4)	Sq'd Dev..P 5) - (3) (4)
10%	–4	16	0.6	9.6
20%	6	36	.4	14.4
			Variance = Total =	24.0
			σ = 4.9	

(b)

Meghna

ER = 30%   σ = 14%   Proportion = 80%

Zeroland

ER = 14%   σ = 4.9%   Proportion = 20%

ER_{mg} (0.8 × 30%) + (0.2 × 14%) = 24% + 2.8% = 26.8%

$σmg$ = 10.89

(c)

The present beta = 1.20

$$\text{Beta of project} = \frac{Cov_{im}}{\sigma^2_{m}} = \frac{r_{im} \, \sigma_i \sigma_m}{\sigma^2_{m}} = \frac{r_{im} \, \sigma_i}{\sigma_{m}}$$

What is the risk of the market (σ_m)?

$$\text{Rearranging, } \sigma_m = \frac{\sigma_i \, r_{im}}{\beta_i}$$

For Meghana

$$σm = \frac{(14)\,(0.8)}{1.2} = 9.3$$

So,

Project beta

$$= \frac{(-0.1)(4.9)}{9.33} = \frac{-0.49}{9.33}$$

$$= -0.05$$

New beta for Meghna:

$$= (0.8 × 1.2) + (0.2 × -0.05)$$

$$= 0.95$$

Therefore, the new project lowers Meghna's beta.

26. Complete the blanks in the following, assuming the relevant equilibrium model to be CAPM with unlimited borrwoing and lending at the riskless rate of interest:

Security Return	Expected Direction	Standard Variance	Residual	β
1	.25	—	.10	2.5
2	—	.30	.06	0.50
3	.15	—	.17	1.00

Ans.:

Given the state

the risk premium from the market portfolio is:

$$\{E(R_m) - R_f\} = \frac{E(R_1) = E(R_3)}{\beta_1 - \beta_2} = \frac{.24 - .18}{2.5 - 1.0}$$

$$= 0.4$$

Knowing this, we can use the information we have for Security 1 to find the risk free rate

$$E(R_1) = R_f + \beta_1 \{E(R_m) - R_f\}$$
$$R_f = E(R_1) - \beta_1\{E(R_m) - R_f\}$$
$$= .25 - (2.5)(.04)$$
$$= .15$$

We can now find the expected return for Security 2

$$E(R_2) \quad = .15 + (.75)(.04)$$
$$= .12$$

The information five for Security 2 allows us to estimate the variance of returns to the market.

$$\sigma^2(R_2) = \beta^2_2 \, \sigma^2(R_m) + \sigma^2(\varepsilon_2)$$

$$\sigma^2(R_m) = \frac{\sigma^2(R_2) - \sigma^2(\varepsilon_2)}{\beta^2_2}$$

$$= \frac{(.30)^2 - (.06)}{(.50)^2}$$
$$= .12$$

The standard deviations of security 1 and 3 can now be found:

$$\sigma^2(R_1) = (2.5)^2(.12) + .10 = .85$$
$$\sigma(R_1) = .92$$
$$\sigma^2(R_2) = (1.0)^2(.12) + .17$$
$$\sigma^2(R_2) = .29$$
$$\sigma = .54$$

The complete table is:

Security Return	Expected Deviction	Standard Variance	Residual	β
1	.24	.92	.10	2.50
2	.12	.30	.06	0.50
3	.18	.29	.17	1.00

27. Complete the following table by assuming the return on the market portfolio is 15 per cent and the return on the zero beta portfolio is 10 per cent. Further also assume the market's standard deviation is 40 per cent and the CAPM with risk-free lending but no risk-free borrowing.

Security Return	Expected Deviation	Standard Variance	Residual	β
A	.12	—	.0525	—
B	.18	—	.0925	—

Ans.:
Using the equation for the security market line where selling the risk-free asset is not allowed, we can find the betas of the two securities:

$$E(R_i) = E(R_z) + \beta\{E(R_m) - E(R_z)\}$$

$$\beta_i = \frac{E(R_i) - E(R_z)}{E(R_m) - E(R_z)}$$

$$\beta_A = \frac{.12 - .10}{.15 - .10} = .4$$

$$\beta_B = \frac{.18 - .10}{.15 - .10} = 1.6$$

With the security betas, we can now get the standard deviations:

$$\sigma^2(R_A) = (.4)^2 (.40)^2 + .0525 = .0256 + .0525 = .0781$$
$$\sigma(R_A) = .28$$
$$\sigma^2(R_B) = (1.6)^2 (.40)^2 + .0925 = .4096 + .0925 = .5021$$
$$\sigma(R_B) = .709$$

28. Given the following data:

Security i	Correlation Coefficient i with M	Standard Deviation of i
ABC	.5.	.25
BCD	.3	.30

$$E(r_M) = .12$$
$$T = .05$$
$$\sigma^2(r_M) = .01.$$

(i) Compute betas for securities ABC and BCD, and for an equally weighted portfolio of stocks A and B.

(ii) Compute the equilibrium expected return according to the CAPM for securities ABC and BCD, and the equally weighted portfolio of securities ABC and BCD.

Ans.:

(i) a. $Cov(r_{ABC}, r_M) = (.5)(.25)(.01)^{.5} = .0125$

$$\beta_{ABC} = \frac{.0125}{.0100} = 1.25$$

b. $Cov(r_{BCD}, r_M) = (.30)(.30)(.01)^{.5} = .009$

$$\beta_{BCD} = \frac{.009}{.010} = .90$$

c. $B_P = (.5)(1.25) + (.5)(.90) = 1.075$

(ii) a. $E(r_1) = .05 + \left[\dfrac{(.12 - .05)}{(.01)^{.5}}(.5)\right].25 = .1375$

b. $E(r_1) = .05 + \left[\dfrac{(.12 - .05)}{(.01)^{.5}}(.3)\right].30 = 1130$

c. $E(r_P) = (.5)(.1375) + (.5)(.1130) = .1253$

29. You are evaluating an investment in two companies whose past ten years of returns are shown below:

Companies	Per cent Return During Year									
	1	2	3	4	5	6	7	8	9	10
FST	37	24	-7	6	18	32	-5	21	18	6
SND	32	29	-12	1	15	30	0	18	27	10

(a) Calculate the standard deviation of each company's returns.
(b) Calculate the correlation coefficient of the companies returns.
(c) If you had placed 50% of your money in each, what would have been the standard deviation of your portfolio and the average yearly return ?
(d) What percentage investment in each would have resulted in the lowest risk ?
(e) Assume that a yearly risk-free-return of 8% was available and that you had held only one of the two companies. Which would have been the better to own?
(f) Graph the risk and return of each fund. Given your answer to part (d), what was the single efficient portfolio of the two ?
(g) Use part (f) to determine :
  - How an average return of 10.8% would have been obtained.
  - How an average return of 17.8% would have been obtained.

Ans.:

(a) Find the average returns :
$$R_{FST} = (37 + 24 + ... + 6)/10 = 15\%$$
$$R_{SND} = (32 + 29 + ... + 10)/10 = 15\%$$
Next, find the SD

$$\sigma_{FST} = \frac{\sqrt{(37-15)^2 + (24-15)^2 + ... + (6-15)^2}}{\sqrt{10}} = 14.0\%$$

$$\sigma_{SND} = \frac{\sqrt{(32-15)^2 + (29-15)^2 + ... + (10-15)^2}}{\sqrt{10}} = 14.3\%$$

(b) To find the Covariance term :

$$Cov. = \frac{\sqrt{(37-15)(32-15) + (24-15)(29-15) + ... + (6-15)(10-15)}}{\sqrt{10}} = 187.4\%$$

The correlation coefficient

$$r = \frac{187.4}{(14.0)(14.3)} = -0.94$$

(c) $\sigma_p = (0.5)^2(14.0)^2 + (0.5)2(14.3)^2 + 2(0.5)(0.5)(14.0)(14.3)(0.94) = 13.9\%$
$E(R_p) = 0.5(15.0) + 0.5(15.0) = 15\%$

(d) Using the minimum variance equation and let W stand for FST:

$$W_{FST} = \frac{c_2^2 - c_1 c_2 r_{1,2}}{\sigma_1^2 + \sigma_2^2 - \sigma_1 \sigma_2 r_{1,2}}$$

$$W_{FST} = \frac{14.3^2 - (14.0)(14.3)(0.94)}{14.0^2 + 14.3^2 - 2(14.0)(14.3)(0.94)} = 67.6\%$$

(e) This part asks which of the funds provided the greater return per unit of risk. The risk-slope of the line:

For FST $= \dfrac{15.0 - 8.0}{14.0} = 0\text{-}5\%$ per unit of σ

For SND $= \dfrac{15.0 - 8.0}{14.3} = 0.49\%$ per unit of α

They were very close, but FST was better.

(f) Both funds have identical average returns. The minimum variance portfolio of $W_{FST} = 67.6\%$ and $W_{SND} = 32.4\%$ would also have had a 15% average return, but its risk would be lower than holding either company in isolation. The minimum standard deviation was 13.9%.

(g) Using 8% as the risk-free rate and the single efficient portfolio in part (f) as the optimal risky portfolio, the following risk/ return relationship was available:

$$E(R_c) = R_f + \sigma_c \left[\frac{E(R_p) - R_f}{\sigma_p} \right]$$

where $\sigma_c = (1 - W_{Rf}) \sigma_p$

$$= 8.0\% + \sigma_c \left[\frac{15.0\% - 8.0\%}{13.9\%} \right]$$

$$= 8.0\% + a_c [0.5036]$$

To earn 10.8%, invest 60% risk-free and 40% it the optimal risky portfolio:

$$10.8\% = 8\% \text{ -(- } (0.4)(13.9\% \times 0.5036)$$

To earn 17.8%, borrow 40% on your equity and invest it with your equity in the optimal risky portfolio:

$$17.8\% = 8.0\% + W(13.9\%)(0.5036)$$
$$= 8.0\% + (1.4)(13.9)(0.5036)$$

30. Given the SML $\overline{R}_i = 0.06 + 0.08\beta_i$, what should the expected return of a security be if it has a β twice as great as a similar security returning 18 per cent?

Solution

$$\overline{R}_i = 0.06 + 0.08\beta = 0.18$$

Solving for β yields

$$\beta = 1.5$$

Therefore, the security's β is $2 \times 1.5 = 3.0$ and the required return is:

$$\overline{R}_i = 0.06 + 0.08 (3.0)$$
$$= 0.30$$

A 30-per cent return is required

31. Assume the assets below are correctly priced according to the security market line. Derive the SML. What is the expected return on an asset with a beta of 2?

$$R_1 = 6\% \qquad \beta_1 = 0.5$$
$$R_2 = 6\% \qquad \beta_2 = 1.5$$

Ans.:

Since the SML in linear, we need only two points:

$$R_i = R_F + \beta_i(R_M - R_F)$$
$$6\% = R_F + 0.5(R_M - R_F) = 0.5\,R_F + 0.5\,R_M$$
$$12\% = R_F + 1.5(R_M - R_F) = -0.5R_F + 1.5\,R_M$$

Adding the two equations to solve simultaneously:

$$18\% = 2.0\,R_M \text{ and } R_M = 9.0\%$$
$$R_F = [6 - 0.5(9)]/.5 = 3\%$$

Hence, the SML is:

$$R_i = 3\% + \beta_i(9 - 3) \text{ or } 3\% + 6\beta_i$$

For beta = 2:

$$R_i = 3 + 2(6) = 15\%$$

32. Assume the SML is given as $R_i = 0.04 + 0.08\beta$ and the estimated betas on two stocks are $\beta_x = 0.5$ and $\beta_y = 2.0$. What must the expected return on the two securities be in order for one to feel that they are a good purchase?

Ans.:

$$R_x = 0.04 + 0.08(0.5) = 0.04 + 0.04 = 0.08$$
$$R_y = 0.04 + 0.08(2.0) = 0.04 + 0.16 = 0.20$$

Hence, $R_x = 8\%$ and $R_y = 20\%$ is required, and must also be expected for a good purchase.

33. Capital market theory and the capital asset pricing model (CAPM) are based on certain specific assumptions; and the CAPM suggests rather specific things about asset pricing.

    (a) What are the basic assumptions underlying capital market theory?
    (b) What happens to the capital market line and the choice of an optimal portfolio if the borrowing rate is allowed to exceed the lending rate?
    (c) What assets lie on both the security market line and the capital market line? What assets should never lie on the capital market line?
    (d) What specifically should a "true believer" in the CAPM do with his money if he seeks to hold a portfolio with a beta of 1.25?

Ans.:

    (a) (1) Investors make decisions based solely upon risk and return, i.e. expected values and standard deviation measures.
        (2) The purchase or sale of a security can be carried out in infinitely divisible units.
        (3) Short selling of shares is permitted.
        (4) Perfect competition in securities markets.
        (5) There are no transaction costs.
        (6) There are no personal income taxes.
        (7) There exists an equal borrowing and lending rate.
        (8) Investors have homogeneous expectations.

    (b) If the borrowing rate exceeds the lending rate, the capital market line will be two lines.
    (c) All efficient portfolios lie along the CML, but only the market portfolio will lie on both CML and the SML. Non-efficient assets will never lie on the CML.

(d) Invest in market portfolio and use leverage (borrowing) to increase the beta from 1.0 to 1.25.

34. The following data are available to you as a portfolio manager:

Security	Return	Expected Beta	Standard Deviation
A	.32	1.70	.50
B	.30	1.40	.35
C	.25	1.10	.40
D	.22	.95	.24
E	.20	1.05	.28
F	.14	.70	.18
XYZ Composite Index	.12	1.00	.20
T-bills	.08	0	0

(a) In terms of a security market line, which of the securities listed above are undervalued? Why?
(b) Assume that a portfolio is constructed using equal portions of the six stocks listed above:
  (1) What is the expected return and risk on such a portfolio?
  (2) What would the expected return and risk be if this portfolio were margined at 40 per cent with the cost of borrowing at 8 per cent?

Ans.:

(a)

Security	Required Returns	Expected Returns	Valued
A	.148	.320	Under
B	.136	.300	Under
C	.124	.250	Under
D	.118	.220	Under
E	.122	.200	Under
F	.108	.140	Under

All are undervalued because their prices are low and their expected returns plot above the SML, or all required returns are less.

(b) (1) The expected return:
$$R_p = (.32 + .30 + .25 + .22 + .20 + .14)/6 = .23883$$
Portfolio beta:
$$\beta_p = (1.7 + 1.4 + 1.10 + .95 + 1.05 + .7)/6 = 1.15$$
Portfolio risk:
$$\sigma_p^2 = [\Sigma(X_i b_i)^2 \sigma_i^2] + [\Sigma X_i^2 e_i^2]$$
$$= [(1/6)^2 (1.7)^2 (.2)^2 + [(1.6)^2 (.5)^2]$$
$$+ [(1/6)^2(1.4)^2 (.2)^2] + [(1/6)^2(.35)^2] + [(1/6)^2(1.1)^2(.2)^2]$$
$$+ [(1/6)^2(.4)^2] + [(1/6)^2(.95)^2(.2)^2] + [(1/6)^2(.24)^2$$

$$+ [(1/6)^2(1.05)^2 \, (.2)^2] + [(1/6)^2(.28)^2] + [(1/6)^2(.7)^2(.2)^2]$$
$$+ [(1/6)^2(.18)^2]$$

$\sigma_p^2 = 0.0289 \, 7449$ and $\sigma_p = 0.17021895$

(2) $R_p = X_m E_m + X_{rf} R_f = 0.23833 \, (1.4) + (-.4)(0.08)$
$= 0.33662 - 0.032$
$= 0.30462$

Risk $= \sigma_p = (1 - X_{rf}) \, \sigma_m = 1.4 \, \sigma_m = 1.4(0.17021895)$
$= 0.2383065$

35. Reddy's stoc has a beta of 1.5. The expected market return is 10 percent and the risk-free rate is 5 per cent. You calculate that the stock will provide a return of 11 per cent. Using the CAPM, is Reddy's stock undervalued or overvalued?

Ans.:

By using the equation:

$$E(R_i) = R_f + [E(R_m) - R_f]\beta_i$$

We get:

The equilibrium expected return $= 5 + (10 - 5)(1.5) = 12.5\%$

Therefore, since the security will provide a return of only 11 per cent, which is less than the return it should provide given its beta (12.5 per cent), the security is overpriced. The security's alpha is negative, as evident from equation

$$E(R_i) = \alpha_i + R_f + \beta_i[E(R_m) - R_f]$$

and it s applicaiton gives us:

$$11 = \alpha + 5 + (10 - 5)(1.5)$$
$$\alpha = 11 - 12.5 = -1.5\%$$

36. The expected return on the market portfolio is 8 per cent and the market risk premium is 5 per cent. Calculate the expected return on a security if

(a) Its historical beta is 0.85.

(b) Its fundamental beta is 1.05.

Market risk premium = expected market return −risk-free rate
$$5\% = 8\% - \text{risk-free rate.}$$

Therefore,

risk-free rate $= 8\% - 5\% = 3\%$

From equation:

$$E(R_i) = R_f + [E(R_m) - R_f]\beta_i$$

1. Using the historical beta,

Expected return on security $= 3\% + (5\%)(0.85) = 7.25\%$

2. Using the fundamental beta,

Expected return on security $= 3\% + (5\%)(1.05) = 8.25\%$

This problem shows how analysis cna be different if there is reason to believe that a firm's risk as measured by beta is likely to differ from what was obtained in the past.

37. You have computed the historical beta of a portfolio to be 1.12. Calculate the adjusted betas using (1) the Value Line adjustment equation and (2) the Merrill Lynch adjustment equation.

Ans.:

Betas as adjusted by Value Line and Merrill Lynch are as follows:

Value Line:

Adjusted Beta = 0.35 + 0.67 (unadjusted beta)

Merrill Lynch:

Adjusted Beta = 0.33743 + 0.66257 (unadjusted beta)

Applying these equations we get:

1. *Value Line:*

    Adjusted beta = 0.35 + 0.67 (1.12) = 1.1004

2. *Merrill Lynch:*

    Adjusted beta = 0.33743 + .66257 (1.12) =1.07951

38. Compare the first five and last four industries listed below. What characteristic seems to determine whether the adjustment factor is positive or negative?

Industry Betas and Adjustment Factors

Industry	Beta	Adjustment Factor
A	.99	−.140
B	1.14	−.099
C	.75	−.288
D	.60	−.237
E	.36	−.827
F	1.27	.062
G.	1.80	.348
H	1.31	.098
I	1.44	.132

Ans.:

The industries with positive adjustment factor are more sensitive to the economy. Their betas could be expected to be higher because the business risk of the firms is higher. In contrest, the industries with negative adjustment factors are in business fields with a lower sensitivity to the economy. Therefore, for any given financial profile, their betas are lower.

39. Suppose that the risk premium on the market portfolio is estimated at 8% with a standard deviation of 22%. What is the risk premium on a portfolio invested 25% in ABC and 75% in XYZ, if both have a beta of 1.15?

Ans.:

$\beta_{ABC} = \beta_{XYZ} = 1.15$. Therefore, whatever the investment proportions, w_{XYZ}, w_{ABC}, the portfolio β, which is

$$\beta_P = w_{ABC}\beta_{ABC} + w_{XYZ}\beta_{XYZ}$$

will equal 1.15.

As the market risk premium, $E(R_M)-R_f$ is .08, the portfolio risk premium will be

$$E(R_p)- R_f = \beta_p[E(R_m)- R_f]$$
$$= 1.15 \times .08 = .092$$

40. Stock XYZ has an expected return of 12% and risk of β = 1. Stock ABC has expected return of 13% and β = 1.5. The market's expected return is 11%, and R_f = 5%.

(a) According to the CAPM, which stock is a better buy?

(b) What is the alpha of each stock?

Ans.:

The alpha of a stock is its expected return in excess of the required by the CAPM.

$$\alpha = E(R) = (R_f + \beta[E(R_M) - R_f)]$$
$$\alpha_{XYZ} = .12 - [.05 + 1.0(.11 - .05)] = .01$$
$$+ \ 1.5(.11 - .05)] = -.01$$

ABC plots below the SML, while XYZ plots above.

41. The risk–free rate is 8% and the expected return on the market portfolio is 16%. A firm considers a project that is expected to have a beta of 1.3.
  (a) What is the required rate of return on the project?
  (b) If the expected IRR of the project is 19%, should it be accepted?

Ans.:

The project–specific required expected return is determined by the project beta coupled with the market risk premium and the risk–free rate. The CAPM tells us that an acceptable expected rate of return for the project is

$$= 8 + 1.3(16 - 8) = 18.4\%$$

which becomes the project's hurdle rate. If the IRR of the project is 19%, then it is desirable. Any project with an IRR equal to or less than 18.4% should be rejected.

42. Suppose that the universe of available risky securities consists of a large number of stocks, identically distributed with $E(R) = 15\%$, $\sigma = 60\%$, and a common correlation coefficient of $r = .5$.
  (a) What is the expected return and standard deviation of an equally weighted risky portfolio of 25 stocks?
  (b) What is the smallest number of stocks necesary to generate an efficient portfolio with a standard deviation equal to or smaller than 43%?
  (c) What is the systematic risk in this universe?
  (d) If T-bills are available and yield 10%, what is the stope of the capital allocation line?

Ans.:

The parameters are $E(R) = .15$, $\sigma = .60$, and the correlation between any pair of stocks is $r = .5$.
  (a) The portfolio expected return is invariant to the size of the portfolio because all stocks have identical expected returns. The standard deviation of a portfolio with $n = 25$ stocks is

$$\sigma_p = [\sigma^2(1/n) + r \times \sigma^2(n - 1)/n]^{\frac{1}{2}}$$
$$= [.60^2/25 + .5 \times .60^2 \times 24/25]^{\frac{1}{2}} = .4327$$

  (b) Because the stocks are identical, efficient portfolios are equally weighted. To obtain a standard deviation of 43%, we need to solve for n:

$$.43^2 = .60^2/n + .5 \times .60^2 \ (n - 1)/n$$
$$.1849n = .3600 + .1800n - .1800$$

Thus we need 37 stocks and will come in slightly under the target.

(c) As n gets very large, the variance of an efficient (equally weighted) portfolio diminishes, leaving only the variance that comes from the covariances among stocks, that is

$$\sigma_p = \sqrt{r \times \sigma^2} = \sqrt{.5 \times .60^2} = .4243$$

Note that with 25 stocks we came within 84 basis points of the systematic risk, that is, the nonsystematic risk of a portfolio of 25 stocks is 84 basis points. With 37 stocks the standard deviation is .4300, of which non-systematic risk is 57 basis points.

(d) If the risk-free is 10%, then the risk premium on any size portfolio is 15 –10 = 5%. The standard deviation of a well-diversified portfolio is (practically) 42.43%, hence the slope of the capital allocation line is

$$S = 5/42.43 = .1178$$

43. Suppose that portfolio P has an expected return of 10%, and β of .5, whereas portfolio Q has an expected return of 15% and β of 1. The risk-free rate, R_f, is 5%.
(a) Find constant, K, for these portfolios, and confirm that they are equal.
(b) Find K for an equally weighted portfolio of P and Q, and show that it equals K for each individual security.

Ans.:

(a) For portfolio P,

$$K = \frac{E(R_f) - R_f}{\beta_p} = \frac{.10 - .05}{.5} = .10$$

For portfolio Q,

$$K = \frac{.15 - .05}{1} = .10$$

(b) The equally weighted portfolio has an expected return of 12.5% and a beta of .75, $K = (.125 = .05)/.75 = .10$.

QUESTIONS

1. Why must the market portfolio be a combinatioin of all securities, each in proportion to market value outstanding?
2. In a perfectly efficient market, a security that is priced currently will have an ex ante alpha of zero in the eyes of well-informed analysis. Therefore, if a person determines that a security has a non-zero ex ante alpha, one of the two conditions must held (i) either he or she is not well informed, or (ii) the market is not efficient. Do you agree
3. Explain the difference between a security characteristic line and the capital market line.
4. Under the CAPM, what is the efficient set called? If there is buying and selling of a risk-free asset, what happens to the efficient set?
5. Are treasury rates comparable with ex post minimum rates of return?
6. Discuss the problems in estimating the market return.
7. In the context of the CAPM with unlimited borrowing andlending at the risk-free rate of interest, explain the meaning of the capital market line.
8. Identify the relationship between the security market line and the characteristic line.
9. If the market portfolio is efficient, what is the relationship between the beta factors for securities and their expected rates of return?

10. Under the CAPM, at what common point do the characteristic lines of individual securities intersect?

11. Compare and contrast the capital market line with the security market line. Include in your discussion the type of assets that will be on both lines and how risk is measured.

12. Discuss how we would arrive at an estimated beta value for a stock based on historical information. Further try to speculate on potential difficulties in using historical information to estimate beta.

13. Discuss the practical and theoretical problems in choosing a proxy for the risk-free asset.

14. The substitution of the intercept from a historical period is fraught with the problems history consistently presents: which period is the one that will be most like the future?

15. Does the approximated market portfolio retain an important role in the reconstructed applications that emerge from recognition of the falsehood of the CAPM.

16. "When the borrowing and lending are different, the notion of market price of the risk is meaningless". Appraise the statement.

17. "In a perfect market, all stocks have the same risk premium." Do you agree with this statement?

18. Can we assume a common identified horizon when investors have different, nonhomogenous horizons?

19. How should the return be calculated? If an index is used, should it be value or equal-weighted?

20. Is the capital market line straight or curved?

21. Is a historical based beta stable enough to use as a proxy for a expectations?

22. Does the risk-free security exist?

23. Over what period should the return be calculated? What proxy should be used for the market?

24. What *is* meant by zero -β portfolio? If more than one zero- β portfolio can be created which one should an investor select? What assumptions are required to create a zero -β portfolio, and how reasonable is the assumption?

25. Suppose that the relevant equilibrium model is the CAPM with unlimited borrowing and lending at a riskless rate of interest. Suppose, further, that you discovered a security that was located *below* the security market line.
    (a) What would you conclude about the pricing of this particular security?
    (b) Describe any changes you would expect to occur in its price.

26. Assume the CAPM with no riskless asset.
    (a) Conrast the capital market line in this model with the capital market line when there *is* a riskless asset that can be bought or sold.
    (b) What is the interpretation of the market portfolio in this model?

27. You choose to invest in the company which is going to turn garbage into vehicle fuel through decomposing gases. The worldwide outlook for natural gas and oil is good for the next 20 years, and the stock of the company is negatively correlated with the market portfolio. If the company has a correlation coefficient of -1.00, what does this mean? If the stock has an expected return of -10 percent, why would you purchae it?

28. Given the CML, discuss and justify the relevant measure of risk for an individual security.

29. What are the two alternative assumptions covered in the chapter that would allow us to claim that investment choices can be evaluated solely on the absis of expected return and variance?

30. In the context of the CAPM with unlimited borrowing and *lending* at the risk-free rate of interest, explain the meaning of the critical market line.

PROBLEMS

1. If the risk-free rate of interest is 6 per cent and the return on the market portfolio is 10 per

centt, what is the equilibrium return on an asset having a beta of 1.4, accoridng to the CAPM (with no constraints on riskless borrowing and lending)?

2. Suppose that the relevant equilibrium model is the CAPM with unlimited borrowing and lending at a riskless rate of interest. Complete the blanks in the following table.

Asset	Expected Return	Standard Deviator	Beta	Residual Variance
A	.08	.10	—	0
B	.12	—	2	.49
C	—	—	1	0
D	.05	—	0	.36

3. Assume the CAPM with risk-free lending but no risk-free borrowing. Suppose the return on the market portfolio is 9 per cent, and the return on a zero beta portfolio is 5 per cent. You have combined two assets in a portfolio with equal weights. The expected returns on the two assets are 7 per cent and 15 per cent. What is the beta of this portfolio?

4. Calculate the expected rate of return for each of the following stocks when the risk free rate is .08 and you expect the market rate to be .17.

Stock	Beta
1	1.23
2	1.52
3	0.76
4	0.84
5	0.62
6	1.06

5. Compute the beta for the XYZ Co. based on the following historic returns:

Year	Sunny Computer	General Index
1	37	18
2	8	31
3	13	-23
4	12	3
5	48	-75
6	11	18

6. Security ABC has a β of 1. If the risk-free rate of interest is 10%, and the market premium is 8%, what is the required rate of return on security ABC according to the SML equation?

Ans.: 0.18

7. The current risk free rate is 12%, and the expected return on the market is 0.18, and security XYZ has a β of 1.2. According to the CAPM, what is the expected return on security XYZ?

8. Suppose the relevant equilibrium model is the CAPM with unlimited borrowing and lending at the riskless rate of interest. Complete the blanks in the following table:

Security Return	Expected Deviation	Standard Variance	β	Residual
X	.15	--	2.0	.10
Y	--	.25	0.75	.04
Z	.09	--	0.50	.17

9. Assume that the risk-free rate is 8% and the market portfolio has an expected return of 15 per cent and a standard deviation of return of 25 per cent. Under equilibrium conditions as described by the CAPM, what would be the expected return for a portfolio having no unsystematic risk and a standard deviation of return of 20 per cent?

10. Assume the CAPM with risk-free lending but no risk-free borrowing. The return on the market portfolio is 10% and the return on the zero β portfolio is 6%. The market's standard deviation is 30%. Complete the following table:

Security Return	Expected Deviation	Standard Variance	β	Residual
A	.16	—	—	0375
B	.08	—	—	.0775

11. Consider the following information on three securities :

Security	β	Correlation of Holding-Period-Return (HPRs) with Market Portfolios Returns MPRs
X	1.2	1.0
Y	-0.8	-0.8
Z	1.6	0.3

(a) Indicate the security(s) with no unsystematic risk.
(b) Based on the CAPM, find out the highest and the lowest expected return securities.

12. BB Group of Industries (BGI) has a β of 1.25 and pays no dividends. The expected market return is 20%, and the risk-free rate is expected to remain constant at 10%. You expected BGI shares to be worth ₹ 50 in one year. Using the CAPM, find the value of the share today.

Ans.: $P_0 = ₹\ 40.82$

13. Security ABC has a β of 0.7 and security KRS has a β of 1.3. The expected rates of return are 10% and 14%, respectively. Find the risk-free rate of return.

Ans.: 5.33%

14. Super Garments has a β of 0.8 and an expected return of 13%. If Hamid Mfg. has a β of 1.6 and the risk-free rate is 9%, what is the expected return on Hamid Mfg.? Under what circumstance will the answer be 26%? Is this a realistic circumstance?

Ans.: 17%

15. Stock ABC has a β of 0.5, stock XYZ has a β of 1.0, and stock RST has a β_p of 1.25. The risk-free risk-free rate is 10%, and the expected market return is 18%.
(a) Find the expected return on stock ABC, XYZ and RST.
(b) Suppose that you construct a portfolio of 40%, ABC 20% XYZ, and 40% RST. Using your answers to part (a), find the expected return on this portfolio.
(c) What is the β of the portfolio specified in part (b).
(d) Using the information in the body of the problem, and your answer to part (c), find the expected return on your portfolio.

Ans.: (a) ABC = 0.14; XYZ = 0.18; RST = 0.20;
(b) 0.172; (c) 0.9; (d) 0.172

16. An investor is able to borrow and lend at the risk-free rate of 10 percent. The market portfolio of securities has an expected return of 18 per cent and a standard deviation of 24 per cent. Determine the expected return and standard deviations of the portfolios : (a) If all wealth is invested in the risk-free asset; (b) if two-thirds is invested in the risk-free asset and one-third in the market portfolio; and (c) if all wealth is invested in the market portfolio. Additionally, the investor borrows an additional one-third of his wealth to invest in the market portfolio.

17. Suppose the risk-free rate is 12% and the expected market return is 20%. ABC company has a β of 0.75, and XYZ company has a β of 1.25.

   (a) Find the expected return on ABC Co. and XYZ Co.

   (b) Suppose that because of a sudden unanticipated increase in inflation, the risk-free rate rises to 16% and the market risk- premium remains at 8%. Find the expected returns on ABC Co. and XYZ Co.

   (c) What is the expected return of a portfolio that has 20% of its value in ABC co. and 80% in XYZ Co.?

Ans.: (a) $E(R_{ABC}) = 0.18; E(R_{XYZ}) = 0.22$

   (b) $E(R_{ABC}) = 0.22; E(R_{XYZ}) = 0.26$

   (c) $\beta_p = 1.15; E(Rp) = 0.252$

18. You invest ₹ 10,000 in Jagan Medicals (β1.5) and ₹ 20,000 in the Super Textiles (β1.2). The risk-free rate is 10%, and the expected market return is 16%.

   (a) What are the β and the expected return of your portfolio?

   (b) You have decided that you want to reduce the β_p of your portfolio to 1.0. What investment would you have to make in Gagan Transport Company (β0.8) to achieve this objective?

   (c) If you decide to invest in risk-free securities to reduce the β of your portfolio to 1.0, what investment would you make in risk-free securities?

   (d) If you decided to invest in Suman Electronics Co. (β – 0.5), what investment would be necessary?.

Ans.: (a) $\beta_p = 1.3; E(R_p) = 0.178$

   (b) ₹ 45,000;

   (c) ₹ 9,000

   (d) ₹ 6,000

19. Zing-Zang Enterprises has a β of 1.50. The risk-free rate is 8 per cent and the expected return on the market portfolio is 15 per cent. The company presently pays a dividend of ₹ 2.50 per share and investors expect it to experience a growth in dividend of 12 per cent per annum for many years to come. Compute the required rate of return on the equity according to the CAPM. What is the present market price of the equity share, assuming the computed required return?

REFERENCES

1. Alexander, Gordon J., and N.L. Chervany, "On the Estimation and Stability of Beta," *Journal of Financial and Quantitative Analysis*, 15 (March 1980)).

2. Arthur A. Eubank, Jr., and J.K. Zumwalt, "Impact of Alternative Length Estimation and Prediction Periods on the Stability of Security and Portfolio Betas," *Journal of Business Research*, 9 (September 1981), 321-25.

3. Baesel, Jerome, "On the assessment of Risk: Some Further Considerations," *Journal of Finance*, 29 (December 1974), 1491-94.

4. Barr Rosenberg and W. McKibben, "The Prediction of Systematic and Specific Risk in Common Stock," *Journal of Financial and Quantitative Analysis*, 8 March 1973), 317-34.

5. Beaver, W., P. Kettler, and M. Scholes, "The Association between Market Determined and Accounting Determined Risk Measures," *Accounting Review*, 45, 231-82.

6. Bey, Roger P., "Market Model Stationarity of Individual Public Utilies," *Journal of Finance and Quantitative Analysis*, 18 (March 1983), 67-85.

7. Bill McDonald, "Functional Forms and the Capital Asset Princing Model, *Journal of Financial and Quantitative Analysis*, 18 (September 1983), 326.

8. Bill McDonald, "Making Sense Out of Unstable Alphas and Betas," *Journal of Portfolio Management*, Winter 1985, p. 20.

9. Black, Fisher, M. Jensen, and M. Scholes, "The Capital Asset Pricing Model: Some Empirical Tests," in *Studies in the Theory of Capital Markets*, ed. M. Jensen, pp. 79-121. New York: Praeger, 1972.

10. Blume, M., On the Assessment of Rism, *"Journal of Finance,* 26 March 1971), Gordeon J. Alexander, and N.L. Chervany, On the estimation of and stability Beta" Journal of Financial and Quantitative Analysis, 15 (March, 1980) 125.

11. Blume, Marshall, "On the Assessment of Risk," *Journal of Finance,* 26 (March 1971), 1-10.

12. Boquist, John, George Racette, and Gary Schlarbaum, "Duration and Risk Assessment for Bonds and Common Stocks," Journal of Finance, 30 (December 1975), 1360-1365.

13. Breen, W.J., and E.M. Lerner, "On the Use of Beta in Regulatory Proceedings," *Bell Journal of Economics and Management Science,* Autumn 1972, pp. 612-21.

14. C. Klemkosky and J.D. Martin, "The Adjustment of Beta Forecasts," *Journal of Financa,* 30 (September 1975), 1123-28, R. Burr Porter and J.R. Ezzell, in "A Note on the Predictive Ability of Beta Coefficients," *Journal of Business Research,* 3 (October 1975), 365-71, also studied the question.

15. Carvell, Steven, and P. Strebel, "A New Beta Incorporating Analysts' Forecasts," *Journal of Financial and Quantitative analysis,* 16 March 1981), 95-112).

16. Copeland and Weston, *Financial Theory and Corporate Policy.*

17. D.J. Thompson, "Sources of Systematic Risk in Common Stock," *Journal of Business,* 46 (1973), 173-87

18. Edwin J. Elton, M. J. Gruber, and M. W. Padburg, "Simple Criteria for Optimal Portfolio Selection," *Journal of Finance,* 31 (December 1976), 1341-57.

19. Elgers, Pieter T., J.R. Haltiner, and W.H. Hawthorne, Beta Regression Tendencies: Statistical and Real Causes," *Journal of Finance,* 33 (December 1978), 1975-84.

20. Elton, Edwin J., M.J. Gruber, and T.J. Urich, "Are Betas Best?" *Journal of Finance,* 33 (December 1978), 1975-84.

21. Eugene F. Fama and J.D. MacBeth, "Risk, Return and Equilibrium: Empirical Tests," *Journal of Political Economy,* 81 (May-June 1973), 607-36.

22. Eugene F. Fama, *Foundations of Finance* (New York: Basic Books, 1976).

23. Eugene Fama and Kenneth French: "The Cross—Section of Expected Stock Returns *"Journal of Finance* (June 1992), pp. 427-446.

24. Fisher Black and M. Scholes, "The Effects of Dividend Yield and Dividend Policy on Common Stock Prices and Returns," *Journal of Financial Economics,* 20 (May 1974), 1-22.

25. Fisher Black, M. Jensen, and M. Scholes, "The Capital Asset Pricing Model: Some Empirical Tests," in *Studies in the Theory of Capital Markets,* ed. M. Jensen (New York: Prager, 1972), pp. 79-121.

26. Fouse, W.L., "Risk and Liquidity: The Keys to Stock Price Behaviour," *Financial Analysts Journal,* 32 (May-June 1976), 35-45.

27. Frank K. Reilly and Rupinder S. Sidhu, "The Many Uses of Bond Duration," *Financial Analysts Journal,* 36 (July-August 1980), 58-72,

28. Fuller, Russell J., and H.S. Kerr, "Estimating the Divisional Cost of Capital: An Analysis of the Pure-Play Technique," *Journal of Finance,* 36 (December 1981), 997-1009.

29. Gordon J. Alexander, and N.L. Chervany, "On the Estimation and Stability of Beta," *Journal of Financial and Quantitative Analysis,* 15 (March 1980), 125.

30. Hamada, Robert S., "The Effect of the Firm's Capital Structure on the Systematic Risk of Common Stocks," *Journal of Finance,* 18 (May 1972), 435-52.

31. Hill, Ned C., and B.K. Stone, "Accounting Betas, Systematic Operating Risk, and Financial Leverage: A Risk-Composition approach to the Determinants of Systematic Risk," *Journal of Financial and Quantitative Analysis,* 15 (September 1980), 595-637.

32. Irving Fisher, *The Theory of Interest,* (New York: Macmillan, 1930).

33. Jack C.Francis and S. H. Archer, *Portfolio Analysis,* 2nd ed. (Englewood Cliffs, N.J.: Prentice-Hall, 1979).

34. Josef Lakonishok and a. C. Shapiro, "Stock Returns, Beta, Variance and Size: An Empirical Analysis," *Financial Analysts Journal*, 40 (July-August 1984), 39.

35. Lawrence Fisher and Jules Kamin, "Forecasting Systematic Risk: Estimates of 'Raw' Beta That Take Account of the Tendency of Beta to Change and the Heteroskedasticity of Residual Returns," *Journal of Financial and quantitative Analysis*, 20 (June 1985), 127-50.

36. Lawrence Kryzanowski and Minh Chau To, "The Telescopic Effect of Past Return Realisations of Ex-Post Beta Estimates," *Financial Review*, 19 (March 1984), 1.

37. Logue, Dennis E., and L.J. Merville, "Financial Policy and Market Expectations," *Financial Management*, 1 (Summer 1972), 37-44.

38. M. Livingston, "Duration and Risk Assessment for Bonds and Common Stocks: A Note, "*Journal of Finance*, 33 (March 1978), 293-95; and John S. Bildersee and G.S. Roberts, "Beta Instability When Interest Rate Levels Change," *Journal of Financial and Quantitative Analysis*, 16 (September 1981), 379-80.

39. M. Miller and M. Scholes, "Dividends and Taxes: Some Empirical Evidence," *Journal of Political Economy*, 90 (June 1982), 1118-41.

40. Marshall Blume and I, Friend, "The Asset Structure of Individual Portfolios," *Journal of Finance*, 30 (May 1975), 601.

41. Melicher, Robert W., and D.F. Rush, "Systematic Risk, Financial Data, and Bond Rating Relationships in a Regulated Industry Environment," *Journal of Finance*, 29 (May 1974), 537-44.

42. Merton Miller and M. S. Scholes, "Dividends and Taxes: Some Empirical Evidence," *Journal of Political Economy*, 90 (June 1982), 1119.

43. Meyers, S., "The Stationarity Problem in the Use of the Market Model of Security Price Behaviour," *Accounting Review*, 48 (April 1973), 318-22.

44. Nai-fu Chen, Richard Roll, Stephen A. Ross, "Economic Forces and the Stock Market: Testing APT and Alternative Asset Pricing Theories" (Working paper No. B-73, University of Chicago, December 1983), p. 38.

45. Ned C. Hill and B.K. Stone, in "Accounting Betas, Systematic Operating Risk, and Financial Leverage: A Risk-Composition Approach to the Determinants of Systematic Risk," *Journal of Financial and Quantitative Analysis*, 15 (September 1980), 595-637.

46. Pamela P. Peterson and D. R. Peterson, "Divergence of Opinion and Return," *Journal of Financial Research*, 5 (Summer 1982), 125-34.

47. Porter, R. Burr, and J.R. Ezzell, "A Note on the Predictive Ability of Beta Coefficients," *Journal, of Business Research*, 3 October 1975) 365-71.

48. R. Lanstein and W.F. Sharpe, "Duration and Security Risk," *Journal of Finance and Quantitative Analysis*, 13 (November 1978), 653-68.

49. Robert D. Arnott, "What Hath MPT Wrought: Which Risks Reap Rewards," *Journal of Portfolio Management*, Fall 1983, p. 6.

50. Robert D. Arnott, "Cluster Analysis and Stock Price Comovement," *Financial Analysts Journal*, 36 (November-December 1980), 59.

51. Robert H. Litzenberger and K. Ramaswamy, "The Effect of Personal Taxes and Dividends Capital Asset Prices," *Journal of Financial Economics*, 7 (1979), 165.

52. Robert Litzenberger and K. Ramaswamy, "The Effect of Personal Taxes and Dividends on Capital Asset Prices," *Journal of Financial Economiocs*, 7 (June 1979), 163-96.

53. Rolf W. Banz, "The Relationship Between Return and Market Value of Common Stocks," *Journal of Financial Economics*, 9 (1981), 17.

54. Ronald Lanstein and W.F. Sharpe, "Duration and Security Risk," *Journal of Financial and Quantitative Analysis*, November 1978, pp. 653-68, for a description of duration as it applies to equities.

55. Rosenberg, Barr, and V. Marathe, "Test of the Capital Asset Pricing Hypothesis." Working Paper No. 32 of the Research Programme in Finance.

56. Rosenberg, Barr, and W. McKibben, "The Prediction of Systematic and Specific Risk in Common Stock," *Journal of Financial and Quantitative Analysis,* 8 (March 1973), 1973), 317-34.

57. S. Bar Yosef and R. Kolodny, "Dividend Policy and Capital Market Theory," *Review of Economics and Statistics,* May 1976, 181-90.

58. Son-Nan Chen, "Beta Nonstationarity, Portfolio Residual Risk and Diversification," *Journal of Financial and Quantitative Analysis,* 16 (March 1981), 95-112.

59. Steve Swindler and P. Vanderheiden, *Journal of Financial Research,* 6 (Summer 1983), 47-50.

60. Thomas E. Copeland and J.F. Weston, *Financial Theory and Corporate Policy,* 2nd ed. (Reading, Mass.: Addison-Wesley, 1983).

61. Tobin, James, "Liquidity Preference as Behaviour toward Risk," *Review of Economic Studies,* 25 (February 1958), 65-86.

62. W.F. Sharpe, *Investments* 2nd ed. (Englewood Cliffs, N.J.: Prentice-Hall, 1981).

63. W.S. Grey, "Discount Rates and Return Forecasts," *Financial Analysts Journal,* 30 (May-June 1974), 55-56.

64. Willard T. Carleton and J. Lakonishok, "Risk and Return on Equity: The Use and Misuese of Historical Estimates," *Financial Analysts Journal,* 41 (January-February 1985), 39.

65. William Beaver and J. Manegold, "The Association between Market-Determined and Accounting-Determined Measures of Systematic Risk: Some Further Evidence," *Journal of Financial and Quantitative Analysis,* 10 (June 1975), 231-84;

29

Factor Models and Arbitrage Pricing Theory

INTRODUCTION

The Capital Asset Pricing Model (CAPM) has been derived under restrictive assumptions, some of which clearly do not hold in reality. Yet, it is possible that the CAPM in its original form is justified on positive grounds if the model actually explain stock price behaviour. Nevertheless, some of the restrictions introduced in the model can be relaxed, leading to a theoretical formula which has a similar structure to that of the CAPM and yet is closer to reality in the sense that the underlying assumptions are less restrictive. Some allow the inclusion of other assets, such as assets with returns denominated in currency other than the investor's home currency. Other non-standard CAPMs incorporate the effect of some investors having an effect on price when they trade, and some are derived from an assumption that investors consider more than the mean and variance of the distribution of returns in making portfolio decisions. There is an alternative to this class of models. The alternative theory is called Arbitrage Pricing Theory (APT). The name arbitrage pricing theory arises from the assumption that investors will arbitrage away any differences in the expected return on assets that have the same risks. Of course, the same assumptions underlies the standard CAPM. The basic assumption of APT is not that investors are mean-variance maximisers, but rather that returns are affected by systematic factors and the return on any asset over time is called the return generating process. Given the belief that there is more than one factor, a goal of security analyst is to identify these factors in the economy and the sensitivities of security returns to movements in these factors. A formal statement of such a relationship is termed a factor model of security returns.

SINGLE FACTOR MODEL

Some investors argue that the return-generating process for securities involves a single factor. Some examples of such a single factor include the growth rate of the Gross National Product and the growth rate in industrial production. In general, a single-factor model can be represented in equation form as follows :

$$\tilde{R}_i = a_i + b_i\,\tilde{F} + \tilde{e}_i \qquad\qquad (1)$$

where :

$\tilde{R}_i$ = the (uncertain) return on security i

a_i, b_i = constants

$\tilde{F}$ = the (uncertain) value of the factor

$\tilde{e}_i$ = the (uncertain) security specific return

If the value of the factor is zero, the return on the security would equal $a_i + \tilde{e}_i$. By

887

convention, the expected value of the security specific component of return is assusmed to be zero. This nearly requires that a_i include the expected portion of the non-factor-related return. This means that the expected return on security i, according to the single-factor model, can be written as :

$$E_i = a_i + b_i E_f \tag{2}$$

where :

E_i = the expected return on security i
E_f = the expected value of the factor while the standard deviation can be determined from :

$$\sigma_f^2 = b_i^2 \sigma\frac{2}{f} + \sigma_{ei}^2 \tag{3}$$

where :

σ_i = the standard deviation of return on security i

The first term on the right-hand side of the equals sign is the factor-related risk, expressed in variance terms. The last term is the non-factor-related (security-specific) risk, also expressed in variance terms.

The characteristic line can now be shown to be an example of a single-factor model where the factor is the return of the market portfolio. As the characteristic line is expressed as :

$$\tilde{R}_i - R_f = \alpha_i + \beta_{im}(\tilde{R}_{im} - R_f) + \tilde{r}_i \tag{4}$$

where α_i and β_{im} are the alpha and beta of the security i, respectively and $\tilde{r}_i$ is a random error term with an expected value of zero. This equation can be rewritten as :

$$\tilde{R}_i = R_f + \alpha_i + \beta_{im}(\tilde{R}_{im} - R_f) + \tilde{r}_i$$
$$= R_f + \alpha_i + \tilde{R}_{im}\beta_{im} - R_f\beta_{im} + \tilde{r}_i$$
$$[\alpha_i + R_f(1 - \beta_{im})] + \beta_{im}\tilde{R}_{im} + \tilde{r}_i \tag{5}$$

Comparing equation (5) with the general form of a single factor model given in equation (1), it can be seen that the characteristic line is an example of a single-factor model when the factor is the return on the market portfolio (that is, $\tilde{F} = \tilde{R}_{im}$). Further more, the term a_i and b_i of the single factor model can be interpreted to be equal to $[\alpha_i + R_f (1 - \beta_{im}]$ and β_{im}, respectively.

As an illustration, assume security i has $\alpha_i = +5\%$ and $\beta_{im'} = .9$. Given a riskfree rate of 8%, the characteristic line of this security is :

$$\tilde{R}_i - 8\% = 5\% + [(\tilde{R}_{im} - 8\%) \times .9] + \tilde{r}_i \tag{6}$$

which can be rewritten as follows :

$$= 8\% + 5\% + [(\tilde{R}_{im} - 8\%) \times .9 + \tilde{r}_i]$$

$$= 8\% + 5\% + [(\tilde{R}_{im} \times .9) - (8\% \times .9) + \tilde{r}_i]$$

$$= 5.8\% + .9\tilde{R}_{im} + \tilde{r}_i \tag{7}$$

Thus, the characteristic line for security i, when rewritten as in equation (7), is similar to a single-factor model of equation (1) where the factor is the return on the market portfolio (that is, $\tilde{F} = \tilde{R}_{im}$), and $a_i = 5.8\%$, $\beta_{im'} = .9$ and $\tilde{e}_i = \tilde{r}_i$. However, there are other examples of single-factor models. An investor may believe that it is more accurate to view security returns as being related to one common factor such as predicted growth rate in GNP. For this investor, R_f is the predicted growth rate in GNP, f is the sensitivity of security b_i to the predicted growth rate in GNP, and a_i is the expected return of security i, if there is zero growth in predicted GNP.

MULTIPLE-FACTOR MODELS

Instead of a single-factor model, a multiple-factor model is needed in a complex world as the security returns are affected by a number of factors, e.g. expectations about future levels of real GNP, expectations about future real interest rates, expectations about future levels of inflation etc. These factors, while they have impact on the return on the market portfolio, may impact on the returns on different securities differently. The general form of a factor model can be written as :

$$\overline{R}_i = a_i + b_{i1}\overline{F}_2 + b_{i2} + ... + b_{im}\overline{F}_m + \overline{e}_i \tag{8}$$

where:

m = the number of factors with the assumption that :

(i) The expected value of each security-specific is zero.

(ii) Security-specific returns are uncorrelated with factors.

(iii) Security-specific returns are uncorrelated with each other.

This is termed as M-factor model. The portfolio can emphasise one or more of the factors by selecting portfolio weights in a particular way. Any portfolio that is formed from these N securities will have a return:

$$\tilde{R}_p = \sum_{i=1}^{n} x_i \tilde{R}_i \tag{9}$$

$$\sum_{i=1}^{n} x_i a_i + \sum_i x_i \beta_{i1}\tilde{F}_{i1} + \sum_i x_i \beta_{i2}\tilde{F}_2 + ... + \sum_{i=1}^{n} x_i \beta_{im}\tilde{F}_{im} + \sum_{i=1}^{n} x_i \tilde{r}_i$$

$$= \sum_{i=1}^{n} x_i a_i + \tilde{F}_{imi} \sum_i x_i \beta_{i1} + \tilde{F}_{im2} \sum_{i=1}^{n} x_i \beta_{i2} + ... + \tilde{F}_{im} \sum_{i=1}^{n} x_i \beta_{im} + \sum_{i=1}^{n} x_i \tilde{r}_i$$

which is influenced by multiple factors. It may be possible to construct a portfolio that is diversified relative to the unique influences r_i, (that is, any x_i is small), yet has its influence concentrated in, say, factor 3.

ARBITRAGE PRICING THEORY (APT) MODEL

The Arbitrage Pricing Theory introduced by Ross provides another model for explaining the relationship between return and risk. The theory relates the expected return of an asset to the return from the risk-free asset and a series of other common factors that systematically enhance or detract from that expected return. In certain respects it is similar to the Capital Asset Model (CAPM), but there are both substantive and subtle differences. Both models assert that every asset must be compensated only according to its systematic risk. One of the major difference is that, in the CAPM, the systematic risk of an asset is defined to be the covariability of the asset with the market portfolio, whereas, in the APT, the systematic risks are defined to be the covariability with not only one factor but also possibly with several economic factors. Another difference is that the CAPM requires the economy to in in equilibrium whereas the APT requires only that the economy has no arbitrage opportunities. It may be noted that absence of arbitrage condition is necessary but not sufficient for the economy to be in equilibrium. One of the key advantage of the APT is that it derives a simple linear pricing relation approximating that in the CAPM without some of the latter's objectionable assumptions. Thus, the APT is a more fundamental relationship than the CAPM in the sense that a rejection of the APT implies the rejection of the CAPM but not vice versa.

Assumptions

The CAPM makes assumptions about investor preferences (more return is preferred to less, and risk must be rewarded), about investors' behaviour (risk is variance of the portfolio, and mean and variance of returns are the normal investor's key considerations), and about the world (investor's forecasts are homogeneous and markets are frictionless).

Of the assumptions made by the CAPM, only three appear needed for the APT:

(i)   Investors seek return tempered by risk: they are risk-averse and seek to maximise their terminal wealth.
(ii) Investors can borrow and lend at the risk-free rate.
(iii) There is no market frictions such as transactions costs, taxes, or restrictions on short-selling.

These three assumptions describe investors' behaviour in general, but fail to describe the factors on which decisions are made. That is an important difference between the two models. The APT does not make any assumption about the distribution of the returns from assets. It does not require that investors make decisions on the basis of the mean and variance, and the troubling CAPM assumption about normalcy of returns is not necessary for the development of the APT. The second assumption, that the risk-free rate is the minimum that an investor would accept for making an investment, is a logical part of any asset pricing model. However, the APT says nothing about the difficult problem of borrowing and lending rates.

While the APT has fewer assumptions than the CAPM, it does have two that are peculiar to it:

(*iv*) Investors agree on the number and identity of the factors that are important systematically in pricing assets.
(*v*) There are no riskless arbitrage profit opportunities.

The first of the unique APT assumptions suggests that asset returns are determined by many factors, not just "the market". The second describes investors' behaviour in the market place: they seek arbitrage opportunities, and through trading strategies designed to capture the riskless profits, eliminate risk. As a consequence, since any market equilibrium must be consistent with no arbitrage profits, every equilibrium will be characterised by a linear relationship between each asset's expected return and its return's response amplitude on the common factors, i.e. *ex ante* and *ex post* the APT is the same. Whereas Roll and Ross assert that a reasonable test of the CAPM must be made with the "true market portfolio", they say that APT yields a statement of relative pricing on subsets of the universe of assets. As a consequence, the APT can be tested by examining only subsets of the set of all actual returns, i.e. it can be tested on any set of data.

Deriving the Arbitrage Pricing Theory

In the derivation of the APT equilibrium model, Ross does not assume risk aversion, and in particular does not assume that investors make their decisions in the mean-variance framework. Instead, he assumes that the securities rate of return R_i are generated by the following process:

$$R_i = ER_i + \beta_i (V - EV) + e_i \qquad (10)$$

Here:

R_i = the rate of return on security i ($i = 1, 2,........n$, where we have securities) with mean ER_i

V = the value of the factor generating the security returns, whose mean is E_i

β_i = a coefficient measuring the effect of changes in factor V on the rate of return R_i

e_i = a random deviation

Note that V is a common factor to all securities i: this may be the GNP, the stock-index, or any other factor which one perceives to be appropriate for generation of securities rates of return.

The basic idea of the APT model is that investors can create a zero-beta portfolio with zero net investment. If the zero-beta portfolio constructed with zero investment yields non-zero (positive) return, a same profit can be made by arbitraging. To be more specific, construct a portfolio with proportions x_i such that:

$$\sum_{i=1}^{n} x_i \beta_i = 0$$

$$\sum_{i=1}^{n} x_i = 0$$

where:

β_i = a coefficient measuring the effect of change in the factor on the rate of return.

The first condition stipulates that this is a zero-beta portfolio, and the second condition indicates that a zero amount is invested in this portfolio. Obviously, such a portfolio can be constructed only when some of the stocks are held short (negative X_i) and some are held long (positive X_i), and the investors receive the proceeds of the short sales investing them in other securities. If we multiply by x_i the return generating process for security i, we get :

$$X_i R_i = x_i ER_i + x_i \beta_i (V - EV) + x_i e_i \tag{11}$$

and some over all the assets (i = 1,2,.. ...n) to obtain the portfolio rate of return:

$$\sum_{i=1}^{n} x_i R_i = \sum_{i=1}^{n} x_i ER_i + (V - EV) \sum_{i=1}^{n} x_i \beta_i + \sum_{i=1}^{n} x_i e_i \tag{12}$$

or

$$R_p = ER_p + (V-EV) \sum_{i=1}^{n} x_i \beta_i + \sum_{i=1}^{n} x_i e_i$$

Here R_p and ER_p stand for the portfolio rate of return and the portfolio mean rate of return, respectively. Since $\sum_{i=1}^{n} x_i \beta_i = 0$ by construction and for a very large portfolio the average random deviation is approximately zero, $\Sigma x_i e_i = 0$ $x_i e_i = 0$ we obtain from (12) a constant rate of return $R_p = ER_p$, i.e., a portfolio with zero variability was constructed with zero net investment. In equilibrium, the mean return on such a portfolio must be zero, $ER_p = 0$. Otherwise, with no risk and no investment, a sure profit can be made by buying (or short selling) such a portfolio. Suppose that this is not so and the mean return is, say, $ER_p = ₹ 300$, and we have $R_p = ER_p = ₹ 300$. With zero investment, one can earn ₹ .300 with certainty. Investors will continue to buy such a portfolio, its price will go up and the rate of return will go down until $R_p = ER_p = 0$. Thus, in equilibrium, no arbitrage opportunities are available.

To sum up, by construction, we have :

$$\sum_{i=1}^{n} x_i = 0$$

$$\sum_{i=1}^{n} x_i \beta_i = 0$$

which implies that

$$ER_p = \sum_{i=1}^{n} x_i ER_i = 0 \text{ and also } R_p = \sum_{i=1}^{n} x_i R_i = 0$$

since the portfolio has zero variability and the mean return is equal to the return itself.

To put the matter somewhat differently, in equilibrium all portfolios of the n assets which satisfy the conditions of using no wealth and having no risk must also earn no return on average.

The above conditions are really statements in linear algebra. Any vector, x, which is orthogonal to the constant vector and to each of the coefficient vectors, b_j ($j = i \ldots k$), must also be orthogonal to the vector of expected returns (n is much greater than the number of factors, k). An algebric consequence of this statement is that the expected vector, E, must be a linear combination of the constant vector and the bj vectors. In algebric terms, there exists $K + 1$ weights, $\lambda_0, \lambda_{11}, \ldots\ldots, \lambda k$ such that

$$E_i = \lambda_0 + \lambda_i b_{i1} + \ldots\ldots + \lambda_i b_i k$$

for all i.   (13)

If there is a riskless asset with return, EO, then :

$$b_{oj} = 0$$

and

$$E_o = \lambda_0,$$

hence we will write :

$$E_i - E_o = \lambda_i b_{ii} + \ldots\ldots + \lambda_k \lambda_{ik}$$

with the understanding that E_o is the riskless rate of return if such an asset exists, and is the common return on all "zero beta" assets, i.e., assets with $b_{ij} = 0$, for all j, whether or not a riskless asset exists. If there is a single factor, then the APT pricing relationship is expected return, E_i, systematic risk, b_i, space :

$$E_i - E_o = \lambda b_i$$

The pricing relationship (13) is the central conclusion of the APT and it will be the cornerstone of empirical testing, but it is natural to ask what interpretation can be given to factor risk premia. By forming portfolios with unit systematic risk on each factor and no risk on other factors, each Xj can be interpreted as

$$\lambda_j = E_j - E_o$$

the excess return or market risk premium on portfolios with only systematic factor j risk. Then (13) can be rewritten as

$$E_i - E_o = (E_i - E_o) b_{i1} + \ldots + (E_k - E_o) b_{ik}$$ (14)

Is the "market portfolio" one such systematic risk factor ? As a well diversified portfolio, indeed a convex combination of diversified portfolios, the market portfolio should not possess much idiosyncratic risk (random deviations). Thus, it might serve as a substitute for one of the factors. Furthermore, individual assets b's calculated against the market portfolio would enter the pricing relationship and the excess return on the market would be the weight on these b's. But, it is important to understand that any well diversified portfolios could be found that approximate the factors better than any single market index. In general, the market portfolio plays no special role whatsoever in the APT, unlike its pivotal role in the CAPM.

Arbitrage pricing theory says nothing about either the magnitudes or the signs of the factor coefficients, or what the factors themselves might be; the model does not give us this guidance, nor did Ross when he first described the model. Neither does the theory say anything about how the identity and magnitude of the factors should be determined. What it says is that, by active trading of securities with different sensitivities to the important factors, investors trade away opportunities for excessive gains: that since there are only a few systematic factors affecting returns, many portfolios are close substitutes for each other and thus will have the same value. Excessive gains come only when, by buying some assets and selling others, the investor hedges his or her portfolio and thereby insulates it from risk without eliminating excess return (the return above the risk free rate). These excessive gains are called arbitrage profits. In efficient markets, excess returns are eliminated by trading, and investors cannot, on average or over time, find opportunities to arbitrage for profits.

A simple example might be useful in demonstrating what an arbitrage profit is, and how an investor could take advantage of it, if it were available. For the sake of simplicity, we will describe a market in which there are only three assets, all sensitive to only one factor – for example, inflation. The sensitivities of each of the assets to the common factor, inflation and the expected returns are shown in Figure-1 and Table-1.

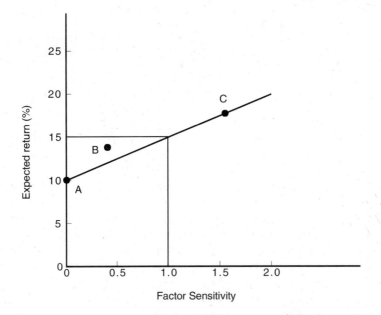

FIGURE 1: FACTOR SENSITIVITY AND EXPECTED RETURNS FOR THREE ASSETS

TABLE 1

Asset	Factor Sensitivity	Expected Return
A	0.0	10%
B	0.5	14.0
C	1.5	17.5

It can be observed that asset B is expected to have a return of 14.0%. Since the return that would usually be expected for an asset with the sensitivity to inflation is 12.5%, asset B promises an excess return of 1.5%. To take advantage of this excess return, and to do so with no risk, an investor can arbitrage among three assets: the investor with ₹ 2000 need only buy ₹ 1000 of asset B and short-sell ₹ 667 of the risk-free security A, and ₹ 333 of asset C. The results of the buying and short-selling activities are shown in Table-2.

TABLE 2

Arbitrage Risk and Return

Action/Amount	Asset	Expected Return	Factor Sensitivity
Buy :			
₹ 1000	B	14.0%	0.5
Short-sell:			
₹ 667	A	(6.7%*)	0.0
₹ 333	C	(5.8%**)	(0.5***)
Total		(12.5%)	(0.5)
Portfolio:			
₹ 2000		1.5%	0.0

* .67 × 10%;   ** .33 × 17.5%;   *** .33 × 1.5

The investor garners the 1.5% excess return, and does so without risk; the factor sensitivity of asset B is offset by the average sensitivity of the short-sold portfolio. An opportunity like this would be similar to finding two bonds, issued by the same company, on the same day, with the same maturities, yields, and other features, offered at two different prices. Obviously inequities offer opportunities to arbitrage. Such opportunities attract investors rapidly, who bid the prices of the assets up or down to eliminate the excess returns. Thus, arbitrage profits are hard to find and capture, and come only when assets are mispriced. Mispricing occurs in two ways. First, the owner of an asset misprices for some reasons, perhaps because of naivete. Second, when there are barriers between markets, and when risk-adjusted rates of return in different markets are different (perhaps because a government lends a support to a particular kind of asset or industry), the few investors who can move between the markets can take advantage of inequalities. Thus, to earn the arbitrage profits, an investor either must be particularly insightful or be one of a few able to move between segmented markets.

The same situation exists when assets are priced on more than one factor. APT allows for as many factors as are important in the pricing of assets. Arbitrage seems intuitively logical, and seems to describe the behaviour of most investors; they are opportunity seekers, believing that opportunities to make profit exist.

PRACTICAL APPLICATIONS OF APT

APT is an interesting alternative to the CAPM and MPT. Since its introduction by Ross, it has been discussed, evaluated, and tested. Based on intuitively sensible ideas, it is an alluring new concept. Are practitioners and academics, therefore, moving away from CAPM ? Since Ross questioned the value of empirical testing of the CAPM, many academics have directed themselves away from the CAPM. Whether that is appropriate or not remaining to be seen since the APT has run into many of the same problems that were discovered during the testing and implementing of the CAPM.

An initial empirical test of the APT was conducted by Roll and Ross (RR). Their methodology was, in a sense, similar to that used by Black, Jensen and Scholes (BJS) in testing the CAPM. They estimated first the factor betas for securities and then the cross-sectional relationship between security betas and average rate of return. RR estimated the factor betas using a statistical technique called factor analysis. The input to factor analysis is the covariance matrix among the returns to the securities in the sample. Factor analysis determines the set of factor betas that best explains the covariance among the securities in the sample.

In a single factor model, the covariance between the rates of return on any two stocks is assumed to be given by the product of (a) the factor beta for the first stock, (b) the factor beta for the second stock, and (c) the variance of the factor. In a multifactor model the covariance is assumed to be given by the sum of a series of such products, one for each of the factors.

Factor analysis makes the working assumptions that the individual factor variables are equal to 1.00, and then finds that set of factor betas for each stock that will make the covariances among the stocks correspond as closely as possible to the sample covariances, as computed directly from the returns. The programme continues to add additional factors until the probability that the next portfolio explains a significant fraction of the covariances between stocks goes below some predetermined level. After estimates of the factor betas are obtained, the next step is to estimate the value of the factor price, associated with each factor. It is done by cross-sectionally relating the factor betas to average return, using a procedure similar to that used by BJS for market betas.

Because of its complexity, factor analysis can only be employed on a relatively small samples of firms. Dhyrymes, Friend, and Gultekin (DFG) found that as the number of securities in the factor analysis increases from fifteen to sixty, the number of significant factors increases from three to seven. As Roll and Ross point out, however, there are many reasons why we should expect this to happen. In any group, say, thirty securities, there may be only one textile company. Investor would not likely find a "textile factor" until he expanded his sample to include more textile companies. They argue that this does not necessarily mean that conducting the tests on small samples is inappropriate, because, unless the factors are pervasive they can be diversified away, and they will not be priced. As such, they are not of interest in testing the theory.

DFG also found that the conclusion as to whether the intercept term is the same or different across different samples depends on the way investor groups the securities. In a later paper DFG, and Gultekin found that the number of "priced" factors increases with the number of securities factor analyses. Overall, these initial empirical results indicate that the APT may be difficult to test by factor analysis. As an alternative to using factor analysis to test the APT, investor can hypothesise that a given set of specified factors explain the covariance matrix among securities. In this approach, investor can use large samples to estimate the factor betas and the factor prices. In employing this procedure, Chen, Roll, and Ross have determined that a large fraction of the covariances among securities can be explained on the basis of unanticipated changes in four specified factors: (*i*) the difference between the yield on a long-term and a short-term treasury bond; (II) the rate of inflation; (*iii*) the difference between the yields as high rated corporate bonds and treasury bonds; and, finally (*iv*) the growth rate in industrial production.

Shanken has raised an even more serious issue about the testability of the APT. He argues that the shares of stock traded in the market place are actually portfolios of the individual units of production in the economy. These portfolios were created through merger and by the adoption of multiple capital budgeting projects by individual firms. Consequently, given a factor structure that explains the covariance among the returns to individual units of production, we may not be able to recognise it on the basis of the portfolio (the stocks traded in the market place).

This point is easy to understand if we suppose a double factor APT is in effect, and both factors are priced. Assume that the stocks in our example are issued by firms that put together portfolios of capital budgeting projects. They may have even merged with other firms in the past. Conceivably, they could disassemble themselves by spinning off divisions or by merging in whole or in part with other firms. They could even reorganise themselves into "portfolios" such that their factor betas were all zero. What would happen to the test of the APT if the firms assembled themselves in this way ? In reality, there are two factors and they are priced, in the sense that they affect expected rates of return. However, if we do a factor analysis on the reorganised firms in our example, we will find their returns are totally uncorrelated, and conclude falsely that there are no factors that are priced. It appears we can not reject the APT on the basis of such a test, because we can never observe the Covariance matrix for the basic units of production units put together on the basis of capital budgeting and merger decisions.

The fact that we can only observe such portfolios may lead us falsely to reject the APT. Suppose again, that we have a two- factor structure with two different factor prices. We test the theory by doing a factor analysis with two separate samples. In the first sample the firms have combined in such a way that their betas with respect to the first factor are zero. The firms in the second sample have combined to make their second factor betas equal to zero. In summing a factor analysis in each sample, investor will conclude that there is only one factor. Moreover, when investor relates factor betas to average returns, investor will conclude that the pricing of the factor is different *as* between the two samples. Investor will incorrectly reject the APT because he, unknowingly, is observing two different factors at work in each of the two samples.

The testability of APT can be called into question in another sense. As the number of companies factor analysed is increased, the number of factors' that investor find explaining the covariance matrix of returns increases as well. Suppose investor takes two groups of fifty stocks, factor analyse each one, find four factors in each, and then look at the cross-sectional relationships between average return and factor betas in each. Investor then announces that he has evidence rejecting the APT. But there may be missing variables in his cross sectional regressions. The missing variables are the betas for the factors that he has failed to capture due to his relatively small sample size of fifty. The variables that are missing may well differ, as between the two samples, accounting for the different risk-free rates of return in the two samples.

Investor may react to this criticism by obtaining more variables by increasing the sample size to 100. He finds more factors, but still different risk free rates of return. He claims that he has rejected the APT, but still the variables are missing. We are in a bind similar to the one we were in with the CAPM. With the CAPM even the best proxies are only a small fraction of the true market portfolio. With the APT, even if the investor increases the sample size to the limits imposed by computing technology, given the requirements of factor analysis, his sample is only a small fraction of the total number of production units in the international economic system. Differences in factor prices and intercepts among samples can always be attributed to missing factors not captured because of small sample size. Moreover, this theory does not tell us the number of factors we should expect to see or the names for any of the factors. Consequently, the number of factors priced by the market is greater than the number he has estimated.

Investors may feel more comfortable if he finds that the number of priced factors increases at a decreasing rate as the sample size increases. This might imply that there may be a point beyond which increasing the sample size will have little impact on his empirical results. Just as any market proxy falls far short of the true market portfolio, any sample size the investor can factor analyse falls far short of the total international population of production units. The number of priced factors may increase at a decreasing rate over the first hundred units, but the investor won't be able to find what happens over the next thousand units.

REVIEW PROBLEMS

1. Given the three portfolios in the table with expected return R_i and sensitivity factors b_{i1} and b_{i2}, what is the equation of the plane in R_i, b_{i2} and b_{i2} space defined by these portfolios ?

Portfolio	Ri	b_{i1}	b_{i2}
A	14.0	0.8	0.8
B	10.8	0.6	0.4
C	11.2	0.4	0.6

Ans:

The information can be used to derive the equation for the risk-return plan by substituting returns and sensitivity-factor information:

$$14 = \lambda_o + 0.8 \lambda_1 + 0.8 \lambda_2 \qquad (i)$$
$$10.8 = \lambda_o + 0.6 \lambda_1 + 0.4 \lambda_2 \qquad (ii)$$
$$11.2 = \lambda_o + 0.4 \lambda_1 + 0.6 \lambda_2 \qquad (iii)$$

Subtract (ii) from (i):
$$3.2 = 0.2 \lambda_1 + 0.4 \lambda_2 \qquad (iv)$$

Subtract (ii) from (iii):
$$0.4 = -0.2 \lambda_1 + 0.2 \lambda_2 \qquad (v)$$

From Equations (iv) and (v) $\lambda_2 = 6$. From Equation (v) $\lambda_1 = 4$.
Finally, from Equation (i), solving for λ_o:

$$\lambda_o = 14 - 0.8 \lambda_1 - 0.8 \lambda_2$$
$$= 14 - 3.2 - 4.8 = 6$$

Hence the equation of the plane describing equilibrium risk- return space can be expressed:

$$E_i = 6 + 4b_{i1} + 6b_{i2}$$

2. Using the portfolios in Review Problem -I, determine how much arbitrage profit, if any, can be made by buying or selling (short) the following portfolios (individually).

Portfolio	R_i (per cent)	b_{i1}	b_{i2}
D	14.0	0.5	0.7
E	15.2	0.8	1.0
F	9.0	0.6	0.5

Ans:

From portfolios A, B and C, the risk/return relationship is
$$r_i = 6 + 4b_{i1} + 6b_{i2}$$

For portfolio D, an equivalent portfolio can be composed from a linear combination of A, B, and C. Given sensitivity factors $b_{i1} = 0.5$ and $b_{i2} = 0.7$, the expected return would be:

$$r_o = 6 + 4(0.5) + 6(0.7)$$
$$= 12.2\%$$

Since 12.2% < 14%, portfolio D is undervalued. A riskless, costless arbitrage profit can be made by buying portfolio D and selling an equivalent amount of a portfolio composed of A, B and C.

For portfolio E, an equivalent portfolio can be constructed with yield:
$$r_{equiv} = 6 + 4(0.8) + 6(1.0)$$
$$= 15.2\%$$

This is exactly the yield of portfolio E; therefore, no arbitrage opportunities remain. For portfolio F:

$$r_{equiv} = 6 + 4(0.6) + 6(0.5)$$
$$= 11.4\%$$

Since 11.4% > 9%, the F portfolio is overpriced. Therefore, portfolio F should be sold and the equivalent portfolio should be bought.

				Risk Factors	
	Initial CF	Ending CF	b_{i1}	b_{i2}	
Portfolio D	−₹ 1,00,00,000	+₹ 11,40,000	0.5	0.7	
Equivalent					
Portfolio	+₹ 1,00,00,000	−₹11,22,000	−0.5	−0.7	
	0	+18,000	0	0	

				Sens. Factors	
	Initial CF	Ending CF	b_{i1}	b_{i2}	
Portfolio F	+₹ 1,00,00,000	−₹10,90,000	−0.8	−1.0	
Equivalent					
Portfolio	−₹ 1,00,00,000	+₹11,14,000	+0.8	+1.0	
	0	24,000	0	0	

A riskless, costless arbitrage profit of ₹24,000 can be made by selling ₹ 1 crore worth of portfolio F and by buying ₹ 1 crore of an equivalent portfolio made up of A, B and C.

3. Assume you have a risk-free rate available equal to 2%. In addition, you have

identified two portfolios of equities which had the following returns over the past five years:

	1	2	3	4	5
Portfolio 1	10.0%	0.0%	10.0%	20.0%	10.0%
Portfolio 2	15.0%	2.5%	15.0%	2.5%	15.0%

(a) Calculate the average return $(\tilde{R}_p)$ on portfolio standard deviation (σ) and correlation of coefficient r_{12} for portfolio 1 and 2.

(b) What is the minimum variance portfolio and what is its standard deviation?

(c) Given a risk-free rate of return of 2%, what is the single *expost* efficient portfolios of risky securities?

(d) Portfolio 1 is smaller and consists *of* A and B securities. The correlation coefficient between A's and B's returns is 0.0. Also $\sigma_B = 2\sigma_A$, $\sigma_A = 7.0711\%$ and $\tilde{R}_A = \tilde{R}_B = 10.0\%$. What then are the optimal X_A and X_B holdings in portfolio 1 ?

(e) Portfolio 1 has a correlation with the single expost efficient portfolio of about 0.70. Since securities A and B are uncorrelated with each other, will they also have identical correlations with the efficient portfolios equal to 0.70 ?

(f) What is the beta of portfolio 1 ?

(g) Use the beta of portfolio 1 to calculate the correlations of securities A and B with the efficient frontier (the single expost efficient portfolio). Calculate the beta estimate for security 1 and 2. (assume the correlation coefficients are identical).

(h) If you were to calculate the market model estimates of the characteristic lines for stock A and B, what would you arrive at ?

(i) Assume you calculate many such market model beta estimates and called them b_i. You then regress the average return on each security $(\tilde{R}_i)$ against these bi values and get :

$$\tilde{R}_i = 2.0\% + 8.0\% \ bi \quad R_2 = 100.0\%$$

Does the linear relationship which perfectly fits the data confirm that the CAPM is correct ?

Ans:

(a) $\tilde{R}_i = (10.0 + 0.0 + 10.0 + 2.0 + 10.0)/5 = 10.0\%$

$\tilde{R}_i = (15.0 + 2.5 + 15.0 + 2.5 + 15.0)/5 = 10.0\%$

$$\sigma_1 = \sqrt{\frac{(10.0-10.0)^2 + \ldots + (10.0-10.0)^2}{\sqrt{5}}} = 6.3246$$

$$\sigma_2 = \sqrt{\frac{(15.0-10.0)^2 + \ldots (15.0-10.0)^2}{\sqrt{5}}} = 6.1237$$

$$r_{12} = \left\{ \frac{(10.0-10.0)(15.0-10.0) + \ldots + (10.0-10.0)(15.0-10.0)}{5} \right\} \times \frac{1}{6.32 \times 6.12} = 0$$

(b) Minimum $X_1 = \dfrac{\sigma_2^2 - \sigma_1\sigma_2 \, r_{12}}{\sigma_1^2 + \sigma_2^2 - 2\sigma_1\sigma_2 \, r_{12}}$

$$= \frac{6.1237^2 - 0.0}{6.3246^2 + 6.1237^2 - 2(0.0)} = 0.484$$

$$X_2 = 1 - X_1 = 0.516$$

$$\sigma_{min} = \sqrt{[(0.484)^2(6.3246)^2 + (0.516)^2(6.1237)^2} = 4.4\%$$

(c) Since portfolios 1 and 2 have the same average return, the minimum variance portfolio from part (b) is the single expost efficient portfolio of risky securities.

$$\text{CML: } E(\tilde{R}_P) = 2.0\% + \sigma_2 \left[\frac{10.5\% - 2.0\%}{4.4\%} \right]$$

$$\text{SML: } E(\tilde{R}_i) = 2.0\% + \beta_{pm}(10.0\% - 2.0\%)$$

(d) Since $r_{AB} = 0$ and $\tilde{R}_A$ and $\tilde{R}_B$ the minimum variance combination of the two is optimal:

$$X_A = \frac{(2 \times 7.0711)^2 - 0.0}{7.0711^2 + (2 \times 7.0711)^2 - 0.0}$$

$$X_A = 0.80$$

$$X_B = 1 - X_A - 0.20$$

(e) No. This would be the case only if securities A and B were perfectly correlated with each other. Otherwise, some of their volatility will be diversified away in portfolio combination of the two and the portfolio will be more highly correlated with the market portfolio (our expost single efficient portfolio of risky securities 1 and 2). Portfolios are more correlated with the market portfolio than single securities.

(f) $\beta_1 = \dfrac{6.3246}{4.4}(0.70) = 1.006$

(g) $\beta_1 = 1.006 = X_A B_A + X_B B_B$

$$= 0.8 \frac{7.0711}{4.4} r + 2.2 \frac{14.1422}{4.4} r$$

Therefore $r = 0$

$$\beta_A = \frac{7.072}{4.4}(0.52) + 0.836 = 0.52$$

$$\beta_B = \frac{14.1422}{4.4}(0.52) = 1.671$$

$$\tilde{R}_{At} = 1.64\% + 0.836(\tilde{R}_{mt} - R_f) + \tilde{r}_{At}$$

$$\tilde{R}_{Bt} = -6.71 + 1.671(\tilde{R}_{mt} - R_f) + \tilde{r}_{Bt}$$

Beta estimates should be the same as in part (g). Alpha estimates are plugged so that average return on the securities is 10% and average return on the market is also 10%.

(i) No. We have here the problem noted by Roll. Whenever an expost efficient portfolio is used to estimate market model betas, the relationship between the average return on each security and its market model beta must be linear and perfectly fit the data. The relationship is mathamatical only and simply says you used an expost efficient portfolio. It does not confirm the CAPM.

4. K. Sundram owns a portfolio with the following characteristics :

Security	Factor 1 Sensitivity	Factor 2 Sensitivity	Proportion	Expected Return
A	1.40	2.50	.30	13%
B	0.90	1.60	.30	18
C	1.00	0.80	.20	10
D	1.30	2.00	.20	12

Assume that returns are generated by a two-factor model and Sundram decides to create an arbitrage portfolio by increasing the holding of security B by 0.05.

(a) What must be the weights of the other three securities in Sundram's portfolio ?

(b) What is the expected return on the arbitrage portfolio?

Ans:

(a) From the conditions required of an arbitrage portfolio, in a four-asset case it must be true that :

$$X_A + X_B + X_C + X_D = 0$$

and

$$b_{A1} X_A + b_{B1} X_B + b_{C1} X_C + b_{D1} X_D = 0$$
$$b_{A2} X_A + b_{B2} X_B + b_{C2} X_C + b_{D2} X_D = 0$$

In this case:

$$X_A + 0.5 + X_C + X_D = 0$$
$$(1.40 \times X_A) + (.90 \times .05) + (1.00 \times Xc) + (130 \times X_D) = 0$$
$$(2.50 \times X_A) + (1.60 \times .05) + (.80 \times Xc) + (2.0 \times X_D) = 0$$

Since:

$$X_A = - X_C - X_D - .05$$

then:

$$[1.40 \times (-X_C - X_D - .05)] + .045 + (1.00 \times Xc) + (2.00 \times X_D) = 0$$
$$[2.50 \times (-X_C - X_D -.05)] + .08 + (.80 \times X_C) + (2.00 \times X_D) = 0$$

Setting these two equations equal to each other and solving for X_c gives:

$$X_A = -.035 - (.692 \times X_D)$$
$$X_C = -.015 - (.308 \times X_D)$$

Substituting these expressions for X_C and X_D into either factor sensitivity equation and solving for X_D gives :

$$X_D = .012$$

Therefore :

$$X_C = -.019 \text{ and } X_A = -.043$$

(b) The expected return on the arbitrage portfolio is then :

$$\tilde{R}_{ap} = (-.043 \times 13\%) + (.05 \times 18\%) + (-.019 \times 10\%) + (.012 \times 12\%) = 0.3\%$$

5. Consider a factor model with earnings yield (or earnings/price ratio) and book-price (or book value/market price ratio) as the two factors. Stock X has an earnings yield of 10% and a book price of 2. Stock Y's earnings yield is 15% and its book value is 0.90. The zero factors of X and Y are 7% and 9% respectively. If theexpected returns of stocks X

and Y are 18% and 16.5% respectively, what are the expected earnings-yield and book price factor values ?

Ans.:

The expected returns on stocks X and Y are :
$$E(R_x) = 18.0\% = 7\% + 10 \times F_1 + 2 \times F_2$$
$$E(R_y) = 16.5\% = 9\% + 15 \times F_2 + .9 \times F_2$$

With two equations and two unknowns, the factor values for earnings yield and book-price can be solved for simultaneously. The solutions are 0.243% for earnings yield and 4.286% for book- price.

6. Based on a two-factor model, consider two securities with the following characteristics :

Characteristic	Security X	Security Y
Factor 1 Sensitivity	1.2	0.15
Factor 2 Sensitivity	2.5	1.80
Nonfactor risk (σ^2_{ei})	20.0	16.0

The standard deviation of factor 1 and factor 2 are 25% and 20% respectively, and the factors have a covariance of 324. What are the standard deviations of securities X and Y? What is their covariance ?

Ans:

Based on a two-factor model, the variance of a security is given by:
$$\sigma = b_{i1}^2\sigma_{F1}^2 + b_{i2}^2\sigma_{F2}^2 + 2b_{i1}b_{i2}\ Cov(F_1,F_2) + \sigma_{ei}^2$$

Therefore, for the two securities in this problem :
$$\begin{aligned}\sigma_x^2 &= [(1.2)^2 \times (25)^2] + (2.5)^2\,(20)^2] + (2 \times 12 \times 25 \times 324) + 20\\ &= [900 + 2500 + 1944 + 20]\\ &= 5364\\ \sigma_x &= 73.24\\ \sigma_y^2 &= [(0.15)^2\,(25)^2] + [(1.80)^2\,(20)^2] + (2 \times 0.15 \times 1.80 \times 324) + 16\\ &= [14.0625 + 1296 + 174.96 + 16] = [1501.0225]\\ \sigma_y &= 38.74\end{aligned}$$

The covariance between two securities in a two-factor world is :
$$\sigma_{ij} = b_{i1}b_{j1}1\,\sigma_{F1}^2 + b_{i2}b_{j2}\,\sigma_{F2}^2 + (b_{i1}b_{j1} + b_{i2}b_{j2})\,Cov.\,(F_1,F_2)$$

In this case :
$$\begin{aligned}\sigma_{xy} &= [(1.2 \times 0.15) \times (25)^2] + [(2.5 \times 1.80) \times (20)^2] + \{[(1.2 \times 1.8) + (25 \times 0.15)] \times 324\}\\ &= \{[(112.5) + (1800)] + [(2.16 + .375) \times 324]\}\\ &= \{[1912.5] + [(2.535) \times 324]\}\\ &= [(1912.5) + (821.34)]\\ &= 2733.84\end{aligned}$$

7. Assuming a one-factor model of the form :
$$\tilde{R}_i = 7\% + b_i F + ei$$

Consider three well diversified portfolios (zero nonfactor risk). The expected value of the factor is 10%.

Portfolio	Factor Sensitivity	Expected Return
A	0.75	14.5%
B	1.00	15.0%
C	1.50	22.0%

Is one of the portfolio's expected return not in line with the factor model relationship ? Can you construct a combination of the other two portfolios that has the same factor sensitivity as the out of line portfolio ? What is the expected return of the combination ? What action would you expect investors to take with respect to these three portfolios ?

Ans:

Given the expected value for the factor of 10% and the stated factor model relationship, then the expected return on the three portfolios should be:

$$\tilde{R}_A = 7\% + 0.75 \times 10\% = 14.5\%$$

$$\tilde{R}_B = 7\% + 1.00 \times 10\% = 17.0\%$$

$$\tilde{R}_C = 7\% + 1.50 \times 10\% = 22\%$$

Thus portfolio B's expected return is 'out of line' with (in this greater than) the factor model relationship.

As portfolio B's factor sensitivity is 1.00, then the issue is what combination of portfolio A and C will yield a factor sensitivity of 1.0. That is:

$$X_A \times 0.75 + X_C \times 1.50 = 1.0$$

It must be that $X_A + X_C = 0$ or $X_C = 1 - X_A$. Thus

$$X_A \times 0.75 + (1 - X_A) \times 1.50 = .75$$
$$0.75 X_A + 1.50 - 1.50 X_A = 1.00$$
$$.75 X_A = .50$$
$$X_A = .67 \text{ and } X_C = .33$$

A portfolio formed of 67 for portfolio A and 33% portfolio C has an expected return of:

$$\tilde{R}_P = .67 \times 14.5\% + .33 \times 22\%$$
$$= 9.715 + 7.26 = 16.975\%$$

Investors can be expected to create arbitrage portfolios by short selling portfolio B and buying a portfolio composed of 67% portfolio A and 33% portfolio C.

8. Assume the CAPM holds and returns are generated by a one- factor model, you are given the following information:

$$\sigma_m^2 = 625 \quad bA = 0.90 \quad bB = 1.25, \quad \text{Cov.}(F, R_m) = 324$$

(a) Calculate the beta coefficients of securities A and B.
(b) If the riskfree rate is 8% and the expected return on the market portfolio is 15%, what is the equilibrium expected return on securities A and B ?

Ans.:

(a) If the CAPM holds and returns are generated by a one-factor model, then:

$$\beta_i = [\text{Cov.}(F, Rm) / \sigma_m^2] \times b_i$$

For Security A:

$$\beta_B = [(324/625) \times .90] = 0.47$$

For Security B:

$$\beta_B = [(324/625) \times 1.25] = 0.65$$

(b) Given that the CAPM holds, the equilibrium expected returns on a security is given by:

$$\tilde{R}_i = R_f + \beta_i(\tilde{R}_m - R_f)$$

In this case:

$$\tilde{R}_A = 8.0\% + [0.47 \times (15.0\% - 8.0\%)]$$
$$= 8.0\% + 3.29\% = 11.29\%$$
$$\tilde{R}_B = 8.0\% + [0.65 \times (15.0\% - 8.0\%)]$$
$$= 8.0\% + 4.55 = 12.55\%$$

9. Assume that security returns are generated by a factor model in which two factors are pervasive. The sensitivities of two securities and of the riskfree asset of each of the two factors is shown below, along with the expected return on each security:

Security	b_{i1}	b_{i2}	Expected Return
A	0.75	0.60	18.0%
B	1.75	1.20	24.0%
R_f	0.00	0.00	12.0%

(a) If R.D. Sharma has ₹ 10,000 to invest and sells short ₹ 5,000 of security B and purchases ₹ 15,000 of security A, what is the sensitivity of Sharma's portfolio to the two factors ?

(b) If Sharma now borrows ₹ 10,000 at the riskfree rate and invest the proceeds of the loan along with the original ₹ 10,000 in securities A and B in the same proportions as described in part (a), what is the sensitivity of the portfolio to the two factors ?

(c) What is the expected return on the portfolio created in part b ?

(d) What is the expected return premium of factor 2 ?

Ans.:

(a) Sharma's position in the two securities are +1.50 in security A and -.50 in security B. As a result, the portfolios sensitivities to the two factors :
$$b_{Prop.1} = 1.50 \times .75 + (-.50) \times 1.75 = 1.125 - 0.875 = 0.25$$
$$b_{prop.2} = 1.50 \times .60 + (-.50) \times 1.20 = 0.90 - 0.60 = 0.30$$

(b) Sharma's position in the two securities are now 3.0 in security A (₹ 30,000/₹10,000), -1.0 in security B (- ₹ 10,000/₹ 10,000), and -1.0 in the riskfree asset (-₹ 10,000/₹ 10,00). Therefore:
$$b_{Prop.1} = 3.0 \times .75 + (-1.0) \times 1.75 + (-1.0) \times 0 = 0.50$$
$$b_{Prop.2} = 3.0 \times .60 + (-1.0) \times 1.20 + (-1.0) \times 0 = 0.60$$

(c) The expected return on the portfolio is given by :
$$\tilde{R}_P = 3.0 \times 1.80\% + (-1.0) \times 24.0\% + (-1.0) \times 12.0\%$$
$$= 54\% - 24\% - 12\% = 18\%$$

(d) The portfolio created in part (b) is a pure factor 2 portfolio. The expected return premium for the factor is the expected return on a pure factor portfolio for that factor less the riskfree rate. Thus :
$$\text{Expected return premium} = 18.0\% - 12.0\% = 6.0\%$$

10. Assume that the CAPM holds and the returns are generated by a two-factor model. You are given the following information:

$$\sigma_m^2 = 225 \quad b_{A1} = .70 \quad b_{B1} = 1.0 \quad \text{Cov.}(F_1, R_m) = 142$$
$$b_{A2} = 1.20 \quad b_{B2} = .80 \quad \text{Cov.} (F_2, R_m) = 350$$

Calculate the beta coefficients of securities A and B.

Ans:

If the CAPM holds and returns are generated by a two-factor model, then :

$$\beta_1 = [\text{Cov.}(F_1, R_m)/\sigma_m^2] \times b_{1i} + [\text{Cov.}(F_2, R_m)/\sigma_m^2] \times b_{2i}$$

For security A :

$$\beta_A = [(142/225)X\ .70] + [(350/225) \times 1.20]$$
$$= [.90 + 1.87] = 2.77$$
$$\beta_B = [(142/225) \times 1.00] + [(350/225) \times 0.80]$$
$$= (0.63 + 1.24) = 1.87$$

11. Assume that the APT model is valid and that the risk-free rate is 4%. Find the stock's actual rate of return if its $e_i = -0.3$ and $a_i = 0.03$, and its required rate of return if its betas with respect to the 5 factors are $\beta_{1i} = 0.5$, $\beta_{2i} = -0.4$, $\beta_{3i} = -0.3$, $\beta_{4i} = -0.2$ and $\beta_{5i} = -0.6$. Assume industrial production growth is 2% higher than expected (i.e. 6% instead of 4%), the T- bill rate drops from 8% to 6.5%; inflation is 3% when it was expected to be 4%; the realised rate of returns on speculative bond was 4% while it was 1% on high grade bonds; and long-term bond return was -5%, representing a drop in the bond's price and an increase in its yield, i.e., a more steeply sloped term structure.

Ans:

Computing the stock's actual rate of return:
$$= .03 + .5\ (.02) - .4\ (-.015) -.3\ (-.01) - 2\ (.03) - .6\ (-.115) -.03$$
$$= .082$$

Computing the stock's required rate of return:
$$= 0.04 + 0.1631\ (0.5) - 0.0015(-0.4) - 0.0075(-0.3) + 0.0865\ (-0.2) - 0.0625\ (-0.6)$$
$$= 0.04 + 0.08155 + 0.0006 + 0.00225 - 0.0173 + 0.0375$$
$$= 0.1446 = 14.46\%$$

12. Assume that an investor has three risky assets with the following parameters:

$$ER_1 = 0.10 \qquad ER_2 = 0.40 \qquad ER_3 = 0.70$$
$$\beta_1 = 1 \qquad \beta_2 = 2 \qquad \beta_3 = 3$$

Construct a zero-beta portfolio with zero investment, i.e.

$$\sum_{i=1}^{3} x_1 \beta_i = 0 \quad \text{and} \quad \sum_{i=1}^{3} x_1 = 0$$

Ans:

Rewriting the two constraints in expanded form:
$$x_1 + x_1 + x_3 = 0$$
or $\quad x_3 = - x_1 - x_2$
and $\quad x_1 \beta_1 + x_2 \beta_2 + x_3 \beta_3 = 0$
or $\quad x_1 + 2x_2 + 3x_3 = 0$

Substituting in the beta equality $x_3 = -x_1 - x_2$ we obtain:
$$x_1 + 2x_2 + 3(-x_1 - x_2) = 0$$
or $\quad -2x_1 - x_2 = 0$

which implies that:

$$x_1 = -\frac{1}{2}x_2$$

Take, for instance, $x_2 = 1$, hence $x_1 = -1/2$ and $x_3 = -x_1 - x_2 = -1 - (-1/2) = -1/2$. For the portfolio $x_1 = -1/2$, $x_2 = 1$ and $x_3 = -1/2$, we have

$$\sum_{i=1}^{n} x_i = 0 \quad \text{and} \quad \sum_{i=1}^{3} x_i \beta_i = 0, \text{ as required.}$$

We also claimed that if $\sum_{i=1}^{n} x_i = 0$ and $\sum_{i=1}^{n} x_i \beta_i = 0$, the rates of return on the individual

assets must adjust so that in equilibrium $ER_p = \sum_{i=1}^{n} x_i ER_i = 0$. We selected ER_i such that

the equilibrium condition holds and no arbitrage profit is available, since:

$$\sum_{i=1}^{n} x_i ER_i = (-1/2) \times 0.10 + 1 \times 0.40 + (-1/2) \times 0.70$$

$$= 0$$

In such a case ER_i can also be written as a linear function of the βi. First, let us find the slope of the line:

$$ER_i = a_o + a_1 \beta_i$$

The slope a_1 is given by:

$$a_1 = \frac{ER_3 - ER_2}{\beta_3 - \beta_2} = \frac{0.70 - 0.40}{3 - 2} = 0.30$$

Hence, $a_1 = 0.3$ Since $ER_3 = a_o + 0.3 \beta_3$ we have $0.7 = a_o + 0.3 \times 3$ which yields $a_o = -0.2$. So, the security 1 will be on the straight line with the coefficients $a_o = -02$, $a_1 = 0.3$ or:

$$ER_i = -0.2 + 0.3 \beta_i$$

Since $\beta_1 = 1$ and $ER_1 = 0.1$, it is easy to verify that security 1 indeed lies on the same straight line. In general, under the conditions of APT, R_i is given as a linear function of β_i.

13. Assume that in a three-factor APT model, the factor betas for a security are -0.8, 3.5, and 1.5 respectively. If the risk-free rate is 4 per cent and the expected returns of the pure factor portfolios are 5 per cent, 6 per cent, and 4.5 per cent, calculate:
   1. the expected risk premiums for each of the factors.
   2. the equilibrium expected return on the security.

Ans.:

1. By applying the equation:

$$\lambda_1 = E(R_P) - \lambda_0$$

We get the expected risk premiums:
Factor 1:   5% −4% = 1%
Factor 2:   6% −4% = 2%
Factor 3:   4% −4% = 0.5%

(2) Using equation $E(R_i) = \lambda_0 - \beta_{i1}[E(R_{P1}) - \lambda_0] - \beta_{i2}[E(R_{P2}) - \lambda_0] - \ldots$

$$\ldots - \beta_{iK}[E(R_{PK}) - \lambda_0]$$

We get the equilibrium expected return on the security is
$$4\% + (-0.8)(1) + (3.5)(2) + (1.5)(0.5) = 10.95\%.$$

14. The sensitivities to unanticipated inflation for three assets are represented by their factor betas as follows:

X	Y	Z
–1.8	2.0	0.55

If you invested equal amounts in the three assets, what would be the inflation beta of the portfolio made up of the three assets?

Ans.:

The weighted inflation beta of the portfolio is
$$(1/3)(–1.8) + (1/3)(2.0) + (1/3)(0.55) = 0.25.$$

QUESTIONS

1. What is the bask assumption behind the APT ? What are the advantages and disadvantages of the APT over the CAPM ?

2. What do you mean by riskless arbitrage opportunity ? Carefully explain why arbitrage opportunities must not exist in an efficient market.

3. The APT expected return relationship looks much like the security market line which was derived in the capital asset pricing model. How would one discriminate between the APT and the CAPM?

4. If the number of assets in the economy is less than finite, what is the implication for the use of APT expected return relationship ?

5. How is the APT model consistent with the CAPM model? What are the fundamental principles underlying the APT Model?

6. What was the finding of Dhrymas, Friend and Gultekin (DFG) concerning the number of factors that were significant in explaining returns?

7. Based on the current theoretical and empirical developments of APT, do you think that this approach offers a practical alternative to the CAPM for individual investors?

8. With regard to the number of different factors that are priced: (a) what do the theoretical results in the APT say about the number of factors? (b) what did the empirical evidence of Roll and Ross indicate about the number of factors.

9. What is meant by the term 'arbitrage profit'? Describe some of the problems associated with empirically testing the APT.

10. In managing money according to the APT, why is the objective to predict the long-term average return and risk to a factor end not to predict the future value for the factor?

11. Explain why you agree or disagree with the following statement: "According to the APT, the contribution of each factor to total volatility is constant over time."

12. In what ways are the underlying assumptions of the APT different from those of the original CAPM?

13. Why are the APT factors necessarily associated with unanticipated changes?

14. Why would you expect the APT factors to be related to fundamental economic variables?

15. Explain what is meant by
  1. a pure factor portfolio
  2. a zero-beta portfolio.

16. Describe how the APT may be utilised in practical investment management.

17. What are the major difficulties and limitations associated with the use of an equilibrium model such as the APT in portfolio practice?

18. "In the CAPM investors should be compensated for accepting systematic risk, for the APT model, investors are rewarded for accepting both systematic risk and systematic risk." Do you agree with this statement?

19. The APT itself does not provide guidance concerning the factors that might expect to determine risk premium. How should the portfolio managers decide which factors to investigate? Why, for example, is the industrial production a reasonable factor to test for a risk premium?

PROBLEMS

1. Suppose you are attempting to estimate an appropriate expected return for a particular equity. Assume the risk-free return is 8 per cent.

   (a) If the expected return on the market is 15 per cent and the equity's beta is 1.2, use the CAPM to calculate the expected return.

   (b) Using the APT approach, the following factors and sensitivity indexes have been identified:

Factor	Market Price of Risk	Sensitivity Index
Unanticipated changes in inflation	6%	1.1
Unanticipated changes in industrial production	2%	0.8
Unanticipated changes in risk premium	3%	1.0
Unanticipated changes in term structure	4%	-0.9

   Use an appropriate APT model to calculate the expected return.

   (c) What explanations can you offer to explain the difference in the two estimates of expected return?

2. An investment consultant determines that the two factors under the APT, which affect the portfolios that he has constructed for his limited clientele, who invest only in chemical securities the rate of inflation and the growth rate of all chemical securities in relation to the growth rate of textiles and cement securities. The consultant determines the market price of the factors to be 0.07 and 0.05, respectively, with zero covariance between the two factors and the zero beta portfolio's expected rate of return is 10 per cent. The beta for his chemical portfolio is 2.5 with respect to both factors. Calculate the expected rate of return for consultant portfolio.

3. Assume a three factor APT model is appropriate and that there are an infinite number of assets. The expected return on a portfolio with zero beta values is 10 percent. You are interested in an equally weighted portfolio of two stocks, A and B. The factor prices are indicated in the table given below, along with the factor betas for A and B. Compute the approximate expected return of the portfolio:

Factor	β_{iA}	β_{iB}	Factor Prices
1	0.2	0.6	0.08
2	0.3	0.8	0.06
3	1.5	1.2	0.05

4. You are given the factor sensitivities on four well-diversified stock portfolio. Both factors 1 and 2 are priced factors.

Portfolio	β_{i1}	β_{i2}	$E(R_i)$
A	0.4	0.6	7.8%
B	6.0	0.4	8.2%
C	1.0	0.0	9.0%
D	0.0	1.0	8.0%

(a) What is meant by priced factors?

(b) Find the percentage to invest in A and B such that the combination has:
— zero factor 2 risk
— zero factor 1 risk

(c) Is portfolio C correctly valued?

(d) Is portfolio D correctly valued?

(e) Create on arbitrage using A, B and D in which ₹ 1,00,000 of D is traded. Show the end-of-period value of this arbitrage for the following actual outcomes of factor 2:

Low	:	$F_2 = 0$
Expected	:	$F_2 = 3$
High	:	$F_2 = 6$

(f) Why is a risk-free rate available in this model?

(g) Why must a fully arbitraged APT model be linear?

5. Suppose that two factors have been deemed appropriate to "explain" returns on stocks, and the covariance between the factors is zero. You have the information below on two stocks, X and Y, and the two factors, 1 and 2. What is the variance of a portfolio consisting of ₹ 1,000 invested in X and ₹ 2,000 invested in Y?

	Beta (Factor 1)	Beta (Factor 2)	Residual Variance
Stock X	1.1	.5	.02
Stock Y	.2	.8	.05

Variance of factor 1 = .15.
Variance of factor 2 = .10.

6. Assume a two-factor APT model is appropriate, and there are an infinite number of assets in the economy. The cross-sectional relationship between expected return and factor betas indicates the price of factor 1 is .15, and the price of factor 2 is –.2. You have estimated factor betas for stock X and Y as follows:

	β_1	β_2
Stock X	1.4	.4
Stock Y	.9	.2

Also, the expected return on an asset having zero betas (with respect to both factors) is .05. According to the APT, what are the approximate equilibrium returns on each of the two stocks?

7. A two-factor model is being employed, one a market factor (Mf) and the other a factor of unexpected changes in the growth of industrial production (Gi).

	Market Beta	Growth Beta	Residual variance
Security A	.5	.25	.07
Security B	.8	.15	.03

Variance of market factor = .15
Variance of the growth factor = .12
Covariance between residuals of securities A and B = .025
Covariance between Mf and Gi = 0

(i) Compute the variance of Security A.

(ii) Assume you had constructed an equally weighted portfolio of securities A and B. Compute the residual variance of the portfolio in two ways:
(a) Making the simplifying assumption of the two-factor model about variance.
(b) Without making the simplifying assumption about residual covariance.

(*iii*)   Compute the market-rate and the growth rate for equally weighted portfolio of securities A and B.

(*iv*)   In an equally weighted portfolio of securities A and B, compute the variance of the portfolio in two ways:

(*a*)   Making the simplifying assumption of the two-factor model about residual covariance.

(*b*)   Without making the simplifying assumption about residual covariance.

8.   The factor betas for four assets representing their sensitivities to two factors are as follows:

	A	B	C	D
Factor 1	1.20	-1.60	-1.30	3.00
Factor 2	-3.70	0.90	-0.30	1.05

Assume if you invest, respectively, 20 percent, 30 percent, 40 percent, and 10 percent of your wealth in these assets, compute the betas of the two factors for the portfolio consisting of the four assets.

9.   An APT model consists of a market factor and an interest rate factor. The expected return on the market portfolio is 7 percent and the expected return on the pure factor portfolio for unanticipated interest rate changes is 5 per cent. If the expected zero-beta of return is 3 per cent, calculate the equilibrium expected return on a security with a market beta of 1.5 and an interest rate beta of -0.50

10.   In a four factor APT model, the factor betas for a security are 1.2, -1.5, 1.1, and 2.8, respectively. The expected returns of the pure factor portfolios for the factor are 8 per cent, 5.5 per cent, 7.5 per cent, and 8.6 per cent. If the risk-free rate is 4.5 per cent, calculate

(1)   the expected risk premiums for each of the factors.

(2)   the equilibrium expected return on the security.

11.   Assume that the following two-index model describes returns

$R_i = a_i + b_{i1} I_1 + b_{i2} I_2 + e_i$

Assume the following three portfolios are observed.

Portfolio	Expected Return	b_{i1}	b_{i2}
X	8.0	1	0.5
Y	9.0	3	0.5
Z	10.0	5	- 0.5

Find the equation of the plane that must describe equilibrium returns.

12.   Refering to the results of problem-11, illustrate the arbitrage opportunities that would exist if a portfolio called ABC with the following properties were observed.

$\overline{R}_{ABC} = 12 \quad b_{ABC_1} = 2 \quad b_{ABC_2} = 0$

REFERENCES

1.   Berry, Michael, Edwin Burrmeister, and Marjorie McElroy: "Sorting Out Risks Using Known APT Factors," *Financial Analysts Journal*, March-April 1988, pp. 29-42.

2.   Born, Jeffery A., "The Arbitrage Pricing Theory, the Market Portfolio and Am-biguity When Performance is Measured by the Security Market Line." Working Paper No. FIN-2-84, University of Kentucky, 1984.

3.   Bower, Dorothy, R.S. Bower, and D.E. Logue, "A Primer on Arbitrage Pric-ing Theory," *Midland Corporate Finance Journal*, 2 (Fall 1984), 31-40.

4.   Breeden, Douglas T., "An Intertemporal Asset Pricing Model with Stochastic Consumption and Investment Opportunities," *Journal of Financial Economics*. 7 (September 1979), 265-96.

5. Brown, Stephen, and M. Weinstein, "A New Approach to Testing Asset Pric-ing Models," *Journal of Finance,* 38 (September 1983), 711-43.

6. Burrmeister, Edwin, and Kent Wall: "The Arbitrage Pricing Theory and Macroeconomic Factor Mea-sures," *The Financial Review,* February 1986, pp. 1 -20.

7. Chen, Nai-fu, "Some Empirical Tests of the Theory of Arbitrage Pricing," *Jour-nal of Finance,* 38 (December 1983), 1393-1414.

8. Chen, Nai-fu, R. Roll, and S.A. Ross, "Economic Forces and the Stock Mar-ket." Working Paper Ser. B-73, University of California at Los Angeles, December 1983.

9. Chen, Nai-fu, Richard Roll, and Stephen Ross: "Economic Forces and the Stock Market," *Journal of Business* 59, July 1986, pp. 386-403.

10. Chen, Nai-fu: "Some Empirical Tests of the Theory of Arbitrage Pricing." *Journal of Finance* 38, December 1983, pp. 1392-1417.

11. Cho, D. Chinhyung, "On Testing the Arbitrage Pricing Theory: Inter-Battery Factor Analysis," *Journal of Finance,* 39 (December 1984), 1485-1502.

12. Connor, Gregory, and Robert Korajczyk: "A Test for the Number of Factors in an Approximate Factor Model," *Journal of Finance,* September 1993, pp. 1263-1291.

13. Dhrymes, Pheobus J., "The Empirical Relevance of Arbitrage Pricing Models," *Journal of Portfolio Management,* Summer 1984.

14. Dhrymes, Pheobus J., I. Friend, and N.B. Gultekin, "A Critical Reexamination of the Empirical Evidence on the Arbitrage Pricing Theory," *Journal of Finance,* 39 (Summer 1984), 35-44.

15. Dhrymes, Pheobus J., I. Friend, M.N. Gultekin, and N.B. Gultekin, "New Tests of the APT and Their Implications," *Journal of Finance,* 40 (July 1985), 659-673.

16. Dybrig, Philip, and Stephen Ross: "Yes, the APT is Testable," *Journal of Finance,* September 1985, pp. 1173-1188.

17. Dybvig, Philip, and Stephen Ross, "Yes, The APT Is Testable," *Journal of Finance,* 40 (September 1985), 1173-. Pari, Robert A., and Son-Nan Chen, "An Empirical Test of the Arbitrage Pric-ing Theory," *Journal of Financial Research,* 7 (Summer 1984), 121-30.

18. Eleswarapu, V., and Marc Reinganum: "The Seasonal Behavior of the Liquidity Premium in Asset Pricing," *Journal of Financial Economics,* December 1993, pp. 373-386.

19. Elton, Edwin J., and Martin J. Gruber: *Modern Portfolio Theory and Investment Analysis,* John Wiley & Sons, New York, 1991.

20. Farrell, J.L., Jr., "Analyzing Covariation of Returns to Determine Homogeneous Stock Groupings," *Journal of Business,* 47 (April 1974), 186-207.

21. ———, *The Multi-Index Model and Practical Portfolio Analysis,* Charlottesville, Va.: Financial Analysts Research Foundation, 1976.

22. ———, "Homogeneous Stock Groupings," *Financial Analysts Journal,* 31 (May-June 1975), 50-62.

23. Fogler, H. Russell, "Common Sense on CAPM, APT, and Correlated Resid-uals," *Journal of Portfolio Management,* Summer 1982, pp. 20-28.

24. Gehr, Adam: "Test of the Arbitrage Pricing Model," Research Report no. 88, Institute for Quantitative Research in Finance, 1979.

25. Hagin, Robert. *Modern Portfolio Theory.* Homewood, Ill.: Dow-Jones-Irwin, 1979.

26. Harrington, Diana R. *Modern Portfolio Theory, the Capital Asset Pricing Model, and Arbitrage Pricing Theory: A User's Guide.* 2d ed. Englewood Cliffs, N.J.: Prentice-Hall, 1987.

27. Jensen, Michael C. "Risk, the Pricing of Capital Assets, and the Evaluation of Investment Portfolios." *Journal of Business* 42, no. 2 (April 1969).

28. Kryzanowski, Lawrence, and Minh Chan To, "General Factor Models and the Structure of Security Returns," *Journal of Financial and Quantitative Anal-ysis,* 18 (March 1983), 31-52.

29. Lehmann, Bruce and David Modest: "The Empirical Foundations of the Arbitrage Pricing Theory," *Journal of Financial Economics,* September 1988.

30. Losq, Etienne, and J. P. D. Chateau, "A Generalization of the CAPM Based on a Property of the Covariance Operator," *Journal of Financial and Quantitative Analysis,* 17 (December 1982), 783-97.

31. Mao, James C.T., "Security Pricing in an Imperfect Capital Market," *Journal of Financial and Quantitative Analysis,* 6 (September 1971), 1105-16.

32. Mayshar, Joram, "Transaction Costs in a Model of Capital Market Equilib-rium," *Journal of Political Economy,* 86 (August 1979), 673-700.

33. Reinganum, Marc, "The Arbitrage Pricing Theory: Some Empirical Results," *Journal of Finance,* 36 (June 1981), 313-21.

34. Roll, Richard. "A Critique of the Asset Pricing Theory's Tests." *Journal of Financial Economics* 4, no. 4 (March 1977).

35. —————,and Stephen Ross. "The Arbitrage Pricing Theory Approach to Strategic Portfolio Planning." *Financial Analysts Journal,* May/June 1984, 14-26.

36. ———, "Regulation, the Capital Asset Pricing Model, and the Arbitrage Pricing Theory," *Public Utilities Fortnightly,* May 26, 1983a, pp. 22-28.

37. ———, "The Arbitrage Pricing Theory Approach to Strategic Portfolio Planning," *Financial Analysts Journal,* 40 (May-June 1984a), 14-26.

38. ———, "The Merits of the Arbitrage Pricing Theory for Portfolio Management." Paper presented at the Institute for Quantitative Research in Finance, Fall 1983b.

39. ———. "An Empirical Investigation of the Arbitrage Pricing Theory." *Journal of Finance,* December 1980, 1073-1103.

40. ———, "A Critical Reexamination of the Empirical Evidence on the Arbitrage Pricing Theory: A Reply," *Journal of Finance,* 39 (June 1984b), 347-50.

41. Ross, S.: "Return, Risk and Arbitrage," in I. Friend and J. Bicksler (eds.), *Risk and Return in Finance,* Ballinger, Cambridge, 1976.

42. ———, "Reply to Dhrymes: APT Is Empirically Relevant," *Journal of Portfolio Management,* Fall 1984, p. 55.

43. ———. "A Simple Approach to the Valuation of Risky Streams." *Journal of Business,* July 1979, 254-286.

44. —————., "The Arbitrage Pricing Theory of Capital Asset Pricing," *Journal of Economic Theory,* 13 (December 1976), 341-60.

45. Shanken, Jay, "The Arbitrage Pricing Theory: Is It Testable?" *Journal of Fi-nance,* 37 (December 1982), 1129-40.

46. ———: "Multi-Bet CAPM or Equilibrium APT?: A Reply," *Journal of Finance.* September 1985, pp. 1189-1196.

47. ———: "Nonsynchronous Data and the Covariance Factor Structure of Returns," *Journal of Finance* June 1987, pp. 221-231.

48. Sharpe, William R, "Factor Models, CAPMs, and the APT," *Journal of Port-folio Management,* Fall 1984, 21-25.

49. Simkowitz, M.A., and W.L. Beedles, "Diversification in a Three-Moment World," *Journal of Finance and Quantitative Analysis,* 13 (December 1978), 924-41.

50. Trycinka. Charles: "On the Number of Factors in the Arbitrage Pricing Model," *Journal of Finance,* June 1986. pp. 347-368.

30

Bond Portfolio Management Strategies

INTRODUCTION

Successful bond portfolio management involves far more than mastering a myriad of technical information. Such information is useful only to the extent that it helps generate higher risk-adjusted returns. In this chapter, we discuss the different types of active bond portfolio strategies, structured portfolio strategies: indexing and liability funding strategies, and the performance measurement and evaluation techniques.

ACTIVE BOND PORTFOLIO STRATEGIES

Active bond portfolio strategies is an investigation of the various sources of return from holding a fixed-income portfolio. Three sources of return are: coupon income, any capital gain (or loss), and reinvestment income. Here we explore the factors that affect one or more of these sources. In general, the factors that affect a portfolio's return are:
1. Changes in the level of interest rates
2. Changes in the shape of the yield curve
3. Changes in yield spreads among bond sectors
4. Changes in the option-adjusted spread; and the
5. Changes in the yield spread (risk premium) for a particular bond

A money manager who pursues an active strategy will position a portfolio to capital on expectations about future interest rates. But the potential outcome (as measured by total return) must be assessed before an active strategy is implemented. The primary reason for this is that the market (collectively) has certain expectations for future interest rates and these expectations are embodied into the market price of bonds. The outcome of a strategy will depend on how a manager's expectation differs from that of the market. Moreover, it does not make a difference if the market's expectation is correct. What is relevant is that the price of a bond embodies those expectations. The same is true for the strategies.

Consequently, while some managers might refer to an "optimal strategy" that should be pursued given certain expectations, that is insufficient information in making an investment decision. If the market's expectations are the same as the manager's, bond prices reflect these expectations. For this reason there is work for evaluating active strategies rather than the blind pursuit of a strategy based merely on general statements such as "if you expect.... you should pursue ... strategy."

Interest-Rate Expectations Strategies

A money manager who believes that he or she can accurately forecast the future level of interest rates will alter the portfolio's sensitivity to interest-rate changes. As duration is a measure of interest-rate sensitivity, this involves increasing a portfolio's duration if interest rates are expected to fall and reducing duration if interest rates are expected to rise. For those managers whose benchmark is a bond index, this means increasing the portfolio duration relative to the benchmark index if interest rates are expected to fall and reducing it if interest rates are expected to rise. The degree to which the duration of the managed portfolio is permitted to diverge from that of the benchmark index may be limited by the client.

A portfolio's duration may be altered by swapping (or exchanging) bonds in the portfolio for new bonds that will achieve the target portfolio duration. Such swaps are commonly referred to as *rate anticipation swaps*. Alternatively, a more efficient means for altering the duration of a bond portfolio is to use interest-rate futures contracts. Buying futures increases a portfolio's duration, while selling futures decreases it.

The key to this active strategy is, of course, an ability to forecast the direction of future interest rates. The interest rates may not be forecasted so that risk-adjusted excess returns can be realised consistently. It is doubtful whether betting on future interest rates will provide a consistently superior return.

While a manager may not pursue an active strategy based strictly on future interest-rate movements, there can be a tendency to make an interest-rate bet to cover inferior performance relative to a benchmark index. For example, suppose that a manager holds himself or herself out to a client as pursuing one of the active strategies and he is to be evaluated over a one-year investment horizon and that three months before the end of the investment horizon, the manager is performing below the client-specified benchmark index. If the manager believes the account will be lost because of under performance, there is an incentive to bet on interest-rate movements. If the manager is correct. The account will be saved, although an incorrect bet will result in under performing the benchmark index by a greater amount. In this case the account might probably be lost regardless of the level of under performance. A client can prevent this type of gaming by a manager by imposing constraints on the degree that the portfolio's duration can vary from that of the benchmark index. Also, in the performance-evaluation stage of the investment management process, decomposing the portfolio's return into the factors that generated the return will highlight the extent to which a portfolio's return is attributable to changes in the level of interest rates.

There are other active strategies that rely on forecasts of future interest-rate levels. Future interest rates, for instance, affect the value of options embedded in callable bonds and the value of prepayment options embedded in mortgage-backed securities. Callable corporate bonds with coupon rates above the expected future interest rate will underperform relative to non-callable bonds or low-coupon bands. This is because of the negative convexity feature of callable bonds. For the wide range of mortgage-backed securities, effect of interest rates on prepayments cause some to benefit from higher future interest rates and others to benefit from lower future interest rates.

Yield Curve Strategies

The yield curve for Treasury securities shows the relationship between their maturities and yields. The shape of this yield curve changes over time. *Yield curve strategies* involve positioning a portfolio to capitalise on expected changes in the shape of the Treasury yield curve.

Types of Shifts in the Yield Curve and Impact on Historical Returns

A shift in the yield curve refers to the relative change in the yield for each Treasury maturity. A *parallel shift in the yield curve* is a shift in which the change in the yield on all maturities is the same. A *nonparallel shift in the yield curve* indicates that the yield for maturities does not change by the same number of basis points.

EXHIBIT-1

Types of Yield Curve Shifts

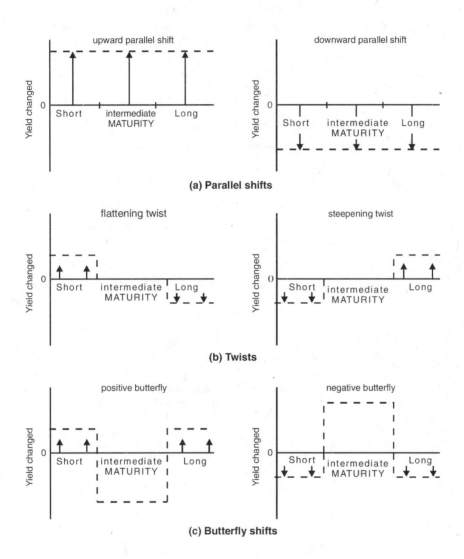

(a) Parallel shifts

(b) Twists

(c) Butterfly shifts

Historically, two types of nonparallel yield curve shifts have been observed: a twist in the slope of the yield curve and a change in the humpedness of the yield curve. All of these shifts are portrayed graphically in Exhibit 1. A twist in the slope of the yield curve refers to a flattening or steepening of the yield curve. In practice, the slope of the yield curve is measured by the spread between some long-term Treasury yield and some short-term Treasury yield.

A flattening of the yield curve indicates that the yield spread between the yield on a long-term and a short-term Treasury has decreased; a *steepening of the yield curve* indicates that the yield spread between a long-term and a short-term Treasury has increased. The other type of nonparallel shift, a change in the humpedness of the yield curve, is referred to as a *butterfly shift*.

Analysis of the three types of yield curve shifts reveals that these shifts are not independent, with the two most common types of yield curve shifts being (1) a downward shift in the yield curve combined with a steepening of the yield curve, and (2) an upward shift in the yield curve combined with a flattening of the yield curve. These two types of shifts in the yield curve are depicted in Exhibit 2. Generally, an upward shift and flattering of the yield curve is correlated with a positive butterfly (less humpedness), while a downward shift and steepening of the yield curve is correlated with a negative butterfly (more humpedness).

EXHIBIT 2

Combinations of Yield Curve Shifts

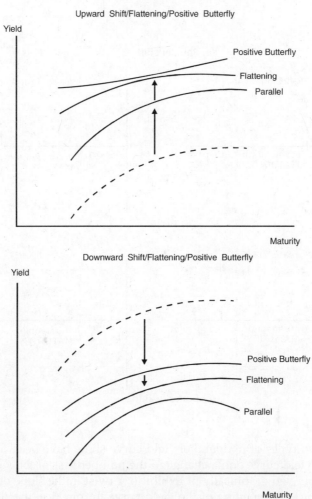

Yield Curve Strategies

In portfolio strategies that seek to capitalise on expectations based on short-term movements in yields, the dominant source of return is the impact on the price of the securities in the portfolio. This means that the maturity of the securities in the portfolio will have an important impact on the portfolio's return. For example, a total return over a one-year investment horizon for a portfolio consisting of securities all maturing in one year will not be sensitive to changes in how the yield curve shifts one year from now. In contrast, the total return over a one-year investment horizon for a portfolio consisting of securities all maturing in 30 years will be sensitive to how the yield curve shifts because one year from now the value of the portfolio will depend on the yield offered on 29-year securities. The long maturity bonds have substantial price volatility when yields change.

When the yield curve shifts, a portfolio consisting of equal proportions of securities maturing in one year and securities maturing in 30 years will have quite a different total return over a one-year investment horizon. The price of the one-year securities in the portfolio will not be sensitive to how the one- year yield has changed, but the price of the 30-year securities will be highly sensitive to how long-term yields have changed. Each of these strategies in depicted in Exhibit-3.

The key point is that for short-term investment horizons, the spacing of the maturity of bonds in the portfolio will have a significant impact on the total return. Consequently, yield curve strategies involve positioning a portfolio with respect to the maturities of the securities across the maturity spectrum included in the portfolio. There are three yield curve strategies: (1) bullet strategies, (2) barbell strategies, and (3) ladder strategies.

In a *bullet strategy,* the portfolio is constructed so that the maturity of the securities in the portfolio are highly concentrated at one point on the yield curve. In a *barbell strategy,* the maturity of the securities included in the portfolio are concentrated at two extreme maturities. Actually, in practice when managers refer to a barbell strategy it is relative to a bullet strategy. For example, a bullet strategy might be to create a portfolio with maturities concentrated around 10 years, while a corresponding barbell strategy might be a portfolio with five- and 20-year maturities. In a *ladder strategy* the portfolio is constructed to have approximately equal amounts of each maturity. So, for example, a portfolio might have equal amounts of securities with one year to maturity, two years to maturity, and so on.

Each of these strategies will result in different performance when the yield curve shift. The actual performance will depend on both the type of shift and the magnitude of the shift. Thus no general statements can be made about the optimal yield curve strategy. The proper way to analyse any portfolio strategy is to look at its potential total return. If a manager wants to assess the outcome of the portfolio for any assumed shift in the Treasury yield curve, this should be done by calculating the potential total return if that shift actually occurs. This can be illustated by looking at the performance of two hypotetical portfolios of Treasury securities assuming different shifts in the Treasury yield curve. The three hypothetical Treasury securities shown in Table-1 are considered for inclusion in our two portfolios. Thus, the Treasury yield curve consists of these three Treasury securities: a short-term security (A, the five-year security), an intermediate-term security (C, the 10-year security), and a long-term security (B, the 20-year security).

Consider the following two yield curve strategies: a bullet strategy and a barbell strategy. We will label the portfolios created based on these two strategies as the "bullet portfolio" and the "barbell portfolio" and they comprise the following:

*   Bullet Portfolio: 100% bond C
*   Barbell portfolio: 50.2% bond A and 49.8% bond B

The bullet portfolio consists of only bond C, the 10-year bond. In our hypothetical portfolio, all the principal is received when bond C matures in 10 years. The barbell portfolio consists of almost an equal amount of the short- and long-term securities. It is

EXHIBIT 3

Yield curve strategies: Bullet, Barbell, and Ladder

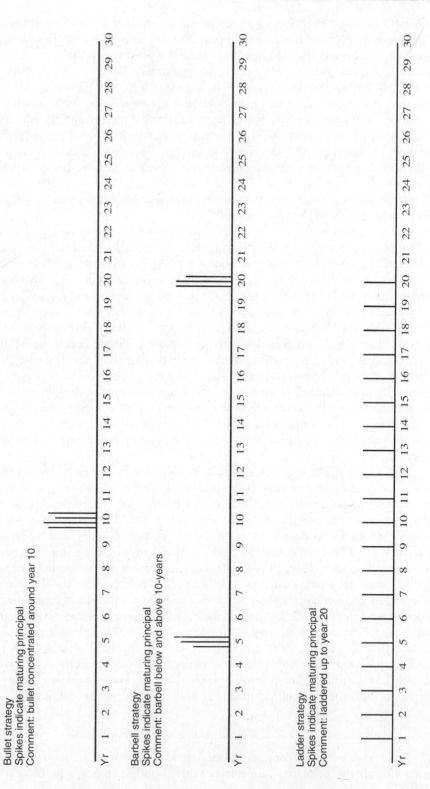

Bullet strategy
Spikes indicate maturing principal
Comment: bullet concentrated around year 10

Barbell strategy
Spikes indicate maturing principal
Comment: barbell below and above 10-years

Ladder strategy
Spikes indicate maturing principal
Comment: laddered up to year 20

the result of a barbell strategy because principal will be received at two ends of the maturity spectrum. Specifically, relative to the bullet portfolio, which in our illustration has all its principal being returned in 10 years, for the barbell portfolio the principal is being returned at shorter (five years) and longer (20 years) dates. As indicated in Table-1, the ₹ duration for the bullet portfolio per 100-basis-point change in yield is 6.434. For the barbell portfolio, the ₹ duration is just the weighted average of the ₹ duration of the two bonds. Therefore,

₹ duration of barbell portfolio = 0.502(4.005) + 0.498(8.882) = 6.434

The ₹ duration of the barbell portfolio is the same as that of the bullet portfolio. (In fact, the barbell portfolio was designed to produce this result.)

Duration is just first approximation of the change in price resulting from a change in interest rates. Convexity provides a second approximation to the price change. For two portfolios with the same ₹ duration, the greater the convexity, the better the performance of a bond or a portfolio when yields change. What is necessary to understand for this illustration is that the larger the ₹ convexity, the greater the ₹ price change due to a portfolio's convexity. As shown in Table-1, the convexity of the bullet portfolio is 55.4506. The ₹ convexity for the barbell portfolio is a weighted average of the ₹ convexity of the two bonds. That is,

₹ Convexity of barbell portfolio = 0.502(19.8164) + 0.498(124.1702) = 71.7846

Therefore, the ₹ convexity of the barbell portfolio is greater than that of the barbell portfolio.

TABLE-1

Three Hypothetical Treasury Securities

Bond	Coupon (%)	Maturity (years)	Price plus Accrued	Yield to Maturity (%)	₹ Duration	₹ Convexity
A	8.50	5	100	8.50	4.005	19.8164
B	9.50	20	100	9.50	8.882	124.1702
C	9.25	10	100	9.25	6.434	55.4506

Similarly, the yield for the two portfolios is not the same. The yield for the bullet portfolio is simply the yield to maturity of bond C, 9.25%. The traditional yield calculation for the barbell portfolio, which is found by taking a weighted average of the yield to maturity of the two bonds included in the portfolio, is 8.998%:

portfolio yield for barbell portfolio 0.502(8.50%) + 0.498(9.50%) = 8.998%

This approach suggests that the yield of the bullet portfolio is 25.2 basis points greater than that of the barbell portfolio (9.25% – 8.998%). Although both portfolios have the same ₹ duration, the yield of the bullet portfolio is greater than the yield of the barbell portfolio. However, the ₹ convexity of the barbell portfolio is greater than that of the bullet portfolio. The difference in the two yields is sometimes referred to as the *cost of convexity* (i.e., giving up yield to get better convexity).

Now, suppose that a portfolio manager with a six-month investment horizon has a choice of investing in the bullet portfolio or the barbell portfolio. Which one should he choose? The manager knows that (I) the two portfolios have the same ₹ duration, (2) the yield for the bullet portfolio is greater than that of the barbell portfolio, and (3) the ₹ convexity of the barbell portfolio is greater than that of the bullet portfolio. Actually, this information is not adequate in making the decision. What is necessary is to assess the potential total return when the yield curve shifts.

Table-2 provides an analysis of the six-month total return of the two portfolios when the yield curve shifts. The numbers reported in the exhibit are the difference in the total return for the two portfolios. Specifically, the following is shown:

difference in ₹ return =   bullet portfolio's total return– barbell portfolio's total return

Thus a positive value means that the bullet portfolio outperformed the barbell portfolio, and a negative sign means that the barbell portfolio outperformed the bullet portfolio.

Let's focus on the second column of Table-2, which is labeled "parallel shift." This is the relative total return of the two portfolios over the six-month investment horizon assuming that the yield curve shifts in a parallel fashion. In this case parallel movement of the yield curve means that the yields for the short-term bond (A), the intermediate-term bond (C), and the long-term bond (B) change by the same number of basis points, shown in the "yield change" column of the table.

Which portfolio is the better investment alternative if the yield curve shifts in a parallel fashion and the investment horizon is six months? The answer depends on the amount by which yields change. Notice that when yields change by less than 100 basis points, the bullet portfolio outperforms the barbell portfolio. The reverse is true if yields change by more than 100 basis points.

This illustration makes two key points. First, even if the yield curve shifts in a parallel fashion, two portfolios with the same ₹ duration will not give the same performance. The reason is that the two portfolios do not have the same convexity. The second point is that while with all other things equal it is better to have more convexity than less. The market charges for convexity in the form of a higher price or a lower yield. But the benefit *of* the greater convexity depends on how much yields change. As can be seen from the second column of Table-2 if market yields change by less than 100 basis points (up or down), the bullet portfolio, which has less convexity, will provide a better total return

Now let's look at what happens if the yield curve does not shift in a parallel fashion. The last two columns of Table-2 show the relative performance of the two portfolios for a nonparallel shift of the yield curve. Specifically, the first nonparallel shift column assumes that if the yield on bond C (the intermediate-term bond) changes by the amount shown in the first column, bond A (the short-term bond) will change by the same amount plus 25 basis points, whereas bond B (the long-term bond) will change by the same amount shown in the first column less 25 basis points. Measuring the steepness of the yield curve as the spread between the long-term yield (yield on bond B) and the short-term yield (yield on Bond A), the spread has decreased by 50 basis points. Such a nonparallel shift means a flattening of the yield curve. As can be seen in Table-2, for this assumed yield curve shift, the barbell outperforms the bullet.

In the last column, the nonparallel shift assumes that for a change in bond C's yield, the yield on bond A will change by the same amount less 25 basis points, whereas that on bond B will change by the same amount plus 25 points. Thus the spread between the long-term yield and the short-term yield has increased by 50 basis points and therefore the yield curve has steepened. In this case the bullet portfolio outperforms the barbell portfolio as long as the yield on bond C does not rise by more than 250 basis points or fall by more than 325 basis points.

TABLE-2
Relative Performance of Bullet Portfolio and Barbell Portfolio over a Six-Month
Investment Horizon[a]

Yield Change	Parallel Shift	Nonparallel Shift[b]	Shift[c] (%)
-5.000	-7.19	-10.69	-3.89
-4.750	-6.28	-9.61	-3.12
-4.500	-5.44	-8.62	-2.44
-4.250	-4.68	-7.71	-1.82
-4.000	-4.00	-6.88	-1.27
-3.750	-3.38	-6.13	-0.78
-3.500	-2.82	-5.44	-0.35
-3.250	-2.32	-4.82	0.03
-3.000	-1.88	-4.26	0.36
-2.750	-1.49	-3.75	0.65
-2.500	-1.15	-3.30	0.89
-2.250	-0.85	-2.90	1.09
-2 000	-0.59	-2.55	1.25
-1.750	-0.38	-2.24	1.37
-1.500	-0.20	-1.97	1.47
-1.250	-0.05	-1.74	1.53
-1.000	0.06	-1.54	1.57
-0.750	0.15	-1.38	1.58
-0.500	0.21	-1.24	1.57
-0.250	0.24	-1.14	1.53
0.000	0.25	-1.06	1.48
0.250	0.24	-1.01	1.41
0.500	0.21	-0.98	1.32
0.750	0.16	-0.97	1.21
1.000	0.09	-0.98	1.09
1.250	0.01	-1.00	0.96
1.500	-0.08	-1.05	0.81
1.750	-0.19	-1.10	0.66
2.000	-0.31	-1.18	0.49
2.250	-0.44	-1.26	0.32
2.500	-0.58	-1.36	0.14
2.750	-0.73	-1.46	-0.05
3.000	-0.88	-1.58	-0.24
3.250	-1.05	-1.70	-0.44
3.500	-1.21	-1.84	-0.64
3.750	-1.39	-1.98	-0.85
4.000	-1.57	-2.12	-1.06
4.250	-1.75	-2.27	-1.27
4.500	-1.93	-2.43	-1.48
4.750	-2.12	-2.58	-1.70
5.000	-2.31	-2.75	-1.92

[a] Performance is based on the difference in total return over a six-month investment horizon. Specifically, bullet portfolio's total return — barbell portfolio's total return Therefore a negative value means that the barbell portfolio outperformed the bullet portfolio.

[b] Change in yield for bond C. Nonparallel shift as follows (flattening of yield curve):
    yield change bond A = yield change bond C + 25 basis points
    yield change bond B = yield change bond C — 25 basis points

[c] Change in yield for bond C. Nonparallel shift as follows (steepening of yield Curve):
    yield change bond A = yield change bond C — 25 basis points
    yield change bond B = yield change bond C + 25 basis points

The key point here is that looking at measures such as yield (yield to maturity or some type of portfolio yield measure), duration, or convexity tells us little about performance over some investment horizon, because performance depends on the magnitude of the change in yields and how the yield curve shifts. Therefore, when a manager wants to position a portfolio based on expectations as to how she, might expect the yield curve to shift, it is imperative to perform total return analysis. For example, in a steepening yield curve environment, it is often stated that a bullet portfolio would be better than a barbell portfolio. As can be from Table-2, it is not the case that a bullet portfolio would out-perform a barbell portfolio. Whether the bullet portfolio outperforms the barbell depends on how much the yield curve steepens. An analysis similar to that in Table-2 based on total return for different degrees of steepening of the yield curve clearly demonstrates to a manager whether a particular yield curve strategy will be superior to another. The same analysis can be performed to assess the potential outcome of a ladder strategy.

Yield Spread Strategies

Yield spread strategies involve positioning a portfolio to capitalise on expected changes in yield spreads between sectors of the bond market. Swapping (or exchanging) one bond for another when the manager believes that the prevailing yield spread between the two bonds in the market is out of line with their historical yield spread, and that the yield spread will realign by the end of the investment horizon, are called *intermarket spread swaps*.

Credit Spreads

Credit or quality spreads change because of expected changes in economic prospects. Credit spreads between Treasury and non-Treasury issues widen in a declining or contracting economy and narrow during economic expansion. The economic rationale is that in a declining or contracting economy, corporations experience a decline in revenue and reduced cash flow, making it difficult for corporate issuers to service their contractual debt obligations. To induce investors to hold non-Treasury securities of lower-quality issuers, the yield spread relative to Treasury securities must widen. The converse is that during economic expansion and brisk economic activity, revenue and cash flow pick up, increasing the likelihood that corporate issuers will have the capacity to service their contractual debt obligations.

Spreads between Callable and Noncallable Securities

Spreads attributable to differences in callable and noncallable bonds and differences in coupons of callable bonds will change as a result of expected changes in (1) the direction of the change in interest rates, and (2) interest-rate volatility. An expected drop in the level of interest rates will widen the yield spread between callable bonds and noncallable bonds as the prospects that the issuer will exercise the call option increase. The reverse is true: The yield spread narrows if interest rates are expected to rise. An increase in interest-rate volatility increases the value of the embedded call option and thereby increases the yield spread between callable bonds and noncallable bonds. Expectations about the direction of the change in interest rates and interest-rate volatility will affect the yield spread between Treasury and mortgage pass-through securities and the yield spread between low-coupon and high-coupon pass-throughs in the same way as it affects the yield spreads for corporates

Importance of Duration Weighting of Yield Spread Strategies

What is critical in assessing yield spread strategies is to compare positions that have the same duration. To understand why, consider two bonds, X and Y. Suppose that the price of bond X is ₹ 80 with a modified duration of 5, while bond Y has a price of ₹ 90 with a modified duration of 4. Since modified duration is the approximate percentage change per 100-basis-point change in yield, a 100-basis-point change in yield for bond X would change its price by about 5%. Based on a price of 80, its price will change by about ₹ 4 per ₹ 80 of market value. Thus its duration for a 100-basis-point change in yield is ₹ 4 per ₹ 80 of market value. Similarly, for bond Y, its ₹ duration for a 1-basis-point change in yield per ₹ 90 of market value can be determined. In this case it is ₹ 3.6. So if bonds X and Y are being considered as alternative investments in a strategy other than one based on anticipating interest-rate movements, the amount of each bond in the strategy should be such that they will both have the same duration.

To illustrate this, suppose that a portfolio manager owns ₹ 10 of par value of bond X, which has a market value of ₹ 8 crore. The duration of bond X per 100-basis-point change in yield for the ₹ 8 crore market value is ₹ 40,00,000. Suppose further that this portfolio manager is considering exchanging bond X that it owns in its portfolio for bond Y. If the portfolio manager wants to have the same interest-rate exposure (i.e. ₹ duration), for bond Y that she currently has for bond X, she will buy a market value amount of bond Y with the same duration. If the portfolio manager purchased ₹ 10 crore of *per value* of bond Y and therefore, ₹ 9 crore of *market value* of bond Y, the price change per 100-basis-point change in yield would be only ₹ 36,00,000. If, instead, the portfolio manager purchased ₹ 10 crore of *market value* of bond Y, the duration per 100-basis-point change in yield would be ₹ 40,00,000. Since bond Y is trading at ₹ 90, ₹ 11.11 crore par value of bond Y must be purchased to keep the ₹ duration of the position from bond Y the same as for bond X.

Failure to adjust a portfolio repositioning based on some expected change in yield spread so as to hold the ₹ duration the same means that the outcome of the portfolio will be affected not only by the expected change in the yield spread but also by a change in the yield level. Thus a manager would be making a conscious yield spread bet and possibly an undesired bet on the level of interest rates.

Individual Security Selection Strategies

There are several active strategies that money managers pursue to identify mispriced securities. The most common strategy identifies an issue as undervalued because either (I) its yield is higher than that of comparably rated issues, or (2) its yield is expected to decline (and price therefore rise) because credit analysis indicates that its rating will improve.

A swap in which a money manager exchanges one bond for another bond that is similar in terms of coupon, maturity, and credit quality, but offers a higher yield, is called a *substitution swap*. This swap depends on a capital market imperfection. Such situations sometimes exist in the bond market owing to temporary market imbalances and the fragmented nature of the non-Treasury bond market. The risk the money manager faces in making a substitution swap is that the bond purchased may not be truly identical to the bond for which it is exchanged. Moreover, typically, bonds will have similar but not identical maturities and coupon. This could lead to differences in the convexity of the two bonds, and any yield spread may reflect the cost of convexity.

STRUCTURED STRATEGIES

Structured strategies generally do not rely on expectations of interest rate movements or change in yield spread relationships. Their objective, instead, is to design a portfolio that will achieve the performance of some predetermined benchmark. The target to achieve may be (1) the return on a specific benchmark index, (2) sufficient funds to satisfy a further single liability, or (3) sufficient funds to satisfy each liability of a future liability stream. The structured bond portfolio strategy used when the target to be achieved is replication of a predetermined benchmark index is called an indexing strategy.

BOND INDEXING

Bond indexing means designing a portfolio so that its performance will match the performance of some bond index. In indexing, performance is measured in terms of total rate of return achieved (or simply, total return) over some investment horizon. Total return over some investment horizon incorporates all three sources of return from holding a portfolio of bonds.

Several factors explain the recent popularity and phenomenal rate of growth of bond indexing. First, the empirical evidence suggests that historically the overall performance of active bond managers has been poor. Secondly, the popularity of bond indexing is because of fall in advisory management fees charged for an indexed portfolio compared to active management advisory fees. Lower nonadvisory fees, such as custodial fees, is the third explanation for the popularity of indexing. Finally, sponsors have greater control over external managers when an indexing strategy is selected. For example, in an actively managed portfolio, a sponsor who specifies a restriction on the portfolio's duration still gives the manager ample leeway to pursue strategies that may significantly underperform the index selected as a benchmark. In contrast, requiring an investment advisor to match an index gives little leeway to the manager and, as a result, should result in performance that does not significantly diverge from a benchmark.

Critics of indexing point out that while an indexing strategy matches the performance of some index, the performance of that index does not necessarily represent optimal performance. Moreover, matching an index does not mean that the manager will satisfy a client's return requirement objective. For example, if the objective of a fund is to have sufficient funds to satisfy a predetermined liability, indexing only reduces the likelihood that performance will not be materially worse than the index. The index's return is not necessarily related to the sponsor's liability. Finally, matching an index means that a money manager is restricted to the sectors of the bond market that are in the index, even though there may be attractive opportunities in market sectors excluded from the index.

At the theoretical level, the index fund approach is supported by the work of Markowitz on the construction of efficient portfolios and by capital market theory as developed by Sharpe Lintner, and Mossin. Markowitz demonstrates how portfolios can be constructed so as to maximise return for a given level of risk. Such portfolios are referred to as efficient portfolios.

The Sharpe-Lintner-Mossin analysis demonstrates that a market portfolio offers the highest level of return per unit of risk in an efficient market. An efficient market is one in which market participants cannot consistently earn abnormal risk-adjusted returns after considering transactions costs. A combination of securities in a portfolio with characteristics, similar to the market is able to capture the efficiency of the market. The theoretical market portfolio consists of all risky assets. The weight of each risky asset in the market portfolio is equal to the ratio of its market value to the aggregate market value of all risky assets. That is, the market portfolio is a capitalisation-weighted (value-weighted) portfolio of all risky assets. Table-3 summarises the advantages and disadvantages of bond indexing.

TABLE-3
Advantages and Disadvantages of Bond Indexing

Advantages	Disadvantages
No dependence on expectations and little risk of underperforming the index	Bond indexes do not reflect optimal performance
Reduced advisory and nonadvisory fees	Bond index may not match the sponsor's liabilities
Greater sponsor control	Restrictions on fund; management ignores opportunities

INDEXING METHODOLOGIES

Once a money manager has decided to pursue an indexing strategy and has selected an index, the next step is to construct a portfolio that will track the index. *Any discrepancy between the performance of the indexed portfolio and the index (whether positive or negative) is referred to as tracking error.* Tracking error has three sources: (1) transaction costs in constructing the indexed portfolio, (2) differences in the composition of the indexed portfolio and the index itself, and (3) discrepancies between prices used by the organisation constructing the index and transaction prices paid by the indexer.

One approach in constructing the indexed portfolio is for the money manager to purchase all the issues in the index according to their weight in the benchmark index. However, substantial tracking error will result from the transactions costs (and other fees) associated with purchasing all the issues and reinvesting cash flow (maturing principal and coupon interest). A broad-based market index may include over 100 issues, so large transactions costs may make this approach impractical. In addition, some issues in the index may not be available at the prices used in constructing the index.

Instead of purchasing all issues in the index, the money manager may purchase just a sample of issues. Although this approach reduces tracking error resulting from high transaction costs, it increases tracking error resulting from the mismatch of the indexed portfolio and the index.

Generally speaking, the fewer the number of issues used to replicate the index, the smaller the tracking error due to transactions costs but the greater the tracking error risk due to the mismatch of the characteristics of the indexed portfolio and the index. In contrast, the more issues purchased to replicate the index, the greater the tracking error due to transactions costs and the smaller the tracking error risk due to the mismatch of the indexed portfolio and the index. Obviously, then, there is a trade-off between tracking error and the number of issues used to construct the indexed portfolio.

There are three methodologies for designing a portfolio to replicate an index: (I) the stratified sampling or cell approach, (2) the optimisation approach, and (3) the variance minimisation approach. For each of these approaches, the initial question that the indexer must ask is: What factors affect a bond index's performance? Each approach assumes that the performance of an individual bond depends on a number of systematic factors that affect the performance of all bonds and on a factor unique to the individual issue. This last risk is diversifiable risk. The objective of the three approaches is to construct an indexed portfolio that eliminates this diversifiable risk.

Stratified Sampling or Cell Approach

Under the *stratified sampling approach to indexing*, the index is divided into cells, each cell representing a different characteristic of the index. The most common characteristics used to break down an index are (I) duration. (2) coupon. (3) maturity, (4) market sectors (Treasury, corporate, mortgage-backed), (5) credit rating, (6) call factors, and (7) sinking fund features. The last two factors are particularly important because the call and sinking fund features of an issue will affect its performance.

For example, suppose that a manager selects the following characteristics to partition a Treasury/agency/corporate bond index:

Characteristic 1: effective duration range: (I) less than or equal to five years, and (2) greater than five years;

Characteristic 2: maturity range: (I) less than five years. (2) between five and 15 years, and (3) greater than or equal to 15 years;

Characteristic 3: market sectors: (I) Treasury, (2) agencies, and (3) corporates;

Characteristic 4: credit rating: (I) triple A, (2) double A, (3) single A, and (4) triple B.

The total number of cells would be equal to 72 (= $2 \times 3 \times 3 \times 4$).

The objective, then, is to select from all the issues in the index one or more issues in each cell that can be used to represent the entire cell. The total amount purchased of the issues from each cell will be based on the percentage of the index's total market value that the cell represents. For example, if 40% of the market value of all the issues in the index is made up of corporate bonds, 40% of the market value of the indexed portfolio should be composed of corporate bond issues.

The number of cells that the indexer uses will depend on the amount of the portfolio to be indexed. A large number of cells would require purchasing odd lots of issues. This increases the cost of buying the issues to represent a cell and thus would increase the tracking error. Reducing the number of cells to overcome this problem increases tracking error risk of index mismatch because the characteristics of the indexed portfolio may differ materially from those of the index.

Optimisation Approach

In the *optimisation approach to indexing*, the money manager seeks to design an indexed portfolio that will match the cell breakdown as just described, and satisfy other constraints, but also optimise some objective. An objective might be to maximise the portfolio yield, to maximise convexity, or to maximise expected total returns. Constraints other than matching the cell breakdown might include not purchasing more than a specified amount of one issuer or group of issuers, or overweighing certain sectors for enhanced indexing.

The computational technique used to derive the optimal solution to the indexing problem in this approach is mathematical programming. When the objective function that the indexer seeks to optimise is a linear function, linear programming (a specific form of mathematical programming) is used. If the objective function is quadratic, the particular mathematical programming technique used is quadratic programming.

Variance Minimisation Approach

The *variance minimisation approach to indexing* is by far the most complex of the methodologies. This approach requires using historical data to estimate the variance of the tracking error. This is done by estimating a price function for every issue in the index. The price function is estimated on the basis of two sets of factors: (I) the cash flows from the issue discounted at the theoretical spot rates, and (2) other factors, such as the duration or sector characteristics. Using a large universe of issues and statistical techniques, the price function is estimated from historical data. Once the price function for each issue is obtained, a variance equation for the tracking error can be constructed. The objective then is to minimise the variance of the tracking error in constructing the indexed portfolio. As the variance is a quadratic function (the difference between the benchmark return and the indexed portfolio's return, squared), quadratic programming is used to find the optimal indexed portfolio in terms of minimised tracking error. The biggest problem with this approach is that-estimating the price function from historical data is very difficult in the Treasury market, let alone the corporate market or the new issue market. Also, the price function may not be stable.

Although the stratified sampling (or cell) approach seems to be the easiest to use. it is extremely difficult to implement when large, diversified portfolios are taken as the benchmark. In this case, many cells are required, and the problem becomes complex. Also, because the handpicking of issues to match each cell is subjective, tracking error may result. Mathematical programming reduces the complexity of the problem when well-defined constraints are employed, allowing the indexer to analyse large quantities of data optimally.

LOGISTICAL PROBLEMS IN IMPLEMENTING AN INDEXING STRATEGY

An indexer faces several logistical problems in constructing an indexed portfolio. First, the prices for each issue used by the organisation that publishes the index may not be execution prices available to the indexer. In fact, they may be materially different from the prices offered by some dealers. In addition, the prices used by organisations reporting the value of indexes are based on bid prices. Dealer ask prices, however, are the ones that the money manager would have to transact at when constructing or rebalancing the indexed portfolio. Thus there will be a bias between the performance of the index and the indexed portfolio that is equal to the bid-ask spread.

Enhanced Indexing

The objective of an *enhanced indexing strategy* is to replicate the total return performance of some predetermined index. In enhanced indexing (also called "indexing plus"), the objective is consistently to exceed the total return performance of the index by an amount sufficient to justify a higher management advisory fee and a higher level of risk of underperforming the index. The total return on the index becomes the minimum total return objective rather than the target total return. Thus enhanced indexing brings active strategies back into the portfolio management process, although they are assumed to employ only low-risk strategies.

LIABILITY FUNDING STRATEGIES

The nature of liabilities as well as regulatory considerations, determines the investment strategy pursued by all institutional investors. By nature, liabilities vary with respect to the amount and timing of their payment. The liabilities will generally fall into one of the four types shown in Table 4.

TABLE 4

Liability Type	Amount of Cash Outlay	Timing of Cash Outlay
I	Known	Known
II	Known	Uncertain
III	Uncertain	Known
IV	Uncertain	Uncertain

Surplus management is a more appropriate description of the activity of asset/liability management of an institution. The economic surplus of any entity is the difference between the market value of all its assets and the market value of its liabilities, that is

economic surplus = market value of assets — market value of liabilities

While the concept of a market value of assets may not seem unusual, one might ask: What is the market value of liabilities? This value is simply the present value of the liabilities, where the liabilities are discounted at an appropriate interest rate. A rise in interest rates will therefore decrease the present value or market value of the liabilities: a decrease in interest rates will increase the present value or market value of liabilities. Thus the economic surplus can be expressed as

economic surplus = market value of assets — present value of liabilities

For example, consider an institution that has a portfolio consisting only of bonds and liabilities. Let's look at what happens to the economic surplus if interest rates rise. This will cause the bonds to decline in value, but it will also cause the liabilities to decline in value. Since both the assets and liabilities decline, the economic surplus can either increase, decrease, or not change. The net effect depends on the relative interest-rate sensitivity of the assets compared to the liabilities. Since duration is a measure of the responsiveness of cash flows to changes in interest rates, a duration can be calculated for liabilities in the same way in which it is calculated for assets. Thus the duration of liabilities measures their responsiveness to a change in interest rates.

Since the net effect on the surplus depends on the duration or interest-rate sensitivity of the assets and liabilities, it is imperative that portfolio managers be able to measure this sensitivity for all assets and liabilities accurately.

Institutional investors must prepare periodic financial statements. These financial statements must be prepared in accordance with *generally accepted accounting principles*. With respect to he financial reporting of assets, there are three possible methods for reporting: (1) amortised cost or historical cost, (2) market value, or (3) the lower of cost or market value. Despite the fact that the real cash flow is the same regardless of the accounting treatment, there can be substantial differences in the financial statements using these three methods. In the *amortised cost method,* the value reported in the balance sheet reflects an adjustment to the acquisition cost for debt securities purchased at a discount or premium from their maturity value. This method is sometimes referred to as *book value accounting.* In the *market value accounting method,* the balance sheet reported value of an asset is its market value. When an asset is reported in the financial statements of an institution at its market value, it is said to be "marked to market." Finally, the *lower of cost* or *market method* requires comparison of market value to the amortised cost, with the lower of these two values reported in the balance sheet. The value reported cannot exceed the amortised cost.

Immunisation of a Portfolio to Satisfy Liabilities

Liability funding strategies involve designing a portfolio to produce sufficient funds to satisfy liabilities whether or not interest rates change. When there is only one future liability to be funded, an immunisation strategy can be used. An immunisation strategy is designed so that as interest rates change, interest-rate risk and reinvestment risk will offset each other in such a way that the minimum accumulated value (or minimum rate of return) becomes the target accumulated value (or target yield). An immunisation strategy requires that a money manager create a bond portfolio with a duration equal to the investment horizon. Because immunisation theory is based on parallel shifts in the yield curve, the risk is that a portfolio will not be immunised even if the duration-matching condition is satisfied. Immunisation risk can be quantified so that a portfolio that minimises this risk can be constructed.

When there are multiple liabilities to be satisfied, either multiperiod immunisation or cash flow matching can be used. Multiperiod immunisation is a duration-matching strategy that exposes the portfolio to immunisation risk. The cash flow—matching strategy does not impose any duration requirement. Although the only risk that the liabilities will not be satisfied is that issues will be called or will default, the cost of a cash flow—matched portfolio may be higher than that of a portfolio constructed using a multiperiod immunisation strategy

Liability funding strategies where the liability payments and the asset cash flows are known with certainty are deterministic models. In a stochastic model, either the liability payments or the asset cash flows, or both, are uncertain. Stochastic models require specification of a probability distribution for the process that generates interest rates.

A combination of active and immunisation strategies can be pursued. Allocation of the portion of the portfolio to be actively managed is based on the immunisation target rate, the minimum return acceptable to the client, and the expected worst-case return from the actively managed portfolio. The key is to calculate the funds required to lock in via immunization a future value at current rates. If T denoter the time left until the horizon date, and r the market interest rate at any particular time, then the value of the fund necessary guarantee an ability to reach the minimum acceptable terminal value / $(1 + r)^t$, because the size of portfolio, if immunized, will grow risk-free to future value by the horizon date. The value becomes the trigger point; if and when the actual portfolio value dips to the trigger point, active management will cease. To illustrate, suppose that interest rate currently are 10% and that a manager's portfolio is worth ₹ 10 crore now. At current rate the manager could lock in, via immunigation techniques, a future value of ₹ 12.10 crore after two years. Now suppose that manager wishes to pursue an active management but is willing to risk losses only to the extent that the terminal value of the portfolio would not drop lower than ₹ 11 crore. Because only ₹ 9.09 crore [₹ 11 crore/ $(1.10)^2$] is required to achieve this minimum acceptable terminal value, and the portfolio currently is worth ₹ 10 crore, the manager can afford to risk some losses at the outset and might start off with an active strategy rather than immediately immunizing.

In a contingent immunisation strategy, a money manager is either actively managing the portfolio or immunising it. Since both strategies are not pursued at the same time, contingent immunisation is not a combination or mixture strategy.

BOND PERFORMANCE MEASUREMENT AND EVALUATION

Performance measurement involves the calculation of the return realised by a portfolio manager over some time interval *which we call the* evaluation period. Performance evaluation *is concerned with two issues. The first is to determine whether the manager added value by outperforming the established benchmark. The second is to determine how the manager achieved the calculated return.*

REQUIREMENTS FOR A BOND PERFORMANCE AND ATTRIBUTION ANALYSIS PROCESS

There are three desired requirements of a bond performance and attribution analysis process. The first is that the process be accurate. For example, there are several ways of measuring portfolio return. The return should recognise the time when each cash flow actually occurs, resulting in a much more accurate measure of the actual portfolio performance. The second requirement is that the process be informative. It should be capable of evaluating the managerial skills that go into fixed-income portfolio management. To be informative, the process must effectively address the key management skills and explain how these can be expressed in terms of realised performance. The final requirement is that the process be simple. Whatever the output of the process, it should be understood by the manager and client, or others who may be concerned with the performance of the portfolio.

To evaluate the performance of a manager, a client must specify a benchmark against which the manager will be measured. There are two types of benchmarks that have been used in evaluating fixed-income portfolio managers: (1) market indexes published by dealer firms and vendors, and (2) normal portfolios.

A *normal portfolio* is a customised benchmark that includes a set of securities that contains all of the securities from which a manager normally chooses, weighted as the manager would weight them in a portfolio. Thus, a normal portfolio is a specialised index. It is argued that normal portfolios are more appropriate benchmarks than market indexes because they control for investment management style thereby representing a passive portfolio against which a manager can be evaluated.

The construction of a normal portfolio for a particular manager is no simple task. The principle is to construct a portfolio that, given the historical portfolios held by the manager, will reflect that manager's style in terms of assets and the weighting of those assets. The construction of a normal portfolio for a manager requires (1) defining the universe of fixed-income securities to be included in the normal portfolio, and (2) determining how these securities to be weighted (i.e. equally weighted or capitalisation weighted).

Defining the set of securities to be included in the normal portfolio begins with discussions between the client and the manager to determine the manager's investment style. Based on these discussions, the universe of all publicly traded securities is reduced to a subset that includes those securities that the manager considers eligible given his or her investment style.

Given these securities, the next question is how they should be weighted in the normal portfolio. The two choices are equal weighting or capitalisation weighting of each security. Various methodologies can be used to determine the weights. These methodologies typically involve a statistical analysis of the historical holdings of a manager and the risk exposure contained in those holdings.

Plan sponsors work with consultants to develop normal portfolios for a manager. The consultants use vendor systems that have been developed for performing the needed statistical analysis and the necessary optimisation programme to create a portfolio exhibiting similar factor positions to replicate the "normal" position of a manager. A plan sponsor must recognise that there is a cost to developing and updating the normal portfolio.

There are some who advocate the responsibility of developing normal portfolios should be left to the manager. However, many clients are reluctant to let their managers control the construction of normal portfolios because they believe that the managers will produce easily beaten, or "slow rabbit," benchmarks.

The role of performance evaluation is to determine if a money manager added value beyond what could have been achieved by a passive strategy in a benchmark portfolio. The analysis requires the establishment of a benchmark. One such benchmark is a normal portfolio. This is a customised benchmark that includes a set of securities that contains the universe of securities that a manager normally selects from and weighted as the manager would weight them in a portfolio. Advocates claim that normal portfolios are more appropriate benchmarks than market indexes because they control for investment management style, thereby representing a passive portfolio against which a manager can be evaluated. It is neither an easy nor a costless process to construct normal portfolios.

In the fixed-income area, returns are attributed to those elements beyond the manager's control, such as the interest-rate environment and duration policy constraints imposed by a client, and those that the management process contributes to such as interest- rate management, sector/quality allocations, and individual bond selection.

REVIEW PROBLEMS

1. A 30-year bond with 8% coupon is currently selling at ₹ 896.81. The investor believes that in 5 years the yield on 25-year bonds will be 8.50%. Should he purchase the 20-year bond which has 10% coupon bond and current yields of 9% but with the expected yield after 5-years to be 8% and selling at ₹ 1092.01 or the 30-year bond? The investor has a five-year time horizon.

Ans: The investor with a five year time horizon would be concerned about the bond's price and the value of the reinvested coupons five year hence. The 30-year 8% coupon bond will provide a stream of coupons of ₹ 40 half-year, which invested at the assumed rate of 4% half-year will accumulate to ₹ 480.24. The bond will sell in five years at a price equal to ₹ 40 x Annuity factor (4.25%, 50) + ₹ 1000 x PV factor (4.25%, 50), or ₹ 948.52, for a capital gain of ₹ 51.71 + ₹ 480.24 = ₹ 531.95, for a five -year return of ₹ 531.95/ ₹ 896.81 = .5932, or 59.32%. The 20 year maturity bond at the end of 5-year have a 15-year maturity. The bond's end-of-period price will be (assuming 30 semi-annual coupon payments

50 x Annuity factor (4%, 30) + 1,000 x PV factor (4%, 30) = ₹ 1172.92

The capital gain on the bond is therefore ₹ 80.91 If all coupon payments are reinvested at 4% per six month period, the value of the 10 semi-annual coupon payments with accumulated interest at the end of the five years will be ₹ 600.31. The total return provided by the bond over the five-year period will be ₹ 80.91 + ₹ 600.31 = ₹ 681.32 for a total five-year holding-period return of ₹ 681.22/₹ 1.092.01 = .624, or 62.4%.

Based on this scenario, the 20-years 10%. coupen bond offers a higher return for a five-year horizon.

2. What would be the trigger point with a three-year horizon, an interest rate of 12%, and a minimm acceptable terminal value of ₹ 10 crore?

   Ans: The trigger point is ₹ 10 crore/$(1.12)^3$ = ₹ 7.118 crore

QUESTIONS

1. What is the essential ingredient in all active portfolio strategies?
2. (a) What is an active portfolio strategy?
   (b) What will determine whether an active or a passive portfolio strategy will be pursued?

3. What are the limitations of using duration and convexity measures in active portfolio strategies?
4. What kinds of risks does duration involve?
5. Explain why you agree or disagree with the following statements:
   (a) "It is always better to have a portfolio with more convexity than one with less convexity."
   (b) "A bullet portfolio will always outperform a barbell portfolio with the same rupee duration if the yield curve steepens."
6. What factors lead to the use of bond indexing? Why does tracking error occur in a bond indexing strategy?
7. What is the stratified sampling or cell approach to indexing?
8. What are the various types of enhanced bond indexing strategies?
9. What is meant by immunising a bond portfolio?
10. (a) Why is basic underlying principle in an immunisation strategy?
    (b) Why may the matching of the maturity of a coupon bond to the maturity of a liability fail to immunise a portfolio?
11. If you expect interest rates to fall, how would you structure your bond portfolio with respect to duration and holding period?
12. How are bonds unique in terms of managing a portfolio of securities? Under what economic conditions might they be more important to some investors?

PROBLEMS

1. Below are two portfolios with a market value of ₹ 500 crore. The bond in both portfolios are trading at par value. The duration of the two portfolios is the same.

Bonds Included in Portfolio I

Issue	Years to Maturity	Par Value (₹ in crore)
A	2.0	₹ 120
B	2.5	130
C	20.0	150
D	20.5	100

Bonds Included in Portfolio II

Issue	Years to Maturity	Par Value (₹ in crore)
E	9.7	₹ 200
F	10.0	230
G	10.2	70

(a) Which portfolio can be characterised as a bullet portfolio?
(b) Which portfolio can be characterised as a barbell portfolio?
(c) Since the two portfolios have the same duration, explain whether their performance will be the same if interest rates change.
(d) If they will not perform the same, how would you go about determining which would perform best assuming that you have a six-month investment horizon?

2. An investor is managing a portfolio of ₹ 10 crore with a target duration of 10 years. He can choose from two bonds: a zero coupon bond with a maturity of 5 years, and a perpetuity, each currently yielding 7%. How much of each bond will the investor hold in his portfolio? How will these fraction changes next year if target duration is now 9 years.

3. What would be the trigger point with a four-year horizon, an invest rate of 10%, and a minimum acceptable value of ₹ 12 crore?

REFERENCES

1. Bierman, Harold. "How Much Diversification is Desirable?" *Journal of Portfolio Management*, Winter 1981, 42-44.

2. Bierwag, G.O., George G. Kaufman, and Alden Toevs. "Immunization Strategies for

Funding Multiple Liabilities." *Journal of Finance and Quantitative Analysis,* March 1983, 113-124.

3. Bierwag, G.O., George G. Kaufman, Robert Schweitzer, and Alden Toevs. "The Art of Risk Management in Bond Portfolios." *Journal of Portfolio Management,* Spring 1981, 27-36.

4. Biger, Nahum, "The Assessment of Inflation and Portfolio Selection," *Journal of Finance.* 45 (July 1975), 451-67.

5. Black, Fisher, "Capital Market Equilibrium with Restricted Borrowing," *Journal of Business,* 45 (July 1972), 444-55.

6. Christy, George A., "A Rationalization of the Stock-Bond Yield Spread," *Quarterly Review of Economics and Business* 7, no. 1 (Spring 1967): 63-70.

7. Cohen, Kalman, and Jerry Pogue: "An Empirical Evaluation of Alternative Portfolio Selection *Models," Journal of Business,* April 1967, pp. 166-193.

8. Dietz, P.O., H.R. Fogler, and D.J. Hardy: "The Challenge of Analyzing Bond Portfolio Returns." *Journal of Portfolio Management,* Spring 1980, pp. 53-58.

9. Dietz, Peter O., H. Russell Fogler, and Donald J. Hardy. "The Challenge of Analyzing Bond Portfolio Returns." *Journal of Portfolio Management* 6, no. 3 (Spring 1980).

10. Fabozzi, Frank J., and Irving M. Pollack, eds. *The Handbook of Fixed Income Securities.* Homewood, Ill.: Dow Jones-Irwin, 1987.

11. Fabozzi, Frank J., and T. Dessa Fabozzi. *Bond Markets, Analyses, and Strategies.* Englewood Cliffs, N.J.: Prentice-Hall, 1989.

12. Fisher, Lawrence, and Roman L. Weil. "Coping with the Risk of Interest Rate Fluctuations: Returns to Bondholders from Naive and Optimal *Strategies." Journal of Business,* October 1971, 408-431.

13. Fong, Gifford, and Oddrick Vasicek: "Fixed Income Performance Attribution." Institute for Quantitative Research in Finance, Spring Seminar 1994, Palm Beach. FL.

14. Fong, Gifford, Charles Pearson, Oldrich Vasicek, and Theresa Conroy. "Fixed-Income Portfolio Performance: Analyzing Sources of Return." In *The Handbook of Fixed-Income Securities,* 3rd ed., edited by Frank J. Fabozzi. Homewood, Ill.: Business One Irwin, 1991.

15. Fong, H. Gifford, and Oldrich Vasicek. "A Risk Minimizing Strategy for Multiple Liability Immunization." *Journal of Finance,* December 1984, 1541-1546.

16. Ibbotson, Roger G., and Rex A. Sinquefield. *Stocks, Bonds, Bills, and Inflation: Historical Returns (1926-1987).* Charlottesville, Va.: Research Foundation of Chartered Financial Analysts, 1989.

17. Leibowitz, Martin: "Goal Oriented Bond Portfolio Management," *Journal of Portfolio Management,* Summer 1979, pp. 13-18.

18. Levy, Haim, and Zvi Leman: "The Benefits of International Diversification in Bonds," *Financial Analysts Journal,* September-October 1988, pp. 56-67.

19. Livingston, M., "Duration and Risk Assessment for Bonds and Common Stocks: A Note," *Journal of Finance,* 33 (March 1978), 293-95.

20. Logue, Dennis E., and L. J. Merville, "Financial Policy and Market Expectations," *Financial Management,* 1 (Summer 1972), 37-44.

21. Longstaff, Francis, and Eduardo Schwartz: "Interest Rate Volatility and Bond Prices," *Financial Analysts Journal,* July-August 1993, pp. 70-74.

22. ———and ———: "Interest Rate Volatility and the Term Structure: A Two-Factor General Equilibrium *Model" Journal of Finance,* September 1992, pp. 1259-1282.

23. McAdams, Lloyd, and Evangelos Karagiannis: "Using Yield Curve Shapes to Manage Bond Portfollios," *Financial Analysts Journal,* May-June 1994, pp. 57-60.

24. McCulloch, J. Huston: "Measuring the Term Structure of Interest Rates," *Journal of Business,* January 1971, pp. 19-31.

25. McEnally, Richard W. "Portfolio Management Policies for Fixed Income Investors." In *Advances in Bond Analysis and Portfolio Strategies,* edited by Frank J. Fabozzi and T. Dessa Garlicki. Chicago: Probus Publishing, 1987.

26. McMillan, T.E., Louis Buck, and James Deegan: "The Fisher Theorem - An Illusion, But Whose?, *Financial Analysts Journal,* November-December 1984, pp. 63-71.

27. Melicher, Robert W., and D. F. Rush, "Systematic Risk, Financial Data, and Bond Rating Relationships in a Regulated Industry Environment," *Journal of Finance,* 29 (May 1974), 537-44.

28. Milne, Robert D. "Determination of Portfolio Policies: Individual Investors." In *Managing Investment Portfolios,* edited by John L. Maginn and Donald L. Tuttle. Boston: Warren, 1983.

29. Price, Lee N. "Choosing between Growth and Yield." *Financial Analysts Journal,* November/December 1981, 57-67.

30. Reilly, Frank K., and Rupinder S. Sidhu, "The Many Uses of Bond Duration," *Financial Analysts Journal,* 36 (July-August 1980), 58-72.

31. Roll, Richard. "Investment Diversification and Bond Maturity." *The Journal of Finance,* March 1971, p. 51.

32. Sharpe, W.F., "Bonds vs. Stocks: Lessons from Capital Market Theory, *Financial Analysts Journal, 29* (November-December 1973), 74-80.

33. Sharpe, William F., "Bonds Versus Stocks: Some Lessons from Capital Market Theory," *Financial Analysts Journal,* November-December 1973, pp. 74-80.

34. Soldofsky, Robert M. "Yield-Risk Performance Measurements." *Financial Analysts Journal,* September-October 1968, p. 130.

35. Strong, Robert A. "Linear Programming Solves Problem: Eases Duration Matching Process." *Pensions and Investment Age,* 17, no. 259, (11 December 1989), 21.

36. Vandell, Robert F., and Mark T. Finn. "Portfolio Objective: Win Big, Lose Little" *Journal of Portfolio Management,* Fall 1981, 37-45.

31

Investment Timing and Performance Measurement

INTRODUCTION

The portfolio building models are the foundation of the modern approach to portfolio management. Along with their successors, they allow the scientific selection of efficient portfolios. Of course, these models do not guarantee investment success because we are dealing with the uncertain future. The best portfolio building model in the world is of little comfort in a stock market crash—except that it may limit portfolio losses. The value of these models is that they give us the opportunity to minimise risk for a given return or maximise return for a given risk.

No matter how the initial portfolio is *built*, it must then be *managed*. Even when the initial selection process results in the best portfolio possible at the time, many influences on portfolio performance can change: investor expectations about future company prospects; interest rate levels; the investor's utility function, wealth level, and attitude toward risk. Changes in these factors mean that investors must consider changing their portfolios. If changes must be made, investors face the problem of *timing*.

Investment timing and performance measurement, then involve this difficult question; Once the original portfolio has been built, what securities should be sold or bought, and when? Portfolio management is really a portfolio revision process in which an investor revises a portfolio from time to time as changing conditions demand. In fact, portfolio selection can be thought of as portfolio revision when the portfolio consists of nothing but cash. True portfolio revision includes not only all of the portfolio selection considerations but such factors as taxes, transaction costs, the investor's opportunity costs, and so on. The problem of when and how to measure the performance and how to revise the portfolio is difficult indeed.

TIMING THE PURCHASES OF SECURITIES

For the majority of investors quality is the first consideration in the selection on investment securities. But after selecting quality companies, one must recognize the importance of timing in their purchase. However, while examining the subject of potential return, the invester may found that stock of excellent quality might still provide a return that was unsatisfactory. The timing concept, very simply, gives recognition to the cyclical characteristics of the securities market.

Many long-term investors, however, invest on the assumption that it makes no difference what price they pay for a stock. In the long run, they reason, the good company will succeed; the price of its stock will go up and will eventually be higher than the purchase price. The buy-and-hold philosophy may be valid if they buy and hold the right stock. However, return can be improved with a fully timed and managed portfolio. With thought, patience, and experience, and without predicting the exact highs and lows of the market, investors can still be successful. Another point that must be brought out in a discussion of timing is that urgency in investment decisions is often unwarranted. An investor is never required to buy a stock at a specific time. The *must-invest* concept has no part in the intelligent process of investment analysis and management. He is always faced with other alternatives— for example, putting funds into bonds or fixed-income securities, or simply holding cash and not making purchases of equity. This is why investment "tips" are so incongruous with the investment decision-making process.

Price Strategies, Timing, and Management

One way to handle the problem of the timing of securities purchases would be to establish price goals for each stock and try to buy the stock at the predetermined price. Then, after the stock is purchased, a selling price and a holding period are determined. This process requires a great deal of patience and presents the danger that one might miss out on some potentially excellent investment securities. Assume, for example, that an investor decides to buy a stock at Rs. 45. The current market price is Rs. 60. But the stock never goes down to Rs. 45 it continues up to Rs. 100. In this case, the goal was impossible, or at least unlikely to occur.

Another danger of waiting for a specific price to be reached is that a change may occur in the fundamental position of the company. A new analysis might reveal that the company was no longer desirable at the original price that was set. This again points up the need for continuous analysis of a company and the portfolio.

An example might help to clarify the good features of the process of price setting as a solution to the timing problem. Assume that an investor wishes to invest Rs. 1,00,000. *How should the investment prograrmme begin and what weight and consideration should be given to timing ?* The *first* step would be to place the funds in a liquid and marketable investment until the investment policy was established. *Second*, the person's investment objectives should be determined. *Third*, a portfolio should be constructed to meet the person's investment needs, considering the risks that the person can assume. *Fourth*, the securities to meet the portfolio requirements should be determined; and *fifth*, the securities should be acquired over the next six months or longer at attractive prices when and if they occur, to meet the yield and return the investor desires. If the stock market is low, it would be possible to invest more quickly. This process emphasizes selection and timing, and it offers one solution to the timing problem.

COMPLEXITIES OF INVESTMENT TIMING

Some of the important aspects that investors must face after completing the initial portfolio selection process are listed below:

Frequency of Revision

An investor may often think a portfolio 'needs' to be changed, but infact this 'need' is based on a forecast of new information. Hence as investor receives new information, he may want to revise the portfolio. The new information could affect overall portfolio strategy in several ways. (1) It now may be possible to increase holdings in stocks with a small volume of trading and therefore more limited marketability. (2) The new funds may permit more diversification than was previously possible. (3) Given an investor's utility function, more funds may be invested in risky assets as the investor becomes wealthier. (4) The new funds available for investment may change the utility function so that the investor becomes more risk averse or less risk averse. The investor may want to move up or down the efficient frontier. On the sell side, the need to liquidate part of the portfolio to provide funds for some alternative use would be a valid reason for portfolio revision.

Other valid reasons for portfolio revision surely exist. The important point is simply that the investor should distinguish between really valid reasons and those strategies that directly and indirectly involve some thoughts of "Beating the market" by anticipating or reaching to perceived events or information.

Should revision be done constantly, every six months, every year, every five years? A trade-off is involved here. The more frequent the revision, the more timely the commitments are. But more expense is involved. Keeping up with economy/market, industry, and company factors is time-consuming and therefore expensive. Frequent revision means higher transaction costs. In a sense they can be ignored when considering portfolio selection models, because they will be incurred regardless of which stocks are selected. However, they become an important issue in portfolio revision discussions since few transaction costs are incurred if few portfolio changes are made. *Finally*, the decisions about when to sell stocks and buy new ones must be made in a portfolio context, not on a case-by-case basis. Each asset must be considered in relation to all other portfolio assets. Portfolio revision may therefore require complete recalculations of portfolio characteristics. A desire to shift into or out of a few securities may result in a "domino effect" because of tight covariance and weighting relationships among securities in the properly constructed portfolio.

Recognising Value

Investment timing is tied in with the question of how to recognise value. The believer in fundamental analysis must assess how the value of an investment is going to be affected by changes in investor expectations and how quickly prices will adjust. Proper timing is worthless if an investor is absolutely correct about the undervalued nature of a security but other investors never recognise its true value. Good timing calls for correctly identifying undervalued securities that will later be recognised as undervalued by the market.

Cyclical Factors

Another aspect of timing involves recognising that various market phenomena move in cycles and trends, such as inflationary surges, interest rates, money supply changes, recessionary periods, and so on. Rapid inflation has obvious implications for portfolio revision strategies. Investors must decide how to allocate funds between debt and equity holdings, and decisions made today cannot be based on the criteria of 10 years ago, when interest rates were high. Over a period, the structural base of an economy change with a different set of parameters occupying center stage.

Cash Flow Changes

Portfolio revision may be heavily influenced by cash flow changes. Forces external to the investment process may periodically influence revision considerations. An individual may have to liquidate securities to meet an alternative need. Institutional investors may be subject to disruptive cash flow problems; for example, retirement benefits may change substantially so that more disbursements than anticipated have to be made. Cash flows from the participants in a pension programme have to be invested frequently.

Rights, Warrants, and Fads

Certain financial considerations may influence portfolio changes in unanticipated ways. A rights offering may be made by a company whose stock is included in the portfolio. Shareholders who want to maintain their proportional ownership of the firm will have to act on the rights. Warrants may be attached to purchased bonds, and they must be held, sold, or exercised. Most have definite expiration dates and must be acted upon at some point. Convertible securities may change considerably in value, making conversion desirable. Conversion will change the previous portfolio mix between debt and equity securities. And so on.

Finally, portfolios are subject to market fads or phases such as the cult of "performance" experienced by institutional investors. The emphasis on performance led to high turnover as institutional portfolio managers attempted to achieve superior returns by aggressive buying and selling. Those managers not participating were considered suspect by observers who equated turnover with performance.

ALTERNATIVE METHODS TO MEASURE THE RETURN ON THE PORTFOLIO

The starting point for evaluating the performance of a money manager is measuring return. This might seem quite simple, but several practical issues make the task complex. For simplicity, we have assumed that no distributions are made from a portfolio during the holding period. Of course, in reality, distributions and withdrawals are common. The return realised on a portfolio for any evaluation period (i.e., a year, month, or week), then, is equal to the sum of (1) the difference between the market value of the portfolio at the end of the evaluation period and the market value at the beginning of the evaluation period and (2) any distributions made from the portfolio. It is important that any capital or income distributions from the portfolio to a client or beneficiary of the portfolio be included.

The rate of return, or simply return, expresses the return in terms of the amount of the market value at the beginning of the evaluation period. Thus, the return can be viewed as the amount (expressed as a fraction of the initial portfolio value)_ that can be withdrawn at the end of the evaluation period while maintaining the initial market value of the portfolio intact.

In equation form, the portfolio's return can be expressed as follows:

$$R_p = \frac{R_{p1} - R_{po} + D}{R_{po}} \qquad (1)$$

Where R_p = the return on the portfolio
R_{p1} = the portfolio market value at the end of the evaluation period
R_{po} = the portfolio market value at the beginning of the evaluation period
D = the each distributions from the portfolio to the client during the evaluation period

To illustrate the calculation of a return assume the following information for an external money manager for a pension plan sponsor: The portfolios' market value at the beginning and end of the evaluation period is Rs. 25 crore and Rs. 28 crores, respectively, and during the evaluation period Rs. 1 crore is distributed to the plan sponsor from investment income. Thus :

R_{P1} = Rs. 28 crore
R_{P0} = Rs. 25 crore
D = Rs. 1 crore

Then,

$$R_p = \frac{\text{Rs. 28 crore - Rs. 25 crore + Rs. 1 crore}}{\text{Rs. 25 crore}}$$

$$= 0.16 = 16\%$$

There are three assumptions in measuring return as given by Equation-1. The first assumption is that cash inflows into the portfolio from dividends and interest that occur during the evaluation period but are not distributed are reinvested in the portfolio. For example, suppose that during the evaluation period Rs. 2 crore is received from dividends. This amount is reflected in the market value of the portfolio at the end of the period.

The second assumption is that if there are distributions from the portfolio, they either occur at the end of the evaluation period or are held in the form of cash until the end of the evaluation period. In our example, Rs. 1 crore is distributed to the plan sponsor. But when did that distribution actually occur? To understand why the timing of the distribution is important, consider two extreme cases: (1) the distribution is made at the end of the evaluation period, as assumed by Equation (1), and (2) the distribution is made at the beginning of the evaluation period. In the first case the fund manager had the use of the Rs. 1 crore to invest for the entire evaluation period. By contrast, in the second case, the fund manager losses the opportunity to invest the funds until the end of the evaluation period. Consequently, the timing of the distribution will affect the return, but this is not considered in Equation (1).

The third assumption is that there is no cash paid into the portfolio by the client. For example, suppose that sometime during the evaluation period the plan sponsor gives an additional Rs. 1.5 crore to the external fund manager to invest. Consequently, the market value of the portfolio at the end of the evaluation period, Rs. 28 crore in our example, would reflect the contribution of Rs. 1.5 crore. Equation (1) does not reflect that the ending market value of the portfolio is affected by the cash paid in by the sponsor. Moreover, the timing of this cash inflow will affect the calculated return.

Thus, while the return calculation for a portfolio using Equation (1) can be determined for an evaluation period of any length of time such as one day, one month, or five years, from a practical point of view the assumptions discussed above limit its application. The longer the evaluation period, the more likely the assumptions will be violated. For example, it is highly likely that there may be more than one distribution to the client and more than one contribution from the client if the evaluation period is five years. Thus, a return calculation made over a long period of time, if longer than a few months, would not be very reliable because of the assumption underlying the calculations that all cash payments and inflows are made and received at the end of the period.

Not only does the violation of the assumptions make it difficult to compare the returns of two fund managers over some evaluation period, but it is also not useful for evaluating performance over different periods. For example, Equation (1) will not give reliable information to compare the performance of a one-month evaluation period and a three-year evaluation period. To make such a comparison, the return must be expressed per unit of time, for example, per year.

The way to handle these practical issues is to calculate the return for a short unit of time such as a month or a quarter. We call the return so calculated the *subperiod return*. To get the return for the evaluation period, the subperiod returns are then averaged. So, for example, if the evaluation period is one year and 12 monthly returns are calculated, the monthly returns are the subperiod returns, and they are averaged to get the one-year return. If a three-year return is sought and 12 quarterly returns can be calculated, quarterly returns are the subperiod returns, and they are averaged to get the three-year return.

It is important to understand just what is to be measured in calculating the return of the portfolio. Conceptually, it would be wise to compare the return of the fund on a unit basis, just as mutual funds must do. They calculate the value of their shares twice each day, and the flow of money into and out of the fund is automatically compensated for in the daily calculations. It is also important to measure return flows into and out of the fund. Adjustments of the time value of money are easily made, and annual returns can be obtained by linking the returns together. Finally, a return formula must be used that accurately reflects the return of the portfolio.

Three methodologies have been used in practice to calculate the average of subperiod returns: 1) The arithmetic average rate of return, 2) the rupee-weighted return and 3) the time-weighted rate of return (also called the geometric rate of return). Box-1 compare the methods side by side.

BOX-1

Three Methods for Averaging Subperiod Returns

Method	Interpretation	Limitations
Arithmetic average (mean) rate of return	• Average value of the withdra- wals (expressed as a fraction of the initial portfolio market value) that can be made at the end of each subperiod while keeping the initial portfolio market value intact	• Overvalues total return when subperiod returns vary greatly • Assumes the mainte- nance of initial market value
Time-weighted (geometric) rate of return	• The compounded rate of growth of the initial portfolio market value during the evaluation period	• Assumes all proceeds are reinvested
Rupee-weighted rate of return (internal) return	• The interest rate that will make the present value of the sum of the subperiod cash flows (plus the terminal market value) equal to the initial market value of the portfolio	• Is affected by client contributions and withd- rawals beyond the control of the money manager

Arithmetic Average (Mean) Rate of Return

The arithmetic average (mean) rate of return is an unweighted average of the subperiods. The general formula is:

$$R_{AP} \quad \frac{R_{P1} + R_{P2} + ... + R_{PN}}{N} \qquad (2)$$

Where

R_{AP} = The arithmetic average rate of return

R_P = The portfolio return for subperiod k as measured by Equation-1, where k - 1, ..., N

N = The number of subperiods in the evaluation period.

For example, if the portfolio return (as measured in Equation-1) were -10%, 20%, and 5% in worth of June, July, and August, respectively, the arithmetic average monthly return is 5%, as show below:

$$R_{AP} = \frac{10 + 0.20 + 0.05}{3} = 0.05 = 5\%$$

There is major problem with using the arithmetic average rate of return. For instance, the initial market value of a portfolio may be ₹ 50 crore and if the market value at the end of the next two months is ₹ 100 crore and ₹ 50 crore, respectively, and there are no distributions or cash inflows form clients for either month, then return from the first month is 100% and the second month is -50%. The arithmetic average rate of return using Equation-2 is the 25%. However, the return is actual over this two month evaluation is zero.

Internal Method—Rupee Weighted

The internal, or rupee-weighted method, calculates the total return of the portfolio without regard to the flow of funds. The basic equation is this:

$$R_{rw} = \frac{R_{p1} - R_{po} + I}{R_{po}} \tag{3}$$

where R_{p1} represents the value of the fund at the end of the period, R_{po} is the value of the fund at the beginning of the period, and 1 is the interest or dividend income received during the period or month. The formula simply tells the internal return for the period. Assume that a portfolio had a value of ₹ 1,00,000 at the beginning of the quarter and ₹ 1,20,000 at the end and that ₹ 300 was received in dividends. The internal rate of return would be:

$$\frac{₹\ 1,20,000 - ₹\ 1,00,000 + ₹\ 300}{₹\ 1,00,000}$$

$$= \frac{₹\ 20,300}{₹\ 1,00,000}$$

$$= 20.3\%$$

However, during the period, ₹ 12,000 was added to the portfolio from outside sources. The internal or rupee weighted return overstated the profitability of the portfolio. In order to assess the performance of the fund correctly, we must change the formula slightly to provide an accurate measure of the return earned on the original amount invested as well as the new capital contributions. To do this we use the time weighted method.

Time-Weighted Rate of Return

To calculate the time-weighted rate of return, we use the formula:

$$R_{rw} = \frac{R_{p1} - (P_o + D)}{R_{po} + (T \times D)} \tag{4}$$

where R_{p1} is the value of the fund at the end of the quarter, R_{po} is the value at the beginning of the quarter, D is the net cash contributed during the quarter, and T is the proportion of the quarter that the cash is being used. Using 90 days per quarter, if the cash were put to work on the 45th day of the quarter, the T in the equation would be 45/90, or 1/2. Assume that the fund in the example above received ₹ 12,000 in contributions as well as ₹ 300 in dividends that must be reinvested. Substituting in the equation, we have:

$$= \frac{₹\,1,20,000 - (₹\,1,00,000 + ₹\,12,300)}{₹\,1,00,000 + (1/2 \times ₹\,12,300)}$$

$$= \frac{₹\,1,20,000 - ₹\,1,12,300}{₹\,1,00,000 + ₹\,6,150}$$

$$= \frac{₹\,7,700}{₹\,1,06,150}$$

$$= .0725$$

The quarterly return, therefore, was 7.25 percent. If this same rate continued for a year, we would link the returns together to find the annual return, as follows:

1.0725 x 1.0725 x 1.0725 x 1.0725 = 1.3231

1.3231 - 1.00 = .3231 = 32.31 percent

Thus the return for the year was 32.31 percent. This method is accurate when funds come in regularly, outside the control of the fund manager, and must be invested.

Time-Weighted Method—Testing Management

In order to test the performance of management, the time-weighted return is found by calculating the return of the fund each time cash is put in or taken out. This provides a series of rates of return that can be linked together. Long periods are obviously weighted more heavily than short periods. This gives an exact time-weighted rate of return. The time-weighted rate is preferable to the rupee-weighted rate, but it is costly to calculate.

Let us see how the manager might influence the results of the portfolio. Assume that the investment period is one quarter, as before. In the preceding case, the manager was required to invest the funds. This time, let's assume that the manager can invest the money or hold it, as he or she sees fit. Let's also assume that the value of the fund at the end of the quarter was ₹ 1,20,000 as before. The return for the investment period would be the same as in time-weighted example—.0725, or 7.25 percent. Now let's assume that the manager decided not to invest the ₹ 12,300 at the middle of the quarter because the market was thought to be overpriced.

We assume that the market moved up in the first half of the quarter and then decreased in the second half. Therefore, instead of investing the ₹ 12,300, the manager held the funds in Treasury bills. If the value of the portfolio is ₹ 1,15,000 at the middle of the quarter and ₹ 12,300 are added, the portfolio dropped to ₹ 1,20,000 at the end of the period. In other words, the portfolio value from ₹ 1,27,300 to ₹ 1,20,000, or ₹ 7,300/₹ 1,27,300 = 5.7 percent. Now, with ₹ 12,300 in reserve in the account, the equity value of the portfolio dropped 5.7 percent, from ₹ 1,15,000 to ₹ 1,08,445, because of the general drop in the market. And the value of the fund at the end of the period is ₹ 1,20,745 (₹ 1,08,445 + ₹ 12,300). Therefore, because of good management, the portfolio has earned an extra ₹ 745. But let's see what it did to the return. The return was:

$$\frac{₹\,1,20,745 - ₹\,1,00,000 + ₹\,12,300}{₹\,1,00,000 + (1/2 \times ₹\,12,300)} = \frac{₹\,8,445}{₹\,1,06,150} = 7.95\%$$

By good management, the fund manager improved the return of the fund from 7.25 percent for the period to 7.95 percent. The assumption is made that the returns are adjusted for the flow of money into the portfolio.

TIMING THE SALE IS CRITICAL

Selection of securities is of primary and paramount importance in portfolio management. Next in importance is buying and selling the securities. This is handled as part of the investor's strategy. The solution is complete management of the portfolio, which includes a recognition of economic trends and of the market cycle as a phenomenon of its own. However, in timing the purchases and sale of securities, management problems are involved. The concept of timing suggests not only that securities be purchased when they are relatively low, but that they be sold when they are relatively high. If the concept of timing has any validity, the idea of selling a security if it appears to be too high is just as reasonable as saying that the stock is low in price and should be purchased.

The solution to the matter of proper timing of the sale rests on expectations about the future. If, based on a reasonable and complete analysis, the present price is excessive compared to future returns from these earnings, then the security should be sold. On the other hand, if expectations about future earnings and return result in a present value that is sufficiently higher than the present price, the investor should consider holding the stock. Future returns should provide the clue of when to buy and sell.

Essentially, the investor must take advantage of the major movements of prices in the marketplace. He must sell securities when they are overpriced relative to future expected earnings, dividends, and price. He must purchase stocks when they are low and hence offer a high return. The only way an investor can "beat" the market index is by managing assets to take advantage of the market—by selling when it is overpriced and buying when it is underpriced.

Guides to Timing the Sale of Securities

The *first* guide to follow in timing the sale of a security is to sell when the security no longer meets the objectives that were originally established. Investment needs frequently change, calling for a change in the type of security that should be held in the portfolio. Assume, for example, that an investor has followed an income-portfolio policy. Later, income needs are satisfied and current income is no longer required. Portfolio policy would shift to an emphasis on growth. This would require the sale of the income shares and purchase of growth shares. The same example could be given for the growth investor who now needs income and must sell growth stocks.

A *second* sign that indicates a time to sell is when the stock market as a whole has moved up to a historic high and the stock itself is selling at an extremely high price. So the investor must judge whether the market is high or low.

A *third* guide in timing the sale of a stock relates to the expectations about the return from the security. When a specific security no longer offers the investor the expectation of a satisfactory return and there is a sharp difference between the analysts' expectations and what can be reasonably obtained, the stock should be sold.

The *fourth* guide to selling under a completely managed portfolio is based on competitive alternatives. The investor should consider selling the stocks held—after all factors are considered, including risk, quality, and taxes—when a compelling alternative investment offers greater returns comparable to risks.

The stock should also be sold when the return is low and the reward-to-risk ratio is unattractive.

ALTERNATIVE SOLUTIONS TO TIMING

Proper investment timing is obviously important. But "Buy low, sell high," like much good advice, is hard to follow. In fact, the Efficient Market Hypothesis says that this ideal strategy cannot even be approached. Many investors do not believe they have the ability to trade stocks and profit. They stress quality and selectivity and develop ways to minimize the effects of timing. Typical solutions to the timing problem 1) the formula plan, 2) rupee-cost averaging, and 3) a buy and hold policy.

FORMULA PLANS

Formula plans are mechanical portfolio timing techniques designed to help the investor make decisions with little forecasting. The plans assume that prices fluctuate cyclically, but that investors cannot predict when these fluctuations will occur. Formula plans attempt to turn price fluctuations into an advantage. They consist of predetermined rules for both buying and selling of the stocks. The selection of a formula plan and the determination of the appropriate ground rules cause the investor to consider and outline his investment objectives and policies. Once the plan is established, the investor is free from making emotional decisions based upon the current attitudes of investors in the stock market.

Formula plans are not, however, a royal road to riches without any weaknesses. *Firstly*, formula plans offer only modest opportunity for capital gains. A fully managed fund will offer a greater potential gains, even though investors might not achieve this goal. *Secondly*, some formula plans do not free the investor from making value judgement as to the relative strength of the stock market. *Thirdly*, a formula plan by its very nature must be inflexible, thus imposing a necessary action by the investor. Investors may choose securities that do not move with the market. After all the beta characteristics of securities are not that stable. *Lastly*, as an effort to solve the timing problem of investing, they make no provisions for what securities should be selected for investment.

TYPES OF FORMULA PLANS

1. Constant-Rupee-Value Plan

The constant rupee value plan specifies that the rupee value of the stock portion of the portfolio will remain constant. Thus, as the value of the stock rises, the investor must automatically sell some of the shares in order to keep the value of his aggressive portfolio constant. If the price of the stock falls, the investor must buy additional stock to keep the value of aggressive portfolio constant. By specifying that the aggressive portfolio will remain constant in money value, the plan also specifies that remainder of the total fund be invested in the conservative fund. The constant-rupee-value plan's major advantage is its simplicity. The investor can clearly see the amount that he needed to have invested. However, the percentage of his total fund that this constant amount will represent in the aggressive portfolio will remain at different levels of his stock's values. The investor must choose predetermined action points some times called revaluation points. The action points are the times at which the investor will make the transfers called for to keep the constant rupee value of the stock portfolio. Of course, the portfolio's value cannot be continuously the same, since this would necessitate constant attention by the investor, innumberable action points, and excessive transaction costs. In fact, the portfolio will have to be allowed to fluctuate to some extent before action taken to readjust its value. The action points may be sent according to prespecified periods of time, percentage changes in some economic or market index, or - mostly ideally - percentage changes in the value of the aggressive portfolio. The tuning of action points can have an important effect on the profits the investor obtains. Action points placed close together cause excessive costs that reduce profits. If the action points are too far apart, however, the investor may completely miss the opportunity to profit from fluctuations that take place between them. Examples will help to clarify the implementation of formula plans. We will use fractional shares and ignore transaction costs to simplify the examples.

Numerical Example

To illustrate the constant rupee value plan, suppose an investor has ₹ 10,000 to invest. The investor decides to begin the plan with balanced portions (₹5,000 aggressive, ₹5,000 defensive) and to rebalance the portfolio whenever the aggressive portion is 20 per cent above or below ₹5,000. On hundred shares of a ₹ 50 each stock and ₹ 5,000 in bonds are purchased. The first column of Table-1 shows stock prices during one cycle of fluctuation below and back up to the original price of ₹50. The fifth column shows the adjustments called for by the 20 per cent signal criterion. The fourth column shows that by the end of the cycle the investor increased the total fund from ₹ 10,000 to ₹ 10,209 even though starting and finishing prices were the same and the stock never rose above the ₹ 50 starting price.

Main limitation of the constant rupee value plan is that it requires some initial forecasting. However, it does not require forecasting the extent to which upward fluctuations may reach. In fact, a forecast of the extent of downward fluctuations is necessary since the conservative portfolio must be large enough so that funds are always available for transfer to the stock portfolio as its value shrinks. This step requires a knowledge of how stock prices might go. Then the required size of the conservative portfolio can be determined if the investor can start his constant rupee fund when the stocks he is acquiring are not priced too far above the lowest values to which they might fluctuate, he can obtain better overall results from a constant- rupee-value plan.

TABLE 1
Constant Rupee Plan

Market Price	Value of Stock Portion ₹	Value of Defensive Portion ₹	Total Portfolio Value ₹	Portfolio Adjustment	Share in stock portion
50	5,000	5,000	10,000		100
44	4,000	5,000	9,400		100
40	4,000	5,000	9,000	Bought	100
40	5,000	4,000	9,000	25 Shares	125
44	5,000	4,000	9,000		125
48	6,000	4,000	10,000	Sold	125
48	5.000	5.000	10.000	20.83 Shares	104.17
50	5,209	5.000	10,209		104.17

2. Constant Ratio Plan

The constant ratio plan goes one step beyond the constant rupee plan by establishing a fixed percentage relationship between the aggressive and defensive components. Under both plans the portfolio is forced to sell stocks as their prices rise and to buy stocks as their prices fall. Under the constant ratio plan, however, both the aggressive and defensive portions remain in constant percentage of the portfolio's total value. The problem posed by re-balancing may mean missing intermediate price movements. The constant ratio plan holder can adjust portfolio balance either at fixed intervals or when the portfolio moves away from the desired ratio by a fixed percentage.

Numerical Example

Table-2 illustrates the constant ratio plan. The chosen ratio of stock to bonds is 1: 1 meaning that the defensive and aggressive portions will each make 50 per cent of the portfolio. Therefore, we divide the initial ₹ 10,000 equally into stock and bond portions. When the stock portion rises or falls by 10 per cent from the desired ratio, the original ratio is restored. The sixth column in the Table-2 indicates the four adjustments required to restore the 50: 50 balance. Even though stock price dropped considerably before rising back to the starting level, this portfolio still made a little bit of money.

The advantage of the constant ratio plan is the automatism with which it forces the manager to adjust counter cyclically his portfolio. This approach does not eliminate the necessary of selecting individual securities, nor does it perform well if the prices of the selected securities do not move with the market. The major limitation for the constant ratio plan, however, is that use of bonds as a haven stocks and bonds are money and capital market instruments, they tend to respond to the same interest rate considerations in the present discounted evaluation framework. This means, at times, they may both rise and decline in value at approximately the same time. There is a limited advantage to be gained from shifting out of the rising stocks into the bonds if, in the downturn, both securities prices decline. If the decline in bond prices is of the same magnitude as that in stock prices, most, if not all, of the gains from the constant ratio plan are eliminated. If the constant ratio plan is used, it must be coordinated between securities that do not tend to move simultaneously in the same direction and in the same magnitude.

TABLE 2
Constant Ratio Plan

Market Price	Value of Stock Portion ₹	Value of Defensive Portion ₹	Total Portfolio Value ₹	Ratio of Stock portion to Defensive Portion	Portfolio Adjustment	Share in Stock Porton
50	5,000	5,000	10,000	1.00		100
48	4,800	5,000	9,000	.96		100
45	4,500	5,000	9,500	.90	Bought	100
45	4,750	4,750	9,500	1.00	55 shares	105.5
40.5	4,273	4,750	9,023	.90	Bought	1055
40.5	4512	4511	9,023	1.00	5.9 shares	111.4
44.5	4,957	4511	9,468	1.10	Sold	111.4
44.5	4,753	4,734	9,469	1.00	5.0 share	106.4
49	5,214	4,734	9,948	1.10	Sold	106.4
49	4,974	4,974	9,948	1.00	4.9 share	101.5
50	5,075	4,974	10,049	1.02		101.5

3. Variable Ratio Plan

Instead of maintaining a constant rupee amount in stocks or a constant ratio of stocks to bonds, the variable ratio plan user steadily lowers the aggressive portion of the total portfolio as stock prices rise, and steadily increases the aggressive portion as stock prices fall. By changing the proportions of defensive aggressive holdings, the investor is in effect buying stock more aggressively as stock prices fall and selling stock more aggressively as stock prices rise.

Numerical Example

Table-3 illustrates another variable ratio plan. Starting price is ₹ 50 per share. The portfolio is divided into two equal portions as before, with ₹ 5,000 in each portion. As the market price drops, the value of the stock portion and the percentage of stock in the total portfolio decline. When the market price reaches ₹ 50, a portfolio adjustment is triggered. The purchase of 57.5 shares raises the stock percentage to 70. As the stock price rises, the value of the stock portion increases until a new portfolio adjustment is triggered. The sale of 51.76 shares reduced the percentage of stock in the portfolio back to 50.

In the example, the portfolio was adjusted for a 20 per cent drop and when the price returned to ₹ 50. Other adjustment criteria would produce different outcomes. The highest under this plan results from the larger transactions in the portfolio's stock portion. The portfolio adjustment section of Table-3 (sixth column) may be compared with the same columns in Table 1 and 2. The variable ratio plan subjects the investor to more risk than the constant ratio plan does. But with accurate forecasts the variable ratio plan designed to take greater advantage of price fluctuations than the constant ratio plan does.

TABLES 3

Variable Ratio Plan

Market Price	Value of Stock Portion ₹	Value of Defensive Portion ₹	Total Portfolio Value ₹	Stock as Percentage of total Portfolio	Portfolio Adjustment	Share in stock portion
50	5,000	5,000	10,000	50		1000
45	4,500	5,000	9,500	47		100
40	4,000	5,000	9,0000	44.5	**Bought**	100
40	6,300	2,700	9,000	70	57.5 Shares	157.5
45	7,088	2,700	9,788	74	**Sold**	157.5
50	7,875	2,700	10,575	74.5	51.76 Shares	157.5
50	5,287	5,287	10,574	50		105.74

A Graphic Illustration

We can graphically illustrate a variable ratio plan as in Figure-1. The solid trend line represents the investor's expectation of future stock prices, zones 1 and 3 represent, respectively, 10 and 20 per cent deviation above the expected trend, and zones 2 and 4 represent, respectively, 10 and 20 per cent deviation below the expected trend. Starting at 40, the portfolio is 50 per cent in stocks and 50 per cent in bonds. Once the actual stock price index passes through a zone such as point **a**, the portfolio is adjusted to the next proportion, in this case 60 per cent bonds and 40 per cent stocks. When the actual stock price index passes through point **b**, the proportion is again 50:50.

Below point **c**, the portfolio is 40 per cent bonds and 60 per cent stocks, and above point **d**, it is again 50: 50. The variable ratio plan does not have to use the trend in the market-prices the same mechanical rules may be used if the deviations from the estimated dividend yield the estimated price/earnings ratio are used. If the dividend yield deviates above (below) the estimated dividend yield by a certain percentage, a higher (lower) ratio of stocks of defensive securities is implemented. A similar system could be based on deviations in the price/earnings ratio.

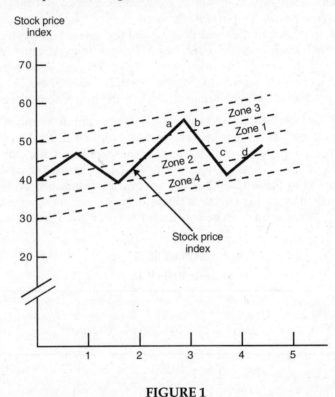

FIGURE 1

The major advantage of this plan is the automatism that it forces on the portfolio manager in emphasizing counter-cyclical portfolio changes. The manager cannot be emotionally swayed by the price swings in the market. The major limitations of the variable ratio plan are in the construction of the appropriate zones, trends, and ratios, the selection of specific securities, and the sub-optimisation of the portfolio. If the trend line is not an accurate portrayal of what does happen, the counter-cyclical emphasis of the portfolio is destroyed. For example, if we foresee a falling trend when it actually rises, the deviations will be above the estimated trend line, and our portfolio will be concentrated in defensive issues during a rising market. If the zero are too small or the rates change the emphasis too rapidly, the portfolio will be concentrated in the defensive securities at a very early stage in the rising market and in the aggressive stocks at a very early stage in a falling market. This naturally limits the portfolio's performance. This approach like all the other formula plans, does not optimise the manager's utility, because it deals only with the timing problem and disregards the other considerations in portfolio analysis.

As conditions change within the market and the economy, the investor may want to switch from one formula plan to another. It is difficult to generalise on the effectiveness and usefulness of formula plans. Some plans used have often been greatly modified, or they have been used over periods that have not permitted fair tests of their worth, the intrinsic worth of the formula plans lies in their taking the investment decision-making process outside the emotions of the investment environment. However, investors must make their predetermined plans on the basis of certain assumptions on historical data. The level of success that formula plans achieve will be dependent on the closeness to which actual future behaviour resembles the pattern that the formula plan anticipates. Formula plans are, therefore, possibly useful in some cases, but they are not a foolproof method of achieving profits.

Advantages of Formula Plans

The major advantage of the formula plan is its automatic character. Once the plan is established, investors are free from making emotional decisions based on the current attitudes of investors in the stock market.

The second advantage is related to timing the sale of stock. Most effort and discussion about timing is concerned with buying securities. The formula plan stresses both buying and selling.

A third advantage of the formula-plan method as a solution to timing is its versatility. It recognizes the defensive and aggressive characteristics of an investment portfolio. As the market moves up, the formula plan results in an increasingly defensive position. When the market declines, the portfolio automatically becomes more aggressive.

Disadvantages of Formula Plans

One disadvantage of the formula plan is that investors must make a value judgment as to the relative height of the stock market for the variable-ratio formula plans. A second disadvantage, related to the first, is that over a sustained market rise, investors would be better off in equity than in a combination of bonds and equity. A third possible criticism is that we might choose securities that do not move with the market. After all, the beta characteristics of equity are not entirely stable. A fourth disadvantage of a formula plan is that it offers only modest opportunity for capital gains. A fully managed fund will offer a greater potential for gain, even though we might not achieve this goal.

RUPEE-COST AVERAGING

Another mechanical investment technique, which is not technically a formula plan, is rupee-cost averaging. It is a simple investment plan which helps the uninformed investor with the timing of his investments. This plan gives no due as to what the investor should buy; it merely simplifies the problem of deciding when to buy. In essence a rupee cost averaging investment programme involves making periodic investments of equal rupee amount. Such a programme leads to the purchase of more shares when their price is cheap than when they are expensive. As a result, the average rupee cost per share is below the average of the intervening prices.

Numerical Example

First, let us examine a stock whose price is not very volatile. If the price fluctuates between ₹ 90 and ₹ 100 per share without any growth and ₹ 1,000 is invested in each period (for example, quarter or year) the results of rupee cost averaging are shown at the top of Table 4.

If a more volatile growth stock is purchased with rupee cost averaging, the results are shown at the bottom of Table 4. The numerical example for the growth stock/

suppose the prices rise from ₹ 60 to ₹ 85 per share while fluctuating. Both examples assume ₹ 1,000 per period is invested.

The results of average cost averaging can be seen most clearly in the last two columns (6 and 7) of Table 4. In both cases the average cost per share (shown in column 6) is below the average of the market prices which occurred on purchase dates (shown in column 7). The examples demonstrate that whatever benefits may be derived from rupee cost averaging are larger for volatile growth stocks than stocks with low volatility. This is due to the fact that more volatile the stock, the more frequently low prices will occur and pull down the average cost per share of shares which are purchased at regular intervals.

TABLE 4

Rupee Cost Averaging Plan

Period	Market Price ₹	No. of Shares for ₹1,000	No. of Shares Purchased	Total Invested ₹	Average Cost/ Shares ₹	Average Market Price ₹
(1)	(2)	(3)	(4)	(5)	(6)=(5)+(4)	(7)
1.	100	10.0	10.0	1,000	100.0	100
2.	90	11.1	21.1	2,000	94.7	95
3.	100	10.0	31.1	3,000	96.4	96.6
4.	90	11.1	42.2	4,000	94.7	95
5.	100	10.0	52.2	5,000	95.9	96
High volatility growth stock						
1.	60	16.7	16.7	1,000	60.0	60.00
2.	80	12.5	29.2	2,000	68.5	70.00
3.	75	13.3	42.5	3,000	70.5	71.66
4.	90	11.1	53.6	4,000	74.5	76.22
5.	85	11.8	65.4	5,000	76.45	78.05

The *advantages of* rupee cost averaging plan are (1) low average price, (2) easy use, (3) fixed limiting considerations, and (4) applicability to both rising and falling markets. The simplicity of the plan is obvious. The manager must decide in advance the sum and the periodic intervals at which he will invest. Once this is decided, the implementation is mechanical. At no other time is a decision about when to invest required. During the price cycle, the cupee cost averaging approach should produce a lower average price paid per share than the average market price.

There are several *limitations of* the plan. The extra transaction costs associated with frequent, small purchases raise the price of the shares. The higher per share commissions and addition add to fees encountered under this plan account for most of this expense. The plan contains no formal indication of when to sell, it is strictly a strategy for buying. It does not eliminate the necessity for selecting the individual stocks that are to be purchased. There is no indication of the appropriate interval between purchases. If the interval is too long, the manager may miss the cyclical fluctuations in market prices and fail to gain the averaging advantage inherent in the plan. The averaging advantage does not yield a profit if the stock price is in a downward trend. If the price is in a downward trend, so that it is continually declining in the extreme, becoming worthless — the opportunity to sell the acquired shares for a profit will not materialise. The present market price may be lower than the previous prices at which any of the shares were acquired, so that if the shares were sold, the investor would have a loss. Further, it is often difficult to obtain the funds during declining markets.

The rupee cost averaging approach depends on a cyclical pattern in stock prices, without which rupee cost averaging would not produce a lower average price. For example, constant or rising stock prices produce only a constant average price or a rising average price with each additional purchase. A constantly declining price may produce a lower average purchase price but provide no profit opportunity. The approach is somewhat limited to a secularly rising stock with intermediary cyclical patterns. Because this has historically been the pattern of most stock prices, the rupee cost averaging method has produced reasonable results. The more volatile stock prices decline and rebound farther, forcing the purchase of more share at a lower price.

The formula timing plans are not designed to yield large returns. Instead they are defensive investment strategies for minimising loss while offering the possibility of modest long-term returns. They help investors to time their investments without a constant dependence on forecasts, by specifying that stocks be bought as prices fall and sold as prices rise. Formula plans are designed for cyclically fluctuating markets. Other price patterns can affect formula plans adversely.

A BUY-AND-HOLD POLICY

An alternative to regular trading periodic portfolio revision is a buy-and-hold strategy. Under this approach, the investor takes a "passive" position and makes few portfolio changes. No real effort is made to find undervalued securities because of the belief that the benefit probably do not justify the costs. Exceptions occur when the investor has particularly good reasons to make a change, such as access to private information or really strong evidence of a coming shift in the market's primary trend. The buy-and-hold strategy is particularly appropriate for a strong believer in the Efficient Market Hypothesis.

The professional manager of a buy-and-hold portfolio may seem to have nothing to do. Actually, the portfolio must still be "managed" but in a different sense. Here are five aspects of the buy-and-hold portfolio manager's activities:

1. *Eliminating unsystematic risk*—The manager should eliminate unsystematic risk by holding enough securities and by holding securities with proper covariances.
2. *Determining systematic risk*—The manager should determine the level of systematic risk appropriate for the investor's purposes.
3. *Considering the investor's tax status*—because the current tax laws permit different treatment of interest, dividends, and capital gains, the manager must consider the tax status of the portfolio's beneficiaries.
5. *Reducing transaction costs*—The manager should consider the effective costs of trading, given the negotiated rates available.

As we know that believers in the Efficient Market Hypothesis maintain that attempts to beat the market are likely to be unsuccessful. Information is quickly impounded into prices so that continuous study of new information is usually valueless. However, up to now this hypothesis has had little impact on most portfolio managers. They continue to believe that somehow they can outperform the market. In fact, all of the formula plans, and in fact all portfolio management policies, must be considered in light of he portfolio holder's option to assume a passive buy-and-hold position. Research costs and transaction costs are minimised in the buy-and-hold portfolio. Any portfolio manager wanting to revise the portfolio for any reason must have confidence that the unavoidable costs of revision will be exceeded by the returns on the revised portfolio.

QUESTIONS

1. What are some trade-offs involved in deciding how often to revise a portfolio?
2. Outline some aspects of investment timing that investors must face after completing the initial portfolio selection process.
3. Describe the two extreme approaches to investment timing. What are the advantages and disadvantages of each? Which end of the continuum of investment timing approaches do you think institutional investors have been on?
4. Name two major constraints on portfolio revision. Do you think they have become more or less stringent in the past few years?
5. What is the premise behind formula plans?
6. What type of investor probably benefits the most from rupee-cost-averaging?
7. What are some weaknesses of rupee-cost-averaging?
8. Which formula plan is most dependent upon the accurate estimation of the long-term trend in stock prices?
9. Assume that you wish to establish a formula plan for the next five years, which you believe will be a period of rising stock prices. From which would you benefit most —a constant rupee value, constant ratio, or variable ratio plan?
10. Why have formula plans declined in popularity?
11. Outline the case for a buy-and-hold strategy.
12. At what point in the building of a portfolio is the impact of rupee cost averaging greatest? Why?
13. "Formula plans aid the investor in overcoming his emotional involvement with the timing of purchase and sales of stock" Comment.
14. Why is it believed that the average cost per share of shares purchased under a rupee cost-averaging plan will be lower than the average price per share of the same stock during the period of the plan's usage? Is this always true? How are action points chosen?
15. Since the defensive portfolio will probably have a low yield, how does it aid the investor using a mechanical formula plan'?
16. Distinguish between time-weighted and Rupee -weighted rate of return .Under what performance measurement circumstances might the rupee-weighted be preferred to time weighted?
17. Do formula plans aid the investor in selecting appropriate securities?
18. Is rupee-cost averaging a formula plan? At what point in the building of a portfolio is the impact of rupee-cost averaging greatest? Prove this by making up an example of your own.
19. What kind of security do you think you would select for your aggressive portfolio?
20. "Portfolios that buy new securities and sell old holdings frequently will outperform portfolios that are managed more passively." Do you agree with this statement?
21. It can be seen from the "evidence on portfolio revision and market timing" in this chapter that there are two potential ways to "beat the market": picking securities that will perform well (as in the quarterly earnings study) and timing portfolio changes by predicting market turning points. Each portfolio manager should choose a strategy depending upon a realistic estimate of personal ability to do these two things (Can) or a lack of ability to do them (Cannot). Given the possible combinations of Can and Cannot for these two factors, indicate what strategies the portfolio manager should follow for each combination. Choose two or the following four strategies for each combination.
    (a) Diversify widely
    (b) Concentrate on securities expected to perform well
    (c) Shift from stocks to cash (or bonds) and/or vary beta of portfolio
    (d) Maintain steady beta based on risk preferences
       — Can: Pick securities

Can: Time market changes
— Can: Pick securities
Cannot: Time market changes
— Can: Pick securities
Cannot: Time market changes
— Cannot: Pick securities
Cannot: Time market changes

22. What is meant by the timing problem in securities investment?
23. One solution to the timing problem is to establish a price we consider to be attractive and then wait until that price is reached. Comment about the advantages and disadvantages of this approach to timing.
24. Explain the concept of rupee averaging and how it might be used in solving the problem of investmet timing. What are the basic advantages and disadvantages of rupee averaging?
25. Explain how formula planning can be used as a tool to solve the timing problem.
26. What are the solutions to the difficult problem of when to sell a security ? Elabo-rate.

PROBLEMS

1. Consider the following mutual fund history:

Share Price

Date	Fund ABC	Fund XYZ
January	₹ 12.45	₹ 11.58
February	13.70	12.45
March	11.50	10.60
April	12.60	11.95
May	14.35	12.75
June	11.75	11.40

(a) Calculate the variance of return for each of the mutual funds.
(b) If you had employed rupee cost averaging programme by making monthly investments of ₹ 2,500, in which fund would you have the most money at the end of the year?

2. Give an example of how rupee cost averaging may cause an investor to forego high returns. Select any stock and calculate the gain or loss from ₹ 1,000 purchases for ten annual periods.

3. WW Company began the year 2010 with a portfolio valued at ₹ 10,00,000/- and made a contribution and a withdrawal from this portfolio over the next three months. Information regarding amounts and dates of these cash flows and the portfolio market value at various dates is shown below:

Date	Contribution(+) or withdrawal(-)	Portfolio Value
31/12/09	Re.0	₹ 10,00,000/
31/1/10	+95,600	9,00,000/
28/2/10	-65,900	12,00,000/
31/3/10	0	13,00,000/

(i) Calculate the rupee—weighted return for the three months period.
(ii) Calculate the time-weighted return for the three months period.
(iii) Why is time-weighted return for the three months period less than the rupee weighted return in this particular problem?

4. If you were using a constant rupee-value-plan and started with a defensive portfolio worth ₹ 20,000 and a stock portfolio consisting of 400 shares of a ₹ 50 stock, at what amounts up and down would you first take action in both portfolios? Assume that you have set your action points at 10 per cent above and below the initial ₹ 20,000 value of the stock portfolio.

5. Suppose that the monthly return for two bond managers is as follows:

Month	Manager I	Manager II
1	9%	25%
2	13%	13%
3	22%	22%
4	-18%	-24%

What is the arithemetic average monthly rate of return for the two managers?

6. What is the time-weighted average monthly rate of return for the two managers in Question 5?

7. Why does the arithemetic average monthly rate of return diverge more from the time-weighted monthly rate of return for manager II than for manager I in Question 5?

8. Karan's portfolio is valued at ₹ 25,00,000 at the beginning of a 31-day month. During the month, Karan withdraws ₹ 1,50,000 from the portfolio on day 12 and contributed ₹ 75,000 on day 21. At month end the portfolio was worth ₹ 24,70,000. What was Karan's Rupee-weighted return for the month?

9. ABC Co. stock price and dividend history is as follows:

Year	2007	2008	2009	2010
Price of Equity share	₹ 350	375	360	380
Dividend	₹ 15	15	15	15

An investor buys 500 share of ABC Co. in 2007, buys another 200 shares at 2008, sells 100 shares in 2009, and sells all remaining shares at in 2010.

i) What are the arithmetic and geometric average time weighted rate of return for the investor?

ii) What is the rupee-weighted rate of return?

REFERENCES

1. Andrews, John R. "The Case for Investing in Growth." *Financial Analysts Journal*, November-December 1970, p. 55.

2. Ankrim. Ernest: "Risk-Adjusted Performance Attribution," *Financial Analysts Journal*, March-April 1992, pp. 75-82.

3. Blume, Marshall, "On the Assessment of Risk," *Journal of Finance*, 26 (March 1971), 1-10.

4. Bookstaber, Richard, and Roger Clarke: "Problems in Evaluating the Performance of Portfolios with Options," *Financial Analysts Journal*, January-February 1985.

5. Bower, Richard, and Donald Wippern, "Risk-Return Measurement in Portfolio Selection and Performance Appraisal Models: Progress Report," *Journal of Financial* and *Quantitative Analysis 4*, no. 4 (December 1969): 417-447.

6. Brealey, Richard A. "How to Combine Active Management with Index Funds." *Journal of Portfolio Management* 12, no. 2 (Winter 1986).

7. Brinson, Gary P., L. Randolph Hood, and Gilbert L. Beebower. "Determinants of Portfolio Performance." *Financial Analysts Journal*, July/August 1986, 39-44.

8. Chang, E.C., and W.G. Lewellen. "Market Timing and Mutual Fund Performance," *Journal of Business*, 1984, 57-72.

9. Chang, Eric C., and Wilbur G. Lewellen. "Market Timing and Mutual Fund Investment Performance." *Journal of Business* 57, no. 1, part 1 (January 1984).

10. Chen, N., T E. Copeland, and D. Mayers. "A Comparison of Single and Multifactor Portfolio Performance Methodologies." *Journal of Financial and Quantitative Analysis* 22, no. 4 (December 1987).

11. Chen. Andrew. Frank Jen. and Stanley Zionts, "The Optimal Portfolio Revision Policy." *Journal of 'Business* 44. No. I (January 1971): 51 61.

12. Cornell, Bradford, and Kevin Green. "The Investment Performance of Low-Grade Bond Funds. *Journal of Finance* 46, no. 1 (March 1991).

13. Cranshaw, T. E., "The Evaluation of Investment Performance," *The Journal of Business.* October 1977, pp. 462-485.

14. Dietz, Peter O., and Jeannette R. Kirschman. "Evaluating Portfolio Performance." In *Managing Investment Portfolios*, 2d ed., edited by John L. Maginn and Donald L. Turtle. Boston: Warren Gorham and Lament, 1990.

15. Ellis, Charles D. "Performance Investing." *Financial Analysts Journal*, September-October 1968, p. 117.

16. Evnine, Jeremy, and Andrew Rudd. "Option Portfolio Risk Analysis." *Journal of Portfolio Management*, Winter 1984, 23-27.

17. Frankfurter, George, "The Effect of 'Market Indexes' on the Ex-post Performance of the Sharpe Portfolio Selection Model," *Journal of Finance* 31 (June 1976): 949-955.

18. Frankfurter, George, Herbert Phillips, and John Seagle, "Performance of the Sharpe Portfolio Selection Model: A Comparison," *Journal of Financial and Quantitative Analysis* 11. No. 2 (June 1976): 195-204.

19. Friend, Irwin, and Marshall Blume, "Measurement of Portfolio Performance Under Uncertainty," *American Economic Review* 60, no. 4 (September 1970): 561-576.

20. Grinblatt, Mark, and Sheridan Titman: "Mutual Fund Performance: An Analysis of Quarterly Portfolio Holdings," *Journal of Business.* July 1989, pp. 393-416.

21. ——and ——: "Performance Measurement without Benchmarks: An Examination of Mutual Fund Returns." *Journal of Business*, January 1993, pp. 47-68.

22. Haugen, B., and N. Baker: "The Inefficiency of the Value-Weighted Index," *Journal of Portfolio Management*, 1989, pp. 42-55.

23. Higgs, Peter, and Stephen Goode: "Target Active Returns and Attribution Analysis," *Financial Analysts Journal, May-June 1993*, pp. 77-80.

24. Ibbotson, R.L. Siegel, and K. Love: "World Wealth: Market Values and Returns," *Journal of Portfolio Management*, Fall 1985, pp. 4-23.

25. Ibbotson, Roger, and Laurence Siegel: "The World Market Wealth Portfolio," *Journal of Portfolio Management*, Winter 1983, pp. 5-17.

26. Jensen, Michael C: "The Performance of Mutual Funds in the Period 1945-1964," *Journal of Finance*, May 1968, pp. 389-416.

27. Korschat, Benjamin. "Measuring Research Analysts Performance." *Financial Analysts Journal*, July-August 1978.

28. Lehman, Bruce, and David Modest: "Mutual Fund Performance Evaluation: A Comparison of Bench-marks and Benchmark Comparisons," *Journal of Finance*, June 1987, pp. 233-265.

29. Rennie, Edward, and Thomas Cowhey: "The Successful Use of Benchmark Portfolios: A Case Study," *Financial Analysts Journal*, September-October 1990, pp. 18-26.

30. Schneider, Theodore H. "Measuring Performance." *Financial Analysts Journal*, May-June 1969, p. 105.

31. Sharpe, W.F.: "Mutual Fund Performance," *Journal of Business*, January 1966, pp. 119-138.

32. Spigelman, Joseph H. "What Basis for Superior Performance?" *Financial Analysts Journal,* May-June 1974, p. 32.

33. Surz, Ronald: "Portfolio Opportunity Distributions: An Innovation in Performance Evaluation," *Journal of Investing,* Summer 1994, pp. 36-41.

34. Tierney, David, and Kenneth Winston: "Defining and Using Dynamic Completeness Funds to Enhance Total Fund Efficiency," *Financial Analysts Journal,* July-August 1990, pp. 49-54.

35. Treynor, J.L. "How to Rate Management of Investment Funds." *Harvard Business Review,* January-February 1965, pp. 63-75.

36. ————. "How to Use Security Analysis to Improve Portfolio Selection." *The Journal of Business* 46 (January 1973).

37. ————. "Long-Term Investing." *Financial Analysts Journal,* May-June 1976, p. 56.

38. Vertin, James R. "The Design and Control of Large Portfolios." The Financial Analysts Federation, Annual Conference, May 1978.

39. Williams, Arthur: *Managing Your Investment Manager,* Dow Jones-Irwin, New York, 1990.

40. Williamson, Peter J. "Measuring Mutual Fund Performance." *Financial Analysts Journal,* November-December 1972, p. 78.

41. ————. "Performance Measurement," in Edward Altman (ed.): *The Financial Handbook,* Wiley, New York, 1980.

32

Performance Evaluation

INTRODUCTION

The management of an investment portfolio requires knowledge, experience, constant research; appraisal and reappraisal of securities markets, sectors within the market, and individual securities. One has to keep trace of the trends in the national economy and the competitive position of different industries. The investor must be familiar with not only those industries in which he invests, but also those in which he does not invest, since they might, in the future, offer attractive outlets for funds. To be successful one requires to combine the skills of a professional analyst with those of a portfolio manager. Not many investors possess the training and experience to carry out an investment programme. Hence arises the management problem and it is in answer to this problem of managing investment portfolios that investment companies have come up.

ALTERNATIVE MEASURES OF PERFORMANCE EVALUATION

Performance evaluation is concerned with two issues: (1) determining whether the money manager added value by outperforming the established benchmark and (2) determining how the fund manager achieved the calculated return. *Did the fund manager achieve the return by market timing, by buying undervalued stocks, by buying low-capitalisation stocks, by overweighting specific industries, etc.?* The decomposition of the performance results to explain the reasons why those results were achieved is called *performance attribution analysis.* Moreover, performance evaluaiton requires the determination of whether a fund manager achieved superior performance (i.e., added value) by skill or by luck.

Basing their research on the Sharpe-Lintner security market model or the CAPM, several researchers have suggested alternative measures of portfolio performance. Although these measures differ from one another, they are closely related, and in fact they represent a common attempt to reduce the two-parameter risk-return dimensions of investment performance to a single measure which incorporates considerations of return with an adjustment for risk. While all agree that the profitability should be measured by the average rate of return, there is no complete agreement regarding the risk index.

TOTAL VARIANCE VS. BETA AS A RISK INDEX

The total variance of a security (or its standard deviation) has nothing to do with measuring risk, at least not for a security included in the context of a well-diversified portfolio. The relevant risk in this case is the security's beta, or the slope of the characteristic line of the security under consideration. Suppose that we plan to compare the performance of various mutual funds. Using beta as the risk index, we explicitly or implicitly assume that in addition to the mutual fund under consideration, investors also diversify their holdings in many other securities, so that overall each investor holds the market portfolio. This assumption is true also for any individual stock or security. For example, if beta is used to evaluate the performance of XYZ stock, this implies the assumption that, in addition to XYZ stock, investors also hold all the other stocks included in the market portfolio. To be more specific, recall that a security's beta is defined as.

$$\hat{\beta}i = Cov(R_i, R_m)/c_m^2$$

where R_i and R_m are the rates of return on security i and on the market portfolio respectively; c_m^2 is the variance of the market portfolio. Since c_m^2 is common to all the stocks, the covariance $Cov(R_i, R_m)$ is the only risk factor which distinguishes the riskiness of one security from another. However, $Cov(R_i, R_m)$ measures the comovements of the rates of return of security i with the market portfolio m. This comovement constitutes an appropriate risk index only if investors actually hold the market portfolio m. If some investors hold a different portfolio k, then for this group of investors the relevant risk index is $Cov\ (R_i, R_k)/c_k^2$, where R_k and c_k^2 are the rates of return and the variance of portfolio k (distinct from the market portfolio m).

To sum up, beta is the appropriate risk index of an individual security or of a portfolio (a mutual fund) only within the framework of the Capital Asset Pricing Model, which asserts that *all investors hold the market portfolio m.*

Let us turn now to the other extreme, when *investors hold only one security* in their portfolio. To be more specific, assume that a group of investors hold only ABC stock. For these investors the beta of ABC measured against the market portfolio (or against any other portfolio) is completely irrelevant as a risk index, since these investors simply do not hold such a highly diversified portfolio. The appropriate risk measure in this extreme case is the variability of the rates of return on ABC stock, normally measured by the stock's "own" total risk (variance) or standard deviation.

The security's "own" variability is particularly appropriate as the risk index for mutual funds. The rationale for this assertion is that most investors who buy mutual fund shares simply leave it to the fund's management to select for them the best diversification strategy. Thus, these investors hold only a single security—the mutual fund shares, a case when the variability of rates of return is precisely the appropriate risk index.

Consider now a more realistic case when some investors hold only one stock in their portfolio (say, ABC), another group of investors hold several securities (a small number) in addition to ABC stock, and the third group hold the entire market portfolio. In this case, there is no single index which properly measures the risk of ABC stock for all investors. The proper risk measure is ABC's variance c_{ABC}^2 for the non-diversifiers, β_{ABC} for the market-portfolio holders, and some complicated combination of c_{ABC}^2 and β_{ABC} for the investors holding a diversified portfolio in which the diversification falls short of that required by the CAPM. Thus, the appropriate risk index depends on the assumed degree of diversification.

Before we turn to the analysis of various mutual funds' performance measures, let us again summarize the aims of this analysis:

(a) Mutual fund managers claim that they have professional knowledge and hence their fund will perform better than a randomly selected "unmanaged" portfolio. If this claim is valid, investors may be willing to allow the fund managers to manage their investments, and will even pay a significant commission for this service. If the claim is false, one would be better off by choosing stocks at random; in this case, even investors who do not possess any knowledge of the stock market should avoid mutual fund shares.

(b) Suppose that mutual funds actually outperform the unmanaged portfolio and it is worthwhile to buy their shares. In this case, we need an index to rank all these funds according to their performance. If past performance indeed predicts future performance, this ranking facilitates the investor's choice among different funds.

(c) The third aim of performance measurement is for internal needs. To be more specific, suppose that the mutual fund management would like to evaluate the investment performance of their professional teams. Then, every few months or few years, they can analyze their investment results in comparison to other funds as well as in comparison to unmanaged portfolios. This evaluation may be used for fixing compensation, and even for such extreme decisions as replacing the professional team should they fail to compete with other teams.

Note that the performance indexes which implicitly assume a single-asset portfolio are appropriate for mutual funds, as investors mostly hold the fund shares without attempting any further diversification on their own. Also most empirical studies use mutual funds data to test if the funds' management is doing better than an unmanaged portfolio.

In what follows we shall focus mainly on three traditional measures of portfolio performance based on the CAPM framework: (a) Treynor's reward-to-volatility ratio, (b) Sharpe's reward-to-variability ratio, and (c) Jensen's performance index.

TREYNOR REWARD-TO-VOLATILITY RATIO

Teynor's portfolio performance measure is based on the concept of characteristics line. It is interpreted as stating the reward (return minus the risk-free rate) in relation to a portfolio's beta risk.

The equation for the *Treynor measure* for the performance of portfolio p, T_p equals[1]

$$T_p = [ER_p - RF]/\beta_p \tag{1}$$

where:

T_p = Treynor's portfolio Index
ER_p = Expected market return on portfolio p
RF = Risk-free rate of interest
β_p = Beta coefficient of portfolio p

The equation (1) stems from the security market line (SML). Which defines a portfolio p as

$$ER_p = RF + \beta_p [ER_M - RF] \tag{2}$$

From Equation 2, the reward for taking risk equals $[ER_p - RF]$. Solving for the reward in Equation 2 gives

$$ER_p - RF = \beta_p [ER_M - RF] \tag{3}$$

Dividing both sides by beta gives

$$[ER_p - RF]/\beta_p = [ER_M - RF] \tag{4}$$

The left-hand side of Equation 4 is simply the Treynor measure for portfolio p, T_p. Note that Equation 4 originated from the *SML*, and $[ER_M - RF]$ is the slope of *SML*. Equation 4 implies that if portfolio *p* lies on *SML*, then the portfolio's Treynor measure,

---

1. Jack Treynor, "How to Rate Management of intrestment Funds," *Harvard Business Review* (January— February 1965), pp. 119-138.

T_p, must equal the slope of the market portfolio's SML, SML_M. In fact, dividing $[ER_M - RF]$ by β_M gives

$$T_M = [ER_M - RF]/\beta_M \tag{5}$$

Because the market portfolio's beta is 1.0 by definition, Equation 5 is equivalent to the right-hand side of Equation 4 or $[ER_M - RF]$. T_p is the slope of the portfolio's SML, SML_p. Therefore, the Treynor measure says that, if the slope of SML_p equals the slope of SML_M (i.e., if T_p equals T_M), then the portfolio must lie on the market SML. Recall that according to SML the performance of any portfolio or security that lies on the line matches the expectations of the CAPM (See Figure-1).

Security Market Line when $T_P = T_M$

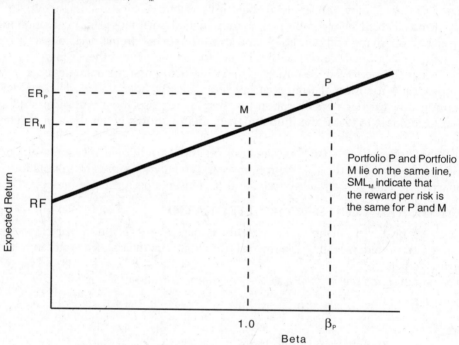

FIGURE 1: SECURITY MARKET LINE WHEN $T_P = T_M$

Suppose that a different portfolio P_1 lies above the SML, as shown in Figure 2. Its slope, calculated by the Treynor measure, would be steeper than that of SML_M:

$$T_{p1} = [ER_{p1} - RF]/\beta_{p1} > [ER_M - RF] = T_M \tag{6}$$

As in the SML analysis, this implies that portfolio P_1 is undervalued; it is outperforming the expectations of SML_M (as defined by the CAPM). Because the SML represents the market portfolio, most interpret this relationship to mean that P_1 is outperforming the market portfolio.

Another interpretation is that the Treynor measure normalises the portfolio's reward by the market's beta of 1.0. Suppose that T_{p1} is 0.245 and T_M is 0.210. This means that at a beta of 1.0, the reward to p1 equals 0.245, whereas the market portfolio's reward equals 0.210. Figure-2 shows this graphically. The Treynor measure compares the rewards of two portfolios, P_1 and M, adjusted to reflect the same risk level. If the reward for P_1 is greater than that for M at the same risk level, P_1 outperforms the market portfolio.

Secuity Market LInes when $T_P > T_M$

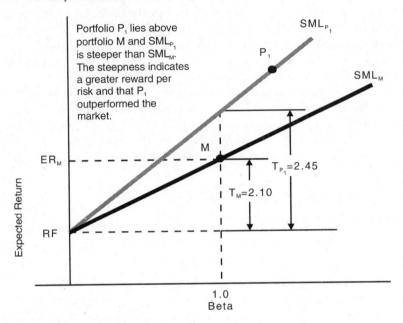

FIGURE 2: SECURITY MARKET LINE WHEN $T_P > T_M$

Finally, if a portfolio P_2 lies below the *SML*, as shown in figure 3, then its slope will be flatter than the slope of the SML_M.

$$T_{p2} = [ER_{p2} - RF]/\beta_{p2} < [ER_M - RF] = T_M \qquad (7)$$

Secuity Market LInes when $T_P < T_M$

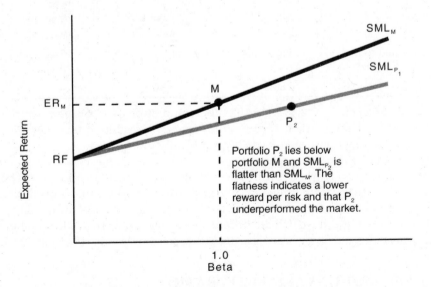

FIGURE 3: SECURITY MARKET LINES WHEN $T_P < T_M$

Portfolio P_2 is overvalued; it underperforms the expectations of the SML, or the market portfolio, because the slope of the market portfolio is the benchmark. Again, if the two portfolios, P_2 and M, and aligned by beta risk of 1.0, then a comparison shows that P_2 generates a smaller reward than M at the same level of beta risk.

Using data provided in Table-1 let's calculate ER_p and the Treynor measure for ABC Fund and a hypothetical Super Index (representing the market portfolio).

First, calculate ER_p as the arithmetic average of return over the years 2001 through 2010; this gives mean returns of 18.53 per cent for ABC fund and 15.61 per cent for the Super Index. The risk-free rate also appears in Table-1 as the return on Treasury bills; its mean equals 5.42 per cent. Now estimate beta by the market model, using the data above. ABC fund's beta is estimated to be 1.05, so the Teynor measure for ABC Fund can be calculated as

$$T_p = [ER]/\beta_p = [18.53\% - 5.42\%]/1.05 = 12.49$$

The Treynor measure for the Super Index equals

$$T_M = [ER_M - RF] = [15.61\% - 5.42\%] = 10.19$$

TABLE 1

Data on a ABC Fund, Super Index, and Treasury Bills

Year	ABC Fund	Super Index	T-Bills
2001	23.7%	18.6%	6.07%
2002	1.0	4.9	5.13
2003	22.8	16.6	6.58
2004	34.6	32.2	8.14
2005	- 4.5	- 3.1	7.50
2006	41.0	30.4	5.59
2007	7.0	7.6	3.46
2008	24.7	10.1	2.90
2009	- 1.8	1.3	3.90
2010	36.8	37.5	4.91
Expected return	18.53%	15.61%	5.42%
Beta	1.05	1.0	0.0
Standard deviation	16.88%	13.93%	—

Because T_p exceeds T_M (12.49 > 10.19), ABC Fund appears to outperform the Super Index, the proxy for the market. Figure 4 illustrates the results of this example. It also indicates how the Treynor measure can be graphically interpreted.

The graph shows the SML_M where a risk-free rate of 5.42 per cent corresponds to a beta equal to zero and a market portfolio return of 15.61 per cent to a 1.0 beta. The graph shows the SML_p based on the same risk-free rate, but with ABC Fund's portfolio beta of 1.05. SML_p is steeper than SML_M. Also, the Treynor measure of 10.19 for the Super Index and 12.49 for ABC Fund measure the differences in their rewards at the 1.0 beta level. ABC Fund provides a 2.30 per cent greater reward (12.49 minus 10.19) at the 1.0 beta level.

SHARPE REWARD-TO-VARIABILITY RATIO

Sharpe's logic for introducing *total risk* instead of beta lies with the assumption behiand the beta risk. Beta risk assumes that a portfolio is well diversified, with no

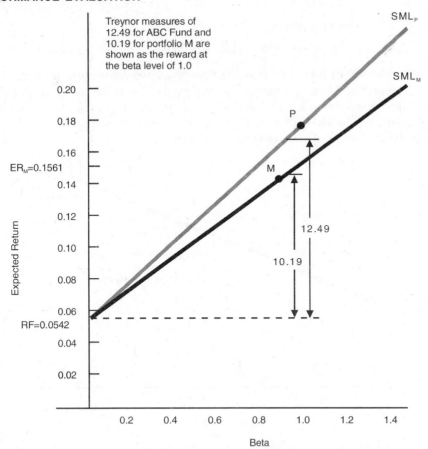

FIGURE 4: GRAPHIC EXAMPLE OF THE TREYNOR MEASURE FOR THE ABC FUND

remaining diversifiable risk. Sharpe argues, however, that a portfolio manager who does not hold a well-diversified portfolio should be penalised for exposing returns to diversifiable risk. Hence, the Sharpe measure adjusts portfolio returns for total risk, σ_p, which includes both systematic (beta) risk and diversifiable risk. Generally, *if mutual funds or other portfolios are well diversified, the Sharpe and Treynor measures will give them the same rankings. If the measures give different rankings, the portfolio ranked higher by Treynor but lower by Sharpe may not be well diversified.* In this way, the Sharpe measure is considered to be more stringent than the Treynor measure.

The *Sharpe measure, S_p,* adjusts portfolio performance by total risk, σ_p, rather than beta risk.[2] The formula is

$$S_p = [ER_p - RF]/\sigma_p \qquad (8)$$

Although Treynor used the SML, the Sharpe measure relies on the capital market line (CML), that is defined as :

$$ER_p = RF + [(ER_m - RF]/\sigma_m]\sigma_p \qquad (9)$$

Again, the reward for taking risk equals $[ER_p - RF]$, which comes from some manipulation of Equation 9:

$$[ER_p - RF] = \{[ER_M - RF]/\sigma_m]\sigma_p \qquad (10)$$

2. William Sharpe, "Mutual Fund Perforamnce," *Journal of Business* (January 1966), pp. 119-138.

Dividing both sides by σ_p gives

$$[ER_p - RF]/\sigma_p = [ER_M - RF]/\sigma_m \tag{11}$$

The left-hand side of Equation 11 is the Sharpe measure for portfolio p, S_p, and the right-hand side is the Sharpe measure for the market portfolio. More important, the right-hand side gives the slope of the CML_M. Again, the logic resembles that for the Treynor measure. If the slope (S_p) of a line, CML_p, equals the slope of the CML_M, then portfolio p must lie on the CML_M as Figure-5 illustrates.

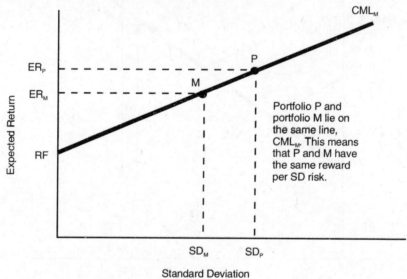

FIGURE 5: CAPITAL MARKET LINE AND THE SHARPE MEASURE

If, however, a portfolio such as p_1 lies above the CML_M, the slope of CML_{p1} (S_{p1}) will be steeper than the slope of the CML_M. This suggests that p_1 outperforms the market. The Sharpe measure adjusts portfolio risk to the equivalent of the market's 1 per cent standard deviation so the analyst can compare the rewards for p_1 and M. Suppose that S_{p1} equals 0.55 and S_M is 0.45; this relationship implies that the reward to p_1 is greater (by 0.10) than the market portfolio's return at the same level of SD_p risk. Figure-6 illustrate this situation.

Suppose that another portfolio, p_2 lies below the CML; its slope (S_{p2}) must be flatter thn the slope of the CML_M. This implies that p_2 underperforms the market. Again, the Sharpe measure shows that the reward to p_2 is less than the market portfolio's reward at the same level of risk, as in Figure-7.

Let's apply the Sharpe measure to ABC Fund and see if the relative performance picture changes. Table-2 reported ER_p for the portfolio ABC Fund, the Super Index, and 30-day Treasury bills, so now we must calculate standard deviations for ABC Fund and the Super Index. The standard deviation of returns on ABC Fund equals 16.88 per cent; for Super Index, the standard deviation is 13.93 percent, as displayed in Table-2. Now, let's calculate the Sharpe measure for ABC Fund:

$$S_p = [ER_p - RF]/\sigma_p = [0.1853 - 0.0542]\ 0.1688 = 0.777$$

The Sharpe measure for the Super Index equals

$$S_M = [ER_M - RF]/\sigma_M = [0.1561 - 0.05421]/0.1393 = 0.732$$

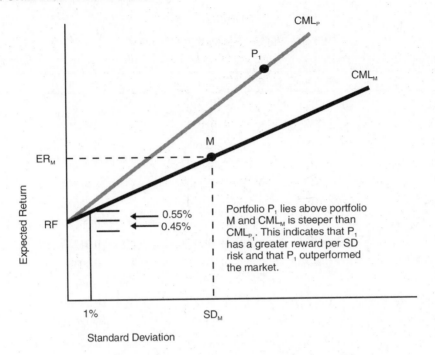

Portfolio P₁ lies above portfolio M and CML_M is steeper than CML_P₁. This indicates that P₁ has a greater reward per SD risk and that P₁ outperformed the market.

FIGURE 6: CAPITAL MARKET LINE AND WHEN $S_P > S_M$

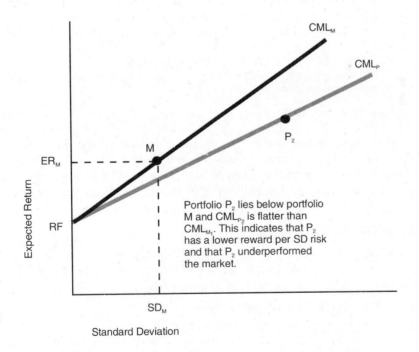

Portfolio P₂ lies below portfolio M and CML_P₂ is flatter than CML_M₁. This indicates that P₂ has a lower reward per SD risk and that P₂ underperformed the market.

FIGURE 7: CAPITAL MARKET LINE AND WHEN $S_P < S_M$

TABLE 2

How to Calculate a Standard Deviation

Using ABC Fund as an example, this table reviews how to calculate a standard deviation.

Year	ABC Fund	Return - M	(Return - M)²
(1)	(2)	(3)	(4)
2001	0.237	0.0517	0.00267
2002	0.010	-0.1753	0.03073
2003	0.228	0.0427	0.00182
2004	0.346	0.1607	0.02582
2005	-0.045	-0.2303	0.53038
2006	0.410	0.2247	0.05049
2007	0.070	-0.1153	0.01329
2008	0.247	0.0617	0.00381
2009	-0.018	-0.2033	0.04133
2010	0.368	0.1827	0.03338
SUM	1.853	SUM	0.02564
Mean	0.1853	SUM / (N - 1)	0.02849

$$\sqrt{0.02849} = 0.16879$$

Step 1: Calculate the arithmetic average or mean of the ABC Fund returns. The mean equals the sum of Colummn 2 divided by the number of returns, N:
M = (Sum of Column 2)/N = 1.853%/10 = 18.53 per cent

Step 2: Create Column 3 by subtracting the mean. M, from each return in Column 2.

Step 3: Create Column 4 by squaring each (Return - M) in Column 3.

Step 4: Sum Column 4 and divide by (N - 1) or (10 - 1). Next, take the square root to find the sample standard deviation, SD:

$$\sqrt{SUM/(N-1)} = \sqrt{0.28488} = 0.16879 \text{ or rounded to } 16.88 \text{ per cent}$$

Because ABC Fund's Sharpe measure is greater than that of the Super Index, the mutual fund appears to outperform the market Super Index. CML_p has a steeper slope than CML_M. Finally, at a 1 per cent level of total risk, σ_p, ABC Fund's reward is 0.045 (0.777 minus 0.732) greater than that of the Super Index. For a graphic display of the results, see Figure-8.

JENSEN'S PERFORMANCE INDEX

Another measure of risk-adjusted return, *Jensen's alpha*, uses the characteristic line estimated by the market model, and again, the CAPM is its benchmark.[3] Let's review the CAPM and then subtract RF from both sides of the equation:

$$ER_p = RF + \beta_p [ER_M - RF] \tag{12}$$
$$ER_p - RF = \beta_p [ER_M - RF] \tag{13}$$

3. Michael Jensen, "Performance of Mutual Funds in the Period 1945-1964," *Journal of Finance* (May 1968), pp. 389-415.

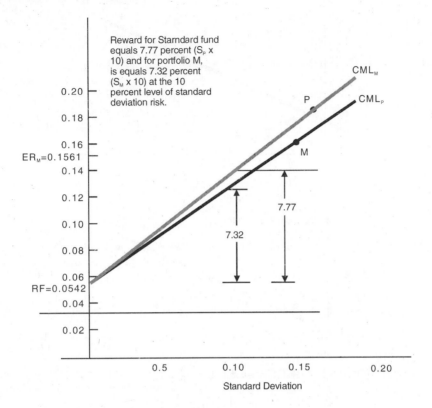

FIGURE 8: GRAPHIC EXAMPLE OF THE SHARPE MEASURE FOR THE STANDARD FUND

Now, let's review the market model and then subtract RF_t from the independent variable, return on the market index, R_{Mt}, and dependent variable, return on a portfolio, R_{pt}. Recall that the market model estimates the α_p and β_p for a regression between R_{mt} and R_{pt}:

$$R_{pt} = \alpha_p + \beta_p (R_{Mt}) + r_{pt} \tag{14}$$
$$(R_{pt} - RF) = \alpha_p + \beta_p (R_{Mt} - RF) + r_{pt} \tag{15}$$

The difference between Equation 14 and 15, subtracting RF from both the independent and dependent variables, leaves the slope the same. The change causes a parallel shift in the market model to a new y-intercept, as figure-9 shows.

The expected value of the regression equation in Equation 15 equals

$$[ER_{pt} - ERF_t] = \alpha_p + \beta_p [ER_{Mt} - ERF_t] + Er_{pt} \tag{16}$$

where α and β are estimated by using least squares estimation technique, ERF_t is the expected risk-free rate, and Er_{pt} is the expected error from the regression. Since the ordinary least squares estimation procedure assume that $Er_{pt} = 0$ and that the expectations operator E is an arithmetic mean, this allows us to rewrite Equation 16 as

$$ER_{pt} - ERF_t = \alpha_p + \beta_p [ER_{Mt} - ERF_t] \tag{17}$$

Now, let's compare Equation 17 with the CAPM, remembering that the ER_p, RF. and ER_M for the CAPM are calculated as arithmetic means using historical data over time. This implies they are equivalent in value to ER_{pt}, ERF_t, and ER_{mt}.

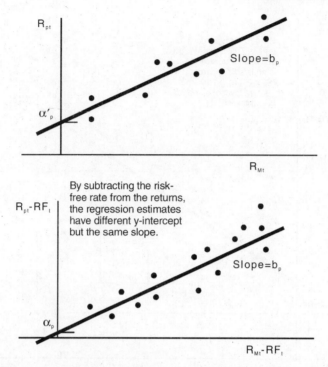

FIGURE 9: MARKET MODEL LESS THE RISK-FREE RATE

$$ER_{pt} - ERF_t = \alpha_p + \beta_p[ER_{Mt} - ERF_t]$$
$$ER_{pt} - RF = 0 + \beta_p[ER_M - RF]$$

The two equations are equivalent only if α_p equals zero. This value is called Jensen's alpha. It equals zero only if the ER_{pt} of portfolio p equals the CAPM equation. This means that p must lie on the SML. This essentially duplicates the SML analysis. In fact, ER_{pt} can be interpreted as the predicted return, PR, in the SML analysis. If α_p equals zero when a portfolio lies on the SML, then α_p must be greater than zero ($\alpha_p > 0$) when a portfolio lies above the SML. Stated differently, $\alpha_p < 0$, then a portfolio must lie below the SML or the actual average return is less than the required CAPM return. Figure-10 compares SML analysis and Jensen's alpha.

Because Jensen's alpha is estimated using regression, the analysis also provides the r-square statistic. In general, r-square indicates how well the independent variable "explains" the dependent variable. More specifically, when the regression equation is in the form of a market model, r-square states the percentage of a security's, or portfolio's, total risk that is systematic. Because one goal of a portfolio is to minimise, or even eliminate, unsystematic risk through diversification, the degree to which r-square approaches 1.0 indicates how well diversified the portfolio is.

An alternative way to calculate Jensen's Alpha is to take an arithmetic mean for the stock's actual returns used for the regression estimation and subtract the CAPM required return. Effectively, subtracting the CAPM equation (Equation 13) from Equation 17, which leaves α_p.

Jensen's α = [Actual mean return for a portfolio] – [CAPM return]   (18)
For ABC Fund, it equals
Jensen's α = [0.1853] – [0.0542 + 1.05 (0.1561 – 0.0542)]
= [0.1853] – [0.1612] = + 0.0241

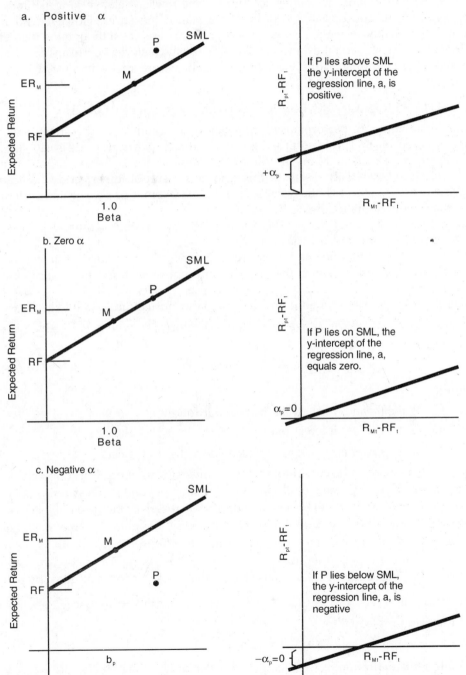

SML Analysis and Jensen's α

Notice the corresponding relationship
between the SML and the regression line.

a.   Positive α

If P lies above SML
the y-intercept of the
regression line, a, is
positive.

b. Zero α

If P lies on SML, the
y-intercept of the
regression line, a,
equals zero.

c. Negative α

If P lies below SML,
the y-intercept of the
regression line, a, is
negative

FIGURE 10: SML ANALYSIS AND JENSEN'S α

Because ABC Fund has a positive α (or α greater than zero), we conclude that it outperforms the market. And to test whether α is statistically greater than zero, t test is to be used.

The three performance measures account for the reward relative to a risk measure and provide more appropriate portfolio performance measures. However, all three portfolio performance measures were applied to historical data, although the theoretical developments were based on ex-ante models. Obviously, historical performance is easier to evaluate than future performance, even though we are really interested in future performance.

DECOMPOSITION OF EXCESS RETURN: FAMA'S APPROACH

The whole notion of performance indexes and the rationale for investing in mutual funds are based on the promise of excess return due to the funds' allegedly superior professional management. Many investors buy mutual fund shares without further diversifying into other risky assets. In this case, as a result of imperfect diversification, the investors are exposed to both systematic and non-systematic risk. The non-systematic risk vanishes only in the following two cases:

(a) the investor perfectly diversifies his portfolio by mixing the mutual fund shares with many other securities; or
(b) the rate of return on the mutual fund is perfectly correlated with the market portfolio; in other words, the mutual fund represents a mean-variance efficient portfolio.

In either case, the excess or abnormal return on the mutual fund i should be measured simply by the actual return $\overline{R}_i$ less the expected return $\overline{R}_i^*$, where $\overline{R}_i^*$ is given by the CAPM formula,

$$\overline{R}_i^* = RF + (\overline{R}_m - RF)\hat{\beta}_i \tag{19}$$

Here

   $\overline{R}_m$ is the mean return on the market portfolio
   RF is the riskless interest rate
   $\hat{\beta}_i$ is the systematic risk as represented by the fund's beta

In cases when either the condition of perfect diversification or of portfolio efficiency does not hold, Fama suggested to decompose the mutual fund's excess return so as to make explicit the investor's exposure to non-systematic risk. Figure-11 illustrates the suggested decomposition. A mutual fund i is marked by the point F in the mean rate of return vs. beta plane. The actual mean rate of return of fund i is $\overline{R}_i$, and the systematic risk is $\hat{\beta}_i$. The straight line in Figure-11 plots the CAPM risk-return relationship, and in equilibrium the fund's rate of return consistent with its risk $\hat{\beta}_i$ should be given by point E on this line, where $\overline{R}_i^* = RF + (\overline{R}_m - RF)\hat{\beta}_i$. Thus, the vertical difference $\overline{R}_i - \overline{R}_i^*$ is the fund's excess return, equal to:

$$\overline{R}_i - \overline{R}_i^* = \overline{R}_i - [RF + (\overline{R}_m - RF)\hat{\beta}_i]$$

Recalling the definition of Jensen's performance index α_i by $\overline{R}_i - RF = \alpha_i + \hat{\beta}_i/(\overline{R}_m - RF)$, we see that the vertical difference $\overline{R}_i - \overline{R}_i^*$ is simply equal to Jensen's index, $\overline{R}_i - \overline{R}_i^* = (\overline{R}_i - RF) - \hat{\beta}_i(\overline{R}_m - RF) = \hat{\alpha}_i$.

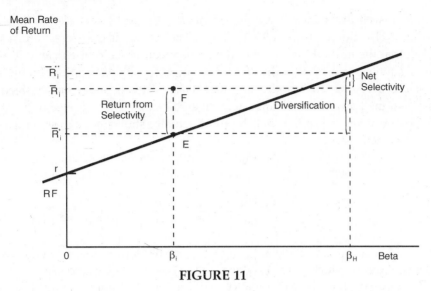

FIGURE 11

As a result of imperfect diversification [condition (a) does not hold], the investor holding only the mutual fund share which promises the excess return $\overline{R}_i - \overline{R}_i^*$ is actually exposed to the fund's total risk c_i^2 given by

$$\sigma_i^2 = \hat{\beta}_i^2\, \sigma_m^2 + \sigma_{ei}^2 \tag{22}$$

and not only to the systematic risk $\hat{\beta}_i$. The non-systematic risk c_{ei}^2 is not "washed out" in this case, since investors rely on the mutual fund diversification strategy and do not diversify their holdings failing to ensure efficiency of their portfolio [condition (b) does not hold either]. It is thus appropriate to ask if the fund's excess return actually compensates the investors for the additional risk associated with imperfect diversification.

To answer this question, we carry out the following decomposition. First, find the hypothetical mutual fund beta, denoted by $\hat{\beta}_H$, in case of perfect correlation with the market portfolio, i.e., when condition (b) holds and the non-systematic risk vanishes so that the total risk is given by:

$$c_i^2 = \beta_H^2 c_m^2 \tag{23}$$

Hence for this hypothetical beta we obtain

$$\hat{\beta}_H = \sigma_i / \sigma_m \tag{24}$$

The actual excess return $\overline{R}_i - \overline{R}_i^*$ is defined by Fama as "return from selectivity". However, at the hypothetical risk level $\hat{\beta}_H$, the required rate of return within the CAPM framework is $\overline{R}_i^{**}$ and the "net" selectivity excess return is thus $\overline{R}_i - \overline{R}_i^{**}$ (which is negative in the specific case shown in Figure-12). Thus, we have the following decomposition of the excess return:

Actual Excess Return   = Diversification + Net Selectivity
(Return from Selectivity)

$$\overline{R}_i - \overline{R}_i^* \;=\; (\tilde{R}_i^{**} - \tilde{R}_i^*) \;+\; \overline{R}_i - \overline{R}_i^{**} \tag{25}$$

Note that the component $(\overline{R}_i^{**} - \overline{R}_i^*)$ is what the investor should get if only the non-diversifiable (systematic) risk is taken into account, namely in the hypothetical case that his portfolio is well-diversified. The component $(\overline{R}_i - \overline{R}_i^{**})$ is the net excess return after the risk is adjusted by moving from $\hat{\beta}_i$ to $\hat{\beta}_H$. The net selectivity is the excess return adjusted for the fact that the mutual fund portfolio may be mean-variance inefficient. It measures the mutual fund's performance adjusted for its imperfect diversification. In our example the net selectivity is negative, indicating that the investor is undercompensated for the extra risk assumed as a result of imperfect diversification. The net selectivity, of course, may also be positive, indicating that the fund actually shows net excess return beyond what could be achieved by wide diversification.

Finally, note that if the mutual fund is *perfectly correlated* with the market portfolio (i.e. the correlation coefficient is $r = 1$ and the portfolio is efficient) we have:

$$\hat{\beta}_i = \frac{Cov(R_i, R_m)}{\sigma_m^2} = \frac{Cov(R_i, R_m)}{\sigma_i \sigma_m} \cdot \frac{\sigma_i}{\sigma_m} = r \cdot \frac{\sigma_i}{\sigma_m} = 1 \cdot \frac{\sigma_i}{\sigma_m} = \frac{\sigma_i}{\sigma_m} = \hat{\beta}_H \qquad (26)$$

The actual beta is equal to the adjusted beta and the return on selectivity is identical to the net selectivity, which in turn is equal to the observed excess return.

To illustrate, consider the performance of TC Investment mutual fund. The estimates of the fund's return parameters, based on *ex-post* data for the ten-year period are the following:

$$\text{Mean rate of return } \overline{R}_{TC} = 20.664\%$$
$$\text{Standard deviation } \sigma_{TC} = 33.758\%$$
$$\text{Systematic risk } \hat{\beta}_{TC} = 1.098$$

The systematic risk was estimated against an unmanaged market portfolio proxy with the following parameter estimates:
$$R_m = 14.360\%$$
$$\sigma_m = 24.473\%$$
The average risk-free interest rate for the period is around 5%.

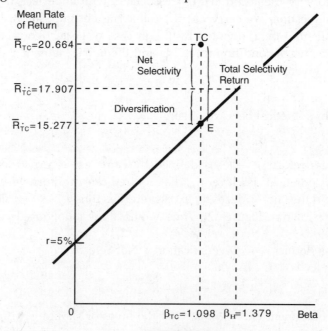

FIGURE 12

Figure-12 plots the fund TC at the point $\hat{\beta}_{TC} = 1.098$, $\overline{R}_{TC} = 20.664\%$ and the equilibrium CAPM risk-return relationship:

$$\overline{R}_i^* = RF + (\overline{R}_m - RF)\hat{\beta}_i = 5 + 9.360\hat{\beta}_i$$

The expected rate of return for $\hat{\beta}_{TC} = 1.098$ is thus:

$$\overline{R}_{TC}^* = 5 + 9.360 \times 1.098 = 15.277$$

and the actual *excess return* is:

$$\overline{R}_{TC} - \overline{R}_{TC}^* = 20.664 - 15.277 = 5.387$$

The fund's total risk is $\sigma_{TC} = 33.758\%$. The hypothetical beta corresponding to the case of perfect diversification with zero non-systematic risk is thus:

$$\hat{\beta}_H = \sigma_{TC}/\sigma_m = \frac{33.758}{24.473} = 1.379$$

The mean rate of return consistent with this risk level in the CAPM framework is calculated from the CAPM relationship above,

$$\overline{R}_{TC}^{**} = 5 + 9.360 \times 1.379 = 17.907$$

and the diversification excess return is thus:

$$\overline{R}_{TC}^{**} - \overline{R}_{TC}^* = 17.907 - 15.277 = 2.630$$

Since the total selectivity excess return is $\overline{R}_i - \overline{R}_i^* = 5.387$, we have here *a positive* net selectivity effect,

$$\overline{R}_{TC} - \overline{R}_{TC}^{**} = (\overline{R}_{TC} - \overline{R}_{TC}^*) - (\overline{R}_{TC}^{**} - \overline{R}_{TC}^*) = 5.387 - 2.630 = 2.757$$

so that the fund actually has more than compensated the investors for the additional imperfect diversification risk.

MEASURING PERFORMANCE USING THE ARBITRAGE PRICING THEORY

The Jensen Index uses the linear relationship of the security market line as a benchmark to measure performance. In the arbitrage pricing theory there is a similar linear relationship between the factor betas and the expected rates of return on securities and portfolios. The relationship for any given portfolio, P, is given by

$$E(r_p) = E(r_z) + \lambda_1 \beta_{1.p} + \lambda_2 \beta_{2.p} + \lambda_n \beta_{n.p} \qquad (27)$$

Expected Portfolio Return = Risk-free Rate + sum of factor risk premiums

Once we have estimates of $E(r_z)$ and the various factor prices, λ, we can use this relationship as a benchmark, measuring performance as the difference between a portfolio's rate of return in a given period and what we would expect it to be, on the basis of the APT equation for expected return. Although there are several ways to do this, we might proceed as follows. The first step is to decide on the number of factors needed to account for the convariances between stocks. Suppose the prior opinion with respect to this question is that there are two, and the factors are unexpected changes in the rate of inflation and the real rate of interest.

The next step is to estimate the factor betas for a cross section of securities. This is done by relating the returns on each security to the unexpected percentage changes in each of the two factors. We are to deal with a three-dimensional space, where we are plotting the security's rates of return on the vertical axis and the unexpected percentage changes in each of the two factors on the two horizontal axes. We slide a plane of best fit through the scatter of points, each point representing the rates of return to the security and the unexpected percentage changes in each of the two factors in a particular period of time, say, a month. The slopes of the plane going down each axis will represent the sensitivity of the security's return to changes in the two factors. These slopes serve as estimates of the two factor betas.

The next step is to estimate the factor prices. This can be done cross sectionally by relating the estimated factor betas to the average rates of return on each stock for the total period examined, in the manner of Black, Jensen, and Scholes. Here, again, we are sliding a line of best fit through a scatter of points in three dimensions. On the vertical axis we have average return, and on the two horizontal axes we have the factor betas for each stock. Each point in the scatter will represent one of the stocks in the population. The point where the plane intercepts the vertical axis will be the estimate of the average rate of return to a stock or portfolio with zero factor risk, r_z. The slope of the plane relative to each horizontal axis serves as the estimates of the two factor prices.

We now have a benchmark to measure performance. The risk-adjusted performance measure is the difference between the portfolio's actual average rate of return for the period and the rate of return given by the position of portfolio on the plane, given estimates of its factor betas. Given the estimated factor betas for the portfolio and the portfolio's average rate of return, it is positioned above the plane.

Note that this performance measure is subject to one of the criticisms levelled at the Jensen Index. It reflects only depth and not breadth of performance. Performance measures based on the APT are also subject to the same types of criticisms that are levied at CAPM-based performance measures. As we know, the APT really makes no predictions about what the factors are. Given the freedom to select factors (or, alternatively, portfolios that represent factors) without restriction, it can be argued that portfolio analyst can literally make the performance of a portfolio anything he wants, it to be. In the case of the CAPM, he can never know whether portfolio performance is due to management skill or to the fact that he has an inaccurate index of the true market portfolio. In the case of APT-based measures, he has similar questions with regard to the selection of the appropriate factors.

MEASURING PERFORMANCE WITHOUT THE USE OF AN ASSET PRICING MODEL

Asset pricing models like CAPM and APT provide us with benchmarks that allegedly tell us if the return to an investment is more or less than sufficient given the investment's risk exposure. However, the power of these benchmarks is weak at best. Given this, it would be useful to have alternative ways of measuring performance that do not rely on asset pricing models.

Grinblatt and Titman have suggested such a procedure. Using their method the portfolio analyst would observe the changes in portfolio weights for individual stocks and see if there is a relationship between the changes and the subsequent returns on the stocks. Do the stocks that the portfolio analyst is taking greater positions in tend to produce relatively high rates of return in the period after weight change is made? This new measure of performance is called the *portfolio change measure* (PCM). To compute a manager's performance over one time period, the portfolio analyst would use the following formula:

$$PCM = r_{i,t} \left(W_{i,t} - W_{i,t-1} \right) \tag{28}$$

where:

$r_{i,t} =$ the rate of return to stock i in period t

$w_{i,t} =$ the percentage of the manager's portfolio invested in stock i at the beginning of period t

$w_{i,t-1} =$ the percentage of the manager's portfolio invested in stock i at the beginning of period t - 1

For each stock in the manager's portfolio, multiply the change in its weight in the previous period by its rate of return in the next period and then sum up all the products to get PCM. If the sum is positive, the manager has tended to increase the weights in the stocks in the portfolio that have subsequently produced high returns relative to the other stocks in the portfolio. Thus, a positive sum would indicate good performance and a negative sum would indicate poor performance.

Here's an example of how the measure works. Suppose a manager has initially invested equally in two stocks, A and B. In the course of the next period, the weight in stock A rises to 75 per cent and the weight in stock B falls to 25 per cent. Thus, the change in the weight for A is + 25 per cent and the corresponding change for B is - 25 per cent in the period following the change, A produces a 20 per cent return while B produces a 10 per cent return. The PCM would be calculated as follows:

$$PCM = 20\% \ (75\% - 50\%) + 10\% \ (25\% - 50\%) = 2.5\%$$

PCM indicates that this manager has a good performance because the manager increased the weight on the stock that subsequently had relatively high return.

Grinblatt and Titman use PCM to measure the performance of 155 mutual funds over the period 1975 through 1984. Their study uses quarterly data, including the quarterly portfolio weights of the mutual funds. For each fund, using the formula for PCM, they sum across all quarters in the time period covered in the study. Then they sum across funds of different types and test to see if the average PCM for a given type of fund is statistically different from zero. They observed that in general, when performance is measured using the previous quarter's changes in weights, performance is neutral, or not significantly different from zero. On the other hand, when performance is measured using the previous year's weight changes, the performance of the funds appears to be good.

Model-free performance measurement has promising advantages. However, we must be careful in assessing the merit of this particular study of mutual fund performance and the PCM measure itself. First, Grinblatt and Titman are careful to point out that all of the mutual funds in their sample survived the entire 10-year period of their study. Ten years is long time considering the life span of many funds. Those that survive that long are likely to have had good performance. The funds with bad performance are likely to go out of business.

Second, PCM examine the relationship between weight changes and the subsequent *relative rates of return* on stocks *in the portfolio*. It may well be the case that the mutual funds tend, as a group, to invest in stocks that underperform the market. PCM is really a measure of the managers' timing abilities relative to the group of stocks they have chosen to invest in. In one sense, this is a deficiency of the measure, but in another, this timing dimension of performance isn't captured in the measures of performance based on CAPM or APT.

Third, in a world characterised by transactions costs and other constraints on trading activity, there may be a real difference between a weight change caused by purchases and sales of shares by the fund and a weight change caused by shifts in the relative market values of different stocks. Fund managers may face constraints on the total volume of trading in their portfolios over the course of a year. This being the case, if an investor trades share of a stock now, he is forgoing options to trade later in the year. Thus, managers may allow relative portfolio weights in their stocks to drift, even though their opinions of the relative merits of the stocks may not have changed. In this sense a change in weights caused by a change in relative market values may not convey the same information about manager opinion as would a change in weights caused by trading activity by the manager.

Fourth, there are technical patterns in a stock's price history that can be used to predict a stock's future relative return. In particular, there are *short-term reversal patterns* in stock returns (if a stock went up relatively fast in the recent past, it has a propensity to produce a relatively small return in the future) that may be related to price pressure caused by trading activity. In addition there are *intermediate-term inertia patterns* (if a stock's performance is relatively good/bad over the last 6 to 12 months, this good/bad relative performance can be expected to continue into the future). These technical patterns in stock returns may create problems with PCM. To illustrate, consider the performance numbers where the weight changes are computed over the preceeding year. Many of those stocks experiencing increases (decreases) in weightings are likely to be doing so because of high relative returns, as opposed to increases (decreases) in the number of shares actually held by the mutual fund. Given intermediate inertia in stock returns, the odds favour high relative returns to these stocks in the next period also. This means that the stocks with positive weight changes will tend to have higher returns than the stocks with negative weight changes. Thus, given the presence of inertia and reversal patterns in security returns, performance under PCM may be significantly related to the length of the periods over which the returns and weight changes are measured.

Finally, although it makes use of available information about the managers' portfolio weights or positions in various stocks, PCM considers only the changes taking place in positions and not the relative magnitude of the positions themselves. Consider, for example, a manager who invests in three stocks, investing 20 per cent in stock A, 20 per cent in stock B, and 60 per cent in stock C. The manager now shifts weightings to 30 per cent in A and 10 per cent in B, maintaining 60 per cent in C. In the next period A produces a 10 per cent return, B a 20 per cent return, and C a 30 per cent return. The manager's PCM is

$$-1\% = 10\% \ (30\% - 20\%) + 20\% \ (10\% - 20\%) + 30\% \ (60\% - 60\%)$$

The manager is penalised for shifting funds to the lowest return stock, but gets no credit for investing the greatest amount of money in the highest return stock.

Given these caveats, an improved version of PCM might discriminate between weight changes caused by shifts in relative market value and changes induced by trading activity. Moreover, rather than multiply the weight changes by the simple return on each stock, one might multiply them by the difference between the stock's return and the return to a benchmark portfolio that has the same non-diversifiable risk as the stock.

APPLICATION OF EVALUATION TECHNIQUES

The answers generated using these performance measures are only as good as the data input. Therefore, it is necessary to be careful in computing the rates of return and take proper account of all inflows and outflows. More important, it is necessary to use judgement in the evaluation process. The above mentioned techniques and methods of evaluating investment performance apply to institutional investors as well as to individual investors. As individual we all know that one of the ways to improve ourselves is to review the past, to see where we made mistakes, and where we can improve. As far as investment is concerned, we should review the past results with respect to the following:

1. *Degree of risk assumed:* Is the portfolio properly diversified, or is it underdiversfied or overly diversified? Do the investor use margin? If so, is it too much? Many individuals' accounts are wiped out because of margin calls and priced sales *of* securities in recession.

2. *Selection of individual securities:* Does the investor have the ability to select undervalued issues ? This can be determined by comparing the percentage gain of the weekly purchased issues with the market performance. If the percentage gain exceeds the market index, it shows that the buyer has made good selections. If one has done this consistently, it shows skill in selecting undervalued issues.

3. *Cyclical and market timing:* Does the investor try to adjust the portfolio into aggressive, neutral, or defensive positions on the basis of anticipating the market savings ? If so, is the investor successful ? On what basis—technical or fundamental factors—does he formulate his anticipation of market savings ? What improvements can be made ? Or would it seem that he should better invest his earning elsewhere ?

4. *Risk-adjusted return :* The investor should compute (*a*) annual rates of return on the portfolio; (*b*) the level of risk assumed in terms of beta of the portfolio or variability of returns, and (*c*) the risk-adjusted returns. Then, the investor should compare the risk adjusted returns with those experienced by the market index, the average of stock funds and balanced mutual funds, etc. An evaluation of a portfolio managed should be done a number of times over different market environments before a final judgement is reached. An evaluation of the portfolio performance by the investor along the lines suggested, if done consistently once every year, should reveal weaknesses and strengths, and provide measures to improve overall ability in managing the investment programme.

PERFORMANCE MEASUREMENT WITH CHANGING PORTFOLIO COMPOSITION

To determine performance levels with any statistical significance, many observations are required even if portfolio return are distributed with constant mean and variance. The problem is compounded and it is harder to assess the performance when mean and variance change under an active managed portfolio strategy since the portfolio manager is to update the portfolio in accordance with the dictates of the financial analysis. Performance evaluation that accounts for frequent revision in portfolio composition is superior by far to evaluation that assumes constant risk characteristics over the entire measurement period. A typical example in the performance measurement with changing portfolio composition is the attempt of the active portfolio managers to time the market, resulting in ever-changing portfolio betas.

In a pure form, market timing involves reallocating funds between a risk-free asset and a market-index portfolio and bills (a risk-free asset). If the weight of the market were constant, then portfolio beta would also be constant, and the characteristic line would plot as a straight line. If market improves and becomes bullish, the investor would shift fund from T-bills to a market-index portfolio. The portfolio beta and the slope of the characteristic line will be higher when R_m is higher, resulting in the curved line.

Treynor and Mazuy added a squared term to the usual linear index model to estimate such a line by:

$$R_p - R_f = a + b\ (R_m - R_f) + c\ (R_m - R_f)^2 + e_p \qquad (29)$$

Where:

R_p = Portfolio return

R_m = Market return

R_f = Risk free asset, T-bills

a, b, and c are estimated by regression analysis. If c turns out to be positive, the characteristic line will be steeper as $R_m - R_f$ is larger, showing the timing ability of the portfolio manager.

Heuriksson and Merton proposed a similar and simpler methodology by suggesting that beta of the portfolio takes only two values: a large value if the market is expected to do well and small value otherwise. Such a characteristic line appears in regression flow as:

$$R_P - R_f = a + b (R_m - R_f) + c (R_m - R_f) D + e_P \qquad (30)$$

Where D is the dummy variable that equals 1 for $Rm > R_f$ and zero otherwise. This implies that beta of the portfolio will be b in bear market and b + c in bull markets. Again, a positive value of c implies market timing ability.

PERFORMANCE ATTRIBUTION PROCEDURES

Portfolio managers frequently revise portfolios and shift funds among sectors and securities. To know the timing and selection ability of the portfolio manager, the overall performance is decomposed into discrete component that may be identified with a particular level of portfolio selection process. Performance attribution studies the difference between a managed portfolio performance against a benchmark portfolio to find the sum of contributions to performance of a series of decisions made at various levels of the portfolio construction process. To illustrate, assume M is a managed portfolio and Z is stated as benchmark portfolio, consisting n asset classes such a equities, bond, and T-bills. For each asset class, a benchmark index portfolio is determined. For exempty NIFTY may be chosen as benchmark for equities. The benchmark portfolio, Z, is set to have fixed weights in each asset class, and its rate of return is given by

$$R_z = \sum_{i=1}^{n} W_{zi} R_{zi} \qquad (31)$$

Where:

W_{zi} = Weight of the Z in asset class i

R_{zi} = Return on the Z portfolio of asset class i

The portfolio manager, based on his capital market expectations, decides weights in each asset class and a portfolio of the securities either each class on the basis of his security analysis which earns R_{Mi} over the evaluation period. The return on the managed portfolio is expressed as:

$$R_M = \sum_{i=1}^{n} W_{Mi} R_{Mi} \qquad (32)$$

Where:

W_{Mi} = Weight of the M in each asset class i

R_{Mi} = Return on the M portfolio of asset class i

The difference between the two rates of return will be:

$$R_M - R_Z = \sum_{i=1}^{n} W_{Mi} R_{Mi} - \sum_{i=1}^{n} W_{Zi} R_{Zi}$$

$$= \sum_{i=1}^{n} (W_{Mi} R_{Mi} - W_{Zi} R_{Zi})$$

The overall performance in the summation of contributions of asset allocation decisions and security selection decisions for each asset class which can be decomposed into a sum of two term as follow.

Contribution from asset allocation	$(W_{Mi} - W_{Zi}) R_{Zi}$
+ Contribution from security selection	$W_{Mi} (R_{Mi} - R_{Zi})$
Total contribution from asset class i	$W_{Mi} R_{Mi} - W_{Zi} R_{Zi}$

The impact of asset allocation is expressed in the first term since it provides the sum measures of deviations of the actual weight from the benchmark weight for that asset class multiplied by the index return for the asset class added to or subtracted from the total performance. The second term of the sum measures the impact of security selection because it shows how the portfolio's manager excess return within the asset class compared to the benchmark return for that class multiplied by the portfolio weight for that class added to or subtracted term total performance. To illustrate this method, consider a portfolio manager invests in equities, bonds and many market securities. The attribution results of the hypothetical portfolio shows the portfolio return over the month is 9.50%. Managed portfolio performance is compared with the passive portfolio strategy. Passive has two attributes. *First,* the allocation of funds under this attribute is sit in accord with a notion of usual, or neutral, allocation across sectors. *Second,* with each passive asset class, the portfolio manager holds an indexed portfolio such as NIFTY for the equity sector. Hence, the portfolio manager using passive strategy as a performance benchmark rules out asset allocation as well as security selective decisions. Risk tolerance of the investors will be the determinant in assigning the weights. For example, a risk-seeker investor will place a large fraction of portfolio in equity market than a risk-averter investor. Any change in weights will take place if the market over-or underperform its usual risk-return profile. In Table-3, the neutral weights have been set at 7% equity, 20% fixed-

TABLE 3

Performance of the Managed Portfolio

Components	Z Performance and Excess Return	
	Z weight	Return of Index during Month (X)
Equity	.70	7.50
Bond	.20	2.50
Cash (Money Market)	.10	0.75
Z = (.70 x 7.50) + (.20 x 2.50) + (.10 x 0.75) = 5.825		
Return of managed portfolio, M =		9.50
- Return of benchmark portfolio, Z =		5.825
Excess return of managed portfolio		3.765

income and 10% cash (money market securities). The benchmark portfolio, Z, returned 3.675% whereas on the managed portfolio, M, the return was 9.50%, an excess of 3.675%. In hypothetical managed portfolio, of the portfolio manager has invest and 80%, 15%, 5% in equity, fixed income, and money market respectively.

To isolate the effect of the manager's asset allocation choice, the performance of a hypothetical portfolio that would have been invested in the indexes for each market with weights 80/15/5 is measured. The return measures the effect of the shift away from the benchmark 78/20/10 weights without allowing for any effects attributable to active management of the securities selected within each market. Table-4 shows that asset allocation contributed 58.75 basis points to the portfolio's overall excess return of 308.75 basis points. The major contributing factor in rupee or performance in this month is because of shifting the finds to equity market by increasing the weight from 70% to 80%.

TABLE 4

Performance Attribution

A. Contribution of Asset Allocation to Performance

Market	Asset Weight in Market	Benchmark Weight in Market	Active or Excess Weight	Market Return (%)	Contribution to Performance (%)
	(1)	(2)	(3)	(4)	(5) = (3) x (4)
Equity	.80	.70	.10	7.50	.7500
Bond	.15	.20	- .05	2.50	- .1250
Cash	.05	.10	- 105	0.75	- .0375
Contribution of Asset allocation					.5875

B. Contribution of Selection to Total Performance

Market	Portfolio Performance	Index Performance	Excess Performance	Portfolio Weight	Contribution (%)
	(1)	(2)	(3)	(4)	(5)
Equity	11.175	7.50	3.675	.80	2.9400
Bond	3.483	2.50	.983	.15	.1475
Contribution of Selection within markets					3.0875

Sector and Security Selection Decisions

Table-4B shows an increase in return of the equity component of the managed portfolio to 11.175% for 7.50%. The return on bond component has also increased to 3.483% from 2.50. This superior return performance in both components in each market sums to the 3.0875% contribution to performance attributable to sector and security selection. Thus the total excess performance of 3.675% on managed portfolio is the sum of advantageous asset allocation across markets (.5875%) and the remaining 3.0875% then is attributable to sector selection and security selection within each market.

STYLE ANALYSIS

Style analysis, introduced by Nobel Laureata William Sharpe, uses a multiple regression model when the factors are category (style) portfolio such as T-bills, bonds, and equities.

A regression of fund return on the style portfolio returns generates residuals that represent the value added of stock selection in each period. These residuals can be used to gauge fund performance relative to similar- style funds. (Because funds are barred from short positions, the regression coefficients are constrained to be either zero or positive and to sum to for so as to represent a complete asset allocation. The R-square of the regression would them measure the percentage of return variability attributed to the effects of security selection).

MORNINGSTAR'S RISK-ADJUSTED RATING (RAR)

The Morningstar RAR method produces results that are similar but not identical to that of the mean /variance-based sharpe ratio. This method compares each fund to a peer group represented by a style portfolio within four asset classes. The peer group for each fund is selected on the basis of the fund's investment universe (e.g., internation, growth versus value, fixed income, and so on) as well as portfolio characteristics such as average price-to-book value, price-earnings ratio, and market capitalisation). Risk-adjusted ratings (RAR) are based on fund returns relative to the peer group and used to award each fund one to five stars based on the rank of its RAR.

THE M² PERFORMANCE MEASURE

Franco Modigliani and his granddaughter proposed a new performance measurement technique in 1997 which they called M². The M² performance measure expresses the relative performance in risk-adjusted basis points. The key is to ensure that the portfolio being evaluated and the benchmark have the same standard deviation. To do this, risk-adjusted portfolio return is calculated by using the following equation:

$$R_{rap} = \frac{S_b}{S_p} R_{ap} + (1 - \frac{S_b}{S_p}) R_f \tag{33}$$

Where:

R_{rap} = Risk adjusted portfolio
R_{ap} = Actual portfolio
σ_b = Benchmark standard deviation
σ_p = Portfolio standard deviation
R_f = Risk free rate

In illustrate, assume portfolio consultant working with an investment company reviews the performance of its investment managers over the past year. Data distribution is given below in Table-5

TABLE-5

	Return	Standard Duration	Sharpe Ratio
ABC Securities	12.07%	0.205	0.335
XYZ Securities	10.87%	0.169	0.335
AYZ Securities	14.56%	0.366	0.256
QQQ Index	12.15%	0.230	0.302
Risk free rate is 5.20 % in last 12 months.			

Performing the calculations, we find

ABC Securities

$$R_{abc} = \frac{0.230}{0.205} \, 12.07\% + \left(1 - \frac{0.230}{0.205}\right) 5.20\%$$

$$= 12.91\%$$

XYZ Securities

$$R_{xyz} = \frac{0.230}{0.169} \, 10.87\% + \left(1 - \frac{0.230}{0.169}\right) 5.20\%$$

$$= 12.91\%$$

ZYZ Securities

$$R_{AYZ} = \frac{0.230}{0.366} \, 14.56\% + \left(1 - \frac{0.230}{0.366}\right) 520\%$$

$$= 12.91\%$$

QQQ Index

$$R_{QQQ} = \frac{0.230}{0.230} \, 12.15\% + \left(1 - \frac{0.230}{0.230}\right) 5.20\%$$

$$= 12.15\%$$

These results show no difference in the returns of ABC and XYZ, both of which outperformed the Index benchmark by 0.76 points (12.91% = 12.15%).

Relative Performance

Performance	Risk-Adjusted Return	Performance
ABC Securities	12.91%	Above Average
XYZ Securities	12.91%	Above Average
QQQ Index	12.15%	Market Average
AYZ Securities	11.08%	Below Average

This is exactly what the Sharpe ratio shows, too. AYZ Securities underperformed the benchmark by 1.07% and underperformed ABC and XYZ by 1.83%.

BOND PORTFOLIO PERFORMANCE EVALUATION

The performance of portfolio of bonds and other types of fixed income securities is often evaluated by comparing their total return (consisting of coupon payments plus capital gains or losses) with those of an index representing a comparable class of securities over some interval of time. Hence, a portfolio that invested in investment-grade long-term corporate bonds would be compared with an investment-grade long-term corporate bond index; a portfolio invested in mortgage-backed securities would be compared with a mortgage-backed securities index, and a high-yield bond fund would be compared with a high-yield bond index.

PERFORMANCE EVALUATION WHEN OPTIONS ARE USED

Use of options in a portfolio usually shifts the return distribution to non-systematical. For instance, writing covered calls causes the distribution to be substantially skewed to the left since the striking price of option creates an upper limit on return of the option writer. Skewness is zero in a normal distribution. And in case the return distribution is non-systematical, Beta and standard deviation lose their theoretical appeal. Since one of the most important assumption in financial theory is that of statistical normality of security returns, this makes the non-normality to be an important consideration in hypothesis testing in technical financial research. However, in most ordinary performance evaluation applications the departure from normality that a well diversified portfolio will experience because of options is modest.

Two alternative methods of performance evaluation in portfolios where options applied are discussed below:

INCREMENTAL RISK-ADJUSTED RETURN (IRAR) FROM OPTIONS

IRAR, a single performance measure, indicates the contribution of an option programme to overall portfolio performance. A positive IRAR indicates above average performance, the negative IRAR indicates that the portfolio would have done better without options.

IRAR form options can be expressed as:

$$IRAR = (O_{sp} - U_{sp})\; c_0 \tag{34}$$

Where:

O_{sp} = Sharpe measure of optioned portfolio
U_{sp} = Sharpe measure of unoptioned portfolio
c_0 = Standard deviation of the optioned portfolio

IRAR, though potentially useful, but can be used inappropriately. A portfolio manager for instance, might use puts to protect against a large fall in stock prices. Such an insurance strategy sets a floor on the possible holding period return and severely truncates the return distribution for the portfolio. In this case, the standard deviation of the optioned portfolio is a poor measure of risk. This is especially true if the portfolio manager is catering to a client who values the ability to set a floor return on investment.

RESIDUAL OPTION SPREAD (ROS)

ROS, an alternative performance measure used in optioned portfolio, calculates the residual option spread for the optioned and unoptioned portfolios. A positive ROS indicates that at the end of the observation period, the use of options may result in a higher terminal wealth than would have resulted from merely holding the stock. A positive ROS does not mean that the incremental return is appropriate, given the new level of risk of the optioned portfolio.

This is not necessarily a problem, though. Covered call writing will always reduce the variance of return on portfolio, so a positive ROS is always evidence of superior risk-adjusted performance in a covered call writing programme. In contrast, put overwriting will always increase the portfolio return variance. No general statement can be made about a positive ROS. We can say that a negative ROS is prima facie evidence of poor performance in a programme of put overwriting.

Portfolio managers use ROS for many reasons. The IRAR and ROS both focus on whether or not an optioned portfolio performance outperform an unoptioned portfolio. Such a measurement can easily overlook important subjective considerations involved in the decision to use options. Using options, as insurance, for instance, sets a floor on the possible holding period return, severally truncating the returns distribution. This means that the standard deviation of the optioned portfolio is a poor measure of risk for this portfolio. Insurance has a value, to sure, but whether portfolio manager can really measure what he wants to measure using only quantitative methods is not clear.

REVIEW PROBLEMS

1. Novex firm is trying to decide between two investment funds. From past performance they were able to calculate the following average returns and standard deviations for these funds. The current risk-free rate is 8 per cent and the firm will use this as a measure of the risk-free rate

	ABC Fund	XYZ Fund
Average return (R) (per cent)	18	16
Standard deviation, σ(per cent)	20	15
Risk-free rate, R_f = 8.0%		

Ans.:

Using the Sharpe performance measure, the risk-return measurement for these two funds are:

$$S_{P_{ABC}} = \frac{0.18 - 0.080}{0.15} = 0.500$$

$$S_{P_{XYZ}} = \frac{0.16 - 0.80}{0.533} = 0.533$$

It is clear that XYZ fund has a slightly better performance and would be the better alternative of the two.

2. With a risk-free rate of 10%, and with the market portfolio having an expected return of 20% with a standard deviation of 8%, what is the Sharpe Index for portfolio X, with a mean of 14% and a standard deviation of 18% and for portfolio Y, having a return of 20% and a standard deviation of 16%? Would you rather be in the market portfolio or one of the other two portfolios?

Ans.:

Portfolio X: $S_p = \dfrac{\tilde{R}_p - R_f}{\sigma_p}$

$$S_p = \frac{14\% - 10\%}{18\%} = 0.222$$

Portfolio Y: $S_p = \dfrac{20\% - 10\%}{16} = 0.625$

Market: $S_p = \dfrac{20\% - 10\%}{8\%} = 1.25$

The market is superior to X and Y.

3. XYZ and ABC are the two mutual funds. XYZ has a sample mean of success .13 and fund ABC has a sample mean of success .18, with the riskier fund ABC having double the beta at 2.0 as fund XYZ. The respective standard deviations are 15% of ABC and 19% of XYZ. The mean return for market index is .12, while the risk-free rate is 8%.

(a) Compute the Jensen Index for each of the funds. What does it indicate?

(b) Compute the Treynor index for the funds. Interpret the results and compare it to the Jensen index.

(c) Compute the Sharpe Index for the funds and the market.

Ans.:

(a) Fund ABC has twice the Jensen Index as Fund XYZ :

Fund XYZ:
$$= 13\% - [8\% + (12\% - 8\%)\ 1.0]$$
$$= 1\%$$

Fund ABC:
$$J = 18\% - [8\% + (12\% - 8\%)\ 2.0] = 2\%$$

(b) The Treynor Index shows the securities performing at the same level :

Fund XYZ:

$$T_p = \frac{\tilde{R}_p - R_f}{\beta_p}$$

$$= \frac{13\% - 8\%}{1.0} = 5$$

Fund ABC:

$$T_p = \frac{\tilde{R}_p - R_f}{\beta_p}$$

$$T_p = \frac{18\% - 8\%}{2.0} = 5$$

(c) The Sharpe Index places Fund ABC ahead of fund XYZ, but by a lesser margin than the Jensen Index:

Fund XYZ :

(Sharpe Index): $$S_p = \frac{\tilde{R}_p - R_f}{\sigma_p}$$

Fund ABC: $$\frac{13\% - 8\%}{15\%} = .333$$

Fund XYZ: $$= \frac{18\% - 8\%}{19\%} = .526$$

Market: $$S_p = \frac{12\% - 8\%}{8\%}$$

$$= .500$$

4. Suppose the standard deviations, betas and average rates of return of several managed portfolio are given below, along with the standard deviation and average rate of return of the market index. The beta of the index is assumed to be 1. Further assume the T-bills rate averaged 7% during the time period performance measurement. Compare these funds on performance using the Sharpe, Treynor and Jensen measures.

Fund	Average Return	Std. Deviation	Beta
A	0.15	0.25	1.25
B	0.12	0.30	0.75
C	0.10	0.20	1.00
$\tilde{R}_m$	0.12	0.25	1.00

Ans.:

Fund A has the best Reward- to- Variability Ratio (Sharpe measure), while Fund B has the best Reward-to- Volatility Ratio (Treynor measure). Fund C is the worst on all these counts. Fund A has a better Reward to Variability ratio than the market 0.32 compared to (0.12 – 0.07)/0.25 = 0.2 Fund A also has a better reward to volatility ratio than the market; 0.64 compared to (0.12 – 0.07) /1 = 0.05. Also, the alpha (Jensen measure) is positive; thus fund A outperformed the market with all measures. Fund B outperformed the market using the Reward-to- Volatility and alpha measures, but not the Reward- to-Variability ratio. Fund C underperformed the market according to all three measures.

Fund	Reward to Variablity	Reward to Volatility	Alpha
A	(0.15 – 0.07)/0.25 = 0.32	(0.15 – 0.07)/1.25 = 0.064	(0.15 – 0.07) – 1.25 (0.12 – 0.07)=0.0175
B	(0.12 – 0.07)/0.30 = 0.167	(0.12 – 0.07)/0.75 = 0.067	(0.12 – 0.07) – 0.75 (0.12 – 0.07)=0.0125
C	(0.10 – 0.07)/0.20 = 0.150	(0.10 – 0.07)/1.00 = 0.03	(0.10 – 0.07) – 1.00 (0.12 – 0.07)=0.0200

5. Suppose you are asked to analyse two portfolios having the following characteristics:

	Observed Return	Beta	Residual Variance
Portfolio A	0.18	2.0	0.03
Portfolio B	0.12	1.5	0.00

The risk-free rate is 0.07. The return on the market portfolio is 0.15. The standard deviation of the market is 0.06.

(a) Compute the Jensen Index for portfolio A and B.

(b) Compute the Sharpe Index for the market portfolio.

(c) Compute the Sharpe Index for portfolios A and B.

(d) Compute the Treynor Index for the portfolios A and B.

Ans.:

(a) Jensen Index:
Portfolio A:
$$= 18\% - [7\% + (15\% - 7\%)\ 2.0]$$
$$= 18\% - [7\% + (8\%)2.0] = -5\%$$

Portfolio B:
$$= 12\% - [7\% + (15\% - 7\%)\ 1.5]$$
$$= 12\% - [7\% + 12\%]$$
$$= -7\%$$

(b) Sharpe Index for Market

$$= \frac{15\% - 7\%}{6\%}$$

$$= 1.33\%$$

(c) Sharpe Index for Portfolios:
Standard deviation of Portfolio A:

$$\sigma_p \quad = \left[\beta_p^2 \sigma_m^2 + \sigma_{ei}^2\right]^{\frac{1}{2}}$$

$$= [(2.0)^2 \,(0.0036 + 0.03)]^{1/2}$$

$$= 34.98\%$$

Sharpe Index for Portfolio A:

$$= \frac{18\% - 7\%}{34.98\%}$$

$$= 0.315$$

Standard deviation for Portfolio B:

$$\sigma_p = [1.5^2 \,(0.0036 + 0.00)]^{1/2}$$

$$= 0.09$$

$$= 9\%$$

Sharpe Index for Portfolio B:

$$= \frac{12\% - 7\%}{9\%}$$

$$= 0.55$$

(d) Treynor Index:

Portfolio A: $\dfrac{18\% - 7\%}{2.0}$

$$= 5.5$$

Portfolio B: $\dfrac{12\% - 7\%}{1.5}$

$$= 3.33$$

6. A variable annuity unit is worth ₹ 50. This is based on 7% annual annuity interest rate for 20 years. If the investor buys 500 units, how much does he invest in the annuity? If the portfolio performance is -6%, how much is the annual payment?

Ans.:

Present value of an Annuity = ₹ $50/0.07(1-[1/1.07]^{20})$

$$= ₹\, 714.3 \,(1 - [0.9346]^{20})$$

$$= ₹\, 714.3 \,(0.7415)$$

$$= ₹\, 529.6 \text{ per unit The cost of 500 units}$$

$$= ₹\, 500 \times ₹\, 529.6$$

$$= ₹\, 2,64,800$$

If the portfolio returns only 6%, the value of an annuity must fall since the base rate is 7%.

Value of Variable Annuity

$$= ₹\, 50 \times [1 + (-0.06 - 0.07)]$$

$$= ₹\, 50 \,[1 - 0.13]$$

$$= ₹\, 43.5$$

Thus the new value of the unit is ₹ 43.5, and the total payment will be 500 × ₹ 43.5 = ₹ 21,750.

7. Fund A has ₹ 10,00,000 under management at time 0. It earns 25% in Period 1. At that time, ₹ 5,00,000 is pulled out by other investors. The remaining capital earns negative 10% during Period 2. What are the fund's time-weighted and rupee-weighted rates of return?

Ans.:

The time-weighted rate of return is calculated as a geometric mean of the individual rates of return. Thus the time-weighted performance is

$$[(1.25 \times 0.90)]^{0.5}-1 = 0.0607$$
$$= 6.07\%$$

The rupee-weighted rate of return is found as the solution to the internal rate of return problem.

$$₹\,10,00,000 = ₹\,5,00,000/(1 + r) + ₹\,6,75,000/(1 + r)^2$$
$$r = 10.88\%$$

8. Consider the following data for a particular sample period:

	Portfolio P	Market M
Average return	0.35	0.28
Beta	1.2	1.0
Standard deviation	0.42	0.30
Nonsystematic risk	0.18	0

Calculate the following performance measures for portfolio P and the market: Sharpe, Jensen, Treynor, Appraisal Ratio. The risk-free rate during the period was 0.06. By which measures did portfolio P outperform the market?

Ans.:

Sharpe:
$$S_p = (0.35 - 0.06)/0.42$$
$$= 0.69$$
$$S_m = (0.28 - 0.06)/0.30$$
$$= 0.733$$

Jensen:
$$J_p = 0.35 - [0.06 + 1.2\,(0.28 - 0.06)]$$
$$= 0.026$$
$$J_m = 0$$

Treynor:
$$T_f = (0.35 - 0.06)/12$$
$$= 0.242$$
$$T_m = (0.28 - 0.06)/1.0$$
$$= 0.22$$

Appraisal Ratio:
$$A_p = J_p/\sigma_{ei} = 0.026/0.18$$
$$= 0.144$$
$$A_m = 0$$

9. Shares of XYZ Co. pay a ₹ 2 dividend at the end of every year on December 31. An investor buys two shares of the stock on January 1 at a price of ₹ 20 each, sells one of those shares for ₹ 22 a year later on the next January 1, and sells the second share an additional year later for ₹ 19. Find the time- and rupee-weighted rates of return on the 2-year investment.

Ans.

Time	Action	Cash Flow
0	Buy two shares	-4
1	Collect dividends; then sell one of the shares	4+22
2	Collect dividend on remaining share, then sell it	2+19

(a) Rupee-weighted return:

$$-40+\frac{26}{(1+r)}+\frac{21}{(+r)^2}=0$$

r = 0.1191 = 11.91%

(b) Time-weighted return:

The rates of return on the stock in the 2 years were

$$r_1 = \frac{2+(22-20)}{20}$$

$$= 0.20$$

$$r_2 = \frac{2+(19-22)}{22}$$

$$= -0.045$$

$(r_1 + r_2)/2 = 0.077$, or 7.7%

10. Suppose that a stock now selling for ₹ 100 will either increase in value by 15% by year-end with probability 0.5, or fall in value by 5% with probability 0.5. The stock pays no dividends.

(a) What are the geometric and arithmatic mean returns on the stock?
(b) What is the expected end-of-year value of the stock?
(c) Which measure of expected return is superior?

Ans.:

(a) Expected geometric return = [(1.15)(0.95)]1/2 – 1 = 0.045
    Expected arithmatic mean return = [0.15 + (–0.05)1/2 = 0.05
(b) The expected stock price is (115 + 95)/2 = 105
(c) The expected rate of return on the stock is 5%, equal to expected arithmatic mean return on the stock.

11. You are presented by a new, feisty client with the following: "I've lived through many a time you'll never see, you young whippersnapper, and if there is one thing I've learned, it's that anyone can have luck now and then. But MANAGEMENT! now that's the key to real success. I've selected two assets for you to assess, my young pup, and I'll take the risky one or the nonrisky, makes no matter. But MANAGEMENT! Find me the one that there's some real talent behind, and you'll have the entire clan's account next week!" You take the paper he hands you, and read the names of the two funds. Doing research into the wee hours of the night, you find that fund A has a sample mean of .13

and fund B has a sample mean of .18, with the riskier fund B having double the beta at 2.0 as a fund A. The respective standard deviations are 15 per cent and 19 per cent. The mean return for your market index is .12 with a standard deviation of .08, while the risk-free rate on the bond market is 8 per cent.

 (a) Compute the Jensen Index for each of the funds. What does it indicate to you?
 (b) Compute the Treynor Index for the fund and the market. Interpret the results.
 (c) Compute the Sharpe Index for the funds and the market.
 (d) What do you say to the client to get the entire clan's account?

Ans.:

 (a) Fund B's Jensen Index is twice that of fund A:

$$\text{Fund } A: \; J_p = \bar{R}_p - [R_f + \beta_p(\bar{R}_m - R_f)]$$
$$= 13\% - [8\% + (12\% - 8\%)\,1.0]$$
$$= 1\%$$
$$\text{Fund } B: \; J_p = 18\% - [8\% + (12\% - 8\%)2.0]$$
$$= 2\%$$

 (b) The Treynor Index shows the securities performing at the same level:

   Fund A:

$$T_p = \frac{R - R_f}{\beta_p}$$

$$= \frac{13\% - 8\%}{1.0} = 5$$

   Fund B

$$= \frac{18\% - 8\%}{2.0} = 5$$

   Market

$$T_p = \frac{12\% - 8\%}{1} = 4$$

 (c) The Sharpe Index places fund B ahead of fund A, but by a lesser margin than the Jensen index:

$$\text{Fund } A: \; S_p = \frac{R_p - R_f}{\sigma_p}$$

$$= \frac{13\% - 8\%}{15\%} = .333$$

$$\text{Fund } B: \; S_p = \frac{18\% - 8\%}{19\%} = .526$$

$$\text{Market}: \; S_p = \frac{12\% - 8\%}{8\%} = .500$$

 (d) Both funds appear to be able to identify undervalued securities because they have positive Jensen indices. Fund B's Jensen is larger, but when considering the investors' ability to lever fund A 1 per cent excess return, they both look pretty much the same in this respect as indicated by their equal Treynor indices. Fund B, however, clearly has the better management because it can capture the excess return while diversifying over many individual issues, as indicated by its superior Sharpe Index. Fund B gets the nod!

12. With a risk-free rate of 5 per cent, and with the market portfolio having an expected return of 10 per cent with a standard deviation of 5 per cent, what is the Sharpe Index for portfolio A, with a return of 8 per cent and a standard deviation of 10 per cent? For portfolio B, having a return of 12 per cent and a standard deviation of 8 per cent? Would you rather be in the market portfolio or one of the other two portfolios?

Ans.:   Portfolio A: $S_p = \dfrac{R_p - R_f}{\sigma_p} = \dfrac{8\% - 5\%}{10\%} = .3$

Portfolio B: $S_p = \dfrac{12\% - 5\%}{8\%} = .875$

Market: $S_p = \dfrac{10\% - 5\%}{5\%} = 1.0$

The market is superior to either A or B.

13. Suppose a manager is holding three stocks, with 25 per cent invested in stock X, 25 per cent invested in stock Y, and 50 per cent invested in stock Z. At the end of the next quarter, the manager's weights are 30 per cent, 20 per cent, and 50 per cent, respectively. In the quarter after that, the stocks produce returns of 15 per cent, 5 per cent, and 30 per cent, respectively. What is the manager's PCM?

Ans.:

The PCM is computed as follows:
.5 = 15% (30% − 25%) + 5% (20% − 15%) + 30% (50% − 50%)

14. TTK Committee manage four mutual funds. The funds are: Balanced, Investment Growth, Fixed Income, and Variable Growth. The data below include annual total return for each fund followed by key statistical measures. The average return on riskless securities during the measurement period was 5 per cent per annum.

	Bal.	Growth	F.I.	V. Growth	XYZ Index
2001	-.085	-.117	-.001	.141	-.116
2002	.028	.032	.056	.035	.077
2003	.100	.201	.030	.255	.190
2004	-.093	-.117	-.014	-.101	-.156
2005	.032	.083	.032	.153	.142
2006	.096	.123	.045	.113	.187
2007	.118	.142	.066	.134	.206
2008	-.072	-.139	.054	-.170	-.076
2009	.166	.235	.071	.240	.224
Return	.0282	.0403	.0373	.0798	.0654
Variance	.009	.020	.001	.021	.023
Beta	.6207	.9127	.1379	.6991	
Rho	.65	.94	.96	.82	

(a) Rank the performance of these portfolios using the Sharpe and Treynor techniques.
(b) Consider the Jensen method of ranking portfolios relative to the market. What is the overall performance of each fund relative to the market.
(c) Which funds had the most unsystematic risk during the evaluation period? Explain.

Ans.:

(a)

	Balanced	Investment Growth	Fixed Income	Variable Growth
Sharpe	.2298	.0686	.4019	.2058
Treynor	.0351	.0106	.0921	.0426
Sharpe ranks	3	2	4	1
Treynor ranks	3	2	4	1

(b) Rank: Variable Growth, Fixed Income, Investment Growth, and Balanced.
(c) Variable Growth most, Investment Growth next, Fixed Income next, Balance next.

$$(e_j^2 = \sigma_j^2 = \beta_j^2 \sigma_I^2)$$

15. Use the following information to answer the questions.

	$E(R_p)$	σ_p	Beta
Mutual fund BAC	0.20	0.10	0.80
Mutual fund XYZ	0.30	0.18	1.50
XYZ Index	0.22	0.12	
Risk-free rate (R_f)	0.05		

i) Calculated the Treynor measure for each mutual fund and the market index.
ii) Calculate the Sharpe measure for each mutual fund and the market index.
iii) Calculate Jensen's alpha for each mutual fund ABC and XYZ.
iv) Determine how the mutual funds performed according to Jensen's alpha.
v) Using the Treynor measure, determine how the funds perform relative to the market.
vi) Using the Sharpe measure, determine how the funds perform relative to the market.
vii) Rank the funds and the market index using the Treynor measure. Rank using the Sharpe measure. Are they consistent in ranking? If so, what does that imply about the funds? If not, what does that imply about the fund?

Ans.:

i) $T_p = \dfrac{ER_p - R_f}{\beta_p}$

$T_{ABC} = \dfrac{20.0 - 5.0}{0.8} = 18.75$

$T_{XYZ} = \dfrac{30.0 - 5.0}{1.5} = 16.67$

$T_m = \dfrac{22.0 - 5.0}{1.0} = 17.00$

ii) $S_p = \dfrac{ER_p - R_f}{\sigma_p}$

$S_{ABC} = \dfrac{0.20 - 0.05}{0.10} = 1.50$

$$S_{XYZ} = \frac{0.30 - 0.05}{0.18} = 1.39$$

$$S_m = \frac{0.22 - 0.05}{0.12} = 1.83$$

iii) Jensen's α = Actual Mean Return – CAPM Return
Mutual fund ABC's α = 0.20 – [0.05 + 0.8(0.22 – 0.05)]
=0.20 – 0.186 = +0.014
Mutual fund XYZ's α = 0.30 - [0.05 + 1.5(0.22-0.05)]
= 0.30 – 0.305 = –0.005

iv) Jensen's α outperform the market if α is greater than zero and it underperform the market if α is less than zero. Mutual fund ABC outperform the market and Mutual fund XYZ underperform the market.

v) Using the Treynor's performance measure, Mutual fund ABC outperform the market because $T_{ABC} > T_m$ and Mutual fund XYZ outperform the market because $T_{XYZ} > T_m$.

vi) Using Sharpe's performance measure, Mutual fund ABC and Mutual fund XYZ underperforum relative to the market because σ_{ABC} and σ_{XYZ} are both less than σ_m.

vii) *Ranking by Treynor:*
i)   Mutual fund ABC
ii) Market
iii) Mutual fund XYZ
Ranking by Sharpe:
i)   Market
ii) Mutual fund ABC
iii) Mutual fund XYZ

Since Sharpe ranks Mutual fund ABC below the market portfolio, it implies that fund ABC must have diversifiable risk in its portfolio. Sharpe penalises funds with diversifiable risk while Treynor assumes it equals zero.

16. Suppose that seven portfolios experienced the following results during a ten-year period:

Portfolio	Average Annual Return %	Standard Deviation %	Correlation with the Market
A	15.6	27.0	.81
B	11.8	18.0	.55
C	8.3	15.2	.38
D	19.0	21.2	.75
E	-6.0	4.0	.45
F	23.5	19.3	.63
G	12.1	8.2	.98
Market	13.0	12.0	
T-bills	6.0		

(a) Rank these portfolios using (1) Sharpe's method, and (2) Treynor's method.
(b) Compare the rankings in part (a) and explain the reasons behind any differences noted.
(c) Did any portfolios outperfrom the market? Why or why not?

Ans.:

(a) 1.

Sharpe's Method

Portfolio	S	Rank
A	.356	4
B	.322	5
C	.151	6
D	.613	3
E	-3.000	7
F	.907	1
G	.744	2

2.

Treynor's Method

Beta	T	Rank
1.8225	5.267	5
.8250	7.030	4
.4813	4.778	6
1.3692	9.495	2
.1500	-80,000	1
1.01130	-17.275	1
.6697	9.109	3

(b) Differences occur for G and D (reversed) and A and B (reversed). The reasons for the differences are based in the standard deviations and correlations with the market. The lower correlation of a pair gives a higher Treynor ranking.

(c) Use $R_M - R_F = 13 - 6 = 7\%$, and then compare $7\beta_P$ to $R_P - R_F$
   A.   9.6 versus 12.7575, Market best.
   B.   5.8 versus 5.7750, B best.
   C.   2.3 versus 3.3690, Market best.
   D.   13.0 versus 9.5840, D best.
   E.   -12.0 versus 1.0500, Market best.
   F.   17.5 versus 7.0910, F best.
   G.   6.1 versus 4.6879, G best.

QUESTIONS

1. What is the essential difference between the Sharpe and Treynor Indexes of portfolio performance? Which do you think is preferable? Why?
2. Portfolios that buy new securities and sell old holdings frequently will outperform portfolios that are managed more passively. Do you agree with this statement?
3. Sharpe's index will rank the performance of a group of investments about the same way that would be ranked if mey were ranked purely in terms of their average holding period return; this is because the average holding return is given more weight than is risk in Sharpe's index. Is this statement true, false or uncertain? Explain.
4. How can the two funds have the same expected rate of return, and yet nearly always

have different realised rates of return?

5. In selecting a measure of performance, why do we want a measure that is insensitive to the risk of investment?

6. Why is the reward- to- variability ratio a more appropriate measure of performance than the expost alpha if the portfolio being assessed represents the entire wealth of the portfolio's owner?

7. How can two funds have the same expected rate of return, and yet nearly always have difference realised rates of return?

8. A Treynor Index adds what factor into its measure of management performance? If you are comparing a levered low-beta portfolio fund to a high-beta portfolio fund, what in general, do you think you will/find—that the low-beta fund or the high-beta fund has the greater Treynor Index?

9. You plot the performance of two portfolios in expected return-beta space in relation to your estimated security market line. You are delighted to find they line up perfectly equidistant above the line and proudly announce to your clientele that you have two well-managed funds and they can be placed in either, depending on their attitudes toward risk. At a later date you discover your estimate of the security market line had too greater slope because you used the wrong risk-free rate; that in fact, the true SML had a very mild incline. What does this do to your evaluations of your two managers?

10. What are the advantages and disadvantages of using portfolio change measure (PCM) to evaluate performance?

11. In selecting a measure of performance, why do we want a measure that is insensitive to the risk of the investment?

12. Discuss the performance are as we want with changing portfolio composition. Explain the performance attribution procedures.

13. Write short notes on:
   (i)   Style Analysis
   (ii)   Morning Stars Risk Adjusted Rate (RAR)
   (iii) M^2 Performance Measure

14. Critically examine M^2 performance measure

15. Explain the performance evaluation when option are used.

PROBLEMS

1. Consider the following performance information on three portfolios:

	Treynor (T_p)	Sharpe (S_p)	Jensen J_p
Portfolio A	-4.0	-5	-5.0
Portfolio B	8.0	1.2	3.0
Portfolio C	4.0	.3	0
XYZ Index	5.0	.6	0

   (a) Rank each of the portfolios using each of the performance measures. Are the rankings consistent for the three techniques?
   (b) Compare each portfolio's performance to the market's performance. Are the comparisons consistent for the three techniques?

2. XYZ Company manages four mutual funds. The funds are: Balanced, Investment Growth, Fixed Income, and Variable Growth. The data below includes annual total return for each fund followed by key statistical measures. The average return on risk-free securities during the measurement period is 8 per cent

(a) Rank the performance of these portfolios using the Sharpe and Treynor Techniques.
(b) Consider the Jensen method of ranking portfolios relative to the market. What is the overall performance of each fund relative to the market?

(c) Which fund had the most unsystematic risk during the evaluation period? Explain.

	Balance	Growth	Fixed Income	Variable Growth	XYZ Index
1995	.166	.235	-.001	-.240	-.076
1994	-0.72	-.139	.056.	-.170	.206
1993	.096	.142	.030	.134	.187
1992	.118	.123	-.014	.113	.142
1991	.032	.083	.032	.153	-.156
1990	-.093	-.117	.045	-.101	.190
1989	.100	.201	.066	.255	.077
1988	.028	.032	.054	.035	-.116
1987	-.085	-.117	.071	.141	.224
Return	.0282	.0403	.0373	0798	.0654
Variance	.009	.020	.001	.021	.023
Beta	.6207	.9127	.1379	.6991	
Rho	.65	.94	.96	.82	

3. Suppose you are asked to analyse two portfolios having the following characteristics:

	Observed r	Betop	Residual variance
Portfolio A	.15	25	.04
Portfolio B	.10	1.5	.00

The risk-free rate is 0.08 and the return on the market portfolio is 15 with the standard deviation of .06. Compute the Jensen, the Treynor and the Sharpe Indexes for portfolios A and B. What would be the Sharpe index for the market portfolio?

4. Here are data on Five mutual funds:

Fund	Return	Standard Deviation	Beta
ABC	16	8	1.50
WER	12	6	0.90
QWA	14	5	1.40
RDS	18	10	0.75
YTR	15	7	1.25

What is the reward- to -variability ratio and the ranking if the risk-free rate is 7 percent?

5. The performance of the Galad Fund, an equity mutual fund, compared with the WWW Index over a ten- year period, is as follows:

	Galad Fund	WWW Index
Average quarterly excess return	0.6%	05%
Standard deviation of quarterly excess return	9.9%	6.6%
Beta	1.10	1.0

A.M. Kar is considering investing in either the Galad Fund or in another mutual fund whose objective is to track the performance of the WWW Index. Which fund would you recommend that Kar select assuming that your decision is based solely on past performance? Justify your answer using various measures of risk- adjusted performance.

6. Consider the following data for a particular sample period:

	Portfolio EWD	Market M
Average return	35	28
Beta	1.2	1.0
Standard Deviation	42	30
Nonsystematic risk	.18	0
Risk-free rate	0.6	

Calculate the following performance measures for portfolio EWD and the market: Sharpe, Jensen (alpha), Treynor, appraisal ratio. By which measures did portfolio EWD out perform the market?

7. Suppose that six portfolios experienced the following results during of 7-year period:

Portfolio	Average Annual Return	Standard Deviation	Correlation with market
A	18.6	27.0	.81
B	14.8	18.0	£5
C	15.1	8.0	.98
D	22.0	21.2	.75
E	-9.0	4.0	.45
F	26.5	19.3	.63
Market Risk	13.0	12.0	
Risk Free Rate	9.0		

(a) Rank these portfolios using (i) Sharpe's method, and (ii) Treynor's method.
(b) Compare the ranking in part (a) and explain the reasons behind the differences,

8. Consider the following mutual fund history:

Share Price

Date	Fund ABC	Fund XYZ
January	₹ 12.45	₹ 11.58
February	13.70	12.45
March	11.50	10.60
April	12.60	11.95
May	14.35	12.75
June	11.75	11.40

(a) Calculate the variance of return for each of the mutual funds.
(b) If you had employed rupee cost averaging programme by making monthly investments of ₹ 2500, in which fund would you have the most money at the end of the year?

9. Refer to problem-8, calculate Jensen's performance index for the two mutual funds. Do the ranking of the two mutual funds by Jensen's performance index the same as the ranking of the two mutual funds by Treynor's performance index?

10. Suppose an investor puts ₹ 10,000 per month into both funds ABC and XYZ in problem-8. Calculate the variance of the two-security portfolio over this period.

11. The following table gives the rate of return on Ever Growth Fund between 1987 and 19%. The riskless interest rate is 7.5%. Calculate Sharpe's performance measure for the mutual fund.

Year	Rate of Return (%)
1987	-14.9
1988	-23.7
1989	-325
1990	15.8
1991	29.6
1992	33.7
1993	20.5
1994	16.6
1995	12.4
1996	18.7
1997	21.9

12. The following table lists annual rates of return on two mutual funds and on the market portfolio. Calculate Treynor's performance index for the mutual funds. The riskless interest rate is 8%. Do the funds outperform the market portfolio?

Year	ABC Fund	Rate of Return (%) XYZ Fund	Market Portfolio
1987	8.6	15.8	18.7
1988	-18.0	-12.0	-15.6
1989	-25.6	-15.8	-18.7
1990	15.8	18.6	215
1991	22.9	35.6	32.8
1992	28.8	405	45.6
1993	20.6	24.6	30.8
1994	21.4	185	25.6
1995	205	15.8	21.7
1996	232	16.7	245
1997	243	17.8	23.7

13. Hypothetical rates of return on two mutual funds and on the market portfolio are as follows (in %):

Year	ABC Fund	FundXYZ	Market Portfolio
1993	20	-20	10
1994	16	18	8
1995	40	60	20
1996	30	36	18
1997	30	40	30

(a) On the assumption that the risk-free rate is 8%, rank the two funds by Jensen and Treynor performance indexes.

(b) Now assume that the risk-free rate falls between the bonds 4% <T> 20% but the precise figure is not known. Rank the two funds by their Treynor's performance index.

14. The following parameters are available for five mutual funds

Fund	A	B	C	D	E
Expected Return (%)	15	18	17	16	20
Beta	05	0.8	0.7	0.6	1.0

(a) Calculate Treynor's performance index and rank the funds on the assumption that risk-free rate is 8% and alternatively that $R_f = 5\%$.

(b) What should be the risk-free rate such that funds A and B will have the same Treynor's performance index?

15. Hypothetical rates of return on two mutual funds and on the market portfolio are as follows (in %):

Year	Mutual Fund ABC	Mutual Fund XYZ	Market Portfolio
2006	-10	+ 15	+ 8
2007	+ 10	-10	-5
2008	+ 20	-10	0
2009	+ 30	+ 20	+ 20
2010	-10	+ 30	+ 20

The risk-free interest rate is 7%.

(a) Which mutual fund shows a higher performance, given that investors hold only one fund in their portfolio?

(b) Which mutual fund shows a higher performance, given that investors further diversify the mutual fund shares with other assets. Compare your results in (a) and (b) above.

16. Ashok Verma is a professional financial planner. His business involves advising clients on comprehensive financial programmees including budgeting, tax matters, and investments. Frequently he advises clients on investment vehicles simply by recommending consideration of mutual funds. These are often appropriate for someone who wants to achieve professional management and diversification at a relatively low cost.

The Galaxy Fund has recently been brought to his attention by the fund's sponsors, who have attempted to sell the merits of the funds to financial advisers such as Verma. In order to carry out a responsible examination, Verma has gathered information on Galaxy as well as several other funds he knows well from past experience.

Exhibit 1 contains comparative annual rates of return on the Galaxy Fund, the XYZ Stock Index, and Treasury bills for 1996-2010. In Exhibit 2 we present data on five other investment companies for the same period.

EXHIBIT 1

Annual Rates of Return Galaxy Fund, XYZ Stock Index, Treasury Bills 1986-2000

Year	Galaxy	XYZ Stock Exchange	Treasury Bills
1996	17.1	10.8	5.4
1997	−14.6	−8.5	6.7
1998	1.7	3.5	6.5
1999	8.0	14.1	4.3
2000	11.5	18.7	4.1
2001	−5.8	−14.5	7.0

2002	−15.6	−26.0	7.9
2003	38.5	36.9	5.8
2004	33.2	23.6	5.0
2005	−7.0	−7.2	5.3
2006	2.9	7.4	6.2
2007	27.4	18.2	10.0
2008	23.0	31.5	11.4
2009	−0.6	−4.9	14.1
2010	21.4	20.4	10.7

EXHIBIT 2

Performance Data for Five Investment Companies, 1996-2010

	Return	Standard Deviation of Return	Beta	R^2
Classic Fund	1.95	20.03	.983	.819
Golden Fund	11.57	18.33	.971	.881
Novex Fund	8.41	22.92	1.169	.816
KDR Fund	9.05	24.04	1.226	.816
Super Top Fund	7.86	15.46	.666	.582

(i) Calculate the necessary ingredients for the Galaxy Fund that are needed for evaluating its performance, using the Sharpe, Treynor, and Jensen Performance Evaluation techniques.

(ii) Rank Parallax along with the other five funds in Exhibit 2 according to the Sharpe, Treynor, and Jensen techniques. How do you reconcile any conflicts in ranking.

REFERENCES

1. Andrews, John R. "The Case for Investing in Growth." *Financial Analysts Journal*, November-December 1970, p. 55.

2. Ankrim. Ernest: "Risk-Adjusted Performance Attribution," *Financial Analysts Journal*, March-April 1992. pp. 75-82.

3. Blume, Marshall, "On the Assessment of Risk," *Journal of Finance*, 26 (March 1971), 1-10.

4. Bookstaber, Richard, and Roger Clarke: "Problems in Evaluating the Performance of Portfolios with Options," *Financial Analysts Journal*, January-February 1985.

5. Bower, Richard, and Donald Wippern, "Risk-Return Measurement in Portfolio Selection and Performance Appraisal Models: Progress Report," *Journal of Financial and Quantitative Analysis* 4, no. 4 (December 1969): 417-447.

6. Brealey, Richard A. "How to Combine Active Management with Index Funds." *Journal of Portfolio Management* 12, no. 2 (Winter 1986).

7. Brinson, Gary P., L. Randolph Hood, and Gilbert L. Beebower. "Determinants of Portfolio Performance." *Financial Analysts Journal*, July/August 1986, 39-44.

8. Chang, E.C., and W.G. Lewellen. "Market Timing and Mutual Fund Performance," *Journal of Business*, 1984, 57-72.

9. Chang, Eric C., and Wilbur G. Lewellen. "Market Timing and Mutual Fund Investment Performance." *Journal of Business* 57, no. 1, part 1 (January 1984).

10. Chen, N., T E. Copeland, and D. Mayers. "A Comparison of Single and Multifactor

Portfolio Perform-ance Methodologies." *Journal of Financial and Quantitative Analysis* 22, no. 4 (December 1987).

11. Chen. Andrew. Frank Jen. and Stanley Zionts, "The Optimal Portfolio Revision Policy." *Journal of 'Business* 44. no. I (January 1971): 51 61.

12. Cornell, Bradford, and Kevin Green. "The Investment Performance of Low-Grade Bond Funds." *Jour-nal of Finance* 46, no. 1 (March 1991).

13. Cranshaw, T. E., "The Evaluation of Investment Performance," *The Journal of Business.* October 1977, pp. 462-485.

14. Dietz, Peter O., and Jeannette R. Kirschman. "Evaluating Portfolio Performance." In *Managing Invest-ment Portfolios,* 2d ed., edited by John L. Maginn and Donald L. Turtle. Boston: Warren Gorham and Lament, 1990.

15. Ellis, Charles D. "Performance Investing." *Financial Analysts Journal,* September-October 1968, p. 117.

16. Evnine, Jeremy, and Andrew Rudd. "Option Portfolio Risk Analysis." *Journal of Portfolio Management,* Winter 1984, 23-27.

17. Frankfurter, George, "The Effect of 'Market Indexes' on the Ex-post Performance of the Sharpe Portfolio Selection Model," *Journal of Finance* 31 (June 1976): 949-955.

18. Frankfurter, George, Herbert Phillips, and John Seagle, "Performance of the Sharpe Portfolio Selection Model: A Comparison," *Journal of Financial and Quantitative Analysis* 11. no. 2 (June 1976): 195-204.

19. Friend, Irwin, and Marshall Blume, "Measurement of Portfolio Performance Under Uncertainty," *American Economic Review* 60, no. 4 (September 1970): 561 -576.

20. Grinblatt, Mark, and Sheridan Titman: "Mutual Fund Performance: An Analysis of Quarterly Portfolio Holdings," *Journal of Business.* July 1989. pp. 393-416.

21. ——and ——: "Performance Measurement without Benchmarks: An Examination of Mutual Fund Returns." *Journal of Business,* January 1993. pp. 47-68.

22. Haugen, B., and N. Baker: "The Inefficiency of the Value-Weighted Index," *Journal of Fortfolio Management,* 1989, pp. 42-55.

23. Higgs, Peter, and Stephen Goode: "Target Active Returns and Attribution Analysis," *Financial Ana-lysts Journal,* May-June 1993, pp. 77-80.

24. Ibbotson, R-L. Siegel, and K. Love: "World Wealth: Market Values and Returns," *Journal of Portfolio Management,* Fall 1985, pp. 4-23.

25. Ibbotson, Roger, and Laurence Siegel: "The World Market Wealth Portfolio," *Journal of Portfolio Management,* Winter 1983, pp. 5-17.

26. Jensen, Michael C: "The Performance of Mutual Funds in the Period 1945-1964," *Journal of Fi-nance,* May 1968, pp. 389-416.

27. Korschat, Benjamin. "Measuring Research Analysts Performance." *Financial Analysts Journal,* July-August 1978.

28. Lehman, Bruce, and David Modest: "Mutual Fund Performance Evaluation: A Comparison of Bench-marks and Benchmark Comparisons," *Journal of Finance,* June 1987, pp. 233-265.

29. Rennie, Edward, and Thomas Cowhey: "The Successful Use of Benchmark Portfolios: A Case Study," *Financial Analysts Journal,* September-October 1990, pp. 18-26.

30. Schneider, Theodore H. "Measuring Performance." *Financial Analysts Journal,* May-June 1969, p. 105.

31. Sharpe, W.F.: "Mutual Fund Performance," *Journal of Business,* January 1966, pp. 119-138.

32. Spigelman, Joseph H. "What Basis for Superior Performance?" *Financial Analysts Journal,* May-June 1974, p. 32.

33. Surz, Ronald: "Portfolio Opportunity Distributions: An Innovation in Performance Evaluation," *Jour-nal of Investing,* Summer 1994, pp. 36-41.

1002

INVESTMENT MANAGEMENT

34. Tierney, David, and Kenneth Winston: "Defining and Using Dynamic Completeness Funds to Enhance Total Fund Efficiency," *Financial Analysts Journal*, July-August 1990, pp. 49-54.

35. Treynor, J.L. "How to Rate Management of Investment Funds." *Harvard Business Review*, January-February 1965, pp. 63-75.

36. ———. "Long-Term Investing." *Financial Analysts Journal*, May-June 1976, p. 56.

37. Vertin, James R. "The Design and Control of Large Portfolios." The Financial Analysts Federation, Annual Conference, May 1978.

38. Williams, Arthur: *Managing Your Investment Manager*, Dow Jones-Irwin, New York, 1990.

39. Williamson, Peter J. "Measuring Mutual Fund Performance." *Financial Analysts Journal*, November-December 1972, p. 78.

40. ———————————: "Performance Measurement," in Edward Altman (ed.): *The Financial Handbook*, Wiley, New York, 1980.

Part V

DERIVATIVES: RISK MANAGEMENT

33

Financial Derivatives Market: A Global Perspective

INTRODUCTION

The past decade has witnessed an explosive growth in the use of financial derivatives by a wide range of corporate and financial institutions. This growth has run in parallel with the increasing direct reliance of companies on the capital markets as the major source of long-term funding. In this respect, derivatives have a vital role to play in enhancing shareholder value by ensuring access to the cheapest source of funds. Active use of derivative instruments allows the overall business risk profile to be modified, thereby providing the potential to improve earnings quality by offsetting undesired risks. Financial institutions use derivatives primarily as a source of revenue, which is, to say the least, a contentious point. However, derivatives can be also seen as powerful risk-management tools. From the risk-management perspective, the same derivatives allow financial institutions and other participants to identify, isolate, and manage separately the market risks of financial instruments and commodities. Used prudently, they offer managers efficient and effective access to techniques for reducing particular risks through hedging, as well as reducing financing costs and increasing yields on assets. Derivatives may be used in market making, position taking, or risk arbitrage, all of which are sources of potential revenue for a financial institution. For example, in theory a profitable market making operation requires the bank to maintain a balanced portfolio while entering into transactions with customers and other market makers. One of the techniques for the risk manager to consider would be to hedge the entire portfolio. Futures and options of the underlying tradeable assets enable the market maker to manage or neutralise market risks to the whole portfolio while generating earnings by providing bid/offer spreads to the market. Similar principles apply for position taking and risk arbitrage.

Despite the clear benefits that the use of derivatives can offer, too often the public—and shareholder—perception of these instruments has been coloured by the intense media coverage of financial disasters where the use of derivatives has been blamed. The impression is usually given that these losses arose from extremely complex and difficult to understand financial strategies. The reality is quite different. When the facts behind the well-reported disasters are analysed almost invariably it is found that the true source of losses was a basic organisational weakness or a failure to observe some simple business controls.

The corollary to this observation is that derivatives can indeed be used safely and successfully provided that a sensible control and management strategy is established and executed. This requires both a deep understanding of how the business is actually conducted (the traditional view of the business process) and how critical areas within the business process can be measured in terms of risk (the new statistical view) and, in turn, implementing various methods for controlling the risks before and after they should happen (the holistic view):

MANAGING DERIVATIVE RISK

Whilst derivative instruments offer countless methods for gaining leveraged exposure to hundreds of markets, it is for this very reason that an independent and formal risk-management and control structure needs to be established. In traditional risk-management terms, *"Even if you have the most sophisticated cash register in the world, who's going to watch the person at the till?"* In order to construct this risk-management and control system, the major types of risk that need to be considered in such a system as discussed below.

TYPES OF DERIVATIVES RISK

The art and science of risk analysis is fundamentally about first identifying potential failures (categorising events into "risk types"), then estimating the frequency of occurrence of these failures, and, finally, determining the magnitude of the consequences ("its value"). The discipline of risk-management takes risk analysis a step further by positively acting on this new found knowledge and thereby, hopefully, reducing the probability of failure. The strategy is that by reducing the probability of failure, the probability of success should increase. In the derivatives business where every instrument is considered "risky," personnel should have a clear grasp of the elementary types of risk which pervade each transaction.

There are many different types of risk which can be considered relevant to any particular derivatives transaction. The following is a list which should be considered by any derivatives risk-management service.

i) *Operational risk:* the risk of loss arising due to procedure errors, omissions or failure of internal control systems.

ii) *Market risk:* the risk of loss arising from adverse market rate movements, e.g. foreign exchange (transaction, translation, or economic), interest rates, commodity and equity prices.

iii) *Interest rate risk:* the change in capital values of an investment resulting from changes in prevailing interest rate levels.

iv) *Systemic risk:* an inherent risk within the inter-bank market, the risk is of a bank finding itself unable to meet its due obligations causing other banks to fail to meet theirs.

v) *Credit risk:* the risk of losses arising from defaults by the counterparty.

vi) *Cashflow risk:* the risk of the institution failing to have sufficient cash resources to meet its obligations, e.g. realised losses being offset by unrealised gains.

vii) *Liquidity risk:* the risk of losses arising from a derivatives market becoming illiquid, or where difficulty or cost issues arise when closing the position.

viii) *Basis risk:* losses arising from the divergence between two prices or rates.

ix) *Aggregation risk (or interconnection risk):* this is the quantification of the problem that some derivatives transactions involve several markets and instruments.

x) *Legal risk: issues* resulting in derivatives contracts becoming unenforceable either by jurisdictional law or by the lack of capacity of the institution.

xi) *Business risk (or specific risk):* the risk, that one transaction or a small group of transactions, causing losses, exposes the firm to risk of failure. This risk can be reduced to the point of insignificance. Diversification is the basic protection strategy. As the number of positions held increases, business risk falls very rapidly. It is very important for institutions to understand that expected rate of return does not fall as a result of diversification. Only the variation around the expected rate of return falls. And, variation is risk!

xii) *Political risk:* this includes tax, trade, regulation, education and social policies. A government's attitude towards capital and business sets the stage for either success or failure of its economy.

xiii) *Audit risk:* the risk of losses arising from failure of the audit function be if internal or external. We hypothesize as a general rule of thumb:

Audit Risk = Inherent risk * Control risk * Non-Sampling detection risk * Sampling detection risk

It is essential that the financial risk review be independent. Equally, the monitoring function should be independent of any front office function to ensure that no conflict of interest or valuation manipulation occurs.

Understanding what types of risks apply where and when is the first task of the risk-management and control function. For example, in an exchange-traded futures contract, the credit and liquidity risk are reduced by the formal exchange mechanism which matches buyers and sellers of futures contracts, and simultaneously guarantees delivery and payment on the contract. However, if there is a weak operational process, comprising inefficient settlement systems, poorly trained and motivated staff, with weak communication lines to the front end of the business, it does not matter what type of derivative is being processed, a high level of operational risk will haunt any transaction. A risk-management policy framework be constructed which takes into account common elements and differences across financial risk-taking activities. This framework must be above all flexible and adaptable to new risks which are discovered or created.

The key requirement, therefore, for any risk-management system is having the infrastructure in place to facilitate the proper identification of not just the size of exposure that exists but also the type of exposure. This reinforces the need for a totally accountable and optimal risk-control system.

AN INTEGRATED APPROACH TO MERGE DERIVATIVE RISKS

The risk issues will be much better served and managed if the elements of risk inherent to the derivatives market are controlled from a centralised source rather than a series of dislocated functions. A close analysis of each risk type also reinforces this by highlighting the existing and potential commonality of risk-control approaches that exist between each area. The following discussion therefore focuses on: i) systemic risk; ii) market risk; iii) credit risk; iv) liquidity risk; v) cashflow management risk; vi) legal risk; and, vii) operational risk.

SYSTEMIC RISK

Systemic risk is the risk that a market disruption causes widespread difficulties to other participants in that market segment or in the financial system as a whole. In other words, it is the risk that a local or organisational problem turns into a global one through a "domino effect." A systemic crisis could start anywhere: from a cascading of asset prices or the demise of a major financial institution. The causal factors are unpredictable and the effects may vary depending on the number and size of firms involved. It would also depend on the general economic environment. Characteristic of a systemic crisis is that market participants start holding back payments, causing gridlock. This can lead to a disruption of payment and settlement systems. As the crisis spreads more broadly it can cause a more general disruption of financial or credit markets.

MARKET RISK

Market risk exposes a company to uncertainty due to movements in factors such as foreign exchange rates, commodity prices, equity prices, and volatilities related to options positions. Evolving from using single-factor models to measure market risk to multiple-factor models such as the Arbitrage Pricing Model and statistical approaches based on parameters involving correlations and standard deviations, market risk quantification is at the core of all activities relating to market risk.

Both regulators and practitioners consider the following activities to be prerequisites for effective market risk management.

   i) *Marking to market:* Measuring the fair value of the organisation's portfolio should be done at least on an intra-day basis with an evolution towards real-time mark to market data.

   ii) *Stress testing/simulation:* Analysis should be performed which tests the valuation effect of the derivatives portfolio under stressful market conditions. Market shifts beyond the parameters of conventional probability-based risk models have occurred in recent years

   iii) *Management reporting:* There is a definite split between the tactical information requirements of the trading room and the strategic level information required by senior management. For example, management may wish to allocate capital in a manner which diversifies the total portfolio but the trader may wish to focus on concentrating capital on particular plays.

   iv) *Risk limit structures:* Risk limit structures using effective risk measurements must be formally introduced and rigorously applied. They must be balanced, however, against business requirements and appetite for risk among senior management and shareholders.

   v) *Risk capital and aggregation:* Establishing a common risk and performance measurement framework across product and functional groups is increasingly recognised as being essential for the comprehensive management of risk.

One of the prominent features of market risk management is how the techniques used there can be transferred to other risk types, thereby facilitating the integration of risk control at an organisational level. Thus, the concept of risk capital is not concerned solely with market risk considerations but can be designed to encompass credit, liquidity, and operational risk elements as well.

CREDIT RISK

It is important to remember that risk-control areas need to manage risk not only on a product basis but also on a counterparty basis. Like other forms of risk inherent in a derivatives portfolio the amount of credit risk that exists in a portfolio depends largely on the size and nature of the products. An exchange-traded futures contract, for example, is likely to have significantly less counterparty exposure than an interest rate swap.

It is also important to differentiate between counterparty risk and credit risk *per se*. A number of factors need to be examined in order to determine the quality of the counterparty's ability to make good its financial obligations. This is part of a bank's normal operations. However, the credit risk *per se* of a portfolio may be traded in the form of credit derivatives. In this case, the main concern would be not so much about the counterparty risk but about issues of liquidity and the widening or thinning of spreads between the buying and selling price of the instruments.

For risk-control purposes there are a variety of methods that an organisation can use to control credit risk, but most techniques can be categorised as either counterparty enhancement tools or part of an ongoing process of credit analysis. Credit enhancement techniques include: *Collateral agreements:* provision for security in case of default; *Netting agreements:* provision setting off total amounts of reciprocal obligations; *Credit guarantees:* third party usually with superior credit rating guarantees principal balance, *Credit triggers:* where outstanding contracts can be terminated if the counterparty's credit rating goes below a certain predetermined level; and, the *Mutual termination options:* which permit either counterparty to terminate unconditionally on a specified date before maturity.

Credit analysis comprises the techniques that are used to measure the ongoing credit risk that the institution is taking, as implied by its portfolio customer mix. It is within the area of credit analysis that there lie significant opportunities for integration with other risk categories, most notably market risk. Conventional credit risk-management procedures include: establishing credit limits; maintaining a database with counterparty ratings information; seeking to avoid excessive concentration among counterparty types; and, the maintaining a list of preferable counterparties.

The most significant aspect of new approaches to credit risk analysis is how they are converging with market risk methodologies. Full-scale integration of market and credit risk is far from a common practice and this is due to tradition as opposed to any practical reason against integration. The advantages of integrating credit risk and market risk analysis range from cost and efficiency issues to improved capital adequacy provision.

A combined area would:

1. ensure a consistent approach between credit and market risk by centralising responsibility for measurement and control policy across the organisation;
2. achieve scale efficiencies by pulling together what are normally two independent and disparate areas;
3. improve risk assessment by aggregating market and credit risk at the product rather than group level.

In derivatives markets the size of the exposure in the event of a counterparty default depends on how the value of the contract has moved, which in turn depends on how the underlying market rates have moved since the trade was executed. However, whilst there is a clear transactional based relationship between credit risk and market risk the two risk elements are not additive. For example, when a derivatives position increases in value there is an increase in credit risk but normally a corresponding reduction in market risk. The situation would be reversed if the position reduced in value.

There are currently a host of quantitative frameworks for credit risk analysis that resemble market risk approaches. Over time, these techniques and their progeny should replace the relatively unsophisticated "gut feet" techniques of traditional credit analysis. These techniques include: using risk adjusted return calculations (similar to value at risk) to measure individual and portfolio level default risk based on expected exposure; applying options theory to credit default analysis; using efficient portfolio theory based on the incremental impact of a deal on the overall level of risk in a portfolio; and, the aggregating risks into a single measurement by the statistical correlation between individual credit risks.

For credit risk control, an approach is required which measures the expected risk-adjusted return on the portfolio before and after the addition of a new deal. In the context of market price risk the common risk denominator is the volatility of price movements, whereas for credit risk the appropriate common denominator is the standard deviation of the distribution of possible credit losses. However, techniques based upon probability distributions of credit default and market price movement can use the same standing data for both market and credit risk.

In short, as the importance of sound credit risk analysis for derivatives has grown, so has the scope for integrating credit and market risk control techniques using a common data platform. A fully integrated market risk and credit risk system is now both feasible and desirable.

LIQUIDITY RISK

Liquidity risk relates to the fluctuation of derivatives instruments according to a number of factors: the size and maturity of the market; the number of participants in the market; market turnover rates; level of market information; split between over-the-counter (OTC) and exchange-traded.

As shown in Table-1, the liquidity of the market governs many of the risk-control approaches relating to the other types of risk. It is therefore difficult to examine liquidity risk in isolation from the other risk types.

TABLE-1

The Risk Continuum

Market conditions	Highly illiquid	Illiquid	Liquid but variable	Liquid
Basis for valuation	Reserve adjusted Book value Supplemented by mark to model	Mark to market Supplemented by mark to market	Mark to market Checked with mark to model Benchmark data	Mark to market
Basis for market, credit and liquidity risk calculations	Loss modelling Scenario analysis based on credit defaults and market shocks	Loss modelling Value at Risk adjusted liquidity	Value at Risk Supplemented by stress testing	Value at Risk Supplemented by stress testing
Ex-ante risk control mechanisms Credit	Pricing and underwriting approval by senior management	Limit approval	Limits Credit enhancements	Limits Credit enhancements
Operational	Documentation of transaction Appraisal of settlement systems for exposure monitoring	Documentation of transaction Appraisal of settlement systems for exposure monitoring	Efficiency measures based on exception reporting	Efficiency measures based on exception reporting
Legal	Consider Ultra Vires* Suitability**	Consider Ultra Vires Suitability	Conform to industry standards)	Conform to Industry standards
Ex-post mechanisms	Risk detection models Testing of mark to model parameters	Risk detection models Testing of mark to model parameters	P&L level and volatility	P&L level and volatility

* *Ultra vires* (Latin for "beyond the power") is the legal doctrine that the contract in question was entered into without the authority of the corporate entity.

** The question of "suitability" is hotly debated. Derivative marketers should be legally responsible for determining the suitability of customers for derivatives transactions, including the commercial question of whether the product was appropriate for the risk in question. Whatever the legal responsibilities are, it would seem prudent and good business sense that the bank itself ask whether the products sold are suitable to the customers' purposes.

Two elements of liquidity risk that arise come from the relative ability of an organisation to transfer its assets into cash and the mismatch between a bank's cash inflows and outflows arising out of derivatives activity. Both these areas can be managed in tandem with credit and market risk requirements and, for most aspects of liquidity risk, using the techniques similar to both areas. One of the major issues related to liquidity is the ability of the bank to transfer the instrument into cash.

Transfer Ability

The ability to transfer derivatives into cash at fair value depends largely on the existence of a secondary market. Clearly, the mix in the derivatives portfolio between OTC and exchange-traded instruments is crucial. OTC instruments such as interest rate swaps do have a secondary market which is growing but as yet is not wholly liquid.

Methods that are used in market risk analysis can also be used to determine the potential cost incurred from closing down a position. Using a VaR methodology, for example, the calculation of liquidity risk would be based on three factors:

1. the transaction costs incurred in liquidation, determined largely by the bid-ask spread and the mean average size of trade for a particular instrument;
2. the cost of exposure of the position while it is being maintained;
3. the cost of hedging the exposure, where possible.

The trade-off between the three components would determine the rate of liquidation that minimises the sum of the overall costs and also pinpoints the liquidity adjusted value at risk of the derivatives portfolio at any one point in time.

In the case of more exotic instruments the effect of liquidity risk on a conventional value at risk calculation can be significant. The cost of close-out of exotic or non-standard derivatives positions must also factor in the cost of liquidity-as it would for emerging market debt instruments. This could significantly magnify the value of risk on these positions. The effect of liquidity on currency positions increased conventional VaR by hundreds of per cent during well-known crises.

Liquidity risk, in the context of *transfer ability*, therefore, must be accounted for as an integral part of the market risk analysis process especially when illiquid transactions form part of the derivatives portfolio.

CASHFLOW MANAGEMENT RISK

Large derivatives portfolios can be subject to sudden cash demands from their ongoing derivatives positions making liquidity management for off-balance sheet products crucial. The method by which banks monitor their derivatives cashflow risk is similar to that used for other banking products, where cash requirements arising from potential price and volatility changes at each point are calculated and then compared to funding availability. Sudden liquidity changes can arise out of either credit risk, through the threat of a counterparty default, or by market risk factors such as a run on a currency. Therefore, the risk manager can use information relating to credit risk analysis and market risk analysis to adjust future cashflow requirements.

LEGAL RISK

The external risk management (ERM) risk area takes into account information supplied by the global database and the legal and compliance teams. It is important to note that senior management will need to be informed of their legal duties and therefore there is a direct communication link from the legal and compliance teams to senior management. The legal and compliance teams will also supply any new legislation and changes to old legislation ("new data") to the global database. The ERM risk area may also wish to interrogate the legal and compliance teams to check whether they have understood the new data from the global data-base and to ensure that their advice to senior management is legally suitable and appropriate.

OPERATIONAL RISK

Operational risk is the most difficult risk area to define and integrate into an enterprise-wide risk-management system. The main reason for this is that operational risk is everywhere within an organisation.

Table-2 shows various types of error and failure that may occur within their respective functions.

TABLE 2
Errors and Failures Causing Risk

Risk category	Functional responsibilities	Examples
PEOPLE	Business line	Human error
	Human resources	Internal fraud
	Security	Staff shortage
TECHNOLOGY	Business line technologies	Technology failure
	Central infrastructure	Outmoded systems
	Data center maintenance	Poor data integrity
REGULATORY	Compliance	Regulator disputes
	Finance and accounting	Misstating accounts
	Legal	

The potential exposures commonly associated with operations are diverse and may relate to: technology choices: batch versus real-time processing; intra-day settlement exposure: no quantification or intra-day or overnight risk; cross-border payment issues; reliance on manual controls; multilateral versus bilateral payment systems; and, timing of payment and delivery. Many of these issues go beyond the organisational level to focus on the effectiveness of settlements and payments organisations such as: bilateral netting and settlement services: FXNET, SWIFT, and VALUENET; multilateral netting and settlement services such as ECHO; and, private sector clearing and payments services such as Euroclear.

Operational risk is relevant to the entire "value chain" of an organisation and cannot be managed simply through a centralised risk-control process. Technology, people, and manual and automated controls throughout the organisation all have a part to play in creating a secure operational environment. However, such is the scale of the potential exposure created by these activities in today's financial system that an operational risk-management function is increasingly seen as an essential to the overall risk-management process.

The question is, then, how can operational concerns be integrated into the integrated risk framework but avoid duplicating the functions of the existing operational controls as well as those of external payments and clearing systems; plus the internal audit function, which is normally concerned with the operational control environment? A solution to this problem may be approached by breaking down aspects of operational risk into their constituent risk elements in an attempt to: qualify the costs involved in specific operational breakdowns; establish the common elements, if any, that are in existence when each breakdown occurs; and, develop a probability-based model for attributing capital to operational risk.

The prerequisites of this type of attributional operational risk system are similar to those utilised in an insurance organisation, namely: gathering information on operational events; seeking expert opinion to estimate loss amounts that are most difficult to quantify; and, sorting each loss type into a relevant category so that correlation analysis can be performed.

In the context of risk management, quantified risk exposures relating to operational events can then be integrated into the overall risk process through: (i) techniques for measuring credit risk and liquidity risk being utilised to calculate the probability of specific operational failures; (ii) responsibility for establishing settlement exposure calculations being given to credit control staff with the information required for this being generated through the centralised data depository or data warehouse; (iii) providing an early warning system for payments, settlements, and other operational risks and so facilitating actionable risk-management designed to mitigate the exposure.

Thus, the operational risk can be mitigated internally through proper controls and procedures and a detailed understanding of all the stages of the operational process. However, in order to be able to quantify the risk there also needs to be a framework for operational risk control. It is this last element that should be controlled and provided by an integrated risk area.

VALUE AT RISK (VaR) ANALYSIS: RISK AGGREGATION

The notion of risk capital is one of the most important developments in risk management in recent years and has become the standard of choice among regulators and sophisticated bankers alike. Essentially risk capital is encapsulated in a class of risk measures, often called value at risk techniques, which are designed to aggregate diverse product and currency positions into a common risk measure. The various risks may be aggregated into a single measure. Value at risk, or VaR, has become a standard in the derivatives industry assisting senior management in both financial institutions and industrial corporations and regulators to under stand the risk exposure of particular derivative instruments. It is important to realise the power and limitations of VaR as well as how the underlying principles of the method can be applied to other forms of risk analysis.

The tendency towards risk aggregation has largely been encapsulated in the increasing use and acceptance of value at risk concepts, which calculate "the expected loss from an adverse market movement within a specific probability over a particular period of time." From this formal definition comes a more intuitive definition of VaR "as the amount of economic or equity capital which must be held to support that particular level of risky business activity".

VALUE AT RISK (VAR): A BIRD'S-EYE VIEW

Value at risk is a probability-weighted aggregation of current results in gains and losses embedded in a trading portfolio, under various market scenarios. VaR typically assumes that no trading occurs during the pricing exercise. In other terms, at least on an instantaneous basis there is zero liquidity in the market.

The daily estimate of value at risk can take the form of a revenues-and-exposures graph as well as of a holding period over 10 days with no risk-reducing trades. The computation should be made at the 99 percent confidence level to be consistent with the 1998 Market Risk Amendment by the Basle Committee.

As seen in Figure-1 the calculation of value at risk assumes a normal distribution of exposures, which is evidently an approximation, whether we talk of individual instruments or of the contents of the whole trading book. A positive aftermath of this approximation is that we can use the concept underpinning the operating characteristics curve (lower part of Figure 1) to estimate the 99 per cent probability that the worst case will not exceed the value derived from computation. This 99 percent level of confidence corresponds to a *Type 1* error, on the OC curve, of 1 percent. This is known as α. In the long run, in 1 percent of cases the VaR estimate will not cover the worst case.

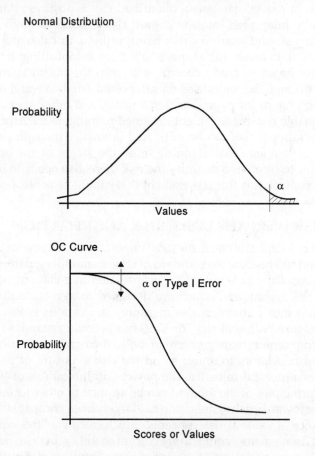

FIGURE 1 : VALUE AT RISK ASSUME A NORMAL DISTRIBUTION OF EXPOSURE, WHICH IS AN APPROXIMATION

In the computation of VaR there may be other errors too that are not statistical in nature, but depend on assumptions and on the correlations. Empirically derived correlations are used for aggregation within each of three basic risk classes: currency exchange, interest rates, and equities. Other classes, too, can be distinguished depending on the business of the bank. Across risk classes, cumulative exposure is computed assuming zero correlation among highly defined risk classes. This is, of course, another approximation reflecting the diversification that might or might not exist in business areas. Hence, depending on the institution and its trading habits, this hypothesis may be weak or outright false.

From a statistical viewpoint, VaR is a scalar *estimate* of an unknown parameter of the loss distribution. Sampling errors can affect the accuracy of point estimates so institutions using VaR must be careful with the hypotheses that they make and the way these hypotheses influence the outcome.

Confidence intervals for the VaR can be derived through a parametric or nonparametric approach taken in connection with a portfolio structure and its distributed returns. Some analysts prefer to compute VaR through interval estimates and choose the use of asymptotic confidence intervals, but the basic methods for VaR calculation are two:

i) Parametric (VaR/P) based on the assumption of a normal distribution of asset and liability prices.

ii) Nonparametric or simulation (VaR/S), which uses Monte Carlo[1] and can lead to stress analysis.

Practical applications of VaR include the measurement of and report on exposure, which is demanded by regulators, as well as the management of market risk. VaR extensions now target credit risk. Senior management can benefit from VaR if it has taken care to appropriately define capital at risk. This has two aspects: i) What's the level of capitalisation-essentially the entrepreneurial capital-that is required by the market? ii) What is the capital at risk-i.e.,the economic capital-*our*bank can afford to put on the block?

Because VaR provides a basis for experimentation, the visibility senior management is after will be achieved iteratively between these two poles of reference. Sophisticated experimental approaches, however, require handling nonlinear distributions for daily changes in market variables; using Monte Carlo simulation; and employing Taylor Series expansion to calculate VaR when distributions are non-normal.

Senior management finds these issues awfully technical. Yet, they are crucial in defining and measuring market risk in an accurate way. Just as important is that the board and senior management understand the role of *backtesting* for tuning the parameters of VaR calculations, as well as the importance of using *stress scenarios* for measurement of catastrophic market risk.

VaR itself is a generic term covering a number of methodologies that are used for a variety of purposes by organisations, all relating to risk management and risk-adjusted performance measurement. Value at risk has become a key component of the analysis of market risk, because it measures what is ultimately of interest from a risk manager's perspective: *the most that can be lost with a given degree of confidence.* However, it is crucial for a risk manager to recognise the inherent limitations in using VaR: something which does not always seem to be the case.

VaR should be seen as a *catalyst* for change towards a more structured risk-analysis approach rather than a "failsafe" measure of risk control. The primary value of VaR as a risk-control tool is that many of the theoretical elements that underpin it can be used to analyse not just market risk exposures but also credit, liquidity, and even operational risk exposure.

The three underlying methodologies commonly used for calculating VaR - historical, parametric, and simulation - each have relative strengths and weaknesses. To counter the inherent weaknesses of the approaches, variations of these standard methodologies have been adopted by different users and in some cases the basic models have been extended to include recognition of more complex characteristics of non-linear risk such as convexity and gamma risk.

Characteristics of VaR Models

The uses of VaR fall broadly into three categories: determination of capital adequacy; performance measurement; and, supporting risk takers and business managers.

Determination of Capital Adequacy

In the regulatory and the supervisory context, the notion that risk capital is the relevant measure for determining capital requirements has become increasingly adopted.

Performance Measurement and Risk Control

For the risk manager, VaR facilitates analyses across time and business areas thereby allowing conclusions to be drawn over the performance of one business over another. However, the risk manager does need to consider the relative strengths and weaknesses of the methodology being used.

VaR is not a Black Box

More than one approach to calculating value at risk should be pursued, using both Monte Carlo simulation techniques in conjunction with a parametric-based approach. The outputs from both systems should then be adjusted to account for the inherent weaknesses in each approach.

The organisational implications of each approach should be taken into account as the accuracy of any risk methodology is heavily dependent on the internal controls and procedures that are in place in each organisation. Central to this is an understanding by senior management of how to use the results generated by these models to enhance the market risk control within the organisation. One final note, as one global head of risk management aptly sums up the proper attitude towards all these various forms of risk measures: *I would prefer a C-rated model with weaknesses and have people with experience and intuition to run our risk management than an A-rated model with a C-rated team of people who don't understand the model and are therefore unable to question the numbers that the system churns out.*

Satisfying Regulatory and Managerial Requirements

The 1966 Market Risk Amendment outlines regulatory specifications for VaR. These are the 99 percent confidence interval a 10-day holding period; a historical observation period of at least one year; a minimum three-month frequency for the update of data sets; and the recognition of correlations across broad risk factors categories, interest rate, currency exchange, equities, and commodities. Another regulatory requirement is a scaling factor for VaR results.

For internal management accounting reasons the bank may also follow another list of "musts". Many institutions have started to internally differentiate between value at risk and capital at risk. Also, for internal management control purposes VaR has started to be endowed with delta/gamma hedging to calculate risk based on a one-day holding period, exponential moving average volatilities, and correlations within risk factors.

This enlarges the implementation horizon of value at risk, and the use of estimates of potential losses in the bank's portfolio for a predetermined probability and holding period. Attention must be paid to the methodology employed to capture all significant risks and meet or exceed industry standards in terms of accuracy and timeliness.

There are number of weaknesses connected to VaR. In real life risk and returns are not normally distributed-as it is assumed. When markets are calm the bell shaped distribution may be acceptable, but in nervous markets it leads to implementation flaws: *Firstly*, VaR models are particularly weak at the edges, because of extreme movements, *Secondly*, outliers occur much more frequently than suggested by the normal distribution.

Thirdly, VaR fails to account for fat fails. Yet, leptokyrtotic distributions very commonly appear with financial time series. The discarding of extreme or repetitive values weakens the benefits obtained from the model. *Fourthly,* VaR incorporates a significant probability of financial disaster-particularly if the 95 per cent level of confidence is used instead of the regulatory 99 percent. Neither the parametric VaR nor the simulation VaR say anything about extreme values: precisely what might happen in the "other" 1 percent, beyond the 99 percent confidence limit. It was found out that in the case of LTCM's near-bankruptcy this other 1 per cent showed a loss of $1.36 billion. Banks should be very careful with extreme events. *Finally,* One major weakness with the *method* (but not necessarily with the model) is the use of meager databases, which leads to meaningless if not outright misleading results.

Challenges with the Test of Hypothesis Used in the Model

Analysts with experience in modeling, and in the computation of credit risk and market risk, have evidence that mapping the market into the computer and doing a rigorous experimentation allows divesification. This brings up a number of other issues relating to management culture, skills requirements, the hypotheses being made, and technological leadership.

A basic but not always appreciated policy is that, in principle, the more diversified is the trading book, the lower the corresponding capital requirements will be. There are regulatory measures, however, that do not permit this flexibility; neither are the available eigenmodels able to serve reliably all sorts of diversification moves.

Beyond the pricing models and the risk models for derivatives, an institution also needs optimisation models that address the contents of the trading book for diversification reasons. Since the algorithms being used most often rest on the normal distribution and its confidence intervals, one of the concerns is the existence of correlations, outliers, and spike volatilities.

Usually spike patterns see to it that data are not normally distributed. Therefore the hypotheses are not substantiated by market facts. Furthermore, because the way to bet is that every distribution has outliers, one of the critical questions is how well model will cope with them. Is it really sensitive to extreme events? Will such events upset its behaviour?

As Dr.Paul Embrechts suggests, we want to have methods for estimating conditional probabilities that account for fat tails. An institution may incur a loss beyond VaR; but how far can it expect it to go? The study of extreme events can be done through extreme value theory. Because extreme events matter, in all likelihood this theory will become an important part of methodology.

The best way to judge models is by what they deliver. Sometime down the line the current linear models based on the normal distribution will become inaccurate. Then they will become unacceptable, if we have not been careful enough to test for outliers in a dual sense; as predictors and as deviators of model behaviour. A similar point can be made about correlations. Usually the algorithms we develop are based on a hypothesis of independent events. This rarely happens in real life, and if we have not been careful about the existence of correlations or their neutralisation, the model will give inadequate results.

The opposite is also true. Fairly frequently the assumption of th existence of correlation is made without the appropriate study and associated tests. It is, for instance, often assumed that the G-10 stock markets move in synergy and that they highly correlate because of globalisation. Yet, a recent study by the Bank of England documents that from 1988 onward the market behaviors of the London Stock Exchange and of the Tokyo Stock

Exchange don't positively correlate in any significant manner. Indeed, it intraday statistics are considered, then sometimes the correlation is negative. Such findings invalidate the hypotheses we sometimes make. They also impact model behaviour, and for this reason they should be kept in perspective. Other issues, too, influence the choice of value at-risk algorithms to be used.

RECENT DEVELOPMENTS IN GLOBAL FINANCIAL DERIVATIVE MARKETS

The past decade has witnessed an explosive growth in the use of financial derivatives by a wide range of corporate and financial institutions. The following factors which have generally been identified as the major driving force behind growth of financial derivatives are the (i) increased volatility in asset prices in financial markets; the increased integration of national financial markets with the international markets; the marked improvement in communication facilities and sharp decline in their costs; the development of more sophisticated risk management strategies; and the innovations in the derivatives markets, which optimally combine the risk and returns over a large number of financial assets, leading to higher returns, reduced risk as well as transaction costs as compared to individual financial assets. The growth in derivatives has run in parallel with the increasing direct reliance of companies on the capital markets as the major source of long-term funding. In this respect, derivatives have a vital role to play in enhancing shareholder value by ensuring access to the cheapest source of funds. Furthermore, active use of derivative instruments allows the overall business risk profile to be modified, thereby providing the potential to improve earnings quality by offsetting undesired risks.

It is estimated that the gross noted outstanding amount of the OTC derivative contracts had reached a peak level of US$ 684 trillion in June 2008; post-Lehman, contracted to US$ 548 trillion. The decline in trading activity reflects a combination of significantly reduced risk appetite expectations of stable low interest rates in major markets and lower hedge fund activity.

Major central banks lowered policy rates to historical lows and interbank money markets became more stable after havinq frozen in September and early October, 2008. Reflecting these developments, after reaching record highs during the crisis, interest rate derivatives turnover decreased to $345 trillion from $458 trillion in the previous quarter. In contrast to the overall picture, a few Asia-Pacific currencies including the New Zealand dollar and the Malaysian ringgit saw an increase in the turnover for interest rate derivatives. This may be partly due to portfolio rebalancing as these currencies weakened vis-a-vis the US dollar.

Activity in equity index derivatives also saw a significant decline in the fourth quarter as markets became less volatile, Towards the end of the fourth quarter both options and futures turnover fell sharply to $58 trillion from a historically high level of $77 trillion in the previous quarter. The significant contraction in part reflects lower hedge fund participation in these markets.

After reaching a record of $7.9 trillion in the previous quarter, foreign exchange derivatives turnover in the fourth quarter plunged to $5.6 trillion The decrease in activity among the main currencies was most pronounced for the US dollar and sterling, followed by the euro and yen segments. The decline was particularly notable for the US dollar segment. Which had been characterised by high turnover since the beginning of the market turmoil in the third quarter of 2007.

Trading in commodity derivatives, observable only in terms of the number of contracts, increased from 411 million contracts in the third quarter to 450 million in the fourth, 10.4% higher than the same quarter in 2007. This ended a one-year period of declining turnover. The increase was due in part to higher turnover for non-precious metals such as copper and aluminium. most likely reflecting uncertainty about future demand.

In the second half of 2008, the financial crisis resulted in a decline in the total notional amounts outstanding of over-the-counter (OTC) derivatives to $592 trillion at end-year, an indication of reduced market activity. Foreign exchange and interest rate derivatives markets both recorded their first significant contractions. Against a background of severely strained credit markets and efforts to improve multilateral netting of offsetting contracts, credit default swap (CDS) markets continued to contract, with outstanding amounts decreasing by more than 25%. Facing significant price drops, outstanding commodity and equity derivatives also declined notably.

Despite the drop in amounts outstanding, significant price movements resulted in notably higher gross market values, which increased to $34 trillion at end-2008. Gross market values, which measure the cost of replacing all existing contracts, can be used to capture derivativesrelated exposures. The higher market values were also reflected in gross replacement costs after taking into account bilateral netting agreements, also referred to as gross credit exposures, which grew by nearly one third to $5 trillion.

The market for interest rate derivatives contracted for the first time in the second half of 2008, with notional amounts outstanding of these instruments falling to $419 trillion. Nonetheless, declining interest rates resulted in almost a doubling of the gross market value. The gross market value of interest rate swaps, by far the largest market segment, reached $17 trillion. The most significant increase took place in the US dollar swap market, where the gross market value nearly tripled.

Amounts outstanding of CDS contracts fell to $42 trillion against a background of severely strained credit markets and increased multilateral netting of offsetting positions by market participants. This was a continuation of the developments which began in the first half of 2008. Single-name contracts outstanding declined to $26 trillion while multi-name contracts, including CDS indices and CDS index tranches, saw a more pronounced decrease to $16 trillion. The composition of market activity across counterparties also changed in the second half of 2008. Outstanding contracts between dealers and other financial institutions as well as between dealers and non-financial institutions saw large declines relative to the inter-dealer market. Despite the lower outstanding amounts, the gross market value of CDS contracts also increased significantly as a result of the credit market turmoil.

Notional amounts outstanding of foreign exchange derivatives decreased to $50 trillion, while their gross market value rose to $4 trillion. The dollar and the euro remained the most important vehicle currencies, followed by the yen and the pound sterling.

Amounts outstanding of commodity derivatives fell by two thirds to $4.4 trillion. The continued declines in commodity prices during the second half of 2008 also had a substantial impact on the gross market value of commodity contracts, which fell to $1.0 trillion.

Outstanding equity derivatives decreased to $6 trillion, well below the levels seen in recent years and a notable change of pace from the increase in the first half of 2008. Reflecting lower outstanding positions and significantly lower equity prices, the gross market values of outstanding equity derivatives saw only a moderate decline.

The first quarter of 2009 saw a continued but limited decline of activity on the international derivatives exchanges. Total turnover based on notional amounts decreased further, to $367 trillion from $380 trillion in the previous quarter. Consistent with a gradual return of risk appetite, however, trading activity on a monthly basis did start to increase towards the end of the quarter. Overall turnover in interest rate derivatives remained largely unchanged at $324 trillion compared to the previous quarter. The moderate change in overall turnover nonetheless reflects differences across regions, with turnover in North America declining notably relative to the previous quarter, while European turnover increased. In contrast to interest derivatives markets, equity derivatives turnover fell for all contract types and all major currencies, including the euro. Against a background of negative economic growth and uncertainty about growth recovery, activity in equity index derivatives declined significantly to $38 trillion. Foreign exchange derivatives turnover also continued to slide. The decrease in activity among the main currencies was most pronounced for the yen and US dollar segments. Turnover in Australian and New Zealand dollar futures, possibly driven by renewed interest in FX carry trades, increased substantially relative to the previous quarter.

In the first half of 2009, notional amounts of all types of over-the-counter (OTC) contracts rebounded somewhat to stand at $605 trillion at the end of June, 10% higher than six months before. In contrast, gross credit exposures fell by 18% from an end-2008 peak to $3.7 trillion. Gross credit exposures take into account bilateral netting agreements but not collateral and provide a measure of counterparty exposures. Gross market values also decreased, by 21% to $25 trillion. However, there was an increase in outstanding amounts which was due in large part to interest rate derivatives. It stood at the end of June 2009 stood at $438 trillion, 13% above the end-2008 level. Gross market values fell by 14% to $15 trillion, with interest rate swaps accounting for most of the decline. The increase in outstanding volumes was concentrated in the US dollar, sterling and euro. The amounts of outstanding forward rate agreements (FRAs) went up 34% to $47 trillion, while option volumes grew by 18% to $49 trillion. Consistent with increased hedging activity, the growth in outstanding volumes was concentrated in longer-dated swap and option contracts, with the latter increasing by over 70%.

Continuing a trend which had begun in the first half of 2008, outstanding notional amounts of CDS contracts fell to $36 trillion at the end of June 2009. One factor was lower activity in the first half of the period, when credit markets were still strained. Activity did, however, increase subsequently. A second important driver was the expansion in the netting of offsetting positions by market participants, in particular the major dealers. In contrast to the declining notional amounts between financial institutions, outstanding contracts between dealers and non-financial customers more than doubled.

In the third quarter of 2009 overall activity on the international derivatives exchanges stabilised, although trading volumes were still only around 60% of the high levels seen before the crisis. Total turnover based on notional amounts was unchanged from the previous quarter, at $425 trillion. Reflecting very low and stable policy rates in many of the largest economies, total activity in derivatives on interest rates declined slightly, to $368 trillion in the third quarter from $376 trillion in the second. This decline was driven by a reduction in options turnover, with the decrease being more visible in the euro segment.

Against a backdrop of higher equity prices, turnover in equity index derivatives went up from $43 trillion to $50 trillion in the third quarter of 2009. This increase was due to rising equity valuations, since turnover in terms of the number of contracts fell slightly, from 1.65 billion to 1.63 billion. The improvement reflected developments in the Korean and other Asian markets, where trading rose significantly, from $16.2 trillion to $19.3 trillion, in the third quarter. Activity in foreign exchange derivatives also continued to grow. This may in part reflect greater FX carry trade activity driven by interest differentials and higher investor confidence. Turnover climbed to $7.2 trillion from $5.9 trillion in the previous quarter. Activity rose in all the main currencies, with a smaller increase for the euro. Turnover also expanded significantly in the New Zealand dollar and the Australian dollar relative to the previous quarter.

The recovery in activity on the international derivatives exchanges continued at a modest pace in the final three months of 2009. Turnover measured by notional amounts went up by 5% to $444 trillion between October and December, 22% higher than at the trough in the first quarter but still well below its peak ($690 trillion) in early 2008. This increase was fairly evenly distributed across risk categories. Open interest, also based on notional amounts, rose in line with turnover, by 6% to $73 trillion.

Turnover in interest rate derivatives went up by 4% to $383 trillion, with considerable variation across currencies. Increasing turnover in contracts denominated in the euro (17%), New Zealand dollar (37%) and Canadian dollar (59%) contrasted with a 10% decline in sterling contracts and stable turnover in futures and options on US and Japanese interest rates.

Higher equity valuations drove up turnover measured by notional amounts in derivatives on stock price indices by 8%, while turnover measured by the number of contracts traded rose by only 3%. Among the few markets with a genuine increase in activity was the Brazilian market, where trading volume measured by notional amounts surged by 58% to $0.7 trillion, just short of its peak of late 2007. In the first quarter of 2009, turnover in Brazilian stock index contracts stood at a mere $0.2 trillion. Much of the recovery in trading activity was driven by increases in stock prices (the Bovespa index gained 11% in the fourth quarter), but the number of contracts traded also went up by 21% in the last quarter, after stagnating in the first three months of the year.

Activity in the market for foreign exchange derivatives strengthened in the final quarter of 2009. Turnover measured by notional amounts rose by 15% to $8 trillion, the highest on record. Open interest increased by 11% to $310 billion. Turnover growth was particularly strong in contracts on the Swiss franc (38%). Most of this appears to reflect higher short-term trading rather than longer-term position-taking, as open interest in derivatives on the franc fell by 17%. There was some support for the notion of the (renewed) attractiveness of FX carry trades. FX carry trades can be implemented in a number of ways, one of which involves a long position in futures or options on a high-yielding currency and a short position in contracts on a low-yielding one. Admittedly, it is impossible to identify the motivations behind individual positions. Even so, it is striking that open interest in two of the most attractive target currencies has increased considerably since the height of the crisis. Open interest in contracts on the Australian dollar rose from $4 billion at the end of 2008 to $13 billion one year later, although much of this increase took place in the first half of the year. Positions in the Brazilian real also expanded considerably (by 26% in the fourth quarter of 2009 alone). The funding currencies have changed from previous episodes of high carry trade activity. Short-term interest rates are low in a number of large economies, which has expanded the number of possible funding currencies. Open interest in the two traditional funding currencies, the Japanese yen and the Swiss franc, fell in the final quarter of 2009. Unfortunately, it is hard to say on the basis of the available data which other currencies have taken their place.

Activity in futures and options on commodities increased at a moderate pace in the final three months of 2009. Turnover measured by the number of contracts traded (notional amounts are not available for this risk category) rose by 7%, although with considerable variation across types of commodities. Trading volumes in contracts on precious metals increased by almost 50%, driven by near doubling of trading in gold contracts on Chinese exchanges. Turnover in contracts on agricultural commodities and energy contracts increased by 5% and 2%, respectively. By contrast, volumes of derivatives on non-precious metals fell by 31%.

Activity on the derivatives exchanges accelerated during the first quarter of 2010. Turnover measured by notional amounts of futures and options on interest rates, stock price indices and foreign exchange increased by 16% quarter on quarter to $514 trillion between January and March. Open interest, expressed in notional amounts outstanding, rose by 12% to $82 trillion. Volumes in the market for derivatives on short-term interest rates surged as market participants revised their expectations about the future path of monetary policy. Turnover in money market contracts went up by 18% to $408 trillion, thus outpacing turnover growth in derivatives on government bonds (up 11% to $11 trillion). Particularly rapid increases in activity were seen in contracts on short-term Brazilian rates, where turnover in futures and options almost doubled to $5.4 trillion, as market participants began to price in higher interest rates. Turnover in contracts on short-term euro interest rates went up by 30% to $162 trillion. In the United States, turnover in futures and options on the overnight federal funds rate – which is closely related to monetary policy – increased by 25% to $28 trillion, whereas turnover in contracts on three-month eurodollar rates rose by 10% to $163 trillion. The main exception to the increase in activity in money market contracts was in the yen segment. Turnover in yen-denominated futures and options fell by 27%, to $2.5 trillion, as investors continued to expect that shortterm interest rates would remain low.

Activity in the market for derivatives on stock price indices remained stable in the first three months of 2010, despite some notable fluctuations in equity prices. Turnover measured in terms of notional amounts increased by 3% to $55 trillion, although this mainly reflected a valuation effect. The number of stock index contracts traded on the international derivatives exchanges barely changed over the period. Investors increased their positions in FX futures and options. Open interest of such contracts increased by 29% to $0.4 trillion, far outpacing growth in turnover (up 11% to $9 trillion). Open interest in contracts with one leg in sterling increased by 57% to $0.02 trillion. As each contract has two legs, open interest and turnover in the various currencies add up to 200% of the total. Open interest in contracts on the Brazilian real rose by 41% to $0.14 trillion. This makes it the second most important currency on the international derivatives exchanges in terms of open positions, behind the US dollar ($0.33 trillion) but ahead of the euro ($0.10 trillion). The importance of the real in the currency segment of the futures and options market is due to the fact that there is comparatively little trading over the counter.

Notional amounts of all over-the-counter (OTC) derivatives increased modestly (2%) in the second half of 2009, reaching $615 trillion by the end of December. The increase was evenly spread among risk categories, with the exception of commodity derivatives and credit default swaps (CDS), where amounts outstanding fell by 21% and 9%, respectively. The decline in reporting banks' gross credit exposures, which provide a measure of counterparty risk, slowed to 6%, after an 18% fall in the first half of 2009. Gross market values also decreased, by 15% to $22 trillion. Notional amounts outstanding of interest rate derivatives rose by 3%, with limited variation between currencies. Increased netting of contracts interacted with a decline in the value of the US dollar during the reporting period to produce the smallest increase since end-2005 (other than the exceptional 16% fall in the second half of 2008, which was partly due to a major correction in sterling and the euro in that period). Market values of interest rate derivatives declined by 9% overall, with notable reductions in US dollar and Canadian dollar contracts (–17% and – 28% respectively).

CDS amounts outstanding contracted again, by almost 10%, due to a combination of factors. A reduction in overall activity and reduced spreads depressed new business, while ongoing netting continued to reduce the volume of outstanding contracts. Market values fell by another 36% for single-name CDS, and by almost 50% for multi-name contracts. The decline in activity was most pronounced for multi-name contracts between reporting dealers (15%), while notional volume between dealers and non-reporters decreased by only 5%. This is consistent with increasing use being made of CCPs, as these contracts are classified as contracts with non-reporting counterparties.

The amounts outstanding of single-name CDS on sovereigns increased by 10% in the second half of the year, as market attention was drawn to the implications of large fiscal deficits in late 2009 and sovereign CDS spreads rose. This increase was driven by inter-dealer positions, which rose by 20%. Data from the Depository Trust & Clearing Corporation (DTCC) suggest that exposures on some sovereign names increased by up to 50% during this period. Nevertheless, at end-2009, total notional amounts outstanding of sovereign CDS remained below their June 2008 peak. In contrast, positions on non-sovereigns (financial and non-financial firms) were down 11%. This was mainly due to reporters' business with non-reporting financial institutions, whose outstanding CDS contracts declined by 17%.

Sizeable increases in the notional amounts outstanding of equity derivatives contrasted with declining replacement values. Rising equity valuations resulted in an increase in notional amounts of contracts on Japanese and other Asian equities by 50–80%, depending on the instrument. At the same time, market values dropped by 10–50% for various instruments. The US equity-linked derivatives segment saw a 17% increase in volume, but in terms of market value positions declined by 5%. Notional amounts and market values for European equities fell by around 20%. Notional amounts of Latin American equity-linked instruments decreased by 69% in the second half of 2009, but market values fell only 34%.

Growth in activity on the derivatives exchanges decelerated somewhat in the second quarter of 2010, compared to the buoyant first quarter. Turnover measured by notional amounts of futures and options on interest rates, stock price indices and foreign exchange increased by 8% quarter on quarter to $555 trillion between April and June, compared to a 16% rise in the previous three months. The relatively modest expansion reflected divergent developments in the United States and Europe. As euro area sovereign bond yield spreads widened relative to German bunds and the euro depreciated against major currencies (10% against the US dollar), turnover in eurodenominated options on these underlying risk types fell by almost 30%, far more than could be accounted for by the valuation effect alone, and turnover in euro futures barely budged. This contrasted with a 35% and 18% surge in all dollar-denominated options and futures, respectively. Open interest of exchange-traded financial derivatives, expressed in notional amounts outstanding, fell by 8% to $75 trillion. While outstanding amounts of instruments denominated in dollars were unchanged, those of eurodenominated contracts dropped by 22% during the quarter, driven primarily by declines in interest rate instruments. Increased basis risk across sovereigns probably contributed to decreased use of exchange-traded derivatives for cross-country hedging of exposures in smaller euro area markets.

The differences in activity growth across currencies were primarily driven by developments in the interest rate segment. Turnover in dollar money market contracts went up by 23% to $235 trillion. By contrast, turnover in contracts on short-term euro rates fell by 15% to $162 trillion. Similarly, turnover growth in derivatives on dollar bonds (up 22% to $20 trillion) contrasted with a 3% turnover decline in long-term euro instruments, although outstanding notional amounts and contract numbers on eurobund options roughly doubled.

Activity in futures and options on stock price indices surged on the back of sharply higher stock price volatility. As stock markets first rose and then declined in the United States and Europe, option-implied volatility rocketed almost to levels last seen in the first quarter of 2009. Equity index derivatives turnover measured in notional amounts went up by 15% to $64 trillion, after having remained almost stable in the first three months of 2010, when implied volatility had declined to the lowest level since early 2009. The number of stock index contracts traded on the international derivatives exchanges increased by around 20% over the period. While turnover measured in notional amounts on US exchanges grew by 22%, that on European exchanges advanced only 5%. Trading volumes on many Asian exchanges also grew, with a particularly sharp increase in India (36%). Turnover in futures and options on exchange rates increased, but amounts outstanding fell. Trading volumes of FX futures went up by 17% to $11 billion, well above the previous peak in the third quarter of 2008. Open interest fell 12% to $188 billion. Option turnover increased by much less (6%), with amounts outstanding falling 8% from the peak reached in the first quarter. Turnover (measured in terms of the number of contracts) on the international commodities exchanges rose by 8%. There was a hefty 32% increase in activity in contracts on precious metals, as gold prices exceeded the previous peak reached in late 2009. Turnover in derivatives on non-precious metals and energy products went up 24% and 13%, respectively, with metal and oil prices dropping a fifth from the high reached at the beginning of the second quarter. Turnover in contracts on agricultural commodities fell 5%.

Sharp movements in asset prices and ongoing efforts to mitigate counterparty risk both had a strong influence on over-the-counter (OTC) derivatives markets in the first half of 2010. The notional amount of outstanding OTC derivatives fell by 3% in dollar terms during this period. However, substantial movements in asset prices, partly related to growing concerns about sovereign risks, drove up the gross market value of these contracts by 15% and the gross credit exposures associated with them by 2%. The smaller rise in gross credit exposures than in gross market values reflects increased netting, which is consistent with greater use of central counterparties (CCPs) in some segments of the market. The ratio of gross credit exposures to gross market values consequently fell to 14.5% at the end of the first half of 2010, down from 16.3% at the end of 2009 and 24.0% at the end of the first half of 2007. There was considerable variation in changes in notional amounts and market values across segments of the OTC derivatives market. Outstanding notional amounts increased for foreign exchange (8%) and equity (5%) derivatives, declined for credit (7%) and commodity (3%) derivatives and were broadly unchanged for interest rate contracts. Gross market values increased for foreign exchange (22%) and interest rate (25%) derivatives, declined for credit (7%) and commodity (16%) contracts and remained stable for equity derivatives.

In the OTC foreign exchange derivatives market, growth in the notional amount of outstanding contracts was supported by particularly strong increases in the volume of contracts linked to the Canadian dollar (20%) and the Swiss franc (23%). The gross market value of outstanding contracts linked to the Swiss franc more than doubled as the currency appreciated by 12% against the euro over the period.

In the interest rate derivatives market, the sharp increase in gross market values was associated with falls in major currency swap rates. The gross market value of derivatives linked to US dollar rates increased particularly strongly (42%), as long-term swap rates declined by more for the US dollar than for several other major currencies.

There were signs of efforts to reduce counterparty risk in the interest rate derivatives market. For example, the notional amount of outstanding interdealer positions decreased by 5% while those between dealers and other financial institutions grew by 2%. This is consistent with positions being shifted to CCPs. In addition, there was a further shortening of the maturity profile of interest rate derivatives.

There were also signs of further efforts to reduce counterparty risk in the credit derivatives market. For example, the 7% fall in the notional amount of outstanding OTC credit derivatives in the first half of 2010 reflected ongoing use of portfolio compression services by market participants as well as increased usage of CCPs. It brought the total decline since the peak in this volume at the end of 2007 to 48%. In addition, the notional amount of outstanding long-term credit derivatives with maturities in excess of five years fell particularly sharply, declining by 22% in the first half of 2010 and by a total of 67% since the end of 2007. This may reflect reduced willingness to commit to counterparties for long periods of time.

Trading activity on the international derivatives exchanges declined in the third quarter of 2010. Turnover measured by notional amounts fell by 21% to $438 trillion between July and September. The decline in volumes affected all major risk categories. Trading in interest rate contracts receded by 23% to $371 trillion, primarily as a result of lower activity in contracts on short-term interest rates (–24%, to $328 trillion). Turnover in futures and options on stock indices fell by 12% to $57 trillion, and that in contracts on exchange rates by 22% to $9 trillion.

Open positions turned out to be more stable than turnover. Open interest in all financial contracts rose by 4% to $78 trillion, although this hides some variation across risk categories. Traders increased their derivatives exposures to stock indices (by 16%, to $6 trillion) and decreased that to exchange rates (by 5%, to $0.4 trillion). Open interest in interest rate contracts remained roughly stable at $71 trillion.

The decline in trading in interest rate contracts affected all major currencies except the yen. Trading volumes of yen-denominated contracts went up by 25% to $7 trillion, with little difference in terms of growth rates between derivatives on short and on long-term rates. By contrast, turnover in futures and options on US dollar interest rates fell by 27% to $185 trillion, mainly owing to lower activity in money market contracts. Trading volumes of interest rate derivatives denominated in the euro and pound sterling dropped by 18% and 29%, respectively, to $130 trillion and $27 trillion.

The decline in turnover in futures and options on stock indices was similarly broad-based as that in the interest rate segment. In most markets, turnover dropped in terms of both notional amounts and the number of contracts traded, suggesting a true reduction in activity and not just valuation effects. China and India were notable exceptions to the decline in trade volumes. Turnover in futures on the Chinese CSI 300 index reached $2.4 trillion, after $1.5 trillion in the second quarter. This makes it the world's fifth most traded stock index contract – only a few months after the contract was first traded in April 2010. Turnover in contracts on Indian equities increased by 10% to $1 trillion.

Market participants increased their positions in some of the classical "carry trade" currencies. Open interest in futures and options on the Australian and New Zealand dollars rose to $21 trillion and $2.1 trillion, respectively. Similarly, open interest in two important funding currencies, the Swiss franc and Japanese yen, increased by 38% and 26%, respectively, to $10 trillion and $37 trillion.

The volume of trade on international derivatives exchanges was higher in the fourth quarter of 2010 than in the previous one. Turnover, measured as the notional amount of traded derivatives contracts, rose by 9% in dollar terms. The bulk of this increase (7.8 percentage points) corresponds to a surge in the turnover of short-term dollar interest rate futures. This rose by 29%, reflecting particularly strong trading in November, when the Federal Reserve Board announced its second round of US Treasury bond purchases. A further notable portion of the increase in derivatives turnover (1.4 percentage points) is due to a 38% rise in trading of Korean equity index options. This was partly offset (−1.3 percentage points) by lower trading of short-term euro interest rate options, which declined by 16%.

Despite the overall increase in turnover on derivatives exchanges, open interest, measured as the notional amount of outstanding contracts, declined by 13%. More than one third of this reduction is explained by a decline in shortterm euro interest rate options, and almost a further one third by declines in short-term interest rate options on both dollar and sterling interest rates. This may reflect decisions by some market participants to shed protection against near-term increases in major-currency interest rates, as expectations of such moves were pushed further into the future during the fourth quarter of 2010.

In interest rate derivatives markets, higher turnover in futures (+14%) contrasted with weaker trading in options (−5%). The rise in futures turnover was driven by the large increase in trading of short-term dollar contracts. In contrast, trading of long-term dollar futures was little changed, despite a marked increase in US Treasury bond futures turnover in November. The fall in options turnover reflects declines in trading of euro and sterling short-dated options of 16% and 19%, respectively.

Heavy trading on Asian exchanges boosted turnover of equity index derivatives (up 15%). In addition to the rise in turnover of Korean equity index options to 59% of total equity index options turnover, trading of Hong Kong and Indian equity index options also expanded rapidly, by 45% and 33%, respectively. Trading of equity index futures on the same regions increased by 15%, 26% and 20%, respectively. Open interest in equity index derivatives fell by 11%, mainly reflecting a 23% decline in open interest in euro area stock index options.

Activity in the market for foreign exchange derivatives increased as higher trading in contracts on the euro more than offset weaker trading in the dollar and sterling. Overall turnover increased by 9%. Trading of both euro futures and options increased by around 20%. In contrast, trading of dollar and sterling options declined by 22% and 26%, respectively. Open interest in foreign exchange derivatives declined by 15%, reflecting widespread falls in contracts linked to major currencies.

Notional amounts outstanding of over-the-counter (OTC) derivatives rose by 3% in the second half of 2010, reaching $601 trillion at end-December. Much of the increase was a direct consequence of the appreciation of major currencies against the US dollar, the currency in which the data are reported. Gross market values of all OTC contracts fell by 14%, driven mainly by the 17% decline in the market value of interest rate contracts. Finally, gross credit exposures dropped by 7% to $3.3 trillion, compared with a 2% increase in the first half of the year.

In the interest rate segment, the largest risk category in the OTC derivatives market by any measure, notional amounts outstanding went up by 3% to $465 trillion, largely owing to exchange rate effects. Contracts on dollar rates dropped by 8%. Positions increased in the euro (10%), yen (7%), Swiss franc (10%) and Swedish krona (14%), but this probably reflected the appreciation of those currencies against the US dollar rather than any genuine increase in activity. Among the major currencies, only the Canadian dollar segment showed a decline. Amounts outstanding of contracts denominated in that currency fell by 4%, despite its 6% appreciation against the US dollar.

Active trading at the shorter end of the FX derivatives market pushed up notional amounts of FX derivatives by 9%, to $58 trillion. Volumes outstanding of contracts with maturities of up to one year went up by 13% and those with maturities of more than five years by 11%. By contrast, amounts outstanding of those with intermediate maturities declined by 6%. Positions in credit default swaps (CDS) remained stable in the second half of 2010. At the end of the year, reporting dealers had contracts with a total face value of $30 trillion on their books, approximately the same as six months earlier. Amounts outstanding with a central counterparty increased from about 10% of the total market at end-June to 15% at end-December 2010. Positions with non-financial customers plummeted to $0.3 trillion, only about 1% of the total. This compares to a peak of 5% reached at the end of December 2009 and just under 3% in the middle of 2010. The sovereign CDS market bucked the downward trend in notional amounts, posting a 6% increase. This followed a 26% gain during the first half of 2010. Positions in non-sovereign CDS declined by 2% in the second half of the year (after falling by 7% in the previous period).

Activity on the international futures and options exchange traded derivatives rose in the first quarter of 2011. Turnover measured by notional amounts increased to $581 trillion, 21% higher than in the previous quarter. Open interest, also measured in notional amounts, expanded by 24% between end-December 2010 and end-March 2011. Activity grew in all market segments except foreign exchange. Turnover in the interest rate segment went up by 23% to $498 trillion. This mainly reflected heavy trading in futures and options on short-term interest rates, whose turnover increased by 23% and 30%, respectively. Trading in contracts on bonds also rose (15%). The growth in activity affected all major currencies except the Japanese yen. Particularly large increases were recorded in the short-term sterling segment, where futures turnover surged by 57% and options turnover by 113% as traders took positions on the changing odds of a Bank of England policy rate increase. In Japan, the odds of a rate change remained low throughout the period, which could explain the 20% drop in turnover at both the long and the short end of the interest rate market.

Trading in futures and options on stock prices indices grew moderately in the first quarter of 2011. Turnover measured by notional amounts rose smartly by 12%, but this overstates the underlying increase in activity. When measured in terms of the number of contracts traded, turnover inched up by merely 4%. That said, there were sizeable discrepancies across regions: trading in stock price indices denominated in Japanese yen surged by 30% (number of contracts) and 41% (notional amounts) over the quarter as a whole. Much of this rise took place after the severe earthquake and tsunami that hit the east coast of Japan on 11 March. Trading in contracts denominated in euros also picked up significantly (number of contracts: 15%, notional amounts: 23%). Sizeable growth in turnover also took place in a number of emerging markets, such as Israel (15% and 17%), India (25% and 15%), Thailand (9% and 22%), Chinese Taipei (32% and 88%) and South Africa (10% and 15%).

Activity in the foreign exchange segment of the international derivatives markets remained stable at $10 trillion in the first quarter of 2011, but this marks sizeable differences across currencies. Turnover in contracts on the Japanese yen went up by 29%. Most of this was short-term trading; open interest rose by merely 9%. Turnover in futures and options on sterling and the Swiss franc rose by 20% each. By contrast, turnover in the Brazilian real (which is traded predominantly on exchanges) fell by 17% and that in the euro by 6%.

The notional amount of interest rate, currency and equity index derivatives traded in the second quarter of 2011 was slightly lower in dollar terms than in the first quarter. Trading volume fell by 3% overall, as turnover of interest rate futures (–1%) and options (–14%) declined, while that of currency (+5%) and equity index (+3%) derivatives increased. Outstanding positions also declined modestly during the quarter, by 2% overall. Turnover of commodity derivatives, measured by number of contracts, was broadly unchanged, while outstanding positions contracted by 3%.

Trading in interest rate derivatives in the second quarter may reflect reduced uncertainty about future interest rates for some of the major currencies. Turnover declined by 4% overall, reflecting falls in trading of futures and options linked to euro (–12%) and sterling (–28%) rates. Outstanding positions also declined in derivatives referencing euro (–20%) and sterling (–19%) rates, while those linked to US dollar rates increased by 13%. This is consistent with declines in probabilities implied by the option prices of euro and, particularly, sterling rate increases during the quarter, as global inflation pressures eased. In contrast, few market participants attached significant probability to near-term changes in the US policy rate at any time during the quarter. Futures linked to yen interest rates also saw declines in trading volumes (–28%) and outstanding positions (–23%). This might reflect greater certainty that rates would remain low to support the Japanese economy following the March earthquake.

A significant portion of trading in currency derivatives may also have been driven by interest rate developments, via amendments to synthetic carry trade positions. Short-term interest rates on the Brazilian real, for example, increased as the Central Bank of Brazil raised its policy rate from 11.75% to 12.25% during the second quarter, having already boosted it by 50 basis points towards the end of the first quarter. This widened the gap vis-à-vis the US policy rate to 12 percentage points. Currency derivatives can be used to speculate that such interest differentials will not be offset by currency movements. Open interest in currency derivatives referencing the Brazilian real almost doubled during the second quarter, boosting the share of such contracts in total currency derivatives positions from 14% to 23%. Open interest in currency derivatives referencing the New Zealand dollar also rose sharply, but from a much lower base.

The modest rise in trading of equity index derivatives in the second quarter was driven by strong turnover growth in the Korean options market. Growth of 18% boosted the share of total equity index transactions accounted for by these options to 36%, up from 31% in the previous quarter. The trades brought about a 15% decline in outstanding Korean options positions, which along with declines in outstanding Japanese futures (–23%) and options (–7%) contributed to an overall decline in open interest in equity index derivatives of 2%. Open interest in North American (–1%) and European (+3%) equity indices were little changed.

Turnover and open interest in commodity derivatives varied across segments of the market. Trading in precious metals futures increased by 13% and open interest rose by 6% during the second quarter, perhaps as investors sought safe havens from sovereign credit and inflation risks. This is consistent with Commodity Futures Trading Commission (CFTC) data, which show that "non-commercial" traders such as asset managers increased their net long positions in gold futures during this quarter. This overall second quarter increase in precious metals open interest was interrupted by a sharp fall in May, however, as silver prices crashed during the early part of the month. Outstanding positions in energy futures (–2%) and options (–4%) also fell in May, coinciding with a correction in oil prices, although positions in energy derivatives were broadly unchanged over the quarter. Trading increased by 4% in agricultural derivatives, while open interest declined by about 11%. Producers and consumers may have felt less need to hold hedging positions after agricultural prices stabilised towards the end of the first quarter, after rising for many months. This is consistent with CFTC data showing lower "commercial" positions in corn and wheat futures.

For the first time since the financial crisis, positions in over-the-counter (OTC) derivatives went up significantly in the first half of 2011. Notional amounts outstanding of contracts in all risk categories rose by 18% to $708 trillion at the end of June, well above the $673 trillion peak in mid-2008. By contrast, gross market values of these contracts fell by 8%, owing mainly to a 10% reduction in the market value of interest rate contracts. Since interest rates remained roughly unchanged over the period since the previous survey, this suggests that a significant number of contracts with large mark to market values have either expired or been terminated. Gross credit exposure dropped by 15% to $3.0 trillion, the lowest since the end of 2007.

Most of the increase in the total amounts outstanding is due to larger (gross) positions on interest rate risk. Notional amounts outstanding of interest rate contracts increased by 19% to $554 trillion. The expansion was evenly split across currencies. Maturities shortened: the amounts outstanding of contracts with remaining maturities of more than five years fell by 6% to $130 trillion, whereas those with maturities of one year or less went up by more than 30% to $247 trillion.

Higher volumes of shorter-maturity contracts also lifted outstanding notional amounts outstanding in FX derivatives. Positions in contracts with maturities of one year or less rose by a quarter, while those with maturities of over five years halved. As a consequence, total amounts outstanding increased by 12% to $65 trillion.

Notional amounts outstanding in the credit default swap (CDS) market increased moderately, reversing the post-crisis downward trend. That said, at $32 trillion at the end of June 2011, notional amounts outstanding of CDS remained well below the peak of $58 trillion at the end of 2007. Multi-name contracts drove the increase, with positions going up by 22% to $14 trillion. Amounts outstanding of single-name CDS remained stable at $18 trillion.

The share of centrally cleared CDS contracts increased slightly. 17% of all CDS by reporting dealers involved a central counterparty (CCP), up from 15% six months before. This means that approximately 9% of all trades were cleared centrally, since a single contract between two CCP members is replaced by separate contracts between the CCP and each of the counterparties. Positions of reporting dealers with non-financial customers shrank by 23% to only $238 billion, following a 63% decline in the second half of 2010. Non-financial customers now hold less than 1% of all CDS, compared with a peak of 5% at the end of December 2009.

Positions in equity and commodity derivatives also increased significantly. Notional amounts outstanding of equity-linked contracts increased by 21%. Positions in equity-linked options were up by 26%, while those in forwards and swaps increased by 11%. Amounts outstanding of commodity contracts grew by 9%, with contracts on gold up 18% and options on precious metals and other commodities up 19%.

Activity on the international derivatives exchanges rebounded in the third quarter of 2011. Turnover measured by notional amounts increased by 7% to $603 trillion between July and September, with very little difference across the types of underlying risk. The increase in turnover more than offset the 3% decline recorded in the second quarter. Open positions continued to contract, falling by 3% to $81 trillion at the end of September, with a particularly large decline in foreign exchange.

Investors taking positions on changes in the medium-term outlook for monetary policy in the euro area and Japan lifted activity in the interest rate segment of the international derivatives exchanges. Turnover in futures and options on interest rates in all currencies increased by 7% to $510 trillion. A sizeable part of the increase was driven by higher turnover in contracts on short-term euro (+30%) and yen (+60%) money market rates. While the near-term outlook for policy rates in these two currencies remained stable during the period, investors began to price in significantly lower rates than before over a one-year horizon. In the euro area, traders mainly demanded options on short-term euro money market rates (70%), whereas trading activity in the corresponding futures contract rose roughly in line with the entire market (+7%). By contrast, with little option trading in short-term yen rates, the entire increase in activity was concentrated in the futures contract.

Activity in futures and options on stock indices rose as equity prices fell in most markets in the third quarter of 2011. Turnover increased by 7% to $81 trillion between July and September, the highest on record. The number of contracts traded, which is independent of valuation effects, went up by 12% over the same period. Trading volumes increased in all major markets apart from Korea, where turnover in won-denominated equity index contracts fell by 20% in dollar terms and 12% in terms of the number of contracts.

Heavier trading in currency futures lifted turnover in exchange-traded FX derivatives. Turnover in FX futures increased by 9% to $10.6 trillion, whereas options turnover remained stable at $0.7 trillion. Open interest in FX contracts plummeted after the Brazilian government introduced a 1% transaction tax on certain FX derivatives. Open positions in contracts traded on Brazilian exchanges fell by 44% (turnover: –6%). The market for futures and options on the Brazilian real is unusually large relative to the OTC market. This makes the real the second most important currency on the international derivatives exchanges in terms of open interest, behind the US dollar but before the euro. As a consequence, the drop in open interest on the Brazilian exchanges fed into a global reduction in open interest in FX products of 17%, despite a 6% increase in positions on all other exchanges.

The introduction of the Brazilian transaction tax triggered a surge in turnover in the real contract listed on the Chicago Mercantile Exchange (68%). That said, at $5.5 billion between July and September 2011, turnover in the Chicago-traded real contracts remains a fraction of that taking place onshore in Brazil ($1.5 trillion) over the same period. Moreover, open interest in the CME's real contract fell by 16% in the third quarter, which suggests that the transaction tax did not result in any significant push of positions offshore.

The notional amount of outstanding over-the-counter (OTC) derivatives fell by 8%, to $648 trillion, in the second half of 2011. But with an increase in price volatility, their market value rose by 40%. Gross credit exposures also increased significantly, by 32%.

The bulk of these changes were in the interest rate market segment. Here, notional amounts outstanding declined by 9%, to $504 trillion. This corresponded closely to cuts to positions in dollar, euro and sterling contracts and to positions with residual maturities of one year or less. Market participants may have perceived little near-term risk of changes in short-term interest rates in these currencies and therefore elected not to replace maturing short-dated contracts. Such a perception would be consistent with the declines in probabilities of near-term increases in policy rates implied by market prices and the proximity of these rates to zero, which limited the scope for cuts. The increase in the market value of outstanding interest rate derivatives was also concentrated in dollar, euro and sterling contracts, for which replacement values increased by 39%, 67% and

71%, respectively. For each of these currencies, swap rates of all maturities fell to low levels by historical standards. This suggests that swap rates moved further away from those prevailing when many outstanding contracts were signed, thus raising their cost of replacement.

The pattern of lower outstanding notional amounts but higher market values was also visible in the credit derivatives market segment. The volume of outstanding positions, which fell by 12%, to $29 trillion, resumed the downward trend that began at the end of 2007. The trend largely reflects the application of portfolio compression services to both bilateral and centrally cleared trades. Even after such compression, outstanding positions with central counterparties (CCPs) still increased from 9% to 11% of the market. After halving the volume of contracts with CCPs, since central clearing replaces original contracts between two counterparties with two contracts, one between the first original counterparty and the CCP and another between the CCP and the second original counterparty. The market value of outstanding positions increased by 18%, as credit default swap premia increased for many sovereigns and other reference entities.

In contrast, the outstanding volume of foreign exchange derivatives changed little, although their market value also increased notably. The gross market value increased by 9%, largely as a result of changes in the values of contracts between the G3 currencies, with the euro depreciating by 5% against the dollar and 8% against the yen in the second half of 2011. In a smaller segment of the market, the gross market value of contracts referencing the Swiss franc fell by 30%, reflecting the Swiss National Bank's decision to try to cap the value of the franc against the euro. This caused the franc to depreciate sharply to just below the cap, reversing a strong appreciation over the preceding several months. Hence, current and expected future values of the exchange rate probably moved back towards the fixed rates locked into many outstanding contracts, thus reducing their cost of replacement. The outstanding volume of foreign exchange contracts referencing the Swiss franc also fell notably, by 16%, perhaps as some market participants who would have incurred losses if the franc appreciated against the euro decided to no longer hedge this risk.

In the smaller equity and commodity segments of the OTC derivatives market, outstanding notional amounts fell somewhat, while market values changed little. The outstanding volume of equity derivatives fell by 13%, reflecting similar proportionate declines in both options and forward and swap positions. The overall decline in commodity derivatives positions was 3%, again with similar proportionate reductions in options and forward and swap positions.

Positions in the OTC derivatives market continued to decline in the first half of 2012. Notional amounts outstanding of the face value of all contracts fell to $639 trillion at the end of June 2012, 10% lower than the high recorded 12 months previously and 1% lower than at end-2011. Gross market values, which measure the cost of replacing existing contracts, dropped by 7% to $25 trillion. Gross credit exposures, which measure reporting dealers' exposure after taking account of legally enforceable netting agreements and thus provide a measure of counterparty risk in the OTC derivatives market; declined to $3.7 trillion.

Smaller positions in the interest rate and credit default swap (CDS) segments more than offset slight increases in foreign exchange and equity-linked contracts. Notional amounts outstanding of interest rate contracts and CDS fell by 2% and 6%, respectively, to $494 trillion and $27 trillion. In contrast, the volume of foreign exchange contracts outstanding rose by 5% to $67 trillion, and that of equity-linked contracts by 6% to $6.3 trillion. Positions in commodity contracts declined slightly (3%) to $3 trillion.

Within the interest rate segment, the trend away from inter-dealer positions towards positions with other finaricial institutions - a category that includes banks and securities firms which are not reporting dealers as well as central counterparties, hedge funds, special purpose vehicles, insurance companies, mutual funds and other financial companies - continued. Notional amounts of inter-dealer positions fell by $18 trillion (12%) to 28% of the total while those with other financial institutions rose by $6 trillion (2%) to 64%. In the mid-2000s, before the financial crisis, inter-dealer positions and positions with other financial institutions were of similar size, each accounting for 40-45% of the market total, Positions with non- financial customers accounted for the remaining 10-15% of the market, but this share has since fallen, to just 8% in mid-2012. This is partly related to the increased use of central counterparties. Interest rate contracts have become increasingly short-term in recent years. Notional amounts of contracts with maturities of more than five years fell by 9% in the first half of 2012 to $117 trillion, or 24% of total interest rate contracts. By contrast, the volume of contracts with a maturity of up to one year went up by 4% to $207 trillion, or 42% of the total. In the mid- and late 2000s, longer-term contracts accounted for up to 35% of all interest rate contracts.

Notional amounts outstanding of CDS continued the decline that started in early 2008. In the first half of 2012, they fell another 6% to $27 trillion, less than half the amount at the end of 2007. Gross market values fell by 25% to $1.2 trillion, The decline in open positions in the CDS market mainty affected contracts referencing non-financial firms. Notional amounts of such contracts fell by 10% to $10 billion. CDS referencing sovereign debt or debt issued by financial institutions remained relatively stable at $3 trillion and $7 trillion, respectively.

THE ROADMAP FOR THE DEVELOPMENT OF DERIVATIVES

The roadmap for the development of derivatives, or for that matter, any new financial product or service, will strive to maintain a balance between the following four objectives:

Efficiency: We can look at the notion of efficiency from two perspectives. For the provider of products and services, it means the ability to do this at the lowest possible cost, with the full benefit of technology and market infrastructure. For the user, efficiency relates to the availability of products and services which address his/her requirements at the lowest possible price.

Stability: From the viewpoint of the financial system, stability requires that aggregate risk is bounded in some way. This requires, in turn, that individual participants be required to mitigate and manage their own risks. However, in situations in which systemic risk goes beyond the aggregate individual risk, additional measures may be warranted.

Transparency: The basic premise is: 'what cannot be measured cannot be managed'. The more market participants know about overall activities and outcomes, the better able they are to make their cost- benefit calculations and act on them, contributing to the overall effectiveness of the market.

Inclusion: Financial development is not an end in itself. It serves the broader purpose of facilitating economic activity, through resource mobilisation and risk management. The more accessible the financial system is to individuals in pursuit of these two objectives, the better.

From this perspective, the approach should be neutral to the form and nature of the product or service; it should be concerned only with whether it is helping to meet the objectives, or at least not detracting from any of them. The emphasise on the objective of inclusion, which, in this context, looks at the desirability of a product in terms of how effectively it might meet the requirements of a very heterogeneous group of producers of various goods and services.

Taking the specific example of OTC fore x products, it is apparent that they remain attractive to a majority of people with forex exposures because they can be customised to the specific characteristics of each transaction. However, the parallel development of the futures market suggests that there may be some complementarities between the two. A hub-and-spoke analogy comes to mind, with OTC products serving as the spokes and the counter-parties to these transactions then aggregating their exposures and managing them with exchange-traded products. Although this phenomenon is not quite prevalent in India at present but this provides a useful way to think about the overall roadmap, with each component playing a legitimate role.

QUESTIONS

1. Discuss the major factors influencing the risk management in a globalised financial derivatives markets.

2. Can all the risks relating to financial derivatives activity be identified, and are they being managed and controlled?

3. Can the market risk methodology be adjusted to measure credit and liquidity to the risk solution being reviewed capable of attributing capital to cover operational and legal risk exposure?

4. To deal with financial derivatives risk, what types of formal structures need to be in place in order to implant a risk culture throughout the whole organisation?

5. Most of the losses from derivatives transactions have come from unclear implementation of risk visions and cultures in approach to risk-management." In the light of the this statement discuss the policies and procedures which can serve as an example of the major types of issue which should be made explicit and implemented by a company.

6. What is the strategic importance of derivatives risk control?

7. Discuss the different types of risk which can be considered relevant to any particular derivatives transaction.

8. How can the integrated risk framework build into its role of activity all the complexity of legal risk?

9. Discuss the growth of financial derivatives in the global financial markets.

10. "The changing nature of financial industry, especially as reflected in developments in the financial derivatives market, provides a considerable opportunities for risk sharing or inter-temporal smothering." What actions can be taken to control or plan for these risks? Can value be produced through risk management strategies? Explain.

11. Discuss the various financial derivatives instruments traded on organised exchanges in world financial markets.

12. "Global networking is no longer a mere metaphor for worldwide activities but now describes in very literal terms the advances in information and communication technology which have been a major driving force behind internationalisation in many areas of life, but especially in the economy. Within the economic sector, in turn, it is in the financial markets that globalisation has been particularly dynamic." Comment.

13. Critically examine the Value-at-Risk (VaR) approach.

14. "Derivatives are sometimes deliberately mispriced in order to conceal losses or to make profits by fraud"" Comment.

REFERENCES

1. Alien, S.L., and A.D. K-leinstein. *Valuing Fixed-Income Investments and Derivative Securities: Cash Flow Analysis and Calculations.* New York: New York Institute of Finance, 1991.

2. Beder, T. "VaR: Seductive but Dangerous," *Financial Analysts Journal,* 51, 5 (1995): 12-24.

3. Cumby, R., S. Figlewski, and J. Hasbrook. "Forecasting Volatilities and Correlations with EGARCH Models," *Journal of Derivatives,* 1, 2 (Winter 1993): 51-63.

4. Dowd, K. *Beyond Value at Risk: The New Science of Risk Management.* New York: Wiley, 1998.

5. Duffie, D., and J. Pan. "An Overview of Value at Risk," *Journal of Derivatives,* 4, 3 (Spring 1997): 7-49.

6. Dunbar, N. *Inventing Money: The Story of Long-Term Capital Management and the Legends Behind It.* Chichester, UK: Wiley, 2000.

7. Engle, R.F. "Autoregressive Conditional Heteroscedasticity with Estimates of the Variance of UK Inflation," *Econometrica* 50 (1982): 987-1008.

8. Frye, J. "Principals of Risk: Finding VAR through Factor-Based Interest Rate Scenarios" in *VAR: Understanding and Applying Value at Risk.* pp. 275-88. London: Risk Publications, 1997.

9. Gastineau, G.L., D.J. Smith, and R. Todd. *Risk Management, Derivatives, and Financial Analysis under SFAS No. 133.* The Research Foundation of AIMR and Blackwell Series in Finance, 2001.

10. Grinblatt, M., and F.A. Longstaff. "Financial Innovation and the Role of Derivatives Securities: An Empirical Analysis of the Treasury Strips Program," *Journal of Finance,* 55,3 (2000): 1415-36.

11. Hendricks. D. "Evaluation of Value-at-Risk Models Using Historical *data* "*Economic Policy Review,* Federal Reserve Bank of New York. 2 (April 1996): 39-69.

12. Hopper, G. "Value at Risk: A New Methodology for Measuring Portfolio Risk," *Business Review,* Federal Reserve Bank of Philadelphia, July/August 1996: 19-29.

13. Hull. J.C., and A. White. "Value at Risk When Daily Changes in Market Variables Are Not Normally Distributed," *Journal of Derivatives,* 5 (Spring 1998): 9-19.

14. Hull. John. *Options, Futures and Other Derivative Securities.* Englewood Cliffs, N.J.: Prentice-Hall, 1989.

15. Jackson, P., D.J. Maude, and W. Perraudin. "Bank Capital and Value at Risk." *Journal of Derivatives,* 4, 3 (Spring 1997): 73-90.

16. Jorion, P. "Risk Management Lessons from Long-Term Capital Management," *European Financial Management,* 6, 3 (September 2000): 277-300.

17. Jorion, P. *Big Bets Gone Bad: Derivatives and Bankruptcy in Orange County.* New York: Academic Press, 1995.

18. Jorion, P. *Value at Risk,* 3rd edn. McGraw-Hill, 2007.

19. Ju, X., and N. Pearson. "Using Value at Risk to Control Risk Taking: How Wrong Can You Be?" *Journal of Risk,* 1 (1999): 5-36.

20. Li, D.X., "On Default Correlation: A Copula Approach," *Journal of Fixed Income,* March 2000: 43-54.

21. Longin, P.M. "Beyond the VaR," *Journal of Derivatives,* 8, 4 (Summer 2001): 36-48.

22. Lowenstein, R. *When Genius Failed: The Rise and Fall of Long-Term Capital Management.* New York: Random House, 2000.

23. Marshall, C., and M. Siegel. "Value at Risk: Implementing a Risk Measurement Standard," *Journal of Derivatives* 4, 3 (Spring 1997): 91-111.

24. Miller, M.H. "Financial Innovation: Achievements and Prospects," *Journal of Applied Corporate Finance,* 4 (Winter 1992): 4-11.

25. Neftci, S.N. "Value at Risk Calculations, Extreme Events and Tail Estimation," *Journal of Derivatives*, 1, 3 (Spring 2000): 23-38.

26. Rawnsley, J.H. *Total Risk: Nick Leeson and the Fall of Barings Bank.* New York: Harper Collins, 1995.

27. Rich, D. "Second Generation VaR and Risk-Adjusted Return on Capital," *Journal of Derivatives*, 10, 4 (Summer 2003): 51-61.

28. Zhang, P.G. *Barings Bankruptcy and Financial Derivatives.* Singapore: World Scientific, 1995.

34

Options

INTRODUCTION

In 1902, a team of French archaeologists uncovered an eight-foot high slab of black stone buried in the desert sand near Susa, Iraq. Carved on the stone in ancient Babylonian script was the world's first complete set of written laws—the famous Code of Hammurabi.

Hammurabi, who lived about 3800 years ago, was the king of Babylon and in his Code he claimed his authority from the Gods. The most common punishment for breaking the Code was death. According to legal scholars, the Code was largely a revision of common law existing at the time; in other words Hammurabi was effectively rubber-stamping the individual 'eye-for-an-eye' codes of personal retribution which were then in use.

But one of Hammurabi's laws, paragraph 48, was different. It doesn't mention punishment, but only says that in the event of a crop disaster, those who owe debts need not pay any interest for one year. The Babylonians used clay tablets for writing on, and in Hammurabi's words, debtors could *'wash the debt tablet in water'*, or erase the loan contract, for the year of the crop failure.

At first sight, paragraph 48 resembles insurance. After all, it refers to debts being payable in grain, while the word 'rent' is used instead of 'interest', suggesting that a typical debtor would have been a farmer paying a mortgage on his property. In a year of crop failure, farmers suffer losses, and like a good politician Hammurabi is insuring them against being unable to pay then debts.

However, paragraph 48 is more subtle than that. Firstly, there is that issue of payment in grain, which suggests farmers were involved. But the Babylonian economy was founded on grain, and while loans were made in silver, it made sense to use grain to repay the debts because it was available everywhere.

And if there is one thing we can be sure about with grain, when the harvest fails, the price goes up because demand outstrips supply. In modern finance, we would say that debtors were 'exposed' to the grain price. This brings us to the second point. Insurance is about losses, which have to be proved before claims can be paid. Yet, paragraph 48 doesn't mention losses, and nor does it mention farmers, who after all might even benefit from inflated grain prices. So it can't be insurance.

Then what is paragraph 48 all about? When a crop failure happened, the debtors had the right to pay nothing that year. The lenders, on the other hand, had no choice in the matter: they had to do without the interest. In other words, the debtors had an option to call upon the lenders to cover their interest payments in the event of crop failure, which effectively put a cap on their grain price exposure.

Paragraph 48 is the earliest written example of an option contract, which is often mistakenly attributed to the Greek philosopher Thales, who lived 1200 years later.

Hammurabi's option derives its value both from the existence of a loan - it's worthless without one - and also from crop failures which impact the price of grain. What's missing from paragraph 48 is how crop failure was defined in practice, and one wonders how often Hammurabi himself was asked to settle disputes between lenders and borrowers seeking to 'wash their tablets'.

What does Hammurabi's option tell us about risk? The risk of crop failure hasn't been removed, but only transferred, to lenders. Being wealthy, the lenders might be better suited to take on the risk. Then again, they might not want to, but disobeying Hammurabi tended to result in excruciating death.

However, Hammurabi doesn't say what the interest rate should be on loans. More recent archaeological research has shown that there was a thriving loan market in ancient Babylon where borrowers could search for the best rate, just as homebuyers do today.

Now imagine that we are lenders in the market of Babylon, and we have just heard that Hammurabi is to make us give an option to every borrower. If we are smart, we should increase the interest rate we charge to compensate us for the extra risk. That involves pricing the option—in other words, charging today for what we might have to pay tomorrow. While there is no historical evidence the Babylonian lenders ever actually did this, the problem is similar to that tackled by Black, Merton and Scholes 3800 later.

OPTION: THE CONCEPT

An option is a type of a contract between two parties when one person grants the other person the right to buy a specific asset at a specific price within a specific time period. Alternatively, the contract may grant the other party the right to sell a specific asset at a specific price within a specific time period. The person who has received the right and thus has a decision to make is known as the option buyer since he or she must pay for the right. The person who has sold the right to the buyer and thus must respond to the buyer's decision is known as the *option writer*.

Generally, stock options are looked upon as a speculative vehicle as in any option there is a risk of loss to both contracting parties — a buyer who uses the option and a seller who makes good the option terms. The optionee might realize no benefit for services performed under the option. The corporation might be required to forego a much larger cash sum during the option period than they wished to pay in cash compensation at the date the option was granted. Yet, the expectation of market increase must be such that it outweighs the expectation of loss and thus provides a desirable speculation acceptable to both parties. It is desirable to the corporation as a means of obtaining valuable services for a minimum current cash outlay, and it is desirable to the optionee as means of obtaining a large amount of income than could otherwise be obtained on a straight cash payment basis.

USES OF OPTIONS

There are a number of reasons for being either a writer or a buyer of options. The writer assures an uncertain amount of risk for a certain amount of money, whereas the buyer assures an uncertain potential gain for a fixed cost. Such a situation can lead to a number of reasons for using options. However, fundamental to either writing or buying an option is the promise that option is fairly valued in terms of the possible outcomes. If the option is not fairly priced then, of course, an additional source of profit or loss is introduced, and the writer or buyer of such a contract may be subject to an additional handicap that will reduce his or her return.

The *reasons for writing option contracts* are varied, but three of the most common are to cash additional income on a securities portfolio, the fact that option buyers are not as sophisticated as writers, and to hedge a long position. It is sometimes argued that option writing is a *source of additional income* for the portfolio of an investor with a large portfolio of securities. Such an approach assumes that the portfolio manager can guess the direction of specific stock prices closely rough to make this strategy worth-while. What cannot be overlooked is that the writer gives up certain rights when the option is written. For example, suppose a call option is written. In this case, the writer would presumably cover the call by giving up securities from his or her portfolio. Hence, the writer is giving up any appreciation beyond the striking price plus the option premium.

Second, it is believed by some that the *buyer of options are not as sophisticated as the writers.* The proponents of this view argue that option writers are the most sophisticated participants in the securities market and view argue that option premiums simply as additional income. However, it should be held that this view pre-supposes that the buyers are *"lambs ready to be shorn"* whether this view is correct or not is unclear, but it follows that over the long-term they may find option writing an unprofitable undertaking.

There are a number of *reasons for buying options;* two of the most common are *leverage and changing the risk complexion of a portfolio.* The term leverage in connection with options indicates buyer being able to control more securities than could be done with realistic margin requirements. In other words, with the use of margins, the buyer of securities can but more securities and hopefully make a greater profit than could be done by taking a basic long position. Puts and calls can be used in much the same fashion and perhaps provide a higher return. For example, suppose an investor has Rs. 50,000 to invest in securities and that call options can be purchased for Rs. 5,000. The remaining Rs. 45,000 can be invested in short-term securities, the interest earned on the short-term securities would reduce the cost of the call options, and if the stock did appreciate, the portfolio would participate in the appreciation.

Another reason of buying options is to *change the risk complexion of a portfolio of securities.* It should be noted that this benefit of options is available not only to buyers but also to writers. Therefore, they permit the portfolio manager to undertake as much or as little risk as he or she feels is appropriate at a point of time. They also give additional flexibility in setting the amount or risk the portfolio manager is willing to accept with respect to a specific portfolio.

TYPES OF OPTIONS

There are two basic types of stock options which can be used separately or combined to derive two additional types of options. Fundamentally, the holder of an option merely possesses the right to buy or sell a specific asset. The option contract specifies between the period of time allowed to exercise this right and the price. The main types of stock options are listed below:

1. Put Option

A put is an option to sell. A put gives its holder the privilege of selling or putting — to a second party a fixed amount of some stock at a stated price on or before a predetermined date.

2. Call Option

Analogously, a call is an option to purchase; its holders has the privilege of purchasing-or-calling from a second party a fixed amount of some stock at a stated price on or before a predetermined day. The standard call contract is not by the individual originating the contract, but his broker who by market practice must be a member firm of the stock exchange. This endorsement guarantees that the contract will be fulfilled and considerably enhances its status as a negotiable instrument.

Therefore puts and calls are securities in end of themselves and can be traded as any other security is traded.

Puts and calls are almost always written on equities, although occasionally preference shares, bonds and warrants become the subject of options. Warrants are themselves a kind of call option, as are stock rights, but they are distinct from the calls that concern since that warrants are issued by corporations themselves as part of financing programmes. Puts and calls, on the other hand, can be created by any individual investor on any stock for which there is a demand for such options.

Puts and calls are the two basic options forms. In addition there are other kinds of options present in today's trading which are combination of puts and calls. These are:

(A) Spread

A spread consists of both a put and a call contract The option price at which the put or call is executed is specified in terms of a number of rupees away from the market price of the stock at time the option is granted. The put may be exercised at a specified number of rupees below the market and the call at the corresponding number of rupees above the market. For example, assume that a spread is bought on XYZ company's equity shares which permits the buyer to buy or sell 100 shares at ₹ 4 per share, or 4 points above or below the current market price within the next 90 days at a premium cost of ₹ 250. If the market price of the equity fluctuates either upward or downward by substantially more than ₹ 7.50 per share including brokerage cost per share, the owner of this contract can make a profit. The ₹ 7.50 per share is computed as follows:

Approximate per share brokerage and the taxes:	₹ 1.00
Cost of contract per 100 share:	₹ 150
Spread from cost:	₹ 4.00
Total:	₹ 7.50

If the fluctuation is less than this spread either on the upside or the downside, the investment is valueless and results in a complete loss to the purchaser.

(B) Straddle

A straddle is similar to a spread except that the execution price of either the put or call option is at the market price of the stock at the time the straddle is granted. In essence, both the straddle and the spread accomplish the same thing.

Two recent additions to the family of options in current trading are the *strip* and the *strap*. A strip is a straddle with a second put added to it having the same dimensions as the first put. A strap is a straddle with a second call added to it. These combination options appear for the most part on the supplying side of the put and the call market. Option buyers tend to buy individual puts and calls, but to obtain these options dealers frequently purchase straddles, spreads, strips and straps for writers.

Exotic Options

The flexibility of OTC derivatives contracts allows unusual contract structures to be traded, including in options. These "exotic" structures may be nonstandard and complex, but they are not necessarily rare, thinly traded, or especially risky. In a standard option, the dealer pays a fee (premium) up front, and receives an option to either buy (call option) or sell (put option) the underlying security at a specified price (strike price). This right may be exercisable only at maturity (European option) or at any time up until maturity (American option). At exercise, the payoff to the option is the difference between the strike price and the price of the underlying security (its intrinsic value). Options with simple structures such as these are known as "plain vanilla" options.

Exotic options can change any or all of these features:

(i) The option may be exercisable at several fixed points in time (Bermuda option).

(ii) The premium can be paid at maturity, rather than at initiation (break forward, Boston option).

(iii) The option can start with a delay (forward start option) (as with some employee incentive stock options).

(iv) The underlying can be another option, rather than an underlying security (compound options); for example, an option on an interest-rate cap (caption) or floor (floortion).

(v) The underlying may be another derivative, for example, a swap (swaption).

(vi) The holder may pick at some point whether the option is a call or put option (chooser option).

(vii) Barrier options are canceled (knockout) or activated (knock-in) when a price threshold is crossed.

(viii) Binary options pay a fixed amount (cash or nothing option) or full asset value (asset or nothing option).

(ix) The payoff may depend on the maximum or minimum price attained by the underlying (look back option) or on the average price of the underlying during the life of the option (Asian option).

(x) During the contract's life, the holder may be able to pick a day, and at expiration receive the maximum of the intrinsic value on that day and the intrinsic value at maturity (shout option).

(xi) The payoff may depend on the prices of several underlying securities (rainbow, basket, exchange options).

(xii) The option may have a payoff that is nonlinear in the underlying price (power caps).

(xiii) The option's payoff may be denominated in a different currency than the underlying (quanto).

(xiv) Many variations either combine one or more of these features, or amount to portfolios of options.

Exotic options raise a number of challenges for the financial institutions that trade them. They can be exceedingly challenging to price; options for which the payoff depends on the price history may not have a closed form solution for the price. In addition, they can be very challenging to hedge. Options are traditionally dynamically hedged by holding a quantity of the underlying security, which is periodically adjusted for changes in the price of the underlying security. Another approach is to hedge using a portfolio of other options constructed to automatically adjust for changes in the underlying security (static hedging). How much of the underlying security is held depends upon how the option's price responds to changes in the underlying; this response can change dramatically for exotic options. Suppose, for example, that when the price of the underlying security rises by 10 per cent, the price of an option on one unit of the underlying rises by 5 per cent in market parlance, the option's delta (change with respect to the underlying) is 0.5. A portfolio of two options, and one unit of the underlying, is then perfectly hedged. However, the value of delta changes with the price of the underlying security. For knockout options, the value of delta declines sharply to zero as the barrier is approached. This has the potential to suddenly unbalance the hedged position and cause a sudden rush of sales or purchases of the underlying security to rebalance the portfolio.

OPTION VALUATION AND PRICING

The value of a put or call depends to a large extent on the market behaviour of the equity (or other financial assets) that underlies the option. Getting a firm grip on the current and expected future value of a put or call is extremely important to option traders and investors. Similarly, to get the most from any options trading programme, it is imperative that investors have an understanding of how options are priced in the market. Continuing to use stock options as a basis of discussion, let's look now at the basic principles of option valuation and pricing, starting with a potential brief review of how profits are derived from puts and calls.

The Profit Potential of Puts and Calls

Although the quoted market price of a put or call is affected by such factors as time to expiration, stock volatility, market interest rates, and supply and demand and conditions, by far the *most* important variable is the *market price behaviour of the underlying equity*. This is the variable that derives any significant moves in the price of the option and which in turn determines the option's profit potential. Thus when the underlying stock moves up in price, *calls do well*; when the price of the underlying stock drops, *puts do well*. Such performance also explains why it is so important to get a good handle on the expected future price behaviour of a stock before an option is bought or sold (written).

The typical price behaviour is illustrated in Figure 1. The diagram on the left depicts a call, and the one on the right shows a put. The *call* diagram is constructed assuring for pay Rs.5000 for a call that carries an exercise price of Rs.50; likewise, the *put* diagram assumes that you can buy a *put* for Rs.5000 and obtain the right to sell the underlying stock at Rs.50 per share. With the call, the diagramme shows what happens to the value of the option when the price of the stock increases; with the put, it shows what happens when the price of the stock falls. Observe that a call does not gain in value until the price of the stock advances past the stated *exercise price* (Rs.50). Also, since it costs Rs.5000 to buy the call, the stock has to move up from Rs.50 to Rs.55 in order for the option investor

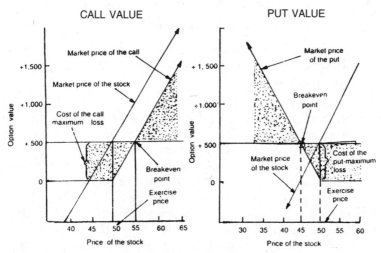

FIGURE 1: THE VALUATION PROPERTIES OF PUT AND CALL OPTIONS

to recover the premium and thereby reach a break-even situation. So long as the stock continues to rise in price, every thing from there on out is profit. Once the premium is recovered, the profit from the call position is limited only by the extent to which the stock price increases over the remaining life of the contract.

In a similar fashion, the value of a *put* is also derived from the price of the underlying stock, except their respective market prices move in opposite directions. Put remains constant until the market price of the corresponding stock drops to the exercise price (Rs.50) on the put. Then as the price continues to fall, the value of the option increases accordingly. The investor do not start making money on the investment until the price of the stock drops below the breakeven point of Rs.45 a share. Beyond that point, the *profit* from the put is defined by the extent to which the price of the underlying stock continues to fall over the remaining life of the contract.

Fundamental Value

The fundamental value of a put or call depends ultimately on the exercise price stated on the option, as well as on the prevailing market price of the underlying equity. More specifically, the *value of a call* is determined according to the following formula:

$$\text{Fundamental value of a call} = \left\{ \begin{array}{ccc} \text{Market price of} & & \text{Strike price in} \\ \text{underlying} & - & \text{the call} \\ \text{equity} & & \end{array} \right\} \times 100$$

$$V = (MP\text{-}SPC) \times 100$$

In other words, the fundamental or underlying value of a call is nothing more than the difference between the market price and strike price. It implies that a call has a value whenever the market price of the underlying equity (or financial asset) *exceeds* the strike price stipulated on the call. For instance, a call carrying a strike price of Rs. 50 on an equity presently trading at Rs.60 has a value of Rs.1,000 [(60 –50) × 100 = Rs.10 × 100]. A put, on the other hand, cannot be valued in the same way, since puts and calls allow the holder to do different things. To find the *value of a put*, simply reverse the order of the equation a bit, so that we have:

$$\text{Fundamental value of a call} = \left\{ \begin{array}{ccc} \text{Strike price} & & \text{Market price of} \\ \text{on the put} & - & \text{the undelying} \\ & & \text{equity} \end{array} \right\} \times 100$$

$$V = (SPP\text{-}MP) \times 100$$

In this case, a put has value so long as the market price of the underlying equity (or financial asset) is less *than the* strike price stipulated on the put.

In-the-Money/Out-of-the-Money

When written, options do not necessarily have to carry strike prices at the prevailing market prices of the underlying equity. And as an option subsequently trades on the listed exchanges, the price of the option will move in response to moves in the price of the underlying equity. When a call has a strike price that is less than the market price of the underlying equity, it has a positive value and is known as an *in-the-money* option. A major portion of the option price in this case is based on (or derived from) the fundamental or intrinsic value of the call. When the strike price exceeds the market price of the equity, the call has no "real" value and is known as an *out-of- the-money* option. Since the option has no intrinsic value, its price is made up solely of investment premium. These terms are much more than convenient, exotic names given to options. A put option, by the way, is in-the-money when its strike price is greater than the market price of the equity; it is out-of-the- money when the market price of the equity exceeds the strike price.

FACTORS DETERMINING OPTION PRICE

The price at which the stock under option may be put or called is the *contract prices.* Sometimes, it is referred to as the *striking price.* During the life of the contract, the contract price remains fixed, except that market practice is for the contract price to be reduced by the amount of any dividend paid or by the value of any stock right which becomes effective during the life of the contract. In purchasing an option the amount the buyer pays for the option privilege is called the *premium,* or sometimes the *option money.* In most option transactions the contract price is the stock market price prevailing at the time the option is written, and the premium becomes the variable over which buyer and seller bargain.

The variety of expiration dates and striking prices offered with option bewilders many investors. *How does anyone select the "best" expiration date and striking price?* The answer depends upon an investor's goals, forecasts of the future and factors listed below:

Volatility

Option premiums deflect the personal beliefs of both buyers and sellers. Buyers of options thrive on changes in stock prices and gladly pay premium for options on volatile stocks. The more stock prices fluctuate in the future, the better their chances, for making money. And the buyers' losses are limited to the amount of the premium. On the other hand, sellers detest volatility, since it can only work against them. As a result, option sellers usually demand much higher prices for writing options on volatile stocks. The willingness of buyers to pay higher premiums combined with the reluctance of sellers to write them produces higher premium on options of more volatile stocks.

Expiration Date

The expiration date of the option also effects the premium. The odds of a stock making a profitable move increase with time. The option buyer resembles a brand jumper. The longer the run, the better the chances of making a good jump. Because buyers benefit from the extended periods of time and sellers suffer, buyers or sellers agree to higher premiums for longer lasting options. For this reason, options are a wasting asset. As time goes on, value of the option decreases, and decline usually occurs at a faster and faster pace.

Striking Prices

Striking prices add a further complication to the analysis of options. The striking price remains the same during the entire life of the option contract The nearer this striking price is to the market price of the underlying stock, the greater the buyer's-chances of making money on the option. In effect the striking price serves as a hurdle placed in front of an investor sprinting after profits. Higher hurdles or striking prices make it more difficult for option buyers to finish the race on time. In fact, many of the runners fall flat on their faces. No wonder calls with striking prices for above the current market prices sell for so little.

Dividends

Dividends also effect option premiums. Generally speaking, firms paying high dividends seldom increase very much in price. So prospective call buyers avoid options on these stocks. Since options writers collect these dividends in addition to their premium income, they naturally prefer to write options on high dividend stocks. Buyers and sellers compromise and agree to lower premiums for high-dividend paying stocks.

Interest Rates

Interest rates have the opposite impact on premiums. At higher interest rates, options writers sacrifice considerable income by holding stocks instead of bonds. As a result, they usually demand and get higher premiums for writing options during times of high interest rates.

The impact of each of these factors depends on whether (1) the option is a put or a call and (2) the option is an American option or a European option. A summary of the effect of each factor on put and call option prices is presented in Table-1.

TABLE 1

Factors that Influence the Option Price

Factor	Effect on an increase of factor on	
	Call Price	Put Price
Current price of underlying stock	Increase	Decrease
Strike price	Decrease	Increase
Time to expiration of option	Increase	Increase
Expected price volatility	Increase	Increase
Short-term interest rate	Increase	Decrease
Anticipated cash dividends	Decrease	Increase

CHARACTERISTICS

In discussing the characteristics of options, the focus is on both the buyer and the writer because what one tends to gain, the other loses as stock price changes. This is true because the option exercise price and the expiration date do not change.

Option Buyer

Optimistic investors purchase calls, with options, they can increase their profit potential by commanding more shares directly. For example, an investor may purchase 100 equity shares of a company at ₹ 25 a share and later sell his shares at ₹ 30 a share. He would earn a gross gain of 20 per cent (5/25) on his outlay. The same investor may also purchase a listed August call option for ₹ 250 instead of buying the share. If the share price rose to ₹ 30, he would sell his option contract for ₹ 450. His gain would be 80% (200/250). The situation can be summarised as follows:

	Call Option	100 shares
March 1 bought	₹ 250	₹ 2500
May 1 sold	450	3000
Gross gain:	200	500
Percent Return	80%	20%

Option Seller

Pessimistic investors purchase puts. For example, an investor might purchase 100 shares at ₹ 232.50 a share and sell a listed call option for ₹ 1580 with an exercising price of ₹255.00. If the price does not move beyond ₹255.00 during the life of the option, the call will not be used. The investor would earn the following returns:

Buy 100 shares	₹ 23, 250
Plus Commission:	₹ 460
Total Cost	₹ 23,710
Sell May Call	₹ 1,580
Less Commission:	₹ 300
Net Proceeds	₹ 1,280
Six months Dividends	₹ 850

Total Receipts:	₹ 2,130
Six month Return:	8.98%

Naked Seller

In this case, the option seller does not own the stock but ensure that his call will be borrowed. For this, he is to deposit say about 50 percent margin with his commission broker. Thus the 50 percent margin would represent the sellers outlay and if there are no dividends to be received the returns are larger.

Deposit 50% margin:	₹ 11,625
Sell May call:	₹ 1,580
Less Commission	₹ 300
Net proceeds:	₹ 1,280
Six months returns:	11.01%

In case the price rises, the naked seller will face a loss. The option will be exercised and naked seller will be forced to purchase shares at a high market price and sell them at a low option price.

Hedging Seller

In this case, the seller establishes a price band in which he will realise a profit. Suppose a speculator believes that XYZ company is likely to increase in value. Instead of buying the stock at its current market price of ₹ 51.50, he buys an August call (giving him the right to purchase 100 shares at ₹ 50) for 2.50 a share, and simultaneously sells an XYZ August ₹ 55 call for ₹1.00 per share. The maximum loss possible on this transaction is the difference between ₹ 250 paid for the August 50 call and the ₹ 100 received from the August 55 call, or ₹ 150. Suppose that by August, the XYZ August call had climbed to 9.25 (370% increase) and the underlying stock rose to ₹ 59.25 (11.51% increase) and the August 55 call increased to ₹ 4.25 (325% increase). In closing out the spread, the investor sustains a loss of ₹ 300 on his written call (₹ 400 - ₹ 100) while earning a profit of ₹ 675 on the purchase call (₹ 925 - ₹ 250) or an overall net gain of ₹ 375 (250%).

Thus, this form of variable hedging creates a band within which an option seller can realise profits.

Appreciation Factor

Listed call options offer a new avenue of analysis — their appreciation factor. Symbolically, it is:

$$A = e/(S-W)$$
$$A = \text{Appreciation factor}$$
$$e = \text{Exercise price of the call option}$$
$$S = \text{Current stock price}$$
$$W = \text{Current option price.}$$

The appreciation factor will work well when the number of shares a call option can purchase is limited to one. When the shares are more than one, both the exercise price and the option price must be divided by the number of shares that can be purchased. For example, a XYZ Corporation August call with an exercise price of ₹ 225 can illustrate an appreciation factor computation. This call sold for ₹ 40 while the equity shares are sold for ₹ 250 per share:

$$A = e/(S-W);$$
$$A = 225/(250-40)$$
$$A = 225/210;$$
$$A = 1.07 \text{ times}$$

This appreciation factor indicates that a price rise in XYZ Corporation equity share the call to yield more than is possible with the equity. The result will be 1.07 times.

BINOMIAL MODEL

The binomial model is a continuous-time model "in the limit". It is called binomial because it assumes that during the most "period of time" share prices will go to only one of two values. Although this assumption might seem to be a strange one on which to develop a practical valuation model, it really is not if the investor thinks of a "period of time" as being very short and of the eventual expiration date as being many periods from now.

We now move on to consider option pricing formula. The basis of this valuation formula is that it is possible to construct a risk-free hedged portfolio by buying shares and writing call options on the shares[1]. As the resulting portfolio is risk free it would be expected that only a risk-free rate of return would be obtained. This then enables *the* investors to obtain a value for the call option.

A general formula for the value of a call option with one period to expiry can be written as

$$V_c = H\left[P_0 - \frac{P_l}{1+r}\right]$$

where V_c is the value of the call option with one period to expiry, r is the risk-free rate of interest, P_0 is the current share price, P_l is the lower value of the share at the end period and $H = (V_u - V_1) / (P_u - P_1)$ is the hedging ratio. V_u is the upper value of the option at the end of the period and V_1 is the lower value of the option at the end of the period; P_u is the upper value of the share at the end of the period.

In the binomial option price formula it is required to value a call one period before expiration. To illustrate, given the following information: present price of share, ₹ 10, exercise price of call option ₹ 10, risk-free interest 25 per cent, assume that the share price will either increase to ₹15 or decrease to ₹ 5 by the exercise date. It should be possible to construct a fully hedged position by buying shares and writing call option.

TABLE 2

Cash Flows in Fully Hedged Position Flows at T

		Possible share prices	
	Flows at 10	₹ 15	₹ 5
Buy one share	-10	15	5
Write two calls	+ 2C	-10	—
		5	5

Table-2 shows the cash flows at the beginning of the period and the end of the period when one share is purchased and two calls written. It can be seen that at the end of the period the net outcome will be same irrespective of whether the ₹ 15 price or the ₹ 5 price prevails. The reason for this is that if the share price at the end of the period is ₹ 15 then the share purchased will be worth ₹ 15 while the holder of the call written will require

1. This is also the base of the more rigorous Black and Scholes formula, In fact, both models are for the European call. Since traded options are of the American variety it may seem that there is more academic than practical merit in this approach. American call is an European call with the additional opportunity to exercise before expiry date. It follows that American call cannot be worth less than an European call having the same expiry date and exercise price. It implies that it never pays to exercise an American call before expiry date provided that the share does not pay dividends or the exercise price is adjusted for dividend payments. The reason for this is that, although the share price might be trading above the exercise price prior to expiry, there is still chance that the price will rise further before expiry. The American call will have two sources of value: the value of an immediate call plus the value of the chance to call from now to expiration date. Therefore provided that an American call will not pay dividends before the expiration date or the exercise price is dividend protected, it can be valued as a European call.

two shares to be delivered for which ₹ 20 will be paid. These shares will have to be purchased in the market at the price of ₹ 15 each and a total cost of ₹ 30 giving a loss of ₹ 10. However, if the price of the exercise date is ₹ 5, then the value of the one share held will be ₹ 5 and the call will go unexercised and will have a value of zero. Because the strategy results in a certain outcome whichever possible share price results, the return on the strategy should be certain return, i.e. the risk-free rate of return. We can, therefore, say

$$(10-2C)\ 1.25\ =\ 5$$
$$C\ =\ ₹\ 3$$

It can be observed from the above equation that investors have a net investment of ₹ 4 i.e. the cost of one share minus the premium received on writing two calls, and as the outcome of this investment is certain, investors would expect to earn the risk-free rate of return. In this case investors required one share for every two calls written. The share-to-option ratio is often called the hedge ratio or option date. In the example, the option rate is 0.5. Options will have to be priced in accordance with this model, otherwise opportunities would occur for dealers to earn riskless profits. Arbitrage activity would ensure that call options are priced in accordance with the formula above.

While the foregoing illustrates the principles of option valuation, it makes the non-realistic assumption that there are only two possible prices for the share at the end of the period. While it would be possible to make the example slightly more realistic, by assuming sub-periods, the calculations would become more complicated without adding greatly to the realism. Fortunately, Black and Scholes have devised an option valuation formula which assumes that a share's returns are normally distributed and this allows for a more realistic assessment of option value.

BLACK-SCHOLES MODEL

Every theory in science starts out with assumptions. When applying his laws of motion, Isaac Newton assumed that the world was frictionless. On Earth, this isn't a very realistic assumption in most situations. However, in space there is virtually no friction, and Newton could use his laws to calculate the motion of the planets - the first time this had been done.

That is how successful theories work - relegating the less important detail to the small print and focusing on the essentials. Up to Newton's time, followers of Aristotle had argued that the planets occupied a purer realm than the corrupted, imperfect Earth, and that different laws applied. Newton showed that the same laws applied to both, while friction could be brought in later on as an extra bit in the equations.

With their option formula, and more importantly the law of dynamic replication that allowed virtually any derivative on earth to be priced. Black, Scholes and Merton could claim to be the Newtons of finance. By leaving aside the details, they could take their idea from one market to the next: from options on stocks to the hidden option on crude oil prices that a company owns when it has oil drilling rights. It really was a universal law of finance.

Fischer Black and Myron Scholes developed a precise model for determining the equilibrium value of an option. The model is widely used by those who deal with options to search for situations where the market price of an option differs substantially from its fair value. In particular, the model provides rich insight into the valuation of debt relation to equity.

Assumptions

The Black Scholes option model is based on following assumptions:
   (i)   There are no transactions costs and no taxes.
   (ii) The risk from interest rate is constant.
   (iii) The market operates continuously.
   (iv) The share prices are continuous, i.e. there are no jumps in the share prices; if one

plots a graph of the share price against time, the graph must be smooth. To be more specific, the share price is log normally distributed for any finite time interval.

(v) The share pays no dividends.

(vi) The option is of European type, that is, options that can be exercised only at maturity.

(vii) Shares can be sold short without penalty and short sellers receive the full proceeds from the transaction.

Given these assumptions, the equilibrium value of an option can be determined. Should the actual price of the option differ from that given by model, the investor could establish a riskless hedged position and a return in excess of the short-term interest rate. As enterprise entered the scene, the excess return would eventually be driven out and the price of the option would equal the value given by the model.

The Specific Model

The Black-Scholes formula for estimating the fair value of a call option (V_c) is

$$V_c = P_s[Nd_1] - \frac{P_x}{e^{(RF)(T)}}[N_{d_2}]$$

$$d_1 = \frac{I_n\left[\frac{P_s}{P_x}\right] + T\left[RF + \frac{\sigma^2}{2}\right]}{\sigma\sqrt{T}}$$

$$d_2 = \frac{I_n\left[\frac{P_s}{P_x}\right] + T\left[RF - \frac{\sigma^2}{2}\right]}{\sigma\sqrt{t}}$$

$$= d_1 - \sigma\sqrt{T}$$

and where P_s = the current price of the share, P_x = the exercise price of the call, $e = 2.7183$, RF = the continuously compounded annual risk-free rate, σ = the standard deviation of the continuously compounded annual rate of return of the share, I_n = the natural log of the bracketed number, T = the time remaining to expiration on an annual basis, and N_{d1} and N_{d2} = the value of the cumulative normal distribution at d_1 and d_2.

To illustrate, consider XYZ share to value a call option. Assume P_s = ₹ 68.125, P_x = ₹ 60.00, RF = 0.1325 per year, and T = 2 months. In addition, the estimated continuous annual standard deviation of returns on XYZ to be 0.4472 (σ^2 = 02). First, d_1 and d_2 would be:

$$d_1 = \frac{I_n\left[\frac{68.125}{60.00}\right] + 2/12\left[0.1325 + \frac{0.2}{2}\right]}{0.4472\sqrt{2/12}} = 0.91$$

$$d_2 = \frac{I_n\left[\frac{68.125}{60.00}\right] + 2/12\left[0.1325 - \frac{0.2}{2}\right]}{0.4472\sqrt{2/12}} = 0.72$$

Second, the value of N_{d1} and N_{d2} must be found. These represent the cumulative probability of the normal standard distribution from $-\infty$ to d_1 and from $-\infty$ to $d_{2,}$ respectively. Consider first d_1. The cumulative probability below the zero mean of the standard normal distribution is 50 percent. The value of d_1 is 0.91, meaning it is 0.91 standard deviation above the zero mean. If we refer to Table 3, which provides the cumulative probabilities of various standard deviations, we find that a standard deviation of 0.91 corresponds to a cumulative probability of 0.3186. In total, N_{d1} would be 05+ 0.3186 = 0.8186. Using a similar procedure for d_2 equal to 0.72 provides an N_{d2}=0.7642. Finally, we can calculate the call option's price by substituting in the equation:

$$V_c = ₹68.125(0.8186(-\frac{₹60}{2.7183^{(0.1325)(0.16667)}}(0.7642)$$

$$= ₹ 10.92$$

TABLE 3

An entry in the table is the proportion under the entire curve which is between $d=0$ and a positive value of d. Areas for negative values of d are obtained by symmetry

d	.00	.01	.02	.03	.04	.05	.06	.07	.08	.09
0.0	.0000	.0040	.0080	.0120	.0160	.0199	.0239	.0279	.0319	.0359
0.1	.0398	.0438	.0478	.0517	.0557	.0596	.0636	.0714	.0675	.0753
0.2	.0793	.0832	.0871	.0910	.0948	.0987	.1026	.1103	.1064	.1141
0.3	.1179	.1217	.1255	.1293	.1331	.1368	.1406	.1480	.1443	.1517
0.4	.1554	.1591	.1628	.1664	.1700	.1736	.1772	.1808	.1844	.1879
0.5	.1915	.1950	.1985	.2019	.2054	.2088	.2123	.2157	.2190	.2224
0.6	.2257	.2291	.2324	.2357	.2389	.2422	.2454	.2486	.2517	.2549
0.7	.2580	.2611	.2642	.2673	.2703	.2734	.2764	.2794	.2823	.2852
0.8	.2881	.2910	.2939	.2967	.2995	.3023	.3051	.3078	.3106	.3133
0.9	.3195	.3186	.3212	.3238	.3289	.3264	.3315	.3340	.3365	.3389
1.0	.3413	.3438	.3461	.3485	.3508	.3531	.3554	.3577	.3599	.3621
1.1	.3643	.3665	.3686	.3708	.3729	.3749	.3770	.3790	.3810	.3830
1.2	.3849	.3869	.3888	.3907	.3925	.3944	.3980	.3962	.3997	.4015
1.3	.4032	.4049	.4066	.4082	.4099	.4115	.4131	.4147	.4162	.4177
1.4	.4192	.4207	.4222	.4236	.4251	.4265	.4279	.4292	.4306	.4319
1.5	.4332	.4345	.4357	.4370	.4382	.4394	.4406	.4418	.4429	.4441
1.6	.4452	.4463	.4474	.4484	.4495	.4505	.4515	.4525	.4535	.4545
1.7	.4554	.4564	.4573	.4582	.4591	.4599	.4608	.4616	.4625	.4633
1.8	.4641	.4649	.4656	.4664	.4671	.4678	.4686	.4693	.4699	.4706
1.9	.4313	.4719	.4726	.4732	.4738	.4744	.4750	.4756	.4761	.4767
2.0	.4772	.4778	.4783	.4788	.4793	.4798	.4803	.4808	.4812	.4817
2.1	.4821	.4826	.4830	.4834	.4838	.4842	.4846	.4850	.4854	.4857
2.2	.4861	.4864	.4868	.4871	.4875	.4878	.4881	.4884	.4887	.4890
2.3	.4893	.4896	.4898	.4901	.4904	.4906	.4609	.4911	.4913	.4916
2.4	.4918	.4920	.4922	.4925	.4927	.4929	.4931	.4932	.4934	.4936
2.5	.4938	.4940	.4941	.4943	.4945	.4946	.4948	.4949	.4951	.4952
2.6	.4953	.4955	.4956	.4957	.4959	.4960	.4961	.4962	.4963	.4964
2.7	.4965	.4966	.4967	.4968	.4969	.4970	.4971	.4972	.4973	.4974
2.8	.4974	.4975	.4976	.4977	.4977	.4978	.4979	.4979	.4980	.4981
2.9	.4981	.4982	.4982	.4983	.4984	.4984	.4985	.4985	.4986	.4986
3.0	.4987	.4987	.4887	.4988	.4988	.4989	.4989	.4989	.4990	.4990

Dividend Adjustment

Cash dividend have three possible impacts on call valuation. *First,* if the dividends are large enough, the calls might be exercised early. *Second,* if dividends are unknown, risk-free hedge portfolio cannot be formed. For these reasons, the calls cannot be valued without relying on investor preference models such as the capital asset pricing model.

However, both these problems are relatively minor for most call options. The *third* case consists of known cash dividends which are not large enough to threaten an early exercise. If this is true, a relatively simple adjustment can be made to the Black-Scholes model.

To illustrate, let D_t represent a known cash dividend to be paid on day t from now. There may be one or more D, values, let only those paid during the option's life are considered. The Black-Scholes model can still be used, but now with an adjusted stock price P^*_s:

$$P^*_s = P_s - \sum_{t=1}^{T} D_t / e^{RF \times t}$$

If known cash dividends equal to ₹ 2.00 are to be paid exactly one and two months from now:

$$P^*_s = ₹\ 68.125 - ₹\ 2.00\ /e^{0.1325\ (0.8333)} - ₹\ 2.00/e\ 0.1325\ (0.16666)$$

$$= ₹\ 64.19$$

Put Valuation

The valuation of an European put can be found by inserting the Black-Scholes call price into the put-call parity model. The result is:

$$P_p = -P_s N_{-d_1} + \frac{P_x}{e^{RF \times T}} N_{-d_2}$$

The cumulative normal density function is evaluated at negative d_1 and d_2 values.

Assume that the stock price is ₹ 40, the put exercise price is ₹ 40, the expiration date is 4 months, the continuous risk- free interest rate is 12%, and the standard deviation of continuously compound stock returns is 30% per year

$$d_1 = \frac{In(₹40 / 40) + 0.12(1 / 3 + 0.09 / 2)}{0.3\sqrt{1/3}}$$

$$= 0.26$$

$$N_{-d1} = 0.3974$$

$$d_2 = 0.26 - 0.3\ \sqrt{1/3} = 0.09$$

$$N_{-d2} = 0.4641$$

$$P_p = -₹\ 40\ (0.3974) + \frac{₹\ 40}{e^{(0.12)(1/3)}} - (0.4641) = ₹\ 1.94$$

DELTA

When options traders or analysts get together, they almost certainly use the term delta early in their conversation. Deltas are an important by-product of the Black-Scholes model, and they provide particularly useful information to investors who use options in portfolios.

Delta is defined as the change in option premium expected from a small change in the strike price, all other things being the same. Symbolically,

$$\Delta = \frac{\Delta C}{\Delta S}$$

where ΔS is a small change in stock price and ΔC is the corresponding change in the call price.

Consider a call option whose delta is 0.6. Suppose that the option price is ₹ 10 and the strike price is ₹ 100. Suppose an investor who has sold 20 option contracts, that is, options to buy 2000 shares. The investor's position could be hedged by buying 0.6×2000 = 1, 200 shares. The gain (loss) on the option position would tend to be offset by the loss (gain) on the stock position. For example, if the stock price goes up by ₹ 2 (producing a gain of ₹ 2, 400 on the shares purchased), the option price will tend to go up by $0.6 \times ₹ 2$ = ₹ 1.2 (producing a loss of ₹ 2, 400 on the options written); if the stock price goes down by ₹ 2 (producing a loss of ₹ 2, 400 on the shares purchased), the option price will tend to go down by ₹ 0.60 (producing a gain of ₹ 2, 400 on the options written).

In the example, the delta of the investor's option is $0.6 \times (-2, 000) = -1, 200$. In other words the investor loses $1, 200 \Delta S$ when the stock price increases by ΔS. The delta of the stock by definition 1.0 and the long position in 1, 200 shares has a delta of+ 1, 200. The delta of the investor's overall position is, therefore, zero. The delta of the asset position offsets the delta of the option position. A position with a delta of zero is referred to as being delta neutral. But delta neutral remains for a relatively short period of time. Black-Scholes valued options by setting up a delta-neutral position and argued that the return on the position should be the risk-free interest rate.

THETA

The *theta of* a portfolio of option, θ, *is the rate of change of the value of the portfolio as time passes with all else remaining the same.* It is sometimes referred to a *time decay of* the portfolio. Theta is almost always negative for an option. (An exception to this could be an in-the-money european put option on a nondividend-paying stock or in-the-money euro-pean call option on a currency with a very high interest rate). This is because as the time to maturity decreases, the option tends to become less valuable.

GAMMA

The gamma of a portfolio on an underlying assets is *the rate of change of the portfolio's delta with respect to the price of the underlying asset.* If gamme is small, delta changes only very slowly, and adjustments to keep a portfolio delta neutral would only be made relatively infrequently. However, if gamma is large in absolute terms, delta is highly sensitive to the price of the underlying asset. It is then quite risky to leave a delta- neutral portfolio unchanged for any length of time.

VEGA

Vega, also referred to as *Kappa* or as Sigma or as *Lambda*, of a portfolio of options is the *rate of change of the value of the portfolio with respect to the volatility of the underlying asset.* If vega is high in absolute terms, volatility changes have relatively little impact on the value of the portfolio.

If a hedger requires a portfolio to be born gamma and vega neutral, at least two traded options dependent on the underlying asset must be used. To illustrate, consider a portfolio that is delta neutral, has a gamma of –5, 000 and a vega of –8, 000. Suppose that a traded option has a gamma of 0.5 and a vega of 2.0 and a delta of 0.6. The portfolio can be traded vega neutral by including a long position in 4, 000 traded options. This would increase delta to 2, 400 and require that 2, 400 units of the asset be sold to maintain delta neutrality. The gamma of the portfolio would change from –5000 to –3000.

To make the portfolio gamma and vega neutral, we suppose that there is a second traded option with a gamma of 0.7, a vega of 1.2 and a delta of 0.5. If W_1 and W_2 are the amounts of the two traded options included in the portfolio, we require that

$$-5, 000+ 0.5\ W_1+ 0.8\ W_2 = 0$$
$$-8, 000+ 2.0\ W_1+ 1.2\ W_2 = 0$$

The solution to these equations is $W_1 = 400, W_2 = 6, 000$. The portfolio can, therefore, be made gamma and vega neutral by including 400 of the first traded options and 6, 000 of the second traded option. The delta of the portfolio after the addition of the positions in me two traded options is $400 \times 0.6+ 6, 000 \times 05 = 3, 240$. Hence, 3, 240 units of the assets would have to be sold to maintain delta stability.

RHO

The rho of a portfolio of options is *the rate of change of the value of the portfolio with respect to the interest rate*. It measures the sensitivity of the value of a portfolio to interest rates.

Theoretically the option traders are continually rebalancing their portfolios to maintain delta neutrality, gamma neutrality, vega neutrality and so on but in practice transaction costs make frequent rebalancing very expensive. Rather than trying to eliminate all risks, an option trader usually concentrates on assessing risks and deciding whether they are acceptable. Portfolio managers are sometimes interested in creating put options synthetically for the purposes of insuring an equity portfolio. They can do this by trading index futures on the portfolio or by trading the portfolio.

The performance of derivatives markets can be analysed on the basis of various parameters like prices, turnover, open interest and cost of carry. The interplay of prices, volumes and open interest indicates the health of the market. Generally, if prices, volumes and open interest are rising, the market is healthy. If the prices are rising, while volume and open interest are falling, then the market is weakening. Volatility is one of the important factors, which is taken into account while pricing options. It is a measure of the amount and speed of price changes, in either direction. Everybody would like to know what future volatility is going to be. Since it is not possible to know future volatility, one tries to estimate it. One way to do this is to look at historical volatility over a certain period of time and try to predict the future movement of the underlying. Alternatively, one could work out implied volatility by entering all parameters into an option pricing model and then solving for volatility. For example, the Black Scholes model solves for the fair price of the option by using the following parameters—days to expiry, strike price, spot price, volatility of underlying, interest rate, and dividend. This model could be used in reverse to arrive at implied volatility by putting the current price of the option prevailing in the market.

Putting it simply, implied volatility is the market's estimate of how volatile the Underlying will be from the present until the option's expiration, and is an important "input for pricing options—when volatility is high, options premiums are relatively expensive; when volatility is low, options premiums are relatively cheap. However, implied volatility estimate can be biased, especially if they are based upon options that are thinly traded.

INDEX OPTIONS

Not all options are written on individual issues of equity. In recent years many new options have been created that have an underlying asset something other than the equity of a particular company. Puts and calls are written on major stock market indexes. The underlying security in this case is the specific market index. When the market index moves in one direction or another, the value of the index option moves accordingly. Since there are no stocks or other financial assets lacking these options, settlement is defined in terms of cash.

Investors who choose to exercise an index option must notify their brokers before certain cutoff time established by their brokerage firm. Contracts size for index options are determined by multiplying the level of index by a multiplier specified by the exchange on which the option is traded. The premium (price) of an index option times the applicable multiplier indicates the total amount paid.

Eligibility Criteria of Stocks

i) The stock shall be chosen from amongst the top 500 stocks in terms of average daily market capitalisation and average daily traded value in the previous six months on a rolling basis.

ii) The stock's median quarter-sigma order size over the last six months shall be not less than ₹ 1 lakh. For this purpose, a stock's, quarter-sigma order size shall mean the order size (in value terms) required to cause a change in the stock price equal to one-quarter of a standard deviation.

iii) The market wide position limit in the stock shall not be less than ₹ 50 crore The marker wide position limit (number of shares) shall be valued taking the closing prices of stocks in the underlying cash market on the date of expiry of contract in the month. The market wide position limit of open position (in terms of the number of underlying stock) on futures and option contracts on a particular underlying stock shall be lower of :

    a) 30 times the average number of shares traded daily, during the previous calendar month, in the relevant underlying security in the underlying segment, OR

    b) 20% of the number of shares held by non-promoters in the relevant underlying security i.e. free-float holding.

iv) If an existing security fails to meet the eligibility criteria for three months consecutively, then no fresh month contract shall be issued on that security,

v) However, the existing unexpired contracts may be permitted to trade till and new strikes may also be introduced in the existing contract months.

Selection Criteria for Unlisted Companies

For unlisted companies coming out with initial public offering, if the net public offer is ₹ 500 crore or more, then the Exchange may consider introducing stock options and stock futures on such stocks at the time of listing in the cash market.

Eligibility Criteria of Index

i) Options contracts on an index can be introduced if all the eligible stocks constitute at least 80% weightage in the index. However, no single ineligible stock in the index shall have a weightage of more than 5% in the index. The index on which futures and options contracts are permitted shall be required to comply with the eligibility criteria on a continuous basis.

ii) The above criteria is applied every month, if the index fails to meet the eligibility criteria for three months consecutively, then no fresh month contract shall be issued on that index, However, the existing unexpired contacts shall be permitted to trade till expiry and new strikes may also be introduced in the existing contracts.

Strike Prices for Option Contracts

NSE introduces option strikes on a daily basis based on the price of the underlying The number of strikes provided in options on Nifty index is related to the range in which previous day's closing value of Nifty index falls.

With regard to options on stocks, CNX IT index and Bank Nifty index the Exchange provides a minimum of seven strike prices for every option type (i.e Call & Put) during the trading month. At any time, there are atleast three strikes in-the-money (ITM), three strikes out-of-the-money (OTM) and one strike at-the-money (ATM).

Nifty Index Level	Strike Interval	Scheme of strikes to be introduced (ITM-ATM-OTM)
upto 1500	10	3-1-3
>1500 upto 2000	10	5-1-5
>2000 upto 2500	10	7-1-7
>2500	10	9-1-9

Settlement of Options Contracts on Index or Individual Securities

Options contracts have three types of settlements, daily premium settlement, interim prercise settlement in the case of option contracts on securities and final settlement.

i) **Daily Premium Settlement for Options:** Buyer of an option is obligated to pay the premium towards the options purchased by him. Similarly, the seller of an option is entitled to receive the premium for the option sold by him. The premium payable amount and the premium receivable amount are netted to compute the net premium payable or receivable amount for each client for each option contract. The CMs who have a premium payable position are required to pay the premium amount to NSCCL which in turn passed on to the members who have a premium receivable position. This is known as daily premium settlement. CMs are also responsible to collect and settle for the premium amounts from the TMs and their clients clearing and settling through them. The pay-in and pay-out of the premium settlement is on T+1 day. The premium payable amount and premium receivable amount are directly credited/debited to the CMs clearing bank account. I

ii) **Interim Exercise Settlement:** Interim exercise settlement takes place only for option contracts on individual securities. An investor can exercise his in- the money options at any time during trading hours, through his trading member. Interim exercise settlement is effected for such options at the close of the trading hours, on the day of exercise. Valid exercised option contracts are assigned to short positions in the option contract with the same series (i.e. having the same underlying, same expiry date and same strike price), on a random basis, at the client level. The CM who has exercised the option receives the exercise settlement value per unit of the option from the CM who has been assigned the option contract.

iii) **Final Exercise Settlement:** Final Exercise settlement is effected for option positions at in the money strike prices existing at the close of trading hours, on the expiration day of an option contract. All long positions at in-the-money strike prices are automatically assigned to short positions in option contracts with the same series on a random basis. Final settlement loss/profit amount for option contracts on Index debited/credited to the relevant CMs clearing bank account onT+1 day. Final settlement loss/profit amount for option contracts on Individual Securities is debited/ credited to the relevant CMs clearing bank account on T+2 day. Open positions, in option contracts, cease to exist after their expiration day.

PORTFOLIO INSURANCE

In the mid 1980s one of the most popular uses of options, procuring portfolio insurance, was developed. Consider an investor who holds a highly diversified portfolio. This investor would like to benefit from any upward movements that may occur in the stock market but would like to be protected from any downward movement. Portfolio insurance is a strategy that may allow investors to alter the amount of risk he or she is willing to accept by giving up some return. In other words, portfolio insurance is a *strategy to protect the value of the portfolio of assets. If the value of assets declines, the insurance or hedge will increase in value to help offset the decline in price of hedged assets. If the price of the assets increases, the increase of the insured portfolio will be less than the increase in the asset but will nevertheless still increase.*

Table 4 illustrates how portfolio insurance works. In this example, the underlying asset is purchase for ₹ 100 and ₹ 5 is spent on portfolio insurance. The minimum amount that the insured investor can realise is ₹ 95, but the uninsured portfolio can fall in value to a low of ₹ 70 if the market falls. If the value of the asset increases, the value of the insured portfolio will increase, but at a smaller rate.

Table 4 shows the three properties of an insured portfolio:

(1) The loss is limited to a prescribed level.
(2) The rate of return on the insured portfolio will be a predictable percentage of the rate of return on the uninsured portfolio.
(3) The investments of the portfolio are restricted to a market index and cash. The expected return on the market index is above the expected return from holding cash, and the insurance is fairly priced. This guarantees that the insured portfolio has a higher expected return than the uninsured portfolio.

In general, portfolio insurance can be thought of as holding two portfolios. The first portfolio can be viewed as the safe or riskless portfolio with value equal to the level of protection desired. This level is called *the floor and* is the lowest value the portfolio can have. For certain strategies this can be held constant or allowed to change over time as market conditions or needs change. The second portfolio consists of difference between the total value of the portfolio and the floor, commonly called *the portfolio cushion.* These assets consist of a leveraged position in risky assets. To insure the portfolio, the cushion

TABLE 4
Mechanics of Portfolio Insurance

Initial investment	₹ 100	
Cost of portfolio insurance	–₹ 5	
Amount of investment going toward securities	95	
Amount invested	= ₹ 100	

Value of Portfolio at year end (in ₹)	Return on uninsured Portfolio (%)	Value of Insured Portfolio (₹)	New return on Insured Portfolio (%)
70	−30	95	−5
75	−25	95	−5
80	−20	95	−5
85	−15	95	−5
90	−10	95	−5
95	−5	95	−5
100	0	95	−5
105	5	100	0
110	10	105	5
115	15	110	10
120	20	115	15
125	25	120	20
130	30	125	25

should be managed so as to fall below zero in value because of the limited-liability property of equity. Table-5 shows the relationship between the total value of the portfolio, the cushion, and the floor. The actual investment or allocation of the portfolio funds between risky and risk-free assets is determined by changing market conditions or the changing requirements of the investor.

TABLE 5
Components of an Insured Portfolio Valued at ₹10,000

Total Portfolio Value ₹10, 000	Asset Allocation ₹10, 000
Cushion ₹2000	Risky, Assets ₹ 5, 000
Floor ₹ 8000	Risk-free Assets ₹ 5000

A simple example of changing the mix between risky and risk- free assets in response to market changes offers the opportunity to demonstrate the dynamic nature of portfolio insurance. As shown in Table 5, half the current portfolio is invested in risky assets and half in risk-free assets. The exposure at this point is ₹ 5000. The cushion is ₹ 2000. If this is a reasonable relationship that the investor wishes to maintain, the relationship between these two, defined as the *multiple,* can be calculated:

$$\text{Multiple} = \frac{\text{Exposure}}{\text{Cushion}}$$

$$M = \frac{E}{C}$$

$$\frac{₹5,000}{₹2,000} = 2.5$$

As the market for the risky assets changes, the exposure and the cushion values change, causing a change in the multiple. Given a predetermined trigger or change in multiple, the portfolio manager can trade to restore the balance between the cusion and the exposure. If, for example, the market value of the risky assets rises 20 percent, the value of the cushion increases to ₹ 3000 and the value of the risky assets rises to ₹ 6000. The total value of the portfolios in the value of risky assets plus the value of the risk-free assets (₹ 5000+ ₹ 6000 or ₹ 11, 000). The value of the floor remains at ₹ 8000 so that the cusion goes to ₹ 3000 (₹ 11, 000 – ₹ 8000). The multiple has fallen to:

$$M = \frac{E}{C} = \frac{₹6,000}{₹3,000} = 2$$

If the target multiple is 2.5, an adjustment must be made by the investor, who must sell some of the risk-free assets and purchase risky assets until the multiple is 2.5. Hence, the investor needs to rebalance the portfolio so that ₹ 7, 500 is invested in risky assets and ₹ 3, 500 is invested in risk-free assets. This mix will restore the multiple to the desired level of 2.5.

$$M = \frac{E}{C} = \frac{₹7,500}{₹3,000} = 2.5$$

Table-6 shows the portfolio after rebalancing.

TABLE 6

Components of an Insured Portfolio after a Market Rise

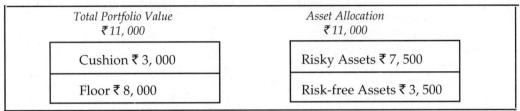

Increasing the portfolio's risky assets as the market rises allows the investor to participate in the bull market. As long as the market continues its rise. the investor continues to shift assets to the risky asset portfolio in the market gain. However, when the market turns bearish and begins to go down, the investor needs to sell off risky assets and invest in risk-free assets. For example, if the market declined by 16-2/3 per cent back to its original level at the beginning of this example, the value of the risky assets would be ₹ 6250. At this new level the multiple would be:

$$M = \frac{E}{C} = \frac{6,250}{1,750} = 3.56$$

The target multiple of 2.5 is below the actual multiple of 3.56, so the investor must sell some of the risky assets and place the proceeds into risk-free assets. The total value of the portfolio has fallen to ₹ 9, 750. The value of the cushion has fallen to 1750. In order to have a multiple of 2.5 the risky assets have to be reduced to:

$$M = \frac{E}{1750} \times 2.5$$

$$E = ₹ 4, 375$$

Hence ₹ 1, 875 of the risky assets must be sold and this amount must be invested in the risk-free assets. Table-7 shows the position of the insured portfolio after this rebalancing.

TABLE 7

Components of an Insured Portfolio Rebalanced after a Market Fall

Total Portfolio Value ₹ 9,750	Asset Allocation ₹ 9,750
Cushion ₹ 1,750	Risky Assets ₹ 3,375
Floor ₹ 8,000	Risk-free Assets ₹ 5,375

As the market falls, the investor sells off risky assets and invests the proceeds in risk-free assets, thereby reducing exposure to a falling market. In general this strategy can best be described as run *with your winners and cut your losses*. Underlying this discussion are the assumptions that the rise and fall of the market takes place over a time interval long enough for the investor to rebalance the position, and that the market has sufficient liquidity to absorb the value of the risky assets.

PUT-CALL PARITY RELATIONSHIP

There is a relationship between the price of a call option and the price of a put option on the same underlying instrument with the same strike prices and the same expiration date. To see this relationship, commonly referred to as the put-call parity relationship, let us assume a put and call option on the same underlying stock (stock XYZ), with month to expiration and with a strike price of ₹100. The price of the underlying stock is assumed to be ₹ 100. The call price and put price are assumed to be ₹ 5 and ₹ 3, respectively. Consider this strategy:

Buy stock XYZ at price of ₹ 100.
Sell a call option at a price of ₹ 5.
Buy a put option at a price of ₹ 3.
The strategy involves:

Long stock XYZ.
Short the call option.
Long the put option.

Table-8 shows the profit and loss profile at the expiration date for this strategy for selected stock prices. For the long stock position, there is no profit. That is because at a price above ₹ 100, stock XYZ will be called from the investor at a price of ₹ 100, and at a price below 100, stock XYZ will be put by the investor at a price of ₹ 100. No matter what stock XYZ's price is at the expiration date, this strategy will produce a profit of ₹ 2 without anybody making any net investment. Ignoring (1) the cost of financing the long position in stock XYZ and the long position and (2) the return from investing the proceeds from the sale of the call, this situation cannot exist in an efficient market. By implementing the strategy to capture the ₹ 2 profit, the actions of market participants will have one or more of the following consequences which tend to eliminate the ₹ 2 profit: (1) the price of the stock **XYZ** will increase, (2) the call option price will drop, and/or (3) the put option price will drop.

TABLE 8

Profit/Loss Profile for a Strategy involving a long position in Stock XYZ, Short Call Option Position, and Long Put option position

Assumptions:

Price of stock XYZ	= ₹ 100
Call option price	= ₹ 5
Put option price	= ₹ 3
Strike price	= ₹ 100
Time to expiration	= 1 month

Price of Stock XYZ at expirate date	Profit from stock XYZ*	Price Received for call	Price paid for put	Overall Profit
₹ 150	0	5	−3	2
0	5	−3	2	
120	0	5	−3	2
110	0	5	−3	2
100	0	5	−3	2
90	0	5	−3	2
80	0	5	−3	2
70	0	5	−3	2

* There is no profit, because at price above ₹ 100, stock XYZ will be called from the investor at price of ₹ 100, and at a price below ₹ 100, stock XYZ will be put by the investor at a price of ₹ 100.

Assuming stock XYZ's price does not change, the call price and the put price will tend toward equality. However, this is true only when we ignore the time value of money (financing cost, opportunity cost, cash payments, and reinvestment income). Also, the illustration does no. consider the possibility of early exercise of the option. Thus, we have been considering a put-call parity relationship applicable for *only* European options.

It can be shown that the put-call parity relationship for an option where the underlying stock makes cash dividend is:

Put option price - call option price = present value of the strike price+ present value of dividends - price of underlying stock.

This relationship is actually the put-call parity relationship for European options; it is approximately true for American options. If this relationship does not hold, arbitrage opportunities exist. That is, portfolios consisting of long and short positions in the stock and related options that provide an extra return with (practical) certainty will exist.

REVIEW PROBLEMS

1. Assume that call options on XYZ Company are to expire today. They have an exercise price of ₹ 70, the share is trading at ₹ 65, and the option is selling at ₹ 7. What is the arbitrage?

Ans:

Write a call option for	₹ 7
Buy the equity for	₹ 65
Hold option open for exercise and receive	₹ 70
Net Arbitrage profit	₹ 12

The value of this call should be zero since it is the expiration date and the equity price is less than the exercise price.

2. You wish to purchase a call option on a local warehouse having an expiration date of one year and an exercise price of ₹ 10,00,000. The warehouse owner will not sell you such an option but is willing to sell the warehouse for ₹ 11,00,000. The current risk-free interest rate is 9% per year, and insurance on a one-year, ₹ 10,00,000 loan would be ₹ 10,000. How would you create a synthetic call option on the warehouse?

Ans:

Buy the warehouse	-	₹ 11,00,000
Obtain a loan		₹ 9,17,431.2
		(PV of ₹ 10,00,000 at 9%)
Purchase insurance	-	₹ 10,000
Net cost of the synthetic call	-	₹ 1,92,568.8

3. Consider the following options on a single stock:

	Calls		Put C
	A	B	
Months of expiration	3	9	3
Continuous yearly risk-free rate (R₁) (Treasury Bills)	10.00%	10%	10.00%
Discrete yearly R_F	10.52%	1052%	10.52%
Standard Deviation of stock returns	40%	40%	40%

Exercise price	₹ 55	₹ 55	₹ 55
Option price	₹ 2.56	—	₹ 6.20
Stock price	₹ 50	₹ 50	₹ 50
Cash Dividend	₹ 0	₹ 0	₹ 0

(a) Why should call B sell for more than call A?

(b) Is the put-call parity model working for options A and C?

(c) How would you trade call A, the stock, and risk-free security in order to replicate the expiration date outcomes of put C?

(d) Calculate the Black-Scholes values of call A and call B.

(e) Interpret what N_{d1} and N_{d2} mean.

Ans:

(a) Call B has longer time to expiration. There is a greater chance that the call will be exercised at a positive value.

(b) ₹ $50 - ₹ 55/ (1.1052^{0.25}) = -₹ 3.64$

Actual difference = ₹ $2.56 - ₹ 6.20 = -₹ 3.64$ Therefore, put-call parity is working.

(c) Buy 1.0 call, sell sort 1.0 stock, but debt now worth ₹ $55/ (1.1052^{0.25})$.

(d) Call A Data

$$d_1 = \frac{\ln (50/55) + 0.25(0.10 + 0.4^2/2)}{0.4\sqrt{0.25}} = -0.25$$

$$d_2 = \frac{\ln (50/55) + 0.25(0.10 + 0.4^2/2)}{0.4\sqrt{0.25}} = -0.45$$

$$N_{d1} = 0.5 - 0.0987 = 0.4013$$

$$N_{d2} = 0.5 - 0.1736 = 0.3264$$

$$V_c = ₹ 50 (0.4013) - \frac{₹ 55}{e^{(0.1)(0.25)}} (0.3264) = ₹ 2.56$$

Call B Data

$$d_1 = \frac{\ln (50/55) + 0.75(0.1 + 0.4^2/2)}{0.4\sqrt{0.75}} = -0.11$$

$$d_2 = d_1 - \sigma\sqrt{T} = -0.23$$

$$N_{d1} = 0.5 + 0.0438 = 0.5438$$

$$N_{d2} = 0.5 - 0.091 = 0.409$$

$$V_c = ₹ 50 (0.5438 - \frac{₹ 55}{e^{(0.1)(0.75)}} (0.409) = ₹ 6.32$$

(e) To replicate the instantaneous payoff of the call, one shall buy N_{d1} shares and issue N_{d2} units of debt which is now worth P_x/e^{RfxT}

4. Consider the information provided below

(a) Calculate the Black-Scholes value of each option.

(b) Taking call A and put E have identical terms, use the put-call parity model to value the put, given the Black-Scholes value of call A. Comment on why the put's value is the same as found in part (a).

(c) Interpret what the term Nd_1 and Nd_2 mean for call A and put E.

	Call Options				Put Options
	A	B	C	D	E
Current Market Price of:					
Option	₹ 16.12	₹ 10.62	₹ 8.31	₹ 10.50	₹ 7.25
Stock	₹ 80	₹ 80	₹ 80	₹ 80	₹ 80
Option Information:					
Exercise Price	₹ 70	₹ 80	₹ 90	₹ 90	₹ 70
Months to Expiration	3	3	3	6	3
Market Information:					
Continuous yearly risk-free return, R_f -Expected cash Dividends	12%	12%	12%	12%	12%
Standard Deviation of	0	0	0	0	0
Stock Returns	60%	60%	60%	60%	60%

Title row: *Options on XYZ Stock*

Ans:

(a) For call A:

$d_1 = (0.13353 + 0.075)/(0.3) = 0.70$

$N_{d1} = 0.7580$

$d_2 = (0.13353 - 0.015)/(0.3) = 0.40$

$N_{d2} = 0.6554$

$$V_c = ₹\ 80\ (0.7580) - \frac{₹70}{e^{(0.12)(0.25)}}\ (0.6554)$$

$$= ₹\ 16.12$$

For Call B:

$d_1 = (0.0 + 0.075)/(0.3) = 0.25$

$N_{d1} = 0.5987$

$d_2 = (0.0 - 0.015)/(0.3) = -0.05$

$N_{d2} = 0.48$

$$V_c = ₹\ 80\ (0.5987)\frac{₹80}{e^{(0.12)(0.25)}}\ (0.48)$$

$$= ₹\ 10.62$$

For call C:

$d_1 = (-0.11778 + 0.075)/(0.3) = -0.14$

$N_{d1} = 0.4443$

$d_2 = (-0.11778 - 0.015)/(0.3) = -0.44$

$N_{d2} = 0.33$

$$V_c = ₹\ 80\ (0.4443)\ \frac{₹90}{e^{(0.12)(0.25)}}\ (0.33) = ₹\ 6.72$$

For call D:

$d_1 = (-0.11778 + 0.015)/(0.4243) = 0.08$

$N_{d1} = 0.5319$

$d_2 = (-0.11778 - 0.03)/(0.4243) = -0.35$

$$N_{d2} = 0.3632$$

$$V_c = ₹\ 80\ (0.5319)\frac{Rs.90}{e^{(0.12)(0.25)}}\ (0.3632) = ₹\ 11.77$$

5. K.L. Anand has written a September 45 naked call option on XYZ software stock. When the option was written, stock sold for ₹ 42 per share. The option premium was ₹ 2.75. Calculate how much margin Anand had to deposit upon writing the call.

Ans:

The margin required on a naked call option is the larger of the two computations:

Method 1

Option premium	₹ 275
= ₹ 2.75 × 100 shares	
20% of stocks's market value	+ ₹ 840
= 20% × ₹ 42 × 100 shares	
Less amount by which call's exercise	
price exceeds stock's market	
price = (₹ 45 – ₹ 42) × 100 shares	– ₹ 300
Total	₹ 815

Method 2

Option premium	₹ 275
= ₹2.75 × 100 shares	
10% of stock's market value	
= 10% × ₹42 × 100 shares	₹ 420
Total	₹ 695

As the margin calculated by Method 1 is greater than that of Method 2, Anand will have to deposit ₹ 815.

6. Vimal Gupta wrote March 175 naked put option on ABC Textile stock. When the option was written, the stock sold for ₹180 per share. The option premium was ₹ 3. How much margin did Vimal have to deposit?

Ans:

The margin required on a naked put option is the larger of two computations:

Method 1

Option premium	
= ₹ 3 × 100 shares	₹ 300
20% of stock's market value	
= 20% × ₹ 180 × 100 shares	₹ 3600
Less amount by which stock's market	
price exceeds put's exercise price	
= (₹ 180 – ₹ 175) × 100 shares	500
Total	₹ 3400

Method 2

Option premium	
₹ 3 × 100 shares	₹ 300
10% less of stock's market value	
= 10% × ₹ 180 × 100	₹ 1800
Total	₹ 2100

As the margin calculated by Method 1 is greater than that of Method 2, Gupta will have to deposit ₹ 3400.

7. An investment home offers a one-year investment yielding either 12 per cent or half of the XYZ Index 100 per cent appreciation, whichever is the greater. The current XYZ Index 100 is 2000 and one year interest rates are 15 per cent.

   (i)   Beyond what value of the XYZ Index 100 does the stock-appreciation-based return exceed the guaranteed minimum return?
   (ii) How could the fund be constructed?
   (iii) What is the price of the implicit option?

Ans:

   (i)   A rise in the XYZ Index 100 to 2480 would provide a 240 index point return for the investor. The 240 amounts to 15 percent. Beyond an index level of 2480 the index-based return would exceed 12 per cent.

   (ii) The institution providing the investment needs to provide 12 percent plus half of any index increase beyond 2480. Depositing 80 percent of the fund at 15 percent per annum would yield a return equal to 12 percent of the whole fund. A call option with a strike price of 2480, and relating to half the size of the fund, would provide a return equal to half the index rise above 2480.

   (iii) Eighty percent of the fund needed to be deposited in order to generate the guaranteed 12 percent return on the whole fund. The interest return on the remaining 20 percent can be used to purchase the option. This interest return amounts to 3 percent of the total fund. The present value of this sum can be used for the option premium, and amounts to about 6 percent of the sum to which the option initially relates (strictly speaking the present value of that 6 percent). So the implicit premium is ₹ 3/ (1.15) for every ₹ 100 of the original investment.

8. Consider the call option on the stock of RDX Company. The stock currently trades for ₹ 22.75 per share. The option has one month to expiration and an exercise price of ₹ 20. The riskless interest rate is 5% (annually), and the variance of RDX's stock is 0.45.

   (a) What is the value of the call option?
   (b) The price exceeds ₹ 2.75. Why?
   (c) Suppose the risk-free interest rate was 7% instead of 5%. Find the option's value. Is this result consistent with your expectation?

Ans:

   (a) ₹ 3.41
   (b) Value of call option ₹ 3.41 > ₹ 2.75 (in option's current intrinsic value) due to the time premium contained in the option's price.
   (c) ₹ 3.43.

9. Given the following:

Price of the equity	₹ 26
Price of the 6-month call at ₹ 25	₹ 4
Price of a six-month call at ₹ 30	₹ 2

   An investor buys the ₹ 25 call and sells the ₹ 20 call. What is the net cash outflow? What are the profits if the stock's price at expiration is ₹ 10, ₹ 15, ₹ 20, ₹ 25, ₹ 26, ₹ 30, or ₹ 40?

Ans:

   Cash outflow   :   ₹ 2.00
   Profit when the price of the

stock is ₹ 20   : – ₹ 2.00
Profit when the price of the
stock is ₹ 40   :   ₹ 3.00

10. A stock sells for ₹ 30. What is the value of a one- year call option according to the Black-Scholes model to buy the stock at ₹ 25, if debt currently yields 10 per cent? (Assume d_1, and $d_2 = 1$).

Ans:

(₹ 30 – ₹ 25)/(1+ 0.1) = ₹ 7.27

11. A call and put exist on the same stock. Each is exercisable at ₹ 50. They trade now for:

Market price of the stock or stock index (P_s) = ₹ 45
Market price of the call (P_c) = ₹ 8
Market price of the put (Pp)   = ₹ 1

Calculate the expiration cash flow, investment value, and net profit from: (i) Buy 1.0 call, (ii) Write 1.0 call; (iii) Buy 1.0 put, and (iv) Write 1.0 put. Do this for expiration date stock prices of ₹ 40, ₹ 45, ₹ 50, ₹ 55 and ₹ 60.

Ans:

(i) through (iv)

	Stock Prices				
	₹ 40	₹ 45	₹ 50	₹ 55	₹ 60
	Expiration date cash flows				
Buy 1.0 call	0	0	0	–50	–50
Write 1.0 call	0	0	0	50	50
Buy 1.0 put	50	50	0	0	0
Write 1.0 put	–50	–50	0	0	0
	Expiration date investment value				
Buy 1.0 call	0	0	0	5	10
Write 1.0 call	0	0	0	–5	–10
Buy 1.0 put	10	5	0	0	0
Write 1.0 put	–10	–5	0	0	0
	Expiration date net profits				
Buy 1.0 call	–8	–8	–8	–3	2
Write 1.0 call	8	8	8	3	–2
Buy 1.0 put	9	4	–1	–1	–1
Write 1.0 put	–9	–4	1	1	1

12. Compute a call option price by applying the Black- Scholes option pricing model on the following values:

Strike price   = ₹ 45
Time remaining to expiration   = 183 days
Current stock price   = ₹ 47
Expected price volatility = standard deviation   = 25
Risk free rate   = 10%

Ans:

Applying the Black-Scholes formula:

$$V_c = P_s [Nd_1] \frac{P_x}{e^{(RF)(T)}} [Nd_2]$$

$$d_1 = \frac{\ln[47/45] + 0.10 + 0.5(0.25)^2]0.5}{0.25\sqrt{0.5}}$$

$$= 0.6172$$

$$d_2 = 0.6172 - 0.25/\sqrt{0.5} = 0.4404$$

From a normal distribution table:

N (0.6172) = 0.7315
and
N (0.4404) = 0.6702

Then

$$C = 47\ (0.7315) - 45\ (e^{-(0.10)(0.5)})\ (0.6702) = ₹\ 5.69$$

13. Refer to problem (12), what will happen to the theoretical option price if the expected price volatility is 40% rather than 25%.

Ans:

Applying the Black-Scholes model:

$$d_1 = \frac{\ln(47/45) + [0.10 + 0.5(0.40)^2]0.5}{0.40\sqrt{0.5}}$$

$$= 0.4719$$

$$d_2 = 0.4719 - 0.40\ \sqrt{0.5}$$

$$= 0.1891$$

From a normal distribution table:

N (0.4719) = 0.6815 and
N (0.1891) = 0.5750

Then

$$C = 47\ (0.6815) - 45\ (e^{-(0.10)(0.5)})\ (0.5750) = ₹\ 7.42$$

Higher the assumed expected price volatility of the underlying stock price, the higher the price of the call option.

14. You are the stock manager of a ₹ 10 crore portfolio which is now invested as follows: ₹ 5 crore in stock similar to the ABC Index 100, and ₹ 5 crore in T-bills. Relevant data on ABC Index 100 calls include:

Price of ABC 100 Spot Index $\qquad$ = ₹ 250

Price of ABC 100 call $\qquad$ = ₹ 15

N_{d1} of call $\qquad$ = 0.75

Beta of ABC 100 Spot Index $\qquad$ = 1.0

How many calls would you trade to change the portfolio's instantaneous beta to : (a) 0.0, (b) 1.0, and (c) 0.6.

Ans:

Beta of ABC 100 Call = (₹ 250/₹ 15) (1.0) (0.75)
$\qquad$ = 12.5

(a) 0= (0.5) (1.0)+ (₹ calls/₹ 10 crore) (12.5)+ 0
₹ calls = −₹ 40,00,000

Calls = 2, 663$\dfrac{2}{3}$ calls written

(b) 1.0 = 0.5 (1.0) + (₹ calls/₹ 10 crore) (12.5) + 0
₹ calls = -₹ 40,00,000

Calls   = ₹ 40,00,000/ (₹ 15 × 100)

= $2,663\frac{2}{3}$ bought

(c) Calls = $533\frac{1}{3}$

15. A call option is the right to buy stock at ₹ 50 a share. Currently the option has six months to expiration, the volatility of the stock (standard deviation) is 0.30, and the rate of interest is 10 percent.

   (a) What is the value of the option according to the Black- Scholes model if the price of the stock is ₹ 45, ₹ 50, or ₹ 55?

   (b) What is the value of the option when the price of the stock is ₹ 50 and the option expires in 6-months, 3- months, or 1-month?

   (c) What is the value of the option when the price of the stock is ₹ 50 and the interest rate is 5%, 10% or 15%?

   (d) What is the value of the option when the price of the stock is ₹ 50 and the volatility of the stock is 0.40, 0.30 or 0.10?

Ans:

   (a) If the price of the stock is ₹ 50, Value of the call: ₹ 2.72

   (b) If the expiration is 6-month, Value of the call: ₹ 5.41

   (c) If the interest rate is 5%, Value of the call: ₹ 4.78

   (d) If the standard deviation is 40% (.4) Value of the call: ₹ 6.74

16. You have been given the following series of monthly returns on a stock. The returns are discrete returns. Calculate the *ex post* estimate of the Black-Scholes standard deviation.

1	2	3	4	5	6	7	8	9	10	11	12
5%	15	2	-8	1	-1	20	5	-8	10	8	0

Ans :

Period	Discrete Returns	Continuous Returns	Difference from Mean Squared
1	5%	4.88%	0.000204
2	15	13.98	0.011078
3	2	1.98	0.000216
4	-8	-8.34	0.013898
5	1	1.00	0.000603
6	-4	-4.08	0.005675
7	20	18.23	0.021849
8	5	4.88	0.000204
9	-8	-8.34	0.013898
10	10	9.53	0.003697
11	8	7.70	0.001802
12	0.0	0.00	0.001191

Average: 3.83%,   3.45%
Sum of squared differences: 0.074315
Sum divided by n-1:   0.006756

Square root = Standard deviation = 8.22%

17. Consider a three month call option on ABC Company's stock with an exercise price of ₹ 45. If ABC is currently selling at ₹ 50 and the risk-free interest rate is 5%, what will be the price of the option? Apply the Black- Scholes model to find call option value by assuming the standard deviation of the rate of return of ABC stock to be 0.4.

Ans:

Applying the Black-Scholes model:

$$d_1 = \frac{\ln\frac{50}{45} + \left[0.05 + \frac{(0.4)^2}{2}\right](0.25)}{0.4\sqrt{0.25}}$$

$$= 0.6893 = 0.69$$

$N(d_1) = 0.5 + 0.2549 = 0.7549$ Similarly,

$$d_2 = 0.6893 - (0.4)\sqrt{0.25} = 0.4893 = 0.49$$

and

$$N(d_2) = 0.5 + 0.1879$$
$$= 0.6879$$

With the appropriate values substituted into the Black- Scholes equation, the call option price is:

$(50) (0.7549) - (45) (e^{-(0.05)(0.25)}) (0.6879) = ₹ 7.18$

18. Assume that cash dividend (D) will be paid on the expiration of a put and call option. Derive the put-call parity model for this case.

Ans:

		Expiration Date	
Transaction	Today	$P_s < P_x$	$P_s > P_x$
Buy 1.0 stock	$-P_s$	$P_s + D$	$P_s + D$
Buy 1.0 put	$-P_p$	$P_x - P_x$	—
Write 1.0 call	P_c	—	$-(P_s - P_x)$
Net	$-(P_s + P_p - P_c)$	$P_x + P$	$P_x + D$

Thus: $P_c - P_p = P_s - (P_x + D) / (1 + RF)$

19. What are the intrinsic values and time premiums paid for the following options:

Option		Price of the Option	Price of the Equity
Calls:	ABC, Inc., 30	₹ 70	₹ 340
	ABC, Inc., 35	₹ 25	₹ 340
Puts:	ABC, Inc., 30	₹ 12.50	₹ 340
	ABC, Inc., 35	₹ 42.50	₹ 340

If the equity sells for ₹ 310 at the expiration date of the preceding options, what are the profits or losses for the writers and the buyers of these options?

Ans:

ABC Calls: ₹ 40 and nil

ABC puts: nil and ₹ 10

If the price of the equity is ₹ 310, the loss to the buyers of the calls are ₹ 60 and ₹ 25.

If the price of the equity is ₹ 310, the profits to the writers of the puts are ₹ 12.50 and ₹ 2.50.

20. The market value of a portfolio which you manage is ₹ 3 crore. You have been asked to use either puts or calls in a portfolio insurance programme. Since the portfolio is similar to the ABC 100 Index, you intend to use ABC 100 Index options. Relevant data are:

    Current spot value of ABC 100   : ₹ 300
    Current (discrete) Risk-free rate   : 10% per year
    Dividend yield on ABC 100   : 2% per year
    (Assume they are paid in exactly six-months from now)

Option Information	Call	Put
Current price	₹ 35	₹ 5
Exercise price	₹ 280	₹ 280
Expiration Date	6-months	6-months
Option Type	Euro	Euro

    (a) Is put-call parity working?
    (b) Illustrate the expiration data values of an insured portfolio using the puts. Do this for ABC 100 value of ₹ 200, ₹ 250, ₹ 300 and ₹ 350.
    (c) Use the calls together with T-bills to create an insured portfolio which has the same minimum floor value as in part (b). Calculate the values for ABC 100 values of ₹ 200, ₹ 250, ₹ 300, and ₹ 350. Compare the results with those obtained for part (b) and explain why they are different.

Ans:

(a) In theory:

$$P_c - P_p = P_s - (P_x + D) / (1 + RF)$$
$$= ₹300 - (₹\,280 + ₹\,3) / (\sqrt{1.1}\,)$$
$$= ₹\,30.17$$

In the markets:

$$P_c - P_p = ₹\,35 - ₹\,5 = ₹\,30$$

Thus, put-call parity is virtually working, but the call is slightly overvalued.

(b) Let N = number of puts to own

$$N\,(₹\,300 + ₹\,5) \times 100 = ₹\,3 \text{ crore}$$
$$N = 983.606557$$

P_s	Stock Value*	Dividends**	Put***	Total
₹ 200	₹ 1,96,72,131	₹ 2, 95,082	₹ 78, 68, 852	₹ 2, 78, 36, 065
250	2, 45, 90, 164	2, 95, 082	29, 50, 820	2, 78, 36, 065
300	2, 95, 08, 197	2, 95, 082	0	2, 98, 03, 278
250	3, 44, 26, 229	2, 95, 082	0	3, 47, 21, 311

   * $N \times P_s \times 100$
 ** $N \times (₹\,300 \times 100) \times 0.01$
*** $N \times (P_x - P_s) \times 100$ if $P_x > P_s$

(c) Buy T-bills with a par value of ₹ 2,78,36,065

Price of one T-bill = ₹ 0.10 crore/$\sqrt{1.1}$) = ₹ 9,53,462.59

Cost of T-bills = ₹ 9,53,462.59 × 27.836065 = ₹ 2,65,40,647

$$\text{Number of calls} = \frac{₹\,3,00,00,000 - ₹\,2,65,40,647}{₹\,3,500} = ₹988.386677$$

P_s	T-bills	Calls	Total
₹ 200	₹ 2, 78, 36, 065	0	₹ 2, 78, 36, 065
250	2, 78, 36, 065	0	2, 78, 36, 065
300	2, 78, 36, 065	₹ 19, 76, 773	2, 98, 12, 838
350	2, 78, 36, 065	69, 18, 707	3, 47, 54, 772

The result of using calls is slightly better since the call was slightly undervalued in the put-call parity model.

21. A particular call is the option to buy equity share at ₹ 25. It expires in six months and currently sells for ₹ 4 when the price of the equity is ₹ 26.

   (a) What is the intrinsic value of the call? What is the time premium paid for the call?

   (b) What will the value of this call be after six months if the price of the equity is ₹ 20, ₹ 25, ₹ 30, and ₹ 40?

   (c) If the price of the equity rises to ₹ 40 at the expiration date of the call, what is the percentage increase in the value of the call?

   (d) If an individual buys the equity and sells this call, what is the cash outflow (i.e. net cost) and what will the profit be on the position after six months if the price of the equity is ₹ 10, ₹ 15, ₹ 20, ₹ 25, ₹ 26, ₹ 30 and ₹ 40?

   (e) If an individual sells this call naked, what will the profit or loss be on me position after six months if the price of the equity is ₹ 20, ₹ 26 and ₹ 40?

Ans:

   (a) Intrinsic value: ₹ 1, time premium: ₹ 3

   (b) *Price of the Equity* — *Value of the Call*
Price of the Equity	Value of the Call
₹ 20	0
25	0
30	5
40	15

   (c) 275 per cent.

   (d) Cash outflow: ₹22
Price of the Equity	Profit
₹ 15	–₹ 7
25	₹ 3
26	₹ 3
30	₹ 3

   (e) ₹ 4, ₹ 3, and –₹ 11.

22. Assume that the new European option contracts are created on XYZ Index of 250. On this hypothetical index, referred as the XYZ 250, each option is a claim to trade on the quoted price of the spot index times 250. It is June 30 and you have gathered the following information about the options:

   Current spot price of XYZ 250 : ₹ 120

   Expected cash dividend on XYZ 250 : ₹ 0

   Current discount rate on 180-day : 7.74%

   T-bills

   Options on the XYZ 250:

	Call	Put
	Call	*Put*
Exercise price	₹ 100	₹ 100
Exercise date	6 months	6 months
Estimated Standard deviation	30%	30%
Current market price	₹ 28	₹ 2

(a) Calculate the yearly continuous and discrete risk-free rates implied in T-bills discounts.

(b) Calculate the Black-Scholes price for the call.

(c) Given the actual market price is different from the Black-Scholes price, what does this suggest about the implied standard deviation actually being priced by market participants?

(d) Is the put-call parity model working properly in current market prices?

(e) You are the manager of a ₹ 10 crore portfolio of stocks which is very similar to the XYZ 250 index. If you were to use the puts to insure a floor value of the stocks in six months:

   (i) How many puts should you buy? (You will sell some of the stock to pay for the puts).

   (ii) What is the minimum portfolio value?

   (iii) Briefly discuss the cost of this portfolio insurance.

(f) You should have also created an insured portfolio by investing ₹ 10 crore in calls and T-bills. Given the answer to part (d), would this be better than using puts?

(g) Given that put-call parity is not working, there is an index arbitrage possible. Illustrate this arbitrage. Assume your trade is ₹ 2.50 crore worth of spot XYZ 250. Show the expiration date pay-offs for spot values of the XYZ 250 at that time of ₹ 100 and ₹ 140.

(h) Why did the problem specify that the options be European options?

Ans:

(a) T-Bills price = 100 -100 (0.0774) (180/360)

$$= 96.13$$

6-month return = (100/96.13) -1

$$= 4.025798\%$$

(1+ 365-day discrete return) = $1.04025798^{(365/180)}$ = 1.0833

365 day continuous return = In (1.0833) = 0.08

(b) d_1 =

$$\frac{\ln(120/100)+(180/365)(0.08+0.3^2/2)}{0.3\sqrt{180/365}}$$

$$= 1.16$$

N_{d1} = 0.8770 N_{d2}= 0.8289

$$P_s = ₹ 120 - (0.8770) = \frac{100}{e^{0.08(180/365)}} (0.8289)$$

$$= ₹ 25.56$$

(c) The implied standard deviation in the market price of ₹ 28 is greater than the 0.3 used in part (b).

(d) $P_c - P_c$ = ₹ 120 – 100/e⁰⁻⁰⁸ (iso/365) = ₹ 23.87

Since the actual call price is ₹ 26, greater than the put, the call is overvalued relative to the put.

(e) (i)   N = Number of puts and units of stock to hold

N = (₹ 2 × 250+ ₹ 120 × 250) = ₹ 10,00,00,000

N = 3,278.6885

(ii) 3, 278 × (₹ 100 × 250) = ₹ 8,19,67,213.13

(iii) There are two costs. First is the direct cost of buying the puts (3, 278.6885 × ₹ 2 × 250 = ₹ 16,39,344). Second is the opportunity cost if the stock increases in value, since the full ₹ 10 crore is not invested in the stock.

(f) No. The call is overvalued. You would prefer strategies which do not involve purchasing the calls.

(g)

	Today	Expiration Data ₹100	₹140
Buy $833\frac{1}{3}$ stock units	-₹ 2,50,00,000	₹ 2,08,33,333	₹ 2,91,66,666
Buy $833\frac{1}{3}$ puts	-4,16,666		
Sell $833\frac{1}{3}$ calls	+ 58,33,333		
Total	-₹ 1,95,83,333	₹ 2,08,33,333	₹ 2,08,33,333
Sell T-bills"	+ 1,95,83,333	-2,03,71,379	2,03,71,379
Net	₹ 0	+₹ 4,61,954	+₹ 4,61,954

* units = ₹ 2,50,00,000/ (₹120 × 250) = $833\frac{1}{3}$

** 1,95,83,333 × $e^{0.08\ (180/365)}$ = ₹ 2,03,71,379

(h) We need to be sure that early exercise does not occur. Since no dividends are to be paid, there would be no danger of early exercises for American calls. However, there is always the potential that American puts would be exercised if the XYZ 250 fell significantly.

23. Refer to problem (22), all net cash flows occur at the expiration date of the options. Is there any way to obtain these net inflows when the arbitrage is initiated? What amount would be received?

Ans:

Sell T-bills, which have a par value of ₹ 2, 08, 33, 333.

24. An analysis of KDR Group suggests that in one year the price of its equity shares will be either ₹ 80 or ₹ 50. They currently sell for ₹ 60. An option that expires in one year with an exercise price of ₹ 60 can be bought for ₹ 10.23. What is one-year risk-free rate?

Ans:

	Value at expiration High	Low	Range
1.0 share	₹ 80	₹ 50	₹ 30
1.0 call	20	0	20

For each 1.0 call sold, buy 2/3 equity share.

2/3 share	₹ 53.33	₹ 33.33
1.0 call (written)	-20.00	0
Net:	₹ 33.33	₹ 33.33

$$\text{So: } (2/3)\,₹\,60 - ₹\,10.23 = \frac{₹\,33.33}{(1+RF)}$$

$$RF = 11.96\%$$

25. You are given the following information: Market price of the stock or stock index (P_s) = ₹ 74; Market price of the put (Pp) = ₹ 5.09; Exercise price of both options (P_x) = ₹ 65; Risk-free rate (RF) = 10%; and, the Expiration = 1 year. Assume that the stock pays no dividends and that the risk-free rate will remain constant.

    (a) What should be the price of a call also exercisable at ₹ 65 with an expiration of one year?

    (b) How could you develop a portfolio of these securities which will have a pay-off in one year which is identical to being long/short the stock? You may not buy or sell the stock?

    (c) How could you develop a portfolio of these securities which will have a pay-off in one year which is identical to writing one put? Again, you may not trade the put.

Ans:

$$P_c = P_s - \frac{P_x}{1+RF} + P_p$$

$$= ₹\,74 - \frac{Rs.65}{1.1} + ₹\,5.09 = ₹\,20.00$$

(b) Identical to being long the stock:
   - Buy call at P_c
   - Buy debt worth P_x / (1+ RF)
   - Sell the put at P_p

Short the stock:
   - Opposite of the above.

(c) Identical to writing one put:
   - Buy the call
   - Sell short the stock
   - Buy debt worth P_x + (1+ RF)

26. Consider the following option quotations on equity of the Milindh Textiles

Option	Strike Price	Calls Dec	Calls Mar	Calls June	Puts Dec	Puts Mar	Puts June
Milindh Textile	55	$8\frac{3}{4}$	9	$9\frac{1}{4}$	$\frac{1}{16}$	$\frac{5}{16}$	$\frac{1}{2}$
$63\frac{1}{4}$	60	$3\frac{1}{2}$	$4\frac{5}{8}$	$5\frac{5}{8}$	$\frac{5}{16}$	1	$1\frac{1}{2}$
$63\frac{1}{4}$	65	$\frac{9}{16}$	$1\frac{3}{4}$	$2\frac{3}{4}$	$2\frac{3}{4}$	$3\frac{1}{2}$	4

    (a) How many different contracts are there that you could trade?

    (b) Look at the June call exercisable at ₹ 55. Assume that you buy the call

Calculate the value of the call and your net profit or loss at the expiration date in late June for each of the following stock prices: ₹ 50, ₹ 55, ₹ 60, ₹ 65, ₹ 70, ₹ 75.

(c) Again, assume that you buy the June/55 call. At what stock price would you not exercise your call at the expiration day? At what prices would you exercise? Why would you exercise even if this results in a net loss?

(d) What is the expiration date break-even stock price of the June/55 call?

(e) What is the immediate value of the June/55 call? Why is the option selling for a higher price?

(f) Repeat parts b through e for the June/65 put.

(g) Why do you suspect that the longer maturity options sell at higher prices?

(h) Assume that you have ₹ 10,000 to purchase either shares of Milindh Textiles or the June/55 calls. Illustrate the greater leverage inherent in owning the calls.

(i) Assume that you buy two puts and three calls, both exercisable in March at ₹ 60. In late March the price of Milindh Textiles stock is ₹ 45. What would you do with your options and what would be your net profit or loss?

(j) Assume that you sell one June/55 call to a buyer of the call What will be your rupee profit or loss at the expiration date for each of the following prices: ₹ 50, ₹ 55, ₹ 60, ₹ 65, ₹ 70, ₹ 75? What does this show? (Compare with part b).

Ans:

(a) There are a total of 18 different option contracts.

(b)

Stock Price	₹ 50	₹ 55	₹ 60	₹ 65	₹ 70	₹ 75
Value of Call	₹ 0	₹ 0	₹ 5	₹ 10	₹ 15	₹ 20
Less: Purchase Price	-925	-935	-9.25	-9.25	-9.25	-9.25
Net Profit	-9.25	-9.25	-4.25	0.75	5.75	10.75

(c) ₹ 55. Don't exercise if the stock can be bought in the security market at a price lower than the exercise price. The reason is very simple; if the stock is selling in the markets at a price lower than the exercise price, why pay the exercise price to purchase it?

Exercise should take place at the exercise date if the stock is selling at a price larger than the exercise price.

This should be done even if the net profit turns out to be a loss. Again, the reason is very simple. If you do not exercise when the stock is worth more than the exercise price, your net loss is equal to the initial amount you originally paid for the option. By exercising, the loss is reduced.

(d) Break-even stock price at expiration date equals the ₹ 55 exercise price plus the ₹ 9.25 original .option price, or ₹ 64.25.

(e) The immediate value is equal to the current stock price (₹ 63.25) minus the exercise price (₹ 55) or ₹ 8.25. This call option is selling at a price ₹ 1.00 higher because of the potential that the stock will sell for more than its current ₹ 63.25 on the expiration date.

(f) Part b repeated

Stock Price	₹ 50	₹ 55	₹ 60	₹ 65	₹ 70	₹ 75
Value of Put	₹ 15	₹ 10	₹ 5	₹ 0	₹ 0	₹ 0
Less: Purchase Price	-4.00	-4.00	-4.00	-4.00	-4.00	-4.00
Net Profit	₹ 11	₹ 6	Re.1	-₹ 4	-₹ 4	-₹ 4

Part c repeated

Don't exercise if stock price is *above* ₹ 65.

Do exercise if stock price is *below* ₹ 65.

Part *d* repeated

Break-even price = ₹ 65 – ₹ 4 = ₹ 61.

Part *e* repeated

Exercise price	₹ 65.00
Less stock price	- 63.25
Immediate value	₹ 1.75

(*g*) Given an exercise price, the longer the maturity the larger the option's price. This is because there is a greater chance that stock prices will be higher (or lower for a put) than current stock prices.

(*h*) *Return on the Purchase of ₹10,000 of Stock (158.1 shares at ₹ 63.25)*

Assumed Stock Price at Expiration:	₹ 50	₹ 55	₹ 60	₹ 65	₹ 70	₹ 75
Ending Value (in thousand ₹)	7.905	8.696	9.486	10.276	11.067	11.858
Less Initial Value	10.000	10.000	10.000	10.000	10.000	10.000
Profit or Loss (₹)	-2.095	-1.304	-0.514	0.276	1.067	1.858
Rate of Return	-20.9%	-13%	-5.1%	2.8%	10.7%	18.6%

Return on the Purchase of ₹ 10, 000 of Calls (1, 081.1 calls at ₹ 9.25)

	₹ 50	₹ 55	₹ 60	₹ 65	₹ 70	₹ 75
Ending Value (in thousand ₹)	0.000	0.000	5.406	10.811	16.216	21.622
Less Initial Value	10.000	10.000	10.000	10.000	10.000	10.000
Profit or Loss	-10.000	-10.000	-4.594	0.811	6.216	11.622
Rate of Return	-100%	-100%	-45.9%	8.1%	62.2%	116.2%

As the stock price increases or decreases, the rate of return earned on the call ownership is more volatile than the stock returns. It is this increased volatility inherent in the call options that is referred to as their greater leverage. A similar result occurs with the ownership of puts except that stock price declines results in positive put profits.

(*i*)

	Initial Purchase Cost	Late March Transaction	Total Value
Buy 2 Puts	₹ 2.000	Exercise	2 (60 – 45) = ₹ 30
Buy 3 Calls	₹ 13.875	Don't Exercise	— 0.0
₹ 15.875	₹ 30		

Net Profit = ₹ 30 - ₹ 15.875

= ₹ 14.125

(*j*) Although for every buyer of an option there must be someone willing to sell (often called "write") the option. A gain (or loss) to the buyer will be a loss (or gain) to the seller.

Stock Price:	₹ 50	₹ 55	₹ 60	₹ 65	₹ 70	₹ 75
Option Buyer Exercises						
You Sell	—	—	₹ 55	₹ 55	₹ 55	₹ 55
You Buy	—	—	-60	-65	-70	-75
	—	—	-5	-10	-15	-20

Original option value received	₹ 9.25	9.25	9.25	9.25	9.25	9.25
Net Profit	₹ 9.25	9.25	4.25	-0.75	-5.75	-1075

Tthe call buyer's profit or loss (from part b) is the call seller's loss or profit.

27. Consider circumstances where possible stock prices at expiration may range from ₹ 10 to ₹ 50 compared with a situation where stock prices may range only from ₹ 20 to ₹ 40. In both cases the expected stock price will be ₹ 30. Suppose that the exercise price on a call option is also ₹ 30. What are the option pay offs, if each outcome is equally likely?

Ans:

High-Volatility Scenario

Stock price	₹ 10	₹ 20	₹ 30	₹ 40	₹ 50
Option pay off	0	0	0	₹ 10	₹ 40

The expected payoff to the option under high-volatility conditions will be ₹ 6 if each outcome is equally likely, with probability 0.2.

Low-Volatility Scenario

Stock price	₹ 20	₹ 25	₹ 30	₹ 35	₹ 40
Option pay off	0	0	0	₹ 5	₹ 10

The expected payoff to the option is half as much, only ₹ 3 with equally likely outcomes i.e. probability 0.2.

28. Refer to problem-27, should a put option also increase in value with the volatility of the stock?

Ans:

Yes. Consider the same scenario as for this call:

Stock price	₹ 10	₹ 20	₹ 30	₹ 40	₹ 50
Option pay off	₹ 20	₹ 10	0	0	0
Stock price	₹ 20	₹ 25	₹ 30	₹ 35	₹ 40
Option pay off	₹ 10	₹ 5	0	0	0

The low volatility scenario yields a lower expected payoff.

29. Apply the Black-Scholes formula to value a call option under the following circumstances:

Stock price	: ₹ 100
Exercise price	: ₹ 95
Interest Rate	: 0.10
Time to Expiration	: 0.25 (3 months)
Standard deviation	: 0.5

Ans:

Applying the Black-Scholes formula:

$$d_1 = \frac{\ln(100/95) + (0.10 + 0.5^2/2) \times 0.25}{0.5\sqrt{0.25}} = 0.43$$

$$d_2 = 0.43 - 0.5/0.25 = 0.18$$

$Nd_1(0.43) = 0.6664$

$Nd_2(0.18) = 0.574$

Thus the value of the call option is:

$= 100 \times 0.6664 - (95\, e^{-0.10 \times 0.25}) \times 0.5714$

$= 66.64 - 52.94 = ₹\, 13.70$

30. Refer to problem -29. Consider the option is selling for ₹ 15 with Black-Scholes value of ₹ 13.70. Is its implied volatility more or less than 0.5?

Ans:

Implied volatility exceeds 0.5. Given a standard deviation of 0.5, the option value is ₹ 13.70. A higher volatility is needed to justify the actual ₹ 15 price.

31. Refer to problem 30. Find the European put option on that stock with identical exercise price and time to maturity.

Ans:

We can derive Black-Scholes European put option values from call option values using the put-call parity theorem. The value of put option:

₹ 13.70+ (₹ 95 e-0$^{0.10 \times 0.25}$) – ₹ 100 = ₹ 6.35

32. What is the elasticity of a put option currently selling for ₹ 4 with exercise price ₹ 120, and hedge ratio -0.4 if the stock price is currently ₹ 122?

Ans:

As Rupee 1 increase in the stock price is a percentage increase of 1/122 = 0.82%. The put option will fall by (0.4 × ₹ 1) = ₹ 0.40, a percentage decrease of ₹ 0.40/₹ 4 = 10%. Elasticity is-10/0.82 =-12.2.

33. Consider the following data:

The market price of the option	₹ 36
The exercise price of the call option	₹ 40
The current annualised market interest rate for T-bills	10%
The time remaining before expiration	90 days (.25 years)
Historical standard deviation	.40
Expected standard deviation	.50 (analysts to expect an increase in stock beta because of a new debt issue)

Apply the Black- Scholes formula developed for deriving the value of American call option.

Ans:

First calculating the option value assuming the historical volatility a =.40:

$$d_1 = \left(\frac{\ln(36/40)+(.10-.5(.4)^2 \ .25}{.4(.25)^{.5}} \right)$$

$$= \left(\frac{-.1054+.045}{.2} \right) = -.302$$

$N(d_1)$ = .3814
$N(d_2)$ = .3079

Option value:

$$(36 (.3814) - (40) (\text{anti In } (.02\ 5)) (.3079)$$
$$= 13.7304 - (40) (.0253) (.3079)$$
$$= 13.7304 - 12.6276 = 1.103$$

Finally, calculating the option value assuming the expected volatility is higher σ =.50:

$$d_1 = \left(\frac{\ln(30/40)+(.10-.5)(.5)^2 .25}{.5(.25)^{.5}} \right)$$

$$= \left(\frac{-.1054-.05625}{.25} \right) = .1966$$

$$d_2 = -.1966 - [.5 \ (.25)^{.5}] = -.4466$$
$$N(d_1) = .4199$$
$$N(d_2) = . \ 3275$$

Option value:

$$(36)(.4199) - (40)(\text{anti In } (.025))(.3275)$$
$$= 15.1164 - (40)(1.0253)(.3275)$$
$$= 15.1164 - 13.4314 = 1.685$$

The result indicates the importance of estimating stock price volatility (from .40 to .50), there is a 53% increase in the value of the option.

34. Suppose an investor wants to calculate the theoretical value of a 3-month (one-fourth of a year) call option with a strike price of ₹ 30 on a stock currently selling for ₹ 28. Treasury bills yield 5%, and σ, the anticipated volatility of the stock returns, is estimated at 25%. Use the Black-Scholes option pricing model to compute the call option's price.

Ans. The first step is to solve for the $N(d_1)$ and (Nd_2).

$$d_1 = \frac{\text{In } (28/30 + (.05 + .25)^2 / 2) \ .25}{.25\sqrt{.25}} = -0.389$$

$$d_2 = -0.389 - .25\sqrt{.25}$$
$$= -0.514$$
$$V_c = 29 \ (.349) - (30e^{-0.5(.25)})(.304)$$
$$= ₹ 1.11$$

35. The following information refers to a 3-month call option on the stock of Best Steel Company.

Price of equity share	₹ 50
Strike price of 3-month call	₹ 40
Market price of the option	₹ 15

    (i) What is the intrinsic value of the option?
    (ii) What is the option's time premium at this price?
    (iii) Is the call in or out of the money?
    (iv) If an investor writes and sells a covered call option, acquiring the covering equity now, how much has he invested?
    (v) What is the most the buyer of the call can lose?
    (vi) What is the most the writer of the call naked can lose?

If just before the option's expiration, Best Steel Co. is selling for ₹ 58.

    (vii) What is the profit or loss from buying the call?
    (viii) What is the profit or loss from writing the call naked?
    (ix) What is the profit or loss from writing the call covered if the covering stock was acquired at the time the call was written?

Solution

    (i) The intrinsic value of the option is = ₹ 50 - ₹ 40 = ₹ 10
    (ii) The time premium is the difference between the option's price and its intrinsic value.

$$\text{Time premium} = ₹ 15 - ₹ 10 = ₹ 5$$

(iii) The call option is *in the money* because it has a positive **intrinsic** value.

(iv) To establish a covered call, the investor buys the stock at its market price and sells an option immediately. The option's price therefore **offsets** the investment in the stock.

Investment = Price of stock - Price of call option = ₹ 50 - ₹ 15 = ₹ 35

(v) The maximum lose to the option buyer can be the option price, ₹ 15 in this case.

(vi) If the buyer exercise the option, the writer off a call will have to buy the stock on the open market. Since in theory, the stock can rise to any price, the naked call writer may lose an infinite amount. In practices a product investor will start purchasing the share when it starts moving up in **order** to **limit** losses.

(vii) The call owner pays the strike price by exercising the option and simultaneously sells the shares at market price. Any resulting gain/loss is reduced by the price paid for the call.

Market price of stock at time of exercise	₹ 58
Less : Strike price	₹ 40
Price of option	55
Gain	₹ 3

(viii) An investor who wrote all naked buys the stock at market price when the option is exercised and sells at the strike price. The result is:

Market price of stock at time of exercise	₹ 58
Plus: Strike Price ₹ 40	₹ 40
Price of option 15	55
Loss	₹ 3

(ix) An investor who wrote a call covered brought the stock at market price when the option was written and sells it at the strike price. The result is improved by the price received for the option.

Market price of stock at time of exercise	₹ 50
Plus: Strike Price	₹ 40
Price of option 15	55
Gain	₹ 5

QUESTIONS

1. Explain why an option has value. State the characteristics of put and call options.
2. How does the price of a call option vary with striking price and the time to maturity?
3. How does the price of a put option vary with the striking price and the time to maturity?
4. "Stock options are for speculators". Comment on this statement.
5. Why would the volatility of an underlying stock be an important consideration when purchasing or selling an option? When purchasing a call option, would a more volatile underlying stock make the option riskier?
6. Illustrate the difference between European and American call options.

7. What are the underlying assumptions of the Black and Scholes option pricing model and why are they needed?

8. Explain what do you understand by the option strategy termed a 'straddle'. Why might an investor use a straddle?

9. Analyse the relative risk and payoff of the following strategies:

   (*a*) buy share; (*b*) buy call; (*c*) buy share and buy put option on the share; (*d*) buy share, buy put and write call; (*e*) sell put; (*f*) buy share and buy call option on the share.

10. Critically appraise the factors which determine the theoretical value of options highlighting any problems that might be encountered in incorporating them in a formal valuation model.

11. Why is writing an in-the-money put more risky than writing an out-of-the money put?

12. Suppose interest rates rise, will an option's delta change if the stock price remains unchanged?

13. Comment on the following statement: Options are nothing more than a side but on the direction stock prices are going to move.

14. Comment on the following statement: An option that is out-of-the-money must have intrinsic value.

15. Comment on the following statement: An option that is in- the money must have intrinsic value.

16. What is meant by the gamma of an option position? Consider the situation of an option writer when the gamma of his or her position is large and negative and the delta is zero. What are the risks?

27. What is portfolio insurance? Identify and explain the various strategies that can be used to insure a portfolio.

18. What is the difference between hedging and portfolio insurance?

19. Consider the following events and indicate how each would affect call and put price. Use (+) to indicate an increase, (-) to indicate a decrease, (0) to indicate no effect, and (?) to indicate indeterminant results. Be prepared to justify each choice. Consider each event in isolation from the other.

	Effect on	
	Call Price	*Put Price*
1. The company pays a large cash dividend		
2. The company pays a large bonus share		
3. Investors become more risk-averse		
4. Inflation expectations increase and cause required returns on risk-free security to increase		
5. Time passes		
6. The firm increases its debt-to-equity ratio		
7. The expected return on the equity		
7. increases, but its risk doesn't		
8. The expected return on the equity increases, but its risk does also, causing the equity price to remain constant.		
9. The company suffers from an unexpected and severe labour strike		

20. How does the price of a call and a put vary with interest rates? Does this relationship vary for American and European put and call? Explain.

21. What is the maximum theoretical value for a European put? Under what conditions does it reach this maximum value? Explain.

22. What is the relationship between the risk of the underlying stock and the call price? Explain in intuitive terms.

23. What relationship holds between time until expiration and the price of a European put?

24. Within the context of the put-call parity relationship, consider the value of a call and put options. What will the value of the put option be if the exercise price is zero? What will the value of the call option be in the same circumstances? What can you say about potential bounds on the value of the call and put options?

25. Using the put-call parity relationship, write the value of call option as a function of the stock price, the risk-free bond, and the put option. Now consider a stock price that is dramatically in excess of the exercise price. What happens to the value of a put and a call as the stock price becomes extremely large relative to the exercise price?

26. What are the shortcomings associated with delta-neutral hedging?

27. Explain how a short and a long spot-asset position be hedged with options.

PROBLEMS

1. Using the binomial pricing model, calculate the hedging ratio and the value of a call option with one year to expiry from the following data: current share price, ₹ 50; exercise price, ₹ 60; value expected at expiration, either ₹ 80 or ₹ 40; risk-free rate of return 10%.

2. Use the Black-Scholes model to calculate the value of a European call option on a non-dividend paying share from the following data: current share price, ₹ 28; exercise price, ₹ 40; expiry date, six months' time; instantaneous standars deviation of return, 05; continuously compounded risk-free rate of interest, 8%.

3. What does it mean to assert that the theta of an option position is -0.1 when time is measured in years? If a trader feels that neither a stock price nor its implied volatility will change, what type of option position is appropriate?

4. What does it mean to assert that the delta of a call option is 0.7? How can a short position in 1000 options be made delta neutral when the delta of each option is 0.7?

5. An investor buys 1000 shares of XYZ Company at ₹ 27 on April 1st. On June 2nd, he writes on 10th July 30 calls for ₹ 3 each. The options are exercised on 20th June and he sells his shares at the exercise price.

   (a) What is the holding period return for the investor?

   (b) What is the internal rate of return using daily compounding?

6. The price of a stock is ₹ 51. You can buy a six- month call at ₹ 50 for ₹ 5 or a six-month put at ₹ 50 for ₹ 2.

   (a) What is the intrinsic value of the call?

   (b) What is the intrinsic value of the put?

   (c) What is the time premium paid for the put?

   (d) What is the time premium paid for the call?

   (e) If the price of the stock falls, what happens to the value of the put?

   (f) What is the maximum you could lose by selling the call covered?

   (g) What is the maximum possible profit if you sell the stock short?

   (h) What is the value of the call?

   (i) What is the profit or loss from buying the put?

   (j) If you had sold the stock short six-months earlier, what would your profit or loss be?

   (k) If you sold the call covered, what would your profit or loss be?

Ans:

(a) ₹ 1	(b) ₹ 0	(c) ₹ 2
(d) ₹ 4 a	(e) Rises	(f) ₹ 46

(g) ₹51   (h) ₹ 8   (i) ₹ 2

(j) –₹ 7   (k) ₹ 4

7. An investor has the following alternative investments and their prices:

Equity share	₹ 50
Six-month call on the Equity at ₹ 50	₹ 4
Six-month ₹ 10, 000 Treasury bills	₹ 9, 600

The investor has ₹ 10, 000 and thus could buy (a) 200 shares of the equity or (b) one call plus the treasury bill. After six-months how much profit or loss will the investor have earned on each alternative (excluding commissions) if the price of the equity is ₹ 60; ₹ 55; ₹ 50; ₹ 45 or ₹ 40? Which alternative is less risky?

Ans: If price of the equity is ₹ 60, make ₹ 2, 000 on the position in the equity versus ₹ 1, 000 in the call and the treasury bill. If the price of the equity is ₹ 40, loss ₹ 2, 000 on the position in the equity versus no loss on the position in the call and the treasury bill.

8. Given that the one-year risk-free interest rate is 8% and XYZ's stock has a standard deviation of 0.31, find the value of a put option with six months to maturity and an exercise price of ₹ 70. XYZ's stock is currently trading for ₹ 68.50 per share.

Ans: Value of call option at expiration = ₹ 6.59

Put option price at expiration = ₹ 5.35

9. Given the following:

Price of the equity	₹ 26
Price of the six-month call at ₹ 25	₹ 2
Price of a six-month call at ₹ 30	₹ 4

An investor buys the ₹ 25 call and sells for ₹ 30 call. What are the profits if the stack's price at expiration is ₹ 20, ₹ 25, ₹ 30, or ₹ 35?

Ans: Profit when the price of the stock is ₹ 20: ₹ 2

Profit when the price of the stock is ₹ 35: ₹ 7

10. A particular put is the option to sell stock at ₹ 40. It expires after 3 months and currently sells for ₹ 2 when the price of the stock is ₹ 42.

(a) If an investor buys this put, what will the profit be after three months if the price of the stock is ₹ 45, ₹ 40 and ₹ 35?

(b) What will the profit be from selling this put after three months if the price of the stock is ₹ 45, ₹ 40 and ₹ 35?

Ans: (a) ₹ 2, – ₹ 2 and ₹ 3

(b) ₹ 2, ₹ 2 and – ₹ 3

11. Chandra Enterprises's current equity price is ₹ 60 per share. The firm operates in a two-state world; that is, there are only two possible outcomes for its share price 1 year hence. If things go well, the share price will increase to ₹ 80, but if things go poorly, the price will fall to ₹ 40. The firm is traded in the options markets and the current price of a 1-year call option with an exercise price of ₹ 60 is ₹ 10.23. What is the 1-year risk-free rate?

Ans: 1.16%

12. RHD Group options are actively traded in the stock market. RHD's current stock price is ₹ 10, with a 0.16 instantaneous variance of returns. The current 6-month risk-free rate is 12%.

(a) What is the value of RHD's 6-month option with an exercise price of ₹ 10 according to the Black-Scholes model?

(b) What would be the effect on the option price if RHD redeployed its assets and thereby reduced its variance of returns to 0.9?

(c) Assume that RHD returns to its initial asset structure; that is, its stock return variance is 0.16. Now assume that RHD's current stock price is ₹ 15. What effect does the stock price increase have on the option value?

(d) Return to base case (part a) values. Now assume that the striking price is ₹ 15. What is the new option value?

Ans: (a) ₹ 1.41 (b) ₹ 1.14 (c) ₹ 5.65 (d) ₹ 0.18.

REFERENCES

1. Abken, Peter. "Interest-Rate Caps, Collars and Floors," *Federal Reserve Bank of Atlanta Economic Review* 72, no. 6 (November-December 1989).

2. Allayannis, G. and J. Weston. "The Use of Foreign Currency Derivatives and Firm Market Value," *Review of Financial Studies*, 14, 1 (Spring 2001): 243-76.

3. Amran, M., and N. Kulatilaka, *Real Options*, Boston, MA: Harvard Business School Press, 1999.

4. Angrist, Stanley W. *Sensible Speculating in Commodities*. New York: Simon & Schuster, 1972.

5. Bailey, Warren. "An Empirical Investigation of the Market for Comex Gold Futures Options." *The Jour-nal of Finance* 42, no. 5 (December 1987).

6. Ball, Clifford A., and Walter N. Torous. "Futures Options and the Volatility of Futures Prices," *The Journal of Finance* 41, no. 4 (September 1986).

7. Black, Fischer. "The Pricing of Commodity Contracts." *Journal of Financial Economics* 3, nos. 1,2 (January-March 1976).

8. Bodnar, G.M., G.S. Hayt, and R.C. Marston. "1998 Wharton Survey of Financial Risk Management by U.S. Non-Financial Firms" *Financial Management*, 2, 4 (1998): 70-91.

9. Bodurtha, James, and Georges Courtadon. "Efficiency Tests of the Foreign Currency Options Market." *The Journal of Finance* 41, no. 1 (March 1986).

10. Bookstaber, Richard. *Option Pricing and Strategies in Investing* (New York: Addison-Wesley, 1986).

11. Briys, Eric, Michel Crouhy, and Rainer Schobel. "The Pricing of Default-Free Interest Rate Caps, Floors and Collars." *The Journal of Finance* 46, no. 5 (December 1991).

12. Brown, G.W. "Managing Foreign Exchange Risk with Derivatives." *Journal of Financial Economics*, 60 (2001): 401-48.

13. Chance, Don M. *An Introduction to Options and Futures*. 2d ed. Hinsdale, III .: Dryden, 1992.

14. Cornell, Bradford, and Marc R. Reinganum. "Forward and Futures Prices: Evidence from the Foreign Exchange Markets." *The Journal of Finance* 36, no. 5 (December 1981).

15. Cox, John C., and Mark Rubinstein. *Options Markets*. Englewood Cliffs, N.J.: Prentice-Hall, 1985.

16. Culp, C. and M.H. Miller. "Metallgesellschaft and the Economics of Synthetic Storage," *Journal of Applied Corporate Finance*, 1, 4 (Winter 1995): 62-76.

17. Dawson, Frederic S. "Risks and Returns in Continuous Option Writing." *Journal of Portfolio Manage-ment* 5, no. 2 (Winter 1979).

18. Ederington, L.H. "The Hedging Performance of the New Futures Market," *Journal of Finance*, 34 (March 1979): 157-70.

19. Edwards, F.R. and M.S. Canter. "The Collapse of Metallgesellschaft: Unhedgeable Risks, Poor Hedging Strategy, or Just Bad Luck?" *Journal of Applied Corporate Finance*, 8, 1 (Spring 1995): 86-105.

20. Einzig, Robert, and Bruce Lange. "Swaps at Transamerica: Applications and Analysis." *Journal of Applied Corporate Finance* 2, no. 4 (Winter 1990).

21. Filer, Herbert. *Understanding Put and Call Options*. New York: Popular Library, 1966.

22. Fisher, Stanley. "Call Option Pricing When the Exercise Price is Uncertain, and the Valuation of Index Bonds," *Journal of Finance*. March 1978.

23. Galai, Dan, and Meir I. Schneller. "Pricing Warrants and the Value of the Firm." *The Journal of Finance* 33, no. 5 (December 1978).

24. Garman, Mark B., and Steven W. Kohlhagen. "Foreign Currency Option Values." *Journal of International Money and Finance* 2, no. 3 (1983).

25. Gastineau, Gary L. *The Options Manual.* 3d ed. New York: McGraw-Hill, 1988.

26. Geczy, C., B.A. Minton, and C. Schrand. "Why Firms Use Currency Derivatives," *Journal of Finance, 52,* 4 (1997): 1323-54.

27. Geske, Robert. "The Valuation of Compound Options." *Journal of Financial Economics* 3, no. 1 (March 1979).

28. Gombola, Michael J., Rodney L. Roenfeldt, and Philip L. Cooley. "Spreading Strategies in CBOE Options: Evidence on Market Performance." *Journal of Financial Research* 1, no. 1 (Winter 1978).

29. Goodman, Laurie S. "The Use of Interest Rate Swaps in Managing Corporate Liabilities." *Journal of Applied Corporate Finance* 2, no. 4 (Winter 1990).

30. Grabbe, J. Orlin. *International Financial Markets.* 2d ed. New York: Elsevier Science Publishing, 1991.

31. Graham, J.R. and C.W. Smith, Jr. "Tax Incentives to Hedge," *Journal of Finance, 54,* 6 (1999): 2241-62.

32. Grube, R. Corwin, Don B. Panton, and J. Michael Terrell. "Risks and Rewards in Covered Call Posi-tions." *Journal of Portfolio Management* 5, no. 2 (Winter 1979).

33. Haushalter, G.D. "Financing Policy, Basis Risk, and Corporate Hedging: Evidence from Oil and Gas Producers," *Journal of Finance, 55,* 1 (2000): 107-52.

34. Hettenhouse, G.W., and D.J. Puglisi. "Investor Experience with *Options," Financial Analysts Journal.* July-Aug. 1975.

35. Hill. Joanne M., and Frank J. Jones. "Equity Trading, Program Trading, Portfolio Insurance, Computer Trading and All That." *Financial Analysts Journal* 44, no. 4 (July-August 1988).

36. Ho, Thomas S.Y., and Alien A. Abrahamson. "Options on Interest Sensitive Securities." In *Financial Options: From Theory to Practice,* edited by S. Figlewski, W.L. Silber, and M.G. Subrahmanyam. Homewood, III.: Business One Irwin, 1990.

37. Hull, John. *Options, Futures and Other Derivative Instruments.* 2nd ed. Englewood Cliffs, N.J.: Prentice-Hall, 1993.

38. Ingersoll, Jonathan E., Jr. "A Contingent Claims Valuation of Convertible Securities." *Journal of Financial Economics* 4, no. 4 (May 1977).

39. Ingersoll, Jonathan E., Jr. "An Examination of Corporate Call Policies on Convertible Securities." *The Journal of Finance* 32, no. 2 (May 1977).

40. Kamphuis, Robert W., Roger C. Kormendi, and J. W. Henry Watson, eds. *Black Monday and the Future of Financial Markets.* Homewood, III.: Irwin, 1989.

41. Kim, Moon, and Allan Young. "Rewards and Risk from Warrant Hedging." *Journal of Portfolio Management* 6, no. 4 (Summer 1980).

42. Kolb, Robert W. *Understanding Futures Markets.* 3rd ed. Miami, FL.: Kolb Publishing, 1991.

43. Latane, Henry A., and Richard J. Rendleman, Jr. "Standard Deviations of Stock Price Ratios Implied in Option Prices." *The Journal of Finance* 31, no. 2 (May 1976).

44. Levi, Maurice D. *International Finance.* 2d ed. New York: McGraw-Hill, 1990.

45. Macbeth, J., and Larry J. Merville. "Tests of the Black-Scholes and Cox Call Option Valuation Models," *Journal of Finance* 35, no. 2 (May 1980).

46. Malkiel, B.G., and R.E. Quandt. *Strategies and Rational Decisions in the Securities Option Market.* Cambridge, Mass.: M.I.T. Press, 1969.

47. Marshall, John F., and Kenneth R. Kapner. *Understanding Swap Finance*. Cincinnati: South-Western Publishing, 1990.

48. Marshall, John F., and Vipul K. Bansal. *Financial Engineering*. Boston: Allyn and Bacon, 1992.

49. Melicher, Ronald W. "A Comment on Financing with Convertible Preferred Stock, 1960-1967." *The Journal of Finance* 26, no. 1 (March 1971).

50. Mello, A.S. and J.E. Parsons. "Hedging and Liquidity," *Review of Financial Studies*, 13 (Spring 2000): 127-53.

51. Merton, R.C. "Theory of Rational Option Pricing," *Bell Journal of Economics and Management Science*. Spring 1973.

52. ————. "The Impact on Option Pricing of Specification Error in the Underlying Stock Price Returns," *Journal of Finance*. May 1976.

53. ——————. "Financial Innovation and Economic Performance." *Journal of Applied Corporate Finance* 4, no. 4 (Winter 1992).

54. ——————., Myron S. Scholes, and Mathew L. Gladstein. "The Returns and Risks of Alternative Call-Option Portfolio Investment Strategies." *Journal of Business* 51 (April 1978).

55. Murray, R.F. "Options as an Investment Tool," *Forbes*. Oct. 1, 1975.

56. Neuberger, A.J. "Hedging Long-Term Exposures with Multiple Short-Term Futures Contracts," *Review of Financial Studies*, 12 (1999): 429-59.

57. Nodding, T.C., and E. zagove. *CBOE Call Options: Your Daily Guide to Portfolio Strategy*. Homewood, III .: Dow Jones-Irwin, 1975.

58. ————. *Advanced Investment Strategies*. Homewood, III .: Dow Johes-Irwin, 1978.

59. Petersen, M.A. and S.R. Thiagarajan, "Risk Management and Hedging: With and Without Derivatives," *Financial Management*, 29, 4 (Winter 2000): 5-30.

60. Prendergast, S.L. *Uncommon Profits Through Stock Purchase War-rants'*. Homewood, III .: Dow Jones-Irwin, 1973.

61. Reback, Robert. "Risk and Return in Option Trading," *Financial Analysts Journal*. July-Aug. 1975.

62. Rendleman, R. "A Reconciliation of Potentially Conflicting Approaches to Hedging with Futures," *Advances in Futures and Options*, 6 (1993): 81-92.

63. Scholes, Myron. "Taxes and the Pricing of Options," *Journal of Finance*. May 1976.

64. Schonbucher, P.J., *Credit Derivatives Pricing Models*. New York: Wiley, 2003.

65. Smith D.J., "Aggressive Corporate Finance: A Close Look at the Procter and Gamble-Bankers Trust Leveraged Swap," *Journal of Derivatives*, 4. 4 (Summer 1997): 67-79.

66. Smith, Clifford W., Jr., and Charles W. Smithson. *The Handbook of Financial Engineering*. Grand Rapids: Harper Business, 1990.

67. ——————————, and D. Sykes Wilford. *Managing Financial Risk*. Grand Rapids: Harper Business, 1990.

68. Stapleton, Richard C., and Marti G. Subrahmanyam. "Interest Rate Caps and Floors." In *Financial Options: From Theory to Practice*, edited by S. Figlewski, W. L. Silber, and M. G. Subrahmanyam. Homewood, III.: Business One Irwin, 1990.

69. Stoll, Hans R., and Robert E. Whaley. "The Dynand cs of Stock Index and Stock Index Futures Returns." *Journal of Financial and Quantitative Analysis* 25, no. 4 (December 1990).

70. Stoll, Hans R., and Robert E. Whaley. *Futures and Options: Theory and Application* Cincinnati: South-western Publishing, 1993.

71. Stulz, R.M. "Optimal Hedging Policies," *Journal of Financial and Quantitative Analysis*, 19 (June 1984): 127-40.

72. Tavakoli, J.M., *Credit Derivatives & Synthetic Structures: A Guide to Instruments and Applications*, 2nd edn. New York: Wiley, 1998. Finnerty, John D. "An Overview of Corporate Securities Innovation." *Journal of Applied Corporate Finance* 4, no. 4 (Winter 1992).

73. Tufano, P. "The Determinants of Stock Price Exposure: Financial Engineering and the Gold Mining Industry," *Journal of Finance*, 53, 3 (1998): 1015-52.

74. —————. "Who Manages Risk? An Empirical Examination of Risk Management Practices in the Gold Mining Industry," *Journal of Finance*, 51,4 (1996): 1097-1138.

75. Wall, Larry D., and John J. Pringle. "Interest Rate Swaps: A Review of the Issues." *Federal Reserve Bank of Atlanta Economic Review* (1988).

76. Whaley, Robert E. "Valuation of American Futures Options: Theory and Empirical Evidence." *The Journal of Finance* 41, no. 1 (March 1986).

77. Young, Robert A. "Convertible Securities: Definitions, Analytical Tools and Practical Investment Strate-gies," in *The Financial Analysts Handbook*. 2d ed., edited by Sumner N. Levine (Homewood, III .: Dow Jones-Irwin, 1988).

35

Convertible Securities

INTRODUCTION

Convertible securities are the oldest hybrid securities. They combine the basic attributes of fixed interest and variable income securities. Individual issues of convertibles are all alike in some characteristics but vary significantly in other attributes. Each convertible security provides that it may be exchanged for another security that convey different rights, privileges, restrictions and limitations. Nearly all convertible securities carry prior rights — those of debt obligation or preference share — plus a privilege to convert into equity of the issuing company. They tend to provide both higher flows of income (i.e. interest or dividends) and smaller price fluctuations than the equity into which they may be converted. Once converted into equity, they cannot be exchanged for bonds/ preference share of the issuing company.

CONVERTIBLE DEBENTURES

The convertible debentures are the most popular form of the hybrid securities. It is a debt issue that can be exchanged for a specified number of equity shares in future. It grants the stable income associated with debentures alongwith the possibility of capital gains of equity shares on conversion.

Features

Convertible debentures or bonds are definitely a far more attractive investment proposition as compared to fixed deposits, given the liquidity, the possible capital appreciation and the higher yield. As compared to equity shares, convertible bond strikes a balance between yield and possibilities of capital loss. Also, investment in equity shares is vulnerable to economic, political and technical factors. Depending on these, the value of the equity share may decrease or increase. In short, a convertible bond combines high return of fixed deposits with the profitability from capital appreciation and the liquidity of equity shares. The main features of convertible debentures are listed below :

1. Conversion Price

The conversion price is the total price at which an ordinary share is issued and allotted to the debenture holder. This includes the premium over the par value. The determination of the conversion price is based on a number of factors including the existing book value, the market price, expected appreciation in the value of equity shares, etc. However, the critical factor is the yield to the investor.

Usually, the conversion price is set well above the market price of the equity shares at the time the convertible bonds are issued. However, it should not be set too high, or the conversion feature will have little value to prospective purchaser. The higher the conversion price, the longer the bond holders will have to wait for the market price of the equity shares to rise enough to push up the market value of the bond. The conversion privilege may thus turn out to be valueless. On the other hand, the conversion price should not be set too low. One purpose of selling a convertible bond issue is to sell equity share, indirectly at a price higher than the current market price. If the conversion price is set below the current market price of the equity shares, then this purpose will be defeated. As the conversion price is lowered, the present value of the conversion privilege is increased. But by lowering the conversion price, the present shareholders are faced with larger sacrifices at some point of time in future because they will be forced to share the earnings of the company with the large number of new shareholders (e.g. bond holders) when conversion takes place.

The aim should be to set the conversion price at a level so that the added rupees gained immediately from the conversion privilege are matched by the present value of the future earnings sacrificed.

2. Conversion Ratio

The conversion ratio is the number of equity shares received in exchange for a convertible bond. In other words, the convertion ratio is :

$$\text{Face Value of the bond} = \frac{\text{Conversion Ratio}}{\text{Conversion Price}}$$

For example on 6th October, 2011, XYZ Company made a public issue of 10,00,000 (at 15% interest rate) convertible bonds of ₹ 450 each for cash at par. Each XYZ Company's bond of ₹ 450 face value, had a conversion price of ₹ 225 meaning that each bond to be converted into two XYZ's share.

$$\text{Conversion ratio of XYZ's Bond} = \frac{₹\ 450}{₹\ 225} = 2 \text{ XYZ's shares.}$$

However, the conversion terms are not necessary constant over time. Many convertible issues provide for increase or "step-ups" in the conversion price at periodic intervals. In this way, the bond converts into fewer shares of equity shares as the time goes by. Usually, the conversion price is adjusted for any stock splits or stock dividends that occur after the securities are sold. If the equity shares were split two for one, for example, the conversion would be halved. This provision protects the convertible bond holder and is known as anti-dilution clause. For example, if XYZ issue bonus shares (stock splits) during the seven-year period the price of ₹ 225 per share will be proportionately reduced.

3. Quantum of Conversion

The quantum to be converted is normally specified in terms of a percentage of the face value of the debenture or bond. The amount to be so converted is translated into the number of equity shares based on the conversion price. Hence the increase in the capital base will be dependent on the percentage conversion and the conversion price. For a specified percentage, the higher the conversion price, lower will be the addition to capital base.

4. Convertible Value

The conversion value is the value of the convertible based on the right to receive equity shares. The conversion value of a convertible is the conversion ratio times the market price per share of the equity. If the XYZ Company share is quoted ₹ 310 on 4th December 2011, on that date the conversion value of the XYZ bond would be ₹ 620.

5. Investment Value — Value Based on Straight Senior Security Value (Also called Bond Value)

A convertible bond/debenture derives value from two sources; its value as a bond/ debenture and its potential value as equity shares if converted. In the case of a bond, we can label the two components of value as the bond value (investment value) and the conversion value. The investment value is the value of the convertible based on its status as a senior security alone without any value. In other words, stripped of the conversion privilege, what is its worth ? The yield obtained by dividing the market price into the interest rate has to be sufficient to satisfy investors without the conversion feature.

For a convertible debenture, the investment value is the market price based on the yield to maturity which will satisfy investors without the conversion feature. Investment value can be estimated with a fair degree of accuracy by a competent security analyst. The analyst first judges the quality by considering all relevant factors; he obtains a sample of all other similar quality non-convertible debentures to obtain the yield that the market would place on the issue without the conversion feature. With this yield related to the interest coupon, he determines the bond value or investment value. However, the investment value may vary over time as a result of change in the quality of the issue due to a change in the company's financial strength or as a result of a general market change in the level of yields on bonds or debentures.

6. Market Price

This is the price the market places on a convertible because of its two features - its conversion value and investment value. The convertible bond can be thought of as a combinatioin of a bond plus an option to buy firm's equity shares. If the value of the equity share rises, the value of the option and hence that of the convertible bond will rise. If the value of the equity falls, the value of the convertible as a bond provides a floor below which the price of the conversion will not fall. This opportunity to be protected from a decline in the equity price by the investment value and yet be able to benefit from a rise in the equity share price causes the convertible to sell at a premium.

7. Premium

This is the amount by which the market price of the convertible is higher than its conversion value or investment/bond value. The investor can reduce his risk by investing in a convertible bond rather than the equity shares of a company. In general, the more volatile the price movements of the shares,the more valuable is the downside protection afforded by the bond value floor. For this reason, the market price of a convertible bond usually is above its conversion value. The difference is known as the premium-over-conversion value.

Moreover, a convertible bond usually will sell at a premium over- bond value, primarily because of the conversion feature. Unless the market price of the share is very low related to the conversion price, the conversion feature usually will have value, in that investors may eventually find it profitable to convert the bond/debenture. To the extent that the conversion feature does have value, the convertible will sell at a premium over its straight bond value. The higher the market price of the equity relative to the conversion price, the greater is to be the premium.

Size of Premium

One of the principal factors which effects the size of the premium is the nearness of the conversion value and the investment value. When they are equal, the premium will be at a maximum. If the conversion value is far above the investment value, the premium will be small because there will be little protection from a decline in the equity price by the investment value. Again, premium will be small if the conversion value is far below the investment values because there would be little chance for the equity shares to move up for enough so that convertible to appreciate above the bond/investment value.

The main factors affecting the size of the premium are listed below :

   (i) The closeness of the conversion value and the investment value ;
  (ii) The outlook for the equity shares:Is it a dull equity without much prospects of growth or does it have real potential ? The greater investor's hope for the equity the greater the premium;
 (iii) The downside risk in the equity : If it is a risky equity that might fall out of bed, there is more reason to pay a premium than for one that has little prospects of a decline. For example, an equity which has an assumed dividend and is selling on a yield basis might have little prospects for a decline;
  (iv) The size of the spread between the yield on the convertible and the equity available through conversion will affect the premium. When the convertible is sold; the yield on the convertible may be large than the yield on the equity. The spread narrows over time with increases in the dividend rate on the equity. When the yield on the equity is larger than the yield on, the convertible, there is less reason for investors to buy the convertible.
   (v) The provisions may dampen or eliminate the premium if they limit the opportunity for the convertible to appreciate with a rise in the equity share price.

Premiums can vary from issue to issue even when the same relationship exists between conversion value and investment value, thereby making valuation of convertible bonds a problem.

Besides the above main reasons for premiums, other factors appear to have at least a modest influence on the premiums. These are:

   (a) Lower transaction costs on convertible bonds relative to those on equity shares, also enhance the attractiveness of these bonds. An investor who wishes to acquire equity shares of a company would incur lower transaction costs by purchasing a convertible bond and converting it into equity shares than he would be purchasing the stock outright. This attraction should exert upward pressure on the premiums-over-conversion value and bond value.
   (b) The duration of the convertible option also should affect the premiums. In general, the longer the duration, the more valuable the option. Unlike other options, however, the duration until expiration is certain owing to the fact that the company can force conversion if the price of the equity shares is high enough.
   (c) Another factor is the dividend on the equity. The greater the dividend, the greater the attraction of the equity vis-a-vis the convertible bond and the lower the premium, all other things the same.
   (d) Yet another influence that may raise premiums is mat certain institutional investors, such as Life Insurance Companies, are very restricted with respect to investing in equity shares. By investing in convertible bonds, they have the benefit of equity shares investment without actually investing in equity shares. All these influences account for the premiums at which convertible bonds sell.

8. Timing of Conversion

This relates to the period during which the conversion option is exerciseable. This can range anywhere from one year from the date of allotment to upto five years.

However, from the company's point of view, the longer duration is preferable from two counts : (a) low pretax financing cost till conversion, *(b)* postponement of earnings dilution and the attendant higher dividend out go.

OBJECTIVES OF CONVERTIBLE DEBENTURES

In general a convertible should not be used unless a company needs equity capital. It could be foolish to incur the potential dilution in earnings per share if equity capital was not needed.

The various purposes of convertible are outlined, below:

1. Sweetener to a Senior Security

Sometimes the addition of the conversion feature becomes necessary to sweeten up a senior security which would otherwise be impossible to sell or difficult to sell at reasonable price. The investor is offered a fixed income obligation with the additional weight of potentials of appreciation through the conversion feature. Some investors go for such a security even though it is weak, provided there are real possibilities of appreciation. This purpose means an admission of financial weakness on the part of the company, but if capital is needed and this is the only way it can be obtained, the use of a convertible may be not only justified, but required.

2. For Extensive Financing Programmes

When the company has such an extensive financing programme that the market will not readily absorb all the equity capital that should be sold in order to keep the capital structure ratios in balance and it would be unwise to postpone long-term financing. A convertible security used for this purpose will permit the capital to be raised by means of long-term security, and the capital structure will *be* strengthened as conversion takes place. In this situation, where equity capital is definitely the goal, the conversion ratio should be attractive enough to assure conversion.

There are number of reasons why a large convertible issue may be more readily absorbed than a similar amount of equity capital. At times, a convertible may be just what the doctor prescribed as far as certain investors' desires are concerned. For example, some investors may not wish to buy a straight debenture or preference shares, but at times might buy a convertible. Furthermore, some institutions might not be interested in a equity, but would buy a senior security combining the equity feature. In designing a convertible to meet such a market demand, it may be necessary to have in mind the special requirements of institutional investors. They may be restricted from buying equity shares, or a convertible issue, if it sells primarily on a parity basis of the equity rather than on its worth as a senior security.

At times, the greater amount that may be borrowed by investors from banks on a convertible debenture may be important in assisting in the sale. Banks may be willing to lend more money on a convertible than on a straight equity and they may be permitted to lend more by law.

3. Refunding Medium

Convertible bonds/debentures may be issued as refunding medium for existing debt, to permit a gradual strengthening of the capital structure. This is perhaps one of the least controversial uses. No additional harm is done to the capital structure if conversion does not take place, unless, of course, the existing debt had a large sinking fund or serial maturity and this is not included in the convertible. Of course, the possible effect on dilution of earning per share must be carefully analysed.

4. Unreasonably Depressed Market Price Per Share

When a company needs to add equity shares to its capital structure, and their market price is unreasonably depressed due to poor earnings, which are expected to improve; a seriously adverse stock market in general; or a large block of the company's stock overhanging in the market, depressing the price unreasonably; the conversion price will be set above the existing market price of the stock at the time of the sale. It will be expected that with an improvement in the market price, conversion will take place. Therefore, the conversion price should be set so as to assure conversion, even if the market price does not improve to the extent anticipated as a result of the natural optimism of the management.

This may be a good reason for the use of convertible, but the other methods of financing should also be explored, such as temporary financing with a bank loan and then repayment through the sale of equity shares. Caution should be used in relying on this purpose to justify a convertible, because most managements have a tendency to think their equity shares price is too low no matter what the price.

5. Dilution

Financing through convertible bonds/debentures may be to permit a gradual dilution of earnings per equity share as conversion takes place rather than heavy dilution, which would result if all the equity shares were sold at one time.

To illustrate suppose that the current market price of the equity shares of ABC corporation is ₹ 320 per share. If the company raises capital with an equity issue, it will have to underprice the issue in order to sell it in the market. Suppose that the company is able to sell the shares through underwriters and realise net proceeds of ₹ 288 per share. If the company wishes to raise ₹ 1440 crore the issue would involve 5 crore shares of additional stock. On the other hand, if ABC corporation sells a convertible issue, it. is able to set the conversion price above the current market price per share. If the conversion premium is 20%, the conversion price would be ₹ 384 per share. Assuming a ₹ 1440 crore issue of convertibles, the number of additional shares after conversion would be ₹ 1440 crore/₹ 384 = 37,50,000.

We see that the potential dilution with a convertible issue is less than that with an equity issue because fewer shares are being added. But this may not be a very good reason for the use of a convertible. The effect of dilution may be anticipated by the investors.

6. Gloomy Conditions in the Stock Market

If the market for either debt or preferred stock is poor and rates required to sell the securities are high, the addition of a conversion feature may be used to sweeten up the security in order to receive a lower rate of interest or dividends. Use of convertibles for this purpose is debatable. As a financing strategy management may wish to finance with convertible securities as opposed to equity shares when its estimates of the firm's future are more favourable than those of the market By so doing, it obtains lesser dilution for existing shareholders than it would if it financed with equity shares. Once management's expecta-tions are realised, the shares prices presumably will rise. Of course, the merit of such a strategy depends upon management's estimates of the future being more accurate than those of the market. When the share is depressed in price, however, it may be wise to avoid both equity shares and convertible financing. Otherwise, it may be trying to slice the bacon too thin, and the company may end up with a convertible which never converts, or converts at the wrong time to cause dilution of earnings per share and thus pressure on the market price of the shares.

7. Credit Rating

Another advantage is for companies with low credit ratings but good prospects of growth. It may be extremely difficult to sell a straight issue of bonds. However, the market may regard a convertible issue of these companies in favourable light, not because of its quality as a bond but because of its quality as equity shares. Convertible securities can be sold during periods of tight money when it may *be* very difficult for even a creditworthy company to sell a straight bond. For these reasons, convertibles are attractive to many firms as a means of financing.

8. Gestation Period

To provide cheap money for a period while the convertible issue is outstanding, perhaps during a period when construction is taking place and then to turn into the more costly type of security, equity shares, at the end of the period, when earnings may materialise, the convertible stock may be issued. This also may be slicing the bacon too thin. There are other methods of handling such a situation, and they should be examined carefully. For example, a bank loan might be used temporarily prior to issuing equity shares.

9. Floatation Cost

Convertible stock can be used as a mechanical aid in issuing equity shares with lower financing costs, since the underwriting fees are less on a convertible than on a straight equity issue, and the conversion price of the shares may be set closer to the market. In view of all the other complications of a convertible this reason alone is hardly a good one.

10. Delay Control

In case the present equity share holders wish to delay temporarily the addition of more shareholders in order to preserve their control, the convertible stock provides the alternative. This is a special situation and one not likely to occur often.

In some situations, a convertible may be used to accomplish more than one of the purposes outlined above, but in deciding whether to use a convertible each purpose should be analysed by itself with its advantages and disadvantages. This should include an analysis of how a convertible will work out with various stock prices each year throughout the life of the convertible, and alternatives for raising the capital with their advantages and disadvantages at the various stock prices. If there are alternatives and they are compared correctly, one of them may prove more advantageous than a convertible issue.

Keep in mind that if a convertible does not convert as planned, the company may be saddled with a senior seniority which might not fit into the capital structure. Furthermore a convertible tends to exert a depressing effect on the market for the equity shares because of the potential dilution which will result when conversion does occur. If it converts at the wrong time, there may be depressing effect on the market when the company would prefer that this not to occur, for example, when more equity is to be offered.

A company will do well to mink of a convertible issue as an emergency type of security and save this slot in its capital structure for this purpose. It is a good form of reserve type of security. A simple rule to follow is that if a company needs equity capital, the market is reasonably receptive and earnings are satisfactory, it should go ahead with the sale of equity and not gamble with a convertible. Anyone who has had experience trying to forecast security prices will readily admit that it is very difficult to tell at what price a share will sell in the future. The more a company needs equity capital in its capitalisation, the less chance it can take on using a convertible and being subject to whims of the stock market to determine whether conversion takes place. If a company can sell shares but wishes to use convertible debentures merely because the market won't afford a high price for the equity shares that company should be thoroughly prepared to justify the position that it can stand the additional debt if no conversion takes place. A company with a very conservative capitalisation is in a better position to play with a convertible for other than emergency purposes. It can better stand the additional senior securities if conversion does not occur.

Companies usually issue convertible bonds with the full expectation that these securities will be converted within a certain length of time. But an investor would convert voluntarily: (i) if the dividends being paid on the equity shares are very attractive, he may sacrifice his senior position in order to obtain the higher dividends; and (ii) if the conversion price were scheduled to increase in the near future, he might convert. Otherwise, he may simply prefer to hold the bond, for its price will increase as the price of the equity shares increases. In addition he receives regular interest. For these reasons and others, many investors do not want to convert their security even though its conversion value is more than what they paid for it.

In order to force conversion, companies issuing convertible bonds usually must call the issue. The *call feature* provides the issuer some control over the timing of the conversion. To do so, the market price of the bond must be significantly higher than the call price, so that the investors will convert rather than accepts the lower call price. To illustrate, suppose that the conversion price of a convertible debenture (₹ 800 face value) were ₹ 40 and that the call price were ₹ 944, for the conversion value of the bond to equal the call price, the market price of the equity must be ₹ 944/20=₹ 47.20 per share. If the bonds are called when the market price is ₹ 47.20, many investors might choose to accept the call price rather convert. The company would then have to redeem many of the bonds for cash, in part defeating the purpose of the original financing. In order to assume almost complete conversion, it might wait to call the debentures, say until the conversion value of bond is 20% above the call price, a value that corresponds to an equity share market price of approximately ₹56.64 a share.

Other means are available to a company for *stimulating* as opposed *to forcing* conversion. By establishing an *acceleration* or *step up* in the conversion price at steady intervals in the future, there is persistent pressure on bond holders to convert, assuming the conversion value of the bond is relatively high. For example, if the conversion price is scheduled to increase from ₹ 40 to ₹ 44.80 at the end of next month, convertible bond holders have an incentive to convert prior to that time, all other things remaining the same. If the holder waits, he receives fewer shares of stock This 'step up' provision must be established at the time of issue of the convertible bond. It cannot be used for purpose of stimulating conversion at a particular moment, in time. Another means for stimulating conversion is to increase the dividend on the equity, thereby making such shares more attractive. In certain cases, the dividend income available on the associated equity shares may exceed interest income on the convertible bond. Although the two stimulants discussed above enhance conversion, invariably a portion of the convertible bond-holders will not convert, owing to the downside protection of the bond, the superior legal claim on assets, and other reasons. Consequently, calling the issue may be the only means for assuring that the issue will be substantially converted.

However, to avoid any undesirable consequences the basic aim of forcing conversion may be included as one of the terms in the bond indenture.

If a company is unable to force or stimulate conversion because the market price of the share has not risen sufficiently to attract the investor to convert the convertible issue, the company is constrained in its ability to obtain new financing and such a convertible issue is said to be *over-hanging*, it is difficult to see another convertible security issue until the present one is converted. The overhanging issue creates apprehension in the market over the investment worthiness of any new issue of convertible and may even create apprehension over the worthiness of a non-convertible security offering.

The *risk of an over-hanging issue* and the loss of flexibility associated with such an issue may offset, at least in fact, the advantage in issuing price of the convertible security over an equity shares offering. With the convertible security issue, it is uncertain when, if even, the security will convert and the company will obtain equity capital. If it were not for this factor, the lower dilution associated with a convertible issue as opposed to an equity issue would always make the convertible issue more attractive. For a growing company, the occurence of an overhanging issue may be a serious problem.

VALUATION OF CONVERTIBLE DEBENTURES

The value of the convertible debenture is related to (1) the value of the equity into which it may be converted and (2) the value of the convertible debenture as a non-convertible debenture instrument. Although each of these factors affects the market, price of the convertible debenture, the importance of each element varies with changing conditions in the security market.

The Convertible Debenture As Equity

The value of convertible debentures in terms of equity into which they may be converted (C_e) depends upon (1) the face or principal amount of the convertible debenture (F), (2) the conversion (or exercise) price of the convertible debenture (P_c), and (3) the market price of the equity (P_s). The face value divided by the conversion price of the convertible debenture gives the number of shares into which the convertible debenture may be converted. For example, if a ₹ 100 convertible debenture may be converted at ₹ 20 per share, then the convertible bond may be converted into 5 shares (₹ 100 + ₹ 20). The number of shares times the market price of a share gives the value of the convertible debenture in terms of equity. If the convertible debenture is convertible into 5 shares and the share sells for ₹ 15 per share, then the convertible bond is worth ₹ 75 in terms of equity (₹ 15 X 5). This theoretical value of the convertible debenture in equity is expressed in Equation-1:

$$C_e = \frac{F}{P_c} \times P_s \qquad\qquad ....(1)$$

and is illustrated in Table-1.

TABLE 1

Relationship Between the Price of Equity and the Value of a Convertible Debenture

Price of the Equity	Shares into which the Convertible Debenture is converted	Value of the Convertible Debenture in terms of Equity
Re. 0	5	0
₹ 5	5	25
₹ 10	5	50
₹15	5	75
₹20	5	100
₹25	5	125

Table 1 shows that the value of the convertible debenture in terms of the equity rises as the price of the equity increases.

The relationship between the price of a convertible debenture and the conversion value of the bond is illustrated in Figure 1. The conversion price of the convertible debenture is given on the vertical axis, and the price of the equity is shown on the horizontal axis. The conversion value of the convertible debenture increases as the price of the equity rises. This is shown in the graph by line $C_{e/}$ which represents the theoretical value of the convertible debenture in terms of equity. If the exercise price of the convertible debenture and the market price of the equity are equal (i.e. $P_c = P^{\wedge}$ which in this case is ₹ 20), then the convertible debenture value as equity equal to the principal amount (i.e. the convertible debenture's face value). As the price of the equity rises above the exercise price of the convertible debenture, the value of the convertible debenture in terms of equity increases to more than the principal amount of the non-convertible debt.

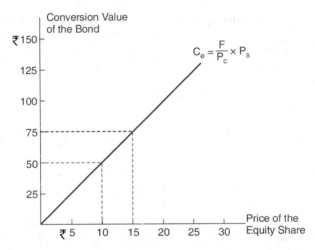

FIGURE 1: THE RELATIONSHIP BETWEEN THE PRICE OF CONVERTIBLE BOND AND THE CONVERSION VALUE OF THE BOND

The theoretical value of convertible debenture as equity sets the minimum market price of a convertible debenture. If the price of the convertible debenture were less than its value as equity, an opportunity to arbitrage would exist. Arbitragers would sell the equity short, purchase the convertible debenture, exercise the conversion feature, and use the shares acquired through the conversion to cover the short sale. The arbitragers would then make a profit equal to the difference between the price of the convertible debenture and the conversion value of the convertible debenture. For example, if the convertible debenture were selling for ₹ 80 when the equity sold for ₹ 20 per share, arbitragers would enter the market. At price ₹ 20 per share, the convertible debenture is worth ₹ 100 in terms of equity. Arbitragers would then sell 5 shares short for ₹ 100. At the same time, they would buy the convertible debenture for ₹ 80 and exercise the option. The arbitrager would acquire the shares through the conversion of the convertible debenture to cover the short position and earn ₹ 20 in profit.

Increase in demand for the convertible debentures would drive up their price. Arbitrage will continue till the price of the convertible debenture is equal to the convertible debenture's value as equity. Because of arbitrage, the market price of a convertible debenture will be at least equal to the conversion value. However, the market price of the convertible debenture is rarely equal to the conversion value of the convertible debenture. The convertible debenture frequently sells for a premium over its conversion value, because the convertible debenture may also have value as debt instruments.

Convertible Debenture As Debt

The value of the convertible debenture as debt (C_D) is related to (1) the annual interest or coupon rate that the convertible debenture pays (I), (2) the current interest rate that is paid on comparable non-convertible debt (R), and (3) the requirement that the principal or face value (F) be retired at maturity (after n number of years) if the convertible debenture is not converted. In terms of present value of a convertible debenture as non- convertible debt is given in Equation-2

$$C_D = \frac{I}{(1+R)^1} + \frac{I}{(1+R)^2} + \frac{I}{(1+R)^3} + ...+ \frac{I}{(1+R)^n} + \frac{F}{(1+R)^n} \qquad ....(2)$$

To illustrate equation (2), assume that the convertible debenture in Table-1 matures in 7 years and pays 15 per cent annually. Non-convertible debt of the same risk class currently yielded 18 per cent. By inserting these values into Equation-2, the value of the convertible debenture as non-convertible debt can be determined.

$$C_D = \frac{₹\ 15}{(1+.18)^1} + \frac{₹\ 15}{(1+.18)^2} + \frac{₹\ 15}{(1+.18)^3} + ...+ \frac{₹\ 15}{(1+.18)^7} + \frac{₹\ 100}{(1+.18)^7}$$

$$C_D = ₹\ 15\ (3.8115) + ₹100\ (0.31392)$$

$$= ₹88.56$$

The relationship between the price of the equity and the value of the convertible debenture as non-convertible debt is illustrated in Figure-2. Horizontal line (C_D) shows that the price ₹88.56 of the convertible debenture would be if it were not converted into equity. The principal amount of the convertible debenture is shown by the broken line F, which is above the line C_D. The principal amount exceeds the value of the convertible debenture as pure debt because the convertible debenture must sell at a discount to be competitive with non- convertible debt.

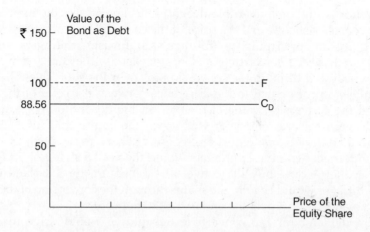

FIGURE 2: THE RELATIONSHIP BETWEEN THE PRICE OF EQUITY SHARE AND THE VALUE BOND AS NONCONVERTIBLE DEBT

The value of the convertible debenture as debt varies with market interest rates. Since interest paid by the convertible debenture is fixed, the value of the convertible debenture as debt varies inversely with interest rates. Table 2 shows that increase in interest rates causes the value of convertible debentures to fall; a decline in interest rates causes this value to rise.

TABLE 2

Relationship between Interest Rates and the Value of a Convertible Debenture

Interest Rate	Coupon Rate	Value of a 7-year Convertible Debenture
12%	15%	₹ 113.69
13%	15%	108.84
14%	15%	104.28
15%	15%	100.00
16%	15%	95.96
17%	15%	92.16
18%	15%	88.56

The value of the convertible debenture as non-convertible debt is important because this value sets a price floor that convertible debenture will command in the market. At the price floor the convertible debenture is competitive with non- convertible debt of the same maturity and degree of risk. If the convertible debenture were to sell below this price, it would offer a yield that is more attractive (i.e. higher) than that of the non-convertible debt. Investors would seek to buy the convertible debenture to attain this higher yield. They would bid up the convertible debenture's price until its yield were comparable to that of non-convertible debt. The price floor would halt any further fall in the price of the convertible debenture even if the value of the equity into which the convertible debenture may be converted were to decline.

The actual minimum price of a convertible debenture conbines its value as equity and its value as debt. This is illustrated in Figure-3, which combines both the values.

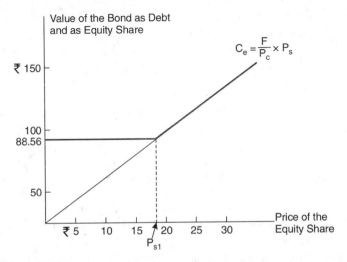

FIGURE 3: THE ACTUAL MINIMUM PRICE OF A CONVERTIBLE BOND.

These values set a minimum price for the convertible debenture, because its price cannot be lower than of these two values. For low equity prices (i.e. equity prices less man P_{sl} in Figure,the minimum price is set by the convertible debenture's value as debt. However, for equity prices greater than P_{sl}, it is the convertible debenture's value as equity that determines the minimum price.

Convertible Debenture's Value As A Hybrid Security

The market price (P_m) of the convertible debenture combines both the conversion value of the convertible debenture and its value as non-convertible debt. If the price of the equity were to decline significantly below the exercise price of the convertible debenture, the market price of the convertible debenture would be influenced primarily by the convertible debenture's value as non- convertible debt. In effect, the convertible debenture would be priced as if it were a pure debt instrument. As the price of the equity rises, the conversion value of the convertible debenture rises and plays an increasingly important role in the determination of the market price of the convertible debenture. At sufficiently high equity prices, the market price of the bond is identical with its conversion value.

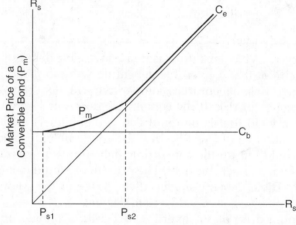

FIGURE 4: DETERMINING THE MARKET PRICE OF A CONVERTIBLE BOND.

These relationships are illustrated in Figure 4. For prices of the equity below P_{sl}, the market price is identical to the convertible debenture's value as non-convertible debt. For prices of the equity above P_{s2} the price of the convertible debenture is identical to its value as equity. At these extreme prices, the convertible debenture may be analysed as if it were either pure debt or equity. For all prices between these two extremes, the market price of the convertible debenture is influenced by the convertible debenture's value both as non-convertible debt and as equity. This dual influence makes the analysis of convertible debentures difficult, since the investor pays a premium over the convertible debenture's value as equity and as debt.

One way to analyse a convertible debenture is to measure the premium over the convertible debenture's value as debt or as equity. For example, if a particular convertible debenture is commanding a higher premium than is paid for similar convertible securities, perhaps this convertible debenture should be sold. Conversely, the convertible debenture may be a good investment if the premium is relatively low. The premiums paid for convertible debenture are illustrated in Table-3. Column 6 gives the premium in terms of equity. This is the difference between the convertible debenture's market price and its value as equity (i.e. the hypothetical value in column 5 minus the value in column 3). This premium declines as the price of the equity rises and plays a more dominant role in the determination of the convertible debenture's price. Column 7 gives the premium in terms of non-convertible debt. This is the difference between the convertible debenture's market price and its value as debt (i.e., the value in column 5 minus the value in column 4). Since the debt element of the convertible debenture is less important, this premium rises as the price of the equity rises.

TABLE 3

Permium Paid for Convertible Debenture

Price of the Share	Shares into which the Convertible Debenture may be Converted	Value of the Convertible Debenture in terms of Equity Shares	Value of the convertible Debenture as non-convertible Debenture	Hypothetical Price of the convertible debeture	Premium in term of equity*	Premium in terms of non-conver-tibledebt**
(1)	(2)	(3)	(4)	(5)	(6)	(7)
0	5	₹ 0	₹88.56	₹88.56	₹88.56	₹0.00
5	5	₹ 25	88.56	88.56	63.56	0.00
10	5	₹ 50	88.56	88.56	38.56	0.00
15	5	₹ 75	88.56	100.00	25.00	11.44
20	5	₹ 100	88.56	120.00	20.00	31.44
25	5	₹ 125	88.56	130.00	5.00	41.44

* Premium in terms of equity is equal to the hypothetical price of the convertible debenture minus the value of the convertible debenture in term of equity.

** The premium in terms of non-convertible debenture is equal to the hypothetical price of the convertible debenture minus the value of the convertible debenture as non-convertible debenture.

Figure-5 illustrates the inverse relationship between the two premiums. The premiums^ are shown by the difference between the line representing the market price (Pm) and the lines representing me value of the convertible debenture in terms of equity (C_e) and the value of the convertible debenture as non- convertible debt (C_D). When title price of the equity is low and the convertible debenture is selling close to its value as debt, the

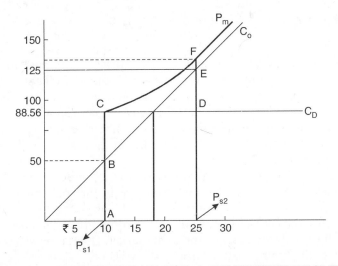

FIGURE 5: PREMIUMS PAID FOR A CONVERTIBLE BOND.

premium above the convertible debenture's intrinsic value as equity is substantial, but the premium above the convertible debenture's value as debt is small. For example, at P_{gl} the price of the equity is ₹ 10, the convertible debenture's value in terms of equity is ₹ 50 (Line ABin Figure-5), and the premium is ₹ 38.56 (Line BC). However, the convertible debenture is selling for its value as non-convertible debt (₹ 88.56), and there is no premium over the value as debt. When the price of the equity is ₹ 25 and the convertible debenture is selling for ₹ 130, the premium in terms of equity is only ₹ 5 (Line EF). However, the convertible debenture's premium over its value as non-convertible debt is ₹ 41.44 (Line DF). Thus, the premium paid for the convertible debenture over its theoretical value as equity declines as the price of the equity rises. This decline in premium is the result of the increasing importance of the conversion value of the convertible debenture's market price and the decreasing importance of the debt element of the convertible debenture's price. The safety feature of the debt diminishes with rise in equity prices. If the price of the equity ceased to rise and started to decline, then the price of the convertible debenture could decline considerably before it reached the floor price set by the non- convertible debt. The safety feature diminishes as the price of equity rises. For example, if the price of the equity declined from ₹ 25 to ₹ 15 (a 40 per cent decline), the price of the convertible debenture could fall from ₹ 130 to ₹ 88.56 (a 31.88 per cent decline). Such a price decline would indicate that the floor value of ₹ 88.56 had little impact on the decline in the price of the convertible debenture.

This decline in the premium also means that the price of the equity will rise more rapidly than the price of the convertible debenture. For example, when the equity's price increased from ₹ 20 to ₹ 25 (a 25 per cent increase), the convertible debenture's price rose from ₹ 120 to ₹ 130 (an 8.33 per cent increase). The reason for this difference in the rate of increase is the declining premium paid for the convertible debenture. Since the premium declines as the price of the equity rises, the rate of increase in the price of the equity must exceed the rate of increase in the price of covertible debentures. Thus, the convertible debentures offer investors the opportunity for some capital growth with less risk.

IMPLICATIONS OF THE CONVERTIBLE BOND ISSUE FOR THE ISSUING COMPANY

The issues affecting a company's decisions in floating an issue of convertible debentures/bonds cover a number of areas. Some of the major issues are discussed below:

1. Timing of Issue

The appropriate timing of convertible issue must be evaluated in relation to the market for the company's equity shares. If it is a poor time to sell equity shares because of depressed market price, it will also be a poor time to sell a convertible issue though the convertible issue can be sold at a conversion price higher than trie price at which an equity issue can be sold. If the management believes that the equity issue is undervalued, it might be best to postpone the convertible issue in the hope that there would be an improvement in the market.

There is a greater dilution when the equity shares are undervalued. It is due both to the depressed market for the stock and to variations in the conversion premium in the market psychology. The greater the prospective growth of a company from the standpoint of market the higher the conversion premium the company can obtain. The conversion premium normally will be lower in a depressed market. The timing of a convertible issue is related closely to the timing of an ordiriary share issue.

2. Dilution of Existing Holding

The issue of debentures may be entirely to the public or to the existing shareholders, or a combination of both. In such situations a factor that is normally taken into consideration is the impact of conversion on the existing holdings of the Indian promoter group and the foreign collaborator if any. Dilution of their holdings would arise if there is a public issue without any reservation for firm allotment to these two groups in proportion or they are not able to subscribe to the rights offer due to any reason whatsoever. Further, any internal decision on not going below a specified percentage for the Indian promoter group or the foreign collaborator subsequent to conversion would necessarily affect the decision on quantum of conversion and the total amount proposed to be raised.

Another factor related to the above is the possible extent to which the financial institutions may acquire shares. If a rights issue is made and there are institutional shareholdings, the extent of their eligibility through rights and additional debentures that may be requested for by the institutions would play a part in determining the extent of their holdings. If a public issue is decided upon, the institutional holdings would be decided by the quantum of their underwriting and the public response to the issue. Probablistic estimate may have to be made on these aspects if the holdings of institutions are deemed to be a critical factor.

3. Yield to the Investor

The yield to the investor would be determined by the quantum of conversion, the conversion price, the market price of the ordinary shares, the timing of conversion and the discount on the debenture after conversion. A rough and ready method of working out the yields is to total up the money realised by the investor by interest, sale of shares at prevailing price, and the sale proceeds of debentures at a discount immediately after conversion and averaging it for the period upto conversion. Again, the market price that is taken into consideration is the price at the time of the issue of debentures and not the anticipated price likely to prevail at the time of conversion.

4. Security

The issue of these debentures can be either secured or unsecured. The security normally offered is a first charge on the fixed assets ranking pari-passu with the existing charges, if any. In such a situation, the major requirement that may have been stipulated by the existing lenders will necessarily have to be taken into account.

Another important issue to be considered is the company Deposit Rules. As per the definition clause in these rules, any amount raised by the issue of bonds or debentures secured by the mortgage of any immovable property of the company or with an option to convert them into shares in the company are exempt from being deemed as deposits provided that in the case of such bonds or debentures secured by the mortgage of any immovable property, the amount of such debentures or bonds shall not exceed the market value of such immovable property. Based on this definition, one aspect to be considered is whether or not unsecured convertible debentures will be deemed as deposits after the expiry of the period for exercising the convertible option. In cases where quantum of conversion is low, issue of unsecured convertible debentures may restrict the quantum of deposits a company can raise. Another possible interpretation is that while determining the except categories of deposits the nature of the debt investment at the time of the issue should be taken into account irrespective of the change that occurs after the expiry of the conversion period. Another aspect is that if the debentures are not secured, a second mortgage would suffice. Provided the issue is marketable otherwise and the market value of the assets exceeds the value of the debentures proposed to be issued. Necessarily any existing outstanding debenture term loans will also have to be taken into account while computing the limit.

5. Liquidity

Convertible bonds are normally quoted on the recognised stock exchanges facilitating dealings. Thus they offer as good a liquidity as the equity share attached with the bond makes them attractive. The same factor also fetches capital appreciation to the bondholders as the bonds may be quoted at a premium on the stock exchange depending upon the price of the equity shares.

6. Capital Gains

This aspect has been looked into and analysed by a number of eminent authorities. Contradictory opinions exist on the aspect. The issue involved is whether capital gains arise on conversion of the debentures into ordinary shares as the specified price of the market value of the share is higher than the conversion price at the time of conversion even though the shares may not be necessarily sold by the investor immediately after conversion.

7. Rights of Public Issue

This is a major issue in so far as distribution of shareholdings after conversion and expenses relating to the issue are concerned. Of course, estimates of the quantum that can be mobilised from the existing shareholders will also be an important factor in taking this decision.

CONVERTIBLE PREFERENCE SHARE

In addition to convertible debentures, companies may issue convertible preference shares. As its name implies, the convertible preference shares may be converted into the equity of the issuing company. Though they are similar to convertible debenture, however, there are some important differences. The differences are primarily the same as those between non- convertible preference share and non-convertible debt. Preference share is treated as an equity investment. Thus, the company is not under any legal obligation to pay the dividend. In addition, the preference share is a perpetual security and does not have to be retired as debt must be.

The value of convertible preference share (like convertible debentures) is related to the price of the equity into which it may be converted and to the value of competitive non-convertible preference share. As with convertible debentures, their values set floors on the price of the convertible preference share. It cannot sell for any significant length of time below its theoretical value as equity. If it did, arbitragers would enter the market and buy the preference share, which would increase its price. Thus, the minimum value of the convertible preference share (like the minimum value of the convertible debenture) must be equal to the conversion price of the equity (P_c). In equation form that is :

$$P_c = P_s \, x \, N \qquad \qquad ....(3)$$

where P_s is the market price of the equity into which the convertible preference share may be converted, and N is the number of equity shares an investor obtains through conversion.

The convertible preference share's value as non-convertible preference share is related to the dividend it pays and to the appropriate discount factor which is the yield earned on competitive non-convertible debt. This is essentially the same as the convertible debenture's value as debt, except that preference share has no definite maturity date. However, this value does not set a floor or the price of a convertible preference share because at that price it is competitive with non-convertible preference share.

As with convertible debentures, the convertible preference share is a hybrid security whose value combines its worth both as equity and as non-convertible preference share. Except for its extreme values, the convertible preference share tends to sell for a premium over its value as equity and its value as straight preference share. Premium on the preference share over the value of equity tends to be smaller. The reason for this reduced premium is that the preference share does not have the element of debt. Its features are more similar to equity than to the features of the convertible debentures. Thus, its price usually commands less of a premium over its value as equity.

SELECTING CONVERTIBLES

Because convertible bonds are a hybrid security, they are more difficult to select than non-convertible bonds. These securities are debt investments and pay a fixed flow of interests income, so they appeal to conservative, income- oriented investors. However, since the bonds sell for a premium over their investment value as debt, investors forgo some of the interest income and safety associated with, non- convertible bonds.

A convertible bond also offers the potential for capital gains if the value of the equity into which the bond may be converted were to rise. Possible capital gains increase the bond's attractiveness to investors seeking capital appreciation. Since the investor pays a premium over the bond's value as equity, the potential from appreciation is less than is available through an investment in the firm's equity. However, the investor who purchases the bond does not collect the interest, which usually exceeds the dividends paid on an equivalent number of shares into which the bond may be converted.

The interest advantage may be seen by considering the 15 percent convertible bond issued by G.K. Stores. Each bond may be converted into 40 shares of equity. The equity shareholders are paid dividends of ₹ 2.50 per share (i.e., the equivalent of ₹ 100 on 40 shares), but the bond paid interest of ₹ 150. The bondholder collected ₹ 50 more in interest income than the equity shareholder collected on an equivalent number of shares.

This additional flow of income offers one way to analyse the premium paid for a convertible bond. If the bond is held for a sufficient amount of time, the additional income will offset the premium. This time period is sometimes referred to as *years to payback* or the *breakeven time*. The following example illustrates how this breakeven time may be computed. Consider a ₹ 1,000 convertible bond with a 14 percent coupon that is convertible into 50 equity shares. The company sells the equity shares for ₹ 16 per equity share and pays a dividend of ₹ 2.00 a share. In terms of equity shares the bond is worth ₹ 800 (50 x ₹ 16) on the equity. The bondholders receive ₹ 140 a year in interest but would receive only ₹ 100 (₹ 2.00 x 50). Thus, purchasing the bond instead of an equivalent number of shares generates ₹ 40 in additional income, which offsets the premium over the bond's value as equity in five years (₹ 200/₹ 40 = 5).

This series of calculations may be summarised as follows:

Market value of the bond	₹ 1,000
Minus bond's conversion value	800
Premium over the conversion value	₹ 200
Bond's annual issue	₹ 140

Minus annual income from equity	₹ 100
Annual income advantage to bond	₹ 40

Premium over the conversion value

$$\text{Payback period} = \frac{\text{Premium over the conversion value}}{\text{Annual income advantage}}$$

$$= \frac{₹\ 200}{₹\ 40} = \text{years}$$

If the additional income offsets the premium paid over the bond's value as equity in a moderate period of time, the convertible bond may be an attractive alternative to the equity. (This, of course, assumes that the equity is also sufficiently attractive and offers the potential for growth). If the time period necessary to overcome the premium is many years, then the bond should not be purchased as an alternative to the equity, but should be viewed solely as a debt investment and analysed as such.

However, it must be noted that this technique is relatively simple and does not consider (i) differences in commission costs to buy bonds instead of equity, (ii) possible growth in cash dividend, which will increase the time period necessary to recapture the premium, and (iii) the time value of money. The premium is paid in the present (i.e., when the bond is purchased) but the flow of interest income occurs in the future. However, this technique does permit the comparisons of various convertible bonds. If the individual computes the time period necessary to recapture the premium for several bonds, he or she may identify specific convertible bonds that are more attractive potential investments.

FUTURE OF THE CONVERTIBLE SECURITIES

The Indian Capital Market during the last few years have seen a spurt in floatation of securities, particularly the convertible securities which have captured the mood and mind of the investors in the country. Besides, the Government and the Reserve Bank of India have also expressed their deep interest in this phenomenon, which should not be allowed to pass off as a "convertibles' wave" but be made a permanent investment channel for mobilising household sayings in the country's investment markets. Accordingly, a concerted effort will need to be made by the Government, financial institutions and other financial intermediaries, sharebroking community and the Stock Exchange authorities for development of convertible market in a sustained manner,

At present the institutional set-up for the debenture market is the same as that of the equity market. The merchant bankers, underwriters and the stock brokers have been organised more or less on an extensive scale and have acquired skill and expertise to handle the issue and the new issue market in respect of these institutions seems to be adequate for expanding base of the primary market. The only limitation in the new issue market is that there is no apex body to guide, regulate and formulate policies in a coordinated manner for orderly floating of the convertible issue. In addition to this, though the existing Stock Exchange provides the facilities of a secondary market for convertibles as for the equities but it's essentially an auction market suitable for trading in speculative scrips. Since, the convertible debentures are devoid of speculative character, they are not suitable to be traded actively in the auction market. Such fixed dated-interest-bearing securities are highly suitable for negotiated bargain or what is called as OTC market. Most of the convertible debentures listed on the stock exchanges have no liquidity and transferability specially because the value of convertible debenture depreciates over the years after the issue. The stock exchange authorities have done precious little to activate the market for convertible debentures.

In order to activate the secondary market for convertible debentures various alternatives will need to be considered. (1) One of the alternative will be that while maintaining the existing status-quo there should be a separate business session exclusively for convertible debentures. However, since the stock exchanges are independent of each other, rule and regulations and other trade practices of the stock exchanges may have to be changed so that the stock-brokers can function effectively in different markets, (2) Another alternative will be to organise a secondary market wherein the public institutions will be buying and selling convertible debentures like units of the UTI, with stock brokers acting as intermediaries they have direct contact with the investors. (3) As another alternative, the OTC market can be developed within the framework of the stock exchanges with the help of resourceful and professionalised stock brokers who should be identified and allowed to operate from different stock exchanges so as to develop a nation-wide convertible debenture market. (4) Another alternative can be to organise a separate market for convertible debentures on the lines of the National Association of Security Dealers Inc. (NASD) as organised in the USA. (5) The role of stockbrokers specially the arbitrageurs, dealers/jobbers has to be recognised and utilised for development of debenture market since without their whole-hearted cooperation and active support such a market cannot be developed. It may also be necessary to provide the cash credit facilities to the brokers dealing in debentures as it will be beyond their means to buy and sell debentures in a big way. (6) Lastly, the convertible securities must be made an attractive investment proposition in relation to other alternativesources like land, building, gold, silver, jewellary, etc. as well as other forms of investment like Company Deposits, National Savings Certificate, etc. Unless the convertible securities offer an adequate and comparable return to the investors, the investing public will not be attracted to buy convertible securities in a big way as a lasting and continuing avenue of investment. In order to make debenture as an attractive investment proposition, the interest rate on convertible debenture will have to be raised to a level comparable to other types of investment. Apart from adopting flexibility in interest rate, there may be differential rates of interest on different types of convertible debentures. The other types of incentives like (a) buy-back provision, (b) introduction of short-dated and long-dated convertible debentures, (c) bearer convertible debentures, (d) floating of serial convertible debentures, index convertible debentures and discount convertible debentures carrying attractive incentives have to be thought of so that the investors can pick and choose according to their requirements. There is also further scope for giving fiscal concessions and introduction of uniform stamp duty on convertible debentures.

To conclude, it may be pointed that raising of finance through issue of convertible securities has to play a major role in financing the corporate sector because of the resource constraint experienced by financial institutions which have been so long providing financial support to private sector companies in the form of long-term loans as well as by making contributions towards equity and preference shares and debentures. The authorities have been extorting the corporate sector to depend more on the market for raising resources. Even the financial institutions, it is learnt, have been informally sounded to be Selective in underwriting the debenture issues. But the scope of raising finances through equity is not unlimited and companies are also averse to expanding their capital base by issuing equity shares to the public. At the same time, the preference shares have little attraction to the investing public as the return on preference shares is comparatively very low and these shares do not appreciate in value and have little price elasticity. In view of these facts, it can be concluded that the market for convertibles must be created and nurtured by painstaking efforts during the coming years to make it a permanent investment channel

REVIEW PROBLEMS

1. A convertible has a maturity of 10 years and pays an annual coupon of ₹100. It has a conversion rate of 100 and the current share price is ₹ll. Conversion can take place on 1st June of the fifth, sixth, seventh and eighth years. The yield curve is flat at 12 per cent per annum.

   (i) Calculate the investment and conversion values of the convertible. What would be the significance for the market value of the convertible if conversion could take place in year five only rather than in any of the four years ?

   (ii) If at the end of the 8th year, one- and two-year interest rates were 5 percent per annum what would you expect the price of the convertible to be at that time?

Ans:

   (i) Investment value :

   $$₹\ 100/1.12 + ₹\ 100/(1.12)^2 + ₹\ 100/(1.12)^3 + ₹\ 100/(1.12)^4 +$$
   $$₹\ 100/(1.12)^5 + ₹\ 100/(1.12)^6 + ₹\ 100/(1.12)^7 + ₹\ 100/(1.12)^8$$
   $$+ ₹\ 100/(1.12)^9 + ₹\ 100/(1.12)^{10}$$
   $$+ ₹\ 1000/(1.12)^{10}$$
   $$= ₹\ 565 + ₹\ 322$$
   $$= ₹\ 887$$

   Conversion value :
   $$= 100 \times ₹\ 11$$
   $$= ₹\ 1100$$

   The ability to convert in year five only would reduce the time to expiry of the option and hence reduce its value. So the convertible would have a lower market value.

   (ii) $₹\ 100/(1.05) + ₹\ 1100/(1.05)^2$
   $$= ₹\ 1093$$

   (Strictly speaking, it would not *be* convertible at the end of the 8th year since the facility to convert would no longer exist).

2. In 2009 Sunny Industries issued ₹ 10 crore of ₹ 100 par value, 15 per cent semi-annual convertible debentures that come due in 2016. The conversion price on these convertibles is ₹ 16 per share. The equity share is selling for ₹ 14 per share on a given date shortly after these convertibles were issued. The straight bonds of the same risk and maturity were yielding 20 per cent on that date. The market price of the convertible was ₹ 95 on that date. Determine the following : (a) Conversion ratio; (fc) Conversion value; (c) Conversion parity price; (d) Conversion premium in absolute terms and (e) Conversion premium in percentage.

Ans:

   (a) Conversion ratio $= \dfrac{₹100}{16} = 6.25$ shares

   (b) Conversion value $= (6.25$ shares $\times ₹\ 14$ per share)
   $$= ₹\ 87.50$$

(c) Conversion parity price $= \dfrac{₹\ 95}{6.25} = ₹\ 15.2 = ₹\ 15.2$

(d) Conversion premium in absolute terms

$$= ₹\ 95 - ₹\ 87.50$$
$$= ₹\ 7.50$$

(e) Conversion premium in percentage

$$= \dfrac{₹\ 95 - ₹87.50}{₹\ 87.50} = 8.57\%$$

3. XYZ company has current earnings of ₹ 5 per share with 50,00,000 issued shares. The company plans to issue 5,00,000 shares of 15%, ₹ 100 par value convertible preference share at par. The preference share is convertible into 4 equity shares for each preference share held. The equity share has a current market price of ₹ 22 per share.

(a) What is the preference share's conversion value ?

(b) What is the conversion premium ?

(c) Assume that total earnings remain same, what will be the effect of the issue on earnings per share before conversion and on a fully diluted basis.

(d) If profits after taxes increase by ₹ 1 crore, what will be the earnings per share before conversion and on a fully diluted basis ?

Ans:

(a) Conversion ratio x Market price per share

$$= 4x\ ₹22$$
$$= ₹88$$

(b) (₹100/₹88) -1 =11.34%

(c) Earnings per share effect:

Before dilution

Total after-tax earnings = ₹5 X 50,00,000	₹2,50,00,000
Preference share dividend	75,00,000
Earnings available to equity shareholders	₹1,75,00,000
No. of shares	50,00,000
Earnings per share	₹3.50

After dilution

Total after-tax earnings	₹2,50,00,000
No. of shares (50,00,000+ 20,00,000)	70,00,000
Earnings per share	3.57

Earnings per share effect with profit increase

Before dilution

Total after-tax earnings	₹ 3,50,00,000
Preference share dividend	75,00,000
Earnings available to equity shareholders	₹ 2,75,00,000
No. of shares	50,00,000

Earnings per share	₹ 5.50

After dilution

Total after-tax earnings	₹ 3,50,00,000
No. of shares (50,00,000 + 20,00,000)	70,00000
Earnings per share	₹ 5.0

4. In 2009, XYZ Company issued ₹ 10 crore of ₹ 100 per value, 15 percent annual convertible debentures that come due in 2024. The conversion price on these convertibles is ₹ 16.75 per share. The equity shares were selling for ₹ 14.75 per share on a given date shortly after the convertibles were issued. These convertibles were yielding 18 percent on that date. The; market price of the convertible was ₹ 97 on that date. Determine the following:

   (a) Conversion ratio
   (b) Conversion value
   (c) Security value
   (d) Conversion premium

Ans:

   (a) Conversion ratio $= \dfrac{₹\ 100}{₹\ 16.75} = 5.97$ shares

   (b) Conversion value $= 5.97$ shares x ₹ 14.75 per share
   $= ₹\ 88.058$

   (c) Security value:

   $$= \sum_{t=1}^{15} \frac{₹\ 15}{(1+.18)^t} + \frac{₹\ 100}{(1+.18)^t}$$

   $= ₹\ 15\ (5.0916) + [₹\ 100\ (.0835)]$
   $= ₹\ 76.3740 + 8.35$
   $= ₹\ 84.724$

   (d) Conversion premium :
   $= ₹\ 97 - ₹\ 88.06$
   $= ₹\ 8.94$

5. Randhawa Fertilizers issued in 2008 some ₹ 1000 par value 14 percent convertible debentures that come due in 2014. The conversion price on these convertibles is ₹ 40 per share. The price of the equity is now ₹ 27.75 per share. These convertibles are now yielding 20 percent. The market price of the convertible is ₹ 875. Determine the following:

   (a) Conversion ratio
   (b) Conversion value
   (c) Security value
   (d) Conversion parity price
   (e) Conversion premium

Ans:

   (a) Conversion ratio $= \dfrac{₹\ 1000}{₹\ 40} = 25$ shares

(b) Conversion value = 25 shares x ₹ 27.75 per share
= ₹ 681.25

(c) Security value $= \sum_{t=1}^{7} \dfrac{₹\,140}{(1+.20)^t} + \dfrac{₹\,1,000}{(1+.20)^7}$

= ₹ 140 (3.8046) + ₹ 1000 (.2791)
= ₹ 53.2644 + 279.1
= ₹ 332.3644

(d) Conversion parity price $= \dfrac{\text{Market price of convertible bond}}{\text{Conversion ratio}}$

$= \dfrac{₹\,875}{25} = ₹\,35$

(e) Conversion premium = ₹ 875 - ₹ 332.3644
= ₹ 542.6356

6. D.D. Group has current earning of ₹ 32 a share with 5,00,000 shares outstanding. The company plans to issue 2,00,000 shares at 12 percent, ₹ 100 par value convertible preference shares at par. Each preference share is convertible into 2 shares of equity. The equity share has a current market price of ₹ 42 per share.
   (a) What is the preference share's conversion value?
   (b) What is its conversion premium?
   (c) Assuming that total earnings stay the same, what will be the effect of the issue on earnings per share before conversion and on a fully diluted basis?
   (d) If profits after taxes increase by ₹ 40 crore, what will be EPS before conversion and on a diluted basis?

Ans:

(a) Conversion ratio x market price per share:
2 x ₹ 42 = ₹ 84.
(b) (₹ 100/₹ 84) -1 = 19.05%
(c) *Earnings per share effect:*

Total after-tax earnings (₹ 32 x 5,00,000)	₹ 1,60,00,000
Dividend on preference shares	24,00,000
Earnings available to equity shareholders	₹ 1,36,00,000
Number of shares	5,00,000
Earning per share	₹ 27.20
Total after-tax earnings	₹ 1,60,00,000
Number of shares (5,00,000 + 4,00,000)	9,00,000
'Earnings per share	₹ 17.78

(d) *Earnings per share effect with profit increase:*

Total after-tax earnings	₹ 2,00,00,000
Dividend to preference shareholders	24,00,000
Earnings available to equity shareholders	₹ 1,76,00,000

Number of shares	5,00,000
Earnings per share	₹ 35.20
Total after-tax earnings	₹ 2,00,00,000
Number of shares (5,00,000 + 4,00,000)	9,00,000
Earnings per share	₹ 22.22

7. Hyderabad Steel Manufacturing plans to issue ₹ 10 crore in 14 percent convertible debentures. Currently the equity is selling at ₹ 40 per equity share, and the company believes it could obtain a conversion premium (issuing price in excess of conversion value) of approximately 25%. The call price of the debenture in the 3 years is ₹ 1125 per bond, after which it drops to ₹ 1050 in the next two years and to ₹ 1000 in the last two years. To allow for fluctuations in the market price of the equity, the company does not want to call the debentures until their conversion value is at least 20% in excess of the call price. EPS are expected to grow at 18.25% compound annual rate in the foreseeable future, and the company envisions no change in its price/earnings ratio.
   (a) Determine the expected length of time that must elapse before the company is in a position to force conversion.
   (b) Is the issuance of a convertible security a good idea for the company?

Ans:
   (a) Conversion price   = ₹ 40 x 1.25
                          = ₹ 50.00
       Call price per share the first 3 years:
                          ₹ 50.00 x 1.125
                          = ₹ 56.25

       Price to which the equity share must rise before company will be in a position to face conversion:
                          ₹ 56.25 x 1.20
                          = ₹ 67.50

       Increase from present price:
                          ₹ 67.50/₹ 40
                          = 1.6875

       At an 18.25% compound growth rate, EPS will grow to approximately 1.6875 in 3 years. (This is simply $\{1.1825\}^3$). If the price earnings ratio stay the same, it will take approximately 3 years before the company will be in a position to force conversion.
   (b) This period may seem to be somewhat longer man the market participants have come to expect for convertible security. Still it is not far out of line and the company may wish to go ahead. However, if uncertainty as to EPS increases with the length of time in the future, there may be considerable risk of an overhanging issue. This may cause the company to reconsider.

8. The earnings per share on equity of HD Industries (HDI) are ₹ 2.50. The company's dividend payout is 50 percent of the earnings and sells at a P/E ratio of 30. The company wishes to offer ₹ 10 crore of 14 percent, 7-year convertible debentures

with an initial conversion premium of 25 percent and a call price of ₹ 110. HDI currently has 1 crore equity shares outstanding and has a 50 percent tax rate.

(a) What is the conversion price?

(b) What is the conversion ratio per ₹ 1,000 debenture?

(c) What is the initial conversion value of each debenture?

(d) How many new equity shares must be issued if all debentures are converted?

(e) If HDI can increase operating earnings from ₹ 10 crores to ₹ 11 crore per year with the proceeds of the debenture issue, compute the new SPS and earnings retained before and after conversion.

Ans:

(a)

EPS	=	₹ 2.50
P/E Ratio	=	30
Price per share	=	₹ 75.00
Premium (20%)		₹ 15.00
Conversion price		₹ 90.00

(b) Face value per bond   = ₹ 1,000
    Divide: Conversion price = ₹ 90

    Conversion ratio   = 11.1111 shares per bond

(c) Conversion value   = 11.11 x ₹ 75
                            = ₹ 833.25

(d) 1,00,000 debentures (₹ 1,000 face value) x 11.1111
    Conversion ratio   = 11,11,111 new shares

(e)

	Original	Before Conversion	After Conversion
Operating Earnings	₹10,00,00,000	₹ 11,00,00,000	₹ 11,00,00,000
Less: Interest	—	1,40,00,000	—
Net Income Before Taxes	₹ 10,00,00,000	₹ 9,60,00,000	₹11,00,00,000
Less: Tax	5,00,00,000	4,80,00,000	5,50,00,000
Net Income	₹ 5,00,00,000	4,80,00,000	5,50,00,000
Less dividend (.5)	2,50,00,000	2,40,00,000	2,75,00,000
Earnings Retained	₹ 2,50,00,000	₹ 2,40,00,000	₹ 2,75,00,000
EPS	₹2.50	₹ 2.40	₹ 2.50

9. Refer to problem (8), assume that the HDI Could sell ₹ 10 crore in straight debt at 15 per cent as an alternative to the convertible issue. Compute the EPS and earnings retained after issuance of the straight debt under the assumption of a ₹ 1 crore increase in operating earnings and compare your answers with those obtained in part (e).

Ans:

Operating earning	₹ 11,00,00,000
Less: Interest	1,50,00,000
Net Income before taxes	₹ 9,50,00,000
Less: Taxes	4,75,00,000
Net Income	₹ 4,75,00,000
Less: Dividend	2,37,50,000
Earnings Retained	2,37,50,000
EPS	₹ 2.16

10. Haryana Group of Industries (HGI) has issued a 15%, 7-year convertible debenture. Each ₹ 1,000 debenture is convertible into 25 equity shares. The company also has straight debt issue outstanding of the same approximate maturity, so it is an easy matter to determine the straight bond value of the convertible issue. The market price of HGI is volatile. Over the last year, the following was observed:

	Observations				
	1	2	3	4	5
Market price per share	₹50	₹ 40	₹45	₹ 30	₹ 25
Straight bond value	750	700	710	₹ 620	₹ 570
Market price convertible debenture	1,280	1,110	1,140	875	770

(a) Compute the premium over conversion value (in rupees) and the premium-over straight bond value for each observation.

(b) Compare the two premiums. What do the relationship tell with respect to the valuation of the convertible debenture?

Ans:

Premium over conversion value:

	Observations				
	1	2	3	4	5
Market price of convertible	₹ 1,280	₹ 1,110	₹ 1,140	₹875	₹770
Conversion value (share price x 25)	1,250	100	1,125	750	625
Premium	₹30	₹ 110	₹ 15	₹ 125	₹ 145
Straight bond value	750	700	710	620	570
Premium over bond value	₹ 530	₹ 410	₹ 430	₹ 255	₹ 200

(b) At high equity prices, the convertible debenture sells at a substantial premium over its book value, but only at a slight premium over its conversion value. Here the convertible sells mainly for its equity attraction, and the bond feature is negligible importance. Also, there is a danger of a call, where the security will be worth only its conversion value. As share price declines from a high of ₹ 50, the premium over conversion value increases. The option feature remains a factor, but increasingly the straight bond value becomes important as the premium over bond value declines. As share price drops, particularly below ₹ 40, the bond value falls in keeping with greater default risk. At ₹ 25 share price, the premium over book value goes down to ₹ 200. The security sells in an important way for its bond value protection, though the other option still has round value, as evidenced by the premium over bond value.

11. The following year, Haryana Group of Industries falls on further hard times (Refer to Problem 10). Its market price drops to ₹ 20 per share and the market price of the convertible debentures to ₹ 600. The straight bond value goes to ₹ 520. Determine the premium-over-conversion value and the premium-over-bond value. What can you say about the bond-value floor?

Ans:

At ₹ 20 a share, the conversion value is ₹ 500 and premium over the conversion value is ₹ 100 and the premium over the bond value is ₹ 80. As the stock price has weakened, due to probable financial difficulty, the bond value floor has fallen. Much less downside protection is given. While some of the variation in bond value may be due to changing interest rates in bond market, most is due to changing perception of default risk. At price lower than ₹ 20 a share, the convertible will sell mainly for its bond feature.

QUESTIONS

1. Why should a company issue convertible securities instead of straight bonds or equity shares ?

2. Explain the following terms : Conversion ratio, Conversion price, Conversion value, and Conversion parity.

3. What are the critical variables in determining the yield on a convertible debenture? How can values for these variables be estimated ?

4. What is meant by the "floor" for a convertible bond ?

5. It is possible to calculate a yield to maturity for a convertible debenture; however, it is often argued that the yield to maturity is not an appropriate yield concept to apply to a convertible bond. Do you agree ?

6. For convertible debentures, what is meant by the premium over the market value floor ? In theory, this premium should progressively decline and finally disappear over time. Why?

7. Investors want to purchase convertible debenture because they feel this investment instrument has all the advantages, but none of the risks of equity and straight debenture. What is your response?

8. What are the straight bond values of the following convertible debentures ?

    (a) A 15 per cent coupon convertible debenture with 7-year to maturity where a straight bond of this maturity would yield 20%.

    (b) A12 per cent coupon convertible bond with 4-years to maturity when the straight bond would yield 15%.

9. Discuss the advantages and disadvantages of a convertible preference share for an investor.

10. Under what conditions is a convertible security deemed attractive?

11. What are some of the analytical procedures for the analysis of convertible preference shares ?

12. Under what circumstances will convertible securities, in general, likely decline in prices ?

13. Investing in convertibles is often referred to as a hedging strategy. Explain how convertibles may (or may not) provide a portfolio hedge under the following conditions:

(a) Interest rates and equity share prices are expected to decline.

(b) Interest rates are expected to remain stable, equity share prices to increase.

(c) Interest rates and equity share prices are expected to increase.

(d) The investor is not sure about the future directions of interest rates and equity share prices.

14. Explain the likely behaviour of the premium on a convertible debenture as the debenture approaches maturity.

15. Explain why it is necessary to examine both the bond and stock properties of a convertible debenture when determining its investment appeal.

16. What is the difference between conversion parity and conversion value ? How would you describe the payback to period or a convertible ? What is the bond investment value of a convertible and what does it reveal ?

17. Explain the limitations of using premium over straight value as a measure of the downside risk of a convertible security.

PROBLEMS

1. Kandla Agro issued some ₹100 par value, 15 per cent convertible debentures that come due in 2011. The conversion price on these convertible is ₹ 45 per share. The price of the equity is now ₹ 36 per share. The straight bond of the same risk and maturity are yielding at present 18%. The market price of the convertible is now ₹ 87.50. Determine the conversion ratio, the conversion value, the conversion parity price, the conversion premium in absolute amount and the conversionjjremium in percentage.

2. Bengal Industries has issued a 15%, 7-year convertible debenture. Each ₹ 100 debenture is convertible into 5 equity shares. The company also has a straight debt issue of the same approximate maturity, so it is easy matter to determine straight bond value of the convertible issue. The market price of the Bengal Industries is volatile. Over the last year, the following was observed:

	Observations				
	1	2	3	4	5
Market price per share	₹ 30	₹ 50	₹ 35	₹ 22	₹ 15
Straight bond value	69	79	65	60	55
Market price of convertible Debenture	106	114	89	74	64

(a) Compute the premium-over-conversion value and the premium-over straight-bond value for each of the observations.

(b) Compare the two premiums either visually or by graph. What does the relationship tell you with respect to the valuation of the convertible debenture?

3. RSD Enterprises has earnings per share of ₹ 3.50, has a dividend payout of two-thirds, and sells at a P/E ratio of 16. RSD wishes to offer ₹ 10 crore of 15 per cent, 7-year convertible debentures with an initial conversion premium of 20 per cent and a call price of ₹ 105. RSD currently has 1 crore shares issued and has a 50 per cent tax rate. Compute the conversion price and the conversion ratio of each debenture. How many new equity shares must be issued if all debentures are converted ? If RSD can increase operating earnings by ₹ 1 crore per year with the proceeds of the debenture issue, compute the new earnings per share and earnings retained before and after conversion.

4. An investor owns 100 shares of KDR ₹ 40 convertible preference. The price as of December 28, 2008, was ₹ 717.50. The preference share is convertible into 2.11 equity shares. The equity share is selling on the market for ₹ 287.50. The equity price in the preference share was ₹ 318.10, which means the convertible preference share was selling at a premium of almost 18%. Assume that the price of the share in five years was expected to increase 20%, and the preference share was to continue to sell at an 18% premium.

   (a) What annual return would the investor earn ?

   (b) What annual average return would the investor earn if the increase in equity share price was only 10 per cent and the premium remained at 18 per cent ?

   (c) What annual average return would the investor earn with a 5% decrease in the share price ? The premium remains at 18%.

   (d) Based on your answer to (a), (b) and (c) above, calculate variability of return and comment on the riskiness of the investment.

5. Angoora Enterprises has a convertible debenture with a coupon yield of 14% and matures in 2008. The convertible is priced at ₹ 80, and the equity share is currently trading at a price of ₹ 18.50. The conversion ratio is 6.00.

   (a) Calculate the conversion price.

   (b) Calculate the conversion value.

   (c) Calculate the premium.

   (d) Is the convertible priced to reflect its conversion value or its straight value ?

6. Consider the following hypothetical convertible bond :

   Par value = ₹ 1000; Coupon rate = 9.5%; Market price of convertible bond = ₹ 1,000;

   Conversion ratio = 37.783;

   Estimated straight value of bond = ₹ 510;

   Yield to maturity of straight bond = 18.7%

   Assume that the price of the equity share is ₹ 23 and that the dividend per share is ₹ 0.75 per share.

   (a) Calculate conversion value; market conversion price; conversion premium per share, conversion premium ratio; premium over straight value; yield advantage of bond; and, finally, the premium payback period.

   (b) Suppose that the price of the equity share increases from ₹ 23 to ₹ 46.

   — What will be the approximate return realised from investing in the convertible bond ?

   — Why would be the return on investing directly in the equity be higher than investing in the convertible bond ?

   — What would be return realised if ₹ 23 had been invested in the equity ?

7. Two bonds have the following terms:

	Bond ABC		Bond XYZ
Principal	₹ 1,000	Principal	₹ 1,000
Coupon	8%	Coupon	7.6%
Maturty	10 years	Maturty	10 years

   Bond XYZ has an additional feature, it may be redeemed at par after 5 years (i.e., it has a put feature). Both bonds were initially sold for their face amounts (i.e., ₹ 1,000).

   (a) If interest rates fall to 7 percent, what will be the price of each bond?

   (b) If interest rates rise to 9 percent, what will be the price of each bond from its initial price?

(c) Bond XYZ requires the investor to forgo ₹ 4 a year (i.e., ₹ 40 if the bond is in existence for 10-years). If interest rates are 8 percent, what is the present value of this forgone interest? If the bond has lacked the put feature but had a coupon of 7.6 percent and a term to maturity of 10-years, it would sell for ₹ 973.16 when interest rates were 8 percent. What, then, is the implied cost of the put option?

Ans: (a)   Bond ABC : ₹ 1070;   (b)   Bond XYZ: ₹ 946;   (c)   ₹ 26.84

8. Sundaram Industries needs to raise ₹ 2.50 crore to construct production facilities for a new model diskette drive. The firm's straight non-convertible debentures currently yield 14%. Its equity sells for ₹ 30 per share; the last dividend was ₹ 2.00, and the expected growth rate is a constant 9%. Investment bankers have tentatively proposed that the firm raise the ₹ 2.50 crore by issuing convertible debentures. Those convertibles would have a ₹ 1,000 par value, carrying a coupon rate of 10%, have a 7-year maturity, and be convertible into 20 equity shares. The bonds would be non-callable for 3 years, after which they would be callable at a price of ₹ 1030; this call price would decline by ₹ 10 per year in year 4 and each year thereafter. Management has called convertibles in the past (and presumably it will call them again in the future), once they were eligible for call, when the bond's conversion value was about 20% above the bond's par value (nor their call price).

(a)   What is the expected rate of return on the proposed convertible issue?

(b)   Do you think that these bonds could be successfully offered to the public at par? That is, does ₹ 1,000 seem to be an equilibrium price in view of the stated terms? If not, suggest the type of change that would have to be made to cause the bonds to trade at ₹ 1,000 in the secondary market, assuming no change in capital market conditions.

9. Compute the straight bond values of the following convertible bonds:

(a)   A 12% coupon convertible bond with 4 years to maturity where a straight bond of this maturity would yield 15%.

(b)   A15% coupon convertible bond with 10 years to maturity when the straight bond would yield 18%.

10. The following information concerns a convertible bond: Coupon: 6% (₹ 60 per 1,000 bond); Exercise price: ₹25; Maturity date: 20 years; Call price: ₹ 1,040; Price of the equity share : ₹ 30.

(a)   If the bond were non-convertible, what would be the approximate value if comparable interest rates were 12 percent?

(b)   Into how many shares can the bond be converted?

(c)   What is the value of the bond in terms of equity?

(d)   What is the current minimum price that the bond will command?

(e)   What do investors receive if they do not convert the bond when it is called?

Ans: (a)   ₹ 552;   (b)   40 shares;   (c)   ₹ 1,200;

(d)   ₹ 1,200 value as equity;   (e)   ₹ 1,040.

11. Two firms have equity shares and convertible bonds outstanding. Information concerning these securities is as follows:

	Firm ABC	Firm XYZ
EQUITY		
Price of Equity Share	₹46	₹30
Cash dividend	None	Re.l
Principal	₹ 1,000	₹ 1,000

CONVERTIBLE BOND		
Conversion price	₹50	₹33
(20 shares)		
(30 shares)		
Maturity date	10 years	10 years
Coupon rate	7.5%	7.5%
Market price	₹ 1,100	₹ 1,100

(a) What is the value of each bond in terms of equity?

(b) What is the premium paid over each bond's value as equity?

(c) What is each bond's income advantage over the equity into which the bond may be converted?

(d) How long will it take for the income advantage to offset the premium determined in part (b)?

(e) If after 4-years firm ABC's equity sells for ₹ 65 and the firm calls the bond, what is the holding period return and the annual rate of return earned on an investment in the equity or in the bond?

Ans: (c) ABC : ₹ 75

(d) ABC : 2.4 years

(e) Annual Return : 10.7%

12. Partha Cement Company has grown rapidly during the past 5 years. Recently, its commercial bank urged the company to consider increasing its permanent financing. Its bank loan under a line of credit has risen to ₹ 2.50 crore; carrying a 14 percent interest rate. Partha has been 30 to 60 days in paying trade creditors.

Discussions with the bank have resulted in the decision to raise ₹ 5 crore at this time. The bank has assured the firm that the following alternatives are feasible (flotation costs will be ignored):

Alternative I: Sell equity share at ₹ 80.

Alternative II: Sell convertible bonds at 14% coupon, convertible into 10 shares of equity for each ₹ 1000 bond (that is, the conversion price is ₹ 100 per share).

Alternative III: Sell debentures at 14 percent coupon, each ₹ 1000 bond carrying 10 warrants to buy each equity share at ₹ 100.

R.S. Partha, the Chairman, owns 80 percent of the equity and wishes to maintain control of the company. Ten lakh (one million) shares are outstanding. The following are estimates of Partha's latest financial statements:

Balance Sheet		
Current liabilities	₹ 4 crore	₹ 4 crore
Equity, par ₹ 10	₹ 1 crore	₹ 1 crore
Retained Earnings	₹ 0.5 crore	₹ 0.5 crore
Total claims	₹ 5.5. crore Total Assets	₹ 5.5 crore

Income Statement	
Sales	₹ 1 1.25 crore
All costs except interest	10.00
EBIT	₹ 1.25 crore
Interest	0.35
EBT	₹ .90

Taxes (40%)	.36
Net Income	₹ .54 crore
Shares issued	10,00,000
EPS	₹5.4
P/E	15.83%
Market price per share	₹ 85.47

(a) Show Partha's control position under each alternative,.assuming that he does not purchase additional shares.

(b) What, is the effect on EPS of each alternative, if it is assumed that profits before interest and taxes will be 20 percent of total assets?

(c) What will be the debt ratio under each alternative?

(d) Which of the three alternatives would you recommend to Partha, and why?

Ans: (a) Plan 1:49%; Plan II: 53%; Plan III: 53%.

(b) Plan I: ₹ 5.90; Plan II: ₹ 6.40; Plan III: ₹ 8.80

(c) Plan 1:19%; Plan II: 19%; Plan III: 50%.

13. MADHAV Textiles has the following convertible bond issued: Coupon 14%; Principal: ₹ 1,000; Maturity: 7 years; Conversion price: ₹40; Call price: ₹ 1,000 plus one year's interest. The bond's credit rating is A. Other bonds" issued by the company have a AA rating. Comparable AA rated bonds yield 18 percent, and A rated bonds yield 20 percent. The firm's equity share is selling for ₹ 60 and pays a dividend of ₹ 5 a share. The convertible bond is selling for par (₹ 1,000).

(a) What is the value of the bond in terms of equity?

(b) What is the premium paid over the bond's value as equity?

(c) What is the bond's income advantage?

(d) Given a bond's income advantage, how long must the investor hold the bond to overcome the premium over the bond's value as equity?

(e) What is the probability that the firm will currently call the bond?

(f) If the price of the bond rises to ₹ 1,350 at the end of three years, what is the total percentage return (i.e., the holding period return) the investor earns on the equity and on the bond?·

(g) If after three years the price of the equity has risen annually by 15 percent, what must have happened to the price of the bond?

(h) Why is the holding period return if the stock is split two for one, what impact will that have on the price of a convertible bond?

(i) If the price of the bond rises to ₹ 1,350 at the end of the three years, what is the annualised return the investor earns? Does this return exceed the return earned on the equity?

(j) If the convertible bond is held to maturity, what does the investor receive? What is the annualised return?

(k) If the price of the equity rises to ₹ 90 a share while interest rates on A-rated bonds rise to 16 percent, what impact does the increase in interest rates have on this convertible bond?

14. Suppose a company simultaneously issues ₹ 5 crore of convertible bonds with a coupon rate of 12.50 percent and ₹ 5 crore of non-convertible bonds with a coupon rate of 14 percent. Both bonds have the same maturity. Does the fact that the convertible issue has the lower coupon rate suggest that it is less risky than the non-convertible bond? Is the cost of capital lower on the convertible than on the non-convertible bond? Explain.

15. Given the following information concerning a convertible bond: Principal : ₹ 1,000; Coupon: 5%; Maturity : 15 years; Call price: ₹ 1,050; Conversion price: ₹ 37 (i.e., 27 shares); Market price of the equity share: ₹ 32; Market price of the bond: ₹ 1,040.

    (a) What is the current yield of the bond?

    (b) What is the value of the bond based on the market price of the equity?

    (c) What is the value of the equity based on the market price of the bond?

    (d) What is the premium in terms of the equity that the investor pays when he or she purchases the convertible bond instead of the equity?

    (e) Non-convertible bonds are selling with a yield to a maturity of 7 percent. If this bond lacked the conversion feature, what would be the approximate price of the bond?

    (f) What *is* the premium in terms of debt that the investor pays when he or she purchases the convertible bond instead of a non-convertible bond?

    (g) If the price of the equity should double, would the price of the convertible bond double?

    (h) If the price of the equity share should decline by 50 percent, would the price of the convertible bond decline by the same percentage?

    (i) What is the probability that the company will call this bond?

    (j) Why are investors willing to pay the premiums mentioned in parts (d) and (f)?

Ans: (a) 4.8%;   (b) ₹ 864;   (c) ₹ 38.52;   (d) ₹ 176;

        (e) ₹ 817;   (f) ₹ 223;   (g) At least ₹ 1,728;

        (h) At least ₹ 817   (i) Virtually nil.

16. Desai Group was planning to finance an expansion in August 2010. The principal executives of the company all agreed that an individual group such as these should finance growth by means of equity rather than by debt. However, they felt that the price of the group's equity did not reflect its true worth, so they decided to sell a convertible security. They considered a convertible debenture but feared the burden of fixed interest charges if the equity did not rise in price to make conversion attractive. They decided on an issue of convertible preference shares, which would pay a dividend of ₹ 2.10 per share. The equity share was selling for ₹ 42 at the time. Management projected earnings for 2010 at ₹ 3 per share and expected a future growth of 10% a year in 2011 and beyond. It was agreed by the investment bankers and the management that the equity would sell at 14 times earnings, the current price/earning ratio.

    (a) Which conversion price should be set by the issuer? The conversion ratio will be 1.0; that is, each share of convertible preference can be converted into one equity share. Therefore, the convertible's par value (and also the issue price) will be equal to the conversion price, which in turn will be determined as a percentage over the current market price of the equity. Your answer will be a guess, but make it a reasonable one.

    (b) Should the preference share include a call provision? Why?

17. Given the following information concerning ABC Industries convertible preference shares: One share of preference is convertible into 0.50 shares of equity; price of equity share: ₹ 24; price of convertible preference share: ₹ 14.

    (a) What is the value of preference share in terms of equity?

    (b) What is the premium over the preference share's value as equity?

    (c) If the preference share is perpetual and comparable preference share offers a dividend yield of 15 percent, what would be the minimum price of this stock if it were not converted?

    (d) If the price of the equity share rose to ₹ 40, what would be the minimum increase in the value of the preference share that you would expect?

REFERENCES

1. Altman, Edward I. "The Convertible Debt Market: Are Returns Worth the Risk? *Financial Analysts Journal* July/August 1989): 23-31.

2. Bacon, Peter W., and Edward L. Winn, Jr., "The Impact of Forced Conversion on Stock Prices," *Journal of Finance,* December 1969, pp. 871-874.

3. Baurnol, William J., Burton G. Malkiel, and Richard E. Quandt, "The Valuation of Convertible Securities," *Quarterly Journal of Economics,* February 1966, pp. 48 59.

4. Brennan. M.J., and E.S. Schwartz, "Convertible Bonds: Valuation and Optimal Strat-egies for Call and Conversion," *Journal of Finance* 32:5 (December 1977), pp. 1699-1715.

5. Brigham, Eugene F., "An Analysis of Convertible Debentures: Theory and Some Em-pirical Evidence," *Journal of Finance,* March 1966, pp. 35-54.

6. Calamos, John P. *Investing in Convertible Securities.* Chicago, III .: Longman Financial Ser-vices Publishing, 1988.

7. Frank, Werner G., and Jerry J. Weygandt. "A Prediction Model for Convertible De-bentures." *Journal of Accounting Research,* Spring 1971, pp. 116-126.

8. Gepts, Stefaan J. *Valuation and Selection of Convertible Bonds.* Westport, Conn.: Greenwood Press, 1987.

9. Ingcrsoll, Jonathan, "An Examination of Corporate Call Policies on Convertible Secu-rities," *Journal of Finance* 32 (May 1977), pp. 463-478.

10. Jennings, Edward H., "An Estimate of Convertible Bond Premiums," *Journal of 'Fi-nancial and Quantitative Analysis.* January 1974, pp. 33-56. Also "Reply: An Estimate of Convertible Bond Premiums," *Journal of Financial and Quantitative Analysis,* June 1975. pp. 375-376.

11. Kaplan, Stanley A., "Piercing the Corporate Boilerplate: Antidilution Clauses in Con-vertible Securities," *University of Chicago Law Review,* Autumn 1965, pp. 1 -30.

12. Liebowitz, Martin L.. "Convertible Securities," *Financial Analysts Journal,* November December 1974, pp. 57-67.

13. Miller, Alexander B., "How to Call Your Convertibles," *Harvard business Review.* May-June 1971. pp. 66 70.

14. Noddings, Thomas. *Investor's Guide to Convertible Bonds.* Homewood, III .: Dow Jones-Irwin, 1982.

15. Pinches, George E. "Financing with Convertible Preferred Stocks, 1960-1967." *The Journal of Finance,* March 1970, p. 53.

16. Schwartz, William. "Convertibles Get Realistic Image." *Financial Analysts Journal,* July-August 1967, p. 55.

17. Soldofsky, R.M. "Convertible Preferred Stock: Renewed Life in an Old Form." *The Business Lawyer,* July 1969, pp. 1385-92.

36

Warrants

INTRODUCTION

A warrant like a call option, is a right to buy a share of a specified company at a certain price during a given time period. While the call option is issued by an individual, the warrant is issued by the company and its proceeds are part of equity. If a warrant is exercised, it increases the number of shares of the company and thus dilutes the equities of its shareholders.

Equity shares warrants may come into being in various ways. The most typical of these include the following:

1. Through the sale of equity shares and the warrants together as a unit.
2. Through exchange as a result of reorganisation.
3. Through sale to underwriters at a nominal price as part of their actual compensation.
4. Through separate public sale (rare).
5. Through attachment as a bonus to senior securities.

The way a warrant comes into being may give some indication as to the future performance of the equity shares of the company in question and, consequently, to the future value of the warrant. Warrants that result from re-organisations, when shareholders and other junior security holders are given warrants in the reorganised company for their old securities, may be suspect. The fact that the company had to be reorganised might give some indication as to the future uncertainty for the equity shares and hence the warrant.

CONSIDERATIONS FOR SHARES ISSUED THROUGH WARRANTS

The consideration received for the share issued on the exercise of warrants is composed of three parts: cash received on exercise of the warrants, cash proceeds of sale of the warrants, and consideration for the earlier financing supplied to the corporation. The financing expense that the corporation incurs for the use of funds other than equity funds is a part of the total consideration received for the shares issued. Another part of the financing expense results from the benefit the corporation derives from arranging for the future sale of an equity security at a price higher than its market price on the date the purchase privilege is granted. A corporation may improve its later financial position over the period from the selling shares at a lower current market price. However, separating the components of the financing expense is impossible, and a corporation should account for the expense in total.

The fair value of shares issued on the exercise of warrants is the most reasonably determinable measure of the total consideration that a corporation receives for the shares. That measure conforms with the arrangements agreed to by both parties to the warrant transaction — the corporation is obliged to deliver securities of unknown value at an indefinite date for a fixed sum. The difference between the total consideration for the shares issued and the cash received represents a cost of corporate financing. A corporation should record the total consideration received as contributed equity at the date the shares are issued In theory at least the warrants provide some of the additional benefits to both the corporation as well as to the investor. These are listed below:

(A) Gains to the Corporation

A corporation sells warrants and receives funds, which it may use to finance operations, but assumes no obligation to pay interest and repay principal, as it would for borrowed funds and grant no dividends and other rights, as it would for equity funds from shareholders. The obligation of the corporation is to deliver an equity shares when the holder of a warrant elects to pay the additional designated price. The amount of the ultimate corporate obligation is uncertain at the time a warrant is sold, but the corporation is willing to assume an unfixed liability to gain the advantage of obtaining funds from other than credit or equity sources.

The corporation has in effect, accomplished two things: (a) It has obtained funds without incurring current expenses for their issue; and, (b) It has insured that the cash consideration for an equity security issued later will exceed its current market price. One may fairly assume that in the absence of these benefits a corporation would not sell warrants with the accompanying uncertain liabilities but instead would obtain loans or sell securities at the market price.

Warrants may be issued without a cash consideration. Those issued for other than cash consideration are usually for services such as those of underwriters and promoters. The value of the consideration received in the form of services should be measured and recorded as a corporate liability for outstanding warrants in the same manner as for warrants sold for cash. The nature of the transactions is the same; the only difference is the nature of the consideration received.

(B) Gains to the Investor

The purchaser of a share warrant advances funds to a corporation and accepts an uncertain return that depends entirely on the later market price of the share that he is privileged to purchase. He forgoes a current return in the form of dividends or interest on his investment. If the price of the share rises, his warrant may be valuable and his return spectacular. Conversely, the share purchase privilege may later convey no advantage, and the warrant may have no value. In theory, however, the warrants provide the following benefits to the buyer:

(1) Instead of locking up money in a slab of a company's ordinary shares, the investor can buy warrants giving him rights to buy the same number of shares at a known price sometime in the future for, normally, a fraction of the cost. This means that he releases his capital to pursue other investment opportunities.

(2) The second benefit provided by warrants is that of liquidity. Buying warrants does not mean to lock up cash for a period of years. The existence of an active market in which you can buy and sell warrants means that you can turn them into cash if need there be.

(3) A third benefit is that, despite the fact that warrants can produce much greater capital gains opportunities when the stock market is recovering from a really vicious bear market, the price of warrants does not fall in the same downward spiral as shares in a bear market. The reason for this is that the warrant price, being normally a fraction of the price of the related ordinary share, sooner or later falls to a point beyond which it can fall no further. It joins the ranks of the "penny stocks", and even though the price of the

ordinary share still has some way to fall, the price of the warrant cannot become a negative amount so losses the company which has issued it stays solvent. So when the market turns, the warrants can chalk up really spectacular gains in the initial buying rush as the professionals sense the opportunity to make a massive capital gain by buying warrants giving the rights to shares at a set price.

GEARING EFFECT

The opportunities for big capital gains are provided by the "gearing effect". The price of warrants moves in the same direction as the price of the shares to which they are linked. However, in percentage terms, the price of warrants moves up faster in a bull market and goes down faster in a bear market, before stopping at the "penny stock" floor. To take a practical example of the gearing effect at work, suppose a share worth ₹ 10 in the market has related warrants entitling the holder to buy shares in the company at ₹ 10 at the end of five years, and these warrants are quoted in the market at ₹ 3.50. If the ordinary share price rises to ₹ 11 (an increase of 10%), the effect of this rise be to push up the value of the warrants to ₹ 4.00 (an increase of 14.3%). Thus the warrant price would have gone up faster than the share price, but the same would be true in reverse in a downward movement; the fall would be corresponding steeper.

The *'volatility factor'* bandied about by the warrant market experts just means price fluctuations with another psuedo scientific name. It is supposed to provide some indication of how speculative the warrants are in the light of the frequency of the price movements (volatility) of the underlying share to which the warrant is linked, *the more volatile the share price, the more attractive are the warrants, because they present the holder with more frequent opportunities to buy and sell and so increase the rate of his capital gains opportunities* (or, it should be stressed, the rate of his capital losses).

The best way to evaluate warrants is not to attach too much importance to gearing ratios and volatility factors but to use common sense and always bear in mind that warrants are a gambler's market. *Warrants, like racehorses, fundamentally have a set of odds attached to them.* The high risk-reward ratio could be assessed just well by a bookmaker as by a warrant expert at 16-7 against or 5-4 on, if he took the trouble to discover just, what ingredients make up *the form.*

The Three Golden Rules to Remember

(a) the warrant market is a gambler's market;
(b) ask yourself if the warrant you are buying gives you a good deal in common sense terms; and
(c) work out the likely effect on the warrant price of the movement in the underlying shareprice.

VALUATION OF WARRANT

The value of a warrant is determined in a manner similar to that used for call options. However, because the warrant is issued by the firm, the additional shares of stock that are created when the warrant is exercised add a slight wrinkle to the analysis. Let us consider an all equity firm with N_s shares, each worth $S(t)$. Thus, the value of the firm, $V(t)$, equals $N_s S(t)$. Let the firm issue N_w warrants with an exercise price of X and a conversion ratio of 1. For simplicity assume that the warrants are European-style and that the firm uses the proceeds of the warrant to finance a zero net present value project.

Now suppose it is the expiration day and the value of the firm is $V(T)$. If the warrants are exercised, the warrant holders will inject new capital into the firm and the new value of the firm will be

$$V(T)^* = V(T) + N_w X$$

where $V(T)$ is the value of the firm before the warrants are exercised and $V(T)^*$ is the value of the firm immediately after the warrants are exercised. Define $q = N_w/N_s$, which is a measure of the dilution effect from the issuance of new shares. Then we can write $V(T)^*$ as

$$V(T)^* = N_s S(T) + q N_s X$$

After the warrants are exercised, the new stock price will adjust to $S(T)^*$, which is equal to the new value of the firm, $V(T)^*$, divided by the total number of shares, $N_s + N_w$. Substituting for $V(T)^*$, we get

$$S(T)^* = \frac{V(T)^*}{N_w + N_s} = \frac{N_s S(T) + q N_s X}{N_w + N_s}$$

$$= \frac{S(T) + qX}{1 + q}$$

The warrant holder will exercise the warrant if the stock price after exercise, $S(T)^*$, exceeds the exercise price. Thus, exercise will occur if

$$\frac{S(T) + qX}{1 + q} > X$$

$$\frac{S(T) + qX - X - qX}{1 + q} > 0$$

which means $S(T) > X$. Thus, the exercise decision of the warrant holder is the same as that of a call holder. The value of the warrant at expiration is

$$W(T) = Max(0, S(T)^* - X)$$

$$= \frac{1}{1 + q} Max(0, S(T) - X)$$

This means the value of the warrant today is simply

$$W(t) = \frac{C(t)}{1 + q}$$

So the warrant is like $1/(1 + q)$ calls. Thus, if the condition of European exercise is met, we can value the warrant by using the Black-Scholes model and then dividing the computed value by $1 + q$.

Consider the following example. A firm has assets valued at ₹ 1,000, no debt, and 50 shares outstanding, which means each share is worth ₹ 20 The risk-free interest rate is 8 per cent. The firm issues 10 warrants that have an exercise price of ₹ 30 and expire in 5 years. The expected standard deviation of the stock's return is .4.

If we used the Black-Scholes model to determine the value of a 5-year call option on the stock with an exercise price of ₹ 30, a stock price of ₹ 20, a risk-free rate of .08, and a standard deviation of .4, we would obtain a value of ₹ 6.87. The value of q is $10/50 = .2$. Thus we would divide ₹ 6.87 by 1.2 and obtain ₹ 5.73 as the value of the warrant.

Now let us consider what happens at the time of exercise. Table 1 contains the results of two outcomes. The first shows the results if the warrants are exercised, while the other presents the results if the warrants expire unexercised. In the first case, the value of the firm is at ₹ 1,800 when the warrants expire. This means that the stock price before the warrants are exercised is ₹ 36. Recall that warrant holders will exercise under the same conditions that holders of ordinary calls will exercise. Since ₹ 36 is greater than the exercise price of ₹ 30, the warrant holders will exercise. Thus. the firm will issue 10 new shares, and warrant holders will contribute ₹ 300 of new capital. The firm will now be worth ₹ 2.100 and will have 60 shares of stock outstanding so each share will be worth ₹ 35. If the firm is worth only ₹ 800 at expiration, the stock price will be only ₹ 16 so the warrant holders will not exercise.

TABLE 1
Effect of Exercise of Warrants with ₹ 30 Exercise Price

$V(T)$	₹ 1,800	₹ 800
$S(T)$	₹ 36	₹ 16
New shares issued	10	0
Total shares	60	50
New capital contributed	₹ 300	0
$V(T)^*$	₹ 2,100	₹ 800
$S(T)^*$	₹ 35	₹ 16

TABLE 2
Warrant Price Movements Relative to Stock Price Movements

$V(t) = 1,000;\ N_s = 50;\ N_w = 10;\ S(t) = 20;\ r = .08;\ X = 30;\ T - t = 5;\ \text{s-} = .4$

Stock price	10.00	15.00	20.00	25.00	30.00
Warrant price	1.24	3.18	5.73	8.71	11.98
Percentage change in stock price	−50.00	-25.00	—	25.00	50.00
Percentage change in warrant price	−78.36	-44.50	—	52.01	109.08

Warrants offer investors significant leverage because for a small initial investment, the holder of a warrant can earn very large rates of return from smaller stock price increases as shown in Table 2 for our sample warrant. A stock price of ₹ 20 is the base, and we demonstrate what happens to warrant price changes when we have stock price movements 5 and 10 points in both directions. Note that the percentage price change for the warrant is always greater than the percentage price change for the stock. This is the leverage effect of the warrants that is essentially the same as the leverage effect in ordinary.

LAPSE OF WARRANTS

Warrant holders may find that the price of the share does not reach or exceed the designated purchase price during the privilege period. Under these considerations, a warrant holder will not exercise his warrant unless he wishes to acquire the shares for reasons other than financial returns, such as to obtain control. The proceeds of sale or other considerations received for warrant should not be shown as contingent equity financing after the end of the privilege period. The consideration and the transaction determine the disposition of the carrying amounts of the warrants.

The purchaser of a warrant pays for the privilege of later purchasing the shares at less than its market price at the later date. The corporation assumes an uncertain obligation for costs as a part of the financing arrangements. If the earnings and future prospects of a corporation or general market conditions do not produce a market price for its shares that is high enough to attract exercise of the warrants, the corporation incurs no additional expenses but benefits to the extent of the consideration received for warrants. The warrant provisions are a part of the overall equity financing and all results, expenses as well as benefits, should be recognised as a part of financing costs. A corporation receives consideration for potential equity financing—equity never materialises.

Therefore the carry amount of warrants that expire unexercised should be transferred to and increase retained earnings. By adopting that procedure, a corporation recognises the results, both benefits and costs of equity financing arrangements as changes in retained earnings. Contingent equity financing was not converted to shareholder interests and the carrying amount of the warrant accrues to the benefit of the existing shareholders.

Unexercised warrants issued originally as a part of credit financing arrangements are an exception to the accounting recommended in the last paragraph. The carrying amount of warrants unexercised at the end of the privilege period should reduce the expenses of credit financing including in net income.

A share subscription right and a share purchase warrant are similar in that each entitles the holder to exercise the privilege of purchasing shares at a stated price. Although the forms of the instruments are similar, differences between the two privileges conveyed to the holders result from different purposes and cause differences in the substance of related transactions.

The primary differences in the two privileges are that:

(*i*) one share may be purchased ordinarily with one warrant but with several rights;

(*ii*) rights to purchase shares are usually issued to existing shareholders but warrants may be sold separately or with other securities as a unit, may be issued separately without cash consideration;

(*iii*) the purchase price fixed by rights is usually less than the current market price of the stock and the purchase price fixed by warrants is normally greater than the market price of the stock at the date the warrants are issued; and

(*iv*) the privilege to purchase usually extends much longer under warrants than under rights.

The purchase price of shares specified by a warrant may vary before its expiration, usually higher price at later dates.

WARRANTS ATTACHED TO DEBENTURE

Some corporations issue debentures as a unit with non- detachable share purchase warrants. A provision that the warrants may be exercised only be surrendering debentures equal to the purchase price of the privilege shares makes the financial terms of the unit equivalent to those of convertible debentures. The debt obligation may be satisfied by issuing shares on the exercise of the warrants the same as on the exercise of a conversion privilege. The share purchase warrants and conversion privilege are both integral parts of the debt financing arrangements. The consideration for the additional shares issued under both arrangements should be measured by the fair value of the share, and the debt financing costs should be measured by the difference between the fair value of the share distributed and the consideration received at the time of sale of the debenture or the unit.

A difference between convertible debentures and debentures with share purchase warrants attached is that one arrangement involves a simple security and the other two securities. When warrants are used as partial compensation for investment bankers or as a 'sweetener' for other uses, no indication is given about the future performance of the warrant. The use of the warrant as a sweetener for the sale of another issue, particularly debenture or other forms of bonds issue, is an alternative to issuing a convertible security. Several *advantages* exist for the purchaser of a senior security with warrants attached over the senior issue convertible into equity shares.

First, the holder has the option of selling the warrant and retaining the original issue, the convertible holder obviously cannot do this.

Second, the life of the warrant cannot be reduced or terminated at the option of the company, whereas many convertible issues are callable after a period of time.

Finally, because of the speculative attractiveness attaching to warrants alone they usually command a greater premium in the market over their realisable value than would a convertible issue.

SIMILARITIES BETWEEN OPTIONS AND WARRANTS

The basic characteristics of stock options are similar to those of stock purchase warrants, and the obligations of an issuing corporation are the same for each security. The primary differences are that most warrants have transferable privileges and involve outsiders and their financing of the corporation, but most stock options have non-transferable privileges and involve employees and their services to the corporation with corporate financing a minor factor. The similarities mean that the same accounting principles apply to the exercise of each type of privilege because the impacts on corporate equity are similar. The differences mean that analysing and recording stock option transactions may be more complex and that services of employees ordinarily affect net income.

Stock options may be granted to other than employees of a corporation. Sometimes a corporation issues options to underwriters as a compensation for their past services. The nature of the issuance and exercise of options issued to outsiders is the same as that for non-transferable stock purchase warrants. Therefore, the accounting for the stock options should correspond to that for warrants issued for the same purchase.

Although definition of a *warrant* i.e., an option to buy a stated number of shares of equity at a specified price at any time during the life of the warrant, is quite similar to the description of a call option, there are several important differences. First, when originally issued, the life of a warrant is usually much longer than that of a call option. Although the listed options markets have recently introduced long-term options, the typical exchange-traded call option has a term to expiration that ranges from 3 to 9 months. In contrast, a warrant generally has an original term to maturity of at least 2 years, and most are between 5 and 10 years. Some are much longer including a few perpetual warrants.

A second major difference is that warrants are usually issued by the company on whose stock the warrant is written. As a result when the warrant is exercised, the investor buys the stock from the company, and the proceeds from the sale are new capital to the issuing firm.

Because these options could have value if the stock price increases as expected, warrants are often used by companies as sweeteners to make new issues of debt or equity more attractive. When offering a new stock or bond issue, the warrant is often attached and after the initial purchase it can be detached and traded on the stock exchange or the OTC market. At the same time, whenever the warrant is exercised, it provides a major source of new equity capital for the company.

Investors are generally interested in warrants because of the leverage possibilities, as we will discuss. Also, investors should be aware that warrants do not pay dividends and the warrant holder has no voting rights. Further, the investor should be sure that a warrant offers protection to the warrant holder against dilution in the case of stock dividends or stock splits whereby either the exercise price is reduced or the number of shares that can be acquired is increased.

REVIEW PROBLEMS

1. Novex Industries currently has some warrants issued that allow the holder to purchase, with one warrant, one equity share at ₹ 18.275 per share. If the equity share was selling at ₹ 25 per share and the warrants were selling for ₹ 9.50, what would be: (a) the minimum price and (b) the warrant premium?

Ans:

(a) Minimum price = (Market price of equity share - Exercise price)

$$\times \text{(Exercise Ratio)}$$

$$= (₹25.00-₹ 18.275) \times (1.0)$$
$$= ₹ 6.725$$

(b) Warrant premium = (Market price of warrant)- (Minimum price of warrant)
$$= ₹ 9.50-₹ 6.725 = ₹ 2.775$$

2. Petro Tech has issued some warrants that allow the holder to purchase, with one warrant, one equity share at ₹ 28.50. If the equity share is selling at ₹ 37.50 and warrants were selling for ₹ 10.50, what would be the (a) minimum price and (b) warrant premium?

Ans:

Minimum price   = (Market price of equity share - Exercise price)

$$\text{(Exercise Ratio)}$$

$$= (₹ 37.50- ₹ 28.50) (1.0) = ₹ 9.00$$
Warrant premium = (Market price of warrant-Minimum price of warrant)
$$= (₹ 10.50-Rs-9.00) = ₹ 1.50$$

3. Trimurti Enterprises has warrants issued that allow the holder to purchase 4 shares of a stock for a total of ₹ 80 for each warrant. Currently, the market price per share of Trimurti equity is ₹ 16 . Investors hold the following probabilistic benefits about the stock 6 months hence:

Market price per share	₹ 10	₹ 16.20	₹ 20	₹ 23	₹ 27
Probability	.10	.20	.30	.25	.15

(a) What is the present theoretical value of the warrant?
(b) What is the expected value of the stock price 6 months hence?
(c) What is the expected value of theoretical value of the warrant 6 months hence?
(d) Would you expect the present market price of the warrant to equal its theoretical value? If not, why not?

Ans:

(a) 4 (₹ 16) - ₹ 80 = - ₹ 16,
or   zero as the warrant can not have a negative value.
(b) (.10) (₹ 10)+.20 (₹ 16)+ .30 (₹ 20)+.25 (₹ 23)+.15 (₹ 27)
$$= ₹ 20.00$$
(c) For market price per share of ₹ 20 or less, the theoretical value of the warrant

will be zero. Therefore the expected value of the theoretical value of the warrant six month hence is:

.10 (0)+ .20 (0)+.30 (0)+.25 (₹ 92 - ₹ 80)+.15 (₹ 108 - ₹ 80)

= ₹ 13.20

(d) As this amount is positive, we can expect the warrant to sell at some positive price, presumably less than ₹ 13.20. Therefore the warrant is worth more than its current theoretical value of zero.

QUESTIONS

1. What is a warrant? What is the chief attraction of a warrant? Describe the leverage feature of a warrant and note why leverage is so attractive to investors?

2. What factors are important in determining the investment appeal of warrant? Why is the price of the warrant itself so important in the investment decision?

3. Explain the difference between a convertible security and a warrant. What factors affect the size of the warrant premium.

4. What is the primary advantage to an investor of a warrant compared to a call option?

5. What are the major differences between a warrant and call option?

6. Identify the factors that influence the value of a warrant.

7. What condition must exist at expiration for the holder of a warrant to decide to exercise it?

PROBLEMS

1. Assume that one warrant gives the holder the right to buy one equity share at an exercise price of ₹ 45. What is the value of this warrant if the current market price of the equity share is ₹ 51? At what premium (₹ and %) would the warrants be trading if they were quoted in the market at a price of ₹ 4?

2. A warrant carries an exercise price of ₹ 20, assume it takes three warrants to buy one share of equity. At what price would the warrant be trading if it is sold at a 20 per cent premium, while the market price of the equity was ₹ 35 per share? What holding period return would an investor make if he buys these warrants (at a 20% premium) when the stock is trading at ₹ 35, and sells them some time later when the equity share is at ₹ 48 and premium on the warrant has dropped to 15%?

3. ABC Corporation has warrants that allow the holder to purchase three shares for a total ₹ 60 for each warrant. Currently the market price per share of XYZ equity is ₹ 18. Investors hold the following probabilistic beliefs about the equity 6 months hence:

Market price per share	₹16	₹ 18	₹ 22	₹ 20	₹ 24
Probability	.20	.15	.20	.30	.15

(a) What is the present theoretical value of the warrant-?

(b) What is the expected value of equity price 6 months hence?

(c) What is the expected value of the theoretical value of the warrant 6 months hence?

(d) Would you expect the present market price of the warrant to equal its theoretical value?

4. Alpha company has a warrant that enables the holder to acquire 2 shares of equity for ₹ 16 a share for each warrant held. The present market price of the equity share is ₹ 19.50 and the expected standard deviation of its continuously compounded return is .20. The warrant has 2 years until expiration. The current risk-free rate is 10 per cent.

(a) If one values the warrant as a European option and uses the Black-Scholes option pricing model, what is the value of the warrant. Assume that the added equity shares upon exercise of the warrants are small relative to the number of shares in the market and that no adjustments to the Black-Scholes formula are necessary.

(b) What would happen to the value of the warrant if the standard deviation were .40? Why does this occur?

5. Kinet Enterprises has some warrants that allow the purchase of equity shares at the price of ₹ 24.50 per share. These warrants are somewhat unusual in that one warrant allows for the purchase of 2.50 equity shares at the exercise price of ₹ 24.50 per share. Given that the warrants were selling for ₹ 4.50 each, and the equity share was selling for ₹ 6.75 per share, determine the minimum and the warrant premium as of that date.

6. Venkat is a highly successful businessman in Delhi. The box manufacturing firm he and his wife Kanta founded several years ago has prospered. Because he is a self employed, he is building his own retirement fund. So far he has accumulated a substantial sum of his investment account, mostly by following an aggressive investment posture, he does this because, as he puts it, "you never know when the bottom's gonna fall out in the business." Venkat has been following the stock of Ganga Paper Products (GPP) and after conducting extensive analysis, feels that the stock is about ready to move. Specifically, he believes that within the next six months, GPP could go about ₹ 80 per share, from its current level of ₹ 52.50. The stock pays annual dividends of ₹ 2.50 per share, and Venkat figures he would receive two quarterly dividend payments over his six-month investment horizon. In studying the company, Venkat has learned that it has some warrants outstanding (they mature in five years and carry an exercise price of ₹ 40); also, it has six-month call options (with ₹ 45 and ₹ 52 striking prices) listed on the BSE. Each warrant is good for one share of stock, and they are currently trading at ₹ 18; the BSE calls are quoted at ₹ 12 for the options with ₹ 45 striking prices, and ₹ 8 for the ₹ 52 options.

(a) How many alternative investment vehicles does Venkat have if he wants to invest in GPP for no more than six months? What if he has a two -year investment horizon?

(b) Using a six-month holding period and assuming the stock does indeed rise to ₹ 80 over this time frame:

  (i) Find the market price of the warrants at the end of the holding period, given that they then trade at premium of 10 percent.

  (ii) Find the value of both calls, given that at the end of holding period neither contains any investment premium.

  (iii) Determine the holding period return for each of the four investments alternatives open to Venkat.

(c) Which course of action would you recommend if Venkat simply wants to maximise profits? Would your answer change if other factors like comparative risk exposure were considered along with return? Explain.

7. A warrant with an expiration date of two years is an option to buy stock at ₹ 24. The current market price of stock is ₹ 35, and the market price of the warrant is ₹ 15.

(a) What is the warrant intrinsic value?

(b) What is the time premium paid for the warrant?

(c) If after two years the stock is selling for ₹ 50, what is the price of the warrant? What is the percentage increase in the value of the stock and the value of the warrant?

(d) If after two years the stock is selling for ₹ 22, what is the price of the warrant? What is the percentage decrease in the value of the stock and the value of the warrant?

Ans: (a) ₹ 11;   (b) ₹ 4;   (c) ₹ 26 (73.3%) increase in the warrant;
           (d) ₹ 0 (100%) decrease in the warrant.

8. Many warrants were issued attached to bonds. In some cases the warrant holders could use the bond instead of (i.e., in lieu of) cash to exercise the warrant. If a warrant is the option to buy stock at ₹ 10 a share and currently sells for ₹ 4 when the stock sells for ₹ 13 and and a ₹ 1, 000 bond (which may be used in lieu of cash) sells for ₹ 700, what would you do and why would you do it? Ans: Arbitrage profit: ₹ 200

9. Rao Industries has warrants issued that permit the holders to purchase one equity share per warrant at a price of ₹ 25.

   (a) Calculate the expiration value of the firm's warrants if the equity share sells at each of the following prices:

        (i) ₹ 20,   (ii) ₹ 25,(iii) ₹ 30,   (iv) ₹ 100.

   (b) At what approximate price do you think the warrants would actually sell under each condition indicated above? What premium is each condition indicated above? What premium is implied in your price? Your answer is a guess, but your price and premiums should bear a reasonable relation to one another.

   (c) How would each of the following factors affect your estimates of the warrant's prices and premiums in Part (b)?

       (1) The life of the warrant.

       (2) Expected variability in the stock's price.

       (3) The expected growth rate in the stack's EPS.

       (4) The company announces a change in dividend policy: whereas it formerly paid no dividends, henceforth it will pay out all earnings as dividends.

   (d) Assume the firm's stock now sells for ₹ 20 per share. The company wants to sell some 20-year, annual interest, ₹ 1, 000 par value bonds. Each bond will have attached 50 warrants, each exercisable into 1 equity share at an exercise price of ₹ 25. The firm's straightbond yield 12%. Regardless of your answer to Part (b), assume that each warrant will have a market value of ₹ 3 when the stock sells at ₹ 20. What coupon interest rate, and rupees coupon, must the company set on the bonds with warrants if they are to clear the market?

Ans: (a)   (1)-₹ 5, or ₹ 0;   (2) ₹ 0;   (3) ₹ 5;   (4) ₹ 75

             (d)   10%; ₹ 100

10. A firm has 100,000 shares of stock outstanding priced at ₹ 35. It has no debt. The firm issues 10,000 warrants, each allowing the purchase of one share of stock at a price of ₹ 50. The warrants expire in 5 years. The standard deviation of the stock is .34, and the risk-free rate is 5.2 per cent.

   (a) Estimate the value of the warrants.

   (b) Determine the price of the stock at expiration assuming the warrants were exercised 1 if the value of the firm is ₹ 52,00,000.

   (c) Reconsider the information in parts a and b. Determine the percentage increase in; the value of the warrants from the value you obtained in part a and the value of the warrant at expiration, which you obtained in b. Compare this to the percentage.

REFERENCES

1. Ansbacher, Max G. *The New Options Market.* New York: Walker, 1979, revised edition.

2. Black, Fisher, "Fact and Fantasy in the Use of Options," *Financial Analysts Journal* 31, no. 4 (July-August 1975).

3. —————————-, and M. Scholes."The Pricing of Options and Corporate Liabilities," *The Journal of Political Economy.* May-June 1973.

4. Boness, A. James: "Elements of a Theory of Stock-Option Value," *Journal of Political Economy,* April 1964, pp. 163-175.

5. Boyle, Phelin, and David Emanuel: "Discretely Adjusted Option Hedges," *Journal of Financial Eco-nomics,* September 1980, pp. 259-282.

6. Chance, Don M.: "Translating the Greek: The Real Meaning of Call Option Derivatives," *Financial Analysts Journal,* July—August 1994, pp. 43-49.

7. Chen, K.C., R. Stephan Sears, and Manuchehr Shahrokhi. "Pricing Nikkei Put Warrants: Some Empiri-cal Evidence." *Journal of Futures Markets* 15, no. 3 (Fall 1992).

8. Cox, John C., and Mark Rubinstein. *Options Markets.* Englewood Cliffs, N.J.: Prentice-Hall, 1985.

9. Cunnion, J.D. *How to Get Maximum Leverage from Puts and Calls.* Larchmont, N.Y.: Business Reports, Inc., 1966.

10. Dimson, Elroy. "Instant Option Valuation," *Financial Analysts Jour-nal.* May-June 1977.

11. Elton, E.J., and M.J. Gruber. "The Economic Value of the Call Option." *The Journal of Finance,* September 1972, pp. 891-902.

12. Engle, R.F., and V. Ng, "Measuring and Testing the Impact of News on Volatility," *Journal of Finance,* 48 (1993): 1749-78.

13. Figlewski, Stephen, N.K. Chidamburan, and Scott Kaplan: "Evaluating the Performance of the Protective Put Strategy," *Financial Analysts Journal,* July-August 1993, pp. 46-56.

14. Figlewski, Stephen, William L. Silber, and Marti G. Subrahmanyam. eds. *Financial Options: From Theory to Practice.* Homewood, III.: Business One Irwin, 1990.

15. Gastineau, Gary: *The Stock Options Manual,* McGraw-Hill, New York, 1990.

16. Gulp, Michael. "A Catalog of Option Strategies," *The Outlook.* Nov. 15, 1976.

17. Hettenhouse, George W., and Donald J. Puglisi, "Investor Experience with Put and Call Options." *Financial Analysts Journal* 31. no. 4 (July-August 1975): 53-58.

18. Katz, Richard. "The Profitability of Put and Call Option Writing," *Industrial Management Review:* Fall 1963, pp. 55-69.

19. Malkiel, Burton G., and Richard E. Quandt: *Strategies and Rational Decisions in the Securities Options Market,* M.I.T. Press, Cambridge, MA, 1969.

20. Manaster, Steven, and Richard Rendleman, Jr. "Option Prices as Predictors of Equilibrium Stock Prices." *The Journal of Finance* 37, no. 4 (September 1982).

21. Merton, Robert C.: "Theory of Rational Option Pricing," *Bell Journal of Economics and Management Science,* Spring 1973, pp. 141-183.

22. Pozen, Robert C.: "The Purchase of Protective Puts by Financial Institutions," *Financial Analysts Journal,* July-August 1978, pp. 47-60.

23. Reback, Robert, "Risk and Return in Option Trading," *Financial Analysts Journal* 31, no. 4 (July August 1975): 42-52.

24. Rendleman, Richard J., Jr. "Optimal Long-Run Option Investment Strategies." *Financial Management* 10,no. 1 (Spring 1981).

25. Ritchken, Peter. *Options: Theory, Strategy, Applications.* (Glenview, III .: Scott, Foresman, 1989.)

26. Slivka, Ronald T. "Risk and Return for Option Investment Strategies," *Financial Analysts Journal* 36, no. 35 (September-October 1980).

27. Smith, Clifford W, Jr. "Option Pricing: A Review." *Journal of Financial Economics* 3, no. 12 (January-March 1976).

28. Stoll, Hans R., "The Relationship Between Put and Call Option Prices," *The Journal of Finance,* December 1969. pp. 801-824.

29. Stulz, R.: "Options on the Minimum or the Maximum of Two Risky Assets," *Journal Of Financial Economies* 10, 1982. pp. 161-185.

37

Futures

INTRODUCTION

Like Hammurabi's option, future help to manage risk. Futures contracts are products created by exchanges. A futures contract is an agreement that requires a party to a agreement either to sell or buy something at a designated future date at a predetermined price. As the value of a futures contract is derived from the value of the underlying instrument, they are commonly called derivative instruments. The basic economic function of futures markets is to provide an opportunity for market participants to hedge against the risk of adverse price movement.

Prior to 1972, only futures contracts involving traditional agricultural commodities, imported foodstuffs, or industrial commodities were traded. Collectively, such futures contracts are known as commodity futures. And, the futures contracts based on a financial instrument or a financial index are known as financial futures. Financial futures can be classified as stock index futures, interest rate futures, and currency futures. The purpose of this chapter is to provide an introduction of financial futures contracts. More detailed strategies employing futures contracts will be discussed in later chapters.

FUTURES MARKETS

In the past several years, derivatives market has attracted many new and inexperienced entrants. The spectacular growth of the new futures markets in interest rates and stock market indexes has generated a demand for a unified economic theory of the effects of futures markets - in commodities, financial instruments, stock market indexes and foreign exchange - upon the intertemporal allocation of resources.

The basic assumption of the investment theory is that investors are risk averse. If risk is to be equated with uncertainty, can we question the validity of this assumption? What evidence is there? As living, functional proof of the appropriateness of the risk aversion assumption, there exists entire market whose sole underlying purpose is to allow investors to display their uncertainties about the future. These particular markets, with primary focus on the future, are called just *that future markets*. These markets allow for the transfer of risk from hedgers (risk averse individuals), a key element necessary for the existence of futures markets is the balance between the number of hedgers and operators who are willing to transfer and accept risk.

What economic theory of futures markets can explain this phenomena? Keynes viewed the futures market as one where commercial firms hold inventories of commodities and sell futures to transfer the risk of price fluctuations. 'Speculators' are on the other side of the market and purchase these futures at a discount below the expected price. The magnitude of this discount is the risk premium demanded by the speculators. His theory of **'normal backwardation'** has been the subject of controversy. Set of theories of futures markets, based upon the capital asset pricing model (CAPM) or the intertemporal CAPM, are incapable of explaining the essential features of futures markets.

The quality of positive economic theory must be judged by its ability to explain with precision clarity and simplicity the key elements of a complex economic phenomenon. Theories which ignore or cannot explain the basic characteristics cannot qualify as relevant or good theories of futures markets. The main characteristics of futures markets, to be explained by a good economic theory are: (*i*) There is only a small number of actively traded products with futures contracts. The trading unit is large and indivisible; (*ii*) Almost all of the open interest is concentrated in the nearby contract, which has a maturity of no more than three months; (*iii*) The success ratio of new contracts is about 25 per cent in world financial markets. Some new contracts succeed and then, which seem to have similar useful features, fail; (*iv*) Futures are seldom used by fanners. Instead, they are forward contracts. The main users of agricultural futures are intermediaries (dealers) in the marketing process; (*v*) There are both commercial and non-commercial users of futures contracts in interest rates and foreign exchange. The commercial users are to a large extent dealers: intermediaries in the marketing process; (*vi*) The position of the commercials and dealers in interest rate futures are almost evenly divided between long and short positions; (*vii*) The main use of futures by the commercials is to hedge corresponding cash and forward positions; (*viii*) The positions of the non-commercials are almost entirely speculative positions; (*ix*) In foreign exchange futures, the positions of the commercials are unbalanced. In some currencies they are net short and in others they are net long. However, their positions are primarily hedging against corresponding cash and forward positions. The non-commercial positions are overwhelmingly speculative positions; and, finally, futures are used in the underwriting of fixed income securities but not in equity underwriting.

Each of these characteristics entail risk. The spectacular growth of the derivatives market and the heavy losses incurred recently by several firms undertaking derivative transactions have reinforced concerns about the possible risks involved. Need to accelerate the implementation of sound risk management practices is well recognised to maintain the stability of the derivatives market. With pools of high-yield-seeking capital growing rapidly, with the technology of international capital markets making it cheaper and easier to alter the composition of portfolios at short notice, and with institutional fund managers under continuing pressure to deliver high performance, the importance of systemic risk control management cannot be over- emphasised.

The economic theory of futures markets focus upon the inter-related questions. *How do the futures markets affect the intertemporal allocation of resources? To what extent do these markets post relevant information concerning supply and demand at a later date? How do these markets affect the risk premiums that producers charge, when the prices of output or of input are uncertain? These questions can be combined into the following: How do futures markets affect the supply functions of output, when there is price uncertainty? What are the welfare effects of the futures markets? To what extent does the diversity in the forecasting ability of the futures speculators simply result in transfers of wealth among themselves and to what extent does it affect the output produced, the price paid by the consumer and the variance of that price? How does the existence of futures markets affect the level of expected production and the variance of the price paid by consumers, relative to the situation that would prevail if there were no futures markets? How can we evaluate the extent to which a particular futures market change the economic welfare? Does trading in financial instruments serve any economic purpose?*

These questions are of great interest to the policy makers as well as to the academics. Extensive trading in financial futures and increased volatility in security prices and interest rates affect the formation of real capital in the economy (particularly that of a long-term nature) and the structure of liquidity in the credit market.

FUTURES CONTRACTS AND FUTURE TRADING

The future contract is an agreement to buy or sell an asset at a certain time in the future for a certain price. Equities, bonds, hybrid securities and currencies are the commodities of the investment business. They are traded on organised exchanges in which a clearing house interposes itself between buyer and seller and guarantees all transactions, so that the identity of the buyer or seller is a matter of indifference to the opposite party. Futures contracts protect those who use these commodities in their business.

Futures trading is to enter into contracts to buy or sell financial instruments, dealing in commodities or other financial instruments, for forward delivery or settlement, on standardised terms. The major functions performed by future markets are: they facilitate stockholding; they facilitate the shifting of risk; they act as a mechanism for collection and dissemination of information; and they perform a forward pricing function. To perform these functions for future trading, the customary condition is that there must be variation in the price of the actual commodity under consideration; second, there must exist economic agents with commitments in the actuals market; and third, it must be possible to specify a standard grade of the commodity and to measure deviations from this grade. As a result of the first two conditions, some economic agents will face a price risk and there will be a demand for hedging facilities. A futures market established specifically to meet purely speculative demands is possible but is unknown. The third condition, together with standardisation of delivery date and of delivery location and testing procedures, where relevant means that a high degree of contract standardisation is possible. Further, conditions which are thought of necessary for the establishment of futures trading are the presence of speculative capital and financial facilities for payment of margins and contract settlement. In addition, a strong infrastructure is required, including financial, legal and communication systems.

Financial futures contracts exist to provide risk management services to participants. Risk and uncertainty in the form of price volatility and opportunism are major factors giving rise to future trading. Futures trading evolved out of autonomous forward contracting by merchants, dealers and processors, designed to increase business efficiency. Indeed, early futures markets were viewed as delivery markets in which transactions were facilitated by the provision of uniform rules on grade and delivery terms, and the security provided by the clearing houses in guaranteeing individual contracts. This evolution from spot, to forward, to futures contracts suggests a progressive adaptation of institutions to more efficient methods of dealing with price risk. It is frequently argued that a pre-condition for futures trading is a well developed cash market and the breakdown of forward contracting. Futures markets develop because they are a more efficient means of transferring those contract rights attached to price. Spot and forward contracting may become too costly. However, these three contracting modes are not mutually exclusive ways of transacting. Indeed, the development of futures markets improve the efficiency of spot and possibly of forward contracting. It is perhaps best to view futures markets as 'side' markets designed to deal with price volatility that is poorly handled by spot and forward markets. This transactional superiority of futures markets comes mainly from their transaction - cost reducing attributes.

Futures markets, by forming prices relating to forward delivery dates, project their prices into the future. These prices are used by agents to plan future production to price forward contracts for the supply of commodities, and to tender for forward contracts. Agents need not transact on future exchanges to use futures prices in this way, and the information contained in such prices is an externality to them. Agents may also use futures markets in deciding whether to store a commodity (using the forward premium as an indicator of whether storage is expected to be profitable). In addition, futures markets may help agents to decide the timing of inputs purchases and of processing activities according to the expected outcome of hedging. Agents in these latter two categories are, of course, transactors on futures markets. Thus, futures markets perform a forward pricing function, and in these ways futures prices facilitate the allocation of resources between present and future uses.

MARGIN

At the heart of futures market procedures is the system of collateral margins that has evolved as a means to reduce default risks. As opposed to margins or stock accounts, a futures margin payment is hot a form of down payment on the balance due since a futures transaction is not an investment of initial capital in return for a later *payoff*, but rather, in its purest form, is an agreement made at no initial investment. Margin payments are used as a means of gradually settling the losses and gain on the contract and also as collateral against default. Margin payments are made frequently (usually daily) in small amounts relative to the size of the contract, rather man in one large initial lump sum, so as to preserve the basic character of a futures contract as a forward agreement: deferred payments for deferred delivery. Infact, daily cash settlement procedure is an important aspect of the futures markets, integral in maintaining the trading system. Each transaction calls for a good-faith deposit known as initial margin, to be posted with a broker. The minimum amount of initial margin required is set by the exchange based on the price volatility of the underlying product. The value of a contract position is assessed, marked to market, daily and these changes are settled in cash on a daily basis. For example, if a contract prices increase, the longs - who have purchased the contract - would receive cash equal to the value of gains, while the shorts - who have sold contracts - would have to pay in funds equal to the value of losses. This procedure, known as variation margin, keeps the value of each market participant's position current and constitutes to the credit of the futures market. Initial margin ensures that the participants will pay variation-margin deficit. When the system is tied in with the variation- margin vehicle through which daily *marks to market* occur, an individual gains the ability of offset a position at any time without regard to who was initially on the other side of the transaction. This is a key to ease of trading and confidence in the future markets. This makes the possibility of taking a large market position without committing a large amount of capital. For this reason, futures contracts are considered an extremely highly leveraged instrument relative to most financial securities. Although high leverage is often associated with high financial instability and high default risk, futures markets have a history of financial integrity and low default risk. This unusual combination of high leverage with low default risk is largely a property of the intricate, multi-tiered, continually adjusting margining system.

To illustrate how margin works, consider an investor who contacts his or her broker on July 9, 2010, to buy two December 2010 gold futures contracts on the XYZ Commodity Exchange. We suppose that the current futures price is $ 1250 per ounce. Since the contract size is 100 ounces, the investor has contracted to buy a total of 200 ounces at this price. The broker will require the investor to deposit funds in what is termed a *margin account.* The amount that must be deposited at the time the contract is first entered into is known as the *initial margin.* We assume this is $ 5,000 per contract or $ 10,000 in total. At the end of each trading day, the margin account is adjusted to reflect the investor's gain or loss. This is known as *marking to market* the account.

Suppose by the end of July 9, 2010 the futures price has dropped from $ 1250 to $ 1240. The investor has a loss of 500 x 2 or $ 1,000. This is because the 200 ounces of December 2010 gold, which he or she contracted at $ 1250, can be sold for $ 1245. The balance in the margin account would, therefore, be reduced by $ 1,000 to $ 9,000. Similarly, if the price of December 2010 gold rose to $ 1260 by the end of the first day, the balance in the margin account would be increased by $ 2,000 to $ 12,000. A trade is first marked to market at the dose of the day on which it takes place. It is then marked to market at the dose of trading on each subsequent day.

Marking to market is not merely an arrangement between broker and client, however, when there is a $ 2,000 decrease in the future prices so that the margin account of an investor with a long position is reduced by $ 2,000, the investor's broker has to pay the exchange $ 2,000 and the exchange passes the money on to the broker of an investor with a short position. Similarly, when there is an increase in the futures price, brokers for parties with short positions pay money to the exchange and brokers for parties with long positions receive money from the exchange.

The investor is entitled to withdraw any balance in the margin account in excess of the initial margin. To ensure that the balance in the margin account never becomes negative *a maintenance margin,* which is somewhat lower than the initial margin, is set. If the balance in the margin account falls below the maintenance margin, the investor receives a *margin call* and is expected to top up the margin account to the initial margin level the next day. In case the extra funds deposited, known as variation margin, are not provided by the investor, the broker doses out the position by selling the contract. In the case of the investor considered earlier dosing out the position would involve underlying the existing contract by selling 200 ounces of gold for delivery in December 2010. Table-1 illustrates the operation of the margin account for one possible sequence of futures prior in the case of the investor considered earlier. The maintenance margin is assumed for the purpose of the illustration is $ 3,500 per contract or $ 7,000 in total. The contract is entered into on 9 July, 2010 at $ 1,250 and closed out on 30 July, 2010 at $ 1232.

TABLE 1

Operation of Margins for a Long position in Two Gold Futures Contracts

Day	Futures Price $	Daily Gain/ Loss $	Cumulative Gain (Loss)	Margin Account Balance $	Margin Call
July 9	1245	-1000	-1000	9000	
July 10	1249	800	-200	9800	
July 11	1243	-1200	-1400	8600	
July 12	1245	400	-1000	9000	
July 13	1241	-800	-1800	8200	
July 14	1236	-1000	-2800	7200	
July 15	1240	800	-2000	8000	
July 16	1237	-600	-2600	7400	

July 17	1332	-1,000	3,600	6,400	3,600
July 18	1235	600	-3,000	10,600	
July 19	1226	-2,200	-5,200	8,400	
July 22	1220	-1,200	-6,400	7,200	
July 23	1215	-1,000	-7,400	6,200	3,800
July 24	1215	0	-7,400	10,000	
July 25	1220	1,000	-6,400	11,000	
July 26	1230	2,000	-4,400	13,000	
July 29	1235	1,000	-3,400	14,000	
July 30	1232	-600	-4,000	13,400	

On 17 July 2010 the balance in the margin account falls $ 600 below the maintenance margin level. This triggers a margin call from the broker for additional margin of $ 3,200. Table-1 assumes that the investor does in fact provide this margin by close of trading on July 18, 2010. On 23 July the balance in the margin account again falls below the maintenance margin level and a margin call for $ 3,800 is sent out. The investor provides this margin by close of trading on 24 July 2010. On 30 July 2010 the investor decides to close out the position by shorting two contracts. The future price on that day is $ 1232 and the investor has a cumulative loss of $ 4,000.

CLEARINGHOUSE AND CLEARING MARGINS

The trade for an outside party must be executed through a broker, and the broker must, in turn, trade through a member of the exchange. Normally, the two parties to a transaction are located far apart and may not even know each other. This raises the issue of trust and the question of whether the traders will perform as they have promised. To resolve this uncertainty about performance in accordance with the contract terms, each futures exchange has a clearing house. The clearing house is a well- capitalised financial institution that guarantees contract performance to both parties. As soon as the trade is commuted, the clearing house interposes itself between the buyer and seller. At this point, the original buyer and seller have obligations to the clearing house and no obligations to each other.

In the calculation of clearing margins, the exchange clearing house calculates the number of contracts on trading on either a gross or a net basis. Basis is *the difference between the current spot price on an asset and corresponding futures prices.* The gross basis simply adds the total of all long positions entered into by clients to the total of all short positions entered into by clients. The *net basis* allows these to be offset against each other. Suppose a dealing house member has two clients, one with a buy position in 50 contracts, the other with a short position in 30 contracts. Gross margining would calculate the dealing margin would calculate the clearing margin on the basis of 80 contracts; net margining would calculate the clearing margin on the basis of 20 contracts. The whole purpose of the margining system is to reduce the possibility of market participants sustaining losses because of defaults.

STOCK INDEX FUTURES

Stock-index futures offer the investor a medium for expressing an opinion on the general course of the market. In addition, these contracts can be used by portfolio managers in a variety of ways to alter the risk-return distribution of their stock portfolios.[1] For instance, much of a sudden upward surge in the market could be missed by the institutional investor due to the time it takes to get money into the stock market. By purchasing stock- index contracts, the institutional investors can enter the market immediately and then gradually unwind the long futures position as they are able to get more funds invested in the stock. Conversely, after a run up in the value of the stock portfolio (assuming it is well diversified and correlates well with one of the major indexes) a portfolio manager might desire to lock in the profits much after being required to report this quarterly return on the portfolio. By selling an appropriate number of stock index-futures contracts, the institutional investors could offset any losses on the stock portfolio with corresponding gains on the future position.

As a speculation tool, stock index futures represent an inexpensive and highly liquid short-run alternative to speculating on the stock market. Instead of purchasing the stocks that make up an index or proxy portfolio, a bullish (bearish) speculation can take a long (short) position in an index futures contract, than purchase treasury securities to satisfy the major requirements. A long or short speculative futures position is referred to as a pure speculative position, or a naked (outright) position.

HEDGING USING INDEX FUTURES

Stock index futures can be used to hedge the risk in a well-diversified portfolio of stocks. Depending on the underlying asset to be hedged, several different types of hedging models can be applied to stock index futures. The most popular models are:

Naive Hedging Model

A perfect hedge can be attained by using a naive hedging model. The model assumes ideal conditions in which there is no quantity, quality, or timing risk extant; hence, the value of the spot position remains unchanged at expiration. In this model, the number of futures contracts (N_f) is found by dividing the current value of the spot position (V_o) by the price of the future contract (F_o):

$$\text{Naive hedge: } N_f = \frac{V_o}{F_o} \tag{1}$$

A portfolio manager who wants to lock in Rs. 2.50 crore when the futures price on the ABC 200 futures contract[2] is 500 could do so by going short in $N_f = 250$ ABC 200 futures contracts:

$$N_f = \frac{\text{Rs. } 2.50}{(500)\,(200)} = 250 \text{ contracts}$$

---

1. A stock index tracks the changes in the value of a hypothetical portfolio of stocks. The weights of a stock in the portfolio equals the proportion of the portfolio invested in the stock. The stocks in the portfolio can have equal weights or weights that change in some way over time. The percentage increase in the value of a stock index over a small interval of time is usually defined so that it is equal to the percentage increase in the total value of the stocks comprising the portfolio at that time. A stock index is not usually adjusted for cash dividends. In other words, any cash dividends received on the portfolio are ignored when percentage changes in most indices are being calculated. It is worth noting that the weights assigned to individual stocks in the portfolio may not remain fixed even if the hypothetical portfolio of stocks remains fixed. If the price of one particular stock rises more sharply than others in the portfolio the more weight is automatically given to that stock. A corollary to this is that, if the weights of the stock in the specified portfolio are to remain constant over a time, the hypothetical portfolio will change each day. If the price of one particular stock in the portfolio rises more sharply than others, the holding of the stock must be reduced to maintain the weightings.

Under ideal conditions, the combined value of the portfolio and the cash flows from the futures position would be worth ₹ 2.50 crores at the future delivery date.

Stock Index Price-Sensitivity Model

The stock index price-sensitivity model is applied to determine the number of stock index futures contracts that will minimise the variability of the profits from a hedged portfolio consisting of the stock portfolio and stock index future contracts. In this model, the number of futures contracts or hedge ratio that will minimise the variability is:

$$N_f^* = -\beta \frac{V_o}{F_o} \qquad (2)$$

where

V_o = current value of stock portfolio

F_o = price on futures contracts

β = beta of stock portfolio (Negative sign indicates opposite positions in the future contracts and the portfolio)

Thus, if a September ABC 200 futures contract is available at 750, a portfolio manager wanting to hedge a ₹ 2.50 crore portfolio with a beta of 3.0 would need -500 short contracts.[3]

$$N_f^* = \frac{-(3.0)(₹\ 2.50\ \text{crore})}{(200)\ (750)} = -500$$

The stock index price sensitivity model can be extended to determine the optimum number of stock index option contracts needed to hedge a portfolio. When stock index options are used instead of futures to hedge a portfolio, the hedge ratio (N^*) is found by substituting the option's exercise price for the futures price in Equation-2. That is:

$$N^* = \frac{\beta V_o}{X} \qquad (3)$$

To illustrate the use of the price-sensitivity model in short index hedging, consider the case of a stock portfolio manager who in January feels that he may be required to liquidate his stock portfolio in June.

Because of this concern, the manager decides to hedge the value of the stock portfolio by taking a short position in the June ABC 200 futures contract. The portfolio is well diversified with a beta of 3.0 and in January is worth ₹ 2.50 crore when the ABC 200 spot index (S_o) is at 300. Finally, a June ABC 200 futures contract priced at 300 is available.

To hedge the portfolio using the price-sensitivity model, the manager would need to go short in 250 ABC 200 contracts. That is:

$$N_f^* = -3.0 \frac{(₹\ 2.50\ \text{crore})}{(200)\ (750)} = 200\ \text{short contracts}$$

---

2. In the case of hypothetical ABC 200 index, one contract is on 200 times the we are assuming. If the future price of ABC 200 is 250, the value of one contract is 250 x 200 = ₹ 50,000.

3. A diversified portfolio with a beta greater than 1 can be thought of as a leveraged investment in the ABC 200. The number of hypothetical ABC 200 shares would be $N^*g = \beta\ V_o / S_o$, where S_o is the spot ABC 200 index, and the amount of debt used to finance the index stock would be the present value of N^*S_o / V_o. Thus, if the spot ABC 200 index is at 500, a ₹ 2.50 crore portfolio with beta = 3.0 would be the equivalent to buying $N_f = 3.0$ (₹ 2.50 crore) /500 = 1,50,000 index shares at ₹ 500 per share (₹ 7.50 crore) and borrowing an amount equal to the present value of ₹ 7.50 crore - ₹ 2.50 crore = ₹ 5.00 crore

Suppose that instead of locking in a future portfolio value, the portfolio manager wanted portfolio insurance so that he had downside protection in case the market declined but still could profit if the market increased. In terms of the example, if a June 750 ABC 200 put option trading at 100 exists, if the multiple of ABC 200 option is ₹ 1000, then X =
(₹ 1,000) (750) = ₹ 7,50,000. Using the price-sensitivity model, the manager could attain portfolio insurance by buying 100 put contracts (total cost).

$$N_p^* = -3.0 \frac{(₹ \ 2.50 \ \text{crore})}{(750) \ (₹1000)} = 100 \ \text{put contracts}$$

A portfolio manager who is planning to invest a future inflow of cash in a stock portfolio could lock in the purchase price of the portfolio by going long in a stock index futures contract. For example, suppose that in January the portfolio manager in the preceding example was anticipating an inflow of cash in June and was planning to invest the cash in a stock portfolio with beta = 3.0 and currently worth ₹ 2.50 crore. If the June ABC 200 futures contract is at $F_0 = 750$, the manager could hedge the purchase price by going long in 500 contracts:

$$N_f^* = -3.0 \frac{₹ \ 2.50 \ \text{crore}}{(200) \ (750)} = 500 \ \text{long contracts}$$

In addition to an anticipatory hedge, the manager also could lock in a maximum portfolio cost or minimum number of shares with the possibility of lower costs or more shares if the market declines by purchasing an index call option. In terms of an example, if a June 750 ABC 200 call option purchased at 100 exists, if the multiple of ABC 200 options is ₹ 1000, then:

$$N_f^* = -\frac{\beta S_o}{X} = \frac{(3.0) \ (₹2.50 \ \text{crore})}{(750) \ (₹ \ 1000)} = 100$$

MARKET TIMING

Stock index futures can be used to change the beta of a portfolio to profit from an expected change in the market. The number of futures contracts needed to move the portfolio beta (beta$_o$) to target beta (beta$_t$) can be determined via the price-sensitivity model, in which:

$$N_f^* = \frac{V_o}{F_o}(\beta_t - \beta_o)$$

where:
  if $\beta_t > \beta_o$ long in futures
  if $\beta_t < \beta_o$, short in futures

To illustrate, consider the case of a stock portfolio manager who in June is confident the market will increase over next three months, and as a result wants to change his portfolio's beta from its current value of beta$_o$ = 1.50 to beta$_t$= 2.5. Suppose the portfolio currently is worth ₹ 5 crore, the spot ABC 200 index is at 2550, and the price on the September ABC 200 futures contract is 2750. To adjust the portfolio beta from 1.50 to 2.50, the manager would need to buy N_f = 90.91 September ABC 200 index futures:

$$N_f = \frac{V_o}{F_o}(\beta_t - \beta_o)$$

$$\frac{₹.5 \text{ crore})}{(2750) (₹\ 200)}(2.50 - 1.50) = 90.91$$

If the market increases, the portfolio manager will earn higher rates of return from the futures-adjusted portfolio than from the unadjusted portfolio and vice-versa.

SPECULATING ON UNSYSTEMATIC RISK

The price movements of an individual stock are affected by both systematic factors (market factors that affect all stocks) and unsystematic factors (factors unique to the securities of a particular industry or firm). Given this, suppose an investor is very confident that a firm or industry factors in the futures will lead to a stock price increase. However, suppose the investor also is bearish about the market, fearing that a general price decline in all securities would negate the anticipated positive impacts on the stock's price resulting from the specific firm and industry factors. The investor would like to eliminate the stock's systematic factors, leaving his investment exposed only to the unsystematic factors. With index futures (and options), an investor can accomplish *speculating on unsystematic risk* by hedging away the systematic risk of the stock.

To illustrate how speculating on unsystematic risk works, consider the case of a mutual fund that in June identifies the XYZ Company as a good candidate for takeover by a leveraged buyout firm. Based on this expectation, the fund is considering purchasing 50,000 shares of XYZ stock, but it is hesitant because of fear the stock market could decline over the next six months (the time period it is believed the takeover could happen). To hedge against the systematic risk, the fund could go short in December index futures (or purchase December stock put options). In this case, suppose XYZ stock has a beta of 1.5 and is trading at ₹ 20 per share, the spot ABC 200 is at 198, and the December ABC 200 futures contract is at 250. The fund could speculate on the stock's unsystematic risk while hedging the systematic risk by buying 50,000 shares of the XYZ stock and going short on December 12 index futures contracts:

$$N_f = \beta \frac{V_o}{F_o} = -1.5\frac{(50,000)\ (₹\ 20)}{(250)\ (200)}$$

$$= 6 \text{ short contracts.}$$

STOCK INDEX FUTURES PRICING: CARRYING-COST MODEL

The equilibrium futures price on a stock index futures contract can be determined via the carrying-cost model. In terms of the model, the index futures price is equal to the net costs of carrying a spot index portfolio or proxy portfolio to expiration at time E_T. For stock index futures, transportation or storage costs do not exist, but dividends from holding the index portfolio do. Thus the equilibrium price for an index future is:

$$F_o^* = S_o(1+T)^t - D_t \tag{5}$$

where

S_o = current spot index value
D_t = value of stock index dividends at time t.

If the equilibrium condition defined by Equation-4 does not hold, an arbitrage opportunity will exist by taking a position in the spot portfolio and an opposite one in the future contract. For example, if the market price on the future contract $F^m o$ exceeds the equilibrium price, an arbitregeur could earn a riskless profit of $F^m o - F^* o$ with an index arbitrage strategy in which he borrows So at risk-free rate of T, buy the spot index portfolio for S_o, and locks in the selling price on the portfolio at time t by going short in the index futures at $F^m o$.

The carrying-costs model for index futures also can be described as an investment in a riskless stock index portfolio paying a certain dividend. That is, an investor who purchases a spot index portfolio (at S_o) paying a certain dividend worth D_T at t and who then locks in the portfolio's selling price at time t by going short in an index futures contract at F_o will earn a riskless one-period rate of return of:

$$\text{Rate} = \frac{(F_o - S_o) - D}{S_o} \tag{6}$$

Since the investment is riskless, in equilibrium the futures and spot prices should be such that the rate of return on the investment is equal to a riskless rate (if not abnormal rates of return could be earned from this investment). Thus, setting Equation-5 equal to the risk-free rate, then solving for F_o, we obtain the carrying-cost model, and solving for So, we obtain:

$$\frac{F_o - D_1}{(1+T)^t}$$

Hence, if the carrying-cost model holds, then in equilibrium the rate of return from an investment in a spot portfolio with the selling price locked in with a futures contract is equal to the risk-free rate, and the spot portfolio price is equal to the present value of the futures price and the portfolio's dividend, with the discount rate being equal to the risk-free rate.

TRIPLE WITCHING HOUR

The portfolio for large arbitrage profits should keep the market price of the index futures very dose to the theoretical price. The computer-based systems constantly monitor prevailing futures, spot, and treasury bill prices to determine whether a profitable arbitrage is available to generate trade orders. Such trades are variant of what is called a *programme trade*. (A programme trade is a large purchase or sale of many securities at virtually the same moment in time). As a result, market prices rarely move outside a transaction cost bound around the theoretical futures price.

There are two features of index arbitrage which have had dramatic impacts on the delivery date volatility of equity shares. First, the trades are risk-free solely because the futures price must be equal to the spot index value at the moment of delivery - the futures exchange defines the futures price to be so at that time. Therefore, arbitrageurs will maintain their spot stock and futures positions as long as they can on the delivery date, usually until the last hour or two. Second, settlement of the futures is in cash. Delivery of spot stock indexes is not allowed. Therefore, in order to unwind an index arbitrage position, any stock position must be closed directly on the stock exchange floor. If the original arbitrage position had consisted of being long stock, large quantities of stock will have to be sold late in the day of the futures delivery. If stock had originally been sold in the arbitrage, large quantities of stock will have to be purchased.

These two features of the arbitrage have had dramatic impact on stock prices during the futures' delivery date. If the programmes required large stock sales, the value of the Future Index may fall substantially in the last hour of trading. The opposite occurred if the programmes required stock purchases. Arbitrageurs were indifferent to such large price swings in spot stock, since whatever they lost on their spot transactions they simultaneously won on their futures position. For example, assume that in dosing out the arbitrage, large stock sales forced stock prices down. At the same time, however, index futures were being bought. Thus, the arbitrageur was not affected by such price swings.

But the general investing public was harmed. For example, public traders who happened to trade during the last hour of the delivery date often traded substantially different from true equilibrium levels. In addition, the public perception grew that the stock market had become more volatile, solely because of the actions of index arbitregeurs.

This problem was particularly severe when index future delivery dates coincided with expiration dates on stock index options. In this case, arbitrages between the spot index, futures on the index, and options on the index were being dosed out, resulting in abnormally large spot stock trading. Because three stock index positions were being traded at the same time, this time came to be known as the *"Triple Witching Hour"*.

FUTURES VERSUS OPTIONS

Investors occasionally make the mistake of confusing a future contract with an options contract. Some analogies can be made between futures contracts and option contracts. Both involve a predetermined price and contract duration. An option, however, is precisely that: an option. The person holding an option has the right, but not the obligation, to exercise the put or call. If an option has no value at its expiration, the option holder will allow it to expire unexercised. But with futures contracts, a trade must occur if the contract is held until its delivery deadline. Futures contracts do not expire until exercised. One party has promised to deliver an asset, which another party has promised to buy. It is also possible for one or both parties to the trade to transfer their half of the promise to someone else via an offsetting trade.

Figure-1 contracts the situation faced by the buyer and the seller of a call option with the situation faced by the buyer and the seller of a futures contract. Specifically, terminal values for buyers and sellers are shown at least possible moment - the expiration date for the option and the delivery date for the futures contract.

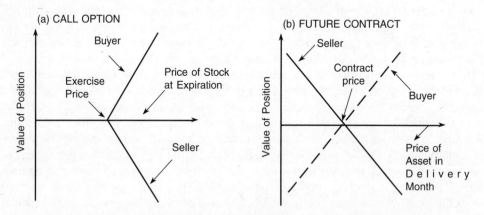

FIGURE 1: TERMINAL VALUES OF POSITION IN CALLS AND FUTURES

As shown in panel (*a*), no matter what the price of the underlying stock, an option buyer cannot lose and an option seller cannot gain on expiration date. Option buyers compensate sellers for putting themselves in this position by paying them a premium when the contract is signed. However, the situation is quite different with a futures contract. As shown in panel (*b*), the buyer may gain or lose, depending on the price of the asset in the delivery month. Whatever the buyer gains or loses, an exactly offsetting loss or gain will be registered by the seller. The higher the contract price (that is, the price of the futures contract when the buyer purchased it from the seller), the greater the likelihood that the buyer will lose and the seller will gain. The lower the contract price, the greater the likelihood that the seller will lose and the buyer will gain.

SYNTHETIC FUTURES

Synthetic futures contract can be enacted even in the case of such assets for which both put and call options are available but future contracts are unavailable. The dearest example involves European options on equity. The purchase of a European call option and the sale of a European put option at the same exercise price and with the same expiration date will provide a value at the expiration that will be related to the stock price at that time. This is shown in Figure-2. Panel (*a*) shows the pay-off associated with the purchase of a call at an exercise price E, whereas panel (*b*) shows the pay-off associated with the sale of a put at the same exercise price. The results obtained by taking *both* positions are shown by the solid line in panel (*c*).

Depending on the prices (i.e. premiums) of the call and the put, this strategy may initially either require a net outflow of cash or provide a net inflow. For comparability with the purchase of a futures contract, this cash flow may be offset with borrowing or lending as required to bring the net investment to zero. The dash line in panel (*c*) shows a case in which the call option costs more than as provided by the sale of that put option. The difference is borrowed, requiring the loan repayment shown in figure. The dashed line thus indicates the net end-of-period payoffs for a strategy requiring no initial outlay. Because these payoffs are equivalent to the payoffs from a futures contract with a contract price equal to F, a synthetic futures contract has been created. In practice, however, the equivalence is not perfect. Moreover, synthetic future is not marked to market on a daily basis. Despite these differences, the existence of well-functioning markets for call and put options will enable investors to create arrangements similar to futures on the underlying asset synthetically.

FUTURES VERSUS FORWARD MARKETS

While futures and forward contacts are similar in many respects, their differences are more important to fully understand the nature and uses of these financial instruments. Both futures and forward contracts specify a transaction to take place at a future date and include precis requirements for the commodity to be delivered, its price, its quantity, the delivery date, and the delivery point. Nevertheless these two types of contracts for future delivery of a commodity and the markets in which they are traded differ in a number of significant ways, some of which are included in Table 2.

Although most investors are unlikely ever to become involved in the forward market, it is important to understand some of the attitudes, particularly as a good deal of the literature on pricing futures contracts typically refers to these contracts interchangeably. Specifically, it might be inferred from Table-2 that differences resulting from liquidity, credit risk, search, margin, taxes and commissions could cause futures and forward contracts not to be price identically. For instance, in dealing with price risk, futures contracts have several transactional advantages relative to spot and forward contracts. Sequential spot contracts, that is spot contracts where the terms of the contract are re-negotiated as events unfold, do not inject any certainty into the transaction. Such a method of contracting is particularly liable to the hazards of opportunism and may deter investment because of the relatively high probability that the contract will be breached. On the other hand, forward and futures contracts inject some certainty into their transaction.

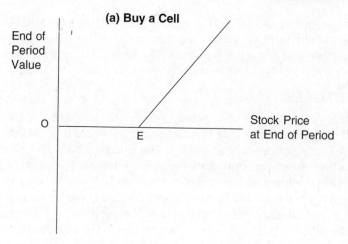

(a) Buy a Cell

End of Period Value

O

E

Stock Price at End of Period

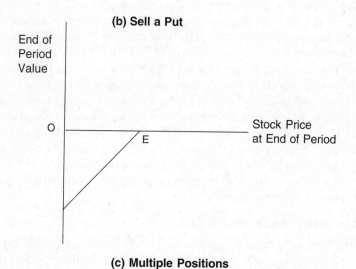

(b) Sell a Put

End of Period Value

O

E

Stock Price at End of Period

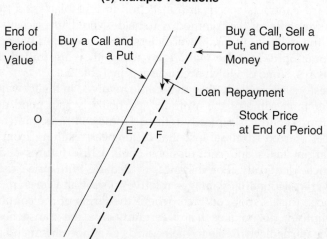

(c) Multiple Positions

End of Period Value

Buy a Call and a Put

Buy a Call, Sell a Put, and Borrow Money

Loan Repayment

O

E   F

Stock Price at End of Period

FIGURE 2

TABLE 2

A Comparison of Futures and Forward Markets

Futures Market	Forward Market
1. Trading is conducted in a competitive arena by "open outcry" of bids, offers, and amounts	1. Trading is done by telex or telephone, with participants generally dealing directly with broker-dealers.
2. Contract terms are standardized with all buyers and sellers negotiating only with respect to price.	2. All contract terms are negotiated privately by the parties.
3. Non-member participants deal through brokers (exchange members who represent them on the exchange floor.	3. Participants deal typically on a principal-to-principal basis.
4. Participants include banks, corporations financial institutions, individual investors, and speculators.	4. Participants are primarily institutions dealing with one other and other interested parties dealing through one or more dealers.
5. The clearing house of the exchange becomes the opposite side to each cleared transactions; therefore, the credit risk for a futures market participant is always the same and there is no need to analyze the credit of other market participants	5. A participant must examine the credit risk and establish credit limits for each opposite party.
6. Margins deposits are to be required of all participants.	6. Typically, no money changes hands until delivery, although a small margin deposit might be required of nondealer customers on certain occasions
7. Settlements are made daily through the exchange clearing house. Gains on open positions may be withdrawn and losses are collected daily.	7. Settlement occurs on date agreed upon between the parties to each transaction.
8. Long and short positions are usually liquidated easily.	8. Forward positions are not as easily offset or transferred to other participants.
9. Settlements are normally made in cash, with only a small percent age of all contracts resulting actual delivery.	9. Most transactions result in delivery.
10. A single, round trip (in and out of the market) commission is charged. It is negotiated between broker and customer and is relatively small in relation to the value of the contract.	10. No commission is typically charged if the transaction is made directly with another dealer. A commission is charged to born buyer and seller, however, if transacted through a broker.
11. Trading is regulated.	11. Trading is mostly unregulated.
12. The delivery price is the spot price.	12. The delivery price is the forward price.

Both share the property that the parties agree to perform the terms of the contract at some future date. In fact, time-dated contracts are generally costlier to enforce than spot contracts. This is due to the absence of the self-enforcing, near simultaneous exchange of value for value characteristic of spot transaction and the greater uncertainty attached both to the eventual outcome and each party's compliance with the terms of forward contracts.

Forward and futures contracts differ, however, in their susceptibility to opportunism, especially in their role of reducing price risk. First forward contracts that cover all feasible contingencies are costly to devise. The information and transaction costs will thus preclude a fully specified forward contract and this contractual incompleteness will give rise to enforcement and execution difficulties. Incomplete contracting has a clear economic justification. Given the cost of tailoring the contract to the particular needs of the parties, it will usually be cost-effective to use standard form contracts. In this regard, organised forward and futures contracting have identical properties. Nevertheless, enforcement and execution difficulties can be expected to pose a more serious problem for forward contracts. This is so for several reasons. First, in forward contracting, individuals will have to incur the expense of determining the reliability risk of the opposite party. To the extent that there are scale economies in such specialisation by identity, forward contracting will be more expensive than organised futures contracting where the exchange ensures the integrity of its members and trading practices. Forward contracts also are subject to high enforcement costs where personal market sanctions are weak. The penalty risk of contract law are costly to enforce and may not deal effectively with all types of breaches.

Another disadvantage of forward contract is that they are tied transactions. The forward contract transfers rights relating to quantity, quality and price. The last, however, may best be separated, especially when the parties are risk averse and their access to insurance markets limited. Price changes have an unfortunate zero-sum quality that increases the likelihood of opportunism. Thus, while forward contracts may inject certainty into the quantity and possibly quality dimensions of future transactions, it is not clear that they are the least cost adaptor to price risk. Depending on the transaction costs in alternative markets, and the strength of governance in each, it may be desirable for both risk-spreading and opportunism-reducing reasons to separate price risk from the other aspects of time-dated transactions. Since spot, forward and futures markets deal in different bundles of rights among different individuals, rights can be divided between those relating to quantity and quality, and those counselling certainty of profits and costs. Forward contracts, especially in personal markets, are best suited to ensuring that contract terms relating to the former are complied with, whereas futures contracts deal with price volatility.

Future contracts permit the price risk to be separated from the reliability risk by removing the former from the set of factors giving rise to opportunism. The governance structure supplied by the exchange authority effectively eliminates reliability risk from futures trading. The seller of a futures contracts incurs a liability not to the buyer, but to the clearing house, and likewise the buyer acquires an asset from the clearing house. The clearing house in effect guarantees all transactions. In addition, the exchange rules, especially regarding its members' contract, severely limit their ability to behave opportunistically. Organised exchanges greatly reduce default and reliability risk from future contracts. This is achieved by transferring transactions overprice risks from a personal to an impersonal market through standard form futures contracts traded in a self-regulated market price.

Future contracts are standard form contracts with only one negotiable term: price. The standardisation of future contracts has significant implications for transaction costs. This is so for several reasons. First, contract standardisation eliminates the costs of bargaining over non-price terms and of enforcing contract provisions. Second, it reduces monitoring costs that are generally incurred in principal-agent relationships. The principal only needs to give his broker instructions as to price and quantity which are easily observed. The monitoring costs in the futures market are, therefore, significantly lower than those in the spot market, where numerous other matters require attention and provide the broker with opportunities to take advantage of the principal. Third, contract standardisation makes all futures contracts of a particular maturity month perfect substitution. The fungibility of futures contracts is not a property shared by forward contracts.

The liquidity and competitive nature of future trading also reduce the waiting costs of brokers and speculators for acceptable bids and offers. One component of the transaction costs of futures trading is the ask-bid spread which in a competitive situation, is directly correlated with the search costs of finding acceptable bids and offers. We may live in the information age, but much of the information we deal with every day is often perplexing. Perhaps most confusing of all is the world of finance. We are deluged with data, analyses and trends - often couched in jargon that makes ones eyes glaze over. We know in a market with incomplete information, buyers and sellers will have to search each other out. The costs of such search activity will differ and will be greater the more geographically dispersed and heterogeneous are buyers and sellers. In fact, the transaction cost arise because the parties to transactions are different individuals with asymmetric information, divergent motives and mutual suspicions and because expenditure of resources can reduce the gap in information and protect the parties against each other. Search costs will not only raise the cost of activities but may preclude otherwise value maximising transactions from taking place. The importance of market liquidity arise not only because it reduces waiting costs, but also because it ensures that competitive pressures exist to keep waiting costs to a minimum for any volume of trade. Competition among the futures traders will have the effect of weeding out these with excessive search costs and poor forecasting ability. Large speculators make consistent profits whereas small traders make losses since the performance difficulties occasioned by opportunism raise the cost of transacting. Each party is confronted by what can be termed a reliability risk - the risk that the other party will default either on the whole transaction or on individual terms in a way that decreases the expected wealth of the non-defaulting party. Reliability risk is an important source of transaction costs because it will pay individuals to guard against opportunism and contract breach. Acquiring information on the reliability of those with whom one transacts yields benefits in he form of reduced losses due to default and incomplete or inferior performance. Degree of success of futures markets can be explained in terms of a net benefits function. The most actively traded commodities have the most variable prices. Choices can be made among contractual arrangements on the basis of maximum net benefit, taking account of transaction costs.

RISK CONTAINMENT MEASURES FOR INDEX FUTURES IN INDIA

The main features of risk containment measures for index futures approved by SEBI are listed below:

1. **Initial Margin Computation:** The initial margin would be computed based on 99% Value at Risk (VaR).
2. **Margins for Calendar Spreads:** A calendar spread is a position at one maturity

which is hedged by an offsetting position at a different maturity, *e.g.*, a short position in six month contract matched by a long position in nine month contract.

   (i)   The margin on calendar spreads shall be at a flat rate of 0.5% per month of spread on the far month contract subject to a minimum margin of 1% and a maximum margin of 3% on the far side of the spread with legs upto 1 year apart.

  (ii)   A calendar spread should be treated as a naked position in the far month contract as the near month contract approaches expiry.

 (iii)   The derivatives exchange should explore the possibility that the trading system could incorporate the ability to place a single order to buy or sell spreads without placing two separate orders for the two legs.

3. **Settlement of Futures Contracts on Index or Individual Securities:** Futures contracts have two types of settlements, the MTM settlement which happens on a continuous basis at the end of each day, and the final settlement which happens on the last trading day of the futures contract.

   (i)   *MTM Settlement for Futures:* All futures contracts for each member are marked-to-market to the daily settlement price of the relevant futures contract at the end of each day. The CMs who have suffered a loss are required to pay the mark-to-market (MTM) loss amount in cash which is in turn passed on to the CMs who have made a MTM profit. This is known as daily mark-to-market settlement. CMs are responsible to collect and settle the daily MTM profits/ losses incurred by the TMs and their clients clearing and settling through them. Similarly, TMs are responsible to collect/pay losses/ profits from/to their clients by the next day. The pay-in and pay-out of the mark-to-market settlement are effected on the day following the trade day (T+l).

   After completion of daily settlement computation, all the open positions are reset to the daily settlement price. Such positions become the open positions for the next day.

  (ii)   *Final Settlement for Futures:* On the expiry day of the futures contracts, after the close of trading hours, NSCCL marks all positions of a CM to the final settlement price and the resulting profit/loss is settled in cash. Final settlement loss/profit amount is debited/credited to the relevant CM's clearing bank account on the day following expiry day of the contract.

 (iii)   *Settlement Prices for Futures:* Daily setdement price on a trading day is the closing price of the respective futures contracts on such day. The closing price for *a* futures contract is currently calculated as the last half an hour weighted average price of the contract in the F&O Segment of NSE. Final settlment price is the the closing price of the relevant underlying index/ security in the capital Market segment of NSE, on the last trading day of the Contract. The closing price of the underlying Index/security is currently its last half an hour weighted average value in the Capital Market Segment of NSE.

4. **Settlement of Interest Rate Futures Contracts:** Daily Mark to Market settlement and Final Mark to Market settlement in respect of admitted deals in Interest Rate Futures Contracts shall be cash settled. All positions (brought forward, created during the day, closed out during the day) of a F&O CM in Futures Contracts, at the close of trading hours on a day, shall be marked to market at the Daily Settlement Price (for Daily Mark to Market Settlement) and settled. All positions (brought forward, created during the day, closed out during the day) of a F&O

Clearing Member in Futures Contracts, at the close of trading hours on the last trading day, shall be marked to market at Final Settlement Price (for Final Settlement) and settled. Daily settlement price shall be the closing price of the relevant futures contract for the trading day. Final settlement price for an interest rate futures contract shall be based on the value of the notional bond determined using the ZCYC computed by the Exchange

(i) *Daily Settlement Price:* Daily Settlement price for an interest rate future contract is the closing price of such interest rate futures contract on the trading day. The closing price for an interest rate futures contract is calculated on the basis of the last half and hour weighted average price of such interest rate futures contract. In absence of trading in the last half an hour, the theoretical price is taken or such other price as may be decided by the relevant authority from time to time. Theoredcal the daily settlement price for unexpired futures contracts shall be the futures prices computed using the (price of the notional bond) spot prices arrived at from the applicable ZCYC Curve. The ZCYC shall be computed by the Exchange or by any other agency as may be nominated in this regard from the prices of Government securities traded on the Exchange or reported on the Negotiated Dealing System of RBI or both taking trades of same day settlement (i.e. t = 0).

In respect of zero coupon notional bond, the price of the bond shall be the present value of the principal payment discounted using discrete discounting for the specified period at the respective zero coupon yield. In respect of the notional T-bill, the settlement price shall be 100 minus the annualized yield for the specified period computed using the zero coupon yield curve. In respect of coupon bearing notional bond, the present value shall be obtained as the sum of present value of the principal payment discounted at the relevant zero coupon yield and the present values of the coupons obtained by discounting each notional coupon payment at the relevant zero coupon yield for that maturity. For this purpose the notional coupon payment date shall be half yearly and commencing from the date of expiry of the relevant futures contract. For computation of futures prices from me price of the notional bond (spot prices) thus arrived the rate of interest may be the relevant MIBOR rate or such other rate *as* may be specified from time to time.

(ii) *Final Settlement Price:* Final settlement price for an interest rate futures contracts on zero coupon notional bond and coupon bearing bond shall be based on the price of the notional bond determined using the zero coupon yield curve.

5. **Reporting and Disclosure:** The derivatives exchange and clearing corporation shall submit quarterly reports to SEBI regarding the functioning of the risk estimation methodology highlighting the specific instances where price moves have been beyond the estimated 99% VaR limits. The clearing corporation/ clearing house shall disclose the details of incidences of failures in collection of margin and/or the settlement dues on a quarterly basis. Failure for this purpose means a shortfall for three consecutive trading days of 50% or more of the liquid net worth of the member.

STRATEGIES FOR FUTURES MARKETS

Today's financial manager must be able to use all of the tools available to control a company's exposure to financial risk. Derivative securities have been very successful innovation in capital markets. Financial futures markets are an increasingly important feature of the world's major financial centres. The introduction of financial futures in the 1970s brought trading volume to previously unheard of levels and entirely changed the character of futures markets. Markets for options, stocks, bonds, index funds, foreign currencies, and other currencies have been propoundly affected by the introduction of related future contracts as well as future options. Recently active financial futures markets have been introduced in developed and developing countries alike. Programme trading, a wide array of most futures contracts as well as futures options, lower transaction costs, increasing trading volume, expanded trading hours, electronic trading, and domestic and international intermarket links continue to tie all of these financial markets into a remarkable a tight and efficient financial trading network. Markets for options, equities, bonds, index funds, foreign currencies, and other currencies have been profoundly affected by the introduction of related future contracts as well as future options.

Futures markets are to provide an opportunity for market participants to hedge against the risk of adverse price movements. Futures are *obligations to* buy or sell a specific commodity on a specific day for a present price. Shares, bonds and currencies are the commodities of the investment business. Just as the dramatic changes in the price rise affect fanners, rice mills and ultimately the consumer so does the changes in interest rates, the relative value of currencies and the direction of the stock market send ripples-and sometimes waves— through the financial community. Futures contracts based on a financial investment or a financial index are known as *financial futures.* Financial futures can be classified as (1) stock index futures; (2) interest rate futures; and (3) currency futures.

In modern life financial engineering approach keep people and business going. Today, futures markets are dominated by large commercial firms who interact with professional risk bearers. Those who want insurance against price risk should either buy options or engage in forward transactions. In the world financial markets, futures markets are used by commercial firms to manage but not to eliminate, the price risks inherent in their ordinary business. Major users of futures markets are dealers and financial intermediaries who are professional risk — bearers. If they did not use the futures markets, the risk premium that they would have to charge their customers would significantly decrease the demand for their services. Anticipating what this approach will cost fuels the futures market.

The investment manager can tailor a given risk position in a variety of ways. Without financial futures, investors would have only one trading location to alter portfolio positions when they get new information that is expected to influence the value of assets - the cash market. If they hear economic war that is expected to impact the value of an asset adversely, investors want to reduce their price risk exposure to that asset. The opposite would be true if the new information is expected to impact the value of an asset favourably; an investor would increase price risk exposure to that asset. There are, of course, transactions costs associated with altering exposure to an asset - explicit costs (commission), and execution costs (bid- ask spread and market impact costs).

Thus, the futures market is an alternative market that investors can use to alter their risk exposure to an asset when new information is acquired. But which market - cash or futures -should the investor employ to alter a position quickly on the receipt of new information? The answer is simple: the one that most efficiently achieve the objective. The factor to consider are liquidity, transactions costs, taxes and leverage advantages of the futures contract.

The market that investors consider more efficient for their investment objective should be the one where prices will first be established that reflect the new economic information. That is, this will be the market where price discovery takes place. Price information is then transmitted to the other market. For many of the financial assets, it is in the futures market that it is easier and less costly to alter a portfolio position. Therefore, it is the futures market that will be the market of choice and will serve as the price discovery market. It is in the futures market that investors send a collective message about how any new information is expected to impact the cash market. How is this message sent to the cash market? It is through arbitrage mechanism which assures that the cash market price will reflect the information that has been collected in the futures market. Since futures price and the cash market price are tied together by the cost of carry if the futures price deviates from the cash market price by more than the cost of carry, arbitrageurs (in attempting to obtain arbitrage profits) would pursue a strategy to bring them back into line.

Some market observers consider that the introduction of a futures market for a financial asset will increase the price volatility of the financial asset in the cash market. That is, some investors believe that, as a result of speculative trading of futures contracts, the cash market instruments does not reflect its fundamental economic value. The implication here is that the price of the financial asset would better reflect its true economic value in the absence of a futures market for that financial asset. This inference may not be justified if, say, the introduction of futures markets lets prices respond more promptly to changes in factors that affect the economic value of a financial asset, and if these factors themselves are subject to large shocks. The greater volatility resulting from an innovation may simply more faithfully reflect the actual variability of factors that affect the economic value of financial assets. In this case, 'more' volatility of a financial asset's price need not be bad but, rather, may be a manifestation of a well-functioning market. Of course, to say that more volatility need not be bad does not mean that it is good. The price volatility greater than what can be justified by relevant new information is undesirable. By definition, it makes price inefficient. This is referred to as 'excess volatility'.

The world financial community has realised the potential of hedging the futures to control risk. Formal identification and evaluation for risk for securities transactions, capital budgeting projects, and other assets and liability decisions had been a major undertaking for the two decades proceeding the introduction of financial futures. However, controlling risk for these situations was a difficult proposition. For example, using either betas or portfolio analysis only allows the investor limited flexibility in changing the amount of risk in the portfolio. Moreover, betas and portfolio risk measures change over time. Finance Managers can employ futures, a more effective and flexible attractive tool to adjust the return and risk characteristics of a cash position. The fluctuations in interest rates, currency values, and stock market price cause severe problems for financial planning and forecasting; future markets are a tool to help alleviate these problems. Futures provide speculators a degree of leverage that is not typically available with other instruments and thus allows speculators to change their risk profile.

Futures markets have two opposite and undeserved reputations. Some groups regard them as pure gambling markets. Others regard them as markets for insurance against risk. Unquestionably, there are amateurs who use futures markets to gamble. They consistently lose money. Futures markets, in fact, are dominated by large firms who interact with professional risk bearers. Those who want insurance against price risk should either buy options or engage in forward transactions. Futures markets are used by firms to manage, but not to eliminate, the price risks inherent in their ordinary business. For example, major users of futures markets are dealers and financial intermediaries who are professional risk bearers. If they did not use the futures markets, the risk premium that they would have to charge their customers would significantly decrease the demand for their services.

There are four basic strategies for using the futures markets: *speculation, hedging, spreading and arbitrage.* The most important distinction between these uses is their different risk-return characteristics. Speculating in futures increases risks by undertaking a futures position with potential high returns but also with the risk of a large loss. Hedging exists when a future position is taken to reduce the risk of a current or anticipated cash position. Spreading involves taking almost offsetting future positions that create a net position that typically possesses significantly less risk than pure speculation, but has lower expected returns. Arbitrage provides a risk-free profit when a trader takes opposite positions in a cash asset and the associated futures counter it when these respective instruments are mispriced in relation to one another.

Speculators wish to take a position in the market. Either they are betting that a price will go up or they are betting that it will go down. In other words, a speculative position can be either a long or a short. A long position occurs when the futures contract is purchased; profits arise when prices increase. A short position when its futures contract is sold; a short trader profits when prices decrease.

Speculative futures positions are very profitable for those who are able to forecast correctly both market direction and the extent of the market move. This profitability is enhanced because the speculator needed to put up only a small percentage of the value of the underlying cash instrument for margin, thereby allowing a significant degree of leverage. Of course, if a speculator forecasts incorrectly, then the mark-to-market rules cause a cash outflow as the futures position deteriorates. Consequently, a speculator needs forecasting ability and substantial knowledge of the underlying cash markets, plus sufficient funds to overcome a short-term (or permanent) loss of funds from losing trades.

There is an important difference between speculating using forward markets and speculating by buying the underlying asset in the spot market. Buying a certain amount of the underlying asset in the spot market requires an initial cash payment equal to the total value of what is bought. Entering into a forward contract on the same amount of the asset requires no initial cash payment. Speculating using forward markets therefore provide an investor with a much higher level of leverage than speculating using spot markets. In the highly leveraged futures markets, minimums are set to ensure that the speculators can affort any potential losses. For this very reason a levy of 15 per cent margin on the contract price has been suggested in the Bombay Stock Exchange plans to introduce futures trading on the exchange parallel to cash transactions on the market. The percentage of margin is to be constant throughout the contract but the amount of margin will vary based on the mark to market price. Members are to pay margins on all futures contracts on a gross basis.

In a volatile market, the speculator needs to establish realistic goals for trades. After reaching these goals, it is best to cover the trade. If a speculator becomes emotionally involved in a position (which generates greed and fear), the ability to make a realistic decision about covering a position is impaired. Some speculators attempt to circumvent such emotional considerations by placing special trading orders with the broker so that the trader is automatically removed from a disadvantageous situation. Although such orders are useful for speculators who are not in constant contact with the market and have specific forecasts of market movements, many active traders believe that recognising the current trend in the market and then adapting to that trend is more important than mechanical position trading.

Whereas speculators wish to take a position in the market, hedgers want to eliminate an exposure to movements in the price of an asset. *Hedging with financial futures is an art as well as a science.* By future hedging, we mean to take a position in futures contracts that offset some of the risk associated with some given market commitment. The essence of hedging is the adoption of a future position that, on average, generates profits when the market value of the commitment is higher than expected. The notion of designing a futures strategy to generate losses under certain circumstances may seem quixotic to some. One must keep in mind the well-repeated adage: "There are no free lunches". One cannot expect trading profits as well as risk reduction (although that sometimes happen). The key is to coordinate losses in futures with gains elsewhere, and vice versa. How does one achieve that kind of coordination? Such futures are not an answer to all investment management problems, but they do provide the finance manager with new means to act upon market decisions. An understanding of the futures contracts and how the futures markets operate is critical to designing a successful hedge strategy. As with any innovative technique, potential hedgers need to take the time to study the markets and determine the risk/return potential for each application.

In order to profit from a spread transaction the trader attempts to determine whether the size of the difference between the prices of the two contracts will increase or decrease. A spread earns a profit if the correct direction of the price difference is forecasted and the appropriate spread transaction is set up in conjunction with the changing price structure of the future contracts.

Spreaders must forecast the relevant factors that cause changes in the spreads. Change in financial futures spread depends upon the behaviour of interest rate. A profitable spread creates a gain on one side of the spread that is larger than the loss on the other side of the spread. A pure speculator would make more money by taking only the profitable side of the market; however, a spread reduces the risk of a position in case the forecast is incorrect. In recognition of the reduced risks, margins on spread positions are much less than the margins on pure long or short positions, and hence the leverage for spreads is increased. Risk is reduced, since both sides of spread usually move in the same direction, even though their prices can change by different amounts.

Arbitrage exists when a trader is able to obtain risk-free profits by taking one position in the cash market and an exact opposite position in the futures market. The arbitrage position is covered later by delivering the cash security into the futures position. The arbitrageur can dose the position prior to delivery if the profit potential has been achieved; this situation occurs principally in the stock index futures market because of the price swings.

Arbitrage keeps the futures and cash prices in line with one another. This relationship between the cash and fair futures prices is expressed by the simple cost of carry pricing. This pricing shows that the fair futures prices is the set of buying the cash asset now and financing this asset until delivery into the futures contract. If the current futures price is higher than the fair price dictated by the cost of carry pricing, then arbitrage is possible by buying the cheaper instrument (the cash) and selling the more expensive instrument (the futures). Alternatively, if the current futures price is less than the fair price, then the arbitrageur purchases futures and sells the cash short. This activity forces the prices of the cash and futures instruments back into their appropriate relationship.

Futures markets reflect the buying and selling activities of many buyers and sellers of the homogeneous contract. Firms often have the power to affect the market price in cash and forward markets because they are merchandising contracts custom-made to the two parties. However, a single party is less able to affect the price in the broad futures market, i.e., the ability of the firm to trade large quantities without affecting the price is one of the main reasons why the new futures markets in financial instruments have flourished.

Futures markets disseminate information quickly, effectively and inexpensively, and thereby reduce monopoly power. In the cash and forward markets, a large firm has a substantial advantage over a smaller firm. The larger firm has more extensive and reliable information concerning current and impending developments. It is difficult for a small firm to gauge the reasonableness of the dealer's offer because the costs of search are high. When there is a futures market, potential buyers and sellers have means of gauging what a broad group of buyers and sellers expect will be the subsequent price of the commodity specified in the futures contract and there is a historic relation between the price of the specific commodity in position and the commodity specified in the futures contract. The parties evaluate the reasonableness of the dealer's offer in terms of its relation to the futures price.

In the future markets, who can beat the market? It is observed in most of the studies that small speculators are big losers, large speculators are small winners, and hedgers are big winners. Since the profits of the large speculators for the individual futures markets are small, the speculators do not earn sufficient profits to compensate for the risk of trading in futures markets. *Why do small trades continue to trade if they consistently lose money?* The possible reason to this may be:- (*i*) small speculators enjoy 'playing the game'; it is exciting, dynamic, and a great conversational topic; (*ii*) small speculators believe they can forecast; in other words they remember their profits but forget their losses; (*iii*) losers drop out, with their places being taken by new small speculators; meanwhile winners become large speculators; (*iv*) the perceived ability of potential large gains is greater than the disutility of small losses with the possibility of large losses discounted as being "unlikely" by the small speculators.

REVIEW PROBLEMS

1. Suppose that you enter into a short futures contract to sell August gold for ₹ 520 per gramme on the XYZ Exchange. The size of the contract is 10 Kg. The initial margin is ₹ 5,00,000 and the maintenance margin is ₹ 3,00,000. What change in the future price will lead to a margin call? What happens if you do not meet the margin call?

Ans.:

There will be a margin call when ₹ 2,00,000 has been lost from the margin account. This will occur when the price of gold increases by ₹ 2,00,000/10 kg. = ₹ 20,000. The price of gold must, therefore, rise to ₹ 540 per gramme for there to be a margin call. If the margin call is not met, your broker closes out your position.

2. A company has a $10 million portfolio with a beta of 1.2. It would like to use futures contracts on the XYZ Index to hedge its risk. The index is currently standing at 270 and each contract is for delivery of $ 500 times the index. What is the hedge that minimizes risk? What should the company do if it wants to reduce the beta of the portfolio to 0.6?

Ans:

The value of the contract is
$$108.46875 \times 1000 = 1,08,468.75$$

The number of contracts that should be shorted is:
$$\frac{60,00,000}{1,08,468.75} \times \frac{8.2}{7.6} = 59.7$$

3. Given the following information, the 7¼ cash bond is to be hedged; the two future instruments are used as the hedging investment, find the two-instruments hedge ratio.

Instruments	Yield	Coupon	Convexity
7½ due in ten years	7.225	6.99	61.88
5-years T-note futures	6.86	4.22	19.99
T-bond futures	7.50	11.52	185.92

Ans.

Using the simultaneous equation approach:

For duration: $X_1 (4.22) + X_2 (11.52) = 6.99$

For convexity : $X_2 (19.99) + X_2 (185.92) = 61.88$

Solving for X_1 in each equation:

$$X_1 = \frac{6.99 - 11.52\, X_2}{4.22}$$

$$X_1 = \frac{6.188 - 185.92\, X_2}{19.99}$$

Solving for X_2 : $X_2 = .218$ (hedge ratio for the T-bond futures)

The Direct Solution Approach

$$X_1 = \frac{(185.92)(6.99) - (61.88)(11.52)}{(185.92)(4.22) - (19.99)(11.52)} = \frac{589.03}{554.30}$$

$$= 1.063 \text{ (hedge ratio for the T-note futures)}$$

$$X_2 = \frac{(61.68)(4.22) - (19.99)(6.99)}{(185.92)(4.22) - (19.99)(11.52)} = \frac{120.56}{554.30}$$

$$= .218 \text{ (hedge ratio for the T-bond futures)}$$

QUESTIONS

1. Explain the importance of the futures markets?
2. How does a futures contract differ from a forward contract?
3. What is the purpose of initial and maintenance margin? How does marking to market affect the amount of funds held in the futures investor's margin account?
4. What is the difference between a long futures position and a short futures position?
5. What is the economic rationale for the existence of futures market?
6. Explain how margins protect investors against the possibility of default.
7. Explain clearly the difference between (a) hedging, (b) speculation and (c) arbitrage.
8. A stock when it is first issued provides funds for a company. Is the same true of a stock option? Discuss.
9. What is the essential difference between a forward contract and a futures contract?
10. What are the functions of a clearing house of a future exchange?
11. What is the investment for a trader who purchases a futures contract?
12. Explain why the futures prices might reasonably thought to equal to expected future spot price?
13. "Options and futures are zero-sum games". What do you think is meant by this statement.

14. Explain why a futures contract can be used for either speculation or hedging.

15. Explain the synthetic futures. Distinguish between a future classified option systems.

16. Carefully explain the difference between a long-hedge and a short-hedge. When would an investor wish to use a long hedge/a short hedge?

17. Carefully explain the function speculators serve in the futures markets.

18. What is the difference between the way in which prices are quoted in the foreign exchange future markets, the foreign exchange forward market, and the foreign exchange spot market?

19. It is sometimes argued that a forward exchange rate is an unbiased predictor of future exchange rates. Under what circumstances is this so?

20. "Stock index futures are an inexpensive and highly liquid short-run alternative to speculating on the stock market". Comment.

21. Discuss the most popular models which can be applied to stock index futures.

22. Discuss the application of carrying-cost model in determining the equilibrium futures price on a stock index futures contract.

23. Describe the roles played by clearinghouses and margin deposits in assuring contract performance.

24. Describe an initial margin, a maintenance margin, and a variation margin.

25. Describe how the vast majority of futures contracts are closed.

PROBLEMS

1. A stock index currently standing at 35. The risk-free interest rate is 8 per cent per annum (with continuous compounding) and the dividend yield on the index is 4 per cent per annum. What should be the futures price for a four-month contract?

2. A company enters into a short futures contract to sell 15,000 tonnes of wheat for ₹ 6,000 per tonne. The initial margin is ₹ 1 crore and the maintenance margin is ₹ 50 lakh. What price change would lead to a margin call? Under what circumstances could ₹ 25 lakh be withdrawn from the margin account?

3. You expect to receive a payment of £ 10,00,000 after six months. The £ is currently worth ₹ 80 (i.e., £1 = ₹ 80), but the six-month futures price is ₹ 76. You expect the price of the £ to decline (i.e., the value of the rupee to rise). If this expectation is fulfilled, you will suffer a loss when the £ are converted into rupee when you receive them six months in the future.

   (a) Given the current price, what is the expected payment in rupee?

   (b) Give the futures price, how much would you receive in rupee?

   (c) If, after six months, the pound is worth ₹ 70, what is your loss from the decline in the value of the pound?

   (d) To avoid this potential loss, you decide to hedge and sell a contract for the future delivery of pounds at the going futures price of ₹ 76. What is the cost to you of this protection from the possible decline in the value of the pound?

   (e) If, after hedging, the price of the pound falls to ₹ 70, what is the maximum amount that you lose? Why is your answer different than your answer to part (C)?

   (f) If, after hedging, the price of the pound rises to ₹ 90, how much do you gain from your position?

4. An investor expects the stock market to decline, but instead of selling the equity short, he decides to sell the stock index futures contract based on the XYZ Stock Exchange Composite Index, the index is currently 138, and the contract has a value that is 500 times the amount of the index. The margin requirement is ₹ 3,500 and the maintenance margin requirement is ₹ 1,000.

(a) When the investor sells the contract, how much must he put up?

(b) What is the value of the contract based on the index?

(c) If after one week of trading the index stands at 140, what has happened to investor's position? How much has he lost or profited?

(d) If the index declined to 136.6 (approximately 1 percent from the starting value), what is investor's percentage profit or loss on his position?

(e) If the investor had purchased the contract instead of selling it, how much would he has invested?

Ans.:   (a) ₹ 3,500   (b) ₹ 69,000   (c) –₹ 1,000

(d) 20 percent profit   (e) ₹ 3,500

5. Assume that on Monday, March 1, you enter a futures contract to buy one March Treasury bond futures contract at ₹ 98,156.25 (98%^{5}/$_{32}$). The initial margin is ₹ 2,500, and the maintenance margin is ₹ 2,000. For simplicity, you do not withdraw excess monies from your margin balance. All margin requirements are met with cash and no interest is earned. You hold your long position through Friday, March 5. Then you sell the contract (a reversing trade at the opening price of ₹ 98,125.00 (98^4/$_{32}$) on Monday, March 8. Presented below is a schedule of assumed prices. Fill in the following information cells. Also be sure to determine your gross profit on the entire transaction.

Trading Date	Settlement Price		Marked to the Market	Other Entries	Account Balance
3/1	₹ 98,000.00	(98^1/$_{32}$)			
3/2	96,250.00	(96^8/$_{32}$)			
3/3	96,750.00	(96^{24}/$_{32}$)			
3/4	98,093.75	(98^3/$_{32}$)			
3/5	98,937.50	(98^{30}/$_{32}$)			
3/8	98,125.00	(98^4/$_{32}$)			

REFERENCES

1. Bear, Robert M., "Margin Levels and the Behavior of Future Prices," *Journal of Finan-cial and Quantitative Analysis*, September 1972, pp. 1907-1930.

2. Chan, Kalok, K.C. Chan, and G. Andrew Karolyi. "Intraday Volatility in the Stock Index and Stock Index Futures Markets." *Review of Financial Studies* 4, no. 4 (1991).

3. Chan, Kalok. "A Further Analysis of the Lead-Lag Relationship Between the Cash Market and Stock Index Futures Market." *The Review of Financial Studies* 5, no. 1 (1992).

4. Chung, Y. Peter. "A Transactions Data Test of Stock Index Futures Market Efficiency and Index Arbi-trage Profitability." *The Journal of Finance* 46, no. 5 (December 1991).

5. Cox, J.C., J.E. Ingersoll, and S.A. Ross. "The Relation between Forward Prices and Futures Prices," *Journal of Financial Economics*, 9 (December 1981): 321-46.

6. Cox, John C., Jonathan E. Ingersoll, Jr. and Stephen A. Ross. "The Relation Between Forward Prices and Futures Prices." *Journal of Financial Economics 9*, no. 4 (December 1981).

7. Duffie, Darrell. *Futures Markets*. Englewood Cliffs, N.J.: Prentice-Hall, 1989.

8. Elton. Edwin J., Martin J. Gruber, and Joel Rentzler. "Intra-Day Tests of the Efficiency of the Treasury Bill Futures Market." *The Review of Economics and Statistics* (66 .no. 1 (February 1984).

9. French, Kenneth. "Pricing Financial Futures." *Journal of Applied Corporate Finance* (winter 1989): 59-66.

10. Ghon, R.S. and R.P. Chang. "Intra-day Arbitrage in Foreign Exchange and Eurocurrency Markets," *Journal of Finance*, 47, 1 (1992): 363-380.

11. Goldman, Ethel R.K. *Computerized Trading Strategies: Programming for the Stock and Futures Markets.* New York: John Wiley & Sons, 1988.

12. Hegde, Shantaram P., and Ben Branch. "An Empirical Analysis of Arbitrage Opportunities in the Treasury Bill Futures Market." *The Journal of Futures Markets* 5. no. 3 (Fall 1985).

13. Hieronymus, Thomas A. *Economics of Futures Trading.* New York: Commodity Research Bureau, 1971.

14. Hieronymus, Thomas A., *Economics of Futures Trading* (New York: Commodity Re-search Bureau, 1971).

15. Jarrow, R.A., and G.S. Oldfield. "Forward Contracts and Futures Contracts," *Journal of Financial Economics, 9* (December 1981): 373-82.

16. Jones, F.J., and R.J. Teweles. In: *The Futures Game,* edited by B. Warwick, 3rd edn. New York: McGraw-Hill, 1998.

17. Kane, E.J. "Market Incompleteness and Divergences between Forward and Futures Interest Rates," *Journal of Finance,* 35 (May 1980): 221-34.

18. Kolb, Robert W. *Understanding Futures Markets.* 3d ed. Miami, Fla.: Kolb, 1991.

19. Lang, R.W., and R.H. rasche. "A Comparison of Yields on Futures Contracts and Implied Forward Rates," *Rev:ew.* Federal Reserve Bank of St. Louis, Dec. 1978.

20. Loosigian, Allan M. *Foreign Exchange Futures.* Homewood, III .: Dow Jones-Irwin, 1981.

21. Loosigian, Allan M. *Interest Rate Futures.* Homewood, III: Dow Jones-Irwin, 1980.

22. Peck, A.E., ed. *Selected Writings on Futures Markets,* vol. 2. Board of Trade of the City of Chicago, 1977.

23. Peterson, Richard L., "Investor Preferences for Futures Straddler," *Journal of Financial and Quantitative Analysis,* March 1977, pp. 105-120.

24. Powers, Mark J., "Does Futures Trading Reduce Price Fluctuations in the Cash Markets?" *American Economic Review,* June 1970, pp. 460-464.

25. Rendleman, Richard J. Jr., and C.E. carabini. "The Efficiency of the Treasury Bill Futures Market," *The Journal of Finance.* Sept. 1979.

26. Richard, S., and S. Sundaresan. "A Continuous-Time Model of Forward and Futures Prices in a Multigood Economy," *Journal of Financial Economics,* 9 (December 1981): 347-72.

27. Rogalski, Richard J., and James K. Seward. "Corporate Issues of Foreign Currency Exchange Warrants." *Journal of Financial Economics* 30, no. 2 (December 1991).

28. Rothstein, Nancy H. *The Handbook of Financial Futures.* New York: McGraw-Hill, 1984.

29. Scholes, Myron S. "The Economics of Hedging and Spreading in Futures Markets." *The Journal of Futures Markets* 1, no. 2 (Summer 1981).

30. Schrock, Nicholas W., "The Theory of Asset Choice: Simultaneous Holding of Short and Long Positions in the Futures Market," *Journal of Political Economy,* (March-April 1971). pp. 270-293.

31. Shakin, Bernard. Interest Rate Futures, *Burron's.* Nov. 13, 1978.

32. Siegel, Daniel, and Diane F. Siegel. *Futures Markets.* Hinsdale, III.: The Dryden Press, 1990.

33. Smith, Courtney D. *How to Make Money in Stock Index Futures.* New York: McGraw-Hill, 1985.

34. Stoll, Hans R., and Robert E. Whaley. *Futures and Options: Theory and Application.* Cincinnati: South-western Publishing, 1993.

35. Telser, Lester G., and Harlow N. Higinbotham, "Organized Futures Markets: Costs and Benefits," *Journal of Political Economy,* October 1977, pp. 969-1000.

36. Working, Holbrook, "New Concepts Concerning Futures Markets and Prices," *Ameri-can Economic Review,* June 1962, pp. 431-459.

38

SWAPS

INTRODUCTION

Today's financial swaps markets owe their origin to the exchange rate instability that followed the demise of Bretton Woods system and to the controls on international capital movements that most countries maintained in those days. Swaps are at the centre of the global financial revolution. Fantastic numbers and growth are talked of. All this is true. But what is also certain is that the current heady acceleration of this market cannot continue. Otherwise, there will be no other activity left-only swapping. Already the shakeout has started. In the "plain vanilla" dollar sector, the profits for brokers and market makers, after costs and allocation of risk capital, are measured in fewer than five basis points. This is before the regulators catch up and force disclosure and capital haircuts. At these spreads the more highly paid must move on — to currency swaps, tax-driven deals, tailored structures and Schlock swaps.

What is certain is that, although the excitement may diminish, swaps are here to stay. Already, swaps have had a major macro economic impact forging the linkage between the Euro and domestic markets, flattening the cash yield curves and reducing central bank monopoly influence on markets. We are all swappers now. And, when you are offered sweet deals, remember the Tibetan saying "Beware of honey offered on a sharp knife". The problem in following the chaotic progress of this very important market is quite simply that "he who knows does not speak, he who speaks does not know." A brief glimpse of how the swap market has matured and a short list of the non-proprietary tools in the swapper's arsenal is presented below:

SWAPS—THE CONCEPT

The essence of a swap contract is the binding of two counterparties to exchange two different payment streams over time, the payment being tied, at least in part, to subsequent — and uncertain — market price developments. In most swaps so far, the prices concerned have been exchange rates or interest rates, but they increasingly reach out to equity indices and physical commodities. All such prices have risk characteristics in common, in quality if not in degree. And for all, the allure of swaps may be expected cost saving, yield enhancement, or hedging or speculative opportunity.

Financial swaps, simple in principle and versatile in practice, are revolutionary, especially for portfolio management. A swap coupled with an existing asset or liability can radically modify effective risk and return. Individually and together with futures, options and other financial derivatives, they allow yield curve and currency risks, and liquidity and geographic market considerations, all to be managed separately and also independently of underlying cash market stocks.

GROWTH OF THE SWAP MARKET

Like most other new "products" in international finance, "swap" transactions are not executed in a physical market. Participants in the swap "market" are many and varied in their location character and motives in exciting swaps. However, the sum total of the activity of participants in the swap market have taken on the character of a classical financial market connected to, and integrating the underlying money, capital and foreign exchange market.

Swap in their current form started in 1981 with the well-publicised currency swaps, and in the following year with dollar interest-rate swaps. The initial deals were characterised by three critical features.

1. *Barter*—two counterparties with exactly offsetting exposures were introduced by a third party. If the credit risk were unequal, the third party — if a bank — might interpose itself or arrange for a bank to do so for a small fee.

2. *Arbitrage driven*—the swap was driven by an arbitrage which gave some profit to all three parties. Generally, this was a credit arbitrage or market-access arbitrage.

3. *Liability driven*—almost all swaps were driven by the need to manage a debt issue on both sides.

The major dramatic change has been the emergence of the large banks as aggressive market makers in dollar interest-rate swaps. Major US banks are in the business of taking credit risk and interest-rate risk. They, therefore, do not need counterparties to do dollar swaps. The net result is that spreads have collapsed and volume has exploded. This means that institutional investors get a better return on their investments and international borrowers pay lower financing costs. This, in turn, result in more competitively priced goods for consumers and in enhanced returns pensioners. Swap therefore have an effect on almost all of us yet they remains an arcane derivative risk management tool, sometimes suspected of providing the international banking system with tools required to bring about destruction.

Although the swap market is now firmly established, there remains a wide divergence among current and potential users as to how exactly a given swap structure works, what risks are entailed when entering into swap transactions and precisely what "the swap market" is and, for that matter, is not.

THE BASIC SWAP STRUCTURES

The growth and continued success of the swap market has been due   small part to the creativity of its participants. As a result, the swap structures currently available and the future potential structures which will in time become just another market "norm" are limited only by the imagination and ingenuity of those participating in the market. Nonetheless, underlying the swap transactions seen in the market today are four basic structures which may now be considered as "fundamental". These structures are:

— the Interest Rate Swap
— the Fixed Rate Currency Swap
— the Currency Coupon Swap
— the Basis Rate Swap

The following is a summary of these fundamental swap structures and some of their primary applications.

THE INTEREST RATE SWAP

The basic structure of an interest rate swap consists of the exchange between two counterparties of fixed rate interest for floating rate interest in the same currency calculated by reference to a mutually agreed notional principal amount. This principal amount, which would normally equate to the underlying assets or liabilities being "swapped" by the counterparties, is applicable solely for the calculation of the interest to be exchanged under the swap. At no time it is physically passed between the counterparties. Through this straightforward swap structure, the counterparties are able to convert an underlying fixed rate asset/liability into a floating rate asset/liability and vice versa.

The majority of interest rate swap transactions are driven by the cost savings to be obtained by each of the counterparties. These cost savings, which are often substantial, result from differentials in the credit standing of the counterparties and other structural considerations.

In general, investors in fixed rate instruments are more sensitive to credit quality than floating rate bank lenders. Accordingly, a greater premium is demanded of issuers of lesser credit quality in the fixed rate debt markets than in the floating rate bank lending market. The counterparties to an interest rate swap may therefore obtain an arbitrage advantage by accessing the market in which they have the greatest relative cost advantage and then entering into an interest rate swap to convert the cost of the funds so raised from a fixed-rate to a floating-rate basis or vice versa.

The credit arbitrage available through the use of an interest rate swap may be illustrated by considering two companies, Company A and Company B with the following profiles (see Exhibit-1).

As expected, Company A with the superior credit quality has a greater relative cost advantage over Company B in the fixed rate debt market Despite the fact that Company A can also raise direct investing rate fluids more   cheaply than Company B, a potential arbitrage therefore costs whereby Company A and Company B may both obtain a cost saving by assessing the markets in which they have the greatest relative cost advantage and entering into an interest rate swap. (see Exhibit-2 and 3).

EXHIBIT-1

	Company A	Company B	Comparative Advantage
Credit Rating	AAA	BBB	
Cost of Raising Direct Fixed Rate Funding	10.80%	12.00%	1.20%
Cost of Raising Direct Floating Rate Funds	6-month LIBOR plus 1/4 %	6-month LIBOR plus 3/4 %	.50%

EXHIBIT-2

	Company A	Company B
Direct Funding Cost		
Fixed Rate Funds Raised Directly by Company A	(10.80%)	
Floating Rate Funds Raised Directly by Company B		(6-month LIBOR+3/4 %)
Swap Payments		

Company A pays Company B Floating Rate Interest	(LIBOR)	LIBOR
Company B pays Company A Fixed Rate Interest	10.90%	(10.90%)
All-in Cost of Funding	LIBOR-1/10%	11.65%
Comparable Cost of Equivalent Direct Funding	LIBRO + 1/4%	12.00%
Saving	35 Basis Points	35 Basis Points

EXHIBIT-3

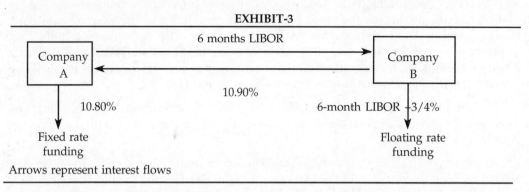

Arrows represent interest flows

This ability to transfer a fixed rate cost advantage to floating rate liabilities has led to many high quality credits issuing fixed rate Eurobonds purely to "swap" and obtain, in many cases, sub-LIBOR funding. The use of this structure in a fixed rate Eurobond issue enables the issuer to obtain substantial funding at points below LIBOR. This most attractive of rates is made possible by (a) the careful timing of the Eurobond issue to ensure its success at the finest of rates and (b) the use of exact hedging and a deferred swap accrual date to ensure the best possible swap terms for the issuer. The "counterparty" to the swap may be a combination of banks and corporate clients. The banks may want to hedge their fixed rate income into a floating rate return that fully matched their floating rate liabilities in order to alleviate interest rate exposure. The corporate clients may want to hedge their floating rate binding into fixed rate liabilities for a size and maturity unavailable in the direct fixed rate debt market. Acting as principal, the intermending may be able to provide both the banks and its corporate clients with swap terms to meet their exact requirements and then subsequently lock the Eurobond issuer into an opposite swap when the Eurobond market is most receptive to the issue.

In addition to the cost advantages, interest rate swaps also provide an excellent mechanism for entities to effectively access markets which are otherwise closed to them — whether by reason of credit quality, lack of name familiarity or excessive use. The ability to obtain the benefits of markets without the need to comply with the prospectus disclosures, credit ratings and other formal requirements provides an additional benefit especially for private companies. An excellent example of the swap market's flexibility in providing benefits is the growth of interest rate swaps using commercial paper as the underlying floating rate basis.

The interest rate swap market also provides finance money with the perfect mechanism for managing interest rate costs and exposure whilst leaving the underlying source of funds unaffected. For example, the cost of fixed rate funding may be reduced in a declining interest rate environment through the use of the interest rate swap technique whilst leaving the underlying funding in place.

THE FIXED RATE CURRENCY SWAP

A fixed rate currency swap consists of the exchange between two counterparties of fixed rate interest in one currency in return for fixed rate interest in another currency. The following three basic steps are common to all currency swaps:-

(a) Initial Exchange of Principal

On the commencement of the swap the counterparties exchange the principal amounts of the swap at an agreed rate of exchange. Although this rate is usually based on the spot exchange rate, a forward rate set in advance of the swap commencement date can also be used. This initial exchange may be on a "notional" basis (i.e. no physical exchange of principal amounts) or alternatively a "physical" exchange.

Whether the initial exchange is on a physical or notional basis its sole importance is to establish the quantum of the respective principal amounts for the purpose of (a) calculating the ongoing payments of interest and (b) the re-exchange of principal amounts under the swap.

(b) Ongoing Exchanges of Interest

Once the principal amounts are established, the counterparties exchange interest payments based on the outstanding principal amounts at the respective fixed interest rates agreed at the outset of the transaction.

(c) Re-exchange of Principal Amounts

On the maturity date the counterparties re-exchange the principal amounts established at the outset. This straightforward, three-step process is standard practice in the swap market and results in the effective transformation of a debt raised in one currency into a fully-hedged fixed-rate liability in another currency.

In principle, the fixed currency swap structure is similar to the conventional long-date forward foreign exchange contract. However, the counterparty nature of the swap market results in a far greater flexibility in respect of both maturity periods and size of the transactions which may be arranged. A currency swap structure also allows for interest rate differentials between the two currencies via periodic payments rather than the lump sum reflected by forward points used in the foreign exchange market. This enables the swap structure to be customised to fit the counterparties exact requirements at attractive rates. For example the cash flows of an underlying bond issue may be matched exactly and invariably.

THE CURRENCY COUPON SWAP

The currency coupon swap is a combination of the interest rate swap and the fixed-rate currency swap. The transaction follows the three basic steps described for the fixed-rate currency swap with the exception that fixed-rate interest in one currency is exchanged for floating rate interest in another currency.

The benefits to be obtained using the currency coupon swap structure are well illustrated by a transaction structured by Bankers Trust. Consider a US Corporate wished to enter into a major leasing contract for a capital project to be sited in the United Kingdom. The Corporate wanted to obtain the advantage of funding through a UK lease which provided lower lease rentals due to the UK tax advantages available to the UK lessor. However, the Corporate was concerned by both the currency and interest rate exposure which would result form the sterling LIBOR based leasing contract The structure provided by Bankers Trust enabled the Corpc ate to obtain the cost benefits available from the UK lease and at the same time conver the underlying lease finance into a fully-hedged fixed-rate dollar liability. Under the structure Bankers Trust paid, on a quarterly basis, the exact payments due on the Corporate's sterling LIBOR based UK lease in return for the Corporate paying an annual amount of fixed US Dollars to Bankers Trust. The amount of the fixed US dollars payable reflected the beneficial level of the US sterling lease payments. As principal, Bankers Trust hedged this position by entering into a number of currency coupon swaps for different maturities and principal amounts to match the amortising structure of the US Corporate's lease.

THE BASIS RATE SWAP

A fast developing area in the international swap markets is the basis rate swap. The structure of the basis rate swap is the same as the straight interest rate swap, with the exception that floating interest calculated on one basis is exchanged for floating interest calculated on a different basis. The forerunner of this type of swap was the US Dollar Prime Rate LIBOR swap. However, an even larger market has developed for the exchange of I month US Dollar LIBOR for 6 month US Dollar LIBOR and more recently US Dollar LIBOR for US Dollar commercial paper at much finer rates than those available on the foreign exchange market.

HOW TO REDUCE SWAP RISK?

Certain precautions can be taken to reduce swap risk by following some of the common approaches. *First, undertake more stringent credit analyses and use greater care in selecting counterparties:* This is best insurance. Having a financially strong counterparty not only minimises the chances of default but also facilitates the transfer of a swap, for either profit, or lack of need, or both. *Second, master agreements:* These stipulate the all swaps between two parties are cross-defaulted to each other; default on any one swap triggers suspension payments on all others covered in the agreement. Such arrangements normally pre-suppose frequent transactions between the parties. They also are most effective in reducing exposure when a balance exists in swap positions between paying and receiving fixed-rate flows, and between notional principal amounts and maturities. Third, *collateralisation:* Collateralisation with marketable securities has become an essential feature of swaps with dubious credits. The right to call can be mutual, more often, it applies only in one direction, depending on the relative strength of the two parties. Many counterparties, however, resist the posting of collateral, since they are often constrained by negative pledge or part *passu* clauses in credit agreements. Fourth, *better documentation:* More protective documentation in swap agreements can provide trigger points for remedial action in advance of actual default. Users could require, for example, that the various tests of financial condition found in credit agreement are incorporated into swaps contracts. Through cross-default or cross- acceleration clauses, users can gain the benefits of such covenants even if they are not specifically set out in the swap contract. Without such protection, one could be worse off On the other hand, if anyone receives protection by demanding such clauses, no one would be better off. Although swap exposure is mutual, a user can expect that its concession of a cross-default clause will not be reciprocated. And, finally, *net settlements:* To minimise risk, a swap user is well advised to insist on settlement of all payments on the same day and on a net basis. A payments lag can leave a user vulnerable to loss of its counterparty defaults before the corresponding payment has been made.

Since global financial integration has become a substantially accomplished fact among the short term cash money markets and the more active of the currency forwards and future markets, these markets are no longer consistently exploitable and offer arbitrage opportunities. Covered interest rate parity (CIRP) holds, more or less, these markets. (CIRP asserts that in free markets, the forward premium or discount on the exchange rate between two currencies should equal the corresponding interest rate differential, apart from transactions costs, political and credit risks and, empirically non-comparability of assets alongwith measurement error). It has taken the maturation of the swaps markets, however, to yield evidence of, or, even bring to pass, a comparable integration of the longer-term capital markets. There, swaps have come to provide a liquid and functionally close substitute for the poorly developed, even absent forwards and futures dimensions. Indeed, CIRP holds about as well as in the long as in the short-term markets.   Thus. swaps have extended the integration of the foreign exchange and interest] rate markets across all maturities. This marks a further attenuation of national policymakers' "independence" or, more accurately. their ability to pursue old fashioned "business as usual". Some one may have been able to conduct monetary and exchange rate policies independently and toward different ends.

Traditional policy tools now have less certain effect — quantitatively for sure and often in their qualitative incidence as well — and policy makers must adapt accordingly. Despite remarkable changes, the various national capital markets are not yet fully integrated, and perhaps may never be so — even presuming ever increasing derivative activity and capital flow across national borders. In particular, investors face differing income and inflation risks in their home countries: allowing too for currency risk, they are bound to make differing evaluation of the expected risks and returns on domestic and foreign assets. Risk aversion, customs, and distrust of foreign entanglements still cause some to cling purely to holdings in their home markets when cross-border diversification makes more sense.

The modern science of risk management reaches out to these broader horizons. The swaps and other derivatives markets offer an increasingly ready means to exploit the opportunities already available. And the application of swaps and derivatives technique to new objects ripe for management, for example in the equities and commodities sectors, is enlarging the opportunity set day by day.

SWAPTIONS

Options on interest rate swaps are referred as swaptions. The buyer of a swaption has the right to enter an interest rate swap agreement by some specified date in the future. The swaption agreement will specify whether the buyer of the swaption will be a fixed-rate receiver or a fixed-rate payer. The writer of the swaption becomes the counterparty to the swap if the buyer exercises.

If the buyer of the swaption has the right to enter into a swap as a fixed-rate payer, the swap is called a *Call swaption*. The writer therefore becomes the fixed-rate receiver/ floating-rate payer. If the buyer of swaption has the right to enter into a swap as a floating-rate payer, the swap is called a *put swaption*. The writer of the swaption therefore becomes the floating-rate receiver/fixed-rate payer.

The strike rate of the swaption indicates the fixed rate that will be swapped versus the floating rate. The swaption will also specify the maturity date of the swap. A swaption may be European or American. Of course, as in all options, the buyer of a swaption pays the writer a premium, although the premium can be structured into the swap terms so that no upfront fee has to be paid.

A swaption can be used to hedge a portfolio strategy that uses an interest rate swap but where the cash flows of the underlying asset or liability are uncertain. The cash flows of the asset will be uncertain if it (*i*) is callable, as in the case of callable bonds, convertible bonds, a loan that can be prepaid etc., and/or (*ii*) exposes the investor/lendor to default risk.

EQUITY CAPS AND FLOORS

An *equity cap* is an agreement in which one party, for an upfront premium, agrees to compensate the other at specific time periods if a designated stock market benchmark is greater than the predetermined level. An *equity* for is an agreement in which one party agrees to pay the other at specific time periods if a specific stock market benchmark is less than a predetermined level. By buying an equity floor and selling an equity cap, a money manager can create an equity collar.

As with equity swaps, these are relatively new derivative contracts. As with interest rate caps and floor, these contracts are nothing more than packages of options and are therefore more transactionally efficient vehicles. They can be customized for any stock market benchmark. However, they are less liquid than exchange-traded options.

REVIEW PROBLEMS

1. An American company has an existing swap agreement with a British company. The original exchange rate was $1.50/£1 (when the swap was agreed) and the current exchange rate is $2/£1. The fixed interest rates for the swap are 10% for sterling and 5% for the US dollar. Interest payments are annual and such payments have just been exchanged. The swap has a remaining life of 3 years. The American company is the recipient of sterling and the payer of dollars. The original sums were $15 million and £10. Interest rates are now equal at 5% p.a. What is the value of the swap to the American company?

Ans.

$B_F = £1m/(1.05) + £1m/(1.05)^2 + £11m/(1.05)^3 = £11.36m$

$B_D = \$0.75m/(1.05) + \$0.75m/(1.05)^2 + \$15.75m/(1.05)^3 + \$15m$

$V = \$2\ B_F - B_D = \$22.72m - \$15m = \$7.72m$

2. Company ABC and XYZ have been offered the following rates per annum on a $ 200 million five-year loan:

	Fixed Rate	Floating Rate
Company ABC	12.0	Libor +0.1%
Company XYZ	13.4	Libor +0.6%

Company ABC requires a floating-rate loan; company XYZ requires a fixed-rate loan. Design a swap that will net a bank acting as intermediary 0.1 percent per annum and be equally attractive the both companies.

Ans.

ABC has a comparative advantage in fixed-rate market but wants to borrow floating. XYZ has a comparative advantage in floating-rate markets but wants to borrow fixed. This provides the basis for the swap. There is a 1.4 percent per annum differential between the fixed rates offered to the two companies and a 0.5% per annum differential between the floating rates offered to the two companies. The total gain to all parties from the swap is, therefore, 1.4 –0.5=0.9% per annum. Since the bank gets 0.1% per annum of this, the swap should make each of ABC and XYZ 0.4% per annum better off. This means that it should lead to ABC borrowing at LIBOR -0.3% and to XYZ borrowing at 13%.

3. XYZ Bank is seeking fixed-rate funding. It is able to finance at a cost of six-month LIBOR +¼% for £100 million for 5 years. The bank is able to swap into a fixed rate at 8.50% versus six-month LIBOR. Treating 6 months as exactly half a year:

(a) Set out the cash flows involved. What will be the all-in cost of funds to XYZ Bank?

(b) Another possibility being considered is the issue of a 'hybrid' instrument which pays 8.50% for the first 3 years and LIBOR —¼% for the remaining 2 years. Given a three-year swap rate of 9% indicate in general terms the method by which the bank would achieve fixed-rate funding.

(c) In principle, without calculating the cash flows involved, does this deal seem attractive?

(d) Briefly outline the risks which would be involved for the bank in such a funding operation.

Ans.

(a) XYZ Bank pays LIBOR +0.25% p.a. for 5 years. The swap involves payment of 8.5% p.a. and receipts of LIBOR.

Interest rates

Inflow	*Outflow*
LIBOR	LIBOR +0.25% + 8.5%

Net interest payment 8.75% p.a.

Cash flows per six-month period

Inflow	*Outflow*
(LIBOR/2) × £100 million	(LIBOR/2)×£100 million + £125,000
	+ £4,250,000

Net outflow $4,375,000 (=all-in cost of funds)

(b) Issues hybrid and enter both the five-year and three-year swaps.

First 3 years

Bank pays 8.5% p.a. on hybrid.

Bank pays 8.5% p.a. on five-year swap.

Bank receives 9% p.a. on three-year swap.

Bank receives LIBOR on five-year swap.

Bank pays LIBOR on three-year swap.

Net interest payment 8% p.a.

Final 2 years

Bank pays LIBOR—0.25% on hybrid.

Bank receives LIBOR on five-year swap.

Bank pays 8.5% p.a. on five-year swap.

Net interest payment 8.25% p.a.

(c) The arrangement in (b), compared with that in (a), saves 0.75% p.a. over the first 3 years and 0.5% p.a. over the final 2 years.

(d) The risks would include default risk on the part of the 2 swap counterparties. There may also be liquidity risk in the event that one or both of the swaps may need be adversed. There could also be legal risk, the legality of one or both swaps may be challenged. Taxation risk means that a change in the tax regulation may adversely affect the benefits from the arrangements. There may may be a country risk if a counterparty is based overseas: payments may be inhibited by an overseas government.

4. Company A wishes to borrow £10 million at a fixed rate for 5 years and has been offered either 11% fixed or six-month LIBOR + 1%. Company B wishes to borrow £10 million at a floating rate for 5 years and has been offered either six-month LIBOR + 0.5% or 10% fixed.

(a) How may they enter into a swap arrangement in which each benefits equally?

(b) What risks may this arrangement generate?

Ans.

(a) By directly borrowing on the required basis, the total interest paid by A and B is:

£10 million × (11% + LIBOR +0.5%)

By borrowing according to comparative advantage, the total interest paid is:

£10 million × (10% + LIBOR +1%)

Borrowing according to comparative advantage provides a total saving of £10 million X¼% to be shared between A and B. Equal sharing means that both have a¼% reduction in interest charge.

There is a number of alternative swap arrangements that would be consistent with this distribution of the interest rate benefit of borrowing according to comparative advantage. For instance, by synthesising a fixed rate borrowing at 10-3/4% (a saving of ¼% relative to borrowing directly at 11%), then B effectively obtains a floating rate loan at LIBOR +¼% (an improvement of ¼% relative to borrowing directly). It may be noted that, conventionally, swaps are quoted in terms of the fixed rate to be exchanged for LIBOR.

(b) B is at risk from LIBOR rising.

A is at risk from an opportunity loss in the event of a fall in LIBOR.

Both are at risk from default by the other.

5. Company AKR wishes to borrow U.S. dollars at a fixed rate of interest. Company RAK wishes to borrow Japanese yen at a fixed rate of interest. The amounts required by the two companies are roughly the same at current exchange rate. The companies have been quoted the following interest rates:

	Yen	Dollars
Company AKR	4.0%	8.6%
Company RAK	5.5%	9.0%

Design a swap that will net a bank, acting as intermediary, 50 basis points per annum. Make the swap equally attractive to the two companies and ensure that all foreign exchange risk is assumed by the bank.

Ans.

AKR has a comparative advantage in yen markets but wants to borrow dollars, RAK has a comparative advantage in dollar markets but wants to borrow yen. This provides the basis for the swap. There is a 1.5% per annum differential between the yen rates and a 0.4 percent per annum differential between the dollar rates. The total gain to all parties from the swap is, therefore, 1.5 –0.4 = 1.1% per annum. Since the bank requires 0.5% per annum, this leaves 0.3% per annum for each of AKR and RAK. The swap should lead to AKR borrowing dollars at 8.6–0.3 = 8.3 percent per annum and to RAK borrowing yen at 5.5 –0.3 = 5.2% per annum.

QUESTIONS

1. In a currency swap, counterparties exchange the same sums at the beginning and the end of the swap penod. Explain how this practice relates to the custom of making interest payments during the life of the swap agreement.

2. Why is an interest rate swap simpler to a futures (or forward) contract?

3. Why can a fixed-rate payer in an interest rate swap be viewed as short the bond market and the floating-rate payer be viewed as long the bond market?

4. How can an interest rate collar be created?

5. In a currency swap, both the final principal and the periodic coupons are exchanged. Why is this unnecessary in an interest-rate swap?

6. Discuss the various precautions which can be taken to reduce swap risk.

7. Why in a standard currency swap, is a fixed rate exchanged for a floating rate? Isn't that making things more complicated by comprising an interest-rate risk with a currency risk?

8. What is a swaption?

9. Explain how you would value a swap that is the exchange of a floating rate in one currency for a fixed rate in another currency.

10. "Companies with high credit risk are the ones that cannot access fixed rate market directly. They are the companies that are most likely to be paying fixed and receiving floating in an interest rate swap". Do you think it increases or decreases the risk of a financial institution's swap portfolio? Assume that companies are most likely to default when interest rates are high.

PROBLEMS

1. A party wants to swap fixed for floating to receive the certificate of deposit (CD) rate for 5 years. The following swap prices are available:

   5-year fixed against LIBOR   8% p.a.

   5-year fixed against CD rate   7.35% p.a.

   Basis swap, pay LIBOR and receive CD rate CD + 50 basis points.

   What alternatives does the party have? What are the costs of these alternatives?

2. A $100 million interest-swap has a remaining life of ten months. Under the terms of the swap, six-month LIBOR is exchanged for 12 percent per annum (compounded semiannually). The average of the bid and ask rate being exchanged for six-month LIBOR in swaps of all maturities is currently 10 percent per annum with continuous compounding. The six-month LIBOR rate was 9.6 percent per annum two months ago. What is the current value of the swap to the party paying floating ? What is its value to the party paying fixed?

3. A currency swap has a remaining life of 15 months. It involves exchanging interest at 14 percent on £20 million for interest at 10 percent on 30 million once a year. The term structure of interest rates in both the U.K and the U.S. is currently flat and if the swap were negotiated today the interest rate exchanged would 8 percent in dollars and 11 percent in sterling. All interest rates are quoted with annual compounding. The current exchange rate is 1.6500. What is the value of the swap to the party paying sterling ? what is the value of the swap to the party paying dollars?

4. For a value date of 1 July 2010 a company entered into a five-year interest rate swap with its bank, under which it has contracted to pay 10% and receive six-month LIBOR, settled semi-annually, on a national principal amount of £10,000,000. It is 1 July 2012 and the swap payments have just settled, so the swap now has exactly 3 years to run. The bank offers to unwind the swap at a rate of 8%. If the company agrees, the transaction will be cancelled by means of a settlement today.

(a) Set out the underlying fixed-rate cash flow that would take place if, instead of cancelling the existing deal, a new deal were made and the 2 deals were to run to maturity. You may assume each interest period has 182.5 days and ignore leap years.

(b) What sum of money would be paid today to cancel the transaction?

(c) To whom?

(d) What assumptions are implicit in the above calculations?

REFERENCES

1. Baz, J., and M. Pascutti. "Alternative Swap Contracts Analysis and Pricing," *Journal of Derivatives*, (Winter 1996): 7-21.

2. Brown, K.C, and D.J. Smith. *Interest Rate and Currency Swaps: A Tutorial*. Association for Investment Management and Research, 1996.

3. Cooper. I., and A. Mello. "The Default Risk in Interest Rate Swaps," *Journal of Finance*, 46, 2 (1991): 597-620.

4. Das, S., *Credit Derivatives: Trading & Management of Credit & Default Risk*, 3rd edn. New York: Wiley, 2005.

5. Dattatreya, R.E., and K. Hotta. *Advanced Interest Rate and Currency Swaps: State-of-the-Art Products, Strategies, and Risk Management Applications*. Irwin, 1993.

6. Flavell, R. *Swaps and Other Instruments*. Chichester: Wiley, 2002.

7. Gupta, A., and M.G. Subrahmanyam. "An Empirical Examination of the Convexity Bias in the Pricing of Interest Rate Swaps," *Journal of Financial Economics*, 55, 2 (2000): 239-79.

8. Hull, J., M. Predescu, and A. White, "Relationship between Credit Default Swap Spreads, Bond Yields, and Credit Rating Announcements," *Journal of Banking and Finance*, 28 (November 2004): 2789-2811.

9. Hull, J.C., and A. White, "Valuation of a CDO and nth to Default Swap without Monte Carlo Simulation," *Journal of Derivatives*, 12, No. 2 (Winter 2004): 8-23.

10. Hull, J.C., and A. White, "Valuing Credit Derivatives Using an Implied Copula Approach," *Journal of Derivatives*, 14, 2 (Winter 2006), 8-28.

11. Laurent, J.-P., and J. Gregory, "Basket Default Swaps, CDOs and Factor Copulas," *Journal of Risk*, 1, 4 (2005), 8-23.

12. Litzenberger, R.H. "Swaps: Plain and Fanciful," *Journal of Finance*, 47, 3 (1992): 831-50.

13. Minton, B.A. "An Empirical Examination of the Basic Valuation Models for Interest Rate Swaps," *Journal of Financial Economics*, 44, 2 (1997): 251-77.

14. Sun, T.S. Sundaresan, and C. Wang. "Interest Rate Swaps: An Empirical Investigation," *Journal of Financial Economics*, 34, 1 (1993): 77-99.

15. Titman, S. "Interest Rate Swaps and Corporate Financing Choices," *Journal of Finance*, 47, 4 (1992): 1503-16.

39

Hedging

INTRODUCTION

Hedging is undertaken to reduce the price risk of a cash or forward position. The managerial goals of a hedging programme are to make a hedging decision and to manage the programme. Although closed related to asset/liability management and often used in conjuction with asset/liability management hedging is a distinct activity. A *hedge* is a position that is taken as a *temporary substitute* for a later position in another asset (or liability) or to protect the value of an existing position in an asset (or liability) until the position can be liquidated. In keeping with accepted terminology, we will describe the position that the firm seeks to hedge, whether it be on the asset side of the balance sheet or on the liabilities side of the balance sheet, as the *cash position.*

Most hedging is done in derivative instruments. The instruments most often used for hedging are futures, forwards, options, and swaps. Futures, forwards, and swaps are off-balance sheet instruments. That is, they do not show up on either the assets side or on the liabilities side of the user's balance sheet. While most hedging is done in off-balance sheet instruments, it is important to note that a hedge can take the form of an on-balance sheet position. This is the case for example, when swap dealers hedge their swap portfolios in Treasury bonds and bills. The key, in this case, is the *temporary* nature of the cash market hedge.

THE OBJECTIVES AND BENEFITS OF HEDGING

In contrast to speculation, hedging is done to reduce risk. But is this desirable? If everyone hedged, would we not simply end up with an economy in which no one takes risks? This would surely lead to economic stagnancy. Moreover, we must wonder whether hedging can actually increase shareholder wealth.

If the famous Modigliani-Miller propositions are correct, then the value of the firm is independent of any financial decisions, which include hedging. Hedging, however, may be desired by the shareholders simply to find a more acceptable combination of return and risk. It can be argued, however, that firms need not hedge since shareholders, if they wanted hedging, could do it themselves. But this ignores several important points. It assumes that shareholders can correctly assess all the firm's hedgeable risks. If a company is exposed to the risk associated with volatile raw materials prices, can the shareholders properly determine the degree of risk? Can they determine the periods over which that risk is greatest? Can they determine the correct number of futures contracts necessary to hedge their share of the total risk? Do they even qualify to open a futures brokerage account? Will their transaction costs be equal to or less than their proportional share of the transaction costs incurred if the firm did the hedging? The answer to each of these questions is "maybe not." It should be obvious that hedging is not something that shareholders can always do as effectively as firms.

In addition, there may be other reasons why firms hedge, such as tax advantages. Low-income firms, for example those that are below the highest corporate tax rate, can particularly benefit from the interaction being also reduces the probability of bankruptcy. This is not necessarily valuable to the shareholders except that it can reduce the expected costs that are incurred if the firm does go bankrupt. Finally, a firm may choose to hedge because its managers' livelihoods may be heavily tied to the performance of the firm. The managers may then benefit from reducing the firm's risk. This may not be in the shareholders' best interest, but it can at least explain why some firms hedge. Finally, hedging may send a signal to potential creditors that the firm is making a concerted effort to protect the value of the underlying assets. This can result in more favourable credit terms and less costly; restrictive covenants.

Many firms, such as financial institutions, are constantly trading over-the-counter financial products like swaps and forwards on behalf of their clients. They offer these services to help their clients manage their risks. These financial institutions then turn around and hedge the risk they have assumed on behalf of their clients. How do they make money? They quote rates and prices to their clients that reflect a spread sufficient to cover their hedging costs and include a profit. In this manner, they become retailers of hedging services.

Hedging benefits society as well as the individual hedger. The ability to transfer risk allows the commodity hedger a more stable estimate of the cost of a product, which translates into a lower and more stable price for the product. Also, users of commodities are able to "lock-in" the future purchase price of the item they need with only a small cash margin "down payment," thereby allowing a reduction in current inventory. This reduction in inventory reduces the cost of business and improves the firm's liquidity, benefits that can be passed on to the consumer. The existence of financial futures allows pension funds to stabilise returns and reduce risk for the pension fund participants, enables financial institutions to reduce risk, and provides the means to create new products in the insurance, loan and investment arenas.

Hedging also is a tool used to offset the market (*systematic*) risk of stock portfolios. Previously, risk management for common stocks concentrated on diversification to eliminate *unsystematic* risk, but until futures and options contracts on stock index futures came into existence there was no effective means for eliminating most of the systematic risk of a stock portfolio. Alternatively, futures are used to adjust the beta of the stock portfolio to the desired value.

Finally, hedging is extremely important for the proper functioning, long-term liquidity, and open interest of a futures market. Thus, viable futures contracts are linked to commercial hedging activity. Although speculative interest provides shorter-term volume, speculative activity can be wagering and uncertain, especially since many speculators hold a position for only several weeks. Market makers on the futures floor provide intraday liquidity, but without speculators and hedgers the market makers soon depart to another pit. Likewise, arbitrageurs provide only limited liquidity for the markets. Hedgers are the key to the market, as is evident when a futures contract stops trading because of a lack of trading volume.

THE HEDGING PROCESS

Hedging is to take a position in futures that "offsets" the price change in the cash asset. Hence, hedging a current long cash position consists of taking a short futures position. In order to determine whether one should sell or buy futures to initiate a hedge, a potential hedger can follow a two-step process:

1. Determine the exposure of the cash position to potential losses; that is, in what direction must cash prices change in order to create a loss? Thus, a loss occurs for a current long cash position when prices decline, whereas a loss occurs for a short cash or an *anticipated* cash position when prices increase.
2. Determine whether a short or a long futures position is needed to offset the potential loss in the cash position.

Before we can understand why a certain hedge is placed or how it works, we must become acquainted with a few basic hedging concepts.

Short Hedge and Long Hedge

The terms *short hedge* and *long hedge* distinguish hedges that involve short and long positions in the futures contract, respectively. A hedger who holds the commodity and is concerned about a decrease in its price might consider hedging it with a short position in futures. If the spot price and futures price move together, the hedge will reduce some of the risk. For example, if the spot price decreases, the futures price also will decrease. Since the hedger is short the futures contract, the futures transaction produces a profit that at least partially offsets the loss on the spot position. This is called a *short hedge* because the hedger is short futures.

Another type of short hedge can be used in anticipation of the future sale of an asset. An example of this occurs when a firm decides that it will need to borrow money at a later date. Borrowing money is equivalent to issuing or selling a bond or promissory note. If interest rates increase before the money is borrowed, the loan will be more expensive. A similar risk exists if a firm has issued a floating rate liability. Since the rate is periodically reset, the firm has contracted for a series of future loans at unknown rates. To hedge this risk, the firm might short an interest rate futures contract. If rates increase, the futures transaction will generate a profit that will at last partially offset the higher interest rate on the loan. Because it is taken out in anticipation of a future transaction in the spot market, this type of hedge is known as an *anticipatory hedge*.

Another type of anticipatory hedge involves an individual who plans to purchase a commodity at a later date. Fearing an increase in the commodity's price, the investor might buy a futures contract. Then, if the price of the commodity increases, the futures price also will increase and produce a profit on the futures position. That profit will at least partially offset the higher cost of purchasing the commodity. This is a long hedge, because the hedger is long in the futures market.

Another type of long hedge might be placed when one is short an asset. Although this hedge is less common, it would be appropriate for someone who has sold short a stock and is concerned that the market will go up. Rather than close out the short position, one might buy a futures and earn a profit on the long position in futures that will at least partially offset the loss on the short position in the stock.

In each of these cases, the hedger held a position in the spot market that was subject to risk. The futures transaction served as a temporary substitute for a spot transaction. Thus, when one holds the spot commodity and is concerned about a price decrease but does not want to sell it, one can execute a short futures trade. Selling the futures contract would substitute for selling the commodity. Table 1 summarises these various hedging situations.

Contract Choice

The choice of futures contract actually consists of four decisions: (1) which futures commodity, (2) which expiration month and (3) whether to be long or short.

TABLE 1

Hedging Situations

Condition Today	Risk	Appropriate Hedge
Hold asset	Asset price may fall	Short hedge
Plan to buy asset	Asset price may rise	Long hedge
Sold short asset	Asset price may rise	Long hedge
Issued floating-rate liability	Interest rates may rise	Short hedge
Plan to issue liability	Interest rates may rise	Short hedge

Note: Short hedge means long spot, short futures; long hedge means short spot, long futures.

Which Futures Commodity?

It is important to select a futures contract on a commodity that is highly correlated with the underlying commodity being hedged. In many cases the choice is obvious, but in some it is not. For example, suppose one wishes to hedge the rate on bank CDs, which are short-term money market instruments issued by commercial banks. There is no bank CD futures contract so the hedger must choose from among some other similar contracts. Liquidity is important, because the hedger must be able to close the contract easily. If the futures contract lacks the necessary liquidity, the hedger should select a contract that has sufficient liquidity and is highly correlated with the spot commodity being hedged. Since both Treasury bills and Eurodollars are short-term money market instruments, their futures contracts, which are quite liquid, would seem appropriate for hedging bank CD rates. Of course, if the hedger wanted the hedging instrument to be identical to the underlying spot asset, he or she could go to the over-the-counter market and request a forward contract, but that would entail some other considerations.

Another factor one should consider is whether the contract is correctly priced. A short hedger will be selling futures contracts and therefore should look for contracts that are overpriced or, in the worst case, correctly priced. A long hedger should hedge by buying underpriced contracts or, in the worst case correctly priced contracts. Sometimes the best hedge can be obtained by using more than one futures commodity.

Which Expiration Month?

Once one has selected the futures commodity, one must decide on the expiration month. As we know, only certain expiration months trade at a given time. For example, in September the Treasury bond futures contract has expirations of December of the current year, March, June, September, and December of the following year, and March, June, and September of the year after that. If the Treasury bond futures contract is the appropriate hedging vehicle, the contract used must come from this group of expirations.

In most cases there will be a time horizon over which the hedge remains in effect. To obtain the maximum reduction in basis risk, a hedger should hold the futures position until as close as possible to expiration. Thus, an appropriate contract expiration would be one that corresponded as closely as possible to the expiration date. However, the general rule of thumb is to avoid holding a futures position in the expiration month. This is because unusual price movements sometimes are observed in the expiration month, and this would pose an additional risk to hedgers. Thus, the hedger should choose an expiration month that is as close as possible to but after the month in which the hedge is terminated. However, this rule used not always be strictly followed since all contracts don't exhibit unusual price behaviour in the expiration month. Infact, the longer the time expiration, the less liquid is the contract. Therefore, the selection of a contract according to this criterion may need to be overruled by the necessity of using a liquid contract. If this happens, one should use a contract with a shorter expiration. When the contract moves into its expiration month, the futures position is closed out and a new position is opened in he next expiration month. This process, called *rolling the hedge forward*, generates some additional risk but can still be quite effective.

Of course, the time horizon problem can be handled perfectly by using a forward contract from the over-the-counter market. In fact some hedgers have horizons of longer than 10 years, which can be hedged only by using forward contracts.

Long or Short?

After selecting the future commodity and expiration month, the hedger must decide whether to be long or short. This decision is critical and there is absolutely no room for a mistake here. If a hedger goes long (or short) when he should have been short (or long), he has doubled the risk. The end result will be a gain or loss twice the amount of the gain or loss of the unhedged position.

The decision of whether to go long or short requires a determination of which type of market move will result in a loss in the spot market. It then requires establishing a futures position that will be profitable while the spot position is losing. Table 2 summarises three methods that will correctly identify the appropriate futures transaction. The first method requires that the hedger identify the worst case scenario and then establish a futures position that will profit if the worst case does occur. The second method requires taking a futures position that is opposite to the current spot position. This is a simple method, but in some cases it is difficult to identify the current spot position. The third method identifies the spot transaction that will be conducted when the hedge is terminated. The futures transaction that will be conducted when the hedge is terminated should be the opposite of this spot transaction. The futures transaction that should be done today should be the opposite of the futures transaction that should be done at the termination of the hedge.

Margin Requirements and Marking to Market

Two other considerations in hedging are the margin requirement and the effect of marking to market. Margin requirements are very small and virtually insignificant in relation to the size of the position being hedged. Moreover, margin requirements for hedges are even smaller than speculative margins. In addition, margins can sometimes be posted with Treasury bills, thus, interest on the money can still be earned. Therefore, the initial amount of margin posted is really not a major factor in hedging.

What is important, however, is the effect of marking to market and the potential for margin calls. Remember that the profit on a futures transaction is supposed to offset the loss on the spot commodity. At least part of the time, there will be profits on the spot commodity and losses on the futures contract. On a given day when the futures contract generates a loss, the hedger must deposit additional margin money to cover that loss. Even if the spot position has generated a profit in excess of the loss on the futures contract, it may be impossible, or at least inconvenient, to withdraw the profit on the spot position to cover the loss on the futures.

TABLE 2

How to Determine Whether to Buy or Sell Futures When Hedging

Worst Case Scenario Method

1. Assuming that the spot and futures markets move together, determine whether long and short positions in futures would be profitable if the market goes up or down.
2. What is the worst that could happen in the sport market?
   a. The spot market goes up.
   b. The spot market goes down.
3. Given your answer in 2, assume that the worst that *can* happen *will* happen.
4. Given your answer in 3, and using your answer in 1, take a futures position that will be profitable.

Current Spot Position Method

1. Determine whether your current position in the spot market is long or short.
   a. If you own or plan to sell an asset, your current position is long.
   b. If you are short an asset, your current position is short.
   c. If you are committed to buying an asset in the future, your current position is short.
   d. If you have issued a floating rate liability, your current position is long.
   e. If you plan to issue a liability, your current position is long
2. Take a futures position that is opposite the position given by your answer in 1.

Anticipated Future Spot Transaction Method

1. Determine what type of sot transaction you will be making when the hedge is terminated.
   a. Sell an asset.
   b. Buy an asset.
   c. Issue (sell) a liability (this includes a liability with a floating rate reset).
2. Given your answer in 1, you will need to terminate a futures position at the horizon date by doing the opposite transaction to the one in 1, e.g., if your answer in 1 is "sell," your answer here is "buy a futures."
3. Given your answer in 2, you will need to open a futures contract today by doing the opposite, e.g., if your answer in 2 is "buy a futures," your answer here should be "sell a futures."

This is one of he major obstacles to more widespread use of futures. Because futures profits and losses are realised immediately and spot profits and losses do not occur until the hedge is terminated, many potential hedgers tend to weigh the losses on the futures position more heavily than the gains on the spot. They also tend to think of hedges on an *ex post* rather than *ex ante* basis. If the hedge produced a profit on the spot position and a loss on the futures position, it would be apparent *after the fact* that the hedge should not have been done. But this would not be known *before the fact*.

Thus, a hedger must be aware that hedging will produce both gains and losses on futures transactions and will require periodic margin calls. The alternative to not meeting a margin call is closing the futures position. It is tempting to do this after a streak of losses and margin calls. If the futures position is closed, however, the hedge will no longer be in effect and the individual or firm will be exposed to the risk in the spot market, which is greater than the risk of the hedge.

Thus the effect of marking to market on the futures price. Infact, the impact is fairly small. If, however, the interest earned or paid on the variation margin is not insignificant, it is possible to take it into account when establishing the optimal number of contracts.

CROSS HEDGES AND CHANGING VOLATILITIES OF AN ASSET POSITION

A crosshedge occurs if the characteristics of the cash asset underlying the futures contract differs from the cash instrument being hedged. A number of factors affect the degree of a crosshedge for a given position. The extent of a stock portfolio crosshedge is affected by the relative stock composition and relative stock weights of the cash and futures positions; any differences in the size between the cash and futures positions also affect the hedge. For a T-bond futures hedge one must consider the effect of the coupon, the time to maturity of the cash position, whether the bond possesses default risk, and the relative size o the underlying cash position. If any of these factors differ from the characteristics of the futures contract or the cheapest-to-deliver cash bond for pricing the futures, then a crosshedge exists. The extent of a crosshedge can be measured by the size of the correlation coefficient between the changes in value of the cash and futures position. The lower the correlation coefficient, the greater the difference in the two positions. When a low correlation exists, the futures contract is not a good instrument to use for hedging purposes.

Crosshedges arising from some of these characteristics, such as coupon differences, have a minimal effect on the performance of the hedge when the cash and futures prices still move nearly in tandem. Crosshedge factors affecting the volatility on the position (e.g., the maturity of the cash bond) are dealt with by adjusting the number of futures contracts employed in the hedge (as shown in the next chapter). However, the effect of quality difference, such as hedging corporate bonds with Treasury bond futures, depends on whether there is a major change in the perceived risk in the economy during the hedge period, which would significantly alter the basis. Consequently, the difficulty of overcoming crosshedge effects depends upon the particular characteristic(s) that differ between the futures and cash positions, whether the factors remain stable over time, and the economic environment at the time of the hedge. For example, hedging one currency with the futures contract of another currency often causes significant crosshedge risk because of the differing economic conditions in the two countries.

Liquidity also can be an issue in *measuring* the basis for a given security, since thinly traded issues often have reported prices that differ from their true prices, especially when the market changes but the thinly traded issue does not trade. Moreover, cash prices typically are reported in terms of bid prices and ask prices rather than transaction prices, and the newspaper prices occur at a different time of day than the close of the futures market; both of these factors affect the *apparent* stability of the basis.

In reality, most hedges involve some type of a crosshedge risk, since the cash asset typically differs from the underlying cash instrument priced by the futures contract. The greater the deviation of any of the factors from the underlying cash instrument, the greater the basis risk. For example, the effect of a large change in the shape of the term structure needs to be considered when the maturities of the cash bond and the cheapest-to-deliver bond for the futures contract differ. The creation of the T-note futures contracts with shorter maturities was undertaken in order to provide a more appropriate hedging vehicle under these circumstances. Also note that care must be taken when hedging the prime rate. Because the prime is an administered rate, it does not usually change in the same manner as market rates; in fact, the prime rate is slow to react to downward changes in interest rates. Hence, it is sometimes difficult to hedge the prime in an effective manner, especially over the short term.

TABLE 3

A Crosshedge

ABC Mutual Fund holds ₹ 5 crore in stocks, with the portfolio configured to match the XYZ 100 index. The Fund's money manager forecasts an increase in volatility in the market, which increases the probability of a major market decline. To reduce risk the money manager sells XYZ 500 futures. Although the XYZ 500 futures do not match the XYZ 100 price movements exactly, the money manager decides that this type of a crosshedge is the best strategy to use in this situation.

Date	Cash Market	Futures Market
Jan 12.	Stock portfolio of ₹ 5 crore, with the XYZ 100 = 325.09	Sell 287 June XYZ 500 futures, with the XYZ 500 futures = 348.20 for a value of ₹ 4,99,66,700
April 26	The XYZ 100 declines to 315.82 for a portfolio value of ₹ 4,85,74,240 = ₹ 5 crore × (315.82/325.09)	Buy back the XYZ 500 futures at 335.25 for a value of ₹ 4,81,08,375
	Change Loss of ₹ 14,25,760	Gain of ₹ 18,58,325 − 287 × 500 × (348.20 − 335.25)

Net gain: ₹ 4,32,565

The crosshedge generates a gain of ₹ 4,32,565. The large deviation between the loss in the cash portfolio and the futures gain shows the relative ineffectiveness of this crosshedge.

Table-3 shows a crosshedge between a cash portfolio mimicking the XYZ 100 cash index and the XYZ 500 futures contract. As shown in the example, crosshedges create net gains or losses that often vary to a greater extent than is the case hen the characteristics of the futures and cash securities are nearly equivalent.

STRATEGIES FOR HEDGING

Hedging typically is associated with reducing risk (reducing price volatility). However, those who employ futures markets have different strategies and different goals in order to implement a hedging programme. Market participants practice four overlapping strategies:

* *Reduction of risk*: the primary use of futures for hedging is to reduce the price variability associated with the cash asset position. Naive, regression, and duration methods determine the appropriate number of futures contracts for a hedge position. The objective of the regression and duration methods is to minimise the risk associated with a cash position.
* *Selective hedging*: hedging only during those time periods when a forecast determines that the cash position will lose money is called selective hedging. If the forecasts are correct then risk is minimised during the hedged periods; meanwhile the asset earns positive returns during the unhedged periods. If the forecasts are incorrect, then risk is not reduced. Many institutions employ some type of market timing to decide when to use selective hedging.
* *"Speculating on the basis"*: when the returns form the hedge are a consideration in whether the hedge will be undertaken, then this approach is equivalent to predicting the change in the basis during the hedge period.
* *Optimal risk-return hedging*: the optimal hedge decision considers both the reduction

in risk *and* the return from the combine cash-futures position. Such an optimal position is associated with portfolio analysis.

The above strategies also can be designated as passive or active strategies. A passive strategy is independent of cash market price/interest rate expectations. Passive strategies depend on the risk attitude of the hedger and the volatility of the cash markets. Active strategies require a forecast of future cash price/interest rates for implementation. The forecast helps the money manager decide when and how much of the cash position to hedge. Thus, an active hedging strategy readjusts the hedging position over time.

The "reduction of risk" strategy listed above is a passive strategy. "Selective hedging" and "speculating on the basis" are active strategies. The "optimal risk-return" strategy can be either a passive or active strategy depending on whether the risk attitude of the hedger or the forecasts of the cash market determine the size of the hedge position.

Avoiding Losses: Sell or Hedge?

A typical question concerning hedging is, "Why should I hedge when I can sell the cash asset if I expect prices to decline?" In fact, selling the cash asset is preferable in some circumstances. The principal rule for deciding whether to make a transaction in the cash market or to hedge in the futures market is

If you can accomplish your goal "effectively" in the cash market, then complete your transaction in that market.

The key to this rule is the word "effectively." In many situations one or more of the following factors cause difficulties if the transaction is completed in the cash market:

* *Liquidity:* the cash market for a given asset often is not liquid for large trades. Thus, the portfolio hedger who sells or buys the cash asset, or the dealer who shorts the asset, causes a significant price change in that security when liquidity does not exist. There is no liquidity problems for trades in most (near-term) financial futures contracts.
* *Cost:* the commissions and size of the bid-ask spread in the cash market often cause the cash transaction to be expensive relative to the same transaction in the futures market. For example, trades in a stock portfolio cost ten times the equivalent trade in futures.
* *Execution:* a futures transaction is initiated much quicker than a cash transaction due to liquidity reasons.
* *Short selling:* a short sale in the cash market typically is expensive.
* *Internal policy or government regulations:* these factors can prevent the desired cash market transaction. For example, a portfolio manager often is required to have a given minimum percentage of assets in bonds rather than in cash or short-term securities, or a financial institution may be prevented from shorting a cash security to obtain an effective cash market hedge.
* *Credit risk:* creating a forward or short sale in the cash market often involves an implicit credit risk on the part of the participants. Futures transactions are completed with the cleaning house, virtually eliminating the credit risk problem.

So far we have examined some basic principles underlying the practice of hedging. The next step is to illustrate how these hedges are executed. We shall look at some examples developed from a variety of economic and financial environments that illustrate several hedging principles.

Short-Term Interest Rate Hedges

Hedging the Future Purchase of a Treasury Bill. Consider the following scenario. On

February 15, a corporate treasurer learns that ₹ 1 crore will be available on May 17. The funds will be needed for long-term investment later in the year, but meanwhile they should be invested in liquid, interest-earning securities. The treasurer decides to purchase 91-day Treasury bills at the weekly auction on May 17.

T-bills are currently offered at a discount of 8.20. The treasurer would like to lock in this rate, but knows that the forward rate would be a more accurate reflection of the rate he would expect to receive when he buys the T-bills. That rate is 8.94. The treasurer knows that there is an active futures contract on Treasury bills that has expirations of March, June, September, and December. The treasurer knows that the risk is that interest rates will fall. Thus, using the worst case scenario method, the treasurer assumes that interest rates will fall. If that happens, Treasury bill futures price will rise. Thus, he knows that he needs to buy futures so that he will profit in the futures market if interest rates fall.

Table-4 presents the anticipatory hedge of a future purchase of a treasury bill The treasurer wants to lock in the yield of 9.6 percent given by the forward price of T-bills. With a ₹ 1 crore position and the futures contract covering ₹ 1 crore of T-bills, the treasurer knows that he needs one contract. Recall that the optimal hedge ratio requires the durations and yields of the spot and futures contracts. Since we are hedging 91-day T-bill futures, the durations are essentially the same: 25. The yield implied by the futures price of 97.83 is 9.31 per cent and the yield on the forward T-bill is 9.60 per cent.

When the hedge is over, the treasurer is glad he did hedge. The T-bills he brought on May 17 yielded only 8.19 per cent, but the futures transaction generated a profit of ₹ 30,500 . This amount effectively reduces the ₹ 98,05,610 he paid for the T-bills, so the effective yield now becomes 9.55 per cent. This hedge worked because the spot and futures T-bill price moved in the same direction. In this case, rates declined. Had rats risen, the T-bills would have been less expensive, thus offering a higher yield. The futures position would have produced a loss, however, and this would have offset some or all of the gain made in the spot market. In that case, the hedge would have been effective, but the treasurer would have wished that the hedge had not been done. The price one pays for hedging is that it will occasionally produce losses on the futures position that will absorb gains made in the spot market.

The above hedge is just one of many types of long hedges one can execute with interest rate futures contracts on short-term instruments. Many types of firms and some individuals determine that they will be investing funds in money market instruments at a later date. As long as the decision to invest the funds is unlikely to be reversed, a hedge is appropriate. This does not mean, however, that one should always hedge. If the hedger believes rates are abnormally low and likely to rise, the hedge will lock in the low rate while money market rates might increase. Thus, the hedger should not blindly hedge in all interest rate environments. Although in an efficient market the hedger should be unable to effectively time the interest rate cycle, it would still be inappropriate for the hedger to ignore his or her own expectations. This will be true for all of the remaining cases.

TABLE 4

Anticipatory Hedge of a Future Purchase of a Treasury Bill

Scenario: On February 15, corporate treasurer learns that ₹ 1 crore will become available on May 17. The treasurer plans to purchase 91-day U.S. Treasury bills at the weekly auction.

Date	Spot Market	Futures Market
February 15	The implied forward price of 91-day T-bills implies a discount of 8.94. Price per ₹ 100 face value $100 - 8.94(91/360) = 97.74.$ Proceeds from ₹ 1 crore face value: ₹ 97,74,000 Implied yield: $(100/97.74)^{365/91} - 1 = 0960$	June T-bill 1MM Index is at 91.32. Price per ₹ 100 face value: $100 - (100 - 91.32)\ 90/360)$ $= 97.83.$ Price per contract: ₹ 97,83,000 *Buy one contract*
May 17	91-day T-bills are selling for a discount of 7.69. Price per ₹ 100 face value: $100 - 7.69(91/360) = 98.0561.$ Proceeds from ₹ 1 crore face value: ₹ 98,05,610 Implied yield: $(100/98,05,610)^{365/91} - 1 = 0819.$	June T-bill 1MM Index is at 92.54. Price per ₹ 100 face value: $100 - 92.54)\ 90/360)$ $= 98.135.$ Price per contract: ₹ 98,13,500 *Sell one contract*

Analysis: When the ₹ 1 crore face value T-bills are purchased on May 17, the treasurer will pay ₹ 98,05,610, which implies a yield of 8.19 per cent, which is much lower than the 9.60 percent implied forward rate in effect at the time the hedge was initiated.

The profit on the futures transactions is

₹ 98,13,500 (sale price of futures)
− ₹ 97,83,000 (purchase price of futures)
_____
₹ 30,500 (profit on futures)

The profit on the futures can be considered as a reduction in the effective rice of the T-bills. This makes the T-bills effectively cost ₹ 97,75,610 − ₹ 30,500 = ₹ 97,45,110

Thus, the treasurer effectively paid ₹ 97,45,110 for ₹ 1 crore face value of T-bills. This implies a return of

(₹ 1 crore/₹ 97,45,110)$^{365/91}$ − .0955.

Thus, the effective return on the T-bills after accounting for the hedge is 9.55 per cent, which is quite close to the 9.60 per cent implied forward rate.

The Long Hedge

A *long hedge* is initiated when a futures contract is purchased in order to reduce the price variability of an *anticipated* future long position. Equivalently, a long hedge "locks-in" the interest rate or price of a cash security that will be purchased in the future, subject to a small adjustment due to the basis risk. Long hedges are sometimes considered speculative, since the hedger is attempting to offset a *projected* position rather than a current position. However, if future cash inflows can be forecasted accurately, if these funds are invested, and if interest rates are forecasted to decline (prices expected to increase), then executing a long hedge locks-in the *current* forward rate existing in the market. Consequently, a long hedge creates profits that offset the subsequent higher price in the cash market. A long hedge is also known as an *anticipatory hedge,* because it is effectively a substitute position for a future cash transaction.

The use of a long hedge serves as an effective *temporary* substitute for the purchase of a cash security, where the cash purchase is undertaken in the future. Thus, if interest rate do decline (prices increase) and no long hedge is executed, then the return on the invested funds will be lower than it would be if a hedge were executed. In other words, a long hedge can prevent an *opportunity loss* on future funds to be invested. An alternative method to look-in a future interest rate (price) when funds are not be available until later is to buy the financial instrument now (e.g., purchase a cash T-bond), and finance that purchase with borrowed funds until money becomes available. In this way the buyer guarantees the long-term yield on the bond. Whether the futures long hedge or the cash financing method is the superior method depends on the relationship of the bond yield to the financing rate, plus any difficulties in arranging financing for the cash transaction or convincing the board of directors of the firm to allow such financing.Table-5 shows how a long hedge is useful in locking-in an effective yield on investment when the funds are not available until a given time in the future. The initiation of a long hedge, as illustrated in Table-5 is made by management either if the firm wishes to reduce risk substantially of if the firm has a better forecast of future interest rates than is available from the forward rate (selective hedging).

Disadvantages of a Long Hedge

Disadvantages of a long hedge are as follows:

* If the financial manager incorrectly forecasts the direction of future interest rates and a long hedge is initiated, then the firm still locks-in the futures yield rather than fully participating in the higher returns available because of the higher interest rates.

* If rates increase instead of fall, then bond prices will fall, causing an immediate cash outflow due to margin calls. This cash outflow will be offset only *over the life of the bond* via a higher yield on investment, or from a higher bond price if the bond recovers in the market and it is sold. Thus, the net investment is the same, but the timing of the accounting profits differs from the investment decision.

* If the futures market already anticipates a fall in interest rates similar to the decrease forecasted by the financial manager, then the futures price reflects this lower rate, negating any return benefit from the long hedge. Specifically, one hedges only against *unanticipated* changes that the futures market has not yet forecasted. Hence, if the eventual cash price increase only to a level *below* the current futures rice, then a loss occurs on the long hedge. Consequently, an increase in return from a long hedge in comparison to the future cash market investment occurs only if the financial manager is a superior forecaster of future interest rates. However, the long hedge does lock-in the currently available long-term futures rate (or a close approximation of this rate), thereby reducing the risk of unanticipated changes in this rate.

* Financial institutions are prohibited from employing long hedges, since their regulatory agencies believe that long hedges are similar to speculation, and these agencies do not want financial institutions to be tempted into affecting the institution's return with highly leveraged "speculative" futures positions.

TABLE 5

Long Hedge

A greeting card company anticipated a large inflow of funds at the end of January when retail outlets pay for the stock of cards sold during the holiday season in December. Management intends to put ₹ 1 crore of these funds into a long-term bond because of the high yields on these investments. The current date is November 1 and the financial manager of the greeting card company projects that the long-term interest rate will fall significantly by the time the firm receives the funds on February 1. Thus, unless a long hedge is initiated now, the financial manager believes that the return on investment will be significantly lower (the cost of the bonds significantly higher) than is currently available via the futures market.

Objective of the long hedge: to benefit from the high long-term interest rates, even though funds are not currently available for investment.

Date	Cash Market	Futures Market
Nov. 1	Bonds at 86-20/32 to yield 9.95%; 8% coupon, 12 years to maturity; ₹ 1 crore to invest February 1	Buy 100 March T-bond futures at 87-16/32 as a long hedge (9.4% projected yield)
Feb. 1	Receive ₹ 1 crore; buy ₹ 1 crore of T-bonds at 100 to yield 8%	Sell futures at 100-2/32 to cover long position (yield 7.9%)
Change	Opportunity loss: ₹ 13,37,500 (₹ 1 crore × 13-12/32%)	Gain: ₹ 12,56,250 (₹1,00,000 × 100 × 12-18/32%)

Net change : ₹ 12,56,250 - ₹ 13,37,500 = – ₹ 81,250

Net yield with futures hedge: 9.83%

The example shows that the purchase of the T-bond futures contracts a gain for the futures instrument and that this gain is used to offset most of the higher future cash T-bond price. To look at it another way, the gain obtained on the futures transaction increases the total yield so that the yield approaches the projected yield given by the futures market on November 1. Although the net loss of ₹ 81,250 on the long hedge shows that the hedge is not perfect, this loss is significantly less than the opportunity loss of ₹ 13,37,250 that occurs without any hedge position.

A Portfolio Hedge

When a money manager forecasts a decline in the price of a portfolio of financial assets *or* does not want the risk associate with those assets, then the money manager can either:

* Do nothing (which creates a loss if the forecast is correct).
* Sell the cash assets.
* Execute a short hedge with a futures contract or alternative hedging instrument.

Typically, a futures hedge provides benefits over simply selling the asset. Hedging the cash asset currently owned is called a *portfolio hedge*. To illustrate, assume a portfolio manager hedges ₹ 1 crore of Treasury bonds when a money manager expects interest rates to increase. By selling T-bond futures short, the money manager profits on the futures side when prices decline (interest rates increase), thereby partially or totally offsetting the loss on the long cash T-bond position as its price declines. The calculations in Table-6 shows how the loss of ₹ 14,46,875 in the value of the cash bond position is reduced to a net loss of ₹ 2,03,125 when the profit from the short sale of the futures contracts is considered. Thus, the hedge reduces the loss on the cash portfolio by nearly 86%.

TABLE 6

A Portfolio Short Hedge

A portfolio manager for long-term Treasury bonds forecasts that interest rates will increase over the next few months (bond prices are expected to fall). The money manager holds a portfolio of ₹ 1 crore May 2011 bonds. A short hedge is implemented in September when long-term rates are at 7.8% and lifted in February after rates rise to 9.1%.

	Cash	*Futures*
Sept. 16	Holds ₹ 1 crore par of May 2011 T-bonds, coupon rate 10-3/4%, yielding 7.8% with a price of 129-13/32	Sells 10 March T-bond futures with a price of 100 (a projected yield of 8.0%)
Feb. 22	Price of bonds has dropped to 144-30/32 with a yield of 9.1%.	Repurchases 10 March T-bond futures at a price of 87-18/32 (where projected yield of 9.4%)
Change in value	Loss of ₹ 14,46,875 (14-15/32 × ₹ 1 crore)	Gain of ₹ 12,43,750 (12-14/32 × ₹ 10,00,000 × 10 or 398× ₹ 312.50 × 10)
	Net loss: ₹ 2,03,125 (i.e., ₹ 14,46,875 - ₹ 12,47,350)	

Many basic trade booklets and publications on futures markets present hedging examples by showing a net loss of zero—that is, a situation in which the gain on the futures position *exactly* offsets the loss on the cash position. This situation is equivalent to having a perfect negative correlation of –1.0 between the cash and futures price changes. Although such a situation would be welcome by hedgers, the reality is that such "perfect hedges" do not exist.

An Asset-Liability Hedge

Financial institutions and the portfolios hedger have different problems. Whereas the portfolio hedger desires to reduce the price risk of a set of assets, the financial institution is concerned about the *relationship* between its assets and liabilities. Specifically, changes in the financial institution's earnings are caused by the relative effect of a change in interest rates on both the assets and liabilities of the institution. If the cost of funds (liabilities) increases, then this cost is partially or completely offset by the additional return from higher interest on assets. Thus, the financial institution is naturally hedged for part of the balance sheet. However, many financial institutions find that it is not possible to reduce the volatility of earnings adequately from this natural asset-liability relationship, since assets often are long-term in nature while liabilities are short-term. This situation creates a "gap" in the maturity relationship, which causes changes in earnings when interest rates change. Hedging this maturity gap is called an asset-liability hedge. Table-7 illustrates a typical asset-liability problem facing a financial institution, how a futures hedge can alleviate this problem. The example begins by showing the problem that occurs when asset returns are fixed for the long term, however, the liability costs very over a much shorter period. It then provides an illustration of how a simple T-bill futures hedge can significantly reduce the volatility of a financial institution's earnings by "locking-in" the future cost of the liability.

TABLE 7

An Asset-Liability Hedge

AAA Savings and Loan has assets in the form of a mortgage portfolio of ₹ 50 crore, with ₹ 30 crore of the portfolio having a 9½% fixed-rate with 20 years to maturity. The other ₹ 200 crore in mortgages are variable-rate loans linked to the 90-day T-bill rate plus a 2% premium, adjustable quarterly. For simplicity, let us assume that the liabilities of AAA consist of ₹ 50 crore of three-month certificates of deposit, where the interest rate is based on the 90-day T-bill rate plus 3/4%.

Since the variable-rate mortgages are repriced at the same time and with the same instrument as the liabilities of the S and L (i.e., both are based on the T-bill rate), this portion of the asset-liability mix does not have a pricing risk. However, the fixed-rate portion of the mortgage portfolio is *not* repriced when the cost of the CDs changes in relation to changing interest rates. This creates a significant potential change in the earnings of the S and L as interest rates change.

PART A: WITHOUT A FUTURES HEDGE

The three-month T-bill rate is 7% on January 15; this rate changes to 11% by April 15. Note the change in the annualised spread between the fixed-rate portion of the mortgages and the liability interest rate from January to April, causing a significant change in earnings.

	Assets	Liabilities	Annualised Spread
Jan. 15	₹ 20 crore variable; 7% T-bill + 2% premium	₹ 20 crore 90-day CD 7-3/4%	9% − 7-3/4% = + 1¼%
	₹ 30 crore fixed, 9½%, 20 year	₹ 30 crore 90-day CD, 7-3/4%	9½% − 7-3/4% = + 1-3/4%
April 15	₹ 20 crore variable, 11% T-bill + 2% premium	₹ 20 crore 90-day CD, 11-3/4%	13% − 11-3/4% = + 1¼%
	₹ 30 crore fixed, 9½%, 20-year	₹ 30 crore 90-day CD, 11-3/4%	9½%−− 11-3/4 = −2¼%

PART B: FUTURES HEDGE FOR FIXED-RATE MORTGAGES

T-bill futures are sold to offset the higher cost of the DCs *to be issued* during July, the CDs being the cost of funds t he S and L. Thus, the hedge is executed in order *to avoid higher costs* from the new CDs.

	Cash Liabilities	Futures
Jan. 15	Current cost: ₹ 30 crore 90-day CDs at 7-3/4%	Sell to hedge cost of new CDs in April: 30 Sept. T-bill futures at 92.60, or 7.40%
April 15	CD's issued: $300MM 90-days CDs at 11-3/4%	Buy back futures: 30 Sept. T-bill futures at 88.90, or 11.10%
Net (three months)	(₹ 30 crore) (4%) (¼ year) = − ₹ 3 crore	(30) futures) 3790 basis points) (₹ 2.50 per basis point) = + ₹ 27,75,000

Net loss with hedge: ₹ 2,25,000

Net loss without hedge: ₹ 30,00,000

The net loss shows the *higher cost of funding* for the financial institution. Note that the hedge given here offsets the higher CD cost for only one quarter, since the T-bill futures are 90-day instruments and a one-to-one hedge between the cash CDs and the T-bill futures is executed. Also, the hedge is not perfect: the cost on the CDs increases more than does the T-bill futures rate, creating a new loss of ₹ 2,25,000 on the combined net position; *however*, this loss is significantly less than the ₹ 30,00,000 that would occur without any hedge.

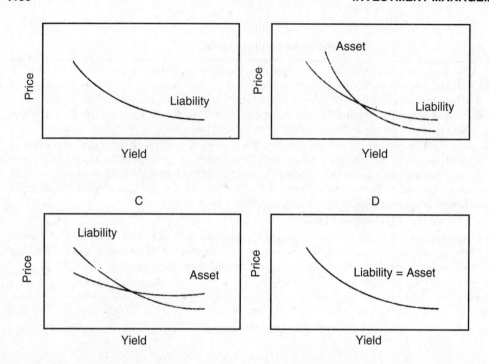

FIGURE 1: INTEREST RATE SENSITIVITY OF ASSETS AND LIABILITIES

Whether it is the problem of hedging the holding period return of a bond or a dedication of assets and liability portfolios, interest rate sensitivity of asset and liability present values (or their market prices) plays a key role in the solution. To amplify this point, let us consider a liability with the price-yield relationship depicted in Panel A of Figure 1. Suppose we wish to hedge this liability with an asset such that the net position is equal to zero. Panels B, C, and D show the price-yield relationship of three different assets. At current interest rates, the market value of the asset is exactly equal to the market value of the liability. Therefore, the position holder is solvent in all the three cases, but only if yield do not change.

To show the effect of changes in interest rates, consider the asset shown in Panel B. At lower yields, the value of the asset is higher than the value of the liability. Therefore, the position holder would be solvent if interest rates were to fall over time. However, the position holder would be insolvent if interest rates were to rise, since the value of the liability would be greater than that of the asset. Panel C shows the case where he reverse holds true. Panel D depicts the case where the position holder will be solvent with respect to all changes in yields.

The motivation to hedge against unexpected changes in interest rates can, in general, arise for two distinct reasons: (1) The desire by investors in fixed-income securities to guarantee holding period returns; and (2) the need for portfolio managers to create dedicated bond portfolios to fulfill specific liabilities over time.

Coupon bonds or series of cash flows are characterised by complex holding period returns. For example, an investor wishing to invest for a period of five years in a coupon-bearing bond yielding 10 per cent cannot be sure of the return over the entire holding period as changes in interest rates result in changes in reinvestment rates. The solution to the holding period return Problem is to invest in a zero coupon bond. Figure 2 depicts the cash flow profiles of five-year zero coupon and coupon-bearing bonds. If the zero coupon bond is held to maturity, the investment return is hedged against all changes in interest rates over the investment horizon. Since there are no cash flows before maturity, a zero coupon bond is not subject to reinvestment risk. In other words, the promised yield, in this case, equals the realise yield.

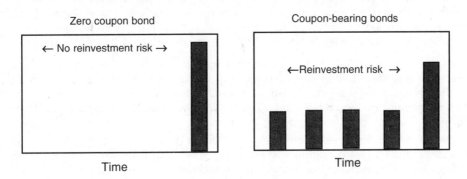

FIGURE 2: ZERO COUPON VERSUS COUPON BOND—CASH FLOWS

Under a coupon-bearing bond, each coupon received is subject to reinvestment risk for the residual life of the bond. The realised yield, in this case, may not equal the promised yield. Since zero coupon bonds are still in relative short supply, investors have to use coupon bonds frequently. However, investors wishing to hedge their holding period returns can use coupon bonds to mimic zero coupon bonds using techniques based on asset sensitivities.

The second motivation to hedge against unexpected changes in interest rates arises from bond portfolio managers' (and indeed banks' and thrifts') desire to create dedicated asset and liability portfolios. For pension funds and insurance companies, this requirement amounts to maintaining their solvency over time. Consider an insurance company with a known stream of nominal liabilities. The problem is to fund these liabilities such that they can be met regardless of subsequent interest rate changes. An obvious way to solve this problem is to purchase assets whose cash flows exactly match those of liabilities. This approach to cash flow dedication is very inflexible and is not always achievable. Even when cash flow dedication is possible, the cost of achieving it may be prohibitive. The solution to this problem depends on the sensitivity of asset and liability present values.

An Inventory Hedge

A dealer is a market maker for an asset or instrument that does not trade on an exchange. The dealer holds inventory of the asset in order to transact trades. For example, bond and currency markets are dealer markets. These dealers trade crore of rupees in government and corporate bonds and foreign currencies each day. An *inventory hedge* occurs when market makers use futures contracts to lock-in the value of their inventory until the market makers can sell the inventory. On occasion, dealers also lock-in the price of assets about to be obtained, especially when bond dealers bid for a new issue of government bonds. Bond and currency dealers routinely use the futures markets to control their risk exposure.

TABLE 8

A Dealer's Inventory Hedge: The IBM Underwriting

In October 1979, IBM offered $1 billion of notes and bonds to the financial market, the largest offering in U.S. corporate history. Solomon Brothers and Merrill Lynch were comanagers of the underwriting, heading a group of 227 members. The underwriters commission on the notes was 5/8% and the bonds provided 7.8%; the spread above the government notes and bonds was only 7 and 12 basis points, respectively. Given that the prime rate had increased five times during the previous month, the commission rate and spread were minimal given the risk being undertaken by the underwriters. The sale began on Thursday, October 4, the same day a Treasury auction took place.

On Saturday, October 6, the Fed announced its famous dictum that it was changing its policy from controlling interest rates to controlling the money supply in order to reduce the rate of inflation. That day the Fed increased the discount rate from 11% to 12%. By October 9 the prime rate had increased one percentage point to 14.5%. By October, 10 the IBM note yield had increased from 9.62% to 10.65% and the bond yield had increased from 9.41% to 10.09%.

When the underwriting syndicate was disbanded on Wednesday, October 10, approximately $650 million of the $ 1 billion offering had been sold, generating $ 5 million in fees. However, the subsequent loss on the remaining $350 million in unsold notes and bonds was $15 million.

The potential loss on the inventory of bonds from the dramatic increase in interest rates was significantly higher than the underwriting commissions on these issues. Solomon Brothers, which took $125 million of the unsold issue, had hedged its inventory position in the futures market by selling T-bond futures. This hedge undoubtedly allowed Solomon to save a significant portion of its revenues from the underwriting. Since this historic underwriting, dealers in bond issues have routinely hedged their inventory position by employing the T-bond and T-note futures markets.

Although the concept and setup for this type of a hedge is equivalent to the portfolio hedge, the motivation differs. Both the portfolio manager and the dealer execute a hedge in order to reduce the price variability of the assets they are holding. However, the portfolio manager could simply sell the cash asset although the dealer *must* keep the current cash inventory in order to transact business. Hence, the money manager completes the portfolio hedge because futures provide important advantages over simply selling the cash asset, including lower transactions costs and greater liquidity; however, a dealer's futures hedge is used to avoid the problems associated with covering an inventory position in the cash market. In particular, covering an inventory position by short selling a similar cash asset can be difficult to execute, and can be very costly or impossible because of the size of the dealer's position. Alternatively, if the dealer is long on some cash assets and short on others (for example, different bond maturities), then the dealer is naturally hedged for part of the inventory. Table-8 shows the classic inventory hedge of the IBM sale of $1 billion of bonds during October 1979; in this case, where the dealer avoided a significant loss by hedging.

REVIEW PROBLEMS

1. It is February 15 and a company expects to borrow ₹ 20 crore for 3 month on April 15. The spot three-month interest rats is 12 p.a., the June three-month rupee futures price is 88, the coefficient of correlation between three-months interest rate changes and changes in the prices of futures maturing 2 months later is 0.95, the standard deviation of spot 3-month interest rate changes is 2, whereas the standard deviation of 3-month interest rate futures prices is 2.5 (for futures maturing in 2 months' time).
   Design a hedge. What sources of possible hedge imperfections are present?

Ans:

The basic hedge would involve dividing the exposure by the size of the futures contract and selling the resulting number of futures contracts:

₹ 20 crore/₹ 0.5 crore = 40 contracts

This number needs to be adjusted for relative volatility:

$$40 \times \text{correlation coefficient} \times \frac{\text{S. D of spot rate}}{\text{S. D of futures prices}}$$

$40 \times 0.95 \times (2/2.5) = 30.4$ contracts.

This number should either be tailed or adjusted for variation margin leverage. If the latter approach is taken, then the previous number of contracts is reduced to

$30.4 \times (1/1.03) \times (1.01)$

Where 1/1.03 offsets interest on variation margin for the 3 month beginning 15 April and 1/1.01 offsets interest on variation margin prior to April 15 (making the simplifying assumption of a constant rate of receipt or payment of variation margin). The hedge would initially sell either futures contracts.

Source of hedge imperfections include basis risk, the possible unrealiability of historical statistics as guides to futures correlation and standard deviations, the inability to trade fraction of contracts, change in interest rates and the uncertainty as to the timing of variation cash flows. Tailing is more accurate than using variation margin leverage.

2. (a) A finance manager needs to borrow ₹ 10 crore for 3 months. It is May 20 and the money is to be borrowed on August 1. How can the finance manager hedge against a rise in interest rates using futures? (Assume ₹ 25 per index point).

    (b) If eurodollar interest rates rise from 6 p.a. to 7% p.a. between May 20 and August 1, what is the loss? If futures prices fell from 93.80 to 92.90 during the same period, how much futures profit would there be from the hedging strategy adopted in part (a)?

    (c) How would the answers to (a) and (b) change if the money was to be borrowed for a year?

Ans:

(a) Sell September 10 eurodollar interest rate futures contracts.

(b) (i) 1% on ₹ 10 crore over 3 months $0.01 \times ₹ 10$ crore $\times 0.25 = ₹ 2,50,000$

    (ii) 90 ticks profit on each of 10 futures contracts at ₹ 25 per tick
          $90 \times 10 \times ₹ 25 = ₹ 22,500$

(c) The best hedge would be a strip hedge involving September 10, December 10, March 10 and June 10 futures contracts. The loss due to the interest rate rise would be 4 times as much, i.e. ₹ 10,00,000. If all futures prices fell by 90 ticks, then the total profit from the futures would be ₹ 22,500 $\times 4 = ₹ 90,000$.

3. An investor has the following portfolio:

	Number of Shares	Share Price (₹)	Share Beta
Andhra Auto	10,000	30	0.9
Bombay Cement	15,000	12	1.2
Calcutta Cotton	12,000	25	1.5
Delhi Tax	20,000	40	0.6

It is 15th February and the March ABC 100 future price is ₹ 300.
- (a) How can the investor hedge the portfolio, with futures? (Assume ₹ 25 per index point).
- (b) What factors might reduce the effectiveness of the measures taken in (a)?

Ans:

Calculate the market exposure of the portfolio by summing the market exposures of individend stocks (market exposure = number of shares × share price × beta):

$$10,000 \times ₹ 30 \times 0.9 = ₹ 2,70,000$$
$$15,000 \times ₹ 12 \times 1.2 = ₹ 2,16,000$$
$$12,000 \times ₹ 25 \times 1.5 = ₹ 4,50,000$$
$$20,000 \times ₹ 40 \times 0.6 = ₹ 4,80,000$$

_____

₹ 14,16,000

_____

The Total market exposure in ₹ 14,16,000. The market exposure provided by one future contract is:

$$300 \times ₹ 25 = ₹ 7,500$$

Hedging the portfolio with futures would involve selling:

₹ 14,16,000 / ₹ 7, 500

= 18.88 contracts.

Since futures contracts are indivisible, this would indicate 18 contracts.

- (b) Factors that could reduce hedge effectiveness include basis risk, the indivisibility of contracts, instability of beta and the presence of firm - or sector - specific risk (i.e. non-systematic risk).
- 4. (a) A finance manager needs to borrow ₹ 4 Crore for 3 month. It is May 20 and the money is to be borrowed on August 1. How can the finance manager hedge against a rise in interest rates using futures?
  - (b) If euro-dollar interest rates rise from 6% p.a. to 7% p.a. between May 20 and August, what is the loss? If futures prices fell from 93.80 to 92.90 during the same period, how much futures profit would there be from the hedging strategy adopted in part (a)? (Assume ₹ 25 per index point).

Ans.:

- (a) Sell September 10 euro-dollar interest rate futures contracts.
- (b) (i) 1% on ₹ 4 crore over 3 months.
  $$0.01 \times ₹ 4,00,00,000 \times 0.25 = ₹ 1,00,000.$$
- (ii) 90 ticks profit on each of 10 futures contracts at ₹ 25 per tick:
  $$90 \times 10 \times ₹ 25 = ₹ 22,500.$$

QUESTIONS

1. Explain the difference between hedging and speculation. Give an example of a short hedger and a long hedger.
2. Why does hedging an equity portfolio using stock index futures work best if the portfolio being hedged is very similar to the underlying stock index of the futures contract?
3. How would you determine the minimum variance hedge ratio?
4. How would a bond portfolio manager deal with the data requirements needed to hedge a portfolio of 50 to 100 separate bonds? How can a regression be used to establish the hedge that has just been issued with a historically unusual coupon rate or

maturity? How can regression be conveniently performed for multiple bond portfolios? How can we rely upon them if an unusual new issue should become the cheapest-to-deliver security for existing futures contracts?

5. Discuss the hedging possibilities in the floatation of debt securities.

6. How would you determine the exposure of the cash position to potential losses?

REFERENCES

1. Andersen, L., J. Sidenius, and S. Basu, "All Your Hedges in One Basket," *Risk*, November 2003.

2. Blume, Marshall E. "On the Assessment of Risk." *The Journal of Finance* XXVI (March 1971), pp. 1-10.

3. Boyle, Phelim P., and Stuart M. Turnbull. "Pricing and Hedging Capped Options." *Journal of Futures Markets 9, no.* 1 (1989).

4. Das, S., *Credit Derivatives: Trading & Management of Credit & Default Risk*, 3rd edn. New York: Wiley, 2005.

5. Hull, J.C., and A. White, "Valuation of a CDO and nth to Default Swap without Monte Carlo Simulation," *Journal of Derivatives*, 12, No. 2 (Winter 2004): 8-23.

6. Hull, J.C., and A. White, "Valuing Credit Derivatives Using an Implied Copula Approach," *Journal of Derivatives*, 14, 2 (Winter 2006), 8-28.

7. Kawaller, I.G., and P.D. Koch. "Meeting the Highly Effective Expectation Criterion for Hedge Accounting," *Journal of Derivatives*, 7, 4 (Summer 2000): 79-87.

8. Laurent, J.-P., and J. Gregory, "Basket Default Swaps, CDOs and Factor Copulas," *Journal of Risk, 1, 4* (2005), 8-23.

9. Perold, Andre, and Evan Schulman: "The Free Lunch in Currency Hedging: Implications for In-vestment Policy and Performance Standards," *Financial Analysts Journal*, May-June 1988. pp. 45-52.

10. Taleb, N.N., *Dynamic Hedging: Managing Vanilla and Exotic Options*. New York: Wiley, 1996.

11. Thomas, Lee: "The Performance of Currency-Hedged Foreign Bonds." *Financial Analysts Journal*, May-June 1989, pp. 25-31.

12. Thomas, Lee: "The Performance of Currency-Hedged Foreign Bonds." *Financial Analysts Journal*, May-June 1989, pp. 25-31.

40

Derivatives: Carry Trades and Speculative Dynamics

INTRODUCTION

The increased degree of financial market integration across various segments of the market as well as countries has made it is easier for contagion of crisis to crisis to travel from one part of the world to the other in a quick manner. This has enhanced the vulnerability of financial systems globally and calls for additional vigilance by financial sector regulators and supervisors in the movement of international finance. A major development engaging attention all over the globe in the recent period has been the turmoil in financial markets in the United States and Europe and the sudden plunge in credit market confidence triggered by the US sub-prime mortgage crisis. The key elements of the current crisis have been the complex nature of the derivatives used; the high degree of leveraging; the underestimation of risk pervading financial markets; the surprisingly sizeable exposures of large financial institutions to some of the debt instruments and derivatives in question; and the speed of contagion. The chapter discusses the financial innovations in the turmoiled financial scenario and the regulatory framework to check the speculative investment strategies in the integrating global financial markets.

ECONOMIC DERIVATIVES

Economic derivatives are financial contracts that allow market participants to take positions on macroeconomic data releases. They are different from the "macro securities", which are meant to insure households and corporations against changes in macroeconomic conditions that may affect their livelihood. By contrast, the economic derivatives focus on short-term data surprises.

Macroeconomic data announcements play an important role in price discovery in financial markets. They are usually scheduled regularly, with a precise date and timing that are known well in advance. The importance of data announcements is underscored by the fact that volatility tends to be markedly higher on release days than on other days. Higher volatility than usual is also observed for a whole range of other financial instruments. Prices move primarily in intervals of just a few minutes around the announcements, reflecting market participants' forceful and instantaneous reaction to the new information.

What are Economic Derivatives?

Economic derivatives are financial instruments which allow traders to take positions directly on the outcome of macroeconomic data releases. Unlike conventional financial instruments, economic derivatives separate the surprise component of announcements (the difference between the outcome and the prior expectation by market participants) from the channel through which such news is transmitted to asset prices.

Economic derivatives were introduced in October 2002 by Deutsche Bank and Goldman Sachs, first on US non-farm payrolls (NFPs) and subsequently also on other releases such as the ISM manufacturing index, US initial jobless claims and retail sales, the euro area harmonised index of consumer prices, and US GDP and international trade balance data. They were initially traded over the counter in Dutch auctions (also known as uniform price auctions), with Goldman Sachs acting as the counterparty. Auctions were subsequently moved to the Chicago Mercantile Exchange (CME) in September 2005, where the clearing house offers the usual services and central counterparty guarantees that are available on an organised exchange.

For each data release, one or more auctions are held, usually on the day of and during the week preceding the announcement. Customers can submit sell and buy offers at a limit price which depends in part on their assessment of the volatility of the underlying macroeconomic data or, in other words, on their estimate that the option will expire in the money. Indicative prices and filled orders are given during the auction, while the final pricing and filled orders are determined at the end of the auction. (Contrary to traditional order-matching systems, where sell orders are matched with buy orders for the same contract, digital options are traded using a pari-mutuel system similar to the one common in sports betting. Under such a system, the premium collected from the holders of out-of-the-money options is paid out to the holders of in-the-money options. This allows prices to be formed even in the absence of matching buy and sell orders, considering the overall inventory of buy and sell orders as one pool of liquidity.)

The main participants in the market are macro and relative value hedge funds, large banks, dealers, proprietary traders and portfolio managers. They follow strategies similar to those in other markets, including directional and volatility-based trading and relative value strategies. Trading of options can be done individually, or in combinations such as spreads, straddles, strangles and risk reversals.

Motives for Trading Economic Announcements

There are several motives for trading economic derivatives. Some market participants may use them to express a view on the outcome of a specific data release while others may want to hedge against the impact of adverse data surprises on their portfolios.

Speculating on the outcomes of data releases is perhaps the most common motive for trading economic derivatives. Economists working in financial markets spend substantial resources on trying to predict such announcements, so it seems natural that they would like to trade on these predictions. That said, there are alternatives to economic derivatives for taking positions on data releases. Using conventional financial instruments to trade announcement risk may enable traders to access a deeper pool of liquidity than the one available in the market for economic derivatives. On the downside, strategies using other instruments may run into difficulties if payoffs react in a different way than predicted to the outcome of an announcement. Such risk is often referred to as "basis risk".

A measure of the basis risk involved in taking positions on NFPs can be obtained by regressing the return of an instrument on the surprise component of the announcement. For economic derivatives, the basis risk is zero by construction. For other contracts, the amount of basis risk depends on the presence of a stable (or at least predictable) relationship between their prices and the surprise component of announcements, as well as on the absence of price changes because of factors other than NFPs.

The attractiveness of economic derivatives for speculating on data releases does not necessarily imply that they are the most appropriate instrument for hedging the announcement risk of a portfolio. This is because hedgers are much less likely than speculators to be interested in unbundling data surprises from the sensitivity of asset prices to macroeconomic data since they presumably care primarily about how the value of their portfolio is affected by releases rather than about announcements per se.

A limited attractiveness of economic derivatives to hedgers could constrain the growth potential of the market. Hedgers might be willing to lose money on average in a market, due to being less well informed than speculators, in order to obtain protection for other positions in their portfolio. A certain amount of uninformed trading is often necessary to sustain a market. In the absence of significant demand by uninformed agents, trading might also be sustained by differences of opinion between highly sophisticated traders. Such differences of opinion may arise from differences in information (although macroeconomic data tend to be publicly available), but might also result from traders having different ways of processing these data.

In the case of economic derivatives, it is not clear which, if any, of the two explanations – the one based on uninformed trading or the one based on differences in opinion – provides a better characterisation of the motives underlying trading in that market. The limited attractiveness of these instruments for hedgers would suggest a restricted role for informational advantages in the sense that some actors are better informed than others. Similarly, differences of opinion would suggest that trading volumes tend to be high when there is a lot of disagreement, which is at odds with the negative correlation between volumes and the dispersion of analyst expectations in the data. However, this might also be due to the short time span of the data.

Economic Derivatives as Indicators of Market Expectations

The market for economic derivatives is of interest to a much broader audience than the limited group of immediate market participants. This is because the prices of these instruments provide useful information about traders' views of the economy. In addition to obtaining market-based mean expectations of data outturns, under some assumptions it is possible to compute the probability distribution underlying expectations. Such information is not available from analyst surveys, which report the *dispersion* of economists' views about data releases but not the uncertainty surrounding those estimates.

In principle, there are two main reasons to believe that the information contained in the prices of economic derivatives is superior to that from surveys. *First,* it is timelier. Auctions are generally conducted on the day of the release or on the previous day, which contrasts with a lag of one week or longer in the case of surveys. *Second,* trading economic derivatives involves real money and is therefore much less likely to be affected by economists misrepresenting their views in order to position themselves relative to consensus forecasts.

On the other hand, market-based forecasts might be distorted by risk premia or by the limited liquidity of the market. Both premia could introduce a wedge between implied expectations and true expectations of market participants, which would distort any inferences of market participants' expectations from prices. Evidence on the existence of such premia may be obtained by running tests for forecast accuracy. These indicate that we cannot fully rule out their presence since the prices of economic derivatives appear to overpredict outturns on average. Economic derivatives allow market participants to trade directly on macroeconomic data releases and unbundle the news component of announcements from the basis risk contained in financial assets traditionally used as proxies. Policymakers can use the prices of ecnomic derivatives to obtain information on the perceptions of market participants about the state of the economy. In contrast to survey-based measures, they are true density forecasts, covering the whole distribution of the "market's view", not just point estimates. This information could be used to track the uncertainly of market participants about the state of the macroeconomy and to monitor the probabilities they attach to tail events. When interpreting the information contained in the prices of economic derivatives, one has to bear in mind that it refers to market participants' perceptions of the current economic situation and not to their expectations of outcomes further ahead. While this may be a limitation when analysing issues such as the transmission mechanism of monetary policy, it may not matter in other settings. For example, the impact of central bank communications might depend on the views of market participants about the current state of the economy, not just on their expectations for the future. That said, it would be useful to have more forward-looking indicators, eg on inflation and growth in the short and medium term, which could complement the information contained in longer-term instruments such as inflation-linked securities.

The potential size of the market for economic derivatives might be limited. In particular, it is not clear whether the market is able to attract a substantial amount of hedging demand, which could serve as a counterweight to highly sophisticated informed traders. In the absence of hedging activity, it is possible that liquidity may dry up in times of limited disagreement between a relatively small number of informed participants.

CARRY TRADE: A SPECULATIVE INVESTMENT STRATEGY

Carry trades are often viewed as a highly speculative investment strategy, to be tried only by the most sophisticated investor. Empirically, however, these trades have been shown to perform well quite consistently for protracted periods and have thus become a fairly common strategy. Confirming this observation is the fact that market participants have created tradable indices as well as various forms of structured FX instruments referencing carry trade strategies. Infact, low exchange rate volatility and persistent interest rate differentials have underpinned significant cross-currency positioning in recent years. These positions have often taken the form of currency carry trades, or leveraged cross-currency trading strategies.

The effect of carry trade activity on exchange rates is typically asymmetric, and can be significant. The build-up of these positions generally contributes to a steady strengthening of target currencies (associated with high interest rates) and a weakening of funding currencies (associated with low interest rates), against the predictions of the uncovered interest parity (UIP) hypothesis. However, when changes in interest rate expectations or volatility lead to a sudden unwinding of carry trades, there is a tendency for target currencies to depreciate and funding currencies to appreciate sharply. Perhaps the best known example is the sharp appreciation of the yen against the US dollar between 6 and 8 October 1998, following a prolonged period of depreciation. This was the sharpest move in major foreign exchange rates since 1974 and was accompanied by a significant spike in volatility: one-month implied volatility reached 40% and bid-ask spreads widened markedly. Market analysts explained the move in terms of a sudden, massive reversal of carry trade positions, despite the lack of an apparent trigger.

What is a Carry Trade?

A currency carry trade is usually defined as a leveraged cross-currency position designed to take advantage of interest rate differentials and low volatility. The strategy involves borrowing funds at a low interest rate in one currency (the funding currency) and buying a higher-yielding asset in another (the target currency). Ex-ante, the strategy is only profitable as long as the gains from interest rate differentials are not expected to be overwhelmed by exchange rate movements in the short to medium term; that is, UIP is not expected to hold. The use of leverage makes these positions particularly sensitive to changes in exchange rates or interest differentials.

Carry Trades Versus Uncovered Interest Parity

The carry trade strategy involves borrowing in a currency with low interest rates (called the funding currency) and investing in one with high interest rates (the target currency). If the target currency does not depreciate vis-à-vis the funding currency during the life of the investment, then the investor earns at least the interest differential. This strategy does not work if uncovered interest parity (UIP) holds. The UIP condition states that higher-yielding currencies will tend to depreciate against lower-yielding ones at a rate equal to the interest differential so that expected returns are equalised in a given currency. Under UIP, any interest differential is offset by currency movements.

In a large body of empirical literature, however, UIP has been failed almost universally at time horizons shorter than five years. Indeed, in many cases the relationship is precisely the opposite of what is predicted by UIP: currencies with high interest rates tend to appreciate while those with low interest rates depreciate.

UIP fails especially when investors hold instruments with maturities that are longer than the investment horizon. This failure of UIP is so well established that the phenomenon is called the "forward premium puzzle". In a world of risk, UIP is almost certainly false. The condition states that expected returns would be equal regardless of risk. Risks clearly vary across currencies, however, and different risks should command different expected returns.

The failure of UIP has been no secret to participants in currency markets. Indeed, the most popular investment strategy in these markets has been the carry trade, which is essentially a bet against UIP. The strategy has become so commonplace that the market has created tradable benchmarks for them and has introduced structured FX instruments referencing these benchmarks.

MEASURING THE RISK IN CARRY TRADES

Risk Measures

Given the distributions of returns for carry trades, what would be the appropriate measure of risk? Here we consider three possible measures: (1) volatility; (2) value-at-risk (VaR); and (3) expected shortfall. Other downside risk measures one could consider are implied volatilities for deep-out-of-themoney call options and risk reversals. While these measures have the advantage of being forward-looking, they also contain risk premia and are therefore potentially misleading measures of risk. Volatility of returns is the most common measure of risk in financial markets and would be most appropriate for normally distributed returns, or at least symmetric return distributions. VaR may be defined as the capital needed to cover a certain level of losses from a financial instrument over a given holding period and for a given confidence level. It is a standard measure of risk in credit markets, where return distributions feature small probabilities of large losses. Expected shortfall is the potential expected loss in situations where losses exceed a given VaR. Both VaR and expected shortfall are measures that focus on downside risk. However, unlike the VaR measure, expected shortfall is considered to be a coherent measure of risk, that is, it always captures benefits from diversification.

Return in Carry Trades

Given the appropriate risk measure, i.e. assuming that the risk measure is what is used by market participants, expected returns would reflect risk. The higher the risk, the higher the expected return. One way to look at this relationship is to consider the ratio of expected returns to risk. The most common is the Sharpe ratio, which is calculated by adding ex post returns form exchange rate movements to those from interest differentials, subtracting the risk-free rate to obtain excess returns and normalising by historical rather than implied volatility. The inclusion of realised exchange rate movements increases the volatility of this ratio relative to the carry-to-risk ratio. A third measure, the carry return index, cumulates the returns form interest rate differentials and exchange rate movements, but does not adjust by any measure of risk.

Over the longer term however, the attractiveness of carry trades relative to other investments is less clear. Risk reversals—or the price difference between two equivalently out-of-the-money options—potentially provide an alternative market indicator of perceived risks in carry trades. If the risk associated with carry trade returns is not generalised uncertainty about future values of the exchange rates, as the carry-to-risk measure implicitly assumes, but rather directional uncertainty, this will be more effectively captured by risk reversals calculated from out-of-the-money options. In addition, the movements in risk reversals tend to post-date large exchange rate movements in periods of high volatility.

In measures that focus on downside risk, however, the pattern of risk-return trade-offs looks different. In the case of both VaR and expected shortfall, the absolute differences between carry trade and equity market strategies, in terms of compensation received per unit of risk, have narrowed considerably (although they remain quite large). More importantly, the differences between carry trades are smaller. This implies that the compensation received per unit of downside risk is similar across carry trade strategies. While this does not show either VaR or expected shortfall to be the better measure of downside risk, the relative uniformity of risk-return ratios across currency pairs for either risk measure suggests that returns for carry trade strategies may be closely aligned to downside risks.

Strategy and Participatns

There are a variety of ways to implement carry trades, each with different implications for what can be traced in different data sources. The simplest approach, which is particularly relevant for investing in emerging market assets, involves exchanging borrowed funds into the target currency in the spot market. The target currency can be held in some short-term asset (such as a bank deposit or short-term government paper) until maturity. Another approach relies on derivative contracts, including foreign exchange futures, forwards and interest rate swaps as well as more complex options. In addition, these strategies are likely to generate hedging activity, which might lead to more trades in the cash or derivatives markets.

These strategies can be implemented with varying degrees of complexity. For example, sophisticated algorithms can be used to decide when to open and close carry trade positions, as opposed to a simple buy and hold strategy. This allows investors to exploit high-frequency movements in exchange rates or interest rate expectations. While this way of implementing carry trades appears to be of secondary importance, it seems to have become more popular in recent years, in line with the growing success of algorithmic trading in foreign exchange markets.

Traditionally, carry trades are used by large financial institutions, such as hedge funds and commodity trading advisors (CTAs). More recently, there has been an increase in the presence of retail investors using margin accounts to take leveraged positions across currencies. For example, data from Gaitame, one provider of foreign exchange margin trading facilities for Japanese retail investors, indicate that the number of accounts it manages increase from less than 2,000 at the beginning of 2003 to almost 120,000 in June 2007, with deposits worth almost 90 billion yen ($0.7 billion). Although the size of these investors in aggregate is still relatively small and the degree of leverage is not likely to be as significant as it is for large financial institutions, their activities have been cited in market commentary as a factor influencing the yen exchange rate over the past year.

It is useful to distinguish the leveraged carry trades from two other investment strategies which are also designed to exploit interest rate differentials. One such strategy involves domestic retail investors trying to diversify their portfolio by purchasing higher-yielding assets denominated in a foreign currency. A second strategy involves households borrowing in lower-yielding foreign currencies to finance purchases of domestic assets. However, unlike the leveraged carry trades of larger institutions, these types of foreign currency exposures are less likely to be unwound quickly in the event of market turbulence.

Tracking Activity

Data on foreign exchange trading can be useful to track the carry trade positions since carry trade activity leaves footprints in the data on futures positions and over-the-counter (OTC) transactions in the spot, swap or forward markets. The effect of carry trade activity on banks' balance sheets will depend on the structure of the trade and the role of the bank in the transaction. Banks can serve as primary market intermediaries, providing loans in the funding currencies and taking deposits in the target currencies used by carry trade investors. At the same time, banks may themselves (via their proprietary trading desks) take outright carry trade positions, possibly generating a rise in liabilities denominated in the funding currencies and in assets denominated in the target currencies. Finally, banks may serve as counterparties in derivatives transactions with carry trade investors, which may or may not appear on balance sheet.

International banking statistics can help to highlight activity which may be linked to carry trades, and to investigate more broadly the flow of capital through the international banking system denominated in the main carry trade funding and target currencies. Although they are one of the few sources of bilateral capital flow data available by currency on a globally consistent basis, these statistics are far from ideal for tracking carry trade activity. *First,* banks report only their on-balance sheet positions. Thus, at best, the statistics will capture carry trade activity executed in the cash markets, or possibly secondary ripples in the cash markets caused by underlying activity in the derivatives markets. Leveraged accounts may rely on instruments like forwards, which do not appear on balance sheet. *Second,* the data do not explicitly distinguish between carry trade positions and other positions, which can reflect other corporate, household or interbank lending and borrowing. *Finally,* the balance sheet implications of carry trades will depend on the type of trade and the role of the bank in the transaction; only the overall net effect of the on-balance sheet components will be evident in the data, making it difficult to explicitly identify activity.

OTC DERIVATIVES

Most foreign exchange trading is done over the counter (OTC) in the form of spot and swap transactions (OTC) derivatives markets have grown rapidly in terms of both size and complexity since 1995. Daily turnover in OTC foreign exchange and interest rate contracts increased from $0.9 trillion in April 1995 to over $4 trillion in April 2007.

Notional amounts outstanding of OTC derivatives of all types increased more than tenfold between 1995 and 2007, to $500 trillion at the end of June 2007, which corresponds to an average rate of growth of over 20% per year. While most of this growth was driven by increasing volumes in fairly standardised ("plain vanilla") contracts, there has also been a proliferation of new products, some of which are highly complex.

The increase in size and complexity of the OTC derivatives markets naturally raises the issue of whether the risks emanating from such contracts are being properly managed. One area which has repeatedly given cause for concern is the post-trading infrastructure of the market, which has often not matched the rise in volumes and the continued development of new and increasingly complex products. The most visible indicator of deficiencies in post-trading processes has been the backlog in trades pending confirmation.

Characteristics of OTC Derivatives and Implications for Post-Trade Processing

OTC derivatives have a number of characteristics that have important implications for post-trade processing. *First,* while OTC transactions may take place on multilateral trading platforms, clearing and settlement is by its very nature bilateral. Information on each trade is often not stored centrally, as in the books of an exchange, but separately at each of the counterparties. Ensuring that this information is consistent is a major challenge. *Second,* OTC derivatives are bilateral contracts, not assets that can be traded freely. Contracts with different counterparties are usually not fungible, which makes it difficult for traders to close positions. One way to circumvent this problem, the novation of trades to another party, was a major factor behind the confirmation backlo. *Novation refers to the replacement of contracts between two initial counterparties with a contract between the remaining party and a third party (the transferee). It is also referred to as assignment or give-up.*

Third, contracts often have long maturities, and counterparties remain exposed to each other until the contract expires. The market for interest rate swaps in the major currencies is reported to be liquid for maturities of up to 30 years, but longer-dated contracts are not unheard of. This makes counterparty risk a much greater concern in OTC derivatives markets than in securities markets. Market participants have developed a variety of measures to handle counterparty risk, for example collateral arrangements, which add to the complexity of post-trade processing.

Fourth, OTC derivatives contracts may themselves be very complex, involving repeated, often state-contingent, payments. Payments that depend on the prices of other assets, possibly in non-linear ways. Furthermore, many contracts are non-standard, often tailored to the needs of a specific customer, which is reflected in the fact that templates for defining OTC derivatives may require up to 10,000 fields in order to be able to handle different contract specifications. By contrast, the templates used to define a typical securities transaction require only half a dozen fields.

Managing Flows of Information

After a deal has been concluded, information on the precise conditions of the contract needs to flow within the firm, from the front office to the middle and back offices, and between counterparties. Errors made during this process, in particular those resulting in discrepancies in the information stored at different counterparties, can result in so-called payment or collateral breaks, when the payments or collateral transfers made by one party do not coincide with those expected by the other party. Even if these breaks are resolved quickly, they do add to the burden of already strained back offices.

Several steps are necessary to capture and confirm trades (see Figure 1). *First,* the details of the trade have to be entered ("captured") into each counterparty's internal system in order to be passed on to the middle and back offices for processing. This is usually done automatically for trades that were executed electronically, but may involve a substantial amount of paperwork for transactions negotiated over the phone.

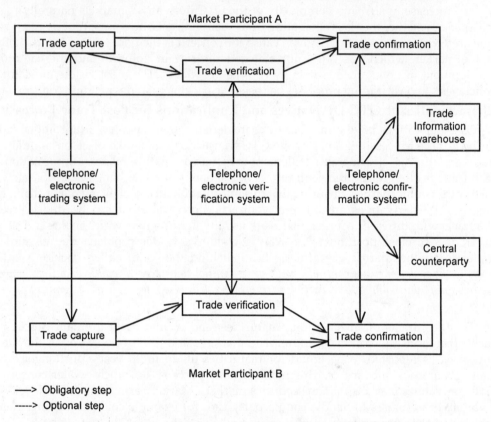

FIGURE 1: FLOWS OF INFORMATION IN OTC DERIVATIVES TRANSACTION

After the trade has been captured, counterparties exchange information on the terms of the trade in order to weed out any discrepancies that could result in payment or collateral breaks at a later point in time. This step is called "confirmation". A confirmation describes all the details of the trade and refers to the master agreement, which sets out the general terms and conditions related to OTC derivatives trades between these two counterparties. A confirmation proposal may either be prepared by both counterparties and then matched (most common for inter-dealer trades), or prepared by only one and affirmed by the other (for trades with investing institutions such as hedge funds). Once counterparties agree on the content of the confirmation, it will serve as the final record of the trade.

Since the confirmation process may take some time, in particular for more complex contracts, some counterparties exchange information on the major terms of the trade before preparing a full confirmation document ("trade verification", also referred to as "economic affirmation"). As with trade capture, the verification and confirmation processes may involve a substantial amount of manual intervention, in particular for trades executed over the phone.

QUESTIONS

1. What are economic derivatives? Can economic derivatives be used as indicators of market expectations? What are the motives for trading economic derivatives?
2. What is a carry trade? Discuss the characteristics of carry trade indices.
3. Critically examine the various approaches to implement carry trades.
4. Given the distribution of returns for carry trades, what would be the appropriate measure of risk?
5. Critically examine the characteristics of OTC derivatives that have important implications for post-trade processing.

REFERENCES

1. Ansbacher, Max G. *The New Options Market*. New York: Walker, 1979, revised edition.
2. Black, Fisher. "Fact and Fantasy in the Use of Options." *Financial Analysts Journal*, July-August 1975, pp. 36-41.
3. Blume, Marshall E. "On the Assessment of Risk." *The Journal of Finance* XXVI (March 1971), pp. 1-10.
4. Boyle, Phelim P., and Stuart M. Turnbull. "Pricing and Hedging Capped Options." *Journal of Futures Markets 9, no.* 1 (1989).
5. Brennan, M.J., and E.S. Schwartz. "The Valuation of American Put Options," *Journal of Finance*. May 1977.
6. Clasing, Henry, *The Dow Jones-Irwin Guide to Put and Call Options* (Homewood, III .: Dow Jones-Irwin, 1975).
7. Cunnion, J.D. *How to Get Maximum Leverage from Puts and Calls*. Larchmont, N.Y.: Business Reports, Inc., 1966.
8. Dimson, Elroy. "Instant Option Valuation" *Financial Analysts Journal*, May-June, 1977.
9. Dowd, K. *Beyond Value at Risk: The New Science of Risk Management*. New York: Wiley, 1998.
10. Duffie, D., and J. Pan. "An Overview of Value at Risk," *Journal of Derivatives*, 4, 3 (Spring 1997): 7-49.
11. Engle, R.F. "Autoregressive Conditional Heteroscedasticity with Estimates of the Variance of UK Inflation," *Econometrica* 50 (1982): 987-1008.
12. Galai. Dan. "Tests of Market Efficiency of the Chicago Board Options Exchange," The *Journal of Business*. April 1977, pp. 167-197.
13. Hettenhouse, George W., and Donald J. Puglisi, "Investor Experience with Put and Call Options." *Financial Analysts Journal* 31. no. 4 (July-August 1975): 53-58.
14. Hull, John. *Options, Futures and Other Derivative Securities*. Englewood Cliffs, N.J.: Prentice-Hall, 1989.
15. Jorion, P. *Big Bets Gone Bad: Derivatives and Bankruptcy in Orange County*. New York: Academic Press, 1995.
16. Katz, Richard. "The Profitability of Put and Call Option Writing," *Industrial Management Review:* Fall 1963, pp. 55-69.
17. Manaster, Steven, and Richard Rendleman, Jr. "Option Prices as Predictors of Equilibrium Stock Prices." *The Journal of Finance* 37, no. 4 (September 1982).
18. Miller, M.H. "Financial Innovation: Achievements and Prospects," *Journal of Applied Corporate Finance, 4* (Winter 1992): 4-11.
19. Nelson, D. "Conditional Heteroscedasticity and Asset Returns: A New Approach," *Econometrica,* 59 (1990): 347-70.
20. Phillips. Susan M., and Clifford W. Smith, Jr. "Trading Costs for Listed Options: The Implications for Market Efficiency." *Journal of Financial Economics* 8, no. 2 (June 1980).
21. Ritchken, Peter. *Options: Theory, Strategy and Applications*. Glenview, III.: Scott-Foresman, 1987.
22. Stoll, Hans R., and Robert E. Whaley. *Futures and Options: Theory and Application*. Cincinnati: South-western Publishing, 1993.

41

Financial Derivatives Market in India

INTRODUCTION

Complex links among financial market participants and institutions are a hallmark of the modern global financial system. Across geographic and market boundaries, agents within the financial system engage in a diverse array of transactions and relationships that connect them to other participants. Indeed, much of the financial innovation that preceded the most recent financial crisis increased both the number and types of connections that linked borrowers and lenders in the economy. The rapid growth in securitization and derivatives markets prior to the crisis provides a stark example of this phenomenon. It is generally believed that the opacity of the derivatives market contributed to the seizure of the financial markets and spread of the financial crisis. Four years after the global financial crisis, the world economy is still struggling to achieve sustained expansion amid major demised risks. Among the measures being discussed world wide to prevent the recurrence of a similar crisis, or, at least to contain the fallout, putting in place an adequately post-trading infrastructure figure prominently. The chapter is to address efforts and experience in relation to derivative trades, structure and regulatory framework and the generic financial innovations proxied by three derivative instruments, giz., Interest Rate Swaps (IRS), Credit Default Swap (CDS) and Interest Rate Futures (IRF).

STRUCTURE OF DERIVATIVES MARKET IN INDIA

The presence and role of derivatives in India, both over-the-counter (OTC) and exchange-traded, has been increasing steadily over the years. These instruments are an important component of the overall financial sector strategy and the broad regulatory objective is to ensure that they are used to their potential in ways that are consistent with both financial development and the contribution of financial markets to economic growth. As instruments for transfer and dispersal of risk. derivatives facilitate socially useful but risky projects, which would not be undertaken in the absence of such risk management framework. Derivatives may either be standard or customized according to the needs of the participants. While the standardized products mostly trade on exchanges, the customized products are traded over the counter (See Box-1). Major exchanges world over have adopt electronic trading platforms that use order-matching technologies to execute trades in a multilateral environment. Trades on exchanges are characterized by anonymity with the exchange clearing house interposing itself as the central counterparty (CCP) along with associated settlement and risk management protocol.

Box-1

EXCHANGE-TRADED *VS.* OTC MARKET

The recent developments in information technology have contributed to the sharp growth in the OTC derivatives markets, over the last few years, accompanied by the modernisation of commercial and investment banking and the globalisation of financial activites. While both exchange-traded and OTC derivative contracts offer many benefits, the former have rigid structures compared with the latter. The episodes of turbulence in financial markets in 1998 revealed the risks posed to market stability originating in features of OTC derivative instruments and markets.

The OTC derivatives markets have the following features, compared to exchange-traded derivatives:

1. The management of counter-party (credit) risk is decentralised and located within individual institutions;

2. There are no formal centralised limits on individual positions, leverage, or margining;

3. There are no formal rules for risk and burden-sharing;

4. There are no formal rules or mechanisms for ensuring market stability and integrity, and for safeguarding the collective interests of market participants; and

5. The OTC contracts are generally not regulated by both a regulatory authority and the exchange's self-regulatory organisation, although they are affected indirectly by national legal systems, banking supervision and market surveillance.

OTC derivative markets in India have a long history, though, in an organised manner, exchange traded derivatives take precedence in time. Commodity derivatives in the form of futures in few select commodities date back to the late nineteenth century. After the government ban on options and cash settlement in futures in 1952, the activity in the commodities market moved to informal forward segment. Futures' trading in several commodities started after the ban was lifted in 2000 and commodity futures exchanges with electronic trading platforms were established. As far as equities are concerned, some form of OTC derivative trading was prevalent in India in the pre-independence days. The Securities Contract Regulation Act, 1956 banned all kinds of derivative trading in equities and it was only in 1999 after the recommendations of two influential committees headed by Shri L.C. Gupta and Shri J.R. Varma that a basis was created for amendment to the said Act. SEBI approved derivatives trading based on Futures Contracts at both BSE and NSE in accordance with the rules/byelaws and regulations of the Stock Exchanges in June 2000. A beginning with equity derivatives has been made with the introduction of stock index futures by BSE and NSE. Stock Index Futures contract allows for the buying and selling of the particular stock index for a specified price at a specified future date. Stock Index Futures, *inter alia*, help in overcoming the problem of asymmetries in information. Information asymmetry is mainly a problem in individual stocks as it is unlkely that a trader has market-wide private information. As such, the asymmetric information component is not likely to be present in a basket of stocks. This provides another rationale for trading in Stock Index Futures. Also, trading in index derivatives involves low transaction cost in comparison with trading in underlying individual stocks comprising the index. While the BSE introduced Stock Index Futures for S&P CNX Nifty comprising 50 scrips. Stock Index Futures in India are available with one month, two month and three month maturities. While derivatives trading based on the Sensitive Index (Sensex) commenced at the BSE on June 9, 2000, derivatives trading based on S&P CNX Nifty commenced at the NSE on June 12, 2000. SIF is the first attempt in the development of derivatives trading. The product base has been increased to include trading in futures and options on S&P CNX Nifty Index, futures and options on CNX IT index, Bank Nifty Index and single securities (118 stock as stipulated by SEBI) and futures on interest rate.

The index futures and index options contracts traded on NSE are based on S&P CNX Nifty Index, CNX IT Index and the CNX Bank Index, while stock futures and options are based on individual securities. Stock Futures and Options are available on 118 securities. Interest rate future contracts are available on Notional 91 day t-bill and Notional 10 year bonds (6% coupon bearing and zero coupon bond). While the index options are European style, stock options arc American style.

At any point of time there are only three contract months available for trading, with 1 month, 2 months and 3 months to expiry. These contracts expire on last Thursday of the expiry month and have a maximum of 3-month expiration cycle. A new contract is introduced on the next trading day following the expiry of the near month contract. All the derivatives contracts are presently cash settled.

The turnover in the derivatives segment has witnessed considerable growth since inception. In the global market, NSE ranks first (1st) in terms of number of contracts traded in the Single Stock Futures, second (2nd) in Asia in terms of number of contracts traded in equity derivatives instrument. Since inception, NSE established itself as the sole market leader in this segment in the country with more than 99.5% market share.

THE REGULATORY FRAMEWORK

Though the statutes do not define over-the-counter derivatives as such, derivatives have been defined in three separate legislations. The Securities Contract Regulation Act, 1956 (through the Securities Laws (Second Amendment) Act,1999), Section 2 (ac) defines a derivative as

> "(A) a security derived from a debt instrument, share, loan, whether secured or unsecured, risk instrument or contract for differences or any other form of security.
> (B) a contract which derives its value from the prices, or index of prices, of underlying securities."

The Forward Contracts (Regulation) Act, 1952, does not define the term derivatives but specific contracts 'forwards' and 'options' (Section 2(c) and Section 2 (g)) as under:

> "'forward contract' means a contract for the delivery of goods and which is not a ready delivery contract"
> "'option in goods' means an agreement, by whatever name called, for the purchase or sale of a right to buy or sell, or a right to buy and sell, goods in future, and includes a teji, a mandi, a teji-mandi, a galli, a put, a call or a put and call in goods"

In the RBI Act, 1934 as amended vide RBI (Amendment) Act 2006, derivatives have been defined in Section 45 (U)(a) as

> "'derivative' means an instrument, to be settled at a future date, whose value is derived from change in interest rate, foreign exchange rate, credit rating or credit index, price of securities (also called 'underlying'), or a combination of more than one of them and includes interest rate swaps, forward rate agreements, foreign currency swaps, foreign currency-rupee swaps, foreign currency options, foreign currency-rupee options or such other instruments as may be specified by the Bank from time to time."

Repurchase agreement or repo, a quasi-derivative instrument comprising a simultaneous spot and forward transaction has been separately defined in Section 45 (U)(c) as

> "'repo' means an instrument for borrowing funds by selling securities with an agreement to repurchase the securities on a mutually agreed future date at an agreed price which includes interest for the funds borrowed."

The RBI Act, 1934, however, makes an exception in so far as its regulatory ambit is concerned with regard to instruments falling under its jurisdiction when they are traded and settled on an exchange (Section 45 W).

"Provided that the directions issued under this sub-section shall not relate to the procedure for execution or settlement of the trades in respect of the transactions mentioned therein, on the Stock Exchanges recognised under section 4 of the Securities Contracts (Regulation) Act, 1956(42 of 1956)."

CLASSIFICATION OF DERIVATIVES

Conventionally, OTC derivative contracts are classified based on the underlying into (a) foreign exchange contracts, (b) interest rate contracts, (c) credit linked contracts, (d) equity linked contracts, and (e) commodity linked contracts. Box-2 depicts the structure of the OTC drivatives market (excluding equity and commonly linked derivatives.

Box-2

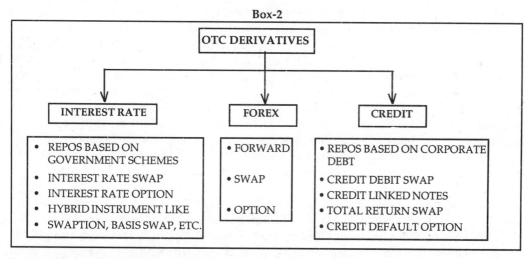

Interest Rate Derivatives in India

The Indian Financial System witnessed wide discussion on the usefulness of derivatives as instruments of risk management in the late 1990's. The origin of recent initiatives for development of derivative market in India can be traced to the L C Gupta Committee (set up by SEBI in November 1996). Though the Committee's main concern was equity based derivatives, it examined the need for financial derivatives in a broader perspective and recommended introduction of interest rate and currency derivatives. The emphasis was on introduction of exchange traded derivatives based on these underlying. It may be recalled that Tarapore Committee on capital account convertibility around the same time had also advocated introduction of currency futures.

Recognising the need for interest rate derivatives in a deregulated interest rate regime, the RBI in 1999 permitted banks, primary dealers (PD) and financial institutions (FI) to undertake transactions in interest rate swaps and forward rate agreements.

A Forward Rate Agreement is (FRA) is a financial contract between two parties to exchange interest payments for a 'notional principal' amount on settlement date, for a specified period from start date to maturity date. An Interest Rate Swap (IRS) is a combination of FRAs in which a fixed interest on a notional principal is exchanged for a floating interest rate equal to the reference rate at periodic intervals over the tenure of the contract.

In the Indian markets, four OTC interest rate products are traded, viz., Overnight Index Swap (OIS) based on overnight MIBOR, a polled rate derived from the overnight unsecured inter-bank market, contracts based on Mumbai Inter-Bank Offered Rate (MIFOR), contracts based on Indian Government Securities Benchmark Rate (INBMK), and contracts based on MIOIS. A typical characteristic of the Indian interest rate market is that unlike in the overseas inter-bank funds markets, there is very little activity in tenors beyond overnight and as such there is no credible interest rate in segments other than overnight. Absence of a liquid 3-month or 6-month funds market has been a hindrance for trading in FRAs as also in swaps based on these benchmarks. Recent emergence of a deep and liquid CD market with significant secondary market trading may perhaps address some of these issues.

In terms of gross notional outstanding, the OIS based on overnight Mumbai Inter-Bank Offered Rate (MIBOR) is the most dominant product traded, accounting for about 90per cent of the outstanding followed by MIFOR which accounts for nearly 10per cent and the remaining two products almost insignificant.

As far as the regulatory regime is concerned, all scheduled commercial banks (SCBs) excluding Regional Rural Banks, primary dealers (PDs) and all-India financial institutions have been allowed to use IRS and FRA for their own balance sheet management as also for the purpose of market making. The non-financial corporations have been allowed to use IRS and FRA to hedge their balance sheet exposures, with a caveat that at least one of the parties in any IRS/FRA transaction should be a RBI regulated entity. In addition to the RBI circular of 1999 which lays down principles for accounting and risk management for positions in IRS/FRA, RBI has, in 2007, released comprehensive guidelines on derivatives comprising general principles for derivatives trading, management of risk and sound corporate governance requirements along with a code of conduct for market makers.

The reporting arrangement in interest rate derivatives in India follows a two tier system. Since at least one party to an OTC interest rate derivatives transaction is a RBI regulated entity, there has been an elaborate prudential reporting requirement in so far as the risk implication of the derivative positions for the entity is concerned. This includes the Price Value of a Base Point (PVBP/PV01) position of IRS contracts including those in the trading book as well as the banking book, notional principal, gross received PV01, gross paid PV01 and net PV01. Regulatory reporting also includes data on benchmark wise details of IRS and credit concentration in derivatives and under the risk based supervision framework, data on credit equivalent, mark-to-market (MTM) value, and daily VaR. These information however are entity specific and cannot be aggregated and therefore do not convey the interconnectedness and cross-counterparty risk implications for the market as a whole.

In 2003, an internal Working Group of the RBI on Rupee derivatives had, inter alia, recommended a centralized clearing system for OTC derivatives through CCIL. Preparatory to introduction of centralized clearing as also to get a better understanding of interest rate derivative market in India, RBI, in 2007, made it mandatory for the RBI regulated entities to report inter-bank/PD transactions in interest rate derivatives (FRAs and IRS) on a platform developed by the CCIL. It was mandated that at the inception, the institutions have to report the transaction level details of all outstanding trades on that date. Subsequently, all inter-bank/PD deals were required to be reported by the banks and PDs on the CCIL platform within 30 minutes of initiating the transaction. The information captured through this reporting system is comprehensive: it includes all details to describe a contract, viz., member name and identification, deal time, reporting member and counterparty reference number, type of transaction (new, amended, cancelled, revised), common identification, swap type (fixed-float, float-fixed, float-float), bank and branch, trade date, effective date, termination date, business day convention, notional principal, fist payment and reset dates, date of reversal of trade, reporting member and counterparty identification, gain/loss on reversal and its settlement date, floating rate benchmark, fixed rate and spread. Further, CCIL's evolution as a repository owed to a regulatory mandate, unlike repositories like DTCC which evolved out of a need to facilitate post trade processing.

An important innovation in OTC derivative markets introduced during the last few years relates to portfolio compression services offered by TriOptima. Since the only way to exit a position in an OTC derivative is to enter into another with opposite pay off, the gross notional outstanding multiplies manifold as a result. Apart from the fact that this does not capture the economic essence of the portfolios, it increases the demand on capital for the regulated entities. TriOptima's TriReduce and TriResolve services reportedly offer multilateral netting with bilateral settlement whereby an entity can extinguish its OTC derivative positions without affecting its MTM value or the PV01. In India too, the service has been used by the IRS portfolio holders with significant reduction in the gross notional positions.

In an attempt to move towards centralised clearing and settlement of IRS transactions, CCIL has introduced a non-guaranteed settlement of these transactions from Nov 27, 2008. It is also in the process of developing TriOptima like trade compression services as also post trade processing services.

The CCIL reporting platform for IRS and FRA did not cover the transactions that the market makers had with their clients and to this extent there remained a gap in information on the interest rate swap market. Since banks were reluctant to share the details of their client transactions with CCIL without detailed protocol about maintenance of client confidentiality, effective from 2009, RBI started collecting information on market makers transactions with their clients. However unlike the reporting of interbank/PD transactions to CCIL, client transaction reporting to RBI is not granular as to transaction particulars but captures the summary of transactions at fortnightly rests. The information collected includes member identification, outstanding contracts as at the beginning of week, notional amount, number of contracts, interest rate range and outstanding contract at the end of the week. Further, bucket-wise details of contracts accounting for 75per cent of notional amount traded are also collected.

Foreign Currency Derivatives

The emergence of the modern foreign exchange market owes to the break-down of the Bretton Woods system in the 1970's and the resultant floating exchange rate regime that came to prevail. The origin of the foreign exchange market in India could be traced to the year 1978 when banks in India were permitted to undertake intra-day trade in foreign exchange. However, it was in the 1990s that the Indian foreign exchange market witnessed far reaching changes along with the shifts in the currency regime in India. The exchange rate of the rupee, that was pegged earlier was floated partially in March 1992 and fully in March 1993 following the recommendations of the Report of the High Level Committee on Balance of Payments. The unification of the exchange rate was instrumental in developing a market-determined exchange rate of the rupee and an important step in the progress towards current account convertibility which was achieved in August 1994.

Over the last decade or so, the foreign exchange market has acquired depth, liquidity and has witnessed increase in turnover. In the USD-INR segment, the daily average turnover increased from USD 7.83 billion in 2005-06 to USD 18.97 billion in 2009-10. The

OTC derivative segment of the forex market includes forwards, forex swaps and forex options. During 2009-10, of the total turnover in the forex market of USD 6.92 trillion, the OTC derivative turnover was USD 3.53 trillion. Of the forex derivatives, the forex swaps are dominant accounting for over 60 per cent of the total turnover during 2009-10. Rupee-forex options, which were allowed in July 2003, have not seen as much trading as the other products.

The foreign exchange market in India has been subject to by a regulatory framework, salient features of which are as under.

a) Need to carry out a foreign exchange transaction, cash or derivative, with an authorized dealer who, in turn, is subject to regulatory covenant,

b) Derivative transactions to be supported by underlying exposures, either specific or based on historical exposures

c) Restriction on dynamic hedging of currency risk

d) Restriction of net open positions that banks/authorized dealers can carry

Broadly three classes of derivatives trade in the foreign exchange market, viz., (outright) forwards, swaps, and options.

Foreign Exchange (Outright) Forwards

A foreign exchange forward contract is an agreement to buy a certain amount of a foreign currency against another currency (in our context, Rupee, the domestic currency) at a rate fixed at the time of entering into the contract. It is used to hedge against the exchange risk arising out of an future exposure, eg., export proceeds, import payments, debt servicing or repayment, etc. The intensity of activity in the forward segment expresses a view of the different class of market participants as to the future path of the exchange rate. A person resident in India may enter into a forward contract with an Authorized Dealer Category-I bank (AD Category I bank) in India to hedge an exposure to exchange risk in respect of a transaction for which sale and/or purchase of foreign exchange is permitted under the Foreign Exchange Management Act, 1999. Outright forward contracts are essentially between banks and their merchant clients and these are much less frequent in the interbank markets, globally as well as in Indian markets. After approval by RBI, CCIL is guaranteeing (December 2009 onwards) the forex forward trades from the trade day to the settlement day acting as a central counterparty. The netting done at CCIL virtually eliminates the credit risk, reduces counterparty exposures and frees the capital which otherwise would have been locked till the settlement of trade.

Swaps

A foreign exchange swap is usually a combination of a spot and a forward transaction, entered into simultaneously. Swaps are mostly inter-bank contracts and are neutral with respect to position as well as impact on the volatility of the exchange rate. Swaps do not have a separate regulatory framework and are covered by the foreign exchange regulations applicable to forward / spot contracts.

A Foreign currency swap is an agreement between two parties to exchange cash flows (viz., the principal and/or interest payments) of a loan in one currency for equivalent cash flows of an equal (in net present value) loan in another. Globally, foreign currency swaps constitute a large segment of foreign currency derivatives. Resident Indians may enter into foreign currency-rupee swap within regulatory limits.

Currency Options

Forex option is a financial derivative under which the buyer of the option has the right but not the obligation to exchange one currency against another at a given point in time at a predetermined exchange rate. Though introduced in the 1990's, the OTC forex options market is not yet very liquid in India. As regards information on the forex options available in the public domain, the Foreign Exchange Dealers' Association of India (FEDAI) publishes foreign currency option volatility rates including ATM volatility, 25-delta risk reversal and 25-delta strangles.

Most of the data of foreign currency derivative is collected by the Foreign Exchange Department (FED) of the RBI. It is important to note that most of the data collection by RBI on foreign exchange markets, for historical reasons, has been motivated by the potential impact of foreign exchange transactions on the volatility of the exchange rate. Each of the AD Category-I banks has to submit daily statements of Foreign Exchange Turnover in Form FTD and Gaps, Position and Cash Balances in Form GPB through the Online Returns Filing System (ORFS). AD Category-I banks have to consolidate the data on cross currency derivative transactions undertaken by residents and submit half-yearly reports (June and December). AD Category-I banks are required to submit a monthly report (as on the last Friday of every month) on the limits granted and utilized by their constituents under the facility of booking forward contracts on past performance basis. AD Category – I banks are required to submit a quarterly report on the forward contracts booked & cancelled by SMEs and Resident Individuals. Apart from the data collected at Foreign Exchange Department (FED), forex forwards data is available at CCIL also, but the data set is not complete as all of the banks are not settling their forex forward deals through CCIL.

a) *Currency Forward:* This data is collected at FED on a daily basis. The FTD report that is submitted online contains both inter-bank and merchant data on transactions in spot, swaps and forwards (including cancellation). CCIL also has a subset of this data as they are undertaking clearing and guaranteed settlement of forex forward and swaps transaction for banks. The data available at CCIL include date of contract, exchange rate, value date, details of buyers and sellers accounts and details of intermediary. Under risk based supervision, DBS collects data on forex forwards including notional principal, credit equivalent, MTM value, PV01 and daily VaR.

b) *Currency swaps:* FED is receiving weekly return on the rupee-foreign currency swaps, where banks are providing data on number of transactions and notional principal amount in USD.

c) *Currency Options:* AD Category-I banks are permitted to offer foreign currency – Rupee options. AD Category-I banks can offer only plain vanilla European options and the transactions undertaken have to be reported to RBI on a weekly basis. The data sent to FED includes trade date, client name, notional amount, option type, strike, maturity, premium and purpose. Further, option position report (weekly) with FED contains net portfolio gamma and net portfolio vega. Strike concentration report includes strike price and bucket-wise (1-week, 2-week, 1-month, 2-months, 3-months and more than 3-months) concentration for a range of 150 paise around the current spot level.

REASONS FOR DERIVATIVE TRANSACTION

A derivatives transaction may be set up for any one of four different reasons: hedging, funding, speculation and arbitrage.

Firstly, firms or financial institutions seek hedged positions in case they cannot directly bear that risk. An example is the protection, through currency options, against currency risk of a relevant investment in a foreign country and currency. Hence, the protection buyer transfers the economic risk related to a market variable (e.g. a possible surge in the price of oil or a currency trend) to other firms or financial institutions willing and effectively prepared to bear the risk (protection seller). In this way, the risk will not be eliminated but simply transferred to other firms that are better equipped to handle it. The possibility to transfer economic risk is linked to the presence of a resilient and safe market infrastructure, where players provide sufficient collateral and countercyclical requirements against the potential default of the counterparty. The use of derivatives in the regular activities of many financial and non-financial institutions has also been widespread during the recent fmancial crisis, as they are essential tools allowing investors to hedge against a Worldwide market.

Secondly, derivatives can be a tool to redistribute funding between financial institutions or within non-financial institutions in a way that best suits the company 's financial needs. For instance, a financial institution issues coupon bonds and decides to rearrange the payments of these periodic coupons with a specific trajectory in order to avoid risks or simply to redistribute risks in a certain way.

Thirdly, derivatives may be also used to speculate on a specific market variable or company trend. As prices reflect the information of informed individuals (arbitrageurs) but only partially, so that those who expend resources to obtain information do receive compensation. Speculative use of derivatives thus includes institutions or traders who invest in information in order to get higher returns from the market. Their trading activity increases the liquidity in the market and - if the information proves to be wrong – speculation may potentially favour 'noise trading,' which can only affect prices for a short time. Uninformed investors buying and selling financial securities at irrational prices, thus creating noise (strange movements) in the price of securities. In effect, trading against fundamentals is costly, even though it is possible and in the short-run it can be even successful. In the end, noise trading helps to create uncertainty on prices, but, at the same time, this leads more uninformed traders to search for information (as they will be compensated), pushing liquidity in the market and improving price discovery (the 'equilibrium of disequilibrium'). Without speculation (or better called 'informed trading'), there would be no counterparties for hedgers. Speculation or informed trading is frequently confused with the intent to manipulate market prices, as the border between investing to obtain and use outside and visible information has, from a regulatory point of view, a 'thin' border with illegal actions intended to obtain inside and sensible information. Therefore, attention should be drawn to the way in which information circulates and how fast it changes in ways that can generate advantages for few participants. Regulators and policy-makers should be less concerned with the particular use of a product or technique as such.

Last but not least, using derivatives as a tool for arbitrage facilitates the mechanism of price formation, aligning in a short interval of time bid/ask spreads. Arbitrageurs operate with a short horizon and are reasonably risk-averse. They aim at making profits without taking relevant risks. Their role is limited to making price formation more efficient, while their systemic impact is not relevant. Frequently, their behaviour can be seen as a response to noise trading rather than as trading on fundamentals. The joint action of arbitrageurs and speculators supports markets in reaching their 'absorptive capacity' (critical level of liquidity). Derivatives instruments and their multiple uses may facilitate efficient market functioning and the revelation of critical information. In effect, CDS (credit default swap) spreads are widely used as a tool for risk management in order to price the credit risk of a specific counterparty.

FACILITATING INSTITUTIONS TO REDUCE COUNTERPARTY RISKS

Although the range of products available and volumes traded in the Indian derivatives market are not comparable to those in the more developed markets and the Indian markets have not seen any upheaval caused by derivatives, the arrangement for reporting of derivative transactions has been existing in India for a long time. While some reports, e.g., those relating to OTC foreign exchange transactions are in summary format, others e.g., reports on OTC interest rate swaps and repo in government bonds captured all details of a transaction and are akin to what is proposed for the repository structure. Nevertheless, the need for consolidation of the reporting arrangements with a view to facilitating a more comprehensive monitoring of the market by the regulator, improving transparency of the market and improving the efficiency of post trade processing infrastructure cannot be overemphasized. Here, a Central Counterparty (CCP) is a financial institution that interposes as an intermediary between security (including derivatives) market participants. This reduces the amount of counterparty risk that market participants are exposed to. A sale is contracted between the seller of a security and the central counter party on one hand and the central counterparty and the buyer on the other. This means that no market participant has a direct exposure to another and if one party defaults, the central counterparty absorbs the loss. Settlement through a central counterparty has been progressively used on most major stock and security exchanges. This eliminates both the risk of direct financial loss though a default and the risk of indirect loss through having to unwind/replace a trade. It is therefore a more complete method of reducing counterparty risk than alternatives such as simple Delivery versus Payment (DVP). It also tends to enhance liquidity in the market by reducing default risk and facilitating anonymous trading. A caveat is however in order in that a CCP based settlement system leads to concentration of risk with the CCP which needs to be appropriately addressed. Collateral benefits of CCP based settlement system include aggregation of the trade data with the CCP which can be shared with the regulators or disseminated to the market.

Unlike the CCP infrastructure, the objective of Trade Repository (TR) is simply to maintain an authoritative electronic database of all open OTC derivative transactions. It collects data derived from centrally or bilaterally clearable transactions as inputted/verified by both parties to a trade. Depending upon the asset class, a TR may also engage in trade lifecycle event management and downstream trade processing services. However, the principal functionality of a TR is its record keeping and reconciliation of definitive copies of trade data . It may be mentioned that other market infrastructure or service providers that centrally maintain market wide OTC derivative contract information (e.g. CCPs) may also provide the function of the TR.

Contracts maintained in a TR can be considered the sole 'official legal record' (the so called 'golden copy') of a transaction depending on legal arrangement in operation in regard to the contract in question. As such, they constitute data usable for various downstream processing. An important attribute of a TR is its ability to interconnect with multiple market participants in support of risk reduction, operational efficiency and cost saving benefits to individual participants and to the market as a whole.

Since information management is the core functionality of a TR, it would be in order to discuss the hierarchy of information and its usage. The typical drawback of the OTC market is that the information concerning any contract is usually available only to the contracting parties. While expanding the scope of availability of information, it is pertinent to distinguish between information available to regulators, to market participants and to public at large. The law usually gives the regulators the right to call for from the entities they regulate, any information including exposures to any single counterparty or groups of counterparties as well as position and risk implication of any class of contract. Information available to the public is usually limited to aggregate data that excludes trade and position data which are sensitive in nature. Such aggregate data is gathered and published by various agencies according to contract types, geographical coverage, etc. The data requirements of market participants are somewhere between that of the regulators and the public.

The regulators can obtain detailed and granular information about the individual positions of the entities they regulate. However, they lack a comprehensive picture of market as a whole. In absence of a TR, it is difficult for regulators to assess even the exact size of the various segments of the OTC derivative market as such information is not readily available. Further, even if the information is pieced together using data from various sources, it would be difficult to compile a complete and meaningful picture due to heterogeneity of data. Secondly, the usual regulatory reporting focuses on the risk sensitivity of the positions and does not cover the composition of the positions. In absence of granular composition of positions, it becomes difficult to ascertain the extent of exposure detailed breakdown of the positions of the counterparties. The situation becomes complex when the trades are between entities regulated by different regulators or between entities in different sovereign jurisdictions. Though this problem may partially be addressed by information sharing agreement amongst the regulators, or by having a single TR, there may still be some issues like data privacy issue, quantum and quality of information in the database, etc.

In absence of a complete picture on the OTC derivative market, the regulators may not be in a position to assess the quantum of risk building up in the system *per se*. Further, the regulator would be oblivious to the inter-linkages of these positions, thereby limiting its ability to detect the risk to the system and to respond to the evolving scenario. Further, the implication for the market participant is also severe as, in absence of complete information, their positions may remain under-collateralised and more importantly, during the time of stress, the market may become completely illiquid due to lack of trust among participants.

A TR is an institution that addresses the above concerns by collecting and aggregating information on individual transactions in OTC derivatives. TRs are a relatively new concept in the financial markets. They were unheard of till as late as 2003 and as such they are still evolving and developing over time. One of the underlying causes behind the introduction of TRs was the rapid expansion of volumes both in terms of the value as well as the number of transactions in the financial markets across the globe. When growth in the financial transactions outpaced existing processing capabilities, it led to backlog of confirmations of the financial transactions.

These backlogs resulted from reliance on inefficient manual confirmation processes that failed to keep up with the rapidly growing volume and because of difficulties in confirming information for trades that end-users transferred to other parties without notifying the original dealer. Although these trades were being entered into the systems that dealers used to manage the risk of loss arising from price changes (market risk) and counterparty defaults (credit risk), the credit derivatives backlogs increased dealers' operational risk by potentially allowing errors that could lead to losses or other problems to go undetected. The increasing number of deal confirmation backlogs started causing worries for all stakeholders including the regulators.

After the electronic trade matching services started making significant difference by bringing down the number of unmatched deals, there was a greater appreciation that for products other than spot market products, say for OTC derivative trades like IRS, only matching services were not of much value unless they are supported by post trade processing services throughout the life cycle of these products. This realization is perhaps the most important driver for the development of TRs and has also resulted in the availability of post trade processing services as an additional functionality provided by such TRs.

In India, RBI initiated measures for transaction-wise reporting of IRS Trades and mandated reporting of all inter-bank trades to Clearing Corporation of India Limited (CCIL) in August 2007. Incidentally, it may be mentioned that Indian financial market has had a well functioning CCP, viz., CCIL, that has been offering CCP-guaranteed settlement for transactions in government securities, a few money market instruments, and forex i.e. dollar-rupee transactions

Impetus for Development Post-Global Financial Crisis (GFC)

During the recent global financial crisis, Depository Trust & Clearing Corporation (DTCC) Deriv/SERV could provide very valuable information on the actual state of exposures in the CDS market to US Regulators. Similarly, after the Lehman crisis, CCIL too could provide precise information to RBI on the IRS exposures of the Lehman subsidiary in India.

Post-crisis analysis of the factors contributing to / accentuating the crisis in light of the experience mentioned above prompted the regulators worldwide to start thinking on improving market infrastructure for OTC products - standardizing them, making centralized clearing mandatory for most plain vanilla products and making reporting in TRs mandatory for all other products. All these developments have provided impetus for rapid development of TRs globally and initiatives are underway in different parts of the world for setting up TRs. (See Box-3).

Box 3

SETTING UP OF TRADE REPOSITORY IN INDIA

The role of TRs in improving transparency of the OTC derivatives markets is well recognised. The regulators World over are attempting to set up TRs. As of now, there are three global swap repositories in existence today - one for OTC equity derivatives operated by DTCC in London, one for OTC interest rate derivatives operated by Tri-Optima in Sweden, and one for credit default swaps operated by DTCC in the USA. There have also been some attempts to set up repositories in the Euro jurisdiction. Nevertheless, the issues relating to the setting up of repositories, their governance structures, regulatory jurisdiction, functionalities, etc. have not yet been crystallized and are being widely discussed. Several organisations, including the Financial Stability Board, the IOSCO, the OTC Derivatives Regulators Forum, the European Central Bank, etc., have come up with documents outlining the areas relating to improvement of the OTC market structure. Apart from a mention in the Dodd Frank act to the effect that data repository should be created to provide regulators and the public with the necessary transparency into the global OTC derivatives markets, there does not seem to be any other regulatory mandate for the repositories.

The issues relating to the repositories fall into two categories. The first covers the structure and organization of the repositories system and the second covers the functionalities of a repository. The pertinent questions regarding the structure of the repository system are (a) whether there should be a single or multiple repository(ies) for each class of OTC derivatives, (b) whether there should be a global repository for each class or multiple repositories across jurisdictions, (c) whether the repository should be a government initiative or private sector initiative and (d) what should be the regulatory regime for the repositories. The second set of issues covers the types, coverage, quality and frequency of transaction data, access to data housed in the TR, services offered by the TRs, and confidentiallty of the data. The latter set of issues is universal and the evolving best practices through the efforts of global bodies such as the OTC Derivatives

Regulator's Forum, FSB, IOSCO can provide the guiding principles for any repository in any jurisdiction.

There is considerable debate on the question whether there should be a single repository across the globe for any given product or there should be several repositories in different jurisdictions for the same product. The problem with more than one repository for a given product lies in data portability and aggregability. The question assumes importance particularly in view of the fact that OTC derivatives are global in nature and the counterparties could be transnational. In such a situation if OTC derivative information about outstanding contracts are fragmented into different repositories in different countries, comprehensive Information for the regulator could be elusive.

As of now, the derivatives market in India is almost entirely domestic and the data aggregability and extra-jurisdictional issues do not apply. Though the non-residents are not allowed in the interest rate swaps market, they have limited access to the foreign exchange derivatives market and are likely to have access to the proposed CDS market. On the other hand, the Indian bank branches abroad do participate in the OTC derivatives markets in the host countries and single named CDS on some of the Indian corporate and banks are also reported to be trading. Even though the domain of the TRs in India would be restricted to products and participants in the domestic markets, it would be desirable to keep in view the data portability and aggregability issues while setting up a repository.

The argument in favour of a single repository for a given class of product is compelling from another perspective. TRs are not 'merely warehouse of information but can significantly contribute to market efficiency through post trade processing service and lifetime event management. If the repositories are fragmented, particularly in a nascent market with limited aclivity, it would not be possible for them to provide any effective post trade service.

A related question in this context is whether multiple class of products may be reported on a single repository. As such, there nothing that prevents a single repository from handling multiple products, provided it has the necessary resources andexpertise. The global experience suggests that a single repository is catering to a particular class of product. e.g., DTCC is Iherepository for credit derivatives, whereas TriOptima deals with interest rate derivatives. It may be mentioned here that such a structure has evolved for historicai reasons and given the large volumes of transaction in each product class, such specialisation is economically feasible and sustainable. On the other hand, in Indian markets, the total volume of transactions is relatively small in any class of derivatives and as such a dedicated repository for each class may pose viability problem.

A regulator can effectively collect all trade information just as *a* repository and disseminate such aggregate/summary information in the public domain as may be necessary for improving market transparency. However, a regulator cannot render post trade processing and event lifecycle management and thus, a TR initiative has necessarily to be a private sector initiative. Though the need for post trade services alone can justify the existence of a TR with information availability to the regulator a useful byproduct, in nascent market such as lndia's with limited trading activity, the evolution of TRs has to necessarily depend on regulatory mandate for reporting of trades with post trade services a later adjunct.

The CCIL, which has been warehousing the transaction details for IRS and also offering guaranteed settlement for severai other financial products, enjoys significant economy of scale and scope in taking up the functionalities of a repository. Firstly, the collection of information on trades is necessary for clearing and settlement, which is the primary activity of CCIL and in which, it has considerable experience over the years. Secondly, it already possesses a comprehensive platform with necessary infrastructure as well as connectivity. These does not seem to be any confiict of interest between the clearing and settlement activities of CCIL and its functioning as a repository. Though the DTCC does not operate a clearing nouse for derivatives, it is involved in clearing activities through its 50 per cent equity interest in New York Portfolio Clearing and three wholly owned subsidiaries which are registered clearing agencies under the Exchange Act, subject to regulation by the SEC. On the other hand, the activities enjoined upon a repository are complete in itself and distinct from that of an institution that does clearing and settlement. Further, repositories, so as to ensure data portability as well as acceptability in foreign jurisdictions, will have to adhere to the best practices as they are formalized. As such, it would be advantageous if there is an institution which functions solely as a TR.

While from a governance and regulatory perspective, there are merits in the case for a dedicated repository without any other collateral activities, there are questions about the economic viability of such an institution. The repository has to make large initial investment in infrastructure for capturing and processing trade data. On the other hand, the only source of income for a repository is the post-trade processing services that it offers to the market participants. In a nascent and developing market like India's, it is highly doubtful whether a repository would be economically viable on its own.

Hence, notwithstanding the desirability of a dedicated repository, it would be expedient if a subsidiary of CCIL is formed to take over and/or commence repository activities. Such an arrangement would both gainfully use the expertise, experience, and infrastructure of CCIL and at the same time satisfy the corporate governance issue.

A related question arises in this context. The international discourse has focused on the merits of a single TR for a given asset class. In certain jurisdictions such as that of India, a question may arise about the merits of a single TR for all asset classes.

The main argument in *favour* of a single TR for all products retates to economic efficiency. Since the reporting infrastructure is same or similar (servers, web connectivity, reporting software etc) it will be cost efficient if a single organization handles the reporting of all asset classes This argument is strengthened in a situation like India's where a particular instrument class may not have sufficient volume to make it viable for a dedicated repository for that instrument class. Second, the availability of the data with a single TR enables the regulator and other users to easily access the posilion/exposure of an entity across all product classes. Third, the supervision and regulation may be easier in case of a single TR than in the case of multiple TRs. Fourth, if two TRs are handling two product classes, they may be using different platforms/ data structures/formats that may pose problem of data portability and aggregability.

The main argument *against* single TR for all asset classes is that it would create a monopoly organization. TR service is a profitable activity and the users are supposed to pay for services provided by the TRs. In case there is a single repository created by regulatory mandate, this will endow pricing power to the institution to the detriment of the reporting institution. Further, if there is a single repository covering all asset classes, under regulatory purview of different regulators, there may be regulatory clashes regarding corporate governance, standards, etc-, of the repository. Moreover, the post trade processing services for different products may demand different competencies. For instance post trade services in case of CDS require life cycle event management; in case interest rate derivatives, trade compression services and in case of forex derivatives, valuation and MIS. It may obviously be difficult for a single TR to house all these diverse expertise and this may act against specialization.

The argument that a single repository for all asset classes would enable the regulator to obtain the exposure of an entity in respect of all the assets is not very strong because the same information can be obtained even when there are different repositories for different asset classes. After ali, the exposure in different asset classes are mutually exclusive and there is no reason why different TRs cannot supply the data concerning the respective asset class at least as quickly. However, the economy and viably arguments strongly suggest that in the present condition the balance is in favour of a single TR for all asset classes in India.

DEVELOPING COMPREHENSIVE REPORTING STRUCTURE FOR OTC FOREX AND INTEREST RATE DERIVATIVES

The financial crisis has underscored the weaknesses in the OTC derivatives markets which need to be addressed for building a resilient financial system less prone to instabilities. The measures that have been suggested to improve the robustness of the OTC derivative markets include the following: (a) Standardization of OTC derivative contracts which would facilitate trading on organised trading platforms, ensure greater comparability of trade information and pave the way for clearing and settlement through

CCP. (b) Robust counterparty risk management either through centralized clearing with a CCP or bilateral collateralization arrangements. (c) Appropriate capital charges on the OTC derivatives positions to capture the risk such positions pose for financial stability and align the incentives of individual market participants with overall financial stability. (d) Improving transparency of the OTC derivatives market from the perspective of regulators, market participants and the general public at large.

At present there is a reporting scheme for various OTC derivative products in India and there is no reason to believe that the reporting scheme has not served the objective of the regulators. In the current perspective, the reporting structure for the OTC derivatives in India needs to be looked at afresh. It is true that the OTC derivatives market in India is not comparable to markets in US and EU jurisdictions, either in the range of products available or in the volume of trades. Moreover, with capital accounts restrictions in place and capital inflows and the prospect of any abrupt reversal continuing to be potential destabilizing factors the regulatory perspective on reporting of OTC derivatives transactions is also different from other jurisdictions. The objective therefore is to consolidate the existing reporting arrangements so as to make it more robust and efficient in the following sense:

a) The information requirement of the regulatory authorities is fully met in a dynamic sense.
b) The burden of reporting on the reporting entities is minimized.
c) The reporting structure supports post trade processing services and seamlessly integrates with any CCP based clearing and settlement, whenever and wherever necessary.
d) The reporting structure facilitates dissemination of price and volume data for the market participants and general public.

Another issue which merits consideration is whether the reporting arrangement should cover only the interbank transactions or also the transactions between banks and their clients. Since the current discussions on OTC derivative transactions reporting are in the backdrop of the global financial crisis, it has to be noted that the liquidity dry-up during the crisis has been attributed to the opacity in OTC derivative transactions between the financial firms; and transactions between banks and other non-financial firms have not been in focus. Nevertheless, some of the proposed OTC market reform measures such as CCP clearing are likely to cover non-financial firms' transactions and this has caused concerns. However, the position obtaining in India in respect of OTC derivatives transactions is different from elsewhere in the sense that for all OTC derivative transactions one of the counterparties has to be necessarily a bank, or a Primary Dealer (PD). In terms of Section 3 of Foreign Exchange Management Act 1999, "... no person shall deal in or transfer any foreign exchange or foreign security to any person not being an authorised person". In terms of Section 45 V of the RBI Act, "... transactions in such derivatives as may be specified by the Bank from time to time, shall be valid, if at least one of the parties to the transaction is the Bank, a scheduled bank, or such other agency falling under regulatory purview of the Bank under the Act, the Banking Regulation Act, 1949(10 of 1949), the Foreign Exchange Management Act, 1999 (42 of 1999), or any other Act or instrument having force of law, as may be specified by the Bank from time to time". Further, in terms of paragraph 3 of the comprehensive guidelines on derivatives, "... at least one party to a derivative transaction is required to be a market maker" while paragraph 5 (i) *ibid.* defines market makers as all commercial banks (excluding local area banks (LABs) and RRBs) and PDs. The implications of the above requirements are two-folds. *First*, when a bank enter into a derivative transaction with a non-financial firm, however systematically important the latter may be and however large the transaction size may be, the bank as a market maker has to do a contra transaction to square its position and as such, the trade between the market makers will in a sense capture the transactions initiated by the non-financial firms. *Second,* the settlement of trades done by non-financial firms will be between those firms and their banks. Since with a high degree of probability, the OTC derivative trade between a non-financial firm and a bank would be preceded by a bank client relationship between them, such a transaction is unlikely to pose a systemic problem though it might lead to disputes.

The Indian financial markets are subject to a capital control framework. While the capital accounts transactions of the non-financial sector has been substantially liberalised, the financial sector is subject to a large number of restrictions. On the other hand, increasing globalisation has led to stronger linkages between the domestic and the international sectors by way of multinational firms, foreign exporters with exposure to Indian markets, etc. The Indian financial system has experienced lumpy and uneven capital flows as well as sudden reversals (as witnessed in the aftermath of Lehmann crisis during Oct 2008 to March 2009). In recent times, there has been significant growth in the non-deliverable forwards (NDF) markets. When the exchange rate is volatile the expectations of the market is expressed through action of non-financial firms (in view of limit on positions of the banks and other financial firms), e.g. cancellation of forward contracts by exporters, increase in booking of forward contracts by importers, etc. As such, it is necessary to have a sense of the activities of the non-financial sector in the OTC derivatives market to take necessary steps to anchor expectations and establish orderly conditions in the market, should there be deviations.

CONSOLIDATING THE REPORTING ARRANGEMENTS OF THE OTC DERIVATIVES

For consolidating the existing reporting arrangement of the permitted OTC derivatives in India, following steps need to be undertaken.

Foreign Exchange OTC Derivatives

The reporting arrangement in the foreign exchange derivatives so far has been geared to the requirements of the regulator, i.e, the RBI. The prices in the forwards market, the dominant segment, are observable almost on a real time basis, because of the electronic trading platforms. It is true that what is disseminated on the newswires are the quoted rates and there may be some difference between the dealt rates and quoted rates, but nevertheless the newswires do give a realistic sense of the trend and liquidity of the market. Moreover, there is an all-encompassing position limit on the banks in place which substantially mitigates the systemic risk posed by OTC derivatives.

Considering the importance of the developments in the foreign exchange forward markets, it is felt that it would be useful to capture the details of the inter-bank forward transactions which will convey a sense of the market's view of the future exchange rate trend. It is true that in a liquid market, the prices incorporate all information. However, in case of a heterogeneous market, information on the activity of the market participants would augment the insight of the regulator. As such, it would be appropriate if all inter-bank forex forward transactions are reported to CCIL which already has a platform for clearing and thence, for capturing the data. In absence of any significant post-trade processing benefits, there may not be enough incentive for banks to report their forward transactions to CCIL in absence of regulatory mandate. It may therefore, be necessary for RBI to issue an appropriate direction.

As the details of forward contracts entered into between banks and their clients do convey the views of the corporate sector on the exchange rate trend, and as such, it is an important input for policy decisions in capital account management and Reserve Bank's intervention strategy. It will be useful to have complete information on the volume and price of transactions rather than anecdotal or summary information. While the details of all forward transactions between corporates and their banks may impose considerable burden on reporting and analysis without providing commensurate insight, it is suggested that arrangements may be put in place for reporting of forward transactions between banks and their clients beyond some threshold, say , USD 100,000. However, banks may be reluctant to report their client trades to a third party; but they have no reservations against reporting such trades to the RBI. The reason for their reluctance stems from client confidentiality and unwillingness to disclose their pricing strategy to a third party. There are fears were that if it becomes known that a particular bank has entered into a large transaction with a customer and will soon be in the market for covering itself, it may be subject to exploitative squeeze by other market participants.

It is true that unlike in case of interbank transactions there is no need for post trade processing services in case of transactions between a bank and its client. The settlement of the trade takes place between the bank and its client in the books of the bank. Thus there may not be any incentive for the banks to report their client trades to a repository.

In the Indian context, it is apparent that the reported client trades are of use only to the Reserve bank (to get a sense of the market and view of the market participants) and that the banks have some reservation about their client trades being known to a third party. From this view, it would follow that the client trades should be reported by the banks only to the regulator. However, it may be feasible if the client trades are reported to an organisation like CCIL with the safeguard that the organisation shall not have any access to these trades and shall only provide the platform for receiving the reports and collating the information into usable formats as decided by RBI from time to time. It may be mentioned that such an arrangement already exists for submission of bids for flotation of government debt through auction which ranks at par with the client trades in terms of confidentiality.

Since the organisation which receives the report of client trade is not going to provide any service to the reporting banks and thus cannot charge for the services, it may not be a commercially feasible operation. It follows that if reporting of client trades is considered imperative from stability viewpoint, if necessary, some form of compensation to the organization may have to be provided for by the beneficiary of the data. The choice between whether RBI itself receives the client trades reporting and whether a designated organisation receives it, subject, of course, to the safeguards mentioned above, depends on expedience.

Forex Option Contracts with Rupee as One of the Currencies

The OTC options market is predominantly between the banks and the end users of the option. The extant regulatory regime distinguishes between banks that are allowed to run an option book and those who are not. The banks that are not allowed to run option book are required to enter into a back to back option contract with another bank for their net options position. Further, corporates are not permitted to write options on a stand alone basis but only as a part of a cost reduction structure, ensuring that there is no net receipt of premium. Unlike in case of linear derivatives where a transaction between a bank and its client usually results in a matching contra transaction in the inter-bank market, in case of options, generally the delta of the option portfolio is reckoned for squaring the position and the squaring is achieved through a spot transaction or a linear derivative.

In keeping with the objective of reporting of all inter-bank OTC derivatives transactions, it is desirable that all forex options contracts between banks should be reported. If CCIL is entrusted with the responsibility of reporting of forward contracts, the economy of scale and scope would favour reporting arrangement for option contracts with CCIL. Besides CCIL should be in a position to offer post-trade processing services such as valuation and MIS reports.

As transactions in the forex options market in India is predominantly between the banks and their clients, regulatory monitoring of the options markets shall not be complete unless the reports include the client transactions as well. As of now, banks permitted to run an option book are required to report transaction-wise details of their options portfolio (inter-bank as well as client trades) at weekly intervals to the Foreign Exchange Department in physical form (some banks report in soft form as well). However, the utility of these reports is limited partly because the reporting is in physical form requiring further data entry and partly because it is periodic. It is therefore suggested that the reporting of option contracts between banks and their clients may be made in a manner similar to the forex forward contracts either to the CCIL with necessary safeguards as to confidentiality or to the Reserve Bank direct.

Cross Currency Options and Other Derivatives

While permissible option contracts are limited to the plain vanilla types when rupee is one of the currencies involved, market participants have considerable latitude in case of cross currency options. Apart from the plain vanilla types, various so called exotic options involving two currencies other than the Rupee can also be contracted. It has been observed that corporate are increasingly using such option contracts. Further, these options are rarely transacted in the interbank market except for the purpose of back-to-back-covering. These contracts have little systemic implications in the sense that they do not contribute to or convey any sense of the volatility of the exchange rate of the rupee. Nevertheless, it would be desirable to cover these options as well in the reporting structure to complete regulatory knowledge of the foreign exchange market. Besides, such reporting may also augment the information requirement for prudential oversight. The suggested arrangement may also be considered for other cross-currency derivatives such as forwards, swaps, etc.

Unlike forex derivatives, the range of OTC interest rate derivatives is rather limited even as the reporting arrangement robust. The only OTC interest rate derivatives permitted are the Forward Rate Agreements (FRA) and Interest Rate Swaps (IRS). IRS is the more actively traded product and at present swaps on three benchmarks – MIBOR, MIFOR and INBMK are traded. Reserve Bank mandated in 2007 that all interbank transactions in FRA and IRS be reported on a platform developed for the purpose by CCIL. The reporting captures all details of the transaction and is on near-real-time basis inasmuch as banks are required to report a transaction within 30 minutes of its conclusion. The data has been available to the Reserve Bank and CCIL has been disseminating some aggregate information on the IRS market. Beyond this, the data bank has so far had no other use as one would expect of a repository arrangement.

The reporting arrangement for IRS and FRA does not cover transactions between banks and their clients. Client transactions constitute a rather small fraction of the interbank market in IRS. Nevertheless, in absence of client trade reporting, the regulator's sense of the market remains incomplete. Recognising the need, Financial Markets

Department has been collecting information on client trades at weekly intervals in soft (worksheet) form. However, this arrangement is at best ad hoc and needs to be put on a more robust footing. It is suggested that the client trades in IRS may also be reported in the same manner as the forex derivatives discussed earlier.

A repo essentially comprises a spot sale (purchase) and forward purchase (sale) of any asset. Thus the second leg of the transaction in a linear derivative like any forward or futures contract. However, a repo is usually looked at from its economic essence viewpoint, i.e., a collateralised borrowing arrangement. Although not treated as a separate class of derivatives, repo transactions have assumed importance because of their twin role in funding an asset position as also facilitating short sale in that asset, if permitted. It may be recalled that the repo market faced severe illiquidity during the crisis and making the repo market more robust is engaging the attention of the regulators.

In Indian markets, there are repo transactions in two assets, viz., the government securities and corporate bonds. A repo-like product, CBLO, operated by the CCIL, where a pool of government securities is created against which units called CBLO are created and allotted to members to be bought (lending of funds) and sold (borrowing of funds) by them is quite popular and commands large volumes. Repos in government securities are partly transacted on an anonymous order matching platform CROMS and partly contracted bilaterally but reported on the RBI's NDS platform. In case of repo in government securities and CBLO, CCIL acts as the central counterparty and hence all transaction level data are available as would be the case in case of a repository. In case of corporate bonds, the trading as well as settlement is bilateral but the transactions are required to be reported to a platform hosted by the FIMMDA.

Thus the reporting arrangement in respect of repo transactions is comprehensive and there is little to suggest for making it more comprehensive. The only issue which merits consideration is that there are three agencies involved in the reporting framework. Since CCIL acts as the central counterparty for all repo trades in government securities, it would be optimal if the reporting of repo transactions outside the CROMS are also reported on a CCIL platform rather than RBI NDS.

Client Trades

The details of a trade reported to a TR is supposed to provide a 'golden copy' of the transaction. It should thus serve as a legally binding contract and dispense with such practices as exchange of confirmation. A reported client trade can serve as a 'golden copy' of contract between the bank and its client only if the transaction is reported by one and confirmed by the other and matched as such by the TR. Therefore, whether the process of reporting and confirmation is an optimal proposition in case of client trades needs to be examined. In case of forex derivatives, the transaction between a bank and its client is invariably extensively documented because the bank has to fulfill its obligation under FEMA for verifying the underlying. As such clients' confirmation of trade reported by banks to TRs may be superfluous. Secondly, the trades between a bank and its client settle in the books of the bank and the systemic implication of such a transaction goes little beyond the bank's credit risk on the client. Thirdly, though technologically feasible, confirmation by numerous and geographically dispersed clients may pose certain problem such as failure of confirmation by clients resulting in unmatched trades.

Although CCPs can broaden the use of derivatives by end users, the rules governing clearing mem-bership could alter financial structures by further concentrating the benefits of these financial transac-tions in a small number of firms. In some CCPs, the clearing members are the same large financial institutions in which trading of OTC derivatives is concentrated, potentially reinforcing a lack of competition in the OTC market if not governed and regulated properly. That said, clearing membership in CCPs typically requires all remaining members to assume the losses imposed by a defaulting member, thereby mutualizing the risks. Even with this mechanism in place, adequately regulating CCPs is very important from the systemic point of view.

Box-4

CHALLENGES IN MIGRATING TO CENTRAL CLEARING

Globally, there is widespread acceptance of the broad objective that OTC derivative products have to migrate to Central clearing. Within the ambit of this broad objective, however, there is recognition of the fact that only products meeting certain conditions can migrate to central clearing. In particular, the features of the product should facilitate management of the risks of the product by a CCP. These features include standardisation; relative lack of complexity in contract terms; sufficient market liquidity; and readily available pricing information. There is, thus, a need for careful assessment and definition of the product scope for mandatory migration to central clearing.

There are also divergent views about the participants to be included under the mandatory central clearing requirement. Views have emerged that the mandatory central clearing requirements should apply only to participants which pose systemic risk and that exemptions/carve outs could be considered for smaller users of derivatives, especially nonfinancial entities. There are also fears that CCP clearing will result in exposures being concentrated in a small number of clearing banks leading to increased systemic risk in case of failure of a clearing member.

A large number of operational issues are also arising. These include issues related to inter-operability across different CCPs in the same jurisdiction and across CCPs in different jurisdictions, cross margining and netting. Each of these issues may, in turn, change the risk profile of individual CCPs while potentially posing systemic risks, which will need to be assessed and managed. There are also divergent views about the participants to be included under the mandatory central clearing requirement. Views have emerged that the mandatory central clearing requirements should apply only to participants which pose systemic risk and that exemptions/carve outs could be considered for smaller users of derivatives, especially nonfinancial entities. There are also fears that CCP clearing will result in exposures being concentrated in a small number of clearing banks leading to increased systemic risk in case of failure of a clearing member.

A large number of operational issues are also arising. These include issues related to inter-operability across different CCPs in the same jurisdiction and across CCPs in different jurisdictions, cross margining and netting. Each of these issues may, in turn, change the risk profile of individual CCPs while potentially posing systemic risks, which will need to be assessed and managed. There are also concerns arising from legal complexity, regulatory uncertainties and inconsistencies, applicability of insolvency regimes and of the default management processes of CCPs and potential increase in collateral requirements.

Yet another set of issues relate to cost considerations. On the one hand, substantial costs are likely to be incurred in providing for the technological and other resources for setting up CCP arrangements and for establishing links and interfaces. On the other, there is also a general consensus among market participants that central clearing is likely to increase the cost of dealing in OTC derivatives. There are fears that the regulatory changes being envisaged for the OTC derivatives market may result in the market itself getting impaired/killed in the medium to long run.

There are views that benefits from central clearing are unlikely to accrue to market participants in the short run even though, in the long run, there are benefits in terms of increased market efficiency as well as lower risks of instability. Regulators around the world are, therefore, exploring the possibility of either mandating the migration to central clearing or incentivising it, or both. The Basel III capital rules, for example, will create an incentive to move to central clearing because exposures to a CCP will generally attract a lower capital charge than other bilateral exposures.

It is also clear that implementation of the G20 reform measures will increase concentration risks vis-à-vis the CCPs. It will, thus, be critical to ensure the compliance of CCPs with the four "safeguards" for a resilient and efficient framework for central clearing: (i) fair and open access by market participants to CCPs, based on transparent and objective criteria; (ii) cooperative oversight arrangements between all relevant authorities, both domestic and international, that result in robust and consistently applied regulation and oversight of global CCPs; (iii) resolution and recovery regimes that ensure the core functions of CCPs are maintained during times of crisis and that consider the interests of all jurisdictions where the CCP is systemically important; and (iv) appropriate liquidity arrangements for CCPs in the currencies they clear.

With regard to margin requirements for noncentrally cleared derivative transactions, there are concerns that the greater collateralisation of such transactions may, in turn, lead to new risks. Margin requirements on non-centrally cleared derivative transactions will mitigate counterparty risks but the underlying collateral may by itself be a source of credit and liquidity risks. There are also concerns about the systemic implications of increased collateral requirements, especially at a time when other regulatory reforms (e.g. Basel III) will also impose demands on similar high quality, liquid collateral.

Significant progress has been made in implementing the OTC derivative reform measures in India. In July 2012, a Trade Repository (TR) for OTC derivative product was launched and, in two phases, reporting of all major foreign exchange OTC derivatives to the TR has commenced. These arrangements will be extended, in phases, to cover foreign currency OTC derivative trades between banks and their clients under a suitable protocol to ensure confidentiality of client trades as also interest rate derivative products including client trades in rupee interest rate swaps (IRS). Further, to enhance the liquidity in the Government Securities and Interest Rate Derivatives Markets, it has been decided to standardise IRS contracts to facilitate centralised clearing and settlement of these contracts.

Infrastructure for the central clearing and guaranteed settlement of foreign exchange forward transactions in the US dollar / Indian rupee segment from the trade date to the settlement date has been in place since December 2009 for inter bank transactions. IRS and forward rate agreements (FRA) in the Indian rupee, which form the bulk of interest rate derivative transactions in the country, are currently being centrally cleared in a non-guaranteed mode. Though, it is not mandatory for market participants to clear their trades through CCP, more than 70 per cent of IRS trades are cleared through CCP. Further guaranteed clearing of foreign exchange forward transactions in the US dollar / Indian rupee segment has been mandated and the migration of transactions in this segment to guaranteed clearing is likely to commence shortly. An "in principle" decision to bring IRS and FRA transactions in the Indian rupee within the ambit of guaranteed settlement has been taken. The risk management framework and procedural aspects proposed by the central counterparty are currently being examined.

Mandatory guaranteed clearing will result in the exposures of banks, which are currently spread across a large number of counterparties, being concentrated against the central counterparty. These exposures are required to be calculated using the current exposure method (the sum of gross positive MTM and potential future credit exposure) and will be subject to the extant exposure limits which prescribe a single borrower exposure limit of 15 per cent of the capital funds of the bank. Mandating settlement of a larger number of derivative products through CCIL is, thus, likely to result in banks' exposures vis-à-vis CCIL breaching the single borrower limit. Given the general consensus that migration to guaranteed clearing will increase settlement costs for participants, incentivising banks to move to guaranteed clearing in the Indian context may also be difficult. Several options could be explored for addressing these issues viz., designing a suitable exposure framework for CCIL which addressed the issue of the single borrower limit; taking recourse to the provisions of the Payment and Settlement Systems Act, 2007 (which defines netting and provides legal recognition for the procedures adopted by the system operator provided the same are approved by the Reserve Bank when it authorises such a system) to permit netting of exposures for capital calculations; examining setting up of additional CCPs; etc. CCIL's eligibility to be treated as a qualified CCP under the new framework issued by the Basel Committee which provides for concessional capital treatment to bank exposures to qualified CCPs would also need to be examined in this connection.

FINANCIAL PRODUCTS INNOVATIONS IN INDIA: *A CRITIQUE*

Generic financial innovation has typically evolved in the form of both on-balance sheet and off-balance sheet derivative instruments. While Collateralized Debt Obligations (CDOs), CDO-squared, CDO-cubed, Credit Linked Notes (CLNs) etc., are the typical examples of on-balance sheet financial innovations. Currency Swaps, Interest Rate Swaps (IRS), Futures, Options, Credit Default Swaps (CDS), .etc., are those of off-balance sheet financial innovations. In both the types, the underlying theory and practice has been the so-called law of one price or, what is the same--- thing as the no-arbitrage argument, involving replication of derivatives cash flows in the cash markets. In other words, a derivative of an underlying cash market asset will be so priced/valued that it is not possible to arbitrage between the cash market and the derivative market, provided the derivative in question is fairly priced/valued. For, if a derivative were priced expensive relative to the underlying asset, an arbitrageur will engage in riskless arbitrage by selling the expensively priced derivative and buying the asset in the cash market by financing it at the going repo rate. In the opposite case, an arbitrageur will engage in riskless arbitrage by shorting the asset in the cash market, investing the proceeds of short sale at the higher going repo rate and buying the relatively cheap derivative until, in equilibrium, the derivative was fairly priced/valued relative to the asset in the cash market. Another way to posit the above is to say that a derivative's cash flows/pay offs can be exactly replicated in the cash market provided, of course, seamless, and frictionless, arbitrage is allowed. Significantly, and interestingly, such seamless and frictionless arbitrage also applies, just as much, to derivatives themselves. Illustratively, a long position in forward can be replicated by buying a call option and selling a put option with the strike prices for both at the current forward price. If the actual forward price is expensive relative to the 'synthetic' forward (call + put options), an arbitrageur will engage in risk-less arbitrage by selling the expensively priced forward and buying the relatively cheap 'synthetic' forward (call + put options) and vice versa.

Interest Rate Swap (IRS) Market

The Report of the Committee on Financial Sector Assessment noted that the notional principal amount of outstanding Interest Rate Swaps (IRS) of all commercial banks increased from ₹ 10 trillion+ as on 31st March 2005 to ₹ 80 trillion+ as of 31st March 2008. However, due to trade compression, involving multilateral early termination, by the Clearing Corporation of India Ltd. (CCIL), the notional principal amount of outstanding IRS of commercial banks declined to ₹ 50 trillion+ as of 30th June 2012. A granular analysis reveals that of all the commercial banks engaging in IRS, public sector banks with about 74% of total bank assets accounted for less than 2% of notional principal amount of outstanding IRS and private sector and foreign banks, with about 19%, and 7%, of total bank assets, accounted for 18%, and 80%, of total notional principal amount of outstanding IRS, respectively. In other words, with combined assets of just ₹ 6 trillion or so, foreign banks accounted for notional principal amount of outstanding IRS of ₹ 40 trillion.

Significantly, it is disturbing to note that, day in, and day out, the IRS yields trade way below yields of comparable maturity Government securities. Specifically, currently the 5 year IRS yield is trading at a negative spread of 120 basis points to 5 year G-Sec. Besides, while the G-Sec yield curve is almost flat, the IRS yield is steeply inverted to the extent of 120 basis points defying term, credit risk and liquidity risk premia which typically characterize a normal yield curve of risk assets. A typical, but fallacious, and vacuous, rationalization offered of this counter-intuitive, warped, wierd and preposterous feature is that while IRS yields are influenced by expected path of future interest rates, those of G-Secs are influenced by their supply. Nothing could be farther from the truth for this rationalization turns the very logic and reason on their head. For, being pure time value of money, G-Secs are influenced by, and immediately price in, inflationary expectations arising from higher fiscal deficit which, in turn, is the cause of additional supply of G-Secs and not the other way round. Thus, here IRS market is completely up side down and running on its head. This is completely anti-thetical to the law of one price, or the no-arbitrage argument. For, if this law held, given hugely negative spreads to Govts., fixed rate receivers, who far exceed, and overwhelmingly outnumber, fixed rate payers, would have engaged in a very simple arbitrage, involving buying corresponding maturity G-Sec in the cash market by financing it in the overnight repo market, and paying fixed, and receiving overnight, in the IRS market. This very normal, and logical, arbitrage would have had the effect of benefiting all the three stake-holders, viz., (a) fixed rate receivers receiving much higher yield than they are currently, (b) Government of India borrowing at much lower cost, and (c) business and industry in general, and infrastructure sector, in particular, getting long-term-fixed-rate-low-cost financing solutions. In other words, this would have been a win-win for all key stake- holders but, the fact of the matter is that, if anything, this is just not happening. As to the explanation of this almost a permanent, structural, though quirky and weird, counter-intuitive, perverse, and preposterous feature of the Indian IRS market, the stock, but specious, refrain is that arbitrage, involving receiving fixed on G-Secs and paying fixed in IRS, is not possible because of the so-called 'basis risk'. But this is totally untenable for the simple reason that 'basis risk' applies just as much to 'hedging' as indeed it does to 'arbitrage'. In other words, 'basis risk' is "arbitrage-hedging" agnostic and, therefore, it inevitably, and incontrovertibly, follows that the IRS market is also not being used even for 'hedging'. If that be so, as indeed it is, the question, especially, but significantly, when one also considers the fact that only 2% of the notional principal amount of the outstanding IRS is accounted for by the real sector i.e. business customers, it begs is what then is 98% of this ₹ 50 trillion+ IRS market being used for. In other words, in the case of the Indian IRS market, what holds instead is the "law-of-two-prices-and-no-arbitrage-argument". In this background, it would be no exaggeration to say that these hugely negative spreads of IRS to G-Secs are as counter-intuitive, quirky, anomalous, warped and preposterous as a father's negative age spread to his son's is. Indeed, in the analytical framework of my Singapore Speech for identifying systemic financial risks, this situation can be reasonably interpreted, in a disturbing and sit-up-and-take-notice manner of speaking, as a veritable IRS 'Super-Bubble', signifying 'huge huge' under-pricing of interest rate/ credit risks. Because a 'bubble', signifying 'huge' under-pricing of risks, is typically diagnosed with spreads of riskier assets to risk-free G-Secs being unusually low, but still positive, whereas, here in the IRS segment, spreads to G-Secs have persistently, and consistently, been negative to the extent of 100 to 150 basis points for 5 year maturity. It thus follows that where the IRS market, instead of being a means to an end of sub serving the real sector is, to all intents and purposes, existing, almost entirely for its own sake to almost complete exclusion of the needs of the real sector, creating a massive "financial sector-real sector imbalance". On this touch-stone, and hallmark, the IRS market in India is then a non-derivative, nay, a financial innovation that never was.

Credit Default Swap (CDS)

Like Interest Rate Swap, or for that matter any other derivative, Credit Default Swap is no exception to cash market replication principle of derivatives pricing. Without going into mathematical gymnastic proper, price of a CDS, in spread terms, is reasonably approximated by the difference between the spread of a reference bond to corresponding maturity G-Sec yield and the spread of IRS to the same maturity G-Sec yield. Thus, if Sc be corporate bond spread and Ss be IRS spread to risk-free G-Sec yield of corresponding maturity, then the fair/theoretical/model value/price of a CDS is approximately equal to Sc minus Ss. Tautologically, since G-Sec yield is common to both spreads, another way to approximate CDS price is simply to take the difference between the yield of the reference bond and the same maturity IRS yield. As this learned audience is aware, finally when the product was launched on 7th December, 2011, it was a stillborn. In fact, its epitaph was written in the warped, anomalous, quirky and preposterous feature of hugely negative IRS yield spreads to corresponding maturity G-Sec yields itself. For, as this discerning audience will readily see from the above formula, because of hugely negative IRS spread, fair price of a CDS would be so high as to make it both pointless, and useless, to buy a reference bond and also hedge it with a CDS. In other words, one is much better off straightaway buying a corresponding maturity risk-free G-Sec itself. Significantly, if actual CDS premium/price/spread is higher than the above theoretical/model price, then an arbitrageur will sell a CDS (which is equivalent to going long the reference corporate bond) and receive this actual spread and short the reference bond and invest the proceeds of short sale at the going corporate bond repo rate and receive fixed, and pay overnight, in an IRS, and do the opposite arbitrage if the actual CDS spread is lower than the theoretical/model spread/price until the arbitrage opportunity disappears and theoretical/model and actual market prices align again. But this arbitrage is just not possible simply because of its complete absence, in the IRS market and, therefore, a desired happening in corporate bond market cannot happen, *inter alia*, to supplement huge infrastructure funding needs of the Indian economy.

Interest Rate Futures (IRFs)

If the CDS was a stillborn, IRF too suffered mortality in its infancy the second time round after its 2003 version which itself was almost a stillborn. For, after their second launch in August 2009, Interest Rate Futures on 10-year notional government bond had seen two settlements, viz. the December 2009 contract and March 2010 contract. Significantly, both traded volumes and Open Interest (OI), witnessed decline over the two settlements, eventually decaying very quickly to zero permanently. In particular, the December 2009 contract, which had a peak Open Interest of ₹ 980 million declined to a pre-settlement Open Interest of ₹ 610 million and settled "entirely" by physical delivery, representing physical settlement of 62% of the peak Open Interest. In contrast, the March 2010 contract, which witnessed a peak Open Interest of ₹ 570 million declined to a pre-settlement Open Interest of ₹ 420 million and also settled entirely by physical delivery, representing physical settlement of 72%. Both these settlements were a far cry from the hall-mark and touch-stone of an efficient, frictionless, seamlessly coupled, and organically connected, physically-settled futures market even where physical delivery typically does not exceed 1% to 3% of the peak Open Interest. This happened because of the inefficient 'disconnect' and 'friction' in the IRF market due to only one way arbitrage viz. buying the cheapest-to-deliver (CTD), with the highest implied repo rate (IRR), by financing the same at the actual repo rate and simultaneously selling futures. In fact, as ascertained from one market participant, who accounted for almost the entire ₹ 600 million worth of physical delivery into the December 2009 contract, the implied repo rate of the CTD was 6.75% as against the actual repo rate of 3.4%, representing a risk-free arbitrage profit of 3.35%. Unlike this, on the other side, for the so-called benchmark, and most expensive-to-deliver, Government security, the IRR was almost zero to negative, suggesting an arbitrage opportunity of short-selling this bond and investing the proceeds of short sale at much higher actual repo rate and buying the futures contract. But this arbitrage could not be engaged in for want of short selling for a period coterminus with that of the futures contract. It is the possibility of this two-way arbitrage, working in the opposite directions, that, like a "good conductor" of 'heat' and 'electricity' in physics, will seamlessly conduct/transmit liquidity from the relatively more liquid (the most-expensive-to-deliver) benchmark government bonds to the so-called illiquid (the cheapest-to-deliver) bonds in the deliverable basket. Here, caution must be observed on this totally misplaced temptation, and impatience, to introduce/launch "cash-settled" IRF, any how, some how, and at any cost, must be firmly, and decisively, resisted for such medicine will be worse than the disease. The reason is that unlike assets such as equity, foreign currencies, commodities which are "homogeneous", government bonds, except , of course, for their same credit risk, are, given their differing coupons and maturities, "heterogeneous" and, therefore, for the cogent arguments adduced above, "physically-settled" contracts will make for seamless transmission/conduction of liquidity from the most liquid benchmark bonds to the relatively less liquid bonds in the deliverable basked and thus impart, and permeate, "much-needed" homogeneity in the entire deliverable basket of government bonds. But that it is perfectly legitimate to have "cash-settled" derivatives contracts in the case of 'homogeneous' assets like equity, currencies and commodities. For any 'cash-settled' derivative, where physical settlement is possible, tends to become a "non-derivative", violating the cardinal principle of arbitrage-free pricing/valuation and, therefore, comes to exist almost entirely for its own sake and to almost complete exclusion of the larger public policy purpose of sub-serving the hedging needs of the real sector, creating a massive "financial sector-real sector imbalance" and, thus, in turn, become the very antithesis of responsible financial innovation.

Market Segmentation

Continuing market segmentation in India is the biggest undoing of an efficient, deep, liquid, organically connected, and seamlessly integrated financial market which is also a 'sine qua non' for effective, efficient and instantaneous monetary transmission. Market fragmentation/segmentation contributes to price distortion and inefficiency. The most tangible and manifest evidence of market segmentation in India is the 'disconnect' between IRS, IRF and government securities markets as reflected in the IRS (bank credit risk) yields being 100 to 125 basis points below G-Sec yields and IRF yields (when last traded) being about 70 basis points higher than their fair value, signifying almost complete absence of arbitrage and thus a pernicious violation of the 'no-arbitrage', or what is the something as, the 'law-of-one-price, argument' which, as the discerning audience is by now well aware, is the most fundamental basis of 'fair value derivatives pricing'. Such manifest 'disconnect' militates against the development of a seamlessly integrated financial market with coupling and organic connect between all the three. However, this market segmentation can be credibly, effectively and decisively addressed if the nuts-and-bolts reforms propositioned below, which are equally also the necessary, and sufficient, conditions, are synchronously orchestrated in all-at-the-same-time-no-piecemeal- and-no-half-way-house manner :

i) For the cogent reasons the totally misplaced temptation, and impatience, to introduce/launch cash settled IRF must be firmly, and decisively, resisted. For else, this will tantamount to "doing the 'easy' and not the 'right' thing" and, in the process, replicating an IRS genie in the IRF/CDS markets which then grows so fast so much that it becomes difficult to put it back into the regulatory bottle.

ii) What must certainly not be done is even to contemplate, much less permit, the most-liquid-single-bond IRF for the very simple reason that this benchmark security represents less than 10% of the current 10-year IRF deliverable basket and would, therefore, at a time, when we are talking about 'inclusion', this will amount to veritable 'exclusion' of 90% of the 10-year Government securities from the benefit of hedging which arguably runs counter to the public policy purpose of IRF providing hedging to as wide a universe of government securities as possible.

iii) What also must certainly not be done is even to contemplate, much less allow, selling/repoing of securities acquired under market repo, another name for 'rehypothecation', if the IMF finding in the wake of the 2007-Global Financial Crisis is anything to go by. The IMF noted that pre-2007, thanks to re-hypothecation, the shadow-banking system in the USA generated funding/liquidity of US $ 4 trillion with the underlying "original collateral" of just US $ 1 trillion, implying astronomical and whopping margins/haircuts of "minus" US $ 3 trillion.

iv) What also must certainly not be done is allocate specific government securities to different Primary Dealers for market making as this will be a "triple whammy" in that this will straight away fragment/segment market, lead to concentration of risk and militate against portfolio diversification.

v) Symmetrical and uniform accounting treatment of both cash and derivatives (IRF/IRS/CDS) markets.

vi) Removal of the 'hedge effectiveness' criterion of 80% to 125% which militates against use of derivatives for hedging purposes for it is better to have 'ineffective' hedge than to have no hedge at all.

vii) Roll-back of the Held to Maturity (HTM) protection i.e. substituting the current "accounting hedge" with "derivative hedge". This is because with HTM, there is no incentive/compulsion whatsoever for use of market-based solutions like IRS/IRF which also require constant monitoring, infrastructure, transaction costs like brokerage and margins etc. Indeed, fears that such roll-back may be disruptive, and disorderly, are totally unfounded if one considers the fact that there is "overwhelming net fixed rate receiving" appetite/ interest in the ₹ 50 trillion+ IRS market which will be even more so with the introduction of IRF, what with the total outstanding amount of dated Government securities at ₹ 30 trillion being much less than the outstanding amount of IRS of ₹ 50 trillion.

viii) Delivery-based short-selling in the cash market for a term co-terminus with that of the futures contract and introduction of term repo, and reverse repo, markets, co-terminus again with the tenure of futures contract for borrowing and lending of cash and G-Secs.

ix) Both for IRS and IRF, actual notional/nominal amount of IRS/IRF must be allowed on duration-weighted basis unlike the current regulation which restricts the maximum notional/nominal amount of hedging instrument to no more than the notional/principal amount of the exposure being hedged resulting in under-hedging of risk.

Learning from the global experience in this regard, it will be of utmost importance that proper disclosure and reporting framework, accounting and valuation policies and clearing & settlement system for these OTC transactions develops concomitantly with the market. In this context, the recent episode of financial turbulence has provoked debate about the measurement, pricing and allocation of risk by way of derivatives, which can have important lessons for India. Some of the important issues are:

(i) Credit Risk Transfer

Over the past decade or so, the business models of global banks have evolved from a "buy-and-hold" to an "originate-to-distribute" model. Instruments to transfer risks from the balance sheets of the originating institution have developed in size and in complexity. Risks have been repackaged and spread throughout the economy. The greater part of these risks is sold to other banks and to leveraged investors, very often the originating bank itself funding the investors. Small and regional banks, in particular, were significant buyers of subprime and other structured products. Insurance companies are also increasingly using such instruments to securitise their liabilities. This wider distribution of credit risks within the global financial system should in principle limit risk concentrations and reduce the risk of a systemic shock.

Recent events, however, suggest some reservations about this positive assessment. One reservation is that banks have become increasingly able to sell quickly even the equity tranches of their loan portfolios (retaining no exposures). This means they have fewer incentives to effectively screen and monitor borrowers. A systematic deterioration in lending and collateral standards would of course entail losses greater than historical experience of default and loss-given-default rates would indicate, and it is not clear that current risk management practices make enough allowance for this. Further the gap between the original borrower and the ultimate investors widened with a number of vehicles in between. Secondly, events may force banks to re-assume risks they had assumed transferred to other parties – either to preserve a bank's reputation (eg related to investment funds sponsored by a bank) or to honour contingency liquidity/credit lines. In a crisis, major banks could therefore end up holding a larger share of exposures that they had planned to securitise.

(ii) Ratings for Structured Products

Ratings on structured finance products provide investors with an independent assessment of risks embedded in them. Given the complexity of such products, some form of expert assessment is desirable. Nevertheless, some investors failed to appreciate that ratings did not purport to cover market risk. And the use of ratings in investment mandates may have tempted some fund managers to "reach for yield" without altering their measured risk exposures. The investment grade status given to tranches of highly leveraged structures has also raised questions. Some have argued that ratings should put more emphasis on the uncertainty associated with the rating of a given structured product – especially those involving the leveraged exposure to market and liquidity risk. Others argue that ratings should cover more than just the dimension of the probability of default.

(iii) Valuation of Financial Assets

A growing share of the assets of financial firms has now to be measured at "fair-value". This fosters more active risk management but also makes reported earnings and capital more sensitive to the volatility of asset prices. In the absence of traded prices, fair-value estimates are determined using a chosen pricing model. An intrinsic problem is that the parameter values used in all such models (especially default correlations and recovery rates) are inevitably matters of judgment given limited historical data. This can bias conclusions as default correlations inevitably rise during periods of market stress, when confidence in mark-to-model prices is undermined. As uncertainty about the true market value of securities with model-driven prices rose, trading in these securities almost ground to a halt. A final aspect is that historical data available before recent events may not have been representative of a full credit cycle. The recent experience may go some way to correcting this shortcoming, and make model-driven estimates more reliable in the future. This could in turn induce a significant change in the behaviour of investors for some time.

(iv) Value at Risk (VaR)

Most financial firms use VaR and stress tests to measure market risks and assign position limits. Despite declining financial market volatility during recent years, most large banks have nevertheless reported a trend rise in the aggregate VaR of their trading book. This presumably implies that they have taken larger positions. This is not necessarily a matter of concern because trading profits and capital increased broadly in line with higher VaRs.

Yet the marked movements in the absolute VaRs of large firms over time does raise questions. These changes could reflect: (a) underlying market volatility; (b) frequent changes in the firm's positioning; or (c) changes in various aspects of methodology. If firms, conscious of methodological shortcomings, frequently modify how they compute their VaRs, changes over time may not be a good guide to changes in underlying risk exposures. This would also make it harder for counterparties to keep accurate track of how underlying risks are evolving.

(v) Stress Tests

Stress tests used by banks probably do not adequately reflect their substantial reliance on liquid capital and money markets for managing, distributing and hedging risks. Some of the problems (eg., difficulties in the leveraged loan market, the valuation of complex products) are not typically incorporated in stress tests. Stress tests at many banks also may fail to adequately capture the potentially significant growth in balance sheet exposures resulting from contingent credit and liquidity facilities. Moreover, stress tests tend to focus on a few risks and thus often fail to capture the potential interactions between many different risk factors. And in such stress tests, banks frequently assume an ability to unwind positions across a wide range of asset classes – including structured credit and other complex products – that may not be feasible in stressed conditions. In addition, attempts to reduce risk exposures during a credit event can further impair market liquidity.

This failure to take into consideration the likelihood that leveraged firms (during a period of market stress) would attempt to reduce exposures in virtually identical ways might explain why large financial shocks have been more frequent during the past 10 years than models predicted – even as underlying macroeconomic conditions have become more stable.

It is thus clear that recent bouts of market uncertainty have been aggravated by the lack of information about the distribution of risks in the global financial system and the risk profiles of individual institutions. New, complex financial instruments have increased linkages across financial institutions and made the assessment of their exposures more difficult. It has also become harder to update the valuation of collateral as market developments have unfolded. Incomplete and differing disclosures also complicate attempts to draw comparisons between them. This insufficient transparency at the firm level probably undermined *ex ante* market discipline. These issues, which have been well-known to the regulators and the industry for some years, become pressing mainly in a crisis. Lending institutions find it difficult, if not impossible, to simultaneously review in a thorough manner a large proportion of their exposures. How effectively *ex post* market discipline is allowed to operate will have a significant impact on the future conduct of financial firms.

To conclude, the derivatives market in India has been expanding rapidly and will continue to grow. While much of the activity is concentrated in foreign and a few private sector banks, increasingly public sector banks are also participating in this market as market makers and not just users. Their participation is dependent on development of skills, adapting technology and developing sound risk management practices. Corporates are also active in these markets. While derivatives are very useful for hedging and risk transfer, and hence improve market efficiency, it is necessary to keep in view the risks of excessive leverage, lack of transparency particularly in complex products, difficulties in valuation, tail risk exposures, counterparty exposure and hidden systemic risk. Clearly there is need for greater transparency to capture the market, credit as well as liquidity risks in off-balance sheet positions and providing capital therefor. From the corporate point of view, understanding the product and inherent risks over the life of the product is extremely important. Further development of the market will also hinge on adoption of international accounting standards and disclosure practices by all market participants, including corporates.

QUESTIONS

1. Define the concept of derivatives. What is the rationale for developing comprehensive reporting framework for OTC derivatives?
2. Discuss the structure of OTC derivatives market.
3. "The financial crisis underscored the importance of a robust and efficient post-trading infrastructure. It is generally believed that the opacity of the over-the-counter (OTC) derivatives market contributed to the seizure of the financial markets and spread of the financial crisis." In the context of the statement, discuss the various measures need to be taken to prevent the resource of a similar crisis, or, at least to contain the fallout.
4. Discuss the various measures required to develop a comprehensive reporting structure for OTC forex and interest rate derivatives.
5. What steps are needed to consolidate the existing reporting arrangements of this permitted OTC derivatives in India?
6. Discuss the role of Trade Reportory in the development of tools that allow regulators and other stakeholders to have access to more information thereby identify emerging risk.
7. Critically, examine the key issues in reporting of the OTC derivative transaction, and suggest optional reporting structure in light thereof.
8. "The real cause of the last global financial crisis was the unsustainable financial sector-real sector imbalance." Do you agree with this statement ?
9. Critically examine the financial innovations proxied by three derivative instruments,

viz., Interest Rate Swap (IRS), Credit Default Swap (CDS) and Interest Rate Future (IRF) as they evolved, or did not evolve in India.

10. "Financial Innovation is not an end in itself, but instead, a means to an end of sub-serving the real sector and in that sense it is consistent with, and a natural fit to puiblic policy purpose of financial sector-real sector balance." Discuss.
11. Discuss the regulatory framework evolved for derivatives market in India.
12. "The job of a derivatives traders is like that of *a bookie once removed, taking bets on people making bets.*" Do you agree with this description about fraudulent trading in derivatives. Why on earth should anyone want to be a *bookie once removed*?

REFERENCES

1. Arora, Dayanand and Rathinam, Francis Xavier (2010): 'OTC *Derivatives Market in India*: Recent Regulatory Initiatives and Open Issues for Market Stability and Development", April 2010.
2. Bank for International Settlements (1996): "OTC derivatives: Settlement Procedures and counterparty risk management", *September 1998.*
3. Bank for International Settlements (2010): "Quarteriy review", *June 2010.*
4. Bank of International Settlement, Triennlal Central Bank Survey, (2010) "Foreign Exchange and Derivatives Market Activity in April 2010 - Preliminary results", *September 2010.*
5. European Commission (2010): "Proposal for a regulation of the European Partiament and of the council on OTC derivatives, Central counterparties and trade repositories", SEC(2010) 1058/2.
6. Committee of European Securities Regulation (2010): "Transaction Reporting on OTC Derivatives and Extension of the Scope of Transaction Reporting Obligations", *Juty 19.*
7. Committee of European Securities Regulation (2009): "Trade Repositories in the European Union", *September 29.*
8. Committee on Payment and Settlement system (2010): "Considerations for trade repositories in OTC derivatives markets-Consuftative report". *May 2010.*
9. Dodd-Frank Wall Street Reform and Consumer Protection Act, USA.
10. European Central Bank (2009): "OTC derivatlves and Post tradlng infrastructures", September 2009.
11. Financial Stability Forum (200B): "Report of the Financial Stability Forum on Enhancing Market and Institutional Resilience", April 7.
12. Financial Services Authority & HM Treasury (2009): "Reforming OTC derivative markets". December 2009.
13. G-20 Leaders' statement. The Pittsburgh summit, September 24-25, 2009.
14. G-20 Toronto summit declaration, *Juna 26-27, 2010.*
15. Gambhir, Neeraj and Goel, Manoj: Foreign Exchange Derivative Market in India - Status and Prospects.
16. Gopinath, Shyamala (2010); "Over-the-counter derivative markets in India - issues and perspectives". Financial Stability Review. BanK of France, July 2010.
17. Huertas, Thomas (2006): "Credit Derivatives. Boon to Mankind or Accident Waiting to Happen", speech at Rhombus Research Annual Conference, London, April 26.
18. International Monetary Fund (2008): Counterparty Rlsk in the Over-The-Counter Derivatives Market, Working Paper -08/258, November 2008.
19. Reserve Bank of India Act. 1934.
20. Reserve Bank of India (2007). "Comprehensive guidelines on derivatives", DBOD No.BP.BC. 86/21.04.157/2006-07, April 20.
21. Reserve Bank of India (2007): Reporting Platform for OTC Interest Rate Derivatives, IDMD/11.08.15/809/ 2007-08, August 23.
22. Reserve Bank of India (2010): "Master Circular on Risk Management and Inter-Bank Dealings", July 1.

42

Derivatives and Commodity Exchange

INTRODUCTION

Commodity exchange in India plays an important role where the prices of any commodity are not fixed, in an organised way. Earlier only the buyer of produce and its seller in the market judged upon the prices. Others never had a say, Today, commodity exchanges are purely speculative in nature. Before discovering the price,'they reach to the producers, end-users, and even the retail investors, at a grassroots level. It brings a price transparency and risk management in the vital market.

A big difference between a typical auction, where a single auctioneer announces the bids, and the Exchange is that people are not only competing to buy but also to sell. By Exchange rules and by law, no one can bid under a higher bid, and no one can offer to sell higher than somone else's lower offer. That keeps the market as efficient as possible, and keeps the traders on their toes to make sure no one gets the purchase or sale before they do. The chapter discusses the evolution and functioning of the three major national demutalised multi-commodity exchanges, turnover on commodity futures markets, and the recent policy initiatives relating to the comodity markets.

EVOLUTION AND FUNCTIONING OF COMMODITY EXCHANGES

Commodity exchanges are those which trade in particular commodities, neglecting the trade of securities, stock index futures and options etc. The Indian experience in commodity futures market dates back to thousand of years. Reference to such markets in India appear in Kautialya's 'Arthasastra,' The words, 'Teji', 'Mandi', 'Gali,' and 'Phatak' have been commonly heard in Indian markets for centuries.

The first organized futures market was however established in 1875 under the aegis of the Bombay Cotton Trade Association to trade in cotton contracts. Derivatives trading were then spread to oilseeds, jute and food grains. The derivatives trading in India however did not have uninterrupted legal 'approval. By the Second World War, i.e., between the 1920's &1940's, futures trading in organized form had commenced in a number of commodities such as - cotton, groundnut, groundnut oil, raw jute, jute goods, castor seed, wheat, rice, sugar, precious metals like gold and silver. During the Second World War futures trading was prohibited under Defence of India Rules.

After independence, the subject of futures trading was placed in the Union list, and Forward Contracts (Regulation) Act, 1952 was enacted. Futures trading in commodities particularly, cotton, oilseeds and bullion, was at its peak during this period. However following the scarcity in various commodities, futures trading in most commodities was prohibited in mid-sixties. There was a time when trading was permitted only two minor commodities, viz., pepper and turmeric.

Deregulation and liberalization following the forex crisis in early 1990s, also triggered policy changes leading to re-introduction of futures trading in commodities in India. The growing realization of imminent globalization under the WTO regime and non-sustainability of the Government support to commodity sector led the Government to explore the alternative of market-based mechanism, viz., futures markets, to protect the commodity sector from price-volatility. In April, 1999 the Government took a landmark decision to remove all the commodities from the restrictive list. Food-grains, pulses and bullion were not exceptions.

The long spell of prohibition had stunted growth and modernization of the surviving traditional commodity exchanges. Therefore, along with liberalization of commodity futures, the Government initiated steps to cajole and incentives the existing Exchanges to modernize their systems and structures. Faced with the grudging reluctance to modernize and slow pace of introduction of fair and transparent "structures by the existing Exchanges, Government allowed setting up of new modern, demutualised Nation-wide Multi-commodity Exchanges with investment support by public and private institutions.

After a gap of almost three decades, Government of India has allowed forward transaction in commodities through Online Commodity Exchanges, a modification of traditional business known as 'Adhat' and 'Vayda Vyapar' to facilitate better risk coverage and delivery of commodities.

COMMODITY FUTURES

A Commodity futures is an agreement between two parties to buy or sell a specified and standardized quantity of a commodity at a certain time in future at a price agreed upon at the time of entering into the contract on the commodity futures exchange. A futures contract is a highly standardized contract with certain distinct features. Futures trading are necessarily organised under the auspices of a market association so that such trading is confined to or conducted through members of the association in accordance with the procedures laid down in the rules and bye-laws of the association. It is invariably entered into for a standard variety known as the 'basis variety' with permission to deliver other identified varieties known as 'tenderable varieties'. The units of price quotation and trading are fixed in these contracts, and parties to the contracts are not capable of altering these units .The delivery periods are specified. The seller in a futures market has the choice to decide whether to deliver goods against outstanding sale contracts. In case he decides to deliver goods, he can do so not only at the location of the association through which trading is organised but also at a number of other pre-specified delivery centres. In futures markets, the actual delivery of goods takes place only in a minimum number of cases. Transactions are mostly squared up before the due date of the contract and contracts are settled by the payment of differences without any physical delivery of goods taking place.

A futures market facilitates offsetting trades without exchanging physical goods until the expiry of a contract. As a result, the futures market attracts hedgers for risk management, and encourages participation of traders (speculators and arbitrageurs) who possess market information and price judgement. While hedgers have long-term perspective of the market, the traders or arbitrageurs prefer an immediate view of the market and these diverging views lead to price discovery for the commodity concerned.

The need for a futures market arises mainly due to the hedging function that it can perform. Commodity markets, like any other financial instrument, involve risk associated with frequent price volatility. The loss due to price volatility can be attributed to the following reasons:

1. **Consumer Preferences:** In the short-term, their influence on price volatility is small since it is a slow process permitting manufacturers, dealers and wholesalers to adjust their inventory in advance.
2. **Changes in supply:** They are abrupt and unpredictable bringing about wild fluctuations in prices. This can be especially noticed in agricultural commodities where the weather plays a major role in affecting the fortunes of people involved in this industry. The, futures market has evolved to neutralize such risks through a mechanism; namely hedging.

Forward/futures trading involves a passage of time between entering into a contract and its performance making thereby the contracts susceptible to risks, uncertainties, etc. Hence there is a need for the regulatory functions to be exercised by an authority that is the Forward Markets Commission (FMC).

PARTICIPANTS OF COMMODITY DERIVATIVES

For a market to succeed, it must have all three kinds of participants - hedgers, speculators and arbitragers. The confluence of these participants ensures liquidity and efficient price discovery on the market. Commodity markets give opportunity for all three kinds of participants.

Hedgers

Many participants in the commodity futures market are hedgers. They use the futures market to reduce a particular risk that they face. This risk might relate to the price of any commodity that the person deals in. The classic hedging example is that of wheat farmer who wants to hedge the risk of fluctuations in the price of wheat around the time that his crop is ready for harvesting. By selling his crop forward, he obtains a hedge by locking in to a predetermined price. Hedging does not necessarily improve the financial outcome; indeed, it could make the outcome worse. What it does however is, that it makes the outcome more certain. Hedgers could be government institutions, private corporations like financial institutions, trading companies and even other participants in the value chain, for instance farmers, extractors, ginners, processors etc., who are influenced by the commodity prices.

There are basically two kinds of hedges that can be taken. A company that wants to sell an asset at a particular time in the future can hedge by taking short futures position. This is called a short hedge. A short hedge is a hedge that requires a short position in futures contracts. A short hedge is appropriate when the hedger already owns the asset, or is likely to own the asset and expects to sell it at some time in the future.

Similarly, a company that knows that it is due to buy an asset in the future can hedge by taking long futures position. This is known as long hedge. A long hedge is appropriate when a company knows it will have to purchase a certain asset in the future and wants to lock in a price now.

Speculators

If hedgers are the people who wish to avoid price risk, speculators are those who are willing to take such risk. These are the people who take positions in the market & assume risks to profit from price fluctuations. In fact the speculators consume market information, make forecasts about the prices & put money in these forecasts. An entity having an opinion on the price movements of a given commodity can speculate using the commodity market. While the basics of speculation apply to any market, speculating in commodities is not as simple as speculating on stocks in the financial market. For a speculator who thinks the shares of a given company will rise, it is easy to buy the shares and hold them for whatever duration he Wants to. However, commodities are bulky products and come with all the costs and procedures of handling these products. The commodities futures markets provide speculators with an easy mechanism to speculate on the price of underlying commodities. To trade commodity futures on the NCDEX, a customer must open a futures trading account with a commodity derivatives broker. Buying futures simply involves putting in the margin money. This enables futures traders to take a position in the underlying commodity without having to actually hold that commodity. With the purchase of futures contract on a commodity, the holder essentially makes a legally binding promise or obligation to buy the underlying security at some point in the future (the expiration date of the contract).

Arbitrage

A central idea in modern economics is the law of one price. This states that in a competitive market, if two assets are equivalent from the point of view of risk and return, they should sell at the same price. If the price of the same asset is different in two markets, there will be operators who will buy in the market where the asset sells cheap and sell in the market where it is costly. This activity termed as arbitrage. The buying cheap and selling expensive continues till prices in the two markets reach equilibrium. Hence, arbitrage helps to equalise prices and restore market efficiency.

The cost-of-carry ensures that futures prices stay in tune with the spot prices of the underlying assets. Whenever the futures price deviates substantially from its fair value, arbitrage opportunities arise. To capture mispricings that result in overpriced futures, the arbitrager must sell futures and buy spot, whereas to capture mispricings that result in underpriced futures, the arbitrager must sell spot and buy futures. In the case of investment commodities, mispricing would result in both, buying the spot and holding it or selling the spot and investing the proceeds. However, in the case of consumption assets which are held primarily for reasons of usage, even if there exists a mispricing, a person who holds the underlying may not want to sell it to profit from the arbitrage.

Commodity swaps allow traders and hedgers to eliminate their exposure to a commodity risk while simultaneously creating an exposure in the money market. Alternatively, as is the case with equity index swaps, they can be used as a way of creating an exposure to commodity risk without actually buying the underlying commodity itself. The effect of this is to change the hedger's or trader's exposure from commodity to money market risk or vice versa.

A gold producer, for example, has a revenue stream which depends upon the value of the gold sold in the marketplace. As the gold price rises, so the producer's revenue increases. If the gold producer wants to fix its return for a given period, then a commodity swap provides it with one means of achieving this. The gold producer contracts to receive a fixed price for a given quantity of gold over a given maturity and agrees in return to pay a floating interest rate. The gold producer will now no longer benefit from a rise in the gold price, but will no longer suffer from its fall. Thus the producer has effectively switched its risk from the gold price to the money market. In essence then, commodity swaps follow the pattern of interest rate, currency and equity swaps in that they allow payers and receivers to change their risk from one market to another.

OBJECTIVES OF COMMODITY FUTURES

Hedging with the objective of transferring risk related to the possession of physical assets through any adverse moments in price. Liquidity and Price discovery to ensure base minimum volume in trading of a commodity through market information and demand supply factors that facilitates a regular and authentic price discovery mechanism.

Maintaining buffer stock and better allocation of resources as it augments reduction in inventory requirement and thus the exposure to risks related with price fluctuation declines. Resources can thus be diversified for investments.

Price stabilization along with balancing demand and supply position. Futures trading leads to predictability in assessing the domestic prices, which maintains stability, thus safeguarding against any short term adverse price movements. Liquidity in Contracts of the commodities traded also ensures in maintaining the equilibrium between demand and supply.

Flexibility, certainty and transparency in purchasing commodities facilitate bank financing. Predictability in prices of commodity would lead to stability, which in turn would eliminate the risks associated with running the business of trading commodities. This would make funding easier and less stringent for banks to commodity market players.

BENEFITS OF COMMODITY FUTURES MARKETS

The primary objectives of any futures exchange are authentic price discovery and an efficient price risk management. The beneficiaries include those who trade in the commodities being offered in the exchange as well as those who have nothing to do with futures trading. It is because of price discovery and risk management through the existence of futures exchanges that a lot of businesses and services are able to function smoothly.

Price Discovery: Based on inputs regarding specific market information, the demand and supply equilibrium, weather forecasts, expert views and comments, inflation rates, Government policies, market dynamics, hopes and fears, buyers and sellers conduct trading at futures exchanges. This transforms in to continuous price discovery mechanism. The execution of trade between buyers and sellers leads to assessment of fair value of a particular commodity that is immediately disseminated on the trading terminal.

Price Risk Management: Hedging is the most common method of price risk management. It is strategy of offering price risk that is inherent in spot market by taking an equal but opposite position in the futures market. Futures markets are used as a mode by hedgers to protect their business from adverse price change which could dent the profitability of their business. Hedging benefits all those who are involved in trading of commodities like farmers, processors, merchandisers, manufacturers, exporters, importers etc.

Import- Export competitiveness: The exporters can hedge their price risk and improve their competitiveness by making use of futures market. A majority of traders which are involved in physical trade internationally intend to buy forwards. The purchases made from the physical market might expose them to the risk of price risk resulting to losses. The existence of futures market would allow the exporters to hedge their proposed purchase by temporarily substituting for actual purchase till the time is ripe to buy in physical market. In the absence of futures market it will be meticulous, time consuming and costly physical transactions.

Predictable Pricing: The demand for certain commodities is highly price elastic. The manufacturers have to ensure that the prices should be stable in order to protect their market share with the free entry of imports. Futures contracts will enable predictability in domestic prices. The manufacturers can, as a result, smooth out the influence of changes in their input prices very easily. With no futures market, the manufacturer can be caught between severe short-term price movements of oils and necessity to maintain price stability, which could only be possible through sufficient financial reserves that could otherwise be utilized for making other profitable investments.

Benefits for farmers/agriculturalists: Price instability has a direct bearing on farmers in the absence of futures market. There would be no need to have large reserves to cover against unfavorable price fluctuations. This would reduce the risk premiums associated with the marketing or processing margins enabling more returns on produce. Storing more and being more active in the markets. The price information accessible to the farmers determines the extent to which traders/processors increase price to them. Since one of the objectives of futures exchange is to make available these prices as far as possible, it is very likely to benefit the farmers. Also, due to the time lag between planning and production, the market-determined price information disseminated by futures exchanges would be crucial for their production decisions.

Credit accessibility: Buyers and sellers can avail of the bank finances for trading in commodities. Many nationalized banks as also some banks in the private sector have come forward to offer credit facilities for commodity trading. More and more banks are likely to fall in line looking at the huge potential that commodity market offers in India. Commodities are less volatile compared to equity market, but more volatile as compared to government securities.

Improved product quality: The existence of warehouses for facilitating delivery with grading facilities along with other related benefits provides a very strong reason to upgrade and enhance the quality of the commodity to grade that is acceptable by the exchange. It ensures uniform standardization of commodity trade, including the terms of quality standard: the quality certificates that are issued by the exchange-certified warehouses have the potential to become the norm for physical trade.

Benefits to Investors: High financial leverage is possible in commodity markets. In case of stocks, an investor needs to put up the full amount of the stock value to buy the stock. With commodities, you control commodity futures contracts with a margin, (usually between 5% to 10% of the value of the commodity). Investor can effectively hedge the risk in price fluctuations of a commodity. Investor can also hedge his risk on investments in stocks and debt markets since commodities provide a choice and provide one more alternative avenue in the investment portfolio. Commodities are usually less volatile compared to equity market, though more volatile as compared to G-Sec's

DIFFERENCE BETWEEN COMMODITY AND FINANCIAL DERIVATIVES

The basic concept of a derivative contract remains the same whether the underlying happens to be a commodity or a financial asset. However there are some features which are very peculiar to commodity derivative markets.

Physical settlement: In the case of financial derivatives, most of these contracts are cash settled. Even in the case of physical settlement, financial assets are not bulky and do not need special facility for storage. Physical settlement of commodity derivatives involves the physical delivery of the underlying commodity, typically at an accredited warehouse. The seller intending to make delivery would have to take the commodities to the designated warehouse and the buyer intending to take delivery would have to go to the designated warehouse and pick up the commodity. The physical settlement of commodities is a complex process. Some of the issues faced in physical settlement of commodities are:-

1) Limits on storage facilities in different states.
2) Restrictions on interstate movement of commodities.
3) State level octroi and duties have an impact on the cost of movement of goods across locations.

Warehousing: One of the main differences between financial and commodity derivatives is the need for warehousing. In case of most exchange-traded financial derivatives, all the positions are cash settled. Cash settlement involves paying up the difference in prices between the time the contract was entered into and the time the contract was closed. In case of commodity derivatives however, there is a possibility of physical settlement, which means that if the seller chooses to hand over the commodity instead of the difference in cash, the buyer must take physical delivery of the underlying asset. This requires the exchange to make an arrangement with warehouses to handle the settlements. The efficacy of the commodities settlements depends on the warehousing system available. Most international commodity exchanges use certified warehouses (CWH) for the purpose of handling physical settlements. Such CWH are required to provide storage facilities for participants in the commodities markets and to certify the quantity and quality of the underlying commodity.

Quality of underlying assets: A derivatives contract is written on a given underlying asset. Variance in quality is not an issue in case of financial derivatives as the physical attribute is missing. When the underlying asset is a commodity, the quality of the underlying asset is of prime importance. There may be quite some variation in the quality of what is available in the marketplace. When the asset is specified, it is therefore important that the exchange stipulate the grade or grades of the commodity that are acceptable. Commodity derivatives demand good standards and quality assurance/ certification procedures. A good grading system allows commodities to be traded by specification. Currently there are various agencies that are responsible for specifying grades for commodities. For example, the Bureau of Indian Standards (BIS) under Ministry of Consumer Affairs specifies standards for processed agricultural commodities whereas AGMARK under the department of rural development under Ministry of Agriculture is responsible for promulgating standards for basic agricultural commodities. Apart from these, there are other agencies like EIA, which specify standards for export oriented commodities.

WORKING OF COMMODITY MARKET

There are two kinds of trades in commodities. The first is the spot trade, in which one pays cash and carries away the goods. The second is futures trade. The underpinning for futures is the warehouse receipt. A person deposits certain amount of say, good X in a ware house and gets a warehouse receipt, which allows him to ask for physical delivery of the good from the warehouse. But some one trading in commodity futures need not necessarily possess such a receipt to strike a deal. A person can buy or sale a commodity future on an exchange based on his expectation of where the price will go. Futures have something called an expiry date, by when the buyer or seller either closes (square off) his account or give/take delivery of the commodity. The broker maintains an account of all dealing parties in which the daily profit or loss due to changes in the futures price is recorded. Squaring off is done by taking an opposite contract so that the net outstanding is nil.

For commodity futures to work, the seller should be able to deposit the commodity at warehouse nearest to him and collect the warehouse receipt. The buyer should be able to take physical delivery at a location of his choice on presenting the warehouse receipt. But at present in India very few warehouses provide delivery for specific commodities. Today Commodity trading system is fully computerized. Traders need not visit a commodity market to speculate. With online commodity trading they could sit in the confines of their home or office and call the shots.

Trading, Settlement and Risk Management of Commodity Futures

The Indian commodity exchanges have witnessed a sharp surge in trade volumes and turnover in recent years. Consequently, the stakes are higher than ever before. Investment in commodity futures is now serving as a noticeable alternative to traditional investments in stock markets. Further, with a progressive FDI policy for commodity markets on the anvil, investor prerequisites include transparency and assurance on the enforcement of future contracts. While the FMC serves as a regulatory body, the exchange defines its own day-to-day functioning, which encompasses setting the norms of trading and settlement, insuring adequate arrangement for surveillance and following the best practices for risk management, which are premeditated to be in line with international standards.

Futures trading in commodities results in transparent and fair price discovery on account of large-scale participation of entities associated with different value chains. This reflects upon the views and expectations of a wide section of investors related to that commodity. It provides an effective platform for price-risk management for all segments of players ranging from producers, traders, processors, exporters/importers and the end-users of a commodity.

The delivery and settlement procedure differs for each commodity in terms of quality implications, place of delivery, options, penalties and margins, and are defined comprehensively by the exchanges. Members of an exchange can perform and clear transactions in only those contracts which are exchange specified and approved by the FMC.

Margin Requirements

With respect to the contracts that are transacted in the exchanges, buyers and sellers will be required to maintain a certain amount as initial margin, including special margin (as applicable) on their respective future positions. These margins vary for each commodity and for different contract months depending upon factors such as market volatility, government policies, macro-economic factors, international price movements, etc.

Margin provisions, subject to margin requirements, are determined by applying the methodology as specified by the exchange and are settled by the clearing house of the exchange. For example, the exchange can levy an initial margin on derivatives contracts using the concept of Value at Risk (VaR) or any other concept as prescribed. Additional margins are levied for deliverable positions on the basis of VaR from the expiry of the contract till the actual settlement date, including a mark-up in case of default. The estimated margin (based on the prescribed methodology) may be on gross position basis, net position basis, client level basis or in any other manner determined by the exchange.

Every clearing member is also required to maintain an appropriate margin account with the clearing house of the exchange against the aggregate open positions cleared by the clearing member in respect of (i) the clearing member's own account, (ii) for other members of the exchange with whom the clearing member has an agreement and, (iii) clients, where applicable.

Margin accounts of all exchange members are marked daily to the market and the exchange members are required to pay the amount prescribed by the clearing house. The entire day's trades and open positions on the exchange are marked to closing price for the respective futures contract, on the basis of which the hypothetical gain or loss is estimated. The investor is required to collect or make compensation for this amount at the end of each trading day. The exchange also prescribes additional or special margins as may be considered necessary during the delivery period and emergencies. Every member of the exchange executing transactions on behalf of clients is required to regularly (time interval is exchange specified) collect the margins from their clients against their open positions.

Relevant authorities also have the right to affect marking to market and settlements through the clearing house more than once during the course of a working day. If deemed fit on account of market risks and other parameters; settlement of differences due on outstanding transactions shall be made by clearing members through the clearing house. This provision prevents the possibility of a potential loss where any of the contracts' participants might default on their contractual obligations. The exchange enforces disciplinary action on any member or a client when they fail to pay the variation margin that is required to maintain the minimum margin requirements. This may even include suspension of the exchange members.

Clearing and Settlement

All futures contracts are settled through the clearing house of each exchange. The settlement, clearing and guaranteeing services of the clearing house can be obtained exclusively by the clearing members. The clearing house also registers the financial performance of the contracts entered into on the exchange. Each exchange has a set eligibility criterion for a person to be qualified as a clearing member.

In order to facilitate smooth clearing and settlement, all exchange members participating in futures trading are required to have bank accounts with designated clearing banks as may be advised by the exchange. All members are required to strictly follow the instructions issued by the exchange regarding the operation of such bank accounts, minimum balance, segregation of clients' fund and own fund, etc. They should also submit an irrevocable mandate in writing, enabling the exchange to debit and credit their settlement account electronically. They are therefore required to keep their accounts adequately funded, to enable the exchange to recover its dues by debiting it.

Each clearing member has to submit all the trades executed by constituent members or clients with whom he has such an agreement and assist the clearing house in a pre-arranged form and manner to effectively manage the clearing facility.

The clearing house processes all transactions submitted and accepts only the net liability of the clearing member to the clearing house. Once a contract is matched and marked to market by the clearing house, the exchange becomes the counter party for all net financial liabilities of the clearing members in specified commodities or contracts in which the exchange has decided to accept the responsibility of guaranteeing the financial obligations.

Delivery

The exchange may prescribe tender days and delivery period for each contract month during which a seller who wishes to tender delivery may issue delivery orders through specific clearing members. Tender days and delivery period end on or before the last day of trading of the relevant contract month.

All contracts outstanding at the end of the last trading day of the contract month of the maturing contract will be closed-out at the due date rate as per the contract specifications. The relevant authority prescribes a penalty on sellers with outstanding positions who fail to issue delivery orders; the exchange may financially compensate the buyers who hold outstanding positions and intended to lift delivery but could not receive delivery orders against such positions due to a failure on the part of the seller.

In Case of Cash Settlement

The, buyer who fails to accept delivery orders is required to pay the difference between the settlement price and the due date rate. In addition, the buyer will have to pay a penalty, as ascertained by the exchange. The seller, who tenders the delivery document, is compensated with the penalty recovered from the buyer, while the delivery is returned to the seller. Failure to pay the dues and penalties relating to such closing out within the stipulated period causes the member to be declared a defaulter, and renders him liable for disciplinary action.

In Case of Physical Delivery

An exchange member desiring to tender goods against an open short position in the maturing contract sends delivery orders to the clearing house through the clearing member up to such time on the stated tender days. The delivery order forms duly signed by the sellers or seller's representative, holding short open positions, should offer the following particulars, in addition to the particulars in the delivery order:

a) *The quality and quantity of goods to be delivered*

b) *Delivery order rate (to be filled in by the clearing house)*

c) *Name of the seller issuing the delivery order*

d) *Period of delivery*

e) *The address or addresses of the warehouse (s) or any storage place where the goods* are kept and the quantity thereof at each warehouse

f) *The name and address of the seller's representative who should be contacted by the buyer for collecting the delivery.*

A seller is entitled to offer delivery only at the exchange determined delivery centres. The delivery can be tendered at these specified centres, strictly as per the contractual delivery procedure. Before tendering delivery, the seller is also required to obtain a certificate from a surveyor empanelled by the exchange and this certificate has to be accompanied with the delivery order being tendered to the clearing house. The surveyor's certificate clearly specifies the quality of the goods tendered and also confirms that such quality is tenderable as per the contract specification of the exchange. In case of non-compliance with any of these conditions, the delivery order is rejected and initiate clearing members shall, in turn, assign the full quantity of goods covered by the delivery orders to their clients holding outstanding long positions.

Additional Practices

To facilitate transparency, a cost-effective trading system and to avoid information asymmetry, other functions of the exchanges, with respect to trading include the determination of the transaction and clearing fees payable by the members of the exchange for trading in different commodities and other charges that may be collected by the exchange from members, registered non-members, participants, approved users, etc. Moreover, the exchange is responsible for fixing the units of trading, the minimum and maximum quantity of contracts traded to be purchased or sold and the limits on price fluctuations permitted in a day or for a particular time period for a particular commodity. This is implemented to avoid acute price volatilities.

With the intention of carrying out periodic and specific checks and inspections related to procedures involved in trading, price manipulation, price distortion and other trading malpractices, major national exchanges have a vigilance committee in place. Commodity-specific experts constitute the senior executives in an exchange to identify such malpractices and maintain an investor-consumer responsive trading environment.

Further, investor awareness in terms of the commodities trade jargon and risk implications form the focal areas of each exchange. Information on these aspects is widely disseminated by the way of online and other media publications, press releases, exchanges' websites, etc. However, the procedure for the same may differ for each exchange. Moreover, the risk disclosure document provides basic and important insight into the risks associated with trading in commodity futures.

STRUCTURE OF THE COMMODITY FUTURES MARKETS IN INDIA

Broadly, the commodities market exists in two distinct forms—the over-the-counter (OTC) market and the exchange-based market. Further, as in equities, there exists the spot and the derivatives segments. Spot markets are essentially OTC markets and participation is restricted to people who are involved with that commodity, such as the farmer, processor, wholesaler, etc. A majority of the derivatives trading takes place through the exchange-based markets with standardised contracts, settlements, etc. The exchange-based markets are essentially derivative markets and are similar to equity derivatives in their working, that is, everything is standardised and a person can purchase *a* contract by paying only a percentage of the contract value. A person can also go short on these exchanges. Moreover, even though there is a provision for delivery, most contracts are squared-off before expiry and are settled in cash. As a result, one can see an active participation by people who are not associated with the commodity.

The commodity futures traded in commodity exchanges are regulated by the Government under the Forward Contracts Regulations Act, 1952 and the rules framed there under. The regulator for the commodities trading is the Forward Markets Commission (FMC), situated at Mumbai, which conies under the Ministry of Consumer Affairs, Food and Public Distribution.

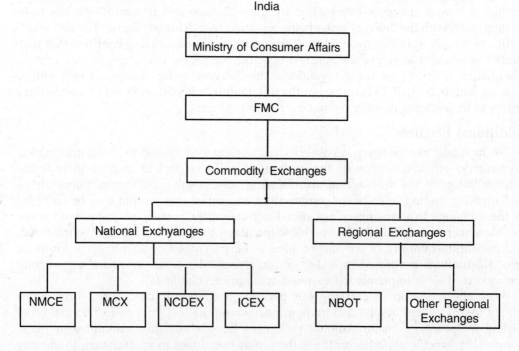

FIGURE 1: STRUCTURE OF COMMODITY FUTURES MARKET IN INDIA

As per the Forward Contracts Regulations Act 1952, the Exchange that organises forward trading in regulated commodities can prepare its own rules (Articles of Association) and bylaws and regulate trading on a day-to-day basis. The FMC approves those rules and byelaws and provides a regulatory overview.

COMMODITY EXCHANGE IN INDIA

Exchange is an association of members which provides all organizational support for carrying out futures trading in a formal environment. These exchanges are managed by the Board of Directors which is composed primarily of the members of the association. There are also representatives of the government and public nominated by the Forward Markets Commission. The majority of members of the Board have been chosen from among the members of the Association who have trading and business interest in the exchange. The Board is assisted by the chief executive officer and his team in day-to-day administration. At present, there are four national level multi-commodity exchanges and a number of recognised commodity futures exchanges in India. The national level multi-commodity exchanges are discussed below:

National Multi-Commodity Exchange of India Limited (NMCE)

In first state-of-the-art dematuralised electronic multi-commodity exchange, National Multi-Commodity Exchange of India Ltd. (NMCE) promoted by commodity-relevant public institutions, viz., Central Warehousing Corporation (CWC), National Agricultural Cooperative Marketing Federation of India (NAFED), Gujarat Agro-Industries Corporation Limited (GAICL), Gujarat State Agricultural Marketing Board (GSAMB), National Institute of Agricultural Marketing (NIAM), and Neptune Overseas Limited (NOL). was granted the National status on permanent basis by the Government of India. While various integral aspects of commodity economy, viz:;warehousing, cooperatives, private and public sector marketing of agricultural commodities, research and training were adequately addressed in structuring the Exchange, finance was still a vital missing link. Punjab National Bank (PNB) took equity of the Exchange to establish that linkage. Even today, NMCE is the only Exchange in India to have such investment and technical support from the commodity relevant institutions. These institutions are represented on the Board of Directors of the Exchange and also on various committees set up by the Exchange to ensure good corporate governance. Some of them have also lent their personnel to provide technical support to the Exchange management. The day-to-day operations of the Exchange are managed by the experienced and qualified professionals with impeccable integrity and expertise. None of them have any trading interest. The structure of NMCE is impossible to replicate in India.

NMCE is unique in many other respects. It is a zero-debt company; following widely accepted prudent accounting and auditing practices. It has robust delivery mechanism making it the most suitable for the participants in the physical commodity markets. The exchange does not compromise on its delivery provisions to attract speculative volume. Public interest rather than commercial interest guide the functioning of the Exchange. It has also established fair and transparent rule-based procedures and demonstrated total commitment towards eliminating any conflicts of interest. It is the only Commodity Exchange in the world to have received ISO 9001:2000 certification from British Standard Institutions (BSI).

NMCE commenced futures trading in 24 commodities on 26th November, 2002 on a national scale and the basket of commodities has grown substantially since then to include cash crops, food grains, plantations, spices, oil seeds, metals & bullion among others. Research Desk of NMCE is constantly in the process of identifying the hedging needs of the commodity economy and the basket of products is likely to grow even further. NMCE has also made immense contribution in raising awareness about and catalyzing implementation of policy reforms in the commodity sector. NMCE was the first Exchange to take up the issue of differential treatment of speculative loss. It was also the first Exchange to enroll participation of high net-worth corporate securities brokers in commodity derivatives market. It was the Exchange, which showed a way to introduce warehouse receipt system within existing legal and regulatory framework. It was the first Exchange to complete the contractual groundwork for dematerialization of the warehouse receipts. Innovation is the way of life at NMCE.

A Close Look At NMCE

NMCE's Exchange solution is a mission critical application which it had then selected in 2002 off the shelf market and then it worked around and built a heavy structure with multiple features and functionalities including its integration with delivery and settlement system & to bring user friendliness and regulatory changes from time to time. Now this is completely different than the original basic application. DTSS is built on C, C++, VC, Power Builder Languages with Sybase as database. This is message based architecture.

When an order is placed on the exchange, the server at NMCE scans through the orders posted on it from all its trading terminals. It then locates and matches the best counter-offers/bids by maintaining anonymity of the counter-parties. Anonymity helps is eliminating formation of cartels and other unfair practices, thereby protecting the efficiency of price- discovery at the Exchange. NMCE was the first commodity exchange to provide trading facility through internet, through Virtual Private Network (VPN).

NMCE follows best international risk management practices. The contracts are marked to market on daily basis. The system of upfront margining based on Value at Risk is followed to ensure financial security of the market. In the event of high volatility in the prices, special intra-day clearing and settlement is held. NMCE has also set up a Trade Guarantee Fund. Well-capitalized in-house clearinghouse assumes counter-party risk of settlement. NMCE was the first to initiate process of dematerialization and electronic transfer of warehoused commodity stocks. The unique strength of NMCE is its settlements via a Delivery Backed System, an imperative in the commodity trading business. These deliveries are executed through a sound and reliable Warehouse Receipt System, leading to guaranteed clearing and settlement.

Multi-Commodity Exchange of India (MCX)

The multi-commodity exchange of India (MCX) was was launched in November 2003 by Financial Technologies (India) Ltd (FTIL), a financial services software firm which secured one of the four licences offered when the Indian government ended a longstanding ban on commodities exchanges in 2002. It has since grown more rapidly than its two main domestic rivals. National Multi-Commodity Exchange (NMCE) and National Commodity and Derivatives Exchange (NCDEX) and is now the market's leading player. It has a state of the art trading platform, which serves the risk management needs of commodity market participants offering widest range of international benchmark commodities as well as domestic commodities. MCX has entered into strategic global alliance with leading global commodity exchanges and has also taken a collaborative approach with several domestic commodity associations and bodies for the overall development of the Indian commodity sector.

MCX also one amongst the leading commodity derivatives exchanges in the world. MCX sets benchmark reference prices for number of primary commodities of national significance in the agriculture, bullion, base metals, energy, emissions and industrial sectors. Being a nation-wide commodity exchange MCX has a robust and scalable infrastructure, offering wide reach & penetration through 1000+ centers, more than 1800 members and 42000 +terminals nationally.

MCX offers a wide spectrum of opportunities to a large cross section of participants including Producers/ Processors, Traders, Corporates, Importers, Exporters, Co-operatives and Industry Associations amongst others. Within 4 years, MCX has brought a paradigm change in the Indian commodities sector through its innovative application of technology, path-breaking ideas, novel products & unique alliances. Today, MCX has become synonymous with innovation as it has consistently done things differently and also adopted new practices to emerge as thought leader in its industry. MCX has successfully put India on the global commodities map, by discovering benchmark commodity prices in the Indian time zone between London & Tokyo. Globally today MCX ranks among the world's top 10 commodity exchanges in terms of number of contracts traded based on FIA for Year 2007. MCX also ranks no. 1 silver, no.2 in natural gas and no.3 in gold, crude oil, and copper futures trading in the world. In addition to being accredited with ISO 9001: 2000 for quality management, MCX has the distinction of achieving the ISO 27001: 2005 certification, the global benchmark for information security management systems.

Currently, there are four categories of membership available at MCX, depending upon the trading and clearing rights.

Trading Member (TM): A Trading Member (TM) is a person having been admitted by the Board as such, who shall have rights to trade on his own account as well as on account of his clients, but shall have no right to clear and settle such trades himself. All such trading members must be affiliated with any one of the Institutional Trading-cum-Clearing Member (ITCM) or Professional Clearing Member (PCM) having clearing rights on the Exchange.

Trading-cum-Clearing Member (TCM): A TCM is entitled to trade on his own account as well as on account of his clients, and clear and settle trades himself. A sole proprietor, partnership firm, a joint Hindu Undivided Family (HUF), a corporate entity, a co-operative society, a public sector organization or any other Government or non-Government entity can become a TCM.

There are two types of TCM memberships, namely, TCM-1 and TCM-2. TCM-1 refers to transferable non-deposit based membership and TCM-2 refers to non-transferable deposit-based membership.

Institutional Trading-cum-Clearing Member (ITCM): Only an Institution/Corporate can be admitted by the exchange as a member, conferring upon them the right to trade and clear through the Clearing House of the Exchange as an ITCM. Moreover, the member may be allowed to make deals for himself as well as on behalf of his clients and clear and settle such deals. Further the ITCMs can also appoint sub-brokers, authorized persons and Trading Members who would be registered as Trading Members on MCX at the request of the ITCM. The ITCM will clear and settle trades on behalf of the sub-brokers, authorized persons and such Trading Members registered on their requests.

Professional Clearing Members: A PCM is entitled to clear and settle traders executed by other members of the exchange. A corporate entity and an institution only can apply for PCM. The member would be allowed to clear and settle trades of such members of the exchange who choose to clear and settle their trades through such PCM.

Types of Margins

Different types of margins as collected by the Exchange are as follows:

Ordinary (Initial) Margin: Ordinary margin requirement is calculated by applying the margin percentage applicable for a contract on the value of the open positions after netting at the level of individual client and grossed across all clients in respect of client positions and on the value of open positions in respect of proprietary positions without any netting off between client and proprietary positions. If a member has open position in different contracts of the same commodity running concurrently, the member is required to pay margin separately on each of these contracts. Similarly, if a member has open position in different commodities, the total amount required is calculated as sum total of margin required in each contract in each commodity separately. The computation methodology in respect of ordinary margin is as follows:

Intra day-During the trading day the margin is calculated on the absolute difference between total sales in value terms and total buy in value terms in respect of all transactions executed in a contract during the day on client/proprietary basis in addition to previous day's open position carried forward at the official closing price of previous day.

End of day-At the end of the trading day, the margin amount is computed on gross position on individual client and proprietary basis in a contract in quantitative terms multiplied by the official closing price.

Special Margin: In case the price fluctuation in a contract during the trading day is more than 50% of the circuit filter limit applicable on that contract compared to the base price of the day, a special margin equivalent to 50% of the circuit filter limit is applied. Such special margin amount is immediately blocked out of available margin deposits of the members having outstanding position in that contract and in case the available margin of a member is not sufficient to cover such special margin required, then a margin call is sent to the member which is required to be remitted by the member immediately. In such case, since the available deposit is already exhausted the member is put in square off mode i.e. the member can square off his outstanding open position. On squaring off or liquidating the outstanding open position to the extent of excess margin utilized, the status of the member gets changed from square off mode to active status. In square off mode member can't create any fresh position... If the price volatility reaches 100% of the circuit filter limit, orders will be accepted by the system only upto the price level equivalent to such circuit filter.

EXHIBIT-1

Multi Commodity Exchange of India Ltd.

Contract Specifications of (Gold (weekly clearing) - Mumbai Contract

Symbol	IGOLD
Description	IGOLDMUMDDM MYY
Contracts available for trading	
Duration of contracts	2 weeks
Commencement of the contracts	Wednesday every week. If Wednesday is a holiday, then subsequent working day
Maturity of the contracts	Tuesday Every week. If Tuesday is a holiday, then preceding working day
No of contracts available concurrently	2

Trading

Trading period	Mondays through Saturdays
Trading session	Monday to Friday: 10.00 a.m. to 1 1 .30 p.m Saturday: 10.00 a.m. to 2.00 p.m.
Trading unit	1 Kg
Quotation/Base Value	10 grams
Price Quote	Ex-Mumbai(inclusive of import duty and octroi but excluding Sales Tax / VAT)
Tick size (minimum price movement)	₹ 1 per 10 grams
Daily price limits	3%
Initial margin	4%
Special Margin	In case of additional volatility, a special margin at such percentage, as deemed fit, will be imposed immediately on both buy and sale side in respect of all outstanding position, which will remain in force for next 2 days, after which the special margin will be relaxed.
Maximum Allowable Open Position	For individual client: 2 MT (i.e. including Gold and Gold HNI contracts) For a member collectively for all clients: 6 MT or 15% of the market-wide open position, whichever is higher (As per FMC letter no. 6/3/2006/ MKT-ll (VOL II) dated August 18, 2006)

Delivery

Delivery unit	1 Kg
Delivery margin	25%
Delivery center(s)	At designated Clearing House facilities of Group 4 Securities at Mumbai
Quality Specifications	995 purity It should be serially numbered Gold bars supplied by LBMA approved suppliers or other suppliers as may be approved by MCX to be submitted alongwith supplier's quality certificate.
If the seller offers delivery of 999 purity	Seller will get a proportionate premium and sale proceeds will be calculated as under: Rate of delivery* 999/ 995 If the quality is less than 995, it is rejected.

Delivery and Settlement Procedure of (Gold and IGold Mini (weekly clearing) Contracts

Delivery Logic	Compulsory Delivery. Any seller having open position on the expiry date fails to deliver on the next day then a penalty as per the penal provision will be imposed to the defaulting seller.
Tender & Delivery period	1st working day after expiry of the contract.
Delivery Notice by Seller	The Seller will deposit gold bars with Group 4 Securities and also submit Delivery notice to the Exchange in a specified format. The Seller is also required to submit the certificate issued by the supplier in original.

Delivery Period margin	25% margin will be imposed on both Buyer and Seller
Exemption from Tender & Delivery Period Margin	Delivery Period margin is exempted if goods tendered on designated tender days of the contract month and seller submits all the documentary evidence to the Exchange.
Mode of Communication	Fax or Courier.
Delivery Order Rate	The delivery order rate shall be the DDR.
Delivery Pay-in	On E+1 working day by 6:00 pm. E means contract expiry day
Funds Pay-in	E+2 working days by 11.00 am
Funds Pay-out	E+2 working days by 5:00 pm
Delivery Pay-out	E+2 working day by 6:00 pm
Buyer's obligation	The buyer shall not refuse taking delivery and such refusal will entail penalty as per the penal provision.
Close out of open positions	All outstanding positions on the expiry of the contract shall be settled by delivery.
Penal Provisions	A penalty of 2.5% of DOR will be imposed on defaulting buyer / seller out of which 2% will be credited to IFF and 0.5% will be credited to the counter party. Additionally, 4% of DOR as a replacement cost will be charged from defaulting buyer / seller out of which 90% will be given to the counter party and 10% will be retained by the Exchange towards administrative expenses.
Verification by the Buyer at the time of release of delivery	At the time of taking delivery, the buyer can open the sealed packets in front of Group 4 personnel. If he is satisfied with the quantity, weight and quality of material, then he will issue receipt of the metals instantly. If he is not satisfied with the metal, he can insist for assaying by any of the approved assayers available at that center. If the buyer chooses for assaying, Group 4 person will carry the goods to the assayers facilities, get it assayed and bring it back to Group 4 facilities along with assayer's certificate. If the assayer's certificate differs from the certificate submitted by the seller in respect of quality or weight materially, then the buyer and seller have to mutually negotiate the final settlement proceeds within 1 day from receipt of assayer's report, however if they do not agree on any mutually acceptable amount within 1 day, then the Exchange will send the goods to a second assayer and in that case, the report received from such assayer will be final and binding on both buyer and seller. The cost of first assaying as well as cost of transportation from Group 4 to assayer's facilities to and fro will be born by the buyer, while the cost of second assaying, if any, will be equally divided between the buyer and seller. The vault charges during such period of first and second assaying, if any, will be born by both the buyers and sellers equally. If the buyer does not opt for assaying at the time of lifting delivery, then he will not have any further recourse to challenge the quantity or quality subsequently and it will be assumed that he has received the quantity and quality as per the bill made by the seller.
Delivery Centers	At designated Clearing House of Group 4 Securities, at Ex-Quote Center.

Legal obligation	The members will provide appropriate tax forms wherever required as per law and as customary and neither of the parties will unreasonably refuse to do so.
Duties, Cess and Levies	In case of Mumbai delivery contracts, prices are inclusive of import duty and octroi, but excluding VAT. In case of Ahmedabad, prices are inclusive of all taxes and levies relating to import duty, customs but excluding Sales Tax / VAT, any other additional tax or surcharge on sales tax, local taxes and octroi. In case of Delhi and Kolkata, prices are inclusive of import duty but excluding VAT. (seller will charge VAT over and above the Delivery Order rate, which is payable by the buyer)
Vault, Insurance and Transportation charges	Borne by the Seller upto Funds Pay-out date. Borne by the Buyer after Funds Pay-out date.

Validation Process

On receipt of delivery, the Group 4 personnel will do the following validations:

a. whether the person carrying Gold is the designated clearing agent of the member;

b. whether the selling member is listed in the statement forwarded by the Exchange as a delivering member

c. whether the quantity being delivered by the seller is exactly the same quantity as communicated by the Exchange;

d. whether the serial no of all the bars is mentioned in the seller's bill;

e. whether the original certificates are accompanied with the Gold Bars

f. whether the serial nos listed in the certificate tally with the nos written inscribed on the bars

g. whether the seller has issued individual bills of relevant quantity in favour of each of the buyer.

Any other validation checks, as they may desire.

Delivery Process

In case any of the above validation fails, the Group 4 Securities will contact the Exchange office and take any further action, only as per instructions received from the Exchange in writing. If all validations are through, then the Group 4 personnel will put the Gold in bag/s and seal the same in front of the customer with unique tamper-proof seal/s. Then the custodian of Group 4 will cut a serially numbered Group 4 receipt (in triplicate consisting of White, Pink and Yellow slips), get the signature of the seller's clearing agent and signing the same for authorization, hand over the Pink slip to seller's clearing agent, send by courier the third copy (Yellow Colour slip) while retaining the White for the records of Group 4 Securities. The receipt details in full are then entered into the package supplied by MCX and is uploaded to MCX server for authorization and further processing. Group 4 in front of the selling member's clearing agent deposit the said metal into a bag and seal it with a tamper-proof unique numbered Group 4 seal and give *a* copy of the same to the customer, send the second one to MCX for its records and third copy of the receipt for its record. The sealed bag will be vaulted in the same condition with Group 4 Securities until further delivery to MCX customer. Even in case if the metal has to be sent to various destinations, it shall be done in same bag only. Each bag shall not contain not more than 20 kg of Gold and where the depository is more than 20 kg, the same will be stored in multiple bags with each having individual seals with unique number. If the metal delivered by a seller has to go to 10 different buyers, 10 individual packets will be made for each buyer and unique numbers will be assigned to each packet.

Quality Adjustment	The price of Gold is on the basis of 995 purity. It should be serially numbered Gold bars supplied by LBMA approved suppliers or other suppliers as may be approved MCX to be submitted alongwith supplier's quality certificate.
	If seller delivers gold of purity more than 995 then he will get a proportionate premium and sale proceeds will be calculated as Rate of delivery * 999/995
	If the quality is less than 995, it is rejected.
Appointment of Clearing Agent of Buyer's and Sellers	For the purpose of effecting delivery of Gold, every member will be entitled to appoint a maximum number of two Clearing Agents, who will be entitled to receive and deliver precious metals on behalf of such member. These Clearing members have to submit requisite form, four photographs, a copy of their ration card / driving license or other document, as may be specified by the Exchange. The Exchange will issue a photo identity card for each Clearing Agent, which will be duly signed and stamped by the Exchange and the member with lamination. At the time of giving or receiving delivery of precious metal, the Clearing Agent will be required to show this Card to Group 4 Securities persons. The Exchange will forward a list of all such Clearing agents to Group 4 Securities in advance.
Intimation about the Clearing Agents	The buyer will be required to inform name of the Clearing agent, who will visit Group 4 Securities office for lifting delivery. This information will be compiled by the Exchange and will be forwarded to Group 4 Securities by 5.00p.m. on E+2 working day.
Endorsement of Delivery Order	The buying member can endorse delivery order to a client or any third party with full disclosure given to MCX. Responsibility for contractual liability would be with the original assignee.
Extension of Delivery Period Due Date Rate	As per Exchange decision due to a force majeure or otherwise Due date rate will be calculated by taking simple average of spot market prices collected from a panel of different entities on the last trading day.
Applicability of Byelaws, Rules and Business Rules	The general provisions of Byelaws, rules and Business Rules of the Exchange and decisions taken by Forward Markets Commission, Board of Directors and Executive Committee of the Exchange in respect of matters specified above will form and integral part of this contract. The Exchange or FMC as the case may be further prescribe additional measures relating to delivery procedures, warehousing, quality certification, margining, risk management from time to time. (The interpretation or clarification given by the Exchange on any terms of this contract shall be final and binding on the members and others.)

Delivery Period Margin: When a contract enters into delivery period towards the end of its life cycle, delivery period margin is imposed. Such margin is applicable on both outstanding buy and sales side, which continues up to the settlement of delivery obligation or expiry of the contract, whichever is earlier. The delivery period margin is calculated at the rate specified for respective commodity multiplied by the net open position held by a member in the expiring contract. When a seller submits delivery documents along with surveyor's certificate, his position is treated as settled and his delivery period margin to such extent is reduced. When a buyer pays money for the delivery allocated to him, his delivery period margin is reduced on such quantity for which he has paid the amount. If delivery does not happen with respect to certain open position and is finally settled by way of difference as per the Due Date Rate, the delivery period margin is released only after final settlement of difference arising out of such closing out as per the Due Date Rate.

MCX launched India's first electricity futures on June 9, 2009. The contracts are weekly and monthly. They trade in units of 24 megawatt hours; the tick size is 1 rupee per megawatt hour. On October 17, 2009, MCX reduced members, transaction feels from Rs. 4 per Rs. 1,00,000 of turnover to Rs. 2.50, eliminating the previous incremented system of fees. MCX experts the new changes to cut members, trading costs by 50%. Exhibit-1 provides the illustration contract specifications at MCX.

National Commodity and Derivatives Exchange (NCDEX) Ltd.

National Commodity and Derivatives Exchange Limited, which is also known as NCDEX, was established by Companies Act, 1956 in the year 2003, shortly after its regulator the FMC made reforms to India's future markets aimed at encouraging growth and competition. Although the exchange was set up on April 23, 2003, it started its' operations from December 15, 2003.

The NCDEX's initial three-way ownership structure later expanded to nine by adding four new Indian partners - Canara Bank, Crisil, Punjab National Bank and Indian Fanners Fertiliser Cooperative (IFCO), and two international ones: New York-based investment bank Goldman Sachs and Atlanta-based Intercontinental Exchange (ICE). In mid-2009 ICE and Goldman Sachs added a tenth partner by agreeing to sell 3% and 2% of their shares respectively to listed India processor Shree Renuka Sugars, giving the three a 5% stake each in NCDEX. The three original shareholders now each hold 15% stakes while Crisil and IFCO hold 12% each and Punjab National and Canara each have 8%.

National Commodity and Derivatives Exchange Limited is a multi commodity exchange. It facilitates commodity trading of Agricultural Commodities like cashew, barley, sugar, coffee, cotton; Precious Metals like gold and silver; Base Metals like aluminium ingot, nickel cathode; Ferrous Metals like sponge iron; Energy Products like furnace oil, brent crude oil and Polymer Products like Polypropylene. In 2008 the NCDEX also launched carbon credits but cannot create a market in them because Indian law ' permits only sellers of such contracts. The exchange is awaiting passage of a key futures-trading bill to widen the scope of Indian derivatives trading to allow buyers.

NCDEX carries out commodity trading at national level.

Barely two years after NCDEX began trading in December 2003 it suffered its first setback when the FCM ordered the exchange to fire an un-named executive after ruling it had violated settlement-price rules on January 2006 contracts for two agricultural commodities. The following year the Indian government banned trading in four different commodities, including wheat and rice, and suspended trading on four others under pressure from a left-wing coalition member, although an election earlier this year has led to some easing of those restrictions. And earlier the NCDEX's bid to reduce its transaction fee was rejected by the FCM as "neither in the interest of the exchange nor of the industry as a whole".

NCDEX has apparently weathered the recent commodities-trading restrictions imposed by the government and volatile markets buffeted by the 2008 financial crisis. In May

2009 the NCDEX and its main national rival, the Multi Commodity Exchange of India (MCX), reintroduced wheat futures trading shortly after the FCM lifted its two-year ban. The NCDEX currently ranks number 34 among the world's largest derivatives exchanges, according the Futures Industry Association - down from number 28 in 2006 - while rival MCX has increased its lead to number 22.

Indian Commodity Exchange Limited (ICEX)

Indian Commodity Exchange Limited (headquartered in Gurgaon) is the latest nation-level commodity exchange which commenced its operations on November 27, 2009 . ICEX is jointly promoted by Indiabulls Financial Services Ltd and MMTC Limited, and has Indian Potash Ltd., KRIBHCO and IDFC among others, as its partners. The exchange has got permission for launching a dozen contracts. ICEX is a screen based on-line derivatives exchange for commodities and has established a reliable, time tested, and a transparent trading platform. It is also in the process of putting in place robust assaying and warehousing facilities in order to facilitate deliveries. Commodities traded at ICEX are : Bullion- Gold, Silver;Minerals- Copper, Nickel Aluminum, Zinc;Oil and Oil seeds-Mustard Seed, Soybean, Soya Oil, Palm Oil ;Pulses- Chana, Spices- Jeera, Turmeric;Fibers and other- Guar seed; Energy- Crude Oil

TURNOVER ON COMMODITY FUTURES MARKETS

Commodities traded in the commodity futures market during 2009 included a variety of agricultural commodities, bullion, crude oil, energy and metal products. Several new commodities were introduced for futures trading in 2009, such as almond, imported thermal coal, carbon credits and platinum. The total value of trades in the commodity futures market rose from Rs 50.34 lakh crore in 2008 to Rs 70.90 lakh crore during 2009. 5.110 The average daily value of trades in the commodity exchanges improved from Rs 16,400 crore during 2008 to Rs 23,200 crore in 2009. Agricultural commodities, bullion and energy accounted for a large share of the commodities traded in the commodity futures market.

TABLE 1

Turnover on Commodity Futures Markets

(Rs crore)

Name of the exchange	*Calendar year*		
	2007	2008'	2009
Multi Commodity Exchange (MCX), Mumbai	27,30,415	42,84,653	59,56,656
National Commodity and Derivatives Exchange (NCDEX)	7,74,965	6,28,074	8,05,720
National Multi Commodity Exchange, (NMCE)	25.056	37,272	1.95,907
Others	1,24,051	83,885	1,32,173
Total	36,54,487	50,33,884	70,90,456

Source: Ministry of Consumer Affairs

The MCX, Mumbai, recorded the highest turnover in terms of value of trade during 2009, followed by the National Commodity & Derivatives Exchange Ltd.(NCDEX) and National Multi Commodity Exchange of India Ltd. (NMCE) respectively.

RECENT POLICY DEVELOPMENTS

Some of the salient features of the policy initiatives relating to the commodity futures markets are listed belows:

1. Regulation and Development of Commodity Futures Markets

The year 2009 began on an optimistic note for the commodity futures market with the revocation of suspension of futures trading in chana, soy oil, rubber and potato in December 2008. This was followed six months later, in May 2009, by the revocation of suspension of trading in wheat. However, futures trading in sugar was suspended on May 26, 2009 for a period of six months till December 31, 2009, which was further extended to September 30, 2010. Agricultural commodity futures staged a remarkable recovery, recording a trading value of Rs 10.88 lakh crore in 2009, displaying growth of 48 per cent over the previous year. During the year, a new national commodity exchange, i.e. the ICEX became operational.

The Forward Markets Commission (FMC), the regulator for commodity futures trading under the provisions of the Forward Contracts (Regulation) Act 1952 continued its efforts to broad-base the market. The emphasis was on participation of physical market participants, especially farmers, as hedgers, to counterbalance the speculative element in price discovery and to increase the awareness level of farmers and other market participants. The Commission undertook various regulatory measures to facilitate hedgers' participation and promote delivery in agricultural commodities, such as introduction of the Exchange of Futures for Physicals (EFP) and Alternate Futures Settlement Mechanism, allowing higher position limits to NAFED to facilitate hedging and delivery by it and introduction of an early delivery system in select commodities. In addition, efforts were made to develop an "aggregation" model in collaboration with commodity exchanges to promote participation of farmers. The FMC also undertook several regulatory initiatives to prevent market manipulation and ensure market integrity, financial integrity and customer protection. Major policy developments initiated by the Forward Markets Commission included the issuance of guidelines for bringing members of the commodity exchanges under the purview of the Money Laundering Act and guidelines for divestment of the equity by the existing national exchanges after five years of their operation. A price dissemination project was initiated by the FMC, under which spot and future prices of agricultural commodities would be made available to fanners on a real-time basis on price ticker boards placed at Agricultural Produce Marketing Committees.

2. Development of Electronic Spot Exchanges

The Government and FMC have allowed the national commodity exchanges to set up three spot exchanges in the country, namely the National Spot Exchange Ltd. (NSEL), NCDEX Spot Exchange Ltd. (NSPOT) and National Agriculture Produce Marketing Company of India Ltd. (NAPMC). During 2009, there was significant expansion of spot exchanges' trading facilities in India. These spot exchanges have created an avenue for direct market linkage among farmers, processors, exporters and end users with a view to reducing the cost of intermediation and enhancing price realization by farmers. They would also provide the most efficient spot price inputs to the futures exchanges. The spot exchanges would encompass the entire spectrum of commodities across the country and would bring home the advantages of an electronic spot trading platform to all market participants in the agricultural and non-agricultural segments. On the agricultural side, the exchanges would enable fanners to trade seamlessly on the platform by providing them real-time access to price information and a simplified delivery process, thereby ensuring them the best possible prices. On the buy side, all users of the commodities in the commodity value chain would have simultaneous access to the exchanges, which would be able to procure at the best possible prices. Therefore, the efficiency levels attained as a result of such seamless spot transactions would result in major benefits for both producers and consumers. Thus the exchanges would enhance the efficiency of the existing OTC markets in the country

So far, Maharashtra, Karnataka. Gujarat, Rajasthan, Orissa and Madhya Pradesh have given licences to the spot exchanges to undertake electronic spot trading. The agricultural commodities traded on the spot exchange platform are cotton, castor seed, desi channa, guar seed, RM seed, wheat, barley, red arecanut, maize, yellow peas. urad. lemon tur, soyabean, jeera, ground nut, sugar, moong and pepper. In the process, farmers' realization has increased by 4-5 per cent. The total turnover of the three exchanges during 2009 was Rs 2,810 crore.

CONSTRAINTS, MAJOR CHALLENGES AND POLICY OPTIONS OF COMMODITY FUTURES

Commodity futures markets are the strength of an agricultural surplus country like India. Commodity exchanges play a pivotal role in ensuring stronger growth, transparency and efficiency of the commodity futures markets. This role is defined by their functions, infrastructure capabilities, trading procedures, settlement and risk management practices. However, Indian commodity exchanges are still at a nascent stage of development as there are numerous bottlenecks hampering their growth. The institutional and policy-level issues associated with commodity exchanges have to be addressed by the government in coordination with the FMC in order to take necessary measures to pave the way for a significant expansion and further development of the commodity futures markets. Some of the major problems associated with commodity markets in India are discussed below:

    I. **Infrastructure:** The lack of efficient and sophisticated infrastructural facilities is the major growth inhibitor of the Indian commodity futures markets. Though some exchanges occupy large premises, they are deficient in terms of the necessary institutional infrastructure, including warehousing facilities, independent and automated clearing houses, transparent trading platforms, etc.

   II. **Warehousing and Standardization:** For commodity derivatives market to work efficiently, it is necessary to have a sophisticated, cost-effective, reliable and convenient warehousing system in the country. The Habibullah (2003) task force admitted, "A sophisticated warehousing industry has yet to come about". Further, independent labs or quality testing centers should be set up in each region to certify the quality, grade and quantity of commodities so that they are appropriately standardized and there are no shocks waiting for the ultimate buyer who takes the physical delivery. Warehouses also need to be conveniently located. For the commodity futures to work effectively, the seller must deposit the commodity traded in a warehouse and the buyer should take physical delivery of the commodity in a warehouse at a location of his , choice. However, at present, only a few warehouses can handle such kind of delivery requests and that too for specific commodities. Because of lack of adequate warehousing facilities that can ensure the quality standards of the commodities traded, traders and farmers still prefer local rural markets for trading the commodities. This factor is hindering the emergence of nation-wide commodity market in India.

  III. Central Warehousing Corporation of India is operating around 500 Warehouses across the country with a storage capacity of about 10.4 million tonnes. This is obviously not adequate for a vast country. To resolve the problem, a Gramin Bhandaran Yojana (Rural Warehousing Plan) has been introduced to construct new and expand the existing rural godowns. Large scale privatization of state warehouses is also being examined.

IV. **Cash versus Physical Settlement:** It is probably due to the inefficiencies in the present warehousing system that only about 1% to 5% of the total commodity derivatives trade in the country is settled in physical delivery. Therefore the warehousing problem obviously has to be handled on a war footing, as a good delivery system is the backbone of any commodity trade. A particularly difficult problem in cash settlement of commodity derivative contracts is that at present, under the Forward Contracts (Regulation) Act 1952, cash settlement of outstanding contracts at maturity is not allowed. In other words, all outstanding contracts at maturity should be settled in physical delivery. To avoid this, participants square off their positions before maturity. So, in practice, most contracts are settled in cash but before maturity. There is a need to modify the law to bring it closer to the widespread practice and save the participants from unnecessary hassles.

V. **Trading System:** Though the operations of national exchanges are carried out through the electronic trading system, a majority of the regional exchanges continue to trade via the open outcry system. In order to attract a greater number of investors towards sector-specific commodities, regional exchanges must introduce the electronic trading system to assure the investors of transparency and fairly priced commodities.

VI. **Trading Conditions:** Towards the growth of any market, the trading conditions or the terms and conditions of contracts play a crucial role. The contracts should be market friendly in terms of attracting both the big and small traders alike. In majority of the contract specifications, it was found that the size is too big for small traders and producers to trade. Unless such finer aspects are dealt with proper attention at the regulatory level and the exchange level, attracting small traders and farmers into commodity futures trading becomes impossible. Especially in a country like India, where corporate farming is absent and predominant section of the farmers own small agricultural lands, meeting the specifications of the contract becomes difficult. Such farmers prefer spot markets rather than commodity markets for trading. Even the small traders refrain from trading owing to the capital constraints.

VII. **Broking Community:** Though a large number of members exist in the exchanges' records, most of them are not involved in trading due to the fact that the business is not highly profitable in comparison to equities. Therefore, it is important to absorb a large number of broking firms that have diversified into stock broking and other related businesses. To attract active traders to commodity futures, the regulatory authority needs to introduce a more stringent code of conduct in setting standards for brokers, imposing capital adequacy norms, defining qualification criteria, etc.

VIII. **Controlled Market:** Price variability is an essential pre-condition for futures markets. Any deviation in the market mechanism or where the free play of supply and demand forces for commodities does not determine commodity prices will dilute the variability of prices and potential risk. For a vibrant futures market, it is imperative that commodity pricing must be left to market forces, without monopolistic government control. However, in India, scores of commodities in which futures trading is permitted are still protected under the ECA, 1955.

IX. **Integration of Regional and National Exchanges:** Another major challenge to the growth of the commodity markets is the number of exchanges itself. Among the 22 commodity exchanges operating in India, majority of the exchanges are specialized in trading a few commodities. As a result of these small exchanges spreading across the nation and specializing in select few commodities, the turnover, volume of trade and the revenues of exchanges are all low. It is very difficult for the exchanges to sustain the momentum and provide value added services to the market functionaries with such low revenues. From a wider standpoint, it is essential to integrate the regional exchanges with the national exchanges to achieve price discovery for regional exchanges to be driven by broad-level prices prevailing at the national exchanges. Secondly, this integration will facilitate the creation of more efficient markets as price discovery will become dependent on domestic demand and supply of commodities. Also the integration of exchanges and clearing house can also solve the problem of warehouses to a significant extent.

X. **Integration of the Spot and Futures Markets:** The integration of the spot and futures market is another critical factor for the expansion of the commodity futures market in India. The spot market in commodities is largely controlled by the state governments. Restrictions exist on stockholding, turnover, and movement of goods, and variations persist in the level of duties levied by the different state governments. This fragments the commodity spot markets and impedes the commodity futures markets from reaching the market players outside the boundaries of the states or zones in which the exchanges are located.

XI. **Commodity Options:** Trading in commodity options contracts has been banned since 1952. The market for commodity derivatives cannot be called complete without the presence of this important derivative. Both futures and options are necessary for the healthy growth of the market. While futures contracts help a participant (say a farmer) to hedge against downside price movements, it does not allow him to reap the benefits of an increase in prices. No doubt there is an immediate need to bring about the necessary legal and regulatory changes to introduce commodity options trading in the country. The matter is said to be under the active consideration of the Government and the options trading may be introduced in the near future.

XII. **The Regulator:** As the market activity pick-up and the volumes rise, the market will definitely need a strong and independent regulator, similar to the Securities and Exchange Board of India (SEBI) that regulates the securities markets. Unlike SEBI which is an independent body, the Forwards Markets Commission (FMC) is under the Department of Consumer Affairs (Ministry of Consumer Affairs, Food and Public Distribution) and depends on it for funds. It is imperative that the Government should grant more powers to the FMC to ensure an orderly development of the commodity markets. The SEBI and FMC also need to work closely with each other due to the inter-relationship between the two markets.

CONVERGENCE OF SECURITIES AND COMMODITY MARKETS

The convergence of commodity futures markets with other derivatives markets will induce eminent economies of scale. It would help in the utilisation of capital and institution building, which has already taken place for the derivatives markets for the purposes of India's agricultural sector. The main expected gains from convergence of securities and commodity markets are listed below:

Gains from convergence

1. Opportunity to speed up development of commodity market: If derivatives in commodities resemble securities, then the developmental challenge of obtaining sound institutions for trading commodity derivatives can be eased by using the stable and mature institutions that are found in the securities markets. The new multi-commodity exchanges have been approved recently and may take some time to pick up speed. If the institutions of the securities markets are used, this would speed up the pace at which modern market institutions become available to farmers, and accelerate the growth rate of the agricultural sector.

2. Commodity derivatives resemble securities: There are strong commonalities between commodity derivatives and securities derivatives. A commodity futures contract is tradable and fungible. Almost all commodity futures contracts are squared off, and do not go to delivery. In this case, the users of commodity futures markets are using the futures for purely financial purposes. Thus, almost all commodity futures contracts are akin to securities; however, there are certain differences with regard to delivery and settlement. In this case, knowledge and procedures for trading in securities is directly pertinent to trading in commodity futures.

3. Economies of scale: Sizable investment has gone into building India's securities infrastructure. This infrastructure can be used to start trading in commodity derivatives at a small incremental cost. Conversely, the viability of the new multi-commodity exchanges would be enhanced if they could trade derivatives on all underlyings. This would serve to reduce the extent to which capital is required in creating the desired institutional capacity for the commodity sector. It is, however, quite possible that convergence would provide economies of scale to some of the leading stock/commodity exchanges, particularly, BSE and NSE only, and other exchanges might see their liquidity migrating to these exchanges.

4. Economies of scope: In risk management, if the clearing corporation holds a single settlement guarantee fund, then it benefits from diversification. Hence, the collateral required in order to obtain a given level of safety is lower when a clearing corporation does novation for a wide variety of products with low correlations, as compared with having separate clearing corporations for each area. Existing SEBI and RBI rules prohibit such integration of the settlement guarantee fund. However, the basic opportunity to reduce the capital requirements of the clearing corporation in this fashion is there, and will be extended if commodity markets are also brought alongside equities, interest rates and credit risk.

5. Possibility of strengthening the commodity spot market: If the commodity futures markets obtain strong liquidity and price discovery in a transparent, anonymous, order matching environment, then this is likely to have a considerable impact upon the underlying spot market, which is likely to remain a fragmented, OTC market for many years. To the extent that convergence helps speed up the migration of commodity futures markets into screen-based, anonymous order matching, this would thus indirectly assist the strengthening of agricultural spot markets.

6. Better serving users: It is useful to emphasise that the convergence approach yields superior efficiency and sophistication, even when a brokerage firm chooses to be highly specialised. In the convergence approach, a brokerage firm that focuses upon cotton would simultaneously be able to access derivatives on cotton, equities trading about firms which deal with cotton, and derivatives on currencies (which are relevant for the currency risk involved in imports and exports of cotton). Thus, even for a brokerage firm that seeks to be a specialist on cotton, the convergence approach gives direct access to a more rich range of traded products as compared with the traditional approach.

7. Impact upon informal market: Presently, a major problem faced with commodity futures trading is a substantial informal market, which is illegal under Indian law. There have been persistent problems in fully eliminating illegal trading given limitations of enforcement mechanisms. The convergence approach offers the possibility of a market-based mechanism through which informal trading can be curbed, except to the extent that the participants choose informal markets to avoid taxation, elaborate paper-work, requirement of maintaining high net worth and service infrastructure and/or to invest black money to satisfy a speculative or gambling instinct. If the legal markets are able to rapidly migrate onto sophisticated, liquid, low-cost platforms, then this would spontaneously pull users into these platforms. Liquidity has a natural monopoly character, and once exchanges achieve a certain minimal critical mass' of liquidity, there are strong incentives for each user of the market to seek the liquidity of exchanges. This is likely to ease the enforcement difficulties faced in eliminating illegal trading.

8. Consequences for government: At present, the Indian government engages in many policy measures, which interact with agricultural spot markets. These policies are unaffected by the convergence question. Whether commodity futures markets are closely integrated with securities markets or not has no impact upon the conduct of policies such as public procurement, support prices, etc. To the extent that convergence helps strengthen price discovery on the commodity futures markets, this would facilitate the design of public policy. If shortages or gluts are expected to take place at a future date, this would be revealed in the futures price well ahead of time. This information signal would help government mount an early response, if desired.

9. Simplicity: There would be important gains for the individuals and firms, if a broad range of derivative products came under a single, simple set of rules and procedures. This includes the operations of the intermediaries, exchanges, regulation, taxation, accounting, IT interfaces, information sources, etc. This would reduce the overhead costs associated with doing transactions on these markets

Divergences, Apprehensions and Concerns

Though the strengths of securities markets and the expected gains of convergence to commodity market are significant, the divergences, apprehensions and concerns are also many, which need to be addressed. Some of these are:

1) Though derivatives in commodities resemble securities and financial futures and provide many of the same economic functions, there are some major differences. First, because financial futures generally have actively traded cash markets, cash prices are generally not "discovered" in the futures market. In fact, futures contracts are often settled from cash or indexes of cash prices. Second, the delivery and settlement process is different. A particularly useful function of exchanges is the facilitation and oversight of contract expirations and the related settlement, delivery or exchange of futures for physicals. Exchanges not only set the terms of delivery, but also oversee the actual delivery as well as the credit verification of members making or taking delivery. In addition, exchanges perform other financial services related to trading, delivery, clearing, and margining. For financial derivatives transactions, exchange delivery mechanisms or oversight are less necessary and can be alternatively accomplished as cash transactions through other institutions or inter-institutional arrangements.

2) There are fears that in the large securities exchanges, there would be a certain lack of focus upon agricultural commodities and the focus would be on organizing derivative trading only in commodities with close semblance to financials, viz., bullion. The most

important policy goal, and policy concern, is safeguarding of the interests of producers - farmers in particular, consumers as well as manufacturers and other functionaries in the supply-chain.

3) Concerns are expressed that unlike securities market, - where the impact of the price volatility is on the willing participants in the market - the impact of the sharp rise or fall in price in commodities is borne by the entire economy, i.e., largely by innocent bystanders.

4) It is apprehended that the possibilities of convergence are limited, insofar as commodity futures trading requires highly specialized knowledge, which is different from that required for securities trading. Unlike the securities market, the factors affecting commodity prices are more complex and commodity-specific. It is also stated that the firms that engage in commodity futures trading differ from the firms that engage in securities trading.

5) There are strong concerns that removing restrictions on stock exchanges from trading commodity derivatives, would affect the viability of the exchanges, which have been granted in-principle approval only recently. These exchanges were required to set up modern infrastructure involving huge investment. Changing the competitive environment so dramatically mid-stream raises the issue of fairness. It is apprehended that the established stock exchanges having huge reserves would easily be able to wipe out competition by leveraging their available resources and infrastructure.

6) Though allowing commodity exchanges to trade securities would appear to be equitable on paper, in reality the existing commodity exchanges will not be able to meet the high regulatory bars set by the SEBI for grant of recognition. This is also true for intermediaries in the commodity derivatives market.

An illustrative statement indicating divergences between the two markets is given below in Table-2.

TABLE 2

Divergences between Security and Commodity Derivatives Markets

Areas	Divergences Action required for convergence
1. Online trading	Besides domain knowledge of commodity markets, agri-products may require different process of online application giving flexibility for outcry system.
	Traditional outcry system may have to be allowed for some time during transition as requested by NBOT, Indore.
2. Cash Basis	Agri-markets do not have liquid cash market to obtain price discovery. Integration of agri-markets and financial sector to speed up.
3. Market Determinants	Agri-products have different shelf life, demand-supply factors, and price determination. Metals notably gold also have different market conditions.
	Standardisation of products and suitable storage facilities need to be build up.
4. Storage of products	Scale and mode of depositing/warehousing | structurally different.
	Warehouse receipt system (WRS) a must for commodity futures.
5. Taxation	Indirect taxation cascades in commodities. IT treatment also different.

	Losses due to speculation not adjusted in corporate taxation in case of commodity futures - only carried forward.
6. Regulation	Compliance of network, capital adequacy, margins, exposure norms different for commodity trading
	Harmonisation possible though separate regulations to continue.
7. Role of banks and Mutual Funds	Under the Banking Regulations Act, Banks are not permitted to trade in commodities derivatives markets.
	Allow Banks to hedge their commodity exposure.
8. Unified Markets	Various State and Central Government laws impede the unification.
	Fragmentation of commodity futures and markets to be overcome through agricultural marketing I reforms.
9. Market awareness	Limited for nascent commodity futures
	Berries will take time to ripen.
10. Centre-State Jurisdiction	Commodities and markets under purview of State
	Inter-state harmonization of
	Governments
	Acts and rules needed.
11. Price Discovery	Mostly in trading pit in commodity futures. Generally cash price quoted at a premium/discount to the futures prices.
	Online trading positions in new exchanges need to be supervised.
12. Base of players	Investors base 25 million and 9000 brokers in securities market. A few thousand brokers in commodity markets.
	Farmers' involvement can help expand the base of commodity futures.

It would be necessary to address the concerns, apprehensions and, if necessary, find graceful transition paths through which the adverse impact upon existing firms and exchanges could be smoothed. Adversely affected entities may have to be given a limited period of time to adapt to the new institutional environment. Attaining growth in commodity market without convergence will need to replicate the infrastructure and regulation resources. This process may be slow. However, till the integration happens, we should expect to see important changes in the existing regional exchanges. Faced with competition from nation-wide exchanges, they would have to improve their technology, transparency and methods of operation in the short run if they are serious about staying in business. Also with the continued acceptance and popularity of institutionalized commodity futures trading, probably the bulk of informal futures trading will slowly be absorbed in the regulated, through-exchange trading as the price and liquidity benefits outweigh the added transaction costs. That would, indeed, be a positive development for all concerned.

Perhaps the biggest event in financial markets around the world - not just commodities or futures markets but securities markets as well - in recent years has been the emergence of Electronic Communication Networks (ECNs). In Indian exchanges, the outcry system has already been replaced by the ECN system. Over time, new products are likely to be introduced in the Indian futures markets. A category of futures that have are extremely popular in developed countries will perhaps make their appearance in India too. These are the weather derivatives, which are now being offered in India as bank products but not actively traded in the bourses. If properly designed such futures can help farmers hedge the climate and rainfall related risks that are concomitant with Indian agriculture. Further an important shift is occurring in the ownership structure and corporate governance of exchanges. Commodity exchanges, like their equity counterparts used to be owned and run by associations of brokers. This raised several transparency and governance issues for exchanges and increased the possibility of price manipulations and unethical practices that Indian markets are so notorious for. Improved corporate governance is essential for the development of commodity futures trading in India and perhaps the first and most important step in that direction is to separate the ownership and management of exchanges from the participating brokers. In other words, the **"self-regulating"** model is likely to give way to for-profit exchanges promoted by outside agencies and financial institutions and run by a team of professionals. Over time, new products are likely to be introduced in the Indian futures markets. A category of futures that have are extremely popular in developed countries will perhaps make their appearance in India too. These are the weather derivatives, which are now being offered in India as bank products but not actively traded in the bourses. If properly designed such futures can help farmers hedge the climate and rainfall related risks that are concomitant with Indian agriculture.

As the Indian economy and financial markets become increasingly integrated with the global markets, its effects are likely to become visible in the commodities futures markets as well. With the increasing role of multi-national corporations in the agricultural and food processing as well as international trade, the connection between commodity prices in India and world prices are becoming increasingly linked. There is also an increasing need for participating clients to hedge and speculate on Indian commodity prices in relation to world prices rather than in isolation. It is reasonable, then, to expect that with time, the linkage between Indian commodity prices and futures prices will be even more connected with world prices and possibly trading itself would be international. In the global scenario, there has been an emergence of alliances of futures markets. It is likely that Indian exchanges would also form partnerships with foreign exchanges allowing more sophisticated instruments enabling Indian traders to better hedge their international risks.

QUESTIONS

1) Critically examine the evolution and function of commodity exchanges in India.
2) Examine the role of major participants in the commodity derivatives.
3) Discuss the commodity futures and the structure of the commodity futures markets in India.
4) Explain the benefits of commodity futures markets.
5) Distingguish between the commodity and financial derivatives. What are the recent trends of turnover on commodity futures markets in India?
6) Explain the working of commodity market.
7) Discuss the objectives of commodity futures markets.
8) Discuss the salient features of the policy initiatives relating to the commodity future markets.
9) Write short note on:
    i)   Multi-Commodity exchange of India
    ii) National Multi-Commodity Exchange of India
    iii) National Commodity and Derivatives Exchange
    iv) Indian Commodity Exchange.

10) Critically examine the gains from convergence of securities and commodity markets. What are the divergences, apprehensions and concerns in that convergence.

REFERENCES

1. Black, Fischer. "The Pricing of Commodity Contracts." *Journal of Financial Economics* 3, nos. 1, 2 (January-March 1976).

2. Dusak, Katherine, "Futures Trading and Investor Returns: An Investigation of Commodity Market Risk Premiums," *Journal of Political Economy* 81, no. 6 (No-vember-December 1973): 1387-1406.

3. Gould, Bruce G. *Dow Jones-Invin Guide To Commodities Trading.* Homewood, Ill.: Dow Jones-Irwin, 1973.

4. Hieronymus, Thomas A., *Economics of Futures Trading* (New York: Commodity Research Bureau, 1971).

5. Labys, Walter, and C.W.J. Granger, *Speculation, Hedging, and Commodity Price Forecasts* (Lexington, Mass.: Heath, 1970).

6. Pindyck, R.S. "Inventor ies and the Short-Run Dynamics of Commodity Prices," *Rand Journal of Economics, 25,*1 (1994): 141-159.

7. Richard, S., and S. Sundaresan. "A Continuous-Time Model of Forward and Futures Prices in a Multigood Economy," *Journal of Financial Economics,* 9 (December 1981): 347-72.

8. Routledge, B.R., D.J. Seppi, and C.S. Spatt. "Equilibrium Forward Curves for Commodities," Journal of Finance, 55, 3 (2000) 1297-1338.

9. Stevenson, Richard A., and Robert M. Bear, "Commodity Futures: Trends or Random Walks," *Journal of Finance 25,* no. 1 (March 1970): 65-81.

10. Telser, Lester G., and Harlow N. Higinbotham, "Or ganized Futures Markets: Costs and Benefits," *Journal of Political Economy,* October 1977, pp. 969-1000.

11. Teweles, R.J., C.V. Harlow, and H.L. Stone. *The Commodity Futures Game, Who Wins? Who Loses? Why?* New York: McGraw-Hill, 1974.

Part VI

INTERNATIONAL FINANCIAL FLOWS

43

World Financial Markets

INTRODUCTION

Financial markets in the recent period have witnessed heightened uncertainty, triggered by a sharp repricing of risk following problems in the US sub-prime mortgage market. Recent financial market developments have unfolded against the backdrop of an expanded period of strong broad-based global growth and overall financial stability. The congruence of favourable macroeconomic conditions, abundant liquidity and low nominal rates generated low perception of financial risks. Investor appetite for high returns in a low interest rate environment encouraged market participants to undertake progressively higher risks, stimulated further technological development for unbundling and distributing risks through financial markets and boosted demand for a range of high yielding and complex financial products. Greater appetite for structured instruments was evident in the rapid rise in the issuance of collateralised debt obligations (CDOs).

No one thought that the financial market could collapse. Sufficient safeguards were in place. There was a safety net: central banks that would lend when needed, deposit insurance and investor protections that freed individuals from worrying about the security of their wealth, regulators and supervisors to watch over individual institutions and keep their managers and owners from taking on too much risk. And the Fed's monetary policy stance before the crisis created the general impression over time that the interest of capital in a free market economy can never be at risk. That encouraged the use of high leverage as a source of sustainable high profits from bubbles, Fed's monetary policy has widely been highlighted by now for its role in supporting the growth of two most unpleasant things - speculation and leverage which in turn contained the potential for a severe financial crisis.

FACTOR LEADING TO FINANCIAL CRISIS

The modern financial system is immensely complex—possibly too complex for any one person to really understand it. Interconnections create systemic risks that are extraordinarily difficult to figure out. The fact that things apparently worked so well (up until the time they did not) gave everyone a fall sense of comfort. And this understandable complacency, born out of booms that make everyone better off, sows the seeds of collapse.

The sudden manifestation of the crisis in 2007 was the result of two important fundamental macroeconomic imbalances that persisted for too long; one, the monetary policy of the Fed Reserve in the Greenspan era and second, the growing global imbalances. Both these factors were clear precursors of unsustainable bubbles which were ignored in general because of the pre-crisis phase of high global growth with low inflation.

What a difference two years make. Since August 2007, the world financial markets has experienced a sequence of critical failures. The massive derailment of the financial sector in advanced economies in mid-September 2008, following the collapse of Lehman Brothers has had a knock on effect on the world economy. The world output is expected to contract by 1.4 per cent in 2009, GDP in the advanced economies is projected to decline by 3.8 per cent in 2009 before growing by a meagre 0.6 per cent in 2010. The GDP of the US and the UK is forecast to witness a fall of 2.6 per cent and 4.2 per cent in 2009 before an anaemic recovery to 0.8 per cent and 0.2 in 2010. respectively. Euro area, on the other hand, is expected to shrink by 4.8 per cent and 0.3 per cent both in 2009 and 2010, respectively. Unemployment in advanced countries is projected to scale higher from 5.8 per cent in 2008 to 8.1 per cent in 2009 and further to 9.2 per cent in 2010. The unemployment in the US is expected to almost double from 5.8 per cent in 2008 to 10.1 per cent in 2010. Spain is forecast to suffer the highest unemployment within the euro area with 19,3 per cent unemployment in 2010. The fiscal stimuli that have been put together in these countries in response led to worsening fiscal positions. In the OECD countries, the fiscal position is set to deteriorate from -3.2 per cent in 2008 to -7.7 per cent in 2009 and further to -8.8 per cent in 2010. The fiscal deficit is poised to more than double in the US. Japan and the euro' area in 2009 and further deteriorate in 2010. By the end of 2010, the ratio of gross government debt to GDP is estimated to reach 98 per cent for the US, 87 per cent for Germany, 80 per cent for France and 73 per cent for the UK. Financial stabilisation in the world has come at a huge cost. Financial stabilisation cost is highest for the US at 12.7 per cent of GDP and lowest for Italy at 0.9 per cent of GDP. For the UK, it is 9.1 per cent, 4.4 per cent for Canada, 3.1 per cent for Germany, and 1.8 per cent for France .

Collapsing growth in advanced economies led to a sharp contraction in economic activity in EMEs, due, *inter alia*, to an unprecedented drop in export demand that coincided, with a significant reversal in international bank lending and foreign portfolio investment. Emerging and developing economies are projected to post a much subdued growth of 1.5 per cent in 2009. notwithstanding an expected pick up in growth momentum during the second half of 2009. Emerging Asia is estimated to grow by 5.5 per cent in 2009 and 7.0 per cent in 2010, owing to improving prospects in China (7.5 per cent and 8.5 per cent) and India (5.4 per cent and 6.5 per cent). African countries are forecast to register much lower growth of 1.8 per cent in 2009 and recover to 4.1 per cent in 2010. On the contrary. Latin America is projected to contract by 2.6 per cent in 2009, before a recovery to 2.3 per cent in 2010. Badly affected by the reversal of capital flows and sharp contraction in commodity exports, countries in central and eastern Europe and in Commonwealth of Independent States are expected to suffer more severe shrinkage of 5.0 per cent and 5.8 per cent, respectively in 2009. These countries are highly dependent on western European banks, which own the majority of banking systems in these countries. Cross-border bank funding has been disrupted as the banking crisis in western Europe intensified. This real sector weakness has been adversely affecting the banking sector in these countries through the negative feedback loop.

It is not, therefore, surprising that governments in virtually all advanced industrial economies have stepped in to provide support to banks and financial institutions, introducing both standalone actions directed at individual distressed institutions and system-wide support programmes (or even multi-programme packages). These measures have included reinforced deposit insurance to help prevent bank runs, capital injections to strengthen banks' capital base, explicit guarantees on liabilities to help banks retain access to wholesale funding, and purchases or guarantees of impaired "legacy" assets to help reduce the exposure of banks to large losses in their asset portfolios. The overall objective of such massive intervention was to avoid widespread bankruptcies of financial intermediaries and to contribute to restoring a normal functioning of financial intermediation.

Government intervention became crucial during the crisis as traditional sources of funding for financial institutions dried up. In particular, financial institutions' issuance of debt securities and equity instruments dropped off considerably in the third and fourth quarters of 2008. Merger and acquisition (M&A) activity in the banking sector, which could have provided a private sector solution to bank restructuring, also remained subdued compared to preceding years. Although large-scale government support may have had side effects - for example, by slowing or even crowding out the revival of non-guaranteed funding and private sector investment in the banking sector - it has no doubt played a crucial role in stabilising banking markets, by meeting funding demands that could not have been fulfilled via the traditional channels during the height of the crisis.

Government Support Measures: What has been done since September 2009?

1. *Recapitalisations:* Governments shore up banks' Tier 1 or Tier 2 capital by injecting resources in the form of common shares, preferred shares, warrants, subordinated debt mandatory convertible notes or silent participations. In doing so, they improve banks capacity to absorb further losses and strengthen protection for banks' creditors, contributing also to reducing the cost of financing on debt markets. Capital injections, by relieving balance sheet constraints, also seek to sustain banks' capacity to lend. Depending on the terms, recapitalisations could dilute existing shareholders' earning rights and depress stock prices. Recapitalisations via common shares also dilute voting rights.

2. *Debt guarantees:* Governments provide explicit guarantees against default on bank debt and other non-deposit liabilities. These measures help banks maintain access to medium-term funding at reasonable cost, offsetting the drying-up of alternative sources of funding (such as securitisation) and the increase in credit spreads. The intended effect is to reduce liquidity risk and lower overall borrowing costs. The potential adverse effects of this type of measure include segmentation and crowding-out of other credit markets and even distortions in the functioning of bond markets.

3. *Asset purchases or guarantees:* Governments assume part or all of the risk of a portfolio of distressed or illiquid assets. Asset guarantees remove the "tail risk" of insured portfolios from banks' balance sheets. Asset purchases improve bank liquidity, and may even provide capital relief, if purchase prices are higher than book values. The purchase of assets at prices below book value would instead imply a forced writedown for the recipient institution.

A Timeline of Events

Action between September 2008 and June 10, 2009 can be divided into five distinct phases:

Phase one (September 2008): Standalone Support Actions for Large Institutions

The earliest interventions were mostly support for single intermediaries. On 16 September, the day after the Lehman Brothers collapse, the first tranche of aid to AIG was accorded, whereby the US Treasury received a majority equity interest in the insurance firm. By late September, the authorities in Europe - where banks had until then been regarded as less vulnerable - also needed to take action. The Dutch and French governments took part in the recapitalisations of Fortis and Dexia, respectively, in concerted actions with the governments of Belgium and Luxembourg.

Phase two (1-16 October 2008): Comprehensive Support Packages

As more and more financial institutions became affected by the crisis, it became apparent that ad hoc interventions to support individual institutions would not be sufficient to restore confidence in the system as a whole. Many countries announced comprehensive rescue packages involving some combination of recapitalisations, debt guarantees and asset purchases.

The announcement of such a large number of comprehensive programmes was in part a result of international coordination, fostered both by the global scale of the crisis and by concerns over potential competitive distortions arising from uncoordinated measures. The G7 meeting on 10 October established guidelines for assistance to systemically relevant institutions; as a follow-up, on 12 October euro area countries adopted an action plan which a few days later was extended to all EU countries and formed the basis for national plans.

Phase Three (November-December 2008): Fewer Programmes, More Standalone Actions

The rollout of new programmes slowed down towards the end of the year, while implementation of existing ones gained pace: as private capital markets suffered heavily from the high uncertainty, government support for capital and debt issuance quickly became crucial to ensure bank financing. In early November, the Swiss authorities announced their readiness to provide guarantees on new bank debt - although no formal framework was set up. Later in the month, the Italian government approved a scheme to inject capital into listed banks. Notably, November saw the emergence of further problems for AIG and Citigroup, prompting further actions from the US authorities: both institutions received a combination of capital injection and asset purchase or guarantee.

Phase Four (January-April 2009): New Packages with More Emphasis on the Assets side

On 19 January 2009, the UK authorities announced new measures, which included an asset protection scheme, whereby the Treasury provided insurance against large credit losses in one or more defined asset portfolios. Two major banks had joined the scheme by the end-March application deadline. On 10 February, the new US administration outlined the Financial Stability Plan, an articulated framework including a compulsory stress test for the 19 biggest banks, a new capital injection programme (*Capital Assistance Program* - CAP) and a legacy asset purchase programme (*Public-Private Investment Program* - PPIP). Under the Plan, those institutions deemed in need of additional capital - and which could not raise capital from private markets - would obtain support from the CAP. The increased emphasis on legacy assets was reflected in standalone actions, which included an asset guarantee scheme (in combination with another capital injection) for Bank of America (on 16 January) and a backstop facility for a portfolio of mortgages held by ING (26 January).

Phase Five (May-10 June 2009): Exiting for Some, Just Getting Started For Others

On 7 May, the main US regulators released the results of the stress test, which required 10 institutions to raise a total of $74.6 billion in capital. In the meantime, in the light of the improved equity market conditions, a number of institutions were able to raise a substantial amount of equity from the market soon afterwards. On 9 June, 10 large banks were also allowed to repay funds previously received under the October scheme (*Capital Purchase Program* - CPP). However, not all CPP recipients were prepared to repay in the near future and, indeed, capital injections continued. In Europe, capital injections through existing programmes or new standalone actions proceeded. The Spanish government has also been considering the creation of a fund to facilitate the restructuring and consolidation of regional banks. In Germany, a "bad bank" draft law was passed in mid-May, creating the possibility for banks to swap their impaired assets for government guaranteed bonds. The debt guarantee programmes in several countries were extended and/or expanded.

CAUTIOUS OPTIMISM ON GRADUAL RECOVERY

Asset prices and economic activity have rebounded from the lows they reached during the financial crisis. The slide in financial market prices triggered by the bankruptcy of Lehman Brothers in September 2008 halted in March 2009, when prices of risky assets began rising, in some cases substantially. Global economic activity stabilised in the middle of that year and began to expand thereafter. The financial imbalances that lie behind the crisis had begun to correct. Banks started to repair their balance sheets and reduce leverage, although the process is far from complete. Households in some of the countries most affected by the crisis was also started to reduce their indebtedness, but debt levels had fallen much less than after previous crises. Overall, between March 2009 and April 2010, equity prices around the world gained strongly, although they remained below their pre-crisis peaks. Credit spreads narrowed to a level roughly in line with their long-term average, implied volatilities fell to their lowest levels since the middle of 2007, and government bond yields, particularly in the United States, rose from the lows reached in late 2008. As tensions in money markets eased and banks became more willing to lend to each other, the spread of Libor above the overnight index swap (OIS) rate dropped sharply from its late 2008 peak.

Many, but not all, of the markets that had seized up during the crisis started to function again. In late 2008, government guarantees had prompted financial institutions to issue bonds, and non-guaranteed issuance followed in 2009. Non-financial corporations placed more bonds in the first half of 2009 than in the six months immediately preceding the crisis, although these gains may have partly reflected the dearth of bank financing. Indeed, bank lending to the private sector in the major advanced economies either stagnated or contracted, and the market for securitised products continued to be weak. In the United States for example, where the bulk of mortgages are securitised, issuance of mortgage-backed securities (MBS) that are not backed by the government remains at depressed levels.

The financial recovery during much of 2009 and early 2010 has been impressive, but it is under threat. Concerns about the sustainability of public finances and bank health triggered bouts of volatility in late 2009 and again in early 2010. However, these were minor compared with the sell-off that took place in April and May 2010, when risky asset prices fell sharply on investor worries about the ability of Greece and, to a lesser extent, Portugal and Spain to service their debts. Policymakers responded with the largest rescue package in history and a new set of central bank emergency measures. These measures succeeded in halting contagion in the euro area, but were not able to restore investor confidence more broadly. In fact, a multi-speed economic recovery interested as the as the decline in global economic activity began to slow in the second quarter of 2009 and gave way to growth towards the middle of the year. The size of both the contraction and the expansion varied greatly across countries. China, India and Poland avoided a contraction altogether – output growth merely slowed and then soon returned to pre-crisis rates. In Australia and Brazil, output contracted briefly but then grew fast to quickly surpass pre-crisis levels. In contrast, by the first quarter of 2010, output in the United States, the euro area, Japan and the United Kingdom remained below its pre-crisis level.

Recovery in Advanced Economies

Throughout much of 2010, the recovery of the major advanced economies followed a somewhat stumbling path. Weak macroeconomic data, in combination with the unfolding of euro area fiscal problems, prompted fears that growth would stall and possibly even reverse. In response, major central banks delayed policy normalisation and provided stimulus by creating or extending extraordinary measures.

In October 2010, the Bank of Japan announced a ¥5 trillion programme to purchase a variety of assets in an effort to lower risk premia and raise asset prices. A month later, the US Federal Reserve began a second round of Treasurybond purchases – the large-scale asset purchase programme commonly known as QE2 – with the intention of adding $600 billion to its holdings by June 2011. Anticipating the Federal Reserve's move, markets had begun bidding up US stock and bond prices long before the early-November announcement. The passage by the US Congress of a further $858 billion stimulus bill in December reinforced the positive market tone. More broadly, an increasingly steady stream of good economic news contributed to the brightening expectations, the rising prices of risky assets and the lowering of implied volatility in Europe, Japan and the United States.

The devastating earthquake and tsunami in Japan in early March 2011 captured world attention but only temporarily dented optimism.

Activity remained strong in major emerging market economies. Mindful of the unevenness of the global recovery, investors continued to shift their portfolios towards emerging markets (centre panel), where equity prices outpaced those in advanced economies (right-hand panel). Differential performance persisted until early 2011, when concerns about overheating and inflation, combined with geopolitical worries linked to unrest in the Middle East and North Africa, prompted a retreat from some emerging markets. While much of the increase in asset prices in the past year reflected improving fundamentals, changing attitudes played a role as well. Market participants had been gradually resuming their willingness to take on risk, as expected in the early stages of a cyclical upturn. A related development was the resurgence of financial innovation, with strong growth in new instruments and vehicles such as synthetic exchange-traded funds, commoditylinked notes and commodity-based hedge funds. At one level, the return of innovation is a positive sign. But the arrival of new products with risks untested by market stress vividly brings back memories of the lead-up to the financial crisis. The revival of risk-taking and innovation therefore poses an important challenge for authorities tasked with maintaining financial stability.

The financial crisis severely tested banking systems, and the deficiencies it revealed warranted a swift and comprehensive official response. The Basel Committee and the FSB introduced a series of strong international measures, capped by the Basel III framework issued in December 2010. The crisis revealed that risk can be transmitted through unexpected channels. Thus, while Basel III responded to the lessons learned from the global financial crisis, it is primarily designed to improve the resilience of all banks regardless of complexity and size and in all jurisdictions.

BASEL III: SHAPING THE REGULATORY REFORM

Learning from the crisis, the focus area to bring about the fastest improvement was the banking system since the severity of the crisis owed much to the fact that the banking sector in many countries had taken on too much risk without a commensurate increase in capital. Furthermore, this inadequate level of capital was of insufficient quality, as the latter had gradually eroded. Basel III tightens capital requirements, encompasses a broader array of risks, and explicitly addresses macroprudential aspects of banking system stability.

Bank Capital

Basel III substantially raises the quality as well as the quantity of capital, with a much greater emphasis on common equity (see Box-1). During the crisis, losses reduced banks' common equity. However, some banks maintained deceptively high ratios of Tier 1 capital to risk-weighted assets through the inclusion of other forms of financial instruments in the capital base. Moreover, non-common Tier 1 capital instruments often did not share in banks' losses through reduced coupon or principal payments and so did not contribute to maintaining the institutions as going concerns in any meaningful way. The artificially high Tier 1 risk-based ratios also meant that banks were building up high levels of leverage. Basel III therefore also introduces a simple leverage ratio that provides a backstop to the risk-based regime. The supplementary ratio, which is a measure of a bank's Tier 1 capital as a percentage of its assets plus off-balance sheet exposures and derivatives, will serve as an additional safeguard against attempts to "game" the risk-based requirements, and will mitigate model risk. By helping contain the build-up of excessive leverage, the leverage ratio is also to complement other macroprudential measures to reduce systemic risk.

BOX 1

Capital Instruments

The global banking system entered the crisis with an insufficient level of high-quality capital. The crisis revealed an inconsistency in how regulatory capital is defined across jurisdictions and the lack of disclosure that would have enabled the market to fully assess and compare the quality of banks' capital. In response, Basel III introduces a harmonised definition of capital that comprises the following components:

- **Common Equity Tier 1–** consists of the bank's common shares and retained earnings less regulatory adjustments (eg the deduction of goodwill). This component of capital fully absorbs losses while the bank remains a going concern. It is therefore the highest-quality component of a bank's capital. A key element of the new definition of capital is the greater focus on Common Equity Tier 1.

- **Additional Tier 1 capital–** consists of preferred shares and other capital instruments that comply with a set of criteria to ensure they can absorb losses while the issuing bank remains a going concern. These criteria include requirements that the instruments be subordinated, have fully discretionary non-cumulative dividends or coupons and have neither a maturity date nor an incentive to redeem.

- **Tier 2 capital–** consists of debt instruments that comply with a set of criteria to ensure they are able to absorb losses when a bank fails (ie when it has become a "gone concern"). These criteria include requirements that the instruments be subordinated, have a minimum original maturity of at least five years and contain no step-ups or other incentives to redeem. Regulatory recognition of these instruments is amortised over the five years before maturity.

During the crisis, a number of distressed banks were rescued by the injection of public sector funds in the form of common equity and other forms of Tier 1 capital. While this had the effect of supporting depositors, it also meant that certain capital instruments did not absorb losses. Therefore, in addition to the characteristics noted above, instruments in Additional Tier 1 and in Tier 2 must have a feature ensuring that they can be written off or converted to common equity when the issuing bank reaches the point of non-viability (ie the point at which the bank is unable to support itself in the private market) as determined by the relevant authority.

The Basel III definition of capital phases out innovative hybrid capital instruments, which provided an incentive to redeem through features such as step-up clauses. It also eliminates Tier 3 capital, which was short-term subordinated debt that was previously permitted to cover market risk.

In addition to the Basel III elements of capital, certain other instruments are being considered in the context of systemically important banks:

- **Contingent capital (also called cocos)**– debt instruments that convert to Common Equity Tier 1 capital through a write-off or conversion to common shares before a bank reaches the point of non-viability.
- **Bail-in-able debt**– debt instruments that convert to Common Equity Tier 1 capital through a writeoff or conversion to common shares when a bank reaches the point of non-viability.

Risk Coverage

The Basel Committee has also improved the risk coverage of the regulatory capital framework for capital market activities – a salient feature of the recent crisis, where trading exposures accounted for much of the build-up of leverage and were an important source of losses. Trading exposures include positions in financial instruments and commodities held either with the intent to trade them or to hedge other trading activities. For purposes of calculating regulatory capital, such positions are subject to the Basel Committee's market risk rules and are said to be held in the "trading book". Weak capital, excessive leverage and inadequate risk coverage prevented the banking system from fully absorbing systemic trading and credit losses. Nor could it cope with the reintermediation of large off-balance sheet exposures that had built up in the shadow banking system. Under Basel III, banks will have to hold more capital against their less liquid, credit-sensitive assets whose holding periods are much longer than traditional trading positions. Trading activities will also be subject to a stressed value-at-risk requirement. In addition, securitisation exposures in the trading book will be subject to capital charges more consistent with those for the banking book. Basel III also imposes higher capital requirements for counterparty credit risk, that is, for the amount that would be lost in the event of default by a counterparty to a financial contract. Moreover, Basel III creates incentives for banks to increase the use of central counterparties (CCPs) – financial institutions that act as intermediaries between market participants (see Box-2) – while ensuring that the risk arising from banks' exposures to CCPs is adequately capitalised.

Liquidity

During the build-up to the crisis, many banks had operated with increasingly thin liquidity margins, placing undue reliance on easy access to market liquidity. At the height of the crisis, counterparties lost confidence in the liquidity of many banking institutions, severely straining their access to funding. Basel III addresses the liquidity deficiencies that the crisis laid bare. The internationally harmonised liquidity framework consists of two minimum regulatory standards: the liquidity coverage ratio (LCR) and the net stable funding ratio (NSFR). They have complementary objectives.

BOX-2

The Role of Financial Market Infrastructures

Transactions in financial markets are conducted either on organised exchanges or over the counter (OTC). After the transaction is concluded, it is passed on to what is commonly known as the post-trade infrastructure. This process starts with the matching of the transaction and ends with its settlement. Settlement typically involves the transfer of money against the delivery of an asset or a financial instrument such as a derivative. In modern financial systems, settlement takes place in financial market infrastructures like large-value payment systems, securities settlement systems and central counterparties (CCPs).

The way these post-trade infrastructures are designed and how they function has important implications for financial stability because they can act as a channel through which disruptions can spread among financial market participants. Put differently, these infrastructures can serve as an important means to mitigate the risks arising from the "interconnectedness" of market participants and can reduce the risk of contagion.

The financial crisis revealed a striking weakness in the way important OTC derivatives, in particular credit default swaps, were processed in the post-trade phase. Many of these transactions were inadequately reported, and the bilateral exposures between counterparties were insufficiently collateralised.

Against this background, authorities from around the world are pushing for two significant changes in the post-trade infrastructure for OTC derivatives. Both should be implemented by the end of 2012.? First, OTC derivatives will need to be reported to a trade repository (TR). A TR is an electronic registry that keeps a record of all relevant details of an OTC derivative transaction over its lifetime. This information can be used in various ways by the reporting institutions, authorities and the public. If all trades are reported to a TR, and the information is made available to the relevant supervisory authorities, then these authorities will be able to attain an overall view of the OTC derivatives markets, including the most important (gross and net) positions taken by the major dealers in these markets. If TRs had existed before the crisis, the build-up of huge derivative positions, such as those at American International Group (AIG), would have been observed much earlier.

Second, clearing OTC derivatives through a CCP instead of bilaterally can bring about several benefits from a financial stability perspective. A CCP interposes itself between the two original counterparties of a financial transaction, becoming the buyer to the seller and the seller to the buyer. In other words, the CCP isolates the original counterparties from each other should one of them default. Thus, it makes financial institutions less interconnected. However, since risks become concentrated in the CCP, the CCP itself needs to be highly robust: it must protect itself against the default of one or more of its members. To that end, the CCP requires its members to adjust their collateral at the CCP at least daily in accordance with the price movements of their positions.

The LCR is designed to bolster the short-term resilience of a bank's liquidity risk profile by ensuring that it has high-quality liquid assets in sufficient quantity to survive a plausibly severe stress scenario lasting for 30 calendar days. The stress scenario, designed by the Basel Committee, incorporates many of the shocks experienced during the crisis. It includes a partial run-off of retail deposits, a partial or complete drying-up of wholesale funding sources, a need to post additional collateral due to a credit rating downgrade, and unscheduled draws on unused credit and liquidity facilities. The NSFR is designed to promote resilience over a longer time horizon by creating additional incentives for banks to use more stable sources of funding on an ongoing basis.

Macroprudential Aspects

Basel III was designed to enhance both bank-specific soundness and wider banking sector stability. Thus, besides its firm-specific approaches, it incorporates macroprudential measures to explicitly address systemic risk.

During the crisis, mounting losses and the resulting strain on capital impaired banks' ability to lend – precisely at the time when economies were most in need of credit. This tendency for the financial system to amplify cyclical effects in the real economy, or procyclicality, combined with the interconnectedness of financial institutions that were considered too big to fail, exacerbated the crisis.

To help mitigate procyclicality in banking and the broader financial system, the new regulatory capital framework provides for building up capital in good times to levels above the minimum requirement. The resulting capital conservation buffer will help banks absorb losses during periods of financial and economic stress. As a bank's capital level moves closer to the minimum requirement, the conservation buffer imposes a progressively tightened constraint on the bank's discretionary distributions, such as dividends. Retaining a bigger proportion of earnings during a downturn will help ensure that capital remains available to support banks' ongoing business operations during the period of stress.

Basel III also introduces a countercyclical buffer. It is based on the observation that private sector credit growth that is out of line with historical experience often ultimately imposes losses on the lenders. The ratio of aggregate credit to GDP will serve as the reference for the build-up of the buffer, which will be implemented through restrictions on capital distributions identical to those that apply to the conservation buffer. Within countries, the authorities will impose this buffer only when they judge that credit growth is resulting in an unacceptable build-up of system-wide risk. Conversely, the buffer will be released when, in the judgment of the authorities, the capital can help absorb banking system losses that pose a risk to financial stability. The ability to run down the buffer without penalties will help reduce the risk of constraining the availability of credit.

The macroprudential elements of Basel III contribute significantly to the development of the broader macroprudential policy framework. From the growth of national and international efforts to develop and implement it (see Box-3), it can be observed that much has been accomplished, more needs to be done, especially on practical implementation of the broad consensus now evident around the framework's core concepts.

BOX-3

National and International Progress on Implementing Macroprudential Policy Frameworks

One of the key lessons of the recent financial crisis is that regulatory policy must have an enhanced macroprudential orientation to comprehensively address systemic financial risks. The national and international work to develop such a macroprudential policy has intensified and continues to grow, building on conceptual efforts by the BIS since the apparent coining of the term "macroprudential" by the Cooke Committee, the forerunner of the Basel Committee, in 1979.

Recent initiatives in a number of international forums have aided the formation of a clear consensus regarding the key features of an effective macroprudential framework. These include:

• effective integration of supervisory information, market intelligence and aggregate indicator data;

• recognition of the importance of domestic and cross-border interlinkages across financial institutions and markets;

• macroprudential instruments matched to the particular risks or imbalances diagnosed;

• macroprudential policy responsibility assigned to an independent central agency or formal committee, either within the central bank or involving the central bank in a key role; clarity of mandate, adequacy of powers and strong accountability; and

• clear macroprudential policy communications that link financial stability assessments to policy decisions and that manage public expectations about the capabilities of macroprudential policy.

Basel III incorporates macroprudential capital elements, and many jurisdictions continue to accumulate practical experience with macroprudential instruments such as loan-to-value ratio caps and reserve requirements. The powers, tools and accountability requirements for macroprudential policy are either well defined or in an advanced stage of development. The imperative now is to get actual policy operations up and running. To do so, key operational issues must be resolved, including the selection, design and calibration of instruments, the translation of risk indicators to instrument settings, and arranging for efficient decision-making by committees encompassing diverse policy interests and knowledge. In short, the development of macroprudential policy is moving from conceptual issues of design to practical questions of implementation.

A stronger, safer banking system allocates credit more efficiently, reduces the risk of a costly financial crisis and stabilises the environment for long-term business decisions. These benefits will begin to be reaped when the reforms are implemented. But the process of implementing the new framework will also impose some costs on banks and their customers as banks adjust their balance sheets and business models.

How much adjustment will be needed? The answer varies substantially across institutions and jurisdictions. In some economies, particularly those affected by the financial crisis, banks are still rebuilding capital and running off certain assets. In others, capital and liquidity levels already meet the new requirements. Regardless of their starting point, all economies will see some adjustment, given the significant qualitative and quantitative changes in supervisory definitions and approaches in Basel III.

Some adjustment within the global banking system is to be expected as banks work to meet the new requirements. The improvements in capital positions since the end of 2009 should mitigate this to some extent. The adjustment will also be eased by improvements in bank profitability and behavioural shifts over the transition period.

In contrast to previous international regulatory initiatives, the formulation of the Basel III proposals was guided by top-down analysis of the potential macroeconomic impact. Thus, alongside their bottom-up efforts to cumulate the impact of higher requirements on individual banks, regulators looked closely at the growth impact during the transition to stronger capital and liquidity requirements as well as the costs and benefits to the economy over the long term.

A CASE OF FRAGILE GLOBAL RECOVERY

The global economic recovery faltered in 2011. For the year as a whole, world output grew by 3.9%, slightly slower than the average growth rate of the decade prior to the financial crisis, but down significantly from 5.3% in 2010. The pace of economic growth in advanced economies halved, to just 1.6% This reflected a significant weakening of the economy in the United States and the United Kingdom and a sharp drop in activity in Japan after the March 2011 earthquake, while growth in the euro area as a whole was broadly unchanged.

Overall, the economic momentum in advanced economies was too weak to generate a robust, self-sustaining recovery. The drag on private consumption persisted. Unemployment remained high, or even increased further. Falling property prices and high levels of debt continued to weigh on household balance sheets in the mature economies hit hardest by the financial crisis. Household sector weakness also weighed on business spending. Very weak public sector finances generally left no room for further fiscal stimulus.

Emerging market economies grew by around 6% in 2011, with the pace of growth moderating only slightly from 2010. Emerging Asia grew at 7.8%, led by China (9.2%) and India (7.2%); Latin America grew at 4.5%. Growth in central and eastern Europe was broadly unchanged at 5.3% for 2011 as a whole. However rapid growth in EMEs was in many cases associated with signs of domestic overheating, including rising inflation, strong credit growth and rising asset prices. Real credit continued to expand rapidly in emerging Asia and Latin America, and real residential property prices rose close to or above previous historical highs in major cities in China and Latin America.

Reflecting the two-speed global expansion, external imbalances remained wide.

Although slightly lower than in 2010, global current account imbalances remained at about 4% of world GDP, which is high by historical standards. Major advanced economies again recorded sizeable current account deficits, with the notable exceptions of Germany and Japan. Current account surpluses in emerging Asia, though shrinking, remained sizeable. Latin America and central and eastern Europe ran current account deficits. The net private capital flow into EMEs in 2011 was still one of the strongest on record. Despite this, few emerging market currencies strengthened significantly against the major currencies, and many depreciated.

The global recovery started to falter in the second quarter of 2011. At that time, indicators of business activity weakened significantly in the United States, followed by those for EMEs; and in the second half of 2011, they deteriorated relatively sharply in Europe. The prices of many growth-sensitive financial assets declined. Major equity indices around the world fell, with the prices of cyclical stocks declining relatively sharply. Corporate bond spreads generally rose, notably for low and sub-investment grade ratings.

These developments reflected two major shocks which exposed underlying weakness in the global economy associated with domestic and external imbalances. *First*, commodity prices, which had already increased significantly, remained high against the backdrop of strong demand from EMEs. This eroded household income in the United States and other advanced economies at a time of high unemployment and ongoing balance sheet repair. In contrast, the main effect in a number of EMEs was higher inflation, which led to policy tightening. *Second*, financial market investors became increasingly wary about the credit quality of several euro area governments and the exposure of European banks to sovereign credit risk. In the second half of 2011, a sharp increase in global risk aversion, fiscal restraint and growing deleveraging pressure on banks sapped demand.

Global growth remained fragile in early 2012. Economic weakness and growing strains in global financial markets towards the end of 2011 triggered a new round of central bank support measures. The Federal Reserve committed to buy an additional $400 billion of long-dated US Treasury securities, funded by sales of shorter-term notes. It also announced that it planned to keep its short-term policy rate at exceptionally low levels until at least the end of 2014. The Bank of Japan and the Bank of England further increased the size of their asset-buying programmes. The central banks of Brazil, China, India, Indonesia, the Philippines and Turkey also loosened monetary policy. In December 2011, the ECB announced offerings of funding to euro area banks for three years, against an expanded set of collateral. Major central banks had already agreed to reduce the prices of currency swap lines between themselves, allowing them to exchange euros for dollars with banks more cheaply than previously.

These measures triggered significant improvements in bank funding markets and financial markets more broadly. The ECB's two auctions of three-year funding in December 2011 and February 2012 allowed euro area banks to prefund much of their unsecured debt redemptions due by 2014. In addition, banks used some of the cash to purchase assets, including euro area sovereign bonds. The yields on these securities declined significantly. More generally, additional policy support helped to boost a wide range of asset prices during the first few months of 2012. The completion of an orderly restructuring of Greek debt in March also removed a downside risk to asset prices.

Global economic activity seemed to recover somewhat in the first quarter of 2012. In the United States, the unemployment rate declined, hand in hand with a significant increase in consumer confidence and spending. In Japan, machinery orders and corporate investment lifted business activity, as the economy continued to rebound from the effects of the March 2011 earthquake. Following a contraction in the last quarter of 2011, GDP in the euro area stabilised. And activity in several EMEs increased at a faster pace, notably in Latin America and Southeast Asia.

That said, sustainable economic growth remained elusive, and economic activity fell in the second quarter. In April and May 2012, a number of economic indicators for the United States were weaker than expected and employment growth slowed again. Indicators of activity in China weakened significantly from the start of 2012, although this partly reflected a response to measures aimed at bringing growth down to more sustainable levels. Output growth also slowed markedly in Brazil and India, notably in the agricultural and manufacturing sectors. In the euro area, output appeared to be contracting again in the second quarter of 2012.

Financial risks in the euro area also intensified in the second quarter of 2012, driven primarily by concerns about the post-election policy orientation of Greece. Deposit and other capital outflows increased from countries perceived as vulnerable to a further deepening of the crisis. In particular, deposit withdrawals from banks in Greece reportedly accelerated in May, 2012. These banks had already lost around one third of their foreign deposits and one quarter of their domestic non-financial deposits. Foreign depositors had also withdrawn funds from banks in Ireland, Italy, Portugal and Spain, while domestic deposits had been more stable. In contrast, deposits at banks in Germany and the Netherlands increased significantly in the first quarter of 2012. Similarly, estimates of overall capital flows show net private outflows from Greece, Ireland, Italy, Portugal and Spain and inflows into Germany and the Netherlands.

REFORM AGENDA

Restoring confidence among private investors is paramount for the stabilization of the financial markets. The policymakers are laying foundations to support that confidence, but numerous technical, legal, and political challenges remain. The urgency of the task is also increasing, as the investors are increasingly buying protection against extreme risks, even if investing in the instruments designed to provide the protection can be costly and may prove ineffective. The realization of extreme risk in 2008 led to a material alteration in investment strategies: strong demand for insurance against tail outcomes (the risk of low-probability but high-impact events). This demand has been relatively price insensitive in the recent past, indicative of a lasting structural shift in investment strategies. New instruments have emerged to satisfy investor demand, the most notable aimed at exploiting the inverse correlation between equity prices and the expected volatility of equity markets. Global tail risks may emanate from one or more sources, such as the euro area crisis or U.S. and Japanese fiscal imbalances. Evaluating the source of specific risks provides policymakers with a guide to areas of potential instability discussed below.

Euro Area Risks: Currency Redenomination Risk

Risks in the euro area are dominated by balance of payments imbalances across member states. Creditor countries are repatriating capital from debtor nations even when the cost of doing so is high, as demonstrated by negative nominal shorter-term interest rates in various countries. Investors are willing to accept negative interest rates as the cost of guarding against a euro breakup and the introduction of national or subregional currencies (currency redenomination risk). Creditor countries expect to see their currencies appreciate substantially, more than offsetting the negative interest rate.

Longer-Term Risks Emerging in Japan

Japan's imbalances are unique in the context of history: very high government debt yet a very large external creditor position. The resolution of these imbalances could have significant implications for both interest rates and exchange rates. The natural expectation leans to a significant increase in bond yields. Interest rate markets do indeed reflect the potential for higher yields in the medium term.

The implications for foreign exchange markets are more complex. As seen during the March 2011 natural disaster in Japan, rapid currency appreciation may occur given the potential for the repatriation of foreign assets. Alternatively, the threat of an erosion of confidence in domestic policy, or, over the longer run, of a deterioration in the current account, might cause substantial depreciation. The market has resolved these two competing forces by anticipating a very high level of medium-term volatility in the dollar-yen exchange rate, well above realized volatility and high relative to past crises.

U.S. Risks: Complacency or Confidence?

The United States has a blend of the imbalances seen in the other major countries. U.S. government debt is high, though not as high as in Japan. The United States is an international net debtor, though not to the same extent as Spain and other countries in the euro area periphery. Nevertheless, markets have a benign expectation for the resolution of U.S. imbalances. Evidence of extreme risks in interest rate and currency markets is absent at virtually all horizons.

While the capacity of the U.S. government to repay its debt is not in doubt, continued growth in macro imbalances would raise the likelihood of a misalignment of policy incentives across internal and external creditors. If the expansion of the Federal Reserve balance sheet is the last-resort policy that prevents a large rise in bond yields, the clearest transmission mechanism is currency depreciation. Medium-term expectations have been, instead, leaning toward a U.S. dollar appreciation.

In the near term, the U.S. sovereign credit default swap curve suggests that the debt ceiling, as well as the fiscal cliff, will be resolved without issue. Uncertainty about a potential technical default as a result of the debt ceiling led to credit risk in short-term default swaps rising above those over longer horizons in July 2011. No such pattern has emerged this time around. In the longer term, option markets are pricing far less fear of a rise in longer-term interest rates compared with Japan.

Financial Stability Implications

Evaluating extreme risks supports financial stability in three important ways. *First*, policymakers can disagree with the market assessment and provide targeted, logical foundations to the contrary both when there is too much and, importantly, too little concern about future imbalances. *Second*, understanding strategies that attempt to insure against extreme risks can reveal potential vulnerabilities in the financial system. Seemingly effective hedges, such as long-term euro interest rate swaps, could further concentrate counterparty exposures, exacerbating risks when extreme events occur. *Third*, changes in investment strategies lead to financial innovation. New products, particularly fast-growing ones where risk diversification is likely to lag innovation, could lead to risks simply being transferred and concentrated, and therefore should be closely monitored.

In recent times, it has been observed that even the focus of the regulatory reform agenda has shifted from the development of standards to rulemaking and implementation of Based III. Some countries are much further behind than others in the implementation process.

The liquidity requirements under Basel III—the liquidity coverage ratio (LCR) and the net stable funding ratio (NSFR)—are still some time away from implementation, with the LCR and NSFR currently within the observation period. Although the LCR rules will be clarified by early 2013, the final shape of the NFSR is less certain, as the implementation date is further out, in 2018. Further, the end-2012 deadline for trading all standardized derivatives contracts through exchanges or electronic trading platforms and clearing them where appropriate through central counterparties (CCPs) is likely to be missed because of lagging implementation at the national level.

The recovery has suffered new setbacks, and uncertainty weighs heavily on the outlook. A key reason is that policies in the major advanced economies have not rebuilt confidence in medium-term prospects. Tail risks, such as those relating to the viability of the euro area or major U.S. fiscal policy mistakes, continue to preoccupy investors. The World Economic Outlook (WEO) forecast thus sees only a gradual strengthening of activity from the relatively disappointing pace of early 2012. Projected global growth is at 3.3 and 3.6 percent in 2012 and 2013, respectively. Output is expected to remain sluggish in advanced economies but still relatively solid in many emerging market and developing economies. Unemployment is likely to stay elevated in many parts of the world. And financial conditions will remain fragile.

The WEO forecast rests on two crucial policy assumptions. The first is that European policymakers will adopt policies that gradually ease financial conditions further in periphery economies. In this regard, the European Central Bank (ECB) has recently done its part. It is now up to national policymakers to move and activate the European Stability Mechanism (ESM), while articulating a credible path and beginning to implement measures to achieve a banking union and greater fiscal integration. The second assumption is that U.S. policymakers will prevent the drastic automatic tax increases and spending cutbacks (the "fiscal cliff") implied by existing budget law, raise the U.S. federal debt ceiling in a timely manner, and make good progress toward a comprehensive plan to restore fiscal sustainability.

More generally, downside risks have increased and are considerable. The IMF staff's fan chart, which uses financial and commodity market data and analyst forecasts to gauge risks—suggests that there is now a 1 in 6 chance of global growth falling below 2 percent, which would be consistent with a recession in advanced economies and low growth in emerging market and developing economies. Ultimately, however, the WEO forecast rests on critical policy action in the euro area and the United States, and it is very difficult to estimate the probability that this action will materialize.

This juncture presents major difficulties for policymakers. In many advanced economies, injections of liquidity are having a positive impact on financial stability and output and employment, but the impact may be diminishing. Many governments have started in earnest to reduce excessive deficits, but because uncertainty is high, confidence is low, and financial sectors are weak, the significant fiscal achievements have been accompanied by disappointing growth or recessions. In emerging market and developing economies, policymakers are conscious of the need to rebuild fiscal and monetary policy space but are wondering how to calibrate policies in the face of major external downside risks.

An effective policy response in the major advanced economies is the key to improving prospects and inspiring more confidence about the future. In the short term, the main tasks are to rule out the tail risk scenarios and adopt concrete plans to bring down public debt over the medium term.

The crisis in the euro area remains the most obvious threat to the global outlook. The ECB has put in place a mechanism to improve the transmission of low policy rates to borrowing costs in the periphery, where investors' fears about the viability of the euro have pushed market rates to very high levels. The periphery economies need to continue to adjust. Governments must meet their commitment to make the euro area firewall more flexible. Specifically, the ESM must intervene in banking systems and provide support to sovereigns, while national leaders must work toward true economic and monetary union. This requires establishing a banking union with a unified financial stability framework and implementing measures toward fiscal integration, on the principle that more area-wide insurance must come with more area-wide control. Unless more action is taken soon, recent improvements in financial markets could prove fleeting.

In emerging market and developing economies, activity has been slowed by policy tightening in response to capacity constraints, weaker demand from advanced economies, and country-specific factors. Policy improvements have raised their resilience to shocks. Since the crisis erupted in 2008, expansionary policies have buffered the negative impact of the weakness in advanced economy markets: fiscal deficits have typically been above precrisis levels, whereas real interest rates have been lower. Domestic credit has grown rapidly. Over the medium term, policymakers will need to ensure that they retain the ability to respond flexibly to shocks by maintaining a sound fiscal position and by keeping inflation and credit growth at moderate rates.

Global imbalances, and the associated vulnerabilities, have diminished, but there is still a need for more decisive policy action to address them. Within the euro area, current account imbalances—the large surpluses in Germany and the Netherlands and the deficits in most periphery economies—need to adjust further. At the global level, the current account positions of the United States, the euro area as a whole, and Japan are weaker than they would be with more sustainable fiscal policies—and the real effective exchange rates of the dollar, euro, and yen are stronger. In contrast, the current account positions of many Asian economies are undesirably strong and their exchange rates undesirably weak. In part, this reflects distortions that hold back consumption. But it also reflects the effect of large-scale official accumulation of foreign exchange.

In general, the policies required to lower current account imbalances and related vulnerabilities suit the interests of the economies concerned. More adjustment in external-deficit economies and more internal demand in external-surplus economies would contribute not only to a safer global economy but also to stronger growth for all. Many external-deficit economies need further fiscal adjustment and strengthened financial sector supervision and regulation. These efforts need to be complemented with structural measures, the details of which differ widely across the external-deficit advanced and emerging market economies but include labor and product market reform, improvements to governance and the business environment, and measures to boost private saving for retirement. The structural measures needed in external-surplus economies with undervalued exchange rates also vary by country but include boosting investment in Germany, reforming the social safety net in China to encourage consumption, and reducing the accumulation of official reserves in many emerging market economies, which would also help rein in high credit and asset price growth.

Going forward, a number of forces—including the crisis itself, ongoing adjustments by market participants, crisis management responses by authorities, and an evolving regulatory reform agenda can be expected to change the structure of the financial intermediation in fundamental ways. Authorities—have made much progress on the reform agenda, but several issues still need the attention of policymakers. While being cognizant of a tendency by government to over-regulate during periods of distress (potentially stifling economic benefits), there are still some regulatory areas that remain unfinished or that may develop and require action because of unintended side effects of reform. The following is a list of those areas and a suggested agenda for further work.

I. Too Important to Fail

i) *A global-level discussion on the pros and cons of direct business activity restrictions,* because the effects of such national initiatives will not stop at the borders. This discussion should address the question of whether imposing higher costs can be expected to lower systemic risks. If not, the questions become, will restraints on activities be more effective? And what might their cross-border implications be?

ii) *Recovery and resolution planning for large institutions.* Progress so far is uneven across economies and, especially for systemically important institutions, faster progress is needed. While a so-called living will is not a panacea for reducing risk at a financial institution, the discipline of constructing such a plan for its own demise can help it sort out its internal structures and enhance its governance mechanisms to control excessive risk taking. If properly implemented, implicit guarantees would be curtailed, lowering the potential use of taxpayer funds.

II. Financial Globalization

i) *Further progress on cross-border resolution.* Globalization works best when the flows are calm and consistent and disruptions can be handled in a fair and transparent manner. Good management by financial institutions with cross-border activities, well-coordinated supervision of cross-border institutions, and transparent methods of dealing with distress are all components of healthy financial globalization. Cross-border resolution remains the most difficult component of any plan to ensure a smooth unwinding of large global institutions—burden sharing and legal commitments are areas for further clarity. The framework for coping with cross-border resolution needs to encourage operating behaviors, both by institutions themselves and by their supervisors, that reduce the likelihood of having to resort to resolution.

III. Shadow Banking

i) *Enhanced monitoring of systemic risks posed by nonbanks.* To the extent that nonbanks act like banks, a common set of prudential standards must be applied to both types of institution. Further monitoring to see where bank-like activities pose systemic concerns needs to continue and be enhanced, since some of the cost pressures on banks mean some activities will undoubtedly move into the nonbank sector.

IV. Complexity and Transparency

i) *Further thought on how to encourage the development of simpler products.* While not inhibiting innovation, we need to have ways to encourage products that can be priced more accurately to reflect risks. Both the producers of such products and their customers should be able to see clearly where risks reside. For example, the new products to securitize counterparty risks warrant close monitoring to ensure that they are transparent to investors and shareholders so they can appropriately price their exposures and to ensure that the products are not offsetting some of the goals of the new banking standards.

ii) *More information to reveal interconnections and the buildup and spillover of risk.* Lack of transparency on counterparty relationships, corporate governance structures, and other potentially risk-ladenconditions blocks investors and counterparties from imposing market discipline and prevents regulators and supervisors from taking early corrective actions.

V. Over-the-counter Derivatives

i) *More consideration of risks in moving OTC derivatives contracts to central counterparties (CCPs).* Current efforts to reduce counterparty exposures through such moves come with some danger that the CCPs themselves will become too important to fail and that the "location" requirements enforced in multiple jurisdictions may create too many CCPs. These institutions could have diverse requirements and levels of oversight that would hinder the benefits of netting, increase the demands for collateral, and unnecessarily increase costs. In general, the international effort to harmonize approaches to reforms in OTC derivatives markets should be reenergized.

VI. Other Conditions

Though they are not part of the regulatory reforms effort, two conditions are essential if the reforms are to bring about a safer financial system: (1) strong supervision in implementing the reforms and (2) a private sector with the incentives to follow them. Without these elements, the reforms will wither and die.

Hence, we cannot overemphasize the importance of the role played by implementation of regulations—both in terms of the final version of rules at the national level and in terms of how those rules are interpreted and enforced within and across institutions. National and regional approaches will vary considerably, and these have the potential to alter the effectiveness of the reforms, not only for themselves but globally as well. Hence, supervision must have a global focus. But with the system remaining complex, and with the set of new (detailed and complex) regulatory initiatives being added, a political and social consensus is needed to give supervisors the will to act and to be intrusive, skeptical, proactive, comprehensive, adaptive, and conclusive.

In addition, the private sector needs to take its share of the responsibility for making financial systems safe for savers and investors—the ultimate beneficiaries. Compensation within institutions should seek to apportion rewards based on both risk and return. Governance structures should be set to support those responsible for ensuring the firm's integrity and soundness. Product development should seek to satisfy customer's bona fide needs in a manner that enables risk-adjusted pricing.

HOW HAS INDIA BEEN HIT BY THE CRISIS?

The contagion of the crisis has spread to India through all the channels – the financial channel, the real channel, and importantly, as happens in all financial crises, the confidence channel.

India's financial markets – equity markets, money markets, forex markets and credit markets – had all come under pressure from a number of directions. First, as a consequence of the global liquidity squeeze, Indian banks and corporates found their overseas financing drying up, forcing corporates to shift their credit demand to the domestic banking sector. Also, in their frantic search for substitute financing, corporates withdrew their investments from domestic money market mutual funds putting redemption pressure on the mutual funds and down the line on non-banking financial companies (NBFCs) where the MFs had invested a significant portion of their funds. This substitution of overseas financing by domestic financing brought both money markets and credit markets under pressure. Second, the forex market came under pressure because of reversal of capital flows as part of the global deleveraging process. Simultaneously, corporates were converting the funds raised locally into foreign currency to meet their external obligations. Both these factors put downward pressure on the rupee. Third, the Reserve Bank's intervention in the forex market to manage the volatility in the rupee further added to liquidity tightening.

In the real sector, the transmission of the global cues to the domestic economy has been quite straight forward – through the slump in demand for exports. The United States, European Union and the Middle East, which account for three quarters of India's goods and services trade are in a synchronized down turn. Service export growth is also likely to slow in the near term as the recession deepens and financial services firms – traditionally large users of outsourcing services – are restructured. Remittances from migrant workers too are likely to slow as the Middle East adjusts to lower crude prices and advanced economies go into a recession.

Beyond the financial and real sectors of transmission the crisis also spread through the confidence channel. In sharp contrast to global financial markets, which went into a seizure on account of a crisis of confidence, Indian financial markets continued to function in an orderly manner. Nevertheless, the tightened global liquidity situation in the period immediately following the Lehman failure in mid-September 2008, coming as it did on top of a turn in the credit cycle, increased the risk aversion of the financial system and made banks cautious about lending

HOW HAS INDIA RESPONDED TO THE CHALLENGE?

The Government and the Reserve Bank of India responded to the challenge in close coordination and consultation. The main plank of the Government response was fiscal stimulus while the Reserve Bank's action comprised monetary accommodation and counter cyclical regulatory forbearance.

The Reserve Bank's policy response was aimed at containing the contagion from the outside – to keep the domestic money and credit markets functioning normally and see that the liquidity stress did not trigger solvency cascades. In particular, RBI targeted three objectives: first, to maintain a comfortable rupee liquidity position; second, to augment foreign exchange liquidity; and third, to maintain a policy framework that would keep credit delivery on track so as to arrest the moderation in growth. This marked a reversal of Reserve Bank's policy stance from monetary tightening in response to heightened inflationary pressures of the previous period to monetary easing in response to easing inflationary pressures and moderation in growth in the current cycle. These measures to meet the above objectives came in several policy packages starting mid-September 2008, on occasion in response to unanticipated global developments and at other times in anticipation of the impact of potential global developments on the Indian markets.

The policy packages included, like in the case of other central banks, bothconventional and unconventional measures. On the conventional side, RBI reduced the policy interest rates aggressively and rapidly, reduced the quantum of bank reserves impounded by the central bank and expanded and liberalised the refinance facilities for export credit. Measures aimed at managing forex liquidity included an upward adjustment of the interest rate ceiling on the foreign currency deposits by non-resident Indians, substantially relaxing the external commercial borrowings (ECB) regime for corporates, and allowing non-banking financial companies and housing finance companies access to foreign borrowing.

The important among the many unconventional measures taken by the Reserve Bank of India are a rupee-dollar swap facility for Indian banks to give them comfort in managing their short-term foreign funding requirements, an exclusive refinance window as also a special purpose vehicle for supporting non-banking financial companies, and expanding the lendable resources available to apex finance institutions for refinancing credit extended to small industries, housing and exports.

Recognising the depth and extraordinary impact of this crisis, the Central Government invoked the emergency provisions of the FRBM Act to seek relaxation from the fiscal targets and launched two fiscal stimulus packages in December 2008 and January 2009. These fiscal stimulus packages, together amounting to about 3 per cent of GDP, included additional public spending, particularly capital expenditure, government guaranteed funds for infrastructure spending, cuts in indirect taxes, expanded guarantee cover for credit to micro and small enterprises, and additional support to exporters. These stimulus packages came on top of an already announced expanded safety-net for rural poor, a farm loan waiver package and salary increases for government staff, all of which too should stimulate demand.

Impact of Policy Measures

Taken together, the measures put in place since mid-September 2008 have ensured that the Indian financial markets continue to function in an orderly manner. The cumulative amount of primary liquidity potentially available to the financial system through these measures is over US$ 75 bln or 7 per cent of GDP. This sizeable easing has ensured a comfortable liquidity position starting mid-November 2008 as evidenced by a number of indicators including the weighted-average call money rate, the overnight money market rate and the yield on the 10-year benchmark government security. Taking the signal from the policy rate cut, many of the big banks have reduced their benchmark prime lending rates. Bank credit has expanded too, faster than it did last year. However, Reserve Bank's rough calculations show that the overall flow of resources to the commercial sector is less than what it was last year. This is because, even though bank credit has expanded, it has not fully offset the decline in non-bank flow of resources to the commercial sector.

However, while evaluating the response to the crisis, it is important to remember that although the origins of the crisis are common around the world, the crisis has impacted different economies differently. Importantly, in advanced economies where it originated, the crisis spread from the financial sector to the real sector. In emerging economies, the transmission of external shocks to domestic vulnerabilities has typically been from the real sector to the financial sector. Countries have accordingly responded to the crisis depending on their specific country circumstances. Thus, even as policy responses across countries are broadly similar, their precise design, quantum, sequencing and timing have varied. In particular, while policy responses in advanced economies have had to contend with both the unfolding financial crisis and deepening recession, in India, the response has been predominantly driven by the need to arrest moderation in economic growth.

These initiatives can be seen within the overall context of the financial sector development in the country, particularly, in the money market, government securities market and the foreign exchange market. With the implementation of these initiatives, we can expect a continuing process of financial market development that aids the overall development process. Similar efforts are being undertaken by the Government and the securities regulator, the Securities and Exchange Board of India along with the Reserve Bank in activating the corporate debt market. As has been experienced elsewhere, among the various financial markets, the corporate debt market is indeed the most difficult to develop for a variety of reasons. A great deal of detailed work needs to be undertaken over a period of time to put in place an appropriate market micro infrastructure, trading platforms, technology and clearing and settlement systems, along with further development of both issuers and buyers. The expansion of the pension fund and insurance industries will progressively result in the presence of a larger financial investor base, which will help in the overall expansion of financial markets and in particular the corporate debt market.

QUESTIONS

1. "Globalisation of financial markets, described as the wave of the future, opens new vistas for international financial managers in financing their worldwide operations." Critically examine the statement.

2. Discuss the factors beyond the diversification benefits which have contributed the increasing popularity of foreign equity investments with institutional portfolio managers.

3. "Increasing interest by investors in foreign equities portends significant implications not only for investors, but also for financial mangers of multinational firms". Discuss.

4. Critically examine the growth prospects and the increasing volatility in the world financial markets.

5. "Strong appetite for risk among global investors and generally favourable macroeconomic conditions fuelled emerging market returns in recent times." Do you agree?

6. Critically examine the validity of the `Decoupling Theory' in the current world financial market scenario.

7. "Before the onset of the crisis, emerging market economics (EMEs) growth had been very strong, but the structure of that growth planted some of the seeds of the recent downturn." Do you agree?

8. The tumult in the global financial markets that began in August 2007 seemed to have had very little effect on the markets of emerging economics. If financial globalisation had indeed deepened, what that apparent disconnect?

9. "Rise in exchange rate-driven capital flows complicates the setting of monetary policy?" Explain the statement in the context of current global financial crisis.

10. How has India been hit by the global financial crisis? How has the government and the RBI responded to the challenge? What is the impact of policy measures?

11. Critically examine the macroprudential elements of Basel III.

12. Restoring confidence among private investors is paramount for the stabilisation of financial markets. What are the sources of specific risks which should be considered by the policymakers while setting the agenda for reform.

REFERENCES

1. Alessi, Lucia, and Carsten Detken, 2009, "Real Time Early Warning Indicators for Costly Asset Price Boom/Bust Cycles—A Role for Global Liquidity," ECB Working Paper Series 1039 (Frankfurt: European Central Bank).

2. Atkins, Charles, Richard Dobbs, Ju-Hon Kwek, Susan Lund, James Manyika, and Charles Roxburgh, 2010, "Debt and Deleveraging: The Global Credit Bubble and Its Economic Consequences," McKinsey Global Institute (New York):

3. Azarchs, Tanya, and Catherine Mattson, 2010, "Industry Outlook: The Worst May Still Be Yet to Come for U.S. Commercial Real Estate Loans," Standard & Poor's Global Credit Portal, February (New York).

4. Bank for International Settlements, 2009a, "Basel II Capital Framework Enhancements Announced by the Basel Committee," BIS Press Release (Basel).

5. ———, 2009b, "Consultative Proposals to Strengthen the Resilience of the Banking Sector Announced by the Basel Committee," BIS Press Releases (Basel).

6. Borio, Claudio, and Mathias Drehmann, 2009, "Towards an Operational Framework for Financial Stability: 'Fuzzy' Measurement and Its Consequences," BIS Working Paper No. 284 (Basel: Bank for International Settlements).

7. Borio, Claudio, and Philip Lowe, 2002, "Asset Prices, Financial and Monetary Stability: Exploring the Nexus," BIS Working Paper No. 114 (Basel: Bank for International Settlements).

8. Committee on the Global Financial System (CGFS), 2007, "Financial Stability and Local Currency Bond Markets," Paper No. 28 (June) (Basel: Bank for International Settlements).

9. Congressional Oversight Panel, 2010, "February Oversight Report: Commercial Real Estate Losses and the Risk to Financial Stability" (Washington).

10. Dattels, Peter, Rebecca McCaughrin, Ken Miyajima, and Jaume Puig Forne, forthcoming, "Can You Map Financial Stability?" IMF Working Paper (Washington: International Monetary Fund).

11. Djankov, Simeon, Oliver Hart, Caralee McLiesh, and Andrei Shleifer, 2008, "Debt Enforcement Around the World," *Journal of Political Economy*, Vol. 116, No. 6, pp1105–149.

12. European Central Bank (ECB), 2009, Financial Stability Review (Frankfurt, December)

13. Gagnon, Joseph, Matthew Raskin, Julie Remache, and Brian Sack, 2010, "Large-Scale Asset Purchases by the Federal Reserve: Did They Work?" Federal Reserve Bank of New York Staff Report No. 441.

14. International Monetary Fund (IMF), 2006, Global Financial Stability Report, World Economic and Financial Surveys (Washington, April).

15. ———, 2007, Global Financial Stability Report, World Economic and Financial Surveys (Washington, April).

16. ———, 2008a, Global Financial Stability Report, World Economic and Financial Surveys (Washington, April).

17. ———, 2008b, World Economic Outlook, World Economic and Financial Surveys (Washington, October).

18. ———, 2008c, "Spain—Staff Report for the 2008 Article IV Consultation," SM/09/34 (Washington).

19. ———, 2009a, Global Financial Stability Report, World Economic and Financial Surveys (Washington, April).

20. ———, 2009b, Global Financial Stability Report, World Economic and Financial Surveys (Washington, October). ———, 2009c, "Japan: Selected Issues," IMF Country Report No. 09/211 (Washington).

21. ———, 2010a, World Economic Outlook, World Economic and Financial Surveys (Washington, April).

22. ———, 2010b, "The State of Public Finances: Cross-Country Fiscal Monitor," IMF Staff Position Note (Washington, May).

23. Kang, Xiaowei, and Dimitris Melas, 2010, "A Fresh Look at the Strategic Equity Allocation of European Institutional Investors," MSCI Barra Research Insight (New York).

24. N'Diaye, Papa M'B. P., 2009, "Macroeconomic Implications for Hong Kong SAR of Accommodative U.S. Monetary Policy," IMF Working Paper No. 09/256 (Washington: International Monetary Fund).

25. Peiris, Shanaka, J., 2010, "Foreign Participation in Emerging Markets' Local Currency Bond Markets," IMF Working Paper No. 10/88 (Washington: International Monetary Fund).

26. Segoviano, Miguel, 2006, "Portfolio Credit Risk and Macroeconomic Shocks: Applications

to Stress Testing Under Data-Restricted Environments," IMF Working Paper No. 06/283 (Washington: International Monetary Fund).

27. Stroebel, Johannes, and John Taylor, 2009, "Estimated Impact of the Fed's Mortgage-Backed Securities Purchase Program," NBER Working Paper 15626 (Cambridge, Massachusetts: National Bureau of Economic Research).

28. Tokuoka, Kiichi, 2010, "The Outlook for Financing Japan's Public Debt," IMF Working Paper No. 10/19 (Washington: International Monetary Fund).

44

International Portfolio Investment

INTRODUCTION

In recent years, economic activity has been characterized by a dramatic increase in the international dimensions of business operations. National economies in all parts of the world have become more closely linked by way of a growing volume of cross-border transactions, not only in terms of goods and services but even more so with respect to financial claims of all kinds. Reduced regulatory barriers between countries, lower cost of communications as well as travel and transportation have resulted in a higher degree of market integration. With respect to real goods and services, this trend towards globalization is clearly reflected in the worldwide growth of exports and imports as a proportion of GDP of individual countries. Consequently, consumption patterns have been internationalized as well, both directly as well as indirectly.

Alongside the increase in international trade one can easily observe the globalization of financial activity. Indeed, the growth of cross-border, or "international", flows of financial assets has outpaced the expansion of trade in goods and services. These developments are underpinned by advances in communication and transportation technology. They make geographic distances less significant, extend both the scope of information as well as the speed with which it is available, thus leading to faster and more efficient global financial operations. By the same token, and not unrelated to the technologically driven developments, policy-induced capital market liberalization such as the abolition of capital and exchange controls in most countries, permits an ever growing volume of international financial flows.

As a consequence, investment opportunities are no longer restricted to domestic markets, but financial capital can now seek opportunities abroad with relative ease. Indeed, international competition for funds has caused an explosive growth in international flows of equities as well as fixed-income and monetary instruments. Emerging markets, in particular, as they have become more and more accessible, have begun to offer seemingly attractive investment alternatives to investors around the globe.

International capital flows are further driven by a divergence in population trends between developed and developing countries. Mature, industrialized countries today are characterized by aging populations with significant needs for private capital accumulation. The underlying demand for savings vehicles is further reinforced by the necessary shift from say-as-you-go pension schemes towards capital market-based arrangements. By the same token, developing countries with their relatively young populations require persistent and high levels of investment in order to create jobs and raise standards of living in line with the aspirations of their impatient populations. All this provides significant incentives for the growth of international markets for all kinds of financial claims in general and securities in particular.

While the environment has undoubtedly become more conducive to international portfolio investment (IPI), the potential benefits for savers/investors have lost none of their attractions. There are the less than perfect correlations between national economies, the possibility of hedging an increasingly international consumption basket, and the participation in exceptional growth opportunities abroad which can now be taken advantage of through IPI. However, there is considerable controversy among investment professionals, both in academia as well as in the financial services industry, on the issue to what extent these intuitively perceived benefits of international portfolio investment are sufficiently significant. When the circumstances of the real world are taken into account, additional risks, costs and other constraints to IPI at best limit the potential advantages, at worst negate the benefits.

PRINCIPLES OF INTERNATIONAL PORTFOLIO INVESTMENT (IPI)

Individuals must allocate their income among current consumption, productive investment, and financial investment. Simplifying these choices by assuming that consumption and productive investment decisions have already been made and thereby omitting potential feedback effects leaves the portfolio decision narrowly defined: how to allocate the remaining wealth to financial and / or real assets so as to maximize the most desirable return, i.e. consumption in the future. Despite this simplification, there is still a bewildering array of forms in which wealth can be held, ranging from non-liquid holdings of real estate, through gold coins and commodity futures, all the way to stocks, bonds, savings accounts, money market securities, and cash equivalents. Investment theory, then, comprises the principles that help investors to rationally allocate their wealth between the different investment alternatives.

In the context of IPI which involves investment not only in domestic, but also in foreign securities, the established investment concepts of portfolio theory and capital market theory must be modified and extended to take into account the international dimension. Whereas the basic principles mostly apply also on an international scale, additional considerations become necessary. An important issue that arises if portfolios are composed of securities from different countries is the choice of a numeraire for measuring risk and expected return. As, a matter, of tradition and/or due to regulation, local currency is used in most cases to calculate these security, characteristics, which means that return and variance values for foreign securities need to be adjusted for currency gains or losses. It has to be noted, however, that foreign goods and services represent a significant proportion of the consumption basket in many countries. Therefore, if purchasing power was to be maintained, the maximization of local currency returns may not be optimal in this regard.

The Capital Asset Pricing Model (CAPM) has been developed with respect to major capital markets in the world. It is well accepted and widely used by professional portfolio managers to analyze the pricing of securities in national financial markets. With integrated capital markets, optimal diversification is realized by forming a global market portfolio, and the riskiness of all securities in the world is measured according to their contribution to the risk of this portfolio. The transfer of the CAPM logic to a global perspective leads to the International Capital Asset Pricing Model (ICAPM) .The extended CAPM takes into account the correlation between national securities markets in determination of securities on a given international market:

$$E(R_j^j) = R_f + \beta_{di}^j[E(R_m) - R_f]$$
(1)

where:

$E(R_j^i)$ = expected rate of return on ith security (or portfolio) in jth country;

$E(R_m)$ = expected market rates of return in j'th country;

β_d^j = the beta coefficient for jth country in terms of domestic country's market rate of return; and

R_f = the risk-free rate in the domestic country.

Equation (1) is a nationalistic model that postulates that security rates of return on each marketplace have in common a national factor, R_m. This national factor R_m is in turn dependent on a single common world factor, R_w^i (return for the world market portfolio), defined:

$$E(R_m) = R_f + \beta_n^j (E(R_w) - R_f)\qquad(2)$$

where β_n^j is the international systematic risk of country j.

From Equation (2), it can be concluded that the lower the correlation between the two markets the lower the β_n^j, the lower the expected return, and the higher the value of international diversification. So it can be inferred that an investor who holds a portfolio of domestic securities would hold an under diversified portfolio with respect to world diversification. Therefore, by holding an international portfolio (or security), the investor can reduce the systematic risk of his portfolio. Assume that the world is one big economy and that markets are fully integrated. Then the risk- (world beta-) adjusted average return across national markets should be similar to those of U.S. markets. The integrated-market theory stipulates that all securities in the world are priced in terms of their global systematic risk. This can be stated as:

$$E(R_j^i) = R_f + \beta_{wn}^j [E(R_w) - R_f]\qquad(3)$$

where:

$E(R_j^i)$ = expected rate of return on ith security (or portfolio) in country j;

R_f = the risk-free rate of interest;

$E(R_w)$ = expected rate of return on the world market portfolio;

β_{wn}^j = $(\rho_{i,n} \sigma_i \sigma_w) / \sigma_n^2$ (correlation coefficient between the rate of return on security i in country j and the world market, times the standard deviation of security i, times the standard deviation of the world market, divided by the variance of the world market portfolio.

The relationship between β_d^j, β_w^j, and β_{wn}^j can be defined:

$$\beta_{wn}^j = \beta_w^j \beta_d^j\qquad(4)$$

Equation (4) indicates that the international systematic risk of a security i in country j (β_{wn}^j) is equal to the product of the national systematic risk of that security (β_d^j) and the international systematic risk (β_w^j).

From the formula it can be inferred that the riskiness of a portfolio results from the covariance of a portfolio rate of return with a national stock-market index. Nevertheless, that index is not the only way to determine the price of a portfolio since the national market now has a relationship with the world market and has a certain influence on the world portfolio. That influence depends on the weight that the nation's financial market index has on the world market index.

The market portfolio is not the only source of risk any more, but exchange rate risk has to be accounted for. As a result, investors take a position composed of the domestic risk-free asset and the common world market portfolio while hedging some of the currency risk.

Although this approach seems to be straightforward, there are subtle problems inherent in the ICAPM, because of the likelihood that many of the assumptions underlying the national market CAPM become very tenuous in an international context. Particularly, as there are many barriers and obstacles to IPI, mean-variance efficiency of all securities cannot be assumed automatically. There is no common real risk-free rate of interest, because of real exchange risk caused by deviations from purchasing power parity (PPP). By the same token, it is difficult to determine a global market portfolio. For national capital markets the use of value-weighted portfolios as benchmarks is quite defensible, but this might not be true in an international context, where financial markets are (a) still segmented to some degree, (b) investors have different risk preferences and (c) expected risk and return change over time. Indeed, the choice of an international benchmark is a controversial issue since there is some evidence, that a global portfolio constructed according to the market capitalization of the individual markets is not mean-variance efficient.

Over time, more sophisticated models have been developed to accommodate special factors of the international context or to improve the realism of the model in general. To illustrate, some approaches account for the fact that the assumption of homogeneity of investor preferences is unlikely to prevail across countries. Further, the scope of securities can be extended to incorporate not only stocks, but also bonds. Moreover, asset pricing in the presence of segmented capital markets has revealed a more complex form of the risk premium which is a function of the type of market imperfection, the characteristics of investors' utility function and their relative wealth.

Whereas the traditional CAPM is based on constant values for the parameters of equities (expected return and variance), there exists increasing evidence to support the hypothesis that these characteristics are time-dependent. Therefore, conditional models have been used to model time-variant measures, i.e. expected return and variance are not assumed to be constant over time. This is because of the assumption that historical information and possibly expectations about interest rates, equity prices etc. are available to the investor, which means in technical terms that e.g. the estimated conditional variance for time t+l depends on the information set available at time t. The simplest of these models are autoregressive conditional heteroscedasticity (ARCH) models, in which the conditional variance is calculated as a weighted average of past squared forecasting errors. In generalized ARCH (or GARCH) models, the conditional variance depends on past error terms as well as on historic conditional variances.

Overall, empirical evidence for an international CAPM is mixed, although there seems to be increasing support for this concept. Testing the ICAPM is difficult as there is limited long-term historical data available on international capital markets, an international benchmark portfolio is hard to determine and it is a challenge to capture the time-variation of the securities' characteristics. In general, conditional ICAPM tests seem to have more explanatory power compared to unconditional models. Empirical studies find, for example, that a CAPM which accounts for foreign-exchange risk premia has more explanatory power with regard to the structure of worldwide rates of return than a model without currency risk factors. Interestingly, not only is financial market information such as interest rates, stock prices, etc. apparently relevant, but also factors external to financial markets e.g. leading indicators of business cycles.

With respect to major capital markets, empirical evidence seems to support the concept of an international asset pricing model and market integration. While emerging markets are characterized by segmentation in early periods, these markets exhibit an increasing degree of integration to the global market as well. Since the degree of market segmentation is constantly changing over time through a dynamic integration process, there exist conceptual problems for all approaches that are based on static assumptions of completely segmented or partially integrated markets.

THE BENEFITS FROM INTERNATIONAL PORTFOLIO INVESTMENT

There are several potential benefits that make it attractive for investors to internationalize their portfolios. These perceived advantages are the driving force and motivation to engage in IPI and will, therefore, be dealt with first, i.e. before looking at the risks and constraints. Specifically, the attractions of IPI are based on (a) the participation in the growth of other (foreign) markets, (b) hedging of the investor's consumption basket, (c) diversification effects and, possibly, (d) abnormal returns due to market segmentation. All else being equal, an investor will benefit from having a greater proportion of wealth invested in foreign securities (1) the higher their expected return, (2) the lower the variation of their returns, (3) the lower the correlation of returns of foreign securities with the investor's home market, and possibly, (4) the greater the share of imported goods and services in her consumption.

Participation in Growth of Foreign Markets

High economic growth usually goes hand in hand with high growth in the country's capital market and thus attracts investors from abroad. IPI allows investors to participate in the faster growth of other countries via the purchase of securities in foreign capital markets. This condition applies particularly to the so-called "emerging markets" of Europe, Latin America, Asia, the Mideast and Africa. Countries are classified as emerging if they have low or medium income according to World Bank statistics, but enjoy rapid rates of economic growth.

Driven by the general economic expansion, the financial markets in these countries have exhibited tremendous growth. This means that the security holdings of investors attained values several times worth the original investment after just a few years. However, investors seeking high growth should not limit their analysis to the fascinating and breath-taking developments in emerging market countries, but also take a close look at some of the well-developed, industrialized countries. These countries can provide interesting investment opportunities as well, because they do not only show above average growth, but are also politically more stable.

Most obvious, emerging markets are small in terms of market capitalization and number of stocks in the respective. Favourable economic development in a country as measured by the real growth rate is frequently associated with high average stock returns. Unfortunately, emerging markets do not only offer high returns, but the risks associated with investments in these countries are frequently higher than in established markets as well.

Moreover, there is political risk which can be observed in many manifestations such as instability of the political system and government, threat of exchange controls, abolishment of non- resident convertibility and free remittance of funds, all the way to risk of nationalization of businesses and loss of property rights. Taking these aspects into consideration, rapid growing developed (as opposed to undeveloped) countries come into focus as the prevailing political stability and a safe regulatory environment in these countries translates into lower risk of the investment. On the other hand, absolute risk itself is normally not what matters but contribution to overall portfolio risk, i.e. the correlation between an individual security's return and total portfolio return. Emerging markets can be very interesting from this perspective, as they often reduce total portfolio risk due to low correlation with mature markets.

Nevertheless, two caveats have to be addressed in the context of investment in stocks from high growth countries. *Firstly*, it could be argued that some of the growth has been already discounted and thus included in the prices of foreign securities. In this case, there would be no or only little advantage to the investor buying these stocks now. Indeed, it is hard to believe that in developed countries the growth of the economy and the financial market would not be anticipated and reflected in securities' prices. On the other hand, global financial markets are not yet fully integrated and still lack market efficiency due to market imperfections such as taxes, investment restrictions, foreign exchange regulations, etc. Consequently, capital asset pricing models that are built on these assumptions may not price the securities in different markets "correctly." Therefore, it might be necessary to distinguish between more and less developed high growth countries. For developed countries, information about economic activity including forecasts for future development should be readily available, and political risk is low. Thus, it seems to be within reason to assume that a large part of the growth is expected and thus reflected in securities' prices. However, actual growth might still be higher than anticipated growth due to the dynamics and complexity of the development, resulting in extraordinary returns compared to markets with less uncertainty about their development. The whole story runs somewhat differently for less developed countries, though. The assessment of emerging markets is an area where information is harder to acquire, more difficult to analyze and evaluate correctly. Thus, the realization of higher returns due to superior knowledge seems to be still possible. This is in line with the results of empirical studies which show that returns in emerging markets are more likely to be influenced by local information than in mature markets. A *second* issue that comes up, assuming that an investment in high growth country stocks can be an attractive opportunity as some of them might not be correctly priced, is the concern that foreign investors may not be able to fully participate in the growth potential ,since they are expropriated by local, dominant managers/shareholders. In many emerging markets, foreign investors not only lack protection from a local, dominant manager/shareholder, but they tend to lose out in conflicts with the local power structure. As a result, foreign investors cannot stop the company from reducing their fair share of the company's success by means of dividend policy, management compensation, transactions with companies owned by controlling shareholders or other corporate decisions favoring the family and political interests of the dominant local shareholders. Corporate governance tends to be a major issue for portfolio investors in emerging markets.

Hedging of Consumption Basket

Since the (international) investor is at the same time a consumer of real goods and services, the return of his (financial) investment must be related to his consumption pattern This is a source of considerable difficulty that bedevils formal models of international portfolio investment. The temptation is to simplify and to assume that goods are homogeneous. This implies that goods are perfect substitutes domestically as well as internationally, If one assumes, realistically, that goods are not perfect substitutes, then' deviations from (a) Purchasing Power Parity (PPP), and (b) the Law of One Price (LOP) are possible.

Future consumption can be curtailed by unexpected inflation which can be caused by exchange rate changes and/or shocks of domestic as well as international demand (monetary policies) and supply (crop failure). Consequently, the type of risk that consumer-investors may face is directly related to their consumption pattern and investment position. The nature of the risk is also affected by the structure of markets for financial assets and real goods and services, for example, whether or not PPP holds. Given that the typical investor can be assumed to consume at least some foreign goods, he may derive benefits from international portfolio investment in that he can hedge his internationalized consumption basket against foreign exchange risk through the investment in foreign assets.

Consumer-investors who consume purely domestic goods and have no international portfolio investment are exposed to unexpected change in the domestic inflation, but not to foreign inflation risk or foreign exchange rate risk. In case consumer-investors have ' made some international portfolio investment, but consume purely domestic goods, they face both domestic inflation and exchange risk, because the investors' wealth is now affected by unexpected changes in the exchange rate. However, this exchange risk is directly translated into inflation risk when PPP holds.

If consumer-investors consume some imported goods (something that will be true for many investors today) but have no foreign securities in their portfolio, they face domestic inflation, foreign inflation, and exchange risk. However, if PPP holds exactly over the investment horizon, then the combination of foreign inflation and exchange rate changes will always be equal to the domestic inflation rate. Thus, consumer-investors only face the domestic inflation risk. In these examples, whenever PPP holds, exchange risk is not a barrier to international portfolio investment.

Finally, in case consumer-investors have some foreign assets in their portfolios and also consume foreign goods, they face domestic inflation, foreign inflation, and exchange risk, because the consumption pattern includes some imported goods. The exchange risk, however, can be hedged through appropriate foreign investment. Therefore, exchange risk on the consumption side could serve as an incentive for international portfolio investment. Again, when PPP holds, the exchange risk is the same as the inflation risk and, thus, there is no incentive for international portfolio investment. Nevertheless, if consumer-investors consume some imported goods and have (proportionately matching) international portfolio investments they are able to hedge the exchange risk. Therefore, regardless of whether PPP holds, they may be able to avoid exchange risk. In addition to hedging the individual consumption basket against exchange rate risk, international portfolio investment can be beneficial to the consumer-investor by reducing "domestic output risk." Through the purchase of securities which are ultimately claims on other countries' output, consumption can in principle be smoothed when output is not highly correlated across countries because of different shocks.

INTERNATIONAL PORTFOLIO DIVERSIFICATION

Benefits from International Portfolio Diversification

The crucial factor determining portfolio risk for a given level of return is the correlation between the returns of the securities that make up that portfolio. *Ceteris paribus,* low as opposed to high correlation between securities means lower portfolio risk (portfolio diversification). Risk-averse investors will always prefer less risk to more. Therefore, they will try to make use of the effect of diversification and select securities with low correlation. Since perfect negative correlation between different securities is rare, the lowest correlations possible will be chosen.

This is the point where foreign securities come into play. Investors who compose their portfolio only of domestic securities restrict themselves to a smaller number of securities to choose from. Since they exclude the large set of foreign stocks, bonds and other securities, they limit the power of diversification a priori and forgo the possibility of further reducing portfolio risk by picking some foreign stocks that exhibit very low correlation with the domestic portfolio.

Portfolio theory indicates that as investors diversify internationally, as long as all of the economies of the world are not perfectly positively correlated with each other they should expect gains from diversification. It is a fact that, given any particular group of assets, various optimal weightings of those assets exist that create portfolios with the maximum possible return for a given level of risk. These are the so-called efficient-frontier portfolios.

The efficient frontier for an internationally diversified portfolio lies above the efficient frontier for portfolios limited to their own domestic market, because the range of potential returns is wider internationally and because the correlations of return are typically lower. As a result, the internationally diversified investor has the potential to achieve a higher level of return than the domestic investor for any given level of risk, or, viewed from a different perspective, to expect a lower variability of return than a domestic investor for any given level of return. These relationships are shown in Figure-1.

FIGURE -1

INTERNATIONAL VERSUS DOMESTIC EFFICIENT FRONTIERS

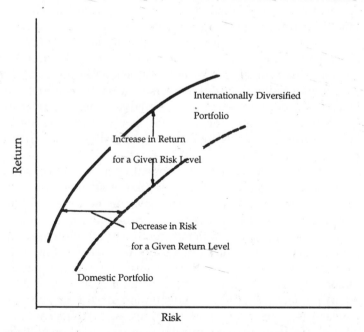

Indeed, there is reason to expect the correlation of returns between foreign securities and domestic securities to be lower than that between only domestic securities. In the latter case, all returns will be partially affected by purely national events, such as real interest rates rising due to a particular government's anti-inflation policy. Within any single country, a strong tendency usually exists for economic phenomena to move more or less in unison, giving rise to periods of relatively high or low economic activity. The reason for this is that the same political authority is responsible for the formulation of economic policies in a particular country. For example, the monetary, fiscal, trade, tax, and industrial policies are all the same for the entire country, but may vary considerably across countries. Thus, regional economic shocks induce large, country-specific variation of returns.

A second explanation for international diversification consists in the industrial diversification argument which is based on the observation that the industrial composition of national markets varies across countries. As industries are less than perfectly correlated, investing in different markets enables the investor to take advantage of diversification effects simply because of the composition of his portfolio with respect to different industries. Thus, at least some international diversification might stem from industrial diversification, which could also explain differences in volatility across markets as some industry sectors tend to be more volatile *ceteris paribus* than others. As a matter of fact, the monetary policies of industrialized countries, if not always other economic policies, have become aligned to an unprecedented degree during the last two decades. For most European countries, this has even been tightly implemented with the introduction of the Euro and the establishment of the European Central Bank. As a result, the power of diversification across national stock markets will be diminished, in contrast to diversification benefits stemming from spreading investment across asset classes (stocks, bonds, etc.) and industries.

Benefits from Market Segmentation

The general benefits of portfolio diversification are by now well recognized, and carry over, in principle, to internationally diversified portfolios. However, troubling questions remain regarding the extent of potential benefits of such international diversification for investors. If the world consists of national securities markets that are assumed to be completely integrated, and where securities can be found whose returns do not show a high, positive correlation with the home market portfolio, investors stand to reap benefits from international portfolio diversification. Increased expected return or decreased variance (risk) become possible. These advantages are referred to as "pure diversification" benefits, stemming from the reduction of risk unrelated to changes in the whole market, i.e. unsystematic risk, which must be distinguished from opportunities associated with segmented markets.

In the context of international portfolio investment, segmentation of securities markets is not an unrealistic assumption. Assuming a degree of segmentation among national securities markets, insights can be gained into the investment flows involving marketable securities between countries. Because investors in different countries seek to construct optimal portfolios, and because that action may require purchases of securities in foreign countries, portfolio theory explains the simultaneous occurrence of investments into and out of a given country. Market segmentation is caused by barriers that are difficult for investors to overcome, such as legal restrictions on international investment, taxes etc.. Segmentation leads to different risk-return tradeoffs and/or different benchmarks (market portfolios) for measuring the riskiness of securities in different capital markets. This phenomenon is further fostered by the natural bias of investors' portfolios towards their home market due to differences in the consumption patterns that limit their demand for foreign securities.

When markets are segmented, the dominant (or optimal) portfolio (that is, the portfolio with minimum variance for a given expected return) may not include all international securities and, therefore, international portfolio investment should be made only on a selective basis. At the same time, investors may receive benefits that have nothing to do with diversification of unsystematic risk.

In order to clarify this important point one may recall that in perfect capital markets all securities are expected to fall on the Security Market Line (SML). In order to focus on any "special" benefits that may be received from international portfolio investment in segmented capital markets, it is useful to simply assume for a moment the existence of a foreign asset that provides no diversification benefit, i.e. that has perfect positive correlation with the domestic market portfolio. One could then measure the degree of riskiness of this asset, using the domestic market portfolio and the position of this asset in relation to the relevant security market line. In case (a) the foreign asset lies above the line, which implies that the foreign asset has a rate of return higher than a similar domestic security and, therefore, that it would be optimal to hold a long position in this security. In case (b) the foreign asset lies below the line and only a short position in this security would provide the investor with extra benefits. In general, there are two reasons why a foreign security may be found above (below) the domestically observed SML: (I) the foreign asset is priced by the standards of investors who are more (less) averse to risk; (2) the rate of return of the foreign security moves more (less) closely with the foreign market portfolio rather than the domestic market portfolio.

Since it is usually costly and risky to overcome barriers to international portfolio investment, it must be noted that the net realized return may not be sufficient to justify the holding (or borrowing) of foreign securities, even if the special benefits of segmented markets are further enhanced by diversification benefits that arise when these assets are less than perfectly correlated with the domestic portfolio.

UNIQUE RISKS OF AND INSTITUTIONAL CONSTRAINTS FOR INTERNATIONAL PORTFOLIO INVESTMENT

Unique Risks of international Portfolio Investment

Unfortunately, there are not only benefits from IPI that simply wait to be taken advantage of, but there are also some unique risks and constraints that arise when extending the scope of securities held to an international scale. These are easily overlooked, but nevertheless have to be included in the analysis when comprehensively assessing the IPI phenomenon since they might influence the investment decision or its implementation considerably.

Currency Risk

The unique international risk can be divided into two components: exchange risk (broadly defined) and political (or country) risk. For example, if an investor considers U.S. dollar-denominated and EUR-denominated Eurobonds listed on the Singapore Exchange, one class of risks is attached to the currency of denomination, dollar or EUR, and another is connected with the political jurisdiction within which the securities are issued or traded.

As foreign assets are denominated, or at least expressed, in foreign currency terms, a portfolio of foreign securities is usually exposed to unexpected changes in the exchange rates of the respective currencies (exchange rate risk or currency risk). These changes can be a source of *additional* risk to the investor, but by the same token can *reduce* risk for the investor. The net effect depends, first of all, on how volatility is measured, in particular whether it is measured in "real" terms against some index of consumption goods, or in nominal terms, expressed in units of a base currency. In any case, the effect *ultimately* depends on the specifics of the portfolio composition, the volatility of the exchange rates, and most importantly on the correlation of returns of the securities and exchange rates, and finally on the correlation between the currencies involved. If total risk of a foreign security is decomposed into the components currency risk and volatility in local- currency value, exchange risk contributes significantly to the total volatility of a security. Nevertheless, total risk is less than the sum of market and currency risk. Moreover, currency risk can be diversified away by investing in securities denominated in many different currencies, preferably with offsetting correlations. Indeed, currency risk itself can be decomposed into the volatility of the currency and the correlation or covariance of exchange rates with local-currency returns. Interestingly, exchange rates and stock markets have shown a tendency to move in the same direction for *major* currencies over *shorter* time periods, implying that currency re-enforces the effect of stock market movements measured in foreign currency. Nevertheless, results of empirical studies show that foreign exchange risk is more than compensated by diversification benefits, i.e. overall portfolio risk can be reduced.

Basically, the issue boils down to the nature of the correlation between returns of securities and currencies in the short and the long run. With respect to large industrialized countries with reputations for monetary discipline, currency values and returns on securities, especially equities, end to exhibit *positive* correlation. In contrast, in countries where monetary policy seems to have an inflationary bias, returns on equities and external currency values tend to be *negatively* correlated. To make things even more complex, countries do not stay immutably in one category or the other over longer periods of time.

In addition to diversification, exchange risk can of course be reduced by means of "hedging," i.e. establishing short or long positions via the use of currency futures and forwards, which represent essentially long or short positions of fixed income instruments, typically with maturities of less than one year. Apart from the extreme position of complete hedging or no hedging, there are many different opinions as to the best way of calculating the hedge ratio. The proposition of a universal hedge ratio that would be the same for all investors in the world appears appealing on first sight, but relies on too restrictive assumptions to be of practical use. More applicable in this sense are approaches that derive the optimal hedge ratio by minimizing the portfolio variance (minimum variance hedge) or maximize the portfolio's risk adjusted return mean-variance hedge). As a matter of fact, the state of knowledge reflects the diversity of practice in the community of professional investors.

Country Risk

The fact that a security is issued or traded in a different and sovereign political jurisdiction than that of the consumer-investor gives rise to what is referred to as country risk or political risk. Country risk in general can be categorized into transfer risks (restrictions on capital flows), operational risks (constraints on management and corporate activity) and ownership-control risks (government policies with regard to ownership/ managerial control). It embraces the possibility of exchange controls, expropriation of assets, changes in tax policy (like withholding taxes being imposed after the investment is undertaken) or other changes in the business environment of the country. In effect, country risk are local government policies that lower the actual (after tax) return on the foreign investment or make the repatriation of dividends, interest, and principal more difficult.

Political risk also includes default risk due to government actions and the general uncertainty regarding political and economic developments in the foreign country. In order to deal with these issues, the investor needs to assess the country's prospects for economic growth, its political developments, and its balance of payments trends. Interestingly, political risk is not unique to developing countries.

In addition to assessing the degree of government intervention in business, the ability of the labour force and the extent of a country's natural resources, the investor needs to appraise the structure, size, and liquidity of its securities markets. Information and data from published financial accounting statements of foreign firms may be limited; moreover, the information available may be difficult to interpret due to incomplete or different reporting practices. This information barrier is another aspect of country risk. Indeed, it is part of a larger issue of corporate governance and the treatment foreign (minority) investors. At this point it is worth noting that in many countries foreign investors are under a cloud of suspicion which often stems from a history of colonial domination.

Perception of country risk is, therefore, a reason for the unwillingness of many international investors to hold a portion of their securities in some of the less developed countries and those that face political turmoil, despite evidence that investments in these countries could contribute to improving the risk-return combination of a portfolio. By the same token, this fact is consistent with the observation of disproportionately large (relative to the share of GNP) holdings of U.S. securities in the portfolios of many non-U.S. mutual funds. Empirical evidence supports the idea that stock markets are perceived differently in terms of political risk. However, the data also show that diversification among politically risky countries improves the risk-return characteristics of portfolios. Even greater benefits result in combining securities from countries with high and low political risk indicating generally low correlation between these groups.

Institutional Constraints for International Portfolio Investment

Institutional constraints are typically government-imposed, and include taxes, foreign exchange controls, and capital market controls, as well as factors such as weak or nonexistent laws protecting the rights of minority stockholders, the lack of regulation to prevent insider trading, or simply inadequate rules on timely and proper disclosure of material facts and information to security holders. Their effect on international portfolio investment appears to be sufficiently important that the theoretical benefits may prove difficult to obtain in practice. This is, of course, the very reason why segmented markets present opportunities for those able to overcome the barriers.

However, when delineating institutional constraints on international portfolio investment, it must be recognized that these barriers are somewhat ambiguous. Depending on one's viewpoint, institutional constraints can turn out to be incentives: what is a constraint in one market (high transaction costs, for example), turns into an incentive for another market. Or, while strict regulation of security issues may be designed for the protection of investors, if administered by an inept bureaucracy it can prove to be a constraint for both issuers and investors.

Taxation

When it comes to international portfolio investment, taxes are both an obstacle as well as an incentive to cross-border activities. Not surprisingly, the issues are complex — in large part because rules regarding taxation are made by individual governments, and there are many of these, all having very complex motivations that reach far beyond simply revenue generation. In the present context, it is not details but a framework or "pattern" of tax considerations affecting IPI that is of foremost interest.

It is obvious then, since tax laws are national, it is individual countries that determine the tax rates paid on various returns from portfolio investment, such as dividends, interest and capital gains. All these rules differ considerably from country to country. Countries also differ in terms of institutional arrangements for investing in securities, but in all countries there are institutional investors which may be tax exempt (e.g. pension funds) or have the opportunity for extensive tax deferral (insurance companies). However, countries do not tax returns from all securities the same way. Income from some securities tends to be exempt in part or totally from income taxes. Interest paid on securities issued by state and municipal entities in the United States, for example, is exempt from Federal income taxes. A number of countries, e.g: Japan, India, etc. provide exemptions on interest income up to a specified amount, but only on interest received from certain domestic securities. Almost all countries tax their resident taxpayers on returns from portfolio investment, whether the underlying securities have been issued and are held abroad or at home. This is known as the worldwide income concept.

There is a significant number of countries, however, who tax returns from foreign securities held abroad *only* when repatriated. The United Kingdom and a number of former dependencies, for example Singapore, belong to this category. Obviously, such rules promote a pattern of IPI where financial wealth is kept "offshore," preferably in jurisdictions that treat foreign investors kindly. Such jurisdictions are frequently referred to "tax havens."

Since such tax havens benefit from the financial industry that caters to investors from abroad, they often make themselves more attractive by adopting law confidentiality provisions, generally referred to as "secrecy laws", protecting the identity of (foreign) investors from the prying eyes of foreign governments, creditors, relatives and others. It is not surprising, therefore, that tax havens are also used by investors from countries that do *not* exempt returns from foreign portfolio investment. Such investors simply forget to declare such returns.

Issues are getting more complex when investors use tax havens not only to shield wealth from the tax and foreign exchange control laws of their home countries. People can also hide financial assets that stem from activities such as theft, robbery, extortion, kidnapping and increasingly proceeds from dealings in prohibited drugs or revenues from large-scale political corruption. In this respect, the term "money laundering" is being used, often involving financial transfers via tax havens, which usually takes the form of transactions that are virtually akin to international portfolio investment. , ,

Developed countries with high tax rates, operating through common organizations, such as the OECD and FATF, have begun aggressive initiatives to minimize the use of tax haven jurisdictions, but the process is not without controversy. While there is little opposition to curtailing financial transactions resulting from criminal activities, a number of (quite reputable) tax haven countries have serious reservations about assisting other countries in enforcing their foreign exchange control laws or confiscatory tax regimes.

The beginning of the new millennium has witnessed major changes being initiated world- wide in this regard. *First* among these, the member countries of the European Union have agreed to introduce a system of reporting foreign investment returns to home countries. *Secondly*, the United States has unilaterally implemented a system of "qualifying foreign financial intermediaries" which effectively makes foreign banks responsible to collect taxes on securities holdings of people who are potentially U.S. taxpayers, assuming they want to continue to do business in U.S. financial markets. *Finally*, under the auspices of the OECD, a general attack on "unfair competition and practices" by tax havens has been initiated, identifying and ultimately sanctioning jurisdictions that do not cooperate with the information request from OECD member countries.

Apart from differences in national tax regimes, barriers to IPI are primarily created by "withholding taxes" that most countries in the world (except tax havens) level on investors residing in other countries, on dividends, interest and royalties paid by their resident borrowers. These withholding taxes are imposed in lieu of income taxes since the country of the payer has no direct way to assess foreign residents on such income. Theoretically such withholding taxes should be creditable against taxes paid by the investor in his own country — provided they are subject to tax there and provided further that they decide to declare such income at home. Given the fact that such tax credits are limited and always fraught with delays and administrative costs, the specter of double taxation is ever present. It is at his point where so called "double taxation agreements" or "tax treaties" among countries play a crucial role for IPI as they reduce or even eliminate with- holding tax rates on a bilateral basis. However, such tax treaties contain increasingly reporting provisions and clauses instituting "administrative cooperation" procedures among the tax authorities involved, which make such treaties as much an obstacle as an incentive to IPI.

The point of all this is that the legal and illegal use of tax haven jurisdictions has led to significant flows of IPI, creating an incentive for such activities by both private and institutional investors, offsetting barriers that otherwise exist. As often, the net effect is difficult to verify empirically; still when everything is said and done, taxes and the uncertainties as well as the associated transactions costs represent one obstacle to IPI.

Foreign Exchange Controls

While the effect of taxation as an obstacle to international portfolio investment is only incidental to its primary purpose, which is to raise revenue, exchange controls are specifically intended to restrain capital flows. Balance of payment reasons or the effort to reserve financial capital for domestic uses lead to these controls. They are accomplished by prohibiting the conversion of domestic funds for foreign moneys for the purpose of acquiring securities abroad.

Purchases of securities are usually the first category of international financial transactions to be subjected to, and the last to be freed from, foreign exchange controls. While countries are quite ready to restrict undesired capital inflows and outflows, they prove reluctant to remove controls when the underlying problem has ceased to exist, or even when economic trends have reversed themselves. The classical example is provided by Japan where, during the early seventies, exchange controls prevented Japanese investors from purchasing foreign securities. At the same time, new measures were taken to prevent further increase in Japanese liabilities through foreign purchases of Japanese securities. At times, countries have resorted to more drastic measures by requiring residents to sell off all or part of their foreign holdings and exchange the foreign currency proceeds for domestic funds.

Capital Market Regulations

Regulations of primary and secondary security markets typically aim at protecting the buyer of financial securities and try to ensure that transactions are carried out on a fair and competitive basis. These functions are usually accomplished through an examining and regulating body, such as the Securities and Exchange Commission (SEC) in the United States, long regarded as exemplary in guarding investor interests. Supervision and control of practices and information disclosure by a relatively impartial body is important for maintaining investors' confidence in a market; it is crucial for foreign investors who will have even less direct knowledge of potential abuses, and whose ability to judge a conditions affecting returns on securities may be very limited.

Most commonly, capital market controls manifest themselves in form of restrictions on the issuance of securities in national capital markets by foreign entities, thereby making foreign securities unavailable to domestic investors. Moreover, some countries put limits on the amount of investment local investors can do abroad or constrain the extent of foreign ownership in national companies. While few industrialized countries nowadays prohibit the acquisition of foreign securities by private investors, institutional investors face a quite different situation. Indeed, there is almost no country where financial institutions, insurance companies, pension funds, and similar fiduciaries are not subject to rules and regulations that make it difficult for them to invest in foreign securities.

Transactions Costs

Transactions costs associated with the purchase of securities in foreign markets tend to be substantially higher compared to buying securities in the domestic market. Clearly, this fact serves as an obstacle to IPI. Trading in foreign markets causes extra costs for financial intermediaries, because access to the market can be expensive, and the same is true for information about prices, market movements, companies and industries, technical equipment and everything else that is necessary to actively participate in trading. Moreover, there is administrative overhead, costs for the data transfer between the domestic bank and its foreign counterpart etc. — be it a bank representative or a local partner institution. Therefore, financial institutions try to pass these, costs on to their customers, i.e. the investor. Simply time differences can be a costly headache, due to the fact that someone has to do transactions at times outside normal business hours. However, transactions costs faced by international investors can be mitigated by the characteristic of "liquidity," providing depth, breadth, and resilience of certain capital markets, thus reducing this constraint and — as a consequence — inducing international portfolio investment to these countries. Issuers from the investors' countries will then have a powerful incentive to list their securities on the exchange(s) of such markets.

The development of efficient institutions, the range of expertise and experience available, the volume of transactions and breath of securities traded, and the readiness with which the market can absorb large, sudden sales or purchases of securities at relatively stable prices all vary substantially from country to country. The U.S. and British markets have a reputation for being superior in these respects, and have attracted a large amount of international portfolio investment as a result. These markets can offer and absorb a wide variety of securities, both with regard to type (bonds, convertibles, preferred shares, ordinary shares, money market instruments, etc.) and with regard to issuer (public authorities, banks, nonbank financial institutions, private companies, foreign and international institutions, etc.).

They offer depth, being able to supply and absorb substantial quantities of different securities at close to the current price, whereas in Continental Europe and Asia one often hears complaints about the "thinness" of the securities markets leading to random volatility of prices. Therefore, all other factors being equal, investors are attracted to markets where transactions are conducted efficiently and at a low cost to borrower and lender, buyer and seller.

Familiarity with Foreign Markets

Finally, investing abroad requires some knowledge about and familiarity with foreign markets. Cultural differences come in many manifestations and flavours such as the way business is conducted, trading procedures, time zones, reporting customs, etc. In order to get a full understanding of the performance of a foreign company and its economic context, a much higher effort has to be made by the part of the investor. He might face high cost of information, and the available information might not be of the same type as at home due to deviations in accounting standards and methods (e.g. with regard to depreciation, provisions, pensions) which make their interpretation more difficult. However, multinational corporations increasingly publish their financial information in English in addition to their local language and adjust the style, presentation and frequency of their disclosure e.g. of earnings estimates to U.S. standards. Moreover, major financial intermediaries provide information about foreign markets and companies to investors as international investment gains importance; the same is true for data services that extend their coverage to foreign corporations.

Sometimes, existing or perceived cultural differences represent more of a psychological barrier than that they are of real nature. As the benefits from international investment/ diversification are known, it might be worthwhile to invest a reasonable amount of time studying foreign markets in order to overcome barriers and take advantage of the gains possible. Indeed, the perception of foreign market risk might be higher than it actually is. To illustrate, just looking at volatility foreign markets might appear very risky on first sight, however, this might not be true when assessing them in a portfolio context as foreign, stocks might eliminate some more diversifiable risk and only add little to total portfolio (market) risk.

CHANNELS FOR INTERNATIONAL PORTFOLIO INVESTMENT

Investors who wish to benefit from the ownership of foreign securities can implement their portfolio strategy in a number of ways, each of which has its peculiar advantages and drawbacks. The most direct way for an investor to acquire foreign securities is to place an order with a securities firm in his home country which would then acquire the securities in the market of the foreign issuer, usually with the aid of a securities broker operating in the foreign country. Furthermore, the investor can establish an investment account with a financial institution in a country other than his residence, and purchase securities either in that country or in the countries of issue.

Because of cost, complex delivery procedures, and the difficulty of securing adequate information about individual securities, the investor might be inclined to buy foreign securities issued or traded in the market of the country in which he resides instead. In this case, he only needs to pay the transaction costs of local brokerage and has the advantage of the protection of local laws and regulations. A preferable alternative to all but large investors consists in indirect investment via mutual funds specializing in foreign securities.

DIRECT FOREIGN PORTFOLIO INVESTMENT

Purchase of Foreign Securities in Foreign Markets

The most direct way to implement international portfolio investment is the purchase of foreign securities directly in the respective local (foreign) market of the issuer. While restrictions on outward IPI have been eliminated by many countries, theoretically foreign investors could place orders through banks or securities brokers — either in the, domestic or foreign country — when they wish to purchase foreign securities. This is true for both outstanding securities and new issues .When the securities have to be purchased in a secondary market, it is usually in the domestic market of the issuing entity, i.e. the borrower.

At this point a number of problems arise. On a technical level, there are difficulties with the delivery of the certificates. Also, there is the expense of making timely payment in foreign funds. Finally, investors may find it difficult to secure good information on the situation of the issuer, conversion and purchase offers, and rights issues, and to collect interest and dividends. Many of these technical problems stem from a lack of international integration of securities markets. Because of a combination of extensive regulation to protect the investing public from fraud, conflict of interest, or gross incompetence, the resistance of entrenched local institutions to competition, especially from abroad, organized securities markets have been less open to securities firms operating on a multinational basis than, say, markets for commercial banking services.

Over the period, there have been many initiatives to reorganize exchanges across borders through mergers and strategic alliances, but progress has been slow because of entrenched interests and nationalistic feelings. The same is true for clearing systems although the publicity in this area is considerably less noisy. All this adds to the cost of international investment.

From a practical perspective, the purchase of foreign securities, can be accomplished by opening an investment account with a brokerage firm abroad. The broker will buy the foreign securities on behalf of the investor and in turn charge commissions for the handling of orders and the management of the account. Such "nonresident accounts" are similar to offshore funds in that they are maintained in a foreign country, outside the control of the country of residence of the investor. These individual investment accounts have been used for decades, particularly by citizens of Western Europe and many less developed countries, who have learned through bitter experience that property rights are precarious and always subject to shifting political fortunes. Further, a situation allowing free, unhindered international transactions in securities is a temporary occurrence at best.

Nonresident accounts have enjoyed long success, especially among the wealthy and upper middle classes. When countries begin to restrict international transactions in general and international portfolio transactions in particular, they usually restrain the activities of their own residents rather than those of foreigners, especially when the foreigners' transactions are not with the local citizens but with other nonresidents.

National authorities are primarily interested in determining their internal economic affairs, even against market forces. However, transactions of foreign investors with other nonresidents do not adversely affect the internal economic conditions of the country concerned. On the contrary, the local financial community gains income, employment, and prestige, and may afford the country a potential source of capital inflows. To interfere with the actions of nonresident investors would offer no more than a one-time advantage at best, and would exact an ongoing cost in foregoing opportunities for what tends to be a lucrative business.

Trading and owning of foreign securities presents, however, several, difficulties and problems to investors. Among these are myriad settlement procedures, a high rate of trade failures, unreliable interest and dividend payments, restrictions on foreign investment, foreign withholding taxes, capital controls, differences in accounting rules and reporting requirements and poor information flow. In order to avoid or overcome these complications, investors might consider the purchase of foreign securities in the domestic market.

Purchase of Foreign Securities in the Domestic Market

In some countries, the possibility exists to purchase foreign securities in the domestic market of the investor. This represents in many respects a convenient alternative to purchasing foreign securities abroad. Foreign securities are available to the investor domestically as well, if the issuing corporation sells its securities not only in the market of the country where it is incorporated, but also in other markets. Such transactions are often accompanied by a listing of the securities usually on one of the exchanges of the country where the securities are placed. Normally, a minimum number of securities must be distributed among local investors a requirement for listing, or alternatively the listing is a prerequisite for the successful placement of a substantial issue. Since the latter part of the 1980s, world financial markets have witnessed a considerable volume of so-called "Global-equity issues" often in connection with the privatization of state-owned enterprises. Local listing fees as well as different disclosure requirements can make multiple listing quite expensive for corporations. The access to local investors may make this effort worthwhile.

All national and international securities markets must deal with the need to organize the physical handling and delivery of traded securities efficiently. In national markets, the trend seems to be moving toward central depositories of one form or another; in some markets, the physical handling and shipping of securities has been virtually eliminated. Instead, a computerized accounting system keeps track of transfers, while the securities themselves are safely tucked away at the central depository usually run by the securities broker's association.

While the basic idea is simple and appealing, it is difficult to implement in some markets, since thorny issues regarding the nature of collateral and the fragmented structure of the securities industry arise. Interestingly, some Continental European countries, whose securities markets do not fare well in comparison with those of the United States, the United Kingdom, or even Canada by most criteria, have transfer systems based on central depositories which seem to be far ahead of those found in these otherwise superior markets.

The problems surrounding the physical transfer of securities multiply when extended to international transactions. Complications range from such mundane matters as the length of mailing time and the unreliability of mail in international transit, to arcane points of contradictory or non- existent provisions in the securities and commercial laws of the different jurisdictions.

In response to these problems, a system of depository receipts (DRs) has been created in most markets where transactions in foreign securities play a significant role. A DR represents a "receipt" issued by a domestic institution for a foreign security which is held in trust in its name abroad. The basic function of the depository company, typically a bank or trust company, is to safeguard the original securities and issue negotiable instruments better suited to the general needs and the specific legal requirements of the investor.

In a market where, by law or by practice, registration of securities is required, the depository company (usually a bank or similar financial institution) will appoint either its own subsidiary or an external correspondent to act as the registered nominee, and will issue DRs in bearer form. Of course, this transformation can work the other way as well, with the foreign trustee holding the original bearers' securities and the depositor company recording the times of the holders of the DRs, making them, in effect, registered securities.

Thus, the basic service that the depository company performs is to "transform" the securities of the original market into negotiable instruments appropriate to the legal environment of the investor's market. In addition, it performs a number of related services. Usually, the depository company will take care of dividend collections and the resulting foreign exchange problems. Further, it will handle rights issues for the investor and make sure that he receives the proceeds. Frequently, the depository company will assist the investor in claiming the withholding tax credits or exemptions. Lastly, the depository company will see to it that the investor receives materials mailed by the corporation that issued the original securities, including proxies, annual reports, and other news, such as the exercise of call provisions, stock splits, and tender offers.

Apart from the bank which issues the DRs, and its related depository institution abroad, large internationally active broker-dealers play an important role in this process: (1) they perform arbitrage by purchasing (selling) the underlying securities abroad, depositing them in (withdrawing them from) the issuing bank's foreign depository in return for the issuance (cancellation) of DRs, whenever there is a sufficient difference between the price, of the DRs vis-à-vis that of the underlying shares; and (2) the broker-dealers also make a market in the DRs which – together with their arbitrage activity — assures a degree of liquidity.

Depository receipt programmes exist in several countries, such as the United States, the Netherlands and the United Kingdom. American depository receipts (ADRs) have to be "sponsored" in order to qualify for listing on the New York or the American Stock Exchange. Sponsored — as opposed to unsponsored — ADRs are supported by the foreign company whose shares back these DRs in that the company takes an active role in the creation and maintenance of their ADR programmes. To illustrate, it pays for the bank's services when a foreign bank requests a depository bank to create ADRs.

Sponsored ADRs are registered with the SEC, and issuers must comply with disclosure requirements similar to U.S. companies which can be quite a costly burden if accounting practices are very different at home, as used to be the case for German or Swiss corporations, for example. This is opposed to unsponsored ADRs, which are issued independently, but generally with the agreement of the foreign company. As they are not registered with the SEC, unsponsored ADRs can only be traded over-the-counter, disclosure of company information is reduced, financial statements might not always be translated into English and accounting data will not conform to U.S. GAAP. Moreover, fees are often not covered by the firm, but passed on to the investor.

DRs are denominated in the local currency of the respective country, thus ADRs show U.S. dollar prices. However, as ADR prices are derived by multiplying the domestic stock price by the exchange rate and adjusting for the appropriate ADR multiple, their value is nevertheless subject to exchange risk as any ordinary stock directly traded in a foreign market. Since ADRs help to eliminate or mitigate problems of international investing such as differences in time zone and language, local market customs, currency exchange, regulation and taxes, they make investing abroad easier and less costly for investors. A potential disadvantage might just consist in lower liquidity of these instruments compared to the actual shares.

INDIRECT FOREIGN PORTFOLIO INVESTMENT

Equity-linked Eurobonds

As it appears difficult and/or costly to invest internationally by purchasing foreign securities directly because of burdensome procedures, lack of information, differences in accounting standards, low liquidity and limited choice of domestically available foreign shares, indirect foreign portfolio investment represents a viable alternative strategy. One way that has been proposed to take this approach is through the acquisition of securities whose value is closely linked to foreign shares such as equity-linked eurobonds. These are basically eurobonds with warrants and convertible eurobonds. They represent hybrid financial instruments that consist of a straight debt component and a call option on the foreign stock. In the case of warrants, these options can and often are separated from the debt instrument and traded individually. With convertible Eurobonds, the two components of the instrument are unchangeably tied to each other.

Due to the equity component of eurobonds with warrants and convertible eurobond the value of these instruments is not only dependent on the movement of interest rates (as straight debt), but changes also with the developments of the underlying equity. Also, for some equity markets that are largely closed to outside investors, warrants or embedded equity options can offer a way to circumvent existing restrictions and open access to these markets through the back door, or avoid settlement problems in underdeveloped markets. Warrants, once separated from the bond, tend to return to their home market and serve as equity options — especially if these instruments are restricted or prohibited. From this perspective, equity-linked eurobonds can be useful instruments in the context of international portfolio investment. Moreover, they represent a means to some institutional investors whose equity investments are restricted to still participate in equity markets.

Purchase of Shares of Multinational Companies

Without barriers to international trade in securities, investors would have easy access to shares of foreign firms. Thus, they could accomplish "homemade" international portfolio diversification themselves, and the acquisition of foreign securities (of companies) by domestic films would not provide benefits that investors could not obtain for themselves. Foreign assets and securities would be priced on the same grounds as domestic assets.

However, because barriers to foreign investment exist, segmented capital markets could be a source of important advantages to multinational companies. In particular, unlike expansion through domestic acquisitions, in many cases foreign acquisitions can add to the value of a MNC. This is because a foreign asset may be acquired at the market value priced in the *segmented* foreign market. The same asset, when made available to domestic investors, could be valued higher because (a) foreign investors are, on average, more risk averse than domestic investors; and/or (b) the foreign asset is perceived to be less risky (i.e., it has a smaller beta) when valuated in the context of the domestic (home) capital market.

Thus, some of the foreign assets that are priced fairly (have a net present value equal to zero) in the context of *the foreign* capital market may command a positive net present value in the context of the *domestic* capital market and, as a result, may add to the wealth of the shareholders of the acquiring firm. It must be noted that this source of advantage has nothing to do with diversification effects per se; it simply involves benefits from arbitrage in markets for risk, i.e. market segmentation. As a rule, companies engaged in international business and foreign operations (MNCs) have better access to foreign firms and securities than domestic investors. This suggests that such companies provide their (domestic) shareholders with the benefits of (indirect) international portfolio diversification.

This view can easily lead to simplistic conclusions. However, if domestic investors already hold well-diversified portfolios (the domestic market portfolio), then a MNC provides diversification benefit if and only if new foreign investments expand the accessible investment opportunity set of domestic investors. The point here is that any *new* real or financial asset, domestic or foreign, would provide a diversification benefit, as long as its return is less than perfectly correlated with the return of the domestic market portfolio (since borrowing is feasible, the expected rate of return is irrelevant).

The size of any single foreign project undertaken by a MNC is insignificant relative to the size of the MNC's domestic market. Thus, it is unlikely that a MNC could affect the risk-return trade-off (the slope of the CML) of the domestic capital market in a significant way. In other words, at the *margin* a MNC cannot provide sizable diversification benefits to investors. It is conceivable, though, that MNCs *as a group*, have, over the years, expanded the investment opportunity set for domestic investors and have thereby provided certain benefits, even though no single MNC could make a marginal contribution for which it is compensated by investors. Of course, the same benefit is provided by any group of companies that creates new assets whose returns are not perfectly positively correlated with the rate of return of the domestic market portfolio.

Foreign portfolio investment could be used as a hedge against exchange risk (due to consumption of foreign goods). One may argue that MNC stocks could be used in a hedge portfolio instead of direct portfolio investment, and in this respect, MNC shares could provide benefits to domestic investors. However, it remains to be seen whether the rates of return on MNC stocks have a significant correlation with prices of consumption goods that are affected by unexpected exchange rate changes.

An alternative approach, which explicitly adjusts for risk, involves the use of the CAPM to find out whether shares of MNCs are priced at a (positive or negative) premium. The basic problem with this method is that in a (domestic) capital market which is reasonably efficient, such information on international involvement is already reflected in stock prices, and shares of MNCs are priced in such a manner that they fall exactly on the security market line. Thus, the stock provides risk-adjusted "abnormal" return only at the time of the arrival of new information about international investment.

One should note, however, that the existence of identical average excess returns does not lead to the conclusion that corporate international diversification has no effect on shareholder wealth. To assess the effect, one needs to examine the behavior of returns around the period of initial diversification or, more precisely, around the period of the arrival of new information regarding foreign expansion.

Others have suggested that relatively high price-earnings ratios of MNCs indicate that investors are willing to pay a premium for their shares. A relatively high price-earnings ratio is usually regarded as an indicator that the company is expected to grow at a relatively high rate, its stock price — reflecting the expectations of the market — being relatively high with respect to its current earnings. Therefore, one could argue that MNCs are "high growth" companies and investors do recognize that feature. However, the rate of growth of a company's earnings is basically a function of its operating strategy and its competitive advantage in the markets for real goods and services, and this aspect is only very indirectly related to foreign investment.

International Mutual Funds

The easiest and most effective way to implement IPI- especially for the individual investor — is to invest in "international" mutual funds. Investing in mutual funds solves the problem of the individual investor to get information about foreign companies/securities, gain market access and deal with all the problems associated with foreign securities trading. Instead, the fund management company takes care of these issues for all investors of the fund with the benefit of economies of scale due to pooled resources. In return, investors are in most cases charged e.g. through up-front fees for the service of the fund and also the management of the portfolio. These costs to the investor are generally less for funds that replicate a local or international index because they have a simple investment strategy that does not require costly and time-intensive research.

The fund industry has undergone dramatic growth, and as a result funds come in a bewildering variety. The investor has to carefully distinguish between the various categories. The first distinction refers to the registration and supervisory regime of the fund: onshore versus offshore. Offshore funds, which are typically incorporated in a tax haven, provide investors with little if any protection beyond the reputation of the sponsoring firm. However, they usually offer anonymity and allow investment managers a great deal of latitude to pursue investment success. This is one of the reasons why almost all hedge funds are incorporated as offshore funds.

Another important dimension of mutual funds is whether they are *open-end* or *closed-end*. The former in contrast to the latter do not limit the number of shares of the funds, i.e. new investors can always enter the fund and are not constrained by the availability of shares in a secondary market. As a consequence, the capital invested in the fund varies considerably over time. Closed- end funds are typically used with respect to markets that are not very liquid. The closed-end structure isolates the fund manager from the problem of having to buy or sell shares in response to new fund purchases or redemptions. However, this structure leads almost invariably to deviations from net asset values (NAV), i.e. premia or discounts.

Whereas the relationship between premium/market price and NAV often appears to be of a random nature, the existence of a (positive) premium seems to be rational for those funds specializing in countries which impose significant foreign investor constraints, such as an illiquid market, substantial information gathering costs or other restrictions on market access. If funds provide a means to investors to circumvent these obstacles, they can be expected to trade at a premium.

QUESTIONS

1) Discuss the principles of International Portfolio Investment.
2) What are the benefits from International Portfolio Investment?
3) Discuss the unique risks of and institutional constraints for International Portfolio Investment.
4) Distinguish between direct and indirect channels for foreign investment.
5) Critically examine the benefits from International Portfolio diversification.
6) Why might a host country try to place severe limits upon foreign portfolio investments from abroad?
7) Discuss the different modes of International Portfolio Investment.

REFERENCES

Adler, M., and B. Dumas. 1983. International Portfolio Choice and Corporate Finance: A Synthesis, Journal of Finance, Vol. 38 (3), 925-984.

Beckers, S., G. Connor, and R. Curds. 1996. National versus Global Influences on Equity Returns, Financial Analyst Journal, Vol. 52(2), 31-39.

Berryessa, N., and E. Kirzner. 1988. Global Investing: The Templeton Way, Homewood: Dow Jones-Irwin.

Bertero, E., and C. Mayer. 1990. Structure and performance: Global interdependence of stock markets around the crash of October 1987, European Economic Review, Vol. 34 (6),1155-1180.

Black, F. 1974. International capital market equilibrium with investment barriers, Journal of Financial Economics, Vol. 1, 337-352.

Botkin, D., and M. Ahern. 1994. Easy Access to Global Securities, Pension World, Vol. 30 (8),30-31.

Brewer, H. L. 198 1. Investor Benefits from Corporate Diversification, Journal of Financial and Quantitative Analysis, Vol. 16 (1), 1 13-126.

Butler, K.C., and D.C. Joaquin. 2000. Are the gains from international portfolio diversification exaggerated? The influence of downside risk in bear markets, Michigan State University Working Paper.

Campbell, J.Y., and J. Ammer. 1993. What Moves the Stock and Bond Markets? A Variance Decomposition for Long-term Asset Returns, Journal of Finance, Vol. 48 (1), 3-38.

Celebuski, M., J. Hill, and J. Kilgannon. 1990. Managing Currency Exposure in International Portfolios, Financial Analysts Journal, Vol. 46 (1), 16-23.

Chan, K.C., G.A. Karolyi, and R.M. Stulz. 1992. Global Financial Markets and the Risk Premium on U.S. Equity, Journal of Financial Economics, Vol. 32 (2), 137-168.

Chang, E., C. Eun, and R. Kolodny. 1995. International Diversification through Closed-End Country Funds, Journal of Banking and Finance, Vol. 19 (7), 1237-1263.

Dumas, B. 1994. A Test of the International CAPM Using Business Cycles Indicators as Instrumental Variables, in J.A. Frankel. ed. The Internationalization of Equity Markets. Chicago: University of Chicago Press.

Dybvig, P.H., and S.A. Ross. 1985a. Differential Information and Performance Measurement Using a Security Market Line, Journal of Finance, Vol. 40 (2), 383-399.

Elton, E., and M. Gruber. 1995. Modern Portfolio Theory and Investment Analysis. New York: Wiley.

Errunza, V., and E. Losq. 1989. Capital flow controls, international asset pricing and investor's welfare: A multi-country framework, Journal of Finance, Vol. 44 (4), 1025-1038.

Eun, C.S. 1994. The Benchmark Beta, CAPM, and Pricing Anomalies, Oxford Economic Papers, Vol. 46 (2), 330-343.

Fama, E.F., and K.R. French. 1993. Common risk factors in the returns on stocks and bonds, Journal of Financial Economics, Vol. 53, 427-465.

Fatemi, A.M. 1984. Shareholder Benefits from Corporate International Diversification, Journal of Finance, Vol. 39 (5), 1325-1344.

Feldstein, M. 1995. Global Capital Flows, The Economist, June 24, 1995, 72-73..

Harvey, CR. 1995. Predictable Risk and Returns in Emerging Markets, Review of Financial Studies, Vol. 8 (3), 773-8 16.

Heston, S.L., and K.G. Rouwenhorst. 1994. Does Industrial Structure Explain the Benefits of International Diversification? Journal of Financial Economics, Vol. 36 (1), 3-27.

Jacquillat, B., and B. Solnik. 1978. Multinationals are Poor Tools for Diversification, Journal of Portfolio Management, Vol. 4 (2), 8-12.

Jorion, P. 1985. International Portfolio Diversification with Estimation Risk, Journal of Business, Vol. 58 (3), 259-278.

Kenen, P.B. 1976. Capital Mobility and Financial Integration: A Survey, Princeton Studies in International Finance No. 39, Princeton University

Krugman, P. 1981. Consumption Preferences, Asset Demands, and Distribution Effects in International Financial Markets, NBER Working Paper No. 651(3).

Larsen, G.A. Jr., and B.G. Resnick. 2000. The optimal construction of internationally diversified equity portfolios hedged against exchange rate uncertainty, European Financial Management, Vol. 5 (4).

Lessard, D.R. 1973. International Portfolio Diversification: A Multivariate Analysis for a Group of Latin American Countries, Journal of Finance, Vol. 28 (6), 6 19-33.

Levi, M.D. 1996. International Finance. 31 ed. McGraw-Hill.

Levich, R.M., and L.R. Thomas. 1993. The merits of active currency risk management: Evidence from international bond portfolios, Financial Analysts Jciurnal, VoL 49 (5), 63-71.

Levy, H., and M. Sarnat. 1970. International Diversification of Investment Portfolios, American Economic Review, Vol. 60 (9), 668-675.

Lin, W.L., R.F. Engel, and T. Ho. 1994. Do bulls and bears move across borders? International transmission of stock returns and volatility, Review of Financial Studies; Vol. 7 (3), 507-538.

Lintner, J. 1965. The Valuation of Risk Assets and the Selection of Risky Investments in Stock Portfolios and Capital Budgets, Review of Economics and Statistics, 13-37.

Markowitz, H.M. 1952. Portfolio Selection, Journal of Finance, Vol. 7 (3), 77-9 1.

Merton, R.C. 1987. A simple model of capital market equilibrium with incomplete information, Journal of Finance, Vol. 42, 483-5 10.

Roll, R. 1992. Industrial Structure and the Comparative Behavior of International Stock Market Indices, Journal of Banking and Finance, Vol. 47 (1), 3-42.

Rosenberg, M. 1990. Why there is no Free Lunch in Currency Hedging, in L. Thomas. ed. The Currency Hedging Debate, London, 83-96.

Rowland, P.F., and L. Tesar. 1998. Multinationals and the gains from international diversification, NBER Working Paper No. 6733.

Sharpe, W. 1964. Capital Asset Pricing: A Theory of Market Equilibrium under Conditions of Risk, Journal of Finance, Vol. 19, 424-447.

Solnik, B. l974b. Why Not Diversify Internationally rather Than Domestically? Financial Analyst Journal, Vol. 30 (4), 48-54.

Sparks, S. 1991. International Investment. **2nd** ed. Addison-Wesley.

Stulz, R.M. 1997. International portfolio flows and security markets. The Ohio State University Working Paper.

Theodossiou, P., and U. Lee. 1993. Mean and Volatility Spillovers Across Major National Stock Markets: Further Empirical Evidence, Journal of Financial Research, Vol. 16 (4), 337-350.

Thomas, S., and M. Wickens. 1993. An International CAPM for Bonds and Equities, Journal of International Money and Finance, Vol. 12 (4), 390-412.

Wallace, A. 1980. Is Beta Dead? Institutional Investor, Vol. 14 (7), 15 1-57.

Williamson, J. 1995. Taming International Portfolio Investment. Washington D.C.: Institute for International Economics.

45

Modern Portfolio Theory-Oriented Approach to Assess the Riskiness of Foreign Claims and Techniques of Portfolio Investment

INTORDUCTION

The theoretical rationale for international portfolio diversification is based on that by holding foreign stocks investors can reduce the variance (risk) of a portfolio of domestic stocks without reducing its expected return. Alternatively, by holding foreign stocks, investors can raise the returns to a domestic portfolio for any given amount of risk. Historically, few developing countries have welcomed foreign acquisition of domestic shares through the stock market. These restrictive features have existed even in countries which have welcomed FDI. Host country reservations are essentially three- fold: first, there is no observable impact of portfolio investment on exports, technology transfer, investment of output; second, portfolio investment can be unstable hot money' — that is, quickly withdrawn at times of national economic difficulty or after achieving a short term speculative gain; third, unrestricted share acquisition could lead to take-overs of local firms which, in most developing countries, are ill-equipped to fight acquisitions from larger and more powerful foreign investors.

In the following sections we will attempt to apply to analysis of the foreign claim portfolios of banks, the theory and the statistical analysis that has transformed perceptions of markets for equity shares and other forms of assets. In the final section we will raise some strategic issues that are already understood by corporate managers making equity invest-ments in developing countries. Aim is to answer the following questions:

- How can one determine the extent to which each new country represented in the asset portfolio adds to the diversification of the portfolio? What distinguishes countries for this purpose? What are the probable sources of covariation among countries?
- How can one determine the extent to which lending into various industries in various foreign countries represents meaningful diversification or more concentration?

GLOBAL ASSET ALLOCATION

Meaningful diversification spreads out the portfolio to reduce risks. However, it will soon become apparent that there are different types of risk, and that strategies that cope well with one type do not necessarily perform well in terms of the others.

We are interested in the earnings or value of a bank's portfolio of investments. It is convenient to proceed as follows. We are now at some date to, and we wish to consider the bank's activities over the period from t_0 to t_1. At date t_0 the bank's portfolio has value $V(t_0)$. At date t_1 it will have value $V(t_1)$ determined by cumulated cash flow over the interval t_0 to t_1, and by the characteristics of the assets in the portfolio at date t_1. Since we have a situation of uncertainty we can represent the distribution $V(t_1)$ as in Figure 1.

What do we mean by the riskiness of the distribution in Figure 1? There is no all-purpose characterization of risk. One has to ask: riskiness to whom? One can suggest at least three perspectives, each of which implies a different measures of risk.

1. A hypothetical, undiversified owner, or anyone else whose career is intimately bound up with the earnings of only this one bank

In this case some summary measures of the dispersion in Figure 1 provide the relevant notion of risk. For example, one might want to use the variance of the returns or terminal value. But note that such a measure is not really comparable across banks. What do we do if we find on comparison of Bank A with Bank B that Bank A's terminal value has higher variance, but also a higher mean? On an intuitive basis, riskiness is supposed to be bad, but in the case of such a comparison the hypothetical owner of Bank A is not necessarily worse off than the hypothetical owner of Bank B.

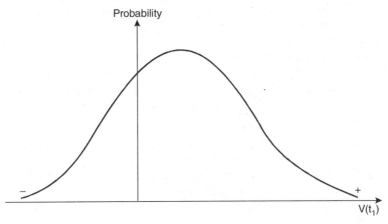

FIGURE 1: PROBABILITY DISTRIBUTION OF THE VALUE OF THE BANK'S CLAIM PORTFOLIO AT FUTURE DATE H

Clearly sometimes it is possible to make comparisons across banks. In our example, if Bank A had a higher variance than Bank B but a mean value the same or lower, we might feel confident in stating that Bank A's portfolio was unambiguously riskier than Bank B's portfolio. There is a general name for such comparisons: we say that the random returns V_B stochastically dominate the random returns V_A if every risk averse individual would prefer the returns V_B to the returns V_A. From the empirical perspective, the most useful form of this principle remains the mean-variance approximation. But note what we have just seen-a stochastic dominance ranking cannot compare all distributions of returns. Only if V_A has mean no higher than V_B and has variance higher than $V_{B'}$, can we say V_A is riskier.

2. A hypothetical stock market investor, who holds a well- diversified portfolio of assets.

Such an individual views the bank's earnings and value in conjunction with the earnings and value of all the other assets in his or her portfolio. The .investor exhibits risk aversion toward the returns from the whole portfolio but not necessarily toward the returns from any one constituent part. To understand this, consider a portfolio containing many small investments, all distributed independently. A greater number of such small invest-ments in a portfolio (holding the mean return on the whole portfolio fixed) lessens the dispersion of the sum of returns. In the limit such a portfolio is riskless, because all the little independent gains and losses cancel out. Thus the holder of a diversified portfolio experi-ences risks from correlation on nonindependence of the returns. If the portfolio of invest-ments held by the bank happens to be distributed independently of the returns on the assets in the portfolio of the investor, the investor will treat the bank as though it yielded its expected value with certainty: i.e., he or she will not demand a risk premium to hold it. If we use the capital asset pricing model as an approximation to the state of affairs in the world of investment, the risk premium exacted by investors is a linear function of the correlation of the value of the bank's earnings with those of the universe of assets, i.e.,

$$E(r_B)-T = \beta_B[E(R)-T]$$

where

$\quad r_B$ = (random) rate of return to an investor in the equity of the bank
$\quad R$ = (random) rate of return to a portfolio of all market assets
$\quad T$ = risk-free rate of return
$\quad \beta_B$ = COV $[r_B,R]/ \sigma^2(r_B])$ is the measure of yield correlation for the bank and the market

In this case we can take the beta of the bank's portfolio as a measure of its riskiness relative to the risk of the market portfolio.

3. A regulatory agency which has the liability for the net debts of the bank should it happen to go bust. In the most general sense, we are interested in the likelihood of the bank's going bad, and in the magnitude of the losses that it incurs should it go bad.

We can approach the measurement of riskiness from this viewpoint in two days. The first is a general characterization of the bankruptcy tail in Figure 2, and the second is estimation of the liability incurred by a regulatory agency if it must make up any losses which result from bankruptcy. The second approach obviously combines the information generated by the first in one particular way.

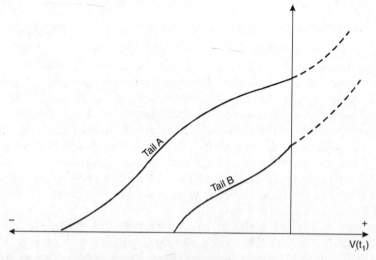

FIGURE 2: A SIMPLE ANALYSIS OF RELATIVE BANKRUPTCY RISK

We will begin with the general characterization. The bankruptcy tail in Figure 2 is that part of the distribution to the left of the $V(t_1)=0$ point. Different portfolios imply tails of different shape. Sometimes it is easy to determine that one distribution is riskier than another.

This is when, on plotting the two distributions, the tails do not cross. Tail B is strictly less risky than Tail A, because the probability of any magnitude of bankruptcy loss is smaller on Tail B than on Tail A. If the tails cross, we must compare a distribution having low probability of large losses with one having higher probability of small losses. There is no universally acceptable ranking by riskiness in such a situation. But a capital market implicitly places a value on the bankruptcy tail. This capital market value is a natural way to compare and rank bankruptcy risks.

What are the practical conclusions to be derived from this discussion? First, whatever the notion of riskiness we choose, we must construct the portfolio return distribution used in Figure 1. Second, the notion of riskiness we adopt dictates which characteristics of the return distribution we wish to operate on by a policy of diversification. If we adopt notion 1, above, we want the affect the general dispersion of the distribution. If we adopt notion 2, we want to affect the correlation of the return on the bank's portfolio with the returns on the universe of traded assets. If we adopt notion 3, we focus only on the lower tail of the return distribution. The contribution of any given project loan or government loan to the reduction of the risk of the portfolio will vary with the notion of risk which is being used. Thus until a decision has been made on the concept of risk that is applicable, no proper answers to the questions posed at the beginning of this section can be provided.

HOW TO GENERATE THE DISTRIBUTION OF PORTFOLIO RETURNS

Consider now how to construct a distribution like that shown in Figure 1 for an actual bank portfolio. We will exhibit a method of generating an estimate of this distribution that also allows immediate evaluation of the impact on any desired measure of risk of adding another project to the portfolio. In principle, if one had a choice of which projects to accept, one could tailor the portfolio to have any desired characteristics. Let us begin by considering the sources of portfolio risk for a bank. Initially we will assume all flows are measured in dollars. Subsequently we will explain how to add an exchange risk component. It is convenient to discuss risks of project lending first, and then to discuss loans to govern-ments.

For convenience we assume that the bank has no equity participation in any projects and is entitled to receive payment of principal and interest if things proceed well, and to liquidate the project at market value in case of default. In order to permit the use of diagrams, we also assume that the projects pay all their returns on one future date, like discount bonds. (This is in no way essential for the calculations.) Let

X_i = total return on project i, measured in dollars

D_i = total payment of principal plus interest due to the bank from project i, a dollar-denominated sum

If the total return exceeds D_i, the bank will be repaid. If the return, X_i is less than D_i, the bank will have to settle for X_i. This is shown in Figure 3, where the thick line shows the probability distribution of the bank's return on the loan. The bank bears risk only when X_i D_i. To compute the bank's risk carrying from a project loan we must first estimate a distribution for X_i, and then superimpose the cutoff, D_i.

In order to consider the overall distribution of X_i it is extremely useful to partition the risk into various sources of factors that contribute to it. Thus, divide projects into a number of categories (for example, copper mining, textile production, logging, plywood production, and so forth). To be useful, the categories must be broad enough to embrace numerous existing and past projects in order to provide a statistically significant sample. Then we may view the returns X_i to a project in category i as being generated by a statistical model of the form:

$$x_i = \beta_{i1} K_1 + \beta_{i2} K_2 + \beta_{i3} K_3 + \varepsilon_i$$

where K_1 = world economy factor. A good proxy for this might be an index of the real GNP of the major trading nations.

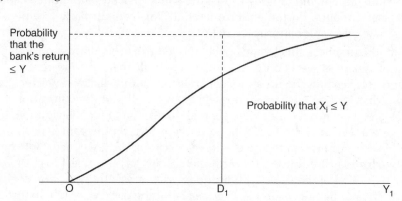

FIGURE 3: CUMULATIVE DISTRIBUTION OF BANK RETURN

K_2 = industry factor. A good proxy for this might be world market price for a raw material, or rate of expansion of world capacity for some manufactured good.

K_3= national factor. One could use an index of GNP of the country in which the project was located, or other suitable variables.

ε_{i1} = residual, uncorrelated error.

$\beta_{i1}, \beta_{i2}, \beta_{i3}$ = impact of the factors on the returns to projects in category i.

Models of this form say that the randomness in X_i is derived from the delta factors. Once the sensitivities beta are estimated, forecasts and characteristics of the randomness in the delta factors automatically generate the characteristics of the distribution of X_i. For example, the forecast variance of X_i is a weighted average of the variances and covariances of the delta factors, the weights being the beta factors specific to category i. Or consider how to estimate the reduction in overall portfolio variance from loans to automobile assembly operations in two different countries. Obviously the world and industry factors and their weights are the same for both. Diversification value can arise only from lack of correlation or negative correlation between the two country factors. It will only be important if the beta impact measures for the country factors are high for the automobile industry. Moreover, if the countries in question are heavy raw material exporters to the major trading nations, their GNPs may have high positive correlation. These considerations become tractable when analysis of this sort is performed.

It should by now be clear how to incorporate exchange rate effects here, if the project is not yielding dollars directly .The exchange rate is a random variable that can be explained in a multifactor model. In the long run the purchasing power parity is the only significant factor, but other things always have transitory effects. One can estimate short-run multifactor equations for exchange rates. These do not provide result sufficiently superior to forward market quotations to permit speculative profits (unfortunately), but they provide forecasts in a form which can be readily integrated with the project factor models. Using these methods one can make a comprehensive analysis of the risk characteristics of a portfolio of pure project loans.

TECHNIQUES OF PORTFOLIO INVESTMENT

(1) COUNTRY FUNDS

Since the New York Stock Exchange-listed Mexico Fund was launched in 1981, country funds have become a cottage industry around the world. At first, they were seen as vehicles for investing in markets which were either dosed to foreign portfolio investors or simply administratively difficult to invest in "stock by stock". Their success was such that the market acquired an enthusiasm for similar vehicles.

As investors grow more informed, innovative variations on the theme have been developed and country funds are becoming increasingly specialised. New funds focus on smaller capitalised stocks, unlisted securities, companies with above- average growth prospects, stocks of companies to be privatised, venture capital and index funds designed to track the performance of certain local stock market indices. The India funds have almost exclusively targetted the large capitalisation companies with high earnings growth potential i.e. the selected few blue- chip, well established companies listed on the Bombay Stock Exchange. Future funds would be attractive to investors when structured to reflect specialised investment strategies such as indicated above.

(a) Setting up a Country Fund

The sponsor or sponsors can be initially any of the following or a combination of them. The government of the country seeking the benefits of obtaining money from the international equity market and having its "flag" firmly planted in London or New York; a professional investment manager seeing attractive investment opportunities for its client and also the opportunity to increase its management fee revenues; an investment bank which sees a marketing opportunity and a continuing relationship with a satisfied host country, as well as an underwriting or placement fee; a major investor or group of investors who see the merits of the country and want an arms length vehicle to follow this through. The sponsor can also be an international agency such as the IFC whose function is to promote markets in developing countries. If a government is the initial sponsor it would have to turn over commercial sponsorship to a market intermediary for implementation (e.g. Unit trust of India (UTI) and the India Funds). The next strategy is setting up a business plan and a structure which will make the fund competitively attractive to investors. *First,* the country must have sound investment prospects and an acceptable financial market infrastructure. *Second,* the fund must be established in such a way that investors will see that the portfolio is well managed, that the administrative structure is prudent and the fees and expenses to be paid by the fund are reasonable. *Third,* the fund's investment objectives and policies must make sense. Weakness on the country side would make the fund shares difficult to sell to investors regardless of the structure of the fund and weakness in the structure would compound the problem.

(b) Structure

These involve such basics as whether the fund should be established as a corporation or trust, etc., where it should be established in terms of attractive regulatory and tax regimes, whether it should be closed-end or open-end and whether it should be a public issue listed on a major stock exchange or an unlisted private placement.

While there is much less discussion of private placement funds than there is of public issues, some of the largest and most successful emerging market funds have been private placements. This is because large institutional investors, especially pension funds, prefer low start-up costs, structural arrangements tailored to their specific requirements and elimination of the risk of having to "mark to market" their shares in the event they trade at a discount to net asset value on a stock exchange. These advantages compensate for lack of liquidity. As start-up costs of public issues range from 6 per cent to 10 per cent compared to from 0.5 per cent to 3 per cent for private placements, the risks of shares of listed funds trading at a discount of net asset value are real. The fiduciaries and the host country also dislike discounts as they reflect on their reputations

There must also be a Custodian to be the physical depository of the fund's assets and the financial controller of disbursements and receipts. In addition, the fund has to have an "Administrator" playing the role of business manager and looking after such routine, but essential, functions as maintaining the books, preparation of financial statements and reporting to regulatory authorities, and so on. Professional investors are more comfortable with fiduciaries in their own country who they know and who they can approach directly and easily. Thus, a fund to be marketed in the US would receive more investor support *if* the investment manager and the custodians were US firms. On the other hand, host country regulations sometimes require local involovement and sometimes the foreign fiduciaries see a serious business need for that local involvement. Finally, the fund must have a board of directors, or some form of outside advisory committee if it does not set up as a company, which combines financial expertise, knowledge of the country and an appropriate degree of independence to represent the interests of shareholders.

(c) Considerations in making the critical decisions

Most of the choices that have to be made in structuring a country fund are self evident. In recognising the objectives that have to be met for a specific fund it is not hard to assess the relative merits of the countries in which the fund vehicle should be established and how it should *be* structured to maximise shareholder interest. The same applies as to which are the appropriate financial intermediaries to fulfil the various fiduciary functions. There are, however, a number of considerations where a different level of judgement has to be applied.

(d) Investment objectives

Domestic mutual funds in the US and European countries have investment objectives ranging from capital gains to income and safety, and achieve them through a variety of strategies. They can offer broad diversification geared to a national index of industry or geographical specialisation. The very nature of emerging markets is such that this wide range of objectives and strategies found in mature markets is difficult, if not impossible. Investors in emerging markets country funds generally expect their money to be fully invested in that country, and diversified in those industries and companies which will produce maximum growth within prudent risk parameters. In some of the larger emerging markets, objectives have become slightly more diverse as the number of funds in them increase. For example, investment policies which emphasise small- or medium-sized companies. The main point is that the investment objectives must reflect the realities of the host country.

(e) Regulatory and taxation environments

Because of the intrinsic international nature of country funds, many tend to be established in tax-haven countries such as Luxembourg, the UK Channel Islands and the Netherlands Antilles, on the assumption that not only will the regulatory environment be less complex but also funds established in their jurisdiction will be tax exempt. This is largely because, especially in the eyes of European and Japanese investors, the US Securities and Exchange Commission (SEC) is perceived to be a somewhat unfriendly regulator with complex requirements involving the need for considerable and expensive legal assistance. The establishment of the Securities and Investments Board in London resulted in the regulatory procedures for the establishment of funds in the UK, especially if they are also listed in London, becoming at least as complicated as those in the US. Luxembourg regulations have also moved in the same direction and, while Japanese investors still appear to prefer Luxembourg incorporated funds, the SEC now looks to be a much more attractive regulator man it was. This is especially the case if the fund's shares are sold principally in the US (which is in any event the country with the largest apetite for such investments). Also, many European investors still feel more comfortable operating under the SEC "umbrella", although listings in European capitals like Paris and Amsterdam do make it possible for certain French and Dutch institutions to invest in such country funds.

Tax regimes are as much a legal issue as a tax issue. However, as a starting point, a country fund must, one way or another, be established under a tax regime where me fund's income is not taxed, to avoid double taxation. Incorporation in the US and registration with the US SEC through the US Investment Company Act of 1940 makes this possible although foreign investors in such funds are subject to a dividend withholding tax. Incorporation in "tax havens" such as Luxembourg and Ireland also ensures the tax-free status, although as European countries' law move closer together, there is always the risk that this may change.

(f) Conflicts of interest

Reference has been made above to the importance of sponsorship and the selection of fiduciaries to carry out the various roles in setting up and operating a fund. At one extreme (most frequently found in the US) the sponsors take pains to ensure that those responsible for marketing the fund's shares initially are independent of the investment manager, and that the custodian and administrator are also independent. At the other extreme, more often found in Europe, funds are promoted by a financial group, the subsidiaries of which handle all of these fiduciary functions and also sometimes carry out transactions for the fund portfolio. While recognising that, in the latter case, regulations usually require "Chinese walls" ensuring mat self- dealing does not take place, prudent investors tend to prefer real independence. This is one of the reasons why funds listed on the New York Stock Exchange tend to have higher premiums or lower discounts than their counterparts listed in London or elsewhere.

(g) Fiduciaries' fees

For public issues, underwriters' fees can vary from 4 per cent to as high as 8 per cent, with the lower range being more usual for European sponsored funds. For private placements they can range from 1 per cent to 3 per cent, depending more on the size of the transactions than the domicile. Investment management fees can range from 0.5 per cent to 2 per cent, depending on the domicile and the size of the issue. Also, management fees can include a performance component. Administrator's fees and custodian's fees can range between 0.15 per cent and 0.25 per cent each, plus certain transaction costs, again depending on the same factors.

The "quality" of a fund is in part a function of these costs of establishing and launching the fund (the start-up expenses) and the ongoing costs (the annual operating expenses) as they have a bearing on performance. The higher the start-up expense, principally underwriting and legal fees, the greater the likelihood of shares selling at a discount in the secondary market. Similarly, operating expenses (those already mentioned which are recorded in the fund's accounts), plus the cost of buying and selling securities (brokerage and other transaction fees and taxes, usually called transaction costs) which are also paid for by the fund but are not included in the fund's accounts, eat into the annual rate of return. If excessive, they can outweigh the benefits to investors of hiring a professional manager to do the work for them. The annual operating expense "benchmark" for large domestic US mutual funds *is* between about 0.5 per cent and 0.75 per cent, also excluding execution costs. However, because of the complexities of dealing in emerging markets, these fund's operating expenses are higher. Only the largest and most efficient emerging markets have operating expenses as low as 1 per cent - most range between 1.5 per cent and 2 per cent.

Another indication of "quality" to investors is when the investment manager acts as a fund's sponsor and places a maximum percentage limit on operating costs (excluding transaction costs) after which the investment manager pays the excess out of its management fee.

(*h*) Size

Hypothetically, a new issue of a country fund which is large gives a better impression of success than one that is small. The host country sees a likelihood of a larger flow of long-term equity capital. The investment banker sees larger underwriting or placement fees and the investment manager can earn a larger management fee. On the other hand, there are risks. If the amount raised is out of proportion to the size of the hose country stock market capitalisation, and especially of its "float" of shares actually available for trading, the manager will have difficulty investing the funds prudently in a reasonable period of time. He runs the risks of driving stock prices up and, under-performing the market. The investment manager, in consultation with the local securities market experts, should establish in advance a maximum size commensurate with the best estimate of what the local market can absorb in the types of stocks it may buy in order to avoid these risks. The manager will also establish a minimum size needed to make the fund an economically viable business. For public issues, investment banks (which principally benefit from the initial fee) have a natural preference for larger issues and, thus, if an initial demand appears to be high they will wish to fill it. However, if they sell shares to too many short-term traders the stock in the after market will move initially to a high premium and then sink rapidly to a discount as the speculators take their profits and as other investors begin to fear the fund has been over-promoted.

(*i*) Controlling costs

As already indicated, start-up and operating costs are measures of both quality and efficiency and thus can have a bearing on the success of a fund offering and its long-term performance. Sponsors, including the larger shareholders, can control most of these costs. Underwriters' and investment managers' fees can be negotiated before contracts are signed. On an ongoing basis, the board of directors of the fund must authorise renewal of all contracts.

Less controllable, however, especially for multi-country funds, are legal expenses and the fiduciaries' due diligence costs which can be quite substantial if the fund has a complex structure. If a fund's domicile is in the same country as that of its underwriter, its investment manager and its custodian, and if most of the shareholders are from the same country, it is possible to negotiate a fairly fixed fee with the attorneys involved as there should only be one representing the fund, one representing the underwriter plus one making representations concerning the host country. If, however, other countries are included in the investment programme and if the investment manager or an underwriter is in a different domicile from that of the fund, legal and due diligence issues arise concerning the different regulatory and tax regimes in each country. This can be compounded for a fund domiciled in a foreign tax haven and with investors from more than one country. Some of these costs are inevitable as there are more issues on which foreign investors will expect clear legal opinions and where fiduciaries will expect warranties and representation from the fund and other fiduciaries as to their legal responsibilities. The costs of addressing these problems are expected to be paid by the fund and thus, ultimately, by its shareholders. Less immediately visible but equally important are the ongoing costs. Leaving aside fiduciaries' fees, these can be substantial because of heavy turnover or because proper care is not exercised in obtaining, "best executions" or both. Directors have an obligation to police these costs as they do other expenses.

It is evident from the foregoing that setting up a country fund involves all the complexities of establishing any new financial service business. Cutting through the details and considering characteristics of the most successful country funds (the Korea Fund, which is listed on the New York Stock Exchange and the Emerging Markets Growth Funds which is a private placement "global" country fund) it is evident that the simple approach is the best approach. That is, to domicile the fund where most of the investors are and to have independent fiduciaries all of which are domiciled in that country. While a closed-end fund cannot really be considered as simple as the standard US or UK open-end mutual fund or unit trust, it is the only practical solution for the smaller and less liquid emerging markets.

(j) Prospects for the future

The IFC believes that, despite the occasional speculative surge or excessive decline, emerging markets will continue to appeal to investors seeking strong fundamentals, good growth prospects and relatively low stock valuations. A number of trends seem likely to emerge. The *first* of these is a shift in the geographic focus of investment away from Asia and towards Europe, especially eastern Europe, and to some countries in Latin America. *Secondly,* the investor base will continue to grow from the present 100 or so large institutions worldwide, as more institutions and funds allocate a specific, if small percentage of their increasing assets to emerging markets. A strong, steady growth of market prices of country funds listed on major exchanges should attract more retail investors as well. *Third,* the emerging markets themselves are likely to grow considerably in depth and breadth. The lack of debt finance from foreign sources combined with high stock prices will lead more companies to take advantage of this lower relative cost of equity financing with a consequent increase in new listings. *Fourth,* the more sophisticated countries will establish second tier markets, as local entrepreneurs and financial institutions from abroad target unlisted companies through venture capital and mezzanine finance funds. *Fifth,* the highest quality companies in the developing countries will raise their capital directly in the international securities markets through listings and cross-listings on the world's major exchanges.

(2) AMERICAN DEPOSITORY RECEIPTS

An American Depository Receipt (ADR) represents an ownership interest in foreign securities. It is a negotiable instrument issued by an American depositary bank certifying that shares of a non-US issuing company are held by the depositary's custodian bank abroad, usually in the home market. Each depositary share represents a multiple or fraction of underlying ordinary shares. If the ratio of ADRs to underlying share is not 1:1, each unit of the ADR is called an American Depository Share (ADS). ADRs could be listed on the New York Stock Exchange, the American Stock Exchange and the National

Association of Securities Dealers Association Quotation (NASDAQ) over-the-counter market or they could be issued as private placement securities under Rule 144a in the US. They are an ideal way for foreign companies to raise funds, expand their international capital base and get name and product exposure in the US.

The shares are issued by the say Indian company to an US intermediary called the depositary in whose name the shares are registered. It is the depositary which subsequently issues the ADRs. The physical possession of the equity shares is with another intermediary, the custodian who is an agent of the depositary (see diagram on next page). The main advantage to the issuer is that he does not assume any exchange risk, though he does enjoy the benefit of foreign exchange collected by way of issue proceeds. The dividend outflow from the company is in rupees. The depositary however pays the dividend in dollars to the investors. By contrast, had the company issued convertible bonds - which gives the holder the right to buy ordinary shares - redemption of the non-convertible portion would be in foreign currency as also interest payment - making exchange rate management - for the issuer - a critical aspect of a convertible bond issue.

Beyond the obvious opportunity of tapping a new source of corporate finance, there are very specific benefits to companies which access the international equity market through ADRs: (1) Because of the low level of stock prices in most developing countries now relative to other markets, a well designed depositary receipt issue could attract a considerably high price per share than a similar issue sold in the domestic market - although in the case of India where stock prices are currently very high, depositary receipts have been issued at a discount. (2) Having the company's name in the international market would make future financings easier as the company would then have a known track record and a broad range of markets to tap. In this connection, most of the world's major global companies, US, Japanese, German, have their shares listed on several leading foreign stock exchanges for this reason. Exxon, IBM, General Electric, General Motors, Sony, Shell, Daimler-Benz and Toyota have listings on four or more foreign stock exchanges.

The third advantage applies especially to companies seeking global markets for their products. Having foreign shareholders and listings of their stocks on the major markets enhances their name recognition in those markets. This prestige helps in locating potential product marketing agents and suppliers.

International issues of ADRs are increasingly popular relative to country funds. As far as the investor is concerned, there are lower management fees and lower execution costs in buying foreign stocks in his own market by way of ADRs. Further, the regulations governing portfolio investments for some institutions in some countries hold that a foreign stock (or Deposit Receipt) listed on the domestic market is regarded as domestic and thus not subject to foreign investment limitations which might be the case if the same stock was bought in its own (foreign) market.

The general criteria companies have to meet to be able to sell equity issues include a current equity market capitalisation of at least US$ 100 mn equivalent (only about a handful of companies would qualify in India); market turnover of at least US$ 1 mn a week in the domestic market; independently audited financial statements and financial disclosure arrangements meeting international standards; a track record of satisfactorily increasing market share, sales and profits; a conservative debt: equity ratio by industry standards; a significant and growing share of export earnings; if it is domestic oriented, domestic market dominance; and finally, the appropriate emphasis on quality, R&D, technology and global competitiveness.

Different investors place different degrees of emphasis on these points. Then, in the final analysis, the current price relative to earnings prospect and compared to similar companies in other countries are usually the decisive factors. Further, while liquidity for an ADR issue is a function of the size of the issue in the market where the ADR is registered, liquidity in the home market is important too as foreign investors like the comfort of knowing the company is also well regarded and traded actively domestically.

The US SEC's Rule 144a - adopted in April 1990 - make foreign private placements easier and cheaper for the issuer as well as more liquid for the professional investor. The total cost of a 144a offer is between a quarter to a half that of an equivalent SEC-registered transaction and the process is much quicker. Moreover, the issuer does not have to register with the SEC and submit onerous periodic disclosure reports. Such registration of securities had discouraged foreign issuers from using the US capital markets in the past.

US investors often prefer ADRs to the foreign securities they represent because : they trade and settle in the US as if they were US securities; they trade in US dollars and dividends are converted into US dollars; investors do not have to make separate custody arrangements for their foreign shares, which can sometimes be more expensive than ADRs; the convenience of buying and selling ADRs as easily as US stocks with 5-business day settlement and no settlement problems because ADRs settle through the Depositary Trust Company. Thus to the US investor, ADRs have become an excellent vehicle which allows them to diversify into the international markets by significantly simplifying the purchase and sale of foreign equities and eliminating costly settlement delays, registration difficulties and dividend payment problems.

Some foreign companies view the creation of an ADR programme as a first step towards entering the US capital markets. The existence of an ADR programme raises the company's profile in the US and makes it easier for the company to list its securities or raise capital at a later date. The SEC's Rule 12g 3-2(*b*), provides an exemption from registration with the SEC for foreign exchange or quoted on NASDAQ, and who have not made a public offering in the US. The company sends the SEC any information that it makes public, sends to its shareholders, or files with its home country regulatory authority. The SEC does not review these documents, but makes them available for inspection by the public. This is a "level one" ADR programme whose aim would be to encourage trading in the company's securities in the US and raise its profile there. And a 144a offering in the private market can be used to test the investment climate, get its stock and story known and follow with a listing or public offering. Along with the capital that can be raised, a 144a deal can also play an important role in building an international following for a company. Although a 144a deal is technically a private placement, it is marketed like a registered public offering, allowing broad distribution. There are over 3500 "qualified institutional buyers" for 144a deals. These are (a) institutions (e.g. pension funds, investment companies) that own or have investment discretion over $ 100 mn; (*b*) banks and savings and loans associations they own or have investment discretion over $ 100 mn and a net worth of at least $ 25 mn; and (c) registered broker-dealers that own or have investment discretion over $ 100 mn.

GLOBAL DEPOSITORY RECEIPTS (GDRS)

In line with the globalisation trends in capital markets, the concept of the ADR has recently expanded beyond the boundary of US markets. At the initiative of Citibank, Global Depository Receipts (GDRs) were introduced in late 1990. A GDR is similar to an ADR, except that it is placed in multiple markets simultaneously and traded under a book-entry settlement system through Eurodollar, CEDEL and the Depositary Trust Company (DTC). In May 1991, Samsung Electronics of Korea became the first developing country company to tap the GDR market. Many recent ADR offerings have involved a GDR component.

The modus operandi for floating a ADR/GDR issue by an Indian company is fairly simple : First, it has to pass a board resolution to adopt the issue and follow it up with a meeting of shareholders who need to approve the issue by passing a special resolution. This requires a minimum vote of 75 per cent. Next, an application has to be sent to the Finance Ministry containing the terms of the issue and the price range. The Ministry's approval approval specifies only the price range. A prospectus is prepared, keeping in mind international disclosure standards. Intermediaries such an overseas underwriters, lead manager, depositary and custodian need to be appointed. The underwriter's job is essentially to market the issue by organising road shows and ensuring the success of the issue. A road show is a presentation made by the issuer to potential investors. During these road shows, an indication of investor response is obtained by an entity called the "book runner". The issuing company decides on the issue price after gauging investor response.

Once the issue is tied up, the company issues shares which are registered in the name of the depositary and lodged physically with the local custodian. The depositary issues the ADR/GDRs to the underwriters who arrange to place them with the final investors. The local custodian holds the shares physically on behalf of the depositary. The depositary arranges to collect the foreign exchange for the issuer and also organises payment of dividends to the investor. The custodian acts as an agent of the depositary and undertakes the administrative work related to the issue in India. The all-in issue cost for the company is estimated at about 5 per cent of the issue size. Once a ADR/GDR is issued, it can be traded freely amongst international investors.

INDIAN DEPOSITORY RECEIPTS (IDRs)

Indian Depository Receipts (IDRs), financial investments similar to the GDRs and ADRs which draw foreign companies to mobilise funds respectively from European and American markets, have been introduced by the department of company affairs (DCA) on February 23, 2004 by issuing the Indian Depository Receipts Rules, 2004 (IDR Rules), under section 605A of the Companies Act, 1956. By introducing IDRs, the government has opened the circular for the foreign companies to raise funds from the Indian capital market as part of its efforts to globalise the Indian finance market and to provide local investors exposure in global companies.

In an IDR, foreign companies issue shares to an Indian Depository, which would, in turn, issue Depository receipts to investors in India. The actual shares underlying the IDRs would be held by an overseas custodian, which will authorise the Indian depository to issue the IDRs. The overseas custodian is required to be a foreign bank having a place of business in India and needs approval from the finance ministry for acting as a custodian. The Indian depository needs to be registered with SEBI.

An IDR issue needs to be approved by SEBI and an application in this regard has to be made a minimum of 90 days before the issue-opening date. The overseas company also has to file a due diligence report and a Prospectus or Letter of Offer with SEBI and the ROC. Further, the overseas company will have to obtain in-principle permission for listing on stock exchanges in India.

The overseas company undertaking the IDR issue needs to have a pre-issue paid-up capital and free reserve of at least $100 million and an average turnover of $500 million during the last three financial years. In addition, overseas companies also need to have earned profits in at least five years preceding the issue and should have declared dividends of at least 10 per cent each year during this period. Further, the pre-issue debt-equity ratio of such company should not be more than 2:1.

The present IDR Rules do not require the overseas company to have a place of business in India. While there was some confusion on this aspect when the concept was introduced in the Companies Act (Amendment) Bill, 1997, the issue has been clarified, both in section 605A of the Companies Act as well as the present IDR Rules. Further, it is also not mandatory for the issuing company to be listed overseas. However, the company would have to agree to the publication of its quarterly audited financial results in Indian newspapers, which may be a difficult condition for privately held companies.

The IDR issue should not be less than Rs 50 crore if the company issuing the IDRs does not receive the minimum subscription of 90% of the issued amount, the company shall forthwith refund the entire subscription amount received.

An issuing company looking to get the nod of SEBI should pay a non-refundable fee of $10,000 along with its application. On being granted the permission, an applicant would have to pay an issue fee of half a per cent of the issue value subject to minimum of Rs 10 lakh where the issue is up to Rs 100 crore. Further, where the issue value exceeds Rs 100 crore, every additional value of issue would be subject to a fee of 0.25 per cent of the issue value.

All IDR issuance should have the prior nod of Sebi. The rules do not require listing of the IDRs in a foreign bourse. An issuing company would only require listing of IDRs in recognised stock exchanges in India.

The rules also stipulate that IDRs shouldn't be redeemed into underlying equity shares before the expiry of the one-year period from the issue date. Further, the IDRs issued by any issuing company in any financial year should not exceed 15% of its paid-up capital and free reserves.

Only qualified institutional investors are allowed to invest in IDRs. NRIs and Flls cannot purchase or possess IDRs unless special permission of the RBI is taken. The minimum investment in IDRs is Rs 2 lakh. Indian companies can also invest in IDRs but it should not exceed the investment limits fixed by their board.

The IDR Rules specify that the repatriation of proceeds of the IDR issue would be subject to prevalent exchange control regulations. Further, although there would be no restriction on the purchase or transfer of the IDRs as the investors would be Indian residents as defined under FEMA, any acquisition of underlying shares would be subject to compliance with the FEMA provisions prevalent at that time.

The IDR route is an addition to the options available to Indian investors for overseas investment — general permission for purchase of shares of listed foreign companies holding at least 10 per cent shares in an Indian listed company; acquisition of shares under the $25,000 route; and investments in Indian mutual funds, which are permitted to invest abroad up to $50 million each.

Indian investors also need to consider the tax implications of investment in the IDRs/underlying equity shares. While the clause relating to IDR issue in the Companies Act (Amendment) Bill, 1997 had a provision stating that the Government would make rules for taxing gains on sale of IDRs, Section 605A introduced in the Companies Act does not contain this requirement.

In the absence of any specific provision in the Income-Tax Act, 1961 (IT Act) for taxing the gain on sale of IDRs, the general rules relating to capital gains taxation should continue to apply. As such, IDRs should be eligible for the beneficial tax rate for Long

Term Capital Gains with a lower holding period of 12 months since IDRs would be a listed security.

However, the tax laws of the foreign jurisdiction where the overseas company is located would also be relevant in this regard. While the IT Act contains a specific provision in Section 47(vii-a) exempting gains on transfers of GDRs between non-residents, it needs to be analysed whether such a provision exists in the country of which the overseas company is a tax resident.

In the case of dividends declared by the overseas company, the same would not be covered under provisions of Section 115-O of the IT Act, which levies a dividend distribution tax on domestic companies. Consequently, such dividend income would not be exempt in the hands of investors. It would be subject to tax withholding in the source country and investors would need to claim tax credit, wherever applicable, on such income. It needs to be noted that a person's residential status under FEMA could be different *vis-a-vis* his tax residence.

As regards conversion of IDRs into shares, while the IT Act exempts conversion of bonds/debentures/deposit certificates into shares under Section 47(x) from an Indian tax perspective, there may need to be incorporated a 'direct' provision for the conversion of IDRs into underlying shares being tax neutral or a scheme, similar to that notified under Section 115AC, specifying the tax treatment relating to IDRs. Further, a similar provision in the tax laws of the overseas jurisdiction may be useful in clarifying the tax implications of such conversion in the overseas jurisdiction.

To summarise, while the IDR Rules can be considered an important step in the direction of India's integration in the global economy, it remains to be seen whether there is an appetite at the end of the issuer as well as the Indian investor.

QUESTIONS

1. Modern portfolio theory helps in the optimal allocation of global resources. Comment?
2. Cite briefly the major objectives behind a company seeking to list its stock in other dun the country of its incorporation. How does multiple listing contribute to the profitability of a company.
3. Discuss the concepts of the ADRs and GDRs.
4. Discuss the regulatory framework of foreign portfolio investment which has been developed by Asian countries ?
5. Why would world capital markets be segmenting ?
6. Are world capital markets efficient ? What factors need to be considered in answering this question ?

REFERENCES

1. Amihud I. and Haim Mendelson: "Liquidity and Stock Returns," *Financial Analysts Journal*, May-June 1986.
2. Andrews, John R. "The Case for Investing in Growth." *Financial Analysts Journal*, November-December 1970, p. 55.
3. Ankrim, Ernest: "Risk-Adjusted Performance Attribution," *Financial Analysts Journal*, March-April 1992. pp. 75-82.
4. Arnott, Robert D.: "What Hath MPT Wrought: Which Risks Reap Rewards," *Journal of Portfolio Management*, Fall 1983, pp. 5-11.
5. Berry, Michael, Edwin Burrmeister, and Marjorie McElroy: "Sorting Out Risks Using Known APT Factors," *Financial Analysts Journal*, March-April 1988, pp. 29-42.
6. Best, M., and R. Grauer: "The Sensitivity of Mean-Variance Efficient Portfolios to Changes in Asset Means: Some Analytical and Computational Results," *Review of Financial Studies*, 1991.

7. Bierman, Harold. "How Much Diversification Is Desirable?" *Journal of Portfolio Management*, Winter 1981, 42-44.

8. ————————————, and Semour Smidt, "Application of the Capital Asset Pricing Model to Multi-period Investments," *Journal of Business Finance and Accounting* 2, no. 3 (Autumn 1975): 327-340.

9. Bierwag, G.O., George G. Kaufman, and Alden Toevs, eds. *Innovations in Bond Portfolio Management: Duration Analysis and Immunization*. Greenwich, Conn.: JAI Press, 1983.

10. ——————————————————————————, and Alden Toevs. "Duration: Its Development and Use in Bond Portfolio Management." *Financial Analysts Journal* 39, no. 4 (July-August 1983).

11. ——————————————————————, and Chulsoon Khang. "Duration and Bond Portfolio Analysis: An Overview." *Journal of Financial and Quantitative Analysis* 13. no. 5 (November 1978).

12. Black, Fischer: "Estimating Expected Return," *Financial Analysts Journal*, Sept-Oct 1993, pp. 36-38.

13. ———————————, Michael C. Jensen, and Myron Scholes: "The Capital Asset Pricing Model: Some Empirical Tests," in Michael C. Jensen (ed.). *Studies in the Theory of Capital Markets, Prages* New York, 1972.

14. Blume, M., and I. Friend, "A New Look at the Capital Asset Pricing Model." *The Journal of Finance*, March 1973, pp. 19-33.

15. Bookstaber, Richard, and Roger Clarke: "Problems in Evaluating the Performance of Portfolios with Options," *Financial Analysts Journal*, January-February 1985.

16. Booth, David, and Eugene Fama: "Diversification Returns and Asset Contributions," *Financial Analysts Journal*, May-June 1992, pp. 26-32.

17. Born, Jeffery A., "The Arbitrage Pricing Theory, the Market Portfolio and Ambiguity When Performance is Measured by the Security Market Line." Working Paper No. FIN-2-84, University of Kentucky, 1984.

18. Bower, Dorothy, R.S. Bower, and D.E. Logue, "A Primer on Arbitrage Pricing Theory," *Midland Corporate Finance Journal*, 2 (Fall 1984), 31-40.

19. Branch, Ben, "The Predictive Power of Stock Market Indicators," *Journal of Financial and Quantitative Analysis*, June 1976, pp. 269-285.

20. Breeden. D.T.: "An Intertemporal Asset Pricing Model with Stochastic Consumption and Investment Opportunities," *Journal of Financial Economics* 7, 1979, pp. 265-269.

21. Brown, Robert G.. "Detection of Turning Points in a Time Series," *Decision Sciences* 2, no. 4 (October 1971): 383-404. "

22. Brown. Stephen: "The Number of Factors in Security *Returns*," *Journal of Finance*. December 1989. pp. 1247-1262.

23. Burrmeister, Edwin, and Kent Wall: "The Arbitrage Pricing Theory and Macroeconomic Factor Measures," *The Financial Review*, February 1986, pp. 1 -20.

24. Callahan, and Rosanne Mohrs: "The Determinants of Systematic Risk: A Synthesis," *The Financial* Review May 1989. pp. 157-182.

25. Carroll, Carolyn, and John Wei: "Risk, Return, and Equilibrium: An Extension," *Journal of Business*, October 1988, pp. 485-500.

26. Chan, Louis and Josef Lakonishok: "Are the Reports of Beta's Death Premature'?.'" *Journal of Portfolio Management*. Summer 1993, pp. 51-62.

27. Chance, Don: "Empirical Estimates of Equivalent Risk Classes and the Effect of Financial Leverage on systematic Risk," *The Financial Review*. Fall 1981. pp. 12-29.

28. Chen, Naifu, "Some Empirical Tests of the Theory of Arbitrage Pricing," *Journal of Finance*, 38 (December 1983), 1393-1414.

29. —————————, R. Roll, and S.A. Ross, "Economic Forces and the Stock Market." Working Paper Ser. B-73, University of California at Los Angeles, December 1983.

30. Chen. Andrew. Frank Jen. and Stanley Zionts, "The Optimal Portfolio Revision Policy." *Journal of 'Business* 44. no. I (January 1971): 51 61.

31. Cho, D. Chinhyung, "On Testing the Arbitrage Pricing Theory: Inter-Battery Factor Analysis," *Journal of Finance,* 39 (December 1984), 1485-1502.

32. Christy, George A., "A Rationalization of the Stock-Bond Yield Spread," *Quarterly Review of Economics and Business* 7, no. 1 (Spring 1967): 63-70.

33. Cohen, Kalman, and Jerry Pogue: "An Empirical Evaluation of Alternative Portfolio Selection *Models," Journal of Business,* April 1967, pp. 166-193.

34. Connor, Gregory, and Robert Korajczyk: "A Test for the Number of Factors in an Approximate Factor Model," *Journal of Finance,* September 1993, pp. 1263-1291.

35. Cumley, Robert, and David Modest: "Testing for Market Timing Ability: A Framework for Forecast Evaluation," *Journal of Financial Economics,* September 1987. pp. 169-190.

36. Dhrymes, Pheobus J., "The Empirical Relevance of Arbitrage Pricing Models," *Journal of Portfolio Management,* Summer 1984.

37. Dietz, Peter O., "Components of a Measurement Model: Rate of Return, Risk, and Timing," *Journal of Finance* 23, no. 2 (May 1968): 267-275.

38. —————————O. "Measurement of Performance of Security Portfolios, Components of a Measurement Model: Rate of Return, Risk and Timing." *The Journal of Finance,* May 1968, p. 267.

39. —————————, H.R. Fogler, and D.J. Hardy: "The Challenge of Analyzing Bond Portfolio Returns." *Journal of Portfolio Management,* Spring 1980, pp. 53-58.

40. Dince, Robert R., "Another View of Formula Planning," *Journal of Finance,* December 1964, pp. 678-688.

41. Eleswarapu, V., and Marc Reinganum: "The Seasonal Behavior of the Liquidity Premium in Asset Pricing," *Journal of Financial Economics,* December 1993, pp. 373-386.

42. Elton, Edwin J., and Martin J. Gruber: *Modern Portfolio Theory and Investment Analysis,* John Wiley & Sons, New York, 1991.

43. Evans, John L., and Stephen H. Archer: "Diversification and the Reduction of Dispersion: An Empir-ical Analysis." *Journal of Finance,* December 1968, pp. 761-767.

44. Fabozzi, Frank J., and Irving M. Pollack, eds. *The Handbook of Fixed Income Securities.* Homewood, III.: Dow Jones-Irwin, 1987.

45. Fabozzi, Frank J., and T. Dessa Fabozzi. *Bond Markets, Analyses, and Strategies.* Englewood Cliffs, N.J.: Prentice-Hall, 1989.

46. Fama, E.F., and J.D. Macbeth. "Risl, Return and Equilibrium: Empirical Tests." *Journal of Political Economy,* May-June 1973, pp. 607-36.

47. —————————: "Components of Investment Performance." *Journal of Finance.* June 1972. pp. 551-67.

48. Farrell, James L., Jr.: "The Multi-Index Model and Practical Portfolio Analysis," Occasional Paper no. 4, Financial Analysts Research Foundation, Charlottesville, VA, 1976.

49. Filatov, Victor, and Peter Rappaport: "Is Complete Hedging Optimal for International Bond Portfolios'?" *Financial Analysts Journal,* July-August 1992, pp. 37-47.

50. Fisher, Lawrence, and Roman L. Weil. "Coping with the Risk of Interest Rate Fluctuations: Returns to Bondholders from Naive and Optimal *Strategies." Journal of Business,* October 1971, 408-431.

51. Fogler, H. Russell, "Common Sense on CAPM, APT, and Correlated Residuals," *Journal of Portfolio Management,* Summer 1982, pp. 20-28.

52. Fong, Gifford, and Oddrick Vasicek: "Fixed Income Performance Attribution." Institute for Quantitative Research in Finance, Spring Seminar 1994, Palm Beach. FL.

53. Fouse, W., and W. Jahnke, and B. Rosenberg: "Is Beta Phlogiston'?" *Financial Analysts Journal*, January-February 1974, pp. 70-80.

54. Francis, J.C, and S.H. Archer. *Portfolio Analysis*. Englewood Cliffs, N.J.: Prentice-Hall, 1971.

55. Friend, I., and M. Blume. "Measurement of Portfolio Performance under Uncertainty." *American Economic Review*, September 1970, pp. 561-75.

56. Fuller, Russell Jr.: "Capital Asset Pricing Theories—Evolution and New Frontiers," Monograph no. 12. Financial Analysts Research Foundation, Charlottesville, VA, 1981.

57. Gehr, Adam: "Test of the Arbitrage Pricing Model," Research Report no. 88, Institute for Quantitative Research in Finance, 1979.

58. Gilster, J.E., Jr., "Capital Market Equilibrium with Divergent Investment Horizon Length Assumptions," *Journal of Finance and Quantitative* Analysis 18 (June 1983), 257-65.

59. Gressis, N.G. Philippatos, and J. Hayya, "Multiperiod Portfolio Analysis and the Inefficiency of the Market Portfolio," *Journal of Finance*, 31 (September 1976), 1115-26.

60. Grinblatt, M., and S. Titman. "Portfolio Performance Evaluation: Old Issues and New Insights," *Review of Financial Studies*, 1989, 393-421.

61. Hagerman, R.L., and E. H. Kim, "Capital Asset Pricing with Price Level Changes," *Journal of Finance and Quantitative* Analysis, 11 (September 1976), 381-92.

62. Harrington, Diana R., "The Changing Use of the Capital Asset Pricing Model in Utility Regulation," *Public Utilities Fortnightly*, August 13, 1980.

63. Henriksson, Roy D. "Market Timing and Mutual Fund Performance: An Empirical Investigation." *Journal of Business*, January 1984, 73-96.

64. Higgs, Peter, and Stephen Goode: "Target Active Returns and Attribution Analysis," *Financial Analysts Journal*, May-June 1993, pp. 77-80.

65. Howe, Jane Tripp. *Junk Bonds: Analysis and Portfolio Strategies*. Chicago: Probus Publishing, 1988.

66. Jacob, Nancy L., and keith V. Smith. "The Value of Perfect Market Forecasts in Portfolio Selection." *The Journal of Finance*, May 1972, p. 355.

67. Jensen, Michael C. "Capital Markets: Theory and Evidence." *Bell Journal of Economics and Management Science*, autumn 1972, pp. 357-98.

68. Jensen, Michael. "The Performance of Mutual Funds in the Period 1945-1965." *Journal of Finance*, May 1968, 389-416.

69. Kryzanowski, Lawrence, and T.M. Chau, "Asset Pricing Models When the Number of Securities Held Is Constrained: A Comparison and Reconciliation of the Mao and Levy Models," *Journal of Financial and Quantitative Analysis*, 17 (March 1982), 63-73.

70. Lakonishok, J. "Performance of Mutual Funds versus Their Expenses," *Journal of Business Research*, Summer 1981, 110-114.

71. Lanstein, Ronald, and W. F. Sharpe, "Duration and Security Risk," *Journal of Financial and Quantitative Analysis*, 13 (November 1978), 653-68.

72. Levitz, Gerald D. "Market Risk in Institutional Portfolios." *Financial Analysts Journal*, January-February 1974, p. 53.

73. Levy, Haim, "Equilibrium in an Imperfect Market: A Constraint on the Number of Securities in the Portfolio," *American Economic Review*, 73 (September 1978), 643-58.

74. Livingston, M., "Duration and Risk Assessment for Bonds and Common Stocks: A Note," *Journal of Finance,* 33 (March 1978), 293-95.

75. Logue, Dennis E., and L. J. Merville, "Financial Policy and Market Expecta-tions," *Financial Management,* 1 (Summer 1972), 37-44.

76. Longstaff, Francis, and Eduardo Schwartz: "Interest Rate Volatility and Bond Prices," *Financial Analysts Journal,* July-August 1993, pp. 70-74.

77. Markowitz, Harry M.,"Portfolio Selection," Journal *of Finance,* March 1952, pp. 77-91.

78. Martin, Robert: "On Market Timing and Investment Performance," *Journal of Business,* July 1981, pp. 363-406.

79. McCulloch, J. Huston: "Measuring the Term Structure of Interest Rates," *Journal of Business,* January 1971, pp. 19-31.

80. McDonald, Bill, "Making Sense Out of Unstable Alphas and Betas," *Journal of Portfolio Management,* Winter 1985, pp. 19-22.

81. McEnally, Richard W. "Portfolio Management Policies for Fixed Income Investors." In *Advances in Bond Analysis and Portfolio Strategies,* edited by Frank J. Fabozzi and T. Dessa Garlicki. Chicago: Probus Publishing, 1987.

82. McMillan, T.E., Louis Buck, and James Deegan: "The Fisher Theorem - An Illusion, But Whose?, *Financial Analysts Journal,* November-December 1984, pp. 63-71.

83. Melicher, Robert W., and D. F. Rush, "Systematic Risk, Financial Data, and Bond Rating Relationships in a Regulated Industry Environment," *Journal of Finance,* 29 (May 1974), 537-44.

84. Merton, R.C.: "An Analytic Derivation of the Efficient Portfolio Frontier," *Journal of Financial and Quantitative Analysis 7,* 1972, pp. 1851-1872.

85. Meyers, S., "The Stationarity Problem in the Use of the Market Model of Security Price Behavior," Accounting *Review,* 48 (April 1973), 318-22.

86. Michaud, R.: "The Markowitz Optimization Enigma: Is Optimized Optimal?" *Financial Analysts Journal,* 1989, pp. 31-42.

87. Milne, Robert D. "Determination of Portfolio Policies: Individual Investors." In *Managing Investment Portfolios,* edited by John L. Maginn and Donald L. Tuttle. Boston: Warren, 1983.

88. Modigliani, Franco, and Gerald Pogue: "An Introduction to Risk and Return," *Financial Analysts Journal,* March-April 1974, pp. 68-86.

89. Moore, Geoffrey and John P. Cullity, "Security Markets and Business Cycles," in *The Financial Analysts Handbook* 2nd ed. (Homewood, III.: Dow Jones-Irwin, 1988).

90. Perold, A.F.: "Large-Scale Portfolio Optimization," *Management Science* 30, pp. 1143-1160.

91. Peterson, D., "Suggests Caution in the Use of Betas," *Financial Analysts Journal,* 28 (May-June 1972), 104.

92. Reilly, Frank, and David Wright: "A Comparison of Published Beta," *Journal of Portfolio Management,* Spring 1988, pp. 64-69. Rosenberg, Barr. "Prediction of Common Stock Betas," *Journal of Portfolio Management,* Winter 1985, pp. 5-14.

93. Reinganum, Marc, "The Arbitrage Pricing Theory: Some Empirical Results," *Journal of Finance,* 36 (June 1981), 313-21.

94. Rennie, Edward, and Thomas Cowhey: "The Successful Use of Benchmark Portfolios: A Case Study," *Financial Analysts Journal,* September-October 1990, pp. 18-26.

95. Roll, R.: "A Critique of the Asset Pricing Theory's Tests." *Journal of Financial Economics,* March 1977, pp. 129-176. Black, Fischer, "Capital Market Equilibrium with Restricted Borrowing," *Journal of Business* 1972, pp. 444-455.

96. —————— and S. A. Ross, "An Empirical Investigation of the Arbitrage Pricing Theory," *Journal of Finance,* 35 (December 1980), 1073-1104.

97. ——————————————: "The Arbitrage Pricing Theory Approach to Strategic Portfolio Planning," *Financial Analysts Journal,* May-June 1984, pp. 14-29.

98. Rosenberg, Barr, and James Guy: "Beta and Investment Fundamentals," *Financial Analysts Journal.* May-June 1976, pp. 60-72.

99. Ross, S.: "Return, Risk and Arbitrage," in I. Friend and J. Bicksler (eds.), *Risk and Return in Finance,* Ballinger, Cambridge, 1976.

100. ——————, "The Arbitrage Pricing Theory of Capital Asset Pricing," *Journal of Economic Theory,* 13 (December 1976), 341-60.

101. Rudd. Andrew, and Barr Rosenberg: "The 'Market Model' in Investment Management," *The Journal of Finance,* May 1980, pp. 597-606.

102. Schneider, Theodore H. "Measuring Performance." *Financial Analysts Journal,* May-June 1969, p. 105.

103. Shanken, Jay, "The Arbitrage Pricing Theory: Is It Testable?" *Journal of Finance,* 37 (December 1982), 1129-40.

104. Sharpe, William F., "Bonds Versus Stocks: Some Lessons from Capital Market Theory," *Financial Analysts Journal,* November-December 1973, pp. 74-80.

105. ——————————: "Mutual Fund Performance," *Journal of Business,* January 1966, pp. 119-138.

106. ——: "Capital Asset Prices: A Theory of Market Equilibrium under Conditions of Risk." *Journal of Finance,* September 1964, pp. 425-442.

107. ——————: "Risk. Market Sensitivity and Diversification." *Financial Analysts Journal,* January-February 1972. pp. 74-79.

108. ——————: *Investments.* Prentice-Hall, Englewood Cliffs, NJ, 1978.

109. ——————: *Portfolio Theory and Capital Markets,* McGraw-Hill, New York, 1970.

110. ——————————: "A Simplified Model for Portfolio Analysis," *Management Science.* January 1963, pp. 277-293.

111. —————————— "Factor Models, CAPMs, and the APT," *Journal of Port-folio Management,* Fall 1984, 21-25.

112. ——————————: " Imputing Expected Security Returns from Portfolio Composition," *Journal of Financial and Quantitative Analysis* 9, 1974, pp. 463—472.

113. Smith. Keith. "Alternative Procedures for Revising Investment Portfolios." *Journal of Financial and Quantitative Analysis* 3. no. 4 (December 1968): 371 404.

114. Soldofsky, Robert M. "Yield-Risk Performance Measurements." *Financial Analysts Journal,* September-October 1968, p. 130.

115. Strong, Robert A. "Linear Programming Solves Problem: Eases Duration Matching Process." *Pensions and Investment Age,* 17, no. 259, (11 December 1989), 21.

116. Surz, Ronald: "Portfolio Opportunity Distributions: An Innovation in Performance Evaluation," *Journal of Investing,* Summer 1994, pp. 36-41.

117. Tierney, David, and Kenneth Winston: "Defining and Using Dynamic Completeness Funds to Enhance Total Fund Efficiency," *Financial Analysts Journal,* July-August 1990, pp. 49-54.

118. Treynor, J.L. "How to Rate Management of Investment Funds." *Harvard Business Review,* January-February 1965, pp. 63-75.

119. Trycinka. Charles: "On the Number of Factors in the Arbitrage Pricing Model," *Journal of Finance,* June 1986. pp. 347-368.

120. Vandell, Robert F. and Jerry L. Stevens, "Evidence of Superior Performance from Timing." *Journal of Portfolio Management* 15, no. 3 (Spring 1989).

121. ─────────────, and Mark T. Finn. "Portfolio Objective: Win Big, Lose Little" *Journal of Portfolio Management*, Fall 1981, 37-45.

122. Vasicek. O.A.. and J.A. McQuown: "The Efficient Market Model." *Financial Analysts Journal*, September-October 1972. pp. 7I-84.

123. Vertin, James R. "The Design and Control of Large Portfolios." The Financial Analysts Federation, Annual Conference, May 1978.

124. Wagner, Jerry, Steven Shellans and Richard Paul, "Market Timing Works Where It Matters Most... in the Real World," *Journal of Portfolio Management* 18, no. 4 (Summer 1992).

125. Williams, Arthur: *Managing Your Investment Manager*, Dow Jones-Irwin, New York, 1990.

126. Williamson, Peter: "Performance Measurement," in Edward Altman (ed.): *The Financial Handbook*, Wiley, New York, 1980.

46

Issues Posed by Foreign
Portfolio Investment

INTRODUCTION

Portfolio investment in developing countries is generally thought of as having desirable properties for investors in industrial countries. Adding portfolio investment in developing countries to a well-diversified portfolio is expected to improve the overall risk-return tradeoff. The quantification of these return and diversification benefits is, however, not straightforward. It is, for example, not clear how integrated developing countries are with industrial countries, how has this changed overtime, and how this depends on barriers to free capital movements. Furthermore, the exact barriers and their opportunity costs in terms of higher cost of capital in developing countries as well as developed countries have not been identified. The objective of this chapter is to discuss the various issues posed by the emergence of substantial flows foreign portfolio investment.

KEY ISSUES

The recent trends in cross-border flows of private capital indicate a declining role of medium-and long term international financial institutions lending and the growing importance of portfolio investment flows. Infact, the revival of capital inflows is treated as though it were a measure of success and an end in itself. However, the sad story of South-East Asia and Latin American involvement in the international capital market should suffice to demonstrate the error of equating capital flows with success. Infact, Latin American countries since independence have borrowed time and again, and encountered debt-servicing problems that dragged down their growth rate: the debt crisis was only the latest episode in a pattern that has been repeated as many as four times. Despite the undoubted potential for capital mobility to increase economic welfare by permitting investment to be reallocated internationally to the area with the highest potential rate of return, it is arguable that the region would have done better had it never borrowed anything. Hence, it is wrong to assume simply that more is better. Rather, the danger of over-borrowing is one of five issues posed by the emergence of portfolio flows. These five issues, are:

Potential Size

In an ideal world, one could anticipate very large capital flows from industrial countries to developing countries over the next half century, while the developing countries completes the demographic transition. During this period the working population of the industrial countries will be fairly stagnant, implying limited investment needs but comparatively high savings, especially in the coming decades as a relatively large proportion of the population is in the pre-retirement high-savings phase of the life-cycle.

Hence one would expect these countries to wish to run current account surpluses, so as to accumulate foreign assets whose income could help them pay the pensions of their increasing population of retirees. In contrast, the developing counties will have growing populations and the opportunity of benefiting from catchup growth, implying high investment needs relative to savings capabilities and the ability to pay high rates of return. An important additional benefit of such capital flows is that they would reduce the pressure for mass migration. Thus there would seem to be clear mutual benefits from large capital flows.

How large is "large"? The conjecture is: as large as is consistent with reasonable certainty that credit worthiness can be maintained. And how *large is that?* The best answer we are able to give at the moment is based on various ad hoc rules of thumb about a maximum prudent level of debt or debt service relative to variables that influence the ability to service debt, such as exports, GNP, or the capital stock. The most famous of such rules of thumb state that the debt/export ratio should not exceed 200 percent, that the debt service ratio (that is, the ratio of debt service to exports) should not exceed 25 per cent, and that the debt/GNP ratio should not exceed 40 per cent. Such rules of thumb doubtless ought to be combined in some way, but they do at least provide a starting point for analysis.

What do these rules of thumb imply about sustainable (desirable) current account deficits? A little algebra can show us Let D = foreign debt and Y = nominal income (expressed in dollars, like the debt mostly is), and use a hat over a variable to signify its rate of change so that D/D is the proportionate rate of change of debt. Consider a typical country, which may expect a long-term growth rate of nominal income of 8 per cent, consisting of 3 per cent inflation and 5 per cent real growth. In steady state the rate of growth of debt must be the same as the rate of growth of nominal income. Then the prudent steady-state current account deficit according to the debt/GNP rule of thumb would be D/Y = (D/D). (D/Y) = 0.08 x 0.4 = 0.032, that is, the steady-state deficit should not exceed 3.2 per cent of GNP. Of course, a country that starts out with a lower debt/GNP ratio than 40 per cent can run a greater deficit for a transitory period, but it is well-advised to prevent the deficit getting too much larger because of the difficulty of adjusting back as the debt limit approaches. (It is appropriate to focus on the debt/GNP ratio for a country with an export/GNP ratio in excess of 20 per cent, and on the debt/export ratio or a country with an export/GNP ratio below 20 per cent, to ensure that both constraints are satisfied).

The total GNP of developing countries, measured at market exchange rates (as is appropriate here since GNP is providing a measure of the size of the domestic economy relative to its foreign obligations), is $ 4.1 trillion (17.7 percent of a gross world product of $ 23 billion). If one accepts five per cent as an estimate of the medium-term potential growth rate of developing countries in general, then a rough estimate of how much capital inflow would be desirable is $ 130 billion per year. That can be compared with the annual flow of portfolio capital that had built up to $ 37 billion by last year, out of a total flow of $ 118 billion (excluding grants).

Portfolio flows are therefore a substantial part of a total flows that now seems close to a best guess estimate of what might be considered optimal. (Admittedly this calculation assume that all developing countries are capable of borrowing all that it would be prudent for them to accept, whereas most of the lower-income countries still have little access to the international capital market). Without portfolio flows, it is difficult to envisage the total flow being as large as desirable. The question therefore arises as to how dependable these flows are. It can be argued, for example, that portfolio lows provide the channel for repatriation of flight capital, which is an inherently transitory phenomenon. While true, the pool from which the flight capital is being drawn is extremely large: the World Bank made an estimate that it amounted to an average of 32 per cent of GDP for 58 developing countries at the end of 1990, which would suggest a total stock of around a trillion dollars for all developing countries.

Furthermore, the other pools from which portfolio flows are drawn (the funds invested in world bond and equity markets) are vast and growing rapidly. Holdings in emerging markets are still marginal: So far less than 0.25 percent of the total assets of institutional investors in industrial countries were laced in emerging markets. The owners of these funds are becoming increasingly predisposed to consider investments in the emerging markets on their merits. Hence there is ample scope for portfolio flows not just to be sustained, but to grow further in coming years.

One other argument for questioning the permanence of recent levels of inflow of portfolio capital is that much of the equity investment has been attracted by the opportunities for buying newly privatised assets, and that the process of privatisation is inherently transitory because in due course there will be nothing left to privatise. This is surely true, although the process of privatisation still has a long way to go in most countries. Moreover, if future growth remains healthy, it will produce a string of new flotations that will offer similar opportunities to investors.

Therefore the potential size issue must be analysed from a wider perspective and the portfolio flows must be potentially large enough to be and remain an important source of external finance to developing countries.

Terms of Lending

This has two main dimensions, maturity and yield. Borrowers have an interest in borrowing long-term (unless they anticipate a forthcoming decline in interest rates), primarily to minimise the danger of a withdrawal of funds precipitating debt difficulties, and in paying little. How well do the various forms of portfolio capital do in meeting these interest? Consider bonds. The terms still evokes in many people's minds the image of long-term fixed-interest bonds that prevailed before the First World War. The present-day reality is different. Most "bonds" nowadays have a maturity of eight years or less, and some of them carry floating interest rates. This means that a large part of the stock of outstanding debt can be withdrawn rather rapidly. It also means that the cost of servicing the bonds does not vary with the borrower's ability to pay (where the interest rate floats, debt service may indeed rise at a time when ability to pay is squeezed, as happened at the beginning of the debt crisis when high world interest rates caused a recession that cut debtors' ability to pay).

In one respect bonds tend to be even more inflexible than bank credits: they lack any mechanism for achieving an agreed rescheduling. Ironically it was precisely this difficulty that made bonds popular with lenders during the 1980s. While it was possible for distressed debtors to maintain debt service on bonds when these were a minute fraction of their total obligations, it will be impossible to do the same if debt difficulties arise in a country with a large proportion of its debt in the form of bonds. Thus creditors are living in something of a fool's paradise.

Money market instruments are short term. An advantage of both money market instruments and bonds is that they are relatively cheap. It is that unless and until it again becomes possible to borrow in the form of long-term (30 years or more) bonds, developing countries would be well-advised to restrain their borrowing in the form of both bonds and money market instruments to rather modest levels. In other words, it is worth paying a premium on the cost of funds in order to get repayment obligations that are better matched to ability to pay and less likely to precipitate debt difficulties.

Equity investment has very different characteristics. It has the advantage of a degree of cyclical sensitivity of the dividends paid, thus helping match debt-service payments to ability to pay. Nor is there as much danger of a disruptive capital outflow. It is true that foreigners may decide at any time that they wish to sell their shares, and that such a desire is quite likely to prove general as the herd instinct takes over. But, unless a sudden desire of foreigners to sell is matched by an increased desire of nationals to buy, the effect will be to depress the stock market rather than to lead to a demand for foreign exchange. One then has to ask whether a decline of the stock market is worse than a loss of foreign exchange reserves: it can be argued that the stock market is a natural place to absorb risk and that the costs of a decline in stock prices are usually modest, with the exception of instances where high stock prices have come to underpin other parts of the financial system.

The cost of equity finance is typically quite high. However, a large part of it usually takes the form of capital gains rather than being a drain on foreign exchange earnings in the short or medium run. Hence equity provides an attractive way in which to borrow.

Macroeconomic Destabilisation

The principal reason for preferring borrowing on long maturity is to limit the danger of a withdrawal of funds leading to debt-servicing difficulties. But there is also a danger of an excessive inflow of funds destabilising macro-economic management. An inflow is excessive when it is so large as to threaten the maintenance of a competitive exchange rate (because of nominal appreciation under a flexible exchange-rate regime or inflation under a fixed exchange-rate regime), and therefore jeopardises the prospects of maintaining export-led growth.

There are various possible reactions to a capital inflow:

i) To allow a nominal appreciation of the currency that will result in the transfer being accomplished, thus in effect accepting market forces rather than the judgment of the authorities as the factor determining the level of transfer.

ii) To engage in unsterilised intervention, which will also result in the transfer being accomplished, though with a delay and with inflation rather than nominal appreciation producing the real appreciation.

iii) To pursue a contractionary fiscal policy, so as to reduce internal absorption and permit a reduction in interest rates that will reduce the incentive for an inflow of capital.

iv) To maintain some controls on capital inflows, such as variable deposit requirements against foreign borrowings, that can be raised when inflows become excessive.

v) To engage in sterilised intervention, thus attempting to resist the transfer, though there is a danger that the market will ultimately overwhelm this attempt.

vi) To manipulate the flow of domestic liquidity into the banking system using excess government savings, which may be regarded as a generalised form of sterilised intervention.

vii) To widen the band of permissible exchange rate fluctuations, so as to allow a temporary appreciation without undermining the confidence of exporters that the exchange rate will remain competitive in the medium term.

viii) To eliminate any remaining subsidies to inward investment, such as free deposit insurance.

One school of thought argues that either the first or second reaction is appropriate, the first corresponding to the flexible and the second to a fixed exchange-rate regime. The implicit judgment is that the authorities should not challenge the presumption that the market knows best, but should rely on the market to limit borrowing/lending to what is prudent. The historical record, including that of the last 20 years, suggests rather strongly that this is not a case where a policy of neglect can be relied on to be benign. Capital markets are precisely those where contagion effects are strongest. Both lenders and borrowers seem to find it easy to convince themselves that times have changed and that past rules of prudence no longer apply, until such time as some event triggers a loss of confidence and causes lenders to decide simultaneously that the debtor is no longer creditworthy. Thus, although many neoclassical economists argue against any governmental concern with the size of capital inflows or the associated current account deficits, their position seems to be unwise.

If one takes the view that government has a duty to try and prevent excessive capital inflows, then it has to select form the remaining six reactions on the above list. The evidence to date suggests that none of them taken individually is likely to be very effective, but that jointly they can constitute a viable programme. Chile provides a great examples which shows that a judicious combination of policies can prevent even strong inflows wreaking havoc with macro management. The maintenance of some capital inflow controls as one of the admissible options, and complete liberalisation should not be introduced prior to (a) evidence that such controls have become completely ineffective (or hopelessly corrupting), or (b) assurance that inflows will not be excessive.

Recipients of Capital Inflows

In retrospect, it is clear that one of the disadvantages of syndicated bank credits is that they channelled funds principally to the public sector, because that was where governments were prepared to provide the sovereign guarantees that most banks demanded. This contributed to the excessive growth in the size of the public sector in many developing countries, and it excluded the private sector, which is now widely regarded as providing the best investment opportunities.

Portfolio capital is very different in this regard. While there is nothing to prevent parastatals from issuing bonds or money market instruments, they can also be issued by the private sector. Equity is issued exclusively by the private sector. Hence, if one regards it as desirable to see a flow of external capital to the private sector, one should welcome the replacement of syndicated bank credits by portfolio flows.

But does it follow that equity investment will necessarily lead to an increase in real investment in the private sector? After all, most stock purchases are on the secondary market rather than involving the purchase of newly issued shares. The first impact is to increase the price of shares rather than the flow of funds to companies that wish to increase investment. Increased wealth of local investors can be expected to lead them to increase their consumption, so that the counterpart to a part of the capital inflow must be expected to be an increase in consumption. However, one expects the same to be true of other forms of capital inflow: a government that is able to borrow abroad will be able to reduce taxes (if nothing else, it will be able to reduce its reliance on the inflation tax) and a part of the counterpart will be increased consumption, expect in a world with full Ricardian equivalence. The other impacts of a foreign equity purchase will tend to increase investment. This might come abut as a result of a lower cost of capital encouraging new equity issues, or it might happen because the sellers of stock decide to increase investment in unquoted assets (such as small business). Thus there remains a presumption that a substantial part of foreign investment in equities will feed through into increased investment in the private sector.

Foreign equity investment (except through the medium of American Depository

Receipts (ADRs), which are traded offshore) has the virtue of stimulating the development of the domestic equity market, which until recently was one of the most underdeveloped parts of the financial system of most developing countries. Bonds and money market instruments, on the other hand, are placed offshore, and hence—like syndicated credits—reduce the incentive for the development of the local financial market.

Financial Innovation

The forms in which capital should and would flow to developing countries as the international capital market revived after the debt crisis is argued that it is neither desirable nor probable that syndicated bank credits would regain the central role that they had in the late 1970s. It is undesirable since they threw too many of the risks on the borrowers and they channeled funds almost exclusively to the public sector. Moreover it is unlikely because the banks had been badly burned and new lenders would demand the chance of upside gains to compensate them for the downside risks that the debt crisis had shown to exist.

What sources might replace the bank? It is suggested that the possibility of both increased flows form traditional private sources, form the public sector, and from innovative private sources. For example, both foreign direct investment and equity (portfolio) investment might increase along with the multilateral development banks (MDBs) (at least the regional development banks) may expand their lending.

However, so far not much action on the more innovative following proposals for private lending has been taken.

i) Investment by multinationals in projects with a return determined by a "quasi-equity" contract, such as production sharing, revenue sharing, or profit sharing.

ii) Lending by banks or other financial institutions on a stand-alone basis for export-oriented projects whose earnings could be escrowed to provide debt service provided that the project prospered.

iii) Long-germ, index-linked bonds issued by a consortium of developing countries [perhaps organised by one of the regional development banks] with a partial guarantee by donors endowing a modest guarantee fund.

iv) Commodity-linked bonds with a yield tied by formula to the prices of major commodities, which would be issued by the exporters of those commodities.

All these proposals still seem to make as much microeconomic sense as they did at the time of debt crisis. On the other hand, the fact that other sources, notably FDI and equity investment (as well as money market instruments and bonds), have grown far more means that there is no longer the same macroeconomic need to foster alternatives. Thus a proper policy stance would seem to be to draw attention once again to these possibilities, to encourage consideration of whether they do not offer microeconomic advantages compared with the current set of instruments, but to avoid any pressure to adopt these proposals.

On the whole, the development of flows of portfolio capital, or more specifically its equity component, seems to be a thoroughly benign event. Equity portfolio capital does not bring with it the access to foreign technology, techniques, and markets that FDI does, but it is capable of channelling funds to the private sector and it has much better risk-sharing properties than do syndicated loans. Moreover, its relatively high cost is at least partly offset by the indefinite postponement of any cash drain because much of the return takes the form of capital gains. Since virtues of bonds and money market insturments are less overwhelming, given that most bonds are still of much shorter maturity than those that prevailed before World War I, The countries should limit their borrowings from these sources, so as to minimise the danger that new debt difficulties will arise This is very pertinent since the sums available in the form of portfolio investment are (in conjunction with likely flows from other sources) large enough to satisfy the prospective borrowing levels that can be undertaken with prudence.

The principal source of concern about portfolio flows is that they may be too much of a good thing. The development of alternative sources of finance, while perhaps still desirable on micro grounds, is less urgent than it seemed during the debt crisis. The market may not automatically regulate capital inflows to a level consistent with macroeconomic prudence, and hence the bubbles will develop. A major challenge for macroeconomic policy in developing countries is to prevent excessive capital inflows which lead to real appreciations that will undermine the prospects for increasing exports, and therefore for sustainable medium-term growth. Success in restraining capital inflows to prudent levels will also help to minimise the danger that a new debt crisis will develop.

PORTFOLIO CAPITAL FLOWS: HOT OR COLD?

Much of the literature implicitly presumes that it is possible to distinguish hot from cold capital flows simply by knowing the nature of the financial instrument being traded or the identity of the transactor. Perhaps the most salient example of this is the presumption that short-term flows are hotter than long-term flows. The basic idea in the literature is that a hot money inflow is likely to disappear or even reverse itself in the near future, whereas a cold money inflow is more likely to persist. Short-term capital inflows are like cars sitting in the parking lot with the engine running.

The notion that one can make inferences about the characteristics of financial flows by just observing their label is not new in economic. There is much conventional wisdom that show capital flows reflect speculative, unstable behaviour while other flows reflect evaluations of long run profitability and are based on fundamental economic condition. The flows of funds approach used by many central banks and others for an analysis of the domestic economy developments is based on labels which are deemed meaningful.

This view has also been an important part of the traditional analysis of international finance for many years. In fact, the structure of balance of payments accounts reflects an implicit theory that different types of capital flows have different economic implications. For example, the distinction between short-term "hot money" and long-term capital flows undoubtedly reflects the view that short-term capital movements are speculative and reversible while long-term capital flows are based on fundamentals and are reversed only when the fundamentals change. The fact that capital control programmes in many countries distinguish between short-and long-term positions also points to the importance attached to this distinction.

Another important distinction found in balance of payments accounts is between official capital flows, including changes in international reserves, and private capital flows. A common view in the context of current capital inflows into developing countries— which is based on labels—is that such flows are fundamentally different form inflows to these same countries in the 1970s because the current inflows are private-to-private transactions not guaranteed by the government of any country.

Finally, it is often argued that direct investment has different implications for the host and recipient countries as compared to other capital flows. For example, direct investment capital flows are often associated with technology transfers and a range of costs and benefits for both countries. An implicit assumption behind these ideas is that the transactions reported in the balance accounts are closely related to the behaviour of interest in the real economy.

This reasoning—based on the label of the flow—at times underlies substantive policy measures. Once a flow is identified as "hot money," it is then seen as requiring some policy response. At various times countries (especially developing countries) have responded with exchange rate management, (sterilised) intervention, fiscal contraction, borrowing taxes, absolute foreign borrowing constraints, and reserve requirements.

There are a number of good reasons to doubt, however, that the micro nature of international capital flows reveals much about the economic importance of such flows. Since many assets are (increasingly becoming) tradable, a distinction between flows based on their terms (for example, short versus long) is (increasingly becoming) less meaningful. A treasury bond with a 30-year maturity can easily be more liquid, and thus lead to a higher volatility of short-term flows than a 30-day time deposit at a commercial bank. And, a short-term asset which is rolled over can in many ways be identical to a long-term asset.

Furthermore, the explicit label given to a flow may not cover its implicit nature. For instance the inflows to developing countries in the 1970s were private capital flows in name, the universal government guarantees of both lenders and borrowers considerably subdued the discipline of the market. In effect the capital flows that helped generate the debt crisis of 1982 should have been considered official capital flows since the private parties undertaking the transactions relied on a government guarantee (and ex post, private claims indeed became the liability of the government). This presumably made private investors less careful than they would have been in the absence of guarantees.

This experience should act as a warning against evaluating capital flows according to their label (for example, the instrument traded or the transactor recorded in the balance of payments statistics). In the past few years inflows to developing countries have taken the form of non-guaranteed portfolio investments and direct investments. If the behaviour behind such investments is different in some important way, it follows that we may not be inviting another debt crisis even if conditions change as they did in 1982. But if the flows are to a significant extent guaranteed by the government, their label "private" may be meaningless. Clearly, in thinking about stability, an important attribute is thus the contingent liability of the government.

The starting point should then also be a clear methodology on how the hypothetical economic implications of different types of capital flows can be identified empirically. If credit markets were perfect and complete, the form of capital flows would not be important. A useful analog here is the Miller-Modigliani theorem from corporate finance. Under a set of strong assumptions, the structure of assets and liabilities among various types of debt and equity have no effect on the value of the firm because investors can offset the structure chosen by the firm in credit markets. If we think of the balance of payments accounts as records of how a country finances its international capital position, it follows that under the Miller-Modigliani assumptions, the structure of capital flows and the structure of the gross international asset and liability positions would be unrelated to the country's net indebtedness.

It might be useful here to look at an analogous issue that has recently been carefully explored in a closed economy context. That issue is whether a "credit crunch" contributed to a downturn in economic activity. This is an interesting hypothesis because it explicitly rests on the view that one type of financial transaction, in this case loans by domestic banks to domestic nonfinancial firms, had important economic effects.

This view is an important part of the (new literature on business cycles, which links financial structures and real activity. This literature provides a useful analytical framework that can be adapted to a discussion of international financial flows. It points out that the importance of changes in bank credit for economic activity, as opposed to bank liabilities or money, is an empirical issue. If good substitutes for bank credit exist in an economy, it follows that a decline in bank credit that is not matched by a decline in money will have no effect on economic activity. Firms would easily substitute other forms of credit, for example commercial paper, to offset the reduction in bank credit. In contrast, if banks have special information about their customers that is not easily transferred to other lenders, a reduction of bank credit will not be easily offset by borrowing from other institutions or markets. In this case an interruption in bank credit could have a depressing effect on expenditures and output.

There are two important lessons from this,. First, meaningful tests of the importance of capital account transactions require a specification of the economic behaviour of interest. Second, a financial transaction is likely to have measurable effects on the specified economic behaviour in cases where the institutional environment, information structures, or other departures from complete markets limit the ability of investors to substitute one type of transaction for another in response to changing incentives.

The view that labels matter can take comfort from the fact that international financial markets are not complete and transactions are subject to a large number of distortions. Many of these are imposed by governments in the form of controls on types of transactions that are considered undesirable. Moreover, subsidies often take the form of a government guarantee of private liabilities, favourable tax treatment on earnings (direct investment), or access to special government facilities (debt equity swaps). Each of these distortions is designed to encourage or discourage a given type of capital transaction.

Furthermore, governments also intervene directly in international capital markets. Developing country governments borrow for long-term objectives and, increasingly, in middle-income countries, to offset short-run pressures on exchange rates and domestic interest rates. A difficulty thus arises in interpreting private capital flows that are sterilised by intervention transactions by the central bank as, to some extent, the composition of private capital flows is conditioned by governments' capital transactions. Clearly a country trying to maintain interest rates above its trading partners in some sense generates the private capital inflow by standing ready to match private inflows with official outflows in the form of increases in reserve assets. Such private inflows are "sustainable" as long as the official capital outflows are "sustainable."

In general, if international capital transactions are effectively distorted by taxes, subsidies and direct intervention, the structure of private capital flows might follow predictable patterns as long as the structure of distortions itself is stable. Over a period the financial transactions are motivated by a variety of economic forces. Over time the institutional framework changes, the behaviour of the official sector probably changes, the exchange rate regime changes, capital control programmes come and go, and banking markets (both on and offshore) develop, fail, and are recapitalised.

The final economic behaviour that seems to provide the most appropriate test for the importance of various capital flows is the net intertemporal trade among countries, conventionally measured by the current account. While there are other interesting candidates, for example, the exchange rate, questions about the sustainability of certain type of capital flows are motivated by concern about the sustainability of a path for changes in net indebtedness to the rest of the world, that is, the mirror image of the cumulative current account balance. Policymakers wish to assess the likelihood of sudden and destabilising changes in the total capital account—not just its components.

On a macro level, national accounts identities state that the sum of all capital flows is equal to the difference between savings and investment. For a given savings investment imbalance, capital flows have to satisfy an adding-up constraint. Unless flows influence domestic investment or domestic savings (or a combination of the two), some substitution between the various flows has to occur, for a given current account, the volatility of one flow will on aggregate be canceled out. The extent of interaction between the various components and the possibility of systematic interactions between components thus needs to be addressed before making inferences from the parts to the whole.

A fundamental difficulty this is that the linkage between current account and any of the capital flows data series might be very weak. For one thing we know that gross capital inflows and outflows are several times larger than net capital flows. Yet it is the net flow that we are interested in when considering sustainability of current account position. It seems clear that the motivation for two-way flows of international capital are very different from the general view that developing countries should be net capital importers and that each type of transaction should show a net inflow.

For example, residents of a small open economy might hold most of their financial wealth in the form of foreign clams since this allows them to diversify their income streams and protect themselves from domestic taxation and income shocks. Offsetting this preference would be the tendency for foreign investors to purchase claims on the country again in order to diversify their risk. This diversification motive for international capital movements might account for much of the recorded flows in balance of payments data.

Moreover, it might be the case that residents of wealthy countries prefer long-term investments such as bonds or loans while residents of developing countries prefer short-term investments such as bank deposits. In this case, we would expect to see short-term capital outflow from developing countries matched by long-term loans to residents of developing countries. These preferences imply nothing about the desired imbalance in the capital or current account.

In fact, the short-term positions of residents might be quite stable if there are relatively few alternative investments. In contrast, the long-term capital inflow to the developing country might take several alternative forms. In one year foreign investors might prefer equities, in another bank loans, and in another bonds. These preferences might in turn reflect subtle changes in tax rules (in the industrial countries) that the analyst would find difficult to identify. The point is that the pattern of financial intermediation might be quite stable for a while but that small differences in the institutional framework, due to either regulation or innovation in credit markets, might alter the form that the intermediation taken in balance of payments statistics.

In general, direct investment is a difficult capital flow to interpret. Balance of payments data on direct investment include short-and long-term capital transactions of a loosely defined set of reporters who own more than a given percent of the equity in a domestic or foreign chartered firm. Because direct investors hold factories and other assets that are impossible to move, it is sometimes assumed that a direct investment inflow is more stable than other forms of capital flows.

This need not be the case. While a direct investor usually has some immovable assets, there is no reason in principle why these cannot be fully offset by domestic liabilities. Clearly, a direct investor can borrow in order to export capital, and thereby generate rapid capital outflows. In most developing countries, there are laws against this, so it would be surprising to see negative flows for foreign domestic investment in a developing country. There could, however, be offsetting movements in other balance of payments accounts or in errors and omissions.

On a micro level, there is also much (anecdotal) evidence that, from the point of view of foreign direct investors, flows with very different classifications are actually close substitutes. Multinationals often substitute between and among the various forms of intercompany transfers (retained earnings, provision of and repatriation of capital, and intercompany loans) and loans from local or foreign banks—for example, to achieve higher profits net of overall taxes. In other cases, flows may be complementary, that is foreign investment may take place through a combination of FDI and portfolio equity investment.

QUESTIONS

1. Are the potential flows of foreign portfolio capital large enough, and can they be sustained long enough, for this source to play a significant role in channelising funds of developing countries.

2. Discuss the various issues posed by foreign portfolio investment to the policy-makers. Is it a measure of success and an end itself?

3. "Short-term capital flows are better than long-term flows." Do you agree?

4. "Short-term capital inflows are like cars sitting in the parking lot with the engine running." Comment.

5. Does foreign portfolio investment channel funds to the agents that are best placed to use them to increase productive investment?

6. Does foreign institutional investors' entry stimulate or retard the development of domestic financial markets?

REFERENCES

1. Berkmen, Pelin, Gaston Gelos, Robert Rennhack, and James Walsh, 2009, "The Global Financial Crisis: Explaining Cross-Country Differences in the Output Impact," IMF Working Paper 09/280 (Washington: International Monetary Fund).

2. Blanchard, Olivier, and Gian Maria Milesie Ferretti, 2009, "Global Imbalances: In Midstream?" IMF Staff Position Note 09/29 (Washington: International Monetary Fund).

3. Brown. Stephen: "The Number of Factors in Security *Returns*," *Journal of Finance*. December 1989. pp. 1247-1262.

4. Callahan, and Rosanne Mohrs: "The Determinants of Systematic Risk: A Synthesis," *The Financial* Review May 1989. pp. 157-182.

5. Cardarelli, Roberto, Selim Elekdag, and Subir Lall, 2009, "Financial Stress, Downturns, and Recoveries," IMF Working Paper 09/100 (Washington: International Monetary Fund).

6. Cargill, Tomas F., Michael M. Hutchison, and Takatoshi Ito, 1997,   *The Political Economy of Japanese Monetary Policy* (Cambridge, Massachusetts: MIT Press).

7. Carroll, Carolyn, and John Wei: "Risk, Return, and Equilibrium: An Extension," *Journal of Business*, October 1988, pp. 485-500.

8. Cashin, Paul, C. John McDermott, and Alasdair Scott, 2002, "Booms and Slumps in World Commodity Prices,"*Journal of Development Economics*, Vol. 69 (October 1), pp. 277–96.

9. Cavallo, Michele, Kate Kisselev, Fabrizio Perry, and Nouriel Roubini, 2004, "Exchange Rate Overshooting and the Costs of Floating" (unpublished).

10. Chen, Naifu, R. Roll, and S.A. Ross, "Economic Forces and the Stock Market." Working Paper Ser. B-73, University of California at Los Angeles, December 1983.

11. Chen. Andrew. Frank Jen. and Stanley Zionts, "The Optimal Portfolio Revision Policy." *Journal of 'Business* 44. no. I (January 1971): 51 61.

12. Claessens, Stijn, Giovanni DellfAriccia, DenizIgan, and Luc Laeven, 2010, "Lessons

and Policy Implications from the Global Financial Crisis," IMF Working Paper 10/44 (Washington: International Monetary Fund).

13. Cumley, Robert, and David Modest: "Testing for Market Timing Ability: A Framework for Forecast Evaluation," *Journal of Financial Economics*, September 1987. pp. 169-190.

14. Decressin, Jörg, and Douglas Laxton, 2009, "Gauging Risks for Deflation," IMF Staff Position Note 09/01 (Washing- ton: International Monetary Fund).

15. Durdu, Ceyhun Bora, Enrique Mendoza, and Marco E. Tererones, 2009, "PrecautionaryDemand for Foreign Assets in Sudden Stop Economies: An Assessment of the New Mercantilism," *Journal of Development Economics*, Vol. 89, No. 2, pp. 194–209.

16. Edwards, Sebastian, 2004, "Thirty Years of Current Account Imbalances, Current Account Reversals and Sudden Stops," NBER Working Paper No. 10276 (Cambridge, Massachussetts: National Bureau of Economic Research).

17. Edwards, Sebastian, 2007, "On Current Account Surpluses and the Correction of Global Imbalances," NBER Working Paper No. 12904 (Cambridge, Massachusetts: National Bureau of Economic Research).

18. Eichengreen, Barry, 2007, *Global Imbalances and the Lessons of Bretton Woods* (Cambridge, Massachusetts: MIT Press).

19. Elekdag, Selim, and Prakash Kannan, 2009, "Incorporating Market Information into the Construction of the Fan Chart," IMF Working Paper 09/178 (Washington: International Monetary Fund).

20. Eleswarapu, V., and Marc Reinganum: "The Seasonal Behavior of the Liquidity Premium in Asset Pricing," *Journal of Financial Economics*, December 1993, pp. 373-386.

21. Elton, Edwin J., and Martin J. Gruber: *Modern Portfolio Theory and Investment Analysis*, John Wiley & Sons, New York, 1991.

22. Fama, E.F., and J.D. Macbeth. "Components of Investment Performance." *Journal of Finance*. June 1972. pp. 551-67.

23. Feyrer, James, 2009, "Trade and Income—Exploiting Time Series in Geography," NBER Working Paper No. 14910 (Cambridge, Massachusetts: National Bureau of Economic Research).

24. Ghosh, Atish R., Jonathan D. Ostry, and Charalambos Tsangarides, 2010, *Exchange Rate Regimes and the Stability of the International Monetary System*, IMF Occasional Paper No.

25. International Monetary Fund (IMF), 2010a, "Strategies for Fiscal Consolidation in the Post-Crisis World" (Washington, February).

26. Jensen, Michael C. "Capital Markets: Theory and Evidence." *Bell Journal of Economics and Management Science*, autumn 1972, pp. 357-98.

27. Klyuev, Vladimir, Phil De Imus, and Krishna Srinivasan,2009, "Unconventional Choices for Unconventional Times: Credit and Quantitative Easing in Advanced Economies," IMF Staff Position Note 09/27 (Washington: International Monetary Fund).

28. Korinek, Anton, and Luis Servén, 2010, "Real Exchange Rate Undervaluation: Static Losses, Dynamic Gains" (unpublished).

29. Kumhof, Michael, Douglas Laxton, Dirk Muir, and Susanna Mursula, 2010, "The Global Integrated Monetary and Fiscal Model (GIMF)— Theoretical Structure," IMF Working Paper 10/34 (Washington: International Monetary Fund).

30. Lee, Jaewoo, Gian Maria MilesiaFerretti, Jonathan Ostry, Alesa sandro Prati, and Luca Antonio Ricci, 2008, *Exchange Rate Assessments: CGER Methodologies*, IMF Occasional Paper No. 261 (Washington: International Monetary Fund).

31. Levitz, Gerald D. "Market Risk in Institutional Portfolios." *Financial Analysts Journal*, January-February 1974, p. 53.

32. Levy, Haim, "Equilibrium in an Imperfect Market: A Constraint on the Number of Securities in the Portfolio," *American Economic Review*, 73 (September 1978), 643 58.

33. Markowitz, Harry M.,"Portfolio Selection," Journal *of Finance,* March 1952, pp. 77-91.

34. McEnally, Richard W. "Portfolio Management Policies for Fixed Income Investors." In *Advances in Bond Analysis and Portfolio Strategies,* edited by Frank J. Fabozzi and T. Dessa Garlicki. Chicago: Probus Publishing, 1987.

35. Modigliani, Franco, and Gerald Pogue: "An Introduction to Risk and Return," *Financial Analysts Journal,* March-April 1974, pp. 68-86.

36. Ostry, Jonathan D., Atish R. Ghosh, Karl Habermeier, Marcos Chamon, Mahvash S. Qureshi, and Dennis B.S. Reinhardt, 2010, "Capital Inflows: Role of Controls," IMF Staff Position Note 10/04 (Washington: International Monetary Fund).

37. Reinhart, Carmen, and Kenneth Rogoff, 2004, "Te Modern History of Exchange Rate Arrangements: A Reinterpretation," *Quarterly Journal of Economics,* Vol. 119 (February), pp. 1–48.

38. Rodrik, Dani, 2008, "Te Real Exchange Rate and Economic Growth," *Brookings Papers on Economic Activity* (Fall), pp. 365–412.

39. Smith. Keith. "Alternative Procedures for Revising Investment Portfolios." *Journal of Financial and Quantitative Analysis* 3. no. 4 (December 1968): 371 404.

40. Surz, Ronald: "Portfolio Opportunity Distributions: An Innovation in Performance Evaluation," *Journal of Investing,* Summer 1994, pp. 36-41.

41. Taylor, John B., 2008, "The Mayekawa Lecture: Te Way Back to Stability and Growth in the Global Economy," presented at the 2008 International Conference "Frontiers in Monetary Policy and Theory," Institute for Monetary and Economic Studies, Bank of Japan, Tokyo, May 28–29.

42. Vandell, Robert F. , and Mark T. Finn. "Portfolio Objective: Win Big, Lose Little" *Journal of Portfolio Management,* Fall 1981, 37-45.

43. Wagner, Jerry, Steven Shellans and Richard Paul, "Market Timing Works Where It Matters Most... in the Real World," *Journal of Portfolio Management* 18, no. 4 (Summer 1992).

44. Williams, Arthur: *Managing Your Investment Manager,* Dow Jones-Irwin, New York, 1990.

45. Woodford, Michael, 2009, "Is an Undervalued Currency the Key to Economic Growth?" Department of Economics Discussion Paper No. 0809-13 (New York: Columbia University).

46. World Bank, 2010, *Global Economic Prospects 2010: Crisis, Finance, and Growth* (Washington).

47. Zarnowitz, Victor, 1992, *Business Cycles: Theory, History, Indicators, and Forecasting,* NBER Studies in Business Cycles, Vol. 27 (Chicago: University of Chicago Press).

47

Foreign Portfolio Investment in India:
Emerging Trends and Policy Developments

INTRODUCTION

In the presence of strong economic and political problems India has embarked on an ambitious path of economic liberalisation. Many countries in recent years have increasingly sought to import foreign technology and accelerate investment as a means of stimulating economic growth. India launched a bold economic reform programme in mid-1991. These reforms include short-term measures which were taken to bring the crisis situation of June 1991 under control, as well as longer term structural reforms aimed at improving efficiency and accelerating economic growth. The longer term reforms include abolition of industrial licensing for most industries, relaxation of regulations relating to foreign direct investment and technical collaboration, measures to improve the efficiency of public sector enterprises, reduction of non-tariff restrictions on imports and steps to achieve convertibility of the rupee in the near future. These reforms greatly increase the role of the market and the private sector, as well as open up the economy to greater external and internal competition. The government has also introduced measures to restore fiscal discipline and restructure the tax system to improve incentives.

The policy package attempts to reduce government intervention in business. The effort includes a re-examination and re-orientation of the role of government and major public sector enterprises. An effort is being made to eliminate a wide range of regulatory controls, remove licensing requirements, and reduce governmental involvement in the financial sector. India is aiming to move away from an inward-oriented economy to one that is better integrated with world markets.

The reform process has changed the country's development policies by increasing the role of market forces, and reducing the role of the public sector. Initially the programme concentrated on macro-economic stabilisation but has now moved on to structural adjustment. The reform plan started under difficult circumstances with the new government facing a large fiscal deficit, very low foreign exchange reserves, and high inflation.

To integrate the Indian economy with global economy, the recent reforms introduced under the new economic policies (NEP) reflect India's determination to facilitate the introduction of foreign capital, management methods, industrial technology and economic information, and its commitment to the modernisation of its economy in the context of open international economic relations, in order to overcome poverty, build a fair society, and achieve true self-sufficiency.

The government has been successful in overcoming the external payment crisis, and in reducing fiscal and balance of payments deficits. The reform programme combines stabilisation and structural policies to slow down demand pressures, address the long-term supply problems, and mobilise external resources for development. The new industrial policy is seen as simpler, more liberal and more transparent. The liberalisation programme is viewed very positively by the business community. However, it is also felt that the process must continue in order for India to compete with the economies of other countries around the world.

It is felt that the Indian Government appears to be committed to economic reforms. The worst may be over for the Indian economy, with real GDP projected to be above 7 per cent and inflation edging downwards. Based on purchasing power parity the IMF has recently ranked India to be the sixth-largest economy in the world.

NEW ECONOMIC POLICY AND FOREIGN INVESTMENT

The far reaching economic reforms in India in the 1990s, witnessed a sharp increase in capital inflows as a result of capital account liberalisation in India and a gradual decrease in home bias in asset allocation in advanced economies. During 1990-91, it was clear that the country was heading for a balance of payment crisis caused by increased absorption due to deficit financed fiscal expansion of the 1980s and the trigger of oil price spike caused by the Gulf War. As foreign exchange reserves dwindled to less than a month's import financing requirements in 1991, global capital taps got switched off and the country faced a real possibility of a first ever sovereign default. Crisis managers got active and averted the default, leaving the country still with a default-free history. The survival stimuli it kindled, unleashed massive economic reforms.

Foreign investment flows, mainly in the form of foreign direct investments, averaged US$118 million during 1990-91 and 1991-92. A significant change in our capital account took place when portfolio investments by foreign institutional investors were permitted in 1992. Hence foreign investment (net) receipts, as a proportion of total capital flows, rose steadily from 1.2 per cent in 1990-91 to reach a peak of 155.2 per cent in 1995-96. Thereafter, it declined to reach a low of 29.4 per cent in 1998-99. After some fluctuations in the interim, such investment (US$17.2 billion) in 2005-06, as a proportion of total capital flows, stood at 71.1 per cent. As a proportion of GDP, foreign investment remained at 0.2 per cent or less till 1992-93. It picked up with reforms to reach 1.6 per cent of GDP in 1996-97, and after some fluctuations in the interim, has remained at about 2 per cent in the latest three years. Net capital inflows during April-December, 2006 touched of US$ 27.3 billion, comprising both debt and non-debt inflows.

During the current decade, foreign investment (net) has been a relatively stable component of total capital flows, fluctuating broadly between 1 per cent and 2 per cent of GDP. However, it seems to have shifted to a higher plane from 2003-04 with average for 2003-04 to 2006-07 roughly double that during 2000-01 to 2002-03. In contrast, the debt flows have fluctuated much more, with a down trend till 2003, which resulted in net outflows in the three years to 2003-04, and a rising trend from 2004-05. The trend in net capital flows since 2003-04 therefore seems to be broadly driven by the rising ratio of debt flows. Variations in debt flows have been primarily due to lumpy repayments on government guaranteed or related External Commercial Borrowing (ECB).

Net capital flows rose from a level of US$ 25.0 billion in 2005-06 to reach US$ 46.4 billion in 2006-07, which implies a growth of 85.8 per cent. The major developments in 2006-07 include: (i) a quantum jump in external commercial borrowings (net); (ii) significant rise in foreign direct investment inflows with a simultaneous rise in outward investment;

(iii) large inflows in the form of nonresident Indian (NRI) deposits; and, (iv) an initial fall in portfolio investment, which was somewhat compensated by a recovery in the latter half of the year 2007. The World Economic Outlook (WEO) reported that many emerging markets and developing countries similarly experienced historically high levels of net foreign exchange inflows. The acceleration in gross flows was sharper than net flows. Net private capital flows to emerging market economies and developing countries, after falling by 18.5 per cent in 2006, have risen by 124.3 per cent to reach US$ 495.4 billion in 2007. Thus, net capital flows into India have been substantial in 2007-08.

Overall, as a proportion of total capital flows and on a net basis, foreign investment has had a mixed trend in the post-reform period. In 2006-07, the proportion stood at 33.5 per cent, down from 62.2 per cent in 2005-06 with negligible growth in foreign investment, year-on-year. The proportion rose to 43.4 per cent in the first half of 2007-08. Of the two major components of foreign investment, namely, FDI and portfolio investment comprising foreign institutional investment (FII), Euro equities and others, the latter had been a major but notso- stable source of foreign investment flows in the period 1993-94 to 2005-06.

During the financial year 2007-08, foreign investment of various components in India recorded increased inflows. The inflows under foreign direct investment (FDI) were US $ 25.5 billion during 2007-08 (April-February) as against US $ 19.6 billion during the corresponding period of the previous year (Table 1). FDI was channelled mainly into manufacturing industries (20.1 per cent), followed by financial services (18.7 per cent) and the construction sector (14.7 per cent). Source-wise, Mauritius, remained the main source of FDI to India during April-February 2007-08, followed by Singapore and the US.

Net inflows by foreign institutional investors (FIIs) aggregated US $ 20.3 billion during the financial year 2007-08. The number of FIIs registered with the SEBI increased from 997 by end-March 2007 to 1,319 by March 31, 2008. Capital inflows through American depository receipts (ADRs)/global depository receipts (GDRs) were US $ 8.7 billion for 2007-08 (April- February).

During the year 2007-08 (April- December), the inflows (net) under external commercial borrowings (ECBs) amounted to US $ 16.3 billion. Net short-term trade credit was US $ 10.8 billion (inclusive of suppliers' credit up to 180 days) in April-December 2007. Out of total short-term trade credit, the suppliers' credit up to 180 days amounted to US $ 4.2 billion during April- December 2007.

NRI deposits registered an inflow of US $ 106 million during 2007-08 (April- February). While there were net inflows under Non-Resident Ordinary Rupee (NRO) account scheme and Non-Resident External Rupee Account NR(E)RA deposits scheme, net outflows took place under Foreign Currency Non-Resident (Banks) [FCNR(B)] deposits segment.

The adverse impact of the global financial market turmoil and liquidity problems on India's BoP was felt in terms of reversal of FIIs inflows and decline in long-term and short-term debt flows. A positive development was, however, turnaround in NRI flows and resilience of FDI inflows in the face of reversal of capital flows, reflecting the attractiveness of India as a long-term investment destination. The capital account balance moderated during April-December 2008 mainly due to higher gross capital outflows coupled with lower gross capital inflows.

The deteriorating external financing conditions also rendered Indian firms' access to external commercial borrowings and trade credits somewhat difficult. The resilience shown by FDI inflows, however, reflects the continued confidence in the Indian economy as a long-term investment destination. There was massive decline in net capital flows from US$ 106.6 billion in 2007-08 (8.8 per cent of GDP) to US$7.2 billion (0.6 per cent of GDP) in 2008-09. The decline was mainly due to net outflows under portfolio investment including foreign institutional investments (FIls), American depository receipts (ADRs)/ global depository receipts (GDRs) (US$ 14.0 billion), banking capital including NRI deposits (US$ 3.2 billion) and short-term trade credit (US$ 1.9 billion). However, notwithstanding these adverse developments, the resilience of FDI inflows (US$ 17.5 billion in 2008-09) reflected the growing perception of India as one of the favourite long-term investment destinations.

All the components under net capital flows, except loans and banking capital, showed improvement during April-September 2009 from their levels in the corresponding period of the previous year. In banking capital, net inflows under non-resident deposits remained higher during April-September 2009 as compared to their previous year's level.Net inward FDI into India remained buoyant at US$ 21.0 billion during April-September 2009 (as against US$ 20.7 billion in April-September 2008) reflecting the continuing liberalization and better growth performance of the Indian economy. During this period, FDI was channeled mainly into manufacturing (21.4 per cent) followed by communication services (12.8 per cent) and the real estate sector (12.6 per cent). Net outward FDI of India at US$ 6.8 billion in April-September 2009 remained at almost the same level as that of the corresponding period of 2008-09. Due to the large inward FDI, the net FDI (inward minus outward) was marginally higher at US$ 14.1 billion in April-September 2009.

The net external commercial borrowings (ECBs) inflow remained lower at US$ 0.7 billion in April-September 2009 than the US $ 3.2 billion in April-September 2008. Banking capital (net) amounted to US$ 1.1 billion in April-September 2009 as compared to US$ 5.0 billion in April-September 2008. Among the components of banking capital, NRI deposits witnessed higher net inflows of US$ 2.9 billion in April-September 2009 as compared to US$ 1.1 billion in April-September 2008. Short-term trade credit recorded a net outflow of US$ 0.6 billion (inclusive of suppliers' credit up to 180 days) during April-September 2009 as against a net inflow of US$4.9 billion during the same period of the previous year. Other capital includes leads and lags in exports, special drawing rights (SDR) allocation, funds held abroad, advances received pending issue of shares under FDI and other capital not included elsewhere (n.i.e). Other capital recorded a lower net outflow of US$ 4.3 billion in April-September 2009 as compared to US$ 10.3 billion in April-September 2008.

FOREIGN PORTFOLIO INVESTMENT

Prior to 1992, only non-resident Indians (NRIs) and overseas corporate bodies (OCBs) were allowed to undertake portfolio investment in India, In line with the recommendation of the High Level Committee on Balance of Payments (Chairman: C. Rangarajan), FIIs were allowed to invest in the Indian debt and equity market. Ceilings on FII investments have been progressively relaxed and at present, aggregate investment by FIIs in a company is allowed within the sectoral cap prescribed for FDI. Apart from equity, FIIs registered under the 100 per cent debt route can invest in debt instruments- both Government as well as corporate, the current aggregate ceiling being US $ 1 billion. Indian corporates are also allowed to access equity capital from foreign sources in the form of ADR/GDR and Euro issues. At present, policies on international offerings on ADRs/GDRs have been liberalised substantially and corporates are allowed to raise funds by way of ADRs/GDRs under an automatic route, subject to specified guidelines.

Two-way fungibility in ADR/GDR issues of Indian companies has been introduced under which investors in India can purchase shares and deposit them with an Indian custodian for issue of ADRs/ GDRs by the overseas depository to the extent of the ADRs/GDRs converted into underlying shares (Box 1).

BOX 1

ADRS/GDRS:FUNGIBILITY AND ALIGNMENT OF SHARE PRICES

The process of convergence of domestic and International share prices becomes more efficient if there is flexibility in conversion of ADRs/GDRs into domestic shares and their re-conversion back, *i.e*, if two-way fungibility is permitted. Empirical findings indicate that spreads between domestic and international equity prices tend to narrow as a result of dual listing although there are periods of divergence. The evidence not only suggests strong inter-linkages across global stock markets but also a stranger relation especially for the technology stocks in the domestic and international stock exchanges.

Except for a brief interlude of 1994-95 and 1998-99, the prices of Indian GDRs/ADRs generally traded at a premium to the domestic share prices, even though many of these instruments were issued at a discount. The premium could be explained in terms of brokerage commission, tax and risk premium on account of exchange rate fluctuations. Also the cost and time involved in conversion of GDRs into domestic shares discouraged market players from effectively using the facility of conversion. The prevalent one-way fungibility also suffered from price volatility and liquidity problems as conversion meant lower float until a fresh issuance. For facilitating conversion/ re-conversion of shares between ADRs/ GDRs and domestic shares and alignment of prices, the two way ADR/GDR fungibility was announced in Union Budget, 2001-02.

The Markov-switching model, used to evaluate impact of two-way fungibility on select scrips in aligning share prices across markets, suggests that industry and country specific factors primarily continue to dominate movements in share prices Two-way fungibility, however, helped in making the share prices across countries more aligned though perfect alignment has not been achieved yet. More significantly, the effect of two-way fungibility was evident: on share prices after nearly a quarter. Partial convertibility limited number of participants, illiquid stocks, differential demand-supply conditions, asymmetry of information, varying disclosure norms across exchanges, non-overlapping trading hours, tax and transactional costs may have led to this fragmentation of markets and a complete alignment of prices may not happen on a real time basis.

Determinants of Portfolio Investment Flows to India

Studies on the determinants of portfolio flows to India find the co-movement between FII flows and the BSE Sensex to be fairly high Contemporaneous domestic stock market return was found to be an important determinant for FII flows A combination of domestic, regional and global variables has been important in determining equity flows to India.

With a view to evaluating the factors influencing FII inflows to India, an empirical exercise was undertaken in a risk-return framework using monthly data. The hypothesis tested was that FIIs compare the return on Indian markets with that on international equity markets. FII investments in domestic markets are expected to be positively related to risk in international markets. Furthermore, opportunity costs measured by the one-month LIBOR rate were taken into cognisance. The results of the first order autocorrelated error regression model suggest that HI flows were positively related to returns on BSE Sensex. FII investments in equities in India were also positively related to risk on Nasdaq as expected. The opportunity cost variable was significant with expected sign.

Another exercise was undertaken based on annual data for the period 1970-71 to

2002-03 to model inflows and outflows on account of portfolio investment in India. The inflows and outflows up to 1992-93 were mainly on account of non-resident Indians. It was only after 1992-93 'that portfolio investment by FIIs was permitted in Indian stock exchanges. Consequently, even though the variability in the BSE Sensitive Index over the variability of the Dow Jones Index was included in the equation, it was not expected to play an, important role in explaining portfolio investments during most of the period in the sample. A one-period lagged exchange rate was included to reflect the impact of an expected depreciation of the Indian rupee on the level of investments. World GDP was included as a proxy for "push" factors. Foreign portfolio investment was found to be very strongly related to world GDP implying that "push" factors were important in attracting foreign portfolio investment, particularly in the 1990s. The outflows on account of portfolio investments are explained in terms of differential in returns in India and abroad, captured, by difference between rate of interest, on Government securities and rate of interest on medium term US Government bonds. The ratio of gross fiscal deficit to GDP was also included to reflect the macro economic conditions in the economy. A dummy variable was included to highlight: the liberalisation period. The results Indicated that even though the interest rate differential, had the expected negative sign it was not significant, possibly because FIIs were not allowed to invest in Indian stock markets during major part of the sample period.

In sum, policies relating to portfolio, investment in. India have been substantially liberalised in the 1990s. India received cross-border portfolio investment to the turn of US $ 2.2 billion per year, on an average, between 1992-93 and 2002-03. The volatility of cross-border 'portfolio investment flows into India has been less than that in respect of other emerging market economies. Empirical estimates indicate that FII flows are positively related to returns on BSE Sensex. FII inflows to India display seasonality, with inflows being significantly higher in the first few months of the calendar year, particularly the month of February.

Trends in Portfolio Investment Flows

FII investments first started flowing to India in 1993. Portfolio investment inflows have since then been substantial, with the lone exception of 1998-99. On an annual average basis, India received, cross-border portfolio investment to the tune of US $ 2.2. billion per year between 1992-93 and 2002-03; the contribution, of FIIs was close to US $ 1.2 billion, on an average. The cumulative FII investment in India is close to US $ 19 billion. FII investments in India account for over 10 per cent of the total market capitalisation of the Indian stock market.

After a subdued performance in 2002-03, portfolio flows rebounded strongly to US$. 11.4 billion in 2003-04. The impressive performance of portfolio investment in 2003-04 was on account of a rapid, influx of FII inflows, driven by the heavily bullish sentiments prevailing in the Indian stock markets.

During the first half of the current year portfolio net inflows dropped sharply to US$ 512 million of such inflows in the-corresponding period of the previous year, but also a mere 4.5 per cent of the total level of such inflows in 2003-04. The decline in portfolio investment in the first half of the current year is attributable to a sharp reduction in FII inflows during the first quarter (April-June), when net portfolio inflows amounted, to only US$ 81 million. The volatility noticed in the Indian stock market in mid-2004, and fresh assessments of risk-return; payoffs by international institutional investors in the wake of 'a rise in US interest rates explain the temporary-reversal in the direction of net ꟻII flows during May-July 2004.

It is noteworthy that while portfolio inflows into India during the first half of 2004-05, at US$ 15.4 billion were much higher than the US$ 9.3 billion in the first half of 2003-04, such outflows from India at US$ 14.8 billion during Apri.l-September 2004-05 were also higher than such outflows of US$ 5.8 billion, in April-September 2003-04, and were, in fact, only about US$ 2 billion less than the total outflow of US$ l6.8 billion in the whole of 2003-04. With resurrection of bullish trends in the Indian stock market from July 2004, portfolio inflows into India also gathered momentum. Though the level of portfolio inflows was lower than in 2005, there was no such outflow from Indian in 2006.

With heightened volatility in Asian and global financial markets in 2006-07, net portfolio inflows into India amounted to US$ 7.1 billion for 2006-07. Portfolio net flows after being negative in the initial months (May-July 2006) picked up momentum in August-November 2006 only to slow down again in March 2007. Euro equities, which were relatively a very small component of portfolio flows (less than US$ 1 billion in the period 1997- 98 to 2004-05), have risen in 2005-06 and 2006- 07 to reach US$ 2.6 billion and US$ 3.8 billion, respectively. In 2006-07, Euro equities constituted 54.3 per cent of the total portfolio net flows. However, this composition was more due to lower net inflows under FII. Portfolio investment inflows in the first six months was US$ 83.4 billion and outflows was US$ 65 billion leaving a net inflow of US$ 18.3 billion, which implies a growth of 1,015.2 per cent, year-on-year.

In the scheme of classification based on duration, portfolio investment flows fall under short term variety. Portfolio investment, primarily comprising foreign institutional investors' (FIIs) investments and American Depository Receipts (ADRs)/Global Depository Receipts (GDRs), witnessed net outflows in April-December 2008 as against net inflows in the corresponding period of the previous year. Outflows under portfolio investment were led by large sales of equities by FIIs in the Indian stock market and slowdown in net inflows under ADRs/GDRs due to drying-up of liquidity in the overseas market. The early signs of the impact of the financial crisis on capital inflows were evident in the portfolio outflows that started in February 2008. There were large capital outflows by portfolio investors during September-October 2008, with concomitant pressures in the foreign exchange market. The impact of the global financial crisis through the financial channel was reflected in the sharp turnaround in the capital flows cycle from a sustained phase of surges in inflows to large outflows, particularly in Q3 (October-December 2008) of 2008-09. On the whole, the adverse impact of the global financial market turmoil was reflected in lower capital inflows during 2008-09. FIIs recorded a net outflow of US $ 15.0 billion as against net inflows of US$ 20.3 billion a year ago. In the financial year, up to April 10,2009, there were net inflows under FIIs to the tune of US $ 0.9 billion as against net outflows of US $ 1.5 billion during the same period last year.

Stronger recovery in India, ahead of the global recovery along with positive sentiments of global investors about India's growth prospects, encouraged a revival in capital flows during 2009-10. The turnaround was mainly driven by large inflows under the FIIs and short-term trade credits. The gross capital inflows at US$ 345.7 billion during 2009-10 were 10.2 per cent higher than the US$ 313.6 billion in 2008-09, while gross capital outflows at US$ 292.3 billion were lower by 4.8 per cent from US$ 306.9 billion in 2008-09. As a result, net capital flows at US$ 53.4 billion (3.8 per cent of GDP) were much higher during 2009-10 as compared to US$ 6.8 billion (0.5 per cent of GPD in 2008-09.

Both inward as well as outward FDI showed declining trend in 2009-10 vis-a-vis 2008-09. The inward FDI declined by 12.4 per cent to US$ 33.1 billion in 2009-10 from US$ 37.8 billion in 2008-09. Similarly outward FDI declined by 19.6 per cent from US$ 17.9 billion in 2008-09 to US$ 14.4 billion 2009-10. Consequently, the net FDI (inward FDI minus outward FDI) was marginally lower at US$ 18.8 billion in 2009-10, as compared with US$ 19.8 billion in 2008-09. The FDI was channelled mainly into manufacturing followed by constructional financial services and the real estate sector.

Portfolio investment witnessed net inflow of US$ 32.4 billion in 2009-10 as against a net outflow of US$ 14.0 billion in 2008-09. The attractive domestic market conditions facilitated net FII inflows of US$ 29.0 billion in 2009-10 (as against net outflows of US$ 15.0 billion in 2008-09). At US$ 3.3 billion, the ADRs/GDRs remained at the same level in 2009-10 as in 2008-09. Net ECBs slowed down to US$ 2.8 billion (US$ 7.9 billion in 2008-09) mainly due to increased repayments.

The net short-term trade credit to India increased significantly to US$ 7.6 billion in 2009-10 from net outflows of US$ 2.0 billion a year earlier, reflecting international confidence in domestic importers. After recording net inflows under non-resident deposits during the first three quarters, there were outflows during the last quarter of the 2009-10. Overall net non-resident deposits inflows stood lower at US$ 2.9 billion during 2009-10 as compared to US$ 2.9 billion during 2009-10 as compared to US$ 4.3 billion during 2008-09.

Net capital inflows increased significantly during 2010-11, mainly due to FII inflows, short-term trade credits and ECBs. The net surplus in the capital account in the first quarter of 2010-11 exceeded the levels of the previous two quarters, as well as the financing need in the current account. There was a compositional shift across different components of capital flows. Foreign investment, which used to be a major constituent of the capital account, showed some moderation, mainly due to the slowdown in Foreign Direct Investment (FDI) inflows. Net inflows by FIIs were also lower during the April-June, 2010-11. FIIs, which were traditionally investing in equity market, started diversifying towards debt markets. The attraction of the debt market could be attributed to the rising interest rate environment in India and the near zero interest rate conditions in advanced countries over an extended period. Strong domestic demand along with the rising interest rate differentials also led to higher net inflows of External Commercial Borrowings (ECBs) during the quarter. Short-term trade credit to India recorded a large net inflow of US$ 5.6 billion in the first quarter of 2010-11 (as against a net outflow of US$ 1.5 billion during the corresponding quarter of 2009-10) in line with the increase in imports associated with strong domestic economic activity and improved conditions in the global financial markets. Banking capital recorded inflows of US$ 4.0 billion during the quarter, mainly due to overseas foreign currency borrowings of banks and net inflows under NRI deposits. Debt flows during the quarter at about US$12 billion accounted for almost 64 per cent of total net capital flows.

In 2010-11 both gross inflows of US$ 499.4 billion outflows of US$ 437.4 billion under the capital account were higher than gross inflows of US$ 345.8 billion and outflows of US$ 294.1 billion in the preceding year. In net terms, capital inflows increased by 20.2 per cent to US$ 62.0 billion (3.7 per cent of GDP) in 2010-11 vis-a-vis US$ 51.6 billion (3.8 per cent of GDP) in 2009-10 mainly on account of trade credit and loans (ECBs and banking capital). The Non-debt flows or foreign investment comprising FDI and portfolio investment (ADRs/GDRs and FIIs) on net basis decreased by 21.4 per cent from US$ 50.4 billion in 2009-10 to US$ 39.7 billion in 2010-11. Decline in foreign investment was offset: by the debt flows component of loans and banking capital which increased by 130.3 per cent from US$ 14.5 billion in 2009-10 to US$ 33.4 billion in 2010-11.

Inward FDI showed a declining trend while outward FDI showed an increasing trend in 2010-11 vis-a-vis 2009-10. Inward FDI declined from US$ 33.1 billion in 2009-10 to US$ 25.9 billion in 2010-11. Sector-wise, deceleration during 2010-11 was mainly on account of lower FDI inflows under manufacturing, financial services, electricity, and construction. Country-wise, investment routed through Mauritius remained the largest component of FDI inflows to India in 2010-11 followed by Singapore and the Netherlands. Outward FDI increased from US$ 15.1 billion in 2009-10 to US$ 16.5 billion in 2010-11. With lower inward FDI and rise in outward FDI, net FDI (inward minus outward) to India stood considerably lower at US$ 9.4 billion during 2010-11 (US$ 18.0 billion a year earlier).

Net portfolio investment flow witnessed marginal decline to US$ 30.3 billion during 2010-11 as against US$ 32.4 billion in 2009-10. This was due to decline in ADRs/GDRs to US$ 2.0 billion in 2010-11 from US$ 3.3 billion in 2009-10, even though FII inflows showed marginal increase to US$ 29.4 billion in 2010-11 from US$ 29.0 billion in 2009-10. Other categories of capital flows, namely debt flows of ECBs, banking capital, and short-H1 of 2010-11 as compared to US$ 9.5 billion during H1 of 2009-10.

Risk aversion in the global financial markets has slackened the pace of capital flows to India. FDI inflows remained robust averaging US$ 4.9 billion per month during April-August 2011 but moderated to US$ 3.2 billion per month during September-November 2011. Pick up in FII flows has been mainly on account of investment in debt instruments. Several measures have been undertaken to improve inflows of external commercial borrowings (ECBs) and NRI deposits. While inflows on account of NR(E)RA and NRO accounts were higher during April-December 2011, the same on account of FCNR (B) accounts were negative. ECBs and FCCBs by Indian companies due for redemption in Q4 of 2011-12 are estimated to be less than US$ 4 billion. Recognising the global macro-economic and financial market conditions, the Reserve Bank raised all-in-cost ceiling on ECBs. The increase in the all-in-cost ceiling, and emphasis on bringing immediately the proceeds of the ECBs meant for rupee expenditure in India, augur well for raising overseas borrowings and financing the CAD. Also, greater flexibility has been given to banks in mobilising nonresident deposits by further deregulating interest rates on NRE and NRO accounts.

Although recent measures by the European Central Bank and other central banks may have eased financing conditions for banks in the euro area, deleveraging by some European banks has begun to affect cross-border lending to the emerging markets. Therefore, actual ECB inflows in the coming quarters would largely depend on risk perception of European banks. If risk aversion persists in the global financial markets, there might be some implications for cost of obtaining external funding.

The exacerbation in CAD during 2011-12 led to depletion of reserves notwithstanding improved capital flows. Since Q1 of 2012-13, concerns about the growth and financial health of euro area countries have further intensified. In addition, signs of weakness in the US and China have also made investors more cautious and driven up global financial market volatility. These factors, combined with weakening domestic macroeconomic conditions, led to a net FII outflow of US$ 1.7 billion in Q1 of 2012-13. Concerns about the domestic business environment appear to be weighing on FDI inflows as well. NRI deposits, however, have picked up. Since concerns about the growth outlook for AEs seem to have prompted investors to reconsider the resilience of emerging market growth as well, the outlook for capital flows to EDEs including India remains subdued. The second quarter of 2012-13 witnessed a turnaround in FII flows. While in Q1 of 2012-13, FIIs disinvested in the equity segment that were partially offset by their net investments in the debt segment, FII investments in Q2 improved distinctly in both segments. There was a surge in portfolio inflows after the reform measures were initiated in mid-September 2012, with net FII investment of over US$ 5.5 billion in a month and a half.

FDI flows to India moderated to US$ 10.7 billion during April-August 2012 compared with US$ 19.6 billion during April-August 2011.

While net inflows under FDl moderated somewhat during April-November 2012, net inflows by foreign institutional investors (FII) have shown a significant uptrend. Net FII inflows during 2012-13 (up to January 18) at US$ 18.8 billion were significantly higher than during the corresponding period of the previous year (US$ 7.6 billion), thus providing temporary comfort for financing of CAD (Table 1). Besides improved global liquidity and sentiment, robust FII inflows were largely the outcome of improved perception about the domestic economy, driven by recent reforms announced by the government since September 2012. These reforms include, inter alla, liberalised FDl norms for the retail, insurance and pension sectors, a roadmap for fiscal consolidation and an increase in FII limits in the corporate and government debt markets. The FII Investment limits in government Securities and corporate bonds were raised by US$ 5 billion each, taking the total investment limit in domestic debt (including corporate debt for infrastructure) to US$ 75 billion. while the increased limit may enhance debt inflows, they do not provide a solution to CAD financing on a sustainable basis.

Much of the recent FII Investment under the G-sec limits has flown into short term T-bills, enhancing the refinancing risks to external debt. On the other hand, a range-bound currency after a bout of depreciation has made the Indian equity market attractive for Flls. Going forward, the implementation and acceleration in domestic reforms would be critical for sustained equity flows to the economy. Though the risk aversion in global markets declined during the previous quarter, the flows could be volatile given the euro area risks.

TABLE 1

Capital Flows

(US$ billon)

Component	2011-12				2012-13		
	Q1	Q2	Q3	04	Q1	Q2	Q3
				Avarage of montnly flows			
1	2	3	4	5	6	7	8
FDI in India	2 4.1	33.1	4 2.3	51.5	62.0	7 3.4	81.9*
FDI by India	1.0	1.0	0.6	1.0	0.7	0.5	0.9*
Flls	0.8	-0.5	0.6	4.7	-0.6	2.6	3.3
ADRs/GDRs	0.1	0.1	0.03	0.01	0.03	0.03	0.0
ECB	1.0	1.6	-0.3	0.8	0.1	0.5	1.3
NRI	0.4	0.9	1.1	1.6	2.2	0.9	0.9*

*: October— November

Benefitting from higher interest rates and a weakening rupee, non-resident Indians (NRIs) nearly doubled their deposits with banks in India during April-November 2012 compared with the corresponding period of 2011-12. Net flow through external Commercial borrowings (ECBs)was higher during Q3 of 2012-13 compared to previous quarter, despite high principal repayments made by the Indian corporate sector. ECBs were mainly raised for the import of capital goods. new projects and the redemption of FCCBs.

INITIATIVES TO ATTRACT FOREIGN INVESTMENT AND EXTERNAL COMMERCIAL BORROWINGS

Expansion of Qualified Foreign Investors (QFIs) Scheme

In Budget 2011-12, the government, for the first time, permitted qualified foreign investors (QFIs), who meet the know-your-customer (KYC) norms, to invest directly in Indian MFs. In January 2012, the government expanded this scheme to allow QFIs to directly invest in Indian equity markets. Taking the scheme forward, as announced in Budget 2012- 13, QFIs have also been permitted to invest in corporate debt securities and MF debt schemes subject to a total overall ceiling of US$ 1 billion. In May 2012, QFIs were allowed to open individual noninterest-bearing rupee bank accounts with authorized dealer banks in India for receiving funds and making payment for transactions in securities they are eligible to invest in. In June 2012, the definition of QFI was expanded to include residents of the member countries of the Gulf Cooperation Council (GCC) and European Commission (EC) as the GCC and EC are the members of the Financial Action Task Force (FATF).

INITIATIVES TO ATTRACT FII INVESTMENT

As regards FII investment in debt securities, there has been progressive enhancement in the quantitative limits for investments in various debt categories. In June 2012, the FII limit for investment in G-Secs (government securities) was enhanced by US $ 5 billion, raising the cap to US $ 20 billion. The scheme for FII investment in long-term infra bonds has been made attractive by gradual reduction in lock-in and residual maturity periods criteria. In November 2012, the limits for FII investment in GSecs and corporate bonds (non-infra category) have been further enhanced by 5 billion each, taking the total limit prescribed for FII investment to US$ 25 billion in G-Secs and US$51 billion for corporate bonds (infra+non-infra). FII debt allocation process has also been reviewed for bringing greater certainty among foreign investors and helping them periodically re-balance their portfolios in sync with international portfolio management practices.

LIBERALIZATION IN EXTERNAL COMMERCIAL BORROWINGS POLICY DURING 2012-13

The important steps taken in the arena of external commercial borrowings (ECB) policy liberalization include:

i)   Enhancing the limit for refinancing rupee loans through ECB from 25 per cent to 40 per cent for Indian companies in the power sector

ii) Allowing ECB for capital expenditure on the maintenance and operation of toll systems for roads and highways so long as they are a part of the original project subject to certain conditions, and also for low cost housing projects

iii) Reducing the withholding tax from 20 per cent to 5 per cent for a period of three years (July 2012- June 2015) on interest payments on ECBs

iv) Introducing a new ECB scheme of US $10 billion for companies in the manufacturing and infrastructure sectors

v)   Permitting the Small Industries Development Bank (SIDBI) as an eligible borrower for accessing ECB for on-lending to the micro, small, and medium enterprises (MSME) sector subject to certain conditions

vi) Permitting the National Housing Bank (NHB)/ Housing Finance Companies to avail themselves of ECBs for financing prospective owners of low cost / affordable housing units

QUESTIONS

1. "New Economic Policy has encouraged the India has encouraged the India companies to explore the euro-market." Comment.
2. Discuss the importants of the NRI investments and Deposits in capital inflows.
3. Comment on the recent steps taken by the Government of India to attrack foreign portfolio investment.
4. Discuss the emerging trends and policy developments on foreign portfolio investments.
5. Critically examine the external commercial borrowings (ECBs) as an additional source of funding for corporate finance.
6. Discuss the special deposit schemes designed to attract the funds from non-residents.

REFERENCES

1. Butler, W.F., and E.C. kavesh. *How Business Economists Forecast*, part 3. Englewood Cliffs, N.J.: Prentice-Hall, 1966.
2. Cardarelli, Roberto, Selim Elekdag, and Subir Lall, 2009, "Financial Stress, Downturns, and Recoveries," IMF Working Paper 09/100 (Washington: International Mon- etary Fund).
3. Cashin, Paul, C. John McDermott, and Alasdair Scott, 2002, "Booms and Slumps in World Commodity Prices,"*Journal of Development Economics*, Vol. 69 (October 1), pp. 277–96.
4. Chen, Nai-fu, R. Roll, and S.A. Ross, "Economic Forces and the Stock Market." Working Paper Ser. B-73, University of California at Los Angeles, December 1983.
5. Claessens, Stijn, Giovanni DellfAriccia, DenizIgan, and Luc Laeven, 2010, "Lessons and Policy Implications from the Global Financial Crisis," IMF Working Paper 10/44 (Washington: International Monetary Fund).
6. Eichengreen, Barry, 2007, *Global Imbalances and the Lessons of Bretton Woods* (Cambridge, Massachusetts: MIT Press).
7. Gooding, Arthur E., "Quantification of Investors' Perceptions of Common Stocks: Risk and Return Dimensions," *Journal of Finance* 30, no. 5 (December 1975): 1301-1316.
8. Gray, William S. III. "The Anatomy of a Stock Market Forecast." *Journal of Portfolio Management* 16, no. 1 (Fall 1989).
9. Keran, Michael W. "Expectations, Money, & the Stock Market," *Review*. Federal Reserve Bank of St. Louis, Jan. 1971.
10. Moor, Roy E. "The Use of Economics in Investment Analysis," *Financial Analysts Journal*. Nov.-Dec. 1971.
11. Moore, Geoffrey H., and Julius Shiskin. *Indicators of Business Expansions and Contractions.* National Bureau of Economic Re-search, 1967.
12. Schwert, William: "Stock Market Volatility," *Financial Analysts Journal*. May-June 1990, pp. 23-34.
13. Siegel, Jeremy J. "Does It Pay Stock Investors to Forecast the Business Cycle?" *The Journal of Port-folio Management* 18, no. 1 (Fall 1991).
14. Spigelman, Joseph H. "What Basis for Superior Performance?" *Financial Analysts Journal*, May-June 1974, p. 32.
15. Tobin, James: " Liquidity Preference as Behavior towards Risk." *Review of Economic Studies*, February 1958. pp. 65-85.
16. Various Issues of Economic Survey(GOI)

17. Wagner, Jerry, Steven Shellans and Richard Paul, "Market Timing Works Where It Matters Most... in the Real World," *Journal of Portfolio Management* 18, no. 4 (Summer 1992).

18. Williams, Arthur: *Managing Your Investment Manager*, Dow Jones-Irwin, New York, 1990.

48

Manias, Panics and Crashes:
Switching Policies in Financial Crises

INTRODUCTION

The jargon of economic and finance contains numerous colourful expressions to denote a market-determined asset price at odds with any reasonable economic explanation. Such words as *tulip menia, bubble, chain letter, Ponzi scheme, panic, crash,* and *financial crises* immediately evokes images of frenjied and probably irrational speculative activity. Many of these terms have emerged from specific speculative episodes which have been sufficiently frequent and important that they underpin a strong current belief among economists that key capital markets sometimes generate irrational and inefficient pricing and allocational outcomes.

Before economists relegate a speculative event to the inexplicable or bubble category, however, we must exhaust all reasonable economic explanation. While such explanations are often not easily generated due to the inherent complexity of economic phenomena, the business of economists is to find clever fundamental market explanation for events; and our methodology should always require that we search intensively for market fundamental explanations.

The perception of an increased probability of large returns might be triggered by genuine economic good news, by a convincing new economic theory about payoffs or by a fraud launched by insiders acting strategically to trick investors. It might also be triggered by the uninfluenced market participants correctly inferring changes in the distribution of dividends by observing price movements generated by the trading of informed indices. While some of these perceptions might in the end prove erroneous, movements in asset prices based on them are fundamental and not just bubble movements. In this chapter we will look at some of the swindlers who prey on get rich quick dream and at the speculative bubbles that are fed by the contagious hopes find/we will examine some reported investments that use financial flim-flam to offer returns that are literally too good to be true. Then we will look at the willingness of people to invest with strangers and in unknown companies. Finally, we will examine some examples of the madness of crowds, instances where investors as a group pushed asset prices to levels that, in retrospect, were far from intrinsic values.

PYRAMIDS AND PONZI SCHEMES

First everyone has received a chain letter, asking the recipient to send money to the person at the top of a list of names, to remove the top name and place his or her name at the bottom, and to send the revised list on to several other people. The letter promises that, if all goes well, soon the mailbox will be overflowing with money. Chain letters are an illegal fraud as are Ponji schemes, pyramids, and related get-rich-quick schemes based on the lausible, but fallacious, chain-letter arguments.

Charles Ponzi's Sleight of Hand

In chain-letter principle can be illustrated by the infamous Charles Ponzi. In 1920, Ponzi promised to pay Massachusetts investors 50 percent interest every forty-five days - com-pounded 8 times a year,$ 1 would grow to $ $1.50^8 = \$ 25.63$, an effective annual rate of return of 2463 percent. His stated plan was to arbitrage the difference between to official and open market price of Spanish pesos he would buy Spanish pesos cheap in the open market, use these pesos to buy international Postage Union Coupons, and then trade the coupons for U.S. postage stamps at the higher official exchange rate. If everything worked as planned, he could buy 10 cents worth of U.S. postage stamps for a penny. (But it was not al all clear how he would convert these stamps back into cash). In practical, he received $ 15 million from investors and appears to have bought only $ 61 in stamps.

If he did not invest the money he received, how could he possibly afford to pay a 50 percent return every forty-five days? He could not. But he could create a temporary illusion of doing so. Suppose that one person invests $ 100, and Ponzi puts the investment in a safe ptece. If Ponzi now finds another two persons to invest $ 100 apiece, then he can pay the first person $ 150, keep $ 150 for himself, and leave the original $ 100 untouched. Now, he has 45 days to find few more people who are willing to invest $ 100, so that he can pay each of the last two investors $ 150 and keep $ 100 for himself. These few investors then can be paid off with the money from 8 new ones, and these 8 from 16 more.

The Fallacy

In a Ponzi scheme, money from new investors is used to pay off earlier ones, and it works as long as there are enough new investors. The problem is that the pool of fish is exhausted surprisingly soon, the twenty-first round requires a million new people, and the thirtieth round requires a billion more. At some point, the scheme runs out of new people and those in the last round (the majority of investors) are left with nothing. A Ponzi scheme merely transfers wealth from late entrants to early entrants.

Ponzi's 1920 scam collapsed after few months when a Boston newspaper discovered that during the time that he supposedly bought $ 15 million in postage coupons, the total amount sold worldwide came to only $ 1 million. Despite his protestations that he could pay off his investors by incorporating and selling shares of stock to other investors, the state of Massachusetts froze his accounts and sent Ponzi to jail for ten years.

A Ponzi scheme is also called a *pyramid deal*, since its working can be visualised by imagining a pyramid with the initial investors at the top and the latest on the bottom; the pyramid collapses when the next round does not materialise. At illegal pyramid parties, people pay a fee to go to one location and pass chain letters among themselves. Even though it is patently obvious that no one goes home richer unless others go home poorer, greed blinds the participants to the likelihood that they will lose money.

Investments That Were Too Good to be True

Ponzi schemes typically lure investors by promising to channel their money to a unique investment or to a fabulous money manager. The best protection is sober reflection and common sense. If it looks too good to be true, it probably is. Of course, greed is powerful emotion and it often tramples common sense. Here are some notorious cases.

A Florida investment advisor raised $ 61 million over a 14- year period beginning in the 1970s by paying investors tax-free returns of upto 15%. As it turned out, the income investors received was not tax-free and, according to a court-appointed receiver, came almost from the cash deposited by new investors - a Ponzi scheme. Another scheme that began in the 1960 was supposed to import low-grade *industrial wine* in U.S. from Europe for salad dressing, earning a minimum 30% return every nine months. There is no such thing afc industrial wine, but this Ponzi scheme lasted 10 years and took in $ 26 million before it collapsed. Again in another Ponzi scheme, J. David Dominelli, a previously obscure stock broker, formed J. David & Co. in 1979 in U.S. Reports of 40% annual returns trading foreign currencies lured investors and millions of dollars, allowing Dominelli to build a financial empire that included six homes, three planes, and dozens of cars. Investors efforts to retrieve their money eventually exposed J. David's as a Ponzi scheme with an $ 80 million deficit and forced the company into bankruptcy in January, 1984. In 1985, Dominelli admitted that he had lied about virtually every aspect of his operation, pleaded guilty to fraud and tax evasion, and was sentenced to 20 years in federal prison.

Millions of dollars have also changed hands in Ponzi schemes disguised as business franchises. The avowed aim of these illegal schemes is to sell some product, such as cosmetics or a diet supplement, but virtually all of the activity involves selling franchises to people hoping to sell franchises to others. The pyramid collapses when it runs out of new people or when it is shut down as an illegal pyramid or lottery. The company founder then retires or moves on and starts another pyramid.

BLIND FAITH AND HIGH HOPES

Investment decisions are based on more than arithmatic calculations and mechanical rules. Inevitably, investors make subjective decisions, influenced by all-too-human emo-tions. It is natural to hope that a clever investment will yield quick and easy wealth. The hope sometimes turns into greed, blurring vision and dulling common sense. And when beggars and showshine boys, barbers and beauticians can tell how to get rich, it is time to remind oneself that there is no more dangerous illusion titan the belief that one can get something for nothing. Unfortunately, people who are trusting (and a bit greedy) often invest in dubious plans recommended by virtual strangers. One cautionery rule is to be wary of any advisor who *is* eager for you to invest If the plan is so good, why does the advisor need your money ? A second rule is that if you do not understand it, don't invest in it.

AGGRESSIVE SALES PEOPLE

Boiler-room operations involves aggressive sales people dialing phone numbers after phone number, trying to persuade gullible people to buy desert lac, take overpriced vacations, or invest in worthless or highly speculative securities.

One of the biggest boiler-room operation ever was exposed in 1988. Based in Switzer-land, it took an estimated $ 250 million from thousands of investors in forty countries, with individual losses ranging from $ 1000 to $ 7,50,000. The scam began with newspaper advertisements offering free samples of an investment newsletter. Those who responded were soon called by a persuasive British or American salesman. According to one attorney, "They all had James Bond-type names - James Church or Charles Snow, or Fleming Windsor. They were very smooth and they all knew how to dose a deal. The salesman would prompt obscure companies that were trading, or had once traded, in the U.S. over-the-counter market. After a purchase, investors received worthless stock certificates, and meaningless computer printout confirming the transaction. Every few months, the boiler room would move to a new Swiss city, to keep ahead of Swiss authorities who might have been alerted by suspicious investors.

A variation is a *bucket shop,* when sales people take orders to buy and sell legitimate securities but do not actually make the trades, because they assume that most of their customers will lose money. Instead of buying at $ 40, returns $ 30 after the sale, and pockets the difference (plus the commission charged for the non-existent transactions). If the customers somehow make money then die bucket shop packs up and moves on before the police arrive.

FALSE PROPHETS

In 1940, an astute observer wrote about the romantic Wall Streeter-and they all romantics, whether they be villains or philanthropists. Else they would never have chosen this business which is a business of dreams. They continued to dream of conquests, coups and power, for themselves or for the people they advise.

These dream draw people to the get-rich-quick games. Faced with great uncertainty and the chance to make millions, people turn to seminars, newsletters, and books that combine the comfort of expert opinion with the excitement produced by unleashed greed. The impounded hopes and wild dreams of investors are also deflated in the ability of small, untested firms to market their securities. Carried to the extreme, the search is for a concept, a story, a hint of growth that will lead other investors to jump or the bandwagon - a few steps after your boarding. As one underwriter put it, *"We're basically selling hope and hopes been teal good to us".* A wonderful example is *How I made Two Million in the Stock Market* (written by a gypsy dancer and, judging from the book itself, the answer to the question is "with a lot of luck"). Some investment games and doom-and-gloom prophets who exploit investor fears and insecurities by predicting the collapse of financial markets, the economy, and, indeed, civilization. The most extreme advise storing water, food and ammunition and selecting a secure cave for survival to the barbaric times ahead. These professional pessimists are unfazed by the continued inaccuracy of their vision. If the prediction of runaway inflation does not work out, they change the forecast to uncontrolled deflation and sell some more books. There is always a market for fear.

SPECULATIVE BUBBLES

From time to time, investors are gripped by what, in retrospect, seems to have been mass hysteria. The price of some commodity or security climbs higher and higher, beyond all reason, a *speculative bubble,* in that nothing justifies the rise in price except the hope that it will go higher still. Then, suddenly, the bubble pops and the price collapses. With hindrights, it is hard to understand why people were so foolish and bought at such crazy prices. Yet paradoxically, at the same time the bubble it seems foolish to sit on the sidelines while others become rich.

Imitative Behaviour

When humans are in an unfamiliar environment — confronted by events they do not fully understand, with consequences they cannot predict — they tend to imitate each other's behaviour. In one interesting psychology experiment, subjects were told that they were testing an experimental vitamin supplement and then injected with spinephrine, a hormone that causes temporary rapid heart beats and hand tremors. Put in a room with actors who supposedly had been given the vitamin supplement too, the subjects typically imitated the actor's behaviour, whether it was light-hearted or depressed.

The same sort of imitative behaviour is observed less formally everyday, in our desire to purchase the latest fashionable doming, entertainment, and automobiles. In financial markets, we have a natural tendency to believe that something is a good investment if others think so too, which leads us to act collectively as an unthinking herd.

The Building of a Bubble

Speculative bubbles generally begin with important events of real economic significance, such as the discovery of gold, an outbreak of war etc. Seeing the profits made by some other investors, others rush to get a piece of the action, pushing prices higher. Soon, greed displaces common sense, and swindlers emerge to part fools from their money. The upward push of prices becomes a speculative bubble in the sense that most of the participants are buying not for the income that their investment might produce but in anticipation that prices will keep rising - a self-fulfilling prophecy as long as there are more buyers then sellers. When everyone is convinced that the investment is a good one, there is no more left who will by and push the price higher still. The bubble burst when buyers no longer outnumber sellers. There is a selling stampede, and prices collapse. In the frantic rush for the exit, very few make it through the door.

Table 1 gives the hypothetical cases of speculative bubbles. In these examples, there is a constant, perpetual annual dividend (or other cash flow) of Rs. 10. At C10 per cent required return, the investment's cash flow is worth Rs.10/.10 = Rs.100 to an investor willing to hold the asset for keeps. What if the market price is Rs.200 ? As Rs.10 dividend on a Rs.200 investment is inadequate, and investors should show it. But what if the price of the asset is Rs. 200 now and is expected to be Rs. 210 a year from ow ? A Rs.10 plus a Rs.10 capital gain will provide the requisite 10 percent return, thus justifying a price of Rs.200. Why will pay Rs. 210 a year from now for a Rs. 10 dividend ? They will if they are confident that the price will keep rising, to be Rs. 221 a year later (A Rs.10 divident plus Rs.ll capital gain is a 10 per cent return on an investment of Rs. 210). By the same logic, Rs. 221 is justified by a price of Rs. 233.10 the year after that. No price is too high, as long as the price can be counted to go higher still. *Does this seem like the Greater Fool Theory?* It is, indeed.

TABLE 1
Two Hypothetical Speculative Bubbles

Year	Annual Dividend	Investment Having a constant Required Return		Investment Having a Rising Required Return	
		Required Return (%)	Price	Required Return (%)	Price
0 ·	Rs.10	10	Rs. 200.0	12	Rs.200.0
1	10	10	210.0	14	214.0
2	10	10	221.0	16	234.0
3	10	10	233.1	18	261.0
4	10	10	244.4	20	298.5
5	10	10	261.0		348.2

A speculative bubble is a run up of prices that is not justified by the underlying economic fundamentals (the present value of an asset's cash flow), but instead is sustained by a belief that prices will keep rising. The bubble bursts when participants are no longer willing to believe in even higher prices. In Table 1, consider what happens in the 5th year if people begin to doubt that the price will continue rising. Even if they think that an asset's price will hold at Rs.261, a Rs.10 dividend is only Rs. 10/Rs. 261 = 3.83% return, far from the requisite 10 per cent. If many rush to sell, putting downward pressure on the price, others may become convinced of an impending capital loss, creating panic selling with no buyer to be found.

The buildup of a speculative bubble is rational in the sense that higher prices today can be rationalised by even higher prices tomorrow. The participants may even be convinced that market prices have strayed far above economic fundamentals but be equally confident that they can get out before the bubble bursts. The inherent uncertainty of speculative bubbles may make them nervous, but that anxiety, too, can be overcome by sufficiently high anticipated prices. The last two columns in Table-1 show the case of a steadily rising required return, to compensate for increasing anxiety about when the bubble will pop. Sufficient bullish price predictions can always satisfy those willing to believe - a point illustrated by Tulipmania.

TULIPMANIA: THE LEGEND

Tulip were virtually unknown in western Europe until 1554, when an ambassador from Vienna brought bulbs back from Turkey. The offspring spered across Europe, catching the fancy of gardners, especially wealthy ones in the Netherlands who were willing to pay handsomely for bulbs that would produce unusual flowers. In 1634, rising prices and rumours that tulips were becoming fashionable in France lured non-gardners into the Dutch tulip market in force, looking for easy money and creating Tulip mania.

With tulip prices rising briskly, it seemed a simple matter to buy a few bulbs and sell them a short while later for a substantial profit. In addition each growing season a bulb can be split into two or three. Could there by any easier way to get rich ? What seems to have escaped notice is that the same potential for multiplying the supply will cause prices to fall when the number of bulbs eventually exceeds demand.

Tulip must be in ground from September until June; so trades made during these months are for future delivery. By 1636, the tulip market was dominated by trading in taverns among non-professionals with little cash or bulbs. As there were no margin requirements, buyers could agree to pay a price beyond their means, anticipating that they would resell the bulbs for a profit before summer delivery.

By November 1636, speculation had spread to even the common tulip varieties, and during January 1637, the prices jumped by a factor of ten or twenty. For instance, a bulb that might have fetched $ 20 in the summer of 1636 traded for $ 160 in January and for $ 2000 a few weeks later. The prices of exotic bulbs topped $ 50,000 and an investor was reported to have paid $ 80,000 for an especially rare bulb. The prices agreed to in the taverns were even higher. Then in February 1637, the market crashed virtually overnight. As people rushed to sell, prices collapsed and buyers vanished, since no one wanted to buy tulips if the prices will be lower tomorrow.

Existing agreements were in limbo until April 1637, when Holland formally suspended all tulip contracts, allowing gardners to sell the bulbs they would dip up that summer at fresh prices. A century later, tulip prices were less than one-thousandth of the prices at the peak of Tulipmania.

STOCK MARKET BUBBLES

There have been several dramatic historical episodes when the stock market was seized by a collective euphoria, as investors seemed to put aside common sense and, instead, were willing to believe whatever was necessary to justify ever higher stock prices. The subsequent, terrifying collapse of prices not only caused fortunes to evaporate, but persuaded many investors that they would never buy stock again. We will look first at an English bubble in the 18th century, then the stock market crash that accompanied the Great Depression, and, finally, at more recent crashes of unprecedented magnitude.

The South Sea Bubble

In 1720, the South Sea Company took over the British government's debt in exchange for exclusive trading privileges with Spain's American colonies. Encouraged by the Com-pany's inventive book keeping, English citizens rushed to invest in this exotic venture. As the price of the South Sea Company's stock soared from £120 on January 28 to £ 400 on May 19, £ 800 on June 4 and £1000 on June 22, the investors became rich, and thousands of other investors rushed to join their ranks. Soon entrepreneurs were offering stock in even more grandiose schemes and were deluged by frantic inventors not wanting to be left out. It scarcely mattered what the scheme was. One promised to build a wheel for perpetual motion. Another was forced for carrying on an undertaking of great advantage, but nobody is to know what it is. *"The shares for this mysterious offering were priced at £100 each, with a promised annual return of £100; after selling all the stock within five hours, the promoter immediately left England and never returned. Yet another stock offer was for the nitvender, or selling of nothing."* When the bubble burst, most of the stock for these myriad ventures became worthless, and fortunes and dreams were lost.

As with all speculative bubbles, there were many believers in the Greater Fool Theory. While some suspected that prices were unreasonable, the market was dominated by people believing that prices would continue to rise, at least until they could sell to the next fool in line. In the spring of 1720, Sir Issac Newton said," *I can calculate the wisdom of the heavenly bodies, but not the madness of people"*, and sold his South Sea shares for a £ 7000 profit. However, later that year, he bought shares again, just before the bubble burst, and lost £20,000. Similarly, when a banker invested £500 in the third offer of South Sea stock (in August 1720), he explained that *"when the rest of the world are mad, we must imitate them in some measure"*. After James Milner, a member of the British Parliament, was bankrupted by the South Sea bubble, he explained that *"I said indeed that ruin must some come upon us but I owe it came two months earlier than I expected"*.

THE GREAT CRASH

The 1920s were an exciting and turbulent decade - for the world economy, for social moves and for the stock markets. In 1924, the Don Jones Industrial Average reached 100. In December 1927, it reached past 200, to 250 in October 1928 and 300 in December. Nine months later, in September 1929, it attained a peak of 386. It seemed as if investors could make money effortlessly by buying stock in rock-solid companies. Between March 1928 and September 1929, American Can went from 77 to 181-7/8, American Telephone from 179-1/2 to 335-5/8, General Electric from 128-3/4 to 396-1/4, and US Steel from 138-1/8 to 279-1/8.

Predicting the future is always treacherous, and history is full of well-informed people making, what, with hindright, are foolish statements. At breakfast before Waterloo, Napo-leon remarked, *"Wellington is a bad General, the English are bad soldiers; we will settle the matter by lunch time"*. In 1899, the Director of the U.S; Patent Office said, *"Everything that can be invented has been invented"*. Thomas Edison believed that *"the phonograph is not of any commercial value"*, and President Hayes said of the telephone, *"That's amazing invention, but who would ever want to use one ?"* Lord Kelvin, a scientist and President of Britain's Royal Society proclaimed, *"Heavier than air flying machines are impossible"*, and "Radio has no future". Harry Warner, the President of Warner Brothers said," *Who the hell wants to hear actors talk!"* and Thomas Watsom, the CEO of IBM said, "I *think there is a world market for almost five computers."*

The stock market and the economy are never easy to predict, and the crash ana the Great Depression were no exceptions. In his final message to Congress on December 4,1928, Calvin Coolidge boasted that *"no Congress of the United States ever assembled on surveying the state of the Union, has met with a more pleasing prospect than that which appears at the present time"*. Herbert Hoover took place office, and in July 1929 predicted that *"the outlook of the world today is for the greatest era of commercial expansion in history"*. On October 17,1929, Fleving Fischer, the greatest American economist of his day, asserted that stocks had reached *'what looks like a permanently high plateau"*.

The five-year bull market was over, and Fisher, could not have been more wrong. After a number of bad days, panic selling hit the market on Thursday, October 24. Terrified investors tried to sell at any price, and stock prices plunged, with the panic heightened by the fact that the ticker tape reporting transactions ran hours late, so that investors had no information about current prices. The market finally steadied in the afternoon when six prominent New York bankers put up $ 40 million apiece to buy stocks. But the market dropped again the following Monday and was hit by panic selling the next day, Black Tuesday, October 29. Again there was an avalanche of sell orders, more than the brokers and ticker tape could process, and more importantly, dwarfing the scattered buy orders. White Sewing Machine, for instance, had recently traded for $ 48; on Monday it dosed at $ 11-1/8. On Black Tuesday, in the complete absence of buy orders, a messanger boy bought shares for $1.

With fits and starts, the market decline continued. By November 13, the Dow had fallen an incredible 48 per cent as the prices of America's premier companies collapsed. American Can was down 53 per cent, and U.S. Steel 46 per cent. Nevertheless, Hoover's optimism persisted. In his December 3, 1929, State of the Union message, he concluded that *"the problems with which we are confronted are the problems of the growth and progess"*. In March 1930, both President Hoover and the Secretary of Commerce predicted that business would be normal by May. In early May, Hoover declared that, *"we have now passed the worst"; in late May, he predicted "recovery by the fall". In* June, he told a group that had come to Washington to urge increased government spending, *"Gentlemen, you have come sixty days too late. The depression is over"*. The President's cheerleading did not reassure the public. In October, the Republican National Chairman complained that *"persons high in Republican circles are beginning to believe that there is some concerted effort on foot to utilise the stock market as a method of discrediting the administration. Every time administration official give out an optimistic statement about business conditions, the market immediately drops"*.

The Dow recovered to nearly 300 in the spring of 1930 but then it began to long, tortuous slide, punctuated by brief, inadequate rallies before finally touching bottom at 42.84 in June 1932 - down 89 per cent from September 1929. It was not until 1956, twenty-seven years later, that the stock market regained its 1929 level.

The Great Depression was more than ajstock-market crash. Between 1929 and 1933, the nation's output fell by one-third, while the unemployment rate rose from 3 per cent to 25 per cent. More than one- third of the nation's banks failed, and household net worth dropped by 30 percent. Behind these aggregate numbers were millions of private tragedies. Many lost life savings in the stock-market crash and in the tidal wave of bank failures. Desperate people moved into shantly settlements (called Hoovervilles), slept under news-papers (Hoover Blankets), and scavenged for food when they could. Edmond

Wilson reported that *'there is not a garbage dump in Chicago which is not hunted by the hungry. Last summer in the hot weather when the smell was sickening and the flies were thick, there was a hundred people a day coming to one of the dumps'*. The Great Depression did not end until the Federal Government began spending nearly $ 100 billion a year during World War II.

Since World War II, indeed, only almost half of sharp stock market declines have been followed by recessions. In the other half, policy makers got the message. The most stable example in 1962, the nearest thing to a crash between 1929 and 1987. The Dow Jones Industrial Average fell 26 per cent in three months compared with 48 per cent in 2 and a half months in 1929. So 1962 was almost half of a Great Crash, but nothing happened in the real economy. The generalised anti-business atmosphere the markets had started to antici-pate did not materialise. Stocks started to recover, and the real economy marched on unhindered. Indeed, with the 1964 tax cuts, it entered one of its best periods of the century which, of course, brings in to 1987.

OCT.' 87 STOCK MARKETS CRASH AND ITS AFTERMATH

Stock markets around the world have gone through a classic financial panic, unique in its high-tech mechanics and the magnitude of the price collapse but no different from those of 1929, 1907 or 1893. The Dow Jones industrial average had dropped 261 points on three days before Black Monday. It fell a further 200 points in an hour and a half Monday morning on heavy volume of 154 million shares, nearly the volume of a normal day, but then rallied. Only in the afternoon did the market take fright. At 2.45 p.m. Dow hovered around 2000, according to Brady Commission. The final plunge to 1738 took just 75 minutes and sucked the average down one point every 17 seconds as some 125 million shares came pouring in. Some $ 500 billion in paper value, a sum equal to the entire GNP of France vanished into thin air. Volumes on the New York Stock Exchange topped 600 million shares, nearly doubling the all time record. Brokers could find only one word to describe the rout, an old word long gone out of fashion but resurrected because no other would do : "panic". The frenzy rose as it spread once again around tine globe. On Tuesday even though some stocks rebounded in early trading — the Dow was up 200 points at 10.30 a.m. — sell orders quickly swamped the exchange and many stocks stopped trading. By 12.15 the Dow was down 30 points (See Graph-I). Trading in futures contracts on the S&P 500, the basis for most programme trading and portfolio insurance, ceased because so many of the underlying stocks had been halted with the futures trading at a record discount from the index's cash-value (see Graph-II). Only the relatively thinly traded futures contract on the Major Market Index, a Chicago Board of Trade contract based on a basket of 20 blue-chip stocks, continued to trade (See Graph-Ill). The sharp rebound at 12.45 - which could have been sparked by relatively little buying — evidently was able to rally the stock market, for the day, but not without narrowly avoiding a complete shut down and, in the words of Brady Report, raising the risk of a *"full-scale financial system breakdown"*.

How close had the system been to disaster ? The words of the President's Task Force are worth quoting in full:

> *"Although Monday was the day of the dramatic stock market decline, it was midday Tuesday that the securities markets and the financial system approached breakdown. First, the ability of securities markets to price equities was in question. There were few buyers in either market and individual stocks ceased to trade Investors began to question the value of equity assets. Second, the more serious, a wide-spread credit breakdown seemed for a time quite possible."*

It was a classic market panic - an example of an event which has occured from time to time throughout financial history. The risk was dispelled largely as a result of the monetary authorities forceful intervention. While the United States was undoubtedly the epicentre of the crash,, with very few exceptions, equity markets were affected worldwide, many recording historically steep single-day price declines.

What set it off? It is not easy to point out any one event or even any combination of events that can explain satisfactorily all that happened at that time. To be sure, from a US

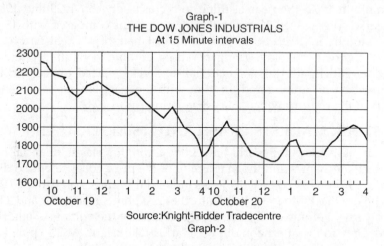

Graph-1
THE DOW JONES INDUSTRIALS
At 15 Minute intervals

Source:Knight-Ridder Tradecentre

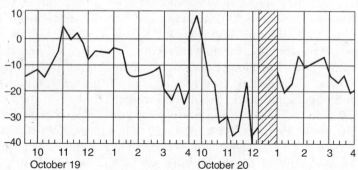

Graph-2

In points, at 15 minute intervals

Note : Trading in future contracts halted between

Source:Knight-Ridder Tradecenter

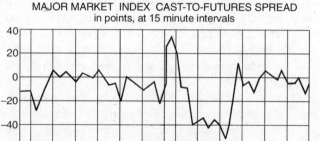

Graph-3
MAJOR MARKET INDEX CAST-TO-FUTURES SPREAD
in points, at 15 minute intervals

Source : Knight-Ridder Tradecenter

perspective the dollar was under pressure in the exchange markets; interest rates, especially long-term rates, had risen; inflationary expectations were building up; and there were strains in the process of international economic policy coordination. While these developments were disturbing, individually and collectively, there was no reason why they should have been decisive and negative, especially since over this same period economic performance was, in several crucial aspects, better than earlier expectations.

Dramatic changes in stock market indexes in 1987 have raised questions about funda-mental shifts in the volatility of share prices. Although volatility in stock prices inevitably results with investors' expectations about corporate earnings and interest rate changes, some observers maintain that innovations in trading techniques have introduced additional volatility into equity markets. Most worrying of all, the big investment funds run on so called *"portfolio insurance'* strategies were starting to become big sellers. Infact, John Phelan, Chairman of the N. Y.S.E., had made no secret of his worries about portfolio insurance. *"At some point in time, you are going to have a first class catastophe"*, he said in March 1987. Seven months later, it happened. As it turned out, the portfolio insurance concept was fatally flawed in two respects. One was that it encouraged investors to buy when shares went up and to sell when shares went down. If there was a trend, the portfolio insurers tended to exaggerate it. The other flaw was that of the concept dependent on what Greenspan calls *"an illusion of liquidity"*, the belief that investors could buy or sell huge lines of stocks or futures without wrecking their prices. This was to be a key element in the October disaster. Portfolio insurance had been one of the fads of the previous two years - the value of pension funds assets managed in this way had jumped from $ 8.5 billion, to more than $ 60 bn. in the space of a year. On the Friday before Black Monday, portfolio insurers sold the equivalent of over $ 2 billion, of stock - but it was nothing like enough. On the basis of the markets decline that week, their computer models dictated that at least $ 12 billion, of equities should have been sold. On a typical computer model, a 10 per cent fall in the market would call for sales of over 20 per cent of one's portfolio. Uncommonly large and concentrated portfolio insurance sales took place in the futures markets on both 19th and 20th October. These sales helped to generate a record drop in the futures price and hence a destablising discount of the futures on the cash index. The discount in turn diverted unprecedented portfolio insurance sales to the cash market. The large losses incurred on outstanding long positions in futures contracts, of the order of US$ 6 billion on the Monday, coupled with the immediate need to meet (variation) margins because of the daily cash settlement rule .(market-to-mar-ket), may have exacerbated forced selling in the stock exchange. The evidence indicates that a number of traders sold stock in anticipation of downward pressure on prices from portfolio insurance sales, as would be especially likely if they perceived the market as overvalued. It has been estimated that, given the price decline during the previous week, the "overhand" of unexecuted portfolio insurance programmes was between $ 8 and 14 billion at the Monday opening. In addition, index arbitrage failed to prevent the formation of persistant and sizeable discount of the futures on the cash index and transmitted selling pressure to the NYSE. The NYSE Report blames part of the Monday fall on the particularly large index arbitrage sales which did take place despite the implementation difficulties. By contrast, the Brady Report argues that it was precisely the failure of index arbitrage dose the discount which precipitated the fall. It stresses the destabilising expectational effect of the discount on the other investors, either in indicating the future value of the cash index or in generating expectations of further arbitrage selling. The SEC Report, on the other hand, remains non-committal on this issue. More generally, it would appear unreasonable to assign much responsibility for the crash to index arbitrage, since the strategy was passively transmitting selling pressure from the futures to the cash market. Rather, attention should be focused on the origin of hedging sales in futures markets - predominantly portfolio insurance and on those mechanisms which artificially magnified the future discount.

In addition to these financial innovations, there was a strong inherent tendency towards expansion which often has nothing to do with the financial needs of the economy for capital formation. By September 1987, the concept of the break-up value, or the value of a company if dismembered and its parts sold, came into prominence as a direct by product of the feverish takeover boom and everything that went with it; arbitrage, leverage, junk bonds, even insider information. Huge takeovers and leveraged buy-outs-in which a company is taken over largely with borrowed money - continued at even higher cash-flow and earnings multiples. What developed was a theory of "private market value" for companies far in excess of stock market value.

In discussing Black Monday, SEC Commissioner Joseph A. Grundfest in an article published in mid-1989 wrote:

> *Had all investors involved in portfolio immence found it possible, and desirable, to satisfy their demand for "insurance" by buying puts instead of relying on dynamic hedges, the market would have had more information about the intensity of investor concern about a downside move. Under these circumstances, there is reason to believe that prices might have not fallen so low on the downside had the market simply been better informed of investors' own concerns. Thus, to the extent position limits on index option forced investors away from the options market and into secret dynamic hedging strategies, the government's position limit restrictions may have unwillingly exacerbated the market's decline.*

Thus, the culprit might not be dynamic hedging/portfolio insurance but, instead, (i) the ability to develop a long-term exchange-traded index options market and *(ii)* government imposition of a regulatory feature - position limits - that impeded the use of the exchange-traded market.   Whether or not one is willing to accept this hypothesis, it should be understood that it is entirely untested and has therefore no empirical underpinning.

THE SCAM

The capital market in India recorded a phenomenal growth since 1980s and the share prices in the stock market touched the peak levels in the years 1991 to 1992. The All India Index Number of share prices computed by the Reserve Bank of India (RBI) on a weekly basis, with the base year 1980-81 equal to 100, recorded an increase from 554.9 in April 1991 and 571.3 in June 1991. The prices continued to rise further and RBI Index moved further to 771.9 in September 1991. By end December 1991, the index touched a level of 805.1. During the same period the Bombay Stock Exchange (BSE) sensitive index with the base year 1978-79 equal to 100 recorded an increase from 1193.61 on 1 April 1991 to 1361.72 on 21 June 1991 and moved up further 1912.35 on 16 September 1991. By end December 1991, presented by the Ministry of Finance in February 1992 reflected, "The market sentiments gathered further bullishness following the fiscal measures announced in the Union Budget for 1991-92 and the new policy initiatives of far-reaching consequences announced in the Industrial Policy Statement in July 1991, and the Trade Policy Statement in August 1991".

Though the share prices in the stock Market registered a slow rate of growth in the months of November and December 1991, the prices started once again booming from early January 1992. The RBI Index rose from 840.7 in January 1992 to 991.2 in February and touched an all time high of 1324.9 in March 1992. The rise in the BSE sensitive index was much more significant in the first quarter of 1992 when the index moved up from 2302.5 in January 1992 to 3047.68 in February and 4285 in March 1992 touching a peak of 4467.32 by 22 April 1992.

The scam is basically a deliberate and clinical misuse of public funds through various types of securities transactions with the aim of illegally siphoning of funds of banks and PSUs to select brokers for speculative returns. The irregularities in the securities and banking transactions, are manifestations of this chronic disorder since they involved not only banks but also the stock market, financial institutions, PSU, the central bank of the country and even the Ministry of Finance, other economic ministries in varying degrees. The most unfortunate aspect has been the emergence of a culture of non-accountability which permeated all sections of the Government and Banking system over the years. The state of the country's system of governance, the persistence of non-adherence to rules, regulations and guidelines, the alarming decay over time in the banking systems has been fully exposed. These grave and numerous irregularities persisted for so long that eventually it was not the observance of regulations but their breach that came to be regarded and defended as *"market practice"*. Through all these years, the ability of the concerned authorities to effectively address themselves to the problems has been tested and found wanting. The consequence of these irregularities in securities and banking transactions are both financial and moral. During the period from July 1991 to May 1992, the most glaring proof of the nexus between the irregularities in banks and the overheating of stock market which came to light is explained by the graphic representation of the BSE Index and the fact that there was *a* sharp increase in securities transactions during the corresponding period of the banks involved in serious irregularities related with the scam. What is more apparent is the systematic and deliberate abuse of the system by certain unscumpulous elements. It is abundantly clear that scam was the result of failure to check irregularities in the banking system and also liberalisation without adequate safeguards. There is also some evidence of collusion of big industrial homes playing an important role. It is because of these elements that the economy of the country had to suffer and while some gained thousands of crores, millions of investors lost their savings. The criminality of the prepetrators of the scam becomes all the more depicable as it was during this period that the country was passing through most trying times, economically and financially. An observation that the Committee has been constrained to make at a number of places that for all these not many have yet been identified end effectively punished.

To quote the Joint Parliamentary Committee (JPC), *"there are several dimensions of this entire episode: the functional one concerns the banks, brokers, PSUs and ministries, etc. Here accountability was largely absent, punishment for a wrong committed, was rare, an ethos of non-implementation prevailed all around."* The second aspect about which the Committee express its grave concern is the supervisory role and responsibility, the supervision failed from top to bottom is both self-evident. What is extremely worrisome is an unhappy side effect. In the entire apparatus of the Governmental machinery, a very demanding approach seems to pervade, that of transferring responsibility downwards. This distressing lack of fibre in the apparatus of governance can only debilitate the state. No system can work through regulations alone, of course, it cannot work if they be flouted; but much more than that, if a system be devoid of the moral quotient, of a commonsense appreciation of right from wrong, of a sense of public duty particularly when entrusted with public funds, then it cannot work.

Scam in the New Millennium

Stock markets around India crashed during March-April 2001. They are yet to recover from the sensex level of around 3000 where the index has been stagnating for the past two years ever since the crash. To probe the irregulaties and mainpulations in the stock market, the government announced the appointment of a joint parliamentary committee (JPC) on April 26, 2001. The JPC unanimous report was submitted to parliament on December 19, 2002.

At the height of the 1999-2000 boom, the sensex had crossed the high watermark of 6000. By April 12, 2001, the sensex had tumbled to 800 points below its early March level and a huge number of skeletons had started tumbling out of the cupboard: i) the involvement of a bewildering number of banks, brokers and corporates in exploiting every available loophole left gaping open by the government and its regulators; ii) rampant irregularities in all major stock exchanges; iii) persistent irregularities in several banks; iv) nexus between banks, brokers and corporates to subvert the integrity of the market; v) Ketan Parkeh's malfeasance; vi) swindles in urban cooperative banks like Madhavpura Mercantile Cooperative Bank in the deputy prime minister's constituency and City Cooperative Bank in the prime minister's constituency; vii) the payments crisis on the Calcutta Stock Exchange; and, finally, viii) misuse of the Mauritius route for investment in our stock markets.

The hardest hit, of course, was the innocent individual investor who had put his trust in the government and its regulators and other agencies to ensure the integrity of the market. It was evident that both the artificial boom and the inevitable bust involved a variety of malpractices. These went unchecked because the ministry of finance and its regulators, in particular the Securities Exchange Board of India (SEBI) and the Reserve Bank of India (RBI), grievously failed in the performance of their duties. The government and its regulators were more concerned with stoking the 'feel good factor' than with ensuring the integrity of the market when the market was dizzily spiralling upwards. They only got concerned when the market collapsed. As the JPC Report remarks: When stock markets were rising, there was general lack of concern to see that such a rise should be in consonance with the integrity of the market and not the consequence of manipulation or other malpractice. On the other hand, when the markets went into a steep fall, there was concern all over.

The small investor enters the market in the expectation that the government and its regulators will ensure the integrity of the market, so that whether the market rises or falls, market behaviour is not the consequence of rigging or other malpractices and irregularities. Of course, no one can stop fraudsters from attempting to deceive ordinary investors. But if there is persistent malpractice, and is known - or should be known - to the government and its regulators, and yet little or nothing is done quickly to restore the integrity to the market, then repeated fraud accompanied by persistent failure on the part of the authorities to close the loopholes becomes a scam. The JPC defines the expression 'scam' in the following terms:

> Individual cases of financial fraud in themselves may not constitute a scam. But persistent and pervasive misappropriation of public funds falling under the purview of statutory regulators and involving issues of good governance becomes a scam.

The issues dealt with in the JPC Report pertain to the 'persistent and pervasive' failure of the key regulators to perform their duties and the failures of 'good governance' pertaining primarily to the failure of the ministry of finance to perform its duties. They also include the failings of the department of company affairs as well as the investigative agencies which fall directly under the prime minister.

The duration of the scam has been defined by the JPC in the following terms:

The events that culminated in the exposure of the scam in March 2001 started approximately 18 months earlier.

As the NDA government took office in March 1998, three years before the 'exposure of the scam', the entire 18 months duration of the scam reflects on the statutory regulators at the time and the ministers responsible at the time for the deficiencies in 'good governance' which led to and pervasively persisted through the duration of the scam.

(i) The failures of regulation have been summed *by* the JPC as follows:

Regulatory authorities should have been able to lay down and implement guidelines and procedures that could prevent such a scam or at least activate red alerts that could lead to early detection, investigation and action against fraud as well as the rectification of any systemic deficiencies discovered.

(ii) The failures of governance have been summed up by the JPC as follows:

Equally, supervisory authorities and coordinating bodies such as the ministry of finance and HLCC (High Level Committee on Financial and Capital Markets) should have been more pro-active and vigilant in recognising that liberalisation requires strong and effective regulation, and greater autonomy for regulators must go hand-in-hand with the accountability of regulators to the country through ministry of finance which, in our scheme of constitutional jurisprudence, is responsible to parliament for the financial health of the economy, including sectors regulated by statutory and other regulators.

(iii) As regards the joint failings of regulation and governance, the JPC has this to say:

Concerted mutual interaction between government and the regulators, especially through the institutional mechanism of HLCC, could have signally contributed to effective pre-emptive and corrective action to forestall or moderate the scam by early detection of wrong-doing.

(iv) The JPC's final judgment then runs as follows:

Clearly, the various regulatory authorities were not able to foresee the situation leading to the scam and prevent it. Nor was adequate attention paid in government circles, particularly the ministry of finance as the custodian of the financial health of the economy and There can be no escaping government's responsibility to parliament and the country.

It is said that stock markets are the indicators of the financial health of the economy. It is a matter of grave concern that in less than three years the stock markets witnessed a second crisis. It was SEBI's job to ferret out the irregularities and defuse them before they below up. This was the primary job of SEBI which they failed to do on time.

Effective regulation is the key to market integrity. What control is to the command economy, regulation is to the market economy. The regulator is not there to see whether the market is going up or down but to ensure that whether the market rises or falls, this reflects market sentiment, not market manipulation or other irregularities. The regulator must also assume that at all times there are fraudsters looking for opportunities to exploit any weaknesses in regulation. The regulator must, therefore, ensure that existing regulations are being strictly observed; more important still, the regulator must be alert to any signals of regulations being subverted or by-passed so that corrective action is taken as quickly as possible. A regulator who waits for the horse to flee before bolting the stable door is not doing its duty. Tragically, the key statutory regulator for the stock exchanges, SEBI, fell flat on its face through both the boom and the bust: Regular inspection and follow-up action of stock exchanges was obviously not implemented properly by SEBI. The JPC have found that SEBI inspections were of very poor quality; that there was little follow-up to the deficiencies uncovered by SEBI's own inspection reports; that SEBI's nominee directors had a very poor record of attending meetings of the boards of stock exchanges; and that SEBI did nothing to correct 'apathy' on the part of the stock exchanges, which are the primary regulators of the stock market.

The JPC, lists five key areas of concern where "SEBI appears to have done nothing particularly substantive": i) monitoring and regulating the massive inflow of some ₹ 50,000 crore from abroad into the stock market; ii) mismatch between the primary and secondary stock market; iii) mismatch between the huge number of listed scrips and the small number of actively traded scrips; iv) rise in private placements to the detriment of the primary market; and v) 'negligence' in checking on whether, bull operators were overtly or covertly obtaining improper bank funding. Little wonder then that fraudsters had a field day deceiving investors while the government prided itself on the 'feel good factor' which pervaded the stock market.

Does the probe by a JPC into the stock market scandal smack of Tokenism? With due respect to on parliamentarians, it surely cannot be the case that they were more competent to investigate irregularities or downright fraud in the stock markets than a body specifically charged with the job. What is it, then, that JPC was likely to find that SEBI was incapable of finding? The answer is perhaps what the parliamentarians are sceptical of is not so much the competence of SEBI in investigating what, if anything, went wrong in the markets, but whether the *watchdog* was fully utilising that competence without fear or favour to use a favourite official expression. The JPC observed that the fault does not lie with SEBI alone: *much that went wrong might have been forestalled* had *the ministry of finance been more insistent on SEBI measuring up.*

THE GLOBAL FINANCIAL CRISIS AND BEYOND

The last four and a half years have been the most turbulent for the global economy since World War II. The crisis that began in a small corner of the financial system, i.e. the sub-prime mortgage market in the United States spread like wildfire to engulf the entire global financial system. The fall of Lehman in September 2008 was the proverbial last straw, making the crisis truly global in terms of outreach, impact and severity for both advanced and developing countries.

Countries have however been affected by the crisis differently and in varying degrees. The response to the crisis, however, has been equally swift, with concerted and coordinated efforts by governments and monetary authorities, through conventional and non-conventional fiscal and monetary instruments. Risks however remain, with rich countries continuing to be more vulnerable to double-dip recession. First, levels of unemployment remains high despite expansionary polices. Second, the extensive use of fiscal policy has meant a sizeable increase in fiscal deficit with the gross public debt to gross domestic product (GDP) ratio in advanced economies likely to rise from 75 to 115 per cent during 2008-2014. Third, the timing of *exit* is important. An early exit could increase the risk of another recession, while late exit could worsen public debt ratios, crowd out private investment and fuel inflationary expectations. Fourth, return of recession could cause havoc. With most policy toolkits already exhausted, public debt ratios skyrocketing and the balance sheets of central banks stretched, little ammunition remains for dealing with another crisis.

As emerging economies are ahead on the recovery curve, a major fallout has been large flows of capital from rich countries seeking to benefit from interest rate differentials and a stock market boom. As such outsized inflows are not supported by economic fundamentals, they are contributing to asset price bubbles and appreciation of domestic currency. A major fallout of the capital inflow is appreciation of domestic currency through creating a supply-demand imbalance in the foreign exchange market. The implication is similar to 'Dutch disease', a concept that owes its origin to offshore natural gas finds in the Netherlands in the 1960s, which led to a surge in capital flows and domestic currency appreciation that made exports uncompetitive and affected domestic industry through cheaper imports. The large inflows are more serious for countries with current account deficits, as domestic currency appreciation generally worsens the deficit. Together with loss of international competitiveness due to pegged exchange rates in some countries, the currency appreciation may make the recovery process more difficult in many emerging economies.

The sharp increase in stock market prices also increases speculative activity, besides contributing to market volatility. The boom and bust cycle in stock markets, since the onset of the crisis, has followed surge and reversal of capital flows to a significant extent. Such price volatility is detrimental for the orderly development of the capital markets and for stock markets to be a viable source for financing capital expenditure.

Another area of asset price bubble is commodities (oil, metals and agricultural), which have emerged as an 'asset class' due to high returns, their role as a hedge against inflation and diversification benefits on account of low correlations. A number of instruments like exchange traded funds (ETFs) are available, which make commodity investment accessible to institutional and individual investors. The rise in the global price of oil, however, could affect nascent recovery in oil- importing emerging economies. Besides, many emerging economies like India are being affected by the high food prices, where apart from domestic supply factors, investment demand appears to be playing a contributory role. A key element in the speculative flows is 'carry trade', which is characterized by borrowing in currencies with low interest and investment in higher interest currencies to take advantage of interest differentials. The carry trade money has also been flowing into stock markets in emerging economies to take advantage of higher returns. Record low interest rates in the US and other advanced countries are reportedly behind the trade. Carry trade and its unwinding have contributed significantly to currency volatility in the international markets during the recent past.

At the international level, the most direct challenge is to improve the regulation of the global financial system. Here, the reform agenda is well known and includes the coordinated, effective regulation of the group of global banks that form the backbone of the international financial system. At a basic level, this would be facilitated by a much deeper knowledge base about the international activities of these banks, which in turn requires much richer data collection, including the full integration of offshore international financial centres into the data matrix on cross-border financial activities. In related fashion, better analytical models of international systemic risk are needed in order to usefully interpret such data and develop appropriatae preventive policy responses.

At the same time, regulatory oversight cannot be an adequate substitute for ensuring that these banks have sufficient incentives to avoid excessive risk taking, while market discipline can also be enhanced through the design of capital structures that increase the incentives for investor monitoring. In addition to enhancing bank safety, it is essential to develop international resolution regimes that can handle failures among this group of banks.

The other main element in international policy reform is the construction of stronger international safety nets. Even with the recent increases in its resources, the lending capacity of the IMF has not kept pace with the growth in cross-border financial positions. Given the costliness of avoidable defaults to the debtor country and, through contagion effects, to the global system, international liquidity provision has to remain a fundamental component in the international financial architecture.

At the same time, the growing size of international balance sheets and the fiscal costs of backstopping international liquidity facilities reinforces the importance of designing bailout systems that limit moral hazard problems. In related fashion, the international system has to be better prepared to deal with insolvency cases, whether it is bankrupt sovereigns or bankrupt banking systems. To this end, the potential gains from establishing an international bankruptcy court could be revisited.

In additional to global-level institutional reform, the very high level of financial integration in Europe (especially within the euro area) calls for the development of regional-level institutions that can help to improve macroeconomic and financial stability. It remains to be seen whether there is sufficient political will to deliver the required European-level institutional reforms.

Still, even if the global and regional financial architectures were much improved, it would remain the case that domestic residents bear the largest costs in the event of a financial crisis. Accordingly, the main responsibility for adapting policy regimes to cope with financial globalisation lies with national governments. In general, domestic policy reforms should be complementary to parallel reforms at the international level.

While operating under the general auspices of international or regional regulatory frameworks, the implementation of financial regulation is set to remain primarily local (with the possible exception of very large financial institutions). A key step is the development of national bank resolution regimes that limit the systemic and fiscal costs of failing banks. In addition, as is well understood, a primary challenge is to develop effective macro-prudential instruments that limit systemic risk. Even more important, national governments have to be willing to actively implement a rigorous macro-prudential framework, even at the risk of committing Type II errors that forestall sustainable expansions in credit growth. A broad macro-prudential framework can include a role for capital controls. Finally, excessive leverage in the non-financial sector (corporates and households) can be further deterred through tax and regulatory policies that do not favour debt financing over equity financing.

In terms of national macroeconomic policy frameworks, two key principles should guide the implementation of monetary and fiscal policies. *First,* the global crisis has provided further evidence of the costs of excessive imbalances (whether excessive domestic credit growth or excessive external deficits). While accepting that it is difficult to draw the line between sustainable and excessive imbalances, a prudential approach would suggest greater activism to lean against the wind. This includes operating a countercyclical fiscal policy that takes into account financial cycles as well as the output cycle. *Second,* it is important to have in place national buffers that can cope with adverse shocks. In terms of monetary regimes for countries with independent currencies, the crisis has revised upwards the prudential level of foreign-currency reserves, even if that level remains far below the scale of reserves currently maintained by some countries. In relation to fiscal policy, a basic message is that the crisis has revised downwards the level of public debt that can be considered "safe" in normal times, in view of the scope for rapid growth in public debt during financial crises.

Moreover, the crisis has shown the importance of a strong public balance sheet in order to adequately address balance sheet problems in other domestic sectors (households, corporates, banks). In addition to maintaining a sufficiently-low public debt, this can involve the accumuiation of a liquid rainy-day fund, since even a low-debt government may find it difficult to borrow during crisis periods.

For those countries still operating under binding financiai account controls, the importance of a robust domestic institutionai and policy framework in effectively managing cross-border financial integration strengthens the case for a gradualist approach to financial account liberalisation. At the same time, the classic tension remains - external account restrictions protect the monopoly power of domestic financial institutions, at the possible cost of lower efficiency and lost growth opportunities. Managing this trade off remains a primary challenge for policy officials in emerging and developing economies.

Finally, there are international externality effects from national policy choices, especially in areas such as the implementation of financial regulation, reserve accumuiation and capital controls. In related fashion, there are international externality effects from national systemic imbalances (banking-system fragilities, external imbalances). Accordingly, an additional role for international institutions is to flag such externalities through monitoring and surveillance frameworks, even if such "soft" financial diplomacy faces natural limits.

QUESTIONS

1. An institutional investor who had been buying before the market crash on October 19, 1987, said that although he believed stocks were overpriced," we followed the *trend is your friend* philosophy." What do you think he meant by the statement? Why is this strategy risky?

2. One observer of the October 19, 1987, crash said that "all the pros knew the portfolio insurance selling was coming; so, the guys with sneakers cut in front of them and tried to sell first.' Comment.

3. Discuss the Ponzi Scheme and Stock Market Bubbles. What are the main factors which build a bubble?

4. What were the main events which led to Great Crash in the stock markets in 1929?

5. "Scam was the result of the *system failure*," Comment.

6. Discuss some of the speculative bubbles.

7. "Speculative bubbles are fed by the contagious hopes find." Do you agree?

REFERENCES

1. Berkmen, Pelin, Gaston Gelos, Robert Rennhack, and James Walsh, 2009, "The Global Financial Crisis: Explaining Cross-Country Differences in the Output Impact," IMF Working Paper 09/280 (Washington: International Monetary Fund).

2. Bratt, E.C. *Business Cycles & Forecasting*, 5th ed. Homewood, III .; R.D. Irwin, 1961.

3. Brown. Stephen: "The Number of Factors in Security *Returns*," *Journal of Finance*. December 1989. pp. 1247-1262.

4. Butler, W.F., and E.C. kavesh. *How Business Economists Forecast*, part 3. Englewood Cliffs, N.J.: Prentice-Hall, 1966.

5. Callahan, and Rosanne Mohrs: "The Determinants of Systematic Risk: A Synthesis," *The Financial* Review May 1989. pp. 157-182.

6. Cardarelli, Roberto, Selim Elekdag, and Subir Lall, 2009, "Financial Stress, Downturns, and Recoveries," IMF Working Paper 09/100 (Washington: International Mon- etary Fund).

7. Cashin, Paul, C. John McDermott, and Alasdair Scott, 2002, "Booms and Slumps in World Commodity Prices,"*Journal of Development Economics*, Vol. 69 (October 1), pp. 277–96.

8. Chen, Nai-fu, R. Roll, and S.A. Ross, "Economic Forces and the Stock Market." Working Paper Ser. B-73, University of California at Los Angeles, December 1983.

9. Claessens, Stijn, Giovanni DellfAriccia, DenizIgan, and Luc Laeven, 2010, "Lessons and Policy Implications from the Global Financial Crisis," IMF Working Paper 10/44 (Washington: International Monetary Fund).

10. Eichengreen, Barry, 2007, *Global Imbalances and the Lessons of Bretton Woods* (Cambridge, Massachusetts: MIT Press).

11. Elekdag, Selim, and Prakash Kannan, 2009, "Incorporating Market Information into the Construction of the Fan Chart," IMF Working Paper 09/178 (Washington: Inter- national Monetary Fund).

12. Fouse, William L., "Risk & Liquidity: The Keys to Stock Price Behavior," *Fi-nancial Analysts Journal*, 32 (May-June 1976), 35-45.

13. Gooding, Arthur E., "Quantification of Investors' Perceptions of Common Stocks: Risk and Return Dimensions," *Journal of Finance* 30, no. 5 (December 1975): 1301-1316.

14. Gray, William S. III. "The Anatomy of a Stock Market Forecast." *Journal of Portfolio Management* 16, no. 1 (Fall 1989).

15. Hamilton, William P. *The Stock Market Barometer.* New York: Richard Kussell Associates, 1960.

16. Jahnke, William W. "The Growth Stock Mania Revisited." *Financial Analysts Journal*, January-February 1975, p. 42.

17. Keran, Michael W. "Expectations, Money, & the Stock Market," *Review.* Federal Reserve Bank of St. Louis, Jan. 1971.

18. Lloyd-Davies, Peter, and Michael Canes, "Stock Prices and the Publication of Second-Hand Information," *Journal of Business*, January 1978, pp. 43-56.

19. Moor, Roy E. "The Use of Economics in Investment Analysis," *Financial Analysts Journal.* Nov.-Dec. 1971.

20. Moore, Geoffrey H., and Julius Shiskin. *Indicators of Business Expansions and Contractions.* National Bureau of Economic Re-search, 1967.

21. Schwert, William: "Stock Market Volatility," *Financial Analysts Journal.* May-June 1990, pp. 23-34.

22. Selihman, Daniel. "Playing the Market with Charts," *Fortune,* Feb. 1962; "The Mystique of Point-and-Figure," *Fortune,* March 1962.

23. Siegel, Jeremy J. "Does It Pay Stock Investors to Forecast the Business Cycle?" *The Journal of Port-folio Management* 18, no. 1 (Fall 1991).

24. Spigelman, Joseph H. "What Basis for Superior Performance?" *Financial Analysts Journal*, May-June 1974, p. 32.

25. Tobin, James: " Liquidity Preference as Behavior towards Risk." *Review of Economic Studies,* Febru-ary 1958. pp. 65-85.

26. Wagner, Jerry, Steven Shellans and Richard Paul, "Market Timing Works Where It Matters Most... in the Real World," *Journal of Portfolio Management* 18, no. 4 (Summer 1992).

27. Williams, Arthur: *Managing Your Investment Manager*, Dow Jones-Irwin, New York, 1990.

49

Success in Investment

INTRODUCTION

Success in most things is relative, and not less so in the field of investment. Success in investment means earning the highest possible return with the constraints imposed by the investor's personal circumstances—age, family needs, liquidity requirements, tax position and acceptability of risk. If possible, performance should be measured against alternative investments, or combinations of investments, available to the investor within those constraints. Genuine success also means winning the battle against inflation, against the fall in the real value of savings and capital. The chapter examines the behavioural aspects of investors, common mistakes mutual fund investors make , the various prevailing myths on financial derivatives— options trading rules, trading secrets of the professionals in the futures, and finally covers a selected list of proverbs of stock markets.

CHARACERISTICS OF SUCCESS

To be successful investor, one should strive to achieve no less than the rate of return consistent with the risk assumed. *But is this success?* If markets are efficient, abnormal returns are not likely to be achieved, and so the best one can hope for a return consistent with the level of risk assumed. The trick is to assess the level of risk we wish to assume and make certain that the collection of assets we buy fulfils our risk expectations. As a reward for assuming this level of risk, we will receive the returns that are consistent with it. If, however, we believe that we do better than the level of return warranted by the level of risk assumed, then success must be measured in these terms. But care must be exercised here. Merely realising higher returns does not indicate success in this sense. We are really talking about outperforming the average of the participant in the market for assets. And if we realise higher return we must be certain that we are not assuming higher risks consistent with those returns in order to measure our success. Thus we are left with two definitions of success.

(i) *Success is achieving the rate of return warranted by the level of risk assumed. Investors expect returns proportional to the risk assumed.*

(ii) *Success is achieving a rate of return in excess of warranted by the level of risk assumed. Investors expect abnormal returns for the risk assumed.*

To be successful under the first definition, an investor must have a rational approach to portfolio construction and management. Reasonably efficient diversification is the key. To be successful under the second definition, an investor must have at least one of the following :

Superior Analytical Skill, Superior Forecasting Ability, Inside Information, Dumb Luck

Whether and to what extent anyone is likely to possess these characteristics and consistently be able to outperform the market by the level of risk assumed is critical issue. The investor should be aware of, but not denoted by, the fact that investment markets, the stock market in particular, are largely dominated by professional investors. As a consequence, grossly under-valued investments are rarely easy to come by. Moreover, he should beware of books subtitled. *How I made a Million in the Stock Market, Get Rich Quick* and statements such as *'You can have a high return with no risk'*. In reasonably efficient markets risk and return go together like bread and butter; in the words of Milton Friedman, there is no such thing as a free lunch.

BEHAVIOURAL ASPECTS IN INVESTMENT FINANCING

The notion of integrating psychological factors with economic factors in the investment process is not new financial economists have been aware for a long time that in laboratory settings, human often make systematic mistakes and choices that cannot be explained by traditional models of choice under uncertainty. Successful speculators do not necessarily have a complete portrait of themselves, warts and all. But, in their own minds, they do have the ability to stop abruptly when their intuition and what is happening out there are suddenly out of kilter. There are a variety of established behaviour patterns that may influence security prices. Anyone involved in the world of security markets and investments should have at least a casual familiarity with these concepts. Some of the most common investment behaviours and statistical and mathematical facts of life which are counter intuitive and hard to believe, even when one knows they are time and may influence investor behaviour, are discussed below.

ESTABLISHED BEHAVIOUR

Representative Heuristic

Investors want to invest in 'good' companies by believing that a well-run company represents a good investment. This is the representativeness heuristic. It takes one character of a company and extends it to other aspects of the firm. However, *a good company is not the same as a good investment*. We cannot determine investment merit if we do not know the stock price.

Loss Aversion

Loss aversion is a fact of life since investors do not like losses and often engage in reducing their psychological impact. To illustrate, assume an investor buys 100 shares at ₹ 80 per share and sees a decline in share price to ₹ 70. The loss is of ₹ 1000 and no amount of rationalization can change it. However, there is a tendency to feel that there are no losses until the shares are sold. Generally, investors, in the expectation that stock might return to earlier prices and recover loss, become attached to the stocks in which they have invested either time, money, or effort. This is *sunk costs effect* psychology. This partially explains why investors may find selling a losing stock so difficult. Investors tendency to be more likely to sell a winning stock then a losing stock is called the *disposition effect*.

Fear of Regret

Investors strive to accumulate pride and show regrets from all their investment decisions. This boosts their confidence and motivate them to keep on trying. They become over confident and make foolish decisions. Fear of regret, closely aligned and loss aversion, make then slow to act. They do not like to make mistakes. They cannot decide on what stock to buy or when to buy. Rather then being unable to decide among attractive alternatives, their focus is on the negative. Whatever they pick might be wrong. If they do not buy a stock they obviously cannot subsequently be sorry they bought it. Later on, though, many investors may have wished that they had entered the stock market sooner and not been afraid of what could be wrong.

Herding

Herding refers to the lemming—like behaviour of investors and analysts looking around, seeing what each other is doing, and heading in that direction. In other word, analysts will recommend a stock simply because other analysts have, and investors will buy a stock because other investors have—they're running with the herd. This happens because capital markets are not efficient.

Analysts should be independent and objective, but it is hard to take a contrarian stance. *You are a hero if your marwick opinion turns out to correct, but you look like a fool if everyone else was right and you were wrong.* Investors like to travel in herd. That's why investment portfolios run by committees may not perform as well as these run by an experienced portfolio manager.

Anchoring

Investment decisions can be influenced by extraneous information contained in the problem statement. This phenomenon represents anchoring. To illustrate, assume two investors, say X and Y, have same information about the company and they are to prefer the fundamental analysis of the investment prospects of the ABC stock, currently selling at ₹ 60. If x has previously purchased it at ₹ 35 and Y has it at ₹ 75, this immaterial fact is likely to colour their decision. A fundamental analyst should agree that any past price of a stock does not influence its current investment merits. The fact remains that investor tend to remember the prices paid for the stock, and this information influences, their subsequent decisions about what to do with it.

Myopic Loss Aversion

Myopic means near-sighted, or short-sighted, in a market sense. Investors have a tendency to assign too much importance to routine daily fluctuation in the market. This results in myopic loss aversion. An investor may start with investment in equity mutual fund. It would not be wise to abandon the mutual fund in favour of government securities just because the first account statement of the equity mutual fund's return for the period is negative. He should not be scared off with fluctuations in equity prices. Many investors would be happier if they looked at their investment portfolio less often. In fact, investors with a relatively long term investment horizon should have a sizeable percentage of funds in equities. Abandoning a long-term investment programme because of normal market behaviour is *suboptional behaviour.*

Illusion of Control

Illusion can be defined as an error that persists even after one recognizes that it is an error. Cosmos are one of the great laboratories of human behaviour. It is observable that a dice shooter by throwing the dice hard pitch to the end of the crap table wants to get a high number whereas a low number demands a nice gentle toss. Realistically, the force of dice throw has nothing to do with the outcome. Psychologists refer to this behaviour as illusion of control. People like to pretend that they are influencing the outcome by method of throwing the dice. Similarly, virtually all investors like to look at the charts. According to the weak form of market efficiency, charts are not helpful in predicting the future prospects for a stock. Still, even the nonbelievers in technical analysis want to see the chart as they find charts to be informative which can help them in decision making process. Illusion of contest may be a partial explanation for this behaviour.

Prospect Theory

Investors, in general, are risk averse. While risk aversion may accurately, describe investor behaviour with gain but it is inaccurate representation of their typical behaviour with losses. Investors often shows risk-seeking behaviour when they face a loss. This is one of the most important dimension of behavioural finance, the prospect theory. This means that investors get increasing utility from higher levels of wealth at a decreasing rate but the shape of their utility function changes when they move from positive into negative territory.

Prospect theory is an explanation for unexpected or abnormal behaviour by a portfolio manager who normally is level headed and reasonable. If a trader income a large loss, prospect theory suggests the trader's 'normal' behaviour will change so that the trader takes additional risk in an attempt to recover the losses. Gambler who has lost big money will always say "I can't quit now, I am too far down'. The implications of this behaviour are that investors may take bigger chances when things have not gone their way.

Mental Accounting

Most of us engage to some degree in practice of mental. This refers to the tendency of putting things in boxes' and track then individually. To illustrate, suppose an individual pays ₹ 500 for a movie, arrive at the theater, and finds that he has lost the ticket. He can buy another ticket for ₹ 500 in just as good a seat. The picture will cost him ₹ 1000. There is another individual case who upon arrival at the theater discovers that he has lost ₹ 500 on the way. He can also get another ticket by paying ₹ 500. Financially, of course, both the individuals are out of ₹ 1000 each but they would be looking at things differently. The explanation lies in mental accounting. Having already paid ₹ 500, the first individual would not buy the ticket second time. However, the second individual would buy as the lost ₹ 500 can be accounted for in variety of ways. The loss need not to be associated with the ticket.

Asset Segregation

Asset segregation refers to the tendency to look at investment decisions individually rather than as part of a group. Investor tend to remember how much price they paid for a particular stock and this become a reference point for buying and selling decision. Most of the investors find it inconvenient to sell a stock for less then the reference point. To illustrate suppose an investor is to select one of the two options for each of two decisions. In the first decision, he has to select either choice A, a sure gain of ₹ 2,800 or choice B, a 30% chance of ₹ 10,000 gain and a 70% choice of winning nothing. Thus, the expected outcome with choice B is (.30) (₹ 10,000) + (70 x ₹ 0) = ₹ 3,000, which is more than the ₹ 2,800 associated with choice A. In the second decision, choice C will give a sure loss of ₹ 7,000 while choice D has a 70% choice of losing ₹ 10,000 and a 30% chance of losing nothing. The choice of D has an expected outcome of (.70) (-₹ 10,000) + (.30) (₹ 0) = -₹ 7,000, the same as that of choice C.

The result show risk *aversion* with Decision 1. Most investors choose A even through B has a higher expected outcome. Decision II, however, shows *risk-seeking* behaviour. A further cross tabulation will show that B and C will give lesser losses.

A&D   :   (100%) (₹ 2,800) + (0) (₹ 10,000) + (.30) (₹ 0) + (.70) x (-₹ 10,000)

= ₹ 2,800 + 0 + 0 – ₹ 7,000 = - ₹ 4,200

B&C   :   (.30) (₹ 10,000) + (.70) (₹ 0) + (100%) (-₹ 7,000)

₹ 3,000 + 0 + 0 -₹7,000 = - ₹ 4,000

But since the investors have a tendency to look at the decision one at a time (asset segregation) and their desire to keep the losses away (loss aversion), they forget that losing ₹ 4,000 is a butter option (B&C) than losing ₹ 4,200 (A&D).

Hindsight Bias

Tendency to remember positive outcomes and repress negative outcome is due to hindsight bias. An investor remember a particular stock on which he made lot of money because of his trading strategy but wouldn't like to dwell on the numerous times he lost.

Overconfidence

Overconfiddence, related to the phenomenon of hindsight bias in some respects, leads to misapprehensions about oneself and to the illusion of control. Investor tend to believe that certain things are more likely then they really are. They start thinking that their understanding of things is more accurate and they can beat the market. In other word, they are above-average stock pickers.

Framing

The concept of framing involves attempts to overlay a situation with an implied sense of gain or loss. A loss seems less painful when it is an increment to a larger loss than when it is considered alone. For example, it is easier to pay ₹ 10,000 for something that may be expected to cost ₹ 9,000 than to pay ₹ 1,000 for something which is expected to be free, even though the economic impact is ₹ 1,000 in both cases.

Availability Heuristic

The availability heuristic is the contention that things that are easier to remember are thought to be more common.

Illusion of Truth

Generally, the people tend to believe things more readily that are easier to understand than things that are more complicated. This is known as illusion of truth. For example, many investor follow a firm's P/E ratio. To most investors, a low P/E ratio seem more desirable. If they are buying, it seems they want a low stock price and high earnings— leading to a low P/E ratio. Similarly stock dividends and cash dividends may not effect shareholder wealth but this is hard to sell because more shares and a cheque for cash are easy notions to grasp.

Biased Expectations

From past experience, one may anticipate certain relationships or characteristics that may not apply outside his frame of reference. This phenomenon reflects biased expectations. For instance, cultural environment may bias one interpretation of the data. A stock may be overpriced or underpriced depending upon society/country.

Reference Dependence

Like other behavioural finance concepts, notion of reference dependence is important. To illustrate, an IPL team management, say XYZ, may offer a cricketer ₹ 2 crore for the next year league matches. Currently, he is getting ₹ 1.90 crore. If the cricketer feels that he deserves ₹ 2.25 crore, he may negotiate with the XYZ but in case the negotiations fail the offer may be withdrawn, the alternative is ABC IPL team. ABC's offer is of ₹ 1.80 crore. If fifty-fifty chances are at negotiations, the cricketer should immediate negotiate and accept the offer of team management of XYZ. Otherwise the favourable negotiations may result in gain of ₹ 25 lacs but the loss in case of loose of contract with XYZ Team will be of ₹ 35 lacs

MISTAKEN STATISTICS

There is a tendency to misinterpret statistics, especially by misjudging the likelihood of an event or series of events.

Round Numbers

Certain random number seem less random than the others, and this belief influences certain investment decisions. To illustrate, investors tend to make disproportionate use of round numbers when placing stop or limit orders. They have the tendency to set the stop price of an even ₹ 50 rather than ₹ 50.20 or ₹ 49.50. This is especially true when stock prices are quoted in fractions. Another example can be a giant lottery wheel with numbers from 1 to 1,000. If one spins the wheel, it may stop at number 1,000. But the chance of any other number is the same, one out of 1,000, or 0.1% For some reason, though, many may find a random outcome like 786 or 687 to be more reasonable than the "unusual" outcome of 1,000.

Extrapolation

Investors have tendency to believe that history will repeat. If the stocks are rising, they will continue to rise there is no way to know, however, that they will continue to do so. A belief that in a sequence of independent event recent occurrences influence the next outcome is known as the *gambler's fallacy*. For instance, someone flips a coin and gets heads ten times in a row, these results will have no influence on the outcome of the next toss.

Percentages Vs. Numbers

Investors need to process and interpret percentages and numbers differently. To illustrate consider the case swineflue in a city of 2 crores population. If The death rate due to this goes up to 40% the last year in the city, a 40% increase in a rare disease is troubling. But from a deeper analysis of the problem if one observes that deaths rose from 100 to 140. This is an increase of 40 persons from the previous year but it is also 40%. The death of 40 persons in a city having a population of 2 crores is not a case of as much concern, but a 40% increase is.

Sample Size

There are many instances where people draw incorrect inferences from statistical data. What, for instance, is the probability that 3 people will have birthday on same day. The number of possible birthday combinations is 365^3, or 4,86,27,125. The number of ways in which the 3 could all have different birthdays in 365 x 365 x 365 = 48,228,180. The means the probability of showed birthday is

$$1 - \frac{4,82,28,180}{4,86,27,125} = 0.82\%$$

Extending the logic, with N people, the probability, that at least two of them will have the same birthday is

$$1 - \frac{365!}{(365-N)!(365^N)}$$

When this expression equal 0.5 there is 50%. That at least 2 people in the groups have the same birthday. When N = 23 the probability is 49.3%; with N = 24 the probability is 53.8%. This means in a group of 23 people the odds are about even that at least 2 of them will have the same birthday. While this is mathematically correct but is difficult to believe. It just does not seen sight.

Apparent Order

The daily state lottery might one up 1, 2, 3, 4, 055. Many people would find this run of five numbers extremely unlikely and someone would probably cry fal. But is this sequence less common than 9, 12, 18, 25, and 30? The answer is no, but the consecutive sequence remain highly suspicious. But a single occurrence of an unlikely event becomes much more likely as the simple size increases. To illustrate, if a coin is flipped 10,000 times and recorded the head and tails. With a binominal even like a coin flip the probability of 10 heads in a row is $(0.5)^{10}$, or $1/1,024$. In a sequency of 10,000 flips, lower the probability of getting 10 heads in a row at some point along the way is quite good. Because the sequence may begin anytime (i.e. with the first flip, the second flip, and so on) there are 9,990 10-flip sequences.

Regression to the Mean

The concept regression to the mean states that given a series of random, independent data observation, an unusual occurrence tends to be followed by a more ordinary event. For example, tall parents usually have slightly shorter children (although they may still be above-average in height). Similarly, good performance tends to be followed by lesser results, and vice versa. In the long run, performance tends to be about average.

Some of the common mistakes which the investors make while investing in mutual funds are listed listed below:

1. Failing to have a good understanding of the objectives, policies and risks of the funds investors buy. This can lead to unsuitable investments and unexpected losses.
2. Investing in the wrong funds, even though they may be in the right categories. Losers will tend to exhibit either high costs, excessive sales charges, or poor management.
3. Using the rear-view mirror approval of buying volatile funds that were top performers over the most recent year or quarter. Funds that beat their peers over the short run usually had to take big risks to get there.
4. Failing to follow a consistent long-term programme of buy- and-held investing.
5. Failing to start planning early enough for retirement, without letting time workfor investors to the greatest extent possible.

SO, WHAT'S THE RECIPE FOR SUCCESS ?

Mutual funds generally don't make investors rich in short- time but if they have patience, they are the best, most convenient way for building up assets over the years. In this regard, the following suggestions are listed to keep in mind.

Step 1: *Let time work for you :* For buyer the money is invested, the more opportunity it has to grow through compounding. ₹100 invested monthly at 10 percent for 10 years compounds to ₹20,655; in 20 years it amounts to ₹ 76,570; in 40 years it swells to ₹ 6,37,678.

Step 2 : *Save maximum :* The simplest, surest way to build wealth is to invest more, regardless of when the initial investment is made. Higher the investment, better will be the return. Putting aside ₹250 instead of ₹100 each month in the preceding example leads to ₹41,310 in 10 years, ₹1,53,139 in 20 years and ₹ 12,75,356 in 40 years.

Step 3: *Invest maximum in equity funds:* Equities provide the best long-term protection against inflation or purchasing-power risk. But the key is to choose funds that suit ones temperament for volatility.

Step 4: *Don't forget the base of investment pyramid :* A large chunk of assets should be kept in stable liquid instruments such as money-market instruments to meet the unexpected media rather than being free to redeem a portion of stock holdings at what could be a bad time. Investors can also use cash to go bargain hunting when especially good values appear.

Step 5: *Avoid the most volatile instruments:* High-risk speculations in options, individual small securities etc. are not worth the potential losses. Money surrendered on highly risky securities is gone forever. It can never go to work for investors where it belonged in the first place - in high quality mutual funds.

Step 6: *Take maximum advantage of tax-deferred compounding :* Comfortable as secure instrument is one of the most important reason for investors to invest. They can hold more assets if they postpone paying taxes on gains.

Step 7: *Don't buy high and sell low :* This is easier said than done. The key is to know how and when to take profits in bull markets and go shopping in bearish environments. Above all, avoid committing a large amount of cash to a fund when the market may be near a peak.

Step 8: *Think twice before making extreme moves :* The biggest risk of market timing is missing bullish surge. The opportunity cost of staying in cash can be enormous.

Step 9: *Think global :* The world is becoming smaller but investment universe is expanding. Globalisation of trade and capital flows is adding an international component to investors portfolio which can pay off in terms of better long-run performance and reduce volatility.

Step 10: *Remember the advantages of indexing:* Passively managed index funds can offer a very low-cost way of staying invested. Better yet, investors can rest assured of not seriously lagging behind the popular market averages.

Step 11: *Don't jump in blindly:* Even though time is important, there is no big rush to put money into a mutual fund. Because of their built-in diversification, most funds move up and down more slowly than individual stocks do. Take time to familiarise with the prospectus and learn about investments with large number of funds now available, investors have got plenty of choices and no need to worry about a high-flyer slipping away.

Step 12: *Don't scatter money too widely:* Too much clutter will only confuse, complicate record keeping, and leads to mediocre results. Stick with a few good funds to meet the needs. Look for good performance in the kinds of portfolios desired, at reasonable cost.

Step 13 : *Keep the assets in balance :* Based on objectives, determine what percentages invested in the different fund categories. Review these weightages at least annually to make sure percentages haven't drifted too far out of line.

Step 14: *Take maximum advantages of fund services:* Learn about and use available fund services to advantage. Automatic investment plans, for example, are a great way to built wealth through a cost-averaging strategy. Withdrawal plans can be helpful for retirees.

Step 15: *Keep good records:* This is an essential by-product of investing, especially when it comes to preparing tax returns. Investors should have complete records on their transactions going back many years.

ACHIEVING SUCCESS IN FINANCIAL DERIVATIVES MARKETS

Financial derivatives have changed the face of finance by creating new ways to understand, measure, and manage financial risks. Ultimately, derivatives offer organizations the opportunity to break financial risks into smaller components and then to buy and sell those components to best meet specific risk-management objectives. Moreover, under a market-oriented philosophy, derivatives allow for the free trading of individual risk components, thereby improving market efficiency. Using financial derivatives should be considered a part of any business's risk-management strategy to ensure that value-enhancing investment opportunities can be pursued. On the other hand, those who oppose financial derivatives fear a financial disaster of tremendous proportions—a disaster that could paralyze the world's financial markets and force governments to intervene to restore stability and prevent massive economic collapse, all at taxpayers' expense. Critics believe that derivatives create risks that are uncontrollable and not well understood. Some critics liken derivatives to gene splicing: potentially useful, but certainly very dangerous, especially if used by a neophyte or a madman without proper safeguards.

Are derivatives a cancerous growth that is slowly but surely destroying global financial markets? Are people who use derivative products irresponsible because they use financial derivatives as part of their overall risk-management strategy? Are financial derivatives the source of the financial fiasco? Some of the common misconceptions about financial derivatives are explored. Believing just one or two of the myths could lead one to advocate tighter legislation and regulatory measures designed to restrict derivative activities and market participants. A careful review of the risks and rewards derivatives offer, however, suggests that regulatory and legislative restrictions are not the answer. To blame organizational failures solely on derivatives is to miss the point. A better answer lies in greater reliance on market forces to control derivative-related risk taking. Indeed, access to risk-management instruments should not be feared but, with caution, embraced to help firms manage the vicissitudes of the market. To consider financial derivatives for inclusion in any corporation 's risk –control arsenal , following certain myths about financial derivatives have been explored .

Myths About Financial Derivatives

Myth Number 1: Derivatives Are New, Complex, High-Tech Financial Products Created by Wall Street's Rocket Scientists

Financial derivatives are not new; they have been around for years. A description of the first known options contract can be found in Aristotle's writings. *Options are just one type of derivative instrument. Derivatives, as their name implies, are contracts that are based on or derived from Aristotle the story of Thales, a poor philosopher from Miletus who developed a "financial device, which involves a principle of universal application." People reproved Thales, saying that his lack of wealth was proof that philosophy was a useless occupation and of no practical value. But Thales knew what he was doing and made plans to prove to others his wisdom and intellect.

Thales had great skill in forecasting and predicted that the olive harvest would be exceptionally good the next autumn. Confident in his prediction, he made agreements with area olive-press owners to deposit what little money he had with them to guarantee him exclusive use of their olive presses when the harvest was ready. Thales successfully negotiated low prices because the harvest was in the future and no one knew whether the harvest would be plentiful or pathetic and because the olive-press owners were willing to hedge against the possibility of a poor yield.

Aristotle's story about Thales ends as one might guess: "When the harvest-time came, and many [presses] were wanted all at once and of a sudden, he let them out at any rate which he pleased, and made a quantity of money. Thus he showed the world that philosophers can easily be rich if they like, but that their ambition is of another sort." So Thales exercised the first known options contracts some 2,500 years ago. He was not obliged to exercise the options. If the olive harvest had not been good, Thales could have let the option contracts expire unused and limited his loss to the original price paid for the options. But as it turned out, a bumper crop came in, so Thales exercised the options and sold his claims on the olive presses at a high profit.some underlying asset,reference rate, or index. Most common financial derivatives, described later, can be classified as one, or a combination, of four types: swaps, forwards, futures, and options that are based on interest rates or currencies.

Most financial derivatives traded today are the "plain vanilla" variety—the simplest form of a financial instrument. But variants on the basic structures have given way to more sophisticated and complex financial derivatives that are much more difficult to measure, manage, and understand. For those instruments, the measurement and control of risks can be far more complicated, creating the increased possibility of unforeseen losses.

Wall Street's "rocket scientists" are continually creating new, complex, sophisticated financial derivative products. However, those products are all built on a foundation of the four basic types of derivatives. Most of the newest innovations are designed to hedge complex risks in an effort to reduce future uncertainties and manage risks more effectively. But the newest innovations require a firm understanding of the tradeoff of risks and rewards. To that end, derivatives users should establish a guiding set of principles to provide a framework for effectively managing and controlling financial derivative activities. Those principles should focus on the role of senior management, valuation and market risk management, credit risk measurement and management, enforceability, operating systems and controls, and accounting and disclosure of risk-management positions.

Myth Number 2: Derivatives Are Purely Speculative, Highly Leveraged Instruments

The job of a derivatives trader is like that of a bookie once removed, taking bets on people making bets. Put another way, this myth is that "derivatives" is a fancy name for gambling. Has speculative trading of derivative products fueled the rapid growth in their use? Are derivatives used only to speculate on the direction of interest rates or currency exchange rates? Of course not. Indeed, the explosive use of financial derivative products in recent years was brought about by three primary forces: more volatile markets, deregulation, and new technologies.

Banks and other financial intermediaries responded to the new environment by developing financial risk-management products designed to better control risk. The first were simple foreign-exchange forwards that obligated one counterparty to buy, and the other to sell, a fixed amount of currency at an agreed date in the future. By entering into a foreign-exchange forward contract, customers could offset the risk that large movements in foreign-exchange rates would destroy the economic viability of their overseas projects. Thus, derivatives were originally intended to beused to effectively hedge certain risks; and, in fact, that was the key that unlocked their explosive development.

Beginning in the early 1980s, a host of new competitors accompanied the deregulation of financial markets, and the arrival of powerful but inexpensive personal computers ushered in new ways to analyze information and break down risk into component parts. To serve customers better, financial intermediaries offered an ever-increasing number of novel products designed to more effectively manage and control financial risks. New technologies quickened the pace of innovation and provided banks with superior methods for tracking and simulating their own derivatives portfolios.

From the simple forward agreements, financial futures contracts were developed. Futures are similar to forwards, except that futures are standardized by exchange clearinghouses, which facilitates anonymous trading in a more competitive and liquid market. In addition, futures contracts are marked to market daily, which greatly decreases counterparty risk—the risk that the other party to the transaction will be unable to meet its obligations on the maturity date.

Around 1980 the first swap contracts were developed. A swap is another forward-based derivative that obligates two counterparties to exchange a series of cash flows at specified settlement dates in the future. Swaps are entered into through private negotiations to meet each firm's specific risk-management objectives. There are two principal types of swaps: interest-rate swaps and currency swaps.

Today interest-rate swaps account for the majority of banks' swap activity, and the fixed-for-floating-rate swap is the most common interest-rate swap. In such a swap, one party agrees to make fixed-rate interest payments in return for floating-rate interest payments from the counterparty, with the interest-rate payment calculations based on a hypothetical amount of principal called the notional amount.

Myth Number 3: The Enormous Size of the Financial Derivatives Market Dwarfs Bank Capital, Thereby Making Derivatives Trading an Unsafe and Unsound Banking Practice

The current financial derivatives market's worth dwarfs bank capital ,thereby making derivatives trading an unsafe and unsound banking practice. However,the often-quoted figures are notional amounts. For derivatives, notional principal is the amount on which interest and other payments are based. Notional principal typically does not change hands; it is simply a quantity used to calculate payments. While notional principal is the most commonly used volume measure in derivatives markets, it is not an accurate measure of credit exposure. A useful proxy for the actual exposure of derivative instruments is replacement-cost credit exposure. That exposure is the cost of replacing the contract at current market values should the counterparty default before the settlement date.

Derivatives help to improve market efficiencies because risks can be isolated and sold to those who are willing to accept them at the least cost. Using derivatives breaks risk into pieces that can be managed independently. Corporations can keep the risks they are most comfortable managing and transfer those they do not want to other companies that are more willing to accept them. From a market-oriented perspective, derivatives offer the free trading of financial risks.

The viability of financial derivatives rests on the principle of comparative advantage—that is, the relative cost of holding specific risks. Whenever comparative advantages exist, trade can benefit all parties involved. And financial derivatives allow for the free trading of individual risk components.

Myth Number 4: Only Large Multinational Corporations and Large Banks Have a Purpose for Using Derivatives

Very large organizations are the biggest users of derivative instruments. However, firms of all sizes can benefit from using them. The economic benefits of derivatives are not dependent on the size of the institution trading them. The decision about whether to use derivatives should be driven, not by the company's size, but by its strategic objectives. The role of any risk-management strategy should be to ensure that the necessary funds are available to pursue value-enhancing investment opportunities. However, it is important that all users of derivatives, regardless of size, understand how their contracts are structured, the unique price and risk characteristics of those instruments, and how they will perform under stressful and volatile economic conditions. A prudent risk-management strategy that conforms to corporate goals and is complete with market simulations and stress tests is the most crucial prerequisite for using financial derivative products.

Myth Number 5: Financial Derivatives Are Simply the Latest Risk-Management Fad

Financial derivatives are important tools that can help organizations to meet their specific risk-management objectives. As is the case with all tools, it is important that the user understand the tool's intended function and that the necessary safety precautions be taken before the tool is put to use.

Builders use power saws when they construct houses. And just as a power saw is a useful tool in building a house—increasing the builder's efficiency and effectiveness—so financial derivatives can be useful tools in helping corporations and banks to be more efficient and effective in meeting their risk-management objectives. But power saws can be dangerous when not used correctly or when used blindly. If users are not careful, they can seriously injure themselves or ruin the project. Likewise, when financial derivatives are used improperly or without a plan, they can inflict pain by causing serious losses or propelling the organization in the wrong direction so that it is ill prepared for the future.

When used properly, financial derivatives can help organizations to meet their risk-management objectives so that funds are available for making worthwhile investments. Again, a firm's decision to use derivatives should be driven by a risk-management strategy that is based on broader corporate objectives.

The most basic questions about a firm's risk-management strategy should be addressed: Which risks should be hedged and which should remain unhedged? What kinds of derivative instruments and trading strategies are most appropriate? How will those instruments perform if there is a large increase or decrease in interest rates? How will those instruments perform if there are wild fluctuations in exchange rates?

Without a clearly defined risk-management strategy, use of financial derivatives can be dangerous. It can threaten the accomplishment of a firm's long-range objectives and result in unsafe and unsound practices that could lead to the organization's insolvency. But when used wisely, financial derivatives can increase shareholder value by providing a means to better control a firm's risk exposures and cash flows.

Clearly, derivatives are here to stay. We are well on our way to truly global financial markets that will continue to develop new financial innovations to improve risk-management practices. Financial derivatives are not the latest risk-management fad; they are important tools for helping organizations to better manage their risk exposures.

Myth Number 6: Derivatives Take Money Out of Productive Processes and Never Put Anything Back

Financial derivatives, by reducing uncertainties, make it possible for corporations to initiate productive activities that might not otherwise be pursued. For example, an Italian company may want to build a manufacturing facility in the United States but is concerned about the project's overall cost because of exchange-rate volatility between the lira and the dollar. To ensure that the company will have the necessary cash available when it is needed for investment, the Italian manufacturer should devise a prudent risk-management strategy that is in harmony with its broader corporate objective of building a manufacturing facility in the United States. As part of that strategy, the Italian firm should use financial derivatives to hedge against foreign-exchange risk. Derivatives used as a hedge can improve the management of cash flows at the individual firm level.

To ensure that productive activities are pursued, corporate finance and treasury groups should transform their operations from mundane bean counting to activist financial risk management. They should integrate a clear set of risk-management goals and objectives into the organization's overall corporate strategy. The ultimate goal is to ensure that the organization has the necessary funds at its disposal to pursue investments that maximize shareholder value. Used properly, financial derivatives can help corporations to reduce uncertainties and promote more productive activities.

Myth Number 7: Only Risk-Seeking Organizations Should Use Derivatives

Financial derivatives can be used in two ways: to hedge against unwanted risks or to *speculate* by taking a position in anticipation of a market movement. Today, the organizations use financial derivatives to actively seek out specific risks and speculate on the direction of interest-rate or exchange-rate movements, or they can use derivatives to hedge against unwanted risks.It is not true that only risk-seeking institutions use derivatives. Indeed, organizations use derivatives as part of their overall risk-management strategy for keeping those risks that they are comfortable managing and selling those that they do not want to others who are more willing to accept them. Even conservatively managed institutions use derivatives to improve their cash-flow management to ensure that the necessary funds are available to meet broader corporate objectives. One could argue that organizations that refuse to use financial derivatives are at greater risk than are those that use them.

When using financial derivatives, however, organizations should be careful to use only those instruments that they understand and that fit best with their corporate risk-management philosophy. It may be prudent to stay away from the more exotic instruments, unless the risk/reward tradeoffs are clearly understood by the firm's senior management and its independent risk-management review team. Exotic contracts should not be used unless there is some obvious reason for doing so.

Myth Number 8: The Risks Associated with Financial Derivatives Are New and Unknown

Financial derivatives are viewed as time bombs for the parties that deal in them and in the economic system.They are financial weapons of mass destruction ,carrying dangers that ,while not latent ,are potential lethal .They could rip guts overnight since the kinds of risks associated with derivatives are no different from those associated with traditional financial instruments, although they can be far more complex. There are credit risks, operating risks, market risks, and so on.

Risks from derivatives originate with the customer. With few exceptions, the risks are man-made, that is, they do not readily appear in nature. For example, when a new homeowner negotiates with a lender to borrow a sum of money, the customer creates risks by the type of mortgage he chooses—risks to himself and the lending company. Financial derivatives allow the lending institution to break up those risks and distribute them around the financial system via secondary markets. Thus, many risks associated with derivatives are actually created by the dealers' customers or by their customers' customers. Those risks have been inherent in our nation's financial system since its inception.

Banks and other financial intermediaries should view themselves as risk managers— blending their knowledge of global financial markets with their clients' needs to help their clients anticipate change and have the flexibility to pursue opportunities that maximize their success. Banking is inherently a risky business. Risk permeates much of what banks do. And, for banks to survive, they must be able to understand, measure, and manage financial risks effectively.

The types of risks faced by corporations today have not changed; rather, they are more complex and interrelated. The increased complexity and volatility of the financial markets have paved the way for the growth of numerous financial innovations that can enhance returns relative to risk. But a thorough understanding of the new financial-engineering tools and their proper integration into a firm's overall risk-management strategy and corporate philosophy can help turn volatility into profitability.

Risk management is not about the elimination of risk; it is about the management of risk: selectively choosing those risks an organization is comfortable with and minimizing those that it does not want. Financial derivatives serve a useful purpose in fulfilling risk-management objectives. Through derivatives, risks from traditional instruments can be efficiently unbundled and managed independently. Used correctly, derivatives can save costs and increase returns.

Myth Number 9: Derivatives Link Market Participants More Tightly Together, Thereby Increasing Systemic Risks

Financial derivative participants can be divided into two groups: end-users and dealers. As end-users, banks use derivatives to take positions as part of their proprietary trading or for hedging as part of their asset/liability management. As dealers, banks use derivatives by quoting bids and offers and committing capital to satisfy customers' needs for managing risk.

In the developmental years of financial derivatives, dealers, for the most part, acted as brokers, finding counterparties with offsetting requirements. Then dealers began to offer themselves as counterparties to intermediate customer requirements. Once a position was taken, a dealer immediately either matched it by entering into an opposing transaction or "warehoused" it—temporarily using the futures market to hedge unwanted risks—until a match could be found.

Today dealers manage portfolios of derivatives and oversee the net, or residual, risk of their overall position. That development has changed the focus of risk management from individual transactions to portfolio exposures and has substantially improved dealers' ability to accommodate a broad spectrum of customer transactions. Because most active derivatives players today trade on portfolio exposures, it appears that financial derivatives do not wind markets together any more tightly than do loans. Derivatives players do not match every trade with an offsetting trade; instead, they continually manage the residual risk of the portfolio. If a counterparty defaults on a swap, the defaulted party does not turn around and default on some other counterparty that offset the original transaction. Instead, a derivatives default is very similar to a loan default. That is why it is important that derivatives players perform with due diligence in determining the financial strength and default risks of potential counterparties.

Myth Number 10: Because of the Risks Associated with Derivatives, Banking Regulators Should Ban Their Use

In fast-changing financial services industry, coercive regulations intended to restrict banks' activities will be unable to keep up with financial innovation. As the lines of demarcation between various types of financial service providers continues to blur, the policy-makers responsible for reforming banking regulation must face the fact that fears about derivatives have proved unfounded. New regulations are unnecessary. Indeed, access to risk-management instruments should not be feared but, with caution, embraced to help firms manage the vicissitudes of the market. To blame organizational failures solely on derivatives is to miss the point. A better answer lies in greater reliance on market forces to control derivative-related risk taking. To that end, banking regulators should emphasize more disclosure of derivatives positions in financial statements and be certain that institutions trading huge derivatives portfolios have adequate capital. In addition, because derivatives could have implications for the stability of the financial system, it is important that users maintain sound risk-management practices.

Innovative Security - Truth or Myth?

Are derivatives the best thing that have ever happened to the corporate treasurer, investment manager, speculator, and passive investor? Many so-called innovative securities are simply new ways of obtaining *leveraged exposure to volatile markets*. One view is that corporates are now able to control their financial destiny more effectively and cheaply than before because they can tailor instruments which minimise or neutralise the risks the manager worries about and increase exposure to what he really wants. If, for example, the corporate manager believes interest rates will strengthen and has exposures in several currencies then the derivatives may offer dozens of products where the currency risk is for the most part neutralised. But these offerings are almost certainly carrying some other form of risk, which the manager may or may not wish to hold. The general rule that risk cannot be eliminated, only altered, continues true - the old saying that there is "No free lunch" rings eternal. Properly used, derivatives have been and will continue to be a source of risk reduction and enhanced investment performance for many participants. Therefore, any manager who is not looking at how derivatives can be employed to manage financial and economic risks, or to enhance yields, is doing his or her investors a disservice. In fact, derivatives have made the world a safer place, not a more dangerous one.

Investment in derivatives should always be preceded by investment in controls. It's not derivatives *per se* that are dangerous. Forms of forwards, futures, options and swaps have been with us for centuries. The root of their risk lies in how and why they are used, and under what framework of control. Uncontrolled derivatives are bound to burn capital.Handling derivatives instruments should be likened to handling dangerous chemicals or, say, nuclear devices. No rational person would believe that an isolated individual could handle these chemicals or devices without a proper system of protocols. A management and control system surrounding the individual who handles these risky instruments is necessary in order to prevent widespread disaster. For end-user effective risk-management, it is necessary to identify the purpose of the use of derivatives (e.g. hedging, efficient portfolio management, proprietary trading, asset liability management, or pure speculation). Thus, whilst interest rate options and futures, swaps, forward rate agreements, caps, collars, floors and more exotic types of derivatives instruments may all be used to alter the level of exposure to movements in interest rates, each instrument will have different levels of risk. Failure to acknowledge the different levels of risk exposure could result in actual losses.

The use of financial derivatives should be integrated into an organization's overall risk-management strategy and be in harmony with its broader corporate philosophy and objectives. There is no need to fear financial derivatives when they are used properly and with the firm's corporate goals as guides.The burden of managing derivatives activities must rest squarely on trading organizations, not the government. Such an approach will promote self-regulation and improve organizations' internal controls through the discipline of market mechanisms. Government guarantees will serve only to strengthen moral-hazard behavior by derivatives traders.

The best regulations are those that guard against the misuse of derivatives, as opposed to those that severely restrict, or even ban, their use. Derivatives-related losses can typically be traced to one or more of the following causes: an overly speculative investment strategy, a misunderstanding of how derivatives reallocate risk, an ineffective internal risk-management audit function, and the absence of systems that simulate adverse market movements and help develop contingency solutions. To address those concerns, supervisory reforms should focus on increasing disclosure of derivatives holdings and the strategies underlying their use, appropriate capital adequacy standards, and sound risk-management guidelines.

For the most part, however, **policymakers** should leave derivatives alone. Derivatives have become important tools that help organizations manage risk exposures. The development of derivatives was brought about by a need to isolate and hedge against specific risks. Derivatives offer a proven method of breaking risk into component pieces and managing those components independently. Almost every organization has inherent in its business and marketplace a unique risk profile that can be better managed through derivatives trading. The freedom to manage risks effectively must not be taken away.

ACHIEVING SUCCESS IN OPTION MARKETS

Options allow the efficient transfer of financial risks and can help to ensure that value-enhancing opportunities are not ignored. Used properly, options can reduce risks and increase returns. At the same time, there is no denying the fact that options also have a dark side. It is important that players in the options markets fully understand the complexity of financial derivatives contracts and the accompanying risks. The participants should be certain that the proper safeguards are built into trading practices and that appropriate incentives are in place so that they are not exposed to unnecessary risks while following the standard rules in options.

TRADING RULES IN OPTIONS

1. Stay away from deep in the money options

The key advantage to buying options are limited risk and high leverage. If an option is too deep in the money, it cuts down on investor's leverage and adds to his risk. He is paying more, and has more to lose, so even the risk is limited it is higher.

The biggest advantage to the option seller is time decay, and with less time the investor has less to gain the easy way (time value decay marches on daily regardless of what the market is doing) and more risk since the intrinsic component is larger.

2. Stay away from deep out of the money options

The illusion is that deep out of the money purchases gives a lot of leverage. In reality they give a lot of hope, promote over-commitment, and offer very little profit opportunity. Yes, they can hit at times, but this is a game of odds, and odds are certainly against an investor if he is buying deep out of the moneys. It may be more realistic to purchase a deep-out of the money option if an investor has a lot of time, but then again he loses some of the leverage because he pays for the time. Surely the odds are in favour when he is to sell deep out of the money options, but the expected reward is minuscule in relation to the risk. The investments could be profitable 99 times out of 100 when selling deep out of the money put options on the stock market, but that crash will come, and when one least expects it. Unless the investor wishes to be "the house", the one who is capitalised enough to cover the powerball lottery, or megabuck jackpot, stay away from deep out of the money.

3. Trade slightly out of the money, at the money, or slightly in the money options

The reasons are the opposite for which one prefers to stay away from the deep options. These have a reasonable chance of providing profitable when buying, one gains from the maximum possible time decay when selling, and they are generally the most liquid of the bunch—which results in a tighter bid/ask spread, which in turn saves on transaction costs. The one variation on this theme has to do with selling options. In this variation it is certainly the fine, or even advantageous, to sell out of the money options with this one caveat—the premium received must warrant the risk. What price might this be? There are no hard and fast rules. One just need to use good judgement.

It is also advisable to use good judgement when cutting losses. This especially involves taking a reasonable or small loss when covering short positions which are not working. However, it also is important to cut losses in long options which are not making money. The fact that most options expire worthless should be strong clue to the buyer to sell out prior to the end in case of non-performance.

4. Know your market

There is a time for all seasons. Option writing can be extremely profitable in dull, flat markets. If the tone changes, cover fast, before that catastrophic loss. If option premiums feel too low to give an adequate cushion of income they probably are. The common wisdom is to "sell flat markets "but this may just be the time to start thinking about buying. Avoid selling in periods of rising volatility, however. Option purchase will start to become more expensive, but then the rising volatility will work in the buyer's favour. Should volatility reach wild proportions, then think about selling. Just make sure that one has adequate margin to take the heat.

5 . Covered all writings is a good strategy for what appears to be a bullish environment, and covered put writings is generally good for what looks like a bearish one

This is one of the few strategies where use of future and options together have the ability to profit on both legs. The strategy works well in a modestly bullish or bearish environment as well. It is not risk free, but is less risky than the outright purchase or sale of futures alone.

6. In "normal" markets, write straddles and strangles

Selling puts and calls works in most market environments. It is a good strategy as long as it is managed properly. "Normal" is a term which cannot be defined specifically. In most cases the premiums received when writing straddles and strangles give an adequate cushion to weather most storms. When the typhoon hits, however, and margin is starting to feel impaired, one should run for the exit door.

7. Look for opportunities to backspread

This is a seldom used strategy, but when used consistently has the potential to make one rich. Recall, this involves selling a call or put at one strike price, and buying a greater number of calls at a higher strike price, or buying a greater number of puts at a lower strike price. Look to establish backspreads for a credit to benefit from time decay, and look only at the market from the potential to move big. This strategy always has a predetermined and limited risk and one of the few which can still prove a mildly profitable when one is dead wrong. The profit is unlimited on a major upside or major downside move.

8. Use options to hedge a profitable future position

The trend-following traders are lucky enough to catch a major move which is showing massive unrealised profits, the great dilemma is when to cash in. An investor inevitably will have to give up a large part of the paper gain if he is to wait for confirmation of a trend change. Yet, top and bottom picking are very hard things to do. There is only one top and only one bottom,in major moves of proportion which could unfold over hundreds of trading sessions. Also, many times, the most important leg of major move comes in the last 48 hours.

Why not use put options to lock in a bull-move profit, and calls for the bear-move profit? Commercial hedgers use options all the time. Trading is a business and this is the prime tool for an individual trader to hedge profit while still showing for additional profits.

These are wonderful tools, these options. Not a panacea, but to a major extent they can offer the best of both the worlds. Constantly be on the alert for ways to use them to your benefit!

TRADING SECRETS OF THE PROFESSIONALS IN FUTURES

Like for success in options , the selected trading secrets of the professionals in future , based more on their failures than their triumphs, have been identified as a world of wisdom. We know that the same mistakes made 50 and 100 years ago continue to the made every day. Technology may change, but human nature never does. Ultimately, the markets are the best teachers, however. A trader may not use all of these secrets, but if he can absorb just a portion, there is no doubt about success. If he disregards, what's presented below, he may lost in the financial desert.

Secret 1: The Trend is Your Friend

So, don't buck it. The way to make the big money is to determine the major trend and then follow it. If the market will not go in the desired direction, then a trader must go its way. When he is in a bear market, and the major trend is down, the plan should be to wait for rallies and sell short; not try to pick the bottom. In a major bear market, he can miss the bottom several times on the way down and end up losing all his money. The same applies (in reverse) in a major bull market. Always go with the tide, never buck it. It is implement to note that in a major bear market it is safer to sell when the market is down 50 points from the top, than when it is down just 10. The reason is, at down 50, all support is gone, and those who bought the breaks have lost all hope, are demoralised, and in a leveraged market are at the point where they are must try to exit the same small door at the same time. The result at times can be an avalanche. There are many examples of markets that have trended long and far, made some people rich and wiped others out. We may hear about the poor traders who lost their money drawn from provident fund, sale of real estate etc. We can almost guarantee that such traders were bull headed and fought the trend until they run out of money.

So, how does a trader do this, stick with the tend and not fight it? Well, it isn't easy. That's why most people don't make money in futures. They need to have strong willpower. Once they can see the trend of the market, they should not change their mind until the "tape" shows the change. In any major move there will, of course, be corrective moves against the trend at times. Some news will developed which will cause a sharp correction, but it will be followed by a more right back in the direction of the major trend. If they listen to this news they will be tempted to liquidate prematurely. Avoid the temptation and listen to no one but the market. One way to do this is to *never* set a fixed price in mind as a profit objective. The majority of people do this, and there's no good reason for it — it's a bad habit based on hope.

Do not set a fixed time to liquidate either. This is the way the amateurs do it. They buy silver at, because their broker told them it's going to ₹ 8000. Well, it gets to ₹ 7800 turns and head south again, and they're still holding looking for ₹ 7800, watching and waiting as their unrealised profit melt. This is just plain bull-headedness. One can seen the opposite as well. The market closes at ₹ 7700, it looks strong and is fundamentally and technically sound. The amateur has his order sitting to sell at ₹ 8000, because this is his price. The market gaps up on the open the next day at ₹ 8100 and his broker is pleased to report he sold

₹ 100 better at this price. However, this is a form of top picking, and who is smarter than the market? The market probably gapped up above ₹

8000 cases like this one, where the open was sharply higher, but was the low of the day. The market never looked back until it hit ₹ 10,000. This is all a version of bucking the trend, which is something not to be recommended. Conditions do change, and one must learn to change his mind when they do. A wise man changes his mind, a fool never. Just be sure if a trader change his position it must be based on sound reasoning. There is no way one can possibly know in advance how much profit to expect. The market determines that. The mission is to determine the trend, hope on for the ride, and stay on until the indicators suggest the trend has changed, *and not before.*

Secret 2: When Market is "cheap" or "Expensive" there Probably is Reason

This one goes hand in hand with "don't buck the trend." The intelligent traders always make money selling short low priced markets which are the public's favourite and in which a large long interest had developed. Alternatively, they cash in on expensive markets when "everyone" is bailing out because the public thought the market high enough for a "healthy" reaction. *Always remember, it's not the price that's important, it's the market action.*

Secret 3: The Best Traders are the Hardest to Do

A trader needs, to have guts and be aggressive on entry. He needs to quickly cut losses when the market is not acting right. *The news will always sound the most bullish at the top, and appear to be the most hopeless at the bottom.* This is why the technical tone of the market is so important. If the news is good, but the market has stopped going up, ask why, and then heed the call. Bottoms can be the most confusing. The accumulation phase, where the smart money is accumulating a position, can be marked by reactions, cross-currents, shakeouts, and false reversals. After the bottom is in place, many traders will be looking for the next break to be a buyer. After all, the market has been so weak so long, the odds favour at least one more break, right? But it never comes. The smart money won't let it. The objective after the bottom is in place is to move the market up to the next level, and the best time to buy may actually feel quite uncomfortable.

Secret 4: Have a Plan Before Trade, and then Work it!

If a trader has a plan and follow it, he avoids the emotionalism which is the major enemy of the trader. He must try to stay calm during the heart of the session, and remain focused. To do this, he has to be totally organised prior to the opening bell. His daily mission, should he decide to accept it, is to make money each day or, barring this, at least not lose much. In normal markets, he should take normal profits. In those unusual markets which occur rarely, he needs to go for abnormal profits. This is one of the keys to success. He must *always limit losses on trades which are not going according to plan.*

This takes willpower and is as essential a quality as having plenty of money. In fact, it is more important than having plenty of money. Money is not to hold on with, this is for the sheep and a trader doesn't want to be sheared. *If big risks are required, don't take the trade, wait for opportunities* where he could enter very close to his risk point. In this way his risk per trade is small in relation to the profit potential.

When it's not going right, *when in doubt, get out.* If a trader has a compass in the middle of the desert, and the oasis is north, he shouldn't get fooled into following the mirage to the west. There is nothing better than getting out *quickly* when one is wrong!

Secret 5: Be Aggressive when Taking Profit and/or Cutting Losses if there is a Good Reason to do so

A good trader will act without hesitation. When something is not right, he will liquidate early to save cash and worry. Never think too much, Just do it! And, doesn't limit his price—go at the market! Many times a market will give one optimal opportunity to act and that's it—go with it. The way to benefit through tuition is to act immediately!

Secret 6: No Regrets

When an intelligent trader liquidates a trade based on sound reasoning, he never regrets his decision. Go on, and if it was a mistake to get out, just learn from it. We all make them. By taking mistakes seriously, one will lose perspective and become too cautious in the future. Try not to think about the price to be entered. This is irrelevant. If the market isn't acting right, don't try to "get out at break even after commissions." This can get very expensive.

Secret 7: Money Management is the Key

Think about this daily. One need not to have a high win to loss ratio, but average win *must* be higher than average loss if one wants to succeed. To do this, there must be (at least some) "big hits" to offset the inevitable numerous (and hopefully small) losses which are going to happen.

It is noted that trader by being able to just cut losses early, by even a small incremental amount per trade, this can make a major difference to the bottom line. This takes decisiveness, so be decisive if the trade is not acting right. Waiting a "few more ticks" is generally not a recipe for success.

One more point there: it is bad practice to cancel or extend a stop loss order. One should never do this. It's OK to cancel a profit taking order at times, but the sooner a loss is stopped the better. When one gets, out of a bad position quickly, and with a minimum of trauma, not only is his capital base maintained, but his judgment will improve. Without a well-defined risk point, there's no judgment, what it's called is hope.

Secret 8: Success Comes Easier When you Specialise

Every market seems to have its own nature, its own personality. Some markets tend to make tops and bottoms with a fast run up and reverse (called an inverted V top or a V bottom). Some have rounding tops and bottoms, some double tops and bottoms, some tops and bottoms with a long consolidation. A trader can read a market better when he becomes, familiar with it's idiosyncrasies. Familiarity comes from concentration and experience. There are plenty of markets out there to be picked up one for each temperament.

Secret 9: Patience Pays!

Some people are in too big a hurry to get rich and as a result they go broke. Don't try to get rich in a few months. Don't try to catch all the fluctuations. Market movements of importance require weeks and even months to get ready. There's generally plenty of time to buy or ell one or two days, or longer, after a big move gets under way. There are times when a man or woman with nerve, knowledge, and a bit of luck can turn a small amount of money into a fortune. However, this cannot be done continually. The best trades come along only rarely. One needs to have patience to wait for the right trades. When they come, one must have the patience to not be overanxious and get in too soon or overtrade. Remember, every act, either opening or closing a trade, must have a sound basis behind it. Never trade for the thrill of it.

One last point on patience: once one is out of the market with a big profit, shouldn't be in too big a hurry to get back in. The best opportunities may be coming, but they're not there every day. One needs the patience to wait. Big account balances lead to the temptation to lay for less than desirable trades. If one makes a good profit, look at it this way: he can now *afford* to wait a few weeks or months for the signs of the next big mover.

Secret 10: Guts are as Important as Patience and More Important the Money!

Some traders are too bold and as a result overtrade. However, some have trouble pulling the trigger. This is a weakness which must be corrected. One must train oneself to trade so there is no hope, no fear. When one enters or exits a position, one should do it decisively and without emotion. This is particularly important after a tough losing streak. Sometimes the traders who suffer a string of losses, through they still have some money left, and when the best opportunity of the year comes along (one they identified) they did not have the guts to act. In cases like this, guts are more valuable than money. Hence, the traders should have the guts to press hard when they are right. They also need the fortitude to cash in when it is most pleasurable.

Secret 11: The "Tape" (The Quote Machine) Will Trick you

It's impossible for the man who stands over "the ticker" day by day to identify a big move before it starts. The tape will fool him every day while accumulation is taking place (and it takes time to accumulate or distribute a large position). The tape the quote machine) is there to fool traders. *"The tape moves in mysterious ways, the multitude to deceive."* Prices can look the weakest/strongest at the strongest/weakest times. Watching quotes all day will cause trader to constantly change his mind and trade too often, and this increases his percentage of being wrong. If he gets in wrong, the quote machine will tend to keep his in wrong longer than he should be because every tick his way will renew his hopes. If he gets in right, and he watches, the screen too closely, there will come a minor move which, in the long run means nothing, which will get him out. As a result he will lose a good position.

Secret 12: Be Skeptical

In other words, it pays to be a *contrarian*. To be successful, a trader needs to be a student of human nature and do the opposite of the general public. Sell on his first clues of weakness, and doesn't wait until "everyone" is bailing out. The tip giver may be good-intentioned, but tips will invariably influence in the wrong direction. Remember, the market doesn't beat a trader rather a trader beats himself. Following tips and not the market is just another sign of human weakness.

Secret 13: Be Time Cognizant

Know how much time the move has taken to get to the point it's at. This is important, because the longer a market moves in one direction, the greater the velocity of the buying or selling will be as the final stage approaches. In many cases, the significant portion of a major move takes place in the final 48 hours. One should watch the volume closely after a market has made a long-term move. Volume tends to run higher than normal at the end of a move. This is the "distribution zone," where the smart money is unloading their position to a public who is frenzied by news.

Actually, it's important to know what "zone" the market is in. Market phases tend to act in a similar manner. Many times, at the bottom, a market can rally on small volume. This indicates there really isn't much for sale. The bottom can follow a period of panicky conditions, pessimism, and apathy. Even the prior bulls will start to sound more cautions, and hint it could get worse before it gets better. It seems nobody is interested in buying. This is the time to watch moving averages closely. If they flash a buy signal, immediately cover shorts and start to buy. Tops ware the opposite of bottoms. It seems nobody notices the market is saturated, yet the market may top going up. After the first break from the top, many times there will be a low volume "failure test of the high." Once the market fails at a lower high, if the trader is not out already, this could be his last best chance to liquidate.

As a general rule, the big money is made in the last stage of a bull market, when prices are feverishly active. The big profits on the short side are made in the last stage of a bear market, when everyone wants to sell and it seems no one wants to be a buyer. It is always darkest before the dawn, and brightest at noon just before the sun starts to recede.

Secret 14: The Market's Reaction to the News is Crucial

It's not the news, but how the market reacts to the news, that's important. In other worlds, it's the news that sets the public perception. Be alert for divergences between the news and market action. It all has to do with *expectation versus reality.* Look for the divergence between what's happening and what people think is supposed to happen. When the big turn comes, the general public will always be looking the wrong way. There are certain ways to analyse reactions to news (or even a lack of news).

Consider the following:

- If bad news is announced, and the market starts to sell off in large volume, it's a good bet the market's going lower.
- If the market doesn't have much of a reaction to good news, it's probably been discounted.
- Moves of importances invariably tend to begin before there is any news to justify the initial price move. Once the move is under way, the emerging fundamentals will slowly come to light. *A big rally (decline) on NO NEWS is always very bullish (bearish).*
- It is generally not good practice to buy after a lot of very bullish news, or to sell after an extremely bearish report. Both good and bad news are many times already discounted in price. Of course, one should always consider whether the trend is down or up when the news is made known. A well-established trend will generally continue regardless of the news.
- When unexpected news occurs (news which the market has not had time to prepare for) and the market opens in a wide range or "gaps" lower or higher, sell out longs, or cover shorts and wait. Watch the market for 30 minutes to an hour. If the market opened sharply lower, with heavy selling, and was not able to trade much lower than that, it's into support and can be bought at the market with a tight risk point. Watch the market closely at this point. Note the tone of the rally. If it is small and the market is able to again fall under the levels made when the bad news came out (or above the good) it is safe to assume the market is going lower (higher).

Secret 15: Never Trade When Sick or Tired

Good health is essential to success. If a trader is not feeling good, he should closed out positions and start over again when he does. Rest is equally essential to success. It is probably a good idea to periodically close out all trades, get entirely out of the market and go on vacation. The market will still be there at return. Some of the most successful traders trade their best right after a vacation. If one sticks to something too long without rest, judgment will become warped. Traders who are continually in the market day in and day out lose their perspective and will ultimately lose.

Secret 16: Overtrading is One of Your Greatest Enemies

Overtrading is the "greatest evil." It is the cause of more losses than anything else. The average novice trader really doesn't have a clue as to how much money is needed to be successful, and he or she invariably buys (or shorts) more than prudence dictates. He may be right in his analysis, or determination of the major trend, but due to too big a position is forced to liquidate at the margin calls. When he's liquidating so are the other novices, and that's when the smart money moves in. The money runs out just at that critical time when it is ripest to enter. The over-trader is exhausted and misses the profit opportunity he had once seen clearly in those more optimistic days.

Be conservative, keep cool, and avoid the temptation to trade more contracts than margin can reasonably support in normal markets. This is especially important at tops and bottoms where the excitement, the rumours, and the news are at fever pitch. Human nature has a tendency towards overconfidence at tops and bottoms. Study charts, and don't let good judgment be influenced by hopes or fears.

Secret 17: Keep a Cool Head During "Blowoffs"

Markets nearly always culminate at the top in the same way. When close to the end of a major move, markets can become wild. Volume is huge, activity is feverish and erratic, and the imagination blossoms. If a trader has the vision to ride the trend to this point his pay day has come. However, in extreme markets men and women of reason lose all sense of proportion. They start to believe the propaganda that the world will literally run out of this or that. It never happens. The history of the world shows that there has never been a time when a great demand for any commodity has not led to a supply in excess of demand.

Extreme markets are *not* the time to pyramid. They are the time to become alert for the end. All good things come to an end, and a trader will be to jump before the big bump. There will be a time when the herd will want to all exit out the same door at the same time. Make sure one should have already left the room. When everyone wants to sell, and all buying support disappears, profits can run into losses fast. In the stock market crash of 1987, profits made in the first ten months of the year were wiped out in three days.

How does a trader turn his paper profits into cash in a runaway market? In blowoff markets the corrections are generally short and sweet. The market is feverish and everyone is bullish (the bears have already thrown in the towel). The public is buying madly. Weeks may go by without a major correction. One will hear of fortunes being made, and if someone is fortunate enough to be on the move, his paper profits will grow geometrically. The end may be near, but nobody can see it. In fact, only about 10 per cent of those with big paper profits will ever cash in near the top.

The Golden Rules in this type of market are: first, it does not pay to take a loss amounting to more than two consecutive days' fluctuations. If the market goes against for two days it's likely to go more. *Secondly, be alert for a morning when the market opens off dramatically without any news.* It may weekly rally, but the rally will fail. This is the first sign of the end. The market has reached the saturation point where it's run out of buyers. Supply has finally overwhelmed demand. *Third, watch for a failure test of the high.* Many times after the first break the market will have a secondary rally which will fail *under* the high. If a trader failes to get out on the first break, this is his last good chance.

Secret 18: Never Let a Good Profit Turn into a Loss

There is one of the trading sins which has ruined many hopes. If a trader has a decent profit in any position, and he is sure it is going to grow, the stop won't be hit. Should the market continue to move in favour, keep moving the stop to lock in some profit. The objective is to always protect principal in every way possible, and when he is fortunate enough to start accumulating paper profits, lock 'em in.

Secret 19: When in Doubt, Get Out!

If it's not acting right, according to plan, get out. If the market has not started to move in favour within a reasonable amount of time, get out. A trader's judgment will deteriorate the longer he hangs on to a losing position and at extremes he will do the wrong thing. One of the old timers once said something to the effect: *"I am prudent enough not to stand in the middle of the railroad tracks while I decide if the headlight I see is a freight train or an illusion."*

Secret 20: Diversify

Distribute risk among a variety of trades and markets. Divide capital into tenths and never risk more than a maximum of 10 per cent on any one trade. One good profit will often totally erase four or five small losers. But if a trader takes big losses and small profits he will have no chance of success. He should concentrating on active, liquid markets which will allow him to enter and exit when he wants to with a minimum of slippage.

Secret 21: Pyramid Correctly

The big money can only be made by a pyramiding a good position in a trending market. A trader has an excellent opportunity to use leverage and his unrealised profits to create a larger position than otherwise possible. Pyramiding takes both courage and self-control. The "weak hands" seldom make the big money, primarily because they do not have the guts to pyramid and maximise the opportunities they are correct about (or they do not have the smarts to do it right).

Be advised, there is a right way and a wrong way to pyramid. The traders should never reverse pyramid (that is, add a greater number of contracts than their initial position as the market moves their way). First risk should be greatest risk. It is generally better to decrease the size of position through the journey, not increase it. In this way, a trader has the opportunity to increase his profitability without dramatically increasing his risk. Other useful pyramid rules are:

- Never try to pyramid after a long advance or decline. The time to begin a pyramid is when the trend first turns up or down after a long move., Technical indicators can help here.
- It is always safer to pyramid after a market moves out of accumulation and/or distribution. In other words, a breakout from consolidation. Remember, the longer the time it takes prior to the breakout, the greater the move one can expect.

Secret 22: Watch for Those "Breakouts from Consolidation"

A trader needs to know what kind of market he is in. In a consolidating market money can be made by scalping small moves back and forth. However, one won't make the big money with this kind of market action, and one should never attempt to pyramid. Big profits can be made in the runs between accumulation and distribution. One can make more money by waiting until a commodity plainly declares its trend, than by getting in before the move starts. Too many traders are fixated on picking the top or bottom and as a result miss the big picture. *Get the idea of prices out of head and concentrate on market action. Forget about picking tops and bottoms.*

The longer the consolidation the better. When a market has remained for a long time in a narrow range, a breakout from the range becomes more significant. The market is telling that a major shift in the supply/demand fundamentals is taking place. Because it has taken a long time to form, there is more fuel available for the coming move. This is the best type of market to play to the hilt!

One last point here: remember there is no Holy Grail and at times there will be false breakouts. Watch for them. It's most likely false if the market again trades into the consolidation range. The best ones will never retrace into the breakout range, but it is OK for a market to trade back to the upper or lower edge of the range before resuming new trend action. There is no question it was false once it breaks through to the other side.

When this happens, a reversal play is the best course of action.

Secret 23: Go with the Relative Strength

It is important to follow the trend of each market and to always buy the strong one and sell the weak one. This is especially important for related markets. Silver and gold are both precious metals and will generally move in the same direction. They will move at different speeds, however. The trader needs to judge a market by its own signs, and always sell the weak one and buy the strong.

Secret 24: Limit Moves are Important Indicators of Support and Resistance

When a market moves "bid limit up," or "offered limit down" (for those market which still have limits), this is a level where a trader theoretically is unable to be a buyer or a seller. There is more demand at the limit up price than available supply, and vice versa. The market should continue in the direction of the limit move. On corrections, it should find support above the limit price (or below if a limit down type move). Watch for this. If a market again trades under the limit bid price, or above the limit offered, *go with the flow*. These are reasonably risked trades, since it is an indication the previous support or resistance is now absent. If anyone can now buy a market where it previously was unable to be brought (of sell where he previously couldn't) this is a major sign of weakness or strength.

Secret 25: Never Average a Loss

This is critical. There are some traders who have had great success averaging down. When a stock they liked got cheaper, they bought more. When the long-term trend turned back up, they make out like bandits. A leveraged market is different, however averaging a loss may work four times out of five, but that fifth will wipe the trader out. It is a bad habit to get into.

Look at it this way: if a trader makes a trade, and it starts to go against him, then he is wrong—at least temporarily. Why buy or sell more to average the loss? When it's getting worse day by day, why should he potentially compound the problem? Stop the loss early before it is eternally too large, and don't make it worse. If a trader could avoid three weaknesses—*overtrading, failing to place a stop loss*, and *averaging a loss*—he will be a success.

GOLDEN RULES FOR SUCCESS IN STOCK MARKETS

Success involves planning—clearly establishing one's objectives and constraints. Investments should be looked at in terms of what they contribute to the overall portfolio, rather than their merits in isolation. Institutional investment will probably play some part, and performance tables are available to give some guidance. But personal direct investment should not be overlooked, particularly in the obvious area of true ownership, and one's own knowledge, skills, hobbies and acquaintances can also be put to advantage.

Remember Francis Bacon's words: *If a man look sharply and attentively, he shall see fortune; for though she be blind, yet she is not so invisible.* More money has been lost in the stock market than one can imagine simply because of the failure of investors to clearly define their objectives and assess their financial temperaments. In analysing the portfolios of individual investors, the most common errors observed *are: firstly*, portfolio is overdiversified, containing so many issues that the investor can not follow closely the developments in those companies; *secondly*, many portfolios suffer from overconcentration in one or two issues; *thirdly*, all too often, the quality of these securities is not consistent with the stated investment goal and usually a portfolio contain too many speculative securities; *fourthly*, many individual investors are afraid to take losses, they want to wait for their stock to come back to the price they paid; *and fifthly*, most investors, without realising it, do not have a plan. They are buying and selling on tips and believe ingoing where the action is instead of sticking to an investment goal; and finally, most serious of all, some investors consider only profit potential and never the risk factor. They try to wait for the bottoms to buy and tops to sell, they don't learn form their mistakes and sight of their financial goals or the time frame of the investment objectives, under pressure of hope, fear, or greed.

Should investor play a winner's game or a loser's game while buying securities? To answer this question, probably the best way to explain it is to use a sport as an illustration. Let us take tennis. To professionals like Wilander or Lendll, tennis is a winner's game. To win, they must deliver the ball to a place where the opponent will find it difficult to return or play at a speed that the opponent cannot keep up with. They win the game by delivering winning shots.

According to sports writers, on the one hand, tennis to amateurs is actually a loser's game. They do not have the strikes that in any way resemble those of Wilander, Lendll, and other professionals. The best strategy to win a game, they, is to keep the ball in play and let the opponent defeat himself by hitting the ball into the net or outside the court. They win the game by losing less than their opponent.

The above analogy clears the distinction between winner's and loser's game. Probably now the investor can guess whether buying securities is a winner's game or a loser's game. Recently, buying securities has became a loser's game even for professionals engaged in institutional investing. For those who are determined to win the loser's game, it is required:

(1) *Play your own game.* Know your policies very well and play according to them all the time.

(2) Do *the things do best.* Make 'fewer' but 'better' investment decisions.

(3) *Concentrate on your defenses.* Most investors spend too little time on sell-decisions.

Sell decisions are as important as buy-decisions. Investors should spent at least equal time in making sell-decision.

The crucial point of the loser's game is to put the balance sheet and the income statement through a fine screen. This is the first step in making sure to avoid a mistake and will help the investor to keep away from letting the excitement make him move too quickly. Remember the old saying/ A fool and his money are quickly parted'.

A SELECTED LIST OF PROVERBS OF STOCK MARKETS

Stock Exchanges are not short of proverbs. Some of them which seem to make good sense are briefly interpreted below to help the investors to grasp their meaning:

1. Turnarounds take seven years

Interpretation: A security believed to be in a turnaround situation may require a longer time to show results than the buyer expects.

2. Buy in haste, repent at leisure

Interpretation: The buyer is warned against making a hasty investment decision.

3. No tree grows to the sky

Interpretation: A high growth rate of sales and earning*? of a company will eventually moderate.

4. Sell your losers and let your runners run

Interpretation: Most traders subscribe to this tenet. They usually use the stop-loss order to get out of positions with small losses. On winning positions, they want to stay in to ride out the full market swing. The method employed is to move the stop-loss order gradually upward when the price of the security is rising.

5. In a bull market, be bullish

Interpretation: The idea to go with the trend. Again, most traders follow this tenet.

6. All growth is temporary

Interpretation: Growth, like other phenomenon, is subject to change. High growth in a company or an industry is not expected to persist forever.

7. The budget will not be balanced in your lifetime

Interpretation: Deficit financing in government may be way of life.

8. Never throw good money after bad

Interpretation: This warns against averaging down, which means buying more shares of a stock when the price of stock declines.

9. Cyclical stocks should be bought when their multiples are high and sold when their multiples are low

Interpretation: The time to buy cyclical stocks is during a recession when earnings are very low and P/E multiples are high. By the same token, the time to sell a cyclical stocks is in prosperity when earnings are high and P/E multiples are low.

10. Successful money managers have brains, nerve and luck

Interpretation: Success does not rest solely on good investment decisions. Luck is also a factor.

11. The market is a discounting mechanism

Interpretation: Buyers and sellers evaluate security prices on the basis of what they can foresee in the economy, industry, and the company. The expected future governs today's prices.

12. What is good for TISCO is good for the country

Interpretation: TISCO represents the leader in a basic, but cyclical industry in the economy. If the TISCO stock is doing well, investors are probably expecting that the economy will do well in the foreseable future.

13. You really should cut your list

Interpretation: This warns against overdiversification.

14. The new high list will do better in the, subsequent six months than the new low list

Interpretation: Most traders subscribe to this tenet, it means that stocks that are doing well now may last for awhile because of momentum. By the same token, those that are doing poorly will likely continue to do poorly for some time.

15. There are no one-decision stocks

Interpretation: There are no stocks that can be safely put away without periodic evaluation. A few years back, when buying growth stocks was very fashionable among institutional investors, the high-growth stocks were labeled as one-decision stocks.

16. To err is human, to hedge divine

Interpretation: The future is unpredictable. The best way to invest is to hedge and control risk> if possible.

17. If the industry leader is overruled, don't buy the dogs

Interpretation: This warns against investing in an industry that is very popular, perhaps overly so. If the industry leader is overvalued, the chances are that other less established companies are also overvalued.

18. Price is a fundamental-it is the only thing you know for sure about a stock

Interpretation: It is difficult to assess the value of a security correctly, because value depends on future estimates which are basically uncertain.

19. Buy on the rumour, sell on the news

Interpretation: When there is a rumour going around, and information is incomplete, then there is a possibility that the price will continue to move upward. When the news becomes official, less informed people may come in to buy, and this is good time to unload.

20. Buy when you can't find a bull

Interpretation: When everybody is pessimistic about a stock or the general market, then prices may be thoroughly depressed. This would be a good time for long-term investors to buy the stock or move into the market.

21. If the idea is right, eighths or quarters won's matter

Interpretation: This means that the buyers should take the time and effort to research a security. If one decides to buy a security after careful research, he should buy the stock at the market. It is unwise to place a buy order at an eighth or a quarter below the market price. In that case, the buyer may not get the stock.

QUESTIONS

1. Understanding stock markets' proverbs help investors in operating successfully.Give interpretations of some of the worldwide proverbs prevalent in stock markets.
2. Most of the losses from derivatives transactions have come from unclear implementation of risk visions and cultures in approach to risk-management." In the light of the this statement discuss the policies and procedures which can serve as an example of the major types of issue which should be made explicit and implemented by a company.
3. What are some common mistakes mutual fund investors make ?
4. Should an investor play a winner's game or a loser's game while buying securities?

5. Discuss the trading secrets of professional in the futures markets.

6. Critically examine the winning rules in the options market.

7. "A fool and his money are quickly parted". Do you agree?

8. "Handling derivatives instruments should be likened to handling dangerous chemicals, or say, nuclear devices. *No* rational person would believe that an isolated individual could handle these chemicals or devices without a proper system of protocols. A management and control system surrounding individual who handles these risky instruments is necessary in order to prevent widespread disaster." Discuss the role of the senior management in the light of this statement.

9. Are derivatives the best thing that have ever happened to the corporate-treasurer, investment manager, speculator, and passive investor?

REFERENCES

1. Aristotle, *Politics*, trans. Benjamin Jowett, vol. 2, *The Great Books of the Western World*, ed. Robert Maynard Hutchins (Chicago: University of Chicago Press, 1952), book 1, chap. 11, p. 453.

2. Group of Thirty Global Derivatives Study Group, "Derivatives: Practices and Principles," July 1993.

3. Gregory P. Wilson, "BAI/McKinsey Survey on the Usage of Derivative Products," Paper presented at Bank Administration Institute Conference on Derivative Products— From A to Z, Chicago, December 6-7, 1993.

4. Kenneth A. Froot, David S. Scharfstein, and Jeremy C. Stein, "A Framework for Risk Management," *Harvard Business Review*, November-December 1994, pp. 91-102.

5. Thomas F. Siems, "Financial Derivatives: Are New Regulations Warranted?" *Financial Industry Studies*, Federal Reserve Bank of Dallas, August 1994, pp. 1-13.

6. Thomas F. Siems, "Derivatives: In the Wake of Disaster," *Financial Industry Issues*, Federal Reserve Bank of Dallas (1995): 2-3.

Index

A

A buy-and-hold Policy, 951
A Portfolio Hedge, 1185
Accounting,
    Beta, 826, 828
    Policies, 582
Active Bond Portfolio Strategies, 913
Active Equity Investment Styles, 310
Adjustment Bonds, 220
ADRs/GDRs, 122
Advance-Decline Ratio, 623
Advantages,
    and Disadvantages of Investing in Mutual
    Fund, 114
    of Listing, 67
Aggregation,
    Risk, 1006
    Sales People, 1363
Alex Kane, 13
Alternative,
    Methods to Measure the Return on the
    Portfolio, 938
    Solutions to Timing, 948, 944
American Depository Receipts (ADRs), 60, 1323
American International Group, 1275
AMFI, 117, 121
An Analysis of the Economy, 563
An Asset-Liability Hedge, 1186
An Integrated Approach to Merge Derivative
    Risks, 1007
An Inventory Hedge, 1189
Analyst's Best Estimate (ABE), 330
Appreciation Factor, 1045
APRs, 554
Arbitrage, 1237
    Pricing Theory (APT), 887
Arbitrageur, 85

ARCH, 1293
Arithmetic Average (Mean) Rate of Return,
    940
As tulip menia, bubble, chain letter, Ponzi scheme,
    1361
ASBA, 212
Asian option, 1040
ASR, 119
Assumed Bonds, 220
Audit risk, 1007
Authorised Capital, 274

B

Babylonian script, 1036
Balanced funds, 114
Bank Capital, 1273
Bank Discount Basis, 552
Bank Discount Yield versus Bond Equivalent
    Yields, 553
Bank-Based and Market-Based Financial
    Systems, 481
Bar Chart, 614
Barbell strategy, 917
Basel III, 1273, 1275, 1276
Basic Margin Formula, 92
Basic Types of Transactions, 89
Basis Rate Swap, 1162
Basis risk, 1006
Bauman's Variable Rate Method, 324
Benefits of,
    Commodity Future Markets, 1238
    Credit Rating, 163
    Private Equity Finance, 381
Benjamin Graham, 14
Bermuda option, 1040
Bernard Baruch, 7
Best rate order, 88

Beta,
    Basics, 836
    Forecasting, 828
Binomial Model, 1046
Black, 895
    Box, 1016
    Monday, 1369
    Scholes Model, 1047
Blind Faith and High Hopes, 1363
Blue chip, 275
Bond,
    Equivalents, Yields, APRs, and EARs, 554
    Features, 217
    Immunization, 236
    Indexing, 924
    Portfolio Performance Evaluation, 982
Book Building, 192
    process, 193
Boston option, 1040
BPLR, 532
Break forward, 1040
Brokerage,
    Charges, 106
    Information, 83
Budliwalla, 84
Bullet strategy, 917
Business,
    and Financial Risk, 16
    Cycle of Private Equity, 380
    Risk, 1006
Butterfly shift, 916
Buy Back, 203

C

Calendar-Based,
    Anomalies, 643
    Trading Strategies, 644
Call,
    Feature, 218
    Option, 1038
    Risk, 222
Call/Notice Money Market, 532
Candlestick Chart, 616
Capital,
    Adequacy, 100
    Asset Pricing Model (CAPM), 336

    Asset Pricing Model, 821
    Expenditure, 586
    Instruments, 1273
    Issues (Control) Act, 1947, 30
    Labour Ratio, 828
    Market (CM), 36
    Stock of Society, 4
    Structure, 584
Caption, 1040
Cardinal utility, 716
Carry Forward Facility and the Theory of Badla, 105
Carry Trade, 1197
Carrying-Cost Model, 1142
Cash,
    Dividend, 283
    Earning Per Share, 584
    Management Services (CMS), 73
Cashflow,
    Management Risk, 1011
    Risk, 1006
CBLO, 529, 530
CCIL, 200, 529, 550
CCPs, 403, 1274, 1281
CDCSS, 39
CDs, 530, 551
Certificates of Deposit, 536
Chakravarty committee, 527
Changing Attitude Towards Equity Ownership, 273
Chaos Theory, 611
Characteristic Lines, 768
Characteristics of,
    SWFs, 451
    the Money Market, 528
    VaR Models, 1016
Charting as a Technical Tool, 613
Chooser option, 1040
Chua's Closed-Form Duration, 232
CIP, 540
Circuit Breakers, 203
CIRP, 1167
CISA, 136
CIV, 111
Cleared, Non-cleared and Permitted Securities, 89

Clearing,
　Banks, 100, 104
　Corporation, 99
　Members, 99, 104
　Process, 99
Clearinghouse and Clearing Margins, 1138
Closed-end Investment Companies, 113
CMB, 538
CML, 824
Code of Hammurabi, 1036
Collateral Trust Bonds, 220
Collateralized fund obligations, 380
Collection Period, 585
Commercial,
　Bills Market, 537
　Paper, 535
Commission broker, 84
Commodity Exchange, 1234
　in India, 1245
Commodity Futures, 1235
Companies Act, 1956, 31
Company Analysis, 581
Complexities of Investment Timing, 936
Compulsory De-listing of Companies, 79
Computation of Net Assets Value (NAV), 124
Concave Utility Function, 719
Concept of coefficient portfolios, 731
Confidence Index, 623
Considerations for Shares Issue Through Warrants, 1121
Consolidated Daily Position, 86
Constant,
　Growth Model, 315
　marginal utility, 717
　Ratio Plan, 945
　Rupee Value Plan, 944
Constructing the Optimal Portfolio, 778
Contract Note, 86
Convergence Among Financial Market Segments, 539
Conversion,
　Price, 1086
　Ratio, 1087
Convertible,
　and Non-Convertible Bonds, 219
　Debentures, 1086

Debenture as Debt, 1096
Debenture's Value as a Hybrid Security, 1098
　Preference Share, 1102
　Value, 1087
Convexity of barbell portfolio, 919
Corner Portfolios, 740
Cost of convexity, 919
Counter Receipt (CR), 35
Country Funds, 1319
CP, 530
Credit Rating,
　Agencies in India, 166
　in India, 161
Credit Risk, 221, 1006
　Transfer, 1230
Credit Spreads, 922
Cross Margining, 211
Crosshedges, 1179
CRR, 529
CSGL, 529
CTCL, 38
CTRs, 122
Currency Coupon Swap, 1162
Currency Derivatives, 37
　Segment (CDS), 36
Current,
　Ratio, 585
　Yield, 223, 266
Custodians, 99, 104
Cyclical stocks, 275

D

Daily Transaction Report, 86
Dealers in non-cleared securities, 84
Decreasing marginal utility, 717
Defensive stock, 275
Delisting, 79
DELTA, 1050
Depositories Act, 1996, 32
Depositories, 100, 104
Depository,
　Participants, 198
　System, 195
Deposits with Companies, 495
Depreciation Methods, 583

Derivatives Market, 446
Determination of Systematic Risk, 825
Developments in the Secondary Capital Market, 40
Dhyrymes, Friend, and Gultekin (DFG), 895
Difference between Commodity and Financial Derivatives, 1239
Direct investments, 380
Disadvantages of Credit Rating, 165
Distribution, 52
Dividend,
    as a Passive Residual, 285
    discount model, 315
DMA, 204
Dominance Principle, 743
Double declining balance, 583
Dow Theory, 608
Duration, 228
    in Value (DV), 234
    of barbell portfolio, 919
DvP, 529

E

EAR, 554
Earning Per Share, 584
Earning Power, 584
ECB, 1278, 1281, 1349
Economic,
    derivatives, 1194
    surplus, 928
Effect of,
    Bonus Rights, Dividends after Transaction, 88
    Book Closing on Delivery, 88
Effective Duration, 233
Efficient Portfolios, 733
EFP, 1255
Eligibility Criteria for,
    IPOs/FPOs, 69
    Trading Membership, 28
Elliott Wave Principle, 611
Equity,
    Caps and floors, 1168
    Funds, 114
Essentials of,
    Margin Trading, 90
    Short Selling, 94

Estimating,
    Beta, 836
    the Market Return, 844
    the Risk-Free Rate, 841
European Stability Mechanism, 1281
Evolution and Functioning of Commodity Exchanges, 1234
Evolution of Private Equity in India, 384
Execution of Order, 86
Exotic Options, 1039

F

Factors Affecting Assigned Ratings, 160
False Prophets, 1364
Fama's Approach, 970
FATF, 1302
FCCBs, 41
Features of,
    an Investment Programme, 14
    Preference Shares, 264
Fibonacci Numbers, 607
FIFO, 582
Filter Rules, 633
FIMMDA, 37
Financial,
    Analysis, 585
    Innovation, 1340
FIPB, 470
Fisher Black, 816
Fisher's ideal price index, 141
Fixed Price process, 193
Fixed Rate Currency Swap, 1162
Floor broker, 84
Floortion, 1040
FOCASS, 39
Foreign Exchange,
    Market, 539
    Risk, 222
Formula Plans, 944
Forward start option, 1040
Fragile Global Recovery, 1277
Functions of a Brokerage Firm, 83
Fund of funds, 380
Future,
    of the Convertible Securities, 1104
    Contracts and Future Trading, 1135
    Markets, 1133

Versus Forward Markets, 1145
Versus Options, 1144

G

GAAP, 1308
GAMBLING, 10
GAMMA, 1051
GAPP, 467
GARCH, 1293
Gearing Effect, 1123
GETFs, 120
Girolamo Cardano, 13
GIVs, 451
Global Asset Allocation, 1314
Global Depository Receipts (GDRs), 1325
Gold, 496
Government Securities Market in India, 405
Greenspan Model, 323
Grodinsky, 573
Gross Profit Margin, 583
Group Rotation Managers, 312
Growth, 275
Funds, 114
Managers, 312
at a Reasonable Price (GARP), 323
Guaranteed Bonds, 220

H

Hand delivery, 87
Harry M. Markowitz, 12, 731
Head and Shoulders Configurations, 618
Hedge funds, 114, 404
Hedgers, 312, 1236
Hedging, 1173
Seller, 1045
Using Index Futures, 1139
Hemline Indicator, 625
Homogeneous Group/Group Rotation Models, 335
HPR, 129
Hybrid security, 263

I

ICICI, 35
IDRBT, 201
IFSD, 29
IIFCL, 473

ILAF, 544
Implications of the Convertible Bond Issues, 1100
Income,
Bonds, 220
Defensive, 275
Funds, 114
Increasing marginal utility, 717
Incremental Risk-Adjusted Return from Option, 983
Indenture, 217
Independent, Captive and Semi-captive funds, 380
Index Linked Bonds, 448
Index Options, 1052
Index: The Concept, 140
Index-based Circuit Filters, 102
Index-linked funds, 114
Indian Commodity Exchange Limited (ICEX), 1254
Indian Depository Receipts (IDRs), 1326
Indian Insurance Industry, 483
Indicators of the Witchcraft Variety, 624
Indifference Curves, 723
Industrial,
Growth Cycle, 573
Analysis, 570
INFINET, 529
ING, 1270
Initial Margin, 92
Computation, 1149
Input-Output Analysis, 578
Insider,
Trading, 201
Transactions, 623
Institutional Underwriters, 53
Interest Rate,
Expectations Strategies, 913
Risk, 18, 221, 1006
Swap, 1162
Internal Method—Rupee Weighted, 941
International Model, 27
In-the-Money/Out-of-the-Money, 1042
Intrinsic Value, 332
vs. Market Price, 333
Inventory,
Pricing, 582
Turnover, 585

Investment Classification of Industries, 580
Investment Company: The Concept, , 110
Investment, speculation and gambling, 3
IPEF, 211
IPOs, 60
    Norms, 194
Irrelavance of Dividends - M M Theory, 286
Issued Capital, 274

J

Jensen and Scholes, 895
Jensen's Performance Index, 966
Jeremy C. Jenks, 325
John C. Clendenin, 318
John Phelan, 1371
Joint,
    Bonds, 220
    Stock, 25
Joseph A. Grundfest, 1372

K

Key Differences Between Closed-End and
    Open-End Fund, 125
Key Provisions in Listing Agreement, 69
Knockout, 1040
Kondratev Wave Theory, 611

L

Ladder strategy, 917
LAF, 529, 530
Lapse of Warrants, 1125
Laspeyres price index, 141
LBOs, 382, 459
LCR, 1280
Leading Stock Market Indexes, 142
Leading, Coincidental, and Lagging Indexes,
    569
Legal Risk, 1006, 1011
Leveraged,
    Funds, 114
    Portfolios, 745
LIFO, 582
    to FIFO, 277
Limited discretionary order, 88
Line Chart, 614
Linear Utility Function, 718
Liquid funds, 114

Liquidity,
    preference theory, 428
    risk, 222, 1006, 1010
Listing: Is it a Legal Requirement?, 68
Long Purchase, 89
Look back option, 1040

M

M&As, 459
Macaulay duration, 230
Macroeconomic Destabilisation, 1338
Maintenance Margin, 92
Marking Margin Transactions, 92
Malkiel's Theorems, 226
Managing Derivative Risk, 1006
Margin(s), 1136
    Trading, 90
    for Calendar Spreads, 1149
Market,
    Anomaly Models, 336
    Based versus Accounting-based Beta
    Forecast, 829
    Breadth Index, 623
    Design of Investment Companies, 111
    Model, 829
    Price, 1088
    rate orders, 88
    risk, 17, 1006
    segmentation theory, 428
    Structure and Activities of PE, 378
    Timers, 312
Marketing, 581
Mark-to-Market Margin, 102
Martin Fridson, 8
Maturity of Equity Shares, 275
MCR, 119
Mean—Variance Model, 731
Measuring,
    Duration, 230
    Performance Using the Arbitrage Pricing,
    973
    Performance without the Use of an Asset,
    974
    the Risk in Carry Trades, 1198
Mechanics of,
    Rights Offering, 278
    Share Trading, 87

Methods of Computing the Stock Indexes, 140

MIBOR, 37

MNC, 1310

Modern portfolio theory, 814

Modified Duration, 232

Money Market Mutual Funds (MMMFs), 538

Morningstar's Risk-Adjusted Rating (RAR), 981

Mortgage or Secured Bonds, 219

Moving Average, 624

MSS, 546, 550, 551

Multi-Commodity Exchange of India (MCX), 1246

Multifactor Models, 335

Multiple-factor Models, 889

Multi-variate analysis, 840

N

Naive Hedging Model, 1139

Naked Seller, 1045

NAPMC, 1255

National Commodity and Derivatives Exchange (NCDEX), 1253

National Multi-Commodity Exchange of India Limited, 1245

National Stock Exchange of India, 36

Nature of Equity Shares, 274

NAV, 118, 1311

NCSS, 39

NDS, 529

NEAT, 37

Net Profit Margin, 583

Net rate orders, 88

Neutral Networks, 613

New Derivative Products, 210

New Economic Policy and Foreign Investment, 1349

New Issue Market: The Concept, 50

NFO, 122

NIBIS, 37

Nicholas Molodovsky, 324

Noncallable Securities, 922

Non-Institutional Underwriting, 53

Nonmarket return, 777

Non-operating Income, 583

Normal backwardation, 1134

NOW, 40

NSCCL imposes, 101

NSCCL, 29, 30, 38, 39, 100

NSE,
    MIBID, 37
    Model, 27

NSEL, 1255

NSFR, 1281

NSPOT, 1255

O

Objectives of,
    Commodity Futures, 1237
    Convertible Debentures, 1090

Oct.' 87 Stock Market Crash and Its Aftermath, 1369

Odd-lot dealer, 84

OECD, 1302

Offshore funds, 114

OFIs, 476

OLS, 838

OLTL, 39

ONICRA — Onida Individual Credit Rating Agency, 180

Open Strata Link (OSL), 38

Open-end Investment Companies, 113

Operating,
    Efficiency, 585
    Rate, 586

Operational risk, 1006, 1012

OPMS, 38

Optimisation Approach, 926

Option,
    Buyer, 1044
    Seller, 1044

Order Confirmation Note, 86

Ordinal utility, 716

Organisational Structure of the Secondary Market, 26

Origination, 52

OTC, 1274
    Derivatives, 1200, 1275

OTCEI, 35

P

Paasche price index, 141

Paid up Capital, 274

PAN, 208

Participants of Commodity Derivatives, 1236
Participating,
  Bonds, 221
  Preference Shares, 264
Pay-in of Funds and Securities, 103
Pay-out of funds and Securities, 103
PCM, 975
PDO, 545
Penny Stocks, 275
Pension Sector, 489
Perfectly,
  Negatively Correlated Returns, 664
  Positively Correlated Returns, 664
Performance Attribution Procedures, 978
Permanent finance, 23
Peter Bernstein, 13
Physical Property, 505
Planning or Holding Period Return, 266
Players in the Private Equity Market, 378
Point-and-Figure Chart, 615
Political risk, 1007
Ponzi Schemes, 1361
Portfolio,
  Capital Flows: Hot or Cold?, 1341
  Characteristic Lines, 775
  Dedication, 708
  Insurance, 1054
  Management Policies, 708
  Monitoring, 700
  Planning Stage, 695
  Risk, 660
Post-Office Small Savings Schemes, 491
Potential Size, 1335
Pre-emptive Right, 277
Present Value Estimation, 313
Prevention of Money Laundering Act, 2002, 32
Price/Book Value [P/BV] Ratio, 327
Price-Cash Flow [P/CF] Ratio, 325
Price-Earnings (P/E) Ratio, 320
Price-Sales (P/S) Ratio, 327
Price-Weighted and Quantity-Weighted Indexes, 140
Primary Dealers, 407
PRISM, 39
Private,
  Equity and Venture Capital, 377

Placement Market, 55
  Subscription, 51
Probabilstic Characteristic Lines, 772
Process of Book Building, 192
Professional Clearing Member: NSCCL, 104
Property Management, 508
Public issues, 51
Purchase of Shares, 87
Purchasing Power Risk, 17, 222
Put,
  Call Parity Relationship, 1057
  Option, 1038
  Valuation, 1050

Q

Quanto, 1040
Quantum of Conversion, 1087
Quick Ratio or Acid Test Ratio, 585

R

Rainbow, basket, exchange options, 1040
Random Valuation Model, 330
Real Estate,
  Fund, 114
  Mutual Funds, 210
  Valuation, 509
Reaons for Issuing Bonds, 217
Recipients of Capital Inflows, 1339
Recovery in Advanced Economies, 1271
Redeeemable,
  and Irredeemable Bonds, 221
  or Callable Preference Shares, 265
Regular and Extra Dividends, 285
Regulation of MUTUAL FUNDS, 116
Reinvestment Risk, 222
REITs, 121, 123
Relative Strength Model, 334
Relevance of Dividends, 289
REMF, 120
Repos, 534
Residual Option Spread (ROS), 983
Return in Carry Trades, 1198
Return on,
  Equity, 584
  Invested Capital, 93, 96
RHO, 1052
Richard Thaler, 12

Right issues, 51

Risk Profile of Private Equity Investment, 381

Risk-Adjusted Excess Return, 835

Risks of Investment, 15

Role of the New Issue Market, 54

ROW, 476

Rudiments of Private Equity, 377

Run Test, 633

Rupee-Cost Averaging, 949

S

Sale of Shares, 87

SEBI, 26

    Act, 1992, 31

SEC, 1303

Securities Contracts (Regulation) Act, 1956, 30

Security,

    Credit Ratings, 159

    Dealer, 85

    Market Plane, 854

Selecting a Broker and a Brokerage Firm, 85

Selecting Convertibles, 1103

Semi-Strong Form, 635

Sensitivity of the Yield Curve, 429

Serial Bonds, 219

Serial Correlations, 633

Setting Real Estate Investment Objectives, 504

Settlement Cycles, 104

Settlement Guarantee Fund, 105

SGL, 529

Shanken, 896

Shape of the Yield Curves, 425

Sharpe Reward-to-Variability Ratio, 962

Short Hedge and Long Hedge, 1175

Short Selling, 94, 743

Silver, 501

Simon Kuznets, 571

Single Factor Model, 887

Single-Index Model (SIM), 768

Sinking Fund,

    Bonds, 219

    Retirement, 265

SIP/STP, 120, 698

Size of Private Equity (PE) Industry, 382

SLAF, 545

SMAC, 204

SML, 1299, 824

Social or Regulatory Risk, 18

Source - and - use - of - funds, 54

Sources of Sovereign Wealth Funds, 451

SPAN, 39

Special,

    delivery, 87

    funds, 114

Speculating,

    on Unsystematic Risk, 1142

    with Short Sales, 97

Speculation, 5

Speculative Bubbles, 1364

Speculators, 1236

Spot delivery, 86

Spread, 623, 1039

SPV, 473

Standard Errors, 839

Static hedging, 1040

Stock Dividend (Bonus Shares), 283

Stock,

    Index Futures, 1138

    Index Price-Sensitivity Model, 1140

    Market Bubbles, 1366

Stop loss order, 88

STP, 120

Straddle, 1039

Straight Line method, 583

Strap, 1039

Strategic Secret of Private Equity, 383

Strategies for Futures Markets, 1151

Stratified Sampling or Cell Approach, 925

Stress Tests, 1231

Strip, 1039

Strong Form, 636

Structure of,

    Industry and State of Competition, 575

    the Commodity Futures Markets in India, 1244

Style Analysis, 980

Sum of the years digit, 583

Sunspots, 625

Support and Resistance Levels, 617

Swaps—The Concept, 1161

Swaption, 1040, 1167

Sweat Equity, 201

Sweetener to a Senior Security, 1090
SWFs, 451
SWP, 120
Synthetic Futures, 1145
Systematic and Unsystematic Risk, 821
Systemic risk, 1006, 1007

T

Tactical Asset Allocation, 699
Takeovers, 202
Taravniwalla or jobber, 84
Target Payout Ratios, 285
Tax Carryover, 583
TCP/IP, 38
Technical,
    Analysis, 604
    Indiators, 622
    vs. Fundamental Analysis, 605
Technicians, 312
Terms of Lending, 1337
Tests of the CAPM, 846
The Primary Securities Market, 189
The Basic Swap Structures, 1162
The Comparative Sales Approach, 510
The Concept of,
    a Yield Curve, 422
    an Industry, 570
    Duration, 229
The Convertible Debenture As Equity, 1094
The Cost Approach, 509
The Expansion Stage, 574
The Fisher Effect, 434
The Fixed Rate Currency Swap, 1165
The Great Crash, 1367
The Hedging Process, 1174
The Income Approach, 510
The January Effect, 643
The M2 Performance Measure, 981
The Normal and Real Interest Rate, 434
The Odd-Lot Ratio, 623
The Pioneering Stage, 573
The Planning or Holding Period Return, 224
The Portfolio Investment Process, 694
The Premium for Default Risk, 432
The Q Ratio, 338
The Security Market Line, 821
The Short Interest Ratio Theory, 622

The South Sea Bubble, 1367
The Stagnation Stage, 574
The Statement of Investment Policy, 698
The Super Bowl Indicator, 624
The Yield Structure of the Government
    Securities, 422
Theoretical Market Line, 846
THETA, 1051
Time-Weighted,
    Method—Testing Management, 942
    Rate of Return, 941
Timing the,
    Purchases of Securities, 935
    Sale is Critical, 943
Top-Down Investment Process, 311
Tracking Activity, 1200
Trade,
    Confirmation, 103
    Recording, 103
Trading Rules, 198
Transaction Costs, 89
Transfer Ability, 1011
Treasury Bills, 538
Trend, 329
    Analysis, 618
Treynor Reward-to-Volatility Ratio, 959
Triangles, Pennants, Wedges and Flags, 621
Triple Witching Hour, 1143
Tulipmania: The Legend, 1366
Types of,
    Derivatives Risk, 1006
    Options, 1038
    Orders, 87
    Rating, 165

U

UIP, 1198
Unbiased expectations theory, 428
Uncorrelated Returns, 665
Underwriting, 52
Unfair Trade Practices, 201
Users and Uses of Market Indexes, 156
Uses of,
    Margin Trading, 94
    Options, 1037
    Short Selling, 96
    the Yield Curve, 430

Utility,
    Functions, 716
    Theory, 716

V

Vaghul committee, 527
Valuation of,
    Convertible Debentures, 1094
    Warrant, 1123
Value at Risk (VaR), 1231
    analysis, 1013
    A Bird's-eye View, 1013
    based margins, 101
Value Managers, 312
Value-Weighted Indexes, 141
Valuing and Financing a Venture, 392
Variable Growth Rate of Dividends, 316
Variable Ratio Plan, 947
Variance Minimisation Approach, 926
VCC, 399
VEGA, 1051
Venture Capital, 384, 391
    Specialisation, 392
Victor Niederhoffer, 5
Volatility Index, 210

Voluntary De-listing of Companies, 79
VSATs, 40

W

Warrant(s), 1121
    Attached to Debenture, 1126
WDM, 28, 29
Weak-Form and the Random Walk, 630
Weekend Effect, 643
WEO, 1281
Wholesale Debt Market, 37
William F. Sharpe, 768
Working Capital Turnover, 585
Working of Commodity Market, 1240

Y

Yield Curve Strategies, 914, 916
Yield to,
    Maturity, 225
    the Call Date, 267
YTM, 424

Z

ZCYC, 423, 424
Zero Growth Model, 315
Zvi Bodie, 13

■ ■ ■